The National Hockey League

Official Guide & Record Book

1989-90

D1737536

Running Press
Philadelphia, Pennsylvania

THE NATIONAL HOCKEY LEAGUE
Official Guide & Record Book/1989-90

Copyright © 1989 by The National Hockey League. Compiled by the NHL Communications Department and the 21 NHL Club Public Relations Directors.

Printed in Canada. All rights reserved under the Pan-American and International Copyright Conventions.

Staff:
Senior editors: Stu Hackel, Gerry Helper, Gary Meagher; Editorial Staff: Ken Arnold, Benny Ercolani, Jane Freer, Suzanne Greenwald, Greg Inglis, Andrew Luks, Michael Santos, Shannon Shay, Sandra Taylor.

Managing Editor: James Duplacey

European Editor: Tom Ratschunas

Contributors:
William Benswanger, Ron Boileau, A. Craig Burnside, Luca Del-Vita, Cindy Douge, Peter Fillman, Filipe Goncalves, David Kaiser, Jan Kerkhof, Al Kowalenko, Neil McDonald, Howard Scheffer, Szymon Szemberg, Amy Woog.

Consulting Publisher: Dan Diamond

Photo Credits:
Special thanks to the Hockey Hall of Fame and Museum, Toronto and to the New York Rangers.

Historical and special event photos: Bruce Bennett, David Bier, Rice Studio, Robert Shaver, Imperial Oil – Turofsky Collection, Hockey Hall of Fame.

Current photos: Graig Abel, Toronto; Joe Angeles, St. Louis; Steve Babineau, Boston; Sol Benjamin, Chicago, Bruce Bennett, NY Islanders, Tony Biegun, Winnipeg, Denis Brodeur, Montreal; Mark Buckner, St. Louis; Denny Cavanaugh, Pittsburgh; Bill Cunningham, Vancouver; Willie Dagenais, Montreal; Bob Fisher, Montreal; Frank Howard, Minnesota; George Kalinsky, NY Rangers; Deborah King, Washington; Jim Mackey, Detroit; Doug MacLellan, Hockey Hall of Fame; Photography Ink, Los Angeles; Andre Pichette, Quebec; Richard Pilling, New Jersey; Wen Roberts, Los Angeles, Al Ruelle, Boston; Harry Scull, Jr., Buffalo; Diane Sobolewski, Hartford; Jim Turner, New Jersey; Brad Watson, Calgary; Bill Wippert, Bufffalo.

Canadian representatives: Cannon Book Distribution Ltd., Toronto 416/252-5207

International representatives: Worldwide Media Services, Inc., 115 East Twenty-third Street, New York, NY 10010.

Typesetting: Q Composition Inc., Toronto
Printing: The Alger Press Limited, Oshawa and Toronto

9 8 7 6 5 4 3 2 1
Digit on the right indicates the number of this printing.

Library of Congress Cataloging-in-Publication Number 88-42749

ISBN 0-89471-737-5

ISSN 0-8286647

This book may be ordered by mail from the publisher.
Please add $2.50 for postage and handling.
But try your bookstore first!
Running Press Book Publishers
125 South Twenty-second Street
Philadelphia, Pennsylvania 19103

Table of Contents

11 CLUBS – records, rosters, management

95 FINAL STATISTICS 1988-89

continued

Table of Contents *continued*

(1989-90 NHL Schedule begins inside front cover)

 Introduction

New features for 1989-90

Welcome to the 1989-90 edition of hockey's most widely-read statistical annual, the *NHL Official Guide & Record Book*. With more information and more photographs than any previous edition, this new *Guide & Record Book* reflects more than forty years of growth and refinement. Since the first *NHL Guide* was published in the late 1940s, the book has grown from a slim pocket digest to the 384-page big-format annual you are reading today.

New features in this edition include:

1. **Career records for Soviet players** are found in the *Guide's* Player and Goaltender Registers. In addition, greatly expanded European statistics are provided for Finnish, Swedish and Czechoslovakian players (pages 207-347, 361-375).

2. **Gretzky & Howe Career Comparison** celebrates the NHL's two all-time leading scorers (page 147).

3. **NHL Individual Award** year-by-year listings have been expanded to include both the winners and runners-up for each major trophy (page 158).

4. **Early Stanley Cup Challenges.** Prior to the formation of the NHL, the Stanley Cup was a challenge competition that was often contested several times a year. Previous lists of Cup winners only noted those challenges where the trophy changed hands. This new listing contains every challenge since the Cup was first presented in 1893 (page 184).

5. **Individual Team Schedule Results** for 1988-89 are found in each team's section at the front of the book. Previous editions did not provide this club-by-club breakdown (pages 11-94).

6. **A General Managers' History** has been added to the Coaching and Captains Histories included in each club's section (pages 11-94).

7. **Coaching Records** have been greatly expanded with the addition of year-by-year junior, college and minor professional coaching statistics for each NHL head coach (pages 11-94).

Active players three-goal-games and several other tables not included in 1988-89 because of space considerations have been restored in this edition.

Special thanks to the 21 public relations departments of the NHL's member clubs. Their co-operation is vital in keeping the *NHL Guide* accurate and up-to-date. We also thank the many hockey fans and members of the media who took time to correspond with us throughout the season. They are listed as contributors on page 2.

ACCURACY remains the *Guide & Record Book's* top priority. We appreciate comments and clarifications from our readers. Please direct these to editors Stu Hackel and Gerry Helper (33rd floor, 650 Fifth Ave., New York, N.Y. 10019-6108) or Gary Meagher (Suite 960, 1155 Metcalfe St., Montreal, Quebec H3B 2W2). Your involvement makes a better book.

Best wishes for an enjoyable NHL season in 1989-90.

National Hockey League

Organized November 22, 1917

Board of Governors

BOARD OF GOVERNORS — Officers
Chairman — William W. Wirtz
Vice-Chairman — Ronald Corey
Secretary — Robert O. Swados

Boston Bruins
(Boston Professional Hockey Association, Inc.)
Jeremy Jacobs — Governor
Harry Sinden — Alternate Governor
Louis Jacobs — Alternate Governor

Buffalo Sabres
(Niagara Frontier Limited Partnership)
Seymour H. Knox III — Governor
Robert O. Swados — Alternate Governor
Gerry Meehan — Alternate Governor

Calgary Flames
(Calgary Flames Hockey Club)
Cliff Fletcher — Governor
Norman N. Green — Alternate Governor
Harley Hotchkiss — Alternate Governor

Chicago Blackhawks
(Chicago Blackhawk Hockey Team, Inc.)
William W. Wirtz — Governor
Arthur M. Wirtz, Jr. — Alternate Governor
Thomas N. Ivan — Alternate Governor

Detroit Red Wings
(Detroit Red Wings, Inc.)
Michael Ilitch — Governor
James Devellano — Alternate Governor
James Lites — Alternate Governor

Edmonton Oilers
(Edmonton Oilers Hockey (Club) Limited)
Peter Pocklington — Governor
Glen Sather — Alternate Governor
Robert Lloyd — Alternate Governor

Hartford Whalers
(Hartford Whalers Hockey Club)
Donald G. Conrad — Governor
Emile Francis — Alternate Governor
Richard Gordon — Alternate Governor

Los Angeles Kings
(Los Angeles Kings Limited)
Bruce McNall — Governor
Rogatien Vachon — Alternate Governor
Roy Mlakar — Alternate Governor

Minnesota North Stars
(Northstar Hockey Partnership)
George Gund III — Governor
Gordon Gund — Alternate Governor
Jack Ferreira — Alternate Governor
Lou Nanne — Alternate Governor

Montreal Canadiens
(Le Club de Hockey Canadien Inc.)
Ronald Corey — Governor
Ron Bowman — Alternate Governor
Serge Savard — Alternate Governor

New Jersey Devils
(Meadowlanders, Inc.)
John J. McMullen — Governor
Louis A. Lamoriello — Alternate Governor
Max McNab — Alternate Governor
John C. Whitehead — Alternate Governor

New York Islanders
(Nassau Sports)
John O. Pickett, Jr. — Governor
William Torrey — Alternate Governor
William Skehan — Alternate Governor
John H. Krumpe — Alternate Governor

New York Rangers
(New York Rangers Hockey Club — a division of
Madison Square Garden Center, Inc.)
Richard Evans — Governor
Michael D. Walker — Alternate Governor
John Diller — Alternate Governor
Ken Munoz — Alternate Governor
Thomas A. Conway — Alternate Governor

Philadelphia Flyers
(Philadelphia Flyers Limited Partnership)
Jay T. Snider — Governor
Edward M. Snider — Alternate Governor
Ronald Rutenberg — Alternate Governor
Ron Ryan — Alternate Governor

Pittsburgh Penguins
(Pittsburgh Penguins, Inc.)
Marie Denise DeBartolo York — Governor
Tony Esposito — Alternate Governor
J. Paul Martha — Alternate Governor

Quebec Nordiques
(Club de Hockey Les Nordiques de Québec)
Société en commandite)
Marcel Aubut — Governor
Maurice Filion — Alternate Governor
Gilles Leger — Alternate Governor

St. Louis Blues
(St. Louis Blues Hockey Club, Inc.)
Michael F. Shanahan — Governor
Jack Quinn — Alternate Governor
Ronald Caron — Alternate Governor

Toronto Maple Leafs
(Maple Leafs Gardens Limited)
Harold E. Ballard — Governor

Vancouver Canucks
(Vancouver Hockey Club, Limited)
Arthur R. Griffiths — Governor
Pat Quinn — Alternate Governor
Frank A. Griffiths — Alternate Governor
Frank W. Griffiths — Alternate Governor

Washington Capitals
(Washington Hockey Limited Partnership)
Abe Pollin — Governor
Richard M. Patrick — Alternate Governor
David Poile — Alternate Governor

Winnipeg Jets
(8 Hockey Ventures, Inc.)
Barry L. Shenkarow — Governor
Bill Davis — Alternate Governor
Michael A. Smith — Alternate Governor

League Offices

MONTREAL
960 Sun Life Building,
1155 Metcalfe Street,
Montreal, Que. H3B 2W2
Phone: 514/871-9220
Executive TWX: 610-421-3260
Central Registry TWX: 610-421-3188

ENVOY ID
Accounting	NHLMTL.ACTG
Auto-delivery station	NHLMTL.AUTO
Central Registry	BON
Computer Operations	NHLMTL.MIS
General	NHLMTL.GNRL
Public Relations	NHLMTL.PR

Telex via CCI NY 7601297
TWX via CCI NY 710-581-5005 MBX: YWX4108
FAX 514/871-1663

NEW YORK
33rd Floor, 650 Fifth Avenue,
New York, N.Y., 10019-6108
Phone: 212/398-1100

ENVOY ID
Accounting	NHLNY.ACTG
Auto-delivery station	NHLNY.AUTO
Broadcasting	NHLNY.TV
General	NHLNY.GNRL
Marketing	NHLNY.MKTG
Public Relations	NHLNY.PR

Telex via CCI NY 7601278
TWX via CCI NY 710-581-5005 MBX: MCY6426
FAX 212/245-8221

TORONTO
Suite 200, 1 Greensboro Drive,
Rexdale, Ont., M9W 1C8
Officiating 416/245-2926
Central Scouting (416) 245-1813; 245-2926
TWX: 610-492-2703

ENVOY ID
Auto-delivery station	NHLTOR.AUTO
Central Scouting	NHLTOR.SCTG
General	NHLTOR.GNRL
Jim Gregory	HOCKEY.OPERATIONS
Officiating	OFFICIATING.TOR

Telex via CCI NY 7601296
TWX via CCI NY 710-581-5005 MBX: DQX1968
FAX 416/245-0375

League Departments

MONTREAL

Administration
Brian O'Neill — Executive Vice President
Madeleine Supino — Secretary
Phil Scheuer — Director of Administration
Nancy Starnino — Secretary
Mike Humes — Administrative Assistant

Central Registry
Garry Lovegrove — Director of Central Registry
Madeleine Supino — Assistant Director
Lisa Rossi — Assistant

Communications
Gary Meagher — Executive Director of Communications
Benny Ercolani — Associate Director of Information/
Statistician
Jane Freer — Assistant Director of Information
Greg Inglis — Researcher

Computer Operations
Mario Carangi — Director of Management Information
Systems
Miranda Ishak — Assistant Director — MIS
Luc Coulombe — Project Leader
Sharon Jardine — Programmer
Johanne Hinds — Operations

Finance
Kenneth G. Sawyer — Vice-President of Finance and
Treasurer
Donald P. Grinton — Director of Accounting
Mary Skiadopoulos — Accounting Supervisor
Steve Hatzepetros — Accountant
Donna Gillman — Accountant
Doris Long — Secretary
Lynne Blagrave — Pension Supervisor
Vivianne Chen — Secretary
Jocelyne Comeau — Accounting Clerk
Vicki Sciortino — Accountant

Office Services
Jean Huard — Printer
Robert Bouchard — Office Assistant
Marcia Golding — Receptionist

OFFICERS
President — John A. Ziegler, Jr.
Executive Vice-President — Brian F. O'Neill
Vice-President/General Counsel — Gilbert Stein
Vice-President of Finance and Treasurer — Kenneth G. Sawyer
Vice-President, Hockey Operations — Jim Gregory
Vice-President, NHL Project Development — Ian Morrison
Vice-President, Broadcasting — Joel Nixon
Vice-President, Marketing/Public Relations — Steve Ryan

NEW YORK
Broadcasting
Joel Nixon — Vice-President, Broadcasting
Stu Hackel — Director of Broadcasting
Lois Cutler — Secretary
Finance
Patricia Cassell-Cooper — Controller
Evelyn Torres — Accounts Payable
Ivonne Merchant — Secretary
Legal Department
Gilbert Stein — Vice-President/General Counsel
Pat Honig — Assistant
Marketing and Communications
Steve Ryan — Vice-President, Marketing and Public Relations
Lucia Ripi — Secretary
Steve Flatow — Director of Marketing/General Manager,
   Promotional Licensing Division
Mary McCarthy — Secretary
Maria Pace — Manager, Client and Team Services
Fred Scalera — General Manager, Retail Licensing Division
Ann Kiely — Secretary
Stu Hackel — General Manager, Publishing & Video Division
Maureen Brady — Director, Events & Service Manager
Gerry Helper — Director of Public Relations
Karen Lechner — Director of Special Events
Michael A. Berger — Editor, Goal Magazine
Shannon Shay — Assistant Director of Information
Suzanne Greenwald — Project Coordinator, Publishing &
   Communications
Office Administration
Mike Christiansen — Office Services Manager
Lola Skaro — Receptionist
Scott Shanes — Administrative Assistant
President's Staff
Susan Rudin — Assistant to the President
John Sohigian — Presidential Liaison Officer
Joanne Blute — Administrative Assistant
Security
Frank Torpey — Director of Security

TORONTO
Jim Gregory — Vice-President of Hockey Operations
Bryan Lewis — Director of Officiating
Wally Harris — Assistant Director of Officiating
Will Norris — Coordinator of Development
Frank Bonello — Director of Central Scouting
Pierre Dorion — Chief Scout
Kevin Prendergast — Central Scouting, Administration
Al Wiseman — Assistant Director of Security
Secretarial Staff
Dorothy Reaves, Mary Keenan, Kelley Bright
Officiating Supervisory Staff
John Ashley, Matt Pavelich, Lou Maschio, Jim Christison,
John D'Amico, Bob Nadin, Sam Sisco
Central Scouting Staff
John Andersen, Mike Donaldson, Gary Eggleston, Laurence
Ferguson, Ron Harris, Tom Martin, Kevin Penny, David Prior,
Marcel Pronovost, Jack Timmins, Barry Trapp
Hockey Hall of Fame
Exhibition Place
Toronto, Ont. M6K 3C3
Phone: 416/595-1345
FAX 416/971-5828
Ian Morrison — President
Esther Richards — Executive Secretary
Jeff Denomme — Director of Administration
Ray Paquet — Exhibit Coordinator
Philip Pritchard — Marketing Services Manager
Joseph Romain — Librarian/Associate Curator
James Duplacey — Associate Curator
M.H. (Lefty) Reid — Historical Consultant
Marilyn Robbins — Receptionist
Raymond Bruce — Security Coordinator
National Hockey League Players' Association
37 Maitland St.
Toronto, Ont. M4Y 1C8
Phone: 416/924-7800
FAX 416/924-3004
Envoy ID NHLPA.TOR
Alan Eagleson — Executive Director
Sam Simpson — Director of Operations

Referees and Linesmen

RON ASSELSTINE . . . Linesman . . . Born: Nov. 6, 1946 in Toronto, Ont. . . . First NHL Game: Oct. 10, 1979 . . . Total NHL Games: 803 . . . In 1989, was selected to work in three NHL-Soviet Super Series games and the 40th NHL All-Star Game in Edmonton. Ron is very active in his community as chairman of the "Make-A-Wish" Foundation and as an Ontario Provincial Police "Auxiliary" Officer. He is married and has two children.

WAYNE BONNEY . . . Linesman . . . Born: May 27, 1953 in Ottawa, Ont. . . . First NHL Game: Oct. 10, 1979 . . . Total NHL Games: 762 . . . Joined the NHL in 1979 and has worked just under 800 games in his 10-year career. In 1988-89, Bonney was selected to work in the 40th NHL All-Star Game in Edmonton. He currently resides in Kirkland, Que., with his wife and daughter and is an avid baseball player.

RYAN BOZAK . . . Linesman . . . Born: Jan. 3, 1947 in Swift Current, Sask. . . . First NHL Game: 1972 . . . Total NHL Games: 1,246 . . . Joined the NHL in 1972 and worked his 1,200th NHL game in 1988-89. He was selected to officiate in the 1983 NHL All-Star Game on Long Island. During the off-season he enjoys golf and tennis and resides in San Diego, CA. Bozak has two children.

GORD BROSEKER . . . Linesman . . . Born: July 8, 1950 in Baltimore, MD . . . First NHL Game: Jan 14, 1975 . . . Total NHL Games: 1,058 . . . Joined the NHL in 1973 and officiated in his 1,000th NHL game in 1988-89. Before beginning his officiating career, he played baseball in the Texas Rangers' organization. Broseker was selected to officiate in the 1986 NHL All-Star Game in Hartford. He currently resides in Richmond, VA, with his wife and daughter.

KEVIN COLLINS . . . Linesman . . . Born: Dec. 15,1950 in Springfield, MA . . . First NHL Game: Oct. 13, 1977 . . . Total NHL Games: 969 . . . Joined the NHL in 1971. He was selected to officiate in the 1988 NHL All-Star Game in St. Louis and has worked in the Stanley Cup Final series for the past three years. Currently residing in Springfield, MA, Collins is married and has three children.

PIERRE CHAMPOUX . . . Linesman . . . Born: Apr. 18, 1963 in Ville St. Pierre, Que. . . . First NHL Game: Oct. 8, 1987 . . . Total NHL Games: 39 . . . Began officiating minor league games at the age of 12 in the Quebec pee wee league. Since then he has worked in two international competitions, having officiated in an exhibition game between the United States and Canada at the Forum and in Canada Cup 1987. During the off-season, Champoux is a part-time firefighter in Ville St. Pierre, Quebec and enjoys playing golf, softball and volleyball. Champoux is single.

MICHAEL CVIK . . . Linesman . . . Born: July 6, 1962 in Calgary, Alta. . . . First NHL Game: Oct. 8, 1987 . . . Total NHL Games: 81 . . . The tallest of the officials at 6'5", began his officiating career in the AAHA in 1978. After working his way through the WHL, he joined the NHL in 1987. During the off-season, Mike participates in the Annual Child Find Bike Ride for Child Find Alberta. He is an avid cyclist and enjoys reading and golf. He is single.

PAT DAPUZZO . . . Linesman . . . Born: Dec. 29, 1958 in Hoboken, NJ . . . First NHL Game: Dec. 5, 1984 . . . Total NHL Games: 333 . . . Officiated in his first NHL game on Dec. 5, 1984, in Madison Square Garden. In 1989, he was selected to officiate in the 88-89 Super Series when the New Jersey Devils faced the Central Red Army on January 2. Pat resides in Bergen, NJ and is single. He is an avid weightlifter and karate enthusiast.

PAUL DEVORSKI . . . Referee . . . Born: Aug. 18, 1958 in Guelph, Ont. . . . Joined the NHL in 1987. He spent 1988-89 working in the AHL and was a stand-by referee for three NHL games. Devorski is a part owner of Gold's Gym in Guelph and plays fastball. He is married.

MARK FAUCETTE . . . Referee . . . Born: June 9, 1958 in Springfield, MA . . . First NHL Game: 1985 . . . Total NHL Games: 26 . . . Joined the NHL in 1985. He resided in Agawam, MA. During the off-season, he organizes softball tournaments to raise funds for Boston Children Hospital's "Jimmy Fund". He is married.

RON FINN . . . Linesman . . . Born: Dec. 1, 1940 in Toronto, Ont. . . . First NHL Game: October 11, 1969 . . . Total NHL Games: 1,559 . . . Has worked in more games than any other active official with 1,559 games through 1988-89. A resident of Brampton, Ont., Finn is also among the leaders in playoff officiating, ranking third with 204 career games. He has worked in two All-Star Games including 1977 (Vancouver) and 1982 (Washington, D.C.). He also worked during Rendez-Vous '87 in Quebec City. Finn was selected to work in the Stanley Cup Finals for the eleventh consecutive year in 1988-89, bringing his career total to 31 games (seventh on the all-time list). He is active in his community during the off-season, working with the Canadian Special Olympics and is an instructor at various officiating schools in Ontario and New Brunswick. Ron is married and has four children.

KERRY FRASER . . . Referee . . . Born: June 30, 1952 in Sarnia, Ont. . . . Total NHL Games: 533 . . . After playing minor league hockey as a youngster, attended the NHL training camp for officials in 1972. Fraser has become one of the League's most experienced and respected referees, as proven by his selection to referee three Stanley Cup Final series (1985, 1986 and 1989). During the off-season, Fraser instructs at the WHL School of Officiating in Calgary and represents drug awareness programs with the RCMP and local police agencies. He is Co-Chairman of a celebrity dinner benefitting the Children's Center and also a golf tournament to aid the Cancer Society. Fraser enjoys sailing and golf. He is married and has six children.

GERARD GAUTHIER . . . Linesman . . . Born: Sept. 5, 1948 in Montreal, Que. . . . First NHL Game: Oct. 16, 1971 . . . Total NHL Games: 1,380 . . . Attended his first NHL training camp in 1971 after two years in junior hockey. He has been selected to work at two NHL All-Star Games in his career; Los Angeles (1981) and Calgary (1985). In addition, he worked in the 1984 Canada Cup. Gauthier has worked in two Stanley Cup Final series in 1982 and 1983. During the off-season, Gauthier enjoys golfing and tennis. He is married and has two children.

TERRY GREGSON . . . Referee . . . Born: Nov. 7 1953 in Guelph, Ont. . . . First NHL Game: Dec. 19, 1981 . . . Total NHL Games: 412 . . . Joined the NHL in 1979 and has worked 412 games in his seven-year career. In 1988, Gregson was selected to officiate at the NHL All-Star Game in St. Louis as well as the Boston vs. Central Red Army Game in Super Series '88-89. Gregson is a Co-Chairman of the Officials' "Make A Wish" Foundation and is an avid traveller and photographer. Gregson is married.

SHANE HEYER . . . Referee . . . Born: Feb. 7,1964 in Summerland, B.C. . . . First NHL Game: Oct. 5, 1988 . . . Total NHL Games: 79 . . . Began officiating in Penticton, B.C., at the age of 10 and was invited to join the NHL program in 1988. In his first year of service, Heyer was selected to work in the December 31 game between the Los Angeles Kings and the Dynamo Riga club during Super Series '88-89. Heyer is single.

BOB HODGES . . . Linesman . . . Born: Aug. 16, 1944 in Galt, Ont. . . . First NHL Game: Oct. 14, 1972 . . . Total NHL Games: 1,175 . . . Hired by the NHL in 1972-73 season at the age of 28, Hodges is one of the NHL's senior officials. He has been chosen to work in the Stanley Cup Finals three times (1982, 1986 and 1987) and officiated at the 1985 All-Star Game in Calgary. During the off-season he works with the Royal Canadian Legion and enjoys hunting, fishing and baseball. Hodges is married and has two children.

RON HOGGARTH . . . Referee . . . Born: Apr. 12, 1948 in Barrie, Ont. . . . First NHL Game: Oct. 16, 1971 . . . Total NHL Games: 825 . . . Began officiating while still a student at McMaster University. He joined the NHL in 1971. In addition to officiating in several Soviet-NHL matches, Hoggarth was selected to referee the 1989 NHL All-Star Game in Edmonton. During the summer, Hoggarth owns and operates KoHo pools in Barrie and is active in golf and tennis. He is married and has two daughters.

Referees and Linesmen continued

DAVE JACKSON . . . Referee . . . Born: Nov. 28, 1964 in Montreal, Que. . . . One of two officials to join the NHL in 1989. He became an NHL trainee at the age of 21 after having attended Ron Fournier's Referee School. In 1988-89, he worked in 42 AHL games, 24 IHL games and six major junior league games. During the off-season, he works in lawn equipment sales. He is active in softball tournaments and is an avid golfer.

SWEDE KNOX . . . Linesman . . . Born: Mar. 2, 1948 in Edmonton, Alta. . . . First NHL Game: Oct. 14, 1972 . . . Total NHL Games: 1,340 . . . Joined the NHL in 1971. In 1982, he was selected to work in the NHL All-Star Game in Washington, D.C. He has been selected to officiate in the Stanley Cup Finals for the last two years. A full-time resident of Edmonton, Swede is married and has two children.

DENNIS LARUE . . . Referee . . . Born: July 14, 1959 in Savannah, GA . . . Attended the USA Hockey Referee Development Camp in 1983 and joined the NHL in 1988. Last season, LaRue worked in the AHL, IHL, CCHA and OHL. During the off-season he is involved in summer camp programs for children and in the Referee Development Program. He is an avid water-skiier and golfer. Dennis is married and has two children.

BRAD LAZAROWICH . . . Linesman . . . Born: Aug. 4, 1962 in Vancouver, B.C. . . . First NHL Game: Oct. 9, 1986 . . . Total NHL Games: 239 . . . Joined the NHL in 1986 and has worked a total of 239 games. In 1988, he was chosen to officiate in Super Series '88-89 (Dynamo Riga vs. Vancouver). During the off-season, Brad is employed by the Delta Corporation in the Water Works division and is an avid bicyclist, golfer and weightlifter. He is married.

RON MARTELL . . . Referee . . . Born: Oct. 21, 1963 in Winnipeg, Man. . . . First NHL Game: Mar. 14, 1984 . . . Total NHL Games: 1 . . . Joined the NHL officially in 1987, although he did officiate in one NHL game in 1984. Due to weather conditions in Winnipeg, Martell was called on to replace the scheduled NHL referee. Martell enjoys playing summer hockey, baseball and works in the promotions department for Blackwoods Beverages in Winnipeg during the off-season.

DON KOHARSKI . . . Referee . . . Born: Dec. 2, 1955 in Halifax, N.S. . . . First NHL Game: Oct. 14, 1977 . . . Total NHL Games: 561 (163 as a linesman) . . . Hired as an official in the WHA at the age of 18. He joined the NHL in 1977 as a linesman, becoming a referee after 163 games. Koharski gained international experience in Canada Cup 1987 and has worked in the Stanley Cup Finals three years consecutively (1986, 1987 and 1988). During the off-season, Koharski is active in the Make-A-Wish Foundation of Burlington, Ont. He also owns and operates his own refereeing school in Burlington. He is married and has two sons.

DAN MAROUELLI . . . Referee . . . Born: July 16, 1955 in Edmonton, Alta. . . . First NHL Game: Nov. 2, 1984 . . . Total NHL Games: 268 . . . Began his officiating career at the age of 13 with the Knights of Columbus. He joined the NHL in 1982. He was selected to officiate the game between Dynamo Riga and Chicago during Super Series '88-89. During the summer, Marouelli works at a number of refereeing schools and owns a small construction business. He is an avid golfer. Dan is married and has three children.

BILL McCREARY . . . Referee . . . Born: Nov. 17, 1955 in Guelph, Ont. . . . First NHL Game: Nov. 3, 1984 . . . Total NHL Games: 260 . . . Joined the NHL in 1982. This season he was selected to referee the Red Army vs. Buffalo Sabres game on January 9 in Super Series '88-89. During the off-season, McCreary is active in golf tournaments and coaching baseball. He also enjoys hunting and fishing. He is married and has two sons.

DAN McCOURT . . . Linesman . . . Born: Aug. 14, 1954 . . . First NHL Game: Dec. 27, 1980 . . . Total NHL Games: 784 . . . Joined the NHL in 1979. During the off-season, he instructs at various officiating schools and is involved with local charities. He enjoys golf, baseball and raquetball. McCourt is engaged to be married.

MIKE McGEOUGH . . . Referee . . . Born: June 20, 1957 in Regina, Sask. . . . Total NHL Games: 20 . . . Began his NHL career in 1987. In 1988-89, he worked 72 games in the AHL and 13 in the NHL. During the off-season, McGeough enjoys golf and bicycling. He instructs at various refereeing schools in the area. He is married and has three children.

RANDY MITTON . . . Linesman . . . Born: Sept. 22, 1950 in Fredericton, N.B. . . . First NHL Game: Dec. 26, 1973 . . . Total NHL Games: 1,143 . . . Became involved in NHL officiating in 1972 after working in the WHL and AHL for two years. He gained international experience as a linesman for the 1987 Canada Cup and was selected to officiate in the 1988 NHL All-Star Game in St. Louis. During the off-season, Mitton is active with the Elks Club and teaches at a number of officiating schools in Western Canada. He is married and has two children.

DENIS MOREL . . . Referee . . . Born: Dec. 13, 1948 in Quebec City, Que. . . . First NHL Game: Jan. 18, 1976 . . . Total NHL Games: 794 . . . Began officiating in Quebec minor leagues before joining the NHL in 1976. He was selected to be the standby referee at the 1983 NHL All-Star Game in Washington D.C. and the 1988 All-Star Game in St. Louis. Morel has also been an official in the Stanley Cup Finals for the past two years (1988 and 1989). During the summer, he is active in the Trois-Rivieres Special Olympics Program and is an instructor at two hockey schools in the area. He enjoys swimming and golf and is an avid reader. He is married and has two children.

BRIAN MURPHY . . . Linesman . . . Born: Dec. 13, 1964 in Dover, NH . . . First NHL Game: Oct. 7, 1988 . . . Total NHL Games: 37 . . . The youngest NHL official. Joined the League in 1988-89 after graduating from the University of New Hampshire with a degree in Business Administration. During his years at University, he worked in the NCAA officiating ranks, including the 1988 NCAA Division I National Championship Game in Lake Placid. During the off-season, Murphy works as a part-time accountant and is an instructor at AHAUS Officiating Development Camps.

DAVE NEWELL . . . Referee . . . Born: Feb. 25, 1945 in Sudbury, Ont. . . . First NHL Game: Mar. 5, 1968 Total NHL Games: 1,126 . . . Joined the NHL in 1967 and now holds the longest tenure of any active official with 22 years in the NHL. He has worked more games than any other active referee with 1,126. He was selected to officiate in the 1980 NHL All-Star Game in Detroit as well as Rendez-Vous '87 in Quebec City. He has served as president of the Officials' Association for nine years. During the off-season, he enjoys fishing, hunting and golf and is active in many local charities. Newell is married and has three children.

MARK PARE . . . Linesman . . . Born: July 26, 1957 in Windsor, Ont. . . . First NHL Game: Oct. 11, 1979 . . . Total NHL Games: 787 . . . Joined the NHL in 1979 after working minor leagues in Windsor. During the off-season, he is a salesman for a food products company. He enjoys golfing. Pare is married and has two children.

JERRY PATEMAN . . . Linesman . . . Born: Jan. 12, 1958 in The Hague, Netherlands . . . First NHL Game: Nov. 10, 1982 . . . Total NHL Games: 204 . . . The only NHL official not born in North America, Pateman started refereeing minor hockey in Chatham, Ont. at the age of 14. He joined the NHL in 1982. During the summer, Pateman works part-time at a food products company and instructs at officiating schools in the area. Pateman now resides in Tecumseh, Ont. with his wife and two children.

LANCE ROBERTS . . . Referee . . . Born: May 28, 1957 in Edmonton, Alta. . . . Joined the NHL in 1987 after beginning his career at the age of 15 in the minor leagues of Alberta. Roberts instructs at the AAHA Development Camp during the summer as well as playing golf and reading. He is married and has one daughter.

DAN SCHACHTE . . . Linesman . . . Born: July 13, 1958 in Madison, WI . . . First NHL Game: October 8, 1982 . . . Total NHL Games: 463 . . . Joined the NHL in 1982. He was chosen to officiate in Super Series '88-89 in the Dynamo Riga vs. Chicago game. During the off-season, Schachte owns and operates a construction business in Madison, WI where he lives with his wife and son. He enjoys hunting, fishing and boating.

ROB SHICK . . . Referee . . . Born: Dec. 4, 1957, in Port Alberni, B.C. . . . First NHL Game: Apr. 6, 1986 . . . Total NHL Games: 108 . . . Joined the NHL in 1984. He is married. During the off-season, he is an avid fastball player and runs a landscaping business in Lethbridge, Alta.

PAUL STEWART . . . Referee . . . Born: Mar. 21, 1955 in Boston, MA . . . First NHL Game: Mar. 27, 1987 . . . Total NHL Games: 100 . . . Joined the NHL in 1985. Shortly after joining the League, he was asked to officiate in the 1987 Canada Cup. Stewart joins Joh Ashley as the only ex-NHL players to become NHL officials. During the off-season, Stewart continues his graduate studies at Northeastern University and is employed in estate planning. He enjoys landscaping, gardening and golf.

LEON STICKLE . . . Linesman . . . Born: Apr. 20, 1948 in Toronto, Ont. . . . First NHL Game: Oct. 17, 1970 . . . Total NHL Games: 1,502 . . . Joined the NHL in 1969 after four years in the minor leagues. In his career, he has worked in three NHL All-Star Games (Montreal, 1975; Buffalo,1978 and Long Island, 1983). He also was selected as an official for the Canada Cup tournament in 1981 and 1984. He has worked in the Stanley Cup Finals six times (1977, 1978, 1980, 1981, 1984 and 1985). During the off-season, Stickle is active with the Ontario and Canadian Special Olympics and coaches minor league baseball. He also enjoys golf. He is married and has three children.

RICHARD TROTTIER . . . Referee . . . Born: Feb. 28, 1957 in Laval, Que. . . . One of two new officials to join the NHL in 1989. He worked in the AHL last season. During his career, he has served as the executive vice-president for the Quebec Esso Cup in 1987-88 and 1988-89 and has been the referee-in-chief for the Quebec Ice Hockey Federation since 1986. During the off-season, he instructs at Ron Fournier's Officiating School and is an avid golfer and raquetball player.

ANDY VANHELLEMOND . . . Referee . . . Born: Feb. 16, 1948 in Winnipeg, Man. . . . First NHL Game: Nov. 22, 1972 . . . Total NHL Games: 1,062 . . . Joined the NHL in 1971 and has become one of the senior NHL officials. He worked in the NHL All-Star Game (1985) and Rendez-Vous '87 in Quebec City. He has been selected to work in the Stanley Cup Final series 13 consecutive years since 1977. During the off-season, vanHellemond enjoys golfing, gardening and baseball.

MARK VINES . . . Linesman . . . Born: Dec. 3, 1960 in Elmira, Ont. . . . First NHL Game: Oct. 13, 1984 . . . Total NHL Games: 403 . . . Joined the NHL in 1984. He has worked 403 games in his five-year career. He attends university during the off-season and is single.

League Presidents

Top: The NHL's first president, Frank Calder, at left, presents the Calder trophy to Boston goaltender Frank Brimsek as the outstanding rookie of 1938-39. Middle: Mervyn "Red" Dutton, president from 1943-46, at right, congratulates Clarence S. Campbell who served as NHL president from 1946 to 1977. Bottom: John A. Ziegler, Jr., president from 1977 to date.

Frank Calder
President, 1917-1943

After an illustrious tenure as secretary of the National Hockey Association, Frank Calder was elected as the first president of the National Hockey League when the League was formed in 1917. He served in this capacity until his death on February 4, 1943.

Born in England in 1877, Calder came to Canada at the turn of the century as a school teacher, but turned to sports writing in 1909. His forthright writing style won him the attention and respect of Montreal Canadiens' owner George Kennedy whose support helped Calder to the position of NHL president.

For nearly 26 years, Calder worked hard to change the League from a small-time circuit to a grand international sports organization. Among his many achievements, Calder guided the NHL through its first expansion into the U.S., including the addition of the Boston Bruins in 1924 and the Chicago Blackhawks, Detroit Cougars and New York Rangers in 1926.

To commemorate his years of service, the League established the Calder Memorial Trophy to honor the rookie of the year at the conclusion of each season. Additionally, Calder was elected to the Hockey Hall of Fame in 1945 as one of its first inductees.

Mervyn "Red" Dutton
President, 1943-46

Born on July 23, 1898 in Russell, Manitoba, Mervyn "Red" Dutton succeeded Frank Calder as the second president of the NHL. For two seasons, 1943-44 and 1944-45, Dutton remained at the head of the League before resuming his career in private business. Most remembered for his rugged playing style, Dutton overcame severe war injuries to skate as a professional for over a decade. After anchoring the defense for Calgary in the Western Hockey League from 1921 to 1925, Dutton signed with the NHL's Montreal Maroons. He stayed with the Maroons through 1930 when he joined the New York Americans. In 1936, he took over coaching and managing that club and remained there until 1942 when the team disbanded.

Upon Frank Calder's death in 1943, Dutton became president of the NHL, a position he maintained until Clarence Campbell assumed the role in 1946. Dutton was elected to the Hockey Hall of Fame in 1958. Currently, the 88-year-old Dutton resides in Calgary, Alberta.

Clarence Campbell
President, 1946-77

Clarence Campbell was a Rhodes Scholar who was born July 9, 1905 in Fleming, Saskatchewan. In 1926, a 20-year-old Campbell graduated from the University of Alberta with bachelor of arts and bachelor of law degrees.

Following his studies at Oxford, England, Campbell returned to Canada to begin his law practise. Forever active in sports, he also became an NHL referee, working 155 regular-season games and twelve Stanley Cup playoff contests through 1939 when he joined the Canadian Armed Forces for the duration of World War II.

On September 5, 1946, Campbell became the NHL's third president succeeding Mervyn "Red" Dutton. Within a year of his appointment, he established the NHL Players' Pension Plan which has since become the prototype for other professional sports leagues.

Campbell led the League through its greatest era of expansion in 1967 when the NHL doubled in size from six to twelve teams. In 1972, he also succeeded in breaking ground in a new era of international competition, when, for the first time in hockey history, Canada's finest NHL talent faced-off against the Soviet Union's elite in an eight-game challenge series.

Elected to the Hockey Hall of Fame in 1966, Campbell also received the Lester Patrick Trophy for "outstanding service to hockey in the United States" in 1972. He retired from the NHL in 1977, but continued to stay close to the League until his death in 1984.

John A. Ziegler, Jr.
President, 1977 to date

John A. Ziegler, Jr., President and Chief Executive Officer of the National Hockey League, was born in Grosse Pointe, Michigan, on February 9, 1934.

He graduated from the University of Michigan in 1957, earning a bachelor of arts and *juris doctor* degrees. Upon graduation he joined the Detroit law firm of Dickinson, Wright, McKean and Cudlip and became a partner in the firm in 1964. In 1969 he left the firm and in September of 1970 he set up his own firm, Ziegler, Dykhouse & Wise. He continued as senior partner in the firm until assuming his present position in September, 1977.

In 1959 he began to do legal work for Olympia Stadium, the Detroit Red Wings and Mr. Bruce Norris. He continued to serve these clients in various capacities until his election as president of the National Hockey League. In 1966 he joined the NHL Board of Governors as an alternate governor for the Detroit Red Wings and, as such, worked on many of the NHL's committees and was involved in various aspects of the League's litigation as well as relations and negotiations with the Players' Association.

In June of 1976, he succeeded William Wirtz as Chairman of the National Hockey League Board of Governors. He was inducted into the Hockey Hall of Fame as a Builder in June, 1987.

An ardent sports fan, Ziegler played amateur hockey in the Detroit area from 1949 to 1969. He has continued to make his home in the Detroit area (Ortonville, Michigan) while maintaining offices in Montreal and New York.

Dirk Graham's 33 goals in 1988-89 were a career high for the Blackhawks' captain.

NHL Attendance

Season	Regular Season Games	Attendance	Playoffs Games	Attendance	Total Attendance
1960-61	210	2,317,142	17	242,000	2,559,142
1961-62	210	2,435,424	18	277,000	2,712,424
1962-63	210	2,590,574	16	220,906	2,811,480
1963-64	210	2,732,642	21	309,149	3,041,791
1964-65	210	2,822,635	20	303,859	3,126,494
1965-66	210	2,941,164	16	249,000	3,190,184
1966-67	210	3,084,759	16	248,336	3,333,095
1967-68[1]	444	4,938,043	40	495,089	5,433,132
1968-69	456	5,550,613	33	431,739	5,982,352
1969-70	456	5,992,065	34	461,694	6,453,759
1970-71[2]	546	7,257,677	43	707,633	7,965,310
1971-72	546	7,609,368	36	582,666	8,192,034
1972-73[3]	624	8,575,651	38	624,637	9,200,288
1973-74	624	8,640,978	38	600,442	9,241,420
1974-75[4]	720	9,521,536	51	784,181	10,305,717
1975-76	720	9,103,761	48	726,279	9,830,040
1976-77	720	8,563,890	44	646,279	9,210,169
1977-78	720	8,526,564	45	686,634	9,213,198
1978-79	680	7,758,053	45	694,521	8,452,574
1979-80[5]	840	10,533,623	63	976,699	11,510,322
1980-81	840	10,726,198	68	966,390	11,692,588
1981-82	840	10,710,894	71	1,058,948	11,769,842
1982-83	840	11,020,610	66	1,088,222	12,028,832
1983-84	840	11,359,386	70	1,107,400	12,466,786
1984-85	840	11,633,730	70	1,107,500	12,741,230
1985-86	840	11,621,000	72	1,152,503	12,773,503
1986-87	840	11,855,880	87	1,383,967	13,239,847
1987-88	840	12,117,512	83	1,336,901	13,454,413
1988-89	840	12,417,969	83	1,327,214	13,745,183

[1] First expansion: Los Angeles, Pittsburgh, California, Philadelphia, St. Louis and Minnesota
[2] Second expansion: Buffalo and Vancouver
[3] Third expansion: Atlanta and New York Islanders
[4] Fourth expansion: Kansas City (Colorado, New Jersey) and Washington
[5] Fifth expansion: Edmonton, Hartford, Quebec and Winnipeg

Kevin Dineen enjoyed his finest pro campaign, beating rival goaltenders 45 times in 1988-89.

Boston Bruins
1988-89 Results: 37w-29L-14T 88 PTS. Second, Adams Division

Randy Burridge, here challenging Chicago goaltender Darren Pang, had his best season in 1988-89, with 31 goals and 30 assists.

Schedule

Home			Away		
Oct.	Thur. 5	Pittsburgh	**Oct.**	Sat. 7	Quebec
	Mon. 9	Montreal		Wed. 11	Montreal
	Thur. 26	Quebec		Fri. 13	Edmonton
	Sat. 28	Hartford		Sun. 15	Vancouver*
Nov.	Thur. 2	Los Angeles		Tues. 17	Los Angeles
	Sat. 4	Buffalo		Fri. 20	Edmonton
	Thur. 9	Edmonton		Sat. 21	Calgary
	Thur. 16	Montreal		Sun. 29	Buffalo
	Sat. 18	New Jersey	**Nov.**	Fri. 10	Washington
	Thur. 23	Toronto		Wed. 15	Hartford
	Thur. 30	Buffalo		Tues. 21	Detroit
Dec.	Sat. 2	St Louis		Sat. 25	Montreal
	Thur. 7	Hartford		Tues. 28	St Louis
	Sat. 9	Washington*	**Dec.**	Sun. 3	Philadelphia
	Sat. 16	Buffalo*		Tues. 5	Quebec
	Thur. 21	Minnesota		Tues. 12	Pittsburgh
	Sat. 23	Detroit*		Wed. 13	Buffalo
	Tues. 26	Toronto		Sun. 17	New Jersey
Jan.	Thur. 4	Winnipeg		Wed. 20	Hartford
	Sat. 6	Washington		Fri. 29	Buffalo
	Thur. 11	Quebec		Sat. 30	Toronto
	Sat. 13	NY Rangers*	**Jan.**	Tues. 2	Pittsburgh
	Mon. 15	Hartford		Sun. 7	Buffalo
	Thur. 18	Calgary		Wed. 17	Hartford
	Thur. 25	NY Islanders		Tues. 23	Quebec
	Sat. 27	Philadelphia*		Mon. 29	Montreal
Feb.	Thur. 1	Montreal	**Feb.**	Sun. 4	Quebec*
	Sat. 3	NY Rangers*		Tues. 6	Detroit
	Thur. 8	Quebec		Wed. 14	Winnipeg
	Sat. 10	NY Islanders*		Sun. 18	Vancouver
	Sun. 11	Vancouver*		Tues. 20	Calgary
Mar.	Thur. 1	Montreal		Thur. 22	Chicago
	Sat. 3	Chicago*		Sat. 24	Minnesota
	Thur. 8	Buffalo		Mon. 26	NY Rangers
	Thur. 15	Winnipeg	**Mar.**	Sun. 4	Chicago*
	Sat. 17	Los Angeles*		Tues. 6	Philadelphia
	Thur. 22	Quebec		Sat. 10	NY Islanders
	Sat. 24	Minnesota*		Sun. 11	Hartford
	Thur. 29	Hartford		Tues. 27	St Louis
Apr.	Sun. 1	New Jersey		Sat. 31	Montreal

* Denotes afternoon game.

Home Starting Times:
Weeknights . . . . 7:35 p.m.
Saturdays and Sundays . . . . 7:05 p.m.
Matinees . . . . 1:35 p.m.

Franchise date: November 1, 1924

66th NHL Season

Year-by-Year Record

Season	GP	Home W	L	T	Road W	L	T	Overall W	L	T	GF	GA	Pts.	Finished	Playoff Result
1988-89	80	17	15	8	20	14	6	37	29	14	289	256	88	2nd, Adams Div.	Lost Div. Final
1987-88	80	24	13	3	20	17	3	44	30	6	300	251	94	2nd, Adams Div.	Lost Final
1986-87	80	25	11	4	14	23	3	39	34	7	301	276	85	3rd, Adams Div.	Lost Div. Semi-Final
1985-86	80	24	9	7	13	22	5	37	31	12	311	288	86	3rd, Adams Div.	Lost Div. Semi-Final
1984-85	80	21	15	4	15	19	6	36	34	10	303	287	82	4th, Adams Div.	Lost Div. Semi-Final
1983-84	80	25	12	3	24	13	3	49	25	6	336	261	104	1st, Adams Div.	Lost Div. Semi-Final
1982-83	80	28	6	6	22	14	4	50	20	10	327	228	110	1st, Adams Div.	Lost Conf. Championship
1981-82	80	24	12	4	19	15	6	43	27	10	323	285	96	2nd, Adams Div.	Lost Div. Final
1980-81	80	26	10	4	11	20	9	37	30	13	316	272	87	2nd, Adams Div.	Lost Prelim. Round
1979-80	80	27	9	4	19	12	9	46	21	13	310	234	105	2nd, Adams Div.	Lost Quarter-Final
1978-79	80	25	10	5	18	13	9	43	23	14	316	270	100	1st, Adams Div.	Lost Semi-Final
1977-78	80	29	6	5	22	12	6	51	18	11	333	218	113	1st, Adams Div.	Lost Final
1976-77	80	27	7	6	22	16	2	49	23	8	312	240	106	1st, Adams Div.	Lost Final
1975-76	80	27	5	8	21	10	9	48	15	17	313	237	113	1st, Adams Div.	Lost Semi-Final
1974-75	80	29	5	6	11	21	8	40	26	14	345	245	94	2nd, Adams Div.	Lost Prelim. Round
1973-74	78	33	4	2	19	13	7	52	17	9	349	221	113	1st, East Div.	Lost Final
1972-73	78	27	10	2	24	12	3	51	22	5	330	235	107	2nd, East Div.	Lost Quarter-Final
1971-72	78	28	4	7	26	9	4	**54**	**13**	**11**	**330**	**204**	**119**	**1st, East Div.**	**Won Stanley Cup**
1970-71	78	33	4	2	24	10	5	57	14	7	399	207	121	1st, East Div.	Lost Quarter-Final
1969-70	76	27	3	8	13	14	11	**40**	**17**	**19**	**277**	**216**	**99**	**2nd, East Div.**	**Won Stanley Cup**
1968-69	76	29	3	6	13	15	10	42	18	16	303	221	100	2nd, East Div.	Lost Semi-Final
1967-68	74	22	9	6	15	18	4	37	27	10	259	216	84	3rd, East Div.	Lost Quarter-Final
1966-67	70	10	21	4	7	22	6	17	43	10	182	253	44	6th,	Out of Playoffs
1965-66	70	15	17	3	6	26	3	21	43	6	174	275	48	5th,	Out of Playoffs
1964-65	70	12	17	6	9	26	0	21	43	6	166	253	48	6th,	Out of Playoffs
1963-64	70	13	15	7	5	25	5	18	40	12	170	212	48	6th,	Out of Playoffs
1962-63	70	7	18	10	7	21	7	14	39	17	198	281	45	6th,	Out of Playoffs
1961-62	70	9	22	4	6	25	4	15	47	8	177	306	38	6th,	Out of Playoffs
1960-61	70	13	17	5	2	25	8	15	42	13	176	254	43	6th,	Out of Playoffs
1959-60	70	21	11	3	7	23	5	28	34	8	220	241	64	5th,	Out of Playoffs
1958-59	70	21	11	3	11	18	6	32	29	9	205	215	73	2nd,	Lost Semi-Final
1957-58	70	15	14	6	12	14	9	27	28	15	199	194	69	4th,	Lost Final
1956-57	70	20	9	6	14	15	6	34	24	12	195	174	80	3rd,	Lost Final
1955-56	70	14	14	7	9	20	6	23	34	13	147	185	59	5th,	Out of Playoffs
1954-55	70	16	10	9	7	16	12	23	26	21	169	188	67	4th,	Lost Semi-Final
1953-54	70	22	8	5	10	20	5	32	28	10	177	181	74	4th,	Lost Semi-Final
1952-53	70	19	10	6	9	19	7	28	29	13	152	172	69	3rd,	Lost Final
1951-52	70	15	12	8	10	17	8	25	29	16	162	176	66	4th,	Lost Semi-Final
1950-51	70	13	12	10	9	18	8	22	30	18	178	197	62	4th,	Lost Semi-Final
1949-50	70	15	12	8	7	20	8	22	32	16	198	228	60	5th,	Out of Playoffs
1948-49	60	18	10	2	11	13	6	29	23	8	178	163	66	2nd,	Lost Semi-Final
1947-48	60	12	8	10	11	16	3	23	24	13	167	168	59	3rd,	Lost Semi-Final
1946-47	60	18	7	5	8	16	6	26	23	11	190	175	63	3rd,	Lost Semi-Final
1945-46	50	11	5	4	13	13	4	24	18	8	167	156	56	2nd,	Lost Final
1944-45	50	11	12	2	5	18	2	16	30	4	179	219	36	4th,	Lost Semi-Final
1943-44	50	15	8	2	4	18	3	19	26	5	223	268	43	5th,	Out of Playoffs
1942-43	50	17	3	5	7	14	4	24	17	9	195	176	57	2nd,	Lost Final
1941-42	48	17	4	3	8	13	3	25	17	6	160	118	56	3rd,	Lost Semi-Final
1940-41	48	15	4	5	12	4	8	**27**	**8**	**13**	**168**	**102**	**67**	**1st,**	**Won Stanley Cup**
1939-40	48	20	3	1	11	9	4	31	12	5	170	98	67	1st,	Lost Semi-Final
1938-39	48	20	2	2	16	8	0	**36**	**10**	**2**	**156**	**76**	**74**	**1st,**	**Won Stanley Cup**
1937-38	48	18	3	3	12	8	4	30	11	7	142	89	67	1st, Amn. Div.	Lost Semi-Final
1936-37	48	9	11	4	14	7	3	23	18	7	120	110	53	2nd, Amn. Div.	Lost Quarter-Final
1935-36	48	15	8	1	7	12	5	22	20	6	92	83	50	2nd, Amn. Div.	Lost Quarter-Final
1934-35	48	17	7	0	9	9	6	26	16	6	129	112	58	1st, Amn. Div.	Lost Semi-Final
1933-34	48	11	11	2	7	14	3	18	25	5	111	130	41	4th, Amn. Div.	Out of Playoffs
1932-33	48	20	2	3	5	13	5	25	15	8	124	88	58	1st, Amn. Div.	Lost Semi-Final
1931-32	48	11	10	3	4	11	9	15	21	12	122	117	42	4th, Amn. Div.	Out of Playoffs
1930-31	44	17	1	5	11	9	1	28	10	6	143	90	62	1st, Amn. Div.	Lost Semi-Final
1929-30	44	23	1	0	15	4	1	38	5	1	179	98	77	1st, Amn. Div.	Lost Final
1928-29	44	16	6	1	10	7	4	**26**	**13**	**5**	**89**	**52**	**57**	**1st, Amn. Div.**	**Won Stanley Cup**
1927-28	44	13	4	5	7	9	6	20	13	11	77	70	51	1st, Amn. Div.	Lost Semi-Final
1926-27	44	15	7	0	6	13	3	21	20	3	97	89	45	2nd, Amn. Div.	Lost final
1925-26	36	10	7	1	7	8	3	17	15	4	92	85	38	4th,	Out of Playoffs
1924-25	30	3	12	0	3	12	0	6	24	0	49	119	12	6th,	Out of Playoffs

1989-90 Player Personnel

FORWARDS	HT	WT	S	Place of Birth	Date	1988-89 Club
BERALDO, Paul	5-11	175	R	Hamilton, Ont.	10/5/67	Boston-Maine
BRICKLEY, Andy	5-11	200	L	Melrose, MA	8/9/61	Boston
BUDA, Dave	6-4	190	L	Mississauga, Ont.	3/14/66	Maine-Northeastern
BURRIDGE, Randy	5-9	180	L	Fort Erie, Ont.	1/7/66	Boston
BYERS, Lyndon	6-1	200	R	Nipawin, Sask.	2/29/64	Boston-Maine
CARPENTER, Bob	6-0	190	L	Beverly, MA	7/13/63	Los Angeles-Boston
CARTER, John	5-10	180	L	Winchester, MA	5/3/63	Boston-Maine
CIMETTA, Robert	6-0	190	L	Toronto, Ont.	2/15/70	Toronto-Boston
CRAWFORD, Lou	6-0	185	L	Belleville, Ont.	11/5/62	Adirondack
CRUICKSHANK, Gord	5-11	185	R	Mississauga, Ont.	5/4/65	Did Not Play
DOURIS, Peter	6-1	195	R	Toronto, Ont.	2/19/66	Peoria
HALL, Dean	6-1	175	L	Winnipeg, Man.	1/14/68	N. Michigan-Seattle
HARLOW, Scott	6-1	185	L	East Bridgewater, MA	10/11/63	Peoria-Maine
JANNEY, Craig	6-1	190	L	Hartford, CT	9/26/67	Boston
JENSEN, David	6-1	195	L	Newton, MA	8/19/65	Maine
JOHNSTON, Greg	6-1	205	R	Barrie, Ont.	1/14/65	Boston-Maine
JOYCE, Bobby	6-1	195	L	St. John, N.B.	7/11/66	Boston
KEKALAINEN, Jarmo	6-0	190	R	Kuopio, Finland	7/3/66	Clarkson
LALONDE, Todd	6-0	190	L	Sudbury, Ont.	8/4/69	Sudbury
LINSEMAN, Ken	5-11	180	L	Kingston, Ont.	8/11/58	Boston
MARKWART, Nevin	5-10	180	L	Toronto, Ont.	12/9/64	Maine
MONTANARI, Mark	5-9	185	L	Toronto, Ont.	6/3/69	Kitchener
NEELY, Cam	6-1	210	R	Comox, B.C.	6/6/65	Boston
NEUFELD, Ray	6-3	210	R	St. Boniface, Man.	4/15/59	Winnipeg-Boston
O'DWYER, Billy	6-0	190	L	South Boston, MA	1/25/60	Boston
PENNEY, Jackson	5-10	180	L	Edmonton, Alta.	2/5/69	Victoria
STEVENSON, Shayne	6-1	190	R	London, Ont.	10/26/70	Kitchener
SWEENEY, Bob	6-3	200	R	Concord, MA	1/25/64	Boston
TOWNSHEND, Graeme	6-2	225	R	Kingston, Jamaica	10/23/65	RPI-Maine
TURCOTTE, Alfie	5-11	185	L	Gary, IN	6/5/65	Moncton
WALZ, Wes	5-10	180	R	Calgary, Alta.	5/15/70	Lethbridge
DEFENSEMEN:						
ALLAIN, Rick	6-0	190	L	Guelph, Ont.	5/20/69	Kitchener
BEERS, Bob	6-2	200	R	Cheektowaga, NY	5/20/67	U/Maine
BLUM, John	6-3	205	R	Detroit, MI	10/8/ 59	Detroit-Adirondack
BOURQUE, Ray	5-11	210	L	Montreal, Que.	12/28/60	Boston
COTE, Alain	6-0	200	R	Montmagny, Que.	4/14/67	Boston-Maine
GALLEY, Garry	6-0	190	L	Montreal, Que.	4/16/63	Boston
HAWGOOD, Greg	5-8	175	L	Edmonton, Alta.	8/10/68	Boston-Maine
KLUZAK, Gord	6-4	215	L	Climax, Sask.	3/4/64	Boston
MOORE, Steve	6-2	185	R	Toronto, Ont.	1/21/67	R.P.I.
PEDERSEN, Allen	6-3	210	L	Ft. Saskatchewan, Alta.	1/13/65	Boston
QUINTAL, Stephane	6-3	215	R	Boucherville, Que.	10/22/68	Boston-Maine
SCHULMAN, Jeff	6-3	210	R	Buffalo, N.Y.	2/15/67	U/Vermont
SHOEBOTTOM, Bruce	6-2	200	L	Windsor, Ont.	8/20/65	Boston-Maine
SWEENEY, Don	5-11	170	L	St. Stephen, N.B.	8/17/66	Boston-Maine
THELVEN, Michael	5-11	185	R	Stockholm, Sweden	1/7/61	Boston
WESLEY, Glen	6-1	195	L	Red Deer, Alta.	10/2/68	Boston
WIEMER, Jim	6-4	210	L	Sudbury, Ont.	1/9/61	Cape Breton-Los Angeles-New Haven

GOALTENDERS	HT	WT	C	Place of Birth	Date	1988-89 Club
CAPRICE, Frank	5-9	165	L	Hamilton, Ont.	5/2/62	Milwaukee
FOSTER, Norm	5-9	175	L	Vancouver, B.C.	2/10/65	Maine
JEFFREY, Mike	6-3	195	R	Kamloops, B.C.	4/6/65	Maine
LEMELIN, Reggie	5-11	170	L	Quebec City, Que.	11/19/54	Boston
MOOG, Andy	5-8	170	L	Penticton, B.C.	2/18/60	Boston
PARSON, Mike	6-0	170	L	Listowel, Ont.	3/12/70	Guelph

Coaching History

Arthur H. Ross, 1924-25 to 1927-28; Cy Denneny, 1928-29; Arthur H. Ross, 1929-30 to 1933-34; Frank Patrick, 1934-35 to 1935-36; Arthur H. Ross, 1936-37 to 1938-39; Ralph (Cooney) Weiland, 1939-40 to 1940-41; Arthur H. Ross, 1941-42 to 1944-45; Aubrey V. (Dit) Clapper, 1945-46 to 1948-49; George (Buck) Boucher, 1949-50; Lynn Patrick, 1950-51 to 1953-54; Lynn Patrick and Milt Schmidt, 1954-55; Milt Schmidt, 1955-56 to 1960-61; Phil Watson, 1961-62; Phil Watson and Milt Schmidt, 1962-63; Milt Schmidt, 1963-64 to 1965-66; Harry Sinden, 1966-67 to 1969-70; Tom Johnson, 1970-71 to 1971-72; Tom Johnson and Bep Guidolin, 1972-73; Bep Guidolin, 1973-74; Don Cherry, 1974-75 to 1978-79; Fred Creighton and Harry Sinden, 1979-80; Gerry Cheevers, 1980-81 to 1983-84; Gerry Cheevers and Harry Sinden, 1984-85; Butch Goring, 1985-86; Butch Goring and Terry O'Reilly, 1986-87; Terry O'Reilly, 1987-88 to 1988-89; Mike Milbury, 1989-90.

Captains' History

No Captain, 1924-25 to 1926-27; Lionel Hitchman, 1927-28 to 1930-31; George Owen, 1931-32; Dit Clapper, 1932-33 to 1937-38; Cooney Weiland, 1938-39; Dit Clapper, 1939-40 to 1945-46; Dit Clapper, John Crawford, 1946-47; John Crawford 1947-48 to 1949-50; Milt Schmidt, 1950-51 to 1953-54; Milt Schmidt, Ed Sanford, 1954-55; Fern Flaman, 1955-56 to 1960-61; Don McKenney, 1961-62, 1962-63; Leo Boivin, 1963-64 to 1965-66; John Bucyk, 1966-67; no captain, 1967-68 to 1972-73; John Bucyk, 1973-74 to 1976-77; Wayne Cashman, 1977-78 to 1982-83; Terry O'Reilly, 1983-84, 1984-85; Ray Bourque, Rick Middleton (co-captains) 1985-86 to 1987-88; Ray Bourque, 1988-89 to date.

1988-89 Scoring

Regular Season

*–Rookie

Pos	#	Player	Team	GP	G	A	Pts	+/–	PIM	PP	SH	GW	OT	S	%
F	8	Cam Neely	BOS	74	37	38	75	14	190	18	0	6	1	235	15.7
F	13	Ken Linseman	BOS	78	27	45	72	15	164	13	1	2	1	159	17.0
F	23	*Craig Janney	BOS	62	16	46	62	20	12	2	0	2	0	95	16.8
F	12	Randy Burridge	BOS	80	31	30	61	19	39	6	2	6	1	189	16.4
D	77	Ray Bourque	BOS	60	18	43	61	20	52	6	0	0	1	243	7.4
D	26	Glen Wesley	BOS	77	19	35	54	23	61	8	1	1	1	181	10.5
F	27	*Bob Joyce	BOS	77	18	31	49	8	46	7	0	3	0	142	12.7
D	38	*Greg Hawgood	BOS	56	16	24	40	4	84	5	0	0	1	132	12.1
F	11	Bob Carpenter	L.A.	39	11	15	26	3	16	3	0	1	0	91	12.1
			BOS	18	5	9	14	4	10	1	0	2	0	46	10.9
			TOTAL	57	16	24	40	7	26	4	0	3	0	137	11.7
F	25	Andy Brickley	BOS	71	13	22	35	4	20	2	0	3	1	98	13.3
F	18	Keith Crowder	BOS	69	15	18	33	6	147	5	0	2	0	121	12.4
D	28	Garry Galley	BOS	78	8	21	29	7–	80	2	1	0	0	145	5.5
F	42	Bob Sweeney	BOS	75	14	14	28	19–	99	2	1	3	0	117	12.0
F	31	*John Carter	BOS	44	12	10	22	1–	24	4	1	0	0	96	12.5
F	39	Greg Johnston	BOS	57	11	10	21	7	32	0	1	5	0	89	12.4
D	22	Michael Thelven	BOS	40	3	18	21	10	71	1	1	0	0	68	4.4
F	19	Ray Neufeld	WPG	31	5	2	7	9–	52	0	0	0	0	47	10.6
			BOS	14	1	3	4	2–	28	0	0	0	0	16	6.3
			TOTAL	45	6	5	11	11–	80	0	0	0	0	63	9.5
D	32	*Don Sweeney	BOS	36	3	5	8	6–	20	0	0	0	0	35	8.6
F	20	*Tom Lehmann	BOS	26	4	2	6	7–	10	1	1	1	0	26	15.4
D	41	Allen Pedersen	BOS	51	0	6	6	3–	69	0	0	0	0	24	.0
D	33	Alain Cote	BOS	31	2	3	5	9–	51	0	0	0	0	45	4.4
D	40	*Bruce Shoebottom	BOS	29	1	3	4	5	44	0	0	0	0	19	5.3
F	34	Lyndon Byers	BOS	49	0	4	4	8–	218	0	0	0	0	25	.0
F	10	Bill O'Dwyer	BOS	19	1	2	3	4–	8	0	0	0	0	18	5.6
F	14	Robert Cimetta	BOS	7	2	0	2	4–	0	0	0	1	0	4	50.0
F	37	Paul Guay	L.A.	2	0	0	0	2–	2	0	0	0	0	2	.0
			BOS	5	0	2	2	0	0	0	0	0	0	1	.0
			TOTAL	7	0	2	2	2–	2	0	0	0	0	3	.0
D	6	Gord Kluzak	BOS	3	0	1	1	2–	2	0	0	0	0	4	.0
F	43	*Ray Podloski	BOS	8	0	1	1	1–	22	0	0	0	0	3	.0
D	21	*Stephane Quintal	BOS	26	0	1	1	5–	29	0	0	0	0	23	.0
G	1	Rejean Lemelin	BOS	40	0	1	1	0	6	0	0	0	0	0	.0
G	35	Andy Moog	BOS	41	0	1	1	0	6	0	0	0	0	0	.0
D	45	*Dale Dunbar	BOS	1	0	0	0	0	0	0	0	0	0	2	.0
F	36	Ron Flockhart	BOS	4	0	0	0	3–	0	0	0	0	0	3	.0
F	30	*Paul Beraldo	BOS	7	0	0	0	2–	4	0	0	0	0	1	.0
F	45	Carl Mokosak	BOS	7	0	0	0	2	31	0	0	0	0	3	.0

Goaltending

No.	Goaltender	GPI	Mins	Avg	W	L	T	EN	SO	GA	SA	S%
1	Rejean Lemelin	40	2392	3.01	19	15	6	3	0	120	1061	.887
35	Andy Moog	41	2482	3.22	18	14	8	0	1	133	1079	.877
	Totals	**80**	**4882**	**3.15**	**37**	**29**	**14**	**3**	**1**	**256**	**2140**	**.880**

Playoffs

Pos	#	Player	Team	GP	G	A	Pts	+/–	PIM	PP	SH	GW	GT	S	%
F	23	*Craig Janney	BOS	10	4	9	13	1	21	0	0	0	0	23	17.4
F	8	Cam Neely	BOS	10	7	2	9	2–	8	4	0	2	0	24	29.2
D	22	Michael Thelven	BOS	10	1	7	8	4	8	0	0	1	0	17	5.9
F	27	*Bob Joyce	BOS	9	5	2	7	0	2	0	0	0	0	13	38.5
F	12	Randy Burridge	BOS	10	5	2	7	6	8	1	1	0	0	22	22.7
F	42	Bob Sweeney	BOS	10	2	4	6	4	19	0	0	0	0	14	14.3
F	19	Ray Neufeld	BOS	10	2	3	5	3	9	0	0	1	0	14	14.3
D	77	Ray Bourque	BOS	10	0	4	4	1–	6	0	0	0	0	40	.0
F	31	*John Carter	BOS	10	1	2	3	1	6	0	0	0	0	16	6.3
F	11	Bob Carpenter	BOS	8	1	1	2	6–	4	1	0	1	0	19	5.3
F	25	Andy Brickley	BOS	10	0	2	2	6–	0	0	0	0	0	6	.0
F	18	Keith Crowder	BOS	10	0	2	2	4	37	0	0	0	0	7	.0
D	38	*Greg Hawgood	BOS	10	0	2	2	3–	2	0	0	0	0	11	.0
D	40	*Bruce Shoebottom	BOS	10	0	2	2	0	35	0	0	0	0	1	.0
D	26	Glen Wesley	BOS	10	0	2	2	0	4	0	0	0	0	14	.0
F	39	Greg Johnston	BOS	10	1	0	1	4–	6	0	1	0	0	16	6.3
G	35	Andy Moog	BOS	6	0	1	1	0	0	0	0	0	0	0	.0
D	28	Garry Galley	BOS	9	0	1	1	2	33	0	0	0	0	16	.0
F	14	*Robert Cimetta	BOS	1	0	0	0	0	15	0	0	0	0	0	.0
F	45	Carl Mokosak	BOS	1	0	0	0	0	0	0	0	0	0	0	.0
F	34	Lyndon Byers	BOS	2	0	0	0	1–	0	0	0	0	0	0	.0
G	1	Rejean Lemelin	BOS	4	0	0	0	0	2	0	0	0	0	0	.0
D	41	Allen Pedersen	BOS	10	0	0	0	2–	2	0	0	0	0	1	.0

Goaltending

No.	Goaltender	GPI	Mins	Avg	W	L	EN	SO	GA	SA	S%
35	Andy Moog	6	359	2.34	4	2	0	0	14	136	.897
1	Rejean Lemelin	4	252	3.81	1	3	0	0	16	112	.857
	Totals	**10**	**612**	**2.94**	**5**	**5**	**0**	**0**	**30**	**248**	**.879**

General Managers' History

Arthur H. Ross, 1924-25 to 1953-54; Lynn Patrick, 1954-55 to 1964-65; Leighton "Hap" Emms, 1965-66 to 1966-67; Milt Schmidt, 1967-68 to 1971-72; Harry Sinden, 1972-73 to date.

Retired Numbers

2	Eddie Shore	1926-1940
3	Lionel Hitchman	1925-1934
4	Bobby Orr	1966-1976
5	Dit Clapper	1927-1947
7	Phil Esposito	1967-1975
9	John Bucyk	1957-1978
15	Milt Schmidt	1936-1955

Club Records

Team

(Figures in brackets for season records are games played; records for fewest points, wins, ties, losses, goals, goals against are for 70 or more games)

Most Points	**121**	1970-71 (78)
Most Wins	**57**	1970-71 (78)
Most Ties	**21**	1954-55 (70)
Most Losses	**47**	1961-62 (70)
Most Goals	**399**	1970-71 (78)
Most Goals Against	**306**	1961-62 (70)
Fewest Points	**38**	1961-62 (70)
Fewest Wins	**14**	1962-63 (70)
Fewest Ties	**5**	1972-73 (78)
Fewest Losses	**13**	1971-72 (78)
Fewest Goals	**147**	1955-56 (70)
Fewest Goals Against	**172**	1952-53 (70)
Longest Winning Streak		
Over-all	**14**	Dec. 3/29-Jan. 9/30
Home	***20**	Dec. 3/29-Mar. 18/30
Away	**8**	Feb. 17-Mar. 8/72
Longest Undefeated Streak		
Over-all	**23**	Dec. 22/40-Feb. 23/41 (15 wins, 8 ties)
Home	**27**	Nov. 22/70-Mar. 20/71 (26 wins, 1 tie)
Away	**15**	Dec. 22/40-Mar. 16/41 (9 wins, 6 ties)
Longest Losing Streak		
Over-all	**11**	Dec. 3/24-Jan. 5/25
Home	***11**	Dec. 8/24-Feb. 17/25
Away	**14**	Dec. 27/64-Feb. 21/65
Longest Winless Streak		
Over-all	**20**	Jan. 28-Mar. 11/62 (16 losses, 4 ties)
Home	**11**	Dec. 8/24-Feb. 17/25 (11 losses)
Away	**14**	Three times
Most Shutouts, Season	**15**	1927-28 (44)
Most Pen. Mins., Season	**2,443**	1987-88 (80)
Most Goals, Game	**14**	Jan. 21/45 (NYR 3 at Bos. 14)

Individual

Most Seasons	**21**	John Bucyk
Most Games	**1,436**	John Bucyk
Most Goals, Career	**545**	John Bucyk
Most Assists, Career	**794**	John Bucyk
Most Points, Career	**1,339**	John Bucyk (545 goals, 794 assists)
Most Pen. Mins., Career	**2,095**	Terry O'Reilly
Most Shutouts, Career	**74**	Tiny Thompson
Longest Consecutive Games Streak	**418**	John Bucyk (Jan. 23/69-Mar. 2/75)
Most Goals, Season	**76**	Phil Esposito (1970-71)
Most Assists, Season	**102**	Bobby Orr (1970-71)
Most Points, Season	**152**	Phil Esposito (1970-71) (76 goals, 76 assists)
Most Pen. Mins., Season	**302**	Jay Miller (1987-88)
Most Points, Defenseman Season	***139**	Bobby Orr (1970-71) (37 goals, 102 assists)
Most Points, Center Season	**152**	Phil Esposito (1970-71) (76 goals, 76 assists)
Most Points, Right Wing Season	**105**	Ken Hodge (1970-71) (43 goals, 62 assists); Ken Hodge (1973-74) (50 goals, 55 assists); Rick Middleton (1983-84) (47 goals, 58 assists)
Most Points, Left Wing Season	**116**	John Bucyk (1970-71) (51 goals, 65 assists)
Most Points, Rookie Season	**92**	Barry Pederson (1981-82) (44 goals, 48 assists)
Most Shutouts, Season	**15**	Hal Winkler (1927-28)
Most Goals, Game	**4**	Several players
Most Assists, Game	**6**	Ken Hodge (Feb. 9/71); Bobby Orr (Jan. 1/73)
Most Points, Game	**7**	Bobby Orr (Nov. 15/73); Phil Esposito (Dec. 19/74); Barry Pederson (Apr. 4/82); Cam Neely (Oct. 16/88)

* NHL Record.

All-time Record vs. Other Clubs

Regular Season

	At Home							On Road							Total						
	GP	W	L	T	GF	GA	PTS	GP	W	L	T	GF	GA	PTS	GP	W	L	T	GF	GA	PTS
Buffalo	64	39	18	7	275	193	85	63	20	32	11	206	242	51	127	59	50	18	481	435	136
**Calgary	32	20	9	3	112	88	43	32	18	12	2	121	117	38	64	38	21	5	233	205	81
Chicago	270	156	82	32	982	758	344	271	89	138	44	721	875	222	541	245	220	76	1703	1633	566
Detroit	273	148	82	43	961	717	339	272	72	148	52	683	910	196	545	220	230	95	1644	1627	535
Edmonton	16	12	2	2	74	42	26	16	7	7	2	55	58	16	32	19	9	4	129	100	42
Hartford	36	24	8	4	152	97	52	36	13	19	4	130	139	30	72	37	27	8	282	236	82
Los Angeles	47	36	8	3	226	125	75	47	27	15	5	182	156	59	94	63	23	8	408	281	134
Minnesota	47	35	5	7	215	107	77	47	27	11	9	182	127	63	94	62	16	16	397	234	140
Montreal	290	131	108	51	854	779	313	289	78	169	42	657	989	198	579	209	277	93	1511	1768	511
New Jersey	26	18	7	1	121	81	37	26	16	2	8	105	66	40	52	34	9	9	226	147	77
NY Islanders	32	17	7	8	124	93	42	32	17	13	2	108	100	36	64	34	20	10	232	193	78
NY Rangers	271	149	84	38	993	754	336	273	102	118	53	764	825	257	544	251	202	91	1757	1579	593
Philadelphia	46	31	9	6	198	137	68	45	19	20	6	138	156	44	91	50	29	12	336	293	112
Pittsburgh	47	36	6	5	220	129	77	47	25	12	10	189	140	60	94	61	18	15	409	269	137
Quebec	36	16	15	5	142	128	37	36	20	13	3	163	144	43	72	36	28	8	305	272	80
St. Louis	45	31	8	6	210	120	68	45	19	17	9	159	139	47	90	50	25	15	369	259	115
Toronto	273	146	80	47	901	733	339	274	84	144	46	703	928	214	547	230	224	93	1604	1661	553
Vancouver	37	32	2	3	172	79	67	37	20	10	7	160	124	47	74	52	12	10	332	203	114
Washington	28	18	7	3	117	71	39	28	14	7	7	109	83	35	56	32	14	10	226	154	74
Winnipeg	16	12	2	2	81	54	26	16	9	6	1	60	55	19	32	21	8	3	141	109	45
Defunct Clubs	164	112	39	13	525	306	237	164	79	67	18	496	440	176	328	191	106	31	1021	746	413
Total	**2096**	**1219**	**588**	**289**	**7655**	**5591**	**2727**	**2096**	**775**	**980**	**341**	**6091**	**6813**	**1889**	**4192**	**1994**	**1568**	**630**	**13746**	**12404**	**4618**

* Totals include those of Kansas City (1974-75, 1975-76) and Colorado (1976-77 through 1981-82)
** Totals include those of Atlanta (1972-73 through 1979-80)

Playoffs

	Series	W	L	GP	W	L	T	GF	GA	Last Mtg.	Round	Result
Buffalo	4	4	0	22	15	7	0	94	70	1989	DSF	W 4-1
Chicago	6	5	1	22	16	5	1	97	63	1978	QF	W 4-0
Detroit	7	4	3	33	19	14	0	96	98	1957	SF	W 4-1
Edmonton	1	0	1	4	0	4	0	12	21	1988	F	L 4-0
Los Angeles	2	2	0	13	8	5	0	56	38	1977	QF	W 4-2
Minnesota	1	0	1	3	0	3	0	13	20	1981	P	L 0-3
Montreal	24	3	21	116	36	80	0	269	372	1989	DF	L 1-4
New Jersey	1	1	0	7	4	3	0	30	19	1988	CF	W 4-3
NY Islanders	2	0	2	11	3	8	0	35	49	1983	CF	L 2-4
NY Rangers	9	6	3	42	22	18	2	114	104	1973	QF	L 1-4
Philadelphia	4	2	2	20	11	9	0	60	57	1978	QF	W 4-1
Pittsburgh	2	2	0	9	7	2	0	37	21	1980	P	W 3-2
Quebec	2	1	1	11	6	5	0	37	36	1983	DSF	W 3-1
St. Louis	2	2	0	8	8	0	0	48	15	1972	SF	W 4-0
Toronto	13	5	8	62	30	31	1	153	150	1974	QF	W 4-0
Defunct Clubs	3	1	2	11	4	5	2	20	20			
Totals	**83**	**38**	**45**	**394**	**189**	**199**	**6**	**1171**	**1153**			

Playoff Results 1989-85

Year	Round	Opponent	Result	GF	GA
1989	DF	Montreal	1-4	13	16
	DSF	Buffalo	4-1	16	14
1988	F	Edmonton	L 0-4	12	21
	CF	New Jersey	W 4-3	30	19
	DSF	Montreal	W 4-1	15	10
	DSF	Buffalo	W 4-2	28	22
1987	DSF	Montreal	L 0-4	11	19
1986	DSF	Montreal	L 0-3	6	10
1985	DSF	Montreal	L 2-3	17	19

Abbreviations: Round: F – Final; **CF** – conference final; **DF** – division final; **DSF** – division semi-final; **SF** – semi-final; **QF** – quarter-final. **P** – preliminary round. **GA** – goals against; **GF** – goals for.

1988-89 Results

Home				Away			
Oct.	6	Toronto	2-1	**Oct**	8	Hartford	6-2
	9	Hartford	3-1		12	Los Angeles	2-6
	25	Montreal	1-1		15	Minnesota	1-5
	27	Quebec	6-2		16	Chicago	10-3
	29	Buffalo	3-3		19	Winnipeg	5-2
Nov.	3	Hartford	3-5		22	St Louis	5-2
	6	Vancouver	4-2		30	Buffalo	3-3
	12	Calgary	1-2	**Nov.**	2	Toronto	7-2
	17	Montreal	2-5		11	NY Rangers	4-4
	20	Detroit	4-5		15	Quebec	5-5
	24	Philadelphia	2-1		18	Detroit	2-5
	26	Chicago	8-2		23	Montreal	0-2
Dec.	1	Minnesota	1-4		29	Philadelphia	1-5
	4	Pittsburgh	3-3	**Dec.**	3	Washington	1-1
	8	Buffalo	2-4		6	NY Islanders	4-3
	10	NY Rangers*	1-1		12	Montreal	1-3
	15	Edmonton	4-3		18	Quebec*	2-4
	17	Quebec*	2-2		21	Hartford	4-3
	22	Montreal	2-4		26	Buffalo	1-2
Jan.	2	St Louis	8-7		29	New Jersey	6-2
	5	NY Islanders	3-5	**Jan.**	7	Montreal	1-3
	12	Montreal	3-5		8	Quebec	4-2
	14	Detroit*	5-5		15	Washington*	4-3
	19	Calgary	2-7		22	Buffalo*	4-6
	21	Buffalo*	5-6		25	Toronto	2-1
	26	St Louis	4-2	**Feb.**	1	Minnesota	4-4
	28	Winnipeg*	3-4		3	Winnipeg	4-2
Feb.	5	Pittsburgh*	2-5		14	Vancouver	2-5
	9	Los Angeles	4-1		15	Los Angeles	7-3
	11	Edmonton*	5-2		18	Calgary	4-3
Mar.	2	Quebec	5-2		19	Edmonton	4-2
	4	Vancouver*	6-4		25	Hartford	9-1
	9	Washington	2-7		28	New Jersey	3-3
	11	Buffalo*	6-6	**Mar.**	5	NY Rangers	5-0
	16	Quebec	2-2		7	NY Islanders	2-1
	18	Philadelphia*	6-3		12	Buffalo	2-3
	19	Hartford	2-3		14	Pittsburgh	8-2
	23	New Jersey	5-3		22	Hartford	2-4
	25	Chicago*	6-3		27	Montreal	2-5
Apr.	2	Hartford	3-2	**Apr.**	1	Quebec*	5-4

* Denotes afternoon game.

Entry Draft
Selections 1989-75

1989
Pick
17 Shayne Stevenson
38 Mike Parson
57 Wes Walz
80 Jackson Penney
101 Mark Montanari
122 Stephen Foster
143 Otto Hascak
164 Rick Allain
185 James Lavish
206 Geoff Simpson
227 David Franzosa

1988
Pick
18 Robert Cimetta
60 Stephen Heinze
81 Joe Juneau
102 Daniel Murphy
123 Derek Geary
165 Mark Krys
186 Jon Rohloff
228 Eric Reisman
249 Doug Jones

1987
Pick
3 Glen Wesley
14 Stephane Quintal
56 Todd Lalonde
67 Darwin McPherson
77 Matt Delguidice
98 Ted Donato
119 Matt Glennon
140 Rob Cheevers
161 Chris Winnes
182 Paul Ohman
203 Casey Jones
224 Eric Lemarque
245 Sean Gorman

1986
Pick
13 Craig Janney
34 Pekka Tirkkonen
76 Dean Hall
97 Matt Pesklewis
118 Garth Premak
139 Paul Beraldo
160 Brian Ferreira
181 Jeff Flaherty
202 Greg Hawgood
223 Steffan Malmquist
244 Joel Gardner

1985
Pick
31 Alain Cote
52 Bill Ranford
73 Jaime Kelly
94 Steve Moore
115 Gord Hynes
136 Per Martinele
157 Randy Burridge
178 Gord Cruickshank
199 Dave Buda
210 Bob Beers
220 John Byce
241 Marc West

1984
Pick
19 Dave Pasin
40 Ray Podloski
61 Jeff Cornelius
82 Robert Joyce
103 Mike Bishop
124 Randy Oswald
145 Mark Thietke
166 Don Sweeney
186 Kevin Heffernan
207 J.D. Urbanic
227 Bill Kopecky
248 Jim Newhouse

1983
Pick
21 Nevin Markwart
42 Greg Johnston
62 Greg Puhalski
82 Alain Larochelle
102 Allen Pederson
122 Terry Taillefor
142 Ian Armstrong
162 Francois Olivier
182 Harri Laurilla
202 Paul Fitzsimmons
222 Norm Foster
242 Greg Murphy

1982
Pick
1 Gord Kluzak
22 Brian Curran
39 Lyndon Byers
60 Dave Reid
102 Bob Nicholson
123 Bob Sweeney
144 John Meulenbrooks
165 Tony Fiore
186 Doug Kostynski
207 Tony Gilliard
228 Tommy Lehmann
249 Bruno Campese

1981
Pick
14 Normand Leveille
35 Luc Dufour
77 Scott McLellan
98 Joe Mantione
119 Bruce Milton
140 Mats Thelin
161 Armel Parisee
182 Don Sylvester
203 Richard Bourque

1980
Pick
18 Barry Pederson
60 Tom Fergus
81 Steve Kasper
102 Randy Hillier
123 Steve Lyons
144 Tony McMurchy
165 Mike Moffat
186 Michael Thelven
207 Jens Ohling

1979
Pick
8 Ray Bourque
15 Brad McCrimmon
36 Doug Morrison
57 Keith Crowder
78 Larry Melnyk
99 Marco Baron
120 Mike Krushelnyski

1978
Pick
16 Al Secord
35 Graeme Nicolson
52 Brad Knelson
68 George Buat
85 Darryl MacLeod
102 Jeff Brubaker
119 Murray Skinner
136 Robert Hehir
153 Craig MacTavish

1977
Pick
16 Dwight Foster
34 Dave Parro
52 Mike Forbes
70 Brian McGregor
88 Doug Butler
106 Keith Johnson
122 Ralph Cox
138 Mario Claude

1976
Pick
16 Clayton Pachal
34 Larry Gloeckner
70 Bob Miller
88 Peter Vandermark
106 Ted Olson

1975
Pick
14 Doug Halward
32 Barry Smith
60 Rick Adduono
68 Denis Daigle
86 Stan Jonathan
104 Matti Hagman
122 Gary Carr
140 Bo Berglund
156 Joe Rando
171 Kevin Nugent

Club Directory

Boston Garden
150 Causeway Street
Boston, Massachusetts 02114
Phone 617/227-3206
FAX 617/523-7184
ENVOY ID
Front Office: BRUINS. GM
Public
Relations: BRUINS. PR
Capacity: 14,448

Executive
Owner and Governor . . . . Jeremy M. Jacobs
Chief Operating Officer . . . . Louis Reif
Alternative Governor . . . . Louis Jacobs
Alternative Governor, President and General
Manager . . . . Harry Sinden
Vice President . . . . Tom Johnson
Assistant to the President . . . . Nate Greenberg
Director of Administration . . . . Dale Hamilton
Administrative Assistant . . . . Carol Gould

Coaching Staff
Assistant General Manager and Coach . . . . . . Mike Milbury
Assistant Coaches . . . . Gordie Clark, Ted Sator
Goaltending Coach . . . . Joe Bertagna
Coach, Maine Mariners (AHL) . . . . Rick Bowness

Scouting Staff
Coordinator of Minor League Player Personnel/
Scouting . . . . Bob Tindall
Director of Player Evaluation . . . . Bart Bradley, Jean Ratelle
Scouting Staff . . . . Jim Morrison (Ontario),
Andre Lachapelle (Quebec),
Joe Lyons (New England),
Don Saatzer (Minnesota),
Lars Waldner (Europe),
Marcel Pelletier (Pro Consultant),
Jean Ratelle (College & High School)

Communications Staff
Director of Media Relations . . . . Heidi Holland
Director of Community Relations, Marketing
Services . . . . Sue Byrne
Director of Player & Alumni Community
Relations . . . . John Bucyk
Administrative Assistant . . . . Marilyn Viola
Video Production . . . . Joe Curnane

Medical and Training Staff
Athletic Trainer . . . . Jim Narrigan
Athletic Therapist . . . . Don Worden
Equipment Manager . . . . Ken Fleger
Assistant Equipment Manager . . . . Eric Anderson
Medical Coordinator . . . . Dr. Richard Weiss
Team Physicians . . . . Dr. John J. Boyle, Dr. Ashby Moncure,
Dr. Bertram Zarins
Team Dentists . . . . Dr. Robert Thomas and Dr. Richard Miner
Team Psychologist . . . . Dr. Fred Neff

Ticketing and Finance Staff
Director of Ticket Operations . . . . Matt Brennan
Assistant Director of Ticket Operations . . . . . . Jim Foley
Receptionist . . . . Linda Bartlett
Controller . . . . John J. Dionne
Accounting Manager . . . . Richard McGlinchey
Accounts Payable . . . . Barbara Johnson

Television and Radio
Broadcasters (TV-38) . . . . Fred Cusick and Derek Sanderson
Broadcasters (NESN) . . . . Fred Cusick, Derek Sanderson and
Dave Shea
Broadcasters (Radio) . . . . Bob Wilson and John Bucyk
TV Channels . . . . New England Sports Network (Home Games)
and WSBK TV-38 (Road Games)
Radio Station . . . . WPLM (99.1 FM, 1390 AM) and
Bruins Radio Network
Dimensions of Rink . . . . 191 feet by 83 feet
Club Colors . . . . Gold, Black and White
Training Camp Site . . . . Wilmington, MA.

General Manager

SINDEN, HARRY JAMES
President and General Manager, Boston Bruins.
Born in Collins Bay, Ont., September 14, 1932.

Harry Sinden never played a game in the NHL but stepped into the Bruins' organization with an impressive coaching background in minor professional hockey and his continued excellence has earned him a place in the Hockey Hall of Fame as one of the true builders in hockey history. In 1965-66 as playing-coach of Oklahoma City Blazers in the CPHL, Sinden led the club to second place in the regular standings and then to eight straight playoff victories for the Jack Adams Trophy. After five years in OHA Senior hockey — including 1958 with the World Amateur Champion Whitby Dunlops — Sinden was named playing-coach in the old Eastern Professional League and its successor, the Central Professional League. Under his guidance, the Bruins of 1967-68 made the playoffs for the first time in nine seasons, finishing third in the East Division, and were nosed out of first place in 1968-69 by Montreal. In 1969-70, Sinden led the Bruins to their first Stanley Cup win since 1940-41. The following season he went into private business but returned to the hockey scene in the summer of 1972 when he was appointed coach of Team Canada. He moulded that group of NHL stars into a powerful unit and led them into an exciting eight-game series against the Soviet national team in September of 1972. Team Canada emerged the winner by a narrow margin with a record of four wins, three losses and one tie. Sinden then returned to the Bruins organization early in the 1972-73 season. Sinden took over as the Bruins' coach in February 1985, after replacing Gerry Cheevers. Boston finished 11-10-3 with Sinden behind the bench before being defeated by Montreal in five games in the Adams Division semi-finals.

Coach

MILBURY, MIKE
Coach, Boston Bruins. Born in Brighton, Mass., June 17, 1952.

Milbury was named the 18th Head Coach of the Bruins on May 16, 1989 after spending two seasons as General Manager and Coach of the Bruins' AHL affiliate—the Maine Mariners. In his first year with the Mariners (1987-88), he led them to the Northern Division Championship and was named the Hockey News' Minor League Coach of the Year and co-winner of the AHL Coach of the Year.

Milbury has spent his entire professional career in the Bruins' organization since signing as a free agent out of Colgate University on November 5, 1974. He first retired as a player on May 6, 1985 and was named the Bruins' assistant coach under Butch Goring, but injuries late in the season saw his return to the Boston blueline. He won his first game as an NHL co-coach with Terry O'Reilly on November 8, 1986 and assumed the title of player-assistant coach on November 14, 1986 when O'Reilly took the head coaching job. His 14-year playing career came to a conclusion on July 16, 1987 when he was named to the Maine position. He finished his playing career with 49-189-238 totals in 754 games, ranking tenth on the Bruins' all-time games played list.

Coaching Record

Season	Team	Games	Regular Season W	L	T	%	Playoffs Games	W	L	%
1987-88	Maine (AHL)	80	44	29	7	.594	10	5	5	.500
1988-89	Maine (AHL)	80	32	40	8	.450	....	....	....	....

Buffalo Sabres

1988-89 Results: 38w-35L-7T 83 PTS. Third, Adams Division

Year-by-Year Record

Season	GP	Home W	L	T	Road W	L	T	W	L	Overall T	GF	GA	Pts.	Finished	Playoff Result
1988-89	80	25	12	3	13	23	4	38	35	7	291	299	83	3rd, Adams Div.	Lost Div. Semi-Final
1987-88	80	19	14	7	18	18	4	37	32	11	283	305	85	3rd, Adams Div.	Lost Div. Semi-Final
1986-87	80	18	18	4	10	26	4	28	44	8	280	308	64	5th, Adams Div.	Out of Playoffs
1985-86	80	23	16	1	14	21	5	37	37	6	296	291	80	5th, Adams Div.	Out of Playoffs
1984-85	80	23	10	7	15	18	7	38	28	14	290	237	90	3rd, Adams Div.	Lost Div. Semi-Final
1983-84	80	25	9	6	23	16	1	48	25	7	315	257	103	2nd, Adams Div.	Lost Div. Semi-Final
1982-83	80	25	7	8	13	22	5	38	29	13	318	285	89	3rd, Adams Div.	Lost Div. Final
1981-82	80	23	8	9	16	18	6	39	26	15	307	273	93	3rd, Adams Div.	Lost Div. Semi-Final
1980-81	80	21	7	12	18	13	9	39	20	21	327	250	99	1st, Adams Div.	Lost Quarter-Final
1979-80	80	27	5	8	20	12	8	47	17	16	318	201	110	1st, Adams Div.	Lost Semi-Final
1978-79	80	19	13	8	17	15	8	36	28	16	280	263	88	2nd, Adams Div.	Lost Prelim. Round
1977-78	80	25	7	8	19	12	9	44	19	17	288	215	105	2nd, Adams Div.	Lost Quarter-Final
1976-77	80	27	8	5	21	16	3	48	24	8	301	220	104	2nd, Adams Div.	Lost Quarter-Final
1975-76	80	28	7	5	18	14	8	46	21	13	339	240	105	2nd, Adams Div.	Lost Quarter-Final
1974-75	80	28	6	6	21	10	9	49	16	15	354	240	113	1st, Adams Div.	Lost Final
1973-74	78	24	10	6	9	24	6	32	34	12	242	250	76	5th, East Div.	Out of Playoffs
1972-73	78	30	6	3	7	21	11	37	27	14	257	219	88	4th, East Div.	Lost Quarter-Final
1971-72	78	11	19	9	5	24	10	16	43	19	203	289	51	6th, East Div.	Out of Playoffs
1970-71	78	16	13	10	8	26	5	24	39	15	217	291	63	5th, East Div.	Out of Playoffs

Schedule

	Home			Away
Oct.	Thur. 5 Quebec		**Oct.**	Sat. 7 Montreal
	Sun. 8 Minnesota			Wed. 11 Toronto
	Fri. 13 Hartford			Sat. 14 Detroit
	Fri. 20 Montreal			Wed. 18 Hartford
	Fri. 27 Toronto			Sat. 21 Pittsburgh
	Sun. 29 Boston			Wed. 25 Minnesota
Nov.	Sun. 5 Los Angeles		**Nov.**	Thur. 2 Montreal
	Fri. 10 Vancouver			Sat. 4 Boston
	Sun. 12 Edmonton			Wed. 8 Hartford
	Wed. 22 NY Rangers			Thur. 16 Calgary
	Sun. 26 Hartford			Fri. 17 Edmonton
Dec.	Fri. 1 New Jersey			Sun. 19 Vancouver
	Sun. 3 St Louis			Sat. 25 Quebec
	Sun. 10 Washington			Tues. 28 Hartford
	Wed. 13 Boston			Thur. 30 Boston
	Sun. 17 Philadelphia		**Dec.**	Tues. 5 NY Islanders
	Fri. 22 Montreal			Thur. 7 Philadelphia
	Tues. 26 Detroit			Sat. 16 Boston*
	Fri. 29 Boston			Wed. 20 NY Rangers
	Sun. 31 NY Islanders			Sat. 23 Quebec
Jan.	Sun. 7 Boston		**Jan.**	Tues. 2 New Jersey
	Fri. 19 Washington			Sat. 6 Montreal
	Fri. 26 Chicago			Thur. 11 Calgary
	Sun. 28 Pittsburgh*			Sat. 13 Vancouver
	Wed. 31 Quebec			Tues. 16 Los Angeles
Feb.	Sun. 4 NY Islanders			Tues. 23 Philadelphia
	Wed. 7 Montreal			Wed. 24 Chicago
	Fri. 9 NY Rangers			Tues. 30 Quebec
	Fri. 16 Montreal		**Feb.**	Sat. 3 Montreal
	Sun. 18 Hartford			Sun. 11 St Louis
	Fri. 23 Hartford			Tues. 13 Chicago
	Sun. 25 Winnipeg			Tues. 20 Winnipeg
Mar.	Sun. 4 Quebec			Wed. 21 Edmonton
	Wed. 14 Los Angeles			Tues. 27 St Louis
	Fri. 16 Toronto		**Mar.**	Sat. 3 Quebec
	Sun. 18 Winnipeg			Tues. 6 Washington
	Wed. 21 Calgary			Thur. 8 Boston
	Sun. 25 New Jersey*			Sat. 10 Hartford
	Thur. 29 Minnesota			Tues. 27 Detroit
Apr.	Sun. 1 Quebec			Sat. 31 Pittsburgh

* Denotes afternoon game.

Home Starting Times:

Weeknights . . . . 7:35 p.m.
Sundays . . . . 7:05 p.m.
Matinees . . . . 2:05 p.m.

Franchise date: May 22, 1970

20th NHL Season

Rick Vaive, acquired in mid-season from Chicago, scored 19 goals in 28 games with the Sabres.

1989-90 Player Personnel

FORWARDS	HT	WT	S	Place of Birth	Date	1988-89 Club
ANDERSSON, Mikael	5-11	183	L	Malmo, Sweden	5/10/66	Rochester-Buffalo
ANDREYCHUK, Dave	6-3	214	R	Hamilton, Ont.	9/29/63	Buffalo
ARNIEL, Scott	6-1	188	L	Kingston, Ont.	7/17/62	Buffalo
AUDETTE, Donald	5-8	182	R	Laval, Que.	9/23/69	Laval
BOYCE, Ian	5-8	177	R	St. Laurent, Que.	1/24/68	U. of Vermont
CAPELLO, Jeff	6-1	195	L	Ottawa, Ont.	9/25/64	Rochester
CORKUM, Bob	6-2	195	R	Salisbury, MA	12/18/67	U. of Maine
DE CARLE, Mike	6-0	180	L	Covina, CA	8/20/66	Lake Superior State
DONNELLY, Mike	5-11	185	L	Detroit, MI	10/10/63	Buffalo-Rochester
FOLIGNO, Mike	6-2	195	R	Sudbury, Ont.	1/29/59	Buffalo
GAGE, Jody	6-0	188	R	Toronto, Ont.	11/29/59	Rochester
GRETZKY, Keith	5-9	160	L	Brantford, Ont.	2/16/67	Roch.-Flint-Kettera (Fin.)
GUAY, Francois	6-0	186	L	Gatineau, Que.	6/8/68	Rochester
HARTMAN, Mike	6-0	183	L	Detroit, MI	2/7/67	Buffalo
HOGUE, Benoit	5-10	177	L	Repentigny, Que.	10/28/66	Buffalo
JACKSON, Jim	5-8	190	R	Oshawa, Ont.	2/1/60	Rochester
KAESE, Trent	5-11	205	R	Nanaimo, B.C.	9/9/67	Rochester
KERR, Kevin	5-10	170	R	North Bay, Ont.	9/18/67	Rochester
LOEWEN, Darcy	5-10	182	L	Calgary, Alta.	2/26/69	Spokane
MacVICAR, Andrew	6-1	195	L	Dartmouth, N.S.	3/12/69	Peterborough
MAGUIRE, Kevin	6-2	200	R	Trenton, Ont.	1/5/63	Buffalo
McCRORY, Scott	5-10	175	R	Sudbury, Ont.	2/27/67	Baltimore
METCALFE, Scott	6-0	195	L	Toronto, Ont.	1/6/67	Buffalo-Rochester
MOGILNY, Alexander	5-11	186	L	Khabarovak, USSR	2/18/69	CSKA (USSR)
NELSON, John	5-10	174	L	Scarborough, Ont.	7/9/69	Toronto
PARKER, Jeff	6-3	194	R	St. Paul, MN	9/7/64	Buffalo-Rochester
PRIESTLAY, Ken	5-10	187	L	Vancouver, B.C.	8/24/67	Buffalo-Rochester
RAY, Robert	6-0	203	L	Stirling, Ont.	6/8/68	Rochester
RUUTTU, Christian	5-11	190	L	Lappeen, Finland	2/20/64	Buffalo
SAVAGE, Joel	5-11	195	R	Surrey, B.C.	12/25/69	Victoria
SHANNON, Darrin	6-2	190	L	Barrie, Ont.	12/8/69	Buffalo
SHEPPARD, Ray	6-1	186	R	Pembroke, Ont.	5/27/66	Buffalo
TKACHUK, Grant	5-10	180	L	La Biche, Alta.	9/24/68	Rochester
TUCKER, John	6-0	200	R	Windsor, Ont.	9/29/64	Buffalo
TURGEON, Pierre	6-1	203	L	Rouyn, Que.	8/29/69	Buffalo
VAIVE, Rick	6-1	192	R	Ottawa, Ont.	5/14/59	Chicago-Buffalo
DEFENSEMEN						
ANDERSON, Shawn	6-1	196	L	Montreal, Que.	2/7/68	Buffalo-Rochester
BASSEGIO, Dave	6-3	210	L	Niagara Falls, Ont.	10/28/67	Yale
BODGER, Doug	6-2	200	L	Chemainua, B.C.	6/18/66	Pittsburgh-Buffalo
DUNN, Richie	6-0	200	L	Boston, Mass.	5/12/57	Buffalo-Rochester
HALKIDIS, Bob	5-11	200	L	Toronto, Ont.	3/5/66	Buffalo-Rochester
HALLER, Kevin	6-2	182	L	Trochu, Alta.	12/5/70	Regina
HOFFORD, Jim	6-0	195	R	Sudbury, Ont.	10/4/64	Rochester
HOUSLEY, Phil	5-10	179	L	St. Paul, Minn.	3/9/64	Buffalo
KRUPP, Uwe	6-6	230	R	Cologne, W. Germ.	6/24/65	Buffalo
LEDYARD, Grant	6-2	190	L	Winnipeg, Man.	11/19/61	Washington-Buffalo
McSWEEN, Don	5-11	194	L	Detroit, MI	6/9/64	Rochester
MILLER, Brad	6-4	200	L	Edmonton, Alta.	7/23/69	Buffalo-Rochester
MOYLAN, Dave	6-1	195	L	Tillsonburg, Ont.	8/13/67	Rochester
PLAYFAIR, Larry	6-4	225	L	Ft. St. James, B.C.	6/23/58	L.A.-Buffalo
RAMSEY, Mike	6-3	187	L	Minneapolis, MN	12/3/60	Buffalo
SMITH, Steve	5-9	195	L	Trenton, Ont.	4/4/63	Buffalo-Rochester
SUTTON, Ken	6-0	184	L	Edmonton, Alta.	5/11/69	Saskatoon
WHITHAM, Shawn	5-11	175	L	Verdun, Que.	3/13/67	Rochester
GOALTENDERS	**HT**	**WT**	**C**	**Place of Birth**	**Date**	**1988-89 Club**
CLOUTIER, Jacques	5-7	167	L	Noranda, Que.	1/3/60	Buffalo
FORD, Brian	5-10	170	R	Edmonton, Alta.	9/22/61	Rochester
LITTMAN, Davis	6-0	175	L	Cranston, RI	6/13/67	Boston College
MALARCHUK, Clint	6-0	190	L	Grande, Alta.	5/1/61	Buffalo
PUPPA, Daren	6-3	197	R	Kirkland Lake, Ont.	3/23/65	Buffalo
WAKALUK, Darcy	5-11	176	L	Pincher Creek, Alta.	3/14/66	Rochester

General Managers' History

George "Punch" Imlach, 1970-71 to 1977-78; John Anderson (acting), 1978-79; Scott Bowman, 1979-80 to 1985-86; Scott Bowman and Gerry Meehan, 1986-87; Gerry Meehan, 1987-88 to date.

Coaching History

"Punch" Imlach, 1970-71; "Punch" Imlach, Floyd Smith and Joe Crozier, 1971-72; Joe Crozier, 1972-73 to 1973-74; Floyd Smith, 1974-75 to 1976-77; Marcel Pronovost, 1977-78; Marcel Pronovost and Bill Inglis, 1978-79; Scott Bowman, 1979-80; Roger Neilson, 1980-81; Jim Roberts and Scott Bowman, 1981-82; Scott Bowman 1981-82 to 1984-85; Jim Schoenfeld and Scott Bowman, 1985-86; Scott Bowman, Craig Ramsay and Ted Sator, 1986-87; Ted Sator, 1987-88 to 1988-89; Rick Dudley, 1989-90.

Captains' History

Floyd Smith, 1970-71; Gerry Meehan, 1971-72 to 1973-74; Jim Schoenfeld, 1974-75 to 1976-77; Danny Gare, 1977-78 to 1980-81; Gil Perreault, 1981-82 to 1986-87; Lindy Ruff, 1986-87 to 1987-88; Lindy Ruff and Mike Foligno, 1988-89; Mike Foligno, 1989-90.

1988-89 Scoring

Regular Season

*–Rookie

Pos	#	Player	Team	GP	G	A	Pts	+/–	PIM	PP	SH	GW	GT	S	%
F	77	Pierre Turgeon	BUF	80	34	54	88	3–	26	19	0	5	0	182	18.7
D	6	Phil Housley	BUF	72	26	44	70	6	47	5	0	3	0	178	14.6
F	21	Christian Ruuttu	BUF	67	14	46	60	13	98	5	0	1	0	149	9.4
F	22	Rick Vaive	CHI	30	12	13	25	5–	60	9	0	1	0	57	21.1
			BUF	28	19	13	32	7	64	7	0	3	0	81	23.5
			TOTAL	58	31	26	57	2	124	16	0	4	0	138	22.5
F	25	Dave Andreychuk	BUF	56	28	24	52	1	40	7	0	3	0	145	19.3
D	8	Doug Bodger	PIT	10	1	4	5	6	7	0	0	0	0	22	4.5
			BUF	61	7	40	47	9	52	6	0	1	0	134	5.2
			TOTAL	71	8	44	52	15	59	6	0	1	0	156	5.1
F	17	Mike Foligno	BUF	75	27	22	49	7–	156	11	0	5	1	144	18.8
F	33	*Benoit Hogue	BUF	69	14	30	44	4–	120	1	2	0	0	114	12.3
F	7	John Tucker	BUF	60	13	31	44	4–	31	3	0	1	0	94	13.8
F	23	Ray Sheppard	BUF	67	22	21	43	7–	15	7	0	4	1	147	15.0
F	9	Scott Arniel	BUF	80	18	23	41	10	46	0	2	3	1	122	14.8
F	65	Mark Napier	BUF	66	11	17	28	4–	33	0	2	1	0	92	12.0
D	3	Grant Ledyard	WSH	61	3	11	14	1	43	1	0	1	0	81	3.7
			BUF	13	1	5	6	1	8	0	0	1	0	25	4.0
			TOTAL	74	4	16	20	2	51	1	0	2	0	106	3.8
F	29	*Jeff Parker	BUF	57	9	9	18	3	82	0	0	2	0	78	11.5
F	19	*Kevin Maguire	BUF	60	8	10	18	9	241	0	0	2	0	35	22.9
D	4	Uwe Krupp	BUF	70	5	13	18	0	55	0	1	0	0	51	9.8
F	20	Mike Hartman	BUF	70	8	9	17	8	316	1	0	0	0	91	8.8
D	5	Mike Ramsey	BUF	56	2	14	16	5	84	0	0	1	0	63	3.2
D	37	Shawn Anderson	BUF	33	2	10	12	3	18	2	0	0	0	26	7.7
F	16	Mike Donnelly	BUF	22	4	6	10	1–	10	0	0	0	0	25	16.0
D	27	Larry Playfair	L.A.	6	0	3	3	3	16	0	0	0	0	4	.0
			BUF	42	0	3	3	10–	110	0	0	0	0	6	.0
			TOTAL	48	0	6	6	7–	126	0	0	0	0	10	.0
D	55	Joe Reekie	BUF	15	1	3	4	6	26	1	0	0	0	14	7.1
G	31	Daren Puppa	BUF	37	0	4	4	0	12	0	0	0	0	0	.0
F	56	Ken Priestlay	BUF	15	2	0	2	8–	2	0	0	0	0	20	10.0
F	32	*Scott Metcalfe	BUF	9	1	1	2	1–	13	0	0	0	0	11	9.1
F	36	Jan Ludvig	BUF	13	0	2	2	1–	39	0	0	0	0	11	.0
G	1	Jacques Cloutier	BUF	36	0	2	2	0	6	0	0	0	0	0	.0
D	26	Richie Dunn	BUF	4	0	1	1	1–	2	0	0	0	0	2	.0
F	14	Mikael Andersson	BUF	14	0	1	1	1–	4	0	0	0	0	12	.0
D	18	Bob Halkidis	BUF	16	0	1	1	1–	66	0	0	0	0	9	.0
G	30	Clint Malarchuk	WSH	42	0	1	1	0	16	0	0	0	0	0	.0
			BUF	7	0	0	0	0	2	0	0	0	0	0	.0
			TOTAL	49	0	1	1	0	18	0	0	0	0	0	.0
F	39	*Trent Kaese	BUF	1	0	0	0	0	0	0	0	0	0	5	.0
G	34	Darren Eliot	BUF	2	0	0	0	0	0	0	0	0	0	0	.0
D	28	*Mark Ferner	BUF	2	0	0	0	2–	2	0	0	0	0	0	.0
F	26	*Darrin Shannon	BUF	3	0	0	0	2–	0	0	0	0	0	0	.0
D	24	*Steve Smith	BUF	3	0	0	0	0	0	0	0	0	0	2	.0
G	35	*Darcy Wakaluk	BUF	6	0	0	0	0	0	0	0	0	0	0	.0
D	44	*Brad Miller	BUF	7	0	0	0	1–	6	0	0	0	0	0	.0

Goaltending

No.	Goaltender	GPI	Mins	Avg	W	L	T	EN	SO	GA	SA	S%
30	Clint Malarchuk	7	326	2.39	3	1	1	0	1	13	142	.908
31	Daren Puppa	37	1908	3.36	17	10	6	1	1	107	961	.889
1	Jacques Cloutier	36	1786	3.63	15	14	0	1	0	108	857	.874
35	*Darcy Wakaluk	6	214	4.21	1	3	0	1	0	15	90	.831
30	Tom Barrasso	10	545	4.95	2	7	0	1	0	45	285	.842
34	Darren Eliot	2	67	6.27	0	0	0	0	0	7	43	.837
	Totals	**80**	**4855**	**3.70**	**38**	**35**	**7**	**4**	**2**	**299**	**2378**	**.874**

Playoffs

Pos	#	Player	Team	GP	G	A	Pts	+/–	PIM	PP	SH	GW	GT	S	%
F	77	Pierre Turgeon	BUF	5	3	5	8	0	2	1	0	0	0	7	42.9
F	17	Mike Foligno	BUF	5	3	1	4	2	21	1	1	1	0	11	27.3
D	6	Phil Housley	BUF	5	1	3	4	0	2	0	0	0	0	10	10.0
F	22	Rick Vaive	BUF	5	2	1	3	5–	8	2	0	0	0	15	13.3
D	3	Grant Ledyard	BUF	5	1	2	3	1–	2	0	0	0	0	13	7.7
F	7	John Tucker	BUF	3	0	3	3	0	0	0	0	0	0	1	.0
F	25	Dave Andreychuk	BUF	5	0	3	3	0	0	0	0	0	0	15	.0
D	8	Doug Bodger	BUF	5	1	1	2	2	11	1	0	0	0	10	10.0
F	65	Mark Napier	BUF	3	1	0	1	0	0	0	0	0	0	2	50.0
F	9	Scott Arniel	BUF	5	1	0	1	2–	4	0	1	0	0	2	50.0
D	5	Mike Ramsey	BUF	5	1	0	1	0	11	1	0	0	0	6	16.7
F	23	Ray Sheppard	BUF	1	0	1	1	1	0	0	0	0	0	2	.0
D	37	Shawn Anderson	BUF	5	0	1	1	4–	4	0	0	0	0	6	.0
D	4	Uwe Krupp	BUF	5	0	1	1	4–	4	0	0	0	0	3	.0
G	30	Clint Malarchuk	BUF	1	0	0	0	0	2	0	0	0	0	0	.0
D	27	Larry Playfair	BUF	1	0	0	0	0	0	0	0	0	0	0	.0
F	21	Christian Ruuttu	BUF	2	0	0	0	1–	2	0	0	0	0	1	.0
F	26	*Darrin Shannon	BUF	2	0	0	0	1–	0	0	0	0	0	1	.0
F	56	Ken Priestlay	BUF	3	0	0	0	3–	2	0	0	0	0	5	.0
G	1	Jacques Cloutier	BUF	4	0	0	0	0	0	0	0	0	0	0	.0
F	20	Mike Hartman	BUF	5	0	0	0	1–	34	0	0	0	0	3	.0
F	33	*Benoit Hogue	BUF	5	0	0	0	1–	17	0	0	0	0	4	.0
F	19	Kevin Maguire	BUF	5	0	0	0	1–	36	0	0	0	0	1	.0
F	29	*Jeff Parker	BUF	5	0	0	0	1–	26	0	0	0	0	3	.0

Goaltending

No.	Goaltender	GPI	Mins	Avg	W	L	EN	SO	GA	SA	S%
1	Jacques Cloutier	4	238	2.52	1	3	1	1	10	108	.907
30	Clint Malarchuk	1	59	5.03	0	1	0	0	5	32	.844
	Totals	**5**	**300**	**3.20**	**1**	**4**	**1**	**1**	**16**	**140**	**.855**

Club Records

Team

(Figures in brackets for season records are games played; records for fewest points, wins, ties, losses, goals, goals against are for 70 or more games)

Most Points	113	1974-75 (80)
Most Wins	49	1974-75 (80)
Most Ties	21	1980-81 (80)
Most Losses	44	1986-87 (80)
Most Goals	354	1974-75 (80)
Most Goals Against	308	1986-87 (80)
		1974-75 (80)
Fewest Points	51	1971-72 (78)
Fewest Wins	16	1971-72 (78)
Fewest Ties	6	1985-86 (80)
Fewest Losses	16	1974-75 (80)
Fewest Goals	203	1971-72 (78)
Fewest Goals Against	201	1979-80 (80)

Longest Winning Streak
Over-all ... 10 Jan. 4-23/84
Home ... 12 Nov. 12/72-Jan. 7/73
Away ... 10 Dec. 10/83-Jan. 23/84

Longest Undefeated Streak
Over-all ... 14 March 6-April 6/80
Home ... 21 Oct. 8/72-Jan. 7/73
Away ... 10 Dec. 10/83-Jan. 23/84 (10 wins)

Longest Losing Streak
Over-all ... 7 Oct. 25-Nov. 8/70
Home ... 5 Feb. 15-Mar. 3/85
Away ... 7 Oct. 14-Nov. 7/70 Feb. 6-27/71

Longest Winless Streak
Over-all ... 10 Nov. 7-Dec. 1/71 (8 losses, 2 ties)
Home ... 6 Feb. 27-Mar. 26/72 (3 losses, 3 ties)

Away ... 23 Oct. 30/71-Feb. 19/72 (15 losses, 8 ties)
Most Shutouts, Season ... 7 1974-75 (80)
Most Pen. Mins., Season ... 2,263 1987-88 (80)
Most Goals, Game ... 14 Jan. 21/75 (Wash. 2 at Buf. 14) Mar. 19/81 (Tor. 4 at Buf. 14)

Individual

Most Seasons	17	Gilbert Perreault
Most Games	1,191	Gilbert Perreault
Most Goals, Career	512	Gilbert Perreault
Most Assists, Career	814	Gilbert Perreault
Most Points, Career	1,326	Gilbert Perreault
Most Pen. Mins., Career	1,388	Larry Playfair
Most Shutouts, Career	14	Don Edwards

Longest Consecutive Games Streak ... 776 Craig Ramsay (Mar. 27/73-Feb. 10/83)
Most Goals, Season ... 56 Danny Gare (1979-80)
Most Assists, Season ... 69 Gilbert Perreault (1975-76)
Most Points, Season ... 113 Gilbert Perreault (1975-76) (44 goals, 69 assists)
Most Pen. Mins., Season ... 316 Mike Hartman (1988-89)
Most Points, Defenseman Season ... 70 Phil Housley (1988-88) (26 goals, 44 assists)
Most Points, Center Season ... 113 Gilbert Perreault (1975-76) (44 goals, 69 assists)
Most Points, Right Wing Season ... 100 René Robert (1974-75) (40 goals, 60 assists)

Most Points, Left Wing Season ... 95 Richard Martin (1974-75) (52 goals, 43 assists)
Most Points, Rookie Season ... 74 Richard Martin (1971-72) (44 goals, 30 assists)
Most Shutouts, Season ... 5 Don Edwards (1977-78) Tom Barrasso (1984-85)
Most Goals, Game ... 5 Dave Andreychuk (Feb. 6/86)
Most Assists, Game ... 5 Gilbert Perreault (Feb. 1/76; Mar. 9/80) Gilbert Perreault (Jan. 4/84)
Most Points, Game ... 7 Gilbert Perreault (Feb. 1/76)

All-time Record vs. Other Clubs

Regular Season

		At Home						On Road						Total					
	GP	W	L	T	GF	GA	PTS	GP	W	L	T	GF	GA	PTS	GP	W	L	T	GF	GA	PTS
Boston	63	32	20	11	242	206	75	64	18	39	7	193	275	43	127	50	59	18	435	481	118
**Calgary	32	18	10	4	136	96	40	31	11	12	8	105	113	30	63	29	22	12	241	209	70
Chicago	38	25	7	6	156	100	56	37	10	21	6	94	120	26	75	35	28	12	250	220	82
Detroit	39	28	5	6	177	93	62	40	16	20	4	121	142	36	79	44	25	10	298	235	98
Edmonton	16	6	7	3	67	68	15	16	3	11	2	44	72	8	32	9	18	5	111	140	23
Hartford	36	18	13	5	145	123	41	36	18	14	4	107	110	40	72	36	27	9	252	233	81
Los Angeles	39	20	12	7	161	119	47	39	18	14	7	137	135	43	78	38	26	14	298	254	90
Minnesota	39	22	9	8	150	103	52	39	18	15	6	126	119	42	78	40	24	14	276	222	94
Montreal	59	25	19	15	180	180	65	59	16	35	8	181	247	40	118	41	54	23	361	427	105
*New Jersey	26	21	2	3	130	70	45	26	19	3	4	114	73	42	52	40	5	7	244	143	87
NY Islanders	32	18	10	4	114	90	40	33	16	12	5	103	97	37	65	34	22	9	217	187	77
NY Rangers	39	24	10	5	178	128	53	38	14	15	9	113	131	37	77	38	25	14	291	259	90
Philadelphia	37	17	14	6	129	112	40	38	7	25	6	93	142	20	75	24	39	12	222	254	60
Pittsburgh	39	21	5	13	178	102	55	39	12	15	12	141	150	36	78	33	20	25	319	252	91
Quebec	36	21	10	5	146	119	47	36	11	21	4	103	141	26	72	32	31	9	249	260	73
St. Louis	37	25	8	4	157	108	54	37	11	21	5	98	140	27	74	36	29	9	255	248	81
Toronto	44	28	14	2	190	124	58	43	18	18	7	153	142	43	87	46	32	9	343	266	101
Vancouver	38	20	10	8	139	106	48	38	11	19	8	124	147	30	76	31	29	16	263	253	78
Washington	28	21	4	3	127	73	45	28	19	4	5	125	77	43	56	40	8	8	252	150	88
Winnipeg	16	13	1	2	80	45	28	16	7	7	2	58	56	16	32	20	8	4	138	101	44
Defunct Clubs	23	13	5	5	94	63	31	23	12	8	3	97	76	27	46	25	13	8	191	139	58
Totals	756	436	195	125	3076	2228	997	756	285	349	122	2430	2705	692	1512	721	544	247	5506	4933	1689

* Totals include those of Kansas City (1974-75, 1975-76) and Colorado (1976-77 through 1981-82)
** Totals include those of Atlanta (1972-73 through 1979-80)

Playoffs

	Series	W	L	GP	W	L	T	GF	GA	Last Mtg.	Round	Result
Boston	4	0	4	22	7	15	0	70	94	1989	DSF	L 1-4
Chicago	2	2	0	9	8	1	0	36	17	1980	QF	W 4-0
Minnesota	2	1	1	7	3	4	0	28	26	1981	QF	L 1-4
Montreal	3	2	1	15	9	6	0	45	52	1983	DSF	W 3-0
NY Islanders	3	0	3	16	4	12	0	45	59	1980	SF	L 2-4
NY Rangers	1	1	0	3	2	1	0	11	6	1978	P	W 2-1
Philadelphia	2	0	2	11	3	8	0	23	35	1978	QF	L 1-4
Pittsburgh	1	0	1	3	1	2	0	9	9	1979	P	L 1-2
Quebec	2	0	2	8	2	6	0	27	35	1985	DSF	L 2-3
St. Louis	1	1	0	3	2	1	0	7	8	1976	P	W 2-1
Vancouver	2	2	0	7	6	1	0	28	14	1981	P	W 3-0
Totals	23	9	14	104	47	57	0	329	355			

Abbreviations: Round: **F** – Final; **CF** – conference final; **DF** – division final; **DSF** – division semi-final; **SF** – semi-final; **QF** – quarter-final. **P** – preliminary round. **GA** – goals against; **GF** – goals for.

Playoff Results 1989-85

Year	Round	Opponent	Result	GF	GA
1989	DSF	Boston	L 1-4	14	16
1988	DSF	Boston	L 2-4	22	28
1985	DSF	Quebec	L 0-3	5	13

1988-89 Results

		Home				Away	
Oct.	6	Montreal	3-2	Oct.	8	Washington	2-6
	12	Pittsburgh	8-5		9	Philadelphia	3-4
	16	Quebec	3-5		14	Quebec	5-4
	21	Montreal	5-3		19	Toronto	2-4
	26	Hartford	1-7		22	Montreal	3-4
	30	Boston	3-3		25	New Jersey	7-4
Nov.	2	NY Rangers	6-4		29	Boston	3-3
	9	Calgary	3-2	Nov.	4	Edmonton	3-7
	13	Edmonton	4-5		5	Calgary	0-9
	25	Chicago	5-4		12	NY Islanders	3-0
	27	Philadelphia	7-3		16	Chicago	2-3
	30	Quebec	6-2		19	Los Angeles	4-5
Dec.	2	Hartford	1-6		22	Vancouver	2-4
	11	Washington	4-6	Dec.	3	Montreal	2-3
	19	Edmonton	5-5		6	Hartford	0-9
	23	Toronto	5-2		8	Boston	4-2
	26	Boston	2-1		14	Winnipeg	3-4
	28	Detroit	4-1		15	Minnesota	2-2
	31	Philadelphia	2-3		21	NY Rangers	5-2
Jan.	4	Hartford	4-5		30	Washington	3-5
	6	New Jersey	4-5	Jan.	6	New Jersey	4-5
	12	Chicago	6-5		7	Toronto	6-1
	15	Calgary	3-2		14	Quebec	1-1
	18	Minnesota	3-3		21	Boston*	6-5
	22	Boston*	6-4		25	Detroit	6-3
	27	Montreal	4-2		28	Montreal	1-2
Feb.	10	Vancouver	4-5		31	Hartford	5-3
	12	St Louis	5-2	Feb.	2	St Louis	3-7
	15	New Jersey	5-3		4	Los Angeles	3-5
	17	Pittsburgh	5-1		9	Hartford	2-5
	19	Detroit*	8-4		14	Pittsburgh	3-7
	22	NY Islanders	7-5		25	Montreal	1-6
	24	Winnipeg	5-4	Mar.	4	Quebec	2-6
Mar.	1	Los Angeles	4-5		8	NY Rangers	2-0
	5	Quebec	2-8		11	Boston*	6-6
	12	Boston*	3-2		16	Hartford	6-1
	22	St Louis	1-2		18	Minnesota	0-3
	24	Vancouver	5-2		20	Winnipeg	4-1
	28	Hartford	4-2		25	Quebec	1-4
	30	Montreal	2-4	Apr.	1	NY Islanders	4-3
Apr.	2	Quebec	4-2				

* Denotes afternoon game.

Entry Draft Selections 1989-75

1989
Pick		
14	Kevin Haller
56	John (Scott) Thomas
77	Doug MacDonald
98	Ken Sutton
107	Bill Pye
119	Mike Barkley
161	Derek Plante
183	Donald Audette
194	Mark Astley
203	John Nelson
224	Todd Henderson
245	Michael Bavis

1988
Pick	
13	Joel Savage
55	Darcy Loewen
76	Keith E. Carney
89	Alexander Mogilny
97	Robert Ray
106	David DiVita
118	Mike McLaughlin
139	Mike Griffith
160	Daniel Ruoho
181	Wade Flaherty
223	Thomas Nieman
244	Robert Wallwork

1987
Pick	
1	Pierre Turgeon
22	Brad Miller
53	Andrew MacVicar
84	John Bradley
85	David Pergola
106	Chris Marshall
127	Paul Flanagan
148	Sean Dooley
153	Tim roberts
169	Grant Tkachuk
190	Ian Herbers
211	David Littman
232	Allan MacIsaac

1986
Pick	
5	Shawn Anderson
26	Greg Brown
47	Bob Corkum
56	Kevin Kerr
68	David Baseggio
89	Larry Rooney
110	Miguel Baldris
131	Mike Hartman
152	Francois Guay
173	Shawn Whitham
194	Kenton Rein
215	Troy Arndt

1985
Pick	
14	Calle Johansson
35	Benoit Hogue
56	Keith Gretzky
77	Dave Moylan
98	Ken Priestlay
119	Joe Reekie
140	Petri Matikainen
161	Trent Kaese
182	Jiri Sejba
203	Boyd Sutton
224	Guy Larose
245	Ken Baumgartner

1984
Pick	
18	Mikael Andersson
39	Doug Trapp
60	Ray Sheppard
81	Bob Halkidis
102	Joey Rampton
123	James Gasseau
144	Darcy Wakaluk
165	Orwar Stambert
207	Brian McKinnon
228	Grant Delcourt
249	Sean Baker

1983
Pick	
5	Tom Barrasso
10	Normand Lacombe
11	Adam Creighton
31	John Tucker
34	Richard Hajdu
74	Daren Puppa
94	Jayson Meyer
114	Jim Hofford
134	Christian Ruuttu
154	Don McSween
174	Tim Hoover
194	Mark Ferner
214	Uwe Krupp
234	Marc Hamelin
235	Kermit Salfi

1982
Pick	
6	Phil Housley
9	Paul Cyr
16	Dave Andreychuk
26	Mike Anderson
30	Jens Johansson
68	Timo Jutila
79	Jeff Hamilton
100	Bob Logan
111	Jeff Parker
121	Jacob Gustavsson
142	Allen Bishop
163	Claude Verrett
184	Rob Norman
205	Mike Craig
226	Jim Plankers

1981
Pick	
17	Jiri Dudacek
38	Hannu Virta
59	Jim Aldred
60	Colin Chisholm
80	Jeff Eatough
83	Anders Wikberg
101	Mauri Eivola
122	Ali Butorac
143	Heikki Leime
164	Gates Orlando
185	Venci Sebeck
206	Warren Harper

1980
Pick	
20	Steve Patrick
41	Mike Moller
56	Sean McKenna
62	Jay North
83	Jim Wiemer
104	Dirk Reuter
125	Daniel Naud
146	Jari Paavola
167	Randy Cunneyworth
188	Dave Beckon
209	John Bader

1979
Pick	
11	Mike Ramsey
32	Lindy Ruff
53	Mark Robinson
55	Jacques Cloutier
74	Gilles Hamel
95	Alan Haworth
116	Rick Knickle

1978
Pick	
13	Larry Playfair
32	Tony McKegney
49	Rob McClanahan
66	Mike Gazdic
82	Randy Ireland
99	Cam MacGregor
116	Dan Eastman
133	Eric Strobel
150	Eugene O'Sullivan

1977
Pick	
14	Ric Seiling
32	Ron Areshenkoff
68	Bill Stewart
86	Richard Sirois
104	Wayne Ramsey

1976
Pick	
33	Joe Kowal
69	Henry Maze
87	Ron Roscoe
105	Don Lemieux

1975
Pick	
17	Bob Sauve
35	Ken Breitenbach
44	Terry Martin
53	Gary McAdam
71	Greg Neeld
89	Don Edwards
107	Jim Minor
125	Grant Rowe
143	Alex Tidey
159	Andy Whitby
174	Len Moher

Coach

DUDLEY, RICK
Coach, Buffalo Sabres. Born in Toronto, Ont., January 31, 1949.

Rick Dudley was named Head Coach of the Sabres on June 16, 1989, marking his return to a club for which he played 279 games between 1972-73 and 1980-81. Dudley's NHL playing career included stints in Buffalo and Winnipeg. He tallied 174 points (75-99-174) in 309 NHL games before ending his playing career in 1981-82.

Dudley's coaching career began in 1982-83 when he assumed the head coaching duties for the Carolina Thunderbirds of the ACHL. He met with instant success as he led his club to the title in his first season. In 1983-84 and 1984-85, Dudley led his team to a first-place finish during the regular-season, before winning another title in 1985-86. Dudley joined the Flint Generals (IHL) in 1986-87 and led them to the Turner Cup Finals in 1987-88. In 1988-89, he was the Head Coach for the New Haven Nighthawks (AHL) where he again led his club to the Final series. In seven years, Dudley compiled a minor league coaching record of 315-157-38 for a .655 winning percentage.

Coaching Record
Season	Team	Games	W	L	T	%	Games	W	L	%
				Regular Season				Playoffs		
1982-83	Carolina (ACHL)	68	51	10	7	.619	8	8	0	1.000
1983-84	Carolina (ACHL)	72	43	24	5	.632	10	5	5	.500
1984-85	Carolina (ACHL)	64	53	11	0	.828	10	8	2	.800
1985-86	Carolina (ACHL)	63	49	14	0	.778	11	8	3	.727
1986-87	Flint (IHL)	82	42	33	7	.555	6	2	4	.333
1987-88	Flint (IHL)	82	42	31	9	.567	16	10	6	.625
1988-89	New Haven (AHL)	80	35	35	10	.500	17	9	8	.529

Club Directory

Memorial Auditorium
Buffalo, N.Y. 14202
Phone 716/856-7300
Outside Buffalo: 800/333-PUCK
GM FAX 716/856-7350
FAX 716/856-7351
ENVOY ID
  Front Office: SABRES. GM
  Public
  Relations: SABRES. PR
Capacity: 16,433

Board of Directors

Chairman of the Board and President	Seymour H. Knox, III
Vice-Chairman of the Board and Counsel	Robert O. Swados
Vice-Chairman of the Board	Robert E. Rich, Jr.
Treasurer	Joseph T.J. Stewart
Board of Directors	Edwin C. Andrews
Niagara Frontier Hockey L.P.	Peter C. Andrews
(includes above listed officers)	George L. Collins, Jr. M.D.
	John B. Fisher
	John Houghton
	Richard W. Rupp
	Howard T. Saperston, Jr.
	Paul A. Schoellkopf
	George Strawbridge, Jr., Arthur Victor, Jr.
Consultant	Northrup R. Knox
Assistant to the President	Seymour H. Knox, IV
Senior Vice-President/Administration	Mitchell Owen
Senior Vice-President/Finance	Robert Pickel
Vice-President/Marketing	George Bergantz
General Manager	Gerry Meehan
Head Coach	Rick Dudley
Assistant Coaches	Don Lever & John Tortorella
Director of Professional Evaluation & Development	Craig Ramsay
Director of Amateur Evaluation & Development	Don Luce
Director of Scouting	Rudy Migay
Coordinator of Minor League Pro. Development	Joe Crozier
Administrative Assistant	Debbie Bonner
Scouting Staff	Don Barrie, Jack Bowman, Larry Carriere, Frank Deegan, Dennis McIvor, Paul Merritt, Mike Racicot, Frank Zywiec
Computer Scouting Analyst	Ken Bass
Head Athletic Trainer	Jim Pizzutelli
Trainer	Rip Simonick
Equipment Supervisor	John Heidinger
Administrative Assistants	Carol McHugh, Verna Wojcik
Controller	Dan DiPofi
Director of Amateur Hockey Development	John Mickler
Director of Communications	Paul Wieland
Director of Community Relations and Promotions	Stan Makowski
Director of Event Sales	Jeffrey Pickel
Director of Information	Budd Bailey
Director of Public Relations	John Gurtler
Director of Sales	Steve Donner
Marketing Associates	John Livsey, Bob Russell
Public Relations Assistant	Steve Rossi
Manager – Sabreland	Shirley Curry
Voice of the Sabres	Ted Darling
Club Doctor	John L. Butsch, M.D.
Orthopedic Consultant	Peter James, M.D.
Club Dentist	Donald DeRose, D.D.S.
Club Staff: Olive Anticola, Evelyn Battleson, Barbara Blendowski, Donna Buyea, Robert M. Dahar, Pat Dudley, Cyndi Dyll, Birgid Haensel, Chris Ivansitz, Mary Jones, John Kreuzer, Sally Lippert, Gerry Magill, Melissa Nitkowski, Mary Onofrio, Cheryl Schoenthaler, Ann Seaman, John Sinclair, Carm Tramont	
Dimensions of Rink	196 feet by 85 feet
Location of Press Box	Suspended from ceiling on west side
Club Colors	Blue, White, Gold
Off-Ice Officials. Hank Olejniczak (Supervisor and Offical Scorer), Tony Caggiano, Sam Costello, Richard Costolnick, Dale Guynn, Robert Kalenik, Don Kwak, Duke Morettin, Jim Murdoch, Stanley Renkas, Clifford Smith, Bill Truman	
Photographer	Bill Wippert
Anthem Singers	Sue Brittain, John Putnam
Public Address Announcer	Milt Ellis
Music	Dave Perry, Jamie Wilson

WNYB-TV (Channel 49) — The Sabres Station

President	Paul A. Mooney
Telephone	716/875-4919

General Manager

MEEHAN, GERARD MARCUS (GERRY)
General Manager, Buffalo Sabres. Born in Toronto, Ont., September 3, 1946.

Gerry Meehan became General Manager of the Sabres midway through the 1986-87 season. He retired as a player in 1979 after ten NHL seasons as a center with six different clubs. He played in Buffalo from 1970 to 1974 and, after his playing career, remained in the Buffalo area, earning an undergraduate degree from Canisius College and a law degree from the University of Buffalo. He practiced law in Buffalo before accepting the post of assistant GM for the Sabres in 1984-85 when he became the first former Buffalo player to move into the club's front office.

Calgary Flames

1988-89 Results: 54w-17L-9T 117 PTS. First, Smythe Division

Year-by-Year Record

		Home			Road			Overall							
Season	GP	W	L	T	W	L	T	W	L	T	GF	GA	Pts.	Finished	Playoff Result
1988-89	**80**	**32**	**4**	**4**	**22**	**13**	**5**	**54**	**17**	**9**	**354**	**226**	**117**	**1st,**	**Smythe Div.**	**Won Stanley Cup**
1987-88	80	26	11	3	22	12	6	48	23	9	397	305	105	1st,	Smythe Div.	Lost Div. Final
1986-87	80	25	13	2	21	18	1	46	31	3	318	289	95	2nd,	Smythe Div.	Lost Div. Semi-Final
1985-86	80	23	11	6	17	20	3	40	31	9	354	315	89	2nd,	Smythe Div.	Lost Final
1984-85	80	23	11	6	18	16	6	41	27	12	363	302	94	3rd,	Smythe Div.	Lost Div. Final
1983-84	80	22	11	7	12	21	7	34	32	14	311	314	82	2nd,	Smythe Div.	Lost Div. Final
1982-83	80	21	12	7	11	22	7	32	34	14	321	317	78	2nd,	Smythe Div.	Lost Div. Final
1981-82	80	20	11	9	9	23	8	29	34	17	334	345	75	3rd,	Smythe Div.	Lost Div. Semi-Final
1980-81	80	25	5	10	14	22	4	39	27	14	329	298	92	3rd,	Patrick Div.	Lost Semi-Final
1979-80	80	18	15	7	17	17	6	35	32	13	282	269	83	4th,	Patrick Div.	Lost Prelim. Round
1978-79	80	25	11	4	16	20	4	41	31	8	327	280	90	4th,	Patrick Div.	Lost Prelim. Round
1977-78	80	20	13	7	14	14	12	34	27	19	274	252	87	3rd,	Patrick Div.	Lost Prelim. Round
1976-77	80	22	11	7	12	23	5	34	34	12	264	265	80	3rd,	Patrick Div.	Lost Prelim. Round
1975-76	80	19	14	7	16	19	5	35	33	12	262	237	82	3rd,	Patrick Div.	Lost Prelim. Round
1974-75	80	24	9	7	10	22	8	34	31	15	243	233	83	4th,	Patrick Div.	Out of Playoffs
1973-74	78	17	15	7	13	19	7	30	34	14	214	238	74	4th,	West Div.	Lost Quarter-Final
1972-73	78	16	16	7	9	22	8	25	38	15	191	239	65	7th,	West Div.	Out of Playoffs

Schedule

	Home			Away
Oct.	Thur. 5 Detroit		**Oct.**	Tues. 10 New Jersey
	Sat. 7 NY Islanders			Wed. 11 NY Rangers
	Sat. 21 Boston			Sat. 14 Washington
	Mon. 23 Washington			Sun. 15 Philadelphia
	Fri. 27 Vancouver			Tues. 17 Quebec
Nov.	Wed. 1 Winnipeg			Wed. 18 Montreal
	Sat. 4 New Jersey			Wed. 25 Los Angeles
	Mon. 6 Edmonton			Sat. 28 Vancouver
	Tues. 14 Los Angeles		**Nov.**	Fri. 3 Edmonton
	Thur. 16 Buffalo			Wed. 8 Los Angeles
	Sat. 18 Chicago			Sat. 11 Minnesota
	Thur. 30 Minnesota			Sun. 12 Winnipeg
Dec.	Sat. 2 Toronto			Mon. 20 Montreal
	Wed. 6 Winnipeg			Tues. 21 Quebec
	Thur. 14 Quebec			Fri. 24 Detroit
	Sat. 16 Pittsburgh			Sat. 25 St Louis
	Wed. 20 Vancouver		**Dec.**	Sun. 10 Winnipeg*
	Fri. 29 Winnipeg			Mon. 11 Edmonton
	Sat. 30 Montreal			Tues. 19 Vancouver
Jan.	Tues. 2 Philadelphia			Sat. 23 Edmonton
	Fri. 5 Hartford			Wed. 27 Los Angeles
	Tues. 9 Edmonton		**Jan.**	Sun. 7 Edmonton
	Thur. 11 Buffalo			Sat. 13 Toronto
	Thur. 25 NY Rangers			Sun. 14 Chicago
	Sat. 27 Minnesota			Tues. 16 St Louis
Feb.	Thur. 1 Vancouver			Thur. 18 Boston
	Tues. 6 Los Angeles			Fri. 19 Hartford
	Tues. 20 Boston			Tues. 30 Vancouver
	Thur. 22 Toronto		**Feb.**	Sat. 3 Los Angeles
	Sun. 25 Edmonton			Sat. 10 Detroit*
Mar.	Thur. 1 Philadelphia			Sun. 11 NY Rangers*
	Sat. 3 Vancouver			Tues. 13 NY Islanders
	Mon. 5 Los Angeles			Thur. 15 Chicago
	Wed. 7 Pittsburgh			Sun. 18 Winnipeg*
	Mon. 12 Winnipeg		**Mar.**	Fri. 9 Vancouver
	Thur. 15 New Jersey			Sun. 11 Winnipeg*
	Sat. 17 Hartford			Wed. 21 Buffalo
	Mon. 19 St Louis			Sat. 24 Pittsburgh*
	Fri. 30 Edmonton			Sun. 25 Washington*
Apr.	Sun. 1 Los Angeles			Tues. 27 NY Islanders

* Denotes afternoon game.

Home Starting Times:
Weeknights . . . . 7:35 p.m.
Saturdays and Sundays . . . . 6:05 p.m.

Franchise date: June 24, 1980.
Transferred from Atlanta

18th NHL Season

Center Doug Gilmour, a face-off specialist acquired by the Flames in September of 1988, was a vital part of the Flames' 117-point regular season and Stanley Cup Championship in 1989.

1989-90 Player Personnel

FORWARDS

	HT	WT	S	Place of Birth	Date	1988-89 Club
BARKOVICH, Rick	5-10	185	L	Kirkland Lake, Ont.	4/25/64	Indianapolis
BERGQVIST, Jonas	5-11	185	L	Sweden	9/26/62	Leksand (Swe.)
BUCYK, Randy	5-11	180	L	Edmonton, Alta.	11/9/62	Salt Lake City
BUREAU, Marc	6-0	190	R	Trois Rivieres, Que.	5/19/66	Salt Lake City
CHERNOMAZ, Rick	5-9	185	R	Selkirk, Man.	9/1/63	Salt Lake-Calgary
DEASLEY, Bryan	6-3	205	L	Toronto, Ont.	11/26/68	Team Canada-Salt Lake
DUMAS, Claude	6-1	185	R	Thetford Mines, Que.	1/10/67	Baltimore
FLEURY, Theoren	5-6	160	R	Oxbow, Sask.	6/29/68	Salt Lake-Calgary
GILMOUR, Doug	5-11	170	L	Kingston, Ont.	6/25/63	Calgary
GRIMSON, Stu	6-5	220	L	Kamloops, B.C.	5/20/65	Salt Lake-Calgary
HAYWARD, Rick	6-0	180	L	Toledo, OH	2/25/66	Salt Lake
HOLMES, Mark	6-2	200	R	Kingston, Jamaica	6/7/64	Salt Lake
HRDINA, Jiri	6-0	195	R	Prague, Czech.	1/5/58	Calgary
HUNTER, Mark	6.0	200	R	Petrolia, Ont.	11/12/62	Calgary
HUNTER, Tim	6-2	202	R	Calgary, Alta.	9/10/60	Calgary
LAPPIN, Peter	5-11	185	R	St. Charles, IL	12/31/65	Salt Lake City
MacLELLAN, Brian	6-3	215	L	Guelph, Ont.	10/27/58	Minnesota-Calgary
MAHONEY, Scott	5-10	190	R	Peterborough, Ont.	4/19/69	Oshawa
MAKAROV, Sergei	5-11	190	R	Chelyabinsk, USSR	6/19/58	CSKA (USSR)
MATTEAU, Stephane	6-3	190	L	Rouyn-Noranda, Que.	9/2/69	Hull
MULLEN, Joe	5-9	180	R	New York, NY	2/26/57	Calgary
NIEUWENDYK, Joe	6-1	195	L	Oshawa, Ont.	9/10/66	Calgary
OTTO, Joel	6-4	220	L	Elk River, MN	10/29/61	Calgary
PATTERSON, Colin	6-2	195	R	Rexdale, Ont.	5/11/60	Calgary
PEPLINSKI, Jim	6-3	209	R	Renfrew, Ont.	10/24/60	Calgary
PICKELL, Doug	5-11	190	L	Sherwood Park, Alta.	5/7/68	Salt Lake City
PRIAKIN, Sergei	6-3	210	L	Moscow, Soviet Union	12/7/63	Soviet Wings-Calgary
RANHEIM, Paul	6-0	195	R	St. Louis, MO	1/25/66	Salt Lake-Calgary
ROBERTS, Gary	6-1	190	L	North York, Ont.	5/23/66	Calgary
SIMARD, Martin	6-3	215	R	Montreal, Que.	6/25/66	Salt Lake
SWEENEY, Tim	5-11	180	L	Boston, MA	4/12/67	Boston College
WENAAS, Jeff	6-0	200	L	Eastend, Sask.	9/1/67	Team Canada-Salt Lake

DEFENSEMEN

	HT	WT	S	Place of Birth	Date	1988-89 Club
BIOTTI, Chris	6-1	200	L	Waltham, MA	4/22/67	Salt Lake City
GLYNN, Brian	6-4	215	L	Iserlohn, W. Germany	11/23/67	Salt Lake-Calgary
GRANT, Kevin	6-3	210	R	Toronto, Ont.	1/9/69	Sudbury-Salt Lake
JOHANSSON, Roger	6-1	185	L	Ljungby, Sweden	4/17/67	Farjestads (Sweden)
LESSARD, Rick	6-2	200	L	Timmins, Ont.	1/9/68	Salt Lake-Calgary
MacINNIS, Al	6-2	196	L	Inverness, N.S.	7/11/63	Calgary
MACOUN, Jamie	6-2	197	L	Newmarket, Ont.	8/17/61	Calgary
McCRIMMON, Brad	5-11	197	L	Dodsland, Sask.	3/29/59	Calgary
MURZYN, Dana	6-2	200	L	Calgary, Alta.	12/9/66	Calgary
NATTRESS, Ric	6-2	210	R	Hamilton, Ont.	5/25/62	Calgary
OLSEN, Darryl	6-0	180	L	Calgary, Alta.	10/7/66	N. Michigan
OLSEN, Mark	6-4	215	L	Burnsville, MN	9/6/66	Colorado College
SABOURIN, Ken	6-3	205	L	Scarborough, Ont.	4/28/66	Salt Lake-Calgary
SUTER, Gary	6-0	190	L	Madison, WI	6/24/64	Calgary
TARRANT, Jerry	6-2	190	L	Burlington, VT	4/3/66	U. of Vermont

GOALTENDERS

	HT	WT	C	Place of Birth	Date	1988-89 Club
COWLEY, Wayne	6-0	185	L	Scarborough, Ont.	12/4/64	Salt Lake City
GUENETTE, Steve	5-10	175	L	Gloucester, Ont.	11/13/65	Pit.-Musk.-Salt Lake
HARVEY, Graeme	6-1	180	L	Green Bay, WI	10/6/69	Sault Ste. Marie
VERNON, Mike	5-9	170	L	Calgary, Alta.	2/24/63	Calgary
WAMSLEY, Rick	5-11	185	L	Simcoe, Ont.	5/25/59	Calgary

Defenseman Al MacInnis won the Conn Smythe Trophy as playoff MVP in 1989. He recorded a League-leading 31 points in post-season play.

1988-89 Scoring

Regular Season

*-Rookie

Pos	#	Player	Team	GP	G	A	Pts	+/-	PIM	PP	SH	GW	GT	S	%
F	7	Joe Mullen	CGY	79	51	59	110	51	16	13	1	7	0	270	18.9
F	12	Hakan Loob	CGY	79	27	58	85	28	44	5	0	4	0	223	12.1
F	39	Doug Gilmour	CGY	72	26	59	85	45	44	11	0	5	1	161	16.1
F	25	Joe Nieuwendyk	CGY	77	51	31	82	26	40	19	3	11	2	215	23.7
D	2	Al MacInnis	CGY	79	16	58	74	38	126	8	0	3	0	277	5.8
D	20	Gary Suter	CGY	63	13	49	62	26	78	8	0	1	0	216	6.0
F	17	Jiri Hrdina	CGY	70	22	32	54	19	26	6	0	2	0	147	15.0
F	29	Joel Otto	CGY	72	23	30	53	12	213	10	2	2	1	123	18.7
F	27	Brian MacLellan	MIN	60	16	23	39	0	104	7	0	0	0	114	14.0
			CGY	12	2	3	5	3	14	0	0	0	0	23	8.7
			TOTAL	72	18	26	44	3	118	7	0	0	0	137	13.1
F	10	Gary Roberts	CGY	71	22	16	30	32	250	1	0	1	2	123	17.9
F	11	Colin Patterson	CGY	74	14	24	38	44	56	0	0	1	0	103	13.6
F	24	Jim Peplinski	CGY	79	13	25	38	6	241	0	0	2	1	103	12.6
F	14	*Theo Fleury	CGY	36	14	20	34	5	46	5	0	3	0	89	15.7
F	22	Mark Hunter	CGY	66	22	8	30	4	194	12	0	2	1	116	19.0
D	34	Jamie Macoun	CGY	72	8	19	27	40	76	0	0	2	0	89	9.0
D	4	Brad McCrimmon	CGY	72	5	17	22	43	96	2	1	2	0	78	6.4
D	5	Dana Murzyn	CGY	63	3	19	22	26	142	0	1	1	0	91	3.3
F	9	Lanny McDonald	CGY	51	11	7	18	1-	26	0	0	3	0	72	15.3
D	55	Rob Ramage	CGY	68	3	13	16	26	156	2	0	0	0	91	3.3
F	19	Tim Hunter	CGY	75	3	9	12	22	375	0	1	1	0	67	4.5
D	6	Ric Nattress	CGY	38	1	8	9	12	47	0	0	0	0	28	3.6
G	30	Mike Vernon	CGY	52	0	4	4	0	18	0	0	0	0		.0
D	3	*Rick Lessard	CGY	6	0	1	1	2-	2	0	0	0	0	2	.0
D	23	*Ken Sabourin	CGY	6	0	1	1	3	26	0	0	0	0	2	.0
D	32	Brian Glynn	CGY	9	0	1	1	1	19	0	0	0	0	4	.0
G	1	*Steve Guenette	PIT	11	0	1	1	0	0	0	0	0	0		.0
			CGY	0	0	0	0		0	0	0	0	0		
			TOTAL	11	0	1	1	0	0	0	0	0	0		.0
G	31	Rick Wamsley	CGY	35	0	1	1	0	8	0	0	0	0		.0
F	15	Rich Chernomaz	CGY	1	0	0	0	1-	0	0	0	0	0	2	.0
F	18	*Stu Grimson	CGY	1	0	0	0	0	5	0	0	0	0	0	.0
F	16	*Serge Priakin	CGY	2	0	0	0	1	2	0	0	0	0	2	.0
D	8	*Dave Reierson	CGY	2	0	0	0	1	2	0	0	0	0	1	.0
F	26	*Paul Ranheim	CGY	5	0	0	0	3-	0	0	0	0	0	4	.0

Goaltending

No.	Goaltender	GPI	Mins	Avg	W	L	T	EN	SO	GA	SA	S%
30	Mike Vernon	52	2938	2.65	37	6	5	0	0	130	1263	.897
31	Rick Wamsley	35	1927	2.96	17	11	4	1	2	95	796	:881
	Totals	80	4871	2.78	54	17	9	1	2	226	2059	.890

Playoffs

Pos	#	Player	Team	GP	G	A	Pts	+/-	PIM	PP	SH	GW	GT	S	%
D	2	Al MacInnis	CGY	22	7	24	31	6	46	5	0	4	1	69	10.1
F	7	Joe Mullen	CGY	21	16	8	24	8	4	6	0	1	0	91	17.6
F	39	Doug Gilmour	CGY	22	11	11	22	12	20	3	0	3	1	49	22.4
F	29	Joel Otto	CGY	22	6	13	19	2	46	2	1	1	1	41	14.6
F	12	Hakan Loob	CGY	22	8	9	17	8	4	2	1	0	0	60	13.3
F	25	Joe Nieuwendyk	CGY	22	10	4	14	0	10	6	0	1	0	57	17.5
F	11	Colin Patterson	CGY	22	3	10	13	10	24	0	0	0	0	24	12.5
F	10	Gary Roberts	CGY	22	5	7	12	9	57	0	0	0	0	29	17.2
D	55	Rob Ramage	CGY	20	1	11	12	5	26	1	0	0	0	46	2.2
F	14	*Theo Fleury	CGY	22	5	6	11	4	24	3	0	3	0	46	10.9
D	34	Jamie Macoun	CGY	22	3	6	9	11	30	0	0	1	0	27	11.1
F	24	Jim Peplinski	CGY	20	1	6	7	3	75	0	0	0	0	22	4.5
F	27	Brian MacLellan	CGY	21	3	2	5	4	19	0	0	1	0	41	7.3
F	22	Mark Hunter	CGY	10	2	2	4	1	23	0	0	0	0	16	12.5
F	9	Lanny McDonald	CGY	14	1	3	4	2	29	0	0	1	0	13	7.7
D	19	Tim Hunter	CGY	19	0	4	4	1	32	0	0	0	0	17	.0
D	20	Gary Suter	CGY	5	0	3	3	3	10	0	0	0	0	16	.0
D	6	Ric Nattress	CGY	19	0	3	3	3	20	0	0	0	0	17	.0
D	5	Dana Murzyn	CGY	21	0	3	3	2	20	0	0	0	0	33	.0
D	4	Brad McCrimmon	CGY	22	0	3	3	4	30	0	0	0	0	30	.0
F	16	*Sergei Priakin	CGY	1	0	0	0	0	0	0	0	0	0	0	.0
D	23	*Ken Sabourin	CGY	1	0	0	0	0	0	0	0	0	0	0	.0
G	31	Rick Wamsley	CGY	1	0	0	0	0	0	0	0	0	0	0	.0
F	17	*Jiri Hrdina	CGY	4	0	0	0	0	0	0	0	0	0	4	.0
G	30	Mike Vernon	CGY	22	0	0	0	0	14	0	0	0	0	0	.0

Goaltending

No.	Goaltender	GPI	Mins	Avg	W	L	EN	SO	GA	SA	S%
30	Mike Vernon	22	1381	2.26	16	5	1	3	52	550	.905
31	Rick Wamsley	1	20	6.00	0	1	0	0	2	10	.800
	Totals	22	1403	2.35	16	6	1	3	55	560	.902

General Manager's History

Cliff Fletcher, 1972-73 to date.

Coaching History

Bernie Geoffrion, 1972-73 to 1973-74; Bernie Geoffrion and Fred Creighton, 1974-75; Fred Creighton, 1975-76 to 1978-79; Al MacNeil, 1979-80 (Atlanta); 1980-81 to 1981-82 (Calgary); Bob Johnson, 1982-83 to 1986-87; Terry Crisp, 1987-88 to date.

Captains' History

Keith McCreary, 1972-73 to 1974-75; Pat Quinn, 1975-76, 1976-77; Tom Lysiak, 1977-78, 1978-79; Jean Pronovost, 1979-80; Brad Marsh, 1980-81; Phil Russell, 1981-82, 1982-83; Lanny McDonald, Doug Risebrough (co-captains), 1983-84; Lanny McDonald, Doug Risebrough, Jim Peplinski (co-captains), 1984-85 to 1986-87; Lanny McDonald, Jim Peplinski (co-captains), 1987-88; Lanny McDonald, Jim Peplinski, Tim Hunter (tri-captains), 1988-89 to date.

Club Records

Team

(Figures in brackets for season records are games played; records for fewest points, wins, ties, losses, goals, goals against are for 70 or more games)

Most Points	117	1988-89 (80)	
Most Wins	54	1988-89 (80)	
Most Ties	19	1977-78 (80)	
Most Losses	38	1972-73 (78)	
Most Goals	397	1987-88 (80)	
Most Goals Against	345	1981-82 (80)	
Fewest Points	65	1972-73 (78)	
Fewest Wins	25	1972-73 (78)	
Fewest Ties	3	1986-87 (80)	
Fewest Losses	17	1988-89 (80)	
Fewest Goals	191	1972-73 (78)	
Fewest Goals Against	226	1988-89 (80)	

Longest Winning Streak
Overall . . . . 10 Oct. 14-
Nov. 3/78
Home . . . . 9 Oct. 17-
Nov. 15/78
. . . . 9 Jan. 3-
Feb. 5/89
Away. . . . . 7 Nov. 10-
Dec. 4/88

Longest Undefeated Streak
Over-all . . . . 13 Nov. 10-
Dec. 8/88
(12 wins, 1 tie)
Home . . . . 17 Oct. 6
Dec. 15/88
(14 wins, 3 ties)
Away. . . . . 9 Feb. 20-
Mar. 21/88
(6 wins, 3 ties)

Longest Losing Streak
Over-all . . . . 11 Dec. 14/85
Jan. 7/86
Home . . . . 4 Four times
Away. . . . . 9 Dec. 1/85
Jan. 12/86

Longest Winless Streak
Over-all . . . . 11 Dec. 14/85-
Jan. 7/86

Home . . . . 6 Nov. 25-Dec. 18/82
Away. . . . . 13 Feb. 3-
Mar. 29/73
(10 losses, 3 ties)
Most Shutouts, Season 8 1974-75 (80)
Most Pen. Mins.,
Season 2,431 1987-88 (80)
Most Goals, Game . . . . 12 Mar. 21/75
(Van. 4 at Atl. 12)

Individual

Most Seasons . . . . 9 Dan Bouchard, Paul
Reinhart, Jim Peplinski
Most Games . . . . 699 Jim Peplinski
Most Goals, Career . . . . . 229 Kent Nilsson
Most Assists, Career . . . . 336 Guy Chouinard, Paul
Reinhart
Most Points, Career . . . . . 562 Kent Nilsson
(229 goals, 333 assists)
Most Pen. Mins., Career . 1,816 Tim Hunter
Most Shutouts, Career . . . 20 Dan Bouchard
Longest Consecutive
Games Streak . . . . . . 257 Brad Marsh
(Oct. 11/78-
Nov. 10/81)
Most Goals, Season . . . . . 66 Lanny McDonald
(1982-83)
Most Assists, Season . . . . . 82 Kent Nilsson
(1980-81)
Most Points, Season . . . . 131 Kent Nilsson
(1980-81)
(49 goals, 82 assists)
Most Pen. Mins., Season . . 375 Tim Hunter
(1988-89)
Most Points, Defenseman
Season . . . . 91 Gary Suter
(1987-88)
(21 goals, 70 assists)
Most Points, Center
Season . . . . 131 Kent Nilsson
(1980-81)
(49 goals, 82 assists)

Most Points, Right Wing
Season . . . . 110 Joe Mullen
(1988-89)
(51 goals, 59 assists)
Most Points, Left Wing
Season . . . . 83 Eric Vail
(1978-79)
(35 goals, 48 assists)
Most Points, Rookie
Season . . . . 92 Joe Nieuwendyk
(1987-88)
(51 goals, 41 assists)
Most Shutouts, Season . . . . . 5 Dan Bouchard
(1973-74)
Phil Myre
(1974-75)
Hakan Loob
(Mar. 12/88)
Most Goals, Game . . . . 5 Joe Nieuwendyk
(Jan. 11/89)
Most Points, Game . . . . . . 6 Guy Chouinard
(Feb. 25/81)
Gary Suter
(Apr. 4/86)
Joe Nieuwendyk
(Nov. 19/87)
(Dec. 13/87)
Joe Mullen
(Jan. 5/89)

All-time Record vs. Other Clubs

Regular Season

	At Home							On Road							Total					
	GP	W	L	T	GF	GA	PTS	GP	W	L	T	GF	GA	PTS	GP	W	L	T	GF	GA	PTS
Boston	32	12	18	2	117	121	26	32	9	20	3	88	112	21	64	21	38	5	205	233	47
Buffalo	31	12	11	8	113	105	32	32	10	18	4	96	136	24	63	22	29	12	209	241	56
Chicago	35	19	10	6	122	103	44	33	8	17	8	95	125	24	68	27	27	14	217	228	68
Detroit	31	20	7	4	138	90	44	31	11	15	5	103	121	27	62	31	22	9	241	211	71
Edmonton	34	16	16	4	166	151	36	36	9	20	7	140	178	25	70	25	36	11	306	329	61
Hartford	19	12	3	4	88	57	25	16	8	6	2	65	57	18	35	20	9	3	153	114	43
Los Angeles	49	32	12	8	246	172	72	51	20	28	3	192	209	43	100	52	40	11	438	381	115
Minnesota	36	19	4	10	136	91	48	34	13	16	5	111	127	31	70	32	20	15	247	218	79
Montreal	30	6	20	5	95	118	17	31	9	17	5	77	112	23	61	15	37	10	172	230	40
*New Jersey	31	23	3	4	146	73	50	31	21	7	3	125	84	45	62	44	10	7	271	157	95
NY Islanders	36	16	10	11	135	117	43	37	8	20	9	98	149	25	73	24	30	20	233	266	68
NY Rangers	37	21	10	6	167	115	48	37	17	16	4	136	134	38	74	38	26	10	303	249	86
Philadelphia	37	19	11	7	156	127	45	38	9	28	1	94	162	19	75	28	39	8	250	289	64
Pittsburgh	31	17	7	7	129	88	41	32	10	14	8	110	115	28	63	27	21	15	239	203	69
Quebec	16	9	3	4	67	45	22	16	8	7	1	48	64	17	32	17	10	5	115	109	39
St. Louis	34	17	14	3	118	98	37	34	16	14	4	129	122	36	68	33	28	7	247	220	73
Toronto	33	19	11	3	144	113	41	32	12	13	7	122	131	31	65	31	24	10	266	244	72
Vancouver	53	37	9	7	246	148	81	53	23	19	11	177	186	57	106	60	28	18	423	334	138
Washington	26	19	5	2	112	59	40	26	12	11	3	101	98	27	52	31	16	5	213	157	67
Winnipeg	34	25	5	4	177	104	54	33	13	14	6	128	140	32	67	38	19	10	305	244	86
Defunct Clubs	13	8	4	1	51	34	17	13	7	3	3	43	33	17	26	15	7	4	94	67	34
Totals	678	378	193	107	2869	2129	863	678	253	323	102	2278	2595	608	1356	631	516	209	5147	4724	1471

* Totals include those of Kansas City (1974-75, 1975-76) and Colorado (1976-77 through 1981-82)

Playoffs

	Series	W	L	GP	W	L	T	GF	GA	Last Mtg.	Round	Result
Chicago	2	2	0	8	7	1	0	30	17	1989	CF	W 4-1
Detroit	1	0	1	2	0	2	0	5	8	1978	P	L 0-2
Edmonton	4	1	3	23	8	15	0	76	110	1988	DF	L 0-4
Los Angeles	4	2	2	14	9	5	0	50	43	1989	DF	W 4-0
Minnesota	1	0	1	6	2	4	0	18	25	1981	SF	L 2-4
Montreal	2	1	1	11	5	6	0	32	31	1989	F	W 4-2
NY Rangers	1	0	1	4	1	3	0	8	14	1980	P	L 1-3
Philadelphia	2	1	1	11	4	7	0	28	43	1981	QF	W 4-3
St. Louis	1	1	0	7	4	3	0	28	22	1986	DF	W 4-3
Toronto	1	0	1	2	0	2	0	5	9	1979	P	L 0-2
Vancouver	4	3	1	18	10	8	0	62	57	1989	DSF	W 4-3
Winnipeg	2	1	1	13	6	7	0	43	45	1987	DSF	L 2-4
Totals	26	12	14	119	56	63	0	395	424			

Playoff Results 1989-85

Year	Round	Opponent	Result	GF	GA
1989	F	Montreal	W 4-2	19	16
	CF	Chicago	W 4-1	15	8
	DF	Los Angeles	W 4-0	22	11
	DSF	Vancouver	W 4-3	26	20
1988	DF	Edmonton	L 0-4	11	18
	DSF	Los Angeles	W 4-1	30	18
1987	DSF	Winnipeg	L 2-4	15	22
1986	F	Montreal	L 1-4	13	15
	CF	St. Louis	W 4-3	28	22
	DF	Edmonton	W 4-3	25	24
	DSF	Winnipeg	W 3-0	15	8
1985	DSF	Winnipeg	L 1-3	13	15

Abbreviations: Round: F – Final; **CF** – conference final; **DF** – division final; **DSF** – division semi-final; **SF** – semi-final; **QF** – quarter-final. **P** – preliminary round. **GA** – goals against; **GF** – goals for.

1988-89 Results

		Home				Away	
Oct.	6	NY Islanders	4-4	Oct.	8	Los Angeles	5-6
	10	Detroit	5-2		22	Toronto	3-3
	14	Edmonton	6-1		23	Philadelphia	5-4
	17	Los Angeles	11-4		25	Pittsburgh	1-6
	19	Minnesota	2-1		30	Vancouver*	1-2
	28	Washington	2-2	Nov.	9	Buffalo	2-3
	31	Chicago	6-3		10	Philadelphia	3-2
Nov.	5	St Louis	6-1		12	Boston	2-1
	5	Buffalo	9-0		15	NY Islanders	5-1
	7	Hartford	6-3		17	New Jersey	5-3
	23	New Jersey	3-2		19	Hartford	5-2
	26	Los Angeles	4-1	Dec.	4	Winnipeg	6-3
	29	Vancouver	3-3		10	Hartford	1-4
Dec.	1	NY Rangers	6-3		12	Toronto	4-4
	6	Quebec	3-2		16	Vancouver	5-3
	8	Edmonton	5-3		20	Los Angeles	3-7
	15	Vancouver	2-0		23	Edmonton	1-4
	29	Montreal	3-4		26	Vancouver	3-2
	31	Winnipeg	4-4	Jan.	8	Edmonton	0-6
Jan.	3	Quebec	5-1		14	Minnesota	1-1
	5	Los Angeles	8-6		15	Buffalo	2-3
	7	Edmonton	7-2		17	Detroit	7-1
	11	Winnipeg	8-3		19	Boston	7-2
	26	NY Rangers	5-3		21	Quebec	3-4
	28	Chicago	5-4		23	Montreal	3-1
Feb.	2	Detroit	3-2		29	Vancouver	4-4
	4	Vancouver	5-2		31	Los Angeles	8-5
	5	Vancouver	5-4	Feb.	9	St Louis	5-3
	18	Boston	3-4		11	Washington	2-1
	20	Washington	6-2		12	Pittsburgh	4-2
	22	Toronto	3-4		15	Winnipeg	6-1
	24	St Louis	4-3		26	Winnipeg*	0-1
	27	Philadelphia	6-3	Mar.	11	Edmonton	5-5
Mar.	2	Montreal	2-3		13	NY Rangers	3-4
	7	Winnipeg	9-5		14	New Jersey	5-1
	9	Pittsburgh	10-3		18	Los Angeles	9-3
	21	NY Islanders	4-1		24	Winnipeg	3-4
	23	Los Angeles	4-2		26	Chicago	7-5
	31	Winnipeg	4-1		27	Minnesota	3-2
Apr.	2	Edmonton*	4-2				

* Denotes afternoon game.

Entry Draft Selections 1989-75

1989
Pick
24 Kent Manderville
42 Ted Drury
50 Veli-Pekka Kautonen
63 Corey Lyons
70 Robert Reichel
84 Ryan O'Leary
105 Francis (Toby) Kearney
147 Alex Nikolic
168 Kevin Wortman
189 Sergei Gomolyakov
210 Dan Sawyer
231 Alexander Yudin
252 Kenneth Kennholt

1988
Pick
21 Jason Muzzatti
42 Todd Harkins
84 Gary Socha
85 Thomas Forslund
90 Scott Matusovich
126 Jonas Bergqvist
147 Stefan Nilsson
168 Troy Kennedy
189 Brett Peterson
210 Guy Darveau
231 Dave Tretowicz
252 Sergey Pryakhin

1987
Pick
19 Bryan Deasley
25 Stephane Matteau
40 Kevin Grant
61 Scott Mahoney
70 Tim Harris
103 Tim Corkery
124 Joe Aloi
145 Peter Ciavaglia
166 Theoren Fleury
187 Mark Osiecki
208 William Sedergren
229 Peter Hasselblad
250 Magnus Svensson

1986
Pick
16 George Pelawa
37 Brian Glynn
79 Tom Quinlan
100 Scott Bloom
121 John Parker
142 Rick Lessard
163 Mark Olsen
184 Warren Sharples
205 Doug Pickell
226 Anders Lindstrom
247 Antonin Stavjana

1985
Pick
17 Chris Biotti
27 Joe Nieuwendyk
38 Jeff Wenaas
59 Lane MacDonald
80 Roger Johansson
101 Esa Keskinen
122 Tim Sweeney
143 Stu Grimson
164 Nate Smith
185 Darryl Olsen
206 Peter Romberg
227 Alexandr Koznevnikov
248 Bill Gregoire

1984
Pick
12 Gary Roberts
33 Ken Sabourin
38 Paul Ranheim
75 Peter Rosol
96 Joel Paunio
117 Brett Hull
138 Kevan Melrose
159 Jiri Hrdina
180 Gary Suter
200 Peter Rucka
221 Stefan Jonsson
241 Rudolf Suchanek

1983
Pick
13 Dan Quinn
51 Brian Bradley
55 Perry Berezan
66 John Bekkers
71 Kevan Guy
77 Bill Claviter
91 Igor Liba
111 Grant Blair
131 Jeff Hogg
151 Chris MacDonald
171 Rob Kivell
191 Tom Pratt
211 Jaroslav Benak
231 Sergei Makarov

1982
Pick
29 Dave Reierson
37 Richard Kromm
51 Jim Laing
65 Dave Meszaros
72 Mark Lamb
93 Lou Kiriakou
114 Jeff Vaive
118 Mats Kihlstrom
135 Brad Ramsden
156 Roy Myllari
177 Ted Pearson
198 Jim Uens
219 Rick Erdall
240 Dale Thompson

1981
Pick
15 Allan MacInnis
56 Mike Vernon
78 Peter Madach
99 Mario Simioni
120 Todd Hooey
141 Rick Heppner
162 Dale Degray
183 George Boudreau
204 Bruce Eakin

1980
Pick
13 Denis Cyr
31 Tony Curtale
32 Kevin LaVallee
39 Steve Konroyd
76 Marc Roy
97 Randy Turnbull
118 John Multan
139 Dave Newsom
160 Claude Drouin
181 Hakan Loob
202 Steve Fletcher

1979
Pick
12 Paul Reinhart
23 Mike Perovich
33 Pat Riggin
54 Tim Hunter
75 Jim Peplinski
96 Brad Kempthorne
117 Glenn Johnson

1978
Pick
11 Brad Marsh
47 Tim Bernhardt
64 Jim MacRae
80 Gord Wappel
97 Greg Meredith
114 Dave Hindmarch
131 Dave Morrison
148 Doug Todd
165 Mark Green
180 Robert Sullivan
196 Berhn Engelbeckt

1977
Pick
20 Miles Zaharko
28 Red Laurence
31 Brian Hill
72 Jim Craig
82 Curt Christofferson
100 Bernard Harbec
118 Bob Gould
133 Jim Bennett
148 Tim Harrer

1976
Pick
8 David Shand
10 Harold Phillipoff
28 Bob Simpson
46 Richard Hodgson
64 Kent Nilsson
82 Mark Earp

1975
Pick
8 Richard Mulhern
26 Rick Bowness
62 Dave Ross
80 Willi Plett
98 Paul Heaver
116 Dale McMullin
134 Rick Piche
150 Nick Sanza
167 Brian O'Connell
181 Joe Augustine
192 Torbjorn Nilsson
216 Gary Gill

Club Directory

Olympic Saddledome
P.O. Box 1540 Station M
Calgary, Alberta T2P 3B9
Phone 403 261-0475
FAX 403 261-0470
ENVOY ID
  Public
  Relations: FLAMES. PR
Capacity: 20.002

Owners
Norman N. Green	Sonia Scurfield
Harley N. Hotchkiss	Byron J. Seaman
Norman L. Kwong	Daryl K. Seaman

President, General Manager, Governor . . . . Cliff Fletcher
Vice-President, Business and Finance. . . . . Clare Rhyasen
Vice-President, Hockey Operations. . . . . Al MacNeil
Vice-President, Corporate &
    Community Relations. . . . . Lanny McDonald
Vice-President, Sales & Broadcasting . . . . Leo Ornest
Assistant to the President . . . . Al Coates
Assistant General Manager. . . . . Doug Risebrough
Controller. . . . . Lynne Tosh
Director of Public Relations. . . . . Rick Skaggs
Head Coach. . . . . Terry Crisp
Assistant Coaches. Paul Baxter, Tom Watt
Goaltending Consultant . . . . Glenn Hall
Salt Lake City Head Coach . . . . Bobby Francis
Salt Lake City Assistant Coach . . . . Jamie Hislop
Chief Scout . . . . Gerry Blair
Co-ordinator of Scouting . . . . Ian McKenzie
Scouts. . . . . Ray Clearwater, Al Godfrey,
                                                          Gerry McNamara, Larry Popein,
                                                          Lou Reycroft
Scouting Staff. . . . . Ben Hays, Garth Malarchuk, David Mayville,
                                                          Lars Norrman, Tom Thompson, Bill White
Executive Secretaries. . . . . Brenda Koyich, Robbie Forand, June Yeates
Assistant Public Relations Director . . . . Mike Burke
Assistant Controller . . . . Dorothy Stuart
Assistant to Vice-President, Sales . . . . Judy Shupe
Advertising Sales . . . . Pat Halls
Ticket Manager. . . . . Ann-Marie Malarchuk
Sport Store Manager . . . . Bruce Wallace
Receptionist . . . . Lynn Horton
Trainer . . . . Jim "Bearcat" Murray
Equipment Manager. . . . . Bobby Stewart
Assistant Trainer . . . . Al Murray
Director of Medicine. . . . . Dr. Terry Groves
Orthopedic Surgeon. . . . . Dr. Lowell Van Zuiden
Team Dentist . . . . Dr. Bill Blair
Consulting Psychologist . . . . Hap Davis, Ph.D.
                                                          and Robert Offenberger, Ph.D.
Location of Press Box . . . . Print/TV—North side; Radio—South Side
Dimensions of Rink . . . . 200 feet by 85 feet
Club Colours . . . . White, Red and Gold
Club Trains at. . . . . Olympic Saddledome
TV Channels . . . . CFAC-TV (Channels 2 & 7)
                                                          CBC-TV (Channels 6 & 9)
Radio . . . . QR-77 Radio (770 AM)

General Manager

FLETCHER, GEORGE CLIFFORD (CLIFF)
General Manager, Calgary Flames. Born in Montreal. Que., August 16, 1935.

Cliff Fletcher's career in professional hockey began in 1956 when he joined the Montreal Canadiens' organization as manager of the Junior "B" Verdun Blues. For the next 10 years, working closely with former Canadien manager Sam Pollock, Fletcher carried out a variety of functions, including coaching and managing the Junior Canadiens and scouting for the parent team. In May, 1966, he joined the St. Louis Blues as Chief Scout for Eastern Canada and remained in that post until June, 1969, when he was appointed Assistant General Manager, a position he held until the end of the 1970-71 season. During his four full seasons with St. Louis, the Blues never failed to reach the playoffs; were Stanley Cup finalists three years in a row and captured two West Division titles. He was named General Manager of the Atlanta Flames, January 10, 1972, and retained the position when the franchise was transferred to Calgary in 1980.

Coach

CRISP, TERRY
Coach, Calgary Flames. Born in Parry Sound, Ont., May 28, 1943.

Terry Crisp, in only his second season behind the Flames' bench, led his club to its finest season in team history; a 54-17-9 record for 117 points, a second consecutive Presidents' Trophy and first ever Stanley Cup Championship. A runner-up for the Adams Trophy in both 1987-88 and 1988-89, Crisp has a .693 winning percentage with the Flames (102-40-18). A former center with the Boston Bruins, St. Louis Blues, New York Islanders and Philadelphia Flyers, Crisp played 11 seasons in the NHL, compiling a 67-134-201 scoring mark in 537 games and contributing to the Flyers' two Stanley Cup seasons in 1974 and 1975. Following his retirement as a player in 1976, he remained with Philadelphia as an assistant coach during 1977-78 and 1978-79. In 1979-80, he was named head coach of the OHL's Sault Ste. Marie Greyhounds, with whom he captured three regular-season titles and two Coach-of the-Year awards in six Junior seasons through 1984-85.

Coaching Record

Season	Team	Games	Regular Season				Games	Playoffs		
			W	L	T	%		W	L	%
1982-83	S.S. Marie (OHL)	70	48	21	1	.693	16	7	6	.531
1983-84	S.S. Marie (OHL)	70	38	28	4	.571	16	8	4	.625
1984-85	S.S. Marie (OHL)	66	54	11	1	.826	16	12	2	.813
1985-86	Moncton (AHL)	80	34	34	12	.500	10	5	5	.500
1986-87	Moncton (AHL)	80	43	31	6	.575	6	2	4	.333
1987-88	**Calgary (NHL)**	**80**	**48**	**23**	**9**	**.656**	**9**	**4**	**5**	**.444**
1988-89	**Calgary (NHL)**	**80**	**54**	**17**	**9**	**.731**	**22**	**16**	**6**	**.727***
	NHL Totals	**160**	**102**	**40**	**18**	**.693**	**31**	**20**	**11**	**.645**

Chicago Blackhawks

1988-89 Results: 27W-41L-12T 66 PTS. Fourth, Norris Division

Schedule

Home

Month	Day	Date	Opponent
Oct.	Thur.	5	St Louis
	Sun.	8	NY Rangers
	Thur.	12	Toronto
	Sun.	15	Detroit
	Thur.	19	Quebec
	Sun.	22	Los Angeles
	Thur.	26	Montreal
	Sun.	29	Washington
Nov.	Thur.	2	Minnesota
	Sun.	5	Winnipeg
	Thur.	9	Pittsburgh
	Sun.	12	Hartford
	Thur.	30	NY Islanders
Dec.	Sun.	3	Detroit
	Wed.	6	Toronto
	Sun.	10	Vancouver
	Sun.	17	Edmonton
	Wed.	20	St Louis
	Fri.	22	Toronto
	Thur.	28	Minnesota
	Sat.	30	Hartford
Jan.	Wed.	3	Edmonton
	Sat.	6	Philadelphia
	Sun.	14	Calgary
	Wed.	17	Minnesota
	Fri.	19	Vancouver
	Wed.	24	Buffalo
Feb.	Tues.	13	Buffalo
	Thur.	15	Calgary
	Sun.	18	Pittsburgh*
	Thur.	22	Boston
	Sun.	25	Philadelphia*
Mar.	Thur.	1	St Louis
	Sun.	4	Boston*
	Sun.	11	St Louis
	Tues.	13	Detroit
	Thur.	22	New Jersey
	Sun.	25	Detroit*
	Thur.	29	Toronto
Apr.	Sun.	1	Minnesota

Away

Month	Day	Date	Opponent
Oct.	Sat.	7	Washington
	Sat.	14	St Louis
	Tues.	17	NY Rangers
	Fri.	20	Winnipeg
	Tues.	24	Detroit
	Sat.	28	New Jersey
	Tues.	31	Quebec
Nov.	Sat.	4	Minnesota
	Sat.	11	NY Islanders
	Thur.	16	Vancouver
	Sat.	18	Calgary
	Sun.	19	Edmonton
	Wed.	22	Los Angeles
	Sun.	26	Minnesota
Dec.	Sat.	9	Pittsburgh
	Wed.	13	Montreal
	Fri.	15	Detroit
	Sat.	23	Toronto
	Tues.	26	St Louis
Jan.	Wed.	10	NY Rangers
	Thur.	11	Philadelphia
	Mon.	15	Toronto
	Fri.	26	Buffalo
	Sat.	27	Hartford
Feb.	Thur.	1	Los Angeles
	Sun.	4	Winnipeg
	Thur.	8	Detroit
	Sat.	10	Minnesota*
	Sat.	17	NY Islanders*
	Tues.	20	St Louis
	Sat.	24	New Jersey*
	Tues.	27	Washington
Mar.	Sat.	3	Boston*
	Wed.	7	Minnesota
	Sat.	10	St Louis
	Thur.	15	Quebec
	Sat.	17	Montreal
	Mon.	19	Toronto
	Sat.	24	Detroit*
	Sat.	31	Toronto

* Denotes afternoon game.

Home Starting Times:

All Games . . . . 7:35 p.m.
Except Matinees . . . . 1:35 p.m.

Franchise date: September 25, 1926

64th NHL Season

Year-by-Year Record

		Home			Road			Overall							
Season	GP	W	L	T	W	L	T	W	L	T	GF	GA	Pts.	Finished	Playoff Result
1988-89	80	16	14	10	11	27	2	27	41	12	297	335	66	4th, Norris Div.	Lost Conf. Championship
1987-88	80	21	17	2	9	24	7	30	41	9	284	328	69	3rd, Norris Div.	Lost Div. Semi-Final
1986-87	80	18	13	9	11	24	5	29	37	14	290	310	72	3rd, Norris Div.	Lost Div. Semi-Final
1985-86	80	23	12	5	16	21	3	39	33	8	351	350	86	1st, Norris Div.	Lost Div. Semi-Final
1984-85	80	22	16	2	16	19	5	38	35	7	309	299	83	2nd, Norris Div.	Lost Conf. Championship
1983-84	80	25	13	2	5	29	6	30	42	8	277	311	68	4th, Norris Div.	Lost Div. Semi-Final
1982-83	80	29	8	3	18	15	7	47	23	10	338	268	104	1st, Norris Div.	Lost Conf. Championship
1981-82	80	20	13	7	10	25	5	30	38	12	332	363	72	4th, Norris Div.	Lost Conf. Championship
1980-81	80	21	11	8	10	22	8	31	33	16	304	315	78	2nd, Smythe Div.	Lost Prelim. Round
1979-80	80	21	12	7	13	15	12	34	27	19	241	250	87	1st, Smythe Div.	Lost Quarter-Final
1978-79	80	18	12	10	11	24	5	29	36	15	244	277	73	1st, Smythe Div.	Lost Quarter-Final
1977-78	80	20	9	11	12	20	8	32	29	19	230	220	83	1st, Smythe Div.	Lost Quarter-Final
1976-77	80	19	16	5	7	27	6	26	43	11	240	298	63	3rd, Smythe Div.	Lost Prelim. Round
1975-76	80	17	15	8	15	15	10	32	30	18	254	261	82	1st, Smythe Div.	Lost Quarter-Final
1974-75	80	24	12	4	13	23	4	37	35	8	268	241	82	3rd, Smythe Div.	Lost Quarter-Final
1973-74	78	20	6	13	21	8	10	41	14	23	272	164	105	2nd, West Div.	Lost Semi-Final
1972-73	78	26	9	4	16	18	5	42	27	9	284	225	93	1st, West Div.	Lost Final
1971-72	78	28	3	8	18	14	7	46	17	15	256	166	107	1st, West Div.	Lost Semi-Final
1970-71	78	30	6	3	19	14	6	49	20	9	277	184	107	1st, West Div.	Lost Final
1969-70	76	26	7	5	19	15	4	45	22	9	250	170	99	1st, East Div.	Lost Semi-Final
1968-69	76	20	14	4	14	19	5	34	33	9	280	246	77	6th, East Div.	Out of Playoffs
1967-68	74	20	13	4	12	13	12	32	26	16	212	222	80	4th, East Div.	Lost Semi-Final
1966-67	70	24	5	6	17	12	6	41	17	12	264	170	94	1st,	Lost Semi-Final
1965-66	70	21	8	6	16	17	2	37	25	8	240	187	82	2nd,	Lost Semi-Final
1964-65	70	20	13	2	14	15	6	34	28	8	224	176	76	3rd,	Lost Final
1963-64	70	26	4	5	10	18	7	36	22	12	218	169	84	2nd,	Lost Semi-Final
1962-63	70	17	9	9	15	12	8	32	21	17	194	178	81	2nd,	Lost Semi-Final
1961-62	70	20	10	5	11	16	8	31	26	13	217	186	75	3rd,	Lost Final
1960-61	**70**	20	6	9	9	18	8	**29**	**24**	**17**	**198**	**180**	**75**	**3rd,**	**Won Stanley Cup**
1959-60	70	18	11	6	10	18	7	28	29	13	191	180	69	3rd,	Lost Semi-Final
1958-59	70	14	12	9	14	17	4	28	29	13	197	208	69	3rd,	Lost Semi-Final
1957-58	70	15	17	3	9	22	4	24	39	7	163	202	55	5th,	Out of Playoffs
1956-57	70	12	15	8	4	24	7	16	39	15	169	225	47	6th,	Out of Playoffs
1955-56	70	9	19	7	10	20	5	19	39	12	155	216	50	6th,	Out of Playoffs
1954-55	70	6	21	8	7	19	9	13	40	17	161	235	43	6th,	Out of Playoffs
1953-54	70	8	21	6	4	30	1	12	51	7	133	242	31	6th,	Out of Playoffs
1952-53	70	14	11	10	13	17	5	27	28	15	169	175	69	4th,	Lost Semi-Final
1951-52	70	9	19	7	8	25	2	17	44	9	158	241	43	6th,	Out of Playoffs
1950-51	70	8	22	5	5	25	5	13	47	10	171	280	36	6th,	Out of Playoffs
1949-50	70	13	18	4	9	20	6	22	38	10	203	244	54	6th,	Out of Playoffs
1948-49	60	13	12	5	8	19	3	21	31	8	173	211	50	5th,	Out of Playoffs
1947-48	60	10	17	3	10	17	3	20	34	6	195	225	46	6th,	Out of Playoffs
1946-47	60	10	17	3	9	20	1	19	37	4	193	274	42	6th,	Out of Playoffs
1945-46	50	15	5	5	8	15	2	23	20	7	200	178	53	3rd,	Lost Semi-Final
1944-45	50	9	14	2	4	16	5	13	30	7	141	194	33	5th,	Out of Playoffs
1943-44	50	15	6	4	7	17	1	22	23	5	178	187	49	4th,	Lost Final
1942-43	50	14	3	8	3	15	7	17	18	15	179	180	49	5th,	Out of Playoffs
1941-42	48	15	8	1	7	15	2	22	23	3	145	155	47	4th,	Lost Quarter-Final
1940-41	48	11	10	3	5	15	4	16	25	7	112	139	39	5th,	Lost Semi-Final
1939-40	48	15	7	2	8	12	4	23	19	6	112	120	52	4th,	Lost Quarter-Final
1938-39	48	5	13	6	7	15	2	12	28	8	91	132	32	7th,	Out of Playoffs
1937-38	**48**	10	10	4	4	15	5	**14**	**25**	**9**	**97**	**139**	**37**	**3rd, Amn. Div.**	**Won Stanley Cup**
1936-37	48	8	13	3	6	14	4	14	27	7	99	131	35	4th, Amn. Div.	Out of Playoffs
1935-36	48	15	7	2	6	12	6	21	19	8	93	92	50	3rd, Amn. Div.	Lost Quarter-Final
1934-35	48	12	9	3	14	8	2	26	17	5	118	88	57	2nd, Amn. Div.	Lost Quarter-Final
1933-34	**48**	13	4	7	7	13	4	**20**	**17**	**11**	**88**	**83**	**51**	**2nd, Amn. Div.**	**Won Stanley Cup**
1932-33	48	12	7	5	4	13	7	16	20	12	88	101	44	4th, Amn. Div.	Out of Playoffs
1931-32	48	13	5	6	5	14	5	18	19	11	86	101	47	2nd, Amn. Div.	Lost Quarter-Final
1930-31	44	14	7	1	10	10	2	24	17	3	108	78	51	2nd, Amn. Div.	Lost Final
1929-30	44	12	9	1	9	9	4	21	18	5	117	111	47	2nd, Amn. Div.	Lost Quarter-Final
1928-29	44	3	13	6	4	16	2	7	29	8	33	85	22	5th, Amn. Div.	Out of Playoffs
1927-28	44	2	18	2	5	16	1	7	34	3	68	134	17	5th, Amn. Div.	Out of Playoffs
1926-27	44	12	8	2	7	14	1	19	22	3	115	116	41	3rd, Amn. Div.	Lost Quarter-Final

Coaching History

Pete Muldoon, 1926-27; Barney Stanley and Hugh Lehman, 1927-28; Herb Gardiner, 1928-29; Tom Shaughnessy and Bill Tobin, 1929-30; Dick Irvin, 1930-31; Dick Irvin and Bill Tobin, 1931-32; Godfrey Matheson, Emil Iverson and Tommy Gorman, 1932-33; Tommy Gorman, 1933-34; Clem Loughlin, 1934-35 to 1936-37; Bill Stewart, 1937-38; Bill Stewart and Paul Thompson, 1938-39; Paul Thompson, 1939-40 to 1943-44; Paul Thompson and Johnny Gottselig, 1944-45; Johnny Gottselig, 1945-46 to 1946-47; Johnny Gottselig and Charlie Conacher, 1947-48; Charlie Conacher, 1948-49 to 1949-50; Ebbie Goodfellow, 1950-51 to 1951-52; Sid Abel, 1952-53 to 1953-54; Frank Eddolls, 1954-55; Dick Irvin, 1955-56; Tommy Ivan, 1956-57; Tommy Ivan and Rudy Pilous, 1957-58; Rudy Pilous, 1958-59 to 1962-63; Billy Reay, 1963-64 to 1975-76; Billy Reay and Bill White, 1976-77; Bob Pulford, 1977-78 to 1978-79; Eddie Johnston, 1979-80; Keith Magnuson, 1980-81; Keith Magnuson and Bob Pulford, 1981-82; Orval Tessier, 1982-83 to 1983-84; Orval Tessier and Bob Pulford, 1984-85; Bob Pulford, 1985-86 to 1986-87; Bob Murdoch, 1987-88; Mike Keenan, 1988-89 to date.

Captains' History

Dick Irvin, 1926-27 to 1928-29; Duke Dutkowski, 1929-30; Ty Arbour, 1930-31; Cy Wentworth, 1931-32; Helge Bostrom, 1932-33; Chuck Gardiner, 1933-34; no captain, 1934-35; Johnny Gottselig, 1935-36 to 1939-40; Earl Seibert, 1940-41, 1941-42; Doug Bentley, 1942-43, 1943-44; Clint Smith 1944-45; John Mariucci, 1945-46; Red Hamill, 1946-47; John Mariucci, 1947-48; Gaye Stewart, 1948-49; Doug Bentley, 1949-50; Jack Stewart, 1950-51, 1951-52; Bill Gadsby, 1952-53, 1953-54; Gus Mortson, 1954-55 to 1956-57; no captain, 1957-58; Eddie Litzenberger, 1958-59 to 1960-61; Pierre Pilote, 1961-62 to 1967-68, no captain, 1968-69; Pat Stapleton, 1969-70; no captain, 1970-71 to 1974-75; Stan Mikita, Pit Martin, 1975-76; Stan Mikita, Pit Martin, Keith Magnuson, 1976-77; Keith Magnuson, 1977-78, 1978-79; Keith Magnuson, Terry Ruskowski, 1979-80; Terry Ruskowski, 1980-81, 1981-82; Darryl Sutter, 1982-83 to 1986-87; Keith Brown, Troy Murray, Denis Savard, 1987-88; Dirk Graham, 1988-89 to date.

1989-90 Player Personnel

FORWARDS	HT	WT	S	Place of Birth	Date	1988-89 Club
BASSEN, Bob	5-10	180	L	Calgary, Alta.	5/6/65	NY Islanders-Chicago
BRACCIA, Rick	6-0	195	L	Revere, MA	9/5/67	Boston College,
CREIGHTON, Adam	6-5	214	L	Burlington, Ont.	6/2/65	Buffalo-Chicago
DAM, Trevor	5-10	208	R	Scarborough, Ont.	4/20/70	London
EAGLES, Mike	5-10	180	L	Sussex, N.B.	3/7/63	Chicago
EGELAND, Tracy	6-1	180		Lethbridge, Alta.	8/20/70	Prince Albert
ELVENAS, Stefan	6-1	183	L	Lund, Sweden	3/30/70	Rogle (Sweden)
ERIKSSON, Tom	5/11	183	R	Umea, Sweden	5/3/66	Djurgarden (Sweden)
GILBERT, Greg	6-1	192	L	Mississauga, Ont.	1/22/62	NY Islanders-Chicago
GRAHAM, Dirk	5-11	190	R	Regina, Sask.	7/29/59	Chicago
GREYERBIEHL, Jason	6-0	175	L	Bramalea, Ont.	3/24/70	Colgate
HUDSON, Mike	6-1	185	L	Guelph, Ont.	2/6/67	Saginaw-Chicago
KOZAK, Mike	6-2	195		Toronto, Ont.	3/14/69	Clarkson Uni.,
LACOUTURE, Bill	6-2	192	R	Framingham, MA	5/28/68	Uni. N. Hampshire
LAFAYETTE, Justin	6-6	200	L	Vancouver, B.C.	1/23/70	Ferris State
LAPPIN, Mike	5-10	175	L	Chicago, IL	1/1/69	Boston U.
LARMER, Steve	5-10	189	L	Peterborough, Ont.	6/16/61	Chicago
LOACH, Lonnie	5-10	181	L	New Liskeard, Ont.	4/14/68	Flint-Saginaw
LUDZIK, Steve	5-11	186	L	Toronto, Ont.	4/3/62	Saginaw-Chicago
LUPZIG, Andreas	6-2	185	L	West Germany	8/5/68	Landshut, Div. 1
MACKEY, David	6-3	190	L	N. Westminster, B.C.	7/24/66	Saginaw-Chicago
MARQUETTE, Dale	5-11	187	L	Prince George, B.C.	3/8/68	Saginaw
McCORMICK, Mike	6-2	220	L	St. Boniface, B.C.	5/14/68	Uni. N. Dakota
MURRAY, Troy	6-1	195	R	Calgary, Alta.	7/31/62	Chicago
NANNE, Marty	6-0	180	R	Edina, MN	7/21/67	Saginaw
NOONAN, Brian	6-1	180	R	Boston, MA	5/29/65	Saginaw-Chicago
PHILLIPS, Guy	6-0	178	R	Brooks, Alta.	2/13/66	Saginaw
POJAR, Jon	6-0	179	L	St. Paul, MN	5/5/70	Colorado College
PRESLEY, Wayne	5-11	172	R	Detroit, MI	3/23/65	Chicago
PULLOLA, Tommi	6-5	202		Vaasa, Finland	5/18/71	SportFin Div. 1 (Fin.)
REILLY, John	6-3	188	L	Lawrence, MA	1/5/68	Boston College
ROENICK, Jeremy	5-11	170	R	Boston, MA	1/17/70	Hull-Chicago
RUCINSKI, Mike	5-11	190	L	Chicago, IL	12/12/63	Saginaw-Chicago
RYCHEL, Warren	6-0	190	L	Tecumseh, Ont.	5/12/67	Saginaw-Chicago
SANDERS, Matt	6-0	180		Ottawa, Ont.	7/17/70	Northeastern
SANDSTROM, Ulf	5-10	180	R	Fagerstad, Sweden	4/24/67	Modo Div. 1 (Sweden)
SANIPASS, Everett	6-1	192	L	Big Cove, N.B.	2/13/68	Saginaw-Chicago
SAVARD, Denis	5-10	167	R	Pt. Gatineau, Que.	2/4/61	Chicago
SECORD, Al	6-1	203	L	Sudbury, Ont.	3/3/58	Toronto-Philadelphia
SUTTER, Duane	6-1	185	R	Viking, Alta.	3/16/60	Chicago
TEPPER, Stephen	6-4	205	R	Santa Ana, Calif.	3/10/69	U. of Maine
THAYER, Chris	6-2	190	R	Exeter, N.H	11/9/67	U. N. Hampshire
THOMAS, Steve	5-10	185	L	Stockport, England	7/15/63	Chicago
TORKKI, Jari	6-0	163	L	Finland	8/11/65	Saginaw-Chicago
VAN DORP, Wayne	6-4	225	L	Vancouver, B.C.	5/19/61	Sag.-Chi.-Rochester
VINCELETTE, Dan	6-1	202	L	Verdun, Que.	8/1/67	Saginaw-Chicago
WERNESS, Lance	6-0	175	R	Burnsville, MN	3/28/69	U. of Minnesota
WILLIAMS, Sean	6-1	182	L	Oshawa, Ont.	1/28/68	Saginaw
WOODCROFT, Craig	6-1	185	L	Toronto, Ont.	12/3/69	Colgate
DEFENSEMEN						
BENNETT, Adam	6-4	206	R	Georgetown, Ont.	3/30/71	Sudbury
BROWN, Keith	6-1	191	R	Cornerbrook, Nfld.	5/6/60	Chicago
CASSIDY, Bruce	5-11	176	L	Ottawa, Ont.	5/20/65	Saginaw-Chicago
CLEARY, Joe	5-11	186	R	Buffalo, NY	1/17/70	Boston College
DAGENAIS, Mike	6-3	198	L	Gloucester, Ont.	7/22/69	Peterborough
DOYON, Mario	6-0	174	R	Quebec City, Que.	8/27/68	Saginaw-Chicago
HAMILTON, Brad	6-0	175	L	Calgary, Alta.	3/30/67	Michigan State
HEED, Jonas	6-0	174	L	Sodertalje, Sweden	1/3/67	Sodertalje (Sweden)
HENTGES, Mathew	6-5	197	L	St. Paul, MN	12/19/69	Merrimac
KURZAWSKI, Mark	6-3	199	R	Chicago, IL	2/25/68	Saginaw
MANSON, Dave	6-2	190	L	Prince Albert, Sask.	1/27/67	Chicago
McGILL, Bob	6-1	190	R	Edmonton, Alta.	4/27/62	Chicago
MOSCALUK, Gary	6-0	195	L	Waskatenau, Alta.	5/23/67	Saginaw
MURRAY, Bob	5-10	186	R	Kingston, Ont.	11/26/54	Saginaw-Chicago
PLAYFAIR, Jim	6-4	200	L	Ft. St. James, B.C.	5/22/64	Saginaw-Chicago
RUSSELL, Cam	6-4	175	L	Halifax, N.S.	1/12/69	Hull
TENZER, Dirk	6-2	193	R	New York, NY	7/26/70	St. Paul's H.S.
TICHY, Milan	6-3	194		Czechoslovakia	9/22/69	Skoda Plzen (Czech)
WILLIAMS, Dan	6-2	180	L	Oak Park, IL	4/15/66	Elmira
WILSON, Doug	6-1	187	L	Ottawa, Ont.	7/5/57	Chicago
WOLF, Todd	6-2	214	L	East Aurora, NY	11/5/67	Colgate
YAWNEY, Trent	6-3	183	L	Hudson Bay, Sask.	9/29/65	Chicago

GOALTENDERS	HT	WT	C	Place of Birth	Date	1988-89 Club
BELFOUR, Ed	5-11	170	L	Carman, Man.	4/21/65	Saginaw-Chicago
CHEVRIER, Alain	5-8	180	L	Cornwall, Ont.	4/23/61	Chicago
DONEGHEY, Michael	6-0	165	L	Boston, MA	7/28/70	Catholic Memorial
PANG, Darren	5-5	155	L	Medford, Ont.	2/17/64	Saginaw-Chicago
WAITE, Jim	6-0	163	R	Sherbrooke, Que.	4/15/69	Saginaw-Chicago

Retired Numbers

1	Glenn Hall	1957-1967
9	Bobby Hull	1957-1972
21	Stan Mikita	1958-1980
35	Tony Esposito	1969-1984

1988-89 Scoring

Regular Season

*–Rookie

Pos	#	Player	Team	GP	G	A	Pts	+/–	PIM	PP	SH	GW	GT	S	%
F	29	Steve Larmer	CHI	80	43	44	87	2	54	19	1	2	0	269	16.0
F	18	Denis Savard	CHI	58	23	59	82	5–	110	7	5	1	1	182	12.6
F	33	Dirk Graham	CHI	80	33	45	78	8	89	5	10	5	1	217	15.2
D	24	Doug Wilson	CHI	66	15	47	62	8	69	4	1	3	0	248	6.0
D	3	Dave Manson	CHI	79	18	36	54	5	352	8	1	0	1	224	8.0
F	19	Troy Murray	CHI	79	21	30	51	0	113	5	2	2	1	156	13.5
F	22	Adam Creighton	BUF	24	7	10	17	5–	44	3	0	1	0	42	16.7
			CHI	43	15	14	29	4–	92	8	0	3	0	113	13.3
			TOTAL	67	22	24	46	9–	136	11	0	4	0	155	14.2
F	32	Steve Thomas	CHI	45	21	19	40	2–	69	8	0	0	0	124	16.9
F	17	Wayne Presley	CHI	72	21	19	40	3–	100	4	3	4	1	132	15.9
D	8	*Trent Yawney	CHI	69	5	19	24	5–	116	3	1	0	0	75	6.7
F	43	*Mike Hudson	CHI	41	7	16	23	12–	20	0	1	0	0	45	15.6
F	14	Greg Gilbert	NYI	55	8	13	21	1	45	0	0	1	0	73	11.0
			CHI	4	0	0	0	1	0	0	0	0	0	2	.0
			TOTAL	59	8	13	21	2	45	0	0	1	0	75	10.7
F	15	Bob Bassen	NYI	19	1	4	5	0	21	0	0	0	0	14	7.1
			CHI	49	4	12	16	5	62	0	0	1	0	37	10.8
			TOTAL	68	5	16	21	5	83	0	0	1	0	51	9.8
F	27	*Jeremy Roenick	CHI	20	9	9	18	4	4	2	0	0	0	52	17.3
D	5	Steve Konroyd	NYI	21	1	5	6	5–	2	0	0	0	0	30	3.3
			CHI	57	5	7	12	11–	40	0	0	1	0	102	4.9
			TOTAL	78	6	12	18	16–	42	0	0	1	0	132	4.5
D	4	Keith Brown	CHI	74	2	16	18	5–	84	1	0	0	0	105	1.9
F	12	Duane Sutter	CHI	75	7	9	16	11–	214	0	0	1	0	83	8.4
F	11	Mike Eagles	CHI	47	5	11	16	8–	44	0	0	0	0	39	12.8
F	10	Brian Noonan	CHI	45	4	12	16	2–	28	2	0	0	1	84	4.8
F	20	Dan Vincelette	CHI	66	11	4	15	9–	119	1	0	0	0	76	14.5
F	7	Everett Sanipass	CHI	50	6	9	15	7–	164	0	0	2	0	51	11.8
D	6	Bob Murray	CHI	15	2	4	6	4–	27	2	0	0	0	19	10.5
G	30	Alain Chevrier	WPG	22	0	4	4	0	2	0	0	0	0	0	.0
			CHI	27	0	0	0	0	0	0	0	0	0	0	.0
			TOTAL	49	0	4	4	0	2	0	0	0	0	0	.0
D	25	Bob McGill	CHI	68	0	4	4	9	155	0	0	0	0	38	.0
F	26	*Dave Mackey	CHI	23	1	2	3	1–	78	0	0	0	0	15	6.7
G	40	Darren Pang	CHI	35	0	3	3	0	4	0	0	0	0	0	.0
F	34	Bill Gardner	CHI	6	1	1	2	2	0	1	0	1	0	4	25.0
D	2	*Mario Doyow	CHI	7	1	1	2	2	6	1	0	0	0	7	14.3
D	37	Bruce Cassidy	CHI	9	0	2	2	5–	4	0	0	0	0	12	.0
F	44	*Jari Torkki	CHI	4	1	0	1	2–	0	1	0	0	0	2	50.0
F	29	Steve Ludzik	CHI	6	1	0	1	0	8	0	0	0	0	7	14.3
F	14	Bill Watson	CHI	3	0	1	1	0	4	0	0	0	0	2	.0
F	16	Mike Stapleton	CHI	7	0	1	1	1–	7	0	0	0	0	6	.0
G	31	*Ed Belfour	CHI	23	0	1	1	0	6	0	0	0	0	0	.0
G	50	*Chris Clifford	CHI	1	0	0	0	0	0	0	0	0	0	0	.0
D	38	*Kevin Paynter	CHI	1	0	0	0	1–	2	0	0	0	0	0	.0
F	36	*Mike Rucinski	CHI	1	0	0	0	0	0	0	0	0	0	0	.0
F	23	*Warren Kychel	CHI	2	0	0	0	1–	17	0	0	0	0	3	.0
D	39	*Jim Playfair	CHI	7	0	0	0	1	28	0	0	0	0	1	.0
F	23	Wayne Van Dorp	CHI	8	0	0	0	1	23	0	0	0	0	4	.0

Goaltending

No.	Goaltender	GPI	Mins	Avg	W	L	T	EN	SO	GA	SA	S%
50	*Chris Clifford	1	4	.00	0	0	0	0	0	0	0	.000
30	Alain Chevrier	27	1573	3.51	13	11	2	2	0	92	740	.875
31	*Ed Belfour	23	1148	3.87	4	12	3	1	0	74	605	.877
40	Darren Pang	35	1644	4.38	10	11	6	1	0	120	915	.869
30	*Jim Waite	11	494	5.22	0	7	1	2	0	43	253	.829
	Totals	**80**	**4874**	**4.12**	**27**	**41**	**12**	**6**	**0**	**335**	**2513**	**.866**

Playoffs

Pos	#	Player	Team	GP	G	A	Pts	+/–	PIM	PP	SH	GW	GT	S	%
F	18	Denis Savard	CHI	16	8	11	19	8	10	2	1	1	0	68	11.8
F	28	Steve Larmer	CHI	16	8	9	17	4	22	3	0	2	0	51	15.7
F	17	Wayne Presley	CHI	14	7	5	12	4	18	1	3	1	0	36	19.4
F	22	Adam Creighton	CHI	15	5	6	11	1–	44	3	1	0	0	31	16.1
D	8	*Trent Yawney	CHI	15	3	6	9	9	20	0	1	0	0	17	17.6
F	19	Troy Murray	CHI	16	3	6	9	1	25	1	0	0	0	20	15.0
F	32	Steve Thomas	CHI	12	3	5	8	2–	10	1	0	2	0	23	13.0
D	3	Dave Manson	CHI	16	0	8	8	2–	84	0	0	0	0	39	.0
F	33	Dirk Graham	CHI	16	2	4	6	3–	38	1	0	0	0	37	5.4
F	14	Greg Gilbert	CHI	15	1	5	6	4	20	0	0	0	0	8	12.5
D	6	Bob Murray	CHI	16	2	3	5	1	22	1	0	0	0	25	8.0
F	12	Duane Sutter	CHI	16	3	1	4	0	15	0	0	2	1	14	21.4
F	27	*Jeremy Roenick	CHI	10	1	3	4	0	7	1	0	1	0	12	8.3
D	4	Keith Brown	CHI	13	1	3	4	1	25	0	0	0	0	13	7.7
D	24	Doug Wilson	CHI	4	1	2	3	1	0	1	0	0	0	11	9.1
F	43	*Mike Hudson	CHI	10	1	2	3	5–	18	1	0	0	0	16	6.3
D	5	Steve Konroyd	CHI	16	2	0	2	1	10	0	1	0	0	19	10.5
F	15	Bob Bassen	CHI	10	1	1	2	1	34	0	0	0	0	7	14.3
G	30	Alain Chevrier	CHI	16	0	1	1	0	0	0	0	0	0	0	.0
F	23	Wayne Van Dorp	CHI	16	0	1	1	1–	17	0	0	0	0	5	.0
D	37	Bruce Cassidy	CHI	1	0	0	0	0	0	0	0	0	0	1	.0
F	10	Brian Noonan	CHI	1	0	0	0	0	0	0	0	0	0	3	.0
G	40	Darren Pang	CHI	2	0	0	0	0	0	0	0	0	0	0	.0
F	7	Everett Sanipass	CHI	3	0	0	0	1–	2	0	0	0	0	2	.0
F	20	Dan Vincelette	CHI	5	0	0	0	0	4	0	0	0	0	3	.0
D	25	Bob McGill	CHI	16	0	0	0	2	33	0	0	0	0	7	.0

Goaltending

No.	Goaltender	GPI	Mins	Avg	W	L	EN	SO	GA	SA	S%
40	Darren Pang	2	10	.00	0	0	0	0	0	4	1.000
30	Alain Chevrier	16	1013	2.61	9	7	1	0	4	484	.909
	Totals	**16**	**1024**	**2.64**	**9**	**7**	**1**	**0**	**45**	**488**	**.908**

Club Records

Team

(Figures in brackets for season records are games played; records for fewest points, wins, ties, losses, goals, goals against are for 70 or more games)

Most Points	107	1970-71 (78)
		1971-72 (78)
Most Wins	49	1970-71 (78)
Most Ties	23	1973-74 (78)
Most Losses	51	1953-54 (70)
Most Goals	351	1985-86 (80)
Most Goals Against	363	1981-82 (80)
Fewest Points	31	1953-54 (70)
Fewest Wins	12	1953-54 (70)
Fewest Ties	7	1953-54 (70)
		1957-58 (70)
Fewest Losses	14	1973-74 (78)
Fewest Goals	*133	1953-54 (70)
Fewest Goals Against	164	1973-74 (78)

Longest Winning Streak

Over-all	8	Dec. 9-26/71
		Jan. 4-21/81
Home	13	Nov. 11-
		Dec. 20/70
Away	7	Dec. 9-29/64

Longest Undefeated Streak

Over-all	15	Jan. 14-
		Feb. 16/67
		(12 wins, 3 ties)
Home	18	Oct. 11-
		Dec. 20/70
		(16 wins, 2 ties)
Away	10	Nov. 2-
		Dec. 16/67
		(8 wins, 2 ties)

Longest Losing Streak

Over-all	13	Feb. 25-
		Oct. 11/51
Home	11	Feb. 8-
		Nov. 22/28
Away	17	Jan. 2-
		Oct. 7/54

Longest Winless Streak

Over-all	21	Dec. 17/50-
		Jan. 28/51
		(18 losses, 3 ties)
Home	*15	Dec. 16/28-
		Feb. 28/29
		(11 losses, 4 ties)
Away	23	Dec. 19/50-
		Oct. 11/51
		(15 losses, 8 ties)

Most Shutouts, Season	15	1969-70 (76)
Most Pen. Mins., Season	2,496	1988-89 (80)
Most Goals, Game	12	Jan. 30/69
		(Chi. 12 at Phil. 0)

Individual

Most Seasons	21	Stan Mikita
Most Games	1,394	Stan Mikita
Most Goals, Career	604	Bobby Hull
Most Assists, Career	926	Stan Mikita
Most Points, Career	1,467	Stan Mikita
		(541 goals, 926 assists)
Most Pen. Mins., Career	1,442	Keith Magnuson
Most Shutouts, Career	74	Tony Esposito
Longest Consecutive Games Streak	560	Steve Larmer
		(1982-83 to present)
Most Goals, Season	58	Bobby Hull
		(1968-69)
Most Assists, Season	87	Denis Savard (81-82, 87-88)
Most Points, Season	131	Denis Savard
		(1987-88)
		(44 goals, 87 assists)
Most Pen. Mins., Season	352	Dave Manson
		(1988-89)
Most Points, Defenseman Season	85	Doug Wilson
		(1981-82)
		(39 goals, 46 assists)

Most Points, Center, Season	131	Denis Savard
		(1987-88)
		(44 goals, 87 assists)
Most Points, Right Wing, Season	92	Jim Pappin
		(1972-73)
		(41 goals, 51 assists)
Most Points, Left Wing, Season	107	Bobby Hull
		(1968-69)
		(58 goals, 49 assists)
Most Points, Rookie, Season	90	Steve Larmer
		(1982-83)
		(43 goals, 47 assists)
Most Shutouts, Season	15	Tony Esposito
		(1969-70)
Most Goals, Game	5	Grant Mulvey
		(Feb. 3/82)
Most Assists, Game	6	Pat Stapleton
		(Mar. 30/69)
Most Points, Game	7	Max Bentley
		(Jan. 28/43)
		Grant Mulvey
		(Feb. 3/82)

* NHL Record.

All-time Record vs. Other Clubs

Regular Season

		At Home						On Road						Total					
	GP	W	L	T	GF	GA	PTS	GP	W	L	T	GF	GA	PTS	GP	W	L	T	GF	GA	Pts
Boston	271	138	89	44	875	721	320	270	82	156	32	758	982	196	541	220	245	76	1633	1703	516
Buffalo	37	21	10	6	120	94	48	38	7	25	6	100	156	20	75	28	35	12	220	250	68
**Calgary	33	17	8	8	125	95	42	35	10	19	6	103	122	26	68	27	27	14	228	217	68
Detroit	290	137	108	45	879	797	319	289	83	179	27	700	993	193	579	220	287	72	1579	1790	512
Edmonton	16	7	7	2	72	78	16	16	4	11	1	58	86	9	32	11	18	3	130	164	25
Hartford	16	8	5	3	74	50	19	16	8	7	1	59	62	17	32	16	12	4	133	112	36
Los Angeles	45	24	15	6	179	138	54	46	21	20	5	158	160	47	91	45	35	11	337	298	101
Minnesota	69	43	18	8	290	181	94	69	31	28	10	246	246	72	138	74	46	18	536	427	166
Montreal	261	87	120	54	699	729	228	261	49	164	48	609	1015	146	522	136	284	102	1308	1744	374
*New Jersey	32	21	7	4	138	89	46	32	14	13	5	105	102	33	64	35	20	9	243	191	79
NY Islanders	34	16	14	4	111	123	36	33	6	16	11	94	128	23	67	22	30	15	205	251	59
NY Rangers	272	123	107	42	831	754	288	272	105	116	52	770	805	262	544	228	223	94	1601	1559	550
Philadelphia	47	22	9	16	160	121	60	47	13	25	8	129	161	34	94	35	34	24	289	282	94
Pittsburgh	46	30	7	9	193	129	69	45	19	22	4	145	159	42	91	49	29	13	338	288	111
Quebec	16	9	6	1	69	57	19	16	4	9	4	58	73	12	32	13	15	5	127	130	31
St. Louis	72	44	18	10	287	210	98	70	23	35	13	225	249	59	142	67	53	23	512	459	157
Toronto	280	136	105	39	847	735	311	281	80	150	48	706	971	208	561	216	255	87	1553	1706	519
Vancouver	43	26	12	5	149	103	57	43	14	19	11	129	129	39	86	40	31	16	278	232	96
Washington	26	15	6	5	114	83	35	26	7	16	3	84	106	17	52	22	22	8	198	189	52
Winnipeg	18	13	4	1	99	58	27	18	7	8	3	73	77	17	36	20	12	4	172	135	44
Defunct Clubs	139	79	40	20	408	267	178	140	52	67	21	316	345	125	279	131	107	41	724	612	303
Totals	2063	1016	715	332	6719	5612	2364	2063	639	1105	319	5625	7127	1597	4126	1655	1820	651	12344	12739	3961

* Totals include those of Kansas City (1974-75, 1975-76) and Colorado (1976-77 through 1981-82)
** Totals include those of Atlanta (1972-73 through 1979-80)

Playoffs

	Series	W	L	GP	W	L	T	GF	GA	Last Mtg.	Round	Result
Boston	6	1	5	22	5	16	1	63	97	1978	QF	L 0-4
Buffalo	2	0	2	9	1	8	0	17	36	1980	QF	L 0-4
Calgary	2	0	2	8	1	7	0	17	30	1989	CF	L 1-4
Detroit	12	7	5	60	33	27	0	187	171	1989	DSF	W 4-2
Edmonton	2	0	2	10	2	8	0	36	69	1985	CF	L 2-4
Los Angeles	1	1	0	5	4	1	0	10	7	1974	QF	W 4-1
Minnesota	4	3	1	20	13	7	0	83	78	1985	DF	W 4-2
Montreal	17	5	12	81	29	50	2	185	261	1976	QF	L 0-4
NY Islanders	2	0	2	6	0	6	0	6	21	1979	QF	L 0-4
NY Rangers	5	4	1	24	14	10	0	66	54	1973	SF	W 4-1
Philadelphia	1	1	0	4	4	0	0	20	8	1971	QF	W 4-0
Pittsburgh	1	1	0	4	4	0	0	14	8	1972	QF	W 4-0
St. Louis	6	5	1	28	19	9	0	92	54	1989	DF	W 4-1
Toronto	7	2	5	25	9	15	1	57	76	1986	DSF	L 0-3
Vancouver	1	0	1	5	1	4	0	13	18	1982	CF	L 1-4
Defunct Clubs	4	2	2	9	5	3	1	16	15			
Totals	73	32	41	320	144	171	5	872	1003			

Abbreviations: Round: F – Final; **CF** – conference final; **DF** – division final; **DSF** – division semi-final; **SF** – semi-final; **QF** – quarter-final. **P** – preliminary round. **GA** – goals against; **GF** – goals for.

Playoff Results 1989-85

Year	Round	Opponent	Result	GF	GA
1989	CF	Calgary	L 1-4	8	15
	DF	St. Louis	W 4-1	19	12
	DSF	Detroit	W 4-2	25	18
1988	DSF	St. Louis	L 4-1	17	21
1987	DSF	Detroit	L 0-4	6	15
1986	DSF	Toronto	L 0-3	9	18
1985	CF	Edmonton	L 2-4	25	44
	DF	Minnesota	W 4-2	31	29
	DSF	Detroit	W 3-0	23	8

1988-89 Results

	Home			Away	
Oct. 6	NY Rangers	2-2	**Oct.** 8	Toronto	4-7
9	Toronto	4-8	15	Hartford	5-7
12	Winnipeg	10-1	18	Detroit	3-4
16	Boston	3-10	20	St Louis	0-2
Nov. 3	Minnesota	4-1	22	Pittsburgh	4-7
6	Los Angeles	3-5	25	Quebec	7-4
9	Montreal	6-6	28	Vancouver	2-5
13	Quebec	5-5	30	Edmonton	5-2
16	Buffalo	3-2	31	Calgary	3-6
20	Vancouver	4-7	**Nov.** 5	Minnesota	5-5
Dec. 11	St Louis	5-2	11	Winnipeg*	6-5
14	Hartford	4-3	19	Montreal	3-5
18	New Jersey	3-5	23	Toronto	3-4
21	Washington	3-4	25	Buffalo	4-5
23	Detroit	7-2	26	Boston	2-8
26	St Louis	1-4	29	Minnesota	2-5
28	Minnesota	4-3	**Dec.** 3	Los Angeles	4-6
Jan. 1	Toronto	3-3	6	Pittsburgh	6-7
8	NY Islanders	3-2	10	Philadelphia*	4-6
11	Detroit	2-2	17	St Louis	0-4
16	Edmonton	2-2	31	NY Rangers*	1-4
18	NY Rangers	4-6	**Jan.** 7	Washington	3-6
30	Toronto	7-1	12	Buffalo	5-6
Feb. 1	Winnipeg	7-4	14	NY Islanders	5-3
5	St Louis	4-5	20	Detroit	3-2
10	NY Islanders	3-1	21	St Louis	2-4
12	Los Angeles*	2-6	24	Vancouver	4-2
15	Washington	7-4	25	Edmonton	6-3
19	Montreal	4-4	28	Calgary	4-5
22	Minnesota	5-5	**Feb.** 4	Toronto	3-1
26	Detroit*	4-4	14	Minnesota	4-2
Mar. 1	Minnesota	5-1	17	Detroit	5-3
5	St Louis	3-3	25	Detroit*	0-5
8	New Jersey	5-7	**Mar.** 4	Toronto	3-3
12	Pittsburgh*	5-6	11	Philadelphia*	2-7
19	Detroit	5-3	15	St Louis	2-3
22	Philadelphia	2-3	16	Minnesota	1-6
26	Calgary	5-7	18	New Jersey*	3-1
29	Quebec	3-1	25	Boston*	3-6
Apr. 2	Toronto	4-3	**Apr.** 1	Hartford	1-6

* Denotes afternoon game.

Entry Draft
Selections 1989-75

1989
Pick
6	Adam Bennett
27	Michael Speer
48	Bob Kellogg
111	Tommi Pullola
132	Tracy Egeland
153	Milan Tichy
174	Jason Greyerbiehl
195	Matt Saunders
216	Mike Kozak
237	Michael Doneghey

1988
Pick
8	Jeremy Roenick
50	Trevor Dam
71	Stefan Elvenas
92	Joe Cleary
113	Justin Lafayette
134	Craig Woodcroft
155	Jon Pojar
176	Mathew Hentges
197	Daniel Maurice
218	Dirk Tenzer
239	Lupzig Andreas

1987
Pick
8	Jimmy Waite
29	Ryan McGill
50	Cam Russell
60	Mike Dagenais
92	Ulf Sandstrom
113	Mike McCormick
134	Stephen Tepper
155	John Reilly
176	Lance Werness
197	Dale Marquette
218	Bill Lacouture
239	Mike Lappin

1986
Pick
14	Everett Sanipass
35	Mark Kurzawski
77	Kucera Frantisek
98	Lonnie Loach
119	Mario Doyon
140	Mike Hudson
161	Marty Nanne
182	Geoff Benic
203	Glen Lowes
224	Chris Thayer
245	Sean Williams

1985
Pick
11	Dave Manson
53	Andy Helmuth
74	Dan Vincelette
87	Rick Herbert
95	Brad Belland
116	Jonas Heed
137	Victor Posa
158	John Reid
179	Richard LaPlante
200	Brad Hamilton
221	Ian Pound
237	Rick Braccia

1984
Pick
3	Ed Olczyk
45	Trent Yawney
66	Tommy Eriksson
90	Timo Lehkonen
101	Darin Sceviour
111	Chris Clifford
132	Mike Stapleton
153	Glen Greenough
174	Ralph Di Fiorie
195	Joakim Persson
216	Bill Brown
224	David Mackey
237	Dan Williams

1983
Pick
18	Bruce Cassidy
39	Wayne Presley
59	Marc Bergevin
79	Tarek Howard
99	Kevin Robinson
115	Jari Torkki
119	Mark Lavarre
139	Scott Birnie
159	Kevin Paynter
179	Brian Noonan
199	Domenic Hasek
219	Steve Pepin

1982
Pick
7	Ken Yaremchuk
28	Rene Badeau
49	Tom McMurchy
70	Bill Watson
91	Brad Beck
112	Mark Hatcher
133	Jay Ness
154	Jeff Smith
175	Phil Patterson
196	Jim Camazzola
217	Mike James
238	Bob Andrea

1981
Pick
12	Tony Tanti
25	Kevin Griffin
54	Darrell Anholt
75	Perry Pelensky
96	Doug Chessell
117	Bill Schafhauser
138	Marc Centrone
159	Johan Mellstrom
180	John Benns
201	Sylvain Roy

1980
Pick
3	Denis Savard
15	Jerome Dupont
28	Steve Ludzik
30	Ken Solheim
36	Len Dawes
57	Troy Murray
58	Marcel Frere
67	Carey Wilson
78	Brian Shaw
99	Kevin Ginnell
120	Steve Larmer
141	Sean Simpson
162	Jim Ralph
183	Don Dietrich
204	Dan Frawley

1979
Pick
7	Keith Brown
28	Tim Trimper
49	Bill Gardner
70	Louis Begin
91	Lowell Loveday
112	Doug Crossman

1978
Pick
10	Tim Higgins
29	Doug Lecuyer
46	Rick Paterson
63	Brian Young
79	Mark Murphy
96	Dave Feamster
113	Dave Mancuso
130	Sandy Ross
147	Mark Locken
164	Glenn Van
179	Darryl Sutter

1977
Pick
6	Doug Wilson
19	Jean Savard
60	Randy Ireland
78	Gary Platt
96	Jack O'Callahan
114	Floyd Lahache
129	Jeff Geiger
144	Stephen Ough

1976
Pick
9	Real Cloutier
27	Jeff McDill
45	Thomas Gradin
63	Dave Debol
81	Terry McDonald
99	John Peterson
115	John Rothstein

1975
Pick
7	Greg Vaydik
25	Daniel Arndt
43	Mike O'Connell
61	Pierre Giroux
79	Bob Hoffmeyer
97	Tom Ulseth
115	Ted Bulley
133	Paul Jensen

Club Directory

Chicago Stadium
1800 W. Madison St.
Chicago, Ill. 60612
Phone 312/733-5300
FAX 312/733-5356
ENVOY ID
  Front Office: HAWKS. GM
  Public
  Relations: HAWKS. PR
Capacity: 17,317

President	William W. Wirtz
Vice-President	Arthur Michael Wirtz, Jr.
Vice-President & Assistant to the President	Thomas N. Ivan
General Manager	Robert J. Pulford
Assistant G.M. & Director of Player Personnel	Jack Davison
Head Coach	Mike Keenan
Assistant Coaches	Jacques Martin, E.J. McGuire
Scouts	Kerry Davison, Michel Dumas, Dave Lucas, Jim Pappin, Don Smith, Jan Spieczny, Jim Walker
Secretary to the General Manager	Cindy Bodnarchuk
Public Relations Director	Jim DeMaria
Asst. PR & Director of Community Relations	Tom Finks
Director of Team Services	Steve Williams
Receptionist	Vicki Stokes
Season Tickets	Mildred Hornik
Club Doctors	Dr. Louis W. Kolb
	Dr. Howard Baim
Club Dentist	Dr. Robert Duresa
Trainers	Lou Varga, Randy Lacey, Mike Gapski
Executive Offices	Chicago Stadium
Largest Hockey Crowd	20,960 on April 10, 1982 vs Minnesota
Location of Press Box	West side of the Stadium
Dimensions of Rink	185 feet by 85 feet
Ends of Rink	Plexi-glass extends above boards around rink
Club Colors	Red, Black and White
Radio Station	WBBM (AM 780)
Television Station	SportsChannel
Broadcasters	Pat Foley, Dale Tallon
Organist	Nancy Faust
Soloist	Wayne Messmer
Public Address Announcer	Harvey Wittenberg

General Manager

PULFORD, ROBERT JESSE (BOB)
General Manager, Chicago Blackhawks.
Born in Newton Robinson, Ont., March 31, 1936.

Bob Pulford was named general-manager and coach of Chicago, July 6, 1977, after five successful seasons as head coach of the Los Angeles Kings. He relinquished the coaching duties to Eddie Johnston prior to the start of the 1979-80 season, but returned behind the bench on February 3, 1982, replacing Keith Magnuson. At the conclusion of the 1981-82 season, Pulford stepped down as coach of the Blackhawks and on June 16, 1982 named Orval Tessier as his successor. After 16 playing seasons in the NHL, Pulford began his coaching career with the Kings in 1972-73. For 14 of those seasons, Pulford was an industrious player with the Toronto Maple Leafs before being traded to Los Angeles where he finished his active career as captain of the Kings. Although he never won an individual award nor was ever selected to an All-Star team, Pulford was recognized as one of the hardest-working centers during the era in which he played. His all-round ability enabled him to be rated one of the League's outstanding penalty-killers. Pulford was named NHL coach-of-the-year in 1974-75 by the NHL Broadcasters' Association.

NHL Coaching Record

			Regular Season				Playoffs			
Season	Team	Games	W	L	T	%	Games	W	L	%
1972-73	Los Angeles	78	31	36	11	.468	....	....	....	....
1973-74	Los Angeles	78	33	33	12	.500	5	1	4	.200
1974-75	Los Angeles	80	42	17	21	.656	3	1	2	.333
1975-76	Los Angeles	80	38	33	9	.531	9	5	4	.556
1976-77	Los Angeles	80	34	31	15	.519	9	4	5	.444
1977-78	Chicago	80	32	29	19	.519	4	0	4	.000
1978-79	Chicago	80	29	36	15	.456	4	0	4	.000
1981-82	Chicago	28	13	13	2	.500	15	8	7	.533
1984-85	Chicago	27	16	7	4	.666	15	9	6	.600
1985-86	Chicago	80	39	33	8	.538	3	0	3	.000
1986-87	Chicago	80	29	37	14	.450	4	0	4	.000
	NHL Totals	**771**	**336**	**305**	**130**	**.520**	**71**	**28**	**43**	**.394**

General Managers' History

Major Frederic McLaughlin, 1926-27 to 1941-42; Bill Tobin, 1942-43 to 1953-54; Tommy Ivan, 1954-55 to 1976-77; Bob Pulford, 1977-78 to date.

Coach

KEENAN, MICHAEL (MIKE)
Head Coach, Chicago Blackhawks.
Born in Toronto, Ont., October 21, 1949.

In his first year with the Blackhawks, Mike Keenan led the club to its best post-season performance in four years. After a slow start, Chicago rebounded as one of the League's most improved teams in the second half of the season, securing a playoff berth and a trip to the Campbell Conference Championship with series wins over Detroit and St. Louis.

Keenan spent four years in the Philadelphia Flyers' organization (1984-85 to 1987-88) before being hired by the Blackhawks on June 9, 1988. While with the Flyers, he led his team to the Stanley Cup Final twice in four years and distinguished himself as the first coach in League history to register 40-or-more wins in his first three seasons. Entering the 1989-90 season, his five-year record stands at 217-143-40 for a .593 winning percentage. Keenan was the head coach for Team Canada in the 1987 Canada Cup and led his club to a 2-1 series victory over the Soviet Union in the Final.

A former team captain of the St. Lawrence University Saints, Keenan began coaching at the Junior B level, winning back-to-back championships in the Metro Toronto League. After leading the OHL's Peterborough Petes to the 1979-80 Memorial Cup Finals, he joined the AHL's Rochester Americans, carrying that team to the 1982-83 Calder Cup title. The following season, 1983-84, immediately preceding his tenure with the Flyers, Keenan posted yet another championship, this time taking the CIAU Canadian college title with the University of Toronto Blues.

Coaching Record

			Regular Season				Playoffs			
Season	Team	Games	W	L	T	%	Games	W	L	%
1979-80	Peterborough (OHL)	68	47	20	1	.699	18	15	3	.833
1980-81	Rochester (AHL)	80	30	42	8	.425	...	...	...	...
1981-82	Rochester (AHL)	80	40	31	9	.556	9	4	5	.444
1982-83	Rochester (AHL)	80	46	25	9	.631	16	12	4	.750
1983-84	U. of Toronto (CIAU)	49	41	5	3	.867	...	...	...	...
1984-85	Philadelphia (NHL)	80	53	20	7	.706	19	12	7	.632
1985-86	Philadelphia (NHL)	80	53	23	4	.688	5	2	3	.400
1986-87	Philadelphia (NHL)	80	46	26	8	.625	26	15	11	.577
1987-88	Philadelphia (NHL)	80	38	33	9	.531	7	3	4	.429
1988-89	Chicago (NHL)	80	27	41	12	.413	16	9	7	.563
	NHL Totals	**400**	**217**	**143**	**40**	**.593**	**73**	**41**	**32**	**.562**

Detroit Red Wings

1988-89 Results: 34w-34L-12T 80 PTS. First, Norris Division

Steve Yzerman re-wrote the Detroit record book with 155 points in 1988-89.

Schedule

Home		Away	
Oct.	Thur. 12 Winnipeg	**Oct.**	Thur. 5 Calgary
	Sat. 14 Buffalo		Sat. 7 Vancouver
	Wed. 18 Minnesota		Sun. 8 Los Angeles
	Tues. 24 Chicago		Sun. 15 Chicago
	Thur. 26 Pittsburgh		Thur. 19 St Louis
Nov.	Wed. 1 Philadelphia		Sat. 21 Hartford
	Fri. 3 Hartford		Sat. 28 Toronto
	Tues. 14 Hartford	**Nov.**	Sat. 4 NY Islanders
	Thur. 16 St Louis		Mon. 6 NY Rangers
	Tues. 21 Boston		Thur. 9 Minnesota
	Fri. 24 Calgary		Sat. 11 Toronto
	Mon. 27 Edmonton		Sat. 18 Quebec
	Wed. 29 Washington	**Dec.**	Fri. 1 Winnipeg
Dec.	Tues. 5 St Louis		Sun. 3 Chicago
	Fri. 8 Minnesota		Sat. 9 Minnesota
	Wed. 13 Toronto		Sat. 16 Montreal
	Fri. 15 Chicago		Sat. 23 Boston*
	Wed. 20 Toronto		Tues. 26 Buffalo
	Sun. 31 New Jersey		Wed. 27 Toronto
Jan.	Tues. 2 Vancouver		Fri. 29 Washington
	Thur. 4 Quebec	**Jan.**	Sat. 6 Minnesota
	Tues. 9 Minnesota		Fri. 12 Winnipeg
	Tues. 23 St Louis		Sat. 13 Minnesota
	Thur. 25 Pittsburgh		Tues. 16 Edmonton
	Wed. 31 Edmonton		Thur. 18 Los Angeles
Feb.	Fri. 2 Toronto		Sat. 27 Quebec
	Tues. 6 Boston	**Feb.**	Sat. 3 St Louis
	Thur. 8 Chicago		Mon. 12 New Jersey
	Sat. 10 Calgary*		Sat. 17 St Louis
	Wed. 14 Los Angeles		Sat. 24 NY Islanders*
	Fri. 16 Philadelphia		Sun. 25 Washington*
	Mon. 19 Montreal	**Mar.**	Sat. 3 Toronto
	Wed. 21 NY Rangers		Mon. 5 NY Rangers
	Wed. 28 NY Islanders		Sat. 10 Montreal
Mar.	Fri. 2 Toronto		Tues. 13 Chicago
	Thur. 8 St Louis		Thur. 15 Pittsburgh
	Tues. 20 Vancouver		Sat. 17 St Louis
	Thur. 22 Minnesota		Sun. 25 Chicago*
	Sat. 24 Chicago*		Sat. 31 New Jersey*
	Tues. 27 Buffalo	**Apr.**	Sun. 1 Philadelphia

* Denotes afternoon game.

Home Starting Times:
Weeknights and Saturdays .... 7:35 p.m.
Sundays .... 7:05 p.m.
Matinees .... 1:05 p.m.

Franchise date: September 25, 1926

64th NHL Season

Year-by-Year Record

Season	GP	Home W	L	T	Road W	L	T	Overall W	L	T	GF	GA	Pts.		Finished	Playoff Result
1988-89	80	20	14	6	14	20	6	34	34	12	313	316	80	1st,	Norris Div.	Lost Div. Semi-Final
1987-88	80	24	10	6	17	18	5	41	28	11	322	269	93	1st,	Norris Div.	Lost Conf. Championship
1986-87	80	20	14	6	14	22	4	34	36	10	260	274	78	2nd,	Norris Div.	Lost Conf. Championship
1985-86	80	10	26	4	7	31	2	17	57	6	266	415	40	5th,	Norris Div.	Out of Playoffs
1984-85	80	19	14	7	8	27	5	27	41	12	313	357	66	3rd,	Norris Div.	Lost Div. Semi-Final
1983-84	80	18	20	2	13	22	5	31	42	7	298	323	69	3rd,	Norris Div.	Lost Div. Semi-Final
1982-83	80	14	19	7	7	25	8	21	44	15	263	344	57	5th,	Norris Div.	Out of Playoffs
1981-82	80	15	19	6	6	28	6	21	47	12	270	351	54	6th,	Norris Div.	Out of Playoffs
1980-81	80	16	15	9	3	28	9	19	43	18	252	339	56	5th,	Norris Div.	Out of Playoffs
1979-80	80	14	21	5	12	22	6	26	43	11	268	306	63	5th,	Norris Div.	Out of Playoffs
1978-79	80	15	17	8	8	24	8	23	41	16	252	295	62	5th,	Norris Div.	Out of Playoffs
1977-78	80	22	11	7	10	23	7	32	34	14	252	266	78	2nd,	Norris Div.	Lost Quarter-Final
1976-77	80	12	22	6	4	33	3	16	55	9	183	309	41	5th,	Norris Div.	Out of Playoffs
1975-76	80	17	15	8	9	29	2	26	44	10	226	300	62	4th,	Norris Div.	Out of Playoffs
1974-75	80	17	17	6	6	28	6	23	45	12	259	335	58	4th,	Norris Div.	Out of Playoffs
1973-74	78	21	12	6	8	27	4	29	39	10	255	319	68	6th,	East Div.	Out of Playoffs
1972-73	78	22	12	5	15	17	7	37	29	12	265	243	86	5th,	East Div.	Out of Playoffs
1971-72	78	25	11	3	8	24	7	33	35	10	261	262	76	5th,	East Div.	Out of Playoffs
1970-71	78	17	15	7	5	30	4	22	45	11	209	308	55	7th,	East Div.	Out of Playoffs
1969-70	76	20	11	7	20	10	8	40	21	15	246	199	95	3rd,	East Div.	Lost Quarter-Final
1968-69	76	23	8	7	10	23	5	33	31	12	239	221	78	5th,	East Div.	Out of Playoffs
1967-68	74	18	15	4	9	20	8	27	35	12	245	257	66	6th,	East Div.	Out of Playoffs
1966-67	70	21	11	3	6	28	1	27	39	4	212	241	58	5th,		Out of Playoffs
1965-66	70	20	8	7	11	19	5	31	27	12	221	194	74	4th,		Lost Final
1964-65	70	25	7	3	15	16	4	40	23	7	224	175	87	1st,		Lost Semi-Final
1963-64	70	23	9	3	7	20	8	30	29	11	191	204	71	4th,		Lost Final
1962-63	70	19	10	6	13	15	7	32	25	13	200	194	77	4th,		Lost Final
1961-62	70	17	11	7	6	22	7	23	33	14	184	219	60	5th,		Out of Playoffs
1960-61	70	15	13	7	10	16	9	25	29	16	195	215	66	4th,		Lost Final
1959-60	70	18	14	3	8	15	12	26	29	15	186	197	67	4th,		Lost Semi-Final
1958-59	70	13	17	5	12	20	3	25	37	8	167	218	58	6th,		Out of Playoffs
1957-58	70	16	11	8	13	18	4	29	29	12	176	207	70	3rd,		Lost Semi-Final
1956-57	70	23	7	5	15	13	7	38	20	12	198	157	88	1st,		Lost Semi-Final
1955-56	70	21	6	8	9	18	8	30	24	16	183	148	76	2nd,		Lost Final
1954-55	**70**	**25**	**5**	**5**	**17**	**12**	**6**	**42**	**17**	**11**	**204**	**134**	**95**	**1st,**		**Won Stanley Cup**
1953-54	**70**	**24**	**4**	**7**	**13**	**15**	**7**	**37**	**19**	**14**	**191**	**132**	**88**	**1st,**		**Won Stanley Cup**
1952-53	70	20	5	10	16	11	8	36	16	18	222	133	90	1st,		Lost Semi-Final
1951-52	**70**	**24**	**7**	**4**	**20**	**7**	**8**	**44**	**14**	**12**	**215**	**133**	**100**	**1st,**		**Won Stanley Cup**
1950-51	70	25	3	7	19	10	6	44	13	13	236	139	101	1st,		Lost Semi-Final
1949-50	**70**	**19**	**9**	**7**	**18**	**10**	**7**	**37**	**19**	**14**	**229**	**164**	**88**	**1st,**		**Won Stanley Cup**
1948-49	60	21	6	3	13	13	4	34	19	7	195	145	75	1st,		Lost Final
1947-48	60	16	9	5	14	9	7	30	18	12	187	148	72	2nd,		Lost Final
1946-47	60	14	10	6	8	17	5	22	27	11	190	193	55	4th,		Lost Semi-Final
1945-46	50	16	5	4	4	15	6	20	20	10	146	159	50	4th,		Lost Semi-Final
1944-45	50	19	5	1	12	9	4	31	14	5	218	161	67	2nd,		Lost Final
1943-44	50	18	5	2	8	13	4	26	18	6	214	177	58	2nd,		Lost Semi-Final
1942-43	**50**	**16**	**4**	**5**	**9**	**10**	**6**	**25**	**14**	**11**	**169**	**124**	**61**	**1st,**		**Won Stanley Cup**
1941-42	48	14	7	3	5	18	1	19	25	4	140	147	42	5th,		Lost Final
1940-41	48	14	5	5	7	11	6	21	16	11	112	102	53	4th,		Lost Final
1939-40	48	11	10	3	5	16	3	16	26	6	90	126	38	5th,		Lost Semi-Final
1938-39	48	14	8	2	4	16	4	18	24	6	107	128	42	5th,		Lost Semi-Final
1937-38	48	8	10	6	4	15	5	12	25	11	99	133	35	4th,	Amn. Div.	Out of Playoffs
1936-37	**48**	**14**	**5**	**5**	**11**	**9**	**4**	**25**	**14**	**9**	**128**	**102**	**59**	**1st,**	**Amn. Div.**	**Won Stanley Cup**
1935-36	**48**	**14**	**5**	**5**	**10**	**11**	**3**	**24**	**16**	**8**	**124**	**103**	**56**	**1st,**	**Amn. Div.**	**Won Stanley Cup**
1934-35	48	11	8	5	8	14	2	19	22	7	127	114	45	4th,	Amn. Div.	Out of Playoffs
1933-34*	48	15	5	4	9	9	6	24	14	10	113	98	58	1st,	Amn. Div.	Lost Final
1932-33	48	17	3	4	8	12	4	25	15	8	111	93	58	2nd,	Amn. Div.	Lost Semi-Final
1931-32	48	14	3	6	3	17	4	18	20	10	95	108	46	3rd,	Amn. Div.	Lost Quarter-Final
1930-31**	44	10	7	5	6	14	2	16	21	7	102	105	39	4th,	Amn. Div.	Out of Playoffs
1929-30	44	9	10	3	5	14	3	14	24	6	117	133	34	4th,	Amn. Div.	Out of Playoffs
1928-29	44	11	6	5	8	10	4	19	16	9	72	63	47	3rd,	Amn. Div.	Lost Quarter-Final
1927-28	44	9	10	3	10	9	3	19	19	6	88	79	44	4th,	Amn. Div.	Out of Playoffs
1926-27***	44	6	15	1	6	13	3	12	28	4	76	105	28	5th,	Amn. Div.	Out of Playoffs

* Team name changed to Red Wings.
** Team name changed to Falcons.
*** Team named Cougars.

1989-90 Player Personnel

FORWARDS	HT	WT	S	Place of Birth	Date	1988-89 Club
BARR, David	6-1	190	R	Toronto, Ont.	11/30/60	Detroit
BISSETT, Tom	6-0	180	L	Seattle, WA	3/13/66	Mich. Tech-Adirondack
BURR, Shawn	6-1	195	L	Sarnia, Ont.	7/1/66	Detroit
CHABOT, John	6-2	200	L	Summerside, P.E.I.	5/18/62	Detroit-Adirondack
EAVES, Murray	5-10	185	R	Calgary, Alta.	5/10/60	Adirondack-Detroit
FEDERKO, Bernie	6-0	180	L	Foam Lake, Sask.	5/12/56	St. Louis
FEDYK, Brent	6-0	195	R	Yorkton, Sask.	3/8/67	Adirondack-Detroit
GALLANT, Gerard	5-10	185	L	Summerside, P.E.I.	9/2/63	Detroit
GRAVES, Adam	5-11	185	L	Toronto, Ont.	4/12/68	Detroit-Adirondack
HABSCHIED, Marc	6-0	185	R	Swift Current, Sask.	3/1/63	Minnesota
HOLLAND, Dennis	5-10	165	L	Vernon, B.C.	1/30/69	Portland
KENNEDY, Sheldon	5-10	170	R	Brandon, Man.	6/15/69	Swift Current
KING, Kris	6-0	193	L	Bracebridge, Ont.	2/18/66	Adirondack-Detroit
KLIMA, Petr	6-0	190	L	Chaomutov, Czech.	12/23/64	Detroit-Adirondack
KOCUR, Joe	6-0	195	R	Calgary, Alta.	12/21/64	Detroit
KOCUR, Kory	5-11	188	R	Kelvington, Sask.	3/6/69	Saskatoon
KRENTZ, Dale	5-11	190	L	Steinbach, Man.	12/19/61	Adirondack-Detroit
McCOSH, Shawn	6-0	188	R	Oshawa, Ont.	6/5/69	Niagara Falls
McKAY, Randy	6-1	185	R	Montreal, Que.	1/25/67	Adirondack-Detroit
McKEGNEY, Tony	6-1	200	L	Montreal, Que.	2/15/58	St. Louis
MERKOSKY, Glenn	5-10	175	L	Edmonton, Alta.	4/8/59	Adirondack
MURPHY, Joe	6-1	190	L	London, Ont.	10/16/67	Detroit-Adirondack
NILL, Jim	6-0	185	R	Hanna, Alta.	4/11/58	Detroit
ROBERTSON Torrie	5-11	200	L	Victoria, B.C.	8/2/61	Hartford-Detroit
SHANK, Daniel	5-10	190	R	Montreal, Que.	5/12/67	Adirondack
SILLINGER, Mike	5-10	191	R	Regina, Sask.	6/29/71	Regina
YZERMAN, Steve	5-11	185	R	Cranbrook, B.C.	5/9/65	Detroit
DEFENSEMEN						
ANGLEHART, Serge	6-2	189	R	Hull, Que.	4/18/70	D'ville-Adirondack
BIGNELL, Greg	6-0	188	L	Kitchener, Ont.	5/9/69	Belleville
BOUGHNER, Bob	5-11	201	R	Windsor, Ont.	3/8/71	Sault Ste. Marie
CHIASSON, Steve	6-1	205	L	Barrie, Ont.	4/14/67	Detroit
DOYLE, Rob	5-11	185	R	Lindsay, Ont.	2/10/64	Adirondack
DUPUIS, Guy	6-2	199	R	Moncton, N.B.	5/10/70	Hull
HOUDA, Doug	6-2	200	R	Blairmore, Alta.	6/3/66	Adirondack-Detroit
KOTSOPOULOS, Chris	6-3	215	R	Scarborough, Ont.	11/27/58	Toronto
KRUPPKE, Gord	6-1	200	R	Slave Lake, Alta.	4/2/69	Prince Albert
MAYER, Derek	6-0	185	R	Rossland, B.C.	5/21/67	Cdn. National Team
MORTON, Dean	6-1	196	R	Peterborough, Ont.	2/27/68	Adirondack
MOKOSAK, John	5-11	200	L	Edmonton, Alta.	9/7/63	Adirondack-Detroit
NORWOOD, Lee	6-1	198	L	Oakland, CA	2/2/60	Detroit
O'CONNELL, Mike	5-9	180	R	Chicago, IL	11/25/55	Detroit
RACINE, Yves	6-0	185	L	Matane, Que.	2/7/69	Victoriaville-Adirondack
SALMING, Borje	6-1	185	L	Kiruna, Sweden	4/17/51	Toronto
SCHENA, Rob	6/1	190	L	Saugess, MA	2/5/67	RPI-Adirondack
SHARPLES, Jeff	6-1	195	L	Terrace, B.C.	7/28/67	Detroit-Adirondack
STARK, Jay	6-0	190	R	Vernon, B.C.	2/29/68	Seattle-Flint
WILKIE, Bob	6-2	200	R	Calgary, Alta.	2/11/69	Swift Current
ZOMBO, Rick	6-1	195	R	DesPlaines, IL	5/8/63	Detroit

GOALTENDERS	HT	WT	C	Place of Birth	Date	1988-89 Club
CHEVELDAE, Tim	5-10	175	L	Melville, Sask.	2/15/68	Adirondack-Detroit
GLICKMAN, Jason	5-9	179	L	Chicago, IL	3/25/69	Hull
HANLON, Glen	6-0	185	R	Brandon, Man.	2/20/57	Detroit
HANSCH, Randy	5-10	165	R	Edmonton, Alta.	2/8/66	Cdn. National Team
REIMER, Mark	5-11	170	L	Calgary, Alta.	3/23/67	Flint-Adirondack
ST. LAURENT, Sam	5-10	190	L	Arvida, Que.	2/16/59	Detroit-Adirondack
STEFAN, Greg	5-11	180	L	Brantford, Ont.	2/11/61	Detroit

Retired Numbers

6	Larry Aurie	1927-1939
9	Gordie Howe	1946-1971

Captains' History

Art Duncan, 1926-27; Reg Noble, 1927-28 to 1929-30; George Hay, 1930-31; Carson Cooper, 1931-32; Larry Aurie, 1932-33; Herbie Lewis, 1933-34; Ebbie Goodfellow, 1934-35; Doug Young, 1935-36 to 1937-38; Ebbie Goodfellow, 1938-39 to 1941-42; Sid Abel, 1942-43; Mud Bruneteau, Bill Hollett (co-captains), 1943-44; Bill Hollett, 1944-45; Bill Hollett, Sid Abel, 1945-46; Sid Abel, 1946-47 to 1951-52; Ted Lindsay, 1952-53 to 1955-56; Red Kelly, 1956-57, 1957-58; Gordie Howe, 1958-59 to 1961-62; Alex Delvecchio, 1962-63 to 1973-74; Marcel Dionne, 1974-75; Danny Grant, Terry Harper, 1975-76; Danny Grant, Dennis Polonich, 1976-77; Dan Maloney, Dennis Hextall, 1977-78; Dennis Hextall, Nick Libett, Paul Woods, 1978-79; Dale McCourt, 1979-80; Errol Thompson, Reed Larson, 1980-81; Reed Larson, 1981-82; Danny Gare, 1982-83 to 1985-86; Steve Yzerman, 1986-87 to date.

1988-89 Scoring

Regular Season

*–Rookie

Pos	#	Player	Team	GP	G	A	Pts	+/–	PIM	PP	SH	GW	GT	S	%
F	19	Steve Yzerman	DET	80	65	90	155	17	61	17	3	7	2	388	16.8
F	17	Gerard Gallant	DET	76	39	54	93	7	230	13	0	7	0	221	17.6
F	21	Adam Oates	DET	69	16	62	78	1–	14	2	0	1	1	127	12.6
F	15	Paul MacLean	DET	76	36	35	71	7	118	16	0	5	1	148	24.3
F	22	Dave Barr	DET	73	27	32	59	12	69	5	2	3	1	140	19.3
D	3	Steve Chiasson	DET	65	12	35	47	6–	149	5	2	0	0	187	6.4
F	11	Shawn Burr	DET	79	19	27	46	5	78	1	4	2	0	149	12.8
D	23	Lee Norwood	DET	66	10	32	42	6	100	4	1	0	0	97	10.3
F	85	Petr Klima	DET	51	25	16	41	5	44	1	0	3	0	145	17.2
D	4	Rick Zombo	DET	75	1	20	21	23	106	1	0	0	0	64	1.6
F	26	Joey Kocur	DET	60	9	9	18	4–	213	1	0	1	0	76	11.8
D	2	Mike O'Connell	DET	66	1	15	16	8–	41	0	0	0	0	49	2.0
F	8	Jim Nill	DET	71	8	7	15	1–	83	0	1	2	0	39	20.5
F	20	Tim Higgins	DET	42	5	9	14	0	62	0	0	0	0	45	11.1
D	34	Jeff Sharples	DET	46	4	9	13	5–	26	3	0	0	0	48	8.3
D	27	Doug Houda	DET	57	2	11	13	17	67	0	0	0	0	38	5.3
F	12	*Adam Graves	DET	56	7	5	12	5–	60	0	0	1	0	60	11.7
F	16	John Chabot	DET	52	2	10	12	18–	6	0	2	0	0	49	4.1
F	14	Torrie Robertson	HFD	27	2	4	6	3–	84	0	0	1	0	21	9.5
			DET	12	2	2	4	1–	63	0	0	0	0	5	40.0
			TOTAL	39	4	6	10	4–	147	0	0	1	0	26	15.4
F	10	Joe Murphy	DET	26	1	7	8	7–	28	0	0	0	0	29	3.4
F	24	Bob Probert	DET	25	4	2	6	11–	106	1	0	0	0	23	17.4
F	28	Dale Krentz	DET	16	3	3	6	3–	4	0	0	1	0	27	11.1
F	18	*Kris King	DET	55	2	3	5	7–	168	0	0	0	0	34	5.9
D	29	Gilbert Delorme	DET	42	1	3	4	11–	51	0	0	0	0	23	4.3
F	7	*Brent Fedyk	DET	5	2	0	2	1–	0	1	0	0	0	6	33.3
G	30	Greg Stefan	DET	46	0	2	2	0	41	0	0	0	0	0	.0
D	5	*John Mokosak	DET	8	0	1	1	0	14	0	0	0	0	0	.0
G	1	Glen Hanlon	DET	39	0	1	1	0	12	0	0	0	0	0	.0
F	38	Jeff Brubaker	DET	1	0	0	0	0	0	0	0	0	0	0	.0
F	35	Miroslav Ihnacak	DET	1	0	0	0	0	0	0	0	0	0	0	.0
G	31	*Tim Cheveldae	DET	2	0	0	0	0	0	0	0	0	0	0	.0
F	14	*Randy McKay	DET	3	0	0	0	1–	0	0	0	0	0	2	.0
G	35	Sam St. Laurent	DET	4	0	0	0	0	0	0	0	0	0	0	.0
D	33	John Blum	DET	6	0	0	0	2–	8	0	0	0	0	3	.0

Goaltending

No.	Goaltender	GPI	Mins	Avg	W	L	T	EN	SO	GA	SA	S%
1	Glen Hanlon	39	2092	3.56	13	14	8	3	1	124	1055	.882
35	Sam St. Laurent	4	141	3.83	0	1	1	0	0	9	91	.901
30	Greg Stefan	46	2499	4.01	21	17	3	4	0	167	1290	.870
31	*Tim Cheveldae	2	122	4.43	0	2	0	0	0	9	74	.878
	Totals	**80**	**4874**	**3.89**	**34**	**34**	**12**	**7**	**1**	**316**	**2510**	**.874**

Playoffs

Pos	#	Player	Team	GP	G	A	Pts	+/–	PIM	PP	SH	GW	GT	S	%
F	19	Steve Yzerman	DET	6	5	5	10	7–	2	2	0	0	0	35	14.3
F	21	Adam Oates	DET	6	0	8	8	1–	2	0	0	0	0	11	.0
F	85	Petr Klima	DET	6	2	4	6	0	19	1	0	0	0	19	10.5
F	22	Dave Barr	DET	6	3	1	4	1	6	1	0	1	0	12	25.0
D	3	Steve Chiasson	DET	5	2	1	3	3–	6	1	0	0	0	18	11.1
F	11	Shawn Burr	DET	6	1	2	3	2	6	0	0	0	0	8	12.5
F	17	Gerard Gallant	DET	6	1	2	3	2–	40	0	0	0	0	12	8.3
D	23	Lee Norwood	DET	6	1	2	3	2	16	1	0	0	0	11	9.1
F	15	Paul MacLean	DET	5	1	1	2	2–	8	0	0	0	0	5	20.0
F	16	John Chabot	DET	6	1	1	2	0	0	0	0	1	0	5	20.0
F	14	Torrie Robertson	DET	6	1	0	1	1–	17	0	0	0	0	2	50.0
F	26	Joey Kocur	DET	3	0	1	1	0	6	0	0	0	0	4	.0
D	29	Gilbert Delorme	DET	6	0	1	1	3	2	0	0	0	0	5	.0
D	27	Doug Houda	DET	6	0	1	1	1–	0	0	0	0	0	3	.0
D	4	Rick Zombo	DET	6	0	1	1	3–	16	0	0	0	0	6	.0
F	20	Tim Higgins	DET	1	0	0	0	0	0	0	0	0	0	0	.0
D	34	Jeff Sharples	DET	1	0	0	0	0	0	0	0	0	0	0	.0
G	1	Glen Hanlon	DET	2	0	0	0	0	0	0	0	0	0	0	.0
F	18	*Kris King	DET	2	0	0	0	0	2	0	0	0	0	0	.0
F	25	*Randy McKay	DET	2	0	0	0	2–	2	0	0	0	0	2	.0
F	12	*Adam Graves	DET	5	0	0	0	1–	4	0	0	0	0	6	.0
G	30	Greg Stefan	DET	5	0	0	0	0	4	0	0	0	0	0	.0
F	8	Jim Nill	DET	6	0	0	0	1–	25	0	0	0	0	2	.0
D	2	Mike O'Connell	DET	6	0	0	0	0	4	0	0	0	0	9	.0

Goaltending

No.	Goaltender	GPI	Mins	Avg	W	L	EN	SO	GA	SA	S%
30	Greg Stefan	5	294	3.67	2	3	0	0	18	151	.881
1	Glen Hanlon	2	78	5.38	0	1	0	0	7	47	.851
	Totals	6	375	4.00	2	4	0	0	25	198	.874

General Managers' History

Art Duncan, 1926-27; Jack Adams, 1927-28 to 1962-63; Sidney Abel, 1963-64 to 1969-70; Sidney Abel and Ned Harkness, 1970-71; Ned Harkness, 1971-72 to 1973-74; Alex Delvecchio, 1974-75 to 1975-76; Alex Delvecchio and Ted Lindsay, 1976-77; Ted Lindsay, 1977-78 to 1979-80; Jimmy Skinner, 1980-81 to 1981-82; Jim Devellano, 1982-83 to date.

Coaching History

Art Duncan, 1926-27; Jack Adams, 1927-28 to 1946-47; Tommy Ivan, 1947-48 to 1953-54; Jimmy Skinner, 1954-55 to 1956-57; Jimmy Skinner and Sid Abel, 1957-58; Sid Abel, 1958-59 to 1967-68; Bill Gadsby, 1968-69; Bill Gadsby and Sid Abel, 1969-70; Ned Harkness and Doug Barkley, 1970-71; Doug Barkley and John Wilson, 1971-72; John Wilson, 1972-73; Ted Garvin and Alex Delvecchio, 1973-74; Alex Delvecchio, 1974-75; Doug Barkley and Alex Delvecchio, 1975-76; Alex Delvecchio and Larry Wilson, 1976-77; Bobby Kromm, 1977-78 to 1978-79; Bobby Kromm and Ted Lindsay, 1979-80; Ted Lindsay and Wayne Maxner, 1980-81; Wayne Maxner and Billy Dea, 1981-82; Nick Polano, 1982-83 to 1984-85; Harry Neale and Brad Park, 1985-86; Jacques Demers, 1986-87 to date.

Club Records

Team

(Figures in brackets for season records are games played; records for fewest points, wins, ties, losses, goals, goals against are for 70 or more games)

Most Points	101	1950-51 (70)
Most Wins	44	1950-51 (70)
		1951-52 (70)
Most Ties	18	1952-53 (70)
		1980-81 (80)
Most Losses	57	1985-86 (80)
Most Goals	322	1987-88 (80)
Most Goals Against	415	1985-86 (80)
Fewest Points	40	1985-86 (80)
Fewest Wins	16	1976-77 (80)
Fewest Ties	4	1966-67 (70)
Fewest Losses	13	1950-51 (70)
Fewest Goals	167	1958-59 (70)
Fewest Goals Against	132	1953-54 (70)

Longest Winning Streak
- Over-all .... 9 — 1950-51; 1954-55
- Home .... 14 — Jan. 21-Mar. 20/65
- Away .... 5 — Three times

Longest Undefeated Streak
- Over-all .... 15 — Nov. 27-Dec. 28/52 (8 wins, 7 ties)
- Home .... 18 — Dec. 26/54-Mar. 20/55 (13 wins, 5 ties)
- Away .... 15 — Oct. 18-Dec. 26/51 (10 wins, 5 ties)

Longest Losing Streak
- Over-all .... 14 — Feb. 24-Mar. 25/82
- Home .... 7 — Feb. 20-Mar. 25/82
- Away .... 14 — Oct. 19-Dec. 21/66

Longest Winless Streak
- Over-all .... 19 — Feb. 26-Apr. 3/77 (18 losses, 1 tie)
- Home .... 10 — Dec. 11/85-Jan. 18/86 (9 losses, 1 tie)

- Away .... 26 — Dec. 15/76-Apr. 3/77 (23 losses, 3 ties)
- Most Shutouts, Season ..... 13 — 1953-54 (70)
- Most. Pen. Mins., Season .... 2,393 — 1985-86 (80)
- Most Goals, Game .... 15 — Jan. 23/44 (NYR at Det. 15)

Individual

Most Seasons	*25	Gordie Howe
Most Games	*1,687	Gordie Howe
Most Goals, Career	*786	Gordie Howe
Most Assists, Career	1,023	Gordie Howe
Most Points, Career	*1,809	Gordie Howe (786 goals, 1,023 assists)
Most Pen. Mins., Career	1,643	Gordie Howe
Most Shutouts, Career	85	Terry Sawchuk

- Longest Consecutive Games Streak .... 548 — Alex Delvecchio (Dec. 13/56-Nov. 11/64)
- Most Goals, Season ...... 65 — Steve Yzerman (1988-89)
- Most Assists, Season ..... 90 — Steve Yzerman (1988-89)
- Most Points, Season .... 155 — Steve Yzerman (1988-89) (65 goals, 90 assists)
- Most Pen. Mins., Season ... 398 — Bob Probert (1987-88)
- Most Points, Defenseman Season .... 74 — Reed Larson (1982-83) (22 goals, 52 assists)
- Most Points, Center, Season .... 155 — Steve Yzerman (1988-89) (65 goals, 90 assists)
- Most Points, Right Wing, Season .... 103 — Gordie Howe (1968-69) (44 goals, 59 assists)
- Most Points, Left Wing, Season .... 105 — John Ogrodnick (1984-85) (55 goals, 50 assists)
- Most Points, Rookie, Season .... 87 — Steve Yzerman (1983-84) (39 goals, 48 assists)
- Most Shutouts, Season ..... 12 — Terry Sawchuk (1951-52; 1953-54; 1954-55); Glenn Hall (1955-56)
- Most Goals, Game .... 6 — Syd Howe (Feb. 3/44)
- Most Assists, Game .... *7 — Billy Taylor (Mar. 16/47)
- Most Points, Game .... 7 — Carl Liscombe (Nov. 5/42); Don Grosso (Feb. 3/44); Billy Taylor (Mar. 16/47)

* NHL Record

All-time Record vs. Other Clubs

Regular Season

	At Home							On Road							Total					
	GP	W	L	T	GF	GA	PTS	GP	W	L	T	GF	GA	PTS	GP	W	L	T	GF	GA	PTS
Boston	272	148	72	52	910	683	348	273	82	148	43	717	961	207	545	230	220	95	1627	1644	555
Buffalo	40	20	16	4	142	121	44	39	5	28	6	93	177	16	79	25	44	10	235	298	60
**Calgary	31	15	11	5	121	103	35	31	7	20	4	90	138	18	62	22	31	9	211	241	53
Chicago	289	179	83	27	993	695	385	290	108	137	45	797	879	261	579	287	220	72	1790	1574	646
Edmonton	16	4	11	1	59	80	9	16	4	10	2	68	94	10	32	8	21	3	127	174	19
Hartford	16	5	5	6	59	50	16	16	5	11	0	53	67	10	32	10	16	6	112	117	26
Los Angeles	51	21	23	7	203	186	49	51	12	29	10	154	214	34	102	33	52	17	357	400	83
Minnesota	64	28	24	12	249	225	68	65	19	35	11	183	255	49	129	47	59	23	432	480	117
Montreal	268	122	94	52	754	685	296	267	62	163	42	597	946	166	535	184	257	94	1351	1631	462
*New Jersey	26	16	8	2	116	80	34	26	8	13	5	74	98	21	52	24	21	7	190	178	55
NY Islanders	15	14	2	1	111	106	32	31	12	19	0	91	128	24	62	27	33	2	202	234	56
NY Rangers	271	154	74	43	946	662	351	270	85	128	57	682	829	227	541	239	202	100	1628	1491	578
Philadelphia	45	19	18	8	150	148	46	45	9	27	9	130	185	27	90	28	45	17	280	333	73
Pittsburgh	51	34	8	9	204	137	77	51	13	35	3	153	223	29	102	47	43	12	357	360	106
Quebec	16	8	7	1	65	62	17	16	3	11	2	52	74	8	32	11	18	3	117	136	25
St. Louis	65	26	29	10	229	201	62	64	15	39	10	171	242	40	129	41	68	20	400	443	102
Toronto	283	146	94	43	828	685	335	283	90	151	42	714	930	222	566	236	245	85	1542	1615	557
Vancouver	37	21	11	5	158	116	47	38	12	20	6	119	157	30	75	33	31	11	277	273	77
Washington	32	14	8	10	122	93	38	32	12	16	4	102	120	28	64	26	24	14	224	213	66
Winnipeg	18	8	7	3	72	75	19	18	6	6	6	48	61	18	36	14	13	9	120	136	37
Defunct Clubs	141	76	40	25	429	307	177	141	49	63	29	363	375	127	282	125	103	54	792	682	304

Totals 2063 1079 657 327 6920 5500 2485 2063 618 1109 336 5451 7153 1572 4126 1697 1766 663 12371 12653 4057

* Totals include those of Kansas City (1974-75, 1975-76) and Colorado (1976-77 through 1981-82)
** Totals include those of Atlanta (1972-73 through 1979-80)

Playoffs

	Series	W	L	GP	W	L	T	GF	GA	Last Mtg.	Round	Result
Boston	7	3	4	33	14	19	0	98	96	1957	SF	L 1-4
Calgary	1	1	0	2	2	0	0	8	5	1978	P	W 2-0
Chicago	12	5	7	60	27	33	0	171	187	1989	DSF	L 2-4
Edmonton	2	0	2	10	2	8	0	26	39	1988	CF	L 1-4
Montreal	12	7	5	62	29	33	0	149	161	1978	QF	L 1-4
NY Rangers	5	4	1	23	13	10	0	57	49	1950	F	W 4-3
St. Louis	2	1	1	9	5	4	0	33	27	1988	DF	W 4-1
Toronto	22	11	11	110	56	54	0	291	289	1988	DSF	W 4-2
Defunct Clubs	4	3	1	10	7	2	1	21	13			
Totals	67	35	32	319	155	163	1	854	866			

Playoff Results 1989-85

Year	Round	Opponent	Result	GF	GA
1989	DSF	Chicago	L 2-4	18	25
1988	CF	Edmonton	L 1-4	16	23
	DF	St. Louis	W 4-1	21	14
	DSF	Toronto	W 4-2	32	22
1987	CF	Edmonton	L 1-4	10	16
	DF	Toronto	W 4-3	20	18
	DSF	Chicago	W 4-0	15	6
1985	DSF	Chicago	L 0-3	8	23

Abbreviations: Round: F – Final; **CF** – conference final; **DF** – division final; **DSF** – division semi-final; **SF** – semi-final; **QF** – quarter-final. **P** – preliminary round. **GA** – goals against; **GF** – goals for.

1988-89 Results

	Home				Away		
Oct.	14	St Louis	8-8	Oct.	6	Los Angeles	2-8
	18	Chicago	4-3		8	Vancouver	3-3
	21	Toronto	2-4		10	Calgary	2-5
	23	New Jersey	3-3		15	Toronto	5-3
	26	Montreal	4-2		29	Minnesota	2-3
	28	Minnesota	4-1	Nov.	9	Minnesota	6-3
Nov.	1	Washington	3-3		12	Philadelphia*	5-4
	4	Philadelphia	3-4		13	NY Rangers	5-3
	6	Edmonton	5-2		16	Hartford	4-3
	18	Boston	5-2		20	Boston	5-4
	23	Los Angeles	3-8	Dec.	3	Quebec	4-6
	25	Winnipeg	6-3		5	Montreal	2-7
	27	Washington	3-4		10	Toronto	8-2
	29	NY Islanders	5-3		17	Pittsburgh	2-3
Dec.	1	Quebec	7-3		22	St Louis	4-4
	9	Toronto	4-3		23	Chicago	2-7
	13	Minnesota	5-4		28	Buffalo	1-4
	16	Los Angeles	4-6		30	Hartford	3-4
	20	St Louis	6-3	Jan.	1	New Jersey	2-5
	31	Hartford	2-3		11	Chicago	2-2
Jan.	4	St Louis	4-2		14	Boston*	5-5
	6	Vancouver	2-2		15	Philadelphia	8-4
	17	Montreal	3-2		22	Washington*	4-3
	17	Calgary	1-7		28	Pittsburgh	5-10
	20	Chicago	2-3	Feb.	2	Calgary	2-3
	25	Buffalo	3-6		3	Edmonton	5-8
	27	Toronto	8-1		5	Winnipeg*	6-2
	30	Quebec	3-4		11	Minnesota	5-1
Feb.	9	New Jersey	3-6		19	Buffalo*	4-8
	13	Winnipeg	2-2		21	NY Islanders	6-5
	15	Minnesota	4-2		26	Chicago*	4-4
	17	Chicago	3-5	Mar.	4	St Louis	5-4
	23	Pittsburgh	6-6		7	Minnesota	3-5
	25	Chicago*	5-0		11	Toronto	3-5
Mar.	1	NY Islanders	6-5		14	Vancouver	2-2
	9	NY Rangers	3-2		15	Edmonton	8-6
	24	Toronto	6-2		18	St Louis	2-3
	27	St Louis	2-3		19	Chicago	3-5
	29	NY Rangers	4-3		25	Toronto	5-6
	31	Minnesota	1-5	Apr.	2	St Louis	2-4

* Denotes afternoon game.

Entry Draft Selections
1989-75

1989
Pick
11	Mike Sillinger
32	Bob Boughner
53	Niklas Lidstrom
74	Sergei Fedorov
95	Shawn McCosh
116	Dallas Drake
137	Scott Zygulski
158	Andy Suhy
179	Bob Jones
200	Greg Bignell
204	Rick Judson
221	Vladimir Konstantinov
242	Joseph Frederick
246	Jason Glickman

1988
Pick
17	Kory Kocur
38	Serge Anglehart
47	Guy Dupuis
59	Petr Hrbek
80	Sheldon Kennedy
143	Kelly Hurd
164	Brian McCormack
185	Jody Praznik
206	Glen Goodall
227	Darren Colbourne
248	Donald Stone

1987
Pick
11	Yves Racine
32	Gordon Kruppke
41	Bob Wilkie
52	Dennis Holland
74	Mark Reimer
95	Radomir Brazda
116	Sean Clifford
137	Mike Gober
158	Kevin Scott
179	Mikko Haapakoski
200	Darin Bannister
221	Craig Quinlan
242	Tomas Jansson

1986
Pick
1	Joe Murphy
22	Adam Graves
43	Derek Mayer
64	Tim Cheveldae
85	Johan Garpenlov
106	Jay Stark
127	Per Djoos
148	Dean Morton
169	Marc Potvin
190	Scott King
211	Tom Bissett
232	Peter Ekroth

1985
Pick
8	Brent Fedyk
29	Jeff Sharples
50	Steve Chiasson
71	Mark Gowans
92	Chris Luongo
113	Randy McKay
134	Thomas Bjur
155	Mike Luckraft
176	Rob Schenna
197	Eerik Hamalainen
218	Bo Svanberg
239	Mikael Lindman

1984
Pick
7	Shawn Burr
28	Doug Houda
49	Milan Chalupa
91	Mats Lundstrom
112	Randy Hansch
133	Stefan Larsson
152	Lars Karlsson
154	Urban Nordin
175	Bill Shibicky
195	Jay Rose
216	Tim Kaiser
236	Tom Nickolau

1983
Pick
4	Steve Yzerman
25	Lane Lambert
46	Bob Probert
68	David Korol
86	Petr Klima
88	Joey Kocur
106	Chris Pusey
126	Bob Pierson
146	Craig Butz
166	Dave Sikorski
186	Stuart Grimson
206	Jeff Frank
226	Charles Chiatto

1982
Pick
17	Murray Craven
23	Yves Courteau
44	Carmine Vani
66	Craig Coxe
86	Brad Shaw
107	Claude Vilgrain
128	Greg Hudas
149	Pat Lahey
170	Gary Cullen
191	Brent Meckling
212	Mike Stern
233	Shaun Reagan

1981
Pick
23	Claude Loiselle
44	Corrado Micalef
86	Larry Trader
107	Gerard Gallant
128	Greg Stefan
149	Rick Zombo
170	Don Leblanc
191	Robert Nordmark

1980
Pick
11	Mike Blaisdell
46	Mark Osborne
88	Mike Corrigan
109	Wayne Crawford
130	Mike Braun
151	John Beukeboom
172	Dave Miles
193	Brian Rorabeck

1979
Pick
3	Mike Foligno
45	Jody Gage
46	Boris Fistric
66	John Ogrodnick
87	Joe Paterson
108	Carmen Cirella

1978
Pick
9	Willie Huber
12	Brent Peterson
28	Glenn Hicks
31	Al Jensen
53	Doug Derkson
62	Bjorn Skaare
78	Ted Nolan
95	Sylvain Locas
112	Wes George
129	John Barrett
146	Jim Malazdrewicz
163	Goeff Shaw
178	Carl Van Harrewyn
194	Ladislav Svozil
208	Tom Bailey
219	Larry Lozinski
224	Randy Betty
226	Brian Crawley
228	Doug Feasby

1977
Pick
1	Dale McCourt
37	Rick Vasko
55	John Hilworth
73	Jim Korn
91	Jim Baxter
109	Randy Wilson
125	Raymond Roy
141	Kip Churchill
155	Lance Gatoni
163	Robert Plumb
170	Alain Belanger
175	Dean Willers
178	Roland Cloutier
181	Edward Hill
184	Val James
185	Grant Morin

1976
Pick
4	Fred Williams
22	Reed Larson
40	Fred Berry
58	Kevin Schamehorn
76	Dwight Schofield
94	Tony Horvath
111	Fernand Leblanc
120	Claude Legris

1975
Pick
5	Rick Lapointe
23	Jerry Rollins
37	Alan Cameron
45	Blair Davidson
50	Clarke Hamilton
59	Mike Wirachowsky
77	Mike Wong
95	Mike Harazny
113	Jean-Luc Phaneuf
131	Steve Carlson
148	Gary Vaughn
164	Jean Thibodeau
176	Dave Hanson
178	Robin Larson

Coach

DEMERS, JACQUES
Coach, Detroit Red Wings. Born in Montreal, Que., August 25, 1944

In 1988-89, Jacques Demers led his club to its third consecutive Norris Division title since he assumed the coaching duties in 1986-87. Demers was the Jack Adams Award winner in 1986-87 and 1987-88, making him the only coach in League history to capture that award twice.

A Montreal native, Demers began coaching in the Quebec Junior League during the late 60's and early 70's. Then, in 1972-73, he jumped to the pro ranks of the newly formed World Hockey Association, in which he piloted the Chicago Cougars and Cincinnati Stingers before joining the WHA's Quebec Nordiques. When Quebec moved into the NHL in 1979-80, Demers remained with the club as coach for one season before taking control of the Nordiques' AHL affiliate in Fredericton. After earning AHL Coach-of-the-Year and Executive-of-the-Year honors in 1982-83, he returned to the NHL as head coach in St. Louis.

Coaching Record

Season	Team	Games	Regular Season W	L	T	%	Playoffs Games	W	L	%
1975-76	Indianapolis (WHA)	80	35	39	6	.475	7	3	4	.429
1976-77	Indianapolis (WHA)	81	36	37	8	.494	9	5	4	.556
1977-78	Cincinnati (WHA)	80	35	42	3	.456	....	....	....	....
1978-79	Quebec (WHA)	80	41	34	5	.544	4	0	4	.000
1979-80	Quebec (NHL)	80	25	44	11	.381	....	....	....	....
1981-82	Fredericton (AHL)	80	20	55	5	.281	....	....	....	....
1982-83	Fredericton (AHL)	80	45	27	8	.544	12	6	6	.500
1983-84	St. Louis (NHL)	80	32	41	7	.444	11	6	5	.545
1984-85	St. Louis (NHL)	80	37	31	12	.538	3	0	3	.000
1985-86	St. Louis (NHL)	80	37	34	9	.519	19	10	9	.526
1986-87	Detroit (NHL)	80	34	36	10	.488	16	9	7	.563
1987-88	Detroit (NHL)	80	41	28	11	.581	16	9	7	.563
1988-89	Detroit (NHL)	80	34	34	12	.500	6	2	4	.333
	NHL Totals	560	240	248	72	.493	71	36	35	.507

Club Directory

Joe Louis Sports Arena
600 Civic Center Drive
Detroit, Michigan 48226
Phone: (313) 567-7333
FAX 313/567-0296
ENVOY ID
  Front Office: DRW. GM
  Public
  Relations: DRW. PR
Capacity: 19,275

Owner and President	Michael Ilitch
Executive Vice-President	James Lites
Secretary-Treasurer	Marian Ilitch
General Counsel	Denise Ilitch-Lites
Vice-President and General Manager	Jim Devellano
Vice-President/Marketing & Ad Sales	Rosanne Kozerski-Brown
Asst. General Manager	Nick Polano
Head Coach	Jacques Demers
Assistant Coaches	Colin Campbell, Dave Lewis, Phil Myre
Goaltending Consultant	Dave Dryden
Director of Scouting	Ken Holland
Pro Scout/NHL Advance Scout	Dan Belisle
Eastern Canada Scout	Wayne Meier
Quebec Scout	Bill Dineen
Director of Scouting/USA	Billy Dea
Europe Scout	Christer Rockstrom
Western USA Scout	Chris Coury
Eastern USA Scout	Jerry Moschella
Northern Ontario Scout	Dave Polano
Director of Public Relations	Bill Jamieson
Director of Finance	Scott Fisher
Director of Advertising Sales	Terry Murphy
Director of Corporate Sales	Gary Vitto
Director of Broadcast Sales	Tony Nagorsen
Director of Marketing	Jeff Cogen
Director of Community Relations	Dave Strader
Director of Season Ticket Sales	Greg Strausser
Director of Arena Operations	John Pettit
Director of Merchandising Sales	Jules Goldman
Director Business & Administration	Nancy Beard
Office Manager	Dave Agius
Box Office Manager	Bob Kerlin
Community Relations/Sports Marketing Manager	Michael Dietz
Group Sales Manager	Robin Moten
Associate Director of Public Relations	Kathy Best
Public Relations Coordinator	Howard Berlin
Physical Therapist	Kirk Vickers
Trainer	Mark Brennan
Assistant Trainer	Larry Wasylon
Team Physicians	Dr. John Finley, D.O., Dr. Collon, M.D.
Team Dentist	Dr. C.J. Regula, D.M.D.
Team Psychologist	Dr. Hugh Bray, Ph.D.
Team Opthamologist	Dr. Charles Slater, M.D.
Assistant to Executive Vice-President	Donna Gregory
P.R. Secretary	Marilyn Rowe
Marketing Secretary	Nancy King
Advertising Secretary	Lori Sbroglia
Administrative Ass't./Finance	Cathy Witzke
Art Director	Beverly Ostrom
Largest crowd	21,019* Nov. 25, 1983; Detroit 5, Pittsburgh 2
Location of Press Box, Radio-TV Booths	Jefferson Ave. side of Arena, top of seats (Row 42)
Location of Media Hospitality Lounge	First floor, in hallway, near Red Wings' dressing room, Atwater St. side of Arena.
Dimensions of Rink	200 feet by 85 feet; S.A.R. Plastic extends above boards all around rink
Club Colors	Red and White
Radio Flagship Station	WJR-AM, 760
TV Stations	Pro-Am Sports System (PASS-Cable) WKBD-TV (Channel 50)
Radio Announcer	Bruce Martyn, Paul Woods
TV Announcers	Dave Strader, Mickey Redmond

*NHL Record

General Manager

DEVELLANO, JAMES (JIM)
General Manager, Detroit Red Wings. Born in Toronto, Ont., January 18, 1943.

Jim Devellano was appointed general manager of the Red Wings on July 12, 1982 after spending several seasons with the New York Islanders. He began his career as a scout for the St. Louis Blues in 1967 and from there moved to join New York in 1972. In his first two years he acted as a scout for the organization and in 1974 was promoted to head scout. In 1979, Devellano held the dual capacities of head scout for the Islanders and general manager for their CHL affiliate Indianapolis Checkers. His results were impressive, and following the 1979-80 season he was named "Hockey News Minor League Executive of the Year". In 1981, Devellano was appointed assistant general manager of the Islanders and held that position until joining the Red Wings.

Edmonton Oilers

1988-89 Results: 38w-34L-8T 84 PTS. Third, Smythe Division

Year-by-Year Record

Season	GP	Home W	L	T	Road W	L	T	Overall W	L	T	GF	GA	Pts.	Finished		Playoff Result
1988-89	80	21	16	3	17	18	5	38	34	8	325	306	84	3rd,	Smythe Div.	Lost Div. Semi-Final
1987-88	80	28	8	4	16	17	7	44	25	11	363	288	99	2nd,	**Smythe Div.**	**Won Stanley Cup**
1986-87	80	29	6	5	21	18	1	50	24	6	372	284	106	1st,	**Smythe Div.**	**Won Stanley Cup**
1985-86	80	32	6	2	24	11	5	56	17	7	426	310	119	1st,	Smythe Div.	Lost Div. Final
1984-85	80	26	7	7	23	13	4	49	20	11	401	298	109	1st,	**Smythe Div.**	**Won Stanley Cup**
1983-84	80	31	5	4	26	13	1	57	18	5	446	314	119	1st,	**Smythe Div.**	**Won Stanley Cup**
1982-83	80	25	9	6	22	12	6	47	21	12	424	315	106	1st,	Smythe Div.	Lost Final
1981-82	80	31	5	4	17	12	11	48	17	15	417	295	111	1st,	Smythe Div.	Lost Div. Semi-Final
1980-81	80	17	13	10	12	22	6	29	35	16	328	327	74	4th,	Smythe Div.	Lost Quarter-Final
1979-80	80	17	14	9	11	25	4	28	39	13	301	322	69	4th,	Smythe Div.	Lost Prelim. Round

Schedule

Home			Away		
Oct.	Wed. 11	Vancouver	**Oct.**	Thur. 5	Vancouver
	Fri. 13	Boston		Sat. 7	Los Angeles
	Sun. 15	Los Angeles		Sun. 22	Winnipeg
	Wed. 18	Winnipeg		Tues. 24	NY Islanders
	Fri. 20	Boston		Wed. 25	NY Rangers
Nov.	Wed. 1	New Jersey		Sat. 28	Quebec
	Fri. 3	Calgary		Sun. 29	Montreal
	Sat. 4	Pittsburgh	**Nov.**	Mon. 6	Calgary
	Wed. 15	Los Angeles		Thur. 9	Boston
	Fri. 17	Buffalo		Sat. 11	Washington
	Sun. 19	Chicago		Sun. 12	Buffalo
	Tues. 21	Vancouver		Fri. 24	Philadelphia*
Dec.	Sat. 2	Minnesota		Sat. 25	NY Islanders
	Sun. 3	Toronto		Mon. 27	Detroit
	Fri. 8	Los Angeles		Thur. 30	Los Angeles
	Mon. 11	Calgary	**Dec.**	Sat. 16	St Louis
	Wed. 13	Quebec		Sun. 17	Chicago
	Thur. 21	Winnipeg		Tues. 19	Minnesota
	Sat. 23	Calgary		Sun. 31	Winnipeg*
	Wed. 27	Philadelphia	**Jan.**	Tues. 2	St Louis
	Fri. 29	Montreal		Wed. 3	Chicago
Jan.	Sat. 6	Hartford		Tues. 9	Calgary
	Sun. 7	Calgary		Thur. 11	Los Angeles
	Tues. 16	Detroit		Tues. 30	Hartford
	Wed. 17	Winnipeg		Wed. 31	Detroit
	Tues. 23	NY Rangers	**Feb.**	Fri. 2	Pittsburgh
	Thur. 25	Los Angeles		Sun. 4	Washington*
	Sat. 27	Vancouver		Tues. 6	New Jersey
Feb.	Sun. 11	Winnipeg		Wed. 7	NY Rangers
	Wed. 14	Washington		Fri. 16	Vancouver
	Sun. 18	Minnesota		Tues. 20	Vancouver
	Wed. 21	Buffalo		Sun. 25	Calgary
	Fri. 23	Toronto		Wed. 28	Los Angeles
Mar.	Sat. 3	Philadelphia	**Mar.**	Fri. 9	Winnipeg
	Sun. 4	Vancouver		Sat. 10	Toronto
	Tues. 6	Pittsburgh		Tues. 13	Quebec
	Sat. 17	New Jersey		Wed. 14	Montreal
	Sun. 18	Hartford		Tues. 27	Vancouver
	Wed. 21	St Louis		Fri. 30	Calgary
	Sat. 24	NY Islanders	**Apr.**	Sun. 1	Winnipeg*

* Denotes afternoon game.

Home Starting Times:
Weeknights .... 7:35 p.m.
Saturdays and Sundays .... 6:05 p.m.

Franchise date: June 22, 1979

11th NHL Season

Mark Messier became the Oilers' fourth team captain in 1988-89.

1989-90 Player Personnel

FORWARDS	HT	WT	S	Place of Birth	Date	1988-89 Club
ANDERSON, Glenn	6-1	190	L	Vancouver, B.C.	10/2/60	Edmonton
BEAULIEU, Nicolas	6-2	200	L	Rimouski, Que.	8/19/68	Cape Breton
BROWN, Dave	6-5	205	R	Saskatoon, Sask.	11/12/62	Philadelphia-Edmonton
BUCHBERGER, Kelly	6-2	205	L	Langenburg, Sask.	12/2/66	Edmonton
CARSON, Jimmy	6-1	200	R	Southfield, MI	7/20/68	Edmonton
CURRIE, Dan	6-2	195	L	Burlington, Ont.	3/15/68	Cape Breton
DRULIA, Stan	5-11	188	R	Elmira, NY	1/5/68	Niagara Falls
ERIKSSON, Peter	6-4	224	R	Kramfors, Sweden	7/12/65	HV-71
GELINAS, Martin	5-11	195	L	Shawinigan, Que.	6/5/70	Edmonton-Hull
GLOVER, Mike	5-11	200	R	Ottawa, Ont.	7/23/68	Cape Breton
HAAS, David	6-2	196	L	Toronto, Ont.	6/23/68	Cape Breton
HUNTER, Dave	5-11	195	L	Petrolia, Ont.	1/1/58	Winnipeg-Edmonton
ISSEL, Kim	6-4	196	R	Regina, Sask.	9/25/67	Cape Breton-Edmonton
JOSEPH, Fabian	5-8	170	L	Sydney, N.S.	12/5/65	Cape Breton
KURRI, Jari	6-1	195	R	Helsinki, Finland	5/18/60	Edmonton
LACOMBE, Normand	5-11	205	R	Pierrefonds, Que.	10/18/64	Edmonton
LAMB, Mark	5-9	180	L	Ponteix, Sask.	8/3/64	Cape Breton-Edmonton
LeBLANC, John	6-1	190	L	Campbellton, N.B.	1/21/64	Milw.-Cape Breton-Edm.
LEHMANN, Tommy	6-1	185	L	Solna, Sweden	2/3/64	Maine
MacTAVISH, Craig	6-1	195	L	London, Ont.	8/15/58	Edmonton
MARTIN, Don	6-0	200	L	London, Ont.	3/29/68	Cape Breton
MATULIK, Ivan	6-1	200	L	Nitra, Czechoslovakia	6/17/68	Cape Breton
McCLELLAND, Kevin	6-2	205	R	Oshawa, Ont.	7/4/62	Edmonton
MESSIER, Mark	6-1	210	L	Edmonton, Alta.	1/18/61	Edmonton
SIMPSON, Craig	6-2	195	R	London, Ont.	2/15/67	Edmonton
SOBERLAK, Peter	6-2	195	L	Kamloops, B.C.	5/12/69	Swift Current
TIKKANEN, Esa	6-1	200	L	Helsinki, Finland	1/25/65	Edmonton
TISDALE, Tim	6-1	186	L	Swift Current, Sask.	5/28/68	Swift Current
VAN ALLEN, Shaun	6-1	200	L	Shaunavon, Sask.	8/29/67	Cape Breton
WARE, Mike	6-5	208	R	York, Ont.	3/22/67	Cape Breton-Edmonton
WILKS, Brian	5-11	180	R	North York, Ont.	2/27/66	N.Haven-L.A.-Cape Breton

DEFENSEMEN	HT	WT	S	Place of Birth	Date	1988-89 Club
BARBE, Mario	6-0	204	L	Cadillac, Que.	3/17/67	Cape Breton
BEUKEBOOM, Jeff	6-4	215	R	Ajax, Ont.	3/28/65	Edmonton-Cape Breton
CHARLESWORTH, Todd	6-1	190	L	Calgary, Alta.	3/22/65	Muskegon
ENGLISH, John	6-2	190	R	Toronto, Ont.	5/3/66	New Haven-Cape Breton
ENNIS, Jim	6-0	198	L	Sherwood Park, Alta.	7/10/67	Cape Breton
FOSTER, Corey	6-3	200	L	Ottawa, Ont.	10/27/69	Peterborough
GREGG, Randy	6-4	215	L	Edmonton, Alta.	2/19/56	Edmonton
HUDDY, Charlie	6-0	210	L	Oshawa, Ont.	6/2/59	Edmonton
JOSEPH, Chris	6-2	210	R	Burnaby, B.C.	9/10/69	Edmonton-Cape Breton
LOWE, Kevin	6-2	195	L	Lachute, Que.	4/15/59	Edmonton
MUNI, Craig	6-3	200	L	Toronto, Ont.	7/19/62	Edmonton
ODELEIN, Selmar	6-0	205	R	Quill Lake, Sask.	4/11/66	Cape Breton-Edmonton
SMITH, Geoff	6-2	190	L	Edmonton, Alta.	3/7/69	North Dakota-Kamloops
SMITH, Steve	6-2	215	L	Glasgow, Scotland	4/30/63	Edmonton

GOALTENDERS	HT	WT	C	Place of Birth	Date	1988-89 Club
BEALS, Darren	6-0	200	R	Dartmouth, N.S.	8/28/68	Cape Breton
FUHR, Grant	5-10	186	R	Spruce Grove, Alta.	9/28/62	Edmonton
GREENLAY, Mike	6-3	200	L	Vitoria, Brazil	9/15/68	Lake Superior-Saskatoon
RANFORD, Bill	5-10	170	L	Brandon, Man.	12/14/66	Edmonton
ROACH, David	5-10	175	L	Burnaby, B.C.	1/10/65	Cape Breton

Retired Numbers

3 Al Hamilton 1972-1980

General Manager's History

Glen Sather, 1979-80 to date.

Coaching History

Glen Sather, 1979-80 to 1988-89; John Muckler, 1989-90.

Captains' History

Ron Chipperfield, 1979-80; Lee Fogolin, 1980-81 to 1982-83; Wayne Gretzky, 1983-84 to 1987-88; Mark Messier, 1988-89 to date.

1988-89 Scoring

Edmonton Oilers

*—Rookie

Pos	#	Player	Team	GP	G	A	Pts	+/−	PIM	PP	SH	GW	GT	S	%
F	17	Jari Kurri	EDM	76	44	58	102	19	69	10	5	8	1	214	20.6
F	12	Jimmy Carson	EDM	80	49	51	100	3	36	19	0	5	1	240	20.4
F	11	Mark Messier	EDM	72	33	61	94	5	130	6	6	4	1	164	20.1
F	10	Esa Tikkanen	EDM	67	31	47	78	10	92	6	8	4	0	151	20.5
F	18	Craig Simpson	EDM	66	35	41	76	3−	80	17	0	4	0	121	28.9
F	9	Glenn Anderson	EDM	79	16	48	64	16−	93	7	0	3	0	212	7.5
F	14	Craig MacTavish	EDM	80	21	31	52	10	55	2	4	2	2	120	17.5
D	22	Charlie Huddy	EDM	76	11	33	44	0	52	5	2	0	1	178	6.2
D	23	Tomas Jonsson	NYI	53	9	23	32	13−	34	4	1	1	0	103	8.7
			EDM	20	1	10	11	12−	22	1	0	0	0	46	2.2
			TOTAL	73	10	33	43	25−	56	5	1	1	0	149	6.7
F	19	Normand Lacombe	EDM	64	17	11	28	2	57	2	0	1	0	71	23.9
F	15	Miroslav Frycer	DET	23	7	8	15	4−	47	2	0	1	0	40	17.5
			EDM	14	5	5	10	2	18	2	0	0	0	33	15.2
			TOTAL	37	12	13	25	2−	65	4	0	1	0	73	16.4
D	4	Kevin Lowe	EDM	76	7	18	25	26	98	0	0	1	0	85	8.2
D	5	Steve Smith	EDM	35	3	19	22	5	97	0	0	0	0	47	6.4
D	24	Kevin McClelland	EDM	79	6	14	20	10−	161	0	0	0	0	43	14.0
D	28	Craig Muni	EDM	69	5	13	18	43	71	0	0	1	0	40	12.5
D	21	Randy Gregg	EDM	57	3	15	18	9	28	1	0	1	0	42	7.1
F	16	*Kelly Buchberger	EDM	66	5	9	14	14−	234	1	0	1	0	57	8.8
D	26	Craig Redmond	EDM	21	3	10	13	10−	12	3	0	0	0	29	10.3
F	27	Dave Hunter	WPG	34	3	1	4	3−	61	0	1	0	0	43	7.0
			EDM	32	3	5	8	5−	22	0	0	0	0	44	6.8
			TOTAL	66	6	6	12	8−	83	0	1	0	0	87	6.9
D	7	Mark Lamb	EDM	20	2	8	10	4	14	1	0	0	0	20	10.0
D	2	*Chris Joseph	EDM	44	4	5	9	9−	54	0	0	0	0	36	11.1
D	37	Doug Halward	DET	18	0	1	1	11−	36	0	0	0	0	5	.0
			EDM	24	0	7	7	3−	25	0	0	0	0	8	.0
			TOTAL	42	0	8	8	14−	61	0	0	0	0	13	.0
D	6	Jeff Beukeboom	EDM	36	0	5	5	2	94	0	0	0	0	26	.0
F	32	Dave Brown	PHI	50	0	3	3	0−	100	0	0	0	0	28	.0
			EDM	22	0	2	2	4−	56	0	0	0	0	14	.0
			TOTAL	72	0	5	5	12−	156	0	0	0	0	42	.0
F	20	*Martin Gelinas	EDM	6	1	2	3	1−	0	0	0	0	0	14	7.1
F	8	John LeBlanc	EDM	2	1	0	1	0	0	0	0	0	0	5	20.0
F	32	*Alan May	EDM	3	1	0	1	0	7	0	0	1	0	3	33.3
D	34	*Mike Ware	EDM	2	0	1	1	1	11	0	0	0	0	0	.0
G	31	Grant Fuhr	EDM	59	0	1	1	0	6	0	0	0	0	0	.0
F	32	Nick Fotiu	EDM	1	0	0	0	1	0	0	0	0	0	1	.0
D	35	*Francois Leroux	EDM	2	0	0	0	1−	0	0	0	0	0	1	.0
D	36	*Selmar Odelein	EDM	2	0	0	0	2	2	0	0	0	0	1	.0
F	33	*Kim Issel	EDM	4	0	0	0	1−	0	0	0	0	0	1	.0
D	34	Glen Cochrane	CHI	6	0	0	0	1−	13	0	0	0	0	1	.0
			EDM	12	0	0	0	2−	52	0	0	0	0	3	.0
			TOTAL	18	0	0	0	3−	65	0	0	0	0	4	.0

Goaltending

No.	Goaltender	GPI	Mins	Avg	W	L	T	EN	SO	GA	SA	S%
30	Bill Ranford	29	1509	3.50	15	8	2	1	1	88	718	.877
31	Grant Fuhr	59	3341	3.83	23	26	6	4	1	213	1714	.875
	Totals	**80**	**4860**	**3.78**	**38**	**34**	**8**	**5**	**2**	**306**	**2432**	**.874**

Playoffs

Pos	#	Player	Team	GP	G	A	Pts	+/−	PIM	PP	SH	GW	GT	S	%
F	11	Mark Messier	EDM	7	1	11	12	1−	8	0	0	0	0	23	4.3
F	17	Jari Kurri	EDM	7	3	5	8	2	6	0	1	0	0	17	17.6
D	5	Steve Smith	EDM	7	2	2	4	3	20	0	0	1	0	6	33.3
F	10	Esa Tikkanen	EDM	7	1	3	4	1−	12	0	0	0	0	17	5.9
F	12	Jimmy Carson	EDM	7	2	1	3	0	6	1	0	1	0	15	13.3
F	19	Normand Lacombe	EDM	7	2	1	3	3	21	0	0	0	0	10	20.0
F	9	Glenn Anderson	EDM	7	1	2	3	1−	8	1	0	0	0	16	6.3
D	4	Kevin Lowe	EDM	7	1	2	3	1−	8	0	0	0	0	11	9.1
D	28	Craig Muni	EDM	7	0	3	3	1−	8	0	0	0	0	4	.0
D	23	Tomas Jonsson	EDM	4	2	0	2	1	6	2	0	0	0	6	33.3
D	22	Charlie Huddy	EDM	7	2	0	2	1	4	1	0	0	0	17	11.8
F	18	Craig Simpson	EDM	7	2	0	2	3−	10	1	0	1	0	10	20.0
D	7	Mark Lamb	EDM	6	0	2	2	1	8	0	0	0	0	4	.0
F	24	Kevin McClelland	EDM	7	0	2	2	3	16	0	0	0	0	7	.0
D	21	Randy Gregg	EDM	7	1	0	1	4	6	0	0	0	0	8	12.5
F	14	Craig MacTavish	EDM	7	0	1	1	1	8	0	0	0	0	10	.0
D	6	Jeff Beukeboom	EDM	1	0	0	0	0	2	0	0	0	0	0	.0
F	8	John LeBlanc	EDM	1	0	0	0	0	0	0	0	0	0	2	.0
D	37	Doug Halward	EDM	2	0	0	0	2−	0	0	0	0	0	0	.0
F	27	Dave Hunter	EDM	6	0	0	0	1	0	0	0	0	0	5	.0
F	32	Dave Brown	EDM	7	0	0	0	2−	0	0	0	0	0	5	.0
G	31	Grant Fuhr	EDM	7	0	0	0	0	0	0	0	0	0	0	.0

Goaltending

No.	Goaltender	GPI	Mins	Avg	W	L	EN	SO	GA	SA	S%
31	Grant Fuhr	7	417	3.45	3	4	1	1	24	227	.899
	Totals	**7**	**420**	**3.57**	**3**	**4**	**1**	**1**	**25**	**227**	**.889**

Club Records

Team

(Figures in brackets for season records are games played; records for fewest points, wins, ties, losses, goals, goals against are for 70 or more

Most Points	119	1983-84 (80)
		1985-86 (80)
Most Wins	57	1983-84 (80)
Most Ties	16	1980-81 (80)
Most Losses	39	1979-80 (80)
Most Goals	.........*446	1983-84 (80)
Most Goals Against	327	1980-81 (80)
Fewest Points	69	1979-80 (80)
Fewest Wins	28	1979-80 (80)
Fewest Ties	5	1983-84 (80)
Fewest Losses	17	1981-82 (80)
		1985-86 (80)
Fewest Goals	301	1979-80 (80)
Fewest Goals Against	284	1986-87 (80)

Longest Winning Streak

Over-all	8	Several times
Home	8	Jan. 19/85-
		Feb. 22/85
Away	7	Dec. 14/83-
		Jan. 11/84

Longest Undefeated Streak

Over-all	15	Oct. 11/84-
		Nov. 9/84
		(12 wins, 3 ties)
Home	12	Oct. 5-
		Dec. 3/83
		(10 wins, 2 ties)
Away	9	Jan. 17-
		Mar. 2/82
		(6 wins, 3 ties)

Longest Losing Streak

Over-all	6	Feb. 29-
		Mar. 9/80
Home	3	Feb. 24-
		Mar. 1/80
Away	9	Nov. 25-
		Dec. 30/80

Longest Winless Streak

Over-all	6	Five times
Home	7	Oct. 24-
		Nov. 19/80
		(3 losses, 4 ties)

Away	9	Nov. 25-
		Dec. 30/80
		(9 losses)
Most Shutouts, Season	3	1984-85 (80)
Most Pen. Mins., Season		
	2,173	1987-88 (80)
Most Goals, Game	13	Nov. 19/83
		(NJ 4 at Edm. 13)

Individual

Most Seasons	10	Kevin Lowe
		Mark Messier
Most Games	760	Kevin Lowe
Most Goals, Career	583	Wayne Gretzky
Most Assists, Career	.*1,086	Wayne Gretzky
Most Points, Career	1,669	Wayne Gretzky
		(583 goals, 1,086 assists)
Most Pen. Mins., Career	.1,285	Kevin McClelland
Most Shutouts, Career	7	Grant Fuhr
Longest Consecutive Games Streak	362	Wayne Gretzky
		(Nov. 2/79-Feb. 3/84)
Most Goals, Season	......*92	Wayne Gretzky
		(1981-82)
Most Assists, Season	...*163	Wayne Gretzky
		(1985-86)
Most Points, Season	....*215	Wayne Gretzky
		(1985-86)
		(52 goals, 163 assists)
Most Pen. Mins., Season	...286	Steve Smith
		(1987-88)
Most Points, Defenseman, Season	138	Paul Coffey
		(1985-86)
		(48 goals, 90 assists)
Most Points, Center, Season	.........*215	Wayne Gretzky
		(1985-86)
		(52 goals, 163 assists)
Most Points, Right Wing, Season	135	Jari Kurri
		(1984-85)
		(71 goals, 64 assists)

Most Points, Left Wing, Season	102	Glen Anderson
		(1985-86)
		(54 goals, 48 assists)
Most Points, Rookie, Season	75	Jari Kurri
		(1980-81)
		(32 goals, 43 assists)
Most Shutouts, Season	4	Grant Fuhr
		(1987-88)
Most Goals, Game	5	Wayne Gretzky
		(Feb. 18/81, Dec. 20/84, Dec. 6/87)
		Jari Kurri (Nov. 19/83)
		Pat Hughes (Feb. 3/84)
Most Assists, Game	.......*7	Wayne Gretzky
		(Feb. 15/80; Dec. 11/85; Feb. 14/86)
Most Points, Game	8	Wayne Gretzky
		(Nov. 19/83)
		Paul Coffey
		(Mar. 14/86)
		Wayne Gretzky
		(Jan. 4/84)

* NHL Record.

All-time Record vs. Other Clubs

Regular Season

	GP	W	L	T	At Home GF	GA	PTS	GP	W	L	T	On Road GF	GA	PTS	GP	W	L	T	Total GF	GA	PTS
Boston	16	7	7	2	58	55	16	16	2	12	2	42	74	6	32	9	19	4	100	129	22
Buffalo	16	11	3	2	72	44	24	16	7	6	3	68	67	17	32	18	9	5	140	111	41
Calgary	36	20	9	7	178	140	47	36	16	16	4	151	166	36	72	36	25	11	329	306	83
Chicago	16	11	4	1	86	58	23	16	7	7	2	78	72	16	32	18	11	3	164	130	39
Detroit	16	10	4	2	94	68	22	16	11	4	1	80	59	23	32	21	8	3	174	127	45
Hartford	16	13	1	2	81	49	28	16	7	7	2	64	71	16	32	20	8	4	145	120	44
Los Angeles	36	22	6	8	214	144	52	36	18	12	6	181	149	42	72	40	18	14	395	293	94
Minnesota	16	10	1	5	89	57	25	16	8	4	4	62	60	20	32	18	5	9	151	117	45
Montreal	16	10	6	0	63	50	20	16	5	9	2	52	61	12	32	15	15	2	115	111	32
New Jersey	18	12	4	2	103	70	26	19	9	9	1	69	69	19	37	21	13	3	172	139	45
NY Islanders	16	9	5	2	64	52	20	16	2	8	6	65	76	10	32	11	13	8	129	128	30
NY Rangers	16	9	6	1	72	57	19	16	10	5	1	74	70	21	32	19	11	2	146	127	40
Philadelphia	16	8	5	3	62	50	19	16	3	12	1	47	75	7	32	11	17	4	109	125	26
Pittsburgh	16	13	2	1	97	56	27	16	10	5	1	82	56	21	32	23	7	2	179	112	48
Quebec	16	12	4	0	95	51	24	16	8	6	2	76	67	18	32	20	10	2	171	118	42
St. Louis	16	11	3	2	82	61	24	16	9	5	2	78	65	20	32	20	8	4	160	126	44
Toronto	16	11	1	4	95	50	26	16	10	5	1	89	68	21	32	21	6	5	184	118	47
Vancouver	36	26	6	4	196	112	56	36	20	11	5	165	131	45	72	46	17	9	31	243	101
Washington	16	8	4	4	71	57	20	16	6	9	1	61	71	13	32	14	13	5	132	128	33
Winnipeg	34	24	8	2	171	113	50	33	21	9	3	176	138	45	67	45	17	5	347	251	95
Totals	**400**	**257**	**89**	**54**	**2043**	**1394**	**568**	**400**	**189**	**161**	**50**	**1760**	**1665**	**428**	**800**	**446**	**250**	**104**	**3803**	**3059**	**996**

Playoffs

	Series	W	L	GP	W	L	T	GF	GA	Last Mtg.	Round	Result
Boston	1	1	0	4	4	0	0	21	12	1988	F	W 4-0
Calgary	4	3	1	23	15	8	0	110	76	1988	DF	W 4-0
Chicago	2	2	0	10	8	2	0	69	36	1985	CF	W 4-2
Detroit	2	2	0	10	8	2	0	16	10	1988	CF	W 4-1
Los Angeles	4	2	2	20	12	8	0	86	79	1989	DSF	L 3-4
Minnesota	1	1	0	4	4	0	0	22	10	1984	CF	W 4-0
Montreal	1	1	0	3	3	0	0	15	6	1981	P	W 3-0
NY Islanders	3	1	2	15	6	9	0	47	58	1984	F	W 4-1
Philadelphia	3	2	1	15	8	7	0	46	43	1987	F	W 4-3
Vancouver	1	1	0	3	3	0	0	17	5	1986	DSF	W 3-0
Winnipeg	5	5	0	19	18	1	0	96	53	1988	DSF	W 4-1
Totals	**27**	**21**	**6**	**126**	**89**	**37**	**0**	**548**	**389**			

Playoff Results 1989-85

Year	Round	Opponent	Result	GF	GA
1989	DSF	Los Angeles	L 3-4	20	25
1988	**F**	**Boston**	**W 4-0**	**21**	**12**
	CF	Detroit	W 4-1	23	16
	DF	Calgary	W 4-0	18	11
	DSF	Winnipeg	W 4-1	25	17
1987	F	**Philadelphia**	W 4-3	19	17
	CF	Detroit	W 4-1	16	10
	DF	Winnipeg	W 4-0	17	9
	DSF	Los Angeles	W 4-1	32	20
1986	DF	Calgary	L 4-3	24	25
	DSF	Vancouver	W 3-0	17	5
1985	F	**Philadelphia**	**W 4-1**	**21**	**14**
	CF	Chicago	W 4-2	44	25
	DF	Winnipeg	W 4-0	22	11
	DSF	Los Angeles	W 3-0	11	7

Abbreviations: Round: F – Final; **CF** – conference final; **DF** – division final; **DSF** – division semi-final; **SF** – semi-final; **QF** – quarter-final. **P** – preliminary round. **GA** – goals against; **GF** – goals for.

Entry Draft
Selections 1989-79

1989
Pick
15	Jason Soules
36	Richard Borgo
78	Josef Beranek
92	Peter White
120	Anatoli Semenov
140	Davis Payne
141	Sergei Yashin
162	Darcy Martini
225	Roman Bozek

1988
Pick
19	Francois Leroux
39	Petro Koivunen
53	Trevor Sim
61	Collin Bauer
82	Cam Brauer
103	Don Martin
124	Len Barrie
145	Mike Glover
166	Shjon Podein
187	Tom Cole
208	Vladimir Zubkov
229	Darin MacDonald
250	Tim Tisdale

1987
Pick
21	Peter Soberlak
42	Brad Werenka
63	Geoff Smith
64	Peter Eriksson
105	Shaun Van Allen
126	Radek Toupal
147	Tomas Srsen
168	Age Ellingsen
189	Gavin Armstrong
210	Mike Tinkham
231	Jeff Pauletti
241	Jesper Duus
252	Igor Viazmikin

1986
Pick
21	Kim Issel
42	Jamie Nichols
63	Ron Shudra
84	Dan Currie
105	David Haas
126	Jim Ennis
147	Ivan Matulik
168	Nicolas Beaulieu
189	Mike Greenlay
210	Matt Lanza
231	Mojmir Bozik
252	Tony Hand

1985
Pick
20	Scott Metcalfe
41	Todd Carnelley
62	Mike Ware
104	Thomas Kapusta
125	Brian Tessier
146	Shawn Tyers
167	Tony Fairfield
188	Kelly Buchberger
209	Mario Barbe
230	Peter Headon
251	John Haley

1984
Pick
21	Selmar Odelein
42	Daryl Reaugh
63	Todd Norman
84	Rich Novak
105	Richard Lambert
106	Emanuel Viveiros
126	Ivan Dornic
147	Heikki Riihijarvi
168	Todd Ewen
209	Joel Curtis
229	Simon Wheeldon
250	Darren Gani

1983
Pick
19	Jeff Beukeboom
40	Mike Golden
60	Mike Flanagan
80	Esa Tikkanen
120	Don Barber
140	Dale Derkatch
160	Ralph Vos
180	Dave Roach
200	Warren Yadlowski
220	John Miner
240	Steve Woodburn

1982
Pick
20	Jim Playfair
41	Steve Graves
62	Brent Loney
83	Jaroslav Pouzar
104	Dwayne Boettger
125	Raimo Summanen
146	Brian Small
167	Dean Clark
188	Ian Wood
209	Grant Dion
230	Chris Smith
251	Jeff Crawford

1981
Pick
8	Grant Fuhr
29	Todd Strueby
71	Paul Houck
92	Phil Drouillard
111	Steve Smith
113	Marc Habscheid
155	Mike Sturgeon
176	Miloslav Horava
197	Gord Sherven

1980
Pick
6	Paul Coffey
48	Shawn Babcock
69	Jari Kurri
90	Walt Poddubny
111	Mike Winther
132	Andy Moog
153	Rob Polmantuin
174	Lars-Gunnar Petersson

1979
Pick
21	Kevin Lowe
48	Mark Messier
69	Glenn Anderson
84	Max Kostovich
105	Mike Toal
126	Blair Barnes

Club Directory

Northlands Coliseum
Edmonton, Alberta T5B 4M9
Phone 403/474-8561
Ticketing 403/471-2191
FAX 403/471-2171
ENVOY ID   OILERS.GM
            OILERS.PR
Capacity: 17,313 (standing 190)

Owner/Governor	Peter Pocklington
Alternate Governor	Glen Sather
General Counsel	Bob Lloyd, Gary Frohlich
President/General Manager	Glen Sather
Assistant General Manager	Bruce MacGregor
Coach	John Muckler
Co-Coach	Ted Green
Assistant Coach	Ron Low
Director of Player Personnel/Chief Scout	Barry Fraser
Scouting Staff	Ace Bailey, Ed Chadwick, Lorne Davis, Bob Freeman, Harry Howell, Matti Vaisanen
Director of Operations (A.H.L.)	John Blackwell
Executive Secretary	Lana Anderson
Receptionist/Secretary	Lori Willoughby

Medical and Training Staff
Athletic Trainer/Therapist	Ken Lowe
Trainer	Barrie Stafford
Assistant Trainer	Lyle Kulchisky
Massage Therapist	Stewart Poirier
Team Physician	Dr. Gordon Cameron
Fitness Consultant	Dr. Art Quinney

Finance
Controller	Werner Baum
Accountants	Lori Bandola, Ellie Merrick, Maureen West

Public Relations
Director of Public Relations	Bill Tuele
Co-ordinator of Publications and Statistics	Steve Knowles
Community Relations/Special Events Mgr.	Trish Kerr
Public Relations Secretary	Fiona Liew

Marketing
Director of Marketing	Stew MacDonald
Marketing Representative/Merchandising Mgr.	Darrell Holowaychuk
Warehouse Supervisor	Mike Kasowski
Marketing Secretary	Heather Hansch

Ticketing
Director of Ticketing Operations	Sheila Stock
Ticketing Operations	Marcia Godwin, Marcella Kinsman, Sheila McCaskill
Location of Press Box	East Side at top (Radio/TV) West Side at top (Media)
Dimensions of Rink	200 feet by 85 feet
Ends of Rink	Herculite extends above boards around rink
Club Colours	Blue, Orange, White
Training Camp Site	Northlands Coliseum, Edmonton, Alberta
Television Channel	CITV (Channel 13) (Cable 8) CBXT TV (Channel 5) (Cable 4)
Radio Station	CFRN (1260 AM)

General Manager

SATHER, GLEN CAMERON
President and General Manager, Edmonton Oilers. Born in High River, Alta., Sept. 2, 1943.

A journeyman left-winger who played for six different teams during his seven-year NHL career, 46-year-old Glen Sather was one of the League's most successful coaches ever before relinquishing his coaching duties on June 12, 1989. He was the 1985-86 Jack Adams Award winner, led his club to four Stanley Cup championships and holds a ten-year winning percentage of .623 (446-250-104). His 446 wins place him sixth on the all-time list in regular season wins. In addition, Sather led his team to 89 play-off victories, fourth on the all-time list. His .706 winning percentage in the playoffs ranks him first.

After closing out his NHL playing career in 1975-76 with an 80-113-193 scoring mark in 660 games, Sather jumped to the Oilers in the World Hockey Association, where he enjoyed his best and last season as a player with totals of 19-34-53 in 81 games. Midway through that 1976-77 campaign, on January 27, 1977, he also assumed the Edmonton coaching duties and led his team to the first of its 11 straight WHA and NHL playoff appearances. Three years later, when the club entered the NHL, Sather took on the added responsibilities of Oilers' President and General Manager, which he currently maintains.

NHL Coaching Record

			Regular Season				Playoffs			
Season	Team	Games	W	L	T	%	Games	W	L	%
1979-80	Edmonton (NHL)	80	28	39	13	.431	3	0	3	.000
1980-81	Edmonton (NHL)	80	29	35	16	.463	9	5	4	.555
1981-82	Edmonton (NHL)	80	48	17	15	.694	5	2	3	.400
1982-83	Edmonton (NHL)	80	47	21	12	.663	16	11	5	.687
1983-84	Edmonton (NHL)	80	57	18	5	.744	19	15	4	.789*
1984-85	Edmonton (NHL)	80	49	20	11	.681	18	15	3	.833*
1985-86	Edmonton (NHL)	80	56	17	7	.744	10	6	4	.600
1986-87	Edmonton (NHL)	80	50	24	6	.663	21	16	5	.762*
1987-88	Edmonton (NHL)	80	44	25	11	.619	18	16	2	.889*
1988-89	Edmonton (NHL)	80	38	34	8	.538	7	3	4	.429
	NHL Totals	**800**	**446**	**250**	**104**	**.623**	**126**	**89**	**37**	**.706**

* Stanley Cup win

Coach

MUCKLER, JOHN
Coach, Edmonton Oilers. Born in Paris, Ont. on April 13, 1934.

John Muckler was named Head Coach of the Oilers on June 12, 1989 after seven years as an assistant and co-coach with Glen Sather. Muckler first joined the Oilers' organization in 1981 when he coached the Oilers' affiliate in the Central Hockey League, the Wichita Wind. Muckler was named an Assistant Coach with Edmonton in 1982 and was elevated to the position of Co-Coach in 1985-86.

Muckler started his coaching career in 1959 as the Head Coach of the Long Island Ducks in the Eastern Hockey League. In 1966, Muckler became Director of Player Personnel with the New York Rangers, followed by a six-year stint as General Manager with various clubs within the Minnesota North Stars system. In 1974-75, he coached the Providence Reds of the AHL before joining Dallas of the CHL in 1978-79. Muckler has been named Coach of the Year in three leagues (EHL, 1963-64; AHL 1974-75; CHL, 1978-79) and has led three teams to league championships (Long Island, 1963-64; Providence, 1974-75 and Dallas 1978-79).

Coaching Record

			Regular Season					Playoffs			
Season	Team	Games	W	L	T	%	Games	W	L	%
1964-65	Long Island (EHL)	72	42	29	1	.590	15	11	4	.733
1965-66	Long Island (EHL)	72	46	23	3	.660	12	7	5	.583
1968-69	**Minnesota (NHL)**	**35**	**6**	**23**	**6**	**.257**	....	....	....	....
1971-72	Cleveland (AHL)	76	32	34	10	.487	6	2	4	.333
1972-73	*Cleveland (AHL)	76	23	44	9	.362	....	....	....	....
1973-74	Providence (AHL)	76	38	26	12	.579	15	9	6	.600
1974-75	Providence (AHL)	76	43	21	12	.645	6	2	4	.333
1975-76	Providence (AHL)	76	34	34	8	.500	3	0	3	.000
1976-77	Providence (AHL)	53	21	30	2	.415	....	....	....	....
1978-79	Dallas (CHL)	76	45	28	3	.612	9	8	1	.889
1981-82	Wichita (CHL)	80	44	33	3	.569	7	3	4	.423
	NHL Totals	**35**	**6**	**23**	**6**	**.257**	....	....	....	....

* Club moved to Jacksonville during regular season.

Hartford Whalers

1988-89 Results: 37w-38L-5T 79 pts. Fourth, Adams Division

Year-by-Year Record

Season	GP	Home			Road			Overall					Pts.	Finished	Playoff Result
		W	L	T	W	L	T	W	L	T	GF	GA			
1988-89	80	21	17	2	16	21	3	37	38	5	299	290	79	4th, Adams Div.	Lost Div. Semi-Final
1987-88	80	21	14	5	14	24	2	35	38	7	249	267	77	4th, Adams Div.	Lost Div. Semi-Final
1986-87	80	26	9	5	17	21	2	43	30	7	287	270	93	1st, Adams Div.	Lost Div. Semi-Final
1985-86	80	21	17	2	19	19	2	40	36	4	332	302	84	4th, Adams Div.	Lost Div. Final
1984-85	80	17	18	5	13	23	4	30	41	9	268	318	69	5th, Adams Div.	Out of Playoffs
1983-84	80	19	16	5	9	26	5	28	42	10	288	320	66	5th, Adams Div.	Out of Playoffs
1982-83	80	13	22	5	6	32	2	19	54	7	261	403	45	5th, Adams Div.	Out of Playoffs
1981-82	80	13	17	10	8	24	8	21	41	18	264	351	60	5th, Adams Div.	Out of Playoffs
1980-81	80	14	17	9	7	24	9	21	41	18	292	372	60	4th, Norris Div.	Out of Playoffs
1979-80	80	22	12	6	5	22	13	27	34	19	303	312	73	4th, Norris Div.	Lost Prelim. Round

Schedule

· Home	Away
Oct. Thur. 5 Montreal	**Oct.** Sun. 8 Quebec
Sat. 7 Minnesota	Fri. 13 Buffalo
Wed. 11 Washington	Thur. 19 NY Rangers
Sat. 14 New Jersey	Mon. 23 Montreal
Wed. 18 Buffalo	Thur. 26 New Jersey
Sat. 21 Detroit	Sat. 28 Boston
Wed. 25 Quebec	**Nov.** Fri. 3 Detroit
Nov. Wed. 1 St Louis	Fri. 10 Winnipeg
Sat. 4 Los Angeles	Sun. 12 Chicago
Wed. 8 Buffalo	Tues. 14 Detroit
Wed. 15 Boston	Sun. 26 Buffalo
Sat. 18 NY Rangers	Thur. 30 St Louis
Wed. 22 Quebec	**Dec.** Sat. 2 Montreal
Sat. 25 Philadelphia	Thur. 7 Boston
Tues. 28 Buffalo	Thur. 14 Philadelphia
Dec. Wed. 6 NY Islanders	Tues. 19 Pittsburgh
Sat. 9 New Jersey	Tues. 26 Quebec
Wed. 13 Los Angeles	Sat. 30 Chicago
Sat. 16 Washington	**Jan.** Fri. 5 Calgary
Wed. 20 Boston	Sat. 6 Edmonton
Sat. 23 Minnesota	Wed. 10 Vancouver
Jan. Wed. 3 Winnipeg	Sat. 13 Los Angeles
Wed. 17 Boston	Mon. 15 Boston
Fri. 19 Calgary	Thur. 25 St Louis
Tues. 23 NY Islanders	**Feb.** Thur. 1 Philadelphia
Sat. 27 Chicago	Sat. 3 Quebec*
Tues. 30 Edmonton	Sun. 4 Montreal
Feb. Fri. 9 Vancouver	Wed. 7 Minnesota
Sat. 10 Toronto	Wed. 14 Toronto
Wed. 21 Quebec	Sat. 17 Montreal
Sat. 24 Winnipeg	Sun. 18 Buffalo
Wed. 28 Montreal	Fri. 23 Buffalo
Mar. Sat. 3 NY Rangers	**Mar.** Fri. 2 Washington
Thur. 8 Toronto	Tues. 6 NY Islanders
Sat. 10 Buffalo	Tues. 13 Vancouver
Sun. 11 Boston	Sat. 17 Calgary
Wed. 21 Quebec	Sun. 18 Edmonton
Sat. 24 Montreal	Tues. 27 Pittsburgh
Sun. 25 Pittsburgh	Thur. 29 Boston
Apr. Sun. 1 Montreal	Sat. 31 Quebec

* Denotes afternoon game.

Home Starting Times:
Weeknights and Saturdays . . . . 7:35 p.m.
Sundays . . . . 7:05 p.m.

Franchise date: June 22, 1979

11th NHL Season

Peter Sidorkiewcz's 3.03 goals-against average earned him the goaltenders' position on the 1988-89 NHL All-Rookie Team.

1989-90 Player Personnel

CENTERS	HT	WT	S	Place of Birth	Date	1988-89 Club
BLACK, James	5-11	185	L	Regina, Sask.	8/15/69	Portland
DOCHUK, Kent	5-11	180	R	Edmonton, Alta.	11/14/69	Seattle
EVASON, Dean	5-10	180	R	Flin Flon, Man.	8/22/64	Hartford
FERRARO, Ray	5-10	185	L	Trail, B.C.	8/23/64	Hartford
FRANCIS, Ron	6-2	200	L	Sault Ste. Marie, Ont.	3/1/63	Hartford
GAUME, Dallas	5-10	180	L	Innisfal, Alta.	8/27/63	Binghamton-Hartford
KASOWSKI, Peter	5-11	180	L	Edmonton, Alta.	3/19/69	Swift Current
KRYGIER, Todd	5-11	180	L	Northville, Mich.	10/12/65	Binghamton
LINDBERG, Chris	6-1	190		Fort Francis, Ont.	4/16/67	U. of Minn.-Duluth
YAKE, Terry	5-11	185	R	New Westminster, B.C.	10/22/68	Binghamton-Hartford

LEFT WINGS						
ANDERSON, John	5-11	200	L	Toronto, Ont.	3/28/57	Hartford
BECHARD, Jerome	5-11	185	L	Regina, Sask.	3/30/69	Moose Jaw
BODAK, Bob	6-2	200	L	Thunder Bay, Ont.	5/28/61	Binghamton-Salt Lake
BOYD, Rick	6-2	215	L	Fort St. John, B.C.	12/20/64	
BUCHANAN, Trevor	6-0	176	L	Thompson, Man.	6/7/69	Kamloops
DANIELS, Scott	6-2	225	L	Prince Albert, B.C.	9/19/69	Regina
GOVEDARIS, Chris	6-0	200	L	Toronto, Ont.	2/2/70	Toronto
KNOPP, Kevin	6-1	190	L	Edmonton, Alta.	10/24/69	Seattle-Swift Cur'nt
LAFORGE, Marc	6-2	210	L	Sudbury, Ont.	1/3/68	Binghamton-Indianapolis
LAWTON, Brian	6-0	190	L	New Brunswick, NJ	6/29/65	NYR-Hartford
MARTIN, Tom	6-2	200	L	Kelowna, B.C.	5/11/64	Minnesota-Hartford
McKENZIE, Jim	6-3	205	L	Gull Lake, Sask.	11/3/69	Victoria
PICARD, Michel	5-11	190	L	Beauport, Que.	11/7/69	Trois-Rivieres
SCEVIOUR, Todd	5-11	195	L	Lacombe, Alta.	2/18/67	
TIPPETT, Dave	5-10	180	L	Moosomin, Sask.	8/25/61	Hartford
TOMLAK, Mike	6-3	205	L	Thunder Bay, Ont.	10/17/64	U. of Western Ontario

RIGHT WINGS						
ATCHEYNUM, Blair	6-2	190	R	Estevan, Sask.	4/20/69	Moose Jaw
BINGHAM, Pat	6-0	185	R	Vancouver, B.C.	10/8/68	Kamloops
BUCSIS, Wayde	6-1	185	L	Prince Albert, Alta.	1/18/68	Prince Albert
DINEEN, Kevin	5-11	190	R	Quebec City, Que.	10/28/63	Hartford
HULL, Jody	6-2	200	R	Cambridge, Ont.	2/2/69	Hartford
KASTELIC, Ed	6-4	215	R	Toronto, Ont.	1/29/64	Binghamton-Hartford
MacDERMID, Paul	6-1	205	R	Chesley, Ont.	4/14/63	Hartford
MOLLER, Mike	6-0	189	R	Calgary, Alta.	6/16/62	Cdn. National
MOORE, John	6-3	205	R	Montreal, Que.	1/9/67	Yale
SAUMIER, Raymond	6-0	195	R	Hull, Que.	2/27/69	Trois-Rivieres
THOMSON, Jim	6-1	205	R	Edmonton, Alta.	12/30/65	Washington-Hartford
VERBEEK, Pat	5-9	190	R	Sarnia, Ont.	5/24/64	New Jersey
YOUNG, Scott	6-0	190	R	Clinton, Mass.	10/1/67	Hartford

DEFENSEMEN						
BABYCH, Dave	6-2	215	L	Edmonton, Alta.	5/23/61	Hartford
BATTICE, John	6-1	182	L	Brampton, Ont.	2/25/69	London
BEAULIEU, Corey	6-2	210	L	Winnipeg, Man.	9/10/69	Moose Jaw
BERTHELSON, Peter	6-2	192	L	Edmonton, Alta.	5/31/69	Lethbridge
BIAFORE, Chad	5-11	185	L	Cranbrook, B.C.	3/28/68	Portland
BURGERS, Martin	6-4	205	L	Diepenveen, Holland	4/21/60	Fort Wayne
BURT, Adam	6-0	190	L	Detroit, Mich.	1/15/69	North Bay-Binghamton-Hartford
CHAPMAN, Brian	6-0	195	L	Brockville, Ont.	2/10/68	Binghamton
COTE, Sylvain	5-11	185	R	Durberger, Que.	1/19/66	Hartford
CULHANE, Jim	6-0	195	L	Haileybury, Ont.	3/13/65	Binghamton
HERCZEG, Don	6-1	210	R	Edmonton, Alta.	6/6/64	Denver-Indianapolis
JENNINGS, Grant	6-3	200	L	Hudson Bay, Sask.	5/5/65	Hartford-Binghamton
LADOUCEUR, Randy	6-2	220	L	Brockville, Ont.	6/30/60	Hartford
MACIVER, Norm	5-11	180	L	Thunder Bay, Ont.	9/8/64	NYR-Hartford
QUENNEVILLE, Joel	6-1	200	L	Windsor, Ont.	9/15/58	Hartford
QUINN, Doug	6-2	205	L	Red Deer, Alta.	4/2/65	
SAMUELSSON, Ulf	6-1	195	L	Fagersta, Sweden	3/26/64	Hartford
SHORT, Mike	6-6	210	L	Scarborough, Ont.		
TUER, Al	6-0	175	L	No. Battleford, Sask.	7/19/63	Binghamton-Hartford

GOALTENDERS	HT	WT	C	Place of Birth	Date	1988-89 Club
EVOY, Sean	6-1	190	L	Sudbury, Ont.	2/11/66	Binghamton
LIUT, Mike	6-2	195	L	Weston, Ont.	1/7/56	Hartford
McKAY, Ross	5-11	175	R	Edmonton, Alta.	3/3/64	Binghamton-Indianapolis
SIDORKIEWICZ, Peter	5-9	180	L	D. Bialostocka, Poland	6/29/63	Hartford
WHITMORE, Kay	5-11	175	L	Sudbury, Ont.	4/10/67	Binghamton-Hartford

Retired Numbers

2	Rick Ley	1979-1981
9	Gordie Howe	1979-1980
19	John McKenzie	1976-1979

1988-89 Scoring

Regular Season

* Rookie

Pos	#	Player	Team	GP	G	A	Pts	+/−	PIM	PP	SH	GW	GT	S	%
F	11	Kevin Dineen	HFD	79	45	44	89	6−	167	20	1	4	0	294	15.3
F	10	Ron Francis	HFD	69	29	48	77	4	36	8	0	4	0	156	18.6
F	26	Ray Ferraro	HFD	80	41	35	76	1	86	11	0	7	0	169	24.3
F	27	*Scott Young	HFD	76	19	40	59	21−	27	6	0	2	0	203	9.4
D	44	Dave Babych	HFD	70	6	41	47	5−	54	4	0	2	0	172	3.5
F	23	Paul MacDermid	HFD	74	17	27	44	1	141	5	0	3	2	113	15.0
F	7	Brian Lawton	NYR	30	7	10	17	2−	39	3	0	0	0	58	12.1
			HFD	35	10	16	26	9−	28	7	0	2	0	70	14.3
			TOTAL	65	17	26	43	11−	67	10	0	2	0	128	13.3
F	15	Dave Tippett	HFD	80	17	24	41	6−	45	1	2	1	0	165	10.3
F	20	John Anderson	HFD	62	16	24	40	15	28	1	0	0	0	132	12.1
D	5	Ulf Samuelsson	HFD	71	9	26	35	23	181	3	0	2	0	122	7.4
F	8	*Jody Hull	HFD	60	16	18	34	6	10	6	0	2	0	82	19.5
D	33	Norm Maciver	NYR	26	0	10	10	3−	14	0	0	0	0	36	.0
			HFD	37	1	22	23	0	24	1	0	0	0	51	2.0
			TOTAL	63	1	32	33	3−	38	1	0	0	0	87	1.1
F	16	Sylvain Turgeon	HFD	42	16	14	30	11−	40	7	0	1	0	122	13.1
F	12	Dean Evason	HFD	67	11	17	28	9−	60	0	0	0	0	95	11.6
F	14	Don Maloney	NYR	31	4	9	13	2	16	0	0	0	0	38	10.5
			HFD	21	3	11	14	1	23	1	0	1	0	34	8.8
			TOTAL	52	7	20	27	3	39	1	0	1	0	72	9.7
D	21	Sylvain Cote	HFD	78	8	9	17	7−	49	1	0	0	0	130	6.2
F	17	Brent Peterson	HFD	66	4	13	17	2	61	0	0	2	0	56	7.1
F	24	Tom Martin	MIN	4	1	1	2	1	4	0	0	0	0	6	16.7
			HFD	38	7	6	13	8	113	0	0	1	0	40	17.5
			TOTAL	42	8	7	15	9	117	0	0	1	0	46	17.4
D	25	*Grant Jennings	HFD	55	3	10	13	17	159	0	0	0	0	39	7.7
D	3	Joel Quenneville	HFD	69	4	7	11	3	32	0	0	0	0	45	8.9
D	4	Jim Pavese	DET	39	3	6	9	1−	130	0	0	0	0	27	11.1
			HFD	5	0	0	0	1−	5	0	0	0	0	6	.0
			TOTAL	44	3	6	9	2−	135	0	0	0	0	33	9.1
D	29	Randy Ladouceur	HFD	75	2	5	7	23−	95	0	0	0	0	56	3.6
G	30	*Peter Sidorkiewicz	HFD	44	0	3	3	0	0	0	0	0	0	0	.0
F	18	*Jim Thomson	WSH	14	2	0	2	3−	53	0	0	0	0	9	22.2
			HFD	5	0	0	0	3−	14	0	0	0	0	3	.0
			TOTAL	19	2	0	2	6−	67	0	0	0	0	12	16.7
F	37	*Dallas Gaume	HFD	4	1	1	2	1	78	0	0	0	0	5	20.0
G	35	*Kay Whitmore	HFD	3	0	2	2	0	4	0	0	0	0	0	.0
F	22	Ed Kastelic	HFD	10	0	2	2	0	15	0	0	0	0	6	.0
D	32	*Brad Shaw	HFD	3	1	0	1	1	0	1	0	0	0	2	50.0
F	38	Mark Reeds	HFD	7	0	1	1	1−	6	0	0	0	0	6	.0
F	38	*Terry Yake	HFD	2	0	0	0	1	0	0	0	0	0	0	.0
D	40	Allan Tuer	HFD	4	0	0	0	2−	23	0	0	0	0	0	.0
D	6	*Adam Burt	HFD	5	0	0	0	1−	6	0	0	0	0	1	.0

Goaltending

No.	Goaltender	GPI	Mins	Avg	W	L	T	EN	SO	GA	SA	S%
30	*Peter Sidorkiewicz	44	2635	3.03	22	18	4	1	4	133	1207	.890
35	*Kay Whitmore	3	180	3.33	2	1	0	0	0	10	96	.896
1	Mike Liut	35	2006	4.25	13	19	1	4	1	142	1027	.861
	Totals	**80**	**4835**	**3.60**	**37**	**38**	**5**	**5**	**5**	**290**	**2330**	**.875**

Playoffs

Pos	#	Player	Team	GP	G	A	Pts	+/−	PIM	PP	SH	GW	GT	S	%
D	44	Dave Babych	HFD	4	1	5	6	1	2	0	0	0	0	16	6.3
F	12	Dean Evason	HFD	4	1	2	3	0	10	0	1	0	0	7	14.3
D	3	Joel Quenneville	HFD	4	0	3	3	2	4	0	0	0	0	4	.0
F	26	Ray Ferraro	HFD	4	2	0	2	2−	4	0	0	0	0	6	33.3
F	27	*Scott Young	HFD	4	2	0	2	4−	4	0	0	0	0	16	12.5
F	23	Paul MacDermid	HFD	4	1	1	2	1−	16	0	0	0	0	5	20.0
F	10	Ron Francis	HFD	4	0	2	2	2−	0	0	0	0	0	10	.0
D	5	Ulf Samuelsson	HFD	4	0	2	2	0	4	0	0	0	0	8	.0
F	16	Sylvain Turgeon	HFD	4	0	2	2	2−	4	0	0	0	0	5	.0
F	7	Brian Lawton	HFD	3	1	0	1	1	0	0	0	0	0	5	20.0
D	32	*Brad Shaw	HFD	3	1	0	1	0	0	0	0	0	0	7	14.3
F	11	Kevin Dineen	HFD	4	1	0	1	0	10	0	0	0	0	10	10.0
D	25	*Grant Jennings	HFD	4	1	0	1	3−	17	1	0	0	0	3	33.3
F	17	Brent Peterson	HFD	2	0	1	1	1−	4	0	0	0	0	3	.0
D	21	Sylvain Cote	HFD	3	0	1	1	3−	4	0	0	0	0	2	.0
F	20	John Anderson	HFD	4	0	1	1	0	2	0	0	0	0	9	.0
F	15	Dave Tippett	HFD	4	0	1	1	3−	0	0	0	0	0	6	.0
F	8	*Jody Hull	HFD	1	0	0	0	0	2	0	0	0	0	0	.0
D	29	Randy Ladouceur	HFD	1	0	0	0	0	10	0	0	0	0	0	.0
D	33	Norm Maciver	HFD	1	0	0	0	2−	2	0	0	0	0	1	.0
F	24	Tom Martin	HFD	1	0	0	0	0	4	0	0	0	0	0	.0
D	4	Jim Pavese	HFD	1	0	0	0	1−	0	0	0	0	0	0	.0
G	30	*Peter Sidorkiewicz	HFD	2	0	0	0	0	0	0	0	0	0	0	.0
G	35	*Kay Whitmore	HFD	2	0	0	0	0	0	0	0	0	0	0	.0
F	14	*Don Maloney	HFD	4	0	0	0	1−	8	0	0	0	0	6	.0

Goaltending

No.	Goaltender	GPI	Mins	Avg	W	L	EN	SO	GA	SA	S%
30	*Peter Sidorkiewicz	2	124	3.87	0	2	0	0	8	45	.822
35	*Kay Whitmore	2	135	4.44	0	2	0	0	10	73	.863
	Totals	**4**	**260**	**4.15**	**0**	**4**	**0**	**0**	**18**	**118**	**.847**

General Managers' History

Jack Kelly, 1979-80 to 1981-82; Emile Francis, 1982-83 to 1988-89; Ed Johnston, 1989-90 to date.

Coaching History

Don Blackburn, 1979-80; Don Blackburn and Larry Pleau, 1980-81; Larry Pleau, 1981-82; Larry Kish and Larry Pleau, 1982- 83; Jack "Tex" Evans, 1983-84 to 1986-87; Jack "Tex" Evans and Larry Pleau, 1987-88; Larry Pleau, 1988-89; Rick Ley, 1989-90.

Captains' History

Rick Ley, 1979-80; Mike Rogers, 1980-81, 1981-82; Russ Anderson, 1982-83; Mark Johnson, 1983-84; Ron Francis, 1984-85 to date.

Club Records

Team

(Figures in brackets for season records are games played; records for fewest points, wins, ties, losses, goals, goals against are for 70 or more games)

Most Points	93	1986-87 (80)
Most Wins	43	1986-87 (80)
Most Ties	19	1979-80 (80)
Most Losses	54	1982-83 (80)
Most Goals	332	1985-86 (80)
Most Goals Against	403	1982-83 (80)
Fewest Points	45	1982-83 (80)
Fewest Wins	19	1982-83 (80)
Fewest Ties	4	1985-86 (80)
Fewest Losses	30	1986-87 (80)
Fewest Goals	249	1987-88 (80)
Fewest Goals Against	267	1987-88 (80)

Longest Winning Streak

Over-all	7	Mar. 16-29/85
Home	5	Mar. 17-29/85
Away	4	Mar. 7-19/86

Longest Undefeated Streak

Over-all	10	Jan. 20-Feb. 10/82 (6 wins, 4 ties)
Home	7	Mar. 15-Apr. 15/83 (5 wins, 2 ties)
Away	6	Jan. 23-Feb. 10/82 (3 wins, 3 ties)

Longest Losing Streak

Over-all	9	Feb. 19/83-Mar. 8/83
Home	6	Feb. 19/83-Mar. 12/83; Feb. 10-Mar. 3/85
Away	13	Dec. 8/82-Feb. 5/83

Longest Winless Streak

Over-all	12	Dec. 18/82-Jan. 11/83 (11 losses, 1 tie)
Home	13	Jan. 15-Mar. 10/85 (11 losses, 2 ties)
Away	15	Nov. 11/79-Jan. 9/80 (11 losses, 4 ties)

Most Shutouts, Season	5	1986-87 (80)
Most Pen. Mins., Season	2,046	1988-89 (80) 1987-88 (80)
Most Goals, Game	11	Feb. 12/84 (Edm. 0 at Hfd. 11)

Individual

Most Seasons	8	Ron Francis, Paul MacDermid
Most Games	567	Ron Francis
Most Goals, Career	219	Blaine Stoughton
Most Assists, Career	433	Ron Francis
Most Points, Career	644	Ron Francis (211 goals, 433 assists)
Most Pen. Mins., Career	1,280	Torrie Robertson
Most Shutouts, Career	10	Mike Liut
Longest Consecutive Games Streak	417	Dave Tippett (Mar. 3/84-Apr. 2/89)
Most Goals, Season	56	Blaine Stoughton (1979-80)
Most Assists, Season	65	Mike Rogers (1980-81)
Most Points, Season	105	Mike Rogers (1979-80) (44 goals, 61 assists) (1980-81) (40 goals, 65 assists)
Most Pen. Mins., Season	358	Torrie Robertson (1985-86)
Most Points, Defenseman Season	69	Dave Babych (1985-86) (14 goals, 55 assists)
Most Points, Center, Season	105	Mike Rogers (1979-80) (44 goals, 61 assists) Mike Rogers (1980-81) (40 goals, 65 assists)
Most Points, Right Wing, Season	100	Blaine Stoughton (1979-80) (56 goals, 44 assists)
Most Points, Left Wing, Season	80	Pat Boutette (1980-81) (28 goals, 52 assists)

Most Points, Rookie, Season	72	Sylvain Turgeon (1983-84) (40 goals, 32 assists)
Most Shutouts, Season	4	Mike Liut (1986-87) Peter Sidorkiewicz (1988-89)
Most Goals, Game	5	Jordy Douglas (Feb. 3/80)
Most Assists, Game	6	Ron Francis (Mar. 5/87)
Most Points, Game	6	Paul Lawless (Jan. 4/87) Ron Francis (Mar. 5/87)

* NHL Record.

All-time Record vs. Other Clubs

Regular Season

			At Home						On Road						Total					
	GP	W	L	T	GF	GA	PTS	GP	W	L	T	GF	GA	PTS	GP	W	L	T	GF	GA	Pts
Boston	36	19	13	4	139	130	42	36	8	24	4	97	152	20	72	27	37	8	236	282	62
Buffalo	36	14	18	4	110	107	32	36	13	18	5	123	145	31	72	27	36	9	233	252	63
**Calgary	16	6	8	2	57	65	14	16	3	12	1	57	88	7	32	9	20	3	114	153	21
Chicago	16	7	8	1	62	59	15	16	5	8	3	50	74	13	32	12	16	4	112	133	28
Detroit	16	11	5	0	67	44	22	16	5	5	6	50	59	16	32	16	10	6	117	103	38
Edmonton	16	7	7	2	71	64	16	16	1	13	2	49	81	4	32	8	20	4	120	145	20
Los Angeles	16	9	5	2	68	68	20	16	5	9	2	64	70	12	32	14	14	4	132	138	32
Minnesota	16	8	8	0	59	57	16	16	5	10	1	56	75	11	32	13	18	1	115	132	27
Montreal	36	12	20	4	115	146	28	36	4	26	6	110	183	14	72	16	46	10	225	329	42
*New Jersey	16	9	3	4	60	48	22	16	7	7	2	70	59	16	32	16	10	6	130	107	38
NY Islanders	16	6	7	3	54	61	15	16	5	10	1	43	69	11	32	11	17	4	97	130	26
NY Rangers	16	9	5	2	65	57	20	16	6	8	2	49	65	14	32	15	13	4	114	122	34
Philadelphia	16	5	7	4	70	75	14	16	2	13	1	42	77	5	32	7	20	5	112	152	19
Pittsburgh	16	10	6	0	81	68	20	16	5	9	2	60	72	12	32	15	15	2	141	140	32
Quebec	36	15	13	8	133	135	38	36	9	23	4	116	171	22	72	24	36	12	249	306	60
St. Louis	16	8	6	2	58	47	18	16	6	8	2	56	61	14	32	14	14	4	114	108	32
Toronto	16	11	3	2	81	51	24	16	10	6	0	71	60	20	32	21	9	2	152	111	44
Vancouver	16	7	5	4	58	59	18	16	4	7	5	44	60	13	32	11	12	9	102	119	31
Washington	16	5	9	2	53	70	12	16	4	11	1	43	61	9	32	9	20	3	96	131	21
Winnipeg	16	9	3	4	75	52	22	16	7	9	0	57	60	14	32	16	12	4	132	112	36
Totals	400	187	159	54	1536	1463	428	400	114	236	50	1307	1742	278	800	301	395	104	2843	3205	706

* Totals include those of Colorado (1979-80, 1980-81, 1981-82)
** Totals include those of Atlanta (1979-80)

Playoffs

	Series	W	L	GP	W	L	T	GF	GA	Last Mtg.	Round	Result
Montreal	4	0	4	20	5	15	0	51	75	1989	DSF	L 0-4
Quebec	2	1	1	9	5	4	0	35	34	1987	DSF	L 2-4
Totals	6	1	5	29	10	19	0	86	109			

Playoff Results 1989-85

Year	Round	Opponent	Result	GF	GA
1989	DSF	Montreal	L 0-4	11	18
1988	DSF	Montreal	L 2-4	19	23
1987	DSF	Quebec	L 2-4	19	27
1986	DF	Montreal	L 3-4	13	16
	DSF	Quebec	W 3-0	16	7

Abbreviations: Round: F – Final; **CF** – conference final; **DF** – division final; **DSF** – division semi-final; **SF** – semi-final; **QF** – quarter-final. **P** – preliminary round. **GA** – goals against; **GF** – goals for.

1988-89 Results

		Home				Away	
Oct.	6	Quebec	2-5	Oct.	9	Boston	1-3
	8	Boston	2-6		12	NY Rangers	4-3
	15	Chicago	7-5		19	Montreal	4-5
	22	Philadelphia	8-6		26	Buffalo	7-1
	29	New Jersey	3-0		28	New Jersey	3-5
Nov.	1	Montreal	3-5	Nov.	3	Boston	5-3
	5	Vancouver	2-3		7	Calgary	3-6
	16	Detroit	3-4		9	Vancouver	1-1
	19	Calgary	2-5		10	Los Angeles	2-7
	23	Quebec	4-3		12	Minnesota	3-1
	30	Montreal	3-6		18	Washington	2-3
Dec.	3	Minnesota	2-4		26	Quebec	4-2
	6	Buffalo	9-0	Dec.	2	Buffalo	6-1
	8	NY Rangers	5-4		14	Chicago	3-4
	10	Calgary	4-1		15	St Louis	3-3
	17	Edmonton	2-4		19	Montreal	1-2
	21	Boston	3-4		23	Philadelphia	4-5
	26	Pittsburgh	3-4		28	Quebec	4-4
	30	Detroit	4-3		31	Detroit	3-2
Jan.	19	Montreal	6-4	Jan.	2	NY Rangers	4-5
	21	Los Angeles	5-4		4	Buffalo	5-4
	25	St Louis	3-3		10	Winnipeg	2-1
	28	Quebec	2-3		14	Los Angeles	6-9
	31	Buffalo	3-5		16	Toronto	3-5
Feb.	9	Buffalo	5-2		18	Montreal	1-3
	11	Winnipeg	7-3		23	Quebec	5-0
	23	Quebec	4-2		27	New Jersey	8-6
	25	Boston	1-9	Feb.	3	Washington	0-1
	26	Pittsburgh	8-6		4	NY Islanders	3-5
Mar.	2	Vancouver	2-1		15	Toronto	4-2
	4	Montreal	1-6		18	Minnesota	4-3
	5	Toronto	3-0		19	Winnipeg	6-7
	8	Edmonton	7-3		21	Edmonton	4-7
	12	Philadelphia	3-3		28	NY Islanders	3-1
	14	NY Islanders	8-2	Mar.	11	Montreal	3-5
	16	Buffalo	1-6		19	Boston	3-2
	18	Washington	2-8		23	Quebec	3-6
	22	Boston	4-2		28	Buffalo	2-4
	25	St Louis	4-0		30	Pittsburgh	9-5
Apr.	1	Chicago	6-1	Apr.	2	Boston	2-3

* Denotes afternoon game.

Entry Draft
Selections 1989-79

1989
Pick	
10	Robert Holik
52	Blair Atcheynum
73	Jim McKenzie
94	James Black
115	Jerome Bechard
136	Scott Daniels
157	Raymond Saumier
178	Michel Picard
199	Trevor Buchanan
220	John Battice
241	Peter Kasowski

1988
Pick	
11	Chris Govedaris
32	Barry Richter
74	Dean Dyer
95	Scott Morrow
116	Corey Beaulieu
137	Kerry Russell
158	Jim Burke
179	Mark Hirth
200	Wayde Bucsis
221	Rob White
242	Dan Slatalla

1987
Pick	
18	Jody Hull
39	Adam Burt
81	Terry Yake
102	Marc Rousseau
123	Jeff St. Cyr
144	Greg Wolf
165	John Moore
186	Joe Day
228	Kevin Sullivan
249	Steve Laurin

1986
Pick	
11	Scott Young
32	Marc Laforge
74	Brian Chapman
95	Bill Horn
116	Joe Quinn
137	Steve Torrel
158	Ron Hoover
179	Robert Glasgow
200	Sean Evoy
221	Cal Brown
242	Brian Verbeek

1985
Pick	
5	Dana Murzyn
26	Kay Whitmore
68	Gary Callaghan
110	Shane Churla
131	Chris Brant
152	Brian Puhalsky
173	Greg Dornbach
194	Paul Tory
215	Jerry Pawlowski
236	Bruce Hill

1984
Pick	
11	Sylvain Cote
110	Mike Millar
131	Mike Vellucci
173	John Devereaux
194	Brent Regan
215	Jim Culhane
236	Pete Abric

1983
Pick	
2	Sylvain Turgeon
20	David Jensen
23	Ville Siren
61	Leif Karlsson
64	Dave MacLean
72	Ron Chyzowski
104	Brian Johnson
124	Joe Reekie
143	Chris Duperron
144	James Falle
164	Bill Fordy
193	Reine Karlsson
204	Allan Acton
224	Darcy Kaminski

1982
Pick	
14	Paul Lawless
35	Mark Paterson
56	Kevin Dineen
67	Ulf Samuelsson
88	Ray Ferraro
109	Randy Gilhen
130	Jim Johannson
151	Mickey Kramptoich
172	Kevin Skilliter
214	Martin Linse
235	Randy Cameron

1981
Pick	
4	Ron Francis
61	Paul MacDermid
67	Michael Hoffman
93	Bill Maguire
103	Dan Bourbonnais
130	John Mokosak
151	Denis Dore
172	Jeff Poeschl
193	Larry Power

1980
Pick	
8	Fred Arthur
29	Michel Galarneau
50	Mickey Volcan
71	Kevin McClelland
100	Darren Jensen
113	Mario Cerri
134	Mike Martin
155	Brent Denat
176	Paul Fricker
197	Lorne Bokshowan

1979
Pick	
18	Ray Allison
39	Stuart Smith
60	Don Nachbaur
81	Ray Neufeld
102	Mark Renaud
123	Dave McDonald

Club Directory

Hartford Civic Center Coliseum
One Civic Center Plaza
Hartford, Connecticut 06103
Phone 203/728-3366
GM FAX 203/247-1274
FAX 203/522-7707
TWX 710-425-8732
ENVOY ID
  Front Office: WHALERS. GM
  Public
  Relations: WHALERS. PR
Capacity: 15,580

Managing General Partner/Governor	Richard Gordon
General Partner/Alternate Governor	Benjamin J. Sisti
Partner/Alternate Governor	Donald G. Conrad
President/Alternate Governor	Emile Francis
Special Assistant to the MGP	Gordie Howe
Vice-President/General Manager	Ed Johnston
Assistant General Manager	Robert W. Crocker
Head Coach	Rick Ley
Assistant Coaches	Jay Leach and Brent Peterson
Director of Player Personnel and Scouting	Ken Schinkel
Scouting Staff	Leo Boivin, Steve Brklacich, Bruce Haralson, Fred Gore, Claude Larose
Head Trainer	Tom Woodcock
Strength Coach	Doug McKenney
Assistant Trainer & Equipment Manager	Skip Cunningham
Executive Vice-President of Finance & Administration	W. David Andrews III
Vice-President of Marketing & Public Relations	William E. Barnes
Treasurer	Michael J. Amendola
Director of Public Relations	Phil Langan
Assistant Director of Public Relations	Mark Willand
Chief Statistician	Frank Polnaszek
Advertising Sales Manager	Rick Francis
Merchandise Manager	Mike Reddy
Ticket Sales Manager	Jeff Morander
Director of Properties/Development	Don Cox
Director of Administration	Camille Beck
Ticket Office Supervisor	Kathy Conran
Club Doctor	Dr. Vincent Turco
Club Dentist	Dr. Walter Kunisch
Radio Play-By-Play	Chuck Kaiton
TV/Cable Play-By-Play	Rick Peckham
Dimensions of Rink	200 feet by 85 feet
Location of Press Box	Center ice, Upper Level, Asylum Street
Location of Broadcast Booth	Center ice, Upper Level, Asylum Street
Location of Press Room	Adjacent to press box, Upper Level, Asylum Street
TV Outlet	WHCT (Channel 18)
Cable TV Outlet	SportsChannel
Radio Outlet	WTIC-AM (1080) Flagship station of the Whalers Radio Network
Team Colors	Green, Blue and White

General Manager

JOHNSTON, ED
Vice-President and General Manager, Hartford Whalers.
Born in Montreal, Que., November 24, 1935.

Ed Johnston was named Vice-President and General Manager of the Whalers on May 11, 1989 after serving in the Pittsburgh Penguins' organization for six years. He was the General Manager of the Penguins from 1982-83 to 1987-88 before being named Assistant General Manager in 1988-89.

Johnston's coaching career began with the Chicago Blackhawks organization. He coached Moncton of the AHL in 1978-79 before taking over as Blackhawks head coach for the 1979-80 campaign. He was head coach of the Penguins for three years (1980-81 to 1982-83). His NHL coaching record is 113-156-54.

Johnston played 11 years with the Boston Bruins and was a member of two NHL Stanley Cup Championship teams. He also played with Toronto, St. Louis and Chicago during his 16-year NHL career and had a 3.25 career goals-against-average and 32 shutouts. Johnston owns the distinction of being the last goaltender to play an entire NHL regular season—having played all 70 games during the 1963-64 season.

NHL Coaching Record

			Regular Season				Playoffs			
Season	Team	Games	W	L	T	%	Games	W	L	%
1979-80	Chicago	80	34	27	19	.544	4	0	4	.000
1980-81	Pittsburgh	80	30	37	13	.456	5	2	3	.400
1981-82	Pittsburgh	80	31	36	13	.469	5	2	3	.400
1982-83	Pittsburgh	80	18	53	9	.281	....	....	....	....
	NHL Totals	**320**	**113**	**156**	**54**	**.438**	**14**	**4**	**10**	**.286**

Coach

LEY, RICK
Coach, Hartford Whalers. Born in Orillia, Ont., November 2, 1948.

Rick Ley was named Head Coach of the Whalers on June 7, 1989 after a seven-year coaching career in the minor leagues. After knee injuries ended his playing career in 1981-82, Ley was named the assistant coach of the Whalers. Mid-way through the 1982-83 season, he was named the head coach of the Binghamton Whalers (AHL). In 1983, Ley left the Whalers' organization to coach the Mohawk Valley Stars of the Atlantic Coast Hockey League. A year later, he was hired by Ed Johnston to coach the Pittsburgh Penguins' IHL affiliate—the Muskegon Lumberjacks. Ley coached Muskegon to first-place finishes each year from 1984-85 to 1987-88. He was the IHL Co-Coach of the Year in 1984-85, led his club to the Turner Cup in 1985-86 and won the regular-season championship in 1987-88. In July of 1988, Ley was hired by the Vancouver Canucks to coach the Milwaukee Admirals (IHL).

Ley was one of the first players to join the New England Whalers of the WHA in 1972-73 after four seasons with the Toronto Maple Leafs. He played 559 career games with the Whalers from 1972-73 to 1980-81, serving as captain for his final six seasons. Ley played in each of the nine WHA All-Star Games and was named the League's top defenseman in 1978-79.

Coaching Record

			Regular Season				Playoffs			
Season	Team	Games	W	L	T	%	Games	W	L	%
1982-83	Binghamton (AHL)	44	22	17	5	.534	5	1	4	.200
1983-84	Mohawk Valley (ACHL)	75	29	39	7	.433	5	1	4	.200
1984-85	Muskegon (IHL)	82	50	29	3	.628	17	11	6	.647
1985-86	Muskegon (IHL)	82	50	32	0	.610	14	12	2	.857
1986-87	Muskegon (IHL)	82	47	30	5	.6C4	15	10	5	.667
1987-88	Muskegon (IHL)	82	58	14	10	.768	6	2	4	.333
1988-89	Milwaukee (IHL)	82	54	23	5	.689	11	5	6	.455

Los Angeles Kings

1988-89 Results: 42w-31L-7T 91 PTS. Second, Smythe Division

Year-by-Year Record

Season	GP	Home W	L	T	Road W	L	T	Overall W	L	T	GF	GA	Pts.	Finished	Playoff Result
1988-89	80	25	12	3	17	19	4	42	31	7	376	335	91	2nd, Smythe Div.	Lost Div. Final
1987-88	80	19	18	3	11	24	5	30	42	8	318	359	70	4th, Smythe Div.	Lost Div. Semi-Final
1986-87	80	20	17	3	11	24	5	31	41	8	318	341	70	4th, Smythe Div.	Lost Div. Semi-Final
1985-86	80	9	27	4	14	22	4	23	49	8	284	389	54	5th, Smythe Div.	Out of Playoffs
1984-85	80	20	14	6	14	18	8	34	32	14	339	326	82	4th, Smythe Div.	Lost Div. Semi-Final
1983-84	80	13	19	8	10	25	5	23	44	13	309	376	59	5th, Smythe Div.	Out of Playoffs
1982-83	80	20	13	7	7	28	5	27	41	12	308	365	66	5th, Smythe Div.	Out of Playoffs
1981-82	80	19	15	6	5	26	9	24	41	15	314	369	63	4th, Smythe Div.	Lost Div. Final
1980-81	80	22	11	7	21	13	6	43	24	13	337	290	99	2nd, Norris Div.	Lost Prelim. Round
1979-80	80	18	13	9	12	23	5	30	36	14	290	313	74	2nd, Norris Div.	Lost Prelim. Round
1978-79	80	20	13	7	14	21	5	34	34	12	292	286	80	3rd, Norris Div.	Lost Prelim. Round
1977-78	80	18	16	6	13	18	9	31	34	15	243	245	77	3rd, Norris Div.	Lost Prelim. Round
1976-77	80	20	13	7	14	18	8	34	31	15	271	241	83	2nd, Norris Div.	Lost Quarter-Final
1975-76	80	22	13	5	16	20	4	38	33	9	263	265	85	2nd, Norris Div.	Lost Quarter-Final
1974-75	80	22	7	11	20	10	10	42	17	21	269	185	105	2nd, Norris Div.	Lost Prelim. Round
1973-74	78	22	13	4	11	20	8	33	33	12	233	231	78	3rd, West Div.	Lost Quarter-Final
1972-73	78	21	11	7	10	25	4	31	36	11	232	245	73	6th, West Div.	Out of Playoffs
1971-72	78	14	23	2	6	26	7	20	49	9	206	305	49	7th, West Div.	Out of Playoffs
1970-71	78	17	14	8	8	26	5	25	40	13	239	303	63	5th, West Div.	Out of Playoffs
1969-70	76	12	22	4	2	30	6	14	52	10	168	290	38	6th, West Div.	Out of Playoffs
1968-69	76	19	14	5	5	28	5	24	42	10	185	260	58	4th, West Div.	Lost Semi-Final
1967-68	74	20	13	4	11	20	6	31	33	10	200	224	72	2nd, West Div.	Lost Quarter-Final

Schedule

Home			Away		
Oct.	Thur. 5	Toronto	Oct.	Fri. 13	Vancouver
	Sat. 7	Edmonton		Sun. 15	Edmonton
	Sun. 8	Detroit		Sat. 21	St Louis
	Wed. 11	NY Islanders		Sun. 22	Chicago
	Tues. 17	Boston		Fri. 27	Winnipeg
	Wed. 25	Calgary		Sun. 29	Winnipeg
Nov.	Wed. 8	Calgary		Tues. 31	Pittsburgh
	Sat. 11	Montreal	Nov.	Thur. 2	Boston
	Sat. 18	Washington		Sat. 4	Hartford
	Wed. 22	Chicago		Sun. 5	Buffalo
	Sat. 25	Vancouver		Tues. 14	Calgary
	Thur. 30	Edmonton		Wed. 15	Edmonton
Dec.	Sat. 2	NY Rangers		Sun. 26	Vancouver
	Wed. 6	Vancouver	Dec.	Fri. 8	Edmonton
	Tues. 19	Winnipeg		Sun. 10	Quebec*
	Thur. 21	Quebec		Mon. 11	Montreal
	Sat. 23	Vancouver		Wed. 13	Hartford
	Wed. 27	Calgary		Fri. 15	New Jersey
	Sat. 30	Philadelphia		Sat. 16	Philadelphia
Jan.	Tues. 9	St Louis	Jan.	Mon. 1	Washington*
	Thur. 11	Edmonton		Tues. 2	NY Islanders
	Sat. 13	Hartford		Thur. 4	New Jersey
	Tues. 16	Buffalo		Sat. 6	Toronto
	Thur. 18	Detroit		Tues. 23	Vancouver
	Sat. 27	NY Rangers		Thur. 25	Edmonton
	Tues. 30	New Jersey	Feb.	Tues. 6	Calgary
Feb.	Thur. 1	Chicago		Sat. 10	Pittsburgh
	Sat. 3	Calgary		Mon. 12	Toronto
	Thur. 8	Winnipeg		Wed. 14	Detroit
	Sat. 17	Quebec		Thur. 15	Minnesota
	Mon. 19	Washington*	Mar.	Fri. 2	Winnipeg
	Wed. 21	Minnesota		Sun. 4	Winnipeg*
	Sat. 24	Vancouver		Mon. 5	Calgary
	Wed. 28	Edmonton		Mon. 12	NY Rangers
Mar.	Wed. 7	Montreal		Wed. 14	Buffalo
	Sat. 10	Pittsburgh*		Sat. 17	Boston*
	Thur. 22	NY Islanders		Sun. 18	Philadelphia
	Sat. 24	St Louis		Tues. 20	Minnesota
	Tues. 27	Winnipeg		Sat. 31	Vancouver
	Thur. 29	Winnipeg	Apr.	Sun. 1	Calgary

* Denotes afternoon game.

Home Starting Times:
All Games . . . . 7:35 p.m.
Except Matinees . . . . 1:05 p.m.

Franchise date: June 5, 1967

23rd NHL Season

Bernie Nicholls became the fifth man in NHL history to score 70 goals in one NHL season.

1989-90 Player Personnel

FORWARDS	HT	WT	S	Place of Birth	Date	1988-89 Club
AIVAZOFF, Micah	6-1	192	L	Powell River, B.C.	5/4/69	Victoria
ALLISON, Mike	6-1	195	R	Ft. Frances, Ont.	3/28/61	Los Angeles
COUTURIER, Sylvain	6-2	205	L	Greenfield Park, Que.	4/23/68	Los Angeles-New Haven
CROWDER, Keith	6-0	190	R	Windsor, Ont.	1/6/59	Boston
DUGUAY, Ron	6-2	200	R	Subdury, Ont.	7/6/57	Los Angeles
DUNCANSON, Craig	6-0	190	L	Naughton, Ont.	3/17/67	Los Angeles-New Haven
ELIK, Todd	6-2	190	L	Brampton, Ont.	4/15/66	Colorado-New Haven
FITZGERALD, Sean	6-1	208	L	West Seneca, NY	1/12/67	Owegeo State
FOX, Jim	5-8	180	R	Coniston, Ont.	5/18/60	Los Angeles
GRETZKY, Wayne	6-0	175	L	Brantford, Ont.	1/26/61	Los Angeles
HORNER, Steve	6-1	195	R	Cowansville, Que.	6/4/66	New Hampshire
KARJALAINEN, Kyosti	6-1	190	L	Gavle, Sweden	6/19/67	Brynas (Sweden)
KASPER, Steve	5-8	175	L	Montreal, Que.	9/28/61	Boston-L.A.
KELLY, Paul	6-0	180	L	Hamilton, Ont.	4/17/67	New Haven-Utica-Flint
KONTOS, Chris	6-1	195	L	Toronto, Ont.	12/10/63	Switzerland-L.A.
KRUSHELNYSKI, Mike	6-2	200	L	Montreal, Que.	4/27/60	Los Angeles
KUDELSKI, Bob	6-1	200	R	Springfield, MA	3/3/64	Los Angeles-New Haven
LINDHOLM, Mikael	6-1	194	L	Gavle, Sweden	12/19/64	Brynas (Sweden)
LOGAN, Robert	6-0	190	R	Montreal, Que.	2/22/64	New Haven
McDONOUGH, Hubie	5-9	180	L	Manchester, NH	7/8/63	New Haven-Los Angeles
McSORLEY, Marty	6-1	220	R	Hamilton, Ont.	5/18/63	Los Angeles
MILLER, Jay	6-2	210	L	Wellesley, MA	7/16/60	Boston-L.A.
NESTER, Kelly	5-9	160	L	Trenton, MI	2/15/69	Hull
NICHOLLS, Bernie	6-0	185	R	Haliburton, Ont.	6/24/61	Los Angeles
PASIN, Dave	6-1	205	R	Edmonton, Alta.	7/8/66	New Haven-Maine
ROBITAILLE, Luc	6-1	190	L	Montreal, Que.	2/17/66	Los Angeles
SAPERGIA, Brent	5-10	195	R	Moose Jaw, Sask.	11/16/62	Indianapolis
STANLEY, Graham	6-2	213		St. Catharines, Ont.	3/19/66	Dalhousie U.
SYKES, Phil	6-0	175	L	Dawson Creek, B.C.	3/18/59	Los Angeles-New Haven
TAYLOR, Dave	6-0	195	R	Levack, Ont.	12/4/55	Los Angeles
TONELLI, John	6-1	200	L	Milton, Ont.	3/23/57	Los Angeles
VAN KESSEL, John	6-4	193	R	Bridgewater, Ont.	12/19/68	North Bay
WALKER, Gord	6-0	175	L	Castlegar, B.C.	8/12/65	Los Angeles-New Haven
WILLIAMS, Darryl	5-11	185	L	Mt. Pearl, Nfld.	2/9/68	Belleville-New Haven
WILSON, Ross	6-3	197	R	The Pas, Man.	6/26/69	Peterborough

DEFENSEMEN	HT	WT	S	Place of Birth	Date	1988-89 Club
BAUMGARTNER, Ken	6-1	200	L	Flin Flon, Man.	3/11/66	Los Angeles-New Haven
BLAKE, Robert	6-3	200		Simcoe, Ont.	12/10/69	Bowling Green
CHAPDELAINE, Rene	6-1	195	R	Weyburn, Sask.	9/27/66	Lake Superior State
DEGRAY, Dale	6-0	200	R	Ottawa, Ont.	9/1/63	Los Angeles
DUCHESNE, Steve	5-11	195	L	Sept-Iles, Que.	6/30/65	Los Angeles
GERMAIN, Eric	6-1	195	L	Quebec City, Que.	6/26/66	New Haven
HOLDEN, Paul	6-3	210	L	Kitchener, Ont.	3/15/70	London
JAQUES, Steve	5-11	186	L	Burnaby, B.C.	2/21/69	Tri-Cities
KENNEDY, Dean	6-2	203	R	Redvers, Sask.	1/18/63	Los Angeles-New Haven
LAIDLAW, Tom	6-1	205	L	Brampton, Ont.	4/15/58	Los Angeles
LARKIN, James	6-1	200	R	Saskatoon, Sask.	2/2/67	Spokane
PANEK, Chris	6-2	205	L	Buffalo, NY	10/13/66	Los Angeles-New Haven
PRAJSLER, Petr	6-2	200	L	Hradec Kralove, Czech.	9/21/65	Los Angeles-New Haven
RICARD, Eric	6-4	220	R	St. Cesaire, Que.	2/16/69	Granby
ROBINSON, Larry	6-3	220	L	Winchester, Ont.	6/2/51	Montreal
THOMPSON, Brent	6-2	175	L	Calgary, Alta.	1/9/71	Medicine Hat
WATTERS, Tim	5-11	180	L	Kamloops, B.C.	7/25/59	Los Angeles
YOUNG, Scott	6-1	195	R	Burlington, Ont.	5/26/65	Colgate-New Haven

GOALTENDERS	HT	WT	C	Place of Birth	Date	1988-89 Club
GOSSELIN, Mario	5-8	160	L	Thetford Mines, Que.	6/15/63	Quebec
HRUDEY, Kelly	5-1	180	L	Edmonton, Alta.	1/13/61	NY Islanders-L.A.
REPP, Carl	6-0	175		Vancouver, B.C.		
STAUBER, Robb	6-0	170	L	Duluth, MN	11/25/67	U. Minnesota

Retired Numbers

30 Rogatien Vachon 1971-1978

General Managers' History

Larry Regan, 1967-68 to 1972-73; Larry Regan and Jake Milford, 1973-74; Jake Milford, 1974-75 to 1976-77; George Maguire, 1977-78 to 1982-83; George Maguire and Rogatien Vachon, 1983-84; Rogatien Vachon, 1984-85 to date.

Coaching History

Leonard "Red" Kelly, 1967-68 to 1968-69; Hal Laycoe and John Wilson, 1969-70; Larry Regan, 1970-71; Larry Regan and Fred Glover, 1971-72; Bob Pulford, 1972-73 to 1976-77; Ron Stewart, 1977-78; Bob Berry, 1978-79 to 1980-81; Parker MacDonald and Don Perry, 1981-82; Don Perry, 1982-83; Don Perry, Rogatien Vachon and Roger Neilson, 1983-84; Pat Quinn, 1984-85 to 1985-86; Pat Quinn and Mike Murphy 1986-87; Mike Murphy and Robbie Ftorek, 1987-88; Robbie Ftorek, 1988-89; Tom Webster, 1989-90.

Captains' History

Bob Wall, 1967-68, 1968-69; Larry Cahan, 1969-70, 1970-71; Bob Pulford, 1971-72, 1972-73; Terry Harper, 1973-74, 1974-75; Mike Murphy, 1975-76 to 1980-81; Dave Lewis, 1981-82, 1982-83; Terry Ruskowski, 1983-84, 1984-85; Dave Taylor, 1985-86 to date.

1988-89 Scoring

Regular Season

*–Rookie

Pos	#	Player	Team	GP	G	A	Pts	+/–	PIM	PP	SH	GW	GT	S	%
F	99	Wayne Gretzky	L.A.	78	54	114	168	15	26	11	5	5	2	303	17.8
F	9	Bernie Nicholls	L.A.	79	70	80	150	30	96	21	8	6	0	385	18.2
F	20	Luc Robitaille	L.A.	78	46	52	98	5	65	10	0	4	0	237	19.4
D	28	Steve Duchesne	L.A.	79	25	50	75	31	92	8	5	2	0	215	11.6
F	27	John Tonelli	L.A.	77	31	33	64	9	110	1	1	3	0	156	19.9
F	18	Dave Taylor	L.A.	70	26	37	63	10	80	7	0	4	0	141	18.4
F	26	Mike Krushelnyski	L.A.	78	26	36	62	9	110	5	0	8	1	143	18.2
F	11	Steve Kasper	BOS	49	10	16	26	2–	49	2	0	0	0	82	12.2
			L.A.	29	9	15	24	0	14	3	2	2	0	48	18.8
			TOTAL	78	19	31	50	2–	63	5	2	2	0	130	14.6
F	10	Mike Allison	L.A.	55	14	22	36	7	122	6	0	2	0	71	19.7
D	24	Dale Degray	L.A.	63	6	22	28	3	97	0	0	1	0	87	6.9
F	33	Marty McSorley	L.A.	66	10	17	27	3	350	2	0	1	0	87	11.5
D	4	Doug Crossman	L.A.	74	10	15	25	11–	53	2	0	0	0	137	7.3
F	23	*Igor Liba	NYR	10	2	5	7	1	15	1	0	0	0	14	14.3
			L.A.	27	5	13	18	4–	21	1	0	0	0	28	17.9
			TOTAL	37	7	18	25	3–	36	2	0	0	0	42	16.7
F	44	Ron Duguay	L.A.	70	7	17	24	23	48	0	0	0	0	80	8.8
D	5	Tim Watters	L.A.	76	3	18	21	17	168	0	0	0	0	62	4.8
D	3	Tom Laidlaw	L.A.	70	3	17	20	30	63	0	0	1	0	31	9.7
F	29	Jay Miller	BOS	37	2	4	6	6–	168	0	0	0	0	14	14.3
			L.A.	29	5	3	8	3–	133	0	0	0	0	16	31.3
			TOTAL	66	7	7	14	9–	301	0	0	0	0	30	23.3
D	6	Dean Kennedy	L.A.	25	2	7	9	14	23	0	0	1	0	18	11.1
			NYR	16	0	1	1	1–	40	0	0	0	0	7	.0
			L.A.	26	1	3	4	4	40	0	0	0	0	20	5.0
			TOTAL	67	3	11	14	17	103	0	0	1	0	45	6.7
D	2	Jim Wiemer	L.A.	9	2	3	5	2	20	0	1	1	0	17	11.8
F	37	Robert Kudelski	L.A.	14	1	3	4	5–	17	0	0	0	0	15	6.7
F	12	*Sylvain Couturier	L.A.	16	1	3	4	3–	2	1	0	0	0	15	6.7
D	22	Ken Baumgartner	L.A.	49	1	3	4	9–	286	0	0	0	0	15	6.7
F	15	Chris Kontos	L.A.	7	2	1	3	2	2	1	0	0	0	9	22.2
F	15	Tim Tookey	L.A.	7	2	1	3	3–	4	0	0	0	0	8	25.0
D	25	*Petr Prajsler	L.A.	2	0	3	3	4	0	0	0	0	0	1	.0
G	32	Kelly Hrudey	NYI	50	0	1	1	0	17	0	0	0	0	1	.0
			L.A.	16	0	2	2	0	2	0	0	0	0	0	.0
			TOTAL	66	0	3	3	0	19	0	0	0	0	1	.0
D	42	Steve Richmond	L.A.	9	0	2	2	2	26	0	0	0	0	1	.0
F	45	*Gord Walker	L.A.	11	1	0	1	2–	2	0	0	0	0	13	7.7
F	39	*Hubie McDonough	L.A.	4	0	1	1	2	0	0	0	0	0	3	.0
F	8	Gilles Hamel	WPG	1	0	0	0	0	0	0	0	0	0	0	.0
			L.A.	11	0	1	1	3–	2	0	0	0	0	11	.0
			TOTAL	12	0	1	1	3–	2	0	0	0	0	11	.0
F	7	Phil Sykes	L.A.	23	0	1	1	3–	8	0	0	0	0	5	.0
G	35	Glenn Healy	L.A.	48	0	1	1	0	28	0	0	0	0	0	.0
D	14	*Jim Hofford	L.A.	1	0	0	0	2	2	0	0	0	0	0	.0
G	1	Bob Janecyk	L.A.	1	0	0	0	0	0	0	0	0	0	0	.0
F	17	Brian Wilks	L.A.	2	0	0	0	0	2	0	0	0	0	2	.0
F	17	Roland Melanson	L.A.	4	0	0	0	0	4	0	0	0	0	0	.0
F	36	*Craig Duncanson	L.A.	5	0	0	0	1–	0	0	0	0	0	1	.0

Goaltending

No.	Goaltender	GPI	Mins	Avg	W	L	T	EN	SO	GA	SA	S%
32	Kelly Hrudey	16	974	2.90	10	4	2	1	1	47	491	.904
*1	Bob Janecyk	1	30	4.00	0	0	0	0	0	2	22	.909
29	*Mark Fitzpatrick	17	957	4.01	6	7	3	3	0	64	566	.886
35	Glenn Healy	48	2699	4.27	25	19	2	7	0	192	1509	.872
31	Roland Melanson	4	178	6.40	1	1	0	0	0	19	109	.826
	Totals	**80**	**4854**	**4.14**	**42**	**31**	**7**	**11**	**1**	**335**	**2697**	**.875**

Playoffs

Pos	#	Player	Team	GP	G	A	Pts	+/–	PIM	PP	SH	GW	OT	S	%
F	99	Wayne Gretzky	LA	11	5	17	22	4–	0	1	1	0	0	42	11.9
F	9	Bernie Nicholls	LA	11	7	9	16	2–	12	3	0	1	0	50	14.0
F	15	Chris Kontos	LA	11	9	0	9	3–	8	6	0	1	0	31	29.0
D	28	Steve Duchesne	LA	11	4	4	8	4–	12	2	0	0	0	23	17.4
F	20	Luc Robitaille	LA	11	2	6	8	0	10	0	0	1	0	24	8.3
F	11	Steve Kasper	LA	11	1	5	6	2–	10	0	0	0	0	18	5.6
F	18	Dave Taylor	LA	11	1	5	6	0	19	1	0	0	0	17	5.9
D	3	Tom Laidlaw	LA	11	2	3	5	3–	6	0	0	0	0	9	22.2
F	26	Mike Krushelnyski	LA	11	1	4	5	7–	4	1	0	0	0	21	4.8
D	2	Jim Wiemer	LA	10	2	1	3	4–	19	0	0	1	0	11	18.2
D	24	Dale DeGray	LA	8	1	2	3	2–	12	1	0	0	0	10	10.0
D	6	Dean Kennedy	LA	11	0	2	2	2–	8	0	0	0	0	4	.0
F	33	Marty McSorley	LA	11	0	2	2	6–	33	0	0	0	0	16	.0
F	10	Mike Allison	LA	7	1	0	1	2–	10	0	0	0	0	6	16.7
D	4	Doug Crossman	LA	2	0	1	1	1	2	0	0	0	0	1	.0
F	29	Jay Miller	LA	11	0	1	1	4–	63	0	0	0	0	6	.0
D	5	Tim Watters	LA	11	0	1	1	1	6	0	0	0	0	7	.0
D	25	*Petr Prajsler	LA	1	0	0	0	1–	0	0	0	0	0	2	.0
F	23	*Igor Liba	LA	2	0	0	0	0	2	0	0	0	0	0	.0
G	35	Glenn Healy	LA	3	0	0	0	0	2	0	0	0	0	0	.0
F	7	Phil Sykes	LA	3	0	0	0	0	8	0	0	0	0	0	.0
D	22	Ken Baumgartner	LA	5	0	0	0	2–	8	0	0	0	0	1	.0
F	27	John Tonelli	LA	6	0	0	0	3–	8	0	0	0	0	11	.0
G	32	Kelly Hrudey	LA	10	0	0	0	0	0	0	0	0	0	0	.0
F	44	Ron Duguay	LA	11	0	0	0	2–	6	0	0	0	0	12	.0

Goaltending

No.	Goaltender	GPI	Mins	Avg	W	L	EN	SO	GA	SA	S%
35	Glenn Healy	3	97	3.71	0	1	0	0	6	59	.898
32	Kelly Hrudey	10	566	3.71	4	6	1	0	35	293	.880
	Totals	**11**	**668**	**3.77**	**4**	**7**	**1**	**0**	**42**	**352**	**.880**

Club Records

Team

(Figures in brackets for season records are games played; records for fewest points, wins, ties, losses, goals, goals against are for 70 or more games)

Most Points	105	1974-75 (80)
Most Wins	43	1980-81 (80)
Most Ties	21	1974-75 (80)
Most Losses	52	1969-70 (76)
Most Goals	376	1988-89 (80)
Most Goals Against	389	1985-86 (80)
Fewest Points	38	1969-70 (76)
Fewest Wins	14	1969-70 (76)
Fewest Ties	7	1988-89 (80)
Fewest Losses	17	1974-75 (80)
Fewest Goals	168	1969-70 (76)
Fewest Goals Against	185	1974-75 (80)

Longest Winning Streak

Over-all	8	Oct. 21-Nov. 7/72
Home	7	Four times
Away	8	Dec. 18/74-Jan. 16/75

Longest Undefeated Streak

Over-all	11	Feb. 28-Mar. 24/74 (9 wins, 2 ties)
Home	10	Oct. 21-Nov. 18/72 (8 wins, 2 ties) Mar. 2-28/74 (8 wins, 2 ties)
Away	11	Oct. 10-Dec. 11/74 (6 wins, 5 ties)

Longest Losing Streak

Over-all	10	Feb. 22-Mar. 9/84
Home	9	Feb. 8-Mar. 12/86
Away	12	Jan. 11-Feb. 15/70

Longest Winless Streak

Over-all	17	Jan. 29-Mar. 5/70 (13 losses, 4 ties)
Home	9	Jan. 29-Mar. 5/70
Away	21	Jan. 11-Apr. 3/70

Most Shutouts, Season	9	1974-75 (80)
Most Pen. Mins., Season	2,124	1987-88 (80)
Most Goals, Game	12	Nov. 28/84 (Van. 1 at L.A. 12)

Individual

Most Seasons	12	Butch Goring, Marcel Dionne, Dave Taylor
Most Games	921	Marcel Dionne
Most Goals, Career	550	Marcel Dionne
Most Assists, Career	757	Marcel Dionne
Most Points Career	1,307	Marcel Dionne
Most Pen. Mins., Career	1,446	Jay Wells
Most Shutouts, Career	32	Rogie Vachon
Longest Consecutive Games Streak	324	Marcel Dionne (Jan. 7/78-Jan. 9/82)
Most Goals, Season	70	Bernie Nicholls (1988-89)
Most Assists, Season	114	Wayne Gretzky (1988-89)
Most Points, Season	168	Wayne Gretzky (1988-89) (54 goals, 114 assists)
Most Pen. Mins., Season	358	Dave Williams (1986-87)
Most Points, Defenseman Season	76	Larry Murphy (1980-81) (16 goals, 60 assists)

Most Points, Center, Season	168	Wayne Gretzky (1988-89) (54 goal, 114 assists)
Most Points, Right Wing, Season	112	Dave Taylor (1980-81) (47 goals, 65 assists)
Most Points, Left Wing, Season	111	Luc Robitaille (1987-88) (53 goals, 58 assists)
Most Points, Rookie, Season	84	Luc Robitaille (1986-87) (45 goals, 39 assists)
Most Shutouts, Season	8	Rogie Vachon (1976-77)
Most Goals, Game	4	Several players
Most Assists, Game	6	Bernie Nicholls (Dec. 1/88)
Most Points, Game	8	Bernie Nicholls (Dec. 1/88)

All-time Record vs. Other Clubs

Regular Season

		At Home							On Road							Total					
	GP	W	L	T	GF	GA	PTS	GP	W	L	T	GF	GA	PTS	GP	W	L	T	GF	GA	Pts
Boston	47	15	27	5	156	182	35	47	8	36	3	125	226	19	94	23	63	8	281	408	54
Buffalo	39	14	18	7	135	137	35	39	12	20	7	119	161	31	78	26	38	14	254	298	66
**Calgary	51	28	20	3	209	192	59	52	12	32	8	172	246	32	103	40	52	11	381	438	91
Chicago	46	20	21	5	160	158	45	45	15	24	6	138	179	36	91	35	45	11	298	337	81
Detroit	51	29	12	10	214	152	68	51	23	21	7	186	203	53	102	52	33	17	400	355	121
Edmonton	36	12	18	6	140	181	30	36	6	22	8	144	214	20	72	18	40	14	293	395	50
Hartford	16	9	5	2	70	64	20	16	5	9	2	68	68	12	32	14	14	4	138	132	32
Minnesota	50	22	14	14	189	156	58	51	13	31	7	134	205	33	101	35	45	21	323	361	91
Montreal	51	13	32	6	151	206	32	51	6	36	9	133	241	21	102	19	68	15	284	447	53
*New Jersey	29	22	1	6	168	89	50	28	13	10	5	107	89	31	57	35	11	11	275	178	81
NY Islanders	31	12	12	7	106	105	31	31	9	18	4	87	119	22	62	21	30	11	193	224	53
NY Rangers	45	18	18	9	149	160	45	45	14	26	5	132	178	33	90	32	44	14	281	338	78
Philadelphia	51	14	30	7	141	173	35	50	13	30	7	129	192	33	101	27	60	14	270	365	68
Pittsburgh	56	34	14	8	209	147	76	57	16	33	8	173	216	40	113	50	47	16	382	363	116
Quebec	16	8	7	1	70	66	17	16	7	7	2	63	68	16	32	15	14	3	133	134	33
St. Louis	50	25	18	7	175	147	57	50	12	33	5	128	191	29	100	37	51	12	303	338	86
Toronto	47	28	14	5	170	128	61	47	12	26	9	153	199	33	94	40	40	14	323	327	94
Vancouver	57	32	16	9	233	170	73	57	20	27	10	196	223	50	114	52	43	19	429	393	123
Washington	32	19	10	3	134	95	41	32	14	13	5	117	135	33	64	33	23	8	251	230	74
Winnipeg	33	11	18	4	140	147	26	34	11	16	7	130	150	29	67	22	34	11	270	297	55
Defunct Clubs	35	27	6	2	141	76	56	34	11	14	9	91	109	31	69	38	20	11	232	185	87
Totals	869	412	331	126	3269	2931	950	869	252	484	133	2725	3612	637	1738	664	815	259	5994	6543	1587

* Totals include those of Kansas City (1974-75, 1975-76) and Colorado (1976-77 through 1981-82)
** Totals include those of Atlanta (1972-73 through 1979-80)

Playoffs

	Series	W	L	GP	W	L	T	GF	GA	Last Mtg.	Round	Result
Boston	2	0	2	13	5	8	0	38	56	1977	QF	L 2-4
Calgary	4	2	2	14	5	9	0	43	50	1989	DF	L 0-4
Chicago	1	0	1	5	1	4	0	7	10	1974	QF	L 1-4
Edmonton	4	2	2	20	8	12	0	79	86	1989	DSF	W 4-3
Minnesota	1	0	1	7	3	4	0	21	26	1968	QF	L 3-4
NY Islanders	1	0	1	4	1	3	0	10	21	1980	P	L 1-3
NY Rangers	2	0	2	6	1	5	0	14	32	1981	P	L 1-3
St. Louis	1	0	1	4	0	4	0	5	16	1969	SF	L 0-4
Toronto	2	0	2	5	1	4	0	9	18	1978	P	L 0-2
Vancouver	1	0	1	5	1	4	0	14	19	1982	DF	L 1-4
Defunct Clubs	1	1	0	4	3	4	0	23	25			
* Totals	20	5	15	90	30	60	0	263	369			

Abbreviations: Round: F – Final; **CF** – conference final; **DF** – division final; **DSF** – division semi-final; **SF** – semi-final; **QF** – quarter-final. **P** – preliminary round. **GA** – goals against; **GF** – goals for.

Playoff Results 1989-85

Year	Round	Opponent	Result	GF	GA
1989	DF	Calgary	L 0-4	11	22
	DSF	Edmonton	W 4-3	25	20
1988	DSF	Calgary	L 4-1	18	30
1987	DSF	Edmonton	L 1-4	20	32
1985	DSF	Edmonton	L 0-3	7	11

1988-89 Results

	Home				Away	
Oct.	6 Detroit	8-2	Oct.	17 Calgary	4-11
	8 Calgary	6-5		19 Edmonton	6-8
	9 NY Islanders	6-5		28 Winnipeg	7-4
	12 Boston	6-2		30 Winnipeg	4-8
	15 Philadelphia	1-4	Nov.	1 Quebec	3-1
	22 Minnesota	8-2		2 Montreal	3-5
	25 Edmonton	4-5		5 Toronto	6-4
Nov.	10 Hartford	7-2		6 Chicago	5-3
	12 Pittsburgh	7-2		12 Philadelphia	6-1
	15 Vancouver	6-4		23 Detroit	8-3
	17 NY Rangers	5-6		26 Calgary	1-4
	19 Buffalo	5-4		27 Vancouver	2-5
	29 New Jersey	9-3	Dec.	10 NY Islanders	4-3
Dec.	1 Toronto	9-3		12 NY Rangers	5-2
	3 Chicago	6-4		14 Pittsburgh	4-5
	6 Winnipeg	4-5		16 Detroit	6-4
	8 Winnipeg	5-5		17 Minnesota	2-3
	20 Calgary	7-3		23 Vancouver	5-2
	21 Minnesota	8-6	Jan.	5 Calgary	6-8
	27 Montreal	2-3		6 Winnipeg	4-4
	29 Vancouver	3-6		8 Winnipeg	4-4
Jan.	10 Edmonton	5-4		17 St Louis	2-5
	12 St Louis	7-4		19 NY Islanders	2-4
	14 Hartford	9-6		21 Hartford	4-5
	26 Vancouver	2-6		24 Washington	4-4
	28 Edmonton	6-7	Feb.	9 Boston	1-4
	31 Calgary	5-8		10 Washington	7-6
Feb.	2 New Jersey	6-6		12 Chicago*	6-2
	4 Buffalo	5-3		24 Edmonton	1-4
	15 Boston	3-7		26 New Jersey	1-1
	18 Quebec	11-3		27 NY Rangers	4-6
	20 Toronto*	5-4	Mar.	1 Buffalo	5-4
	22 Washington	2-7		2 St Louis	4-6
Mar.	4 Philadelphia	6-2		10 Vancouver	2-4
	7 Pittsburgh	3-2		12 Edmonton	6-3
	18 Calgary	3-9		14 Quebec	4-0
	25 Edmonton	4-2		15 Montreal	2-5
	28 Winnipeg	3-3		21 Edmonton	4-3
	29 Winnipeg	2-1		23 Calgary	2-4
Apr.	1 Vancouver	6-4	Apr.	2 Vancouver	5-4

* Denotes afternoon game.

Entry Draft
Selections 1989-75

1989		1985		1981		1976	
Pick		**Pick**		**Pick**		**Pick**	
39	Brent Thompson	9	Craig Duncanson	2	Doug Smith	21	Steve Clippingdale
81	Jim Maher	10	Dan Gratton	39	Dean Kennedy	49	Don Moores
102	Eric Ricard	30	Par Edlund	81	Marty Dallman	67	Bob Mears
103	Thomas Newman	72	Perry Florio	123	Brad Thompson	85	Rob Palmer
123	Daniel Rydmark	93	Petr Prajzler	134	Craig Hurley	103	Larry McRae
144	Ted Kramer	135	Tim Flannigan	144	Peter Sawkins		
165	Sean Whyte	156	John Hyduke	165	Dan Brennan	**1975**	
182	Jim Giacin	177	Steve Horner	186	Allan Tuer	**Pick**	
186	Martin Maskarinec	219	Trent Ciprick	207	Jeff Baikie	16	Tim Young
207	Jim Hiller	240	Marion Howarth			33	Terry Bucyk
228	Steve Jaques			**1980**		69	Andre Leduc
249	Kevin Sneddon	**1984**		**Pick**		87	Dave Miglia
		Pick		4	Larry Murphy	105	Bob Russell
1988		6	Craig Redmond	10	Jim Fox	123	Dave Faulkner
Pick		24	Brian Wilks	33	Greg Terrion	141	Bill Reber
7	Martin Gelinas	48	John English	34	Dave Morrison	157	Sean Sullivan
28	Paul Holden	69	Tom Glavine	52	Steve Bozek	172	Brian Petrovek
49	John Van Kessel	87	Dave Grannis	73	Bernie Nicholls	186	Tom Goddard
70	Rob Blake	108	Greg Strome	94	Alan Graves	197	Mario Viens
91	Jeff Robison	129	Tim Hanley	115	Darren Eliot	203	Chuck Carpenter
109	Micah Aivazoff	150	Shannon Deegan	136	Mike O'Connor	207	Bob Fish
112	Robert Larsson	171	Luc Robitaille	157	Bill O'Dwyer	210	Dave Taylor
133	Jeff Kruesel	192	Jeff Crossman	178	Daryl Evans	213	Robert Shaw
154	Timo Peltomaa	213	Paul Kenny	199	Kim Collins		
175	Jim Larkin	234	Brian Martin				
196	Brad Hyatt			**1979**			
217	Doug Laprade	**1983**		**Pick**			
238	Joe Flanagan	**Pick**		16	Jay Wells		
		47	Bruce Shoebottom	29	Dean Hopkins		
1987		67	Guy Benoit	30	Mark Hardy		
Pick		87	Bob LaForest	50	J.P. Kelly		
4	Wayne McBean	100	Garry Galley	71	John Gibson		
27	Mark Fitzpatrick	107	Dave Lundmark	92	Jim Brown		
43	Ross Wilson	108	Kevin Stevens	113	Jay MacFarlane		
90	Mike Vukonich	127	Tim Burgess				
111	Greg Batters	147	Ken Hammond	**1978**			
132	Kyosti Karjalainen	167	Bruce Fishback	**Pick**			
174	Jeff Gawlicki	187	Thomas Ahlen	77	Paul Mancini		
195	John Preston	207	Jan Blaha	94	Doug Keans		
216	Rostislav Vlach	227	Chad Johnson	111	Don Waddell		
237	Mikael Lindholm			128	Rob Mierkains		
		1982		145	Ric Scully		
1986		**Pick**		162	Brad Thiessen		
Pick		27	Mike Heidt	177	Jim Armstrong		
2	Jimmy Carson	48	Steve Seguin	193	Claude Larochelle		
44	Denis Larocque	64	Dave Gans				
65	Sylvain Couturier	82	Dave Ross	**1977**			
86	Dave Guden	90	Darcy Roy	**Pick**			
107	Robb Stauber	95	Ulf Issakson	84	Julian Baretta		
128	Sean Krakiwsky	132	Victor Nechaev	85	Warren Holmes		
149	Rene Chapdelaine	153	Peter Helander	103	Randy Rudnyk		
170	Trevor Pochipinski	174	Dave Chartier	121	Bob Suter		
191	Paul Kelly	195	John Franzosa				
212	Russ Mann	216	Ray Shero				
233	Brian Hayton	237	Mats Ulander				

Club Directory

The Great Western Forum
3900 West Manchester Blvd.
Box 17013
Inglewood, California 90306
Phone 213/419-3160
FAX 213/673-8927
ENVOY ID
  Front Office: KINGS.GM
  Public Relations: KINGS.PR
Capacity: 16,005

Executive

Governor/President	Bruce McNall
Alternate Governors	Roy A. Mlakar, Rogatien Vachon
Executive Vice-President	Roy A. Mlakar
Executive Secretary to Vice-President	Susie Pulkkila
Vice-President	Steven H. Nesenblatt
Vice-President	Nora J. Rothrock
Vice-President	Susan A. Waks
Vice President, Adminstration/Finance	Robert Moor

Hockey Operations

General Manager	Rogatien Vachon
Administrative Assistant to General Manager	John Wolf
Executive Secretary to General Manager	Marcia Galloway
Special Assistant to General Manager	Ted O'Connor
Director of Player Personnel/Development	Nick Beverley
Coaches	Tom Webster, Rick Wilson, Cap Raeder
Director of Amateur Scouting	Bob Owen
Scouting Staff	Jim Anderson, Serge Blanchard, Jan Lindgren, Joe Mahoney, Mark Miller, Al Murray, Don Perry, Skip Schamehorn, Alex Smart

Medical Staff

Trainers	Pete Demers, Mark O'Neill, Peter Millar
Team Physicians	Dr. Steve Lombardo, Dr. James Tibone
Internist	Dr. Michael Mellman
Team Dentist	Dr. Gordon Knuth
Team Opthalmologist	Dr. Howard Lazerson
Team Hospital	Centinela Hospital Medical Centre

Communications

Director of Community and Public Relations	Scott J. Carmichael
Director of Media Relations	Nick Saleta
Assistant Director of Media Relations	Susan Carpenter
Director of Community Relations/Travel Coordinator	Ron Muniz
Play-by-Play Announcer	Bob Miller
Color Commentator	Nick Nickson
Video Coordinator	Bob Borgen
Radio Station	KLAC (570), KORG (1190), KGIL (1260)
Television	Prime Ticket Cable Network

Marketing and Finance

Controller	Bruce Bargmann
Director of Promotion	Mike Gilbert
Director of Merchandising	Harvey Boles
Accounting Manager	Martin Greenspun
Sales Manager Season and Group Sales	Dennis Metz
Account Executive	Keith Jacobson
Account Executive	Andrew Silverman

Home ice	The Great Western Forum
Dimensions of Rink	200 feet by 85 feet
Supervisor of Off-Ice Officials	Bill Meuris
Public Address Announcer	David Courtney
Colors	Black, White and Silver
Training Camp	Hull, Quebec & The Forum
Location of Press Box	West Side Colonade, Sec. 28, Row 1-10

Coach

WEBSTER, TOM
Coach, Los Angeles Kings. Born in Kirkland Lake, Ont., October 4, 1948.

Tom Webster was named the 16th head coach of the Los Angeles Kings on May 31, 1989 after a two-year stint with the Windsor Spitfires of the OHL. While with Windsor he led his club to the OHL Championship in 1988.

In 1981, Webster led the Adirondack Red Wings of the AHL to a Calder Cup Championship and in 1984 he coached the Tulsa Oilers to the CHL Championship. Webster was the head coach of the New York Rangers for 14 games in 1986-87 before stepping down due to an ear ailment. Webster coached Canada's national junior team to a fourth-place finish at the 1989 World Championships in Alaska.

Drafted by the Boston Bruins in 1967, Webster spent two seasons in the NHL with the Detroit Red Wings (1970-71) and Oakland Seals (1971-72) before joining the New England Whalers of the WHA for seven seasons (1972-79). He completed his NHL career with the Red Wings in 1979-80.

Coaching Record

			Regular Season				Playoffs			
Season	**Team**	**Games**	**W**	**L**	**T**	**%**	**Games**	**W**	**L**	**%**
1979-80	Adirondack (AHL)	80	32	37	11	.469	5	1	4	.200
1980-81	Adirondack (AHL)	80	35	40	5	.469	18	12	6	.667
1981-82	Springfield (AHL)	80	32	43	5	.431	....	....	....	....
1982-83	Tulsa (CHL)	80	32	47	1	.406	....	....	....	....
1983-84	Tulsa (CHL)	68	36	27	5	.566	9	8	1	.889
1984-85	Salt lake (IHL)	82	35	39	8	.476	7	3	4	.429
1986-87	**NY Rangers (NHL)**	14	5	7	2	.429	....	....	....	....
1987-88	Windsor (OHL)	66	50	14	2	.773	12	12	0	1.000
1988-89	Windsor (OHL)	66	25	37	4	.409	4	0	4	.000
	NHL Totals	14	5	7	2	.429	....	....	....	....

General Manager

VACHON, ROGATIEN
General Manager, Los Angeles Kings. Born in Palmorelle, Que., September 8, 1945.

Rogie Vachon was named General Manager of the Kings on Jan. 30, 1984 after spending the first half of the 1983-84 season as an assistant coach to Don Perry. In his first year as GM of the club, Los Angeles improved from 59 points in 1983-84 to 82 points in 1984-85. A veteran of 16 NHL seasons, Vachon spent seven years in a Los Angeles uniform, in addition to Montreal, Detroit and Boston. While with the Canadiens in 1967-68, Vachon shared the Vezina Trophy with Lorne "Gump" Worsley. During his seven-year stint in Los Angeles from 1971 to 1978, Vachon helped the club emerge as one of the NHL's top defensive teams. In 1974-75, his finest season, Vachon was named *Hockey News'* Player of the Year after compiling a 2.24 average and a 27-14-13 record while leading the Kings to their highest point total in team history (105). Following his retirement in 1982, he returned to Los Angeles to instruct the Kings' young goaltenders.

Minnesota North Stars

1988-89 Results: 27w-37L-16T 70 PTS. Third, Norris Division

Schedule

Home		Away	
Oct. Thur. 5 NY Islanders		**Oct.** Sat. 7 Hartford	
Thur. 12 St Louis		Sun. 8 Buffalo	
Sat. 14 Quebec		Tues. 17 NY Islanders	
Wed. 25 Buffalo		Wed. 18 Detroit	
Sat. 28 Philadelphia		Sat. 21 Quebec	
Tues. 31 Toronto		Thur. 26 St Louis	
Nov. Sat. 4 Chicago		**Nov.** Thur. 2 Chicago	
Thur. 9 Detroit		Mon. 6 Toronto	
Sat. 11 Calgary		Wed. 15 New Jersey	
Sun. 12 Toronto		Thur. 16 Philadelphia	
Sat. 18 St Louis		Tues. 21 St Louis	
Wed. 22 Toronto		Thur. 30 Calgary	
Fri. 24 New Jersey		**Dec.** Sat. 2 Edmonton	
Sun. 26 Chicago		Sun. 3 Vancouver	
Dec. Wed. 6 Montreal		Fri. 8 Detroit	
Sat. 9 Detroit		Sat. 16 Toronto	
Tues. 12 Vancouver		Thur. 21 Boston	
Thur. 14 Pittsburgh		Sat. 23 Hartford	
Tues. 19 Edmonton		Tues. 26 Winnipeg	
Sun. 31 St Louis		Thur. 28 Chicago	
Jan. Thur. 4 NY Rangers		Sat. 30 St Louis	
Sat. 6 Detroit		**Jan.** Tues. 9 Detroit	
Thur. 11 NY Islanders		Mon. 15 Montreal	
Sat. 13 Detroit		Wed. 17 Chicago	
Thur. 18 Quebec		Wed. 24 Toronto	
Mon. 29 Winnipeg		Fri. 26 Vancouver	
Wed. 31 Washington		Sat. 27 Calgary	
Feb. Wed. 7 Hartford		**Feb.** Sat. 3 Philadelphia*	
Sat. 10 Chicago*		Sun. 4 NY Rangers*	
Tues. 13 St Louis		Sun. 11 Washington*	
Thur. 15 Los Angeles		Sun. 18 Edmonton	
Sat. 24 Boston		Wed. 21 Los Angeles	
Tues. 27 Winnipeg		**Mar.** Sun. 4 Pittsburgh	
Mar. Sat. 3 Montreal		Mon. 12 Toronto	
Wed. 7 Chicago		Sat. 17 Pittsburgh*	
Sat. 10 NY Rangers*		Thur. 22 Detroit	
Tues. 13 New Jersey		Sat. 24 Boston*	
Sun. 18 Washington		Thur. 29 Buffalo	
Tues. 20 Los Angeles		Sat. 31 St Louis	
Mon. 26 Toronto		**Apr.** Sun. 1 Chicago	

* Denotes afternoon game.

Home Starting Times:
All Games . . . . 7:35 p.m.
Except Matinees . . . . 1:35 p.m.

Franchise date: June 5, 1967

23rd NHL Season

Mike Gartner — a career 400-goal scorer — arrived in Minnesota late in the 1988-89 season.

Year-by-Year Record

Season	GP	Home W	L	T	Road W	L	T	Overall W	L	T	GF	GA	Pts.	Finished		Playoff Result
1988-89	80	17	15	8	10	22	8	27	37	16	258	278	70	3rd,	Norris Div.	Lost Div. Semi-Final
1987-88	80	10	24	6	9	24	7	19	48	13	242	349	51	5th,	Norris Div.	Out of Playoffs
1986-87	80	17	20	3	13	20	7	30	40	10	296	314	70	5th,	Norris Div.	Out of Playoffs
1985-86	80	21	15	4	17	18	5	38	33	9	327	305	85	2nd,	Norris Div.	Lost Div. Semi-Final
1984-85	80	14	19	7	11	24	5	25	43	12	268	321	62	4th	Norris Div.	Lost Div. Final
1983-84	80	22	14	4	17	17	6	39	31	10	345	344	88	1st,	Norris Div.	Lost Conf. Championship
1982-83	80	23	6	11	17	18	5	40	24	16	321	290	96	2nd,	Norris Div.	Lost Div. Final
1981-82	80	21	7	12	16	16	8	37	23	20	346	288	94	1st,	Norris Div.	Lost Div. Semi-Final
1980-81	80	23	10	7	12	18	10	35	28	17	291	263	87	3rd,	Adams Div.	Lost Final
1979-80	80	25	8	7	11	20	9	36	28	16	311	253	88	3rd,	Adams Div.	Lost Semi-Final
1978-79	80	19	15	6	9	25	6	28	40	12	257	289	68	4th,	Adams Div.	Out Of Playoffs
1977-78	80	12	24	4	6	29	5	18	53	9	218	325	45	5th,	Smythe Div.	Out of Playoffs
1976-77	80	17	14	9	6	25	9	23	39	18	240	310	64	2nd,	Smythe Div.	Lost Prelim. Round
1975-76	80	15	22	3	5	31	4	20	53	7	195	303	47	4th,	Smythe Div.	Out of Playoffs
1974-75	80	17	20	3	6	30	4	23	50	7	221	341	53	4th,	Smythe Div.	Out of Playoffs
1973-74	78	18	15	6	5	23	11	23	38	17	235	275	63	7th,	West Div.	Out of Playoffs
1972-73	78	26	8	5	11	22	6	37	30	11	254	230	85	3rd,	West Div.	Lost Quarter-Final
1971-72	78	22	11	6	15	18	6	37	29	12	212	191	86	2nd,	West Div.	Lost Quarter-Final
1970-71	78	16	15	8	12	19	8	28	34	16	191	223	72	4th,	West Div.	Lost Semi-Final
1969-70	76	11	16	11	8	19	11	19	35	22	224	257	60	3rd,	West Div.	Lost Quarter-Final
1968-69	76	11	21	6	7	22	9	18	43	15	189	270	51	6th,	West Div.	Out of Playoffs
1967-68	74	17	12	8	10	20	7	27	32	15	191	226	69	4th,	West Div.	Lost Semi-Final

1989-90 Player Personnel

FORWARDS	HT	WT	S	Place of Birth	Date	1988-89 Club
ARCHIBALD, Dave	6-1	195	L	Vancouver, B.C.	4/14/69	Minnesota
BABE, Warren	6-3	200	L	Medicine Hat, Alta.	9/7/68	Minnesota-Kalamazoo
BALDERIS, Helmut	5-10	181		Soviet Union	6/31/52	Dynamo Riga (USSR)
BARBER, Don	6-1	205	L	Victoria, B.C.	12/2/64	Minnesota-Kalamazoo
BARNETT, Brett	6-3	185	L	Toronto, Ont.	10/12/67	Lake Superior State
BELLOWS, Brian	5-11	195	L	St. Catharines, Ont.	9/1/64	Minnesota
BEREZAN, Perry	6-2	190	R	Edmonton, Alta.	12/5/64	Calgary-Minnesota
BISCHOFF, Grant	5-10	165	L	Anoka, MN	10/26/68	U. of Minnesota
BLUM, Ken	6-1	175	L	Hackensack, NJ	6/8/71	St. Josephs HS
BROOKE, Bob	6-1	200	R	Acton, MA	12/18/60	Minnesota
BROTEN, Neal	5-9	170	L	Roseau, MN	11/29/59	Minnesota
CHURLA, Shane	6-1	200	R	Fernie, B.C.	6/24/65	Calgary-Minnesota
CRAIG, Mike	6-1	180	R	London, Ont.	6/6/71	Oshawa
DePALMA, Larry	6-0	190	L	Trenton, MI	10/27/65	Minnesota
DONATELLI, Clark	5-10	190	L	Providence, R.I.	10/22/65	Did Not Play
DUCHESNE, Gaetan	5-11	200	L	Quebec City, Que.	7/11/62	Quebec
EMMONS, Gary	5-9	180	R	Winnipeg, Man.	12/30/63	Canadian Olympic
EVANS, Kevin	5-11	195	L	Peterborough, Ont.	7/10/65	Kalamazoo
FRASER, Curt	6-1	200	L	Cincinnati, OH	1/12/58	Minnesota
GAGNER, Dave	5-10	185	L	Chatham, Ont.	12/11/64	Minnesota-Kalamazoo
GARBUTT, Murray	6-2	205	L	Hanna, Alta.	6/29/71	Medicine Hat
GARTNER, Mike	6-0	185	R	Ottawa, Ont.	10/29/59	Washington-Minnesota
GAVIN, Stewart	6-0	190	L	Ottawa, Ont.	3/15/60	Minnesota
GOTAAS, Steve	5-9	170	R	Camrose, Alta.	5/10/67	Minnesota-Kalamazoo
HILTNER, Mike	6-1	190	R	St. Cloud, MN	3/22/66	Kalamazoo
HODGE, Ken	6-1	190	L	St. Catharines, Ont.	4/13/66	Minnesota-Kalamazoo
JERRARD, Paul	6-1	185	R	Winnipeg, Man.	4/30/65	Minnesota-Kalamazoo
McCRADY, Scott	6-1	195	R	Calgary, Alta.	10/30/68	Kalamazoo
MODANO, Mike	6-3	190	L	Livonia, MI	6/7/70	Prince Albert
McRAE, Basil	6-2	205	L	Orillia, Ont.	1/5/61	Minnesota
MESSIER, Mitch	6-2	185	R	Regina, Sask.	8/21/65	Minnesota-Kalamazoo
McHUGH, Mike	5-10	190	L	Bowdoin, MA	8/16/65	Minnesota-Kalamazoo
NORTON, Darcy	6-0	175	L	Camrose, Alta.	5/2/67	Kalamazoo
PASEK, Dusan	6-1	200	L	Bratislava, Czech.	9/7/60	Minnesota
QUINTIN, J.F.	6-1	190	L	St. Jean, Que.	5/28/69	Shawinigan
ROBINSON, Scott	6-2	200	L	100 Mile House, B.C.	3/29/64	Kalamazoo
SHIELDS, David	5-9	170	R	Calgary, Alta.	4/24/67	U. of Denver
SMITH, Randy	6-4	200	L	Saskatoon, Sask.	7/7/65	Kalamazoo-Maine
SULLIVAN, Mike	6-2	185	L	Marshfield, MA	2/27/68	Boston University
THYER, Mario	5-11	170	L	Montreal, Que.	9/29/66	U. of Maine
TOMLINSON, Kirk	5-11	190	L	Toronto, Ont.	5/2/68	Kitchener
DEFENSEMEN						
BERGER, Mike	6-0	200	R	Edmonton, Alta.	6/2/67	Minnesota-Kalamazoo
CHAMBERS, Shawn	6-2	210	L	Royal Oaks, MI	10/11/66	Minnesota
GAETZ, Link	6-4	220	L	Vancouver, B.C.	10/2/68	Minnesota-Kalamazoo
GILES, Curt	5-8	175	L	The Pas, Man.	11/30/58	Minnesota
KOLSTAD, Dean	6-6	210	L	Edmonton, Alta.	6/16/68	Minnesota-Kalamazoo
LEITER, Ken	6-1	195	L	Detroit, MI	4/19/61	Minnesota
MacLEOD, Pat	5-11	190	L	Metfort, Sask.	6/15/69	Kamloops
MURPHY, Larry	6-2	210	R	Scarborough, Ont.	3/8/61	Washington-Minnesota
MUSIL, Frantisek	6-3	205	L	Pardubice, Czech.	12/17/64	Minnesota
SCHMIDT, Don	5-10	185	L	Calgary, Alta.	7/13/68	Kamloops
SCHOFIELD, David	6-1	190	R	Wayland, MA	2/17/65	Kalamazoo
SIREN, Ville	6-1	185	L	Tampere, FIN	2/10/64	Pittsburgh-Minnesota
TINORDI, Mark	6-4	205	L	Red Deer, Alta.	5/9/66	Minnesota
VIVEIROS, Emanuel	6-0	175	L	St. Albert, Alta.	1/8/66	Kalamazoo
WILKINSON, Neil	6-3	180	R	Selkirk, Man.	10/16/67	Kalamazoo
ZETTLER, Rob	6-3	190	L	Sept Iles, Que.	3/8/68	Minnesota-Kalamazoo

GOALTENDERS	HT	WT	C	Place of Birth	Date	1988-89 Club
BLUE, John	5-9	170	L	Huntington, CA	2/19/66	Kalamazoo-Virginia
CASEY, Jon	5-10	155	L	Grand Rapids, MN	3/29/62	Minnesota
DYCK, Larry	5-11	170	L	Winkler, Man.	12/15/65	Kalamazoo
FLAHERTY, Wade	5-11	170	L	Terrace, B.C.	1/11/68	Victoria
LOEWEN, Jamie	5-10	165	L	N. Vancouver, B.C.	9/23/68	U. of Alaska, Fairbanks
MYLLYS, Jarmo	5-8	150	L	Savolinna, FIN	5/29/65	Minnesota-Kalamazoo
TAKKO, Kari	6-2	185	L	Uusikaupunki, Finland	6/23/62	Minnesota

General Managers' History

Wren A. Blair, 1967-68 to 1973-74; Jack Gordon, 1974-75 to 1976-77; Lou Nanne, 1977-78 to 1987-88; Jack Ferreira, 1988-89 to date.

Coaching History

Wren Blair, 1967-68; John Muckler and Wren Blair, 1968-69; Wren Blair and Charlie Bruns, 1969-70; Jackie Gordon, 1970-71 to 1972-73; Jackie Gordon and Parker MacDonald, 1973-74; Jackie Gordon and Charlie Burns, 1974-75; Ted Harris, 1975-76 to 1976-77; Ted Harris, André Beaulieu, Lou Nanne, 1977-78; Harry Howell and Glen Sonmor, 1978-79; Glen Sonmor, 1979-80 to 1981-82; Glen Sonmor and Murray Oliver, 1982-83; Bill Mahoney, 1983-84 to 1984-85; Lorne Henning, 1985-86; Lorne Henning and Glen Sonmor, 1986-87; Herb Brooks, 1987-88; Pierre Page, 1988-89 to date.

Captains' History

Bob Woytowich, 1967-68; Elmer Vasko, 1968-69; Claude Larose, 1969-70; Ted Harris, 1970-71 to 1973-74; Bill Goldsworthy, 1974-75, 1975-76; Bill Hogaboam, 1976-77; Nick Beverly, 1977-78; J.P. Parise, 1978-79; Paul Shmyr, 1979-80, 1980-81; Tim Young, 1981-82; Craig Hartsburg, 1982-83; Brian Bellows, Craig Hartsburg, 1983-84; Craig Hartsburg, 1984-85 to 1987-88; Craig Hartsburg and Curt Giles, 1988-89; Curt Giles, 1989-90.

1988-89 Scoring

Regular Season

*–Rookie

Pos	#	Player	Team	GP	G	A	Pts	+/–	PIM	PP	SH	GW	GT	S	%
F	15	Dave Gagner	MIN	75	35	43	78	13	104	11	3	3	2	183	19.1
F	11	Mike Gartner	WSH	56	26	29	55	8	71	6	0	1	1	190	13.7
			MIN	13	7	7	14	3	2	3	0	0	0	33	21.2
			TOTAL	69	33	36	69	11	73	9	0	1	1	223	14.8
F	7	Neal Broten	MIN	68	18	38	56	1	57	4	5	1	1	160	11.3
F	10	Marc Habscheid	MIN	76	23	31	54	2	40	7	3	3	0	182	12.6
F	23	Brian Bellows	MIN	60	23	27	50	14–	55	7	0	4	1	196	11.7
D	8	Larry Murphy	WSH	65	7	29	36	5–	70	3	0	0	0	129	5.4
			MIN	13	4	6	10	5	12	3	0	1	1	31	12.9
			TOTAL	78	11	35	46	0	82	6	0	1	1	160	6.9
D	28	Reed Larson	EDM	10	2	7	9	1	15	0	1	0	0	19	10.5
			NYI	33	7	13	20	8–	35	6	0	1	0	77	9.1
			MIN	11	0	9	9	3–	18	0	0	0	0	19	.0
			TOTAL	54	9	29	38	10–	68	6	1	1	0	115	7.8
F	14	David Archibald	MIN	72	14	19	33	11–	14	7	0	2	0	105	13.3
F	17	Basil McRae	MIN	78	12	19	31	8–	365	4	0	0	0	122	9.8
F	12	Stewart Gavin	MIN	73	8	18	26	3	34	0	1	0	0	129	6.2
D	26	*Shawn Chambers	MIN	72	5	19	24	4–	80	1	2	0	0	131	3.8
D	6	Frantisek Musil	MIN	55	1	19	20	4–	54	0	0	1	0	78	1.3
D	4	Craig Hartsburg	MIN	30	4	14	18	0–	47	1	0	0	0	75	5.3
F	13	Bob Brooke	MIN	57	7	9	16	12–	57	0	1	2	0	77	9.1
D	2	Curt Giles	MIN	76	5	10	15	2	77	0	1	0	0	64	7.8
F	22	*Dusan Pasek	MIN	48	4	10	14	8–	30	1	0	0	0	86	4.7
F	37	*Don Barber	MIN	23	8	5	13	2	8	3	0	2	2	42	19.0
F	23	Perry Berezan	CGY	35	4	4	8	5	23	0	1	0	0	49	8.2
			MIN	16	1	4	5	1	4	0	0	0	0	16	6.3
			TOTAL	51	5	8	13	6	25	0	1	0	0	65	7.7
D	5	Ville Siren	PIT	12	1	0	1	0	14	0	0	0	0	11	9.1
			MIN	38	2	10	12	0	58	0	0	0	0	39	5.1
			TOTAL	50	3	10	13	0	72	0	0	0	0	50	6.0
F	31	Larry Depalma	MIN	43	5	7	12	14–	102	1	0	1	0	42	11.9
F	18	Curt Fraser	MIN	35	5	5	10	15–	76	1	0	0	0	58	8.6
F	16	*Wally Schreiber	MIN	25	2	5	7	5–	10	1	0	1	0	41	4.9
D	40	*Dean Kolstad	MIN	25	1	5	6	5–	42	1	0	0	0	41	2.4
F	29	*Warren Babe	MIN	14	2	3	5	3	19	0	0	0	0	15	13.3
D	24	*Mark Tinordi	MIN	47	2	3	5	9–	107	0	0	0	0	39	5.1
F	34	Steve Gotaas	MIN	12	1	3	4	1–	6	1	0	0	0	18	5.6
F	8	Terry Ruskowski	MIN	3	1	1	2	1	2	0	0	0	0	2	50.0
F	28	*Ken Hodge	MIN	5	1	1	2	1	0	0	0	0	0	6	16.7
D	36	*Link Gaetz	MIN	12	0	2	2	3–	53	0	0	0	0	8	.0
F	27	Shane Churla	CGY	5	0	0	0	3–	25	0	0	0	0	2	.0
			MIN	13	1	0	1	0	54	0	0	0	0	6	16.7
			TOTAL	18	1	0	1	3–	79	0	0	0	0	8	12.5
F	38	*Mitch Messier	MIN	3	0	1	1	1–	0	0	0	0	0	3	.0
F	9	Dennis Maruk	MIN	6	0	1	1	0	2	0	0	0	0	6	.0
G	30	Jon Casey	MIN	55	0	1	1	0	10	0	0	0	0	0	.0
D	34	Mike Berger	MIN	1	0	0	0	1–	2	0	0	0	0	0	.0
F	32	*Kevin Kaminski	MIN	1	0	0	0	0	0	0	0	0	0	0	.0
D	41	*Rob Zettler	MIN	2	0	0	0	1–	0	0	0	0	0	0	.0
F	16	Mike McHugh	MIN	3	0	0	0	1–	2	0	0	0	0	1	.0
D	25	*Paul Jerrard	MIN	5	0	0	0	1–	4	0	0	0	0	8	.0

Goaltending

No.	Goaltender	GPI	Mins	Avg	W	L	T	EN	SO	GA	SA	S%
33	Don Beaupre	1	59	3.05	0	1	0	1	0	3	26	.880
30	Jon Casey	55	2961	3.06	18	17	12	3	1	151	1509	.900
1	Kari Takko	32	1603	3.48	8	15	4	5	0	93	922	.899
35	*Jarmo Myllys	6	238	5.55	1	4	0	0	0	22	138	.841
	Totals	**80**	**4882**	**3.42**	**27**	**37**	**16**	**9**	**1**	**278**	**2595**	**.892**

Playoffs

Pos	#	Player	Team	GP	G	A	Pts	+/–	PIM	PP	SH	GW	GT	S	%
F	23	Brian Bellows	MIN	5	2	3	5	5–	8	2	0	0	0	15	13.3
F	12	Stewart Gavin	MIN	5	3	1	4	1	10	0	0	0	0	12	25.0
F	7	Neal Broten	MIN	5	2	2	4	3–	4	1	1	0	0	14	14.3
F	10	Marc Habscheid	MIN	5	1	3	4	1–	13	0	0	0	0	8	12.5
F	13	Bob Brooke	MIN	5	3	0	3	1–	2	0	0	0	0	7	42.9
F	21	Perry Berezan	MIN	5	1	2	3	0	4	0	0	0	0	4	25.0
F	37	*Don Barber	MIN	4	1	1	2	1	2	0	0	1	0	13	7.7
D	6	Frantisek Musil	MIN	5	1	1	2	0	4	0	0	0	0	9	11.1
D	26	*Shawn Chambers	MIN	3	0	2	2	0	0	0	0	0	0	4	.0
D	8	Larry Murphy	MIN	5	0	2	2	5–	8	0	0	0	0	9	.0
F	22	*Dusan Pasek	MIN	2	1	0	1	1–	0	0	0	0	0	3	33.3
F	34	Steve Gotaas	MIN	3	0	1	1	1	5	0	0	0	0	1	.0
F	14	David Archibald	MIN	5	0	1	1	5–	0	0	0	0	0	9	.0
F	29	*Warren Babe	MIN	2	0	0	0	1–	0	0	0	0	0	1	.0
F	31	Larry Depalma	MIN	2	0	0	0	0	6	0	0	0	0	0	.0
F	9	*Mike Modano	MIN	2	0	0	0	2–	0	0	0	0	0	0	.0
D	28	Reed Larson	MIN	3	0	0	0	2–	4	0	0	0	0	4	.0
G	1	Kari Takko	MIN	3	0	0	0	0	0	0	0	0	0	0	.0
G	30	Jon Casey	MIN	4	0	0	0	0	2	0	0	0	0	0	.0
D	5	Ville Siren	MIN	4	0	0	0	1–	4	0	0	0	0	4	.0
F	11	Mike Gartner	MIN	5	0	0	0	4–	6	0	0	0	0	14	.0
D	2	Curt Giles	MIN	5	0	0	0	1–	4	0	0	0	0	8	.0
F	17	Basil McRae	MIN	5	0	0	0	1–	58	0	0	0	0	4	.0
D	24	*Mark Tinordi	MIN	5	0	0	0	4–	0	0	0	0	0	8	.0

Goaltending

No.	Goaltender	GPI	Mins	Avg	W	L	EN	SO	GA	SA	S%
1	Kari Takko	3	105	4.00	0	1	0	0	7	55	.853
30	Jon Casey	4	211	4.55	1	3	0	0	16	121	.868
	Totals	**5**	**317**	**4.35**	**1**	**4**	**0**	**0**	**23**	**176**	**.869**

Club Records

Team

(Figures in brackets for season records are games played; records for fewest points, wins, ties, losses, goals, goals against are for 70 or more games)

Most Points 96 1982-83 (80)
Most Wins 40 1982-83 (80)
Most Ties 22 1969-70 (76)
Most Losses 53 1975-76, 1977-78 (80)
Most Goals 346 1981-82 (80)
Most Goals Against 344 1983-84 (80)
Fewest Points 45 1977-78 (80)
Fewest Wins 18 1968-69 (76)
      1977-78 (80)
Fewest Ties 7 1974-75 (80)
      1975-76 (80)
Fewest Losses 23 1981-82 (80)
Fewest Goals 189 1968-69 (76)
Fewest Goals Against 191 1971-72 (78)

Longest Winning Streak
  Over-all .... 7 Mar. 16-28/80
  Home .... 11 Nov. 4-
      Dec. 27/72
  Away .... 5 Dec. 2-16/67
      Feb. 5-
      Mar. 5/83

Longest Undefeated Streak
  Over-all .... 12 Feb. 18-
      Mar. 15/82
      (9 wins, 3 ties)
  Home .... 13 Oct. 28-
      Dec. 27/72
      (12 wins, 1 tie)
      Nov. 21-
      Jan. 9/80
      (10 wins, 3 ties)
  Away .... 6 Nov. 30-
      Dec. 16/67
      (5 wins, 1 tie)
      Nov. 7-27/71
      (5 wins, 1 tie)
      Nov. 9-Dec. 3/83
      (5 wins, 1 tie)

Longest Losing Streak
  Over-all .... 10 Feb. 1-20/76

  Home .... 6 Jan. 17-
      Feb. 4/70
  Away .... 8 Oct. 19-
      Nov. 13/75; Jan. 28-
      Mar. 3/88

Longest Winless Streak
  Over-all .... 20 Jan. 15-
      Feb. 28/70
      (15 losses, 5 ties)
  Home .... 12 Jan. 17-
      Feb. 25/70
      (8 losses, 4 ties)
  Away .... 23 Oct. 25/74-
      Jan. 28/75
      (19 losses, 4 ties)
Most Shutouts, Season 7 1972-73 (78)
Most Pen. Mins., Season
    .... 1,936 1986-87 (80)
Most Goals, Game .... 15 Nov. 11/81
      (Wpg. 2 at Minn. 15)

Individual

Most Seasons .... 12 Fred Barrett
Most Games .... 730 Fred Barrett
Most Goals, Career .... 332 Dino Ciccarelli
Most Assists, Career .... 382 Neal Broten
Most Points Career ..... 651 Dino Ciccarelli
      (332 goals, 319 assists)
Most Pen. Mins., Career . 1,000 Brad Maxwell
Most Shutouts, Career ... 26 Cesare Maniago
Longest Consecutive
  Games Streak .... 442 Danny Grant
      (Dec. 4/68-Apr. 7/74)
Most Goals, Season ..... 55 Dino Ciccarelli
      (1981-82)
Most Assists, Season ..... 76 Neal Broten
      (1985-86)
Most Point, Season ..... 114 Bobby Smith
      (1981-82)
      (43 goals, 71 assists)
Most Pen. Mins., Season ... 382 Basil McRae
      (1987-88)

Most Points, Defenseman
  Season .... 77 Craig Hartsburg
      (1981-82)
      (17 goals, 60 assists)
Most Points, Center,
  Season .... 114 Bobby Smith
      (1981-82)
      (43 goals, 71 assists)
Most Points, Right Wing,
  Season .... 107 Dino Ciccarelli
      (1981-82)
      (55 goals, 52 assists)
Most Point, Left Wing,
  Season .... 85 Steve Payne
      (1979-80)
      (42 goals, 43 assists)
Most Points, Rookie,
  Season .... 97 Neal Broten
      (981-82)
      (38 goals, 59 assists)
Most Shutouts, Season ..... 6 Cesare Maniago
      (1967-68)
Most Goals, Game .... 5 Tim Young
      (Jan. 15/79)
Most Assists, Game .... 5 Murray Oliver
      (Oct. 24/71)
Most Points, Game .... 7 Bobby Smith
      (Nov. 11/81)

* NHL Record.

All-time Record vs. Other Clubs

Regular Season

		At Home						On Road						Total				
	GP	W	L	T	GF	GA	PTS	GP	W	L	T	GF	GA	PTS	GP	W	L	T	GF	GA	PTS
Boston	47	11	27	9	127	182	31	47	5	35	7	107	215	17	94	16	62	16	234	397	48
Buffalo	39	15	18	6	119	126	36	39	9	22	8	103	150	26	78	24	40	14	222	276	62
**Calgary	34	16	13	5	127	111	37	33	4	19	10	91	136	18	67	20	32	15	218	247	55
Chicago	69	28	31	10	246	246	66	69	18	43	8	190	290	44	138	46	74	18	436	536	110
Detroit	65	35	19	11	255	187	81	64	24	28	12	225	249	60	129	59	47	23	480	436	141
Edmonton	16	4	8	4	60	62	12	16	1	10	5	57	89	7	32	5	18	9	117	151	19
Hartford	16	10	5	1	75	56	21	16	8	8	0	57	59	16	32	18	13	1	132	115	37
Los Angeles	51	31	13	7	205	134	69	50	14	22	14	156	189	42	101	45	35	21	361	323	111
Montreal	45	11	24	10	118	164	32	45	9	30	6	114	198	24	90	20	54	16	232	362	56
*New Jersey	31	19	6	6	129	75	44	31	13	15	3	104	106	29	62	32	21	9	233	181	73
NY Islanders	33	11	17	5	91	124	27	33	7	18	8	94	136	22	66	18	35	13	185	260	49
NY Rangers	47	14	27	6	142	190	34	47	10	28	9	130	169	29	94	24	55	15	272	359	63
Philadelphia	52	20	20	12	167	179	52	53	8	35	10	114	204	26	105	28	55	22	281	383	78
Pittsburgh	50	29	17	4	196	170	62	50	14	31	5	127	188	33	100	43	48	9	323	358	95
Quebec	16	8	6	2	63	54	18	16	2	12	2	41	81	6	32	10	18	4	104	135	24
St. Louis	73	31	27	15	256	229	77	75	23	37	15	218	267	61	148	54	64	30	474	496	138
Toronto	66	33	25	8	256	223	74	67	23	30	14	228	248	60	133	56	55	22	484	471	134
Vancouver	42	27	8	7	180	115	61	42	13	22	7	128	172	33	84	40	30	14	308	287	94
Washington	26	12	6	8	101	75	32	26	9	11	6	80	85	24	52	21	17	14	181	160	56
Winnipeg	18	10	6	2	82	56	22	18	9	8	1	66	65	19	36	19	14	3	148	121	41
Defunct Clubs	33	19	8	6	123	86	44	32	10	16	6	84	105	26	65	29	24	12	207	191	70
Totals	869	394	331	144	3118	2844	932	869	233	480	156	2514	3401	622	1738	627	811	300	5632	6245	1554

* Totals include those of Kansas City (1974-75, 1975-76) and Colorado (1976-77 through 1981-82)
** Totals include those of Atlanta (1972-73 through 1979-80)

Playoffs

	Series	W	L	GP	W	L	T	GF	GA	Last Mtg.	Round	Result
Boston	1	1	0	3	3	0	0	20	13	1981	P	W 3-0
Buffalo	2	1	1	7	4	3	0	26	28	1981	QF	W 4-1
**Calgary	1	1	0	6	4	2	0	25	18	1981	SF	W 4-2
Chicago	4	1	3	26	7	13	0	78	83	1985	DF	L 2-4
Edmonton	1	0	1	4	0	4	0	10	22	1984	CF	L 0-4
Los Angeles	1	1	0	7	4	3	0	26	21	1968	QF	W 4-3
Montreal	2	1	1	13	6	7	0	37	48	1980	QF	W 4-3
NY Islanders	1	0	1	5	1	4	0	16	26	1981	F	L 1-4
Philadelphia	2	0	2	11	3	8	0	26	41	1980	SF	L 1-4
St. Louis	8	3	5	46	22	24	0	136	135	1989	DSF	L 1-4
Toronto	2	2	0	7	6	1	0	35	26	1983	DSF	W 3-1
Totals	25	11	14	129	60	69	0	435	461			

Playoff Results 1989-85

Year	Round	Opponent	Result	GF	GA
1989	DSF	St. Louis	L 1-4	15	23
1986	DSF	St. Louis	L 2-3	20	18
1985	DF	Chicago	L 2-4	29	33
	DSF	St. Louis	W 3-0	9	5

Abbreviations: Round: **F** – Final; **CF** – conference final; **DF** – division final; **DSF** – division semi-final; **SF** – semi-final; **QF** – quarter-final. **P** – preliminary round. **GA** – goals against; **GF** – goals for.

1988-89 Results

		Home				Away	
Oct.	6	St Louis	3-8	Oct.	8	Montreal	3-4
	13	Philadelphia	6-7		9	Quebec	1-4
	15	Boston	5-1		17	Edmonton	3-3
	26	Toronto	2-3		19	Calgary	1-2
	29	Detroit	3-2		22	Los Angeles	2-8
Nov.	5	Chicago	5-5		28	Detroit	1-4
	9	Detroit	3-6	Nov.	3	Chicago	1-4
	12	Hartford	1-3		10	St Louis	5-5
	17	Vancouver	7-6		14	Toronto	5-4
	19	NY Rangers	1-4		15	Washington	2-4
	23	Edmonton	3-3		26	Toronto	6-3
	25	Toronto	5-3	Dec.	1	Boston	4-1
	29	Chicago	5-2		3	Hartford	4-2
Dec.	7	Montreal	2-2		6	St. Louis	0-3
	10	St Louis	1-3		13	Detroit	4-5
	15	Buffalo	2-2		19	Vancouver	1-5
	17	Los Angeles	3-2		21	Los Angeles	6-8
	26	Winnipeg	5-1		28	Chicago	3-4
	31	St Louis	6-2		30	St Louis	5-5
Jan.	2	Edmonton	2-3	Jan.	10	Philadelphia	2-3
	5	Philadelphia	5-3		15	Winnipeg	4-1
	12	Pittsburgh	2-9		18	Buffalo	3-3
	14	Calgary	1-1		19	Toronto	3-3
	26	Quebec	3-5		21	NY Islanders	6-8
	28	New Jersey	4-4		23	New Jersey	7-2
	30	Washington	4-4	Feb.	4	Quebec*	3-6
Feb.	1	Boston	4-4		5	NY Rangers	5-3
	9	Vancouver	3-2		15	Detroit	2-4
	11	Detroit	1-5		21	Pittsburgh	2-1
	14	Chicago	2-4		22	Chicago	5-5
	18	Hartford	3-4		28	Washington	4-3
	20	Toronto	2-4	Mar.	1	Chicago	1-5
Mar.	4	NY Islanders*	4-3		5	New Jersey	0-2
	7	Detroit	5-3		11	St Louis	2-2
	12	St Louis	5-3		22	NY Rangers	1-3
	14	Toronto	3-5		23	NY Islanders	1-3
	16	Chicago	6-1		25	Montreal	1-1
	18	Buffalo	3-0		29	Toronto	1-3
	20	Pittsburgh	7-2		31	Detroit	5-1
	27	Calgary	2-3	Apr.	2	Winnipeg*	2-3

* Denotes afternoon game.

Entry Draft Selections 1989-75

1989
Pick
- 7 Doug Zmolek
- 28 Mike Craig
- 60 Murray Garbutt
- 75 Jean-Franco Quintin
- 87 Pat MacLeod
- 91 Bryan Schoen
- 97 Rhys Hollyman
- 112 Scott Cashman
- 154 Jonathan Pratt
- 175 Kenneth Blum
- 196 Artur Irbe
- 217 Tom Pederson
- 238 Helmut Balderis

1988
Pick
- 1 Mike Modano
- 40 Link Gaetz
- 43 Shaun Kane
- 64 Jeffrey Stolp
- 148 Ken MacArthur
- 169 Travis Richards
- 190 Ari Matilainen
- 211 Grant Bischoff
- 232 Trent Andison

1987
Pick
- 6 David Archibald
- 35 Scott McCrady
- 48 Kevin Kaminski
- 73 John Weisbrod
- 88 Teppo Kivela
- 109 D'Arcy Norton
- 130 Timo Kulonen
- 151 Don Schmidt
- 172 Jarmo Myllys
- 193 Larry Olimb
- 214 Mark Felicio
- 235 Dave Shields

1986
Pick
- 12 Warren Babe
- 30 Neil Wilkinson
- 33 Dean Kolstad
- 54 Eric Bennett
- 55 Rob Zettler
- 58 Brad Turner
- 75 Kirk Tomlinson
- 96 Jari Gronstand
- 159 Scott Mathias
- 180 Lance Pitlick
- 201 Dan Keczmer
- 222 Garth Joy
- 243 Kurt Stahura

1985
Pick
- 51 Stephane Roy
- 69 Mike Berger
- 90 Dwight Mullins
- 111 Mike Mullowney
- 132 Mike Kelfer
- 153 Ross Johnson
- 174 Tim Helmer
- 195 Gordon Ernst
- 216 Ladislav Lubina
- 237 Tommy Sjodin

1984
Pick
- 13 David Quinn
- 46 Ken Hodge
- 76 Miroslav Maly
- 89 Jiri Poner
- 97 Kari Takko
- 118 Gary McColgan
- 139 Vladimir Kyhos
- 160 Darin MacInnis
- 181 Duane Wahlin
- 201 Mike Orn
- 222 Tom Terwilliger
- 242 Mike Nightengale

1983
Pick
- 1 Brian Lawton
- 36 Malcolm Parks
- 38 Frantisek Musil
- 56 Mitch Messier
- 76 Brian Durand
- 96 Rich Geist
- 116 Tom McComb
- 136 Sean Toomey
- 156 Don Biggs
- 176 Paul Pulis
- 196 Milos Riha
- 212 Oldrich Valek
- 236 Paul Roff

1982
Pick
- 2 Brian Bellows
- 59 Wally Chapman
- 80 Rob Rouse
- 81 Dusan Pasek
- 101 Marty Wiitala
- 122 Todd Carlile
- 143 Victor Zhluktov
- 164 Paul Miller
- 185 Pat Micheletti
- 206 Arnold Kadlec
- 227 Scott Knutson

1981
Pick
- 13 Ron Meighan
- 27 Dave Donnelly
- 31 Mike Sands
- 33 Tom Hirsch
- 34 Dave Preuss
- 41 Jali Wahlsten
- 69 Terry Tait
- 76 Jim Malwitz
- 97 Kelly Hubbard
- 118 Paul Guay
- 139 Jim Archibald
- 160 Kari Kanervo
- 181 Scott Bjugstad
- 202 Steve Kudebeh

1980
Pick
- 16 Brad Palmer
- 32 Don Beaupre
- 53 Randy Velischek
- 79 Mark Huglen
- 100 Dave Jensen
- 121 Dan Zavarise
- 142 Bill Stewart
- 163 Jeff Walters
- 184 Bob Lakso
- 205 Dave Richter

1979
Pick
- 6 Craig Hartsburg
- 10 Tom McCarthy
- 42 Neal Broten
- 63 Kevin Maxwell
- 90 Jim Dobson
- 111 Brian Gualazzi

1978
Pick
- 1 Bobby Smith
- 19 Steve Payne
- 24 Steve Christoff
- 54 Curt Giles
- 70 Roy Kerling
- 87 Bob Bergloff
- 104 Kim Spencer
- 121 Mike Cotter
- 138 Brent Gogol
- 155 Mike Seide

1977
Pick
- 7 Brad Maxwell
- 25 Dave Semenko
- 61 Kevin McCloskey
- 79 Bob Parent
- 97 Jamie Gallimore
- 115 J.P. Sanvido
- 133 Greg Tebbutt
- 151 Keith Hanson

1976
Pick
- 3 Glen Sharpley
- 31 Jim Roberts
- 39 Don Jackson
- 51 Ron Zanussi
- 75 Mike Federko
- 93 Phil Verchota
- 111 Dave Delich
- 129 Jeff Barr

1975
Pick
- 4 Bryan Maxwell
- 40 Paul Harrison
- 41 Alex Pirus
- 58 Steve Jensen
- 76 David Norris
- 94 Greg Clause
- 112 Francois Robert
- 130 Dean Magee
- 148 Terry Angel
- 164 Michel Blais
- 188 Earl Sargent
- 201 Gilles Cloutier

Club Directory

Metropolitan Sports Center
7901 Cedar Avenue South
Bloomington, Minnesota 55425
Phone 612/853-9333
FAX 612/853-9432
GM FAX 612/853-9408
TWX 910-576-2853
ENVOY ID
Front Office: STARS. GM
Public
Relations: STARS. PR
Capacity: 15,093

Co-Chairman of the Board	George Gund III
Co-Chairman of the Board	Gordon Gund
President	Lou Nanne
Vice-President/General Manager	Jack Ferreira
Vice-President, Communications/Sales	Dick Arneson
Vice President, Corporate Relations	Paul Giel
Vice-President, Met Center Operations	Jim Goddard
Vice-President, Marketing	Frank Jirik
Vice-President, Finance	George Wettstaedt
Assistant General Manager	Dean Lombardi
Coach	Pierre Page
Assistant Coaches	Dave Chambers, Craig Hartsburg, Doug Jarvis
Director of Professional Scouting	Chuck Grillo
Director of Amateur Scouting	Les Jackson
U.S. and College Scout	Craig Button
Scouts	Pat Funk, Herb Hammond, Mark Pezzin, Brad Robson, Larry Ross
Public Relations Director	Joe Janasz
Assistant P.R. Director	Joan Preston
Community Relations Manager	Patty Reid
Director of Administration	Peter Jocketty
Director of Marketing	David Shama
Director of Advertising Sales	Wally Shaver
Director of Ticket Sales & Promotions	Conrad Smith
Ticket Manager	Rick Olson
Promotions Manager	Tom Andrews
Advertising Manager	Elaine Waddell
Team Physicians	Dr. George Nagabods, Dr. John Schaeffer, Dr. Jim Schaffausen, Dr. Frank Sidell, Dr. William Simonet
Team Dentists	Dr. Paul Belvedere, Dr. Doug Lambert
Head Athletic Trainer	Dave Surprenant
Team Physical Therapist	Tom Coplin
Athletic Training Consultant	Doc Rose
Assistant Trainer	Dave Smith
Equipment Manager	Mark Baribeau
Executive Offices	Alpha Business Center
Location of Press Boxes	North Side — Press and Radio South Side — TV
Dimensions of Rink	200 feet by 85 feet
Ends of Rink	Unbreakable glass extends above boards all around rink
Club Colors	Green, White, Gold and Black
Club Trains at	Wings' Stadium, Kalamazoo, MI, Met Center and Eden Prairie Community Center
Radio Announcers	Al Shaver and Tom Reid (WAYL-AM, 980)
TV Announcers	Doug McLeod and Tom Reid (KMSP-TV Channel 9)

General Manager

FERREIRA, JACK
General Manager, Minnesota North Stars. Born in Providence, R.I., June 9, 1944

Jack Ferreira was appointed to the position of General Manager of the North Stars on June 14, 1988 after spending two years as Director of Player Development for the New York Rangers. Prior to joining the Rangers' staff in August, 1986, the 45-year-old native of Providence, Rhode Island had worked for seven years as the U.S. and college scout for the Calgary Flames. Ferreira's career in professional hockey began in 1972 as assistant general manager of the New England Whalers of the World Hockey Association.

Coach

PAGE, PIERRE
Coach, Minnesota North Stars. Born in St. Hermas, Que., April 30, 1948.

In his rookie season with the North Stars, Page led his club to a 27-37-16 record (70 points), a 19-point improvement over their 1987-88 record. As the League's second most improved team in 1988-89, the North Stars earned their first playoff berth since 1985-86.

Page, 41, joined the Flames in 1980-81 as an assistant coach to Al MacNeil. He served in that capacity through the 1981-82 season before accepting a position as coach and general manager of the Flames' top minor league affiliate in Denver (two seasons) and later Moncton (one season). In 1985-86, Page returned to Calgary as an assistant to head coach Bob Johnson and remained in that capacity through last season under Terry Crisp.

Before joining the Flames, Page was head coach of the Dalhousie University Tigers of the Canadian University League where in 1978-79, he guided his club to a second place finish in the national final. He has also served as an assistant coach with the 1980 Canadian Olympic Team and the 1981 Team Canada entry in the Canada Cup.

Coaching Record

| Season | Team | Games | Regular Season | | | | Playoffs | | | |
			W	L	T	%	Games	W	L	%
1978-79	Dalhousie (CIAU)									
1982-83	Colorado (CHL)	80	41	36	3	.531	6	2	4	.333
1983-84	Colorado (CHL)	76	48	25	3	.651	6	2	4	.333
1984-85	Moncton (AHL)	80	32	40	8	.450	....	....	....	....
1988-89	**Minnesota (NHL)**	80	27	37	16	.438	5	1	4	.200
	NHL Totals	80	27	37	16	.438	5	1	4	.200

Retired Numbers

19	Bill Masterton	1967-1968

Montreal Canadiens

1988-89 Results: 53W-18L-9T 115 PTS. First, Adams Division

Ryan Walter

Schedule

Home				Away			
Oct.	Sat.	7	Buffalo	**Oct.**	Thur.	5	Hartford
	Wed.	11	Boston		Mon.	9	Boston
	Mon.	16	Washington		Fri.	13	New Jersey
	Wed.	18	Calgary		Sat.	14	Pittsburgh
	Sat.	21	New Jersey		Fri.	20	Buffalo
	Mon.	23	Hartford		Thur.	26	Chicago
	Sat.	28	Pittsburgh		Tues.	31	NY Islanders
	Sun.	29	Edmonton	**Nov.**	Wed.	8	NY Rangers
Nov.	Thur.	2	Buffalo		Thur.	9	St Louis
	Sat.	4	NY Rangers		Sat.	11	Los Angeles
	Mon.	6	St Louis		Thur.	16	Boston
	Wed.	15	Winnipeg		Wed.	22	Philadelphia
	Sat.	18	Toronto		Thur.	30	Quebec
	Mon.	20	Calgary	**Dec.**	Wed.	6	Minnesota
	Sat.	25	Boston		Fri.	8	Winnipeg
	Wed.	29	Quebec		Sat.	9	Toronto
Dec.	Sat.	2	Hartford		Sun.	17	NY Rangers
	Mon.	11	Los Angeles		Fri.	22	Buffalo
	Wed.	13	Chicago		Wed.	27	Vancouver
	Sat.	16	Detroit		Fri.	29	Edmonton
	Sat.	23	Philadelphia		Sat.	30	Calgary
Jan.	Sat.	6	Buffalo	**Jan.**	Tues.	9	Quebec
	Sun.	7	Vancouver		Fri.	12	New Jersey
	Sat.	13	Philadelphia		Fri.	26	Washington
	Mon.	15	Minnesota		Sat.	27	Toronto
	Wed.	17	NY Islanders	**Feb.**	Thur.	1	Boston
	Wed.	24	Quebec		Wed.	7	Buffalo
	Mon.	29	Boston		Fri.	16	Buffalo
Feb.	Sat.	3	Buffalo		Mon.	19	Detroit
	Sun.	4	Hartford		Thur.	22	Quebec
	Sat.	10	Quebec		Wed.	28	Hartford
	Wed.	14	Vancouver	**Mar.**	Thur.	1	Boston
	Sat.	17	Hartford		Sat.	3	Minnesota
	Sat.	24	Pittsburgh		Wed.	7	Los Angeles
	Sun.	25	St Louis		Tues.	13	NY Islanders
Mar.	Sat.	10	Detroit		Wed.	21	Winnipeg
	Wed.	14	Edmonton		Fri.	23	Washington
	Sat.	17	Chicago		Sat.	24	Hartford
	Sun.	18	Quebec		Thur.	29	Quebec
	Sat.	31	Boston	**Apr.**	Sun.	1	Hartford

* Denotes afternoon game.

Home Starting Times:
Weeknights .... 7:35 p.m.
Saturdays .... 8:05 p.m.
Sundays .... 7:05 p.m.

Franchise date: November 22, 1917

73rd NHL Season

Year-by-Year Record

Season	GP	Home W	Home L	Home T	Road W	Road L	Road T	Overall W	Overall L	Overall T	GF	GA	Pts.	Finished		Playoff Result
1988-89	80	30	6	4	23	12	5	53	18	9	315	218	115	1st,	Adams Div.	Lost Final
1987-88	80	26	8	6	19	14	7	45	22	13	298	238	103	1st,	Adams Div.	Lost Div. Final
1986-87	80	27	9	4	14	20	6	41	29	10	277	241	92	2nd,	Adams Div.	Lost Conf. Championship
1985-86	**80**	25	11	4	15	22	3	**40**	**33**	**7**	**330**	**280**	**87**	**2nd,**	**Adams Div.**	**Won Stanley Cup**
1984-85	80	24	10	6	17	17	6	41	27	12	309	262	94	1st,	Adams Div.	Lost Div. Final
1983-84	80	19	19	2	16	21	3	35	40	5	286	295	75	4th,	Adams Div.	Lost Conf. Championship
1982-83	80	25	6	9	17	18	5	42	24	14	350	286	98	2nd,	Adams Div.	Lost Div. Semi-Final
1981-82	80	25	6	9	21	11	8	46	17	17	360	223	109	1st,	Adams Div.	Lost Div. Semi-Final
1980-81	80	31	7	2	14	15	11	45	22	13	332	232	103	1st,	Norris Div.	Lost Prelim. Round
1979-80	80	30	7	3	17	13	10	47	20	13	328	240	107	1st,	Norris Div.	Lost Quarter-Final
1978-79	**80**	29	6	5	23	11	6	**52**	**17**	**11**	**337**	**204**	**115**	**1st,**	**Norris Div.**	**Won Stanley Cup**
1977-78	**80**	32	4	4	27	6	7	**59**	**10**	**11**	**359**	**183**	**129**	**1st,**	**Norris Div.**	**Won Stanley Cup**
1976-77	**80**	33	1	6	27	7	6	**60**	**8**	**12**	**387**	**171**	**132**	**1st,**	**Norris Div.**	**Won Stanley Cup**
1975-76	**80**	32	3	5	26	8	6	**58**	**11**	**11**	**337**	**174**	**127**	**1st,**	**Norris Div.**	**Won Stanley Cup**
1974-75	80	27	8	5	20	6	14	47	14	19	374	225	113	1st,	Norris Div.	Lost Semi-Final
1973-74	78	24	12	3	21	12	6	45	24	9	293	240	99	2nd,	East Div.	Lost Quarter-Final
1972-73	**78**	29	4	6	23	6	10	**52**	**10**	**16**	**329**	**184**	**120**	**1st,**	**East Div.**	**Won Stanley Cup**
1971-72	78	29	3	7	17	13	9	46	16	16	307	205	108	3rd,	East Div.	Lost Quarter-Final
1970-71	**78**	29	7	3	13	16	10	**42**	**23**	**13**	**291**	**216**	**97**	**3rd,**	**East Div.**	**Won Stanley Cup**
1969-70	76	21	9	8	17	13	8	38	22	16	244	201	92	5th,	East Div.	Out of Playoffs
1968-69	**76**	26	7	5	20	12	6	**46**	**19**	**11**	**271**	**202**	**103**	**1st,**	**East Div.**	**Won Stanley Cup**
1967-68	**74**	26	5	6	16	17	4	**42**	**22**	**10**	**236**	**167**	**94**	**1st,**	**East Div.**	**Won Stanley Cup**
1966-67	70	19	9	7	13	16	6	32	25	13	202	188	77	2nd,		Lost Final
1965-66	**70**	23	11	1	18	10	7	**41**	**21**	**8**	**239**	**173**	**90**	**1st,**		**Won Stanley Cup**
1964-65	**70**	20	8	7	16	15	4	**36**	**23**	**11**	**211**	**185**	**83**	**2nd,**		**Won Stanley Cup**
1963-64	70	22	7	6	14	14	7	36	21	13	209	167	85	1st,		Lost Semi-Final
1962-63	70	15	10	10	13	9	13	28	19	23	225	183	79	3rd,		Lost Semi-Final
1961-62	70	26	2	7	16	12	7	42	14	14	259	166	98	1st,		Lost Semi-Final
1960-61	70	24	6	5	17	13	5	41	19	10	254	188	92	1st,		Lost Semi-Final
1959-60	**70**	23	4	8	17	14	4	**40**	**18**	**12**	**255**	**178**	**92**	**1st,**		**Won Stanley Cup**
1958-59	**70**	21	8	6	18	10	7	**39**	**18**	**13**	**258**	**158**	**91**	**1st,**		**Won Stanley Cup**
1957-58	**70**	23	8	4	20	9	6	**43**	**17**	**10**	**250**	**158**	**96**	**1st,**		**Won Stanley Cup**
1956-57	**70**	23	6	6	12	17	6	**35**	**23**	**12**	**210**	**155**	**82**	**2nd,**		**Won Stanley Cup**
1955-56	**70**	29	5	1	16	10	9	**45**	**15**	**10**	**222**	**131**	**100**	**1st,**		**Won Stanley Cup**
1954-55	70	26	5	4	15	13	7	41	18	11	228	157	93	2nd,		Lost Final
1953-54	70	27	5	3	8	19	8	35	24	11	195	141	81	2nd,		Lost Final
1952-53	**70**	18	12	5	10	11	14	**28**	**23**	**19**	**155**	**148**	**75**	**2nd,**		**Won Stanley Cup**
1951-52	70	22	8	5	12	18	5	34	26	10	195	164	78	2nd,		Lost Final
1950-51	70	17	10	8	8	20	7	25	30	15	173	184	65	3rd,		Lost Final
1949-50	70	17	8	10	12	14	9	29	22	19	172	150	77	2nd,		Lost Semi-Final
1948-49	60	19	8	3	9	15	6	28	23	9	152	126	65	3rd,		Lost Semi-Final
1947-48	60	13	13	4	7	16	7	20	29	11	147	169	51	5th,		Out of Playoffs
1946-47	60	19	6	5	15	10	5	34	16	10	189	138	78	1st,		Lost Final
1945-46	**50**	16	6	3	12	11	2	**28**	**17**	**5**	**172**	**134**	**61**	**1st,**		**Won Stanley Cup**
1944-45	50	21	2	2	17	6	2	38	8	4	228	121	80	1st,		Lost Semi-Final
1943-44	**50**	22	0	3	16	5	4	**38**	**5**	**7**	**234**	**109**	**83**	**1st,**		**Won Stanley Cup**
1942-43	60	14	4	7	5	15	5	19	19	12	181	191	50	4th,		Lost Semi-Final
1941-42	48	12	10	2	6	17	1	18	27	3	134	173	39	6th,		Lost Quarter-Final
1940-41	48	11	9	4	5	17	2	16	26	6	121	147	38	6th,		Lost Quarter-Final
1939-40	48	5	14	5	5	19	0	10	33	5	90	167	25	7th,		Out of Playoffs
1938-39	48	8	11	5	7	13	4	15	24	9	115	146	39	6th,		Lost Quarter-Final
1937-38	48	13	4	7	5	13	6	18	17	13	123	128	49	3rd,	Cdn. Div.	Lost Quarter-Final
1936-37	48	16	8	0	8	10	6	24	18	6	115	111	54	1st,	Cdn. Div.	Lost Semi-Final
1935-36	48	5	11	8	6	15	3	11	26	11	82	123	33	4th,	Cdn. Div.	Out of Playoffs
1934-35	48	11	11	2	8	12	4	19	23	6	110	145	44	3rd,	Cdn. Div.	Lost Quarter-Final
1933-34	48	16	6	2	6	14	4	22	20	6	99	101	50	2nd,	Cdn. Div.	Lost Quarter-Final
1932-33	48	15	5	4	3	20	1	18	25	5	92	115	41	3rd,	Cdn. Div.	Lost Quarter-Final
1931-32	48	18	3	3	7	13	4	25	16	7	128	111	57	1st,	Cdn. Div.	Lost Semi-Final
1930-31	**44**	15	3	4	11	7	4	**26**	**10**	**8**	**129**	**89**	**60**	**1st,**	**Cdn. Div.**	**Won Stanley Cup**
1929-30	**44**	13	5	4	8	9	5	**21**	**14**	**9**	**142**	**114**	**51**	**2nd,**	**Cdn. Div.**	**Won Stanley Cup**
1928-29	44	12	4	6	10	3	9	22	7	15	71	43	59	1st,	Cdn. Div.	Lost Semi-Final
1927-28	44	12	7	3	14	4	4	26	11	7	116	48	59	1st,	Cdn. Div.	Lost Semi-Final
1926-27	44	15	5	2	13	9	0	28	14	2	99	67	58	2nd,	Cdn. Div.	Lost Final
1925-26	36	5	12	1	6	12	0	11	24	1	79	108	23	7th,		Out of Playoffs
1924-25	30	10	5	0	7	6	2	17	11	2	93	56	36	3rd,		Lost Cup Playoff
1923-24	**24**	10	2	0	3	9	0	**13**	**11**	**0**	**59**	**48**	**26**	**2nd,**		**Won Stanley Cup**
1922-23	24	10	2	0	3	7	2	13	9	2	73	61	28	2nd,		Lost NHL Playoff
1921-22	24	8	3	1	4	8	0	12	11	1	88	94	25	3rd,		Out of Playoffs
1920-21	24	9	3	0	4	8	0	13	11	0	112	99	26	3rd,		Out of Playoffs
1919-20	24	8	4	0	5	7	0	13	11	0	129	113	26	2nd,		Out of Playoffs
1918-19	18	7	2	0	3	6	0	10	8	0	88	78	20	2nd,		Cup Final but no Decision
1917-18	22	8	3	0	5	6	0	13	9	0	115	84	26	1st and 3rd*		Lost NHL Final

* Season played in two halves with no combined standing at end.
From 1917-18 through 1925-26, NHL champions played against PCHL champions for Stanley Cup.

1989-90 Player Personnel

FORWARDS	HT	WT	S	Place of Birth	Date	1988-89 Club
BRUNET, Benoit	5-11	184	L	Ste-Anne de Bellevue, Que.	8/24/68	Montreal-Sherbrooke
CARBONNEAU, Guy	5-11	180	R	Sept-Iles, Que.	3/18/60	Montreal
CASSELS, Andrew	6-0	167	L	Bramalea, Ont.	7/23/69	Ottawa
CHORSKE, Tom	6-1	185	L	Minneapolis, MN	9/18/66	U. of Minnesota
CORSON, Shayne	6-0	175	L	Barrie, Ont.	8/13/66	Montreal
COURTNALL, Russ	5-11	180	R	Duncan, B.C.	6/2/65	Montreal-Toronto
CRISTOFOLI, Ed	6-2	205	L	Trail, B.C.	5/14/67	Denver
DESJARDINS, Martin	5-11	165	L	Ste-Rose, Que.	1/28/67	Sherbrooke
FERGUSON, John Jr.	6-0	175	L	Winnipeg, Man.	7/7/67	Providence
GILCHRIST, Brent	5-11	175	L	Moose Jaw, Sask.	4/3/67	Montreal-Sherbrooke
KEANE, Mike	5-10	175	R	Winnipeg, Man.	5/28/67	Montreal
LEBEAU, Stéphan	5-10	180	R	Sherbrooke, Que.	2/28/68	Montreal-Sherbrooke
LEMIEUX, Claude	6-1	206	R	Buckingham, Que.	7/16/65	Montreal
LEMIEUX, Jocelyn	5-10	200	L	Mont-Laurier, Que.	11/18/67	Montreal-Sherbrooke
MARTINSON, Steven	6-1	205	L	Minnetonka, MN	6/21/59	Montreal-Sherbrooke
McPHEE, Mike	6-1	200	L	Rivière-Bourgeois, N.S.	7/14/60	Montreal
NASLUND, Mats	5-7	160	L	Timra, Sweden	10/31/59	Montreal
NESICH, Jim	5-11	170	R	Dearborn, MI	2/22/66	Sherbrooke
PEDERSON, Mark	6-2	190	L	Prelate, Sask.	1/14/68	Sherbrooke
RICHER, Stéphane J.J.	6-2	200	R	Ripon, Que.	6/7/66	Montreal
ROBERGE, Mario	5-11	185	L	Québec, Que.	1/23/64	Sherbrooke
ROBERGE, Serge	6-1	195	R	Québec, Que.	3/31/65	Sherbrooke
SAUMIER, Marc	5-8	185	R	Hull, Que.	4/18/67	Sherbrooke-Peoria
SKRUDLAND, Brian	6-0	188	L	Peace River, Alta.	7/31/63	Montreal
SMITH, Bobby	6-4	210	L	North-Sydney, N.S.	2/12/58	Montreal
THIBAUDEAU, Gilles	5-10	180	L	Montréal, Que.	3/4/63	Montreal
WALTER, Ryan	6-0	195	L	New Westminster, B.C.	4/23/58	Montreal
WOODLEY, Dan	5-11	185	R	Oklahoma City, OK	12/29/67	Sherbrooke-Milwaukee

DEFENSEMEN	HT	WT	S	Place of Birth	Date	1988-89 Club
BISHOP, Mike	6-2	185	L	Sarnia, Ont.	6/15/66	Colgate
BISSON, Steve	6-1	193	L	Ottawa, Ont.	5/24/68	Sherbrooke-North Bay
CHARRON, Eric	6-3	192	L	Verdun, Que.	1/14/70	Sherbrooke-Verdun
CHELIOS, Chris	6-1	186	R	Chicago, IL	1/25/62	Montreal
DAIGNEAULT, Jean-Jacques	5-11	185	L	Montréal, Que.	10/12/65	Sherbrooke-Hershey
DESJARDINS, Eric	6-1	185	R	Rouyn, Que.	6/14/69	Montreal-Cdn. Jr. Olympic
DUFRESNE, Donald	6-1	190	R	Québec, Que.	4/10/67	Montreal-Sherbrooke
GAUTHIER, Luc	5-9	195	R	Longueuil, Que.	4/19/64	Sherbrooke
GREEN, Rick	6-3	210	L	Belleville, Ont.	2/20/56	Montreal
LEFEBVRE, Sylvain	6-2	187	L	Richmond, Que.	10/14/67	Sherbrooke
LUDWIG, Craig	6-3	217	L	Rhinelander, WI	3/15/61	Montreal
LUMME, Jyrki	6-1	190	L	Tampere, Finland	7/16/66	Montreal-Sherbrooke
ODELEIN, Lyle	5-10	185	L	Quill Lake, Sask.	7/21/68	Sherbrooke-Flint
RICHARDS, Todd	6-0	180	R	Robindale, MN	10/20/66	U. of Minnesota
RICHER, Stéphane J.G.	5-11	200	R	Hull, Que.	4/23/66	Sherbrooke
SCHNEIDER, Mathieu	5-11	180	L	Woonsockett, RI	6/12/69	Cornwall
SVOBODA, Petr	6-1	170	L	Most, Cze.	2/14/66	Montreal

GOALTENDERS	HT	WT	C	Place of Birth	Date	1988-89 Club
BERGERON, Jean-Claude	6-2	181	L	Hauterive, Que.	10/14/68	Sherbrooke-Verdun
EXELBY, Randy	5-9	170	L	Toronto, Ont.	8/13/65	Montreal-Sherbrooke
GRAVEL, François	6-2	185	R	Ste-Foy, Que.	10/21/68	Sherbrooke
HAYWARD, Brian	5-10	175	L	Georgetown, Ont.	6/25/60	Montreal
ROY, Patrick	6-0	174	L	Québec, Que.	10/5/65	Montreal

1987-88 Scoring

Regular Season

*–Rookie

Pos	#	Player	Team	GP	G	A	Pts	+/–	PIM	PP	SH	GW	GT	S	%
F	26	Mats Naslund	MTL	77	33	51	84	34	14	14	0	4	0	165	20.0
F	15	Bobby Smith	MTL	80	32	51	83	25	69	6	0	3	0	195	16.4
D	24	Chris Chelios	MTL	80	15	58	73	35	185	8	0	6	0	206	7.3
F	44	Stephane Richer	MTL	68	25	35	60	4	61	11	0	6	0	214	11.7
F	21	Guy Carbonneau	MTL	79	26	30	56	37	44	1	2	10	0	142	18.3
F	32	Claude Lemieux	MTL	69	29	22	51	14	136	7	0	3	0	220	13.2
F	27	Shayne Corson	MTL	80	26	24	50	1–	193	10	0	3	1	133	19.5
D	25	Petr Svoboda	MTL	71	8	37	45	28	147	4	0	1	0	131	6.1
F	6	Russ Courtnall	TOR	9	1	1	2	2–	4	0	1	0	0	11	9.1
			MTL	64	22	17	39	11	15	7	0	3	0	136	16.2
			TOTAL	73	23	18	41	9	19	7	1	3	0	147	15.6
F	35	Mike McPhee	MTL	73	19	22	41	14	74	1	1	1	1	154	12.3
F	39	Brian Skrudland	MTL	71	12	29	41	22	84	1	1	5	0	98	12.2
F	12	*Mike Keane	MTL	69	16	19	35	9	69	5	0	1	0	90	17.8
F	11	Ryan Walter	MTL	78	14	17	31	23	48	1	1	0	0	104	13.5
D	19	Larry Robinson	MTL	74	4	26	30	23	22	0	0	0	0	79	5.1
F	41	*Brent Gilchrist	MTL	49	8	16	24	9	16	0	0	2	0	68	11.8
F	23	Bob Gainey	MTL	49	10	7	17	13	34	1	0	2	0	65	15.4
D	17	Craig Ludwig	MTL	74	3	13	16	33	73	0	1	1	1	83	3.6
D	5	Rick Green	MTL	72	1	14	15	19	25	0	0	0	0	42	2.4
D	28	*Eric Desjardins	MTL	36	2	12	14	9	26	1	0	0	0	39	5.1
F	29	Gilles Thibaudeau	MTL	32	6	6	12	5	6	1	0	0	0	42	14.3
G	33	Patrick Roy	MTL	48	0	6	6	0	2	0	0	0	0	0	.0
D	20	*Jyrki Lumme	MTL	21	1	3	4	3	10	1	0	0	0	18	5.6
F	8	*Steve Martinson	MTL	25	1	0	1	1–	87	0	0	1	0	8	12.5
F	47	*Stephane Lebeau	MTL	1	0	1	1	1	2	0	0	0	0	1	.0
F	45	Jocelyn Lemieux	MTL	1	0	1	1	1–	0	0	0	0	0	0	.0
F	43	*Benoit Brunet	MTL	2	0	1	1	0	0	0	0	0	0	1	.0
D	34	*Donald Dufresne	MTL	13	0	1	1	3	43	0	0	0	0	5	.0
G	37	*Randy Exelby	MTL	1	0	0	0	0	0	0	0	0	0	0	.0

Goaltending

No.	Goaltender	GPI	Mins	Avg	W	L	T	EN	SO	GA	SA	S%
37	*Randy Exelby	1	3	.00	0	0	0	0	0	0	1	1.000
33	Patrick Roy	48	2744	2.47	33	5	6	2	4	113	1228	.908
1	Brian Hayward	36	2091	2.90	20	13	3	2	1	101	894	.887
	Totals	**80**	**4849**	**2.70**	**53**	**18**	**9**	**4**	**5**	**218**	**2123**	**.897**

Playoffs

Pos	#	Player	Team	GP	G	A	Pts	+/–	PIM	PP	SH	GW	GT	S	%
F	15	Bobby Smith	MTL	21	11	8	19	1	46	5	0	1	1	40	27.5
D	24	Chris Chelios	MTL	21	4	15	19	2	28	1	0	2	0	53	7.5
F	26	Mats Naslund	MTL	21	4	11	15	5	6	1	0	0	0	54	7.4
F	6	Russ Courtnall	MTL	21	8	5	13	12	18	1	0	2	1	53	15.1
D	25	Petr Svoboda	MTL	21	1	11	12	3–	16	0	0	0	0	23	4.3
F	44	Stephane Richer	MTL	21	6	5	11	5–	14	2	0	3	1	47	12.8
F	35	Mike McPhee	MTL	20	4	7	11	2–	30	0	0	1	0	35	11.4
F	39	Brian Skrudland	MTL	21	3	7	10	3	40	0	0	0	0	24	12.5
D	19	Larry Robinson	MTL	21	2	8	10	9	12	0	0	0	0	15	13.3
F	21	Guy Carbonneau	MTL	21	4	5	9	3	10	0	1	0	0	34	11.8
F	27	Shayne Corson	MTL	21	4	5	9	3	65	2	0	2	0	28	14.3
F	11	Ryan Walter	MTL	21	3	5	8	2	6	0	1	2	1	35	8.6
F	32	Claude Lemieux	MTL	18	4	3	7	0	58	1	0	1	0	46	8.7
F	12	*Mike Keane	MTL	21	4	3	7	4	17	2	0	0	0	21	19.0
F	23	Bob Gainey	MTL	16	1	4	5	0	8	0	0	0	0	14	7.1
D	34	*Donald Dufresne	MTL	6	1	1	2	2	4	0	0	0	0	2	50.0
F	41	*Brent Gilchrist	MTL	9	1	1	2	0	10	0	0	0	0	6	16.7
D	28	*Eric Desjardins	MTL	14	1	1	2	0	6	1	0	0	0	21	4.8
D	5	Rick Green	MTL	21	1	1	2	0	6	0	0	0	0	9	11.1
G	33	Patrick Roy	MTL	19	0	2	2	0	16	0	0	0	0	0	.0
D	17	Craig Ludwig	MTL	21	0	2	2	10	24	0	0	0	0	18	.0
F	8	*Steven Martinson	MTL	1	0	0	0	1–	10	0	0	0	0	1	.0
G	1	Brian Hayward	MTL	2	0	0	0	0	0	0	0	0	0	0	.0

Goaltending

No.	Goaltender	GPI	Mins	Avg	W	L	EN	SO	GA	SA	S%
33	Patrick Roy	19	1206	2.09	13	6	2	2	42	528	.920
1	Brian Hayward	2	124	3.39	1	1	0	0	7	54	.870
	Totals	**21**	**1336**	**2.29**	**14**	**7**	**2**	**2**	**51**	**582**	**.912**

Retired Numbers

2	Doug Harvey	1947-1961
4	Jean Béliveau	1950-1971
7	Howie Morenz	1923-1937
9	Maurice Richard	1942-1960
10	Guy Lafleur	1971-1984
16	Henri Richard	1955-1975

General Managers' History

Joseph Cattarinich, 1909-1910; George Kennedy, 1910-11 to 1919-20; Leo Dandurand, 1920-21 to 1934-35; Ernest Savard, 1935-36; Cecil Hart, 1936-37 to 1938-39; Jules Dugal, 1939-40; Tom P. Gorman, 1941-42 to 1945-46; Frank J. Selke, 1946-47 to 1963-64; Sam Pollock, 1964-65 to 1977-78; Irving Grundman, 1978-79 to 1982-83; Serge Savard, 1983-84 to date.

Coaching History

George Kennedy, 1917-18 to 1919-20; Léo Dandurand, 1920-21 to 1924-25; Cecil Hart, 1925-26 to 1931-32; Newsy Lalonde, 1932-33 to 1933-34; Newsy Lalonde and Léo Dandurand, 1934-35; Sylvio Mantha, 1935-36; Cecil Hart, 1936-37 to 1937-38; Cecil Hart and Jules Dugal, 1938-39; "Babe" Siebert, 1939*; Pit Lepine, 1939-40; Dick Irvin 1940-41 to 1954-55; Toe Blake, 1955-56 to 1967-68; Claude Ruel, 1968-69 to 1969-70; Claude Ruel and Al MacNeil, 1970-71; Scott Bowman, 1971-72 to 1978-79; Bernie Geoffrion and Claude Ruel, 1979-80; Claude Ruel, 1980-81; Bob Berry, 1981-82 to 1982-83; Bob Berry and Jacques Lemaire, 1983-84; Jacques Lemaire, 1984-85; Jean Perron, 1985-86 to 1987-88; Pat Burns, 1988-89 to date.

* Named coach in summer but died before 1939-40 season began.

Captains' History

Newsy Lalonde, 1917-18 to 1920-21; Sprague Cleghorn, 1921-22 to 1924-25; Bill Couture, 1925-26; Sylvio Mantha, 1926-27 to 1931-32; George Hainsworth, 1931-32; Sylvio Mantha, 1932-33 to 1935-36; Babe Seibert, 1936-37 to 1938-39; Walter Buswell, 1939-40; Toe Blake, 1940-41 to 1946-47; Toe Blake, Bill Durnan (co-captains) 1947-48; Emile Bouchard, 1948-49 to 1955-56; Maurice Richard, 1956-57 to 1959-60; Doug Harvey, 1960-61; Jean Beliveau, 1961-62 to 1970-71; Henri Richard, 1971-72 to 1974-75; Yvan Cournoyer, 1975-76 to 1978-79; Serge Savard, 1979-80, 1980-81; Bob Gainey, 1981-82 to date.

Club Records

Team

(Figures in brackets for season records are games played; records for fewest points, wins, ties, losses, goals, goals against are for 70 or more games)

Most Points	*132	1976-77 (80)
Most Wins	*60	1976-77 (80)
Most Ties	23	1962-63 (70)
Most Losses	40	1983-84 (80)
Most Goals	387	1976-77 (80)
Most Goals Against	295	1983-84 (80)
Fewest Points	65	1950-51 (70)
Fewest Wins	25	1950-51 (70)
Fewest Ties	5	1983-84 (80)
Fewest Losses	*8	1976-77 (80)
Fewest Goals	155	1952-53 (70)
Fewest Goals Against	*131	1955-56 (70)

Longest Winning Streak
Over-all .... 12 Jan. 6-
Feb. 3/68
Home .... 13 Nov. 2/43-
Jan. 8/44
Jan. 30-
Mar. 26/77
Away .... 8 Dec. 18/77-
Jan. 18/78
Jan. 21-
Feb. 21/82

Longest Undefeated Streak
Over-all .... 28 Dec. 12/77-
Feb. 23/78
(23 wins, 5 ties)
Home .... *34 Nov. 1/76-
Apr. 2/77
(28 wins, 6 ties)
Away .... *23 Nov. 27/74-
Mar. 12/75
(14 wins, 9 ties)

Longest Losing Streak
Over-all .... 12 Feb. 13/26-
Mar. 13/26
Home .... 7 Dec. 16/39-
Jan. 18/40
Away .... 10 Dec. 1/25-
Feb. 2/26

Longest Winless Streak
Over-all .... 12 Feb. 13-
Mar. 13/26
(12 losses)
Nov. 28-
Dec. 29/35
(8 losses, 4 ties)
Home .... *15 Dec. 16/39-
Mar. 7/40
(12 losses, 3 ties)
Away .... 12 Oct. 20-
Dec. 13/51
(8 losses, 4 ties)

Most Shutouts, Season *22 1928-29 (44)
Most Pen. Mins., Season . 1,842
Most Goals, Game .... *16 Mar. 3/20
(Mtl. 16 at Que. 3)

Individual

Most Seasons	20	Henri Richard
Most Games	1,256	Henri Richard
Most Goals Career	544	Maurice Richard
Most Assists, Career	728	Guy Lafleur
Most Points Career	1,246	Guy Lafleur
		(518 goals, 728 assists)
Most Pen. Mins., Career	2,174	Chris Nilan
Most Shutouts, Career	75	George Hainsworth

Longest Consecutive
Games Streak .... 560 Doug Jarvis
(Oct. 8/75-Apr. 4/82)
Most Goals, Season ...... 60 Steve Shutt
(1976-77)
Guy Lafleur
(1977-78)
Most Assists, Season ..... 82 Peter Mahovlich
(1974-75)
Most Points, Season ..... 136 Guy Lafleur
(1976-77)
(56 goals, 80 assists)
Most Pen. Mins., Season ... 358 Chris Nilan
(1984-85)

Most Points, Defenseman
Season .... 85 Larry Robinson
(1976-77)
(19 goals, 66 assists)
Most Points, Center,
Season .... 117 Peter Mahovlich
(1974-75)
(35 goals, 82 assists)
Most Points, Right Wing,
Season .... 136 Guy Lafleur
(1976-77)
(56 goals, 80 assists)
Most Points, Left Wing,
Season .... 110 Mats Naslund
(1985-86)
(43 goals, 67 assists)
Most Points, Rookie,
Season .... 71 Mats Naslund
(1982-83)
(26 goals, 45 assists)
Kjell Dahlin
(1985-86)
(32 goals, 39 assists)
Most Shutouts, Season .... *22 George Hainsworth
(1928-29)
Most Goals, Game .... 6 Newsy Lalonde
(Jan. 10/20)
Most Assists, Game .... 6 Elmer Lach
(Feb. 6/43)
Most Points, Game .... 8 Maurice Richard
5G-3A
(Dec. 28/44)
Bert Olmstead
4G-4A
(Jan. 9/54)

* NHL Record.

All-time Record vs. Other Clubs

Regular Season

		At Home							On Road							Total				
	GP	W	L	T	GF	GA	PTS	GP	W	L	T	GF	GA	PTS	GP	W	L	T	GF	GA	PTS
Boston	289	169	78	42	989	657	380	290	108	131	51	779	854	267	579	277	209	93	1768	1511	647
Buffalo	59	35	16	8	247	181	78	59	19	25	15	180	180	53	118	54	41	23	427	361	131
**Calgary	31	17	9	5	112	77	39	31	20	6	5	118	95	45	62	37	15	10	230	172	84
Chicago	261	164	49	48	1015	609	376	261	120	87	54	729	699	294	522	284	136	102	1744	1308	670
Detroit	267	163	62	42	946	596	368	268	94	122	52	685	754	240	535	257	184	94	1631	1350	608
Edmonton	16	9	5	2	61	52	20	16	6	10	0	50	63	12	32	15	15	2	111	115	32
Hartford	36	26	4	6	183	110	58	36	20	12	4	146	115	44	72	46	16	10	329	225	102
Los Angeles	51	36	6	9	241	133	81	51	32	13	6	206	151	70	102	68	19	15	447	284	151
Minnesota	45	30	9	6	198	114	66	45	24	11	10	164	118	58	90	54	20	16	362	232	124
*New Jersey	26	20	3	3	117	65	43	26	20	6	0	131	66	40	52	40	9	3	248	131	83
NY Islanders	31	18	7	6	118	93	42	32	13	16	3	96	112	29	63	31	23	9	214	205	71
NY Rangers	262	174	54	34	1039	606	382	261	106	105	50	764	751	262	523	280	159	84	1803	1357	644
Philadelphia	45	27	9	9	179	124	63	45	19	15	11	139	118	49	90	46	24	20	318	242	112
Pittsburgh	51	42	4	5	261	128	89	51	28	15	8	194	149	64	102	70	19	13	455	277	153
Quebec	36	23	8	5	159	112	51	36	14	20	2	122	131	30	72	37	28	7	281	243	81
St. Louis	45	34	7	4	205	114	72	45	24	9	12	162	114	60	90	58	16	16	367	228	132
Toronto	308	187	82	39	1092	755	413	308	108	156	44	803	928	260	616	295	238	83	1895	1683	673
Vancouver	38	30	6	2	190	99	62	37	25	4	8	149	87	58	75	55	10	10	339	186	120
Washington	32	24	3	5	160	63	53	32	15	11	6	115	80	36	64	39	14	11	275	143	89
Winnipeg	16	14	2	0	90	39	28	16	8	5	3	68	51	19	32	22	7	3	158	90	47
Defunct Clubs	231	148	58	25	779	469	321	230	98	97	35	586	606	231	461	246	155	60	1365	1075	552
Totals	2176	1390	481	305	8381	5196	3085	2176	921	876	379	6386	6222	2221	4352	2311	1357	684	14767	11418	5306

Playoffs

	Series	W	L	GP	W	L	T	GF	GA	Last Mtg.	Round	Result
Boston	24	21	3	116	80	36	0	372	269	1989	DF	W 4-1
Buffalo	3	1	2	15	6	9	0	52	45	1983	DSF	L 0-3
Calgary	2	1	1	11	6	5	0	31	32	1989	F	L 2-4
Chicago	17	12	5	81	50	29	2	261	185	1976	QF	W 4-0
Detroit	12	5	7	62	33	29	0	161	149	1978	QF	W 4-1
Edmonton	1	0	1	3	0	3	0	6	15	1981	P	L 0-3
Hartford	4	4	0	20	15	5	0	75	51	1989	DSF	W 4-0
Minnesota	2	1	1	13	7	6	0	48	37	1980	QF	L 3-4
NY Islanders	3	2	1	17	10	7	0	48	44	1984	CF	L 2-4
NY Rangers	13	7	6	55	32	21	2	171	139	1986	CF	W 4-1
Philadelphia	4	3	1	21	14	7	0	72	52	1989	CF	W 4-2
Quebec	4	2	2	25	13	12	0	87	69	1987	DF	W 4-3
St. Louis	3	3	0	12	12	0	0	42	14	1977	QF	W 4-0
Toronto	13	7	6	67	39	28	0	203	148	1979	QF	W 4-0
Vancouver	1	1	0	5	4	1	0	20	9	1975	QF	W 4-1
Defunct Clubs	3	1	2	6	1	2	3	5	9			
Totals	109	71	38	529	322	200	7	1654	1267			

Playoff Results 1989-85

Year	Round	Opponent	Result	GF	GA
1989	F	Calgary	L 2-4	16	19
	CF	Philadelphia	W 4-2	17	8
	DF	Boston	W 4-1	16	13
	DSF	Hartford	W 4-0	18	11
1988	DF	Boston	L 1-4	10	15
	DSF	Hartford	W 4-2	23	19
1987	CF	Philadelphia	L 2-4	22	22
	DF	Quebec	W 4-3	27	21
	DSF	Boston	W 4-0	19	11
1986	F	Calgary	W 4-1	15	13
	CF	NY Rangers	W 4-1	15	10
	DF	Hartford	W 4-3	17	13
	DSF	Boston	W 3-0	10	6
1985	DF	Quebec	L 3-4	24	24
	DSF	Boston	W 3-2	19	17

Abbreviations: Round: F – Final; CF – conference final; DF – division final; DSF – division semi-final; SF – semi-final; QF – quarter-final. P – preliminary round. GA – goals against; GF – goals for.

General Manager

SAVARD, SERGE A.
Managing Director, Montreal Canadiens. Born in Montreal, Que., January 22, 1946.
When Serge Savard was named Managing Director of the Montreal Canadiens on April 28, 1983, he took over a club that finished in fourth place with 75 points. In 1984-85, the Canadiens were vastly improved, finishing first with 94 points. Evidence of Savard's front office efforts were visible throughout the organization where he spent 14 of his 16 NHL seasons as a standout defenseman and an important part of eight Stanley Cup winning teams. As a player, Savard captured the Conn Smythe Trophy as the most valuable player in the 1969 Stanley Cup playoffs and was recipient of the Bill Masterton Trophy in 1978-79 for his dedication, perserverance and sportsmanship to the game of hockey. He was acquired by the Winnipeg Jets in the 1981 Waiver Draft and closed out his playing career with two seasons as a leader and teacher to the young Jets' team which showed remarkable improvement during Savard's term. In the 1960's, Savard twice suffered multiple leg fractures and most experts doubted he would ever play again. He was named to the NHL's Second All-Star Team in 1978-79.

Coach

BURNS, PAT
Coach, Montreal Canadiens. Born in St-Henri, Que., April 4, 1952.
Pat Burns, in his rookie season as head coach of the Montreal Canadiens, led the team to its best regular-season finish since 1978-79, posting a 53-18-9 record for 115 points. After leading his club to the Stanley Cup Finals, Burns was named the 1988-89 recipient of the Jack Adams Award, only the third rookie coach in League history to receive that honor. Following 17 years of service with the Gatineau (Quebec) and Ottawa Police Departments, Burns began his rise to the NHL coaching ranks by assuming the head coaching position with the Hull Olympiques of the Quebec Major Hockey League in 1983-84. In 1985-86, his best year at Hull, he led the Olympiques to the Memorial Cup Final after finishing the regular-season with a 54-18-0 record. Later that year he served as an assistant coach to Bert Templeton for Team Canada at the 1986 World Junior Hockey Championships in Czechoslovkia. Burns' pro coaching career began in 1987-88 when he guided the Canadiens' top minor league affiliate, the AHL Sherbrooke Canadiens, to a 42-34-4 regular-season record.

Coaching Record

Season	Team	Games	Regular Season W	L	T	%	Playoffs Games	W	L	%
1983-84	Hull (QMJHL)	70	25	45	0	.357	....	....	....	....
1984-85	Hull (QMJHL)	68	33	34	1	.493	5	1	4	.200
1985-86	Hull (QMJHL)	72	54	18	0	.750	15	15	0	1.000
1986-87	Hull (QMJHL)	70	26	39	5	.407	8	4	4	.500
1987-88	Sherbrooke (AHL)	80	42	34	4	.550	6	2	4	.333
1988-89	**Montreal (NHL)**	**80**	**53**	**18**	**9**	**.719**	**21**	**14**	**7**	**.667**
	NHL Totals	**80**	**53**	**18**	**9**	**.719**	**21**	**14**	**7**	**.667**

Entry Draft Selections 1989-75

1989
Pick
13 Lindsay Vallis
30 Patrice Brisebois
41 Steve Larouche
51 Pierre Sevigny
83 Andre Racicot
104 Marc Deschamps
146 Craig Ferguson
167 Patrick Lebeau
188 Roy Mitchell
209 Ed Henrich
230 Justin Duberman
251 Steve Cadieux

1988
Pick
20 Eric Charron
34 Martin St. Amour
46 Neil Carnes
83 Patrik Kjellberg
93 Peter Popovic
104 Jean-Claude Bergeron
125 Patrik Carnback
146 Tim Chase
167 Sean Hill
188 Haris Vitolinis
209 Juri Krivohija
230 Kevin Dahl
251 Dave Kunda

1987
Pick
17 Andrew Cassels
33 John Leclair
38 Eric Desjardins
44 Mathieu Schneider
58 Francois Gravel
80 Kris Miller
101 Steve McCool
122 Les Kuntar
143 Rob Kelley
164 Will Geist
185 Eric Tremblay
206 Barry McKinlay
227 Ed Ronan
248 Bryan Herring

1986
Pick
15 Mark Pederson
27 Benoit Brunet
57 Jyrkki Lumme
78 Brent Bobyck
94 Eric Aubertin
99 Mario Milani
120 Steve Bisson
141 Lyle Odelin
162 Rick Hayward
183 Antonin Routa
204 Eric Bohemier
225 Charlie Moore
246 Karel Svoboda

1985
Pick
12 Jose Charbonneau
16 Tom Chorske
33 Todd Richards
47 Rockey Dundas
75 Martin Desjardins
79 Brent Gilchrist
96 Tom Sagissor
117 Donald Dufresne
142 Ed Cristofoli
163 Mike Claringbull
184 Roger Beedon
198 Maurice Mansi
205 Chad Arthur
226 Mike Bishop
247 John Ferguson Jr.

1984
Pick
5 Peter Svoboda
9 Shayne Corson
29 Stephane Richer
51 Patrick Roy
54 Graeme Bonar
65 Lee Brodeur
95 Gerald Johannson
116 Jim Nesich
137 Scott MacTavish
158 Brad McCaughey
179 Eric Demers
199 Ron Annear
220 Dave Tanner
240 Troy Crosby

1983
Pick
17 Alfie Turcotte
26 Claude Lemieux
27 Sergio Momesso
35 Todd Francis
45 Daniel Letendre
78 John Kordic
98 Dan Wurst
118 Arto Javanainen
138 Vladislav Tretiak
158 Rob Bryden
178 Grant MacKay
198 Thomas Rundquist
218 Jeff Perpich
238 Jean Guy Bergeron

1982
Pick
19 Alain Heroux
31 Jocelyn Gauvreau
32 Kent Carlson
33 David Maley
40 Scott Sandelin
61 Scott Harlow
69 John Devoe
103 Kevin Houle
117 Ernie Vargas
124 Michael Dark
145 Hannu Jarvenpaa
150 Steve Smith
166 Tom Kolioupoulos
187 Brian Williams
208 Bob Emery
229 Darren Acheson
250 Bill Brauer

1981
Pick
7 Mark Hunter
18 Gilbert Delorme
19 Jan Ingman
32 Lars Eriksson
40 Chris Chelios
46 Dieter Hegen
82 Kjell Dahlin
88 Steve Rooney
124 Tom Anastos
145 Tom Kurvers
166 Paul Gess
187 Scott Ferguson
208 Danny Burrows

1980
Pick
1 Doug Wickenheiser
27 Ric Nattress
40 John Chabot
45 John Newberry
61 Craig Ludwig
82 Jeff Teal
103 Remi Gagne
124 Mike McPhee
145 Bill Norton
166 Steve Penney
187 John Schmidt
208 Scott Robinson

1979
Pick
27 Gaston Gingras
37 Mats Naslund
43 Craig Levie
44 Guy Carbonneau
58 Rick Wamsley
79 Dave Orleski
100 Yvon Joly
121 Greg Moffatt

1978
Pick
8 Dan Geoffrion
17 Dave Hunter
30 Dale Yakiwchuk
36 Ron Carter
42 Richard David
69 Kevin Reeves

1977
Pick
10 Mark Napier
18 Normand Dupont

36 Mike Boyd
103 Keith Acton
120 Jim Lawson
137 Larry Landon
154 Kevin Constantine
171 John Swain
186 Daniel Metivier
201 Vjacselev Fetisov
212 Jeff Mars
222 Greg Tignanelli
225 George Goulakos
227 Ken Moodie
229 Serge Leblanc
230 Bob Magnuson
231 Chris Nilan
232 Rick Wilson
233 Louis Sleigher
234 Doug Robb

36 Rod Langway
43 Alain Cote
46 Pierre Lagace
49 Moe Robinson
54 Gord Roberts
64 Bob Holland
90 Gaetan Rochette
108 Bill Himmelright
124 Richard Sevigny
137 Keith Hendrickson
140 Mike Reilly
152 Barry Barrett
154 Sid Tanchak
160 Mark Holden
162 Craig Laughlin
167 Daniel Poulin
169 Tom McDonnell
173 Cary Farelli
174 Carey Walker
176 Mark Wells
177 Stan Palmer

179 Jean Belisle
180 Bob Daly
182 Bob Boileau
183 John Costello

1976
Pick
12 Peter Lee
13 Rod Schutt
18 Bruce Baker
36 Barry Melrose
54 Bill Baker
72 Ed Clarey
90 Maurice Barrette
108 Pierre Brassard
118 Rich Gosselin
123 John Gregory
125 Bruce Horsch
127 John Tavella
129 Mark Davidson
131 Bill Wells
133 Ron Wilson

1975
Pick
9 Robin Sadler
15 Pierre Mondou
22 Brian Engblom
34 Kelly Greenbank
51 Paul Woods
52 Pat Hughes
70 Dave Gorman
88 Jim Turkiewicz
106 Michel Lachance
124 Tim Burke
142 Craig Norwich
158 Paul Clarke
173 Bob Ferriter
187 David Bell
198 Carl Jackson
204 Michel Brisebois
208 Roger Bourque
211 Jim Lundquist
214 Don Madson
215 Bob Bain

Club Directory

Montreal Forum
2313 St. Catherine Street West
Montreal, Quebec H3H 1N2
Phone 514/932-2582
FAX (Hockey) 514/932-8736
P.R. 514/932-8285
ENVOY ID
Front Office: CANADIEN.
GM
Public CANADIEN.
Relations: PR
Capacity: 16,197

Owner: The Molson Companies Limited

Chairman of the Board, President and Governor — Ronald Corey
Managing Director and Alternate Governor. . . . . — Serge Savard
Senior Vice-President, Corporate Affairs . . . . . . — Jean Béliveau
Vice-President, Forum Operations . . . . — Aldo Giampaolo
Vice-President, Finance and Administration . . . . — Fred Steer
Vice President, Planning and Development . . . . . — Louis-Joseph Regimbal
Assistant to the Managing Director . . . . — Jacques Lemaire
Assistant to the Managing Director, Director of Recruitment and Managing Director of Le Canadien de Sherbrooke . . . . — André Boudrias
Head Coach. . . . . — Pat Burns
Assistant Coach . . . . — Jacques Laperrière
Goaltending Instructor . . . . — François Allaire
Director of Player Development and Scout. . . . . — Claude Ruel
Chief Scout . . . . — Doug Robinson
Scouting Staff. . . . . — Neil Armstrong, Scott Baker, Pat Flannery, Kevin Houle, Pierre Mondou, Gerry O'Flaherty, Richard Scammell, Eric Taylor, Jean-Claude Tremblay, Del Wilson
Farm Team (AHL) . . . . — Le Canadien de Sherbrooke
Head Coach. . . . . — Jean Hamel
Director of Operations and Assistant Coach . . . . — Claude Larose

Medical and Training Staff
Club Physician . . . . — Dr. D.G. Kinnear
Head Sports Therapist . . . . — Gaetan Lefebvre
Assistant to the Head Sports Therapist . . . . — John Shipman
Head Trainer . . . . — Eddy Palchak
Assistant Trainers . . . . — Pierre Gervais, Sylvain Toupin

Marketing
EFFIX Inc. . . . . — François-Xavier Seigneur
Director of Advertising Sales . . . . — Floyd Curry
Director of Boutiques Souvenirs . . . . — Maurice Corey

Communications
Director of Public Relations . . . . — Claude Mouton
Director of Press Relations . . . . — Michèle Lapointe
Director of Special Events . . . . — Camil Desroches
Computer Supervisor . . . . — Sylvain Roy

Finance
Controller. . . . . — Dennis McKinley
Administrative Supervisor . . . . — Dave Poulton
Accountants . . . . — Françoise Brault, Gilles Viens

Forum
Director of Concessions . . . . — Yvon Gosselin
Director of Purchasing . . . . — Robert Loiseau
Director of Security . . . . — Bob Leblanc
Forum Superintendent . . . . — René Massicotte
Superintendent Assistant . . . . — Alain Gauthier

Ticketing
Box Office Supervisor . . . . — René St-Jacques
Box Office Manager. — Doug Foster

Executive Secretaries
President (Lise Beaudry)/Managing Director (Donna Stuart)/Senior V.P., C.A. (Louise Richer)/ V.P. Forum Operations (Trudy Hughes)/V.P. Finance (Susan Cryans)/Public Rel. (Normande Herget)/Press Rel. (Frédérique Cardinal)

Location of Press Box . . . . — suspended above ice — west side
Location of Radio and TV booth. . . . . — suspended above ice — east side
Club trains at . . . . — Montreal Forum

Play-by-Play — Radio/TV . . . . — Dick Irvin (English)
Claude Quenneville, Richard Garneau, Pierre Rinfret (French)
TV Channels . . . . — CBMT (6), CFTM (10), CBFT (2)
Radio Stations . . . . — CBF (690), CFCF (600)

New Jersey Devils

1988-89 Results: 27w-41L-12T 66 PTS. Fifth, Patrick Division

Year-by-Year Record

Season	GP	Home W	L	T	Road W	L	T	Overall W	L	T	GF	GA	Pts.	Finished	Playoff Result
1988-89	80	17	18	5	10	23	7	27	41	12	281	325	66	5th, Patrick Div.	Out of Playoffs
1987-88	80	23	16	1	15	20	5	38	36	6	295	296	82	4th, Patrick Div.	Lost Conf. Championship
1986-87	80	20	17	3	9	28	3	29	45	6	293	368	64	6th, Patrick Div.	Out of Playoffs
1985-86	80	17	21	2	11	28	1	28	49	3	300	374	59	6th, Patrick Div.	Out of Playoffs
1984-85	80	13	21	6	9	27	4	22	48	10	264	346	54	5th, Patrick Div.	Out of Playoffs
1983-84	80	10	28	2	7	28	5	17	56	7	231	350	41	5th, Patrick Div.	Out of Playoffs
1982-83	80	11	20	9	6	29	5	17	49	14	230	338	48	5th, Patrick Div.	Out of Playoffs
1981-82	80	14	21	5	4	28	8	18	49	13	241	362	49	5th, Smythe Div.	Out of Playoffs
1980-81	80	15	16	9	7	29	4	22	45	13	258	344	57	5th, Smythe Div.	Out of Playoffs
1979-80	80	12	20	8	7	28	5	19	48	13	234	308	51	6th, Smythe Div.	Out of Playoffs
1978-79	80	8	24	8	7	29	4	15	53	12	210	331	42	4th, Smythe Div.	Out of Playoffs
1977-78	80	17	14	9	2	26	12	19	40	21	257	305	59	2nd, Smythe Div.	Lost Prelim. Round
1976-77	80	12	20	8	8	26	6	20	46	14	226	307	54	5th, Smythe Div.	Out of Playoffs
1975-76	80	8	24	8	4	32	4	12	56	12	190	351	36	5th, Smythe Div.	Out of Playoffs
1974-75	80	12	20	8	3	34	3	15	54	11	184	328	41	5th, Smythe Div.	Out of Playoffs

Schedule

Home

Oct. Sat. 7 Pittsburgh
Tues. 10 Calgary
Fri. 13 Montreal
Wed. 18 Philadelphia
Fri. 20 Vancouver
Thur. 26 Hartford
Sat. 28 Chicago
Nov. Wed. 8 Quebec
Sat. 11 Philadelphia*
Wed. 15 Minnesota
Fri. 17 NY Rangers
Tues. 28 NY Islanders
Dec. Sat. 2 Washington
Fri. 8 Pittsburgh
Wed. 13 NY Islanders
Fri. 15 Los Angeles
Sun. 17 Boston
Sat. 23 St Louis
Wed. 27 Washington
Fri. 29 NY Rangers
Jan. Tues. 2 Buffalo
Thur. 4 Los Angeles
Mon. 8 Winnipeg
Wed. 10 Pittsburgh
Fri. 12 Montreal
Wed. 24 Washington
Fri. 26 Toronto
Feb. Tues. 6 Edmonton
Mon. 12 Detroit
Fri. 16 NY Rangers
Thur. 22 Winnipeg
Sat. 24 Chicago*
Mar. Fri. 2 Pittsburgh
Tues. 6 St Louis
Thur. 8 NY Islanders
Sat. 10 Quebec
Tues. 20 Philadelphia
Tues. 27 Washington
Thur. 29 NY Rangers
Sat. 31 Detroit*

Away

Oct. Thur. 5 Philadelphia
Sat. 14 Hartford
Sat. 21 Montreal
Mon. 23 Toronto
Tues. 31 Vancouver
Nov. Wed. 1 Edmonton
Sat. 4 Calgary
Sun. 12 Philadelphia
Sat. 18 Boston
Wed. 22 Pittsburgh
Fri. 24 Minnesota
Sat. 25 Winnipeg
Dec. Fri. 1 Buffalo
Wed. 6 NY Rangers
Sat. 9 Hartford
Tues. 12 NY Islanders
Tues. 19 NY Islanders
Fri. 22 Philadelphia
Tues. 26 NY Rangers
Sun. 31 Detroit
Jan. Sat. 13 Quebec
Tues. 16 Washington
Tues. 23 Pittsburgh
Sun. 28 NY Islanders*
Tues. 30 Los Angeles
Feb. Sun. 4 Vancouver
Fri. 9 Washington
Sat. 10 St Louis
Sat. 17 Toronto
Mon. 19 NY Rangers*
Sun. 25 NY Islanders*
Wed. 28 Pittsburgh
Mar. Sun. 4 Washington*
Tues. 13 Minnesota
Thur. 15 Calgary
Sat. 17 Edmonton
Thur. 22 Chicago
Sat. 24 Philadelphia*
Sun. 25 Buffalo*
Apr. Sun. 1 Boston

* Denotes afternoon game.

Home Starting Times:
All Games . . . . 7:45 p.m.
Except Matinees . . . . 1:35 p.m.

Franchise date: June 30, 1982. Transferred from Denver to New Jersey, Previously transferred from Kansas City to Denver, Colorado.

 **16th NHL Season**

John MacLean led the Devils with 42 goals and 45 assists in 1988-89.

1989-90 Player Personnel

FORWARDS	HT	WT	S	Place of Birth	Date	1988-89 Club
ANDERSON, Perry	6-1	225	L	Barrie, Ont.	10/14/61	New Jersey
BRADY, Neil	6-3	190	L	Montreal, Que.	4/12/68	Utica
BROTEN, Aaron	5-10	180	L	Roseau, MN	11/14/60	New Jersey
BROWN, Doug	5-11	180	R	Southboro, MA	6/12/64	New Jersey-Utica
BUDY, Tim	6-0	190	L	Selkirk, Man.	2/14/67	Utica-Colorado Coll.
CHRISTIAN, Jeff	6-1	185	L	Burlington, Ont.	7/30/70	London
CICHOCKI, Chris	5-11	185	R	Detroit, MI	9/7/63	New Jersey-Utica
CONACHER, Pat	5-8	190	L	Edmonton, Alt.	5/1/59	New Jersey
CROWDER, Troy	6-4	215	R	Sudbury, Ont.	5/3/68	Utica
GUAY, Paul	5-11	185	R	Providence, R.I.	9/2/63	New Haven-L.A.-Bos.-Maine
GUERIN, Bill	6-2	190	R	Wilbraham, MA	11/9/70	Springfield
JOHNSON, Mark	5-9	170	L	Madison, WI	9/22/57	New Jersey
KORN, Jim	6-4	220	L	Hopkins, MN	7/28/57	New Jersey
LANTHIER, Jean-Marc	6-2	195	R	Montreal, Que.	3/27/63	Utica-Maine
MacLEAN, John	6-0	200	R	Oshawa, Ont.	11/20/64	New Jersey
MADILL, Jeff	5-11	195	R	Oshawa, Ont.	6/21/67	Utica
MALEY, David	6-2	205	L	Beaver Dam, WI	4/24/63	New Jersey
MILLER, Jason	6-1	180	L	Edmonton, Alta.	3/1/71	Medicine Hat
MORRIS, Jon	6-0	175	R	Lowell, MA	5/6/66	New Jersey
MULLER, Kirk	6-0	205	L	Kingston, Ont.	2/8/66	New Jersey
OJANEN, Janne	6-2	190	L	Tampere, Finland	4/9/68	New Jersey-Utica
PODDUBNY, Walt	6-1	205	L	Thunder Bay, Ont.	2/14/60	Quebec
ROONEY, Steve	6-2	200	L	Canton, MA	6/28/62	New Jersey
SAPERGIA, Brett	5-10	195	R	Moose Jaw, Sask.	11/16/62	Indianapolis-Switz.
SHANAHAN, Brendan	6-3	205	R	Mimico, Ont.	1/23/69	New Jersey
SIMON, Jason	6-1	190	L	Sarnia, Ont.	3/21/69	Windsor
SKALDE, Jarrod	6-0	180	L	Niagara Falls, Ont.	2/26/71	Oshawa
STEWART, Al	6-0	195	L	Fort St. John, B.C.	1/31/64	New Jersey-Utica
SUNDSTROM, Patrik	6-0	195	L	Skelleftea, Sweden	12/14/61	New Jersey
SUNDSTROM, Peter	6-0	180	L	Skelleftea, Sweden	12/14/61	Washington
TODD, Kevin	5-10	180	L	Winnipeg, Man.	5/4/63	New Jersey-Utica
TURGEON, Sylvain	6-0	195	L	Noranda, Que.	1/17/65	Hartford
VILGRAIN, Claude	6-1	195	R	Port-au-Prince, Haiti	3/1/63	New Jersey-Utica-Milwaukee
YSEBAERT, Paul	6-1	185	L	Sarnia, Ont.	5/15/66	Utica

DEFENSEMEN	HT	WT	S	Place of Birth	Date	1988-89 Club
ALBELIN, Tommy	6-1	200	L	Stockholm, Sweden	5/21/64	New Jersey-Quebec
DANEYKO, Ken	6-0	210	L	Windsor, Ont.	4/16/64	New Jersey
DRIVER, Bruce	6-0	185	L	Toronto, Ont.	4/29/62	New Jersey
FETISOV, Viacheslav	6-1	200	L	Moscow, USSR	5/20/58	ZSKA (Soviet)
HUSCROFT, Jamie	6-2	200	L	Creston, B.C.	1/9/67	New Jersey-Utica
KURVERS, Tom	6-0	205	L	Minneapolis, MN	9/14/62	New Jersey
LANIEL, Marc	6-1	190	L	Oshawa, Ont.	1/16/68	Utica
MARCINYSHYN, Dave	6-3	210	L	Edmonton, Alta.	2/4/67	Utica
O'CONNOR, Myles	5-11	165	L	Calgary, Alta.	4/2/67	Utica-Michigan
RUOTSALAINEN, Reijo	5-8	170	R	Oulu, Finland	4/1/60	Bern (Swiss)
STARIKOV, Sergei	5-10	215	L	Chelyabinsk, USSR	12/4/58	ZSKA (Soviet)
VELISCHEK, Randy	6-1	200	L	Montreal, Que.	2/10/62	New Jersey
WEINRICH, Eric	6-1	210	L	Roanoke, VA	12/19/66	New Jersey-Utica
WOLANIN, Craig	6-3	210	L	Grosse Pointe, MI	7/27/67	New Jersey
WOODS, Bob	6-0	170	L	Leroy, Sask.	1/24/68	Utica-Brandon

GOALTENDERS	HT	WT	C	Place of Birth	Date	1988-89 Club
BILLINGTON, Craig	5-10	165	L	London, Ont.	9/11/66	New Jersey-Utica
BURKE, Sean	6-3	205	L	Windsor, Ont.	1/29/67	New Jersey
MELANSON, Roland	5-10	180	L	Moncton, N.B.	6/28/60	L.A.-New Haven
TERRERI, Chris	5-9	160	L	Providence, RI	11/15/64	New Jersey-Utica

1988-89 Scoring

Regular Season
*–Rookie

Pos	#	Player	Team	GP	G	A	Pts	+/-	PIM	PP	SH	GW	GT	S	%
F	15	John MacLean	N.J.	74	42	45	87	26	127	14	0	4	2	266	15.8
F	9	Kirk Muller	N.J.	80	31	43	74	23−	119	12	1	4	0	182	17.0
F	17	Patrik Sundstrom	N.J.	65	28	41	69	22	36	12	1	1		156	17.9
D	5	Tom Kurvers	N.J.	74	16	50	66	11	38	5	0	0	1	190	8.4
F	10	Aaron Broten	N.J.	80	16	43	59	7−	81	4	0	2	0	179	9.0
F	11	Brendan Shanahan	N.J.	68	22	28	50	2	115	9	0	0	1	152	14.5
F	16	Pat Verbeek	N.J.	77	26	21	47	18−	189	9	0	1	0	175	14.9
F	12	Mark Johnson	N.J.	40	13	25	38	1	24	4	0	2	0	95	13.7
D	26	Tommy Albelin	QUE	14	2	4	6	6−	27	1	0	1	0	16	12.5
			N.J.	46	7	24	31	18	67	2	1	2	0	98	8.5
			TOTAL	60	9	28	37	12	94	2	1	2	0	114	7.9
D	14	Jim Korn	N.J.	65	15	16	31	3−	212	4	0	3	1	65	5.2
D	7	Jack O'Callahan	N.J.	36	5	21	26	0	51	5	0	0	1	96	5.2
F	24	Doug Brown	N.J.	63	15	10	25	7−	15	4	0	2	0	110	13.6
D	2	Joe Cirella	N.J.	80	3	19	22	14−	155	0	1	1	0	84	3.6
F	19	Claude Loiselle	N.J.	74	7	14	21	10−	209	0	1	1	0	92	7.6
D	27	Randy Velischek	N.J.	80	4	14	18	2−	70	0	1	0	0	77	5.2
D	23	Bruce Driver	N.J.	27	1	15	16	0	24	1	0	0	1	69	1.4
F	32	Pat Conacher	N.J.	55	7	5	12	7−	14	0	1	1	0	59	11.9
F	20	Anders Carlsson	N.J.	47	4	8	12	3	20	0	0	0	0	42	9.5
F	8	David Maley	N.J.	68	5	6	11	27−	249	0	0	0	0	63	7.9
D	6	Craig Wolanin	N.J.	56	3	8	11	9−	69	0	0	0	0	70	4.3
D	3	Ken Daneyko	N.J.	80	5	5	10	22−	283	1	0	0	0	108	4.6
F	25	Perry Anderson	N.J.	39	3	2	5	8−	128	0	0	0	0	36	8.3
F	18	Steve Rooney	N.J.	25	3	1	4	9−	79	0	0	1	0	23	13.0
F	22	*Paul Ysebaert	N.J.	5	0	4	4	2	0	0	0	0	0	4	.0
G	1	*Sean Burke	N.J.	62	0	3	3	0	54	0	0	0	0	0	.0
F	22	*Jon Morris	N.J.	4	0	2	2	0	0	0	0	0	0	2	.0
F	26	*Allan Stewart	N.J.	6	0	2	2	2−	15	0	0	0	0	4	.0
D	4	*Jamie Huscroft	N.J.	15	0	2	2	3−	51	0	0	0	0	3	.0
F	21	George McPhee	N.J.	1	0	1	1	1	2	0	0	0	0	1	.0
F	29	*Chris Cichocki	N.J.	2	0	1	1	0	0	0	0	0	0	2	.0
F	29	*Janne Ojanen	N.J.	3	0	1	1	1−	2	0	0	0	0	1	.0
F	21	*Kevin Todd	N.J.	1	0	0	0	1−	0	0	0	0	0	0	.0
D	29	*Corey Foster	N.J.	2	0	0	0	0	0	0	0	0	0	2	.0
D	4	*Eric Weinrich	N.J.	2	0	0	0	1−	0	0	0	0	0	3	.0

Goaltending

No.	Goaltender	GPI	Mins	Avg	W	L	T	EN	SO	GA	SA	S%
30	*Chris Terreri	8	402	2.69	0	4	2	1	0	18	170	.893
1	*Sean Burke	62	3590	3.84	22	31	9	7	3	230	1823	.873
28	Bob Sauve	15	720	4.67	4	5	1	2	0	56	333	.831
31	Craig Billington	3	140	4.71	1	1	0	0	0	11	65	.831
	Totals	80	4873	4.00	27	41	12	10	3	325	2391	.864

Kirk Muller

General Managers' History
(Kansas City) Sidney Abel, 1974-75 to 1975-76; (Colorado) Ray Miron, 1976-77 to 1981-82; Billy MacMillan, 1982-83; Billy MacMillan and Max McNab, 1983-84; Max McNab 1984-85 to 1986-87; Lou Lamoriello, 1987-88 to date.

Coaching History
(Kansas City) Bep Guidolin, 1974-75; Bep Guidolin, Sid Abel, and Eddie Bush, 1975-76; (Colorado) John Wilson, 1976-77; Pat Kelly, 1977-78; Pat Kelly, Aldo Guidolin, 1978-79; Don Cherry, 1979-80; Bill MacMillan, 1980-81; Bert Marshall and Marshall Johnston, 1981-82; (New Jersey) Bill MacMillan, 1982-83; Bill MacMillan and Tom McVie, 1983-84; Doug Carpenter, 1984-85 to 1986-87; Doug Carpenter and Jim Schoenfeld, 1987-88; Jim Schoenfeld, 1988-89 to date.

Captains' History
Simon Nolet, 1974-75 to 1976-77; Wilf Paiement, 1977-78; Gary Croteau, 1978-79; Mike Christie, Rene Robert, Lanny McDonald, 1979-80; Lanny McDonald, 1980-81; Lanny McDonald, Rob Ramage, 1981-82; Don Lever, 1982-83; Don Lever, Mel Bridgman, 1983-84; Mel Bridgman, 1984-85, 1985-86; Kirk Muller, 1987-88 to date.

Club Records

Team

(Figures in brackets for season records are games played; records for fewest points, wins, ties, losses, goals, goals against are for 70 or more games)

Most Points	.82	1987-88 (80)
Most Wins	.38	1987-88 (80)
Most Ties	*21	1977-78 (80)
	14	1982-83 (80)
Most Losses	*56	1983-84 (80)
		1975-76 (80)
Most Goals	.300	1985-86 (80)
Most Goals Against	.374	1985-86 (80)
Fewest Points	*36	1975-76 (80)
	41	1983-84 (80)
Fewest Wins	*12	1975-76 (80)
	17	1982-83 (80)
		1983-84 (80)
Fewest Ties	3	1985-86 (80)
Fewest Losses	.36	1987-88 (80)
Fewest Goals	*184	1974-75 (80)
	230	1982-83 (80)
Fewest Goals Against	.296	1987-88 (80)

Longest Winning Streak
Over-all .... 5 Mar. 27-Apr. 3/88
Home .... 8 Oct. 9-Nov. 7/87
Away .... 3 Dec. 2-9/79; Mar. 12-24/88

Longest Undefeated Streak
Over-all .... 8 Mar. 20-Apr. 3/88 (7 wins, 1 tie)
Home .... 6 Feb. 24-Mar. 19/78 (3 wins, 3 ties)
Away .... 6 Jan. 20-Feb. 9/89 (3 wins, 3 ties)

Longest Losing Streak
Over-all .... *14 Dec. 30/75-Jan. 29/76
10 Oct. 14-Nov. 4/83
Home .... 9 Dec. 22/85-Feb. 6/86
Away .... 12 Oct. 19/83-Dec. 1/83

Longest Winless Streak
Over-all .... *27 Feb. 12-Apr. 4/76 (21 losses, 6 ties)
18 Oct. 20-Nov. 26/82 (14 losses 4 ties)

Home .... *14 Feb. 12-Mar. 30/76 (10 losses, 4 ties)
Feb. 4-Mar. 31/79 (12 losses, 2 ties)
9 Dec. 22/85-Feb. 6/86 (9 losses)
Away .... *32 Nov. 12/77-Mar. 15/78 (22 losses, 10 ties)
14 Dec. 26/82-Mar. 5/83 (13 losses, 1 tie)

Most Shutouts, Season 3 1988-89 (80)
Most Pen. Mins., Season 2,494 1988-89 (80)
Most Goals, Game .... 9 Apr. 1/79 (St.L. 5 at Col. 9) Feb. 12/82 (Que. 2 at Col. 9) Apr. 6/86 (NYI 7 at N.J. 9)

Individual

Most Seasons .... *8 Mike Kitchen
7 Aaron Broten
Most Games .... .599 Aaron Broten
Most Goals, Career ..... .170 Pat Verbeek
Most Assists, Career ..... .299 Aaron Broten
Most Points, Career ..... .451 Aaron Broten (152 goals, 299 assists)
Most Pen. Mins., Career . .943 Pat Verbeek
Most Shutouts, Career ...... .4 Sean Burke
Longest Consecutive Games Streak .... .266 Aaron Broten (Dec. 6/82-Feb. 15/86)
Most Goals, Season ...... .47 Pat Verbeek (1987-88)
Most Assists, Season ..... .57 Aaron Broten, Kirk Muller (1987-88)
Most Points, Season ..... .94 Kirk Muller (1987-88) (37 goals, 57 assists)
Most Pen. Mins., Season . . .239 Ken Daneyko (1987-88)
Most Points, Defenseman Season .... .66 Tom Kurvers (1988-89) (16 goals, 50 assists)
Most Points, Center Season .... .94 Kirk Muller (1987-88) (37 goals, 57 assists)

Most Points, Right Wing, Season .... *87 Wilf Paiement (1977-78) (31 goals, 56 assists)
87 John MacLean (1988-89) (42 goals, 45 assists)
Most Points, Left Wing, Season .... .83 Aaron Broten (1987-88) (26 goals, 57 assists)
Most Points, Rookie, Season .... *60 Barry Beck (1977-78) (22 goals, 38 assists)
54 Kirk Muller (1984-85) (17 goals, 37 assists)
Most Shutouts, Season ..... .3 Sean Burke (1988-89)
Most Goals, Game .... .4 Bob MacMillan (Jan. 8/82) Pat Verbeek (Feb. 28/88)
Most Assists, Game .... .5 Kirk Muller (Mar. 25/87) Greg Adams (Oct. 10/86) Tom Kurvers (Feb. 13/89)
Most Points, Game .... .6 Kirk Muller (Nov. 29/86) (3 goals, 3 assists)

* – Record includes Kansas City Scouts and Colorado Rockies from 1974-75 through 1981-82

All-time Record vs. Other Clubs

Regular Season

	At Home						On Road						Total					
	GP	W	L	T	GF	GA	PTS	GP	W	L	T	GF	GA	PTS	GP	W	L	T	GF	GA	PTS
Boston	26	2	16	8	66	105	12	26	7	18	1	81	121	15	52	9	34	9	147	226	27
Buffalo	26	3	19	4	73	114	10	26	2	21	3	70	130	7	52	5	40	7	143	244	17
**Calgary	31	7	21	3	84	125	17	30	3	23	4	69	146	10	61	10	44	7	153	271	27
Chicago	32	13	14	5	93	98	31	32	7	20	5	73	127	19	64	20	34	10	166	225	50
Detroit	26	13	8	5	98	76	31	26	8	16	2	81	116	18	52	21	24	7	179	192	49
Edmonton	19	9	9	1	69	69	19	18	4	12	2	70	103	10	37	13	21	3	139	172	29
Hartford	16	7	7	2	59	70	16	16	3	9	4	48	60	10	32	10	16	6	107	130	26
Los Angeles	28	10	13	5	89	107	25	29	1	22	6	89	168	8	57	11	35	11	178	275	33
Minnesota	31	15	13	3	106	104	33	31	6	19	6	75	129	18	62	21	32	9	181	233	51
Montreal	26	6	20	0	66	131	12	26	3	20	3	65	117	9	52	9	40	3	131	248	21
NY Islanders	43	13	24	6	141	187	32	42	1	37	4	101	216	6	85	14	61	10	242	403	38
NY Rangers	43	15	24	4	152	180	34	42	13	25	4	141	190	30	85	28	49	8	293	370	64
Philadelphia	42	16	23	3	147	181	35	42	4	35	3	79	194	11	84	20	58	6	226	375	46
Pittsburgh	39	18	14	7	147	141	43	41	14	24	3	149	177	31	80	32	38	10	296	318	74
Quebec	16	6	9	1	64	64	13	16	4	10	2	54	79	10	32	10	19	3	118	143	23
St. Louis	32	11	14	7	100	97	29	32	7	22	3	101	147	17	64	18	36	10	201	244	46
Toronto	26	9	8	9	98	85	27	26	5	19	2	85	121	12	52	14	27	11	183	206	39
Vancouver	35	13	16	6	102	122	32	34	6	17	11	103	131	23	69	19	33	17	205	253	55
Washington	40	14	20	6	129	132	34	40	7	30	3	114	186	17	80	21	50	9	243	318	51
Winnipeg	15	5	6	4	49	52	14	17	2	13	2	40	73	6	32	7	19	6	89	125	20
Defunct Clubs	8	4	2	2	25	17	10	8	2	3	3	21	27	7	16	6	5	5	44	46	17
Totals	600	209	300	91	1957	2257	509	600	109	415	76	1709	2758	294	1200	318	715	167	3664	5017	803

** Totals include those of Atlanta (1974-75 through 1979-80)

Playoffs

	Series	W	L	GP	W	L	T	GF	GA	Last Mtg.	Round	Result
Boston	1	0	1	7	3	4	0	30	19	1988	CF	L 3-4
NY Islanders	1	1	0	6	4	2	0	23	18	1988	DSF	W 4-2
Philadelphia	1	0	1	2	0	2	0	3	6	1978	P	L 0-2
Washington	1	1	0	7	4	3	0	25	23	1988	DF	W 4-3
Totals	4	2	2	22	11	11	0	81	66			

Abbreviations: Round: F – Final; **CF** – conference final; **DF** – division final; **DSF** – division semi-final; **SF** – semi-final; **QF** – quarter-final. **P** – preliminary round. **GA** – goals against; **GF** – goals for.

Playoff Results 1989-85

Year	Round	Opponent	Result	GF	GA
1988	CF	Boston	L 3-4	19	30
	DF	Washington	W 4-3	25	23
	DSF	NY Islanders	W 4-2	23	18

1988-89 Results

	Home				Away	
Oct.	14 Montreal	3-7	Oct.	6 Philadelphia	1-4
	19 Vancouver	0-4		8 Quebec	5-3
	21 Pittsburgh	6-4		10 NY Rangers	5-0
	25 Buffalo	4-7		15 Washington	5-8
	28 Hartford	5-3		23 Detroit	3-3
Nov.	1 Philadelphia	3-2		29 Hartford	0-3
	3 Winnipeg	3-3	Nov.	12 Washington	6-3
	6 NY Rangers	6-5		15 St Louis	4-2
	9 Edmonton	2-3		20 Philadelphia	1-7
	11 NY Islanders	3-3		23 Calgary	2-3
	17 Calgary	3-5		25 Vancouver	2-2
	19 Washington	2-3		29 Los Angeles	3-9
Dec.	3 Philadelphia*	3-5	Dec.	4 Philadelphia	2-6
	7 Washington	5-1		10 Pittsburgh	4-4
	9 NY Islanders	6-5		17 NY Islanders	2-5
	13 St Louis	4-3		18 Chicago	5-3
	15 Toronto	6-3		21 Winnipeg	5-3
	23 Pittsburgh	2-2		26 NY Rangers*	1-5
	27 NY Rangers	5-7		31 Pittsburgh	6-8
	29 Boston	2-6	Jan.	9 NY Rangers	5-4
Jan.	6 Buffalo	5-4		11 Montreal	0-1
	7 Detroit	5-2		17 Quebec	4-7
	13 NY Islanders	3-5		20 Washington	6-5
	15 Edmonton	1-0		24 NY Islanders	2-2
	19 Quebec	4-5		28 Minnesota	4-4
	23 Minnesota	2-7	Feb.	2 Los Angeles	6-6
	27 Hartford	6-8		5 Edmonton*	4-2
Feb.	13 Toronto	8-1		9 Detroit	6-3
	24 Philadelphia	2-6		11 Montreal	4-5
	26 Los Angeles	1-1		15 Buffalo	3-5
	28 Boston	3-3		17 Winnipeg	2-3
Mar.	3 NY Rangers	6-3		18 Toronto	3-5
	5 Minnesota	2-0		20 NY Rangers*	4-7
	14 Calgary	1-5	Mar.	1 Pittsburgh	1-4
	16 Pittsburgh	1-2		7 St Louis	2-6
	18 Chicago*	1-3		8 Chicago	7-5
	20 Vancouver	3-1		11 NY Islanders	2-3
	27 Philadelphia	5-3		23 Boston	3-5
	29 NY Islanders	4-5		25 Pittsburgh	4-5
Apr.	2 Washington	7-4	Apr.	1 Washington	4-6

* Denotes afternoon game.

Entry Draft
Selections 1989-75

1989
Pick
5	Bill Guerin
18	Jason Miller
26	Jarrod Skalde
47	Scott Pellerin
89	Mike Heinke
110	David Emma
152	Sergei Starikow
173	Andre Faust
215	Jason Simon
236	Peter Larsson

1988
Pick
12	Corey Foster
23	Jeff Christian
54	Zdenek Ciger
65	Matt Ruchty
75	Scott Luik
96	Chris Nelson
117	Chad Johnson
138	Chad Erickson
159	Bryan Lafort
180	Sergei Svetlov
201	Bob Woods
207	Alexander Semak
222	Charles Hughes
243	Michael Pohl

1987
Pick
2	Brendan Shanahan
23	Rickard Persson
65	Brian Sullivan
86	Kevin Dean
107	Ben Hankinson
128	Tom Neziol
149	Jim Dowd
170	John Blessman
191	Peter Fry
212	Alain Charland

1986
Pick
3	Neil Brady
24	Todd Copeland
45	Janne Ojanen
62	Marc Laniel
66	Anders Carlsson
108	Troy Crowder
129	Kevin Todd
150	Ryan Pardoski
171	Scott McCormack
192	Frederic Chabot
213	John Andersen
236	Doug Kirton

1985
Pick
3	Craig Wolanin
24	Sean Burke
32	Eric Weinrich
45	Myles O'Connor
66	Gregg Polak
108	Bill McMillan
129	Kevin Schrader
150	Ed Krayer
171	Jamie Huscroft
192	Terry Shold
213	Jamie McKinley
234	David Williams

1984
Pick
2	Kirk Muller
23	Craig Billington
44	Neil Davey
74	Paul Ysebaert
86	Jon Morris
107	Kirk McLean
128	Ian Ferguson
149	Vladimir Kames
170	Mike Roth
190	Mike Peluso
211	Jarkko Piiparinen
231	Chris Kiene

1983
Pick
6	John MacLean
24	Shawn Evans
87	Chris Terreri
108	Gordon Mark
129	Greg Evtushevski
150	Vjacselev Fetisov
171	Jay Octeau
192	Alexi Chernykh
213	Allan Stewart
234	Aleksei Kasatonov

1982
Pick
8	Rocky Trottier
18	Ken Daneyko
43	Pat Verbeek
54	Dave Kasper
85	Scott Brydges
106	Mike Moher
127	Paul Fulcher
148	John Hutchings
169	Alan Hepple
190	Brent Shaw
207	Tony Gilliard
211	Scott Fusco
232	Dan Dorian

1981
Pick
5	Joe Cirella
26	Rich Chernomaz
48	Ullie Hiemer
66	Gus Greco
87	Doug Speck
108	Bruce Driver
129	Jeff Larmer
150	Tony Arima
171	Tim Army
192	John Johannson

1980
Pick
19	Paul Gagne
22	Joe Ward
64	Rick LaFerriere
85	Ed Cooper
106	Aaron Broten
127	Dan Fascinato
148	Andre Hidi
169	Shawn MacKenzie
190	Bob Jansch

1979
Pick
1	Rob Ramage
64	Steve Peters
85	Gary Dillon
106	Bob Attwell

1978
Pick
4	Mike Gillis
27	Merlin Malinowski
41	Paul Messier
58	Dave Watson
73	Tim Thomlison
74	Rod Guimont
91	John Hynes
108	Andy Clark
125	John Oliver
142	Kevin Krook
159	Jeff Jensen
174	Bo Ericsson
190	Jari Viitala
204	Ulf Zetterstrom

1977
Pick
2	Barry Beck
38	Doug Berry
47	Randy Pierce
92	Daniel Lempe
110	Rick Doyle
126	Joe Contini
142	Jack Hughes

1976
Pick
11	Paul Gardner
38	Mike Kitchen
74	Rick McIntyre
92	Larry Skinner

1975
Pick
2	Barry Dean
20	Don Cairns
38	Neil Lyseng
56	Ron Delorme
74	Terry McDonald
92	Eric Sanderson
110	Bill Oleschuk
128	Joe Baker
145	Scott Williams

Club Directory

Byrne Meadowlands Arena
P.O. Box 504
East Rutherford, N.J. 07073
Phone 201/935-6050
GM FAX 201/507-0711
FAX 201/935-2127
ENVOY ID
  Front Office: DEVILS. GM
  Public
  Relations: DEVILS. PR
Capacity: 19,040

Chairman	John J. McMullen
President & General Manager	Louis A. Lamoriello
Executive Vice-President	Max McNab
Vice-President, Communications & Advertising	Larry Brooks
Vice-President, Marketing/Sales	Jerry Dailey
Vice-President, Operations/Human Resources	Peter McMullen
Vice-President, Finance	Chris Modrzynski

Hockey Club Personnel

Director of Player Personnel	Marshall Johnston
Head Coach	Jim Schoenfeld
Assistant Coach	John Cunniff
Goaltending Coach/Scout	Bob Bellemore
Assistant Director of Player Personnel	David Conte
Scouting Staff	Tim Burke, Claude Carrier, Glen Dirk, Milt Fisher, Frank Jay, Dan Labraaten, Russ LeClair, Ed Thomlinson, Les Widdifield
Special Assignment Scout	Bob Sauve
Athletic Trainer	Ted Schuch
Equipment Specialists	Jeff Croop, Dave Baglio
Strength Coach	Dimitri Lopuchin
Team Orthopedists	Dr. Barry Fisher, Dr. Len Jaffe
Team Internist	Dr. Richard Commentucci
Team Cardiologist	Dr. Joseph Niznik
Team Dentist	Dr. H. Hugh Gardy
Exercise Physiologist	Dr. Garrett Caffrey
Massage Therapist	Bob Huddleston
Administrative Assistants to the President/GM	Marie Carnevale, Charlotte Smaldone
Staff Assistant	Angela Gorgone

Communications Department

Director, Public & Media Relations	David Freed
Public Relations Assistants	Mike Levine, Tom Shine
Secretary, Marketing & P.R.	Linda Germano
Secretary	Karen Lynch
Receptionist	Jelsa Belotta

Finance Department

Assistant Controller	Gene Amore
Staff Accountant	Eric Mandelbaum
Accounts Payable	George Arsenault
Secretary	Eileen Musikant

Sales

Regional Sales Managers	Ken Ferriter, Joe Ehrline, Don Gleeson, John Glynn, Melanie Padovano

Tickets

Director, Ticket Operations	Terry Farmer
Assistant Director, Ticket Operations	Scott Tanfield

Team Photographers	Steve Crandall, Jim Turner
Location of Press Box	Section 108, center ice
Location of Broadcast Booth	Front, Section 234
Dimensions of Rink	200 feet by 85 feet
Club Colors	Red, Green and White
Television Outlet	SportsChannel
Television Announcers	Gary Thorne (play-by-play); Peter McNab (color)
Flagship Radio Station	WABC (770 AM)
Radio Announcers	Chris Moore (play-by-play); Larry Brooks (color)

General Manager

LAMORIELLO, LOU
President and General Manager, New Jersey Devils.
Born in Providence, Rhode Island, October 21, 1942.

Lou Lamoriello is entering his third season as President and General Manager of the Devils following a more than 20-year association with Providence College as a player, coach and administrator. A member of the varsity hockey Friars during his undergraduate days, he became an assistant coach with the college club after graduating in 1963. Lamoriello was later named head coach and in the ensuing 15 years, led his teams to a 248-179-13 record, a .578 winning percentage and appearances in 10 post-season tournaments, including the 1983 NCAA Final Four. Lamoriello also served a five-year term as Athletic Director at Providence and was a co-founder of Hockey East, one of the strongest collegiate hockey conferences in the U.S. He remained as Athletic Director until he was hired as President of the Devils on April 30, 1987. He assumed the dual responsibility of General Manager on September 10, 1987.

Coach

SCHOENFELD, JIM
Head Coach, New Jersey Devils. Born in Galt, Ontario, September 4, 1952.

In his first full season as Head Coach of the Devils, Schoenfeld led his club to a 27-41-12 record (66 points). Schoenfeld took the coaching reins on January 26, 1988 and led the Devils to their most successful season in 1987-88, bringing them to the Wales Conference Championship.

Schoenfeld brings the same enthusiasm and leadership to coaching as he demonstrated as a player for 13 seasons with Buffalo, Detroit and Boston. He posted 51-204-255 career totals with 1,132 penalty minutes in 719 regular-season games and appeared in two NHL All-Star Games and the 1979 Challenge Cup.

The 37-year-old native of Galt began his coaching career in 1984-85 by guiding the Rochester Americans, Buffalo's top minor league affiliate, to a league record 11 consecutive wins to start the season. However, 25 games into the season, he rejoined the Sabres as a player for the remainder of the year. In 1985-86 he received his first NHL head coaching assignment when Buffalo General Manager Scotty Bowman hired Schoenfeld. He was replaced by Bowman behind the bench, however, after posting a 19-19-5 record in 43 games.

Coaching Record

Team	Season	Regular Season					Playoffs			
		Games	W	L	T	%	Games	W	L	%
1984-85	Rochester (AHL)	25	17	6	2	.720	....	....	....	....
1985-86	Buffalo (NHL)	43	19	19	5	.500	....	....	....	....
1987-88	New Jersey (NHL)	30	17	12	1	.583	20	11	9	.550
1988-89	New Jersey (NHL)	80	27	41	12	.413	....	....	....	....
	NHL Totals	153	63	72	18	.471	20	11	9	.550

New York Islanders
1988-89 Results: 28w-47L-5T 61 PTS. Sixth, Patrick Division

Year-by-Year Record

Season	GP	Home W	L	T	Road W	L	T	Overall W	L	T	GF	GA	Pts.		Finished	Playoff Result
1988-89	80	19	18	3	9	29	2	28	47	5	265	325	61	6th,	Patrick Div.	Out of Playoffs
1987-88	80	24	10	6	15	21	4	39	31	10	308	267	88	1st,	Patrick Div.	Lost Div. Semi-Final
1986-87	80	20	15	5	15	18	7	35	33	12	279	281	82	3rd,	Patrick Div.	Lost Div. Final
1985-86	80	22	11	7	17	18	5	39	29	12	327	284	90	3rd,	Patrick Div.	Lost Div. Semi-Final
1984-85	80	26	11	3	14	23	3	40	34	6	345	312	86	3rd,	Patrick Div.	Lost Div. Final
1983-84	80	28	11	1	22	15	3	50	26	4	357	269	104	1st,	Patrick Div.	Lost Final
1982-83	**80**	**26**	**11**	**3**	**16**	**15**	**9**	**42**	**26**	**12**	**302**	**226**	**96**	**2nd,**	**Patrick Div.**	**Won Stanley Cup**
1981-82	**80**	**33**	**3**	**4**	**21**	**13**	**6**	**54**	**16**	**10**	**385**	**250**	**118**	**1st,**	**Patrick Div.**	**Won Stanley Cup**
1980-81	**80**	**23**	**6**	**11**	**25**	**12**	**3**	**48**	**18**	**14**	**355**	**260**	**110**	**1st,**	**Patrick Div.**	**Won Stanley Cup**
1979-80	**80**	**26**	**9**	**5**	**13**	**19**	**8**	**39**	**28**	**13**	**281**	**247**	**91**	**2nd,**	**Patrick Div.**	**Won Stanley Cup**
1978-79	80	31	3	6	20	12	8	51	15	14	358	214	116	1st,	Patrick Div.	Lost Semi-Final
1977-78	80	29	3	8	19	14	7	48	17	15	334	210	111	1st,	Patrick Div.	Lost Quarter-Final
1976-77	80	24	11	5	23	10	7	47	21	12	288	193	106	2nd,	Patrick Div.	Lost Semi-Final
1975-76	80	24	8	8	18	13	9	42	21	17	297	190	101	2nd,	Patrick Div.	Lost Semi-Final
1974-75	80	22	6	12	11	19	10	33	25	22	264	221	88	3rd,	Patrick Div.	Lost Semi-Final
1973-74	78	13	17	9	6	24	9	19	41	18	182	247	56	8th,	East Div.	Out of Playoffs
1972-73	78	10	25	4	2	35	2	12	60	6	170	347	30	8th,	East Div.	Out of Playoffs

Schedule

	Home		Away
Oct.	Sat. 14 Philadelphia	**Oct.**	Thur. 5 Minnesota
	Tues. 17 Minnesota		Sat. 7 Calgary
	Sat. 21 Vancouver		Mon. 9 Vancouver*
	Tues. 24 Edmonton		Wed. 11 Los Angeles
	Sat. 28 NY Rangers		Fri. 20 Washington
	Tues. 31 Montreal		Fri. 27 NY Rangers
Nov.	Sat. 4 Detroit	**Nov.**	Thur. 2 Pittsburgh
	Tues. 7 Washington		Sun. 5 Philadelphia
	Thur. 9 Quebec		Sun. 12 NY Rangers
	Sat. 11 Chicago		Sat. 18 Pittsburgh
	Tues. 14 Philadelphia		Wed. 22 Washington
	Thur. 16 Toronto		Tues. 28 New Jersey
	Tues. 21 Winnipeg		Thur. 30 Chicago
	Sat. 25 Edmonton	**Dec.**	Sat. 2 Winnipeg
Dec.	Tues. 5 Buffalo		Wed. 6 Hartford
	Sat. 9 NY Rangers		Wed. 13 New Jersey
	Tues. 12 New Jersey		Fri. 15 Washington
	Sat. 16 NY Rangers		Sat. 30 Quebec
	Tues. 19 New Jersey		Sun. 31 Buffalo
	Sat. 23 Pittsburgh*	**Jan.**	Wed. 10 Toronto
	Thur. 28 St Louis		Thur. 11 Minnesota
Jan.	Tues. 2 Los Angeles		Wed. 17 Montreal
	Sat. 6 Quebec		Fri. 19 Winnipeg
	Sat. 13 Washington		Tues. 23 Hartford
	Tues. 16 Vancouver		Thur. 25 Boston
	Sat. 27 Pittsburgh*	**Feb.**	Sun. 4 Buffalo
	Sun. 28 New Jersey*		Tues. 6 Pittsburgh
	Tues. 30 St Louis		Thur. 8 Philadelphia
Feb.	Fri. 2 Washington		Sat. 10 Boston*
	Tues. 13 Calgary		Sun. 18 Philadelphia*
	Sat. 17 Chicago*		Thur. 22 Pittsburgh
	Sat. 24 Detroit*		Wed. 28 Detroit
	Sun. 25 New Jersey*	**Mar.**	Fri. 2 NY Rangers
Mar.	Tues. 6 Hartford		Sat. 3 St Louis
	Sat. 10 Boston		Thur. 8 New Jersey
	Tues. 13 Montreal		Thur. 15 Philadelphia
	Sat. 17 NY Rangers*		Tues. 20 Washington
	Sun. 18 Pittsburgh*		Thur. 22 Los Angeles
	Tues. 27 Calgary		Sat. 24 Edmonton
	Sat. 31 Philadelphia		Wed. 28 Toronto

* Denotes afternoon game.

Home Starting Times:
Weeknights & Saturdays .... 7:35 p.m.
Matinees .... 2:05 p.m.
Except Sat. Oct. 14 .... 5:05 p.m.
Sun. Jan. 28 .... 1:05 p.m.

Franchise date: June 6, 1972

 18th NHL Season

Pat LaFontaine's 45 goals and 43 assists made him the Islanders' top scorer in 1988-89.

1989-90 Player Personnel

FORWARDS	HT	WT	Place of Birth	Date	1988-89 Club
BYRAM, Shawn	6-2	204	Neepawa, Man.	9/12/68	Springfield
CHYZOWSKI, David	6-1	190	Edmonton, Alta.	7/11/71	Kamloops
CLARK, Kerry	6-1	190	Kelvington, Sask.	8/21/68	Springfield
DALGARNO, Brad	6-3	215	Vancouver, B.C.	8/11/67	NY Islanders
DALLMAN, Rod	5-11	185	Quesnel, B.C.	1/26/67	Springfield
DIMAIO, Rob	5-8	175	Calgary, Alta.	2/19/68	NYI-Springfield
DOUCET, Wayne	6-2	203	Etobicoke, Ont.	6/19/70	Springfield-Kingston
ENS, Kelly	6-2	194	Saskatoon, Sask.	6/15/69	Lethbridge
EWEN, Dean	6-1	185	St. Albert, Alta.	2/28/69	Springfield-Seattle
FITZGERALD, Tom	6-1	193	Melrose, MA	8/28/68	NYI-Springfield
FLATLEY, Patrick	6-2	197	Toronto, Ont.	10/3/63	NYI-Springfield
FRASER, Iain	5-1	175	Scarborough, Ont.	8/10/69	Oshawa
GAUCHER, Yves	5-11	189	Valleyfield, Que.	7/14,68	Chicoutimi
GREEN, Travis	6-0	196	Creston, B.C.	12/20/70	Spokane
GRIEVE, Brent	6-1	202	Oshawa, Ont.	5/9/69	Oshawa
HENRY, Dale	6-0	205	Prince Albert, Sask.	9/24/64	NYI-Springfield
HUBER, Phil	5-10	194	Calgary, Alta.	1/10/69	Kamloops
KERR, Alan	5-11	195	Hazelton, B.C.	3/28/64	NY Islanders
KING, Derek	6-1	210	Hamilton, Ont.	2/11/67	NYI-Springfield
KUSHNER, Dale	6-1	205	Terrace, B.C.	6/13/66	Springfield
LAUER, Brad	6-0	195	Humboldt, Sask.	10/27/66	NYI-Springfield
LaFONTAINE, Pat	5-10	177	St. Louis, MO	2/22/65	NY Islanders
LeBRUN, Sean	6-2	200	Prince George, B.C.	5/2/69	Tri-Cities
MAKELA, Mikko	6-2	193	Tampere, Fin.	2/28/65	NY Islanders
MALONEY, Don	6-1	197	Lindsay, Ont.	9/5/58	NYR-Hartford
McLELLAN, Todd	5-11	185	Melville, Sask.	10/3/67	Springfield
STEVENS, Mike	5-10	195	Kitchener, Ont.	12/30/65	NYI-Springfield
SUTTER, Brent	5-11	180	Viking, Alta.	6/10/62	NY Islanders
TROTTIER, Bryan	5-11	195	Val Marie, Sask.	7/17/56	NY Islanders
VOLEK, David	6-0	185	Prague, Czech.	6/18/66	NY Islanders
VUKOTA, Mick	6-2	195	Saskatoon, Sask.	9/14/66	NYI-Springfield
WALSH, Mike	6-2	195	New York, NY	4/3/62	NYI-Springfield
WOOD, Randy	6-0	195	Princeton, NJ	10/12/63	NYI-Springfield
YOUNG, Steve	6-3	200	Calgary, Atla.	5/17/69	Moose Jaw

DEFENSEMEN					
BERG, Bill	6-1	190	St. Catharines, Ont.	10/21/67	NYI-Springfield
BERGEVIN, Marc	6-0	185	Montreal, Que.	8/11/65	NYI-Chicago
BRASSARD, Andre	6-0	190	Arvida, Que.	4/18/68	Trois Rivieres
CHEVELDAYOFF, Kevin	6-0	202	Saskatoon, Sask.	2/4/70	Brandon
CHYNOWETH, Dean	6-2	190	Calgary, Alta.	10/30/68	NY Islanders
CROSSMAN, Doug	6-2	190	Peterborough, Ont.	6/30/60	Los Angeles
DIDUCK, Gerald	6-2	207	Edmonton, Alta.	4/6/65	NY Islanders
EVANS, Shawn	6-3	195	Kingston, Ont.	9/7/65	Springfield
FINLEY, Jeff	6-2	185	Edmonton, Alta.	4/14/67	NYI-Springfield
LAMMENS, Hank	6-1	190	Brockville, Ont.	2/21/66	Springfield
McBEAN, Wayne	6-2	185	Calgary, Alta.	2/21/69	NYI-L.A.-New Haven
NORTON, Jeff	6-2	190	Cambridge, MA	11/25/65	NY Islanders
NYLUND, Gary	6-4	210	Surrey, B.C.	10/28/63	NYI-Chicago
PILON, Richard	6-0	202	Saskatoon, Sask.	4/30/68	NY Islanders
PRYOR, Chris	5-11	210	St. Paul, MN	1/31/61	NYI-Springfield
REEKIE, Joe	6-3	215	Petawawa, Ont.	2/22/65	Buffalo-Rochester
SMITH, Vern	6-1	190	Winnipeg, Man.	5/30/64	Springfield

GOALTENDERS	HT	WT	Place of Birth	Date	1988-89 Club
FITZPATRICK, Mark	6-2	190	Toronto, Ont.	11/13/68	L.A.-New Haven-NYI
HACKETT, Jeff	6-1	175	London, Ont.	6/1/68	NYI-Springfield
HEALY, Glenn	5-9	183	Pickering, Ont.	8/23/62	Los Angeles
LORENZ, Danny	5-10	167	Murrayeville, B.C.	12/12/69	Springfield-Seattle
MANELUK, George	5-11	185	Winnipeg, Man.	7/25/67	Springfield

1988-89 Scoring

Regular Season

*–Rookie

Pos	#	Player	Team	GP	G	A	Pts	+/-	PIM	PP	SH	GW	GT	S	%
F	16	Pat LaFontaine	NYI	79	45	43	88	8 −	26	16	0	4	0	288	15.6
F	21	Brent Sutter	NYI	77	29	34	63	12 −	77	17	2	2	0	187	15.5
F	25	*Dave Volek	NYI	77	25	34	59	11 −	24	9	0	7	0	229	10.9
F	19	Bryan Trottier	NYI	73	17	28	45	7 −	44	5	0	3	0	163	10.4
F	24	Mikko Makela	NYI	76	17	28	45	16 −	22	4	0	0	0	126	13.8
F	27	Derek King	NYI	60	14	29	43	10	14	4	0	0	0	103	13.6
F	10	Alan Kerr	NYI	71	20	18	38	5 −	144	6	0	4	0	147	13.6
D	4	Gerald Diduck	NYI	65	11	21	32	9	155	6	0	0	0	132	8.3
D	8	*Jeff Norton	NYI	69	1	30	31	24 −	74	1	0	0	0	126	.8
F	11	Randy Wood	NYI	77	15	13	28	18 −	44	0	0	1	0	115	13.0
F	26	Patrick Flatley	NYI	41	10	15	25	5 −	31	2	1	1	0	72	13.9
F	17	Brad Dalgarno	NYI	55	11	10	21	8 −	86	2	0	1	0	83	13.3
D	36	Gary Nylund	CHI	23	3	2	5	−	63	0	0	0	0	26	11.5
			NYI	46	4	8	12	15 −	74	0	0	0	0	48	8.3
			TOTAL	69	7	10	17	19 −	137	0	0	0	0	74	9.5
D	39	Marc Bergevin	CHI	11	0	0	0	3 −	18	0	0	0	0	9	.0
			NYI	58	2	13	15	2	62	1	0	0	0	56	3.6
			TOTAL	69	2	13	15	1 −	80	1	0	0	0	65	3.1
D	47	*Richard Pilon	NYI	62	0	14	14	9 −	242	0	0	0	0	47	.0
F	40	Raimo Helminen	NYI	24	1	11	12	15 −	4	1	0	0	0	22	4.5
F	59	*Tom Fitzgerald	NYI	23	3	5	8	1	10	0	0	1	0	24	12.5
F	12	Rich Kromm	NYI	20	1	6	7	3 −	4	0	0	0	0	12	8.3
D	28	Wayne McBean	L.A.	33	0	5	5	9 −	23	0	0	0	0	19	.0
			NYI	19	0	1	1	4 −	12	0	0	0	0	17	.0
			TOTAL	52	0	6	6	13 −	35	0	0	0	0	36	.0
F	32	Brad Lauer	NYI	14	3	2	5	2 −	2	0	0	0	0	21	14.3
F	20	Dale Henry	NYI	22	2	2	4	4 −	66	0	0	0	0	20	10.0
F	38	*Mick Vukota	NYI	48	2	2	4	17 −	237	0	0	0	0	19	10.5
D	6	Ken Morrow	NYI	34	1	3	4	7 −	32	0	0	0	0	27	3.7
D	58	*Bill Berg	NYI	7	1	2	3	2 −	10	1	0	0	0	10	10.0
F	53	*Mike Walsh	NYI	13	2	0	2	7 −	4	0	0	1	0	11	18.2
G	29	*Mark Fitzpatrick	L.A.	17	0	1	1	0	0	0	0	0	0	0	.0
			NYI	11	0	1	1	0	2	0	0	0	0	0	.0
			TOTAL	28	0	2	2	0	4	0	0	0	0	0	.0
F	55	Mike Stevens	NYI	9	1	0	1	1 −	14	0	0	0	0	9	11.1
F	34	Rob Dimaio	NYI	16	1	0	1	6 −	30	0	0	1	0	16	6.3
G	1	*Jeff Hackett	NYI	13	0	1	1	0	0	0	0	0	0	0	.0
F	44	*Rod Dallman	NYI	1	0	0	0	0	15	0	0	0	0	1	.0
D	37	*Jeff Finley	NYI	4	0	0	0	1 −	6	0	0	0	0	1	.0
D	2	*Dean Chynoweth	NYI	6	0	0	0	4 −	48	0	0	0	0	0	.0
D	35	Chris Pryor	NYI	7	0	0	0	6 −	25	0	0	0	0	2	.0
G	31	Billy Smith	NYI	17	0	0	0	0	8	0	0	0	0	0	.0

Goaltending

No.	Goaltender	GPI	Mins	Avg	W	L	T	EN	SO	GA	SA	S%
1	*Jeff Hackett	13	662	3.53	4	7	0	0	0	39	329	.881
29	*Mark Fitzpatrick	11	627	3.92	3	5	2	0	0	41	313	.869
30	Kelly Hrudey	50	2800	3.92	18	24	3	6	0	183	1457	.874
31	Billy Smith	17	730	4.44	3	11	0	2	0	54	364	.851
	Totals	**80**	**4832**	**4.04**	**28**	**47**	**5**	**8**	**0**	**325**	**2463**	**.868**

General Manager's History

William A. Torrey, 1972-73 to date.

Coaching History

Phil Goyette and Earl Ingarfield, 1972-73; Al Arbour, 1973-74 to 1985-86; Terry Simpson, 1986-87 to 1987-88; Terry Simpson and Al Arbour, 1988-89; Al Arbour, 1989-90.

Captains' History

Ed Westfall, 1972-73 to 1975-76; Ed Westfall, Clark Gillies, 1976-77; Clark Gillies, 1977-78, 1978-79; Denis Potvin, 1979-80 to 1986-87; Brent Sutter, 1987-88 to date.

Right winger Brad Dalgarno

Club Records

Team

(Figures in brackets for season records are games played; records for fewest points, wins, ties, losses, goals, goals against are for 70 or more games)

Most Points 118 1981-82 (80)
Most Wins 54 1981-82 (80)
Most Ties 22 1974-75 (80)
Most Losses 60 1972-73 (78)
Most Goals 385 1981-82 (80)
Most Goals Against 347 1972-73 (78)
Fewest Points 30 1972-73 (78)
Fewest Wins 12 1972-73 (78)
Fewest Ties 4 1983-84 (80)
Fewest Losses 15 1978-79 (80)
Fewest Goals 170 1972-73 (78)
Fewest Goals Against 190 1975-76 (80)
Longest Winning Streak
Over-all . . . . *15 Jan. 21/82-
Feb. 21/82
Jan. 12-26/80
Home . . . . .14 Jan. 2/82-
Feb. 27/82
Away . . . . 8 Feb. 27/81
Mar. 31/81
Longest Undefeated Streak
Over-all . . . . .15 Jan. 21-
Feb. 21/82
(15 wins)
Nov. 4-
Dec. 4/80
(13 wins, 2 ties)
Home . . . . .23 Oct. 17/78-
Jan. 27/79
(19 wins, 4 ties)
Jan. 2/82-
Apr. 3/82
(21 wins, 2 ties)
Away . . . . 8 Four times
Longest Losing Streak
Over-all . . . . .12 Dec. 27/72-
Jan. 18/73

Home . . . . 5 Jan. 2-23/73
Feb. 28-
Mar. 19/74
Away . . . . .15 Jan. 20-
Apr. 1/73
Longest Winless Streak
Over-all . . . . .15 Nov. 22-
Dec. 23/72
(12 losses, 3 ties)
Home . . . . 7 Oct. 14-
Nov. 21/72
(6 losses, 1 tie)
Nov. 28-
Dec. 23/72
(5 losses, 2 ties)
Away . . . . .20 Nov. 3/72-
Jan. 13/73
(19 losses, 1 tie)
Most Shutouts, Season 10 1975-76 (80)
Most Pen. Mins., Season . 1,857 1986-87 (80)
Most Goals, Game . . . . . . .11 Dec. 20/83
(NYI 11 at Pit. 3)
Mar. 3/84
(Tor. 6 at NYI 11)

Individual

Most Seasons . . . . .17 Billy Smith
Most Games . . . . 1,064 Bryan Trottier
Most Goals, Career . . . . .573 Mike Bossy
Most Assists, Career . . . .842 Bryan Trottier
Most Points, Career . . . 1,329 Bryan Trottier
(487 goals, 842 assists)
Most Pen. Mins., Career . 1,466 Garry Howatt
Most Shutouts, Career . . . . .25 Glenn Resch
Longest Consecutive
Games Streak . . . . . . .576 Bill Harris
(Oct. 7/72-Nov. 30/79)
Most Goals, Season . . . . . .69 Mike Bossy
(1978-79)

Most Assists, Season . . . . .87 Bryan Trottier
(1978-79)
Most Points, Season . . . .147 Mike Bossy
(1981-82)
(64 goals, 83 assists)
Most Pen. Mins., Season . . .356 Brian Curran
(1986-87)
Most Points, Defenseman,
Season . . . . .101 Denis Potvin
(1978-79)
(31 goals, 70 assists)
Most Points, Center,
Season . . . . .134 Bryan Trottier
(1978-79)
(47 goals, 87 assists)
Most Points, Right Wing,
Season . . . . *147 Mike Bossy
(1981-82)
(64 goals, 83 assists)
Most Points, Left Wing,
Season . . . . .100 John Tonelli
(1984-85)
(42 goals, 58 assists)
Most Points, Rookie,
Season . . . . .95 Bryan Trottier
(1975-76)
(32 goals, 63 assists)
Most Shutouts, Season . . . . .7 Glenn Resch
(1975-76)
Most Goals, Game . . . . .5 Bryan Trottier
(Dec. 23/78)
Bryan Trottier
(Feb. 13/82)
Most Assists, Game . . . . . . .6 Mike Bossy
(Jan. 6/81)
Most Points, Game . . . . . . .8 Bryan Trottier
(Dec. 23/78)

* NHL Record.

All-time Record vs. Other Clubs

Regular Season

	At Home						On Road						Total						
	GP	W	L	T	GF	GA	PTS	GP	W	L	T	GF	GA	PTS	GP	W	L	T	GF	GA	PTS
Boston	32	13	17	2	100	108	28	32	7	17	8	93	124	22	64	20	34	10	193	232	50
Buffalo	33	12	16	5	97	103	29	32	10	18	4	90	114	24	65	22	34	9	187	217	53
**Calgary	37	20	8	9	149	98	49	37	10	16	11	117	135	31	74	30	24	20	266	233	80
Chicago	33	16	6	11	128	96	43	34	14	16	4	123	111	32	67	30	22	15	251	207	75
Detroit	31	19	12	0	128	88	38	31	14	15	2	106	111	30	62	33	27	2	234	199	68
Edmonton	16	8	2	6	76	65	22	16	5	9	2	52	64	12	32	13	11	8	128	129	34
Hartford	16	10	5	1	69	43	21	16	7	6	3	61	54	17	32	17	11	4	130	97	38
Los Angeles	31	18	9	4	119	87	40	31	12	12	7	105	106	31	62	30	21	11	224	193	71
Minnesota	33	18	7	8	136	94	44	33	17	11	5	124	91	39	66	35	18	13	260	185	83
Montreal	32	16	13	3	112	90	35	31	7	18	6	93	118	20	63	23	31	9	205	214	55
*New Jersey	42	37	1	4	216	101	78	43	24	13	6	187	141	54	85	61	14	10	403	242	132
NY Rangers	53	35	15	3	234	167	73	55	16	35	4	168	220	36	108	51	50	7	402	387	109
Philadelphia	53	27	17	9	212	158	63	54	17	31	6	162	198	40	107	44	48	15	374	356	103
Pittsburgh	48	30	11	7	208	142	67	47	17	20	10	159	169	44	95	47	31	17	367	311	111
Quebec	16	10	5	1	72	57	21	16	7	8	1	53	63	15	32	17	13	2	125	120	36
St. Louis	34	21	4	9	139	72	51	33	16	11	6	116	112	38	67	37	15	15	255	184	89
Toronto	32	19	11	2	143	101	40	33	15	15	3	121	116	33	65	34	26	5	264	217	73
Vancouver	33	20	5	8	136	88	48	34	17	15	2	111	109	36	67	37	20	10	247	197	84
Washington	43	32	10	1	195	123	65	42	20	15	7	148	128	47	85	52	25	8	343	251	112
Winnipeg	16	8	3	5	66	51	21	16	10	5	1	63	47	21	32	18	8	6	129	98	42
Defunct Clubs	14	11	1	2	75	33	24	12	4	4	4	35	41	12	26	15	5	6	110	74	36
Totals	678	400	178	100	2810	1971	900	678	266	310	102	2287	2372	634	1356	666	488	202	5097	4343	1534

* Totals include those of Kansas City (1974-75, 1975-76) and Colorado (1976-77 through 1981-82)
** Totals include those of Atlanta (1972-73 through 1979-80)

Playoffs

	Series	W	L	GP	W	L	T	GF	GA	Last Mtg.	Round	Result
Boston	2	2	0	11	8	3	0	49	35	1983	CF	W 4-2
Buffalo	3	3	0	16	12	4	0	59	45	1980	SF	W 4-2
Chicago	2	2	0	6	6	0	0	21	6	1979	QF	W 4-0
Edmonton	3	2	1	15	9	6	0	58	47	1984	F	L 1-4
Los Angeles	1	1	0	4	3	1	0	21	10	1980	P	W 3-1
Minnesota	1	1	0	5	4	1	0	26	16	1981	F	W 4-1
Montreal	3	1	2	17	7	10	0	44	48	1984	CF	W 4-2
New Jersey	1	0	1	6	2	4	0	18	23	1988	DSF	L 2-4
NY Rangers	6	5	1	30	19	11	0	113	88	1984	DSF	W 3-2
Philadelphia	4	1	3	25	11	14	0	69	83	1987	DF	L 3-4
Pittsburgh	2	2	0	12	7	5	0	43	31	1982	DSF	W 3-2
Quebec	1	1	0	4	4	0	0	18	9	1982	CF	W 4-0
Toronto	2	1	1	10	6	4	0	23	20	1981	P	W 3-0
Vancouver	2	2	0	6	6	0	0	26	14	1982	F	W 4-0
Washington	5	4	1	24	14	10	0	76	65	1987	DSF	W 4-3
Totals	38	28	10	191	118	73	0	674	541			

Playoff Results 1989-85

Year	Round	Opponent	Result	GF	GA
1988	DSF	New Jersey	L 2-4	18	23
1987	DF	Philadelphia	L 3-4	16	23
	DSF	Washington	W 4-3	19	18
1986	DSF	Washington	L 0-3	4	11
1985	DF	Philadelphia	L 1-4	11	16
	DSF	Washington	W 3-2	14	12

Abbreviations: Round: F – Final; **CF** – conference final; **DF** – division final; **DSF** – division semi-final; **SF** – semi-final; **QF** – quarter-final. **P** – preliminary round. **GA** – goals against; **GF** – goals for.

1988-89 Results

		Home				Away	
Oct.	15	Montreal	2-1	Oct.	6	Calgary	4-4
	18	Vancouver	3-2		7	Edmonton	1-5
	22	Quebec	7-3		9	Los Angeles	5-6
	25	Toronto	3-4		10	Vancouver	3-2
Nov.	1	Winnipeg	1-8		27	Philadelphia	2-5
	5	Washington	4-3		29	Quebec	2-3
	8	NY Rangers	4-3	Nov.	4	Washington	2-4
	12	Buffalo	0-3		11	New Jersey	3-3
	15	Calgary	1-5		16	Montreal	4-5
	19	Pittsburgh	6-3		23	Washington	6-7
	22	Washington	2-4		27	NY Rangers	3-5
	26	NY Rangers	4-6		29	Detroit	3-5
Dec.	6	Boston	3-4	Dec.	1	St Louis	0-8
	10	Los Angeles	3-4		3	Pittsburgh	2-4
	15	Pittsburgh	2-8		9	New Jersey	3-5
	17	New Jersey	5-2		14	NY Rangers	1-2
	22	Philadelphia	2-4		20	Pittsburgh	3-5
	31	Washington	6-4		26	Toronto	4-3
Jan.	3	Philadelphia	1-4	Jan.	5	Boston	5-3
	7	NY Rangers	1-5		8	Chicago	2-3
	14	Chicago	3-5		10	Pittsburgh	3-5
	17	Pittsburgh	5-2		13	New Jersey	5-3
	19	Los Angeles	4-2		28	Philadelphia*	4-7
	21	Minnesota	8-6		30	NY Rangers	3-7
	24	New Jersey	2-2	Feb.	5	Quebec	3-2
	26	Winnipeg	8-6		10	Chicago	1-3
Feb.	2	Toronto	1-4		11	St Louis	0-5
	4	Hartford	5-3		19	Philadelphia*	4-5
	14	Edmonton	5-3		22	Buffalo	5-7
	16	St Louis	7-3	Mar.	1	Detroit	5-6
	18	Philadelphia	3-2		4	Minnesota*	3-4
	21	Detroit	5-6		5	Winnipeg*	4-3
	25	Pittsburgh	5-5		13	Montreal	5-3
	28	Hartford	1-3		14	Hartford	2-8
Mar.	7	Boston	1-2		18	Vancouver	1-2
	9	Philadelphia	4-4		19	Edmonton	2-3
	11	New Jersey	3-2		21	Calgary	1-4
	23	Minnesota	3-1		26	Washington*	2-3
	28	Washington	5-4		29	New Jersey	5-4
Apr.	1	Buffalo	3-4	Apr.	2	NY Rangers	6-4

* Denotes afternoon game.

Entry Draft
Selections 1989-75

1989
Pick
2	Dave Chyzowski
23	Travis Green
44	Jason Zent
65	Brent Grieve
86	Jace Reed
90	Steve Young
99	Kevin O'Sullivan
128	Jon Larson
133	Brett Harkins
149	Phil Huber
170	Matthew Robbins
191	Vladimir Malakhov
212	Kelly Ens
233	Iain Fraser

1988
Pick
16	Kevin Cheveldayoff
29	Wayne Doucet
37	Sean Le Brun
58	Danny Lorenz
79	Andre Brassard
100	Paul Rutherford
111	Pavel Gross
121	Jason Rathbone
142	Yves Gaucher
163	Marty McInnis
184	Jeff Blumer
205	Jeff Kampersal
226	Phillip Neururer
247	Joe Capprini

1987
Pick
13	Dean Chynoweth
34	Jeff Hackett
55	Dean Ewen
76	George Maneluk
97	Petr Vlk
118	Rob Dimaio
139	Knut Walbye
160	Jeff Saterdalen
181	Shawn Howard
202	John Herlihy
223	Michael Erickson
244	Will Averill

1986
Pick
17	Tom Fitzgerald
38	Dennis Vaske
59	Bill Berg
80	Shawn Byram
101	Dean Sexsmith
104	Todd McLellan
122	Tony Schmalzbauer
138	Will Anderson
143	Richard Pilon
164	Peter Harris
185	Jeff Jablonski
206	Kerry Clark
227	Dan Beaudette
248	Paul Thompson

1985
Pick
6	Brad Dalgarno
13	Derek King
34	Brad Lauer
55	Jeff Finley
76	Kevin Herom
89	Tommy Hedlund
97	Jeff Sveen
118	Rod Dallman
139	Kurt Lackten
160	Hank Lammens
181	Rich Wiest
202	Real Arsenault
223	Mike Volpe
244	Tony Grenier

1984
Pick
20	Duncan MacPherson
41	Bruce Melanson
62	Jeff Norton
70	Doug Wieck
83	Ari Eerik Haanpaa
104	Mike Murray
125	Jim Wilharm
146	Kelly Murphy
167	Franco Desantis
187	Tom Warden
208	David Volek
228	Russ Becker
249	Allister Brown

1983
Pick
3	Pat LaFontaine
16	Gerald Diduck
37	Garnet McKechney
57	Mike Neill
65	Mikko Makela
84	Bob Caulfield
97	Ron Viglasi
117	Darin Illikainen
137	Jim Sprenger
157	Dale Henry
177	Kevin Vescio
197	Dave Shellington
217	John Bjorkman
237	Peter McGeough

1982
Pick
21	Patrick Flatley
42	Vern Smith
63	Garry Lacey
84	Alan Kerr
105	Rene Breton
126	Roger Kortko
147	John Tiano
168	Todd Okerlund
189	Gord Paddock
210	Eric Faust
231	Pat Goff
252	Jim Koudys

1981
Pick
21	Paul Boutilier
42	Gord Dineen
57	Ron Handy
63	Neal Coulter
84	Todd Lumbard
94	Jacques Sylvestre
126	Chuck Brimmer
147	Teppo Virta
168	Bill Dowd
189	Scott MacLellan
210	Dave Randerson

1980
Pick
17	Brent Sutter
38	Kelly Hrudey
59	Dave Simpson
68	Monty Trottier
80	Greg Gilbert
101	Ken Leiter
122	Dan Revell
143	Mark Hamway
164	Morrison Gare
185	Peter Steblyk
206	Glen Johannesen

1979
Pick
17	Duane Sutter
25	Tomas Jonsson
38	Bill Carroll
59	Roland Melanson
80	Tom Lockridge
101	Glen Duncan
122	John Gibb

1978
Pick
15	Steve Tambellini
34	Randy Johnston
51	Dwayne Lowdermilk
84	Greg Hay
101	Kelly Davis
118	Richard Pepin
135	David Cameron
152	Paul Joswiak
169	Scott Cameron
184	Chris Lowdall
199	Gunnar Persson

1977
Pick
15	Mike Bossy
33	John Tonelli
50	Hector Marini
51	Bruce Andres
69	Steve Stoyanovich
87	Markus Mattsson
105	Steve Letzgus
121	Harold Luckner

1976
Pick
14	Alex McKendry
32	Mike Kaszycki
50	Garth McGuigan
68	Ken Morrow
86	Mike Hordy
104	Yvon Vautour

1975
Pick
11	Pat Price
29	David Salvian
47	Joe Fortunato
65	Andre Lepage
83	Denis McLean
101	Mike Sleep
119	Richie Hansen
137	Bob Sunderland
153	Dan Blair
168	Joey Girardin
183	Geoff Green
194	Kari Makkonen

Club Directory

**Nassau Veterans'
Memorial Coliseum**
Uniondale, N.Y. 11553
Phone 516/794-4100
GM FAX 516/794-4346
FAX 516/794-8083
TWX 510-222-5575 (PR)
510-600-6914 (EXEC)
ENVOY ID
  Front Office: ISLANDERS. GM
  Public
  Relations: ISLANDERS. PR
Capacity: 16,297

Owner	John O. Pickett, Jr.
Chairman of the Board and General Manager	William A. Torrey
President	John H. Krumpe
General Counsel	William M. Skehan
Vice-President/Administration	Joseph H. Dreyer
Vice-President/Finance	Aurthur J. McCarthy
Vice-President/Media Sales	Arthur Adler
Head Coach	Al Arbour
Assistant Coach	Lorne Henning
Asst. Coach/Dir. of Hockey Administration	Darcy Regier
Assistant General Manager/Director of Scouting	Gerry Ehman
Scouting Staff	Harry Boyd, Richard Green, Earl Ingarfield, Hal Laycoe, Bert Marshall, Mario Saraceno, Jack Vivian
Publicity Director	Greg Bouris
Assistant Publicity Director	Catherine Schutte
Publicity Assistant	Steven Blinn
Communications Consultant	Barney Kremenko
Editor, Islander News	Chris Botta
Controller	Ralph Sellitti
Director of Public Affairs	Jill Knee
Director of Sales	Jim Johnson
Director of Special Projects	Bob Nystrom
Administrative Assistants	
Owner	Rosemarie LaNasa, Carol Ann Kelly
Chairman of the Board and General Manager	Joanne Holewa, Jill Murphy
Athletic Trainer	Mark Aldridge
Assistant Trainers	Terry Murphy, Jim Pickard
Team Orthopedists	Jeffrey Minkoff, M.D., Barry Fisher, M.D.
Team Internist	George J. Gilbert, Jr., M.D.
Team Dentist	Bruce Michnick, D.D.S., Jan Sherman, D.D.S.
Team Photographer	Bruce Bennett
Location of Press Box	East Side of Building
Dimensions of Rink	200 feet by 85 feet
Ends of Rink	Herculite extends above boards around rink
Club Colors	Blue, Orange and White
Training Camp Site/Practice Facility	Cantiague Park, Hicksville, NY
Television Announcers	Jiggs McDonald, Ed Westfall, Stan Fischler
Television Station	SportsChannel
Radio Station	WEVD (1050 AM), WBAB (1240 AM)

General Manager
TORREY, WILLIAM ARTHUR (BILL)
President and General Manager, New York Islanders.
Born in Montreal, Que., June 23, 1934.

Although he never played professionally, Bill Torrey has been a valuable addition to professional hockey and was named winner of the 1983 Lester Patrick Trophy for his contribution to hockey in the United States. He attended St. Lawrence University in Canton, N.Y. where he played for the varsity team and graduated in 1957 with a Bachelor of Science degree. He joined the Pittsburgh Hornets of the American Hockey League in 1960 and served with that club until 1965, first as Director of Public Relations and later as Business Manager. In September 1968, Torrey moved to the California Seals of the NHL as Executive Vice-President and during his tenure, the Seals went from last place in the West Division to playoff berths the following two seasons. On February 15, 1972, he was appointed General Manager of the New York Islanders and has moulded the franchise into one of the greatest in the history of professional sports. His most satisfying season was 1979-80 when the Islanders won their first of four consecutive Stanley Cup titles.

Coach
ARBOUR, AL
Coach, New York Islanders. Born in Sudbury, Ont., November 1, 1932.

Al Arbour was named Head Coach of the Islanders on June 26, 1989 after serving as the Vice-President in charge of player development for three years. Arbour returned to the Islander bench on December 7, 1988 after Terry Simpson was relieved of his duties. Arbour coached 53 games, leading his squad to a 21-29-3 record in that span.

Arbour, 56, began his coaching career with the St. Louis Blues in 1970 and coached parts of three seasons there before joining the Islanders at the start of the 1973-74 season. Arbour has coached 1,198 regular-season games and has a career record of 615-386-197 with a winning percentage of .596. In the playoffs, Arbour has coached 182 games, posting a record of 113-69 with a .621 winning percentage. Arbour enters the 1989-90 season ranking third on the NHL's all-time regular season wins list and is only one win behind Scotty Bowman on the NHL's all-time playoff win list.

Coaching Record

			Regular Season					Playoffs			
Season	Team	Games	W	L	T	%		Games	W	L	%
1970-71	St. Louis (NHL)	50	21	15	14	.560		....	....	....	....
1971-72	St. Louis (NHL)	44	19	19	6	.500		11	4	7	.364
1972-73	St. Louis (NHL)	13	2	6	5	.346		....	....	....	....
1973-74	NY Islanders (NHL)	78	19	41	18	.358		....	....	....	....
1974-75	NY Islanders (NHL)	80	33	25	22	.550		....	....	....	....
1975-76	NY Islanders (NHL)	80	42	21	17	.631		13	7	6	.538
1976-77	NY Islanders (NHL)	80	47	21	12	.663		12	8	4	.666
1977-78	NY Islanders (NHL)	80	48	17	15	.694		7	3	4	.429
1978-79	NY Islanders (NHL)	80	51	15	14	.725		10	6	4	.600
1979-80	NY Islanders (NHL)	80	39	28	13	.589		21	15	6	.714*
1980-81	NY Islanders (NHL)	80	48	18	14	.600		18	15	3	.833*
1981-82	NY Islanders (NHL)	80	54	16	10	.738		19	15	4	.789*
1982-83	NY Islanders (NHL)	80	42	26	12	.600		20	15	5	.750*
1983-84	NY Islanders (NHL)	80	50	26	4	.650		21	12	9	.571
1984-85	NY Islanders (NHL)	80	40	34	6	.538		10	4	6	.400
1985-86	NY Islanders (NHL)	80	39	29	12	.563		3	0	3	.000
1988-89	NY Islanders (NHL)	53	21	29	3	.425		....	....	....	....
	NHL Totals	1189	615	386	197	.596		182	113	69	.621

* Stanley Cup win

New York Rangers

1988-89 Results: 37W-35L-8T 82 PTS. Third, Patrick Division

Brian Leetch set a team record for points by a rookie defenseman with 71.

Schedule

Home		Away	
Oct. Wed. 11 Calgary		**Oct.** Fri. 6 Winnipeg	
Sun. 15 Pittsburgh		Sun. 8 Chicago	
Tues. 17 Chicago		Fri. 13 Washington	
Thur. 19 Hartford		Sat. 21 Philadelphia	
Mon. 23 Vancouver		Sat. 28 NY Islanders	
Wed. 25 Edmonton		**Nov.** Sat. 4 Montreal	
Fri. 27 NY Islanders		Tues. 14 Pittsburgh	
Mon. 30 Philadelphia		Fri. 17 New Jersey	
Nov. Thur. 2 Quebec		Sat. 18 Hartford	
Mon. 6 Detroit		Wed. 22 Buffalo	
Wed. 8 Montreal		Sat. 25 Toronto	
Sun. 12 NY Islanders		Wed. 29 Winnipeg	
Mon. 20 Winnipeg		**Dec.** Fri. 1 Vancouver	
Sun. 26 Quebec		Sat. 2 Los Angeles	
Dec. Wed. 6 New Jersey		Sat. 9 NY Islanders	
Sun. 10 Philadelphia		Sat. 16 NY Islanders	
Wed. 13 St Louis		Sat. 23 Washington	
Sun. 17 Montreal		Wed. 27 Pittsburgh	
Wed. 20 Buffalo		Fri. 29 New Jersey	
Tues. 26 New Jersey		**Jan.** Thur. 4 Minnesota	
Sun. 31 Pittsburgh*		Sat. 6 St Louis	
Jan. Wed. 3 Washington		Sat. 13 Boston*	
Mon. 8 Pittsburgh		Thur. 18 Pittsburgh	
Wed. 10 Chicago		Tues. 23 Edmonton	
Sun. 14 Philadelphia		Thur. 25 Calgary	
Wed. 31 St Louis		Sat. 27 Los Angeles	
Feb. Sun. 5 Minnesota*		**Feb.** Sat. 3 Boston*	
Wed. 7 Edmonton		Fri. 9 Buffalo	
Sun. 11 Calgary*		Tues. 13 Philadelphia	
Wed. 14 Pittsburgh		Fri. 16 New Jersey	
Mon. 19 New Jersey*		Wed. 21 Detroit	
Mon. 26 Boston		Fri. 23 Washington	
Wed. 28 Washington		**Mar.** Sat. 3 Hartford	
Mar. Fri. 2 NY Islanders		Thur. 8 Philadelphia	
Mon. 5 Detroit		Sat. 10 Minnesota*	
Mon. 12 Los Angeles		Wed. 14 Toronto	
Sun. 18 Vancouver		Sat. 17 NY Islanders*	
Wed. 21 Toronto		Tues. 27 Quebec	
Sun. 25 Philadelphia*		Thur. 29 New Jersey	
Apr. Sun. 1 Washington		Sat. 31 Washington	

* Denotes afternoon game.

Home Starting Times:
All Games . . . . 7:35 p.m.
Matinees . . . . 1:35 p.m.

Franchise date: May 15, 1926

64th NHL Season

Year-by-Year Record

		Home			Road			Overall							
Season	GP	W	L	T	W	L	T	W	L	T	GF	GA	Pts.	Finished	Playoff Result
1988-89	80	21	17	2	16	18	6	37	35	8	82	310	307	3rd, Patrick Div.	Lost Div. Semi-Final
1987-88	80	22	13	5	14	21	5	36	34	10	300	283	82	5th, Patrick Div.	Out of Playoffs
1986-87	80	18	18	4	16	20	4	34	38	8	307	323	76	4th, Patrick Div.	Lost Div. Semi-Final
1985-86	80	20	18	2	16	20	4	36	38	6	280	276	78	4th, Patrick Div.	Lost Conf. Championship
1984-85	80	16	18	6	10	26	4	26	44	10	295	345	62	4th, Patrick Div.	Lost Div. Semi-Final
1983-84	80	27	12	1	15	17	8	42	29	9	314	304	93	4th, Patrick Div.	Lost Div. Semi-Final
1982-83	80	24	13	3	11	22	7	35	35	10	306	287	80	4th, Patrick Div.	Lost Div. Final
1981-82	80	19	15	6	20	12	8	39	27	14	316	306	92	2nd, Patrick Div.	Lost Div. Final
1980-81	80	17	13	10	13	23	4	30	36	14	312	317	74	4th, Patrick Div.	Lost Semi-Final
1979-80	80	22	10	8	16	22	2	38	32	10	308	284	86	3rd, Patrick Div.	Lost Quarter-Final
1978-79	80	19	13	8	21	16	3	40	29	11	316	292	91	3rd, Patrick Div.	Lost Final
1977-78	80	18	15	7	12	22	6	30	37	13	279	280	73	4th, Patrick Div.	Lost Prelim. Round
1976-77	80	17	18	5	12	19	9	29	37	14	272	310	72	4th, Patrick Div.	Out of Playoffs
1975-76	80	16	16	8	13	26	1	29	42	9	262	333	67	4th, Patrick Div.	Out of Playoffs
1974-75	80	21	11	8	16	18	6	37	29	14	319	276	88	2nd, Patrick Div.	Lost Prelim. Round
1973-74	78	26	7	6	14	17	8	40	24	14	300	251	94	3rd, East Div.	Lost Semi-Final
1972-73	78	26	8	5	21	15	3	47	23	8	297	208	102	3rd, East Div.	Lost Semi-Final
1971-72	78	26	7	6	22	11	6	48	17	13	317	192	109	2nd, East Div.	Lost Final
1970-71	78	30	2	7	19	16	4	49	18	11	259	177	109	2nd, East Div.	Lost Semi-Final
1969-70	76	22	8	8	16	14	8	38	22	16	246	189	92	4th, East Div.	Lost Quarter-Final
1968-69	76	27	7	4	14	19	5	41	26	9	231	196	91	3rd, East Div.	Lost Quarter-Final
1967-68	74	22	8	7	17	15	5	39	23	12	226	183	90	2nd, East Div.	Lost Quarter-Final
1966-67	70	18	12	5	12	16	7	30	28	12	188	189	72	4th,	Lost Semi-Final
1965-66	70	12	16	7	6	25	4	18	41	11	195	261	47	6th,	Out of Playoffs
1964-65	70	8	19	8	12	19	4	20	38	12	179	246	52	5th,	Out of Playoffs
1963-64	70	14	13	8	8	25	2	22	38	10	186	242	54	5th,	Out of Playoffs
1962-63	70	12	17	6	10	19	6	22	36	12	211	233	56	5th,	Out of Playoffs
1961-62	70	16	11	8	10	21	4	26	32	12	195	207	64	4th,	Lost Semi-Final
1960-61	70	15	15	5	7	23	5	22	38	10	204	248	54	5th,	Out of Playoffs
1959-60	70	10	15	10	7	23	5	17	38	15	187	247	49	6th,	Out of Playoffs
1958-59	70	14	16	5	12	16	7	26	32	12	201	217	64	5th,	Out of Playoffs
1957-58	70	14	15	6	18	10	7	32	25	13	195	188	77	2nd,	Lost Semi-Final
1956-57	70	15	12	8	11	18	6	26	30	14	184	227	66	4th,	Lost Semi-Final
1955-56	70	20	7	8	12	21	2	32	28	10	204	203	74	3rd,	Lost Semi-Final
1954-55	70	10	12	13	7	23	5	17	35	18	150	210	52	5th,	Out of Playoffs
1953-54	70	18	12	5	11	19	5	29	31	10	161	182	68	5th,	Out of Playoffs
1952-53	70	11	14	10	6	23	6	17	37	16	152	211	50	6th,	Out of Playoffs
1951-52	70	16	13	6	7	21	7	23	34	13	192	219	59	5th,	Out of Playoffs
1950-51	70	14	11	10	6	18	11	20	29	21	169	201	61	5th,	Out of Playoffs
1949-50	70	19	12	4	9	19	7	28	31	11	170	189	67	4th,	Lost Final
1948-49	60	13	12	5	5	19	6	18	31	11	133	172	47	6th,	Out of Playoffs
1947-48	60	11	12	7	10	14	6	21	26	13	176	201	55	4th,	Lost Semi-Final
1946-47	60	11	14	5	11	18	1	22	32	6	167	186	50	5th,	Out of Playoffs
1945-46	50	8	12	5	5	16	4	13	28	9	144	191	35	6th,	Out of Playoffs
1944-45	50	7	11	7	4	18	3	11	29	10	154	247	32	6th,	Out of Playoffs
1943-44	50	4	17	4	2	22	1	6	39	5	162	310	17	6th,	Out of Playoffs
1942-43	50	7	13	5	4	18	3	11	31	8	161	253	30	6th,	Out of Playoffs
1941-42	48	15	8	1	14	9	1	29	17	2	177	143	60	1st,	Lost Semi-Final
1940-41	48	13	7	4	8	12	4	21	19	8	143	125	50	4th,	Lost Semi-Final
1939-40	48	17	4	3	10	7	7	**27**	**11**	**10**	**136**	**77**	**64**	**2nd,**	**Won Stanley Cup**
1938-39	48	13	8	3	13	8	3	26	16	6	149	105	58	2nd,	Lost Semi-Final
1937-38	48	15	5	4	12	10	2	27	15	6	149	96	60	2nd, Amn. Div.	Lost Quarter-Final
1936-37	48	9	7	8	10	13	1	19	20	9	117	106	47	3rd, Amn. Div.	Lost Final
1935-36	48	11	6	7	8	11	5	19	17	12	91	96	50	4th, Amn. Div.	Out of Playoffs
1934-35	48	11	8	5	11	12	1	22	20	6	137	139	50	3rd, Amn. Div.	Lost Semi-Final
1933-34	48	11	7	6	10	12	2	21	19	8	120	113	50	3rd, Amn. Div.	Lost Quarter-Final
1932-33	48	12	7	5	11	10	3	**23**	**17**	**8**	**135**	**107**	**54**	**3rd, Amn. Div.**	**Won Stanley Cup**
1931-32	38	13	7	4	10	10	4	23	17	8	134	112	54	1st, Amn. Div.	Lost Final
1930-31	44	10	9	3	9	7	6	19	16	9	106	87	47	3rd, Amn. Div.	Lost Semi-Final
1929-30	44	11	5	6	6	12	4	17	17	10	136	143	44	3rd, Amn. Div.	Lost Semi-Final
1928-29	44	12	6	4	9	7	6	21	13	10	72	65	52	2nd, Amn. Div.	Lost Final
1927-28	44	10	8	4	9	8	5	**19**	**16**	**9**	**94**	**79**	**47**	**2nd, Amn. Div.**	**Won Stanley Cup**
1926-27	44	13	5	4	12	8	2	25	13	6	95	72	56	1st, Amn. Div.	Lost Quarter-Final

1989-90 Player Personnel

FORWARDS	HT	WT	S	Place of Birth	Date	1988-89 Club
BERGERON, Martin	6-0	180	L	Verdun, Que.	1/20/68	Drumm'dville-Denver
BROTEN, Paul	5-11	175	R	Roseau, MN	10/27/65	Denver
CHYZOWSKI, Barry	6-0	170	R	Edmonton, Alta.	5/25/68	Denver
CYR, Paul	5-11	205	L	Port Alberni, B.C.	10/31/63	NY Rangers
DAHLEN, Ulf	6-2	196	L	Ostersund, Sweden	1/12/67	NY Rangers
DIONNE, Marcel	5-8	190	R	Drummondville, Que.	8/3/51	Denver-NY Rangers
ERIXON, Jan	6-0	196	L	Skelleftea, Sweden	7/8/62	NY Rangers
GAGNE, Simon	6-4	202	R	Montreal, Que.	9/29/68	Denver
GOLDEN, Mike	6-1	195	R	Boston, MA	6/14/65	Denver
GRAHAM, Robb	6-4	205	R	Bellevue, WA	4/7/68	Denver
GRANATO, Tony	5-10	175	R	Dowhers Grove, IL	7/25/64	NY Rangers
JANSSENS, Mark	6-3	195	L	Surrey, B.C.	5/19/68	NYR-Denver
KISIO, Kelly	5-9	180	R	Peace River, Alta.	9/18/59	NY Rangers
LACROIX, Daniel	6-2	185	L	Montreal, Que	3/11/69	Granby-Denver
LAFRENIERE, Jason	5-11	185	R	St. Catharines, Ont.	12/6/66	Denver-NY Rangers
LATOS, James	6-1	200	R	Wakaw, Sask.	1/4/66	NY Rangers-Denver
McRAE, Chris	6-0	180	L	Newmarket, Ont.	8/26/65	Toronto-N'mkt.-Denver
MILLEN, Corey	5-7	170	R	Cloquet, MN	4/29/64	Ambri (Switz.)
MILLER, Kevin	5-10	180	R	Lansing, MI	9/2/65	NY Rangers-Denver
MULLEN, Brian	5-10	180	L	New York, NY	3/16/62	NY Rangers
NILAN, Chris	6-0	205	R	Boston, MA	2/9/58	NY Rangers
OGRODNICK, John	6-0	206	L	Ottawa, Ont.	6/20/59	NY Rangers
PATERSON, Joe	6-2	207	L	Toronto, Ont.	6/25/60	Denver-New Hav'n- NYR
POESCHEK, Rudy	6-1	210	R	Kamloops, B.C.	9/29/66	Denver-NY Rangers
RUFF, Lindy	6-2	200	L	Warburg, Alta.	2/17/60	Buffalo-NY Rangers
SANDSTRÖM, Tomas	6-2	204	L	Jakobstad, Finland	9/4/64	NY Rangers
TURCOTTE, Darren	6-0	185	L	Boston, MA	3/2/68	Denver-NY Rangers
WALTER, Bret	6-1	195	R	Calgary, Alta.	4/28/69	Denver
WHEELDON, Simon	5-11	180	L	Nelson, B.C.	10/2/68	NY Rangers-Denver
WILSON, Carey	6-2	205	R	Winnipeg, Man.	5/19/62	Hartford-NY Rangers
DEFENSEMEN						
BLOEMBERG, Jeff	6-2	200	R	Listowel, Ont.	1/31/68	NY Rangers-Denver
BROCHU, Stephane	6-1	185	L	Sherbrooke, Que.	8/15/67	NY Rangers-Denver
FIORENTINO, Peter	6-1	200	R	Niagara Falls, Ont.	12/22/68	Sault Ste. Marie-Denver
GRESCHNER, Ron	6-2	208	L	Goodsoil, Sask.	12/22/54	NY Rangers
HARDY, Mark	5-11	195	L	Semaden, Switzerland	2/1/59	Minnesota-NY Rangers
HORAVA, Miloslav	6-0	190	L	Kladno, Czech.	8/18/61	Kladno (Czech.)-NYR
HURLBUT, Mike	6-2	195		Massena, NY	10/7/66	St. Lawrence-Denver
LAROCQUE, Denis	6-1	195	L	Hawkesbury, Ont.	10/5/67	New Haven-Denver
LAVIOLETTE, Peter	6-2	200	L	Franklin, MA	7/12/64	NY Rangers-Denver
LEETCH, Brian	5-11	185	L	Corpus Christi, TX	3/3/68	NY Rangers
MORE, Jayson	6-1	190	R	Souris, Man.	1/12/69	NY Rangers-Denver
PATRICK, James	6-2	192	R	Winnipeg, Man.	6/14/63	NY Rangers
PETIT, Michel	6-1	205	R	St. Malo, Que.	2/12/64	NY Rangers
ROCHEFORT, Normand	6-1	200	L	Trois-Rivieres, Que.	1/28/61	NY Rangers
SHAW, David	6-2	204	R	St. Thomas, Ont.	5/25/64	NY Rangers
SHUDRA, Ron	6-2	192	L	Winnipeg, Man.	11/28/67	Cape Breton-Denver

GOALTENDERS	HT	WT	C	Place of Birth	Date	1988-89 Club
BROWER, Scott	6-0	185	L	Viking, Alta.	9/26/64	Denver
FROESE, Bob	5-11	178	L	St. Catharines, Ont.	6/30/58	NY Rangers
RICHTER, Mike	5-10	185	L	Abington, PA	9/22/66	Denver
SCOTT, Ron	5-8	155	L	Guelph, Ont.	7/21/60	Denver
VANBIESBROUCK, J.	5-8	179	L	Detroit, MI	9/4/63	NY Rangers

Coaching History

Lester Patrick, 1926-27 to 1938-39; Frank Boucher, 1939-40 to 1947-48; Frank Boucher and Lynn Patrick, 1948-49; Lynn Patrick, 1949-50; Neil Colville, 1950-51; Neil Colville and Bill Cook, 1951-52; Bill Cook, 1952-53; Frank Boucher and Murray Patrick, 1953-54; Murray Patrick, 1954-55; Phil Watson, 1955-56 to 1958-59; Phil Watson and Alf Pike, 1959-60; Alf Pike, 1960-61; Doug Harvey, 1961-62; Murray Patrick and George Sullivan, 1962-63; George Sullivan, 1963-64 to 1964-65; George Sullivan and Emile Francis, 1965-66; Emile Francis, 1966-67 to 1967-68; Bernie Geoffrion and Emile Francis, 1968-69; Emile Francis, 1969-70 to 1972-73; Larry Popein and Emile Francis, 1973-74; Emile Francis, 1974-75; Ron Stewart and John Ferguson, 1975-76; John Ferguson, 1976-77; Jean-Guy Talbot, 1977-78; Fred Shero, 1978-79 to 1979-80; Fred Shero and Craig Patrick, 1980-81; Herb Brooks, 1981-82 to 1983-84; Herb Brooks and Craig Patrick, 1984-85; Ted Sator, 1985-86; Ted Sator, Tom Webster, Phil Esposito 1986-87; Michel Bergeron, 1987-88; Michel Bergeron and Phil Esposito, 1988-89; Roger Neilson, 1989-90.

Captains' History

Bill Cook, 1926-27 to 1936-37; Art Coulter, 1937-38 to 1941-42; Ott Heller, 1942-43 to 1944-45; Neil Colville 1945-46 to 1948-49; Buddy O'Connor, 1949-50; Frank Eddolls, 1950-51; Frank Eddolls, Allan Stanley, 1951-52; Allan Stanley, 1952-53; Allan Stanley, Don Raleigh, 1953-54; Don Raleigh, 1954-55; Harry Howell, 1955-56, 1956-57; George Sullivan, 1957-58 to 1960-61; Andy Bathgate, 1961-61, 1962-63; Andy Bathgate, Camille Henry, 1963-64; Camille Henry, Bob Nevin, 1964-65; Bob Nevin 1965-66 to 1970-71; Vic Hadfield, 1971-72 to 1973-74; Brad Park, 1974-75; Brad Park, Phil Esposito, 1975-76; Phil Esposito, 1976-77, 1977-78; Dave Maloney, 1978-79, 1979-80; Dave Maloney, Walt Tkaczuk, Barry Beck, 1980-81; Barry Beck, 1981-82 to 1985-86; Ron Greschner, 1986-87; Ron Greschner and Kelly Kisio, 1987-88; Kelly Kisio, 1988-89 to date.

1988-89 Scoring

Regular Season

*–rookie

Pos	#	Player	Team	GP	G	A	Pts	+/–	PIM	PP	SH	GW	GT	S	%
F	28	Tomas Sandstrom	NYR	79	32	56	88	5	148	11	2	4	0	240	13.3
F	17	Carey Wilson	NYR	34	11	11	22	12–	14	4	0	2	0	56	19.6
			NYR	41	21	34	55	1	45	10	0	3	0	108	19.4
			TOTAL	75	32	45	77	11–	59	14	0	5	0	164	19.5
D	2	*Brian Leetch	NYR	68	23	48	71	8	50	8	3	1	1	268	8.6
F	19	Brian Mullen	NYR	78	29	35	64	7	60	8	3	5	1	217	13.4
F	18	*Tony Granato	NYR	78	36	27	63	17	140	4	4	3	2	234	15.4
F	11	Kelly Kisio	NYR	70	26	36	62	14	91	2	0	4	0	128	20.3
D	3	James Patrick	NYR	68	11	36	47	3	41	6	0	2	1	147	7.5
F	10	Guy Lafleur	NYR	67	18	27	45	1	12	6	0	2	0	122	14.8
F	9	Ulf Dahlen	NYR	56	24	19	43	6–	50	8	0	1	1	147	16.3
F	25	John Ogrodnick	NYR	60	13	29	42	0	14	1	0	1	0	149	8.7
F	23	Lucien DeBlois	NYR	73	9	24	33	6–	107	0	0	2	0	117	7.7
D	24	Michel Petit	NYR	69	8	25	33	15–	154	5	0	1	0	132	6.1
F	15	Jason Lafreniere	NYR	38	8	16	24	3–	6	3	0	0	0	42	19.0
F	16	Marcel Dionne	NYR	37	7	16	23	6–	20	4	0	0	0	74	9.5
D	44	Lindy Ruff	BUF	63	6	11	17	17–	86	0	0	0	0	69	8.7
			NYR	13	0	5	5	6–	31	0	0	0	0	19	.0
			TOTAL	76	6	16	22	23–	117	0	0	0	0	88	6.8
D	14	Mark Hardy	MIN	15	2	4	6	1–	26	0	0	1	0	19	10.5
			NYR	45	2	12	14	8–	45	0	0	0	0	51	3.9
			TOTAL	60	4	16	20	9–	71	0	0	1	0	70	5.7
D	21	David Shaw	NYR	63	6	11	17	14	88	3	1	1	0	85	7.1
F	20	Jan Erixon	NYR	44	4	11	15	3–	27	0	0	2	0	41	9.8
F	30	Chris Nilan	NYR	38	7	7	14	8–	177	0	0	1	0	39	17.9
D	4	Ron Greschner	NYR	58	1	10	11	9	94	0	0	0	0	49	2.0
F	8	*Darren Turcotte	NYR	20	7	3	10	0	4	2	0	2	0	49	14.3
F	26	*Kevin Miller	NYR	24	3	5	8	1–	2	0	0	1	0	40	7.5
D	5	Normand Rochefort	NYR	11	1	5	6	0	18	0	0	1	0	14	7.1
D	29	*Rudy Poeschek	NYR	52	0	2	2	8–	199	0	0	0	0	17	.0
G	34	John Vanbiesbrouck	NYR	56	0	2	2	0	30	0	0	0	0	0	.0
D	6	*Miroslav Horava	NYR	6	0	1	1	2–	0	0	0	0	0	7	.0
F	41	Simon Wheeldon	NYR	6	0	1	1	1–	2	0	0	0	0	2	.0
F	27	Joe Paterson	NYR	20	0	1	1	3–	84	0	0	0	0	8	.0
G	33	Bob Froese	NYR	30	0	1	1	0	6	0	0	0	0	0	.0
D	32	*Stephane Brochu	NYR	1	0	0	0	1	0	0	0	0	0	1	.0
F	22	Paul Cyr	NYR	1	0	0	0	0	2	0	0	0	0	0	.0
F	44	*Jim Latos	NYR	1	0	0	0	1–	0	0	0	0	0	0	.0
D	40	*Jayson More	NYR	1	0	0	0	1–	0	0	0	0	0	0	.0
F	47	*Mark Janssens	NYR	5	0	0	0	4–	0	0	0	0	0	0	.0
D	38	*Jeff Aldenberg	NYR	9	0	0	0	2	0	0	0	0	0	9	.0
D	39	*Peter Laviolette	NYR	12	0	0	0	2	6	0	0	0	0	2	.0

Goaltending

No.	Goaltender	GPI	Mins	Avg	W	L	T	EN	SO	GA	SA	S%
34	John Vanbiesbrouck	56	3207	3.69	28	21	4	4	0	197	1666	.881
33	Bob Froese	30	1621	3.78	9	14	4	4	1	102	791	.870
	Totals	**80**	**4844**	**3.80**	**37**	**35**	**8**	**8**	**1**	**307**	**2457**	**.875**

Playoffs

Pos	#	Player	Team	GP	G	A	Pts	+/–	PIM	PP	SH	GW	GT	S	%
D	2	*Brian Leetch	NYR	4	3	2	5	4–	2	2	0	0	0	25	12.0
F	28	Thomas Sandstrom	NYR	4	3	2	5	3–	12	2	0	0	0	12	25.0
F	17	Carey Wilson	NYR	4	1	2	3	4–	2	0	0	0	0	12	8.3
F	25	John Ogrodnick	NYR	3	2	0	2	2–	0	1	0	0	0	9	22.2
F	18	*Tony Granato	NYR	4	1	1	2	1–	21	0	0	0	0	16	6.3
D	24	Michel Petit	NYR	4	0	2	2	4–	27	0	0	0	0	8	.0
D	21	David Shaw	NYR	4	0	2	2	3–	30	0	0	0	0	7	.0
F	10	Guy Lafleur	NYR	4	1	0	1	3–	0	1	0	0	0	10	10.0
G	33	Bob Froese	NYR	2	0	1	1	0	0	0	0	0	0	0	.0
F	19	Brian Mullen	NYR	3	0	1	1	2	4	0	0	0	0	4	.0
F	20	Jan Erixon	NYR	4	0	1	1	3–	2	0	0	0	0	3	.0
D	4	Ron Greschner	NYR	4	0	1	1	1–	6	0	0	0	0	11	.0
D	14	Mark Hardy	NYR	4	0	1	1	3–	31	0	0	0	0	7	.0
F	30	Chris Nilan	NYR	4	0	1	1	2–	28	0	0	0	0	8	.0
D	3	James Patrick	NYR	4	0	1	1	1–	2	0	0	0	0	6	.0
G	35	*Mike Richter	NYR	1	0	0	0	0	0	0	0	0	0	0	.0
F	8	*Darren Turcotte	NYR	1	0	0	0	1–	0	0	0	0	0	0	.0
D	44	Lindy Ruff	NYR	2	0	0	0	2–	17	0	0	0	0	1	.0
G	34	John Vanbiesbrouck	NYR	2	0	0	0	0	0	0	0	0	0	0	.0
F	15	Jason Lafreniere	NYR	3	0	0	0	3–	17	0	0	0	0	3	.0
F	9	Ulf Dahlen	NYR	4	0	0	0	3–	0	0	0	0	0	5	.0
F	23	Lucien DeBlois	NYR	4	0	0	0	1–	4	0	0	0	0	4	.0
F	11	Kelly Kisio	NYR	4	0	0	0	1–	9	0	0	0	0	7	.0

Goaltending

No.	Goaltender	GPI	Mins	Avg	W	L	EN	SO	GA	SA	S%
34	John Vanbiesbrouck	2	107	3.36	0	1	1	0	6	55	.889
35	Mike Richter	1	58	4.14	0	1	0	0	4	30	.867
33	Bob Froese	2	72	6.67	0	2	0	0	8	51	.843
	Totals	**4**	**240**	**4.75**	**0**	**4**	**1**	**0**	**19**	**136**	**.859**

General Managers' History

Lester Patrick, 1927-28 to 1945-46; Frank Boucher, 1946-47 to 1954-55; Murray "Muzz" Patrick, 1955-56 to 1963-64; Emile Francis, 1964-65 to 1974-75; Emile Francis and John Ferguson, 1975-76; John Ferguson, 1976-77 to 1977-78; John Ferguson and Fred Shero, 1978-79; Fred Shero, 1979-80; Fred Shero and Craig Patrick, 1980-81; Craig Patrick, 1981-82 to 1985-86; Phil Esposito, 1986-87 to 1988-89; Neil Smith, 1989-90.

Retired Numbers

1	Eddie Giacomin	1965-1976
7	Rod Gilbert	1960-1978

Club Records

Team

(Figures in brackets for season records are games played; records for fewest points, wins, ties, losses, goals, goals against are for 70 or more games)

Most Points **109** 1970-71 (78)
 1971-72 (78)
Most Wins **49** 1970-71 (78)
Most Ties **21** 1950-51 (70)
Most Losses **44** 1984-85 (80)
Most Goals **319** 1974-75 (80)
Most Goals Against **345** 1984-85 (80)
Fewest Points **47** 1965-66 (70)
Fewest Wins **17** 1952-53; 54-55; 59-60 (70)
Fewest Ties **6** 1985-86 (80)
Fewest Losses **17** 1971-72 (78)
Fewest Goals **150** 1954-55 (70)
Fewest Goals Against **177** 1970-71 (78)

Longest Winning Streak
Over-all . . . .**10** Dec. 19/39-
 Jan. 13/40
Home . . . .**14** Dec. 19/39-
 Feb. 25/40
Away . . . . **7** Jan. 12-
 Feb. 12/35
 Oct. 28-
 Nov. 29/78

Longest Undefeated Streak
Over-all . . . .**19** Nov. 23/39-
 Jan. 13/40
 (14 wins, 5 ties)
Home . . . .**26** Mar. 29/70-
 Feb. 2/71
 (19 wins, 7 ties)
Away . . . .**11** Nov. 5/39-
 Jan. 13/40
 (6 wins, 5 ties)

Longest Losing Streak
Over-all . . . .**11** Oct. 30-
 Nov. 27/43
Home . . . . **7** Oct. 20-
 Nov. 14/76
Away . . . .**10** Oct. 30-
 Dec. 23/43

Longest Winless Streak
Over-all . . . .**21** Jan. 23-
 Mar. 19/44
 (17 losses, 4 ties)
Home . . . .**10** Jan. 30-
 Mar. 19/44
 (7 losses, 3 ties)
Away . . . .**16** Oct. 9-
 Dec. 20/52
 (12 losses, 4 ties)
Most Shutouts, Season **13** 1928-29 (44)
Most. Pen. Mins., Season . **1,981**
Most Goals, Game . . . .**12** Nov. 21/71
 (Cal. 1 at NYR 12)

Individual

Most Seasons . . . .**17** Harry Howell
Most Games . . . . **1,160** Harry Howell
Most Goals, Career . . . . .**406** Rod Gilbert
Most Assists, Career . . . .**615** Rod Gilbert
Most Points, Career . . . .**1,021** Rod Gilbert
 (406 goals, 615 assists)
Most Pen. Mins., Career . **1,173** Ron Greschner
Most Shutouts, Career . . . .**49** Ed Giacomin
Longest Consecutive
 Games Streak . . . .**560** Andy Hebenton
 (Oct. 7/55-Mar. 24/63)
Most Goals, Season . . . . . .**50** Vic Hadfield
 (1971-72)
Most Assists, Season . . . . .**65** Mike Rogers
 (1981-82)
Most Points, Season . . . . .**109** Jean Ratelle
 (1971-72)
 (46 goals, 63 assists)
Most Pen. Mins., Season . . .**231** Barry Beck
 (1980-81)
Most Points, Defenseman
 Season . . . .**82** Brad Park
 (1973-74)
 (25 goals, 57 assists)
Most Points, Center,
 Season . . . .**109** Jean Ratelle
 (1971-72)
 (46 goals, 63 assists)

Most Points, Right Wing,
 Season . . . .**97** Rod Gilbert
 (1971-72)
 (43 goals, 54 assists)
 Rod Gilbert
 (1974-75)
 (36 goals, 61 assists)
Most Points, Left Wing,
 Season . . . .**106** Vic Hadfield
 (1971-72)
 (50 goals, 56 assists)
Most Points, Rookie,
 Season . . . .**76** Mark Pavelich
 (1981-82)
 (33 goals, 43 assists)
Most Shutouts, Season . . . . .**13** John Ross Roach
 (1928-29)
Most Goals, Game . . . .**5** Don Murdoch
 (Oct. 12/76)
 Mark Pavelich
 (Feb. 23/83)
Most Assists, Game . . . .**5** Walt Tkaczuk
 (Feb. 12/72)
 Rod Gilbert
 (Mar. 2/75; Mar. 30/75;
 Oct. 8/76)
 Don Maloney
 (Jan. 3/87)
Most Points, Game . . . .**7** Steve Vickers
 (Feb. 18/76)

All-time Record vs. Other Clubs

Regular Season

			At Home							On Road							Total				
	GP	W	L	T	GF	GA	PTS	GP	W	L	T	GF	GA	PTS	GP	W	L	T	GF	GA	PTS
Boston	273	118	102	53	825	764	289	271	84	149	38	754	993	206	544	202	251	91	1579	1757	495
Buffalo	38	15	14	9	131	113	39	39	10	24	5	128	178	25	77	25	38	14	259	291	64
**Calgary	37	16	17	4	134	136	36	37	10	21	6	115	167	26	74	26	38	10	249	303	62
Chicago	272	115	105	52	805	770	282	272	107	123	42	754	831	256	544	222	228	94	1559	1601	538
Detroit	270	129	85	56	829	689	314	271	73	154	44	662	946	190	541	202	239	100	1491	1635	504
Edmonton	16	5	10	1	70	74	11	16	6	9	1	57	72	13	32	11	19	2	127	146	24
Hartford	16	8	6	2	65	49	18	16	5	9	2	57	65	12	32	13	15	4	122	114	30
Los Angeles	45	26	14	5	178	132	57	45	18	19	8	160	149	45	90	44	32	14	338	281	102
Minnesota	47	28	10	9	169	130	65	47	27	14	6	190	142	60	94	55	24	15	359	272	125
Montreal	261	105	106	50	751	764	260	262	54	174	34	606	1039	142	523	159	280	84	1357	1803	402
*New Jersey	42	25	13	4	190	141	54	43	24	15	4	180	152	52	85	49	28	8	370	293	106
NY Islanders	55	35	16	4	220	168	74	53	15	35	3	167	234	33	108	50	51	7	387	402	107
Philadelphia	67	26	23	18	213	202	70	68	23	34	11	194	236	57	135	49	57	29	407	438	127
Pittsburgh	61	33	21	7	257	203	73	62	31	21	10	232	211	72	123	64	42	17	489	414	145
Quebec	16	10	3	3	68	45	23	16	4	9	3	68	76	11	32	14	12	6	136	121	34
St. Louis	47	40	3	4	212	105	84	48	21	20	7	156	147	49	95	61	23	11	368	252	133
Toronto	262	108	100	54	796	769	270	261	75	148	38	668	899	188	523	183	248	92	1464	1668	458
Vancouver	40	30	7	3	180	100	63	39	27	10	2	162	125	56	79	57	17	5	342	225	119
Washington	43	22	16	5	195	160	49	42	14	20	8	142	171	36	85	36	36	13	337	331	85
Winnipeg	16	8	7	1	82	74	17	16	8	6	2	60	62	18	32	16	13	3	142	136	35
Defunct Clubs	139	87	30	22	460	290	196	139	82	34	23	441	291	187	278	169	64	45	901	581	383
Totals	**2063**	**989**	**708**	**366**	**6830**	**5878**	**2344**	**2063**	**718**	**1047**	**298**	**5953**	**7186**	**1734**	**4126**	**1707**	**1755**	**664**	**12783**	**13064**	**4078**

* Totals include those of Kansas City (1974-75, 1975-76) and Colorado (1976-77 through 1981-82)
** Totals include those of Atlanta (1972-73 through 1979-80)

Playoffs

	Series	W	L	GP	W	L	T	GF	GA	Last Mtg.	Round	Result
Boston	9	3	6	42	18	22	2	104	114	1973	QF	W 4-1
Buffalo	1	0	1	3	1	2	0	6	11	1978	P	L 1-2
Calgary	1	1	0	4	3	1	0	14	8	1980	P	W 3-1
Chicago	5	1	4	24	10	14	0	54	66	1973	SF	L 1-4
Detroit	5	1	4	23	10	13	0	49	57	1950	F	L 3-4
Los Angeles	2	2	0	6	5	1	0	32	14	1981	P	W 3-1
Montreal	13	6	7	55	21	32	2	139	171	1986	CF	L 1-4
NY Islanders	6	1	5	30	11	19	0	88	113	1984	DSF	L 2-3
Philadelphia	8	4	4	38	19	19	0	130	119	1987	DSF	L 2-4
Pittsburgh	1	0	1	4	0	4	0	11	19	1989	DSF	L 0-4
St. Louis	1	1	0	6	4	2	0	29	22	1981	QF	W 4-2
Toronto	8	5	3	35	19	16	0	86	86	1971	QF	W 4-2
Washington	1	1	0	6	4	2	0	20	25	1986	DF	W 4-2
Defunct Clubs	9	6	3	22	11	7	4	43	29			
Totals	**70**	**32**	**38**	**298**	**136**	**154**	**8**	**805**	**854**			

Playoff Results 1989-85

Year	Round	Opponent	Result	GF	GA
1989	DSF	Pittsburgh	L 0-4	11	19
1987	DSF	Philadelphia	L 2-4	13	22
1986	CF	Montreal	L 1-4	10	15
	DF	Washington	W 4-2	20	25
	DSF	Philadelphia	W 3-2	18	15
1985	DSF	Philadelphia	L 0-3	10	14

Abbreviations: Round: F – Final; **CF** – conference final; **DF** – division final; **DSF** – division semi-final; **SF** – semi-final; **QF** – quarter-final. **P** – preliminary round. **GA** – goals against; **GF** – goals for.

1988-89 Results

		Home				Away	
Oct.	10	New Jersey	0-5	**Oct.**	6	Chicago	2-2
	12	Hartford	3-4		8	St Louis	4-2
	16	Vancouver	3-2		21	Washington	4-1
	19	Washington	5-1		29	Philadelphia	6-5
	23	Quebec	8-2	**Nov.**	2	Buffalo	4-6
	26	Philadelphia	4-3		6	New Jersey	5-6
	30	Pittsburgh	9-2		8	NY Islanders	3-4
Nov.	9	Philadelphia	5-3		15	Philadelphia	3-3
	11	Boston	4-4		17	Los Angeles	6-5
	13	Detroit	3-5		19	Minnesota	4-1
	21	Montreal	2-4		23	Pittsburgh	2-8
	27	NY Islanders	5-3		26	NY Islanders	6-4
Dec.	12	Los Angeles	2-5		29	Winnipeg	4-3
	14	NY Islanders	2-1	**Dec.**	1	Calgary	3-6
	19	Washington	3-1		4	Edmonton	6-10
	21	Buffalo	2-5		6	Vancouver	5-3
	26	New Jersey*	5-1		8	Hartford	4-5
	31	Chicago*	4-1		10	Boston*	1-1
Jan.	2	Hartford	5-4		17	Montreal	3-6
	4	Washington	3-3		23	Washington	2-2
	9	New Jersey	4-5		27	New Jersey	7-5
	15	Pittsburgh*	6-4	**Jan.**	7	NY Islanders	5-1
	30	NY Islanders	7-3		14	Pittsburgh*	4-4
Feb.	1	Washington	3-4		18	Chicago	6-4
	5	Minnesota	3-5		19	St Louis	5-0
	9	Winnipeg	4-3		21	Vancouver	5-4
	12	Edmonton	1-3		23	Edmonton	3-2
	17	Toronto	6-10		26	Calgary	3-5
	20	New Jersey*	7-4		28	Toronto	1-1
	22	Philadelphia	4-6	**Feb.**	4	Montreal	5-7
	25	Los Angeles	6-4		14	Philadelphia	1-3
Mar.	1	Toronto	7-4		18	Pittsburgh	5-3
	5	Boston	0-5		25	Quebec	7-2
	8	Buffalo	0-2	**Mar.**	3	New Jersey	3-6
	13	Calgary	4-3		9	Detroit	2-3
	15	Winnipeg	3-6		11	Washington	2-4
	20	St Louis	7-4		18	Quebec	3-8
	22	Minnesota	3-1		25	Philadelphia	1-6
	26	Pittsburgh	4-6		29	Detroit	3-4
Apr.	2	NY Islanders	4-6	**Apr.**	1	Pittsburgh	2-5

* Denotes afternoon game.

Entry Draft
Selections 1989-75

1989
Pick
20	Steven Rice
40	Jason Prosofsky
45	Rob Zamuner
49	Louie Debrusk
67	Jim Cummins
88	Aaron Miller
118	Joby Messier
139	Greg Leahy
160	Greg Spenrath
181	Mark Bavis
202	Roman Oksyuta
223	Steve Locke
244	Ken MacDermid

1988
Pick
22	Troy Mallette
26	Murray Duval
68	Tony Amonte
99	Martin Bergeron
110	Dennis Vial
131	Mike Rosati
152	Eric Couvrette
173	Shorty Forrest
194	Paul Cain
202	Eric Fenton
215	Peter Fiorentino
236	Keith Slifstien

1987
Pick
10	Jayson More
31	Daniel Lacroix
46	Simon Gagne
69	Michael Sullivan
94	Eric O'Borsky
115	Ludek Cajka
136	Clint Thomas
157	Charles Wiegand
178	Eric Burrill
199	David Porter
205	Brett Barnett
220	Lance Marciano

1986
Pick
9	Brian Leetch
51	Bret Walter
53	Shawn Clouston
72	Mark Janssens
93	Jeff Bloemberg
114	Darren Turcotte
135	Robb Graham
156	Barry Chyzowski
177	Pat Scanlon
198	Joe Ranger
219	Russell Parent
240	Soren True

1985
Pick
7	Ulf Dahlen
28	Mike Richter
49	Sam Lindstahl
70	Pat Janostin
91	Brad Stephan
112	Brian McReynolds
133	Neil Pilon
154	Lary Bernard
175	Stephane Brochu
196	Steve Nemeth
217	Robert Burakovski
238	Rudy Poeschek

1984
Pick
14	Terry Carkner
35	Raimo Helminen
77	Paul Broten
98	Clark Donatelli
119	Kjell Samuelsson
140	Thomas Hussey
161	Brian Nelson
182	Ville Kentala
188	Heinz Ehlers
202	Kevin Miller
223	Tom Lorentz
243	Scott Brower

1983
Pick
12	Dave Gagner
33	Randy Heath
49	Vesa Salo
53	Gordie Walker
73	Peter Andersson
93	Jim Andonoff
113	Bob Alexander
133	Steve Orth
153	Peter Marcov
173	Paul Jerrard
213	Bryan Walker
233	Ulf Nilsson

1982
Pick
15	Chris Kontos
36	Tomas Sandstrom
57	Corey Millen
78	Chris Jensen
120	Tony Granato
141	Sergei Kapustin
160	Brian Glynn
162	Jan Karlsson
183	Kelly Miller
193	Simo Saarinen
204	Bob Lowes
225	Andy Otto
246	Dwayne Robinson

1981
Pick
9	James Patrick
30	Jan Erixon
50	Peter Sundstrom
51	Mark Morrison
72	John Vanbiesbrouck
114	Eric Magnuson
135	Mike Guentzel
156	Ari Lahtenmaki
177	Paul Reifenberger
198	Mario Proulx

1980
Pick
14	Jim Malone
35	Mike Allison
77	Kurt Kleinendorst
98	Scot Kleinendorst
119	Reijo Ruotsalainen
140	Bob Scurfield
161	Bart Wilson
182	Chris Wray
203	Anders Backstrom

1979
Pick
13	Doug Sulliman
34	Ed Hospodar
76	Pat Conacher
97	Dan Makuch
118	Stan Adams

1978
Pick
26	Don Maloney
43	Ray Markham
44	Dean Turner
59	Dave Silk
60	Andre Dore
76	Mike McDougall
93	Tom Laidlaw
110	Dan Clark
127	Greg Kostenko
144	Brian McDavid
161	Mark Rodrigues
176	Steve Weeks
192	Pierre Daigneault
206	Chris McLaughlin
217	Todd Johnson
223	Dan McCarthy

1977
Pick
8	Lucien DeBlois
13	Ron Duguay
26	Mike Keating
44	Steve Baker
62	Mario Marois
80	Benoit Gosselin
98	John Bethel
116	Robert Sullivan
131	Lance Nethery
146	Alex Jeans
157	Peter Raps
164	Mike Brown
171	Mark Miller

1976
Pick
6	Don Murdoch
24	Dave Farrish
42	Mike McEwen
60	Claude Periard
78	Doug Gaines
96	Barry Scully
112	Remi Levesque

1975
Pick
12	Wayne Dillon
30	Doug Soetaert
49	Greg Hickey
66	Bill Cheropita
84	Larry Huras
102	Randy Koch
120	Claude Larose
138	Bill Hamilton
154	Bud Stefanski
169	Daniel Beaulieu
184	John McMorrow
195	Tom McNamara
200	Steve Roberts
201	Paul Dionne
205	Cecil Luckern
209	John Corriveau
212	Tom Funke

General Manager

SMITH, NEIL
General Manager, New York Rangers. Born in Toronto, Ont., January, 9 1954.

Smith, 35-years-old, joined the Rangers on July 17, 1989 after seven seasons with the Detroit Red Wings and two with the New York Islanders. After serving as a scout for the Islanders in 1980-81 and 1981-82, Smith joined the Red Wings. While with the Red Wings, Smith held several positions including Director of Scouting and Player Development. He also served as General Manager of the Adirondack Red Wings (AHL), leading that club to two Calder Cups (1985-86 and 1988-89).

A former All-American defenseman from Western Michigan University, Smith was drafted in 1974 by the New York Islanders. After receiving his degree in Communications and Business, Smith played two seasons in the IHL—1978-79 with the Kalamazoo Wings and Saginaw Gears and 1979-80 with the Dayton Gems, Milwaukee Admirals and Muskegon Mohawks.

Coach

NEILSON, ROGER PAUL
Coach, New York Rangers. Born in Toronto, Ont., June 16, 1934.

Roger Neilson began his coaching career as a 17-year-old with a neighborhood baseball team in his native Toronto. He began scouting Ontario prospects for the Montreal Canadiens before becoming coach of the Peterborough Petes of the OHA in 1966. He remained in Peterborough for ten seasons, winning one OHA championship while finishing lower than third in regular-season play only twice. He made his pro coaching debut with the Dallas Black Hawks of the CHL in 1976-77 and moved up to the NHL with the Toronto Maple Leafs in 1977-78. He joined the Buffalo Sabres in 1979-80 as associate coach under Scotty Bowman. He acted as the Sabres' bench coach for part of this campaign and for all of 1980-81. He became associate coach of the Vancouver Canucks under Harry Neale in 1981-82 and coached five games late in the season when Neale was serving a suspension. He also guided the Canucks in the 1982 playoffs and in 1982-83. In 1983-84, he coached the Los Angeles Kings for the last 28 games of the regular season. He served as co-coach of the Chicago Blackhawks from 1984-85 through 1986-87 before taking on special scouting assignments for the Blackhawks. He also has provided television commentary on Canadian NHL telecasts.

Club Directory

Madison Square Garden
4 Pennsylvania Plaza
New York, New York 10001
Phone 212/563-8000
GM FAX 212/967-5954
PR FAX 212/563-8101
ENVOY ID
Front Office: RANGERS. GM
Public
Relations: RANGERS. PR
Capacity: 16,651

Executive Management
President and Governor	Richard Evans
Executive Vice-President	Jack Diller*
Vice-President & General Manager	Neil Smith*
Vice-President & General Counsel	Kenneth W. Munoz*
Senior Vice-President, Marketing & Communications	Michael D. Walker*
Vice-President, Communications	John Halligan
Assistant Vice-President, Legal Affairs	Kevin Billet
Director, Marketing	Kevin Kennedy

Team Management
Assistant General Manager/Operations	Gord Stellick
Assistant General Manager/Player Development	Larry Pleau
Coach	Roger Neilson
Assistant Coaches	Wayne Cashman, Ron Smith
Development Coach	Paul Theriault
Scouting Staff	Al Cerrone, John Chapman, Tony Feltrin, Lou Jankowski, George Kozak, David McNab, Dan Summers
Manager of Team Services	Matthew Loughran
Hockey Assistant	Bill Short
Executive Administratiave Assistant	Maggie McLoughlin
Adminstrative Assistant	Janet Ungarten
Secretary	Linda Olmstead

Medical/Training Staff
Team Physician/Ortho Surgeon	Barton Nisonson, M.D.
Medical Consultants	Peter Bruno, Howard Chester, Anthony Maddalo, Irwin Miller, James A. Nicholas, Ronald Weissman,
Medical Trainer/Strength Conditioning	Dave Smith
Trainers	Jacques Cayer, Joe Murphy
Equipment Manager	Scott Luhrmann
Locker-room Assistant	Benny Petrizzi

Public Relations
Public Relations Manager	Barry Watkins
Public Relations Assistant	Ginger Killian
Statistician	Arthur Friedman

Home Ice	Madison Square Garden
Press Facilities	33rd Street
Television Facilities	31st Street
Radio Facilities	33rd Street
Rink Dimensions	200 feet by 85 feet
Ends and Sides of Rink	Herculite Tempered Plate Glass
Club Colors	Blue, Red, and White
Training Camp	Rye, New York
TV Announcers	Bruce Beck, John Davidson, Sam Rosen
Radio Announcers	Marv Albert, Sal Messina
Television Outlets	Madison Square Garden Cable Network
Radio Outlet	WFAN (66 AM)

*-alternate governors

The New York Rangers Hockey Club is part of the
MSG Sports Group of Madison Sqaure Garden Corporation
A Paramount Communications Company

Coaching Record

Season	Team	Games	Regular Season W	L	T	%	Playoffs Games	W	L	%
1966-67	Peterborough (OHA)					UNAVAILABLE				
1967-68	Peterborough (OHA)	54	27	18	9	.583				
1968-69	Peterborough (OHA)	54	29	13	12	.648				
1969-70	Peterborough (OHA)	54	29	13	12	.648				
1970-71	Peterborough (OHA)	62	41	13	8	.726				
1971-72	Peterborough (OHA)	63	34	20	9	.611				
1972-73	Peterborough (OHA)	63	42	13	8	.730				
1973-74	Peterborough (OHA)	70	35	21	14	.600				
1974-75	Peterborough (OHA)	70	37	20	13	.621				
1975-76	Peterborough (OHA)	66	18	37	11	.356				
1976-77	Dallas (CHL)	76	35	25	16	.566				
1977-78	**Toronto (NHL)**	**80**	**41**	**29**	**10**	**.575**	**13**	**6**	**7**	**.462**
1978-79	**Toronto (NHL)**	**80**	**34**	**33**	**13**	**.506**	**6**	**2**	**4**	**.333**
1979-80	**Buffalo (NHL)**	**26**	**14**	**6**	**6**	**.654**	....	....	....	....
1980-81	**Buffalo (NHL)**	**80**	**39**	**20**	**21**	**.619**	**8**	**4**	**4**	**.500**
1981-82	**Vancouver (NHL)**	**5**	**4**	**0**	**1**	**.900**	**17**	**11**	**6**	**.647**
1982-83	**Vancouver (NHL)**	**80**	**30**	**35**	**15**	**.469**	**4**	**1**	**3**	**.250**
	Los Angeles (NHL)	**28**	**8**	**17**	**3**	**.339**				
	NHL Totals	**427**	**187**	**166**	**74**	**.525**	**48**	**24**	**24**	**.500**

Philadelphia Flyers

1988-89 Results: 36w-36L-8T 80 PTS. Fourth, Patrick Division

Year-by-Year Record

Season	GP	Home W	L	T	Road W	L	T	Overall W	L	T	GF	GA	Pts.	Finished		Playoff Result
1988-89	80	22	15	3	14	21	5	36	36	8	307	285	80	4th,	Patrick Div.	Lost Conf. Championship
1987-88	80	20	14	6	18	19	3	38	33	9	292	292	85	3rd,	Patrick Div.	Lost Div. Semi-Final
1986-87	80	29	9	2	17	17	6	46	26	8	310	245	100	1st,	Patrick Div.	Lost Final
1985-86	80	33	6	1	20	17	3	53	23	4	335	241	110	1st,	Patrick Div.	Lost Div. Semi-Final
1984-85	80	32	4	4	21	16	3	53	20	7	348	241	113	1st,	Patrick Div.	Lost Final
1983-84	80	25	10	5	19	16	5	44	26	10	350	290	98	3rd,	Patrick Div.	Lost Div. Semi-Final
1982-83	80	29	8	3	20	15	5	49	23	8	326	240	106	1st,	Patrick Div.	Lost Div. Semi-Final
1981-82	80	25	10	5	13	21	6	38	31	11	325	313	87	3rd.	Patrick Div.	Lost Div. Semi-Final
1980-81	80	23	9	8	18	15	7	41	24	15	313	249	97	2nd,	Patrick Div.	Lost Quarter-Final
1979-80	80	27	5	8	21	7	12	48	12	20	327	254	116	1st,	Patrick Div.	Lost Final
1978-79	80	26	10	4	14	15	11	40	25	15	281	248	95	2nd,	Patrick Div.	Lost Quarter-Final
1977-78	80	29	6	5	16	14	10	45	20	15	296	200	105	2nd,	Patrick Div.	Lost Semi-Final
1976-77	80	33	6	1	15	10	15	48	16	16	323	213	112	1st,	Patrick Div.	Lost Semi-Final
1975-76	80	36	2	2	15	11	14	51	13	16	348	209	118	1st,	Patrick Div.	Lost Final
1974-75	**80**	**32**	**6**	**2**	**19**	**12**	**9**	**51**	**18**	**11**	**293**	**181**	**113**	**1st,**	**Patrick Div.**	**Won Stanley Cup**
1973-74	**78**	**28**	**6**	**5**	**22**	**10**	**7**	**50**	**16**	**12**	**273**	**164**	**112**	**1st,**	**West Div.**	**Won Stanley Cup**
1972-73	78	27	8	4	10	22	7	37	30	11	296	256	85	2nd,	West Div.	Lost Semi-Final
1971-72	78	19	13	7	7	25	7	26	38	14	200	236	66	5th,	West Div.	Out of Playoffs
1970-71	78	20	10	9	8	23	8	28	33	17	207	225	73	3rd,	West Div.	Lost Quarter-Final
1969-70	76	11	14	13	6	21	11	17	35	24	197	225	58	5th,	West Div.	Out of Playoffs
1968-69	76	14	16	8	6	19	13	20	35	21	174	225	61	3rd,	West Div.	Lost Quarter-Final
1967-68	74	17	13	7	14	19	4	31	32	11	173	179	73	1st,	West Div.	Lost Quarter-Final

Schedule

Home				Away			
Oct.	Thur.	5	New Jersey	**Oct.**	Fri.	6	Washington
	Thur.	12	Quebec		Sun.	8	Winnipeg
	Sun.	15	Calgary		Sat.	14	NY Islanders
	Sat.	21	NY Rangers		Wed.	18	New Jersey
	Tues.	24	St Louis		Sat.	28	Minnesota
Nov.	Sun.	5	NY Islanders		Mon.	30	NY Rangers
	Thur.	9	Toronto	**Nov.**	Wed.	1	Detroit
	Sun.	12	New Jersey		Sat.	4	Toronto
	Thur.	16	Minnesota		Sat.	11	New Jersey*
	Sat.	18	Winnipeg*		Tues.	14	NY Islanders
	Wed.	22	Montreal		Sat.	25	Hartford
	Fri.	24	Edmonton*		Tues.	28	Pittsburgh
	Thur.	30	Pittsburgh	**Dec.**	Fri.	1	Washington
Dec.	Sun.	3	Boston		Sat.	9	Quebec*
	Tues.	5	Washington		Sun.	10	NY Rangers
	Thur.	7	Buffalo		Sun.	17	Buffalo
	Thur.	14	Hartford		Sat.	23	Montreal
	Sat.	16	Los Angeles		Wed.	27	Edmonton
	Tues.	19	Washington		Sat.	30	Los Angeles
	Fri.	22	New Jersey		Sun.	31	Vancouver
Jan.	Thur.	11	Chicago	**Jan.**	Tues.	2	Calgary
	Thur.	18	Vancouver		Thur.	4	St Louis
	Tues.	23	Buffalo		Sat.	6	Chicago
	Thur.	25	Winnipeg		Sat.	13	Montreal
Feb.	Thur.	1	Hartford		Sun.	14	NY Rangers
	Sat.	3	Minnesota*		Tues.	16	Pittsburgh
	Thur.	8	NY Islanders		Sat.	27	Boston*
	Sun.	11	Pittsburgh		Sun.	28	Washington*
	Tues.	13	NY Rangers		Tues.	30	Pittsburgh
	Thur.	15	Toronto	**Feb.**	Fri.	16	Detroit
	Sun.	18	NY Islanders*		Tues.	20	Pittsburgh
Mar.	Tues.	6	Boston		Thur.	22	St Louis
	Thur.	8	NY Rangers		Sun.	25	Chicago*
	Sat.	10	Washington		Wed.	28	Vancouver
	Thur.	15	NY Islanders	**Mar.**	Thur.	1	Calgary
	Sun.	18	Los Angeles		Sat.	3	Edmonton
	Thur.	22	Pittsburgh		Sat.	17	Quebec
	Sat.	24	New Jersey*		Tues.	20	New Jersey
	Thur.	29	Washington		Sun.	25	NY Rangers*
Apr.	Sun.	1	Detroit		Sat.	31	NY Islanders

* Denotes afternoon game.

Home Starting Times:

Weeknights & Saturdays . . . . 7:35 p.m.
Sundays . . . . 7:05 p.m.
Matinees . . . . 1:05 p.m.
Except Sat. Feb. 3, ... 11:05 a.m.
Sun. Feb. 18, ... 1:35 p.m.

Franchise date: June 5, 1967

23rd NHL Season

Tim Kerr overcame a series of shoulder injuries to lead the Flyers with 48 goals in 69 games.

1989-90 Player Personnel

FORWARDS	HT	WT	S	Place of Birth	Date	1988-89 Club
ACTON, Keith	5-8	170	L	Stouffville, Ont.	4/15/58	Edmonton-Flyers
BERUBE, Craig	6-1	205	L	Calihoo, Alta.	11/17/65	Flyers
BIGGS, Don	5-8	185	R	Mississauga, Ont.	4/7/65	Hershey
BOIVIN, Claude	6-2	200	L	St. Foy, Que.	3/1/70	Drummondville
BULLARD, Mike	6-2	195	L	Ottawa, Ont.	3/10/61	St. Louis-Flyers
CRAVEN, Murray	6-2	185	L	Medicine Hat, Alta.	7/20/64	Flyers
DOBBIN, Brian	5-11	205	R	Petrolia, Ont.	8/18/66	Flyers-Hershey
EKLUND, Pelle	5-10	175	L	Stockholm, Sweden	3/22/63	Flyers
FLETCHER, Steve	6-3	205	L	Montreal, Que.	3/31/62	Moncton-Hershey
FREER, Mark	5-10	180	L	Peterborough, Ont.	7/14/68	Hershey-Flyers
HARDING, Jeff	6-3	220	R	Toronto, Ont.	4/6/69	Hershey-Flyers
HARPER, Warren	6-1	200	L	Prince Albert, Sask.	5/10/63	Hershey
HAWLEY, Kent	6-3	215	L	Kingston, Ont.	2/20/68	Hershey
HORACEK, Tony	6-4	210	L	Vancouver, B.C.	2/3/67	Hershey-Indianapolis
JENSEN, Chris	5-10	170	R	Fort St. John, B.C.	10/28/63	Hershey
KERR, Tim	6-3	230	R	Windsor, Ont.	1/5/60	Flyers
KYPREOS, Nick	6-0	195	L	Toronto, Ont.	6/4/66	Hershey
MELLANBY, Scott	6-1	205	R	Montreal, Que.	6/11/66	Flyers
NACHBAUR, Don	6-2	195	L	Kitimat, B.C.	1/30/59	Hershey-Flyers
POULIN, Dave	5-11	190	L	Timmins, Ont.	12/17/58	Flyers
PROPP, Brian	5-11	190	L	Lanigan, Sask.	2/15/59	Flyers
RENDALL, Bruce	6-1	190	L	Thunder Bay, Ont.	4/18/67	Hershey-Indianapolis
SEABROOKE, Glen	6-0	190	L	Peterborough, Ont.	9/11/67	Hershey-Flyers
SIMPSON, Reid	6-1	211	L	Flin Flan, Man.	5/21/69	Prince Albert
SINISALO, Ilkka	6-0	200	R	Valeakoski, Finland	7/10/58	Flyers
SMITH, Derrick	6-2	215	L	Scarborough, Ont.	1/22/65	Flyers
SULLIMAN, Doug	5-9	190	L	Glace Bay, N.S.	8/29/59	Flyers
SUTTER, Ron	6-0	180	R	Viking, Alta.	12/2/63	Flyers
TOCCHET, Rick	6-0	205	R	Scarborough, Ont.	4/9/64	Flyers
TOOKEY, Tim	5-11	190	L	Edmonton, Alta.	8/29/60	L.A.-New Haven-Muskegon

DEFENSEMEN	HT	WT	S	Place of Birth	Date	1988-89 Club
BARON, Murray	6-3	210	L	Prince George, B.C.	6/1/67	U. of N. Dakota-Hershey
CARKNER, Terry	6-3	212	L	Smiths Falls, Ont.	3/7/66	Flyers
CHYCHRUN, Jeff	6-4	212	R	LaSalle, Que.	5/3/66	Flyers
FENYVES, Dave	5-11	192	L	Dunnville, Ont.	4/29/60	Hershey-Flyers
HOWE, Mark	5-11	185	L	Detroit, MI	5/28/55	Flyers
HUFFMAN, Kerry	6-2	200	L	Peterborough, Ont.	1/3/68	Flyers-Hershey
MANTHA, Moe	6-2	210	R	Lakewood, OH	1/21/61	Minnesota-Flyers
MURPHY, Gord	6-2	190	R	Willowdale, Ont.	2/23/67	Flyers
PADDOCK, Gord	6-0	187	R	Hamiota, Man.	2/15/64	Hershey
RUMBLE, Darren	6-1	200	L	Barrie, Ont.	1/23/69	Kitchener
SABOL, Shawn	6-2	215	L	Fargo, N.D.	7/13/66	Hershey
SAMUELSSON, Kjell	6-6	235	R	Tyringe, Sweden	10/18/58	Flyers
SANDELIN, Scott	6-0	180	R	Hibbing, MN	8/8/64	Sherbrooke-Hershey
STEVENS, John	6-1	195	L	Completon, N.B.	5/4/66	Hershey
STOTHERS, Mike	6-4	212	L	Toronto, Ont.	2/22/62	Hershey
WELLS, Jay	6-1	210	L	Paris, Ont.	5/18/59	Flyers

GOALTENDERS	HT	WT	C	Place of Birth	Date	1988-89 Club
D'AMOUR, Marc	5-9	190	L	Sudbury, Ont.	4/29/61	Hershey-Flyers
GILMOUR, Darryl	6-0	170	L	Winnipeg, Man.	2/13/67	Hershey
HEXTALL, Ron	6-3	192	L	Brandon, Man.	5/3/64	Flyers
HOFFORT, Bruce	5-10	185	L	N. Battleford, Sask.	7/30/66	Lake Superior St.
LaFOREST, Mark	5-11	190	L	Welland, Ont.	7/10/62	Flyers-Hershey
PEETERS, Pete	6-1	195	L	Edmonton, Alta.	8/17/57	Washington
PERREAULT, Jocelyn	6-3	196	L	Montreal, Que.	1/8/66	Hershey
ROUSSEL, Dominic	6-1	185	L	Hull, Que.	2/22/70	Shawinigan
WREGGET, Ken	6-1	195	L	Brandon, Man.	3/25/64	Toronto-Flyers

Retired Numbers

1	Bernie Parent	1967-1971 and 1973-1979
4	Barry Ashbee	1970-1974
16	Bobby Clarke	1969-1984

General Managers' History

Normand Robert Poile, 1967-68 to 1969-70; Keith Allen, 1970-71 to 1982-83; Bob McCammon, 1983-84; Bobby Clarke, 1984-85 to date.

Coaching History

Keith Allen, 1967-68 to 1968-69; Vic Stasiuk, 1969-70 to 1970-71; Fred Shero, 1971-72 to 1977-78; Bob McCammon and Pat Quinn, 1978-79; Pat Quinn, 1979-80 to 1980-81; Pat Quinn and Bob McCammon, 1981-82; Bob McCammon, 1982-83 to 1983-84; Mike Keenan, 1984-85 to 1987-88; Paul Holmgren, 1988-89 to date.

Captains' History

Lou Angotti, 1967-68; Ed Van Impe, 1968-69 to 1971-72; Ed Van Impe, Bob Clarke, 1972-73; Bob Clarke, 1973-74 to 1978-79; Mel Bridgman, 1979-80, 1980-81; Bill Barber, 1981-82; Bill Barber, Bob Clarke, 1982-83; Bob Clarke, 1983-84; Dave Poulin, 1984-85 to date.

1988-89 Scoring

Regular Season

*–rookie

Pos	#	Player	Team	GP	G	A	Pts	+/–	PIM	PP	SH	GW	GT	S	%
F	12	Tim Kerr	PHI	69	48	40	88	4–	73	25	0	2	1	236	20.3
F	22	Rick Tocchet	PHI	66	45	36	81	1–	183	16	1	5	3	220	20.5
F	26	Brian Propp	PHI	77	32	46	78	16	37	13	2	5	1	245	13.1
F	9	Per-Erik Eklund	PHI	79	18	51	69	5	23	8	1	2	0	121	14.9
F	10	Mike Bullard	STL	20	4	12	16	1	46	2	0	0	0	52	7.7
			PHI	54	23	26	49	1	60	8	0	3	0	137	16.8
			TOTAL	74	27	38	65	2	106	10	0	3	0	189	14.3
F	19	Scott Mellanby	PHI	76	21	29	50	13–	183	11	0	3	0	202	10.4
F	14	Ron Sutter	PHI	55	26	22	48	25	80	4	1	2	0	106	24.5
D	29	Terry Carkner	PHI	78	11	32	43	6–	149	2	1	1	0	84	13.1
F	25	Keith Acton	EDM	46	11	15	26	9	47	0	1	1	0	74	14.9
			PHI	25	3	10	13	1	64	0	1	0	0	38	7.9
			TOTAL	71	14	25	39	10	111	0	2	1	0	112	12.5
D	2	Mark Howe	PHI	52	9	29	38	7	45	5	1	1	0	95	9.5
F	32	Murray Craven	PHI	51	9	28	37	4	52	0	0	2	0	89	10.1
F	20	Dave Poulin	PHI	69	18	17	35	4	49	1	5	4	0	81	22.2
D	3	*Gordon Murphy	PHI	75	4	31	35	7–	68	3	0	1	0	116	3.4
F	24	Derrick Smith	PHI	74	16	14	30	4–	43	0	1	3	0	115	13.9
D	7	Jay Wells	PHI	67	2	19	21	3–	184	0	0	0	0	67	3.0
D	8	Moe Mantha	MIN	16	1	6	7	1	10	1	0	0	0	32	3.1
			PHI	30	3	8	11	5–	33	2	0	0	0	71	4.2
			TOTAL	46	4	14	18	4–	43	3	0	0	0	103	3.9
D	28	Kjell Samuelsson	PHI	69	3	14	17	13	140	0	1	0	0	60	5.0
F	21	Al Secord	TOR	40	5	10	15	13–	71	1	0	1	0	52	9.6
			PHI	20	1	0	1	7–	38	0	0	0	0	15	6.7
			TOTAL	60	6	10	16	20–	109	1	0	1	0	67	9.0
F	15	Doug Sulliman	PHI	52	6	6	12	8–	8	0	1	1	0	52	11.5
D	5	Kerry Huffman	PHI	29	0	11	11	0	31	0	0	0	0	23	.0
G	27	Ron Hextall	PHI	64	0	8	8	0	113	0	0	0	0	5	.0
F	23	Ilkka Sinisalo	PHI	13	1	6	7	6	2	0	0	0	0	15	6.7
D	6	*Jeff Chychrun	PHI	80	1	4	5	11	245	0	0	1	0	53	1.9
G	33	Mark LaForest	PHI	17	0	4	4	0	4	0	0	0	0	0	.0
G	35	Ken Wregget	TOR	32	0	3	3	0	20	0	0	0	0	0	.0
			PHI	3	0	0	0	0	0	0	0	0	0	0	.0
			TOTAL	35	0	3	3	0	20	0	0	0	0	0	.0
F	10	Magnus Roupe	PHI	7	1	1	2	1	10	0	0	0	0	15	6.7
F	17	Craig Berube	PHI	53	1	1	2	15–	199	0	0	0	0	31	3.2
F	42	Don Nachbaur	PHI	15	1	0	1	1–	37	0	0	0	0	10	10.0
D	39	Dave Fenyves	PHI	1	0	1	1	0	0	0	0	0	0	0	.0
F	11	Glen Seabrooke	PHI	3	0	1	1	1–	0	0	0	0	0	0	.0
F	37	*Mark Freer	PHI	5	0	1	1	0	0	0	0	0	0	1	.0
F	18	Brian Dobbin	PHI	14	0	1	1	6–	8	0	0	0	0	13	.0
G	49	*Marc D'Amour	PHI	1	0	0	0	0	0	0	0	0	0	0	.0
F	34	*Jeff Harding	PHI	6	0	0	0	1	29	0	0	0	0	11	.0

Goaltending

No.	Goaltender	GPI	Mins	Avg	W	L	T	EN	SO	GA	SA	S%
49	*Marc D'Amour	1	19	.00	0	0	0	1	0	0	14	1.000
27	Ron Hextall	64	3756	3.23	30	28	6	5	0	202	1860	.891
33	Mark LaForest	17	933	4.12	5	7	2	0	0	64	497	.871
35	Ken Wregget	3	130	6.00	1	1	0	0	0	13	73	.822
	Totals	**80**	**4854**	**3.52**	**36**	**36**	**8**	**6**	**0**	**285**	**2444**	**.883**

Playoffs

Pos	#	Player	Team	GP	G	A	Pts	+/–	PIM	PP	SH	GW	GT	S	%
F	12	Tim Kerr	PHI	19	14	11	25	1	27	8	0	2	0	54	25.9
F	26	Brian Propp	PHI	18	14	9	23	8	14	5	1	1	0	52	26.9
D	2	Mark Howe	PHI	19	0	15	15	14	10	0	0	0	0	33	.0
F	22	Rick Tocchet	PHI	16	6	6	12	0	69	2	0	1	0	58	10.3
F	10	Mike Bullard	PHI	19	3	9	12	0	32	1	0	0	0	36	8.3
F	20	Dave Poulin	PHI	19	6	5	11	5	16	0	2	2	1	27	22.2
F	9	Per-Erik Eklund	PHI	19	3	8	11	4–	2	3	0	1	0	22	13.6
F	14	Ron Sutter	PHI	19	1	9	10	5	51	0	0	0	0	39	2.6
F	19	Scott Mellanby	PHI	19	4	5	9	2	28	0	0	0	0	45	8.9
D	3	*Gordon Murphy	PHI	19	2	7	9	0	13	1	0	1	0	32	6.3
F	24	Derrick Smith	PHI	19	5	2	7	3	12	0	2	1	0	39	12.8
D	29	Terry Carkner	PHI	19	1	5	6	1–	28	0	1	0	0	21	4.8
F	25	Keith Acton	PHI	16	2	3	5	0	18	0	0	0	0	10	20.0
D	28	Kjell Samuelsson	PHI	19	1	3	4	13	24	0	0	0	0	16	6.3
F	21	Al Secord	PHI	14	0	4	4	2	31	0	0	0	0	8	.0
F	23	Ilkka Sinisalo	PHI	8	1	1	2	1–	0	0	1	1	0	7	14.3
D	7	Jay Wells	PHI	18	0	2	2	1–	51	0	0	0	0	14	.0
D	6	*Jeff Chychrun	PHI	19	0	2	2	3–	65	0	0	0	0	16	.0
G	27	Ron Hextall	PHI	15	1	0	1	0	28	0	1	0	0	1	100.0
F	32	Murray Craven	PHI	1	0	0	0	1–	2	0	0	0	0	2	.0
D	8	Moe Mantha	PHI	1	0	0	0	0	0	0	0	0	0	2	.0
F	18	Brian Dobbin	PHI	2	0	0	0	0	17	0	0	0	0	1	.0
F	15	Doug Sulliman	PHI	4	0	0	0	0	0	0	0	0	0	2	.0
G	35	Ken Wregget	PHI	5	0	0	0	0	16	0	0	0	0	0	.0
F	17	Craig Berube	PHI	16	0	0	0	0	56	0	0	0	0	2	.0

Goaltending

No.	Goaltender	GPI	Mins	Avg	W	L	EN	SO	GA	SA	S%
35	Ken Wregget	5	268	2.24	2	2	1	0	10	139	.928
27	Ron Hextall	15	886	3.32	8	7	0	0	49	445	.890
	Totals	**19**	**1156**	**3.12**	**10**	**9**	**1**	**0**	**60**	**584**	**.897**

Club Records

Team

(Figures in brackets for season records are games played; records for fewest points, wins, ties, losses, goals, goals against are for 70 or more games)

Most Points	118	1975-76 (80)
Most Wins	53	1984-85 (80)
		1985-86 (80)
Most Ties	*24	1969-70 (76)
Most Losses	38	1971-72 (78)
Most Goals	350	1983-84 (80)
Most Goals Against	313	1981-82 (78)
Fewest Points	58	1969-70 (76)
Fewest Wins	17	1969-70 (76)
Fewest Ties	4	1985-86 (80)
Fewest Losses	12	1979-80 (80)
Fewest Goals	173	1967-68 (74)
Fewest Goals Against	164	1973-74 (78)

Longest Winning Streak
Over-all ... 13 Oct. 19-Nov. 17/85
Home ... *20 Jan. 4-
Apr. 3/76
Away ... 8 Dec. 22/82-
Jan. 16/83

Longest Undefeated Streak
Over-all ... *35 Oct. 14/79-
Jan. 6/80
(25 wins, 10 ties)
Home ... 26 Oct. 11/79-
Feb. 3/80
(19 wins, 7 ties)
Away ... 16 Oct. 20/79-
Jan. 6/80
(11 wins, 5 ties)

Longest Losing Streak
Over-all ... 6 Mar. 25-
Apr. 4/70
Home ... 5 Jan. 30-
Feb. 15/69
Away ... 8 Oct. 25-
Nov. 26/72

Longest Winless Streak
Over-all ... 11 Nov. 21-
Dec. 14/69
(9 losses, 2 ties)
Dec. 10/70-
Jan. 3/71
(9 losses, 2 ties)
Home ... 8 Dec. 19/68-
Jan. 18/69
(4 losses, 4 ties)
Away ... 19 Oct. 23/71-
Jan. 27/72
(15 losses, 4 ties)

Most Shutouts, Season ... 13 1974-75 (80)
Most Pen. Mins., Season
... *2,621 1980-81 (80)
Most Goals, Game ... 13 Mar. 22/84
(Phi. 13 at Pit. 4)
Oct. 18/84
(Van. 2 at Phil. 13)

Individual

Most Seasons ... 15 Bobby Clarke
Most Games ... 1,144 Bobby Clarke
Most Goals, Career ... 420 Bill Barber
Most Assists, Career ... 852 Bobby Clarke
Most Points, Career ... 1,210 Bobby Clarke
(358 goals, 852 assists)
Most Pen Mins., Career ... 1,600 Paul Holmgren
Most Shutouts, Career ... 50 Bernie Parent
Longest Consecutive
Game Streak ... 287 Rick MacLeish
(Oct. 6/72-Feb. 5/76)
Most Goals, Season ... 61 Reggie Leach
(1975-76)
Most Assists, Season ... 89 Bobby Clarke
(1974-75; 1975-76)
Most Points, Season ... 119 Bobby Clarke
(1975-76)
(30 goals, 89 assists)

Most Pen. Mins., Season ... *472 Dave Schultz
(1974-75)
Most Points, Defenseman,
Season ... 82 Mark Howe
(1985-86)
(24 goals, 58 assists)
Most Points, Center,
Season ... 119 Bobby Clarke
(1975-76)
(30 goals, 89 assists)
Most Points, Right Wing,
Season ... 98 Tim Kerr
(1984-85)
(54 goals, 44 assists)
Most Points, Left Wing,
Season ... 112 Bill Barber
(1975-76)
(50 goals, 62 assists)
Most Points, Rookie,
Season ... 76 Dave Poulin
(1983-84)
(31 goals, 45 assists)
Most Shutouts, Season ... 12 Bernie Parent
(1973-74; 1974-75)
Most Goals, Game ... 4 Rick MacLeish
(Feb. 13/73; Mar. 4/72)
Tom Bladon
(Dec. 11/77)
Tim Kerr
(Oct. 25/84, Jan. 17/85,
Feb. 9/85, Nov. 20/86)
Brian Propp
(Dec. 2/86)
Rick Tocchet
(Feb. 27/88)
Most Assists, Game ... 5 Bobby Clarke
Apr. 1/76
Most Points, Game ... 8 Tom Bladon
(Dec. 11/77)

* NHL Record.

All-time Record vs. Other Clubs

Regular Season

	At Home						On Road						Total					
	GP	W	L	T	GF	GA	PTS	GP	W	L	T	GF	GA	PTS	GP	W	L	T	GF	GA	PTS
Boston	45	20	19	6	156	138	46	46	9	31	6	137	198	24	91	29	50	12	293	336	70
Buffalo	38	25	7	6	142	93	56	37	14	17	6	112	129	34	75	39	24	12	254	222	90
**Calgary	38	28	9	1	162	94	57	37	11	19	7	127	156	29	75	39	28	8	289	250	86
Chicago	47	26	13	8	161	129	60	47	9	22	16	121	160	34	94	35	35	24	282	289	94
Detroit	45	27	9	9	185	130	63	45	18	19	8	148	150	44	90	45	28	17	333	280	107
Edmonton	16	12	3	1	75	47	25	16	5	8	3	50	62	13	32	17	11	4	125	109	38
Hartford	16	13	2	1	77	42	27	16	7	5	4	75	70	18	32	20	7	5	152	112	45
Los Angeles	50	30	13	7	192	129	67	51	30	14	7	173	141	67	101	60	27	14	365	270	134
Minnesota	53	35	8	10	204	114	80	52	20	20	12	179	167	52	105	55	28	22	383	281	132
Montreal	45	15	19	11	118	139	41	45	9	27	9	124	179	27	90	24	46	20	242	318	68
*New Jersey	42	35	4	3	194	79	73	42	23	16	3	181	147	49	84	58	20	6	375	226	122
NY Islanders	53	30	17	6	198	162	66	54	18	27	9	158	212	45	107	48	44	15	356	374	111
NY Rangers	68	34	23	11	236	194	79	67	23	26	18	202	213	64	135	57	49	29	438	407	143
Pittsburgh	68	55	7	6	316	154	116	66	27	26	13	206	206	67	134	82	33	19	522	360	183
Quebec	16	12	2	2	68	41	26	16	6	4	6	58	52	18	32	18	6	8	126	93	44
St. Louis	53	36	9	8	209	120	80	53	25	21	7	155	151	57	106	61	30	15	364	271	137
Toronto	45	29	9	7	188	110	65	46	16	17	13	146	161	45	91	45	26	20	334	271	110
Vancouver	39	29	10	0	188	114	58	39	21	10	8	150	112	50	78	50	20	8	338	226	108
Washington	42	28	11	3	176	112	59	43	21	15	7	164	148	49	85	49	26	10	340	260	108
Winnipeg	16	14	2	0	83	43	28	16	8	7	1	61	57	17	32	22	9	1	144	100	45
Defunct Clubs	34	24	4	6	137	67	54	35	14	8	10	102	89	34	69	37	18	14	239	156	88
Totals	869	557	200	112	3465	2251	1226	869	333	365	171	2829	2960	837	1738	890	565	283	6294	5211	2063

* Totals include those of Kansas City (1974-75, 1975-76) and Colorado (1976-77 through 1981-82)
** Totals include those of Atlanta (1972-73 through 1979-80)

Playoffs

	Series	W	L	GP	W	L	T	GF	GA	Last Mtg.	Round	Result
Boston	4	2	2	20	9	11	0	57	60	1978	QF	L 1-4
Buffalo	2	2	0	11	8	3	0	35	23	1978	QF	W 4-1
Calgary	2	1	1	11	7	4	0	43	28	1981	QF	L 3-4
Chicago	1	0	1	4	0	4	0	8	20	1971	QF	L 0-4
Edmonton	3	1	2	15	7	8	0	43	46	1987	F	L 3-4
Minnesota	2	2	0	11	8	3	0	41	26	1980	SF	W 4-1
Montreal	4	1	3	21	6	15	0	52	72	1989	CF	L 2-4
*New Jersey	1	1	0	2	2	0	0	6	3	1978	P	W 2-0
NY Islanders	4	3	1	25	14	11	0	83	69	1987	DF	W 4-3
NY Rangers	8	4	4	38	19	19	0	119	130	1987	DSF	W 4-2
Pittsburgh	1	1	0	7	4	3	0	31	24	1989	DF	W 4-3
Quebec	2	2	0	11	7	4	0	39	29	1985	CF	W 4-2
St. Louis	2	0	2	11	3	8	0	20	34	1969	QF	L 0-4
Toronto	3	3	0	17	12	5	0	67	47	1977	QF	W 4-2
Vancouver	1	1	0	3	2	1	0	15	9	1979	P	W 2-1
Washington	3	1	2	16	7	9	0	55	65	1989	DSF	W 4-2
Totals	43	25	18	223	116	107	0	714	685			

Playoff Results 1989-85

Year	Round	Opponent	Result	GF	GA
1989	CF	Montreal	L 2-4	8	17
	DF	Pittsburgh	W 4-3	31	24
	DSF	Washington	W 4-2	25	19
1988	DSF	Washington	L 3-4	25	31
1987	F	Edmonton	L 3-4	17	19
	CF	Montreal	W 4-2	22	22
	DF	NY Islanders	W 4-3	23	16
	DSF	NY Rangers	W 4-2	22	13
1986	DSF	NY Rangers	L 2-3	15	18
1985	F	Edmonton	L 1-4	14	21
	CF	Quebec	W 4-2	17	12
	DF	NY Islanders	W 4-1	16	11
	DSF	NY Rangers	W 3-0	14	10

Abbreviations: Round: F – Final; CF – conference final; DF – division final; DSF – division semi-final; SF – semi-final; QF – quarter-final. P – preliminary round. GA – goals against; GF – goals for.

1988-89 Results

		Home					Away	
Oct.	6	New Jersey	4-1	Oct.	13	Minnesota	7-6
	9	Buffalo	4-3		15	Los Angeles	4-1
	20	Quebec	5-2		18	Pittsburgh	2-4
	23	Calgary	4-5		22	Hartford	6-8
	27	NY Islanders	5-2		26	NY Rangers	3-4
	29	NY Rangers	5-6	Nov.	1	New Jersey	2-3
Nov.	3	Vancouver	2-5		4	Detroit	4-3
	6	Pittsburgh	5-4		9	NY Rangers	3-5
	10	Calgary	2-3		19	Quebec	5-6
	12	Detroit*	4-5		24	Boston	1-2
	15	NY Rangers	3-3		26	Pittsburgh	3-4
	17	St Louis	1-3		27	Buffalo	3-7
	20	New Jersey	7-1	Dec.	3	New Jersey*	5-3
	22	Los Angeles	1-6		6	Washington	3-4
	29	Boston	5-1		17	Toronto	7-1
Dec.	1	Montreal	2-2		22	NY Islanders	4-2
	4	New Jersey	6-2		27	Washington	3-4
	8	Pittsburgh	4-3		29	Pittsburgh	3-2
	10	Chicago*	6-4		31	Buffalo	3-2
	15	Washington	4-1	Jan.	3	NY Islanders	4-1
	18	Winnipeg	5-1		5	Minnesota	3-5
	23	Hartford	5-4		7	St Louis	4-7
Jan.	10	Minnesota	3-2		17	Vancouver	3-5
	12	Quebec	7-2		20	Edmonton	1-1
	15	Detroit	4-8		21	Winnipeg	7-3
	26	Washington	0-1	Feb.	5	Washington*	3-1
	28	NY Islanders*	7-4		11	Toronto	3-4
Feb.	2	Pittsburgh	3-5		18	NY Islanders	2-3
	9	Edmonton	1-3		22	NY Rangers	6-4
	12	Vancouver	2-3		24	New Jersey	6-2
	14	NY Rangers	3-1		27	Calgary	3-6
	16	Montreal	4-7	Mar.	1	Winnipeg	4-4
	19	NY Islanders*	5-4		4	Los Angeles	2-6
Mar.	7	Edmonton	4-4		9	NY Islanders	4-4
	11	Chicago*	7-2		12	Hartford	3-3
	16	St Louis	3-4		18	Boston*	3-6
	19	Toronto	8-6		22	Chicago	3-2
	25	NY Rangers	6-1		24	Washington	1-6
	30	Washington	5-4		27	New Jersey	3-5
Apr.	2	Pittsburgh	5-6	Apr.	1	Montreal	2-2

* Denotes afternoon game.

Entry Draft Selections 1989-75

1989
Pick
33	Greg Johnson
34	Patrik Juhlin
72	Reid Simpson
117	Niklas Eriksson
138	John Callahan Jr.
159	Sverre Sears
180	Glen Wisser
201	Al Kummu
222	Matt Brait
243	James Pollio

1988
Pick
14	Claude Boivin
35	Pat Murray
56	Craig Fisher
63	Dominic Roussel
77	Scott Lagrand
98	Edward O'Brien
119	Gordie Frantti
140	Jamie Cooke
161	Johan Salle
182	Brian Arthur
203	Jeff Dandreta
224	Scott Billey
245	Drahomir Kadlec

1987
Pick
20	Darren Rumble
30	Jeff Harding
62	Martin Hostak
83	Tomaz Eriksson
104	Bill Gall
125	Tony Link
146	Mark Strapon
167	Darryl Ingham
188	Bruce McDonald
209	Steve Morrow
230	Darius Rusnak
251	Dale Roehl

1986
Pick
20	Kerry Huffman
23	Jukka Seppo
28	Kent Hawley
83	Mark Bar
125	Steve Scheifele
146	Sami Wahlsten
167	Murray Baron
188	Blaine Rude
209	Shawn Sabol
230	Brett Lawrence
251	Daniel Stephano

1985
Pick
21	Glen Seabrooke
42	Bruce Rendall
48	Darryl Gilmour
63	Shane Whelan
84	Paul Marshall
105	Daril Holmes
126	Ken Alexander
147	Tony Horacek
168	Mike Cusack
189	Gordon Murphy
231	Rod Williams
252	Paul Maurice

1984
Pick
22	Greg Smyth
27	Scott Mellanby
37	Jeff Chychrun
43	Dave McLay
47	John Stevens
79	Dave Hanson
100	Brian Dobbin
121	John Dzikowski
142	Tom Allen
163	Luke Vitale
184	Bill Powers
205	Daryn Fersovitch
247	Juraj Bakos

1983
Pick
41	Peter Zezel
44	Derrick Smith
81	Alan Bourbeau
101	Jerome Carrier
121	Rick Tocchet
141	Bobby Mormina
161	Per-Erik Eklund
181	Rob Nichols
201	William McCormick
221	Brian Jopling
241	Harold Duvall

1982
Pick
4	Ron Sutter
46	Miroslav Dvorak
47	Bill Campbell
77	Mikael Hjalm
98	Todd Bergen
119	Ron Hextall
140	Dave Brown
161	Alain Lavigne
182	Magnus Roupe
203	Tom Allen
224	Rick Gal
245	Mark Vichorek

1981
Pick
16	Steve Smith
37	Rich Costello
47	Barry Tobobondung
58	Ken Strong
65	David Michayluk
79	Ken Latta
100	Justin Hanley
121	Andre Villeneuve
137	Vladimir Svitek
142	Gil Hudon
163	Steve Taylor
184	Len Hachborn
205	Steve Tsujiura

1980
Pick
21	Mike Stothers
42	Jay Fraser
63	Paul Mercier
84	Taras Zytynsky
105	Dan Held
126	Brian Tutt
147	Ross Fitzpatrick
168	Mark Botell
189	Peter Dineen
195	Bob O'Brien
210	Andy Brickley

1979
Pick
14	Brian Propp
22	Blake Wesley
35	Pelle Lindbergh
56	Lindsay Carson
77	Don Gillen
98	Thomas Eriksson
119	Gord Williams

1978
Pick
6	Behn Wilson
7	Ken Linseman
14	Dan Lucas
33	Mike Simurda
37	Gord Salt
50	Glen Cochrane
67	Russ Wilderman
83	Brad Tamblyn
100	Mark Taylor
117	Mike Ewanouski
126	Jerry Price
134	Darren Switzer
151	Greg Francis
167	Rick Berard
168	Don Lucia
182	Mark Berge
183	Ken Moore
195	Jim Olson
198	Anton Stastny

1977
Pick
17	Kevin McCarthy
35	Tom Gorence
53	Dave Hoyda
67	Yves Guillemette
71	Rene Hamelin
89	Dan Clark
107	Alain Chaput
123	Richard Dalpe
135	Pete Peeters
136	Clint Eccles
139	Mike Greeder
150	Tom Bauer
151	Mike Bauman
153	Bruce Crowder
158	Bob Nicholson
159	Dave Isherwood
161	Steve Jones
165	Jim Trainor
166	Barry Duench
168	Rob McNais
172	Mike Laycock

1976
Pick
17	Mark Suzor
35	Drew Callander
53	Craig Hammer
71	Dave Hynek
89	Robin Lang
107	Paul Klasinski
117	Ray Kurpis

1975
Pick
1	Mel Bridgman
54	Bob Ritchie
72	Rick St. Croix
90	Gary Morrison
108	Paul Holmgren
126	Dana Decker
160	Viktor Khatulev
175	Duffy Smith

1974
Pick
35	Don McLean
53	Bob Sirois
71	Randy Andreachuk
89	Dennis Sobchuk
107	Willie Friesen
125	Rejean Lemelin
142	Steve Short
159	Peter McKenzie
174	Marcel Labrosse
189	Scott Jesse
201	Richard Guay
211	Brad Morrow
219	Craig Arvidson

1973
Pick
20	Larry Goodenough
26	Brent Leavins
40	Bob Stumpf
42	Mike Clarke
58	Dale Cook
74	Michel Latreille
90	Doug Ferguson
106	Tom Young
122	Norm Barnes
137	Dan O'Donohue
153	Brian Dick

1972
Pick
7	Bill Barber
23	Tom Bladon
39	Jimmy Watson
55	Al MacAdam
71	Darryl Fedorak
87	Dave Hastings
103	Serge Beaudoin
119	Pat Russell
135	Ray Boutin

Club Directory

The Spectrum
Pattison Place
Philadelphia, PA 19148
Phone 215/465-4500
PR FAX 215/389-9403
Pres. & GM FAX 215/389-9409
TWX 910-997-2239
ENVOY ID
Front Office: FLYERS. GM
Public
Relations: FLYERS. PR
Capacity: 17,423

Board of Directors
Ed Snider, Jay Snider, Joe Scott, Keith Allen, Fred Shabel, Bob Clarke, Sylvan Tobin

Majority Ownership	Ed Snider and family
Limited Partners	Sylvan and Fran Tobin
Chairman of the Board Emeritus	Joe Scott
President	Jay Snider
Executive Vice-President	Keith Allen
Vice-President and General Manager	Bob Clarke
Assistant General Manager	John Paddock
Head Coach	Paul Holmgren
Assistant Coaches	Mike Eaves, Andy Murray
Goaltending Instructor	Bernie Parent
Physical Conditioning Coach	Pat Croce, LPT, ATC
Director of Pro Scouting	Bill Barber
Chief Scout	Jerry Melnyk
Scouts	Walt Atanas, Inge Hammarstrom, Kevin Maxwell, Jim McMahon, Doug Overton, Dennis Patterson, Bob Perry, Glen Sonmor, Red Sullivan, Ron Woody
Executive Vice-President, Administration	Ron Ryan
Vice-President, Sales	Jack Betson
Marketing Assistant	Lynn McGoldrick
Vice-President, Communications	John Brogan
Director of Public Relations	Rodger Gottlieb
Director of Media Relations	Mark Piazza
Director of Community Relations	Linda Panasci
Controller	Bob Baer
Accounting Manager	Jeff Niessea
Accountant	Susann Schaffer
Accounting Clerk	Karen Rehm
Accounts Payable Clerk	Michelle Stanek
Director of Team Services	Joe Kadlec
Computer Analyst, Hockey Dept.	Michael Blair
Executive Assistants/Secretaries	Ileen Forcine, Barbara Gottesman, Dianna Taylor, Robin Walther
Ticket Manager	Ceil Baker
Ticket Office Assistant	Carmen Moses
Video Coordinator	Leon Friedrich
Product Development and Sales	Jeff Landis
Archivist	Mott Linn
Receptionist	Dolores McDermott
P.A. Announcer	Lou Nolan
Team Physician	Jeff Hartzell, M.D.
Orthopedic Surgeon	John Gregg, M.D.
Oral Surgeon	Everett Borghesani, D.D.S.
Ophthalmologist	Lewis Karp, M.D.
Trainer	Dave Settlemyre
Assistant Trainer	Kurt Mundt
Equipment Manager	Jim Evers
Dimensions of rink	200 feet by 85 feet
Location of Press Box	Mid-ice, North side, concourse level
Club colors	Orange, Black and White
Training camp site and Practice Center	The Coliseum, Voorhees, NJ
TV Announcers	Mike Emrick, Bill Clement, Steve Coates
Radio Announcers	Gene Hart, Bobby Taylor
TV Stations	WGBS-TV (Ch. 57), PRISM
Radio Station	WIP-610 (AM)

General Manager

CLARKE, ROBERT EARLE (BOB)
General Manager, Philadelphia Flyers. Born in Flin Flon, Man., August 13, 1949.
After 15 seasons with the Flyers, Bob Clarke retired as a player to become the General Manager of the Philadelphia club. In 1984-85, his first season, as GM, the Flyers finished with 113 points and reached the Stanley Cup finals. As a player, the former Philadelphia captain led his club to Stanley Cup championships in 1974 and 1975 and captured numerous individual awards, including the Hart Trophy as the League's Most Valuable Player in 1973, 1975 and 1976. The four-time All-Star also received the Masterton Memorial Trophy (perseverence and dedication) in 1972 and Frank J. Selke Trophy (top defensive forward) in 1983. Drafted 17th overall in the 1969 Amateur Draft from the Flin Flon Bombers, Clarke appeared in 1,144 regular-season games, scoring 358 goals, 852 assists for 1,210 points. He also added 119 points in 136 playoff games.

Coach

HOLMGREN, PAUL
Coach, Philadelphia Flyers. Born in St. Paul,MN., December 2, 1955.
After serving as an assistant coach for the Flyers for three years, Holmgren assumed the Head Coaching duties on June 1, 1988. In his first NHL season, he led Philadelphia to a 36-36-8 record (80 points) and the Wales Conference Championship series where they lost to Montreal.

Always a Philadelphia fan favorite, the St. Paul native played 500 of his 527 career NHL games in a Flyers' uniform, accumulating 138-171-309 scoring totals and setting an all-time club record with 1,600 penalty minutes. Holmgren was traded to the North Stars on February 23, 1984, where he played a total of 27 games over two years before retiring following the 1984-85 season. On July 22, 1985, he rejoined the Flyers as an assistant coach.

Coaching Record

Season	Team	Games	Regular Season W	L	T	%	Playoffs Games	W	L	%
1988-89	Philadelphia (NHL)	80	36	36	8	.500	19	10	9	.526
	NHL Totals	80	36	36	8	.500	19	10	9	.526

Pittsburgh Penguins

1988-89 Results: 40w-33L-7T 87 PTS. Second, Patrick Division

Year-by-Year Record

		Home			Road				Overall					
Season	GP	W	L	T	W	L	T	W	L	T	GF	GA	Pts.	Finished	Playoff Result
1988-89	80	24	13	3	16	20	4	40	33	7	347	349	87	2nd,	Patrick Div.	Lost Div. Final
1987-88	80	22	12	6	14	23	3	36	35	9	319	316	81	6th,	Patrick Div.	Out of Playoffs
1986-87	80	19	15	6	11	23	6	30	38	12	297	290	72	5th,	Patrick Div.	Out of Playoffs
1985-86	80	20	15	5	14	23	3	34	38	8	313	305	76	5th,	Patrick Div.	Out of Playoffs
1984-85	80	17	20	3	7	31	2	24	51	5	276	385	53	6th,	Patrick Div.	Out of Playoffs
1983-84	80	7	29	4	9	29	2	16	58	6	254	390	38	6th,	Patrick Div.	Out of Playoffs
1982-83	80	14	22	4	4	31	5	18	53	9	257	394	45	6th,	Patrick Div.	Out of Playoffs
1981-82	80	21	11	8	10	25	5	31	36	13	310	337	75	4th,	Patrick Div.	Lost Div. Semi-Final
1980-81	80	21	16	3	9	21	10	30	37	13	302	345	73	3rd,	Norris Div.	Lost Prelim. Round
1979-80	80	20	13	7	10	24	6	30	37	13	251	303	73	3rd,	Norris Div.	Lost Prelim. Round
1978-79	80	23	12	5	13	19	8	36	31	13	281	279	85	2nd,	Norris Div.	Lost Quarter-Final
1977-78	80	16	15	9	9	22	9	25	37	18	254	321	68	4th,	Norris Div.	Out of Playoffs
1976-77	80	22	12	6	12	21	7	34	33	13	240	252	81	3rd,	Norris Div.	Lost Prelim. Round
1975-76	80	23	11	6	12	22	6	35	33	12	339	303	82	3rd,	Norris Div.	Lost Prelim. Round
1974-75	80	25	5	10	12	23	5	37	28	15	326	289	89	3rd,	Norris Div.	Lost Quarter-Final
1973-74	78	15	18	6	13	23	3	28	41	9	242	273	65	5th,	West Div.	Out of Playoffs
1972-73	78	24	11	4	8	26	5	32	37	9	257	265	73	5th,	West Div.	Out of Playoffs
1971-72	78	18	15	6	8	23	8	26	38	14	220	258	66	4th,	West Div.	Lost Quarter-Final
1970-71	78	18	12	9	3	25	11	21	37	20	221	240	62	6th,	West Div.	Out of Playoffs
1969-70	76	17	13	8	9	25	4	26	38	12	182	238	64	2nd,	West Div.	Lost Semi-Final
1968-69	76	12	20	6	8	25	5	20	45	11	189	252	51	5th,	West Div.	Out of Playoffs
1967-68	74	15	12	10	12	22	3	27	34	13	195	216	67	5th,	West Div.	Out of Playoffs

Schedule

Home			Away		
Oct.	Tues. 10 Winnipeg	**Oct.**	Thur. 5 Boston		
	Sat. 14 Montreal		Sat. 7 New Jersey		
	Tues. 17 Toronto		Sun. 15 NY Rangers		
	Wed. 18 St Louis		Thur. 26 Detroit		
	Sat. 21 Buffalo		Sat. 28 Montreal		
	Wed. 25 Toronto	**Nov.**	Sat. 4 Edmonton		
	Tues. 31 Los Angeles		Sun. 5 Vancouver		
Nov.	Thur. 2 NY Islanders		Thur. 9 Chicago		
	Tues. 14 NY Rangers		Sat. 11 St Louis		
	Thur. 16 Quebec		Fri. 24 Washington		
	Sat. 18 NY Islanders		Thur. 30 Philadelphia		
	Wed. 22 New Jersey	**Dec.**	Sat. 2 Quebec		
	Sat. 25 Washington		Fri. 8 New Jersey		
	Tues. 28 Philadelphia		Thur. 14 Minnesota		
Dec.	Wed. 6 Washington		Sat. 16 Calgary		
	Sat. 9 Chicago		Sat. 23 NY Islanders*		
	Tues. 12 Boston		Tues. 26 Washington		
	Tues. 19 Hartford		Sun. 31 NY Rangers*		
	Thur. 21 Washington	**Jan.**	Mon. 8 NY Rangers		
	Wed. 27 NY Rangers		Wed. 10 New Jersey		
Jan.	Tues. 2 Boston		Fri. 12 Washington		
	Thur. 4 Vancouver		Thur. 25 Detroit		
	Sat. 6 Winnipeg		Sat. 27 NY Islanders*		
	Tues. 16 Philadelphia		Sun. 28 Buffalo*		
	Thur. 18 NY Rangers	**Feb.**	Sat. 3 Toronto		
	Tues. 23 New Jersey		Sun. 11 Philadelphia		
	Tues. 30 Philadelphia		Wed. 14 NY Rangers		
Feb.	Fri. 2 Edmonton		Fri. 16 Winnipeg		
	Tues. 6 NY Islanders		Sun. 18 Chicago*		
	Thur. 8 Washington		Sat. 24 Montreal		
	Sat. 10 Los Angeles		Mon. 26 Quebec		
	Tues. 20 Philadelphia	**Mar.**	Fri. 2 New Jersey		
	Thur. 22 NY Islanders		Tues. 6 Edmonton		
	Wed. 28 New Jersey		Wed. 7 Calgary		
Mar.	Sun. 4 Minnesota		Sat. 10 Los Angeles*		
	Thur. 15 Detroit		Sun. 11 Vancouver*		
	Sat. 17 Minnesota*		Sun. 18 NY Islanders*		
	Sat. 24 Calgary*		Thur. 22 Philadelphia		
	Tues. 27 Hartford		Sun. 25 Hartford		
	Sat. 31 Buffalo		Thur. 29 St Louis		

* Denotes afternoon game.

Home Starting Times:
All Games .... 7:35 p.m.
Except Matinees .... 1:35 p.m.
Sat., Oct. 14 .... 8:05 p.m.

Franchise date: June 5, 1967

23rd
NHL
Season

Mario Lemieux captured his second consecutive Art Ross Trophy in 1988-89, leading all scorers with 85 goals, 114 assists and 199 points.

1989-90 Player Personnel

FORWARDS

	HT	WT	Place of Birth	Date	1988-89 Club
AITKEN, Brad	6-2	200	Scarborough, Ont.	10/30/67	Muskegon
BOURQUE, Phil	6-1	203	Chelmsford, MA	6/8/62	Pittsburgh
BROWN, Rob	5-11	185	Kingston, Ont.	4/10/68	Pittsburgh
CALLANDER, Jock	6-1	188	Regina, Sask.	4/23/61	Pittsburgh-Muskegon
CAPUANO, Dave	6-2	188	Warwick, RI	7/27/68	U. of Maine
CULLEN, John	5-10	187	Puslinch, Ont.	8/2/64	Pittsburgh
DANIELS, Jeff	6-1	197	Oshawa, Ont.	6/24/68	Muskegon
ERREY, Bob	5-10	177	Montreal, Que.	9/21/64	Pittsburgh
FRAWLEY, Dan	6-1	195	Sturgeon Falls, Ont.	6/2/62	Pittsburgh-Muskegon
GAUTHIER, Daniel	6-2	176	Charlemagne, Que.	5/17/70	Victoriaville
GIFFIN, Lee	6-0	181	Chatham, Ont.	4/1/67	Muskegon
GILHEN, Randy	5-10	190	Zweibrucken, W. Ger.	6/13/63	Winnipeg
HANNAN, Dave	5-10	185	Sudbury, Ont.	11/26/61	Pittsburgh-Indianapolis
HEWARD, Jamie	6-2	185	Regina, Sask.	3/30/71	Regina
KACHOWSKI, Mark	5-10	196	Edmonton, Alta.	2/20/65	Pittsburgh-Muskegon
LEACH, Jamie	6-1	198	Winnipeg, Man.	8/25/69	Niagara Falls
LEMIEUX, Mario	6-4	210	Montreal, Que.	10/5/65	Pittsburgh
LONEY, Troy	6-3	205	Bow Island, Alta.	9/21/63	Pittsburgh
MAJOR, Mark	6-3	227	Toronto, Ont.	3/20/70	North Bay-Kingston
McBAIN, Andrew	6-1	195	Toronto, Ont.	2/18/65	Winnipeg
MICHAYLUK, Dave	5-10	180	Wakaw, Sask.	5/18/62	Muskegon
MICK, Troy	5-11	180	Barnaby, B.C.	3/30/69	Portland
MULVENNA, Glenn	5-11	182	Calgary, Alta.	2/18/67	Muskegon
QUINN, Dan	5-11	177	Ottawa, Ont.	6/1/65	Pittsburgh
RECCHI, Mark	5-10	189	Kamloops, B.C.	2/1/68	Muskegon-Pittsburgh
SMART, Jason	6-4	212	Prince George, B.C.	1/23/70	Saskatoon-Pr. Albert
STEVENS, Kevin	6-3	210	Brockton, MA	4/15/65	Pittsburgh
WILSON, Mitch	5-8	189	Kelowna, B.C.	2/15/62	Muskegon
ZEMLAK, Richard	6-2	190	Wynyard, Sask.	3/3/63	Min.-K'zoo-Pit.-Musk.

DEFENSEMEN

	HT	WT	Place of Birth	Date	1988-89 Club
BUSKAS, Rod	6-1	207	Wetaskiwin, Alta.	1/7/61	Pittsburgh
CAUFIELD, Jay	6-4	240	Philadelphia, PA	7/17/60	Pittsburgh
COFFEY, Paul	6-1	205	Weston, Ont.	6/1/61	Pittsburgh
DAHLQUIST, Chris	6-1	196	Fridley, MN	12/14/62	Pittsburgh-Muskegon
DELORME, Gilbert	6-1	205	Boucherville, Que.	11/25/62	Detroit
DINEEN, Gord	6-0	195	Toronto, Ont.	9/21/62	Min.-Pit.-K'zoo
FARRELL, Scott	5-11	190	Richmond, B.C.	4/15/70	Spokane
HILLIER, Randy	6-1	186	Toronto, Ont.	3/30/60	Pittsburgh
HOBSON, Doug	6-0	185	Prince Albert, Sask.	4/9/68	Muskegon
JOHNSON, Jim	6-1	190	New Hope, MN	8/9/62	Pittsburgh
KYTE, Jim	6-5	210	Ottawa, Ont.	3/21/64	Winnipeg
LAUS, Paul	6-1	200	Beamsville, Ont.	9/26/70	Niagara Falls
MERSCH, Mike	6-2	210	Skokie, IL	9/29/64	Muskegon-Flint
PAEK, Jim	6-1	194	Seoul, Korea	4/7/67	Muskegon
PANCOE, Don	6-1	188	St. George, Ont.	2/23/69	Hamilton
STANTON, Paul	6-0	185	Boston, MA	6/22/67	U. Wisconsin
STOLK, Darren	6-4	201	Taber, Alta.	7/22/68	Lethbridge
TAYLOR, Randy	6-2	195	Cornwall, Ont.	7/30/65	Flint-Indianapolis
WAVER, Jeff	5-10	189	St. Boniface, Man.	9/28/68	Hamilton-Muskegon
WOLF, Andrew	5-11	196	Richmond, B.C.	5/29/69	Victoria
ZALAPSKI, Zarley	6-1	204	Edmonton, Alta.	4/22/68	Pittsburgh

GOALTENDERS

	HT	WT	Place of Birth	Date	1988-89 Club
BARRASSO, Tom	6-3	207	Boston, MA	3/31/65	Buffalo-Pittsburgh
PIETRANGELO, Frank	5-10	182	Niagara Falls, Ont.	12/17/64	Pittsburgh-Muskegon
RACINE, Bruce	6-0	160	Cornwall, Ont.	8/9/66	Muskegon
YOUNG, Wendell	5-9	183	Halifax, N.S.	8/1/63	Pittsburgh

Retired Numbers

21   Michel Briere   1969-1970

General Managers' History

Jack Riley, 1967-68 to 1969-70; Leonard "Red" Kelly, 1970-71 to 1971-72; Jack Riley, 1972-73 to 1973-74; Jack Button, 1974-75; Wren A. Blair, 1975-76 to 1976-77; Baz Bastien, 1977-78 to 1982-83; Ed Johnston, 1983-84 to 1987-88; Tony Esposito, 1988-89 to date.

Coaching History

George Sullivan, 1967-68 to 1968-69; Red Kelly, 1969-70 to 1971-72; Red Kelly and Ken Schinkel, 1972-73; Ken Schinkel and Marc Boileau, 1973-74; Marc Boileau, 1974-75; Marc Boileau and Ken Schinkel, 1975-76; Ken Schinkel, 1976-77; John Wilson, 1977-78 to 1979-80; Eddie Johnston, 1980-81 to 1982-83; Lou Angotti, 1983-84; Bob Berry, 1984-85 to 1986-87; Pierre Creamer, 1987-88; Gene Ubriaco, 1988-89 to date.

Captains' History

Ab McDonald, 1967-68; no captain, 1968-69 to 1972-73; Ron Schock, 1973-74 to 1976-77; Jean Pronovost, 1977-78; Orest Kindrachuk, 1978-79 to 1980-81; Randy Carlyle, 1981-82 to 1983-84; Mike Bullard, 1984-85, 1985-86; Terry Ruskowski, 1986-87; Dan Frawley and Mario Lemieux, 1987-88; Mario Lemieux, 1988-89 to date.

1988-89 Scoring

Regular Season

*—rookie

Pos	#	Player	Team	GP	G	A	Pts	+/−	PIM	PP	SH	GW	GT	S	%
F	66	Mario Lemieux	PIT	76	85	114	199	41	100	31	13	8	1	313	27.2
F	44	Rob Brown	PIT	68	49	66	115	27	118	24	0	6	0	169	29.0
D	77	Paul Coffey	PIT	75	30	83	113	10−	193	11	0	2	0	342	8.8
F	10	Dan Quinn	PIT	79	34	60	94	37−	102	16	0	4	0	200	17.0
F	12	Bob Errey	PIT	76	26	32	58	40	124	0	3	5	0	130	20.0
F	11	John Cullen	PIT	79	12	37	49	25−	112	8	0	0	0	121	9.9
F	33	*Zarley Zalapski	PIT	58	12	33	45	9	57	5	1	2	1	95	12.6
F	15	Randy Cunneyworth	PIT	70	25	19	44	22−	156	10	0	1	0	163	15.3
F	29	Phil Bourque	PIT	80	17	26	43	22−	97	5	2	3	0	153	11.1
F	32	Dave Hannan	PIT	72	10	20	30	12−	157	2	1	3	0	72	13.9
D	23	Randy Hillier	PIT	68	1	23	24	4−	141	0	1	0	0	37	2.7
F	24	Troy Loney	PIT	69	10	6	16	5−	165	0	0	1	1	90	11.1
F	6	Jim Johnson	PIT	76	2	14	16	7	163	1	0	0	0	70	2.9
F	25	*Kevin Stevens	PIT	24	12	3	15	8−	19	4	0	3	0	52	23.1
F	14	Jock Callander	PIT	30	6	5	11	3−	20	2	0	0	0	35	17.1
G	35	Tom Barrasso	BUF	10	0	3	3	0	21	0	0	0	0	0	.0
			PIT	44	0	5	5	0	49	0	0	0	0	0	.0
			TOTAL	54	0	8	8	0	70	0	0	0	0	0	.0
F	28	Dan Frawley	PIT	46	3	4	7	1−	66	0	0	1	0	37	8.1
F	22	Steve Dykstra	PIT	65	1	6	7	12−	126	0	0	0	0	38	2.6
D	4	Chris Dahlquist	PIT	43	1	5	6	8−	42	0	0	0	0	27	3.7
D	7	Rod Buskas	PIT	52	1	5	6	2−	105	0	0	0	0	15	6.7
D	16	*Jay Caufield	PIT	58	1	4	5	4−	285	0	0	0	0	10	10.0
D	5	Gord Dineen	MIN	2	0	1	1	4	2	0	0	0	0	7	.0
			PIT	38	1	2	3	5−	42	0	0	0	0	25	4.0
			TOTAL	40	1	3	4	9−	44	0	0	0	0	32	3.1
F	27	Scott Bjugstad	PIT	24	3	0	3	12−	4	0	0	1	0	21	14.3
F	19	Dave McLlwain	PIT	24	1	2	3	11−	4	0	0	0	0	14	7.1
F	26	Mark Kachowski	PIT	12	1	1	2	1	43	0	0	0	0	3	33.3
F	8	*Mark Recchi	PIT	15	1	1	2	2−	0	0	0	0	0	11	9.1
G	1	Wendell Young	PIT	22	0	2	2	0	4	0	0	0	0	0	.0
G	31	*Rich Tabaracci	PIT	1	0	0	0	0	0	0	0	0	0	0	.0
F	20	Perry Ganchar	PIT	3	0	0	0	3−	0	0	0	0	0	3	.0
G	40	*Frank Pietrangelo	PIT	15	0	0	0	0	0	0	0	0	0	0	.0
F	18	Richard Zemlak	MIN	3	0	0	1	0	13	0	0	0	0	1	.0
			PIT	31	0	0	0	4−	135	0	0	0	0	3	.0
			TOTAL	34	0	0	0	3−	138	0	0	0	0	3	.0

Goaltending

No.	Goaltender	GPI	Mins	Avg	W	L	T	EN	SO	GA	SA	S%
40	*Frank Pietrangelo	15	669	4.04	5	3	0	1	0	45	409	.890
35	Tom Barrasso	44	2406	4.04	18	15	7	4	0	162	1445	.888
30	*Steve Guenette	11	574	4.29	5	6	0	0	0	41	308	.867
1	Wendell Young	22	1150	4.80	12	9	0	0	0	92	673	.863
31	*Rich Tabaracci	1	33	7.27	0	0	0	0	0	4	21	.810
	Totals	80	4844	4.32	40	33	7	5	0	349	2856	.878

Playoffs

Pos	#	Player	Team	GP	G	A	Pts	+/−	PIM	PP	SH	GW	GT	S	%
F	66	Mario Lemieux	PIT	11	12	7	19	1−	16	7	1	0	0	41	29.3
D	77	Paul Coffey	PIT	11	2	13	15	7−	31	2	0	1	0	48	4.2
F	25	*Kevin Stevens	PIT	11	3	7	10	1−	16	0	0	0	0	21	14.3
F	10	Dan Quinn	PIT	11	6	3	9	6−	10	4	0	1	0	39	15.4
F	11	*John Cullen	PIT	11	3	6	9	4	28	0	0	0	0	20	15.0
F	33	*Zarley Zalapski	PIT	11	1	8	9	2−	13	1	0	0	0	30	3.3
F	44	Rob Brown	PIT	11	5	3	8	2−	22	1	0	3	0	17	29.4
4	15	Randy Cunneyworth	PIT	11	3	5	8	1−	26	1	0	1	0	20	15.0
F	14	Jock Callander	PIT	10	2	5	7	6	10	0	0	0	0	14	14.3
F	29	Phil Bourque	PIT	11	4	1	5	2	66	0	0	1	1	11	36.4
D	6	Jim Johnson	PIT	11	0	5	5	7	44	0	0	0	0	10	.0
F	24	Troy Loney	PIT	11	1	3	4	3	24	0	0	0	0	12	8.3
F	12	Bob Errey	PIT	11	1	2	3	1	12	0	0	0	0	23	4.3
F	19	Dave McLlwain	PIT	3	0	1	1	0	6	0	0	0	0	7	.0
F	32	Dave Hannan	PIT	8	0	1	1	0	4	0	0	0	0	5	.0
D	23	Randy Hillier	PIT	9	0	1	1	1−	49	0	0	0	0	8	.0
G	35	Tom Barrasso	PIT	11	0	1	1	0	8	0	0	0	0	0	.0
F	22	Steve Dykstra	PIT	1	0	0	0	0	2	0	0	0	0	0	.0
G	1	Wendell Young	PIT	1	0	0	0	0	0	0	0	0	0	0	.0
F	18	Richard Zemlak	PIT	1	0	0	0	0	10	0	0	0	0	0	.0
D	4	Chris Dahlquist	PIT	2	0	0	0	0	28	0	0	0	0	0	.0
D	16	*Jay Caufield	PIT	9	0	0	0	2−	28	0	0	0	0	0	.0
D	7	Rod Buskas	PIT	10	0	0	0	1−	23	0	0	0	0	0	.0

Goaltending

No.	Goaltender	GPI	Mins	Avg	W	L	EN	SO	GA	SA	S%
1	Wendell Young	1	39	1.54	0	0	0	0	1	11	.909
35	Tom Barrasso	11	631	3.80	7	4	1	0	40	389	.897
	Totals	11	672	3.75	7	4	1	0	42	400	.895

Club Records

Team

(Figures in brackets for season records are games played; records for fewest points, wins, ties, losses, goals, goals against are for 70 or more games)

Most Points	89	1974-75 (80)
Most Wins	40	1988-89 (80)
Most Ties	20	1970-71 (78)
Most Losses	58	1983-84 (80)
Most Goals	347	1988-89 (80)
Most Goals Against	394	1982-83 (80)
Fewest Points	38	1983-84 (80)
Fewest Wins	16	1983-84 (80)
Fewest Ties	6	1983-84 (80)
Fewest Losses	28	1974-75 (80)
Fewest Goals	182	1969-70 (76)
Fewest Goals Against	216	1967-68 (74)

Longest Winning Streak

Over-all .... 7 Oct. 9-
Oct. 22/86

Home .... 9 Feb. 26-
Apr. 5/75

Away .... 4 Oct. 14-
Nov. 2/84;
Jan. 16-
Jan. 23/88

Longest Undefeated Streak

Over-all .... 11 Feb. 7-28/76
(7 wins, 4 ties)

Home .... 20 Nov. 30/74-
Feb. 22/75
(12 wins, 8 ties)

Away .... 7 Mar. 13-27/79
(5 wins, 2 ties)

Longest Losing Streak

Over-all .... 11 Jan. 22/83-
Feb. 10/83

Home .... 7 Oct. 8-29/83

Away .... 18 Dec. 23/82-
Mar. 4/83

Longest Winless Streak

Over-all .... 18 Jan. 2/83-
Feb. 10/83
(17 losses, 1 tie)

Home .... 11 Oct. 8-
Nov. 19/83
(9 losses, 2 ties)

Away .... 18 Oct. 25/70-
Jan. 14/71
(11 losses, 7 ties)
Dec. 23/82-
Mar. 4/83
(18 losses)

Most Shutouts, Season 6 1967-68 (74)
1976-77 (80)

Most. Pen. Mins., Season *2,670 1988-89*

Most Goals, Game .... 12 Mar. 15/75
(Wash. 1 at Pit. 12)

Individual

Most Seasons	11	Rick Kehoe
Most Games	753	Jean Pronovost
Most Goals, Career	316	Jean Pronovost
Most Assists, Career	415	Mario Lemieux
Most Points, Career	715	Mario Lemieux

(300 goals, 415 assists)

Most Pen. Mins., Career ...946 Rod Buskas
Most Shutouts, Career .....11 Les Binkley

Longest Consecutive
Games Streak ....320 Ron Schock
(Oct. 24/73-Apr. 3/77)

Most Goals, Season ......85 Mario Lemieux
(1988-89)

Most Assists, Season ....114 Mario Lemieux
(1988-89)

Most Points, Season ....199 Mario Lemieux
(1988-89)

Most Pen. Mins., Season ...407 Paul Baxter
(1981-82)

Most Points, Defenseman,
Season ....113 Paul Coffey
(1988-89)
(30 goals, 83 assists)

Most Points, Center,
Season ....199 Mario Lemieux
(1988-89)
(85 goals, 114 assists)

Most Points, Right Wing,
Season ....115 Rob Brown
(1988-89)
(49 goals, 66 assists)

Most Points, Left Wing,
Season ....82 Lowell MacDonald
(1973-74)
(43 goals, 39 assists)

Most Points, Rookie,
Season ....100 Mario Lemieux
(1984-85)
(43 goals, 57 assists)

Most Shutouts, Season .....6 Les Binkley
(1967-68)

Most Goals, Game ....5 Mario Lemieux
(Dec. 31/88)

Most Assists, Game ....6 Ron Stackhouse
(Mar. 8/75)
Greg Malone
(Nov. 28/79)
Mario Lemieux
(Oct. 15/88)

Most Points, Game ....8 Mario Lemieux
(Oct. 15/88,
Dec. 31/88)

* NHL Record.

All-time Record vs. Other Clubs

Regular Season

		At Home						On Road						Total					
	GP	W	L	T	GF	GA	PTS	GP	W	L	T	GF	GA	PTS	GP	W	L	T	GF	GA	PTS
Boston	47	12	25	10	140	189	34	47	6	36	5	129	220	17	94	18	61	15	269	409	51
Buffalo	39	15	12	12	150	141	42	39	5	21	13	102	178	23	78	20	33	25	252	319	65
**Calgary	32	14	10	8	115	110	36	31	7	17	7	88	129	21	63	21	27	15	203	239	57
Chicago	45	22	19	4	159	145	48	46	7	30	9	129	193	23	91	29	49	13	288	338	71
Detroit	51	35	13	3	223	150	73	51	8	34	9	137	204	25	102	43	47	12	360	354	98
Edmonton	16	5	10	1	56	82	11	16	2	13	1	56	97	5	32	7	23	2	112	179	16
Hartford	16	9	5	2	72	60	20	16	6	10	0	68	81	12	32	15	15	2	140	141	32
Los Angeles	57	33	16	8	216	173	74	56	14	34	8	147	209	36	113	47	50	16	363	382	110
Minnesota	50	31	14	5	188	127	67	50	17	29	4	170	196	38	100	48	43	9	358	323	105
Montreal	51	15	28	8	149	194	38	51	4	42	5	128	261	13	102	19	70	13	277	455	51
*New Jersey	41	24	14	3	177	149	51	39	14	18	7	141	147	35	80	38	32	10	318	296	86
NY Islanders	47	20	17	10	169	159	50	48	11	30	7	142	208	29	95	31	47	17	311	367	79
NY Rangers	62	21	31	10	211	232	52	61	21	33	7	203	257	49	123	42	64	17	414	489	101
Philadelphia	66	26	27	13	206	206	65	68	7	55	6	154	316	20	134	33	82	19	360	522	85
Quebec	16	8	6	2	65	70	18	16	7	9	0	58	75	14	32	15	15	2	123	145	32
St. Louis	50	22	17	11	185	149	55	51	13	33	5	136	196	31	101	35	50	16	321	345	86
Toronto	47	24	18	5	175	150	53	47	16	21	10	156	187	42	94	40	39	15	331	337	95
Vancouver	37	23	8	6	167	130	52	37	17	17	3	144	139	37	74	40	25	9	311	269	89
Washington	48	22	20	6	201	165	50	49	19	27	3	178	217	41	97	41	47	9	379	382	91
Winnipeg	16	10	6	0	64	52	20	16	9	7	0	62	63	18	32	19	13	0	126	115	38
Defunct Clubs	35	22	6	7	148	93	51	34	13	10	11	108	101	37	69	35	16	18	256	194	88
Totals	869	413	322	134	3236	2926	960	869	223	526	120	2636	3674	566	1738	636	848	254	5872	6600	1526

* Totals include those of Kansas City (1974-75, 1975-76) and Colorado (1976-77 through 1981-82)
** Totals include those of Atlanta (1972-73 through 1979-80)

Playoffs

	Series	W	L	GP	W	L	T	GF	GA	Last Mtg.	Round	Result
Boston	2	0	2	9	2	7	0	21	37	1980	P	L 2-3
Buffalo	1	1	0	3	2	1	0	9	9	1979	P	W 2-1
Chicago	1	0	1	4	0	4	0	8	14	1972	QF	L 0-4
NY Islanders	2	0	2	12	5	7	0	31	43	1982	DSF	L 2-3
NY Rangers	1	1	0	4	4	0	0	19	11	1989	DSF	W 4-0
Philadelphia	1	0	1	7	3	4	0	24	31	1989	DF	L 3-4
St. Louis	3	1	2	13	6	7	0	40	45	1981	P	L 2-3
Toronto	2	0	2	6	2	4	0	13	21	1977	P	L 1-2
Defunct Clubs	1	1	0	4	4	0	0	13	6			
Totals	14	4	10	62	28	34	0	185	217			

Playoff Results 1989-85

Year	Round	Opponent	Result	GF	GA
1989	DF	Philadelphia	L 3-4	24	31
	DSF	NY Rangers	W 4-0	19	11

Abbreviations: Round: F – Final; **CF** – conference final; **DF** – division final; **DSF** – division semi-final; **SF** – semi-final; **QF** – quarter-final. **P** – preliminary round. **GA** – goals against; **GF** – goals for.

1988-89 Results

	Home			Away	
Oct.	11 Washington	8-7	Oct.	7 Washington	6-4
	15 St Louis	9-2		12 Buffalo	5-8
	18 Philadelphia	4-2		21 New Jersey	4-6
	22 Chicago	7-4		27 St Louis	3-4
	25 Calgary	6-1		29 Montreal	5-4
Nov.	1 Vancouver	5-3		30 NY Rangers	2-9
	3 Quebec	2-6	Nov.	6 Philadelphia	4-5
	8 Edmonton	3-7		12 Los Angeles	2-7
	10 Toronto	5-1		13 Vancouver	4-2
	23 NY Rangers	8-2		16 Toronto	5-8
	26 Philadelphia	4-3		19 NY Islanders	3-6
	30 Washington	6-4		25 Washington	5-3
Dec.	3 NY Islanders	4-2	Dec.	4 Boston	3-3
	6 Chicago	7-6		8 Philadelphia	3-4
	10 New Jersey	4-4		15 NY Islanders	8-2
	14 Los Angeles	5-4		21 Toronto	6-1
	17 Detroit	3-2		23 New Jersey	2-2
	20 NY Islanders	5-3		26 Hartford	4-3
	29 Philadelphia	2-3	Jan.	2 Washington*	0-8
	31 New Jersey	8-6		12 Minnesota	9-2
Jan.	7 Vancouver	5-7		15 NY Rangers*	4-6
	10 NY Islanders	5-3		17 NY Islanders	2-5
	14 NY Rangers*	4-4		20 Winnipeg	3-7
	25 Winnipeg	5-4		21 Edmonton	7-4
	28 Detroit	10-5	Feb.	2 Philadelphia	5-3
	31 Montreal	1-5		5 Boston*	5-2
Feb.	3 St Louis	3-3		11 Quebec	1-8
	9 Buffalo	5-2		17 Buffalo	1-5
	12 Calgary	2-4		23 Detroit	6-6
	14 Buffalo	7-3		25 NY Islanders	5-5
	18 NY Rangers	3-5		26 Hartford	6-8
	21 Philadelphia	1-2	Mar.	3 Washington	2-4
Mar.	1 New Jersey	4-1		7 Los Angeles	2-3
	5 Edmonton	2-4		9 Calgary	3-10
	14 Boston	2-8		10 Winnipeg	5-1
	18 Montreal	2-7		12 Chicago*	6-5
	22 Washington	4-5		16 New Jersey	2-1
	25 New Jersey	5-4		20 Minnesota	2-7
	30 Hartford	5-9		26 NY Rangers	6-4
Apr.	1 NY Rangers	5-2	Apr.	2 Philadelphia	6-5

* Denotes afternoon game.

Entry Draft Selections 1989-75

1989
Pick
16	Jamie Heward
37	Paul Laus
58	John Brill
79	Todd Nelson
100	Tom Nevers
121	Mike Markovich
126	Mike Needham
142	Patrick Schafhauser
163	Dave Shute
184	Andrew Wolf
205	Greg Hagen
226	Scott Farrell
247	Jason Smart

1988
Pick
4	Darrin Shannon
25	Mark Major
62	Daniel Gauthier
67	Mark Recchi
88	Greg Andrusak
130	Troy Mick
151	Jeff Blaeser
172	Rob Gaudreau
193	Donald Pancoe
214	Cory Laylin
235	Darren Stolk

1987
Pick
5	Chris Joseph
26	Richard Tabaracci
47	Jamie Leach
68	Risto Kurkinen
89	Jeff Waver
110	Shawn McEachern
131	Jim Bodden
152	Jiri Kucera
173	Jack MacDougall
194	Daryn McBride
215	Mark Carlson
236	Ake Lilljebjorn

1986
Pick
4	Zarley Zalapski
25	Dave Capuano
46	Brad Aitken
67	Rob Brown
88	Sandy Smith
109	Jeff Daniels
130	Doug Hobson
151	Steve Rohlik
172	Dave McLlwain
193	Kelly Cain
214	Stan Drulia
235	Rob Wilson

1985
Pick
2	Craig Simpson
23	Lee Giffin
58	Bruce Racine
86	Steve Gotaas
107	Kevin Clemens
114	Stuart Marston
128	Steve Titus
149	Paul Stanton
170	Jim Paek
191	Steve Shaunessy
212	Doug Greschuk
233	Gregory Choules

1984
Pick
1	Mario Lemieux
9	Doug Bodger
16	Roger Belanger
64	Mark Teevens
85	Arto Javanainen
127	Tom Ryan
169	John Del Col
189	Steve Hurt
210	Jim Steen
250	Mark Ziliotto

1983
Pick
15	Bob Errey
22	Todd Charlesworth
58	Mike Rowe
63	Frank Pietrangelo
103	Patrick Emond
123	Paul Ames
163	Marty Ketola
183	Alec Haidy
203	Garth Hildebrand
223	Dave Goertz

1982
Pick
10	Rich Sutter
38	Tim Hrynewich
52	Troy Loney
94	Grant Sasser
136	Grant Couture
157	Peter Derkson
178	Greg Gravel
199	Stu Wenaas
220	Chris McCauley
241	Stan Bautch

1981
Pick
28	Steve Gatzos
49	Tom Thornbury
70	Norm Schmidt
109	Paul Edwards
112	Rod Buskas
133	Geoff Wilson
154	Mitch Lamoureaux
175	Dean Defazio
196	David Hannan

1980
Pick
9	Mike Bullard
51	Randy Boyd
72	Tony Feltrin
93	Doug Shedden
114	Pat Graham
156	Robert Geale
177	Brian Lundberg
198	Steve McKenzie

1979
Pick
31	Paul Marshall
52	Bennett Wolf
73	Brian Cross
94	Nick Ricci
115	Marc Chorney

1978
Pick
25	Mike Meeker
61	Shane Pearsall
75	Rob Garner

1977
Pick
30	Jim Hamilton
48	Kim Davis
66	Mark Johnson
102	Greg Millen

1976
Pick
2	Blair Chapman
19	Greg Malone
29	Peter Marsh
47	Morris Lukowich
65	Greg Redquist
83	Brendan Lowe
101	Vic Sirko

1975
Pick
13	Gord Laxton
31	Russ Anderson
49	Paul Baxter
67	Stu Younger
85	Kim Clackson
103	Peter Morris
121	Mike Will
139	Tapio Levo
155	Byron Shutt
170	Frank Salive
185	John Glynne
196	Lex Hudson
202	Dan Tsubouchi
206	Bronislav Stankovsky
217	Kelly Secord

Club Directory

Civic Arena
Pittsburgh, PA 15219
Phone 412/642-1800
FAX 412/642-1925
ENVOY ID
Front Office: PENS. GM.
Public
Relations   PENS. PR
Capacity: 16,025

Chairman of the Board	Edward J. DeBartolo, Sr.
President	Marie Denise DeBartolo York
Vice-President & General Manager	Tony Esposito
General Counsel	J. Paul Martha
Head Coach	Gene Ubriaco
Assistant Coaches	Rick Kehoe, Rick Paterson
Trainer	Skip Thayer
Conditioning Coach	John Welday
Equipment Manager	Steve Latin
Ontario/Central Collegiate Scouts	Greg Malone, Les Binkley
Minnesota Scout	John Gill
Business Manager	Rick McLaughlin
Purchasing Agent	Dana Backstrom
Director of Press Relations	Cindy Himes
Assistant Director of Press Relations	Harry Sanders
Director of Marketing	Tinsy Labrie
Director of Ticket Sales	Jeff Mercer
Ticket Manager	Carol Coulson
Team Physicians	Dr. Chip Burke, Dr. John McCarthy, Dr. Mary Lynn Scovazzo
Team Dentists	Dr. Ronald Linaburg, Dr. Raymond Rainka
Executive Office	Gate 7, Civic Arena
Location of Press Box	East Side of Building
Dimensions of Rink	200 feet by 85 feet
Club Colors	Black, Gold and White
Club Trains at	Pittsburgh, PA
Radio Station	KDKA (1020 AM)
Play-by-Play Announcer	Mike Lange
Television Station	WPGH-TV (53)
Television Commentators	Mike Lange & Paul Steigerwald

General Manager

ESPOSITO, TONY
Vice-President and General Manger, Pittsburgh Penguins. Born in Sault Ste. Marie, Ont., April 23, 1943.

Tony Esposity joined the Penguins organization on April 14, 1988 as their Director of Hockey Operations as well as Vice-President and General Manager. Esposito enjoyed a 16-year NHL playing career with the Montreal Canadiens and Chicago Blackhawks that ended with his retirement in 1983-84.

After 13 games with the Canadiens in 1968-69, Espositio was acquired by the Blackhawks in the Intra-League Draft. In 1969-70, his first full NHL season, Espositio's list of accomplishments was indeed impressive — Vezina Trophy, Calder Trophy and a berth on the NHL First All-Star Team as the Blackhawks captured the Prince of Wales Trophy after a first place finish. In addition, he posted a 2.17 average in 63 games and his 15 shutouts was the second highest total recorded in League history. Espositio went on to appear in 886 career games, registering a 423-307-151 record, 2.92 average and 76 shutouts. He won the Vezina Trophy a total of three times and was named to an NHL All-Star Team on five occasions, including three First Team berths.

Coach

UBRIACO, GENE
Coach, Pittsburgh Penguins. Born in Sault Ste. Marie, Ont., December 26, 1937.

Gene Ubriaco took over head coaching duties for the Penguins on June 28, 1988 and led the club to their best season since 1974-75 with a 40-33-7 record (87 points) and a second-place Patrick Division finish. In their first post-season play since 1981-82, the Penguins advanced to the Division Finals before losing to the Philadelphia Flyers.

The 51-year-old native of Sault Ste. Marie came to the Penguins from the AHL's Baltimore Skipjacks, where he coached from 1982-83 to 1987-88. He also served as that organization's vice-president and general manager during the 1987-88 season.

A left winger during his playing career, Ubriaco spent seven years in the AHL with Rochester, Hershey and Pittsburgh before making his NHL debut with the Penguins in 1967-68, their inaugural NHL season. He later played for the Oakland Seals and Chicago Blackhawks, retiring following the 1969-70 season. In 177 career NHL games, Ubriaco posted scoring totals of 39-35-74.

Ubriaco's coaching career began in 1972-73 as an assistant coach at Lake Superior State College. Since 1974-75, he has coached in the United States Hockey League, the Eastern Hockey League, the Central Hockey League and the American League, winning Coach of the Year honors at various times in each league.

Coaching Record

			Regular Season					Playoffs			
Season	Team	Games	W	L	T	%	Games	W	L	%
1979-80	Baltimore (EHL)	70	41	25	4	.614	10	5	5	.500
1980-81	Baltimore (EHL)	72	29	36	7	.451	....	....	....	....
1981-82	Nashville (CHL)	80	41	35	4	.538	3	0	3	.000
1982-83	Birmingham (CHL)	80	41	37	2	.525	13	6	7	.462
1983-84	Baltimore (AHL)	80	46	24	10	.638	10	6	4	.600
1984-85	Baltimore (AHL)	80	45	27	8	.613	15	10	5	.667
1985-86	Baltimore (AHL)	76	24	44	8	.368	....	....	....	....
1986-87	Baltimore (AHL)	81	36	37	8	.494	....	....	....	....
1987-88	Baltimore (AHL)	80	13	58	9	.219	....	....	....	....
1988-89	**Pittsburgh (NHL)**	**80**	**40**	**33**	**7**	**.544**	**11**	**7**	**4**	**.636**
	NHL Totals	**80**	**40**	**33**	**7**	**.544**	**11**	**7**	**4**	**.636**

Quebec Nordiques

1988-89 Results: 27w-46l-7t 61 pts. Fifth, Adams Division

Year-by-Year Record

Season	GP	Home W	L	T	Road W	L	T	Overall W	L	T	GF	GA	Pts.	Finished	Playoff Result
1988-89	80	16	20	4	11	26	3	27	46	7	269	342	61 5th,	Adams Div.	Out of Playoffs
1987-88	80	15	23	2	17	20	3	32	43	5	271	306	69 5th,	Adams Div.	Out of Playoffs
1986-87	80	20	13	7	11	26	3	31	39	10	267	276	72 4th,	Adams Div.	Lost Div. Final
1985-86	80	23	13	4	20	18	2	43	31	6	330	289	92 1st,	Adams Div.	Lost Div. Semi-Final
1984-85	80	24	12	4	17	18	5	41	30	9	323	275	91 2nd,	Adams Div.	Lost Conf. Championship
1983-84	80	24	11	5	18	17	5	42	28	10	360	278	94 3th,	Adams Div.	Lost Div. Final
1982-83	80	23	10	7	11	24	5	34	34	12	343	336	80 4th,	Adams Div.	Lost Div. Semi-Final
1981-82	80	24	13	3	9	18	13	33	31	16	356	345	82 4th,	Adams Div.	Lost Conf. Championship
1980-81	80	18	11	11	12	21	7	30	32	18	314	318	78 4th,	Adams Div.	Lost Prelim. Round
1979-80	80	17	16	7	8	28	4	25	44	11	248	313	61 5th,	Adams Div.	Out of Playoffs

Schedule

	Home		Away
Oct.	Sat. 7 Boston	Oct.	Thur. 5 Buffalo
	Sun. 8 Hartford		Thur. 12 Philadelphia
	Tues. 17 Calgary		Sat. 14 Minnesota
	Sat. 21 Minnesota		Thur. 19 Chicago
	Sat. 28 Edmonton		Wed. 25 Hartford
	Tues. 31 Chicago		Thur. 26 Boston
Nov.	Sat. 4 St Louis*	Nov.	Thur. 2 NY Rangers
	Sun. 5 Washington*		Wed. 8 New Jersey
	Sat. 11 Vancouver		Thur. 9 NY Islanders
	Tues. 14 Winnipeg		Thur. 16 Pittsburgh
	Sat. 18 Detroit		Wed. 22 Hartford
	Tues. 21 Calgary		Sun. 26 NY Rangers
	Sat. 25 Buffalo		Wed. 29 Montreal
	Thur. 30 Montreal	Dec.	Wed. 13 Edmonton
Dec.	Sat. 2 Pittsburgh		Thur. 14 Calgary
	Tues. 5 Boston		Sun. 17 Vancouver
	Sat. 9 Philadelphia*		Thur. 21 Los Angeles
	Sun. 10 Los Angeles*	Jan.	Wed. 3 Toronto
	Sat. 23 Buffalo		Thur. 4 Detroit
	Tues. 26 Hartford		Sat. 6 NY Islanders
	Sat. 30 NY Islanders		Thur. 11 Boston
Jan.	Tues. 9 Montreal		Tues. 16 Winnipeg
	Sat. 13 New Jersey		Thur. 18 Minnesota
	Tues. 23 Boston		Wed. 24 Montreal
	Sat. 27 Detroit		Wed. 31 Buffalo
	Tues. 30 Buffalo	Feb.	Tues. 6 Washington
Feb.	Sat. 3 Hartford*		Thur. 8 Boston
	Sun. 4 Boston*		Sat. 10 Montreal
	Tues. 13 Vancouver		Thur. 15 St Louis
	Thur. 22 Montreal		Sat. 17 Los Angeles
	Sat. 24 St Louis		Wed. 21 Hartford
	Mon. 26 Pittsburgh		Wed. 28 Toronto
Mar.	Sat. 3 Buffalo	Mar.	Sun. 4 Buffalo
	Tues. 13 Edmonton		Wed. 7 Winnipeg
	Thur. 15 Chicago		Fri. 9 Washington
	Sat. 17 Philadelphia		Sat. 10 New Jersey
	Sat. 24 Toronto		Sun. 18 Montreal
	Tues. 27 NY Rangers		Wed. 21 Hartford
	Thur. 29 Montreal		Thur. 22 Boston
	Sat. 31 Hartford	Apr.	Sun. 1 Buffalo

* Denotes afternoon game.

Home Starting Times:

All Games .... 7:35 p.m.
Except Matinees .... 2:05 p.m.

Franchise date: June 22, 1979

11th
NHL
Season

Mario Marois returned to Quebec after more than two seasons with the Winnipeg Jets.

1989-90 Player Personnel

FORWARDS

	HT	WT	Place of Birth	Date	1988-89 Club
BAILLARGEON, Joel	6-2	215	Quebec, Que.	10/6/64	Quebec-Halifax
BAKER, Jamie	5-11	180	Nepean, Ont.	8/31/66	St. Lawrence University
BERGER, Phil	6-0	190	Dearborn, MI	12/3/66	N. Michigan
DEBLOIS, Lucien	5-11	200	Joliette, Que.	6/21/57	New York Rangers
DORE, Daniel	6-3	202	Ferme-Neuve, Que.	4/9/70	Drummondville
FORTIER, Marc	6-0	192	Windsor, Que.	2/26/66	Quebec-Halifax
GILLIS, Paul	5-11	198	Toronto, Ont.	12/31/63	Quebec
GOULET, Michel	6-1	195	Péribonka, Que.	4/21/60	Quebec
HOPKINS, Dean	6-1	210	Cobourg, Ont.	6/6/59	Quebec-Halifax
HOUGH, Mike	6-1	192	Montréal, Que.	2/6/63	Quebec-Halifax
JACKSON, Jeff	6-1	195	Dresden, Ont.	4/24/65	Quebec
JARVI, Iiro	6-1	198	Helsinki, Finland	3/23/65	Quebec
KAMINSKI, Kevin	5-9	170	Churchbridge, Sask.	3/13/69	Saskatoon
KIMBLE, Darin	6-2	205	Swift Current, Sask.	11/22/68	Quebec-Halifax
LAFLEUR, Guy	6-0	185	Thurso, Que.	9/20/51	NY Rangers
LATTA, David	6-1	190	Thunder Bay, Ont.	1/3/67	Quebec-Halifax
LOISELLE, Claude	5-11	195	Ottawa, Ont.	5/29/63	New Jersey
McRAE, Ken	6-1	195	Winchester, Ont.	4/23/68	Quebec-Halifax
MAILHOT, Jacques	6-2	208	Shawinigan, Que.	12/5/61	Quebec-Halifax
MAJOR, Bruce	6-3	180	Vernon, B.C.	1/3/67	U. of Maine
MIDDENDORF, Max	6-4	210	Syracuse, NY	12/18/67	Halifax
MILLER, Keith	6-2	215	Toronto, Ont.	3/18/67	Fort Wayne
MORIN, Stephane	6-0	174	Montreal, Que.	3/27/69	Chicoutimi
QUINNEY, Ken	5-10	186	New Westminster, B.C.	5/23/65	Halifax
ROUTHIER, Jean-Marc	6-2	190	Quebec, Que.	2/2/68	Halifax
SAKIC, Joe	5-11	185	Burnaby, B.C.	7/7/69	Quebec
SASSO, Tom	6-1	190	Maiden, MA	11/20/66	Johnstown
SEVERYN, Brent	6-2	210	Vegreville, Alta.	2/22/66	Halifax
SHAUNESSY, Scott	6-4	220	Newport, RI	1/22/64	Quebec-Halifax
STASTNY, Peter	6-1	199	Bratislava, Czeh.	9/18/56	Quebec
STIENBURG, Trevor	6-1	200	Kingston, Ont.	5/13/66	Quebec
VERMETTE, Mark	6-1	203	Cochenour, Ont.	10/3/67	Quebec-Halifax

DEFENSEMEN

	HT	WT	Place of Birth	Date	1988-89 Club
BROWN, Jeff	6-1	202	Ottawa, Ont.	4/30/66	Quebec
BZDEL, Gérald	6-1	196	Wynyard, Sask.	3/13/68	Halifax
CIRELLA, Joe	6-3	210	Hamilton, Ont.	5/9/63	New Jersey
ESPE, David	6-0	185	St. Paul, MI	11/3/66	U. of Minnesota
FINN, Steven	6-0	198	Laval, Que.	8/20/66	Quebec
FOGARTY, Brian	6-2	198	Brantford, Ont.	6/11/69	Niagara Falls
GRONSTRAND, Jari	6-3	197	Tampere, Finland	11/14/62	Quebec-Halifax
GUERARD, Stephane	6-2	198	Ste-Elizabeth, Que	4/12/68	Halifax
JULIEN, Claude	6-0	198	Blind River, Ont.	4/23/60	Halifax
LESCHYSHYN, Curtis	6-1	205	Thompson, Man.	9/21/69	Quebec
MAROIS, Mario	5-11	190	Quebec, Que.	12/15/57	Quebec-Winnipeg
MOLLER, Randy	6-2	207	Red Deer, Alta.	8/23/63	Quebec
PICARD, Robert	6-2	212	Montreal, Que	5/25/57	Quebec
RICHARD, Jean-Marc	5-11	178	St. Raymond, Que.	10/8/66	Halifax
SMYTH, Greg	6-3	212	Oakville, Ont.	4/23/66	Quebec-Halifax
SPROTT, Jim	6-1	200	Oakville, Ont.	4/11/69	London

GOALTENDERS

	HT	WT	Place of Birth	Date	1988-89 Club
BRUNETTA, Mario	6-3	180	Quebec, Que.	1/25/67	Quebec-Halifax
FISET, Stephane	6-0	175	Montreal, Que.	6/17/70	Victoriaville
GORDON, Scott	5-9	175	Brockton, MA	2/6/63	Johnstown
MYLNIKOV, Sergei	5-10	175	Chelyabinsk, USSR	10/6/58	Chelyabinsk (USSR)
TUGNUTT, Ron	5-11	155	Scarborough, Ont.	10/22/67	Quebec-Halifax

1988-89 Scoring

Regular Season

*rookie

Pos	#	Player	Team	GP	G	A	Pts	+/−	PIM	PP	SH	GW	GT	S	%
F	26	Peter Stastny	QUE	72	35	50	85	23 −	117	13	0	5	0	195	17.9
F	75	Walt Poddubny	QUE	72	38	37	75	18 −	107	14	0	2	1	197	19.3
D	22	Jeff Brown	QUE	78	21	47	68	22 −	62	13	1	1	0	276	7.6
F	16	Michel Goulet	QUE	69	26	38	64	20 −	67	11	0	2	0	162	16.0
F	88	*Joe Sakic	QUE	70	23	39	62	36 −	24	10	0	2	1	148	15.5
F	11	*Iiro Jarvi	QUE	75	11	30	41	13 −	40	1	0	1	0	109	10.1
F	23	Paul Gillis	QUE	79	15	25	40	14 −	163	5	0	1	0	97	15.5
F	9	Marc Fortier	QUE	57	20	19	39	18 −	45	2	2	2	1	90	22.2
F	20	Anton Stastny	QUE	55	7	30	37	19 −	12	3	0	0	0	84	8.3
F	14	Gaetan Duchesne	QUE	70	8	21	29	0	56	2	1	1	0	110	7.3
D	21	Randy Moller	QUE	74	7	22	29	2	136	2	0	0	0	117	6.0
D	24	Robert Picard	QUE	74	7	14	21	28 −	61	2	1	1	1	102	6.9
F	18	Mike Hough	QUE	46	9	10	19	7 −	39	1	3	3	0	51	17.6
F	12	*Ken McRae	QUE	37	6	11	17	9 −	68	1	0	2	0	47	12.8
D	44	Mario Marois	WPG	7	1	1	2	6 −	17	1	0	0	0	10	10.0
			QUE	42	2	11	13	15 −	101	0	0	0	0	61	3.3
			TOTAL	49	3	12	15	21 −	118	1	0	0	0	71	4.2
D	46	*Curtis Leschyshyn	QUE	71	4	9	13	32 −	71	1	1	0	0	58	6.9
F	27	*Dave Latta	QUE	24	4	8	12	8 −	4	1	0	1	0	30	13.3
F	25	Jeff Jackson	QUE	33	4	6	10	5 −	28	0	1	2	0	40	10.0
F	19	Alain Cote	QUE	55	2	8	10	1 −	14	0	1	0	0	31	6.5
F	17	Trevor Stienberg	QUE	55	6	3	9	17 −	125	1	0	0	0	65	9.2
D	29	Steven Finn	QUE	77	2	6	8	21 −	235	0	1	0	0	86	2.3
F	15	*Darin Kimble	QUE	26	3	1	4	5 −	149	0	0	0	0	21	14.3
F	7	Lane Lambert	QUE	13	2	2	4	2 −	23	0	0	0	0	19	10.5
D	5	*Jari Gronstrand	QUE	25	1	3	4	9 −	14	0	0	0	0	18	5.6
F	10	*Mark Vermette	QUE	12	0	4	4	7 −	7	0	0	0	0	10	.0
D	2	Bobby Dollas	QUE	16	0	3	3	11 −	16	0	0	0	0	11	.0
G	1	*Ron Tugnutt	QUE	26	0	3	3	0	2	0	0	0	0	0	.0
F	15	Dean Hopkins	QUE	5	0	2	2	1	4	0	0	0	0	6	.0
G	33	Mario Gosselin	QUE	39	0	2	2	0	6	0	0	0	0	0	.0
D	4	Greg Smyth	QUE	10	0	1	1	9 −	70	0	0	0	0	3	.0
G	1	Bob Mason	QUE	22	0	1	1	0	2	0	0	0	0	0	.0
F	18	Scott Shaunessy	QUE	4	0	0	0	0	16	0	0	0	0	0	.0
F	38	*Joel Baillargeon	QUE	5	0	0	0	3 −	4	0	0	0	0	2	.0
G	30	Mario Brunetta	QUE	5	0	0	0	0	0	0	0	0	0	0	.0
F	28	*Jacques Mailhot	QUE	5	0	0	0	0	33	0	0	0	0	0	.0

Goaltending

No.	Goaltender	GPI	Mins	Avg	W	L	T	EN	SO	GA	SA	S%
1	*Ron Tugnutt	26	1367	3.60	10	10	3	1	0	82	756	.891
33	Mario Gosselin	39	2064	4.24	11	19	3	0	0	146	1105	.868
1	Bob Mason	22	1168	4.73	5	14	1	1	0	92	627	.853
30	Mario Brunetta	5	226	5.04	1	3	0	1	0	19	117	.836
	Totals	80	4841	4.24	27	46	7	3	0	342	2605	.869

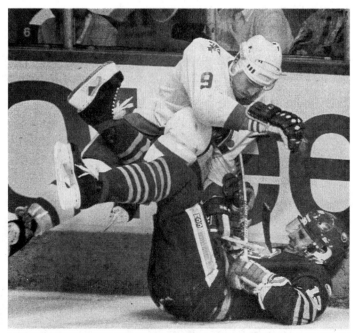

Marc Fortier, a 20-goal scorer for the Nordiques in 1988-89, tangles with the Sabres' Doug Smith.

Retired Numbers

3	J.C. Tremblay	1972-1979
8	Marc Tardif	1979-1983

General Managers' History

Maurice Filion, 1979-80 to 1987-88; Martin Madden 1988-89 to date.

Coaching History

Jacques Demers, 1979-80; Maurice Filion and Michel Bergeron, 1980-81; Michel Bergeron, 1981-82 to 1986-87; André Savard and Ron Lapointe, 1987-88; Ron Lapointe, and Jean Perron, 1988-89; Michel Bergeron, 1989-90.

Captains' History

Marc Tardif, 1979-80, 1980-81; Robbie Ftorek, Andre Dupont, 1981-82; Mario Marois, 1982-83 to 1984-85; Mario Marois, Peter Stastny, 1985-86; Peter Stastny, 1986-87 to date.

Club Records

Team

(Figures in brackets for season records are games played; records for fewest points, wins, ties, losses, goals, goals against are for 70 or more games)

Most Points	94	1983-84 (80)
Most Wins	43	1985-86 (80)
Most Ties	18	1980-81 (80)
Most Losses	46	1988-89 (80)
Most Goals	360	1983-84 (80)
Most Goals Against	345	1981-82 (80)
Fewest Points	61	1979-80 (80)
		1988-89 (80)
Fewest Wins	25	1979-80 (80)
Fewest Ties	5	1987-88 (80)
Fewest Losses	28	1983-84 (80)
Fewest Goals	248	1979-80 (80)
Fewest Goals Against	275	1984-85 (80)

Longest Winning Streak
Over-all .... 7 Nov. 24-
 Dec. 10/83
Home .... 10 Nov. 26/83-
 Jan. 10/84
Away .... 5 Feb. 28-
 Mar. 24, 1986

Longest Undefeated Streak
Over-all .... 11 Mar. 10-31/81
 (7 wins, 4 ties)
Home .... 14 Nov. 19/83
 Jan. 21/84
 (11 wins, 3 ties)
Away .... 8 Feb. 17/81-
 Mar. 22/81
 (6 wins, 2 ties)

Longest Losing Streak
Over-all .... 7 Feb. 9-23/80
Home .... 4 Mar. 12-30/80
Away .... 9 Feb. 2-
 Mar. 19/80;
 Feb. 18-
 Mar. 4/86;
 Mar. 19-
 Apr. 2/88

Longest Winless Streak
Over-all .... 13 Oct. 12-
 Nov. 11/80
 (9 losses, 4 ties)
Home .... 8 Dec. 23/80-
 Jan. 28/81
 (4 losses, 4 ties)

Away .... 13 Jan. 11-
 Mar. 19/80
 (12 losses, 1 tie)
Most Shutouts, Season 6 1985-86 (80)
Most Pen. Mins., Season
.... 2,042 1987-88 (80)
Most Goals, Game .... 12 Feb. 1/83
 (Hfd. 3 at Que. 12)
 Oct. 20/84
 (Que. 12 at Tor. 3)

Individual

Most Seasons .... 10 Michel Goulet,
 Alain Côté
Most Games .... 756 Michel Goulet
Most Goals, Career .... 440 Michel Goulet
Most Assists, Career .... 630 Peter Stastny
Most Points, Career .... 986 Peter Stastny
 (356 goals, 630 assists)
Most Pen. Mins., Career 1,545 Dale Hunter
Most Shutouts, Career .... 6 Mario Gosselin
Longest Consecutive
 Games Streak ....312 Dale Hunter
 (Oct. 9/80-Mar. 13/84)
Most Goals, Season .... 57 Michel Goulet
 (1982-83)
Most Assists, Season .... 93 Peter Stastny
 (1980-81, 1981-82)
Most Points, Season ....139 Peter Stastny
 (1981-82)
 (46 goals, 93 assists)
Most Pen. Mins., Season ...301 Gord Donnelly
 (1987-88)
Most Points, Defenseman,
 Season .... 68 Jeff Brown
 (1988-89)
 (21 goals, 47 assists)
Most Points, Center,
 Season .... 139 Peter Stastny
 (1981-82)
 (46 goals, 93 assists)
Most Points, Right Wing,
 Season .... 103 Jacques Richard
 (1980-81)
 (52 goals, 51 assists)

Most Points, Left Wing,
 Season .... 121 Michel Goulet
 (1983-84)
 (56 goals, 65 assists)
Most Points, Rookie,
 Season .... 109 Peter Stastny
 (1980-81)
 (39 goals, 70 assists)
Most Shutouts, Season .... 4 Clint Malarchuk
 (1985-86)
Most Goals, Game .... 4 Michel Goulet
 (Dec. 14/85;
 Mar. 17/86
 Peter Stastny
 (Feb. 22/81;
 Feb. 11/89)
Most Assists, Game .... 5 Anton Stastny
 (Feb. 22/81)
 Michel Goulet
 (Jan. 3/84)
Most Points, Game .... 8 Peter Stastny
 (Feb. 22/81)
 Anton Stastny
 (Feb. 22/81)

* NHL Record.

All-time Record vs. Other Clubs

Regular Season

	At Home						On Road						Total					
	GP	W	L	T	GF	GA	PTS	GP	W	L	T	GF	GA	PTS	GP	W	L	T	GF	GA	PTS
Boston	36	13	20	3	144	163	29	36	15	16	5	128	142	35	72	28	36	8	272	305	64
Buffalo	36	21	11	4	141	103	46	36	10	21	5	119	146	25	72	31	32	9	260	249	71
**Calgary	16	7	8	1	64	59	15	16	3	9	4	45	67	10	32	10	17	5	109	126	25
Chicago	16	8	4	4	73	58	20	16	6	9	1	57	69	13	32	14	13	5	130	127	33
Detroit	16	11	3	2	74	45	24	16	7	8	1	62	65	15	32	18	11	3	136	110	39
Edmonton	16	6	8	2	67	76	14	16	4	12	0	51	95	8	32	10	20	2	118	171	22
Hartford	36	23	9	4	171	116	50	36	13	15	8	135	133	34	72	36	24	12	306	249	84
Los Angeles	16	7	7	2	68	63	16	16	7	8	1	66	70	15	32	14	15	3	134	133	31
Minnesota	16	12	2	2	81	41	26	16	6	8	2	54	63	14	32	18	10	4	135	104	40
Montreal	36	20	14	2	131	122	42	36	8	23	5	112	159	21	72	28	37	7	243	281	63
*New Jersey	16	10	4	2	79	54	22	16	9	6	1	64	64	19	32	19	10	3	143	118	41
NY Islanders	16	8	7	1	63	53	17	16	5	10	1	57	72	11	32	13	17	2	120	125	28
NY Rangers	16	9	4	3	76	68	21	16	3	10	3	45	68	9	32	12	14	6	121	136	30
Philadelphia	16	4	6	6	52	58	14	16	2	12	2	41	68	6	32	6	18	8	93	126	20
Pittsburgh	16	9	7	0	75	58	18	16	6	8	2	70	65	14	32	15	15	2	145	123	32
St. Louis	16	9	5	2	62	49	20	16	3	12	1	52	71	7	32	12	17	3	114	120	27
Toronto	16	9	3	4	68	55	22	16	8	6	2	70	50	18	32	17	9	6	138	105	40
Vancouver	16	5	7	4	47	49	14	16	6	10	0	68	73	12	32	11	17	4	115	122	26
Washington	16	6	6	4	57	61	16	16	6	8	2	62	60	18	32	12	14	6	119	121	34
Winnipeg	16	7	7	2	67	64	16	16	5	7	4	63	63	14	32	12	14	6	130	127	30
Totals	400	204	142	54	1660	1415	462	400	134	216	50	1421	1663	318	800	338	358	104	3081	3078	780

* Totals include those of Colorado Rockies (1979-80, 1980-81 and 1981-82)
** Totals include those of Atlanta (1979-80)

Playoffs

	Series	W	L	GP	W	L	T	GF	GA
Boston	2	1	1	11	5	6	0	36	37
Buffalo	2	2	0	8	6	2	0	35	27
Hartford	2	1	1	9	4	5	0	34	35
Montreal	4	2	2	25	12	13	0	74	82
NY Islanders	1	0	1	4	0	4	0	9	18
Philadelphia	2	0	2	11	4	7	0	29	39
Totals	13	6	7	68	31	37	0	217	238

Playoff Results 1989-85

Year	Round	Opponent	Result	GF	GA
			Last Mtg. Round Result		
	1983	DSF	L 1-3		
	1985	DSF	W 3-2		
	1987	DSF	W 4-2		
	1987	DF	L 3-4		
	CF	L 0-4			
	1985	CF	L 2-4		
1987	DF	Montreal	L 3-4	21	27
	DSF	Hartford	W 4-2	27	19
1986	DSF	Hartford	L 0-3	7	16
1985	CF	Philadelphia	L 2-4	12	17
	DF	Montreal	W 4-3	24	24
	DSF	Buffalo	W 3-2	22	22

Abbreviations: Round: **F** – Final; **CF** – conference final; **DF** – division final; **DSF** – division semi-final; **SF** – semi-final; **QF** – quarter-final. **P** – preliminary round. **GA** – goals against; **GF** – goals for.

1988-89 Results

		Home				Away	
Oct.	8	New Jersey	3-5	Oct.	6	Hartford	5-2
	9	Minnesota	4-1		12	Montreal	6-5
	14	Buffalo	4-5		16	Buffalo	5-3
	25	Chicago	4-7		20	Philadelphia	2-5
	29	NY Islanders	4-7		22	NY Islanders	3-7
Nov.	1	Los Angeles	1-3		23	NY Rangers	2-8
	5	St Louis	2-5		27	Boston	2-6
	8	Winnipeg	4-8	Nov.	3	Pittsburgh	6-2
	15	Boston	5-5		10	Washington	1-4
	19	Philadelphia	6-5		12	St Louis	3-4
	24	Montreal	5-3		13	Chicago	5-5
	26	Hartford	2-4		23	Hartford	3-4
	28	Edmonton	4-7		30	Buffalo	2-6
Dec.	3	Detroit	6-4	Dec.	1	Detroit	3-7
	13	Washington	1-4		6	Calgary	2-3
	15	Montreal	6-4		7	Edmonton	3-8
	18	Boston*	4-2		9	Vancouver	4-2
	28	Hartford	4-4		17	Boston*	2-2
	29	Toronto	5-6		21	Montreal	4-6
Jan.	8	Boston	2-4		23	Winnipeg	5-4
	10	Washington	4-4		31	Toronto	1-6
	14	Buffalo	1-1	Jan.	3	Calgary	1-5
	17	New Jersey	7-4		4	Edmonton	2-4
	21	Calgary	4-3		12	Philadelphia	2-7
	23	Hartford	0-5		19	New Jersey	5-4
Feb.	2	Montreal	1-6		26	Minnesota	3-5
	4	Minnesota*	6-3		28	Hartford	3-2
	5	NY Islanders	2-3		30	Detroit	4-3
	11	Pittsburgh	8-1	Feb.	9	Pittsburgh	2-5
	21	Winnipeg	4-3		13	Montreal	3-2
	25	NY Rangers	2-7		16	Vancouver	2-3
	28	Vancouver	2-3		18	Los Angeles	3-11
Mar.	4	Buffalo	6-2		23	Hartford	2-4
	7	Toronto	4-6	Mar.	2	Boston	2-5
	9	Montreal	2-5		5	Buffalo	8-2
	14	Los Angeles	0-4		16	Boston	2-2
	18	NY Rangers	8-3		22	Montreal	0-8
	23	Hartford	6-3		29	Chicago	1-3
	25	Buffalo	4-1		30	St Louis	3-4
Apr.	1	Boston*	4-5	Apr.	2	Buffalo	2-4

* Denotes afternoon game.

Entry Draft
Selections 1989-79

1989
Pick
1	Mats Sundin
22	Adam Foote
43	Stephane Morin
54	John Tanner
68	Niclas Andersson
76	Eric Dubois
85	Kevin Kaiser
106	Dan Lambert
127	Sergei Mylnikov
148	Paul Krake
169	Viacheslav Bykov
190	Andrei Khumutov
211	Byron Witkowski
232	Noel Rahn

1988
Pick
3	Curtis Leschyshyn
5	Daniel Dore
24	Stephane Fiset
45	Petri Aaltonen
66	Darin Kimble
87	Stephane Venne
108	Ed Ward
129	Valeri Kamensky
150	Sakari Lindfors
171	Dan Wiebe
213	Alexei Gusarov
234	Claude Lapointe

1987
Pick
9	Bryan Fogarty
15	Joe Sakic
51	Jim Sprott
72	Kip Miller
93	Rob Mendel
114	Garth Snow
135	Tim Hanus
156	Jake Enebak
177	Jaroslav Sevcik
183	Ladislav Tresl
198	Darren Nauss
219	Mike Williams

1986
Pick
18	Ken McRae
39	Jean-M Routhier
41	Stephane Guerard
81	Ron Tugnutt
102	Gerald Bzdel
117	Scott White
123	Morgan Samuelsson
134	Mark Vermette
144	Jean-Francois Nault
165	Keith Miller
186	Pierre Millier
207	Chris Lappin
228	Martin Latreille
249	Sean Boudreault

1985
Pick
15	David Latta
36	Jason Lafreniere
57	Max Middendorf
65	Peter Massey
78	David Espe
99	Bruce Major
120	Andy Akervik
141	Mike Oliverio
162	Mario Brunetta
183	Brit Peer
204	Tom Sasso
225	Gary Murphy
246	Jean Bois

1984
Pick
15	Trevor Stienburg
36	Jeff Brown
57	Steve Finn
78	Terry Perkins
120	Darren Cota
141	Henrik Cedegren
162	Jyrki Maki
183	Guy Ouellette
203	Ken Quinney
244	Peter Loob

1983
Pick
32	Yves Heroux
52	Bruce Bell
54	Iiro Jarvi
92	Luc Guenette
112	Brad Walcott
132	Craig Mack
152	Tommy Albelin
172	Wayne Groulx
192	Scott Shaunessy
232	Bo Berglund
239	Dinorich Kokrement

1982
Pick
13	David Shaw
34	Paul Gillis
55	Mario Gosselin
76	Jiri Lala
97	Phil Stanger
131	Daniel Poudrier
181	Mike Hough
202	Vincent Lukac
223	Andre Martin
244	Jozef Lukac
248	Jan Jasko

1981
Pick
11	Randy Moller
53	Jean-Marc Gaulin
74	Clint Malarchuk
95	Ed Lee
116	Mike Eagles
158	Andre Cote
179	Marc Brisebois
200	Kari Takko

1980
Pick
24	Normand Rochefort
66	Jay Miller
108	Mark Kumpel
129	Gaston Therrien
150	Michel Bolduc
171	Christian Tanguay
192	William Robinson

1979
Pick
20	Michel Goulet
41	Dale Hunter
62	Lee Norwood
83	Anton Stastny
104	Pierre Lacroix
125	Scott McGeown

General Manager

MADDEN, MARTIN
General Manager, Quebec Nordiques. Born in Quebec City, Que., June 5, 1943.

On June 27, 1988, the Quebec Nordiques named Martin Madden as the club's general manager. Madden had previously served as the Nordiques' director of scouting. Originally hired by the Philadelphia Flyers as a scout, Madden was a part of the Flyers when that organization won the Stanley Cup in 1974 and 1975. He later joined the NHL's Central Scouting Bureau and, in 1978-79, became general manager of the Quebec Remparts of the QMJHL.

His involvement with the Nordiques began in 1979 when he was retained as a consultant to aid in preparation for the NHL Expansion Draft. The next year, he was appointed assistant general manager and director of scouting for the Nordiques, assuming these positions just prior to the start of the 1980-81 season.

Coach

BERGERON, JOSEPH ROBERT (MICHEL)
Coach, Quebec Nordiques. Born in Montreal, Que., June 12, 1946.

Michel Bergeron returned to coach the Nordiques on April 14, 1989 after two years with the New York Rangers. He returns to the team with which he began his NHL coaching career in 1980-81 and posted a 253-222-79 record in 554 games.

After managing midget teams in his native Montreal, the 43-year-old Bergeron broke into Junior hockey in 1974-75 as coach of the Trois-Rivieres Draveurs in the QMJHL. He piloted the Draveurs for six seasons, leading that club to back-to-back Memorial Cup Championships in 1977-78 and 1978-79.

In 1980-81, Bergeron joined the Nordiques' organization, taking over as coach shortly after the start of the season. On June 18, 1987, the New York Rangers dealt their 1988 first round draft choice to Quebec in exchange for the services of Michel Bergeron.

Coaching Record

Season	Team	Games	Regular Season				Playoffs			
			W	L	T	%	Games	W	L	%
1974-75	Trois-Rivieres (QMJHL)	72	34	25	13	.563	6	2	4	.333
1975-76	Trois-Rivieres (QMJHL)	72	36	31	5	.535	10	5	5	.500
1976-77	Trois-Rivieres (QMJHL)	72	38	24	10	.597	6	2	4	.333
1977-78	Trois-Rivieres (QMJHL)	72	47	18	7	.701	17	13	4	.765
1978-79	Trois-Rivieres (QMJHL)	72	58	8	6	.847	17	14	3	.824
1979-80	Trois-Rivieres (QMJHL)	72	36	27	9	.563	7	3	4	.429
1980-81	**Quebec (NHL)**	74	29	29	16	.500	5	2	3	.400
1981-82	**Quebec (NHL)**	80	33	31	16	.512	16	7	9	.437
1982-83	**Quebec (NHL)**	80	34	34	12	.500	4	1	3	.250
1983-84	**Quebec (NHL)**	80	42	28	10	.588	9	5	4	.556
1984-85	**Quebec (NHL)**	80	41	30	9	.569	18	9	9	.500
1985-86	**Quebec (NHL)**	80	43	31	6	.575	3	0	3	.000
1986-87	**Quebec (NHL)**	80	31	39	10	.450	13	7	6	.538
1987-88	NY Rangers (NHL)	80	36	34	10	.513	....	....	....	....
1988-89	NY Rangers (NHL)	78	37	33	8	.526	....	....	....	....
	NHL Totals	712	326	289	97	.526	68	31	37	.456

Club Directory

Colisée de Québec
2205 Ave du Colisée
Québec City, Quebec
G1L 4W7
Phone 418/529-8441
GM FAX 418/529-7446
FAX 418/529-1052
ENVOY ID
Front Office: NORDIQUES. GM
Public
Relations: NORDIQUES. PR
Marketing: NORDIQUES. MKTG
Capacity: 15,399

President and Governor	Marcel Aubut
Alternate Governors	Maurice Filion, Gilles Léger, Martin Madden
Executive Secretaries to the President	Louise Marois, Nicole Vandal

Hockey Club Personnel
General Manager	Martin Madden
Head Coach	Michel Bergeron
Associate Coaches	Alain Chainey, Guy Lapointe
Goaltending Coach	Serge Aubry
Vice-President/Hockey Operations	Maurice Filion
Director of Farm Club System	Gilles Léger
Scout – Professional hockey and special assignments	Simon Nolet
Chief Scout	Pierre Gauthier
Assistant to the Chief Scout	Darwin Bennett
Supervisor of Player Development	André Savard
Scouts	Don Boyd, P.A. Fontaine, Michel Georges, Mark Kelley, Guy Lafrance, Bob Mancini, Frank Moberg, Don Paarup, Calle Törnquist
Physiotherapist	Jacques Lavergne
Trainers	René Lacasse, René Lavigueur, Brian Turpin
Team Physician	Dr. Pierre Beauchemin
Executive Secretaries – hockey department	Liza Boivin, Suzanne Lussier

Administration and Finance
Vice President/Administration and Finance	Jean Laflamme
Director of Finance	Mario Rancourt
Assistant to the Director of Finance	Raynald Larose
General Counsel	Jean Pelletier
Executive Secretary	Josette Gagné

Marketing and Communications
Vice-President/Marketing and Communications	Jean-D. Legault
Supervisor of Public Relations	Marius Fortier
Supervisor of Press Relations	Jean Martineau
Coordinator of statistics and fan relations	Nicole Bouchard
Coordinator of research and development	Céline Porlier
Marketing Coordinator	Bernard Thiboutot
Graphic Communications Coordinator	Daniel Gagné
Director of Sales & Promotions	André Lestourneau
Supervisor of Novelties & Souvenirs	André Pelletier
Executive Secretaries – Marketing	Michelle Métivier, Nicole Sampaio
Executive Secretary	Jozée Paré
Team Photographer	André Pichette

Location of Press Box	East & West side of building, upper level
Dimensions of Rink	200 feet by 85 feet
Club Colors	Blue, White and Red
Training Camp Site	Québec City
Radio Station	CHRC 80
Radio Announcers	Alain Crête, Michel Carrier
TV Station	CFAP (2) Quatre-Saisons
TV Announcers	André Côté, Claude Bédard

Joe Sakic had an outstanding debut for the Nordiques, recording 62 points on 23 goals and 39 assists.

St. Louis Blues

1988-89 Results: 33w-35L-12T 78 PTS. Second, Norris Division

Year-by-Year Record

Season	GP	Home W	L	T	Road W	L	T	Overall W	L	T	GF	GA	Pts.	Finished	Playoff Result
1988-89	80	22	11	7	11	24	5	33	35	12	275	285	78	2nd, Norris Div.	Lost Div. Final
1987-88	80	18	17	5	16	21	3	34	38	8	278	294	76	2nd, Norris Div.	Lost Div. Final
1986-87	80	21	12	7	11	21	8	32	33	15	281	293	79	1st, Norris Div.	Lost Div. Semi-Final
1985-86	80	23	11	6	14	23	3	37	34	9	302	291	85	3rd, Norris Div.	Lost Conf. Championship
1984-85	80	21	12	7	16	19	5	37	31	12	299	288	86	1st, Norris Div.	Lost Div. Semi-Final
1983-84	80	23	14	3	9	27	4	32	41	7	293	316	71	2nd, Norris Div.	Lost Div. Final
1982-83	80	16	16	8	9	24	7	25	40	15	285	316	65	4th, Norris Div.	Lost Div. Semi-Final
1981-82	80	22	14	4	10	26	4	32	40	8	315	349	72	3rd Norris Div.	Lost Div. Final
1980-81	80	29	7	4	16	11	13	45	18	17	352	281	107	1st, Smythe Div.	Lost Quarter-Final
1979-80	80	20	13	7	14	21	5	34	34	12	266	278	80	2nd, Smythe Div.	Lost Prelim. Round
1978-79	80	14	20	6	4	30	6	18	50	12	249	348	48	3rd, Smythe Div.	Out of Playoffs
1977-78	80	12	20	8	8	27	5	20	47	13	195	304	53	4th, Smythe Div.	Out of Playoffs
1976-77	80	22	13	5	10	26	4	32	39	9	239	276	73	1st, Smythe Div.	Lost Quarter-Final
1975-76	80	20	12	8	9	25	6	29	37	14	249	290	72	3rd, Smythe Div.	Lost Prelim. Round
1974-75	80	23	13	4	12	18	10	35	31	14	269	267	84	2nd, Smythe Div.	Lost Prelim. Round
1973-74	78	16	16	7	10	24	5	26	40	12	206	248	64	6th, West Div.	Out of Playoffs
1972-73	78	21	11	7	11	23	5	32	34	12	233	251	76	4th, West Div.	Lost Quarter-Final
1971-72	78	17	17	5	11	22	6	28	39	11	208	247	67	3rd, West Div.	Lost Semi-Final
1970-71	78	23	7	9	11	18	10	34	25	19	223	208	87	2nd, West Div.	Lost Quarter-Final
1969-70	76	24	9	5	13	18	7	37	27	12	224	179	86	1st, West Div.	Lost Final
1968-69	76	21	8	9	16	17	5	37	25	14	204	157	88	1st, West Div.	Lost Final
1967-68	74	18	12	7	9	19	9	27	31	16	177	191	70	3rd, West Div.	Lost Final

Schedule

	Home			Away	
Oct.	Sat. 7	Toronto	**Oct.**	Thur. 5	Chicago
	Sat. 14	Chicago		Thur. 12	Minnesota
	Thur. 19	Detroit		Wed. 18	Pittsburgh
	Sat. 21	Los Angeles		Tues. 24	Philadelphia
	Thur. 26	Minnesota		Tues. 31	Washington
	Sat. 28	Washington	**Nov.**	Wed. 1	Hartford
Nov.	Thur. 9	Montreal		Sat. 4	Quebec*
	Sat. 11	Pittsburgh		Mon. 6	Montreal
	Tues. 21	Minnesota		Wed. 15	Toronto
	Sat. 25	Calgary		Thur. 16	Detroit
	Tues. 28	Boston		Sat. 18	Minnesota
	Thur. 30	Hartford		Thur. 23	Winnipeg
Dec.	Thur. 7	Toronto	**Dec.**	Sat. 2	Boston
	Sat. 9	Vancouver		Sun. 3	Buffalo
	Sat. 16	Edmonton		Tues. 5	Detroit
	Tues. 26	Chicago		Mon. 11	Toronto
	Sat. 30	Minnesota		Wed. 13	NY Rangers
Jan.	Tues. 2	Edmonton		Mon. 18	Toronto
	Thur. 4	Philadelphia		Wed. 20	Chicago
	Sat. 6	NY Rangers		Sat. 23	New Jersey
	Tues. 16	Calgary		Thur. 28	NY Islanders
	Thur. 18	Toronto		Sun. 31	Minnesota
	Thur. 25	Hartford	**Jan.**	Tues. 9	Los Angeles
	Sat. 27	Winnipeg		Fri. 12	Vancouver
Feb.	Sat. 3	Detroit		Sun. 14	Winnipeg
	Tues. 6	Toronto		Tues. 23	Detroit
	Sat. 10	New Jersey		Tues. 30	NY Islanders
	Sun. 11	Buffalo		Wed. 31	NY Rangers
	Thur. 15	Quebec	**Feb.**	Wed. 7	Toronto
	Sat. 17	Detroit		Tues. 13	Minnesota
	Tues. 20	Chicago		Sat. 24	Quebec
	Thur. 22	Philadelphia		Sun. 25	Montreal
	Tues. 27	Buffalo	**Mar.**	Thur. 1	Chicago
Mar.	Sat. 3	NY Islanders		Tues. 6	New Jersey
	Sat. 10	Chicago		Thur. 8	Detroit
	Thur. 15	Vancouver		Sun. 11	Chicago
	Sat. 17	Detroit		Tues. 13	Washington
	Tues. 27	Boston		Mon. 19	Calgary
	Thur. 29	Pittsburgh		Wed. 21	Edmonton
	Sat. 31	Minnesota		Sat. 24	Los Angeles

* Denotes afternoon game.

Home Starting Times:
Weeknights & Saturdays . . . . 7:35 p.m.
Sundays . . . . 6:05 p.m.

Franchise date: June 5, 1967.

23rd NHL Season

Peter Zezel had 36 assists in 52 games with the St. Louis Blues.

1988-89 Player Personnel

FORWARDS	HT	WT	S	Place of Birth	Date	1988-89 Club
BRIND'AMOUR, Rod	6-1	200	L	Ottawa, Ont.	8/9/70	Michigan State
CAVALLINI, Gino	6-1	215	L	Toronto, Ont.	11/24/62	St. Louis
CHASE, Kelly	5-11	200	R	Porcupine, Sask.	10/25/67	Peoria
COXE, Craig	6-5	220	L	Chula Vista, CA	1/21/64	St. Louis
DUCOLON, Toby	6-0	195	R	St. Albans, VT	6/18/66	Peoria
EVANS, Doug	5-9	170	L	Peterborough, Ont.	6/2/63	St. Louis
EWEN, Todd	6-2	220	R	Saskatoon, Sask.	3/22/66	St. Louis
HRKAC, Tony	5-11	170	L	Thunder Bay, Ont.	7/7/66	St. Louis
HULL, Brett	5-12	195	R	Belleville, Ont.	9/9/64	St. Louis
LOWRY, Dave	6-1	195	L	Sudbury, Ont.	2/14/65	St. Louis
MacLEAN, Paul	6-2	205	R	Grostenquin, France	3/9/58	Detroit
MacLEAN, Terry	6-1	178	L	Montreal, Que.	1/14/68	Peoria
MEAGHER, Rick	5-8	175	L	Belleville, Ont.	11/4/53	St. Louis
MIEHM, Kevin	6-2	190	L	Kitchener, Ont.	9/10/69	Oshawa
MOMESSO, Sergio	6-3	215	L	Montreal, Que.	9/4/65	St. Louis
OATES, Adam	5-11	185	R	Weston, Ont.	8/27/62	Detroit
O'BRIEN, David	6-1	180	R	Brighton, MA	9/13/66	Binghamton
OSBORNE, Keith	6-1	180	R	Toronto, Ont.	4/2/69	Niagara Falls
RAGLAN, Herb	6-0	200	R	Peterborough, Ont.	8/5/67	St. Louis
SMITH, Darin	6-2	204	L	Vineland Station, Ont.	2/20/67	Peoria
THOMLINSON, Dave	6-1	185	L	Edmonton, Alta.	10/22/66	Peoria
TUTTLE, Steve	6-1	180	R	Vancouver, B.C.	1/5/66	St. Louis
VESEY, Jim	6-3	200	R	Columbus, MA	10/29/65	Peoria
WOLAK, Mike	5-10	155	L	Utica, NY	4/29/68	Windsor
ZEZEL, Peter	5-11	200	L	Toronto, Ont.	4/22/65	Philadelphia-St. Louis

DEFENSEMEN	HT	WT	S	Place of Birth	Date	1988-89 Club
BENNING, Brian	6-1	195	L	Edmonton, Alta.	6/10/66	St. Louis
CAVALLINI, Paul	6-2	210	L	Toronto, Ont.	10/13/65	St. Louis
DeGAETANO, Phil	6-1	203	R	Flushing, NY	8/9/63	Peoria
DIRK, Robert	6-4	210	L	Regina, Sask.	8/20/66	Peoria
FEATHERSTONE, Glen	6-4	210	L	Toronto, Ont.	7/8/68	St. Louis
LALOR, Mike	6-3	200	L	Buffalo, NY	3/8/63	Montreal-St. Louis
LAVOIE, Dominic	6-2	195	R	Montreal, Que.	11/21/67	Peoria
McPHERSON, Darwin	6-1	195	L	Flin Flon, Man.	5/16/68	Saskatoon
PALUCH, Scott	6-3	185	L	Chicago, IL	3/9/66	Peoria
PLAVSIC, Adrien	6-1	190	L	Montreal, Que.	1/13/70	Cdn. National
RICHTER, Dave	6-5	225	L	St. Boniface, Man.	4/8/60	St. Louis
ROBERTS, Gordie	6-1	190	L	Detroit, MI	10/2/57	St. Louis
ROBINSON, Rob	6-1	210	L	St. Catharines, Ont.	4/19/67	Miami Ohio
SKARDA, Randy	6-1	195	R	St. Paul, MN	5/5/68	U. of Minnesota
TILLEY, Tom	6-0	180	L	Trenton, Ont.	3/28/65	St. Louis
TWIST, Tony	6-0	212	L	Sherwood Park, Alta.	5/9/68	Peoria
WILSON, Rik	6-0	210	R	Long Beach, CA	6/19/63	Villach (Aus.)

GOALTENDERS	HT	WT	C	Place of Birth	Date	1988-89 Club
JABLONSKI, Pat	6-0	175	R	Toledo, OH	6/20/67	Peoria
JOSEPH, Curtis	5-10	170	L	Keswick, Ont.	4/29/67	U. of Wisconsin
MILLEN, Greg	5-9	175	L	Toronto, Ont.	6/25/57	St. Louis
RIENDEAU, Vincent	5-10	190	L	St. Hyacinthe, Que.	4/20/66	St. Louis

1988-89 Scoring

Regular Season
*-Rookie

Pos	#	Player	Team	GP	G	A	Pts	+/-	PIM	PP	SH	GW	GT	S	%
F	16	Brett Hull	STL	78	41	43	84	17 –	33	16	0	6	1	305	13.4
F	9	Peter Zezel	PHI	26	4	13	17	13 –	15	0	0	0	0	34	11.8
			STL	52	17	36	53	1 –		27	5	1	4	0	115	14.8
			TOTAL	78	21	49	70	14 –	42	5	1	4	0	149	14.1
F	24	Bernie Federko	STL	66	22	45	67	20 –	54	9	0	6	2	115	19.1
F	7	Cliff Ronning	STL	64	24	31	55	3	18	16	0	1	0	150	16.0
F	28	Greg Paslawski	STL	75	26	26	52	8	18	8	0	3	0	179	14.5
F	18	Tony Hrkac	STL	70	17	28	45	10 –	8	5	0	1	0	133	12.8
F	17	Gino Cavallini	STL	74	20	23	43	2	79	1	0	4	1	153	13.1
F	10	Tony McKegney	STL	71	25	17	42	1 –	58	7	0	2	0	154	16.2
D	2	Brian Benning	STL	66	8	26	34	23 –	102	3	0	0	0	91	8.8
F	22	Rick Meagher	STL	78	15	14	29	9	53	0	1	1	0	109	13.8
F	27	Sergio Momesso	STL	53	9	17	26	1 –	139	0	0	0	0	81	11.1
D	4	Gordie Roberts	STL	77	2	24	26	7	90	0	0	0	0	52	3.8
F	35	*Steve Tuttle	STL	53	13	12	25	3	6	0	1	3	0	82	15.9
D	14	Paul Cavallini	STL	65	4	20	24	25	128	0	0	0	0	93	4.3
D	20	*Tom Tilley	STL	70	1	22	23	1	47	0	0	0	0	77	1.3
D	26	Mike Lalor	MTL	12	1	4	5	1 –	15	0	0	1	0	12	8.3
			STL	36	1	14	15	15	54	0	0	1	0	40	2.5
			TOTAL	48	2	18	20	14	69	0	0	2	0	52	3.8
F	32	Doug Evans	STL	53	7	12	19	3	81	0	1	0	1	48	14.6
F	25	Herb Raglan	STL	50	7	10	17	8 –	144	0	0	0	0	86	8.1
D	23	Gaston Gingras	STL	52	3	10	13	1	6	2	0	0	0	98	3.1
F	21	Todd Ewen	STL	34	4	5	9	4	171	0	0	0	0	22	18.2
F	15	Craig Coxe	STL	41	0	7	7	3	127	0	0	0	0	15	.0
F	12	Dave Lowry	STL	21	3	3	6	1	11	0	1	0	0	22	13.6
F	33	Dave Richter	STL	66	1	5	6	21 –	99	0	0	0	0	23	4.3
F	33	Jim Vesey	STL	5	1	1	2	1 –	7	0	0	0	0	5	20.0
D	36	*Glen Featherstone	STL	18	0	2	2	3 –	22	0	0	0	0	9	.0
D	34	*Robert Dirk	STL	9	0	1	1	3 –	11	0	0	0	0	7	.0
G	30	*Vincent Riendeau	STL	32	0	1	1	0	4	0	0	0	0	0	.0
D	34	*Dominic Lavoie	STL	1	0	0	0	2	0	0	0	0	0	1	.0
D	6	Tim Bothwell	STL	22	0	0	0	4	14	0	0	0	0	10	.0

Goaltending

No.	Goaltender	GPI	Mins	Avg	W	L	T	EN	SO	GA	SA	S%
29	Greg Millen	52	3019	3.38	22	20	7	3	6	170	1411	.879
30	*Vincent Riendeau	32	1842	3.52	11	15	5	4	0	108	836	.870
	Totals	80	4871	3.51	33	35	12	7	6	285	2247	.873

Playoffs

Pos	#	Player	Team	GP	G	A	Pts	+/-	PIM	PP	SH	GW	GT	S	%
F	9	Peter Zezel	STL	10	6	6	12	2 –	4	1	1	1	0	31	19.4
F	24	Bernie Federko	STL	10	4	8	12	2 –	0	2	0	0	0	19	21.1
F	16	Brett Hull	STL	10	5	5	10	4 –	6	1	0	2	1	43	11.6
D	4	Gordie Roberts	STL	10	1	7	8	3	8	0	0	0	0	18	5.6
F	27	Sergio Momesso	STL	10	2	5	7	0	24	0	0	0	0	23	8.7
F	22	Rick Meagher	STL	10	3	2	5	4	6	0	0	1	1	16	18.8
F	12	Dave Lowry	STL	10	0	5	5	4	4	0	0	0	0	18	.0
D	14	Paul Cavallini	STL	10	2	2	4	0	14	0	0	0	0	20	10.0
F	7	Cliff Ronning	STL	7	1	3	4	0	0	1	0	0	0	15	6.7
F	28	Greg Paslawski	STL	9	2	1	3	3 –	2	1	0	0	0	22	9.1
F	35	*Steve Tuttle	STL	6	1	2	3	4	0	0	0	0	0	4	25.0
F	32	Doug Evans	STL	7	1	2	3	2	16	0	0	0	0	3	33.3
F	25	Herb Raglan	STL	8	1	2	3	2	13	0	0	0	0	11	9.1
D	20	*Tom Tilley	STL	10	1	2	3	7	17	0	0	0	0	16	6.3
F	19	*Rod Brind'Amour	STL	5	2	0	2	4	0	0	0	0	0	4	50.0
F	18	Tony Hrkac	STL	4	1	1	2	2 –	0	0	0	1	1	8	12.5
D	2	Brian Benning	STL	7	1	1	2	2 –	11	1	0	0	0	6	16.7
D	26	Mike Lalor	STL	10	1	1	2	1	14	1	0	0	0	11	9.1
F	17	Gino Cavallini	STL	9	0	2	2	2	17	0	0	0	0	13	.0
F	10	Tony McKegney	STL	3	0	1	1	1	0	0	0	0	0	4	.0
D	23	Gaston Gingras	STL	7	0	1	1	2 –	2	0	0	0	0	18	.0
F	21	Todd Ewen	STL	2	0	0	0	1	21	0	0	0	0	4	.0
D	36	*Glen Featherstone	STL	6	0	0	0	0	25	0	0	0	0	1	.0
G	29	Greg Millen	STL	10	0	0	0	0	2	0	0	0	0	0	.0

Goaltending

No.	Goaltender	GPI	Mins	Avg	W	L	EN	SO	GA	SA	S%
29	Greg Millen	10	649	3.14	3	5	0	0	34	308	.890
	Totals	10	651	3.13	5	5	0	0	34	308	.890

Tony Hrkac (18) prepares to feather a pass to teammate Brett Hull (16).

General Managers' History
Lynn Patrick, 1967-68 to 1968-69; Scotty Bowman, 1969-70 to 1970-71; Lynn Patrick, 1971-72; Sidney Abel, 1972-73; Charles Catto, 1973-74; Gerry Ehman, 1974-75; Dennis Ball, 1975-76; Emile Francis, 1976-77 to 1982-83; Ron Caron, 1983-84 to date.

Coaching History
Lynn Patrick and Scott Bowman, 1967-68; Scott Bowman, 1968-69 to 1969-70; Al Arbour and Scott Bowman, 1970-71; Sid Abel, Bill McCreary, Al Arbour, 1971-72; Al Arbour and Jean-Guy Talbot, 1972-73; Jean-Guy Talbot and Lou Angotti, 1973-74; Lou Angotti, Lynn Patrick and Garry Young, 1974-75; Garry Young, Lynn Patrick and Leo Boivin, 1975-76; Emile Francis, 1976-77; Leo Boivin and Barclay Plager, 1977-78; Barclay Plager, 1978-79; Barclay Plager and Red Berenson, 1979-80; Red Berenson, 1980-81; Red Berenson and Emile Francis, 1981-82; Barclay Plager and Emile Francis, 1982-83; Jacques Demers, 1983-84 to 1985-86; Jacques Martin, 1986-87 to 1987-88. Brian Sutter, 1988-89 to date.

Captains' History
Al Arbour, 1967-68 to 1969-70; Red Berenson, Barclay Plager, 1970-71; Barclay Plager, 1971-72 to 1975-76; no captain, 1976-77; Red Berenson, 1977-78; Barry Gibbs, 1978-79; Brian Sutter, 1979-80 to 1987-88; Bernie Federko, 1988-89 to date.

Retired Numbers

3	Bob Gassoff	1973-1977
8	Barclay Plager	1967-1977

Club Records

Team

(Figures in brackets for season records are games played; records for fewest points, wins, ties, losses, goals, goals against are for 70 or more games)

Most Points	.107	1980-81 (80)
Most Wins	.45	1980-81 (80)
Most Ties	.19	1970-71 (78)
Most Losses	.50	1978-79 (80)
Most Goals	.352	1980-81 (80)
Most Goals Against	.349	1981-82 (80)
Fewest Points	.48	1978-79 (80)
Fewest Wins	.18	1978-79 (80)
Fewest Ties	.7	1983-84 (80)
Fewest Losses	.18	1980-81 (80)
Fewest Goals	.177	1967-68 (74)
Fewest Goals Against	.157	1968-69 (76)

Longest Winning Streak

Over-all	7	Jan. 21 Feb. 3/80
Home	7	Nov. 28- Dec. 29/81
Away	4	Dec. 16/73- Jan. 8/74; Jan. 21-Feb. 3/88

Longest Undefeated Streak

Over-all	12	Nov. 10- Dec. 8/68 (5 wins, 7 ties)
Home	11	Feb. 12- Mar. 19/69 (5 wins, 6 ties) Feb. 7- Mar. 29/75 (9 wins, 2 ties)
Away	6	Dec. 9-26/87 (4 wins, 3 ties)

Longest Losing Streak

Over-all	7	Nov. 12-26/67 and Feb. 12-25/89
Home	5	Nov. 19- Dec. 6/77
Away	10	Jan. 20/82- Mar. 8/82

Longest Winless Streak

Over-all	12	Jan. 17- Feb. 15/78 (10 losses, 2 ties)
Home	7	Dec. 28/82- Jan. 25/83 (6 losses, 1 tie)
Away	17	Jan. 23- Apr. 7/74 (14 losses, 3 ties)

Most Shutouts, Season	13	1968-69 (76)
Most Pen. Mins., Season	1,919	1987-88 (80)
Most Goals, Game	10	Feb. 2/82 (Wpg. 6 at St. L. 10) Dec. 1/84 (Det. 5 at St. L. 10)

Individual

Most Seasons	13	Bernie Federko
Most Games	927	Bernie Federko
Most Goals, Career	352	Bernie Federko
Most Assists, Career	721	Bernie Federko
Most Points, Career	1,073	Bernie Federko
Most Pen. Mins., Career	1,777	Brian Sutter
Most Shutouts, Career	16	Glenn Hall
Longest Consecutive Games Streak	662	Garry Unger (Feb. 7/71-Apr. 8/79)
Most Goals, Season	54	Wayne Babych (1980-81)
Most Assists, Season	73	Bernie Federko (1980-81)
Most Points, Season	107	Bernie Federko (1983-84, 1984-85) (41 goals, 66 assists)
Most Pen. Mins., Season	306	Bob Gassoff (1975-76)
Most Points, Defenseman Season	66	Rob Ramage (1985-86) (10 goals, 56 assists)

Most Points, Center, Season	107	Bernie Federko (1983-84) (41 goals, 66 assists)
Most Points, Right Wing, Season	96	Wayne Babych (1980-81) (54 goals, 42 assists)
Most Points, Left Wing, Season	85	Chuck Lefley (1975-76) (43 goals, 42 assists)
Most Points, Rookie, Season	73	Jorgen Pettersson (1980-81) (37 goals, 36 assists)
Most Shutouts, Season	8	Glenn Hall (1968-69)
Most Goals, Game	6	Red Berenson (Nov. 7/68)
Most Assists, Game	4	Several players
Most Points, Game	7	Red Berenson (Nov. 7/68) Garry Unger (Mar. 13/71)

All-time Record vs. Other Clubs

Regular Season

	At Home						On Road						Total					
	GP	W	L	T	GF	GA	PTS	GP	W	L	T	GF	GA	PTS	GP	W	L	T	GF	GA	PTS
Boston	45	17	19	9	139	159	43	45	8	33	6	120	210	22	90	25	52	15	259	369	65
Buffalo	37	21	11	5	140	98	47	37	8	25	4	108	157	20	74	29	36	9	248	255	67
**Calgary	34	14	16	4	122	109	32	34	14	17	3	98	118	31	68	28	33	7	220	227	63
Chicago	70	34	23	13	249	225	81	72	18	43	10	210	287	46	142	52	66	23	459	512	127
Detroit	64	39	15	10	242	168	88	65	29	24	10	201	229	68	129	68	39	20	443	397	156
Edmonton	16	5	9	2	65	78	12	16	3	12	1	61	82	8	32	8	21	4	126	160	20
Hartford	16	8	6	2	61	56	18	16	6	10	—	47	58	14	32	14	16	4	108	114	32
Los Angeles	50	33	12	5	191	128	71	50	18	23	7	147	175	43	100	51	35	12	338	303	114
Minnesota	75	37	23	15	267	218	89	73	27	32	15	229	256	69	148	64	55	30	496	474	158
Montreal	45	9	24	12	114	162	30	45	7	34	4	114	205	18	90	16	58	16	228	367	48
*New Jersey	32	22	7	3	147	101	47	32	14	9	7	97	100	35	64	36	16	10	244	201	82
NY Islanders	33	11	16	6	112	116	28	34	4	20	9	72	139	17	67	15	36	15	184	255	45
NY Rangers	48	20	21	7	147	156	47	47	3	39	4	105	212	10	95	23	60	11	252	368	57
Philadelphia	53	21	25	7	151	155	49	53	9	37	8	120	209	26	106	30	62	15	271	364	75
Pittsburgh	51	33	13	5	196	136	71	50	17	23	11	149	185	45	101	50	36	16	345	321	116
Quebec	16	12	3	1	71	52	25	16	5	8	2	49	62	12	32	17	11	3	120	114	37
Toronto	65	40	15	10	228	174	90	64	18	41	7	193	254	43	129	58	56	17	421	428	133
Vancouver	43	26	11	6	171	124	58	43	18	20	5	135	140	41	86	44	31	11	306	264	99
Washington	26	11	8	7	111	82	29	26	10	15	2	83	99	22	52	21	23	9	194	181	51
Winnipeg	18	8	4	6	81	61	22	18	3	9	5	53	67	11	36	11	13	11	134	128	33
Defunct Clubs	32	25	4	3	131	55	53	33	11	10	12	95	100	34	65	36	14	15	226	155	87
Totals	**869**	**446**	**285**	**138**	**3136**	**2613**	**1030**	**869**	**250**	**484**	**135**	**2486**	**3344**	**635**	**1738**	**696**	**769**	**273**	**5622**	**5957**	**1665**

* Totals include those of Kansas City (1974-75, 1975-76) and Colorado (1976-77 through 1981-82)
** Totals include those of Atlanta (1972-73 through 1979-80)

Playoffs

	Series	W	L	GP	W	L	T	GF	GA	Last Mtg.	Round	Result
Boston	2	0	2	8	0	8	0	15	48	1972	SF	L 0-4
Buffalo	1	0	1	3	1	2	0	8	7	1976	P	L 1-2
Calgary	1	0	1	7	3	4	0	22	28	1986	CF	L 3-4
Chicago	6	1	5	38	9	19	0	75	109	1989	DF	L 1-4
Detroit	2	1	1	9	4	5	0	27	33	1988	DF	L 1-4
Los Angeles	1	1	0	4	4	0	0	16	5	1969	SF	W 4-0
Minnesota	8	5	3	46	24	22	0	135	136	1989	DSF	W 4-1
Montreal	3	0	3	12	0	12	0	14	42	1977	QF	L 0-4
NY Rangers	1	0	1	6	2	4	0	22	29	1981	QF	L 2-4
Philadelphia	2	2	0	11	8	3	0	34	20	1969	QF	W 4-0
Pittsburgh	3	2	1	13	7	6	0	45	40	1981	P	W 3-2
Toronto	2	1	1	13	6	7	0	35	37	1987	DSF	L 2-4
Winnipeg	1	1	0	4	3	1	0	20	13	1982	DSF	W 3-1
Totals	**33**	**14**	**19**	**164**	**71**	**93**	**0**	**468**	**549**			

Playoff Results 1989-85

Year	Round	Opponent	Result	GF	GA
1989	DF	Chicago	L 1-4	12	19
	DSF	Minnesota	W 4-1	23	15
1988	DF	Detroit	L 1-4	14	21
	DSF	Chicago	W 4-1	21	17
1987	DSF	Toronto	L 2-4	11	15
1986	CF	Calgary	L 3-4	22	28
	DF	Toronto	W 4-3	24	22
	DSF	Minnesota	W 3-2	18	20
1985	DSF	Minnesota	L 0-3	5	9

Abbreviations: Round: F – Final; **CF** – conference final; **DF** – division final; **DSF** – division semi-final; **SF** – semi-final; **QF** – quarter-final. **P** – preliminary round. **GA** – goals against; **GF** – goals for.

1988-89 Results

		Home					Away	
Oct.	8	NY Rangers	2-4	Oct.	6	Minnesota	8-3
	20	Chicago	2-0		12	Toronto	4-2
	22	Boston	2-5		14	Detroit	8-8
	27	Pittsburgh	4-3		15	Pittsburgh	2-9
	29	Toronto	3-2	Nov.	2	Edmonton	4-5
Nov.	10	Minnesota	5-5		3	Calgary	1-6
	12	Quebec	4-3		5	Quebec	5-2
	15	New Jersey	2-4		7	Montreal	3-3
	19	Vancouver	2-3		17	Philadelphia	3-1
	24	Edmonton	2-4		21	Toronto	0-4
	26	Winnipeg	4-4		29	Washington	3-4
Dec.	1	NY Islanders	8-0	Dec.	10	Minnesota	3-1
	3	Toronto	3-0		11	Chicago	2-5
	6	Minnesota	3-0		13	New Jersey	3-4
	8	Montreal	1-5		19	Toronto	3-4
	15	Hartford	3-3		20	Detroit	3-6
	17	Chicago	4-0		26	Chicago	4-1
	22	Detroit	4-4		28	Winnipeg	2-6
	30	Minnesota	5-5		31	Minnesota	2-6
Jan.	7	Philadelphia	7-4	Jan.	2	Boston	7-8
	17	Los Angeles	5-2		4	Detroit	2-4
	19	NY Rangers	0-5		12	Los Angeles	4-7
	21	Chicago	4-2		15	Vancouver	1-2
	28	Washington	4-4		25	Hartford	3-3
	31	Winnipeg	5-3		26	Boston	2-4
Feb.	2	Buffalo	7-3	Feb.	3	Pittsburgh	3-3
	9	Calgary	3-5		5	Chicago	5-4
	11	NY Islanders	5-0		12	Buffalo	2-5
	14	Washington	3-5		16	NY Islanders	3-7
	18	Montreal	2-4		21	Vancouver	0-2
Mar.	2	Los Angeles	6-4		24	Calgary	3-4
	4	Detroit	4-5		25	Edmonton	3-5
	7	New Jersey	6-2		27	Toronto	7-5
	9	Toronto	4-1	Mar.	5	Chicago	3-3
	11	Minnesota	2-2		12	Minnesota	3-5
	14	Chicago	3-2		16	Philadelphia	4-3
	18	Detroit	3-2		20	NY Rangers	4-7
	30	Quebec	4-3		22	Buffalo	2-1
Apr.	1	Toronto	4-3		25	Hartford	0-4
	2	Detroit	4-2		27	Detroit	3-2

* Denotes afternoon game.

Entry Draft
Selections 1989-75

1989
Pick
9 Jason Marshall
31 Rick Corriveau
55 Denny Felsner
93 Daniel Laperriere
114 David Roberts
124 Derek Frenette
135 Jeff Batters
156 Kevin Plager
177 John Roderick
198 John Valo
219 Brian Lukowski

1988
Pick
9 Rod Brind' Amour
30 Adrien Plavsic
51 Rob Fournier
72 Jaan Luik
105 Dave Lacourte
114 Dan Fowler
135 Matt Hayes
156 John McCoy
177 Tony Twist
198 Bret Hedican
219 Heath Deboer
240 Michael Francis

1987
Pick
12 Keith Osborne
54 Kevin Miehm
59 Robert Nordmark
75 Darin Smith
82 Andy Rymsha
117 Rob Robinson
138 Tobb Crabtree
159 Guy Hebert
180 Robert Dumas
201 David Marvin
207 Andy Cesarski
222 Dan Rolfe
243 Ray Savard

1986
Pick
10 Jocelyn Lemieux
31 Mike Posma
52 Tony Hejna
73 Glen Featherstone
87 Michael Wolak
115 Mike O'Toole
136 Andy May
157 Randy Skarda
178 Martyn Ball
199 Rod Thacker
220 Terry MacLean
234 Bill Butler
241 David Obrien

1985
Pick
37 Herb Raglan
44 Nelson Emerson
54 Ned Osmond
100 Dan Brooks
121 Rick Burchill
138 Pat Jablonski
159 Scott Brickey
180 Jeff Urban
201 Vince Guidotti
222 Ron Saatzer
243 Dave Jecha

1984
Pick
26 Brian Benning
32 Tony Hrkac
50 Toby Ducolon
53 Robert Dirk
56 Alan Perry
71 Graham Herring
92 Scott Paluch
113 Steve Tuttle
134 Cliff Ronning
148 Don Porter
155 Jim Vesey
176 Daniel Jomphe
196 Tom Tilley
217 Mark Cupolo
237 Mark Lanigan

1983
DID NOT DRAFT

1982
Pick
50 Mike Posavad
92 Scott Machej
113 Perry Ganchar
134 Doug Gilmour
155 Chris Delaney
176 Matt Christensen
197 John Shumski
218 Brian Ahern
239 Peter Smith

1981
Pick
20 Marty Ruff
36 Hakin Nordin
62 Gordon Donnelly
104 Mike Hickey
125 Peter Aslin
146 Erik Holmberg
167 Alain Vigneault
188 Dan Wood
209 Richard Zemlak

1980
Pick
12 Rik Wilson
54 Jim Pavese
75 Bob Brooke
96 Alain Lemieux
117 Perry Anderson
138 Roger Hagglund
159 Par Rabbitt
180 Peter Lindberg
201 John Smyth

1979
Pick
2 Perry Turnbull
65 Bob Crawford
86 Mark Reeds
107 Gilles Leduc

1978
Pick
3 Wayne Babych
39 Steve Harrison
72 Kevin Willison
89 Jim Nill
106 Steve Stockman
109 Paul MacLean
123 Denis Houle
140 Tony Meagher
143 Rick Simpson
157 Jim Lockhurst
160 Bob Froese
170 Dan Lerg
173 Risto Siltanen
175 Dan Hermansson
181 Jean-Francois Boutin
185 John Sullivan
188 Serge Menard
191 Don Boyd
197 Paul Stasiuk
200 Gerhard Truntschka
203 Victor Shkurdjuk
205 Carl Bloomberg
207 Terry Kitching
209 Brian O'Connor
210 Brian Crombeen
211 Mike Pidgeon
214 John Cochrane
216 Joe Casey
218 Jim Farrell
221 Blair Wheeler

1977
Pick
9 Scott Campbell
27 Neil Labatte
45 Tom Roulston
63 Tony Currie
81 Bruce Hamilton
99 Gary McMonagle
117 Matti Forss
132 Raimo Hirvonen
147 Bjorn Olsson

1976
Pick
7 Bernie Federko
20 Brian Sutter
25 John Smrke
43 Jim Kirkpatrick
56 Mike Liut
61 Paul Skidmore
97 Nels Goddard
113 Mike Eaves
121 Jacques Soquel
124 Dave Dornself
126 Brad Wilson
128 Dan Hoene
130 Goran Lindblom
132 Jim Bales
134 Anders Hakansson
135 Johani Wallenius

1975
Pick
27 Ed Staniowski
36 Jamie Masters
63 Rick Bourbonnais
81 Jim Gustafson
99 Jack Brownschidle
117 Doug Lindskog
135 Vic Lamby
151 David McNab

Club Directory

St. Louis Arena
5700 Oakland Avenue
St. Louis, MO 63110
Phone 314/781-5300
Night line 314/781-5352
GM FAX 314/645-1573
FAX 314/645-1340
ENVOY ID
Front Office: BLUES. GM
Public
Relations: BLUES. PR
Capacity: 17,188

Board of Directors
Michael F. Shanahan, Jerome V. LaBarbera, Phil McCarty, Bob Mohrman, Jack Quinn

Management
Chairman of the Board. . . . . Michael F. Shanahan
Vice-Chairman . . . . Jerome V. LaBarbera
President. . . . . Jack Quinn
Vice-President/General Manager . . . . Ronald Caron
Vice-President/Director of Public Relations and
Marketing. . . . . Susie Mathieu
Director of Sales . . . . Bruce Affleck
Director of Finance and Administration . . . . Jerry Jasiek
Secretary/General Counsel . . . . Timothy Wolf

Hockey Staff
Head Coach. . . . . Brian Sutter
Assistant Coach . . . . Bob Berry
Assistant Coach . . . . Joe Micheletti
Head Coach, Peoria Rivermen (IHL). . . . . . . Wayne Thomas
Director of Player Development . . . . Bob Plager
Director of Scouting . . . . Ted Hampson
Assistant Director of Scouting/Head Eastern
Canada and U.S. Scout. . . . . Jack Evans
Head Western Canada and U.S. Scout . . . . . . Pat Ginnell
Administrative Assistant . . . . Sue Profeta

Medical Training Staff
Orthopedic Surgeon. . . . . Dr. Jerome Gilden
Internist. . . . . Dr. Aaron Birenbaum
Team Dentist . . . . Dr. Leslie Rich
Head Trainer . . . . Mike Folga
Equipment Manager. . . . . Frank Burns
Conditioning Consultant . . . . Mackie Shilstone

Front Office Staff
Director of Alumni Services . . . . Norm Mackie
Controller. . . . . Margaret Steinmeyer
Accountant. . . . . Rita Russell
Assistant Director of Public Relations/Media
Relations . . . . Mark Niebling
Assistant Director of Public Relations/
Publications . . . . Jeff Trammel
Assistant Director of Promotions/Community
Relations . . . . Tracy Lovasz
Merchandise Manager . . . . George Pavlik
Sales Staff. . . . . John Casson, Wes Edwards, Tammy Iuli,
                                                    Jill Mann
Executive Secretary. . . . . Lynn Diederichsen
Public Relations/Marketing Secretary . . . . . . Donna Quirk
Receptionist . . . . Pam Barrett
Largest Hockey Attendance. . . . . 20,009 (March 31/73)
Location of Press Box . . . . East side of building,
                                                    upper level
Club Colors . . . . Blue, Gold, Red and White
Training Camp . . . . Brentwood Ice Rink, St. Louis Mo.
Radio Station . . . . KMOX Radio
Television Station . . . . KPLR-TV (Channel 11)
Broadcasters . . . . Bruce Affleck, John Kelly, Ken Wilson

General Manager

CARON, RON
Vice-President General Manager and Alternate Governor, St. Louis Blues.
Born in Hull, Que., December 19, 1929

Ron Caron joined the St. Louis Blues on August 13, 1983 after a 26-year association with the Montreal Canadiens' organization. He joined the Canadiens in 1957 on a part-time scouting basis after coaching in the amateur ranks. In 1966, Caron was promoted to a full-time position as chief scout of the Montreal Junior Canadiens and was instrumental in assembling two Memorial Cup championship teams. In 1968, he was named chief scout of the parent club and served as an assistant to former manager Sam Pollock. In 1969 he added the responsibilities of general manager of the Montreal Voyageurs of the AHL and maintained that role until 1978 when he was named Director of Scouting and Player Personnel for the Canadiens. Caron remained with the Montreal organization until the conclusion of the 1982-83 campaign.

Coach

SUTTER, BRIAN
Coach, St. Louis Blues. Born in Viking, Alta., October 7, 1956.

Brian Sutter, 33, became the youngest head coach in the NHL on June 20, 1988 when he was named to that position with the Blues. In his rookie season behind the bench, Sutter led the Blues to a 33-35-12 record, second place in the Norris Division and their second consecutive appearance in the Division Finals.

The Blues' second choice, 20th overall, in the 1976 Amateur Draft, Brian was the first of a record six brothers to play in the NHL. After a junior career with Lethbridge of the Western Junior League, Sutter turned pro in 1976 and played in only 38 games in the minor leagues (Kansas City, CHL) before making his NHL debut with the Blues. From 1979-80 until his retirement last season, Sutter served as captain of the St. Louis club. He also appeared in three NHL All-Star Games (1982, 1983 and 1985) and ranks second on the Blues' all-time list in games played (779), goals (303), assists (333) and points (636).

Coaching Record

| Team | Seasons | Regular Season | | | | | Playoffs | | | |
		Games	W	L	T	%	Games	W	L	%
1988-89	St. Louis (NHL)	80	33	35	12	.488	10	5	5	.500
	NHL Totals	80	33	35	12	.488	10	5	5	.500

Toronto Maple Leafs

1988-89 Results: 28w-46L-6T 62 PTS. Fifth, Norris Division

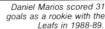

Daniel Marios scored 31 goals as a rookie with the Leafs in 1988-89.

Schedule

Home

Oct.
- Wed. 11 Buffalo
- Sat. 14 Winnipeg
- Wed. 18 Vancouver
- Sat. 21 Washington
- Mon. 23 New Jersey
- Sat. 28 Detroit

Nov.
- Sat. 4 Philadelphia
- Mon. 6 Minnesota
- Sat. 11 Detroit
- Wed. 15 St Louis
- Sat. 25 NY Rangers

Dec.
- Sat. 9 Montreal
- Mon. 11 St Louis
- Sat. 16 Minnesota
- Mon. 18 St Louis
- Sat. 23 Chicago
- Wed. 27 Detroit
- Sat. 30 Boston

Jan.
- Wed. 3 Quebec
- Sat. 6 Los Angeles
- Mon. 8 Washington
- Wed. 10 NY Islanders
- Sat. 13 Calgary
- Mon. 15 Chicago
- Wed. 24 Minnesota
- Sat. 27 Montreal

Feb.
- Sat. 3 Pittsburgh
- Wed. 7 St Louis
- Mon. 12 Los Angeles
- Wed. 14 Hartford
- Sat. 17 New Jersey
- Wed. 28 Quebec

Mar.
- Sat. 3 Detroit
- Sat. 10 Edmonton
- Mon. 12 Minnesota
- Wed. 14 NY Rangers
- Sat. 17 Winnipeg
- Mon. 19 Chicago
- Wed. 28 NY Islanders
- Sat. 31 Chicago

Away

Oct.
- Thur. 5 Los Angeles
- Sat. 7 St Louis
- Thur. 12 Chicago
- Tues. 17 Pittsburgh
- Wed. 25 Pittsburgh
- Fri. 27 Buffalo
- Tues. 31 Minnesota

Nov.
- Fri. 3 Washington
- Thur. 9 Philadelphia
- Sun. 12 Minnesota
- Thur. 16 NY Islanders
- Sat. 18 Montreal
- Wed. 22 Minnesota
- Thur. 23 Boston
- Wed. 29 Vancouver

Dec.
- Sat. 2 Calgary
- Sun. 3 Edmonton
- Wed. 6 Chicago
- Thur. 7 St Louis
- Wed. 13 Detroit
- Wed. 20 Detroit
- Fri. 22 Chicago
- Tues. 26 Boston

Jan.
- Thur. 18 St Louis
- Fri. 26 New Jersey
- Wed. 31 Winnipeg

Feb.
- Fri. 2 Detroit
- Tues. 6 St Louis
- Sat. 10 Hartford
- Thur. 15 Philadelphia
- Thur. 22 Calgary
- Fri. 23 Edmonton
- Mon. 26 Vancouver

Mar.
- Fri. 2 Detroit
- Thur. 8 Hartford
- Fri. 16 Buffalo
- Wed. 21 NY Rangers
- Sat. 24 Quebec
- Mon. 26 Minnesota
- Thur. 29 Chicago

* Denotes afternoon game.

Home Starting Times:
- Weeknights .... 7:35 p.m.
- Saturdays .... 8:05 p.m.
- Sundays .... 7:05 p.m.

Franchise date: November 22, 1917

73rd NHL Season

Year-by-Year Record

Season	GP	Home W	Home L	Home T	Road W	Road L	Road T	Overall W	Overall L	Overall T	GF	GA	Pts.	Finished	Playoff Result
1988-89	80	15	20	5	13	26	1	28	46	6	259	342	62 5th,	Norris Div.	Out of Playoffs
1987-88	80	14	20	6	7	29	4	21	49	10	273	345	52 4th,	Norris Div.	Lost Div. Semi-Final
1986-87	80	22	14	4	10	28	2	32	42	6	286	319	70 4th,	Norris Div.	Lost Div. Final
1985-86	80	16	21	3	9	27	4	25	48	7	311	386	57 4th,	Norris Div.	Lost Div. Final
1984-85	80	10	28	2	10	24	6	20	52	8	253	358	48 5th,	Norris Div.	Out of Playoffs
1983-84	80	17	16	7	9	29	2	26	45	9	303	287	61 5th,	Norris Div.	Out of Playoffs
1982-83	80	20	15	5	8	25	7	28	40	12	293	330	68 3rd,	Norris Div.	Lost Div. Semi-Final
1981-82	80	12	20	8	8	24	8	20	44	16	298	380	56 5th,	Norris Div.	Out of Playoffs
1980-81	80	14	21	5	14	16	10	28	37	15	322	367	71 5th,	Adams Div.	Lost Prelim. Round
1979-80	80	17	19	4	18	21	1	35	40	5	304	327	75 4th,	Adams Div.	Lost Prelim. Round
1978-79	80	20	12	8	14	21	5	34	33	13	267	252	81 3rd,	Adams Div.	Lost Quarter-Final
1977-78	80	21	13	6	20	16	4	41	29	10	271	237	92 3rd,	Adams Div.	Lost Semi-Final
1976-77	80	18	13	9	15	19	6	33	32	15	301	285	81 3rd,	Adams Div.	Lost Quarter-Final
1975-76	80	23	12	5	11	19	10	34	31	15	294	276	83 3rd,	Adams Div.	Lost Quarter-Final
1974-75	80	19	12	9	12	21	7	31	33	16	280	309	78 3rd,	Adams Div.	Lost Quarter-Final
1973-74	78	21	11	7	14	16	9	35	27	16	274	230	86 4th,	East Div.	Lost Quarter-Final
1972-73	78	20	12	7	7	29	3	27	41	10	247	279	64 6th,	East Div.	Out of Playoffs
1971-72	78	21	11	7	12	20	7	33	31	14	209	208	80 4th,	East Div.	Lost Quarter-Final
1970-71	78	24	9	6	13	24	2	37	33	8	248	211	82 4th,	East Div.	Lost Quarter-Final
1969-70	76	18	13	7	11	21	6	29	34	13	222	242	71 6th,	East Div.	Out of Playoffs
1968-69	76	20	8	10	15	18	5	35	26	15	234	217	85 4th,	East Div.	Lost Quarter-Final
1967-68	74	24	9	4	9	22	6	33	31	10	209	176	76 5th,	East Div.	Out of Playoffs
1966-67	**70**	21	8	6	11	19	5	**32**	**27**	**11**	**204**	**211**	**75 3rd,**		**Won Stanley Cup**
1965-66	70	22	9	4	12	16	7	34	25	11	208	187	79 3rd,		Lost Semi-Final
1964-65	70	17	15	3	13	11	11	30	26	14	204	173	74 4th,		Lost Semi-Final
1963-64	**70**	22	7	6	11	18	6	**33**	**25**	**12**	**192**	**172**	**78 3rd,**		**Won Stanley Cup**
1962-63	**70**	21	8	6	14	15	6	**35**	**23**	**12**	**221**	**180**	**82 1st,**		**Won Stanley Cup**
1961-62	**70**	25	5	5	12	17	6	**37**	**22**	**11**	**232**	**180**	**85 2nd,**		**Won Stanley Cup**
1960-61	70	21	6	8	18	13	4	39	19	12	234	176	90 2nd,		Lost Semi-Final
1959-60	70	20	9	6	15	17	3	35	26	9	199	195	79 2nd,		Lost Final
1958-59	70	17	13	5	10	19	6	27	32	11	189	201	65 4th,		Lost Final
1957-58	70	12	16	7	9	22	4	21	38	11	192	226	53 6th,		Out of Playoffs
1956-57	70	12	16	7	9	18	8	21	34	15	174	192	57 5th,		Out of Playoffs
1955-56	70	19	10	6	5	23	7	24	33	13	153	181	61 4th,		Lost Semi-Final
1954-55	70	14	10	11	10	14	11	24	24	22	147	135	70 3rd,		Lost Semi-Final
1953-54	70	22	6	7	10	18	7	32	24	14	152	131	78 3rd,		Lost Semi-Final
1952-53	70	17	12	6	10	18	7	27	30	13	156	167	67 5th,		Out of Playoffs
1951-52	70	17	10	8	12	15	8	29	25	16	168	157	74 3rd,		Lost Semi-Final
1950-51	**70**	22	8	5	19	8	8	**41**	**16**	**13**	**212**	**138**	**95 2nd,**		**Won Stanley Cup**
1949-50	70	18	9	8	13	18	4	31	27	12	176	173	74 3rd,		Lost Semi-Final
1948-49	**60**	12	8	10	10	17	3	**22**	**25**	**13**	**147**	**161**	**57 4th,**		**Won Stanley Cup**
1947-48	**60**	22	3	5	10	12	8	**32**	**15**	**13**	**182**	**143**	**77 1st,**		**Won Stanley Cup**
1946-47	**60**	20	8	2	11	11	8	**31**	**19**	**10**	**209**	**172**	**72 2nd,**		**Won Stanley Cup**
1945-46	50	10	13	2	9	11	5	19	24	7	174	185	45 5th,		Out of Playoffs
1944-45	**50**	13	9	3	11	13	1	**24**	**22**	**4**	**183**	**161**	**52 3rd,**		**Won Stanley Cup**
1943-44	50	13	11	1	10	12	3	23	23	4	214	174	50 3rd,		Lost Semi-Final
1942-43	50	17	6	2	5	13	7	22	19	9	198	159	53 3rd,		Lost Semi-Final
1941-42	**48**	18	6	0	9	12	3	**27**	**18**	**3**	**158**	**136**	**57 2nd,**		**Won Stanley Cup**
1940-41	48	16	5	3	12	9	3	28	14	6	145	99	62 2nd,		Lost Semi-Final
1939-40	48	15	3	6	10	14	0	25	17	6	134	110	56 3rd,		Lost Final
1938-39	48	13	8	3	6	12	6	19	20	9	114	107	47 3rd,		Lost Final
1937-38	48	13	6	5	11	9	4	24	15	9	151	127	57 1st,	Cdn. Div.	Lost Final
1936-37	48	14	9	1	8	12	4	22	21	5	119	115	49 3rd,	Cdn. Div.	Lost Quarter-Final
1935-36	48	15	4	5	8	15	1	23	19	6	126	106	52 2nd,	Cdn. Div.	Lost Final
1934-35	48	16	6	2	14	8	2	30	14	4	157	111	64 1st,	Cdn. Div.	Lost Final
1933-34	48	19	2	3	7	11	6	26	13	9	174	119	61 1st,	Cdn. Div.	Lost Semi-Final
1932-33	48	16	4	4	8	14	2	24	18	6	119	111	54 1st,	Cdn. Div.	Lost Final
1931-32	**48**	17	4	3	6	14	4	**23**	**18**	**7**	**155**	**127**	**53 2nd,**	**Cdn. Div.**	**Won Stanley Cup**
1930-31	44	15	4	3	7	9	6	22	13	9	118	99	53 2nd,	Cdn. Div.	Lost Quarter-Final
1929-30	44	10	8	4	7	13	2	17	21	6	116	124	40 4th,	Cdn. Div.	Out of Playoffs
1928-29	44	15	5	2	6	13	3	21	18	5	85	69	47 3rd,	Cdn. Div.	Lost Semi-Final
1927-28	44	9	8	5	9	10	3	18	18	8	89	88	44 4th,	Cdn. Div.	Out of Playoffs
1926-27*	44	10	10	2	5	14	3	15	24	5	79	94	35 5th,	Cdn. Div.	Out of Playoffs
1925-26	36	11	5	2	1	16	1	12	21	3	92	114	27 6th,		Out of Playoffs
1924-25	30	10	5	0	9	6	0	19	11	0	90	84	38 2nd,		Lost NHL S-Final
1923-24	24	7	5	0	3	9	0	10	14	0	59	85	20 3rd,		Out of Playoffs
1922-23	24	10	1	1	3	9	0	13	10	1	82	88	27 3rd,		Out of Playoffs
1921-22	**24**	8	4	0	5	6	1	**13**	**10**	**1**	**98**	**97**	**27 2nd,**		**Won Stanley Cup**
1920-21	24	9	3	0	6	6	0	15	9	0	105	100	30 1st,		Lost NHL Playoffs
1919-20**	24	8	4	0	4	8	0	12	12	0	119	106	24 3rd,		Out of Cup Playoffs
1918-19	18	5	4	0	0	9	0	5	13	0	64	92	10 3rd,		Out of Playoffs
1917-18*	**22**	10	1	0	3	8	0	**13**	**9**	**0**	**108**	**109**	**26 2nd and 1st**		**Won Stanley Cup**

* Name changed from St. Patricks to Maple Leafs.
** Name changed from Arenas to St. Patricks.
*** Season played in two halves with no combined standing at end.

1989-90 Player Personnel

FORWARDS

Name	HT	WT	S	Place of Birth	Date	1988-89 Club
ARMSTRONG, Tim	5-11	170	R	Toronto, Ont.	5/12/67	Newmarket-Toronto
BEAN, Tim	6-1	190	L	Saulte Ste. Marie, Ont.	3/9/67	Newmarket
BELLEFEUILLE, Brian	6-2	185	L	Natick, MA	3/21/67	University of Maine
BLAISDELL, Mike	6-1	195	L	Moose Jaw, Sask.	1/18/60	Newmarket-Toronto
BRENNAN, Stephen	6-1	190	R	Winchester, MA	3/22/67	Clarkson
CLARK, Wendel	5-11	194	L	Kelvington, Sask.	10/25/66	Toronto
DAMPHOUSSE, Vincent	6-1	190	L	Montreal, Que.	12/17/67	Toronto
DAOUST, Dan	5-11	170	L	Montreal, Que.	2/29/60	Toronto-Newmarket
DOERS, Michael	6-0	175	R	Madison, WI	6/17/71	Northwood Prep.
DOMI, Tahir (Tie)	5-10	200	R	Windsor, Ont.	11/1/69	Peterborough
EASTWOOD, Michael	6-2	190	R	Ottawa, Ont.	7/1/67	Western Michigan Univ.
FERGUS, Tom	6-3	210	L	Chicago, IL	6/16/62	Toronto
FRANCESCHETTI, Lou	6-0	190	L	Toronto, Ont.	3/28/58	Washington
GAGNE, Paul	5-10	180	L	Iroquois Falls, Ont.	2/6/62	Newmarket-Toronto
HULST, Kent	6-0	180	L	St. Thomas, Ont.	4/8/68	Belleville
IHNACAK, Peter	6-1	200	R	Poprad, Czech.	5/3/57	Toronto-Newmarket
JACKSON, Mike	6-0	192	R	Mississauga, Ont.	2/4/69	Toronto (OHL)
JARVIS, Wes	5-11	185	L	Toronto, Ont.	5/30/58	Newmarket
JOBE, Trevor	6-1	192	L	Lethbridge, Alta.	5/14/67	Newmarket
KORDIC, John	6-1	190	R	Edmonton, Alta.	3/22/65	Toronto
LAWLESS, Paul	5-11	180	L	Scarborough, Ont.	9/2/64	Milwaukee-Toronto
LAXDAL, Derek	6-2	178	R	St. Boniface, Man.	2/21/66	Newmarket-Toronto
LEEMAN, Gary	5-11	175	R	Toronto, Ont.	2/19/64	Toronto
MAROIS, Daniel	6-1	180	R	Montreal, Que.	10/3/68	Toronto
McINTYRE, John	6-1	175	L	Ravenswood, Ont.	4/29/69	Guelph-Newmarket
McKENNA, Sean	6-0	185	R	Asbestos, Que.	3/7/62	Newmarket-Toronto
MERKLER, Keith	6-2	205	L	Syosset, NY	4/23/71	Portledge
MOES, Mike	5-11	190		Burlington, Ont.	3/30/67	University of Michigan
OLCZYK, Ed	6-1	200	L	Chicago, IL	8/16/66	Toronto
OSBORNE, Mark	6-2	205	L	Toronto, Ont.	8/13/61	Toronto
PEARSON, Rob	6-1	173	R	Oshawa, Ont.	8/3/71	Belleville
PEARSON, Scott	6-1	203	L	Cornwall, Ont.	12/19/69	Niagara Falls-Toronto
REID, Dave	6-0	205	L	Toronto, Ont.	5/15/64	Toronto
REYNOLDS, Bobby	5-11	175	L	Flint, MI	7/14/67	Michigan State
SACCO, Joe	6-1	180	R	Medford, MA	2/4/69	Boston Univ.
SEROWICK, Jeff	6-0	190	R	Manchester, NH	10/1/67	Providence College
SHEDDEN, Doug	6-0	185	R	Wallaceburg, Ont.	4/29/61	Newmarket-Toronto
ST. LAURENT, Jeffrey	6-2	175	R	Sanford, MA	5/16/71	Berwick
THORNTON, Scott	6-2	200	L	London, Ont.	1/9/71	Belleville

DEFENSEMEN

Name	HT	WT	S	Place of Birth	Date	1988-89 Club
BANCROFT, Steve	6-1	214	L	Toronto, Ont.	10/6/70	Belleville
BLAD, Brian	6-2	195	L	Brockville, Ont.	7/22/67	Newmarket
BUCKLEY, David	6-4	195	L	Newton, MA	1/27/66	Boston College
BURKE, David	6-1	182	L	Detroit, MI	10/15/70	Cornell
CAPUANO, Jack	6-2	210	L	Cranston, RI	7/7/66	Newmarket
CARNEY, Keith	6-1	175	L	Cumberland, RI	2/7/71	Mount St. Charles
CROWLEY, Edward (Ted)	6-2	188	R	Concord, MA	5/3/70	Lawrence Academy
CURRAN, Brian	6-5	215	L	Toronto, Ont.	11/5/63	Toronto
DELAY, Mike	6-0	190	L	Boston, MA	8/31/69	Boston College
ESAU, Leonard	6-3	190	R	Meadow Lake, Sask.	3/16/68	St. Cloud College
GILL, Todd	6-1	185	L	Brockville, Ont.	11/9/65	Toronto
HAMMOND, Ken	6-1	190	L	Port Credit, Ont.	8/22/63	Tor.-Edm.-NYR
HEPPLE, Alan	5-9	200	L	Blaydon-on-Tyne, U.K.	8/16/63	Newmarket
HOTHAM, Greg	5-11	185	R	London, Ont.	3/7/56	Newmarket
IAFRATE, Al	6-3	215	L	Dearborn, MI	3/21/66	Toronto
JENSEN, Chris	5-10	160	R	Fort St. John B.C.	10/28/63	Univ. of Wisconsin
LANGILLE, Derek	6-0	184	L	Toronto, Ont.	6/25/69	North Bay
RAMAGE, Rob	6-2	195	R	Byron, Ont.	1/11/59	Calgary
RICHARDSON, Luke	6-4	210	L	Ottawa, Ont.	3/26/69	Toronto
ROOT, Bill	6-0	210	R	Toronto, Ont.	9/6/59	Newmarket
SACCO, David	5-9	162	R	Malden, MA	7/31/70	Boston Univ.
SHANNON, Darryl	6-2	190	L	Barrie, Ont.	6/21/68	Newmarket-Toronto
SLANINA, Peter	6-2	185	R	Czechoslovakia	12/16/59	USZ Kosice (Czech.)
SPANGLER, Ken	5-11	190	R	Edmonton, Alta.	5/2/67	Flint-Baltimore
TAYLOR, Scott	6-0	180	R	Toronto, Ont.	3/23/68	Oshawa
VEITCH, Darren	6-0	190	R	Saskatoon, Sask.	4/24/60	Toronto
WEINRICH, Alex	6-0	178		Lewiston, MA	3/12/69	Merrimack

GOALTENDERS

Name	HT	WT	C	Place of Birth	Date	1988-89 Club
ANDERSON, Dean	5-10	175	L	Oshawa, Ont.	7/14/66	Newmarket
BERNHARDT, Tim	5-9	160	L	Sarnia, Ont.	1/17/58	Newmarket
BESTER, Allan	5-7	150	L	Hamilton, Ont.	3/26/64	Toronto
GREGORIO, Mike	6-3	195	L	Reading, MA	8/17/69	Kent State
ING, Peter	6-2	165	L	Toronto, Ont.	4/28/69	London-Windsor
REESE, Jeff	5-9	150	R	Brantford, Ont.	3/24/66	Newmarket-Toronto
RHODES, Damian	6-0	165	L	St. Paul, MN	5/28/69	Michigan Tech.

1988-89 Scoring

Regular Season

* rookie

Pos	#	Player	Team	GP	G	A	Pts	+/−	PIM	PP	SH	GW	GT	S	%
F	16	Ed Olczyk	TOR	80	38	52	90	0	75	11	2	4	1	249	15.3
F	11	Gary Leeman	TOR	61	32	43	75	5	66	7	1	3	0	195	16.4
F	10	Vincent Damphousse	TOR	80	26	42	68	8−	75	6	0	4	0	190	13.7
F	19	Tom Fergus	TOR	80	22	45	67	38−	48	10	1	3	0	151	14.6
F	32	*Dan Marois	TOR	76	31	23	54	4	76	7	0	4	1	146	21.2
F	12	Mark Osborne	TOR	75	16	30	46	5−	112	5	0	1	0	118	13.6
D	33	Al Iafrate	TOR	65	13	20	33	3	72	1	2	3	1	105	12.4
F	14	Dave Reid	TOR	77	9	21	30	12	22	1	1	0	0	87	10.3
D	23	Todd Gill	TOR	59	11	14	25	3−	72	0	0	1	0	92	12.0
F	18	Craig Laughlin	TOR	66	10	13	23	22−	41	0	0	0	0	87	11.5
D	21	Borje Salming	TOR	63	3	17	20	7	86	1	0	0	0	58	5.2
F	15	Peter Ihnacak	TOR	26	2	16	18	3	10	0	0	0	0	30	6.7
D	3	Brad Marsh	TOR	80	1	15	16	16−	79	0	0	0	0	69	1.4
F	35	*Derek Laxdal	TOR	41	9	6	15	11−	65	1	0	0	0	41	22.0
D	26	Chris Kotsopoulos	TOR	57	1	14	15	4−	44	0	0	0	0	66	1.5
F	24	Dan Daoust	TOR	68	7	5	12	20−	54	0	2	1	0	66	10.6
F	17	Wendel Clark	TOR	15	7	4	11	3−	66	3	0	1	0	30	23.3
D	25	Darren Veitch	TOR	37	3	7	10	17−	16	1	0	0	0	69	4.3
D	4	Rick Lanz	TOR	32	1	9	10	17−	18	0	0	1	0	56	1.8
D	2	Luke Richardson	TOR	55	2	7	9	15−	106	0	0	0	0	59	3.4
F	41	Paul Gagne	TOR	16	3	2	5	8−	6	1	0	1	0	14	21.4
D	28	Brian Curran	TOR	47	1	4	5	0	185	0	0	0	0	18	5.6
D	34	*Darryl Shannon	TOR	14	1	3	4	5	6	0	0	0	0	16	6.3
F	27	John Kordic	MTL	6	0	0	0	1−	13	0	0	0	0	2	.0
			TOR	46	1	2	3	13−	185	0	0	0	0	33	3.0
			TOTAL	52	1	2	3	14−	198	0	0	0	0	35	2.9
D	29	Ken Hammond	EDM	5	0	1	1	2−	8	0	0	0	0	1	.0
			NYR	3	0	0	0	3−	0	0	0	0	0	2	.0
			TOR	14	0	2	2	13−	12	0	0	0	0	9	.0
			TOTAL	22	0	3	3	18−	20	0	0	0	0	12	.0
G	30	Allan Bester	TOR	43	0	2	2	0	2	0	0	0	0	0	.0
F	22	Mike Blaisdell	TOR	9	1	0	1	5−	4	0	0	0	0	8	12.5
F	8	*Tim Armstrong	TOR	11	1	0	1	2−	6	0	0	0	0	5	20.0
F	34	Ken Yaremchuk	TOR	11	1	0	1	4−	2	0	0	0	0	13	7.7
F	8	Sean McKenna	TOR	3	0	1	1	2−	0	0	0	0	0	1	.0
F	18	*Scott Pearson	TOR	9	0	1	1	0	2	0	0	0	0	8	.0
F	37	Doug Shedden	TOR	1	0	0	0	1−	0	0	0	0	0	2	.0
F	29	*Chris McRae	TOR	3	0	0	0	0	12	0	0	0	0	0	.0
F	15	*Marty Dallman	TOR	4	0	0	0	0	0	0	0	0	0	2	.0
F	20	Paul Lawless	TOR	7	0	0	0	2−	0	0	0	0	0	11	.0
G	1	*Jeff Reese	TOR	10	0	0	0	0	4	0	0	0	0	0	.0

Goaltending

No.	Goaltender	GPI	Mins	Avg	W	L	T	EN	SO	GA	SA	S%
30	Allan Bester	43	2460	3.80	17	20	3	5	2	156	1420	.890
31	Ken Wregget	32	1888	4.42	9	20	2	1	0	139	1037	.866
1	Jeff Reese	10	486	4.94	2	6	1	1	0	40	286	.860
	Totals	**80**	**4846**	**4.23**	**28**	**46**	**6**	**7**	**2**	**342**	**2743**	**.875**

Tom Fergus

General Managers' History

Conn Smythe, 1927-28 to 1956-57; Hap Day, 1957-58; George "Punch" Imlach, 1958-59 to 1968-69; Jim Gregory, 1969-70 to 1978-79; Punch Imlach, 1979-80 to 1980-81; Punch Imlach and Gerry McNamara, 1981-82; Gerry McNamara, 1982-83 to 1987-88; Gord Stellick, 1988-89.

Retired Numbers

5	Bill Barilko	1946-1951
6	Irwin "Ace" Bailey	1927-1934

Coaching History

Conn Smythe, 1927-28 to 1929-30; Conn Smythe and Art Duncan, 1930-31; Art Duncan and Dick Irvin, 1931-32; Dick Irvin, 1932-33 to 1939-40; Hap Day, 1940-41 to 1949-50; Joe Primeau, 1950-51 to 1952-53; "King" Clancy, 1953-54 to 1955-56; Howie Meeker, 1956-57; Billy Reay, 1957-58; Billy Reay and "Punch" Imlach, 1958-59; "Punch" Imlach, 1959-60 to 1968-69; John McLellan, 1969-70 to 1970-71; John McLellan and "King" Clancy, 1971-72; John McLellan, 1972-73; Red Kelly, 1973-74 to 1976-77; Roger Neilson, 1977-78 to 1978-79; Floyd Smith, Dick Duff and "Punch" Imlach, 1979-80; "Punch" Imlach, Joe Crozier and Mike Nykoluk, 1980-81; Mike Nykoluk, 1981-82 to 1983-84; Dan Maloney, 1984-85 to 1985-86; John Brophy, 1986-87 to 1987-88; John Brophy and George Armstrong, 1988-89; Doug Carpenter, 1989-90.

Captains' History

Hap Day, 1927-28 to 1936-37; Charlie Conacher, 1937-38; Red Horner, 1938-39, 1939-40; Syl Apps, 1940-41 to 1942-43; Bob Davidson, 1943-44-45; Syl Apps, 1945-46 to 1947-48; Ted Kennedy, 1948-49 to 1954-55; Sid Smith, 1955-56; Ted Kennedy, Jim Thomson, 1956-57; George Armstrong, 1958-59 to 1968-69; Dave Keon, 1969-70 to 1974-75; Darryl Sittler, 1975-76 to 1980-81; Rick Vaive, 1981-82 to 1985-86; no captain, 1986-87 to date.

Club Records

Team

(Figures in brackets for season records are games played; records for fewest points, wins, ties, losses, goals, goals against are for 70 or more games)

Most Points	95	1950-51 (70)
Most Wins	41	1950-51 (70)
		1977-78 (80)
Most Ties	22	1954-55 (70)
Most Losses	52	1984-85 (80)
Most Goals	322	1980-81 (80)
Most Goals Against	387	1983-84 (80)
Fewest Points	48	1984-85 (80)
Fewest Wins	20	1981-82, 1984-85 (80)
Fewest Ties	5	1979-80 (80)
Fewest Losses	16	1950-51 (70)
Fewest Goals	146	1954-55 (70)
Fewest Goals Against	*131	1953-54 (70)

Longest Winning Streak

Over-all	9	Jan. 30-Feb. 28/25
Home	9	Nov. 11-Dec. 26/53
Away	7	Nov. 14-Dec. 15/40 Dec. 4/60-Jan. 5/61

Longest Undefeated Streak

Over-all	11	Oct. 15-Nov. 8/50 (8 wins, 3 ties)
Home	18	Nov. 28/33-Mar. 10/34 (15 wins, 3 ties) Oct. 31/53-Jan. 23/54 (16 wins, 2 ties)
Away	9	Nov. 30/47-Jan. 11/48 (4 wins, 5 ties)

Longest Losing Streak

Over-all	10	Jan. 15-Feb. 8/67
Home	7	Nov. 10-Dec. 5/84 Jan. 26-Feb. 25/85
Away	11	Feb. 20/-Apr. 1/88

Longest Winless Streak

Over-all	15	Dec. 26/87-Jan. 25/88 (11 losses, 4 ties)
Home	11	Dec. 19/87-Jan. 25/88 (7 losses, 4 ties)
Away	18	Oct. 6/82-Jan. 5/83 (14 losses, 4 ties)

Most Shutouts, Season	13	1953-54 (70)
Most Pen. Mins., Season	1,888	1981-82 (80)
Most Goals, Game	14	Mar. 16/57 (NYR 1 at Tor. 14)

Individual

Most Seasons	20	George Armstrong
Most Games	1,187	George Armstrong
Most Goals, Career	389	Darryl Sittler
Most Assists, Career	620	Borje Salming
Most Points, Career	916	Darryl Sittler (389 goals, 527 assists)
Most Pen. Mins., Career	1,670	Dave Williams
Most Shutouts, Career	62	Turk Broda
Longest Consecutive Games Streak	486	Tim Horton (Feb. 11/61-Feb. 4/68)
Most Goals, Season	54	Rick Vaive (1981-82)
Most Assists, Season	72	Darryl Sittler (1977-78)
Most Points, Season	117	Darryl Sittler (1977-78) (45 goals, 72 assists)

Most Pen. Mins., Season	351	Dave Williams (1977-78)
Most Points, Defenseman Season	79	Ian Turnbull (1976-77) (22 goals, 57 assists)
Most Points, Center Season	117	Darryl Sittler (1977-78) (45 goals, 72 assists)
Most Points, Right Wing, Season	97	Wilf Paiement (1980-81) (40 goals, 57 assists)
Most Points, Left Wing, Season	84	Frank Mahovlich (1960-61) (48 goals, 36 assists)
Most Points, Rookie, Season	66	Peter Ihnacak (1982-83) (28 goals, 38 assists)
Most Shutouts, Season	13	Harry Lumley (1953-54)
Most Goals, Game	6	Corb Denneny (Jan. 26/21) Darryl Sittler (Feb. 7/76)
Most Assists, Game	6	Babe Pratt (Jan. 8/44)
Most Points, Game	*10	Darryl Sittler (Feb. 7/76)

* NHL Record.

All-time Record vs. Other Clubs

Regular Season

		At Home						On Road						Total					
	GP	W	L	T	GF	GA	PTS	GP	W	L	T	GF	GA	PTS	GP	W	L	T	GF	GA	PTS
Boston	274	144	84	46	928	703	334	273	80	146	47	733	901	207	547	224	230	93	1661	1604	541
Buffalo	43	18	18	7	142	153	43	44	14	28	2	124	190	30	87	32	46	9	266	343	73
**Calgary	32	13	12	7	131	122	33	33	11	19	3	113	144	25	65	24	31	10	244	266	58
Chicago	281	153	80	48	971	706	354	280	105	136	39	735	847	249	561	258	216	87	1706	1553	603
Detroit	283	151	90	42	930	727	344	283	94	146	43	685	828	231	566	245	236	85	1615	1555	575
Edmonton	16	5	10	1	68	89	11	16	1	11	4	50	95	6	32	6	21	5	118	184	17
Hartford	16	6	10	0	60	71	12	16	3	11	2	51	81	8	32	9	21	2	111	152	20
Los Angeles	47	26	12	9	199	153	61	47	14	28	5	128	170	33	94	40	40	14	327	323	94
Minnesota	67	30	23	14	248	228	74	66	25	33	8	223	256	58	133	55	56	22	471	484	132
Montreal	308	156	108	44	928	803	356	308	82	187	39	755	1092	203	616	238	295	83	1683	1895	559
*New Jersey	26	19	5	2	121	85	40	26	8	9	9	85	98	25	52	27	14	11	206	183	65
NY Islanders	33	15	15	3	116	121	33	32	11	19	2	101	143	24	65	26	34	5	217	264	57
NY Rangers	261	148	75	38	899	668	334	262	100	108	54	769	796	254	523	248	183	92	1668	1464	588
Philadelphia	46	17	16	13	161	146	47	45	9	29	7	110	188	25	91	26	45	20	271	334	72
Pittsburgh	47	21	16	10	187	156	52	47	18	24	5	150	175	41	94	39	40	15	337	331	93
Quebec	16	6	8	2	50	70	14	16	3	9	4	55	68	10	32	9	17	6	105	138	24
St. Louis	64	39	18	7	254	193	85	65	15	40	10	174	228	40	129	54	58	17	428	421	125
Vancouver	38	16	14	8	147	135	40	38	11	20	7	125	135	29	76	27	34	15	272	270	69
Washington	28	15	9	4	127	97	34	28	10	16	2	81	111	22	56	25	25	6	208	208	56
Winnipeg	18	5	12	1	72	91	11	18	7	10	1	81	87	15	36	12	22	2	153	178	26
Defunct Clubs	232	158	53	21	860	515	337	233	84	120	29	607	745	197	465	242	173	50	1467	1260	534
Totals	2176	1161	688	327	7599	6032	2649	2176	705	1149	322	5935	7378	1732	4352	1866	1837	649	13534	13410	4381

* Totals include those of Kansas City (1974-75, 1975-76) and Colorado (1976-77 through 1981-82)
** Totals include those of Atlanta (1972-73 through 1979-80)

Playoffs

	Series	W	L	GP	W	L	T	GF	GA	Last Mtg.	Round	Result
Boston	13	8	5	62	31	30	1	150	153	1974	QF	L 0-4
Calgary	1	1	0	2	2	0	0	9	5	1979	P	W 2-0
Chicago	7	5	2	25	15	9	1	76	57	1986	DSF	W 3-0
Detroit	22	11	11	110	54	56	0	289	291	1988	DSF	L 2-4
Los Angeles	2	2	0	5	4	1	0	18	9	1978	P	W 2-0
Minnesota	2	0	2	7	1	6	0	26	35	1983	DSF	L 1-3
Montreal	13	6	7	67	28	39	0	138	184	1979	QF	L 0-4
NY Islanders	2	1	1	10	4	6	0	20	23	1981	P	L 0-3
NY Rangers	8	3	5	35	16	19	0	86	86	1971	QF	L 2-4
Philadelphia	3	0	3	17	5	12	0	47	67	1977	QF	L 2-4
Pittsburgh	2	2	0	6	4	2	0	21	13	1977	P	W 2-1
St. Louis	2	1	1	13	7	6	0	37	35	1987	DSF	W 4-2
Defunct Clubs	4	3	1	10	5	4	1	20	16			
Totals	81	43	38	369	176	190	3	937	984			

Playoff Results 1989-85

Year	Round	Opponent	Result	GF	GA
1988	DSF	Detroit	L 2-4	22	32
1987	DF	Detroit	L 3-4	18	20
	DSF	St. Louis	W 4-2	15	11
1986	DF	St. Louis	L 3-4	22	24
	DSF	Chicago	W 3-0	18	9

Abbreviations: Round: F – Final; **CF** – conference final; **DF** – division final; **DSF** – division semi-final; **SF** – semi-final; **QF** – quarter-final. **P** – preliminary round. **GA** – goals against; **GF** – goals for.

1988-89 Results

	Home			Away	
Oct. 8	Chicago	7-4	**Oct.** 6	Boston	1-2
12	St Louis	2-4	9	Chicago	8-4
15	Detroit	3-5	14	Washington	3-1
19	Buffalo	4-2	17	Montreal	6-2
22	Calgary	3-3	21	Detroit	4-2
Nov. 2	Boston	2-7	25	NY Islanders	4-3
5	Los Angeles	4-6	26	Minnesota	3-2
12	Edmonton	2-6	29	St Louis	2-3
14	Minnesota	4-5	**Nov.** 10	Pittsburgh	1-5
16	Pittsburgh	8-5	18	Winnipeg	0-3
21	St Louis	4-0	19	Edmonton	1-9
23	Chicago	4-3	25	Minnesota	3-5
26	Minnesota	3-6	**Dec.** 1	Los Angeles	3-9
Dec. 10	Detroit	2-8	3	St Louis	0-3
12	Calgary	4-4	9	Detroit	3-4
14	Edmonton	2-8	15	New Jersey	3-6
17	Philadelphia	1-7	23	Buffalo	2-5
19	St Louis	4-3	29	Quebec	6-5
21	Pittsburgh	1-6	**Jan.** 1	Chicago	3-3
26	NY Islanders	3-4	6	Washington	0-3
31	Quebec	6-1	21	Montreal	3-4
Jan. 7	Buffalo	1-6	27	Detroit	1-8
9	Vancouver	3-0	30	Chicago	1-7
11	Washington	2-3	**Feb.** 2	NY Islanders	4-1
14	Montreal	3-5	13	New Jersey	1-8
16	Hartford	5-3	17	NY Rangers	10-6
19	Minnesota	3-3	20	Los Angeles*	4-5
25	Boston	1-2	22	Calgary	4-3
28	NY Rangers	1-1	23	Vancouver	1-2
Feb. 4	Chicago	1-3	25	Minnesota	4-2
11	Philadelphia	4-3	**Mar.** 1	NY Rangers	4-7
18	Hartford	2-4	3	Hartford	0-3
18	New Jersey	5-3	7	Quebec	6-4
27	St Louis	5-7	9	St Louis	1-4
Mar. 4	Chicago	3-3	12	Winnipeg	7-9
11	Detroit	5-3	14	Minnesota	5-3
18	Winnipeg	2-10	19	Philadelphia	6-8
22	Vancouver	5-3	24	Detroit	2-6
25	Detroit	6-5	**Apr.** 1	St Louis	3-4
29	Minnesota	3-1	2	Chicago	3-4

* Denotes afternoon game.

Entry Draft Selections 1989-75

1989
Pick
3	Scott Thornton
12	Rob Pearson
21	Steve Bancroft
66	Matt Martin
96	Keith Carney
108	David Burke
125	Michael Doers
129	Keith Merkler
150	Derek Langille
171	Jeffrey St. Laurent
192	Justin Tomberlin
213	Mike Jackson
234	Steve Chartrand

1988
Pick
6	Scott Pearson
27	Tie Domi
48	Peter Ing
69	Ted Crowley
87	Leonard Esau
132	Matt Mallgrave
153	Roger Elvenas
174	Mike Delay
195	David Sacco
216	Mike Gregorio
237	Peter Deboer

1987
Pick
7	Luke Richardson
28	Daniel Marois
49	John McIntyre
71	Joe Sacco
91	Mike Eastwood
112	Damian Rhodes
133	Trevor Jobe
154	Chris Jensen
175	Brian Blad
196	Ron Bernacci
217	Ken Alexander
238	Alex Weinrich

1986
Pick
6	Vincent Damphousse
36	Darryl Shannon
48	Sean Boland
69	Kent Hulst
90	Scott Taylor
111	Stephane Giguere
132	Danny Hie
153	Stephen Brennan
174	Brian Bellefeuille
195	Sean Davidson
216	Mark Holick
237	Brian Hoard

1985
Pick
1	Wendel Clark
22	Ken Spangler
43	Dave Thomlinson
64	Greg Vey
85	Jeff Serowik
106	Jiri Latal
127	Tim Bean
148	Andy Donahue
169	Todd Whittemore
190	Bob Reynolds
211	Tim Armstrong
232	Mitch Murphy

1984
Pick
4	Al Iafrate
25	Todd Gill
67	Jeff Reese
88	Jack Capuano
109	Joe Fabian
130	Joe McInnis
151	Derek Laxdal
172	Dan Turner
192	David Buckley
213	Mikael Wurst
233	Peter Slanina

1983
Pick
7	Russ Courtnall
28	Jeff Jackson
48	Allan Bester
83	Dan Hodgson
128	Cam Plante
148	Paul Bifano
168	Cliff Albrecht
184	Greg Rolston
188	Brian Ross
208	Mike Tomlak
228	Ron Choules

1982
Pick
3	Gary Nylund
24	Gary Leeman
25	Peter Ihnacak
45	Ken Wregget
73	Vaclav Ruzicka
87	Eduard Uvara
99	Sylvain Charland
108	Ron Dreger
115	Craig Kales
129	Dom Campedelli
139	Jeff Triano
171	Miroslav Ihnacak
192	Leigh Verstraete
213	Tim Loven
234	Jim Appleby

1981
Pick
6	Jim Benning
24	Gary Yaremchuk
55	Ernie Godden
90	Normand LeFrancois
102	Barry Brigley
132	Andrew Wright
153	Richard Turmel
174	Greg Barber
195	Marc Magnan

1980
Pick
25	Craig Muni
26	Bob McGill
43	Fred Boimistruck
74	Stewart Gavin
95	Hugh Larkin
116	Ron Dennis
137	Russ Adam
158	Fred Perlini
179	Darwin McCutcheon
200	Paul Higgins

1979
Pick
9	Laurie Boschman
51	Normand Aubin
72	Vincent Tremblay
93	Frank Nigro
114	Bill McCreary

1978
Pick
21	Joel Quenneville
48	Mark Kirton
65	Bob Parent
81	Jordy Douglas
92	Mel Hewitt
98	Normand Lefebvre
115	John Scammell
132	Kevin Reinhart
149	Mike Waghorne
166	Laurie Cuvelier

1977
Pick
11	John Anderson
12	Trevor Johansen
24	Bob Gladney
29	Rockey Saganiuk
65	Dan Eastman
83	John Wilson
101	Roy Sommer
119	Lynn Jorgenson

1976
Pick
30	Randy Carlyle
48	Alain Belanger
52	Gary McFayden
66	Tim Williams
84	Greg Hotham
102	Dan Dkjakalovic

1975
Pick
6	Don Ashby
24	Doug Jarvis
42	Bruce Boudreau
78	Ted Long
96	Kevin Campbell
114	Mario Rouillard
132	Ron Wilson
149	Paul Evans
165	Jean Latendresse
166	Paul Crowley
179	Dan D'Alvise
180	Jack Laine
188	Ken Holland

1974
Pick
13	Jack Valiquette
31	Dave Williams
49	P. Alexandersson
67	Peter Driscoll
85	Mike Palmateer
103	Bill Hassard
121	Kevin Devine
139	Kevin Kemp

1973
Pick
4	Lanny McDonald
10	Bob Neely
15	Ian Turnbull
52	Francois Rochon
68	Gord Titcomb
84	Doug Marit
100	Dan Follett
116	Les Burgess
132	Dave Pay
144	Lee Palmer
147	Bob Peace

1972
Pick
11	George Ferguson
27	Randy Osburn
43	Denis Deslauriers
59	Brian Bowles
75	Michel Plante
91	Dave Shardlow
107	Monte Miron
123	Peter Williams
139	Pat Boutette
143	Gary Schofield

Club Directory

Maple Leaf Gardens
60 Carlton Street
Toronto, Ontario M5B 1L1
Phone 416/977-1641
FAX 416/977-5364
ENVOY ID
    Front Office: LEAFS. GM
    Public
    Relations: LEAFS. PR
Capacity: 16,182 (standing 200)

Board of Directors
Harold E. Ballard	Jake Dunlap, Q.C.	Douglas H. Roxborough
Norman Bosworth	Edward Lawrence	Steve Stavro
Donald Giffin	Paul McNamara, Q.C.	

President, Managing Director and Governor . . . Harold E. Ballard
Chairman of the Board. . . . . Paul McNamara, Q.C.
Alternate Governor . . . . George Armstrong
General Manager . . . . TBA
Coach . . . . Doug Carpenter
Assistant Coach . . . . Garry Lariviere
Chief Scout . . . . Floyd Smith
Scouts. . . . . George Armstrong, Johnny Bower, Jim Bzdell,
    Frank Currie, Dick Duff, Jack Gardiner,
    Bob Johnson, Dan Marr, Doug Woods
Director of Public Relations . . . . Bob Stellick
Executive Assistant . . . . Pat Park
Administrative Assistants . . . . Ellen Salnek, Mary Speck
Trainers. . . . . Guy Kinnear, Dan Lemelin, Brian Papineau
Treasurer. . . . . Donald Crump
Box Office Manager . . . . I.M. (Patty) Patoff
Building Superintendent . . . . Donald MacKenzie
Team Doctors. . . . . Dr. Dave Hastings, Dr. Simon McGrail,
    Dr. Murray Urowitz, Dr. Leith Douglas,
    Dr. Ernie Lewis, Dr. Michael Easterbrook,
    Dr. Earl Bogoch
Dimensions of rink. . . . . 200 feet by 85 feet
Club Colours . . . . Home - Blue and White
Press Box . . . . East Side
Play-by-Play TV broadcasters . . . . Ron McLean, Harry Neale,
    Bob Cole, Joe Bowen
    (CBC-TV 5 and Global TV)
Radio Network . . . . TBS
Radio Play-by-Play broadcaster . . . . Joe Bowen

Allan Bester

Coach

CARPENTER, DOUG
Coach, Toronto Maple Leafs. Born in Cornwall, Ont., July 1, 1942.

47-year-old Doug Carpenter was named coach of the Maple Leafs on August 16, 1989, returning to the organization that saw him launch his career as a coach in professional hockey. A graduate of Montreal's McGill University in 1962 and Loyola College in 1967, Carpenter spent eight seasons as a minor league defenseman/left-winger in the Eastern and International Leagues (1966-74) before becoming head coach of the Cornwall Royals of the Quiebec Junior League in 1978-79. After leading Cornwall to the Memorial Cup in 1979-80, he was hired by the Toronto Maple Leafs as coach of their top minor league affiliates. These included New Brunswick (AHL) in 1980-81, Cincinnati (CHL) in 1981-82 and St. Catharines (AHL) in 1982-83 and 1983-84.

He moved up to the NHL as coach of the New Jersey Devils in 1984-85. After his rookie season with New Jersey, Carpenter was named head coach of Team Canada at the 1985 World Championships in Czechoslovakia, where his squad defeated the Soviet Union 3-1 for Canada's first win against the Soviets in an IIHF championship since 1961. Carpenter's Canadian team went onto win a silver medal. Carpenter coached the improving young Devils club for 3½ seasons until January of 1988. He coached Halifax of the AHL in 1988-89.

Coaching Record
Team		Regular Season					Playoffs				
		Games	W	L	T	%	Games	W	L	T	%
1978-79	Cornwall (QJHL)	72	29	36	7	.451	7	3	4		.429
1979-80	Cornwall (QJHL)	72	41	25	6	.611	17	12	5		.706
1980-81	New Brunswick (AHL)	80	37	33	10	.525	13	7	6		.538
1981-82	Cincinnati (CHL)	80	46	30	4	.600	4	1	3		.250
1982-83	St. Catharines (AHL)	80	33	41	6	.450	....	....	....	....	....
1983-84	St. Catharines (AHL)	79	43	30	6	.5832	7	3	4		.429
1984-85	**New Jersey (NHL)**	**80**	**22**	**48**	**10**	**.338**	....	....	....	....	....
1985-86	**New Jersey (NHL)**	**80**	**28**	**49**	**3**	**.369**	....	....	....	....	....
1986-87	**New Jersey (NHL)**	**80**	**29**	**45**	**6**	**.400**	....	....	....	....	....
1987-88	**New Jersey (NHL)**	**50**	**21**	**24**	**5**	**.470**	....	....	....	....	....
1988-89	Halifax (AHL)	80	42	30	8	.575	4	0	4		.000
	NHL Totals	**290**	**100**	**166**	**24**	**.386**	....	....	....	....	....

Vancouver Canucks
1988-89 Results: 33w-39L-8T 74 PTS. Fourth, Smythe Division

Year-by-Year Record

Season	GP	Home W	L	T	Road W	L	T	Overall W	L	T	GF	GA	Pts.	Finished	Playoff Result
1988-89	80	19	15	6	14	24	2	33	39	8	251	253	74	4th, Smythe Div.	Lost Div. Semi-Final
1987-88	80	15	20	5	10	26	4	25	46	9	272	320	59	5th, Smythe Div.	Out of Playoffs
1986-87	80	17	19	4	12	24	4	29	43	8	282	314	66	5th, Smythe Div.	Out of Playoffs
1985-86	80	17	18	5	6	26	8	23	44	13	282	333	59	4th, Smythe Div.	Lost Div. Semi-Final
1984-85	80	15	21	4	10	25	5	25	46	9	284	401	59	5th, Smythe Div.	Out of Playoffs
1983-84	80	20	16	4	12	23	5	32	39	9	306	328	73	3rd, Smythe Div.	Lost Div. Semi-Final
1982-83	80	20	12	8	10	23	7	30	35	15	303	309	75	3rd, Smythe Div.	Lost Div. Semi-Final
1981-82	80	20	8	12	10	25	5	30	33	17	290	286	77	2nd, Smythe Div.	Lost Stanley Cup Final
1980-81	80	17	12	11	11	20	9	28	32	20	289	301	76	3rd, Smythe Div.	Lost Prelim. Round
1979-80	80	14	17	9	13	20	7	27	37	16	256	281	70	3rd, Smythe Div.	Lost Prelim. Round
1978-79	80	15	18	7	10	24	6	25	42	13	217	291	63	2nd, Smythe Div.	Lost Prelim. Round
1977-78	80	13	15	12	7	28	5	20	43	17	239	320	57	3rd, Smythe Div.	Out of Playoffs
1976-77	80	13	21	6	12	21	7	25	42	13	235	294	63	4th, Smythe Div.	Out of Playoffs
1975-76	80	22	11	7	11	21	8	33	32	15	271	272	81	2nd, Smythe Div.	Lost Prelim. Round
1974-75	80	23	12	5	15	20	5	38	32	10	271	254	86	1st, Smythe Div.	Lost Quarter-Final
1973-74	78	14	18	7	10	25	4	24	43	11	224	296	59	7th, East Div.	Out of Playoffs
1972-73	78	17	18	4	5	29	5	22	47	9	233	339	53	7th, East Div.	Out of Playoffs
1971-72	78	14	20	5	6	30	3	20	50	8	203	297	48	7th, East Div.	Out of Playoffs
1970-71	78	17	18	4	7	28	4	24	46	8	229	296	56	6th, East Div.	Out of Playoffs

Schedule

Home		Away	
Oct. Thur. 5 Edmonton		**Oct.** Wed. 11 Edmonton	
Sat. 7 Detroit		Wed. 18 Toronto	
Mon. 9 NY Islanders*		Fri. 20 New Jersey	
Fri. 13 Los Angeles		Sat. 21 NY Islanders	
Sun. 15 Boston*		Mon. 23 NY Rangers	
Sat. 28 Calgary		Fri. 27 Calgary	
Tues. 31 New Jersey		**Nov.** Wed. 8 Winnipeg	
Nov. Fri. 3 Winnipeg		Fri. 10 Buffalo	
Sun. 5 Pittsburgh		Sat. 11 Quebec	
Tues. 14 Washington		Tues. 21 Edmonton	
Thur. 16 Chicago		Sat. 25 Los Angeles	
Sun. 19 Buffalo		**Dec.** Wed. 6 Los Angeles	
Sun. 26 Los Angeles		Sat. 9 St Louis	
Wed. 29 Toronto		Sun. 10 Chicago	
Dec. Fri. 1 NY Rangers		Tues. 12 Minnesota	
Sun. 3 Minnesota		Wed. 13 Winnipeg	
Fri. 15 Winnipeg		Wed. 20 Calgary	
Sun. 17 Quebec		Sat. 23 Los Angeles	
Tues. 19 Calgary		**Jan.** Tues. 2 Detroit	
Wed. 27 Montreal		Thur. 4 Pittsburgh	
Sun. 31 Philadelphia		Fri. 5 Washington	
Jan. Wed. 10 Hartford		Sun. 7 Montreal	
Fri. 12 St Louis		Tues. 16 NY Islanders	
Sat. 13 Buffalo		Thur. 18 Philadelphia	
Tues. 23 Los Angeles		Fri. 19 Chicago	
Fri. 26 Minnesota		Sat. 27 Edmonton	
Tues. 30 Calgary		**Feb.** Thur. 1 Calgary	
Feb. Sun. 4 New Jersey		Fri. 2 Winnipeg	
Tues. 6 Winnipeg		Fri. 9 Hartford	
Fri. 16 Edmonton		Sun. 11 Boston*	
Sun. 18 Boston		Tues. 13 Quebec	
Tues. 20 Edmonton		Wed. 14 Montreal	
Mon. 26 Toronto		Sat. 24 Los Angeles	
Wed. 28 Philadelphia		**Mar.** Sat. 3 Calgary	
Mar. Fri. 9 Calgary		Sun. 4 Edmonton	
Sun. 11 Pittsburgh*		Thur. 15 St Louis	
Tues. 13 Hartford		Sat. 17 Washington	
Sun. 25 Winnipeg		Sun. 18 NY Rangers	
Tues. 27 Edmonton		Tues. 20 Detroit	
Sat. 31 Los Angeles		Fri. 23 Winnipeg	

* Denotes afternoon game.

Home Starting Times:
Weeknights .... 7:35 p.m.
Saturdays .... 5:05 p.m.
Sundays .... 7:05 p.m.
Matinees .... 2:05 p.m.

Franchise date: May 22, 1970.

**20th
NHL
Season**

Defenseman Paul Reinhart had 50 assists in 64 games for the Canucks.

1989-90 Player Personnel

FORWARDS

	HT	WT	S	Place of Birth	Date	1988-89 Club
ADAMS, Greg	6-3	190	L	Nelson, B.C.	8/1/63	Vancouver
ADAMS, Greg C.	6-2	200	L	Duncan, B.C.	5/31/60	Edmonton-Vancouver
BAKOVIC, Peter	6-2	200	R	Thunder Bay, Ont.	1/31/65	Milwaukee
BOZEK, Steve	5-11	180	L	Kelowna, B.C.	11/26/60	Vancouver
BRADLEY, Brian	5-10	180	R	Kitchener, Ont.	1/21/65	Vancouver
BRUCE, Dave	5-11	185	R	Thunder Bay, Ont.	10/7/64	Vancouver
CHARBONNEAU, Jose	6-0	195	R	Ferme-Neuve, Que.	11/21/66	MtL.-Sher.-Van.-Milw.
CRAWFORD, Marc	5-11	185	L	Belleville, Ont.	2/13/61	Milwaukee
DeBOER, Peter	6-0	195	R	Windsor, Ont.	6/13/68	Windsor-Milwaukee
HAWKINS, Todd	6-1	195	R	Kingston, Ont.	8/2/66	Vancouver-Milwaukee
JOHNSON, Steve	6-1	190	R	Grand Forks, ND	3/3/66	Milwaukee
LARIONOV, Igor	5-9	165	L	Voskresensk, USSR	12/3/60	CSKA (USSR)
LENARDON, Tim	6-2	185	L	Trail, B.C.	5/11/62	Utica-Milwaukee
LINDEN, Trevor	6-4	200	R	Medicine Hat, Alta.	4/11/70	Vancouver
MAZUR, Jay	6-2	205	R	Hamilton, Ont.	1/22/65	Milwaukee-Vancouver
MURPHY, Rob	6-3	205	L	Hull, Que.	4/7/69	Van-Drummondville-Mil
PEDERSON, Barry	5-11	185	L	Big River, Sask.	3/13/61	Vancouver
ROHLICEK, Jeff	6-0	180	L	Park Ridge, IL	1/27/66	Milwaukee-Vancouver
SANDLAK, Jim	6-3	219	R	Kitchener, Ont.	12/12/66	Vancouver
SKRIKO, Petri	5-10	180	L	Lapeenranta, Finland	3/12/62	Vancouver
SMITH, Doug	5-11	186	R	Ottawa, Ont.	5/17/63	Edm-Cape Breton-Van.
SMYL, Stan	5-8	195	R	Glendon, Alta.	1/28/58	Vancouver
STANLEY, Daryl	6-2	200	R	Winnipeg, Man.	12/2/62	Vancouver
STERN, Ronnie	6-0	195	R	St. Agathe, Que.	1/11/67	Vancouver-Milwaukee
STREET, Keith	6-0	170	R	Moose Jaw, Sask.	3/18/65	Milwaukee
SUTTER, Rich	5-11	190	L	Viking, Alta.	12/2/63	Vancouver
TANTI, Tony	5-9	185	L	Toronto, Ont.	10/9/63	Vancouver
VARGAS, Ernie	6-1	180	L	St. Paul, MN	3/1/64	Milwaukee

DEFENSEMEN

	HT	WT	S	Place of Birth	Date	1988-89 Club
AGNEW, Jim	6-1	190	L	Hartney, Man.	3/21/66	Milwaukee
BENNING, Jim	6-0	185	L	Edmonton, Alta.	4/29/63	Vancouver
BUTCHER, Garth	6-0	200	R	Regina, Sask.	1/8/63	Vancouver
GUY, Kevan	6-3	202	R	Edmonton, Alta.	7/16/65	Vancouver
HERNIMAN, Steve	6-4	210	L	Windsor, Ont.	6/9/68	Kitchener
HUNT, Curtis	6-0	195	L	North Battleford, Sask.	1/28/67	Milwaukee
KIDD, Ian	5-11	195	R	Gresham, OR	5/11/64	Vancouver-Milwaukee
LIDSTER, Doug	6-1	200	R	Kamloops, B.C.	10/18/60	Vancouver
MELNYK, Larry	6-0	195	L	Saskatoon, Sask.	2/21/60	Vancouver
NORDMARK, Robert	6-1	200	R	Lulea, Sweden	8/20/62	Vancouver
REINHART, Paul	5-11	200	R	Kitchener, Ont.	1/8/60	Vancouver
SNEPSTS, Harold	6-3	210	L	Edmonton, Alta.	10/24/54	Vancouver
VALIMONT, Carl	6-1	200	L	Southington, CT	3/1/66	Milwaukee
VEILLEUX, Steve	6-0	198	R	Lachenaie, Que.	3/9/69	Trois-Rivieres-Milw.

GOALTENDERS

	HT	WT	S	Place of Birth	Date	1988-89 Club
GAMBLE, Troy	5-11	195	L	New Glasgow, N.S.	4/7/67	Vancouver-Milwaukee
McKICHAN, Steve	5-11	180	L	Strathroy, Ont.	9/29/67	Miami-Ohio
McLEAN, Kirk	6-0	185	L	Willowdale, Ont.	6/26/66	Vancouver
WEEKS, Steve	5-11	170	L	Scarborough, Ont.	6/30/58	Vancouver

1988-89 Scoring

Regular Season
* rookie

Pos	#	Player	Team	GP	G	A	Pts	+/-	PIM	PP	SH	GW	GT	S	%
F	26	Petri Skriko	VAN	74	30	36	66	3-	57	9	0	5	0	204	14.7
F	16	*Trevor Linden	VAN	80	30	29	59	10-	41	10	1	2	0	186	16.1
D	23	Paul Reinhart	VAN	64	7	50	57	4-	44	3	0	1	0	133	5.3
F	9	Tony Tanti	VAN	77	24	25	49	10-	69	8	0	3	1	211	11.4
F	10	Brian Bradley	VAN	71	18	27	45	5-	42	6	0	3	0	151	11.9
F	7	Barry Pederson	VAN	62	15	26	41	5	22	7	1	0	0	98	15.3
D	6	Robert Nordmark	VAN	80	6	35	41	4-	97	5	0	1	0	156	3.8
F	19	Jim Sandlak	VAN	72	20	20	40	8	99	9	0	4	1	164	12.2
F	14	Steve Bozek	VAN	71	17	18	35	1	64	0	2	2	0	138	12.3
F	8	Greg Adams	VAN	61	19	14	33	21-	24	9	0	2	0	144	13.2
F	15	Rich Sutter	VAN	75	17	15	32	3	122	1	3	4	0	125	13.6
F	12	Stan Smyl	VAN	75	7	18	25	0	102	1	0	0	0	89	7.9
D	3	Doug Lidster	VAN	63	5	17	22	4-	78	3	0	0	0	116	4.3
D	5	Garth Butcher	VAN	78	0	20	20	4	227	0	0	0	0	101	.0
F	22	Dan Hodgson	VAN	23	4	13	17	3	25	0	0	1	0	38	10.5
F	22	Greg C. Adams	EDM	49	4	5	9	1	82	0	0	1	0	49	8.2
			VAN	12	4	2	6	2	35	2	0	0	0	22	18.2
			TOTAL	61	8	7	15	3	117	2	0	1	0	71	11.3
F	25	David Bruce	VAN	53	7	7	14	16-	65	1	0	2	0	86	8.1
D	24	Larry Melnyk	VAN	74	3	11	14	3	82	0	1	1	0	59	5.1
D	4	Jim Benning	VAN	65	3	9	12	4-	48	1	0	0	0	55	5.5
F	21	Doug Smith	EDM	19	1	1	2	1	9	0	0	0	0	15	6.7
			VAN	10	3	4	7	3	4	1	0	1	0	12	25.0
			TOTAL	29	4	5	9	2	13	1	0	1	0	27	14.8
D	27	Harold Snepsts	VAN	59	0	8	8	3-	69	0	0	0	0	27	.0
F	28	Mel Bridgman	VAN	15	4	3	7	4-	10	2	0	0	0	17	23.5
F	17	*Jose Charbonneau	MTL	9	1	3	4	1	6	0	0	0	0	15	6.7
			VAN	13	0	1	1	3-	6	0	0	0	0	16	.0
			TOTAL	22	1	4	5	4	12	0	0	0	0	31	3.2
D	29	Daryl Stanley	VAN	20	3	1	4	3	14	0	0	1	0	12	25.0
D	2	Kevan Guy	VAN	45	2	2	4	14-	34	0	0	0	0	40	5.0
F	18	Ken Berry	VAN	13	2	1	3	2	5	0	0	0	0	10	20.0
F	20	*Ronnie Stern	VAN	17	1	0	1	4-	49	0	0	0	0	13	7.7
D	29	Randy Boyd	VAN	2	0	1	1	-	0	0	0	0	0	6	.0
F	21	*Rob Murphy	VAN	8	0	1	1	2-	2	0	0	0	0	10	.0
G	1	Kirk McLean	VAN	42	0	1	1	0	6	0	0	0	0	0	.0
D	32	*Ian Kidd	VAN	1	0	0	0	-	0	0	0	0	0	0	.0
F	33	Jay Mazur	VAN	1	0	0	0	-	0	0	0	0	0	1	.0
F	34	*Jeff Rohlicek	VAN	2	0	0	0	-	4	0	0	0	0	2	.0
F	17	*Todd Hawkins	VAN	4	0	0	0	-	9	0	0	0	0	2	.0
G	35	*Troy Gamble	VAN	5	0	0	0	-	0	0	0	0	0	0	.0

Goaltending

No.	Goaltender	GPI	Mins	Avg	W	L	T	EN	SO	GA	SA	S%
35	*Troy Gamble	5	302	2.38	2	3	0	2	0	12	140	.913
31	Steve Weeks	35	2056	2.98	11	19	5	7	0	102	953	.892
1	Kirk McLean	42	2477	3.08	20	17	3	3	4	127	1169	.891
	Totals	**80**	**4856**	**3.13**	**33**	**39**	**8**	**12**	**4**	**253**	**2262**	**.888**

Playoffs

Pos	#	Player	Team	GP	G	A	Pts	+/-	PIM	PP	SH	GW	GT	S	%
F	10	Brian Bradley	VAN	7	3	4	7	2	10	1	0	0	0	10	30.0
F	16	*Trevor Linden	VAN	7	3	4	7	1-	8	2	1	0	0	11	27.3
F	26	Petri Skriko	VAN	7	1	5	6	0	4	0	0	0	0	13	7.7
D	6	Robert Nordmark	VAN	7	3	2	5	1-	8	2	0	0	0	10	30.0
F	8	Greg Adams	VAN	7	2	3	5	1-	2	0	0	0	0	18	11.1
D	23	Paul Reinhart	VAN	7	2	3	5	3-	4	1	0	2	1	20	10.0
F	9	Tony Tanti	VAN	7	0	5	5	2-	4	0	0	0	0	16	.0
F	15	Rich Sutter	VAN	7	2	1	3	1	12	0	0	0	0	13	15.4
F	28	Mel Bridgman	VAN	7	1	2	3	1-	10	1	0	0	0	3	33.3
F	19	Jim Sandlak	VAN	6	1	1	2	1-	4	0	0	0	0	10	10.0
D	5	Garth Butcher	VAN	7	1	1	2	5	22	0	0	1	0	9	11.1
D	3	Doug Lidster	VAN	7	1	1	2	1	9	0	0	0	0	13	7.7
F	14	Steve Bozek	VAN	7	0	2	2	1	4	0	0	0	0	7	.0
F	20	*Ronnie Stern	VAN	3	0	1	1	0	17	0	0	0	0	6	.0
D	27	Harold Snepsts	VAN	7	0	1	1	2-	6	0	0	0	0	7	.0
D	2	Kevan Guy	VAN	1	0	0	0	-	0	0	0	0	0	1	.0
D	4	Jim Benning	VAN	3	0	0	0	-	0	0	0	0	0	0	.0
G	31	Steve Weeks	VAN	3	0	0	0	-	0	0	0	0	0	0	.0
D	24	Larry Melnyk	VAN	7	0	0	0	2-	2	0	0	0	0	3	.0
F	21	Doug Smith	VAN	4	0	0	0	-	6	0	0	0	0	5	.0
G	1	Kirk McLean	VAN	5	0	0	0	-	0	0	0	0	0	0	.0
F	22	Greg C. Adams	VAN	7	0	0	0	2-	21	0	0	0	0	15	.0
F	12	Stan Smyl	VAN	7	0	0	0	1-	9	0	0	0	0	4	.0

Goaltending

No.	Goaltender	GPI	Mins	Avg	W	L	EN	SO	GA	SA	S%
31	Steve Weeks	3	140	3.43	1	1	0	0	8	79	.899
1	Kirk McLean	5	302	3.53	2	3	0	0	18	167	.892
	Totals	**7**	**442**	**3.53**	**3**	**4**	**0**	**0**	**26**	**246**	**.894**

Trevor Linden was one of the NHL's finest first-year players in 1988-89, scoring 30 goals for the Canucks.

General Managers' History

Normand Robert Poile, 1970-71 to 1972-73; Hal Laycoe, 1973-74; Phil Maloney, 1974-75 to 1976-77; Jake Milford, 1977-78 to 1981-82; Harry Neale, 1982-83 to 1984-85; Jack Gordon, 1985-86 to 1986-87; Pat Quinn, 1987-88 to date.

Coaching History

Hal Laycoe, 1970-71 to 1971-72; Vic Stasiuk, 1972-73; Bill McCreary and Phil Maloney, 1973-74; Phil Maloney, 1974-75 to 1975-76; Phil Maloney and Orland Kurtenbach, 1976-77; Orland Kurtenbach, 1977-78; Harry Neale, 1978-79 to 1981-82; Harry Neale and Roger Neilson, 1981-82; Roger Neilson 1982-83, 1983-84; Harry Neale, 1983-84; Bill Laforge, 1984-85; Tom Watt, 1985-86, 1986-87; Bob McCammon, 1987-88 to date.

Captains' History

Orland Kurtenbach, 1970-71 to 1973-74; no captain, 1974-75; Andre Boudrias, 1975-76; Chris Oddleifson, 1976-77; Don Lever, 1977-78; Don Lever, Kevin McCarthy, 1978-79; Kevin McCarthy, 1979-80, 1980-81; Stan Smyl, 1981-82 to date.

Retired Numbers

11	Wayne Maki	1971-1973

Club Records

Team
(Figures in brackets for season records are games played; records for fewest points, wins, ties, losses, goals, goals against are for 70 or more games)

Most Points	.86	1974-75 (80)
Most Wins	.38	1974-75 (80)
Most Ties	.20	1980-81 (80)
Most Losses	.50	1971-72 (78)
Most Goals	306	1983-84 (80)
Most Goals Against	401	1984-85 (80)
Fewest Points	.48	1971-72 (78)
Fewest Wins	.20	1971-72 (78)
Fewest Ties	.8	1970-71 (78)
		1971-72 (78)
		1988-89 (80)
Fewest Losses	.32	1974-75 (80)
		1975-76 (80)
		1980-81 (80)
Fewest Goals	203	1971-72 (78)
Fewest Goals Against	253	1988-89 (80)

Longest Winning Streak
Over-all ... .7 Feb. 10-23/89
Home ... .8 Feb. 27/83-
Mar. 21/83
Jan. 31-
Mar. 10/89
Away ... .3 Eight times

Longest Undefeated Streak
Over-all ... .10 Mar. 5-25/77
(5 wins, 5 ties)
Home ... .12 Oct. 29-
Dec. 17/74
(11 wins, 1 tie)
Jan. 29-
Mar. 18/89
(10 wins, 2 ties)
Away ... .5 Three times

Longest Losing Streak
Over-all ... .9 Three times
Home ... .6 Dec. 18/70-
Jan. 20/71
Nov. 3-18/78
Away ... .12 Nov. 28/81-
Feb. 6/82

Longest Winless Streak
Over-all ... .13 Nov. 9-
Dec. 7/73
(10 losses, 3 ties)
Home ... .11 Dec. 18/70-
Feb. 6/71
(10 losses, 1 tie)
Away ... .20 Jan. 2/86-
Apr. 2/86
(14 losses, 6 ties)
Most Shutouts, Season 8 1974-75 (80)
Most Pen. Mins., Season
... 1,917 1986-87 (80)
Most Goals, Game ... .11 Mar. 28/71
(Cal. 5 at Van. 11)
Nov. 25/86
(Van. 11 at L.A. 5)

Individual

Most Seasons ... .11 Stan Smyl,
Harold Snepsts
Most Games ... 804 Stan Smyl
Most Goals, Career ... 259 Stan Smyl
Most Assists, Career ... 384 Stan Smyl
Most Points, Career ... 643 Stan Smyl
(259 goals, 384 assists)
Most Pen. Mins., Career
... 1,418 Harold Snepsts
Most Shutouts, Career ... .11 Gary Smith
Longest Consecutive
Games Streak ... 437 Don Lever
(Oct. 7/72-Jan. 14/78)
Most Goals, Season ... .45 Tony Tanti
(1983-84)
Most Assists, Deason ... .62 André Boudrias
(1974-75)
Most Points, Season ... .91 Patrik Sundstrom
(1983-84)
(38 goals, 53 assists)
Most Pen. Mins., Season ... .343 Dave Williams
(1980-81)

Most Points, Defenseman,
Season ... .63 Doug Lidster
(1986-87)
(12 goals, 51 assists)
Most Points, Center,
Season ... .91 Patrik Sundstrom
(1983-84)
(38 goals, 53 assists)
Most Points, Right Wing,
Season ... .88 Stan Smyl
(1982-83)
(38 goals, 50 assists)
Most Points, Left Wing,
Season ... .81 Darcy Rota
(1982-83)
(42 goals, 39 assists)
Most Points, Rookie,
Season ... .60 Ivan Hlinka
(1981-82)
(23 goals, 37 assists)
Most Shutouts, Season ... .6 Gary Smith
(1974-75)
Most Goals, Game ... .4 Several players
Most Assists, Game ... .6 Patrik Sundstrom
(Feb. 29/84)
Most Points, Game ... .7 Patrik Sundstrom
(Feb. 29/84)

All-time Record vs. Other Clubs

Regular Season

	At Home						On Road						Total					
	GP	W	L	T	GF	GA	PTS	GP	W	L	T	GF	GA	PTS	GP	W	L	T	GF	GA	PTS
Boston	37	10	20	7	124	160	27	37	2	32	3	79	172	7	74	12	52	10	203	332	34
Buffalo	38	19	11	8	147	124	46	38	10	20	8	106	139	28	76	29	31	16	253	263	74
**Calgary	53	19	23	11	186	177	49	53	9	37	7	148	246	25	106	28	60	18	334	423	74
Chicago	43	18	14	11	129	129	47	43	12	26	5	103	149	29	86	30	40	16	232	278	76
Detroit	38	20	12	6	157	119	46	37	11	21	5	116	158	27	75	31	33	11	273	277	73
Edmonton	36	11	20	5	131	165	27	36	6	26	4	112	196	16	72	17	46	9	243	361	43
Hartford	16	7	4	5	60	44	19	16	5	7	4	59	58	14	32	12	11	9	119	102	33
Los Angeles	57	27	20	10	223	196	64	57	16	32	9	170	233	41	114	43	52	19	393	429	105
Minnesota	42	22	13	7	172	128	51	42	8	27	7	115	180	23	84	30	40	14	287	308	74
Montreal	37	4	25	8	87	149	16	38	6	30	2	99	190	14	75	10	55	10	186	339	30
*New Jersey	34	17	6	11	131	103	45	35	16	13	6	122	102	38	69	33	19	17	253	205	83
NY Islanders	34	15	17	2	109	113	32	33	5	20	8	88	136	18	67	20	37	10	197	249	50
NY Rangers	39	10	27	2	125	162	22	40	7	30	3	100	180	17	79	17	57	5	225	342	39
Philadelphia	39	10	21	8	112	150	28	39	10	29	0	114	188	20	78	20	50	8	226	338	48
Pittsburgh	37	17	17	3	139	144	37	37	8	23	6	130	167	22	74	25	40	9	269	311	59
Quebec	16	10	6	0	73	68	20	16	7	5	4	49	47	18	32	17	11	4	122	115	38
St. Louis	43	20	18	5	140	135	45	43	11	26	6	124	171	28	86	31	44	11	264	306	73
Toronto	38	20	11	7	135	125	47	38	14	16	8	135	147	36	76	34	27	15	270	272	83
Washington	26	12	11	3	91	87	27	26	9	15	2	80	87	20	52	21	26	5	171	174	47
Winnipeg	34	20	10	4	139	110	44	33	9	19	5	125	137	23	67	29	29	9	264	247	67
Defunct Clubs	19	14	3	2	82	48	30	19	10	8	1	71	68	21	38	24	11	3	153	116	51
Totals	756	322	309	125	2692	2636	769	756	191	462	103	2245	3151	485	1512	513	771	228	4937	5787	1254

* Totals include those of Kansas City (1974-75, 1975-76) and Colorado (1976-77 through 1981-82)
** Totals include those of Atlanta (1972-73 through 1979-80)

Playoffs

	Series	W	L	GP	W	L	T	GF	GA	Last Mtg.	Round	Result
Buffalo	2	0	2	7	1	6	0	14	28	1981	P	L 0-3
**Calgary	4	1	3	18	8	10	0	57	62	1989	DSF	L 3-4
Chicago	1	1	0	5	4	1	0	18	13	1982	CF	W 4-1
Edmonton	1	0	1	3	0	3	0	5	17	1986	DSF	L 0-3
Los Angeles	1	1	0	5	4	1	0	19	14	1982	DF	W 4-1
Montreal	1	0	1	5	1	4	0	9	20	1975	QF	L 1-4
NY Islanders	2	0	2	6	0	6	0	14	26	1982	F	L 0-4
Philadelphia	1	0	1	3	1	2	0	9	15	1979	P	L 1-2
Totals	13	3	10	22	19	33	0	145	195			

** Totals include those of Atlanta (1972-73 through 1979-80)

Playoff Results 1989-85

Year	Round	Opponent	Result	GF	GA
1989	DSF	Calgary	L 3-4	20	26
1986	DSF	Edmonton	L 0-3	5	17

Abbreviations: Round: F – Final; **CF** – conference final; **DF** – division final; **DSF** – division semi-final; **SF** – semi-final; **QF** – quarter-final. **P** – preliminary round. **GA** – goals against; **GF** – goals for.

Entry Draft
Selections 1989-75

1989
Pick
8	Jason Herter
29	Robert Woodward
71	Brett Hauer
113	Pavel Bure
134	James Revenberg
155	Rob Sangster
176	Sandy Moger
197	Gus Morschauser
218	Hayden O'Rear
239	Darcy Cahill
248	Jan Bergman

1988
Pick
2	Trevor Linden
33	Leif Rohlin
44	Dane Jackson
107	Corrie D'Alessio
122	Phil Von Stefenelli
128	Dixon Ward
149	Greg Geldart
170	Roger Akerstrom
191	Paul Constantin
212	Chris Wolanin
233	Steffan Nilsson

1987
Pick
24	Rob Murphy
45	Steve Veilleux
66	Doug Torrel
87	Sean Fabian
108	Gary Valk
129	Todd Fanning
150	Viktor Tuminev
171	Craig Daly
192	John Fletcher
213	Roger Hansson
233	Neil Eisenhut
234	Matt Evo

1986
Pick
7	Dan Woodley
49	Don Gibson
70	Ronnie Stern
91	Eric Murano
112	Steve Herniman
133	Jon Helgeson
154	Jeff Noble
175	Matt Merton
196	Marc Lyons
217	Todd Hawkins
238	Vladimir Krutov

1985
Pick
4	Jim Sandlak
25	Troy Gamble
46	Shane Doyle
67	Randy Siska
88	Robert Kron
109	Martin Hrstka
130	Brian McFarlane
151	Hakan Ahlund
172	Curtis Hunt
193	Carl Valimont
214	Igor Larionov
235	Darren Taylor

1984
Pick
10	J.J. Daigneault
31	Jeff Rolicek
52	Dave Saunders
55	Landis Chaulk
58	Mike Stevens
73	Brian Bertuzzi
94	Brett MacDonald
115	Jeff Korchinski
136	Blaine Chrest
157	Jim Agnew
178	Rex Grant
198	Ed Lowney
219	Doug Clarke
239	Ed Kister

1983
Pick
9	Cam Neely
30	Dave Bruce
50	Scott Tottle
70	Tim Lorentz
90	Doug Quinn
110	Dave Lowry
130	Terry Maki
150	John Labatt
170	Allan Measures
190	Roger Grillo
210	Steve Kayser
230	Jay Mazur

1982
Pick
11	Michel Petit
53	Yves Lapointe
71	Shawn Kilroy
116	Taylor Hall
137	Parie Proft
158	Newell Brown
179	Don McLaren
200	Al Raymond
221	Steve Driscoll
242	Shawn Green

1981
Pick
10	Garth Butcher
52	Jean-Marc Lanthier
73	Wendell Young
105	Moe Lemay
115	Stu Kulak
136	Bruce Holloway
157	Petri Skriko
178	Frank Caprice
199	Rejean Vignola

1980
Pick
7	Rick Lanz
49	Andy Schliebener
70	Marc Crawford
91	Darrel May
112	Ken Berry
133	Doug Lidster
154	John O'Connor
175	Patrik Sundstrom
196	Grant Martin

1979
Pick
5	Rick Vaive
26	Brent Ashton
47	Ken Ellacott
68	Art Rutland
89	Dirk Graham
110	Shane Swan

1978
Pick
4	Bill Derlago
22	Curt Fraser
40	Stan Smyl
56	Harold Luckner
57	Brad Smith
90	Gerry Minor
107	Dave Ross
124	Steve O'Neill
141	Charlie Antetomaso
158	Richard Martens

1977
Pick
4	Jere Gillis
22	Jeff Bandura
40	Glen Hanlon
56	Dave Morrow
58	Murray Bannerman
76	Steve Hazlett
94	Brian Drumm
112	Ray Creasey

1976
Pick
26	Bob Manno
44	Rob Flockhart
62	Elmer Ray
80	Rick Durston
98	Rob Tudor
114	Brad Rhiness
122	Stu Ostlund

1975
Pick
10	Rick Blight
28	Brad Gassoff
46	Norm Lapointe
64	Glen Richardson
82	Doug Murray
100	Bob Watson
118	Brian Shmyr
136	Allan Fleck
152	Bob McNiece
182	Sid Veysey

Coach
McCAMMON, BOB
Coach, Vancouver Canucks. Born in Kenora, Ont., April 14, 1941.

Bob McCammon was named head coach of the Canucks on June 22, 1987. After a rebuilding year in 1987-88, McCammon led the Canucks to a 33-39-8 record in 1988-89, marking a 15-point improvement in their performance. They earned their first playoff berth since 1985-86 and McCammon was the runner-up for the Jack Adams Award.

After retiring from his 11-year minor league playing career with the Port Huron Flags in 1972-73, McCammon remained with the IHL club as coach through 1976-77. The following season, he joined the Philadelphia Flyers' organization as coach of the Maine Mariners, their top farm club in the AHL, leading them to the AHL's Calder Cup championship and earning Coach-of-the-Year honors.

In 1978-79, the Flyers named McCammon to their head coaching position and then guided the NHL team to a 22-17-11 record in 50 games before returning to Maine in mid-season. In each of the next three years, he piloted the Mariners to 40 or more wins and again won AHL Coach-of-the-Year honors in 1980-81.

Late in the 1981-82 season, McCammon worked his way back to the Flyers as head coach and was promoted to general manager/head coach in 1983-84. In 218 NHL games with Philadelphia, he compiled a record of 119-68-31 for a .617 winning percentage.

In 1985-86, McCammon was named to an assistant coaching position with the Edmonton Oilers and later became that club's Head of Player Development.

Coaching Record
Season	Team	Games	Regular Season W	L	T	%	Playoffs Games	W	L	%
1973-74	Port Huron (IHL)	76	29	44	3	.401	....	....	....	....
1974-75	Port Huron (IHL)	76	35	38	3	.480	5	1	4	.200
1975-76	Port Huron (IHL)	78	36	31	11	.532	15	8	7	.533
1976-77	Port Huron (IHL)	78	27	43	8	.397	....	....	....	....
1977-78	Maine (AHL)	80	43	28	9	.594	12	8	4	.667
1978-79	Philadelphia (NHL)	50	22	17	11	.550	....	....	....	....
1978-79	Maine (AHL)	30	17	8	5	.650	11	8	3	.727
1979-80	Maine (AHL)	80	41	28	11	.581	12	6	6	.500
1980-81	Maine (AHL)	80	45	28	7	.606	20	10	10	.500
1981-82	Maine (AHL)	79	40	23	6	.544	....	....	....	....
	Philadelphia (NHL)	8	4	2	2	.625	4	1	3	.250
1982-83	**Philadelphia (NHL)**	**80**	**49**	**23**	**8**	**.663**	**3**	**0**	**3**	**.000**
1983-84	**Philadelphia (NHL)**	**80**	**44**	**26**	**10**	**.613**	**3**	**0**	**3**	**.000**
1987-88	**Vancouver (NHL)**	**80**	**25**	**46**	**9**	**.369**	**....**	**....**	**....**	**....**
1988-89	**Vancouver (NHL)**	**80**	**33**	**39**	**8**	**.463**	**7**	**3**	**4**	**.429**
	NHL Totals	**378**	**177**	**153**	**48**	**.532**	**17**	**4**	**13**	**.235**

Club Directory

Pacific Coliseum
100 North Renfrew Street
Vancouver, B.C. V5K 3N7
Phone 604/254-5141
FAX 604/251-5123
GM FAX 604/251-5514
ENVOY ID
Front Office: CANUCKS. GM
Public
Relations: CANUCKS. PR
Capacity: 16,160

Northwest Sports Enterprises Ltd.
Board of Directors

J. Lawrence Dampier	W.L. McEwen	Andrew E. Saxton
Arthur R. Griffiths	David S. Owen	Peter W. Webster
Frank A. Griffiths, C.A.	Senator Ray Perrault	Sydney W. Welsh
F.W. Griffiths	J. Raymond Peters	D.A. Williams, C.A.
Coleman E. Hall	Peter Paul Saunders	D. Alexander Farac (Sec.)
Senator E.M. Lawson		

Chairman.	Frank A. Griffiths, C.A.
Vice-Chairman	Arthur R. Griffiths
President and General Manager.	Pat Quinn
Vice-President and Director of Hockey Operations	Brian Burke
Vice-President and Director of Marketing and Communications	Glen Ringdal
Senior Advisor	Jack Gordon
Head Coach.	Bob McCammon
Assistant Coaches.	Jack McIlhargey, Mike Murphy
Goaltending Consultant	Cesare Maniago
Director of Public and Media Relations	Darcy Rota
Director of Scouting	Mike Penny
Director of Pro Scouting	Murray Oliver
Scouting Staff.	Scott Carter, Ron Delorme, Paul MacIntosh, Jack McCartan, Ed McColgan, Jim Paatenko, Ken Slater
Director of Publishing.	Norm Jewison
Director of Hockey Information.	Frank Bohmer
Director of Community Relations & Ticket Sales	Lynn Harrison
Director of Sales	Duke Dickson
Sales Coordinator	Gail Nishi
Box Office Manager.	Fiona Hayes
Executive Secretary, Pres. & GM.	Jette Sandeford
Executive Secretary, Vice-President,	Patti Timms
Trainers.	Larry Ashley, Pat O'Neill, Ed Georgica
Strength Coach.	Wayne Wilson
Manager of Food and Beverage Operations.	Terreeia Rauffman
Souvenir Shop Manager.	Irene Parker
Club Doctors	Dr. David Harris, Dr. Ross Davidson
Club Dentist.	Dr. Ken Walters, Dr. David Lawson
Club Colours.	White, Black, Red and Gold
Club Trains at:	Parksville, B.C.
Play-by-Play Broadcaster	Jim Robson (radio and TV)
Radio Station.	CKNW (980)
TV Channel	CBC (2), BCTV (8)

General Manager
QUINN, PAT
President and General Manager, Vancouver Canucks.
Born in Hamilton, Ont., January 29, 1943.

Pat Quinn took up management responsibilities with the Vancouver Canucks in 1987-88 after coaching in Los Angeles from 1984 to 1987 and in Philadelphia from 1978 to 1982. In Philadelphia, Quinn was awarded the Jack Adams award for leading the Flyers to the Stanley Cup finals in 1979-80. He started his coaching career with the Maine Mariners of the AHL and eventually was promoted to the head coaching job with Philadelphia. An NHL defenseman himself, Quinn played in over 600 games over nine years.

NHL Coaching Record
Season	Team	Games	Regular Season W	L	T	%	Playoffs Games	W	L	%
1978-79	Philadelphia	30	18	8	4	.667	8	3	5	.375
1979-80	Philadelphia	80	48	12	20	.725	19	13	6	.684
1980-81	Philadelphia	80	41	24	15	.606	12	6	6	.500
1981-82	Philadelphia	72	34	29	9	.535	....	....	....	....
1984-85	Los Angeles	80	34	32	14	.513	3	0	3	.000
1985-86	Los Angeles	80	23	49	8	.338	....	....	....	....
1986-87	Los Angeles	42	18	20	4	.476	....	....	....	....
	NHL Totals	**464**	**216**	**174**	**74**	**.545**	**42**	**22**	**20**	**.524**

Washington Capitals

1988-89 Results: 41w-29L-10t 92 pts. First, Patrick Division

Year-by-Year Record

Season	GP	Home			Road			Overall					Pts.	Finished		Playoff Result
		W	L	T	W	L	T	W	L	T	GF	GA				
1988-89	80	25	12	3	16	17	7	41	29	10	305	259	92	1st,	Patrick Div.	Lost Div. Semi-Final
1987-88	80	22	14	4	16	19	5	38	33	9	281	249	85	2nd,	Patrick Div.	Lost Div. Final
1986-87	80	22	15	3	16	17	7	38	32	10	285	278	86	2nd,	Patrick Div.	Lost Div. Semi-Final
1985-86	80	30	8	2	20	15	5	50	23	7	315	272	107	2nd,	Patrick Div.	Lost Div. Final
1984-85	80	27	11	2	19	14	7	46	25	9	322	240	101	2nd,	Patrick Div.	Lost Div. Semi-Final
1983-84	80	26	11	3	22	16	2	48	27	5	308	226	101	2nd,	Patrick Div.	Lost Div. Final
1982-83	80	22	12	6	17	13	10	39	25	16	306	283	94	3rd,	Patrick Div.	Lost Div. Semi-Final
1981-82	80	16	16	8	10	25	5	26	41	13	319	338	65	5th,	Patrick Div.	Out of Playoffs
1980-81	80	16	17	7	10	19	11	26	36	18	286	317	70	5th,	Patrick Div.	Out of Playoffs
1979-80	80	20	14	6	7	26	7	27	40	13	261	293	67	5th,	Patrick Div.	Out of Playoffs
1978-79	80	15	19	6	9	22	9	24	41	15	273	338	63	4th,	Norris Div.	Out of Playoffs
1977-78	80	10	23	7	7	26	7	17	49	14	195	321	48	5th,	Norris Div.	Out of Playoffs
1976-77	80	17	15	8	7	27	6	24	42	14	221	307	62	4th,	Norris Div.	Out of Playoffs
1975-76	80	6	26	8	5	33	2	11	59	10	224	394	32	5th,	Norris Div.	Out of Playoffs
1974-75	80	7	28	5	1	39	0	8	67	5	181	446	21	5th,	Norris Div.	Out of Playoffs

Schedule

Home				Away			
Oct.	Fri.	6	Philadelphia	**Oct.**	Wed.	11	Hartford
	Sat.	7	Chicago		Mon.	16	Montreal
	Fri.	13	NY Rangers		Sat.	21	Toronto
	Sat.	14	Calgary		Mon.	23	Calgary
	Fri.	20	NY Islanders		Wed.	25	Winnipeg
	Tues.	31	St Louis		Sat.	28	St Louis
Nov.	Fri.	3	Toronto		Sun.	29	Chicago
	Fri.	10	Boston	**Nov.**	Sun.	5	Quebec*
	Sat.	11	Edmonton		Tues.	7	NY Islanders
	Wed.	22	NY Islanders		Tues.	14	Vancouver
	Fri.	24	Pittsburgh		Sat.	18	Los Angeles
Dec.	Fri.	1	Philadelphia		Sat.	25	Pittsburgh
	Fri.	15	NY Islanders		Wed.	29	Detroit
	Sat.	23	NY Rangers	**Dec.**	Sat.	2	New Jersey
	Tues.	26	Pittsburgh		Tues.	5	Philadelphia
	Fri.	29	Detroit		Wed.	6	Pittsburgh
Jan.	Mon.	1	Los Angeles*		Sat.	9	Boston*
	Fri.	5	Vancouver		Sun.	10	Buffalo
	Fri.	12	Pittsburgh		Sat.	16	Hartford
	Tues.	16	New Jersey		Tues.	19	Philadelphia
	Tues.	23	Winnipeg		Thur.	21	Pittsburgh
	Fri.	26	Montreal		Wed.	27	New Jersey
	Sun.	28	Philadelphia*	**Jan.**	Wed.	3	NY Rangers
Feb.	Sun.	4	Edmonton*		Sat.	6	Boston
	Tues.	6	Quebec		Mon.	8	Toronto
	Fri.	9	New Jersey		Wed.	10	Winnipeg
	Sun.	11	Minnesota*		Sat.	13	NY Islanders
	Fri.	23	NY Rangers		Fri.	19	Buffalo
	Sun.	25	Detroit*		Wed.	24	New Jersey
	Tues.	27	Chicago		Wed.	31	Minnesota
Mar.	Fri.	2	Hartford	**Feb.**	Fri.	2	NY Islanders
	Sun.	4	New Jersey*		Thur.	8	Pittsburgh
	Tues.	6	Buffalo		Wed.	14	Edmonton
	Fri.	9	Quebec		Mon.	19	Los Angeles*
	Tues.	13	St Louis		Wed.	28	NY Rangers
	Sat.	17	Vancouver	**Mar.**	Sat.	10	Philadelphia
	Tues.	20	NY Islanders		Sun.	18	Minnesota
	Fri.	23	Montreal		Tues.	27	New Jersey
	Sun.	25	Calgary*		Thur.	29	Philadelphia
	Sat.	31	NY Rangers	**Apr.**	Sun.	1	NY Rangers

* Denotes afternoon game.

Home Starting Times:
Saturdays and Mondays
  through Thursdays . . . . 7:35 p.m.
Fridays . . . . 8:05 p.m.
Sundays . . . . 1:35 p.m.
Except Wed. Nov. 22 . . . . 8:05 p.m.
  Mon. Jan. 1 . . . . 1:35 p.m.
  Sun. Jan. 28 . . . . 12:05 p.m.

Franchise date: June 11, 1974

**16th
NHL
Season**

Rod Langway has been Washington's "Secretary of Defense" for seven seasons.

1989-90 Player Personnel

FORWARDS

	HT	WT	S	Place of Birth	Date	1988-89 Club
BAWA, Robin	6-2	214	R	Chemainos, B.C.	3/26/66	Baltimore
BERGLAND, Tim	6-2	194	R	Crookston, MN	1/11/65	Baltimore
CHRISTIAN, Dave	5-11	195	R	Warroad, MN	5/12/59	Washington
CICCARELLI, Dino	5-10	175	R	Sarnia, Ont.	2/8/60	Min.-Wsh.
CORRIVEAU, Yvon	6-1	215	L	Welland, Ont.	2/8/67	Wsh.-Balt.
COURTNALL, Geoff	6-1	190	L	Victoria, B.C.	8/18/62	Washington
DICKIE, Gary	5-11	187		Regina, Sask.	11/19/68	Regina
DRUCE, John	6-1	200	L	Peterborough, Ont.	2/23/66	Washington
GERVAIS, Victor	5-9	172		Prince George, B.C.	3/13/69	Seattle
GOULD, Bob	5-10	185	R	Petrolia, Ont.	9/2/57	Washington
GREENLAW, Jeff	6-1	230	L	Toronto, Ont.	2/28/68	Baltimore
HOLLETT, Steve	6-0	200	L	St. Johns, Nfld.	6/12/67	Fort Wayne
HOLOEIN, Dean	6-0	197	R	Melfort, Sask.	4/16/69	Saskatoon
HUNTER, Dale	5-10	198	L	Petrolia, Ont.	7/31/60	Washington
LARTER, Tyler	5-10	190	L	Charlottetown, P.E.I.	3/12/68	Baltimore
LEACH, Steve	5-11	198	R	Cambridge, MA	1/16/66	Washington
LINDAL, Kirby	5-10	180	R	Humboldt, Sask.	1/12/68	Medicine Hat
LORENTZ, Dave	5-9	182	L	Kitchener, Ont.	3/16/69	Peterborough
MALTAIS, Steve	6-2	204	L	Arvida, Que.	1/25/69	Cornwall
MAY, Alan	6-1	200	R	Barrhead, Man.	1/14/65	Cape Breton-New Haven
McEWEN, Dennis	5-11	191	R	Elliot Lake, Ont.	1/30/68	London
MILLAR, Mike	5-11	175	L	St. Catharines, Ont.	4/28/65	Wsh.-Balt.
MILLER, Kelly	5-11	196	L	Detroit, MI.	3/3/63	Washington
MURRAY, Rob	6-0	185	R	Toronto, Ont.	4/4/67	Baltimore
PIVONKA, Michal	6-2	198	L	Kladno, Czech.	1/28/66	Balt.-Washington
PURVES, John	6-0	201	R	Toronto, Ont.	2/12/68	North Bay
RICHARD, Mike	5-10	194	L	Scarborough, Ont.	7/9/66	Baltimore
RIDLEY, Mike	6-1	200	L	Winnipeg, Man.	7/8/63	Washington
SAVAGE, Reggie	5-10	179	L	Montreal, Que.	5/1/70	Victoriaville
SEFTEL, Steve	6-2	196	L	Kitchener, Ont.	5/14/68	Baltimore
TAYLOR, Tim	5-11	178	L	Stratford, Ont.	2/6/69	London
WICKENHEISER, Doug	6-1	200	L	Regina, Sask.	3/30/61	NYR-Wsh.-Team Canada-Balt.

DEFENCEMEN

	HT	WT	S	Place of Birth	Date	1988-89 Club
BABCOCK, Bobby	6-1	222	L	Toronto, Ont.	8/3/68	Cornwall
BALLANTYNE, Jeff	6-1	203	L	Elmira, Ont.	1/7/69	Ottawa
BARTLEY, Wade	6-0	190	R	Killarney, Man.	5/18/70	U.N. Dakota
DOLLAS, Bobby	6-2	212	L	Montreal, Que.	1/31/65	Quebec-Halifax
FELIX, Chris	5-10	191	R	Bramalea, Ont.	5/27/64	Balt.-Wsh.
FERNER, Mark	6-0	193	L	Regina, Sask.	9/5/65	Buf.-Rochester
HATCHER, Kevin	6-4	225	R	Detroit, MI	9/9/66	Washington
HOHENBERGER,	6-0	185	R	Villach, Austria	2/8/69	
HOULDER, Bill	6-3	212	L	Thunder Bay, Ont.	3/11/67	Wsh.-Balt.
JOHANSSON, Calle	5-11	205	L	Goteborg, Sweden	2/14/67	Buffalo-Washington
KLEINENDORST, Scot	6-3	215	L	Grand Rapids, MN	1/16/60	Hartford-Washington
KUMMU, Ryan	6-3	205	L	Kitchener, Ont.	6/5/67	R.P.I.
LANGWAY, Rod	6-3	224	L	Formosa	5/3/57	Washington
MATHIESON, Jim	6-1	209	R	Kindersley, Sask.	1/24/70	Regina
PAYNTER, Kent	6-0	186	L	Summerside, P.E.I.	4/27/65	Saginaw
ROUSE, Bob	6-1	210	R	Surrey, B.C.	6/18/64	Min.-Wsh.
SHEEHY, Neil	6-2	214	R	International Falls, MN	2/9/60	Cgy.-Hfd.
SMITH, Dennis	5-11	192	L	Detroit, MI	7/27/64	Adirondack
STEVENS, Scott	6-1	215	L	Kitchener, Ont.	4/1/64	Washington
TUTT, Brian	6-1	195	L	Small Well, Alta.	6/9/62	Balt.-Team Canada
WHISTLE, Rob	6-2	195	R	Thunder Bay, Ont.	4/4/61	Baltimore

GOALTENDERS

	HT	WT	C	Place of Birth	Date	1988-89 Club
BEAUPRE, Don	5-9	165	L	Waterloo, Ont.	9/19/61	K'zoo.-Min.-Balt.-Wsh.
DAFOE, Byron	5-11	175	L	Duncan, B.C.	2/25/71	Portland
HRIVNAK, Jim	6-2	185	L	Montreal, Que.	5/20/68	Merrimack-Balt.
KOLZIG, Olaf	6-3	207	L	Johannesburg, S. Africa	4/9/70	Tri-Cities
MASON, Bob	6-1	180	R	International Falls, MN	4/22/61	Quebec-Halifax
RAYMOND, Alain	5-10	180	R	Rimouski, Que.	6/24/65	Baltimore
SIMPSON, Shawn	5-11	183	R	Gloucester, Ont.	8/10/68	Baltimore

1988-89 Scoring

Regular Season
*rookie

Pos	#	Player	Team	GP	G	A	Pts	+/-	PIM	PP	SH	GW	GT	S	%
F	17	Mike Ridley	WSH	80	41	48	89	17	49	16	0	9	9	187	21.9
F	14	Geoff Courtnall	WSH	79	42	38	80	11	112	16	0	6	0	239	17.6
F	22	Dino Ciccarelli	MIN	65	32	27	59	16-	64	13	0	5	1	208	15.4
			WSH	11	12	3	15	10	12	3	0	3	0	39	30.8
			TOTAL	76	44	30	74	6-	76	16	0	8	1	247	17.8
F	16	Bengt Gustafsson	WSH	72	18	51	69	13	18	5	4	6	0	107	16.8
D	3	Scott Stevens	WSH	80	7	61	68	1	225	6	0	3	0	195	3.6
F	27	Dave Christian	WSH	80	34	31	65	2	12	16	1	1	2	177	19.2
F	32	Dale Hunter	WSH	80	20	37	57	3-	219	9	0	3	0	138	14.5
F	10	Kelly Miller	WSH	78	19	21	40	13	45	2	1	3	0	121	15.7
D	4	Kevin Hatcher	WSH	62	13	27	40	19	101	3	0	2	0	148	8.8
F	21	Stephen Leach	WSH	74	11	19	30	4	94	4	0	0	0	145	7.6
F	20	Michal Pivonka	WSH	52	8	19	27	9	30	1	0	1	0	73	11.0
D	6	Calle Johansson	BUF	47	2	11	13	7-	33	0	0	1	0	53	3.8
			WSH	12	1	7	8	1	4	1	0	0	0	22	4.5
			TOTAL	59	3	18	21	6-	37	1	0	1	0	75	4.0
D	5	Rod Langway	WSH	76	2	19	21	12	65	0	0	0	0	80	2.5
D	8	Bob Rouse	MIN	66	4	13	17	5-	124	1	1	0	0	66	6.1
			WSH	13	0	2	2	2	36	0	0	0	0	19	.0
			TOTAL	79	4	15	19	3-	160	1	1	0	0	85	4.7
F	23	Bob Gould	WSH	75	5	13	18	2-	65	0	1	0	0	91	5.5
F	25	Lou Franceschetti	WSH	63	7	10	17	4-	123	0	0	0	0	55	12.7
F	19	*John Druce	WSH	48	8	7	15	7	62	0	0	1	0	59	13.6
F	9	Mike Millar	WSH	18	6	3	9	4	4	3	0	1	0	37	16.2
F	19	Doug Wickenheiser	NYR	1	1	0	1	1	0	0	0	0	0	4	25.0
			WSH	16	2	5	7	0	4	1	0	0	0	29	6.9
			TOTAL	17	3	5	8	1	4	1	0	0	0	33	9.1
D	28	*Chris Felix	WSH	21	0	8	8	1	8	0	0	0	0	18	.0
D	15	Neil Sheehy	WSH	72	3	4	7	1-	179	0	0	0	0	22	13.6
F	12	Peter Sundstrom	WSH	35	4	2	6	5-	12	0	0	1	0	39	10.3
F	26	Yvon Corriveau	WSH	33	3	2	5	0	62	0	0	0	0	39	7.7
	34	Bill Houlder	WSH	8	0	3	3	7	4	0	0	0	0	5	.0
D	29	Scot Kleinendorst	HFD	24	0	1	1	11-	36	0	0	0	0	7	.0
			WSH	3	0	1	1	0	10	0	0	0	0	0	.0
			TOTAL	27	0	2	2	11-	46	0	0	0	0	7	.0
D	39	Kent Carlson	WSH	2	1	0	1	2	0	0	0	0	1	1	100.0
G	1	Pete Peeters	WSH	33	0	1	1	0	8	0	0	0	0	0	.0
D	22	*Shawn Cronin	WSH	1	0	0	0	0	0	0	0	0	0	0	.0
G	33	Don Beaupre	MIN	1	0	0	0	0	0	0	0	0	0	0	.0
			WSH	11	0	0	0	0	6	0	0	0	0	0	.0
			TOTAL	12	0	0	0	0	6	0	0	0	0	0	.0

Goaltending

No.	Goaltender	GPI	Mins	Avg	W	L	T	EN	SO	GA	SA	S%
1	Pete Peeters	35	1854	2.85	20	7	3	0	4	88	790	.889
33	Don Beaupre	11	578	2.91	5	4	0	1	1	28	269	.896
30	Clint Malarchuk	42	2428	3.48	16	18	7	1	1	141	1145	.877
	Totals	80	4865	3.19	41	29	10	2	6	259	2204	.882

Playoffs

Pos	#	Player	Team	GP	G	A	Pts	+/-	PIM	PP	SH	GW	GT	S	%
F	14	Geoff Courtnall	WSH	6	2	5	7	2	12	1	0	0	0	19	10.5
F	22	Dino Ciccarelli	WSH	6	3	3	6	2-	12	3	0	0	0	16	18.8
F	16	Bengt Gustafsson	WSH	4	2	3	5	5-	6	1	0	0	0	8	25.0
D	4	Kevin Hatcher	WSH	6	1	4	5	3-	20	1	0	0	0	19	5.3
D	3	Scott Stevens	WSH	6	1	4	5	2-	11	0	0	0	0	16	6.3
F	17	Mike Ridley	WSH	6	0	5	5	2	0	0	0	0	0	9	.0
F	20	Michal Pivonka	WSH	6	3	1	4	0	10	0	0	1	0	17	17.6
F	32	Dale Hunter	WSH	6	0	4	4	3	27	0	0	0	0	7	.0
D	6	Calle Johansson	WSH	6	1	2	3	2-	0	1	0	0	0	13	7.7
D	8	Bob Rouse	WSH	6	2	0	2	3	4	0	0	0	0	9	22.2
F	27	Dave Christian	WSH	6	1	1	2	3-	0	1	0	0	0	21	4.8
F	23	Bob Gould	WSH	6	0	2	2	1-	0	0	0	0	0	4	.0
F	25	Lou Franceschetti	WSH	6	1	0	1	2-	8	0	0	1	0	4	25.0
F	21	Stephen Leach	WSH	6	1	0	1	2-	12	1	0	0	0	9	11.1
F	10	Kelly Miller	WSH	6	1	0	1	6-	2	0	0	1	1	14	7.1
D	28	*Chris Felix	WSH	1	0	1	1	0	0	0	0	0	0	0	.0
F	26	Yvon Corriveau	WSH	1	0	0	0	1-	0	0	0	0	0	0	.0
F	19	*John Druce	WSH	1	0	0	0	0	0	0	0	0	0	0	.0
F	18	Doug Wickenheiser	WSH	5	0	0	0	1-	2	0	0	0	0	3	.0
D	5	Rod Langway	WSH	6	0	0	0	4-	6	0	0	0	0	10	.0
G	1	Pete Peeters	WSH	6	0	0	0	0	2	0	0	0	0	0	.0
D	15	Neil Sheehy	WSH	6	0	0	0	4-	19	0	0	0	0	3	.0

Goaltending

No.	Goaltender	GPI	Mins	Avg	W	L	EN	SO	GA	SA	S%
1	Pete Peeters	6	359	4.01	2	4	1	0	24	164	.853
	Totals	6	361	4.16	2	4	1	0	25	164	.847

Retired Numbers

7	Yvon Labre	1973-1981

General Managers' History
Milt Schmidt, 1974-75 to 1975-76; Max McNab, 1976-77 to 1980-81; Roger Crozier, 1981-82; David Poile, 1982-83 to date.

Coaching History
Jim Anderson, George Sullivan, Milt Schmidt, 1974-75; Milt Schmidt and Tom McVie, 1975-76; Tom McVie, 1976-77 to 1977-78; Danny Belisle, 1978-79; Danny Belisle and Gary Green, 1979-80; Gary Green, 1980-81; Gary Green and Bryan Murray, 1981-82; Bryan Murray, 1982-83 to date.

Captains' History
Doug Mohns, 1974-75; Bill Clement, Yvon Labre, 1975-76; Yvon Labre, 1976-77, 1977-78; Guy Charron, 1978-79; Ryan Walter, 1979-80 to 1981-82; Rod Langway, 1982-83 to date.

Club Records

Team

(Figures in brackets for season records are games played; records for fewest points, wins, ties, losses, goals, goals against are for 70 or more games)

Most Points 107 1985-86 (80)
Most Wins 50 1985-86 (80)
Most Ties 18 1980-81 (80)
Most Losses *67 1974-75 (80)
Most Goals 322 1984-85 (80)
Most Goals Against *446 1974-75 (80)
Fewest Points *21 1974-75 (80)
Fewest Wins *8 1974-75 (80)
Fewest Ties 5 1974-75 (80)
                           1983-84 (80)
Fewest Losses 23 1985-86 (80)
Fewest Goals 181 1974-75 (80)
Fewest Goals Against . . .226 1983-84 (80)

Longest Winning Streak
  Over-all . . . . .10 Jan. 27-
                          Feb. 18/84
  Home . . . . .8 Mar. 3-
                          April 1/89
  Away . . . . .6 Feb. 26-
                          Apr. 1/84

Longest Undefeated Streak
  Over-all . . . . .14 Nov. 12-
                          Dec. 23/82
                          (9 wins, 5 ties)
                          Jan. 17-Feb. 18/84
                          (13 wins, 1 tie)
  Home . . . . .12 Nov. 7/82-
                          Dec. 14/82
                          (9 wins, 3 ties)
  Away . . . . .10 Nov. 24/82-
                          Jan. 8/83

Longest Losing Streak
  Over-all . . . . *17 Feb. 18-
                          Mar. 26/75
  Home . . . . *11 Feb. 18-
                          Mar. 30/75
  Away . . . . *37 Oct. 9/74-
                          Mar. 26/75

Longest Winless Streak
  Over-all . . . . .25 Nov. 29/75-
                          Jan. 21/76
                          (22 losses, 3 ties)
  Home . . . . .14 Dec. 3/75-
                          Jan. 21/76
                          (11 losses, 3 ties)

Away . . . . *37 Oct. 9/74-
                          Mar. 26/75
                          (37 losses)
Most Shutouts, Season 8 1983-84 (80)
Most Pen. Mins., Season
. . . . 1,932 1981-82 (80)
Most Goals, Game . . . . . . .11 Dec. 11/81
                        (Tor. 2 at Wash. 11)

Individual

Most Seasons . . . . .9 Mike Gartner
Most Games . . . . .756 Mike Gartner
Most Goals, Career . . . . .397 Mike Gartner
Most Assists, Career . . . .392 Mike Gartner
Most Points, Career . . . . .789 Mike Gartner
                        (397 goals, 392 assists)
Most Pen. Mins., Career   Scott Stevens
. . . . 1,476
Most Shutouts, Career . . . . .8 Al Jensen
Longest Consecutive
  Games Streak . . . . . . .422 Bob Carpenter

Most Goals, Season . . . . . .60 Dennis Maruk
                        (1981-82)
Most Assists, Season . . . . .76 Dennis Maruk
                        (1981-82)
Most Points, Season . . . . .136 Dennis Maruk
                        (1981-82)
                        (60 goals, 76 assists)
Most Pen. Mins., Season . . .285 Scott Stevens
                        (1986-87)
Most Points, Defenseman,
  Season . . . . .81 Larry Murphy
                        (1986-87)
                        (23 goals, 58 assists)
Most Points, Center,
  Season . . . . .136 Dennis Maruk
                        (1981-82)
                        (60 goals, 76 assists)
Most Points, Right Wing,
  Season . . . . .102 Mike Gartner
                        (1984-85)
                        (50 goals, 52 assists)

Most Points, Left Wing,
  Season . . . . .87 Ryan Walter
                        (1981-82)
                        (38 goals, 49 assists)
Most Points, Rookie,
  Season . . . . .67 Bobby Carpenter
                        (1981-82)
                        (32 goals, 35 assists)
                        Chris Valentine
                        (1981-82)
                        (30 goals, 37 assists)
Most Shutouts, Season . . . . .4 Al Jensen, Pat Riggin
                        (1983-84)
                        Clint Malarchuk
                        (1987-88)
                        Pete Peeters
                        (1988-89)
Most Goals, Game . . . . .5 Bengt Gustafsson
                        (Jan. 8/84)
Most Assists, Game . . . . . . .6 Mike Ridley
                        (Jan. 7/89)
Most Points, Game . . . . . . .7 Dino Ciccarelli
                        (Mar. 18/89)

* NHL Record.

All-time Record vs. Other Clubs

Regular Season

	At Home						On Road						Total					
	GP	W	L	T	GF	GA	PTS	GP	W	L	T	GF	GA	PTS	GP	W	L	T	GF	GA	PTS
Boston	28	7	14	7	83	109	21	28	7	18	3	71	117	17	56	14	32	10	154	226	38
Buffalo	28	4	19	5	77	125	13	28	4	21	3	73	127	11	56	8	40	8	150	252	24
**Calgary	26	11	12	3	98	101	25	26	5	19	2	59	112	12	52	16	31	5	157	213	37
Chicago	26	16	7	3	106	84	35	26	6	15	5	83	114	17	52	22	22	8	189	198	52
Detroit	32	16	12	4	120	96	36	32	8	14	10	93	122	26	64	24	26	14	213	218	62
Edmonton	16	9	6	1	71	61	19	16	4	8	4	57	71	12	32	13	14	5	128	132	31
Hartford	16	11	4	1	61	43	23	16	9	5	2	70	53	20	32	20	9	3	131	96	43
Los Angeles	32	13	14	5	135	117	31	32	10	19	3	95	134	23	64	23	33	8	230	251	54
Minnesota	26	11	9	6	85	80	28	26	6	12	8	75	101	20	52	17	21	14	160	181	48
Montreal	32	11	15	6	80	115	28	32	3	24	5	63	160	11	64	14	39	11	143	275	39
*New Jersey	40	30	7	3	186	114	63	40	20	14	6	132	129	46	80	50	21	9	318	243	109
NY Islanders	42	15	20	7	128	148	37	43	10	32	1	123	195	21	85	25	52	8	251	343	58
NY Rangers	42	20	14	8	171	142	48	43	16	22	5	160	195	37	85	36	36	13	331	337	85
Philadelphia	43	15	21	7	148	164	37	42	11	28	3	112	176	25	85	26	49	10	260	340	62
Pittsburgh	49	27	19	3	217	178	57	48	20	22	6	165	201	46	97	47	41	9	382	379	103
Quebec	16	6	8	2	60	62	14	16	6	6	4	61	57	16	32	12	14	6	121	119	30
St. Louis	26	14	10	2	99	83	30	26	8	11	7	82	111	23	52	22	21	9	181	194	53
Toronto	28	16	10	2	111	81	34	28	9	15	4	97	127	22	56	25	25	6	208	208	56
Vancouver	26	15	9	2	87	80	32	26	11	12	3	87	91	25	52	26	21	5	174	171	57
Winnipeg	16	12	3	1	81	49	25	16	5	6	5	62	55	15	32	17	9	6	143	104	40
Defunct Clubs	10	2	8	0	28	42	4	10	4	5	1	30	39	9	20	6	13	1	58	81	13
Totals	**600**	**281**	**241**	**78**	**2232**	**2074**	**640**	**600**	**182**	**328**	**90**	**1850**	**2487**	**454**	**1200**	**463**	**569**	**168**	**4082**	**4561**	**1094**

* Totals include those of Kansas City (1974-75, 1975-76) and Colorado (1976-77 through 1981-82)
** Totals include those of Atlanta (1974-75 through 1979-80) and (1976-77 through 1981-82)

Playoffs

	Series	W	L	GP	W	L	T	GF	GA	Last Mtg.	Round	Result
New Jersey	1	0	1	7	3	4	0	23	25	1988	DF	L 3-4
NY Islanders	5	1	4	24	10	14	0	65	76	1987	DSF	L 3-4
NY Rangers	1	0	1	6	2	4	0	25	20	1986	DF	L 2-4
Philadelphia	3	2	1	16	9	7	0	65	55	1989	DSF	L 2-4
Totals	**10**	**3**	**7**	**53**	**24**	**29**	**0**	**178**	**176**			

Playoff Results 1989-85

Year	Round	Opponent	Result	GF	GA
1989	DSF	Philadelphia	L 2-4	19	25
1988	DF	New Jersey	L 3-4	25	23
	DSF	Philadelphia	W 4-3	31	25
1987	DSF	NY Islanders	L 3-4	18	19
1986	DF	NY Rangers	L 2-4	25	20
	DSF	NY Islanders	W 3-0	11	4
1985	DSF	NY Islanders	L 2-3	12	14

Abbreviations: Round: F – Final; **CF** – conference final; **DF** – division final; **DSF** – division semi-final; **SF** – semi-final;
QF – quarter-final. **P** – preliminary round. **GA** – goals against; **GF** – goals for.

1988-89 Results

		Home				Away	
Oct.	7	Pittsburgh	4-6	Oct.	11	Pittsburgh	7-8
	8	Buffalo	6-2		19	NY Rangers	1-5
	14	Toronto	1-3		23	Winnipeg*	2-3
	15	New Jersey	8-5		25	Vancouver	4-3
	21	NY Rangers	1-4		28	Calgary	2-2
Nov.	4	NY Islanders	4-2		29	Edmonton	3-4
	10	Quebec	4-1	Nov.	1	Detroit	3-3
	12	New Jersey	3-6		5	NY Islanders	3-4
	15	Minnesota	4-2		19	New Jersey	3-2
	18	Hartford	3-2		22	NY Islanders	4-2
	23	NY Islanders	7-6		27	Detroit	4-3
	25	Pittsburgh	3-5		30	Pittsburgh	4-6
	29	St Louis	4-3	Dec.	7	New Jersey	1-5
Dec.	3	Boston	1-1		10	Montreal	0-0
	6	Philadelphia	4-3		11	Buffalo	6-4
	17	Winnipeg	6-3		13	Quebec	4-1
	23	NY Rangers	2-2		15	Philadelphia	1-4
	27	Philadelphia	4-3		19	NY Rangers	1-3
	30	Buffalo	5-3		21	Chicago	4-3
Jan.	2	Pittsburgh*	8-0		31	NY Islanders	4-6
	6	Toronto	3-0	Jan.	4	NY Rangers	3-3
	7	Chicago	6-3		10	Quebec	4-4
	13	Edmonton	5-3		11	Toronto	3-2
	15	Boston*	3-4		26	Philadelphia	1-0
	20	New Jersey	5-6		28	St Louis	4-4
	22	Detroit*	3-4		30	Minnesota	4-4
	24	Los Angeles	4-4	Feb.	1	NY Rangers	4-3
Feb.	3	Hartford	1-0		14	St Louis	5-3
	5	Philadelphia*	1-3		15	Chicago	4-7
	10	Los Angeles	6-7		17	Edmonton	8-2
	11	Calgary	1-2		19	Vancouver	2-3
	28	Minnesota	3-4		20	Calgary	2-6
Mar.	3	Pittsburgh	4-2		22	Los Angeles	7-2
	5	Vancouver*	3-0	Mar.	8	Montreal	2-3
	11	NY Rangers	4-2		9	Boston	7-2
	14	Winnipeg	6-3		18	Hartford	8-2
	17	Montreal	4-1		22	Pittsburgh	5-4
	24	Philadelphia	6-1		28	NY Islanders	4-5
	26	NY Islanders*	3-2		30	Philadelphia	4-5
Apr.	1	New Jersey	6-4	Apr.	2	New Jersey	4-7

* Denotes afternoon game.

General Manager

POILE, DAVID
Vice-President and General Manager, Washington Capitals.
Born in Toronto, Ont., February 14, 1949.

David Poile was named to the position of General Manager of the Capitals on August 30, 1982 and quickly built the franchise into a solid Stanley Cup contender. During his inaugural campaign (1982-83), he led the Caps' to their first winning season (39-25-16) and a first-time berth in the Stanley Cup playoffs. He received *The Sporting News* "Executive of the Year" award in 1982-83 for his efforts and duplicated the feat in 1983-84 following the Capitals' 48-27-5 season. Poile, a graduate of Northeastern University with a degree in Business Administration, began his professional hockey management career in 1972 as an Administrative Assistant for the Atlanta Flames organization where he served until joining the Washington franchise. A former collegiate hockey star at Northeastern, he won MVP and scoring honors during his senior year.

Coach

MURRAY, BRYAN CLARENCE
Coach, Washington Capitals. Born in Shawville, Que., December 5, 1942.

In less than eight full seasons behind the Washington Capitals bench, Bryan Murray has achieved more success than any other coach in the team's 15-year history. In 1988-89, Murray reached two milestones — he coached his 600th NHL game (Feb. 1) and won his 300th regular-season game (Dec. 17) and led the Capitals to their first Patrick Division regular-season title with a record of 41-29-10 (92 points).

A graduate of McGill University, he took over the last-place Regina Pats and carried the team to the WHL championship in 1979-80. His one-year success in Regina translated into a professional coaching job in 1980-81 with the Capitals' AHL farm team, the Hershey Bears, whom he guided to their best season in over 40 years. That first-year effort netted him the Hockey News Minor League Coach-of-the-Year honors. Although he began the 1981-82 campaign in Hershey, Murray was promoted to Washington on November 11, 1981.

Coaching Record

Team		Games	W	L	T	%	Games	W	L	%
				Regular Season				**Playoffs**		
1979-80	Regina (WHL)	72	47	24	1	.660	22	16	6	.727
1980-81	Hershey (AHL)	80	47	24	9	.644	10	6	4	.600
1981-82	Washington (NHL)	16	25	28	13	.477	....	....	....	....
1982-83	Washington (NHL)	10	39	25	16	.588	4	1	3	.250
1983-84	Washington (NHL)	80	48	27	5	.631	8	4	4	.500
1984-85	Washington (NHL)	80	46	25	9	.631	5	2	3	.400
1985-86	Washington (NHL)	80	50	23	7	.669	9	5	4	.556
1986-87	Washington (NHL)	80	38	32	10	.538	7	3	4	.429
1987-88	Washington (NHL)	80	38	33	9	.531	14	7	7	.500
1988-89	Washington (NHL)	80	41	29	10	.575	6	2	4	.333
	NHL Totals	626	325	222	79	.582	53	24	29	.453

Entry Draft Selections 1989-75

1989
Pick
19 Olaf Kolzig
35 Byron Dafoe
59 Jim Mathieson
61 Jason Woolley
82 Trent Klatt
145 Dave Lorentz
166 Dean Holoien
187 Victor Gervais
208 Jiri Vykoukal
229 Andri Sidorov
250 Ken House

1988
Pick
15 Reginald Savage
36 Tim Taylor
41 Wade Bartley
57 Duane Derksen
78 Rob Krauss
120 Dimitri Hristich
141 Keith Jones
144 Brad Schlegal
162 Todd Hilditch
183 Petr Pavlas
192 Mark Sorensen
204 Claudio Scremin
225 Chris Venkus
246 Ron Pascucci

1987
Pick
36 Jeff Ballantyne
57 Steve Maltais
78 Tyler Larter
99 Pat Beauchesne
120 Rich Defreitas
141 Devon Oleniuk
162 Thomas Sjogren
204 Chris Clarke
225 Milos Vanik
240 Dan Brettschneider
246 Ryan Kummu

1986
Pick
19 Jeff Greenlaw
40 Steve Seftel
60 Shawn Simpson
61 Jimmy Hrivnak
82 Erin Ginnell
103 John Purves
124 Stefan Nilsson
145 Peter Choma
166 Lee Davidson
187 Tero Toivola
208 Bobby Bobcock
229 John Schratz
250 Scott McCrory

1985
Pick
19 Yvon Corriveau
40 John Druce
61 Robert Murray
82 Bill Houlder
83 Larry Shaw
103 Claude Dumas
124 Doug Stromback
145 Jamie Nadjiwan
166 Mark Haarmann
187 Steve Hollett
208 Dallas Eakins
229 Steve Hrynewich
250 Frank DiMuzio

1984
Pick
17 Kevin Hatcher
34 Steve Leach
59 Michal Pivonka
80 Kris King
122 Vito Cramarossa
143 Timo Iijima
164 Frank Joo
185 Jim Thomson
205 Paul Cavallini
225 Mikhail Tatarinov
246 Per Schedrin

1983
Pick
75 Tim Bergland
95 Martin Bouliane
135 Dwaine Hutton
155 Marty Abrams
175 David Cowan
195 Yves Beaudoin
215 Alain Raymond
216 Anders Huss

1982
Pick
5 Scott Stevens
58 Milan Novy
89 Dean Evason
110 Ed Kastelic
152 Wally Schreiber
173 Jamie Reeves
194 Juha Nurmi
215 Wayne Prestage
236 John Holden
247 Marco Kallas

1981
Pick
3 Bob Carpenter
45 Eric Calder
68 Tony Kellin
89 Mike Siltala
91 Peter Sidorkiewicz
110 Jim McGeough
131 Risto Jalo
152 Gaetan Duchesne
173 George White
194 Chris Valentine

1980
Pick
5 Darren Veitch
47 Dan Miele
55 Torrie Robertson
89 Timo Blomqvist
110 Todd Bidner
131 Frank Perkins
152 Bruce Raboin
173 Peter Andersson
194 Tony Camazzola

1979
Pick
4 Mike Gartner
24 Errol Rausse
67 Harvie Pocza
88 Tim Tookey
109 Greg Theberge

1978
Pick
2 Ryan Walter
18 Tim Coulis
20 Paul Mulvey
23 Paul MacKinnon
38 Glen Currie
45 Jay Johnston
55 Bengt Gustafsson
71 Lou Franceschetti
88 Vince Magnan
105 Mats Hallin
122 Rick Sirois
139 Denis Pomerleau
156 Barry Heard
172 Mark Toffolo
187 Paul Hogan
189 Steve Barger
202 Rod Pacholsuk
213 Wes Jarvis
215 Ray Irwin

1977
Pick
3 Robert Picard
21 Mark Lofthouse
39 Eddy Godin
57 Nelson Burton
75 Denis Turcotte
93 Perry Schnarr
111 Rollie Bouton
127 Brent Tremblay
143 Don Micheletti
165 Archie Henderson

1976
Pick
1 Rick Green
15 Greg Carroll
37 Tom Rowe
55 Al Glendinning
73 Doug Patey
91 Jim Bedard
109 Dale Rideout
119 Allan Dumba

1975
Pick
18 Alex Forsyth
19 Peter Scammurra
55 Blair MacKasey
73 Craig Crawford
91 Roger Swanson
109 Clark Jantzie
127 Mike Fryia
144 Jim Ofrim
161 Mal Zinger

Club Directory

Capital Centre
Landover, Maryland 20785
Phone 301/386-7000
TWX 710/600-7017
GM FAX 301/386-7082
ENVOY ID
   Front Office: CAPS. GM
   Public
   Relations: CAPS. PR
Capacity: 18,130

Board of Directors
Abe Pollin — Chairman
David P. Bindeman
Stewart L. Bindeman
James E. Cafritz
A. James Clark
Albert Cohen
J. Martin Irving
James T. Lewis
R. Robert Linowes
Arthur K. Mason
Dr. Jack Meshel
David M. Osnos
Richard M. Patrick

Management
Chairman & Governor . . . . Abe Pollin
President & Alternate Governor . . . . Richard M. Patrick
Vice-President and General Manager . . . . . David Poile
Legal Counsel and Alternate Governors . . . . . . David M. Osnos, Peter F. O'Malley
Vice-President and Comptroller . . . . Edmund Stelzer

Coaching Staff
Head Coach . . . . Bryan Murray
Assistant Coaches . . . . Rob Laird, Doug MacLean
Head Coach, Baltimore (AHL) . . . . Terry Murray

Scouting Staff
Director of Player Personnel and Recruitment . . . Jack Button
Chief U.S. Scout . . . . Jack Barzee
Chief Eastern Scout . . . . Jack Ferguson
Chief Western Scout . . . . Barry Trotz
Scouting Coordinator . . . . Hugh Rogers
Scouts . . . . Gilles Cote, Fred Devereaux, Bruce Hamilton, Eje Johansson, Richard Rothermel, Bob Schmidt, John Stanton, Dan Sylvester, Darryl Young

Training Staff
Head Trainer . . . . Stan Wong
Assistant Trainer/Head Equipment Mgr. . . . . . . Doug Shearer
Assistant Equipment Mgr. . . . . Craig Leydig
Strength and Conditioning Coach . . . . Frank Costello
Team Nutritionist . . . . Dr. Pat Mann

Front Office Staff
Vice-President of Marketing . . . . Lew Strudler
Director of Public Relations . . . . Lou Corletto
Assistant Director of Marketing . . . . Debi Angus
Director of Community Relations . . . . Yvon Labre
Director of Promotions . . . . Charles Copeland
Director of Season Subscriptions . . . . Joanne Kowalski
Assistant Comptroller . . . . Aggie Ballard
Public Relations Assistant . . . . David Ferry
Administrative Assistant to the
General Manager . . . . Pat Young
Administrative Assistant to the
V.P. of Marketing . . . . Karen Merewitz
Administrative Assistant to the PR Director . . . . Julie Hensley
Administrative Assistant to the Comptroller . . . . Sharon Baxter
Administrative Assistant to the Sales Dept. . . . . Janice Toepper
Partial Plans Administrator . . . . Stephanie Rhine
Corporate Sales Manager . . . . Kerry Gregg
Regional Sales Managers . . . . Jerry Murphy, Ron Potter, Paul Van
Telemarketing Supervisor . . . . John Oakes
Accounting Assistants . . . . David Berman, Crystal Coffren, Melanie Sakacs
Secretary to the Marketing Dept. . . . . Renee D'Abate
Receptionist . . . . Nancy Woodall
Assistant to the Hockey Dept. . . . . Todd Button

Operations Staff
Director of Telescreen . . . . Brad Froman
Director of Television . . . . Ernie Fingers
Director of Production . . . . Bill Harpole
Manager of Production . . . . Mike Long

Medical Team
Team Physicians . . . . Dr. Stephen S. Haas, Dr. Carl C. MacCartee, Jr. Dr. Frank S. Melograna
Team Dentist . . . . Dr. Howard Salob
Team Psychologist . . . . Dr. Jim McGee
Organist . . . . Chris Mitchell
Anthem Singer . . . . Glenn Cunningham
Public Address Announcer . . . . Marv Brooks
Dimensions of Rink . . . . 200 feet by 85 feet
Team Nickname . . . . Capitals
Club Colors . . . . Red, White and Blue
Training Camp . . . . Alexandria, Virginia
Radio Station . . . . WMAL (630 AM), WCAO (600 AM)
TV Stations . . . . WDCA-TV (Channel 20), Home Team Sports (Cable)

Winnipeg Jets

1988-89 Results: 26W-42L-12T 64 PTS. Fifth, Smythe Division

Year-by-Year Record

		Home			Road			Overall						
Season	GP	W	L	T	W	L	T	W	L	T	GF	GA	Pts.	Finished	Playoff Result
1988-89	80	17	18	5	9	24	7	26	42	12	300	355	64	5th, Smythe Div.	Out of Playoffs
1987-88	80	20	14	6	13	22	5	33	36	11	292	310	77	3rd, Smythe Div.	Lost Div. Semi-Final
1986-87	80	25	12	3	15	20	5	40	32	8	279	271	88	3rd, Smythe Div.	Lost Div. Final
1985-86	80	18	19	3	8	28	4	26	47	7	295	372	59	3rd, Smythe Div.	Lost Div. Semi-Final
1984-85	80	21	13	6	22	14	4	43	27	10	358	332	96	2nd, Smythe Div.	Lost Div. Final
1983-84	80	17	15	8	14	23	3	31	38	11	340	374	73	4th, Smythe Div.	Lost Div. Semi-Final
1982-83	80	22	16	2	11	23	6	33	39	8	311	333	74	4th, Smythe Div.	Lost Div. Semi-Final
1981-82	80	18	13	9	15	20	5	33	33	14	319	332	80	2nd, Norris Div.	Lost Div. Semi-Final
1980-81	80	7	25	8	2	32	6	9	57	14	246	400	32	6th, Smythe Div.	Out of Playoffs
1979-80	80	13	19	8	7	30	3	20	49	11	214	314	51	5th, Smythe Div.	Out of Playoffs

Schedule

Home			Away		
Oct.	Fri.	6 NY Rangers	**Oct.**	Tues.	10 Pittsburgh
	Sun.	8 Philadelphia		Thur.	12 Detroit
	Fri.	20 Chicago		Sat.	14 Toronto
	Sun.	22 Edmonton		Wed.	18 Edmonton
	Wed.	25 Washington	**Nov.**	Wed.	1 Calgary
	Fri.	27 Los Angeles		Fri.	3 Vancouver
	Sun.	29 Los Angeles		Sun.	5 Chicago
Nov.	Wed.	8 Vancouver		Tues.	14 Quebec
	Fri.	10 Hartford		Wed.	15 Montreal
	Sun.	12 Calgary		Sat.	18 Philadelphia*
	Thur.	23 St Louis		Mon.	20 NY Rangers
	Sat.	25 New Jersey		Tues.	21 NY Islanders
	Wed.	29 NY Rangers	**Dec.**	Wed.	6 Calgary
Dec.	Fri.	1 Detroit		Fri.	15 Vancouver
	Sat.	2 NY Islanders		Tues.	19 Los Angeles
	Fri.	8 Montreal		Thur.	21 Edmonton
	Sun.	10 Calgary*		Fri.	29 Calgary
	Wed.	13 Vancouver	**Jan.**	Wed.	3 Hartford
	Tues.	26 Minnesota		Thur.	4 Boston
	Sun.	31 Edmonton*		Sat.	6 Pittsburgh
Jan.	Wed.	10 Washington		Mon.	8 New Jersey
	Fri.	12 Detroit		Wed.	17 Edmonton
	Sun.	14 St Louis		Tues.	23 Washington
	Tues.	16 Quebec		Thur.	25 Philadelphia
	Fri.	19 NY Islanders		Sat.	27 St Louis
	Wed.	31 Toronto		Mon.	29 Minnesota
Feb.	Fri.	2 Vancouver	**Feb.**	Tues.	6 Vancouver
	Sun.	4 Chicago		Thur.	8 Los Angeles
	Wed.	14 Boston		Sun.	11 Edmonton
	Fri.	16 Pittsburgh		Thur.	22 New Jersey
	Sun.	18 Calgary*		Sat.	24 Hartford
	Tues.	20 Buffalo		Sun.	25 Buffalo
Mar.	Fri.	2 Los Angeles		Tues.	27 Minnesota
	Sun.	4 Los Angeles*	**Mar.**	Mon.	12 Calgary
	Wed.	7 Quebec		Thur.	15 Boston
	Fri.	9 Edmonton		Sat.	17 Toronto
	Sun.	11 Calgary*		Sun.	18 Buffalo
	Wed.	21 Montreal		Sun.	25 Vancouver
	Fri.	23 Vancouver		Tues.	27 Los Angeles
Apr.	Sun.	1 Edmonton*		Thur.	29 Los Angeles

* Denotes afternoon game.

Home Starting Times:

Weeknights . . . . 7:35 p.m.
Saturdays & Sundays . . . . 7:05 p.m.
Matinees . . . . 2:35 p.m.
Except Sun. Dec 31. . . . . 4:05 p.m.

Franchise date: June 22, 1979

**11th
NHL
Season**

Randy Carlyle continues to anchor the Jets' defense.

1989-90 Player Personnel

FORWARDS	HT	WT	S	Place of Birth	Date	1988-89 Club
ASHTON, Brent	6-1	210	L	Saskatoon, Sask.	5/18/60	Winnipeg
BARNES, Stu	5-10	175	R	Edmonton, Alta.	12/25/70	Tri-Cities
BORREL, John	6-2	190	R	Shakopee, MN	3/23/67	Lowell Univ.
BORSATO Luciano	5-10	165	R	Richmond Hill, Ont.	1/7/66	Clarkson Univ.
BOSCHMAN, Laurie	6-0	185	L	Major, Sask.	6/4/60	Winnipeg
CIRONE, Jason	5-9	184	L	Toronto, Ont.	2/21/71	Cornwall Royals
COLE, Danton	5-11	189	C	Lansing, MI	1/10/67	Michigan State
CUNNEYWORTH, Randy	6-0	180	L	Etobicoke, Ont.	5/10/61	Pittsburgh
DiPIETRO, Paul	5-9	190	R	Sault Ste. Marie, Ont.	9/8/70	Sudbury
DONNELLY, Gord	6-1	202	R	Montreal, Que.	4/5/62	Quebec-Winnipeg
DRAPER, Kris	5-11	188	L	Toronto, Ont.	5/24/71	Cdn. Olympic
DUNCAN, Iain	6-1	180	L	Weston, Ont.	8/4/63	Winnipeg
ELYNUIK, Pat	6-0	185	R	Foam Lake, Sask.	10/30/67	Winnipeg
ENDEAN, Craig	5-11	175	L	Kamloops, B.C.	4/13/68	Moncton-Ft. Wayne
FENTON, Paul	5-11	180	L	Springfield, MA	12/22/64	Los Angeles-Winnipeg
HANNIGAN, Jason	6-0	188	R	Stoney Creek, Ont.	1/13/69	Cornwall
HAWERCHUK, Dale	5-11	185	L	Toronto, Ont.	3/4/63	Winnipeg
HEISE, Kevin	6-1	169	L	Regina, Sask.	9/9/68	Lethbridge (1987-88)
HUGHES, Brent	5-11	190	L	New Westminister, B.C.	4/5/66	Moncton-Winnipeg
HUNT, Brian	6-1	184	L	Toronto, Ont.	2/12/69	Oshawa
JONES, Brad	6-0	180	L	Sterling Heights, MI	6/26/65	Winnipeg-Moncton
JONES, Ron	6-3	197	R	Detroit, MI	2/7/69	London
JOSEPH, Tony	6-4	203	R	Cornwall, Ont.	3/1/69	Oshawa
KULAK, Stu	5-10	180	R	Edmonton, Alta.	3/10/63	Moncton
KUMPEL, Mark	6-0	190	R	Wakefield, MA	3/7/61	Moncton
LAROSE, Guy	5-9	175	L	Hull, Que.	7/31/67	Moncton
McLLWAIN, Dave	6-0	190	L	Seafort, Ont.	1/9/67	Muskegon-Pittsburgh
McREYNOLDS, Brian	6-1	180	L	Penetanguishene, Ont.	1/5/65	Cdn. Olympic
MEADMORE, Neil	6-4	190	R	Winnipeg, Man.	10/23/59	Moncton
PASLAWSKI, Greg	5-11	190	R	Kindersley, Sask.	8/25/61	St. Louis
PELTOLA, Pekka	6-2	196	R	Helsinki, Finland	6/24/65	HPK Finland
SCHNEIDER, Scott	6-1	180	R	Rochester, MN	5/18/65	Moncton
SELANNE, Teemu	6-0	176	R	Helsinki, Finland	7/3/70	Jokerit (Finland)
SMAIL, Doug	5-9	175	L	Moose Jaw, Sask.	9/2/57	Winnipeg
STEEN, Thomas	5-10	195	L	Tockmark, Sweden	6/8/60	Winnipeg
WARUS, Mike	6-1	190	R	Sudbury, Ont.	1/16/64	Moncton
WILSON, Ron	5-9	175	L	Toronto, Ont.	5/13/56	Moncton

DEFENSEMEN	HT	WT	S	Place of Birth	Date	1988-89 Club
BERRY, Brad	6-2	190	L	Bashaw, Alta.	4/1/65	Winnipeg
BLOMSTEN, Arto	6-1	190	L	Vasa, Finland	3/16/65	Djurgardens Swe.
CARLYLE, Randy	5-10	200	L	Sudbury, Ont.	4/19/56	Winnipeg
CRONIN, Shawn	6-2	210	R	Flushing, MI	8/20/63	Baltimore
ELLETT, Dave	6-1	200	L	Cleveland, OH	3/30/64	Winnipeg
FLICHEL, Todd	6-3	195	R	Osgoode, Ont.	9/14/64	Moncton
GALLOWAY, Kyle	5-11	170	L	Winnipeg, Man.	11/10/69	U. of Manitoba
GOSSELIN, Guy	5-10	190	R	Rochester, MN	1/6/64	Moncton
HERVEY, Matt	5-11	205	R	Whittier CA	5/16/66	Moncton
MARCHMENT, Bryan	6-11	198	L	Scarborough, Ont.	5/1/69	Belleville
NORTON, Chris	6-23	200	R	Oakville, Ont.	3/11/65	Moncton
NUMMINEN, Teppo	6-1	190	R	Tampere, Finland	7/3/68	Winnipeg
OLAUSSON, Fredrik	6-2	200	R	Vaxsjo, Sweden	10/5/66	Winnipeg
TAGLIANETTI, Peter	6-2	200	L	Framingham, MA	9/16/63	Winnipeg

GOALTENDERS	HT	WT	C	Place of Birth	Date	1988-89 Club
BEAUREGARD, Stephane	5-11	182	R	Cowansville, Que.	1/10/68	Moncton-Ft. Wayne
BERTHIAUME, Dan	5-9	150	L	Longueil, Que.	1/26/66	Winnipeg
DRAPER, Tom	5-11	180	L	Outrement, Que.	11/20/66	Moncton
ESSENSA, Bob	6-0	160	L	Toronto, Ont.	1/14/65	Ft. Wayne-Winnipeg
FURLAN, Frank	5-9	160	L	Sherwood Park, AB	3/8/68	Tri-Cities
O'NEILL, Mike	5-7	160	L	Montreal, Que.	11/3/67	Yale University
REDDICK, Eldon	5-8	170	L	Halifax, N.S.	10/6/64	Winnipeg
TABARACCI, Rich	5-10	185	L	Toronto, Ont.	1/2/69	Cornwall Royals

1988-89 Scoring

Regular Season
* rookie

Pos	#	Player	Team	GP	G	A	Pts	+/-	PIM	PP	SH	GW	GT	S	%
F	10	Dale Hawerchuk	WPG	75	41	55	96	30-	28	14	3	4	1	239	17.2
F	25	Thomas Steen	WPG	80	27	61	88	14	80	9	1	2	1	173	15.6
F	20	Andrew McBain	WPG	80	37	40	77	35-	71	20	1	3	2	180	20.6
F	7	Brent Ashton	WPG	75	31	37	68	5-	36	7	1	1	0	180	17.2
D	4	Fredrik Olausson	WPG	75	15	47	62	6	32	4	0	1	0	178	8.4
D	2	Dave Ellett	WPG	75	22	34	56	18-	62	9	2	5	0	209	10.5
F	15	*Pat Elynuik	WPG	56	26	25	51	5	29	5	0	6	0	100	26.0
F	19	Iain Duncan	WPG	57	14	30	44	17-	74	1	0	0	0	91	15.4
D	8	Randy Carlyle	WPG	78	6	38	44	19-	78	2	0	2	0	124	4.8
F	16	Laurie Boschman	WPG	70	10	26	36	17-	163	3	0	1	0	113	8.8
F	12	Doug Smail	WPG	47	14	15	29	12	52	0	2	0	0	68	20.6
F	11	Paul Fenton	L.A.	21	2	3	5	1-	6	0	0	0	0	26	7.7
			WPG	59	14	9	23	15-	33	1	0	0	0	109	12.8
			TOTAL	80	16	12	28	16-	39	1	0	0	0	135	11.9
F	22	Gord Donnelly	QUE	16	4	0	4	8-	46	1	0	0	0	14	28.6
			WPG	57	6	10	16	12-	228	0	0	0	0	53	11.3
			TOTAL	73	10	10	20	20-	274	1	0	0	0	67	14.9
D	32	Peter Taglianetti	WPG	66	1	14	15	23-	226	1	0	0	0	72	1.4
D	27	*Teppo Numminen	WPG	69	1	14	15	11-	36	0	1	0	1	85	1.2
D	6	Jim Kyte	WPG	74	3	9	12	25-	190	0	0	0	0	56	5.4
F	38	Brad Jones	WPG	22	6	5	11	0	6	0	1	0	1	25	24.0
F	23	Hannu Jarvenpaa	WPG	53	4	7	11	14-	41	1	0	0	0	27	14.8
D	29	Brad Berry	WPG	38	0	9	9	8-	45	0	0	0	0	21	.0
F	39	Randy Gilhen	WPG	64	5	3	8	24-	38	0	1	1	0	76	6.6
F	46	*Brent Hughes	WPG	28	3	2	5	7-	82	0	1	0	0	37	8.1
F	13	Alfie Turcotte	WPG	14	1	3	4	6-	2	0	0	0	0	10	10.0
F	17	Stu Kulak	WPG	18	2	0	2	6-	24	1	0	0	0	18	11.1
F	18	*Markku Kyllonen	WPG	9	0	2	2	3-	2	0	0	0	0	7	.0
F	47	*Anthony Joseph	WPG	2	1	0	1	1	0	0	0	0	0	4	25.0
F	36	Moe Lemay	BOS	12	0	0	0	5-	23	0	0	0	0	6	.0
			WPG	10	1	0	1	3-	14	0	0	0	0	15	6.7
			TOTAL	22	1	0	1	8-	37	0	0	0	0	21	4.8
F	26	*Guy Larose	WPG	3	0	1	1	1-	6	0	0	0	0	2	.0
G	33	Eldon Reddick	WPG	41	0	1	1	1	6	0	0	0	0	0	.0
F	15	*Darren Boyko	WPG	1	0	0	0	0	0	0	0	0	0	1	.0
D	47	*Todd Flichel	WPG	1	0	0	0	1-	0	0	0	0	0	0	.0
G	37	*Tom Draper	WPG	2	0	0	0	0	0	0	0	0	0	0	.0
D	42	*Matt Hervey	WPG	2	0	0	0	2	4	0	0	0	0	1	.0
D	3	*Bryan Marchment	WPG	2	0	0	0	2	2	0	0	0	0	1	.0
D	41	Paul Boutilier	WPG	3	0	0	0	2-	4	0	0	0	0	4	.0
D	40	*Steve Fletcher	WPG	3	0	0	0	1-	5	0	0	0	0	1	.0
G	30	Daniel Berthiaume	WPG	9	0	0	0	0	0	0	0	0	0	0	.0

Goaltending

No.	Goaltender	GPI	Mins	Avg	W	L	T	EN	SO	GA	SA	S%
35	*Bob Essensa	20	1102	3.70	6	8	3	2	1	68	574	.881
33	Eldon Reddick	41	2109	4.10	11	17	7	3	0	144	1132	.872
31	Alain Chevrier	22	1092	4.29	8	8	2	2	1	78	554	.859
30	Daniel Berthiaume	9	443	5.96	0	8	0	2	0	44	255	.826
37	*Tom Draper	2	120	6.00	1	1	0	0	0	12	66	.818
	Totals	80	4880	4.36	26	42	12	9	2	355	2581	.862

Retired Numbers
9 Bobby Hull 1972-1980

General Managers' History
John Ferguson, 1979-80 to 1987-88; John Ferguson and Mike Smith, 1988-89; Mike Smith, 1989-90 to date.

Coaching History
Tom McVie, 1979-80; Tom McVie and Bill Sutherland, 1980-81; Tom Watt, 1981-82 to 1982-83; Tom Watt, John Ferguson and Barry Long, 1983-84; Barry Long, and John Ferguson, 1985-86. Dan Maloney, 1986-87 to 1987-88, Dan Maloney and Rick Bowness 1988-89; Bob Murdoch, 1989-90.

Captains' History
Lars-Erik Sjoberg, 1979-80; Morris Lukowich, 1980-81; Dave Christian, 1981-82; Dave Christian, Lucien DeBlois, 1982-83; Dale Hawerchuk, 1984-85 to date.

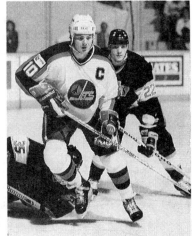

Dale Hawerchuk reached the 40-goal plateau for the seventh time in his eight-year NHL career in 1988-89.

Club Records

Team

(Figures in brackets for season records are games played; records for fewest points, wins, ties, losses, goals, goals against are for 70 or more games)

Most Points	.96	1984-85 (80)
Most Wins	.43	1984-85 (80)
Most Ties	.14	1980-81 (80)
		1981-82 (80)
Most Losses	.57	1980-81 (80)
Most Goals	.358	1984-85 (80)
Most Goals Against	.400	1980-81 (80)
Fewest Points	.32	1980-81 (80)
Fewest Wins	.9	1980-81 (80)
Fewest Ties	.8	1982-83 (80)
Fewest Losses	.27	1984-85 (80)
Fewest Goals	.214	1979-80 (80)
Fewest Goals Against	.271	1986-87 (80)

Longest Winning Streak

Over-all	.9	Mar. 8-27/85
Home	.6	Feb. 28-Mar. 24/82
		Dec. 2-22/84
Away	.8	Feb. 25-Apr. 6/85

Longest Undefeated Streak

Over-all	.13	Mar. 8-Apr. 7/85 (10 wins, 3 ties)
Home	.11	Dec. 23/83 Feb. 5/84 (6 wins, 5 ties)
Away	.9	Feb. 25-Apr. 7/85 (8 wins, 1 tie)

Longest Losing Streak

Over-all	.10	Nov. 30-Dec. 20/80
Home	.4	Four times
Away	.9	Dec. 26/79-Jan. 20/80

Longest Winless Streak

Over-all	*30	Oct. 19-Dec. 20/80 (23 losses, 7 ties)
Home	.14	Oct. 19-Dec. 14/80 (9 losses, 5 ties)
Away	.18	Oct. 10-Dec. 20/80 (16 losses, 2 ties)
Most Shutouts, Season	.3	1981-82 (80)

Most Pen. Mins., Season	2,278	1987-88 (80)
Most Goals, Game	.12	Feb. 25/85 (Wpg. 12 at NYR. 5)

Individual

Most Seasons	.9	Doug Smail
Most Games	.634	Dale Hawerchuk
Most Goals, Career	.353	Dale Hawerchuk
Most Assists, Career	.495	Dale Hawerchuk
Most Points, Career	.848	Dale Hawerchuk
Most Pen. Mins., Career	1,235	Laurie Boschman
Most Shutouts, Career	.3	Markus Mattson
Longest Consecutive Games Streak	.475	Dale Hawerchuk (Dec. 19/82-Dec. 10/89)
Most Goals, Season	.53	Dale Hawerchuk (1984-85)
Most Assists, Season	.77	Dale Hawerchuk (1984-85)
Most Points, Season	.130	Dale Hawerchuk (1984-85) (53 goals, 77 assists)
Most Pen. Mins., Season	.287	Jimmy Mann (1979-80)
Most Points, Defenseman Season	.74	David Babych (1982-83) (13 goals, 61 assists)
Most Points, Center, Season	.130	Dale Hawerchuk (1984-85) (53 goals, 77 assists)
Most Points, Right Wing, Season	.101	Paul Maclean (1984-85) (41 goals, 60 assists)
Most Points, Left Wing, Season	.92	Morris Lukowich (1981-82) (43 goals, 49 assists)
Most Points, Rookie, Season	.103	Dale Hawerchuk (1981-82) (45 goals, 58 assists)

Most Shutouts, Season	.2	Markus Mattsson (1979-80) Doug Soetaert (1981-82) Dan Bouchard (1985-86) Daniel Berthiaume (1987-88)
Most Goals, Game	.5	Willy Lindstrom (Mar. 2/82)
Most Assists, Game	.5	Dale Hawerchuk (Mar. 6/84, Mar. 18/89)
Most Points, Game	.6	Willy Lindstrom (Mar. 2/82) Dale Hawerchuk (Dec. 14/83, Mar. 18/89) Thomas Steen (Oct. 24/84)

* NHL Record.

All-time Record vs. Other Clubs

Regular Season

			At Home							On Road							Total				
	GP	W	L	T	GF	GA	PTS	GP	W	L	T	GF	GA	PTS	GP	W	L	T	GF	GA	Pts
Boston	16	6	9	1	55	60	13	16	2	12	2	54	81	6	32	8	21	3	109	141	19
Buffalo	16	7	7	2	56	58	16	16	1	13	2	45	80	4	32	8	20	4	101	138	20
**Calgary	33	14	13	6	140	128	34	34	5	25	4	104	177	14	67	19	38	10	244	305	48
Chicago	18	8	7	3	77	73	19	18	4	13	1	58	99	9	36	12	20	4	135	172	28
Detroit	18	6	6	6	61	56	18	18	7	8	3	75	72	17	36	13	14	9	136	128	35
Edmonton	33	9	21	3	138	176	21	34	8	24	2	113	171	18	67	17	45	5	251	347	39
Hartford	16	9	7	0	60	57	18	16	3	9	4	52	75	10	32	12	16	4	112	132	28
Los Angeles	34	16	11	7	150	130	39	33	18	11	4	147	140	40	67	34	22	11	297	270	79
Minnesota	18	8	9	1	65	66	17	18	6	10	2	56	82	14	36	14	19	3	121	148	31
Montreal	16	5	8	3	51	68	13	16	2	14	0	39	90	4	32	7	22	3	90	158	17
*New Jersey	17	13	2	2	73	40	28	15	6	5	4	52	49	16	32	19	7	6	125	89	44
NY Islanders	16	5	10	1	47	63	11	16	3	8	5	51	66	11	32	8	18	6	98	129	22
NY Rangers	16	6	8	2	62	60	14	16	7	8	1	74	82	15	32	13	16	3	136	142	29
Philadelphia	16	7	8	1	57	61	15	16	2	14	0	43	83	4	32	9	22	1	100	144	19
Pittsburgh	16	7	9	0	63	62	14	16	6	10	0	52	64	12	32	13	19	0	115	126	26
Quebec	16	7	5	4	63	63	18	16	7	7	2	64	67	16	32	14	12	6	127	130	34
St. Louis	18	10	3	5	67	53	25	18	4	8*	6	61	81	14	36	14	11	11	128	134	39
Toronto	18	10	7	1	87	81	21	18	12	5	1	91	72	25	36	22	12	2	178	153	46
Vancouver	33	19	9	5	137	125	43	34	10	20	4	110	139	24	67	29	29	9	247	264	67
Washington	16	6	5	5	55	62	17	16	3	12	1	49	81	7	32	9	17	6	104	143	24
Totals	**400**	**178**	**164**	**58**	**1564**	**1542**	**414**	**400**	**116**	**236**	**48**	**1390**	**1851**	**280**	**800**	**294**	**400**	**106**	**2954**	**3393**	**694**

* Totals include of Colorado Rockies (1979-80, 1980-81 and 1981-82)
** Totals include those of Atlanta Flames (1979-80)

Playoffs

	Series	W	L	GP	W	L	T	GF	GA	Last Mtg.	Round	Result
Calgary	3	2	1	13	7	6	0	45	45	1987	DSF	W 4-2
Edmonton	5	0	5	19	1	18	0	53	96	1988	DSF	L 1-4
St. Louis	1	0	1	4	1	3	0	13	20	1982	DSF	L 1-3
Totals	9	2	7	36	9	27	0	111	159			

Playoff Results 1989-85

Year	Round	Opponent	Result	GF	GA
1988	DSF	Edmonton	L 1-4	17	25
1987	DF	Edmonton	L 0-4	9	17
	DSF	Calgary	W 4-2	22	15
1985	DSF	Calgary	L 0-3	8	15
1985	DF	Edmonton	L 0-4	11	22
	DSF	Calgary	W 3-1	15	13

Abbreviations: Round: F – Final; **CF** – conference final; **DF** – division final; **DSF** – division semi-final; **SF** – semi-final; **QF** – quarter-final. **GA** – goals against; **GF** – goals for.

1988-89 Results

		Home				Away	
Oct.	14	Vancouver	4-3	Oct.	6	Vancouver	2-2
	16	Edmonton	3-3		9	Edmonton	4-5
	19	Boston	2-5		12	Chicago	1-10
	23	Washington*	3-2	Nov.	1	NY Islanders	8-1
	28	Los Angeles	4-7		3	New Jersey	3-3
	30	Los Angeles	8-4		5	Montreal	2-7
Nov.	11	Chicago*	5-6		8	Quebec	8-4
	13	Montreal	7-3		16	Edmonton	2-1
	18	Toronto	3-0		25	Detroit	3-3
	20	Edmonton	7-4		26	St Louis	4-4
	29	NY Rangers	3-4	Dec.	6	Los Angeles	5-4
Dec.	2	Vancouver	6-3		8	Los Angeles	5-5
	4	Calgary	3-6		10	Edmonton	7-6
	14	Buffalo	4-3		11	Vancouver	6-8
	21	New Jersey	5-5		17	Washington	3-6
	23	Quebec	4-5		18	Philadelphia	1-5
	28	St Louis	6-2		26	Minnesota	1-5
Jan.	4	Vancouver	4-2		31	Calgary	4-4
	6	Los Angeles	4-4	Jan.	11	Calgary	3-8
	8	Los Angeles	4-4		13	Vancouver	3-1
	10	Hartford	1-2		25	Pittsburgh	4-5
	15	Minnesota	1-4		26	NY Islanders	6-8
	18	Edmonton	4-9		28	Boston*	4-3
	20	Pittsburgh	7-3		31	St Louis	3-5
	21	Philadelphia	3-7	Feb.	1	Chicago	4-7
Feb.	3	Boston	2-4		9	NY Rangers	3-3
	5	Detroit*	2-6		11	Hartford	3-7
	15	Calgary	1-6		13	Detroit	2-2
	17	New Jersey	3-2		21	Quebec	3-4
	19	Hartford	7-6		22	Montreal	3-6
	26	Calgary*	1-0		24	Buffalo	4-5
Mar.	1	Philadelphia	4-4	Mar.	7	Calgary	5-9
	3	Edmonton	4-7		8	Vancouver	0-3
	5	NY Islanders*	3-4		14	Washington	3-6
	10	Pittsburgh	1-5		15	NY Rangers	6-3
	12	Toronto	9-7		18	Toronto	10-2
	20	Buffalo	1-4		23	Edmonton	4-5
	24	Calgary	3-4		28	Los Angeles	3-3
	26	Vancouver*	3-7		29	Los Angeles	1-2
Apr.	2	Minnesota*	3-2		31	Calgary	1-4

* Denotes afternoon game.

Entry Draft
Selections 1988-79

1989
Pick
4	Stu Barnes
25	Dan Ratushny
46	Jason Cirone
62	Kris Draper
64	Mark Brownschidle
69	Allain Roy
109	Dan Bylsma
130	Pekka Peltola
131	Doug Evans
151	Jim Solly
172	Stephane Gauvin
193	Joe Larson
214	Bradley Podiak
235	Gennenya Davydov
240	Sergei Kharin

1988
Pick
10	Teemu Selanne
31	Russell Romaniuk
52	Stephane Beauregard
73	Brian Hunt
94	Anthony Joseph
101	Benoit Lebeau
115	Ronald Jones
127	Markus Akerblom
136	Jukka Marttila
157	Mark Smith
178	Mike Helber
199	Pavei Kostichkin
220	Kevin Heise
241	Kyle Galloway

1987
Pick
16	Bryan Marchment
37	Patrik Eriksson
79	Don McLennan
96	Ken Gernander
100	Darrin Amundson
121	Joe Harwell
142	Todd Hartje
163	Markku Kyllonen
184	Jim Fernholz
226	Roger Rougelot
247	Hans Goran Elo

1986
Pick
8	Pat Elynuik
29	Teppo Numminen
50	Esa Palosaari
71	Hannu Jarvenpaa
92	Craig Endean
113	Robertson Bateman
155	Frank Furlan
176	Mark Green
197	John Blue
218	Matt Cote
239	Arto Blomsten

1985
Pick
18	Ryan Stewart
39	Roger Ohman
60	Dan Berthiaume
81	Fredrik Olausson
102	John Borrell
123	Danton Cole
144	Brent Mowery
165	Tom Draper
186	Nevin Kardum
207	Dave Quigley
228	Chris Norton
249	Anssi Melametsa

1984
Pick
30	Peter Douris
68	Chris Mills
72	Sean Clement
93	Scott Schneider
114	Gary Lorden
135	Luciano Borsato
156	Brad Jones
177	Gord Whitaker
197	Rick Forst
218	Mike Warus
238	Jim Edmonds

1983
Pick
8	Andrew McBain
14	Bobby Dollas
29	Brad Berry
43	Peter Taglianetti
69	Bob Essensa
89	Harry Armstrong
109	Joel Baillargeon
129	Iain Duncan
149	Ron Pessetti
169	Todd Flichel
189	Cory Wright
209	Eric Cormier
229	Jamie Husgen

1982
Pick
12	Jim Kyte
74	Tom Martin
75	Dave Ellett
96	Tim Mishler
138	Derek Ray
159	Guy Gosselin
180	Tom Ward
201	Mike Savage
222	Bob Shaw
243	Jan Urban Ericson

1981
Pick
1	Dale Hawerchuk
22	Scott Arniel
43	Jyrki Seppa
64	Kirk McCaskill
85	Marc Behrend
106	Bob O'Connor
127	Peter Nilsson
148	Dan McFaul
169	Greg Dick
190	Vladimir Kadlec
211	Dave Kirwin

1980
Pick
2	David Babych
23	Moe Mantha
44	Murray Eaves
65	Guy Fournier
86	Glen Ostir
107	Ron Loustel
128	Brian Mullen
135	Mike Lauen
149	Sandy Beadle
170	Ed Christian
191	Dave Chartier

1979
Pick
19	Jimmy Mann
40	Dave Christian
61	Bill Whelton
82	Pat Daley
103	Thomas Steen
124	Tim Watters

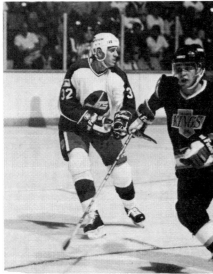

Peter Taglianetti

Club Directory

Winnipeg Arena
15-1430 Maroons Road
Winnipeg, Manitoba R3G 0L5
Phone 204/783-5387
Mktg, PR FAX 204/788-4668
ENVOY ID
General
Manager: JETS. GM
Public
Relations: JETS. PR
Marketing: JETS, MAR
Capacity: 15,405

Board of Directors
Barry L. Shenkarow	Marvin Shenkarow	Harvey Secter
Jerry Kruk	Don Binda	Bill Davis
Harvey Johnson		

President & Governor . . . . Barry L. Shenkarow
Alternate Governors . . . . Michael Smith, Bill Davis

Hockey Operations
Vice-President & General Manager . . . . Michael Smith
Assistant General Manager/Director of Hockey
Operations . . . . Dennis McDonald
Coach . . . . Bob Murdoch
Assistant Coaches . . . . Clare Drake, Alpo Suhonen
GM/Head Coach, Moncton (AHL) . . . . Dave Farrish
Assistant Coach, Moncton (AHL) . . . . Ron Wilson
Director of Scouting . . . . Bill Lesuk
Assistant Director of Scouting . . . . Joe Yannetti
Scouts . . . . Connie Broden, Tom Savage
Executive Ass't. to Vice-President &
G.M. . . . . Pat MacDonald
Administrative Ass't - Hockey Operations/
Finance . . . . Loris Enns

Finance and Administration
Director of Finance & Administration . . . . Don Binda
Accountant and Office Manager . . . . Glenda Leiske
Ticket Manager . . . . Dianne Gabbs
Accounting Clerks . . . . Trish Benson, Bryan Braun
Administrative Assistant/Novelty Operations   Lynda Sweetland
Receptionist . . . . Sherry Larson

Public Relations
Director of Public Relations . . . . Murray Harding
Director of Media Relations . . . . Mike O'Hearn
Director of Community Relations . . . . Lori Summers
Administrative Ass't., P.R. . . . . Sharon Harding
Statistician/Public Relations Assistant . . . . . . Bruce Barton
Administrative Ass't., Community Relations . . . Lisa Winslow
Administrative Ass't., Goals for Kids . . . . Anne-Marie Blake

Marketing
Vice-President of Marketing and P.R. . . . . Madeline Hanson
Director of Sales . . . . Val Overwater
Marketing Assistant . . . . Val Kuhn
Account Representatives . . . . Gord Dmytriw, Mike Miguez
Merchandising Manager . . . . Chris Newman
Administrative Assistant/Sales . . . . Sherri Wilson
Sales Representative . . . . Paul Haarstad

Dressing Room
Athletic Therapists . . . . Chuck Badcock, Jim Ramsay
Equipment Manager . . . . Craig Heisinger
Assistant Equipment Manager . . . . Phil Walker
Team Physician . . . . Dr. Wayne Hildahl
Team Dentist . . . . Dr. Gene Solmundson
Team Colors . . . . Blue, Red and White
Dimensions of Rink . . . . 200 feet by 85 feet
Training Camp . . . . Saskatoon, SK and Winnipeg
Press Box Location . . . . East Side
TV Channel . . . . CKY-TV
Radio Station . . . . CKY AM 580
Play-by-Play . . . . Curt Keilback (TV and Radio)
Color Commentary . . . . Mike O'Hearn (Radio)

General Manager

MIKE SMITH
General Manager, Winnipeg Jets. Born on August 31, 1945 in Potsdam, New York.

Mike Smith was appointed General Manager of the club on December 3, 1988 after ten years of service within the Jets organization. He had held the position of Assistant General Manager and Director of Scouting since 1984.

Smith began his NHL career in 1976-77 when he was an assistant coach with the New York Rangers under John Ferguson. After two seasons in New York, he assumed the same coaching duties with the Colorado Rockies. When the Jets entered the League in 1979-80, Smith was hired as General Manager of their CHL franchise in Tulsa. In 1980-81, midway through the season, Smith was asked to come to Winnipeg to be head coach. In 1981-82 he became the team's Director of Recruiting.

Coach

MURDOCH, ROBERT JOHN (BOB)
Head Coach, Winnipeg Jets. Born in Kirkland Lake, Ont., November 20, 1946.

Bob Murdoch joined the Jets on May 25, 1989. After eight years in the Calgary Flames organization, including three as a player and five as an assistant coach, former NHL defenseman Murdoch joined the Chicago Blackhawks where he coached in 1987-88.

An alumnus of the University of Waterloo in Ontario, Murdoch opened his 12-year NHL playing career with the 1970-71 Stanley Cup champion Montreal Canadiens. After earning another championship ring in 1972-73, he was dealt by Montreal to the Los Angeles Kings, with whom he played until 1978-79, when the Flames acquired his services. At the conclusion of his playing days, Murdoch had registered scoring totals of 60-218-278 in 757 games.

Coaching Record

| Season | Team | Games | Regular Season | | | | Games | Playoffs | | | |
			W	L	T	%		W	L	%
1987-88	Chicago (NHL)	80	30	41	9	.431	5	1	4	.200
	NHL Totals	80	30	41	9	.431	5	1	4	.200

1988-89 Final Statistics

Standings

Abbreviations: GA – goals against; **GF** – goals for; **GP** – games played; **L** – losses; **PTS** – points; **T** – ties; **W** – wins; **%** – percentage of games won.

CLARENCE CAMPBELL CONFERENCE

Norris Division

	GP	W	L	T	GF	GA	PTS	%
Detroit	80	34	34	12	313	316	80	.500
St. Louis	80	33	35	12	275	285	78	.488
Minnesota	80	27	37	16	258	278	70	.438
Chicago	80	27	41	12	297	335	66	.413
Toronto	80	28	46	6	259	342	62	.388

Smythe Division

	GP	W	L	T	GF	GA	PTS	%
Calgary	80	54	17	9	354	226	117	.731
Los Angeles	80	42	31	7	376	335	91	.569
Edmonton	80	38	34	8	325	306	84	.525
Vancouver	80	33	39	8	251	253	74	.463
Winnipeg	80	26	42	12	300	355	64	.400

PRINCE OF WALES CONFERENCE

Adams Division

	GP	W	L	T	GF	GA	PTS	%
Montreal	80	53	18	9	315	218	115	.719
Boston	80	37	29	14	289	256	88	.550
Buffalo	80	38	35	7	291	299	83	.519
Hartford	80	37	38	5	299	290	79	.494
Quebec	80	27	46	7	269	342	61	.381

Patrick Division

	GP	W	L	T	GF	GA	PTS	%
Washington	80	41	29	10	305	259	92	.575
Pittsburgh	80	40	33	7	347	349	87	.544
NY Rangers	80	37	35	8	310	307	82	.513
Philadelphia	80	36	36	8	307	285	80	.500
New Jersey	80	27	41	12	281	325	66	.413
NY Islanders	80	28	47	5	265	325	61	.381

Joe Mullen led the Calgary Flames in scoring during the 1988-89 season with a career-high 110 points.

INDIVIDUAL LEADERS

Goal Scoring

Player	Team	GP	G
Mario Lemieux	Pit.	76	85
Bernie Nicholls	L.A.	79	70
Steve Yzerman	Det.	80	65
Wayne Gretzky	L.A.	78	54
Joe Nieuwendyk	Cgy.	77	51
Joe Mullen	Cgy.	79	51

Assists

Player	Team	GP	A
Mario Lemieux	Pit.	76	114
Wayne Gretzky	L.A.	78	114
Steve Yzerman	Det.	80	90
Paul Coffey	Pit.	75	83
Bernie Nicholls	L.A.	79	80

Power Play Goals

Player	Team	GP	PP
Mario Lemieux	Pit.	76	31
Tim Kerr	Phi.	69	25
Rob Brown	Pit.	68	24
Bernie Nicholls	L.A.	79	21
Kevin Dineen	Hfd.	79	20
Andrew McBain	Wpg.	80	20

Short-Hand Goals

Player	Team	GP	SH
Mario Lemieux	Pit.	76	13
Dirk Graham	Chi.	80	10
Esa Tikkanen	Edm.	67	8
Bernie Nicholls	L.A.	79	8
Mark Messier	Edm.	72	6

Game-Winning Goals

Player	Team	GP	GW
Joe Nieuwendyk	Cgy.	77	11
Guy Carbonneau	Mtl.	79	10
Mike Ridley	Wsh.	80	9
Dino Ciccarelli	Min.-Wsh.	76	8
Jari Kurri	Edm.	76	8
Mario Lemieux	Pit.	76	8
Mike Krushelnyski	L.A.	78	8

Game-Tying Goals

Player	Team	GP	GT
Rick Tocchet	Phi.	66	3

Thirteen players with two each.

Shots

Player	Team	GP	S
Steve Yzerman	Det.	80	388
Bernie Nicholls	L.A.	79	385
Paul Coffoy	Pit.	75	342
Mario Lemieux	Pit.	76	313
Brett Hull	StL.	78	305
Wayne Gretzky	L.A.	78	303
Kevin Dineen	Hfd.	79	294

First Goals

Player	Team	GP	FG
Mario Lemieux	Pit.	76	10
Dave Christian	Wsh.	80	10
Steve Larmer	Chi.	80	10
Patrik Sundstrom	N.J.	65	9
Stephane Richer	Mtl.	68	8
Geoff Courtnall	Wsh.	79	8
Steve Yzerman	Det.	80	8

Shooting Percentage
(minimum 80 shots)

Player	Team	GP	G	S	%
Rob Brown	Pit.	68	49	169	29.0
Craig Simpson	Edm.	66	35	121	28.9
Mario Lemieux	Pit.	76	85	313	27.2
*Pat Elynuik	Wpg.	56	26	100	26.0
Ron Sutter	Phi.	55	26	106	24.5

Plus/Minus

Player	Team	GP	+/-
Joe Mullen	Cgy.	79	51
Doug Gilmour	Cgy.	72	45
Colin Patterson	Cgy.	74	44
Craig Muni	Edm.	69	43
Brad McCrimmon	Cgy.	72	43
Gary Suter	Cgy.	75	39

Individual Leaders

Abbreviations: ***** – rookie eligible for Calder Trophy; **A** – assists; **G** – goals; **GP** – games played; **GT** – game-tying goals; **GW** – game-winning goals; **PIM** – penalties in minutes; **PP** – power play goals; **Pts** – points; **S** – shots on goal; **SH** – short-handed goals; **%** – percentage of shots resulting in goals; **+/–** – difference between Goals For (**GF**) scored when a player is on the ice with his team at even strength or short-handed and Goals Against (**GA**) scored when the same player is on the ice with his team at even strength or on a power play.

Individual Scoring Leaders for Art Ross Trophy

Player	Team	GP	G	A	Pts	+/–	PIM	PP	SH	GW	GT	S	%
Mario Lemieux	Pittsburgh	76	85	114	199	41	100	31	13	8	1	313	27.2
Wayne Gretzky	Los Angeles	78	54	114	168	15	26	11	5	5	2	303	17.8
Steve Yzerman	Detroit	80	65	90	155	17	61	17	3	7	2	388	16.8
Bernie Nicholls	Los Angeles	79	70	80	150	30	96	21	8	6	0	385	18.2
Rob Brown	Pittsburgh	68	49	66	115	27	118	24	0	6	0	169	29.0
Paul Coffey	Pittsburgh	75	30	83	113	10–	193	11	0	2	0	342	8.8
Joe Mullen	Calgary	79	51	59	110	51	16	13	1	7	0	270	18.9
Jari Kurri	Edmonton	76	44	58	102	19	69	10	5	8	1	214	20.6
Jimmy Carson	Edmonton	80	49	51	100	3	36	19	0	5	1	240	20.4
Luc Robitaille	Los Angeles	78	46	52	98	5	65	10	0	4	0	237	19.4
Dale Hawerchuk	Winnipeg	75	41	55	96	30–	28	14	3	4	1	239	17.2
Dan Quinn	Pittsburgh	79	34	60	94	37–	102	16	0	4	0	200	17.0
Mark Messier	Edmonton	72	33	61	94	5–	130	6	6	4	1	164	20.1
Gerard Gallant	Detroit	76	39	54	93	7	230	13	0	7	0	221	17.6
Ed Olczyk	Toronto	80	38	52	90	0	75	11	2	4	1	249	15.3
Kevin Dineen	Hartford	79	45	44	89	6–	167	20	1	4	0	294	15.3
Mike Ridley	Washington	80	41	48	89	17	49	16	0	9	0	187	21.9
Tim Kerr	Philadelphia	69	48	40	88	4–	73	25	0	3	1	236	20.3
Pat LaFontaine	NY Islanders	79	45	43	88	8–	26	16	0	4	0	288	15.6
Pierre Turgeon	Buffalo	80	34	54	88	3–	26	19	0	5	0	182	18.7
Tomas Sandstrom	NY Rangers	79	32	56	88	5	148	11	2	4	0	240	13.3
Thomas Steen	Winnipeg	80	27	61	88	14	80	9	1	2	1	173	15.6
Steve Larmer	Chicago	80	43	44	87	2	54	19	1	2	0	269	16.0
John MacLean	New Jersey	74	42	45	87	26	127	14	0	4	2	266	15.8

Defensemen Scoring Leaders

Player	Team	GP	G	A	Pts	+/–	PIM	PP	SH	GW	GT	S	%
Paul Coffey	Pittsburgh	75	30	83	113	10–	193	11	0	2	0	342	8.8
Steve Duchesne	Los Angeles	79	25	50	75	31	92	8	5	2	0	215	11.6
Al MacInnis	Calgary	79	16	58	74	38	126	8	0	3	0	277	5.8
Chris Chelios	Montreal	80	15	58	73	35	185	8	0	6	0	206	7.3
*Brian Leetch	NY Rangers	68	23	48	71	8	50	8	3	1	1	268	8.6
Phil Housley	Buffalo	72	26	44	70	6	47	5	0	3	0	178	14.6
Jeff Brown	Quebec	78	21	47	68	22–	62	13	1	1	0	276	7.6
Scott Stevens	Washington	80	7	61	68	1	225	6	0	3	0	195	3.6
Tom Kurvers	New Jersey	74	16	50	66	11	38	5	0	0	1	190	8.4
Doug Wilson	Chicago	66	15	47	62	8	69	4	1	3	0	248	6.0
Fredrik Olausson	Winnipeg	75	15	47	62	6	32	4	0	1	0	178	8.4
Gary Suter	Calgary	63	13	49	62	26	78	8	0	1	0	216	6.0

CONSECUTIVE SCORING STREAKS

Goals

Games	Player	Team	G
10	Bernie Nicholls	Los Angeles	17
9	Rick Tocchet	Philadelphia	13
9	Steve Yzerman	Detroit	12
8	Gerard Gallant	Detroit	8
7	Mario Lemieux	Pittsburgh	15
7	Jimmy Carson	Edmonton	12
7	Ray Ferraro	Hartford	9
6	*Tony Granato	NY Rangers	10
6	Steve Thomas	Chicago	8
6	Steve Yzerman	Detroit	8
6	Pat LaFontaine	NY Islanders	7
6	Steve Yzerman	Detroit	6

Assists

Games	Player	Team	A
9	Mario Lemieux	Pittsburgh	20
9	Steve Duchesne	Los Angeles	12
8	Steve Yzerman	Detroit	15
8	Wayne Gretzky	Los Angeles	11
8	Thomas Steen	Winnipeg	10
8	Dave Taylor	Los Angeles	8

Points

Games	Player	Team	G	A	Pts
28	Steve Yzerman	Detroit	29	36	65
23	Wayne Gretzky	Los Angeles	18	33	51
17	Bernie Nicholls	Los Angeles	25	17	42
16	Wayne Gretzky	Los Angeles	8	25	33
15	Mario Lemieux	Pittsburgh	20	24	44
15	Carey Wilson	Hfd.-NYR	8	17	25
15	Geoff Courtnall	Washington	12	11	23
13	Rob Brown	Pittsburgh	14	15	29
13	Bernie Nicholls	Los Angeles	9	20	29
13	Luc Robitaille	Los Angeles	10	14	24
13	Steve Larmer	Chicago	9	13	22
13	Esa Tikkanen	Edmonton	7	14	21

Esa Tikkanen led the Edmonton Oilers with eight short-handed goals in 1988-89.

Scott Young, left, had a fine rookie campaign for the Hartford Whalers, totaling 59 points on 19 goals and 40 assists. Bob Joyce, right, a former NCAA All-Star, led all Bruins' rookies with seven power-play goals in 1988-89.

Individual Rookie Scoring Leaders

Scoring Leaders

Rookie	Team	GP	G	A	Pts	+/−	PIM	PP	SH	GW	GT	S	%
Brian Leetch	NY Rangers	68	23	48	71	8	50	8	3	1	1	268	8.6
Tony Granato	NY Rangers	78	36	27	63	17	140	4	4	3	2	234	15.4
Joe Sakic	Quebec	70	23	39	62	36 −	24	10	0	2	1	148	15.5
Craig Janney	Boston	62	16	46	62	20	12	2	0	2	0	95	16.8
Trevor Linden	Vancouver	80	30	29	59	10 −	41	10	1	2	0	186	16.1
Dave Volek	NY Islanders	77	25	34	59	11 −	24	9	0	7	0	229	10.9
Scott Young	Hartford	76	19	40	59	21 −	27	6	0	2	0	203	9.4
Dan Marois	Toronto	76	31	23	54	4 −	76	7	0	4	1	146	21.2
Jiri Hrdina	Calgary	70	22	32	54	19	26	6	0	2	0	147	15.0
Pat Elynuik	Winnipeg	56	26	25	51	5	29	5	0	6	0	100	26.0

Goal Scoring

Rookie	Team	GP	G
Tony Granato	NYR	78	36
Dan Marois	Tor.	76	31
Trevor Linden	Van.	80	30
Pat Elynuik	Wpg.	56	26
Dave Volek	NYI	77	25

Assists

Rookie	Team	GP	A
Brian Leetch	NYR	68	48
Craig Janney	Bos.	62	46
Scott Young	Hfd.	76	40
Joe Sakic	Que.	70	39
John Cullen	Pit.	79	37

Power Play Goals

Name	Team	GP	PP
Joe Sakic	Que.	70	10
Trevor Linden	Van.	80	10
Dave Volek	NYI	77	9
Brian Leetch	NYR	68	8
John Cullen	Pit.	79	8

Short Hand Goals

Name	Team	GP	SH
Tony Granato	NYR	78	4
Brian Leetch	NYR	68	3
Benoit Hogue	Buf.	69	2
Shawn Chambers	Min.	72	2

Game Winning Goals

Name	Team	GP	GW
Dave Volek	NYI	77	7
Pat Elynuik	Wpg.	56	6
Dan Marois	Tor.	76	4

Game Tying Goals

Name	Team	GP	GT
Dan Barber	Min.	23	2
Tony Granato	NYR	78	2

Shots

Rookie	Team	GP	S
Brian Leetch	NYR	68	268
Tony Granato	NYR	78	234
Dave Volek	NYI	77	229
Scott Young	Hfd.	76	203
Trevor Linden	Van.	80	186

First Goals

Rookie	Team	GP	FG
Benoit Hogue	Buf.	69	5
Jiri Hrdina	Cgy.	70	5
Trevor Linden	Van.	80	5

Shooting Percentage
(minimum 80 shots)

Rookie	Team	GP	G	S	%
Pat Elynuik	Wpg.	56	26	100	26.0
Dan Marois	Tor.	76	31	146	21.2
Jody Hull	Hfd.	60	16	82	19.5
Mike Keane	Mtl.	69	16	90	17.8
Craig Janney	Bos.	62	16	95	16.8

Plus/Minus

Name	Team	GP	+/−
Craig Janney	Bos.	62	20
Jiri Hrdina	Cgy.	70	19
Grant Jennings	Hfd.	55	17
Tony Granato	NYR	78	17
Jeff Chychrun	Phi.	80	11

CONSECUTIVE ROOKIE SCORING STREAKS

Goals

Games	Rookie	Team	G
6	Tony Granato	NY Rangers	10
5	Don Barber	Minnesota	7

Assists

Games	Rookie	Team	A
7	Brian Leetch	NY Rangers	11
7	Pat Elynuik	Winnipeg	10
6	Scott Young	Hartford	9
6	Zarley Zalapski	Pittsburgh	8
6	Tony Granato	NY Rangers	6
5	Brian Leetch	NY Rangers	8
5	Greg Hawgood	Boston	7
5	Benoit Hogue	Buffalo	7
5	Joe Sakic	Quebec	7
5	Shawn Chambers	Minnesota	6
5	Bob Joyce	Boston	6
5	Jeff Norton	NY Islanders	5

Points

Games	Rookie	Team	G	A	Pts
12	Joe Sakic	Quebec	10	7	17
9	Scott Young	Hartford	2	11	13
8	Dan Marois	Toronto	8	3	11
7	Brian Leetch	NY Rangers	3	11	14
7	Pat Elynuik	Winnipeg	3	10	13
7	Scott Young	Hartford	3	6	9
6	Tony Granato	NY Rangers	10	6	16
6	Zarley Zalapski	Pittsburgh	1	8	9
6	Craig Janney	Boston	3	5	8
6	Bob Joyce	Boston	2	6	8

Three-or-More-Goal Games

Player	Team	Date	Final Score	G
Greg Adams	Vancouver	Oct. 12	VAN 6 EDM 2	3
Glenn Anderson	Edmonton	Nov. 19	TOR 1 EDM 9	4
John Anderson	Hartford	Feb. 11	WPG 3 HFD 7	3
Dave Andreychuk	Buffalo	Oct. 12	PIT 5 BUF 8	3
Brent Ashton	Winnipeg	Feb. 19	HFD 6 WPG 7	3
*Don Barber	Minnesota	Mar. 16	CHI 1 MIN 6	3
Dave Barr	Detroit	Feb. 21	DET 6 NYI 5	3
Brian Bellows	Minnesota	Nov. 25	TOR 3 MIN 5	3
Rob Brown	Pittsburgh	Oct. 15	STL 2 PIT 9	3
Rob Brown	Pittsburgh	Nov. 25	PIT 5 WSH 3	3
Rob Brown	Pittsburgh	Jan. 28	DET 5 PIT 10	3
Rob Brown	Pittsburgh	Feb. 05	PIT 5 BOS 2	3
Randy Burridge	Boston	Feb. 09	L.A. 1 BOS 4	3
Randy Burridge	Boston	Mar. 04	VAN 4 BOS 6	3
Jimmy Carson	Edmonton	Dec. 04	NYR 6 EDM 10	3
Dave Christian	Washington	Oct. 15	N.J. 5 WSH 8	3
Dino Ciccarelli	Minnesota	Nov. 17	VAN 6 MIN 7	3
Dino Ciccarelli	Minnesota	Dec. 31	STL 2 MIN 6	3
Dino Ciccarelli	Washington	Mar. 18	WSH 8 HFD 2	4
Shayne Corson	Montreal	Feb. 04	NYR 5 MTL 7	3
Shayne Corson	Montreal	Mar. 22	QUE 0 MTL 8	3
Geoff Courtnall	Washington	Mar. 09	WSH 7 BOS 2	3
Adam Creighton	Buffalo	Nov. 02	NYR 4 BUF 6	3
Adam Creighton	Chicago	Feb. 19	MTL 4 CHI 4	3
Vincent Damphousse	Toronto	Oct. 17	TOR 6 MTL 2	3
Kevin Dineen	Hartford	Mar. 08	EDM 3 HFD 7	3
Steve Duchesne	Los Angeles	Mar. 02	L.A. 4 STL 1	3
Iain Duncan	Winnipeg	Nov. 20	EDM 4 WPG 7	3
Bernie Federko	St Louis	Feb. 27	STL 7 TOR 5	3
Tom Fergus	Toronto	Nov. 21	STL 0 TOR 4	3
Ray Ferraro	Hartford	Nov. 26	HFD 4 QUE 2	3
Mike Foligno	Buffalo	Jan. 31	BUF 5 HFD 3	3
Ron Francis	Hartford	Jan. 27	HFD 8 N.J. 6	3
Dave Gagner	Minnesota	Nov. 14	MIN 5 TOR 4	3
Dave Gagner	Minnesota	Jan. 21	MIN 6 NYI 8	3
Gerard Gallant	Detroit	Jan. 04	STL 2 DET 4	3
*Tony Granato	NY Rangers	Oct. 30	PIT 2 NYR 9	4
*Tony Granato	NY Rangers	Jan. 14	NYR 4 PIT 2	3
*Tony Granato	NY Rangers	Jan. 18	NYR 6 CHI 4	3
Wayne Gretzky	Los Angeles	Feb. 04	BUF 3 L.A. 5	3
Wayne Gretzky	Los Angeles	Feb. 12	L.A. 6 CHI 2	3
Dale Hawerchuk	Winnipeg	Nov. 08	WPG 8 QUE 4	3
Dale Hawerchuk	Winnipeg	Jan. 26	WPG 6 NYI 8	3
*Jiri Hrdina	Calgary	Oct. 17	L.A. 4 CGY 11	3
*Jiri Hrdina	Calgary	Nov. 07	HFD 3 CGY 6	4
*Jody Hull	Hartford	Feb. 26	PIT 3 HFD 8	3
Mark Hunter	Calgary	Jan. 19	CGY 7 BOS 2	4
Mark Hunter	Calgary	Mar. 07	WPG 5 CGY 9	3
Mark Hunter	Calgary	Mar. 18	CGY 9 L.A. 3	3
Tim Kerr	Philadelphia	Nov. 12	DET 5 PHI 4	3
Tim Kerr	Philadelphia	Jan. 21	PHI 7 WPG 3	3
Tim Kerr	Philadelphia	Feb. 22	PHI 6 NYR 4	3
Jari Kurri	Edmonton	Nov. 08	EDM 7 PIT 3	3
Jari Kurri	Edmonton	Dec. 07	QUE 3 EDM 8	3
Guy Lafleur	NY Rangers	Feb. 27	L.A. 4 NYR 6	3
Pat LaFontaine	NY Islanders	Jan. 14	CHI 5 NYI 3	3
Pat LaFontaine	NY Islanders	Jan. 21	MIN 5 NYI 8	3
Gary Leeman	Toronto	Mar. 19	TOR 6 PHI 8	3
Claude Lemieux	Montreal	Oct. 14	MTL 7 N.J. 3	3
Mario Lemieux	Pittsburgh	Oct. 11	WSH 7 PIT 8	3
Mario Lemieux	Pittsburgh	Oct. 18	PHI 2 PIT 4	3
Mario Lemieux	Pittsburgh	Dec. 21	PIT 6 TOR 1	3
Mario Lemieux	Pittsburgh	Dec. 31	N.J. 6 PIT 8	5
Mario Lemieux	Pittsburgh	Jan. 10	NYI 3 PIT 5	3
Mario Lemieux	Pittsburgh	Feb. 14	BUF 3 PIT 7	3
Mario Lemieux	Pittsburgh	Mar. 12	PIT 6 CHI 5	3
Mario Lemieux	Pittsburgh	Mar. 25	N.J. 4 PIT 5	3
Mario Lemieux	Pittsburgh	Mar. 30	HFD 9 PIT 5	4
*Trevor Linden	Vancouver	Nov. 17	VAN 6 MIN 7	3
*Trevor Linden	Vancouver	Nov. 22	BUF 2 VAN 4	3
Ken Linseman	Boston	Mar. 14	BOS 8 PIT 2	3
John MacLean	New Jersey	Dec. 07	WSH 1 N.J. 4	3
John MacLean	New Jersey	Dec. 09	NYI 5 N.J. 6	3
John MacLean	New Jersey	Dec. 15	TOR 3 N.J. 6	3
*Dan Marois	Toronto	Feb. 17	TOR 10 NYR 6	3
*Dan Marois	Toronto	Mar. 07	TOR 6 QUE 4	3
Andrew McBain	Winnipeg	Nov. 20	EDM 4 WPG 7	3
Tony McKegney	St Louis	Oct. 14	STL 8 DET 4	3
Mark Messier	Edmonton	Feb. 21	HFD 4 EDM 7	4
Brian Mullen	NY Rangers	Oct. 19	WSH 1 NYR 5	3
Joe Mullen	Calgary	Nov. 05	BUF 0 CGY 9	3
Joe Mullen	Calgary	Jan. 05	L.A. 6 CGY 8	4
Joe Mullen	Calgary	Jan. 31	CGY 8 L.A. 5	3
Joe Mullen	Calgary	Mar. 26	CGY 7 CHI 5	3
Mats Naslund	Montreal	Nov. 26	EDM 5 MTL 7	3
Mats Naslund	Montreal	Mar. 18	MTL 7 PIT 2	3
Cam Neely	Boston	Oct. 16	BOS 10 CHI 3	3
Bernie Nicholls	Los Angeles	Oct. 28	L.A. 7 WPG 4	3
Bernie Nicholls	Los Angeles	Nov. 22	L.A. 6 PHI 1	3
Bernie Nicholls	Los Angeles	Jan. 12	STL 1 L.A. 7	3
Bernie Nicholls	Los Angeles	Apr. 01	VAN 4 L.A. 6	3
Joe Nieuwendyk	Calgary	Jan. 11	WPG 3 CGY 8	5
Joe Nieuwendyk	Calgary	Jan. 31	CGY 8 L.A. 5	3
Ed Olczyk	Toronto	Mar. 25	DET 5 TOR 6	3
Walt Poddubny	Quebec	Nov. 03	QUE 6 PIT 2	3
Brian Propp	Philadelphia	Oct. 13	PHI 7 MIN 6	3
Mike Ridley	Washington	Oct. 11	WSH 7 PIT 8	4
Mike Ridley	Washington	Dec. 06	PHI 3 WSH 4	3
Luc Robitaille	Los Angeles	Oct. 06	DET 2 L.A. 8	3
*Joe Sakic	Quebec	Oct. 22	QUE 3 NYI 7	3
*Joe Sakic	Quebec	Nov. 24	MTL 3 QUE 5	3
Jim Sandlak	Vancouver	Mar. 26	VAN 7 WPG 3	3
Brendan Shanahan	New Jersey	Feb. 13	TOR 1 N.J. 8	3
Craig Simpson	Edmonton	Feb. 25	STL 3 EDM 5	3
Derrick Smith	Philadelphia	Dec. 10	CHI 4 PHI 6	3
Peter Stastny	Quebec	Feb. 11	PIT 1 QUE 8	4
Peter Stastny	Quebec	Mar. 18	NYR 3 QUE 8	3
Thomas Steen	Winnipeg	Mar. 18	WPG 10 TOR 2	3
Tony Tanti	Vancouver	Jan. 07	VAN 7 PIT 5	3
Dave Taylor	Los Angeles	Dec. 01	TOR 3 LA 9	3
Esa Tikkanen	Edmonton	Nov. 12	EDM 6 TOR 2	3
Rick Tocchet	Philadelphia	Nov. 20	N.J. 1 PHI 7	3
Rick Tocchet	Philadelphia	Dec. 17	PHI 7 TOR 1	3
John Tonelli	Los Angeles	Dec. 20	CGY 3 L.A. 7	3
*Darren Turcotte	NY Rangers	Mar. 01	TOR 4 NYR 7	3
Rick Vaive	Chicago	Oct. 12	WPG 1 CHI 10	3
Pat Verbeek	New Jersey	Feb. 13	TOR 1 N.J. 8	3
Steve Yzerman	Detroit	Nov. 04	PHI 4 DET 3	3
Steve Yzerman	Detroit	Nov. 12	DET 5 PHI 4	3

NOTE: 119 Three-or-more-goal games recorded in 1988-89.

Mario Lemieux had nine three-or-more goal games in the 1988-89 season.

Goaltending Leaders

Minimum 25 games

Goals Against Average

Goaltender	Team	GPI	MINS	GA	AVG
Patrick Roy	Montreal	48	2744	113	2.47
Mike Vernon	Calgary	52	2938	130	2.65
Pete Peeters	Washington	33	1854	88	2.85
Brian Hayward	Montreal	36	2091	101	2.90
Rick Wamsley	Calgary	35	1927	95	2.96

Wins

Goaltender	Team	GPI	MINS	W	L	T
Mike Vernon	Calgary	52	2938	37	6	5
Patrick Roy	Montreal	48	2744	33	5	6
Ron Hextall	Philadelphia	64	3756	30	28	6
John Vanbiesbrouck	NY Rangers	56	3207	28	21	4
Kelly Hrudey	NYI-L.A.	66	3774	28	28	5

Save Percentage

Goaltender	Team	GPI	MINS	GA	SA	S%	W	L	T
Patrick Roy	Montreal	48	2744	113	1228	.908	33	5	6
Jon Casey	Minnesota	55	2961	151	1509	.900	18	17	12
Kari Takko	Minnesota	32	1603	93	922	.899	8	15	4
Mike Vernon	Calgary	52	2938	130	1263	.897	37	6	5
Steve Weeks	Vancouver	35	2056	102	953	.892	11	19	5

Shutouts

Goaltender	Team	GPI	MINS	SO	W	L	T
Greg Millen	St. Louis	52	3019	6	22	20	7
Pete Peeters	Washington	33	1854	4	20	7	3
Kirk McLean	Vancouver	42	2477	4	20	17	3
*Peter Sidorkiewicz	Hartford	44	2635	4	22	18	4
Patrick Roy	Montreal	48	2744	4	33	5	6

Kelly Hrudey, traded to Los Angeles on February 22, 1989, won 10 of his 16 starts in goal for the Kings.

Team Statistics

TEAMS' HOME-AND-ROAD RECORD

Norris Division

			Home								Road					
	GP	W	L	T	GF	GA	PTS	%	GP	W	L	T	GF	GA	PTS	%
DET	40	20	14	6	157	140	46	.575	40	14	20	6	156	176	34	.425
STL	40	22	11	7	148	117	51	.638	40	11	24	5	127	168	27	.338
MIN	40	17	15	8	141	135	42	.525	40	10	22	8	117	143	28	.350
CHI	40	16	14	10	165	153	42	.525	40	11	27	2	132	182	24	.300
TOR	40	15	20	5	133	165	35	.438	40	13	26	1	126	177	27	.338
Total	**200**	**90**	**74**	**36**	**744**	**710**	**216**	**.540**	**200**	**59**	**119**	**22**	**658**	**846**	**140**	**.350**

Smythe Division

	GP	W	L	T	GF	GA	PTS	%	GP	W	L	T	GF	GA	PTS	%
CGY	40	32	4	4	200	103	68	.850	40	22	13	5	154	123	49	.613
L.A.	40	25	12	3	215	169	53	.663	40	17	19	4	161	166	38	.475
EDM	40	21	16	3	172	150	45	.563	40	17	18	5	153	156	39	.488
VAN	40	19	15	6	122	111	44	.550	40	14	24	2	129	142	30	.375
WPG	40	17	18	5	153	167	39	.488	40	9	24	7	147	188	25	.313
Total	**200**	**114**	**65**	**21**	**862**	**700**	**249**	**.623**	**200**	**79**	**98**	**23**	**744**	**775**	**181**	**.453**

Adams Division

	GP	W	L	T	GF	GA	PTS	%	GP	W	L	T	GF	GA	PTS	%
MTL	40	30	6	4	162	104	64	.800	40	23	12	5	153	114	51	.638
BOS	40	17	15	8	141	135	42	.525	40	20	14	6	148	121	46	.575
BUF	40	25	12	3	167	141	53	.663	40	13	23	4	124	158	30	.375
HFD	40	21	17	2	156	145	44	.550	40	16	21	3	143	145	35	.438
QUE	40	16	20	4	150	160	36	.450	40	11	26	3	119	182	25	.313
Total	**200**	**109**	**70**	**21**	**776**	**685**	**239**	**.598**	**200**	**83**	**96**	**21**	**687**	**720**	**187**	**.468**

Patrick Division

	GP	W	L	T	GF	GA	PTS	%	GP	W	L	T	GF	GA	PTS	%
WSH	40	25	12	3	159	117	53	.663	40	16	17	7	146	142	39	.488
PIT	40	24	13	3	185	159	51	.638	40	16	20	4	162	190	36	.450
NYR	40	21	17	2	160	147	44	.550	40	16	18	6	150	160	38	.475
PHI	40	22	15	3	166	134	47	.588	40	14	21	5	141	151	33	.413
N.J.	40	17	18	5	143	149	39	.488	40	10	23	7	138	176	27	.338
NYI	40	19	18	3	141	149	41	.513	40	9	29	2	124	176	20	.250
Total	**240**	**128**	**93**	**19**	**954**	**855**	**275**	**.573**	**240**	**81**	**128**	**31**	**861**	**995**	**193**	**.402**
Total	**840**	**441**	**302**	**97**	**3336**	**2950**	**979**	**.583**	**840**	**302**	**441**	**97**	**2950**	**3336**	**701**	**.417**

TEAMS' DIVISIONAL RECORD

Norris Division

		Against Own Division									Against Other Divisions						
	GP	W	L	T	GF	GA	PTS	%	GP	W	L	T	GF	GA	PTS	%
DET	32	15	13	4	129	110	34	.531	48	19	21	8	184	206	46	.479
STL	32	18	8	6	117	98	42	.656	48	15	27	6	158	187	36	.375
MIN	32	10	16	6	106	119	26	.406	48	17	21	10	152	159	44	.458
CHI	32	12	13	7	107	110	31	.484	48	15	28	5	190	225	35	.365
TOR	32	12	17	3	105	127	27	.422	48	16	29	3	154	215	35	.365
Total	**160**	**67**	**67**	**26**	**564**	**564**	**160**	**.500**	**240**	**82**	**126**	**32**	**838**	**992**	**196**	**.408**

Smythe Division

	GP	W	L	T	GF	GA	PTS	%	GP	W	L	T	GF	GA	PTS	%
CGY	32	21	7	4	155	103	46	.719	48	33	10	5	199	123	71	.740
L.A.	32	12	16	4	134	157	28	.438	48	30	15	3	242	178	63	.656
EDM	32	13	17	2	126	136	28	.438	48	25	17	6	199	170	56	.583
VAN	32	13	16	3	114	110	29	.453	48	20	23	5	137	143	45	.469
WPG	32	11	14	7	119	142	29	.453	48	15	28	5	181	213	35	.365
Total	**160**	**70**	**70**	**20**	**648**	**648**	**160**	**.500**	**240**	**123**	**93**	**24**	**958**	**827**	**270**	**.563**

Adams Division

	GP	W	L	T	GF	GA	PTS	%	GP	W	L	T	GF	GA	PTS	%
MTL	32	23	8	1	129	82	47	.734	48	30	10	8	186	136	68	.708
BOS	32	9	16	7	101	105	25	.391	48	28	13	7	188	151	63	.656
BUF	32	14	14	4	101	122	32	.500	48	24	21	3	190	177	51	.531
HFD	32	13	18	1	109	116	27	.422	48	24	20	4	190	174	52	.542
QUE	32	12	15	5	107	122	29	.453	48	15	31	2	162	220	32	.333
Total	**160**	**71**	**71**	**18**	**547**	**547**	**160**	**.500**	**240**	**121**	**95**	**24**	**916**	**858**	**266**	**.554**

Patrick Division

	GP	W	L	T	GF	GA	PTS	%	GP	W	L	T	GF	GA	PTS	%
WSH	35	16	17	2	131	134	34	.486	45	25	12	8	174	125	58	.644
PIT	35	19	12	4	152	142	42	.600	45	21	21	3	195	207	45	.500
NYR	35	17	14	4	141	131	38	.543	45	20	21	4	169	176	44	.489
PHI	35	19	14	2	137	110	40	.571	45	17	22	6	170	175	40	.444
N.J.	35	12	19	4	130	151	28	.400	45	15	22	8	151	174	38	.422
NYI	35	12	19	4	123	146	28	.400	45	16	28	1	142	179	33	.367
Total	**210**	**95**	**95**	**20**	**814**	**814**	**210**	**.500**	**270**	**114**	**126**	**30**	**1001**	**1036**	**258**	**.478**

TEAM STREAKS

Consecutive Wins

Games	Team	From	To
9	Montreal	Dec. 17	Jan. 7
8	Calgary	Jan. 31	Feb. 15
8	Washington	Mar. 9	Mar. 26
7	NY Rangers	Oct. 16	Oct. 30
7	Detroit	Nov. 6	Nov. 20
7	Calgary	Nov. 10	Nov. 26
7	Philadelphia	Dec. 8	Dec. 23
7	Vancouver	Feb. 10	Feb. 23
6	Edmonton	Feb. 21	Mar. 5
5	Los Angeles	Nov. 5	Nov. 15
5	Washington	Nov. 15	Nov. 23
5	Montreal	Nov. 16	Nov. 23
5	Pittsburgh	Nov. 23	Dec. 3
5	Minnesota	Nov. 25	Dec. 3
5	Calgary	Dec. 1	Dec. 8
5	Pittsburgh	Dec. 14	Dec. 21
5	NY Rangers	Jan. 15	Jan. 23
5	Montreal	Jan. 28	Feb. 11
5	Buffalo	Feb. 15	Feb. 24
5	Montreal	Mar. 2	Mar. 11

Consecutive Home Wins

Games	Team	From	To
9	Calgary	Jan. 3	Feb. 5
8	Philadelphia	Dec. 4	Jan. 12
8	Montreal	Dec. 12	Jan. 21
8	Vancouver	Jan. 31	Mar. 10
8	Washington	Mar. 3	Apr. 1
6	Pittsburgh	Oct. 11	Nov. 1
6	NY Rangers	Oct. 16	Nov. 9
6	Calgary	Oct. 31	Nov. 26
6	Pittsburgh	Nov. 10	Dec. 6
6	Montreal	Nov. 16	Dec. 5
6	Washington	Dec. 27	Jan. 13
6	Buffalo	Feb. 12	Feb. 24
6	Calgary	Mar. 7	Apr. 2
5	Montreal	Feb. 22	Mar. 11
5	St. Louis	Mar. 14	Apr. 2

Consecutive Road Wins

Games	Team	From	To
7	Calgary	Nov. 10	Dec. 4
6	Toronto	Oct. 9	Oct. 26
5	Detroit	Nov. 9	Nov. 20
5	Montreal	Dec. 22	Jan. 1
5	Calgary	Jan. 31	Feb. 15
4	Los Angeles	Nov. 5	Nov. 23
4	Edmonton	Nov. 8	Nov. 13
4	NY Rangers	Jan. 18	Jan. 23
4	Montreal	Jan. 31	Feb. 18
4	Boston	Feb. 15	Feb. 25

Consecutive Undefeated

Games	Team	W	T	From	To
13	Calgary	12	1	Nov. 10	Dec. 8
12	Calgary	11	1	Jan. 23	Feb. 15
9	Montreal	6	3	Nov. 26	Dec. 12
9	Montreal	9	0	Dec. 17	Jan. 7
9	Buffalo	7	2	Jan. 7	Jan. 27
9	Boston	8	1	Feb. 15	Mar. 7
8	Boston	5	3	Oct. 16	Nov. 2
8	Pittsburgh	6	2	Dec. 10	Dec. 26
8	Washington	8	0	Mar. 9	Mar. 26
7	NY Rangers	7	0	Oct. 16	Oct. 30
7	Detroit	7	0	Nov. 6	Nov. 20
7	Pittsburgh	6	1	Nov. 23	Dec. 6
7	Philadelphia	7	0	Dec. 8	Dec. 23
7	NY Rangers	5	2	Dec. 23	Jan. 7
7	Washington	5	2	Jan. 2	Jan. 13
7	Vancouver	7	0	Feb. 10	Feb. 23
7	Edmonton	6	1	Feb. 21	Mar. 7

Consecutive Home Undefeated

Games	Team	W	T	From	To
18	Montreal	16	2	Nov. 2	Jan. 21
17	Calgary	14	3	Oct. 6	Dec. 15
12	Vancouver	10	2	Jan. 29	Mar. 18
11	Washington	9	2	Nov. 29	Jan. 13
10	Pittsburgh	9	1	Nov. 10	Dec. 20
10	Philadelphia	9	1	Nov. 29	Jan. 12
10	Calgary	9	1	Dec. 31	Feb. 5
8	Washington	8	0	Mar. 3	Apr. 1
8	St Louis	7	1	Mar. 7	Apr. 2
7	NY Rangers	6	1	Oct. 16	Nov. 11
6	Pittsburgh	6	0	Oct. 11	Nov. 1
6	St Louis	3	3	Dec. 15	Jan. 17
6	Minnesota	2	4	Jan. 14	Feb. 9
6	Buffalo	6	0	Feb. 12	Feb. 24
6	Chicago	2	4	Feb. 15	Mar. 5
6	Calgary	6	0	Mar. 7	Apr. 2

Consecutive Road Undefeated

Games	Team	W	T	From	To
8	NY Rangers	6	2	Dec. 23	Jan. 23
8	Washington	4	4	Jan. 4	Feb. 14
7	Boston	4	3	Oct. 16	Nov. 15
7	Calgary	7	0	Nov. 10	Dec. 4
7	Calgary	6	1	Jan. 23	Feb. 15
7	Boston	6	1	Feb. 15	Mar. 7
6	Toronto	6	0	Oct. 9	Oct. 26
6	New Jersey	3	3	Jan. 20	Feb. 9
5	Detroit	5	0	Nov. 9	Nov. 20
5	Montreal	5	0	Dec. 22	Jan. 1
5	Montreal	4	1	Jan. 31	Feb. 19

Zarley Zalapski's inspired play on the Pittsburgh Penguins' defense earned him a spot on the 1988-89 MasterCard/ NHL All-Rookie Team.

Team Penalties

Abbreviations: GP - games played; **PEN** - total penalty minutes, including bench penalties; **BMI** - total bench minor minutes; **AVG** - average penalty minutes/calculated by dividing total penalty minutes by games played.

Team	GP	PEN	BMI	AVG
MTL	80	1537	8	19.2
VAN	80	1569	10	19.6
HFD	80	1672	10	20.9
STL	80	1675	14	20.9
TOR	80	1740	14	21.8
NYI	80	1822	18	22.8
WSH	80	1836	12	23.0
WPG	80	1843	10	23.0
NYR	80	1891	14	23.6
BOS	80	1929	10	24.1
EDM	80	1931	20	24.1
MIN	80	1972	12	24.7
QUE	80	2004	10	25.1
BUF	80	2034	18	25.4
L.A.	80	2215	32	27.7
DET	80	2245	10	28.1
PHI	80	2317	12	29.0
CGY	80	2444	10	30.6
CHI	80	2496	30	31.2
N.J	80	2499	24	31.2
PIT	80	2670	16	33.4
TOTAL	**840**	**42341**	**314**	**50.4**

TEAMS' POWER-PLAY RECORDS

Abbreviations: ADV – total advantages; **PPGF** – power-play goals for; **%** – arrived by dividing number of power-play goals by total advantages.

Home

	Team	GP	ADV	PPGF	%
1	CGY	40	200	61	30.5
2	PHI	40	201	54	26.9
3	BUF	40	197	52	26.4
4	WPG	40	183	45	24.6
5	NYI	40	186	43	23.1
6	MIN	40	197	45	22.8
7	DET	40	182	41	22.5
8	WSH	40	245	55	22.4
9	L.A.	40	238	53	22.3
10	PIT	40	270	60	22.2
11	QUE	40	208	44	21.2
12	VAN	40	211	44	20.9
13	CHI	40	240	49	20.4
14	EDM	40	217	44	20.3
15	MTL	40	183	37	20.2
16	TOR	40	185	36	19.5
17	N.J.	40	246	46	18.7
18	STL	40	179	33	18.4
19	BOS	40	224	41	18.3
20	HFD	40	225	41	18.2
21	NYR	40	229	39	17.0
TOTAL		**840**	**4446**	**963**	**21.7**

Road

Team	GP	ADV	PPGF	%
PIT	40	221	59	26.7
PHI	40	166	44	26.5
HFD	40	193	46	23.8
QUE	40	184	41	22.3
NYI	40	192	42	21.9
MTL	40	198	43	21.7
CHI	40	194	42	21.6
STL	40	191	41	21.5
BOS	40	205	44	21.5
WSH	40	198	41	20.7
NYR	40	228	46	20.2
WPG	40	174	34	19.5
CGY	40	205	40	19.5
EDM	40	202	39	19.3
DET	40	170	32	18.8
L.A.	40	157	29	18.5
N.J.	40	220	39	17.7
VAN	40	199	34	17.1
MIN	40	195	33	16.9
BUF	40	183	26	14.2
TOR	40	149	20	13.4
TOTAL	**840**	**4024**	**815**	**20.3**

Overall

Team	GP	ADV	PPGF	%
PHI	80	367	98	26.7
CGY	80	405	101	24.9
PIT	80	491	119	24.2
NYI	80	378	85	22.5
WPG	80	357	79	22.1
QUE	80	392	85	21.7
WSH	80	443	96	21.7
MTL	80	381	80	21.0
CHI	80	434	91	21.0
HFD	80	418	87	20.8
L.A.	80	395	82	20.8
DET	80	352	73	20.7
BUF	80	380	78	20.5
STL	80	370	74	20.0
MIN	80	392	78	19.9
BOS	80	429	85	19.8
EDM	80	419	83	19.8
VAN	80	410	78	19.0
NYR	80	457	85	18.6
N.J.	80	466	85	18.2
TOR	80	334	56	16.8
TOTAL	**840**	**8470**	**1778**	**21.0**

SHORT HAND GOALS FOR

Home

	Team	GP	SHGF
1	CHI	40	16
2	PIT	40	14
3	EDM	40	13
4	DET	40	11
5	L.A.	40	10
6	PHI	40	8
7	QUE	40	8
8	TOR	40	7
9	NYR	40	7
10	CGY	40	6
11	MIN	40	6
12	WPG	40	5
13	BOS	40	4
14	WSH	40	4
15	MTL	40	4
16	STL	40	4
17	VAN	40	3
18	N.J.	40	3
19	HFD	40	2
20	BUF	40	2
21	NYI	40	0
TOTAL		**840**	**137**

Road

Team	GP	SHGF
EDM	40	14
L.A.	40	12
MIN	40	11
WPG	40	10
CHI	40	9
PHI	40	8
PIT	40	7
NYR	40	6
BOS	40	6
BUF	40	5
VAN	40	5
QUE	40	4
NYI	40	4
N.J.	40	4
DET	40	4
CGY	40	4
TOR	40	3
WSH	40	3
MTL	40	2
STL	40	1
HFD	40	1
TOTAL	**840**	**123**

Overall

Team	GP	SHGF
EDM	80	27
CHI	80	25
L.A.	80	22
PIT	80	21
MIN	80	17
PHI	80	16
DET	80	15
WPG	80	15
NYR	80	13
QUE	80	12
BOS	80	10
TOR	80	10
CGY	80	10
VAN	80	8
BUF	80	7
N.J.	80	7
WSH	80	7
MTL	80	6
STL	80	5
NYI	80	4
HFD	80	3
TOTAL	**840**	**260**

TEAMS' PENALTY KILLING RECORDS

Abbreviations: TSH – times short-handed; **PPGA** – power-play goals against; **%** – arrived by dividing – times short minus power-play goals against — by times short.

Home

	Team	GP	TSH	PPGA	%
1	EDM	40	210	30	85.7
2	CGY	40	210	34	83.8
3	DET	40	197	32	83.8
4	L.A.	40	202	34	83.2
5	STL	40	175	30	82.9
6	MIN	40	219	39	82.2
7	WSH	40	174	31	82.2
8	PHI	40	208	38	81.7
9	MTL	40	149	28	81.2
10	QUE	40	180	34	81.1
11	VAN	40	151	30	80.1
12	CHI	40	248	51	79.4
13	NYR	40	174	37	78.7
14	BOS	40	170	37	78.2
15	HFD	40	181	40	77.9
16	PIT	40	237	53	77.6
17	BUF	40	194	46	76.3
18	WPG	40	158	38	75.9
19	TOR	40	179	46	74.3
20	N.J.	40	226	58	74.3
21	NYI	40	182	49	73.1
TOTAL		**840**	**4024**	**815**	**79.7**

Road

Team	GP	TSH	PPGA	%
BOS	40	204	30	85.3
HFD	40	196	30	84.7
MTL	40	177	30	83.1
CGY	40	247	44	82.2
BUF	40	216	40	81.5
PHI	40	224	42	81.3
VAN	40	190	36	81.1
MIN	40	222	43	80.6
EDM	40	242	48	80.2
WPG	40	216	44	79.6
DET	40	229	47	79.5
WSH	40	188	42	77.7
L.A.	40	205	46	77.6
QUE	40	205	48	76.6
N.J.	40	241	57	76.3
PIT	40	245	58	76.3
NYR	40	197	48	75.6
NYI	40	208	54	74.0
TOR	40	180	52	71.1
STL	40	181	53	70.7
CHI	40	233	71	69.5
TOTAL	**840**	**4446**	**963**	**78.3**

Overall

Team	GP	TSH	PPGA	%
CGY	80	457	78	82.9
EDM	80	452	78	82.7
MTL	80	326	58	82.2
BOS	80	374	67	82.1
PHI	80	432	80	81.5
DET	80	426	79	81.5
HFD	80	377	70	81.4
MIN	80	441	82	81.4
VAN	80	341	66	80.6
L.A.	80	407	80	80.3
WSH	80	362	73	79.8
BUF	80	410	86	79.0
QUE	80	385	82	78.7
WPG	80	374	82	78.1
NYR	80	371	85	77.1
PIT	80	482	111	77.0
STL	80	356	83	76.7
N.J.	80	467	115	75.4
CHI	80	481	122	74.6
NYI	80	390	103	73.6
TOR	80	359	98	72.7
TOTAL	**840**	**8470**	**1778**	**79.0**

SHORT HAND GOALS AGAINST

Home

	Team	GP	SHGA
1	BOS	40	2
2	CGY	40	2
3	DET	40	2
4	BUF	40	3
5	MIN	40	3
6	QUE	40	4
7	WPG	40	4
8	NYI	40	4
9	CHI	40	4
10	WSH	40	5
11	N.J.	40	5
12	PHI	40	6
13	L.A.	40	7
14	MTL	40	7
15	STL	40	7
16	PIT	40	7
17	VAN	40	9
18	NYR	40	9
19	EDM	40	10
20	TOR	40	10
21	HFD	40	12
TOTAL		**840**	**123**

Road

Team	GP	SHGA
BOS	40	2
NYI	40	3
PHI	40	3
TOR	40	4
STL	40	5
VAN	40	5
MTL	40	6
DET	40	6
MIN	40	6
CGY	40	6
HFD	40	6
L.A.	40	6
EDM	40	7
QUE	40	8
NYR	40	8
WSH	40	8
WPG	40	9
PIT	40	9
BUF	40	9
N.J.	40	10
CHI	40	11
TOTAL	**840**	**137**

Overall

Team	GP	SHGA
BOS	80	4
NYI	80	7
CGY	80	8
DET	80	8
PHI	80	9
MIN	80	9
QUE	80	12
BUF	80	12
STL	80	12
MTL	80	13
L.A.	80	13
WPG	80	13
WSH	80	13
TOR	80	14
VAN	80	14
N.J.	80	15
CHI	80	16
PIT	80	16
NYR	80	17
EDM	80	17
HFD	80	18
TOTAL	**840**	**260**

Overtime Results

1988-89
Home Team Wins: 26
Visiting Team Wins: 26

Team	1988-89				1987-88				1986-87				1985-86				1984-85				1983-84			
	GP	W	L	T	GP	W	L	T	GP	W	L	T	GP	W	L	T	GP	W	L	T	GP	W	L	T
Boston	19	3	2	14	14	4	4	6	12	2	3	7	17	2	3	12	18	4	4	10	7	1	0	6
Buffalo	13	2	4	7	12	0	1	11	13	1	4	8	9	1	2	6	17	0	3	14	13	5	1	7
Calgary	17	5	3	9	15	2	4	9	4	1	0	3	12	1	2	9	14	1	1	12	18	4	0	14
Chicago	17	2	3	12	15	4	2	9	15	1	0	14	12	3	1	8	12	2	3	7	9	0	1	8
Detroit	16	3	1	12	16	2	3	11	17	2	5	10	13	2	5	6	14	0	2	12	11	3	1	7
Edmonton	15	4	3	8	16	3	2	11	14	5	3	6	14	5	2	7	12	0	1	11	9	4	0	5
Hartford	10	1	4	5	12	3	2	7	9	2	0	7	7	1	2	4	17	4	4	9	15	2	3	10
Los Angeles	14	6	1	7	12	1	3	8	12	2	2	8	14	3	3	8	19	3	2	14	17	1	3	13
Minnesota	17	0	1	16	16	1	2	13	14	2	2	10	15	4	2	9	15	1	2	12	18	5	3	10
Montreal	11	2	0	9	16	1	2	13	16	2	4	10	14	1	6	7	18	3	3	12	7	1	1	5
New Jersey	17	1	4	12	12	4	2	6	13	3	4	6	10	4	3	3	12	0	2	10	15	1	7	7
NY Islanders	11	3	3	5	13	3	0	10	20	5	3	12	17	4	1	12	15	1	8	6	10	3	3	4
NY Rangers	10	1	1	8	11	0	1	10	19	5	6	8	13	0	7	6	17	2	5	10	17	5	3	9
Philadelphia	14	1	5	8	13	1	3	9	10	5	1	4	9	4	1	4	9	1	1	7	14	3	1	10
Pittsburgh	10	2	1	7	16	5	2	9	21	5	4	12	14	3	3	8	8	3	0	5	12	1	5	6
Quebec	10	2	1	7	9	2	2	5	14	0	4	10	11	4	1	6	14	3	2	9	15	0	5	10
St. Louis	16	3	1	12	14	2	4	8	21	4	2	15	17	5	3	9	15	2	1	12	11	3	1	7
Toronto	11	1	4	6	13	1	2	10	13	3	4	6	17	4	6	7	15	5	2	8	13	1	3	9
Vancouver	14	2	4	8	11	0	2	9	10	2	0	8	16	1	2	13	17	7	1	9	16	3	4	9
Washington	16	2	4	10	15	2	4	9	17	5	2	10	11	4	0	7	12	3	0	9	9	1	3	5
Winnipeg	20	6	2	12	21	8	2	11	11	2	1	8	8	0	1	7	14	3	1	10	24	7	6	11
Totals	149	52		97	146	49		97	148	55		93	135	56		79	152	48		104	140	54		86

1988-89 Penalty Shots

Scored

Brent Ashton (Winnipeg) scored against Kirk McLean (Vancouver) in 8-6 loss at Vancouver, December 11.

Joe Nieuwendyk (Calgary) scored against Steve Weeks (Vancouver) in 5-3 win at Vancouver, December 16.

Craig MacTavish (Edmonton) scored against Mike Vernon (Calgary) in 4-1 win at Edmonton, December 23.

Mario Lemieux (Pittsburgh) scored against Chris Terreri (New Jersey) in 8-6 win at Pittsburgh, December 31.

Doug Evans (St. Louis) scored against Daniel Berthiaume (Winnipeg) in 5-3 win at St. Louis, January 31.

Steve Yzerman (Detroit) scored against Bob Essensa (Winnipeg) in 2-2 tie at Detroit, February 13.

Mario Lemieux (Pittsburgh) scored against Kelly Hrudey (Los Angeles) in 3-2 loss at Los Angeles, March 7.

Jock Callender (Pittsburgh) scored against Patrick Roy (Montreal) in 7-2 loss at Pittsburgh, March 18.

Stopped

Miroslav Frycer (Detroit) unsuccessful against **Don Beaupre** (Minnesota) in 4-1 win at Minnesota, October 28.

Ray Bourque (Boston) unsuccessful against **John Vanbiesbrouck** (New York Rangers) in 4-4 tie at New York, November 11.

Dino Ciccarelli (Minnesota) unsuccessful against **Allan Bester** (Toronto) in 6-3 win at Toronto, November 26.

Guy Lafleur (New York Rangers) unsuccessful against **Eldon Reddick** (Winnipeg) in 4-3 win at Winnipeg, November 29.

Joe Nieuwendyk (Calgary) unsuccessful against **Jeff Reese** (Toronto) in 4-4 tie at Toronto, December 12.

Dale Hawerchuk (Winnipeg) unsuccessful against **Clint Malarchuk** (Washington) at Washington, December 17.

Michel Goulet (Quebec) unsuccessful against **Allan Bester** (Toronto) in 6-5 loss at Quebec, December 29.

Greg Adams (Vancouver) unsuccessful against **Allan Bester** (Toronto) in 3-0 loss at Toronto, January 9.

Luc Robitaille (Los Angeles) unsuccessful against **Sean Burke** (New Jersey) in 6-6 tie at Los Angeles, February 2.

Steve Tuttle (St. Louis) unsuccessful against **Alain Chevrier** (Chicago) in 5-4 win at Chicago, February 5.

Greg Paslawski (St. Louis) unsuccessful against **Clint Malarchuk** (Washington) in 5-3 win at St. Louis, February 14.

Mike Foligno (Buffalo) unsuccessful against **Glen Hanlon** (Detroit) in 8-4 win at Buffalo, February 19.

Hakan Loob (Calgary) unsuccessful against **Jeff Reese** (Toronto) in 4-3 loss at Calgary, February 22.

Steve Larmer (Chicago) unsuccessful against **Kari Takko** (Minnesota) in 5-5 tie at Chicago, February 22.

Anton Stastny (Quebec) unsuccessful against **Allan Bester** (Toronto) in 6-4 loss at Quebec, March 7.

Kirk Muller (New Jersey) unsuccessful against **Mike Vernon** (Calgary) in 5-1 loss at New Jersey, March 14.

Petr Klima (Detroit) unsuccessful against **Jon Casey** (Minnesota) in 5-1 loss at Detroit, March 31.

Anders Carlsson (New Jersey) unsuccessful against **Don Beaupre** (Washington) in 7-4 win at New Jersey, April 2.

Summary

26 penalty shots resulted in 8 goals.

DIVISION/CONFERENCE RECORDS

Clarence Campbell Conference

Norris vs Smythe

GP	W	L	T	GF	GA	PTS	%
75	21	43	11	255	326	53	.353

Smythe vs Norris

GP	W	L	T	GF	GA	PTS	%
75	43	21	11	326	255	97	.647

Campbell vs Wales Conference

GP	W	L	T	GF	GA	PTS	%
330	141	155	34	1215	1238	316	.479

Prince of Wales Conference

Adams vs Patrick

GP	W	L	T	GF	GA	PTS	%
90	47	33	10	364	319	104	.578

Patrick vs Adams

GP	W	L	T	GF	GA	PTS	%
90	33	47	10	319	364	76	.422

Wales vs Campbell Conference

GP	W	L	T	GF	GA	PTS	%
330	155	141	34	1238	1215	344	.521

NHL Record Book

All-Time Standings of NHL Teams
(ranked by percentage)

Team	Games	Won	Lost	Tied	Goals For	Goals Against	Points	%
Edmonton	800	446	250	104	3,803	3,059	996	.623
Montreal	4,352	2,311	1,357	684	14,767	11,418	5,306	.610
Philadelphia	1,738	890	565	283	6,294	5,211	2,063	.593
NY Islanders	1,356	666	488	202	5,097	4,343	1,534	.566
Buffalo	1,512	721	544	247	5,506	4,933	1,689	.559
Boston	4,192	1,994	1,568	630	13,746	12,404	4,618	.551
**Calgary	1,356	631	516	209	5,147	4,471	1,471	.542
Toronto	4,352	1,866	1,837	649	13,534	13,410	4,381	.503
NY Rangers	4,126	1,707	1,755	664	12,783	13,064	4,078	.494
Detroit	4,126	1,697	1,766	663	12,371	12,658	4,057	.492
Quebec	800	338	358	104	3,081	3,078	780	.488
Chicago	4,126	1,655	1,820	651	12,344	12,739	3,961	.480
St. Louis	1,738	696	769	273	5,622	5,957	1,665	.479
Los Angeles	1,738	664	815	259	5,994	6,543	1,587	.457
Washington	1,200	463	569	168	4,082	4,561	1,094	.456
Minnesota	1,738	627	811	300	5,632	6,245	1,554	.447
Hartford	800	301	395	104	2,843	3,205	706	.441
Pittsburgh	1,738	636	848	254	5,872	6,600	1,526	.439
Winnipeg	800	294	400	106	2,954	3,393	694	.434
Vancouver	1,512	513	771	228	4,937	5,785	1,254	.415
*New Jersey	1,200	318	715	167	3,677	5,028	803	.335

* Totals included those of Kansas City (1974-75, 1975-76) and Colorado (1976-77 through 1981-82)
** Totals include those of Atlanta (1972-73 through 1979-80)

Year-By-Year Final Standings & Leading Scorers

Note: Assists not tabulated until 1926-27.
*Stanley Cup winner.

1917-18

Team	GP	W	L	T	GF	GA	PTS
Montreal	22	13	9	0	115	84	26
*Toronto	22	13	9	0	108	109	26
Ottawa	22	9	13	0	102	114	18
**Mtl. Wanderers	6	1	5	0	17	35	2

**Montreal Arena burned down and Wanderers forced to withdraw from League. Canadiens and Toronto each counted a win for defaulted games with Wanderers.

Leading Scorers

Player	Team	GP	G
Malone, Joe	Montreal	20	44
Denneny, Cy	Ottawa	22	36
Noble, Reg	Toronto	20	28
Lalonde, Newsy	Montreal	14	23
Denneny, Corbett	Toronto	21	20
Pitre, Didier	Montreal	19	17
Cameron, Harry	Toronto	20	17

1918-19

Team	GP	W	L	T	GF	GA	PTS
Ottawa	18	12	6	0	71	54	24
Montreal	18	10	8	0	88	78	20
Toronto	18	5	13	0	65	92	10

Leading Scorers

Player	Team	GP	G
Cleghorn, Odie	Montreal	17	24
Lalonde, Newsy	Montreal	17	21
Denneny, Cy	Ottawa	18	18
Nighbor, Frank	Ottawa	18	17
Pitre, Didier	Montreal	17	15
Skinner, Alf	Toronto	17	13
Darragh, Jack	Ottawa	14	12

1919-20

Team	GP	W	L	T	GF	GA	PTS
*Ottawa	24	19	5	0	121	64	38
Montreal	24	13	11	0	129	113	26
Toronto	24	12	12	0	119	106	24
Quebec	24	4	20	0	91	177	8

Leading Scorers

Player	Team	GP	G
Malone, Joe	Quebec	24	39
Lalonde, Newsy	Montreal	23	37
Nighbor, Frank	Ottawa	23	25
Denneny, Corbett	Toronto	23	25
Noble, Reg	Toronto	24	24
Darragh, Jack	Ottawa	22	24
Arbour, Amos	Montreal	20	21

Howie Morenz won two scoring titles in his career, and finished among the top ten point leaders in 10 consecutive seasons.

1920-21

Team	GP	W	L	T	GF	GA	PTS
Toronto	24	15	9	0	105	100	30
*Ottawa	24	14	10	0	97	75	28
Montreal	24	13	11	0	112	99	26
Hamilton	24	6	18	0	92	132	12

Leading Scorers

Player	Team	GP	G
Dye, Cecil	Tor.-Ham.	24	35
Denneny, Cy	Ottawa	24	34
Lalonde, Newsy	Montreal	24	32
Malone, Joe	Hamilton	20	28
Denneny, Corbett	Toronto	20	19
Noble, Reg	Toronto	24	19
Nighbor, Frank	Ottawa	24	19

1921-22

Team	GP	W	L	T	GF	GA	PTS
Ottawa	24	14	8	2	106	84	30
*Toronto	24	13	10	1	98	97	27
Montreal	24	12	11	1	88	94	25
Hamilton	24	7	17	0	88	105	14

Leading Scorers

Player	Team	GP	G
Broadbent, Harry	Ottawa	24	30
Dye, Cecil	Toronto	24	30
Denneny, Cy	Ottawa	22	28
Malone, Joe	Hamilton	24	23
Cleghorn, Odie	Montreal	23	21
Denneny, Corbett	Toronto	24	20
Cameron, Harry	Toronto	24	18

1922-23

Team	GP	W	L	T	GF	GA	PTS
*Ottawa	24	14	9	1	77	54	29
Montreal	24	13	9	2	73	61	28
Toronto	24	13	10	1	82	88	27
Hamilton	24	6	18	0	81	110	12

Leading Scorers

Player	Team	GP	G
Dye, Cecil	Toronto	22	26
Boucher, Billy	Montreal	24	25
Denneny, Cy	Ottawa	24	23
Cleghorn, Odie	Montreal	24	18
Adams, Jack	Toronto	23	18
Roach, Mickey	Hamilton	23	17
Wilson, Cully	Hamilton	23	15

1923-24

Team	GP	W	L	T	GF	GA	PTS
Ottawa	24	16	8	0	74	54	32
*Montreal	24	13	11	0	59	48	26
Toronto	24	10	14	0	59	85	20
Hamilton	24	9	15	0	63	68	18

Leading Scorers

Player	Team	GP	G
Denneny, Cy	Ottawa	21	22
Burch, Billy	Hamilton	24	16
Boucher, Billy	Montreal	23	16
Dye, Cecil	Toronto	19	16
Joliat, Aurel	Montreal	24	15
Boucher, George	Ottawa	21	13
Adams, Jack	Toronto	22	13
Morenz, Howie	Montreal	24	13

1924-25

Team	GP	W	L	T	GF	GA	PTS
Hamilton	30	19	10	1	90	60	39
Toronto	30	19	11	0	90	84	38
Montreal	30	17	11	2	93	56	36
Ottawa	30	17	12	1	83	66	35
Mtl. Maroons	30	9	19	2	45	65	20
Boston	30	6	24	0	49	119	12

Leading Scorers

Player	Team	GP	G
Dye, Cecil	Toronto	29	38
Morenz, Howie	Montreal	30	30
Joliat, Aurel	Montreal	24	29
Denneny, Cy	Ottawa	28	22
Adams, Jack	Toronto	27	21
Burch, Billy	Hamilton	27	21
Green, Redvers	Hamilton	30	19

1925-26

Team	GP	W	L	T	GF	GA	PTS
Ottawa	36	24	8	4	77	42	52
*Mtl. Maroons	36	20	11	5	91	73	45
Pittsburgh	36	19	16	1	82	70	39
Boston	36	17	15	4	92	85	38
NY Americans	36	12	20	4	68	89	28
Toronto	36	12	21	3	92	114	27
Montreal	36	11	24	1	79	108	23

Leading Scorers

Player	Team	GP	G
Stewart, Nels	Mtl. Maroons	36	34
Cooper, Carson	Boston	36	28
Herberts, Jimmy	Boston	36	26
Denneny, Cy	Ottawa	36	24
Morenz, Howie	Montreal	31	23
Adams, Jack	Toronto	36	22
Burch, Billy	New York	36	19

1926-27

Canadian Division

Team	GP	W	L	T	GF	GA	PTS
*Ottawa	44	30	10	4	86	69	64
Montreal	44	28	14	2	99	67	58
Mtl. Maroons	44	20	20	4	71	68	44
NY Americans	44	17	25	2	82	91	36
Toronto	44	15	24	5	79	94	35

American Division

Team	GP	W	L	T	GF	GA	PTS
New York	44	25	13	6	95	72	56
Boston	44	21	20	3	97	89	45
Chicago	44	19	22	3	115	116	41
Pittsburgh	44	15	26	3	79	108	33
Detroit	44	12	28	4	76	105	28

Leading Scorers

Player	Team	GP	G	A	PTS	PIM
Cook, Bill	New York	44	33	4	37	58
Irvin, Dick	Chicago	43	18	18	36	34
Morenz, Howie	Montreal	44	25	7	32	49
Fredrickson, Frank	Bos., Det.	41	18	13	31	46
Dye, Cecil	Chicago	41	25	5	30	14
Bailey, Ace	Toronto	42	15	13	28	82
Boucher, Frank	New York	44	13	15	28	17
Burch, Billy	NY Americans	43	19	8	27	40
Oliver, Harry	Boston	42	18	6	24	17
Keats, Gordon	Bos., Det.	42	16	8	24	52

Dick Irvin Sr. whose coaching career in Toronto, Montreal and Chicago spanned 26 years, reached the Finals a record 16 times.

1927-28

Canadian Division

Team	GP	W	L	T	GF	GA	PTS
Montreal	44	26	11	7	116	48	59
Mtl. Maroons	44	24	14	6	96	77	54
Ottawa	44	20	14	10	78	57	50
Toronto	44	18	18	8	89	88	44
NY Americans	44	11	27	6	63	128	28

American Division

Team	GP	W	L	T	GF	GA	PTS
Boston	44	20	13	11	77	70	51
*New York	44	19	16	9	94	79	47
Pittsburgh	44	19	17	8	67	76	46
Detroit	44	19	19	6	88	79	44
Chicago	44	7	34	3	68	134	17

Leading Scorers

Player	Team	GP	G	A	PTS	PIM
Morenz, Howie	Montreal	43	33	18	51	66
Joliat, Aurel	Montreal	44	28	11	39	105
Boucher, Frank	New York	44	23	12	35	15
Hay, George	Detroit	42	22	13	35	20
Stewart, Nels	Mtl. Maroons	41	27	7	34	104
Gagne, Art	Montreal	44	20	10	30	75
Cook, Fred	New York	44	14	14	28	45
Carson, Bill	Toronto	32	20	6	26	36
Finnigan, Frank	Ottawa	38	20	5	25	34
Cook, Bill	New York	43	18	6	24	42
Keats, Gordon	Chi., Det.	38	14	10	24	60

1928-29

Canadian Division

Team	GP	W	L	T	GF	GA	PTS
Montreal	44	22	7	15	71	43	59
NY Americans	44	19	13	12	53	53	50
Toronto	44	21	18	5	85	69	47
Ottawa	44	14	17	13	54	67	41
Mtl. Maroons	44	15	20	9	67	65	39

American Division

Team	GP	W	L	T	GF	GA	PTS
*Boston	44	26	13	5	89	52	57
New York	44	21	13	10	72	65	52
Detroit	44	19	16	9	72	63	47
Pittsburgh	44	9	27	8	46	80	26
Chicago	44	7	29	8	33	85	22

Leading Scorers

Player	Club	GP	G	A	PTS	PIM
Bailey, Ace	Toronto	44	22	10	32	78
Stewart, Nels	Mtl. Maroons	44	21	8	29	74
Cooper, Carson	Detroit	43	18	9	27	14
Morenz, Howie	Montreal	42	17	10	27	47
Blair, Andy	Toronto	44	12	15	27	41
Boucher, Frank	New York	44	10	16	26	8
Oliver, Harry	Boston	43	17	6	23	24
Cook, Bill	New York	43	15	8	23	41
Ward, Jimmy	Mtl. Maroons	43	14	8	22	46

1929-30

Canadian Division

Team	GP	W	L	T	GF	GA	PTS
Mtl. Maroons	44	23	16	5	141	114	51
*Montreal	44	21	14	9	142	114	51
Ottawa	44	21	15	8	138	118	50
Toronto	44	17	21	6	116	124	40
NY Americans	44	14	25	5	113	161	33

American Division

Team	GP	W	L	T	GF	GA	PTS
Boston	44	38	5	1	179	98	77
Chicago	44	21	18	5	117	111	47
New York	44	17	17	10	136	143	44
Detroit	44	14	24	6	117	133	34
Pittsburgh	44	5	36	3	102	185	13

Leading Scorers

Name	Club	GP	G	A	PTS	PIM
Weiland, Ralph	Boston	44	43	30	73	27
Boucher, Frank	New York	42	26	36	62	16
Clapper, Aubrey	Boston	44	41	20	61	48
Cook, Bill	New York	44	29	30	59	56
Kilrea, Hec	Ottawa	44	36	22	58	72
Stewart, Nels	Mtl. Maroons	44	39	16	55	81
Morenz, Howie	Montreal	44	40	10	50	72
Himes, Norm	NY Americans	44	28	22	50	15
Lamb, Joe	Ottawa	44	29	20	49	119
Gainor, Norm	Boston	42	18	31	49	39

1930-31

Canadian Division

Team	GP	W	L	T	GF	GA	PTS
*Montreal	44	26	10	8	129	89	60
Toronto	44	22	13	9	118	99	53
Mtl. Maroons	44	20	18	6	105	106	46
NY Americans	44	18	16	10	76	74	46
Ottawa	44	10	30	4	91	142	24

American Division

Team	GP	W	L	T	GF	GA	PTS
Boston	44	28	10	6	143	90	62
Chicago	44	24	17	3	108	78	51
New York	44	19	16	9	106	87	47
Detroit	44	16	21	7	102	105	39
Philadelphia	44	4	36	4	76	184	12

Leading Scorers

Player	Club	GP	G	A	PTS	PIM
Morenz, Howie	Montreal	39	28	23	51	49
Goodfellow, Ebbie	Detroit	44	25	23	48	32
Conacher, Charlie	Toronto	37	31	12	43	78
Bailey, Ace	Toronto	40	23	19	42	46
Cook, Bill	New York	43	30	12	42	39
Primeau, Joe	Toronto	38	9	32	41	18
Stewart, Nels	Mtl. Maroons	42	25	14	39	75
Boucher, Frank	New York	44	12	27	39	20
Weiland, Ralph	Boston	44	25	13	38	14
Cook, Fred	New York	44	18	17	35	72
Joliat, Aurel	Montreal	43	13	22	35	73

1931-32

Canadian Division

Team	GP	W	L	T	GF	GA	PTS
Montreal	48	25	16	7	128	111	57
*Toronto	48	23	18	7	155	127	53
Mtl. Maroons	48	19	22	7	142	139	45
NY Americans	48	16	24	8	95	142	40

American Division

Team	GP	W	L	T	GF	GA	PTS
New York	48	23	17	8	134	112	54
Chicago	48	18	19	11	86	101	47
Detroit	48	18	20	10	95	108	46
Boston	48	15	21	12	122	117	42

Leading Scorers

Player	Club	GP	G	A	PTS	PIM
Jackson, Harvey	Toronto	48	28	25	53	63
Primeau, Joe	Toronto	46	13	37	50	25
Morenz, Howie	Montreal	48	24	25	49	46
Conacher, Charlie	Toronto	44	34	14	48	66
Cook, Bill	New York	48	34	14	48	33
Trottier, Dave	Mtl. Maroons	48	26	18	44	94
Smith, Reg	Mtl. Maroons	43	11	33	44	49
Siebert, Albert	Mtl. Maroons	48	21	18	39	64
Joliat, Aurel	Montreal	48	15	24	39	46
Clapper, Aubrey	Boston	48	17	22	39	21

Hooley Smith played on Stanley Cup winners with the Ottawa Senators and Montreal Maroons during his 17-year NHL career.

1932-33

Canadian Division

Team	GP	W	L	T	GF	GA	PTS
Toronto	48	24	18	6	119	111	54
Mtl. Maroons	48	22	20	6	135	119	50
Montreal	48	18	25	5	92	115	41
NY Americans	48	15	22	11	91	118	41
Ottawa	48	11	27	10	88	131	32

American Division

Team	GP	W	L	T	GF	GA	PTS
Boston	48	25	15	8	124	88	58
Detroit	48	25	15	8	111	93	58
*New York	48	23	17	8	135	107	54
Chicago	48	16	20	12	88	101	44

Leading Scorers

Player	Club	GP	G	A	PTS	PIM
Cook, Bill	New York	48	28	22	50	51
Jackson, Harvey	Toronto	48	27	17	44	43
Northcott, Lawrence	Mtl. Maroons	48	22	21	43	30
Smith, Reg	Mtl. Maroons	48	20	21	41	66
Haynes, Paul	Mtl. Maroons	48	16	25	41	18
Joliat, Aurel	Montreal	48	18	21	39	53
Barry, Marty	Boston	48	24	13	37	40
Cook, Fred	New York	48	22	15	37	35
Stewart, Nels	Boston	47	18	18	36	62
Shore, Eddie	Boston	48	8	27	35	102
Boucher, Frank	New York	47	7	28	35	4
Morenz, Howie	Montreal	46	14	21	35	32
Gagnon, Johnny	Montreal	48	12	23	35	64

1933-34

Canadian Division

Team	GP	W	L	T	GF	GA	PTS
Toronto	48	26	13	9	174	119	61
Montreal	48	22	20	6	99	101	50
Mtl. Maroons	48	19	18	11	117	122	49
NY Americans	48	15	23	10	104	132	40
Ottawa	48	13	29	6	115	143	32

American Division

Team	GP	W	L	T	GF	GA	PTS
Detroit	48	24	14	10	113	98	58
*Chicago	48	20	17	11	88	83	51
New York	48	21	19	8	120	113	50
Boston	48	18	25	5	111	130	41

Leading Scorers

Player	Club	GP	G	A	PTS	PIM
Conacher, Charlie	Toronto	42	32	20	52	38
Primeau, Joe	Toronto	45	14	32	46	8
Boucher, Frank	New York	48	14	30	44	4
Barry, Marty	Boston	48	27	12	39	12
Dillon, Cecil	New York	48	13	26	39	10
Stewart, Nels	Boston	48	21	17	38	68
Jackson, Harvey	Toronto	38	20	18	38	38
Joliat, Aurel	Montreal	48	22	15	37	27
Smith, Reg	Mtl. Maroons	47	18	19	37	58
Thompson, Paul	Chicago	48	20	16	36	17

1934-35

Canadian Division

Team	GP	W	L	T	GF	GA	PTS
Toronto	48	30	14	4	157	111	64
*Mtl. Maroons	48	24	19	5	123	92	53
Montreal	48	19	23	6	110	145	44
NY Americans	48	12	27	9	100	142	33
St. Louis	48	11	31	6	86	144	28

American Division

Team	GP	W	L	T	GF	GA	PTS
Boston	48	26	16	6	129	112	58
Chicago	48	26	17	5	118	88	57
New York	48	22	20	6	137	139	50
Detroit	48	19	22	7	127	114	45

Leading Scorers

Player	Club	GP	G	A	PTS	PIM
Conacher, Charlie	Toronto	47	36	21	57	24
Howe, Syd	St.L., Det.	50	22	25	47	34
Aurie, Larry	Detroit	48	17	29	46	24
Boucher, Frank	New York	48	13	32	45	2
Jackson, Harvey	Toronto	42	22	22	44	27
Chapman, Art	NY Americans	47	9	34	43	4
Lewis, Herb	Detroit	47	16	27	43	26
Schriner, David	NY Americans	48	18	22	40	6
Barry, Marty	Boston	48	20	20	40	33
Stewart, Nels	Boston	47	21	18	39	45
Thompson, Paul	Chicago	48	16	23	39	20

Eddie Shore, one of the game's greatest defensemen, won four Hart Trophies during 14 years in the NHL.

1935-36

Canadian Division

Team	GP	W	L	T	GF	GA	PTS
Mtl. Maroons	48	22	16	10	114	106	54
Toronto	48	23	19	6	126	106	52
NY Americans	48	16	25	7	109	122	39
Montreal	48	11	26	11	82	123	33

American Division

Team	GP	W	L	T	GF	GA	PTS
*Detroit	48	24	16	8	124	103	56
Boston	48	22	20	6	92	83	50
Chicago	48	21	19	8	93	92	50
New York	48	19	17	12	91	96	50

Leading Scorers

Player	Club	GP	G	A	PTS	PIM
Schriner, David	NY Americans	48	19	26	45	8
Barry, Marty	Detroit	48	21	19	40	16
Thompson, Paul	Chicago	45	17	23	40	19
Romnes, Doc	Chicago	48	13	25	38	6
Thoms, Bill	Toronto	48	23	15	38	29
Conacher, Charlie	Toronto	44	23	15	38	74
Smith, Reg	Mtl. Maroons	47	19	19	38	75
Chapman, Art	NY Americans	47	10	28	38	14
Lewis, Herb	Detroit	45	14	23	37	25
Northcott, Lawrence	Mtl. Maroons	48	15	21	36	41

1936-37

Canadian Division

Team	GP	W	L	T	GF	GA	PTS
Montreal	48	24	18	6	115	111	54
Mtl. Maroons	48	22	17	9	126	110	53
Toronto	48	22	21	5	119	115	49
NY Americans	48	15	29	4	122	161	34

American Division

Team	GP	W	L	T	GF	GA	PTS
*Detroit	48	25	14	9	128	102	59
Boston	48	23	18	7	120	110	53
New York	48	19	20	9	117	106	47
Chicago	48	14	27	7	99	131	35

Leading Scorers

Player	Club	GP	G	A	PTS	PIM
Schriner, David	NY Americans	48	21	25	46	17
Apps, Syl	Toronto	48	16	29	45	10
Barry, Marty	Detroit	48	17	27	44	6
Aurie, Larry	Detroit	45	23	20	43	20
Jackson, Harvey	Toronto	46	21	19	40	12
Gagnon, Johnny	Montreal	48	20	16	36	38
Gracie, Bob	Mtl. Maroons	47	11	25	36	18
Stewart, Nels	Bos., NYA	43	23	12	35	37
Thompson, Paul	Chicago	47	17	18	35	28
Cowley, Bill	Boston	46	13	22	35	4

1937-38

Canadian Division

Team	GP	W	L	T	GF	GA	PTS
Toronto	48	24	15	9	151	127	57
NY Americans	48	19	18	11	110	111	49
Montreal	48	18	17	13	123	128	49
Mtl. Maroons	48	12	30	6	101	149	30

American Division

Team	GP	W	L	T	GF	GA	PTS
Boston	48	30	11	7	142	89	67
New York	48	27	15	6	149	96	60
*Chicago	48	14	25	9	97	139	37
Detroit	48	12	25	11	99	133	35

Leading Scorers

Player	Club	GP	G	A	PTS	PIM
Drillon, Gord	Toronto	48	26	26	52	4
Apps, Syl	Toronto	47	21	29	50	9
Thompson, Paul	Chicago	48	22	22	44	14
Mantha, Georges	Montreal	47	23	19	42	12
Dillon, Cecil	New York	48	21	18	39	6
Cowley, Bill	Boston	48	17	22	39	8
Schriner, David	NY Americans	49	21	17	38	22
Thoms, Bill	Toronto	48	14	24	38	14
Smith, Clint	New York	48	14	23	37	0
Colville, Neil	New York	45	17	19	36	11
Stewart, Nels	NY Americans	48	19	17	36	29

1938-39

Team	GP	W	L	T	GF	GA	PTS
*Boston	48	36	10	2	156	76	74
New York	48	26	16	6	149	105	58
Toronto	48	19	20	9	114	107	47
NY Americans	48	17	21	10	119	157	44
Detroit	48	18	24	6	107	128	42
Montreal	48	15	24	9	115	146	39
Chicago	48	12	28	8	91	132	32

Leading Scorers

Player	Club	GP	G	A	PTS	PIM
Blake, Hector	Montreal	48	24	23	47	10
Schriner, David	NY Americans	48	13	31	44	20
Cowley, Bill	Boston	34	8	34	42	2
Barry, Marty	Detroit	48	13	28	41	4
Smith, Clint	New York	48	21	20	41	2
Anderson, Tom	NY Americans	48	13	27	40	14
Apps, Syl	Toronto	44	15	25	40	4
Gottselig, Johnny	Chicago	48	16	23	39	15
Haynes, Paul	Montreal	47	5	33	38	27
Carr, Lorne	NY Americans	46	19	18	37	16
Colville, Neil	New York	48	18	19	37	12
Conacher, Roy	Boston	47	26	11	37	12
Watson, Phil	New York	48	15	22	37	42

1939-40

Team	GP	W	L	T	GF	GA	PTS
Boston	48	31	12	5	170	98	67
*New York	48	27	11	10	136	77	64
Toronto	48	25	17	6	134	110	56
Chicago	48	23	19	6	112	120	52
Detroit	48	16	26	6	90	126	38
NY Americans	48	15	29	4	106	140	34
Montreal	48	10	33	5	90	167	25

Leading Scorers

Player	Club	GP	G	A	PTS	PIM
Schmidt, Milt	Boston	48	22	30	52	37
Dumart, Woody	Boston	48	22	21	43	16
Bauer, Bob	Boston	48	17	26	43	2
Drillon, Gord	Toronto	43	21	19	40	13
Cowley, Bill	Boston	48	13	27	40	24
Hextall, Bryan	New York	48	24	15	39	52
Colville, Neil	New York	48	19	19	38	22
Howe, Syd	Detroit	46	14	23	37	17
Armstrong, Murray	NY Americans	48	16	20	36	12
Blake, Hector	Montreal	48	17	19	36	48

1940-41

Team	GP	W	L	T	GF	GA	PTS
*Boston	48	27	8	13	168	102	67
Toronto	48	28	14	6	145	99	62
Detroit	48	21	16	11	112	102	53
New York	48	21	19	8	143	125	50
Chicago	48	16	25	7	112	139	39
Montreal	48	16	26	6	121	147	38
NY Americans	48	8	29	11	99	186	27

Leading Scorers

Player	Club	GP	G	A	PTS	PIM
Cowley, Bill	Boston	46	17	45	62	16
Hextall, Bryan	New York	48	26	18	44	16
Drillon, Gord	Toronto	42	23	21	44	2
Apps, Syl	Toronto	41	20	24	44	6
Patrick, Lynn	New York	48	20	24	44	12
Howe, Syd	Detroit	48	20	24	44	8
Colville, Neil	New York	48	14	28	42	28
Wiseman, Eddie	Boston	48	16	24	40	10
Bauer, Bobby	Boston	48	17	22	39	2
Schriner, David	Toronto	48	24	14	38	6
Conacher, Roy	Boston	40	24	14	38	7
Schmidt, Milt	Boston	44	13	25	38	23

1941-42

Team	GP	W	L	T	GF	GA	PTS
New York	48	29	17	2	177	143	60
*Toronto	48	27	18	3	158	136	57
Boston	48	25	17	6	160	118	56
Chicago	48	22	23	3	145	155	47
Detroit	48	19	25	4	140	147	42
Montreal	48	18	27	3	134	173	39
NY Americans	48	16	29	3	133	175	35

Leading Scorers

Player	Club	GP	G	A	PTS	PIM
Hextall, Bryan	New York	48	24	32	56	30
Patrick, Lynn	New York	47	32	22	54	18
Grosso, Don	Detroit	48	23	30	53	13
Watson, Phil	New York	48	15	37	52	48
Abel, Sid	Detroit	48	18	31	49	45
Blake, Hector	Montreal	47	17	28	45	19
Thoms, Bill	Chicago	47	15	30	45	8
Drillon, Gord	Toronto	48	23	18	41	6
Apps, Syl	Toronto	38	18	23	41	0
Anderson, Tom	NY Americans	48	12	29	41	54

1942-43

Team	GP	W	L	T	GF	GA	PTS
*Detroit	50	25	14	11	169	124	61
Boston	50	24	17	9	195	176	57
Toronto	50	22	19	9	198	159	53
Montreal	50	19	19	12	181	191	50
Chicago	50	17	18	15	179	180	49
New York	50	11	31	8	161	253	30

Leading Scorers

Player	Club	GP	G	A	PTS	PIM
Bentley, Doug	Chicago	50	33	40	73	18
Cowley, Bill	Boston	48	27	45	72	10
Bentley, Max	Chicago	47	26	44	70	2
Patrick, Lynn	New York	50	22	39	61	28
Carr, Lorne	Toronto	50	27	33	60	15
Taylor, Billy	Toronto	50	18	42	60	2
Hextall, Bryan	New York	50	27	32	59	28
Blake, Hector	Montreal	48	23	36	59	28
Lach, Elmer	Montreal	45	18	40	58	14
O'Connor, Herb	Montreal	50	15	43	58	2

1943-44

Team	GP	W	L	T	GF	GA	PTS
*Montreal	50	38	5	7	234	109	83
Detroit	50	26	18	6	214	177	58
Toronto	50	23	23	4	214	174	50
Chicago	50	22	23	5	178	187	49
Boston	50	19	26	5	223	268	43
New York	50	6	39	5	162	310	17

Leading Scorers

Player	Club	GP	G	A	PTS	PIM
Cain, Herb	Boston	48	36	46	82	4
Bentley, Doug	Chicago	50	38	39	77	22
Carr, Lorne	Toronto	50	36	38	74	9
Liscombe, Carl	Detroit	50	36	37	73	17
Lach, Elmer	Montreal	48	24	48	72	23
Smith, Clint	Chicago	50	23	49	72	4
Cowley, Bill	Boston	36	30	41	71	12
Mosienko, Bill	Chicago	50	32	38	70	10
Jackson, Art	Boston	49	28	41	69	8
Bodnar, Gus	Toronto	50	22	40	62	18

1944-45

Team	GP	W	L	T	GF	GA	PTS
Montreal	50	38	8	4	228	121	80
Detroit	50	31	14	5	218	161	67
*Toronto	50	24	22	4	183	161	52
Boston	50	16	30	4	179	219	36
Chicago	50	13	30	7	141	194	33
New York	50	11	29	10	154	247	32

Leading Scorers

Player	Club	GP	G	A	PTS	PIM
Lach, Elmer	Montreal	50	26	54	80	37
Richard, Maurice	Montreal	50	50	23	73	36
Blake, Hector	Montreal	49	29	38	67	15
Cowley, Bill	Boston	49	25	40	65	2
Kennedy, Ted	Toronto	49	29	25	54	14
Mosienko, Bill	Chicago	50	28	26	54	4
Carveth, Joe	Detroit	50	26	28	54	6
DeMarco, Albert	New York	50	24	30	54	10
Smith, Clint	Chicago	50	23	31	54	0
Howe, Syd	Detroit	46	17	36	53	6

Syd Howe played for five teams in his first six NHL seasons before arriving in Detroit and helping the Red Wings to three Stanley Cup Championships.

Ted Lindsay, here being checked by Neil Colville and Billy Moe of the Rangers, helped the Wings win four Stanley Cups in the 1950s.

1945-46

Team	GP	W	L	T	GF	GA	PTS
*Montreal	50	28	17	5	172	134	61
Boston	50	24	18	8	167	156	56
Chicago	50	23	20	7	200	178	53
Detroit	50	20	20	10	146	159	50
Toronto	50	19	24	7	174	185	45
New York	50	13	28	9	144	191	35

Leading Scorers

Player	Club	GP	G	A	PTS	PIM
Bentley, Max	Chicago	47	31	30	61	6
Stewart, Gaye	Toronto	50	37	15	52	8
Blake, Hector	Montreal	50	29	21	50	2
Smith, Clint	Chicago	50	26	24	50	2
Richard, Maurice	Montreal	50	27	21	48	50
Mosienko, Bill	Chicago	40	18	30	48	12
DeMarco, Albert	New York	50	20	27	47	20
Lach, Elmer	Montreal	50	13	34	47	34
Kaleta, Alex	Chicago	49	19	27	46	17
Taylor, Billy	Toronto	48	23	18	41	14
Horeck, Pete	Chicago	50	20	21	41	34

1946-47

Team	GP	W	L	T	GF	GA	PTS
Montreal	60	34	16	10	189	138	78
*Toronto	60	31	19	10	209	172	72
Boston	60	26	23	11	190	175	63
Detroit	60	22	27	11	190	193	55
New York	60	22	32	6	167	186	50
Chicago	60	19	37	4	193	274	42

Leading Scorers

Player	Club	GP	G	A	PTS	PIM
Bentley, Max	Chicago	60	29	43	72	12
Richard, Maurice	Montreal	60	45	26	71	69
Taylor, Billy	Detroit	60	17	46	63	35
Schmidt, Milt	Boston	59	27	35	62	40
Kennedy, Ted	Toronto	60	28	32	60	27
Bentley, Doug	Chicago	52	21	34	55	18
Bauer, Bob	Boston	58	30	24	54	4
Conacher, Roy	Detroit	60	30	24	54	6
Mosienko, Bill	Chicago	59	25	27	52	2
Dumart, Woody	Boston	60	24	28	52	12

1947-48

Team	GP	W	L	T	GF	GA	PTS
*Toronto	60	32	15	13	182	143	77
Detroit	60	30	18	12	187	148	72
Boston	60	23	24	13	167	168	59
New York	60	21	26	13	176	201	55
Montreal	60	20	29	11	147	169	51
Chicago	60	20	34	6	195	225	46

Leading Scorers

Player	Club	GP	G	A	PTS	PIM
Lach, Elmer	Montreal	60	30	31	61	72
O'Connor, Buddy	New York	60	24	36	60	8
Bentley, Doug	Chicago	60	20	37	57	16
Stewart, Gaye	Tor., Chi.	61	27	29	56	83
Bentley, Max	Chi., Tor.	59	26	28	54	14
Poile, Bud	Tor., Chi.	58	25	29	54	17
Richard, Maurice	Montreal	53	28	25	53	89
Apps, Syl	Toronto	55	26	27	53	12
Lindsay, Ted	Detroit	60	33	19	52	95
Conacher, Roy	Chicago	52	22	27	49	4

1948-49

Team	GP	W	L	T	GF	GA	PTS
Detroit	60	34	19	7	195	145	75
Boston	60	29	23	8	178	163	66
Montreal	60	28	23	9	152	126	65
*Toronto	60	22	25	13	147	161	57
Chicago	60	21	31	8	173	211	50
New York	60	18	31	11	133	172	47

Leading Scorers

Player	Club	GP	G	A	PTS	PIM
Conacher, Roy	Chicago	60	26	42	68	8
Bentley, Doug	Chicago	58	23	43	66	38
Abel, Sid	Detroit	60	28	26	54	49
Lindsay, Ted	Detroit	50	26	28	54	97
Conacher, Jim	Det., Chi.	59	26	23	49	43
Ronty, Paul	Boston	60	20	29	49	11
Watson, Harry	Toronto	60	26	19	45	0
Reay, Billy	Montreal	60	22	23	45	33
Bodnar, Gus	Chicago	59	19	26	45	14
Peirson, John	Boston	59	22	21	43	45

1949-50

Team	GP	W	L	T	GF	GA	PTS
*Detroit	70	37	19	14	229	164	88
Montreal	70	29	22	19	172	150	77
Toronto	70	31	27	12	176	173	74
New York	70	28	31	11	170	189	67
Boston	70	22	32	16	198	228	60
Chicago	70	22	38	10	203	244	54

Leading Scorers

Player	Club	GP	G	A	PTS	PIM
Lindsay, Ted	Detroit	69	23	55	78	141
Abel, Sid	Detroit	69	34	35	69	46
Howe, Gordie	Detroit	70	35	33	68	69
Richard, Maurice	Montreal	70	43	22	65	114
Ronty, Paul	Boston	70	23	36	59	8
Conacher, Roy	Chicago	70	25	31	56	16
Bentley, Doug	Chicago	64	20	33	53	28
Peirson, John	Boston	57	27	25	52	49
Prystai, Metro	Chicago	65	29	22	51	31
Guidolin, Bep	Chicago	70	17	34	51	42

1950-51

Team	GP	W	L	T	GF	GA	PTS
Detroit	70	44	13	13	236	139	101
*Toronto	70	41	16	13	212	138	95
Montreal	70	25	30	15	173	184	65
Boston	70	22	30	18	178	197	62
New York	70	20	29	21	169	201	62
Chicago	70	13	47	10	171	280	36

Leading Scorers

Player	Club	GP	G	A	PTS	PIM
Howe, Gordie	Detroit	70	43	43	86	74
Richard, Maurice	Montreal	65	42	24	66	97
Bentley, Max	Toronto	67	21	41	62	34
Abel, Sid	Detroit	69	23	38	61	30
Schmidt, Milt	Boston	62	22	39	61	33
Kennedy, Ted	Toronto	63	18	43	61	32
Lindsay, Ted	Detroit	67	24	35	59	110
Sloan, Tod	Toronto	70	31	25	56	105
Kelly, Red	Detroit	70	17	37	54	24
Smith, Sid	Toronto	70	30	21	51	10
Gardner, Cal	Toronto	66	23	28	51	42

1951-52

Team	GP	W	L	T	GF	GA	PTS
*Detroit	70	44	14	12	215	133	100
Montreal	70	34	26	10	195	164	78
Toronto	70	29	25	16	168	157	74
Boston	70	25	29	16	162	176	66
New York	70	23	34	13	192	219	59
Chicago	70	17	44	9	158	241	43

Leading Scorers

Player	Club	GP	G	A	PTS	PIM
Howe, Gordie	Detroit	70	47	39	86	78
Lindsay, Ted	Detroit	70	30	39	69	123
Lach, Elmer	Montreal	70	15	50	65	36
Raleigh, Don	New York	70	19	42	61	14
Smith, Sid	Toronto	70	27	30	57	6
Geoffrion, Bernie	Montreal	67	30	24	54	66
Mosienko, Bill	Chicago	70	31	22	53	10
Abel, Sid	Detroit	62	17	36	53	32
Kennedy, Ted	Toronto	70	19	33	52	33
Schmidt, Milt	Boston	69	21	29	50	57
Peirson, John	Boston	68	20	30	50	30

1952-53

Team	GP	W	L	T	GF	GA	PTS
Detroit	70	36	16	18	222	133	90
*Montreal	70	28	23	19	155	148	75
Boston	70	28	29	13	152	172	69
Chicago	70	27	28	15	169	175	69
Toronto	70	27	30	13	156	167	67
New York	70	17	37	16	152	211	50

Leading Scorers

Player	Club	GP	G	A	PTS	PIM
Howe, Gordie	Detroit	70	49	46	95	57
Lindsay, Ted	Detroit	70	32	39	71	111
Richard, Maurice	Montreal	70	28	33	61	112
Hergesheimer, Wally	New York	70	30	29	59	10
Delvecchio, Alex	Detroit	70	16	43	59	28
Ronty, Paul	New York	70	16	38	54	20
Prystai, Metro	Detroit	70	16	34	50	12
Kelly, Red	Detroit	70	19	27	46	8
Olmstead, Bert	Montreal	69	17	28	45	83
Mackell, Fleming	Boston	65	27	17	44	63
McFadden, Jim	Chicago	70	23	21	44	29

1953-54

Team	GP	W	L	T	GF	GA	PTS
*Detroit	70	37	19	14	191	132	88
Montreal	70	35	24	11	195	141	81
Toronto	70	32	24	14	152	131	78
Boston	70	32	28	10	177	181	74
New York	70	29	31	10	161	182	68
Chicago	70	12	51	7	133	242	31

Leading Scorers

Player	Club	GP	G	A	PTS	PIM
Howe, Gordie	Detroit	70	33	48	81	109
Richard, Maurice	Montreal	70	37	30	67	112
Lindsay, Ted	Detroit	70	26	36	62	110
Geoffrion, Bernie	Montreal	54	29	25	54	87
Olmstead, Bert	Montreal	70	15	37	52	85
Kelly, Red	Detroit	62	16	33	49	18
Reibel, Earl	Detroit	69	15	33	48	18
Sandford, Ed	Boston	70	16	31	47	42
Mackell, Fleming	Boston	67	15	32	47	60
Mosdell, Ken	Montreal	67	22	24	46	64
Ronty, Paul	New York	70	13	33	46	18

1954-55

Team	GP	W	L	T	GF	GA	PTS
*Detroit	70	42	17	11	204	134	95
Montreal	70	41	18	11	228	157	93
Toronto	70	24	24	22	147	135	70
Boston	70	23	26	21	169	188	67
New York	70	17	35	18	150	210	52
Chicago	70	13	40	17	161	235	43

Leading Scorers

Player	Club	GP	G	A	PTS	PIM
Geoffrion, Bernie	Montreal	70	38	37	75	57
Richard, Maurice	Montreal	67	38	36	74	125
Beliveau, Jean	Montreal	70	37	36	73	58
Reibel, Earl	Detroit	70	25	41	66	15
Howe, Gordie	Detroit	64	29	33	62	68
Sullivan, George	Chicago	69	19	42	61	51
Olmstead, Bert	Montreal	70	10	48	58	103
Smith, Sid	Toronto	70	33	21	54	14
Mosdell, Ken	Montreal	70	22	32	54	82
Lewicki, Danny	New York	70	29	24	53	8

1955-56

Team	GP	W	L	T	GF	GA	PTS
*Montreal	70	45	15	10	222	131	100
Detroit	70	30	24	16	183	148	76
New York	70	32	28	10	204	203	74
Toronto	70	24	33	13	153	181	61
Boston	70	23	34	13	147	185	59
Chicago	70	19	39	12	155	216	50

Leading Scorers

Player	Club	GP	G	A	PTS	PIM
Beliveau, Jean	Montreal	70	47	41	88	143
Howe, Gordie	Detroit	70	38	41	79	100
Richard, Maurice	Montreal	70	38	33	71	89
Olmstead, Bert	Montreal	70	14	56	70	94
Sloan, Tod	Toronto	70	37	29	66	100
Bathgate, Andy	New York	70	19	47	66	59
Geoffrion, Bernie	Montreal	59	29	33	62	66
Reibel, Earl	Detroit	68	17	39	56	10
Delvecchio, Alex	Detroit	70	25	26	51	24
Creighton, Dave	New York	70	20	31	51	43
Gadsby, Bill	New York	70	9	42	51	84

1956-57

Team	GP	W	L	T	GF	GA	PTS
Detroit	70	38	20	12	198	157	88
*Montreal	70	35	23	12	210	155	82
Boston	70	34	24	12	195	174	80
New York	70	26	30	14	184	227	66
Toronto	70	21	34	15	174	192	57
Chicago	70	16	39	15	169	225	47

Leading Scorers

Player	Club	GP	G	A	PTS	PIM
Howe, Gordie	Detroit	70	44	45	89	72
Lindsay, Ted	Detroit	70	30	55	85	103
Beliveau, Jean	Montreal	69	33	51	84	105
Bathgate, Andy	New York	70	27	50	77	60
Litzenberger, Ed	Chicago	70	32	32	64	48
Richard, Maurice	Montreal	63	33	29	62	74
McKenney, Don	Boston	69	21	39	60	31
Moore, Dickie	Montreal	70	29	29	58	56
Richard, Henri	Montreal	63	18	36	54	71
Ullman, Norm	Detroit	64	16	36	52	47

1957-58

Team	GP	W	L	T	GF	GA	PTS
*Montreal	70	43	17	10	250	158	96
New York	70	32	25	13	195	188	77
Detroit	70	29	29	12	176	207	70
Boston	70	27	28	15	199	194	69
Chicago	70	24	39	7	163	202	55
Toronto	70	21	38	11	192	226	53

Leading Scorers

Player	Club	GP	G	A	PTS	PIM
Moore, Dickie	Montreal	70	36	48	84	65
Richard, Henri	Montreal	67	28	52	80	56
Bathgate, Andy	New York	65	30	48	78	42
Howe, Gordie	Detroit	64	33	44	77	40
Horvath, Bronco	Boston	67	30	36	66	71
Litzenberger, Ed	Chicago	70	32	30	62	63
Mackell, Fleming	Boston	70	20	40	60	72
Beliveau, Jean	Montreal	55	27	32	59	93
Delvecchio, Alex	Detroit	70	21	38	59	22
McKenney, Don	Boston	70	28	30	58	22

1958-59

Team	GP	W	L	T	GF	GA	PTS
*Montreal	70	39	18	13	258	158	91
Boston	70	32	29	9	205	215	73
Chicago	70	28	29	13	197	208	69
Toronto	70	27	32	11	189	201	65
New York	70	26	32	12	201	217	64
Detroit	70	25	37	8	167	218	58

Leading Scorers

Player	Club	GP	G	A	PTS	PIM
Moore, Dickie	Montreal	70	41	55	96	61
Beliveau, Jean	Montreal	64	45	46	91	67
Bathgate, Andy	New York	70	40	48	88	48
Howe, Gordie	Detroit	70	32	46	78	57
Litzenberger, Ed	Chicago	70	33	44	77	37
Geoffrion, Bernie	Montreal	59	22	44	66	30
Sullivan, George	New York	70	21	42	63	56
Hebenton, Andy	New York	70	33	29	62	8
McKenney, Don	Boston	70	32	30	62	20
Sloan, Tod	Chicago	59	27	35	62	79

1959-60

Team	GP	W	L	T	GF	GA	PTS
*Montreal	70	40	18	12	255	178	92
Toronto	70	35	26	9	199	195	79
Chicago	70	28	29	13	191	180	69
Detroit	70	26	29	15	186	197	67
Boston	70	28	34	8	220	241	64
New York	70	17	38	15	187	247	49

Leading Scorers

Player	Club	GP	G	A	PTS	PIM
Hull, Bobby	Chicago	70	39	42	81	68
Horvath, Bronco	Boston	68	39	41	80	60
Beliveau, Jean	Montreal	60	34	40	74	57
Bathgate, Andy	New York	70	26	48	74	28
Richard, Henri	Montreal	70	30	43	73	66
Howe, Gordie	Detroit	70	28	45	73	46
Geoffrion, Bernie	Montreal	59	30	41	71	36
McKenney, Don	Boston	70	20	49	69	28
Stasiuk, Vic	Boston	69	29	39	68	121
Prentice, Dean	New York	70	32	34	66	43

1960-61

Team	GP	W	L	T	GF	GA	PTS
Montreal	70	41	19	10	254	188	92
Toronto	70	39	19	12	234	176	90
*Chicago	70	29	24	17	198	180	75
Detroit	70	25	29	16	195	215	66
New York	70	22	38	10	204	248	54
Boston	70	15	42	13	176	254	43

Leading Scorers

Player	Club	GP	G	A	PTS	PIM
Geoffrion, Bernie	Montreal	64	50	45	95	29
Béliveau, Jean	Montreal	69	32	58	90	57
Mahovlich, Frank	Toronto	70	48	36	84	131
Bathgate, Andy	New York	70	29	48	77	22
Howe, Gordie	Detroit	64	23	49	72	30
Ullman, Norm	Detroit	70	28	42	70	34
Kelly, Red	Toronto	64	20	50	70	12
Moore, Dickie	Montreal	57	35	34	69	62
Richard, Henri	Montreal	70	24	44	68	91
Delvecchio, Alex	Detroit	70	27	35	62	26

1961-62

Team	GP	W	L	T	GF	GA	PTS
Montreal	70	42	14	14	259	166	98
*Toronto	70	37	22	11	232	180	85
Chicago	70	31	26	13	217	186	75
New York	70	26	32	12	195	207	64
Detroit	70	23	33	14	184	219	60
Boston	70	15	47	8	177	306	38

Leading Scorers

Player	Club	GP	G	A	PTS	PIM
Hull, Bobby	Chicago	70	50	34	84	35
Bathgate, Andy	New York	70	28	56	84	44
Howe, Gordie	Detroit	70	33	44	77	54
Mikita, Stan	Chicago	70	25	52	77	97
Mahovlich, Frank	Toronto	70	33	38	71	87
Delvecchio, Alex	Detroit	70	26	43	69	18
Backstrom, Ralph	Montreal	66	27	38	65	29
Ullman, Norm	Detroit	70	26	38	64	54
Hay, Bill	Chicago	60	11	52	63	34
Provost, Claude	Montreal	70	33	29	62	22

1962-63

Team	GP	W	L	T	GF	GA	PTS
*Toronto	70	35	23	12	221	180	82
Chicago	70	32	21	17	194	178	81
Montreal	70	28	19	23	225	183	79
Detroit	70	32	25	13	200	194	77
New York	70	22	36	12	211	233	56
Boston	70	14	39	17	198	281	45

Leading Scorers

Player	Club	GP	G	A	PTS	PIM
Howe, Gordie	Detroit	70	38	48	86	100
Bathgate, Andy	New York	70	35	46	81	54
Mikita, Stan	Chicago	65	31	45	76	69
Mahovlich, Frank	Toronto	67	36	37	73	56
Richard, Henri	Montreal	67	23	50	73	57
Beliveau, Jean	Montreal	69	18	49	67	68
Bucyk, John	Boston	69	27	39	66	36
Delvecchio, Alex	Detroit	70	20	44	64	8
Hull, Bobby	Chicago	65	31	31	62	27
Oliver, Murray	Boston	65	22	40	62	38

1963-64

Team	GP	W	L	T	GF	GA	PTS
Montreal	70	36	21	13	209	167	85
Chicago	70	36	22	12	218	169	84
*Toronto	70	33	25	12	192	172	78
Detroit	70	30	29	11	191	204	71
New York	70	22	38	10	186	242	54
Boston	70	18	40	12	170	212	48

Leading Scorers

Player	Club	GP	G	A	PTS	PIM
Mikita, Stan	Chicago	70	39	50	89	146
Hull, Bobby	Chicago	70	43	44	87	50
Beliveau, Jean	Montreal	68	28	50	78	42
Bathgate, Andy	NYR, Tor.	71	19	58	77	34
Howe, Gordie	Detroit	69	26	47	73	70
Wharram, Ken	Chicago	70	39	32	71	18
Oliver, Murray	Boston	70	24	44	68	41
Goyette, Phil	New York	67	24	41	65	15
Gilbert, Rod	New York	70	24	40	64	62
Keon, Dave	Toronto	70	23	37	60	6

1964-65

Team	GP	W	L	T	GF	GA	PTS
Detroit	70	40	23	7	224	175	87
*Montreal	70	36	23	11	211	185	83
Chicago	70	34	28	8	224	176	76
Toronto	70	30	26	14	204	173	74
New York	70	20	38	12	179	246	52
Boston	70	21	43	6	166	253	48

Leading Scorers

Player	Club	GP	G	A	PTS	PIM
Mikita, Stan	Chicago	70	28	59	87	154
Ullman, Norm	Detroit	70	42	41	83	70
Howe, Gordie	Detroit	70	29	47	76	104
Hull, Bobby	Chicago	61	39	32	71	32
Delvecchio, Alex	Detroit	68	25	42	67	16
Provost, Claude	Montreal	70	27	37	64	28
Gilbert, Rod	New York	70	25	36	61	52
Pilote, Pierre	Chicago	68	14	45	59	162
Bucyk, John	Boston	68	26	29	55	24
Backstrom, Ralph	Montreal	70	25	30	55	41
Esposito, Phil	Chicago	70	23	32	55	44

1965-66

Team	GP	W	L	T	GF	GA	PTS
*Montreal	70	41	21	8	239	173	90
Chicago	70	37	25	8	240	187	82
Toronto	70	34	25	11	208	187	79
Detroit	70	31	27	12	221	194	74
Boston	70	21	43	6	174	275	48
New York	70	18	41	11	195	261	47

Leading Scorers

Player	Club	GP	G	A	PTS	PIM
Hull, Bobby	Chicago	65	54	43	97	70
Mikita, Stan	Chicago	68	30	48	78	58
Rousseau, Bobby	Montreal	70	30	48	78	20
Beliveau, Jean	Montreal	67	29	48	77	50
Howe, Gordie	Detroit	70	29	46	75	83
Ullman, Norm	Detroit	70	31	41	72	35
Delvecchio, Alex	Detroit	70	31	38	69	16
Nevin, Bob	New York	69	29	33	62	10
Richard, Henri	Montreal	62	22	39	61	47
Oliver, Murray	Boston	70	18	42	60	30

1966-67

Team	GP	W	L	T	GF	GA	PTS
Chicago	70	41	17	12	264	170	94
Montreal	70	32	25	13	202	188	77
*Toronto	70	32	27	11	204	211	75
New York	70	30	28	12	188	189	72
Detroit	70	27	39	4	212	241	58
Boston	70	17	43	10	182	253	44

Leading Scorers

Player	Club	GP	G	A	PTS	PIM
Mikita, Stan	Chicago	70	35	62	97	12
Hull, Bobby	Chicago	66	52	28	80	52
Ullman, Norm	Detroit	68	26	44	70	26
Wharram, Ken	Chicago	70	31	34	65	21
Howe, Gordie	Detroit	69	25	40	65	53
Rousseau, Bobby	Montreal	68	19	44	63	58
Esposito, Phil	Chicago	69	21	40	61	40
Goyette, Phil	New York	70	12	49	61	6
Mohns, Doug	Chicago	61	25	35	60	58
Richard, Henri	Montreal	65	21	34	55	28
Delvecchio, Alex	Detroit	70	17	38	55	10

1967-68
East Division

Team	GP	W	L	T	GF	GA	PTS
*Montreal	74	42	22	10	236	167	94
New York	74	39	23	12	226	183	90
Boston	74	37	27	10	259	216	84
Chicago	74	32	26	16	212	222	80
Toronto	74	33	31	10	209	176	76
Detroit	74	27	35	12	245	257	66

West Division

Team	GP	W	L	T	GF	GA	PTS
Philadelphia	74	31	32	11	173	179	73
Los Angeles	74	31	33	10	200	224	72
St. Louis	74	27	31	16	177	191	70
Minnesota	74	27	32	15	191	226	69
Pittsburgh	74	27	34	13	195	216	67
Oakland	74	15	42	17	153	219	47

Leading Scorers

Player	Club	GP	G	A	PTS	PIM
Mikita, Stan	Chicago	72	40	47	87	14
Esposito, Phil	Boston	74	35	49	84	21
Howe, Gordie	Detroit	74	39	43	82	53
Ratelle, Jean	New York	74	32	46	78	18
Gilbert, Rod	New York	73	29	48	77	12
Hull, Bobby	Chicago	71	44	31	75	39
Ullman, Norm	Det., Tor.	71	35	37	72	28
Delvecchio, Alex	Detroit	74	22	48	70	14
Bucyk, John	Boston	72	30	39	69	8
Wharram, Ken	Chicago	74	27	42	69	18

1968-69
East Division

Team	GP	W	L	T	GF	GA	PTS
*Montreal	76	46	19	11	271	202	103
Boston	76	42	18	16	303	221	100
New York	76	41	26	9	231	196	91
Toronto	76	35	26	15	234	217	85
Detroit	76	33	31	12	239	221	78
Chicago	76	34	33	9	280	246	77

West Division

Team	GP	W	L	T	GF	GA	PTS
St. Louis	76	37	25	14	204	157	88
Oakland	76	29	36	11	219	251	69
Philadelphia	76	20	35	21	174	225	61
Los Angeles	76	24	42	10	185	260	58
Pittsburgh	76	20	45	11	189	252	51
Minnesota	76	18	43	15	189	270	51

Leading Scorers

Player	Club	GP	G	A	PTS	PIM
Esposito, Phil	Boston	74	49	77	126	79
Hull, Bobby	Chicago	74	58	49	107	48
Howe, Gordie	Detroit	76	44	59	103	58
Mikita, Stan	Chicago	74	30	67	97	52
Hodge, Ken	Boston	75	45	45	90	75
Cournoyer, Yvan	Montreal	76	43	44	87	31
Delvecchio, Alex	Detroit	72	25	58	83	8
Berenson, Red	St. Louis	76	35	47	82	43
Beliveau, Jean	Montreal	69	33	49	82	55
Mahovlich, Frank	Detroit	76	49	29	78	38
Ratelle, Jean	New York	75	32	46	78	26

Members of the "Scooter Line" (left to right):
Ken Wharram, Stan Mikita and Doug Mohns
finished in the top ten in 1965-66.

1969-70

East Division

Team	GP	W	L	T	GF	GA	PTS
Chicago	76	45	22	9	250	170	99
*Boston	76	40	17	19	277	216	99
Detroit	76	40	21	15	246	199	95
New York	76	38	22	16	246	189	92
Montreal	76	38	22	16	244	201	92
Toronto	76	29	34	13	222	242	71

West Division

Team	GP	W	L	T	GF	GA	PTS
St. Louis	76	37	27	12	224	179	86
Pittsburgh	76	26	38	12	182	238	64
Minnesota	76	19	35	22	224	257	60
Oakland	76	22	40	14	169	243	58
Philadelphia	76	17	35	24	197	225	58
Los Angeles	76	14	52	10	168	290	38

Leading Scorers

Player	Club	GP	G	A	PTS	PIM
Orr, Bobby	Boston	76	33	87	120	125
Esposito, Phil	Boston	76	43	56	99	50
Mikita, Stan	Chicago	76	39	47	86	50
Goyette, Phil	St. Louis	72	29	49	78	16
Tkaczuk, Walt	New York	76	27	50	77	38
Ratelle, Jean	New York	75	32	42	74	28
Berenson, Red	St. Louis	67	33	39	72	38
Parise, Jean-Paul	Minnesota	74	24	48	72	72
Howe, Gordie	Detroit	76	31	40	71	58
Mahovlich, Frank	Detroit	74	38	32	70	59
Balon, Dave	New York	76	33	37	70	100
McKenzie, John	Boston	72	29	41	70	114

1970-71

East Division

Team	GP	W	L	T	GF	GA	PTS
Boston	78	57	14	7	399	207	121
New York	78	49	18	11	259	177	109
*Montreal	78	42	23	13	291	216	97
Toronto	78	37	33	8	248	211	82
Buffalo	78	24	39	15	217	291	63
Vancouver	78	24	46	8	229	296	56
Detroit	78	22	45	11	209	308	55

West Division

Team	GP	W	L	T	GF	GA	PTS
Chicago	78	49	20	9	277	184	107
St. Louis	78	34	25	19	223	208	87
Philadelphia	78	28	33	17	207	225	73
Minnesota	78	28	34	16	191	223	72
Los Angeles	78	25	40	13	239	303	63
Pittsburgh	78	21	37	20	221	240	62
California	78	20	53	5	199	320	45

Leading Scorers

Player	Club	GP	G	A	PTS	PIM
Esposito, Phil	Boston	78	76	76	152	71
Orr, Bobby	Boston	78	37	102	139	91
Bucyk, John	Boston	78	51	65	116	8
Hodge, Ken	Boston	78	43	62	105	113
Hull, Bobby	Chicago	78	44	52	96	32
Ullman, Norm	Toronto	73	34	51	85	24
Cashman, Wayne	Boston	77	21	58	79	100
McKenzie, John	Boston	65	31	46	77	120
Keon, Dave	Toronto	76	38	38	76	4
Beliveau, Jean	Montreal	70	25	51	76	40
Stanfield, Fred	Boston	75	24	52	76	12

1971-72

East Division

Team	GP	W	L	T	GF	GA	PTS
*Boston	78	54	13	11	330	204	119
New York	78	48	17	13	317	192	109
Montreal	78	46	16	16	307	205	108
Toronto	78	33	31	14	209	208	80
Detroit	78	33	35	10	261	262	76
Buffalo	78	16	43	19	203	289	51
Vancouver	78	20	50	8	203	297	48

West Division

Team	GP	W	L	T	GF	GA	PTS
Chicago	78	46	17	15	256	166	107
Minnesota	78	37	29	12	212	191	86
St. Louis	78	28	39	11	208	247	67
Pittsburgh	78	26	38	14	220	258	66
Philadelphia	78	26	38	14	200	236	66
California	78	21	39	18	216	288	60
Los Angeles	78	20	49	9	206	305	49

Leading Scorers

Player	Club	GP	G	A	PTS	PIM
Esposito, Phil	Boston	76	66	67	133	76
Orr, Bobby	Boston	76	37	80	117	106
Ratelle, Jean	New York	63	46	63	109	4
Hadfield, Vic	New York	78	50	56	106	142
Gilbert, Rod	New York	73	43	54	97	64
Mahovlich, Frank	Montreal	76	43	53	96	36
Hull, Bobby	Chicago	78	50	43	93	24
Cournoyer, Yvan	Montreal	73	47	36	83	15
Bucyk, John	Boston	78	32	51	83	4
Clarke, Bobby	Philadelphia	78	35	46	81	87
Lemaire, Jacques	Montreal	77	32	49	81	26

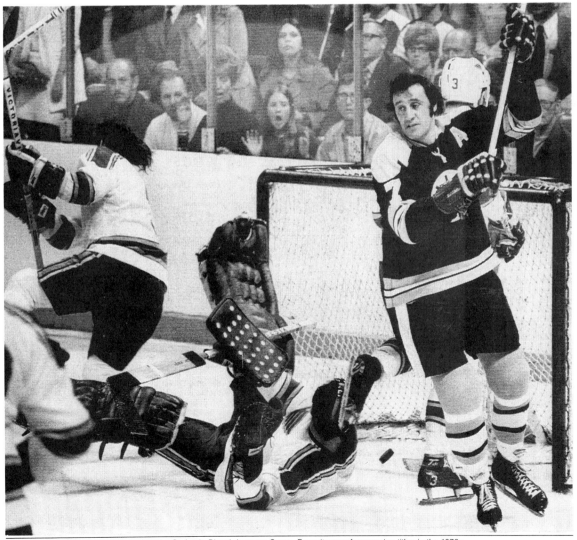

Phil Esposito celebrates a goal against the St. Louis Blues' Jacques Caron. Esposito won four scoring titles in the 1970s.

Mickey Redmond scored 52 goals in 1972-73, becoming the first Detroit Red Wing to reach the 50-goal plateau in a single season.

Rick MacLeish had a 50-goal, 100-point season in 1972-73.

1972-73

East Division

Team	GP	W	L	T	GF	GA	PTS
*Montreal	78	52	10	16	329	184	120
Boston	78	51	22	5	330	235	107
NY Rangers	78	47	23	8	297	208	102
Buffalo	78	37	27	14	257	219	88
Detroit	78	37	29	12	265	243	86
Toronto	78	27	41	10	247	279	64
Vancouver	78	22	47	9	233	339	53
NY Islanders	78	12	60	6	170	347	30

West Division

Team	GP	W	L	T	GF	GA	PTS
Chicago	78	42	27	9	284	225	93
Philadelphia	78	37	30	11	296	256	85
Minnesota	78	37	30	11	254	230	85
St. Louis	78	32	34	12	233	251	76
Pittsburgh	78	32	37	9	257	265	73
Los Angeles	78	31	36	11	232	245	73
Atlanta	78	25	38	15	191	239	65
California	78	16	46	16	213	323	48

Leading Scorers

Player	Club	GP	G	A	PTS	PIM
Esposito, Phil	Boston	78	55	75	130	87
Clarke, Bobby	Philadelphia	78	37	67	104	80
Orr, Bobby	Boston	63	29	72	101	99
MacLeish, Rick	Philadelphia	78	50	50	100	69
Lemaire, Jacques	Montreal	77	44	51	95	16
Ratelle, Jean	NY Rangers	78	41	53	94	12
Redmond, Mickey	Detroit	76	52	41	93	24
Bucyk, John	Boston	78	40	53	93	12
Mahovlich, Frank	Montreal	78	38	55	93	51
Pappin, Jim	Chicago	76	41	51	92	82

1973-74

East Division

Team	GP	W	L	T	GF	GA	PTS
Boston	78	52	17	9	349	221	113
Montreal	78	45	24	9	293	240	99
NY Rangers	78	40	24	14	300	251	94
Toronto	78	35	27	16	274	230	86
Buffalo	78	32	34	12	242	250	76
Detroit	78	29	39	10	255	319	68
Vancouver	78	24	43	11	224	296	59
NY Islanders	78	19	41	18	182	247	56

West Division

Team	GP	W	L	T	GF	GA	PTS
*Philadelphia	78	50	16	12	273	164	112
Chicago	78	41	14	23	272	164	105
Los Angeles	78	33	33	12	233	231	78
Atlanta	78	30	34	14	214	238	74
Pittsburgh	78	28	41	9	242	273	65
St. Louis	78	26	40	12	206	248	64
Minnesota	78	23	38	17	235	275	63
California	78	13	55	10	195	342	36

Leading Scorers

Player	Club	GP	G	A	PTS	PIM
Esposito, Phil	Boston	78	68	77	145	58
Orr, Bobby	Boston	74	32	90	122	82
Hodge, Ken	Boston	76	50	55	105	43
Cashman, Wayne	Boston	78	30	59	89	111
Clarke, Bobby	Philadelphia	77	35	52	87	113
Martin, Rick	Buffalo	78	52	34	86	38
Apps, Syl	Pittsburgh	75	24	61	85	37
Sittler, Darryl	Toronto	78	38	46	84	55
MacDonald, Lowell	Pittsburgh	78	43	39	82	14
Park, Brad	NY Rangers	78	25	57	82	148
Hextall, Dennis	Minnesota	78	20	62	82	138

1974-75

PRINCE OF WALES CONFERENCE

Norris Division

Team	GP	W	L	T	GF	GA	PTS
Montreal	80	47	14	19	374	225	113
Los Angeles	80	42	17	21	269	185	105
Pittsburgh	80	37	28	15	326	289	89
Detroit	80	23	45	12	259	335	58
Washington	80	8	67	5	181	446	21

Adams Division

Team	GP	W	L	T	GF	GA	PTS
Buffalo	80	49	16	15	354	240	113
Boston	80	40	26	14	345	245	94
Toronto	80	31	33	16	280	309	78
California	80	19	48	13	212	316	51

CLARENCE CAMPBELL CONFERENCE

Patrick Division

Team	GP	W	L	T	GF	GA	PTS
*Philadelphia	80	51	18	11	293	181	113
NY Rangers	80	37	29	14	319	276	88
NY Islanders	80	33	25	22	264	221	88
Atlanta	80	34	31	15	243	233	83

Smythe Division

Team	GP	W	L	T	GF	GA	PTS
Vancouver	80	38	32	10	271	254	86
St. Louis	80	35	31	14	269	267	84
Chicago	80	37	35	8	268	241	82
Minnesota	80	23	50	7	221	341	53
Kansas City	80	15	54	11	184	328	41

Leading Scorers

Player	Club	GP	G	A	PTS	PIM
Orr, Bobby	Boston	80	46	89	135	101
Esposito, Phil	Boston	79	61	66	127	62
Dionne, Marcel	Detroit	80	47	74	121	14
Lafleur, Guy	Montreal	70	53	66	119	37
Mahovlich, Pete	Montreal	80	35	82	117	64
Clarke, Bobby	Philadelphia	80	27	89	116	125
Robert, Rene	Buffalo	74	40	60	100	75
Gilbert, Rod	NY Rangers	76	36	61	97	22
Perreault, Gilbert	Buffalo	68	39	57	96	36
Martin, Rick	Buffalo	68	52	43	95	72

1975-76
PRINCE OF WALES CONFERENCE
Norris Division

Team	GP	W	L	T	GF	GA	PTS
*Montreal	80	58	11	11	337	174	127
Los Angeles	80	38	33	9	263	265	85
Pittsburgh	80	35	33	12	339	303	82
Detroit	80	26	44	10	226	300	62
Washington	80	11	59	10	224	394	32

Adams Division

	GP	W	L	T	GF	GA	PTS
Boston	80	48	15	17	313	237	113
Buffalo	80	46	21	13	339	240	105
Toronto	80	34	31	15	294	276	83
California	80	27	42	11	250	278	65

CLARENCE CAMPBELL CONFERENCE
Patrick Division

	GP	W	L	T	GF	GA	PTS
Philadelphia	80	51	13	16	348	209	118
NY Islanders	80	42	21	17	297	190	101
Atlanta	80	35	33	12	262	237	82
NY Rangers	80	29	42	9	262	333	67

Smythe Division

	GP	W	L	T	GF	GA	PTS
Chicago	80	32	30	18	254	261	82
Vancouver	80	33	32	15	271	272	81
St. Louis	80	29	37	14	249	290	72
Minnesota	80	20	53	7	195	303	47
Kansas City	80	12	56	12	190	351	36

Leading Scorers

Player	Club	GP	G	A	PTS	PIM
Lafleur, Guy	Montreal	80	56	69	125	36
Clarke, Bobby	Philadelphia	76	30	89	119	136
Perreault, Gilbert	Buffalo	80	44	69	113	36
Barber, Bill	Philadelphia	80	50	62	112	104
Larouche, Pierre	Pittsburgh	76	53	58	111	33
Ratelle, Jean	Bos., NYR	80	36	69	105	18
Mahovlich, Pete	Montreal	80	34	71	105	76
Pronovost, Jean	Pittsburgh	80	52	52	104	24
Sittler, Darryl	Toronto	79	41	59	100	90
Apps, Syl	Pittsburgh	80	32	67	99	24

1976-77
PRINCE OF WALES CONFERENCE
Norris Division

Team	GP	W	L	T	GF	GA	PTS
*Montreal	80	60	8	12	387	171	132
Los Angeles	80	34	31	15	271	241	83
Pittsburgh	80	34	33	13	240	252	81
Washington	80	24	42	14	221	307	62
Detroit	80	16	55	9	183	309	41

Adams Division

	GP	W	L	T	GF	GA	PTS
Boston	80	49	23	8	312	240	106
Buffalo	80	48	24	8	301	220	104
Toronto	80	33	32	15	301	285	81
Cleveland	80	25	42	13	240	292	63

CLARENCE CAMPBELL CONFERENCE
Patrick Division

	GP	W	L	T	GF	GA	PTS
Philadelphia	80	48	16	16	323	213	112
NY Islanders	80	47	21	12	288	193	106
Atlanta	80	34	34	12	264	265	80
NY Rangers	88	29	37	14	272	310	72

Smythe Division

	GP	W	L	T	GF	GA	PTS
St. Louis	80	32	39	9	239	276	73
Minnesota	80	23	39	18	240	310	64
Chicago	80	26	43	11	240	298	63
Vancouver	80	25	42	13	235	294	63
Colorado	80	20	46	14	226	307	54

Leading Scorers

Player	Club	GP	G	A	PTS	PIM
Lafleur, Guy	Montreal	80	56	80	136	20
Dionne, Marcel	Los Angeles	80	53	69	122	12
Shutt, Steve	Montreal	80	60	45	105	28
MacLeish, Rick	Philadelphia	79	49	48	97	42
Perreault, Gilbert	Buffalo	80	39	56	95	30
Young, Tim	Minnesota	80	29	66	95	58
Ratelle, Jean	Boston	78	33	61	94	22
McDonald, Lanny	Toronto	80	46	44	90	77
Sittler, Darryl	Toronto	73	38	52	90	89
Clarke, Bobby	Philadelphia	80	27	63	90	71

1977-78
PRINCE OF WALES CONFERENCE
Norris Division

Team	GP	W	L	T	GF	GA	PTS
*Montreal	80	59	10	11	359	183	129
Detroit	80	32	34	14	252	266	78
Los Angeles	80	31	34	15	243	245	77
Pittsburgh	80	25	37	18	254	321	68
Washington	80	17	49	14	195	321	48

Adams Division

	GP	W	L	T	GF	GA	PTS
Boston	80	51	18	11	333	218	113
Buffalo	80	44	19	17	288	215	105
Toronto	80	41	29	10	271	237	92
Cleveland	80	22	45	13	230	325	57

CLARENCE CAMPBELL CONFERENCE
Patrick Division

	GP	W	L	T	GF	GA	PTS
NY Islanders	80	48	17	15	334	210	111
Philadelphia	80	45	20	15	296	200	105
Atlanta	80	34	27	19	274	252	87
NY Rangers	80	30	37	13	279	280	73

Smythe Division

	GP	W	L	T	GF	GA	PTS
Chicago	80	32	29	19	230	220	83
Colorado	80	19	40	21	257	305	59
Vancouver	80	20	43	17	239	320	57
St. Louis	80	20	47	13	195	304	53
Minnesota	80	18	53	9	218	325	45

Leading Scorers

Player	Club	GP	G	A	PTS	PIM
Lafleur, Guy	Montreal	79	60	72	132	26
Trottier, Bryan	NY Islanders	77	46	77	123	46
Sittler, Darryl	Toronto	80	45	72	117	100
Lemaire, Jacques	Montreal	76	36	61	97	14
Potvin, Denis	NY Islanders	80	30	64	94	81
Bossy, Mike	NY Islanders	73	53	38	91	6
O'Reilly, Terry	Boston	77	29	61	90	211
Perreault, Gilbert	Buffalo	79	41	48	89	20
Clarke, Bobby	Philadelphia	71	21	68	89	83
McDonald, Lanny	Toronto	74	47	40	87	54
Paiement, Wilf	Colorado	80	31	56	87	114

1978-79
PRINCE OF WALES CONFERENCE
Norris Division

Team	GP	W	L	T	GF	GA	PTS
*Montreal	80	52	17	11	337	204	115
Pittsburgh	80	36	31	13	281	279	85
Los Angeles	80	34	34	12	292	286	80
Washington	80	24	41	15	273	338	63
Detroit	80	23	41	16	252	295	62

Adams Division

	GP	W	L	T	GF	GA	PTS
Boston	80	43	23	14	316	270	100
Buffalo	80	36	28	16	280	263	88
Toronto	80	34	33	13	267	252	81
Minnesota	80	28	40	12	257	289	68

CLARENCE CAMPBELL CONFERENCE
Patrick Division

	GP	W	L	T	GF	GA	PTS
NY Islanders	80	51	15	14	358	214	116
Philadelphia	80	40	25	15	281	248	95
NY Rangers	80	40	29	11	316	292	91
Atlanta	80	41	31	8	327	280	90

Smythe Division

	GP	W	L	T	GF	GA	PTS
Chicago	80	29	36	15	244	277	73
Vancouver	80	25	42	13	217	291	63
St. Louis	80	18	50	12	249	348	48
Colorado	80	15	53	12	210	331	42

Leading Scorers

Player	Club	GP	G	A	PTS	PIM
Trottier, Bryan	NY Islanders	76	47	87	134	50
Dionne, Marcel	Los Angeles	80	59	71	130	30
Lafleur, Guy	Montreal	80	52	77	129	28
Bossy, Mike	NY Islanders	80	69	57	126	25
MacMillan, Bob	Atlanta	79	37	71	108	14
Chouinard, Guy	Atlanta	80	50	57	107	14
Potvin, Denis	NY Islanders	73	31	70	101	58
Federko, Bernie	St. Louis	74	31	64	95	14
Taylor, Dave	Los Angeles	78	43	48	91	124
Gillies, Clark	NY Islanders	75	35	56	91	68

Dave Taylor had back-to-back 100-point seasons for the Los Angeles Kings in 1980-81 and 1981-82.

1979-80
PRINCE OF WALES CONFERENCE
Norris Division

Team	GP	W	L	T	GF	GA	PTS
Montreal	80	47	20	13	328	240	107
Los Angeles	80	30	36	14	290	313	74
Pittsburgh	80	30	37	13	251	303	73
Hartford	80	27	34	19	303	312	73
Detroit	80	26	43	11	268	306	63

Adams Division

Team	GP	W	L	T	GF	GA	PTS
Buffalo	80	47	17	16	318	201	110
Boston	80	46	21	13	310	234	105
Minnesota	80	36	28	16	311	253	88
Toronto	80	35	40	5	304	327	75
Quebec	80	25	44	11	248	313	61

CLARENCE CAMPBELL CONFERENCE
Patrick Division

Team	GP	W	L	T	GF	GA	PTS
Philadelphia	80	48	12	20	327	254	116
*NY Islanders	80	39	28	13	281	247	91
NY Rangers	80	38	32	10	308	284	86
Atlanta	80	35	32	13	282	269	83
Washington	80	27	40	13	261	293	67

Smythe Division

Team	GP	W	L	T	GF	GA	PTS
Chicago	80	34	27	19	241	250	87
St. Louis	80	34	34	12	266	278	80
Vancouver	80	27	37	16	256	281	70
Edmonton	80	28	39	13	301	322	69
Winnipeg	80	20	49	11	214	314	51
Colorado	80	19	48	13	234	308	51

Leading Scorers

Player	Club	GP	G	A	PTS	PIM
Dionne, Marcel	Los Angeles	80	53	84	137	32
Gretzky, Wayne	Edmonton	79	51	86	137	21
Lafleur, Guy	Montreal	74	50	75	125	12
Perreault, Gilbert	Buffalo	80	40	66	106	57
Rogers, Mike	Hartford	80	44	61	105	10
Trottier, Bryan	NY Islanders	78	42	62	104	68
Simmer, Charlie	Los Angeles	64	56	45	101	65
Stoughton, Blaine	Hartford	80	56	44	100	16
Sittler, Darryl	Toronto	73	40	57	97	62
MacDonald, Blair	Edmonton	80	46	48	94	6
Federko, Bernie	St. Louis	79	38	56	94	24

1980-81
PRINCE OF WALES CONFERENCE
Norris Division

Team	GP	W	L	T	GF	GA	PTS
Montreal	80	45	22	13	332	232	103
Los Angeles	80	43	24	13	337	290	99
Pittsburgh	80	30	37	13	302	345	73
Hartford	80	21	41	18	292	372	60
Detroit	80	19	43	18	252	339	56

Adams Division

Team	GP	W	L	T	GF	GA	PTS
Buffalo	80	39	20	21	327	250	99
Boston	80	37	30	13	316	272	87
Minnesota	80	35	28	17	291	263	87
Quebec	80	30	32	18	314	318	78
Toronto	80	28	37	15	322	367	71

CLARENCE CAMPBELL CONFERENCE
Patrick Division

Team	GP	W	L	T	GF	GA	PTS
*NY Islanders	80	48	18	14	355	260	110
Philadelphia	80	41	24	15	313	249	97
Calgary	80	39	27	14	329	298	92
NY Rangers	80	30	36	14	312	317	74
Washington	80	26	36	18	286	317	70

Smythe Division

Team	GP	W	L	T	GF	GA	PTS
St. Louis	80	45	18	17	352	281	107
Chicago	80	31	33	16	304	315	78
Vancouver	80	28	32	20	289	301	76
Edmonton	80	29	35	16	328	327	74
Colorado	80	22	45	13	258	344	57
Winnipeg	80	9	57	14	246	400	32

Leading Scorers

Player	Club	GP	G	A	PTS	PIM
Gretzky, Wayne	Edmonton	80	55	109	164	28
Dionne, Marcel	Los Angeles	80	58	77	135	70
Nilsson, Kent	Calgary	80	49	82	131	26
Bossy, Mike	NY Islanders	79	68	51	119	32
Taylor, Dave	Los Angeles	72	47	65	112	130
Stastny, Peter	Quebec	77	39	70	109	37
Simmer, Charlie	Los Angeles	65	56	49	105	62
Rogers, Mike	Hartford	80	40	65	105	32
Federko, Bernie	St. Louis	78	31	73	104	47
Richard, Jacques	Quebec	78	52	51	103	39
Middleton, Rick	Boston	80	44	59	103	16
Trottier, Bryan	NY Islanders	73	31	72	103	74

1981-82
CLARENCE CAMPBELL CONFERENCE
Norris Division

Team	GP	W	L	T	GF	GA	PTS
Minnesota	80	37	23	20	346	288	94
Winnipeg	80	33	33	14	319	332	80
St. Louis	80	32	40	8	315	349	72
Chicago	80	30	38	12	332	363	72
Toronto	80	20	44	16	298	380	56
Detroit	80	21	47	12	270	351	54

Smythe Division

Team	GP	W	L	T	GF	GA	PTS
Edmonton	80	48	17	15	417	295	111
Vancouver	80	30	33	17	290	286	77
Calgary	80	29	34	17	334	345	75
Los Angeles	80	24	41	15	314	369	63
Colorado	80	18	49	13	241	362	49

PRINCE OF WALES CONFERENCE
Adams Division

Team	GP	W	L	T	GF	GA	PTS
Montreal	80	46	17	17	360	223	109
Boston	80	43	27	10	323	285	96
Buffalo	80	39	26	15	307	273	93
Quebec	80	33	31	16	356	345	82
Hartford	80	21	41	18	264	351	60

Patrick Division

Team	GP	W	L	T	GF	GA	PTS
*NY Islanders	80	54	16	10	385	250	118
NY Rangers	80	39	27	14	316	306	92
Philadelphia	80	38	31	11	325	313	87
Pittsburgh	80	31	36	13	310	337	75
Washington	80	26	41	13	319	338	65

Leading Scorers

Player	Club	GP	G	A	PTS	PIM
Gretzky, Wayne	Edmonton	80	92	120	212	26
Bossy, Mike	NY Islanders	80	64	83	147	22
Stastny, Peter	Quebec	80	46	93	139	91
Maruk, Dennis	Washington	80	60	76	136	128
Trottier, Bryan	NY Islanders	80	50	79	129	88
Savard, Denis	Chicago	80	32	87	119	82
Dionne, Marcel	Los Angeles	78	50	67	117	50
Smith, Bobby	Minnesota	80	43	71	114	82
Ciccarelli, Dino	Minnesota	76	55	51	106	138
Taylor, Dave	Los Angeles	78	39	67	106	130

1982-83
CLARENCE CAMPBELL CONFERENCE
Norris Division

Team	GP	W	L	T	GF	GA	PTS
Chicago	80	47	23	10	338	268	104
Minnesota	80	40	24	16	321	290	96
Toronto	80	28	40	12	293	330	68
St. Louis	80	25	40	15	285	316	65
Detroit	80	21	44	15	263	344	57

Smythe Division

Team	GP	W	L	T	GF	GA	PTS
Edmonton	80	47	21	12	424	315	106
Calgary	80	32	34	14	321	317	78
Vancouver	80	30	35	15	303	309	75
Winnipeg	80	33	39	8	311	333	74
Los Angeles	80	27	41	12	308	365	66

PRINCE OF WALES CONFERENCE
Adams Division

Team	GP	W	L	T	GF	GA	PTS
Boston	80	50	20	10	327	228	110
Montreal	80	42	24	14	350	286	98
Buffalo	80	38	29	13	318	285	89
Quebec	80	34	34	12	343	336	80
Hartford	80	19	54	7	261	403	45

Patrick Division

Team	GP	W	L	T	GF	GA	PTS
Philadelphia	80	49	23	8	326	240	106
*NY Islanders	80	42	26	12	302	226	96
Washington	80	39	25	16	306	283	94
NY Rangers	80	35	35	10	306	287	80
New Jersey	80	17	49	14	230	338	48
Pittsburgh	80	18	53	9	257	394	45

Leading Scorers

Player	Club	GP	G	A	PTS	PIM
Gretzky, Wayne	Edmonton	80	71	125	196	59
Stastny, Peter	Quebec	75	47	77	124	78
Savard, Denis	Chicago	78	35	86	121	99
Bossy, Mike	NY Islanders	79	60	58	118	20
Dionne, Marcel	Los Angeles	80	56	51	107	22
Pederson, Barry	Boston	77	46	61	107	47
Messier, Mark	Edmonton	77	48	58	106	72
Goulet, Michel	Quebec	80	57	48	105	51
Anderson, Glenn	Edmonton	72	48	56	104	70
Nilsson, Kent	Calgary	80	46	58	104	10
Kurri, Jari	Edmonton	80	45	59	104	22

Bernie Federko was the first man to record 50-or-more assists in 10 consecutive NHL seasons.

1983-84
CLARENCE CAMPBELL CONFERENCE
Norris Division

Team	GP	W	L	T	GF	GA	PTS
Minnesota	80	39	31	10	345	344	88
St. Louis	80	32	41	7	293	316	71
Detroit	80	31	42	7	298	323	69
Chicago	80	30	42	8	277	311	68
Toronto	80	26	45	9	303	387	61

Smythe Division

Team	GP	W	L	T	GF	GA	PTS
*Edmonton	80	57	18	5	446	314	119
Calgary	80	34	32	14	311	314	82
Vancouver	80	32	39	9	306	328	73
Winnipeg	80	31	38	11	340	374	73
Los Angeles	80	23	44	13	309	376	59

PRINCE OF WALES CONFERENCE
Adams Division

Team	GP	W	L	T	GF	GA	PTS
Boston	80	49	25	6	336	261	104
Buffalo	80	48	25	7	315	257	103
Quebec	80	42	28	10	360	278	94
Montreal	80	35	40	5	286	295	75
Hartford	80	28	42	10	288	320	66

Patrick Division

Team	GP	W	L	T	GF	GA	PTS
NY Islanders	80	50	26	4	357	269	104
Washington	80	48	27	5	308	226	101
Philadelphia	80	44	26	10	350	290	98
NY Rangers	80	42	29	9	314	304	93
New Jersey	80	17	56	7	231	350	41
Pittsburgh	80	16	58	6	254	390	38

Leading Scorers

Player	Club	GP	G	A	PTS	PIM
Gretzky, Wayne	Edmonton	74	87	118	205	39
Coffey, Paul	Edmonton	80	40	86	126	104
Goulet, Michel	Quebec	75	56	65	121	76
Stastny, Peter	Quebec	80	46	73	119	73
Bossy, Mike	NY Islanders	67	51	67	118	8
Pederson, Barry	Boston	80	39	77	116	64
Kurri, Jari	Edmonton	64	52	61	113	14
Trottier, Bryan	NY Islanders	68	40	71	111	59
Federko, Bernie	St. Louis	79	41	66	107	43
Middleton, Rick	Boston	80	47	58	105	14

1984-85
CLARENCE CAMPBELL CONFERENCE
Norris Division

Team	GP	W	L	T	GF	GA	PTS
St. Louis	80	37	31	12	299	288	86
Chicago	80	38	35	7	309	299	83
Detroit	80	27	41	12	313	357	66
Minnesota	80	25	43	12	268	321	62
Toronto	80	20	52	8	253	358	48

Smythe Division

Team	GP	W	L	T	GF	GA	PTS
*Edmonton	80	49	20	11	401	298	109
Winnipeg	80	43	27	10	358	332	96
Calgary	80	41	27	12	363	302	94
Los Angeles	80	34	32	14	339	326	82
Vancouver	80	25	46	9	284	401	59

PRINCE OF WALES CONFERENCE
Adams Division

Team	GP	W	L	T	GF	GA	PTS
Montreal	80	41	27	12	309	262	94
Quebec	80	41	30	9	323	275	91
Buffalo	80	38	28	14	290	237	90
Boston	80	36	34	10	303	287	82
Hartford	80	30	41	9	268	318	69

Patrick Division

Team	GP	W	L	T	GF	GA	PTS
Philadelphia	80	53	20	7	348	241	113
Washington	80	46	25	9	322	240	101
NY Islanders	80	40	34	6	345	312	86
NY Rangers	80	26	44	10	295	345	62
New Jersey	80	22	48	10	264	346	54
Pittsburgh	80	24	51	5	276	385	53

Leading Scorers

Player	Club	GP	G	A	PTS	PIM
Gretzky, Wayne	Edmonton	80	73	135	208	52
Kurri, Jari	Edmonton	73	71	64	135	30
Hawerchuk, Dale	Winnipeg	80	53	77	130	74
Dionne, Marcel	Los Angeles	80	46	80	126	46
Coffey, Paul	Edmonton	80	37	84	121	97
Bossy, Mike	NY Islanders	76	58	59	117	38
Ogrodnick, John	Detroit	79	55	50	105	30
Savard, Denis	Chicago	79	38	67	105	56
Gartner, Mike	Washington	80	50	52	102	7

1985-86
CLARENCE CAMPBELL CONFERENCE
Norris Division

Team	GP	W	L	T	GF	GA	PTS
Chicago	80	39	33	8	351	349	86
Minnesota	80	38	33	9	327	305	85
St. Louis	80	37	34	9	302	291	83
Toronto	80	25	48	7	311	386	57
Detroit	80	17	57	6	266	415	40

Smythe Division

Team	GP	W	L	T	GF	GA	PTS
Edmonton	80	56	17	7	426	310	119
Calgary	80	40	31	9	354	315	89
Winnipeg	80	26	47	7	295	372	59
Vancouver	80	23	44	13	282	333	59
Los Angeles	80	23	49	8	284	389	54

PRINCE OF WALES CONFERENCE
Adams Division

Team	GP	W	L	T	GF	GA	PTS
Quebec	80	43	31	6	330	289	92
*Montreal	80	40	33	7	330	280	87
Boston	80	37	31	12	311	288	86
Hartford	80	40	36	4	332	302	84
Buffalo	80	37	37	6	296	291	80

Patrick Division

Team	GP	W	L	T	GF	GA	PTS
Philadelphia	80	53	23	4	335	241	110
Washington	80	50	23	7	315	272	107
NY Islanders	80	39	29	12	327	284	90
NY Rangers	80	36	38	6	280	276	78
Pittsburgh	80	34	38	8	313	305	76
New Jersey	80	28	49	3	300	374	59

Leading Scorers

Player	Club	GP	G	A	PTS	PIM
Gretzky, Wayne	Edmonton	80	52	163	215	52
Lemieux, Mario	Pittsburgh	79	48	93	141	43
Coffey, Paul	Edmonton	79	48	90	138	120
Kurri, Jari	Edmonton	78	68	63	131	22
Bossy, Mike	NY Islanders	80	61	62	123	14
Stastny, Peter	Quebec	76	41	81	122	60
Savard, Denis	Chicago	80	47	69	116	111
Naslund, Mats	Montreal	80	43	67	110	16
Hawerchuk, Dale	Winnipeg	80	46	59	105	44
Broten, Neal	Minnesota	80	29	76	105	47

Barry Pederson had a 116-point season for the Bruins in 1983-84.

Dino Ciccarelli had his second 50-goal campaign in 1986-87, scoring 52 times for the North Stars.

1986-87

CLARENCE CAMPBELL CONFERENCE

Norris Division

Team	GP	W	L	T	GF	GA	PTS
St. Louis	80	32	33	15	281	293	79
Detroit	80	34	36	10	260	274	78
Chicago	80	29	37	14	290	310	72
Toronto	80	32	42	6	286	319	70
Minnesota	80	30	40	10	296	314	70

Smythe Division

Team	GP	W	L	T	GF	GA	PTS
*Edmonton	80	50	24	6	372	284	106
Calgary	80	46	31	3	318	289	95
Winnipeg	80	40	32	8	279	271	88
Los Angeles	80	31	41	8	318	341	70
Vancouver	80	29	43	8	282	314	66

PRINCE OF WALES CONFERENCE

Adams Division

Team	GP	W	L	T	GF	GA	PTS
Hartford	80	43	30	7	287	270	93
Montreal	80	41	29	10	277	241	92
Boston	80	39	34	7	301	276	85
Quebec	80	31	39	10	267	276	72
Buffalo	80	28	44	8	280	308	64

Patrick Division

Team	GP	W	L	T	GF	GA	PTS
Philadelphia	80	46	26	8	310	245	100
Washington	80	38	32	10	285	278	86
NY Islanders	80	35	33	12	279	281	82
NY Rangers	80	34	38	8	307	323	76
Pittsburg	80	30	38	12	297	290	72
New Jersey	80	29	45	6	293	368	64

Leading Scorers

Player	Club	GP	G	A	PTS	PIM
Gretzky, Wayne	Edmonton	79	62	121	183	28
Kurri, Jari	Edmonton	79	54	54	108	41
Lemieux, Mario	Pittsburgh	63	54	53	107	57
Messier, Mark	Edmonton	77	37	70	107	73
Gilmour, Doug	St. Louis	80	42	63	105	58
Ciccarelli, Dino	Minnesota	80	52	51	103	92
Hawerchuk, Dale	Winnipeg	80	47	53	100	54
Goulet, Michel	Quebec	75	49	47	96	61
Kerr, Tim	Philadelphia	75	58	37	95	57
Bourque, Ray	Boston	78	23	72	95	36

1987-88

CLARENCE CAMPBELL CONFERENCE

Norris Division

Team	GP	W	L	T	GF	GA	PTS
Detroit	80	41	28	11	322	269	93
St. Louis	80	34	38	8	278	294	76
Chicago	80	30	41	9	284	326	69
Toronto	80	21	49	10	273	345	52
Minnesota	80	19	48	13	242	349	51

Smythe Division

Team	GP	W	L	T	GF	GA	PTS
Calgary	80	48	23	9	397	305	105
*Edmonton	80	44	25	11	363	288	99
Winnipeg	80	33	36	11	292	310	77
Los Angeles	80	30	42	8	318	359	68
Vancouver	80	25	46	9	272	320	59

PRINCE OF WALES CONFERENCE

Adams Division

Team	GP	W	L	T	GF	GA	PTS
Montreal	80	45	22	13	298	238	103
Boston	80	44	30	6	300	251	94
Buffalo	80	37	32	11	283	305	85
Hartford	80	35	38	7	249	267	77
Quebec	80	32	43	5	271	306	69

Patrick Division

Team	GP	W	L	T	GF	GA	PTS
NY Islanders	80	39	31	10	308	267	88
Washington	80	38	33	9	281	249	85
Philadelphia	80	38	33	9	292	282	85
New Jersey	80	38	36	6	295	296	82
NY Rangers	80	36	34	10	300	283	82
Pittsburgh	80	36	35	9	319	316	81

Leading Scorers

Player	Club	GP	G	A	PTS	PIM
Lemieux, Mario	Pittsburgh	76	70	98	168	92
Gretzky, Wayne	Edmonton	64	40	109	149	24
Savard, Denis	Chicago	80	44	87	131	95
Hawerchuk, Dale	Winnipeg	80	44	77	121	59
Robitaille, Luc	Los Angeles	80	53	58	111	82
Stastny, Peter	Quebec	76	46	65	111	69
Messier, Mark	Edmonton	77	37	74	111	103
Carson, Jimmy	Los Angeles	80	55	52	107	45
Loob, Hakan	Calgary	80	50	56	106	47
Goulet, Michel	Quebec	80	48	58	106	56

1988-89

CLARENCE CAMPBELL CONFERENCE

Norris Division

Team	GP	W	L	T	GF	GA	PTS
Detroit	80	34	34	12	313	316	80
St. Louis	80	33	35	12	275	285	78
Minnesota	80	27	37	16	258	278	70
Chicago	80	27	41	12	297	335	66
Toronto	80	28	46	6	259	342	62

Smythe Division

Team	GP	W	L	T	GF	GA	PTS
*Calgary	80	54	17	9	354	226	117
Los Angeles	80	42	31	7	376	335	91
Edmonton	80	38	34	8	325	306	84
Vancouver	80	33	39	8	251	253	74
Winnipeg	80	26	42	12	300	355	64

PRINCE OF WALES CONFERENCE

Adams Division

Team	GP	W	L	T	GF	GA	PTS
Montreal	80	53	18	9	315	218	115
Boston	80	37	29	14	289	256	88
Buffalo	80	38	35	7	291	299	83
Hartford	80	37	38	5	299	290	79
Quebec	80	27	46	7	269	342	61

Patrick Division

Team	GP	W	L	T	GF	GA	PTS
Washington	80	41	29	10	305	259	92
Pittsburgh	80	40	33	7	347	349	87
NY Rangers	80	37	35	4	310	307	82
Philadelphia	80	36	36	8	307	285	80
New Jersey	80	27	41	12	281	325	66
NY Islanders	80	28	47	5	265	325	61

Leading Scorers

Player	Club	GP	G	A	PTS	PIM
Lemieux, Mario	Pittsburgh	76	85	114	199	100
Gretzky, Wayne	Los Angeles	78	54	114	168	26
Yzerman, Steve	Detroit	80	65	90	155	61
Nicholls, Bernie	Los Angeles	79	70	80	150	96
Brown, Rob	Pittsburgh	68	49	66	115	118
Coffey, Paul	Pittsburgh	75	30	83	113	193
Mullen, Joe	Calgary	79	51	59	110	16
Kurri, Jari	Edmonton	76	44	58	102	69
Carson, Jimmy	Edmonton	80	49	51	100	36
Robitaille, Luc	Los Angeles	78	46	52	98	65

Note: Detailed statistics for 1988-89 are listed in the Final Statistics, 1988-89 section of the **NHL Guide & Record Book.**

NHL History

1917 — National Hockey League organized November 22 in Montreal following suspension of operations by the National Hockey Association of Canada Limited (NHA). Montreal Canadiens, Montreal Wanderers, Ottawa Senators and Quebec Bulldogs attended founding meeting. Delegates decided to use NHA rules.

Toronto Arenas were later admitted as fifth team; Quebec decided not to operate during the first season. Quebec players allocated to remaining four teams.

Frank Calder elected president and secretary-treasurer.

First NHL games played December 19, with Toronto only arena with artificial ice. Clubs played 22-game split schedule.

1918 — Emergency meeting held January 3 due to destruction by fire of Montreal Arena which was home ice for both Canadiens and Wanderers.

Wanderers withdrew, reducing the NHL to three teams; Canadiens played remaining home games at 3,250-seat Jubilee rink.

Quebec franchise sold to P.J. Quinn of Toronto on October 18 on the condition that the team operate in Quebec City for 1918-19 season. Quinn did not attend the November League meeting and Quebec did not play in 1918-19.

1919-20 — NHL reactivated Quebec Bulldogs franchise. Former Quebec players returned to the club. New Mount Royal Arena became home of Canadiens. Toronto Arenas changed name to St. Patricks. Clubs played 24-game split schedule.

1920-21 — H.P. Thompson of Hamilton, Ontario made application for the purchase of an NHL franchise. Quebec franchise shifted to Hamilton with other NHL teams providing players to strengthen the club.

1921-22 — Split schedule abandoned. First and second place teams at the end of full schedule to play for championship.

1922-23 — Clubs agreed that players could not be sold or traded to clubs in any other league without first being offered to all other clubs in the NHL. In March, Foster Hewitt broadcast radio's first hockey game.

1923-24 — Ottawa's new 10,000-seat arena opened. First U.S. franchise granted to Boston for following season.

Dr. Cecil Hart Trophy donated to NHL to be awarded to the player judged most useful to his team.

1924-25 — Canadian Arena Company of Montreal granted a franchise to operate Montreal Maroons. NHL now six team league with two clubs in Montreal. Inaugural game in new Montreal Forum played November 29, 1924 as Canadiens defeated Toronto 7-1. Forum was home rink for the Maroons, but no ice was available in the Canadiens arena November 29, resulting in shift to Forum.

Hamilton finished first in the standings, receiving a bye into the finals. But Hamilton players, demanding $200 each for additional games in the playoffs, went on strike. The NHL suspended all players, fining them $200 each. Stanley Cup finalist to be the winner of NHL semi-final between Toronto and Canadiens.

Prince of Wales and Lady Byng trophies donated to NHL.

Clubs played 30-game schedule.

1925-26 — Hamilton club dropped from NHL. Players signed by new New York Americans franchise. Franchise granted to Pittsburgh.

Clubs played 36-game schedule.

1926-27 — New York Rangers granted franchise April 17, 1926. Chicago Black Hawks and Detroit Cougars granted franchises May 15, 1926. NHL now ten-team league with an American and a Canadian division.

Stanley Cup came under the control of NHL. In previous seasons, winners of the now-defunct Western or Pacific Coast leagues would play NHL champion in Cup finals.

Toronto franchise sold to a new company controlled by Hugh Aird and Conn Smythe. Name changed from St. Patricks to Maple Leafs.

Clubs played 44-game schedule.

The Montreal Canadiens donated the Vezina Trophy to be awarded to the team allowing the fewest goals-against in regular season play. The winning team would, in turn, present the trophy to the goaltender playing in the greatest number of games during the season.

1929-30 — Detroit franchise changed name from Cougars to Falcons.

1930-31 — Pittsburgh transferred to Philadelphia for one season. Pirates changed name to Philadelphia Quakers. Trading deadline for teams set at February 15 of each year. NHL approved operation of farm teams by Rangers, Americans, Falcons and Bruins. Four-sided electric arena clock first demonstrated.

1931-32 — Philadelphia dropped out. Ottawa withdrew for one season. New Maple Leaf Gardens completed. Clubs played 48-game schedule.

1932-33 — Franchise application received from St. Louis but refused because of additional travel costs. Ottawa team resumed play.

1933-34 — Detroit franchise changed name from Falcons to Red Wings. First All-Star Game played as a benefit for injured player Ace Bailey. Stanley Cup champion Leafs defeated All-Stars 7-3 in Toronto.

1934-35 — Ottawa franchise transferred to St. Louis. Team called St. Louis Eagles and consisted largely of Ottawa's players.

1935-36 — Ottawa-St. Louis franchise terminated. Montreal Canadiens finished season with very poor record. To strengthen the club, NHL gave Canadiens first call on the services of all French-Canadian players for three seasons.

1937-38 — Second benefit all-star game staged November 2 in Montreal in aid of the family of the late Canadiens star Howie Morenz.

Montreal Maroons withdrew from the NHL on June 22, 1938, leaving seven clubs in the League.

1938-39 — Expenses for each club regulated at $5 per man per day for meals and $2.50 per man per day for accommodation.

1939-40 — Benefit All-Star Game played October 29, 1939 in Montreal for the children of the late Albert (Babe) Siebert.

1940-41 — Ross-Tyer puck adopted as the official puck of the NHL. Early in the season it was apparent that this puck was too soft. The Spalding puck was adopted in its place.

After the playoffs, Arthur Ross, NHL governor from Boston, donated a perpetual trophy to be awarded annually to the player voted outstanding in the league.

1941-42 — New York Americans changed name to Brooklyn Americans.

1942-43 — Brooklyn Americans withdrew from NHL, leaving six teams: Boston, Chicago, Detroit, Montreal, New York and Toronto. Playoff format saw first-place team play third-place team and second play fourth.

Clubs played 50-game schedule.

Frank Calder, president of the NHL since its inception, died in Montreal. Mervyn "Red" Dutton, former manager of the New York Americans, became president. The NHL commissioned the Calder Memorial Trophy to be awarded to the League's outstanding rookie each year.

1945-46 — Philadelphia, Los Angeles and San Francisco applied for NHL franchises.

The Philadelphia Arena Company of the American Hockey League applied for an injunction to prevent the possible operation of an NHL franchise in that city.

1946-47 — Mervyn Dutton retired as president of the NHL prior to the start of the season. He was succeeded by Clarence S. Campbell.

Individual trophy winners and all-star team members to receive $1,000 awards.

Playoff guarantees for players introduced.

Clubs played 60-game schedule.

1947-48 — The first annual All-Star Game for the benefit of the players' pension fund was played when the All-Stars defeated the Stanley Cup Champion Toronto Maple Leafs 4-3 in Toronto on October 13, 1947.

Ross Trophy, awarded to the NHL's outstanding player since 1941, to be awarded annually to the League's scoring leader.

Philadelphia and Los Angeles franchise applications refused.

National Hockey League Pension Society formed.

1949-50 — Clubs played 70-game schedule.

First intra-league draft held April 30, 1950. Clubs allowed to protect 30 players. Remaining players available for $25,000 each.

1951-52 — Referees included in the League's pension plan.

1952-53 — In May of 1952, City of Cleveland applied for NHL franchise. Application denied. In March of 1953, the Cleveland Barons of the AHL challenged the NHL champions for the Stanley Cup. The NHL governors did not accept this challenge.

1953-54 — The James Norris Memorial Trophy presented to the NHL for annual presentation to the League's best defenseman.

Intra-league draft rules amended to allow teams to protect 18 skaters and two goaltenders, claiming price reduced to $15,000.

1954-55 — Each arena to operate an "out-of-town" scoreboard. Referees and linesmen to wear shirts of black and white vertical stripes. Teams agree to wear white uniforms at home and colored uniforms on the road.

1956-57 — Standardized signals for referees and linesmen introduced.

1960-61 — Canadian National Exhibition, City of Toronto and NHL reach agreement for the construction of a Hockey Hall of Fame on the CNE grounds. Hall opens on August 26, 1961.

1963-64 — Player development league established with clubs operated by NHL franchises located in Minneapolis, St. Paul, Indianapolis, Omaha and, beginning in 1964-65, Tulsa. First universal amateur draft took place. All players of qualifying age (17) unaffected by sponsorship of junior teams available to be drafted.

1964-65 — Conn Smythe Trophy presented to the NHL to be awarded annually to the outstanding player in the Stanley Cup playoffs.

Minimum age of players subject to amateur draft changed to 18.

1965-66 — NHL announced expansion plans for a second six-team division to begin play in 1967-68.

1966-67 — Fourteen applications for NHL franchises received.

Lester Patrick Trophy presented to the NHL to be awarded annually for outstanding service to hockey in the United States.

NHL sponsorship of junior teams ceased, making all players of qualifying age not already on NHL-sponsored lists eligible for the amateur draft.

1967-68 — Six new teams added: California Seals, Los Angeles Kings, Minnesota North Stars, Philadelphia Flyers, Pittsburgh Penguins, St. Louis Blues. New teams to play in West Division. Remaining six teams to play in East Division.

Minimum age of players subject to amateur draft changed to 20.

Clubs played 74-game schedule.

Clarence S. Campbell Trophy awarded to team finishing the regular season in first place in West Division.

California Seals changed name to Oakland Seals on December 8, 1967.

1968-69 — Clubs played 76-game schedule.

Amateur draft expanded to cover any amateur player of qualifying age throughout the world.

1970-71 — Two new teams added: Buffalo Sabres and Vancouver Canucks. These teams joined East Division: Chicago switched to West Division.

Clubs played 78-game schedule.

1971-72 — Playoff format amended. In each division, first to play fourth; second to play third.

1972-73 — Soviet Nationals and Canadian NHL stars play eight-game pre-season series. Canadians win 4-3-1.

Two new teams added. Atlanta Flames join West Division; New York Islanders join East Division.

1974-75 — Two new teams added: Kansas City Scouts and Washington Capitals. Teams realigned into two nine-team conferences, the Prince of Wales made up of the Norris and Adams Divisions, and the Clarence Campbell made up of the Smythe and Patrick Divisions.

Clubs played 80-game schedule.

1976-77 — California franchise transferred to Cleveland. Team named Cleveland Barons. Kansas City franchise transferred to Denver. Team named Colorado Rockies.

1977-78 — Clarence S. Campbell retires as NHL president. Succeeded by John A. Ziegler, Jr.

1978-79 — Cleveland and Minnesota franchises merge, leaving NHL with 17 teams. Merged team placed in Adams Division, playing home games in Minnesota.

Minimum age of players subject to amateur draft changed to 19.

1979-80 — Four new teams added: Edmonton Oilers, Hartford Whalers, Quebec Nordiques and Winnipeg Jets.

Minimum age of players subject to entry draft changed to 18.

1980-81 — Atlanta franchise shifted to Calgary, retaining "Flames" name.

1981-82 — Unbalanced schedule adopted.

1982-83 — Colorado Rockies franchise shifted to East Rutherford, New Jersey. Team named New Jersey Devils.

Major Rule Changes

1910-11 — Game changed from two 30-minute periods to three 20-minute periods.

1911-12 — National Hockey Association (forerunner of the NHL) originated six-man hockey, replacing seven-man game.

1917-18 — Goalies permitted to fall to the ice to make saves. Previously a goaltender was penalized for dropping to the ice.

1918-19 — Penalty rules amended. For minor fouls, substitutes not allowed until penalized player had served three minutes. For major fouls, no substitutes for five minutes. For match fouls, no substitutes allowed for the remainder of the game.

With the addition of two lines painted on the ice twenty feet from center, three playing zones were created, producing a forty-foot neutral center ice area in which forward passing was permitted. Kicking the puck was permitted in this neutral zone.

Tabulation of assists began.

1921-22 — Goaltenders allowed to pass the puck forward up to their own blue line.

Overtime limited to twenty minutes.

Minor penalties changed from three minutes to two minutes.

1923-24 — Match foul defined as actions deliberately injuring or disabling an opponent. For such actions, a player was fined not less than $50 and ruled off the ice for the balance of the game. A player assessed a match penalty may be replaced by a substitute at the end of 20 minutes. Match penalty recipients must meet with the League president who can assess additional punishment.

1925-26 — Delayed penalty rules introduced. Each team must have a minimum of four players on the ice at all times.

Two rules were amended to encourage offense: No more than two defensemen permitted to remain inside a team's own blue line when the puck has left the defensive zone. A faceoff to be called for ragging the puck unless short-handed.

Team captains only players allowed to talk to referees.

Goaltender's leg pads limited to 12-inch width.

Timekeeper's gong to mark end of periods rather than referee's whistle. Teams to dress a maximum of 12 players for each game from a roster of no more than 14 players.

1926-27 — Blue lines repositioned to sixty feet from each goal-line, thereby enlarging the neutral zone and standardizing distance from blueline to goal.

Uniform goal nets adopted throughout NHL with goal posts securely fastened to the ice.

1927-28 — To further encourage offense, forward passes allowed in defending and neutral zones and goaltender's pads reduced in width from 12 to 10 inches.

Game standardized at three twenty-minute periods of stop-time separated by ten-minute intermissions.

Teams to change ends after each period.

Ten minutes of sudden-death overtime to be played if the score is tied after regulation time.

Minor penalty to be assessed to any player other than a goaltender for deliberately picking up the puck while it is in play. Minor penalty to be assessed for deliberately shooting the puck out of play.

The Art Ross goal net adopted as the official net of the NHL.

Maximum length of hockey sticks limited to 53 inches measured from heel of blade to end of handle. No minimum length stipulated.

Home teams given choice of goals to defend at start of game.

1928-29 — Forward passing permitted in defensive and neutral zones and into attacking zone if pass receiver is in neutral zone when pass is made. No forward passing allowed inside attacking zone.

Minor penalty to be assessed to any player who delays the game by passing the puck back into his defensive zone.

Ten-minute overtime without sudden-death provision to be played in games tied after regulation time. Games tied after this overtime period declared a draw.

Exclusive of goaltenders, team to dress at least 8 and no more than 12 skaters.

1929-30 — Forward passing permitted inside all three zones but not permitted across either blue line.

Kicking the puck allowed, but a goal cannot be scored by kicking the puck in.

No more than three players including the goaltender may remain in their defensive zone when the puck has gone up ice. Minor penalties to be assessed for the first two violations of this rule in a game; major penalties thereafter.

Goaltenders forbidden to hold the puck. Pucks caught must be cleared immediately. For infringement of this rule, a faceoff to be taken ten feet in front of the goal with no player except the goaltender standing between the faceoff spot and the goal-line.

Highsticking penalties introduced.

Maximum number of players in uniform increased from 12 to 15.

December 21, 1929 — Forward passing rules instituted at the beginning of the 1929-30 season more than doubled number of goals scored. Partway through the season, these rules were further amended to read, "No attacking player allowed to precede the play when entering the opposing defensive zone." This is similar to modern offside rule.

1930-31 — A player without a complete stick ruled out of play and forbidden from taking part in further action until a new stick is obtained. A player who has broken his stick must obtain a replacement at his bench.

A further refinement of the offside rule stated that the puck must first be propelled into the attacking zone before any player of the attacking side can enter that zone; for infringement of this rule a faceoff to take place at the spot where the infraction took place.

1931-32 — Though there is no record of a team attempting to play with two goaltenders on the ice, a rule was instituted which stated that each team was allowed only one goaltender on the ice at one time.

Attacking players forbidden to impede the movement or obstruct the vision of opposing goaltenders.

Defending players with the exception of the goaltender forbidden from falling on the puck within 10 feet of the net.

1932-33 — Each team to have captain on the ice at all times.

If the goaltender is removed from the ice to serve a penalty, the manager of the club to appoint a substitute.

Match penalty with substitution after five minutes instituted for kicking another player.

1933-34 — Number of players permitted to stand in defensive zone restricted to three including goaltender.

Visible time clocks required in each rink.

Two referees replace one referee and one linesman.

1934-35 — Penalty shot awarded when a player is tripped and thus prevented from having a clear shot on goal, having no player to pass to other than the offending player. Shot taken from inside a 10-foot circle located 38 feet from the goal. The goaltender must not advance more than one foot from his goal-line when the shot is taken.

1937-38 — Rules introduced governing icing the puck.

Penalty shot awarded when a player other than a goaltender falls on the puck within 10 feet of the goal.

1938-39 — Penalty shot modified to allow puck carrier to skate in before shooting.

One referee and one linesman replace two referee system.

Blue line widened to 12 inches.

Maximum number of players in uniform increased from 14 to 15.

1939-40 — A substitute replacing a goaltender removed from ice to serve a penalty may use a goaltender's stick and gloves but no other goaltending equipment.

1940-41 — Flooding ice surface between periods made obligatory.

1941-42 — Penalty shots classified as minor and major. Minor shot to be taken from a line 28 feet from the goal. Major shot, awarded when a player is tripped with only the goaltender to beat, permits the player taking the penalty shot to skate right into the goalkeeper and shoot from point-blank range.

One referee and two linesmen employed to officiate games.

For playoffs, standby minor league goaltenders employed by NHL as emergency substitutes.

1942-43 — Because of wartime restrictions on train scheduling, regular-season overtime was discontinued on November 21, 1942.

Player limit reduced from 15 to 14. Minimum of 12 men in uniform abolished.

1943-44 — Red line at center ice introduced to speed up the game and reduce offside calls. This rule is considered to mark the beginning of the modern era in the NHL.

Delayed penalty rules introduced.

1945-46 — Goal indicator lights synchronized with official time clock required at all rinks.

1946-47 — System of signals by officials to indicate infractions introduced.

Linesmen from neutral cities employed for all games.

1947-48 — Goal awarded when a player with the puck has an open net to shoot at and a thrown stick prevents the shot on goal. Major penalty to any player who throws his stick in any zone other than defending zone. If a stick is thrown by a player in his defending zone but the thrown stick is not considered to have prevented a goal, a penalty shot is awarded.

All playoff games played until a winner determined, with 20-minute sudden-death overtime periods separated by 10-minute intermissions.

1949-50 — Ice surface painted white.

Clubs allowed to dress 17 players exclusive of goaltenders.

Major penalties incurred by goaltenders served by a member of the goaltender's team instead of resulting in a penalty shot.

1950-51 — Each team required to provide an emergency goaltender in attendance with full equipment at each game for use by either team in the event of illness or injury to a regular goaltender.

1951-52 — Visiting teams to wear basic white uniforms; home teams basic colored uniforms.

Goal crease enlarged from 3 × 7 feet to 4 × 8 feet.

Number of players in uniform reduced to 15 plus goaltenders.

Faceoff circles enlarged from 10-foot to 15-foot radius.

1952-53 — Teams permitted to dress 15 skaters on the road and 16 at home.

1953-54 — Number of players in uniform set at 16 plus goaltenders.

1954-55 — Number of players in uniform set at 18 plus goaltenders up to December 1 and 16 plus goaltenders thereafter.

1956-57 — Player serving a minor penalty allowed to return to ice when a goal is scored by opposing team.

1959-60 — Players prevented from leaving their benches to enter into an altercation. Substitutions permitted providing substitutes do not enter into altercation.

1960-61 — Number of players in uniform set at 16 plus goaltenders.

1961-62 — Penalty shots to be taken by the player against whom the foul was committed. In the event of a penalty shot called in a situation where a particular player hasn't been fouled, the penalty shot to be taken by any player on the ice when the foul was committed.

1964-65 — No bodily contact on faceoffs.

In playoff games, each team to have its substitute goaltender dressed in his regular uniform except for leg pads and body protector. All previous rules governing standby goaltenders terminated.

1965-66 — Teams required to dress two goaltenders for each regular-season game.

1966-67 — Substitution allowed on coincidental major penalties.

Between-periods intermissions fixed at 15 minutes.

1967-68 — If a penalty incurred by a goaltender is a co-incident major, the penalty to be served by a player of the goaltender's team on the ice at the time the penalty was called.

1970-71 — Home teams to wear basic white uniforms; visiting teams basic colored uniforms.

Limit of curvature of hockey stick blade set at 1/2 inch.

Minor penalty for deliberately shooting the puck out of the playing area.

1971-72 — Number of players in uniform set at 17 plus 2 goaltenders.

Third man to enter an altercation assessed an automatic game misconduct penalty.

1972-73 — Minimum width of stick blade reduced to 2 inches from 2-1/2 inches.

1974-75 — Bench minor penalty imposed if a penalized player does not proceed directly and immediately to the penalty box.

1976-77 — Rule dealing with fighting amended to provide a major and game misconduct penalty for any player who is clearly the instigator of a fight.

1977-78 — Teams requesting a stick measurement to be assessed a minor penalty in the event that the measured stick does not violate the rules.

1981-82 — If both of a team's listed goaltenders are incapacitated, the team can dress and play any eligible goaltender who is available.

1982-83 — Number of players in uniform set 18 plus 2 goaltenders.

1983-84 — Five-minute sudden-death overtime to be played in regular-season games that are tied at the end of regulation time.

1985-86 — Substitutions allowed in the event of co-incidental minor penalties.

Team Records

BEST WINNING PERCENTAGE, ONE SEASON:
.875—**Boston Bruins,** 1929-30. 38w-5L-1T. 77PTS in 44GP
.830—Montreal Canadiens, 1943-44. 38w-5L-7T. 83PTS in 50GP
.825—Montreal Canadiens, 1976-77. 60w-8L-12T. 132PTS in 80GP
.806—Montreal Canadiens, 1977-78. 59w-10L-11T. 129PTS in 80GP
.800—Montreal Canadiens, 1944-45. 38w-8L-4T. 80PTS in 50GP

MOST POINTS, ONE SEASON:
132 — **Montreal Canadiens,** 1976-77. 60w-8L-12T. 80GP
129 — Montreal Canadiens, 1977-78. 59w-10L-11T. 80GP
127 — Montreal Canadiens, 1975-76. 58w-11L-11T. 80GP

FEWEST POINTS, ONE SEASON:
8 — **Quebec Bulldogs,** 1919-20. 4w-20L-0T. 24GP
10 — Toronto Arenas, 1918-19. 5w-13L-0T. 18GP
12 — Hamilton Tigers, 1920-21. 6w-18L-0T. 24GP
— Hamilton Tigers, 1922-23. 6w-18L-0T. 24GP
— Boston Bruins, 1924-25. 6w-24L-0T. 30GP
— Philadelphia Quakers, 1930-31. 4w-36L-4T. 44GP

FEWEST POINTS, ONE SEASON (MINIMUM 70-GAME SCHEDULE):
21 — **Washington Capitals,** 8w-67L-5T. 80GP
30 — New York Islanders, 1972-73. 12w-60L-6T. 78GP
31 — Chicago Black Hawks, 1953-54. 12w-51L-7T. 70GP

MOST WINS, ONE SEASON:
60 — **Montreal Canadiens,** 1976-77. 80GP
59 — Montreal Canadiens, 1977-78. 80GP
58 — Montreal Canadiens, 1975-76. 80GP

FEWEST WINS, ONE SEASON:
4 — **Quebec Bulldogs,** 1919-20. 24GP
— **Philadelphia Quakers,** 1930-31. 44GP
5 — Toronto Arenas, 1918-19. 18GP
— Pittsburgh Pirates, 1929-30. 44GP

FEWEST WINS, ONE SEASON (MINIMUM 70-GAME SCHEDULE):
8 — **Washington Capitals,** 1974-75. 80GP
9 — Winnipeg Jets, 1980-81 80GP
11 — Washington Capitals, 1975-76. 80GP

MOST LOSSES, ONE SEASON:
67 — **Washington Capitals,** 1974-75. 80GP
60 — New York Islanders, 1972-73. 78GP
59 — Washington Capitals, 1975-76. 80GP

FEWEST LOSSES, ONE SEASON:
5 — **Ottawa Senators,** 1919-20. 24GP
— **Boston Bruins,** 1929-30. 44GP
— **Montreal Canadiens,** 1943-44. 50GP

FEWEST LOSSES, ONE SEASON (MINIMUM 70-GAME SCHEDULE):
8 — **Montreal Canadiens,** 1976-77. 80GP
10 — Montreal Canadiens, 1972-73. 78GP
— Montreal Canadiens, 1977-78. 80GP
11 — Montreal Canadiens, 1975-76. 80GP

MOST TIES, ONE SEASON:
24 — **Philadelphia Flyers,** 1969-70. 76GP
23 — Montreal Canadiens, 1962-63. 70GP
— Chicago Black Hawks, 1973-74. 78GP

FEWEST TIES, ONE SEASON (Since 1926-27):
1 — **Boston Bruins,** 1929-30. 44GP
2 — New York Americans, 1926-27. 44GP
— Montreal Canadiens, 1926-27. 44GP
— Boston Bruins, 1938-39. 48GP
— New York Rangers, 1941-42. 48GP

FEWEST TIES, ONE SEASON (MINIMUM 70-GAME SCHEDULE):
3 — **New Jersey Devils,** 1985-86. 80GP
— **Calgary Flames,** 1986-87. 80GP
4 — Detroit Red Wings, 1966-67. 70GP
— New York Islanders, 1983-84. 80GP
— Hartford Whalers, 1985-86. 80GP
— Philadelphia Flyers, 1985-86. 80GP

MOST HOME WINS, ONE SEASON:
36 — **Philadelphia Flyers,** 1975-76. 40GP
33 — Boston Bruins, 1970-71. 39GP
— Boston Bruins, 1973-74. 39GP
— Montreal Canadiens, 1976-77. 40GP
— Philadelphia Flyers, 1976-77. 40GP
— New York Islanders, 1981-82. 40GP
— Philadelphia Flyers,1985-86. 40GP

MOST ROAD WINS, ONE SEASON:
27 — **Montreal Canadiens,** 1976-77. 40GP
— **Montreal Canadiens,** 1977-78. 40GP
26 — Boston Bruins, 1971-72. 39GP
— Montreal Canadiens, 1975-76. 40GP
— Edmonton Oilers, 1983-84. 40GP

MOST HOME LOSSES, ONE SEASON:
29 — **Pittsburgh Penguins,** 1983-84. 40GP
28 — Washington Capitals, 1974-75. 40GP
— New Jersey Devils, 1983-84. 40GP
27 — Los Angeles Kings, 1985-86. 40GP

*Denis Potvin was a key member of the
record-setting New York Islander teams
of the early 1980s.*

MOST ROAD LOSSES, ONE SEASON:
 39 — **Washington Capitals,** 1974-75. 40GP
 37 — California Seals, 1973-74. 39GP
 35 — New York Islanders, 1972-73. 39GP

MOST HOME TIES, ONE SEASON:
 13 — **New York Rangers,** 1954-55. 35GP
  — **Philadelphia Flyers,** 1969-70. 38GP
  — **California Seals,** 1971-72. 39GP
  — **California Seals,** 1972-73. 39GP
  — **Chicago Black Hawks,** 1973-74. 39GP
 12 — New York Islanders, 1974-75. 40GP
  — Vancouver Canucks, 1977-78. 40GP
  — Buffalo Sabres, 1980-81. 40GP
  — Minnesota North Stars, 1981-82. 40GP
  — Vancouver Canucks, 1981-82. 40GP

MOST ROAD TIES, ONE SEASON:
 15 — **Philadelphia Flyers,** 1976-77. 40GP
 14 — Montreal Canadiens, 1952-53. 35GP
  — Montreal Canadiens, 1974-75. 40GP
  — Philadelphia Flyers, 1975-76. 40GP

FEWEST HOME WINS, ONE SEASON:
 2 — **Chicago Black Hawks,** 1927-28. 22GP
 3 — Boston Bruins, 1924-25. 15GP
  — Chicago Black Hawks, 1928-29. 22GP
  — Philadelphia Quakers, 1930-31. 22GP

FEWEST HOME WINS, ONE SEASON (MINIMUM 70-GAME SCHEDULE):
 6 — **Chicago Black Hawks,** 1954-55. 35GP
  — **Washington Capitals,** 1975-76. 40GP
 7 — Boston Bruins, 1962-63. 35GP
  — Washington Capitals, 1974-75. 40GP
  — Winnipeg Jets, 1980-81. 40GP
  — Pittsburgh Penguins, 1983-84. 40GP

FEWEST ROAD WINS, ONE SEASON:
 0 — **Toronto Arenas,** 1918-19. 9GP
  — **Quebec Bulldogs,** 1919-20. 12GP
  — **Pittsburgh Pirates,** 1929-30. 22GP
 1 — Hamilton Tigers, 1921-22. 12GP
  — Toronto St. Patricks, 1925-26. 18GP
  — Philadelphia Quakers, 1930-31. 22GP
  — New York Americans, 1940-41. 24GP
  — Washington Capitals, 1974-75. 40GP

FEWEST ROAD WINS, ONE SEASON (MINIMUM 70-GAME SCHEDULE):
 1 — **Washington Capitals,** 1974-75. 40GP
 2 — Boston Bruins, 1960-61. 35GP
  — Los Angeles Kings, 1969-70. 38GP
  — New York Islanders, 1972-73. 39GP
  — California Seals, 1973-74. 39GP
  — Winnipeg Jets, 1980-81. 40GP

FEWEST HOME LOSSES, ONE SEASON:
 0 — **Ottawa Senators,** 1922-23. 12GP
  — **Montreal Canadiens,** 1943-44. 25GP
 1 — Toronto Arenas, 1917-18. 11GP
  — Ottawa Senators, 19. 9GP
  — Ottawa Senators, 1919-20. 12GP
  — Toronto St. Patricks, 1922-23. 12GP
  — Boston Bruins, 1929-30 and 1930-31. 22GP
  — Montreal Canadiens, 1976-77. 40GP

FEWEST HOME LOSSES, ONE SEASON (MINIMUM 70-GAME SCHEDULE):
 1 — **Montreal Canadiens,** 1976-77. 40GP
 2 — Montreal Canadiens, 1961-62. 35GP
  — New York Rangers, 1970-71. 39GP
  — Philadelphia Flyers, 1975-76. 40GP

FEWEST ROAD LOSSES, ONE SEASON:
 3 — **Montreal Canadiens,** 1928-29. 22GP
 4 — Ottawa Senators, 1919-20. 12GP
  — Montreal Canadiens, 1927-28. 22GP
  — Boston Bruins, 1929-30. 20GP
  — Boston Bruins, 1940-41. 24GP

FEWEST ROAD LOSSES, ONE SEASON (MINIMUM 70-GAME SCHEDULE):
 6 — **Montreal Canadiens,** 1972-73. 39GP
  — **Montreal Canadiens,** 1974-75. 40GP
  — **Montreal Canadiens,** 1977-78. 40GP
 7 — Detroit Red Wings, 1951-52. 35GP
  — Montreal Canadiens, 1976-77. 40GP
  — Philadelphia Flyers, 1979-80. 40GP

FEWEST HOME TIES, ONE SEASON:
 0 — **Boston Bruins,** 1926-27. 22GP
  — **Boston Bruins,** 1929-30. 22GP
  — **Boston Bruins,** 1934-35. 24GP
  — **Montreal Canadiens,** 1936-37. 24GP
  — **Toronto Maple Leafs,** 1941-42. 24GP

FEWEST HOME TIES, ONE SEASON (MINIMUM 70-GAME SCHEDULE):
 1 — **Montreal Canadiens,** 1955-56. 35GP
  — **Montreal Canadiens,** 1965-66. 35GP
  — **California Seals,** 1970-71. 39GP
  — **Philadelphia Flyers,** 1976-77. 40GP
  — **New York Islanders,** 1983-84. 40GP
  — **New York Rangers,** 1983-84. 40GP
  — **Buffalo Sabres,** 1985-86. 40GP
  — **Philadelphia Flyers,** 1985-86. 40GP
  — **New Jersey Devils,** 1987-88. 40GP

FEWEST ROAD TIES, ONE SEASON:
 0 — **Montreal Canadiens,** 1926-27. 22GP
  — **New York Americans,** 1926-27. 22GP
  — **Boston Bruins,** 1938-39. 24GP
  — **Toronto Maple Leafs,** 1939-40. 24GP
  — **Montreal Canadiens,** 1939-40. 24GP
  — **Boston Bruins,** 1964-65. 35GP
  — **California Seals,** 1973-74. 39GP
  — **Washington Capitals,** 1974-75. 40GP

FEWEST ROAD TIES, ONE SEASON (MINIMUM 70-GAME SCHEDULE):
 0 — **Boston Bruins,** 1964-65. 35GP
  — **California Seals,** 1973-74. 39GP
  — **Washington Capitals,** 1974-75. 40GP
 1 — Chicago Black Hawks, 1953-54. 35GP
  — Detroit Red Wings, 1966-67. 35GP
  — New York Rangers, 1975-76. 40GP
  — Toronto Maple Leafs, 1979-80. 40GP
  — Buffalo Sabres, 1983-84. 40GP
  — Edmonton Oilers, 1983-84. 40GP
  — New Jersey Devils, 1985-86. 40GP
  — Edmonton Oilers, 1986-87. 40GP
  — Calgary Flames, 1986-87. 40GP
  — Toronto Maple Leafs, 1988-89. 40GP

LONGEST WINNING STREAK:
 15 Games — **New York Islanders,** Jan. 21, 1982 - Feb. 20, 1982.
 14 Games — Boston Bruins, Dec. 3, 1929 - Jan. 9, 1930.
 13 Games — Boston Bruins, Feb. 23, 1971 - March 20, 1971.
        — Philadelphia Flyers, Oct. 19, 1985 - Nov. 17, 1985.

LONGEST WINNING STREAK FROM START OF SEASON:
 8 Games — **Toronto Maple Leafs,** 1934-35.
        — **Buffalo Sabres,** 1975-76.
 7 Games — Edmonton Oilers, 1983-84.
        — Quebec Nordiques, 1985-86.
        — Pittsburgh Penguins, 1986-87.

LONGEST HOME WINNING STREAK FROM START OF SEASON:
 11 Games — **Chicago Black Hawks, 1963-64**
 10 Games — Ottawa Senators, 1925-26
 9 Games — Montreal Canadiens, 1953-54
        — Chicago Black Hawks, 1971-72
 8 Games — Boston Bruins, 1983-84
        — Philadelphia Flyers, 1986-87
        — New Jersey Devils, 1987-88

LONGEST WINNING STREAK, INCLUDING PLAYOFFS:
 15 Games — **Detroit Red Wings,** Feb. 27, 1955 - April 5, 1955. Nine regular-season games, six playoff games.

LONGEST HOME WINNING STREAK (ONE SEASON):
 20 Games — **Boston Bruins,** Dec. 3, 1929 - Mar. 18, 1930.
        — **Philadelphia Flyers,** Jan. 4, 1976 - April 3, 1976.

LONGEST HOME WINNING STREAK, INCLUDING PLAYOFFS:
 24 Games — **Philadelphia Flyers,** Jan. 4, 1976 - April 25, 1976. 20 regular-season games, 4 playoff games.

LONGEST ROAD WINNING STREAK (ONE SEASON):
 10 Games — **Buffalo Sabres,** Dec. 10, 1983 - Jan. 23, 1984.
 8 Games — Boston Bruins, Feb. 17, 1972 - Mar. 8, 972.
        — Los Angeles Kings, Dec. 18, 1974 - Jan. 16, 1975.
        — Montreal Canadiens, Dec. 18, 1977 - Jan. 18. 1978.
        — New York Islanders, Feb. 27, 1981 - March 29, 1981.
        — Montreal Canadiens, Jan. 21, 1982 - Feb. 21, 1982.
        — Philadelphia Flyers, Dec. 22, 1982 - Jan. 16, 1983.
        — Winnipeg Jets, Feb. 25, 1985 - Apr. 6, 1985.
        — Edmonton Oilers, Dec. 9, 1986 - Jan. 17, 1987.

LONGEST UNDEFEATED STREAK (ONE SEASON):
 35 Games — **Philadelphia Flyers,** Oct. 14, 1979 - Jan. 6, 1980. 25w-10T.
 28 Games — Montreal Canadiens, Dec. 18, 1977 - Feb. 23, 1978. 23w-5T.
 23 Games — Boston Bruins, Dec. 22, 1940 - Feb. 23, 1941. 15w-8T.
        — Philadelphia Flyers, Jan. 29, 1976 - Mar. 18, 1976. 17w-6T.

LONGEST UNDEFEATED STREAK FROM START OF SEASON:
 15 Games — **Edmonton Oilers,** 1984-85. 12w-3T
 14 Games — Montreal Canadiens, 1943-44. 11w-3T
 13 Games — Montreal Canadiens, 1972-73. 9w-4T

LONGEST HOME UNDEFEATED STREAK (ONE SEASON):
 34 Games — **Montreal Canadiens,** Nov. 1, 1976 - Apr. 2, 1977. 28w-6T.
 27 Games — Boston Bruins, Nov. 22, 1970 - Mar. 20, 1971. 26w-1T.

LONGEST HOME UNDEFEATED STREAK, INCLUDING PLAYOFFS:
 38 Games — **Montreal Canadiens,** Nov. 1, 1976 - April 26, 1977. 28w-6T in regular season and 4w in playoffs).

Wayne Gretzky and Paul Coffey were vital parts of Edmonton Oiler teams that scored 400 or more goals in five consecutive seasons from 1981-82 to 1985-86.

LONGEST ROAD UNDEFEATED STREAK (ONE SEASON):
23 Games — Montreal Canadiens, Nov. 27, 1974 - Mar. 12, 1975. 14w-9т.
17 Games — Montreal Canadiens, Dec. 18, 1977 - March 1, 1978. 14w-3т.
16 Games — Philadelphia Flyers, Oct. 20, 1979 - Jan. 6, 1980. 11w-5т.

LONGEST LOSING STREAK (ONE SEASON):
17 Games — Washington Capitals, Feb. 18, 1975 - Mar. 26, 1975.
15 Games — Philadelphia Quakers, Nov. 29, 1930 - Jan. 8, 1931.

LONGEST LOSING STREAK FROM START OF SEASON:
11 Games — New York Rangers, 1943-44.
7 Games — Montreal Canadiens, 1938-39.
— Chicago Black Hawks, 1947-48.
— Washington Capitals, 1983-84.

LONGEST HOME LOSING STREAK (ONE SEASON):
11 Games — Boston Bruins, Dec. 8, 1924 - Feb. 17, 1925.
— **Washington Capitals,** Feb. 18, 1975 - Mar. 30, 1975.

LONGEST ROAD LOSING STREAK (ONE SEASON):
37 Games — Washington Capitals, Oct. 9, 1974 - Mar. 26, 1975.

LONGEST WINLESS STREAK (ONE SEASON):
30 Games — Winnipeg Jets, Oct. 19, 1980 - Dec. 28, 1980. 23L-7т.
27 Games — Kansas City Scouts, Feb. 12, 1976 - April 4, 1976. 21L-6т.
25 Games — Washington Capitals, Nov. 29, 1975 - Jan. 21, 1976. 22L-3т.

LONGEST WINLESS STREAK FROM START OF SEASON:
15 Games — New York Rangers, 1943-44. 14L-1т
12 Games — Pittsburgh Pirates, 1927-28. 9L-3т
11 Games — Minnesota North Stars, 1973-74. 5L-6т

LONGEST HOME WINLESS STREAK (ONE SEASON):
15 Games — Chicago Black Hawks, Dec. 16, 1928 - Feb. 28, 1929. 11L-4т.
— **Montreal Canadiens,** Dec. 16, 1939 - Mar. 7, 1940. 12L-3т.

LONGEST ROAD WINLESS STREAK (ONE SEASON):
37 Games — Washington Capitals, Oct. 9, 1974 - Mar. 26, 1975. 37L-0т.

LONGEST NON-SHUTOUT STREAK:
264 Games — Calgary Flames, Nov. 12, 1981 - Jan. 9, 1985.
252 Games — Los Angeles Kings, Mar. 15, 1986 - Apr. 2, 1989.
230 Games — Quebec Nordiques, Feb. 10, 1980 - Jan. 13, 1983.
229 Games — Edmonton Oilers, Mar. 15, 1981 - Feb. 11, 1984.
228 Games — Chicago Black Hawks, Mar. 14, 1970 - Feb. 21, 1973.

LONGEST NON-SHUTOUT STREAK INCLUDING PLAYOFFS:
264 Games — Los Angeles Kings, Mar. 15 1986 - Apr. 6, 1989.
(5 playoff games in 1987; 5 in 1988; 2 in 1989)
262 Games — Chicago Black Hawks, Mar. 14, 1970 - Feb. 21, 1973. (8 playoff games in 1970; 18 in 1971; 8 in 1972).
251 Games — Quebec Nordiques, Feb. 10, 1980 - Jan. 13, 1983. (5 playoff games in 1981; 16 in 1982).
235 Games — Boston Bruins, Oct. 26, 1977 - Feb. 20, 1980. (15 playoff games in 1978; 11 in 1979).

MOST CONSECUTIVE GAMES SHUT OUT:
8 — Chicago Black Hawks, 1928-29.

MOST SHUTOUTS, ONE SEASON:
22 — Montreal Canadiens, 1928-29. All by George Hainsworth. 44GP
16 — New York Americans, 1928-29. Roy Worters had 13; Flat Walsh 3. 44GP
15 — Ottawa Senators, 1925-26. All by Alex Connell. 36GP
— Ottawa Senators, 1927-28. All by Alex Connell. 44GP
— Boston Bruins, 1927-28. All by Hal Winkler. 44GP
— Chicago Black Hawks, 1969-70. All by Tony Esposito. 76GP

MOST GOALS, ONE SEASON:
446—Edmonton Oilers, 1983-84. 80GP
426—Edmonton Oilers, 1985-86. 80GP
424—Edmonton Oilers, 1982-83. 80GP
417—Edmonton Oilers, 1981-82. 80GP
401—Edmonton Oilers, 1984-85. 80GP

HIGHEST GOALS-PER-GAME AVERAGE, ONE SEASON:
5.58—Edmonton Oilers, 1983-84. 446G in 80GP.
5.38—Montreal Canadiens, 1919-20. 129G in 24GP.
5.33—Edmonton Oilers, 1985-86. 426G in 80GP.
5.30—Edmonton Oilers, 1982-83. 424G in 80GP.
5.23—Montreal Canadiens, 1917-18. 115G in 22GP.

FEWEST GOALS, ONE SEASON:
33—Chicago Black Hawks, 1928-29. 44GP
45—Montreal Maroons, 1924-25. 30GP
46—Pittsburgh Pirates, 1928-29. 44GP

FEWEST GOALS, ONE SEASON (MINIMUM 70-GAME SCHEDULE):
133—Chicago Black Hawks, 1953-54. 70GP
147—Toronto Maple Leafs, 1954-55. 70GP
—Boston Bruins, 1955-56. 70GP
150—New York Rangers, 1954-55. 70GP

LOWEST GOALS-PER-GAME AVERAGE, ONE SEASON:
.75—Chicago Black Hawks, 1928-29, 33G in 44GP.
1.05—Pittsburgh Pirates, 1928-29. 46G in 44GP.
1.20—New York Americans, 1928-29. 53G in 44GP.

MOST GOALS AGAINST, ONE SEASON:
446—Washington Capitals, 1974-75. 80GP
415—Detroit Red Wings, 1985-86. 80GP
403—Hartford Whalers, 1982-83. 80GP
401—Vancouver Canucks, 1984-85. 80GP
400—Winnipeg Jets, 1980-81. 80GP

HIGHEST GOALS-AGAINST-PER-GAME AVERAGE, ONE SEASON:
7.38—Quebec Bulldogs, 1919-20, 177GA vs. in 24GP.
6.20—New York Rangers, 1943-44, 310GA vs. in 50GP.
5.58—Washington Capitals, 1974-75, 446GA vs. in 80GP.

Bob Bourne scored 238 goals in his 12 seasons with the New York Islanders.

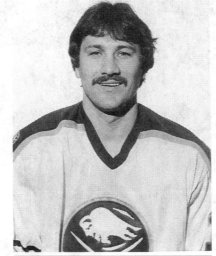

Gil Perreault holds 10 team scoring records for the Buffalo Sabres.

FEWEST GOALS AGAINST, ONE SEASON:
42—Ottawa Senators, 1925-26. 36GP
43—Montreal Canadiens, 1928-29. 44GP
48—Montreal Canadiens, 1923-24. 24GP
—Montreal Canadiens, 1927-28. 44GP

FEWEST GOALS AGAINST, ONE SEASON (MINIMUM 70-GAME SCHEDULE):
131—Toronto Maple Leafs, 1953-54. 70GP
—Montreal Canadiens, 1955-56. 70GP
132—Detroit Red Wings, 1953-54. 70GP
133—Detroit Red Wings, 1951-52 70GP

LOWEST GOALS-AGAINST-PER-GAME AVERAGE, ONE SEASON:
.98—Montreal Canadiens, 1928-29. 43GA vs. in 44GP.
1.05—Montreal Canadiens, 1927-28. 48GA vs. in 44GP.
1.17—Ottawa Senators, 1925-26. 42GA vs. in 36GP.

MOST POWER-PLAY GOALS, ONE SEASON:
120—Pittsburgh Penguins, 1988-89. 80GP
111—New York Rangers, 1987-88. 80GP
110—Pittsburgh Penguins, 1987-88. 80GP
—Winnipeg Jets, 1987-88, 80GP
109—Calgary Flames, 1987-88. 80GP
103—Los Angeles Kings, 1987-88. 80GP
101—Calgary Flames, 1988-89. 80GP

MOST POWER-PLAY GOALS AGAINST, ONE SEASON:
122—Chicago Blackhawks, 1988-89. 80GP
120—Pittsburgh Penguins, 1987-88. 80GP
115—New Jersey Devils, 1988-89. 80GP
111—Detroit Red Wings, 1985-86. 80GP
—Pittsburgh Penguins, 1988-89. 80GP
110—Pittsburgh Penguins, 1982-83. 80GP
108—Minnesota North Stars, 1987-88. 80GP
103—New Jersey Devils, 1985-86. 80GP
—Los Angeles Kings, 1985-86. 80GP
—New York Islanders, 1988-89. 80GP

MOST SHORTHAND GOALS, ONE SEASON:
36 — Edmonton Oilers, 1983-84. 80GP
28 — Edmonton Oilers, 1986-87. 80GP
27 — Edmonton Oilers, 1985-86. 80GP
— Edmonton Oilers, 1988-89. 80GP

MOST SHORTHAND GOALS AGAINST, ONE SEASON:
22 — Pittsburgh Penguins, 1984-85. 80GP
21 — Calgary Flames, 1984-85. 80GP
20 — Minnesota North Stars, 1982-83. 80GP
— Quebec Nordiques, 1985-86. 80GP

MOST ASSISTS, ONE SEASON:
737—Edmonton Oilers, 1985-86. 80GP
736—Edmonton Oilers, 1983-84. 80GP
723—Edmonton Oilers, 1982-83. 80GP

FEWEST ASSISTS, ONE SEASON:
45 — New York Rangers, 1926-27. 44GP

FEWEST ASSISTS, ONE SEASON (MINIMUM 70-GAME SCHEDULE):
206—Chicago Black Hawks, 1953-54. 70GP

MOST SCORING POINTS, ONE SEASON:
1,182 — Edmonton Oilers, 1983-84. 80GP
1,163 — Edmonton Oilers, 1985-86. 80GP
1,129 — Edmonton Oilers, 1982-83. 80GP

MOST 50-OR-MORE-GOAL SCORERS, ONE SEASON:
3 — Edmonton Oilers, 1983-84. Wayne Gretzky, 87; Glenn Anderson, 54; Jari Kurri, 52 80GP.
— **Edmonton Oilers,** 1985-86. Jari Kurri, 68; Glenn Anderson, 54; Wayne Gretzky, 52. 80GP.
2 — Boston Bruins, 1970-71. Phil Esposito, 76; John Bucyk, 51. 78GP.
— Boston Bruins, 1973-74. Phil Esposito, 68; Ken Hodge, 50. 78GP.
— Philadelphia Flyers, 1975-76. Reggie Leach, 61; Bill Barber, 50. 80GP.
— Pittsburgh Penguins, 1975-76. Pierre Larouche, 53; Jean Pronovost, 52. 80GP
— Montreal Canadiens, 1976-77. Steve Shutt, 60; Guy Lafleur, 56. 80GP
— Los Angeles Kings, 1979-80. Charlie Simmer, 56; Marcel Dionne, 53. 80GP
— Montreal Canadiens, 1979-80. Pierre Larouche, 50; Guy Lafleur, 50. 80GP
— Los Angeles Kings, 1980-81. Marcel Dionne, 58; Charlie Simmer, 56. 80GP
— Edmonton Oilers, 1981-82. Wayne Gretzky, 92; Mark Messier, 50. 80GP
— New York Islanders, 1981-82. Mike Bossy, 64; Bryan Trottier, 50. 80GP
— Edmonton Oilers, 1984-85. Wayne Gretzky, 73; Jari Kurri, 71. 80GP
— Washington Capitals, 1984-85. Bob Carpenter, 53; Mike Gartner, 50. 80GP
— Edmonton Oilers, 1986-87. Wayne Gretzky, 62; Jari Kurri, 54. 80GP
— Calgary Flames, 1987-88. Joe Nieuwendyk, 51; Hakan Loob, 50. 80GP
— Los Angeles Kings, 1987-88. Jimmy Carson, 55; Luc Robitaille, 53. 80GP
— Los Angeles Kings, 1988-89. Bernie Nicholls, 70; Wayne Gretzky, 54. 80GP
— Calgary Flames, 1988-89. Joe Nieuwendyk, 51; Joe Mullen, 51. 80GP

MOST 40-OR-MORE-GOAL SCORERS, ONE SEASON:
4 — Edmonton Oilers, 1982-83. Wayne Gretzky, 71; Glenn Anderson, 48; Mark Messier, 48; Jari Kurri, 45. 80GP
— **Edmonton Oilers,** 1983-84. Wayne Gretzky, 87; Glenn Anderson, 54; Jari Kurri, 52; Paul Coffey, 40. 80GP
— **Edmonton Oilers,** 1984-85. Wayne Gretzky, 73; Jari Kurri, 71; Mike Krushelnyski, 43; Glenn Anderson, 42. 80GP
— **Edmonton Oilers,** 1985-86. Jari Kurri, 68; Glenn Anderson, 54; Wayne Gretzky, 52; Paul Coffey, 48. 80GP
— **Calgary Flames,** 1987-88. Joe Nieuwendyk, 51; Hakan Loob, 50; Mike Bullard, 48; Joe Mullen, 40. 80GP
3 — Boston Bruins, 1970-71. Phil Esposito, 76; John Bucyk, 51; Ken Hodge, 43. 78GP
— New York Rangers, 1971-72. Vic Hadfield, 50; Jean Ratelle, 46; Rod Gilbert, 43. 78GP
— Buffalo Sabres, 1975-76. Danny Gare, 50; Rick Martin, 49; Gilbert Perreault, 44. 80GP
— Montreal Canadiens, 1979-80. Guy Lafleur, 50; Pierre Larouche, 50; Steve Shutt, 47. 80GP
— Buffalo Sabres, 1979-80. Danny Gare, 56; Rick Martin, 45; Gilbert Perreault, 40. 80GP
— Los Angeles Kings, 1980-81. Marcel Dionne, 58; Charlie Simmer, 56; Dave Taylor, 47. 80GP
— Los Angeles Kings, 1984-85. Marcel Dionne, 46; Bernie Nicholls, 46; Dave Taylor, 41. 80GP
— New York Islanders, 1984-85. Mike Bossy, 58; Brent Sutter, 42; John Tonelli; 42. 80GP
— Chicago Blackhawks, 1985-86. Denis Savard, 47; Troy Murray, 45; Al Secord, 40. 80GP
— Chicago Blackhawks, 1987-88. Denis Savard, 44; Rick Vaive, 43; Steve Larmer, 41. 80GP
— Edmonton Oilers, 1987-88. Craig Simpson, 43; Jari Kurri, 43; Wayne Gretzky, 40. 80GP
— Los Angeles Kings, 1988-89. Bernie Nicholls, 70; Wayne Gretzky 54; Luc Robitaille, 46. 80GP

MOST 30-OR-MORE GOAL SCORERS, ONE SEASON:
6 — **Buffalo Sabres,** 1974-75. Rick Martin, 52; René Robert, 40; Gilbert Perreault, 39; Don Luce, 33; Rick Dudley, Danny Gare, 31 each. 80GP
— **New York Islanders,** 1977-78, Mike Bossy, 53; Bryan Trottier, 46; Clark Gillies, 35; Denis Potvin, Bob Nystrom, Bob Bourne, 30 each. 80GP
— **Winnipeg Jets,** 1984-85. Dale Hawerchuk, 53; Paul MacLean, 41; Thomas Steen, 30; Laurie Boschman, 32; Brian Mullen, 32; Doug Smail, 31. 80GP
5 — Chicago Black Hawks, 1968-69. 76GP
— Boston Bruins, 1970-71. 78GP
— Montreal Canadiens, 1971-72. 78GP
— Philadelphia Flyers, 1972-73. 78GP
— Boston Bruins, 1973-74. 78GP
— Montreal Canadiens, 1974-75. 80GP
— Montreal Canadiens, 1975-76. 80GP
— Pittsburgh Penguins, 1975-76. 80GP
— New York Islanders, 1978-79. 80GP
— Detroit Red Wings, 1979-80. 80GP
— Philadelphia Flyers, 1979-80. 80GP
— New York Islanders, 1980-81. 80GP
— St. Louis Blues, 1980-81. 80GP
— Chicago Black Hawks, 1981-82. 80GP
— Edmonton Oilers, 1981-82. 80GP
— Montreal Canadiens, 1981-82. 80GP
— Washington Capitals, 1981-82. 80GP
— Edmonton Oilers, 1982-83. 80GP
— Edmonton Oilers, 1983-84. 80GP
— Edmonton Oilers, 1984-85. 80GP
— Edmonton Oilers, 1985-86. 80GP
— Edmonton Oilers, 1986-87. 80GP
— Edmonton Oilers, 1987-88. 80GP
— Edmonton Oilers, 1988-89. 80GP

MOST 20-OR-MORE GOAL SCORERS, ONE SEASON:
11 — **Boston Bruins,** 1977-78; Peter McNab, 41; Terry O'Reilly, 29; Bobby Schmautz, Stan Jonathan, 27 each; Jean Ratelle, Rick Middleton, 25 each; Wayne Cashman, 24; Gregg Sheppard, 23; Brad Park, 22; Don Marcotte, Bob Miller, 20 each. 80GP
10 — Boston Bruins, 1970-71. 78GP
— Montreal Canadiens, 1974-75. 80GP
— St. Louis Blues, 1980-81. 80GP

MOST 100 OR-MORE-POINT SCORERS, ONE SEASON:
4 — **Boston Bruins,** 1970-71, Phil Esposito, 76G-76A-152PTS; Bobby Orr, 37G-102A-139PTS; John Bucyk, 51G-65A-116PTS; Ken Hodge, 43G-62A-105PTS. 78GP
— **Edmonton Oilers,** 1982-83, Wayne Gretzky, 71G-125A-196PTS; Mark Messier, 48G-58A-106PTS; Glenn Anderson, 48G-58A-104PTS; Jari Kurri, 45G-59A-104PTS. 80GP.
— **Edmonton Oilers,** 1983-84, Wayne Gretzky, 87G-118A-205PTS; Paul Coffey, 40G-86A-126PTS; Jari Kurri, 52G-61A-113PTS; Mark Messier, 37G-64A-101PTS. 80GP.
— **Edmonton Oilers,** 1985-86, Wayne Gretzky, 52G-163A-215PTS; Paul Coffey, 48G-90A-138PTS; Jari Kurri, 68G-63A-131PTS; Glenn Anderson, 54G-48A-102PTS. 80GP.
3 — Boston Bruins, 1973-74, Phil Esposito, 68G-77A-145PTS; Bobby Orr, 32G-90A-122PTS; Ken Hodge, 50G-55A-105PTS. 78GP
— New York Islanders, 1978-79, Bryan Trottier, 47G-87A-134PTS; Mike Bossy, 69G-57A-126PTS; Denis Potvin, 31G-70A-101PTS. 80GP
— Los Angeles Kings, 1980-81, Marcel Dionne, 58G-77A-135PTS; Dave Taylor, 47 G-65A-112PTS; Charlie Simmer, 56G-49A-105PTS. 80GP
— Edmonton Oilers, 1984-85, Wayne Gretzky, 73G-135A-208PTS; Jari Kurri, 71G-64A-135PTS; Paul Coffey, 37G-84A-121PTS. 80GP
— New York Islanders, 1984-85. Mike Bossy, 58G-59A-117PTS; Brent Sutter, 42G-60A-102PTS; John Tonelli, 42G-58A-100PTS. 80GP
— Edmonton Oilers, 1986-87, Wayne Gretzky, 62G-121A-183PTS; Jari Kurri, 54G-54A-108PTS; Mark Messier, 37G-70A-107PTS. 80GP
— Pittsburgh Penguins, 1988-89, Mario Lemieux, 85G-114A-199PTS; Rob Brown, 49G-66A-115PTS; Paul Coffey, 30G-83A-113PTS. 80GP

MOST PENALTY MINUTES, ONE SEASON:
2,670 – Pittsburgh Penguins, 1988-89. 80GP
2,621 – Philadelphia Flyers, 1980-81. 80GP
2,499 – New Jersey Devils, 1988-89. 80GP
2,496 – Chicago Blackhawks, 1988-89. 80GP

MOST GOALS, BOTH TEAMS, ONE GAME:
21 — **Montreal Canadiens, Toronto St. Patricks,** at Montreal, Jan. 10, 1920. Montreal won 14-7.
— **Edmonton Oilers, Chicago Blackhawks,** at Chicago, Dec. 11, 1985. Edmonton won 12-9.
20 — Edmonton Oilers, Minnesota North North Stars, at Edmonton, Jan. 4, 1984. Edmonton won 12-8.
— Toronto Maple Leafs, Edmonton Oilers, at Toronto, Jan. 8, 1986. Toronto won 11-9.
19 — Montreal Wanderers, Toronto Arenas, at Montreal, Dec. 19, 1917. Montreal won 10-9.
— Montreal Canadiens, Quebec Bulldogs, at Quebec City, March 3, 1920, Montreal won 16-3.
— Montreal Canadiens, Hamilton Tigers, at Montreal, Feb. 26, 1921. Canadiens won 13-6.
— Boston Bruins, New York Rangers, at Boston, March 4, 1944, Boston won 10-9.
— Boston Bruins, Detroit Red Wings, at Detroit, March 16, 1944. Detroit won 10-9.
— Vancouver Canucks, Minnesota North Stars, at Vancouver, Oct. 7, 1983. Vancouver won 10-9.

MOST GOALS, ONE TEAM, ONE GAME:
16 — **Montreal Canadiens,** March 3, 1920, at Quebec City. Defeated Quebec Bulldogs 16-3.

MOST CONSECUTIVE GOALS, ONE TEAM, ONE GAME:
15 — **Detroit Red Wings,** Jan. 23, 1944, at Detroit. Defeated New York Rangers 15-0.

MOST POINTS, BOTH TEAMS, ONE GAME:
62 — **Edmonton Oilers, Chicago Blackhawks,** at Chicago, Dec. 11, 1985. Edmonton won 12-9. Edmonton had 24A, Chicago, 17.
53 — Quebec Nordiques, Washington Capitals at Washington, Feb. 22, 1981. Quebec won 11-7. Quebec had 22A, Washington, 13.
— Edmonton Oilers, Minnesota North Stars, at Edmonton, Jan. 4, 1984. Edmonton had 20A, Minnesota 13.
— Minnesota North Stars, St. Louis Blues, at St. Louis, Jan. 27, 1984. Minnesota won 10-8. Minnesota had 19A, St. Louis 16.
52 — Montreal Maroons, New York Americans, at New York, Feb. 18, 1936. 8-8 tie. New York had 20A, Montreal 16. (3A allowed for each goal.)
— Vancouver Canucks, Minnesota North Stars, at Vancouver, Oct. 7, 1983. Vancouver won 10-9. Vancouver had 16A, Minnesota 17.

MOST POINTS, ONE TEAM, ONE GAME:
40 — **Buffalo Sabres,** Dec. 21, 1975, at Buffalo. Buffalo defeated Washington Capitals 14-2, receiving 26A.
39 — Minnesota North Stars, Nov. 11, 1981, at Minnesota. Minnesota defeated Winnipeg 15-2, receiving 24A.
36 — Detroit Red Wings, Jan. 23, 1944, at Detroit. Detroit defeated New York Rangers 15-0, receiving 22A.
— Toronto Maple Leafs, March 16, 1957, at Toronto. Toronto defeated New York Rangers 14-1, receiving 23A.
— Buffalo Sabres, Feb. 25, 1978, at Cleveland. Buffalo defeated Cleveland Barons 13-3, receiving 24A.
— Edmonton Oilers, Dec. 11, 1985, at Chicago. Edmonton defeated Chicago 12-9, receiving 24A.

MOST SHOTS, BOTH TEAMS, ONE GAME:
141— New York Americans, Pittsburgh Pirates, Dec. 26, 1925. Americans, who won game 3-1, had 73 shots; Pirates, 68 shots.

MOST SHOTS, ONE TEAM, ONE GAME:
73— **New York Americans, Dec. 26, 1925,** at New York. Americans defeated Pittsburgh Pirates 3-1.
72— Boston Bruins, Dec. 10, 1970, at Boston. Bruins defeated Buffalo 8-2.

MOST PENALTIES, BOTH TEAMS, ONE GAME: (AND)
MOST PENALTY MINUTES, BOTH TEAMS, ONE GAME:
84 Penalties; 406 Minutes — **Minnesota North Stars, Boston Bruins** at Boston, Feb. 26, 1981. Minnesota received 18 minors, 13 majors, 4 10-minute misconducts and 7 game misconducts; a total 42 penalties and 211PIM. Boston received 20 minors, 13 majors, 3 10-minute misconducts and 6 game misconducts; a total 42 penalties and 195PIM.

MOST PENALTIES, ONE TEAM, ONE GAME:
42 — **Minnesota North Stars,** Feb. 26, 1981, at Boston. Minnesota received 18 minors, 13 majors, 4 10-minute misconducts and 7 game misconducts.
— **Boston Bruins,** Feb. 26, 1981, at Boston vs. Minnesota. Boston received 20 minors, 13 majors, 3 10-minute misconducts and 7 game misconducts.

MOST PENALTY MINUTES, ONE TEAM, ONE GAME:
211— **Minnesota North Stars,** Feb. 26, 1981, at Boston. Minnesota received 18 minors, 13 majors, 4 10-minute misconducts and 7 game misconducts.

MOST GOALS, BOTH TEAMS, ONE PERIOD:
12 — **Buffalo Sabres, Toronto Maple Leafs,** at Buffalo, March 19, 1981, second period. Buffalo scored 9 goals, Toronto 3, during 14-4 win by Buffalo.
— **Edmonton Oilers, Chicago Blackhawks,** at Chicago, Dec. 11, 1985, second period. Edmonton scored 6 goals, Chicago 6, during 12-9 win by Edmonton.
10 — New York Rangers, New York Americans, at New York, March 16, 1939, third period. Rangers scored seven goals, Americans three. Rangers won game 11-5.
— Toronto Maple Leafs, Detroit Red Wings, at Detroit, March 17, 1946, third period. Toronto scored six goals, Detroit four. Toronto won game 11-7.
— Vancouver Canucks, Buffalo Sabres, at Buffalo, Jan. 8, 1976, third period. Sabres scored six goals, Canucks four. Buffalo won game 8-5.
— Buffalo Sabres, Montreal Canadiens, at Montreal, Oct. 26, 1982, first period. Canadiens scored five goals, Sabres five. Tie game 7-7.
— Boston Bruins, Quebec Nordiques, at Quebec, Dec. 7, 1982, second period. Nordiques scored six goals, Bruins four. Quebec won game 10-5.
— Calgary Flames, Vancouver Canucks, at Vancouver, Jan. 16, 1987, first period. Canucks scored six goals, Flames four. Vancouver won game 9-5.
— Winnipeg Jets, Detroit Red Wings, at Detroit, Nov. 25, 1987, third period. Detroit scored seven goals, Winnipeg three. Detroit won game 10-8.
— Chicago Blackhawks, St. Louis Blues, at St. Louis, Mar. 15, 1988, third period. Chicago scored five goals, St. Louis five. Tie game 7-7.

MOST GOALS, ONE TEAM, ONE PERIOD:
9 — **Buffalo Sabres,** March 19, 1981, at Buffalo vs. Toronto Maple Leafs, second period. Buffalo won 14-4.
8 — Detroit Red Wings, Jan. 23, 1944, at Detroit, third period during 15-0 win over New York Rangers.
— Boston Bruins, March 16, 1969, at Boston, second period during 11-3 win over Toronto Maple Leafs.
— New York Rangers, Nov. 21, 1971, at New York, third period during 12-1 win over California Seals.
— Philadelphia Flyers, March 31, 1973, at Philadelphia, second period during 10-2 win over New York Islanders.
— Buffalo Sabres, Dec. 21, 1975, at Buffalo, third period during 14-2 win over Washington Capitals.
— Minnesota North Stars, Nov. 11, 1981, at Minnesota, second period during 15-2 win over Winnipeg.

MOST POINTS, BOTH TEAMS, ONE PERIOD:
35 — **Edmonton, Oilers, Chicago Blackhawks,** at Chicago, Dec. 11, 1985, second period. Edmonton had 6G, 12A; Chicago, 6G, 11A. Edmonton won game 12-9.
31 — **Buffalo Sabres, Toronto Maple Leafs,** at Buffalo, March 19, 1981, second period. Buffalo had 9G, 14A; Toronto, 3G, 5A. Buffalo won game 14-4.
29 — **Winnipeg Jets, Detroit Red Wings,** at Detroit, Nov. 25, 1987, third period. Detroit had 7G, 13A; Winnipeg had 3G, 6A. Detroit won game 10-8.
— **Chicago Blackhawks, St. Louis Blues,** at St. Louis, Mar. 15, 1988, third period. St. Louis had 5G, 10A; Chicago had 5G, 9A. Tie game 7-7.

MOST POINTS, ONE TEAM, ONE PERIOD:
23 — **New York Rangers,** Nov. 21, 1971, at New York, third period during 12-1 win over California Seals. New York scored 8G and 15A.
— **Buffalo Sabres,** Dec. 21, 1975, at Buffalo, third period during 14-2 win over Washington Capitals. Buffalo scored 8G and 15A.
— **Buffalo Sabres,** March 19, 1981, at Buffalo vs. Toronto in second period. 9G, 14A. Buffalo won 14-4.
22 — **Detroit Red Wings,** Jan. 23, 1944, at Detroit, third period during 15-0 win over New York Rangers. Detroit scored 8G and 14A.
— **Boston Bruins,** March 16, 1969, at Boston, second period during 11-3 win over Toronto Maple Leafs. Boston scored 8G and 14A.
— **Minnesota North Stars,** Nov. 11, 1981, at Minnesota, second period during 15-2 win over Winnipeg. Minnesota scored 8G and 14A.

MOST SHOTS, ONE TEAM, ONE PERIOD:
37 — **Boston Bruins,** March 4, 1941, at Boston, first period. Boston defeated Chicago 3-2.

MOST PENALTIES, BOTH TEAMS, ONE PERIOD:
67 — **Minnesota North Stars, Boston Bruins,** at Boston, Feb. 26, 1981, first period. Minnesota received 15 minors, 8 majors, 4 10-minute misconducts and 7 game misconducts, a total 34 penalties. Boston had 16 minors, 8 majors, 3 10-minute misconducts and 6 game misconducts, a total 33 penalties.

MOST PENALTY MINUTES, BOTH TEAMS, ONE PERIOD:
372—**Los Angeles Kings, Philadelphia Flyers** at Philadelphia, March 11, 1979, first period. Philadelphia received 4 minors, 8 majors, 6 10-minute misconducts and 8 game misconducts for 188 minutes. Los Angeles received 2 minors, 8 majors, 6 10-minute misconducts and 8 game misconducts for 184 minutes.

MOST PENALTIES, ONE TEAM, ONE PERIOD:
34 — **Minnesota North Stars,** Feb. 26, 1981, at Boston, first period. 15 minors, 8 majors, 4 10-minute misconducts, 7 game misconducts.

MOST PENALTY MINUTES, ONE TEAM, ONE PERIOD:
188—**Philadelphia Flyers,** March 11, 1979, at Philadelphia vs. Los Angeles, first period. Flyers received 4 minors, 8 majors, 6 10-minute misconducts and 8 game misconducts.

FASTEST SIX GOALS, BOTH TEAMS
6 Goals; 3 Minutes, 15 Seconds — Montreal Canadiens, Toronto Maple Leafs, at Montreal, Jan. 4, 1944, first period. Montreal scored 4G, Toronto 2. Montreal won game 6-3.

FASTEST FIVE GOALS, BOTH TEAMS:
1 Minute, 24 Seconds — Chicago Black Hawks, Toronto Maple Leafs, at Toronto, Oct. 15, 1983, second period. Scorers were: Gaston Gingras, Toronto, 16:49; Denis Savard, Chicago, 17:12; Steve Larmer, Chicago, 17:27; Savard, 17:42; and John Anderson, Toronto, 18:13. Toronto won game 10-8.
1 Minute, 39 Seconds — Detroit Red Wings, Toronto Maple Leafs, at Toronto, Nov. 15, 1944, third period. Scorers were: Ted Kennedy, Toronto, 10:36 and 10:55; Hal Jackson, Detroit, 11:48; Steve Wochy, Detroit, 12:02; Don Grosso, Detroit, 12:15. Detroit won game 8-4.

FASTEST FIVE GOALS, ONE TEAM:
2 Minutes, 7 Seconds — Pittsburgh Penguins, at Pittsburgh, Nov. 22, 1972, third period. Scorers: Bryan Hextall, 12:00; Jean Pronovost, 12:18; Al McDonough, 13:40; Ken Schinkel, 13:49; Ron Schock, 14:07. Pittsburgh defeated St. Louis Blues 10-4.
2 Minutes, 55 Seconds — Boston Bruins, at Boston, Dec. 19, 1974. Scorers: Bobby Schmautz, 19:13 (first period); Ken Hodge, 0:18; Phil Esposito, 0:43; Don Marcotte, 0:58; John Bucyk, 2:08 (second period). Boston defeated New York Rangers 11-3.

FASTEST FOUR GOALS, BOTH TEAMS:
53 Seconds — Chicago Black Hawks, Toronto Maple Leafs, at Toronto, Oct. 15, 1983, second period. Scorers were: Gaston Gingras, Toronto, 16:49; Denis Savard, Chicago, 17:12; Steve Larmer, Chicago, 17:27; and Savard at 17:42. Toronto won game 10-8.
1 Minute, 1 Second — Colorado Rockies, New York Rangers, at New York, Jan. 15, 1980, first period. Scorers were: Doug Sulliman, Rangers, 7:52; Ed Johnstone, Rangers, 7:57; Warren Miller, Rangers, 8:20; Rob Ramage, Colorado, 8:53. Colorado 6, Rangers 6.
1 Minute, 5 Seconds — Montreal Canadiens, Toronto Maple Leafs, at Toronto, March 16, 1966, second period. Scorers were: Jean Beliveau, Montreal, 5:00; Dave Keon, Toronto, 5:21; Jean Beliveau, Montreal, 5:43; Ralph Backstrom, Montreal, 6:05. Montreal won game 7-2.

FASTEST FOUR GOALS, ONE TEAM:
1 Minute, 20 Seconds — Boston Bruins, at Boston, Jan. 21, 1945, second period. Scorers were: Bill Thoms at 6:34; Frank Mario at 7:08 and 7:27; and Ken Smith at 7:54. Boston defeated New York Rangers 14-3.

Danny Gare scored 354 goals in his 13-year career with Buffalo, Detroit and Edmonton.

FASTEST THREE GOALS, BOTH TEAMS:
15 Seconds — Minnesota North Stars, New York Rangers, at Minnesota, Feb. 10, 1983, second period. Scorers were: Mark Pavelich, New York, 19:18; Ron Greschner, New York, 19:27; Willi Plett, Minnesota, 19:33. Minnesota won game 7-5.
18 Seconds — Montreal Canadiens, New York Rangers, at Montreal, Dec. 12, 1963, first period. Scorers were: Dave Balon, Montreal, 0:58; Gilles Tremblay, Montreal, 1:04; Camille Henry, New York, 1:16. Montreal won game 6-4.
18 Seconds — California Golden Seals, Buffalo Sabres, at California, Feb. 1, 1976, third period. Scorers were: Jim Moxey, California, 19:38; Wayne Merrick, California, 19:45; Danny Gare, Buffalo, 19:56. Buffalo won game 9-5.

FASTEST THREE GOALS, ONE TEAM:
20 Seconds — Boston Bruins, Feb. 25, 1971, vs. Vancouver Canucks, third period. John Bucyk scored at 4:50, Ed Westfall at 5:02 and Ted Green at 5:10. Bruins won game 8-3.
21 Seconds — Chicago Black Hawks, at New York, Mar. 23, 1952, third period. Bill Mosienko scored all three goals, at 6:09, 6:20 and 6:30. Chicago defeated Rangers 7-6.

FASTEST THREE GOALS FROM START OF PERIOD, BOTH TEAMS:
1 Minute, 5 Seconds — Hartford Whalers, Montreal Canadiens, at Montreal, March 11, 1989, second period. Scorers were: Kevin Dineen, Hartford, 0:11; Guy Carbonneau, Montreal, 0:36; Petr Svoboda, Montreal, 1:05. Montreal won game 5-3.

FASTEST TWO GOALS, BOTH TEAMS:
2 Seconds — St. Louis Blues, Boston Bruins, at Boston, Dec. 19, 1987, third period. Scorers were: Ken Linseman, Boston, at 19:50; Doug Gilmour, St. Louis, at 19:52. St. Louis won game 7-5.
3 Seconds — Chicago Blackhawks, Minnesota North Stars, at Minnesota, November 5, 1988, third period. Scorers were: Steve Thomas, Chicago, at 6:03; Dave Gagner, Minnesota, at 6:06. Chicago and Minnesota tied 5-5.

FASTEST TWO GOALS, ONE TEAM:
4 Seconds — Montreal Maroons, at Montreal, Jan. 3, 1931, third period. Nels Stewart scored both goals, at 8:24 and 8:28. Maroons defeated Boston 5-3.
— **Buffalo Sabres,** at Buffalo, Oct. 17, 1974, third period. Scorers were: Lee Fogolin at 14:55 and Don Luce at 14:59. Buffalo defeated California 6-1.
— **Toronto Maple Leafs,** December 29, 1988, third period. Scorers were: Ed Olczyk at 5:24 and Gary Leeman at 5:28. Toronto won game 6-5.
5 Seconds — New York Rangers, at New York, March 5, 1961, first period. Pat Hannigan at 2:18 and Andy Bathgate at 2:23. Rangers defeated Detroit 4-3.
— **Montreal Canadiens,** at Montreal, Feb. 20, 1971, third period. Pete Mahovlich scored both goals, at 12:16 and 12:21. Montreal defeated Chicago 7-1.
— **New York Rangers,** at New York, Jan. 14, 1980, first period. Scorers were: Doug Sulliman at 7:52 and Ed Johnstone at 7:57. New York and Colorado tied 6-6.
— **Buffalo Sabres,** Dec. 7, 1980, at Buffalo, second period. Gilles Hamel scored at 2:32 and Ric Seiling at 2:37. Buffalo defeated Pittsburgh Penguins 10-1.
— **Chicago Black Hawks,** Jan. 1, 1931, at Philadelphia, third period. Vic Desjardins scored at 1:15 Frank Ingram at 1:20. Chicago defeated Philadelphia 10-3.
— **Toronto Maple Leafs,** Jan. 23, 1987, at Winnipeg, first period. Miroslav Frycer scored at 11:18 and Greg Terrion at 11:23. Winnipeg defeated Toronto 7-5.

FASTEST TWO GOALS FROM START OF PERIOD, BOTH TEAMS:
14 Seconds — New York Rangers, Quebec Nordiques, at Quebec, Nov. 5, 1983, third period. Scorers: Andre Savard, Quebec, 8 seconds; Pierre Larouche, NY Rangers, 14 seconds. Rangers and Quebec tied 4-4.
35 Seconds — Boston Bruins, Pittsburgh Penguins, at Boston, Feb. 10, 1973, second period. Scorers: Lowell MacDonald, Pittsburgh, 7 seconds; Phil Esposito, Boston, 35 seconds. Boston won 6-3.
36 Seconds — Hartford Whalers, Montreal Canadiens, at Montreal, March 11, 1989, second period. Scorers: Kevin Dineen, Hartford, 11 seconds; Guy Carbonneau, Montreal 36 seconds. Montreal won game 5-3.

FASTEST TWO GOALS FROM START OF GAME, ONE TEAM:
24 Seconds — Edmonton Oilers, March 28, 1982, at Los Angeles. Mark Messier, at 14 seconds and Dave Lumley, at 24 seconds, scored in first period. Edmonton won 6-2.
29 Seconds — Pittsburgh Penguins, Dec. 6, 1981, at Pittsburgh against Chicago. George Ferguson at 17 seconds, and Greg Malone, at 29 seconds, scored in first period. Pittsburgh won 6-4.
32 Seconds — Calgary Flames, Mar. 11, 1987, at Hartford. Doug Risebrough scored at 9 seconds and Colin Patterson, at 32 seconds, in first period. Calgary won 6-1.

FASTEST TWO GOALS FROM START OF PERIOD, ONE TEAM:
21 Seconds — Chicago Black Hawks, Nov. 5, 1983, at Minnesota, second period. Ken Yaremchuk scored at 12 seconds and Darryl Sutter at 21 seconds. Minnesota defeated Chicago 10-5.
30 Seconds — Washington Capitals, Jan. 27, 1980, at Washington, second period. Mike Gartner scored at 8 seconds and Bengt Gustafsson at 30 seconds. Washington defeated New York Islanders 7-1.
31 Seconds —Buffalo Sabres, Jan. 10, 1974, at Buffalo, Rene Robert, at 21 seconds and Rick Martin, at 31 seconds, in third period as Buffalo defeated NY Rangers 7-2.
— New York Islanders, Feb. 22, 1986, at New York, third period Roger Kortko at 10 seconds and Bob Bourne at 31 seconds. New York defeated Detroit 5-2.

Individual Records

Career

MOST SEASONS:
26 — Gordie Howe, Detroit Red Wings, 1946-47 – 1970-71; Hartford Whalers, 1979-80.
23 — Alex Delvecchio, Detroit Red Wings, 1951-52 – 1973-74.
— John Bucyk, Detroit, Boston, 1955-56 – 1977-78.
22 — Tim Horton, Toronto, New York Rangers, Pittsburgh, Buffalo, 1952-53 – 1973-74.
— Dean Prentice, New York Rangers, Boston, Detroit, Pittsburgh, Minnesota, 1952-53 – 1973-74.
— Doug Mohns, Boston, Chicago, Minnesota, Atlanta, Washington, 1953-54 – 1974-75.
— Stan Mikita, Chicago Black Hawks, 1958-59 – 1979-80.

MOST GAMES:
1,767 — Gordie Howe, Detroit Red Wings, 1946-47 – 1970-71; Hartford Whalers, 1979-80.
1,549 — Alex Delvecchio, Detroit Red Wings, 1950-51 – 1973-74.
1,540 — John Bucyk, Detroit, Boston, 1955-56 – 1977-78.

MOST GOALS:
801 — Gordie Howe, Detroit Red Wings, Hartford Whalers, in 26 seasons, 1,767GP.
731 — Marcel Dionne, Detroit Red Wings, Los Angeles Kings, New York Rangers, in 18 seasons, 1,348GP.
717 — Phil Esposito, Chicago Black Hawks, Boston Bruins, New York Rangers, in 18 seasons, 1,282GP.
637 — Wayne Gretzky, Edmonton Oilers, Los Angeles Kings, in 10 seasons, 774GP.
610 — Bobby Hull, Chicago Black Hawks, Winnipeg Jets, Hartford Whalers, in 16 seasons, 1,063GP.

HIGHEST GOALS-PER-GAME AVERAGE, CAREER
(AMONG PLAYERS WITH 200 OR MORE GOALS):
.823 — Wayne Gretzky, Edmonton, Los Angeles, 637G, 774GP from 1979-80 – 1988-89.
.815 — Mario Lemieux, Pittsburgh, 300G, 368GP from 1984-85 – 1988-89.
.767 — Cy Denneny, Ottawa, Boston, 250G, 326GP from 1917-18 – 1928-29.
.762 — Mike Bossy, NY Islanders, 573G, 752GP from 1977-78 – 1986-87.
.738 — Babe Dye, Toronto, Chicago, NY Americans, 200G, 271GP from 1919-20 – 1930-31.

MOST ASSISTS:
1,200 — Wayne Gretzky, Edmonton, Los Angeles, in 10 seasons, 774GP.
1,049 — Gordie Howe, Detroit, Hartford in 26 seasons, 1,767GP.
1,040 — Marcel Dionne, Detroit, Los Angeles, NY Rangers in 18 seasons, 1,348GP.
926 — Stan Mikita, Chicago, in 22 seasons, 1,394GP.
873 — Phil Esposito, Chicago, Boston, NY Rangers in 18 seasons, 1,282GP.

HIGHEST ASSIST-PER-GAME AVERAGE, CAREER
(AMONG PLAYERS WITH 300 OR MORE ASSISTS):
1.550 — Wayne Gretzky, Edmonton, Los Angeles, 1,200A, 774GP from 1979-80 – 1988-89.
1.128 — Mario Lemieux, Pittsburgh Penguins, 415A, 368GP from 1984-85 – 1988-89.
.982 — Bobby Orr, Boston, Chicago, 645A, 657GP from 1966-67 – 1978-79.
.933 — Peter Stastny, Quebec, 630A, 675GP from 1980-81 – 1988-89.
.911 — Paul Coffey, Edmonton, Pittsburgh, 595A, 653GP from 1980-81 – 1988-89.
.901 — Denis Savard, Chicago, 609A, 676GP from 1980-81 – 1988-89.

MOST POINTS:
1,850 — Gordie Howe, Detroit, Hartford, in 26 seasons, 1,767GP (801G-1049A).
1,837 — Wayne Gretzky, Edmonton, Los Angeles, in 10 seasons, 774GP (637G-1200A).
1,771 — Marcel Dionne, Detroit, Los Angeles, NY Rangers, in 18 seasons, 1,348GP (731G-1,040A).
1,590 — Phil Esposito, Chicago, Boston, NY Rangers in 18 seasons, 1,282GP (717G-873A).
1,467 — Stan Mikita, Chicago in 22 seasons, 1,394GP (541G-926A).

MOST GOALS BY A CENTER, CAREER
731 — Marcel Dionne, Detroit, Los Angeles, NY Rangers, in 18 seasons.
717 — Phil Esposito, Chicago, Boston, NY Rangers, in 18 seasons.
637 — Wayne Gretzky, Edmonton, Los Angeles, in 10 seasons.
541 — Stan Mikita, Chicago, in 22 seasons.
512 — Gilbert Perreault, Buffalo, in 17 seasons.
507 — Jean Beliveau, Montreal, in 20 seasons.

MOST ASSISTS BY A CENTER, CAREER;
1,200 — Wayne Gretzky, Edmonton, Los Angeles, in 10 seasons.
1,040 — Marcel Dionne, Detroit, Los Angeles, NY Rangers, in 18 seasons.
926 — Stan Mikita, Chicago, in 22 seasons.
873 — Phil Esposito, Chicago, Boston, NY Rangers, in 18 seasons.
852 — Bobby Clarke, Philadelphia, in 15 seasons.

MOST POINTS BY A CENTER, CAREER:
1,837 — Wayne Gretzky, Edmonton, Los Angeles, in 10 seasons.
1,771 — Marcel Dionne, Detroit, Los Angeles, NY Rangers, in 18 seasons.
1,590 — Phil Esposito, Chicago, Boston, NY Rangers, in 18 seasons.
1,467 — Stan Mikita, Chicago, in 22 seasons
1,329 — Bryan Trottier, NY Islanders, in 14 seasons.
1,326 — Gilbert Perreault, Buffalo, in 17 seasons.

MOST GOALS BY A LEFT WING, CAREER:
610 — Bobby Hull, Chicago, Winnipeg, Hartford, in 16 seasons.
556 — John Bucyk, Detroit, Boston, in 23 seasons.
533 — Frank Mahovlich, Toronto, Detroit, Montreal, in 18 seasons.
440 — Michel Goulet, Quebec, in 10 seasons.
424 — Steve Shutt, Montreal, Los Angeles, in 13 seasons.
420 — Bill Barber, Philadelphia, in 12 seasons.

Stan Mikita holds Chicago Blackhawk records for most seasons, games played, career assists and career points.

Wayne Cashman played all of his 17-year NHL career with the Bruins, appearing in 1,074 games before retiring in 1983.

Now with Detroit, Borje Salming recorded 620 assists in 16 seasons with Toronto.

MOST ASSISTS BY A LEFT WING, CAREER:
813 — **John Bucyk,** Detroit, Boston, in 23 seasons.
570 — Frank Mahovlich, Toronto, Detroit, Montreal, in 18 seasons.
560 — Bobby Hull, Chicago, Winnipeg, Hartford, in 16 seasons.
516 — Wayne Cashman, Boston, in 17 seasons.
472 — Ted Lindsay, Detroit, Chicago, in 17 seasons.
469 — Dean Prentice, NY Rangers, Boston, Detroit, Pittsburgh, Minnesota, in 22 seasons.

MOST POINTS BY A LEFT WING, CAREER:
1,369 — **John Bucyk,** Detroit, Boston, in 23 seasons.
1,170 — Bobby Hull, Chicago, Winnipeg, Hartford, in 16 seasons.
1,103 — Frank Mahovlich, Toronto, Detroit, Montreal, in 18 seasons.
900 — Michel Goulet, Quebec, in 10 seasons.
883 — Bill Barber, Philadelphia, in 12 seasons.
860 — Dean Prentice, NY Rangers, Boston, Detroit, Pittsburgh, Minnesota, in 22 seasons.

MOST GOALS BY A RIGHT WING, CAREER:
801 — **Gordie Howe,** Detroit, Hartford, in 26 seasons.
573 — Mike Bossy, NY Islanders, in 10 seasons.
544 — Maurice Richard, Montreal, in 18 seasons.
536 — Guy Lafleur, Montreal, NY Rangers in 15 seasons.

MOST ASSISTS BY A RIGHT WING, CAREER:
1,049 — **Gordie Howe,** Detroit, Hartford, in 26 seasons.
755 — Guy Lafleur, Montreal, NY Rangers, in 15 seasons.
624 — Andy Bathgate, NY Rangers, Toronto, Detroit, Pittsburgh in 17 seasons.
615 — Rod Gilbert, NY Rangers, in 18 seasons.

MOST POINTS BY A RIGHT WING, CAREER:
1,850 — **Gordie Howe,** Detroit, Hartford, in 26 seasons.
1,291 — Guy Lafleur, Montreal, NY Rangers, in 15 seasons.
1,126 — Mike Bossy, NY Islanders, in 10 seasons.
1,021 — Rod Gilbert, NY Rangers, in 18 seasons.

MOST GOALS BY A DEFENSEMAN, CAREER:
310 — **Denis Potvin,** NY Islanders, in 15 seasons.
270 — Bobby Orr, Boston, Chicago, in 12 seasons.
254 — Paul Coffey, Edmonton, Pittsburgh in 9 seasons.
248 — Doug Mohns, Boston, Chicago, Minnesota, Atlanta, Washington, in 22 seasons.
222 — Reed Larson, Detroit, Boston, Edmonton, NY Islanders, Minnesota, in 13 seasons.
213 — Brad Park, NY Rangers, Boston, Detroit, in 17 seasons.

MOST ASSISTS BY A DEFENSEMAN, CAREER:
742 — **Denis Potvin,** NY Islanders, in 15 seasons.
686 — Larry Robinson, Montreal, in 17 seasons.
683 — Brad Park, NY Rangers, Boston, Detroit, in 17 seasons.
645 — Bobby Orr, Bosotn, Chicago, in 12 seasons.
620 — Borje Salming, Toronto, in 16 seasons.

MOST POINTS BY A DEFENSEMAN, CAREER:
1,052 — **Denis Potvin,** NY Islanders, in 15 seasons.
915 — Bobby Orr, Boston, Chicago, in 12 seasons.
896 — Brad Park, NY Rangers, Boston, Detroit, in 17 seasons.
883 — Larry Robinson, Montreal, in 17 seasons.
849 — Paul Coffey, Edmonton, Pittsburgh, in 9 seasons.

MOST OVERTIME GOALS, CAREER:
7 — **Mario Lemieux,** Pittsburgh.
6 — Jari Kurri, Edmonton.
5 — Paul MacLean, St. Louis, Winnipeg.

MOST OVERTIME ASSISTS, CAREER:
9 — **Bernie Federko,** St. Louis.
8 — Wayne Gretzky, Edmonton.
6 — Dale Hawerchuk, Winnipeg.
— Mario Lemieux, Pittsburgh.
— Paul MacLean, St. Louis, Winnipeg, Detroit.

MOST OVERTIME POINTS, CAREER:
13 — **Mario Lemieux,** Pittsburgh, 7G-6A
11 — Paul MacLean, St. Louis, Winnipeg. 5G-6A
10 — Dale Hawerchuk, Winnipeg. 4G-6A
9 — Jari Kurri, Edmonton. 6G-3A
— Wayne Gretzky, Edmonton, Los Angeles. 1G-8A
— Bernie Federko, St. Louis. 9A

HIGHEST POINTS-PER-GAME AVERAGE, CAREER:
(AMONG PLAYERS WITH 500 OR MORE POINTS):
2.373 — **Wayne Gretzky,** Edmonton, Los Angeles, 1,837PTS (637G-1,200A), 774GP from 1979-80 – 1988-89.
1.943 — Mario Lemieux, Pittsburgh, 715PTS (300G-415A), 368GP from 1984-85 – 1988-89.
1.497 — Mike Bossy, NY Islanders, 1,126PTS (573G-553A), 752GP from 1978-79 – 1986-87.
1.461 — Peter Stastny, Quebec, 986PTS (356G-630A), 675GP from 1980-81 – 1988-89.
1.405 — Jari Kurri, Edmonton, 950PTS (441G-509A), 676GP from 1980-81 – 1988-89.
1.393 — Bobby Orr, Boston, Chicago, 915PTS (270G-645A), 657GP from 1966-67 – 1978-79.

MOST PENALTY MINUTES:
3,966 — **Dave Williams,** Toronto, Vancouver, Detroit, Los Angeles, Hartford, in 14 seasons, 962GP.
2,572 — Willi Plett, Atlanta, Calgary, Minnesota, Boston, in 12 seasons, 834GP
2,447 — Chris Nilan, Monteal, NY Rangers, in 10 seasons, 566GP.
2,294 — Dave Schultz, Philadelphia, Los Angeles, Pittsburgh, Buffalo, in 9 seasons, 533GP.
2,212 — Bryan Watson, Montreal, Detroit, California, Pittsburgh, St. Louis, Washington, in 16 seasons, 878GP.

*Alex Delvecchio ranks second in all-time games played,
suiting up 1,549 times with Detroit in his 23-year career.*

*Terry Sawchuk, who joined the Toronto Maple Leafs in 1964,
played a key role in the Leafs' Stanley Cup victory of 1967.*

MOST GAMES, INCLUDING PLAYOFFS:
1,924 — Gordie Howe, Detroit, Hartford, 1,767 regular-season and 157 playoff games.
1,670 — Alex Delvecchio, Detroit, 1,549 regular-season and 121 playoff games.
1,664 — John Bucyk, Detroit, Boston, 1,540 regular-season and 124 playoff games.

MOST GOALS, INCLUDING PLAYOFFS:
869 — Gordie Howe, Detroit, Hartford, 801 regular-season goals and 68 playoff goals.
778 — Phil Esposito, Chicago, Boston, NY Rangers, 717 regular-season and 61 playoff goals.
752 — Marcel Dionne, Detroit, Los Angeles, NY Rangers, 731 regular-season and 21 playoff goals.
723 — Wayne Gretzky, Edmonton, Los Angeles, 637 regular-season and 86 playoff goals.

MOST ASSISTS, INCLUDING PLAYOFFS:
1,388 — Wayne Gretzky, Edmonton, Los Angeles, 1,200 regular-season and 188 playoff assists.
1,141 — Gordie Howe, Detroit, Hartford, 1,049 regular-season and 92 playoff assists.
1,064 — Marcel Dionne, Detroit, Los Angeles, NY Rangers, 1,040 regular-season and 24 playoff assists.
1,017 — Stan Mikita, Chicago, 926 regular-season and 91 playoff assists.
949 — Phil Esposito, Chicago, Boston, NY Rangers, 873 regular-season and 76 playoff assists.

MOST POINTS, INCLUDING PLAYOFFS:
2,111 — Wayne Gretzky, Edmonton, Los Angeles, 1,837 regular-season and 274 playoff points.
2,010 — Gordie Howe, Detroit, Hartford, 1,850 regular-season and 160 playoff points.
1,816 — Marcel Dionne, Detroit, Los Angeles, NY Rangers, 1,771 regular-season and 45 playoff points.
1,727 — Phil Esposito, Chicago, Boston, NY Rangers, 1,590 regular-season and 137 playoff points.
1,617 — Stan Mikita, Chicago, 1,467 regular-season and 150 playoff points.

MOST PENALTY MINUTES, INCLUDING PLAYOFFS:
4,421 — Dave Williams, Toronto, Vancouver, Los Angeles, 3,966 in regular season; 455 in playoffs.
3,038 — Willi Plett, Atlanta, Calgary, Minnesota, Boston, 2,572 in regular-season; 466 in playoffs.
2,882 — Chris Nilan, Montreal, NY Rangers, 2,447 in regular-season; 435 in playoffs.
2,706 — Dave Schultz, Philadelphia, Los Angeles, Pittsburgh, Buffalo, 2,294 regular season; 412 in playoffs.
2,448 — Dale Hunter, Quebec, Washington, 2,004 in regular-season; 444 in playoffs.
2,338 — Andre Dupont, NY Rangers, St. Louis, Philadelphia, Quebec, 1,986 regular-season; 352 in playoffs.

MOST CONSECUTIVE GAMES:
962 — Doug Jarvis, Montreal, Washington, Hartford, from Oct. 8, 1975 – Apr. 5, 1987.
914 — Garry Unger, Toronto, Detroit, St. Louis, Atlanta from Feb. 24, 1968, – Dec. 21, 1979.
776 — Craig Ramsay, Buffalo Sabres, from March 27, 1973, – Feb. 10, 1983.
630 — Andy Hebenton, NY Rangers, Boston nine complete 70-game seasons from 1955-56 – 1963-64.
580 — John Wilson, Detroit, Chicago, Toronto, from Feb. 10, 1952 – Mar. 20, 1960.

MOST GAMES APPEARED IN BY A GOALTENDER, CAREER:
971 — Terry Sawchuk, Detroit, Boston, Toronto, Los Angeles, NY Rangers from 1949-50 - 1969-70.
906 — Glenn Hall, Detroit, Chicago, St. Louis from 1952-53 hrough 1970-71.
886 — Tony Esposito, Montreal, Chicago from 1968-69 - 1983-84.
860 — Lorne "Gump" Worsley, NY Rangers, Montreal, Minnesota from 1952-53 - 1973-74.

MOST CONSECUTIVE COMPLETE GAMES BY A GOALTENDER:
502 — Glenn Hall, Detroit, Chicago. Played 502 games from beginning of 1955-56 season - first 12 games of 1962-63. In his 503rd straight game, Nov. 7, 1962, at Chicago, Hall was removed from the game against Boston with a back injury in the first period.

MOST SHUTOUTS BY A GOALTENDER, CAREER:
103 — Terry Sawchuk, Detroit, Boston, Toronto, Los Angeles, NY Rangers in 20 seasons.
94 — George Hainsworth, Montreal Canadiens, Toronto in 10 seasons.
84 — Glenn Hall, Detroit, Chicago, St. Louis in 16 seasons.

MOST GAMES SCORING THREE-OR-MORE GOALS:
45 — Wayne Gretzky, Edmonton, in 10 seasons, 32 three-goal games, 9 four-goal games, 4 five-goal games.
39 — Mike Bossy, NY Islanders, in 10 seasons, 30 three-goal games, 9 four-goal games.
32 — Phil Esposito, Chicago, Boston, NY Rangers, in 18 seasons, 27 three-goal games, 5 four-goal games.
28 — Bobby Hull, Chicago, Winnipeg, Hartford, in 16 seasons, 24 three-goal games, 4 four-goal games.
— Marcel Dionne, Detroit, Los Angeles, NY Rangers, in 18 seasons, 25 three-goal games, 3 four-goal games.
26 — Cy Denneny, Ottawa Senators in 12 seasons. 20 three-goal games, 5 four-goal games, 1 six-goal game.
— Maurice Richard, Montreal, in 18 seasons, 23 three-goal games, 2 four-goal games, 1 five-goal game.

MOST 20-OR-MORE GOAL SEASONS:
22 — Gordie Howe, Detroit, Hartford in 26 seasons.
17 — Marcel Dionne, Detroit, Los Angeles, NY Rangers, in 18 seasons.
16 — Phil Esposito, Chicago, Boston, NY Rangers, in 18 seasons.
— Norm Ullman, Detroit, Toronto, in 19 seasons.
— John Bucyk, Detroit, Boston, in 22 seasons.
15 — Frank Mahovlich, Toronto, Detroit, Montreal in 17 seasons.
— Gilbert Perreault, Buffalo, in 17 seasons.

MOST CONSECUTIVE 20-OR-MORE GOAL SEASONS:
22 — Gordie Howe, Detroit, 1949-50 – 1970-71.
17 — Marcel Dionne, Detroit, Los Angeles, NY Rangers, 1971-72 – 1987-88.
16 — Phil Esposito, Chicago, Boston, NY Rangers, 1964-65 – 1979-80.
14 — Maurice Richard, Montreal, 1943-44 – 1956-57.
— Stan Mikita, Chicago Black Hawks, 1961-62 — 1974-75.
13 — Guy Lafleur, Montreal, 1971-72 – 1983-84.
— Bryan Trottier, NY Islanders, 1975-76 – 1987-88.

MOST 30-OR-MORE GOAL SEASONS:
14 — Gordie Howe, Detroit, in 25 seasons.
— Marcel Dionne, Detroit, Los Angeles, NY Rangers, in 18 seasons.
13 — Bobby Hull, Chicago, in 16 seasons.
— Phil Esposito, Chicago, Boston, NY Rangers, in 18 seasons.

MOST CONSECUTIVE 30-OR-MORE GOAL SEASONS:
13 — Bobby Hull, Chicago Blackhawks, 1959-60 – 1971-72.
— Phil Esposito, Boston, NY Rangers, 1967-68 – 1979-80.
12 — Marcel Dionne, Detroit, Los Angeles,1974-75 – 1985-86.
10 — Darryl Sittler, Toronto, Philadelphia, 1973-74 – 1982-83.
— Mike Bossy, NY Islanders, 1977-78 – 1986-87.
— Mike Gartner, Washington, Minnesota, 1979-80 – 1988-89.
— Wayne Gretzky, Edmonton, Los Angeles, 1979-80 – 1988-89.
9 — Steve Shutt, Montreal, 1974-75 – 1982-83.
— Lanny McDonald, Toronto, Colorado, Calgary, 1975-76 – 1983-84.
— Bryan Trottier, NY Islanders, 1975-76 – 1983-84.
— Jari Kurri, Edmonton, 1980-81 – 1988-89.
— Rick Vaive, Toronto, Chicago, Buffalo, 1980-81 – 1988-89.
8 — Garry Unger, St. Louis, 1971-72 – 1978-79.
— Glenn Anderson, Edmonton, 1980-81 – 1987-88.
— Michel Goulet, Quebec, 1980-81 – 1987-88.
— Dale Hawerchuk, Winnipeg, 1981-82 – 1988-89.

MOST 40-OR-MORE GOAL SEASONS:
10 — Marcel Dionne, Detroit, Los Angeles, NY Rangers, in 18 seasons.
— Wayne Gretzky, Edmonton, Los Angeles, in 10 seasons.
9 — Mike Bossy, NY Islanders, in 10 seasons.
8 — Bobby Hull, Chicago, Winnipeg, Hartford, in 16 seasons.
— Phil Esposito, Chicago, Boston, NY Rangers, in 18 seasons.
7 — Michel Goulet, Quebec, in 9 seasons.
— Jari Kurri, Edmonton, in 9 seasons.
— Dale Hawerchuk, Winnipeg, in 8 seasons.
6 — Guy Lafleur, Montreal Canadiens, in 13 seasons.
— Lanny McDonald, Toronto, Colorado, Calgary in 13 seasons.
— Joe Mullen, St. Louis, Calgary in 8 seasons.
5 — Gordie Howe, Detroit, Hartford, in 26 seasons.
— Richard Martin, Buffalo, Los Angeles, in 10 seasons.
— Bryan Trottier, NY Islanders, in 13 seasons.
— Rick Middleton, NY Rangers, Boston, in 14 seasons.
— Mike Gartner, Washington, in 9 seasons.
— Peter Stastny, Quebec, in 8 seasons.
— Dino Ciccarelli, Minnesota, Washington, in 9 seasons.
— Tim Kerr, Philadelphia, in 9 seasons.
— Mario Lemieux, Phittsburgh, in 5 seasons.

MOST CONSECUTIVE 40-OR-MORE GOAL SEASONS:
10 — Wayne Gretzky, Edmonton, Los Angeles, 1979-80 – 1988-89.
9 — Mike Bossy, NY Islanders, 1977-78 – 1985-86.
7 — Phil Esposito, Boston, 1968-69 – 1974-75.
— Michel Goulet, Quebec, 1981-82 – 1987-88.
— Jari Kurri, Edmonton, 1982-83 – 1988-89.
6 — Guy Lafleur, Montreal, 1974-75 – 1979-80.
— Joe Mullen, St. Louis, Calgary, 1983-84 – 1988-89.
5 — Rick Middleton, Boston, 1979-80 – 1984-85.
— Marcel Dionne, Los Angeles, 1978-79 – 1982-83.
— Dale Hawerchuk, Winnipeg, 1984-85 – 1988-89.
— Mario Lemieux, Pittsburgh, 1984-85 – 1988-89.
4 — Bobby Hull, Chicago, 1965-66 – 1968-69.
— Lanny McDonald, Toronto, Colorado, 1976-77 – 1979-80.
— Blaine Stoughton, Hartford, 1979-80 – 1982-83.
— Glenn Anderson, Edmonton, 1982-83 – 1985-86.
— Tim Kerr, Philadelphia, 1983-84 – 1986-87.
— Dino Ciccarelli, Minnesota, Washington, 1985-86 – 1988-89.

MOST 50-OR-MORE GOAL SEASONS:
9 — Mike Bossy, NY Islanders, in 10 seasons.
— Wayne Gretzky, Edmonton, Los Angeles, in 10 seasons.
6 — Guy Lafleur, Montreal, in 13 seasons.
— Marcel Dionne, Detroit, Los Angeles, NY Rangers, in 17 seasons.
5 — Bobby Hull, Chicago, Winnipeg, Hartford, in 16 seasons.
— Phil Esposito, Chicago, Boston, NY Rangers, in 18 seasons.

MOST CONSECUTIVE 50-OR-MORE GOAL SEASONS:
9 — Mike Bossy, NY Islanders, 1977-78 – 1985-86.
8 — Wayne Gretzky, Edmonton, 1979-80 – 1986-87.
6 — Guy Lafleur, Montreal Canadiens, 1974-75 – 1979-80.
5 — Phil Esposito, Boston, 1970-71 – 1974-75.
— Marcel Dionne, Los Angeles, 1978-79 – 1982-83.

MOST 100-OR-MORE POINT SEASONS:
10 — Wayne Gretzky, Edmonton, Los Angeles, 1979-80 – 1988-89.
8 — Marcel Dionne, Detroit, 1974-75; Los Angeles, 1976-77; 1978-79 – 1982-83; 1984-85.
7 — Mike Bossy, NY Islanders, 1978-79; 1980-81 – 1985-86.
— Peter Stastny, Quebec, 1980-81 – 1986-87; 1987-88.
6 — Phil Esposito, Chicago, 1968-69; 1970-71 – 1974-75.
— Bobby Orr, Boston, 1969-70 – 1974-75.
— Guy Lafleur, Montreal, 1974-75 – 1979-80.
— Bryan Trottier, NY Islanders, 1977-78 – 1981-82; 1983-84.
— Dale Hawerchuk, Winnipeg, 1981-82; 1983-84 – 1987-88.
— Jari Kurri, Edmonton, 1982-83 – 1986-87; 1988-89.

MOST CONSECUTIVE 100-OR-MORE POINT SEASONS:
10 — Wayne Gretzky, Edmonton, Los Angeles, 1979-80 – 1988-89.
6 — Bobby Orr, Boston, 1969-70 – 1974-75.
— Guy Lafleur, Montreal, 1974-75 – 1979-80.
— Mike Bossy, NY Islanders,1980-81 – 1985-86.
— Peter Stastny, Quebec, 1980-81 – 1985-86.
5 — Phil Esposito, Boston, 1970-71 – 1974-75.
— Bryan Trottier, NY Islanders, 1977-78 – 1981-82.
— Marcel Dionne, Los Angeles, 1978-79 – 1982-83.
— Jari Kurri, Edmonton, 1982-83 – 1986-87.
— Dale Hawerchuk, Winnipeg, 1983-84 – 1987-88.
— Mario Lemieux, Pittsburgh, 1984-85 – 1988-89.

Rick Middleton had five consecutive 40-goal seasons for the Bruins from 1979-80 to 1984-85.

Single Season

MOST GOALS, ONE SEASON:
92 — Wayne Gretzky, Edmonton, 1981-82. 80 game schedule.
87 — Wayne Gretzky, Edmonton, 1983-84. 80 game schedule.
85 — Mario Lemieux, Pittsburgh, 1988-89. 80 game schedule.
76 — Phil Esposito, Boston, 1970-71. 78 game schedule.
73 — Wayne Gretzky, Edmonton, 1984-85. 80 game schedule.
71 — Jari Kurri, Edmonton, 1984-85 80 game schedule.
 — Wayne Gretzky, Edmonton, 1982-83. 80 game schedule.
70 — Mario Lemieux, Pittsburgh, 1987-1988. 80 game schedule.
 — Bernie Nicholls, Los Angeles, 1988-89. 80 game schedule.
69 — Mike Bossy, NY Islanders, 1978-79. 80 game schedule.
68 — Phil Esposito, Boston, 1973-74. 78 game schedule.
 — Mike Bossy, NY Islanders, 1980-81. 80 game schedule.
 — Jari Kurri, Edmonton, 1985-86. 80 game schedule.

MOST ASSISTS, ONE SEASON:
163 — Wayne Gretzky, Edmonton , 1985-86. 80 game schedule.
135 — Wayne Gretzky, Edmonton, 1984-85. 80 game schedule.
125 — Wayne Gretzky, Edmonton, 1982-83. 80 game schedule.
121 — Wayne Gretzky, Edmonton, 1986-87. 80 game schedule.
120 — Wayne Gretzky, Edmonton, 1981-82. 80 game schedule.
118 — Wayne Gretzky, Edmonton, 1983-84. 80 game schedule.
114 — Wayne Gretzky, Los Angeles, 1988-89. 80 game schedule.
 — Mario Lemieux, Pittsburgh, 1988-89. 80 game schedule.
109 — Wayne Gretzky, Edmonton, 1980-81. 80 game schedule.
 — Wayne Gretzky, Edmonton, 1987-88. 80 game schedule.
102 — Bobby Orr, Boston, 1970-71. 78 game schedule.

MOST POINTS, ONE SEASON:
215 — Wayne Gretzky, Edmonton, 1985-86. 80 game schedule.
212 — Wayne Gretzky, Edmonton, 1981-82. 80 game schedule.
208 — Wayne Gretzky, Edmonton, 1984-85. 80 game schedule.
205 — Wayne Gretzky, Edmonton, 1983-84. 80 game schedule.
199 — Mario Lemieux, Pittsburgh, 1988-89. 80 game schedule.
196 — Wayne Gretzky, Edmonton, 1982-83. 80 game schedule.
183 — Wayne Gretzky, Edmonton, 1986-87. 80 game schedule.
168 — Mario Lemieux, Pittsburgh, 1987-88, 80 game schedule.
 — Wayne Gretzky, Los Angeles, 1988-89. 80 game schedule.
164 — Wayne Gretzky, Edmonton, 1980-81. 80 game schedule.
155 — Steve Yzerman, Detroit, 1988-89. 80 game schedule.
152 — Phil Esposito, Boston, 1970-71. 78 game schedule.
150 — Bernie Nicholls, Los Angeles, 1988-89. 80 game schedule.

MOST GAMES SCORING AT LEAST THREE GOALS, ONE SEASON:
10 — Wayne Gretzky, Edmonton, 1981-82. 6 three-goal games, 3 four-goal games, 1 five-goal game.
 — **Wayne Gretzky,** Edmonton, 1983-84. 6 three-goal games, 4 four-goal games.
9 — Mike Bossy, NY Islanders, 1980-81. 6 three-goal games, 3 four-goal games.
 — Mario Lemieux, Pittsburgh, 1988-89. 7 three-goal games, 1 four-goal game, 1 five-goal game.
7 — Joe Malone, Montreal, 1917-18. 2 three-goal games, 2 four-goal games, 3 five-goal games.
 — Phil Esposito, Boston, 1970-71. 7 three-goal games.
 — Rick Martin, Buffalo, 1975-76. 6 three-goal games, 1 four-goal game.

HIGHEST GOALS-PER-GAME AVERAGE, ONE SEASON (AMONG PLAYERS WITH 20-OR-MORE GOALS):
2.20 — Joe Malone, Montreal, 1917-18, with 44G in 20GP.
1.64 — Cy Denneny, Ottawa, 1917-18, with 36G in 22GP.
 — Newsy Lalonde, Montreal, 1917-18, with 23G in 14GP.
1.63 — Joe Malone, Quebec, 1919-20, with 39G in 24GP.

HIGHEST ASSISTS-PER-GAME AVERAGE, ONE SEASON (AMONG PLAYERS WITH 35-OR-MORE ASSISTS):
2.04 — Wayne Gretzky, Edmonton, 1985-86, with 163A in 80GP.
1.70 — Wayne Grezky, Edmonton, 1987-88, with 109A in 64GP.
1.69 — Wayne Gretzky, Edmonton, 1984-85, with 135A in 80GP.
1.59 — Wayne Gretzky, Edmonton, 1983-84, with 118A in 74GP.
1.56 — Wayne Gretzky, Edmonton, 1982-83, with 125A in 80GP.
1.53 — Wayne Gretzky, Edmonton, 1986-87, with 121A in 79GP.
1.50 — Wayne Gretzky, Edmonton, 1981-82, with 120A in 80GP.
1.50 — Mario Lemieux, Pittsburgh, 1988-89, with 114A in 76GP.
1.46 — Wayne Gretzky, Los Angeles, 1988-89, with 114A in 78GP.
1.36 — Wayne Gretzky, Edmonton, 1980-81, with 109A in 80GP.
1.31 — Bobby Orr, Boston, 1970-71, with 102A in 78GP.
1.27 — Mario Lemieux, Pittsburgh, 1987-88, with 98A in 77GP.
1.22 — Bobby Orr, Boston, 1973-74, with 90A in 74GP.
1.17 — Bobby Clarke, Philadelphia, 1975-76, with 89A in 76GP.

HIGHEST POINTS-PER-GAME AVERAGE, ONE SEASON (AMONG PLAYERS WITH 50-OR-MORE POINTS):
2.77 — Wayne Gretzky, Edmonton, 1983-84, with 205PTS in 74GP.
2.69 — Wayne Gretzky, Edmonton, 1985-86, with 215PTS in 80GP.
2.65 — Wayne Gretzky, Edmonton, 1981-82, with 212PTS in 80GP.
2.62 — Mario Lemieux, Pittsburgh, 1988-89, with 199PTS in 78GP.
2.60 — Wayne Gretzky, Edmonton, 1984-85, with 208PTS in 80GP.
2.45 — Wayne Gretzky, Edmonton, 1982-83, with 196PTS in 80GP.
2.33 — Wayne Gretzky, Edmonton, 1987-88, with 149PTS in 64GP.
2.32 — Wayne Gretzky, Edmonton, 1986-87, with 183PTS in 79GP.
2.18 — Mario Lemieux, Pittsburgh, 1987-88 with 168PTS in 77GP.
2.15 — Wayne Gretzky, Los Angeles, 1988-89, with 168PTS in 78GP.
2.05 — Wayne Gretzky, Edmonton, 1980-81, with 164PTS in 80GP.
1.97 — Bill Cowley, Boston, 1943-44, with 71PTS in 36GP.
1.95 — Phil Esposito, Boston, 1970-71, with 152PTS in 78GP.

Rick Martin, a member of the Sabres' "French Connection" line, scored a career-high 95 points in 1974-75.

MOST GOALS, ONE SEASON, INCLUDING PLAYOFFS:

100 — **Wayne Gretzky,** Edmonton, 1983-84, 87G in 74 regular-season games and 13G in 19 playoff games.
97 — Wayne Gretzky, Edmonton, 1981-82, 92G in 80 regular-season games and 5G in 5 playoff games.
— Mario Lemieux, Pittsburgh, 1988-89, 85G in 76 regular-season games and 12G in 11 playoff games.
90 — Wayne Gretzky, Edmonton, 1984-85, 73G in 80 regular season games and 17G in 18 playoff games.
— Jari Kurri, Edmonton, 1984-85, 71G in 80 regular season games and 19G in 18 playoff games.
85 — Mike Bossy, NY Islanders, 1980-81, 68G in 79 regular-season games and 17G in 18 playoff games.
83 — Wayne Gretzky, Edmonton, 1982-83, 71G in 80 regular-season games and 12G in 16 playoff games.
81 — Mike Bossy, NY Islanders, 1981-82, 64G in 80 regular-season games and 17G in 19 playoff games.
80 — Reggie Leach, Philadelphia, 1975-76, 61G in 80 regular-season games and 19G in 16 playoff games.

MOST ASSISTS, ONE SEASON, INCLUDING PLAYOFFS:

174 — **Wayne Gretzky,** Edmonton, 1985-86, 163A in 80 regular-season games and 11A in 10 playoff games.
165 — Wayne Gretzky, Edmonton, 1984-85, 135A in 80 regular-season games and 30A in 18 playoff games.
151 — Wayne Gretzky, Edmonton, 1982-83, 125A in 80 regular-season games and 26A in 16 playoff games.
150 — Wayne Gretzky, Edmonton, 1986-87, 121A in 79 regular-season games and 29A in 21 playoff games.
140 — Wayne Gretzky, Edmonton, 1983-84, 118A in 74 regular-season games and 22A in 19 playoff games.
— Wayne Gretzky, Edmonton, 1987-88, 109A in 64 regular-season games and 31A in 19 playoff games.
131 — Wayne Gretzky, Los Angeles, 1988-89, 114A in 78 regular-season games and 17A in 11 playoff games.
127 — Wayne Gretzky, Edmonton, 1981-82, 120A in 80 regular-season games and 7A in 5 playoff games.
123 — Wayne Gretzky, Edmonton, 1980-81, 109A in 80 regular-season games and 14A in 9 playoff games.
121 — Mario Lemieux, Pittsburgh, 1988-89, 114A in 76 regular-season games and 7A in 11 playoff games.
109 — Bobby Orr, Boston, 1970-71, 102A in 78 regular-season games and 7A in 7 playoff games.
— Paul Coffey, Edmonton, 1984-85, 84A in 80 regular-season games and 25A in 18 playoff games.

MOST POINTS, ONE SEASON, INCLUDING PLAYOFFS:

255 — **Wayne Gretzky,** Edmonton, 1984-85, 208PTS in 80 regular-season games and 47PTS in 18 playoff games.
240 — Wayne Gretzky, Edmonton, 1983-84, 205PTS in 74 regular-season games and 35PTS in 19 playoff games.
234 — Wayne Gretzky, Edmonton, 1982-83, 196PTS in 80 regular-season games and 38PTS in 16 playoff games.
— Wayne Gretzky, Edmonton, 1985-86, 215PTS in 80 regular-season games and 19PTS in 10 playoff games.
224 — Wayne Gretzky, Edmonton, 1981-82, 212PTS in 80 regular-season games and 12PTS in 5 playoff games.
218 — Mario Lemieux, Pittsburgh, 1988-89, 199PTS in 76 regular-season games and 19PTS in 11 playoff games.
217 — Wayne Gretzky, Edmonton, 1986-87, 183PTS in 79 regular-season games and 34PTS in 21 playoff games.
192 — Wayne Gretzky, Edmonton, 1987-88, 149PTS in 64 regular-season games and 43PTS in 19 playoff games.
190 — Wayne Gretzky, Los Angeles, 1988-89, 168PTS in 78 regular-season games and 22PTS in 11 playoff games.
185 — Wayne Gretzky, Edmonton, 1980-81, 164PTS in 80 regular-season games and 21PTS in 9 playoff games.

MOST GOALS, ONE SEASON, BY A DEFENSEMAN:

48 — **Paul Coffey,** Edmonton, 1985-86. 80 game schedule.
46 — Bobby Orr, Boston, 1974-75. 80 game schedule.
40 — Paul Coffey, Edmonton, 1983-84. 80 game schedule.
39 — Doug Wilson, Chicago, 1981-82. 80 game schedule.
37 — Bobby Orr, Boston, 1970-71. 78 game schedule.
— Bobby Orr, Boston, 1971-72. 78 game schedule.
— Paul Coffey, Edmonton, 1984-85 80 game schedule..
33 — Bobby Orr, Boston, 1969-70. 76 game schedule.
32 — Bobby Orr, Boston, 1973-74. 78 game schedule.
31 — Denis Potvin, NY Islanders, 1975-76. 80 game schedule.
— Denis Potvin, NY Islanders, 1978-79. 80 game schedule.
— Raymond Bourque, Boston, 1983-84. 80 game schedule.
— Phil Housley, Buffalo, 1983-84. 80 game schedule.
30 — Denis Potvin, NY Islanders, 1979-80. 80 game schedule.
— Paul Coffey, Pittsburgh, 1988-89. 80 game schedule.

MOST GOALS, ONE SEASON, BY A CENTER:

92 — **Wayne Gretzky,** Edmonton, 1981-82. 80 game schedule.
87 — Wayne Gretzky, Edmonton, 1983-84. 80 game schedule.
85 — Mario Lemieux, Pittsburgh, 1988-89. 80 game schedule.
76 — Phil Esposito, Boston, 1970-71. 78 game schedule.
73 — Wayne Gretzky, Edmonton, 1984-85. 80 game schedule.
71 — Wayne Gretzky, Edmonton, 1982-83. 80 game schedule.
70 — Mario Lemieux, Pittsburgh, 1987-88. 80 game schedule.
— Bernie Nicholls, Los Angeles, 1988-89. 80 game schedule.

MOST GOALS, ONE SEASON, BY A RIGHT WINGER:

71 — **Jari Kurri,** Edmonton, 1984-85. 80 game schedule.
69 — Mike Bossy, NY Islanders, 1978-79. 80 game schedule.
— Jari Kurri, Edmonton, 1985-86. 80 game schedule..
68 — Mike Bossy, NY Islanders, 1980-81. 80 game schedule.
66 — Lanny McDonald, Calgary, 1982-83. 80 game schedule.
64 — Mike Bossy, NY Islanders, 1981-82. 80 game schedule.
61 — Reggie Leach, Philadelphia, 1975-76. 80 game schedule.
60 — Guy Lafleur, Montreal, 1977-78. 80 game schedule.
— Mike Bossy, NY Islanders, 1982-83. 80 game schedule.
58 — Mike Bossy, NY Islanders, 1984-85. 80 game schedule.
— Tim Kerr, Philadelphia, 1986-87. 80 game schedule.
56 — Guy Lafleur, Montreal, 1975-76, 1976-77. 80 game schedule.
— Blaine Stoughton, Hartford, 1979-80. 80 game schedule.
— Danny Gare, Buffalo, 1979-80. 80 game schedule.

MOST GOALS, ONE SEASON, BY A LEFT WINGER:

60 — **Steve Shutt,** Montreal, 1976-77. 80 game schedule.
58 — Bobby Hull, Chicago, 1968-69. 76 game schedule.
57 — Michel Goulet, Quebec, 1982-83. 80 game schedule.
56 — Charlie Simmer, Los Angeles, 1979-80. 80 game schedule.
— Charlie Simmer, Los Angeles, 1980-81. 80 game schedule.
— Michel Goulet, Quebec, 1983-84. 80 game schedule.
55 — Michel Goulet, Quebec, 1984-85. 80 game schedule.
— John Ogrodnick, Detroit, 1984-85. 80 game schedule.
54 — Bobby Hull, Chicago, 1965-66. 70 game schedule.
— Al Secord, Chicago, 1982-83. 80 game schedule.

Bobby Orr set an NHL record for defensemen with 102 assists in the 1970-71 season.

MOST GOALS, ONE SEASON, BY A ROOKIE:

53 — **Mike Bossy,** NY Islanders, 1977-78. 80 game schedule.
51 — Joe Nieuwendyk, Calgary, 1987-88. 80 game schedule.
45 — Dale Hawerchuk, Winnipeg, 1981-82. 80 game schedule.
— Luc Robitaille, Los Angeles, 1986-87. 80 game schedule.
44 — Richard Martin, Buffalo, 1971-72. 80 game schedule.
— Barry Pederson, Boston, 1981-82. 80 game schedule.
43 — Steve Larmer, Chicago, 1982-83. 80 game schedule.
— Mario Lemieux, Pittsburgh, 1984-85. 80 game schedule.
40 — Darryl Sutter, Chicago, 1980-81. 80 game schedule.
— Sylvain Turgeon, Hartford, 1983-84. 80 game schedule.
— Warren Young, Pittsburgh, 1984-85. 80 game schedule.

MOST GOALS, ONE SEASON, BY A ROOKIE DEFENSEMAN:

23 — **Brian Leetch,** NY Rangers, 1988-89. 80 game schedule.
22 — Barry Beck, Colorado, 1977-78. 80 game schedule.
19 — Reed Larson, Detroit, 1977-78. 80 game schedule.
— Phil Housley, Buffalo, 1982-83. 80 game schedule.

MOST ASSISTS, ONE SEASON, BY A DEFENSEMAN:

102 — **Bobby Orr,** Boston, 1970-71. 78 game schedule.
90 — Paul Coffey, Edmonton, 1985-86. 80 game schedule.
90 — Bobby Orr, Boston, 1973-74. 78 game schedule.
89 — Bobby Orr, Boston, 1974-75. 80 game schedule.

MOST ASSISTS, ONE SEASON, BY A CENTER:
163 — Wayne Gretzky, Edmonton, 1985-86. 80 game schedule.
135 — Wayne Gretzky, Edmonton, 1984-85. 80 game schedule.
125 — Wayne Gretzky, Edmonton, 1982-83. 80 game schedule.
121 — Wayne Gretzky, Edmonton, 1986-87. 80 game schedule.
120 — Wayne Gretzky, Edmonton, 1981-82. 80 game schedule.
118 — Wayne Gretzky, Edmonton, 1983-84. 80 game schedule.
114 — Wayne Gretzky, Edmonton, 1988-89. 80 game schedule.
    — Mario Lemieux, Pittsburgh, 1988-89. 80 game schedule.
109 — Wayne Gretzky, Edmonton, 1980-81. 80 game schedule.
    — Wayne Gretzky, Edmonton, 1987-88. 80 game schedule.

MOST ASSISTS, ONE SEASON, BY A RIGHT WINGER:
83 — Mike Bossy, NY Islanders, 1981-82. 80 game schedule.
80 — Guy Lafleur, Montreal, 1976-77. 80 game schedule.
77 — Guy Lafleur, Montreal, 1978-79. 80 game schedule.

MOST ASSISTS, ONE SEASON, BY A LEFT WINGER:
67 — Mats Naslund, Montreal, 1985-86. 80 game schedule.
65 — John Bucyk, Boston, 1970-71. 78 game schedule.
    — Michel Goulet, Quebec, 1983-84. 80 game schedule.
64 — Mark Messier, Edmonton, 1983-84. 80 game schedule.
62 — Bill Barber, Philadelphia, 1975-76. 80 game schedule.
60 — Anton Stastny, Quebec, 1982-83. 80 game schedule.
59 — Wayne Cashman, Boston, 1973-74. 78 game schedule.
    — Mats Naslund, Montreal, 1987-88. 80 game schedule.

MOST ASSISTS, ONE SEASON, BY A ROOKIE:
70 — Peter Stastny, Quebec, 1980-81. 80 game schedule.
63 — Bryan Trottier, NY Islanders, 1975-76. 80 game schedule.
60 — Larry Murphy, Los Angeles, 1980-81. 80 game schedule.

MOST ASSISTS, ONE SEASON, BY A ROOKIE DEFENSEMAN:
60 — Larry Murphy, Los Angeles, 1980-81. 80 game schedule.
55 — Chris Chelios, Montreal, 1984-85. 80 game schedule.
50 — Stefan Persson, NY Islanders, 1977-78. 80 game schedule.
    — Gary Suter, Calgary, 1985-86, 80 game schedule..
48 — Raymond Bourque, Boston, 1979-80. 80 game schedule.
    — Brian Leetch, NY Rangers, 1988-89. 80 game schedule.

MOST POINTS, ONE SEASON, BY A DEFENSEMAN:
139 — Bobby Orr, Boston, 1970-71. 78 game schedule.
138 — Paul Coffey, Edmonton,1985-86. 80 game schedule.
135 — Bobby Orr, Boston, 1974-75. 80 game schedule.
126 — Paul Coffey, Edmonton, 1983-84. 80 game schedule.
122 — Bobby Orr, Boston, 1973-74. 78 game schedule.

Grant Fuhr assisted on 14 goals in 1983-84, establishing a new point record for goaltenders.

MOST POINTS, ONE SEASON, BY A CENTER:
215 — Wayne Gretzky, Edmonton, 1985-86. 80 game schedule.
212 — Wayne Gretzky, Edmonton, 1981-82. 80 game schedule.
208 — Wayne Gretzky, Edmonton, 1984-85. 80 game schedule.
205 — Wayne Gretzky, Edmonton, 1983-84. 80 game schedule.
199 — Mario Lemieux, Pittsburgh, 1988-89. 80 game schedule.
196 — Wayne Gretzky, Edmonton, 1982-83. 80 game schedule.
183 — Wayne Gretzky, Edmonton, 1986-87. 80 game schedule.
168 — Mario Lemieux, Pittsburgh, 1987-88. 80 game schedule.
    — Wayne Gretzky, Los Angeles, 1988-89. 80 game schedule.
164 — Wayne Gretzky, Edmonton, 1980-81. 80 game schedule.
155 — Steve Yzerman, Detroit, 1988-89. 80 game schedule.

MOST POINTS, ONE SEASON, BY A RIGHT WINGER:
147 — Mike Bossy, NY Islanders, 1981-82. 80 game schedule.
136 — Guy Lafleur, Montreal, 1976-77. 80 game schedule.
135 — Jari Kurri, Edmonton, 1984-85. 80 game schedule.
132 — Guy Lafleur, Montreal, 1977-78. 80 game schedule.

MOST POINTS, ONE SEASON, BY A LEFT WINGER:
121 — Michel Goulet, Quebec, 1983-84. 80 game schedule.
116 — John Bucyk, Boston, 1970-71. 78 game schedule.
112 — Bill Barber, Philadelphia, 1975-76. 80 game schedule.
111 — Luc Robitaille, Los Angeles, 1987-88. 80 game schedule.
110 — Mats Naslund, Montreal, 1985-86. 80 game schedule.
107 — Bobby Hull, Chicago, 1968-69. 76 game schedule.

MOST POINTS, ONE SEASON, BY A ROOKIE:
109 — Peter Stastny, Quebec, 1980-81. 80 game schedule.
103 — Dale Hawerchuk, Winnipeg, 1981-82. 80 game schedule.
100 — Mario Lemieux, Pittsburgh, 1984-85. 80 game schedule.
97 — Neal Broten, Minnesota, 1981-82. 80 game schedule.

MOST POINTS, ONE SEASON, BY A ROOKIE DEFENSEMAN:
76 — Larry Murphy, Los Angeles, 1980-81. 80 game schedule.
71 — Brian Leetch, NY Rangers, 1988-89. 80 game schedule.
68 — Gary Suter, Calgary, 1985-86. 80 game schedule.
66 — Phil Housley, Buffalo, 1982-83. 80 game schedule.
65 — Raymond Bourque, Boston, 1979-80. 80 game schedule.
64 — Chris Chelios, Montreal, 1984-85. 80 game schedule.

MOST POINTS, ONE SEASON, BY A GOALTENDER:
14 — Grant Fuhr, Edmonton, 1983-84. (14A)
8 — Mike Palmateer, Washington, 1980-81. (8A)
    — Grant Fuhr, Edmonton, 1987-88 (8A)
7 — Ron Hextall, Philadelphia, 1987-88 (1G-6A)
6 — Gilles Meloche, California, 1974-75. (6A)
    — Grant Fuhr, Edmonton, 1981-82. (6A)
    — Ron Hextall, Philadelphia, 1986-87. (6A)

MOST POWER-PLAY GOALS, ONE SEASON:
34 — Tim Kerr, Philadelphia, 1985-86. 80 game schedule.
31 — Joe Nieuwendyk, Calgary, 1987-88. 80 game schedule.
    — Mario Lemieux, Pittsburgh, 1988-89. 80 game schedule.
29 — Michel Goulet, Quebec, 1987-88. 80 game schedule.
28 — Phil Esposito, Boston, 1971-72. 78 game schedule.
    — Mike Bossy, NY Islanders, 1980-81. 80 game schedule.
    — Michel Goulet, Quebec, 1985-86. 80 game schedule.

MOST SHORTHAND GOALS, ONE SEASON:
13 — Mario Lemieux, Pittsburgh, 1988-89. 80 game schedule.
12 — Wayne Gretzky, Edmonton, 1983-84. 80 game schedule.
11 — Wayne Gretzky, Edmonton, 1984-85. 80 game schedule.
10 — Marcel Dionne, Detroit, 1974-75. 80 game schedule.
    — Mario Lemieux, Pittsburgh, 1987-88. 80 game schedule.
    — Dirk Graham, Chicago, 1988-89. 80 game schedule.

MOST SHOTS ON GOAL, ONE SEASON:
550 — Phil Esposito, Boston, 1970-71. 78 game schedule.
426 — Phil Esposito, Boston, 1971-72. 78 game schedule.
414 — Bobby Hull, Chicago, 1968-69. 76 game schedule.

MOST PENALTY MINUTES, ONE SEASON:
472 — Dave Schultz, Philadelphia, 1974-75.
407 — Paul Baxter, Pittsburgh, 1981-82.
405 — Dave Schultz, Los Angeles, 1977-78.

MOST SHUTOUTS, ONE SEASON:
22 — George Hainsworth, Montreal, 1928-29. 44GP
15 — Alex Connell, Ottawa, 1925-26. 36GP
    — Alex Connell, Ottawa, 1927-28. 44GP
    — Hal Winkler, Boston, 1927-28. 44GP
    — Tony Esposito, Chicago, 1969-70. 63GP
14 — George Hainsworth, Montreal, 1926-27. 44GP

LONGEST UNDEFEATED STREAK BY A GOALTENDER:
32 Games — Gerry Cheevers, Boston, 1971-72. 24w-8T.
31 Games — Pete Peeters, Boston, 1982-83. 26w-5T.
27 Games — Pete Peeters, Philadelphia, 1979-80. 22w-5T.
23 Games — Frank Brimsek, Boston, 1940-41. 15w-8T.
    — Glenn Resch, NY Islanders, 1978-79. 15w-8T.
    — Grant Fuhr, Edmonton, 1981-82. 15w-8T.

MOST GAMES, ONE SEASON, BY A GOALTENDER:
75 — Grant Fuhr, Edmonton, 1987-88.
73 — Bernie Parent, Philadelphia, 1973-74.
72 — Gary Smith, Vancouver, 1974-75.
    — Don Edwards, Buffalo, 1977-78.
71 — Gary Smith, California, 1970-71.
    — Tony Esposito, Chicago, 1974-75.

MOST WINS, ONE SEASON, BY A GOALTENDER:
47 — **Bernie Parent**, Philadelphia, 1973-74.
44 — Bernie Parent, Philadelphia, 1974-75.
 — Terry Sawchuk, Detroit, 1950-51.
 — Terry Sawchuk, Detroit, 1951-52.

LONGEST WINNING STREAK, ONE SEASON, BY A GOALTENDER:
17 — **Gilles Gilbert**, Boston, 1975-76.
14 — Don Beaupre, Minnesota, 1985-86.
 — Ross Brooks, Boston, 1973-74.
 — Tiny Thompson, Boston, 1929-30.

MOST GOALS, 50 GAMES FROM START OF SEASON:
61 — **Wayne Gretzky**, Edmonton, 1981-82. Oct. 7, 1981 - Jan. 22, 1982. (80-game schedule)
 — **Wayne Gretzky**, Edmonton, 1983-84. Oct. 5, 1983 - Jan. 25, 1984. (80-game schedule)
54 — Mario Lemieux, Pittsburgh. Oct. 7, 1988 - Jan. 31, 1989. (80-game schedule)
53 — Wayne Gretzky, Edmonton, 1984-85. Oct. 11, 1984 - Jan. 28, 1985. (80-game schedule)
50 — Maurice Richard, Montreal, 1944-45. Oct. 28, 1944 - March 18, 1945. (50-game schedule)
 — Mike Bossy, NY Islanders, 1980-81. Oct. 11, 1980 - Jan. 24, 1981. (80-game schedule)

LONGEST CONSECUTIVE POINT-SCORING STREAK FROM START OF SEASON:
51 Games — **Wayne Gretzky**, Edmonton, 1983-84. 61G-92A-153PTS during streak which was stopped by goaltender Markus Mattsson and the Los Angeles Kings on Jan. 28, 1984.

LONGEST CONSECUTIVE POINT SCORING STREAK:
51 Games — **Wayne Gretzky**, Edmonton, 1983-84. 61G-92A-153PTS during streak.
39 Games — Wayne Gretzky, Edmonton, 1985-86. 33G-75A-108PTS during streak.
30 Games — Wayne Gretzky, Edmonton, 1982-83. 24G52A76PTS during streak.
28 Games — Guy Lafleur, Montreal, 1976-77. 19G-42A-61PTS during streak.
 — Wayne Gretzky, Edmonton, 1984-85. 20G-43A-63PTS during streak.
 — Mario Lemieux, Pittsburgh, 1985-86. 21G-38A-59PTS during streak.
 — Paul Coffey, Edmonton, 1985-86. 16G-39A-55PTS during a streak.
 — Steve Yzerman, Detroit, 1988-89. 29G-36A-65PTS during streak.

LONGEST CONSECUTIVE POINT-SCORING STREAK BY A DEFENSEMAN:
28 Games — **Paul Coffey**, Edmonton, 1985-86. 16G-39A-55PTS during streak.
19 Games — Ray Bourque, Boston, 1987-88. 6G-21A-27PTS during streak.
17 Games — Ray Bourque, Boston, 1984-85. 4G-24A-28PTS during streak.
16 Games — Gary Suter, Calgary, 1987-88. 8G-17A-25PTS during streak.
15 Games — Bobby Orr, Boston, 1973-74. 8G-15A-23PTS during streak.
15 Games — Bobby Orr, Boston, 1970-71. 10G-23A-33PTS during streak.

LONGEST CONSECUTIVE GOAL-SCORING STREAK:
16 Games — **Harry (Punch) Broadbent**, Ottawa Senators, 1921-22. 25 goals during streak.
14 Games — Joe Malone, Montreal Canadiens, 1917-18. 35 goals during streak.
13 Games — Newsy Lalonde, Montreal Canadiens, 1920-21. 24 goals during streak.
 — Charlie Simmer, Los Angeles Kings, 1979-80. 17 goals during streak.
12 Games — Cy Denneny, Ottawa Senators, 1917-18. 23 goals during streak.
 — Dave Lumley, Edmonton Oilers, 1981-82. 15 goals during streak.
11 Games — Babe Dye, Toronto St. Patricks, Hamilton Tigers, 1920-21. 22 goals during streak.
 — Babe Dye, Toronto St. Patricks, 1921-22. 15 goals during streak.
 — Marcel Dionne, Los Angeles, 1982-83. 14 goals during streak.

LONGEST CONSECUTIVE ASSIST-SCORING STREAK:
17 Games — **Wayne Gretzky**, Edmonton Oilers, 1983-84. 38A during streak.
 — **Paul Coffey**, Edmonton Oilers, 1985-86. 27A during streak.
15 Games — Jari Kurri, Edmonton Oilers, 1983-84. 21A during streak.
14 Games — Stan Mikita, Chicago Black Hawks, 1967-68. 18A during streak.
 — Bobby Orr, Boston Bruins, 1970-71. 23A during streak.
 — Jude Drouin, Minnesota North Stars, 1971-72. 21A during streak.
 — Wayne Gretzky, Edmonton Oilers, 1981-82. 26A during streak.
 — Wayne Gretzky, Edmonton Oilers, 1985-86. 39A during streak.
 — Mario Lemieux, Pittsburgh Penguins, 1985-86. 23A during streak.
12 Games — Norm Ullman, Toronto Maple Leafs, 1970-71. 15A during streak.
 — Pete Mahovlich, Montreal Canadiens, 1974-75. 18A during streak.
 — Bobby Clarke, Philadelphia Flyers, 1975-76. 20A during streak.
 — Bobby Clarke, Philadelphia Flyers, 1977-78. 16A during streak.
 — Guy Lafleur, Montreal Canadiens, 1979-80. 15A during streak.
 — Wayne Gretzky, Edmonton Oilers, 1982-83. 20A during streak.
 — Barry Pederson, Boston Bruins, 1982-83. 15A during streak.
 — Wayne Gretzky, Edmonton Oilers, 1985-86. 24A during streak.
 — Ken Linseman, Boston Bruins, 1985-86. 19A during streak.

LONGEST SHUTOUT SEQUENCE BY A GOALTENDER:
461 Minutes, 29 Seconds — **Alex Connell**, Ottawa Senators, 1927-28, six consecutive shoutouts. (Forward passing not permitted in attacking zones in 1927-1928.)
343 Minutes, 5 Seconds — George Hainsworth, Montreal Canadiens, 1928-29, four consecutive shutouts.
324 Minutes, 40 Seconds — Roy Worters, New York Americans, 1930-31, four consecutive shutouts.
309 Minutes, 21 Seconds — Bill Durnan, Montreal Canadiens, 1948-49, four consecutive shutouts.

Single Game

MOST GOALS, ONE GAME:
7 — **Joe Malone**, Quebec Bulldogs, Jan. 31, 1920, at Quebec City. Quebec 10, Toronto St. Pats 6.
6 — Newsy Lalonde, Montreal Canadiens, Jan. 10, 1920, at Montreal. Canadiens 14, Toronto St. Pats 7.
 — Joe Malone, Quebec Bulldogs, March 10, 1920, at Quebec City. Quebec 10, Ottawa Senators 4.
 — Corb Denneny, Toronto St. Patricks, Jan. 26, 1921, at Toronto. Toronto 10, Hamilton Tigers 3.
 — Cy Denneny, Ottawa Senators, March 7, 1921, at Ottawa. Ottawa 12, Hamilton Tigers 5.
 — Syd Howe, Detroit Red Wings, Feb. 3, 1944, at Detroit. Detroit 12, New York Rangers 2.
 — Red Berenson, St. Louis Blues, Nov. 7, 1968, at Philadelphia. St. Louis 8, Philadelphia 0.
 — Darryl Sittler, Toronto Maple Leafs, Feb. 7, 1976, at Toronto. Toronto 11, Boston 4.

MOST GOALS, ONE ROAD GAME:
6 — **Red Berenson**, St. Louis Blues, Nov. 7, 1968, at Philadelphia. St. Louis 8, Philadelphia 0.
5 — Joe Malone, Montreal Canadiens, Dec. 19, 1917, at Ottawa. Montreal 9, Ottawa 4.
 — Redvers Green, Hamilton Tigers, Dec. 5, 1924, at Toronto. Hamilton 10, Toronto 3.
 — Babe Dye, Toronto St. Patricks, Dec. 22, 1924, at Boston. Toronto 10, Boston 2.
 — Harry Broadbent, Montreal Maroons, Jan. 7, 1925, at Hamilton. Montreal 6, Hamilton 2.
 — Don Murdoch, New York Rangers, Oct. 12, 1976, at Minnesota. New York 10, Minnesota 4.
 — Tim Young, Minnesota North Stars, Jan. 15, 1979, at New York Rangers. Minnesota 8, New York 1.
 — Willy Lindstrom, Winnipeg Jets, March 2, 1982, at Philadelphia. Winnipeg 7, Philadelphia 6.
 — Bengt Gustafsson, Washington Capitals, Jan. 8, 1984, at Philadelphia. Washington 7, Philadelphia 1.
 — Dave Andreychuk, Buffalo Sabres, Feb. 6, 1986, at Boston. Buffalo 8, Boston 6.

MOST ASSISTS, ONE GAME:
7 — **Billy Taylor**, Detroit Red Wings, March 16, 1947, at Chicago. Detroit 10, Chicago 6.
 — **Wayne Gretzky**, Edmonton Oilers, Feb. 15, 1980, at Edmonton. Edmonton 8, Washington 2.
 — **Wayne Gretzky**, Edmonton Oilers, Dec. 11, 1985, at Chicago. Edmonton 12, Chicago 9.
 — **Wayne Gretzky**, Edmonton Oilers, Feb. 14, 1986, at Edmonton. Edmonton 8, Quebec 2.
6 — Elmer Lach, Montreal Canadiens, Feb. 6, 1943, at Montreal. Montreal 8, Boston 3.
 — Walter (Babe) Pratt, Toronto Maple Leafs, Jan. 8, 1944, at Toronto. Toronto 12, Boston 3.
 — Don Grosso, Detroit Red Wings, Feb. 3, 1944, at Detroit. Detroit 12, New York Rangers 2.
 — Pat Stapleton, Chicago Black Hawks, March 30, 1969, at Chicago 9, Detroit Red Wings 5.
 — Ken Hodge, Boston Bruins, Feb. 9, 1971, at Boston. Boston 6, New York Rangers 3.
 — Bobby Orr, Boston Bruins, Jan. 1, 1973, at Vancouver, Boston 8, Vancouver 2.
 — Ron Stackhouse, Pittsburgh, March 8, 1974, at Pittsburgh. Pittsburgh 8, Philadelphia 2.
 — Greg Malone, Pittsburgh, Nov. 28, 1979, at Pittsburgh. Pittsburgh 7, Quebec 2.
 — Mike Bossy, New York Islanders, Jan. 6, 1981, at New York. Islanders 6, Toronto 3.
 — Guy Chouinard, Calgary Flames, Feb. 25, 1981, at Calgary. Calgary 11, NY Islanders 4.
 — Mark Messier, Edmonton Oilers, Jan. 4, 1984, at Edmonton. Edmonton 12, Minnesota 8.
 — Patrik Sundstrom, Vancouver Canucks, Feb 29, 1984, at Pittsburgh. Vancouver 9, Pittsburgh 5.
 — Wayne Gretzky, Edmonton Oilers, Dec. 20, 1985, at Edmonton. Edmonton 9, Los Angeles 4.
 — Paul Coffey, Edmonton Oilers, Mar. 14, 1986 at Edmonton. Edmonton 12, Detroit 3.
 — Gary Suter, Calgary Flames, Apr. 4, 1986 at Calgary. Calgary 9, Edmonton 3.
 — Mario Lemieux, Pittsburgh Penguins, Oct. 15, 1988, at Pittsburgh. Pittsburgh 9, St. Louis 2.
 — Bernie Nicholls, Los Angeles Kings, Dec. 1, 1988, at Los Angeles. Los Angeles 9, Toronto 3.
 — Mario Lemieux, Pittsburgh Penguins, Dec. 31, 1988 at Pittsburgh. Pittsburgh 8, New Jersey 6.

MOST ASSISTS, ONE ROAD GAME:
7 — **Billy Taylor**, Detroit Red Wings, March 16, 1947, at Chicago. Detroit 10, Chicago 6.
 — **Wayne Gretzky**, Edmonton Oilers, Dec. 11, 1985, at Chicago. Edmonton 12, Chicago 9.
6 — Bobby Orr, Boston Bruins, Jan. 1, 1973, at Vancouver. Boston 8, Vancouver 2.
 — Patrik Sundstrom, Vancouver Canucks, Feb. 29, 1984, at Pittsburgh. Vancouver 9, Pittsburgh 5.

MOST POINTS, ONE GAME:
- 10 — **Darryl Sittler,** Toronto Maple Leafs, Feb. 7, 1976, at Toronto, 6G-4A. Toronto 11, Boston 4.
- 8 — Maurice Richard, Montreal Canadiens, Dec. 28, 1944, at Montreal, 5G-3A. Montreal 9, Detroit 1.
  - Bert Olmstead, Montreal Canadiens, Jan. 9, 1954, at Montreal, 4G-4A. Montreal 12, Chicago 1.
  - Tom Bladon, Philadelphia Flyers, Dec. 11, 1977, at Philadelphia, 4G-4A. Philadelphia 11, Cleveland 1.
  - Bryan Trottier, New York Islanders, Dec. 23, 1978, at New York, 5G-3A. NY Rangers 4 NY Islanders 9.
  - Peter Stastny, Quebec Nordiques, Feb. 22, 1981, at Washington, 4G-4A. Quebec 11, Washington 7.
  - Anton Stastny, Quebec Nordiques, Feb. 22, 1981, at Washington, 3G-5A. Quebec 11, Washington 7.
  - Wayne Gretzky, Edmonton Oilers, Nov. 19, 1983, at Edmonton, 3G-5A. Edmonton 13, New Jersey 4.
  - Wayne Gretzky, Edmonton Oilers, Jan. 4, 1984, at Edmonton, 4G-4A. Edmonton 12 Minnesota 8.
  - Paul Coffey, Edmonton Oilers, Mar. 14, 1986, at Edmonton, 2G-6A. Edmonton 12, Detroit 3.
  - Mario Lemieux, Pittsburgh Penguins, Oct. 15, 1988, at Pittsburgh, 2G, 6A. Pittsburgh 9, St. Louis 2.
  - Mario Lemieux, Pittsburgh Penguins, Dec. 31, 1988, at Pittsburgh, 5G, 3A. Pittsburgh 8, New Jersey 6.
  - Bernie Nicholls, Los Angeles Kings, Dec. 1, 1988, at Los Angeles, 2G, 6A. Los Angeles 9, Toronto 3.
- 7— Joe Malone, Quebec Bulldogs, Jan. 31, 1920, at Quebec City, 7G. Quebec 10, Toronto St. Patrick 6.
  - Frank Fredrickson, Pittsburgh Pirates, Nov. 19, 1929, at Pittsburgh, 2G-5A. Pittsburgh 10, Toronto 5.
  - Carl Liscombe, Detroit Red Wings, Nov. 5, 1942, at Detroit, 3G-4A. Detroit 12, New York Rangers 5.
  - Max Bentley, Chicago Black Hawks, Jan. 28, 1943, at Chicago, 4G-3A. Chicago 10, New York Rangers 1.
  - Don Grosso, Detroit Red Wings, Feb. 3, 1944, at Detroit, 1G-6A. Detroit 12, New York Rangers 2.
  - Billy Taylor, Detroit Red Wings, March 16, 1947, at Chicago. 7A. Detroit 10, Chicago 6.
  - Jean Béliveau, Montreal Canadiens, March 7, 1959, at Montreal, 4G-3A. Montreal 10, Detroit 2.
  - Red Berenson, St. Louis Blues, Nov. 7, 1968, at Philadelphia, 6G-1A. St. Louis 8, Philadelphia 0.
  - Garry Unger, St. Louis Blues, March 13, 1971, at St. Louis, 3G-4A. St. Louis 9, Buffalo Sabres 0.
  - Rick MacLeish, Philadelphia Flyers, March 4, 1973, at Philadelphia, 4G-3A. Philadelphia 10, Toronto 0.
  - Bobby Orr, Boston Bruins, Nov. 15, 1973, at Boston, 3G-4A. Boston 10, NY Rangers 2.
  - Phil Esposito, Boston Bruins, Dec. 19, 1974, at Boston, 3G-4A. Boston 11, NY Rangers 3.
  - Yvan Cournoyer, Montreal Canadiens, Feb. 15, 1975, at Montreal, 5G-2A. Montreal 12, Chicago 3.
  - Gilbert Perreault, Buffalo Sabres, Feb. 1, 1976, at California, 2G-5A. Buffalo 9, California 5.
  - Steve Vickers, New York Rangers, Feb. 18, 1976, at New York, 3G-4A. New York Rangers 11, Washington 4.
  - Darryl Sittler, Toronto Maple Leafs, Oct. 14, 1978, at Toronto, 3G-4A. Toronto 10, NY Islanders 7.
  - Wayne Gretzky, Edmonton Oilers, Feb. 15, 1980, at Edmonton, 7A. Edmonton 8, Washington 2.
  - Wayne Gretzky, Edmonton Oilers, Feb. 18, 1981, at Edmonton. 5G-2A. Edmonton 9, St. Louis 2.
  - Bobby Smith, Minnesota North Stars, Nov. 11, 1981, at Minnesota, 4G-3A. Winnipeg 2, Minnesota 15.
  - Wayne Gretzky, Edmonton Oilers, Dec. 19, 1981, at Edmonton, 3G-4A. Minnesota 6, Edmonton 9.
  - Grant Mulvey, Chicago Black Hawks, Feb. 3, 1982, at Chicago, 5G-2A. St. Louis 5, Chicago 9.
  - Barry Pederson, Boston Bruins, April 4, 1982, at Boston, 3G-4A. Hartford 2, Boston 7.
  - Peter Stastny, Quebec Nordiques, April 4, 1982, at Buffalo, 3G-4A. Quebec 7, Buffalo 4.
  - Wayne Gretzky, Edmonton Oilers, Nov. 6, 1983, at Winnipeg, 4G-3A. Edmonton 8, Winnipeg 5.
  - Patrik Sundstrom, Vancouver Canucks, Feb. 29, 1984, at Pittsburgh, 1G-6A. Vancouver 9, Pittsburgh 5.
  - Wayne Gretzky, Edmonton Oilers, Dec. 11, 1985, at Chicago, 7A. Edmonton 12, Chicago 9.
  - Wayne Gretzky, Edmonton Oilers, Feb. 14, 1986, at Edmonton, 7A. Edmonton 8, Quebec 2.
  - Cam Neely, Boston Bruins, Oct. 16, 1988, at Chicago, 3G, 4A. Boston 10, Chicago 3.
  - Mario Lemieux, Pittsburgh Penguins, Jan. 21, 1989, at Edmonton, 2G, 5A. Pittsburgh 7, Edmonton 4.
  - Wayne Gretzky, Los Angeles Kings, Feb. 18, 1989, at Los Angeles, 2G, 5A. Los Angeles 11, Quebec 3.
  - Dino Ciccarelli, Washington Capitals, March 18, 1989, at Hartford, 4G, 3A. Washington 8, Hartford 2.

MOST POINTS, ONE ROAD GAME:
- 8 — **Peter Stastny,** Quebec Nordiques, Feb. 22, 1981, at Washington, 4G-4A. Quebec 11, Washington 7.
  - **Anton Stastny,** Quebec Nordiques, Feb. 22, 1981, at Washington, 3G-5A. Quebec 11, Washington 7.
- 7 — Billy Taylor, Detroit Red Wings, March 16, 1947, at Chicago, 7A. Detroit 10, Chicago. 6.
  - Red Berenson, St. Louis Blues, Nov. 7, 1968, at Philadelphia, 6G-1A. St. Louis 8, Philadelphia 0.
  - Gilbert Perreault, Buffalo Sabres, Feb. 1, 1976, at California, 2G-5A. Buffalo 9, California 5.
  - Peter Stastny, Quebec Nordiques, April 1, 1982, at Boston, 3G-4A. Quebec 8, Boston 5.
  - Wayne Gretzky, Edmonton Oilers, Nov. 6, 1984, at Winnipeg, 4G-3A. Edmonton 8, Winnipeg 5.
  - Patrik Sundstrom, Vancouver Canucks, Feb. 29, 1984, at Pittsburgh, 1G-6A. Vancouver 9, Pittsburgh 5.
  - Wayne Gretzky, Edmonton Oilers, Dec. 11, 1985, at Chicago. 7A, Edmonton 12, Chicago 9.
  - Mario Lemieux, Pittsburgh Penguins, Jan. 21, 1989, at Edmonton, 2G, 5A. Pittsburgh 7, Edmonton 4.
  - Cam Neely, Boston Bruins, Oct. 16, 1988, at Chicago, 3G, 4A. Boston 10, Chicago 3.
  - Dino Ciccarelli, Washington Capitals, March 18, 1989, at Hartford, 4G, 3A. Washington 8, Hartford 2.

Ian Turnbull's five goals on February 2, 1977 set a new single-game record for goals by a defensemen.

MOST GOALS, ONE GAME, BY A DEFENSEMAN:
- 5 — **Ian Turnbull,** Toronto Maple Leafs, Feb. 2, 1977, at Toronto. Toronto 9, Detroit 1.
- 4 — Harry Cameron, Toronto Arenas, Dec. 26, 1917, at Toronto. Toronto 7, Montreal Canadiens 5.
  - Harry Cameron, Montreal Canadiens, March 3, 1920, at Quebec City. Montreal 16, Quebec Bulldogs 3.
  - Sprague Cleghorn, Montreal Canadiens, Jan. 14, 1922, at Montreal. Montreal 10, Hamilton Tigers 6.
  - Johnny McKinnon, Pittsburgh Pirates, Nov. 19, 1929, at Pittsburgh. Pittsburgh 10, Toronto 5.
  - Hap Day, Toronto Maple Leafs, Nov. 19, 1929, at Pittsburgh. Pittsburgh 10, Toronto 5.
  - Tom Bladon, Philadelphia Flyers, Dec. 11, 1977, at Philadelphia. Philadelphia 11, Cleveland 1.
  - Ian Turnbull, Los Angeles Kings, Dec. 12, 1981, at Los Angeles. Los Angeles 7, Vancouver 5.

MOST GOALS BY ONE PLAYER IN HIS FIRST NHL GAME:
3 — **Alex Smart,** Montreal Canadiens, Jan. 14, 1943, at Montreal. Canadiens 5, Chicago 1.
— **Real Cloutier,** Quebec Nordiques, Oct. 10, 1979, at Quebec. Atlanta 5, Quebec 3.

MOST GOALS, ONE GAME, BY A PLAYER IN HIS FIRST NHL SEASON:
5 — **Howie Meeker,** Toronto Maple Leafs, Jan. 8, 1944, at Toronto. Toronto 10, Chicago 4.
— **Don Murdoch,** New York Rangers, Oct. 12, 1976, at Minnesota. NY Rangers 10, Minnesota 4.

MOST ASSISTS, ONE GAME, BY A DEFENSEMAN:
6 — **Babe Pratt,** Toronto Maple Leafs, Jan. 8, 1944, at Toronto. Toronto 12, Boston 3.
— **Pat Stapleton,** Chicago Black Hawks, March 30, 1969, at Chicago. Chicago 9, Detroit 5.
— **Bobby Orr,** Boston Bruins, Jan. 1, 1973, at Vancouver, Boston 8, Vancouver 2.
— **Ron Stackhouse,** Pittsburgh Penguins, March 8, 1975, at Pittsburgh. Pittsburgh 8, Philadelphia 2.
— **Paul Coffey,** Edmonton Oilers, Mar. 14, 1986, at Edmonton. Edmonton 12, Detroit 3.
— **Gary Suter,** Calgary Flames, Apr. 4, 1986, at Calgary. Calgary 9, Edmonton 3.

MOST ASSISTS BY ONE PLAYER IN HIS FIRST NHL GAME:
4 — **Earl (Dutch) Reibel,** Detroit Red Wings, Oct. 8, 1953, at Detroit. Detroit 4, New York Rangers 1.
— **Roland Eriksson,** Minnesota North Stars, Oct. 6, 1976, at New York. Rangers 6, Minnesota 5.
3 — **Al Hill,** Philadelphia Flyers, Feb. 14, 1977, at Philadelphia. Philadelphia 6, St. Louis 4.

MOST ASSISTS, ONE GAME, BY A PLAYER IN HIS FIRST NHL SEASON:
7 — **Wayne Gretzky,** Edmonton Oilers, Feb. 15, 1980, at Edmonton. Edmonton 8, Washington 2.
6 — Gary Suter, Calgary Flames, Apr. 4, 1986, at Calgary. Calgary 9, Edmonton 3.
5 — Jim McFadden, Detroit Red Wings, Nov. 23, 1947, at Chicago. Detroit 9, Chicago 3.
— Mark Howe, Hartford Whalers, Jan. 30, 1980, at Hartford. Hartford 8, Boston 3.
— Anton Stastny, Quebec Nordiques, Feb. 22, 1981, at Washington. Quebec 11, Washington 7.
— Mark Osborne, Detroit Red Wings, Feb. 7, 1982, at Detroit. St. Louis 5, Detroit 8.

MOST POINTS, ONE GAME, BY A DEFENSEMAN:
8 — **Tom Bladon,** Philadelphia Flyers, Dec. 11, 1977, at Philadelphia. 4G-4A. Philadelphia 11, Cleveland 1.
— **Paul Coffey,** Edmonton Oilers, Mar. 14, 1986, at Edmonton. 2G-6A. Edmonton 12, Detroit 3.
7 — Bobby Orr, Boston Bruins, Nov. 15, 1973, at Boston, 3G-4A. Boston 10, NY Rangers 2.

MOST POINTS BY ONE PLAYER IN HIS FIRST NHL GAME:
5 — **Al Hill,** Philadelphia Flyers, Feb. 14, 1977, at Philadelphia. 2G-3A. Philadelphia 6, St. Louis 4.
4 — Alex Smart, Montreal Canadiens, Jan. 14, 1943, at Montreal, 3G-1A. Canadiens 5, Chicago 1.
— Earl (Dutch) Reibel, Detroit Red Wings, Oct. 8, 1953, at Detroit. 4A. Detroit 4, New York Rangers 1.
— Roland Eriksson, Minnesota North Stars, Oct. 6, 1976 at New York. 4A. Rangers 5, Minnesota 5.

MOST POINTS, ONE GAME, BY A PLAYER IN HIS FIRST NHL SEASON:
8 — **Peter Stastny,** Quebec Nordiques, Feb. 22, 1981, at Washington. 4G-4A. Quebec 11, Washington 7.
— **Anton Stastny,** Quebec Nordiques, Feb. 22, 1981, at Washington. 3G-5A. Quebec 11, Washington 7.
7 — Wayne Gretzky, Edmonton Oilers, Feb. 15, 1980, at Edmonton. 7A. Edmonton 8, Washington 2.
6 — Wayne Gretzky, Edmonton Oilers, March 29, 1980, at Toronto. 2G-4A. Edmonton 8, Toronto 5.
— Gary Suter, Calgary Flames, Apr. 4, 1986, at Calgary. Calgary 9, Edmonton 3.

MOST PENALTIES, ONE GAME:
9 — **Jim Dorey,** Toronto Maple Leafs, Oct. 16, 1968, at Toronto against Pittsburgh. 4 minors, 2 majors, 2 10-minute misconducts, 1 game misconduct.
— **Dave Schultz,** Pittsburgh Penguins, Apr. 6, 1978, at Detroit, 5 minors, 2 majors, 2 10-minute misconducts.
— **Randy Holt,** Los Angeles Kings, Mar. 11, 1979, at Philadelphia. 1 minor, 3 majors, 2 10-minute misconducts, 3 game misconducts.
— **Russ Anderson,** Pittsburgh Penguins, Jan. 19, 1980, at Pittsburgh. 3 minors, 3 majors, 3 game misconducts.
— **Kim Clackson,** Quebec Nordiques, March 8, 1981, at Quebec. 4 minors, 3 majors, 2 game misconducts.
— **Terry O'Reilly, Boston Bruins,** Dec. 19, 1984 at Hartford. 5 minors, 3 majors, 1 game misconduct.
— **Larry Playfair,** Los Angeles Kings, Dec. 9, 1986, at NY Islanders. 6 minors, 2 majors, 1 10-minute misconduct.

MOST PENALTY MINUTES, ONE GAME:
67 — **Randy Holt,** Los Angeles Kings, Mar. 11, 1979, at Philadelphia. 1 minor, 3 majors, 2 10-minute misconducts, 3 game misconducts.
55 — Frank Bathe, Philadelphia Flyers, March 11, 1979, at Philadelphia. 3 majors, 2 10-minute misconducts, 2 game misconducts.
51 — Russ Anderson, Pittsburgh Penguins, Jan. 19, 1980, at Pittsburgh. 3 minors, 3 majors, 3 game misconducts.

MOST GOALS, ONE PERIOD:
4 — **Harvey (Busher) Jackson,** Toronto Maple Leafs, Nov. 20, 1934, at St. Louis, third period. Toronto 5, St. Louis Eagles 2.
— **Max Bentley,** Chicago Black Hawks, Jan. 28, 1943, at Chicago, third period. Chicago 10, New York Rangers 1.
— **Clint Smith,** Chicago Black Hawks, March 4, 1945, at Chicago, third period. Chicago 6, Montreal Canadiens 4.
— **Red Berenson,** St. Louis Blues, Nov. 7, 1968, at Philadelphia, second period. St. Louis 8, Philadelphia Flyers 0.
— **Wayne Gretzky,** Edmonton Oilers, Feb. 18, 1981, at Edmonton, third period. Edmonton 9, St. Louis 2.
— **Grant Mulvey,** Chicago Black Hawks, Feb. 3, 1982, at Chicago, first period. Chicago 9, St. Louis 5.
— **Bryan Trottier,** New York Islanders, Feb 13, 1982, at New York, second period. Islanders 8 Philadelphia 2.
— **Al Secord,** Chicago Black Hawks, Jan. 7, 1987 at Chicago, second period. Chicago 6, Toronto Maple Leafs 4.
— **Joe Nieuwendyk,** Calgary Flames, Jan. 11, 1989, at Calgary, second period. Calgary 8, Winnipeg 3.

MOST ASSISTS, ONE PERIOD:
5 — **Dale Hawerchuk,** Winnipeg Jets, Mar. 6, 1984, at Los Angeles, second period. Winnipeg 7, Los Angeles 3.
4 — Buddy O'Connor, Montreal Canadiens, Nov. 8, 1942, at Montreal, third period. Montreal 10, New York Rangers 4.
— Doug Bentley, Chicago Black Hawks, Jan. 28, 1943, at Chicago, third period. Chicago 10, New York Rangers 1.
— Joe Carveth, Detroit Red Wings, Jan. 23, 1944, at Detroit, third period. Detroit 15, New York Rangers 0.
— Phil Watson, Montreal Canadiens, March 18, 1944, at Montreal, third period. Montreal 11, New York Rangers 4.
— Bill Mosienko, Chicago Black Hawks, March 4, 1945, at Chicago, third period. Chicago 6, Montreal Canadiens 4.
— Jean-Claude Tremblay, Montreal Canadiens, Dec. 29, 1962, at Montreal, second period. Montreal 5, Detroit 1.
— Phil Goyette, New York Rangers, Oct. 20, 1963, at New York, first period. New York 5, Boston 1
— Jim Wiste, Chicago Black Hawks, Nov. 9, 1969, at Chicago, third period. Chicago 9, Toronto 0.
— Cliff Koroll, Chicago Black Hawks, Dec. 16, 1970, at Chicago, second period. Chicago 8, St. Louis Blues 3.
— Syl Apps, Jr., Pittsburgh Penguins, March 24, 1971, at Pittsburgh, third period. Pittsburgh 8, Detroit Red Wings 2.
— Bobby Orr, Boston Bruins, Feb. 15, 1972, at Boston, first period. Boston 6, California 1.
— Jim Pappin, Chicago Black Hawks, March 24, 1973, at Chicago, second period. Chicago 7, Atlanta 0.
— Ron Stackhouse, Pittsburgh Penguins, March 8, 1975, at Pittsburgh, second period. Pittsburgh 8, Philadelphia 2.
— Chuck Lefley, St. Louis Blues, March 6, 1976, third period. St. Louis 7, Chicago 4.
— Clark Gillies, New York Islanders, Dec. 23, 1978, at New York, second period. New York Rangers 4 at New York Islanders 9.
— Brad Park, Boston Bruins, Mar. 17, 1979, at Boston, first period. Boston 4, Chicago 2.
— Mark Howe, Hartford Whalers, Jan. 30. 1980, at Hartford, second period. Hartford 8, Boston 2.
— Paul Mulvey, Washington Capitals, March 5, 1980, at Washington, first period. Washington 7, St. Louis 4.
— Mike Bossy, New York Islanders, Feb. 13, 1982, at New York, second period. Islanders 8, Philadelphia 2.
— Wayne Gretzky, Edmonton Oilers, Feb. 4, 1983, at Edmonton, first period. Edmonton 7, Montreal 3.
— Mark Messier, Edmonton Oilers, Jan. 4, 1984, at Edmonton, second period. Edmonton 12, Minnesota 8.
— Wayne Gretzky, Edmonton Oilers, October 26, 1984, at Edmonton, second period. Edmonton 8, Los Angeles 3.
— Wayne Gretzky, Edmonton Oilers, March 31, 1985, at Chicago, 3rd period. Edmonton 7, Chicago 3.
— Wayne Gretzky, Edmonton Oilers, Oct. 30, 1985, at Edmonton, second period. Edmonton 7, Winnipeg 3.
— Paul Gagne, New Jersey Devils, Feb. 9, 1986, at Hartford, third period. New Jersey 6, Hartford 3.
— Wayne Gretzky, Edmonton Oilers, Feb. 14, 1986, at Edmonton, third period. Edmonton 8, Quebec 3.
— Gary Suter, Calgary Flames, Apr. 4, 1986, at Calgary, second period. Calgary 9, Edmonton 3.
— Wayne Gretzky, Edmonton Oilers, Oct. 15, 1986, at Edmonton, third period. Edmonton 5, Quebec 2.
— Scott Stevens, Washington Capitals, Mar. 13, 1987, at Washington, third period. Washington 5, Toronto 2.
— Anton Stastny, Quebec Nordiques, Apr. 4, 1987, at Quebec, second period. Quebec 8, New Jersey 4.
— Wayne Gretzky, Edmonton Oilers, Nov. 14, 1987, at St. Louis, third period. Edmonton 6, St. Louis 5.
— Wayne Gretzky, Edmonton Oilers, Mar. 4, 1988, at Edmonton, first period. Philadelphia 4, Edmonton 7.
— Wayne Gretzky, Edmonton Oilers, Mar. 7, 1988, at Winnipeg, second period. Edmonton 6, Winnipeg 0.
— Glen Wesley, Boston Bruins, Oct. 16, 1988, at Chicago, second period. Boston 10, Chicago 3.
— Dave Babych, Hartford Whalers, Oct. 26, 1988, at Buffalo, third period. Hartford 7, Buffalo 1.
— Bengt Gustafsson, Washington Capitals, Nov. 23, 1988 at Washington, second period. Washington 7, NY Islanders 6.
— Wayne Gretzky, Los Angeles Kings, March 4, 1989, at Los Angeles, second period. Los Angeles 6, Philadelphia 2.

Dave "Tiger" Williams (22), battles the Sabres' Jerry Korab (4) for a rebound. Williams later played for Vancouver, Detroit, Los Angeles and Hartford. With the Kings, he scored at the :07 mark of the first period against the Whalers — the third-fastest goal from the start of an NHL game.

MOST POINTS, ONE PERIOD:
6 — Bryan Trottier, New York Islanders, Dec. 23, 1978, at New York, second period. 3G, 3A. New York Rangers 4 at New York Islanders 9.
5 — Les Cunningham, Chicago Black Hawks, Jan. 28, 1940, at Chicago, third period. 2G, 3A. Chicago 8, Montreal Canadiens 1.
— Max Bentley, Chicago Black Hawks, Jan. 28, 1943, at Chicago, third period. 4G, 1A, Chicago 10, New York Rangers 1.
— Leo Labine, Boston Bruins, Nov. 28, 1954, at Boston, second period, 3G, 2A. Boston 6, Detroit 2.
— Darryl Sittler, Toronto Maple Leafs, Feb. 7, 1976, at Toronto, second period. 3G, 2A. Toronto 11, Boston 4.
— Dale Hawerchuk, Winnipeg Jets, Mar. 6, 1984, at Los Angeles, second period. 5A. Winnipeg 7 Los Angeles 3.
— Jari Kurri, Edmonton Oilers, October 26, 1984 at Edmonton, 2nd period. Edmonton 8, Los Angeles 2.
— Pat Elynuik, Winnipeg Jets, Jan. 20, 1989, at Winnipeg, second period. 2G, 3A. Winnipeg 7, Pittsburgh 3.

FASTEST GOAL BY A ROOKIE IN HIS FIRST NHL GAME:
15 Seconds — Gus Bodnar, Toronto Maple Leafs, Oct. 30, 1943. Toronto 5, NY Rangers 2.
18 Seconds — Danny Gare, Buffalo Sabres, Oct. 10, 1974. Buffalo 9, Boston 5.
36 Seconds — Al Hill, Philadelphia Flyers, Feb. 14, 1977. Philadelphia 6, St. Louis 4.

FASTEST GOAL FROM START OF GAME:
5 Seconds — Bryan Trottier, New York Islanders, Mar. 22, 1984, at Boston. NY Islanders 3, Boston 3
— Doug Smail, Winnipeg Jets, Dec. 20, 1981, at Winnipeg. Winnipeg 5, St. Louis 4.
6 Seconds — Henry Boucha, Detroit Red Wings, Jan. 28, 1973, at Montreal. Detroit 4, Montreal 2
— Jean Pronovost, Pittsburgh Penguins, March 25, 1976, at St. Louis. St. Louis 5, Pittsburgh 2
7 Seconds — Charlie Conacher, Toronto Maple Leafs, Feb. 6, 1932, at Toronto. Toronto 6, Boston 0
— Danny Gare, Buffalo Sabres, Dec. 17, 1978, at Buffalo. Buffalo 6, Vancouver 3
— Dave Williams, Los Angeles Kings, Feb. 14, 1987 at Los Angeles. Los Angeles 5, Harford 2.
8 Seconds — Ron Martin, New York Americans, Dec. 4, 1932, at New York. NY Americans 4, Montreal 2
— Chuck Arnason, Colorado Rockies, Jan. 28, 1977, at Atlanta. Colorado 3, Atlanta 3
— Wayne Gretzky, Edmonton Oilers, Dec. 14, 1983, at New York. Edmonton 9, NY Rangers 4
— Gaetan Duchesne, Washington Capitals, Mar. 14, 1987, at St. Louis. Washington 3, St. Louis 4.
— Tim Kerr, Philadelphia Flyers, March 7, 1989, at Philadelphia. Philadelphia 4, Edmonton 4.

FASTEST GOAL FROM START OF A PERIOD:
4 Seconds — Claude Provost, Montreal Canadiens, Nov. 9, 1957, at Montreal, second period. Montreal 4, Boston 2.
— Denis Savard, Chicago Blackhawks, Jan. 12, 1986, at Chicago, third period. Chicago 4, Hartford 2.

FASTEST TWO GOALS:
4 Seconds — Nels Stewart, Montreal Maroons, Jan. 3, 1931, at Montreal at 8:24 and 8:28, third period. Montreal 5, Boston 3.
5 Seconds — Pete Mahovlich, Montreal Canadiens, Feb. 20, 1971, at Montreal at 12:16 and 12:21, third period. Montreal 7, Chicago 1.
6 Seconds — Jim Pappin, Chicago Black Hawks, Feb. 16, 1972, at Chicago at 2:57 and 3:03, third period. Chicago 3, Philadelphia 3.
— Ralph Backstrom, Los Angeles Kings, Nov. 2, 1972, at Los Angeles at 8:30 and 8:36, third period. Los Angeles 5, Boston 2.
— Lanny McDonald, Calgary Flames, Mar. 22, 1984, at Calgary at 16:23 and 16:29, first period. Detroit 6, Calgary 4.
— Sylvain Turgeon, Hartford Whalers, Mar. 28, 1987, at Hartford at 13:59 and 14:05, second period. Hartford 5, Pittsburgh 4.

FASTEST THREE GOALS:
21 Seconds — Bill Mosienko, Chicago Black Hawks, March 23, 1952, at New York, against goaltender Lorne Anderson. Mosienko scored at 6:09, 6:20 and 6:30, third period, all with both teams at full strength. Chicago 7, NY Rangers 6.
44 Seconds — Jean Béliveau, Montreal Canadiens, Nov. 5, 1955, at Montreal against goaltender Terry Sawchuk of Boston Bruins. Béliveau scored at 00:42, 1:08 and 1:26 of second period, all with Montreal holding a 6-4 man advantage. Montreal 4, Boston 2.

FASTEST THREE ASSISTS:
21 Seconds — Gus Bodnar, Chicago Black Hawks, March 23, 1952, at New York, Bodnar assisted on Bill Mosienko's three goals at 6:09, 6:20, 6:30 of third Period. Chicago 7, NY Rangers 6.
44 Seconds — Bert Olmstead, Montreal Canadiens, Nov. 5, 1955, at Montreal against Boston Bruins. Olmstead assisted on Jean Béliveau's three goals at 00:42, 1:08 and 1:26 of second period. Montreal 4, Boston 2.

MOST PENALTIES, ONE PERIOD:
9 — Randy Holt, Los Angeles Kings, Mar. 11, 1979, at Philadelphia, first period. 1 minor, 3 majors, 2 10-minute misconducts, 3 game misconducts.

MOST PENALTY MINUTES, ONE PERIOD:
67 — Randy Holt, Los Angeles Kings, Mar. 11, 1979, at Philadelphia, first period. 1 minor, 3 majors, 2 10-minute misconducts, 3 game misconducts.

Top 100 All-Time Goal-Scoring Leaders

*active player

(figures in parentheses indicate ranking of top 10 by goals per game)

Player		Seasons	Games	Goals	Goals per game
1. Gordie Howe	Det.	25	1,687	**786**	.466
	Hfd.	1	80	15	.188
	Total	26	1,767	**801**	.453
*2. Marcel Dionne	Det.	4	309	139	.450
	L.A.	11¾	921	550	.597
	NYR	2¼	118	42	.356
	Total	18	1,348	**731**	.542
3. Phil Esposito	Chi.	4	235	74	.315
	Bos.	8¼	625	459	.734
	NYR	5¾	422	184	.436
	Total	18	1,282	**717**	.559(10)
*4. Wayne Gretzky	Edm.	9	696	583	.838
	L.A.	1	78	54	.692
	Total	10	774	**637**	.823 (1)
5. Bobby Hull	Chi.	15	1,036	604	.583
	Wpg.	⅔	18	4	.222
	Hfd.	⅓	9	2	.222
	Total	16	1,063	**610**	.574 (7)
6. Mike Bossy	NYI	10	752	**573**	.762 (3)
7. John Bucyk	Det.	2	104	11	.106
	Bos.	21	1,436	545	.380
	Total	23	1,540	**556**	.361
8. Maurice Richard	Mtl.	18	978	**544**	.556
9. Stan Mikita	Chi.	22	1,394	**541**	.388
*10. Guy Lafleur	Mtl.	14	961	518	.539
	NYR.	1	67	18	.269
	Total	15	1,028	**536**	.521
11. Frank Mahovlich, Tor., Det., Mtl., ...		18	1,181	**533**	.451
12. Gilbert Perreault, Buf.		17	1,191	**512**	.430
13. Jean Beliveau, Mtl.		20	1,125	**507**	.451
*14. Lanny McDonald, Tor., Col., Cgy.		16	1,111	**500**	.450
15. Jean Ratelle, NYR, Bos.		21	1,281	**491**	.383
16. Norm Ullman, Det., Tor.		20	1,410	**490**	.348
*17. Bryan Trottier, NYI		14	1,064	**487**	.458
18. Darryl Sittler, Tor., Phi., Det.		15	1,096	**484**	.442
19. Alex Delvecchio, Det.		23	1,549	**456**	.294
*20. Rick Middleton, NYR, Bos.		14	1,005	**448**	.446
*21. Jari Kurri, Edm.		9	676	**441**	.652 (4)
*22. Michel Goulet, Que.		10	756	**440**	.582 (6)
23. Yvan Cournoyer, Mtl.		16	968	**428**	.442
24. Steve Shutt, Mtl., L.A.		13	930	**424**	.456
25. Bill Barber, Phi.		12	903	**420**	.465
26. Garry Unger, Tor., Det., St. L., Atl., L.A., Edm.		16	1,105	**413**	.374
27. Rod Gilbert, NYR		18	1,065	**406**	.381
*28. Mike Gartner, Wsh., Min.		10	771	**404**	.524
29. Dave Keon, Tor., Hfd.		18	1,296	**396**	.305
30. Pierre Larouche, Pit., Mtl., Hfd., NYR		14	812	**395**	.486
31. Bernie Geoffrion, Mtl., NYR		16	883	**393**	.445
32. Jean Pronovost, Pit., Atl., Wsh.		14	998	**391**	.392
33. Dean Prentice, NYR, Bos., Det., Pit., Min.		22	1,378	**391**	.284
*34. Rick Vaive, Van., Tor., Chi., Buf.		10	715	**386**	.540
35. Richard Martin, Buf., L.A.		11	685	**384**	.561 (9)
36. Reggie Leach, Bos., Cal., Phi., Det.		13	934	**381**	.408
37. Ted Lindsay, Det., Chi.		17	1,068	**379**	.355
38. Butch Goring, L.A., NYI, Bos.		16	1,107	**375**	.339
*39. Dave Taylor, L.A.		12	822	**373**	.454
40. Rick Kehoe, Tor., Pit.		14	906	**371**	.409
41. Jacques Lemaire, Mtl.		12	853	**366**	.429
42. Peter McNab, Buf., Bos., Van., N.J.		14	954	**363**	.381
43. Rick MacLeish, Phi., Hfd., Pit., Det.		14	846	**349**	.413
44. Ivan Boldirev, Bos., Cal., Atl., Van., Det., Chi.		15	1,052	**361**	.343
45. Bobby Clarke, Phi.		15	1,144	**358**	.313
46. Henri Richard, Mtl.		20	1,256	**358**	.285
*47. Peter Stastny, Que.		9	675	**356**	.527
*48. Brian Propp, Phi.		9	750	**356**	.475
*49. Dennis Maruk, Cal., Cle., Wsh., Min.		13	882	**356**	.404
50. Wilf Paiement, K.C., Col., Tor., Que., NYR, Buf.		14	946	**356**	.386
*51. Glenn Anderson, Edm.		9	681	**355**	.521
52. Danny Gare, Buf., Det., Edm.		13	827	**354**	.428
*53. Dale Hawerchuk, Wpg.		8	634	**353**	.557
*54. Bernie Federko, St. L.		13	927	**352**	.380
55. Andy Bathgate, NYR, Tor., Det., Pit.		16	1,069	**349**	.326
*56. Dino Ciccarelli, Min., Wsh.		9	613	**344**	.561 (8)
*57. Charlie Simmer, Cal., Cle., L.A., Bos., Pit.		14	712	**342**	.480
*58. Mark Messier, Edm.		10	719	**335**	.466
59. Ron Ellis, Tor.		16	1,034	**332**	.321
60. Ken Hodge, Chi., Bos., NYR		13	881	**328**	.372
*61. Tim Kerr, Phi.		9	534	**324**	.607 (5)
62. Nels Stewart, Mtl. M, Bos., NYA		15	654	**324**	.495
*63. Denis Savard, Chi.		9	676	**324**	.479
64. Pit Martin, Det., Bos., Chi., Van.		17	1,101	**324**	.294
65. Vic Hadfield, NYR, Pit.		16	1,002	**323**	.322
66. Clark Gillies, NYI, Buf.		14	958	**319**	.333
*67. Bobby Smith, Min., Mtl.		11	838	**316**	.377

Rod Gilbert battled through several serious injuries to score 404 goals in his 18-year career with the Rangers.

Player	Seasons	Games	Goals	Goals per game
68. Don Lever, Van., Atl., Cgy., Col., N.J., Buf.	15	1,020	**313**	.307
*69. Denis Potvin, NYI	15	1,060	**310**	.292
70. Bob Nevin, Tor., NYR, Min., L.A.	18	1,128	**307**	.272
71. Joey Mullen, St. L., Cgy.	8	568	**305**	.537
*72. John Ogrodnick, Det., Que., NYR	10	695	**305**	.439
*73. Mike Foligno, Det., Buf.	10	758	**305**	.402
74. Brian Sutter, St. L.	12	779	**303**	.389
75. Dennis Hull, Chi., Det.	14	959	**303**	.316
76. Mario Lemieux, Pit.	5	368	**300**	.815 (2)
77. George Armstrong, Tor.	20	1,187	**296**	.249
78. Tom Lysiak, Atl., Chi.	13	919	**292**	.318
*79. Mike Bullard, Pit., Cgy. St. L., Phi.	9	592	**288**	.486
80. Peter Mahovlich, Det., Mtl., Pit.	16	884	**288**	.326
81. Tony McKegney, Buf., Que., Min., St. L.	12	791	**285**	.360
82. Paul MacLean, St. L., Wpg., Det.	8	599	**284**	.474
83. Rene Robert, Pit., Buf., Col., Tor.	12	744	**284**	.382
84. Bill Goldsworthy, Bos., Min., NYR	14	771	**283**	.367
85. Dick Duff, Tor., NYR, Mtl., L.A., Buf.	18	1,030	**283**	.275
*86. John Anderson, Tor., Que., Hfd.	12	814	**282**	.346
87. Bob Pulford, Tor., L.A.	16	1,079	**281**	.260
88. Red Kelly, Det., Tor.	20	1,316	**281**	.214
89. Camille Henry, NYR, Chi., St. L.	12	727	**279**	.384
90. Jim Pappin, Tor., Chi., Cal., Cle.	14	767	**278**	.362
91. Ralph Backstrom, Mtl., L.A., Chi.	16	1,032	**278**	.362
92. John Tonelli, NYI, Cgy., L.A.	11	832	**277**	.333
93. Wayne Cashman, Bos.	17	1,027	**277**	.270
94. Ron Stewart, Tor., Bos., St. L., NYR, Van., NYI	21	1,353	**276**	.204
*95. Ron Duguay, NYR, Det., Pit., L.A.	12	869	**274**	.315
96. Murray Oliver, Det., Bos., Tor., Min.	17	1,127	**274**	.243
97. Howie Morenz, Mtl., Chi., NYR	14	550	**273**	.496
98. Bobby Schmautz, Chi., Bos., Van., Edm., Col.	13	764	**271**	.355
99. Aurel Joliat, Mtl.	16	654	**270**	.413
100. Bobby Orr, Bos., Chi.	12	657	**270**	.411

Top 100 All-Time Assist Leaders

John Bucyk

Bobby Clarke

*active player
(figures in parentheses indicates ranking of top 10 in order of assists per game)

Player	Seasons	Games	Assists	Assists per game
*1. Wayne Gretzky . . . Edm.	9	696	1,086	1.560 (1)
L.A.	1	78	114	1.462
Total	10	774	1,200	1.550
2. Gordie Howe . . . . Det.	25	1,687	1,023	.606
Hfd.	1	80	26	.325
Total	26	1,767	1,049	.594
*3. Marcel Dionne . . . Det.	4	309	227	.735
L.A.	11¾	921	757	.822
NYR	2¼	118	56	.475
Total	18	1,348	1,040	.772(10)
4. Stan Mikita . . . . . . Chi.	22	1,394	926	.664
5. Phil Esposito . . . . Chi.	4	235	100	.426
Bos.	8¼	625	553	.885
NYR	5¾	422	220	.521
Total	18	1,282	873	.681
6. Bobby Clarke . . . . Phi.	15	1,144	852	.745
*7. Bryan Trottier . . . . NYI	14	1,064	842	.791 (7)
8. Alex Delvecchio . . Det.	23	1,549	825	.533
9. Gilbert Perreault . . Buf.	17	1,191	814	.683
10. John Bucyk . . . . . Det.	2	104	19	.183
Bos.	21	1,436	794	.553
Total	23	1,540	813	.528
11. Jean Ratelle, NYR, Bos.	21	1,281	776	.606
*12. Guy Lafleur, Mtl., NYR	15	1,028	755	.734
13. Denis Potvin, NYI	15	1,060	742	.700
14. Norm Ullman, Det., Tor.	20	1,410	739	.524
*15. Bernie Federko, St. L.	13	927	721	.778 (9)
16. Jean Beliveau, Mtl.	20	1,125	712	.633
17. Henri Richard, Mtl.	20	1,256	688	.548
*18. Larry Robinson, Mtl.	16	1,202	686	.571
19. Brad Park, NYR, Bos., Det.	17	1,113	683	.614
20. Bobby Orr, Bos., Chi.	12	657	645	.982 (3)
21. Darryl Sittler, Tor., Phi., Det.	15	1,096	637	.581
*22. Peter Stastny, Que.	9	675	630	.933 (4)
23. Andy Bathgate, NYR, Tor., Det., Pit.	17	1,069	624	.584
*24. Borje Salming, Tor.	16	1,099	620	.564
25. Rod Gilbert, NYR	18	1,065	615	.577
*26. Denis Savard, Chi.	9	676	609	.901 (6)
*27. Paul Coffey, Edm., Pit.	9	653	595	.911 (5)
*28. Bobby Smith, Min., Mtl.	11	838	590	.704
29. Dave Keon, Tor., Hfd.	18	1,296	590	.455
30. Frank Mahovlich, Tor., Det., Mtl.	18	1,181	570	.483
31. Bobby Hull, Chi., Wpg., Hfd.	16	1,063	560	.527
32. Mike Bossy, NYI	10	752	553	.735
*33. Dave Taylor, L.A.	12	822	551	.670
34. Tom Lysiak, Atl., Chi.	13	919	551	.600
*35. Ray Bourque, Bos.	10	718	545	.759
36. Red Kelly, Det., Tor.	20	1,316	542	.412
*37. Rick Middleton, NYR, Bos.	14	1,005	540	.537
38. Dennis Maruk, Cal., Cle., Wsh., Min.	13	882	521	.591
39. Wayne Cashman, Bos.	17	1,027	516	.502
40. Butch Goring, L.A., NYI, Bos.	16	1,107	513	.463
*41. Jari Kurri, Edm.	9	676	509	.753
*42. Mark Messier, Edm.	10	719	506	.704
*43. Lanny McDonald, Tor., Col., Cgy.	16	1,111	506	.455
44. Ivan Boldirev, Bos., Cal., Chi., Atl., Van., Det.	15	1,052	505	.480
*45. Ken Linseman, Phi., Edm., Bos.	11	741	497	.671
*46. Dale Hawerchuk, Wpg.	8	634	495	.781 (8)
47. Peter Mahovlich, Mtl., Pit., Det.	16	884	486	.550

Player	Seasons	Games	Goals	Goals per game
48. Pit Martin, Det., Bos., Chi., Van.	17	1,101	485	.441
*49. Doug Wilson, Chi.	11	817	475	.581
50. Ken Hodge, Chi., Bos., NYR	13	881	472	.536
51. Ted Lindsay, Det., Chi.	17	1,068	472	.442
52. Jacques Lemaire, Mtl.	12	853	469	.550
53. Dean Prentice, NYR, Bos., Det., Pit., Min.	22	1,378	469	.340
54. Phil Goyette, Mtl., NYR, St. L., Buf.	16	941	467	.496
*55. Brian Propp, Phi.	10	750	464	.619
56. Bill Barber, Phi.	12	903	463	.513
*57. Reed Larson, Det., Bos., Edm., NYI, Min.	13	903	463	.513
58. Doug Mohns, Bos., Chi., Min., Atl., Wsh.	22	1,390	462	.332
*59. Michel Goulet, Que.	10	756	460	.608
60. Bobby Rousseau, Mtl., Min., NYR	15	942	458	.486
61. Wilf Paiement, K.C., Col., Tor., Que., NYR, Buf.	14	946	458	.484
*62. Randy Carlyle, Tor., Pit., Wpg.	13	862	455	.528
63. Murray Oliver, Det., Bos., Tor., Min.	17	1,127	454	.403
64. Doug Harvey, Mtl., NYR, Det., St. L.	19	1,113	452	.406
65. Guy Lapointe, Mtl., St. L., Bos.	16	884	451	.510
66. Walt Tkaczuk, NYR	14	945	451	.477
67. Peter McNab, Buf., Bos., Van., N.J.	14	954	450	.472
*68. Mel Bridgman, Phi., Cgy., N.J., Det., Van.	14	977	449	.460
*69. John Tonelli, NYI, Cgy., L.A.	11	832	447	.537
*70. Mark Howe, Hfd., Phi.	10	706	440	.623
71. Bill Gadsby, Chi., NYR, Det.	20	1,248	437	.350
72. Yvan Cournoyer, Mtl.	16	968	435	.449
*73. Ron Francis, Hfd.	8	567	433	.764
74. Bernie Geoffrion, Mtl., NYR	16	883	429	.486
75. Pierre Larouche, Pit., Mtl., Hfd., NYR	14	812	427	.526
76. Syl Apps, Jr., NYR, Pit., L.A.	10	727	423	.582
77. Kent Nilsson, Atl., Cgy., Min., Edm.	8	547	422	.771
*78. Ron Greschner, NYR	15	927	422	.455
79. Bert Olmstead, Chi., Mtl., Tor.	14	848	421	.496
80. Maurice Richard, Mtl.	18	978	421	.430
*81. Larry Murphy, L.A., Wsh., Min.	9	708	420	.593
82. Craig Ramsay, Buf.	14	1,070	420	.393
83. Bob Nevin, Tor., NYR, Min., L.A.	18	1,128	419	.371
84. Rene Robert, Pit., Buf., Col., Tor.	12	744	418	.562
85. Pierre Pilote, Chi., Tor.	14	890	418	.470
86. Carol Vadnais, Mtl., Oak., Cal., Bos., NYR, N.J.	17	1,087	418	.385
87. George Armstrong, Tor.	21	1,187	417	.351
*88. Mario Lemieux, Pit.	5	368	415	1.128 (2)
*89. Glenn Anderson, Edm.	9	681	414	.608
90. Rick MacLeish, Phi., Hfd., Pit., Det.	14	846	410	.485
91. Elmer Lach, Mtl.	14	664	408	.614
92. Fred Stanfield, Chi., Bos., Min., Buf.	14	914	405	.443
93. Tim Horton, Tor., NYR, Pit., Buf.	22	1,446	403	.279
94. Terry O'Reilly, Bos.	14	891	402	.451
*95. Dave Babych, Wpg., Hfd.	9	659	401	.608
*96. Mike Gartner, Wsh., Min.	10	771	399	.518
97. Red Berenson, Mtl., NYR, St. L., Det.	17	987	397	.402
98. Rick Kehoe, Tor., Pit.	14	906	396	.437
99. Eddie Westfall, Bos., NYI	18	1,227	394	.322
100. Steve Shutt, Mtl., L.A.	13	930	393	.422

Top 100 All-Time Point Leaders

* active player

(figures in parentheses indicate ranking of top 10 by points per game)

Player		Seasons	Games	Goals	Assists	Points	Points per game	
1. Gordie Howe	Det.	25	1,687	786	1,023	1,809	1.072	
	Hfd.	1	80	15	26	41	.513	
	Total	26	1,767	801	1,049	**1,850**	1.047	
*2. Wayne Gretzky	Edm.	9	696	583	1,086	**1,669**	2.398	
	L.A.	1	78	54	114	168		
	Total	10	774	637	1,200	**1,837**	2.373	(1)
*3. Marcel Dionne	Det.	4	309	139	227	366	1.184	
	LA	11¾	921	550	757	1,307	1.419	
	NYR	2¼	118	42	56	98	.831	
	Total	18	1,348	731	1,040	**1,771**	1.314	(9)
4. Phil Esposito	Chi.	4	235	74	100	174	.740	
	Bos.	8¼	625	459	553	1,012	1.619	
	NYR	5¾	422	184	220	404	.957	
	Total	18	1,282	717	873	**1,590**	1.240	
5. Stan Mikita	Chi.	22	1,394	541	926	**1,467**	1.052	
6. John Bucyk	Det.	2	104	11	19	30	.288	
	Bos.	21	1,436	545	794	1,339	.932	
	Total	23	1,540	556	813	**1,369**	.889	
*7. Bryan Trottier	NYI	14	1,064	487	842	**1,329**	1.249	
8. Gilbert Perreault	Buf.	17	1,191	512	814	**1,326**	1.113	
*9. Guy Lafleur	Mtl.	14	961	518	728	**1,246**	1.296	
	NYR	1	67	18	27	45	.672	
	Total	15	1,028	536	755	**1,291**	1.256	
10. Alex Delvecchio	Det.	24	1,549	456	825	**1,281**	.827	
11. Jean Ratelle	NYR, Bos.	21	1,281	491	776	**1,267**	.989	
12. Norm Ullman	Det., Tor.	20	1,410	490	739	**1,229**	.872	
13. Jean Beliveau	Mtl.	20	1,125	507	712	**1,219**	1.084	
14. Bobby Clarke	Phi.	15	1,144	358	852	**1,210**	1.057	
15. Bobby Hull	Chi., Wpg., Hfd.	16	1,063	610	560	**1,170**	1.101	
16. Mike Bossy	NYI	10	752	573	553	**1,126**	1.497	(3)
17. Darryl Sittler	Tor., Phi., Det.	15	1,096	484	637	**1,121**	1.023	
18. Frank Mahovlich	Tor., Det., Mtl.	18	1,181	533	570	**1,103**	.934	
*19. Bernie Federko	St. L.	13	927	352	721	**1,073**	1.157	
20. Denis Potvin	NYI	15	1,060	310	742	**1,052**	.992	
21. Henri Richard	Mtl.	20	1,256	358	688	**1,046**	.833	
22. Rod Gilbert	NYR	18	1,065	406	615	**1,021**	.959	
*23. Lanny McDonald	Tor., Col., Cgy.	16	1,111	500	506	**1,006**	.905	
24. Rick Middleton	Bos., NYR	14	1,005	448	540	**988**	.983	
*25. Peter Stastny	Que.	9	675	356	630	**986**	1.461	(4)
26. Dave Keon	Tor., Hfd.	18	1,296	396	590	**986**	.761	
27. Andy Bathgate	NYR, Tor., Det., Pit.	17	1,069	349	624	**973**	.910	
28. Maurice Richard	Mtl.	18	978	544	421	**965**	.987	
*29. Jari Kurri	Edm.	9	676	441	509	**950**	1.405	(5)
*30. Denis Savard	Chi.	9	676	324	609	**933**	1.380	(7)
*31. Dave Taylor	L.A.	12	822	373	551	**924**	1.124	
32. Bobby Orr	Bos., Chi.	12	657	270	645	**915**	1.393	(6)
*33. Bobby Smith	Min., Mtl.	11	838	316	590	**906**	1.081	
*34. Michel Goulet	Que.	10	756	440	460	**900**	1.190	
35. Brad Park	NYR, Bos., Det.	17	1,113	213	683	**896**	.805	
36. Butch Goring	L.A., NYI, Bos.	16	1,107	375	513	**888**	.802	
37. Bill Barber	Phi.	12	903	420	463	**883**	.978	
*38. Larry Robinson	Mtl.	16	1,202	197	686	**883**	.735	
39. Dennis Maruk	Cal., Cle., Wsh., Min.	13	882	356	521	**877**	.994	
40. Ivan Boldirev	Bos., Cal., Chi., Atl., Van., Det.	15	1,052	361	505	**866**	.823	
41. Yvan Cournoyer	Mtl.	16	968	428	435	**863**	.892	
42. Dean Prentice	NYR, Bos., Det., Pit., Min.	22	1,378	391	469	**860**	.624	
43. Ted Lindsay	Det., Chi.	17	1,068	379	472	**851**	.797	
*44. Paul Coffey	Edm., Pit.	9	653	254	595	**849**	1.300	(10)
*45. Dale Hawerchuk	Wpg.	9	634	353	495	**848**	1.338	(8)
46. Tom Lysiak	Atl., Chi.	13	919	292	551	**843**	.917	
*47. Mark Messier	Edm.	10	719	335	506	**841**	1.170	
48. Jacques Lemaire	Mtl.	12	853	366	469	**835**	.979	
49. Red Kelly	Det., Tor.	20	1,316	281	542	**823**	.625	
50. Pierre Larouche	Pit., Mtl., Hfd., NYR	14	812	395	427	**822**	1.012	
51. Bernie Geoffrion	Mtl., NYR	16	883	393	429	**822**	.931	
*52. Brian Propp	Phi.	10	750	356	464	**820**	1.093	
53. Steve Shutt	Mtl., L.A.	13	930	424	393	**817**	.878	
54. Wilf Paiement	K.C., Col., Tor., Que., NYR, Buf., Pit.	14	946	356	458	**814**	.860	
55. Peter McNab	Buf., Bos., Van., N.J.	14	954	363	450	**813**	.852	
56. Pit Martin	Det., Bos., Chi., Van.	17	1,101	324	485	**809**	.800	
57. Garry Unger	Tor., Det., St. L., Atl., L.A., Edm.	16	1,105	413	391	**804**	.728	
*58. Mike Gartner	Wsh., Min.	10	771	404	399	**803**	1.042	
59. Ken Hodge	Chi., Bos., NYR	13	881	328	472	**800**	.908	
60. Wayne Cashman	Bos.	17	1,027	277	516	**793**	.772	
61. Jean Pronovost	Pit., Atl., Wsh.	14	998	391	383	**774**	766	
62. Peter Mahovlich	Det., Mtl., Pit.	16	884	288	485	**773**	.874	

The "Big M", Frank Mahovlich, won the Calder Trophy as the NHL's top rookie in 1958.

Player		Seasons	Games	Goals	Assists	Points	Points per game
*63. Glenn Anderson	Edm.	9	681	355	414	**769**	1.129
*64. Borje Salming	Tor.	16	1,099	148	620	**768**	.699
65. Rick Kehoe	Tor., Pit.	14	906	371	396	**767**	.846
66. Rick MacLeish	Phi., Hfd., Pit., Det.	14	846	349	410	**759**	.897
*67. Ray Bourque	Bos.	10	718	211	545	**756**	1.053
*68. Ken Linseman	Phi., Edm., Bos.	10	741	238	497	**735**	.992
69. Murray Oliver	Det., Bos., Tor., Min.	17	1,127	274	454	**728**	.646
70. Bob Nevin	Tor., NYR, Min., L.A.	18	1,128	307	419	**726**	.644
*71. John Tonelli	NYI, Cgy., L.A.	11	832	277	447	**724**	.870
*72. Mario Lemieux	Pit.	5	368	300	415	**715**	1.943
73. George Armstrong	Tor.	21	1,187	296	417	**713**	.601
74. Vic Hadfield	NYR, Pit.	16	1,002	323	289	**712**	.711
*75. Charlie Simmer	Cal., Cle., L.A., Bos., Pit.	14	712	342	369	**711**	.999
76. Doug Mohns	Bos., Chi., Min., Atl., Wsh.	22	1,390	248	462	**710**	.511
77. Bobby Rousseau	Mtl., Min., NYR	15	942	245	458	**703**	.746
78. Rene Robert	Tor., Pit., Buf., Col.	12	744	284	418	**702**	.944
79. Richard Martin	Buf., L.A.	11	685	384	317	**701**	1.023
*80. Mel Bridgman	Phi., Chi., N.J., Det., Van.	14	977	252	449	**701**	.718
81. Clark Gillies	NYI, Buf.	14	958	319	378	**697**	.728
82. Kent Nilsson	Atl., Cgy., Min., Edm.	8	547	263	422	**685**	1.252
83. Danny Gare	Buf., Det., Edm.	13	827	354	331	**685**	.828
*84. Reed Larson	Det., Bos., Edm., NYI, Min.	13	903	222	463	**685**	.759
*85. Rick Vaive	Van., Tor., Chi., Buf.	10	715	386	298	**684**	.957
*86. Bernie Nicholls	L.A.	8	555	300	383	**683**	1.231
87. Don Lever	Van., Atl., Cgy., Col., N.J., Buf.	15	1,020	313	367	**680**	.667
88. Walt Tkaczuk	NYR	14	945	227	451	**678**	.717
89. Phil Goyette	Mtl., NYR, St. L., Buf.	16	941	207	467	**674**	.716
90. Craig Ramsay	Buf.	14	1,070	252	420	**672**	.628
*91. Dino Ciccarelli	Min., Wsh.	9	613	344	322	**666**	1.086
*92. Doug Wilson	Chi.	12	817	191	475	**666**	.815
93. Reggie Leach	Bos., Cal., Phi., Det.	13	934	381	285	**666**	.713
94. Red Berenson	Mtl., NYR, St. L., Det.	17	987	261	397	**658**	.756
*95. John Ogrodnick	Det., Que., NYR	10	695	305	352	**657**	.945
*96. Joe Mullen	St. L., Cgy.	8	568	305	349	**657**	1.151
97. Dennis Hull	Chi., Det.	14	959	303	351	**654**	.682
*98. Ron Francis	Hfd.	8	567	211	433	**644**	1.136
*99. Stan Smyl	Van.	11	804	259	384	**643**	.800
100. Bob Pulford	Tor., L.A.	16	1,079	281	362	**643**	.596

All-Time Games Played Leaders

(Regular Season)

	Player	Team	Seasons	GP
1.	**Gordie Howe**	Detroit	25	1,687
		Hartford	1	80
		Total	**26**	**1,767**
2.	**Alex Delvecchio**	**Detroit**	**24**	**1,549**
3.	**John Bucyk**	Detroit	2	104
		Boston	21	1,436
		Total	**23**	**1,540**
4.	**Tim Horton**	Toronto	17	1,185
		New York	1½	93
		Pittsburgh	1	44
		Buffalo	2	124
		Total	**21½**	**1,446**
5.	**Harry Howell**	NY Rangers	17	1,160
		California	1½	83
		Los Angeles	2½	168
		Total	**21**	**1,411**
6.	**Norm Ullman**	Detroit	12½	875
		Toronto	7½	535
		Total	**20**	**1,410**
7.	**Stan Mikita**	**Chicago**	**22**	**1,394**
8.	**Doug Mohns**	Boston	11	710
		Chicago	6½	415
		Minnesota	2½	162
		Atlanta	1	28
		Washington	1½	75
		Total	**22**	**1,390**
9.	**Dean Prentice**	NY Rangers	10½	666
		Boston	3	170
		Detroit	3½	230
		Pittsburgh	2	144
		Minnesota	3	168
		Total	**22**	**1,378**
10.	**Ron Stewart**	Toronto	13	838
		Boston	2	126
		St. Louis	½	19
		NY Rangers	4	306
		Vancouver	1	42
		NY Islanders	½	22
		Total	**21**	**1,353**
*11.	**Marcel Dionne**	Detroit	4	309
		Los Angeles	11¾	67
		NY Rangers	2¼	118
		Total	**18**	**1,348**
12.	**Red Kelly**	Detroit	12	846
		Toronto	7½	470
		Total	**20**	**1,316**
13.	**Dave Keon**	Toronto	15	1,062
		Hartford	3	234
		Total	**18**	**1,296**
14.	**Phil Esposito**	Chicago	4	235
		Boston	8½	625
		NY Rangers	5⅓	422
		Total	**18**	**1,282**
15.	**Jean Ratelle**	NY Rangers	15⅓	862
		Boston	5⅔	419
		Total	**21**	**1,281**
16.	**Henri Richard**	**Montreal**	**20**	**1,256**
17.	**Bill Gadsby**	Chicago	8½	468
		NY Rangers	6½	457
		Detroit	5	323
		Total	**20**	**1,248**
18.	**Allan Stanley**	NY Rangers	7	307
		Chicago	2	111
		Boston	2	129
		Toronto	9	633
		Philadelphia	1	64
		Total	**21**	**1,244**
19.	**Eddie Westfall**	Boston	11	734
		NY Islanders	7	493
		Total	**18**	**1,227**
20.	**Eric Nesterenko**	Toronto	5	206
		Chicago	16	1,013
		Total	**21**	**1,219**
21.	**Marcel Pronovost**	Detroit	15	983
		Toronto	5	223
		Total	**20**	**1,206**
*22.	**Larry Robinson**	**Montreal**	**17**	**1,202**
23.	**Gilbert Perreault**	**Buffalo**	**17**	**1,191**
24.	**George Armstrong**	**Toronto**	**21**	**1,187**
25.	**Frank Mahovlich**	Toronto	12	720
		Detroit	2½	198
		Montreal	3½	263
		Total	**18**	**1,181**
26.	**Don Marshall**	Montreal	10	585
		NY Rangers	7	479
		Buffalo	1	62
		Toronto	1	50
		Total	**19**	**1,176**
*27.	**Bob Gainey**	**Montreal**	**16**	**1,160**
28.	**Leo Boivin**	Toronto	2½	137
		Boston	11	717
		Detroit	1½	85
		Pittsburgh	1½	114
		Minnesota	1½	97
		Total	**18**	**1,150**

Guy Lafleur's comeback in 1988-89 enabled him to reach the milestone mark of 1,000 games played.

	Player	Team	Seasons	GP
29.	**Bobby Clarke**	**Philadelphia**	**15**	**1,144**
30.	**Butch Goring**	Los Angeles	10¾	736
		NY Islanders	4¾	359
		Boston	½	39
		Total	**16**	**1,134**
31.	**Bob Nevin**	Toronto	6	250
		NY Rangers	7	505
		Minnesota	2	138
		Los Angeles	3	235
		Total	**18**	**1,128**
32.	**Murray Oliver**	Detroit	1½	101
		Boston	6½	429
		Toronto	3	226
		Minnesota	5	371
		Total	**16**	**1,127**
33.	**Jean Beliveau**	**Montreal**	**18**	**1,125**
34.	**Doug Harvey**	Montreal	14	890
		NY Rangers	3	151
		Detroit	1	2
		St. Louis	1	70
		Total	**19**	**1,113**
35.	**Brad Park**	NY Rangers	7½	465
		Boston	7½	501
		Detroit	2	147
		Total	**17**	**1,113**
*36.	**Lanny McDonald**	Toronto	6½	477
		Colorado	1¾	142
		Calgary	6¾	441
		Total	**16**	**1,111**
37.	**Garry Unger**	Toronto	½	15
		Detroit	3	196
		St. Louis	8	662
		Atlanta	1	79
		Los Angeles	½	58
		Edmonton	2⅓	75
		Total	**16**	**1,105**
38.	**Pit Martin**	Detroit	3⅓	119
		Boston	1⅔	111
		Chicago	10⅓	740
		Vancouver	1⅔	131
		Total	**17**	**1,101**
*39.	**Borje Salming**	**Toronto**	**16**	**1,099**
40.	**Darryl Sittler**	Toronto	11½	844
		Philadelphia	2½	191
		Detroit	1	61
		Total	**15**	**1,096**
41.	**Carol Vadnais**	Montreal	2	42
		Oakland	2	152
		California	2	94
		Boston	3½	263
		NY Rangers	6⅔	485
		New Jersey	1	51
		Total	**17**	**1,087**
42.	**Bob Pulford**	Toronto	14	947
		Los Angeles	2	132
		Total	**16**	**1,079**

	Player	Team	Seasons	GP
43.	**Craig Ramsay**	**Buffalo**	**14**	**1,070**
44.	**Andy Bathgate**	NY Rangers	11	719
		Toronto	1	70
		Detroit	2	130
		Pittsburgh	2	150
		Total	**16**	**1,069**
45.	**Ted Lindsay**	Detroit	14	862
		Chicago	3	206
		Total	**17**	**1,068**
46.	**Terry Harper**	Montreal	10	554
		Los Angeles	3	234
		Detroit	4	252
		St. Louis	1	11
		Colorado	1	15
		Total	**19**	**1,066**
47.	**Rod Gilbert**	**NY Rangers**	**16**	**1,065**
*48	**Bryan Trottier**	**NY Islanders**	**14**	**1,064**
49.	**Bobby Hull**	Chicago	15	1,036
		Winnipeg	⅔	18
		Hartford	⅓	9
		Total	**16**	**1,063**
50.	**Denis Potvin**	**NY Islanders**	**15**	**1,060**
51.	**Jean Guy Talbot**	Montreal	12	791
		Minnesota	⅓	4
		Detroit	⅓	32
		St. Louis	2⅓	172
		Buffalo	1	57
		Total	**17**	**1,056**
52.	**Ivan Boldirev**	Boston	⅓	13
		California	2⅔	191
		Chicago	5⅔	384
		Atlanta	1⅓	65
		Vancouver	2⅔	216
		Detroit	2½	183
		Total	**15**	**1,052**
53.	**Eddie Shack**	NY Rangers	2	141
		Toronto	8½	504
		Boston	2	120
		Los Angeles	1½	84
		Buffalo	1½	111
		Pittsburgh	1½	87
		Total	**17**	**1,047**
54.	**Serge Savard**	Montreal	15	917
		Winnipeg	2	123
		Total	**17**	**1,040**
55.	**Ron Ellis**	**Toronto**	**16**	**1,034**
55.	**Ralph Backstrom**	Montreal	13	844
		Los Angeles	2⅔	172
		Chicago	⅓	16
		Total	**16**	**1,032**
57.	**Dick Duff**	Toronto	9½	582
		NY Rangers	1	43
		Montreal	5	305
		Los Angeles	½	39
		Buffalo	2	61
		Total	**18**	**1,030**
*58	**Guy Lafleur**	Montreal	14	961
		NY Rangers	1	67
		Total	**15**	**1,028**
59.	**Wayne Cashman**	**Boston**	**17**	**1,027**
60.	**Jim Neilson**	NY Rangers	12	810
		California	2	213
		Cleveland	2	115
		Total	**16**	**1,023**
61.	**Don Lever**	Vancouver	7⅔	593
		Atlanta	⅓	28
		Calgary	1⅓	85
		Colorado	⅔	59
		New Jersey	3	216
		Buffalo	1	39
		Total	**15**	**1,020**
62.	**Phil Russell**	Chicago	6¾	504
		Atlanta	1¼	93
		Calgary	3	229
		New Jersey	2¾	172
		Buffalo	1¼	18
		Total	**15**	**1,016**
63.	**Dave Lewis**	NY Islanders	6¾	514
		Los Angeles	3¼	221
		New Jersey	3	209
		Detroit	2	64
		Total	**15**	**1,008**
64.	**Jim Roberts**	Montreal	9⅔	611
		St. Louis	5⅓	395
		Total	**15**	**1,006**
65.	**Claude Provost**	**Montreal**	**15**	**1,005**
66.	**Rick Middleton**	NY Rangers	2	124
		Boston	12	881
		Total	**14**	**1,005**
67.	**Vic Hadfield**	NY Rangers	13	839
		Pittsburgh	3	163
		Total	**16**	**1,002**

* Active player

Goaltending Records

All-Time Shutout Leaders

Goaltender	Team	Seasons	Games	Shutouts
Terry Sawchuk (1949-1970)	Detroit	14	734	85
	Boston	2	102	11
	Toronto	3	91	4
	Los Angeles	1	36	2
	NY Rangers	1	8	1
	Total	21	971	**103**
George Hainsworth (1926-1937)	Montreal	7½	317	75
	Toronto	3½	145	19
	Total	11	464	**94**
Glenn Hall (1952-1971)	Detroit	4	148	17
	Chicago	10	618	51
	St. Louis	4	140	16
	Total	18	906	**84**
Jacques Plante (1952-1973)	Montreal	11	556	58
	NY Rangers	2	98	5
	St. Louis	2	69	10
	Toronto	2½	106	7
	Boston	½	8	2
	Total	18	837	**82**
Tiny Thompson (1928-1940)	Boston	10⅓	467	74
	Detroit	1⅔	85	7
	Total	12	552	**81**
Alex Connell (1925-1937)	Ottawa	8	292	63
	Detroit	1	48	6
	NY Americans	1	1	0
	Mtl. Maroons	2	75	11
	Total	12	416	**80**
Tony Esposito (1968-1984)	Montreal	1	13	2
	Chicago	15	873	74
	Total	16	886	**76**
Lorne Chabot (1926-1937)	NY Rangers	2	80	21
	Toronto	5	215	33
	Montreal	1	47	8
	Chicago	1	48	8
	Mtl. Maroons	1	16	2
	NY Americans	1	6	1
	Total	11	412	**73**
Harry Lumley (1943-1960)	Detroit	7	324	26
	Chicago	2	134	5
	Toronto	4	267	34
	Boston	3	78	6
	Total	16	803	**71**
Roy Worters (1925-1937)	Pittsburgh Pirates	3	123	22
	NY Americans	9	364	44
	*Montreal		1	0
	Total	12	488	**66**
Turk Broda (1936-1952)	Toronto	12	628	**62**

Goaltender	Team	Seasons	Games	Shutouts
Clint Benedict (1917-1926)	Ottawa	7	158	19
	Mtl. Maroons	6	202	39
	Total	13	360	**58**
John Roach (1921-1935)	Toronto	7	223	13
	NY Rangers	4	89	30
	Detroit	3	180	15
	Total	14	492	**58**
Bernie Parent (1965-1979)	Boston	2	57	1
	Philadelphia	9½	486	50
	Toronto	1½	65	4
	Total	13	608	**55**
Ed Giacomin (1965-1978)	NY Rangers	10	539	49
	Detroit	3	71	5
	Total	13	610	**54**
David Kerr (1930-1941)	Mtl. Maroons	3	102	11
	NY Americans	1	1	0
	NY Rangers	7	324	40
	Total	11	427	**51**
Rogie Vachon (1966-1982)	Montreal	5½	206	13
	Los Angeles	6⅔	389	32
	Detroit	2	109	4
	Boston	2	91	2
	Total	16	795	**51**
Ken Dryden (1970-1979)	Montreal	8	397	**46**
Gump Worsley (1952-1974)	NY Rangers	10	582	24
	Montreal	6½	171	16
	Minnesota	4½	107	3
	Total	21	860	**43**
Chuck Gardiner (1927-1934)	Chicago	7	316	**42**
Frank Brimsek (1938-1950)	Boston	9	445	35
	Chicago	1	70	5
	Total	10	515	**40**
Johnny Bower (1953-1970)	NY Rangers	3	77	5
	Toronto	12	475	32
	Total	15	552	**37**
Bill Durnan (1943-1950)	Montreal	7	383	**34**
Eddie Johnston (1962-1978)	Boston	11	444	27
	Toronto	1	26	1
	St. Louis	3⅔	118	4
	Chicago	⅓	4	0
	Total	16	502	**32**
Roger Crozier (1963-1977)	Detroit	7	313	20
	Buffalo	6	202	10
	Washington	1	3	0
	Total	14	518	**30**
Cesare Maniago (1960-1978)	Toronto	⅓	7	0
	Montreal	⅓	14	0
	NY Rangers	2	34	2
	Minnesota	9	420	26
	Vancouver	2	93	2
	Total	14	568	**30**

*Played 1 game for Canadiens in 1929-30.

Ten or More Shutouts, One Season

Number of Shutouts	Goaltender	Team	Season	Length of Schedule
22	George Hainsworth	Montreal	1928-29	44
15	Alex Connell	Ottawa	1925-26	36
	Alex Connell	Ottawa	1927-28	44
	Hal Winkler	Boston	1927-28	44
	Tony Esposito	Chicago	1969-70	76
14	George Hainsworth	Montreal	1926-27	44
13	Clint Benedict	Mtl. Maroons	1926-27	44
	George Hainsworth	Montreal	1927-28	44
	Roy Worters	NY Americans	1927-28	44
	John Roach	NY Rangers	1928-29	44
	Roy Worters	NY Americans	1928-29	44
12	Alex Connell	Ottawa	1926-27	44
	Tiny Thompson	Boston	1928-29	44
	Lorne Chabot	Toronto	1928-29	44
	Chuck Gardiner	Chicago	1930-31	44
	Terry Sawchuk	Detroit	1951-52	70
	Terry Sawchuk	Detroit	1953-54	70
	Terry Sawchuk	Detroit	1954-55	70
	Glenn Hall	Detroit	1955-56	70
	Bernie Parent	Philadelphia	1973-74	78
	Bernie Parent	Philadelphia	1974-75	80
11	Lorne Chabot	NY Rangers	1927-28	44
	Harry Holmes	Detroit	1927-28	44
	Clint Benedict	Mtl. Maroons	1928-29	44
	Joe Miller	Pittsburgh Pirates	1928-29	44
	Tiny Thompson	Boston	1932-33	48
	Terry Sawchuk	Detroit	1950-51	70
10	Lorne Chabot	NY Rangers	1926-27	44
	Roy Worters	Pittsburgh Pirates	1927-28	44
	Clarence Dolson	Detroit	1928-29	44
	John Roach	Detroit	1932-33	48
	Chuck Gardiner	Chicago	1933-34	48
	Tiny Thompson	Boston	1935-36	48
	Frank Brimsek	Boston	1938-39	48
	Bill Durnan	Montreal	1948-49	60
	Gerry McNeil	Montreal	1952-53	70
	Harry Lumley	Toronto	1952-53	70
	Tony Esposito	Chicago	1973-74	78
	Ken Dryden	Montreal	1976-77	80

All-Time Win Leaders

(Minimum 200 Wins)

Wins	Goaltender	GP	MINS	Losses	Ties	%
435	Terry Sawchuk	971	57,114	337	188	.545
434	Jacques Plante	837	49,533	246	137	.600
423	Tony Esposito	886	52,585	307	151	.563
407	Glenn Hall	906	53,464	327	165	.540
355	Rogie Vachon	795	46,298	291	115	.519
335	Gump Worsley	862	50,232	353	150	.476
332	Harry Lumley	804	48,097	324	143	.502
305	*Bill Smith	680	38,426	233	105	.526
302	Turk Broda	629	38,167	224	101	.560
289	Ed Giacomin	610	35,693	206	97	.553
286	Dan Bouchard	655	37,919	232	113	.523
284	Tiny Thompson	553	34,174	194	75	.581
270	Bernie Parent	608	35,136	197	121	.544
262	Gilles Meloche	761	44,007	342	126	.427
258	Ken Dryden	397	23,352	57	74	.743
252	Frank Brimsek	514	31,210	182	80	.568
251	Johnny Bower	549	32,016	196	90	.539
251	*Mike Liut	570	33,037	232	68	.500
247	George Hainsworth	465	29,415	146	74	.611
236	*Pete Peeters	439	25,289	135	45	.589
236	Eddie Johnston	591	34,182	256	87	.473
231	Glenn Resch	571	32,279	224	82	.476
230	Gerry Cheevers	418	24,394	94	74	.671
218	John Roach	491	30,423	204	69	.514
211	*Grant Fuhr	389	22,051	106	48	.604
208	Bill Durnan	383	22,945	112	62	.624
208	Don Edwards	459	26,181	155	77	.537
206	Lorne Chabot	411	25,309	140	65	.580
206	Roger Crozier	518	28,566	197	74	.469

Active Shutout Leaders

Goaltender	Teams	Seasons	Games	Shutouts
Bill Smith	Los Angeles, NY Islanders	18	680	22
Mike Liut	St. Louis, Hartford	10	570	20
Pete Peeters	Phi., Bos., Wsh.	11	439	19
Greg Millen	Pit., Hfd., St. L.	11	542	16
Tom Barrasso	Buffalo, Pittsburgh	7	310	13
Bob Froese	Philadelphia, NY Rangers	7	227	13
Glen Hanlon	Van., St. L., NYR, Det.	12	413	12
Clint Malarchuk	Que., Wsh., Buf.	7	243	11
Rick Wamsley	Mtl., St. L., Cgy.	9	322	10
Rejean Lemelin	Atl., Cgy., Bos.	11	413	9
Patrick Roy	Montreal	4	187	9
Robert Sauve	Buf., Chi., N.J.	13	420	8
Al Jensen	Det., Wsh., L.A.	7	179	8

Active Goaltending Leaders

(Ranked by winning percentage; minimum 250 games played)

Goaltender	Teams	Seasons	GP	W	L	T	Winning %
Andy Moog	Edmonton, Boston	9	282	165	69	29	.637
Grant Fuhr	Edmonton	8	389	211	106	48	.604
Pete Peeters	Phi., Bos., Wsh.	11	439	236	135	45	.589
Rick Wamsley	Mtl., St. L., Cgy.	9	322	165	109	35	.567
Bill Smith	Los Angeles, NY Islanders	18	680	305	233	105	.526
Rejean Lemelin	Atl., Cgy., Bos.	11	413	187	122	58	.523
Tom Barrasso	Buffalo, Pittsburgh	7	310	142	117	35	.515
Pat Riggin	Atl., Cgy., Wsh., Bos., Pit.	10	350	153	120	52	.511
Kelly Hrudey	NY Islanders, Los Angeles	6	257	116	94	28	.506
Robert Sauve	Buf., Chi., N.J.	13	420	182	154	58	.502
Mike Liut	St. Louis, Hartford	10	570	251	232	68	.500
Rollie Melanson	NY Islanders, Los Angeles	9	281	124	103	33	.500
Brian Hayward	Winnipeg, Monteal	7	277	124	111	27	.496
John Vanbiesbrouck	NY Rangers	7	269	119	109	24	.487
Don Beaupre	Minnesota, Washington	9	327	131	129	45	.469
Greg Stefan	Detroit	8	292	114	122	30	.442
Greg Millen	Pit., Hfd., St. L.	11	542	193	256	81	.431
Glen Hanlon	Van., St. L., NYR, Det.	12	413	148	178	53	.423
Richard Brodeur	NYI, Van., Hfd.	10	385	131	176	62	.421

Andy Moog has won 165 of 282 games played in the NHL for a league-leading percentage of .637.

Goals Against Average Leaders

Season	Goaltender and Club	GP	MINS.	GA	SO	AVG.	Team GP	Totals GA
1988-89	Patrick Roy, Montreal	48	2744	113	4	2.47	80	218
	Brian Hayward, Montreal	36	2091	101	1	2.90		
1987-88	Brian Hayward, Montreal	39	2247	107	2	2.86	80	238
	Patrick Roy, Montreal	45	2586	125	3	2.90		
1986-87	Brian Hayward, Montreal	37	2178	102	1	2.81	80	241
	Patrick Roy, Montreal	46	2686	131	1	2.93		
1985-86	Bob Froese, Philadelphia	51	2728	116	5	2.55	80	241
	Darren Jensen, Philadelphia	29	1436	88	2	3.68		
1984-85	Tom Barrasso, Buffalo	54	3248	144	5	2.66	80	237
	Bob Sauve, Buffalo	27	1564	84	0	3.22		
1983-84	Pat Riggin, Washington	41	2299	102	4	2.66	80	226
	Al Jensen, Washington	43	2414	117	4	2.91		
1982-83	Roland Melanson, NY Islanders	44	2460	109	1	2.66	80	231
	Billy Smith, NY Islanders	41	2340	112	1	2.87		
1981-82	Denis Herron, Montreal	27	1547	68	3	2.64	80	223
	Rick Wamsley, Montreal	38	2206	101	2	2.75		
1980-81	Richard Sevigny, Montreal	33	1777	71	2	2.40	80	232
	Michel Larocque, Montreal	28	1623	82	1	3.03		
	Denis Herron, Montreal	25	1147	67	1	3.50		
1979-80	Bob Sauvé, Buffalo	32	1880	74	4	2.36	80	201
	Don Edwards, Buffalo	49	2920	125	2	2.57		
1978-79	Ken Dryden, Montreal	47	2814	108	5	2.30	80	204
	Michel Larocque, Montreal	34	1986	94	3	2.84		
1977-78	Ken Dryden, Montreal	52	3071	105	5	2.05	80	183
	Michel Larocque, Montreal	30	1729	77	1	2.67		
1976-77	Michel Larocque, Montreal	26	1525	53	4	2.09	80	171
	Ken Dryden, Montreal	56	3275	117	10	2.14		
1975-76	Ken Dryden, Montreal	62	3580	121	8	2.03	80	174
1974-75	Bernie Parent, Philadelphia	68	4041	137	12	2.03	80	181
1973-74	Bernie Parent, Philadelphia	73	4314	136	12	1.89	78	164
	Tony Esposito, Chicago	70	4143	141	10	2.04	78	164
1972-73	Ken Dryden, Montreal	54	3165	119	6	2.26	78	184
1971-72	Tony Esposito, Chicago	48	2780	82	9	1.76	78	166
	Gary Smith, Chicago	28	1540	62	5	2.41		
1970-71	Ed Giacomin, NY Rangers	45	2641	95	8	2.15	78	177
	Gilles Villemure, NY Rangers	34	2039	78	4	2.29		
1969-70	Tony Esposito, Chicago	63	3763	136	15	2.17	76	170
1968-69	Jacques Plante, St. Louis	37	2139	70	5	1.96	76	157
	Glenn Hall, St. Louis	41	2354	85	8	2.17		
1967-68	Lorne Worsley, Montreal	40	2213	73	6	1.98	74	167
	Rogatien Vachon, Montreal	39	2227	92	4	2.48		
1966-67	Glenn Hall, Chicago	32	1664	66	2	2.38	70	170
	Denis DeJordy, Chicago	44	2536	104	4	2.46		
1965-66	Lorne Worsley, Montreal	51	2899	114	2	2.36	70	173
	Charlie Hodge, Montreal	26	1301	56	1	2.58		
1964-65	Johnny Bower, Toronto	34	2040	81	3	2.38	70	173
	Terry Sawchuk, Toronto	36	2160	92	1	2.56		
1963-64	Charlie Hodge, Montreal	62	3720	140	8	2.26	70	167
1962-63	Glenn Hall, Chicago	66	3910	166	5	2.51	70	178
1961-62	Jacques Plante, Montreal	70	4200	166	4	2.37	70	166
1960-61	Johnny Bower, Toronto	58	3480	145	2	2.50	70	176
1959-60	Jacques Plante, Montreal	69	4140	175	3	2.54	70	178
1958-59	Jacques Plante, Montreal	67	4000	144	9	2.18	70	158
1957-58	Jacques Plante, Montreal	57	3446	119	9	2.11	70	158
1956-57	Jacques Plante, Montreal	61	3660	123	9	2.02	70	155
1955-56	Jacques Plante, Montreal	64	3840	119	7	1.86	70	131
1954-55	Terry Sawchuk, Detroit	68	4080	132	12	1.94	70	134
1953-54	Harry Lumley, Toronto	69	4140	128	13	1.85	70	131
1952-53	Terry Sawchuk, Detroit	63	3780	120	9	1.90	70	133
1951-52	Terry Sawchuk, Detroit	70	4200	133	12	1.90	70	133
1950-51	Al Rollins, Toronto	40	2367	70	5	1.75	70	138
1949-50	Bill Durnan, Montreal	64	3840	141	8	2.20	70	150
1948-49	Bill Durnan, Montreal	60	3600	126	10	2.10	60	126
1947-48	Turk Broda, Toronto	60	3600	143	5	2.38	60	143
1946-47	Bill Durnan, Montreal	60	3600	138	4	2.30	60	138
1945-46	Bill Durnan, Montreal	40	2400	104	4	2.60	50	134
1944-45	Bill Durnan, Montreal	50	3000	121	1	2.42	50	121
1943-44	Bill Durnan, Montreal	50	3000	109	2	2.18	50	109
1942-43	Johnny Mowers, Detroit	50	3000	124	6	2.48	50	124
1941-42	Frank Brimsek, Boston	47	2820	115	3	2.44	48	118
1940-41	Turk Broda, Toronto	48	2880	99	5	2.06	48	99
1939-40	Dave Kerr, NY Rangers	48	2880	77	8	1.60	48	77
1938-39	Frank Brimsek, Boston	44	2640	70	10	1.59	48	76
1937-38	Tiny Thompson, Boston	48	2880	89	7	1.85	48	89
1936-37	Normie Smith, Detroit	48	2880	102	6	2.13	48	102
1935-36	Tiny Thompson, Boston	48	2880	83	10	1.73	48	83
1934-35	Lorne Chabot, Chicago	48	2880	88	8	1.83	48	88
1933-34	Chuck Gardiner, Chicago	48	2880	83	10	1.73	48	83
1932-33	Tiny Thompson, Boston	48	2880	88	11	1.83	48	88
1931-32	Chuck Gardiner, Chicago	48	2880	101	4	2.10	48	101
1930-31	Roy Worters, NY Americans	44	2640	74	8	1.68	44	74
1929-30	Tiny Thompson, Boston	44	2640	98	3	2.23	44	98
1928-29	George Hainsworth, Montreal	44	2640	43	22	0.98	44	43
1927-28	George Hainsworth, Montreal	44	2640	48	13	1.09	44	48
1926-27	George Hainsworth, Montreal	44	2640	67	14	1.52	44	67

* Goaltender(s) with lowest goals-against average awarded Vezina Trophy up to and including 1980-81 season. Beginning with 1982-83 season, William Jennings Trophy awarded.

Goaltender Ed Giacomin had his number (1) retired by the Rangers in 1989.

All-Time Penalty-Minute Leaders

(Regular season. Minimum 1,500 minutes)

Player	Team	Seasons	Games	Penalty Minutes	Mins. per game
Dave Williams,	Tor., Van., Det., L.A., Hfd.	13	962	3,966	4.12
Willi Plett,	Atl., Cgy., Minn., Bos.	12	834	2,572	3.08
*Chris Nilan,	Mtl., NYR	10	566	2,447	4.32
Dave Schultz,	Phi., L.A., Pit., Buf.	9	535	2,294	4.29
Bryan Watson,	Mtl., Det., Cal., Pit., St. L., Wsh.	16	878	2,212	2.52
Terry O'Reilly,	Boston	14	891	2,095	2.35
Phil Russell,	Chi., Atl., Cgy., N.J., Buf.	15	1,016	2,038	2.01
*Dale Hunter,	Que., Wsh.	8	682	2,004	2.94
Andre Dupont,	NYR, St. L., Phi., Que.	13	810	1,986	2.45
*Al Secord,	Chi., Tor., Phi.	10	723	1,962	2.71
*Harold Snepsts,	Van., Min., Det.	15	933	1,923	2.06
*Laurie Boschman,	Tor., Edm., Wpg.	10	720	1,861	2.58
Garry Howatt,	NYI, Hfd., N.J.	12	720	1,836	2.55
Carol Vadnais,	Mtl., Oak., Cal., Bos., NYR, N.J.	17	1,087	1,813	1.67
*Tim Hunter,	Calgary	7	414	1,816	4.39
Ted Lindsay,	Det., Chi.	17	1,068	1,808	1.69
*Larry Playfair,	Buf., L.A.	10	684	1,810	2.65
Brian Sutter,	St. L.	12	779	1,786	2.29
Wilf Paiement,	K.C., Col., Tor., Que., NYR, Buf.	13	923	1,718	1.86
Gordie Howe,	Det., Hfd.	26	1,767	1,685	.95
Paul Holmgren,	Phi., Min.	9	527	1,684	3.23
*Mike Foligno,	Buffalo	10	758	1,656	2.18
*Torrie Robertson,	Wsh., Hfd., Det.	8	400	1,639	4.10
*Jay Wells,	L.A., Phi.	10	671	1,630	2.43
Jerry Korab,	Chi., Van., Buf., L.A.	15	975	1,629	1.67
*Mel Bridgman,	Phi., Cgy., N.J., Det., Van.	14	977	1,625	1.66
*Jim Korn,	Det., Tor., Buf., N.J.	9	551	1,625	2.95
*Rob Ramage,	Col., St. L., Cgy.	10	755	1,620	2.15
Tim Horton,	Tor., NYR, Pit., Buf.	24	1,446	1,611	1.11
Paul Baxter,	Que., Pit., Cgy.	8	472	1,564	3.31
*Glen Cochrane,	Phi., Van., Chi., Edm.	9	411	1,556	3.79
Mike Milbury,	Boston	12	754	1,552	2.06
Dave Hutchison,	L.A., Tor., Chi., N.J.	10	584	1,550	2.65
Doug Risebrough,	Mtl., Cal.	13	740	1,542	2.08
Bill Gadsby,	Chi., NYR, Det.	20	1,248	1,539	1.23
*Ken Linseman,	Phi., Edm., Bos.	11	741	1,535	2.07

* Active player

Bryan Murray, left, has spent his entire NHL coaching career at the helm of the Washington Capitals. In his 33-year career in hockey, Bob Pulford, right, has been active as a player, coach and general manager.

Coaching Records

(Minimum 600 regular-season games. Ranked by number of games coached.)

Coach	Team	Seasons	Games	Wins	Losses	Ties	%*
Dick Irvin	Chicago	1930-31; 55-56	114	43	56	15	.443
	Toronto	1931-40	427	216	152	59	.575
	Montreal	1940-55	896	431	313	152	.566
	Total		**1,437**	**690**	**521**	**226**	**.559**
Scott Bowman	St. Louis	1967-71	238	110	83	45	.557
	Montreal	1971-79	634	419	110	105	.744
	Buffalo	1979-07	404	210	134	60	.594
	Total		**1,276**	**739**	**327**	**210**	**.661**
Al Arbour	St. Louis	1970-73	107	42	40	25	.509
	NY Islanders	1973-86; 88-89	1,092	573	346	172	.603
	Total		**1,198**	**615**	**386**	**197**	**.596**
Billy Reay	Toronto	1957-59	90	26	50	14	.367
	Chicago	1963-77	1,012	516	335	161	.589
	Total		**1,102**	**542**	**385**	**175**	**.571**
Jack Adams	Detroit	1927-44	**964**	**413**	**390**	**161**	**.512**
Sid Abel	Chicago	1952-54	140	39	79	22	.357
	Detroit	1957-68; 69-70	810	340	338	132	.501
	St. Louis	1971-72	10	3	6	1	.350
	Kansas City	1975-76	3	0	3	0	.000
	Total		**963**	**382**	**426**	**155**	**.477**
Punch Imlach	Toronto	1958-69; 79-81	840	391	311	138	.548
	Buffalo	1970-72	119	32	62	25	.374
	Total		**959**	**423**	**373**	**163**	**.526**
Toe Blake	Montreal	1955-68	**914**	**500**	**255**	**159**	**.634**
Glen Sather	Edmonton	1979-89	**800**	**446**	**250**	**104**	**.623**
Emile Francis	NY Rangers	1965-75	654	347	209	98	.606
	St. Louis	1976-77, 81-83	124	46	64	14	.427
	Total		**778**	**393**	**273**	**112**	**.577**
Bob Pulford	Los Angeles	1972-77	396	178	150	68	.535
	Chicago	1977-79; 1981-82; 84-87	375	158	155	62	.504
	Total		**771**	**336**	**305**	**130**	**.520**

Coach	Team	Seasons	Games	Wins	Losses	Ties	%*
Milt Schmidt	Boston	1954-61; 62-66	726	245	360	121	.421
	Washington	1974-76	43	5	33	5	.174
	Total		**769**	**250**	**393**	**126**	**.407**
Red Kelly	Los Angeles	1967-69	150	55	75	20	.433
	Pittsburgh	1969-73	274	90	132	52	.423
	Toronto	1973-77	318	133	123	62	.516
	Total		**742**	**278**	**330**	**134**	**465**
Fred Shero	Philadelphia	1971-78	554	308	151	95	.642
	NY Rangers	1978-81	180	82	74	24	.522
	Total		**734**	**390**	**225**	**119**	**.612**
Art Ross	Boston	1924-45	**728**	**361**	**277**	**90**	**.558**
Michel Bergeron	Quebec	1980-87	554	253	222	79	.528
	NY Rangers	1987-89	156	73	77	18	.526
	Total		**712**	**326**	**289**	**97**	**.526**
Bob Berry	Los Angeles	1978-81	240	107	94	39	.527
	Montreal	1981-84	223	116	71	36	.601
	Pittsburgh	1984-87	240	88	127	25	.419
	Total		**703**	**311**	**292**	**100**	**.514**
Bryan Murray	Washington	1981-89	**626**	**325**	**222**	**79**	**.582**
Jack Evans	California	1975-76	80	27	42	11	.406
	Cleveland	1976-78	160	47	87	26	.375
	Hartford	1983-88	374	163	174	37	.485
	Total		**614**	**237**	**303**	**74**	**.446**
Tommy Ivan	Detroit	1947-54	470	262	118	90	.653
	Chicago	1956-58	140	40	78	22	.364
	Total		**610**	**302**	**196**	**112**	**.587**
Lester Patrick	NY Rangers	1926-39	**604**	**281**	**216**	**107**	**.554**

* % arrived at by dividing possible points into actual points.

One Season Scoring Records

Goals-Per-Game Leaders, One Season
(Among players with 20 goals or more in one season)

Player	Team	Season	Games	Goals	Average
Joe Malone	Montreal	1917-18	20	44	2.20
Newsy Lalonde	Montreal	1917-18	14	23	1.64
Cy Denneny	Ottawa	1917-18	22	36	1.64
Joe Malone	Quebec	1919-20	24	39	1.63
Newsy Lalonde	Montreal	1919-20	23	37	1.61
Cecil Dye	Toronto, Hamilton	1920-21	24	35	1.46
Cy Denneny	Ottawa	1920-21	24	34	1.42
Odie Cleghorn	Montreal	1918-19	17	24	1.41
Reg Noble	Toronto	1917-18	20	28	1.40
Joe Malone	Hamilton	1920-21	20	28	1.40
Newsy Lalonde	Montreal	1920-21	24	32	1.33
Cecil Dye	Toronto	1924-25	29	38	1.31
Cy Denneny	Ottawa	1921-22	22	28	1.27
Harry Broadbent	Ottawa	1921-22	24	30	1.25
Cecil Dye	Toronto	1921-22	24	30	1.25
Newsy Lalonde	Montreal	1918-19	17	21	1.25
Aurel Joliat	Montreal	1924-25	24	29	1.21
Wayne Gretzky	Edmonton	1983-84	74	87	1.18
Cecil Dye	Toronto	1922-23	22	26	1.18
Wayne Gretzky	Edmonton	1981-82	80	92	1.15
Mario Lemieux	Pittsburgh	1988-89	76	85	1.12
Jack Darragh	Ottawa	1919-20	22	24	1.09
Frank Nighbor	Ottawa	1919-20	23	25	1.09
Corb Denneny	Toronto	1919-20	23	25	1.09
Amos Arbour	Montreal	1919-20	20	21	1.05
Cy Denneny	Ottawa	1923-24	21	22	1.05
Billy Boucher	Montreal	1922-23	24	25	1.04
Maurice Richard	Montreal	1944-45	50	50	1.00
Howie Morenz	Montreal	1924-25	30	30	1.00
Cy Denneny	Ottawa	1924-25	28	28	1.00
Reg Noble	Toronto	1919-20	24	24	1.00
Cooney Weiland	Boston	1929-30	44	43	.98
Phil Esposito	Boston	1970-71	78	76	.97
Jari Kurri	Edmonton	1984-85	73	71	.97

Assists-Per-Game Leaders, One Season
(Among players with 35 assists or more in one season)

Player	Team	Season	Games	Assists	Average
Wayne Gretzky	Edmonton	1985-86	80	163	2.04
Wayne Gretzky	Edmonton	1987-88	64	109	1.70
Wayne Gretzky	Edmonton	1984-85	80	135	1.68
Wayne Gretzky	Edmonton	1983-84	74	118	1.59
Wayne Gretzky	Edmonton	1982-83	80	125	1.56
Wayne Gretzky	Edmonton	1986-87	79	121	1.53
Wayne Gretzky	Edmonton	1981-82	80	120	1.50
Mario Lemieux	Pittsburgh	1988-89	76	114	1.50
Wayne Gretzky	Los Angeles	1988-89	78	114	1.46
Wayne Gretzky	Edmonton	1980-81	80	109	1.36
Bobby Orr	Boston	1970-71	78	102	1.31
Mario Lemieux	Pittsburgh	1987-88	77	98	1.27
Bobby Orr	Boston	1973-74	74	90	1.22
Mario Lemieux	Pittsburgh	1985-86	79	93	1.18
Bobby Clarke	Philadelphia	1975-76	76	89	1.17
Peter Stastny	Quebec	1981-82	80	93	1.16
Bobby Orr	Boston	1969-70	76	87	1.15
Paul Coffey	Edmonton	1985-86	79	90	1.14
Bryan Trottier	NY Islanders	1978-79	76	87	1.14
Bobby Orr	Boston	1972-73	63	72	1.14
Bill Cowley	Boston	1943-44	36	41	1.14
Steve Yzerman	Detroit	1988-89	80	90	1.13
Paul Coffey	Pittsburgh	1988-89	75	83	1.11
Bobby Clarke	Philadelphia	1974-75	80	89	1.11
Bobby Orr	Boston	1974-75	80	89	1.11
Denis Savard	Chicago	1982-83	78	86	1.10
Wayne Gretzky	Edmonton	1979-80	79	86	1.09
Denis Savard	Chicago	1981-82	80	87	1.09
Denis Savard	Chicago	1987-88	80	87	1.09
Paul Coffey	Edmonton	1983-84	80	86	1.08
Elmer Lach	Montreal	1944-45	50	54	1.08
Peter Stastny	Quebec	1985-86	76	81	1.07
Bobby Orr	Boston	1971-72	76	80	1.05
Marcel Dionne	Los Angeles	1979-80	80	84	1.05
Phil Esposito	Boston	1968-69	74	77	1.04
Mike Bossy	NY Islanders	1981-82	80	83	1.04
Bryan Trottier	NY Islanders	1983-84	68	71	1.04
Kent Nilsson	Calgary	1980-81	80	82	1.03
Peter Stastny	Quebec	1982-83	75	77	1.03
Pete Mahovlich	Montreal	1974-75	80	82	1.02
Bernie Nicholls	Los Angeles	1988-89	79	80	1.01
Guy Lafleur	Montreal	1979-80	74	75	1.01
Guy Lafleur	Montreal	1976-77	80	80	1.00
Bryan Trottier	NY Islanders	1977-78	77	77	1.00
Mike Bossy	NY Islanders	1983-84	67	67	1.00
Jean Ratelle	NY Rangers	1971-72	63	63	1.00
Guy Chouinard	Calgary	1980-81	52	52	1.00
Elmer Lach	Montreal	1943-44	48	48	1.00

Cooney Weiland scored 43 goals in 44 games in 1929-30.

Peter Stastny set a NHL record for assists by a rookie with 70 in 1980-81.

Points-Per-Game Leaders, One Season
(Among players with 50 points or more in one season)

Player	Team	Season	Games	Points	Average	Player	Team	Season	Games	Points	Average
Wayne Gretzky	Edmonton	1983-84	74	205	2.77	Guy Lafleur	Montreal	1977-78	78	132	1.69
Wayne Gretzky	Edmonton	1985-86	80	215	2.69	Guy Lafleur	Montreal	1979-80	74	125	1.69
Wayne Gretzky	Edmonton	1981-82	80	212	2.65	Rob Brown	Pittsburgh	1988-89	68	115	1.69
Mario Lemieux	Pittsburgh	1988-89	76	199	2.62	Jari Kurri	Edmonton	1985-86	78	131	1.68
Wayne Gretzky	Edmonton	1984-85	80	208	2.60	Phil Esposito	Boston	1972-73	78	130	1.67
Wayne Gretzky	Edmonton	1982-83	80	196	2.45	Cooney Weiland	Boston	1929-30	44	73	1.66
Wayne Gretzky	Edmonton	1987-88	64	149	2.33	Peter Stastny	Quebec	1982-83	75	124	1.65
Wayne Gretzky	Edmonton	1986-87	79	183	2.32	Bobby Orr	Boston	1973-74	74	122	1.65
Mario Lemieux	Pittsburgh	1987-88	77	168	2.18	Kent Nilsson	Calgary	1980-81	80	131	1.64
Wayne Gretzky	Los Angeles	1988-89	78	168	2.15	Marcel Dionne	Los Angeles	1978-79	80	130	1.63
Wayne Gretzky	Edmonton	1980-81	80	164	2.05	Bryan Trottier	NY Islanders	1983-84	68	111	1.63
Bill Cowley	Boston	1943-44	36	71	1.97	Dale Hawerchuk	Winnipeg	1984-85	80	130	1.63
Phil Esposito	Boston	1970-71	78	152	1.95	Charlie Simmer	Los Angeles	1980-81	65	105	1.62
Steve Yzerman	Detroit	1988-89	80	155	1.94	Guy Lafleur	Montreal	1978-79	80	129	1.61
Bernie Nicholls	Los Angeles	1988-89	79	150	1.90	Bryan Trottier	NY Islanders	1981-82	80	129	1.61
Phil Esposito	Boston	1973-74	78	145	1.86	Phil Esposito	Boston	1974-75	79	127	1.61
Jari Kurri	Edmonton	1984-85	73	135	1.85	Peter Stastny	Quebec	1985-86	76	122	1.61
Mike Bossy	NY Islanders	1981-82	80	147	1.84	Michel Goulet	Quebec	1983-84	75	121	1.61
Bobby Orr	Boston	1970-71	78	139	1.78	Bryan Trottier	NY Islanders	1977-78	77	123	1.60
Mario Lemieux	Pittsburgh	1985-86	79	141	1.78	Bobby Orr	Boston	1972-73	63	101	1.60
Jari Kurri	Edmonton	1983-84	64	113	1.77	Elmer Lach	Montreal	1944-45	50	80	1.60
Bryan Trottier	NY Islanders	1978-79	76	134	1.76	Guy Chouinard	Calgary	1980-81	52	83	1.60
Mike Bossy	NY Islanders	1983-84	67	118	1.76	Steve Yzerman	Detroit	1987-88	64	102	1.59
Paul Coffey	Edmonton	1985-86	79	138	1.75	Mike Bossy	NY Islanders	1978-79	80	126	1.58
Phil Esposito	Boston	1971-72	76	133	1.75	Paul Coffey	Edmonton	1983-84	80	126	1.58
Peter Stastny	Quebec	1981-82	80	139	1.74	Bobby Orr	Boston	1969-70	76	120	1.58
Wayne Gretzky	Edmonton	1979-80	79	137	1.73	Charlie Simmer	Los Angeles	1979-80	64	101	1.58
Jean Ratelle	NY Rangers	1971-72	63	109	1.73	Marcel Dionne	Los Angeles	1984-85	80	126	1.58
Marcel Dionne	Los Angeles	1979-80	80	137	1.71	Bobby Clarke	Philadelphia	1975-76	76	119	1.57
Herb Cain	Boston	1943-44	48	82	1.71	Guy Lafleur	Montreal	1975-76	80	125	1.56
Dennis Maruk	Washington	1981-82	80	136	1.70	Dave Taylor	Los Angeles	1980-81	72	112	1.56
Guy Lafleur	Montreal	1976-77	80	136	1.70	Denis Savard	Chicago	1982-83	78	121	1.55
Phil Esposito	Boston	1968-69	74	126	1.70	Mike Bossy	NY Islanders	1985-86	80	123	1.54
Guy Lafleur	Montreal	1974-75	70	119	1.70	Bobby Orr	Boston	1971-72	76	117	1.54
Mario Lemieux	Pittsburgh	1986-87	63	107	1.70	Doug Bentley	Chicago	1943-44	50	77	1.54
Bobby Orr	Boston	1974-75	80	135	1.69	Mike Bossy	NY Islanders	1984-85	76	117	1.54
Marcel Dionne	Los Angeles	1980-81	80	135	1.69	Marcel Dionne	Los Angeles	1976-77	80	122	1.53
						Paul Coffey	Pittsburgh	1988-89	75	113	1.51

Penalty Leaders

Season	Player and Club	Games Played	Penalties in Minutes	Season	Player and Club	Games Played	Penalties in Minutes
1988-89	Tim Hunter, Calgary	75	375	1957-58	Lou Fontinato, New York Rangers	70	152
1987-88	Bob Probert, Detroit	74	398	1956-57	Gus Mortson, Chicago	70	147
1986-87	Dave Williams, Los Angeles	76	358	1955-56	Lou Fontinato, New York Rangers	70	202
1985-86	Joey Kocur, Detroit	59	377	1954-55	Fern Flaman, Boston	70	150
1984-85	Chris Nilan, Montreal	77	358	1953-54	Gus Mortson, Chicago	68	132
1983-84	Chris Nilan, Montreal	76	338	1952-53	Maurice Richard, Montreal	70	112
1982-83	Randy Holt, Washington	70	275	1951-52	Gus Kyle, Boston	69	127
1981-82	Paul Baxter, Pittsburgh	76	409	1950-51	Gus Mortson, Toronto	60	142
1980-81	Dave Williams, Vancouver	77	343	1949-50	Bill Ezinicki, Toronto	67	144
1979-80	Jimmy Mann, Winnipeg	72	287	1948-49	Bill Ezinicki, Toronto	52	145
1978-79	Dave Williams, Toronto	77	298	1947-48	Bill Barilko, Toronto	57	147
1977-78	Dave Schultz, L.A., Pit.	74	405	1946-47	Gus Mortson, Toronto	60	133
1976-77	Dave Williams, Toronto	77	338	1945-46	Jack Stewart, Detroit	47	73
1975-76	Steve Durbano, Pit., K.C.	69	370	1944-45	Pat Egan, Boston	48	86
1974-75	Dave Schultz, Philadelphia	76	472	1943-44	Mike McMahon, Montreal	42	98
1973-74	Dave Schultz, Philadelphia	73	348	1942-43	Jimmy Orlando, Detroit	40	89*
1972-73	Dave Schultz, Philadelphia	76	259	1941-42	Jimmy Orlando, Detroit	48	81**
1971-72	Bryan Watson, Pittsburgh	75	212	1940-41	Jimmy Orlando, Detroit	48	99
1970-71	Keith Magnuson, Chicago	76	291	1939-40	Red Horner, Toronto	30	87
1969-70	Keith Magnuson, Chicago	76	213	1938-39	Red Horner, Toronto	48	85
1968-69	Forbes Kennedy, Phi., Tor.	77	219	1937-38	Red Horner, Toronto	47	82*
1967-68	Barclay Plager, St. Louis	49	153	1936-37	Red Horner, Toronto	48	124
1966-67	John Ferguson, Montreal	67	177	1935-36	Red Horner, Toronto	43	167
1965-66	Reg Fleming, New York Rangers	69	166	1934-35	Red Horner, Toronto	46	125
1964-65	Carl Brewer, Toronto	70	177	1933-34	Red Horner, Toronto	42	126*
1963-64	Vic Hadfield, New York Rangers	69	151	1932-33	Red Horner, Toronto	48	144
1962-63	Howie Young, Detroit	64	273	1931-32	Red Dutton, New York Americans	47	107
1961-62	Lou Fontinato, Montreal	54	167	1930-31	Harvey Rockburn, Detroit	42	118
1960-61	Pierre Pilote, Chicago	70	165	1929-30	Joe Lamb, Ottawa	44	119
1959-60	Carl Brewer, Toronto	67	150	1928-29	Red Dutton, Montreal Maroons	44	139
1958-59	Ted Lindsay, Chicago	70	184	1927-28	Eddie Shore, Boston	44	165
				1926-27	Nels Stewart, Montreal Maroons	44	133

* Match Misconduct penalty not included in total penalty minutes.
** Three Match Misconduct penalties not included in total penalty minutes.
1946-47 was the first season that a Match penalty was automatically written into the player's total penalty minutes as 20 minutes. Now all penalties, Match, Game Misconduct, and Misconduct, are written as 10 minutes.

Active NHL Players' Three-or-More-Goal Games

Regular Season

Teams named are the ones the players were with at the time of their multiple-scoring games. Players listed alphabetically.

Player	Team	3-Goals	4-Goals	5-Goals
Acton, Keith	Mtl., Min.	3	—	—
Adams, Greg	Washington	1	1	—
Adams, Gregory C.	Vancouver	1	—	—
Allison, Mike	NY Rangers	1	—	—
Anderson, Glenn	Edmonton	16	3	—
Anderson, John	Tor., Hfd.	4	—	—
Anderson, Perry	New Jersey	1	—	—
Andreychuk, Dave	Buffalo	4	—	1
Arniel, Scott	Winnipeg	1	—	—
Ashton, Brent	Que., Wpg.	6	—	—
Barber, Don	Minnesota	1	—	—
Barr, Dave	St. L., Det.	2	—	—
Bellows, Brian	Minnesota	2	1	—
Bjugstad, Scott	Minnesota	3	—	—
Boschman, Laurie	Winnipeg	2	—	—
Bourque, Raymond	Boston	1	—	—
Bozek, Steve	Los Angeles	2	—	—
Brickley, Andy	Pittsburgh	1	—	—
Bridgman, Mel	Calgary	1	—	—
Brooke, Bob	NY Rangers	1	—	—
Broten, Aaron	New Jersey	1	—	—
Broten, Neal	Minnesota	5	—	—
Brown, Rob	Pittsburgh	4	—	—
Bullard, Mike	Pittsburgh	7	—	—
Burr, Shawn	Detroit	1	—	—
Burridge, Randy	Boston	2	—	—
Carbonneau, Guy	Montreal	—	1	—
Carpenter, Bob	Washington	1	1	—
Carson, Jimmy	L.A., Edm.	5	1	—
Chabot, John	Pittsburgh	1	—	—
Christian, Dave	Wpg., Wsh.	2	—	—
Ciccarelli, Dino	Min., Wsh.	13	2	—
Clark, Wendel	Toronto	1	1	—
Coffey, Paul	Edmonton	4	1	—
Carson, Shayne	Montreal	2	—	—
Cote, Alain	Quebec	1	—	—
Courtnall, Geoff	Bos., Wsh.	1	—	—
Courtnall, Russ	Toronto	1	—	—
Craven, Murray	Philadelphia	2	—	—
Creighton, Adam	Buf., Chi.	2	—	—
Crowder, Keith	Boston	2	—	—
Cunneyworth, Randy	Pittsburgh	1	1	—
Cyr, Paul	Buffalo	1	—	—
Dahlen, Ulf	NY Rangers	1	—	—
Damphousse, Vincent	Toronto	1	—	—
Daoust, Dan	Toronto	1	—	—
DeBlois, Lucien	Winnipeg	1	—	—
Dineen, Kevin	Hartford	3	—	—
Dionne, Marcel	Los Angeles	25	3	—
Duchesne, Steve	Los Angeles	1	—	—
Duguay, Ron	NYR, Det.	9	—	—
Duncan, Iain	Winnipeg	1	—	—
Evason, Dean	Hartford	1	—	—
Federko, Bernie	St. Louis	11	—	—
Fergus, Tom	Toronto	4	—	—
Ferraro, Ray	Hartford	4	—	—
Flatley, Patrick	NY Islanders	—	1	—
Foligno, Mike	Det., Buf.	8	—	—
Francis, Ron	Hartford	6	1	—
Fraser, Curt	Chicago	1	—	—
Frycer, Miroslav	Que., Tor.	8	1	—
Gagne, Paul	New Jersey	1	—	—
Gagner, Dave	Minnesota	2	—	—
Gainey, Bob	Montreal	1	—	—
Gallant, Gerard	Detroit	4	—	—
Gartner, Mike	Washington	10	2	—
Gilbert, Greg	NY Islanders	2	—	—
Gillis, Paul	Quebec	1	—	—
Gilmour, Doug	St. Louis	2	—	—
Gould, Bobby	Calgary	1	—	—
Goulet, Michel	Quebec	11	2	—
Granato, Tony	NY Rangers	2	1	—
Greschner, Ron	NY Rangers	1	—	—
Gretzky, Wayne	Edmonton	33	8	4
Gustafsson, Bengt	Washington	1	—	1
Hamel, Gilles	Buffalo	1	—	—
Hannan, Dave	Edmonton	1	—	—
Hartsburg, Craig	Minnesota	1	—	—
Hawerchuk, Dale	Winnipeg	11	—	—
Higgins, Tim	Detroit	1	—	—
Housley, Phil	Buffalo	2	—	—
Howe, Mark	Hartford	1	—	—
Hrdina, Jiri	Calgary	1	1	—
Hull, Brett	Calgary	1	—	—
Hull, Jody	Hartford	1	—	—
Hunter, Dale	Quebec	3	—	—
Hunter, Mark	St. L., Cgy.	5	1	—
Ihnacak, Peter	Toronto	1	—	—
Janney, Craig	Boston	1	—	—
Johnson, Mark	Hfd., NJ	5	—	—

Denis Savard has had 10 ''hat-tricks'' in his NHL career.

Player	Team	3-Goals	4-Goals	5-Goals
Kasper, Steve	Boston	3	—	—
Kerr, Tim	Philadelphia	13	4	—
Klima, Petr	Detroit	3	—	—
Korn, Jim	Toronto	1	—	—
Krushelnyski, Mike	Edmonton	1	—	—
Kurri, Jari	Edmonton	18	1	1
Lafleur, Guy	Mtl., NYR	16	1	—
LaFontaine, Pat	NY Islanders	4	—	—
Lambert, Lane	Detroit	2	—	—
Larmer, Steve	Chicago	4	—	—
Larson, Reed	Detroit	3	—	—
Lawless, Paul	Hartford	1	—	—
Lawton, Brian	Minnesota	2	—	—
Leeman, Gary	Toronto	2	—	—
Lemieux, Claude	Montreal	1	—	—
Lemieux, Mario	Pittsburgh	15	5	1
Linden, Trevor	Vancouver	2	—	—
Linseman, Ken	Phi., Edm., Bos.	3	—	—
Loob, Hakan	Calgary	5	1	—
Ludzik, Steve	Chicago	1	—	—
MacLean, John	New Jersey	4	—	—
MacLean, Paul	Winnipeg	6	1	—
MacLellan, Brian	LA, NYR, Min.	2	1	—
MacTavish, Craig	Edmonton	1	—	—
Makela, Mikko	NY Islanders	1	—	—
Maloney, Don	NY Rangers	4	—	—
Marois, Daniel	Toronto	2	—	—
Maruk, Dennis	Cal., Cle., Wsh.	8	4	—
McBain, Andrew	Winnipeg	1	—	—
McDonald, Lanny	Tor., Col., Cgy.	16	—	—
McKegney, Tony	Buf., Que., Min., St.L.	7	1	—
McKenna, Sean	Buffalo	1	—	—
McPhee, Mike	Montreal	2	—	—
Meagher, Rick	Hartford	1	—	—
Messier, Mark	Edmonton	8	2	—
Momesso, Sergio	Montreal	1	—	—
Mullen, Brian	Wpg., NYR	2	—	—
Mullen, Joe	St. L., Cgy.	4	2	—
Muller, Kirk	New Jersey	3	—	—
Murray, Troy	Chicago	3	—	—
Napier, Mark	Montreal	1	1	—
Naslund, Mats	Montreal	4	1	—
Neely, Cam	Boston	5	—	—
Neufeld, Ray	Winnipeg	3	—	—
Nicholls, Bernie	Los Angeles	12	2	—
Nieuwendyk, Joe	Calgary	3	2	1
Ogrodnick, John	Detroit	6	—	—
Olczyk, Ed	Toronto	1	—	—
Osborne, Mark	Detroit	1	—	—
Otto, Joel	Calgary	1	—	—
Paslawski, Greg	St. Louis	2	—	—
Pederson, Barry	Boston	6	1	—
Peplinski, Jim	Calgary	1	1	—
Poddubny, Walt	Tor., Que.	4	—	—
Poulin, Dave	Philadelphia	5	—	—

Player	Team	3-Goals	4-Goals	5-Goals
Presley, Wayne	Chicago	1	—	—
Probert, Bob	Detroit	1	—	—
Propp, Brian	Philadelphia	3	1	—
Quinn, Dan	Pittsburgh	3	—	—
Reeds, Mark	St. Louis	1	—	—
Reinhart, Paul	Calgary	1	—	—
Richer, Stephane	Montreal	2	1	—
Ridley, Mike	NYR, Wsh.	2	1	—
Robertson, Torrie	Hartford	1	—	—
Robinson, Larry	Montreal	1	—	—
Robitaille, Luc	Los Angeles	5	—	—
Ronning, Cliff	St. Louis	1	—	—
Ruff, Lindy	Buffalo	1	1	—
Ruskowski, Terry	Pittsburgh	1	—	—
Sakic, Joe	Quebec	2	—	—
Salming, Borje	Toronto	1	—	—
Sandlak, Jim	Vancouver	1	—	—
Sandstrom, Tomas	NY Rangers	3	1	—
Savard, Denis	Chicago	10	—	—
Secord, Al	Chicago	3	2	—
Shanahan, Brendan	New Jersey	1	—	—
Shedden, Doug	Pittsburgh	2	—	—
Sheppard, Ray	Buffalo	2	—	—
Sinisalo, Ilkka	Philadelphia	3	—	—
Simpson, Craig	Pit., Edm.	3	—	—
Skriko, Petri	Vancouver	4	1	—
Smail, Doug	Winnipeg	2	—	—
Smith, Derrick	Philadelphia	1	—	—
Smith, Bobby	Minnesota	5	1	—
Smyl, Stan	Vancouver	7	—	—
Stastny, Anton	Quebec	3	—	—
Stastny, Peter	Quebec	13	2	—
Steen, Thomas	Winnipeg	3	—	—
Sulliman, Doug	Hartford	2	—	—
Sundstrom, Patrik	Vancouver	2	—	—
Sundstrom, Peter	NY Rangers	2	—	—
Sutter, Brent	NY Islanders	5	—	—
Tanti, Tony	Vancouver	9	1	—
Taylor, Dave	Los Angeles	6	1	—
Thomas, Steve	Chicago	1	—	—
Tikkanen, Esa	Edmonton	1	—	—
Tocchet, Rick	Philadelphia	4	1	—
Tonelli, John	NYI, L.A.	4	—	1
Trottier, Bryan	NY Islanders	13	1	2
Tucker, John	Buffalo	1	—	—
Turcotte, Darren	NY Rangers	1	—	—
Turgeon, Sylvain	Hartford	3	—	—
Vaive, Rick	Tor., Chi.	10	3	—
Verbeek, Pat	New Jersey	4	1	—
Walter, Ryan	Montreal	1	—	—
Wickenheiser, Doug	Mtl., St. L.	2	—	—
Wilson, Carey	Calgary	2	—	—
Yzerman, Steve	Detroit	6	—	—
Zezel, Peter	Philadelphia	1	—	—

Gordie Howe and Wayne Gretzky: The NHL's All-Time Leading Scorers

Entering the 1989-90 season, Gordie Howe and Wayne Gretzky ranked first and second on the NHL's list of career scoring leaders. Gretzky, who trailed Howe by only 13 points as the season commenced, was about to surpass what had long been considered to be a mark that no other player would equal.

Both Howe and Gretzky's careers celebrate NHL excellence:

Howe's 1,850 points were scored in 26 seasons spanning the lowest-scoring era in the modern NHL. Howe was a presence in each of his 1,767 games played, from his NHL debut as an 18-year old in 1946 to his last season, 1979-80 with Hartford, when he played 80 games and scored 15 goals at age 51. In between, he won the Art Ross and Hart Trophies six times each and was named to the NHL All-Star Team on 21 occasions. He scored 100 points in the first season this feat was accomplished, recording 44G-59A–103PTS in 1968-69.

Gretzky has rewritten the records section of this book in his ten-year NHL career. With 1,837 points scored in 774 games, Gretzky holds or shares nine career and 20 regular-season records. With 274 points in 131 playoff games, he holds or shares an additional 15 post-season records as well. Gretzky is the only NHLer to score 200-or-more points in a season, and has done so four times. His 92 goals in 1981-82 set an NHL record, as did his 163 assists in 1985-86. He is a nine-time Hart Trophy winner and has won the Art Ross Trophy on eight occasions. He is a ten-time NHL All-Star.

CAREER COMPARISON

	Gordie Howe	Wayne Gretzky
REGULAR SEASON		
Points	1850	1837
Goals	801	637
Assists	1049	1200
Games Played	1767	774
Seasons	26	10
PLAYOFFS		
Points	160	274
Goals	68	86
Assists	92	188
Games Played	157	131
Seasons	20	10
Hart Trophy	6	9
Art Ross Trophy	6	8
Playoff Scoring Leader	6	5
First All-Star Team	12	7
Second All-Star Team	9	3

HOWE, GORDON

Right wing. Shoots right. 6′, 205 lbs.
Born, Floral, Sask., March 31, 1928.
Last amateur club: Saskatoon Lions Club Juveniles.

			Regular Schedule					Playoffs				
Season	Club	Lea	GP	G	A	TP	PIM	GP	G	A	TP	PIM
1945-46	Omaha	USHL	51	22	26	48	53	6	2	1	3	15
1946-47	Detroit	NHL	58	7	15	22	52	5	0	0	0	18
1947-48	Detroit	NHL	60	16	28	44	63	10	1	1	2	11
1948-49a	Detroit	NHL	40	12	25	37	57	11	*8	3	*11	19
1949-50a	Detroit	NHL	70	35	33	68	69	1	0	0	0	7
1950-51bc	Detroit	NHL	70	*43	*43	*86	74	6	4	3	7	4
1951-52bcd	Detroit	NHL	70	*47	39	*86	78	8	2	*5	*7	2
1952-53bcd	Detroit	NHL	70	*49	*46	*95	57	6	2	5	7	2
1953-54bc	Detroit	NHL	70	33	*48	*81	109	12	4	5	9	*31
1954-55	Detroit	NHL	64	29	33	62	68	11	*9	11	*20	24
1955-56a	Detroit	NHL	70	38	41	79	100	10	3	9	12	8
1956-57bcd	Detroit	NHL	70	*44	45	*89	72	5	2	5	7	6
1957-58bd	Detroit	NHL	64	33	44	77	40	4	1	1	2	0
1958-59a	Detroit	NHL	70	32	46	78	57	....	....	....	....	....
1959-60bd	Detroit	NHL	70	28	45	73	46	6	1	5	6	4
1960-61a	Detroit	NHL	64	23	49	72	30	11	4	11	*15	10
1961-62a	Detroit	NHL	70	33	44	77	54	....	....	....	....	....
1962-63bcd	Detroit	NHL	70	*38	48	*86	100	11	7	9	*16	22
1963-64a	Detroit	NHL	69	26	47	73	70	14	*9	10	*19	16
1964-65a	Detroit	NHL	70	29	47	76	104	7	4	2	6	20
1965-66b	Detroit	NHL	70	29	46	75	83	12	4	6	10	12
1966-67ae	Detroit	NHL	69	25	40	65	53	....	....	....	....	....
1967-68b	Detroit	NHL	74	39	43	82	53	....	....	....	....	....
1968-69b	Detroit	NHL	76	44	59	103	58	....	....	....	....	....
1969-70b	Detroit	NHL	76	31	40	71	58	4	2	0	2	2
1970-71	Detroit	NHL	63	23	29	52	38	....	....	....	....	....
1971-72	Did Not Play.											
1972-73	Did Not Play.											
1973-74	Houston	WHA	70	31	69	100	46	13	3	*14	17	34
1974-75	Houston	WHA	75	34	65	99	84	13	8	12	20	20
1975-76	Houston	WHA	78	32	70	102	76	17	4	8	12	31
1976-77	Houston	WHA	62	24	44	68	57	11	5	3	8	11
1977-78	New England	WHA	76	34	62	96	85	14	5	5	10	15
1978-79	New England	WHA	58	19	24	43	51	10	3	1	4	4
1979-80	Hartford	NHL	80	15	26	41	42	3	1	1	2	2
	NHL Totals		1767	801	1049	1860	1685	157	68	92	160	220
	WHA Totals		419	174	334	508	399	78	28	43	71	115

a Second All-Star Team (right wing).
b First All-Star Team (right wing).
c Won Art Ross Trophy.
d Won Hart Memorial Trophy.
e Won Lester Patrick Trophy.

Wayne Gretzky's year-by-year statistics are found on page 250.

Gordie Howe challenges Toronto's Johnny Bower, October, 1963.

Wayne Gretzky

Rookie Scoring Records

Top Goal-Scoring Rookies

(30 Goals or More)

	Rookie	Team	Position	Season	GP	G	A	PTS
1.	*Mike Bossy	NY Islanders	Right wing	1977-78	73	**53**	38	91
2.	*Joe Niewendyk	Calgary	Center	1987-88	75	**51**	41	92
3.	*Dale Hawerchuk	Winnipeg	Center	1981-82	80	**45**	58	103
4.	*Luc Robitaille	Los Angeles	Left wing	1986-87	79	**45**	39	84
5.	Barry Pederson	Boston	Center	1981-82	80	**44**	48	92
	Rick Martin	Buffalo	Left wing	1971-72	73	**44**	30	74
7.	*Steve Larmer	Chicago	Right wing	1982-83	80	**43**	47	90
	*Mario Lemieux	Pittsburgh	Center	1984-85	73	**43**	57	100
9.	Darryl Sutter	Chicago	Left wing	1980-81	76	**40**	22	62
	Sylvain Turgeon	Hartford	Left wing	1983-84	76	**40**	32	72
	Warren Young	Pittsburgh	Left wing	1984-85	80	**40**	32	72
12.	Anton Stastny	Quebec	Left wing	1980-81	80	**39**	46	85
	Steve Yzerman	Detroit	Center	1983-84	80	**39**	48	87
	*Peter Stastny	Quebec	Center	1980-81	77	**39**	70	109
	*Eric Vail	Atlanta	Left wing	1974-75	72	**39**	21	60
16.	Neal Broten	Minnesota	Center	1981-82	73	**38**	59	97
	*Gilbert Perreault	Buffalo	Center	1970-71	78	**38**	34	72
18.	Jimmy Carson	Los Angeles	Centre	1986-87	80	**37**	42	79
	Jorgen Pettersson	St. Louis	Left wing	1980-81	62	**37**	36	73
	Mike Bullard	Pittsburgh	Center	1981-82	75	**37**	27	64
21.	Mike Foligno	Detroit	Right wing	1979-80	80	**36**	35	71
	Tony Granato	NY Rangers	Right wing	1988-89	78	**36**	27	63
	Paul MacLean	Winnipeg	Right wing	1981-82	74	**36**	25	61
24.	Marian Stastny	Quebec	Right wing	1981-82	74	**35**	54	89
	Brian Bellows	Minnesota	Right wing	1982-83	80	**35**	30	60
26.	Nels Stewart	Mtl. Maroons	Center	1925-26	36	**34**	8	42
	*Danny Grant	Minnesota	Left wing	1968-69	75	**34**	31	65
	Norm Ferguson	Oakland	Right wing	1968-69	76	**34**	20	54
	Brian Propp	Philadelphia	Left wing	1979-80	80	**34**	41	75
	Wendel Clark	Toronto	Left wing	1985-86	66	**34**	11	45
31.	Mark Pavelich	NY Rangers	Center	1981-82	79	**33**	43	76
	*Willi Plett	Atlanta	Right wing	1976-77	64	**33**	23	56
	Dale McCourt	Detroit	Center	1977-78	76	**33**	39	72
	Ron Flockhart	Philadelphia	Center	1981-82	72	**33**	39	72
	Steve Bozek	Los Angeles	Center	1981-82	71	**33**	23	56
36.	Jari Kurri	Edmonton	Left wing	1980-81	75	**32**	43	75
	Bill Mosienko	Chicago	Right wing	1943-44	50	**32**	38	70
	Don Murdoch	NY Rangers	Right wing	1976-77	59	**32**	24	56
	Michel Bergeron	Detroit	Right wing	1975-76	72	**32**	27	59
	*Bryan Trottier	NY Islanders	Center	1975-76	80	**32**	63	95
	Kjell Dahlin	Montreal	Right wing	1985-86	77	**32**	39	71
	Petr Klima	Detroit	Left wing	1985-86	74	**32**	24	56
43.	Danny Gare	Buffalo	Right wing	1974-75	78	**31**	31	62
	Pierre Larouche	Pittsburgh	Center	1974-75	79	**31**	37	68
	Dave Poulin	Philadelphia	Center	1983-84	73	**31**	45	76
	Daniel Marios	Toronto	Right wing	1988-89	76	**31**	23	54
46.	Trevor Linden	Vancouver	Right wing	1988-89	80	**30**	29	59

* Calder Trophy Winner.

Eric Vail scored 39 goals for the Atlanta Flames in 1974-75, his inaugural NHL campaign.

All-Time Top Point-Scoring Rookies

	Rookie	Team	Position	Season	GP	G	A	PTS
1.	*Peter Stastny	Quebec	Center	1980-81	77	39	70	**109**
2.	*Dale Hawerchuk	Winnipeg	Center	1981-82	80	45	58	**103**
3.	*Mario Lemieux	Pittsburgh	Center	1984-85	73	43	57	**100**
4.	Neal Broten	Minnesota	Center	1981-82	73	38	59	**97**
5.	*Bryan Trottier	NY Islanders	Center	1975-76	80	32	63	**95**
6.	*Joe Nieuwendyk	Calgary	Center	1987-88	75	51	41	**92**
	Barry Pederson	Boston	Center	1981-82	80	44	48	**92**
8.	*Mike Bossy	NY Islanders	Right wing	1977-78	73	53	38	**91**
9.	*Steve Larmer	Chicago	Right wing	1982-83	80	43	47	**90**
10.	Marian Stastny	Quebec	Right wing	1981-82	74	35	54	**89**
11.	Steve Yzerman	Detroit	Center	1983-84	80	39	48	**87**
12.	Anton Stastny	Quebec	Left wing	1980-81	80	39	46	**85**
13.	*Luc Robitaille	Los Angeles	Left wing	1986-87	79	45	39	**84**
14.	Jimmy Carson	Los Angeles	Center	1986-87	80	37	42	**79**
15.	Marcel Dionne	Detroit	Center	1971-72	78	28	49	**77**
16.	Mark Pavelich	NY Rangers	Center	1981-82	79	33	43	**76**
	Larry Murphy	Los Angeles	Defense	1980-81	80	16	60	**76**
	Dave Poulin	Philadelphia	Center	1983-84	73	31	45	**76**
19.	Jari Kurri	Edmonton	Left wing	1980-81	75	32	43	**75**
	Brian Propp	Philadelphia	Left wing	1979-80	80	34	41	**75**
	Denis Savard	Chicago	Center	1980-81	76	28	47	**75**
22.	Rick Martin	Buffalo	Left wing	1971-72	73	44	30	**74**
	*Bobby Smith	Minnesota	Center	1978-79	80	30	44	**74**
24.	Jorgen Pettersson	St. Louis	Left wing	1980-81	62	37	36	**73**
25.	*Gilbert Perreault	Buffalo	Center	1970-71	78	38	34	**72**
	Ron Flockhart	Philadelphia	Center	1981-82	72	33	39	**72**
	Dale McCourt	Detroit	Center	1977-78	76	33	39	**72**
	Sylvain Turgeon	Hartford	Left wing	1983-84	76	40	32	**72**
	Warren Young	Pittsburgh	Left wing	1984-85	80	40	32	**72**
	Carey Wilson	Calgary	Center	1984-85	74	24	48	**72**
31.	Dave Christian	Winnipeg	Center	1980-81	80	28	43	**71**
	Mike Foligno	Detroit	Right wing	1979-80	80	36	35	**71**
	Mats Naslund	Montreal	Left wing	1982-83	74	26	45	**71**
	Kjell Dahlin	Montreal	Right wing	1985-86	77	32	39	**71**
	*Brian Leetch	NY Rangers	Defense	1988-89	68	23	48	**71**
35.	Bill Mosienko	Chicago	Right wing	1943-44	50	32	38	**70**
36.	Roland Eriksson	Minnesota	Center	1976-77	80	25	44	**69**
37.	Pierre Larouche	Pittsburgh	Center	1974-75	79	31	37	**68**
	Ron Francis	Hartford	Center	1981-82	59	25	43	**68**
	Jude Drouin	Minnesota	Center	1970-71	75	16	52	**68**
	*Gary Suter	Calgary	Defense	1985-86	80	18	50	**68**
41.	Bobby Carpenter	Washington	Center	1981-82	80	32	35	**67**
	Chris Valentine	Washington	Center	1981-82	60	30	37	**67**
	Tom Webster	Detroit	Right wing	1970-71	78	30	37	**67**
	Mark Osborne	Detroit	Left wing	1981-82	80	26	41	**67**
45.	Peter Ihnacak	Toronto	Center	1982-83	80	28	38	**66**
	Phil Housley	Buffalo	Defense	1982-83	77	19	47	**66**
	Per-Erik Eklund	Philadelphia	Center	1985-86	70	15	51	**66**
48.	Brian Bellows	Minnesota	Right wing	1982-83	78	35	30	**65**
	*Danny Grant	Minnesota	Left wing	1968-69	75	34	31	**65**
	Mike Krushelnyski	Boston	Center	1982-83	79	23	42	**65**
	*Raymond Bourque	Boston	Defense	1979-80	80	17	48	**65**
	Mike Ridley	NY Rangers	Center	1985-86	80	22	43	**65**
	Christian Ruuttu	Buffalo	Center	1986-87	76	22	43	**65**

* Calder Trophy Winner.

Five-or-more-Goal Games

Player	Team	Date	Score		Opposing Goaltender
SEVEN GOALS					
Joe Malone	Quebec Bulldogs	Jan. 31/20	Tor. 6	at Que. 10	Ivan Mitchell
SIX GOALS					
Newsy Lalonde	Montreal	Jan. 10/20	Tor. 7	at Mtl. 14	Ivan Mitchell
Joe Malone	Quebec Bulldogs	Mar. 10/20	Ott. 4	at Que. 10	Clint Benedict
Corb Denneny	Toronto St. Pats	Jan. 26/21	Ham. 3	at Tor. 10	Howard Lockhart
Cy Denneny	Ottawa Senators	Mar. 7/21	Ham. 5	at Ott. 12	Howard Lockhart
Syd Howe	Detroit	Feb. 3/44	NYR 2	at Det. 12	Ken McAuley
Red Berenson	St. Louis	Nov. 7/68	St. L. 8	at Phil 0	Doug Favell
Darryl Sittler	Toronto	Feb. 7/76	Bos. 4	at Tor. 11	Dave Reece
FIVE GOALS					
Joe Malone	Montreal	Dec. 19/17	Mtl. 9	at Ott. 4	Clint Benedict
Harry Hyland	Mtl. Wanderers	Dec. 19/17	Tor. 9	at Mtl. 10	Arthur Brooks
Joe Malone	Montreal	Jan. 12/18	Ott. 4	at Mtl. 9	Clint Benedict
Joe Malone	Montreal	Feb. 2/18	Tor. 2	at Mtl. 11	Harry Holmes
Mickey Roach	Toronto St. Pats	Mar. 6/20	Que. 2	at Tor. 11	Frank Brophy
Newsy Lalonde	Montreal	Feb. 16/21	Ham. 5	at Mtl. 10	Howard Lockhart
Babe Dye	Toronto St. Pats	Dec. 16/22	Mtl. 2	at Tor. 7	Georges Vezina
Redvers Green	Hamilton Tigers	Dec. 5/24	Ham. 10	at Tor. 3	John Roach
Babe Dye	Toronto St. Pats	Dec. 22/24	Tor. 10	at Bos. 2	Charlie Stewart
Harry Broadbent	Mtl. Maroons	Jan. 7/25	Mtl. 6	at Ham. 2	Vernon Forbes
Pit Lepine	Montreal	Dec. 14/29	Ott. 4	at Mtl. 6	Alex Connell
Howie Morenz	Montreal	Mar. 18/30	NYA 3	at Mtl. 8	Roy Worters
Charlie Conacher	Toronto	Jan. 19/32	NYA 3	at Tor. 11	Roy Worters
Ray Getliffe	Montreal	Feb. 6/43	Bos. 3	at Mtl. 8	Frank Brimsek
Maurice Richard	Montreal	Dec. 28/44	Det. 1	at Mtl. 9	Harry Lumley
Howie Meeker	Toronto	Jan. 8/47	Chi. 4	at Tor. 10	Paul Bibeault
Bernie Geoffrion	Montreal	Feb. 19/55	NYR 2	at Mtl. 10	Gump Worsley
Bobby Rousseau	Montreal	Feb. 1/64	Det. 3	at Mtl. 9	Roger Crozier
Yvan Cournoyer	Montreal	Feb. 15/75	Chi. 3	at Mtl. 12	Mike Veisor
Don Murdoch	NY Rangers	Oct. 12/76	NYR 10	at Min. 4	Gary Smith
Ian Turnbull	Toronto	Feb. 2/77	Det. 1	at Tor. 9	Ed Giacomin (2) Jim Rutherford (3)
*Bryan Trottier	NY Islanders	Dec. 23/78	NYR 4	at NYI 9	Wayne Thomas (4) John Davidson (1)
Tim Young	Minnesota	Jan. 15/79	Min. 8	at NYR 1	Doug Soetaert (3) Wayne Thomas (2)
*John Tonelli	NY Islanders	Jan. 6/81	Tor. 3	at NYI 6	Jiri Crha (5)
*Wayne Gretzky	Edmonton	Feb. 18/81	St.L. 2	at Edm. 9	Mike Liut (3) Ed Staniowski (2)
*Wayne Gretzky	Edmonton	Dec. 30/81	Phi. 5	at Edm. 7	Pete Peeters (4) Empty Net (1)
Grant Mulvey	Chicago	Feb. 3/82	St.L. 5	at Chi. 9	Mike Liut (4) Gary Edwards (1)
*Bryan Trottier	NY Islanders	Feb. 13/82	Phi. 2	at NYI 8	Pete Peeters
Willy Lindstrom	Winnipeg	Mar. 2/82	Wpg. 7	at Phi. 6	Pete Peeters
Mark Pavelich	NY Rangers	Feb. 23/83	Hfd. 3	at NYR 11	Greg Millen
*Jari Kurri	Edmonton	Nov. 19/83	NJ. 4	at Edm. 13	Glenn Resch (3) Ron Low (2)
*Bengt Gustafsson	Washington	Jan. 8/84	Wash. 7	at Phi. 1	Pelle Lindbergh
Pat Hughes	Edmonton	Feb. 3/84	Cgy. 5	at Edm. 10	Don Edwards (3) Rejean Lemelin (2)
*Wayne Gretzky	Edmonton	Dec. 15/84	Edm. 8	at St. L. 2	Rick Wamsley (4) Mike Liut(1)
*Dave Andreychuk	Buffalo	Feb. 6/86	Buf. 8	at Bos. 6	Pat Riggin (1) Doug Keans (4)
*Wayne Gretzky	Edmonton	Dec. 6/87	Min. 4	at Edm. 10	Don Beaupre (4) Kari Takko (1)
*Mario Lemieux	Pittsburgh	Dec. 31/88	N.J. 6	at Pit. 8	Bob Sauve (3) Chris Terreri (2)
*Joe Nieuwendyk	Calgary	Jan. 11/89	Wpg. 3	at Cgy. 8	Daniel Berthiaume (5)

* Active.

50-Goal Seasons

Player	Team	Date of 50th Goal	Score		Goaltender	Player's Game No.	Team Game No.	Total Goals	Total Games	Age When First 50th Scored (Yrs. & Mos.)
Maurice Richard	Mtl.	18-3-45	Mtl. 4	at Bos. 2	Harvey Bennett	50	50	50	50	23.7
Bernie Geoffrion	Mtl.	16-3-61	Tor. 2	at Mtl. 5	Cesare Maniago	62	68	50	64	30.1
Bobby Hull	Chi.	25-3-62	Chi. 1	at NYR 4	Gump Worsley	70	70	50	70	23.2
Bobby Hull	Chi.	2-3-66	Det. 4	at Chi. 5	Hank Bassen	52	57	54	65	
Bobby Hull	Chi.	18-3-67	Chi. 5	at Tor. 9	Bruce Gamble	63	66	52	66	
Bobby Hull	Chi.	5-3-69	NYR 4	at Chi. 4	Ed Giacomin	64	66	58	74	
Phil Esposito	Bos.	20-2-71	Bos. 4	at L.A. 5	Denis DeJordy	58	58	76	78	29.0
John Bucyk	Bos.	16-3-71	Bos. 11	at Det. 4	Roy Edwards	69	69	51	78	35.1
Phil Esposito	Bos.	20-2-72	Bos. 3	at Chi. 1	Tony Esposito	60	60	66	76	
Bobby Hull	Chi.	2-4-72	Det. 1	at Chi. 6	Andy Brown	78	78	50	78	
Vic Hadfield	NYR	2-4-72	Mtl. 6	at NYR 5	Denis DeJordy	78	78	50	78	31.6
Phil Esposito	Bos.	25-3-73	Buf. 1	at Bos. 6	Roger Crozier	75	75	55	78	
Mickey Redmond	Det.	27-3-73	Det. 8	at Tor. 1	Ron Low	73	75	52	76	25.3
Rick MacLeish	Phi.	1-4-73	Phi. 4	at Pit. 5	Cam Newton	78	78	50	78	23.2
Phil Esposito	Bos.	20-2-74	Bos. 5	at Min. 5	Cesare Maniago	56	56	68	78	
Mickey Redmond	Det.	23-3-74	NYR 3	at Det. 5	Ed Giacomin	69	71	51	76	
Ken Hodge	Bos.	6-4-74	Bos. 2	at Mtl. 6	Michel Larocque	75	77	50	76	29.10
Rick Martin	Buf.	7-4-74	St.L. 2	at Buf. 5	Wayne Stephenson	78	78	52	78	22.9
Phil Esposito	Bos.	8-2-75	Bos. 8	at Det. 5	Jim Rutherford	54	54	61	79	
Guy Lafleur	Mtl.	29-3-75	K.C. 1	at Mtl. 4	Denis Herron	66	76	53	70	23.6
Danny Grant	Det.	2-4-75	Wsh. 3	at Det. 8	John Adams	78	78	50	80	29.2
Rick Martin	Buf.	3-4-75	Bos. 2	at Buf. 4	Ken Broderick	67	79	52	68	
Reggie Leach	Phi.	14-3-76	Atl. 1	at Phi. 6	Daniel Bouchard	69	69	61	80	25.11
Jean Pronovost	Pit.	24-3-76	Bos. 5	at Pit. 5	Gilles Gilbert	74	74	52	80	31.3
Guy Lafleur	Mtl.	27-3-76	K.C. 2	at Mtl. 8	Denis Herron	76	76	56	80	
Bill Barber	Phi.	3-4-76	Buf. 2	at Phi. 5	Al Smith	79	79	50	80	23.9
Pierre Larouche	Pit.	3-4-76	Wash. 5	at Pit. 4	Ron Low	75	79	53	76	20.5
Danny Gare	Buf.	4-4-76	Tor. 2	at Buf. 5	Gord McRae	79	80	50	79	21.11
Steve Shutt	Mtl.	1-3-77	Mtl. 5	at NYI 4	Glenn Resch	65	65	60	80	24.8
Guy Lafleur	Mtl.	6-3-77	Mtl. 1	at Buf. 4	Don Edwards	68	68	56	80	
Marcel Dionne	L.A.	2-4-77	Min. 2	at L.A. 7	Pete LoPresti	79	79	53	80	25.8
Guy Lafleur	Mtl.	8-3-78	Wsh. 3	at Mtl. 4	Jim Bedard	63	65	60	78	
Mike Bossy	NYI	1-4-78	Wsh. 2	at NYI 3	Bernie Wolfe	69	76	53	73	21.2
Mike Bossy	NYI	24-2-79	Det. 1	at NYI 3	Rogie Vachon	58	58	69	80	
Marcel Dionne	L.A.	11-3-79	L.A. 3	at Phi. 6	Wayne Stephenson	68	68	59	80	
Guy Lafleur	Mtl.	31-3-79	Pit. 3	at Mtl. 5	Denis Herron	76	76	52	80	
Guy Chouinard	Atl.	6-4-79	NYR 2	at Atl. 9	John Davidson	79	79	50	80	22.5
Marcel Dionne	L.A.	12-3-80	L.A. 2	at Pit. 4	Nick Ricci	70	70	53	80	
Mike Bossy	NYI	16-3-80	NYI 6	at Chi. 1	Tony Esposito	68	71	51	75	
Charlie Simmer	L.A.	19-3-80	Det. 3	at L.A. 4	Jim Rutherford	57	73	56	64	26.0
Pierre Larouche	Mtl.	25-3-80	Chi. 4	at Mtl. 8	Tony Esposito	72	75	50	73	
Danny Gare	Buf.	27-3-80	Det. 1	at Buf. 10	Jim Rutherford	71	75	56	76	
Blaine Stoughton	Hfd.	28-3-80	Hfd. 4	at Van. 4	Glen Hanlon	75	75	56	80	27.0
Guy Lafleur	Mtl.	2-4-80	Mtl. 7	at Det. 2	Rogie Vachon	72	78	50	74	
Wayne Gretzky	Edm.	2-4-80	Min. 1	at Edm. 1	Gary Edwards	78	79	51	79	19.2
Reggie Leach	Phi.	3-4-80	Wsh. 2	at Phi. 4	(empty net)	75	79	50	76	
Mike Bossy	NYI	24-1-81	Que. 3	at NYI 7	Ron Grahame	50	50	68	79	
Charlie Simmer	L.A.	26-1-81	L.A. 7	at Que. 5	Michel Dion	51	51	56	65	
Marcel Dionne	L.A.	8-3-81	L.A. 4	at Wpg. 1	Markus Mattsson	68	68	58	80	
Wayne Babych	St.L.	12-3-81	St.L. 3	at Mtl. 4	Richard Sevigny	70	68	54	78	22.9
Wayne Gretzky	Edm.	15-3-81	Edm. 3	at Cgy. 3	Pat Riggin	69	69	55	80	
Rick Kehoe	Pit.	16-3-81	Pit. 7	at Edm. 6	Eddie Mio	70	70	55	80	29.7
Jacques Richard	Que.	29-3-81	Mtl. 0	at Que. 4	Richard Sevigny	76	75	52	78	28.6
Dennis Maruk	Wsh.	5-4-81	Det. 2	at Wsh. 7	Larry Lozinski	80	80	50	80	25.3
Wayne Gretzky	Edm.	30-12-81	Phi. 5	at Edm. 7	(empty net)	39	39	92	80	
Dennis Maruk	Wsh.	21-2-82	Wpg. 3	at Wsh. 6	Doug Soetaert	61	61	60	80	
Mike Bossy	NYI	4-3-82	Tor. 1	at NYI 10	Michel Larocque	66	66	64	80	
Dino Ciccarelli	Min.	8-3-82	St.L. 1	at Min. 8	Mike Liut	67	68	55	76	21.7
Rick Vaive	Tor.	24-3-82	St.L. 3	at Tor. 4	Mike Liut	72	75	54	77	22.10
Rick Middleton	Bos.	28-3-82	Bos. 5	at Buf. 9	Paul Harrison	72	77	51	75	
Blaine Stoughton	Hfd.	28-3-82	Min. 5	at Hfd. 2	Gilles Meloche	76	76	52	80	29.1
Marcel Dionne	L.A.	30-3-82	Cgy. 7	at L.A. 5	Pat Riggin	75	77	50	78	
Mark Messier	Edm.	31-3-82	L.A. 3	at Edm. 7	Mario Lessard	78	79	50	78	21.3
Bryan Trottier	NYI	3-4-82	Phi. 3	at NYI 6	Pete Peeters	79	79	50	80	25.9
Lanny McDonald	Cgy.	18-2-83	Cgy. 1	at Buf. 5	Bob Sauve	60	60	66	80	30.0
Wayne Gretzky	Edm.	19-2-83	Edm. 10	at Pit. 7	Nick Ricci	60	60	71	80	
Michel Goulet	Que.	5-3-83	Que. 7	at Hfd. 3	Mike Veisor	67	67	57	80	22.11
Mike Bossy	NYI	12-3-83	Wsh. 2	at NYI 6	Al Jensen	70	71	60	79	
Marcel Dionne	L.A.	17-3-83	Que. 3	at L.A. 4	Daniel Bouchard	71	71	56	80	
Al Secord	Chi.	20-3-83	Tor. 3	at Chi. 7	Mike Palmateer	73	73	54	80	25.0
Rick Vaive	Tor.	30-3-83	Tor. 4	at Det. 2	Gilles Gilbert	76	78	51	78	
Wayne Gretzky	Edm.	7-1-84	Hfd. 3	at Edm. 5	Greg Millen	42	42	87	74	
Michel Goulet	Que.	8-3-84	Que. 8	at Pit. 6	Denis Herron	63	69	56	75	
Rick Vaive	Tor.	14-3-84	Min. 3	at Tor. 3	Gilles Meloche	69	72	52	76	
Mike Bullard	Pit.	14-3-84	Pit. 6	at L.A. 7	Markus Mattsson	71	72	51	76	23.0
Jari Kurri	Edm.	15-3-84	Edm. 2	at Mtl. 3	Rick Wamsley	57	73	52	64	23.10
Glenn Anderson	Edm.	21-3-84	Hfd. 3	at Edm. 5	Greg Millen	76	76	54	80	23.6
Tim Kerr	Phi.	22-3-84	Pit. 4	at Phi. 13	Denis Herron	74	75	54	79	24.3
Mike Bossy	NYI	31-3-84	NYI 3	at Wsh. 1	Pat Riggin	67	79	51	67	

Vic Hadfield

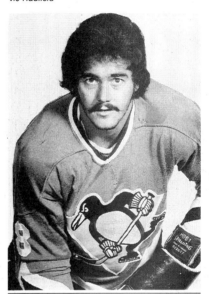

Rick Kehoe

Danny Grant

Hakan Loob

Lanny McDonald

Bobby Hull

50-Goal Seasons continued

Player	Team	Date of 50th Goal		Score		Goaltender	Player's Game No.	Team Game No.	Total Goals	Total Games	Age When First 50th Scored (Yrs. & Mos.)
Wayne Gretzky	Edm.	26-1-85	Pit. 3	at Edm. 6		Denis Herron	49	49	73	80	
Jari Kurri	Edm.	3-2-85	Hfd. 3	at Edm. 6		Greg Millen	50	53	71	73	
Mike Bossy	NYI	5-3-85	Phi. 5	at NYI 4		Bob Froese	61	65	58	76	
Tim Kerr	Phi.	7-3-85	Wsh. 6	at Phi. 9		Pat Riggin	63	65	54	74	
John Ogrodnick	Det.	13-3-85	Det. 6	at Edm. 7		Grant Fuhr	69	69	55	79	25.9
Bob Carpenter	Wsh.	21-3-85	Wsh. 2	at Mtl. 3		Steve Penney	72	72	53	80	21.9
Michel Goulet	Que.	26-3-85	Buf. 3	at Que. 4		Tom Barrasso	62	73	55	69	
Dale Hawerchuk	Wpg.	29-4-85	Chi. 5	at Wpg. 5		W. Skorodenski	77	77	53	80	21.1
Mike Gartner	Wsh.	7-4-85	Pit. 3	at Wsh. 7		Brian Ford	80	80	50	80	25.5
Jari Kurri	Edm.	4-3-86	Edm. 6	at Van. 2		Richard Brodeur	63	65	68	78	
Mike Bossy	NYI	11-3-86	Cgy. 4	at NYI 8		Rejean Lemelin	67	67	61	80	
Glenn Anderson	Edm.	14-3-86	Det. 3	at Edm. 12		Greg Stefan	63	71	54	72	
Michel Goulet	Que.	17-3-86	Que. 8	at Mtl. 6		Patrick Roy	67	72	53	75	
Wayne Gretzky	Edm.	18-3-86	Wpg. 2	at Edm. 6		Brian Hayward	72	72	52	80	
Tim Kerr	Phi.	20-3-86	Pit. 1	at Phi. 5		Roberto Romano	68	72	58	76	
Wayne Gretzky	Edm.	2-4-87	Edm. 6	at Min. 5		Don Beaupre	55	55	62	79	
Tim Kerr	Phi.	3-17-87	NYR 1	at Phi. 4		J. Vanbiesbrouck	67	71	58	75	
Jari Kurri	Edm.	3-17-87	N.J. 4	at Edm. 7		Craig Billington	69	70	54	79	
Mario Lemieux	Pit.	3-12-87	Que. 3	at Pit. 6		Mario Gosselin	53	70	54	63	21.5
Dino Ciccarelli	Min.	3-7-87	Pit. 7	at Min. 3		Gilles Meloche	66	66	52	80	
Mario Lemieux	Pit.	2-2-88	Wsh. 2	at Pit. 3		Pete Peeters	51	54	70	77	
Steve Yzerman	Det.	1-3-88	Buf. 4	at Det. 4		Tom Barrasso	64	64	50	64	22.10
Joe Nieuwendyk	Cgy.	12-3-88	Buf. 4	at Cgy. 10		Tom Barrasso	66	70	51	75	21.5
Craig Simpson	Edm.	15-3-88	Buf. 4	at Edm. 6		Jacques Cloutier	71	71	56	80	21.1
Jimmy Carson	L.A.	26-3-88	Chi. 5	at L.A. 9		Darren Pang	77	77	55	88	19.7
Luc Robitaille	L.A.	1-4-88	L.A. 6	at Cgy. 3		Mike Vernon	79	79	53	80	21.10
Hakan Loob	Cgy.	3-4-88	Min. 1	at Cgy. 4		Don Beaupre	80	80	50	80	27.9
Stephane Richer	Mtl.	3-4-88	Mtl. 4	at Buf. 4		Tom Barrasso	72	80	50	72	21.10
Mario Lemieux	Pit.	20-1-89	Pit. 3	at Wpg. 7		Eldon Reddick	44	46	85	76	
Bernie Nicholls	L.A.	28-1-89	Edm. 7	at L.A. 6		Grant Fuhr	51	51	70	79	27.7
Steve Yzerman	Det.	5-2-89	Det. 6	at Wpg. 2		Eldon Reddick	55	55	65	80	
Wayne Gretzky	L.A.	4-3-89	Phi. 2	at L.A. 6		Ron Hextall	66	67	54	78	
Joe Nieuwendyk	Cgy.	21-3-89	NYI 1	at Cgy. 4		Mark Fitzpatrick	72	74	51	77	
Joe Mullen	Cgy.	31-3-89	Wpg. 1	at Cgy. 4		Bob Essensa	78	79	51	79	32.1

Players' 500th Goals

Player	Team	Date	Game No.	Score		Opposing Goaltender	Total Goals	Total Games
Maurice Richard	Montreal	Oct. 19/57	863	Chi. 1	at Mtl. 3	Glenn Hall	544	978
Gordie Howe	Detroit	Mar. 14/62	1,045	Det. 2	at NYR 3	Gump Worsley	801	1,767
Bobby Hull	Chicago	Feb. 21/70	861	NYR. 2	at Chi. 4	Ed Giacomin	610	1,063
Jean Béliveau	Montreal	Feb. 11/71	1,101	Minn. 2	at Mtl. 6	Gilles Gilbert	507	1,125
Frank Mahovlich	Montreal	Mar. 21/73	1,105	Van. 2	at Mtl. 3	Dunc Wilson	533	1,181
Phil Esposito	Boston	Dec. 22/74	803	Det. 4	at Bos. 5	Jim Rutherford	717	1,282
John Bucyk	Boston	Oct. 30/75	1,370	St. L. 2	at Bos. 3	Yves Bélanger	556	1,540
Stan Mikita	Chicago	Feb. 27/77	1,221	.Van. 4	at Chi. 3	Cesare Maniago	541	1,394
*Marcel Dionne	Los Angeles	Dec. 14/82	887	L.A. 2	at Wash. 7	Al Jensen	731	1,348
*Guy Lafleur	Montreal	Dec. 20/83	918	Mtl. 6	at N.J. 0	Glenn Resch	536	1,028
Mike Bossy	NY Islanders	Jan. 2/86	647	Bos. 5	at NYI 7	empty net	573	752
Gilbert Perreault	Buffalo	Mar. 9/86	1,159	NJ 3	at Buf. 4	Alain Chevrier	512	1,191
*Wayne Gretzky	Edmonton	Nov. 22/86	575	Van. 2	at Edm. 5	Troy Gamble	637	774
*Lanny McDonald	Calgary	Mar. 21/89	1,107	NYI 1	at Cgy. 4	Mark Fitzpatrick	500	1,111

Players' 1,000th Points

Player	Team	Date	Game No.	G or A	Score		Total Points G A PTS	Total Games
Gordie Howe	Detroit	Nov. 27/60	938	(A)	Tor. 0	at Det. 2	801–1,049–1,850	1,767
Jean Béliveau	Montreal	Mar. 3/68	911	(G)	Mtl. 2	at Det. 5	507–712–1,219	1,125
Alex Delvecchio	Detroit	Feb. 16/69	1,143	(A)	LA 3	at Det. 6	456–825–1,281	1,549
Norm Ullman	Toronto	Oct. 16/71	1,113	(A)	NYR 5	at Tor. 3	490–739–1,229	1,410
Bobby Hull	Chicago	Dec. 12/71	909	(A)	Minn. 3	at Chi. 5	610–560–1,170	1,063
John Bucyk	Boston	Nov. 9/72	1,144	(G)	Det. 3	at Bos. 8	556–813–1,369	1,540
Frank Mahovlich	Montreal	Feb. 13/73	1,090	(A)	Phi. 7	at Mtl. 6	533–570–1,103	1,181
Stan Mikita	Chicago	Nov. 3/73	986	(A)	Chi. 4	at Minn. 5	541–926–1,467	1,394
Henri Richard	Montreal	Dec. 20/73	1,194	(A)	Mtl. 2	at Buf. 2	358–688–1,046	1,256
Phil Esposito	Boston	Feb. 15/74	745	(A)	Bos. 4	at Van. 2	717–873–1,590	1,282
Rod Gilbert	NY Rangers	Feb. 19/77	1,027	(G)	NYR 2	at NYI 5	406–615–1,021	1,065
Jean Ratelle	Boston	Apr. 3/77	1,007	(A)	Tor. 4	at Bos. 7	491–776–1,267	1,281
Bobby Clarke	Philadelphia	Mar. 19/81	922	(G)	Phi. 5	at Bos. 3	358–852–1,210	1,144
*Marcel Dionne	Los Angeles	Jan. 7/81	740	(G)	L.A. 5	at Hfd. 3	731–1,040–1,771	1,348
*Guy Lafleur	Montreal	March 4/81	720	(G)	Mtl. 9	at Wpg. 3	536–755–1,291	1,028
Gilbert Perreault	Buffalo	Apr. 3/82	871	(A)	Buf. 5	at Mtl. 4	512–814–1,326	1,191
Darryl Sittler	Philadelphia	Jan. 20/83	927	(A)	Cgy 2	at Phi. 5	484–637–1,121	1,096
*Wayne Gretzky	Edmonton	Dec. 19/84	424	(A)	L.A. 3	at Edm. 7	637–1,200–1,837	774
*Bryan Trottier	NY Islanders	Jan. 29/85	726	(G)	Min. 4	at NYI 4	487–842–1,329	1,064
Mike Bossy	NY Islanders	Jan. 24/86	656	(A)	NYI 7	at Tor. 5	573–553–1,126	752
Denis Potvin	NY Islanders	Apr. 4/87	987	(A)	Buf. 6	at NYI 6	310–742–1,052	1,060
*Bernie Federko	St. Louis	Mar. 19/88	855	(A)	Hfd. 5	at St.L. 3	352–721–1,073	927
*Lanny McDonald	Calgary	Mar. 7/89	1,101	(G)	Wpg. 5	at Cgy. 9	500–506–1,006	1,111

* Active

100-Point Seasons

Player	Team	Date of 100th Point	G or A	Score	Player's Game No.	Team Game No.	Points G - A — PTS	Total Games	Age when first 100th point scored (Yrs. & Mos.)
Phil Esposito	Bos.	2-3-69	(G)	Pit. 0 at Bos. 4	60	62	49-77 — 126	74	27.1
Bobby Hull	Chi.	20-3-69	(G)	Chi. 5 at Bos. 5	71	71	58-49 — 107	76	30.2
Gordie Howe	Det.	30-3-69	(G)	Det. 5 at Chi. 9	76	76	44-59 — 103	76	41.0
Bobby Orr	Bos.	15-3-70	(G)	Det. 5 at Bos. 5	67	67	33-87 — 120	76	22.11
Phil Esposito	Bos.	6-2-71	(A)	Buf. 3 at Bos. 4	51	51	76-76 — 152	78	
Bobby Orr	Bos.	22-2-71	(A)	Bos. 4 at L.A. 5	58	58	37-102 — 139	78	
John Bucyk	Bos.	13-3-71	(A)	Bos. 6 at Van. 3	68	68	51-65 — 116	78	35.10
Ken Hodge	Bos.	21-3-71	(A)	Buf. 7 at Bos. 5	72	72	43-62 — 105	78	26.9
Jean Ratelle	NYR	18-2-72	(A)	NYR 2 at Cal. 2	58	58	46-63 — 109	63	31.4
Phil Esposito	Bos.	19-2-72	(A)	Bos. 6 at Min. 4	59	59	66-67 — 133	76	
Bobby Orr	Bos.	2-3-72	(A)	Van. 3 at Bos. 7	64	64	37-80 — 117	76	
Vic Hadfield	NYR	25-3-72	(A)	NYR 3 at Mtl. 3	74	74	50-56 — 106	78	31.5
Phil Esposito	Bos.	3-3-73	(A)	Bos. 1 at Mtl. 5	64	64	55-75 — 130	78	
Bobby Clarke	Phi.	29-3-73	(G)	Atl. 2 at Phi. 4	76	76	37-67 — 104	78	23.7
Bobby Orr	Bos.	31-3-73	(G)	Bos. 3 at Tor. 7	62	77	29-72 — 101	63	
Rick MacLeish	Phi.	1-4-73	(G)	Phi. 4 at Pit. 5	78	78	50-50 — 100	78	23.3
Phil Esposito	Bos.	13-2-74	(A)	Bos. 9 at Cal. 6	53	53	68-77 — 145	78	
Bobby Orr	Bos.	12-3-74	(A)	Buf. 0 at Bos. 4	62	66	32-90 — 122	74	
Ken Hodge	Bos.	24-3-74	(A)	Mtl. 3 at Bos. 6	72	72	50-55 — 105	76	
Phil Esposito	Bos.	8-2-75	(A)	Bos. 8 at Det. 5	54	54	61-66 — 127	79	
Bobby Orr	Bos.	13-2-75	(A)	Bos. 1 at Buf. 3	57	57	46-89 — 135	80	
Guy Lafleur	Mtl.	7-3-75	(G)	Wsh. 4 at Mtl. 8	56	66	53-66 — 119	70	24.6
Pete Mahovlich	Mtl.	9-3-75	(G)	Mtl. 5 at NYR 3	67	67	35-82 — 117	80	29.5
Marcel Dionne	Det.	9-3-75	(A)	Det. 5 at Phi. 8	67	67	47-74 — 121	80	23.7
Bobby Clarke	Phi.	22-3-75	(A)	Min. 0 at Phi. 4	72	72	27-89 — 116	80	
René Robert	Buf.	5-4-75	(A)	Buf. 4 at Tor. 2	74	80	40-60 — 100	74	26.4
Guy Lafleur	Mtl.	10-3-76	(G)	Mtl. 5 at Chi. 1	69	69	56-69 — 125	80	
Bobby Clarke	Phi.	11-3-76	(A)	Buf. 1 at Phi. 6	64	68	30-89 — 119	76	
Bill Barber	Phi.	18-3-76	(A)	Van. 2 at Phi. 3	71	71	50-62 — 112	80	23.8
Gilbert Perreault	Buf.	21-3-76	(A)	K.C. 1 at Buf. 3	73	73	44-69 — 113	80	25.4
Pierre Larouche	Pit.	24-3-76	(G)	Bos. 5 at Pit. 5	70	74	53-58 — 111	76	20.4
Pete Mahovlich	Mtl.	28-3-76	(A)	Mtl. 2 at Bos. 2	77	77	34-71 — 105	80	
Jean Ratelle	Bos.	30-3-76	(G)	Buf. 4 at Bos. 4	77	77	36-69 — 105	80	
Jean Pronovost	Pit.	3-4-76	(A)	Wsh. 5 at Pit. 4	79	79	52-52 — 104	80	30.4
Darryl Sittler	Tor.	3-4-76	(A)	Bos. 4 at Tor. 2	78	79	41-59 — 100	79	26.7
Guy Lafleur	Mtl.	26-2-77	(A)	Clev. 3 at Mtl. 5	63	63	56-80 — 136	80	
Marcel Dionne	L.A.	5-3-77	(G)	Pit. 3 at L.A. 3	67	67	53-69 — 122	80	
Steve Shutt	Mtl.	27-3-77	(A)	Mtl. 6 at Det. 0	77	77	60-45 — 105	80	24.9
Bryan Trottier	NYI	25-2-78	(A)	Chi. 1 at NYI 7	59	60	46-77 — 123	77	21.7
Guy Lafleur	Mtl.	28-2-78	(G)	Det. 3 at Mtl. 9	59	61	60-72 — 132	78	
Darryl Sittler	Tor.	12-3-78	(A)	Tor. 7 at Pit. 1	67	67	45-72 — 117	80	
Guy Lafleur	Mtl.	27-2-79	(A)	Mtl. 3 at NYI 7	61	61	52-77 — 129	80	
Bryan Trottier	NYI	6-3-79	(A)	Buf. 3 at NYI 2	59	63	47-87 — 134	76	
Marcel Dionne	L.A.	8-3-79	(G)	L.A. 4 at Buf. 6	66	66	59-71 — 130	80	
Mike Bossy	NYI	11-3-79	(G)	NYI 4 at Bos. 4	66	66	69-57 — 126	80	22.2
Bob MacMillan	Atl.	15-3-79	(A)	Atl. 4 at Phi. 5	68	69	37-71 — 108	79	26.6
Guy Chouinard	Atl.	30-3-79	(G)	L.A. 3 at Atl. 5	75	75	50-57 — 107	80	22.5
Denis Potvin	NYI	8-4-79	(A)	NYI 5 at NYR 2	73	80	31-70 — 101	73	25.5
Marcel Dionne	L.A.	6-2-80	(A)	L.A. 3 at Hfd. 7	53	53	53-84 — 137	80	
Guy Lafleur	Mtl.	10-2-80	(A)	Mtl. 3 at Bos. 2	55	55	50-75 — 125	74	
Wayne Gretzky	Edm.	24-2-80	(A)	Bos. 4 at Edm. 2	61	62	51-86 — 137	79	19.2
Bryan Trottier	NYI	30-3-80	(A)	NYI 9 at Que. 6	75	77	42-62 — 104	78	
Gilbert Perreault	Buf.	1-4-80	(A)	Buf. 5 at Atl. 2	77	77	40-66 — 106	80	
Mike Rogers	Hfd.	4-4-80	(A)	Que. 2 at Hfd. 9	79	79	44-61 — 105	80	25.5
Charlie Simmer	L.A.	5-4-80	(G)	Van. 5 at L.A. 3	64	80	56-45 — 101	64	26.0
Blaine Stoughton	Hfd.	6-4-80	(A)	Det. 3 at Hfd. 5	80	80	56-44 — 100	80	27.0
Wayne Gretzky	Edm.	6-2-81	(G)	Wpg. 4 at Edm. 10	53	53	55-109 — 164	80	
Marcel Dionne	L.A.	12-2-81	(A)	L.A. 5 at Chi. 5	58	58	58-77 — 135	80	
Charlie Simmer	L.A.	14-2-81	(A)	Bos. 5 at L.A. 4	59	59	56-49 — 105	65	
Kent Nilsson	Cgy.	27-2-81	(G)	Hfd. 1 at Cgy. 5	64	64	49-82 — 131	80	24.6
Mike Bossy	NYI	3-3-81	(G)	Edm. 8 at NYI 8	65	66	68-51 — 119	79	
Dave Taylor	L.A.	14-3-81	(G)	Min. 4 at L.A. 10	63	70	47-65 — 112	72	25.3
Mike Rogers	Hfd.	22-3-81	(G)	Tor. 3 at Hfd. 3	74	74	40-65 — 105	80	
Bernie Federko	St.L.	28-3-81	(A)	Buf. 4 at St.L. 7	74	76	31-73 — 104	78	24.10
Rick Middleton	Bos.	28-3-81	(A)	Chi. 2 at Bos. 5	76	76	44-59 — 103	80	27.4
Jacques Richard	Que.	29-3-81	(G)	Mtl. 0 at Que. 4	75	76	52-51 — 103	78	28.6
Bryan Trottier	NYI	29-3-81	(G)	NYI 5 at Wsh. 4	69	76	31-72 — 103	73	
Peter Stastny	Que.	29-3-81	(A)	Mtl. 0 at Que. 4	73	76	39-70 — 109	77	24.6
Wayne Gretzky	Edm.	27-12-81	(G)	L.A. 3 at Edm. 10	38	38	92-120 — 212	80	
Mike Bossy	NYI	13-2-82	(A)	Phi. 2 at NYI 8	55	55	64-83 — 147	80	
Peter Stastny	Que.	16-2-82	(A)	Wpg. 3 at Que. 7	60	60	46-93 — 139	80	25.5
Dennis Maruk	Wsh.	20-2-82	(G)	Wsh. 3 at Min. 7	60	60	60-76 — 136	80	26.3
Bryan Trottier	NYI	23-2-82	(A)	Chi. 1 at NYI 5	61	61	50-79 — 129	80	
Denis Savard	Chi.	27-2-82	(A)	Chi. 5 at L.A. 3	64	64	32-87 — 119	80	21.1
Bobby Smith	Min.	3-3-82	(A)	Det. 4 at Min. 6	66	66	43-71 — 114	80	24.1
Marcel Dionne	L.A.	6-3-82	(A)	L.A. 6 at Hfd. 7	64	66	50-67 — 117	78	
Dave Taylor	L.A.	20-3-82	(A)	Pit. 5 at L.A. 7	71	72	39-67 — 106	78	
Dale Hawerchuk	Wpg.	24-3-82	(G)	L.A. 3 at Wpg. 5	74	74	45-58 — 103	80	18.11
Dino Ciccarelli	Min.	27-3-82	(A)	Min. 6 at Bos. 5	72	76	55-52 — 107	76	21.8
Glenn Anderson	Edm.	28-3-82	(G)	Edm. 6 at L.A. 2	78	78	38-67 — 105	80	21.7
Mike Rogers	NYR	2-4-82	(G)	Pit. 7 at NYR 5	79	79	38-65 — 103	80	

Charlie Simmer

Jean Ratelle

Jean Pronovost

John Tonelli

Glenn Anderson

Jimmy Carson

100-Point Seasons continued

Player	Team	Date of 100th Point	G or A	Score		Player's Game No.	Team Game No.	Points G-A PTS	Total Games	Age when first 100th point scored (Yrs. & Mos.)
Wayne Gretzky	Edm.	5-1-83	(A)	Edm. 8	at Wpg. 3	42	42	71-125 - 196	80	
Mike Bossy	NYI	3-3-83	(A)	Tor. 1	at NYI. 5	66	67	60-58 — 118	79	
Peter Stastny	Que.	5-3-83	(A)	Hfd. 3	at Que. 10	62	67	47-77 — 124	75	
Denis Savard	Chi.	6-3-83	(G)	Mtl. 4	at Chi. 5	65	67	35-86 — 121	78	
Mark Messier	Edm.	23-3-83	(G)	Edm. 4	at Wpg. 7	73	76	48-58 — 106	77	22.2
Barry Pederson	Bos.	26-3-83	(A)	Hfd. 4	at Bos. 7	73	76	46-61 — 107	77	22.0
Marcel Dionne	L.A.	26-3-83	(A)	Edm. 9	at L.A. 3	75	75	56-51 — 107	80	
Michel Goulet	Que.	27-3-83	(A)	Que. 6	at Buf. 6	77	77	57-48 — 105	80	22.11
Glenn Anderson	Edm.	29-3-83	(A)	Edm. 7	at Van. 4	70	78	48-56 — 104	72	
Jari Kurri	Edm.	29-3-83	(A)	Edm. 7	at Van. 4	78	78	45-59 — 104	80	22.10
Kent Nilsson	Cgy.	29-3-83	(G)	L.A. 3	at Cgy. 5	78	78	46-58 — 104	80	
Wayne Gretzky	Edm.	18-12-83	(G)	Edm. 7	at Wpg. 5	34	34	87-118 — 205	74	
Paul Coffey	Edm.	4-3-84	(A)	Mtl. 1	at Edm. 6	68	68	40-86 — 126	80	22.9
Michel Goulet	Que.	4-3-84	(A)	Que. 1	at Buf. 1	62	67	56-65 — 121	75	
Jari Kurri	Edm.	7-3-84	(A)	Chi. 4	at Edm. 7	53	69	52-61 — 113	64	
Peter Stastny	Que.	8-3-84	(A)	Que. 8	at Pit. 6	69	69	46-73 — 119	80	
Mike Bossy	NYI	8-3-84	(G)	Tor. 5	at NYI 9	56	68	51-67 — 118	67	
Barry Pederson	Bos.	14-3-84	(A)	Bos. 4	at Det. 2	71	71	39-77 — 116	80	
Bryan Trottier	NYI	18-3-84	(G)	NYI 4	at Hfd. 5	62	73	40-71 — 111	68	
Bernie Federko	St.l.	20-3-84	(A)	Wpg. 3	at St.L. 9	75	76	41-66 — 107	79	
Rick Middleton	Bos.	27-3-84	(A)	Bos. 6	at Que. 4	77	77	47-58 — 105	80	
Dale Hawerchuk	Wpg.	27-3-84	(G)	Wpg. 3	at L.A. 3	77	77	37-65 — 102	80	
Mark Messier	Edm.	27-3-84	(G)	Edm. 9	at Cgy. 2	72	79	37-64 — 101	73	
Wayne Gretzky	Edm.	29-12-84	(A)	Det. 3	at Edm. 6	35	35	73-135 — 208	80	
Jari Kurri	Edm.	29-1-85	(A)	Edm. 4	at Cgy. 2	48	51	71-64 — 135	73	
Mike Bossy	NYI	23-2-85	(G)	Bos. 1	at NYI 7	56	60	58-59 — 117	76	
Dale Hawerchuk	Wpg.	25-2-85	(A)	Wpg. 12	at NYR 5	64	64	53-77 — 130	80	
Marcel Dionne	L.A.	5-3-85	(A)	Pit. 0	at L.A. 6	66	66	46-80 — 126	80	
Brent Sutter	NYI	12-3-85	(A)	NYI 6	at St. L. 5	68	68	42-60 — 102	72	22.10
John Ogrodnick	Det.	22-3-85	(A)	NYR 3	at Det. 5	73	73	55-50 — 105	79	25.9
Paul Coffey	Edm.	26-3-85	(G)	Edm. 7	at NYI 5	74	74	37-84 — 121	80	
Denis Savard	Chi.	29-3-85	(A)	Chi. 5	at Wpg. 5	75	76	38-67 — 105	79	
Peter Stastny	Que.	2-4-85	(A)	Bos. 4	at Que. 6	74	77	32-68 — 100	75	
Bernie Federko	St.L.	4-4-85	(A)	NYR 5	at St.L. 4	74	78	30-73 — 103	76	
John Tonelli	NYI	6-4-85	(G)	NJ 5	at NYI 5	80	80	42-58 — 100	80	28.1
Paul MacLean	Wpg.	6-4-85	(A)	Wpg. 6	at Edm. 5	78	79	41-60 — 101	79	27.1
Mike Gartner	Wsh.	7-4-85	(G)	Pit. 3	at Wsh. 7	80	80	50-52 — 102	80	25.6
Bernie Nicholls	L.A.	6-4-85	(A)	Van. 4	at L.A. 4	80	80	46-54 — 100	80	22.9
Mario Lemieux	Pit.	7-4-85	(G)	Pit. 3	at Wsh. 7	73	80	43-57 — 100	73	19.6
Wayne Gretzky	Edm.	4-1-86	(A)	Hfd. 3	at Edm. 4	39	39	52-163 — 215	80	
Mario Lemieux	Pit.	15-2-86	(A)	Van. 4	at Pit. 9	55	56	48-93 — 141	79	
Paul Coffey	Edm.	19-2-86	(A)	Tor. 5	at Edm. 9	59	60	48-90 — 138	79	
Jari Kurri	Edm.	2-3-86	(G)	Phi. 1	at Edm. 2	62	64	68-63 — 131	78	
Peter Stastny	Que.	1-3-86	(A)	Buf. 8	at Que. 4	66	68	41-81 — 122	76	
Mike Bossy	NYI	8-3-86	(G)	Wsh. 6	at NYI 2	65	65	61-62 — 123	80	
Denis Savard	Chi.	12-3-86	(A)	Buf. 7	at Chi. 6	69	69	47-69 — 116	80	
Mats Naslund	Mtl.	13-3-86	(A)	Mtl. 2	at Bos. 3	70	70	43-67 — 110	80	26.4
Michel Goulet	Que.	24-3-86	(A)	Que. 1	at Min. 0	70	75	53-50 — 103	75	
Glenn Anderson	Edm.	25-3-86	(G)	Edm. 7	at Det. 2	66	74	54-48 — 102	72	
Neal Broten	Min.	26-3-86	(A)	Min. 6	at Tor. 1	76	76	29-76 — 105	80	26.4
Dale Hawerchuk	Wpg.	31-3-86	(A)	Wpg. 5	at L.A. 2	78	78	46-59 — 105	80	
Bernie Federko	St.L.	5-4-86	(G)	Chi. 5	at St.L. 7	79	79	34-68 — 102	80	
Wayne Gretzky	Edm.	1-11-87	(A)	Cgy. 3	at Edm. 5	42	42	62-121 — 183	79	
Jari Kurri	Edm.	3-14-87	(A)	Buf. 3	at Edm. 5	67	68	54-54 — 108	79	
Mario Lemieux	Pit.	3-18-87	(A)	St.L. 4	at Pit. 5	55	72	54-53 — 107	63	
Mark Messier	Edm.	3-19-87	(A)	Edm. 4	at Cgy. 5	71	71	37-70 — 107	77	
Doug Gilmour	St.L.	4-2-87	(A)	Buf. 3	at St.L. 5	78	78	42-63 — 105	80	23.10
Dino Ciccarelli	Min.	3-30-87	(A)	NYR 6	at Min. 5	78	78	52-51 — 103	80	
Dale Hawerchuk	Wpg.	4-5-87	(A)	Wpg. 3	at Cgy. 1	80	80	47-53 — 100	80	
Mario Lemieux	Pit.	20-1-88	(G)	Plt. 8	at Chi. 3	45	48	70-98 — 168	77	
Wayne Gretzky	Edm.	11-2-88	(A)	Edm. 7	at Van. 2	43	56	40-109 — 149	64	
Denis Savard	Chi.	12-2-88	(A)	St.L. 3	at Chi. 4	57	57	44-87 — 131	80	
Dale Hawerchuk	Wpg.	23-2-88	(G)	Wpg. 4	at Pit. 3	61	61	44-77 — 121	80	
Steve Yzerman	Det.	27-2-88	(A)	Det. 4	at Que. 5	63	63	50-52 — 102	64	22.10
Peter Stastny	Que.	8-3-88	(A)	Hfd. 4	at Que. 6	63	67	46-65 — 111	76	
Mark Messier	Edm.	15-3-88	(A)	Buf. 4	at Edm. 6	68	71	37-74 — 111	77	
Jimmy Carson	L.A.	26-3-88	(A)	Chi. 5	at L.A. 9	77	77	55-52 — 107	80	19.8
Hakan Loob	Cgy.	26-3-88	(A)	Van. 1	at Cgy. 6	76	76	50-56 — 106	80	27.9
Mike Bullard	Cgy.	26-3-88	(A)	Van. 1	at Cgy. 6	76	76	48-55 — 103	79	27.1
Michel Goulet	Que.	27-3-88	(A)	Pit. 6	at Que. 3	76	76	48-58 — 106	80	
Luc Robitaille	L.A.	30-3-88	(G)	Cgy. 7	at L.A. 9	78	78	53-58 — 111	80	22.1
Mario Lemieux	Pit.	31-12-88	(A)	N.J. 6	at Pit. 8	36	38	85-114-199	76	
Wayne Gretzky	L.A.	21-1-89	(A)	L.A. 4	at Hfd. 5	47	48	54-114-168	78	
Steve Yzerman	Det.	27-1-89	(G)	Tor. 1	at Det. 5	50	50	65-90-155	80	
Bernie Nicholls	L.A.	21-1-89	(A)	L.A. 4	at Hfd. 5	48	48	70-80-150	79	
Rob Brown	Pit.	16-3-89	(A)	Pit. 2	at N.J. 1	60	72	49-66-115	68	20.11
Paul Coffey	Pit.	20-3-89	(A)	Pit. 2	at Min. 7	69	74	30-83-113	75	
Joe Mullen	Cgy.	23-3-89	(A)	L.A. 2	at Cgy. 4	74	75	51-59-110	79	32.1
Jari Kurri	Edm.	29-3-89	(A)	Edm. 5	at Van. 2	75	79	44-58-102	76	
Jimmy Carson	Edm.	2-4-89	(A)	Edm. 2	at Cgy. 4	80	80	49-51-100	80	

Individual Awards

Hart Memorial Trophy

Art Ross Trophy

Calder Memorial Trophy

James Norris Memorial Trophy

HART MEMORIAL TROPHY

An annual award "to the player adjudged to be the most valuable to his team". Winner selected in poll by Professional Hockey Writers' Association in the 21 NHL cities at the end of the regular schedule. The winner receives $3,000 and the runner-up $1,000.

History: The Hart Memorial Trophy was presented by the National Hockey League in 1960 after the original Hart Trophy was retired to the Hockey Hall of Fame. The original Hart Trophy was donated to the NHL in 1923 by Dr. David A. Hart, father of Cecil Hart, former manager-coach of the Montreal Canadiens.

1988-89 Winner: Wayne Gretzky, Los Angeles Kings
Runners-up: Mario Lemieux, Pittsburgh Penguins
Steve Yzerman, Detroit Red Wings

Los Angeles Kings center Wayne Gretzky became the first player in League history to win the same award nine times by capturing the Hart Memorial Trophy, awarded to "the player adjudged to be the most valuable to his team".

Gretzky amassed 267 of a maximum 315 points, including 40 of 63 first-place votes, to outdistance Penguins' center Mario Lemieux and Red Wings' center Steve Yzerman, who finished with 187 and 109 points, respectively. Gretzky was the only player to be named on all 63 Hart Trophy ballots.

During the 1988-89 regular season, Gretzky ranked second in scoring with 168 points (54-114-168). At season's end, he ranked fourth on the NHL's all-time goal scoring list with 637, first in career assists with 1,200 and only 13 points shy of Gordie Howe's all-time points record with 1,837 in ten seasons. Gretzky led the Kings to their best season since 1980-81 as they posted 91 points (a 23-point improvement over 1987-88) and a fourth-place overall finish.

ART ROSS TROPHY

An annual award "to the player who leads the league in scoring points at the end of the regular season." Overall winner receives $3,000 and the overall runner-up $1,000.

History: Arthur Howie Ross, former manager-coach of Boston Bruins, presented the trophy to the National Hockey League in 1947. If two players finish the schedule with the same number of points, the trophy is awarded in the following manner: 1. Player with most goals. 2. Player with fewer games played. 3. Player scoring first goal of the season.

1988-89 Winner: Mario Lemieux, Pittsburgh Penguins
Runners-up: Wayne Gretzky, Los Angeles Kings
Steve Yzerman, Detroit Red Wings

Mario Lemieux won his second consecutive Art Ross Trophy as the NHL's regular-season scoring champion. His 85 goals and 114 assists gave him 199 points in 76 games played. Lemieux became only the second player in League history, joining Wayne Gretzky, to score more than 70 goals in a season twice. In addition to establishing a League record for shorthand goals in a season (13), he was named the Dodge/NHL Performer of the Week five times and Dodge Performer of the Month three times.

CALDER MEMORIAL TROPHY

An annual award "to the player selected as the most proficient in his first year of competition in the National Hockey League". Winner selected in poll by Professional Hockey Writers' Association at the end of the regular schedule. The winner receives $3,000 and the runner-up $1,000.

History: From 1936-37 until his death in 1943, Frank Calder, NHL President, bought a trophy each year to be given permanently to the outstanding rookie. After Calder's death, the NHL presented the Calder Memorial Trophy in his memory and the trophy is to be kept in perpetuity. To be eligible for the award, a player cannot have played more than 25 games in any single preceding season nor in six or more games in each of any two preceding seasons in any major professional league.

1988-89 Winner: Brian Leetch, New York Rangers
Runners-up: Trevor Linden, Vancouver Canucks
Tony Granato, New York Rangers

New York Rangers' defenseman Brian Leetch, who received 268 of a possible 315 points, including 42 first-place votes, edged Canucks' center Trevor Linden (206) and Rangers' right wing Tony Granato (56) to capture the Calder Memorial Trophy awarded to the "player selected as the most proficient in his first season"

Leetch led all rookies in scoring in 1988-89 with 71 points (23-48-71) in 68 games. He ranked fifth among League defensemen in scoring and fell just five points shy of the NHL record for most points by a rookie defenseman set by Larry Murphy in 1980-81. The former NCAA All-American (1987) set a League record for most goals by a rookie defenseman (23) and also set club records for most goals, assists and points by a freshman defenseman.

JAMES NORRIS MEMORIAL TROPHY

An annual award "to the defense player who demonstrates throughout the season the greatest all-round ability in the position." Winner selected in poll by Professional Hockey Writers' Association at the end of the regular schedule. The winner receives $3,000 and the runner-up $1,000.

History: The James Norris Memorial Trophy was presented in 1953 by the four children of the late James Norris in memory of the former owner-president of the Detroit Red Wings.

1988-89 Winner: Chris Chelios, Montreal Canadiens
Runners-up: Paul Coffey, Pittsburgh Penguins
Al MacInnis, Calgary Flames

Chris Chelos of the Montreal Canadiens received 226 of a possible 315 points, including 37 first-place votes, to capture the James Norris Memorial Trophy as the defenseman demonstrating "the greatest all-around ability in the position". Two-time winner, Paul Coffey of Pittsburgh, finished second in the voting with 115 votes while the Flames' Al MacInnis finished third with 57 points.

Chelios became the first U.S.-born player to win the Norris Trophy since its inception in 1954. The 27-year-old native of Chicago finished third in team scoring with 73 points (15-58-73), while placing fourth among defensive scoring leaders. The Montreal Canadiens notched the best defensive record in the League, allowing only 218 goals. Chelios recorded eight power-play goals and six game-winners while recording a plus-minus rating of plus-35 through 80 games.

Vezina Trophy

Lady Byng Memorial Trophy

Frank J. Selke Trophy

Conn Smythe Trophy

VEZINA TROPHY

An annual award "to the goalkeeper adjudged to be the best at his position" as voted by the general managers of each of the 21 clubs. Over-all winner receives $3,000, runner-up $1,000.

History: Leo Dandurand, Louis Letourneau and Joe Cattarinich, former owners of the Montreal Canadiens, presented the trophy to the National Hockey League in 1926-27 in memory of Georges Vezina, outstanding goalkeeper of the Canadiens who collapsed during an NHL game November 28, 1925, and died of tuberculosis a few months later. Until the 1981-82 season, the goalkeeper(s) of the team allowing the fewest number of goals during the regular-season were awarded the Vezina Trophy.

1988-89 Winner: Patrick Roy, Montreal Canadiens
Runners-up: Mike Vernon, Calgary Flames
Kirk McLean, Vancouver Canucks

Montreal Canadiens' goaltender Patrick Roy received 87 of a potential 105 points, including 15 first-place votes, to capture his first Vezina Trophy, awarded annually to the "goaltender adjudged to be the best in his position". Mike Vernon of the Flames placed second with 54 points, while Kirk McLean of the Canucks was third with 17 points.

Roy led the League in save percentage (.908) and goals-against-average (2.47), while posting a 33-5-6 record. He did not lost a home game during the 1988-89 regular-season, posting a 25-0-4 record at the Forum and finishing the regular-season with a 17-game undefeated streak. Roy and teammate Brian Hayward have captured the Jennings Trophy for three consecutive seasons, allowing only 218 goals against in 1988-89.

LADY BYNG MEMORIAL TROPHY

An annual award "to the player adjudged to have exhibited the best type of sportsmanship and gentlemanly conduct combined with a high standard of playing ability." Winner selected in poll by Professional Hockey Writers' Association at the end of the regular schedule. The winner receives $3,000 and the runner-up $1,000.

History: Lady Byng, wife of Canada's Governor-General at the time, presented the Lady Byng Trophy in 1925. After Frank Boucher of New York Rangers won the award seven times in eight seasons, he was given the trophy to keep and Lady Byng donated another trophy in 1936. After Lady Byng's death in 1949, the National Hockey League presented a new trophy, changing the name to Lady Byng Memorial Trophy.

1988-89 Winner: Joe Mullen, Calgary Flames
Runners-up: Wayne Gretzky, Los Angeles Kings
Mats Naslund, Montreal Canadiens

Joe Mullen received 254 of a potential 315 votes to outdistance center Wayne Gretzky of the Los Angeles Kings (114 points) and the 1987-88 winner Mats Naslund of the Canadiens (59 points) to capture the Lady Byng Trophy, awarded to the player "who exhibits the best type of sportsmanship and gentlemanly conduct combined with a high standard of playing ability."

Mullen, who captured the Lady Byng Trophy in 1986-87 as well, enjoyed his finest season ever with 110 points (51-59-110) to lead the Flames in scoring. In 79 games, the native of New York registered a total of 16 penalty minutes. He recorded 13 power-play goals and seven game-winners in 1988-89, while leading the League in plus-minus with a plus-51 rating. In 568 career games, Mullen has accumulated only 116 minutes in penalties.

FRANK J. SELKE TROPHY

An annual award "to the forward who best excels in the defensive aspects of the game." Winner selected in poll by Professional Hockey Writers' Association at the end of the regular schedule. The winner receives $3,000 and the runner-up $1,000.

History: Presented to the National Hockey League in 1977 by the Board of Governors of the NHL in honour of Frank J. Selke, one of the great architects of NHL championship teams.

1988-89 Winner: Guy Carbonneau, Montreal Canadiens
Runners-up: Esa Tikkanen, Edmonton Oilers
Colin Patterson, Calgary Flames

Center Guy Carbonneau of the Canadiens amassed 222 of a potential 315 points, including 36 first-place votes, to capture his second consecutive Frank J. Selke Trophy, presented to the "forward who best excels at the defensive aspects of the game." Carbonneau outdistanced left wing Esa Tikkanen of the Oilers and right wing Colin Patterson of the Flames, each of whom finished with 73 points.

Carbonneau is only the second player to win the Selke Trophy more than once in his career, joining former teammate Bob Gainey, the winner from 1977-78 to 1980-81, in that respect. Carbonneau recorded 56 points (26-30-56) in 79 games this season, his second highest career point total. He led the Canadiens with two shorthanded goals and ten game-winning goals and posted a plus-minus rating of plus-37. The Canadiens allowed the fewest goals (218) and the fewest power-play goals (58) during the season.

CONN SMYTHE TROPHY

An annual award "to the most valuable player for his team in the playoffs." Winner selected by the Professional Hockey Writers' Association at the conclusion of the final game in the Stanley Cup Finals. The winner receives $3,000.

History: Presented by Maple Leaf Gardens Limited in 1964 to honor Conn Smythe, the former coach, manager, president and owner-governor of the Toronto Maple Leafs.

1988-89 Winner: Al MacInnis, Calgary Flames

Al MacInnis became the first defenseman since 1978 (Larry Robinson) to capture the Conn Smythe Trophy. He led his team to series victories over the Vancouver Canucks, Los Angeles Kings, Chicago Blackhawks and Montreal Canadiens en route to Calgary's first Stanley Cup in club history.

Leading all playoff scorers with 31 points, MacInnis established a record for defensemen by scoring points in 17 consecutive playoff games, totalling seven goals and 19 assists from April 13 to May 25. The streak ties him with Wayne Gretzky for second place all-time behind Bryan Trottier (18 games). He became the first defenseman ever to lead post-season scoring, his 24 assists ranking second among all defensemen for assists in one playoff year, just one shy of Paul Coffey's record of 25 (1985).

William M. Jennings
Trophy

Jack Adams
Award

Bill Masterton
Trophy

Lester Patrick
Trophy

WILLIAM M. JENNINGS TROPHY

An annual award "to the goalkeeper(s) having played a minimum of 25 games for the team with the fewest goals scored against it." Winners selected on regular-season play. Overall winner receives $3,000, runner-up $1,000. Leader at end of first half of season and leader in second half each receive $250.

History: The Jennings Trophy was presented in 1981-82 by the National Hockey League's Board of Governors to honor the late William M. Jennings, longtime governor and president of the New York Rangers and one of the great builders of hockey in the United States.

**1988-89 Winners: Brian Hayward and Patrick Roy, Montreal Canadiens
Runners-up: Mike Vernon and Rick Wamsley, Calgary Flames**

Combining for a League-leading 2.70 goals-against-average, Hayward and Roy captured their third consecutive Jennings Trophy. Together they backstopped the Canadiens to the best defensive record, allowing only 218 goals.

Roy led the League in goals-against-average (2.47) and save percentage (.908) while posting a 33-5-6 record. Hayward placed fourth in the League with a 2.90 average and registered a 20-13-3 record.

JACK ADAMS AWARD

An annual award presented by the National Hockey League Broadcasters' Association to "the NHL coach adjudged to have contributed the most to his team's success." Winner selected by poll among members of the NHL Broadcasters' Association at the end of the regular season. The winner receives $1,000 from the NHLBA.

History: The award was presented by the NHL Broadcasters' Association in 1974 to commemorate the late Jack Adams, coach and general manager of Detroit Red Wings, whose lifetime dedication to hockey serves as an inspiration to all who aspire to further the game.

**1988-89 Winner: Pat Burns, Montreal Canadiens
Runners-up: Bob McCammon, Vancouver Canucks
Terry Crisp, Calgary Flames**

Pat Burns, head coach of the Canadiens, became only the third rookie coach (Pat Quinn, 1980: Mike Keenan, 1985) in NHL history to capture the Jack Adams Trophy awarded to the "NHL coach adjudged to have contributed the most to his team's success". Burns outdistanced Bob McCammon of the Canucks and Terry Crisp of the Flames to earn the award.

Burns led his club to its best regular-season finish since 1978-79 in his freshman season behind the bench. As the 17th head coach of the Canadiens, he posted a 53-18-9 record for 115 points and a second place overall finish behind the Flames.

BILL MASTERTON MEMORIAL TROPHY

An annual award under the trusteeship of the Professional Hockey Writers' Association to "the National Hockey League player who best exemplifies the qualities of perseverance, sportsmanship and dedication to hockey." Winner selected by poll among the 21 chapters of the PHWA at the end of the regular season. A $2,500 grant from the PHWA is awarded annually to the Bill Masterton Scholarship Fund, based in Bloomington, MN, in the name of the Masterton Trophy winner.

History: The trophy was presented by the NHL Writers' Association in 1968 to commemorate the late William Masterton, a player of the Minnesota North Stars, who exhibited to a high degree the qualities of perseverance, sportsmanship and dedication to hockey, and who died January 15, 1968.

1988-89 Winner: Tim Kerr, Philadelphia Flyers

Fifth on the Flyers' all-time regular-season scoring list, with 329 goals and 249 assists for 578 points in 533 games, Kerr posted four consecutive 50-goal seasons from 1983-84 through 1986-87 to become only the seventh player in League history to accomplish the feat. Kerr becomes the second Flyer to win the Masterton Trophy, along with Bob Clarke in 1972. After playing in only eight games during the 1987-88 season due to a severe shoulder injury, Kerr returned in 1988-89 to lead his team in points (88) and goals (48). In addition, Kerr led his team in many offensive categories during post-season play, including: points (25, 2nd in the NHL), goals (14, 2nd in the NHL) and power-play goals (8, first in the NHL and one goal shy of a League record).

LESTER PATRICK TROPHY

An annual award "for outstanding service to hockey in the United States." Eligible recipients are players, officials, coaches, executives and referees. Winner selected by an award committee consisting of the President of the NHL, an NHL Governor, a representative of the New York Rangers, a member of the Hockey Hall of Fame Builder's section, a member of the Hockey Hall of Fame Player's section, a member of the U.S. Hockey Hall of Fame, a member of the NHL Broadcasters' Association and a member of the Professional Hockey Writers' Association. Each except the League President is rotated annually. The winner receives a miniature of the trophy.

History: Presented by the New York Rangers in 1966 to honor the late Lester Patrick, longtime general manager and coach of the New York Rangers, whose teams finished out of the playoffs only once in his first 16 years with the club.

1988-89 Winners: Dan Kelly, Lou Nanne, Bud Poile and Lynn Patrick.

The late Dan Kelly began his broadcasting career at the age of 19, calling hockey action as well as football and baseball at CJET Radio in Smiths Falls, Ontario. He became the sports director at CKSO Radio in 1958-59 in Sudbury where he was the voice of the Sudbury Wolves. He joined CBC-TV in 1959 and worked hockey and Canadian football, before joining Hockey Night in Canada in 1965-66. Two years later, Kelly moved to St. Louis and became the voice of the Blues. Kelly had done extensive national television work during the past two decades, including: NHL/CBS Game of the Week (1969-72), NHL-TV Network Game (1977-79), USA Cable Network (1981-85) and ESPN Cable (1985-87).

Lou Nanne has been an integral part of Minnesota hockey for more than 25 years. He attended the University of Minnesota, and was the only defenseman to win the WCHA scoring title. A naturalized U.S. citizen, he captained the U.S. Olympic Hockey Team in 1968. He then spent ten seasons as a player with the Minnesota North Stars, appearing at right wing and defense. On February 10, 1978, Nanne was appointed coach and general manager of the North Stars. He built a team that advanced to the Stanley Cup Finals in 1981. During the past year, Nanne relinquished his general manager duties to concentrate on his role as President of the North Stars. He also has been active at the League level, serving on the Marketing and Public Relations Committee as well as being a former chairman of the General Managers Committee.

Born in Fort William, Ontario in 1924, Bud Poile has been involved with professional hockey since 1942. After a seven-year NHL career as a player, Poile began his management career by serving as player-coach of Tulsa of the United States Hockey League in 1950. In 1952, he began a 10-year coaching stint with the Edmonton Flyers of the Western Hockey League before becoming general manager of San Francisco's WHL franchise for four years. Poile was named the Philadelphia Flyers' first general manager in 1967 and was appointed to a similar post with the Vancouver Canucks in 1970. Poile became executive vice-president of the World Hockey Association in 1974, and two years later became president of the Central Hockey League, a position he held until 1983. He has been President of the International Hockey League since 1984, a post from which he retired following the 1988-89 season.

The late Lynn Patrick, a member of the 1939-40 Stanley Cup Champion New York Rangers, played 10 NHL seasons (he retired in 1946) for the Rangers, twice leading the team in scoring. His front office involvement began when he became general manager and coach of the New Haven Ramblers of the American Hockey League. He returned to the NHL as the Rangers' head coach during the 1948-49 season and, the following year, led the team to the Stanley Cup Finals before losing in seven games to Detroit. In 1950 he became coach of the Boston Bruins and spent a total of 10 seasons in the Bruins' front office. Patrick was named general manager of the expansion St. Louis Blues in 1966, and led the Blues to the Stanley Cup Finals in each of their first three seasons. He remained with the Blues until 1977 and was elected to the Hockey Hall of Fame in 1980.

King Clancy Memorial Trophy

Lester B. Pearson Award

Budweiser/NHL Man of The Year

Trico Goaltender Award

Presidents' Trophy

KING CLANCY MEMORIAL TROPHY

An annual award "to the player who best exemplifies leadership qualities on and off the ice and has made a noteworthy humanitarian contribution in his community". The winner receives $3,000 and the runner-up $1,000.

History: The King Clancy Memorial Trophy was presented to the National Hockey League by the Board of Governors in 1988 to honor the late Frank "King" Clancy.

1988-89 Winner: Bryan Trottier, New York Islanders
Runners-up: Kevin Lowe, Edmonton Oilers
Ryan Walter, Montreal Canadiens

Bryan Trottier of the New York Islanders became the second recipient of the King Clancy Memorial Trophy, awarded "to the player who best exemplifies leadership qualities on and off the ice and has made a noteworthy humanitarian contribution in his community."

Trottier, in his 14 seasons with the Islanders, has established himself as their all-time leader in games played, assists and total points. In addition to serving as the alternate captain of the Islanders, he was selected by his peers to represent them as the President of the National Hockey League Players' Association. Off the ice, Trottier is actively involved in the Long Island community. He works closely with Special Olympics, the Easter Seals Society, Big Brothers/Sisters, Foster Grandparents, the Make-A-Wish Foundation, the Long Island "Just Say No To Drugs" campaign, Athletes Helping Athletes and a national campaign to promote reading. He owns and operates the Bryan Trottier Skating Academy in Port Washington, Long Island where he is the head instructor during the off-season.

LESTER B. PEARSON AWARD

An annual award presented to the NHL's outstanding player as selected by the members of the National Hockey League Players' Association. The winner receives $3,000 and the runner-up $1,500.

History: The award was presented in 1970-71 by the NHLPA in honor of the late Lester B. Pearson, former Prime Minister of Canada.

1988-89 Winner: Steve Yzerman, Detroit Red Wings

Yzerman finished the regular-season with a career high 155 points (65-90-155) leading his team to its second consecutive Norris Division regular-season title. He ranked third among League scorers in goals, assists and points and was first in shots (388). He became only the fourth player in League history to have recorded 150-or-more points in a season, joining Wayne Gretzky, Mario Lemieux and Phil Esposito. Yzerman recorded the season's longest point-scoring streak, posting 65 points (29-36-65) in 28 games from November 1 to January 4. He registered at least one point in 70 of his 80 games played and recorded his 500th NHL point in his 400th NHL game on January 15.

NHL AWARD MONEY BREAKDOWN

(All team awards are based on units of 21 per team except Presidents' Trophy which is based on 20 units.)

Stanley Cup Playoffs		Individual Shares	Total
Division Semi-Final Losers	(8 teams)	$ 3,000	$ 504,000
Division Final Losers	(4 teams)	6,000	504,000
Conference Championship Losers	(2 teams)	11,000	462,000
Stanley Cup Championship Losers		18,000	378,000
Stanley Cup Winners		25,000	525,000
TOTAL PLAYOFF AWARD MONEY			$2,373,000
Final Standings, Regular Season			
Presidents' Trophy (Team's share $100,000)		$5,000	$200,000
Division Winners	(4 teams)	5,000	420,000
Second Place	(4 teams)	2,500	210,000
TOTAL CHAMPIONSHIP POOL			$830,000
Individual Awards			
First Team All-Stars		$5,000	$30,000
Second Team All-Stars		2,000	12,000
All-Star Game winners' share		1,000	20,000
All-Star Game losers' share		750	15,000
Individual Award Winners		3,000	30,000
Individual Award Runners-up		1,000	10,000
TOTAL INDIVIDUAL AWARD MONEY			$117,000

BUDWEISER/NHL MAN OF THE YEAR

An annual award **to the player recognized in the local community as a positive role model through his conduct on and off the ice. This includes involvement with local youth groups, charities and causes, as well as recognition among his peers and fans as a player who extols sportsmanlike qualities while maximizing his efforts toward improving his play and that of the team.** The winner is selected by a special committee of distinguished NHL officials and management executives. The Bud/NHL Man of the Year recognizes one player from each of the local media representatives. Each nominated player receives a check for $1,000 to be given to his favorite charity. The winner receives $21,000 to be distributed to his favorite charities.

1988-89 Winner: Lanny McDonald, Calgary Flames
Runners-up: Kevin Lowe, Edmonton Oilers
Mike Gartner, Minnesota North Stars

Veteran right winger Lanny McDonald was named the recipient of the second Budweiser/NHL Man of the Year award (35 points), oudistancing Kevin Lowe of the Oilers and Mike Gartner of the North Stars to capture the honor.

McDonald, 36, has earned the reputation as one of the most prolific scorers in NHL history during his 16 pro seasons. He achieved his three lifelong goals in 1988-89 when he scored his 500th career goal, 1000th career point and helped the Flames to their first Stanley Cup in club history. McDonald has been a model of consistency during his NHL tenure. He has scored 30 or more goals nine times during his career and in 1982-83, he scored a club record 66 goals. That season he won the Bill Masterton Trophy for perseverance, dedication and sportsmanship, and was named to the Second All-Star Team at right wing.

McDonald has been actively involved in several charities, including the Canadian Special Olympics, the Alberta Children's Hospital in Calgary, Ronald McDonald House and the Foothills Hospital Burn Unit Foundation. He was also Calgary's nominee for the Budweiser/NHL Man of the Year Award in 1988.

TRICO GOALTENDER AWARD

An annual award **to the goaltender with the best save percentage during the regular schedule.** The winner receives $10,000 to benefit the charitable organization of his choice. The runners-up each receive $1,000 to be presented in their names to the charity of their choice.

History: The award was presented to the National Hockey League in 1988-89 by Trico to recognize the goaltender with the best save percentage during the regular schedule.

1988-89 Winner: Patrick Roy, Montreal Canadiens
Runners-up: Jon Casey, Minnesota North Stars
Mike Vernon, Calgary Flames

Roy finished the regular season with a .908 save percentage by stopping 1,115 shots of 1,228 faced. He finished the season with a League-leading 2.47 goals-against-average and was undefeated in 29 home games (25-0-4). The 21-year-old winner of the Vezina Trophy as the League's top goaltender also captured his third consecutive Jennings Trophy along with teammate Brian Hayward. Together, the duo led the League with a 2.70 goals-against-average.

Team Award

PRESIDENTS' TROPHY

An annual award to the club finishing the regular-season with the best overall record. The winner receives $200,000, to be split evenly between the team and its players. Based on 20 players in each game during the regular-season, a player who appears in all 80 games receives $5,000. Players appearing in less than 80 games receive pro-rated amounts.

History: Presented to the National Hockey League in 1985-86 by the NHL Board of Governors to recognize the team compiling the top regular-season record.

1988-89 Winner: Calgary Flames
Runners-up: Montreal Canadiens
Washington Capitals

The Calgary Flames won the 1988-89 Presidents' Trophy with the NHL's best regular-season record of 54-17-9 for 117 points. The Montreal Canadiens finished second at 53-18-9 for 115 points, while the Washington Capitals had the third best regular-season mark at 41-29-10 for 92 points.

Dodge Ram Tough Award

DODGE PERFORMANCE OF THE YEAR

An annual award for which both individuals and teams are eligible **to honor an outstanding performance in the NHL.** The winner is selected by a panel of Professional Hockey Writers' Association members and is awarded $5,000 to benefit youth hockey.

History: The award was first presented in 1987-88 to honor the team or outstanding individual performance of the year in the NHL.

1988-89 Winner: Wayne Gretzky, Los Angeles Kings

Gretzky received the award in recognition of his leading the Los Angeles Kings to second place in the Smythe Division. Gretzky recorded his tenth straight 100-point season, ninth 50-goal season, shared the League lead in assists with 114, and helped the Kings score a club record 376 goals. His efforts helped make the Kings the most improved NHL team during the 1988-89 season. Other nominations included two for Pittsburgh's Mario Lemieux, one for becoming only the second player in NHL history to score more than 80 goals in a season and the other for his five-goal game versus the New Jersey Devils on December 31, 1988. Detroit's Steve Yzerman was nominated for playing in all 80 games, producing career high point totals (65-90-155) and leading Detroit to their second consecutive Norris Division title. The fifth nomination went to the New York Rangers' Guy Lafleur for returning to the NHL after a four-year retirement.

DODGE RAM TOUGH AWARD

An annual award presented **to the player who wins the overall Ram Tough statistical category (combined total of power play, shorthanded, game-winning and game-tying goals)**. Dodge Truck presents each individual team winner $1,000 to be donated to the youth hockey association of his choice.

History: The award was presented to the NHL in 1987-88 by Dodge to recognize the League leader in Ram Tough statistics.

1988-89 Winner: Mario Lemieux, Pittsburgh Penguins
Runner-up: Bernie Nicholls, Los Angeles Kings

Lemieux's record-setting 53 Dodge Ram Tough ranking shattered last year's mark of 42. The Penguins' center notched 31 power-play, a League-record 13 shorthanded, eight game-winning and one game-tying goal. He was involved in 79 (31-48-79) of the Penguins' NHL-record 119 power-play goals. Individual team leaders included: Cam Neely, Boston Bruins; Pierre Turgeon, Buffalo Sabres; Joe Nieuwendyk, Calgary Flames; Steve Larmer, Chicago Blackhawks; Steve Yzerman, Detroit Red Wings; Jimmy Carson, Edmonton Oilers; Kevin Dineen, Hartford Whalers; Bernie Nicholls, Los Angeles Kings; Dave Gagner, Minnesota North Stars; Mats Naslund, Montreal Canadiens; John MacLean, New Jersey Devils; Brent Sutter, New York Islanders; Carey Wilson, New York Rangers; Tim Kerr, Philadelphia Flyers; Walt Poddubny, Quebec Nordiques; Brett Hull, St. Louis Blues; Ed Olczyk, Toronto Maple Leafs; Petri Skriko, Vancouver Canucks; Mike Ridley, Washington Capitals; Andrew McBain, Winnipeg Jets.

DODGE PERFORMER OF THE YEAR AWARD

An annual award presented by Dodge to the National Hockey League's **most outstanding performer in the regular-season.** The winner receives the Dodge vehicle of his choice.

History: The award was first presented in 1984-85 to recognize the NHL's top player. Dodge also sponsors the Performer of the Week and Performer of the Month awards, donating $500 and $1,000, respectively, to youth hockey organizations across North America in the recipients' honor.

1988-89 Winner: Mario Lemieux, Pittsburgh Penguins

During the regular season the 23-year-old Lemieux led the League in goals (85) and shared the League lead in assists (114) on his way to his second consecutive Art Ross Trophy (scoring leader). Lemieux joins Wayne Gretzky as the only other NHL player to score more than 70 goals in a season twice. Lemieux captured five Dodge/NHL Peformer of the Week and three Dodge/NHL Performer of the Month awards to tie a single-season record set by Gretzky during the 1983-84 season.

1988-89 Dodge/NHL Award Winners

Performer of the Week

Week Ending	Player	Club	Youth Hockey Recipient
October 16	Wayne Gretzky	Los Angeles	So. Cal. Youth Hockey (CA)
	Mario Lemieux	Pittsburgh	Bethel Park High School (PA)
October 23	Ken Wregget	Toronto	Valley Midget Wildcats (N.S.)
October 30	Mario Lemieux	Pittsburgh	Pittsburgh Amateur Hockey (PA)
November 6	Doug Gilmour	Calgary	Alton Minor Hockey (PA)
November 13	Esa Tikkanen	Edmonton	Confederation Hockey Club (Alta.)
November 20	Alain Chevrier	Winnipeg	Cornwall Minor Hockey (Ont.)
November 27	Steve Weeks	Vancouver	North Van. Minor Hockey (B.C.)
December 4	Bernie Nicholls	Los Angeles	Haliburton High School Hockey (Ont.)
December 11	John MacLean	New Jersey	Oshawa Minor Hockey (Ont.)
December 18	Ron Hextall	Philadelphia	Hockey Central (PA.)
December 25	Mario Lemieux	Pittsburgh	Pittsburgh Amateur Hockey (PA)
January 1	Mario Lemieux	Pittsburgh	Pittsburgh Amateur Hockey (PA)
January 8	Pete Peeters	Washington	Mornville Minor Hockey (Alta.)
January 15	Brian Hayward	Montreal	Georgetown Minor Hockey (Ont.)
January 22	Tony Granato	NY Rangers	American Hearing Impaired Hockey (NY)
January 29	Mike Vernon	Calgary	Southwood Royals (Alta.)
February 5	Wayne Gretzky	Los Angeles	Brantford Bantams (Ont.)
February 12	Doug Gilmour	Calgary	Kingston Minor Hockey (Ont.)
February 19	Ray Bourque	Boston	South Boston Youth Hockey (MA)
February 26	Tim Kerr	Philadelphia	Bristol Blazers (PA)
March 5	Grant Fuhr	Edmonton	Edmonton Hockey Association (Alta.)
March 12	Geoff Courtnall	Washington	Racquet Club of Victoria (B.C.)
March 19	Dino Ciccarelli	Washington	Sarnia Minor Hockey (Ont.)
	Kirk McLean	Vancouver	Don Mills Flyers (Ont.)
March 26	Mario Lemieux	Pittsburgh	Pittsburgh Amateur Hockey (PA)
April 3	Kirk Muller	New Jersey	Kingston Minor Hockey (Ont.)

Performer of the Month

Month	Player	Club	Youth Hockey Recipient
October	Mario Lemieux	Pittsburgh	Pittsburgh Amateur Hockey (PA)
November	Steve Yzerman	Detroit	Detroit Hockey Association (MI)
December	Mario Lemieux	Pittsburgh	Pittsburgh Amateur Hockey (PA)
January	Mike Vernon	Calgary	South Calgary Community Assn. (Alta.)
February	Patrick Roy	Montreal	Canadiens Family Foundation (Que.)
March	Mario Lemieux	Pittsburgh	Pittsburgh Amateur Hockey (PA)

Performer of the Year

Year	Player	Club	Youth Hockey Recipient
1988-89	Mario Lemieux	Pittsburgh	Pittsburgh Amateur Hockey (PA)

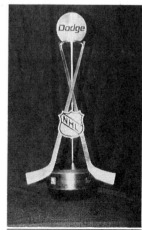

Dodge Performance of The Year

Dodge Performer of The Year Award

NATIONAL HOCKEY LEAGUE INDIVIDUAL AWARD WINNERS

ART ROSS TROPHY

	Winner	Runner-up
1989	Mario Lemieux, Pit.	Wayne Gretzky, L.A.
1988	Mario Lemieux, Pit.	Wayne Gretzky, Edm.
1987	Wayne Gretzky, Edm.	Jari Kurri, Edm.
1986	Wayne Gretzky, Edm.	Mario Lemieux, Pit.
1985	Wayne Gretzky, Edm.	Jari Kurri, Edm.
1984	Wayne Gretzky, Edm.	Paul Coffey, Edm.
1983	Wayne Gretzky, Edm.	Peter Stastny, Que.
1982	Wayne Gretzky, Edm.	Mike Bossy, NYI
1981	Wayne Gretzky, Edm.	Marcel Dionne, L.A.
1980	Marcel Dionne, L.A.	Wayne Gretzky, Edm.
1979	Bryan Trottier, NYI	Marcel Dionne, L.A.
1978	Guy Lafleur, Mtl.	Bryan Trottier, NYI
1977	Guy Lafleur, Mtl.	Marcel Dionne, L.A.
1976	Guy Lafleur, Mtl.	Bobby Clarke, Phi.
1975	Bobby Orr, Bos.	Phil Esposito, Bos.
1974	Phil Esposito, Bos.	Bobby Orr, Bos.
1973	Phil Esposito, Bos.	Bobby Clarke, Phi.
1972	Phil Esposito, Bos.	Bobby Orr, Bos.
1971	Phil Esposito, Bos.	Bobby Orr, Bos.
1970	Bobby Orr, Bos.	Phil Esposito, Bos.
1969	Phil Esposito, Bos.	Bobby Hull, Chi.
1968	Stan Mikita, Chi.	Phil Esposito, Bos.
1967	Stan Mikita, Chi.	Bobby Hull, Chi.
1966	Bobby Hull, Chi.	Stan Mikita, Chi.
1965	Stan Mikita, Chi.	Norm Ullman, Det.
1964	Stan Mikita, Chi.	Bobby Hull, Chi.
1963	Gordie Howe, Det.	Andy Bathgate, NYR
1962	Bobby Hull, Chi.	Andy Bathgate, NYR
1961	Bernie Geoffrion, Mtl.	Jean Beliveau, Mtl.
1960	Bobby Hull, Chi.	Bronco Horvath, Bos.
1959	Dickie Moore, Mtl.	Jean Beliveau, Mtl.
1958	Dickie Moore, Mtl.	Henri Richard, Mtl.
1957	Gordie Howe, Det.	Ted Lindsay, Det.
1956	Jean Beliveau, Mtl.	Gordie Howe, Det.
1955	Bernie Geoffrion, Mtl.	Maurice Richard, Mtl.
1954	Gordie Howe, Det.	Maurice Richard, Mtl.
1953	Gordie Howe, Det.	Ted Lindsay, Det.
1952	Gordie Howe, Det.	Ted Lindsay, Det.
1951	Gordie Howe, Det.	Maurice Richard, Mtl.
1950	Ted Lindsay, Det.	Sid Abel, Det.
1949	Roy Conacher, Chi.	Doug Bentley, Chi.
1948	Elmer Lach, Mtl.	Buddy O'Connor, NYR
1947*	Max Bentley, Chi.	Maurice Richard, Mtl.
1946	Max Bentley, Chi.	Gaye Stewart, Tor.
1945	Elmer Lach, Mtl.	Maurice Richard, Mtl.
1944	Herbie Cain, Bos.	Doug Bentley, Chi.
1943	Doug Bentley, Chi.	Bill Cowley, Bos.
1942	Bryan Hextall, NYR	Lynn Patrick, NYR
1941	Bill Cowley, Bos.	Bryan Hextall, NYR
1940	Milt Schmidt, Bos.	Woody Dumart, Bos.
1939	Toe Blake, Mtl.	Dave Schriner, NYA
1938	Gordie Drillon, Tor.	Syl Apps, Tor.
1937	Dave Schriner, NYA	Syl Apps, Tor.
1936	Dave Schriner, NYA	Marty Barry, Det.
1935	Charlie Conacher, Tor.	Syd Howe, St.L-Det.
1934	Charlie Conacher, Tor.	Joe Primeau, Tor
1933	Bill Cook, NYR	Harvey Jackson, Tor.
1932	Harvey Jackson, Tor.	Joe Primeau, Tor.
1931	Howie Morenz, Mtl.	Ebbie Goodfellow, Det.
1930	Cooney Weiland, Bos.	Frank Boucher, NYR
1929	Ace Bailey, Tor.	Nels Stewart, Mtl.M
1928	Howie Morenz, Mtl.	Aurel Joliat, Mtl.
1927	Bill Cook, NYR	Dick Irvin, Chi.
1926	Nels Stewart, Mtl.M.	Carson Cooper, Bos.
1925	Babe Dye, Tor.	Howie Morenz, Mtl.
1924	Cy Denneny, Ott.	Babe Dye, Tor.
1923	Babe Dye, Tor.	Billy Boucher, Mtl.
1922	Punch Broadbent, Ott.	Babe Dye, Tor.
1921	Newsy Lalonde, Mtl.	Cy Denneny, Ott.
1920	Joe Malone, Que.	Newsy Lalonde, Mtl.
1919	Newsy Lalonde, Mtl.	Newsy Lalonde, Mtl.
1918	Joe Malone, Mtl.	Cy Denneny, Ott.

* Scoring leader prior to inception of Art Ross Trophy in 1947-48

HART TROPHY

	Winner	Runner-up
1989	Wayne Gretzky, L.A.	Mario Lemieux, Pit.
1988	Mario Lemieux, Pit.	Grant Fuhr, Edm.
1987	Wayne Gretzky, Edm.	Raymond Bourque, Bos.
1986	Wayne Gretzky, Edm.	Mario Lemieux, Pit.
1985	Wayne Gretzky, Edm.	Dale Hawerchuk, Wpg.
1984	Wayne Gretzky, Edm.	Rod Langway, Wash.
1983	Wayne Gretzky, Edm.	Pete Peeters, Bos.
1982	Wayne Gretzky, Edm.	Bryan Trottier, NYI
1981	Wayne Gretzky, Edm.	Mike Liut, St.L.
1980	Wayne Gretzky, Edm.	Marcel Dionne, L.A.
1979	Bryan Trottier, NYI	Guy Lafleur, Mtl
1978	Guy Lafleur, Mtl.	Bryan Trottier, NYI
1977	Guy Lafleur, Mtl.	Bobby Clarke, Phi.
1976	Bobby Clarke, Phi.	Denis Potvin, NYI
1975	Bobby Clarke, Phi.	Rogatien Vachon, L.A.
1974	Phil Esposito, Bos.	Bernie Parent, Phi.
1973	Bobby Clarke, Phi.	Phil Esposito, Bos.
1972	Bobby Orr, Bos.	Ken Dryden, Mtl.
1971	Bobby Orr, Bos.	Phil Esposito, Bos.
1970	Bobby Orr, Bos.	Tony Esposito, Chi.
1969	Phil Esposito, Bos.	Jean Beliveau, Mtl.
1968	Stan Mikita, Chi.	Jean Beliveau, Mtl.
1967	Stan Mikita, Chi.	Ed Giacomin, NYR
1966	Bobby Hull, Chi.	Jean Beliveau, Mtl.
1965	Bobby Hull, Chi.	Norm Ullman, Det.
1964	Jean Beliveau, Mtl.	Bobby Hull, Chi.
1963	Gordie Howe, Det.	Stan Mikita, Chi.
1962	Jacques Plante, Mtl.	Doug Harvey, NYR
1961	Bernie Geoffrion, Mtl.	Johnny Bower, Tor.
1960	Gordie Howe, Det.	Bobby Hull, Chi.
1959	Andy Bathgate, NYR	Gordie Howe, Det.
1958	Gordie Howe, Det.	Andy Bathgate, NYR
1957	Gordie Howe, Det.	Jean Beliveau, Mtl.
1956	Jean Beliveau, Mtl.	Tod Sloan, Tor.
1955	Ted Kennedy, Tor.	Harry Lumley, Tor.
1954	Al Rollins, Chi.	Red Kelly, Det.
1953	Gordie Howe, Det.	Al Rollins, Chi.
1952	Gordie Howe, Det.	Elmer Lach, Mtl.
1951	Milt Schmidt, Bos.	Maurice Richard, Mtl.
1950	Charlie Rayner, NYR	Ted Kennedy, Tor.
1949	Sid Abel, Det.	Bill Durnan, Mtl.
1948	Buddy O'Connor, NYR	Frank Brimsek, Bos.
1947	Maurice Richard, Mtl.	Milt Schmidt, Bos.
1946	Max Bentley, Chi.	Gaye Stewart, Tor.
1945	Elmer Lach, Mtl.	Maurice Richard, Mtl.
1944	Babe Pratt, Tor.	Bill Cowley, Bos.
1943	Bill Cowley, Bos.	Doug Bentley, Chi.
1942	Tom Anderson, NYA	Syl Apps, Tor.
1941	Bill Cowley, Bos.	Dit Clapper, Bos.
1940	Ebbie Goodfellow, Det.	Syl Apps, Tor.
1939	Toe Blake, Mtl.	Syl Apps, Tor.
1938	Eddie Shore, Bos.	Paul Thompson, Chi.
1937	Babe Siebert, Mtl.	Lionel Conacher, Mtl.M
1936	Eddie Shore, Bos.	Hooley Smith, Mtl.M
1935	Eddie Shore, Bos.	Charlie Conacher, Tor.
1934	Aurel Joliat, Mtl.	Lionel Conacher, Chi.
1933	Eddie Shore, Bos.	Bill Cook, NYR
1932	Howie Morenz, Mtl.	Joe Primeau, Tor.
1931	Howie Morenz, Mtl.	Eddie Shore, Bos.
1930	Nels Stewart, Mtl.M.	Lionel Hitchman, Bos.
1929	Roy Worters, NYA	Ace Bailey, Tor.
1928	Howie Morenz, Mtl.	Roy Worters, Pit.
1927	Herb Gardiner, Mtl.	Bill Cook, NYR
1926	Nels Stewart, Mtl.M.	Sprague Cleghorn, Bos.
1925	Billy Burch, Ham.	Howie Morenz, Mtl.
1924	Frank Nighbor, Ott.	Sprague Cleghorn, Mtl.

LADY BYNG TROPHY

	Winner	Runner-up
1989	Joe Mullen, Cgy.	Wayne Gretzky, L.A.
1988	Mats Naslund, Mtl.	Wayne Gretzky, Edm.
1987	Joe Mullen, Cal.	Wayne Gretzky, Edm.
1986	Mike Bossy, NYI	Jari Kurri, Edm.
1985	Jari Kurri, Edm.	Joe Mullen, St.L.
1984	Mike Bossy, NYI	Rick Middleton, Bos.
1983	Mike Bossy, NYI	Rick Middleton, Bos.
1982	Rick Middleton, Bos.	Mike Bossy, NYI
1981	Rick Kehoe, Pit.	Wayne Gretzky, Edm.
1980	Wayne Gretzky, Edm.	Marcel Dionne, L.A.
1979	Bob MacMillan, Atl.	Marcel Dionne, L.A.
1978	Butch Goring, L.A.	Peter McNab, Bos.
1977	Marcel Dionne, L.A.	Jean Ratelle, Bos.
1976	Jean Ratelle, NYR-Bos.	Jean Pronovost, Pit.
1975	Marcel Dionne, Det.	John Bucyk, Bos.
1974	John Bucyk, Bos.	Lowell MacDonald, Pit.
1973	Gilbert Perreault, Buf.	Jean Ratelle, NYR
1972	Jean Ratelle, NYR	John Bucyk, Bos.
1971	John Bucyk, Bos.	Dave Keon, Tor.
1970	Phil Goyette, St.L.	John Bucyk, Bos.
1969	Alex Delvecchio, Det.	Ted Hampson, Oak.
1968	Stan Mikita, Chi.	John Bucyk, Bos.
1967	Stan Mikita, Chi.	Dave Keon, Tor.
1966	Alex Delvecchio, Det.	Bobby Rousseau, Mtl.
1965	Bobby Hull, Chi.	Alex Delvecchio, Det.
1964	Ken Wharram, Chi.	Dave Keon, Tor.
1963	Dave Keon, Tor.	Camille Henry, NYR
1962	Dave Keon, Tor.	Claude Provost, Mtl.
1961	Red Kelly, Tor.	Norm Ullman, Det.
1960	Don McKenney, Bos.	Andy Hebenton, NYR
1959	Alex Delvecchio, Det.	Andy Hebenton, NYR
1958	Camille Henry, NYR	Don Marshall, Mtl.
1957	Andy Hebenton, NYR	Earl Reibel, Det.
1956	Earl Reibel, Det.	Floyd Curry, Mtl.
1955	Sid Smith, Tor.	Danny Lewicki, NYR
1954	Red Kelly, Det.	Don Raleigh, NYR
1953	Red Kelly, Det.	Wally Hergesheimer, NYR
1952	Sid Smith, Tor.	Red Kelly, Det.
1951	Red Kelly, Det.	Woody Dumart, Bos.
1950	Edgar Laprade, NYR	Red Kelly, Det.
1949	Bill Quackenbush, Det.	Harry Watson, Tor.
1948	Buddy O'Connor, NYR	Syl Aps, Tor.
1947	Bobby Bauer, Bos.	Syl Apps, Tor.
1946	Toe Blake, Mtl.	Clint Smith, Chi.
1945	Bill Mosienko, Chi.	Syd Howe, Det.
1944	Clint Smith, Chi.	Herb Cain, Bos.
1943	Max Bentley, Chi.	Buddy O'Connor, Mtl.
1942	Syl Apps, Tor.	Gordie Drillon, Tor.
1941	Bobby Bauer, Bos.	Gordie Drillon, Tor.
1940	Bobby Bauer, Bos.	Clint Smith, NYR
1939	Clint Smith, NYR	Marty Barry, Det.
1938	Gordie Drillon, Tor.	Clint Smith, NYR
1937	Marty Barry, Det.	Gordie Drillon, Tor.
1936	Doc Romnes, Chi.	Dave Schriner, NYA
1935	Frank Boucher, NYR	Russ Blinco, Mtl.M
1934	Frank Boucher, NYR	Joe Primeau, Tor.
1933	Frank Boucher, NYR	Joe Primeau, Tor.
1932	Joe Primeau, Tor.	Frank Boucher, NYR
1931	Frank Boucher, NYR	Normie Himes, NYA
1930	Frank Boucher, NYR	Normie Himes, NYA
1929	Frank Boucher, NYR	Harry Darragh, Pit.
1928	Frank Boucher, NYR	George Hay, Det.
1927	Billy Burch, NYA	Dick Irvin, Chi.
1926	Frank Nighbor, Ott.	Billy Burch, NYA
1925	Frank Nighbor, Ott.	none

LESTER B. PEARSON AWARD WINNERS

1989	Steve Yzerman	Detroit
1988	Mario Lemieux	Pittsburgh
1987	Wayne Gretzky	Edmonton
1986	Mario Lemieux	Pittsburgh
1985	Wayne Gretzky	Edmonton
1984	Wayne Gretzky	Edmonton
1983	Wayne Gretzky	Edmonton
1982	Wayne Gretzky	Edmonton
1981	Mike Liut	St. Louis
1980	Marcel Dionne	Los Angeles
1979	Marcel Dionne	Los Angeles
1978	Guy Lafleur	Montreal
1977	Guy Lafleur	Montreal
1976	Guy Lafleur	Montreal
1975	Bobby Orr	Boston
1974	Bobby Clarke	Phi.
1973	Phil Esposito	Boston
1972	Jean Ratelle	NY Rangers
1971	Phil Esposito	Boston

WILLIAM M. JENNINGS TROPHY WINNERS

	Winner	Runner-up
1989	Patrick Roy, Mtl.	Mike Vernon, Cgy.
	Brian Hayward	Rick Wamsley
1988	Patrick Roy, Mtl.	Clint Malarchuk, Wsh.
	Brian Hayward	Pete Peters
1987	Patrick Roy, Mtl.	Ron Hextall, Phi.
	Brian Hayward	
1986	Bob Froese, Phi.	Al Jensen, Wsh.
	Darren Jensen	Pete Peeters
1985	Tom Barrasso, Buf.	Pat Riggin, Wsh.
	Bob Sauve	
1984	Al Jensen, Wsh.	Tom Barrasso, Buf.
	Pat Riggin	Bob Sauve
1983	Roland Melanson, NYI	Pete Peeters, Bos.
	Bill Smith	
1982	Rick Wamsley, Mtl.	Billy Smith, NYI
	Denis Herron	Roland Melanson

BILL MASTERTON TROPHY WINNERS

1989	Tim Kerr	Philadelphia
1988	Bob Bourne	Los Angeles
1987	Doug Jarvis	Hartford
1986	Charlie Simmer	Boston
1985	Anders Hedberg	NY Rangers
1984	Brad Park	Detroit
1983	Lanny McDonald	Calgary
1982	Glenn Resch	Colorado
1981	Blake Dunlop	St. Louis
1980	Al MacAdam	Minnesota
1979	Serge Savard	Montreal
1978	Butch Goring	Los Angeles
1977	Ed Westfall	NY Islanders
1976	Rod Gilbert	NY Rangers
1975	Don Luce	Buffalo
1974	Henri Richard	Montreal
1973	Lowell MacDonald	Pittsburgh
1972	Bobby Clarke	Philadelphia
1971	Jean Ratelle	NY Rangers
1970	Pit Martin	Chicago
1969	Ted Hampson	Oakland
1968	Claude Provost	Montreal

VEZINA TROPHY

	Winner	Runner-up
1989	Patrick Roy, Mtl.	Mike Vernon, Cgy.
1988	Grant Fuhr, Edm.	Tom Barrasso, Buf.
1987	Ron Hextall, Phi.	Mike Liut, Hfd.
1986	John Vanbiesbrouck, NYR	Bob Froese, Phi.
1985	Pelle Lindbergh, Phi.	Tom Barrasso, Buf.
1984	Tom Barrasso, Buf.	Rejean Lemelin, Cgy.
1983	Pete Peeters, Bos.	Roland Melanson, NYI
1982	Bill Smith, NYI	Grant Fuhr, Edm.
1981	Richard Sevigny, Mtl.	Pete Peeters, Phi.
	Denis Herron, Mtl.	Rick St. Croix, Phi.
	Michel Larocque, Mtl.	
1980	Bob Sauve, Buf.	Gerry Cheevers, Bos.
	Don Edwards, Buf.	Gilles Gilbert, Bos.
1979	Ken Dryden, Mtl.	Glenn Resch, NYI
	Michel Larocque, Mtl.	Bill Smith, NYI
1978	Ken Dryden, Mtl.	Bernie Parent, Phi.
	Michel Larocque	Wayne Stephenson, Phi.
1977	Ken Dryden, Mtl.	Glenn Resch, NYI
	Michel Larocque, Mtl.	Bill Smith, NYI
1976	Ken Dryden, Mtl.	Glenn Resch, NYI
		Bill Smith, NYI
1975	Bernie Parent, Phi.	Rogie Vachon, L.A.
		Gary Edwards, L.A.
1974	Bernie Parent, Phi. (tie)	Gilles Gilbert, Bos.
	Tony Esposito, Chi. (tie)	
1973	Ken Dryden, Mtl.	Ed Giacomin, NYR
		Gilles Villemure, NYR
1972	Tony Esposito, Chi.	Cesare Maniago, Min.
	Gary Smith, Chi.	Lorne Worsley, Min.
1971	Ed Giacomin, NYR	Tony Esposito, Chi.
	Gilles Villemure, NYR	
1970	Tony Esposito, Chi.	Jacques Plante, St.L.
		Ernie Wakely, St.L.
1969	Jacques Plante, St.L.	Ed Giacomin, NYR
	Glenn Hall, St.L.	
1968	Lorne Worsley, Mtl.	Johnny Bower, Tor.
	Rogatien Vachon, Mtl.	Bruce Gamble, Tor.
1967	Glenn Hall, Chi.	Charlie Hodge, Mtl.
	Denis Dejordy, Chi.	
1966	Lorne Worsley, Mtl.	Glenn Hall, Chi.
	Charlie Hodge, Mtl.	
1965	Terry Sawchuk, Tor.	Roger Crozier, Det.
	Johnny Bower, Tor.	
1964	Charlie Hodge, Mtl.	Glenn Hall, Chi.
1963	Glenn Hall, Chi.	Johnny Bower, Tor.
		Don Simmons, Tor.
1962	Jacques Plante, Mtl.	Johnny Bower, Tor.
1961	Johnny Bower, Tor.	Glenn Hall, Chi.
1960	Jacques Plante, Mtl.	Glenn Hall, Chi.
1959	Jacques Plante, Mtl.	Johnny Bower, Tor.
		Ed Chadwick, Tor.
1958	Jacques Plante, Mtl.	Lorne Worsley, NYR
		Marcel Paille, NYR
1957	Jacques Plante, Mtl.	Glenn Hall, Det.
1956	Jacques Plante, Mtl.	Glenn Hall, Det.
1955	Terry Sawchuk, Det.	Harry Lumley, Tor.
1954	Harry Lumley, Tor.	Terry Sawchuk, Det.
1953	Terry Sawchuk, Det.	Gerry McNeil, Mtl.
1952	Terry Sawchuk, Det.	Al Rollins, Tor.
1951	Al Rollins, Tor.	Terry Sawchuk, Det.
1950	Bill Durnan, Mtl.	Harry Lumley, Det.
1949	Bill Durnan, Mtl.	Harry Lumley, Det.
1948	Turk Broda, Tor.	Harry Lumley, Det.
1947	Bill Durnan, Mtl.	Turk Broda, Tor.
1946	Bill Durnan, Mtl.	Frank Brimsek, Bos.
1945	Bill Durnan, Mtl.	Frank McCool, Tor. (tie)
		Harry Lumley, Det. (tie)
1944	Bill Durnan, Mtl.	Paul Bibeault, Tor.
1943	Johnny Mowers, Det.	Turk Broda, Tor.
1942	Frank Brimsek, Bos.	Turk Broda, Tor.
1941	Turk Broda, Tor.	Frank Brimsek, Bos. (tie)
		Johnny Mowers, Det. (tie)
1940	Dave Kerr, NYR	Frank Brimsek, Bos.
1939	Frank Brimsek, Bos.	Dave Kerr, NYR
1938	Tiny Thompson, Bos.	Dave Kerr, NYR
1937	Normie Smith, Det.	Dave Kerr, NYR
1936	Tiny Thompson, Bos.	Mike Karakas, Chi.
1935	Lorne Chabot, Chi.	Alex Connell, Mtl.M
1934	Charlie Gardiner, Chi.	Wilf Cude, Det.
1933	Tiny Thompson, Bos.	John Roach, Det.
1932	Charlie Gardiner, Chi.	Alex Connell, Det.
1931	Roy Worters, NYA	Charlie Gardiner, Chi.
1930	Tiny Thompson, Bos.	Charlie Gardiner, Chi.
1929	George Hainsworth, Mtl.	Tiny Thompson, Bos.
1928	George Hainsworth, Mtl.	Alex Connell, Ott.
1927	George Hainsworth, Mtl.	Clint Benedict, Mtl.M

CALDER MEMORIAL TROPHY WINNERS

	Winner	Runner-up
1989	Brian Leetch, NYR	Trevor Linden, Van.
1988	Joe Nieuwendyk, Cal.	Ray Sheppard, Buf.
1987	Luc Robitaille, L.A.	Ron Hextall, Phi.
1986	Gary Suter, Cal.	Wendel Clark, Tor.
1985	Mario Lemieux, Pit.	Chris Chelios, Mtl.
1984	Tom Barrasso, Buf.	Steve Yzerman, Det.
1983	Steve Larmer, Chi.	Phil Housley, Buf.
1982	Dale Hawerchuk, Wpg.	Barry Pederson, Bos.
1981	Peter Stastny, Que.	Larry Murphy, L.A.
1980	Ray Bourque, Bos.	Mike Foligno, Det.
1979	Bobby Smith, Min	Ryan Walter, Wsh.
1978	Mike Bossy, NYI	Barry Beck, Col.
1977	Willi Plett, Atl.	Don Murdoch, NYR
1976	Bryan Trottier, NYI	Glenn Resch, NYI
1975	Eric Vail, Atl.	Pierre Larouche, Pit.
1974	Denis Potvin, NYI	Tom Lysiak, Atl.
1973	Steve Vickers, NYR	Bill Barber, Phi.
1972	Ken Dryden, Mtl.	Rick Martin, Buf.
1971	Gilbert Perreault, Buf.	Jude Drouin, Min.
1970	Tony Esposito, Chi.	Bill Fairbairn, NYR
1969	Danny Grant, Min.	Norm Ferguson, Oak.
1968	Derek Sanderson, Bos.	Jacques Lemaire, Mtl.
1967	Bobby Orr, Bos.	Ed Van Impe, Chi.
1966	Brit Selby, Tor.	Bert Marshall, Det.
1965	Roger Crozier, Det.	Ron Ellis, Tor.
1964	Jacques Laperriere, Mtl.	John Ferguson, Mtl.
1963	Kent Douglas, Tor.	Doug Barkley, Det.
1962	Bobby Rousseau, Mtl.	Cliff Pennington, Bos.
1961	Dave Keon, Tor.	Bob Nevin, Tor.
1960	Bill Hay, Chi.	Murray Oliver, Det.
1959	Ralph Backstrom, Mtl.	Carl Brewer, Tor.
1958	Frank Mahovlich, Tor.	Bobby Hull, Chi.
1957	Larry Regan, Bos.	Ed Chadwick, Tor.
1956	Glenn Hall, Det.	Andy Hebenton, NYR
1955	Ed Litzenberger, Chi.	Don McKenney, Bos.
1954	Camille Henry, NYR	Earl Reibel, Det.
1953	Lorne Worsley, NYR	Gordie Hannigan, Tor.
1952	Bernie Geoffrion, Mtl.	Hy Buller, NYR
1951	Terry Sawchuk, Det.	Al Rollins, Tor.
1950	Jack Gelineau, Bos.	Phil Maloney, Bos.
1949	Pentti Lund, NYR	Allan Stanley, NYR
1948	Jim McFadden, Det.	Pete Babando, Bos.
1947	Howie Meeker, Tor.	Jimmy Conacher, Det.
1946	Edgar Laprade, NYR	
1945	Frank McCool, Tor.	Ken Smith, Bos.
1944	Gus Bodnar, Tor.	Bill Durnan, Mtl.
1943	Gaye Stewart, Tor.	
1942	Grant Warwick, NYR	
1941	Johnny Quilty, Mtl.	Johnny Mowers, Det.
1940	Kilby MacDonald, NYR	
1939	Frank Brimsek, Bos.	
1938	Cully Dahlstrom, Chi.	
1937	Syl Apps, Tor.	
1936	Mike Karakas, Chi.	
1935	Dave Schriner, NYA	
1934	Russ Blinko, Mtl.M	
1933	Carl Voss, Det.	

JAMES NORRIS TROPHY WINNERS

	Winner	Runner-up
1989	Chris Chelios, Mtl	Paul Coffey, Pit.
1988	Ray Bourque, Bos.	Scott Stevens, Wsh.
1987	Ray Bourque, Bos.	Mark Howe, Phi.
1986	Paul Coffey, Edm.	Mark Howe, Phi.
1985	Paul Coffey, Edm.	Ray Bourque, Bos.
1984	Rod Langway, Wash.	Paul Coffey, Edm.
1983	Rod Langway, Wash.	Mark Howe, Phi.
1982	Doug Wilson, Chi.	Ray Bourque, Bos.
1981	Randy Carlyle, Pit.	Denis Potvin, NYI
1980	Larry Robinson, Mtl.	Borje Salming, Tor.
1979	Denis Potvin, NYI	Larry Robinson, Mtl.
1978	Denis Potvin, NYI	Brad Park, Bos.
1977	Larry Robinson, Mtl.	Borje Salming, Tor.
1976	Denis Potvin, NYI	Brad Park, NYR-Bos.
1975	Bobby Orr, Bos.	Denis Potvin, NYI
1974	Bobby Orr, Bos.	Brad Park, NYR
1973	Bobby Orr, Bos.	Guy Lapointe, Mtl.
1972	Bobby Orr, Bos.	Brad Park, NYR
1971	Bobby Orr, Bos.	Brad Park, NYR
1970	Bobby Orr, Bos.	Brad Park, NYR
1969	Bobby Orr, Bos.	Tim Horton, Tor.
1968	Bobby Orr, Bos.	J.C. Tremblay, Mtl
1967	Harry Howell, NYR	Pierre Pilote, Chi.
1966	Jacques Laperriere, Mtl.	Pierre Pilote, Chi.
1965	Pierre Pilote, Chi.	Jacques Laperriere, Mtl.
1964	Pierre Pilote, Chi.	Tim Horton, Tor.
1963	Pierre Pilote, Chi.	Carl Brewer, Tor.
1962	Doug Harvey, NYR	Pierre Pilote, Chi.
1961	Doug Harvey, Mtl.	Marcel Pronovost, Det.
1960	Doug Harvey, Mtl.	Allan Stanley, Tor.
1959	Tom Johnson, Mtl.	Bill Gadsby, NYR
1958	Doug Harvey, Mtl.	Bill Gadsby, NYR
1957	Doug Harvey, Mtl.	Red Kelly, Det.
1956	Doug Harvey, Mtl.	Bill Gadsby, NYR
1955	Doug Harvey, Mtl.	Red Kelly, Det.
1954	Red Kelly, Det.	Doug Harvey, Mtl.

JACK ADAMS AWARD WINNERS

	Winner	Runner-up
1989	Pat Burns, Mtl.	Bob McCammon, Van.
1988	Jacques Demers, Det.	Terry Crisp, Cgy.
1987	Jacques Demers, Det.	Jack Evans, Hfd.
1986	Glen Sather, Edm.	Jacques Demers, St.L.
1985	Mike Keenan, Phi.	Barry Long, Wpg.
1984	Bryan Murray, Wash.	Scott Bowman, Buf.
1983	Orval Tessier, Chi.	
1982	Tom Watt, Wpg.	
1981	Gordon (Red) Berenson, St.L.	Bob Berry, L.A.
1980	Pat Quinn, Phi.	
1979	Al Arbour, NYI	Fred Shero, NYR
1978	Bobby Kromm, Det.	Don Cherry, Bos.
1977	Scott Bowman, Mtl.	Tom McVie, Wsh.
1976	Don Cherry, Bos.	
1975	Bob Pulford, L.A.	
1974	Fred Shero, Phi.	

Willi Plett, NHL Calder Trophy winner, 1977.

LESTER PATRICK TROPHY WINNERS

1989	Dan Kelly
	Lou Nanne
	*Lynn Patrick
	Bud Poile
1988	Keith Allen
	Fred Cusick
	Bob Johnson
1987	*Hobey Baker
	Frank Mathers
1986	John MacInnes
	Jack Riley
1985	Jack Butterfield
	Arthur M. Wirtz
1984	John A. Ziegler Jr.
	*Arthur Howie Ross
1983	Bill Torrey
1982	Emile P. Francis
1981	Charles M. Schulz
1980	Bobby Clarke
	Edward M. Snider
	Frederick A. Shero
	1980 U.S. Olympic Hockey Team
1979	Bobby Orr
1978	Philip A. Esposito
	Tom Fitzgerald
	William T. Tutt
	William W. Wirtz
1977	John P. Bucyk
	Murray A. Armstrong
	John Mariucci
1976	Stanley Mikita
	George A. Leader
	Bruce A. Norris
1975	Donald M. Clark
	William L. Chadwick
	Thomas N. Ivan
1974	Alex Delvecchio
	Murray Murdoch
	*Weston W. Adams, Sr.
	*Charles L. Crovat
1973	Walter L. Bush, Jr.
1972	Clarence S. Campbell
	John Kelly
	Ralph "Cooney" Weiland
	*James D. Norris
1971	William M. Jennings
	*John B. Sollenberger
	*Terrance G. Sawchuk
1970	Edward W. Shore
	*James C. V. Hendy
1969	Robert M. Hull
	*Edward J. Jeremiah
1968	Thomas F. Lockhart
	*Walter A. Brown
	*Gen. John R. Kilpatrick
1967	Gordon Howe
	*Charles F. Adams
	*James Norris, Sr.
1966	J.J. "Jack" Adams
	* awarded posthumously

CONN SMYTHE TROPHY WINNERS

1989	Al MacInnis	Calgary
1988	Wayne Gretzky	Edmonton
1987	Ron Hextall	Philadelphia
1986	Patrick Roy	Montreal
1985	Wayne Gretzky	Edmonton
1984	Mark Messier	Edmonton
1983	Bill Smith	NY Islanders
1982	Mike Bossy	NY Islanders
1981	Butch Goring	NY Islanders
1980	Bryan Trottier	NY Islanders
1979	Bob Gainey	Montreal
1978	Larry Robinson	Montreal
1977	Guy Lafleur	Montreal
1976	Reggie Leach	Philadelphia
1975	Bernie Parent	Philadelphia
1974	Bernie Parent	Philadelphia
1973	Yvan Cournoyer	Montreal
1972	Bobby Orr	Boston
1971	Ken Dryden	Montreal
1970	Bobby Orr	Boston
1969	Serge Savard	Montreal
1968	Glenn Hall	St. Louis
1967	Dave Keon	Toronto
1966	Roger Crozier	Detroit
1965	Jean Béliveau	Montreal

KING CLANCY MEMORIAL TROPHY WINNERS

1989	Bryan Trottier	NY Islanders
1988	Lanny McDonald	Calgary

FRANK J. SELKE TROPHY WINNERS

	Winner	Runner-up
1989	Guy Carbonneau, Mtl.	Esa Tikkanen, Edm.
1988	Guy Carbonneau, Mtl.	Steve Kasper, Bos.
1987	Dave Poulin, Phi.	Guy Carbonneau, Mtl.
1986	Troy Murray, Chi.	Ron Sutter, Phi.
1985	Craig Ramsay, Buf.	Doug Jarvis, Wsh.
1984	Doug Jarvis, Wash.	Bryan Trottier, NYI
1983	Bobby Clarke, Phi.	Jari Kurri, Edm.
1982	Steve Kasper, Bos.	Bob Gainey, Mtl.
1981	Bob Gainey, Mtl.	Craig Ramsay, Buf.
1980	Bob Gainey, Mtl.	Craig Ramsay, Buf.
1979	Bob Gainey, Mtl.	Don Marcotte, Bos.
1978	Bob Gainey, Mtl.	Craig Ramsay, Buf.

BUD MAN OF THE YEAR AWARD WINNERS

1989	Lanny McDonald	Calgary
1988	Bryan Trottier	NY Islanders

TRICO GOALTENDER AWARD WINNER

1989	Patrick Roy	Montreal

DODGE PERFORMER OF THE YEAR AWARD WINNERS

1989	Mario Lemieux	Pittsburgh
1988	Mario Lemieux	Pittsburgh
1987	Wayne Gretzky	Edmonton
1986	Wayne Gretzky	Edmonton
1985	Wayne Gretzky	Edmonton

DODGE PERFORMANCE OF THE YEAR AWARD WINNERS

1989	Wayne Gretzky	Los Angeles
1988	Mario Lemieux	Pittsburgh

DODGE RAM TOUGH AWARD WINNERS

1989	Mario Lemieux	Pittsburgh
1988	Joe Nieuwendyk	Calgary

Ken Dryden, who won the Conn Smythe Trophy as playoff MVP in 1971, relaxes in the pose that became his trademark.

NHL Amateur and Entry Draft

History

Year	Site	Date	Total Players Drafted
1963	Queen Elizabeth Hotel	June 5	21
1964	Queen Elizabeth Hotel	June 11	24
1965	Queen Elizabeth Hotel	April 27	11
1966	Mount Royal Hotel	April 25	24
1967	Queen Elizabeth Hotel	June 7	18
1968	Queen Elizabeth Hotel	June 13	24
1969	Queen Elizabeth Hotel	June 12	84
1970	Queen Elizabeth Hotel	June 11	116
1971	Queen Elizabeth Hotel	June 10	117
1972	Queen Elizabeth Hotel	June 8	152
1973	Mount Royal Hotel	May 15	168
1974	NHL Montreal Office	May 28	247
1975	NHL Montreal Office	June 3	217
1976	NHL Montreal Office	June 1	135
1977	NHL Montreal Office	June 14	185
1978	Queen Elizabeth Hotel	June 15	234
1979	Queen Elizabeth Hotel	August 9	126
1980	Montreal Forum	June 11	210
1981	Montreal Forum	June 10	211
1982	Montreal Forum	June 9	252
1983	Montreal Forum	June 8	242
1984	Montreal Forum	June 9	250
1985	Toronto Convention Centre	June 15	252
1986	Montreal Forum	June 21	252
1987	Joe Louis Sports Arena	June 13	252
1988	Montreal Forum	June 11	252
1989	Metropolitan Sports Center	June 17	252

* The NHL Amateur Draft became the NHL Entry Draft in 1979

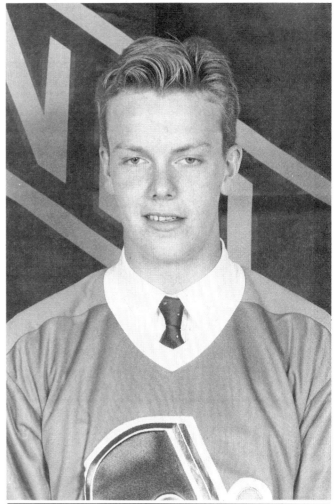

Mats Sundin became the first European player to be chosen first overall in the NHL Entry Draft when he was selected by the Quebec Nordiques on June 17, 1989.

First Selections

Year	Player	Pos	Drafted By	Drafted From	Age
1969	Rejean Houle	LW	Montreal	Montreal Jr. Canadiens	19.7
1970	Gilbert Perreault	C	Buffalo	Montreal Jr. Canadiens	19.7
1971	Guy Lafleur	RW	Montreal	Quebec Remparts	19.8
1972	Billy Harris	RW	NY Islanders	Toronto Marlboros	20.4
1973	Denis Potvin	D	NY Islanders	Ottawa 67's	19.7
1974	Greg Joly	D	Washington	Regina Pats	20.0
1975	Mel Bridgman	C	Philadelphia	Victoria Cougars	20.1
1976	Rick Green	D	Washington	London Knights	20.3
1977	Dale McCourt	C	Detroit	St. Catharines Fincups	20.4
1978	Bobby Smith	C	Minnesota	Ottawa 67's	20.4
1979	Bob Ramage	D	Colorado	London Knights	20.5
1980	Doug Wickenheiser	C	Montreal	Regina Pats	19.2
1981	Dale Hawerchuk	C	Winnipeg	Cornwall Royals	18.2
1982	Gord Kluzak	D	Boston	Nanaimo Islanders	18.3
1983	Brian Lawton	C	Minnesota	Mount St. Charles HS	18.11
1984	Mario Lemieux	C	Pittsburgh	Laval Voisins	18.8
1985	Wendel Clark	LW/D	Toronto	Saskatoon Blades	18.7
1986	Joe Murphy	C	Detroit	Michigan State	18.8
1987	Pierre Turgeon	C	Buffalo	Granby Bisons	17.10
1988	Mike Modano	C	Minnesota	Prince Albert Raiders	18.0
1989	Mats Sundin	RW	Quebec	Nacka (Sweden)	18.4

Draft Summary

Following is a summary of the number of players drafted from the Ontario Hockey League (OHL), Western Hockey League (WHL), Quebec Major Junior Hockey League (QMJHL), United States Colleges, United States High Schools, European Leagues and other Leagues throughout North America since 1969:

	OHL	WHL	QMJHL	US Coll.	US HS	International	Other
1969	36	20	11	7	0	1	9
1970	51	22	13	16	0	0	13
1971	41	28	13	22	0	0	13
1972	46	44	30	21	0	0	11
1973	56	49	24	25	0	0	14
1974	69	66	40	41	0	6	24
1975	45	54	28	59	0	6	25
1976	47	33	18	26	0	8	3
1977	42	44	40	49	0	5	5
1978	59	48	22	71	0	15	19
1979	48	37	19	15	0	7	2
1980	73	41	24	42	7	13	10
1981	59	36	28	21	17	32	18
1982	60	55	17	20	47	35	18
1983	57	41	24	14	35	34	37
1984	55	38	16	22	44	40	35
1985	59	43	15	20	48	30	37
1986	66	32	22	22	40	28	42
1987	32	36	17	40	69	38	20
1988	33	30	22	48	56	39	24
1989	39	44	16	48	47	38	20
Total	1073	841	459	649	409	375	399

Ontario Hockey League

Club	'69	'70	'71	'72	'73	'74	'75	'76	'77	'78	'79	'80	'81	'82	'83	'84	'85	'86	'87	'88	'89	Total
Peterborough	5	5	4	5	9	4	3	1	4	6	9	10	3	5	7	3	9	2	5	2	2	103
Toronto	3	7	6	5	6	8	4	4	7	5	4	10	2	6	4	4	3	4	1	2	2	97
Oshawa	5	4	3	5	5	7	6	6	1	3	3	2	9	5	5	6	6	6	3	3	4	97
Kitchener	1	6	2	8	4	13	3	1	3	4	4	4	5	5	8	4	6	3	2	1	7	94
London	4	9	1	5	6	6	3	5	4	3	6	2	5	5	3	7	1	3	2	6	3	89
Ottawa	2	4	3	4	6	5	6	5	5	5	3	8	4	9	2	2	3	3	2	–	–	81
S.S. Marie	–	–	–	–	4	5	2	5	1	5	3	3	8	1	6	4	5	7	1	3	3	66
Hamilton	2	3	5	4	6	4	7	3	–	8	1	–	–	–	3	6	4	3	–	–	–	59
Kingston	–	–	–	–	4	4	6	4	9	2	8	5	2	1	3	3	4	1	1	–	–	57
Sudbury	–	–	–	–	6	6	4	5	4	4	3	7	2	4	–	2	5	3	1	–	1	57
St. Catharines	5	5	8	5	4	7	3	4	6	–	–	–	–	–	–	–	–	–	–	–	–	47
Niagara Falls	4	2	1	4	–	–	–	2	3	5	8	6	6	–	–	–	–	–	–	–	4	45
Windsor	–	–	–	–	–	2	1	4	2	3	5	3	2	2	3	7	0	5	2	–	–	41
Brantford	–	–	–	–	–	–	–	–	3	8	5	2	7	2	–	–	–	–	–	–	–	27
Cornwall	–	–	–	–	–	–	–	–	–	–	–	–	–	7	4	3	2	2	3	3	2	26
Guelph	–	–	–	–	–	–	–	–	–	–	–	–	–	–	1	5	3	8	2	–	4	23
Belleville	–	–	–	–	–	–	–	–	–	–	–	–	–	–	3	4	4	5	2	–	4	22
North Bay	–	–	–	–	–	–	–	–	–	–	–	–	–	–	4	4	3	3	3	3	1	21
Montreal	5	6	8	1	–	–	–	–	–	–	–	–	–	–	–	–	–	–	–	–	–	20

Year	Total Ontario Drafted	Total Players Drafted	Ontario %
1969	36	84	42.9
1970	51	116	44.0
1971	41	117	35.0
1972	46	152	30.3
1973	56	168	33.3
1974	69	247	27.9
1975	45	217	20.7
1976	47	135	34.8
1977	42	185	22.7
1978	59	234	25.2
1979	48	126	38.1
1980	73	210	34.8
1981	59	211	28.0
1982	60	252	23.8
1983	57	242	23.6
1984	55	250	22.0
1985	59	252	23.4
1986	66	252	26.2
1987	32	252	12.7
1988	33	252	13.1
1989	39	252	15.5
Total	**1073**	**4206**	**25.5**

Western Hockey League

Club	'69	'70	'71	'72	'73	'74	'75	'76	'77	'78	'79	'80	'81	'82	'83	'84	'85	'86	'87	'88	'89	Total
Regina	–	–	5	5	1	8	5	3	1	4	1	3	5	6	8	4	4	3	2	–	5	75
Portland	–	–	–	–	–	–	–	4	8	7	8	6	7	7	5	1	4	3	1	4	–	68
Saskatoon	1	–	1	3	8	4	5	3	4	1	2	2	3	5	5	3	1	5	4	4	3	67
Calgary	3	5	2	7	4	8	4	4	3	–	2	5	4	3	3	3	2	2	–	–	–	66
Victoria	–	–	–	2	2	5	7	4	3	3	1	8	6	2	3	4	2	1	2	4	4	63
New Westm'r	–	–	–	6	8	7	9	5	8	6	5	1	–	–	2	1	1	2	1	–	–	62
Medicine Hat	–	–	–	4	6	4	5	3	5	4	–	4	2	1	2	1	6	2	5	1	4	59
Brandon	–	3	1	5	2	7	4	–	3	1	10	5	2	2	1	3	2	1	3	3	–	58
Kamloops	–	–	–	–	–	4	4	4	4	–	–	–	–	2	4	4	4	4	3	1	5	43
Lethbridge	–	–	–	–	–	–	2	3	5	4	1	4	7	2	1	5	1	–	3	3	–	41
Flin Flon	4	4	5	2	4	7	4	3	1	5	–	–	–	–	–	–	–	–	–	–	–	39
Winnipeg	3	2	4	2	5	4	4	–	4	–	–	1	4	1	–	–	–	–	–	–	–	34
Edmonton	4	4	5	6	6	2	3	2	–	2	–	–	–	–	–	–	–	–	–	–	–	34
Seattle	–	–	–	–	–	4	2	3	–	6	–	2	2	1	2	4	2	–	–	–	–	28
Prince Albert	–	–	–	–	–	–	–	–	–	–	4	2	2	6	6	1	3	3	–	–	–	27
Swift Current	1	–	1	–	3	6	–	–	–	–	–	–	–	–	–	–	–	5	2	2	–	20
Billings	–	–	–	–	4	3	4	2	–	–	–	–	–	–	–	–	–	–	–	–	–	13
Estevan	4	4	4	–	–	–	–	–	–	–	–	–	–	–	–	–	–	–	–	–	–	12
Kelowna	–	–	–	–	–	–	–	–	–	–	–	–	–	2	4	4	–	–	–	–	–	10
Moose Jaw	–	–	–	–	–	–	–	–	–	–	–	–	–	–	1	3	–	3	–	–	–	7
Nanaimo	–	–	–	–	–	–	–	–	–	–	–	5	1	–	–	–	–	–	–	–	–	6
Spokane	–	–	–	–	–	–	–	–	–	–	–	–	–	–	–	–	–	1	3	2	–	6
Tri-Cities	–	–	–	–	–	–	–	–	–	–	–	–	–	–	–	–	–	–	–	4	–	4
Vancouver	–	–	2	–	–	–	–	–	–	–	–	–	–	–	–	–	–	–	–	2	–	2

Year	Total Western Drafted	Total Players Drafted	Western %
1969	20	84	23.8
1970	22	116	19.0
1971	28	117	23.9
1972	44	152	28.9
1973	49	168	29.2
1974	66	247	26.7
1975	54	217	24.9
1976	33	135	24.4
1977	44	185	23.8
1978	48	234	20.5
1979	37	126	29.4
1980	41	210	19.5
1981	36	211	17.1
1982	55	252	21.8
1983	41	242	16.9
1984	38	250	15.2
1985	41	252	17.1
1986	32	252	12.7
1987	36	252	14.3
1988	30	252	11.9
1989	44	252	17.5
Total	**841**	**4206**	**20.0**

International

Country	'69	'70	'71	'72	'73	'74	'75	'76	'77	'78	'79	'80	'81	'82	'83	'84	'85	'86	'87	'88	'89	Total
Sweden	–	–	–	–	–	5	2	5	2	8	6	9	13	14	10	14	20	9	15	14	9	155
Finland	1	–	–	–	1	3	2	3	2	–	4	13	5	9	10	5	10	6	7	3	–	84
Czechoslovakia	–	–	–	–	–	1	1	–	4	13	9	13	8	6	11	5	8	–	–	–	–	79
Soviet Union	–	–	–	–	–	1	–	2	–	–	3	5	1	1	1	2	–	11	18	–	–	45
West Germany	–	–	–	–	–	–	2	–	2	–	1	2	1	–	1	–	2	–	–	–	–	11
Denmark	–	–	–	–	–	–	–	–	–	–	–	–	–	–	–	–	–	1	1	–	–	2
Norway	–	–	–	–	–	–	–	–	–	–	–	–	–	–	–	–	–	2	–	–	–	2
Switzerland	–	–	–	1	–	–	–	–	–	–	–	–	–	–	–	–	–	–	–	–	–	1
Scotland	–	–	–	–	–	–	–	–	–	–	–	–	–	–	–	–	1	–	–	–	–	1

Year	Total International Drafted	Total Players Drafted	International %
1969	1	84	1.2
1970	0	116	0
1971	0	117	0
1972	0	152	0
1973	0	168	0
1974	7	247	2.8
1975	6	217	2.8
1976	8	135	5.9
1977	5	185	2.7
1978	15	234	6.4
1979	7	126	5.5
1980	13	210	6.2
1981	32	211	15.2
1982	35	252	13.9
1983	34	242	14.0
1984	40	250	17.6
1985	30	252	12.0
1986	28	252	11.1
1987	38	252	15.1
1988	39	252	15.5
1989	38	252	15.1
Total	**375**	**4206**	**8.9**

Quebec Major Junior Hockey League

Club	'69	'70	'71	'72	'73	'74	'75	'76	'77	'78	'79	'80	'81	'82	'83	'84	'85	'86	'87	'88	'89	Total
Quebec	1	1	2	4	6	6	1	3	7	1	3	2	2	1	2	2	2	–	–	–	–	47
Cornwall	2	1	2	6	4	8	1	3	1	6	1	5	5	–	–	–	–	–	–	–	–	45
Shawinigan	3	2	1	6	1	5	3	–	3	–	–	2	2	5	5	2	–	2	1	–	2	45
Sherbrooke	–	2	2	4	3	7	5	6	3	4	1	5	2	–	–	–	–	–	–	–	–	44
Trois Rivieres	–	1	2	2	2	3	2	6	3	2	2	2	1	3	–	3	–	1	3	3	–	43
Montreal	–	–	–	–	4	4	8	1	3	2	4	3	–	3	–	–	–	–	–	–	–	32
Chicoutimi	–	–	–	–	–	1	–	5	1	1	3	6	1	3	–	3	1	2	2	1	–	30
Hull	–	–	–	–	3	2	2	3	–	–	3	1	–	3	1	–	4	3	2	2	–	29
Sorel	2	3	1	3	1	8	1	1	3	–	–	–	5	–	–	–	–	–	–	–	–	28
Drummondville	2	4	1	4	2	1	–	–	–	–	–	–	–	–	1	2	2	2	4	1	–	26
Verdun	–	1	1	2	–	–	–	–	–	1	3	3	–	–	3	3	–	3	0	3	1	24
Granby	–	–	–	–	–	–	–	–	–	–	–	–	2	1	3	2	2	4	–	2	–	16
Laval	–	–	–	–	–	–	–	–	–	–	–	–	–	–	–	5	3	1	3	–	–	12
St. Jean	–	–	–	–	–	–	–	–	–	–	–	–	–	–	2	–	1	1	0	3	1	8
Longueuil	–	–	–	–	–	–	–	–	–	–	–	–	–	–	–	1	2	1	2	1	–	7
Victoriaville	–	–	–	–	–	–	–	–	–	–	–	–	–	–	–	–	–	–	–	4	–	4
St. Jerome	1	–	1	–	–	–	–	–	–	–	–	–	–	–	–	–	–	–	0	–	–	2

Year	Total Quebec Drafted	Total Players Drafted	Quebec %
1969	11	84	13.1
1970	13	116	11.2
1971	13	117	11.1
1972	30	152	19.7
1973	24	168	14.3
1974	40	247	16.2
1975	28	217	12.9
1976	18	135	13.3
1977	40	185	21.6
1978	22	234	9.4
1979	19	126	15.1
1980	24	210	11.4
1981	28	211	13.3
1982	17	252	6.7
1983	24	242	9.9
1984	16	250	6.4
1985	15	252	5.9
1986	22	252	8.7
1987	17	252	6.7
1988	22	252	8.7
1989	16	252	6.3
Total	**459**	**4206**	**10.9**

United States Colleges

Club	'69	'70	'71	'72	'73	'74	'75	'76	'77	'78	'79	'80	'81	'82	'83	'84	'85	'86	'87	'88	'89	Total
Minnesota	1	3	2	–	–	9	4	4	5	5	2	3	1	1	1	–	–	2	1	1	1	46
Michigan Tech	–	–	3	1	2	5	4	4	1	2	1	4	–	1	–	2	2	2	1	1	2	38
Wisconsin	–	1	2	4	5	4	4	2	3	–	1	–	3	2	–	1	1	–	1	1	1	35
Denver	1	3	2	4	2	3	1	2	2	2	2	1	–	1	–	–	1	2	4	1	1	35
Boston U.	–	4	–	–	1	1	1	4	5	1	–	1	–	1	1	2	2	3	1			29
North Dakota	2	3	3	1	4	2	1	–	1	2	3	3	1	–	1	–	–	–	2			29
Michigan	1	–	–	–	2	2	3	3	1	4	–	4	–	–	–	1	1	–	1	2	3	28
Providence	–	–	–	–	–	–	3	2	3	4	–	5	4	1	2	–	1	1	–	–	–	26
New Hampshire	–	–	–	1	1	3	6	–	4	1	1	2	1	1	1	2	–	–	1	–		25
Michigan State	–	–	1	–	1	1	1	1	–	–	–	2	–	2	–	2	–	1	1	4	4	21
Cornell	–	–	–	2	1	1	–	1	1	1	–	1	1	1	–	1	2	–	1	2	5	21
Clarkson	–	–	2	2	1	–	2	–	2	2	1	1·	1	1	1	–	–	1	1	1		20
Notre Dame	–	–	2	3	–	–	7	2	–	3	1	1	–	–	–	–	–	–	–	–	–	19
Colorado	2	1	–	–	1	3	1	2	2	–	1	–	–	3	–	1	–	1	–	–		18
Boston College	–	1	–	–	–	–	1	1	–	5	–	2	1	1	–	–	1	2	–	2		17
Harvard	–	–	2	–	–	–	2	–	2	2	–	–	1	1	–	2	–	1	1	2		16
Bowling Green	–	–	–	–	–	1	3	2	1	1	1	1	–	1	–	–	–	–	–	3	2	16
RPI	–	–	–	–	1	–	–	–	1	3	–	1	2	1	1	–	1	2	2	–	–	15
Northern Mich.	–	–	–	–	–	–	–	–	4	–	1	1	–	–	–	–	–	4	1	2		15
Lake Superior	–	–	–	2	1	1	1	–	3	–	–	–	–	1	–	3	–	3	2			15
Vermont	–	–	–	1	–	4	1	1	–	1	1	–	1	1	2	–	1	–	–	1		14
St. Lawrence	–	–	–	–	1	–	1	3	–	–	3	–	1	1	1	1	1	1				14
W. Michigan	–	–	–	–	–	–	–	2	–	2	–	2	–	2	2	–	2	1	1	1		13
Brown	–	–	–	–	1	2	1	3	2	–	1	–	–	–	–	–	–	–	–	–		10
Yale	–	–	1	–	1	–	2	1	–	–	–	–	–	–	1	2	–	1				9
Miami of Ohio	–	–	–	–	–	–	–	–	–	–	–	–	–	–	1	2,	4	2				9
Minn.-Duluth	–	2	1	–	–	–	1	1	–	1	–	–	–	–	–	–	–	2	1			9
Ohio State	–	–	–	–	–	2	1	–	–	–	1	–	2	2	–							8
Maine	–	–	–	–	–	–	–	–	1	1	–	1	–	3	2							8
Northeastern	–	–	–	–	1	–	1	–	1	–	1	–	1	1	–	1						7
St. Louis	–	–	–	–	1	2	–	1	3	–	–	–	–	–	–	–	1					7
Princeton	–	–	–	–	1	–	1	–	1	1	1	–	1	1	–	1						7
U. of Ill.-Chi.	–	–	–	–	–	–	–	–	–	–	–	–	1	2	1	2						6
Colgate	–	–	–	1	–	–	2	1	–	–	–	–	–	1	1							6
Pennsylvania	–	–	1	2	1	–	–	1	–	–	–											5
Union College	–	–	–	–	–	–	4	–	–	–	–											4
Lowell	–	–	–	–	1	1	–	1	1	–	–											4
Dartmouth	–	–	1	–	–	1	–	1	1	–	1	–	–									4
Ferris State	–	–	–	–	–	–	–	–	–	–	–	2	1	1								4
Merrimack	–	–	–	–	–	–	1	–	–	–	1	–	1	–								3
Babson College	–	–	–	–	–	–	–	–	–	–	1	1	1	–								3
Alaska-Anchorage	–	–	–	–	–	–	–	–	–	–	–	–	–	2								2
Salem State	–	–	–	–	1	–	–	–	–	–												1
Bemidji State	–	1	–	–	–	–	–	–	–													1
San Diego U.	–	–	–	–	–	–	1	–	–													1
Greenway	–	–	–	–	–	–	–	–	1													1
St. Anselen College	–	–	–	–	–	–	–	1	–													1
Hamilton College	–	–	–	–	–	–	–	1	–													1
St. Thomas	–	–	–	–	–	–	–	1	–													1
St. Cloud State	–	–	–	–	–	–	–	1	–													1
Amer. Int'l College	–	–	–	–	–	–	–	–	1	1												1

Year	Total College Drafted	Total Players Drafted	College %
1969	7	84	8.3
1970	16	116	13.8
1971	22	117	18.8
1972	21	152	13.8
1973	25	168	14.9
1974	41	247	16.6
1975	59	217	26.7
1976	26	135	19.3
1977	49	185	26.5
1978	71	234	32.0
1979	15	126	11.9
1980	42	210	20.0
1981	21	211	10.0
1982	20	252	7.9
1983	14	242	5.8
1984	22	250	8.8
1985	20	252	7.9
1986	22	252	8.7
1987	40	252	15.9
1988	48	252	19.0
1989	48	252	19.0
Total	**649**	**4206**	**15.4**

1989 Entry Draft

Transferred draft choice notation:
Example: L.A.-Phi. represents a draft choice transferred **from** Los Angeles **to** Philadelphia.

Pick	Player	Claimed By	Amateur Club	Position
ROUND # 1				
1	SUNDIN, Mats	Que.	Nacka	RW
2	CHYZOWSKI, Dave	NYI	Kamloops	LW
3	THORNTON, Scott	Tor.	Belleville	C
4	BARNES, Stu	Wpg.	Tri-Cities	C
5	GUERIN, Bill	N.J.	Springfield Jr. B	RW
6	BENNETT, Adam	Chi.	Sudbury	D
7	ZMOLEK, Doug	Min.	John Marshall	D
8	HERTER, Jason	Van.	U. of North Dakota	D
9	MARSHALL, Jason	St.L.	Vernon T-II Jr. A	D
10	HOLIK, Robert	Hfd.	Jihlava	C
11	SILLINGER, Mike	Det.	Regina	C
12	PEARSON, Rob	Phi.-Tor.	Belleville	RW
13	VALLIS, Lindsay	NYR-Mtl.	Seattle	RW
14	HALLER, Kevin	Buf.	Regina	D
15	SOULES, Jason	Edm.	Niagara Falls	D
16	HEWARD, Jamie	Pit.	Regina	RW
17	STEVENSON, Shayne	Bos.	Kitchener	RW
18	MILLER, Jason	L.A.-Edm. N.J.	Medicine Hat	C
19	KOLZIG, Olaf	Wsh.	Tri-Cities	G
20	RICE, Steven	Mtl.-NYR	Kitchener	RW
21	BANCROFT, Steve	Cgy.-Tor.	Belleville	D
ROUND # 2				
22	FOOTE, Adam	Que.	Sault-Ste-Marie	D
23	GREEN, Travis	NYI	Spokane	C
24	MANDERVILLE, Kent	Tor.-Cgy.	Notre Dame T-II Jr. A	LW
25	RATUSHNY, Dan	Wpg.	Cornell University	D
26	SKALDE, Jarrod	N.J.	Oshawa	C
27	SPEER, Michael	Chi.	Guelph	D
28	CRAIG, Mike	Min.	Oshawa	RW
29	WOODWARD, Robert	Van.	Deerfield	LW
30	BRISEBOIS, Patrice	St.L.-Mtl.	Laval	D
31	CORRIVEAU, Rick	Hfd.-St.L.	London	D
32	BOUGHNER, Bob	Det.	Sault-Ste-Marie	D
33	JOHNSON, Greg	Phi.	Thunder Bay Jr. A	C
34	JUHLIN, Patrik	NYR-Phi.	Vasteras	LW
35	DAFOE, Byron	Buf.-Wsh.	Portland	G
36	BORGO, Richard	Edm.	Kitchener	RW
37	LAUS, Paul	Pit.	Niagara Falls	D
38	PARSON, Mike	Bos.	Guelph	G
39	THOMPSON, Brent	L.A.	Medicine Hat	D
40	PROSOFSKY, Jason	Wsh.-NYR	Medicine Hat	RW
41	LAROUCHE, Steve	Mtl.	Trois-Rivieres	C
42	DRURY, Ted	Cgy.	Fairfield Prep	C
ROUND # 3				
43	MORIN, Stephane	Que.	Chicoutimi	C
44	ZENT, Jason	NYI	Nichols	LW
45	ZAMUNER, Rob	Tor.-NYR	Guelph	C
46	CIRONE, Jason	Wpg.-N.J.-Wpg.	Cornwall	C
47	PELLERIN, Scott	N.J.	University of Maine	LW
48	KELLOGG, Bob	Chi.	Springfield Jr. B	D
49	DEBRUSK, Louie	Min.-NYR	London	LW
50	KAUTONEN, Veli-Pekka	Van.-Cgy.	IFK Helsinki	D
51	SEVIGNY, Pierre	St.L.-Mtl.	Verdun	LW
52	ATCHEYNUM, Blair	Hfd.	Moose Jaw	RW
53	LIDSTROM, Niklas	Det.	Vasteras	D
54	TANNER, John	Phi.-Que.	Peterborough	G
55	FELSNER, Denny	NYR-Wpg.-St.L.	Michigan University	LW
56	THOMAS, John (Scott)	Buf.	Nichols	RW
57	WALZ, Woc	Edm. Bos.	Lethbridge	C
58	BRILL, John	Pit.	Grand Rapids	RW
59	MATHIESON, Jim	Bos.-Wsh.	Regina	D
60	GARBUTT, Murray	L.A.-Min.	Medicine Hat	C
61	WOOLLEY, Jason	Wsh.	Michigan State	D
62	DRAPER, Kris	Mtl.-St.L.-Wpg.	Canadian Olympic	C
63	LYONS, Corey	Cgy.	Lethbridge	RW
ROUND # 4				
64	BROWNSCHIDLE, Mark	Que.-Wpg.	Boston University	D
65	GRIEVE, Brent	NYI	Oshawa	LW
66	MARTIN, Matt	Tor.	Avon Old Farms	D
67	CUMMINS, Jim	Wpg.-NYR	Michigan State	RW
68	ANDERSSON, Niclas	N.J.-Que.	Frolunda	RW
69	ROY, Allain	Chi.-Wpg.	Harvard University	G
70	REICHEL, Robert	Min.-Cgy.	Litvinov	C
71	HAUER, Brett	Van.	Richfield	D
72	SIMPSON, Reid	St.L.-Phi.	Prince Albert	LW
73	McKENZIE, Jim	Hfd.	Victoria	LW
74	FEDOROV, Sergei	Det.	CSKA-Russia	C
75	QUINTIN, Jean-Francois	Phi.-Min.	Shawinigan	C
76	DUBOIS, Eric	NYR-Que.	Laval	D
77	MacDONALD, Doug	Buf.	U. of Wisconsin	C
78	BERANEK, Josef	Edm.	Litvinov	C
79	NELSON, Todd	Pit.	Prince Albert	D
80	PENNEY, Jackson	Bos.	Victoria	C
81	MAHER, Jim	L.A.	Illinois-Chicago	D
82	KLATT, Trent	Wsh.	Osseo	C
83	RACICOT, Andre	Mtl.	Granby	G
84	O'LEARY, Ryan	Cgy.	Hermantown	C

1989 Entry Draft (continued)

ROUND # 5

Pick	Player	Claimed By	Amateur Club	Position
85	KAISER, Kevin	Que.	U. Minnesota-Duluth	LW
86	REED, Jace	NYI	Grand Rapids	D
87	MacLEOD, Pat	Tor.-Min.	Kamloops	D
88	MILLER, Aaron	Wpg.-NYR	Niagara Jr. A	D
89	HEINKE, Mike	N.J.	Avon Old Farms	D
90	YOUNG, Steve	Chi.-NYI	Moose Jaw	RW
91	SCHOEN, Bryan	Min.	Minnetonka	G
92	WHITE, Peter	Van.-Edm.	Michigan State	LW
93	LAPERRIERE, Daniel	St.L.	St. Lawrence U.	D
94	BLACK, James	Hfd.	Portland	C
95	McCOSH, Shawn	Det.	Niagara Falls	C
96	CARNEY, Keith	Phi.-Tor.	Mount St. Charles	D
97	HOLLYMAN, Rhys	NYR-Min.	Miami-Ohio	D
98	SUTTON, Ken	Buf.	Saskatoon	D
99	O'SULLIVAN, Kevin	Edm.-NYI	Catholic Memorial	D
100	NEVERS, Tom	Pit.	Edina	C
101	MONTANARI, Mark	Bos.	Kitchener	C
102	RICARD, Eric	L.A.	Granby	D
103	NEWMAN, Thomas	Wsh.-L.A.	Blaine	D
104	DESCHAMPS, Marc	Mtl.	Cornell University	D
105	KEARNEY, Francis (Toby)	Cgy.	Belmont Hill	LW

ROUND # 6

Pick	Player	Claimed By	Amateur Club	Position
106	LAMBERT, Dan	Que.	Swift Current	D
107	PYE, Bill	NYI-Buf.	Northern Michigan U.	G
108	BURKE, David	Tor.	Cornell University	D
109	BYLSMA, Dan	Wpg.	Bowling Green	LW
110	EMMA, David	N.J.	Boston College	C
111	PULLOLA, Tommi	Chi.	Sport Fin Div I	G
112	CASHMAN, Scott	Min.	Kanata T-II Jr. A	G
113	BURE, Pavel	Van.	USSR	RW
114	ROBERTS, David	St.L.	Avon Old Farms	LW
115	BECHARD, Jerome	Hfd.	Moose Jaw	LW
116	DRAKE, Dallas	Det.	Northern Michigan U.	C
117	ERIKSSON, Niklas	Phi.	Sweden	C
118	MESSIER, Joby	NYR	Michigan State	D
119	BARKLEY, Mike	Buf.	University of Maine	RW
120	SEMENOV, Anatoli	Edm.	Moscow Dynamo	LW
121	MARKOVICH, Mike	Pit.	University of Denver	D
122	FOSTER, Stephen	Bos.	Catholic Memorial	D
123	RYDMARK, Daniel	L.A.	Farjestad	C
124	FRENETTE, Derek	Wsh.-St.L.	Ferris State	LW
125	DOERS, Michael	Mtl.-Tor.	Northwood Prep	RW
126	NEEDHAM, Mike	Cgy.-Pit.	Kamloops	RW

ROUND # 7

Pick	Player	Claimed By	Amateur Club	Position
127	MYLNIKOV, Sergei	Que.	Tractor Tjelsabinsky	G
128	LARSON, Jon	NYI	Roseau	D
129	MERKLER, Keith	Tor.	Portledge	LW
130	PELTOLA, Pekka	Wpg.	HPK Finland	RW
131	EVANS, Doug	N.J.-Wpg.	Michigan University	LW
132	EGELAND, Tracy	Chi.	Prince Albert	LW
133	HARKINS, Brett	Min.-NYI	Detroit Comp. Jr. A	LW
134	REVENBERG, James	Van.	Windsor	RW
135	BATTERS, Jeff	St.L.	Alaska-Anchorage	D
136	DANIELS, Scott	Hfd.	Regina	LW
137	ZYGULSKI, Scott	Det.	Culver Mil. Academy	D
138	CALLAHAN JR., John	Phi.	Belmont Hill	D
139	LEAHY, Greg	NYR	Portland	C
140	PAYNE, Davis	Buf.-Tor.	Michigan Tech U.	LW
141	YASHIN, Sergei	Edm.	Moscow Dynamo	LW
142	SCHAFHAUSER, Patrick	Pit.	Hill-Murray	D
143	HASCAK, Otto	Bos.	Dukla Trencin	RW
144	KRAMER, Ted	L.A.	Michigan University	RW
145	LORENTZ, Dave	Wsh.	Peterborough	LW
146	FERGUSON, Craig	Mtl.	Yale University	C
147	NIKOLIC, Alex	Cgy.	Cornell University	LW

ROUND # 8

Pick	Player	Claimed By	Amateur Club	Position
148	KRAKE, Paul	Que.	Alaska-Anchorage	G
149	HUBER, Phil	NYI	Kamloops	LW
150	LANGILLE, Derek	Tor.	North Bay	D
151	SOLLY, Jim	Wpg.	Bowling Green	C
152	STARIKOW, Sergei	N.J.	Zska Moscow	D
153	TICHY, Milan	Chi.	Skoda Plzen	D
154	PRATT, Jonathan	Min.	Pingree	C
155	SANGSTER, Rob	Van.	Kitchener	LW
156	PLAGER, Kevin	St.L.	Parkway North	RW
157	SAUMIER, Raymond	Hfd.	Trois-Rivieres	RW
158	SUHY, Andy	Det.	Western Michigan	D
159	SEARS, Sverre	Phi.	Belmont Hill	D
160	SPENRATH, Greg	NYR	Tri-Cities	LW
161	PLANTE, Derek	Buf.	Cloquet	C
162	MARTINI, Darcy	Edm.	Michigan Tech U.	D
163	SHUTE, Dave	Pit.	Victoria	C
164	ALLAIN, Rick	Bos.	Kitchener	D
165	WHYTE, Sean	L.A.	Guelph	C
166	HOLOIEN, Dean	Wsh.	Saskatoon	D
167	LEBEAU, Patrick	Mtl.	St-Jean	LW
168	WORTMAN, Kevin	Cgy.	Amer. Int'l College	D

ROUND # 9

Pick	Player	Claimed By	Amateur Club	Position
169	BYKOV, Viacheslav	Que.	Zska Moscow	C
170	ROBBINS, Matthew	NYI	New Hampton	C
171	ST. LAURENT, Jeffrey	Tor.	Berwick	RW
172	GAUVIN, Stephane	Wpg.	Cornell University	LW
173	FAUST, Andre	N.J.	Princeton University	C
174	GREYERBIEHL, Jason	Chi.	Colgate University	LW
175	BLUM, Kenneth	Min.	St. Joseph	C
176	MOGER, Sandy	Van.	Lake Superior	RW
177	RODERICK, John	St.L.	Rindge & Latin	D
178	PICARD, Michel	Hfd.	Trois-Rivieres	LW
179	JONES, Bob	Det.	Sault-Ste-Marie	D
180	WISSER, Glen	Phi.	Philadelphia Jr. B	RW
181	BAVIS, Mark	NYR	Cushing Academy	C
182	GIACIN, Jim	Buf.-L.A.	Culver Mil. Academy	C
183	AUDETTE, Donald	Edm.-Buf.	Laval	RW
184	WOLF, Andrew	Pit.	Victoria	D
185	LAVISH, James	Bos.	Deerfield Academy	RW
186	MASKARINEC, Martin	L.A.	Sparta Praha	D
187	GERVAIS, Victor	Wsh.	Seattle	C
188	MITCHELL, Roy	Mtl.	Portland	D
189	GOMOLYAKOV, Sergei	Cgy.	Tractor Tselsabinsk	C

ROUND # 10

Pick	Player	Claimed By	Amateur Club	Position
190	KHUMUTOV, Andrei	Que.	Zska Moscow	RW
191	MALAKHOV, Vladimir	NYI	Zska Moscow	D
192	TOMBERLIN, Justin	Tor.	Greenway	C
193	LARSON, Joe	Wpg.	Minnetonka	C
194	ASTLEY, Mark	N.J.-Buf.	Lake Superior	D
195	SAUNDERS, Matt	Chi.	Northeastern U.	LW
196	IRBE, Artur	Min.	Dynamo Riga	G
197	MORSCHAUSER, Gus	Van.	Kitchener	G
198	VALO, John	St.L.	Detroit Comp. Jr. A	D
199	BUCHANAN, Trevor	Hfd.	Kamloops	LW
200	BIGNELL, Greg	Det.	Belleville	D
201	KUMMU, Al	Phi.	Humboldt T-II Jr. A	D
202	OKSYUTA, Roman	NYR	Himik	RW
203	NELSON, John	Buf.	Toronto	C
204	JUDSON, Rick	Edm.-Det.	Illinois-Chicago	LW
205	HAGEN, Greg	Pit.	Hill-Murray	D
206	SIMPSON, Geoff	Bos.	Estevan T-II Jr. A	D
207	HILLER, Jim	L.A.	Melville T-II Jr. A	RW
208	VYKOUKAL, Jiri	Wsh.	Olomouc	D
209	HENRICH, Ed	Mtl.	Nichols	D
210	SAWYER, Dan	Cgy.	Ramapo Rangers Jr.	D

ROUND # 11

Pick	Player	Claimed By	Amateur Club	Position
211	WITKOWSKI, Byron	Que.	Nipiwan T-II Jr. A	LW
212	ENS, Kelly	NYI	Lethbridge	C
213	JACKSON, Mike	Tor.	Toronto	RW
214	PODIAK, Bradley	Wpg.	Wayzata	LW
215	SIMON, Jason	N.J.	Windsor	LW
216	KOZAK, Mike	Chi.	Clarkson University	RW
217	PEDERSON, Tom	Min.	U. of Minnesota	D
218	O'REAR, Hayden	Van.	Lathrop	D
219	LUKOWSKI, Brian	St.L.	Niagara Jr. A	G
220	BATTICE, John	Hfd.	London	D
221	KONSTANTIVOV, Vladimir	Det.	Zska Moscow	D
222	BRAIT, Matt	Phi.	St. Michael's Jr. B	D
223	LOCKE, Steve	NYR	Niagara Falls	LW
224	HENDERSON, Todd	Buf.	Thunder Bay Jr. A	G
225	BOZEK, Roman	Edm.	Budejovice CSSR	RW
226	FARRELL, Scott	Pit.	Spokane	D
227	FRANZOSA, David	Bos.	Boston College	LW
228	JAQUES, Steve	L.A.	Tri-Cities	D
229	SIDOROV, Andri	Wsh.		
230	DUBERMAN, Justin	Mtl.	U. of North Dakota	RW
231	YUDIN, Alexander	Cgy.	Dynamo Moscow	D

ROUND # 12

Pick	Player	Claimed By	Amateur Club	Position
232	RAHN, Noel	Que.	Edina	C
233	FRASER, Iain	NYI	Oshawa	C
234	CHARTRAND, Steve	Tor.	Drummondville	LW
235	DAVYDOV, Genneyna	Wpg.	Zska Moscow	RW
236	LARSSON, Peter	N.J.	Sodertalje	C
237	DONEGHEY, Michael	Chi.	Catholic Memorial	G
238	BALDERIS, Helmut	Min.	Dynamo Riga	RW
239	CAHILL, Darcy	Van.	Cornwall	C
240	KHARIN, Sergei	St.L.-Wpg.	Krylja Moscow	RW
241	KASOWSKI, Peter	Hfd.	Swift Current	C
242	FREDERICK, Joseph	Det.	Madison Jr. A	RW
243	POLLIO, James	Phi.	Vermont Academy	LW
244	MacDERMID, Ken	NYR	Hull	LW
245	BAVIS, Michael	Buf.	Cushing Academy	RW
246	GLICKMAN, Jason	Edm.-Det.	Hull	G
247	SMART, Jason	Pit.	Saskatoon	C
248	BERGMAN, Jan	Bos.-Van.	Sodertalje	D
249	SNEDDON, Kevin	L.A.	Harvard University	D
250	HOUSE, Ken	Wsh.	Miami-Ohio	C
251	CADIEUX, Steve	Mtl.	Shawinigan	C
252	KENNHOLT, Kenneth	Cgy.	Djurgarden	D

Draft Choices, 1988-69

1988

FIRST ROUND

Selection	Claimed By	Amateur Club
1. MODANO, Mike	Min.	Prince Albert
2. LINDEN, Trevor	Van.	Medicine Hat
3. LESCHYSHYN, Curtis	Que.	Saskatoon
4. SHANNON, Darrin	Pit.	Windsor
5. DORE, Daniel	Que.	Drummondville
6. PEARSON, Scott	Tor.	Kingston
7. GELINAS, Martin	L.A.	Hull
8. ROENICK, Jeremy	Chi.	Thayer Academy
9. BRIND'AMOUR, Rod	St.L.	Notre Dame Jr.A
10. SELANNE, Teemu	Wpg.	Jokerit (Finland)
11. GOVEDARIS, Chris	Hfd.	Toronto
12. FOSTER, Corey	N.J.	Peterborough
13. SAVAGE, Joel	Buf.	Victoria
14. BOIVIN, Claude	Phi.	Drummondville
15. SAVAGE, Reginald	Wsh.	Victoriaville
16. CHEVELDAYOFF, Kevin	NYI	Brandon
17. KOCUR, Kory	Det.	Saskatoon
18. CIMETTA, Robert	Bos.	Toronto
19. LEROUX, Francois	Edm.	St. Jean
20. CHARRON, Eric	Mtl.	Trois-Rivieres
21. MUZZATTI, Jason	Cgy.	Michigan State

SECOND ROUND

Selection	Claimed By	Amateur Club
22. MALLETTE, Troy	NYR	Sault Ste. Marie
23. CHRISTIAN, Jeff	N.J.	London
24. FISET, Stephane	Que.	Victoriaville
25. MAJOR, Mark	Pit.	North Bay
26. DUVAL, Murray	NYR	Spokane
27. DOMI, Tie	Tor.	Peterborough
28. HOLDEN, Paul	L.A.	London
29. DOUCET, Wayne	NYI	Hamilton
30. PLAVSIC, Adrien	St.L.	U. of New Hampshire
31. ROMANIUK, Russell	Wpg.	St. Boniface Jr. A
32. RICHTER, Barry	Hfd.	Culver Academy
33. ROHLIN, Leif	Van.	VIK (Sweden)
34. ST. AMOUR, Martin	Mtl.	Verdun
35. MURRAY, Pat	Phi.	Michigan State
36. TAYLOR, Tim	Wsh.	London
37. LE BRUN, Sean	NYI	New Westminster
38. ANGLEHART, Serge	Det.	Drummondville
39. KOIVUNEN, Petro	Edm.	K-Espoo (Finland)
40. GAETZ, Link	Min.	Spokane
41. BARTLEY, Wade	Wsh.	Dauphin Jr. A
42. HARKINS, Todd	Cgy.	Miami-Ohio

1987

FIRST ROUND

Selection	Claimed By	Amateur Club
1. TURGEON, Pierre	Buf.	Granby
2. SHANAHAN, Brendan	N.J.	London
3. WESLEY, Glen	Bos.	Portland
4. McBEAN, Wayne	L.A.	Medicine Hat
5. JOSEPH, Chris	Pit.	Seattle
6. ARCHIBALD, David	Min.	Portland
7. RICHARDSON, Luke	Tor.	Peterborough
8. WAITE, Jimmy	Chi.	Chicoutimi
9. FOGARTY, Bryan	Que.	Kingston
10. MORE, Jayson	NYR	New Westminster
11. RACINE, Yves	Det.	Longueuil
12. OSBORNE, Keith	St.L.	North Bay
13. CHYNOWETH, Dean	NYI	Medicine Hat
14. QUINTAL, Stephane	Bos.	Granby
15. SAKIC, Joe	Que.	Swift Current
16. MARCHMENT, Bryan	Wpg.	Belleville
17. CASSELS, Andrew	Mtl.	Ottawa
18. HULL, Jody	Hfd.	Peterborough
19. DEASLEY, Bryan	Cgy.	U. of Michigan
20. RUMBLE, Darren	Phi.	Kitchener
21. SOBERLAK, Peter	Edm.	Swift Current

SECOND ROUND

Selection	Claimed By	Amateur Club
22. MILLER, Brad	Buf.	Regina
23. PERSSON, Rickard	N.J.	Ostersund, Sweden
24. MURPHY, Rob	Van.	Laval
25. MATTEAU, Stephane	Cgy.	Hull
26. TABARACCI, Richard	Pit.	Cornwall
27. FITZPATRICK, Mark	L.A.	Medicine Hat
28. MAROIS, Daniel	Tor.	Chicoutimi
29. DOMI, Dan	Chi.	Swift Current
30. HARDING, Jeff	Phi.	St. Michael's Jr. B
31. LACROIX, Daniel	NYR	Granby
32. KRUPPKE, Gordon	Det.	Prince Albert
33. LECLAIR, John	Mtl.	Bellows Academy
34. HACKETT, Jeff	NYI	Oshawa
35. McCRADY, Scott	Min.	Medicine Hat
36. BALLANTYNE, Jeff	Wsh.	Ottawa
37. ERIKSSON, Patrik	Wpg.	Brynas, Sweden
38. DESJARDINS, Eric	Mtl.	Granby
39. BURT, Adam	Hfd.	North Bay
40. GRANT, Kevin	Cgy.	Kitchener
41. WILKIE, Bob	Det.	Swift Current
42. WERENKA, Brad	Edm.	N. Michigan

1986

FIRST ROUND

Selection	Claimed By	Amateur Club
1. MURPHY, Joe	Det.	Michigan State
2. CARSON, Jimmy	L.A.	Verdun Juniors
3. BRADY, Neil	N.J.	Medicine Hat Tigers
4. ZALAPSKI, Zarley	Pit.	Team Canada
5. ANDERSON, Shawn	Buf.	Team Canada
6. DAMPHOUSSE, Vincent	Tor.	Laval Olympiques
7. WOODLEY, Dan	Van.	Portland Winterhawks
8. ELYNUIK, Pat	Wpg.	Prince Albert Raiders
9. LEETCH, Brian	NYR	Avon Old Farms HS
10. LEMIEUX, Jocelyn	St.L.	Laval Olympiques
11. YOUNG, Scott	Hfd.	Bos. University
12. BABE, Warren	Min.	Lethbridge Broncos
13. JANNEY, Craig	Bos.	Bos. College
14. SANIPASS, Everett	Chi.	Verdun Juniors
15. PEDERSON, Mark	Mtl.	Medicine Hat Tigers
16. PELAWA, George	Cgy.	Bemidji HS
17. FITZGERALD, Tom	NYI	Austin Prep
18. McRAE, Ken	Que.	Sudbury Wolves
19. GREENLAW, Jeff	Wsh.	Team Canada
20. HUFFMAN, Kerry	Phi.	Guelph Platers
21. ISSEL, Kim	Edm.	Prince Albert Raiders

SECOND ROUND

Selection	Claimed By	Amateur Club
22. GRAVES, Adam	Det.	Windsor Spitfires
23. SEPPO, Jukka	Phi.	Vasa Sport, (Finland)
24. COPELAND, Todd	N.J.	Belmont Hill HS
25. CAPUANO, Dave	Pit.	Mt. St. Charles HS
26. BROWN, Greg	Buf.	St. Mark's
27. BRUNET, Benoit	Mtl.	Hull Olympiques
28. HAWLEY, Kent	Phi.	Ottawa 67's
29. NUMMINEN, Teppo	Wpg.	Tappara, (Finland)
30. WILKINSON, Neil	Min.	Selkirk Settlers
31. POSMA, Mike	St.L.	Buf. Jr. Sabres
32. LaFORGE, Marc	Hfd.	Kingston Canadians
33. KOLSTAD, Dean	Min.	Prince Albert Raiders
34. TIRKKONEN, Pekka	Bos.	Sapko, (Finland)
35. KURZAWSKI, Mark	Chi.	Windsor Spitfires
36. SHANNON, Darryl	Tor.	Windsor Spitfires
37. GLYNN, Brian	Cgy.	Saskatoon Blades
38. VASKE, Dennis	NYI	Armstrong HS
39. ROUTHIER, Jean-M	Que.	Hull Olympiques
40. SEFTEL, Steve	Wsh.	Kingston Canadians
41. GUERARD, Stephane	Que.	Shawinigan Cataractes
42. NICHOLS, Jamie	Edm.	Portland Winter Hawks

1985

FIRST ROUND

Selection	Claimed By	Amateur Club
1. CLARK, Wendel	Tor.	Saskatoon Blades
2. SIMPSON, Craig	Pit.	Michigan State
3. WOLANIN, Craig	N.J.	Kitchener Rangers
4. SANDLAK, Jim	Van.	London Knights
5. MURZYN, Dana	Hfd.	Cgy. Wranglers
6. DALGARNO, Brad	NYI	Hamilton Steelhawks
7. DAHLEN, Ulf	NYR	Ostersund (Sweden)
8. FEDYK, Brent	Det.	Regina Pats
9. DUNCANSON, Craig	L.A.	Sudbury Wolves
10. GRATTON, Dan	L.A.	Oshawa Generals
11. MANSON, David	Chi.	Prince Albert Raiders
12. CHARBONNEAU, Jose	Mtl.	Drummondville
13. KING, Derek	NYI	Sault Greyhounds
14. JOHANSSON, Carl	Buf.	V. Frolunda (Sweden)
15. LATTA, Dave	Que.	Kitchener Rangers
16. CHORSKE, Tom	Mtl.	Minneapolis HS
17. BIOTTI, Chris	Cgy.	Belmont Hill HS
18. STEWART, Ryan	Wpg.	Kamloops Blazers
19. CORRIVEAU, Yvon	Wsh.	Tor. Marlboros
20. METCALFE, Scott	Edm.	Kingston Canadians
21. SEABROOKE, Glen	Phi.	Peterborough Petes

SECOND ROUND

Selection	Claimed By	Amateur Club
22. SPANGLER, Ken	Tor.	Cgy. Wranglers
23. GIFFIN, Lee	Pit.	Oshawa Generals
24. BURKE, Sean	N.J.	Tor. Marlboros
25. GAMBLE, Troy	Van.	Medicine Hat Tigers
26. WHITMORE, Kay	Hfd.	Peterborough Petes
27. NIEUWENDYK, Joe	Cgy.	Cornell Big Red
28. RICHTER, Mike	NYR	Northwood Prep
29. SHARPLES, Jeff	Det.	Kelowna Wings
30. EDLUND, Par	L.A.	Bjorkloven (Sweden)
31. COTE, Alain	Bos.	Que. Remparts
32. WEINRICH, Eric	N.J.	North Yarmouth
33. RICHARD, Todd	Mtl.	Armstrong HS
34. LAUER, Brad	NYI	Regina Pats
35. HOGUE, Benoit	Buf.	St Jean Castors
36. LAFRENIERE, Jason	Que.	Hamilton Steelhawks
37. RAGLAN, Herb	St.L.	Kingston Canadians
38. WENAAS, Jeff	Cgy.	Medicine Hat Tigers
39. OHMAN, Roger	Wpg.	Leksand Jr. (Sweden)
40. DRUCE, John	Wsh.	Peterborough Petes
41. CARNELLEY, Todd	Edm.	Kamloops Blazers
42. RENDALL, Bruce	Phi.	Chatham Maroons

Derek King was the New York Islanders' first selection, 13th overall, in the 1985 NHL Amateur Draft.

1984

FIRST ROUND

Selection	Claimed By	Amateur Club
1. LEMIEUX, Mario	Pit.	Laval Voisins
2. MULLER, Kirk	N.J.	Team Canada-Guelph
3. OLCZYK, Ed	Chi.	Team USA
4. IAFRATE, Al	Tor.	Team USA-Belleville
5. SVOBODA, Petr	Mtl.	Czechoslovakia Jr.
6. REDMOND, Craig	L.A.	Team Canada
7. BURR, Shawn	Det.	Kitchener Rangers
8. CORSON, Shayne	Mtl.	Brantford Alexanders
9. BODGER, Doug	Pit.	Kamloops Jr. Oilers
10. DAIGNEAULT, J.J.	Van.	Canada-Longueuil
11. COTE, Sylvain	Hfd.	Que. Remparts
12. ROBERTS, Gary	Cgy.	Ottawa 67's
13. QUINN, David	Min.	Kent High School
14. CARKNER, Terry	NYR	Peterborough Petes
15. STIENBURG, Trevor	Que.	Guelph Platers
16. BELANGER, Roger	Pit.	Kingston Canadians
17. HATCHER, Kevin	Wsh.	North Bay Centennials
18. ANDERSSON, Bo Mikael	Buf.	V. Frolunda (Sweden)
19. PASIN, Dave	Bos.	Prince Albert Raiders
20. MACPHERSON, Duncan	NYI	Saskatoon Blades
21. ODELEIN, Selmar	Edm.	Regina Pats

SECOND ROUND

Selection	Claimed By	Amateur Club
22. SMYTH, Greg	Phi.	London Knights
23. BILLINGTON, Craig	N.J.	Belleville Bulls
24. WILKS, Brian	L.A.	Kitchener Rangers
25. GILL, Todd	Tor.	Windsor Spitfires
26. BENNING, Brian	St.L.	Portland Winter Hawks
27. MELLANBY, Scott	Phi.	Henry Carr Jr. B
28. HOUDA, Doug	Det.	Cgy. Wranglers
29. RICHER, Stephane	Mtl.	Granby Bisons
30. DOURIS, Peter	Wpg.	U. of N. Hampshire
31. ROHLICEK, Jeff	Van.	Portland Winter Hawks
32. HRKAC, Anthony	St.L.	Orillia Jr. A
33. SABOURIN, Ken	Cgy.	Sault Greyhounds
34. LEACH, Stephen	Wsh.	Matignon High School
35. HELMINEN, Raimo Ilmari	NYR	Ilves (Finland)
36. BROWN, Jeff	Que.	Sudbury Wolves
37. CHYCHRUN, Jeff	Phi.	Kingston Canadians
38. RANHEIM, Paul	Cgy.	Edina Hornets HS
39. TRAPP, Doug	Buf.	Regina Pats
40. PODLOSKI, Ray	Bos.	Portland Winter Hawks
41. MELANSON, Bruce	NYI	Oshawa Generals
42. REAUGH, Daryl	Edm.	Kamloops Jr. Oilers

1983

FIRST ROUND

Selection	Claimed By	Amateur Club
1. LAWTON, Brian	Min.	Mount St. Charles HS
2. TURGEON, Sylvain	Hfd.	Hull Olympiques
3. LAFONTAINE, Pat	NYI	Verdun Juniors
4. YZERMAN, Steve	Det.	Peterborough Petes
5. BARRASSO, Tom	Buf.	Acton-Boxboro HS
6. MacLEAN, John	N.J.	Oshawa Generals
7. COURTNALL, Russ	Tor.	Victoria Cougars
8. McBAIN, Andrew	Wpg.	North Bay Centennials
9. NEELY, Cam	Van.	Portland Winter Hawks
10. LACOMBE, Normand	Buf.	University of New Hampshire
11. CREIGHTON, Adam	Buf.	Ottawa 67's
12. GAGNER, Dave	NYR	Brantford Alexanders
13. QUINN, Dan	Cgy.	Belleville Bulls
14. DOLLAS, Bobby	Wpg.	Laval Voisins
15. ERREY, Bob	Pit.	Peterborough Petes
16. DIDUCK, Gerald	NYI	Lethbridge Broncos
17. TURCOTTE, Alfie	Mtl.	Portland Winter Hawks
18. CASSIDY, Bruce	Chi.	Ottawa 67's
19. BEUKEBOOM, Jeff	Edm.	Sault Greyhounds
20. JENSEN, David	Hfd.	Lawrence Academy
21. MARKWART, Nevin	Bos.	Regina Pats

SECOND ROUND

Selection	Claimed By	Amateur Club
22. CHARLESWORTH, Todd	Pit.	Oshawa Generals
23. SIREN, Ville	Hfd.	Ilves (Finland)
24. EVANS, Shawn	N.J.	Peterborough Petes
25. LAMBERT, Lane	Det.	Saskatoon Blades
26. LEMIEUX, Claude	Mtl.	Trois Rivieres Draveurs
27. MOMESSO, Sergio	Mtl.	Shawinigan Cataractes
28. JACKSON, Jeff	Tor.	Brantford Alexanders
29. BERRY, Brad	Wpg.	St. Albert Saints
30. BRUCE, Dave	Van.	Kitchener Rangers
31. TUCKER, John	Buf.	Kitchener Rangers
32. HEROUX, Yves	Que.	Chicoutimi Sagueneens
33. HEATH, Randy	NYR	Portland Winter Hawks
34. HAJDU, Richard	Buf.	Kamloops Jr. Oilers
35. FRANCIS, Todd	Mtl.	Brantford Alexanders
36. PARKS, Malcolm	Min.	St. Albert Saints
37. McKECHNEY, Grant	NYI	Kitchener Rangers
38. MUSIL, Frantisek	Min.	Czech. National Team
39. PRESLEY, Wayne	Chi.	Kitchener Rangers
40. GOLDEN, Mike	Edm.	Reading High School
41. ZEZEL, Peter	Phi.	Tor. Malboros
42. JOHNSTON, Greg	Bos.	Tor. Malboros

1982

FIRST ROUND

Selection	Claimed By	Amateur Club
1. KLUZAK, Gord	Bos.	Nanaimo Islanders
2. BELLOWS, Brian	Min.	Kitchener Rangers
3. NYLUND, Gary	Tor.	Portland Winter Hawks
4. SUTTER, Ron	Phi.	Lethbridge Broncos
5. STEVENS, Scott	Wsh.	Kitchener Rangers
6. HOUSLEY, Phil	Buf.	S. St. Paul High School
7. YAREMCHUK, Ken	Chi.	Portland Winter Hawks
8. TROTTIER, Rocky	N.J.	Nanaimo Islanders
9. CYR, Paul	Buf.	Victoria Cougars
10. SUTTER, Rich	Pit.	Lethbridge Broncos
11. PETIT, Michel	Van.	Sherbrooke Castors
12. KYTE, Jim	Wpg.	Cornwall Royals
13. SHAW, David	Que.	Kitchener Rangers
14. LAWLESS, Paul	Hfd.	Windsor Spitfires
15. KONTOS, Chris	NYR	Tor. Marlboros
16. ANDREYCHUK, Dave	Buf.	Oshawa Generals
17. CRAVEN, Murray	Det.	Medicine Hat Tigers
18. DANEYKO, Ken	N.J.	Seattle Breakers
19. HEROUX, Alain	Mtl.	Chicoutimi Sagueneens
20. PLAYFAIR, Jim	Edm.	Portland Winter Hawks
21. FLATLEY, Pat	NYI	University of Wisconsin

SECOND ROUND

Selection	Claimed By	Amateur Club
22. CURRAN, Brian	Bos.	Portland Winter Hawks
23. COURTEAU, Yves	Det.	Laval Voisins
24. LEEMAN, Gary	Tor.	Regina Pats
25. IHNACAK, Peter	Tor.	Czech National Team
26. ANDERSON, Mike	Buf.	N. St. Paul High School
27. HEIDT, Mike	L.A.	Cgy. Wranglers
28. BADEAU, Rene	Chi.	Que. Remparts
29. REIERSON, Dave	Cgy.	Prince Albert Raiders
30. JOHANSSON, Jens	Buf.	Pitea (Sweden)
31. GAUVREAU, Jocelyn	Mtl.	Granby Bisons
32. CARLSON, Kent	Mtl.	St. Lawrence University
33. MALEY, David	Mtl.	Edina High School
34. GILLIS, Paul	Que.	Niagara Falls Flyers
35. PATERSON, Mark	Hfd.	Ottawa 67's
36. SANDSTROM, Tomas	NYR	Farjestads (Sweden)
37. KROMM, Richard	Cgy.	Portland Winter Hawks
38. HRYNEWICH, Tim	Pit.	Sudbury Wolves
39. BYERS, Lyndon	Bos.	Regina Pats
40. SANDELIN, Scott	Mtl.	Hibbing High School
41. GRAVES, Steve	Edm.	Sault Greyhounds
42. SMITH, Vern	NYI	Lethbridge Broncos

1981

FIRST ROUND

Selection	Claimed By	Amateur Club
1. HAWERCHUK, Dale	Wpg.	Cornwall Royals
2. SMITH, Doug	L.A.	Ottawa 67's
3. CARPENTER, Bobby	Wsh.	St. John's High School
4. FRANCIS, Ron	Hfd.	Sault Greyhounds
5. CIRELLA, Joe	Col.	Oshawa Generals
6. BENNING, Jim	Tor.	Portland Winter Hawks
7. HUNTER, Mark	Mtl.	Brantford Alexanders
8. FUHR, Grant	Edm.	Victoria Cougars
9. PATRICK, James	NYR	U. of North Dakota
10. BUTCHER, Garth	Van.	Regina Pats
11. MOLLER, Randy	Que.	Lethbridge Broncos
12. TANTI, Tony	Chi.	Oshawa Generals
13. MEIGHAN, Ron	Min.	Niagara Falls Flyers
14. LEVEILLE, Normand	Bos.	Chicoutimi Sagueneens
15. MacINNIS, Allan	Cgy.	Kitchener Rangers
16. SMITH, Steve	Phi.	Sault Greyhounds
17. DUDACEK, Jiri	Buf.	Kladno (Czech.)
18. DELORME, Gilbert	Mtl.	Chicoutimi Sagueneens
19. INGMAN, Jan	Mtl.	Sweden
20. RUFF, Marty	St.L.	Lethbridge Broncos
21. BOUTILIER, Paul	NYI	Sherbrooke Castors

SECOND ROUND

Selection	Claimed By	Amateur Club
22. ARNIEL, Scott	Wpg.	Cornwall Royals
23. LOISELLE, Claude	Det.	Windsor Spitfires
24. YAREMCHUK, Gary	Tor.	Portland Winter Hawks
25. GRIFFIN, Kevin	Chi.	Portland Winter Hawks
26. CHERNOMAZ, Rich	Col.	Victoria Cougars
27. DONNELLY, Dave	Min.	St. Albert Saints
28. GATZOS, Steve	Pit.	Sault Greyhounds
29. STRUEBY, Todd	Edm.	Regina Pats
30. ERIXON, Jan	NYR	Skelleftea (Sweden)
31. SANDS, Mike	Min.	Sudbury Wolves
32. ERIKSSON, Lars	Mtl.	Brynas (Sweden)
33. HIRSCH, Tom	Min.	Patrick Henry HS
34. PREUSS, Dave	Min.	St. Thomas Academy
35. DUFOUR, Luc	Bos.	Chicoutimi Sagueneens
36. NORDIN, Hakan	St.L.	Farjestads (Sweden)
37. COSTELLO, Rich	Phi.	Natick High School
38. VIRTA, Hannu	Buf.	TPS Finland
39. KENNEDY, Dean	L.A.	Brandon Wheat Kings
40. CHELIOS, Chris	Mtl.	Moose Jaw Canucks
41. WAHLSTEN, Jali	Min.	TPS Finland
42. DINEEN, Gord	NYI	Sault Greyhounds

1980

FIRST ROUND

Selection	Claimed By	Amateur Club
1. WICKENHEISER, Doug	Mtl.	Regina Pats
2. BABYCH, Dave	Wpg.	Portland Winter Hawks
3. SAVARD, Denis	Chi.	Mtl. Juniors
4. MURPHY, Larry	L.A.	Peterborough Petes
5. VEITCH, Darren	Wsh.	Regina Pats
6. COFFEY, Paul	Edm.	Kitchener Rangers
7. LANZ, Rick	Van.	Oshawa Generals
8. ARTHUR, Fred	Hfd.	Cornwall Royals
9. BULLARD, Mike	Pit.	Brantford Alexanders
10. FOX, Jimmy	L.A.	Ottawa 67's
11. BLAISDELL, Mike	Det.	Regina Pats
12. WILSON, Rik	St.L.	Kingston Canadians
13. CYR, Denis	Cgy.	Mtl. Juniors
14. MALONE, Jim	NYR	Tor. Marlboros
15. DUPONT, Jerome	Chi.	Tor. Marlboros
16. PALMER, Brad	Min.	Victoria Cougars
17. SUTTER, Brent	NYI	Red Deer Rustlers
18. PEDERSON, Barry	Bos.	Victoria Cougars
19. GAGNE, Paul	Col.	Windsor Spitfires
20. PATRICK, Steve	Buf.	Brandon Wheat Kings
21. STOTHERS, Mike	Phi.	Kingston Canadians

SECOND ROUND

Selection	Claimed By	Amateur Club
22. WARD, Joe	Col.	Seattle Breakers
23. MANTHA, Moe	Wpg.	Tor. Marlboros
24. ROCHEFORT, Normand	Que.	Que. Remparts
25. MUNI, Craig	Tor.	Kingston Canadians
26. McGILL, Bob	Tor.	Victoria Cougars
27. NATTRESS, Ric	Mtl.	Brantford Alexanders
28. LUDZIK, Steve	Chi.	Niagara Falls Flyers
29. GALARNEAU, Michel	Hfd.	Hull Olympiques
30. SOLHEIM, Ken	Chi.	Medicine Hat Tigers
31. CURTALE, Tony	Cgy.	Brantford Alexanders
32. LaVALLEE, Kevin	Cgy.	Brantford Alexanders
33. TERRION, Greg	L.A.	Brantford Alexanders
34. MORRISON, Dave	L.A.	Peterborough Petes
35. ALLISON, Mike	NYR	Sudbury Wolves
36. DAWES, Len	Chi.	Victoria Cougars
37. BEAUPRE, Don	Min.	Sudbury Wolves
38. HRUDEY, Kelly	NYI	Medicine Hat Tigers
39. KONROYD, Steve	Cgy.	Oshawa Generals
40. CHABOT, John	Mtl.	Hull Olympiques
41. MOLLER, Mike	Buf.	Lethbridge Broncos
42. FRASER, Jay	Phi.	Ottawa 67's

1979

FIRST ROUND

Selection	Claimed By	Amateur Club
1. RAMAGE, Rob	Col.	London Knights
2. TURNBULL, Perry	St.L.	Portland Winter Hawks
3. FOLIGNO, Mike	Det.	Sudbury Wolves
4. GARTNER, Mike	Wsh.	Niagara Falls Flyers
5. VAIVE, Rick	Van.	Sherbrooke Castors
6. HARTSBURG, Craig	Min.	Sault Greyhounds
7. BROWN, Keith	Chi.	Portland Winter Hawks
8. BOURQUE, Raymond	Bos.	Verdun Black Hawks
9. BOSCHMAN, Laurie	Tor.	Brandon Wheat Kings
10. McCARTHY, Tom	Min.	Oshawa Generals
11. RAMSEY, Mike	Buf.	University of Min.
12. REINHART, Paul	Atlanta	Kitchener Rangers
13. SULLIMAN, Doug	NYR	Kitchener Rangers
14. PROPP, Brian	Phi.	Brandon Wheat Kings
15. McCRIMMON, Brad	Bos.	Brandon Wheat Kings
16. WELLS, Jay	L.A.	Kingston Canadians
17. SUTTER, Duane	NYI	Lethbridge Broncos
18. ALLISON, Ray	Hfd.	Brandon Wheat Kings
19. MANN, Jimmy	Wpg.	Sherbrooke Beavers
20. GOULET, Michel	Que.	Que. Remparts
21. LOWE, Kevin	Edm.	Que. Remparts

SECOND ROUND

Selection	Claimed By	Amateur Club
22. WESLEY, Blake	Phi.	Portland Winter Hawks
23. PEROVICH, Mike	Atlanta	Brandon Wheat Kings
24. RAUSSE, Errol	Wsh.	Seattle Breakers
25. JONSSON, Tomas	NYI	MoDo AIK (Sweden)
26. ASHTON, Brent	Van.	Saskatoon Blades
27. GINGRAS, Gaston	Mtl.	Hamilton Fincups
28. TRIMPER, Tim	Chi.	Peterborough Petes
29. HOPKINS, Dean	L.A.	London Knights
30. HARDY, Mark	L.A.	Mtl. Juniors
31. MARSHALL, Paul	Pit.	Brantford Alexanders
32. RUFF, Lindy	Buf.	Lethbridge Broncos
33. RIGGIN, Pat	Atlanta	London Knights
34. HOSPODAR, Ed	NYR	Ottawa 67's
35. LINDBERGH, Pelle	Phi.	Solna (Sweden)
36. MORRISON, Doug	Bos.	Lethbridge Broncos
37. NASLUND, Mats	Mtl.	Brynas IFK (Sweden)
38. CARROLL, Billy	NYI	London Knights
39. SMITH, Stuart	Hfd.	Peterborough Petes
40. CHRISTIAN, Dave	Wpg.	U. of North Dakota
41. HUNTER, Dale	Que.	Sudbury Wolves
42. BROTEN, Neal	Min.	University of Min.

1978

FIRST ROUND

Selection	Claimed By	Amateur Club
1. SMITH, Bobby	Min.	Ottawa 67's
2. WALTER, Ryan	Wsh.	Seattle Breakers
3. BABYCH, Wayne	St.L.	Portland Winter Hawks
4. DERLAGO, Bill	Van.	Brandon Wheat Kings
5. GILLIS, Mike	Col.	Kingston Canadians
6. WILSON, Behn	Phi.	Kingston Canadians
7. LINSEMAN, Ken	Phi.	Kingston Canadians
8. GEOFFRION, Danny	Mtl.	Cornwall Royals
9. HUBER, Willie	Det.	Hamilton Fincups
10. HIGGINS, Tim	Chi.	Ottawa 67's
11. MARSH, Brad	Atl.	London Knights
12. PETERSON, Brent	Det.	Portland Winter Hawks
13. PLAYFAIR, Larry	Buf.	Portland Winter Hawks
14. LUCAS, Danny	Phi.	Sault Greyhounds
15. TAMBELLINI, Steve	NYI	Lethbridge Broncos
16. SECORD, Al	Bos.	Hamilton Fincups
17. HUNTER, Dave	Mtl.	Sudbury Wolves
18. COULIS, Tim	Wsh.	Hamilton Fincups

SECOND ROUND

Selection	Claimed By	Amateur Club
19. PAYNE, Steve	Min.	Ottawa 67's
20. MULVEY, Paul	Wsh.	Portland Winter Hawks
21. QUENNEVILLE, Joel	Tor.	Windsor Spitfires
22. FRASER, Curt	Van.	Victoria Cougars
23. MacKINNON, Paul	Wsh.	Peterborough Petes
24. CHRISTOFF, Steve	Min.	University of Min.
25. MEEKER, Mike	Pit.	Peterborough Petes
26. MALONEY, Don	NYR	Kitchener Rangers
27. MALINOWSKI, Merlin	Col.	Medicine Hat Tigers
28. HICKS, Glenn	Det.	Flin Flon Bombers
29. LECUYER, Doug	Chi.	Portland Winter Hawks
30. YAKIWCHUK, Dale	Mtl.	Portland Winter Hawks
31. JENSEN, Al	Det.	Hamilton Fincups
32. McKEGNEY, Tony	Buf.	Kingston Canadians
33. SIMURDA, Mike	Phi.	Kingston Canadians
34. JOHNSTON, Randy	NYI	Peterborough Petes
35. NICOLSON, Graeme	Bos.	Cornwall Royals
36. CARTER, Ron	Mtl.	Sherbrooke Castors

1977

FIRST ROUND

Selection	Claimed By	Amateur Club
1. McCOURT, Dale	Det.	St. Catharines Fincups
2. BECK, Barry	Col.	New Westminster
3. PICARD, Robert	Wsh.	Mtl. Jrs.
4. GILLIS, Jere	Van.	Sherbrooke Castors
5. CROMBEEN, Mike	Cle.	Kingston Canadians
6. WILSON, Doug	Chi.	Ottawa 67's
7. MAXWELL, Brad	Min.	New Westminster
8. DEBLOIS, Lucien	NYR	Sorel Black Hawks
9. CAMPBELL, Scott	St.L.	London Knights
10. NAPIER, Mark	Mtl.	Tor. Marlboros
11. ANDERSON, John	Tor.	Tor. Marlboros
12. JOHANSON, Trevor	Tor.	Tor. Marlboros
13. DUGUAY, Ron	NYR	Sudbury Wolves
14. SEILING, Ric	Buf.	St. Catharines Fincups
15. BOSSY, Mike	NYI	Laval Nationales
16. FOSTER, Dwight	Bos.	Kitchener Rangers
17. McCARTHY, Kevin	Phi.	Wpg. Monarchs
18. DUPONT, Norm	Mtl.	Montreal Jrs.

SECOND ROUND

Selection	Claimed By	Amateur Club
19. SAVARD, Jean	Chi.	Que. Remparts
20. ZAHARKO, Miles	Atl.	New Westminster
21. LOFTHOUSE, Mark	Wsh.	New Westminster
22. BANDURA, Jeff	Van.	Portland Winter Hawks
23. CHICOINE, Daniel	Cle.	Sherbrooke Castors
24. GLADNEY, Bob	Tor.	Oshawa Generals
25. SEMENKO, Dave	Min.	Brandon Wheat Kings
26. KEATING, Mike	NYR	St. Catherines Fincups
27. LABATTE, Neil	St.L.	Tor. Marlboros
28. LAURENCE, Don	Atl.	Kitchener Rangers
29. SAGANIUK, Rocky	Tor.	Lethbridge Broncos
30. HAMILTON, Jim	Pit.	London Knights
31. HILL, Brian	Atl.	Medicine Hat Tigers
32. ARESHENKOFF, Ron	Buf.	Medicine Hat Tigers
33. TONELLI, John	NYI	Tor. Marlboros
34. PARRO, Dave	Bos.	Saskatoon Blades
35. GORENCE, Tom	Phi.	U. of Minnesota
36. LANGWAY, Rod	Mtl.	U. of N. Hampshire

1976

FIRST ROUND

Selection	Claimed By	Amateur Club
1. GREEN, Rick	Wsh.	London Knights
2. CHAPMAN, Blair	Pit.	Saskatoon Blades
3. SHARPLEY, Glen	Min.	Hull Festivals
4. WILLIAMS, Fred	Det.	Saskatoon Blades
5. JOHANSSON, Bjorn	Cal.	Sweden
6. MURDOCH, Don	NYR	Medicine Hat Tigers
7. FEDERKO, Bernie	St.L.	Saskatoon Blades
8. SHAND, Dave	Atl.	Peterborough Petes
9. CLOUTIER, Real	Chi.	Que. Remparts
10. PHILLIPOFF, Harold	Atl.	New Westminster
11. GARDNER, Paul	K.C.	Oshawa Generals
12. LEE, Peter	Mtl.	Ottawa 67's
13. SCHUTT, Rod	Mtl.	Sudbury Wolves
14. McKENDRY, Alex	NYI	Sudbury Wolves
15. CARROLL, Greg	Wsh.	Medicine Hat Tigers
16. PACHAL, Clayton	Bos.	New Westminster
17. SUZOR, Mark	Phi.	Kingston Canadians
18. BAKER, Bruce	Mtl.	Ottawa 67's

SECOND ROUND

Selection	Claimed By	Amateur Club
19. MALONE, Greg	Pit.	Oshawa Generals
20. SUTTER, Brian	St.L.	Lethbridge Broncos
21. CLIPPINGDALE, Steve	L.A.	New Westminster
22. LARSON, Reed	Det.	University of Min.
23. STENLUND, Vern	Cal.	London Knights
24. FARRISH, Dave	NYR	Sudbury Wolves
25. SMRKE, John	St.L.	Tor. Marlboros
26. MANNO, Bob	Van.	St. Catharines Hawks
27. McDILL, Jeff	Chi.	Victoria Cougars
28. SIMPSON, Bobby	Atl.	Sherbrooke Castors
29. MARSH, Peter	Pit.	Sherbrooke Castors
30. CARLYLE, Randy	Tor.	Sudbury Wolves
31. ROBERTS, Jim	Min.	Ottawa 67's
32. KASZYCKI, Mike	NYI	Sault Greyhounds
33. KOWAL, Joe	Buf.	Hamilton Fincups
34. GLOECKNER, Larry	Bos.	Victoria Cougars
35. CALLANDER, Drew	Phi.	Regina Pats
36. MELROSE, Barry	Mtl.	Kamloops Chiefs

1975

FIRST ROUND

Selection	Claimed By	Amateur Club
1. BRIDGMAN, Mel	Phi.	Victoria Cougars
2. DEAN, Barry	K.C.	Medicine Hat Tigers
3. KLASSEN, Ralph	Cal.	Saskatoon Blades
4. MAXWELL, Brian	Min.	Medicine Hat Tigers
5. LAPOINTE, Rick	Det.	Victoria Cougars
6. ASHBY, Don	Tor.	Cgy. Centennials
7. VAYDIK, Greg	Chi.	Medicine Hat Tigers
8. MULHERN, Richard	Atl.	Sherbrooke Beavers
9. SADLER, Robin	Mtl.	Edm. Oil Kings
10. BLIGHT, Rick	Van.	Brandon Wheat Kings
11. PRICE, Pat	NYI	Saskatoon Blades
12. DILLON, Wayne	NYR	Tor. Marlboros
13. LAXTON, Gord	Pit.	New Westminster
14. HALWARD, Doug	Bos.	Peterborough Petes
15. MONDOU, Pierre	Mtl.	Montreal Juniors
16. YOUNG, Tim	L.A.	Ottawa 67's
17. SAUVE, Bob	Buf.	Laval Nationales
18. FORSYTH, Alex	Wsh.	Kingston Canadians

SECOND ROUND

Selection	Claimed By	Amateur Club
19. SCAMURRA, Peter	Wsh.	Peterborough Petes
20. CAIRNS, Don	K.C.	Victoria Cougars
21. MARUK, Dennis	Cal.	London Knights
22. ENGBLOM, Brian	Mtl.	University of Wisconsin
23. ROLLINS, Jerry	Det.	Wpg. Jr. Jets
24. JARVIS, Doug	Tor.	Peterborough Petes
25. ARNDT, Daniel	Chi.	Saskatoon Blades
26. BOWNASS, Rick	Atl.	Montreal Juniors
27. STANIOWSKI, Ed	St.L.	Regina Pats
28. GASSOFF, Brad	Van.	Kamloops Chiefs
29. SALVIAN, David	NYI	St. Catharines Hawks
30. SOETAERT, Doug	NYR	Edm. Oil Kings
31. ANDERSON, Russ	Pit.	U. of Minnesota
32. SMITH, Barry	Bos.	New Westminster
33. BUCYK, Terry	L.A.	Lethbridge Broncos
34. GREENBANK, Kelvin	Mtl.	Wpg. Jr. Jets
35. BREITENBACH, Ken	Buf.	St. Catharines Hawks
36. MASTERS, Jamie	St.L.	Ottawa 67's

Mel Bridgman, claimed by the Philadelphia Flyers, was the first player selected in the 1975 Amateur Draft.

1974

FIRST ROUND

Selection	Claimed By	Amateur Club
1. JOLY, Greg	Wsh.	Regina Pats
2. PAIEMENT, Wilfred	K.C.	St. Catharines Hawks
3. HAMPTON, Rick	Cal.	St. Catharines Hawks
4. GILLIES, Clark	NYI	Regina Pats
5. CONNOR, Cam	Mtl.	Flin Flon Bombers
6. HICKS, Doug	Min.	Flin Flon Bombers
7. RISEBROUGH, Doug	Mtl.	Kitchener Rangers
8. LAROUCHE, Pierre	Pit.	Sorel Black Hawks
9. LOCHEAD, Bill	Det.	Oshawa Generals
10. CHARTRAW, Rick	Mtl.	Kitchener Rangers
11. FOGOLIN, Lee	Buf.	Oshawa Generals
12. TREMBLAY, Mario	Mtl.	Montreal Juniors
13. VALIQUETTE, Jack	Tor.	Sault Greyhounds
14. MALONEY, Dave	NYR	Kitchener Rangers
15. McTAVISH, Gord	Mtl.	Sudbury Wolves
16. MULVEY, Grant	Chi.	Cgy. Centennials
17. CHIPPERFIELD, Ron	Cal.	Brandon Wheat Kings
18. LARWAY, Don	Bos.	Swift Current Broncos

SECOND ROUND

Selection	Claimed By	Amateur Club
19. MARSON, Mike	Wsh.	Sudbury Wolves
20. BURDON, Glen	K.C.	Regina Pats
21. AFFLECK, Bruce	Cal.	University of Denver
22. TROTTIER, Bryan	NYI	Swift Current Broncos
23. SEDLBAUER, Ron	Van.	Kitchener Rangers
24. NANTAIS, Rick	Min.	Que. Remparts
25. HOWE, Mark	Bos.	Tor. Marlboros
26. HESS, Bob	St.L.	New Westminster
27. COSSETTE, Jacques	Pit.	Sorel Black Hawks
28. CHOUINARD, Guy	Atl.	Que. Remparts
29. GARE, Danny	Buf.	Cgy. Centennials
30. MacGREGOR, Gary	Mtl.	Cornwall Royals
31. WILLIAMS, Dave	Tor.	Swift Current Broncos
32. GRESCHNER, Ron	NYR	New Westminster
33. LUPIEN, Gilles	Mtl.	Montreal Juniors
34. DAIGLE, Alain	Chi.	Trois Rivières Draveurs
35. McLEAN, Don	Phi.	Sudbury Wolves
36. STURGEON, Peter	Bos.	Kitchener Rangers

1973

FIRST ROUND

Selection	Claimed By	Amateur Club
1. POTVIN, Denis	NYI	Ottawa 67's
2. LYSIAK, Tom	Atl.	Medicine Hat Tigers
3. VERVERGAERT, Dennis	Van.	London Knights
4. McDONALD, Lanny	Tor.	Medicine Hat Tigers
5. DAVIDSON, John	St.L.	Cgy. Centennials
6. SAVARD, Andre	Bos.	Que. Remparts
7. STOUGHTON, Blaine	Pit.	Flin Flon Bombers
8. GAINEY, Bob	Mtl.	Peterborough Petes
9. DAILEY, Bob	Van.	Tor. Marlboros
10. NEELEY, Bob	Tor.	Peterborough Petes
11. RICHARDSON, Terry	Det.	New Westminster
12. TITANIC, Morris	Buf.	Sudbury Wolves
13. ROTA, Darcy	Chi.	Edm. Oil Kings
14. MIDDLETON, Rick	NYR	Oshawa Generals
15. TURNBULL, Ian	Tor.	Ottawa 67's
16. MERCREDI, Vic	Atl.	New Westminster

SECOND ROUND

Selection	Claimed By	Amateur Club
17. GOLDUP, Glen	Mtl.	Tor. Marlboros
18. DUNLOP, Blake	Min.	Ottawa 67's
19. BORDELEAU, Paulin	Van.	Tor. Marlboros
20. GOODENOUGH, Larry	Phi.	London Knights
21. VAIL, Eric	Atl.	Sudbury Wolves
22. MARRIN, Peter	Mtl.	Tor. Marlboros
23. BIANCHIN, Wayne	Pit.	Flin Flon Bombers
24. PESUT, George	St.L.	Saskatoon Blades
25. ROGERS, John	Min.	Edm. Oil Kings
26. LEVINS, Brent	Phi.	Swift Current Broncos
27. CAMPBELL, Colin	Pit.	Peterborough Petes
28. LANDRY, Jean	Buf.	Que. Remparts
29. THOMAS, Reg	Chi.	London Knights
30. HICKEY, Pat	NYR	Hamilton Red Wings
31. JONES, Jim	Bos.	Peterborough Petes
32. ANDRUFF, Ron	Mtl.	Flin Flon Bombers

1972

FIRST ROUND

Selection	Claimed By	Amateur Club
1. HARRIS, Billy	NYI	Tor. Marlboros
2. RICHARD, Jacques	Atl.	Que. Remparts
3. LEVER, Don	Van.	Niagara Falls Flyers
4. SHUTT, Steve	Mtl.	Tor. Marlboros
5. SCHOENFELD, Jim	Buf.	Niagara Falls Flyers
6. LAROCQUE, Michel	Mtl.	Ottawa 67's
7. BARBER, Bill	Phi.	Kitchener Rangers
8. GARDNER, Dave	Mtl.	Tor. Marlboros
9. MERRICK, Wayne	St.L.	Ottawa 67's
10. BLANCHARD, Albert	NYR	Kitchener Rangers
11. FERGUSON, George	Tor.	Tor. Marlboros
12. BYERS, Jerry	Min.	Kitchener Rangers
13. RUSSELL, Phil	Chi.	Edm. Oil Kings
14. VAN BOXMEER, John	Mtl.	Guelph Juniors
15. MacMILLAN, Bobby	NYR	St. Catharines Hawks
16. BLOOM, Mike	Bos.	St. Catharines Hawks

SECOND ROUND

Selection	Claimed By	Amateur Club
17. HENNING Lorne	NYI	New Westminster
18. BIALOWAS, Dwight	Atl.	Regina Pats
19. McSHEFFREY, Brian	Van.	Ottawa 67's
20. KOZAK, Don	L.A.	Edm. Oil Kings
21. SACHARUK, Larry	NYR	Saskatoon Blades
22. CASSIDY, Tom	Cal.	Kitchener Rangers
23. BLADON, Tom	Phi.	Edm. Oil Kings
24. LYNCH, Jack	Pit.	Oshawa Generals
25. CARRIERE, Larry	Buf.	Loyola College
26. GUITE, Pierre	Det.	St. Catharines Hawks
27. OSBURN, Randy	Tor.	London Knights
28. WEIR, Stan	Cal.	Medicine Hat Tigers
29. OGILVIE, Brian	Chi.	Edm. Oil Kings
30. LUKOWICH, Bernie	Pit.	New Westminster
31. VILLEMURE, Rene	NYR	Shawinigan Bruins
32. ELDER, Wayne	Bos.	London Knights

1971

FIRST ROUND

Selection	Claimed By	Amateur Club
1. LAFLEUR, Guy	Mtl.	Que. Remparts
2. DIONNE, Marcel	Det.	St. Catharines Hawks
3. GUEVREMONT, Jocelyn	Van.	Mtl. Junior Canadiens
4. CARR, Gene	St.L.	Flin Flon Bombers
5. MARTIN, Rick	Buf.	Mtl. Junior Canadiens
6. JONES, Ron	Bos.	Edm. Oil Kings
7. ARNASON, Chuck	Mtl.	Flinflon Bombers
8. WRIGHT, Larry	Phi.	Regina Pats
9. PLANTE, Pierre	Phi.	Drummondville Rangers
10. VICKERS, Steve	NYR	Tor. Marlboros
11. WILSON, Murray	Mtl.	Ottawa 67's
12. SPRING, Dan	Chi.	Edm. Oil Kings
13. DURBANO, Steve	NYR	Tor. Marlboros
14. O'REILLY, Terry	Bos.	Oshawa Generals

SECOND ROUND

Selection	Claimed By	Amateur Club
15. BAIRD, Ken	Cal.	Flin Flon Bombers
16. BOUCHA, Henry	Det.	U.S. Nationals
17. LALONDE, Bobby	Van.	Mtl. Junior Canadiens
18. McKENZIE, Brian	Pit.	St. Catharines Hawks
19. RAMSAY, Craig	Buf.	Peterborough Petes
20. ROBINSON, Larry	Mtl.	Kitchener Rangers
21. NORRISH, Rod	Min.	Regina Pats
22. KEHOE, Rick	Tor.	Hamilton Red Wings
23. FORTIER, Dave	Tor.	St. Catharines Hawks
24. DEGUISE, Michel	Mtl.	Sorel Eperviers
25. FRENCH, Terry	Mtl.	Ottawa 67's
26. KRYSKOW, Dave	Chi.	Edm. Oil Kings
27. WILLIAMS, Tom	NYR	Hamilton Red Wings
28. RIDLEY, Curt	Bos.	Portage Terriers

1970

FIRST ROUND

Selection	Claimed By	Amateur Club
1. PERREAULT, Gilbert	Buf.	Mtl. Junior Canadiens
2. TALLON, Dale	Van.	Tor. Marlboros
3. LEACH, Reg	Bos.	Flin Flon Bombers
4. MacLEISH, Rick	Bos.	Peterborough Petes
5. MARTINIUK, Ray	Mtl.	Flin Flon Bombers
6. LEFLEY, Chuck	Mtl.	Canadian Nationals
7. POLIS, Greg	Pit.	Estevan Bruins
8. SITTLER, Darryl	Tor.	London Knights
9. PLUMB, Ron	Bos.	Peterborough Petes
10. ODDLEIFSON, Chris	Oak.	Wpg. Jets
11. GRATTON, Norm	NYR	Mtl. Junior Canadiens
12. LAJEUNESSE, Serge	Det.	Mtl. Junior Canadiens
13. STEWART, Bob	Bos.	Oshawa Generals
14. MALONEY, Dan	Chi.	London Knights

SECOND ROUND

Selection	Claimed By	Amateur Club
15. DEADMARSH, Butch	Buf.	Brandon Wheat Kings
16. HARGREAVES, Jim	Van.	Wpg. Jets
17. HARVEY, Fred	Min.	Hamilton Red Wings
18. CLEMENT, Bill	Phi.	Ottawa 67's
19. LAFRAMBOISE, Pete	Oak.	Ottawa 67's
20. BARRETT, Fred	Min.	Tor. Marlboros
21. STEWART, John	Pit.	Flin Flon Bombers
22. THOMPSON, Errol	Tor.	Charlottetown Royals
23. KEOGAN, Murray	St.L.	U. of Minnesota
24. McDONOUGH, Al	L.A.	St. Catharines Hawks
25. FRENCH, Mike	NYR	Ottawa 67's
26. MURPHY, Mike	NYR	Tor. Marlboros
27. GUINDON, Bobby	Det.	Mtl. Junior Canadiens
28. BOUCHARD, Dan	Bos.	London Knights
29. ARCHAMBAULT, Mike	Chi.	Drummondville Rangers

1969

FIRST ROUND

Selection	Claimed By	Amateur Club
1. HOULE, Rejean	Mtl.	Mon. Junior Canadiens
2. TARDIF, Marc	Mtl.	Mon. Junior Canadiens
3. TANNAHILL, Don	Bos.	Niagara Falls Flyers
4. SPRING, Frank	Bos.	Edm. Oil Kings
5. REDMOND, Dick	Min.	St. Catharines Hawks
6. CURRIER, Bob	Phi.	Cornwall Royals
7. FEATHERSTONE, Tony	Oak.	Peterborough Petes
8. DUPONT, André	NYR	Mtl. Junior Canadiens
9. MOSER, Ernie	Tor.	Estevan Bruins
10. RUTHERFORD, Jim	Det.	Hamilton Red Wings
11. BOLDIREV, Ivan	Bos.	Oshawa Generals
12. JARRY, Pierre	NYR	Ottawa 67's
13. BORDELEAU, J.-P.	Chi.	Mtl. Junior Canadiens
14. O'BRIEN, Dennis	Min.	St. Catharines Hawks

SECOND ROUND

Selection	Claimed By	Amateur Club
15. KESSELL, Rick	Pit.	Oshawa Generals
16. HOGANSON, Dale	L.A.	Estevan Bruins
17. CLARKE, Bobby	Phi.	Flin Flon Bombers
18. STACKHOUSE, Ron	Oak.	Peterborough Petes
19. LOWE, Mike	St.L.	Loyola College
20. BRINDLEY, Doug	Tor.	Niagara Falls Flyers
21. GARWASIUK, Ron	Det.	Regina Pats
22. QUOQUOCHI, Art	Bos.	Mtl. Junior Canadiens
23. WILSON, Bert	NYR	London Knights
24. ROMANCHYCH, Larry	Chi.	Flin Flon Bombers
25. GILBERT, Gilles	Min.	London Knights
26. BRIERE, Michel	Pit.	Shawinigan Falls
27. BODDY, Greg	L.A.	Edm. Oil Kings
28. BROSSART, Bill	Phi.	Estevan Bruins

NHL All-Stars

Leading NHL All-Stars — 1930-89

Player	Pos	Team	NHL Seasons	First Team Selections	Second Team Selections	Total Selections
Howe, Gordie	RW	Detroit	26	12	9	21
Richard, Maurice	RW	Montreal	18	8	6	14
Hull, Bobby	LW	Chicago	15	10	2	12
Harvey, Doug	D	Mtl-NYR	19	10	1	11
*Gretzky, Wayne	C	Edmonton	10	7	3	10
Beliveau, Jean	C	Montreal	20	6	4	10
*Bourque, Ray	D	Boston	10	6	4	10
Seibert, Earl	D	NYR-Chi	15	4	6	10
Orr, Bobby	D	Boston	12	8	1	9
Lindsay, Ted	LW	Detroit	17	8	1	9
Hall, Glenn	G	Chi-St.L.	18	6	3	9
Mahovlich, Frank	LW	Tor-Det-Mtl	20	3	6	9
Shore, Eddie	D	Boston	14	7	1	8
Mikita, Stan	C	Chicago	22	6	2	8
Kelly, Red	D	Detroit	20	6	2	8
Esposito, Phil	C	Boston	18	6	2	8
Pilote, Pierre	D	Chicago	14	5	3	8
Brimsek, Frank	G	Boston	10	2	6	8
Bossy, Mike	RW	NY Islanders	10	5	3	8
Potvin, Denis	D	NY Islanders	15	5	2	7
Park, Brad	D	NYR-Boston	16	5	2	7
Plante, Jacques	G	Mtl-Tor	18	3	4	7
Gadsby, Bill	D	Chi-NYR-Det	20	3	4	7
Sawchuk, Terry	G	Detroit	21	3	4	7
Durnan, Bill	G	Montreal	7	6	0	6
Lafleur, Guy	RW	Montreal	12	6	0	6
Dryden, Ken	G	Montreal	8	5	1	6
*Coffey, Paul	D	Edm-Pit	9	3	3	6
*Robinson, Larry	D	Montreal	17	3	3	6
Clapper, Dit	D	Boston	20	3	3	6
Horton, Tim	D	Toronto	24	3	3	6
*Salming, Borje	D	Toronto	16	1	5	6
Cowley, Bill	C	Boston	13	4	1	5
Jackson, Harvey	LW	Toronto	15	4	1	5
Conacher, Charlie	RW	Toronto	12	3	2	5
Stewart, Jack	D	Detroit	12	3	2	5
Lach, Elmer	C	Montreal	14	3	2	5
Quackenbush, Bill	D	Det-Bos	14	3	2	5
Blake, Toe	LW	Montreal	15	3	2	5
Reardon, Ken	D	Montreal	7	2	3	5
Kurri, Jari	RW	Edmonton	9	2	3	5
Apps, Syl	C	Toronto	10	2	3	5
Giacomin, Ed	G	NY Rangers	13	2	3	5

*—Active

Position Leaders in All-Star Selections

Position	Player	First Team	Second Team	Total
GOAL	Glenn Hall	7	4	11
	Frank Brimsek	2	6	8
	Jacques Plante	3	4	7
	Terry Sawchuk	3	4	7
	Bill Durnan	6	0	6
	Ken Dryden	5	1	6
DEFENSE	Doug Harvey	10	1	11
	*Ray Bourque	6	4	10
	Earl Seibert	4	6	10
	Bobby Orr	8	1	9
	Eddie Shore	7	1	8
	Red Kelly	6	2	8
	Pierre Pilote	5	3	8
LEFT WING	Bobby Hull	10	2	12
	Ted Lindsay	8	1	9
	Frank Mahovlich	3	6	9
	Harvey Jackson	4	1	5
	Toe Blake	3	2	5
RIGHT WING	Gordie Howe	12	9	21
	Maurice Richard	8	6	14
	Mike Bossy	5	3	8
	Guy Lafleur	6	0	6
	Charlie Conacher	3	2	5
CENTER	*Wayne Gretzky	7	3	10
	Jean Beliveau	6	4	10
	Stan Mikita	6	2	8
	Phil Esposito	6	2	8
	Bill Cowley	4	1	5
	Elmer Lach	3	2	5
	Syl Apps	2	3	5

* — Active

Active Players' All-Star Selection Records

	First Team Selections	Second Team Selections	Total
GOALTENDERS			
Tom Barrasso	(1) 1983-84.	(1) 1984-85	2
Grant Fuhr	(1) 1987-88.	(1) 1981-82.	2
Mike Liut	(1) 1980-81.	(1) 1986-87	2
Patrick Roy	(1) 1988-89.	(1) 1987-88.	2
Bill Smith	(1) 1981-82.	(0)	1
Pete Peeters	(1) 1982-83.	(0)	1
J. Vanbiesbrouck	(1) 1985-86.	(0)	1
Ron Hextall	(1) 1986-87.	(0)	1
R. Melanson	(0)	(1) 1982-83.	1
Pat Riggin	(0)	(1) 1983-84.	1
Bob Froese	(0)	(1) 1985-86.	1
Mike Vernon	(0)	(1) 1988-89.	1
DEFENSEMEN			
Ray Bourque	(6) 1979-80; 1981-82; 1983-84; 1984-85; 1986-87; 1987-88.	(4) 1980-81; 1982-83; 1985-86; 1988-89.	10
Borje Salming	(1) 1976-77.	(5) 1974-75; 1975-76; 1977-78; 1978-79; 1979-80.	6
Larry Robinson	(3) 1976-77; 1978-79; 1979-80.	(3) 1977-78; 1980-81; 1985-86.	6
Paul Coffey	(3) 1984-85; 1985-86; 1988-89.	(3) 1981-82; 1982-83; 1983-84	6
Mark Howe	(3) 1982-83; 1985-86; 1986-87.	(0)	3
Rod Langway	(2) 1982-83; 1983-84	(1) 1984-85.	3
Randy Carlyle	(1) 1980-81.	(0)	1
Doug Wilson	(1) 1981-82.	(1) 1984-85.	2
Scott Stevens	(1) 1987-88.	(0)	1
Chris Chelios	(1) 1988-89.	(0)	1
Brian Engblom	(0)	(1) 1981-82.	1
Larry Murphy	(0)	(1) 1986-87.	1
Al MacInnis	(0)	(2) 1986-87; 1988-89.	2
Gary Suter	(0)	(1) 1987-88.	1
Brad McCrimmon	(0)	(1) 1987-88.	1
CENTERS			
Wayne Gretzky	(7) 1980-81; 1981-82; 1982-83; 1983-84; 1984-85; 1985-86; 1986-87.	(3) 1979-80; 1987-88; 1988-89.	10
Marcel Dionne	(2) 1976-77; 1979-80.	(2) 1978-79; 1980-81.	4
Bryan Trottier	(2) 1977-78; 1978-79.	(2) 1981-82; 1983-84.	4
Mario Lemieux	(2) 1987-88; 1988-89.	(2) 1985-86; 1986-87.	4
Denis Savard	(0)	(1) 1982-83.	1
Dale Hawerchuk	(0)	(1) 1984-85.	1
RIGHT WING			
Mike Bossy	(5) 1980-81; 1981-82; 1982-83; 1983-84; 1985-86.	(3) 1977-78; 1978-79; 1984-85.	8
Jari Kurri	(2) 1984-85; 1986-87.	(3) 1983-84; 1985-86; 1988-89.	5
L. McDonald	(0)	(2) 1976-77; 1982-83.	2
Hakan Loob	(1) 1987-88.	(0)	1
Joe Mullen	(1) 1988-89.	(0)	1
Dave Taylor	(0)	(1) 1980-81.	1
Rick Middleton	(0)	(1) 1981-82.	1
Tim Kerr	(0)	(1) 1986-87.	1
Cam Neely	(0)	(1) 1987-88.	1
LEFT WING			
Michel Goulet	(3) 1983-84; 1985-86; 1986-87.	(2) 1982-83; 1987-88.	5
Mark Messier	(2) 1981-82; 1982-83.	(1) 1983-84.	3
Luc Robitaille	(2) 1987-88; 1988-89.	(1) 1986-87.	3
Clark Gillies	(2) 1977-78; 1978-79.	(0)	2
Charlie Simmer	(2) 1979-80; 1980-81.	(0)	2
John Tonelli	(0)	(2) 1981-82; 1984-85.	2
John Ogrodnick	(1) 1984-85.	(0)	1
Mats Naslund	(0)	(1) 1985-86.	1
Gerard Gallant	(0)	(1) 1988-89.	1

Don Beaupre stretches to the limit to corral this shot in the 1981 All-Star Game, as Ray Bourque looks on.

All-Star Teams
1930 - 89

Voting for the NHL All-Star Team is conducted among the representatives of the Professional Hockey Writers' Association at the end of the season.

Following is a list of the First and Second All-Star Teams since their inception in 1930-31.

1988-89

First Team		Second Team
Roy, Patrick, Mtl.	G	Vernon, Mike, Cgy.
Chelios, Chris, Mtl.	D	MacInnis, Al, Cgy.
Coffey, Paul, Pit.	D	Bourque, Ray, Bos.
Lemieux, Mario, Pit.	C	Gretzky, Wayne, L.A.
Mullen, Joe, Cgy.	RW	Kurri, Jari, Edm.
Robitaille, Luc, L.A.	LW	Gallant, Gerard, Det.

1987-88

First Team		Second Team
Fuhr, Grant, Edm.	G	Roy, Patrick, Mtl.
Bourque, Raymond, Bos.	D	Suter, Gary, Cgy.
Stevens, Scott, Wsh.	D	McCrimmon, Brad, Cgy.
Lemieux, Mario, Pit.	C	Gretzky, Wayne, Edm.
Loob, Hakan, Cgy.	RW	Neely, Cam, Bos.
Robitaille, Luc, L.A.	LW	Goulet, Michel, Que.

1986-87

First Team		Second Team
Hextall, Ron, Phi.	G	Liut, Mike, Hfd.
Bourque, Raymond, Bos.	D	Murphy, Larry, Wsh.
Howe, Mark, Phi.	D	MacInnis, Al, Cgy.
Gretzky, Wayne, Edm.	C	Lemieux, Mario, Pit.
Kurri, Jari, Edm.	RW	Kerr, Tim, Phi.
Goulet, Michel, Que.	LW	Robitaille, Luc, L.A.

1985-86

First Team		Second Team
Vanbiesbrouck, J., NYR	G	Froese, Bob Phi.
Coffey, Paul, Edm.	D	Robinson, Larry, Mtl.
Howe, Mark, Phi.	D	Bourque, Raymond, Bos.
Gretzky, Wayne, Edm.	C	Lemieux, Mario, Pit.
Bossy, Mike, NYI	RW	Kurri, Jari, Edm.
Goulet, Michel, Que.	LW	Naslund, Mats, Mtl.

1984-85

First Team		Second Team
Lindbergh, Pelle, Phi.	G	Barrasso, Tom Buf.
Coffey, Paul, Edm.	D	Langway, Rod, Wsh.
Bourque, Raymond, Bos.	D	Wilson, Doug, Chi.
Gretzky, Wayne, Edm.	C	Hawerchuk, Dale, Wpg.
Kurri, Jari, Edm.	RW	Bossy, Mike, NYI
Ogrodnick, John, Det.	LW	Tonelli, John, NYI

1983-84

First Team		Second Team
Barrasso, Tom, Buf.	G	Riggin, Pat Wsh.
Langway, Rod, Wsh.	D	Coffey, Paul, Edm.
Bourque, Raymond, Bos.	D	Potvin, Denis, NYI
Gretzky, Wayne, Edm.	C	Trottier, Bryan, NYI
Bossy, Mike, NYI	RW	Kurri, Jari, Edm.
Goulet, Michel, Que.	LW	Messier, Mark, Edm.

1982-83

First Team		Second Team
Peeters, Pete, Bos.	G	Melanson, Roland, NYI
Howe, Mark, Phi.	D	Bourque, Raymond, Bos.
Langway, Rod, Wsh.	D	Coffey, Paul, Edm.
Gretzky, Wayne, Edm.	C	Savard, Denis, Chi.
Bossy, Mike, NYI	RW	McDonald, Lanny, Cgy.
Messier, Mark, Edm.	LW	Goulet, Michel, Que.

1981-82

First Team		Second Team
Smith, Bill, NYI	G	Fuhr, Grant, Edm.
Wilson, Doug, Chi.	D	Coffey, Paul, Edm.
Bourque, Raymond, Bos.	D	Engblom, Brian, Mtl.
Gretzky, Wayne, Edm.	C	Trottier, Bryan, NYI
Bossy, Mike, NYI	RW	Middleton, Rick, Bos.
Messier, Mark, Edm.	LW	Tonelli, John, NYI

1980-81

First Team		Second Team
Liut, Mike, St.L.	G	Lessard, Mario, L.A.
Potvin, Denis, NYI	D	Robinson, Larry, Mtl.
Carlyle, Randy, Pit.	D	Bourque, Raymond, Bos.
Gretzky, Wayne, Edm.	C	Dionne, Marcel, L.A.
Bossy, Mike, NYI	RW	Taylor, Dave, L.A.
Simmer, Charlie, L.A.	LW	Barber, Bill, Phi.

1979-80

First Team		Second Team
Esposito, Tony, Chi.	G	Edwards, Don, Buf.
Robinson, Larry, Mtl.	D	Salming, Borje, Tor.
Bourque, Raymond, Bos.	D	Schoenfeld, Jim, Buf.
Dionne, Marcel, L.A.	C	Gretzky, Wayne, Edm.
Lafleur, Guy, Mtl.	RW	Gare, Danny, Buf.
Simmer, Charlie, L.A.	LW	Shutt, Steve, Mtl.

1978-79

First Team		Second Team
Dryden, Ken, Mtl.	G	Resch, Glenn, NYI
Potvin, Denis, NYI	D	Salming, Borje, Tor.
Robinson, Larry, Mtl.	D	Savard, Serge, Mtl.
Trottier, Bryan, NYI	C	Dionne, Marcel, L.A.
Lafleur, Guy, Mtl.	RW	Bossy, Mike, NYI
Gillies, Clark, NYI	LW	Barber, Bill, Phi.

1977-78

First Team		Second Team
Dryden, Ken, Mtl.	G	Edwards, Don, Buf.
Potvin, Denis, NYI	D	Robinson, Larry, Mtl.
Park, Brad, Bos.	D	Salming, Borje, Tor.
Trottier, Bryan, NYI	C	Sittler, Darryl, Tor.
Lafleur, Guy, Mtl.	RW	Bossy, Mike, NYI
Gillies, Clark, NYI	LW	Shutt, Steve, Mtl.

1976-77

First Team		Second Team
Dryden, Ken, Mtl.	G	Vachon, Rogatien, L.A.
Robinson, Larry, Mtl.	D	Potvin, Denis, NYI
Salming, Borje, Tor.	D	Lapointe, Guy, Mtl.
Dionne, Marcel, L.A.	C	Perreault, Gilbert, Buf.
Lafleur, Guy, Mtl.	RW	McDonald, Lanny, Tor.
Shutt, Steve, Mtl.	LW	Martin, Richard, Buf.

1975-76

First Team		Second Team
Dryden, Ken, Mtl.	G	Resch, Glenn, NYI
Potvin, Denis, NYI	D	Salming, Borje, Tor.
Park, Brad, Bos.	D	Lapointe, Guy, Mtl.
Clarke, Bobby, Phi.	C	Perreault, Gilbert, Buf.
Lafleur, Guy, Mtl.	RW	Leach, Reggie, Phi.
Barber, Bill, Phi.	LW	Martin, Richard, Buf.

1974-75

First Team		Second Team
Parent, Bernie, Phi.	G	Vachon, Rogie, L.A.
Orr, Bobby, Bos.	D	Lapointe, Guy, Mtl.
Potvin, Denis, NYI	D	Salming, Borje, Tor.
Clarke, Bobby, Phi.	C	Esposito, Phil, Bos.
Lafleur, Guy, Mtl.	RW	Robert, René, Buf.
Martin, Richard, Buf.	LW	Vickers, Steve, NYR

1973-74

First Team		Second Team
Parent, Bernie, Phi.	G	Esposito, Tony, Chi.
Orr, Bobby, Bos.	D	White, Bill, Chi.
Park, Brad, NYR	D	Ashbee, Barry, Phi.
Esposito, Phil, Bos.	C	Clarke, Bobby, Phi.
Hodge, Ken, Bos.	RW	Redmond, Mickey, Det.
Martin, Richard, Buf.	LW	Cashman, Wayne, Bos.

1972-73

First Team		Second Team
Dryden, Ken, Mtl.	G	Esposito, Tony, Chi.
Orr, Bobby, Bos.	D	Park, Brad, NYR
Lapointe, Guy, Mtl.	D	White, Bill, Chi.
Esposito, Phil, Bos.	C	Clarke, Bobby, Phi.
Redmond, Mickey, Det.	RW	Cournoyer, Yvan, Mtl.
Mahovlich, Frank, Mtl.	LW	Hull, Dennis, Chi.

1971-72

First Team		Second Team
Esposito, Tony, Chi.	G	Dryden, Ken, Mtl.
Orr, Bobby, Bos.	D	White, Bill, Chi.
Park, Brad, NYR	D	Stapleton, Pat, Chi.
Esposito, Phil, Bos.	C	Ratelle, Jean, NYR
Gilbert, Rod, NYR	RW	Cournoyer, Yvan, Mtl.
Hull, Bobby, Chi.	LW	Hadfield, Vic, NYR

1970-71

First Team		Second Team
Giacomin, Ed, NYR	G	Plante, Jacques, Tor.
Orr, Bobby, Bos.	D	Park, Brad, NYR
Tremblay, J.C., Mtl.	D	Stapleton, Pat, Chi.
Esposito, Phil, Bos.	C	Keon, Dave, Tor.
Hodge, Ken, Bos.	RW	Cournoyer, Yvan, Mtl.
Bucyk, John, Bos.	LW	Hull, Bobby, Chi.

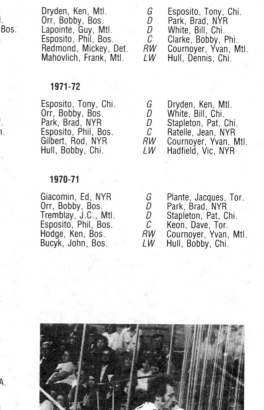

Larry Robinson takes Clark Gillies heavily into the boards during first period action in the 1978 All-Star Game. Robinson's Wales Conference team won the contest 3-2 in overtime.

First Team		Second Team

1969-70

First Team		Second Team
Esposito, Tony, Chi.	G	Giacomin, Ed, NYR
Orr, Bobby, Bos.	D	Brewer, Carl, Det.
Park, Brad, NYR	D	Laperrière, Jacques, Mtl.
Esposito, Phil, Bos.	C	Mikita, Stan, Chi.
Howe, Gordie, Det.	RW	McKenzie, John, Bos.
Hull, Bobby, Chi.	LW	Mahovlich, Frank, Det.

1968-69

First Team		Second Team
Hall, Glenn, St.L.	G	Giacomin, Ed, NYR
Orr, Bobby, Bos.	D	Green, Ted, Bos.
Horton, Tim, Tor.	D	Harris, Ted, Mtl.
Esposito, Phil, Bos.	C	Béliveau, Jean, Mtl.
Howe, Gordie, Det.	RW	Cournoyer, Yvan, Mtl.
Hull, Bobby, Chi.	LW	Mahovlich, Frank, Det.

1967-68

First Team		Second Team
Worsley, Lorne, Mtl.	G	Giacomin, Ed, NYR
Orr, Bobby, Bos.	D	Tremblay, J.C., Mtl.
Horton, Tim, Tor.	D	Neilson, Jim, NYR
Mikita, Stan, Chi.	C	Esposito, Phil, Bos.
Howe, Gordie, Det.	RW	Gilbert, Rod, NYR
Hull, Bobby, Chi.	LW	Bucyk, John, Bos.

1966-67

First Team		Second Team
Giacomin, Ed, NYR	G	Hall, Glenn, Chi.
Pilote, Pierre, Chi.	D	Horton, Tim, Tor.
Howell, Harry, NYR	D	Orr, Bobby, Bos.
Mikita, Stan, Chi.	C	Ullman, Norm, Det.
Wharram, Ken, Chi.	RW	Howe, Gordie, Det.
Hull, Bobby, Chi.	LW	Marshall, Don, NYR

1965-66

First Team		Second Team
Hall, Glenn, Chi.	G	Worsley, Lorne, Mtl.
Laperrière, Jacques, Mtl.	D	Stanley, Allan, Tor.
Pilote, Pierre, Chi.	D	Stapleton, Pat, Chi.
Mikita, Stan, Chi.	C	Béliveau, Jean, Mtl.
Howe, Gordie, Det.	RW	Rousseau, Bobby, Mtl.
Hull, Bobby, Chi.	LW	Mahovlich, Frank, Tor.

1964-65

First Team		Second Team
Crozier, Roger, Det.	G	Hodge, Charlie, Mtl.
Pilote, Pierre, Chi.	D	Gadsby, Bill, Det.
Laperrière, Jacques, Mtl.	D	Brewer, Carl, Tor.
Ullman, Norm, Det.	C	Mikita, Stan, Chi.
Provost, Claude, Mtl.	RW	Howe, Gordie, Det.
Hull, Bobby, Chi.	LW	Mahovlich, Frank, Tor.

1963-64

First Team		Second Team
Hall, Glenn, Chi.	G	Hodge, Charlie, Mtl.
Pilote, Pierre, Chi.	D	Vasko, Elmer, Chi.
Horton, Tim, Tor.	D	Laperrière, Jacques, Mtl.
Mikita, Stan, Chi.	C	Béliveau, Jean, Mtl.
Wharram, Ken, Chi.	RW	Howe, Gordie, Det.
Hull, Bobby, Chi.	LW	Mahovlich, Frank, Tor.

1962-63

First Team		Second Team
Hall, Glenn, Chi.	G	Sawchuk, Terry, Det.
Pilote, Pierre, Chi.	D	Horton, Tim, Tor.
Brewer, Carl, Tor.	D	Vasko, Elmer, Chi.
Mikita, Stan, Chi.	C	Richard, Henri, Mtl.
Howe, Gordie, Det.	RW	Bathgate, Andy, NYR
Mahovlich, Frank, Tor.	LW	Hull, Bobby, Chi.

1961-62

First Team		Second Team
Plante, Jacques, Mtl.	G	Hall, Glenn, Chi.
Harvey, Doug, NYR	D	Brewer, Carl, Tor.
Talbot, Jean-Guy, Mtl.	D	Pilote, Pierre, Chi.
Mikita, Stan, Chi.	C	Keon, Dave, Tor.
Bathgate, Andy, NYR	RW	Howe, Gordie, Det.
Hull, Bobby, Chi.	LW	Mahovlich, Frank, Tor.

1960-61

First Team		Second Team
Bower, Johnny, Tor.	G	Hall, Glenn, Chi.
Harvey, Doug, Mtl.	D	Stanley, Allan, Tor.
Pronovost, Marcel, Det.	D	Pilote, Pierre, Chi.
Béliveau, Jean, Mtl.	C	Richard, Henri, Mtl.
Geoffrion, Bernie, Mtl.	RW	Howe, Gordie, Det.
Mahovlich, Frank, Tor.	LW	Moore, Dickie, Mtl.

1959-60

First Team		Second Team
Hall, Glenn, Chi.	G	Plante, Jacques, Mtl.
Harvey, Doug, Mtl.	D	Stanley, Allan, Tor.
Pronovost, Marcel, Det.	D	Pilote, Pierre, Chi.
Béliveau, Jean, Mtl.	C	Horvath, Bronco, Bos.
Howe, Gordie, Det.	RW	Geoffrion, Bernie, Mtl.
Hull, Bobby, Chi.	LW	Prentice, Dean, NYR

1958-59

First Team		Second Team
Plante, Jacques, Mtl.	G	Sawchuk, Terry, Det.
Johnson, Tom, Mtl.	D	Pronovost, Marcel, Det.
Gadsby, Bill, NYR	D	Harvey, Doug, Mtl.
Béliveau, Jean, Mtl.	C	Richard, Henri, Mtl.
Bathgate, Andy, NYR	RW	Howe, Gordie, Det.
Moore, Dickie, Mtl.	LW	Delvecchio, Alex, Det.

1957-58

First Team		Second Team
Hall, Glenn, Chi.	G	Plante, Jacques, Mtl.
Harvey, Doug, Mtl.	D	Flaman, Fern, Bos.
Gadsby, Bill, NYR	D	Pronovost, Marcel, Det.
Richard, Henri, Mtl.	C	Béliveau, Jean, Mtl.
Howe, Gordie, Det.	RW	Bathgate, Andy, NYR
Moore, Dickie, Mtl.	LW	Henry, Camille, NYR

1956-57

First Team		Second Team
Hall, Glenn, Det.	G	Plante, Jacques, Mtl.
Harvey, Doug, Mtl.	D	Flaman, Fern, Bos.
Kelly, Red, Det.	D	Gadsby, Bill, NYR
Béliveau, Jean, Mtl.	C	Litzenberger, Eddie, Chi.
Howe, Gordie, Det.	RW	Richard, Maurice, Mtl.
Lindsay, Ted, Det.	LW	Chevrefils, Real, Bos.

1955-56

First Team		Second Team
Plante, Jacques, Mtl.	G	Hall, Glenn, Det.
Harvey, Doug, Mtl.	D	Kelly, Red, Det.
Gadsby, Bill, NYR	D	Johnson, Tom, Mtl.
Béliveau, Jean, Mtl.	C	Sloan, Tod, Tor.
Richard, Maurice, Mtl.	RW	Howe, Gordie, Det.
Lindsay, Ted, Det.	LW	Olmstead, Bert, Mtl.

1954-55

First Team		Second Team
Lumley, Harry, Tor.	G	Sawchuk, Terry, Det.
Harvey, Doug, Mtl.	D	Goldham, Bob, Det.
Kelly, Red, Det.	D	Flaman, Fern, Bos.
Béliveau, Jean, Mtl.	C	Mosdell, Ken, Mtl.
Richard, Maurice, Mtl.	RW	Geoffrion, Bernie, Mtl.
Smith, Sid, Tor.	LW	Lewicki, Danny, NYR

1953-54

First Team		Second Team
Lumley, Harry, Tor.	G	Sawchuk, Terry, Det.
Kelly, Red, Det.	D	Gadsby, Bill, Chi.
Harvey, Doug, Mtl.	D	Horton, Tim, Tor.
Mosdell, Ken, Mtl.	C	Kennedy, Ted, Tor.
Howe, Gordie, Det.	RW	Richard, Maurice, Mtl.
Lindsay, Ted, Det.	LW	Sandford, Ed, Bos.

1952-53

First Team		Second Team
Sawchuk, Terry, Det.	G	McNeil, Gerry, Mtl.
Kelly, Red, Det.	D	Quackenbush, Bill, Bos.
Harvey, Doug, Mtl.	D	Gadsby, Bill, Chi.
Mackell, Fleming, Bos.	C	Delvecchio, Alex, Det.
Howe, Gordie, Det.	RW	Richard, Maurice, Mtl.
Lindsay, Ted, Det.	LW	Olmstead, Bert, Mtl.

1951-52

First Team		Second Team
Sawchuk, Terry, Det.	G	Henry, Jim, Bos.
Kelly, Red, Det.	D	Buller, Hy, NYR
Harvey, Doug, Mtl.	D	Thomson, Jim, Tor.
Lach, Elmer, Mtl.	C	Schmidt, Milt, Bos.
Howe, Gordie, Det.	RW	Richard, Maurice, Mtl.
Lindsay, Ted, Det.	LW	Smith, Sid, Tor.

1950-51

First Team		Second Team
Sawchuk, Terry, Det.	G	Rayner, Chuck, NYR
Kelly, Red, Det.	D	Thomson, Jim, Tor.
Quackenbush, Bill, Bos.	D	Reise, Leo, Det.
Schmidt, Milt, Bos.	C	Abel, Sid, Det.
	(tied)	Kennedy, Ted, Tor.
Howe, Gordie, Det.	RW	Richard, Maurice, Mtl.
Lindsay, Ted, Det.	LW	Smith, Sid, Tor.

1949-50

First Team		Second Team
Durnan, Bill, Mtl.	G	Rayner, Chuck, NYR
Mortson, Gus, Tor.	D	Reise, Leo, Det.
Reardon, Kenny, Mtl.	D	Kelly, Red, Det.
Abel, Sid, Det.	C	Kennedy, Ted, Tor.
Richard, Maurice, Mtl.	RW	Howe, Gordie, Det.
Lindsay, Ted, Det.	LW	Leswick, Tony, NYR

1948-49

First Team		Second Team
Durnan, Bill, Mtl.	G	Rayner, Chuck, NYR
Quackenbush, Bill, Det.	D	Harmon, Glen, Mtl.
Stewart, Jack, Det.	D	Reardon, Kenny, Mtl.
Abel, Sid, Det.	C	Bentley, Doug, Chi.
Richard, Maurice, Mtl.	RW	Howe, Gordie, Det.
Conacher, Roy, Chi.	LW	Lindsay, Ted, Det.

1947-48

First Team		Second Team
Broda, W. "Turk", Tor.	G	Brimsek, Frank, Bos.
Quackenbush, Bill, Det.	D	Reardon, Kenny, Mtl.
Stewart, Jack, Det.	D	Colville, Neil, NYR
Lach, Elmer, Mtl.	C	O'Connor, "Buddy", NYR
Richard, Maurice, Mtl.	RW	Poile, "Bud", Chi.
Lindsay, Ted, Det.	LW	Stewart, Gaye, Chi.

1946-47

First Team		Second Team
Durnan, Bill, Mtl.	G	Brimsek, Frank, Bos.
Reardon, Kenny, Mtl.	D	Stewart, Jack, Det.
Bouchard, Emile, Mtl.	D	Quackenbush, Bill, Det.
Schmidt, Milt, Bos.	C	Bentley, Max, Chi.
Richard, Maurice, Mtl.	RW	Bauer, Bobby, Bos.
Bentley, Doug, Chi.	LW	Dumart, Woody, Bos.

1945-46

First Team		Second Team
Durnan, Bill, Mtl.	G	Brimsek, Frank, Bos.
Crawford, Jack, Bos.	D	Reardon, Kenny, Mtl.
Bouchard, Emile, Mtl.	D	Stewart, Jack, Det.
Bentley, Max, Chi.	C	Lach, Elmer, Mtl.
Richard, Maurice, Mtl.	RW	Mosienko, Bill, Chi.
Stewart, Gaye, Tor.	LW	Blake, "Toe", Mtl.
Irvin, Dick, Mtl.	Coach	Gottselig, John, Chi.

1944-45

First Team		Second Team
Durnan, Bill, Mtl.	G	Karakas, Mike, Chi.
Bouchard, Emile, Mtl.	D	Harmon, Glen, Mtl.
Hollett, Bill, Det.	D	Pratt, "Babe", Tor.
Lach, Elmer, Mtl.	C	Cowley, Bill, Bos.
Richard, Maurice, Mtl.	RW	Mosienko, Bill, Chi.
Blake, "Toe", Mtl.	LW	Howe, Syd, Det.
Irvin, Dick, Mtl.	Coach	Adams, Jack, Det.

1943-44

First Team		Second Team
Durnan, Bill, Mtl.	G	Bibeault, Paul, Tor.
Seibert, Earl, Chi.	D	Bouchard, Emile, Mtl.
Pratt, "Babe", Tor.	D	Clapper, "Dit", Bos.
Cowley, Bill, Bos.	C	Lach, Elmer, Mtl.
Carr, Lorne, Tor.	RW	Richard, Maurice, Mtl.
Bentley, Doug, Chi.	LW	Cain, Herb, Bos.
Irvin, Dick, Mtl.	Coach	Day, C.H., "Hap", Tor.

1942-43

First Team		Second Team
Mowers, Johnny, Det.	G	Brimsek, Frank, Bos.
Seibert, Earl, Chi.	D	Crawford, Johnny, Bos.
Stewart, Jack, Det.	D	Hollett, Bill, Bos.
Cowley, Bill, Bos.	C	Apps, Syl, Tor.
Carr, Lorne, Tor.	RW	Hextall, Bryan, NYR
Bentley, Doug, Chi.	LW	Patrick, Lynn, NYR
Adams, Jack, Det.	Coach	Ross, Art, Bos.

First Team		Second Team	First Team		Second Team	First Team		Second Team

1941-42

First Team			Second Team
Brimsek, Frank, Bos.	G		Broda, W. "Turk", Tor.
Seibert, Earl, Chi.	D		Egan, Pat, NYA
Anderson, Tommy, NYA	D		McDonald, Bucko, Tor.
Apps, Syl, Tor.	C		Watson, Phil, NYR
Hextall, Bryan, NYR	RW		Drillon, Gord, Tor.
Patrick, Lynn, NYR	LW		Abel, Sid, Det.
Boucher, Frank, NYR	Coach		Thompson, Paul, Chi.

1940-41

First Team			Second Team
Broda, W. "Turk", Tor.	G		Brimsek, Frank, Bos.
Clapper, "Dit", Bos.	D		Seibert, Earl, Chi.
Stanowski, Wally, Tor.	D		Heller, Ott, NYR
Cowley, Bill, Bos.	C		Apps, Syl, Tor.
Hextall, Bryan, NYR	RW		Bauer, Bobby, Bos.
Schriner, Dave, Tor.	LW		Dumart, Woody, Bos.
Weiland, "Cooney", Bos.	Coach		Irvin, Dick, Mtl.

1939-40

First Team			Second Team
Kerr, Dave, NYR	G		Brimsek, Frank, Bos.
Clapper, "Dit", Bos.	D		Coulter, Art, NYR
Goodfellow, Ebbie, Det.	D		Seibert, Earl, Chi.
Schmidt, Milt, Bos.	C		Colville, Neil, NYR
Hextall, Bryan, NYR	RW		Bauer, Bobby, Bos.
Blake, "Toe", Mtl.	LW		Dumart, Woody, Bos.
Thompson, Paul, Chi.	Coach		Boucher, Frank, NYR

1938-39

First Team			Second Team
Brimsek, Frank, Bos.	G		Robertson, Earl, NYA
Shore, Eddie, Bos.	D		Seibert, Earl, Chi.
Clapper, "Dit", Bos.	D		Coulter, Art, NYR
Apps, Syl, Tor.	C		Colville, Neil, NYR
Drillon, Gord, Tor.	RW		Bauer, Bobby, Bos.
Blake, "Toe", Mtl.	LW		Gottselig, Johnny, Chi.
Ross, Art, Bos.	Coach		Dutton, "Red", NYA

1937-38

First Team			Second Team
Thompson, "Tiny", Bos.	G		Kerr, Dave, NYR
Shore, Eddie, Bos.	D		Coulter, Art, NYR
Seibert, "Babe", Mtl.	D		Seibert, Eart, Chi.
Cowley, Bill, Bos.	C		Apps, Syl, Tor.
Dillon, Cecil, NYR	RW		Dillon, Cecil, NYR
Drillon, Gord, Tor.	(tied)		Drillon, Gord, Tor.
Thompson, Paul, Chi.	LW		Blake, Toe, Mtl.
Patrick, Lester, NYR	Coach		Ross, Art, Bos.

1936-37

First Team			Second Team
Smith, Norm, Det.	G		Cude, Wilf, Mtl.
Siebert, "Babe", Mtl.	D		Seibert, Earl, Chi.
Goodfellow, Ebbie, Det.	D		Conacher, Lionel, Mtl. M.
Barry, Marty, Det.	C		Chapman, Art, NYA
Aurie, Larry, Det.	RW		Dillon, Cecil, NYR
Jackson, Harvey, Tor.	LW		Schriner, Dave, NYA
Adams, Jack, Det.	Coach		Hart, Cecil, Mtl.

1935-36

First Team			Second Team
Thompson, "Tiny", Bos.	G		Cude, Wilf, Mtl.
Shore, Eddie, Bos.	D		Seibert, Earl, Chi.
Seibert, "Babe", Mtl.	D		Goodfellow, Ebbie, Det.
Smith, "Hooley", Mtl. M.	C		Thoms, Bill, Tor.
Conacher, Charlie, Tor.	RW		Dillon, Cecil, NYR
Schriner, Dave, NYA	LW		Thompson, Paul, Chi.
Patrick, Lester, NYR	Coach		Gorman, T.P., Mtl. M.

1934-35

First Team			Second Team
Chabot, Lorne, Chi.	G		Thompson, "Tiny", Bos.
Shore, Eddie, Bos.	D		Wentworth, Cy, Mtl. M.
Seibert, Earl, NYR	D		Coulter, Art, Chi.
Boucher, Frank, NYR	C		Weiland, "Cooney", Det.
Conacher, Charlie, Tor.	RW		Clapper, "Dit", Bos.
Jackson, Harvey, Tor.	LW		Joliat, Aurel, Mtl.
Patrick, Lester, NYR	Coach		Irvin, Dick, Tor.

1933-34

First Team			Second Team
Gardiner, Charlie, Chi.	G		Worters, Roy, NYA
Clancy, "King", Tor.	D		Shore, Eddie, Bos.
Conacher, Lionel, Chi.	D		Johnson, "Ching", NYR
Boucher, Frank, NYR	C		Primeau, Joe, Tor.
Conacher, Charlie, Tor.	RW		Cook, Bill, NYR
Jackson, Harvey, Tor.	LW		Joliat, Aurel, Mtl.
Patrick, Lester, NYR	Coach		Irvin, Dick, Tor.

1932-33

First Team			Second Team
Roach, John Ross, Det.	G		Gardiner, Charlie, Chi.
Shore, Eddie, Bos.	D		Clancy, "King", Tor.
Johnson, "Ching", NYR	D		Conacher, Lionel, Mtl. M.
Boucher, Frank, NYR	C		Morenz, Howie, Mtl.
Cook, Bill, NYR	RW		Conacher, Charlie, Tor.
Northcott, "Baldy", Mtl M.	LW		Jackson, Harvey, Tor.
Patrick, Lester, NYR	Coach		Irvin, Dick, Tor.

1931-32

First Team			Second Team
Gardiner, Charlie, Chi.	G		Worters, Roy, NYA
Shore, Eddie, Bos.	D		Mantha, Sylvio, Mtl.
Johnson, "Ching", NYR	D		Clancy, "King", Tor.
Morenz, Howie, Mtl.	C		Smith, "Hooley", Mtl. M.
Cook, Bill, NYR	RW		Conacher, Charlie, Tor.
Jackson, Harvey, Tor.	LW		Joliat, Aurel, Mtl.
Patrick, Lester, NYR	Coach		Irvin, Dick, Tor.

1930-31

First Team			Second Team
Gardiner, Charlie, Chi.	G		Thompson, "Tiny", Bos.
Shore, Eddie, Bos.	D		Mantha, Sylvio, Mtl.
Clancy, "King", Tor.	D		Johnson, "Ching", NYR
Morenz, Howie, Mtl.	C		Boucher, Frank, NYR
Cook, Bill, NYR	RW		Clapper, "Dit", Bos.
Joliet, Aurel, Mtl.	LW		Cook, "Bun", NYR
Patrick, Lester, NYR	Coach		Irvin, Dick, Chi.

The 1948 First All-Star Team: (left to right), coach Tommy Ivan, "Black" Jack Stewart, Elmer Lach, Bill Quackenbush, "Turk" Broda, NHL president Clarence Campbell, Maurice Richard and Ted Lindsay.

MASTERCARD/NHL ALL-ROOKIE TEAM

Voting for the NHL's All-Rookie Team is conducted among the representatives of the Professional Hockey Writers' Association at the end of the season. The rookie all-star team was first selected for the 1982-83 season.

1988-89

Peter Sidorkiewicz, Hartford	Goal
Brian Leetch, NY Rangers	Defense
Zarley Zalapski, Pittsburgh	Defense
Trevor Linden, Vancouver	Center
Tony Granato, NY Rangers	Right Wing
David Volek, NY Islanders	Left Wing

1987-88

Darren Pang, Chicago	Goal
Glen Wesley, Boston	Defense
Calle Johansson, Buffalo	Defense
Joe Nieuwendyk, Calgary	Center
Ray Sheppard, Buffalo	Right Wing
Iain Duncan, Winnipeg	Left Wing

1986-87

Ron Hextall, Philadelphia	Goal
Steve Duchesne, Los Angeles	Defense
Brian Benning, St. Louis	Defense
Jimmy Carson, Los Angeles	Center
Jim Sandlak, Vancouver	Right Wing
Luc Robitaille, Los Angeles	Left Wing

1985-86

Patrick Roy, Montreal	Goal
Gary Suter, Calgary	Defense
Dana Murzyn, Hartford	Defense
Mike Ridley, NY Rangers	Center
Kjell Dahlin, Montreal	Right Wing
Wendel Clark, Toronto	Left Wing

1984-85

Steve Penney, Montreal	Goal
Chris Chelios, Montreal	Defense
Bruce Bell, Quebec	Defense
Mario Lemieux, Pittsburgh	Center
Tomas Sandstrom, NYR	Right Wing
Warren Young, Pittsburgh	Left Wing

1983-84

Tom Barrasso, Buffalo	Goal
Thomas Eriksson, Philadelphia	Defense
Jamie Macoun, Calgary	Defense
Steve Yzerman, Detroit	Center
Hakan Loob, Calgary	Right Wing
Sylvain Turgeon, Hartford	Left Wing

1982-83

Pelle Lindbergh, Philadelphia	Goal
Scott Stevens, Washington	Defense
Phil Housley, Buffalo	Defense
Dan Daoust, Montreal/Toronto	Center
Steve Larmer, Chicago	Right Wing
Mats Naslund, Montreal	Left Wing

David Volek, left winger on the 1988-89 MasterCard/NHL All-Rookie Team.

All-Star Game Results

Year	Venue	Score	Coaches	Attendance
1989	Edmonton	Campbell 9, Wales 5	Glen Sather, Terry O'Reilly	17,503
1988	St. Louis	Wales 6, Campbell 5 OT	Mike Keenan, Glen Sather	17,878
1986	Hartford	Wales 4, Campbell 3 OT	Mike Keenan, Glen Sather	15,100
1985	Calgary	Wales 6, Campbell 4	Al Arbour, Glen Sather	16,825
1984	New Jersey	Wales 7, Campbell 6	Al Arbour, Glen Sather	18,939
1983	NY Islanders	Campbell 9, Wales 3	Roger Neilson, Al Arbour	15,230
1982	Washington	Wales 4, Campbell 2	Al Arbour, Glen Sonmor	18,130
1981	Los Angeles	Campbell 4, Wales 1	Pat Quinn, Scott Bowman	15,761
1980	Detroit	Wales 6, Campbell 3	Scott Bowman, Al Arbour	21,002
1978	Buffalo	Wales 3, Campbell 2 OT	Scott Bowman, Fred Shero	16,433
1977	Vancouver	Wales 4, Campbell 3	Scott Bowman, Fred Shero	15,607
1976	Philadelphia	Wales 7, Campbell 5	Floyd Smith, Fred Shero	16,436
1975	Montreal	Wales 7, Campbell 1	Bep Guidolin, Fred Shero	16,080
1974	Chicago	West 6, East 4	Billy Reay, Scott Bowman	16,426
1973	New York	East 5, West 4	Tom Johnson, Billy Reay	16,986
1972	Minnesota	East 3, West 2	Al MacNeil, Billy Reay	15,423
1971	Boston	West 2, East 1	Scott Bowman, Harry Sinden	14,790
1970	St. Louis	East 4, West 1	Claude Ruel, Scott Bowman	16,587
1969	Montreal	East 3, West 3	Toe Blake, Scott Bowman	16,260
1968	Toronto	Toronto 4, All-Stars 3	Punch Imlach, Toe Blake	15,753
1967	Montreal	Montreal 3, All-Stars 0	Toe Blake, Sid Abel	14,284
1965	Montreal	All-Stars 5, Montreal 2	Billy Reay, Toe Blake	13,529
1964	Toronto	All-Stars 3, Toronto 2	Sid Abel, Punch Imlach	14,232
1963	Toronto	All-Stars 3, Toronto 3	Sid Abel, Punch Imlach	14,034
1962	Toronto	Toronto 4, All-Stars 1	Punch Imlach, Rudy Pilous	14,236
1961	Chicago	All-Stars 3, Chicago 1	Sid Abel, Rudy Pilous	14,534
1960	Montreal	All-Stars 2, Montreal 1	Punch Imlach, Toe Blake	13,949
1959	Montreal	Montreal 6, All-Stars 1	Toe Blake, Punch Imlach	13,818
1958	Montreal	Montreal 6, All-Stars 3	Toe Blake, Milt Schmidt	13,989
1957	Montreal	All-Stars 5, Montreal 3	Milt Schmidt, Toe Blake	13,003
1956	Montreal	All-Stars 1, Montreal 1	Jim Skinner, Toe Blake	13,095
1955	Detroit	Detroit 3, All-Stars 1	Jim Skinner, Dick Irvin	10,111
1954	Detroit	All-Stars 2, Detroit 2	King Clancy, Jim Skinner	10,689
1953	Montreal	All-Stars 3, Montreal 1	Lynn Patrick, Dick Irvin	14,153
1952	Detroit	1st team 1, 2nd team 1	Tommy Ivan, Dick Irvin	10,680
1951	Toronto	1st team 2, 2nd team 2	Joe Primeau, Hap Day	11,469
1950	Detroit	Detroit 7, All-Stars 1	Tommy Ivan, Lynn Patrick	9,166
1949	Toronto	All-Stars 3, Toronto 1	Tommy Ivan, Hap Day	13,541
1948	Chicago	All-Stars 3, Toronto 1	Tommy Ivan, Hap Day	12,794
1947	Toronto	All-Stars 4, Toronto 3	Dick Irvin, Hap Day	14,169

There was no All-Star contest during the calendar year of 1966 since the game was moved from the start of season to mid-season. In 1979, the Challenge Cup series between the Soviet Union and Team NHL replaced the All-Star Game. In 1987, Rendez-Vous '87, two games between the Soviet Union and Team NHL replaced the All-Star Game.

1988-89 All-Star Game Summary

February 7, 1989 at Edmonton — Campbell 9, Wales 5

PLAYERS ON ICE: **Campbell Conference** — *Fuhr, Vernon, Ellett, Manson, *Lowe, Suter, Reinhart, *Duchesne, J. Mullen, Nicholls, Leeman, Messier, Carson, Hull, *Kurri, Yzerman, Ciccarelli, *Robitaille, Nieuwendyk, *Gretzky. Coach: Sather.

Wales Conference — Lemelin, *Burke, Stevens, Housley, *Coffey, Robinson, Wesley, *R. Bourque, *Neely, K. Dineen, J. MacLean, B. Smith, LaFontaine, Ridley, B. Mullen, Tocchet, McPhee, R. Brown, *M. Lemieux, Poddubny, *Naslund (injured). Coach: O'Reilly.

* Indicates voted to respective All-Star Team by fans.

GOALTENDERS	Campbell:	Fuhr	30 minutes	3 goals against
		Vernon	30 minutes	2 goals against
	Wales:	Lemelin	30 minutes	3 goals against
		Burke	30 minutes	6 goals against

SUMMARY
First Period

1.	Campbell	Kurri	(Gretzky, Robitaille)	1:07
2.	Campbell	Gretzky	(Duchesne)	4:33
3.	Wales	Neely	(Lemieux, Stevens)	9:47 PPG
4.	Wales	Poddubny	(Ridley, Robinson)	10:38

PENALTIES: Messier (C) 9:35.

Second Period

5.	Wales	Wesley	(LaFontaine, B. Mullen)	3:16
6.	Campbell	J. Mullen	(Messier, Nieuwendyk)	7:57
7.	Campbell	Yzerman	(Duchesne, Ciccarelli)	17:21
8.	Campbell	Leeman	(Carson)	17:35

PENALTIES: Bourque (W) 13:44.

Third Period

9.	Wales	Poddubny	(Tocchet, Robinson)	4:40
10.	Campbell	J. Mullen	(Manson)	6:53
11.	Wales	Ridley	(Bourque, Tocchet)	9:35
12.	Campbell	Robitaille	(Kurri, Gretzky)	12:18
13.	Campbell	Carson	(Leeman, Hull)	14:35
14.	Campbell	Messier	(Nieuwendyk, J. Mullen)	17:14

PENALTIES: None.

SHOTS ON GOAL BY:

Campbell Conference	13	10	14	—	37
Wales Conference	14	9	15	—	38

Attendance: 17, 503

All-Star Game Records 1947 through 1989

TEAM RECORDS

MOST GOALS, BOTH TEAMS, ONE GAME:
14 – Campbell 9, Wales 5, 1989 at Edmonton
13 – Wales 7, Campbell 6, 1984 at New Jersey
12 – Campbell 9, Wales 3, 1983 at NY Islanders
   – Wales 7, Campbell 5, 1976 at Philadelphia
11 – Wales 6, Campbell 5, 1988 at St. Louis
10 – West 6, East 4, 1974 at Chicago
   – Wales 6, Campbell 4, 1985 at Calgary

FEWEST GOALS, BOTH TEAMS, ONE GAME:
2 – NHL All-Stars 1, Montreal Canadiens 1, 1956 at Montreal
   – First Team All-Stars 1, Second Team All-Stars 1, 1952 at Detroit
3 – West 2, East 1, 1971 at Boston
   – Montreal Canadiens 3, NHL All-Stars 0, 1967 at Montreal
   – NHL All-Stars 2, Montreal Canadiens 1, 1960 at Montreal

MOST GOALS, ONE TEAM, ONE GAME:
9 – Campbell 9, Wales 3, 1983 at NY Islanders
   Campbell 9, Wales 5, 1989 at Edmonton
7 – Wales 7, Campbell 5, 1976 at Philadelphia
   – Wales 7, Campbell 1, 1975 at Montreal
   – Detroit Red Wings 7, NHL All-Stars 1, 1950 at Detroit
   – Wales 7, Campbell 6, 1984 at New Jersey

FEWEST GOALS, ONE TEAM, ONE GAME:
0 – NHL All-Stars 0, Montreal Canadiens 3, 1967 at Montreal
1 – 17 times (1981, 1975, 1971, 1970, 1962, 1961, 1960, 1959, both teams
   1956, 1955, 1953, both teams 1952, 1950, 1949, 1948)

MOST SHOTS, BOTH TEAMS, ONE GAME (SINCE 1955):
81 – 1968 at Toronto – NHL All-Stars 3 (40 shots),
                          Toronto Maple Leafs 4 (41 shots)
75 – 1955 at Detroit   – NHL All-Stars 1 (31 shots),
                          Detroit Red Wings 3 (44 shots)
   – 1989 at   Campbell 9 (37 shots),
      Edmonton   Wales 5 (38 shots)
74 – 1963 at Toronto – NHL All-Stars 3 (38 shots),
                          Toronto Maple Leafs 3 (36 shots)

FEWEST SHOTS, BOTH TEAMS, ONE GAME (SINCE 1955):
52 – 1978 at Buffalo   – Campbell 2 (12 shots)
                          Wales 3 (40 shots)
53 – 1960 at Montreal – NHL All-Stars 2 (27 shots)
                          Montreal Canadiens 1 (26 shots)
55 – 1956 at Montreal – NHL All-Stars 1 (28 shots)
                          Montreal Canadiens 1 (27 shots)
55 – 1971 at Boston   – West 2 (28 shots)
                          East 1 (27 shots)

MOST SHOTS, ONE TEAM, ONE GAME (SINCE 1955):
44 – 1955 at Detroit – Detroit Red Wings (3-1 vs. NHL All-Stars)
44 – 1970 at St. Louis – East (4-1 vs. West)
43 – 1981 at Los Angeles – Campbell (4-1 vs. Wales)
42 – 1976 at Philadelphia – Wales (7-5 vs. Campbell)

FEWEST SHOTS, ONE TEAM, ONE GAME (SINCE 1955):
12 – 1978 at Buffalo – Campbell (2-3 vs. Wales)
17 – 1970 at St. Louis – West (1-4 vs. East)
23 – 1961 at Chicago – Chicago Black Hawks (1-3 vs. NHL All-Stars)
24 – 1976 at Philadelphia – Campbell (5-7 vs. Wales)

MOST POWER-PLAY GOALS, BOTH TEAMS, ONE GAME (SINCE 1950):
3 – 1953 at Montreal   NHL All-Stars 3 (2 power-play goals),
                          Montreal Canadiens 1 (1 power-play goal)
3 – 1954 at Detroit   NHL All-Stars 2 (1 power-play goal)
                          Detroit Red Wings 2 (2 power-play goals)
3 – 1958 at Montreal   NHL All-Stars 3 (1 power-play goal)
                          Montreal Canadiens 6 (2 power-play goals)

FEWEST POWER-PLAY GOALS, BOTH TEAMS, ONE GAME (SINCE 1950):
0 – 13 times (1952, 1959, 1960, 1967, 1968, 1969, 1972, 1973, 1976, 1980,
   1981, 1984, 1985)

FASTEST TWO GOALS, BOTH TEAMS, FROM START OF GAME:
37 seconds – 1970 at St. Louis – Jacques Laperriere of East scored at 20
seconds and Dean Prentice of West scored at 37 seconds. Final score: East 4,
West 1.

4:08 – 1963 at Toronto – Frank Mahovlich scored for Toronto Maple Leafs at 2:22
of first period and Henri Richard scored at 4:08 for NHL All-Stars. Final score: NHL
All-Stars 3, Toronto Maple Leafs 3.

4:19 – 1980 at Detroit – Larry Robinson scored at 3:58 for Wales and Steve
Payne scored at 4:19 for Wales. Final score: Wales 6, Campbell 3.

FASTEST TWO GOALS, BOTH TEAMS:
10 seconds – 1976 at Philadelphia – Dennis Ververgaert scored at 4:33 and at
4:43 of third period for Campbell . Final score: Wales 7, Campbell 5.
14 seconds – 1989 at Edmonton. Steve Yzerman and Gary Leeman scored at
17:21 and 17:35 of second period for Campbell. Final score: Campbell 9, Wales 5.
17 seconds – 1970 at St. Louis – Jacques Laperriere of East scored at 20
seconds of first period and Dean Prentice of West scored at 37 seconds. Final
score: East 4, West 1.
17 seconds – 1973 at New York – Paul Henderson of East scored at 19:12 of
second period and Pit Martin of West scored at 19:29. Final score: East 5, West 4.

FASTEST THREE GOALS, BOTH TEAMS:
1:32 – 1980 at Detroit – all by Wales – Ron Stackhouse scored at 11:40 of third
period, Craig Hartsburg scored at 12:40 and Reed Larson scored at 13:12. Final
score: Wales 6, Campbell 3.
2:01 – 1976 at Philadelphia – Curt Bennett scored at 16:59 of first period for
Campbell ; Pete Mahovlich scored at 18:31 for Wales ; Brad Park scored at 19:00
for Wales . Final score: Wales 7, Campbell 5.
2:55 – 1964 at Toronto – Leo Boivin scored at 10:47 of second period for NHL All-
Stars; Kent Douglas scored at 11:45 for Toronto; Jean Beliveau scored at 13:52
for All-Stars. Final score: NHL All-Stars 3, Toronto Maple Leafs 2.

FASTEST FOUR GOALS, BOTH TEAMS:
4:26 – 1980 at Detroit – all by Wales – Ron Stackhouse scored at 11:40 of third
period; Craig Hartsburg scored at 12:40; Reed Larson scored at 13:12; Real
Cloutier scored at 16:06. Final score: Wales 6, Campbell 3.
5:14 – 1983 at NY Islanders – Don Maloney scored at 14:04 of third period for
Wales; Wayne Gretzky scored at 15:32 for Campbell; Rick Vaive scored at 17:15
for Campbell; Gretzky scored at 19:18 for Campbell. Final score: Campbell 9,
Wales 3.
6:44 – 1983 at NY Islanders – Wayne Gretzky scored at 10:31 of third period for
Campbell; Don Maloney scored at 14:04 for Wales; Gretzky scored at 15:32 for
Campbell; Rick Vaive scored at 17:15 for Campbell. Final score: Campbell 9,
Wales 3.

FASTEST TWO GOALS, ONE TEAM, FROM START OF GAME:
4:19 – 1980 at Detroit – Wales – Larry Robinson scored at 3:58 and Steve Payne
scored at 4:19. Final score: Wales 6, Campbell 3.
4:38 – 1971 at Boston – West – Chico Maki scored at 36 seconds and Bobby Hull
scored at 4:38. Final score: West 2, East 1.
5:25 – 1953 at Montreal – NHL All-Stars – Wally Hergesheimer scored at 4:06 and
5:25. Final score: NHL All-Stars 3, Montreal Canadiens 1.
5:31 – 1985 at Calgary – Wales – Ron Francis scored at 1:40 and Tim Kerr
scored at 5:31. Final score: Wales 6, Campbell 4.

FASTEST TWO GOALS, ONE TEAM:
10 seconds – 1976 at Philadelphia – Campbell – Dennis Ververgaert scored at
4:33 and at 4:43 of third period. Final score: Wales 7, Campbell 5.
14 seconds – 1989 at Edmonton. Steve Yzerman and Gary Leeman scored at
17:21 and 17:35 of second period for Campbell. Final score: Campbell 9, Wales 5.
21 seconds – 1980 at Detroit – Wales – Larry Robinson scored at 3:58 of first
period and Steve Payne scored at 4:19. Final score: Wales 6, Campbell 3.
29 seconds – 1976 at Philadelphia – Campbell – Denis Potvin scored at 14:17 of
third period and Steve Vickers scored at 14:46. Final score: Wales 7, Campbell 5.
29 seconds – 1976 at Philadelphia – Wales – Pete Mahovlich scored at 18:31 of
first period and Brad Park scored at 19:00. Final score: Wales 7, Campbell 5.

FASTEST THREE GOALS, ONE TEAM:
1:32 – 1980 at Detroit – Wales – Ron Stackhouse scored at 11:40 of third period;
Craig Hartsburg scored at 12:40; Reed Larson scored at 13:12.
Final score: Wales 6, Campbell 3.
3:05 – 1984 at New Jersey – Wales – Rick Middleton scored at 14:49 of first
period; Mats Naslund at 16:40; Pierre Larouche at 17:14.
Final score: Wales 7, Campbell 6.
3:26 – 1980 at Detroit – Wales – Craig Hartsburg scored at 12:40 of third period;
Reed Larson scored at 13:12; Real Cloutier scored at 13:06.
Final score: Wales 6, Campbell 3.
3:46 – 1983 at NY Islanders – Campbell – Wayne Gretzky scored at 15:32 of third
period; Rick Vaive scored at 17:15; Gretzky scored at 19:18.
Final score: Campbell 9, Wales 3.

FASTEST FOUR GOALS, ONE TEAM:
4:26 – 1980 at Detroit – Wales – Ron Stackhouse scored at 11:40 of third period; Craig Hartsburg scored at 12:40; Reed Larson scored at 13:12; Real Cloutier scored at 16:06. Final score: Wales 6, Campbell 3.
7:25 – 1976 at Philadelphia – Wales – Al MacAdam scored at 9:34 of second period; Guy Lafleur scored at 11:54; Marcel Dionne scored at 13:51; Dan Maloney scored at 16:59. Final score: Wales 7, Campbell 5.
8:03 – 1975 at Montreal – Wales – Phil Esposito scored at 19:16 of second period; Syl Apps scored at 3:25 of third period; Terry O'Reilly scored at 5:43; Bobby Orr scored at 7:19. Final score: Wales 7, Campbell 1.

MOST GOALS, BOTH TEAMS, ONE PERIOD:
7 – 1983 at NY Islanders – Third period – Campbell (6), Wales (1)
Final score: Campbell 9, Wales 3.
6 – 1989 at Edmonton – Third period – Campbell (4), Wales (2).
Final score: Campbell 9, Wales 5.
5 – 1962 at Toronto – First period – Toronto (4), NHL All-Stars (1).
Final score: Toronto Maple Leafs 4, NHL All-Stars 1.
5 – 1965 at Montreal – Second period – NHL All-Stars (3), Montreal (2).
Final score: NHL All-Stars 5, Montreal Canadiens 2.
5 – 1973 at New York – Second period – East (3), West (2).
Final score: East 5, West 4.
5 – 1974 at Chicago – Third period – West (3), East (2).
Final score: West 6, East 4.
5 – 1980 at Detroit – Third period – Wales (4), Campbell (1).
Final score: Wales 6, Campbell 3.

MOST GOALS, ONE TEAM, ONE PERIOD:
6 – 1983 at NY Islanders – Third period – Campbell.
Final score: Campbell 9, Wales 3.
5 – 1984 at New Jersey – First period – Wales.
Final score: Wales 7, Campbell 6.
4 – 1959 at Montreal – Third period – Montreal Canadiens. Final score: Montreal Canadiens 6, NHL All-Stars 1.
4 – 1962 at Toronto – First period – Toronto Maple Leafs. Final score: Toronto Maple Leafs 4, NHL All-Stars 1.
4 – 1976 at Philadelphia – Second period – Wales.
Final score: Wales 7, Campbell 5.
4 – 1976 at Philadelphia – Third period – Campbell.
Final score: Wales 7, Campbell 5.
4 – 1980 at Detroit – Third period – Wales. Final score: Wales 6, Campbell 3.
4 – 1989 at Edmonton – Third period – Campbell. Final score: Campbell 9, Wales 5.

MOST SHOTS, BOTH TEAMS, ONE PERIOD:
30 – 1959 at Montreal – Second period – NHL All-Stars (16), Montreal (14).
Final score: Montreal Canadiens 6, NHL All-Stars 1
29 – 1955 at Detroit – Third period – Detroit Red Wings (18), NHL All- Stars (11).
Final score: Detroit Red Wings 3, NHL All-Stars 1
29 – 1968 at Toronto – Second period – Toronto Maple Leafs (18), NHL All- Stars (11). Final score: Toronto Maple Leafs 4, NHL All-Stars 3
29 – 1980 at Detroit – Third period – Wales (17), Campbell (12).
Final score: Wales 6, Campbell 3
29 – 1989 at Edmonton – Third period – Wales (15). Campbell (14).
Final score: Campbell 9, Wales 5.

MOST SHOTS, ONE TEAM, ONE PERIOD:
20 – 1970 at St. Louis – Third period – East. Final score: East 4, West 1
18 – 1955 at Detroit – Third period – Detroit Red Wings.
Final score: Detroit Red Wings 3, NHL All-Stars 1
18 – 1968 at Toronto – Second period – Toront Maple Leafs.
Final score: Toronto Maple Leafs 4, NHL All-Stars 3
18 – 1981 at Los Angeles – First period – Campbell.
Final score: Campbell 4, Wales 1

FEWEST SHOTS, BOTH TEAMS, ONE PERIOD:
9 – 1971 at Boston – Third period – East (2), West (7). Final score: West 2, East 1
9 – 1980 at Detroit – Second period – Campbell (4), Wales (5).
Final score: Wales 6, Campbell 3.
13 – 1982 at Washington – Third period – Campbell (6), Wales (7).
Final score: Wales 4, Campbell 2.
14 – 1978 at Buffalo – First period – Campbell (7), Wales (7).
Final score: Wales 3, Campbell 2.
14 – 1986 at Hartford – First period – Campbell (6), Wales (8).
Final score: Wales 4, Campbell 3.

FEWEST SHOTS, ONE TEAM, ONE PERIOD:
2 – 1971 at Boston – Third period – East
Final score: West 2, East 1
2 – 1978 at Buffalo – Second period – Campbell
Final score: Wales 3, Campbell 2
3 – 1978 at Buffalo – Third period – Campbell
Final score: Wales 3, Campbell 2
4 – 1955 at Detroit – First period – NHL All-Stars
Final score: Detroit Red Wings 3, NHL All-Stars 1
4 – 1980 at Detroit – Second period – Campbell
Final score: Wales 6, Campbell 3

On February 14, 1934, in Toronto, the Maple Leafs played a collection of stars from other teams for the benefit of Ace Bailey, whose brilliant career had come to an abrupt end the year before. The Leafs won this first All-Star Game 7-3.

INDIVIDUAL RECORDS
Career

MOST GAMES PLAYED:
23 – Gordie Howe from 1948 through 1980
15 – Frank Mahovlich from 1959 through 1974
13 – Jean Beliveau from 1953 through 1969
 – Alex Delvecchio from 1953 through 1967
 – Doug Harvey from 1951 through 1969
 – Maurice Richard from 1947 through 1959

MOST GOALS:
10 – Gordie Howe in 23GP
 – **Wayne Gretzky** in 9GP
8 – Frank Mahovlich in 15GP
7 – Maurice Richard in 13GP
5 – Bobby Hull in 12GP
 – Ted Lindsay in 11GP
 – Denis Potvin in 8GP
 – Mario Lemieux in 4GP

MOST ASSISTS:
9 – Gordie Howe in 23GP
7 – Doug Harvey in 13GP
 – Guy Lafleur in 5GP
6 – Red Kelly in 11GP
 – Norm Ullman in 11GP
 – Mats Naslund in 3GP

MOST POINTS:
19 – Gordie Howe (10G-9A in 23GP)
13 – Frank Mahovlich (8G-5A in 15GP)
 – Wayne Gretzky (10G-3A in 9GP)
10 – Bobby Hull (5G-5A in 12GP)
 – Ted Lindsay (5G-5A in 11GP)
 – Mario Lemieux (5G-5A in 4GP)
9 – Maurice Richard (7G-2A in 13GP)
 – Henri Richard (4G-5A in 10GP)
 – Denis Potvin (5G-4A in 8GP)
8 – Norm Ullman (2G-6A in 11GP)
 – Guy Lafleur (1G-7A in 5GP)
 – Doug Harvey (1G-7A in 13GP)

MOST PENALTY MINUTES:
27 – Gordie Howe in 23GP
21 – Gus Mortson in 9GP
16 – Harry Howell in 7GP

MOST POWER-PLAY GOALS:
6 – Gordie Howe in 23GP
3 – Bobby Hull in 12GP
2 – Maurice Richard in 13GP

Game

MOST GOALS, ONE GAME:
4 – Wayne Gretzky, Campbell, 1983
3 – Ted Lindsay, Detroit Red Wings, 1950
 – Mario Lemieux, Wales, 1988
2 – Wally Hergesheimer, NHL All-Stars, 1953
 – Earl Reibel, Detroit Red Wings, 1955
 – Andy Bathgate, NHL All-Stars, 1958
 – Maurice Richard, Montreal Canadiens, 1958
 – Frank Mahovlich, Toronto Maple Leafs, 1963
 – Gordie Howe, NHL All-Stars, 1965
 – John Ferguson, Montreal Canadiens, 1967
 – Frank Mahovlich, East All-Stars, 1969
 – Greg Polis, West All-Stars, 1973
 – Syl Apps, Wales, 1975
 – Dennis Ververgaert, Campbell, 1976
 – Richard Martin, Wales, 1977
 – Lanny McDonald, Wales, 1977
 – Mike Bossy, Wales, 1982
 – Pierre Larouche, Wales, 1984
 – Mario Lemieux, Wales 1985
 – Brian Propp, Wales, 1986
 – Joe Mullen, Campbell, 1989

MOST ASSISTS, ONE GAME:
5 – Mats Naslund, Wales, 1988
4 – Raymond Bourque, Wales, 1985
3 – Dickie Moore, Montreal Canadiens, 1958
 – Doug Harvey, Montreal Canadiens, 1959
 – Guy Lafleur, Wales, 1975
 – Pete Mahovlich, Wales, 1976
 – Mark Messier, Campbell, 1983
 – Rick Vaive, Campbell, 1984
 – Mark Johnson, Wales, 1984
 – Don Maloney, Wales, 1984
 – Mike Krushelnyski, Campbell, 1985

MOST POINTS, ONE GAME:
6 – Mario Lemieux, Wales, 1988 (3G-3A)
5 – Mats Naslund, Wales, 1988 (5A)
4 – Ted Lindsay, Detroit Red Wings, 1950 (3G-1A)
 – Gordie Howe, NHL All-Stars, 1965 (2G-2A)
 – Pete Mahovlich, Wales, 1976 (1G-3A)
 – Wayne Gretzky, Campbell, 1983 (4G)
 – Don Maloney, Wales, 1984 (1G-3A)
 – Raymond Bourque, Wales, 1985 (4A)

MOST GOALS, ONE PERIOD:
4 – Wayne Gretzky, Campbell, Third period, 1983
2 – Ted Lindsay, Detroit Red Wings, First period, 1950
 – Wally Hergesheimer, NHL All-Stars, First period, 1953
 – Andy Bathgate, NHL All-Stars, Third period, 1958
 – Frank Mahovlich, Toronto Maple Leafs, First period, 1963
 – Dennis Ververgaert, Campbell, Third period, 1976
 – Richard Martin, Wales, Third period, 1977

MOST ASSISTS, ONE PERIOD:
3 – Mark Messier, Clarence Campbell, Third period, 1983
2 – By several players

MOST POINTS, ONE PERIOD:
4 – Wayne Gretzky, Campbell, Third period, 1983 (4G)
3 – Gordie Howe, Detroit, Second period, 1965 (1G-2A)
 – Pete Mahovlich, Wales, First period, 1976 (1G-2A)
 – Mark Messier, Campbell, Third period, 1983 (4A)
 – Mario Lemieux, Wales, Second period, 1988 (1G-2A)

FASTEST GOAL FROM START OF GAME:
19 seconds – Ted Lindsay, Detroit Red Wings, 1950
20 seconds – Jacques Laperriere, East All-Stars, 1970
36 seconds – Chico Maki, West All-Stars, 1971
37 seconds – Dean Prentice, West All-Star, 1970
45 seconds – Kent Nilsson, Campbell , 1981

FASTEST GOAL FROM START OF A PERIOD:
19 seconds – Ted Lindsay, Detroit Red Wings, 1950 (first period)
20 seconds – Jacques Laperriere, East , 1970 (first period)
26 seconds – Wayne Gretzky, Campbell, 1982 (second period)
28 seconds – Maurice Richard, NHL All-Stars, 1947 (third period)
33 seconds – Bert Olmstead, Montreal Canadiens, 1957 (second period)

FASTEST TWO GOALS FROM START OF GAME:
5:25 – Wally Hergesheimer, NHL All-Stars, 1953. Scored at 4:06 and 5:25 of first period.
12:11 – Frank Mahovlich, Toronto Maple Leafs, 1963. Scored at 2:22 and 12:11 of first period.

FASTEST TWO GOALS FROM START OF A PERIOD:
4:43 – Dennis Ververgaert, Campbell , 1976. Scored at 4:33 and 4:43 of third period.
5:25 – Wally Hergesheimer, NHL All-Stars, 1953. Scored at 4:06 and 5:25 of first period.
12:11 – Frank Mahovlich, Toronto Maple Leafs, 1963. Scored at 2:22 and 12:11 of first period.
13:54 – Andy Bathgate, NHL All-Stars, 1958. Scored at 3:55 and 13:54 of third period.

FASTEST TWO GOALS:
10 seconds – Dennis Ververgaert, Campbell, 1976. Scored at 4:33 and 4:43 of third period.
1:19 – Wally Hergesheimer, NHL All-Stars, 1953. Scored at 4:06 and 5:25 of first period.
4:09 – Mike Bossy, Wales, 1982. Scored at 17:10 of second period and 1:19 of third period.

Goaltenders

MOST GAMES PLAYED:
13 – Glenn Hall from 1955-1969
11 – Terry Sawchuk from 1950-1968
 8 – Jacques Plante from 1956-1970
 6 – Tony Esposito from 1970-1980
 – Ed Giacomin from 1967-1973

MOST GOALS AGAINST:
22 – Glenn Hall in 13GP
19 – Terry Sawchuk in 11GP
18 – Jacques Plante in 8GP
14 – Turk Broda in 4GP

BEST GOALS-AGAINST-AVERAGE AMONG THOSE WITH AT LEAST TWO GAMES PLAYED:
0.68 – Gilles Villemure in 3GP
1.02 – Frank Brimsek in 2GP
1.59 – Johnny Bower in 4GP
1.64 – Lorne "Gump" Worsley in 4GP
1.98 – Gerry McNeil in 3GP
2.03 – Don Edwards in 2GP
2.44 – Terry Sawchuk in 11GP

MOST MINUTES PLAYED:
467 – Terry Sawchuk in 11GP
421 – Glenn Hall in 13GP
370 – Jacques Plante in 8GP
209 – Turk Broda in 4GP
182 – Ed Giacomin in 6GP
165 – Tony Esposito in 6GP

NHL and Soviet Clubs to Play 21 Games in 1989-90

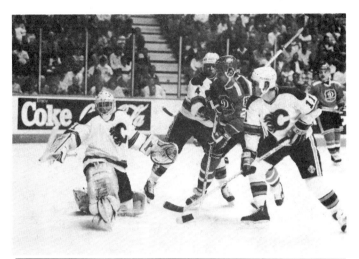

Calgary Flames vs. Dynamo Riga, December 27, 1988.

Beginning on December 4, 1989, Soviet club teams will begin a 21-game exhibition tour against NHL opponents. This tour will be the seventh occasion one or more Soviet clubs have played NHL teams in North America. This season's Super Series features four Soviet teams, and will see one game played by each NHL club. The four Soviet teams will be named in the fall of 1989.

Fifty games have been played between Soviet and NHL clubs since December, 1975. The Soviets lead the combined series, with a record of 28 wins, 16 losses and 6 ties.

Soviet/NHL cooperation continues to grow. In 1989, Soviet players signed contracts with NHL teams with the approval of the Soviet Ice Hockey Federation. As well, the Calgary Flames and Washington Capitals played pre-season exhibition games in the Soviet Union.

Super Series 1989-90 Schedule

Monday	Dec. 4	at	Los Angeles
Wednesday	Dec. 6	at	Edmonton
Friday	Dec. 8	at	Calgary
Monday	Dec. 11	at	Detroit
Tuesday	Dec. 12	at	Washington
Thursday	Dec. 14	at	St. Louis
Tuesday	Dec. 26	at	NY Islanders
Wednesday	Dec. 27	at	Hartford
		at	Winnipeg
Friday	Dec. 29	at	Pittsburgh
		at	Vancouver
Sunday	Dec. 31	at	Quebec
		at	Toronto
Monday	Jan. 1	at	NY Rangers
Tuesday	Jan. 2	at	Minnesota
Wednesday	Jan. 3	at	Buffalo
Thursday	Jan. 4	at	Montreal
Saturday	Jan. 6	at	New Jersey
Sunday	Jan. 7	at	Chicago
Tuesday	Jan. 9	at	Boston
		at	Philadelphia

NHL-Soviet Game Record, 1972-1989

Date	Venue	Score	Goaltenders
9/2/72	Montreal	Soviet Union 7, Team Canada 3	Tretiak – Dryden
9/4/72	Toronto	Team Canada 4, Soviet Union 1	Esposito – Tretiak
9/6/72	Winnipeg	Soviet Union 4, Team Canada 4	Tretiak – Esposito
9/8/72	Vancouver	Soviet Union 5, Team Canada 3	Tretiak – Dryden
9/22/72	Moscow	Soviet Union 5, Team Canada 4	Tretiak – Esposito
9/26/72	Moscow	Team Canada 3, Soviet Union 2	Dryden – Tretiak
9/26/72	Moscow	Team Canada 4, Soviet Union 3	Esposito – Tretiak
9/28/72	Moscow	Team Canada 6, Soviet Union 5	Dryden – Tretiak
12/28/75	New York	Red Army 7, NY Rangers 3	Tretiak – Davidson
12/29/75	Pittsburgh	Soviet Wings 7, Pittsburgh 4	Sidelnikov – Plasse
12/31/75	Montreal	Montreal 3, Red Army 3	Dryden – Tretiak
1/4/76	Buffalo	Buffalo 12, Soviet Wings 6	Desjardins – Kylikov, Sidelnikov
1/7/76	Chicago	Soviet Wings 4, Chicago 2	Sidelnikov – Esposito
1/8/76	Boston	Red Army 5, Boston 2	Tretiak – Gilbert
1/10/76	New York	Soviet Wings 2, NY Islanders 1	Sidelnikov – Resch
1/11/76	Philadelphia	Philadelphia 4, Red Army 1	Stephenson – Tretiak
9/9/76	Philadelphia	Soviet Union 5, Team U.S.A. 0	Tretiak – Curran
9/11/76	Toronto	Team Canada 3, Soviet Union 1	Vachon – Tretiak
12/28/77	Vancouver	Vancouver 2, Spartak 0	Ridley – Pashkov
1/3/78	Denver	Spartak 8, Colorado 3	Pashkov – Favell, McKenzie
1/5/78	St. Louis	Spartak 2, St. Louis 1	Doroshenko – Johnston, Myre
1/6/78	Montreal	Montreal 5, Spartak 2	Dryden, Larocque – Pashkov
1/8/78	Atlanta	Spartak 2, Atlanta 1	Doroshenko – Belanger
12/31/78	Minnesota	Soviet Wings 8, Minnesota 5	Myshkin – Edwards, LoPresti
1/2/79	Philadelphia	Philadelphia 4, Soviet Wings 4	Parent – Myshkin
1/4/79	Detroit	Detroit 6, Soviet Wings 5	Rutherford, Vachon – Myshkin
1/9/79	Boston	Soviet Wings 4, Boston 1	Sidelnikov – Cheevers, Pettie
2/8/79	New York	Team NHL 4, Soviet Union 2	Dryden – Tretiak
2/10/79	New York	Soviet Union 5, Team NHL 4	Tretiak – Dryden
2/11/79	New York	Soviet Union 6, Team NHL 0	Myshkin – Cheevers
12/26/79	Vancouver	Vancouver 6, Dynamo 2	Ridley – Myshkin
12/27/79	New York	Red Army 5, NY Rangers 2	Tretiak – Baker, Davidson
12/29/79	New York	Red Army 3, NY Islanders 2	Tretiak – Smith
12/31/79	Montreal	Montreal 4, Red Army 2	Sevigny – Tretiak
1/2/80	Winnipeg	Dynamo 7, Winnipeg 0	Myshkin – Hamel, Middlebrook
1/3/80	Buffalo	Buffalo 6, Red Army 1	Edwards – Tretiak
1/4/80	Edmonton	Dynamo 4, Edmonton 1	Myshkin – Mio
1/6/80	Quebec	Red Army 6, Quebec 4	Tretiak – Dion
1/8/80	Washington	Washington 5, Dynamo 5	Inness – Myshkin
9/5/81	Edmonton	Soviet Union 4, Team U.S.A. 1	Tretiak – Esposito
9/9/81	Montreal	Team Canada 7, Soviet Union 3	Liut – Myshkin
9/13/81	Montreal	Soviet Union 8, Team Canada 1	Tretiak – Liut
12/28/82	Edmonton	Edmonton 4, Soviet Union 3	Moog – Myshkin
12/30/82	Quebec	Soviet Union 3, Quebec 0	Tretiak – Bouchard
12/31/82	Montreal	Soviet Union 5, Montreal 0	Tretiak – Sevigny
1/2/83	Calgary	Calgary 3, Soviet Union 2	Edwards, Lemelin – Myshkin
1/4/83	Minnesota	Soviet Union 6, Minnesota 3	Tretiak – Mattson, Beaupre
1/6/83	Philadelphia	Soviet Union 5, Philadelphia 1	Tretiak – Lindbergh
9/8/84	Edmonton	Soviet Union 2, Team U.S.A. 1	Myshkin – Barrasso
9/10/84	Edmonton	Soviet Union 5, Team Canada 3	Tyzhnykh – Lemelin
9/13/84	Calgary	Team Canada 3, Soviet Union 2	Peeters – Myshkin
12/26/85	Los Angeles	Red Army 5, Los Angeles 2	Mylnikov Janecyk
12/27/85	Edmonton	Red Army 6, Edmonton 3	Mylnikov – Moog
12/29/85	Quebec	Quebec 5, Red Army 1	Malarchuk – Mylnikov
12/29/85	Calgary	Calgary 4, Dynamo 3	Vernon – Myshkin
12/31/85	Montreal	Red Army 6, Montreal 1	Mylnikov – Soetaert, Roy
1/2/86	St. Louis	Red Army 4, St. Louis 2	Mylnikov – Millen, Wamsley
1/4/86	Minnesota	Red Army 4, Minnesota 3	Mylnikov – Casey
1/4/86	Pittsburgh	Dynamo 3, Pittsburgh 3	Myshkin – Herron
1/6/86	Boston	Dynamo 6, Boston 4	Myshkin – Keans
1/8/86	Buffalo	Dynamo 7, Buffalo 4	Myshkin – Cloutier
2/11/87	Quebec	NHL All-Stars 3, Soviet Union 2	Fuhr – Belosheykin
2/13/87	Quebec	Soviet Union 5, NHL All-Stars 3	Belosheykin – Fuhr
9/4/87	Hartford	Soviet Union 5, Team USA 1	Mylnikov – Barrasso
9/6/87	Hamilton, Ont.	Team Canada 3, Soviet Union 3	Fuhr – Belosheykin
9/11/87	Montreal	Soviet Union 6, Team Canada 5	Mylnikov – Fuhr
9/13/87	Hamilton, Ont.	Soviet Union 4, Team Canada 3	Fuhr – Belosheykin
9/15/87	Hamilton, Ont.	Team Canada 6, Soviet Union 5	Fuhr – Mylnikov
12/26/88	Quebec	Red Army 5, Quebec 5	Mylnikov – Mason
12/27/88	Calgary	Dynamo Riga 2, Calgary 2	Irbe – Wamsley
12/28/88	Edmonton	Edmonton 2, Dynamo Riga 1	Irbe – Fuhr
12/29/88	NY Islanders	Red Army 3, NY Islanders 2	Mylnikov – Smith, Hrudey
12/30/88	Vancouver	Vancouver 6, Dynamo Riga 1	Irbe – McLean
12/31/88	Boston	Red Army 5, Boston 4	Mylnikov – Lemelin
12/31/88	Los Angeles	Dynamo Riga 5, Los Angeles 2	Irbe – Fitzpatrick
1/2/89	New Jersey	Red Army 5, New Jersey 0	Mylnikov – Terreri
1/4/89	Pittsburgh	Pittsburgh 4, Red Army 2	Mylnikov, Goloshumov – Pietrangelo, Young
1/4/89	Chicago	Chicago 4, Dynamo Riga 1	Irbe – Belfour
1/5/89	St. Louis	St. Louis 5, Dynamo Riga 0	Irbe – Jablonski
1/7/89	Minnesota	Dynamo Riga 2, Minnesota 1	Irbe – Myllys
1/7/89	Hartford	Red Army 6, Hartford 3	Goloshumov – Liut
1/9/89	Buffalo	Buffalo 6, Red Army 5	Goloshumov, Mylnikov – Cloutier, Puppa

Hockey Hall of Fame

Location: Toronto's Exhibition Park, on the shore of Lake Ontario, adjacent to Ontario Place and Exhibition Stadium. The Hockey Hall of Fame building is in the middle of Exhibition Place, directly north of the stadium.

Telephone: (416) 595-1345.

Hours: Mid-May to mid-August - 10 am to 7 pm Tuesday through Sunday; Mondays 10 am to 5 pm. Mid-August to Labor Day - Hours vary during annual Exhibition. September after Labor Day to mid-May - 10 am to 4:30 pm. Also closed Christmas Day, New Year's Day and the day prior to the annual Exhibition.

Admission: Adults $3, Seniors & Students $1. Group rates, and reduced rate during Exhibition.

History: The Hockey Hall of Fame building was completed May 1, 1961, and officially opened August 26, 1961, by the Prime Minister of Canada, John G. Diefenbaker, and U.S. ambassador to Canada, Livingston T. Merchant. The six member clubs of the NHL operating at the time provided the funds required for construction. The City of Toronto, owner of the grounds, provided an ideal site, and the Canadian National Exhibition Association, as administrator of the park area, agreed to service and maintain the building in perpetuity for the purposes of the Hockey Hall of Fame. Hockey exhibits are provided and financed by the NHL with co-operative support of the Canadian Amateur Hockey Association. Staff and most administration costs are underwritten by the NHL.

Eligibility Requirements: Any person who is, or has been distinguished in hockey as a player, executive or referee/linesman, shall be eligible for election. Player and referee/linesman candidates will normally have completed their active participating careers three years prior to election, but in exceptional cases this period may be shortened by the Hockey Hall of Fame Board of Directors. Veteran player candidates must have concluded their careers as active players in the sport of hockey for at least 25 years. Candidates for election as executives and referees/linesmen shall be nominated only by the Board of Directors and upon election shall be known as Builders or referees/linesmen. Candidates for election as players shall be chosen on the basis of "playing ability, integrity, character and their contribution to their team and the game of hockey in general."

Honor Roll: There are 272 Honored Members of the Hockey Hall of Fame. Of the total, 189 are listed as players, 72 as Builders and 11 as Referees/Linesmen. Ian (Scotty) Morrison is President of the Hall.

(Year of election to the Hall is indicated in brackets after the Members' names).

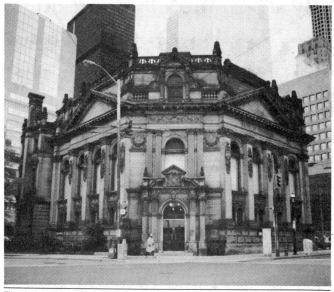

The Hockey Hall of Fame is relocating to a site in the heart of downtown Toronto. Combining the old with the new, the Hall of Fame will have exhibit space in both the historic Bank of Montreal Building (1885), pictured above, and in the concourse of BCE Place, a new development bounded by Yonge, Front, Bay and Wellington Streets. Projected opening date for the new Hall of Fame is 1991-92.

PLAYERS

Abel, Sidney Gerald (1969)
*Adams, John James "Jack" (1959)
Apps, Charles Joseph Sylvanus "Syl" (1961)
Armstrong, George Edward (1975)
Bailey, Irvine Wallace "Ace" (1975)
*Bain, Donald H. "Dan" (1945)
*Baker, Hobart "Hobey" (1945)
*Barry, Martin J. "Marty" (1965)
Bathgate, Andrew James "Andy" (1978)
Beliveau, Jean Arthur (1972)
*Benedict, Clinton S. (1965)
Bentley, Douglas Wagner (1964)
*Bentley, Maxwell H. L. (1966)
Blake, Hector "Toe" (1966)
Boivin, Leo Joseph (1986)
*Boon, Richard R. "Dickie" (1952)
Bouchard, Emile Joseph "Butch" (1966)
*Boucher, Frank (1958)
*Boucher, George "Buck" (1960)
Bower, John William (1976)
*Bowie, Russell (1945)
Brimsek, Francis Charles (1966)
*Broadbent, Harry L. "Punch" (1962)
*Broda, Walter Edward "Turk" (1967)
Bucyk, John Paul (1981)
*Burch, Billy (1974)
*Cameron, Harold Hugh "Harry" (1962)
Cheevers, Gerald Michael "Gerry" (1985)
*Clancy, Francis Michael "King" (1958)
*Clapper, Aubrey "Dit" (1945)
Clarke, Robert "Bobby" (1987)
*Cleghorn, Sprague (1958)
Colville, Neil MacNeil (1967)
*Conacher, Charles W. (1961)
*Connell, Alex (1958)
*Cook, William Osser (1952)
Coulter, Arthur Edmund (1974)
Cournoyer, Yvan Serge (1982)
Cowley, William Mailes (1968)
*Crawford, Samuel Russell "Rusty" (1962)
*Darragh, John Proctor "Jack" (1962)
*Davidson, Allan M. "Scotty" (1950)
Day, Clarence Henry "Hap" (1961)
Delvecchio, Alex (1977)
Denneny, Cyril "Cy" (1959)
*Drillon, Gordon Arthur (1975)
*Drinkwater, Charles Graham (1950)

Dryden, Kenneth Wayne (1983)
*Dunderdale, Thomas (1974)
*Durnan, William Ronald (1964)
*Dutton, Mervyn A. "Red" (1958)
*Dye, Cecil Henry "Babe" (1970)
Esposito, Anthony James "Tony" (1988)
Esposito, Philip Anthony (1984)
*Farrell, Arthur F. (1965)
*Foyston, Frank (1958)
*Frederickson, Frank (1958)
Gadsby, William Alexander (1970)
*Gardiner, Charles Robert "Chuck" (1945)
*Gardiner, Herbert Martin "Herb" (1958)
*Gardner, James Henry "Jimmy" (1962)
Geoffrion, Jos. A. Bernard "Boom Boom" (1972)
*Gerard, Eddie (1945)
Giacomin, Edward "Eddie" (1987)
Gilbert, Rodrigue Gabriel "Rod" (1982)
*Gilmour, Hamilton Livingstone "Billy" (1962)
*Goheen, Frank Xavier "Moose" (1952)
*Goodfellow, Ebenezer R. "Ebbie" (1963)
*Grant, Michael "Mike" (1950)
*Green, Wilfred "Shorty" (1962)
*Griffis, Silas Seth "Si" (1950)
*Hainsworth, George (1961)
Hall, Glenn Henry (1975)
*Hall, Joseph Henry (1961)
Harvey, Douglas Norman (1973)
*Hay, George (1958)
*Hern, William Milton "Riley" (1962)
*Hextall, Bryan Aldwyn (1969)
Holmes, Harry "Hap" (1972)
*Hooper, Charles Thomas "Tom" (1962)
Horner, George Reginald "Red" (1965)
*Horton, Miles Gilbert "Tim" (1977)
Howe, Gordon (1972)
*Howe, Sydney Harris (1965)
Howell, Henry Vernon "Harry" (1979)
Hull, Robert Marvin (1983)
*Hutton, John Bower "Bouse" (1962)
*Hyland, Harry M. (1962)
*Irvin, James Dickenson "Dick" (1958)
*Jackson, Harvey "Busher" (1971)
*Johnson, Ernest "Moose" (1952)
*Johnson, Ivan "Ching" (1958)
Johnson, Thomas Christian (1970)
*Joliat, Aurel (1947)

*Keats, Gordon "Duke" (1958)
Kelly, Leonard Patrick "Red" (1969)
Kennedy, Theodore Samuel "Teeder" (1966)
Keon, David Michael (1986)
Lach, Elmer James (1966)
Lafleur, Guy Damien (1988)
*Lalonde, Edouard Charles "Newsy" (1950)
Laperriere, Jacques (1987)
*Laviolette, Jean Baptiste "Jack" (1962)
*Lehman, Hugh (1958)
Lemaire, Jacques Gerard (1984)
*LeSueur, Percy (1961)
Lewis, Herbert A. (1989)
Lindsay, Robert Blake Theodore "Ted" (1966)
Lumley, Harry (1980)
*MacKay, Duncan "Mickey" (1952)
Mahovlich, Frank William (1981)
*Malone, Joseph "Joe" (1950)
*Mantha, Sylvio (1960)
*Marshall, John "Jack" (1965)
*Maxwell, Fred G. "Steamer" (1962)
*McGee, Frank (1945)
*McGimsie, William George "Billy" (1962)
*McNamara, George (1958)
Mikita, Stanley (1983)
Moore, Richard Winston (1974)
*Moran, Patrick Joseph "Paddy" (1958)
*Morenz, Howie (1945)
*Mosienko, William "Billy" (1965)
*Nighbor, Frank (1945)
*Noble, Edward Reginald "Reg" (1962)
*O'Connor, Herbert William "Buddy" (1988)
*Oliver, Harry (1967)
Olmstead, Murray Bert "Bert" (1985)
Orr, Robert Gordon (1979)
Parent, Bernard Marcel (1984)
Park, Douglas Bradford "Brad" (1988)
*Patrick, Joseph Lynn (1980)
*Patrick, Lester (1945)
*Phillips, Tommy (1945)
Pilote, Joseph Albert Pierre Paul (1975)
*Pitre, Didier "Pit" (1962)
*Plante, Joseph Jacques Omer (1978)
*Pratt, Walter "Babe" (1966)
*Primeau, A. Joseph (1963)
Pronovost, Joseph René Marcel (1978)
*Pulford, Harvey (1945)

Quackenbush, Hubert George "Bill" (1976)
*Rankin, Frank (1961)
Ratelle, Joseph Gilbert Yvan Jean "Jean" (1985)
Rayner, Claude Earl "Chuck" (1973)
Reardon, Kenneth Joseph (1966)
Richard, Joseph Henri (1979)
Richard, Joseph Henri Maurice "Rocket" (1961)
*Richardson, George Taylor (1950)
*Roberts, Gordon (1971)
*Ross, Arthur Howie (1945)
*Russel, Blair (1965)
*Russell, Ernest (1965)
*Ruttan, J.D. "Jack" (1962)
Savard, Serge A. (1986)
*Sawchuk, Terrance Gordon "Terry" (1971)
*Scanlan, Fred (1965)
Schmidt, Milton Conrad "Milt" (1961)
Schriner, David "Sweeney" (1962)
Seibert, Earl Walter (1963)
*Seibert, Oliver Levi (1961)
*Shore, Edward W. "Eddie" (1945)
*Siebert, Albert C. "Babe" (1964)
*Simpson, Harold Edward "Bullet Joe" (1962)
Sittler, Daryl Glen (1989)
*Smith, Alfred E. (1962)
*Smith, Reginald "Hooley" (1972)
*Smith, Thomas James (1973)
Stanley, Allan Herbert (1981)
*Stanley, Russell "Barney" (1962)
*Stewart, John Sherratt "Black Jack" (1964)
*Stewart, Nelson "Nels" (1962)
*Stuart, Bruce (1961)
*Stuart, Hod (1945)
*Taylor, Frederic "Cyclone" (O.B.E.) (1945)
*Thompson, Cecil R. "Tiny" (1959)
Tretiak, Vladislav (1989)
*Trihey, Col. Harry J. (1950)
Ullman, Norman Victor Alexander "Norm" (1982)
*Vezina, Georges (1945)
*Walker, John Phillip "Jack" (1960)
*Walsh, Martin "Marty" (1962)
*Watson, Harry E. (1962)
*Weiland, Ralph "Cooney" (1971)
*Westwick, Harry (1962)
*Whitcroft, Fred (1962)
*Wilson, Gordon Allan "Phat" (1962)
Worsley, Lorne John "Gump" (1980)
*Worters, Roy (1969)

BUILDERS

*Adams, Charles Francis (1960)
*Adams, Weston W. (1972)
*Ahearn, Thomas Franklin "Frank" (1962)
*Ahearne, John Francis "Bunny" (1977)
*Allan, Sir Montague (C.V.O.) (1945)
Ballard, Harold Edwin (1977)
*Bauer, Father David (1989)
*Bickell, John Paris (1978)
*Brown, George V. (1961)
*Brown, Walter A. (1962)
Buckland, Frank (1975)
Butterfield, Jack Arlington (1980)
*Calder, Frank (1945)
*Campbell, Angus D. (1964)
*Campbell, Clarence Sutherland (1966)
*Cattarinich, Joseph (1977)
*Dandurand, Joseph Viateur "Leo" (1963)
Dilio, Francis Paul (1964)
*Dudley, George S. (1958)
*Dunn, James A. (1968)
Eagleson, Robert Alan (1989)
Francis, Emile (1982)
*Gibson, Dr. John L. "Jack" (1976)
*Gorman, Thomas Patrick "Tommy" (1963)
Hanley, William (1986)
*Hay, Charles (1974)
*Hendy, James C. (1968)
*Hewitt, Foster (1965)
*Hewitt, William Abraham (1945)
*Hume, Fred J. (1962)
*Imlach, George "Punch" (1984)
Ivan, Thomas N. (1974)
*Jennings, William M. (1975)
Juckes, Gordon W. (1979)
*Kilpatrick, Gen. John Reed (1960)
*Leader, George Alfred (1969)
LeBel, Robert (1970)
*Lockhart, Thomas F. (1965)
*Loicq, Paul (1961)
*Mariucci, John (1985)
*McLaughlin, Major Frederic (1963)
*Milford, John "Jake" (1984)
Molson, Hon. Hartland de Montarville (1973)
*Nelson, Francis (1945)
*Norris, Bruce A. (1969)
*Norris, Sr., James (1958)
*Norris, James Dougan (1962)
*Northey, William M. (1945)
*O'Brien, John Ambrose (1962)
*Patrick, Frank (1958)
*Pickard, Allan W. (1958)
Pilous, Rudy (1985)
Pollock, Samuel Patterson Smyth (1978)
*Raymond, Sen. Donat (1958)
*Robertson, John Ross (1945)
*Robinson, Claude C. (1945)
*Ross, Philip D. (1976)
*Selke, Frank J. (1960)
Sinden, Harry James (1983)
*Smith, Frank D. (1962)
*Smythe, Conn (1958)
Snider, Edward M. (1988)
*Stanley of Preston, Lord (G.C.B.) (1945)
*Sutherland, Cap. James T. (1945)
Tarasov, Anatoli V. (1974)
*Turner, Lloyd (1958)
Tutt, William Thayer (1978)
Voss, Carl Potter (1974)
*Waghorn, Fred C. (1961)
*Wirtz, Arthur Michael (1971)
Wirtz, William W. "Bill" (1976)
Ziegler, John A. Jr. (1987)

REFEREES/LINESMEN

Ashley, John George (1981)
Chadwick, William L. (1964)
*Elliott, Chaucer (1961)
*Hayes, George William (1988)
*Hewitson, Robert W. (1963)
*Ion, Fred J. "Mickey" (1961)
Pavelich, Matt (1987)
*Rodden, Michael J. "Mike" (1962)
*Smeaton, J. Cooper (1961)
Storey, Roy Alvin "Red" (1967)
Udvari, Frank Joseph (1973)

*Deceased

United States Hockey Hall of Fame

The United States Hockey Hall of Fame is located in Eveleth, Minnesota, 60 miles north of Duluth, on Highway 53. The facility is open Monday to Saturday 9 a.m. to 5 p.m. and Sundays noon to 5 p.m. from the day after Labor Day until June 14. During the remaining summer period the Monday to Saturday hours are 9 a.m. to 8 p.m. and Sundays 10 a.m. to 8 p.m.; Adult $2.50; Seniors $2.25; Juniors $1.50; and Children 7-12 $1.25; Children under 6 free. Group rates available.

The Hall was dedicated and opened on June 21, 1973, largely as the result of the work of D. Kelly Campbell, Chairman of the Eveleth Civic Association's Project H Committee. The National Hockey League contributed $100,000 towards the construction of the building. There are now 70 enshrinees consisting of 45 players, 10 coaches, 14 administrators, and one referee. New members are inducted annually in October and must have made a significant contribution toward hockey in the United States through the vehicle of their careers. Mitch Batinich and Archie Rauzi are Co-directors of the Hall.

PLAYERS

*Abel, Clarence "Taffy"
*Baker, Hobart "Hobey"
Bartholome, Earl
Bessone, Peter
Blake, Robert
Brimsek, Frank
*Chaisson, Ray
Chase, John P.
Christian, Roger
Christian, William "Bill"
Cleary, Robert
Cleary, William
*Conroy, Anthony
Dahlstrom, Carl "Cully"
DesJardins, Victor
Desmond, Richard
Dill, Robert
Everett, Doug
*Garrison, John B.
Garrity, Jack
*Goheen, Frank "Moose"
Harding, Austin "Austie"
Iglehart, Stewart
Johnson, Virgil
Karakas, Mike
Kirrane, Jack
Lane, Myles J.
*Linder, Joseph
*LoPresti, Sam L.
*Mariucci, John
Mayasich, John
McCartan, Jack
Moe, William
Moseley, Fred
*Murray, Hugh "Muzz" Sr.
*Nelson, Hubert "Hub"
Olson , Eddie
*Owen, Jr., George
*Palmer, Winthrop
Paradise, Robert
Purpur, Clifford "Fido"
Riley, William
*Romnes, Elwin "Doc"
Rondeau, Richard
Williams, Thomas
*Winters, Frank "Coddy"
Yackel, Ken

COACHES

*Almquist, Oscar
*Gordon, Malcolm K.
Heyliger, Victor
*Jeremiah, Edward J.
*Kelley, John "Snooks"
Riley, Jack
Ross, Larry
*Thompson, Clifford. R.
*Stewart, William
*Winsor, Alfred "Ralph"

ADMINISTRATORS

*Brown, George V.
*Brown, Walter A.
Bush, Walter
Clark, Donald
*Gibson, J.C. "Doc"
*Jennings, William M.
*Kahler, Nick
*Lockhart, Thomas F.
Marvin, Cal
Ridder, Robert
Trumble, Harold
*Tutt, William Thayer
Wirtz, William W. "Bill"
*Wright, Lyle Z.

REFEREE

Chadwick, William

*Deceased

Jubilant members of the 1960 U.S. Olympic hockey team celebrate their upset 3-2 gold medal victory over the Soviet Union at Squaw Valley, California. U.S. Hall of Fame inductees Jack Riley (coach), Bill Cleary (forward), John Mayasich (defense) and Jack McCartan (goaltender) were members of this team.

Results

1989 Stanley Cup Playoffs

Prince of Wales Conference

DIVISION SEMI-FINALS
(Best of seven series)

Series 'A'
Wed. Apr. 5	Hartford 2	at Montreal 6
Thur. Apr. 6	Hartford 2	at Montreal 3
Sat. Apr. 8	Montreal 5	at Hartford 4*
Sun. Apr. 9	Montreal 4	at Hartford 3**

* Stephane Richer scored at 5:01 of overtime
** Russ Courtnall scored at 15:12 of overtime
Montreal won series 4-0

Series 'B'
Wed. Apr. 5	Buffalo 6	at Boston 0
Thur. Apr. 6	Buffalo 3	at Boston 5
Sat. Apr. 8	Boston 4	at Buffalo 2
Sun. Apr. 9	Boston 3	at Buffalo 2
Tue. Apr. 11	Buffalo 1	at Boston 4

Boston won series 4-1

Series 'C'
Wed. Apr. 5	Philadelphia 2	at Washington 3
Thur. Apr. 6	Philadelphia 3	at Washington 2
Sat. Apr. 8	Washington 4	at Philadelphia 3*
Sun. Apr. 9	Washington 2	at Philadelphia 5
Tue. Apr. 11	Philadelphia 8	at Washington 5
Thur. Apr. 13	Washington 3	at Philadelphia 4

* Kelly Miller scored at 0:51 of overtime
Philadelphia won series 4-2

Series 'D'
Wed. Apr. 5	NY Rangers 1	at Pittsburgh 3
Thur. Apr. 6	NY Rangers 4	at Pittsburgh 7
Sat. Apr. 8	Pittsburgh 5	at NY Rangers 3
Sun. Apr. 9	Pittsburgh 4	at NY Rangers 3

Pittsburgh won series 4-0

DIVISION FINALS
(Best-of-seven series)

Series 'I'
Mon. Apr. 17	Boston 2	at Montreal 3
Wed. Apr. 19	Boston 2	at Montreal 3*
Fri. Apr. 21	Montreal 5	at Boston 4
Sun. Apr. 23	Montreal 2	at Boston 3
Tues. Apr. 25	Boston 2	at Montreal 3

* Bobby Smith scored at 12:24 of overtime
Montreal won series 4-1

Series 'J'
Mon. Apr. 17	Philadelphia 3	at Pittsburgh 4
Wed. Apr. 19	Philadelphia 4	at Pittsburgh 2
Fri. Apr. 21	Pittsburgh 4	at Philadelphia 3*
Sun. Apr. 23	Pittsburgh 1	at Philadelphia 4
Tues. Apr. 25	Philadelphia 7	at Pittsburgh 10
Thur. Apr. 27	Pittsburgh 2	at Philadelphia 6
Sat. Apr. 29	Philadelphia 4	at Pittsburgh 1

* Phil Bourque scored at 12:08 of overtime
Philadelphia won series 4-3

CONFERENCE CHAMPIONSHIPS
(Best-of-seven series)

Series 'M'
Mon. May 1	Philadelphia 3	at Montreal 1
Wed. May 3	Philadelphia 0	at Montreal 3
Fri. May 5	Montreal 5	at Philadelphia 1
Sun. May 7	Montreal 3	at Philadelphia 0
Tues. May 9	Philadelphia 2	at Montreal 1*
Thur. May 11	Montreal 4	at Philadelphia 2

* Dave Poulin scored at 5:02 of overtime
Montreal won series 4-2

Clarence Campbell Conference

Series 'E'
Wed. Apr. 5	Chicago 2	at Detroit 3
Thur. Apr. 6	Chicago 5	at Detroit 4*
Sat. Apr. 8	Detroit 2	at Chicago 4
Sun. Apr. 9	Detroit 2	at Chicago 3
Tue. Apr. 11	Chicago 4	at Detroit 6
Thur. Apr. 13	Detroit 1	at Chicago 7

* Duane Sutter scored at 14:36 of overtime
Chicago won series 4-2

Series 'F'
Wed. Apr. 5	Minnesota 3	at St. Louis 4*
Thur. Apr. 6	Minnesota 3	at St. Louis 4**
Sat. Apr. 8	St. Louis 5	at Minnesota 3
Sun. Apr. 9	St. Louis 4	at Minnesota 5
Tue. Apr. 11	Minnesota 1	at St. Louis 6

* Brett Hull scored at 11:55 of overtime
** Rick Meagher scored at 5:30 of overtime
St. Louis won series 4-1

Series 'G'
Wed. Apr. 5	Vancouver 4	at Calgary 3*
Thur. Apr. 6	Vancouver 2	at Calgary 5
Sat. Apr. 8	Calgary 4	at Vancouver 0
Sun. Apr. 9	Calgary 3	at Vancouver 5
Tue. Apr. 11	Vancouver 0	at Calgary 4
Thur. Apr. 13	Calgary 3	at Vancouver 6
Sat. Apr. 15	Vancouver 3	at Calgary 4**

* Paul Reinhart scored at 2:47 of overtime
** Joel Otto scored at 19:21 of overtime
Calgary won series 4-3

Series 'H'
Wed. Apr. 5	Edmonton 4	at Los Angeles 3
Thur. Apr. 6	Edmonton 2	at Los Angeles 5
Sat. Apr. 8	Los Angeles 0	at Edmonton 4
Sun. Apr. 9	Los Angeles 3	at Edmonton 4
Tue. Apr. 11	Edmonton 2	at Los Angeles 4
Thur. Apr. 13	Los Angeles 4	at Edmonton 1
Sat. Apr. 15	Edmonton 3	at Los Angeles 6

Los Angeles won series 4-3

Series 'K'
Tues. Apr. 18	Chicago 3	at St. Louis 1
Thur. Apr. 20	Chicago 4	at St. Louis 5*
Sat. Apr. 22	St. Louis 2	at Chicago 5
Mon. Apr. 24	St. Louis 2	at Chicago 3
Wed. Apr. 26	Chicago 4	at St. Louis 2

* Tony Hrkac scored at 33:49 of overtime
Chicago won series 4-1

Series 'L'
Tues. Apr. 18	Los Angeles 3	at Calgary 4*
Thur. Apr. 20	Los Angeles 3	at Calgary 8
Sat. Apr. 22	Calgary 5	at Los Angeles 2
Mon. Apr. 24	Calgary 5	at Los Angeles 3

* Doug Gilmour scored at 7:47 of overtime
Calgary won series 4-0

Series 'N'
Tues. May 2	Chicago 0	at Calgary 3
Thur. May 4	Chicago 4	at Calgary 2
Sat. May 6	Calgary 5	at Chicago 2
Mon. May 8	Calgary 2	at Chicago 1*
Wed. May 10	Chicago 1	at Calgary 3

* Al MacInnis scored at 15:05 of overtime
Calgary won series 4-1

STANLEY CUP CHAMPIONSHIP
(Best-of-seven series)

Series 'O'
Sun. May 14	Montreal 2	at Calgary 3
Wed. May 17	Montreal 4	at Calgary 2
Fri. May 19	Calgary 3	at Montreal 4*
Sun. May 21	Calgary 4	at Montreal 2
Tues. May 23	Montreal 2	at Calgary 3
Thur. May 25	Calgary 4	at Montreal 2

* Ryan Walter scored at 38:08 of overtime
Calgary won series 4-2

Mike Vernon, seen here defending against Montreal's Mats Naslund in the Stanley Cup Championship series, registered three shutouts and 16 wins in the 1989 playoffs.

Team Playoff Records

	GP	W	L	GF	GA	%
Calgary	22	16	6	82	55	.727
Montreal	21	14	7	67	51	.667
Philadelphia	19	10	9	64	60	.526
Chicago	16	9	7	52	45	.563
Pittsburgh	11	7	4	43	42	.636
St. Louis	10	5	5	35	34	.500
Boston	10	5	5	29	30	.500
Los Angeles	11	4	7	36	42	.364
Vancouver	7	3	4	20	26	.429
Edmonton	7	3	4	20	25	.429
Washington	6	2	4	19	25	.333
Detroit	6	2	4	18	25	.333
Minnesota	5	1	4	15	23	.200
Buffalo	5	1	4	14	16	.200
Hartford	4	0	4	11	18	.000
NY Rangers	4	0	4	11	19	.000

Individual Leaders

Abbreviations: * – rookie eligible for Calder Trophy; **A** – assists; **G** – goals; **GP** – games played; **GT** – game-tying goals; **GW** – game-winning goals; **PIM** – penalties in minutes; **PP** – power play goals; **PTS** – points; **S** – shots on goal; **SH** – short-handed goals; **%** – percentage of shots resulting in goals; **+/–** – difference between Goals For (**GF**) scored when a player is on the ice with his team at even strength or short-handed and Goals Against (**GA**) scored when the same player is on the ice with his team at even strength or on a power play.

Playoff Scoring Leaders

Player	Team	GP	G	A	Pts	+/–	PIM	PP	SH	GW	OT	S	%
Al MacInnis	Calgary	22	7	24	31	6	46	5	0	4	1	69	10.1
Tim Kerr	Philadelphia	19	14	11	25	1	27	8	0	2	0	54	25.9
Joe Mullen	Calgary	21	16	8	24	8	4	6	0	1	0	91	17.6
Brian Propp	Philadelphia	18	14	9	23	8	14	5	1	1	0	52	26.9
Doug Gilmour	Calgary	22	11	11	22	12	20	3	0	3	1	49	22.4
Wayne Gretzky	Los Angeles	11	5	17	22	4–	0	1	1	0	0	42	11.9
Mario Lemieux	Pittsburgh	11	12	7	19	1–	16	7	1	0	0	41	29.3
Bobby Smith	Montreal	21	11	8	19	4	46	5	0	1	1	40	27.5
Denis Savard	Chicago	16	8	11	19	8	10	2	1	1	0	68	11.8
Joel Otto	Calgary	22	6	13	19	2	46	2	1	1	1	41	14.6
Chris Chelios	Montreal	21	4	15	19	2	28	1	0	2	0	53	7.5
Steve Larmer	Chicago	16	8	9	17	4	22	3	0	2	0	51	15.7
Hakan Loob	Calgary	22	8	9	17	8	4	2	2	1	0	60	13.3
Bernie Nicholls	Los Angeles	11	7	9	16	2–	12	3	0	1	0	50	14.0
Mats Naslund	Montreal	21	4	11	15	5	6	1	0	0	0	54	7.4
Paul Coffey	Pittsburgh	11	2	13	15	7–	31	2	0	1	0	48	4.2
Mark Howe	Philadelphia	19	0	15	15	14	10	0	0	0	0	33	.0
Joe Nieuwendyk	Calgary	22	10	4	14	0	10	6	0	1	0	57	17.5
Russ Courtnall	Montreal	21	8	5	13	12	18	1	0	2	1	53	15.1
*Craig Janney	Boston	10	4	9	13	1	21	0	0	0	0	23	17.4
Colin Patterson	Calgary	22	3	10	13	10	24	0	0	0	0	24	12.5

Playoff Defensemen Scoring Leaders

Player	Team	GP	G	A	Pts	+/–	PIM	PP	SH	GW	OT	S	%
Al MacInnis	Calgary	22	7	24	31	6	46	5	0	4	1	69	10.1
Chris Chelios	Montreal	21	4	15	19	2	28	1	0	2	0	53	7.5
Paul Coffey	Pittsburgh	11	2	13	15	7–	31	2	0	1	0	48	4.2
Mark Howe	Philadelphia	19	0	15	15	14	10	0	0	0	0	33	.0
Rob Ramage	Calgary	20	1	11	12	5	26	1	0	0	0	46	2.2
Petr Svoboda	Montreal	21	1	11	12	3–	16	0	0	0	0	23	4.3
Larry Robinson	Montreal	21	2	8	10	9	12	0	0	0	0	15	13.3
*Trent Yawney	Chicago	15	3	6	9	9	20	0	1	0	0	17	17.6
Jamie Macoun	Calgary	22	3	6	9	11	30	0	0	1	0	27	11.1
*Gordon Murphy	Philadelphia	19	2	7	9	0	13	1	0	1	0	32	6.3

Goal Scoring

Name	Team	GP	G
Joe Mullen	Calgary	21	16
Brian Propp	Philadelphia	18	14
Tim Kerr	Philadelphia	19	14
Mario Lemieux	Pittsburgh	11	12
Bobby Smith	Montreal	21	11
Doug Gilmour	Calgary	22	11

Assists

Name	Team	GP	A
Al MacInnis	Calgary	22	24
Wayne Gretzky	Los Angeles	11	17
Mark Howe	Philadelphia	19	15
Chris Chelios	Montreal	21	15
Paul Coffey	Pittsburgh	11	13
Joel Otto	Calgary	22	13

Power Play Goals

Name	Team	GP	PP
Tim Kerr	Philadelphia	19	8
Mario Lemieux	Pittsburgh	11	7
Chris Kontos	Los Angeles	11	6
Joe Mullen	Calgary	21	6
Joe Nieuwendyk	Calgary	22	6

Short-Handed Goals

Name	Team	GP	SH
Wayne Presley	Chicago	14	3
Dave Poulin	Philadelphia	19	2
Derrick Smith	Philadelphia	19	2
Hakan Loob	Calgary	22	2

Game-Winning Goals

Name	Team	GP	GW
Al MacInnis	Calgary	22	4
Rob Brown	Pittsburgh	11	3
Stephane Richer	Montreal	21	3
*Theoren Fleury	Calgary	22	3
Doug Gilmour	Calgary	22	3

Overtime Goals

Name	Team	GP	OT
Tony Hrkac	St. Louis	4	1
Kelly Miller	Washington	6	1
Paul Reinhart	Vancouver	7	1
Brett Hull	St. Louis	10	1
Rick Meagher	St. Louis	10	1
Phil Bourque	Pittsburgh	11	1
Duane Sutter	Chicago	16	1
Dave Poulin	Philadelphia	19	1
Russ Courtnall	Montreal	21	1
Stephane Richer	Montreal	21	1
Bobby Smith	Montreal	21	1
Ryan Walter	Montreal	21	1
Doug Gilmour	Calgary	22	1
Al MacInnis	Calgary	22	1
Joel Otto	Calgary	22	1

Shots

Name	Team	GP	S
Joe Mullen	Calgary	21	91
Al MacInnis	Calgary	22	69
Denis Savard	Chicago	16	68
Hakan Loob	Calgary	22	60
Rick Tocchet	Philadelphia	16	58

First Goals

Name	Team	GP	FG
Randy Burridge	Boston	10	4
Mario Lemieux	Pittsburgh	11	4
Chris Kontos	Los Angeles	11	3
Stephane Richer	Montreal	21	3
Joe Nieuwendyk	Calgary	22	3

Plus/Minus

Name	Team	GP	+/–
Mark Howe	Philadelphia	19	14
K. Samuelsson	Philadelphia	19	13
Russ Courtnall	Montreal	21	12
Doug Gilmour	Calgary	22	12
Jamie Macoun	Calgary	22	11

Playoff Goaltending

(Minimum 420 Minutes)

Goals Against Average

Goaltender	Team	GPI	Mins.	GA	AVG
Patrick Roy	Montreal	19	1206	42	2.09
Mike Vernon	Calgary	22	1381	52	2.26
Alain Chevrier	Chicago	16	1013	44	2.61
Greg Millen	St. Louis	10	649	34	3.14
Ron Hextall	Philadelphia	15	886	49	3.32

Wins

Goaltender	Team	GPI	Mins.	W	L
Mike Vernon	Calgary	22	1381	16	5
Patrick Roy	Montreal	19	1206	13	6
Alain Chevrier	Chicago	16	1013	9	7
Ron Hextall	Philadelphia	15	886	8	7
Tom Barrasso	Pittsburgh	11	631	7	4

Save Percentage

Goaltender	Team	GPI	Mins.	GA	SA	S%	W	L
Patrick Roy	Montreal	19	1206	42	528	.920	13	6
Alain Chevrier	Chicago	16	1013	44	484	.909	9	7
Mike Vernon	Calgary	22	1381	52	550	.905	16	5
Tom Barrasso	Pittsburgh	11	631	40	389	.897	7	4

Shutouts

Goaltender	Team	GPI	Mins.	SO	W	L
Mike Vernon	Calgary	22	1381	3	16	5
Patrick Roy	Montreal	19	1206	2	13	6
Jacques Cloutier	Buffalo	4	238	1	1	3
Grant Fuhr	Edmonton	7	417	1	3	4

Brian Propp scored 14 goals in 18 games during the 1989 playoffs.

Team Penalties

Abbreviations: GP – games played; **PEN** – total penalty minutes, including bench penalites; **BMI** – total bench penalty minutes; **AVG** – average penalty minutes per game.

Team	Games	PEN	BMI	AVG
STL	10	216	6	21.6
MTL	21	456	6	21.7
BOS	10	229	2	22.9
VAN	7	160	2	22.9
EDM	7	161	2	23.0
L.A.	11	270	2	24.5
CGY	22	563	0	25.6
WSH	6	155	0	25.8
HFD	4	111	0	27.8
MIN	5	144	0	28.8
CHI	16	484	6	30.3
DET	6	187	0	31.2
PHI	19	612	2	32.2
BUF	5	188	0	37.6
PIT	11	452	2	41.1
NYR	4	214	0	53.5
TOTAL	82	4602	30	56.1

Team Statistics

TEAMS' HOME-AND-ROAD RECORD

			Home						Road			
	GP	W	L	GF	GA	%	GP	W	L	GF	GA	%
CGY	12	9	3	44	28	.750	10	7	3	38	27	.700
MTL	11	7	4	31	26	.636	10	7	3	36	25	.700
PHI	9	4	5	28	28	.444	10	6	4	36	32	.600
CHI	7	5	2	25	16	.714	9	4	5	27	29	.444
PIT	6	4	2	27	23	.667	5	3	2	16	19	.600
STL	6	4	2	22	18	.667	4	1	3	13	16	.250
BOS	5	3	2	16	17	.600	5	2	3	13	13	.400
L.A.	6	3	3	23	21	.500	5	1	4	13	21	.200
VAN	3	2	1	11	10	.667	4	1	3	9	16	.250
EDM	3	2	1	9	7	.667	4	1	3	11	18	.250
WSH	3	1	2	10	13	.333	3	1	2	9	12	.333
DET	3	2	1	13	11	.667	3	0	3	5	14	.000
MIN	2	1	1	8	9	.500	3	0	3	7	14	.000
BUF	2	0	2	4	7	.000	3	1	2	10	9	.333
HFD	2	0	2	7	9	.000	2	0	2	4	9	.000
NYR	2	0	2	6	9	.000	2	0	2	5	10	.000
TOTAL	82	47	35	284	252	.573	82	35	47	252	284	.427

TEAMS' POWER PLAY RECORD

Abbreviations: ADV-advantages; **PPGF**-power play goals for; **%**-arrived by dividing number of power-play goals by total advantages.

			Home						Road						Overall		
	Team	GP	ADV	PPGF	%	Team	GP	ADV	PPGF	%	Team	GP	ADV	PPGF	%
1	L.A.	6	36	12	33.3	NYR	2	11	4	36.4	L.A.	11	54	15	27.8
2	PIT	6	41	10	24.4	PHI	10	43	12	27.9	PIT	11	70	16	22.9
3	WSH	3	25	5	20.0	BUF	3	16	4	25.0	CGY	22	131	28	21.4
4	CGY	12	67	13	19.4	EDM	4	21	5	23.8	WSH	6	43	9	20.9
5	CHI	7	48	9	18.8	CGY	10	64	15	23.4	PHI	19	96	20	20.8
6	VAN	3	24	4	16.7	WSH	3	18	4	22.2	NYR	4	29	6	20.7
7	BOS	9	25	4	16.0	MIN	3	9	2	22.2	BUF	5	31	6	19.4
8	PHI	9	53	8	15.1	PIT	5	29	6	20.7	MIN	5	16	3	18.8
9	MIN	2	7	1	14.3	MTL	10	44	9	20.5	EDM	7	32	6	18.8
10	STL	6	37	5	13.5	DET	3	21	4	19.0	CHI	16	90	16	17.8
11	BUF	2	15	2	13.3	L.A.	5	18	3	16.7	MTL	21	97	16	16.5
12	MTL	11	53	7	13.2	CHI	9	42	7	16.7	DET	6	37	6	16.2
13	HFD	2	8	1	12.5	STL	4	19	3	15.8	VAN	7	44	7	15.9
14	DET	3	16	2	12.5	VAN	4	20	3	15.0	STL	10	56	8	14.3
15	NYR	2	18	2	11.1	BOS	5	22	2	9.1	BOS	10	47	6	12.8
16	EDM	3	11	1	9.1	HFD	2	7	0	.0	HFD	4	15	1	6.7
	TOTAL	82	484	86	17.8		82	404	83	20.5		82	888	169	19.0

TEAMS' PENALTY KILLING RECORD

Abbreviations: TSH-Total short-handed; **PPGA**-power play goals against; **%** arrived by dividing-times short minus power-play goals against-by times short.

			Home						Road						Overall		
	Team	GP	TSH	PPGA	%	Team	GP	TSH	PPGA	%	Team	GP	TSH	PPGA	%
1	MTL	11	46	4	91.3	CGY	10	68	7	89.7	MTL	21	88	9	89.8
2	EDM	3	9	1	88.9	CHI	9	54	6	88.9	CGY	22	126	18	85.7
3	HFD	2	8	1	87.5	MTL	10	42	5	88.1	CHI	16	99	15	84.8
4	STL	6	22	3	86.4	BOS	5	22	3	86.4	STL	10	38	6	84.2
5	BUF	2	11	2	81.8	MIN	3	20	3	85.0	BOS	10	44	7	84.1
6	BOS	5	22	4	81.8	PIT	5	40	6	85.0	BUF	5	30	5	83.3
7	CGY	12	58	11	81.0	BUF	3	19	3	84.2	MIN	5	30	5	83.3
8	MIN	2	10	2	80.0	L.A.	5	24	4	83.3	L.A.	11	57	11	80.7
9	CHI	7	45	9	80.0	STL	4	16	3	81.3	PHI	19	119	26	78.2
10	L.A.	6	33	7	78.8	WSH	3	20	4	80.0	HFD	4	18	4	77.8
11	PHI	9	50	11	78.0	NYR	2	14	3	78.6	NYR	4	27	6	77.8
12	NYR	2	13	3	76.9	PHI	10	69	15	78.3	PIT	11	69	17	75.4
13	VAN	3	20	5	75.0	DET	3	23	6	73.9	WSH	6	34	9	73.5
14	DET	3	14	4	71.4	HFD	2	10	3	70.0	DET	6	37	10	73.0
15	WSH	3	14	5	64.3	VAN	4	16	5	68.8	VAN	7	36	10	72.2
16	PIT	6	29	11	62.1	EDM	4	27	10	63.0	EDM	7	36	11	69.4
	TOTAL	82	404	83	79.5		82	484	86	82.2		82	888	169	81.0

Stanley Cup Record Book

THE STANLEY CUP

Awarded annually to the team winning the National Hockey League's best-of-seven final playoff round. It is symbolic of the World's Professional Hockey Championship.

The first four teams in each division at the end of the regular schedule advance to the playoffs. In each division, the first-place team opposes the fourth-place club while the second and third-place teams meet, all in best-of-seven Division Semi-Finals. The winners oppose the other winners in each division in best-of-seven Division Final Series. The division winners then play the opposite winners in each of the two conferences in best-of-seven Conference Championships. The Prince of Wales Conference champions then meet the Clarence Campbell Conference champions in the best-of-seven Stanley Cup Championship Series.

History: The Stanley Cup, the oldest trophy competed for by professional athletes in North America, was donated by Frederick Arthur, Lord Stanley of Preston and son of the Earl of Derby, in 1893. Lord Stanley purchased the trophy for 10 guineas ($50 at that time) for presentation to the amateur hockey champions of Canada. Since 1910, when the National Hockey Association took possession of the Stanley Cup, the trophy has been the symbol of professional hockey supremacy. It has been competed for only by NHL teams since 1926 and has been under the exclusive control of the NHL since 1946.

1988-89 Winner: Calgary Flames

The Calgary Flames won their first Stanley Cup Championship by defeating the Montreal Canadiens in six games.

The Flames won game one in Calgary and, after dropping games two and three, went on to win three straight games to become the first visiting team to clinch the Cup against the Canadiens in the Montreal Forum. Conn Smythe Trophy winner Al MacInnis led the way for the Flames with 31 points in post-season play.

Stanley Cup Winners Prior to Formation of NHL in 1917

Season	Champion	Challenger
1916-17	Seattle Metropolitans	Montreal Canadiens
1915-16	Montreal Canadiens	Portland Rosebuds
1914-15	Vancouver Millionaires	Ottawa Senators
1913-14	Toronto Blueshirts	Victoria Cougars
		Montreal Canadiens
1912-13**	Quebec Bulldogs	Sydney Miners
1911-12	Quebec Bulldogs	Moncton Victorias
1910-11	Ottawa Senators	Port Arthur Bearcats
		Galt
1909-10	Montreal Wanderers	Berlin Union Jacks
		Edmonton Eskimos
		Galt
1908-09	Ottawa Senators	(no challenger)
1907-08	Montreal Wanderers	Edmonton Eskimos
		Toronto Trolley Leaguers
		Winnipeg Maple Leafs
		Ottawa Victorias
1906-07	Montreal Wanderers (March)	Kenora Thistles
1906-07	Kenora Thistles (January)	Montreal Wanderers
1905-06	Montreal Wanderers	New Glasgow Cubs
		Ottawa Silver Seven
1905-06	Ottawa Silver Seven	Montreal Wanderers
		Smith's Falls
		Queen's University
1904-05	Ottawa Silver Seven	Rat Portage Thistles
		Dawson City Nuggets
1903-04	Ottawa Silver Seven	Brandon Wheat Kings
		Montreal Wanderers
		Toronto Marlboros
		Winnipeg Rowing Club
1902-03	Ottawa Silver Seven	Rat Portage Thistles
		Montreal Victorias
1902-03	Montreal A.A.A.	Winnipeg Victorias
1901-02	Montreal A.A.A.	Winnipeg Victorias
1901-02	Winnipeg Victorias	Toronto Wellingtons
1900-01	Winnipeg Victorias	Montreal Shamrocks
1899-1900	Montreal Shamrocks	Halifax Crescents
		Winnipeg Victorias
1898-99	Montreal Shamrocks	Queen's University
1898-99	Montreal Victorias	Winnipeg Victorias
1897-98	Montreal Victorias	(no challenger)
1896-97	Montreal Victorias	Ottawa Capitals
1895-96	Montreal Victorias	Winnipeg Victorias
1895-96	Winnipeg Victorias	Montreal Victorias
1894-95	Montreal Victorias	(no challenger)
1893-94	Montreal A.A.A.	Ottawa Generals
1892-93	Montreal A.A.A.	(no challenger)

**Victoria defeated Quebec in unofficial challenge series.

STANLEY CUP WINNERS AND FINALISTS

Season	Champion	Finalist	GP in Final
1988-89	Calgary Flames	Montreal Canadiens	6
1987-88	Edmonton Oilers	Boston Bruins	4
1986-87	Edmonton Oilers	Philadelphia Flyers	7
1985-86	Montreal Canadiens	Calgary Flames	5
1984-85	Edmonton Oilers	Philadelphia Flyers	5
1983-84	Edmonton Oilers	New York Islanders	5
1982-83	New York Islanders	Edmonton Oilers	4
1981-82	New York Islanders	Vancouver Canucks	4
1980-81	New York Islanders	Minnesota North Stars	5
1979-80	New York Islanders	Philadelphia Flyers	6
1978-79	Montreal Canadiens	New York Rangers	5
1977-78	Montreal Canadiens	Boston Bruins	6
1976-77	Montreal Canadiens	Boston Bruins	4
1975-76	Montreal Canadiens	Philadelphia Flyers	4
1974-75	Philadelphia Flyers	Buffalo Sabres	6
1973-74	Philadelphia Flyers	Boston Bruins	6
1972-73	Montreal Canadiens	Chicago Black Hawks	6
1971-72	Boston Bruins	New York Rangers	6
1970-71	Montreal Canadiens	Chicago Black Hawks	7
1969-70	Boston Bruins	St. Louis Blues	4
1968-69	Montreal Canadiens	St. Louis Blues	4
1967-68	Montreal Canadiens	St. Louis Blues	4
1966-67	Toronto Maple Leafs	Montreal Canadiens	6
1965-66	Montreal Canadiens	Detroit Red Wings	6
1964-65	Montreal Canadiens	Chicago Black Hawks	7
1963-64	Toronto Maple Leafs	Detroit Red Wings	7
1962-63	Toronto Maple Leafs	Detroit Red Wings	5
1961-62	Toronto Maple Leafs	Chicago Black Hawks	6
1960-61	Chicago Black Hawks	Detroit Red Wings	6
1959-60	Montreal Canadiens	Toronto Maple Leafs	4
1958-59	Montreal Canadiens	Toronto Maple Leafs	5
1957-58	Montreal Canadiens	Boston Bruins	6
1956-57	Montreal Canadiens	Boston Bruins	5
1955-56	Montreal Canadiens	Detroit Red Wings	5
1954-55	Detroit Red Wings	Montreal Canadiens	7
1953-54	Detroit Red Wings	Montreal Canadians	7
1952-53	Montreal Canadiens	Boston Bruins	5
1951-52	Detroit Red Wings	Montreal Canadiens	4

Season	Champion	Finalist	GP in Final
1950-51	Toronto Maple Leafs	Montreal Canadiens	5
1949-50	Detroit Red Wings	New York Rangers	7
1948-49	Toronto Maple Leafs	Detroit Red Wings	4
1947-48	Toronto Maple Leafs	Detroit Red Wings	4
1946-47	Toronto Maple Leafs	Montreal Canadiens	6
1945-46	Montreal Canadiens	Boston Bruins	5
1944-45	Toronto Maple Leafs	Detroit Red Wings	7
1943-44	Montreal Canadiens	Chicago Black Hawks	4
1942-43	Detroit Red Wings	Boston Bruins	4
1941-42	Toronto Maple Leafs	Detroit Red Wings	7
1940-41	Boston Bruins	Detroit Red Wings	4
1939-40	New York Rangers	Toronto Maple Leafs	6
1938-39	Boston Bruins	Toronto Maple Leafs	5
1937-38	Chicago Black Hawks	Toronto Maple Leafs	4
1936-37	Detroit Red Wings	New York Rangers	5
1935-36	Detroit Red Wings	Toronto Maple Leafs	4
1934-35	Montreal Maroons	Toronto Maple Leafs	3
1933-34	Chicago Black Hawks	Detroit Red Wings	4
1932-33	New York Rangers	Toronto Maple Leafs	4
1931-32	Toronto Maple Leafs	New York Rangers	3
1930-31	Montreal Canadiens	Chicago Black Hawks	5
1929-30	Montreal Canadiens	Boston Bruins	2
1928-29	Boston Bruins	New York Rangers	2
1927-28	New York Rangers	Montreal Maroons	5
1926-27	Ottawa Senators	Boston Bruins	4
1925-26	Montreal Maroons	Victoria Cougars	4
1924-25	Victoria Cougars	Montreal Canadiens	4
1923-24	Montreal Canadiens	Vancouver, Calgary	2,2
1922-23	Ottawa Senators	Vancouver, Edmonton	3,2
1921-22	Toronto St. Pats	Vancouver Millionaires	5
1920-21	Ottawa Senators	Vancouver Millionaires	5
1919-20	Ottawa Senators	Seattle Metropolitans	5
1918-19	No decision*	No decision*	5
1917-18	Toronto Arenas	Vancouver Millionaires	5

* In the spring of 1919 the Montreal Canadiens travelled to Seattle to meet Seattle, PCHL champions. After five games had been played — teams were tied at 2 wins and 1 tie — the series was called off by the local Department of Health because of the influenza epidemic and the death from influenza of Joe Hall.

Championship Trophies

PRINCE OF WALES TROPHY

Beginning with the 1981-82 season, the club which advances to the Stanley Cup Finals as the winner of the Wales Conference is presented with the Prince of Wales Trophy.

History: His Royal Highnesss, the Prince of Wales, donated the trophy to the National Hockey League in 1924. From 1927-28 through 1937-38, the award was presented to the team finishing first in the American Division of the NHL. From 1938-39, when the NHL reverted to one section, to 1966-67, it was presented to the team winning the NHL championship. With expansion in 1967-68, it again became a divisional trophy through the 1973-74 season. Beginning in 1974-75, it was awarded to the regular-season winner of the conference bearing the name of the trophy. Starting with the 1981-82 season the trophy was presented to the playoff champion in the Wales Conference.

1988-89 Winner: Montreal Canadiens

The Montreal Canadiens captured their fourth Prince of Wales Trophy in the last decade on May 11, with a 4-2 series win over the Philadelphia Flyers. After losing the first game at home, the Canadiens took a commanding 3-1 lead in the series through Game Four. In a 2-1 overtime win the Flyers forced the series back to Philadelphia, where the Canadiens perservered with a 4-2 decision.

Prince of Wales Trophy

PRINCE OF WALES TROPHY WINNERS

1988-89	**Montreal Canadiens**	1955-56	Montreal Canadiens
1987-88	Boston Bruins	1954-55	Detroit Red Wings
1986-87	Philadelphia Flyers	1953-54	Detroit Red Wings
1985-86	Montreal Canadiens	1952-53	Detroit Red Wings
1984-85	Philadelphia Flyers	1951-52	Detroit Red Wings
1983-84	New York Islanders	1950-51	Detroit Red Wings
1982-83	New York Islanders	1949-50	Detroit Red Wings
1981-82	New York Islanders	1948-49	Detroit Red Wings
1980-81	Montreal Canadiens	1947-48	Toronto Maple Leafs
1979-80	Buffalo Sabres	1946-47	Montreal Canadiens
1978-79	Montreal Canadiens	1945-46	Montreal Canadiens
1977-78	Montreal Canadiens	1944-45	Montreal Canadiens
1976-77	Montreal Canadiens	1943-44	Montreal Canadiens
1975-76	Montreal Canadiens	1942-43	Detroit Red Wings
1974-75	Buffalo Sabres	1941-42	New York Rangers
1973-74	Boston Bruins	1940-41	Boston Bruins
1972-73	Montreal Canadiens	1939-40	Boston Bruins
1971-72	Boston Bruins	1938-39	Boston Bruins
1970-71	Boston Bruins	1937-38	Boston Bruins
1969-70	Chicago Black Hawks	1936-37	Detroit Red Wings
1968-69	Montreal Canadiens	1935-36	Detroit Red Wings
1967-68	Montreal Canadiens	1934-35	Boston Bruins
1966-67	Chicago Black Hawks	1933-34	Detroit Red Wings
1965-66	Montreal Canadiens	1932-33	Boston Bruins
1964-65	Detroit Red Wings	1931-32	New York Rangers
1963-64	Montreal Canadiens	1930-31	Boston Bruins
1962-63	Toronto Maple Leafs	1929-30	Boston Bruins
1961-62	Montreal Canadiens	1928-29	Boston Bruins
1960-61	Montreal Canadiens	1927-28	Boston Bruins
1959-60	Montreal Canadiens	1926-27	Ottawa Senators
1958-59	Montreal Canadiens	1925-26	Montreal Maroons
1957-58	Montreal Canadiens	1924-25	Montreal Canadiens
1956-57	Detroit Red Wings		

CLARENCE S. CAMPBELL BOWL

Beginning with the 1981-82 season, the club which advances to the Stanley Cup Finals as the winner of the Campbell Conference championship is presented with the Clarence S. Campbell Bowl.

History: Presented by the member clubs in 1968 for perpetual competition by the National Hockey League in recognition of the services of Clarence S. Campbell, President of the NHL from 1946 to 1977. From 1967-68 through 1973-74, the trophy was awarded to the champions of the West Division. The trophy itself is a hallmark piece made of sterling silver and was crafted by a British silversmith in 1878.

1988-89 Winner: Calgary Flames

The Calgary Flames won their second Campbell Conference Championship in four years with a 4-1 series win over the Chicago Blackhawks. The Flames, boasting the League's best regular-season record, split the first two games of the series with the Blackhawks before winning three straight to capture the conference title.

Clarence S. Campbell Bowl

CLARENCE S. CAMPBELL BOWL WINNERS

1988-89	**Calgary Flames**	1976-77	Philadelphia Flyers
1987-88	Edmonton Oilers	1975-76	Philadelphia Flyers
1986-87	Edmonton Oilers	1974-75	Philadelphia Flyers
1985-86	Calgary Flames	1973-74	Philadelphia Flyers
1984-85	Edmonton Oilers	1972-73	Chicago Black Hawks
1983-84	Edmonton Oilers	1971-72	Chicago Black Hawks
1982-83	Edmonton Oilers	1970-71	Chicago Black Hawks
1981-82	Vancouver Canucks	1969-70	St. Louis Blues
1980-81	New York Islanders	1968-69	St. Louis Blues
1979-80	Philadelphia Flyers	1967-68	Philadelphia Flyers
1978-79	New York Islanders		
1977-78	New York Islanders		

Stanley Cup

Stanley Cup Winners:

Rosters and Final Series Scores

1988-89 — Calgary Flames — Mike Vernon, Rick Wamsley, Al MacInnis, Brad McCrimmon, Dana Murzyn, Ric Nattress, Joe Mullen, Lanny McDonald (Co-captain), Gary Roberts, Colin Patterson, Hakan Loob, Theoren Fleury, Jiri Hrdina, Tim Hunter (Ass't. captain), Gary Suter, Mark Hunter, Jim Peplinski (Co-captain), Joe Nieuwendyk, Brian MacLellan, Joel Otto, Jamie Macoun, Doug Gilmour, Rob Ramage. Norman Green, Harley Hotchkiss, Norman Kwong, Sonia Scurfield, B.J. Seaman, D.K. Seaman (Owners), Cliff Fletcher (President and General Manager), Al MacNeil (Ass't General Manager), Al Coates (Ass't to the President), Terry Crisp (Head Coach), Doug Risebrough, Tom Watt (Ass't Coaches), Glenn Hall (Goaltending Consultant), Jim Murray (Trainer), Bob Stewart (Equipment Manager), Al Murray (Ass't Trainer).
Scores: May 14 at Calgary — Calgary 3, Montreal 2; May 17 at Calgary — Montreal 4, Calgary 2; May 19 at Montreal — Montreal 4, Calgary 3; May 21 at Montreal — Calgary 4, Montreal 2; May 23 at Calgary — Calgary 3, Montreal 2; May 25 at Montreal — Calgary 4, Montreal 2.

1987-88 — Edmonton Oilers — Keith Acton, Glenn Anderson, Jeff Beukeboom, Geoff Courtnall, Grant Fuhr, Randy Gregg, Wayne Gretzky, Dave Hannan, Charlie Huddy, Mike Krushelnyski, Jari Kurri, Normand Lacombe, Kevin Lowe, Craig MacTavish, Kevin McClelland, Marty McSorley, Mark Messier, Craig Muni, Bill Ranford, Craig Simpson, Steve Smith, Esa Tikkanen, Peter Pocklington (Owner), Glen Sather (General Manager/Coach), John Muckler (Co-Coach), Ted Green (Ass't Coach), Barry Fraser (Director of Player Personnel), Bill Tuele (Director of Public Relations), Dr. Gordon Cameron (Team Physician), Peter Millar (Athletic Therapist), Barrie Stafford (Trainer), Juergen Mers (Message Therapist), Lyle Kulchisky (Ass't Trainer).
Scores: May 18 at Edmonton — Edmonton 2, Boston 1; May 20 at Edmonton — Edmonton 4, Boston 2; May 22 at Boston — Edmonton 6, Boston 3; May 24 at Boston — Boston 3, Edmonton 3 (suspended due to power failure); May 26 at Edmonton — Edmonton 6, Boston 3.

1986-87 — Edmonton Oilers — Glenn Anderson, Jeff Beukeboom, Kelly Buchberger, Paul Coffey, Grant Fuhr, Randy Gregg, Wayne Gretzky, Charlie Huddy, Dave Hunter, Mike Krushelnyski, Jari Kurri, Moe Lemay, Kevin Lowe, Craig MacTavish, Kevin McClelland, Marty McSorley, Mark Messier, Andy Moog, Craig Muni, Kent Nilsson, Jaroslav Pouzar, Reijo Ruotsalainen, Steve Smith, Esa Tikkanen, Peter Pocklington (Owner), Glen Sather (General Manager/ Coach), John Muckler (Co-Coach), Ted Green (Ass't. Coach), Ron Low (Ass't. Coach), Bruce MacGregor (Ass't. General Manager), Barry Fraser (Director of Player Personnel), Peter Millar (Athletic Therapist), Barrie Stafford (Trainer), Lyle Kulchisky (Ass't Trainer).
Scores: May 17 at Edmonton — Edmonton 4, Philadelphia 3; May 20 at Edmonton — Edmonton 3, Philadelphia 2; May 22 at Philadelphia — Philadelphia 5, Edmonton 3; May 24 at Philadelphia — Edmonton 4, Philadelphia 1; May 26 at Edmonton — Philadelphia 4, Edmonton 3; May 28 at Philadelphia — Philadelphia 3, Edmonton 2; May 31 at Edmonton — Edmonton 3, Philadelphia 1.

1985-86 — Montreal Canadiens — Bob Gainey, Doug Soetaert, Patrick Roy, Rick Green, David Maley, Ryan Walter, Serge Boisvert, Mario Tremblay, Bobby Smith, Craig Ludwig, Tom Kurvers, Kjell Dahlin, Larry Robinson, Guy Carbonneau, Chris Chelios, Petr Svoboda, Mats Naslund, Lucien DeBlois, Steve Rooney, Gaston Gingras, Mike Lalor, Chris Nilan, John Kordic, Claude Lemieux, Mike McPhee, Brian Skrudland, Stephane Richer, Ronald Corey (President), Serge Savard (General Manager), Jean Perron (Coach), Jacques Laperriere (Ass't. Coach), Jean Beliveau (Vice President), Francois-Xavier Seigneur (Vice President), Fred Steer (Vice President), Jacques Lemaire (Ass't. General Manager), Andre Boudrias (Ass't. General Manager), Claude Ruel, Yves Belanger (Athletic Therapist), Gaetan Lefebvre (Ass't. Athletic Therapist), Eddy Palchek (Trainer), Sylvain Toupin (Ass't. Trainer).
Scores: May 16 at Calgary — Calgary 5, Montreal 3; May 18 at Calgary — Montreal 3, Calgary 2; May 20 at Montreal — Montreal 5, Calgary 3; May 22 at Montreal — Montreal 1, Calgary 0; May 24 at Calgary — Montreal 4, Calgary 3.

1984-85 — Edmonton Oilers — Glenn Anderson, Bill Carrol, Paul Coffey, Lee Fogolin, Grant Fuhr, Randy Gregg, Wayne Gretzky, Charlie Huddy, Pat Hughes, Dave Hunter, Don Jackson, Mike Krushelnyski, Jari Kurri, Willy Lindstrom, Kevin Lowe, Dave Lumley, Kevin McClelland, Larry Melnyk, Mark Messier, Andy Moog, Mark Napier, Jaroslav Pouzar, Dave Semenko, Esa Tikkanen, Peter Pocklington (Owner), Glen Sather (General Manager/Coach), John Muckler (Ass't. Coach), Ted Green (Ass't. Coach), Bruce MacGregor (Ass't. General Manager), Barry Fraser (Director of Player Personnel/Chief Scout), Peter Millar (Athletic Therapist), Barrie Stafford, Lyle Kulchisky (Trainers)
Scores: May 21 at Philadelphia — Philadelphia 4, Edmonton 1; May 23 at Philadelphia — Edmonton 3, Philadelphia 1; May 25 at Edmonton — Edmonton 4, Philadelphia 3; May 28 at Edmonton — Edmonton 5, Philadelphia 3; May 30 at Edmonton — Edmonton 8, Philadelphia 3.

1983-84 — Edmonton Oilers — Glenn Anderson, Paul Coffey, Pat Conacher, Lee Fogolin, Grant Fuhr, Randy Gregg, Wayne Gretzky, Charlie Huddy, Pat Hughes, Dave Hunter, Don Jackson, Jari Kurri, Willy Lindstrom, Ken Linseman, Kevin Lowe, Dave Lumley, Kevin McClelland, Mark Messier, Andy Moog, Jaroslav Pouzar, Dave Semenko, Peter Pocklington (Owner), Glen Sather (General Manager/Coach), John Muckler (Ass't. Coach), Ted Green (Ass't. Coach), Bruce MacGregor (Ass't. General Manager), Barry Fraser (Director of Player Personnel/Chief Scout), Peter Millar (Athletic Therapist), Barrie Stafford (Trainer)
Scores: May 10 at New York — Edmonton 1, NY Islanders 0; May 12 at New York — NY Islanders 6, Edmonton 1; May 15 at Edmonton — Edmonton 7, NY Islanders 2; May 17 at Edmonton — Edmonton 7, NY Islanders 2; May 19 at Edmonton — Edmonton 5, NY Islanders 2.

1982-83 — New York Islanders — Mike Bossy, Bob Bourne, Paul Boutilier, Bill Carroll, Greg Gilbert, Clark Gillies, Butch Goring, Mats Hallin, Tomas Jonsson, Anders Kallur, Gord Lane, Dave Langevin, Mike McEwen, Roland Melanson, Wayne Merrick, Ken Morrow, Bob Nystrom, Stefan Persson, Denis Potvin, Bill Smith, Brent Sutter, Duane Sutter, John Tonelli, Bryan Trottier, Al Arbour (coach), Lorne Henning (ass't coach), Bill Torrey (general manager), Ron Waske, Jim Pickard (trainers)
Scores: May 10 at Edmonton — NY Islanders 2, Edmonton 0; May 12 at Edmonton — NY Islanders 6, Edmonton 3; May 14 at New York — NY Islanders 5, Edmonton 1; May 17 at New York — NY Islanders 4, Edmonton 2

1981-82 — New York Islanders — Mike Bossy, Bob Bourne, Bill Carroll, Butch Goring, Greg Gilbert, Clark Gillies, Tomas Jonsson, Anders Kallur, Gord Lane, Dave Langevin, Hector Marini, Mike McEwen, Roland Melanson, Wayne Merrick, Ken Morrow, Bob Nystrom, Stefan Persson, Denis Potvin, Bill Smith, Brent Sutter, Duane Sutter, John Tonelli, Bryan Trottier, Al Arbour (coach), Lorne Henning (ass't coach), Bill Torrey (general manager), Ron Waske, Jim Pickard (trainers)
Scores: May 8 at New York — NY Islanders 6, Vancouver 5; May 11 at New York — NY Islanders 6, Vancouver 4; May 13 at Vancouver — NY Islanders 3, Vancouver 0; May 16 at Vancouver — NY Islanders 3, Vancouver 1

1980-81 — New York Islanders — Denis Potvin, Mike McEwen, Ken Morrow, Gord Lane, Bob Lorimer, Stefan Persson, Dave Langevin, Mike Bossy, Bryan Trottier, Butch Goring, Wayne Merrick, Clark Gillies, John Tonelli, Bob Nystrom, Bill Carroll, Bob Bourne, Hector Marini, Anders Kallur, Duane Sutter, Garry Howatt, Lorne Henning, Bill Smith, Roland Melanson, Al Arbour (coach), Bill Torrey (general manager), Ron Waske, Jim Pickard (trainers).
Scores: May 12 at New York — NY Islanders 6, Minnesota 3; May 14 at New York — NY Islanders 6, Minnesota 3; May 17 at Minnesota — NY Islanders 7, Minnesota 5; May 19 at Minnesota— Minnesota 4, NY Islanders 2; May 21 at New York — NY Islanders 5, Minnesota 1.

1979-80 — New York Islanders — Gord Lane, Jean Potvin, Bob Lorimer, Denis Potvin, Stefan Persson, Ken Morrow, Dave Langevin, Duane Sutter, Garry Howatt, Clark Gillies, Lorne Henning, Wayne Merrick, Bob Bourne, Steve Tambellini, Bryan Trottier, Mike Bossy, Bob Nystrom, John Tonelli, Anders Kallur, Butch Goring, Alex McKendry, Glenn Resch, Billy Smith, Al Arbour (coach), Bill Torrey (general manager), Ron Waske, Jim Pickard (trainers).
Scores: May 13 at Philadelphia — NY Islanders 4, Philadelphia 3; May 15 at Philadelphia — Philadelphia 8, NY Islanders 3; May 17 at Long Island — NY Islanders 6, Philadelphia 2; May 19 at Long Island — NY Islanders 5, Philadelphia 2; May 22 at Philadelphia — Philadelphia 6, NY Islanders 3; May 24 at Long Island — NY Islanders 5, Philadelphia 4.

1978-79 — Montreal Canadiens — Ken Dryden, Larry Robinson, Serge Savard, Guy Lapointe, Brian Engblom, Gilles Lupien, Rick Chartraw, Guy Lafleur, Steve Shutt, Jacques Lemaire, Yvan Cournoyer, Rejean Houle, Pierre Mondou, Bob Gainey, Doug Jarvis, Yvon Lambert, Doug Risebrough, Pierre Larouche, Mario Tremblay, Cam Connor, Pat Hughes, Rod Langway, Mark Napier, Michel Larocque, Richard Sevigny, Scotty Bowman (coach), Irving Grundman (managing director), Eddy Palchak, Pierre Meilleur (trainers).
Scores: May 13 at Montreal — NY Rangers 4, Montreal 1; May 15 at Montreal — Montreal 6, NY Rangers 2; May 17 at New York — Montreal 4, NY Rangers 1; May 19 at New York — Montreal 4, NY Rangers 3; May 21 at Montreal — Montreal 4, NY Rangers 1.

1977-78 — Montreal Canadiens — Ken Dryden, Larry Robinson, Serge Savard, Guy Lapointe, Bill Nyrop, Pierre Bouchard, Brian Engblom, Gilles Lupien, Rick Chartraw, Guy Lafleur, Steve Shutt, Jacques Lemaire, Yvan Cournoyer, Rejean Houle, Pierre Mondou, Bob Gainey, Doug Jarvis, Yvon Lambert, Doug Risebrough, Pierre Larouche, Mario Tremblay, Michel Larocque, Scotty Bowman (coach), Sam Pollock (general manager), Eddy Palchak, Pierre Meilleur (trainers).
Scores: May 13 at Montreal — Montreal 4, Boston 1; May 16 at Montreal — Montreal 3, Boston 2; May 18 at Boston — Boston 4, Montreal 0; May 21 at Boston — Boston 4, Montreal 3; May 23 at Montreal — Montreal 4, Boston 1; May 25 at Boston — Montreal 4, Boston 1.

1976-77 — Montreal Canadiens — Ken Dryden, Guy Lapointe, Larry Robinson, Serge Savard, Jimmy Roberts, Rick Chartraw, Bill Nyrop, Pierre Bouchard, Brian Engblom, Yvan Cournoyer, Guy Lafleur, Jacques Lemaire, Steve Shutt, Pete Mahovlich, Murray Wilson, Doug Jarvis, Yvon Lambert, Bob Gainey, Doug Risebrough, Mario Tremblay, Rejean Houle, Pierre Mondou, Mike Polich, Michel Larocque, Scotty Bowman (coach), Sam Pollock (general manager), Eddy Palchak, Pierre Meilleur (trainers).
Scores: May 7 at Montreal — Montreal 7, Boston 3; May 10 at Montreal — Montreal 3, Boston 0; May 12 at Boston — Montreal 4, Boston 2; May 14 at Boston — Montreal 2, Boston 1.

1975-76 — Montreal Canadiens — Ken Dryden, Serge Savard, Guy Lapointe, Larry Robinson, Bill Nyrop, Pierre Bouchard, Jim Roberts, Guy Lafleur, Steve Shutt, Pete Mahovlich, Yvan Cournoyer, Jacques Lemaire, Yvon Lambert, Bob Gainey, Doug Jarvis, Doug Risebrough, Murray Wilson, Mario Tremblay, Rick Chartraw, Michel Larocque, Scotty Bowman (coach), Sam Pollock (general manager), Eddy Palchak, Pierre Meilleur (trainers).
Scores: May 9 at Montreal — Montreal 4, Philadelphia 3; May 11 at Montreal — Montreal 2, Philadelphia 1; May 13 at Philadelphia — Montreal 3, Philadelphia 2; May 16 at Philadelphia — Montreal 5, Philadelphia 3.

1974-75 — Philadelphia Flyers — Bernie Parent, Wayne Stephenson, Ed Van Impe, Tom Bladon, André Dupont, Joe Watson, Jim Watson, Ted Harris, Larry Goodenough, Rick MacLeish, Bobby Clarke, Bill Barber, Reggie Leach, Gary Dornhoefer, Ross Lonsberry, Bob Kelly, Terry Crisp, Don Saleski, Dave Schultz, Orest Kindrachuk, Bill Clement, Fred Shero (coach), Keith Allen (general manager), Frank Lewis, Jim McKenzie (trainers).
Scores: May 15 at Philadelphia — Philadelphia 4, Buffalo 1; May 18 at Philadelphia — Philadelphia 2, Buffalo 1; May 20 at Buffalo — Buffalo 5, Philadelphia 4; May 22 at Buffalo — Buffalo 4, Philadelphia 2; May 25 at Philadelphia — Philadelphia 5, Buffalo 1; May 27 at Buffalo — Philadelphia 2, Buffalo 0.

1973-74 — Philadelphia Flyers — Bernie Parent, Ed Van Impe, Tom Bladon, André Dupont, Joe Watson, Jim Watson, Barry Ashbee, Bill Barber, Dave Schultz, Don Saleski, Gary Dornhoefer, Terry Crisp, Bobby Clarke, Simon Nolet, Ross Lonsberry, Rick MacLeish, Bill Flett, Orest Kindrachuk, Bill Clement, Bob Kelly, Bruce Cowick, Al MacAdam, Bobby Taylor, Fred Shero (coach), Keith Allen (general manager), Frank Lewis, Jim McKenzie (trainers).
Scores: May 7 at Boston — Boston 3, Philadelphia 2; May 9 at Boston — Philadelphia 3, Boston 2; May 12 at Philadelphia — Philadelphia 4, Boston 1; May 14 at Philadelphia — Philadelphia 4, Boston 2; May 16 at Boston — Boston 5, Philadelphia 1; May 19 at Philadelphia — Philadelphia 1, Boston 0.

1972-73 — Montreal Canadiens — Ken Dryden, Guy Lapointe, Serge Savard, Larry Robinson, Jacques Laperriere, Bob Murdoch, Pierre Bouchard, Jim Roberts, Yvan Cournoyer, Frank Mahovlich, Jacques Lemaire, Pete Mahovlich, Marc Tardif, Henri Richard, Rejean Houle, Guy Lafleur, Chuck Lefley, Claude Larose, Murray Wilson, Steve Shutt, Michel Plasse, Scotty Bowman (coach), Sam Pollock (general manager), Ed Palchak, Bob Williams (trainers).
Scores: April 29 at Montreal — Montreal 8, Chicago 3; May 1 at Montreal — Montreal 4, Chicago 1; May 3 at Chicago — Chicago 7, Montreal 4; May 6 at Chicago — Montreal 4, Chicago 0; May 8 at Montreal — Chicago 8, Montreal 7; May 10 at Chicago — Montreal 6, Chicago 4.

Terry Crisp played on two Stanley Cup winners with the Philadelphia Flyers in 1973-74 and 1974-75.

1971-72 — Boston Bruins — Gerry Cheevers, Ed Johnston, Bobby Orr, Ted Green, Carol Vadnais, Dallas Smith, Don Awrey, Phil Esposito, Ken Hodge, John Bucyk, Mike Walton, Wayne Cashman, Garnet Bailey, Derek Sanderson, Fred Stanfield, Ed Westfall, John McKenzie, Don Marcotte, Garry Peters, Chris Hayes, Tom Johnson (coach), Milt Schmidt (general manager), Dan Canney, John Forristall (trainers).
Scores: April 30 at Boston — Boston 6, New York Rangers 5; May 2 at Boston — Boston 2, New York 1; May 4 at New York — New York 5, Boston 2; May 7 at New York — Boston 3, New York 2; May 9 at Boston — New York 3, Boston 2; May 11 at New York — Boston 3, New York 0.

1970-71 — Montreal Canadiens — Ken Dryden, Rogatien Vachon, Jacques Laperriere, Jean-Claude Tremblay, Guy Lapointe, Terry Harper, Pierre Bouchard, Jean Beliveau, Marc Tardif, Yvan Cournoyer, Rejean Houle, Claude Larose, Henri Richard, Phil Roberto, Pete Mahovlich, Leon Rochefort, John Ferguson, Bobby Sheehan, Jacques Lemaire, Frank Mahovlich, Bob Murdoch, Chuck Lefley, Al MacNeil (coach), Sam Pollock (general manager), Yvon Belanger, Ed Palchak (trainers).
Scores: May 4 at Chicago — Chicago 2, Montreal 1; May 6 at Chicago — Chicago 5, Montreal 3; May 9 at Montreal — Montreal 4, Chicago 2; May 11 at Montreal — Montreal 5, Chicago 2; May 13 at Chicago — Chicago 2, Montreal 0; May 16 at Montreal — Montreal 4, Chicago 3; May 18 at Chicago — Montreal 3, Chicago 2.

1969-70 — Boston Bruins — Gerry Cheevers, Ed Johnston, Bobby Orr, Rick Smith, Dallas Smith, Bill Speer, Gary Doak, Don Awrey, Phil Esposito, Ken Hodge, John Bucyk, Wayne Carleton, Wayne Cashman, Derek Sanderson, Fred Stanfield, Ed Westfall, John McKenzie, Jim Lorentz, Don Marcotte, Bill Lesuk, Dan Schock, Harry Sinden (coach), Milt Schmidt (general manager), Dan Canney, John Forristall (trainers).
Scores: May 3 at St. Louis — Boston 6, St. Louis 1; May 5 at St. Louis — Boston 6, St. Louis 2; May 7 at Boston — Boston 4, St. Louis 1; May 10 at Boston — Boston 4, St. Louis 3.

1968-69 — Montreal Canadiens — Lorne Worsley, Rogatien Vachon, Jacques Laperriere, Jean-Claude Tremblay, Ted Harris, Serge Savard, Terry Harper, Larry Hillman, Jean Beliveau, Ralph Backstrom, Dick Duff, Yvan Cournoyer, Claude Provost, Bobby Rousseau, Henri Richard, John Ferguson, Christian Bordeleau, Mickey Redmond, Jacques Lemaire, Lucien Grenier, Tony Esposito, Claude Ruel (coach), Sam Pollock (general manager), Larry Aubut, Eddy Palchak (trainers).
Scores: April 27 at Montreal — Montreal 3, St. Louis 1; April 29 at Montreal — Montreal 3, St. Louis 1; May 1 at St. Louis — Montreal 4, St. Louis 0; May 4 at St. Louis — Montreal 2, St. Louis 1.

1967-68 — Montreal Canadiens — Lorne Worsley, Rogatien Vachon, Jacques Laperriere, Jean-Claude Tremblay, Ted Harris, Serge Savard, Terry Harper, Carol Vadnais, Jean Beliveau, Gilles Tremblay, Ralph Backstrom, Dick Duff, Claude Larose, Yvan Cournoyer, Claude Provost, Bobby Rousseau, Henri Richard, John Ferguson, Danny Grant, Jacques Lemaire, Mickey Redmond, Toe Blake (coach), Sam Pollock (general manager), Larry Aubut, Eddy Palchak (trainers).
Scores: May 5 at St. Louis — Montreal 3, St. Louis 2; May 7 at St. Louis — Montreal 1, St. Louis 0; May 9 at Montreal — Montreal 4, St. Louis 3; May 11 at Montreal — Montreal 3, St. Louis 2.

1966-67 — Toronto Maple Leafs — Johnny Bower, Terry Sawchuk, Larry Hillman, Marcel Pronovost, Tim Horton, Bob Baun, Aut Erickson, Allan Stanley, Red Kelly, Ron Ellis, George Armstrong, Pete Stemkowski, Dave Keon, Mike Walton, Jim Pappin, Bob Pulford, Brian Conacher, Eddie Shack, Frank Mahovlich, Milan Marcetta, Larry Jeffrey, Bruce Gamble, Punch Imlach (manager-coach), Bob Haggart (trainer).
Scores: April 20 at Montreal — Toronto 2, Montreal 6; April 22 at Montreal — Toronto 3, Montreal 0; April 25 at Toronto — Toronto 3, Montreal 2; April 27 at Toronto — Toronto 2, Montreal 6; April 29 at Montreal — Toronto 4, Montreal 1; May 2 at Toronto — Toronto 3, Montreal 1.

1965-66 — Montreal Canadiens — Lorne Worsley, Charlie Hodge, Jean-Claude Tremblay, Ted Harris, Jean-Guy Talbot, Terry Harper, Jacques Laperriere, Noel Price, Jean Beliveau, Ralph Backstrom, Dick Duff, Gilles Tremblay, Claude Larose, Yvan Cournoyer, Claude Provost, Bobby Rousseau, Henri Richard, Dave Balon, John Ferguson, Leon Rochefort, Jim Roberts, Toe Blake (coach), Sam Pollock (general manager), Larry Aubut, Andy Galley (trainers).
Scores: April 24 at Montreal — Detroit 3, Montreal 2; April 26 at Montreal — Detroit 5, Montreal 2; April 28 at Detroit — Montreal 4, Detroit 2; May 1 at Detroit — Montreal 2, Detroit 1; May 3 at Montreal — Montreal 5, Detroit 1; May 5 at Detroit — Montreal 3, Detroit 2.

1964-65 — Montreal Canadiens — Lorne Worsley, Charlie Hodge, Jean-Claude Tremblay, Ted Harris, Jean-Guy Talbot, Terry Harper, Jacques Laperriere, Jean Gauthier, Noel Picard, Jean Beliveau, Ralph Backstrom, Dick Duff, Claude Larose, Yvan Cournoyer, Claude Provost, Bobby Rousseau, Henri Richard, Dave Balon, John Ferguson, Red Berenson, Jim Roberts, Toe Blake (coach), Sam Pollock (general manager), Larry Aubut, Andy Galley (trainers).
Scores: April 17 at Montreal — Montreal 3, Chicago 2; April 20 at Montreal — Montreal 2, Chicago 0; April 22 at Chicago — Montreal 1, Chicago 3; April 25 at Chicago — Montreal 1, Chicago 5; April 27 at Montreal — Montreal 6, Chicago 0; April 29 at Chicago — Montreal 1, Chicago 2; May 1 at Montreal — Montreal 4, Chicago 0.

1963-64 — Toronto Maple Leafs — Johnny Bower, Carl Brewer, Tim Horton, Bob Baun, Allan Stanley, Larry Hillman, Al Arbour, Red Kelly, Gerry Ehman, Andy Bathgate, George Armstrong, Ron Stewart, Dave Keon, Billy Harris, Don McKenney, Jim Pappin, Bob Pulford, Eddie Shack, Frank Mahovlich, Eddie Litzenberger, Punch Imlach (manager-coach), Bob Haggert (trainer).
Scores: April 11 at Toronto — Toronto 3, Detroit 2; April 14 at Toronto — Toronto 3, Detroit 4; April 16 at Detroit — Toronto 3, Detroit 4; April 18 at Detroit — Toronto 4, Detroit 2; April 21 at Toronto — Toronto 1, Detroit 2; April 23 at Detroit — Toronto 4, Detroit 3; April 25 at Toronto — Toronto 4, Detroit 0.

1962-63 — Toronto Maple Leafs — Johnny Bower, Don Simmons, Carl Brewer, Tim Horton, Kent Douglas, Allan Stanley, Bob Baun, Larry Hillman, Red Kelly, Dick Duff, George Armstrong, Bob Nevin, Ron Stewart, Dave Keon, Billy Harris Bob Pulford, Eddie Shack, Ed Litzenberger, Frank Mahovlich, John MacMillan, Punch Imlach (manager-coach), Bob Haggert (trainer).
Scores: April 9 at Toronto — Toronto 4, Detroit 2; April 11 at Toronto — Toronto 4, Detroit 2; April 14 at Detroit — Toronto 2, Detroit 3; April 16 at Detroit — Toronto 4, Detroit 2; April 18 at Toronto — Toronto 3, Detroit 1.

1961-62 — Toronto Maple Leafs — Johnny Bower, Don Simmons, Carl Brewer, Tim Horton, Bob Baun, Allan Stanley, Al Arbour, Larry Hillman, Red Kelly, Dick Duff, George Armstrong, Frank Mahovlich, Bob Nevin, Ron Stewart, Bill Harris, Bert Olmstead, Bob Pulford, Eddie Shack, Dave Keon, Ed Litzenberger, John MacMillan, Punch Imlach (manager-coach), Bob Haggert (trainer).
Scores: April 10 at Toronto — Toronto 4, Chicago 1; April 12 at Toronto — Toronto 3, Chicago 2; April 15 at Chicago — Toronto 0, Chicago 3; April 17 at Chicago — Toronto 1, Chicago 4; April 19 at Toronto — Toronto 8, Chicago 4; April 22 at Chicago — Toronto 2, Chicago 1.

1960-61 — Chicago Black Hawks — Glenn Hall, Al Arbour, Pierre Pilote, Elmer Vasko, Jack Evans, Dollard St. Laurent, Reg Fleming, Tod Sloan, Ron Murphy, Eddie Litzenberger, Bill Hay, Bobby Hull, Ab McDonald, Eric Nesterenko, Ken Wharram, Earl Balfour, Stan Mikita, Murray Balfour, Chico Maki, Tommy Ivan (manager), Rudy Pilous (coach), Nick Garen (trainer).
Scores: April 6 at Chicago — Chicago 3, Detroit 2; April 8 at Detroit — Detroit 3, Chicago 1; April 10 at Chicago — Chicago 3, Detroit 1; April 12 at Detroit — Detroit 2, Chicago 1; April 14 at Chicago — Chicago 6, Detroit 3; April 16 at Detroit — Chicago 5, Detroit 1.

1959-60 — Montreal Canadiens — Jacques Plante, Charlie Hodge, Doug Harvey, Tom Johnson, Bob Turner, Jean-Guy Talbot, Albert Langlois, Ralph Backstrom, Jean Beliveau, Marcel Bonin, Bernie Geoffrion, Phil Goyette, Bill Hicke, Don Marshall, Ab McDonald, Dickie Moore, André Pronovost, Claude Provost, Henri Richard, Maurice Richard, Frank Selke (manager), Toe Blake (coach), Hector Dubois, Larry Aubut (trainers).
Scores: April 7 at Montreal — Canadiens 4, Toronto 2; April 9 at Montreal — Canadiens 2, Toronto 1; April 12 at Toronto — Canadiens 5, Toronto 2; April 14 at Toronto — Canadiens 4, Toronto 0.

1958-59 — Montreal Canadiens — Jacques Plante, Charlie Hodge, Doug Harvey, Tom Johnson, Bob Turner, Jean-Guy Talbot, Albert Langlois, Bernie Geoffrion, Ralph Backstrom, Bill Hicke, Maurice Richard, Dickie Moore, Claude Provost, Ab McDonald, Henri Richard, Marcel Bonin, Phil Goyette, Don Marshall, André Pronovost, Jean Béliveau, Frank Selke (manager), Toe Blake (coach), Hector Dubois, Larry Aubut (trainers).
Scores: April 9 at Montreal — Canadiens 5, Toronto 3; April 11 at Montreal — Canadiens 3, Toronto 1; April 14 at Toronto — Toronto 3, Canadiens 2; April 16 at Toronto — Canadiens 3, Toronto 2; April 18 at Montreal — Canadiens 5, Toronto 3.

1957-58 — Montreal Canadiens — Jacques Plante, Gerry McNeil, Doug Harvey, Tom Johnson, Bob Turner, Dollard St-Laurent, Jean-Guy Talbot, Albert Langlois, Jean Béliveau, Bernie Geoffrion, Maurice Richard, Dickie Moore, Claude Provost, Floyd Curry, Bert Olmstead, Henri Richard, Marcel Bonin, Phil Goyette, Don Marshall, André Pronovost, Connie Broden, Frank Selke (manager), Toe Blake (coach), Hector Dubois, Larry Aubut (trainers).
Scores: April 8 at Montreal — Canadiens 2, Boston 1; April 10 at Montreal — Boston 5, Canadiens 2; April 13 at Boston — Canadiens 3, Boston 0; April 15 at Boston — Boston 3, Canadiens 1; April 17 at Montreal — Canadiens 3, Boston 2; April 20 at Boston — Canadiens 5, Boston 3.

1956-57 — Montreal Canadiens — Jacques Plante, Gerry McNeil, Doug Harvey, Tom Johnson, Bob Turner, Dollard St. Laurent, Jean-Guy Talbot, Jean Béliveau, Bernie Geoffrion, Floyd Curry, Dickie Moore, Maurice Richard, Claude Provost, Bert Olmstead, Henri Richard, Phil Goyette, Don Marshall, André Pronovost, Connie Broden, Frank Selke (manager), Toe Blake (coach), Hector Dubois, Larry Aubut (trainers).
Scores: April 6, at Montreal — Canadiens 5, Boston 1; April 9, at Montreal — Canadiens 1, Boston 0; April 11, at Boston — Canadiens 4, Boston 2; April 14, at Boston — Boston 2, Canadiens 0; April 16, at Montreal — Canadiens 5, Boston 1.

1955-56 — Montreal Canadiens — Jacques Plante, Doug Harvey, Emile Bouchard, Bob Turner, Tom Johnson, Jean-Guy Talbot, Dollard St. Laurent, Jean Béliveau, Bernie Geoffrion, Bert Olmstead, Floyd Curry, Jackie Leclair, Maurice Richard, Dickie Moore, Henri Richard, Ken Mosdell, Don Marshall, Claude Provost, Frank Selke (manager), Toe Blake (coach), Hector Dubois (trainer).
Scores: March 31, at Montreal — Canadiens 6, Detroit 4; April 3, at Montreal — Canadiens 5, Detroit 1; April 5, at Detroit — Detroit 3, Canadiens 1; April 8, at Detroit — Canadiens 3, Detroit 0; April 10, at Montreal — Canadiens 3, Detroit 1.

1954-55 — Detroit Red Wings — Terry Sawchuk, Red Kelly, Bob Goldham, Marcel Pronovost, Ben Woit, Jim Hay, Larry Hillman, Ted Lindsay, Tony Leswick, Gordie Howe, Alex Delvecchio, Marty Pavelich, Glen Skov, Earl Reibel, John Wilson, Bill Dineen, Vic Stasiuk, Marcel Bonin, Jack Adams (manager), Jimmy Skinner (coach), Carl Mattson (trainer).
Scores: April 3, at Detroit — Detroit 4, Canadiens 2; April 5, at Detroit — Detroit 7, Canadiens 1, April 7 at Montreal — Canadiens 4, Detroit 2; April 9, at Montreal — Canadiens 5, Detroit 3; April 10, at Detroit — Detroit 5, Canadiens 1; April 12, at Montreal — Canadiens 6, Detroit 3; April 14, at Detroit — Detroit 3, Canadiens 1.

1953-54 — Detroit Red Wings — Terry Sawchuk, Red Kelly, Bob Goldham, Ben Woit, Marcel Pronovost, Al Arbour, Keith Allen, Ted Lindsay, Tony Leswick, Gordie Howe, Marty Pavelich, Alex Delvecchio, Metro Prystai, Glen Skov, John Wilson, Bill Dineen, Jim Peters, Earl Reibel, Vic Stasiuk, Jack Adams (manager), Tommy Ivan (coach), Carl Mattson (trainer).
Scores: April 4, at Detroit — Detroit 3, Canadiens 1; April 6, at Detroit — Canadiens 3, Detroit 1; April 8, at Montreal — Detroit 5, Canadiens 2; April 10, at Montreal — Detroit 2, Canadiens 0; April 11, at Detroit — Canadiens 1, Detroit 0; April 13, at Montreal — Canadiens 4, Detroit 1; April 16, at Detroit — Detroit 2, Canadiens 1.

1952-53 — Montreal Canadiens — Gerry McNeil, Jacques Plante, Doug Harvey, Emile Bouchard, Tom Johnson, Dollard St. Laurent, Bud MacPherson, Maurice Richard, Elmer Lach, Bert Olmstead, Bernie Geoffrion, Floyd Curry, Paul Masnick, Billy Reay, Dickie Moore, Ken Mosdell, Dick Gamble, Johnny McCormack, Lorne Davis, Calum McKay, Eddie Mazur, Frank Selke (manager), Dick Irvin (coach), Hector Dubois (trainer).
Scores: April 9, at Montreal — Canadiens 4, Boston 2; April 11, at Montreal — Boston 4, Canadiens 1; April 12, at Boston — Canadiens 3, Boston 0; April 14, at Boston — Canadiens 7, Boston 3; April 16, at Montreal — Canadiens 1, Boston 0.

1951-52 — Detroit Red Wings — Terry Sawchuk, Bob Goldham, Ben Woit, Red Kelly, Leo Reise, Marcel Pronovost, Ted Lindsay, Tony Leswick, Gordie Howe, Metro Prystai, Marty Pavelich, Sid Abel, Glen Skov, Alex Delvecchio, John Wilson, Vic Stasiuk, Larry Zeidel, Jack Adams (manager) Tommy Ivan (coach), Carl Mattson (trainer).
Scores: April 10, at Montreal — Detroit 3, Canadiens 1; April 12 at Montreal — Detroit 2, Canadiens 1; April 13, at Detroit — Detroit 3, Canadiens 0; April 15, at Detroit — Detroit 3, Canadiens 0.

1950-51 — Toronto Maple Leafs — Turk Broda, Al Rollins, Jim Thomson, Gus Mortson, Bill Barilko, Bill Juzda, Fern Flaman, Hugh Bolton, Ted Kennedy, Sid Smith, Tod Sloan, Cal Gardner, Howie Meeker, Harry Watson, Max Bentley, Joe Klukay, Danny Lewicki, Ray Timgren, Fleming Mackell, Johnny McCormack, Bob Hassard, Conn Smythe (manager), Joe Primeau (coach), Tim Daly (trainer).
Scores: April 11, at Toronto — Toronto 3, Canadiens 2; April 14, at Toronto — Canadiens 3, Toronto 2; April 17, at Montreal — Toronto 2, Canadiens 1; April 19, at Montreal — Toronto 3, Canadiens 2; April 21, at Toronto — Toronto 3, Canadiens 2.

1949-50 — Detroit Red Wings — Harry Lumley, Jack Stewart, Leo Reise, Clare Martin, Al Dewsbury, Lee Fogolin, Marcel Pronovost, Red Kelly, Ted Lindsay, Sid Abel, Gordie Howe, George Gee, Jimmy Peters, Marty Pavelich, Jim McFadden, Pete Babando, Max McNab, Gerry Couture, Joe Carveth, Steve Black, John Wilson, Larry Wilson, Jack Adams (manager), Tommy Ivan (coach), Carl Mattson (trainer).
Scores: April 11, at Detroit — Detroit 4, Rangers 1; April 13, at Toronto* — Rangers 3, Detroit 1; April 15, at Toronto — Detroit 4, Rangers 0; April 18, at Detroit — Rangers 4, Detroit 3; April 20, at Detroit — Rangers 2, Detroit 1; April 22, at Detroit — Detroit 5, Rangers 4; April 23, at Detroit — Detroit 4, Rangers 3.

* Ice was unavailable in Madison Square Garden and Rangers elected to play second and third games on Toronto ice.

1948-49 — Toronto Maple Leafs — Turk Broda, Jim Thomson, Gus Mortson, Bill Barilko, Garth Boesch, Bill Juzda, Ted Kennedy, Howie Meeker, Vic Lynn, Harry Watson, Bill Ezinicki, Cal Gardner, Max Bentley, Joe Klukay, Sid Smith, Don Metz, Ray Timgren, Fleming Mackell, Harry Taylor, Bob Dawes, Tod Sloan, Conn Smythe (manager), Hap Day (coach), Tim Daly (trainer).

Scores: April 8, at Detroit — Toronto 3, Detroit 2; April 10, at Detroit — Toronto 3, Detroit 1; April 13, at Toronto — Toronto 3, Detroit 1; April 16, at Toronto — Toronto 3, Detroit 1.

1947-48 — Toronto Maple Leafs — Turk Broda, Jim Thomson, Wally Stanowski, Garth Boesch, Bill Barilko. Gus Mortson, Phil Samis, Syl Apps, Bill Ezinicki, Harry Watson, Ted Kennedy, Howie Meeker, Vic Lynn, Nick Metz, Max Bentley, Joe Klukay, Les Costello, Don Metz, Sid Smith, Conn Smythe (manager), Hap Day (coach), Tim Daly (trainer).
Scores: April 7, at Toronto — Toronto 5, Detroit 3; April 10, at Toronto — Toronto 4, Detroit 2; April 11, at Detroit — Toronto 2, Detroit 0; April 14, at Detroit — Toronto 7, Detroit 2.

1946-47 — Toronto Maple Leafs — Turk Broda, Garth Boesch, Gus Mortson, Jim Thomson, Wally Stanowski, Bill Barilko, Harry Watson, Bud Poile, Ted Kennedy, Syl Apps, Don Metz, Nick Metz, Bill Ezinicki, Vic Lynn, Howie Meeker, Gaye Stewart, Joe Klukay, Gus Bodnar, Bob Goldham, Conn Smythe (manager), Hap Day (coach), Tim Daly (trainer).
Scores: April 8, at Montreal — Canadiens 6, Toronto 0; April 10, at Montreal — Toronto 4, Canadiens 0; April 12, at Toronto — Toronto 4, Canadiens 2; April 15, at Toronto — Toronto 2, Canadiens 1; April 17, at Montreal — Canadiens 3, Toronto 1; April 19, at Toronto — Toronto 2, Canadiens 1.

1945-46 — Montreal Canadiens — Elmer Lach, Toe Blake, Maurice Richard, Bob Fillion, Dutch Hiller, Murph Chamberlain, Ken Mosdell, Buddy O'Connor, Glen Harmon, Jim Peters, Emile Bouchard, Bill Reay, Ken Reardon, Leo Lamoureux, Frank Eddolls, Gerry Plamondon, Bill Durnan, Tommy Gorman (manager), Dick Irvin (coach), Ernie Cook (trainer).
Scores: March 30, at Montreal — Canadiens 4, Boston 3; April 2, at Montreal — Canadiens 3, Boston 2; April 4, at Boston — Canadiens 4, Boston 2; April 7, at Boston — Boston 3, Canadiens 2; April 9, at Montreal — Canadiens 6, Boston 3.

1944-45 — Toronto Maple Leafs — Don Metz, Frank McCool, Wally Stanowski, Reg Hamilton, Elwyn Morris, Johnny McCreedy, Tommy O'Neill, Ted Kennedy, Babe Pratt, Gus Bodnar, Art Jackson, Jack McLean, Mel Hill, Nick Metz, Bob Davidson, Dave Schriner, Lorne Carr, Conn Smythe (manager), Frank Selke (business manager), Hap Day (coach), Tim Daly (trainer).
Scores: April 6, at Detroit — Toronto 1, Detroit 0; April 8, at Detroit — Toronto 2, Detroit 0; April 12, at Toronto — Toronto 1, Detroit 0; April 14, at Toronto — Detroit 5, Toronto 3; April 19, at Detroit — Detroit 2, Toronto 0; April 21, at Toronto — Detroit 1, Toronto 0; April 22, at Detroit — Toronto 2, Detroit 1.

1943-44 — Montreal Canadiens — Toe Blake, Maurice Richard, Elmer Lach, Ray Getliffe, Murph Chamberlain, Phil Watson, Emile Bouchard, Glen Harmon, Buddy O'Connor, Jerry Heffernan, Mike McMahon, Leo Lamoureux, Fernand Majeau, Bob Fillion, Bill Durnan, Tommy Gorman (manager), Dick Irvin (coach), Ernie Cook (trainer).
Scores: April 4, at Montreal — Canadiens 5, Chicago 1; April 6, at Chicago — Canadiens 3, Chicago 1; April 9 at Chicago — Canadiens 3, Chicago 2; April 13, at Montreal — Canadiens 5, Chicago 4.

1942-43 — Detroit Red Wings — Jack Stewart, Jimmy Orlando, Sid Abel, Alex Motter, Harry Watson, Joe Carveth, Mud Bruneteau, Eddie Wares, Johnny Mowers, Cully Simon, Don Grosso, Carl Liscombe, Connie Brown, Syd Howe, Les Douglas, Hal Jackson, Joe Fisher, Jack Adams (manager), Ebbie Goodfellow (playing-coach), Honey Walker (trainer).
Scores: April 1, at Detroit — Detroit 6, Boston 2; April 4, at Detroit — Detroit 4, Boston 3; April 7, at Boston — Detroit 4, Boston 0; April 8, at Boston — Detroit 2, Boston 0.

Rangers' goalie Dave Kerr smothers this scoring attempt by the Leafs' Red Heron in the second game of the 1940 Stanley Cup Finals.

1941-42 — Toronto Maple Leafs — Wally Stanowski, Syl Apps, Bob Goldham, Gord Drillon, Hank Goldup, Ernie Dickens, Dave Schriner, Bucko McDonald, Bob Davidson, Nick Metz, Bingo Kampman, Don Metz, Gaye Stewart, Turk Broda, Johnny McCreedy, Lorne Carr, Pete Langelle, Billy Taylor, Conn Smythe (manager), Hap Day (coach), Frank Selke (business manager), Tim Daly (trainer).
Scores: April 4, at Toronto — Detroit 3, Toronto 2; April 7, at Toronto — Detroit 4, Toronto 2; April 9, at Detroit — Detroit 5, Toronto 2; April 12, at Detroit — Toronto 4, Detroit 3; April 14, at Toronto — Toronto 9, Detroit 3; April 16, at Detroit — Toronto 3, Detroit 0; April 18, at Toronto — Toronto 3, Detroit 1.

1940-41 — Boston Bruins — Bill Cowley, Des Smith, Dit Clapper, Frank Brimsek, Flash Hollett, John Crawford, Bobby Bauer, Pat McCreavy, Herb Cain, Mel Hill, Milt Schmidt, Woody Dumart, Roy Conacher, Terry Reardon, Art Jackson, Eddie Wiseman, Art Ross (manager), Cooney Weiland (coach), Win Green (trainer).
Scores: April 6, at Boston — Detroit 2, Boston 3; April 8, at Boston — Detroit 1, Boston 2; April 10, at Detroit — Boston 4, Detroit 2; April 12, at Detroit — Boston 3, Detroit 1.

1939-40 — New York Rangers — Dave Kerr, Art Coulter, Ott Heller, Alex Shibicky, Mac Colville, Neil Colville, Phil Watson, Lynn Patrick, Clint Smith, Muzz Patrick, Babe Pratt, Bryan Hextall, Kilby Macdonald, Dutch Hiller, Alf Pike, Sanford Smith, Lester Patrick (manager), Frank Boucher (coach), Harry Westerby (trainer).
Scores: April 2, at New York — Rangers 2, Toronto 1; April 3, at New York — Rangers 6, Toronto 2; April 6, at Toronto — Rangers 1, Toronto 2; April 9, at Toronto — Rangers 0, Toronto 3; April 11, at Toronto — Rangers 2, Toronto 1; April 13, at Toronto — Rangers 3, Toronto 2.

1938-39 — Boston Bruins — Bobby Bauer, Mel Hill, Flash Hollett, Roy Conacher, Gord Pettinger, Milt Schmidt, Woody Dumart, Jack Crawford, Ray Getliffe, Frank Brimsek, Eddie Shore, Dit Clapper, Bill Cowley, Jack Portland, Red Hamill, Cooney Weiland, Art Ross (manager-coach), Win Green (trainer).
Scores: April 6, at Boston — Toronto 1, Boston 2; April 9, at Boston — Toronto 3, Boston 2; April 11, at Toronto — Toronto 1, Boston 3; April 13 at Toronto — Toronto 0, Boston 3.

1937-38 — Chicago Black Hawks — Art Wiebe, Carl Voss, Hal Jackson, Mike Karakas, Mush March, Jack Shill, Earl Seibert, Cully Dahlstrom, Alex Levinsky, Johnny Gottselig, Lou Trudel, Pete Palangio, Bill MacKenzie, Doc Romnes, Paul Thompson, Roger Jenkins, Bert Connolly, Virgil Johnson, Paul Goodman, Bill Stewart (manager-coach), Eddie Froelich (trainer).
Scores: April 5, at Toronto — Chicago 3, Toronto 1; April 7, at Toronto — Chicago 1, Toronto 5; April 10 at Chicago — Chicago 2, Toronto 1; April 12, at Chicago — Chicago 4, Toronto 1.

1936-37 — Detroit Red Wings — Normie Smith, Pete Kelly, Larry Aurie, Herbie Lewis, Hec Kilrea, Mud Bruneteau, Syd Howe, Wally Kilrea, Jimmy Franks, Bucko McDonald, Gordon Pettinger, Ebbie Goodfellow, Johnny Gallagher, Scotty Bowman, Johnny Sorrell, Marty Barry, Earl Robertson, Johnny Sherf, Howard Mackie, Jack Adams (manager-coach), Honey Walker (trainer).
Scores: April 6, at New York — Detroit 1, Rangers 5; April 8, at Detroit — Detroit 4, Rangers 2; April 11, at Detroit — Detroit 0, Rangers 1; April 13, at Detroit — Detroit 1, Rangers 0; April 15, at Detroit — Detroit 3, Rangers 0.

1935-36 — Detroit Red Wings — Johnny Sorrell, Syd Howe, Marty Barry, Herbie Lewis, Mud Bruneteau, Wally Kilrea, Hec Kilrea, Gordon Pettinger, Bucko McDonald, Scotty Bowman, Pete Kelly, Doug Young, Ebbie Goodfellow, Normie Smith, Jack Adams (manager-coach), Honey Walker (trainer).
Scores: April 5, at Detroit — Detroit 3, Toronto 1; April 7, at Detroit — Detroit 9, Toronto 4; April 9, at Toronto — Detroit 3, Toronto 4; April 11, at Toronto — Detroit 3, Toronto 1.

1934-35 — Montreal Maroons — Marvin (Cy) Wentworth, Alex Connell, Toe Blake, Stew Evans, Earl Robinson, Bill Miller, Dave Trottier, Jimmy Ward, Larry Northcott, Hooley Smith, Russ Blinco, Allan Shields, Sammy McManus, Gus Marker, Bob Gracie, Herb Cain, Tommy Gorman (manager), Lionel Conacher (coach), Bill O'Brien (trainer).
Scores: April 4, at Toronto — Montreal 3, Toronto 2; April 6, at Toronto — Montreal 3, Toronto 1; April 9, at Montreal — Montreal 4, Toronto 1.

1933-34 — Chicago Black Hawks — Taffy Abel, Lolo Couture, Lou Trudel, Lionel Conacher, Paul Thompson, Leroy Goldsworthy, Art Coulter, Don McFayden, Tommy Cook, Doc Romnes, Johnny Gottselig, Mush March, Johny Sheppard, Chuck Gardiner (captain), Bill Kendall, Tommy Gorman (manager-coach), Eddie Froelich (trainer).
Scores: April 3, at Detroit — Detroit 1, Chicago 2; April 5, at Detroit — Detroit 1, Chicago 4; April 8, at Chicago — Detroit 5, Chicago 2; April 10, at Chicago — Detroit 0, Chicago 1.

1932-33 — New York Rangers — Ching Johnson, Butch Keeling, Frank Boucher, Art Somers, Babe Siebert, Bun Cook, Andy Aitkinhead, Ott Heller, Ozzie Asmundson, Gord Pettinger, Doug Brennan, Cecil Dillon, Bill Cook (captain), Murray Murdock, Earl Seibert, Lester Patrick (manager-coach), Harry Westerby (trainer).
Scores: April 4, at New York — Toronto 1, Rangers 5; April 8, at Toronto — Toronto 1, Rangers 3; April 11, at Toronto — Toronto 3, Rangers 2; April 13, at Toronto — Toronto 0, Rangers 1.

1931-32 — Toronto Maple Leafs — Charlie Conacher, Harvey Jackson, King Clancy, Andy Blair, Red Horner, Lorne Chabot, Alex Levinsky, Joe Primeau, Hal Darragh, Hal Cotton, Frank Finnigan, Hap Day, Ace Bailey, Bob Gracie, Fred Robertson, Earl Miller, Conn Smythe (manager), Dick Irvin (coach), Tim Daly (trainer).
Scores: April 5 at New York — Toronto 6, New York Rangers 4; April 7, at Boston* — Toronto 6, New York Rangers 2; April 9, at Toronto — Toronto 6, New York Rangers 4.

* Ice was unavailable in Madison Square Garden and Rangers elected to play the second game on neutral ice.

1930-31 — Montreal Canadiens — George Hainsworth, Wildor Larochelle, Marty Burke, Sylvio Mantha, Howie Morenz, Johnny Gagnon, Aurel Joliat, Armand Mondou, Pit Lepine, Albert Leduc, Georges Mantha, Art Lesieur, Nick Wasnie, Bert McCaffrey, Gus Rivers, Jean Pusie, Leo Dandurand (manager), Cecil Hart (coach), Ed Dufour (trainer).
Scores: April 3, at Chicago — Canadiens 2, Chicago 1; April 5, at Chicago — Canadiens 1, Chicago 2; April 9, at Montreal — Canadiens 2, Chicago 3; April 11, at Montreal — Canadiens 4, Chicago 2; April 14, at Montreal — Canadiens 2, Chicago 0.

1929-30 — Montreal Canadiens — George Hainsworth, Marty Burke, Sylvio Mantha, Howie Morenz, Bert McCaffrey, Aurel Joliat, Albert Leduc, Pit Lepine, Wildor Larochelle, Nick Wasnie, Gerald Carson, Armand Mondou, Georges Mantha, Gus Rivers, Leo Dandurand (manager), Cecil Hart (coach), Ed Dufour (trainer).
Scores: April 1 — Canadiens 3, Boston 0; April 3 — Canadiens 4, Boston 3.

1928-29 — Boston Bruins — Cecil (Tiny) Thompson, Eddie Shore, Lionel Hitchman, Perk Galbraith, Eric Pettinger, Frank Fredrickson, Mickey Mackay, Red Green, Dutch Gainor, Harry Oliver, Eddie Rodden, Dit Clapper, Cooney Weiland, Lloyd Klein, Cy Denneny, Bill Carson, George Owen, Myles Lane, Art Ross (manager-coach), Win Green (trainer).
Scores: March 28 — Rangers 0, Boston 2; March 29 — Rangers 1, Boston 2.

1927-28 — New York Rangers — Lorne Chabot, Taffy Abel, Leon Bourgault, Ching Johnson, Bill Cook, Bun Cook, Frank Boucher, Billy Boyd, Murray Murdock, Paul Thompson, Alex Gray, Joe Miller, Patsy Callighen, Lester Patrick (manager-coach), Harry Westerby (trainer).
Scores: April 5 — Rangers 0, Maroons 2; April 7 — Rangers 2, Maroons 1; April 10 — Rangers 0, Maroons 2; April 12 — Rangers 1, Maroons 0; April 14 — Rangers 2, Maroons 1.

1926-27 — Ottawa Senators — Alex Connell, King Clancy, George (Buck) Boucher, Ed Gorman, Frank Finnigan, Alex Smith, Hooley Smith, Cy Denneny, Frank Nighbor, Jack Adams, Milt Halliday, Dave Gil (manager-coach).
Scores: April 7 — Boston 0, Ottawa 0; April 9 — Boston 1, Ottawa 3; April 11 — Boston 1, Ottawa 1; April 13 — Boston 1, Ottawa 3.

1925-26 — Montreal Maroons — Clint Benedict, Reg Noble, Frank Carson, Dunc Munro, Nels Stewart, Harry Broadbent, Babe Siebert, Dinny Dinsmore, Bill Phillips, Hobart (Hobie) Kitchen, Sammy Rothschiel, Albert (Toots) Holway, Shorty Horne, Bern Brophy, Eddie Gerard (manager-coach), Bill O'Brien (trainer).
Scores: at Montreal, Maroons 3, Victoria 0; Maroons 3, Victoria 0; Victoria 3, Maroons 2; Maroons 2, Victoria 0. Total goals: Montreal 10, Victoria 3.

The series in the spring of 1926 ended the annual playoffs between the champions of the east and the champions of the west. The west coast league disbanded, selling its players to Chicago, Detroit and New York Rangers. Since 1926-27 the annual play-offs in the National Hockey League have decided the Stanley Cup champions.

1924-25 — Victoria Cougars — Harry (Happy) Holmes, Clem Loughlin, Gordie Fraser, Frank Fredrickson, Jack Walker, Harold (Gizzy) Hart, Harold (Slim) Halderson, Frank Foyston, Wally Elmer, Harry Meeking, Jocko Anderson, Lester Patrick (manager-coach).
Scores: at Victoria, Victoria 5, Montreal Canadiens 2; Victoria 3, Canadiens 1; Canadiens 4, Victoria 2; Victoria 6, Canadiens 1. Total goals: Victoria 16, Canadiens 8.

1923-24 — Montreal Canadiens — Georges Vezina, Sprague Cleghorn, Billy Couture, Howie Morenz, Aurel Joliat, Billy Boucher, Odie Cleghorn, Sylvio Mantha, Bobby Boucher, Billy Bell, Billy Cameron, Joe Malone, Fortier, Leo Dandurand (manager-coach).
Scores: at Montreal, Canadiens 3, Vancouver 2; Canadiens 2, Vancouver 1. Total goals, Canadiens 5, Vancouver 3. Canadiens 6, Calgary 1; (the second game was transferred to Ottawa to benefit from an artificial ice surface) Canadiens 3, Calgary 0. Total goals: Canadiens 9, Calgary 1. [Because of an agreement between the NHL and the two western Leagues (WCHL and PCHA) Canadiens had to play the champions of each league in the Stanley Cup series in 1924.]

1922-23 — Ottawa Senators — George (Buck) Boucher, Lionel Hitchman, Frank Nighbor, King Clancy, Harry Helman, Clint Benedict, Jack Darragh, Eddie Gerard, Cy Denneny, Harry Broadbent, Tommy Gorman (manager), Pete Green (coach), F. Dolan (trainer).
Scores: at Vancouver, Ottawa 1, Vancouver 0; Vancouver 4, Ottawa 1; Ottawa 3, Vancouver 2; Ottawa 5, Vancouver 1. Ottawa also met and defeated Edmonton Eskimos, Champions of the WCHL. The scores: Ottawa 2, Edmonton 1; Ottawa 1, Edmonton 0. Total goals: Ottawa 10, Vancouver 7; Ottawa 3, Edmonton 1.

1921-22 — Toronto St. Pats — Ted Stackhouse, Corb Denneny, Rod Smylie, Lloyd Andrews, John Ross Roach, Harry Cameron, Bill (Red) Stuart, Cecil (Babe) Dye, Ken Randall, Reg Noble, Eddie Gerard (borrowed for one game from Ottawa), Stan Jackson, Nolan Mitchell, Charlie Querrie (manager), Eddie Powers (coach).
Scores: at Toronto, Vancouver 4, Toronto 3; Toronto 2, Vancouver 1; Vancouver 3, Toronto 0; Toronto 6, Vancouver 0; Toronto 5, Vancouver 1. Total goals: Toronto 16, Vancouver 9.

1920-21 — Ottawa Senators — Jack McKell, Jack Darragh, Morley Bruce, George (Buck) Boucher, Eddie Gerard, Clint Benedict, Sprague Cleghorn, Frank Nighbor, Harry Broadbent, Cy Denneny, Leth Graham, Tommy Gorman (manager), Pete Green (coach), F. Dolan (trainer).
Scores: at Vancouver, Vancouver 2, Ottawa 1; Ottawa 4, Vancouver 3; Ottawa 3, Vancouver 2; Vancouver 3, Ottawa 2; Ottawa 2, Vancouver 1; Total goals: Ottawa 12, Vancouver 11.

1919-20 — Ottawa Senators — Jack McKell, Jack Darragh, Morley Bruce, Horrace Merrill, George (Buck) Boucher, Eddie Gerard, Clint Benedict, Sprague Cleghorn, Frank Nighbor, Harry Broadbent, Cy Denneny, Price, Tommy Gorman (manager), Pete Green (coach).
Scores: at Ottawa, Ottawa 3, Seattle 2; Ottawa 3, Seattle 0; Seattle 3, Ottawa 1. Mild weather ruined natural ice surface at Ottawa rink and necessitated the transfer of two games of the series to Toronto's artificial rink. At Toronto — Seattle 5, Ottawa 2; Ottawa 6, Seattle 1. Total goals: Ottawa 15, Seattle 11.

1918-19 — No decision, Series halted by Spanish influenza epidemic, illness of several players and death of Joe Hall of Montreal Canadiens from flu. Five games had been played when the series was halted, each team having won two and tied one. The results are shown:
Scores: at Seattle, Seattle 7, Canadiens 0; Canadiens 4, Seattle 2; Seattle 7, Canadiens 2; Seattle 0, Canadiens 0 (20 minutes overtime); Canadiens 4, Seattle 3 (15:57 overtime). Total goals: Seattle 19, Canadiens 10.

1917-18 — Toronto Arenas — Rusty Crawford, Harry Meeking, Ken Randall, Corb Denneny, Harry Cameron, Jack Adams, Alf Skinner, Harry Mummery, Harry (Happy) Holmes, Reg Noble, Sammy Hebert, Jack Coughlin, Neville, Charlie Querrie (manager), Dick Carroll (coach), Frank Carroll (trainer).
Scores: at Toronto, Toronto 5, Vancouver 3; Vancouver 6, Toronto 4; Toronto 6, Vancouver 3; Vancouver 8, Toronto 1; Toronto 2, Vancouver 1. Total goals: Vancouver 21, Toronto 18.

1916-17 — Seattle Metropolitans — Harry (Happy) Holmes, Ed Carpenter, Cully Wilson, Jack Walker, Bernie Morris, Frank Foyston, Roy Rickey, Jim Riley, Bobby Rowe (captain), Peter Muldoon (manager).
Scores: at Seattle, Montreal Canadiens 8, Seattle 4; Seattle 6, Canadiens 1; Seattle 4, Canadiens 1; Seattle 9, Canadiens 1. Total goals: Seattle 23, Canadiens 11.

1915-16 — Montreal Canadiens — Georges Vezina, Bert Corbeau, Jack Laviolette, Newsy Lalonde, Louis Berlinguette, Goldie Prodgers, Howard McNamara, Didier Pitre, Skene Ronan, Amos Arbour, Skinner Poulin, Jack Fournier, George Kennedy (manager).
Scores: at Montreal, Portland 2, Canadiens 0; Canadiens 2, Portland 1; Canadiens 6, Portland 3; Portland 6, Canadiens 5; Canadiens 2, Portland 1. Total goals: Canadiens 15, Portland 13.

1914-15 — Vancouver Millionaires — Kenny Mallen, Frank Nighbor, Fred (Cyclone) Taylor, Hughie Lehman, Lloyd Cook, Mickey MacKay, Barney Stanley, Jim Seaborn, Si Griffis (captain), Jean Matz, Frank Patrick (playing manager).
Scores: at Vancouver, Vancouver 6, Ottawa 2; Vancouver 8, Ottawa 3; Vancouver 12, Ottawa 3. Total goals: Vancouver 26, Ottawa 8.

1913-14 — Toronto Blueshirts — Con Corbeau, F. Roy McGiffen, Jack Walker, George McNamara, Cully Wilson, Frank Foyston, Harry Cameron, Harry (Happy) Holmes, Alan M. Davidson (captain), Harriston, Jack Marshall (playing-manager), Frank and Dick Carroll (trainers).
Scores: at Toronto, Toronto 5, Victoria 2; Toronto 6, Victoria 5 (15 minutes overtime); Toronto 2, Victoria 1. Total goals: Toronto 13, Victoria 8.

1912-13 — Quebec Bulldogs — Joe Malone, Joe Hall, Paddy Moran, Harry Mummery, Tommy Smith, Jack Marks, Russell Crawford, Billy Creighton, Jeff Malone, Rocket Power, M.J. Quinn (manager), D. Beland (trainer).
Scores: at Quebec, March 8-10; Quebec 14, Sydney 3; Quebec 6, Sydney 2 (Quebec won best-of-three series 2-0). Victoria challenged Quebec but the Bulldogs refused to put the Stanley Cup in competition so the two teams played an exhibition series with Victoria winning two games to one by scores of 7-5, 3-6, 6-1. It was the first meeting between the Eastern champions and the Western champions. The following year, and until the Pacific Coast League disbanded after the 1926 playoffs, the Cup went to the winner of the series between East and West.

1911-12 — Quebec Bulldogs — Goldie Prodgers, Joe Hall, Walter Rooney, Paddy Moran, Jack Marks, Jack MacDonald, Eddie Oatman, Leonard, Joe Malone (captain), C. Nolan (coach), M.J. Quinn (manager), D. Beland (trainer).
Scores: at Quebec, Quebec 9, Moncton 3; Quebec 8, Moncton 0 (best-of-three series). Total goals: Quebec 17, Moncton 3. [Prior to 1912, teams could challenge the Stanley Cup champions for the title, thus there was more than one Championship Series played in most of the seasons between 1894 and 1911.]

1910-11 — Ottawa Senators — Hamby Shore, Percy LeSueur, Jack Darragh, Bruce Stuart, Marty Walsh, Bruce Ridpath, Fred Lake, Albert (Dubby) Kerr, Alex Currie, Horace Gaul.
Scores: at Ottawa, March 13, Ottawa 7, Galt 4. March 16, Ottawa 13, Port Arthur 4.

1909-10 — Montreal Wanderers — Cecil W. Blackford, Ernie (Moose) Johnson, Ernie Russell, Riley Hern, Harry Hyland, Jack Marshall, Frank (Pud) Glass (captain), Jimmy Gardner, R. R. Boon (manager).
Scores: at Montreal, March 12, Montreal 7, Berlin (Kitchener) 3.

1908-09 — Ottawa Senators — Fred Lake, Percy LeSueur, Fred (Cyclone) Taylor, H.L. (Billy) Gilmour, Albert Kerr, Edgar Dey, Marty Walsh, Bruce Stuart (captain).
Scores: Ottawa, as champions of the Eastern Canada Hockey Association took over the Stanley Cup in 1909 and, although a challenge was accepted by the Cup trustees from Winnipeg Shamrocks but could not be arranged because of the lateness of the season, no other challenges were made in 1909. The following season — 1909-10 — however, the Senators accepted two challenges as defending Cup Champions. The first was against Galt in a two-game, total-point series, and the second against Edmonton, also a two-game, total-point series. Details follow: at Ottawa, Jan. 5, Ottawa 12, Galt 3; Jan. 7, Ottawa 3, Galt 1. At Ottawa, Jan. 18, Ottawa 8, Edmonton 4; Jan. 20, Ottawa 13, Edmonton 7.

1907-08 — Montreal Wanderers — Riley Hern, Art Ross, Walter Small, Frank (Pud) Glass, Bruce Stuart, Ernie Russell, Ernie (Moose) Johnson, Cecil Blachford (captain), Tom Hooper, Larry Gilmour, Ernie Liffiton, R.R. Boon (manager).
Scores: Wanderers accepted four challenges for the Cup: at Montreal, Jan. 9, Wanderers 9, Ottawa Vics 3; Jan. 13, Wanderers 13, Ottawa 1. (Wanderers won two-game, total point series). At Montreal, March 10, Wanderers 11, Winnipeg Maple Leafs 5; March 12, Wanderers 9, Winnipeg 2 (Wanderers won two-game, total-point series). At Montreal, March 14 (sudden death), Wanderers 6, Toronto Maple Leafs (of Toronto Trolley League) 4. At start of following season, 1908-09, Wanderers were challenged by Edmonton. The results: At Montreal, Dec. 28, Wanderers 7, Edmonton 3; Dec. 30, Edmonton 7, Wanderers 6. (Wanderers won two-game, total-point series).

1906-07 — (March) — Montreal Wanderers — W. S. (Billy) Strachan, Riley Hern, Lester Patrick, Hod Stuart, Frank (Pud) Glass, Ernie Russell, Cecil Blachford (captain), Ernie (Moose) Johnson, Rod Kennedy, Jack Marshall, R. R. Boon (manager).
Scores: (March) — at Winnipeg, March 23, Wanderers 7, Kenora Thistles 2; March 25, Kenora 6, Wanderers 5 (Wanderers won two-game, total-point series).

1906-07 — (January) — Kenora Thistles — Eddie Geroux, Art Ross, Si Griffis, Tom Hooper, Billy McGimsie, Roxy Beaudro, Tom Phillips.
Scores: (January) — At Montreal, Jan. 17, Kenora 4, Wanderers 2; Jan. 21, Kenora 8, Wanderers 6. (Kenora won two-game, total-point series).

1905-06 — Montreal Wanderers — H. Menard, Billy Strachan, Rod Kennedy, Lester Patrick, Frank (Pud) Glass, Ernie Russell, Ernie (Moose) Johnson, Cecil Blachford (captain), Josh Arnold, R. R. Boon (manager).
Scores: at Montreal, March 14, Wanderers 9, Ottawa Silver Seven 1; March 17 at Ottawa, Ottawa 9, Wanderers 3 (Wanderers won two-game, total-point series). Wanderers accepted a challenge from New Glasgow, N.S., prior to the start of the 1906-07 season. The result: at Montreal, Dec. 27, Wanderers 10, New Glasgow 3; Dec. 29, Wanderers 7, New Glasgow 2.

1904-05 — Ottawa Silver Seven — Dave Finnie, Harvey Pulford (captain), Arthur Moore, Harry Westwick, Frank McGee, Alf Smith (playing coach), Billy Gilmour, Frank White, Horace Gaul, Hamby Shore, Allen.
Scores: at Ottawa, March 7, Rat Portage (Kenora) 9, Ottawa 3; March 9, Ottawa 4, Rat Portage 2; March 11, Ottawa 5, Rat Portage 4 (Ottawa won best-of-three series). As defending Cup champions, Ottawa was challenged twice during the following season, 1905-06, and accepted both. Here are the results: at Ottawa, Feb. 27, 28, Ottawa 16, Queen's University 7; Ottawa 12, Queen's 7 (Ottawa won two-game, total-point series). At Ottawa, March 6, 8, Ottawa 6, Smiths Falls 5; Ottawa 8, Smiths Falls 2 (Ottawa won two-game, total-point series).

1903-04 — Ottawa Silver Seven — S. C. (Suddy) Gilmour, Arthur Moore, Frank McGee, J.B. (Bouse) Hutton, H.L. (Billy) Gilmour, Jim McGee, Harry Westwick, E. H. (Harvey) Pulford (captain), Scott, A. T. (Alf) Smith (playing coach).
Scores: at Montreal, March 2, Wanderers 5, Ottawa 5. Following the tie game, a new two-game series was ordered to be played in Ottawa but Wanderers refused unless the tie-game was replayed in Montreal. When no settlement could be reached, the series was abandoned and Ottawa retained the Cup and accepted a two-game challenge from Brandon. The results: (both games at Ottawa), March 9, Ottawa 6, Brandon 3; March 11, Ottawa 9, Brandon 3. As defending Cup champions, Ottawa was challenged by Dawson City Klondikers and the two-game series was played at Ottawa the following season, 1904-05, Jan. 13 and 16. The results: Ottawa 9, Dawson City 2; Ottawa 23, Dawson City 2.

1902-03 — Ottawa Silver Seven — S. C. (Suddy) Gilmour, P.T. (Percy) Sims, J. B. (Bouse) Hutton, D. J. (Dave) Gilmour, H. L. (Billy) Gilmour, Harry Westwick, Frank McGee, F. H. Wood, A. A. Fraser, Charles D. Spittal, E. H. (Harvey) Pulford (captain), Arthur Moore, A. T. (Alf) Smith (coach.)
Scores: at March 7, Montreal Victorias 1, Ottawa 1; at Ottawa, March 10, Ottawa 8, Montreal Vics 0 (Ottawa won two-game, total-point series). Ottawa was then challenged by Rat Portage in a two-game series. The results: at Ottawa, March 12, 14, Ottawa 6, Rat Portage 2; Ottawa 4, Rat Portage 2. The following season, 1903-04, Ottawa as defending Cup champions, accepted two more challenges. The results: at Ottawa, Dec. 30, 1903, Ottawa 9, Winnipeg Rowing Club 1; Jan. 1, 1904, Winnipeg 6, Ottawa 2; Jan. 4, Ottawa 2, Winnipeg 0 (Ottawa won best-of-three series). At Ottawa, Feb. 23, Ottawa 6, Toronto Marlboroughs 3; Feb. 25, Ottawa 11, Toronto 2 (Ottawa won two-game, total-point series).

1901-02 — Montreal AAA — Tom Hodge, R. R. (Dickie) Boon, W.C. (Billy) Nicholson, Art Hooper, W. J. (Billy) Bellingham, Charles A. Liffiton, Jack Marshall, Roland Elliott, Jim Gardner.
Scores: at Winnipeg, March 13, Winnipeg Victorias 1, Montreal 0; March 15, Montreal 5, Winnipeg 0; March 17, Montreal 2, Winnipeg 1 (Montreal won best-of-three series). Winnipeg challenged Montreal the following season, 1902-03, and, as defending Cup champions, Montreal accepted. The results: At Montreal, Jan. 29, Montreal 8, Winnipeg 1; Jan. 31, Winnipeg 2, Montreal 2 (27 minutes overtime); Feb. 2, Winnipeg 4, Montreal 2; Feb. 4, Montreal 4, Winnipeg 1.

1900-01 — Winnipeg Victoria — Burke Wood, Jack Marshall, A.B. (Tony) Gingras, Charles W. Johnstone, R. M. (Rod) Flett, Magnus L. Flett, Danny Bain (captain), A. Brown.
Scores: at Montreal, Jan. 29, Winnipeg 4, Montreal Shamrocks 3; Jan. 31, Winnipeg 2, Montreal 1 (4 minutes overtime) (Winnipeg won best-of-three series). The following season, 1901-02, Winnipeg, as defending Cup champions, defeated Toronto Wellingtons. The results: At Winnipeg, Jan. 21, Winnipeg 5, Toronto 3; Jan. 23, Winnipeg 5, Toronto 3 (Winnipeg won best-of-three series).

Early Playoff Records

1893-1918
Team Records

MOST GOALS, BOTH TEAMS, ONE GAME:
25 — **Ottawa Silver Seven, Dawson City** at Ottawa, Jan. 16, 1905. Ottawa 23, Dawson City 2. Ottawa won best-of-three series 2-0.

MOST GOALS, ONE TEAM, ONE GAME:
23 — **Ottawa Silver Seven** at Ottawa, Jan. 16, 1905. Ottawa defeated Dawson City 23-2.

MOST GOALS, BOTH TEAMS, BEST-OF-THREE SERIES:
42 — **Ottawa Silver Seven, Queen's** at Ottawa, 1906. Ottawa defeated Queen's 16-7, Feb. 27, and 12-7, Feb. 28.

MOST GOALS, ONE TEAM, BEST-OF-THREE SERIES:
32 — **Ottawa Silver Seven** in 1905 at Ottawa. Defeated Dawson City 9-2, Jan. 13, and 23-2, Jan. 16.

MOST GOALS, BOTH TEAMS, BEST-OF-FIVE SERIES:
39 — **Toronto Arenas, Vancouver** at Toronto, 1918. Arenas won 5-3, Mar. 20; 6-3, Mar. 26; 2-1, Mar. 30. Vancouver won 6-4, Mar. 23, and 8-1, Mar. 28. Toronto scored 18 goals; Vancouver 21.

MOST GOALS, ONE TEAM, BEST-OF-FIVE SERIES:
26 — **Vancouver** in 1915 at Vancouver. Defeated Ottawa Senators 6-2, Mar. 22; 8-3, Mar. 24; and 12-3, Mar. 26.

Individual Records
MOST GOALS IN PLAYOFFS:
63 — **Frank McGee, Ottawa Silver Seven,** in 22 playoff games. Seven goals in four games, 1903; 21 goals in eight games, 1904; 18 goals in four games, 1905; 17 goals in six games, 1906.

MOST GOALS, ONE PLAYOFF SERIES:
15 — **Frank McGee, Ottawa Silver Seven,** in two games in 1905 at Ottawa. Scored one goal, Jan. 13, in 9-2 victory over Dawson City and 14 goals, Jan. 16, in 23-2 victory.

Fred "Cyclone" Taylor played on the 1915 Stanley Cup-winning Vancouver Millionaires.

MOST GOALS, ONE PLAYOFF GAME:
14 — **Frank McGee, Ottawa Silver Seven,** Jan. 16, 1905 at Ottawa in 23-2 victory over Dawson City.

FASTEST THREE GOALS:
40 Seconds — **Marty Walsh, Ottawa Senators,** at Ottawa, March 16, 1911, at 3:00, 3:10, and 3:40 of third period. Ottawa defeated Port Arthur 13-4.

All-Time NHL Playoff Formats

1917-18 — The regular-season was split into two halves. The winners of both halves faced each other in a two-game, total-goals series for the NHL championship and the right to meet the PCHA champion in the best-of-five Stanley Cup Finals.

1918-19 — Same as 1917-18, except that the Stanley Cup Finals was extended to a best-of-seven series.

1919-20 — Same as 1917-1918, except that Ottawa won both halves of the split regular-season schedule to earn an automatic berth into the best-of-five Stanley Cup Finals against the PCHA champions.

1921-22 — The top two teams at the conclusion of the regular-season faced each other in a two-game, total-goals series for the NHL championship. The NHL champion then moved on to play the winner of the PCHA-WCHL playoff series in the best-of-five Stanley Cup Finals.

1922-23 — The top two teams at the conclusion of the regular-season faced each other in a two-game, total-goals series for the NHL championship. The NHL champion then moved on to play the PCHA champion in the best-of-three Stanley Cup Semi-Finals, and the winner of the Semi-Finals played the WCHL champion, which had been given a bye, in the best-of-three Stanley Cup Finals.

1923-24 — The top two teams at the conclusion of the regular-season faced each other in a two-game, total-goals series for the NHL championship. The NHL champion then moved on to play the loser of the PCHA-WCHL playoff (the winner of the PCHA-WCHL playoff earned a bye into the Stanley Cup Finals) in the best-of-three Stanley Cup Semi-Finals. The winner of this series met the PCHA-WCHL playoff winner in the best-of-three Stanley Cup Finals.

1924-25 — The first place team (Hamilton) at the conclusion of the regular-season was supposed to play the winner of a two-game, total goals series between the second (Toronto) and third (Montreal) place clubs. However, Hamilton refused to abide by this new format, demanding greater compensation than offered by the League. Thus, Toronto and Montreal played their two-game, total-goals series, and the winner (Montreal) earned the NHL title and then played the WCHL champion (Victoria) in the best-of-five Stanley Cup Finals.

1925-26 — The format which was intended for 1924-25 went into effect. The winner of the two-game, total-goals series between the second and third place teams squared off against the first place team in the two-game, total-goals NHL championship series. The NHL champion then moved on to play the WHL champion in the best-of-five Stanley Cup Finals.

After the 1925 season, the NHL was the only major professional hockey league still in existence and consequently took over sole control of the Stanley Cup competition.

1926-27 — The 10-team league was divided into two divisions — Candian and American — of five teams apiece. In each division, the winner of the two-game, total-goals series between the second and third place teams faced the first place team in a two-game, total-goals series for the division title. The two division title winners then met in the best-of-five Stanley Cup Finals.

1928-29 — Both first place teams in the two divisions played each other in a best-of-five series. Both second place teams in the two divisions played each other in a two-game, total-goals series as did the two third place teams. The winners of these latter two series then played each other in a best-of-three series for the right to meet the winner of the series between the two first place clubs. This Stanley Cup Finals was a best-of-three.

Series A: First in Canadian Division versus first in American (best-of-five)
Series B: Second in Canadian Division versus second in American (two-game, total-goals)
Series C: Third in Canadian Division versus third in American (two-game, total-goals)
Series D: Winner of Series B versus winner of Series C (best-of-three)
Series E: Winner of Series A versus winner of Series D (best of three) for Stanley Cup

1931-32 — Same as 1928-29, except that Series D was changed to a two-game, total-goals series.

1936-37 — Same as 1928-29, except that Series A and E were both best-of-five and Series B, C, and D were each best-of-three.

Stanley Cup Standings
1918-89

Team	Yrs.	Series	Won	Lost	Games	Won	Lost	Tied	GF	GA	Cup Wins	Winning %
Montreal	64	119 *	77	41	539	340	212	8	1681	1317	22**	.612
Toronto	53	87	47	40	391	184	203	4	935	974	13	.476
Boston	50	83	38	44	384	189	199	6	1159	1132	5	.487
Chicago	44	73	32	40	304	144	171	5	882	1003	3	.452
NY Rangers	40	70	32	37	294	136	154	8	805	854	3	.476
Detroit	39	67	35	31	313	155	163	1	854	866	7	.490
Philadelphia	20	43	25	17	204	116	107	0	714	685	2	.520
St. Louis	19	33	14	18	154	71	93	0	468	547	0	.429
Calgary***	15	26	12	14	97	59	60	0	395	424	1	.443
Los Angeles	15	20	5	14	79	30	60	0	263	369	0	.329
NY Islanders	14	38	28	10	191	118	73	0	674	540	4	.618
Minnesota	14	25	11	13	124	60	69	0	435	461	0	.476
Buffalo	14	23	9	13	99	47	57	0	329	355	0	.465
Edmonton	10	27	21	5	119	89	37	0	527	377	5	.723
Pittsburgh	10	14	4	9	51	28	34	0	178	217	0	412
Vancouver	10	13	3	9	45	19	33	0	145	195	0	.356
Quebec	7	13	6	7	68	31	37	0	217	238	0	.456
Washington	7	11	4	6	47	24	29	0	178	176	0	.468
Winnipeg	7	9	2	7	36	9	27	0	111	159	0	.250
Hartford	5	6	1	4	25	10	19	0	86	109	0	.400
New Jersey****	2	4	2	2	22	11	11	0	70	77	0	.500

* 1919 final incomplete due to influenza epidemic.
** Canadiens also won the Stanley Cup in 1916.
*** Includes totals of Atlanta 1974-80.
**** Includes totals of Colorado 1976-82.

1938-39 — With the NHL reduced to seven teams, the two-division system was replaced by one seven-team league. Based on final regular-season standings, the following playoff format was adopted:

Series A: First versus Second (best-of-seven)
Series B: Third versus Fourth (best-of-three)
Series C: Fifth versus Sixth (best-of-three)
Series D: Winner of Series B versus winner of Series C (best-of-three)
Series E: Winner of Series A versus winner of Series D (best-of-seven)

1942-43 — With the NHL reduced to six teams (the "original six"), only the top four finishers qualified for playoff action. The best-of-seven Semi-Finals pitted Team #1 vs Team #3 and Team #2 vs Team #4. The winners of each Semi-Final series met in the best-of-seven Stanley Cup Finals.

1967-68 — When it doubled in size from 6 to 12 teams, the NHL once again was divided into two divisions — East and West — of six teams apiece. The top four clubs in each division qualified for the playoffs (all series were best-of-seven):

Series A: Team #1 (East) vs Team #3 (East)
Series B: Team #2 (East) vs Team #4 (East)
Series C: Team #1 (West) vs Team #3 (West)
Series D: Team #2 (West) vs Team #4 (West)

Series E: Winner of Series A vs winner of Series B
Series F: Winner of Series C vs winner of Series D
Series G: Winner of Series E vs Winner of Series F

1970-71 — Same as 1967-68 except that Series E matched the winners of Series A and D, and Series F matched the winners of Series B and C.

1971-72 — Same as 1970-71, except that Series A and C matched Team #1 vs Team #4, and Series B and D matched #2 vs Team #3.

1974-75 — With the League now expanded to 18 teams in four divisions, a completely new playoff format was introduced. First, the #2 and #3 teams in each of the four divisions were pooled together in the Preliminary round. These eight (#2 and #3) clubs were ranked #1 to #8 based on regular-season record:

Series A: Team #1 vs Team #8 (best-of-three)
Series B: Team #2 vs Team #7 (best-of-three)
Series C: Team #3 vs Team #6 (best-of-three)
Series D: Team #4 vs Team #5 (best-of-three)

The winners of this Preliminary round then pooled together with the four division winners, which had received byes into this Quarter-Final round. These eight teams were again ranked #1 to #8 based on regular-season record:

Series E: Team #1 vs Team #8 (best-of-seven)
Series F: Team #2 vs Team #7 (best-of-seven)
Series G: Team #3 vs Team #6 (best-of-seven)
Series H: Team #4 vs Team #5 (best-of-seven)

The four Quarter-Finals winners, which moved on to the Semi-Finals, were then ranked #1 to #4 based on regular season record:

Series I: Team #1 vs Team #4 (best-of-seven)
Series J: Team #2 vs Team #3 (best-of-seven)
Series K: Winner of Series I vs winner of Series J (best-of-seven)

1977-78 — Same as 1974-75, except that the Preliminary round consisted of the #2 teams in the four divisions and the next four teams based on regular-season record (not their standings within their divisions).

1979-80 — With the addition of four WHA franchises, the League expanded its playoff structure to include 16 of its 21 teams. The four first place teams in the four divisions automatically earned playoff berths. Among the 17 other clubs, the top 12, according to regular-season record, also earned berths. All 16 teams were then pooled together and ranked #1 to #16 based on regular-season record:

Series A: Team #1 vs Team #16 (best-of-five)
Series B: Team #2 vs Team #15 (best-of-five)
Series C: Team #3 vs Team #14 (best-of-five)
Series D: Team #4 vs Team #13 (best-of-five)
Series E: Team #5 vs Team #12 (best-of-five)
Series F: Team #6 vs Team #11 (best-of-five)
Series G: Team #7 vs Team #10 (best-of-five)
Series H: Team #8 vs Team # 9 (best-of-five)

The eight Preliminary round winners, ranked #1 to #8 based on regular-season record, moved on to the Quarter-Finals:

Series I: Team #1 vs Team #8 (best-of-seven)
Series J: Team #2 vs Team #7 (best-of-seven)
Series K: Team #3 vs Team #6 (best-of-seven)
Series L: Team #4 vs Team #5 (best-of-seven)

The eight Quarter-Finals winners, ranked #1 to #4 based on regular-season record, moved on to the semi-finals:

Series M: Team #1 vs Team #4 (best-of-seven)
Series N: Team #2 vs Team #3 (best-of-seven)
Series O: Winner of Series M vs winner of Series N (best-of-seven)

1981-82 — (Current format) The first four teams in each division earn playoff berths. In each division, the first-place team opposes the fourth-place team and the second-place team opposes the third-place team in a best-of-five Division Semi-Final series (DSF). In each division, the two winners of the DSF meet in a best-of-seven Division Final series (DF). The two winners in each conference meet in a best-of-seven Conference Final series (CF). In the Prince of Wales Conference, the Adams Division winner opposes the Patrick Division winner; in the Clarence Campbell Conference, the Smythe Division winner opposes the Norris Division winner. The two CF winners meet in a best-of-seven Stanley Cup Final series.

1986-87 — Division Semi-Final series changed from best-of-five to best-of-seven.

Team Records

1918-1989

MOST STANLEY CUP CHAMPIONSHIPS:
22 — Montreal Canadiens 1924-30-31-44-46-53-56-57-58-59-60-65-66-68-69-71-73-76-77-78-79-86
13 — Toronto Maple Leafs 1918-22-32-42-45-47-48-49-51-62-63-64-67
7 — Detroit Red Wings 1936-37-43-50-52-54-55

MOST FINAL SERIES APPEARANCES:
31 — Montreal Canadiens in 72-year history.
21 — Toronto Maple Leafs in 72-year history.
18 — Detroit Red Wings in 63-year history.

MOST YEARS IN PLAYOFFS:
64 — Montreal Canadiens in 72-year history.
53 — Toronto Maple Leafs in 72-year history.
50 — Boston Bruins in 65-year history.

MOST CONSECUTIVE STANLEY CUP CHAMPIONSHIPS:
5 — Montreal Canadiens (1956-57-58-59-60)
4 — New York Islanders (1980-81-82-83)
— Montreal Canadiens (1976-77-78-79)

MOST CONSECUTIVE FINAL SERIES APPEARANCES:
10 — Montreal Canadiens (1951-60, inclusive)

MOST CONSECUTIVE PLAYOFF APPEARANCES:
22 — Boston Bruins (1968-89, inclusive)
21 — Montreal Canadiens (1949-69, inclusive)
20 — Detroit Red Wings (1939-58, inclusive)

MOST GOALS BOTH TEAMS, ONE PLAYOFF SERIES:
69 — Edmonton Oilers, Chicago Black Hawks in 1985 Campbell Conference Final. Edmonton won best-of-seven series 4-2, outscoring Chicago 44-25.
62 — Chicago Black Hawks, Minnesota North Stars in 1985 Norris Division Final. Chicago won best-of-seven series 4-2, outscoring Minnesota 33-29.
60 — Edmonton Oilers, Calgary Flames in 1984 Smythe Division Final. Edmonton won best-of-seven series 4-3, outscoring Calgary 33-27.

MOST GOALS ONE TEAM, ONE PLAYOFF SERIES:
44 — Edmonton Oilers in 1985 Campbell Conference Final. Edmonton won best-of-seven series 4-2, outscoring Chicago 44-25.
35 — Edmonton Oilers in 1983 Smythe Division Final. Edmonton won best-of-seven series 4-1, outscoring Calgary 35-13.

MOST GOALS, BOTH TEAMS, THREE-GAME SERIES:
33 — Minnesota North Stars, Boston Bruins in 1981 Preliminary Round. Minnesota won best-of-five series 3-0, outscoring Boston 20-13.
31 — Chicago Black Hawks, Detroit Red Wings in 1985 Norris Division Semi-Final. Chicago won best-of-five series 3-0, outscoring Detroit 23-8.
28 — Toronto Maple Leafs, New York Rangers in 1932 Final. Toronto won best-of-five series 3-0, outscoring New York 18-10.

MOST GOALS, ONE TEAM, THREE-GAME SERIES:
23 — Chicago Black Hawks in 1985 Norris Division Semi-Final. Chicago won best-of-five series 3-0, outscoring Detroit 23-8.
20 — Minnesota North Stars in 1981 Preliminary Round. Minnesota won best-of-five series 3-0, outscoring Boston 20-13.
— New York Islanders in 1981 Preliminary Round. New York won best-of-five series 3-0, outscoring Toronto 20-4.

MOST GOALS, BOTH TEAMS, FOUR-GAME SERIES:
36 — Boston Bruins, St. Louis Blues in 1972 Semi-Final. Boston won best-of-seven series 4-0, outscoring St. Louis 28-8.
35 — New York Rangers, Los Angeles Kings in 1981 Preliminary Round. New York won best-of-five series 3-1, outscoring Los Angeles 23-12.

MOST GOALS, ONE TEAM, FOUR-GAME SERIES:
28 — Boston Bruins in 1972 Semi-Final. Boston won best-of-seven series 4-0, outscoring St. Louis 28-8.

MOST GOALS, BOTH TEAMS, FIVE-GAME SERIES:
52 — Edmonton Oilers, Los Angeles Kings in 1987 Smythe Division Semi-Final. Edmonton won best-of-seven series 4-1, outscoring Los Angeles 32-20.
50 — Los Angeles Kings, Edmonton Oilers in 1982 Division Semi-Final. Los Angeles won best-of-five series 3-2, outscoring Edmonton 27-23.
48 — Edmonton Oilers, Calgary Flames in 1983 Smythe Division Final. Edmonton won best-of-seven series 4-1, outscoring Calgary 35-13.
— Calgary Flames, Los Angeles Kings in 1988 Smythe Division Semi-Final. Calgary won best-of-seven series 4-1, outscoring Los Angeles 30-18.

MOST GOALS, ONE TEAM, FIVE-GAME SERIES:
35 — Edmonton Oilers in 1983 Smythe Division Final. Edmonton won best-of-seven series 4-1, outscoring Calgary 35-13.
32 — Edmonton Oilers in 1987 Smythe Division Semi-Final. Edmonton won best-of-seven series 4-1, outscoring Los Angeles 32-20.
28 — New York Rangers in 1979 Quarter-Final. New York won best-of-seven series 4-1, outscoring Philadelphia 28-8.
27 — Philadelphia Flyers in 1980 Semi-Final. Philadelphia won best-of-seven series 4-1, outscoring Minnesota 27-14.
— Los Angeles Kings, in 1982 Division Semi-Final. Los Angeles won best-of-five series 3-2, outscoring Edmonton 27-23.

MOST GOALS, BOTH TEAMS, SIX-GAME SERIES:
69 — Edmonton Oilers, Chicago Black Hawks in 1985 Campbell Conference Final. Edmonton won best-of-seven series 4-2, outscoring Chicago 44-25.
62 — Chicago Black Hawks, Minnesota North Stars in 1985 Norris Division Final. Chicago won best-of-seven series 4-2, outscoring Minnesota 33-29.
56 — Montreal Canadiens, Chicago Black Hawks in 1973 Final. Montreal won best-of-seven series 4-2, outscoring Chicago 33-23.

MOST GOALS, ONE TEAM, SIX-GAME SERIES:
44 — Edmonton Oilers in 1985 Campbell Conference Final vs. Chicago. Edmonton won best-of-seven series 4-2, outscoring Chicago 44-25.
33 — Chicago Black Hawks in 1985 Norris Division Final vs. Minnesota. Chicago won best-of-seven series 4-2, outscoring Minnesota 33-29.
— Montreal Canadiens in 1973 Final. Montreal won best-of-seven series 4-2, outscoring Chicago 33-23.

MOST GOALS, BOTH TEAMS, SEVEN-GAME SERIES:
60 — Edmonton Oilers, Calgary Flames in 1984 Smythe Division Final. Edmonton won best-of-seven series 4-3, outscoring Calgary 33-27.

MOST GOALS, ONE TEAM, SEVEN-GAME SERIES:
33 — Philadelphia Flyers in 1976 Quarter-Final against Toronto. Philadelphia won best-of-seven series 4-3, outscoring Toronto 33-23.
— Boston Bruins in 1983 Adams Division Final vs. Buffalo. Boston won best-of-seven series 4-3, outscoring Buffalo 33-23.
— Edmonton Oilers in 1984 Smythe Division Final against Calgary. Edmonton won best-of-seven series 4-3, outscoring Calgary 33-27.

FEWEST GOALS, BOTH TEAMS, TWO-GAME SERIES:
1 — New York Rangers, New York Americans, in 1929 Semi-Final. Rangers defeated Americans 1-0 in two-game, total-goal series.
— Montreal Maroons, Chicago Black Hawks in 1935 Semi-Final. Montreal defeated Chicago 1-0 in two-game, total-goal series.

FEWEST GOALS, ONE TEAM, TWO-GAME SERIES:
0 — Montreal Maroons in 1937 Semi-Final. Lost best-of-three series 2-0 to New York Rangers while being outscored 5-0.
— New York Americans in 1939 Quarter-Final. Lost best-of-three series 2-0 to Toronto while being outscored 6-0.
— New York Americans in 1929 Semi-Final. Lost two-game total series 1-0 against New York Rangers.
— Chicago Black Hawks in 1935 Semi-Final. Lost two-game total goal series 1-0 against Montreal Maroons.

FEWEST GOALS, BOTH TEAMS, THREE-GAME SERIES:
7 — Boston, Montreal Canadiens in 1929 Semi-Final. Boston won best-of-five series 3-0, outscoring Montreal 5-2.

FEWEST GOALS, ONE TEAM, THREE-GAME SERIES:
0 — Montreal Maroons in 1936 Semi-Final. Lost best-of-five series 3-0 to Detroit and were outscored 6-0.

FEWEST GOALS, BOTH TEAMS, FOUR-GAME SERIES:
9 — Toronto, Boston in 1935 Semi-Final. Toronto won best-of-five series 3-1, outscoring Boston 7-2.

FEWEST GOALS, ONE TEAM, FOUR-GAME SERIES:
2 — Boston Bruins in 1935 Semi-Final. Toronto won best-of-five series 3-1, outscoring Boston 7-2.
— Montreal Canadiens in 1952 Final. Detroit won best-of-seven series 4-0, outscoring Montreal 11-2.

FEWEST GOALS, BOTH TEAMS, FIVE-GAME SERIES:
11 — New York Rangers, Montreal Maroons in 1928 Final. New York won best-of-five series 3-2, while outscored by Maroons 6-5.

FEWEST GOALS, ONE TEAM, FIVE-GAME SERIES:
5 — New York Rangers in 1928 Final. New York won best-of-five series 3-2, while outscored by Montreal Maroons 6-5.

FEWEST GOALS, BOTH TEAMS, SIX-GAME SERIES:
22 — Toronto, Boston in 1951 Semi-Final. Toronto won best-of-seven series 4-1 with one tie, outscoring Boston 17-5.

FEWEST GOALS, ONE TEAM, SIX-GAME SERIES:
5 — Boston Bruins in 1951 Semi-Final. Toronto won best-of-seven series 4-1 with one tie, outscoring Boston 17-5.

FEWEST GOALS, BOTH TEAMS, SEVEN-GAME SERIES:
18 — Toronto, Detroit in 1945 Final. Toronto won best-of-seven series 4-3; teams tied in scoring 9-9.

FEWEST GOALS, ONE TEAM, SEVEN-GAME SERIES:
9 — Toronto Maple Leafs, in 1945 Final. Toronto won best-of-seven series 4-3; teams tied in scoring 9-9.
— Detroit Red Wings, in 1945 Final. Toronto won best-of-seven series 4-3; teams tied in scoring 9-9.

MOST GOALS, BOTH TEAMS, ONE GAME:
18 — **Los Angeles, Edmonton** at Edmonton, April 7, 1982. Los Angeles 10, Edmonton 8. Los Angeles won best-of-five Division Semi-Final series 3-2.
17 — Pittsburgh, Philadelphia at Pittsburgh, April 25, 1989. Pittsburgh 10, Philadelphia 7. Philadelphia won best-of-seven Patrick Division Final 4-3.
16 — Edmonton, Los Angeles at Edmonton, April 9, 1987. Edmonton 13, Los Angeles 3. Edmonton won best-of-seven Smythe Division Semi-Final 4-1.
15 — Chicago, Montreal at Montreal, May 8, 1973. Chicago 8, Montreal 7. Montreal won best-of-seven Final series 4-2.
— Minnesota North Stars, Boston Bruins, at Boston, April 9, 1981. Minnesota 9, Boston 6, Minnesota won best-of-five Preliminary Round series 3-0.
— Edmonton, Chicago at Edmonton, May 14, 1985. Edmonton 10, Chicago 5. Edmonton won best-of-seven Campbell Conference Final series 4-2.

MOST GOALS, ONE TEAM, ONE GAME:
13 — **Edmonton Oilers** at Edmonton, April 9, 1987. Edmonton 13, Los Angeles 3. Edmonton won best-of-seven Smythe Division Semi-Final 4-1.
11 — Montreal Canadiens at Montreal, March 30, 1944. Canadiens 11, Toronto 0. Canadiens won best-of-seven Semi-Final 4-1.
— Edmonton Oilers at Edmonton May 4, 1985. Edmonton 11, Chicago 2. Edmonton won best-of-seven Campbell Conference Final 4-2.

MOST GOALS, BOTH TEAMS, ONE PERIOD:
9 — **New York Rangers, Philadelphia Flyers,** April 24, 1979, at Philadelphia, third period. Rangers won game 8-3 scoring six of nine third-period goals.
8 — Chicago, Montreal at Montreal, May 8, 1973, in the second period. Chicago won game 8-7 scoring five of eight second-period goals.
— Chicago, Edmonton at Chicago, May 12, 1985 in the first period. Chicago won game 8-6, scoring five of eight first-period goals.
— Edmonton, Winnipeg at Edmonton, April 6, 1988 in the third period. Edmonton won game 7-4, scoring six of eight third period goals.
— Hartford, Montreal at Hartford, April 10, 1988 in the third period. Hartford won game 7-5, scoring five of eight third period goals.

MOST GOALS, ONE TEAM, ONE PERIOD:
7 — **Montreal Canadiens,** March 30, 1944, at Montreal in third period, during 11-0 win against Toronto.

LONGEST OVERTIME:
116 Minutes, 30 Seconds — **Detroit, Montreal Maroons** at Montreal, March 24-25, 1936. Detroit 1, Maroons 0. Mud Bruneteau scored, assisted by Hec Kilrea, at 16:30 of sixth overtime period, or after 176 minutes, 30 seconds from start of game, which ended at 2:25 a.m. Detroit won best-of-five semi-final 3-0.

SHORTEST OVERTIME:
9 Seconds — **Montreal Canadiens, Calgary Flames,** at Calgary, May 18, 1986. Montreal won game 3-2 on Brian Skrudland's goal and captured the best-of-seven Final series 4-1.
11 Seconds — **New York Islanders, New York Rangers,** at NY Rangers, April 11, 1975. NY Islanders won game 4-3 on Jean-Paul Parise's goal and captured the best-of-three series 2-1.

MOST OVERTIME GAMES, ONE PLAYOFF YEAR:
16 — **1982.** Of 71 games played, 16 went into overtime: one in Division Semi-Final won by Quebec 3-2 against Montreal; two in Division Semi-Final won by NY Islanders 3-2 against Pittsburgh; one in Division Semi-Final won by Chicago 3-1 against Minnesota; two in Division Semi-Final won by Los Angeles 3-2 against Edmonton; one in Division Semi-Final won by Vancouver 3-0 against Calgary; two in Division Semi-Final won by Quebec 4-3 against Boston; one in Division Final won by NY Islanders 4-2 against NY Rangers; one in Division Final won by Chicago 4-2 against St. Louis; two in Division Final won by Vancouver 4-1 against Los Angeles; one in Conference Championship won by NY Islanders 4-0 against Quebec; one in Conference Championship won by Vancouver 4-1 against Chicago; one in Stanley Cup Championship won by NY Islanders 4-0 against Vancouver.

FEWEST OVERTIME GAMES, ONE PLAYOFF YEAR:
0 — **1963.** None of the 16 games went into overtime, the only year since 1926 that no overtime was required in any playoff series.

MOST OVERTIME-GAME VICTORIES, ONE TEAM, ONE PLAYOFF YEAR:
6 — **New York Islanders,** 1980. One against Los Angeles in the Preliminary Round; two against Boston in the Quarter-Final; one against Buffalo in the Semi-Final; and two against Philadelphia in the Final. Islanders played 21 games.

MOST OVERTIME GAMES, FINAL SERIES:
5 — **Toronto, Montreal Canadiens** in 1951. Toronto defeated Canadiens 4-1 in best-of-seven series.

MOST OVERTIME GAMES, SEMI-FINAL SERIES:
4 — **Toronto, Boston** in 1933. Toronto won best-of-five series 3-2.
— **Boston, New York Rangers** in 1939. Boston won best-of-seven series 4-3.
— **St. Louis, Minnesota** in 1968. St. Louis won best-of-seven series 4-3.

MOST GAMES PLAYED BY ALL TEAMS, ONE PLAYOFF YEAR:
87 — **1987.** There were 44 Division Semi-Final, 25 Division Final, 11 Conference Championships and 7 Stanley Cup Final games.
83 — **1988.** There were 46 Division Semi-Final, 27 Division Final, 12 Conference Championship and 4 Stanley Cup Final games.
82 — **1989.** There were 44 Division Semi-Final, 21 Division Final, 11 Conference Championship and 6 Stanley Cup Final games.
72 — **1986.** There were 28 Division Semi-Final, 27 Division Final, 12 Conference Championship and 5 Stanley Cup Final games.

MOST GAMES PLAYED, ONE TEAM, ONE PLAYOFF YEAR:
26 — **Philadelphia Flyers,** 1987. Won Patrick DSF 4-2 against NY Rangers, Patrick DF 4-3 against NY Islanders, Wales CC 4-2 against Montreal, and lost Final 4-3 against Edmonton.
22 — Calgary Flames,1986. Won Smythe DSF 3-0 against Winnipeg, Smythe DF 4-3 against Edmonton, Campbell CC 4-3 against St. Louis and lost Final 4-1 against Montreal.
— Boston Bruins, 1988. Won Adams DSF 4-2 against Buffalo, Adams DF 4-1 against Montreal, Wales CC 4-3 against New Jersey and lost Final 4-0 against Edmonton.
— Calgary Flames, 1989. Won Smythe DSF 4-3 against Vancouver, Smythe DF 4-0 against Los Angeles, Campbell CC 4-1 against Chicago and Final 4-2 against Montreal.

MOST ROAD VICTORIES, ONE TEAM, ONE PLAYOFF YEAR:
8 — **New York Islanders,** 1980. Won two at Los Angeles in a Preliminary Round series; three at Boston in a Quarter-Final series; two at Buffalo in a Semi-Final series; and one at Philadelphia in the Final series.

MOST HOME VICTORIES, ONE TEAM, ONE PLAYOFF YEAR:
11 — **Edmonton Oilers,** 1988
10 — Edmonton Oilers, 1985 in 10 home-ice games.
— Montreal Canadiens, 1986.
9 — Philadelphia Flyers, 1974
— New York Islanders, 1981
— New York Islanders, 1983
— Edmonton Oilers, 1984
— Calgary Flames, 1989

MOST ROAD VICTORIES, ALL TEAMS, ONE PLAYOFF YEAR:
46 — **1987.** Of 87 games played, road teams won 46 (22 DSF, 14 DF, 8 CC and 2 Stanley Cup).

MOST CONSECUTIVE PLAYOFF GAME VICTORIES:
12 — **Edmonton Oilers.** Streak began May 15, 1984 at Edmonton with a 7-2 win over New York Islanders in third game of Final series, and ended May 9, 1985 when Chicago Black Hawks defeated Edmonton 5-2 at Chicago. Included in the streak were three wins over the Islanders, in 1984, three over the Los Angeles Kings, four over the Winnipeg Jets and two over the Black Hawks, all in 1985.
11 — Montreal Canadiens. Streak began April 16, 1959, at Toronto with 3-2 win in fourth game of Final series, won by Canadiens 4-1, and ended March 23, 1961, when Chicago defeated Canadiens 4-3 in second game of Semi-Final series. Included in streak were eight straight victories in 1960.
— Montreal Canadiens. Streak began April 28, 1968, at Montreal with 4-3 win in fifth game of Semi-Final series, won by Canadiens 4-2, and ended April 17, 1969, at Boston when Bruins defeated them 5-0 in third game of Semi-Final series. Included in the streak were four straight wins over St. Louis in the 1968 Final and four straight wins over New York Rangers in a 1969 Quarter-Final series.
— Boston Bruins. Streak began April 14, 1970, at Boston with 3-2 victory over New York Rangers in fifth game of a Quarter-Final series, won by Bruins 4-2. It continued with a four-game victory over Chicago in the 1970 Semi-Final and a four-game win over St. Louis in the 1970 Final. Boston then won the first game of a 1971 Quarter-Final series against Montreal. Canadiens ended the streak April 8, 1971, at Boston with a 7-5 victory.
— Montreal Canadiens. Streak started May 6, 1976, at Montreal with 5-2 win in fifth game of a Semi-Final series against New York Islanders, won by Montreal 4-1. Continued with a four-game sweep over Philadelphia in the 1976 Final and a four-game win against St. Louis in the 1977 Quarter-Final. Canadiens won the first two games of a 1977 Semi-Final series against the Islanders before Islanders ended the streak, April 2, 1977 at Long Island with a 5-3 victory.

MOST CONSECUTIVE VICTORIES, ONE PLAYOFF YEAR:
10 — **Boston Bruins** in 1970. Bruins won last two games of best-of-seven Quarter-Final against New York Rangers to win series 4-2 and then defeated Chicago 4-0 in best-of-seven Semi-Final and St. Louis 4-0 in best-of-seven Final.

Gerry Cheevers backstopped the Boston Bruins into the Stanley Cup winners' circle in 1970 and 1972.

LONGEST PLAYOFF LOSING STREAK:
16 Games — Chicago Black Hawks. Streak started in 1975 Quarter-Final against Buffalo when Hawks lost last two games. Then Hawks lost four games to Montreal in 1976 Quarter-Final; two games to New York Islanders in 1977 Preliminary Round; four games to Boston in 1978 Quarter-Final and four games to New York Islanders in 1979 Quarter-Final. Streak ended on April 8, 1980 when Chicago defeated St. Louis 3-2 in the opening game of their 1980 Preliminary Round series.

12 Games — Toronto Maple Leafs. Streak started on April 16, 1979 as Toronto lost four straight games in a Quarter-Final series against Montreal. Continued with three-game Preliminary Round defeats versus Philadelphia and NY Islanders in 1980 and 1981 respectively. Toronto failed to qualify for the 1982 playoffs and lost the first two games of a 1983 Division Semi-Final against Minnesota. Toronto ended the streak with a 6-3 win against the North Stars on April 9, 1983.

10 Games — New York Rangers. Streak started in 1968 Quarter-Final against Chicago when Rangers lost last four games and continued through 1969 (four straight losses to Montreal in Quarter-Final) and 1970 (two straight losses to Boston in Quarter-Final) before ending with a 4-3 win against Boston, at New York, April 11, 1970.
— Philadelphia Flyers. Streak started on April 18, 1968, the last game in the 1968 Quarter-Final series against St. Louis, and continued through 1969 (four straight losses to Chicago in Quarter-Final) and 1973 (opening game loss to Minnesota in Quarter-Final) before ending with a 4-1 win against Minnesota, at Philadelphia, April 5, 1973.

MOST SHUTOUTS, ONE PLAYOFF YEAR, ALL TEAMS:
8 — **1937.** Of 17 games played, New York Rangers had four, Detroit three, Boston one.
— **1975.** Of 51 games played, Philadelphia had five, Montreal two, New York Islanders one.
— **1980.** Of 67 games played, Buffalo had three, Philadelphia two, Montreal, NY Islanders and Minnesota one each.
— **1984.** Of 70 games played, Montreal had 3, Edmonton, Minnesota, NY Rangers, St. Louis and Vancouver one each.

FEWEST SHUTOUTS, ONE PLAYOFF YEAR, ALL TEAMS:
0 — **1959.** Of 18 games played.

MOST SHUTOUTS, BOTH TEAMS, ONE SERIES:
5 — **1945 Final, Toronto, Detroit.** Toronto had three shutouts, Detroit two. Toronto won best-of-seven series 4-3.
— **1950 Semi-Final, Toronto, Detroit.** Toronto had three shutouts, Detroit two. Detroit won best-of-seven series 4-3.

MOST PENALTIES, BOTH TEAMS, ONE SERIES:
219 — **New Jersey, Washington** in 1988 Patrick DF won by New Jersey 4-3. New Jersey received 98 minors, 11 majors, 9 misconducts and 1 match penalty. Washington received 80 minors, 11 majors, 8 misconducts and 1 match penalty.

MOST PENALTY MINUTES, BOTH TEAMS, ONE SERIES:
656 — **New Jersey, Washington** in 1988 Patrick DF won by New Jersey 4-3. New Jersey had 351 minutes; Washington 305.

MOST PENALTIES, ONE TEAM, ONE SERIES:
119 — **New Jersey** in 1988 Patrick DF versus Washington. New Jersey received 98 minors, 11 majors, 9 misconducts and 1 match penalty.

MOST PENALTY MINUTES, ONE TEAM, ONE SERIES:
317 — **Hartford Whalers** in 1987 Adams DSF won by Quebec 4-2.

MOST PENALTY MINUTES, BOTH TEAMS, ONE GAME:
267 Minutes — **New York Rangers, Los Angeles Kings,** at Los Angeles, April 9, 1981. Rangers received 31 penalties for 142 minutes; Los Angeles 28 penalties for 125 minutes. Los Angeles won game 5-4.

MOST PENALTIES, BOTH TEAMS, ONE GAME:
62 — **New Jersey, Washington,** at New Jersey, April 22, 1988. New Jersey received 32 penalties; Washington 30. New Jersey won game 10-4.

MOST PENALTIES, ONE TEAM, ONE GAME:
32 — **New Jersey Devils,** at Washington, April 22,1988. New Jersey won game 10-4.
31 — New York Rangers, at Los Angeles, April 9, 1981. Kings won game 5-4.
30 — Philadelphia Flyers, at Toronto, April 15, 1976. Toronto won game 5-4.

MOST PENALTY MINUTES, ONE TEAM, ONE GAME:
142 — **New York Rangers,** at Los Angeles, April 9, 1981. Los Angeles won game 5-4.

MOST PENALTIES, BOTH TEAMS, ONE PERIOD:
43 — **New York Rangers, Los Angeles Kings,** April 9, 1981, at Los Angeles, first period. Rangers had 24 penalties; Los Angeles 19. Los Angeles won game 5-4.

MOST PENALTY MINUTES, BOTH TEAMS, ONE PERIOD:
248 — **New York Islanders, Boston Bruins,** April 17, 1980, first period, at Boston. Each team received 124 minutes. Islanders won 5-4.

MOST PENALTIES, ONE TEAM, ONE PERIOD: (AND) MOST PENALTY MINUTES, ONE TEAM, ONE PERIOD:
24 Penalties; 125 Minutes — **New York Rangers,** April 9, 1981, at Los Angeles, first period. Los Angeles won game 5-4.

FEWEST PENALTIES, BOTH TEAMS, BEST-OF-SEVEN SERIES:
19 — **Detroit, Toronto** in 1945 Final, won by Toronto 4-3. Detroit received 10 minors. Toronto 9 minors.

FEWEST PENALTIES, ONE TEAM, BEST-OF-SEVEN SERIES:
9 — **Toronto Maple Leafs** in 1945 Final, won by Leafs 4-3 against Detroit.

MOST POWER-PLAY GOALS BY ALL TEAMS, ONE PLAYOFF YEAR:
196 — **1988** in 83 games.

MOST POWER-PLAY GOALS, ONE TEAM, ONE PLAYOFF YEAR:
31 — **New York Islanders,** 1981. 6 against Toronto in Preliminary Round, won by Islanders 3-0; 13 against Edmonton in Quarter-Final, won by Islanders 4-2; 7 against NY Rangers in Semi-Final, won by Islanders 4-0; and 5 in Final against Minnesota, won by Islanders 4-1.
30 — Edmonton Oilers, 1988 in 18 games.

MOST POWER-PLAY GOALS, BOTH TEAMS, ONE SERIES:
21 — **New York Islanders, Philadelphia Flyers** in 1980 Final Series, won by Islanders 4-2. Islanders had 15 and Flyers 6.
— **New York Islanders, Edmonton Oilers** in 1981 Quarter-Final, won by Islanders 4-2. Islanders had 13 and Oilers 8.
— **Philadelphia Flyers, Pittsburgh Penguins** in 1989 Patrick DF, won by Philadelphia 4-3. Flyers had 11 and Penguins 10.
20 — Toronto, Philadelphia in 1976 Quarter-Final series won by Philadelphia 4-3. Toronto had 12 power-play goals; Philadelphia 8.

MOST POWER-PLAY GOALS, ONE TEAM, ONE SERIES:
15 — **New York Islanders** in 1980 Final Series against Philadelphia. Islanders won series 4-2.
13 — New York Islanders in 1981 Quarter-Final against Edmonton. Islanders won series 4-2.
— Calgary Flames in 1986 Conference Championship against St. Louis. Calgary won series 4-3.
12 — Toronto Maple Leafs in 1976 Quarter-Final series won by Philadelphia 4-3.

MOST POWER-PLAY GOALS, BOTH TEAMS, ONE GAME:
7 — **Minnesota North Stars, Edmonton Oilers,** April 28, 1984 at Minnesota. Minnesota had 4, Edmonton 3. Edmonton won game 8-5.
— **Philadelphia Flyers, New York Rangers,** April 13, 1985 at New York. Philadelphia had 4, New York 3. Philadelphia won game 6-5.
— **Edmonton Oilers, Chicago Black Hawks,** May 14, 1985 at Edmonton. Chicago had 5, Edmonton 2. Edmonton won game 10-5.
— **Vancouver Canucks, Calgary Flames,** April 9, 1989 at Vancouver. Vancouver had 4, Calgary 3. Vancouver won game 5-3.
6 — Detroit Red Wings, Montreal Canadiens, March 23, 1939, at Detroit. Detroit had four power-play goals, Montreal two. Detroit won game 7-3.
— Boston Bruins, April 2, 1969, at Boston against Toronto Maple Leafs. Boston won game 10-0, scoring six power-play goals.
— Boston Bruins, Chicago Black Hawks, April 21, 1974, at Boston. Each had three power-play goals. Boston won game 8-6.
— Philadelphia, Toronto, April 15, 1976, at Toronto. Toronto had five power-play goals, Philadelphia had one. Toronto won game 5-4.
— New York Islanders, Edmonton Oilers, April 17, 1981, at New York. Islanders had four, Edmonton two power-play goals. Islanders won game 6-3.
— New York Rangers, Philadelphia Flyers, April 8, 1982, at New York. Rangers had four, Philadelphia two power-play goals. New York won game 7-3.

MOST POWER-PLAY GOALS, ONE TEAM, ONE GAME:
6 — **Boston Bruins,** April 2, 1969, at Boston against Toronto Maple Leafs. Boston won game 10-0.

MOST POWER-PLAY GOALS, BOTH TEAMS, ONE PERIOD:
5 — **Minnesota North Stars, Edmonton Oilers,** April 28, 1984, second period, at Minnesota. North Stars had four and Oilers one. Edmonton won game 8-5.
— **Vancouver Canucks, Calgary Flames,** April 9, 1989, third period at Vancouver. Canucks had three and Flames two. Vancouver won game 5-3.

MOST POWER-PLAY GOALS, ONE TEAM, ONE PERIOD:
4 — **Toronto Maple Leafs,** March 26, 1936, second period against Boston at Toronto. Toronto won game 8-3.
— **Minnesota North Stars,** April 28, 1984, second period against Edmonton. Oilers won game 8-5.

MOST SHORTHAND GOALS BY ALL TEAMS, ONE PLAYOFF YEAR:
33 — **1988,** in 83 games.

MOST SHORTHAND GOALS, ONE TEAM, ONE PLAYOFF YEAR:
10 — **Edmonton Oilers 1983,** in 16 games.
9 — New York Islanders, 1981, in 19 games.
8 — Philadelphia Flyers, 1989, in 19 games.
7 — New York Islanders, 1980, in 21 games.
7 — Chicago Blackhawks, 1989, in 16 games.

MOST SHORTHAND GOALS, BOTH TEAMS, ONE SERIES:
7 — **Boston Bruins (4), New York Rangers (3),** in 1958 semi-final, won by Boston 4-2.
— **Edmonton Oilers (5), Calgary Flames (2),** in 1983 Smythe Division Final won by Edmonton 4-1.

MOST SHORTHAND GOALS, ONE TEAM, ONE SERIES:
5 — Edmonton Oilers in 1983 best-of-seven Smythe Division Final won by Edmonton 4-1.
— **New York Rangers** in 1979 against Philadelphia Flyers in best-of-seven Quarter-Final, won by Rangers 4-1.
4 — Boston Bruins in 1958 against New York Rangers in best-of-seven Semi-Final series, won by Boston 4-2.
— **Minnesota North Stars** in 1981 against Calgary Flames in best-of-seven Semi-Final, won by Minnesota 4-2.
— **Chicago Blackhawks** in 1989 against Detroit Red Wings in best-of-seven Norris Division Semi-Final won by Chicago 4-2.
— **Philadelphia Flyers** in 1989 against Pittsburgh Penguins in best-of-seven Patrick Division Final won by Philadelphia 4-3.

MOST SHORTHAND GOALS, BOTH TEAMS, ONE GAME:
4 — New York Islanders, New York Rangers, April 17, 1983 at NY Rangers. The Islanders scored 3 shorthand goals, Rangers 1. The Rangers won 7-6.
— **Boston Bruins, Minnesota North Stars,** April 11, 1981, at Minnesota. Boston had 3 shorthand goals, Minnesota 1. Minnesota won 6-3.
3 — Toronto Maple Leafs, Detroit Red Wings, April 5, 1947, at Toronto. Toronto had 2 shorthand goals, Detroit 1. Toronto won 6-1.
— **New York Rangers,** Boston Bruins, April 1, 1958, at Boston. New York had 2 shorthand goals, Boston 1. New York won 5-2.
— **Minnesota North Stars,** Philadelphia Flyers, May 4, 1980, at Minnesota. Minnesota had 2 shorthand goals, Philadelphia 1. Philadelphia won 5-3.
— **Edmonton Oilers,** Winnipeg Jets, April 9, 1988 at Winnipeg. Winnipeg had 2 shorthand goals, Edmonton 1. Winnipeg won 6-4.
— **New Jersey Devils,** New York Islanders, April 14, 1988 at New Jersey. NY Islanders had 2 shorthand goals, New Jersey 1. New Jersey won 6-5.

MOST SHORTHAND GOALS, ONE TEAM, ONE GAME:
3 — Boston Bruins, April 11, 1981, at Minnesota. Minnesota won 6-3.

MOST SHORTHAND GOALS, BOTH TEAMS, ONE PERIOD:
3 — Toronto Maple Leafs, Detroit Red Wings, April 5, 1947, at Toronto, first period. Toronto scored two short-hand goals; Detroit one. Toronto won game 6-1.

MOST SHORTHAND GOALS ONE TEAM, ONE PERIOD:
2 — Toronto Maple Leafs, April 5, 1947, at Toronto against Detroit, first period. Toronto won game 6-1.
— **Toronto Maple Leafs,** April 13, 1965, at Toronto against Montreal, first period. Montreal won game 4-3.
— **Boston Bruins,** April 20, 1969, at Boston against Montreal, first period. Boston won game 3-2.
— **Boston Bruins,** April 8, 1970, at Boston against New York Rangers, second period. Boston won game 8-2.
— **Boston Bruins,** April 30, 1972, at Boston against New York Rangers, first period. Boston won game 6-5.
— **Chicago Black Hawks,** May 3, 1973, at Chicago against Montreal, first period. Chicago won game 7-4.
— **Montreal Canadiens,** April 23, 1978, at Detroit, first period. Montreal won game 8-0.
— **New York Islanders,** April 8, 1980, at New York against Los Angeles, second period. Islanders won 8-1.
— **Los Angeles Kings,** April 9, 1980, at New York Islanders, first period. Los Angeles won 6-3.
— **Boston Bruins,** April 13, 1980, at Pittsburgh, second period. Boston won 8-3.
— **Minnesota North Stars,** May 4, 1980, at Minnesota against Philadelphia, second period. Flyers won 5-3.
— **Boston Bruins,** April 11, 1981, at Minnesota, third period. Minnesota won 6-3.
— **New York Islanders,** May 12, 1981, at New York, first period. Islanders defeated Minnesota 6-3.
Montreal Canadiens, April 7, 1982, at Montreal, third period. Montreal defeated Quebec 5-1.
— **Edmonton Oilers,** April 24, 1983, at Edmonton, third period. Edmonton defeated Chicago 8-4.
— **Winnipeg Jets,** April 14, 1985, at Calgary, second period. Winnipeg defeated Calgary 5-3.
— **Boston Bruins,** April 6, 1988 at Boston against Buffalo, first period. Boston won 7-3.
— **New York Islanders,** April 14, 1988 at New Jersey, third period. New Jersey won 6-5.

FASTEST TWO GOALS, BOTH TEAMS:
5 Seconds — Pittsburgh, Buffalo at Buffalo, April 14, 1979. Gilbert Perreault scored for Buffalo at 12:59 and Jim Hamilton for Pittsburgh at 13:04 of first period. Pittsburgh won game 4-3 and best-of-three Preliminary Round 2-1.
8 seconds — Minnesota, St. Louis at Minnesota, April 9, 1989. Bernie Federko scored for St. Louis at 2:28 of third period and Perry Berezan at 2:36 for Minnesota. Minnesota won game 5-4, and St. Louis won best-of-seven Norris Division Semi-Final 4-1.
9 seconds — NY Islanders, Washington at Washington, April 10, 1986. Bryan Trottier scored for New York at 18:26 of second period and Scott Stevens at 18:35 for Washington. Washington won game 5-2, and won best-of-five Division Semi-Final 3-0.
11 Seconds — Buffalo, Quebec at Buffalo, April 14, 1985. Phil Housley scored for Buffalo at 17:36 of second period and Mike Gillis at 17:47 for Quebec. Buffalo won game 7-4, and Quebec won best-of-five Division Semi-Final 3-2.

FASTEST TWO GOALS, ONE TEAM:
5 Seconds — Detroit Red Wings at Detroit, April 11, 1965, against Chicago. Norm Ullman scored at 17:35 and 17:40, 2nd period. Detroit won game 4-2. Chicago won best-of-seven Semi-Final 4-3.

FASTEST THREE GOALS, BOTH TEAMS:
21 Seconds — Edmonton, Chicago at Edmonton, May 7, 1985. Behn Wilson scored for Chicago at 19:22 of third period, Jari Kurri at 19:36 and Glenn Anderson at 19:43 for Edmonton. Edmonton Won game 7-3 and best-of-seven Conference Final 4-2.
36 Seconds — Los Angeles, Edmonton at Edmonton, April 7, 1982. Steve Bozek of Los Angeles scored at 6:00 of first period, Tom Roulston of Edmonton scored at 6:16, Risto Siltanen of Edmonton scored at 6:36. Los Angeles won game 10-8 and best-of-five Division Semi-Final 3-2.
38 Seconds — Toronto, Montreal at Toronto, April 13, 1965. Red Kelly of Toronto scored at 3:11 of first period, John Ferguson of Montreal at 3:32 and Ron Ellis of Toronto at 3:49. Montreal won game 4-3 in overtime and best-of-seven semi-final series 4-2.
— Boston, Philadelphia at Philadelphia, April 26, 1977. Mike Milbury of Boston scored at 15:01 of second period; Gary Dornhoefer of Philadelphia at 15:16; and Jean Ratelle of Boston at 15:39. Boston won game 5-4 and best-of-seven semi-final series 4-0.

FASTEST THREE GOALS, ONE TEAM:
23 Seconds — Toronto Maple Leafs at Toronto, April 12, 1979, against Atlanta Flames. Darryl Sittler scored at 4:04 and 4:16 and Ron Ellis at 4:27, first period. Leafs won game 7-4 and best-of-three Preliminary Round 2-0.
28 Seconds — New York Rangers at New York, April 12, 1986. Jim Wiemer scored at 12:29 of third period, Bob Brooke at 12:43 and Ron Greschner at 13:07. Rangers won game 5-2 and the best-of-five division semi-final 3-2.
56 Seconds — Montreal Canadiens at Detroit, April 6, 1954. Dickie Moore scored at 15:03 of first period, Maurice Richard at 15:28 and again at 15:59. Canadiens won game 3-1 but Detroit won best-of-seven Final 4-3.

FASTEST FOUR GOALS, BOTH TEAMS:
1 Minute, 33 Seconds — Philadelphia, Toronto at Philadelphia, April 20, 1976. Don Saleski of Philadelphia scored at 10:04 of second period; Bob Neely of Toronto at 10:42; Gary Dornhoefer of Philadelphia at 11:24 and Don Saleski again at 11:37. Philadelphia won game 7-1 and best-of-seven Quarter-Final series 4-3.
1 minute, 34 seconds — Montreal, Calgary at Montreal, May 20, 1986. Joel Otto of Calgary scored at 17:59 of first period; Bobby Smith of Montreal at 18:25; Mats Naslund of Montreal at 19:17 and Bob Gainey of Montreal at 19:33. Montreal won game 5-3 and best-of-seven Final series 4-1.
1 Minute, 38 Seconds — Boston, Philadelphia at Philadelphia, April 26, 1977. Gregg Sheppard of Boston scored at 14:01 of second period; Mike Milbury of Boston at 15:01; Gary Dornhoefer of Philadelphia at 15:16 and Jean Ratelle of Boston at 15:39. Boston won game 5-4 and best-of-seven Semi-Final series 4-0.

FASTEST FOUR GOALS, ONE TEAM:
2 Minutes, 35 Seconds — Montreal Canadiens at Montreal, March 30, 1944, against Toronto. Toe Blake scored at 7:58 of third period and again at 8:37, Maurice Richard at 9:17, Ray Getliffe at 10:33. Canadiens won game 11-0 and best-of-seven Semi-Final 4-0.

FASTEST FIVE GOALS, BOTH TEAMS:
3 Minutes, 6 Seconds — Chicago, Minnesota, at Chicago April 21, 1985. Keith Brown scored for Chicago at 1:12, second period; Ken Yaremchuk, Chicago, at 1:27; Dino Ciccarelli, Minnesota, 2:48; Tony McKegney, Minnesota, 4:07; and Curt Fraser, Chicago, 4:18. Chicago won game 6-2.
3 Minutes, 20 Seconds — Minnesota, Philadelphia, at Philadelphia, April 29, 1980. Paul Shmyr scored for Minnesota at 13:20, first period; Steve Christoff, Minnesota, at 13:59; Ken Linseman, Philadelphia, at 14:54; Tom Gorence, Philadelphia, at 15:36; and Linseman, at 16:40. Minnesota won game 6-5.
4 Minutes, 19 Seconds — Toronto, New York Rangers at Toronto, April 9, 1932. Ace Bailey scored for Toronto at 15:07 of third period, Fred Cook at 16:32 for Rangers, Bob Gracie of Toronto at 17:36, Frank Boucher of Rangers at 18:26 and again at 19:26. Toronto won game 6-4 and best-of-five Final 3-0.

FASTEST FIVE GOALS, ONE TEAM:
3 Minutes, 36 Seconds — Montreal Canadiens at Montreal, March 30, 1944, against Toronto. Toe Blake scored at 7:58 of third period and 8:37, Maurice Richard at 9:17, Ray Getliffe at 10:33 and Buddy O'Connor at 11:34. Canadiens won game 11-0 and best-of-seven Semi-Final 4-0.

MOST THREE-OR-MORE GOAL GAMES BY ALL TEAMS,
ONE PLAYOFF YEAR:
12 — 1983 in 66 games.
12 — 1988 in 83 games.
11 — 1985 in 70 games.

MOST THREE-OR-MORE GOAL GAMES, ONE TEAM, ONE PLAYOFF YEAR:
6 — Edmonton Oilers in 16 games, 1983.
— **Edmonton Oilers** in 18 games, 1985.

Individual Records

Career

MOST YEARS IN PLAYOFFS:
20 — Gordie Howe, Detroit, Hartford (1947-58 incl.; 60-61; 63-66 incl.; 70 and 80)
19 — Red Kelly, Detroit, Toronto
18 — Stan Mikita, Chicago Black Hawks
   — Henri Richard, Montreal Canadiens

MOST CONSECUTIVE YEARS IN PLAYOFFS:
17 — Brad Park, New York Rangers, Boston, Detroit (1969-1985 inclusive).
16 — Jean Beliveau, Montreal Canadiens (1954-69, inclusive).

MOST PLAYOFF GAMES:
203 — Larry Robinson, Montreal Canadiens
185 — Denis Potvin, New York Islanders
182 — Bob Gainey, Montreal Canadiens
180 — Henri Richard, Montreal Canadiens
171 — Bryan Trottier, New York Islanders

MOST POINTS IN PLAYOFFS (CAREER):
274 — Wayne Gretzky, Edmonton Oilers, 86 goals, 188 assists
177 — Jari Kurri, Edmonton Oilers, 82 goals, 95 assists
176 — Jean Beliveau, Montreal Canadiens, 79 goals, 97 assists
169 — Mark Messier, Edmonton Oilers, 67 goals, 102 assists
   — Bryan Trottier, New York Islanders, 63 goals, 106 assists

MOST GOALS IN PLAYOFFS (CAREER):
86 — Wayne Gretzky, Edmonton Oilers, Los Angeles Kings
85 — Mike Bossy, New York Islanders
82 — Maurice Richard, Montreal Canadiens
   — Jari Kurri, Edmonton Oilers

MOST GAME-WINNING GOALS IN PLAYOFFS (CAREER):
18 — Maurice Richard, Montreal Canadiens
17 — Mike Bossy, New York Islanders
16 — Wayne Gretzky, Edmonton Oilers, Los Angeles Kings
15 — Jean Beliveau, Montreal Canadiens
   — Yvan Cournoyer, Montreal Canadiens

MOST OVERTIME GOALS IN PLAYOFFS (CAREER):
6 — Maurice Richard, Montreal Canadiens. (1 in 1946; 3 in 1951; 1 in 1957; 1 in 1958.)
4 — Bob Nystrom, New York Islanders
   — Dale Hunter, Quebec Nordiques, Washington Capitals
3 — Mel Hill, Boston Bruins
   — Rene Robert, Buffalo Sabres
   — Danny Gare, Buffalo Sabres
   — Jacques Lemaire, Montreal Canadiens
   — Bobby Clarke, Philadelphia Flyers
   — Terry O'Reilly, Boston Bruins
   — Mike Bossy, New York Islanders
   — Steve Payne, Minnesota North Stars
   — Ken Morrow, New York Islanders
   — Lanny McDonald, Toronto Maple Leafs, Calgary Flames
   — Glenn Anderson, Edmonton Oilers
   — Peter Stastny, Quebec Nordiques

MOST POWER-PLAY GOALS IN PLAYOFFS (CAREER):
35 — Mike Bossy, New York Islanders
27 — Denis Potvin, New York Islanders
26 — Jean Beliveau, Montreal Canadiens
22 — Bobby Hull, Chicago Black Hawks
   — Phil Esposito, Chicago, Boston, NY Rangers
21 — Bernie Geoffrion, Montreal Canadiens, NY Rangers

MOST SHORTHAND GOALS IN PLAYOFFS (CAREER):
10 — Mark Messier, Edmonton Oilers
   — Wayne Gretzky, Edmonton Oilers, Los Angeles Kings
8 — Ed Westfall, Boston Bruins, New York Islanders
6 — Dave Keon, Toronto Maple Leafs
   — Derek Sanderson, Boston Bruins
5 — Lorne Henning, New York Islanders
   — Bob Bourne, New York Islanders
   — Anders Kallur, New York Islanders

MOST THREE-OR-MORE-GOAL GAMES IN PLAYOFFS (CAREER):
7 — Maurice Richard, Montreal Canadiens. Four three-goal games; two four-goal games; one five-goal game.
   — **Wayne Gretzky, Edmonton Oilers.** Two four-goal games; five three-goal games.
6 — Jari Kurri, Edmonton Oilers. One four-goal game; five three-goal games.
5 — Mike Bossy, New York Islanders. Four three-goal games; one four-goal game.

MOST ASSISTS IN PLAYOFFS (CAREER):
188 — Wayne Gretzky, Edmonton Oilers, Los Angeles Kings
109 — Larry Robinson, Montreal Canadiens
108 — Denis Potvin, New York Islanders
106 — Bryan Trottier, New York Islanders
102 — Mark Messier, Edmonton Oilers

MOST PENALTY MINUTES IN PLAYOFFS (CAREER):
466 — Willi Plett, Atlanta, Calgary, Minnesota, Boston
455 — Dave Williams, Toronto, Vancouver, Los Angeles
444 — Dale Hunter, Quebec, Washington
   — Chris Nilan, Montreal, New York Rangers
412 — Dave Schultz, Philadelphia, Los Angeles, Buffalo

Brad Park never missed the playoffs in his 17-year career, but never played on a Stanley Cup winner.

MOST SHUTOUTS IN PLAYOFFS (CAREER):
14 — Jacques Plante, Montreal Canadiens, St. Louis Blues in 16 playoff years.
13 — Turk Broda, Toronto Maple Leafs
12 — Terry Sawchuk, Detroit, Toronto, Los Angeles

MOST PLAYOFF GAMES APPEARED IN BY A GOALTENDER (CAREER):
132 — Bill Smith, NY Islanders
115 — Glenn Hall, Detroit, Chicago, St. Louis
112 — Jacques Plante, Montreal, St. Louis, Toronto, Boston
   — Ken Dryden, Montreal
106 — Terry Sawchuk, Detroit, Toronto, Los Angeles, New York Rangers

MOST MINUTES PLAYED BY A GOALTENDER (CAREER):
7,645 — Bill Smith, NY Islanders
6,899 — Glenn Hall, Detroit, Chicago, St. Louis
6,841 — Ken Dryden, Montreal
6,651 — Jacques Plante, Montreal, St. Louis, Toronto, Boston

Single Playoff Year

MOST POINTS, ONE PLAYOFF YEAR:
47 — Wayne Gretzky, Edmonton, in 1985. 17 goals, 30 assists in 18 games.
43 — Wayne Gretzky, Edmonton, in 1988. 12 goals, 31 assists in 19 games.
38 — Wayne Gretzky, Edmonton, in 1983. 12 goals, 26 assists in 16 games.
37 — Paul Coffey, Edmonton, in 1985. 12 goals, 25 assists in 18 games.
35 — Mike Bossy, NY Islanders, in 1981. 17 goals, 18 assists in 18 games.
   — Wayne Gretzky, Edmonton, in 1984. 13 goals, 22 assists in 19 games.
   — Mark Messier, Edmonton, in 1988. 11 goals, 23 assists in 19 games.
34 — Wayne Gretzky, Edmonton, in 1987. 5 goals, 29 assists in 21 games.
33 — Rick Middleton Boston, in 1983. 11 goals, 22 assists in 17 games.
32 — Barry Pederson, Boston, in 1983. 14 goals, 18 assists in 17 games.

MOST POINTS BY A DEFENSEMAN, ONE PLAYOFF YEAR:
37 — Paul Coffey, Edmonton, in 1985. 12 goals, 25 assists in 18 games.
31 — Al MacInnis, Calgary, in 1989. 7 goals, 24 assists in 18 games.
25 — Denis Potvin, NY Islanders, in 1981. 8 goals, 17 assists in 18 games.
24 — Bobby Orr, Boston, in 1972. 5 goals, 19 assists in 15 games.

MOST POINTS BY A ROOKIE, ONE PLAYOFF YEAR:
21 — Dino Ciccarelli, Minnesota North Stars, in 1981. 14 goals, 7 assists in 19 games.
20 — Don Maloney, New York Rangers, in 1979. 7 goals, 13 assists in 18 games.

LONGEST CONSECUTIVE POINT-SCORING STREAK, ONE PLAYOFF YEAR:
18 games — Bryan Trottier, NY Islanders, 1981. 11 goals, 18 assists, 29 points.
17 games — Wayne Gretzky, Edmonton, 1988. 12 goals, 29 assists, 41 points.
   — Al MacInnis, Calgary, 1989. 7 goals, 19 assists, 24 points.

**LONGEST CONSECUTIVE POINT-SCORING STREAK,
MORE THAN ONE PLAYOFF YEAR:**
27 games — Bryan Trottier, New York Islanders, 1980, 1981 and 1982. 7 games in 1980 (3 goals, 5 assists, 8 points), 18 games in 1981 (11 goals, 18 assists, 29 points), and two games in 1982 (2 goals, 3 assists, 5 points) Total points, 42.
19 games — Wayne Gretzky, Edmonton Oilers, Los Angeles Kings 1988 and 1989. 17 games in 1988 (12 goals, 29 assists, 41 points with Edmonton), 2 games in 1989 (1 goal, 2 assists, 3 points with Los Angeles). Total points, 44.
18 games — Phil Esposito, Boston Bruins, 1970 and 1971. 13 goals, 20 assists, 33 points.

MOST GOALS, ONE PLAYOFF YEAR:
19 — Reggie Leach, Philadelphia Flyers, 1976. 16 games.
  — Jari Kurri, Edmonton Oilers, 1985. 18 games.
17 — Mike Bossy, New York Islanders, 1981. 18 games.
  — Steve Payne, Minnesota North Stars, 1981. 19 games.
  — Mike Bossy, New York Islanders, 1982. 19 games.
  — Mike Bossy, New York Islanders, 1983. 19 games
  — Wayne Gretzky, Edmonton Oilers, 1985. 18 games.

MOST GOALS BY A DEFENSEMAN, ONE PLAYOFF YEAR:
12 — Paul Coffey, Edmonton Oilers, 1985. 18 games.
9 — Bobby Orr, Boston Bruins, 1970. 14 games.
  — Brad Park, Boston Bruins, 1978. 15 games.
8 — Denis Potvin, New York Islanders, 1981. 18 games.
  — Raymond Bourque, Boston Bruins, 1983. 17 games.
  — Denis Potvin, New York Islanders, 1983. 20 games.
  — Paul Coffey, Edmonton Oilers, 1984. 19 games

MOST GOALS BY A ROOKIE, ONE PLAYOFF YEAR:
14 — Dino Ciccarelli, Minnesota North Stars, 1981. 19 games.
10 — Claude Lemieux, Montreal Canadiens, 1986. 20 games.
9 — Pat Flatley, NY Islanders, 1984. 21 games
8 — Steve Christoff, Minnesota North Stars, 1980. 14 games.
  — Brad Palmer, Minnesota North Stars, 1981. 19 games.
  — Mike Krushelnyski, Boston Bruins, 1983. 17 games.
  — Bob Joyce, Boston Bruins, 1988. 23 games.

MOST GAME-WINNING GOALS, ONE PLAYOFF YEAR:
5 — Mike Bossy, New York Islanders, 1983. 19 games.
  — Jari Kurri, Edmonton Oilers, 1987. 21 games.

MOST OVERTIME GOALS, ONE PLAYOFF YEAR:
3 — Mel Hill, Boston Bruins, 1939. All against New York Rangers in best-of-seven Semi-Final, won by Boston 4-3.
  — Maurice Richard, Montreal Canadiens, 1951. 2 against Detroit Red Wings in best-of-seven Semi-Final, won by Montreal 4-2; 1 against Toronto Maple Leafs in best-of-seven Final, won by Toronto 4-1.

MOST POWER-PLAY GOALS, ONE PLAYOFF YEAR:
9 — Mike Bossy, New York Islanders, 1981. 18 games against Toronto, Edmonton, NY Rangers and Minnesota.
8 — Tim Kerr, Philadelphia Flyers, 1989. 19 games.
7 — Michel Goulet, Quebec Nordiques, 1985. 17 games.
  — Mark Messier, Edmonton Oilers, 1988. 19 games.
  — Mario Lemieux, Pittsburgh Penguins, 1989. 11 games.
6 — Andy Bathgate, Detroit Red Wings, 1966. 12 games.
  — Bobby Hull, Chicago Black Hawks, 1971. 18 games.
  — Jacques Lemaire, Montreal Canadiens, 1979. 16 games.
  — Mike Bossy, New York Islanders, 1980. 21 games.
  — Denis Potvin, New York Islanders, 1981. 18 games.
  — Steve Payne, Minnesota North Stars, 1981. 19 games.
  — Mike Bossy, New York Islanders, 1982. 19 games.
  — Mike Bossy, New York Islanders, 1983. 19 games.
  — Joe Mullen, Calgary Flames, 1989. 21 games.
  — Joe Nieuwendyk, Calgary Flames, 1989. 22 games.

MOST SHORTHAND GOALS, ONE PLAYOFF YEAR:
3 — Derek Sanderson, Boston Bruins, 1969. 1 against Toronto in Quarter-Final, won by Boston 4-0; 2 against Montreal in Semi-Final, won by Montreal, 4-2.
  — Bill Barber, Philadelphia Flyers, 1980. All against Minnesota in Semi-Final, won by Philadelphia 4-1.
  — Lorne Henning, New York Islanders, 1980. 1 against Boston in Quarter-Final won by NYI 4-1; 1 against Buffalo in Semi-Final, won by NYI 4-2, 1 against Philadelphia in Final, won by NYI 4-2.
  — Wayne Gretzky, Edmonton Oilers, 1983. 2 against Winnipeg in Division Semi-Final won by Edmonton 3-0; 1 against Calgary in Division Final, won by Edmonton 4-1.
  — Wayne Presley, Chicago Blackhawks, 1989. All against Detroit in Division Semi-Final won by Chicago 4-2.
MOST THREE-OR-MORE GOAL GAMES, ONE PLAYOFF YEAR:
4 — Jari Kurri, Edmonton Oilers, 1985. 1 four-goal game, 3 three-goal games.
3 — Mark Messier, Edmonton Oilers, 1983. 3 three-goal games.
  — Mike Bossy, New York Islanders, 1983. 3 three-goal games
2 — Maurice Richard, Montreal Canadiens, 1944. 1 five-goal game; 1 three-goal game.
  — Doug Bentley, Chicago Black Hawks, 1944. 2 three-goal games.
  — Norm Ullman, Detroit Red Wings, 1964. 2 three-goal games.
  — Phil Esposito, Boston Bruins, 1970. 2 three-goal games.
  — Pit Martin, Chicago Black Hawks, 1973. 2 three-goal games.
  — Rick MacLeish, Philadelphia Flyers, 1975. 2 three-goal games.
  — Lanny McDonald, Toronto Maple Leafs, 1977. 1 three-goal game; 1 four-goal game.
  — Wayne Gretzky, Edmonton Oilers, 1981. 2 three-goal games.
  — Wayne Gretzky, Edmonton Oilers, 1985. 2 three-goal games.
  — Wayne Gretzky, Edmonton Oilers, 1983. 2 four-goal games.
  — Petr Klima, Detroit Red Wings, 1988. 2 three-goal games.

LONGEST CONSECUTIVE GOAL-SCORING STREAK, ONE PLAYOFF YEAR:
9 Games — Reggie Leach, Philadelphia Flyers, 1976. Streak started April 17 at Toronto and ended May 9 at Montreal. He scored one goal in each of seven games; two in one game; and five in another; a total 14 goals.

MOST ASSISTS, ONE PLAYOFF YEAR:
31 — Wayne Gretzky, Edmonton Oilers, 1988. 19 games.
30 — Wayne Gretzky, Edmonton Oilers, 1985. 18 games.
29 — Wayne Gretzky, Edmonton Oilers, 1987. 21 games.
26 — Wayne Gretzky, Edmonton Oilers, 1983. 16 games.
25 — Paul Coffey, Edmonton Oilers, 1985. 18 games.
24 — Al MacInnis, Calgary Flames, 1989. 22 games.

MOST ASSISTS BY A DEFENSEMAN, ONE PLAYOFF YEAR:
25 — Paul Coffey, Edmonton Oilers, 1985. 18 games.
24 — Al MacInnis, Calgary Flames, 1989. 22 games.
19 — Bobby Orr, Boston Bruins, 1972. 15 games.
18 — Ray Bourque, Boston Bruins, 1988. 23 games.
17 — Larry Robinson, Montreal Canadiens, 1978. 15 games.
  — Denis Potvin, New York Islanders, 1981. 18 games.
  — Charlie Huddy, Edmonton Oilers, 1985. 18 games.

MOST MINUTES PLAYED BY A GOALTENDER, ONE PLAYOFF YEAR:
1,540 — Ron Hextall, Philadelphia Flyers, 1987. 26 games.
1,381 — Mike Vernon, Calgary Flames, 1989. 22 games.
1,229 — Mike Vernon, Calgary Flames, 1986. 21 games.
1,221 — Ken Dryden, Montreal Canadiens, 1971. 20 games.
1,218 — Patrick Roy, Montreal Canadiens, 1986. 20 games.
1,206 — Patrick Roy, Montreal Canadiens, 1989. 19 games.

MOST WINS BY A GOALTENDER, ONE PLAYOFF YEAR:
16 — Grant Fuhr, Edmonton Oilers, 1988. 19 games.
  — Mike Vernon, Calgary Flames, 1989. 22 games.
15 — Bill Smith, New York Islanders, 1980. 20 games.
  — Bill Smith, New York Islanders, 1982. 18 games.
  — Grant Fuhr, Edmonton, Oilers, 1985. 18 games.
  — Patrick Roy, Montreal Canadiens, 1986. 20 games.
  — Ron Hextall, Philadelphia Flyers, 1987. 26 games.
14 — Bill Smith, New York Islanders, 1981. 17 games.
14 — Grant Fuhr, Edmonton Oilers, 1987. 19 games.

MOST CONSECUTIVE WINS BY A GOALTENDER, ONE PLAYOFF YEAR:
10 — Gerry Cheevers, Boston Bruins, 1970. 2 wins against NY Rangers in Quarter-Final, won by Boston 4-2; 4 wins against Chicago in Semi-Final, won by Boston 4-0; and 4 wins against St. Louis in Final, won by Boston 4-0.

MOST SHUTOUTS, ONE PLAYOFF YEAR:
4 — Clint Benedict, Montreal Maroons, 1928. 9 games.
  — Dave Kerr, New York Rangers, 1937. 9 games.
  — Frank McCool, Toronto Maple Leafs, 1945. 13 games.
  — Terry Sawchuk, Detroit Red Wings, 1952. 8 games.
  — Bernie Parent, Philadelphia Flyers, 1975. 17 games.
  — Ken Dryden, Montreal Canadiens, 1977. 14 games.

MOST CONSECUTIVE SHUTOUTS:
3 — Frank McCool, Toronto Maple Leafs, 1945. McCool shut out Detroit Red Wings 1-0, April 6; 2-0, April 8; 1-0, April 12. Toronto won the best-of-seven Final 4-3.

LONGEST SHUTOUT SEQUENCE:
248 Minutes, 32 Seconds — Norm Smith, Detroit Red Wings, 1936. In best-of-five Semi-Final, Smith shut out Montreal Maroons 1-0, March 24, in 116:30 overtime; shut out Maroons 3-0 in second game, March 26; and was scored against at 12:02 of first period, March 29, by Gus Marker. Detroit won series 3-0.

One-Series Records

MOST POINTS IN FINAL SERIES:
13 — Wayne Gretzky, Edmonton Oilers, in 1988, during 4 games plus suspended game vs. Boston. 3 goals, 10 assists.
12 — Gordie Howe, Detroit Red Wings, in 1955, during 7 games vs. Montreal. 5 goals, 7 assists.
  — Yvan Cournoyer, Montreal Canadiens, in 1973, during 6 games vs. Chicago. 6 goals, 6 assists.
  — Jacques Lemaire, Montreal Canadiens, in 1973, during 6 games vs. Chicago. 3 goals, 9 assists.

MOST GOALS IN FINAL SERIES:
7 — Jean Beliveau, Montreal Canadiens, in 1956, during 5 games vs. Detroit.
  — Mike Bossy, New York Islanders, in 1982, during 4 games vs. Vancouver.
  — Wayne Gretzky, Edmonton Oilers, in 1985, during 5 games vs. Philadelphia.

MOST ASSISTS IN FINAL SERIES:
10 — Wayne Gretzky, Edmonton Oilers, in 1988, during 4 games plus suspended game vs. Boston.
9 — Jacques Lemaire, Montreal Canadiens, in 1973, during 6 games vs. Chicago.
  — Wayne Gretzky, Edmonton Oilers, in 1987, during 7 games vs. Philadelphia.

MOST POINTS IN ONE SERIES (OTHER THAN FINAL):
19 — **Rick Middleton, Boston Bruins,** in 1983, during 7 games vs. Buffalo. 5 goals, 14 assists.
18 — **Wayne Gretzky,** Edmonton Oilers, in 1985, during 6 games vs. Chicago. 4 goals, 14 assists.
16 — Barry Pederson, Boston Bruins, in 1983, during 7 games vs. Buffalo. 7 goals, 9 assists.
15 — Jari Kurri, Edmonton Oilers, in 1985, during 6 games vs. Chicago. 12 goals, 3 assists.
— Wayne Gretzky, Edmonton Oilers, in 1987, during 5 games vs. Los Angeles. 2 goals, 13 assists.
— Tim Kerr, Philadelphia Flyers, in 1989, during 7 games vs. Pittsburgh. 10 goals, 5 assists.

MOST GOALS IN ONE SERIES (OTHER THAN FINAL):
12 — **Jari Kurri, Edmonton Oilers,** in 1985, during 6 games vs. Chicago.
10 — Tim Kerr, Philadelphia Flyers, in 1989, during 7 games vs. Pittsburgh.
9 — Reggie Leach, Philadelphia, in 1976, during 5 games vs. Boston.
— Bill Barber, Philadelphia, in 1980, during 5 games vs. Minnesota.
— Mike Bossy, New York Islanders, in 1983, during 6 games vs. Boston.
— Mario Lemieux, Pittsburgh Penguins, in 1989, during 7 games vs. Philadelphia.

MOST ASSISTS IN ONE SERIES (OTHER THAN FINAL):
14 — **Rick Middleton, Boston,** in 1983, during 7 games vs. Buffalo.
— **Wayne Gretzky, Edmonton,** in 1985, during 6 games vs. Chicago.
13 — Wayne Gretzky, Edmonton, in 1987, during 5 games vs. Los Angeles.
11 — Mark Messier, Edmonton, in 1989, during 7 games vs. Los Angeles.
10 — Fleming Mackell, Boston, in 1958 during 6 games vs. NY Rangers.
— Stan Mikita, Chicago, in 1962, during 6 games vs. Montreal.
— Bob Bourne, NY Islanders, in 1983, during 6 games vs. NY Rangers.
— Wayne Gretzky, Edmonton, in 1988, during 5 games vs. Winnipeg.
— Wayne Gretzky, Edmonton, in 1988, during 5 games vs. Winnipeg.

MOST OVERTIME GOALS, ONE PLAYOFF SERIES:
3 — **Mel Hill, Boston Bruins,** 1939, in Semi-Final series vs. New York Rangers, won by Boston 4-3. Hill scored at 59:25 overtime March 21 for a 2-1 win; at 8:24, March 23 for a 3-2 win; and at 48:00 April 2 for a 2-1 win.

MOST POWER-PLAY GOALS, ONE PLAYOFF SERIES:
6 — **Chris Kontos, Los Angeles,** 1989, Smythe DSF vs. Edmonton, won by Los Angeles 4-3.
5 — Andy Bathgate, Detroit, 1966, SF vs. Chicago, won by Detroit 4-2.
— Denis Potvin, NY Islanders, 1981, QF vs. Edmonton, won by Islanders 4-2.
— Ken Houston, Calgary, 1981, QF vs. Philadelphia, won by Calgary 4-3.
— Rick Vaive, Chicago, 1988, Norris DSF vs. St. Louis, won by St. Louis 4-1.
— Tim Kerr, Philadelphia, 1989, Patrick DF vs. Pittsburgh, won by Philadelphia 4-3.
— Mario Lemieux, Pittsburgh, 1989, Patrick DF vs. Philadelphia won by Philadelphia 4-3.

MOST SHORTHAND GOALS, ONE PLAYOFF SERIES:
3 — **Bill Barber, Philadelphia,** 1980, SF vs. Minnesota, won by Philadelphia 4-1.
— **Wayne Presley, Chicago,** 1989, Norris DSF vs. Detroit, won by Chicago 4-2.
2 — Mac Colville, NY Rangers, 1940, SF vs. Boston, won by New York 4-2.
— Jerry Toppazzini, Boston, 1958, SF vs. New York Rangers, won by Boston 4-2.
— Dave Keon, Toronto, 1963, Final Series vs. Detroit, won by Toronto 4-1.
— Bob Pulford, Toronto, 1964, Final Series vs. Detroit, won by Toronto 4-3.
— Serge Savard, Montreal, 1968, Final Series vs. St. Louis, won by Montreal 4-0.
— Derek Sanderson, Boston, 1969, SF vs. Montreal, won by Montreal 4-2.
— Bryan Trottier, NY Islanders, 1980, Preliminary Round vs. Los Angeles, won by Islanders 3-1.
— Bobby Lalonde, Boston, 1981, Preliminary Round vs. Minnesota, won by Minnesota 3-0.
— Butch Goring, NY Islanders, 1981, SF vs. New York Rangers, won by Islanders 4-0.
— Wayne Gretzky, Edmonton, 1983, Smythe DSF vs. Winnipeg, won by Oilers 3-0.
— Mark Messier, Edmonton, 1983, Smythe DF vs. Calgary, won by Oilers 4-1.
— Jari Kurri, Edmonton, 1983, Campbell CF vs. Chicago, won by Oilers 4-0.
— Wayne Gretzky, Edmonton, 1985, Smythe DF vs. Winnipeg, won by Oilers 4-0.
— Kevin Lowe, Edmonton, 1987, Final Series vs. Philadelphia, won by Edmonton 4-3.
— Bob Gould, Washington, 1988, Patrick DSF vs. Philadelphia, won by Washington 4-3.
— Dave Poulin, Philadelphia, 1989, Patrick DF vs. Pittsburgh, won by Philadelphia 4-3.

MOST THREE-OR-MORE-GOAL GAMES, ONE PLAYOFF SERIES:
3 — **Jari Kurri, Edmonton** 1985, Campbell Conference Championship vs. Chicago. Kurri scored three goals May 7 in 7-3 win at Edmonton; three goals May 14 in 10-5 win at Edmonton; and four goals May 16 in 8-2 win at Chicago.
2 — Doug Bentley, Chicago, 1944, Semi-Final vs. Detroit, won by Chicago 4-1. Bentley scored three goals March 28 at Chicago in 7-1 win and three goals March 30 at Detroit in 5-2 win.
— Norm Ullman, Detroit, 1964, Semi-Final vs. Chicago, won by Detroit 4-3. Ullman scored three goals March 29 at Chicago in 5-4 win and three goals April 7 at Detroit in 7-1 win.
— Mark Messier, Edmonton, 1983, Smythe DF vs. Calgary. Messier scored three goals April 14 in 6-3 win at Edmonton and three goals April 17 in 10-2 win at Calgary.
— Mike Bossy, NY Islanders, 1983, Wales Conference Final vs. Boston. Bossy scored three goals May 3 in 8-3 win at New York and four goals in 8-4 win May 7 at New York.

Single Playoff Game Records

MOST POINTS, ONE GAME:
8 — **Patrik Sundstrom, New Jersey Devils,** April 22, 1988 at New Jersey during 10-4 win. Sundstrom had three goals, 5 assists.
— **Mario Lemieux, Pittsburgh Penguins,** April 25, 1989 at Pittsburgh during 10-7 win over Philadelphia. Lemieux had 5 goals, 3 assists.
7 — Wayne Gretzky, Edmonton Oilers, April 17, 1983 at Calgary during 10-2 win. Gretzky had 4 goals, 3 assists.
— Wayne Gretzky, Edmonton Oilers, April 25, 1985 at Winnipeg during 8-3 win. Gretzky had 3 goals, 4 assists.
— Wayne Gretzky, Edmonton Oilers, April 9, 1987, at Edmonton during 13-3 win over Los Angeles. Gretzky had one goal, six assists.
6 — Dickie Moore, Montreal Canadiens, March 25, 1954, at Montreal during 8-1 win over Boston. Moore had 2 goals, 4 assists.
— Phil Esposito, Boston Bruins, April 2, 1969, at Boston during 10-0 win over Toronto. Esposito had 4 goals, 2 assists.
— Darryl Sittler, Toronto Maple Leafs, April 22, 1976, at Toronto during 8-5 win over Philadelphia. Sittler had 5 goals, 1 assist.
— Guy Lafleur, Montreal Canadiens, April 11, 1977, at Montreal during 7-2 victory vs. St. Louis. Lafleur had 3 goals, 3 assists.
— Mikko Leinonen, New York Rangers, April 8, 1982, at New York during 7-3 win over Philadelphia. Leinonen had 6 assists.
— Paul Coffey, Edmonton Oilers, May 14, 1985 at Edmonton during 10-5 win over Chicago. Coffey had 1 goal, 5 assists.
— John Anderson, Hartford Whalers, April 12, 1986 at Hartford during 9-4 win over Quebec. Anderson had 2 goals, 4 assists.

MOST POINTS BY A DEFENSEMAN, ONE GAME:
6 — **Paul Coffey, Edmonton Oilers,** May 14, 1985 at Edmonton. 1 goal, 5 assists. Edmonton won 10-5.
5 — Eddie Bush, Detroit Red Wings, April 9, 1942, at Toronto. 1 goal, 4 assists. Detroit won 5-2.
— Bob Dailey, Philadelphia Flyers, May 1, 1980, at Philadelphia vs. Minnesota North Stars. 1 goal, 4 assists. Flyers won 7-0.
— Denis Potvin, New York Islanders, April 17, 1981, at New York vs. Edmonton Oilers. 3 goals, 2 assists. Islanders won 6-3.

MOST GOALS, ONE GAME:
5 — **Maurice Richard, Montreal Canadiens,** March 23, 1944, at Montreal. Final score: Canadiens 5, Toronto 1.
— **Darryl Sittler, Toronto Maple Leafs,** April 22, 1976, at Toronto. Final score: Toronto 8, Philadelphia 5.
— **Reggie Leach, Philadelphia Flyers,** May 6, 1976, at Philadelphia. Final score: Philadelphia 6, Boston 3.
— **Mario Lemieux, Pittsburgh Penguins,** April 25, 1989 at Pittsburgh. Final score: Pittsburgh 10, Philadelphia 7.

MOST GOALS BY A DEFENSEMAN, ONE GAME:
3 — **Bobby Orr, Boston Bruins,** April 11, 1971 at Montreal. Final score: Boston 5, Montreal 2.
— **Dick Redmond, Chicago Black Hawks,** April 4, 1973 at Chicago. Final score: Chicago 7, St. Louis 1.
— **Denis Potvin, NY Islanders,** April 17, 1981 at Long Island. Final score: NY Islanders 6, Edmonton 3.
— **Paul Reinhart, Calgary Flames,** April 14, 1983 at Edmonton. Final score: Edmonton 6, Calgary 3.
— **Paul Reinhart, Calgary,** April 8, 1984 at Vancouver. Final score: Calgary 5, Vancouver 1.
— **Doug Halward, Vancouver Canucks,** April 7, 1984 at Vancouver. Final score: Vancouver 7, Calgary 0.

Defenseman Bob Dailey had a five-point night in the playoffs with one goal and four assists on May 1, 1980.

MOST POWER-PLAY GOALS, ONE GAME:

3 — **Syd Howe, Detroit Red Wings,** March 23, 1939, at Detroit vs. Montreal Canadiens. Detroit won 7-3.
— **Sid Smith, Toronto Maple Leafs,** April 10, 1949, at Toronto vs. Detroit Red Wings. Toronto won 3-1.
— **Phil Esposito, Boston Bruins,** April 2, 1969, at Boston vs. Toronto Maple Leafs. Boston won 10-0.
— **John Bucyk, Boston Bruins,** April 21, 1974, at Boston vs. Chicago Black Hawks. Boston won 8-6.
— **Denis Potvin, New York Islanders,** April 17, 1981, at New York vs. Edmonton Oilers. Islanders won 6-3.
— **Tim Kerr, Philadelphia Flyers,** April 13, 1985, at New York vs. Rangers. Philadelphia won 6-5.
— **Jari Kurri, Edmonton Oilers,** April 9, 1987, at Edmonton vs. Los Angeles Kings. Edmonton Won 13-3.
— **Mark Johnson, New Jersey Devils,** April 22, 1988, at New Jersey vs. Washington. New Jersey won 10-4.

MOST SHORTHAND GOALS, ONE GAME:

2 — **Dave Keon, Toronto Maple Leafs,** April 18, 1963, at Toronto, in 3-1 win vs. Detroit.
— **Bryan Trottier, New York Islanders,** April 8, 1980 at Long Island, in 8-1 win vs. Los Angeles.
— **Bobby Lalonde, Boston Bruins,** April 11, 1981 at Minnesota. Final score: Minnesota 6, Boston 3.
— **Wayne Gretzky, Edmonton Oilers,** April 6, 1983 at Edmonton, in 6-3 win vs. Winnipeg.
— **Jari Kurri, Edmonton, Oilers,** April 24, 1983, at Edmonton. Final score: Edmonton 8, Chicago 4.

MOST ASSISTS, ONE GAME:

6 — **Mikko Leinonen, New York Rangers,** April 8, 1982, at New York. Final score: NY Rangers 7, Philadelphia 3.
— **Wayne Gretzky, Edmonton Oilers,** April 9, 1987, at Edmonton. Final score: Edmonton 13, Los Angeles 3.
5 — Toe Blake, Montreal Canadiens, March 23, 1944, at Montreal. Final score: Montreal 5, Toronto 1.
— Maurice Richard, Montreal Canadiens, March 27, 1956, at Montreal. Final score: Montreal, 7, NY Rangers 0.
— Bert Olmstead, Montreal Canadiens, March 30, 1957, at Montreal. Final score: Montreal 8, NY Rangers 3.
— Don McKenney, Boston Bruins, April 5, 1958, at Boston. Final score: Boston 8, NY Rangers 2.
— Stan Mikita, Chicago Black Hawks, April 4, 1973, at Chicago. Final score: Chicago 7, St. Louis 1.
— Wayne Gretzky, Edmonton Oilers, April 8, 1981, at Montreal. Final score: Edmonton 6, Montreal 3.
— Paul Coffey, Edmonton Oilers, May 14, 1985, at Edmonton. Fianl score: Edmonton 10, Chicago 5.
— Doug Gilmour, St. Louis Blues, April 15, 1986, at Minnesota. Final score: St. Louis 6, Minnesota 3.
— Patrik Sundstrom, New Jersey Devils, April 22, 1988, at New Jersey. Final score: New Jersey 10, Washington 4.

MOST PENALTY MINUTES, ONE GAME:

42 — **Dave Schultz, Philadelphia Flyers,** April 22, 1976, at Toronto. One minor, two majors, one 10-minute misconduct and two game-misconducts. Final score: Toronto 8, Philadelphia 5.

MOST PENALTIES, ONE GAME:

8 — **Forbes Kennedy, Toronto Maple Leafs,** April 2, 1969, at Boston. Four minors, two majors, one 10-minute misconduct, one game misconduct. Final score: Boston 10, Toronto 0.
— **Kim Clackson, Pittsburgh Penguins,** April 14, 1980, at Boston. Five minors, two majors, one 10-minute misconduct.

MOST POINTS, ONE PERIOD:

4 — **Maurice Richard, Montreal Canadiens,** March 29, 1945, at Montreal vs. Toronto. Third period, three goals, one assist. Final score: Montreal 10, Toronto 3.
— **Dickie Moore, Montreal Canadiens,** March 25, 1954, at Montreal vs. Boston. First period, two goals, two assists. Final score: Montreal 8, Boston 1.
— **Barry Pederson, Boston Bruins,** April 8, 1982, at Boston vs. Buffalo. Second period, three goals, one assist. Final score: Boston 7, Buffalo 3.
— **Peter McNab, Boston Bruins,** April 11, 1982, at Buffalo. Second period, one goal, three assists. Final score: Boston 5, Buffalo 2.
— **Tim Kerr, Philadelphia Flyers,** April 13, 1985 at New York. Second period, four goals. Final score: Philadelphia 6, Rangers 5.
— **Ken Linseman, Boston Bruins,** April 14, 1985 at Boston vs. Montreal. Second period, two goals, two assists. Final score: Boston 7, Montreal 6.
— **Wayne Gretzky, Edmonton Oilers,** April 12, 1987, at Edmonton vs. Los Angeles. Third period, one goal, three assists. Final score: Edmonton 6, Los Angeles 3.
— **Glenn Anderson, Edmonton Oilers,** April 6, 1988, at Edmonton vs. Winnipeg. Third period, three goals, one assist. Final score: Edmonton 7, Winnipeg 4.
— **Mario Lemieux, Pittsburgh Penguins,** April 25, 1989, at Pittsburgh vs. Philadelphia. First period, four goals. Final score: Pittsburgh 10, Philadelphia 7.

MOST GOALS, ONE PERIOD:

4 — **Tim Kerr, Philadelphia Flyers,** April 13, 1985, at New York vs. Rangers, second period. Final score: Philadelphia 6, Rangers 5.
— **Mario Lemieux, Pittsburgh Penguins,** April 25, 1989, at Pittsburgh vs. Philadelphia, first period. Final score: Pittsburgh 10, Philadelphia 7.
3 — Harvey (Busher) Jackson, Toronto Maple Leafs, April 5, 1932, at New York vs. Rangers, second period. Final score: Toronto 6, Rangers 4.
— Maurice Richard, Montreal Canadiens, March 23, 1944, at Montreal vs. Toronto, second period. Final score: Montreal 5, Toronto 1.
— Maurice Richard, Montreal Canadiens, March 29, 1945, at Montreal vs. Toronto, third period. Final score: Montreal 10, Toronto 3.
— Maurice Richard, Montreal Canadiens, April 6, 1957 at Montreal vs. Boston, second period. Final score: Montreal 5, Boston 1.
— Ted Lindsay, Detroit Red Wings, April 5, 1955, at Detroit vs. Canadiens, second period. Final score: Detroit 7, Montreal 1.
— Red Berenson, St. Louis Blues, April 15, 1969, at St. Louis vs. Los Angeles, second period. Final score: St. Louis 4, Los Angeles 0.
— Jacques Lemaire, Montreal Canadiens, April 20, 1971, at Montreal vs. Minnesota, second period. Final score: Montreal 7, Minnesota 2.
— Rick MacLeish, Philadelphia Flyers, April 11, 1974, at Philadelphia vs. Atlanta, second period. Final score: Philadelphia 5, Atlanta 1.
— Tom Williams, Los Angeles Kings, April 14, 1974, at Los Angeles vs. Chicago, third period. Final score: Los Angeles 5, Chicago 1.
— Darryl Sittler, Toronto Maple Leafs, April 22, 1976, at Toronto vs. Philadelphia, second period. Final score: Toronto 8, Philadelphia 5.
— Reggie Leach, Philadelphia Flyers, May 6, 1976, at Philadelphia vs. Boston, second period. Final score: Philadelphia 6, Boston 3.
— Bobby Schmautz, Boston Bruins, April 11, 1977, at Boston vs. Los Angeles, first period. Final score: Boston 8, Los Angeles 3.
— George Ferguson, Toronto Maple Leafs, April 11, 1978, at Toronto vs. Los Angeles, third period. Final score: Toronto 7, Los Angeles 3.
— Barry Pederson, Boston Bruins, April 8, 1982, at Boston vs. Buffalo, second period. Final score: Boston 7, Buffalo 3.
— Peter Stastny, Quebec Nordiques, April 5, 1983, at Boston, first period. Final score: Boston 4, Quebec 3.
— Wayne Gretzky, Edmonton Oilers, April 6, 1983 at Edmonton, second period. Final score: Edmonton 6, Winnipeg 3.
— Mike Bossy, NY Islanders, May 7, 1983 at Long Island, second period. Final score: NY Islanders 8, Boston 4.
— Dave Andreychuk, Buffalo Sabres, April 14, 1985, at Buffalo vs. Quebec, third period. Final score: Buffalo 7, Quebec 4.
— Wayne Gretzky, Edmonton Oilers, May 25, 1985, at Edmonton vs. Philadelphia, first period. Final score: Edmonton 4, Philadelphia 3.
— Glenn Anderson, Edmonton Oilers, April 6, 1988, at Edmonton vs. Winnipeg, third period. Final score: Edmonton 7, Winnipeg 4.
— Tim Kerr, Philadelphia Flyers, April 19, 1989, at Pittsburgh vs. Penguins, first period. Final score: Philadelphia 4, Pittsburgh 2.

MOST POWER PLAY GOALS, ONE PERIOD:

3 — **Tim Kerr, Philadelphia Flyers,** April 13, 1985 at New York, second period in 6-5 win vs. Rangers.
2 — Charlie Conacher, Toronto Maple Leafs, March 26, 1936, second period at Toronto in 8-3 win vs. Boston.
— Syd Howe, Detroit Red Wings, March 23, 1939, third period at Detroit in 7-3 win vs. Montreal Canadiens.
— Mac Colville, New York Rangers, March 22, 1942, third period at New York in 4-2 win by Toronto Maple Leafs.
— Sid Smith, Toronto Maple Leafs, April 10, 1949, first period at Toronto in 3-1 win vs. Detroit Red Wings.
— Maurice Richard, Montreal Canadiens, April 6, 1954, first period at Detroit in 3-1 win by Montreal.
— Bernie Geoffrion, Montreal Canadiens, April 7, 1955, first period at Montreal in 4-2 win vs. Detroit Red Wings.
— Don McKenney, Boston Bruins, March 29, 1958, first period at Boston in 5-0 win vs. New York Rangers.
— Floyd Smith, Detroit Red Wings, April 10, 1966, first period at Chicago in 7-0 win by Detroit.
— Gilles Tremblay, Montreal Canadiens, April 14, 1966, second period at Toronto in 4-1 win by Montreal.
— Rosaire Paiement, Philadelphia Flyers, April 13, 1968, third period at Philadelphia in 6-1 win vs. St. Louis Blues.
— Jean Béliveau, Montreal Canadiens, April 20, 1968, second period at Montreal in 4-1 win vs. Chicago Black Hawks.
— Phil Esposito, Boston Bruins, April 2, 1969, second period at Boston in 10-0 win vs. Toronto Maple Leafs.
— John Bucyk, Boston Bruins, April 23, 1970, second period at Boston in 5-2 win vs. Chicago Black Hawks.
— Bobby Hull, Chicago Black Hawks, April 10, 1971, third period at Philadelphia in 3-2 Chicago win.
— John McKenzie, Boston Bruins, April 23, 1972, second period at St. Louis during 7-2 Boston win.
— Brad Park, New York Rangers, May 4, 1972, first period at New York in 5-2 win vs. Boston Bruins.
— Pit Martin, Chicago Black Hawks, April 4, 1973, third period at Chicago in 7-1 win vs. St. Louis Blues.
— John Bucyk, Boston Bruins, April 21, 1974, first period at Boston in 8-6 win vs. Chicago Black Hawks.
— Rick MacLeish, Philadelphia Flyers, May 13, 1975, first period at Philadelphia in 4-1 win vs. New York Islanders.
— Denis Potvin, New York Islanders, April 17, 1981, at New York in 6-3 win vs. Edmonton Oilers.
— Mike Bossy, New York Islanders, May 5, 1981, first period at New York Rangers in 5-2 Islander win.
— Marcel Dionne, Los Angeles Kings, April 7, 1982, second period at Edmonton in 10-8 win.
— Denis Savard, Chicago Black Hawks, April 19, 1982, first period at Chicago in 7-4 win vs. St. Louis Blues.
— Larry Murphy, Washington Capitals, April 10, 1985, second period at Washington vs. New York Islanders in 4-3 Capitals win.

— Denis Savard, Chicago Blackhawks, April 10, 1986 at Chicago, first period in 6-4 Toronto win.
— Dan Quinn, Calgary Flames, May 12, 1986 at St. Louis, second period in 6-5 St. Louis win.
— Jari Kurri, Edmonton Oilers, April 9, 1987, at Edmonton in 13-3 win vs. Los Angeles.
— Mark Johnson, New Jersey Devils, April 22, 1988, at New Jersey in 10-4 win vs. Washington.
— Brian Propp, Philadelphia Flyers, April 6, 1989, at Washington, third period in 3-2 Philadelphia win.
— Tim Kerr, Philadelphia Flyers, April 19, 1989, at Pittsburgh, first period in 4-2 Philadelphia win.
— Tim Kerr, Philadelphia Flyers, April 23, 1989 at Philadelphia, second period in 4-1 Philadelphia win vs. Pittsburgh.
— Mario Lemieux, Pittsburgh Penguins, April 25, 1989, at Pittsburgh, first period in 10-7 Pittsburgh win vs. Philadelphia.

MOST SHORTHAND GOALS, ONE PERIOD:
2 — **Bryan Trottier, New York Islanders,** April 8, 1980, second period at New York in 8-1 win vs. Los Angeles Kings.
— **Bobby Lalonde, Boston Bruins,** April 11, 1981, third period at Minnesota in 6-3 win by North Stars.
— **Jari Kurri, Edmonton Oilers,** April 24, 1983, third period at Edmonton in 8-4 win vs. Chicago Black Hawks.

Bob Gainey's goal seven seconds into a 1977 playoff game vs. the Islanders ranks as the second-fastest in playoff history.

FASTEST GOAL FROM START OF GAME:
6 Seconds — **Don Kozak, Los Angeles Kings,** April 17, 1977, at Los Angeles vs. Boston and goaltender Gerry Cheevers during 7-4 Los Angeles victory.
7 Seconds — Bob Gainey, Montreal Canadiens, May 5, 1977, at New York vs. Islanders and goaltender Glenn Resch. Montreal won game 2-1.
— Terry Murray, Philadelphia Flyers, April 12, 1981, at Quebec vs. goaltender Dan Bouchard. Quebec won game 4-3 in overtime.
8 Seconds — Stan Smyl, Vancouver Canucks, April 7, 1982, at Vancouver vs. Calgary and goaltender Pat Riggin. Vancouver won game 5-3.

FASTEST GOAL FROM START OF PERIOD (OTHER THAN FIRST):
6 Seconds — **Pelle Eklund, Philadelphia Flyers,** April 25, 1989, at Pittsburgh vs. goaltender Tom Barrasso, second period. Pittsburgh won game 10-7.
9 Seconds — Bill Collins, Minnesota North Stars, April 9, 1968, at Minnesota vs. Los Angeles and goaltender Wayne Rutledge, third period. Minnesota won game 7-5.
— Dave Balon, Minnesota North Stars, April 25, 1968, at St. Louis vs. goaltender Glenn Hall, third period. Minnesota won game 5-1.
— Murray Oliver, Minnesota North Stars, April 8, 1971, at St. Louis vs. goaltender Ernie Wakely, third period. St. Louis won game 4-2.
— Clark Gillies, New York Islanders, April 15, 1977, at Buffalo vs. goaltender Don Edwards, third period. Islanders won game 4-3.
— Eric Vail, Atlanta Flames, April 11, 1978, at Atlanta vs. Detroit and goaltender Ron Low, third period. Detroit won game 5-3.
— Stan Smyl, Vancouver Canucks, April 10, 1979, at Philadelphia vs. goaltender Wayne Stephenson, third period. Vancouver won game 3-2.
— Wayne Gretzky, Edmonton Oilers, April 6, 1983, at Edmonton vs. goaltender Brian Hayward, second period. Edmonton won game 6-3.
— Mark Messier, Edmonton Oilers, April 16, 1984, at Calgary vs. goaltender Don Edwards, third period. Edmonton won game 5-3.
— Brian Skrudland, Montreal Canadiens, May 18, 1986 at Calgary vs. Calgary and goaltender Mike Vernon, overtime. Montreal won game 3-2.

FASTEST TWO GOALS FROM START OF GAME:
1 Minute, 8 Seconds — **Dick Duff, Toronto Maple Leafs,** April 9, 1963, at Toronto vs. Detroit and goaltender Terry Sawchuk. Duff scored at 49 seconds and 1:08. Final score: Toronto 4, Detroit 2.

FASTEST TWO GOALS FROM START OF PERIOD:
35 Seconds — **Pat LaFontaine, NY Islanders,** May 19, 1984 at Edmonton vs. goaltender Andy Moog. LaFontaine scored at 13 and 35 seconds of third period. Final score: Edmonton 5, NY Islanders 2.

MOST ASSISTS, ONE PERIOD:
3 — **Nick Metz, Toronto Maple Leafs,** March 25, 1941, at Toronto vs. Boston, second period. Final score: Toronto 7, Boston 2.
— **Toe Blake, Montreal Canadiens,** March 23, 1944, at Montreal vs. Toronto, second period. Final score: Montreal 5, Toronto 1.
— **Toe Blake, Montreal Canadiens,** April 13, 1944, at Montreal vs. Chicago, third period. Final score: Montreal 5, Chicago 4.
— **Elmer Lach, Montreal Canadiens,** March 30, 1944, at Montreal vs. Toronto, third period. Final score: Montreal 11, Toronto 0.
— **Bobby Bauer, Boston Bruins,** March 24, 1946, at Boston vs. Detroit, third period. Final score: Boston 5, Detroit 2.
— **Jean Béliveau, Montreal Canadiens,** March 25, 1954, at Montreal vs. Boston, first period. Final score: Montreal 8, Boston 1.
— **Jean Béliveau, Montreal Canadiens,** April 27, 1971, at Montreal vs. Minnesota, third period. Final score: Montreal 6, Minnesota 1.
— **Maurice Richard, Montreal Canadiens,** March 27, 1956, at Montreal vs. Rangers, second period. Final score: Montreal 7, Rangers 0.
— **Doug Harvey, Montreal Canadiens,** April 6, 1957, at Montreal vs. Boston, second period. Final score: Canadiens 5, Boston 1.
— **Doug Harvey, Montreal Canadiens,** April 2, 1959, at Montreal vs. Chicago, first period. Final score: Montreal 4, Chicago 2.
— **Don McKenney, Boston Bruins,** April 5, 1958, at Boston vs. Rangers, third period. Final score: Boston 8, Rangers 2.
— **Dickie Moore, Montreal Canadiens,** April 2, 1959, at Montreal vs. Chicago, first period. Final score: Montreal 4, Chicago 2.
— **Henri Richard, Montreal Canadiens,** April 7, 1960, at Montreal vs. Toronto, first period. Final score: Montreal 4, Toronto 2.
— **Bobby Rousseau, Montreal Canadiens,** May 1, 1965, at Montreal vs. Chicago, first period. Final score: Montreal 4, Chicago 0.
— **Alex Delvecchio, Detroit Red Wings,** April 14, 1966, at Detroit vs. Chicago, third period. Final score: Detroit 5, Chicago 1.
— **Ab McDonald, St. Louis Blues,** April 21, 1970, at St. Louis, vs. Pittsburgh, first period. Final score: St. Louis 4, Pittsburgh 1.
— **Bobby Orr, Boston Bruins,** April 8, 1971, at Boston vs. Montreal, second period. Final score: Montreal 7, Boston 5.
— **Bobby Orr, Boston Bruins,** April 9, 1972, at Toronto, third period. Final score: Boston 5, Toronto 4.
— **Danny Grant, Minnesota North Stars,** April 22, 1971, at Montreal, first period. Final score: Minnesota 6, Montreal 3.
— **Jean Ratelle, New York Rangers,** April 22, 1971, at New York vs. Chicago, first period. Final score: New York 4, Chicago 1.
— **Barry Ashbee, Philadelphia Flyers,** April 5, 1973, at Philadelphia vs. Minnesota, second period. Final score: Philadelphia 4, Minnesota 1.
— **Pat Stapleton, Chicago Black Hawks,** April 29, 1973, at Montreal, first period. Final score: Montreal 8, Chicago 3.
— **Jean-Paul Parise, New York Islanders,** April 17, 1975, at New York vs. Pittsburgh, third period. Final score: Pittsburgh 6, NY Islanders 4.
— **Wayne Gretzky, Edmonton Oilers,** April 8, 1981, at Montreal, first period. Final score: Edmonton 6, Montreal 3.
— **Wayne Gretzky, Edmonton Oilers,** April 24, 1983, at Edmonton, third period. Final score: Chicago 4, Edmonton 8.
— **Peter McNab, Boston Bruins,** April 11, 1982, at Buffalo, second period. Final score: Boston 5, Buffalo 2.
— **Mikko Leinonen, New York Rangers,** April 8, 1982, at New York, second period. Final score: Rangers 7, Philadelphia 3.
— **Joe Mullen, St. Louis Blues,** April 11, 1982, at St. Louis, first period. Final score: St. Louis 8, Winnipeg 2.
— **Bob Bourne, New York Islanders,** April 14, 1983 at Long Island, third period. Final score: NY Islanders 4, NY Rangers 1.
— **Rick Middleton, Boston Bruins,** April 18, 1983 at Buffalo, third period. Final score: Boston 6, Buffalo 2.
— **Raymond Bourque, Boston Bruins,** April 20, 1983 at Boston, first period. Final score: Boston 9, Buffalo 0.
— **Steve Payne, Minnesota North Stars,** April 26, 1984 at Edmonton, second period. Final score: Edmonton 4, Minnesota 3.
— **Peter Zezel, Philadelphia Flyers,** April 13, 1985 at New York, second period. Final score: Philadelphia 6, Rangers 5.
— **Raymond Bourque, Boston Bruins,** April 14, 1985 at Boston, second period. Final score: Boston 7, Montreal 6.
— **Tim Kerr, Philadelphia Flyers,** April 21, 1985 at Philadelphia, first period. Final score: Philadelphia 5, New York Islanders 2.
— **Wayne Gretzky, Edmonton Oilers,** April 25, 1985 at Winnipeg, second period. Final score: Edmonton 8, Winnipeg 3.
— **Randy Gregg, Edmonton Oilers,** May 4, 1985 at Edmonton, third period. Final score: Edmonton 11, Chicago 2.
— **Paul Coffey, Edmonton Oilers,** May 4, 1985 at Edmonton, second period. Final score: Edmonton 11 Chicago 2.
— **Wayne Gretzky, Edmonton Oilers,** April 9, 1987 at Edmonton, first period. Final score: Edmonton 13, Los Angeles 3.
— **Wayne Gretzky, Edmonton Oilers,** April 12, 1987, at Edmonton, third period. Final score: Edmonton 6, Los Angeles 3.
— **Glenn Anderson, Edmonton Oilers,** May 13, 1987, at Edmonton, third period. Final score: Edmonton 6, Detroit 3.
— **Mark Messier, Edmonton Oilers,** April 6, 1988, at Edmonton. Final score: Edmonton 7, Winnipeg 4.
— **Ray Bourque, Boston Bruins,** May 6, 1988, at New Jersey, second period. Final score: Boston 6, New Jersey 1.
— **Mario Lemieux, Pittsburgh Penguins,** April 25, 1989 at Pittsburgh, second period. Final score: Pittsburgh 10, Philadelphia 7.

MOST PENALTIES, ONE PERIOD AND MOST PENALTY MINUTES, ONE PERIOD:
6 Penalties; 39 Minutes — **Ed Hospodar, NY Rangers,** April 9, 1981 at Los Angeles, first period. Two minors, one major, one 10-minute misconduct, two game misconducts. Final score: Los Angeles 5, NY Rangers 4.

FASTEST TWO GOALS:
5 Seconds — **Norm Ullman, Detroit Red Wings,** at Detroit, April 11, 1965, vs. Chicago and goaltender Glenn Hall. Ullman scored at 17:35 and 17:40 of second period. Detroit won game 4-2.

Jari Kurri holds down second spot on the all-time playoff point list with 177 points in 124 games.

All-Time Playoff Goal Leaders since 1918

(40 or more goals)

Player	Teams	Yrs.	GP	G
*Wayne Gretzky	Edm., L.A.	10	131	86
Mike Bossy	NY Islanders	10	129	85
*Jari Kurri	Edmonton	9	121	82
Maurice Richard	Montreal	15	133	82
Jean Beliveau	Montreal	17	162	79
Goldie Howe	Det., Hfd.	20	157	68
*Mark Messier	Edmonton	10	126	67
*Glenn Anderson	Edmonton	9	124	65
Yvan Cournoyer	Montreal	12	147	64
*Bryan Trottier	NY Islanders	13	171	63
Bobby Hull	Chi., Hfd.	14	119	62
Phil Esposito	Chi., Bos., NYR	15	130	61
Stan Mikita	Chicago	18	155	59
*Guy Lafleur	Mtl., NYR	14	128	58
Bernie Geoffrion	Mtl., NYR	16	131	58
Denis Potvin	NY Islanders	14	185	56
Rick MacLeish	Phi., Pit., Det.	11	114	54
*Bobby Smith	Min., Mtl.	10	143	54
Bill Barber	Philadelphia	11	129	53
*Brian Propp	Philidelphia	11	116	52
Frank Mahovlich	Tor., Det., Mtl.	14	137	51
Steve Shutt	Mtl., LA.	10	96	50
Henri Richard	Montreal	18	180	49
Reggie Leach	Philadelphia	8	96	47
Ted Lindsay	Det., Chi.	16	133	47
Clark Gillies	NYI, Buf.	13	164	47
*Denis Savard	Chicago	9	79	46
Dickie Moore	Mtl., Tor., St. L.	14	135	46
**Rick Middleton	NYR, Bos.	12	114	45
*Lanny McDonald	Tor., Cgy.	13	117	44
*Ken Linseman	Phi., Edm., Bos.	10	111	43
Bobby Clarke	Philadelphia	13	136	42
*Joe Mullen	St.L., Cgy.	7	75	41
John Bucyk	Det., Bos.	14	124	41
Peter McNab	Bos., Van.	10	107	40
*Bob Bourne	NYI, L.A.	13	139	40

* — Active player.

All-Time Playoff Assist Leaders since 1918

(60 or more assists)

Player	Teams	Yrs.	GP	A
*Wayne Gretzky	Edm. L.A.	10	131	188
*Larry Robinson	Montreal	16	203	109
Denis Potvin	NY Islanders	14	185	108
*Bryan Trottier	NY Islanders	13	171	106
*Mark Messier	Edmonton	10	126	102
Jean Beliveau	Montreal	17	162	97
*Jari Kurri	Edmonton	9	124	95
Gordie Howe	Det., Hfd.	20	157	92
Stan Mikita	Chicago	18	155	91
Brad Park	NYR, Bos., Det.	16	159	90
*Glenn Anderson	Edmonton	9	124	83
*Paul Coffey	Edm., Pits.	8	105	80
*Bobby Smith	Min., Mtl.	10	143	80
Henri Richard	Montreal	18	180	80
Jacques Lemaire	Montreal	11	145	78
Bobby Clarke	Philadelphia	13	136	77
*Ken Linseman	Phi., Edm., Bos.	10	111	76
*Guy Lafleur	Mtl., NYR	14	128	76
Phil Esposito	Chi., Bos., NYR	15	130	76
Mike Bossy	NY Islanders	10	129	75
Gilbert Perreault	Buffalo	11	85	70
Alex Delvecchio	Detroit	14	121	69
*John Tonelli	NYI, Cgy., L.A.	11	150	69
Bobby Hull	Chi., Hfd.	14	119	67
Frank Mahovlich	Tor., Det., Mtl.	14	137	67
Bobby Orr	Boston	8	74	66
*Bernie Federko	St. Louis	11	91	66
Jean Ratelle	NYR, Bos.	14	120	66
Dickie Moore	Mtl., Tor., St. L.	14	135	64
Doug Harvey	Mtl., NYR, St. L.	15	137	64
Yvan Cournoyer	Montreal	12	147	63
John Bucyk	Det., Bos.	14	124	62

* — Active player.

All-Time Playoff Point Leaders since 1918

(100 or more points)

Player	Teams	Yrs.	GP	G	A	Pts.
*Wayne Gretzky	Edm., L.A.	10	131	86	188	274
*Jari Kurri	Edmonton	9	124	82	95	177
Jean Beliveau	Montreal	17	162	79	97	176
*Mark Messier	Edmonton	10	126	67	102	169
*Bryan Trottier	NY Islanders	13	171	63	106	169
Denis Potvin	NY Islanders	14	185	56	108	164
Mike Bossy	NY Islanders	10	129	85	75	160
Gordie Howe	Det., Hfd.	20	157	68	92	160
Stan Mikita	Chicago	18	155	59	91	150
*Glenn Anderson	Edmonton	9	124	65	83	148
Jacques Lemaire	Montreal	11	145	61	78	139
Phil Esposito	Chi., Bos., NYR	15	130	61	76	137
*Guy Lafleur	Mtl, NYR	14	128	58	76	134
*Larry Robinson	Montreal	16	203	25	109	134
*Bobby Smith	Min., Mtl.	10	143	54	80	134
Bobby Hull	Chi., Hfd.	14	119	62	67	129
Henri Richard	Montreal	18	180	49	80	129
Yvan Cornoyer	Montreal	12	147	64	63	127
Maurice Richard	Montreal	15	133	82	44	126
Brad Park	NYR, Bos., Det.	17	162	35	90	125
*Ken Linseman	Phi., Edm., Bos.	10	111	43	76	119
Bobby Clarke	Philadelphia	13	136	42	77	119
*Paul Coffey	Edm., Pit.	8	105	38	80	118
Frank Mahovlich	Tor., Det., Mtl.	14	137	51	67	118
Bernie Geoffrion	Mtl., NYR	16	131	58	59	117
*Brian Propp	Philadelphia	11	116	52	60	112
Dickie Moore	Mtl., Tor., St. L.	14	135	46	64	106
Bill Barber	Philadelphia	11	129	53	55	108
Rick MacLeish	Phi., Pit., Det.	11	114	54	53	107
*John Tonelli	NYI, Cgy., L.A.	11	150	37	69	106
Alex Delveccio	Detroit	14	121	35	69	104
John Bucyk	Det., Bos.	14	124	41	62	103
Gilbert Perreault	Buffalo	14	90	33	70	103

* — Active player.

Three-or-more-Goal Games, Playoffs 1927 – 1989

Player	Team	Date	City	Total Goals	Opposing Goaltender	Score	
Maurice Richard (7)	Mtl.	Mar. 23/44	Mtl.	5	Paul Bibeault	Mtl. 5	Tor. 1
		Apr. 7/44	Chi.	3	Mike Karakas	Mtl. 3	Chi. 1
		Mar. 29/45	Mtl.	4	Frank McCool	Mtl. 10	Tor. 3
		Apr. 14/53	Bos.	3	Gord Henry	Mtl. 7	Bos. 3
		Mar. 20/56	Mtl.	3	Lorne Worsley	Mtl. 7	NYR 1
		Apr. 6/57	Mtl.	4	Don Simmons	Mtl. 5	Bos. 1
		Apr. 1/58	Det.	3	Terry Sawchuk	Mtl. 4	Det. 3
Wayne Gretzky (7)	Edm.	Apr. 11/81	Edm.	3	Richard Sevigny	Edm. 6	Mtl. 2
		Apr. 19/81	Edm.	3	Billy Smith	Edm. 5	NYI 2
		Apr. 6/83	Edm.	4	Brian Hayward	Edm. 6	Wpg. 3
		Apr. 17/83	Cgy.	4	Rejean Lemelin	Edm. 10	Cgy. 2
		Apr. 25/85	Wpg.	3	Bryan Hayward (2) Marc Behrend (1)	Edm. 8	Wpg. 3
		May 25/85	Edm.	3	Pelle Lindbergh	Edm. 4	Phi. 3
		Apr. 24/86	Cgy.	3	Mike Vernon	Edm. 7	Cgy. 4
Jari Kurri (6)	Edm.	Apr. 4/84	Edm.	3	Doug Soetaert (1) Mike Veisor (2)	Edm. 9	Wpg. 2
		Apr. 25/85	Wpg.	3	Bryan Hayward (1) Marc Behrend (1)	Edm. 8	Wpg. 3
		May 7/85	Edm.	3	Murray Bannerman	Edm. 7	Chi. 3
		May 14/85	Edm.	3	Murray Bannerman	Edm. 10	Chi. 5
		May 16/85	Chi.	4	Murray Bannerman	Edm. 8	Chi. 2
		Apr. 9/87	Edm.	4	Roland Melanson (2) Daren Eliot (2)	Edm. 13	L.A. 3
Mike Bossy (5)	NYI	Apr. 16/79	NYI	3	Tony Esposito	NYI 6	Chi. 2
		May 8/82	NYI	3	Richard Brodeur	NYI 6	Van. 5
		Apr. 10/83	Wsh.	3	Al Jensen	NYI 6	Wsh. 2
		May 3/83	NYI	3	Pete Peeters	NYI 8	Bos. 3
		May 7/83	NYI	3	Pete Peeters	NYI 8	Bos. 3
Phil Esposito (4)	Bos.	Apr. 2/69	Bos.	4	Bruce Gamble	Bos. 10	Tor. 0
		Apr. 8/70	Bos.	3	Ed Giacomin	Bos. 8	NYR 2
		Apr. 19/70	Chi.	3	Tony Esposito	Bos. 6	Chi. 3
		Apr. 8/75	Bos.	3	Tony Esposito (2) Michel Dumas (1)	Bos. 8	Chi. 2
Bernie Geoffrion (3)	Mtl.	Mar. 27/52	Mtl.	3	Jim Henry	Mtl. 4	Bos. 0
		Apr. 7/55	Mtl.	3	Terry Sawchuk	Mtl. 4	Det. 2
		Mar. 30/57	Mtl.	3	Lorne Worsley	Mtl. 8	NYR 3
Norm Ullman (3)	Det.	Mar. 29/64	Chi.	3	Glenn Hall	Det. 5	Chi. 4
		Apr. 7/64	Det.	3	Glenn Hall (2) Denis DeJordy (1)	Det. 7	Chi. 2
		Apr. 11/65	Det.	3	Glenn Hall	Det. 4	Chi. 2
John Bucyk (3)	Bos.	May 3/70	St. L.	3	Jacques Plante (1) Ernie Wakely (2)	Bos. 6	St.L. 1
		Apr. 20/72	Bos.	3	Jacques Caron (1) Ernie Wakely (2)	Bos. 10	St.L. 2
		Apr. 21/74	Bos.	3	Tony Esposito	Bos. 8	Chi. 6
Rick MacLeish (3)	Phil	Apr. 11/74	Phil	3	Phil Myre	Phi. 6	Atl. 1
		Apr. 13/75	Phil	3	Gord McRae	Phi. 6	Tor. 3
		May 13/75	Phil	3	Glenn Resch	Phi. 4	NYI 1
Mark Messier (3)	Edm.	Apr. 14/83	Edm.	4	Rejean Lemelin	Edm. 6	Cgy. 3
		Apr. 17/83	Cgy.	3	Rejean Lemelin (1) Don Edwards (2)	Edm. 10	Cgy. 2
		Apr. 26/83	Edm.	3	Murray Bannerman	Edm. 8	Chi. 2
Denis Savard (3)	Chi.	Apr. 19/82	Chi.	3	Mike Liut	Chi. 7	StL. 4
		Apr. 10/86	Chi.	4	Ken Wregget	Tor. 6	Chi. 4
		Apr. 9/88	Chi.	3	Greg Millen	Chi. 6	St.L. 3
Tim Kerr (3)	Phi.	Apr. 13/85	NYR	4	Glen Hanlon	Phi. 6	NYR 5
		Apr. 20/87	Phi.	3	Kelly Hrudey	Phi. 4	NYI 2
		Apr. 19/89	Pit.	3	Tom Barrasso	Phi. 4	Pit. 2
Ted Kennedy (2)	Tor.	Apr. 14/45	Tor.	3	Harry Lumley	Det. 5	Tor. 3
		Mar. 27/48	Tor.	4	Frank Brimsek	Tor. 5	Bos. 3
Doug Bentley (2)	Chi.	Mar. 28/44	Chi.	3	Connie Dion	Chi. 7	Det. 1
		Mar. 30/44	Det.	3	Connie Dion	Chi. 5	Det. 2
Toe Blake (2)	Mtl.	Mar. 22/38	Mtl.	3	Mike Karakas	Mtl. 6	Chi. 4
		Mar. 26/46	Chi.	3	Mike Karakas	Mtl. 7	Chi. 2
Dino Ciccarelli (2)	Min.	May 5/81	Min.	3	Pat Riggin	Min. 7	Cgy. 4
		Apr. 10/82	Min.	3	Murray Bannerman	Min. 7	Chi. 1
Bobby Hull (2)	Chi.	Apr. 7/63	Det.	3	Terry Sawchuk	Det. 7	Chi. 4
		Apr. 9/72	Pitt	3	Jim Rutherford	Chi. 6	Pit. 5
F. St. Marseille (2)	St. L.	Apr. 28/70	St.L	3	Al Smith	St.L. 5	Pit. 0
		Apr. 6/72	Min.	3	Cesare Maniago	Min. 6	St.L. 1
Pit Martin (2)	Chi.	Apr. 4/73	Chi.	3	W. Stephenson	Chi. 7	St.L. 1
		May 10/73	Chi.	3	Ken Dryden	Mtl. 6	Chi. 4
Yvan Cournoyer (2)	Mtl.	Apr. 5/73	Mtl.	3	Dave Dryden	Mtl. 7	Buf. 3
		Apr. 11/74	Mtl.	3	Ed Giacomin	Mtl. 4	NYR 1
Lanny McDonald (2)	Tor.	Apr. 9/77	Pitt	3	Denis Herron	Tor. 5	Pit. 2
		Apr. 17/77	Tor.	4	W. Stephenson	Phi. 6	Tor. 5
Guy Lafleur (2)	Mtl.	May 1/75	Mtl.	3	Roger Crozier (1) Gerry Desjardins (2)	Mtl. 7	Buf. 0
		Apr. 11/77	Mtl.	3	Ed Staniowski	Mtl. 7	St.L. 2
Butch Goring (2)	L.A.	Apr. 9/77	L.A.	3	Phil Myre	L.A. 4	Atl. 2
	NYI	May 17/81	Min.	3	Gilles Meloche	NYI 7	Min. 5
Bryan Trottier (2)	NYI	Apr. 8/80	NYI	3	Doug Keans	NYI 8	L.A. 1
		Apr. 9/81	NYI	3	Michel Larocque	NYI 5	Tor. 1
Bill Barber (2)	Phil	May 4/80	Min.	4	Gilles Meloche	Phi. 5	Min. 3
		Apr. 22/81	Phi.	3	Dan Bouchard	Phi. 8	Que. 5
Paul Reinhart (2)	Cgy	Apr. 14/83	Edm.	3	Andy Moog	Edm. 6	Cgy. 3
		Apr. 8/84	Van	3	Richard Brodeur	Cgy. 5	Van. 1
Brian Propp (2)	Phi.	Apr. 22/81	Phi.	3	Pat Riggin	Phi. 9	Cgy. 4
		Apr. 21/85	Phi.	3	Billy Smith	Phi. 5	NYI 2

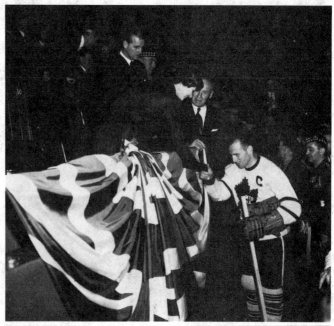

Ted Kennedy (here meeting Her Royal Highness, Princess Elizabeth) scored two hat-tricks in his playoff career.

Player	Team	Date	City	Total Goals	Opposing Goaltender	Score	
Peter Stastny (2)	Que.	Apr. 5/83	Bos.	3	Pete Peeters	Bos. 4	Que. 3
		Apr. 11/87	Que.	3	Mike Liut (2) Steve Weeks (1)	Que. 5	Hfd. 1
Michel Goulet (2)	Que.	Apr. 23/85	Que.	3	Steve Penney	Que. 7	Mtl. 6
		Apr. 12/87	Que.	3	Mike Liut	Que. 4	Hfd. 1
Glenn Anderson (2)	Edm.	Apr. 26/83	Edm.	4	Murray Bannerman	Edm. 8	Chi. 2
		Apr. 6/88	Wpg.	3	Daniel Berthiaume	Edm. 7	Wpg. 4
Petr Klima (2)	Det.	Apr. 7/88	Tor.	3	Alan Bester (2) Ken Wregett (1)	Det. 6	Tor. 2
		Apr. 21/88	St.L.	3	Greg Millen	Det. 6	St.L. 0
Perk Galbraith	Bos.	Mar. 31/27	Bos.	3	Hugh Lehman	Bos. 4	Chi. 4
Busher Jackson	Tor.	Apr. 5/32	NYR	3	John Ross Roach	Tor. 6	NYR 4
Frank Boucher	NYR	Apr. 9/32	Tor.	3	Lorne Chabot	Tor. 6	NYR 4
Charlie Conacher	Tor.	Mar. 26/36	Tor.	3	Tiny Thompson	Tor. 8	Bos. 3
Syd Howe	Det.	Mar. 23/39	Det.	3	Claude Bourque	Det. 7	Mtl. 3
Bryan Hextall	NYR	Apr. 3/40	NYR	3	Turk Broda	NYR 6	Tor. 2
Joe Benoit	Mtl.	Mar. 22/41	Mtl.	3	Sam LoPresti	Mtl. 4	Chi. 3
Syl Apps	Tor.	Mar. 25/41	Tor.	3	Frank Brimsek	Tor. 7	Bos. 2
Jack McGill	Bos.	Mar. 29/42	Bos.	3	Johnny Mowers	Det. 6	Bos. 4
Don Metz	Tor.	Apr. 14/42	Tor.	3	Johnny Mowers	Tor. 9	Det. 3
Mud Bruneteau	Det.	Apr. 1/43	Det.	3	Frank Brimsek	Det. 6	Bos. 2
Don Grosso	Det.	Apr. 7/43	Bos.	3	Frank Brimsek	Det. 4	Bos. 0
Carl Liscombe	Det.	Apr. 3/45	Bos.	4	Paul Bibeault	Det. 5	Bos. 3
Billy Reay	Mtl.	Apr. 1/47	Bos.	3	Frank Brimsek	Mtl. 5	Bos. 1
Gerry Plamondon	Mtl.	Mar. 24/49	Det.	3	Harry Lumley	Mtl. 4	Det. 1
Sid Smith	Tor.	Apr. 10/49	Det.	3	Harry Lumley	Tor. 3	Det. 1
Pentti Lund	NYR	Apr. 2/50	NYR	3	Bill Durnan	NYR 4	Mtl. 1
Ted Lindsay	Det.	Apr. 5/55	Det.	4	Charlie Hodge (1) Jacques Plante (3)	Det. 7	Mtl. 1
Gordie Howe	Det.	Apr. 10/55	Det.	3	Jacques Plante	Det. 5	Mtl. 1
Phil Goyette	Mtl.	Mar. 25/58	Mtl.	3	Terry Sawchuk	Mtl. 8	Det. 1
Jerry Toppazzini	Bos.	Apr. 5/58	Bos.	3	Lorne Worsley	Bos. 8	NYR 2
Bob Pulford	Tor.	Apr. 19/62	Tor.	3	Glenn Hall	Tor. 8	Chi. 4
Dave Keon	Tor.	Apr. 9/64	Mtl.	3	Charlie Hodge	Tor. 3	Mtl. 1
Henri Richard	Mtl.	Apr. 20/67	Mtl.	3	Terry Sawchuk (1) Johnny Bower (1)	Mtl. 6	Tor. 2
Rosaire Paiement	Phi.	Apr. 13/68	Phi.	3	Glenn Hall (1) Seth Martin (2)	Phi. 6	St. L. 1
Jean Beliveau	Mtl.	Apr. 20/68	Mtl.	3	Denis DeJordy	Mtl. 4	Chi. 1
Red Berenson	St. L.	Apr. 15/69	St. L.	3	Gerry Desjardins	St. L. 4	L.A. 0
Ken Schinkel	Pit.	Apr. 11/70	Oak.	3	Gary Smith	Pit. 5	Oak. 2
Jim Pappin	Chi.	Apr. 11/71	Chi.	3	Bruce Gamble	Chi. 6	Phi. 2
Bobby Orr	Bos.	Apr. 11/71	Mtl.	3	Ken Dryden	Bos. 5	Mtl. 2
Jacques Lemaire	Mtl.	Apr. 20/71	Mtl.	3	Lorne Worsley	Mtl. 7	Min. 2
Vic Hadfield	NYR	Apr. 22/71	NYR	3	Tony Esposito	NYR 4	Chi. 1
Fred Stanfield	Bos.	Apr. 18/72	Bos.	3	Jacques Caron	Bos. 6	St. L. 1
Ken Hodge	Bos.	Apr. 30/72	Bos.	3	Ed Giacomin	Bos. 6	NYR 5
Steve Vickers	NYR	Apr. 10/73	Bos.	3	Ross Brooks (2) Ed Johnston (1)	NYR 6	Bos. 4
Dick Redmond	Chi.	Apr. 4/73	Chi.	3	Wayne Stephenson	Chi. 7	St. L. 1
Tom Williams	L.A.	Apr. 14/74	L.A.	3	Mike Veisor	L.A. 5	Chi. 1
Marcel Dionne	L.A.	Apr. 15/76	L.A.	3	Gilles Gilbert	L.A. 6	Bos. 4
Don Saleski	Phi.	Apr. 20/76	Phil	3	Wayne Thomas	Phi. 7	Tor. 1
Darryl Sittler	Tor.	Apr. 22/76	Tor.	5	Bernie Parent	Tor. 8	Phi. 5

Fleming Mackell led all playoff scorers in the 1958 playoffs with five goals and 14 assists.

Leading Playoff Scorers, 1927 – 1989

Season	Player and Club	Games Played	Goals	Assists	Points
1988-89	Al MacInnis, Calgary	22	7	24	31
1987-88	Wayne Gretzky, Edmonton	19	12	31	43
1986-87	Wayne Gretzky, Edmonton	21	5	29	34
1985-86	Doug Gilmour, St. Louis	19	9	12	21
	Bernie Federko, St. Louis	19	7	14	21
1984-85	Wayne Gretzky, Edmonton	18	17	30	47
1983-84	Wayne Gretzky, Edmonton	19	13	22	35
1982-83	Wayne Gretzky, Edmonton	16	12	26	38
1981-82	Bryan Trottier, NY Islanders	19	6	23	29
1980-81	Mike Bossy, NY Islanders	18	17	18	35
1979-80	Bryan Trottier, NY Islanders	21	12	17	29
1978-79	Jacques Lemaire, Montreal	16	11	12	23
	Guy Lafleur, Montreal	16	10	13	23
1977-78	Guy Lafleur, Montreal	15	10	11	21
	Larry Robinson, Montreal	15	4	17	21
1976-77	Guy Lafleur, Montreal	14	9	17	26
1975-76	Reggie Leach, Philadelphia	16	19	5	24
1974-75	Rick MacLeish, Philadelphia	17	11	9	20
1973-74	Rick MacLeish, Philadelphia	17	13	9	22
1972-73	Yvan Cournoyer, Montreal	17	15	10	25
1971-72	Phil Esposito, Boston	15	9	15	24
	Bobby Orr, Boston	15	5	19	24
1970-71	Frank Mahovlich, Montreal	20	14	13	27
1969-70	Phil Esposito, Boston	14	13	14	27
1968-69	Phil Esposito, Boston	10	8	10	18
1967-68	Bill Goldsworthy, Minnesota	14	8	7	15
1966-67	Jim Pappin, Toronto	12	7	8	15
1965-66	Norm Ullman, Detroit	12	6	9	15
1964-65	Bobby Hull, Chicago	14	10	7	17
1963-64	Gordie Howe, Detroit	14	9	10	19
1962-63	Gordie Howe, Detroit	11	7	9	16
	Norm Ullman, Detroit	11	4	12	16
1961-62	Stan Mikita, Chicago	12	6	15	21
1960-61	Gordie Howe, Detroit	11	4	11	15
	Pierre Pilote, Chicago	12	3	12	15
1959-60	Henri Richard, Montreal	8	3	9	12
	Bernie Geoffrion, Montreal	8	2	10	12
1958-59	Dickie Moore, Montreal	11	5	12	17
1957-58	Fleming Mackell, Boston	12	5	14	19
1956-57	Bernie Geoffrion, Montreal	11	11	7	18
1955-56	Jean Béliveau, Montreal	10	12	7	19
1954-55	Gordie Howe, Detroit	11	9	11	20
1953-54	Dickie Moore, Montreal	11	5	8	13
1952-53	Ed Sanford, Boston	11	8	3	11
1951-52	Ted Lindsay, Detroit	8	5	2	7
	Floyd Curry, Montreal	11	4	3	7
	Metro Prystai, Detroit	8	2	5	7
	Gordie Howe, Detroit	8	2	5	7
1950-51	Maurice Richard, Montreal	11	9	4	13
	Max Bentley, Toronto	11	2	11	13
1949-50	Pentti Lund, NY Rangers	12	6	5	11
1948-49	Gordie Howe, Detroit	11	8	3	11
1947-48	Ted Kennedy, Toronto	9	8	6	14
1946-47	Maurice Richard, Montreal	10	6	5	11
1945-46	Elmer Lach, Montreal	9	5	12	17
1944-45	Joe Carveth, Detroit	14	5	6	11
1943-44	Toe Blake, Montreal	9	7	11	18
1942-43	Carl Liscombe, Detroit	10	6	8	14
1941-42	Don Grosso, Detroit	12	8	6	14
1940-41	Milt Schmidt, Boston	11	5	6	11
1939-40	Phil Watson, NY Rangers	12	3	6	9
	Neil Colville, NY Rangers	12	2	7	9
1938-39	Bill Cowley, Boston	12	3	11	14
1937-38	Johnny Gottselig, Chicago	10	5	3	8
1936-37	Marty Barry, Detroit	10	4	7	11
1935-36	Buzz Boll, Toronto	9	7	3	10
1934-35	Baldy Northcott, Mtl. Maroons	7	4	1	5
	Harvey Jackson, Toronto	7	3	2	5
	Marvin Wentworth, Mtl. Maroons	7	3	2	5
1933-34	Larry Aurie, Detroit	9	3	7	10
1932-33	Cecil Dillon, NY Rangers	8	8	2	10
1931-32	Frank Boucher, NY Rangers	7	3	6	9
1930-31	Cooney Weiland, Boston	5	6	3	9
1929-30	Marty Barry, Boston	6	3	3	6
	Cooney Weiland, Boston	6	1	5	6
1928-29	Andy Blair, Toronto	4	3	0	3
	Butch Keeling, NY Rangers	6	3	0	3
	Ace Bailey, Toronto	4	1	2	3
1927-28	Frank Boucher, NY Rangers	9	7	3	10
1926-27	Harry Oliver, Boston	8	4	2	6
	Perk Galbraith, Boston	8	3	3	6
	Frank Fredrickson, Boston	8	2	4	6

Player	Team	Date	City	Total Goals	Opposing Goaltender	Score	
Reggie Leach	Phi.	May 6/76	Phi.	5	Gilles Gilbert	Phi. 6	Bos. 3
Jim Lorentz	Buf.	Apr. 7/77	Min.	3	Pete LoPresti (2)		
					Gary Smith (1)	Buf. 7	Min. 1
Bobby Schmautz	Bos.	Apr. 11/77	Bos.	3	Rogatien Vachon	Bos. 8	L.A. 3
Billy Harris	NYI	Apr. 23/77	Mtl.	3	Ken Dryden	Mtl. 4	NYI 3
George Ferguson	Tor.	Apr. 11/78	Tor.	3	Rogatien Vachon	Tor. 7	L.A. 3
Jean Ratelle	Bos.	May 3/79	Bos.	3	Ken Dryden	Bos. 4	Mtl. 3
Stan Jonathan	Bos.	May 8/79	Bos.	3	Ken Dryden	Bos. 5	Mtl. 2
Ron Duguay	NYR	Apr. 20/80	NYR	3	Pete Peeters	NYR 4	Phi. 2
Steve Shutt	Mtl.	Apr. 22/80	Mtl.	3	Gilles Meloche	Mtl. 6	Min. 2
Gilbert Perreault	Buf.	May 6/80	NYI	3	Billy Smith (2)		
					ENG (1)	Buf. 7	NYI 4
Paul Holmgren	Phi.	May 15/80	Phil	3	Billy Smith	Phi. 8	NYI 3
Steve Payne	Min.	Apr. 8/81	Bos.	3	Rogatien Vachon	Min. 5	Bos. 4
Denis Potvin	NYI	Apr. 17/81	NYI	3	Andy Moog	NYI 6	Edm. 3
Barry Pederson	Bos.	Apr. 8/82	Bos.	3	Don Edwards	Bos. 7	Buf. 3
Duane Sutter	NYI	Apr. 15/83	NYI	3	Glen Hanlon	NYI 5	NYR 0
Doug Halward	Van.	Apr. 7/84	Van.	3	Rejean Lemelin (2)		
					Don Edwards (1)	Van. 7	Cgy. 0
Jorgen Pettersson	St. L	Apr. 8/84	Det.	3	Ed Mio	St. L. 3	Det. 2
Clark Gillies	NYI	May 12/84	NYI	3	Grant Fuhr	NYI 6	Edm. 1
Ken Linseman	Bos.	Apr. 14/85	Bos.	3	Steve Penney	Bos. 7	Mtl. 6
Dave Andreychuk	Buf.	Apr. 14/85	Buf.	3	Dan Bouchard	Que. 4	Buf. 7
Peter Zezel	Phi.	Apr. 13/86	NYR	3	J. Vanbiesbrouck	Phi. 7	NYR 1
Greg Paslawski	StL.	Apr. 15/86	Min.	3	Don Beaupre	St. L. 6	Min. 3
Doug Risebrough	Cgy.	May 4/86	Cgy.	3	Rick Wamsley	Cgy. 8	St.L. 2
Cam Neely	Bos.	Apr. 9/87	Mtl.	3	Patrick Roy	Mtl. 4	Bos. 3
Mike McPhee	Mtl.	Apr. 11/87	Bos.	3	Doug Keans	Mtl. 5	Bos. 4
John Ogrodnick	Que.	Apr. 14/87	Hfd.	3	Mike Liut	Que. 7	Hfd. 5
Pelle-Erik Eklund	Phi.	May 10/87	Mtl.	3	Patrick Roy (1)		
					Bryan Hayward (2)	Phi. 6	Mtl. 3
Peter Stastny	Que.	Apr. 11/87	Que.	3	Mike Liut (2)		
					Steve Weeks (1)	Que. 5	Hfd. 1
Michel Goulet	Que.	Apr. 12/87	Que.	3	Mike Liut	Que. 4	Hfd. 1
Tim Kerr	Phi.	Apr. 20/87	Phi.	3	Kelly Hrudey (2)		
					Billy Smith (1)	Phi. 4	NYI 2
John Tucker	Buf.	Apr. 9/88	Bos.	4	Andy Moog	Buf. 6	Bos. 2
Tony Hrkac	St.L.	Apr. 10/88	St.L.	4	Darren Pang	St.L. 6	Chi. 5
Hakan Loob	Cgy.	Apr. 10/88	Cgy.	3	Glenn Healy	Cgy. 7	L.A. 3
Ed Olczyk	Tor.	Apr. 12/88	Tor.	3	Greg Stefan (2)		
					Glen Hanlon (1)	Tor. 6	Det. 5
Aaron Broten	N.J.	Apr. 20/88	N.J.	3	Pete Peeters	N.J. 5	Wsh. 2
Mark Johnson	N.J.	Apr. 22/88	Wsh.	4	Pete Peeters	N.J. 10	Wsh. 4
Patrik Sundstrom	N.J.	Apr. 22/88	Wsh.	3	Pete Peeters (2)		
					Clint Malarchuk (1)	N.J. 10	Wsh. 4
Esa Tikkanen	Edm.	May. 22/88	Edm.	3	Rejean Lemelin	Edm. 6	Bos. 3
Bob Brooke	Min.	Apr. 5/89	St. L.	3	Greg Millen	St.L. 4	Min. 3
Chris Kontos	L.A.	Apr. 6/89	L.A.	3	Grant Fuhr	L.A. 5	Edm. 2
Mario Lemieux	Pit.	Apr. 25/89	Pit.	5	Ron Hextall	Pit. 10	Phi. 7
Wayne Presley	Chi.	Apr. 13/89	Chi.	3	Greg Stefan (1)		
					Glen Hanlon (2)	Chi. 7	Det. 1
Steve Yzerman	Det.	Apr. 6/89	Det.	3	Alain Chevrier	Chi. 5	Det. 4
Peter Zezel	St. L.	Apr. 11/89	St. L.	3	Jon Casey (2)		
					Kari Takko (1)	St. L. 6	Min. 1

Overtime Games since 1927

Abbreviations: Teams/Cities: — **Atl.** - Atlanta; **Bos.** - Boston; **Buf.** - Buffalo; **Cgy.** - Calgary; **Chi.** - Chicago; **Col.** - Colorado; **Det.** - Detroit; **Edm.** - Edmonton; **Hfd.** - Hartford; **L.A.** - Los Angeles; **Min.** - Minnesota; **Mtl.** - Montreal; **Mtl.M.** - Montreal Maroons; **N.J.** - New Jersey; **NY** - New York; **NYA** - NY Americans; **NYI** - New York Islanders; **NYR** - New York Rangers; **Oak.** - Oakland; **Ott.** - Ottawa; **Phi.** - Philadelphia; **Pit.** - Pittsburgh; **Que.** - Quebec; **St.L.** - St. Louis; **Tor.** - Toronto; **Van.** - Vancouver; **Wpg.** - Winnipeg; **Wsh.** - Washington.

SERIES — **CF** - conference final; **DF** - division; **DSF** - division semi-final; **F** - final; **P** preliminary round; **QF** - quarter final; **SF** - semi-final.

Date	City	Series	Score		Scorer	Overtime	Series Winner
Mar. 31/27	Mtl.	QF	Mtl. 1	Mtl. M. 0	Howie Morenz	12:05	Mtl.
Apr. 7/27	Bos.	F	Ott. 0	Bos. 0	no scorer	20:00	Ott.
Apr. 11/27	Ott.	F	Bos. 1	Ott. 1	no scorer	20:00	Ott.
Apr. 3/28	Mtl.	QF	Mtl. M. 1	Mtl. 0	Russ Oatman	8:20	Mtl. M.
Apr. 7/28	Mtl.	F	NYR 2	Mtl. M. 1	Frank Boucher	7:05	NYR
Mar. 21/29	NY	QF	NYR 1	NYA 0	Butch Keeling	29:50	NYR
Mar. 26/29	Tor.	SF	NYR 2	Tor. 1	Frank Boucher	2:03	NYR
Mar. 20/30	Mtl.	SF	Bos. 2	Mtl. M. 1	Harry Oliver	45:35	Bos.
Mar. 25/30	Bos.	SF	Mtl. M. 1	Bos. 0	Archie Wilcox	26:27	Bos.
Mar. 26/30	Mtl.	QF	Chi. 2	Mtl. 2	Howie Morenz (Mtl.)	51:43	Mtl.
Mar. 28/30	Mtl.	SF	Mtl. 2	NYR 1	Gus Rivers	68:52	Mtl.
Mar. 24/31	Bos.	SF	Bos. 5	Mtl. 4	Cooney Weiland	18:56	Mtl.
Mar. 26/31	Chi.	QF	Chi. 2	Tor. 1	Steward Adams	19:20	Chi.
Mar. 28/31	Mtl.	SF	Mtl. 4	Bos. 3	Georges Mantha	5:10	Mtl.
Apr. 1/31	Mtl.	SF	Mtl. 3	Bos. 2	Wildor Larochelle	19:00	Mtl.
Apr. 5/31	Chi.	F	Chi. 2	Mtl. 1	Johnny Gottselig	24:50	Mtl.
Apr. 9/31	Mtl.	F	Chi. 3	Mtl. 2	Cy Wentworth	53:50	Mtl.
Mar. 26/32	Mtl.	SF	NYR 4	Mtl. 3	Fred Cook	59:32	NYR
Apr. 2/32	Tor.	SF	Tor. 3	Mtl. M. 2	Bob Gracie	17:59	Tor.
Mar. 25/33	Bos.	SF	Bos. 2	Tor. 1	Marty Barry	14:14	Tor.
Mar. 28/33	Bos.	SF	Tor. 1	Bos. 0	Busher Jackson	15:03	Tor.
Mar. 30/33	Tor.	SF	Bos. 2	Tor. 1	Eddie Shore	4:23	Tor.
Apr. 3/33	Tor.	SF	Tor. 1	Bos. 0	Ken Doraty	104:46	Tor.
Apr. 13/33	Tor.	F	NYR 1	Tor. 0	Bill Cook	7:33	NYR
Mar. 22/34	Tor.	SF	Det. 2	Tor. 1	Herbie Lewis	1:33	Det.
Mar. 25/34	Chi.	QF	Chi. 1	Mtl. 1	Mush March (Chi)	11:05	Chi.
Apr. 3/34	Det.	F	Chi. 2	Det. 1	Paul Thompson	21:05	Chi.
Apr. 10/34	Chi.	F	Chi. 1	Det. 0	Mush March	30:05	Chi.
Mar. 23/35	Bos.	SF	Bos. 1	Tor. 0	Dit Clapper	33:26	Tor.
Mar. 26/35	Chi.	QF	Mtl. M. 1	Chi. 0	Baldy Northcott	4:02	Mtl. M
Mar. 30/35	Tor.	SF	Tor. 2	Bos. 1	Pep Kelly	1:36	Tor.
Apr. 4/35	Tor.	F	Mtl. M. 3	Tor. 2	Dave Trottier	5:20	Mtl. M.
Mar. 24/36	Mtl.	SF	Det. 1	Mtl. M. 0	Mud Bruneteau	116:30	Det.
Apr. 9/36	Tor.	F	Tor. 4	Det. 3	Buzz Boll	0:31	Det.
Mar. 25/37	NY	QF	NYR 2	Tor. 1	Babe Pratt	13:05	NYR
Apr. 1/37	Mtl.	SF	Det. 2	Mtl. 1	Hec Kilrea	51:49	Det.
Mar. 22/38	NY	QF	NYA 2	NYR 1	Johnny Sorrell	21:25	NYA
Mar. 25/38	Tor.	SF	Tor. 1	Bos. 0	George Parsons	21:31	Tor.
Mar. 26/38	Mtl.	QF	Chi. 3	Mtl. 2	Paul Thompson	11:49	Chi.
Mar. 27/38	NY	QF	NYA 3	NYR 2	Lorne Carr	60:40	NYA
Mar. 29/38	Bos.	SF	Tor. 3	Bos. 2	Gord Drillon	10:04	Tor.
Mar. 31/38	Chi.	SF	Chi. 1	NYA 0	Cully Dahlstrom	33:01	Chi.
Mar. 21/39	NY	SF	Bos. 2	NYR 1	Mel Hill	59:25	Bos.
Mar. 23/39	Bos.	SF	Bos. 3	NYR 2	Mel Hill	8:24	Bos.
Mar. 26/39	Det.	QF	Det. 1	Mtl. 0	Marty Barry	7:47	Det.
Mar. 30/39	Bos.	SF	NYR 2	Bos. 1	Snuffy Smith	17:19	Bos.
Apr. 1/39	Tor.	SF	Tor. 5	Det. 4	Gord Drillon	5:42	Tor.
Apr. 2/39	Bos.	SF	Bos. 2	NYR 1	Mel Hill	48:00	Bos.
Apr. 9/39	Bos.	F	Tor. 3	Bos. 2	Doc Romnes	10:38	Bos.
Mar. 19/40	Det.	QF	Det. 2	NYA 1	Syd Howe	0:25	Det.
Mar. 19/40	Tor.	QF	Tor. 3	Chi. 2	Syl Apps	6:35	Tor.
Apr. 2/40	NY	F	NYR 2	Tor. 1	Alf Pike	15:30	NYR
Apr. 11/40	Tor.	F	NYR 2	Tor. 1	Muzz Patrick	31:43	NYR
Apr. 13/40	Tor.	F	NYR 3	Tor. 2	Bryan Hextall	2:07	NYR
Mar. 20/41	Det.	QF	Det. 2	NYR 1	Gus Giesebrecht	12:01	Det.
Mar. 22/41	Mtl.	QF	Mtl. 4	Chi. 3	Charlie Sands	34:04	Chi.
Mar. 29/41	Bos.	SF	Tor. 2	Bos. 1	Pete Langelle	17:31	Bos.
Mar. 30/41	Chi.	SF	Det. 2	Chi. 1	Gus Giesebrecht	9:15	Det.
Mar. 22/42	Chi.	QF	Bos. 2	Chi. 1	Des Smith	9:51	Bos.
Mar. 21/43	Bos.	SF	Bos. 5	Mtl. 4	Don Gallinger	12:30	Bos.
Mar. 23/43	Det.	SF	Tor. 3	Det. 2	Jack McLean	70:18	Det.
Mar. 25/43	Mtl.	SF	Bos. 3	Mtl. 2	Harvey Jackson	3:20	Bos.
Mar. 30/43	Tor.	SF	Det. 3	Tor. 2	Adam Brown	9:21	Det.
Mar. 30/43	Bos.	SF	Bos. 5	Mtl. 4	Ab DeMarco	3:41	Bos.
Apr. 13/44	Mtl.	F	Mtl. 5	Chi. 4	Toe Blake	9:12	Mtl.
Mar. 27/45	Tor.	SF	Tor. 4	Mtl. 3	Gus Bodnar	12:36	Tor.
Mar. 29/45	Det.	SF	Det. 3	Bos. 2	Mud Bruneteau	17:12	Det.
Apr. 21/45	Tor.	F	Det. 1	Tor. 0	Ed Bruneteau	14:16	Tor.
Mar. 28/46	Bos.	SF	Bos. 4	Det. 3	Don Gallinger	9:51	Bos.
Mar. 30/46	Mtl.	F	Mtl. 4	Bos. 3	Maurice Richard	9:08	Mtl.
Apr. 2/46	Mtl.	F	Mtl. 3	Bos. 2	Jim Peters	16:55	Mtl.
Apr. 7/46	Bos.	F	Bos. 3	Mtl. 2	Terry Reardon	15:13	Mtl.
Mar. 26/47	Tor.	SF	Tor. 3	Det. 2	Howie Meeker	3:05	Tor.
Mar. 27/47	Mtl.	SF	Mtl. 2	Bos. 1	Ken Mosdell	5:38	Mtl.
Apr. 3/47	Mtl.	SF	Mtl. 4	Bos. 3	John Quilty	36:40	Mtl.
Apr. 15/47	Tor.	F	Tor. 2	Mtl. 1	Syl Apps	16:36	Tor.
Mar. 24/48	Tor.	SF	Tor. 5	Bos. 4	Nick Metz	17:03	Tor.
Mar. 22/49	Det.	SF	Det. 2	Mtl. 1	Max McNab	44:52	Det.
Mar. 24/49	Det.	SF	Mtl. 4	Det. 3	Gerry Plamondon	2:59	Det.
Mar. 26/49	Tor.	SF	Bos. 5	Tor. 4	Woody Dumart	16:14	Tor.
Apr. 8/49	Det.	F	Tor. 3	Det. 2	Joe Klukay	17:31	Tor.
Apr. 4/50	Tor.	SF	Det. 2	Tor. 1	Leo Reise	20:38	Det.
Apr. 4/50	Mtl.	SF	Mtl. 3	NYR 2	Elmer Lach	15:19	Mtl.
Apr. 9/50	Det.	SF	Det. 1	Tor. 0	Leo Reise	8:39	Det.
Apr. 18/50	Det.	F	NYR 4	Det. 3	Don Raleigh	8:34	Det.
Apr. 20/50	Det.	F	NYR 2	Det. 1	Don Raleigh	1:38	Det.
Apr. 23/50	Det.	F	Det. 4	NYR 3	Pete Babando	28:31	Det.
Mar. 27/51	Det.	SF	Mtl. 3	Det. 2	Maurice Richard	61:09	Mtl.
Mar. 29/51	Det.	SF	Mtl. 1	Det. 0	Maurice Richard	42:20	Mtl.
Mar. 31/51	Tor.	SF	Bos. 1	Tor. 1	no scorer	20:00	Tor.
Apr. 11/51	Tor.	F	Tor. 3	Mtl. 2	Sid Smith	5:51	Tor.
Apr. 14/51	Tor.	F	Mtl. 3	Tor. 2	Maurice Richard	2:55	Tor.
Apr. 17/51	Mtl.	F	Tor. 2	Mtl. 1	Ted Kennedy	4:47	Tor.
Apr. 19/51	Mtl.	F	Tor. 3	Mtl. 2	Harry Watson	5:15	Tor.
Apr. 21/51	Tor.	F	Tor. 3	Mtl. 2	Bill Barilko	2:53	Tor.
Apr. 6/52	Bos.	SF	Mtl. 3	Bos. 2	Paul Masnick	27:49	Mtl.
Mar. 29/53	Bos.	SF	Bos. 2	Det. 1	Jack McIntyre	12:29	Bos.
Mar. 29/53	Chi.	SF	Chi. 2	Mtl. 1	Al Dewsbury	5:18	Mtl.
Apr. 16/53	Mtl.	F	Mtl. 1	Bos. 0	Elmer Lach	1:22	Mtl.
Apr. 1/54	Det.	SF	Det. 4	Tor. 3	Ted Lindsay	21:01	Det.
Apr. 11/54	Det.	F	Mtl. 1	Det. 0	Ken Mosdell	5:45	Det.
Apr. 16/54	Det.	F	Det. 2	Mtl. 1	Tony Leswick	4:29	Det.
Mar. 29/55	Bos.	SF	Mtl. 4	Bos. 3	Don Marshall	3:05	Mtl.
Mar. 24/56	Tor.	SF	Det. 5	Tor. 4	Ted Lindsay	4:22	Det.
Mar. 28/57	NY	SF	NYR 4	Mtl. 3	Andy Hebenton	13:38	Mtl.
Apr. 4/57	Mtl.	SF	Mtl. 4	NYR 3	Maurice Richard	1:11	Mtl.
Mar. 27/58	NY	SF	Bos. 4	NYR 3	Jerry Toppazzini	4:46	Bos.
Mar. 30/58	Det.	SF	Mtl. 2	Det. 1	André Pronovost	11:52	Mtl.
Apr. 17/58	Mtl.	F	Mtl. 3	Bos. 2	Maurice Richard	5:45	Mtl.
Mar. 28/59	Tor.	SF	Tor. 3	Bos. 2	Gerry Ehman	5:02	Tor.
Mar. 31/59	Tor.	SF	Tor. 3	Bos. 2	Frank Mahovlich	11:21	Tor.
Apr. 14/59	Tor.	F	Tor. 3	Mtl. 2	Dick Duff	10:06	Mtl.
Mar. 26/60	Mtl.	SF	Mtl. 4	Chi. 3	Doug Harvey	8:38	Mtl.
Mar. 27/60	Det.	SF	Tor. 5	Det. 4	Frank Mahovlich	43:00	Tor.
Mar. 29/60	Det.	SF	Det. 2	Tor. 1	Gerry Melnyk	1:54	Tor.
Mar. 22/61	Tor.	SF	Tor. 3	Det. 2	George Armstrong	24:51	Det.
Mar. 26/61	Chi.	SF	Chi. 2	Mtl. 1	Murray Balfour	52:12	Chi.
Apr. 5/62	Tor.	SF	Tor. 3	NYR 2	Red Kelly	24:23	Tor.
Apr. 2/64	Det.	SF	Chi. 3	Det. 2	Murray Balfour	8:21	Det.
Apr. 14/64	Tor.	F	Det. 3	Tor. 2	Larry Jeffrey	7:52	Tor.
Apr. 23/64	Det.	F	Tor. 4	Det. 3	Bobby Baun	1:43	Tor.
Apr. 6/65	Tor.	SF	Tor. 3	Mtl. 2	Dave Keon	4:17	Mtl.
Apr. 13/65	Tor.	SF	Mtl. 4	Tor. 3	Claude Provost	16:33	Mtl.
May 5/66	Det.	F	Mtl. 3	Det. 2	Henri Richard	2:20	Mtl.
Apr. 13/67	NY	SF	Mtl. 2	NYR 1	John Ferguson	6:28	Mtl.
Apr. 25/67	Tor.	F	Tor. 3	Mtl. 2	Bob Pulford	28:26	Tor.
Apr. 10/68	St. L.	QF	St. L. 3	Phi. 2	Larry Keenan	24:10	St. L.
Apr. 16/68	St. L.	QF	Phi. 2	St. L. 1	Don Blackburn	31:38	St. L.
Apr. 16/68	Min.	QF	Min. 4	L.A. 3	Milan Marcetta	9:11	Min.
Apr. 22/68	Min.	SF	Min. 3	St. L. 2	Parker MacDonald	3:41	St. L.
Apr. 27/68	St. L.	SF	St. L. 4	Min. 3	Gary Sabourin	1:32	St. L.
Apr. 28/68	Mtl.	SF	Mtl. 4	Chi. 3	Jacques Lemaire	2:14	Mtl.
Apr. 29/68	St. L.	SF	St. L. 3	Min. 2	Bill McCreary	17:27	St. L.
May 3/68	St. L.	SF	St. L. 2	Min. 1	Ron Schock	22:50	St. L.
May 5/68	St. L.	F	Mtl. 3	St. L. 2	Jacques Lemaire	1:41	Mtl.
May 9/68	Mtl.	F	Mtl. 4	St. L. 3	Bobby Rousseau	1:13	Mtl.
Apr. 2/69	Oak.	QF	L.A. 5	Oak. 4	Ted Irvine	0:19	L.A.
Apr. 10/69	Mtl.	SF	Mtl. 3	Bos. 2	Ralph Backstrom	0:42	Mtl.
Apr. 13/69	Mtl.	SF	Mtl. 4	Bos. 3	Mickey Redmond	4:55	Mtl.
Apr. 24/69	Bos.	SF	Mtl. 2	Bos. 1	Jean Béliveau	31:28	Mtl.
Apr. 12/70	Oak.	QF	Pit. 3	Oak. 2	Michel Briere	8:28	Pit.
May 10/70	Bos.	F	Bos. 4	St. L. 3	Bobby Orr	0:40	Bos.
Apr. 15/71	Tor.	QF	NYR 2	Tor. 1	Bob Nevin	9:07	NYR
Apr. 18/71	Chi.	SF	NYR 2	Chi. 1	Pete Stemkowski	1:37	Chi.
Apr. 27/71	Chi.	SF	Chi. 3	NYR 2	Bobby Hull	6:35	Chi.
Apr. 29/71	NY	SF	NYR 3	Chi. 2	Pete Stemkowski	41:29	Chi.
May 4/71	Chi.	F	Chi. 2	Mtl. 1	Jim Pappin	21:11	Mtl.
Apr. 6/72	Bos.	OF	Tor. 4	Bos. 3	Jim Harrison	2:58	Bos.
Apr. 6/72	Min.	QF	Min. 6	St. L. 5	Bill Goldsworthy	1:36	St. L.
Apr. 9/72	Pit.	QF	Chi. 6	Pit. 5	Pit Martin	0:12	Chi.
Apr. 16/72	Min.	QF	St. L. 2	Min. 1	Kevin O'Shea	10:07	St. L.
Apr. 01/73	Mtl.	QF	Buf. 3	Mtl. 2	René Robert	9:18	Mtl.
Apr. 10/73	Phi.	QF	Phi. 3	Min. 2	Gary Dornhoefer	8:35	Phi.
Apr. 14/73	Mtl.	SF	Phi. 5	Mtl. 4	Rick MacLeish	2:56	Mtl.
Apr. 17/73	Mtl.	SF	Mtl. 4	Phi. 3	Larry Robinson	6:45	Mtl.
Apr. 14/74	Tor.	QF	Bos. 4	Tor. 3	Ken Hodge	1:27	Bos.
Apr. 14/74	Atl.	QF	Phi. 4	Atl. 3	Dave Schultz	5:40	Phi.
Apr. 16/74	Mtl.	QF	NYR 3	Mtl. 2	Ron Harris	4:07	NYR
Apr. 23/74	Chi.	Sf	Chi. 4	Bos. 3	Jim Pappin	3:48	Bos.
Apr. 28/74	NY	SF	NYR 2	Phi. 1	Rod Gilbert	4:20	Phi.
May 9/74	Bos.	F	Phi. 3	Bos. 2	Bobby Clarke	12:01	Phi.
Apr. 8/75	L.A.	P	L.A. 3	Tor. 2	Mike Murphy	8:53	Tor.
Apr. 10/75	Tor.	P	Tor. 3	L.A. 2	Blaine Stoughton	10:19	Tor.
Apr. 10/75	Chi.	P	Chi. 4	Bos. 3	Ivan Boldirev	7:33	Chi.
Apr. 11/75	NY	P	NYI 4	NYR 3	Jean-Paul Parise	0:11	NYI
Apr. 19/75	Tor.	QF	Phi. 4	Tor. 3	André Dupont	1:45	Phi.
Apr. 17/75	Chi.	QF	Chi. 5	Buf. 4	Stan Mikita	2:31	Buf.
Apr. 22/75	Mtl.	QF	Mtl. 5	Van. 4	Guy Lafleur	17:06	Mtl.
May 1/75	Phi.	SF	Phi. 5	NYI 4	Bobby Clarke	2:56	Phi.
May 7/75	NYI	SF	NYI 4	Phi. 3	Jude Drouin	1:53	Phi.
Apr. 27/75	Buf.	SF	Buf. 6	Mtl. 5	Danny Gare	4:42	Buf.
May 6/75	Buf.	SF	Buf. 5	Mtl. 4	René Robert	5:56	Buf.
May 20/75	Buf.	F	Buf. 5	Phi. 4	René Robert	18:29	Phi.
Apr. 8/76	Buf.	P	Buf. 3	St. L. 2	Danny Gare	11:43	Buf.
Apr. 9/76	Buf.	P	Buf. 2	St. L. 1	Don Luce	14:27	Buf.
Apr. 13/76	Bos.	QF	L.A. 3	Bos. 2	Butch Goring	0:27	Bos.

Date	City	Series	Score		Scorer	Overtime	Series Winner
Apr. 13/76	Buf.	QF	Buf. 3	NYI 2	Danny Gare	14:04	NYI
Apr. 22/76	L.A.	QF	L.A. 4	Bos. 3	Butch Goring	18:28	Bos.
Apr. 29/76	Phi.	SF	Phi. 2	Bos. 1	Reggie Leach	13:38	Phi.
Apr. 15/77	Tor.	QF	Phi. 4	Tor. 3	Rick MacLeish	2:55	Phi.
Apr. 17/77	Tor.	QF	Phi. 6	Tor. 5	Reggie Leach	19:10	Phi.
Apr. 24/77	Phi.	SF	Bos. 4	Phi. 3	Rick Middleton	2:57	Bos.
Apr. 26/77	Phi.	SF	Bos. 5	Phi. 4	Terry O'Reilly	30:07	Bos.
May 3/77	Mtl.	SF	NYI 4	Mtl. 3	Billy Harris	3:58	Mtl.
May 14/77	Bos.	F	Mtl. 2	Bos. 1	Jacques Lemaire	4:32	Mtl.
Apr. 11/78	Phi.	P	Phi. 3	Col. 2	Mel Bridgman	0:23	Phi.
Apr. 13/78	NY	P	NYR 4	Buf. 3	Don Murdoch	1:37	Buf.
Apr. 19/78	Bos.	QF	Bos. 4	Chi. 3	Terry O'Reilly	1:50	Bos.
Apr. 19/78	NYI	QF	NYI 3	Tor. 2	Mike Bossy	2:50	Tor.
Apr. 21/78	Chi.	QF	Bos. 4	Chi. 3	Peter McNab	10:17	Bos.
Apr. 25/78	NYI	QF	NYI 2	Tor. 1	Bob Nystrom	8:02	Tor.
Apr. 29/78	NYI	QF	Tor. 2	NYI 1	Lanny McDonald	4:13	Tor.
May 2/78	Bos.	SF	Bos. 3	Phi. 2	Rick Middleton	1:43	Bos.
May 16/78	Mtl.	F	Mtl. 3	Bos. 2	Guy Lafleur	13:09	Mtl.
May 21/78	Bos.	F	Bos. 4	Mtl. 3	Bobby Schmautz	6:22	Mtl.
Apr. 12/79	L.A.	P	NYR 2	L.A. 1	Phil Esposito	6:11	NYR
Apr. 14/79	Buf.	P	Pit. 4	Buf. 3	George Ferguson	0:47	Pit.
Apr. 16/79	Phi.	QF	Phi. 3	NYR 2	Ken Linseman	0:44	NYR
Apr. 18/79	NYI	QF	NYI 1	Chi. 0	Mike Bossy	2:31	NYI
Apr. 21/79	Tor.	QF	Mtl. 4	Tor. 3	Cam Connor	25:25	Mtl.
Apr. 22/79	Tor.	QF	Mtl. 5	Tor. 4	Larry Robinson	4:14	Mtl.
Apr. 28/79	NYI	SF	NYI 4	NYR 3	Denis Potvin	8:02	NYR
May 3/79	NY	SF	NYI 3	NYR 2	Bob Nystrom	3:40	NYR
May 3/79	Bos.	SF	Bos. 4	Mtl. 3	Jean Ratelle	3:46	Mtl.
May 10/79	Mtl.	SF	Mtl. 5	Bos. 4	Yvon Lambert	9:33	Mtl.
May 19/79	NY	F	Mtl. 4	NYR 3	Serge Savard	7:25	Mtl.
Apr. 8/80	NY	P	NYR 2	Atl. 1	Steve Vickers	0:33	NYR
Apr. 8/80	Phi.	P	Phi. 4	Edm. 3	Bobby Clarke	8:06	Phi.
Apr. 8/80	Chi.	P	Chi. 3	St. L. 2	Doug Lecuyer	12:34	Chi.
Apr. 11/80	Hfd.	P	Mtl. 4	Hfd. 3	Yvon Lambert	0:29	Mtl.
Apr. 11/80	Tor.	P	Min. 4	Tor. 3	Al MacAdam	0:32	Min.
Apr. 11/80	L.A.	P	NYI 4	L.A. 3	Ken Morrow	6:55	NYI
Apr. 11/80	Edm.	P	Phi. 3	Edm. 2	Ken Linseman	23:56	Phi.
Apr. 16/80	Bos.	QF	NYI 2	Bos. 1	Clark Gillies	1:02	NYI
Apr. 17/80	Bos.	QF	NYI 5	Bos. 4	Bob Bourne	1:24	NYI
Apr. 21/80	NYI	QF	Bos. 4	NYI 3	Terry O'Reilly	17:13	NYI
May 1/80	Buf.	SF	NYI 2	Buf. 1	Bob Nystrom	21:20	NYI
May 13/80	Phi.	F	NYI 4	Phi. 3	Denis Potvin	4:07	NYI
May 24/80	NYI	F	NYI 5	Phi. 4	Bob Nystrom	7:11	NYI
Apr. 8/81	Buf.	P	Buf. 3	Van. 2	Alan Haworth	5:00	Buf.
Apr. 8/81	Bos.	P	Min. 5	Bos. 4	Steve Payne	3:34	Min.
Apr. 11/81	Chi.	P	Cgy. 5	Chi. 4	Willi Plett	35:17	Cgy.
Apr. 12/81	Que.	P	Que. 4	Phi. 3	Dale Hunter	:37	Phi.
Apr. 14/81	St. L.	P	St. L. 4	Pit. 3	Mike Crombeen	25:16	St. L.
Apr. 16/81	Buf.	QF	Min. 4	Buf. 3	Steve Payne	0:22	Min.
Apr. 20/81	Min.	QF	Buf. 5	Min. 4	Craig Ramsay	16:32	Min.
Apr. 20/81	Edm.	QF	NYI 5	Edm. 4	Ken Morrow	5:41	NYI
Apr. 7/82	Min.	DSF	Chi. 3	Min. 2	Greg Fox	3:34	Chi.
Apr. 8/82	Edm.	DSF	Edm. 3	L.A. 2	Wayne Gretzky	6:20	L.A.
Apr. 8/82	Van.	DSF	Van. 2	Cgy. 1	Dave Williams	14:20	Van.
Apr. 10/82	Pit.	DSF	Pit. 2	NYI 1	Rick Kehoe	4:14	NYI
Apr. 10/82	L.A.	DSF	L.A. 6	Edm. 5	Daryl Evans	2:35	L.A.
Apr. 13/82	Mtl.	DSF	Que. 3	Mtl. 2	Dale Hunter	0:22	Que.
Apr. 13/82	NY	DSF	Pit. 3	NY14	John Tonelli	6:19	L.A.
Apr. 16/82	Van.	DF	L.A. 3	Van. 2	Steve Bozek	4:33	Van.
Apr. 18/82	Que.	DF	Que. 3	Bos. 2	Wilf Paiement	11:44	Que.
Apr. 18/82	NY	DF	NYI 4	NYR 3	Bryan Trottier	3:00	NYI
Apr. 18/82	L.A.	DF	Van. 4	L.A. 3	Colin Campbell	1:23	Van.
Apr. 21/82	St. L.	DF	St. L. 3	Chi. 2	Bernie Federko	3:28	Chi.
Apr. 23/82	Que.	DF	Bos. 6	Que. 5	Peter McNab	10:54	Que.
Apr. 27/82	Chi.	CF	Van. 2	Chi. 1	Jim Nill	28:58	Van.
May 1/82	Que.	CF	NYI 5	Que. 4	Wayne Merrick	16:52	NYI
May 8/82	NYI	SCF	NYI 6	Van. 5	Mike Bossy	19:58	NYI
Apr. 5/83	Bos.	DSF	Bos. 4	Que. 3	Barry Pederson	1:46	Bos.
Apr. 6/83	Cgy.	DSF	Cgy. 4	Van. 3	Eddy Beers	12:27	Cgy.
Apr. 7/83	Min.	DSF	Min. 5	Tor. 4	Bobby Smith	5:03	Min.
Apr. 10/83	Tor.	DSF	Min. 5	Tor. 4	Dino Ciccarelli	8:05	Min.
Apr. 10/83	Van.	DSF	Cgy. 4	Van. 3	Greg Meredith	1:06	Cgy.
Apr. 18/83	Min.	DF	Chi. 4	Min. 3	Rich Preston	10:34	Chi.
Apr. 24/83	Bos.	DF	Bos. 3	Buf. 3	Brad Park	1:52	Bos.
Apr. 5/84	Edm.	DSF	Edm. 5	Wpg. 4	Randy Gregg	0:21	Edm.
Apr. 7/84	Det.	DSF	St. L. 4	Det. 3	Mark Reeds	37:07	St. L.
Apr. 8/84	Det.	DSF	St. L. 3	Det. 2	Jorgen Pettersson	2:42	St. L.
Apr. 10/84	NYI	DSF	NYI 3	NYR 2	Ken Morrow	8:56	NYI
Apr. 13/84	Min.	DF	St. L. 4	Min. 3	Doug Gilmour	16:16	Min.
Apr. 13/84	Edm.	DF	Cgy. 6	Edm. 5	Carey Wilson	3:42	Edm.
Apr. 13/84	NYI	DF	NYI 5	Wash. 4	Anders Kallur	7:35	NYI
Apr. 16/84	Mtl.	DF	Que. 4	Mtl. 3	Bo Berglund	3:00	Mtl.
Apr. 20/84	Cgy.	DF	Cgy. 5	Edm. 4	Lanny McDonald	1:04	Edm.
Apr. 22/84	Min.	DF	Min. 4	St. L. 3	Steve Payne	6:00	Min.
Apr. 10/85	NYR	DSF	NYR 4	Phi. 5	Mark Howe	8:01	Phi.
Apr. 10/85	Wsh.	DSF	NYI 3	Wsh. 4	Alan Haworth	2:28	NYI
Apr. 11/85	Wsh.	DSF	NYI 1	Wsh. 2	Mike Gartner	1:23	NYI
Apr. 10/85	Edm.	DSF	L.A. 2	Edm. 3	Lee Fogolin	3:01	Edm.
Apr. 13/85	L.A.	DSF	Edm. 4	L.A. 3	Glenn Anderson	0:46	Edm.
Apr. 10/85	Wpg.	DSF	Cgy. 4	Wpg. 5	Brian Mullen	7:56	Wpg.
Apr. 18/85	Mtl.	DF	Que. 2	Mtl. 1	Mark Kumpel	12:23	Que.
Apr. 23/85	Que.	DF	Que. 7	Mtl. 6	Dale Hunter	18:36	Que.
Apr. 25/85	Min.	DF	Chi. 7	Min. 6	Darryl Sutter	1:57	Chi.
Apr. 28/85	Chi.	DF	Chi. 4	Min. 5	Dennis Maruk	1:14	Chi.
Apr. 30/85	Min.	DF	Chi. 6	Min. 5	Darryl Sutter	15:41	Chi.
May 2/85	Mtl.	DF	Que. 3	Mtl. 2	Peter Stastny	2:22	Que.
May 5/85	Que.	CF	Phi. 1	Que. 2	Peter Stastny	6:20	Phi.
Apr. 9/86	Que.	DSF	Hfd. 3	Que. 2	Sylvain Turgeon	2:36	Hfd.
Apr. 12/86	Wpg.	DSF	Cgy. 4	Wpg. 3	Lanny McDonald	8:25	Cgy.

Date	City	Series	Score		Scorer	Overtime	Series Winner
Apr. 17/86	Wsh.	DF	NYR 4	Wsh. 3	Brian MacLellan	1:16	NYR
Apr. 20/86	Edm.	DF	Edm.. 6	Cgy. 5	Glenn Anderson	1:04	Cgy.
Apr. 23/86	Hfd.	DF	Hfd. 2	Mtl. 1	Kevin Dineen	1:07	Mtl.
Apr. 23/86	NYR	DF	NYR 6	Wash. 5	Bob Brooke	2:40	NYR
Apr. 26/86	St L.	DF	St L. 4	Tor. 3	Mark Reeds	7:11	St L.
Apr. 29/86	Mtl.	DF	Mtl. 2	Hfd. 1	Claude Lemieux	5:55	Mtl.
May 5/86	NYR	CF	Mtl. 4	NYR 3	Claude Lemieux	9:41	Mtl.
May 12/86	St L.	CF	St L. 6	Cgy. 5	Doug Wickenheiser	7:30	Cgy.
May 18/86	Cgy.	F	Mtl. 3	Cgy. 2	Brian Skrudland	0:09	Mtl.
Apr. 8/87	Hfd.	DSF	Hfd. 3	Que. 2	Paul MacDermid	2:20	Que.
Apr. 9/87	Mtl.	DSF	Mtl. 4	Bos. 3	Mats Naslund	2:28	Mtl.
Apr. 9/87	St. L.	DSF	Tor. 3	St. L. 2	Rick Lanz	10:17	Tor.
Apr. 11/87	Wpg.	DSF	Cgy. 3	Wpg. 2	Mike Bullard	3:53	Wpg.
Apr. 11/87	Chi.	DSF	Det. 4	Chi. 3	Shawn Burr	4:51	Det.
Apr. 16/87	Que.	DSF	Que. 5	Hfd. 4	Peter Stastny	6:05	Que.
Apr. 18/87	Wsh.	DSF	NYI 3	Wsh. 2	Pat LaFontaine	68:47	NYI
Apr. 21/87	Edm.	DF	Edm. 3	Wpg. 2	Glenn Anderson	0:36	Edm.
Apr. 26/87	Que.	DF	Mtl. 3	Que. 2	Mats Naslund	5:30	Mtl.
Apr. 27/87	Tor.	DF	Tor. 3	Det. 2	Mike Allison	9:31	Det.
May 4/87	Phi.	CF	Phi. 4	Mtl. 3	Ilkka Sinisalo	9:11	Phi.
May 20/87	Edm.	F	Edm. 3	Phi. 2	Jari Kurri	6:50	Edm.
Apr. 6/88	NYI	DSF	NYI 4	N.J. 3	Pat LaFontaine	6:11	N.J.
Apr. 10/88	Phi.	DSF	Phi. 5	Wsh. 4	Murray Craven	1:18	Wsh.
Apr. 10/88	N.J.	DSF	NYI 5	N.J. 4	Brent Sutter	15:07	N.J.
Apr. 10/88	Buf.	DSF	Buf. 6	Bos. 5	John Tucker	5:32	Bos.
Apr. 12/88	Det.	DSF	Tor. 6	Det. 5	Ed Olczyk	0:34	Det.
Apr. 16/88	Wsh.	DF	Wsh. 5	Phi. 4	Dale Hunter	5:57	Wsh.
Apr. 21/88	Cgy.	CF	Edm. 5	Cgy. 4	Wayne Gretzky	7:54	Edm.
May 4/88	Bos.	CF	N.J. 3	Bos. 2	Doug Brown	17:46	Bos.
May 9/88	Det.	CF	Edm. 4	Det. 3	Jari Kurri	11:02	Edm.
Apr. 5/89	St. L.	DSF	Min. 3	St. L. 4	Brett Hull	11:55	St. L.
Apr. 5/89	Cgy.	DSF	Van. 4	Cgy. 3	Paul Reinhart	2:47	Cgy.
Apr. 6/89	St. L.	DSF	Min. 3	St. L. 4	Rick Meagher	5:30	St. L.
Apr. 6/89	Det.	DSF	Chi. 5	Det. 4	Duane Sutter	14:36	Chi.
Apr. 8/89	Hfd.	DSF	Mtl. 5	Hfd. 4	Stephane Richer	5:01	Mtl.
Apr. 8/89	Phi.	DSF	Wsh. 4	Phi. 3	Kelly Miller	0:51	Phi.
Apr. 9/89	Hfd.	DSF	Mtl. 4	Hfd. 3	Russ Courtnall	15:12	Mtl.
Apr. 15/89	Cgy.	DSF	Van. 3	Cgy. 4	Joel Otto	19:21	Cgy.
Apr. 18/89	Cgy.	DF	L.A. 3	Cgy. 4	Doug Gilmour	7:47	Cgy.
Apr. 19/89	Mtl.	DF	Bos. 2	Mtl. 3	Bobby Smith	12:24	Mtl.
Apr. 20/89	St. L.	DF	Chi. 4	St. L. 5	Tony Hrkac	33:49	Chi.
Apr. 21/89	Phi.	DF	Pit. 4	Phi. 3	Phil Bourque	12:08	Phi.
May 8/89	Chi.	CF	Cgy. 2	Chi. 1	Al MacInnis	15:05	Cgy.
May 9/89	Mtl.	CF	Phi. 2	Mtl. 1	Dave Poulin	5:02	Mtl.
May 19/89	Mtl.	F	Cgy. 3	Mtl. 4	Ryan Walter	38:08	Cgy.

Ten Longest Overtime Games

Mar. 24/36	Mtl.	SF	Det. 1	Mtl. M. 0	Mud Bruneteau	116:30	Det.
Apr. 3/33	Tor.	SF	Tor. 1	Bos. 0	Ken Doraty	104:46	Tor.
Mar. 23/43	Det.	SF	Tor. 3	Det. 2	Jack McLean	70:18	Det.
Mar. 28/30	Mtl.	SF	Mtl. 2	NYR 1	Gus Rivers	68:52	Mtl.
Apr. 18/87	Wsh.	DSF	NYI 3	Wsh. 2	Pat LaFontaine	68:47	NYI
Mar. 27/51	Det.	SF	Mtl. 3	Det. 2	Maurice Richard	61:09	Mtl.
Mar. 26/32	Mtl.	SF	NYR 4	Mtl. 3	Fred Cook	59:32	NYR
Mar. 21/39	NY	SF	Bos. 2	NYR 1	Mel Hill	59:25	Bos.
Apr. 9/31	Mtl.	F	Chi. 3	Mtl. 2	Cy Wentworth	53:50	Mtl.
Mar. 26/61	Chi.	SF	Chi. 2	Mtl. 1	Murray Balfour	52:12	Chi.

Overtime Record of Current Teams

(Listed by number of OT games played)

	Overall				Home					Road				
Team	GP	W	L	T	GP	W	L	T	Last OT Game	GP	W	L	T	Last OT Game
Montreal	95	50	43	2	44	25	16	1	May 19/89	51	23	27	1	Apr. 9/89
Boston	77	30	44	3	35	17	17	1	May 4/88	42	13	27	2	Apr. 19/89
Toronto	74	36	37	1	47	22	24	1	Apr. 27/87	27	14	13	0	Apr. 12/88
Detroit	47	20	27	0	29	10	19	0	Apr. 6/89	18	10	8	0	Apr. 27/87
NY Rangers	46	23	23	0	19	9	10	0	May 5/86	27	14	13	0	Apr. 17/86
Chicago	43	21	20	2	22	12	9	1	May 8/89	21	9	11	1	Apr. 20/89
Philadelphia	34	18	16	0	13	8	5	0	Apr. 21/89	21	10	11	0	May 9/89
NY Islanders	31	24	7	0	13	11	2	0	Apr. 6/88	18	13	5	0	Apr. 10/88
St. Louis	26	15	11	0	13	11	2	0	Apr. 20/89	13	4	9	0	Apr. 9/87
Minnesota	23	10	13	0	12	5	7	0	Apr. 30/85	11	5	6	0	Apr. 20/89
*Calgary	20	10	10	0	8	4	4	0	Apr. 18/89	12	6	6	0	May 19/89
Buffalo	16	10	6	0	11	8	3	0	Apr. 10/88	5	2	3	0	Apr. 24/83
Quebec	15	9	6	0	9	5	4	0	Apr. 26/87	6	4	2	0	Apr. 8/87
Los Angeles	15	6	9	0	7	3	4	0	Apr. 13/85	8	3	5	0	Apr. 18/89
Edmonton	15	9	6	0	9	6	3	0	May 20/87	6	3	3	0	May 9/88
Vancouver	11	4	7	0	3	1	2	0	Apr. 10/83	8	3	5	0	Apr. 15/89
Washington	9	4	5	0	5	3	2	0	Apr. 16/88	4	1	3	0	Apr. 8/89
Hartford	8	3	5	0	5	2	3	0	Apr. 9/89	3	1	2	0	Apr. 16/87
Pittsburgh	7	4	3	0	2	1	1	0	Apr. 10/82	5	3	2	0	Apr. 21/89
Winnipeg	5	2	3	0	3	1	2	0	Apr. 11/87	2	1	1	0	Apr. 21/87
**New Jersey	4	1	3	0	1	0	1	0	Apr. 10/88	3	1	2	0	May 4/88

* Totals include those of Atlanta 1974-80.
** Totals include those of Kansas City and Colorado 1975-82.

Stanley Cup Coaching Records

Coaches listed in order of total games coached in playoffs. Minimum: 65 games.

Coach	Team	Years	Series	W	L	G	W	L	T	Cups	%
Irvin, Dick	Chicago	1	3	2	1	9	5	3	1	0	.611
	Toronto	9	20	12	8	66	33	32	1	1	.508
	Montreal	14	22	11	11	115	62	53	0	3	.539
	TOTALS	**24**	**45**	**25**	**20**	**190**	**100**	**88**	**2**	**4**	**.532**
Bowman, Scott	St. Louis	4	10	6	4	52	26	26	0	0	.500
	Montreal	8	19	16	3	98	70	28	0	5	.714
	Buffalo	5	8	3	5	36	18	18	0	0	.500
	TOTALS	**17**	**37**	**25**	**12**	**186**	**114**	**72**	**0**	**5**	**.612**
Arbour, Al	St. Louis	1	2	1	1	11	4	7	0	0	.364
	NY Islanders	12	35	27	8	171	109	62	0	4	.637
	TOTALS	**13**	**37**	**28**	**9**	**182**	**113**	**69**	**0**	**4**	**.621**
Sather, Glen	Edmonton	10	27	21	6	*126	89	37	0	4	.706
Blake, Toe	Montreal	13	23	18	5	119	82	37	0	8	.689
Reay, Billy	Chicago	12	22	10	12	117	57	60	0	0	.487
Shero, Fred	Philadelphia	6	16	12	4	83	48	35	0	2	.578
	NY Rangers	2	5	3	2	25	13	12	0	0	.520
	TOTALS	**8**	**21**	**15**	**6**	**108**	**61**	**47**	**0**	**2**	**.565**
Adams, Jack	Detroit	15	27	15	12	105	52	52	1	3	.500
Francis, Emile	NY Rangers	9	14	5	9	75	34	41	0	0	.453
	St. Louis	3	4	1	3	18	6	12	0	0	.333
	TOTALS	**12**	**18**	**6**	**12**	**93**	**40**	**53**	**0**	**0**	**.430**
Imlach, Punch	Toronto	11	17	10	7	92	44	48	0	4	.478
Day, Hap	Toronto	9	14	10	4	80	49	31	0	5	.613
Abel, Sid	Chicago	1	1	0	1	7	3	4	0	0	.429
	Detroit	8	12	4	8	69	29	40	0	0	.420
	TOTALS	**9**	**13**	**4**	**9**	**76**	**32**	**44**	**0**	**0**	**.421**
Keenan, Mike	Philadelphia	4	10	6	4	57	32	25	0	0	.561
	Chicago	1	3	2	1	16	9	7	0	0	.563
	TOTALS	**5**	**13**	**8**	**5**	**73**	**41**	**32**	**0**	**0**	**.562**
Demers, Jacques	St. Louis	3	6	3	3	33	16	17	0	0	.485
	Detroit	3	7	4	3	38	20	18	0	0	.526
	TOTALS	**6**	**13**	**7**	**6**	**71**	**36**	**35**	**0**	**0**	**.507**
Ross, Art	Boston	12	19	9	10	70	32	33	5	2	.493
Bergeron, Michel	Quebec	7	13	6	7	68	31	37	0	0	.456
Ivan, Tommy	Detroit	7	12	8	4	67	36	31	0	3	.537
Pulford, Bob	Los Angeles	4	6	2	4	26	11	15	0	0	.423
	Chicago	5	9	4	5	41	17	24	0	0	.415
	TOTALS	**9**	**15**	**6**	**9**	**67**	**28**	**39**	**0**	**0**	**.418**
Patrick, Lester	NY Rangers	12	24	14	10	65	31	26	8	2	.538

* Does not include suspended game, May 24, 1988.

Jacques Demers has guided the Detroit Red Wings into the playoffs in three straight years.

Penalty Shots in Stanley Cup Playoff Games

Date	Player	Goaltender	Scored	Final Score	Series	
Mar. 25/37	Lionel Conacher, Mtl. Maroons	Tiny Thompson, Boston	No	Mtl. 0 at Bos.	4	QF
Apr. 15/37	Alex Shibicky, NY Rangers	Earl Robertson, Detroit	No	NYR 0 at Det.	3	F
Apr. 13/44	Virgil Johnson, Chicago	Bill Durnan, Montreal	No	Chi. 4 at Mtl.	5*	F
Apr. 9/68	Wayne Connelly, Minnesota	Terry Sawchuk, Los Angeles	Yes	L.A. 5 at Min.	7	QF
Apr. 27/68	Jim Roberts, St. Louis	Cesare Maniago, Minnesota	No	St. L. 4 at Min.	3	SF
May 16/71	Frank Mahovlich, Montreal	Tony Esposito, Chicago	No	Chi. 3 at Mtl.	4	F
May 7/75	Bill Barber, Philadelphia	Glenn Resch, NY Islanders	No	Phi. 3 at NYI	4	SF
Apr. 20/79	Mike Walton, Chicago	Glenn Resch, NY Islanders	No	NYI 4 at Chi.	4	QF
Apr. 9/81	Peter McNab, Boston	Don Beaupre, Minnesota	No	Min. 5 at Bos.	4*	P
Apr. 17/81	Anders Hedberg, NY Rangers	Mike Liut, St. Louis	Yes	NYR 6 at St. L.	4	QF
Apr. 9/83	Denis Potvin, NY Islanders	Pat Riggin, Washington	No	NYI 5 at Wsh.	2	DSF
Apr. 28/84	Wayne Gretzky, Edmonton	Don Beaupre, Minnesota	Yes	Edm. 8 at Min.	3	CF
May 1/84	Mats Naslund, Montreal	Bill Smith, NY Islanders	No	Mtl. 1 at NYI	3	CF
Apr. 14/85	Bob Carpenter, Washington	Bill Smith, NY Islanders	No	Wsh. 4 at NYI.	6	DF
May 28/85	Ron Sutter, Philadelphia	Grant Fuhr, Edmonton	No	Phi. 3 at Edm.	5	F
May 30/85	Dave Poulin, Philadelphia	Grant Fuhr, Edmonton	No	Phi. 3 at Edm.	8	F
Apr. 9/88	John Tucker, Buffalo	Andy Moog, Boston	Yes	Bos. 2 at Buf	6	DSF
Apr. 9/88	Petr Klima, Detroit	Allan Bester, Toronto	Yes	Det. 6 at Tor.	3	DSF
Apr. 8/89	Neal Broten, Minnesota	Greg Millen, St. Louis	Yes	St.L. 5 at Min.	3	DSF

* Game was decided in overtime, but shot taken during regulation time.

Glen Sather has a .706 winning percentage as a coach in the playoffs.

1989-90 Player Register

Note: The 1989-1990 Player Register lists forwards and defensemen only. Goaltenders are listed separately. The Player Register lists every skater who appeared in an NHL game in the 1988-89season, every skater drafted in the first two rounds of the 1988 and 1989 Entry Drafts and other players on NHL Reserve Lists. Trades and roster changes are current as of August 10, 1989.

Abbreviations: A – assists; **G** – goals; **GP** – games played; **Lea** – league; **PIM** – penalties in minutes; **TP** – total points; * – league-leading total.
Pronunciation courtesy of the NHL Broadcasters' Association

Goaltender Register begins on page 361.

LEAGUES:

ACHL	Atlantic Coast Hockey League
AHL	American Hockey League
AJHL	Alberta Junior Hockey League
AUAA	Atlantic Universities Athletic Association
BCJHL	British Columbia Junior Hockey League
CCHA	Central Collegiate Hockey Association
CHL	Central Hockey League
COJHL	Central Ontario Junior Hockey League
CWUAA	Canada West Universities Athletic Association
ECAC	Eastern Collegiate Athletic Association
EHL	Eastern Hockey League
GPAC	Great Plains Athletic Conference
H.E.	Hockey East
HS	High School
IHL	International Hockey League
MJHA	(New York) Metropolitan Junior Hockey Association
MJHL	Manitoba Junior Hockey League
NAHL	North American Hockey League
NHL	National Hockey League
OHA	Ontario Hockey Association
OHL	Ontario Hockey League
OPJHL	Ontario Provincial Junior Hockey League
OUAA	Ontario Universities Athletic Association
QJHL, QMJHL	Quebec Major Junior Hockey League
SHL	Southern Hockey League
SJHL	Saskatchewan Junior Hockey League
SOHL	Southern Ontario Hockey League
USHL	United States Hockey League
WCHA	Western Collegiate Hockey Association
WHA	World Hockey Association
WHL	Western Hockey League

AALTONEN, PETRI

Center. Shoots left. 5'9", 175 lbs.   Born, Tampere, Finland, May 31, 1970.
(Quebec's 4th choice, 45th overall, in 1988 Entry Draft).

			Regular Season					Playoffs				
Season	Club	Lea	GP	G	A	TP	PIM	GP	G	A	TP	PIM
1986-87	IFK Helsinki	Fin. Jr.	30	8	5	13	24	4	0	0	0	0
1987-88	IFK Helsinki	Fin. Jr.	34	37	20	57	25	....	....	....	....	....
1988-89	IFK Helsinki	Fin.	2	0	0	0	0	....	....	....	....	....

ACTON, KEITH EDWARD

Center. Shoots left. 5'8", 170 lbs.   Born, Stouffville, Ont., April 15, 1958.
(Montreal's 8th choice, 103rd over-all, in 1978 Amateur Draft).

			Regular Season					Playoffs				
Season	Club	Lea	GP	G	A	TP	PIM	GP	G	A	TP	PIM
1976-77	Peterborough	OHA	65	52	69	121	93	4	1	4	5	6
1977-78	Peterborough	OHA	68	42	86	128	52	21	10	8	18	16
1978-79	Nova Scotia	AHL	79	15	26	41	22	10	4	2	6	4
1979-80	**Montreal**	**NHL**	2	0	1	1	0	....	....	....	....	....
	Nova Scotia	AHL	75	45	53	98	38	6	1	2	3	8
1980-81	**Montreal**	**NHL**	61	15	24	39	74	2	0	0	0	6
1981-82	**Montreal**	**NHL**	78	36	52	88	88	5	0	4	4	16
1982-83	**Montreal**	**NHL**	78	24	26	50	63	3	0	0	0	0
1983-84	**Montreal**	**NHL**	9	3	7	10	4	....	....	....	....	....
	Minnesota	**NHL**	62	17	38	55	60	15	4	7	11	12
1984-85	**Minnesota**	**NHL**	78	20	38	58	90	9	4	4	8	6
1985-86	**Minnesota**	**NHL**	79	26	32	58	100	5	0	3	3	6
1986-87	**Minnesota**	**NHL**	78	16	29	45	56	....	....	....	....	....
1987-88	**Minnesota**	**NHL**	46	8	11	19	74	....	....	....	....	....
	Edmonton	**NHL**	26	3	6	9	21	7	2	0	2	16
1988-89	**Edmonton**	NHl	46	11	15	26	47	....	....	....	....	....
	Philadelphia	**NHL**	25	3	10	13	64	16	2	3	5	18
	NHL Totals		668	182	289	471	741	62	12	21	33	80

Played in NHL All-Star Game (1982)
Traded to **Minnesota** by **Montreal** with Mark Napier and Toronto's third round choice (Ken Hodge) in 1984 Entry Draft — Montreal's property via earlier transaction — for Bobby Smith, October 28, 1983. Traded to **Edmonton** by **Minnesota** for Moe Mantha, January 22, 1988. Traded to **Philadelphia** by **Edmonton** with Edmonton's fifth-round choice in 1991 Entry Draft for Dave Brown, February 7, 1989.

ADAMS, GREG

Center. Shoots left. 6'3", 185 lbs.   Born, Nelson, B.C., August 1, 1963.

			Regular Season					Playoffs				
Season	Club	Lea	GP	G	A	TP	PIM	GP	G	A	TP	PIM
1981-82	Kelowna	BCJHL	45	31	42	73	24	....	....	....	....	....
1982-83	N. Arizona	NCAA	29	14	21	35	19	....	....	....	....	....
1983-84	N. Arizona	NCAA	26	44	29	73	24	....	....	....	....	....
1984-85	**New Jersey**	**NHL**	36	12	9	21	14	....	....	....	....	....
	Maine	AHL	41	15	20	35	12	11	3	4	7	0
1985-86	**New Jersey**	**NHL**	78	35	42	77	30	....	....	....	....	....
1986-87	**New Jersey**	**NHL**	72	20	27	47	19	....	....	....	....	....
1987-88	**Vancouver**	**NHL**	80	36	40	76	30	....	....	....	....	....
1988-89	**Vancouver**	**NHL**	61	19	14	33	24	7	2	3	5	2
	NHL Totals		327	122	132	254	117	7	2	3	5	2

Played in NHL All-Star Game (1988)
Signed as a free agent by **New Jersey**, June 25, 1984. Traded to **Vancouver** by **New Jersey** with Kirk McLean for Patrik Sundstrom and Vancouver's fourth round choice (Matt Ruchty) in 1988 Entry Draft, September 10, 1987.

ADAMS, GREGORY CHARLES (GREG)

Left wing. Shoots left. 6'2", 200 lbs.   Born, Duncan, B.C., May 31, 1960.

			Regular Season					Playoffs				
Season	Club	Lea	GP	G	A	TP	PIM	GP	G	A	TP	PIM
1978-79	Victoria	WHL	71	23	31	54	151	14	5	0	5	59
1979-80	Victoria	WHL	71	62	48	110	212	16	9	11	20	71
1980-81	**Philadelphia**	**NHL**	6	3	0	3	8	....	....	....	....	....
	Maine	AHL	71	19	20	39	158	20	2	3	5	89
1981-82	**Philadelphia**	**NHL**	33	4	15	19	105	....	....	....	....	....
	Maine	AHL	45	16	21	37	241	4	0	3	3	28
1982-83	**Hartford**	**NHL**	79	10	13	23	216	....	....	....	....	....
1983-84	**Washington**	**NHL**	57	2	6	8	133	1	0	0	0	0
1984-85	**Washington**	**NHL**	51	6	12	18	72	5	0	0	0	9
	Binghamton	AHL	28	9	16	25	58	....	....	....	....	....
1985-86	**Washington**	**NHL**	78	18	38	56	152	9	1	3	4	27
1986-87	**Washington**	**NHL**	67	14	30	44	184	7	1	3	4	58
1987-88	**Washington**	**NHL**	78	15	12	27	153	14	0	5	5	58
1988-89	**Edmonton**	**NHL**	49	4	5	9	82	....	....	....	....	....
	Vancouver	**NHL**	12	4	2	6	35	7	0	0	0	21
	NHL Totals		510	80	133	213	1140	43	2	11	13	153

Signed as a free agent by **Philadelphia**, September 28, 1979. Traded to **Hartford** by **Philadelphia** with Ken Linseman and Philadelphia's first (David Jensen) and third (Leif Karlsson) round choices in the 1983 Entry Draft for Mark Howe and Hartford's third round (Derrick Smith) choice in the 1983 Entry Draft, August 20, 1982. Traded to **Washington** by **Hartford** for Torrie Robertson, October 3, 1983. Traded to **Edmonton** by **Washington** for the rights to Geoff Courtnall, July 22, 1988. Traded to **Vancouver** by **Edmonton** with Doug Smith for Jean LeBlanc and Vancouver's fifth-round choice (Peter White) in 1989 Entry Draft, March 7, 1989.

AGNEW, JIM

Defense. Shoots left. 6'1", 190 lbs.   Born, Hartney, Man., March 21, 1966.
(Vancouver's 10th choice, 157th over-all, in 1984 Entry Draft).

			Regular Season					Playoffs				
Season	Club	Lea	GP	G	A	TP	PIM	GP	G	A	TP	PIM
1982-83	Brandon	WHL	14	1	1	2	9	....	....	....	....	....
1983-84	Brandon	WHL	71	6	17	23	107	12	0	1	1	39
1984-85	Brandon	WHL	19	3	15	18	82	....	....	....	....	....
	Portland	WHL	44	5	24	29	223	6	0	2	2	44
1985-86a	Portland	WHL	70	6	30	36	286	9	0	1	1	48
1986-87	**Vancouver**	**NHL**	4	0	0	0	0	....	....	....	....	....
1986-87	Fredericton	AHL	67	0	5	5	261	....	....	....	....	....
1987-88	**Vancouver**	**NHL**	10	0	1	1	16	....	....	....	....	....
	Fredericton	AHL	63	2	8	10	188	14	0	2	2	43
1988-89	Milwaukee	IHL	47	2	10	12	181	11	0	2	2	34
	NHL Totals		14	0	1	1	16	....	....	....	....	....

a WHL First All-Star Team, West Division (1986)

AITKEN, BRAD

Left wing. Shoots left. 6'3", 200 lbs.   Born, Scarborough. Ont., October 30, 1967.
(Pittsburgh's 3rd choice, 46th over-all, in 1986 Entry Draft).

			Regular Season					Playoffs				
Season	Club	Lea	GP	G	A	TP	PIM	GP	G	A	TP	PIM
1985-86	S.S. Marie	OHL	58	17	47	64	88	....	....	....	....	....
1986-87	S.S. Marie	OHL	52	27	38	65	86	4	1	2	3	5
1987-88	**Pittsburgh**	**NHL**	5	1	1	2	0	....	....	....	....	....
	Muskegon	IHL	74	32	31	63	128	1	0	0	0	0
1988-89	Muskegon	IHL	74	35	30	65	139	13	5	5	10	75
	NHL Totals		5	1	1	2	0	....	....	....	....	....

ALBELIN, TOMMY

Defense. Shoots left. 6'1", 198 lbs. Born, Stockholm, Sweden, May 21, 1964.
(Quebec's 7th choice, 152nd overall, in 1983 Entry Draft).

			Regular Season					Playoffs				
Season	Club	Lea	GP	G	A	TP	PIM	GP	G	A	TP	PIM
1982-83	Djurgarden	Swe.	19	2	5	7	4	6	1	0	1	2
1983-84	Djurgarden	Swe.	30	9	5	14	26	4	0	1	1	2
1984-85	Djurgarden	Swe.	32	9	8	17	22	8	2	1	3	4
1985-86	Djurgarden	Swe.	35	4	8	12	26	....	....	....	....	....
1986-87	Djurgarden	Swe.	33	7	5	12	49	2	0	0	0	0
1987-88	Quebec	NHL	60	3	23	26	47	....	....	....	....	....
1988-89	Quebec	NHL	14	2	4	6	27	....	....	....	....	....
	New Jersey	NHL	46	7	24	31	40	....	....	....	....	....
	Halifax	AHL	8	2	5	7	4	....	....	....	....	....
	NHL Totals		120	12	51	63	114	....	....	....	....	....

Traded to **New Jersey** by **Quebec** for New Jersey's fourth-round choice (Niclas Andersson) in 1989 Entry Draft, December 12, 1988.

ALLISON, DAVID BRYAN (DAVE)

Defense. Shoots right. 6'1", 200 lbs. Born, Fort Frances, Ont., April 14, 1959.

			Regular Season					Playoffs				
Season	Club	Lea	GP	G	A	TP	PIM	GP	G	A	TP	PIM
1976-77	Cornwall	QJHL	63	2	11	13	180	12	0	4	4	60
1977-78	Cornwall	QJHL	60	9	29	38	302	5	2	3	5	32
1978-79	Cornwall	QJHL	66	7	31	38	407	7	1	6	7	34
1979-80	Nova Scotia	AHL	49	1	12	13	119	4	0	0	0	46
1980-81	Nova Scotia	AHL	70	5	12	17	298	6	0	0	0	15
1981-82	Nova Scotia	AHL	78	8	25	33	*332	9	0	3	3	*84
1982-83	Nova Scotia	AHL	70	3	22	25	180	7	0	2	2	2
1983-84	Montreal	NHL	3	0	0	0	12	....	....	....	....	....
	Nova Scotia	AHL	53	2	18	20	155	6	0	3	3	25
1984-85	Sherbrooke	AHL	4	0	1	1	19	....	....	....	....	....
	Nova Scotia	AHL	68	4	18	22	175	6	0	2	2	15
1985-86	Muskegon	IHL	66	7	30	37	247	14	2	9	11	46
1986-87	Muskegon	IHL	67	11	35	46	337	15	4	3	7	20
1987-88	Newmarket	AHL	48	1	9	10	166	....	....	....	....	....
1988-89	Halifax	AHL	12	1	2	3	29	....	....	....	....	....
	Indianapolis	IHL	34	0	7	7	105	....	....	....	....	....
	NHL Totals		3	0	0	0	12	....	....	....	....	....

Signed as a free agent by **Montreal**, October 4, 1979.

ALLISON, MICHAEL EARNEST (MIKE)

Left wing. Shoots right. 6', 200 lbs. Born, Fort Frances, Ont., March 28, 1961.
(NY Rangers' 2nd choice, 35th over-all, in 1980 Entry Draft).

			Regular Season					Playoffs				
Season	Club	Lea	GP	G	A	TP	PIM	GP	G	A	TP	PIM
1978-79	Sudbury	OHA	59	24	32	56	41	10	4	2	6	18
1979-80	Sudbury	OHA	67	24	71	95	74	9	8	6	14	6
1980-81	NY Rangers	NHL	75	26	38	64	83	14	3	1	4	20
1981-82	Springfield	AHL	2	0	0	0	0	....	....	....	....	....
	NY Rangers	NHL	48	7	15	22	74	10	1	3	4	18
1982-83	Tulsa	CHL	6	2	2	4	2	....	....	....	....	....
	NY Rangers	NHL	39	11	9	20	37	8	0	5	5	10
1983-84	NY Rangers	NHL	45	8	12	20	64	5	0	1	1	6
1984-85	NY Rangers	NHL	31	9	15	24	17	....	....	....	....	....
1985-86	NY Rangers	NHL	28	2	13	15	22	16	0	2	2	38
	New Haven	AHL	9	6	6	12	4	....	....	....	....	....
1986-87	Toronto	NHL	71	7	16	23	66	13	3	5	8	15
1987-88	Toronto	NHL	15	0	3	3	10	....	....	....	....	....
	Los Angeles	NHL	37	16	12	28	57	5	0	0	0	16
1988-89	Los Angeles	NHL	55	14	22	36	122	7	1	0	1	10
	NHL Totals		444	100	155	255	552	78	8	17	25	133

Traded to **Toronto** by **NY Rangers** for Walt Poddubny, August 18, 1986. Traded to **Los Angeles** by **Toronto** for Sean McKenna, December 14, 1987.

ALLISON, RAYMOND PETER (RAY)

Right wing. Shoots right. 5'10", 195 lbs. Born, Cranbrook, B.C., March 4, 1959.
(Hartford's 1st choice, 18th over-all, in 1979 Entry Draft).

			Regular Season					Playoffs				
Season	Club	Lea	GP	G	A	TP	PIM	GP	G	A	TP	PIM
1975-76	Brandon	WHL	36	9	17	26	50	5	2	1	3	0
1976-77	Brandon	WHL	71	45	92	137	198	14	9	11	20	37
1977-78	Brandon	WHL	71	74	86	160	254	8	7	8	15	35
1978-79	Brandon	WHL	62	60	93	153	191	22	18	19	37	28
1979-80	Springfield	AHL	13	6	9	15	18	....	....	....	....	....
	Hartford	NHL	64	16	12	28	13	2	0	1	1	0
1980-81	Hartford	NHL	6	1	0	1	0	....	....	....	....	....
	Binghamton	AHL	74	31	39	70	81	1	0	1	1	0
1981-82	Maine	AHL	26	15	13	28	75	....	....	....	....	....
	Philadelphia	NHL	51	17	37	54	104	3	2	0	2	2
1982-83	Philadelphia	NHL	67	21	30	51	57	3	0	1	1	12
1983-84	Philadelphia	NHL	37	8	13	21	47	3	0	1	1	4
1984-85	Philadelphia	NHL	11	1	1	2	2	1	0	0	0	2
	Hershey	AHL	49	17	22	39	61	....	....	....	....	....
1985-86	Hershey	AHL	77	32	46	78	131	18	4	6	10	28
1986-87	Philadelphia	NHL	2	0	0	0	0	....	....	....	....	....
	Hershey	AHL	78	29	55	84	57	5	3	1	4	12
1987-88	Hershey	AHL	....	....	....	....	....	9	2	9	11	17
1988-89	Hershey	AHL	15	6	11	17	18	12	4	7	11	6
	NHL Totals		238	64	93	157	223	12	2	3	5	20

Traded to **Philadelphia** by **Hartford** with Fred Arthur and Hartford's first (Ron Sutter), second (Peter Ihnacak, which was later transferred to **Toronto**) and third-round (Miroslav Dvorak) choices in the 1982 Entry Draft for Rick MacLeish, Blake Wesley, Don Gillen and Philadelphia's first (Paul Lawless), second (Mark Paterson) and third-round (Kevin Dineen) choices in the 1982 Entry Draft, July 3, 1981.

ALOI, JOSEPH (JOE)

Defense. Shoots right. 6'2", 205 lbs. Born, New Haven, CT, October 10, 1968.
(Calgary's 7th choice, 124th overall, in 1987 Entry Draft).

			Regular Season					Playoffs				
Season	Club	Lea	GP	G	A	TP	PIM	GP	G	A	TP	PIM
1986-87	Hull	QMJHL	58	2	5	7	166	8	0	0	0	13
1987-88	Hull	QMJHL	66	0	18	18	171	19	0	2	2	39
1988-89	Hull	QMJHL	40	0	12	12	108	....	....	....	....	....

AMUNDSON, DARRIN

Center. Shoots right. 6'2", 175 lbs.Born, Duluth, MN, November 13, 1968.
(Winnipeg's 5th choice, 100th overall, in 1987 Entry Draft).

			Regular Season					Playoffs				
Season	Club	Lea	GP	G	A	TP	PIM	GP	G	A	TP	PIM
1986-87	Duluth East	HS	24	20	37	57	....	....	....	....	....	....
1987-88	Minn.-Duluth	WCHA	16	0	6	6	4	....	....	....	....	....
1988-89	Minn.-Duluth	WCHA	37	5	11	16	23	....	....	....	....	....

ANDERSON, GLENN CHRIS

Right wing. Shoots left. 6'1", 190 lbs. Born, Vancouver, B.C., October 2, 1960.
(Edmonton's 3rd choice, 69th over-all, in 1979 Entry Draft).

			Regular Season					Playoffs				
Season	Club	Lea	GP	G	A	TP	PIM	GP	G	A	TP	PIM
1978-79	U. of Denver	WCHA	40	26	29	55	58	....	....	....	....	....
1979-80	Seattle	WHL	7	5	5	10	4	....	....	....	....	....
	Cdn. Olympic	...	49	21	21	42	46	....	....	....	....	....
1980-81	Edmonton	NHL	58	30	23	53	24	9	5	7	12	12
1981-82	Edmonton	NHL	80	38	67	105	71	5	2	5	7	8
1982-83	Edmonton	NHL	72	48	56	104	70	16	10	10	20	32
1983-84	Edmonton	NHL	80	54	45	99	65	19	6	11	17	33
1984-85	Edmonton	NHL	80	42	39	81	69	18	10	16	26	38
1985-86	Edmonton	NHL	72	54	48	102	90	10	8	3	11	14
1986-87	Edmonton	NHL	80	35	38	73	65	21	14	13	27	59
1987-88	Edmonton	NHL	80	38	50	88	58	19	9	16	25	49
1988-89	Edmonton	NHL	79	16	48	64	93	7	1	2	3	8
	NHL Totals		681	355	414	769	605	124	65	83	148	253

Played in NHL All-Star Game (1984-86, 1988)

ANDERSON, JOHN MURRAY

Right wing. Shoots left. 5'11", 200 lbs. Born, Toronto, Ont., March 28, 1957.
(Toronto's 1st choice, 11th over-all, in 1977 Amateur Draft).

			Regular Season					Playoffs				
Season	Club	Lea	GP	G	A	TP	PIM	GP	G	A	TP	PIM
1973-74	Toronto	OHA	38	22	22	44	6	....	....	....	....	....
1974-75	Toronto	OHA	70	49	64	113	31	22	16	14	30	14
1975-76	Toronto	OHA	39	26	25	51	19	10	7	4	11	7
1976-77a	Toronto	OHA	64	57	62	119	42	6	3	5	8	0
1977-78	Toronto	NHL	17	1	2	3	2	2	0	0	0	0
	Dallas	CHL	55	22	23	45	6	13	*11	8	*19	2
1978-79	Toronto	NHL	71	15	11	26	10	6	0	2	2	0
1979-80	Toronto	NHL	74	25	28	53	22	3	1	1	2	0
1980-81	Toronto	NHL	75	17	26	43	31	2	0	0	0	0
1981-82	Toronto	NHL	69	31	26	57	30	....	....	....	....	....
1982-83	Toronto	NHL	80	31	49	80	24	4	2	4	6	0
1983-84	Toronto	NHL	73	37	31	68	22	....	....	....	....	....
1984-85	Toronto	NHL	75	32	31	63	27	....	....	....	....	....
1985-86	Quebec	NHL	65	21	28	49	26	....	....	....	....	....
	Hartford	NHL	14	8	17	25	2	10	5	8	13	0
1986-87	Hartford	NHL	76	31	44	75	19	6	1	2	3	0
1987-88	Hartford	NHL	63	17	32	49	20	....	....	....	....	....
1988-89	Hartford	NHL	62	16	24	40	28	4	0	1	1	2
	NHL Totals		814	282	349	631	263	37	9	18	27	2

a OHA First All-Star Team (1977)

Traded to **Quebec** by **Toronto** for Brad Maxwell, August 21, 1985. Traded to **Hartford** by **Quebec** for Risto Siltanen, March 8, 1986.

ANDERSON, PERRY LYNN

Left wing. Shoots left. 6'1", 225 lbs. Born, Barrie, Ont., October 14, 1961.
(St. Louis' 5th choice, 117th over-all, in 1980 Entry Draft).

			Regular Season					Playoffs				
Season	Club	Lea	GP	G	A	TP	PIM	GP	G	A	TP	PIM
1978-79	Kingston	OHA	61	6	13	19	85	5	2	1	3	6
1979-80	Kingston	OHA	63	17	16	33	52	3	0	0	0	6
1980-81	Kingston	OHA	38	9	13	22	118	....	....	....	....	....
	Brantford	OHA	31	8	27	35	43	6	4	2	6	15
1981-82	Salt Lake	CHL	71	32	32	64	117	2	1	0	1	2
	St. Louis	NHL	5	1	2	3	0	10	2	0	2	4
1982-83	St. Louis	NHL	18	5	2	7	14	....	....	....	....	....
	Salt Lake	CHL	57	23	19	42	140	....	....	....	....	....
1983-84	Montana	CHL	8	7	3	10	34	....	....	....	....	....
	St. Louis	NHL	50	7	5	12	195	9	0	0	0	27
1984-85	St. Louis	NHL	71	9	9	18	146	3	0	0	0	7
1985-86	New Jersey	NHL	51	7	12	19	91	....	....	....	....	....
1986-87	New Jersey	NHL	57	10	9	19	107	....	....	....	....	....
	Maine	AHL	9	5	4	9	42	....	....	....	....	....
1987-88	New Jersey	NHL	60	4	6	10	222	10	0	0	0	113
1988-89	New Jersey	NHL	39	3	6	9	128	....	....	....	....	....
	NHL Totals		351	46	51	97	903	32	2	0	2	151

Traded to **New Jersey** by **St. Louis** for Rick Meagher and New Jersey's 12th round choice (Bill Butler) in 1986 Entry Draft, August 29, 1985.

ANDERSON, SHAWN

Defense. Shoots left. 6'1", 196 lbs. Born, Montreal, Que., February 7, 1968.
(Buffalo's 1st choice, 5th over-all, in 1986 Entry Draft).

			Regular Season					Playoffs				
Season	Club	Lea	GP	G	A	TP	PIM	GP	G	A	TP	PIM
1984-85	Lac St. Louis	Midget	42	23	42	65	100	....	....	....	....	....
1985-86	Maine	H.E.	16	5	8	13	22	....	....	....	....	....
	Cdn. Olympic	....	49	4	14	18	38	....	....	....	....	....
1986-87	**Buffalo**	**NHL**	**41**	**2**	**11**	**13**	**23**	....	....	....	....	....
	Rochester	AHL	15	2	5	7	11	....	....	....	....	....
1987-88	**Buffalo**	**NHL**	**23**	**1**	**2**	**3**	**17**	....	....	....	....	....
	Rochester	AHL	22	5	16	21	19	6	0	0	0	0
1988-89	**Buffalo**	**NHL**	**33**	**2**	**10**	**12**	**18**	**5**	**0**	**1**	**1**	**4**
	Rochester	AHL	31	5	14	19	24	....	....	....	....	....
	NHL Totals		**97**	**5**	**23**	**28**	**58**	**5**	**0**	**1**	**1**	**4**

ANDERSSON, BO MIKAEL

Center. Shoots left. 5'11", 185 lbs. Born, Malmo, Sweden, May 10, 1966.
(Buffalo's 1st choice, 18th over-all, in 1984 Entry Draft).

			Regular Season					Playoffs				
Season	Club	Lea	GP	G	A	TP	PIM	GP	G	A	TP	PIM
1982-83	V. Frolunda	Swe.	1	1	0	1	0	....	....	....	....	....
1983-84	V. Frolunda	Swe.	18	0	3	6	....	....	....	....	....	....
1984-85	V. Frolunda	Swe.	30	16	11	27	18	6	3	2	5	2
1985-86	**Buffalo**	**NHL**	**32**	**1**	**9**	**10**	**4**	....	....	....	....	....
	Rochester	AHL	20	10	4	14	6	....	....	....	....	....
1986-87	**Buffalo**	**NHL**	**16**	**0**	**3**	**3**	**0**	....	....	....	....	....
1986-87	Rochester	AHL	42	6	20	26	14	9	1	2	3	2
1987-88	**Buffalo**	**NHL**	**37**	**3**	**20**	**23**	**10**	**1**	**1**	**0**	**1**	**0**
	Rochester	AHL	35	12	24	36	16	....	....	....	....	....
1988-89	**Buffalo**	**NHL**	**14**	**0**	**1**	**1**	**4**	....	....	....	....	....
	Rochester	AHL	56	18	33	51	12	....	....	....	....	....
	NHL Totals		**99**	**4**	**33**	**37**	**18**	**1**	**1**	**0**	**1**	**0**

ANDERSSON, PETER

Defense. Shoots left. 6', 185 lbs. Born, Orebro, Sweden, August 29, 1965.
(NY Rangers' 5th choice, 73rd overall, in 1983 Entry Draft).

			Regular Season					Playoffs				
Season	Club	Lea	GP	G	A	TP	PIM	GP	G	A	TP	PIM
1981-82	Orebro	Swe. 2	31	8	5	13	30	2	0	0	0	0
1982-83	Orebro	Swe. 2	25	10	10	20	16	2	1	2	3	2
1983-84	Farjestad	Swe.	36	4	7	11	22	....	....	....	....	....
1984-85	Farjestad	Swe.	35	5	12	17	24	3	0	1	1	4
1985-86	Farjestad	Swe.	34	6	10	16	18	8	2	2	4	10
1986-87	Farjestad	Swe.	33	9	8	17	32	7	2	1	3	6
1987-88	Farjestad	Swe.	39	12	20	32	44	9	2	12	14	8
1988-89	Farjestad	Swe.	33	6	17	23	44	....	....	....	....	....

ANDREYCHUK, DAVID (DAVE)

Center. Shoots right. 6'3", 215 lbs. Born, Hamilton, Ont., September 29, 1963.
(Buffalo's 3rd choice, 16th over-all, in 1982 Entry Draft).

			Regular Season					Playoffs				
Season	Club	Lea	GP	G	A	TP	PIM	GP	G	A	TP	PIM
1980-81	Oshawa	OHA	67	22	22	44	80	10	3	2	5	20
1981-82	Oshawa	OHL	67	57	43	100	71	3	1	4	5	16
1982-83	Oshawa	OHL	14	8	24	32	6	....	....	....	....	....
	Buffalo	**NHL**	**43**	**14**	**23**	**37**	**16**	**4**	**1**	**0**	**1**	**4**
1983-84	**Buffalo**	**NHL**	**78**	**38**	**42**	**80**	**42**	**2**	**0**	**1**	**1**	**2**
1984-85	**Buffalo**	**NHL**	**64**	**31**	**30**	**61**	**54**	**5**	**4**	**2**	**6**	**4**
1985-86	**Buffalo**	**NHL**	**80**	**36**	**51**	**87**	**61**	....	....	....	....	....
1986-87	**Buffalo**	**NHL**	**77**	**25**	**48**	**73**	**46**	....	....	....	....	....
1987-88	**Buffalo**	**NHL**	**80**	**30**	**48**	**78**	**112**	**6**	**2**	**4**	**6**	**0**
1988-89	**Buffalo**	**NHL**	**56**	**28**	**24**	**52**	**40**	**5**	**0**	**3**	**3**	**0**
	NHL Totals		**478**	**202**	**266**	**468**	**371**	**22**	**7**	**10**	**17**	**10**

ANGLEHART, SERGE

Defense. Shoots right. 6'2", 190 lbs. Born, Hull, Que., April 10, 1970.
(Detroit's 2nd choice, 38th overall, in 1988 Entry Draft).

			Regular Season					Playoffs				
Season	Club	Lea	GP	G	A	TP	PIM	GP	G	A	TP	PIM
1986-87	Outaouais	Midget	41	4	27	31	102	....	....	....	....	....
1987-88	Drummondville	QMJHL	44	1	8	9	122	17	0	3	3	19
1988-89	Drummondville	QMJHL	39	6	15	21	89	3	0	0	0	37
	Adirondack	AHL	....	....	....	....	....	2	0	0	0	0

ARABSKI, ROB

Center. Shoots right. 6', 185 lbs. Born, Brantford, Ont., July 17, 1968.

			Regular Season					Playoffs				
Season	Club	Lea	GP	G	A	TP	PIM	GP	G	A	TP	PIM
1985-86	Guelph	OHL	54	9	8	17	13	20	8	9	17	4
1986-87	Guelph	OHL	64	29	60	89	36	....	....	....	....	....
1987-88	Guelph	OHL	60	25	41	66	50	....	....	....	....	....
1988-89	Guelph	OHL	61	18	51	69	51	7	6	9	15	8

Signed as a free agent by **Washington**, October 17, 1986.

ARCHIBALD, DAVE

Center. Shoots left. 6'1", 190 lbs. Born, Chilliwack, B.C., April 14, 1969.
(Minnesota's 1st choice, 6th overall, in 1987 Entry Draft).

			Regular Season					Playoffs				
Season	Club	Lea	GP	G	A	TP	PIM	GP	G	A	TP	PIM
1984-85	Portland	WHL	47	7	11	18	10	3	0	2	2	0
1985-86	Portland	WHL	70	29	35	64	56	15	6	7	13	11
1986-87	Portland	WHL	65	50	57	107	40	20	10	18	28	11
1987-88	**Minnesota**	**NHL**	**78**	**13**	**20**	**33**	**26**	....	....	....	....	....
1988-89	**Minnesota**	**NHL**	**72**	**14**	**19**	**33**	**14**	**5**	**0**	**1**	**1**	**0**
	NHL Totals		**150**	**27**	**39**	**66**	**40**	**5**	**0**	**1**	**1**	**0**

ARMSTRONG, TIM

Center. Shoots right. 5'11", 170 lbs. Born, Toronto, Ont., May 12, 1967
(Toronto's 11th choice, 211th over-all, in 1985 Entry Draft).

			Regular Season					Playoffs				
Season	Club	Lea	GP	G	A	TP	PIM	GP	G	A	TP	PIM
1984-85	Toronto	OHL	63	17	45	62	28	5	5	2	7	0
1985-86	Toronto	OHL	64	35	69	104	36	4	1	3	4	9
1986-87	Newmarket	AHL	5	3	0	3	2	....	....	....	....	....
	Toronto	OHL	66	29	55	84	61	....	....	....	....	....
1987-88	Newmarket	AHL	78	19	40	59	26	....	....	....	....	....
1988-89	**Toronto**	**NHL**	**11**	**1**	**0**	**1**	**6**	....	....	....	....	....
	Newmarket	AHL	37	16	24	40	38	....	....	....	....	....
	NHL Totals		**11**	**1**	**0**	**1**	**6**	....	....	....	....	....

ARNIEL, SCOTT (ar-NEEL)

Center. Shoots left. 6'1", 190 lbs. Born, Kingston, Ont., September 17, 1962.
(Winnipeg's 2nd choice, 22nd over-all, in 1981 Entry Draft).

			Regular Season					Playoffs				
Season	Club	Lea	GP	G	A	TP	PIM	GP	G	A	TP	PIM
1980-81	Cornwall	QJHL	68	52	71	123	102	19	14	19	33	24
1981-82	Cornwall	OHL	24	18	26	44	43	....	....	....	....	....
	Winnipeg	**NHL**	**17**	**1**	**8**	**9**	**14**	**3**	**0**	**0**	**0**	**0**
1982-83	**Winnipeg**	**NHL**	**75**	**13**	**5**	**18**	**46**	**2**	**0**	**0**	**0**	**0**
1983-84	**Winnipeg**	**NHL**	**80**	**21**	**35**	**56**	**68**	**2**	**0**	**0**	**0**	**5**
1984-85	**Winnipeg**	**NHL**	**79**	**22**	**22**	**44**	**81**	**8**	**1**	**2**	**3**	**9**
1985-86	**Winnipeg**	**NHL**	**80**	**18**	**25**	**43**	**40**	**3**	**0**	**0**	**0**	**12**
1986-87	**Buffalo**	**NHL**	**63**	**11**	**14**	**25**	**59**	....	....	....	....	....
1987-88	**Buffalo**	**NHL**	**73**	**17**	**23**	**40**	**61**	**6**	**0**	**1**	**1**	**5**
1988-89	**Buffalo**	**NHL**	**80**	**18**	**23**	**41**	**46**	**5**	**1**	**0**	**1**	**4**
	NHL Totals		**547**	**121**	**155**	**276**	**415**	**29**	**2**	**3**	**5**	**35**

Traded to **Buffalo** by **Winnipeg** for Gilles Hamel, June 21, 1986.

ASHTON, BRENT KENNETH

Left wing. Shoots left. 6'1", 210 lbs. Born, Saskatoon, Sask., May 18, 1960.
(Vancouver's 2nd choice, 26th over-all, in 1979 Entry Draft).

			Regular Season					Playoffs				
Season	Club	Lea	GP	G	A	TP	PIM	GP	G	A	TP	PIM
1977-78	Saskatoon	WHL	46	38	26	64	47	....	....	....	....	....
1978-79	Saskatoon	WHL	62	64	55	119	80	11	14	4	18	5
1979-80	**Vancouver**	**NHL**	**47**	**5**	**14**	**19**	**11**	**4**	**1**	**0**	**1**	**6**
1980-81	**Vancouver**	**NHL**	**77**	**18**	**11**	**29**	**57**	**3**	**0**	**0**	**0**	**0**
1981-82	**Colorado**	**NHL**	**80**	**24**	**36**	**60**	**26**	....	....	....	....	....
1982-83	**New Jersey**	**NHL**	**76**	**14**	**19**	**33**	**47**	....	....	....	....	....
1983-84	**Minnesota**	**NHL**	**68**	**7**	**10**	**17**	**54**	**12**	**1**	**2**	**3**	**22**
1984-85	**Minnesota**	**NHL**	**29**	**4**	**7**	**11**	**15**	....	....	....	....	....
	Quebec	**NHL**	**49**	**27**	**24**	**51**	**38**	**18**	**6**	**4**	**10**	**13**
1985-86	**Quebec**	**NHL**	**77**	**26**	**32**	**58**	**64**	**3**	**2**	**1**	**3**	**9**
1986-87	**Quebec**	**NHL**	**46**	**25**	**19**	**44**	**17**	....	....	....	....	....
	Detroit	**NHL**	**35**	**15**	**16**	**31**	**22**	**16**	**4**	**9**	**13**	**6**
1987-88	**Detroit**	**NHL**	**73**	**26**	**27**	**53**	**50**	**16**	**7**	**5**	**12**	**10**
1988-89	**Winnipeg**	**NHL**	**75**	**31**	**37**	**68**	**36**	....	....	....	....	....
	NHL Totals		**732**	**222**	**252**	**474**	**437**	**72**	**21**	**21**	**42**	**66**

Traded to **Winnipeg** by **Vancouver** with Vancouver's fourth-round choice (Tom Martin) in the 1982 Entry Draft as compensation for Vancouver's signing of Ivan Hlinka, July 15, 1981. Traded to **Colorado** by **Winnipeg** with Winnipeg's third round choice (Dave Kasper) in 1982 Entry Draft for Lucien DeBlois, July 15, 1981. Traded to **Minnesota** by **New Jersey** for Dave Lewis, October 3, 1983. Traded to **Quebec** by **Minnesota** with Brad Maxwell for Tony McKegney and Bo Berglund, December 14, 1984. Traded to **Detroit** by **Quebec** with Gilbert Delorme and Mark Kumpel for Basil McRae, John Ogrodnick and Doug Shedden, January 17, 1987. Traded to **Winnipeg** by **Detroit** for Paul MacLean, June 13, 1988.

AVERILL, WILLIAM

Defense. Shoots right. 5'11", 175 lbs. Born, Wayland, MA, December 20, 1968.
(NY Islanders' 12th choice, 244th overall, in 1987 Entry Draft).

			Regular Season					Playoffs				
Season	Club	Lea	GP	G	A	TP	PIM	GP	G	A	TP	PIM
1986-87	Belmont Hill	HS	22	6	19	25	....	....	....	....	....	....
1987-88	Northeastern	H.E.	36	2	23	25	36	....	....	....	....	....
1988-89	Northeastern	H.E.	36	4	16	20	40	....	....	....	....	....

BABCOCK, BOBBY

Defense. Shoots left. 6', 225 lbs. Born, Agincourt, Ont., August 3, 1968.
(Washington's 11th choice, 208th overall, in 1986 Entry Draft).

			Regular Season					Playoffs				
Season	Club	Lea	GP	G	A	TP	PIM	GP	G	A	TP	PIM
1985-86	S.S. Marie	OHL	50	1	7	8	188	....	....	....	....	....
1986-87	S.S. Marie	OHL	62	7	8	15	243	4	0	0	0	11
1987-88	Cornwall	OHL	50	0	18	18	150	....	....	....	....	....
1988-89	Cornwall	OHL	42	0	9	9	163	18	1	3	4	29

BABE, WARREN

Left wing. Shoots left. 6'3", 200 lbs. Born, Medicine Hat, Alta., September 7, 1968
(Minnesota's 1st choice, 12th overall, in 1986 Entry Draft).

			Regular Season					Playoffs				
Season	Club	Lea	GP	G	A	TP	PIM	GP	G	A	TP	PIM
1985-86	Lethbridge	WHL	63	33	24	57	125	....	....	....	....	....
1986-87	Swift Current	WHL	16	8	12	20	19	....	....	....	....	....
	Kamloops	WHL	52	28	45	73	109	11	4	6	10	8
1987-88	**Minnesota**	**NHL**	**6**	**0**	**1**	**1**	**4**	....	....	....	....	....
	Kalamazoo	IHL	6	0	0	0	7	....	....	....	....	....
	Kamloops	WHL	32	17	19	36	73	18	5	12	17	42
1988-89	**Minnesota**	**NHL**	**14**	**2**	**3**	**5**	**19**	**2**	**0**	**0**	**0**	**0**
	Kalamazoo	IHL	62	18	24	42	102	6	1	4	5	24
	NHL Totals		**20**	**2**	**4**	**6**	**23**	**2**	**0**	**0**	**0**	**0**

BABYCH, DAVID MICHAEL (DAVE) (BAB-itch)

Defense. Shoots left. 6'2", 215 lbs. Born, Edmonton, Alta., May 23, 1961.
(Winnipeg's 1st choice, 2nd over-all, in 1980 Entry Draft).

			Regular Season					Playoffs				
Season	Club	Lea	GP	G	A	TP	PIM	GP	G	A	TP	PIM
1978-79	Portland	WHL	67	20	59	79	63	25	7	22	29	22
1979-80ab	Portland	WHL	50	22	60	82	71	8	1	10	11	2
1980-81	Winnipeg	NHL	69	6	38	44	90	....	....	....	....	....
1981-82	Winnipeg	NHL	79	19	49	68	92	4	1	2	3	29
1982-83	Winnipeg	NHL	79	13	61	74	56	3	0	0	0	0
1983-84	Winnipeg	NHL	66	18	39	57	62	3	1	1	2	0
1984-85	Winnipeg	NHL	78	13	49	62	78	8	2	7	9	6
1985-86	Winnipeg	NHL	19	4	12	16	14	....	....	....	....	....
	Hartford	NHL	62	10	43	53	36	8	1	3	4	14
1986-87	Hartford	NHL	66	8	33	41	44	6	1	1	2	14
1987-88	Hartford	NHL	71	14	36	50	54	6	3	2	5	2
1988-89	Hartford	NHL	70	6	41	47	54	4	1	5	6	2
	NHL Totals		659	111	401	512	580	42	10	21	31	67

a WHL First All-Star Team (1980)
b Named WHL's Top Defenseman (1980)

Played in NHL All-Star Game (1983, 1984)

Traded to **Hartford** by **Winnipeg** for Ray Neufeld, November 21, 1985.

BAILLARGEON, JOEL (BIGH uhr ZHAN)

Left Wing. Shoots left. 6'1", 205 lbs. Born, Quebec City, Que., October 6, 1964.
(Winnipeg's 5th choice, 109th over-all, in 1983 Entry Draft).

			Regular Season					Playoffs				
Season	Club	Lea	GP	G	A	TP	PIM	GP	G	A	TP	PIM
1981-82	Trois Rivieres	QMJHL	26	1	3	4	47	22	1	1	2	58
1982-83	Trois Rivieres	QMJHL	29	4	5	9	197	....	....	....	....	....
	Hull	QMJHL	25	15	7	22	76	7	0	1	1	16
1983-84	Chicoutimi	QMJHL	60	48	35	83	184	....	....	....	....	....
	Sherbrooke	AHL	8	0	0	0	26	....	....	....	....	....
1984-85	Granby	QMJHL	32	25	24	49	160	....	....	....	....	....
1985-86	Sherbrooke	AHL	56	6	12	18	115	....	....	....	....	....
1986-87	Winnipeg	NHL	11	0	1	1	15	....	....	....	....	....
	Sherbrooke	AHL	44	9	18	27	137	6	2	2	4	27
	Fort Wayne	IHL	4	1	1	2	37	....	....	....	....	....
1987-88	Winnipeg	NHL	4	0	1	1	12	....	....	....	....	....
	Moncton	AHL	48	8	14	22	133	....	....	....	....	....
1988-89	Quebec	NHL	5	0	0	0	4	....	....	....	....	....
	Halifax	NHL	53	11	19	30	122	4	1	0	1	26
	NHL Totals		20	0	2	2	31	....	....	....	....	....

Traded to **Quebec** by **Winnipeg** for future considerations, July 29, 1988.

BAKER, JAMIE

Center. Shoots right. 5'11", 180 lbs. Born, Nepean, Ont., August 31, 1966.
(Quebec's 2nd choice, 8th overall, in 1988 Supplemental Draft).

			Regular Season					Playoffs				
Season	Club	Lea	GP	G	A	TP	PIM	GP	G	A	TP	PIM
1985-86	St. Lawrence	ECAC	31	9	16	25	52	....	....	....	....	....
1986-87	St. Lawrence	ECAC	32	8	24	32	59	....	....	....	....	....
1987-88	St. Lawrence	ECAC	34	26	24	50	38	....	....	....	....	....
1988-89	St. Lawrence	ECAC	13	11	16	27	16	....	....	....	....	....

BAKOVIC, PETER GEORGE (BAK oh VIHK)

Right Wing. Shoots right. 6'2", 200 lbs. Born, Thunder Bay, Ont., January 31, 1965.

			Regular Season					Playoffs				
Season	Club	Lea	GP	G	A	TP	PIM	GP	G	A	TP	PIM
1983-84	Windsor	OHL	63	12	31	43	161	3	0	2	2	14
1984-85	Windsor	OHL	58	26	48	74	259	3	0	0	0	12
1985-86	Moncton	AHL	80	18	36	54	349	10	2	2	4	30
1986-87	Moncton	AHL	77	17	34	51	280	6	3	3	6	54
1987-88	Vancouver	NHL	10	2	0	2	48	....	....	....	....	....
	Salt Lake	IHL	39	16	27	43	221	....	....	....	....	....
1988-89	Milwaukee	IHL	40	16	14	30	211	11	4	4	8	46
	NHL Totals		10	2	0	2	48	....	....	....	....	....

Signed as a free agent by **Calgary**, October 10, 1985. Traded to **Vancouver** by **Calgary** with Brian Bradley and Kevin Guy for Craig Coxe, March 6, 1988.

BALL, MARTYN

Left wing. Shoots left. 6'2", 175 lbs. Born, Toronto, Ont., June 12, 1968.
(St. Louis' 9th choice, 178th overall, in 1986 Entry Draft).

			Regular Season					Playoffs				
Season	Club	Lea	GP	G	A	TP	PIM	GP	G	A	TP	PIM
1985-86	St. Michael's	Jr.B	36	20	16	36	54	....	....	....	....	....
1986-87	St. Lawrence	ECAC	31	11	2	13	14	....	....	....	....	....
1987-88	St. Lawrence	ECAC	33	5	15	20	18	....	....	....	....	....
1988-89	St. Lawrence	ECAC	36	11	15	26	40	....	....	....	....	....

BALLANTYNE, JEFF

Defense. Shoots left. 6'1", 203 lbs. Born, Elmira, Ont., January 7, 1969.
(Washington's 1st choice, 36th overall, in 1987 Entry Draft).

			Regular Season					Playoffs				
Season	Club	Lea	GP	G	A	TP	PIM	GP	G	A	TP	PIM
1986-87	Ottawa	OHL	65	2	13	15	75	5	0	0	0	9
1987-88	Ottawa	OHL	DID NOT PLAY — INJURED									
1988-89	Ottawa	OHL	61	3	21	24	155	9	0	0	0	24

BANNISTER, DARIN

Defense. Shoots right. 6', 185 lbs. Born, Calgary, Alta., January 16, 1967.
(Detroit's 11th choice, 200th overall, in 1987 Entry Draft).

			Regular Season					Playoffs				
Season	Club	Lea	GP	G	A	TP	PIM	GP	G	A	TP	PIM
1986-87	Ill.-Chicago	CCHA	38	4	16	20	38	....	....	....	....	....
1987-88	Ill.-Chicago	CCHA	39	2	26	28	96	....	....	....	....	....
1988-89	Ill.-Chicago	CCHA	41	7	26	33	88	....	....	....	....	....

BARBE, MARIO (BARB)

Defense. Shoots left. 6'1", 209 lbs. Born, Cadillac, Que., March 17, 1967.
(Edmonton's 9th choice, 209th overall, in 1985 Entry Draft).

			Regular Season					Playoffs				
Season	Club	Lea	GP	G	A	TP	PIM	GP	G	A	TP	PIM
1984-85	Chicoutimi	QMJHL	64	2	13	15	211	14	0	2	2	36
1985-86	Granby	QMJHL	70	5	25	30	261	....	....	....	....	....
1986-87	Granby	QMJHL	65	7	25	32	356	7	1	5	6	38
1987-88	Granby	QMJHL	45	8	10	18	294	5	1	4	5	16
1988-89	Cape Breton	AHL	70	1	11	12	137	....	....	....	....	....

BARBER, DON

Left wing. Shoots left. 6'1", 205 lbs. Born, Victoria, B.C., December 2, 1964.
(Edmonton's 5th choice, 120th over-all, in 1983 Entry Draft).

			Regular Season					Playoffs				
Season	Club	Lea	GP	G	A	TP	PIM	GP	G	A	TP	PIM
1984-85	Bowling Green	CCHA	39	15	22	37	44	....	....	....	....	....
1985-86	Bowling Green	CCHA	35	21	22	43	64	....	....	....	....	....
1986-87	Bowling Green	CCHA	43	29	34	63	107	....	....	....	....	....
1987-88	Bowling Green	CCHA	38	18	47	65	62	....	....	....	....	....
1988-89	Minnesota	NHL	23	8	5	13	8	4	1	1	2	2
	Kalamazoo	IHL	39	14	17	31	23	....	....	....	....	....
	NHL Totals		23	8	5	13	8	4	1	1	2	2

Traded to **Minnesota** by **Edmonton** with Marc Habscheid and Emanuel Viveiros for Gord Sherven and Don Biggs, December 20, 1985.

BARKOVICH, RICHARD (RICK)

Center. Shoots right. 5'10", 190 lbs. Born, Kirkland Lake, Ont., April 25, 1964.

			Regular Season					Playoffs				
Season	Club	Lea	GP	G	A	TP	PIM	GP	G	A	TP	PIM
1986-87	Brantford	Sr.	35	31	32	63	22	....	....	....	....	....
1987-88	Salt Lake	IHL	79	34	25	59	65	17	9	11	20	18
1988-89	Indianapolis	IHL	78	32	35	67	81	....	....	....	....	....

Signed as a free agent by **Calgary**, October 10, 1987.

BARNETT, BRETT

Right wing. Shoots left. 6'3", 185 lbs. Born, Toronto, Ont., October 12, 1967.
(NY Rangers' 11th choice, 205th overall, in 1987 Entry Draft).

			Regular Season					Playoffs				
Season	Club	Lea	GP	G	A	TP	PIM	GP	G	A	TP	PIM
1987-88	Lake Superior	CCHA	44	16	23	39	124	....	....	....	....	....
1988-89	Lake Superior	CCHA	30	15	11	26	104	....	....	....	....	....

Rights traded to **Minnesota** by **NY Rangers** with Paul Jerrard, the rights to Mike Sullivan, and Los Angeles' third-round choice (Murray Garbutt) in 1989 Entry Draft - acquired March 10, 1987 by Minnesota - for Brian Lawton, Igor Liba and the rights to Eric Bennett, October 11, 1988.

BARON, MURRAY

Defense. Shoots left. 6'3", 210 lbs. Born, Prince George, B.C., June 1, 1967.
(Philadelphia's 7th choice, 167th overall, in 1986 Entry Draft).

			Regular Season					Playoffs				
Season	Club	Lea	GP	G	A	TP	PIM	GP	G	A	TP	PIM
1985-86	Vernon	BCJHL	46	12	32	44	0	....	....	....	....	....
1986-87	North Dakota	WCHA	41	4	10	14	62	....	....	....	....	....
1987-88	North Dakota	WCHA	41	1	10	11	95	....	....	....	....	....
1988-89	Hershey	AHL	9	0	3	3	8	....	....	....	....	....
	North Dakota	WCHA	40	2	6	8	92	....	....	....	....	....

BARR, DAVID (DAVE)

Right wing. Shoots right. 6'1", 195 lbs. Born, Edmonton, Alta., November 30, 1960.

			Regular Season					Playoffs				
Season	Club	Lea	GP	G	A	TP	PIM	GP	G	A	TP	PIM
1979-80	Lethbridge	WHL	60	16	38	54	47	....	....	....	....	....
1980-81	Lethbridge	WHL	72	26	62	88	106	....	....	....	....	....
1981-82	Erie	AHL	76	18	48	66	29	....	....	....	....	....
	Boston	NHL	2	0	0	0	0	5	1	0	1	0
1982-83	Baltimore	AHL	72	27	51	78	67	....	....	....	....	....
	Boston	NHL	10	1	1	2	7	10	0	0	0	2
1983-84	NY Rangers	NHL	6	0	0	0	2	....	....	....	....	....
	St. Louis	NHL	1	0	0	0	0	....	....	....	....	....
	Tulsa	CHL	50	28	37	65	24	....	....	....	....	....
1984-85	St. Louis	NHL	75	16	18	34	32	2	0	0	0	2
1985-86	St. Louis	NHL	72	13	38	51	70	11	1	1	2	14
1986-87	St. Louis	NHL	2	0	0	0	0	....	....	....	....	....
	Hartford	NHL	30	2	4	6	19	....	....	....	....	....
	Detroit	NHL	37	13	13	26	49	13	1	0	1	14
1987-88	Detroit	NHL	51	14	26	40	58	16	5	7	12	22
1988-89	Detroit	NHL	73	27	32	59	69	6	3	1	4	6
	NHL Totals		359	86	132	218	306	63	11	9	20	60

Signed as free agent by **Boston**, September 28, 1981. Traded to **NY Rangers** by **Boston** for Dave Silk, October 5, 1983. Traded to **St. Louis** by **NY Rangers** with NY Rangers' third-round choice (Alan Perry) in the 1984 Entry Draft for Larry Patey and Bob Brooke, March 5, 1984. Traded to **Hartford** by **St. Louis** for Tim Bothwell, October 21, 1986. Traded to **Detroit** by **Hartford** for Randy Ladouceur, January 12, 1987.

BARTEL, ROBIN DALE

Defense. Shoots left. 6', 200 lbs. Born, Drake, Sask., May 16, 1961

			Regular Season					Playoffs				
Season	Club	Lea	GP	G	A	TP	PIM	GP	G	A	TP	PIM
1980-81	Prince Albert	SJHL	86	22	63	85	....	....	....	....	....	....
1981-82	Prince Albert	SJHL	83	17	73	90	....	....	....	....	....	....
1982-83a	U. of Sask.	CWUAA	27	6	7	13	36	....	....	....	....	....
1983-84	Cdn. National	...	51	4	6	10	50	....	....	....	....	....
	Cdn. Olympic	...	6	0	1	1	4	....	....	....	....	....
1984-85	Moncton	AHL	41	4	11	15	54	....	....	....	....	....
1985-86	**Calgary**	**NHL**	**1**	**0**	**0**	**0**	**0**	**6**	**0**	**0**	**0**	**16**
	Moncton	AHL	74	4	21	25	100	3	0	0	0	0
1986-87	**Vancouver**	**NHL**	**40**	**0**	**1**	**1**	**14**	....	....	....	....	....
	Fredericton	AHL	10	0	2	2	15	....	....	....	....	....
1987-88	Fredericton	AHL	37	1	10	11	54	3	0	0	0	9
1988-89	Moncton	AHL	23	0	4	4	19	10	0	1	1	18
	Milwaukee	IHL	26	1	5	6	59	....	....	....	....	....
	NHL Totals		**41**	**0**	**1**	**1**	**14**	**6**	**0**	**0**	**0**	**16**

a CWUAA Freshman of the Year, Second All-Star Team (1983)

Signed as a free agent by **Calgary**, July 1, 1985. Signed as a free agent by **Vancouver**, June 27, 1986.

BARTLEY, WADE

Defense. Shoots right. 6'1", 190 lbs. Born, Killarney, Man., May 16, 1970.
(Washington's 3rd choice, 41st overall, in 1988 Entry Draft).

			Regular Season					Playoffs				
Season	Club	Lea	GP	G	A	TP	PIM	GP	G	A	TP	PIM
1986-87	Dauphin	MJHL	36	4	24	28	55	....	....	....	....	....
1987-88	Dauphin	MJHL	47	10	64	74	104	....	....	....	....	....
1988-89	North Dakota	WCHA	32	1	1	2	8	....	....	....	....	....

BASSEGIO, DAVID

Defense. Shoots left. 6'3", 210 lbs. Born, Niagara Falls, Ont., October 28, 1967.
(Buffalo's 5th choice, 68th overall, in 1986 Entry Draft).

			Regular Season					Playoffs				
Season	Club	Lea	GP	G	A	TP	PIM	GP	G	A	TP	PIM
1985-86	Yale	ECAC	30	7	17	24	54	....	....	....	....	....
1986-87	Yale	ECAC	29	8	17	25	52	....	....	....	....	....
1987-88	Yale	ECAC	24	4	22	26	67	....	....	....	....	....
1988-89a	Yale	ECAC	28	10	23	33	41	....	....	....	....	....

a ECAC Second All-Star Team (1989)

BASSEN, BOB

Center. Shoots left. 5'10", 180 lbs. Born, Calgary, Alta., May 6, 1965.

			Regular Season					Playoffs				
Season	Club	Lea	GP	G	A	TP	PIM	GP	G	A	TP	PIM
1982-83	Medicine Hat	WHL	4	3	2	5	0	3	0	0	0	4
1983-84	Medicine Hat	WHL	72	29	29	58	93	14	5	11	16	12
1984-85a	Medicine Hat	WHL	65	32	50	82	143	10	2	8	10	39
1985-86	**NY Islanders**	**NHL**	**11**	**2**	**1**	**3**	**6**	**3**	**0**	**1**	**1**	**0**
	Springfield	AHL	54	13	21	34	111	....	....	....	....	....
1986-87	**NY Islanders**	**NHL**	**77**	**7**	**10**	**17**	**89**	**14**	**1**	**2**	**3**	**21**
1987-88	**NY Islanders**	**NHL**	**77**	**6**	**16**	**22**	**99**	**6**	**0**	**1**	**1**	**23**
1988-89	**NY Islanders**	**NHL**	**19**	**1**	**4**	**5**	**21**	....	....	....	....	....
	Chicago	**NHL**	**49**	**4**	**12**	**16**	**62**	**10**	**1**	**1**	**2**	**34**
	NHL Totals		**233**	**20**	**43**	**63**	**277**	**33**	**2**	**5**	**7**	**78**

a WHL First All-Star Team (1985)

Signed as a free agent by **NY Islanders**, October 19, 1984.Traded to **Chicago** by **NY Islanders** with Steve Konroyd for Marc Bergevin and Gary Nylund, November 25, 1988.

BATEMAN, ROBERTSON (ROB)

Right wing. Shoots right. 6', 175 lbs. Born, LaSalle, Que., January 2, 1968.
(Winnipeg's 6th choice, 113th overall, in 1986 Entry Draft).

			Regular Season					Playoffs				
Season	Club	Lea	GP	G	A	TP	PIM	GP	G	A	TP	PIM
1985-86	St Laurent	HS	41	2	13	15	73	....	....	....	....	....
1986-87	U. of Vermont	ECAC	32	2	3	5	78	....	....	....	....	....
1987-88	U. of Vermont	ECAC	34	1	3	4	64	....	....	....	....	....
1988-89	U. of Vermont	ECAC	32	1	4	5	38	....	....	....	....	....

BAUER, COLLIN

Defense. Shoots left. 6'1", 175 lbs. Born, Edmonton, Alta., September 6, 1970.
(Edmonton's 4th choice, 61st overall, in 1988 Entry Draft).

			Regular Season					Playoffs				
Season	Club	Lea	GP	G	A	TP	PIM	GP	G	A	TP	PIM
1986-87	Saskatoon	WHL	61	1	25	26	37	11	0	6	6	10
1987-88	Saskatoon	WHL	70	9	53	62	66	10	2	5	7	16
1988-89a	Saskatoon	WHL	61	17	62	79	71	8	1	8	9	8

a WHL East All-Star Team (1989)

BAUMGARTNER, KEN

Defense. Shoots left. 6'1", 200 lbs. Born, Flin, Flon, Man., March 11, 1966
(Buffalo's 12th choice, 245th over-all, in 1985 Entry Draft).

			Regular Season					Playoffs				
Season	Club	Lea	GP	G	A	TP	PIM	GP	G	A	TP	PIM
1984-85	Prince Albert	WHL	60	3	9	12	252	13	1	3	4	89
1985-86	Prince Albert	WHL	70	4	23	27	277	20	3	9	12	112
1986-87	New Haven	AHL	13	0	3	3	99	6	0	0	0	60
1987-88	**Los Angeles**	**NHL**	**30**	**2**	**3**	**5**	**189**	**5**	**0**	**1**	**1**	**28**
	New Haven	AHL	48	1	5	6	181	....	....	....	....	....
1988-89	**Los Angeles**	**NHL**	**49**	**1**	**3**	**4**	**288**	**5**	**0**	**0**	**0**	**8**
	New Haven	AHL	10	1	3	4	26	....	....	....	....	....
	NHL Totals		**79**	**3**	**6**	**9**	**477**	**10**	**0**	**1**	**1**	**36**

Traded to **Los Angeles** by **Buffalo** with Sean McKenna and Larry Playfair for Brian Engblom and Doug Smith, January 29, 1986.

BAWA, ROBIN (BAH-wuh)

Right wing. Shoots right. 6'2", 214 lbs. Born, Chemainus, B.C., March 26, 1966.

			Regular Season					Playoffs				
Season	Club	Lea	GP	G	A	TP	PIM	GP	G	A	TP	PIM
1982-83	Kamloops	WHL	66	10	24	34	17	7	1	2	3	0
1983-84	Kamloops	WHL	64	16	28	44	40	13	4	2	6	4
1984-85	Kamloops	WHL	52	6	19	25	45	15	4	9	13	14
1985-86	Kamloops	WHL	63	29	43	72	78	16	5	13	18	4
1986-87a	Kamloops	WHL	62	57	56	113	91	13	6	7	13	22
1987-88	Fort Wayne	IHL	55	12	27	39	239	6	1	3	4	24
1988-89	Baltimore	AHL	75	23	24	47	205	....	....	....	....	....

a WHL West All-Star Team (1987)

Signed as a free agent by **Washington**, May 22, 1987.

BEAN, TIM

Left wing. Shoots left. 6'1", 190 lbs. Born, Sault Ste. Marie, Ont., March 9, 1967.
(Toronto's 7th choice, 127th over-all, in 1985 Entry Draft).

			Regular Season					Playoffs				
Season	Club	Lea	GP	G	A	TP	PIM	GP	G	A	TP	PIM
1983-84	Belleville	OHL	63	12	13	25	131	3	0	0	0	0
1984-85	Belleville	OHL	31	10	11	21	60	....	....	....	....	....
	North Bay	OHL	28	11	13	24	61	8	2	5	7	8
1985-86	North Bay	OHL	66	32	34	66	129	10	5	5	10	22
1986-87	North Bay	OHL	65	24	39	63	134	21	4	12	16	65
1987-88	Newmarket	AHL	76	12	16	28	118	....	....	....	....	....
1988-89	Newmarket	AHL	44	4	12	16	55	....	....	....	....	....
	Flint	IHL	3	1	3	4	4	....	....	....	....	....

BEAUCHESNE, PAT

Defense. Shoots left. 6'2", 204 lbs. Born, Albertville, Sask., February 12, 1967.
(Washington's 4th choice, 99th overall, in 1987 Entry Draft).

			Regular Season					Playoffs				
Season	Club	Lea	GP	G	A	TP	PIM	GP	G	A	TP	PIM
1984-85	Medicine Hat	WHL	53	1	9	10	85	....	....	....	....	....
1985-86	Medicine Hat	WHL	4	0	0	0	10	....	....	....	....	....
	Moose Jaw	WHL	64	3	13	16	116	13	0	2	2	23
1986-87	Moose Jaw	WHL	69	11	33	44	151	9	2	7	9	16
1987-88	Moose Jaw	WHL	54	1	19	20	190	....	....	....	....	....
1988-89	Baltimore	AHL	2	0	0	0	4	....	....	....	....	....

BEAUDETTE, DAN

Center. Shoots right. 6'3", 202 lbs. Born, St. Paul, MN, February 18, 1968.
(NY Islanders 13th choice, 227th overall, in 1986 Entry Draft).

			Regular Season					Playoffs				
Season	Club	Lea	GP	G	A	TP	PIM	GP	G	A	TP	PIM
1985-86	St. Thomas	HS	23	21	15	36	18	....	....	....	....	....
1986-87	Miami-Ohio	CCHA	31	5	9	14	26	....	....	....	....	....
1987-88	Miami-Ohio	CCHA	29	3	3	6	12	....	....	....	....	....
1988-89	Miami-Ohio	CCHA	34	5	13	18	32	....	....	....	....	....

BEAULIEU, NICOLAS (BOWL-ec-oh)

Left wing. Shoots left. 6', 200 lbs. Born, Rimouski, Que., April 19, 1968.
(Edmonton's 8th choice, 168th overall, in 1986 Entry Draft).

			Regular Season					Playoffs				
Season	Club	Lea	GP	G	A	TP	PIM	GP	G	A	TP	PIM
1985-86	Drummondville	QMJHL	70	11	20	31	93	23	0	1	1	11
1986-87	Drummondville	QMJHL	69	19	34	53	198	8	0	1	1	8
1987-88	Laval	QMJHL	64	39	56	95	240	14	3	13	16	37
1988-89	Cape Breton	AHL	60	10	13	23	85	....	....	....	....	....

BECK, BRAD

Defense. Shoots right. 5'11", 180 lbs. Born, Vancouver, B.C., February 10, 1964.
(Chicago's 5th choice, 91st over-all, in 1982 Entry Draft).

			Regular Season					Playoffs				
Season	Club	Lea	GP	G	A	TP	PIM	GP	G	A	TP	PIM
1981-82	Penticton	BCJHL	52	13	32	45	116	....	....	....	....	....
1982-83	Michigan State	CCHA	42	5	15	20	40	....	....	....	....	....
1983-84	Michigan State	CCHA	42	2	7	9	67	....	....	....	....	....
1984-85	Michigan State	CCHA	42	5	18	23	62	....	....	....	....	....
1985-86	Michigan State	CCHA	41	3	15	18	40	....	....	....	....	....
1986-87	Saginaw	IHL	82	10	24	34	114	10	0	2	2	24
1987-88	Saginaw	IHL	80	8	22	30	159	9	0	2	2	4
1988-89	Indianapolis	IHL	34	4	15	19	103	....	....	....	....	....
	Assat	Fin.	16	1	4	5	22	5	0	0	0	12

BEERS, BOB

Defense. Shoots right. 6'2", 200 lbs. Born, Cheektowaga, NY, May 20, 1967.
(Boston's 10th choice, 210th overall, in 1985 Entry Draft).

			Regular Season					Playoffs				
Season	Club	Lea	GP	G	A	TP	PIM	GP	G	A	TP	PIM
1985-86	N. Arizona	NCAA	28	11	39	50	96	....	....	....	....	....
1986-87	U. of Maine	H.E.	38	0	13	13	45	....	....	....	....	....
1987-88	U. of Maine	H.E.	41	3	11	14	72	....	....	....	....	....
1988-89ab	U. of Maine	H.E.	44	10	27	37	53	....	....	....	....	....

a Hockey East Second All-Star Team (1989)
b NCAA East Second All-American Team (1989)

BELL, BRUCE
Defense. Shoots left. 6', 190 lbs.   Born, Toronto, Ont., February 15, 1965.
(Quebec's 2nd choice, 52nd over-all, in 1983 Entry Draft).

			Regular Season					Playoffs				
Season	Club	Lea	GP	G	A	TP	PIM	GP	G	A	TP	PIM
1981-82	S. S. Marie	OHL	67	11	18	29	63	12	0	2	2	24
1982-83	S. S. Marie	OHL	5	0	2	2	2	....	....	....	....	....
	Windsor	OHL	61	10	35	45	39	3	0	4	4	0
1983-84a	Brantford	OHL	63	7	41	48	55	6	0	3	3	16
1984-85b	Quebec	NHL	75	6	31	37	44	16	2	2	4	21
1985-86	St. Louis	NHL	75	2	18	20	43	14	0	2	2	13
1986-87	St. Louis	NHL	45	3	13	16	18	4	1	1	2	7
1987-88	NY Rangers	NHL	13	1	2	3	8	....	....	....	....	....
	Colorado	IHL	65	11	34	45	107	4	2	3	5	0
1988-89	Halifax	AHL	12	0	6	6	0	2	0	1	1	2
	Adirondack	AHL	9	1	4	5	4	....	....	....	....	....
	NHL Totals		208	12	64	76	113	34	3	5	8	41

a OHL First All-Star Team (1984)
b NHL All-Rookie Team (1985)
Traded to **St. Louis** by **Quebec** for Gilbert Delorme, October 2, 1985. Traded to **NY Rangers** by **St. Louis** with future considerations for Tony McKegney and Rob Whistle, May 28, 1987. Traded to **Quebec** by **NY Rangers** with Jari Gronstrand, Walt Poddubny and NY Rangers' fourth round choice (Eric Dubois) in 1989 Entry Draft for Jason Lafreniere and Normand Rochefort, August 1, 1988.

BELLEFEUILLE, BRIAN
Left wing. Shoots left. 6'2", 185 lbs.   Born, Natick, MA, March 21, 1967.
(Toronto's 9th choice, 174th overall, in 1986 Entry Draft).

			Regular Season					Playoffs				
Season	Club	Lea	GP	G	A	TP	PIM	GP	G	A	TP	PIM
1985-86	Canterbury	HS	31	57	58	115	0	....	....	....	....	....
1986-87	Ill.-Chicago	CCHA	2	0	0	0	2	....	....	....	....	....
1987-88	U. of Maine	H.E.	15	2	2	4	30	....	....	....	....	....
1988-89	U. of Maine	H.E.	36	5	10	15	32	....	....	....	....	....

BELLOWS, BRIAN
Right wing. Shoots right. 5'11", 200 lbs.   Born, St. Catharines, Ont., September 1, 1964.
(Minnesota's 1st choice, 2nd over-all, in 1982 Entry Draft).

			Regular Season					Playoffs				
Season	Club	Lea	GP	G	A	TP	PIM	GP	G	A	TP	PIM
1980-81a	Kitchener	OHA	66	49	67	116	23	16	14	13	27	13
1981-82bc	Kitchener	OHL	47	45	52	97	23	15	16	13	29	11
1982-83	Minnesota	NHL	78	35	30	65	27	9	5	4	9	18
1983-84	Minnesota	NHL	78	41	42	83	66	16	2	12	14	6
1984-85	Minnesota	NHL	78	26	36	62	72	9	2	4	6	9
1985-86	Minnesota	NHL	77	31	48	79	46	5	5	0	5	16
1986-87	Minnesota	NHL	65	26	27	53	34	....	....	....	....	....
1987-88	Minnesota	NHL	77	40	41	81	81	....	....	....	....	....
1988-89	Minnesota	NHL	60	23	27	50	55	5	2	3	5	8
	NHL Totals		513	222	251	473	381	44	16	23	39	57

a OHA Third All-Star Team (1981)
b OHL First All-Star Team (1982)
c Most Sportsmanlike Player, Memorial Cup Tournament (1982)
Played in NHL All-Star Game (1984, 1988)

BENAK, JAROSLAV
Defense. Shoots left. 6', 185 lbs.   Born, Hrdec Brod, Czechoslovakia, April 3, 1964.
(Calgary's 13th choice, 211th overall, in 1983 Entry Draft).

			Regular Season					Playoffs				
Season	Club	Lea	GP	G	A	TP	PIM	GP	G	A	TP	PIM
1986-87	Dukla Jihlava	Czech.	34	1	6	7		....	....	....	....	....
1987-88	Dukla Jihlava	Czech.	26	2	8	10		....	....	....	....	....
1988-89	Dukla Jihlava	Czech.	28	1	6	7		....	....	....	....	....

BENIC, GEOFF
Left wing. Shoots left. 6'2", 200 lbs.   Born, Toronto, Ont., September 1, 1968.
(Chicago's 8th choice, 182nd overall, in 1986 Entry Draft).

			Regular Season					Playoffs				
Season	Club	Lea	GP	G	A	TP	PIM	GP	G	A	TP	PIM
1985-86	Windsor	OHL	59	3	7	10	77	14	0	1	1	10
1986-87	Windsor	OHL	63	9	7	16	169	14	2	1	3	22
1987-88	Windsor	OHL	46	2	4	6	149	12	0	0	0	16
1988-89	Indianapolis	IHL	10	1	0	1	51	....	....	....	....	....

BENNETT, ERIC (RIC)
Left wing. Shoots left. 6'3", 200 lbs.   Born, Springfield, MA, July 24, 1967.
(Minnesota's 4th choice, 54th over-all, in 1986 Entry Draft).

			Regular Season					Playoffs				
Season	Club	Lea	GP	G	A	TP	PIM	GP	G	A	TP	PIM
1985-86	Wilbraham	HS	57	9	40	49	95	9	1	5	6	14
1986-87	Providence	H.E.	32	15	12	27	34	....	....	....	....	....
1987-88	Providence	H.E.	33	9	16	25	70	....	....	....	....	....
1988-89a	Providence	H.E.	32	14	32	46	74	....	....	....	....	....

a NCAA East Second All-American Team (1989)
Rights traded to **NY Rangers** by **Minnesota** with Brian Lawton and Igor Liba for Paul Jerrard and Mark Tinordi, the rights to Bret Barnett and Mike Sullivan, and Los Angeles' third-round choice (Murray Garbutt) in 1989 Entry Draft - acquired March 10, 1987 by Minnesota - October 11, 1988.

BENNING, BRIAN
Defense. Shoots left. 6', 195 lbs.   Born, Edmonton, Alta., June 10, 1966.
(St. Louis' 1st choice, 26th over-all, in 1984 Entry Draft).

			Regular Season					Playoffs				
Season	Club	Lea	GP	G	A	TP	PIM	GP	G	A	TP	PIM
1982-83	St. Albert	AJHL	57	8	38	46	229	....	....	....	....	....
1983-84	Portland	WHL	38	6	41	47	108	....	....	....	....	....
1984-85	St. Louis	NHL	4	0	2	2	0	....	....	....	....	....
	Kamloops	WHL	17	3	18	21	26	....	....	....	....	....
1985-86	St. Louis	NHL	....					6	1	2	3	13
	Cdn. Olympic	....	60	6	13	19	43	....	....	....	....	....
1986-87a	St. Louis	NHL	78	13	36	49	110	6	0	4	4	9
1987-88	St. Louis	NHL	77	8	29	37	107	10	1	6	7	25
1988-89	St. Louis	NHL	66	8	26	34	102	7	1	1	2	11
	NHL Totals		225	29	93	122	319	29	3	13	16	58

a NHL All-Rookie Team (1987)

BENNING, JAMES (JIM)
Defense. Shoots left. 6', 185 lbs.   Born, Edmonton, Alta., April 29, 1963.
(Toronto's 1st choice, 6th over-all, in 1981 Entry Draft).

			Regular Season					Playoffs				
Season	Club	Lea	GP	G	A	TP	PIM	GP	G	A	TP	PIM
1979-80	Portland	WHL	71	11	60	71	42	8	3	9	12	6
1980-81ab	Portland	WHL	72	28	111	139	61	9	1	5	6	16
1981-82	Toronto	NHL	74	7	24	31	46	....	....	....	....	....
1982-83	Toronto	NHL	74	5	17	22	47	4	1	1	2	2
1983-84	Toronto	NHL	79	12	39	51	66	....	....	....	....	....
1984-85	Toronto	NHL	80	9	35	44	55	....	....	....	....	....
1985-86	Toronto	NHL	52	4	21	25	71	....	....	....	....	....
1986-87	Toronto	NHL	5	0	0	0	4	....	....	....	....	....
	Newmarket	AHL	10	1	5	6	0	....	....	....	....	....
	Vancouver	NHL	54	2	11	13	40	....	....	....	....	....
1987-88	Vancouver	NHL	77	7	26	33	58	....	....	....	....	....
1988-89	Vancouver	NHL	65	3	9	12	48	3	0	0	0	0
	NHL Totals		560	49	182	231	435	7	1	1	2	2

a WHL First All-Star Team (1981)
b Named WHL's Top Defenseman (1981)
Traded to **Vancouver** by **Toronto** with Dan Hodgson for Rick Lanz, December 2, 1986

BERALDO, PAUL
Right wing. Shoots right. 5'11", 175 lbs.   Born, Hamilton, Ont., October 5, 1967.
(Boston's 6th choice, 139th overall, in 1986 Entry Draft).

			Regular Season					Playoffs				
Season	Club	Lea	GP	G	A	TP	PIM	GP	G	A	TP	PIM
1985-86	S.S. Marie	OHL	61	15	13	28	48	....	....	....	....	....
1986-87	S.S. Marie	OHL	63	39	51	90	117	4	3	2	5	6
1987-88	Boston	NHL	3	0	0	0	0	....	....	....	....	....
	Maine	AHL	62	22	15	37	112	2	0	0	0	19
1988-89	Boston	NHL	7	0	0	0	4	....	....	....	....	....
	Maine	AHL	73	25	28	53	134	....	....	....	....	....
	NHL Totals		10	0	0	0	4	....	....	....	....	....

BEREZAN, PERRY EDMUND   (BEAR-a-zan)
Center. Shoots right. 6'2", 190 lbs.   Born, Edmonton, Alta., December 5, 1964.
(Calgary's 3rd choice, 56th over-all, in 1983 Entry Draft).

			Regular Season					Playoffs				
Season	Club	Lea	GP	G	A	TP	PIM	GP	G	A	TP	PIM
1983-84	North Dakota	WCHA	44	28	24	52	29	....	....	....	....	....
1984-85a	North Dakota	WCHA	42	23	35	58	32	....	....	....	....	....
	Calgary	NHL	9	3	2	5	4	2	1	0	1	4
1985-86	Calgary	NHL	55	12	21	33	39	8	1	1	2	6
1986-87	Calgary	NHL	24	5	3	8	24	2	0	2	2	7
1987-88	Calgary	NHL	29	7	12	19	66	8	0	2	2	13
1988-89	Calgary	NHL	35	4	4	8	23	....	....	....	....	....
	Minnesota	NHL	16	1	4	5	4	5	1	2	3	4
	NHL Totals		168	32	46	78	160	25	3	7	10	34

a WCHA Second All-Star Team (1985)
Traded to **Minnesota** by **Calgary** with Shane Churla for Brian MacLellan and Minnesota's fourth-round choice (Robert Reichel) in 1989 Entry Draft, March 4, 1989.

BERG, BILL
Defense. Shoots left. 6'1", 190 lbs.   Born, St. Catharines, Ont., October 21, 1967.
(NY Islanders' 3rd choice, 59th over-all, in 1986 Entry Draft).

			Regular Season					Playoffs				
Season	Club	Lea	GP	G	A	TP	PIM	GP	G	A	TP	PIM
1984-85	Grimsby	OPJHL	42	10	22	32	153	....	....	....	....	....
1985-86	Toronto	OHL	64	3	35	38	143	4	0	0	0	19
	Springfield	AHL	4	1	1	2	4	....	....	....	....	....
1986-87	Toronto	OHL	57	3	15	18	138	....	....	....	....	....
1987-88	Springfield	AHL	76	6	26	32	148	....	....	....	....	....
	Peoria	IHL	5	0	1	1	8	7	0	3	3	31
1988-89	NY Islanders	NHL	7	1	2	3	10	....	....	....	....	....
	Springfield	AHL	69	17	32	49	122	....	....	....	....	....
	NHL Totals		7	1	2	3	10	....	....	....	....	....

BERGER, MIKE
Defense. Shoots right. 6', 200 lbs.   Born, Edmonton, Alta., June 2, 1967.
(Minnesota's 2nd choice, 69th over-all, in 1985 Entry Draft).

			Regular Season					Playoffs				
Season	Club	Lea	GP	G	A	TP	PIM	GP	G	A	TP	PIM
1982-83	Lethbridge	WHL	1	0	0	0	0	....	....	....	....	....
1983-84	Lethbridge	WHL	41	2	9	11	60	5	0	1	1	7
1984-85	Lethbridge	WHL	58	9	31	40	85	4	0	3	3	9
1985-86	Spokane	WHL	57	9	40	49	95	9	1	5	6	14
1986-87	Indianapolis	IHL	4	0	3	3	4	6	0	1	1	13
	Spokane	WHL	65	26	49	75	80	2	0	0	0	2
1987-88	Minnesota	NHL	29	3	1	4	65	....	....	....	....	....
	Kalamazoo	IHL	36	5	10	15	94	6	2	0	2	8
1988-89	Minnesota	NHL	1	0	0	0	2	....	....	....	....	....
	Kalamazoo	IHL	67	9	16	25	96	6	0	2	2	8
	NHL Totals		30	3	1	4	67	....	....	....	....	....

BERGER, PHILIP

Left wing. Shoots left. 6', 190 lbs.   Born, Dearborn, MI, December 3, 1966.
(Quebec's 1st choice, 3rd overall, in 1988 Supplemental Draft).

				Regular Season					Playoffs			
Season	Club	Lea	GP	G	A	TP	PIM	GP	G	A	TP	PIM
1985-86	N. Michigan	WCHA	21	5	2	7	20	....	....	....	....	....
1986-87	N. Michigan	WCHA	24	11	10	21	6	....	....	....	....	....
1987-88a	N. Michigan	WCHA	38	40	32	72	22	....	....	....	....	....
1988-89b	N. Michigan	WCHA	44	30	33	63	24	....	....	....	....	....

a WCHA First All-Star Team (1988)
b WCHA Second All-Star Team (1989)

BERGEVIN, MARC

Defense. Shoots right. 6', 185 lbs.   Born, Montreal, Que., August 11, 1965.
(Chicago's 3rd choice, 59th over-all, in 1983 Entry Draft).

				Regular Season					Playoffs			
Season	Club	Lea	GP	G	A	TP	PIM	GP	G	A	TP	PIM
1982-83	Chicoutimi	QMJHL	64	3	27	30	113	....	....	....	....	....
1983-84	Chicoutimi	QMJHL	70	10	35	45	125	....	....	....	....	....
	Springfield	AHL	7	0	1	1	2	....	....	....	....	....
1984-85	Springfield	AHL	....	....	....	....	....	4	0	0	0	0
	Chicago	**NHL**	60	0	6	6	54	6	0	3	3	2
1985-86	Chicago	NHL	71	7	7	14	60	3	0	0	0	0
1986-87	Chicago	NHL	66	4	10	14	66	3	1	0	1	2
1987-88	Chicago	NHL	58	1	6	7	85	....	....	....	....	....
	Saginaw	IHL	10	2	7	9	20	....	....	....	....	....
1988-89	Chicago	NHL	11	0	0	0	18	....	....	....	....	....
	NY Islanders	NHL	58	2	13	15	62	....	....	....	....	....
	NHL Totals		324	14	42	56	345	12	1	3	4	4

Traded to **NY Islanders** by **Chicago** with Gary Nylund for Steve Konroyd and Bob Bassen, November 25, 1988.

BERGLAND, TIM

Right wing. Shoots right. 6'3", 195 lbs.   Born, Crookston, MN, January 11, 1965.
(Washington's 1st choice, 75th over-all, in 1983 Entry Draft).

				Regular Season					Playoffs			
Season	Club	Lea	GP	G	A	TP	PIM	GP	G	A	TP	PIM
1983-84	U. Minnesota	WCHA	24	4	11	15	4	....	....	....	....	....
1984-85	U. Minnesota	WCHA	34	5	9	14	8	....	....	....	....	....
1985-86	U. Minnesota	WCHA	48	11	16	27	26	....	....	....	....	....
1986-87	U. Minnesota	WCHA	49	18	17	35	48	....	....	....	....	....
1987-88	Fort Wayne	IHL	13	2	1	3	9	....	....	....	....	....
	Binghamton	AHL	63	21	26	47	31	4	0	0	0	0
1988-89	Baltimore	AHL	78	24	29	53	39	....	....	....	....	....

BERNARD, LARRY

Left wing. Shoots left. 6'2", 195 lbs.   Born, Prince George, B.C., April 16, 1967.
(NY Rangers' 8th choice, 154th over-all, in 1985 Entry Draft).

				Regular Season					Playoffs			
Season	Club	Lea	GP	G	A	TP	PIM	GP	G	A	TP	PIM
1984-85	Seattle	WHL	63	18	26	44	66	....	....	....	....	....
1985-86	Seattle	WHL	54	17	25	42	64	5	1	3	4	10
1986-87	Seattle	WHL	70	40	46	86	159	....	....	....	....	....
1987-88	Colorado	IHL	64	14	13	27	68	9	0	3	3	18
1988-89	Denver	IHL	21	4	5	9	44	....	....	....	....	....
	Kalamazoo	IHL	45	9	16	25	47	1	0	0	0	5

Traded to **Minnesota** by **NY Rangers** with NY Ranger's fifth-round choice (Rhys Hollyman) in 1989 Entry Draft for Mark Hardy, December 9, 1988.

BERRY, BRAD

Defense. Shoots left. 6'2", 190 lbs.   Born, Bashaw, Alta., April 1, 1965.
(Winnipeg's 3rd choice, 29th over-all, in 1983 Entry Draft).

				Regular Season					Playoffs			
Season	Club	Lea	GP	G	A	TP	PIM	GP	G	A	TP	PIM
1982-83	St. Albert	AJHL	55	9	33	42	97	....	....	....	....	....
1983-84	North Dakota	WCHA	32	2	7	9	8	....	....	....	....	....
1984-85	North Dakota	WCHA	40	4	26	30	26	....	....	....	....	....
1985-86	North Dakota	WCHA	40	6	29	35	26	....	....	....	....	....
	Winnipeg	NHL	13	1	0	1	10	3	0	0	0	0
1986-87	Winnipeg	NHL	52	2	8	10	60	7	0	1	1	14
1987-88	Winnipeg	NHL	48	0	6	6	75	....	....	....	....	....
	Moncton	AHL	10	1	3	4	14	....	....	....	....	....
1988-89	Winnipeg	NHL	38	0	9	9	45	....	....	....	....	....
	Moncton	AHL	38	3	16	19	39	....	....	....	....	....
	NHL Totals		151	3	23	26	190	10	0	1	1	14

BERRY, KENNETH E. (KEN)

Left wing. Shoots left. 5'8", 175 lbs.   Born, Burnaby, B.C., June 21, 1960.
(Vancouver's 5th choice, 112th overall, in 1980 Entry Draft).

				Regular Season					Playoffs			
Season	Club	Lea	GP	G	A	TP	PIM	GP	G	A	TP	PIM
1979-80	Cdn. National	....	57	19	20	39	48	....	....	....	....	....
	Cdn. Olympic	....	6	4	1	5	8	....	....	....	....	....
1980-81	U. of Denver	WCHA	40	22	34	56	74	....	....	....	....	....
	Wichita	CHL	9	7	6	13	13	17	2	4	6	28
1981-82	**Edmonton**	**NHL**	15	2	3	5	9	....	....	....	....	....
	Wichita	CHL	58	28	29	57	70	....	....	....	....	....
1982-83	Moncton	AHL	76	24	26	50	80	....	....	....	....	....
1983-84	Moncton	AHL	53	18	20	38	75	....	....	....	....	....
	Edmonton	**NHL**	13	2	3	5	10	....	....	....	....	....
1984-85	Nova Scotia	AHL	71	30	27	57	40	6	2	2	4	2
1985-86	Bayreuth	W.Ger.	33	27	25	52	88	....	....	....	....	....
	Cdn. National	....	8	1	2	3	20	....	....	....	....	....
1986-87	Cdn. National	....	52	17	27	44	60	....	....	....	....	....
1987-88	Cdn. National	....	59	18	15	33	47	....	....	....	....	....
	Cdn. Olympic	....	8	2	4	6	4	....	....	....	....	....
	Vancouver	**NHL**	14	2	3	5	6	....	....	....	....	....
1988-89	**Vancouver**	**NHL**	13	2	1	3	5	....	....	....	....	....
	Milwaukee	IHL	5	4	4	8	2	....	....	....	....	....
	NHL Totals		55	8	10	18	30	....	....	....	....	....

Traded to **Edmonton** by **Vancouver** with Garry Lariviere for Blair MacDonald and Lars-Gunnar Petersson, March 10, 1981. Signed as a free agent by **Vancouver**, March 1, 1988.

BERUBE, CRAIG   (buh ROO bee)

Left wing. Shoots left. 6'1", 205 lbs.   Born, Calihoo, Alta., December 17, 1965.

				Regular Season					Playoffs			
Season	Club	Lea	GP	G	A	TP	PIM	GP	G	A	TP	PIM
1982-83	Kamloops	WHL	4	0	0	0	0	....	....	....	....	....
1983-84	N. Westminster	WHL	70	11	20	31	104	8	1	2	3	5
1984-85	N. Westminster	WHL	70	25	44	69	191	10	3	2	5	4
1985-86	Kamloops	WHL	32	17	14	31	119	....	....	....	....	....
	Medicine Hat	WHL	34	14	16	30	95	25	7	8	15	102
1986-87	**Philadelphia**	**NHL**	7	0	0	0	57	5	0	0	0	17
	Hershey	AHL	63	7	17	24	325	....	....	....	....	....
1987-88	**Philadelphia**	**NHL**	27	3	2	5	108	....	....	....	....	....
	Hershey	AHL	31	5	9	14	119	....	....	....	....	....
1988-89	**Philadelphia**	**NHL**	53	1	1	2	199	16	0	0	0	56
	Hershey	AHL	7	0	2	2	19	....	....	....	....	....
	NHL Totals		87	4	3	7	364	21	0	0	0	73

Signed as a free agent by **Philadelphia**, March 19, 1986.

BEUKEBOOM, JEFF   (BOO-ka-boom)

Defense. Shoots right. 6'4", 215 lbs.   Born, Ajax, Ont., March 28, 1965.
(Edmonton's 1st choice, 19th over-all, in 1983 Entry Draft).

				Regular Season					Playoffs			
Season	Club	Lea	GP	G	A	TP	PIM	GP	G	A	TP	PIM
1981-82	Newmarket	OPJHL	49	5	30	35	218	....	....	....	....	....
1982-83	S. S. Marie	OHL	70	0	25	25	143	16	1	4	5	46
1983-84	S. S. Marie	OHL	61	6	30	36	178	16	1	7	8	43
1984-85a	S. S. Marie	OHL	37	4	20	24	85	16	4	6	10	47
1985-86	**Edmonton**	**NHL**	....	....	....	....	....	1	0	0	0	4
	Nova Scotia	AHL	77	9	20	29	175	....	....	....	....	....
1986-87	**Edmonton**	**NHL**	44	3	8	11	124	....	....	....	....	....
	Nova Scotia	AHL	14	1	7	8	35	....	....	....	....	....
1987-88	**Edmonton**	**NHL**	73	5	20	25	201	7	0	0	0	16
1988-89	**Edmonton**	**NHL**	36	0	5	5	94	1	0	0	0	2
	Cape Breton	AHL	8	0	4	4	36	....	....	....	....	....
	NHL Totals		153	8	33	41	419	9	0	0	0	22

a OHL First All-Star Team (1985)

BIGGS, DON

Center. Shoots right. 5'8", 175 lbs.   Born, Mississauga, Ont., April 7, 1965.
(Minnesota's 9th choice, 156th over-all, in 1983 Entry Draft).

				Regular Season					Playoffs			
Season	Club	Lea	GP	G	A	TP	PIM	GP	G	A	TP	PIM
1981-82	Missisauga	Midget	54	49	67	116	125	....	....	....	....	....
1982-83	Oshawa	OHL	70	22	53	75	145	16	3	6	9	17
1983-84	Oshawa	OHL	58	31	60	91	149	7	4	4	8	18
1984-85	**Minnesota**	**NHL**	1	0	0	0	0	....	....	....	....	....
	Springfield	AHL	6	0	3	3	0	2	1	0	1	0
	Oshawa	OHL	60	48	69	117	105	5	3	4	7	6
1985-86	Springfield	AHL	28	15	16	31	46	....	....	....	....	....
	Nova Scotia	AHL	47	6	23	29	36	....	....	....	....	....
1986-87	Nova Scotia	AHL	80	22	25	47	165	5	1	2	3	4
1987-88	Hershey	AHL	77	38	41	79	151	12	5	*11	*16	22
1988-89	Hershey	AHL	76	36	67	103	158	11	5	9	14	30
	NHL Totals		1	0	0	0	0	....	....	....	....	....

Traded to **Edmonton** by **Minnesota** with Gord Sherven for Marc Habscheid, Don Barber and Emanuel Viveiros, December 20, 1985.

BIOTTI, CHRIS

Defense. Shoots left. 6'3", 200 lbs.   Born, Waltham, MA., April 22, 1967.
(Calgary's 1st choice, 17th over-all, in 1985 Entry Draft).

				Regular Season					Playoffs			
Season	Club	Lea	GP	G	A	TP	PIM	GP	G	A	TP	PIM
1983-84	Belmont	HS	23	10	20	30		....	....	....	....	....
1984-85	Belmont	HS	25	13	24	37	....	....	....	....	....	....
1985-86	Harvard	ECAC	15	3	5	8	18	....	....	....	....	....
1986-87	Harvard	ECAC	30	1	6	7	23	....	....	....	....	....
1987-88	Salt Lake	IHL	72	5	19	24	73	12	2	3	5	33
1988-89	Salt Lake	IHL	57	6	14	20	44	12	3	4	7	16

BISCHOFF, GRANT

Left wing. Shoots left. 5'10", 165 lbs.   Born, Anoka, MN, October 26, 1968.
(Minnesota's 8th choice, 211th overall, in 1988 Entry Draft).

				Regular Season					Playoffs			
Season	Club	Lea	GP	G	A	TP	PIM	GP	G	A	TP	PIM
1987-88	U. Minnesota	WCHA	44	15	22	37	14	....	....	....	....	....
1988-89	U. Minnesota	WCHA	47	21	16	37	14	....	....	....	....	....

BISHOP, MICHAEL

Defense. Shoots left. 6'2", 185 lbs.   Born, Sarnia, Ont., June 15, 1966.
(Montreal's 14th choice, 226th over-all, in 1985 Entry Draft).

				Regular Season					Playoffs			
Season	Club	Lea	GP	G	A	TP	PIM	GP	G	A	TP	PIM
1985-86	Colgate	ECAC	17	5	6	11	47	....	....	....	....	....
1986-87	Colgate	ECAC	30	7	17	24	68	....	....	....	....	....
1987-88	Colgate	ECAC	31	8	24	32	49	....	....	....	....	....
1988-89a	Colgate	ECAC	31	8	13	21	92	....	....	....	....	....

a ECAC Second All-Star Team (1989)

BISSETT, TOM   (BISS-it)

Center. Shoots left. 6', 180 lbs.   Born, Seattle, WA, March 13, 1966.
(Detroit's 11th choice, 211th overall, in 1986 Entry Draft).

				Regular Season					Playoffs			
Season	Club	Lea	GP	G	A	TP	PIM	GP	G	A	TP	PIM
1985-86	Michigan Tech.	WCHA	40	12	21	33	18	....	....	....	....	....
1986-87	Michigan Tech.	WCHA	40	16	19	35	12	....	....	....	....	....
1987-88	Michigan Tech.	WCHA	41	18	26	44	20	....	....	....	....	....
1988-89	Adirondack	AHL	5	0	1	1	0	....	....	....	....	....
	Michigan Tech.	WCHA	42	19	28	47	16	....	....	....	....	....

BISSON, STEVE

Defense. Shoots left. 6'1", 193 lbs. Born, Ottawa, Ont., May 24, 1968.
(Montreal's 7th choice, 120th overall, in 1986 Entry Draft).

			Regular Season					Playoffs				
Season	Club	Lea	GP	G	A	TP	PIM	GP	G	A	TP	PIM
1985-86	S.S. Marie	OHL	66	3	23	26	44	....	....	....	....	....
1986-87	S.S. Marie	OHL	52	5	15	20	38	4	1	1	2	4
1987-88	Cornwall	OHL	64	10	59	69	89	10	0	7	7	10
1988-89	Sherbrooke	AHL	4	0	3	3	4	....	....	....	....	....
	North Bay	OHL	37	8	16	24	83	11	5	7	12	10

BJUGSTAD, SCOTT (BYOOK-stad)

Center. Shoots left. 6'1", 185 lbs. Born, St. Paul, MN, June 2, 1961.
(Minnesota's 13th choice, 181st over-all, in 1981 Entry Draft).

			Regular Season					Playoffs				
Season	Club	Lea	GP	G	A	TP	PIM	GP	G	A	TP	PIM
1979-80	U. Minnesota	WCHA	18	2	2	4	2	....	....	....	....	....
1980-81	U. Minnesota	WCHA	35	12	23	25	34	....	....	....	....	....
1981-82	U. Minnesota	WCHA	36	29	14	43	24	....	....	....	....	....
1982-83a	U. Minnesota	WCHA	26	21	35	56	12	....	....	....	....	....
1983-84	U.S. National	...	54	31	20	51	28	....	....	....	....	....
	U.S. Olympic	...	6	3	2	5	6	....	....	....	....	....
	Minnesota	**NHL**	**5**	**0**	**0**	**0**	**2**	....	....	....	....	....
	Salt Lake	CHL	15	10	8	18	6	5	3	4	7	0
1984-85	**Minnesota**	**NHL**	**72**	**11**	**4**	**15**	**32**	....	....	....	....	....
	Springfield	AHL	5	2	3	5	2	....	....	....	....	....
1985-86	**Minnesota**	**NHL**	**80**	**43**	**33**	**76**	**24**	**5**	**0**	**1**	**1**	**0**
1986-87	**Minnesota**	**NHL**	**39**	**4**	**9**	**13**	**43**	....	....	....	....	....
	Springfield	AHL	11	4	6	10	7	....	....	....	....	....
1987-88	**Minnesota**	**NHL**	**33**	**10**	**12**	**22**	**15**	....	....	....	....	....
1988-89	**Pittsburgh**	**NHL**	**24**	**3**	**0**	**3**	**4**	....	....	....	....	....
	Kalamazoo	IHL	4	5	0	5	4	....	....	....	....	....
	NHL Totals		**253**	**71**	**58**	**129**	**120**	**5**	**0**	**1**	**1**	**0**

a WCHA First All-Star Team (1983)

Traded to **Pittsburgh** by **Minnesota** with Gord Dineen for Ville Siren and Steve Gotaas, December 17, 1988.

BJUHR, THOMAS (BYOOR)

Right wing. Shoots left. 6'1", 205 lbs. Born, Stockholm, Sweden, August 28, 1966.
(Detroit's 7th choice, 134th overall, in 1985 Entry Draft).

			Regular Season					Playoffs				
Season	Club	Lea	GP	G	A	TP	PIM	GP	G	A	TP	PIM
1984-85	AIK	Swe. Jr.	33	38	18	56	28	....	....	....	....	....
	AIK	Swe.	3	1	0	1	0	....	....	....	....	....
1985-86	AIK	Swe.	14	0	1	1	8	....	....	....	....	....
1986-87	Portland	WHL	39	28	26	54	23	....	....	....	....	....
1987-88	Adirondack	AHL	58	4	2	6	21	....	....	....	....	....
1988-89	AIK	Swe.	34	8	9	17	40	....	....	....	....	....

BLAD, BRIAN

Defense. Shoots left. 6', 185 lbs. Born, Brockville, Ont., July 22, 1967.
(Toronto's 9th choice, 175th overall, in 1987 Entry Draft).

			Regular Season					Playoffs				
Season	Club	Lea	GP	G	A	TP	PIM	GP	G	A	TP	PIM
1986-87	Windsor	OHL	15	1	1	2	30	....	....	....	....	....
	Belleville	OHL	20	1	5	6	43	....	....	....	....	....
1987-88	Milwaukee	IHL	28	1	6	7	45	....	....	....	....	....
	Newmarket	AHL	39	0	4	4	74	....	....	....	....	....
1988-89	Newmarket	AHL	59	2	4	6	149	5	0	1	1	5

BLAESER, JEFFREY

Left wing. Shoots left. 6'3", 190 lbs. Born, Parma, OH, May 11, 1970.
(Pittsburgh's 7th choice, 151st overall, in 1988 Entry Draft).

			Regular Season					Playoffs				
Season	Club	Lea	GP	G	A	TP	PIM	GP	G	A	TP	PIM
1987-88	St. John's Prep	HS	18	14	20	34	....	....	....	....	....	....
1988-89	Yale	ECAC	31	8	19	27	12	....	....	....	....	....

BLAISDELL, MICHAEL WALTER (MIKE) (BLAZE-dell)

Right wing. Shoots right. 6'1", 195 lbs. Born, Moose Jaw, Sask., January 18, 1960.
(Detroit's 1st choice, 11th over-all, in 1980 Entry Draft).

			Regular Season					Playoffs				
Season	Club	Lea	GP	G	A	TP	PIM	GP	G	A	TP	PIM
1977-78	Regina	WHL	6	5	5	10	2	13	4	7	11	0
1978-79	U. Wisconsin	WCHA	20	7	1	8	4	....	....	....	....	....
1979-80	Regina	WHL	63	71	38	109	62	18	16	9	25	26
1980-81	**Detroit**	**NHL**	**32**	**3**	**6**	**9**	**10**	....	....	....	....	....
	Adirondack	AHL	41	10	4	14	8	12	2	2	4	5
1981-82	**Detroit**	**NHL**	**80**	**23**	**32**	**55**	**48**	....	....	....	....	....
1982-83	**Detroit**	**NHL**	**80**	**18**	**23**	**41**	**22**	....	....	....	....	....
1983-84	**NY Rangers**	**NHL**	**36**	**5**	**6**	**11**	**31**	....	....	....	....	....
	Tulsa	CHL	32	10	8	18	23	9	6	6	12	6
1984-85	**NY Rangers**	**NHL**	**12**	**1**	**0**	**1**	**11**	....	....	....	....	....
	New Haven	AHL	64	21	23	44	41	....	....	....	....	....
1985-86	**Pittsburgh**	**NHL**	**66**	**15**	**14**	**29**	**36**	....	....	....	....	....
1986-87	**Pittsburgh**	**NHL**	**10**	**1**	**1**	**2**	**2**	....	....	....	....	....
	Baltimore	AHL	43	12	12	24	47	....	....	....	....	....
1987-88	**Toronto**	**NHL**	**18**	**3**	**2**	**5**	**2**	**6**	**1**	**2**	**3**	**10**
	Newmarket	AHL	57	25	28	53	30	....	....	....	....	....
1988-89	**Toronto**	**NHL**	**9**	**1**	**0**	**1**	**4**	....	....	....	....	....
	Newmarket	AHL	40	16	7	23	48	....	....	....	....	....
	NHL Totals		**343**	**70**	**84**	**154**	**166**	**6**	**1**	**2**	**3**	**10**

Traded to **NY Rangers** by **Detroit** with Willie Huber and Mark Osborne for Ron Duguay, Eddie Mio and Eddie Johnstone, June 13, 1983. Claimed by **Pittsburgh** from **NY Rangers** in NHL Waiver Draft, October 7, 1985. Signed as a free agent by **Toronto**, July 10, 1987.

BLAKE, ROBERT

Defense. Shoots right. 6'3", 200 lbs. Born, Simcoe, Ont., December 10, 1969.
(Los Angeles' 4th choice, 70th overall, in 1988 Entry Draft).

			Regular Season					Playoffs				
Season	Club	Lea	GP	G	A	TP	PIM	GP	G	A	TP	PIM
1987-88	Bowling Green	CCHA	43	5	8	13	88	....	....	....	....	....
1988-89a	Bowling Green	CCHA	46	11	21	32	140	....	....	....	....	....

a ECAC Second All-Star Team (1989)

BLESSMAN, JOHN

Defense. Shoots left. 6'3", 210 lbs. Born, Toronto, Ont., April 27, 1967.
(New Jersey's 8th choice, 170th overall, in 1987 Entry Draft).

			Regular Season					Playoffs				
Season	Club	Lea	GP	G	A	TP	PIM	GP	G	A	TP	PIM
1984-85	Toronto	OHL	25	1	3	4	42	5	0	0	0	0
1985-86	Toronto	OHL	64	2	13	15	116	4	0	0	0	11
1986-87	Toronto	OHL	61	6	24	30	130	....	....	....	....	....
1987-88	Utica	AHL	24	0	2	2	50	....	....	....	....	....
	Toronto	OHL	23	8	11	19	64	4	0	4	4	0
1988-89	Utica	AHL	26	2	3	5	46	....	....	....	....	....
	Indianapolis	IHL	31	2	5	7	60	....	....	....	....	....

BLOEMBERG, JEFF

Defense. Shoots right. 6'1", 205 lbs. Born, Listowel, Ont., January 31, 1968.
(NY Ranger's 5th choice, 93rd overall, in 1986 Entry Draft).

			Regular Season					Playoffs				
Season	Club	Lea	GP	G	A	TP	PIM	GP	G	A	TP	PIM
1985-86	North Bay	OHL	60	2	11	13	76	8	1	2	3	9
1986-87	North Bay	OHL	60	5	13	18	91	21	1	6	7	13
1987-88	Colorado	IHL	5	0	0	0	0	11	1	0	1	8
	North Bay	OHL	46	9	26	35	60	4	1	4	5	2
1988-89	**NY Rangers**	**NHL**	**9**	**0**	**0**	**0**	**0**	....	....	....	....	....
	Denver	IHL	64	7	22	29	55	1	0	0	0	0
	NHL Totals		**9**	**0**	**0**	**0**	**0**	....	....	....	....	....

BLOMSTEN, ARTO

Defense. Shoots left. 6'1", 190 lbs. Born, Vasa, Finland, March 16, 1965.
Last amateur club: Djurgardens (Sweden).
(Winnipeg's 11th choice, 239th overall, in 1986 Entry Draft).

			Regular Season					Playoffs				
Season	Club	Lea	GP	G	A	TP	PIM	GP	G	A	TP	PIM
1983-84	Djurgarden	Swe.	3	0	0	0	4	....	....	....	....	....
1984-85	Djurgarden	Swe.	18	3	1	4	2	8	0	0	0	8
1985-86	Djurgarden	Swe.	8	0	3	3	8	....	....	....	....	....
1986-87	Djurgarden	Swe.	29	2	4	6	28	....	....	....	....	....
1987-88	Djurgarden	Swe.	39	12	6	18	36	2	1	0	1	0
1988-89	Djurgarden	Swe.	40	10	9	19	38	....	....	....	....	....

BLOOM, SCOTT

Left wing. Shoots left. 5'11", 195 lbs. Born, Edina, MN, February 8, 1968.
(Calgary's 4th choice, 100th overall, in 1986 Entry Draft).

			Regular Season					Playoffs				
Season	Club	Lea	GP	G	A	TP	PIM	GP	G	A	TP	PIM
1986-87	U. Minnesota	WCHA	44	6	11	17	28	....	....	....	....	....
1987-88	U. Minnesota	WCHA	40	10	11	21	58	....	....	....	....	....
1988-89	U. Minnesota	WCHA	19	2	5	7	22	....	....	....	....	....

BLUM, JOHN JOSEPH

Defense. Shoots right. 6'3", 205 lbs. Born, Detroit, MI, October 8, 1959.

			Regular Season					Playoffs				
Season	Club	Lea	GP	G	A	TP	PIM	GP	G	A	TP	PIM
1980-81	Michigan	WCHA	38	9	43	52	93	....	....	....	....	....
1981-82	Wichita	CHL	78	8	33	41	247	7	0	3	3	24
1982-83	**Edmonton**	**NHL**	**5**	**0**	**3**	**3**	**24**	....	....	....	....	....
	Moncton	AHL	76	10	30	40	219	....	....	....	....	....
1983-84	Moncton	AHL	57	3	22	25	202	....	....	....	....	....
	Edmonton	**NHL**	**4**	**0**	**1**	**1**	**2**	....	....	....	....	....
	Boston	**NHL**	**12**	**1**	**1**	**2**	**30**	**3**	**0**	**0**	**0**	**4**
1984-85	**Boston**	**NHI**	**75**	**3**	**13**	**16**	**263**	**5**	**0**	**0**	**0**	**13**
1985-86	**Boston**	**NHL**	**61**	**1**	**7**	**8**	**80**	**3**	**0**	**0**	**0**	**6**
	Moncton	AHL	12	1	5	6	37	....	....	....	....	....
1986-87	**Washington**	**NHL**	**66**	**2**	**8**	**10**	**133**	**6**	**0**	**1**	**1**	**4**
1987-88	**Boston**	**NHL**	**19**	**0**	**1**	**1**	**70**	**3**	**0**	**1**	**1**	**0**
	Maine	AHL	43	5	18	23	136	8	0	6	6	35
1988-89	**Detroit**	**NHL**	**6**	**0**	**0**	**0**	**8**	....	....	....	....	....
	Adirondack	AHL	56	1	19	20	168	12	0	1	1	18
	NHL Totals		**248**	**7**	**34**	**41**	**610**	**20**	**0**	**2**	**2**	**27**

Signed as free agent by **Edmonton**, May 5, 1981. Traded to **Boston** by **Edmonton** for Larry Melnyk, March 6, 1984. Claimed by **Washington** from **Boston** in NHL Waiver Draft, October 6, 1986. Traded to **Boston** by **Washington** for Boston's seventh round choice (Brad Schlegal) in 1988 Entry Draft, June 1, 1987. Signed as a free agent by **Detroit**, August 12, 1988.

BOBYCK, BRENT

Left wing. Shoots left. 5'10", 175 lbs. Born, Regina, Sask., April 26, 1968.
(Montreal's 4th choice, 78th overall, in 1986 Entry Draft).

			Regular Season					Playoffs				
Season	Club	Lea	GP	G	A	TP	PIM	GP	G	A	TP	PIM
1985-86	Notre Dame	HS	50	40	50	90	50	....	....	....	....	....
1986-87	North Dakota	WCHA	46	8	11	19	16	....	....	....	....	....
1987-88	North Dakota	WCHA	41	10	20	30	43	....	....	....	....	....
1988-89	North Dakota	WCHA	28	11	8	19	16	....	....	....	....	....

BODAK, ROBERT PETER

Left wing. Shoots left. 6'2", 195 lbs. Born, Thunder Bay, Ont., May 28, 1961.

			Regular Season					Playoffs				
Season	Club	Lea	GP	G	A	TP	PIM	GP	G	A	TP	PIM
1983-84	Lakehead U	GPAC	22	23	24	47	18	....	....	....	....	....
1984-85	Springfield	AHL	79	20	25	45	52	4	1	0	1	2
1985-86	Springfield	AHL	4	0	0	0	4	....	....	....	....	....
	Moncton	AHL	58	27	15	42	114	10	3	3	6	0
1986-87	Moncton	AHL	48	11	20	31	75	6	1	1	2	18
1987-88	**Calgary**	**NHL**	**3**	**0**	**0**	**0**	**22**	....	....	....	....	....
	Salt Lake	IHL	44	12	10	22	117	18	1	3	4	74
1988-89	Binghamton	AHL	44	15	25	40	135	....	....	....	....	....
	Salt Lake	IHL	4	0	0	0	2	....	....	....	....	....
	NHL Totals		**3**	**0**	**0**	**0**	**22**	....	....	....	....	....

Signed as a free agent by **Calgary**, January 28, 1986.

BODDEN, JAMES (JIM)

Center. Shoots right. 5'10", 180 lbs. Born, Dundas, Ont., October 26, 1967.
(Pittsburgh's 7th choice, 131st overall, in 1987 Entry Draft).

			Regular Season					Playoffs				
Season	Club	Lea	GP	G	A	TP	PIM	GP	G	A	TP	PIM
1986-87	Chatham	SOHL	30	32	31	63	14	....	....	....	....	....
1987-88	Miami-Ohio	CCHA	38	10	14	24	30	....	....	....	....	....
1988-89	Miami-Ohio	CCHA	33	11	10	21	15	....	....	....	....	....

BODGER, DOUG

Defense. Shoots left. 6'2", 200 lbs. Born, Chemainus, B.C., June 18, 1966
(Pittsburgh's 2nd choice, 9th over-all, in 1984 Entry Draft).

			Regular Season					Playoffs				
Season	Club	Lea	GP	G	A	TP	PIM	GP	G	A	TP	PIM
1982-83a	Kamloops	WHL	72	26	66	92	98	7	0	5	5	2
1983-84	Kamloops	WHL	70	21	77	98	90	17	2	15	17	12
1984-85	**Pittsburgh**	**NHL**	**65**	**5**	**26**	**31**	**67**	....	....	....	....	....
1985-86	**Pittsburgh**	**NHL**	**79**	**4**	**33**	**37**	**63**	....	....	....	....	....
1986-87	**Pittsburgh**	**NHL**	**76**	**11**	**38**	**49**	**52**	....	....	....	....	....
1987-88	**Pittsburgh**	**NHL**	**69**	**14**	**31**	**45**	**103**	....	....	....	....	....
1988-89	**Pittsburgh**	**NHL**	**10**	**1**	**4**	**5**	**7**	....	....	....	....	....
	Buffalo	**NHL**	**61**	**7**	**40**	**47**	**52**	**5**	**1**	**1**	**2**	**11**
	NHL Totals		**360**	**42**	**172**	**214**	**344**	**5**	**1**	**1**	**2**	**11**

a WHL Second All-Star Team (1983)

Traded to **Buffalo** by **Pittsburgh** with Darrin Shannon for Tom Barrasso and Buffalo's third-round choice in 1990 Entry Draft, November 12, 1988.

BOIVIN, CLAUDE

Left wing. Shoots left. 6'2", 200 lbs. Born, Ste. Foy, Que., March 1, 1970.
(Philadelphia's 1st choice, 14th overall, in 1988 Entry Draft).

			Regular Season					Playoffs				
Season	Club	Lea	GP	G	A	TP	PIM	GP	G	A	TP	PIM
1986-87	Ste. Foy	Midget	39	12	27	39	90	....	....	....	....	....
1987-88	Drummondville	QMJHL	63	23	26	49	233	17	5	3	8	74
1988-89	Drummondville	QMJHL	63	20	36	56	218	4	0	2	2	27

BONAR, GRAEME

Right Wing. Shoots right. 6'3", 210 lbs. Born, Toronto, Ont., January 21, 1966.
(Montreal's 5th choice, 54th over-all, in 1984 Entry Draft).

			Regular Season					Playoffs				
Season	Club	Lea	GP	G	A	TP	PIM	GP	G	A	TP	PIM
1983-84	S. S. Marie	OHL	65	15	39	54	80	16	6	4	10	15
1984-85a	S. S. Marie	OHL	66	66	71	137	93	16	13	20	33	10
1985-86b	Peterborough	OHL	56	53	40	93	41	16	11	10	21	15
1986-87	Sherbrooke	AHL	21	6	6	12	7	....	....	....	....	....
1987-88	Baltimore	AHL	6	2	1	3	0	....	....	....	....	....
	Sherbrooke	AHL	8	1	1	2	2	....	....	....	....	....
	Saginaw	IHL	11	6	4	10	2	....	....	....	....	....
1988-89	Rochester	AHL	1	0	0	0	0	....	....	....	....	....
	Flint	IHL	3	1	0	1	0	....	....	....	....	....
	Indianapolis	IHL	38	11	8	19	19	....	....	....	....	....
	Cdn. National	....	4	2	0	2	2	....	....	....	....	....

a OHL First All-Star Team (1985)
b OHL Second All-Star Team (1986)

BORGO, RICHARD

Right wing. Shoots right. 5'11", 190 lbs. Born, Thunder Bay, Ont., September 25, 1970.
(Edmonton's 2nd choice, 36th overall, in 1989 Entry Draft).

			Regular Season					Playoffs				
Season	Club	Lea	GP	G	A	TP	PIM	GP	G	A	TP	PIM
1987-88	Kitchener	OHL	64	24	22	46	81	4	0	4	4	0
1988-89	Kitchener	OHL	66	23	23	46	75	5	0	1	1	4

BORRELL, JOHN

Right wing. Shoots right. 6'2", 190 lbs. Born, Shakopee, MN, March 23, 1967.
(Winnipeg's 5th choice, 102nd over-all, in 1985 Entry Draft).

			Regular Season					Playoffs				
Season	Club	Lea	GP	G	A	TP	PIM	GP	G	A	TP	PIM
1985-86	U. of Lowell	H.E.	41	3	15	18	12	....	....	....	....	....
1986-87	U. of Lowell	H.E.	34	5	10	15	43	....	....	....	....	....
1987-88	U. of Lowell	H.E.	29	2	8	10	34	....	....	....	....	....
1988-89	U. of Lowell	H.E.	29	8	8	16	24	....	....	....	....	....

BORSATO, LUCIANO

Center. Shoots right. 5'10", 165 lbs. Born, Richmond Hill, Ont., January 7, 1966.
(Winnipeg's 6th choice, 135th over-all, in 1984 Entry Draft).

			Regular Season					Playoffs				
Season	Club	Lea	GP	G	A	TP	PIM	GP	G	A	TP	PIM
1984-85	Clarkson	ECAC	33	15	17	32	37	....	....	....	....	....
1985-86	Clarkson	ECAC	28	14	17	31	44	....	....	....	....	....
1986-87	Clarkson	ECAC	31	16	41	57	55	....	....	....	....	....
1987-88ab	Clarkson	ECAC	33	15	29	44	38	....	....	....	....	....
	Moncton	AHL	3	1	1	2	0	....	....	....	....	....
1988-89	Moncton	AHL	6	2	5	7	4	....	....	....	....	....
	Tappara	Fin.	44	31	36	67	69	7	0	3	3	4

a ECAC Second All-Star Team (1988)
b NCAA East Second All-American Team (1988)

BOSCHMAN, LAURIE JOSEPH (BOSH-man)

Center. Shoots left. 6', 185 lbs. Born, Major, Sask., June 4, 1960.
(Toronto's 1st choice, 9th over-all, in 1979 Entry Draft).

			Regular Season					Playoffs				
Season	Club	Lea	GP	G	A	TP	PIM	GP	G	A	TP	PIM
1976-77	Brandon	WHL	3	0	1	1	0	12	1	1	2	17
1977-78	Brandon	WHL	72	42	57	99	227	8	2	5	7	45
1978-79a	Brandon	WHL	65	66	83	149	215	22	11	23	34	56
1979-80	**Toronto**	**NHL**	**80**	**16**	**32**	**48**	**78**	**3**	**1**	**1**	**2**	**18**
1980-81	New Brunswick	AHL	4	4	1	5	47	....	....	....	....	....
	Toronto	**NHL**	**53**	**14**	**19**	**33**	**178**	**3**	**0**	**0**	**0**	**7**
1981-82	**Toronto**	**NHL**	**54**	**9**	**19**	**28**	**150**	....	....	....	....	....
	Edmonton	**NHL**	**11**	**2**	**3**	**5**	**37**	**3**	**0**	**1**	**1**	**4**
1982-83	**Edmonton**	**NHL**	**62**	**8**	**12**	**20**	**183**	....	....	....	....	....
	Winnipeg	**NHL**	**12**	**3**	**5**	**8**	**36**	**3**	**0**	**1**	**1**	**12**
1983-84	**Winnipeg**	**NHL**	**61**	**28**	**46**	**74**	**234**	**3**	**0**	**1**	**1**	**5**
1984-85	**Winnipeg**	**NHL**	**80**	**32**	**44**	**76**	**180**	**8**	**2**	**1**	**3**	**21**
1985-86	**Winnipeg**	**NHL**	**77**	**27**	**42**	**69**	**241**	**3**	**0**	**1**	**1**	**6**
1986-87	**Winnipeg**	**NHL**	**80**	**17**	**24**	**41**	**152**	**10**	**2**	**3**	**5**	**32**
1987-88	**Winnipeg**	**NHL**	**80**	**25**	**23**	**48**	**229**	**5**	**1**	**3**	**4**	**9**
1988-89	**Winnipeg**	**NHL**	**70**	**10**	**26**	**36**	**163**	....	....	....	....	....
	NHL Totals		**720**	**191**	**295**	**486**	**1861**	**41**	**6**	**12**	**18**	**114**

a WHL First All-Star Team (1979)

Traded to **Edmonton** by **Toronto** for Walt Poddubny and Phil Drouilliard, March 8, 1982. Traded to **Winnipeg** by **Edmonton** for Willy Lindstrom, March 7, 1983.

BOTHWELL, TIMOTHY (TIM)

Defense. Shoots left. 6'3", 190 lbs. Born, Vancouver, B.C., May 6, 1955.

			Regular Season					Playoffs				
Season	Club	Lea	GP	G	A	TP	PIM	GP	G	A	TP	PIM
1976-77	Brown U.	ECAC	27	7	27	34	40	....	....	....	....	....
1977-78	Brown U.	ECAC	29	9	26	35	48	....	....	....	....	....
1978-79	**NY Rangers**	**NHL**	**1**	**0**	**0**	**0**	**2**	....	....	....	....	....
	New Haven	AHL	66	15	33	48	44	10	4	6	10	8
1979-80	New Haven	AHL	22	6	7	13	25	....	....	....	....	....
	NY Rangers	**NHL**	**45**	**4**	**6**	**10**	**20**	**9**	**0**	**0**	**0**	**8**
1980-81	**NY Rangers**	**NHL**	**3**	**0**	**1**	**1**	**0**	....	....	....	....	....
	New Haven	AHL	73	10	53	63	98	4	1	2	3	6
1981-82	**NY Rangers**	**NHL**	**13**	**0**	**3**	**3**	**10**	....	....	....	....	....
	Springfield	AHL	10	0	4	4	7	....	....	....	....	....
1982-83	**St. Louis**	**NHL**	**61**	**4**	**11**	**15**	**34**	....	....	....	....	....
1983-84	Montana	CHL	4	0	3	3	0	....	....	....	....	....
	St. Louis	**NHL**	**62**	**2**	**13**	**15**	**65**	**11**	**0**	**2**	**2**	**14**
1984-85	**St. Louis**	**NHL**	**79**	**4**	**22**	**26**	**62**	**3**	**0**	**0**	**0**	**2**
1985-86	**Hartford**	**NHL**	**62**	**2**	**8**	**10**	**53**	**10**	**0**	**0**	**0**	**8**
1986-87	**Hartford**	**NHL**	**4**	**1**	**0**	**1**	**0**	....	....	....	....	....
	St. Louis	**NHL**	**72**	**5**	**16**	**21**	**46**	**6**	**0**	**0**	**0**	**6**
1987-88	**St. Louis**	**NHL**	**78**	**6**	**13**	**19**	**76**	**10**	**0**	**1**	**1**	**18**
1988-89	**St. Louis**	**NHL**	**22**	**0**	**0**	**0**	**14**	....	....	....	....	....
	Peoria	IHL	14	0	7	7	14	....	....	....	....	....
	NHL Totals		**502**	**28**	**93**	**121**	**382**	**49**	**0**	**3**	**3**	**56**

Signed as free agent by **NY Rangers**, June 8, 1978. Claimed by **St. Louis** from **NY Rangers** in NHL Waiver Draft, October 4, 1982. Rights sold to **Hartford** by **St. Louis**, October 4, 1985. Traded to **St. Louis** by **Hartford** for Dave Barr, October 21, 1986.

BOUDREAU, BRUCE ALLAN (BOO-droh)

Center. Shoots left. 5'9", 175 lbs. Born, Toronto, Ont., January 9, 1955.
(Toronto's 3rd choice, 42nd over-all, in 1975 Amateur Draft).

			Regular Season					Playoffs				
Season	Club	Lea	GP	G	A	TP	PIM	GP	G	A	TP	PIM
1973-74	Toronto	OHA	53	46	67	113	51	....	....	....	....	....
1974-75	Toronto	OHA	69	*68	97	*165	52	22	12	*28	40	26
1975-76	Minnesota	WHA	30	3	6	9	4	....	....	....	....	....
	Johnstown	NAHL	34	25	35	60	14	....	....	....	....	....
1976-77	Dallas	CHL	58	*37	34	71	40	1	1	1	2	0
	Toronto	**NHL**	**15**	**2**	**5**	**7**	**4**	**3**	**0**	**0**	**0**	**0**
1977-78	**Toronto**	**NHL**	**40**	**11**	**18**	**29**	**12**	....	....	....	....	....
	Dallas	CHL	22	13	9	22	11	....	....	....	....	....
1978-79	**Toronto**	**NHL**	**26**	**4**	**3**	**7**	**2**	....	....	....	....	....
	New Brunswick	AHL	49	20	38	58	20	5	1	1	2	8
1979-80	**Toronto**	**NHL**	**2**	**0**	**0**	**0**	**2**	....	....	....	....	....
	New Brunswick	AHL	75	36	54	90	47	17	6	7	13	23
1980-81	**Toronto**	**NHL**	**39**	**10**	**14**	**24**	**18**	**2**	**1**	**0**	**1**	**0**
	New Brunswick	AHL	40	17	41	58	22	8	6	5	11	14
1981-82	**Toronto**	**NHL**	**12**	**0**	**2**	**2**	**6**	....	....	....	....	....
	Cincinnati	CHL	65	42	61	103	42	4	3	1	4	8
1982-83	St. Catharines	AHL	80	50	72	122	65	....	....	....	....	....
	Toronto	**NHL**	....	....	....	....	....	**4**	**1**	**0**	**1**	**0**
1983-84	St. Catharines	AHL	80	47	62	109	44	7	0	5	5	11
1984-85	Baltimore	AHL	17	4	7	11	4	15	3	9	12	4
1985-86	**Chicago**	**NHL**	**7**	**1**	**0**	**1**	**2**	....	....	....	....	....
	Nova Scotia	AHL	65	30	36	66	36	....	....	....	....	....
1986-87	Nova Scotia	AHL	78	35	47	82	40	5	3	3	6	4
1987-88abc	Springfield	AHL	80	42	*74	*116	84	....	....	....	....	....
1988-89	Springfield	AHL	50	28	36	64	42	....	....	....	....	....
	Newmarket	AHL	20	7	16	23	12	4	0	1	1	6
	NHL Totals		**141**	**28**	**42**	**70**	**46**	**9**	**2**	**0**	**2**	**0**

a AHL First All-Star Team (1988)
b Won Fred Hunt Award (Sportsmanship-AHL) (1988)
c Won John Sollenberger Trophy (Top Scorer-AHL) (1988)

Claimed by **Toronto** as fill in Expansion Draft, June 13, 1979. Signed as a free agent by **Chicago**, October 10, 1985.

BOUDREAULT, SEAN

Left wing. Shoots left. 6', 170 lbs. Born, Midfield, RI, February 22, 1967.
(Quebec's 14th choice, 249th overall, in 1986 Entry Draft).

			Regular Season					Playoffs				
Season	Club	Lea	GP	G	A	TP	PIM	GP	G	A	TP	PIM
1986-87	U. of Lowell	H.E.	DID NOT PLAY - INJURED					....	....	....	....	
1987-88	U. of Lowell	H.E.	3	0	1	1	4	....	....	....	....	....
1988-89	U. of Lowell	H.E.	14	0	1	1	12	....	....	....	....	....

BOUGHNER, BOB

Defense. Shoots right. 5'11", 200 lbs. Born, Windsor, Ont., March 8, 1971.
(Detroit's 2nd choice, 32nd overall, in 1989 Entry Draft).

			Regular Season					Playoffs				
Season	Club	Lea	GP	G	A	TP	PIM	GP	G	A	TP	PIM
1987-88	St. Mary's	OHA	36	4	18	22	177	....	....	....	....	....
1988-89	S.S. Marie	OHL	64	6	15	21	182	....	....	....	....	....

BOURBEAU, ALLEN (bore-Boe)

Center. Shoots right. 5'10", 180 lbs. Born, Teaticket, MA, May 17, 1965.
(Philadelphia's 3rd choice, 81st overall, in 1983 Entry Draft).

			Regular Season					Playoffs				
Season	Club	Lea	GP	G	A	TP	PIM	GP	G	A	TP	PIM
1985-87	Harvard	ECAC	25	24	19	43	26	....	....	....	....	....
1986-87	Harvard	ECAC	33	23	34	57	46	....	....	....	....	....
1987-88	U.S. National	....	45	18	20	38	26	....	....	....	....	....
	U.S. Olympic	....	5	3	1	4	2	....	....	....	....	....
1988-89a	Harvard	ECAC	33	11	43	54	48	....	....	....	....	....

a ECAC Second All-Star Team (1989)

BOURGEOIS, CHARLES MARC (CHARLIE) (BUHR-zhwah)

Defense. Shoots right. 6'4", 215 lbs. Born, Moncton, N.B., November 19, 1959.

			Regular Season					Playoffs				
Season	Club	Lea	GP	G	A	TP	PIM	GP	G	A	TP	PIM
1980-81	U. of Moncton	AUAA	24	8	23	31	....	6	4	6	10	....
1981-82	Oklahoma City	CHL	13	2	2	4	17	....	....	....	....	....
	Calgary	NHL	54	2	13	15	112	3	0	0	0	7
1982-83	Calgary	NHL	15	2	3	5	21	....	....	....	....	....
	Colorado	CHL	51	10	18	28	128	6	2	3	5	30
1983-84	Colorado	CHL	54	12	32	44	133	....	....	....	....	....
	Calgary	NHL	17	1	3	4	35	8	0	1	1	27
1984-85	Calgary	NHL	47	2	10	12	134	4	0	0	0	17
1985-86	Calgary	NHL	29	5	5	10	128	....	....	....	....	....
	St. Louis	NHL	31	2	7	9	116	19	2	2	4	116
1986-87	St. Louis	NHL	66	2	12	14	164	6	0	0	0	27
1987-88	St. Louis	NHL	30	0	1	1	78	....	....	....	....	....
	Hartford	NHL	1	0	0	0	0	....	....	....	....	....
1988-89	Binghamton	AHL	76	9	35	44	239	....	....	....	....	....
	NHL Totals		290	16	54	70	788	40	2	3	5	194

Signed as free agent by **Calgary**, April 19, 1981. Traded to **St. Louis** by **Calgary** with Eddy Beers and Gino Cavallini for Joe Mullen, Terry Johnson and Rik Wilson, February 1, 1986. Traded to **Hartford** by **St. Louis** with Hartford's third round choice (Blair Atcheynum) in 1989 Entry Draft — acquired earlier by St. Louis in Mark Reeds deal — for Hartford's second round choice ((Rick Corriveau) in 1989 Entry Draft, March 8, 1988.

BOURQUE, PHILLIPPE RICHARD (PHIL) (BORK)

Left wing. Shoots left. 6'1", 200 lbs. Born, Chelmsford, MA, June 8, 1962.

			Regular Season					Playoffs				
Season	Club	Lea	GP	G	A	TP	PIM	GP	G	A	TP	PIM
1980-81	Kingston	OHL	47	4	4	8	46	6	0	0	0	10
1981-82	Kingston	OHL	67	11	40	51	111	4	0	0	0	0
1982-83	Baltimore	AHL	65	1	15	16	93	....	....	....	....	....
1983-84	Pittsburgh	NHL	5	0	1	1	12	....	....	....	....	....
	Baltimore	AHL	58	5	17	22	96	....	....	....	....	....
1984-85	Baltimore	AHL	79	6	15	21	164	13	2	5	7	23
1985-86	Pittsburgh	NHL	4	0	0	0	2	....	....	....	....	....
	Baltimore	AHL	74	8	18	26	226	....	....	....	....	....
1986-87	Pittsburgh	NHL	22	2	3	5	32	....	....	....	....	....
	Baltimore	AHL	49	15	16	31	183	....	....	....	....	....
1987-88	Pittsburgh	NHL	21	4	12	16	20	....	....	....	....	....
ab	Muskegon	IHL	52	16	36	52	66	6	1	2	3	16
1988-89	Pittsburgh	NHL	80	17	26	43	97	11	4	1	5	66
	NHL Totals		132	23	42	65	163	11	4	1	5	66

a IHL First All-Star Team (1988)
b Won Governor's Trophy (Outstanding Defenseman-IHL) (1988)

Signed as free agent by **Pittsburgh**, October 4, 1982.

BOURQUE, RAYMOND JEAN (BORK)

Defense. Shoots left. 5'11", 210 lbs. Born, Montreal, Que., December 28, 1960.
(Boston's 1st choice, 8th over-all, in 1979 Entry Draft).

			Regular Season					Playoffs				
Season	Club	Lea	GP	G	A	TP	PIM	GP	G	A	TP	PIM
1976-77	Sorel	QJHL	69	12	36	48	61	....	....	....	....	....
1977-78	Verdun	QJHL	72	22	57	79	90	4	2	1	3	0
1978-79	Verdun	QJHL	63	22	71	93	44	11	3	16	19	18
1979-80ab	Boston	NHL	80	17	48	65	73	10	2	9	11	27
1980-81c	Boston	NHL	67	27	29	56	96	3	0	1	1	2
1981-82b	Boston	NHL	65	17	49	66	51	9	1	5	6	16
1982-83c	Boston	NHL	65	22	51	73	20	17	8	15	23	10
1983-84b	Boston	NHL	78	31	65	96	57	3	0	2	2	0
1984-85b	Boston	NHL	73	20	66	86	53	5	0	3	3	4
1985-86c	Boston	NHL	74	19	58	77	68	3	0	0	0	0
1986-87bd	Boston	NHL	78	23	72	95	36	4	1	2	3	0
1987-88bd	Boston	NHL	78	17	64	81	72	23	3	18	21	26
1988-89c	Boston	NHL	60	18	43	61	52	10	0	4	4	6
	NHL Totals		718	211	545	756	578	87	15	59	74	91

a Won Calder Memorial Trophy (1980)
b NHL First All-Star Team (1980, 1982, 1984, 1985, 1987, 1988)
c NHL Second All-Star Team (1981, 1983, 1989)
d Won James Norris Memorial Trophy (1987, 1988)

Played in NHL All-Star Game (1981-86, 1988-89)

BOUTILIER, PAUL ANDRE (boot-LEER)

Defense. Shoots left. 6', 200 lbs. Born, Sydney, N.S., May 3, 1963.
(NY Islanders' 1st choice, 21st over-all, in 1981 Entry Draft).

			Regular Season					Playoffs				
Season	Club	Lea	GP	G	A	TP	PIM	GP	G	A	TP	PIM
1980-81	Sherbrooke	QJHL	72	10	29	39	95	14	3	7	10	10
1981-82	NY Islanders	NHL	1	0	0	0	0	....	....	....	....	....
ab	Sherbrooke	QJHL	57	20	60	80	62	21	7	31	38	12
1982-83	St. Jean	QJHL	22	5	14	19	30	....	....	....	....	....
	NY Islanders	NHL	29	4	5	9	24	2	0	0	0	2
1983-84	Indianapolis	CHL	50	6	17	23	56	....	....	....	....	....
	NY Islanders	NHL	28	0	11	11	36	21	1	7	8	10
1984-85	NY Islanders	NHL	78	12	23	35	90	10	0	2	2	16
1985-86	NY Islanders	NHL	77	4	30	34	100	3	0	0	0	2
1986-87	Boston	NHL	52	5	9	14	84	....	....	....	....	....
	Minnesota	NHL	10	2	4	6	8	....	....	....	....	....
1987-88	NY Rangers	NHL	4	0	1	1	6	....	....	....	....	....
	New Haven	AHL	9	0	3	3	10	....	....	....	....	....
	Colorado	IHL	9	2	6	8	4	....	....	....	....	....
	Winnipeg	NHL	6	0	0	0	6	5	0	0	0	15
	Moncton	AHL	41	9	29	38	40	....	....	....	....	....
1988-89	Winnipeg	NHL	3	0	0	0	4	....	....	....	....	....
c	Moncton	AHL	77	6	54	60	101	10	2	7	9	4
	NHL Totals		288	27	83	110	358	41	1	9	10	45

a QMJHL First All-Star Team (1982)
b Named QMJHL's Top Defenseman (1982)
c AHL First All-Star Team (1989)

Acquired by **Boston** as compensation for signing of free agent Brian Curran, August 6, 1987. Traded to **Minnesota** by **Boston** for Minnesota's fourth round choice (Darwin McPherson) in 1987 Entry Draft, March 10, 1987. Traded to **NY Rangers** by **Minnesota** with Jari Gronstrand for Jay Caulfield and Dave Gagne, October 8, 1987. Traded to **Winnipeg** by **NY Rangers** for future considerations, December 16, 1987.

BOYCE, MICHAEL

Defense. Shoots left. 6'2", 210 lbs. Born, Oshawa, Ont., September 3, 1964.

			Regular Season					Playoffs				
Season	Club	Lea	GP	G	A	TP	PIM	GP	G	A	TP	PIM
1984-85	Merrimack	NCAA	25	8	8	16	27	....	....	....	....	....
1985-86	Merrimack	NCAA	33	7	17	24	24	....	....	....	....	....
1986-87	Merrimack	NCAA	36	9	28	37	42	....	....	....	....	....
1987-88	Merrimack	NCAA	40	8	45	53	56	....	....	....	....	....
1988-89	New Haven	AHL	10	0	1	1	2	....	....	....	....	....
	Denver	IHL	21	0	5	5	29	....	....	....	....	....

Signed as a free agent by **Philadelphia**, April 29, 1988. Traded to **NY Rangers** by **Philadelphia** for Chris Jensen, September 28, 1988. Traded to **Los Angeles** by **NY Rangers** with Igor Liba, Todd Elik and future considerations for Dean Kennedy and Denis Larocque, December 12, 1988.

BOYD, RANDY KEITH

Defense. Shoots left. 5'11", 190 lbs. Born, Coniston, Ont., January 23, 1962.
(Pittsburgh's 2nd choice, 51st over-all, in 1980 Entry Draft).

			Regular Season					Playoffs				
Season	Club	Lea	GP	G	A	TP	PIM	GP	G	A	TP	PIM
1979-80	Ottawa	OHA	65	3	21	24	148	11	0	2	2	13
1980-81a	Ottawa	OHA	64	11	43	54	225	7	2	3	5	35
1981-82	Ottawa	OHL	26	9	29	38	51	....	....	....	....	....
	Pittsburgh	NHL	23	0	2	2	49	3	0	0	0	11
1982-83	Baltimore	AHL	21	5	10	15	43	....	....	....	....	....
	Pittsburgh	NHL	56	4	14	18	71	....	....	....	....	....
1983-84	Pittsburgh	NHL	5	0	1	1	6	....	....	....	....	....
	Baltimore	AHL	20	6	13	19	21	....	....	....	....	....
	Chicago	NHL	23	0	4	4	16	....	....	....	....	....
	Springfield	AHL	27	2	11	13	48	4	0	2	2	34
1984-85	Chicago	NHL	3	0	0	0	6	3	0	1	1	7
	Milwaukee	IHL	68	18	55	73	162	....	....	....	....	....
1985-86	NY Islanders	NHL	55	2	12	14	79	3	0	0	0	2
1986-87	NY Islanders	NHL	30	7	17	24	37	4	0	1	1	6
	Springfield	AHL	48	9	30	39	96	....	....	....	....	....
1987-88	Vancouver	NHL	60	7	16	23	64	....	....	....	....	....
1988-89	Vancouver	NHL	2	0	1	1	0	....	....	....	....	....
bc	Milwaukee	IHL	73	24	55	79	218	9	0	6	6	26
	NHL Totals		257	20	67	87	328	13	0	2	2	26

a OHA First All-Star Team (1981)
b IHL First All-Star Team (1989)
c Won Governor's Trophy (Outstanding Defenseman-IHL)

Traded to **Chicago** by **Pittsburgh** for Greg Fox, December 6, 1983. Claimed by **NY Islanders** from **Chicago** in NHL Waiver Draft, October 7, 1985. Claimed by **Vancouver** in NHL Waiver Draft, October 5, 1987.

BOYKO, DARREN

Center. Shoots right. 5'9", 170 lbs. Born, Winnipeg, Man., January 16, 1964.

			Regular Season					Playoffs				
Season	Club	Lea	GP	G	A	TP	PIM	GP	G	A	TP	PIM
1981-82	Winnipeg	WHL	65	35	37	72	14	....	....	....	....	....
1982-83	Winnipeg	WHL	72	49	81	130	8	3	0	2	2	0
1983-84	U. of Toronto	OUAA	40	33	51	84	24	9	7	10	17	4
1984-85	U. of Toronto	OUAA	39	31	53	84	42	2	1	0	1	6
1985-86	IFK Helsinki	Fin.	36	18	26	44	8	....	....	....	....	....
1986-87	IFK Helsinki	Fin.	44	22	13	35	44	....	....	....	....	....
1987-88	IFK Helsinki	Fin.	44	14	40	54	16	....	....	....	....	....
1988-89	IFK Helsinki	Fin.	34	15	15	30	10	....	....	....	....	....
	Winnipeg	NHL	1	0	0	0	0	....	....	....	....	....
	Moncton	AHL	18	3	7	10	2	4	0	0	0	0
	NHL Totals		1	0	0	0	0	....	....	....	....	....

Signed as a free agent by **Winnipeg**, May 16, 1988.

BOZEK, STEVEN MICHAEL (STEVE)

Left wing. Shoots left. 5'11", 175 lbs. Born, Kelowna, B.C., November 26, 1960.
(Los Angeles' 5th choice, 52nd over-all, in 1980 Entry Draft).

			Regular Season					Playoffs				
Season	Club	Lea	GP	G	A	TP	PIM	GP	G	A	TP	PIM
1979-80	N. Michigan	CCHA	41	42	47	89	32	....	....	....	....	....
1980-81	N. Michigan	CCHA	44	35	55	90	0	....	....	....	....	....
1981-82	**Los Angeles**	**NHL**	**71**	**33**	**23**	**56**	**68**	**10**	**4**	**1**	**5**	**6**
1982-83	**Los Angeles**	**NHL**	**53**	**13**	**13**	**26**	**14**	....	....	....	....	....
1983-84	**Calgary**	**NHL**	**46**	**10**	**10**	**20**	**16**	**10**	**3**	**1**	**4**	**15**
1984-85	**Calgary**	**NHL**	**54**	**13**	**22**	**35**	**6**	**3**	**1**	**0**	**1**	**4**
1985-86	**Calgary**	**NHL**	**64**	**21**	**22**	**43**	**24**	**14**	**2**	**6**	**8**	**32**
1986-87	**Calgary**	**NHL**	**71**	**17**	**18**	**35**	**22**	**4**	**1**	**0**	**1**	**2**
1987-88	**Calgary**	**NHL**	**26**	**3**	**7**	**10**	**12**	....	....	....	....	....
	St. Louis	**NHL**	**7**	**0**	**0**	**0**	**2**	**7**	**1**	**1**	**2**	**6**
1988-89	**Vancouver**	**NHL**	**71**	**17**	**18**	**35**	**64**	**7**	**0**	**2**	**2**	**4**
	NHL Totals		**463**	**127**	**133**	**260**	**228**	**55**	**12**	**11**	**23**	**69**

Traded to **Calgary** by **Los Angeles** for Carl Mokosak and Kevin LaVallee, June 20, 1983. Traded to **St. Louis** by **Calgary** with Brett Hull for Rob Ramage and Rick Wamsley, March 7, 1988. Traded to **Calgary** by **St. Louis** with Mark Hunter,DougGilmour and Michael Dark for Mike Bullard, Craig Coxe andTim Corkery, September 6, 1988. Traded to **Vancouver** by **Calgary** with PaulReinhart for Vancouver's third-round pick (Veli-Pekka Kautonen) in 1989 Entry Draft, September 6, 1988.

BOZON, PHILIPPE

Left wing. Shoots left. 5'10", 175 lbs. Born, Charmonix, France, November 30, 1966.

			Regular Season					Playoffs				
Season	Club	Lea	GP	G	A	TP	PIM	GP	G	A	TP	PIM
1984-85	St. Jean	QMJHL	67	32	50	82	82	5	0	5	5	4
1985-86a	St. Jean	QMJHL	65	59	52	111	72	10	10	6	16	16
	Peoria	IHL	....	....	....	....	....	5	1	0	1	0
1986-87	Peoria	IHL	28	4	11	15	17	....	....	....	....	....
	St. Jean	QMJHL	25	20	21	41	75	8	5	5	10	30
1987-88	Mont-Blanc	France	18	11	15	26	34	10	15	6	21	6
1988-89		DID NOT PLAY										

a QMJHL Second All-Star Team (1986).

Signed as a free agent by **St. Louis**, September 29, 1985.

BRACCIA, RICK

Left wing. Shoots left. 6', 195 lbs. Born, Revere, MA., September 5, 1967.
(Chicago's 12th choice, 242nd over-all, in 1985 Entry Draft).

			Regular Season					Playoffs				
Season	Club	Lea	GP	G	A	TP	PIM	GP	G	A	TP	PIM
1985-86	Boston College	H.E.	9	0	3	3	20	....	....	....	....	....
1986-87	Boston College	H.E.	30	4	5	9	52	....	....	....	....	....
1987-88	Boston College	H.E.	11	2	2	4	10	....	....	....	....	....
1988-89	Boston College	H.E.	36	3	7	10	78	....	....	....	....	....

BRADLEY, BRIAN WALTER RICHARD

Center. Shoots right. 5'10", 170 lbs. Born, Kitchener, Ont., January 21, 1965.
(Calgary's 2nd choice, 51st over-all, in 1983 Entry Draft).

			Regular Season					Playoffs				
Season	Club	Lea	GP	G	A	TP	PIM	GP	G	A	TP	PIM
1982-83	London	OHL	67	37	82	119	37	3	1	0	1	0
1983-84	London	OHL	49	40	60	100	24	4	2	4	6	0
1984-85	London	OHL	32	27	49	76	22	8	5	10	15	4
1985-86	**Calgary**	**NHL**	**5**	**0**	**1**	**1**	**0**	**1**	**0**	**0**	**0**	**0**
	Moncton	AHL	59	23	42	65	40	10	6	9	15	4
1986-87	**Calgary**	**NHL**	**40**	**10**	**18**	**28**	**16**	....	....	....	....	....
	Moncton	AHL	20	12	16	28	8	....	....	....	....	....
1987-88	**Vancouver**	**NHL**	**11**	**3**	**5**	**8**	**6**	....	....	....	....	....
	Cdn. National	.....	47	8	19	37	42	....	....	....	....	....
	Cdn. Olympic	.....	7	0	4	4	0	....	....	....	....	....
1988-89	**Vancouver**	**NHL**	**71**	**18**	**27**	**45**	**42**	**7**	**3**	**4**	**7**	**10**
	NHL Totals		**127**	**31**	**51**	**82**	**64**	**8**	**3**	**4**	**7**	**10**

Traded to **Vancouver** by **Calgary** with Peter Bakovic and Kevin Guy for Craig Coxe, March 6, 1988.

BRADY, NEIL

Center. Shoots left. 6'3", 195 lbs. Born, Montreal, Que., April 12, 1968.
(New Jersey's 1st choice, 3rd over-all, in 1986 Entry Draft).

			Regular Season					Playoffs				
Season	Club	Lea	GP	G	A	TP	PIM	GP	G	A	TP	PIM
1984-85	Calgary	Midget	37	25	50	75	75	....	....	....	....	....
	Medicine Hat	WHL	....	....	....	....	....	3	0	0	0	2
1985-86a	Medicine Hat	WHL	72	21	60	81	104	21	9	11	20	23
1986-87	Medicine Hat	WHL	57	19	64	83	126	18	1	4	5	25
1987-88	Medicine Hat	WHL	61	16	35	51	110	15	0	3	3	19
1988-89	Utica	AHL	75	16	21	37	56	4	0	3	3	0

a WHL Rookie of the Year (1986)

BRANT, CHRIS

Left wing. Shoots left. 6'1", 190 lbs. Born, Belleville, Ont., August 26, 1965.
(Hartford's 5th choice, 131st over-all, in 1985 Entry Draft).

			Regular Season					Playoffs				
Season	Club	Lea	GP	G	A	TP	PIM	GP	G	A	TP	PIM
1982-83	Kingston	OHL	67	1	17	18	53	....	....	....	....	....
1983-84	Kingston	OHL	7	4	4	8	14	....	....	....	....	....
	S.S. Marie	OHL	60	9	12	21	50	15	1	2	3	10
1984-85	S.S. Marie	OHL	52	16	33	49	110	16	8	9	17	15
1985-86	Binghamton	AHL	73	7	6	13	45	6	0	1	1	19
1986-87	Salt Lake	IHL	67	27	38	65	107	17	11	10	21	23
1987-88	Binghamton	AHL	66	18	29	47	74	4	3	0	3	6
1988-89	Binghamton	AHL	65	28	28	56	138	....	....	....	....	....

BRAUER, CAM

Defense. Shoots left. 6'3", 205 lbs. Born, Calgary, Alta., January 4, 1970.
(Edmonton's 5th choice, 82nd overall, in 1988 Entry Draft).

			Regular Season					Playoffs				
Season	Club	Lea	GP	G	A	TP	PIM	GP	G	A	TP	PIM
1987-88	RPI	ECAC	18	0	1	1	4	....	....	....	....	....
1988-89	Regina	WHL	49	0	9	9	59	....	....	....	....	....

BRAZDA, RADOMIR

Defense. Shoots right. 6'2", 175 lbs. Born, Pardubice, Czechoslovakia, October 11, 1967.
(Detroit's 6th choice, 95th overall, in 1987 Entry Draft).

			Regular Season					Playoffs				
Season	Club	Lea	GP	G	A	TP	PIM	GP	G	A	TP	PIM
1986-87	Tesla Par.	Czech.	31	1	1	2	....	....	....	....	....	....
1987-88	Tesla Par.	Czech.	11	1	2	3	....	....	....	....	....	....
1988-89	Dukla Trencin	Czech.	35	1	1	2	....	....	....	....	....	....

BRENNAN, STEPHEN

Right wing. Shoots right. 6'1", 190 lbs. Born, Winchester, MA, March 22, 1967.
(Toronto's 8th choice, 153rd overall, in 1986 Entry Draft).

			Regular Season					Playoffs				
Season	Club	Lea	GP	G	A	TP	PIM	GP	G	A	TP	PIM
1986-87	Clarkson	ECAC	29	3	3	6	17	....	....	....	....	....
1987-88	Clarkson	ECAC	12	4	0	4	18	....	....	....	....	....
1988-89	Clarkson	ECAC	25	3	4	7	42	....	....	....	....	....

BRICKLEY, ANDY

Center. Shoots left. 5'11", 200 lbs. Born, Melrose, MA, August 9, 1961.
(Philadelphia's 10th choice, 210th over-all, in 1980 Entry Draft).

			Regular Season					Playoffs				
Season	Club	Lea	GP	G	A	TP	PIM	GP	G	A	TP	PIM
1979-80	N. Hampshire	ECAC	27	15	17	32	8	....	....	....	....	....
1980-81	N. Hampshire	ECAC	31	27	25	52	16	....	....	....	....	....
1981-82ab	N. Hampshire	ECAC	35	26	27	53	6	....	....	....	....	....
1982-83	**Philadelphia**	**NHL**	**3**	**1**	**1**	**2**	**0**	....	....	....	....	....
c	Maine	AHL	76	29	54	83	10	17	9	5	14	0
1983-84	Springfield	AHL	7	1	5	6	2	....	....	....	....	....
	Baltimore	AHL	4	0	5	5	2	....	....	....	....	....
	Pittsburgh	**NHL**	**50**	**18**	**20**	**38**	**9**	....	....	....	....	....
1984-85	**Pittsburgh**	**NHL**	**45**	**7**	**15**	**22**	**10**	....	....	....	....	....
	Baltimore	AHL	31	13	14	27	8	15	10	8	18	0
1985-86	Maine	AHL	60	26	34	60	20	5	0	4	4	0
1986-87	**New Jersey**	**NHL**	**51**	**11**	**12**	**23**	**8**	....	....	....	....	....
1987-88	**New Jersey**	**NHL**	**45**	**8**	**14**	**22**	**14**	**4**	**0**	**1**	**1**	**4**
	Utica	AHL	9	5	8	13	4	....	....	....	....	....
1988-89	**New Jersey**	**NHL**	**71**	**13**	**22**	**35**	**20**	....	....	....	....	....
	NHL Totals		**265**	**58**	**84**	**142**	**61**	**4**	**0**	**1**	**1**	**4**

a ECAC First All-Star Team (1982)
b NCAA All-American Team (1982)
c AHL Second All-Star Team (1983)

Traded to **Pittsburgh** by **Philadelphia** with Mark Taylor, Ron Flockhart, Philadephia's first round (Roger Belanger) and third round (Mike Stevens — later transferred to Vancouver) choices in 1984 Entry Draft for Rich Sutter and Pittsburgh's second round (Greg Smyth) and third round (David McLay) choices in 1984 Entry Draft, October 23, 1983. Signed as a free agent by **New Jersey**, July 8, 1986. Claimed by **Boston** in NHL Waiver Draft, October 3, 1988,

BRIDGMAN, MELVIN JOHN (MEL) (BRIJ-man)

Center. Shoots left. 6', 190 lbs. Born, Trenton, Ont., April 28, 1955.
(Philadelphia's 1st choice and 1st over-all in 1975 Amateur Draft).

			Regular Season					Playoffs				
Season	Club	Lea	GP	G	A	TP	PIM	GP	G	A	TP	PIM
1972-73	Victoria	WHL	4	1	1	2	0	....	....	....	....	....
1973-74	Victoria	WHL	62	26	39	65	149	....	....	....	....	....
1974-75a	Victoria	WHL	66	66	91	*157	175	12	12	6	18	34
1975-76	**Philadelphia**	**NHL**	**80**	**23**	**27**	**50**	**86**	**16**	**6**	**8**	**14**	**31**
1976-77	**Philadelphia**	**NHL**	**70**	**19**	**38**	**57**	**120**	**7**	**1**	**0**	**1**	**8**
1977-78	**Philadelphia**	**NHL**	**76**	**16**	**32**	**48**	**203**	**12**	**1**	**7**	**8**	**36**
1978-79	**Philadelphia**	**NHL**	**76**	**24**	**35**	**59**	**184**	**8**	**1**	**2**	**3**	**17**
1979-80	**Philadelphia**	**NHL**	**74**	**16**	**31**	**47**	**136**	**19**	**2**	**9**	**11**	**70**
1980-81	**Philadelphia**	**NHL**	**77**	**14**	**37**	**51**	**195**	**12**	**2**	**4**	**6**	**39**
1981-82	**Philadelphia**	**NHL**	**9**	**7**	**5**	**12**	**47**	....	....	....	....	....
	Calgary	**NHL**	**63**	**26**	**49**	**75**	**94**	**3**	**2**	**0**	**2**	**14**
1982-83	**Calgary**	**NHL**	**79**	**19**	**31**	**50**	**103**	**9**	**3**	**4**	**7**	**33**
1983-84	**New Jersey**	**NHL**	**79**	**23**	**38**	**61**	**121**	....	....	....	....	....
1984-85	**New Jersey**	**NHL**	**80**	**22**	**39**	**61**	**105**	....	....	....	....	....
1985-86	**New Jersey**	**NHL**	**78**	**23**	**40**	**63**	**80**	....	....	....	....	....
1986-87	**New Jersey**	**NHL**	**51**	**8**	**31**	**39**	**80**	....	....	....	....	....
	Detroit	**NHL**	**13**	**2**	**2**	**4**	**19**	**16**	**5**	**2**	**7**	**28**
1987-88	**Detroit**	**NHL**	**57**	**6**	**11**	**17**	**42**	**16**	**4**	**1**	**5**	**12**
	Adirondack	AHL	2	1	2	3	0	....	....	....	....	....
1988-89	**Vancouver**	**NHL**	**15**	**4**	**3**	**7**	**10**	**7**	**1**	**2**	**3**	**10**
	NHL Totals		**977**	**252**	**449**	**701**	**1625**	**125**	**28**	**39**	**67**	**298**

a Shared WHL First All-Star Team (1975) with Bryan Trottier (Lethbridge)

Traded to **Calgary** by **Philadelphia** for Brad Marsh, November 11, 1981. Traded to **New Jersey** by **Calgary** with Phil Russell for Steve Tambellini and Joel Quenneville, June 21, 1983. Traded to **Detroit** by **New Jersey** for Chris Cichocki and Detroit's third-round choice (later transferred to Buffalo — Andrew MacVicar) in 1987 Entry Draft, March 9, 1987.

BRILL, JOHN

Right wing. Shoots left. 6'3", 180 lbs. Born, St. Paul, MN, December 3, 1970.
(Pittsburgh's 3rd choice, 58th overall, in 1989 Entry Draft).

			Regular Season					Playoffs				
Season	Club	Lea	GP	G	A	TP	PIM	GP	G	A	TP	PIM
1987-88	Grand Rapids	HS	28	15	13	28	....	....	....	....	....	....
1988-89	Grand Rapids	HS	25	23	29	52	28	....	....	....	....	....

BRIND'AMOUR, ROD

Center. Shoots left. 6'1", 200 lbs. Born, Ottawa, Ont., August 9, 1970.
(St. Louis' 1st choice, 9th overall, in 1988 Entry Draft).

			Regular Season					Playoffs				
Season	Club	Lea	GP	G	A	TP	PIM	GP	G	A	TP	PIM
1986-87	Notre Dame	Midget	33	38	50	88	66	....	....	....	....	....
1987-88	Notre Dame	SJHL	56	46	61	107	136	....	....	....	....	....
1988-89a	Michigan	CCHA	42	27	32	59	63	....	....	....	....	....
	St. Louis	**NHL**	....	....	....	....	....	**5**	**2**	**0**	**2**	**4**
	NHL Totals		....	....	....	....	....	**5**	**2**	**0**	**2**	**4**

a CCHA Freshman of the Year (1989)

BRISEBOIS, PATRICE

Defense. Shoots right. 6'1", 175 lbs.   Born, Montreal, Que., January 27, 1971.
(Montreal's 2nd choice, 30th overall, in 1989 Entry Draft).

			Regular Season					Playoffs				
Season	Club	Lea	GP	G	A	TP	PIM	GP	G	A	TP	PIM
1987-88	Laval	QMJHL	48	10	34	44	95	6	0	2	2	2
1988-89	Laval	QMJHL	50	20	45	65	95	17	8	14	22	45

BROCHU, STEPHANE

Defense. Shoots left. 6'1", 185 lbs.   Born, Sherbrooke, Que., August 15, 1967.
(NY Rangers' 9th choice, 175th over-all, in 1985 Entry Draft).

			Regular Season					Playoffs				
Season	Club	Lea	GP	G	A	TP	PIM	GP	G	A	TP	PIM
1984-85	Quebec	QMJHL	59	2	16	18	56	4	0	2	2	2
1985-86	St. Jean	QMJHL	63	14	27	41	121	3	1	0	1	2
1986-87	St. Jean	QMJHL	DID NOT PLAY - INJURED					8	0	2	2	11
1987-88	St. Jean	QMHL	29	4	35	39	88					
	Colorado	IHL	52	4	10	14	70	12	3	3	6	13
1988-89	NY Rangers	NHL	1	0	0	0	0	....				
	Denver	IHL	67	5	14	19	109	3	0	0	0	0
	NHL Totals		1	0	0	0	0	....		....		

BROOKE, ROBERT W. (BOB)

Center. Shoots right. 6'1", 200 lbs.   Born, Melrose, MA, December 18, 1960.
(St. Louis' 3rd choice, 75th over-all, in 1980 Entry Draft).

			Regular Season					Playoffs				
Season	Club	Lea	GP	G	A	TP	PIM	GP	G	A	TP	PIM
1979-80	Yale	ECAC	24	7	22	29	38	....		....		
1980-81	Yale	ECAC	27	12	30	42	59	....		....		
1981-82	Yale	ECAC	25	12	30	42	60	....		....		
1982-83ab	Yale	ECAC	21	10	27	37	48	....		....		
1983-84	U.S. National	....	54	7	18	25	75	....		....		
	U.S. Olympic	....	6	1	2	3	10	....		....		
	NY Rangers	NHL	9	1	2	3	4	5	0	0	0	7
1984-85	NY Rangers	NHL	72	7	9	16	79	3	0	0	0	8
1985-86	NY Rangers	NHL	79	24	20	44	111	16	6	9	15	28
1986-87	NY Rangers	NHL	15	3	5	8	20	....		....		
	Minnesota	NHL	65	10	18	28	78	....		....		
1987-88	Minnesota	NHL	77	5	20	25	108	....		....		
1988-89	Minnesota	NHL	57	7	9	16	57	5	3	0	3	2
	NHL Totals		374	57	83	140	457	29	9	9	18	45

a ECAC First All-Star Team (1983)
b NCAA All-American First Team (1983)
Rights traded to **NY Rangers** by **St. Louis** with Larry Patey for Dave Barr, NY Rangers' third round choice (Alan Perry) in 1984 Entry Draft and cash, March 5, 1984. Traded to **Minnesota** by **NY Rangers** with NY Rangers' rights to Minnesota's fourth-round choice (Jeffery Stolp) in 1988 Entry Draft previously acquired by NY Rangers in Mark Pavelich deal for Curt Giles, Tony McKegney and Minnesota's second-round choice (Troy Mallette) in 1988 Entry Draft, November 13, 1986.

BROOKS, DAN

Defense. Shoots right. 6'3", 210 lbs.   Born, St. Paul, MN, April 26, 1967.
(St. Louis' 4th choice, 100th overall, in 1985 Entry Draft).

			Regular Season					Playoffs				
Season	Club	Lea	GP	G	A	TP	PIM	GP	G	A	TP	PIM
1986-87	U. of Denver	WCHA	7	0	0	0	4	....		....		
1987-88	U. of Denver	WCHA	27	1	2	3	14	....		....		
1988-89	U. of Denver	WCHA	41	0	6	6	36	....		....		

BROTEN, AARON   (BRAH tuhn)

Center. Shoots left. 5'10", 180 lbs.   Born, Roseau, MN, November 14, 1960.
(Colorado's 5th choice, 106th over-all, in 1980 Entry Draft).

			Regular Season					Playoffs				
Season	Club	Lea	GP	G	A	TP	PIM	GP	G	A	TP	PIM
1979-80	U. Minnesota	WCHA	41	25	47	72	8	....		....		
1980-81	U. Minnesota	WCHA	45	*47	*59	*106	24	....		....		
	Colorado	NHL	2	0	0	0	0	....		....		
1981-82	Fort Worth	CHL	19	15	21	36	11	....		....		
	Colorado	NHL	58	15	24	39	6	....		....		
1982-83	Wichita	CHL	4	0	4	4	0	....		....		
	New Jersey	NHL	73	16	39	55	28	....		....		
1983-84	New Jersey	NHL	80	13	23	36	36	....		....		
1984-85	New Jersey	NHL	80	22	35	57	38	....		....		
1985-86	New Jersey	NHL	66	18	25	43	26	....		....		
1986-87	New Jersey	NHL	80	26	53	79	36	....		....		
1987-88	New Jersey	NHL	80	26	57	83	80	20	5	11	16	20
1988-89	New Jersey	NHL	80	16	43	59	81	....		....		
	NHL Totals		599	152	299	451	331	20	5	11	16	20

BROTEN, NEAL LaMOY   (BRAH tuhn)

Center. Shoots left. 5'9", 170 lbs.   Born, Roseau, MN, November 29, 1959.
(Minnesota's 3rd choice, 42nd over-all, in 1979 Entry Draft).

			Regular Season					Playoffs				
Season	Club	Lea	GP	G	A	TP	PIM	GP	G	A	TP	PIM
1978-79	U. Minnesota	WCHA	40	21	50	71	18	....		....		
1979-80	U.S. National	...	55	25	30	55	20	....		....		
	U.S. Olympic	...	7	2	1	3	2	....		....		
1980-81ab	U. Minnesota	WCHA	36	17	54	71	56	....		....		
	Minnesota	NHL	3	2	0	2	12	19	1	7	8	9
1981-82	Minnesota	NHL	73	38	60	98	42	4	0	2	2	0
1982-83	Minnesota	NHL	79	32	45	77	43	9	1	6	7	10
1983-84	Minnesota	NHL	76	28	61	89	43	16	5	5	10	4
1984-85	Minnesota	NHL	80	19	37	56	39	9	2	5	7	10
1985-86	Minnesota	NHL	80	29	76	105	47	5	3	2	5	2
1986-87	Minnesota	NHL	46	18	35	53	33	....		....		
1987-88	Minnesota	NHL	54	9	30	39	32	....		....		
1988-89	Minnesota	NHL	68	18	38	56	57	5	2	2	4	4
	NHL Totals		559	193	382	575	348	67	14	29	43	39

Played in NHL All-Star Game (1983-86)
a WCHA First All-Star Team (1981)
b Won Hobey Baker Memorial Trophy (Top U.S. College Player) (1981)

BROTEN, PAUL   (BRAH tuhn)

Center. Shoots right. 5'11", 170 lbs.   Born, Roseau, MN, October 27, 1965.
(NY Rangers 3rd choice, 77th over-all, in 1984 Entry Draft).

			Regular Season					Playoffs				
Season	Club	Lea	GP	G	A	TP	PIM	GP	G	A	TP	PIM
1984-85	U. Minnesota	WCHA	44	8	8	16	26	....		....		
1985-86	U. Minnesota	WCHA	38	6	16	22	24	....		....		
1986-87	U. Minnesota	WCHA	48	17	22	39	52	....		....		
1987-88	U. Minnesota	WCHA	38	18	21	39	42	....		....		
1988-89	Denver	IHL	77	28	31	59	133	4	0	2	2	6

BROWN, CAL

Defense. Shoots left. 6', 195 lbs.   Born, Calgary, Alta., January 13, 1967.
(Hartford's 10th choice, 221st overall, in 1986 Entry Draft).

			Regular Season					Playoffs				
Season	Club	Lea	GP	G	A	TP	PIM	GP	G	A	TP	PIM
1986-87	Colorado	WCHA	41	7	17	24	80	....		....		
1987-88	Colorado	WCHA	34	7	11	18	94	....		....		
1988-89	Colorado	WCHA	37	2	27	29	63	....		....		

BROWN, DAVID

Right wing. Shoots right. 6'5", 205 lbs.   Born, Saskatoon, Sask., October 12, 1962.
(Philadelphia's 7th choice, 40th over-all, in 1982 Entry Draft).

			Regular Season					Playoffs				
Season	Club	Lea	GP	G	A	TP	PIM	GP	G	A	TP	PIM
1980-81	Spokane	WHL	9	2	2	4	21	....		....		
1981-82	Saskatoon	WHL	62	11	33	44	344	5	1	0	1	4
1982-83	Philadelphia	NHL	2	0	0	0	5	....		....		
	Maine	AHL	71	8	6	14	418	16	0	0	0	107
1983-84	Springfield	AHL	59	17	14	31	150	....		....		
	Philadelphia	NHL	19	1	5	6	98	2	0	0	0	12
1984-85	Philadelphia	NHL	57	3	6	9	165	11	0	0	0	59
1985-86	Philadelphia	NHL	76	10	7	17	277	5	0	0	0	16
1986-87	Philadelphia	NHL	62	7	3	10	274	26	1	2	3	59
1987-88	Philadelphia	NHL	47	12	5	17	114	7	1	0	1	27
1988-89	Philadelphia	NHL	50	0	3	3	100	....		....		
	Edmonton	NHL	22	0	2	2	56	7	0	0	0	6
	NHL Totals		335	33	31	64	1089	58	2	2	4	179

Traded to **Edmonton** by **Philadelphia** for Keith Acton and Edmonton's fifth-round choice in 1991 Entry Draft, February 7, 1989.

BROWN, DOUG

Right wing. Shoots right. 5'11", 180 lbs.   Born, Southboro, MA, July 12, 1964.

			Regular Season					Playoffs				
Season	Club	Lea	GP	G	A	TP	PIM	GP	G	A	TP	PIM
1982-83	Boston College	ECAC	22	9	8	17	0	....		....		
1983-84	Boston College	ECAC	38	11	10	21	6	....		....		
1984-85	Boston College	H.E.	45	37	31	68	10	....		....		
1985-86	Boston College	H.E.	38	16	40	56	16	....		....		
1986-87	New Jersey	NHL	4	0	1	1	0	....		....		
	Maine	AHL	73	24	34	58	15	....		....		
1987-88	New Jersey	NHL	70	14	11	25	20	19	5	1	6	6
	Utica	AHL	2	0	2	2	2	....		....		
1988-89	New Jersey	NHL	63	15	10	25	15	....		....		
	Utica	AHL	4	1	4	5	0	....		....		
	NHL Totals		137	29	22	51	35	19	5	1	6	6

Signed as a free agent by **New Jersey**, August 6, 1986.

BROWN, GREG

Defense. Shoots right. 5'11", 180 lbs.   Born, Hartford, CT, March 7, 1968.
(Buffalo's 2nd choice, 26th over-all, in 1986 Entry Draft).

			Regular Season					Playoffs				
Season	Club	Lea	GP	G	A	TP	PIM	GP	G	A	TP	PIM
1985-86	St. Mark's	HS	19	22	28	50	50	....		....		
1986-87	Boston College	H.E.	37	10	27	37	22	....		....		
1987-88	U.S. National	....	55	6	29	35	22	....		....		
	U.S. Olympic	....	6	0	4	4	2	....		....		
1988-89abc	Boston College	H.E.	40	9	34	43	24	....		....		

a Hockey East First All-Star Team (1989)
b Hockey East Player of the Year (1989)
c NCAA East First All-American Team (1989)

BROWN, JEFF

Defense. Shoots right. 6'1", 202 lbs.   Born, Ottawa, Ont., April 30, 1966.
(Quebec's 2nd choice, 36th over-all, in 1984 Entry Draft).

			Regular Season					Playoffs				
Season	Club	Lea	GP	G	A	TP	PIM	GP	G	A	TP	PIM
1982-83	Sudbury	OHL	65	9	37	46	39	....		....		
1983-84	Sudbury	OHL	68	17	60	77	39	....		....		
1984-85	Sudbury	OHL	56	16	48	64	26	....		....		
1985-86	Quebec	NHL	8	3	2	5	6	1	0	0	0	0
a	Sudbury	OHL	45	22	28	50	24	4	0	2	2	11
	Fredericton	AHL	....					1	0	1	1	0
1986-87	Quebec	NHL	44	7	22	29	16	13	3	3	6	2
	Fredericton	AHL	26	2	14	16	16	....		....		
1987-88	Quebec	NHL	78	16	36	52	64	....		....		
1988-89	Quebec	NHL	78	21	47	68	62	....		....		
	NHL Totals		208	47	107	154	148	14	3	3	6	2

a OHL First All-Star Team (1986)

BROWN, KEITH JEFFREY

Defense. Shoots right. 6'1", 195 lbs. Born, Corner Brook, Nfld., May 6, 1960.
(Chicago's 1st choice, 7th over-all, in 1979 Entry Draft).

			Regular Season					Playoffs				
Season	Club	Lea	GP	G	A	TP	PIM	GP	G	A	TP	PIM
1977-78a	Portland	WHL	72	11	53	64	51	8	0	3	3	2
1978-79bc	Portland	WHL	70	11	85	96	75	25	3	*30	33	21
1979-80	**Chicago**	**NHL**	**76**	**2**	**18**	**20**	**27**	**6**	**0**	**0**	**0**	**4**
1980-81	**Chicago**	**NHL**	**80**	**9**	**34**	**43**	**80**	**3**	**0**	**2**	**2**	**2**
1981-82	**Chicago**	**NHL**	**33**	**4**	**20**	**24**	**26**	**4**	**0**	**2**	**2**	**5**
1982-83	**Chicago**	**NHL**	**50**	**4**	**27**	**31**	**20**	**7**	**0**	**0**	**0**	**11**
1983-84	**Chicago**	**NHL**	**74**	**10**	**25**	**35**	**94**	**5**	**0**	**1**	**1**	**10**
1984-85	**Chicago**	**NHL**	**56**	**1**	**22**	**23**	**55**	**11**	**2**	**7**	**9**	**31**
1985-86	**Chicago**	**NHL**	**70**	**11**	**29**	**40**	**87**	**3**	**0**	**1**	**1**	**9**
1986-87	**Chicago**	**NHL**	**73**	**4**	**23**	**27**	**86**	**4**	**0**	**1**	**1**	**6**
1987-88	**Chicago**	**NHL**	**24**	**3**	**6**	**9**	**45**	**5**	**0**	**2**	**2**	**10**
1988-89	**Chicago**	**NHL**	**74**	**2**	**16**	**18**	**84**	**13**	**1**	**3**	**4**	**25**
	NHL Totals		**610**	**50**	**220**	**270**	**604**	**61**	**3**	**19**	**22**	**113**

a Shared WHL's Rookie of the Year with John Ogrodnick (New Westminster) (1978)
b Named WHL's Top Defenseman (1979)
c WHL First All-Star Team (1979)

BROWN, ROB

Center. Shoots left. 5'11", 170 lbs. Born, Kingston, Ont., April 10, 1968.
(Pittsburgh's 4th choice, 67th overall, in 1986 Entry Draft).

			Regular Season					Playoffs				
Season	Club	Lea	GP	G	A	TP	PIM	GP	G	A	TP	PIM
1984-85	Kamloops	WHL	60	29	50	79	95	15	8	8	26	28
1985-86ab	Kamloops	WHL	69	58	115	173	171	16	18	28	46	14
1986-87abc	Kamloops	WHL	63	76	136	212	101	5	6	5	11	6
1987-88	**Pittsburgh**	**NHL**	**51**	**24**	**20**	**44**	**56**	....	....	....	....	....
1988-89	**Pittsburgh**	**NHL**	**68**	**49**	**66**	**115**	**118**	**11**	**5**	**3**	**8**	**22**
	NHL Totals		**119**	**73**	**86**	**159**	**174**	**11**	**5**	**3**	**8**	**22**

a WHL Player of the Year (1987)
b WHL First All-Star Team (1987)
c Canadian Major Junior Player of the Year (1987)

Played in NHL All-Star Game (1989)

BRUBAKER, JEFFREY J. (JEFF) (BREW-bake-er)

Left wing. Shoots left. 6'2", 210 lbs. Born, Frederick, MD, February 24, 1958.
(Boston's 6th choice, 102nd over-all, in 1978 Amateur Draft).

			Regular Season					Playoffs				
Season	Club	Lea	GP	G	A	TP	PIM	GP	G	A	TP	PIM
1976-77	Peterborough	OHA	26	0	5	5	143	4	0	2	2	7
1977-78	Peterborough	OHA	68	20	24	44	307	21	6	5	11	52
1978-79	Rochester	AHL	57	4	10	14	253	....	....	....	....	....
	New England	WHA	12	0	0	0	19	3	0	0	0	12
1979-80	**Hartford**	**NHL**	**3**	**0**	**1**	**1**	**2**	....	....	....	....	....
	Springfield	AHL	50	12	13	25	165	....	....	....	....	....
1980-81	**Hartford**	**NHL**	**43**	**5**	**3**	**8**	**93**	....	....	....	....	....
	Binghamton	AHL	33	18	11	29	138	....	....	....	....	....
1981-82	**Montreal**	**NHL**	**3**	**0**	**1**	**1**	**32**	**2**	**0**	**0**	**0**	**27**
	Nova Scotia	AHL	60	28	12	40	256	6	2	1	3	32
1982-83	Nova Scotia	AHL	78	31	27	58	183	7	1	1	2	25
1983-84	**Calgary**	**NHL**	**4**	**0**	**0**	**0**	**19**	....	....	....	....	....
	Colorado	CHL	57	16	19	35	218	6	3	1	4	15
1984-85	**Toronto**	**NHL**	**68**	**8**	**4**	**12**	**209**	....	....	....	....	....
1985-86	**Toronto**	**NHL**	**21**	**0**	**0**	**0**	**67**	....	....	....	....	....
	Edmonton	**NHL**	**4**	**1**	**0**	**1**	**12**	....	....	....	....	....
	Nova Scotia	AHL	19	4	3	7	41	....	....	....	....	....
1986-87	Nova Scotia	AHL	47	10	16	26	80	....	....	....	....	....
	Hershey	AHL	12	1	2	3	30	3	2	0	2	10
1987-88	**NY Rangers**	**NHL**	**31**	**2**	**0**	**2**	**78**	....	....	....	....	....
	Colorado	IHL	30	12	10	22	53	13	2	2	4	21
1988-89	**Detroit**	**NHL**	**1**	**0**	**0**	**0**	**0**	....	....	....	....	....
	Adirondack	AHL	63	3	10	13	137	....	....	....	....	....
	NHL Totals		**178**	**16**	**9**	**25**	**512**	....	....	....	....	....

Rights transferred to **Hartford** by **Boston**, June 22, 1979. Claimed by **Montreal** from **Hartford** in NHL Waiver Draft, October 5, 1981. Claimed by **Quebec** from **Montreal** in NHL Waiver Draft, October 3, 1983. Claimed by **Calgary** from **Quebec** in NHL Waiver Draft, October 3, 1983. Signed as a free agent by **Edmonton,** June 21, 1984. Claimed by **Toronto** from **Edmonton** in NHL Waiver Draft, October 9, 1984. Claimed on waivers by **Edmonton** from **Toronto**, December 5, 1985. Traded to **Philadelphia** by **Edmonton** for Dom Campedelli, March 9, 1987. Sold to **NY Rangers** by **Philadelphia**, July 21, 1987.

BRUCE, DAVID

Right wing/Center. Shoots right. 5'11", 187 lbs. Born, Thunder Bay, Ont., October 7, 1964.
(Vancouver's 2nd choice, 30th over-all, in 1983 Entry Draft).

			Regular Season					Playoffs				
Season	Club	Lea	GP	G	A	TP	PIM	GP	G	A	TP	PIM
1982-83	Kitchener	OHL	67	36	35	71	199	12	7	9	16	27
1983-84	Kitchener	OHL	62	52	40	92	203	10	5	8	13	20
1984-85	Fredericton	AHL	56	14	11	25	104	5	0	0	0	37
1985-86	**Vancouver**	**NHL**	**12**	**0**	**1**	**1**	**14**	**1**	**0**	**0**	**0**	**0**
	Fredericton	AHL	66	25	16	41	151	2	0	1	1	12
1986-87	**Vancouver**	**NHL**	**50**	**9**	**7**	**16**	**109**	....	....	....	....	....
	Fredericton	AHL	17	7	6	13	73	....	....	....	....	....
1987-88	**Vancouver**	**NHL**	**28**	**7**	**3**	**10**	**57**	....	....	....	....	....
	Fredericton	AHL	30	27	18	45	115	....	....	....	....	....
1988-89	**Vancouver**	**NHL**	**53**	**7**	**7**	**14**	**65**	....	....	....	....	....
	NHL Totals		**143**	**23**	**18**	**41**	**245**	**1**	**0**	**0**	**0**	**0**

BRUMWELL, JAMES (MURRAY)

Defense. Shoots left. 6'2", 190 lbs. Born, Calgary, Alta., March 31, 1960.

			Regular Season					Playoffs				
Season	Club	Lea	GP	G	A	TP	PIM	GP	G	A	TP	PIM
1978-79	Billings	WHL	61	11	32	43	62	....	....	....	....	....
1979-80	Billings	WHL	67	18	54	72	50	....	....	....	....	....
1980-81	**Minnesota**	**NHL**	**1**	**0**	**0**	**0**	**0**	....	....	....	....	....
	Oklahoma City	CHL	79	12	43	55	79	3	0	0	0	4
1981-82	**Minnesota**	**NHL**	**21**	**0**	**3**	**3**	**18**	**2**	**0**	**0**	**0**	**2**
	Nashville	CHL	55	4	21	25	66	....	....	....	....	....
1982-83	Wichita	CHL	11	4	1	5	4	....	....	....	....	....
	New Jersey	**NHL**	**59**	**5**	**14**	**19**	**34**	....	....	....	....	....
1983-84	**New Jersey**	**NHL**	**42**	**7**	**13**	**20**	**14**	....	....	....	....	....
	Maine	AHL	35	4	25	29	16	17	1	5	6	15
1984-85	Maine	AHL	64	8	31	39	12	10	4	5	9	19
1985-86	**New Jersey**	**NHL**	**1**	**0**	**0**	**0**	**0**	....	....	....	....	....
	Maine	AHL	66	9	28	37	35	5	0	3	3	2
1986-87	**New Jersey**	**NHL**	**1**	**0**	**0**	**0**	**2**	....	....	....	....	....
	Maine	AHL	69	10	38	48	30	....	....	....	....	....
1987-88	**New Jersey**	**NHL**	**3**	**0**	**1**	**1**	**2**	....	....	....	....	....
a	Utica	AHL	77	13	53	66	44	....	....	....	....	....
1988-89	Utica	AHL	73	5	29	34	29	5	0	0	0	2
	NHL Totals		**128**	**12**	**31**	**43**	**70**	**2**	**0**	**0**	**0**	**2**

a AHL Second All-Star Team (1988)

Signed as free agent by **Minnesota**, August 7, 1980. Claimed by **New Jersey** from **Minnesota** in Waiver Draft, October 4, 1982.

BRUNET, BENOIT

Left wing. Shoots left. 5'10", 180 lbs. Born, Ste-Anne de Bellevue, Que., August 24, 1968.
(Montreal's 2nd choice, 27th over-all, in 1986 Entry Draft).

			Regular Season					Playoffs				
Season	Club	Lea	GP	G	A	TP	PIM	GP	G	A	TP	PIM
1985-86	Hull	QMJHL	71	33	37	70	81	....	....	....	....	....
1986-87a	Hull	QMJHL	60	43	67	110	105	6	7	5	12	8
1987-88	Hull	QMJHL	62	54	89	143	131	10	3	10	13	11
1988-89	**Montreal**	**NHL**	**2**	**0**	**1**	**1**	**0**	....	....	....	....	....
b	Sherbrooke	AHL	73	41	76	117	95	6	2	0	2	4
	NHL Totals		**2**	**0**	**1**	**1**	**0**	....	....	....	....	....

a QMJHL Second All-Star Team (1987)
b AHL First All-Star Team (1989)

BRYDEN, ROB

Left wing. Shoots left. 6'3", 205 lbs. Born, Toronto, Ont., April 5, 1963.
(Montreal's 10th choice, 158th over-all, in 1983 Entry Draft).

			Regular Season					Playoffs				
Season	Club	Lea	GP	G	A	TP	PIM	GP	G	A	TP	PIM
1983-84	W. Michigan	CCHA	36	17	12	29	60	....	....	....	....	....
1984-85	W. Michigan	CCHA	39	18	19	37	59	....	....	....	....	....
1985-86	W. Michigan	CCHA	44	23	28	51	85	....	....	....	....	....
1986-87a	W. Michigan	CCHA	43	46	32	78	82	....	....	....	....	....
1987-88	Sherbrooke	AHL	66	21	16	37	75	5	1	0	1	9
1988-89	Sherbrooke	AHL	13	8	2	10	15	6	3	0	3	6
	Flint	IHL	28	14	12	26	22	....	....	....	....	....

a CCHA Second All-Star Team (1987).

BRYDGES, PAUL

Center. Shoots right. 5'11", 180 lbs. Born, Guelph, Ont., June 21, 1965.

			Regular Season					Playoffs				
Season	Club	Lea	GP	G	A	TP	PIM	GP	G	A	TP	PIM
1982-83	Guelph	OHL	56	13	13	26	27	....	....	....	....	....
1983-84	Guelph	OHL	68	27	23	50	37	....	....	....	....	....
1984-85	Guelph	OHL	57	22	24	46	39	....	....	....	....	....
1985-86	Guelph	OHL	62	17	40	57	88	19	10	15	25	22
1986-87	**Buffalo**	**NHL**	**15**	**2**	**2**	**4**	**6**	....	....	....	....	....
	Rochester	AHL	54	13	17	30	54	1	0	0	0	0
1987-88	Rochester	AHL	69	15	16	31	86	7	1	1	2	4
1988-89	Rochester	AHL	51	8	3	11	36	....	....	....	....	....
	NHL Totals		**15**	**2**	**2**	**4**	**6**	....	....	....	....	....

Signed as a free agent by **Buffalo**, June 11, 1986.

BUCHBERGER, KELLY (BUCK-ber-ger)

Left wing. Shoots left. 6'2", 205 lbs. Born, Langenburg, Sask., December 2, 1966.
(Edmonton's 8th choice, 188th over-all, in 1985 Entry Draft).

			Regular Season					Playoffs				
Season	Club	Lea	GP	G	A	TP	PIM	GP	G	A	TP	PIM
1984-85	Moose Jaw	WHL	51	12	17	29	114	....	....	....	....	....
1985-86	Moose Jaw	WHL	72	14	22	36	206	13	11	4	15	37
1986-87	**Edmonton**	**NHL**	....	....	....	....	....	**3**	**0**	**1**	**1**	**5**
	Nova Scotia	AHL	70	12	20	32	257	5	0	1	1	23
1987-88	**Edmonton**	**NHL**	**19**	**1**	**0**	**1**	**81**	....	....	....	....	....
	Nova Scotia	AHL	49	21	23	44	206	2	0	0	0	11
1988-89	**Edmonton**	**NHL**	**66**	**5**	**9**	**14**	**234**	....	....	....	....	....
	NHL Totals		**85**	**6**	**9**	**15**	**315**	**3**	**0**	**1**	**1**	**5**

BUCKLEY, DAVID

Defense. Shoots left. 6'4", 195 lbs. Born, Newton, MA, January 27, 1966.
(Toronto's 9th choice, 192nd over-all, in 1984 Entry Draft).

			Regular Season					Playoffs				
Season	Club	Lea	GP	G	A	TP	PIM	GP	G	A	TP	PIM
1985-86	Boston College	H.E.	22	0	2	2	4	....	....	....	....	....
1986-87	Boston College	H.E.	34	3	5	8	9	....	....	....	....	....
1987-88	Boston College	H.E.	33	1	8	9	40	....	....	....	....	....
1988-89	Boston College	H.E.	40	3	7	10	48	....	....	....	....	....

BUCYK, RANDY (BYOO-sik)

Center. Shoots left. 5'11", 185 lbs. Born, Edmonton, Alta., November 9, 1962.

			Regular Season					Playoffs				
Season	Club	Lea	GP	G	A	TP	PIM	GP	G	A	TP	PIM
1980-81	Northeastern	ECAC	31	18	17	35	0	....	....	....	....	....
1981-82	Northeastern	ECAC	33	19	17	36	10	....	....	....	....	....
1982-83	Northeastern	ECAC	28	16	20	36	16	....	....	....	....	....
1983-84	Northeastern	ECAC	29	16	13	29	11	....	....	....	....	....
1984-85	Sherbrooke	AHL	62	21	26	47	20	8	0	0	0	20
1985-86	Sherbrooke	AHL	43	18	33	51	22	....	....	....	....	....
	Montreal	**NHL**	**17**	**4**	**2**	**6**	**8**	**2**	**0**	**0**	**0**	**0**
1986-87	Sherbrooke	AHL	70	24	39	63	28	17	3	11	14	2
1987-88	**Calgary**	**NHL**	**2**	**0**	**0**	**0**	**0**	....	....	....	....	....
	Salt Lake	IHL	75	37	45	82	68	19	7	8	15	12
1988-89	Salt Lake	IHL	79	28	59	87	24	14	5	5	10	4
	Cdn. National	....	4	0	0	0	2	....	....	....	....	....
	NHL Totals		**19**	**4**	**2**	**6**	**8**	**2**	**0**	**0**	**0**	**0**

Signed as a free agent by **Montreal**, January 15, 1986. Signed as a free agent by **Calgary**, June 29, 1987.

BUDA, DAVID

Center. Shoots left. 6'4", 190 lbs. Born, Mississauga, Ont., March 14, 1966.
(Boston's 9th choice, 199th over-all, in 1985 Entry Draft).

			Regular Season					Playoffs				
Season	Club	Lea	GP	G	A	TP	PIM	GP	G	A	TP	PIM
1985-86	Northeastern	H.E.	39	4	4	8	39	....	....	....	....	....
1986-87	Northeastern	H.E.	37	15	15	30	32	....	....	....	....	....
1987-88	Northeastern	H.E.	37	21	16	37	66	....	....	....	....	....
1988-89a	Northeastern	H.E.	35	23	23	46	45	....	....	....	....	....
	Maine	AHL	5	3	1	4	2	....	....	....	....	....

a Hockey East First All-Star Team (1989)

BUDY, TIMOTHY (TIM)

Left wing. Shoots left. 6', 190 lbs. Born, Selkirk, Man., February 14, 1967.
(New Jersey's 1st choice, 17th overall, in 1988 Supplemental Draft).

			Regular Season					Playoffs				
Season	Club	Lea	GP	G	A	TP	PIM	GP	G	A	TP	PIM
1985-86	Colorado Coll.	WCHA	40	9	8	17	30	....	....	....	....	....
1986-87	Colorado Coll.	WCHA	42	17	20	37	40	....	....	....	....	....
1987-88	Colorado Coll.	WCHA	38	14	15	29	28	....	....	....	....	....
1988-89	Colorado	WCHA	40	23	23	46	54	....	....	....	....	....
	Utica	AHL	3	0	0	0	2	....	....	....	....	....

BULLARD, MICHAEL BRIAN (MIKE) (BULL-ard)

Center. Shoots left. 5'10", 185 lbs. Born, Ottawa, Ont., March 10, 1961.
(Pittsburgh's 1st choice, 9th over-all, in 1980 Entry Draft).

			Regular Season					Playoffs				
Season	Club	Lea	GP	G	A	TP	PIM	GP	G	A	TP	PIM
1978-79	Brantford	OHA	66	43	56	99	66	....	....	....	....	....
1979-80a	Brantford	OHA	66	66	84	150	86	11	10	6	16	29
1980-81b	Brantford	OHA	42	47	60	107	55	6	4	5	9	10
	Pittsburgh	**NHL**	**15**	**1**	**2**	**3**	**19**	**4**	**3**	**3**	**6**	**0**
1981-82	**Pittsburgh**	**NHL**	**75**	**36**	**27**	**63**	**91**	**5**	**1**	**1**	**2**	**4**
1982-83	**Pittsburgh**	**NHL**	**57**	**22**	**22**	**44**	**60**	....	....	....	....	....
1983-84	**Pittsburgh**	**NHL**	**76**	**51**	**41**	**92**	**57**	....	....	....	....	....
1984-85	**Pittsburgh**	**NHL**	**68**	**32**	**31**	**63**	**75**	....	....	....	....	....
1985-86	**Pittsburgh**	**NHL**	**77**	**41**	**42**	**83**	**69**	....	....	....	....	....
1986-87	**Pittsburgh**	**NHL**	**14**	**2**	**10**	**12**	**17**	....	....	....	....	....
	Calgary	**NHL**	**57**	**28**	**26**	**54**	**34**	**6**	**4**	**3**	**7**	**2**
1987-88	**Calgary**	**NHL**	**79**	**48**	**55**	**103**	**68**	**6**	**0**	**2**	**2**	**6**
1988-89	**St. Louis**	**NHL**	**20**	**4**	**12**	**16**	**46**	....	....	....	....	....
	Philadelphia	**NHL**	**54**	**23**	**26**	**49**	**60**	**19**	**3**	**9**	**12**	**32**
	NHL Totals		**592**	**288**	**294**	**582**	**596**	**40**	**11**	**18**	**29**	**44**

a OHA Third All-Star Team (1979)
b OHA Second All-Star Team (1980)

Traded to **Calgary** by **Pittsburgh** for Dan Quinn, November 12, 1986. Traded to **St. Louis** by **Calgary** with Craig Coxe and Tim Corkery for Mark Hunter, Doug Gilmour, Steve Bozek and Michael Dark, September 6, 1988. Traded to **Philadelphia** by **St. Louis** for Peter Zezel, November 29, 1988.

BURAKOVSKI, ROBERT

Right wing. Shoots right. 5'10", 165 lbs. Born, Malmo, Sweden, November 24, 1966.
(NY Rangers' 11th choice, 217th overall, in 1985 Entry Draft).

			Regular Season					Playoffs				
Season	Club	Lea	GP	G	A	TP	PIM	GP	G	A	TP	PIM
1985-86	Leksand	Swe.	19	4	3	7	4	....	....	....	....	....
1986-87	Leksand	Swe.	36	21	15	36	26	....	....	....	....	....
1987-88	Leksand	Swe.	36	10	11	21	10	....	....	....	....	....
1988-89	Leksand	Swe.	40	23	20	43	44	10	6	7	13	4

BUREAU, MARC (BEWR oh)

Right wing. Shoots right. 6', 195 lbs. Born, Trois-Rivieres, Que., May 19, 1966.

			Regular Season					Playoffs				
Season	Club	Lea	GP	G	A	TP	PIM	GP	G	A	TP	PIM
1983-84	Chicoutimi	QMJHL	56	6	16	22	14	....	....	....	....	....
1984-85	Granby	QMJHL	68	50	70	120	29	....	....	....	....	....
1985-86	Chicoutimi	QMJHL	63	36	62	98	69	9	3	7	10	10
1986-87	Longueuil	QMJHL	66	54	58	112	68	20	17	20	37	12
1987-88	Salt Lake	IHL	69	7	20	27	86	7	0	3	3	8
1988-89	Salt Lake	IHL	76	28	36	64	119	14	7	5	12	31

Signed as a free agent by **Calgary**, May 19, 1987.

BURKE, JAMES

Defense. Shoots left. 6'2", 200 lbs. Born, Newton, MA, January 3, 1968.
(Hartford's 7th choice, 158th overall, in 1988 Entry Draft).

			Regular Season					Playoffs				
Season	Club	Lea	GP	G	A	TP	PIM	GP	G	A	TP	PIM
1986-87	U. of Maine	HE	23	0	0	0	18	....	....	....	....	....
1987-88	U. of Maine	HE	41	2	10	12	34	....	....	....	....	....
1988-89	U. of Maine	HE	41	1	7	8	56	....	....	....	....	....

BURNIE, STUART

Right wing. Shoots right. 5'11", 185 lbs. Born, Orilla, Ont., May 7, 1962.

			Regular Season					Playoffs				
Season	Club	Lea	GP	G	A	TP	PIM	GP	G	A	TP	PIM
1982-83	W. Michigan	CCHA	36	12	7	19	50	....	....	....	....	....
1983-84	W. Michigan	CCHA	42	26	13	39	73	....	....	....	....	....
1984-85	W. Michigan	CCHA	39	21	16	37	49	....	....	....	....	....
1985-86a	W. Michigan	CCHA	42	43	36	79	78	....	....	....	....	....
1986-87	Springfield	AHL	76	21	30	51	62	....	....	....	....	....
1987-88	Springfield	AHL	78	33	22	55	98	....	....	....	....	....
1988-89	Springfield	AHL	74	28	36	64	49	....	....	....	....	....

a CCHA Second All-Star Team (1986)

Signed as a free agent by **NY Islanders**, September 5, 1986.

BURR, SHAWN

Center. Shoots left. 6'1", 195 lbs. Born, Sarnia, Ont., July 1, 1966.
(Detroit's 1st choice, 7th over-all, in 1984 Entry Draft).

			Regular Season					Playoffs				
Season	Club	Lea	GP	G	A	TP	PIM	GP	G	A	TP	PIM
1982-83	Sarnia	Midget	52	50	85	135	125	....	....	....	....	....
1983-84	Kitchener	OHL	68	41	44	85	50	16	5	12	17	22
1984-85	**Detroit**	**NHL**	**9**	**0**	**0**	**0**	**2**	....	....	....	....	....
	Adirondack	AHL	4	0	0	0	2	....	....	....	....	....
	Kitchener	OHL	48	24	42	66	50	4	3	3	6	2
1985-86	**Detroit**	**NHL**	**5**	**1**	**0**	**1**	**4**	....	....	....	....	....
	Adirondack	AHL	3	2	2	4	2	17	5	7	12	32
a	Kitchener	OHL	59	60	67	127	104	5	2	3	5	8
1986-87	**Detroit**	**NHL**	**80**	**22**	**25**	**47**	**107**	**16**	**7**	**2**	**9**	**20**
1987-88	**Detroit**	**NHL**	**78**	**17**	**23**	**40**	**97**	**9**	**3**	**1**	**4**	**14**
1988-89	**Detroit**	**NHL**	**79**	**19**	**27**	**46**	**78**	**6**	**1**	**2**	**3**	**6**
	NHL Totals		**251**	**59**	**75**	**134**	**288**	**31**	**11**	**5**	**16**	**40**

a OHL Second All-Star Team (1986)

BURRIDGE, RANDY

Left Wing. Shoots left. 5'9", 180 lbs. Born, Fort Erie, Ont., January 7, 1966.
(Boston's 7th choice, 157th over-all, in 1985 Entry Draft).

			Regular Season					Playoffs				
Season	Club	Lea	GP	G	A	TP	PIM	GP	G	A	TP	PIM
1983-84	Peterborough	OHL	55	6	7	13	44	8	3	2	5	7
1984-85	Peterborough	OHL	66	49	57	106	88	17	9	16	25	18
1985-86	Peterborough	OHL	17	15	11	26	23	3	1	3	4	2
	Boston	**NHL**	**52**	**17**	**25**	**42**	**17**	**3**	**0**	**4**	**4**	**12**
	Moncton	AHL	....	....	....	....	....	3	0	2	2	2
1986-87	**Boston**	**NHL**	**23**	**1**	**4**	**5**	**16**	**2**	**1**	**0**	**1**	**2**
	Moncton	AHL	47	26	41	67	139	3	1	2	3	30
1987-88	**Boston**	**NHL**	**79**	**27**	**28**	**55**	**105**	**23**	**2**	**10**	**12**	**16**
1988-89	**Boston**	**NHL**	**80**	**31**	**30**	**61**	**39**	**10**	**5**	**2**	**7**	**6**
	NHL Totals		**234**	**75**	**87**	**163**	**177**	**38**	**8**	**16**	**24**	**36**

BURT, ADAM

Defense. Shoots left. 6', 195 lbs. Born, Detroit, MI, January 15, 1969.
(Hartford's 2nd choice, 39th overall, in 1987 Entry Draft).

			Regular Season					Playoffs				
Season	Club	Lea	GP	G	A	TP	PIM	GP	G	A	TP	PIM
1985-86	North Bay	OHL	49	0	11	11	81	10	0	0	0	24
1986-87	North Bay	OHL	57	4	27	31	138	24	1	6	7	68
1987-88	Binghamton	AHL	....	....	....	....	....	2	1	1	2	0
a	North Bay	OHL	66	17	53	70	176	2	0	3	3	6
1988-89	**Hartford**	**NHL**	**5**	**0**	**0**	**0**	**6**	....	....	....	....	....
	Binghamton	AHL	5	0	2	2	13	....	....	....	....	....
	North Bay	OHL	23	4	11	15	45	12	2	12	14	12
	NHL Totals		**5**	**0**	**0**	**0**	**6**	....	....	....	....	....

a OHL Second All-Star Team (1988)

BUSKAS, ROD

Defense. Shoots right. 6'1", 200 lbs. Born, Wetaskiwin, Alta., January 7, 1961.
(Pittsburgh's 5th choice, 112th over-all, in 1981 Entry Draft).

			Regular Season					Playoffs				
Season	Club	Lea	GP	G	A	TP	PIM	GP	G	A	TP	PIM
1978-79	Billings	WHL	1	0	0	0	0	....	....	....	....	....
	Medicine Hat	WHL	34	1	12	13	60	....	....	....	....	....
1979-80	Medicine Hat	WHL	72	7	40	47	284	....	....	....	....	....
1980-81	Medicine Hat	WHL	72	14	46	60	164	5	1	1	2	8
1981-82	Erie	AHL	69	1	18	19	78	....	....	....	....	....
1982-83	**Pittsburgh**	**NHL**	**41**	**2**	**2**	**4**	**102**	....	....	....	....	....
	Baltimore	AHL	31	2	8	10	45	....	....	....	....	....
1983-84	**Pittsburgh**	**NHL**	**47**	**2**	**4**	**6**	**60**	....	....	....	....	....
	Baltimore	AHL	33	2	12	14	100	10	1	3	4	22
1984-85	**Pittsburgh**	**NHL**	**69**	**2**	**7**	**9**	**191**	....	....	....	....	....
1985-86	**Pittsburgh**	**NHL**	**72**	**2**	**7**	**9**	**159**	....	....	....	....	....
1986-87	**Pittsburgh**	**NHL**	**68**	**3**	**15**	**18**	**123**	....	....	....	....	....
1987-88	**Pittsburgh**	**NHL**	**76**	**4**	**8**	**12**	**206**	....	....	....	....	....
1988-89	**Pittsburgh**	**NHL**	**52**	**1**	**5**	**6**	**105**	**10**	**0**	**0**	**0**	**23**
	NHL Totals		**425**	**16**	**48**	**64**	**946**	**10**	**0**	**0**	**0**	**23**

BUTCHER, GARTH

Defense. Shoots right. 6', 200 lbs. Born, Regina, Sask., January 8, 1963.
(Vancouver's 1st choice, 10th over-all, in 1981 Entry Draft).

			Regular Season					Playoffs				
Season	Club	Lea	GP	G	A	TP	PIM	GP	G	A	TP	PIM
1979-80	Regina	WHL	13	0	4	4	20	....	....	....	....	....
1980-81a	Regina	WHL	69	9	77	86	230	11	5	17	22	60
1981-82a	Regina	WHL	65	24	68	92	318	19	3	17	20	95
	Vancouver	NHL	5	0	0	0	9	1	0	0	0	0
1982-83	Vancouver	NHL	55	1	13	14	105	3	1	0	1	2
1983-84	Vancouver	NHL	28	2	0	2	34	....	....	....	....	....
	Fredericton	AHL	25	4	13	17	43	6	0	2	2	19
1984-85	Vancouver	NHL	75	3	9	12	152	....	....	....	....	....
	Fredericton	AHL	3	1	0	1	11	....	....	....	....	....
1985-86	Vancouver	NHL	70	4	7	11	188	3	0	0	0	0
1986-87	Vancouver	NHL	70	5	15	20	207	....	....	....	....	....
1987-88	Vancouver	NHL	80	6	17	23	285	....	....	....	....	....
1988-89	Vancouver	NHL	78	0	20	20	227	7	1	1	2	22
	NHL Totals		461	21	81	102	1207	14	2	1	3	22

a WHL First All-Star Team (1981, 1982)

BUTLER, BILL

Left wing. Shoots left. 6'2", 195 lbs. Born, Boston, MA, March 3, 1967.
(St. Louis' 12th choice, 234th overall, in 1986 Entry Draft).

			Regular Season					Playoffs				
Season	Club	Lea	GP	G	A	TP	PIM	GP	G	A	TP	PIM
1985-86	Northwood	HS	17	14	16	30	12	....	....	....	....	....
1986-87	U. of Vermont	ECAC	32	0	7	7	14	....	....	....	....	....
1987-88	U. of Vermont	ECAC	26	1	3	4	10	....	....	....	....	....
1988-89	U. of Vermont	ECAC	10	1	6	7	8	....	....	....	....	....

BYCE, JOHN

Center. Shoots left. 6'1", 180 lbs. Born, Madison, WI, August 9, 1967.
(Boston's 11th choice, 220th overall, in 1985 Entry Draft).

			Regular Season					Playoffs				
Season	Club	Lea	GP	G	A	TP	PIM	GP	G	A	TP	PIM
1986-87	U. Wisconsin	WCHA	40	1	4	5	12	....	....	....	....	....
1987-88	U. Wisconsin	WCHA	41	22	12	34	18	....	....	....	....	....
1988-89a	U. Wisconsin	WCHA	42	27	28	55	16	....	....	....	....	....

a WCHA Second All-Star Team (1989)

BYERS, LYNDON

Right wing. Shoots right. 6'1", 200 lbs. Born, Nipawin, Sask., February 29, 1964.
(Boston's 3rd choice, 39th over-all, in 1982 Entry Draft).

			Regular Season					Playoffs				
Season	Club	Lea	GP	G	A	TP	PIM	GP	G	A	TP	PIM
1981-82	Regina	WHL	57	18	25	43	169	20	5	6	11	48
1982-83	Regina	WHL	70	32	38	70	153	5	1	1	2	16
1983-84	Boston	NHL	10	2	4	6	32	....	....	....	....	....
	Regina	WHL	58	32	57	89	154	23	17	18	35	78
1984-85	Boston	NHL	33	3	8	11	41	....	....	....	..	....
	Hershey	AHL	27	4	6	10	55	....	....	....	....	....
1985-86	Boston	NHL	5	0	2	2	9	....	....	....	....	....
	Moncton	AHL	14	2	4	6	26	....	....	....	....	....
	Milwaukee	IHL	8	0	2	2	22	....	....	....	....	....
1986-87	Boston	NHL	18	2	3	5	53	1	0	0	0	0
	Moncton	AHL	27	5	5	10	63	....	....	....	....	....
1987-88	Boston	NHL	53	10	14	24	236	11	1	2	3	62
	Maine	AHL	2	0	1	1	18	....	....	....	....	....
1988-89	Boston	NHL	49	0	4	4	218	2	0	0	0	0
	Maine	AHL	4	1	3	4	2	....	....	....	....	....
	NHL Totals		168	17	35	52	589	14	1	2	3	62

BYRAM, SHAWN

Left wing. Shoots left. 6'2", 204 lbs. Born, Neepawa, Man., September 12, 1968.
(NY Islanders' 4th choice, 80th overall, in 1986 Entry Draft).

			Regular Season					Playoffs				
Season	Club	Lea	GP	G	A	TP	PIM	GP	G	A	TP	PIM
1985-86	Regina	WHL	46	7	6	13	45	9	0	1	1	11
1986-87	Prince Albert	WHL	67	19	21	40	147	7	1	1	2	10
1987-88	Prince Albert	WHL	61	23	28	51	178	10	5	2	7	27
1988-89	Springfield	AHL	45	5	11	16	195	....	....	....	....	....
	Indianapolis	IHL	1	0	0	0	2	....	....	....	....	....

BZDEL, GERALD (bizz-DEL)

Defense. Shoots right. 6'1", 196 lbs. Born, Wynyard, Sask., March 13, 1968.
(Quebec's 5th choice, 102nd overall, in 1986 Entry Draft).

			Regular Season					Playoffs				
Season	Club	Lea	GP	G	A	TP	PIM	GP	G	A	TP	PIM
1985-86	Regina	WHL	72	2	15	17	107	10	0	3	3	14
1986-87	Regina	WHL	13	0	3	3	38	....	....	....	....	....
	Seattle	WHL	48	4	12	16	137	....	....	....	....	....
1987-88	Moose Jaw	WHL	72	4	17	21	217	....	....	....	....	....
1988-89	Halifax	AHL	36	1	3	4	46	....	....	....	....	....

CAIN, KELLY

Center. Shoots left. 5'6", 180 lbs. Born, Toronto, Ont., April 19, 1968.
(Pittsburgh's 10th choice, 193rd overall, in 1986 Entry Draft).

			Regular Season					Playoffs				
Season	Club	Lea	GP	G	A	TP	PIM	GP	G	A	TP	PIM
1983-84	St. Michael's	Jr.B	30	26	29	55	56	....	....	....	....	....
1985-86	London	OHL	62	46	51	97	87	5	1	0	1	7
1986-87	London	OHL	5	4	3	7	18	....	....	....	....	....
	Kitchener	OHL	28	18	19	37	48	....	....	....	....	....
	Kingston	OHL	12	3	5	8	15	....	....	....	....	....
1987-88a	Windsor	OHL	66	57	76	133	66	12	6	15	21	
1988-89	S.S. Marie	OHL	22	16	25	41	18	....	....	....	....	....
	London	OHL	25	22	27	49	9	21	20	22	42	12

a OHL Third All-Star Team (1988)

CAIN, PAUL

Center. Shoots right. 5'10", 180 lbs. Born, Toronto, Ont., April 6, 1969.
(NY Rangers' 9th choice, 194th overall, in 1988 Entry Draft).

			Regular Season					Playoffs				
Season	Club	Lea	GP	G	A	TP	PIM	GP	G	A	TP	PIM
1987-88	Cornwall	OHL	21	14	9	23	41	7	0	2	2	0
1988-89	Cornwall	OHL	44	19	47	66	26	12	5	9	14	6

CAJKA, LUDEK

Defense. Shoots right. 6'3", 192 lbs. Born, Cesky Tesin, Czechoslovakia, November 3, 1963.
(NY Rangers' 6th choice, 115th overall, in 1987 Entry Draft).

			Regular Season					Playoffs				
Season	Club	Lea	GP	G	A	TP	PIM	GP	G	A	TP	PIM
1986-87	Dukla Jihlava	Czech.	34	4	5	9	....	....	....	....	....	....
1987-88	Gottwaldov	Czech.	33	4	5	9	....	....	....	....	....	....
1988-89	Gottwaldov	Czech.	44	6	16	22	....	....	....	....	....	....

CALLAGHAN, GARY

Center. Shoots left. 5'11", 175 lbs. Born, Oshawa, Ont., August 12, 1967.
(Hartford's 3rd choice, 68th over-all, in 1985 Entry Draft).

			Regular Season					Playoffs				
Season	Club	Lea	GP	G	A	TP	PIM	GP	G	A	TP	PIM
1984-85	Belleville	OHL	57	24	25	49	42	14	2	4	6	5
1985-86	Belleville	OHL	53	29	16	45	42	24	4	6	10	28
1986-87	Kitchener	OHL	56	30	30	60	23	4	2	3	5	0
1987-88	Binghamton	AHL	4	2	2	4	0	....	....	....	....	....
	Milwaukee	IHL	71	14	20	34	38	....	....	....	....	....
1988-89	Binghamton	AHL	72	23	17	40	33	....	....	....	....	....

CALLANDER, JOHN (JOCK)

Center. Shoots right. 6'1", 185 lbs. Born, Regina, Sask., April 23, 1961.

			Regular Season					Playoffs				
Season	Club	Lea	GP	G	A	TP	PIM	GP	G	A	TP	PIM
1979-80	Regina	WHL	39	9	11	20	25	18	8	5	13	0
1980-81	Regina	WHL	72	67	86	153	37	11	6	7	13	14
1981-82	Regina	WHL	71	79	111	*190	59	20	13	*26	39	37
1982-83	Salt Lake	CHL	68	20	27	47	26	6	0	1	1	9
1983-84	Montana	CHL	72	27	32	59	69	....	....	....	....	....
	Toledo	IHL	2	0	0	0	0	....	....	....	....	....
1984-85	Muskegon	IHL	82	39	68	107	86	17	T13	21	33	
1985-86a	Muskegon	IHL	82	39	72	111	121	14	12	11	23	12
1986-87bcd	Muskegon	IHL	82	54	82	136	110	15	13	7	20	23
1987-88	Pittsburgh	NHL	41	11	16	27	45	....	....	....	....	....
	Muskegon	IHL	31	20	36	56	49	6	2	3	5	25
1988-89	Pittsburgh	NHL	30	6	5	11	20	10	2	5	7	10
	Muskegon	IHL	48	25	39	64	40	7	5	5	10	30
	NHL Totals		71	17	21	38	65	10	2	5	7	10

a IHL Playoff MVP (1986)
b IHL First All-Star Team (1987)
c Shared James Gatschene Memorial Trophy (MVP-IHL) with Jeff Pyle (1987)
d Shared Leo P. Lamoreau Memorial Trophy (Top Scorer-IHL) with Jeff Pyle (1987)

Signed as free agent by **St. Louis**, September 28, 1981. Signed as a free agent by **Pittsburgh**, July 31, 1987.

CAPELLO, JEFF

Left wing. Shoots left. 6'1", 195 lbs. Born, Ottawa, Ont., September 25, 1964.
(Buffalo's 1st choice, 5th overall, in 1986 Supplemental Draft).

			Regular Season					Playoffs				
Season	Club	Lea	GP	G	A	TP	PIM	GP	G	A	TP	PIM
1983-84	U. of Vermont	ECAC	27	6	15	21	20	....	....	....	....	....
1984-85	U. of Vermont	ECAC	29	8	10	18	16	....	....	....	....	....
1985-86	U. of Vermont	ECAC	31	9	17	26	36	....	....	....	....	....
1986-87	U. of Vermont	ECAC	32	17	26	43	56	....	....	....	....	....
1987-88	Rochester	AHL	69	15	23	38	53	7	1	4	5	4
1988-89	Rochester	AHL	39	6	7	13	22	....	....	....	....	....

CAPUANO, DAVE

Right wing/Center. Shoots left. 6'2", 190 lbs. Born, Warwick, RI, July 27, 1968.
(Pittsburgh's 2nd choice, 25th over-all, in 1986 Entry Draft).

			Regular Season					Playoffs				
Season	Club	Lea	GP	G	A	TP	PIM	GP	G	A	TP	PIM
1985-86	Mt. St. Charles	HS	25	43	42	85	10	....	....	....	....	....
1986-87	U. of Maine	H.E.	38	18	41	59	14	....	....	....	....	....
1987-88abc	U. of Maine	H.E.	42	*34	*51	*85	51	....	....	....	....	....
1988-89ac	U. of Maine	H.E.	41	37	30	67	38	....	....	....	....	....

a NCAA East First All-American Team (1988, 1989)
b NCAA All-Tournament Team (1988)
c Hockey East First All-Star Team (1988, 1989)

CAPUANO, JACK

Defense. Shoots left. 6'2", 210 lbs. Born, Cranston, RI, July 7, 1966.
(Toronto's 4th choice, 67th over-all, in 1984 Entry Draft).

			Regular Season					Playoffs				
Season	Club	Lea	GP	G	A	TP	PIM	GP	G	A	TP	PIM
1985-86	U. of Maine	H.E.	39	9	18	27	51	....	....	....	....	....
1986-87a	U. of Maine	H.E.	42	10	34	44	20	....	....	....	....	....
1987-88bc	U. of Maine	H.E.	43	13	37	50	87	....	....	....	....	....
1988-89	Newmarket	AHL	74	5	16	21	52	1	0	0	0	0

a Hockey East Second All-Star Team (1987)
b NCAA East First All-American Team (1988)
c Hockey East First All-Star Team (1988)

CARBONNEAU, GUY (KAR buhn oh, GEE)

Center. Shoots right. 5'11", 175 lbs. Born, Sept Iles, Que., March 18, 1960.
(Montreal's 4th choice, 44th over-all, in 1979 Entry Draft).

			Regular Season					Playoffs				
Season	Club	Lea	GP	G	A	TP	PIM	GP	G	A	TP	PIM
1976-77	Chicoutimi	QJHL	59	9	20	29	8	4	1	0	1	0
1977-78	Chicoutimi	QJHL	70	28	55	83	60	....	....	....	....	....
1978-79	Chicoutimi	QJHL	72	62	79	141	47	4	2	1	3	4
1979-80	Chicoutimi	QJHL	72	72	110	182	66	12	9	15	24	28
	Nova Scotia	AHL	....	....	....	....	....	2	1	1	2	2
1980-81	**Montreal**	**NHL**	**2**	**0**	**1**	**1**	**0**	....	....	....	....	....
	Nova Scotia	AHL	78	35	53	88	87	6	1	3	4	9
1981-82	Nova Scotia	AHL	77	27	67	94	124	9	2	7	9	8
1982-83	**Montreal**	**NHL**	**77**	**18**	**29**	**47**	**68**	**3**	**0**	**0**	**0**	**2**
1983-84	**Montreal**	**NHL**	**78**	**24**	**30**	**54**	**75**	**15**	**4**	**3**	**7**	**12**
1984-85	**Montreal**	**NHL**	**79**	**23**	**34**	**57**	**43**	**12**	**4**	**3**	**7**	**8**
1985-86	**Montreal**	**NHL**	**80**	**20**	**36**	**56**	**57**	**20**	**7**	**5**	**12**	**35**
1986-87	**Montreal**	**NHL**	**79**	**18**	**27**	**45**	**68**	**17**	**3**	**8**	**11**	**20**
1987-88a	**Montreal**	**NHL**	**80**	**17**	**21**	**38**	**61**	**11**	**0**	**4**	**4**	**2**
1988-89a	**Montreal**	**NHL**	**79**	**26**	**30**	**56**	**44**	**21**	**4**	**5**	**9**	**10**
	NHL Totals		**554**	**146**	**208**	**354**	**416**	**99**	**22**	**28**	**50**	**89**

a Won Frank J. Selke Trophy (1988, 1989)

CARKNER, TERRY

Defense. Shoots left. 6'3", 212 lbs. Born, Smiths Falls, Ont., March 7, 1966.
(NY Rangers' 1st choice, 14th over-all, in 1984 Entry Draft).

			Regular Season					Playoffs				
Season	Club	Lea	GP	G	A	TP	PIM	GP	G	A	TP	PIM
1982-83	Brockville	OPJHL	47	8	32	40	94	....	....	....	....	....
1983-84	Peterborough	OHL	58	4	19	23	77	8	0	6	6	13
1984-85a	Peterborough	OHL	64	14	47	61	125	17	2	10	12	11
1985-86b	Peterborough	OHL	54	12	32	44	106	16	1	7	8	17
1986-87	**NY Rangers**	**NHL**	**52**	**2**	**13**	**15**	**118**	**1**	**0**	**0**	**0**	**0**
	New Haven	AHL	12	2	6	8	56	3	1	0	1	0
1987-88	**Quebec**	**NHL**	**63**	**3**	**24**	**27**	**159**	....	....	....	....	....
1988-89	**Philadelphia**	**NHL**	**78**	**11**	**32**	**43**	**149**	**19**	**1**	**5**	**6**	**28**
	NHL Totals		**193**	**16**	**69**	**85**	**426**	**20**	**1**	**5**	**6**	**28**

a OHL Second All-Star Team (1985)
b OHL First All-Star Team (1986)

Traded to **Quebec** by **NY Rangers** with Jeff Jackson for John Ogrodnick and David Shaw September, 30 1987. Traded to **Philadelphia** by **Quebec** for Greg Smyth and Philadelphia's third round choice (John Tanner) in the 1989 Entry Draft, July 25, 1988.

CARLSON, KENT

Defense. Shoots left. 6'3", 200 lbs. Born, Concord, NH, January 11, 1962.
(Montreal's 3rd choice, 32nd over-all, in 1982 Entry Draft).

			Regular Season					Playoffs				
Season	Club	Lea	GP	G	A	TP	PIM	GP	G	A	TP	PIM
1981-82	St. Lawrence	ECAC	28	8	14	22	0	....	....	....	....	....
1982-83	St. Lawrence	ECAC	36	10	23	33	56	....	....	....	....	....
1983-84	**Montreal**	**NHL**	**65**	**3**	**7**	**10**	**73**	....	....	....	....	....
1984-85	**Montreal**	**NHL**	**18**	**1**	**1**	**2**	**33**	....	....	....	....	....
	Sherbrooke	AHL	13	1	4	5	7	2	1	1	2	0
1985-86	**Montreal**	**NHL**	**2**	**0**	**0**	**0**	**0**	....	....	....	....	....
	Sherbrooke	AHL	35	11	15	26	79	....	....	....	....	....
	St. Louis	**NHL**	**26**	**2**	**3**	**5**	**42**	**5**	**0**	**0**	**0**	**11**
1986-87		DID NOT PLAY - INJURED										
1987-88	**St. Louis**	**NHL**	....	....	....	....	....	**3**	**0**	**0**	**0**	**2**
	Peoria	IHL	52	5	16	21	88	....	....	....	....	....
1988-89	**Washington**	**NHL**	**2**	**1**	**0**	**1**	**0**	....	....	....	....	....
	Baltimore	AHL	28	2	8	10	69	....	....	....	....	....
	NHL Totals		**113**	**7**	**11**	**18**	**148**	**8**	**0**	**0**	**0**	**13**

Traded to **St. Louis** by **Montreal** for Graham Herring and St. Louis' fifth-round choice (Eric Aubertin) in 1986 Entry Draft, January 31, 1986. Traded to **Winnipeg** by **St. Louis** with St. Louis' Twelfth-round choice (Sergei Kharin) in 1989 Entry Draft and St. Louis' fourth-round choice in 1990 Entry Draft for Peter Douris, September 29, 1988. Traded to **Washington** by **Winnipeg** for future considerations, October 11, 1988.

CARLSSON, ANDERS

Center. Shoots left. 5'11", 185 lbs. Born, Gavle, Sweden, November 25, 1960.
(New Jersey's 5th choice, 66th over-all, in 1986 Entry Draft).

			Regular Season					Playoffs				
Season	Club	Lea	GP	G	A	TP	PIM	GP	G	A	TP	PIM
1978-79	Brynas	Swe.	1	0	0	0	2	....	....	....	....	....
1979-80	Brynas	Swe.	17	0	1	1	2	1	0	0	0	0
1980-81	Brynas	Swe.	36	8	8	16	36	....	....	....	....	....
1981-82	Brynas	Swe.	35	5	5	10	22	....	....	....	....	....
1982-83	Brynas	Swe.	35	18	13	31	26	....	....	....	....	....
1983-84	Brynas	Swe.	35	8	26	34	34	....	....	....	....	....
1984-85	Sodertalje	Swe.	36	20	14	34	18	8	0	3	3	4
1985-86	Sodertalje	Swe.	36	12	26	38	20	7	2	4	6	0
1986-87	**New Jersey**	**NHL**	**48**	**2**	**18**	**20**	**14**	....	....	....	....	....
	Maine	AHL	6	0	6	6	2	....	....	....	....	....
1987-88	**New Jersey**	**NHL**	**9**	**1**	**0**	**1**	**0**	**3**	**1**	**0**	**1**	**2**
	Utica	AHL	33	12	22	34	16	....	....	....	....	....
1988-89	**New Jersey**	**NHL**	**47**	**4**	**8**	**12**	**20**	....	....	....	....	....
	Utica	AHL	7	2	4	6	4	....	....	....	....	....
	NHL Totals		**104**	**7**	**26**	**33**	**34**	**3**	**1**	**0**	**1**	**2**

CARLSSON, LEIF

Defense. Shoots left. 6'1", 205 lbs. Born, Ludvika, Sweden, February 18, 1965.
(Hartford's 4th choice, 61st overall, in 1983 Entry Draft).

			Regular Season					Playoffs				
Season	Club	Lea	GP	G	A	TP	PIM	GP	G	A	TP	PIM
1983-84	Farjestad	Swe.	19	3	0	3	10	....	....	....	....	....
1984-85	Farjestad	Swe.	36	4	8	12	24	3	0	0	0	0
1985-86	Farjestad	Swe.	36	7	6	13	22	7	1	3	4	4
1986-87	Farjestad	Swe.	33	9	4	13	18	7	2	2	4	10
1987-88	Farjestad	Swe.	40	10	14	24	26	9	2	1	3	4
1988-89	Farjestad	Swe.	39	6	6	12	38	....	....	....	....	....

CARLYLE, RANDY ROBERT

Defense. Shoots left. 5'10", 200 lbs. Born, Sudbury, Ont., April 19, 1956.
(Toronto's 1st choice, 30th over-all, in 1976 Amateur Draft).

			Regular Season					Playoffs				
Season	Club	Lea	GP	G	A	TP	PIM	GP	G	A	TP	PIM
1974-75	Sudbury	OHA	67	17	47	64	118	15	3	6	9	21
1975-76a	Sudbury	OHA	60	15	64	79	126	17	6	13	19	50
1976-77	Dallas	CHL	26	2	7	9	63	....	....	....	....	....
	Toronto	**NHL**	**45**	**0**	**5**	**5**	**51**	**9**	**0**	**1**	**1**	**20**
1977-78	Dallas	CHL	21	3	14	17	31	....	....	....	....	....
	Toronto	**NHL**	**49**	**2**	**11**	**13**	**31**	**7**	**0**	**1**	**1**	**8**
1978-79	**Pittsburgh**	**NHL**	**70**	**13**	**34**	**47**	**78**	**7**	**0**	**0**	**0**	**12**
1979-80	**Pittsburgh**	**NHL**	**67**	**8**	**28**	**36**	**45**	**5**	**1**	**0**	**1**	**4**
1980-81bc	**Pittsburgh**	**NHL**	**76**	**16**	**67**	**83**	**136**	**5**	**4**	**5**	**9**	**9**
1981-82	**Pittsburgh**	**NHL**	**73**	**11**	**64**	**75**	**131**	**5**	**1**	**3**	**4**	**16**
1982-83	**Pittsburgh**	**NHL**	**61**	**15**	**41**	**56**	**110**	....	....	....	....	....
1983-84	**Pittsburgh**	**NHL**	**50**	**3**	**23**	**26**	**82**	....	....	....	....	....
	Winnipeg	**NHL**	**5**	**0**	**3**	**3**	**2**	**3**	**0**	**2**	**2**	**4**
1984-85	**Winnipeg**	**NHL**	**71**	**13**	**38**	**51**	**98**	**8**	**1**	**5**	**6**	**13**
1985-86	**Winnipeg**	**NHL**	**68**	**16**	**33**	**49**	**93**	....	....	....	....	....
1986-87	**Winnipeg**	**NHL**	**71**	**16**	**26**	**42**	**93**	**10**	**1**	**5**	**6**	**18**
1987-88	**Winnipeg**	**NHL**	**78**	**15**	**44**	**59**	**210**	**5**	**0**	**2**	**2**	**10**
1988-89	**Winnipeg**	**NHL**	**78**	**6**	**38**	**44**	**78**	....	....	....	....	....
	NHL Totals		**862**	**134**	**455**	**589**	**1238**	**64**	**8**	**24**	**32**	**114**

a OHA Second All-Star Team (1976)
b Won James Norris Memorial Trophy (1981)
c NHL First All-Star Team (1981)

Played in NHL All-Star Game (1981-83, 1985)

Traded to **Pittsburgh** by **Toronto** with George Ferguson for Dave Burrows, June 14, 1978. Traded to **Winnipeg** by **Pittsburgh** for Winnipeg's first round choice (Doug Bodger) in 1984 Entry Draft and future considerations (Moe Mantha), March 5, 1984.

CARNBACK, PATRIK

Left wing. Shoots left. 6', 180 lbs. Born, Goteborg, Sweden, February 1, 1968.
(Montreal's 7th choice, 125th overall, in 1988 Entry Draft).

			Regular Season					Playoffs				
Season	Club	Lea	GP	G	A	TP	PIM	GP	G	A	TP	PIM
1986-87	V. Frolunda	Swe.	28	3	1	4	....	....	....	....	....	....
1987-88	V. Frolunda	Swe.	33	16	19	35	....	....	....	....	....	....
1988-89	V. Frolunda	Swe.	53	39	36	75	52	....	....	....	....	....

CARNELLEY, TODD

Defense. Shoots right. 5'11", 195 lbs. Born, St. Albert, Alta., September 18, 1966.
(Edmonton's 2nd choice, 41st over-all, in 1985 Entry Draft).

			Regular Season					Playoffs				
Season	Club	Lea	GP	G	A	TP	PIM	GP	G	A	TP	PIM
1983-84	Kamloops	WHL	70	7	23	30	66	17	0	6	6	4
1984-85a	Kamloops	WHL	56	18	29	47	69	15	8	19	27	19
1985-86	Kamloops	WHL	44	3	23	26	63	16	3	6	9	20
1986-87	Muskegon	IHL	71	4	29	33	75	2	0	0	0	0
1987-88	Milwaukee	IHL	46	5	10	15	43	....	....	....	....	....
1988-89	Cdn. National	....	6	1	1	2	12	....	....	....	....	....

a WHL First All-Star Team, West Division (1985)

CARNEY, KEITH E.

Defense. Shoots left. 6'1", 200 lbs. Born, Pawtucket, RI, February 3, 1970.
(Buffalo's 3rd choice, 76th overall, in 1988 Entry Draft).

			Regular Season					Playoffs				
Season	Club	Lea	GP	G	A	TP	PIM	GP	G	A	TP	PIM
1987-88	Mt. St. Charles	HS	18	12	43	55	....	....	....	....	....	....
1988-89	U. of Maine	HE	40	4	22	26	24	....	....	....	....	....

CARPENTER, ROBERT (BOB)

Center. Shoots left. 6', 190 lbs. Born, Beverly, MA, July 13, 1963.
(Washington's 1st choice, 3rd over-all, in 1981 Entry Draft).

			Regular Season					Playoffs				
Season	Club	Lea	GP	G	A	TP	PIM	GP	G	A	TP	PIM
1980-81	St. John's	HS	18	14	24	38	....	....	....	....	....	....
1981-82	**Washington**	**NHL**	**80**	**32**	**35**	**67**	**69**	....	....	....	....	....
1982-83	**Washington**	**NHL**	**80**	**32**	**37**	**69**	**64**	**4**	**1**	**0**	**1**	**2**
1983-84	**Washington**	**NHL**	**80**	**28**	**40**	**68**	**51**	**8**	**2**	**1**	**3**	**25**
1984-85	**Washington**	**NHL**	**80**	**53**	**42**	**95**	**87**	**5**	**1**	**4**	**5**	**8**
1985-86	**Washington**	**NHL**	**80**	**27**	**29**	**56**	**105**	**9**	**5**	**4**	**9**	**12**
1986-87	**Washington**	**NHL**	**22**	**5**	**7**	**12**	**21**	....	....	....	....	....
	NY Rangers	**NHL**	**28**	**2**	**8**	**10**	**20**	....	....	....	....	....
	Los Angeles	**NHL**	**10**	**2**	**3**	**5**	**6**	**5**	**1**	**2**	**3**	**2**
1987-88	**Los Angeles**	**NHL**	**71**	**19**	**33**	**52**	**84**	**5**	**1**	**1**	**2**	**0**
1988-89	**Los Angeles**	**NHL**	**39**	**11**	**15**	**26**	**16**	....	....	....	....	....
	Boston	**NHL**	**18**	**5**	**9**	**14**	**10**	**8**	**1**	**1**	**2**	**4**
	NHL Totals		**588**	**216**	**258**	**474**	**533**	**44**	**12**	**13**	**25**	**53**

Played in NHL All-Star Game (1985)

Traded to **NY Rangers** by **Washington** with Washington's second-round choice (Jason Prosofsky) in 1989 Entry Draft for Bob Crawford, Kelly Miller and Mike Ridley, January 1, 1987. Traded to **Los Angeles** by **NY Rangers** with Tom Laidlaw for Jeff Crossman, Marcel Dionne and Los Angeles' third-round choice in 1989 Entry Draft (Draft choice acquired by **Minnesota**, October 12, 1988. **Minnesota** selected Murray Garbutt.) Traded to **Boston** by **Los Angeles** for Steve Kasper, January 23, 1989.

CARSON, JIMMY

Center. Shoots right. 6', 200 lbs.　Born, Southfield, MI, July 20, 1968.
(Los Angeles' 1st choice, 2nd over-all, in 1986 Entry Draft).

			Regular Season					Playoffs				
Season	Club	Lea	GP	G	A	TP	PIM	GP	G	A	TP	PIM
1985-86a	Verdun	QMJHL	69	70	83	153	46	5	2	6	8	0
1986-87b	Los Angeles	NHL	80	37	42	79	22	5	1	2	3	6
1987-88	Los Angeles	NHL	80	55	52	107	45	5	5	3	8	4
1988-89	Edmonton	NHL	80	49	51	100	36	7	2	1	3	6
	NHL Totals		240	141	145	286	103	17	8	6	14	16

a QMJHL Second All-Star Team (1986)
b Named to NHL All-Rookie Team (1987)
Played in NHL All-Star Game (1989)

Traded to **Edmonton** by **Los Angeles** with Martin Gelinas, Los Angeles' first round choices in 1989, (acquired by **New Jersey**, June 17, 1989. **New Jersey** selected Jason Miller), 1991 and 1993 Entry Drafts and cash for Wayne Gretzky, Mike Krushelnyski and Marty McSorley, August 9, 1988.

CARSON, LINDSAY WARREN

Center. Shoots left. 6'2", 195 lbs.　Born, Oxbow, Sask., November 21, 1960.
(Philadelphia's 4th choice, 56th over-all, in 1979 Entry Draft).

			Regular Season					Playoffs				
Season	Club	Lea	GP	G	A	TP	PIM	GP	G	A	TP	PIM
1978-79	Saskatoon	WHL	37	21	29	50	56	....	....	....	....	....
	Billings	WHL	30	13	22	35	50	....	....	....	....	....
1979-80	Billings	WHL	70	42	66	108	101	....	....	....	....	....
1980-81	Maine	AHL	79	11	25	36	84	20	4	12	16	45
1981-82	Philadelphia	NHL	18	0	1	1	32	....	....	....	....	....
	Maine	AHL	54	20	31	51	92	4	0	0	0	12
1982-83	Philadelphia	NHL	78	18	19	37	67	1	0	0	0	0
1983-84	Springfield	AHL	5	2	4	6	5	....	....	....	....	....
	Philadelphia	NHL	16	1	3	4	10	1	0	0	0	5
1984-85	Philadelphia	NHL	77	20	19	39	123	17	0	3	3	24
1985-86	Philadelphia	NHL	50	9	12	21	84	1	0	0	0	5
1986-87	Philadelphia	NHL	71	11	15	26	141	24	3	5	8	22
1987-88	Philadelphia	NHL	36	2	7	9	37	....	....	....	....	....
	Hartford	NHL	27	5	4	9	30	5	1	2	3	0
1988-89	Binghamton	AHL	24	4	10	14	35	....	....	....	....	....
	NHL Totals		373	66	80	146	524	49	4	10	14	56

Traded to **Hartford** by **Philadelphia** for Paul Lawless, January 22, 1988.

CARTER, JOHN

Left wing. Shoots left. 5'10", 175 lbs.　Born, Winchester, MA, May 3, 1963.

			Regular Season					Playoffs				
Season	Club	Lea	GP	G	A	TP	PIM	GP	G	A	TP	PIM
1982-83	RPI	ECAC	29	16	22	38	33	....	....	....	....	....
1983-84	RPI	ECAC	38	35	39	74	52	....	....	....	....	....
1984-85	RPI	ECAC	37	43	29	72	52	....	....	....	....	....
1985-86	RPI	ECAC	27	23	18	41	68	....	....	....	....	....
	Boston	NHL	3	0	0	0	0	....	....	....	....	....
1986-87	Boston	NHL	8	0	1	1	0	....	....	....	....	....
	Moncton	AHL	58	25	30	55	60	6	2	3	5	5
1987-88	Boston	NHL	4	0	1	1	2	....	....	....	....	....
	Maine	AHL	76	38	38	76	145	10	4	4	8	44
1988-89	Boston	NHL	44	12	10	22	24	10	1	2	3	6
	Maine	AHL	24	13	6	19	12	....	....	....	....	....
	NHL Totals		59	12	12	24	26	10	1	2	3	6

Signed as a free agent by **Boston**, May 3, 1986.

CASSELS, ANDREW

Center. Shoots left. 6', 165 lbs.　Born, Bramalea, Ont., July 23, 1969.
(Montreal's 1st choice, 17th overall, in 1987 Entry Draft).

			Regular Season					Playoffs				
Season	Club	Lea	GP	G	A	TP	PIM	GP	G	A	TP	PIM
1986-87a	Ottawa	OHL	66	26	66	92	28	11	5	9	14	7
1987-88bc	Ottawa	OHL	61	48	*103	*151	39	16	8	*24	*32	13
1988-89c	Ottawa	OHL	56	37	97	134	66	12	5	10	15	10

a OHL Rookie of the Year (1987)
b OHL Player of the Year (1988)
c OHL First All-Star Team (1988,1989)

CASSIDY, BRUCE

Defense. Shoots left. 5'11", 175 lbs.　Born, Ottawa, Ont., May 20, 1965.
(Chicago's 1st choice, 18th over-all, in 1983 Entry Draft).

			Regular Season					Playoffs				
Season	Club	Lea	GP	G	A	TP	PIM	GP	G	A	TP	PIM
1981-82	Hawkesbury	COJHL	37	13	30	43	32	....	....	....	....	....
1982-83	Ottawa	OHL	70	25	86	111	33	9	3	9	12	10
1983-84	Chicago	NHL	1	0	0	0	0	....	....	....	....	....
a	Ottawa	OHL	67	27	68	95	58	13	6	16	22	6
1984-85	Ottawa	OHL	28	13	27	40	15	....	....	....	....	....
1985-86	Chicago	NHL	1	0	0	0	0	....	....	....	....	....
	Nova Scotia	AHL	4	0	0	0	0	....	....	....	....	....
1986-87	Chicago	NHL	2	0	0	0	0	....	....	....	....	....
	Nova Scotia	AHL	19	2	8	10	4	....	....	....	....	....
	Cdn. Olympic	....	12	3	6	9	4	....	....	....	....	....
	Saginaw	IHL	10	2	13	15	6	2	1	1	2	0
1987-88	Chicago	NHL	21	3	10	13	6	....	....	....	....	....
	Saginaw	IHL	60	9	37	46	59	10	2	3	5	19
1988-89	Chicago	NHL	9	0	2	2	4	1	0	0	0	0
	Saginaw	IHL	72	16	64	80	80	6	0	2	2	6
	NHL Totals		34	3	12	15	10	1	0	0	0	0

a OHL Second All-Star Team (1984).

CAUFIELD, JAY

Defense. Shoots right. 6'4", 230 lbs.　Born, Philadelphia, PA, July 17, 1960.

			Regular Season					Playoffs				
Season	Club	Lea	GP	G	A	TP	PIM	GP	G	A	TP	PIM
1984-85	North Dakota	WCHA	1	0	0	0	0	....	....	....	....	....
1985-86	Toledo	IHL	30	5	4	9	54	....	....	....	....	....
	New Haven	AHL	40	2	3	5	40	1	0	0	0	0
1986-87	NY Rangers	NHL	13	2	1	3	45	3	0	0	0	12
	Flint	IHL	12	4	3	7	59	....	....	....	....	....
	New Haven	AHL	13	0	0	0	43	....	....	....	....	....
1987-88	Minnesota	NHL	1	0	0	0	0	....	....	....	....	....
	Kalamazoo	IHL	65	5	10	15	273	6	0	1	1	47
1988-89	Pittsburgh	NHL	58	1	4	5	285	9	0	0	0	28
	NHL Totals		72	3	5	8	330	12	0	0	0	40

Signed as a free agent by **NY Rangers**, October 8, 1985. Traded to **Minnesota** by **NY Rangers** with Dave Gagne for Jari Gronstrand and Paul Boutilier, October 8,1987. Claimed by **Pittsburgh** in NHL Waiver Draft, Oct. 3, 1988.

CAVALLINI, GINO JOHN

Left wing. Shoots left. 6'1", 215 lbs.　Born, Toronto, Ont., November 24, 1962.

			Regular Season					Playoffs				
Season	Club	Lea	GP	G	A	TP	PIM	GP	G	A	TP	PIM
1981-82	St. Michael's	Jr. B	33	22	33	55	50	....	....	....	....	....
1982-83	Bowling Green	CCHA	40	8	16	24	52	....	....	....	....	....
1983-84	Bowling Green	CCHA	43	25	23	48	16	....	....	....	....	....
1984-85	Calgary	NHL	27	6	10	16	14	3	0	0	0	4
	Moncton	AHL	51	29	19	48	28	....	....	....	....	....
1985-86	Calgary	NHL	27	7	7	14	26	....	....	....	....	....
	Moncton	AHL	4	3	2	5	7	....	....	....	....	....
	St. Louis	NHL	30	6	5	11	36	17	4	5	9	10
1986-87	St. Louis	NHL	80	18	26	44	54	6	3	1	4	2
1987-88	St. Louis	NHL	64	15	17	32	62	10	5	5	10	19
1988-89	St. Louis	NHL	74	20	23	43	79	9	0	2	2	17
	NHL Totals		302	72	88	160	271	45	12	13	25	52

Signed as a free agent by **Calgary**, May 16, 1984. Traded to **St. Louis** by **Calgary** with Eddy Beers and Charles Bourgeois for Joe Mullen, Terry Johnson and Rik Wilson, February 1, 1986.

CAVALLINI, PAUL

Defense. Shoots left. 6'2", 210 lbs.　Born, Toronto, Ont., October 13, 1965.
(Washington's 10th choice, 205th over-all, in 1984 Entry Draft).

			Regular Season					Playoffs				
Season	Club	Lea	GP	G	A	TP	PIM	GP	G	A	TP	PIM
1984-85	Providence	H.E.	37	4	10	14	52	....	....	....	....	....
1985-86	Binghamton	AHL	15	3	4	7	20	6	0	2	2	56
	Cdn. Olympic	....	52	1	11	12	95	....	....	....	....	....
1986-87	Washington	NHL	6	0	2	2	8	....	....	....	....	....
	Binghamton	AHL	66	12	24	36	188	13	2	7	9	35
1987-88	Washington	NHL	24	2	3	5	66	....	....	....	....	....
	St. Louis	NHL	48	4	7	11	86	10	1	6	7	26
1988-89	St. Louis	NHL	65	4	20	24	128	10	2	2	4	14
	NHL Totals		143	10	32	42	288	20	3	8	11	40

Traded to **St. Louis** by **Washington** for Montreal's second round choice (Wade Bartley) in 1988 Entry Draft — St. Louis' property via earlier deal — December 11, 1987.

CESARSKI, ANDREW

Defense. Shoots left. 6'4", 200 lbs.　Born, Ft. Monmouth, NJ, September 21, 1968.
(St. Louis' 11th choice, 207th overall, in 1987 Entry Draft).

			Regular Season					Playoffs				
Season	Club	Lea	GP	G	A	TP	PIM	GP	G	A	TP	PIM
1987-88	Princeton	ECAC	28	2	3	5	34	....	....	....	....	....
1988-89	Princeton	ECAC	26	6	10	16	34	....	....	....	....	....

CHABOT, JOHN DAVID　(sha-BAWT)

Center. Shoots left. 6'2", 200 lbs.　Born, Summerside, P.E.I., May 18, 1962.
(Montreal's 3rd choice, 40th over-all, in 1980 Entry Draft).

			Regular Season					Playoffs				
Season	Club	Lea	GP	G	A	TP	PIM	GP	G	A	TP	PIM
1979-80	Hull	QMJHL	68	26	57	83	28	4	1	2	3	0
1980-81	Hull	QMJHL	70	27	62	89	24	....	....	....	....	....
	Nova Scotia	AHL	1	0	0	0	0	2	0	0	0	0
1981-82ab	Sherbrooke	QMJHL	62	34	*109	143	42	19	6	26	32	6
1982-83	Nova Scotia	AHL	76	16	73	89	19	7	1	3	4	0
1983-84	Montreal	NHL	56	18	25	43	13	11	1	4	5	0
1984-85	Montreal	NHL	10	1	6	7	2	....	....	....	....	....
	Pittsburgh	NHL	67	8	45	53	12	....	....	....	....	....
1985-86	Pittsburgh	NHL	77	14	31	45	6	....	....	....	....	....
1986-87	Pittsburgh	NHL	72	14	22	36	8	....	....	....	....	....
1987-88	Detroit	NHL	78	13	44	57	10	16	4	15	19	2
1988-89	Detroit	NHL	52	2	10	12	6	6	1	1	2	0
	Adirondack	AHL	8	3	12	15	0	....	....	....	....	....
	NHL Totals		412	70	183	253	57	33	6	20	26	2

a QMJHL First All-Star Team (1982)
b QMJHL Most Valuable Player (1982)
Traded to **Pittsburgh** by **Montreal** for Ron Flockhart, November 9, 1984. Signed as a free agent by **Detroit**, June 25, 1987.

CHAMBERS, SHAWN

Defense. Shoots left. 6'2", 210 lbs.　Born, Sterling Heights, MI, October 11, 1966.
(Minnesota's 1st choice, 4th overall, in 1987 Supplemental Draft).

			Regular Season					Playoffs				
Season	Club	Lea	GP	G	A	TP	PIM	GP	G	A	TP	PIM
1986-87	Alaska-Fair.	G.N.	28	8	29	37	84	....	....	....	....	....
	Seattle	WHL	28	8	25	33	58	....	....	....	....	....
	Ft. Wayne	IHL	12	2	6	8	0	10	1	4	5	5
1987-88	Minnesota	NHL	19	1	7	8	21	....	....	....	....	....
	Kalamazoo	IHL	19	1	6	7	22	....	....	....	....	....
1988-89	Minnesota	NHL	72	5	19	24	80	3	0	2	2	0
	NHL Totals		91	6	26	32	101	3	0	2	2	0

CHANNELL, CRAIG

Defense. Shoots left. 5'11", 190 lbs. Born, Moncton, N.B., April 24, 1962.

			Regular Season					Playoffs				
Season	Club	Lea	GP	G	A	TP	PIM	GP	G	A	TP	PIM
1979-80	Seattle	WHL	70	3	21	24	191	12	0	0	0	22
1980-81	Seattle	WHL	71	9	66	75	181	5	0	2	2	4
1981-82	Seattle	WHL	71	9	79	88	244	10	0	11	11	22
1982-83	Sherbrooke	AHL	65	0	15	15	109	....				
1983-84	Sherbrooke	AHL	80	5	18	23	112	....				
1984-85	Sherbrooke	AHL	1	0	0	0	0	....				
	Fort Wayne	IHL	78	10	35	45	110	8	0	5	5	33
1985-86	Fort Wayne	IHL	69	7	28	35	116	15	3	12	15	41
1986-87	Fort Wayne	IHL	81	12	42	54	90	11	2	1	3	29
1987-88	Fort Wayne	IHL	81	11	29	40	108	6	0	1	1	15
1988-89a	Fort Wayne	IHL	79	5	25	30	168	11	0	7	7	32

a IHL Second All-Star Team (1989)

Signed as a free agent by **Winnipeg**, November 9, 1981.

CHAPDELAINE, RENE

Defense. Shoots right. 6'1", 195 lbs. Born, Weyburn, Sask., September 27, 1966.
(Los Angeles' 7th choice, 149th overall, in 1986 Entry Draft).

			Regular Season					Playoffs				
Season	Club	Lea	GP	G	A	TP	PIM	GP	G	A	TP	PIM
1985-86	Lake Superior	CCHA	32	1	4	5	47	....				
1986-87	Lake Superior	CCHA	28	1	5	6	51	....				
1987-88	Lake Superior	CCHA	35	1	9	10	44	....				
1988-89	Lake Superior	CCHA	46	4	9	13	62	....				

CHAPMAN, BRIAN

Defense. Shoots left. 6', 195 lbs. Born, Brockville, Ont., February 10, 1968.
(Hartford's 3rd choice, 74th overall, in 1986 Entry Draft).

			Regular Season					Playoffs				
Season	Club	Lea	GP	G	A	TP	PIM	GP	G	A	TP	PIM
1985-86	Belleville	OHL	66	6	31	37	168	24	2	6	8	54
1986-87	Belleville	OHL	54	4	32	36	142	6	1	1	2	10
1987-88	Belleville	OHL	63	11	57	68	180	6	1	4	5	13
1988-89	Binghamton	AHL	71	5	25	30	216	....				

CHARBONNEAU, JOSE   (CHAR-bo-no, Joe-zee)

Right wing. Shoots right. 6', 195 lbs. Born, Ferme-Neuve, Que., November 21, 1966.
(Montreal's 1st choice, 12th over-all, in 1985 Entry Draft).

			Regular Season					Playoffs				
Season	Club	Lea	GP	G	A	TP	PIM	GP	G	A	TP	PIM
1983-84	Drummondville	QMJHL	65	31	59	90	110	....				
1984-85	Drummondville	QMJHL	46	34	40	74	91	12	5	10	15	20
1985-86	Drummondville	QMJHL	57	44	45	89	158	23	16	20	36	40
1986-87	Sherbrooke	AHL	72	14	27	41	94	16	5	12	17	17
1987-88	**Montreal**	**NHL**	16	0	2	2	6	8	0	0	0	4
	Sherbrooke	AHL	55	30	35	65	108	....				
1988-89	**Montreal**	**NHL**	9	1	3	4	6	....				
	Sherbrooke	AHL	33	13	15	28	95	....				
	Vancouver	**NHL**	13	0	1	1	6	....				
	Milwaukee	IHL	13	8	5	13	46	10	3	2	5	23
	NHL Totals		**38**	**1**	**6**	**7**	**18**	**8**	**0**	**0**	**0**	**4**

Traded to **Vancouver** by **Montreal** for Dan Woodley, January 25, 1989.

CHARLESWORTH, TODD

Defense. Shoots left. 6'1", 190 lbs. Born, Calgary, Alta., March 22, 1965.
(Pittsburgh's 2nd choice, 22nd over-all, in 1983 Entry Draft).

			Regular Season					Playoffs				
Season	Club	Lea	GP	G	A	TP	PIM	GP	G	A	TP	PIM
1981-82	Gloucester	COJHL	50	13	24	37	67	....				
1982-83	Oshawa	OHL	70	6	23	29	55	17	0	4	4	20
1983-84	**Pittsburgh**	**NHL**	10	0	0	0	8	....				
	Oshawa	OHL	57	11	35	46	54	7	0	4	4	4
1984-85	**Pittsburgh**	**NHL**	67	1	8	9	31	....				
1985-86	**Pittsburgh**	**NHL**	2	0	1	1	0	....				
	Baltimore	AHL	19	1	3	4	10	....				
	Muskegon	IHL	51	9	27	36	78	14	3	8	11	14
1986-87	**Pittsburgh**	**NHL**	1	0	0	0	0	....				
	Baltimore	AHL	75	5	21	26	64	....				
1987-88	**Pittsburgh**	**NHL**	6	2	0	2	2	....				
	Muskegon	IHL	64	9	31	40	49	5	0	0	0	18
1988-89a	Muskegon	IHL	74	10	53	63	85	14	2	13	15	8
	NHL Totals		**86**	**3**	**9**	**12**	**41**	....				

a IHL Second All-Star Team (1989)

CHARRON, ERIC

Defense. Shoots left. 6'3", 195 lbs. Born, Verdun, Que., January 14, 1970.
Last amateur club: Trois Rivieres Draveurs (QMJHL).
(Montreal's 1st choice, 20th overall, in 1988 Entry Draft).

			Regular Season					Playoffs				
Season	Club	Lea	GP	G	A	TP	PIM	GP	G	A	TP	PIM
1986-87	Lac St. Louis	Midget	41	1	8	9	92	....				
1987-88	Trois Rivieres	QMJHL	67	3	13	16	135	....				
1988-89	Verdun	QMJHL	67	4	31	35	177	....				
	Sherbrooke	AHL	1	0	0	0	0	....				

CHASE, KELLY WAYNE

Right wing. Shoots right. 5'11", 200 lbs. Born, Porcupine Plain, Sask., October 25, 1967.

			Regular Season					Playoffs				
Season	Club	Lea	GP	G	A	TP	PIM	GP	G	A	TP	PIM
1985-86	Saskatoon	WHL	57	7	18	25	172	10	3	4	7	37
1986-87	Saskatoon	WHL	68	17	29	46	285	11	2	8	10	37
1987-88	Saskatoon	WHL	70	21	34	55	343	9	3	5	8	32
1988-89	Peoria	IHL	38	14	7	21	278	....				

Signed as a free agent by **St. Louis**, February 23, 1988.

CHASE, TIMOTHY

Center. Shoots left. 6'1", 175 lbs. Born, Gaithersburg, MD, March 23, 1970.
(Montreal's 8th choice, 146th overall, in 1988 Entry Draft).

			Regular Season					Playoffs				
Season	Club	Lea	GP	G	A	TP	PIM	GP	G	A	TP	PIM
1987-88	Tabor	HS	28	20	20	40	....					
1988-89	Tabor	HS	22	21	20	41	18	....				

CHEEVERS, ROBERT

Center. Shoots right. 6'2", 195 lbs. Born, North Andover, MA, October 29, 1968.
(Boston's 7th choice, 140th overall, in 1987 Entry Draft).

			Regular Season					Playoffs				
Season	Club	Lea	GP	G	A	TP	PIM	GP	G	A	TP	PIM
1986-87	Boston College	H.E.	10	1	2	3	6	....				
1987-88	Boston College	H.E.	29	3	3	6	6	....				
1988-89	Boston College	H.E.	4	0	0	0	0	....				

CHELIOS, CHRIS   (CHELL-EE-ohs)

Defense. Shoots right. 6'1", 186 lbs. Born, Chicago, Illinois, January 25, 1962.
(Montreal's 5th choice, 40th over-all, in 1981 Entry Draft).

			Regular Season					Playoffs				
Season	Club	Lea	GP	G	A	TP	PIM	GP	G	A	TP	PIM
1980-81	Moose Jaw	SJHL	54	23	64	87	175	....				
1981-82	U. Wisconsin	WCHA	43	6	43	49	50	....				
1982-83ab	U. Wisconsin	WCHA	26	9	17	26	50	....				
1983-84	U.S. National	...	60	14	35	49	58	....				
	U.S. Olympic	...	6	0	4	4	8	....				
	Montreal	NHL	12	0	2	2	12	15	1	9	10	17
1984-85c	Montreal	NHL	74	9	55	64	87	9	2	8	10	17
1985-86	Montreal	NHL	41	8	26	34	67	20	2	9	11	49
1986-87	Montreal	NHL	71	11	33	44	124	17	4	9	13	38
1987-88	Montreal	NHL	71	20	41	61	172	11	3	1	4	29
1988-89de	Montreal	NHL	80	15	58	73	185	21	4	15	19	28
	NHL Totals		**349**	**63**	**215**	**278**	**647**	**93**	**16**	**51**	**67**	**178**

a WCHA Second All-Star Team (1983)
b NCAA All-Tournament Team (1983)
c NHL All-Rookie Team (1985)
d NHL First All-Star Team (1989)
e Won Norris Trophy (1989)
Played in NHL All-Star Game (1985)

CHERNOMAZ, RICHARD (RICH)   (CHAIR-noh-maz)

Right wing. Shoots right. 5'9", 175 lbs. Born, Selkirk, Man., September 1, 1963.
(Colorado's 2nd choice, 26th over-all, in 1981 Entry Draft).

			Regular Season					Playoffs				
Season	Club	Lea	GP	G	A	TP	PIM	GP	G	A	TP	PIM
1980-81	Victoria	WHL	72	49	64	113	92	15	11	15	26	38
1981-82	Colorado	NHL	2	0	0	0	0	....				
	Victoria	WHL	49	36	62	98	69	4	1	2	3	13
1982-83a	Victoria	WHL	64	71	53	124	113	12	10	5	15	18
1983-84	New Jersey	NHL	7	2	1	3	2	....				
	Maine	AHL	69	17	29	46	39	2	0	1	1	0
1984-85	New Jersey	NHL	3	0	2	2	2	....				
	Maine	AHL	64	17	34	51	64	10	2	2	4	4
1985-86	Maine	AHL	78	21	28	49	82	5	0	0	0	2
1986-87	New Jersey	NHL	25	6	4	10	8	....				
	Maine	AHL	58	35	27	62	65	....				
1987-88	Calgary	NHL	2	1	0	1	0	....				
b	Salt Lake	IHL	73	48	47	95	122	18	4	14	18	30
1988-89	Calgary	NHL	1	0	0	0	0	....				
	Salt Lake	IHL	81	33	68	101	122	14	7	5	12	47
	NHL Totals		**40**	**9**	**7**	**16**	**12**	....				

a WHL First All-Star Team (1983)
b IHL Second All-Star Team (1988)
Signed as a free agent by **Calgary**, August 15, 1987.

CHEVELDAYOFF, KEVIN

Defense. Shoots right. 6', 200 lbs. Born, Saskatoon, Sask., February 4, 1970.
(New York Islanders' 1st choice, 16th overall, in 1988 Entry Draft).

			Regular Season					Playoffs				
Season	Club	Lea	GP	G	A	TP	PIM	GP	G	A	TP	PIM
1986-87	Brandon	WHL	70	0	16	16	259	....				
1987-88	Brandon	WHL	71	3	29	32	265	4	0	2	2	20
1988-89	Brandon	WHL	40	4	12	16	135	....				

CHIASSON, STEVE   (CHASE-on)

Defense. Shoots left. 6'1", 205 lbs. Born, Barrie, Ont., April 14, 1967.
(Detroit's 3rd choice, 50th over-all, in 1985 Entry Draft).

			Regular Season					Playoffs				
Season	Club	Lea	GP	G	A	TP	PIM	GP	G	A	TP	PIM
1984-85	Guelph	OHL	61	8	22	30	139	....				
1985-86	Guelph	OHL	54	12	30	42	126	18	10	10	20	37
1986-87	**Detroit**	**NHL**	45	1	4	5	73	2	0	0	0	19
1987-88	**Detroit**	**NHL**	29	2	9	11	57	9	2	2	4	31
	Adirondack	AHL	23	6	11	17	58	....				
1988-89	**Detroit**	**NHL**	65	12	35	47	149	5	2	1	3	6
	NHL Totals		**139**	**15**	**48**	**63**	**279**	**16**	**4**	**3**	**7**	**56**

CHITARONI, MARIO BRIAN

Center. Shoots right. 5'8", 170 lbs. Born, Haileybury, Ont., March 11, 1966.

			Regular Season					Playoffs				
Season	Club	Lea	GP	G	A	TP	PIM	GP	G	A	TP	PIM
1987-88	Flint	IHL	80	49	47	96	156	12	9	8	17	60
1988-89	Flint	IHL	21	10	11	21	59	....				
	New Haven	AHL	54	12	24	36	97	16	2	7	9	57

Signed as a free agent by **Los Angeles**, July 1, 1988.

CHORSKE, TOM

Left wing. Shoots right. 6'1", 185 lbs. Born, Minneapolis, MN, September 18, 1966.
(Montreal's 2nd choice, 16th over-all, in 1985 Entry Draft).

			Regular Season					Playoffs				
Season	Club	Lea	GP	G	A	TP	PIM	GP	G	A	TP	PIM
1984-85	Mpls. S.W.	HS	23	44	26	70	24					
1985-86	U. Minnesota	WCHA	39	6	4	10	16					
1986-87	U. Minnesota	WCHA	47	20	22	42	20					
1987-88	U.S. National	....	36	9	16	25	24					
1988-89a	U. Minnesota	WCHA	37	25	24	49	28					

a WCHA First All-Star Team (1989)

CHRISTIAN, DAVID (DAVE)

Right wing. Shoots right. 6', 175 lbs. Born, Warroad, MN, May 12, 1959.
(Winnipeg's 2nd choice, 40th over-all, in 1979 Entry Draft).

			Regular Season					Playoffs				
Season	Club	Lea	GP	G	A	TP	PIM	GP	G	A	TP	PIM
1977-78	North Dakota	WCHA	38	8	16	24	14					
1978-79	North Dakota	WCHA	40	22	24	46	22					
1979-80	U.S. National	...	59	10	20	30	26					
	U.S. Olympic	...	7	0	8	8	6					
	Winnipeg	NHL	15	8	10	18	2					
1980-81	Winnipeg	NHL	80	28	43	71	22					
1981-82	Winnipeg	NHL	80	25	51	76	28	4	0	1	1	2
1982-83	Winnipeg	NHL	55	18	26	44	23	3	0	0	0	0
1983-84	Washington	NHL	80	29	52	81	28	8	5	4	9	5
1984-85	Washington	NHL	80	26	43	69	14	5	1	1	2	0
1985-86	Washington	NHL	80	41	42	83	15	9	4	4	8	0
1986-87	Washington	NHL	76	23	27	50	8	7	1	3	4	6
1987-88	Washington	NHL	80	37	21	58	26	14	5	6	11	6
1988-89	Washington	NHL	80	34	31	65	12	6	1	1	2	0
	NHL Totals		**706**	**269**	**346**	**615**	**178**	**56**	**17**	**20**	**37**	**19**

Traded to **Washington** by **Winnipeg** for Washington's first round choice (Bob Dollas) in the 1983 Entry Draft, June 8, 1983.

CHRISTIAN, JEFF

Left wing. Shoots left. 6'1", 185 lbs. Born, Burlington, Ont., July 30, 1970.
(New Jersey's 2nd choice, 23rd overall, in 1988 Entry Draft).

			Regular Season					Playoffs				
Season	Club	Lea	GP	G	A	TP	PIM	GP	G	A	TP	PIM
1986-87	Dundas	OPJHL	29	20	34	54	42					
1987-88	London	OHL	64	15	29	44	154	9	1	5	6	27
1988-89	London	OHL	64	27	30	57	221	20	3	4	7	56

CHURLA, SHANE

Right wing. Shoots right. 6'1", 200 lbs. Born, Fernie, B.C., June 24, 1965.
(Hartford's 4th choice, 110th over-all, in 1985 Entry Draft).

			Regular Season					Playoffs				
Season	Club	Lea	GP	G	A	TP	PIM	GP	G	A	TP	PIM
1983-84	Medicine Hat	WHL	48	3	7	10	115	14	1	5	6	41
1984-85	Medicine Hat	WHL	70	14	20	34	370	9	1	0	1	55
1985-86	Binghamton	AHL	52	4	10	14	306	3	0	0	0	22
1986-87	Hartford	NHL	20	0	1	1	78	2	0	0	0	42
	Binghamton	AHL	24	1	5	6	249					
1987-88	Hartford	NHL	2	0	0	0	14					
	Binghamton	AHL	25	5	8	13	168					
	Calgary	NHL	29	1	5	6	132	7	0	1	1	17
1988-89	Calgary	NHL	5	0	0	0	25					
	Salt Lake	IHL	32	3	13	16	278					
	Minnesota	NHL	13	1	0	1	54					
	NHL Totals		**69**	**2**	**6**	**8**	**303**	**9**	**0**	**1**	**1**	**59**

Traded to **Calgary** by **Hartford** with Dana Murzyn for Neil Sheehy, Carey Wilson, and the rights to Lane MacDonald, January 3, 1988. Traded to **Minnesota** by **Calgary** with Perry Berezan for Brian MacLellan and Minnesota's fourth-round choice (Robert Reichel) in 1989 Entry Draft, March 4, 1989.

CHYCHRUN, JEFF (CHICK-run)

Defense. Shoots right. 6'4", 212 lbs. Born, LaSalle, Que., May 3, 1966.
(Philadelphia's 3rd choice, 37th over-all, in 1984 Entry Draft).

			Regular Season					Playoffs				
Season	Club	Lea	GP	G	A	TP	PIM	GP	G	A	TP	PIM
1982-83	Nepean	COJHL	44	3	10	13	59					
1983-84	Kingston	OHL	63	1	13	14	137					
1984-85	Kingston	OHL	58	4	10	14	206					
1985-86	Kingston	OHL	61	4	21	25	127	10	2	1	3	17
	Hershey	AHL	....	....	....	....	....	4	0	1	1	9
	Kalamazoo	IHL	....	....	....	....	....	3	1	0	1	0
1986-87	Philadelphia	NHL	1	0	0	0	4					
	Hershey	AHL	74	1	17	18	239	4	0	0	0	10
1987-88	Philadelphia	NHL	3	0	0	0	4					
	Hershey	AHL	55	0	5	5	210	12	0	2	2	44
1988-89	Philadelphia	NHL	80	1	4	5	245	19	0	2	2	65
	NHL Totals		**84**	**1**	**4**	**5**	**253**	**19**	**0**	**2**	**2**	**65**

CHYNOWETH, DEAN

Defense. Shoots right. 6'2", 190 lbs. Born, Calgary, Alta., October 30, 1968.
(NY Islanders' 1st choice, 13th overall, in 1987 Entry Draft).

			Regular Season					Playoffs				
Season	Club	Lea	GP	G	A	TP	PIM	GP	G	A	TP	PIM
1985-86	Medicine Hat	WHL	69	3	12	15	208	17	3	2	5	52
1986-87	Medicine Hat	WHL	67	3	18	21	285	13	4	2	6	28
1987-88	Medicine Hat	WHL	64	1	21	22	274	16	0	6	6	87
1988-89	NY Islanders	NHL	6	0	0	0	48					
	NHL Totals		**6**	**0**	**0**	**0**	**48**					

CHYZOWSKI, BARRY

Center. Shoots right. 6', 170 lbs. Born, Edmonton, Alta., May 25, 1968.
(NY Rangers' 8th choice, 156th overall, in 1986 Entry Draft).

			Regular Season					Playoffs				
Season	Club	Lea	GP	G	A	TP	PIM	GP	G	A	TP	PIM
1985-86	St. Albert	AJHL	45	39	34	73	33					
1986-87	Minn.-Duluth	WCHA	39	5	11	16	16					
1987-88	Minn.-Duluth	WCHA	41	22	34	56	14					
1988-89	Denver	IHL	69	12	21	33	48	3	0	0	0	4

a WHL West All-Star Team (1989)

CHYZOWSKI, DAVE

Left wing. Shoots left. 6'1", 190 lbs. Born, Edmonton, Alta., July 11, 1971.
(NY Islanders' 1st choice, 2nd overall, in 1989 Entry Draft).

			Regular Season					Playoffs				
Season	Club	Lea	GP	G	A	TP	PIM	GP	G	A	TP	PIM
1987-88	Kamloops	WHL	66	16	17	33	117	18	2	4	6	26
1988-89a	Kamloops	WHL	68	56	48	104	139	16	15	13	28	32

a WHL West All-Star Team (1989)

CIAVAGLIA, PETER

Center. Shoots left. 5'10", 165 lbs. Born, Albany, NY, July 15, 1969.
(Calgary's 7th choice, 145th overall, in 1987 Entry Draft).

			Regular Season					Playoffs				
Season	Club	Lea	GP	G	A	TP	PIM	GP	G	A	TP	PIM
1986-87	Nichols	HS	23	53	84	137	....					
1987-88	Harvard	ECAC	30	10	23	33	16					
1988-89a	Harvard	ECAC	34	15	48	63	36					

a ECAC Second All-Star Team (1989)

CICCARELLI, DINO (SIHS uh REHL ee)

Right wing. Shoots right. 5'10", 180 lbs. Born, Sarnia, Ont., February 8, 1960.

			Regular Season					Playoffs				
Season	Club	Lea	GP	G	A	TP	PIM	GP	G	A	TP	PIM
1977-78a	London	OHA	68	72	70	142	49	9	6	10	16	6
1978-79	London	OHA	30	8	11	19	35	7	3	5	8	0
1979-80	London	OHA	62	50	53	103	72	5	2	6	8	15
1980-81	Oklahoma City	CHL	48	32	25	57	45					
	Minnesota	NHL	32	18	12	30	29	19	14	7	21	25
1981-82	Minnesota	NHL	76	55	51	106	138	4	3	1	4	2
1982-83	Minnesota	NHL	77	37	38	75	94	9	4	6	10	11
1983-84	Minnesota	NHL	79	38	33	71	58	16	4	5	9	27
1984-85	Minnesota	NHL	51	15	17	32	41	9	3	3	6	8
1985-86	Minnesota	NHL	75	44	45	89	51	5	0	1	1	6
1986-87	Minnesota	NHL	80	52	51	103	88					
1987-88	Minnesota	NHL	67	41	45	86	79					
1988-89	Minnesota	NHL	65	32	27	59	64					
	Washington	NHL	11	12	3	15	12	6	3	3	6	12
	NHL Totals		**613**	**344**	**322**	**666**	**654**	**68**	**31**	**26**	**57**	**91**

a OHA Second All-Star Team (1978)

Played in NHL All-Star Game (1982, 1983,1989)

Signed as free agent by **Minnesota**, September 28, 1979. Traded to **Washington** by **Minnesota** with Bob Rouse for Mike Gartner and Larry Murphy, March 7, 1989.

CICHOCKI, CHRIS (chih HAH kee)

Right wing. Shoots right. 5'11", 185 lbs. Born, Detroit, MI, September 17, 1963.
Last amateur club: Michigan Tech University Huskies (CCHA)

			Regular Season					Playoffs				
Season	Club	Lea	GP	G	A	TP	PIM	GP	G	A	TP	PIM
1982-83	Michigan Tech	CCHA	36	12	10	22	10					
1983-84	Michigan Tech	CCHA	40	25	20	45	36					
1984-85	Michigan Tech	CCHA	40	30	24	54	14					
1985-86	Detroit	NHL	59	10	11	21	21					
	Adirondack	AHL	9	4	4	8	6					
1986-87	Detroit	NHL	2	0	0	0	2					
	Adirondack	AHL	55	31	34	65	27					
	Maine	AHL	7	2	2	4	0					
1987-88	New Jersey	NHL	5	1	0	1	2					
	Utica	AHL	69	36	30	66	66					
1988-89	New Jersey	NHL	2	0	1	1	2					
	Utica	AHL	59	32	31	63	50	5	0	1	1	2
	NHL Totals		**68**	**11**	**12**	**23**	**27**					

Signed as a free agent by **Detroit**, June 28, 1985. Traded to **New Jersey** by **Detroit** with Detroit's third-round choice (later transferred to Buffalo - Andrew MacVicar) in 1987 Entry Draft for Mel Bridgman, March 9, 1987.

CIGER, ZDENKO

Left wing. Shoots left. 6'3", 195 lbs. Born, Martin, Czech., October 19, 1969.
(New Jersey's 3rd choice, 54th overall, in 1988 Entry Draft).

			Regular Season					Playoffs				
Season	Club	Lea	GP	G	A	TP	PIM	GP	G	A	TP	PIM
1988-89	Dukla Trencin	Czech.	32	15	21	36	18					

CIMETTA, ROBERT

Left wing. Shoots left. 6', 190 lbs. Born, Toronto, Ont., February 15, 1970.
(Boston's 1st choice, 18th overall, in 1988 Entry Draft).

			Regular Season					Playoffs				
Season	Club	Lea	GP	G	A	TP	PIM	GP	G	A	TP	PIM
1986-87	Toronto	OHL	66	21	35	56	65					
1987-88	Toronto	OHL	64	34	42	76	90	4	2	2	4	7
1988-89	Boston	NHL	7	2	0	2	0	1	0	0	0	15
a	Toronto	OHL	58	*55	47	102	89	6	3	3	6	0
	NHL Totals		**7**	**2**	**0**	**2**	**0**	**1**	**0**	**0**	**0**	**15**

a OHL First All-Star Team (1989)

CIRELLA, JOE (suh REHL uh)

Defense. Shoots right. 6'3", 210 lbs. Born, Hamilton, Ont., May 9, 1963.
(Colorado's 1st choice, 5th over-all, in 1981 Entry Draft).

			Regular Season					Playoffs				
Season	Club	Lea	GP	G	A	TP	PIM	GP	G	A	TP	PIM
1980-81	Oshawa	OHA	56	5	31	36	220	11	0	2	2	41
1981-82	**Colorado**	**NHL**	**65**	**7**	**12**	**19**	**52**	....	....	....	....	....
	Oshawa	OHL	3	0	1	1	0	11	7	10	17	32
1982-83	**New Jersey**	**NHL**	**2**	**0**	**1**	**1**	**4**	....	....	....	....	....
a	Oshawa	OHL	56	13	55	68	110	17	4	16	20	37
1983-84	**New Jersey**	**NHL**	**79**	**11**	**33**	**44**	**137**	....	....	....	....	....
1984-85	**New Jersey**	**NHL**	**66**	**6**	**18**	**24**	**141**	....	....	....	....	....
1985-86	**New Jersey**	**NHL**	**66**	**6**	**23**	**29**	**147**	....	....	....	....	....
1986-87	**New Jersey**	**NHL**	**65**	**9**	**22**	**31**	**111**	....	....	....	....	....
1987-88	**New Jersey**	**NHL**	**80**	**8**	**31**	**39**	**191**	**19**	**0**	**7**	**7**	**49**
1988-89	**New Jersey**	**NHL**	**80**	**3**	**19**	**22**	**155**	....	....	....	....	....
	NHL Totals		**503**	**50**	**159**	**209**	**938**	**19**	**0**	**7**	**7**	**49**

a OHL First All-Star Team (1983)

Played in NHL All-Star Game (1984)

Traded to **Quebec** by **New Jersey** with Claude Loiselle for Walt Poddubny and future considerations, June 17, 1989.

CIRONE, JASON

Center. Shoots left. 5'9", 185 lbs. Born, Toronto, Ont., February 21, 1971.
(Winnipeg's 3rd choice, 46th overall, in 1989 Entry Draft).

			Regular Season					Playoffs				
Season	Club	Lea	GP	G	A	TP	PIM	GP	G	A	TP	PIM
1987-88	Cornwall	OHL	53	12	11	23	41	11	1	2	3	4
1988-89	Cornwall	OHL	64	39	44	83	67	17	19	8	27	14

CLARK, KERRY

Right wing. Shoots right. 6'1", 190 lbs. Born, Kelvington, Sask., August 21, 1968.
(NY Islanders' 12th choice, 206th overall, in 1986 Entry Draft).

			Regular Season					Playoffs				
Season	Club	Lea	GP	G	A	TP	PIM	GP	G	A	TP	PIM
1985-86	Saskatoon	WHL	62	9	12	21	162	13	2	2	4	33
1986-87	Saskatoon	WHL	54	12	10	22	229	8	0	1	1	23
1987-88	Saskatoon	WHL	67	15	11	26	241	10	2	2	4	16
1988-89	Springfield	AHL	63	7	7	14	264	....	....	....	....	....
	Indianapolis	IHL	3	0	1	1	12	....	....	....	....	....

CLARK, WENDEL

Left Wing. Shoots left. 5'11", 194 lbs. Born, Kelvington, Sask., October 25, 1966.
(Toronto's 1st choice, 1st over-all, in 1985 Entry Draft).

			Regular Season					Playoffs				
Season	Club	Lea	GP	G	A	TP	PIM	GP	G	A	TP	PIM
1983-84	Saskatoon	WHL	72	23	45	68	225	....	....	....	....	....
1984-85a	Saskatoon	WHL	64	32	55	87	253	3	3	3	6	7
1985-86b	**Toronto**	**NHL**	**66**	**34**	**11**	**45**	**227**	**10**	**5**	**1**	**6**	**47**
1986-87	**Toronto**	**NHL**	**80**	**37**	**23**	**60**	**271**	**13**	**6**	**5**	**11**	**38**
1987-88	**Toronto**	**NHL**	**28**	**12**	**11**	**23**	**80**	....	....	....	....	....
1988-89	**Toronto**	**NHL**	**15**	**7**	**4**	**11**	**66**	....	....	....	....	....
	NHL Totals		**189**	**90**	**49**	**139**	**644**	**23**	**11**	**6**	**17**	**85**

a WHL First All-Star Team, East Division (1985)
b NHL All-Rookie Team (1986)

Played in NHL All-Star Game (1986)

CLARKE, CHRISTOPHER

Defense. Shoots left. 6', 180 lbs. Born, Arnprior, Ont., August 6, 1967.
(Washington's 8th choice, 204th overall, in 1987 Entry Draft).

			Regular Season					Playoffs				
Season	Club	Lea	GP	G	A	TP	PIM	GP	G	A	TP	PIM
1987-88	W. Michigan	CCHA	42	7	32	39	64	....	....	....	....	....
1988-89	W. Michigan	CCHA	38	3	21	24	65	....	....	....	....	....

CLARKE, DOUG

Defense. Shoots left. 6', 190 lbs. Born, Toronto, Ont., February 29, 1964.
(Vancouver's 13th choice, 219th over-all, in 1984 Entry Draft).

			Regular Season					Playoffs				
Season	Club	Lea	GP	G	A	TP	PIM	GP	G	A	TP	PIM
1982-83	St.Michael's	Jr. B	35	3	20	23	83	....	....	....	....	....
1983-84	Colorado	WCHA	33	5	25	30	62	....	....	....	....	....
1984-85	Colorado	WCHA	37	12	36	48	77	....	....	....	....	....
1985-86	Cdn. National	....	72	7	7	14	38	....	....	....	....	....
1986-87	Colorado	WCHA	37	11	37	48	73	....	....	....	....	....
1987-88	Salt Lake	IHL	71	11	26	37	14	19	4	9	13	10
1988-89	Salt Lake	IHL	35	5	7	12	20	....	....	....	....	....

CLEARY, JOSEPH

Defense. Shoots right. 5'11", 185 lbs. Born, Buffalo, NY, January 17, 1970.
(Chicago's 5th choice, 92nd overall, in 1988 Entry Draft).

			Regular Season					Playoffs				
Season	Club	Lea	GP	G	A	TP	PIM	GP	G	A	TP	PIM
1986-87	Cushing Aca.	HS	....	15	30	45	....	....	....	....	....	....
1987-88	Stratford	OPJHL	41	20	37	57	160	....	....	....	....	....
1988-89	Boston College	HE	38	5	7	12	36	....	....	....	....	....

CLEMENT, SEAN (CLEM-ent)

Defense. Shoots left. 6'2", 185 lbs. Born, Winnipeg, Man., February 26, 1966.
(Winnipeg's 3rd choice, 72nd over-all, in 1984 Entry Draft).

			Regular Season					Playoffs				
Season	Club	Lea	GP	G	A	TP	PIM	GP	G	A	TP	PIM
1984-85	Michigan State	CCHA	44	5	13	18	24	....	....	....	....	....
1985-86	Michigan State	CCHA	40	4	7	11	40	....	....	....	....	....
1986-87	Michigan State	CCHA	41	3	11	14	70	....	....	....	....	....
1987-88	Michigan State	CCHA	42	3	12	15	92	....	....	....	....	....
1988-89	Moncton	AHL	65	2	8	10	64	....	....	....	....	....

CLEMENTS, SCOTT

Defense. Shoots left. 6'1", 205 lbs. Born, Sudbury, Ont., May 1, 1962.

			Regular Season					Playoffs				
Season	Club	Lea	GP	G	A	TP	PIM	GP	G	A	TP	PIM
1984-85	St. Catharines	AHL	13	1	8	9	19	....	....	....	....	....
1985-86	St. Catharines	AHL	53	1	10	11	43	....	....	....	....	....
	Fredericton	AHL	20	0	2	2	4	6	1	2	3	2
1986-87	Newmarket	AHL	70	1	14	15	77	....	....	....	....	....
1987-88	Newmarket	AHL	76	3	11	14	53	....	....	....	....	....
1988-89	Indianapolis	IHL	23	2	6	8	35	....	....	....	....	....

Signed as a free agent by **Toronto**, May 24, 1985.

CLIFFORD, SEAN

Defense. Shoots left. 6'1", 200 lbs. Born, North Bay, Ont., May 11, 1967.
(Detroit's 7th choice, 116th overall, in 1987 Entry Draft).

			Regular Season					Playoffs				
Season	Club	Lea	GP	G	A	TP	PIM	GP	G	A	TP	PIM
1985-86	Ohio State	CCHA	12	0	2	2	18	....	....	....	....	....
1986-87	Ohio State	CCHA	42	3	8	11	107	....	....	....	....	....
1987-88	Ohio State	CCHA	40	1	6	7	121	....	....	....	....	....
1988-89	Ohio State	CCHA	17	1	7	8	18	....	....	....	....	....

CLOUSTON, SHAUN

Right wing. Shoots left. 6', 210 lbs. Born, Viking, Alta., April 28, 1968.
(NY Rangers' 3rd choice, 53rd over-all, in 1986 Entry Draft).

			Regular Season					Playoffs				
Season	Club	Lea	GP	G	A	TP	PIM	GP	G	A	TP	PIM
1985-86	Alberta	CWUAA	53	18	21	39	75	....	....	....	....	....
1986-87	Portland	WHL	70	6	25	31	93	19	0	5	5	45
1987-88	Portland	WHL	68	29	50	79	144	....	....	....	....	....
1988-89	Portland	WHL	72	45	47	92	150	19	7	10	17	28

Signed as a free agent by **Vancouver**, May 27, 1989.

COCHRANE, GLEN MACLEOD

Defense. Shoots left. 6'2", 205 lbs. Born, Cranbrook, B.C., January 29, 1958.
(Philadelphia's 6th choice, 50th over-all, in 1978 Amateur Draft).

			Regular Season					Playoffs				
Season	Club	Lea	GP	G	A	TP	PIM	GP	G	A	TP	PIM
1976-77	Calgary	WHL	35	1	5	6	105	....	....	....	....	....
	Victoria	WHL	36	1	7	8	60	4	0	0	0	31
1977-78	Victoria	WHL	72	7	40	47	311	13	1	5	6	51
1978-79	**Philadelphia**	**NHL**	**1**	**0**	**0**	**0**	**0**	....	....	....	....	....
	Maine	AHL	76	1	22	23	320	10	3	4	7	24
1979-80	Maine	AHL	77	1	11	12	269	8	2	0	2	83
1980-81	Maine	AHL	38	4	13	17	201	....	....	....	....	....
	Philadelphia	**NHL**	**31**	**1**	**8**	**9**	**219**	**6**	**1**	**1**	**2**	**18**
1981-82	**Philadelphia**	**NHL**	**63**	**6**	**12**	**18**	**329**	**2**	**0**	**0**	**0**	**2**
1982-83	**Philadelphia**	**NHL**	**77**	**2**	**22**	**24**	**237**	**3**	**0**	**0**	**0**	**4**
1983-84	**Philadelphia**	**NHL**	**67**	**7**	**16**	**23**	**225**	....	....	....	....	....
1984-85	**Philadelphia**	**NHL**	**18**	**0**	**3**	**3**	**100**	....	....	....	....	....
	Hershey	AHL	9	0	8	8	35	....	....	....	....	....
1985-86	**Vancouver**	**NHL**	**49**	**0**	**3**	**3**	**125**	**2**	**0**	**0**	**0**	**5**
1986-87	**Vancouver**	**NHL**	**14**	**0**	**0**	**0**	**52**	....	....	....	....	....
1987-88	**Chicago**	**NHL**	**73**	**1**	**8**	**9**	**204**	**5**	**0**	**0**	**0**	**2**
1988-89	**Chicago**	**NHL**	**6**	**0**	**0**	**0**	**13**	....	....	....	....	....
	Edmonton	**NHL**	**12**	**0**	**0**	**0**	**52**	....	....	....	....	....
	NHL Totals		**411**	**17**	**72**	**89**	**1556**	**18**	**1**	**1**	**2**	**31**

Traded to **Vancouver** by **Philadelphia** for Vancouver's third round choice in 1986 Entry Draft, March 12, 1985. Claimed by **Chicago** in NHL Waiver Draft, October 5, 1987. Claimed on waivers by **Edmonton** from **Chicago** , November 7, 1988.

COFFEY, PAUL DOUGLAS

Defense. Shoots left. 6'1", 205 lbs. Born, Weston, Ont., June 1, 1961.
(Edmonton's 1st choice, 6th over-all, in the 1980 Entry Draft).

			Regular Season					Playoffs				
Season	Club	Lea	GP	G	A	TP	PIM	GP	G	A	TP	PIM
1978-79a	S. S. Marie	OHA	68	17	72	89	103	....	....	....	....	....
1979-80b	S. S. Marie	OHA	23	10	21	31	63	....	....	....	....	....
	Kitchener	OHA	52	19	52	71	130	....	....	....	....	....
1980-81	**Edmonton**	**NHL**	**74**	**9**	**23**	**32**	**130**	**9**	**4**	**3**	**7**	**22**
1981-82c	**Edmonton**	**NHL**	**80**	**29**	**60**	**89**	**106**	**5**	**1**	**1**	**2**	**6**
1982-83c	**Edmonton**	**NHL**	**80**	**29**	**67**	**96**	**87**	**16**	**7**	**7**	**14**	**14**
1983-84c	**Edmonton**	**NHL**	**80**	**40**	**86**	**126**	**104**	**19**	**8**	**14**	**22**	**21**
1984-85de	**Edmonton**	**NHL**	**80**	**37**	**84**	**121**	**97**	**18**	**12**	**25**	**37**	**44**
1985-86de	**Edmonton**	**NHL**	**79**	**48**	**90**	**138**	**120**	**10**	**1**	**9**	**10**	**30**
1986-87	**Edmonton**	**NHL**	**59**	**17**	**50**	**67**	**49**	**17**	**3**	**8**	**11**	**30**
1987-88	**Pittsburgh**	**NHL**	**46**	**15**	**52**	**67**	**93**	....	....	....	....	....
1988-89e	**Pittsburgh**	**NHL**	**75**	**30**	**83**	**113**	**195**	**11**	**2**	**13**	**15**	**31**
	NHL Totals		**653**	**254**	**595**	**849**	**981**	**105**	**38**	**80**	**118**	**198**

a OHA Third All-Star Team (1979)
b OHA Second All-Star Team (1980)
c NHL Second All-Star Team (1982, 1983, 1984).
d Won James Norris Memorial Trophy (1985, 1986)
e NHL First All-Star Team (1985, 1986, 1989)

Played in NHL All-Star Game (1982-86, 1988-89)

Traded to **Pittsburgh** by **Edmonton** with Dave Hunter and Wayne Van Dorp for Craig Simpson, Dave Hannan, Moe Mantha and Chris Joseph, November 24, 1987.

COLBOURNE, DARREN

Right wing. Shoots left. 5'11", 185 lbs. Born, Corner Brook, Nfld., January 5, 1968.
(Detroit's 10th choice, 227th overall, in 1988 Entry Draft).

			Regular Season					Playoffs				
Season	Club	Lea	GP	G	A	TP	PIM	GP	G	A	TP	PIM
1986-87	Oshawa	OHL	17	3	2	5	18	....	....	....	....	....
	Cornwall	OHL	41	17	25	42	33	5	1	2	3	2
1987-88	Cornwall	OHL	61	47	51	98	66	11	7	4	11	11
1988-89	Cornwall	OHL	62	51	46	97	49	18	6	15	21	10

COLE, DANTON

Right wing. Shoots right. 5'10", 180 lbs.   Born, Pontiac, MI, January 10, 1967.
(Winnipeg's 6th choice, 123rd over-all, in 1985 Entry Draft).

			Regular Season					Playoffs				
Season	Club	Lea	GP	G	A	TP	PIM	GP	G	A	TP	PIM
1985-86	Michigan State	CCHA	43	11	10	21	22	....	....	....	....	....
1986-87	Michigan State	CCHA	44	9	15	24	16	....	....	....	....	....
1987-88	Michigan State	CCHA	46	20	36	56	38	....	....	....	....	....
1988-89	Michigan State	CCHA	47	29	33	62	46	....	....	....	....	....

CONACHER, PATRICK JOHN (PAT)   (CON-a-kur)

Center. Shoots left. 5'8", 190 lbs.   Born, Edmonton, Alta., May 1, 1959.
(NY Rangers' 4th choice, 76th over-all, in 1979 Entry Draft).

			Regular Season					Playoffs				
Season	Club	Lea	GP	G	A	TP	PIM	GP	G	A	TP	PIM
1977-78	Billings	WHL	72	31	44	75	105	20	15	14	29	22
1978-79	Billings	WHL	39	25	37	62	50	....	....	....	....	....
	Saskatoon	WHL	33	15	32	47	37	....	....	....	....	....
1979-80	New Haven	AHL	53	11	14	25	43	7	1	1	2	4
	NY Rangers	**NHL**	17	0	5	5	4	3	0	1	1	2
1980-81			DID NOT PLAY									
1981-82	Springfield	AHL	77	23	22	45	38	....	....	....	....	....
1982-83	**NY Rangers**	**NHL**	5	0	1	1	4	....	....	....	....	....
	Tulsa	CHL	63	29	28	57	44	....	....	....	....	....
1983-84	Moncton	AHL	28	7	16	23	30	....	....	....	....	....
	Edmonton	**NHL**	45	2	8	10	31	3	1	0	1	2
1984-85	Nova Scotia	AHL	68	20	45	65	44	6	3	2	5	0
1985-86	**New Jersey**	**NHL**	2	0	2	2	2	....	....	....	....	....
	Maine	AHL	69	15	30	45	83	5	1	1	2	11
1986-87	Maine	AHL	56	12	14	26	47	....	....	....	....	....
1987-88	**New Jersey**	**NHL**	24	2	5	7	12	17	2	2	4	14
	Utica	AHL	47	14	33	47	32	....	....	....	....	....
1988-89	**New Jersey**	**NHL**	55	7	5	12	14	....	....	....	....	....
	NHL Totals		148	11	26	37	67	23	3	3	6	18

Signed as free agent by **Edmonton**, October 4, 1983. Signed as a free agent by **New Jersey**, August 14, 1985.

COOKE, JAMES

Right wing. Shoots right. 6'2", 205 lbs.   Born, Toronto, Ont., November 5, 1968.
(Philadelphia's 8th choice, 140th overall, in 1988 Entry Draft).

			Regular Season					Playoffs				
Season	Club	Lea	GP	G	A	TP	PIM	GP	G	A	TP	PIM
1987-88	Bramalea	OPJHL	37	26	44	70	....					
1988-89	Colgate	ECAC	28	13	11	24	26					

COPELAND, TODD

Defense. Shoots left. 6'2", 210 lbs.   Born, Ridgewood, NJ, May 18, 1967.
(New Jersey's 2nd choice, 24th over-all, in 1986 Entry Draft).

			Regular Season					Playoffs				
Season	Club	Lea	GP	G	A	TP	PIM	GP	G	A	TP	PIM
1984-85	Belmont-Hill	HS	23	8	25	33	18	....	....	....	....	....
1985-86	Belmont-Hill	HS	19	4	19	23	19	....	....	....	....	....
1986-87	U. of Michigan	CCHA	34	2	11	13	59	....	....	....	....	....
1987-88	U. of Michigan	CCHA	41	3	10	13	58	....	....	....	....	....
1988-89	U. of Michigan	CCHA	39	5	14	19	102	....	....	....	....	....

CORKERY, TIM

Defense. Shoots right. 6'4", 210 lbs.   Born, Ponoka, Alta., February 17, 1967.
(Calgary's 6th choice, 103rd over-all, in 1987 Entry Draft).

			Regular Season					Playoffs				
Season	Club	Lea	GP	G	A	TP	PIM	GP	G	A	TP	PIM
1986-87	Ferris State	CCHA	40	3	7	10	120	....	....	....	....	....
1987-88	Ferris State	CCHA	40	0	6	6	108	....	....	....	....	....
1988-89	Ferris State	CCHA	23	2	5	7	53	....	....	....	....	....

Traded to **St. Louis** by **Calgary** with Mike Bullard and Craig Coxe for Mark Hunter, Doug Gilmour, Steve Bozek and Michael Dark, September 6, 1988.

CORKUM, BOB

Right wing. Shoots right. 6'2", 195 lbs.   Born, Salisbury, MA, December 18, 1967.
(Buffalo's 3rd choice, 57th over-all, in 1986 Entry Draft).

			Regular Season					Playoffs				
Season	Club	Lea	GP	G	A	TP	PIM	GP	G	A	TP	PIM
1984-85	Triton Regional	HS	18	35	36	71	....	....	....	....	....	....
1985-86	U. of Maine	H.E.	39	7	26	33	53	....	....	....	....	....
1986-87	U. of Maine	H.E.	35	18	11	29	24	....	....	....	....	....
1987-88	U. of Maine	H.E.	40	14	18	32	64	....	....	....	....	....
1988-89	U. of Maine	H.E.	45	17	31	48	64	....	....	....	....	....

CORRIVEAU, RICK

Defense. Shoots left. 5'11", 205 lbs.   Born, Welland, Ont., January 6, 1971.
(St. Louis' 2nd choice, 31st overall, in 1989 Entry Draft).

			Regular Season					Playoffs				
Season	Club	Lea	GP	G	A	TP	PIM	GP	G	A	TP	PIM
1987-88a	London	OHL	62	19	47	66	51	12	4	10	14	18
1988-89	London	OHL	12	4	10	14	21	1	0	0	0	0

a OHL Rookie of the Year (1988)

CORRIVEAU, YVON

Left wing. Shoots left. 6'2", 205 lbs.   Born, Welland, Ont., February 8, 1967.
(Washington's 1st choice, 19th over-all, in 1985 Entry Draft).

			Regular Season					Playoffs				
Season	Club	Lea	GP	G	A	TP	PIM	GP	G	A	TP	PIM
1983-84	Welland	OPJHL	36	16	21	37	51	....	....	....	....	....
1984-85	Toronto	OHL	59	23	28	51	65	3	0	0	0	5
1985-86	**Washington**	**NHL**	2	0	0	0	0	4	0	3	3	2
	Toronto	OHL	59	54	36	90	75	4	1	1	2	0
	Toronto	OHL	23	14	19	33	23	....	....	....	....	....
1986-87	**Washington**	**NHL**	17	1	1	2	24	....	....	....	....	....
	Binghamton	AHL	7	0	0	0	2	8	0	1	1	0
1987-88	**Washington**	**NHL**	44	10	9	19	84	13	1	2	3	30
	Binghamton	AHL	35	15	14	29	64	....	....	....	....	....
1988-89	**Washington**	**NHL**	33	3	2	5	62	1	0	0	0	0
	Baltimore	AHL	33	16	23	39	129	....	....	....	....	....
	NHL Totals		96	14	12	26	170	18	1	5	6	32

CORSON, SHAYNE

Center. Shoots left. 6', 175 lbs.   Born, Barrie, Ont., August 13, 1966
(Montreal's 2nd choice, 8th over-all, in 1984 Entry Draft).

			Regular Season					Playoffs				
Season	Club	Lea	GP	G	A	TP	PIM	GP	G	A	TP	PIM
1982-83	Barrie	OPJHL	23	13	29	42	87	....	....	....	....	....
1983-84	Brantford	OHL	66	25	46	71	165	6	4	1	5	26
1984-85	Hamilton	OHL	54	27	63	90	154	11	3	7	10	19
1985-86	**Montreal**	**NHL**	3	0	0	0	2	....	....	....	....	....
	Hamilton	OHL	47	41	57	98	153	....	....	....	....	....
1986-87	**Montreal**	**NHL**	55	12	11	23	144	17	6	5	11	30
1987-88	**Montreal**	**NHL**	71	12	27	39	152	3	1	0	1	12
1988-89	**Montreal**	**NHL**	80	26	24	50	193	21	4	5	9	65
	NHL Totals		209	50	62	112	491	41	11	10	21	107

COTE, ALAIN   (koh-TAY)

Left wing. Shoots left. 5'10", 200 lbs.   Born, Matane, Que., May 3, 1957.
(Montreal's 4th choice, 43rd over-all, in 1977 Amateur Draft).

			Regular Season					Playoffs				
Season	Club	Lea	GP	G	A	TP	PIM	GP	G	A	TP	PIM
1975-76	Chicoutimi	QJHL	72	35	49	84	93	5	3	3	6	2
1976-77	Chicoutimi	QJHL	56	42	45	87	86	8	1	5	6	14
1977-78	Hampton	AHL	36	15	17	32	38	....	....	....	....	....
	Quebec	WHA	27	3	5	8	8	11	1	2	3	0
1978-79	Quebec	WHA	79	14	13	27	23	4	0	0	0	2
1979-80	**Quebec**	**NHL**	41	5	11	16	13	....	....	....	....	....
	Syracuse	AHL	6	0	5	5	9	....	....	....	....	....
1980-81	Rochester	AHL	23	1	6	7	14	....	....	....	....	....
	Quebec	**NHL**	51	8	18	26	64	4	0	0	0	6
1981-82	**Quebec**	**NHL**	79	15	16	31	82	16	1	2	3	8
1982-83	**Quebec**	**NHL**	79	12	28	40	45	4	0	3	3	0
1983-84	**Quebec**	**NHL**	77	19	24	43	41	9	0	2	2	17
1984-85	**Quebec**	**NHL**	80	13	22	35	31	18	5	5	10	11
1985-86	**Quebec**	**NHL**	78	13	21	34	29	3	1	0	1	0
1986-87	**Quebec**	**NHL**	80	12	24	36	38	13	2	3	5	2
1987-88	**Quebec**	**NHL**	76	4	18	22	26	....	....	....	....	....
1988-89	**Quebec**	**NHL**	55	2	8	10	14	....	....	....	....	....
	NHL Totals		696	103	190	293	383	67	9	15	24	44
	WHA Totals		106	17	18	35	31	15	1	2	3	2

Reclaimed by **Montreal** from **Quebec** prior to Expansion Draft, June 9, 1979. Claimed by **Quebec** from **Montreal** in Expansion Draft, June 13, 1979.

COTE, ALAIN GABRIEL   (koh-TAY)

Defense. Shoots right. 6', 200 lbs.   Born, Montmagny, Que., April 14, 1967.
(Boston's 1st choice, 31st over-all, in 1985 Entry Draft).

			Regular Season					Playoffs				
Season	Club	Lea	GP	G	A	TP	PIM	GP	G	A	TP	PIM
1983-84	Quebec	QMJHL	60	3	17	20	40	5	1	3	4	8
1984-85	Quebec	QMJHL	68	9	25	34	173	4	0	1	1	12
1985-86	Granby	QMJHL	22	4	12	16	48	....	....	....	....	....
	Boston	**NHL**	32	0	6	6	14	....	....	....	....	....
1986-87	**Boston**	**NHL**	3	0	0	0	0	....	....	....	....	....
	Granby	QMJHL	43	7	24	31	185	4	0	3	3	2
1987-88	**Boston**	**NHL**	2	0	0	0	0	....	....	....	....	....
	Maine	AHL	69	9	34	43	108	9	2	4	6	19
1988-89	**Boston**	**NHL**	31	2	3	5	51	....	....	....	....	....
	Maine	AHL	37	5	16	21	111	....	....	....	....	....
	NHL Totals		68	2	9	11	65	....	....	....	....	....

COTE, SYLVAIN   (koh-TAY)

Defense. Shoots right. 5'11", 185 lbs.   Born, Quebec City, Que., January 19, 1966.
(Hartford's 1st choice, 11th over-all, in 1984 Entry Draft).

			Regular Season					Playoffs				
Season	Club	Lea	GP	G	A	TP	PIM	GP	G	A	TP	PIM
1982-83	Quebec	QMJHL	66	10	24	34	50	....	....	....	....	....
1983-84	Quebec	QMJHL	66	15	50	65	89	5	1	1	2	0
1984-85	**Hartford**	**NHL**	67	3	9	12	17	....	....	....	....	....
1985-86	**Hartford**	**NHL**	2	0	0	0	0	....	....	....	....	....
a	Hull	QMJHL	26	10	33	43	14	13	6	28	34	22
	Binghamton	AHL	12	2	4	6	0	....	....	....	....	....
1986-87	**Hartford**	**NHL**	67	2	8	10	20	2	0	2	2	2
1987-88	**Hartford**	**NHL**	67	7	21	28	30	6	1	1	2	4
1988-89	**Hartford**	**NHL**	78	8	9	17	49	3	0	1	1	4
	NHL Totals		281	20	47	67	116	11	1	4	5	10

a QMJHL First All-Star Team (1986).

COURTNALL, GEOFF

Left wing. Shoots left. 6', 170 lbs. Born, Victoria, B.C., August 18, 1962.

			Regular Season					Playoffs				
Season	Club	Lea	GP	G	A	TP	PIM	GP	G	A	TP	PIM
1980-81	Victoria	WHL	11	3	4	7	6	15	2	1	3	7
1981-82	Victoria	WHL	72	35	57	90	100	4	1	0	1	2
1982-83	Victoria	WHL	71	41	73	114	186	12	6	7	13	42
1983-84	**Boston**	**NHL**	**4**	**0**	**0**	**0**	**0**	....	....	....	....	....
	Hershey	AHL	74	14	12	26	51	....	....	....	....	....
1984-85	**Boston**	**NHL**	**64**	**12**	**16**	**28**	**82**	**5**	**0**	**2**	**2**	**7**
	Hershey	AHL	9	8	4	12	4	....	....	....	....	....
1985-86	**Boston**	**NHL**	**64**	**21**	**16**	**37**	**61**	**3**	**0**	**0**	**0**	**2**
	Moncton	AHL	12	8	8	16	6	....	....	....	....	....
1986-87	**Boston**	**NHL**	**65**	**13**	**23**	**36**	**117**	**1**	**0**	**0**	**0**	**0**
1987-88	**Boston**	**NHL**	**62**	**32**	**26**	**58**	**108**	....	....	....	....	....
	Edmonton	**NHL**	**12**	**4**	**4**	**8**	**15**	**19**	**0**	**3**	**3**	**23**
1988-89	**Washington**	**NHL**	**79**	**42**	**38**	**80**	**112**	**6**	**2**	**5**	**7**	**12**
	NHL Totals		**350**	**124**	**123**	**247**	**495**	**34**	**2**	**10**	**12**	**44**

Signed as free agent by **Boston**, July 6, 1983. Traded to **Edmonton** by **Boston** with Bill Ranford and future considerations for Andy Moog, March 8, 1988. Rights traded to **Washington** by **Edmonton** for Greg Adams, July 22, 1988.

COURTNALL, RUSSELL (RUSS)

Center. Shoots right. 5'11", 180 lbs. Born, Duncan, B.C., June 2, 1965.
(Toronto's 1st choice, 7th over-all, in 1983 Entry Draft).

			Regular Season					Playoffs				
Season	Club	Lea	GP	G	A	TP	PIM	GP	G	A	TP	PIM
1981-82	Notre Dame	Midget	28	13	28	41	....	....	....	....	....	....
1982-83	Victoria	WHL	60	36	61	97	33	12	11	7	18	6
1983-84	Cdn. Olympic	...	16	4	7	11	10	....	....	....	....	....
	Victoria	WHL	32	29	37	16	63	....	....	....	....	....
	Toronto	**NHL**	**14**	**3**	**9**	**12**	**6**	....	....	....	....	....
1984-85	**Toronto**	**NHL**	**69**	**12**	**10**	**22**	**44**	....	....	....	....	....
1985-86	**Toronto**	**NHL**	**73**	**22**	**38**	**60**	**52**	**10**	**3**	**6**	**9**	**8**
1986-87	**Toronto**	**NHL**	**79**	**29**	**44**	**73**	**90**	**13**	**3**	**4**	**7**	**11**
1987-88	**Toronto**	**NHL**	**65**	**23**	**26**	**49**	**47**	**6**	**2**	**1**	**3**	**0**
1988-89	**Toronto**	**NHL**	**9**	**1**	**1**	**2**	**4**	....	....	....	....	....
	Montreal	**NHL**	**64**	**22**	**17**	**39**	**15**	**21**	**8**	**5**	**13**	**18**
	NHL Totals		**373**	**112**	**145**	**257**	**258**	**50**	**16**	**16**	**32**	**37**

Traded to **Montreal** by **Toronto** for John Kordic and Montreal's sixth-round choice (Michael Doers) in 1989 Entry Draft, November 7, 1988.

COUTURIER, SYLVAIN (kew-TUR-ee-ay)

Left wing. Shoots left. 6'2", 205 lbs. Born, Greenfield Park, Que., April 23, 1968.
(Los Angeles' 3rd choice, 65th overall, in 1986 Entry Draft).

			Regular Season					Playoffs				
Season	Club	Lea	GP	G	A	TP	PIM	GP	G	A	TP	PIM
1985-86	Laval	QMJHL	68	21	37	58	64	14	1	7	8	28
1986-87	Laval	QMJHL	67	39	51	90	77	13	12	14	26	19
1987-88a	Laval	QMJHL	67	70	67	137	115	....	....	....	....	....
1988-89	**Los Angeles**	**NHL**	**16**	**1**	**3**	**4**	**2**	....	....	....	....	....
	New Haven	AHL	44	18	20	38	33	10	2	2	4	11
	NHL Totals		**16**	**1**	**3**	**4**	**2**	....	....	....	....	....

a QMJHL Third All-Star Team (1988)

COUVRETTE, ERIC

Left wing. Shoots left. 6', 185 lbs. Born, Pointe Claire, Que., March 11, 1969.
(NY Rangers' 7th choice, 152nd overall, in 1988 Entry Draft).

			Regular Season					Playoffs				
Season	Club	Lea	GP	G	A	TP	PIM	GP	G	A	TP	PIM
1987-88	St. Jean	QMJHL	55	34	60	94	37	7	1	5	6	2
1988-89	St. Jean	QMJHL	55	24	54	78	62	4	0	0	0	0

COXE, CRAIG

Center. Shoots left. 6'4", 220 lbs. Born, Chula Vista, CA, January 21, 1964.
(Detroit's 4th choice, 66th over-all, in 1982 Entry Draft)

			Regular Season					Playoffs				
Season	Club	Lea	GP	G	A	TP	PIM	GP	G	A	TP	PIM
1982-83	Belleville	OHL	64	14	27	41	102	4	1	2	3	2
1983-84	Belleville	OHL	45	17	28	45	90	3	2	0	2	4
1984-85	**Vancouver**	**NHL**	**9**	**0**	**0**	**0**	**49**	....	....	....	....	....
	Fredericton	AHL	62	8	7	15	242	4	2	1	3	16
1985-86	**Vancouver**	**NHL**	**57**	**3**	**5**	**8**	**176**	**3**	**0**	**0**	**0**	**2**
1986-87	**Vancouver**	**NHL**	**15**	**1**	**0**	**1**	**31**	....	....	....	....	....
	Fredericton	AHL	46	1	12	13	168	....	....	....	....	....
1987-88	**Vancouver**	**NHL**	**64**	**5**	**12**	**17**	**186**	....	....	....	....	....
	Calgary	**NHL**	**7**	**2**	**3**	**5**	**32**	**2**	**1**	**0**	**1**	**16**
1988-89	**St. Louis**	**NHL**	**41**	**0**	**7**	**7**	**127**	....	....	....	....	....
	Peoria	IHL	8	2	7	9	38	....	....	....	....	....
	NHL Totals		**193**	**11**	**27**	**38**	**401**	**5**	**1**	**0**	**1**	**18**

Signed as a free agent by **Vancouver**, June 26, 1984. Traded to **Calgary** by **Vancouver** for Brian Bradley and Peter Bakovic, March 6, 1988. Traded to **St. Louis** by **Calgary** with Mike Bullard and Tim Corkery for Mark Hunter, Doug Giolmour, Steve Bozek and Michael Dark, September 6, 1988.

CRABTREE, TODD

Defense. Shoots right. 6'2", 170 lbs. Born, Georgetown, MA, May 11, 1968.
(St. Louis' 6th choice, 138th overall, in 1987 Entry Draft).

			Regular Season					Playoffs				
Season	Club	Lea	GP	G	A	TP	PIM	GP	G	A	TP	PIM
1987-88	Babson	NCAA	30	6	4	10	18	....	....	....	....	....
1988-89	Babson	NCAA	14	1	2	3	12	....	....	....	....	....

CRAIG, MIKE

Right wing. Shoots right. 6', 180 lbs. Born, London, Ont., June 6, 1971.
(Minnesota's 2nd choice, 28th overall, in 1989 Entry Draft).

			Regular Season					Playoffs				
Season	Club	Lea	GP	G	A	TP	PIM	GP	G	A	TP	PIM
1987-88	Oshawa	OHL	61	6	10	16	39	7	0	1	1	11
1988-89	Oshawa	OHL	63	36	36	72	34	6	3	1	4	6

CRAVEN, MURRAY

Left wing. Shoots left. 6'2", 190 lbs. Born, Medicine Hat, Alta., July 20, 1964.
(Detroit's 1st choice, 17th over-all, in 1982 Entry Draft).

			Regular Season					Playoffs				
Season	Club	Lea	GP	G	A	TP	PIM	GP	G	A	TP	PIM
1980-81	Medicine Hat	WHL	69	5	10	15	18	5	0	0	0	2
1981-82	Medicine Hat	WHL	72	35	46	81	49	....	....	....	....	....
1982-83	Medicine Hat	WHL	28	17	29	46	35	....	....	....	....	....
	Detroit	**NHL**	**31**	**4**	**7**	**11**	**6**	....	....	....	....	....
1983-84	**Detroit**	**NHL**	**15**	**0**	**4**	**4**	**6**	....	....	....	....	....
	Medicine Hat	WHL	48	38	56	94	53	4	5	3	8	4
1984-85	**Philadelphia**	**NHL**	**80**	**26**	**35**	**61**	**30**	**19**	**4**	**6**	**10**	**11**
1985-86	**Philadelphia**	**NHL**	**78**	**21**	**33**	**54**	**34**	**5**	**0**	**3**	**3**	**4**
1986-87	**Philadelphia**	**NHL**	**77**	**19**	**30**	**49**	**38**	**12**	**3**	**1**	**4**	**9**
1987-88	**Philadelphia**	**NHL**	**72**	**30**	**46**	**76**	**58**	**7**	**2**	**5**	**7**	**4**
1988-89	**Philadelphia**	**NHL**	**51**	**9**	**28**	**37**	**52**	**1**	**0**	**0**	**0**	**0**
	NHL Totals		**404**	**109**	**183**	**292**	**224**	**44**	**9**	**15**	**24**	**28**

Traded to **Philadelphia** by **Detroit** with Joe Paterson for Darryl Sittler, October 10, 1984.

CRAWFORD, LOUIS

Left wing. Shoots left. 6', 185 lbs. Born, Belleville, Ont., November 5, 1962.
Last amateur club: Kitchener Rangers (OHL).

			Regular Season					Playoffs				
Season	Club	Lea	GP	G	A	TP	PIM	GP	G	A	TP	PIM
1980-81	Kitchener	OHA	53	2	7	9	134	....	....	....	....	....
1981-82	Kitchener	OHL	64	11	17	28	243	15	3	4	7	71
1982-83	Rochester	AHL	64	5	11	16	142	13	1	1	2	7
1983-84	Rochester	AHL	76	7	6	13	234	17	2	4	6	87
1984-85	Rochester	AHL	70	8	7	15	213	1	0	0	0	10
1985-86	Nova Scotia	AHL	78	8	11	19	214	....	....	....	....	....
1986-87	Nova Scotia	AHL	35	3	4	7	48	....	....	....	....	....
1987-88	Nova Scotia	AHL	65	15	15	30	170	4	1	2	3	9
1988-89	Adirondack	AHL	74	23	23	46	179	9	0	6	6	32

Signed as free agent by **Buffalo**, August 23, 1984.

CRAWFORD, MARC JOSEPH JOHN

Left wing. Shoots left. 5'11", 185 lbs. Born, Belleville, Ont., February 13, 1961.
(Vancouver's 3rd choice, 70th over-all, in 1980 Entry Draft).

			Regular Season					Playoffs				
Season	Club	Lea	GP	G	A	TP	PIM	GP	G	A	TP	PIM
1979-80	Cornwall	QJHL	54	27	36	63	127	12	12	12	24	31
1980-81	Cornwall	QJHL	63	42	57	99	242	19	20	15	35	27
1981-82	Dallas	CHL	34	13	21	34	71	....	....	....	....	....
	Vancouver	**NHL**	**40**	**4**	**8**	**12**	**29**	**14**	**1**	**0**	**1**	**11**
1982-83	**Vancouver**	**NHL**	**41**	**4**	**5**	**9**	**28**	**3**	**0**	**1**	**1**	**25**
	Fredericton	AHL	30	15	9	24	59	9	1	3	4	10
1983-84	**Vancouver**	**NHL**	**19**	**0**	**1**	**1**	**9**	....	....	....	....	....
	Fredericton	AHL	56	9	22	31	96	7	4	2	6	23
1984-85	Fredericton	AHL	65	12	29	41	177	5	0	1	1	10
	Vancouver	**NHL**	**1**	**0**	**0**	**0**	**4**	....	....	....	....	....
1985-86	**Vancouver**	**NHL**	**54**	**11**	**14**	**25**	**92**	**3**	**0**	**1**	**1**	**8**
	Fredericton	AHL	26	10	14	24	55	....	....	....	....	....
1986-87	**Vancouver**	**NHL**	**21**	**0**	**3**	**3**	**67**	....	....	....	....	....
	Fredericton	AHL	25	8	11	19	21	....	....	....	....	....
1987-88	Fredericton	AHL	43	5	13	18	90	2	0	0	0	14
1988-89	Milwaukee	IHL	53	23	30	53	166	11	2	5	7	26
	NHL Totals		**176**	**19**	**31**	**50**	**229**	**20**	**1**	**2**	**3**	**44**

CREIGHTON, ADAM (KRAY-ton)

Center. Shoots left. 6'5", 214 lbs. Born, Burlington, Ont., June 2, 1965.
(Buffalo's 3rd choice, 11th over-all, in 1983 Entry Draft).

			Regular Season					Playoffs				
Season	Club	Lea	GP	G	A	TP	PIM	GP	G	A	TP	PIM
1981-82	Ottawa	OHL	60	15	27	42	73	17	7	1	8	40
1982-83	Ottawa	OHL	68	44	46	90	88	9	0	2	2	12
1983-84	**Buffalo**	**NHL**	**7**	**2**	**2**	**4**	**4**	....	....	....	....	....
	Ottawa	OHL	56	42	49	91	79	13	16	11	27	28
1984-85	**Buffalo**	**NHL**	**30**	**2**	**8**	**10**	**33**	....	....	....	....	....
	Rochester	NHL	6	5	3	8	2	5	2	1	3	20
	Ottawa	OHL	10	4	14	18	23	5	6	2	8	11
1985-86	**Buffalo**	**NHL**	**19**	**1**	**1**	**2**	**2**	....	....	....	....	....
	Rochester	AHL	32	17	21	38	27	....	....	....	....	....
1986-87	**Buffalo**	**NHL**	**56**	**18**	**22**	**40**	**26**	....	....	....	....	....
1987-88	**Buffalo**	**NHL**	**36**	**10**	**17**	**27**	**87**	....	....	....	....	....
1988-89	**Buffalo**	**NHL**	**24**	**7**	**10**	**17**	**44**	....	....	....	....	....
	Chicago	**NHL**	**43**	**15**	**14**	**29**	**92**	**15**	**5**	**6**	**11**	**44**
	NHL Totals		**215**	**55**	**74**	**129**	**288**	**15**	**5**	**6**	**11**	**44**

Traded to **Chicago** by **Buffalo** for Rick Vaive, December 26, 1988.

CRISTOFOLI, ED

Center. Shoots left. 6'2", 205 lbs. Born, Trail, B.C., May 14, 1967.
(Montreal's 9th choice, 142nd over-all, in 1985 Entry Draft).

			Regular Season					Playoffs				
Season	Club	Lea	GP	G	A	TP	PIM	GP	G	A	TP	PIM
1985-86	U. of Denver	WCHA	46	10	9	19	32	....	....	....	....	....
1986-87	U. of Denver	WCHA	40	14	15	29	52	....	....	....	....	....
1987-88	U. of Denver	WCHA	38	12	27	39	64	....	....	....	....	....
1988-89	U. of Denver	WCHA	43	20	19	39	50	....	....	....	....	....

CRONIN, SHAWN

Defense. Shoots right. 6'2", 210 lbs. Born, Flushing, MI, August 20, 1963.

			Regular Season					Playoffs				
Season	Club	Lea	GP	G	A	TP	PIM	GP	G	A	TP	PIM
1983-84	Ill-Chicago	CCHA	32	0	4	4	41	....	....	....	....	....
1984-85	Ill-Chicago	CCHA	31	2	6	8	52	....	....	....	....	....
1985-86	Ill-Chicago	CCHA	35	3	8	11	70	....	....	....	....	....
1986-87	Salt Lake	IHL	53	8	16	24	118	....	....	....	....	....
	Binghamton	AHL	12	0	1	1	60	10	0	0	0	41
1987-88	Binghamton	AHL	65	3	8	11	212	4	0	0	0	15
1988-89	**Washington**	**NHL**	**1**	**0**	**0**	**0**	**0**	....	....	....	....	....
	Baltimore	AHL	75	3	9	12	267	....	....	....	....	....
	NHL Totals		**1**	**0**	**0**	**0**	**0**	....	....	....	....	....

Signed as a free agent by **Hartford**, March, 1986. Signed as a free agent by **Philadelphia**, June 12, 1989. Traded to **Winnipeg** by **Philadelphia** for future considerations, July 21, 1989.

CROSSMAN, DOUGLAS (DOUG)

Defense. Shoots left. 6'2", 190 lbs. Born, Peterborough, Ont., May 30, 1960.
(Chicago's 6th choice, 112th over-all, in 1979 Entry Draft).

			Regular Season					Playoffs				
Season	Club	Lea	GP	G	A	TP	PIM	GP	G	A	TP	PIM
1978-79	Ottawa	OHA	67	12	51	63	65	4	1	3	4	0
1979-80	Ottawa	OHA	66	20	96	116	48	11	7	6	13	19
1980-81	**Chicago**	**NHL**	**9**	**0**	**2**	**2**	**2**	....	....	....	....	....
	New Brunswick	AHL	70	13	43	56	90	13	5	6	11	36
1981-82	**Chicago**	**NHL**	**70**	**12**	**28**	**40**	**24**	**11**	**0**	**3**	**3**	**4**
1982-83	**Chicago**	**NHL**	**80**	**13**	**40**	**53**	**46**	**13**	**3**	**7**	**10**	**6**
1983-84	**Philadelphia**	**NHL**	**78**	**7**	**28**	**35**	**63**	**3**	**0**	**0**	**0**	**0**
1984-85	**Philadelphia**	**NHL**	**80**	**4**	**33**	**37**	**65**	**19**	**4**	**6**	**10**	**38**
1985-86	**Philadelphia**	**NHL**	**80**	**6**	**37**	**43**	**55**	**5**	**0**	**1**	**1**	**4**
1986-87	**Philadelphia**	**NHL**	**78**	**9**	**31**	**40**	**29**	**26**	**4**	**14**	**18**	**31**
1987-88	**Philadelphia**	**NHL**	**76**	**9**	**29**	**38**	**43**	**7**	**1**	**1**	**2**	**8**
1988-89	**Los Angeles**	**NHL**	**74**	**10**	**15**	**25**	**53**	**2**	**0**	**1**	**1**	**2**
	New Haven	AHL	3	0	0	0	0	....	....	....	....	....
	NHL Totals		**625**	**70**	**243**	**313**	**380**	**86**	**12**	**33**	**45**	**83**

Traded to **Philadelphia** by **Chicago** with Chicago's second round choice (Scott Mellanby) in the 1984 Entry Draft for Behn Wilson, June 8, 1983. Traded to **Los Angeles** by **Philadelphia** for Jay Wells, September 29, 1988. Traded to **NY Islanders** by **Los Angeles** to complete February 22, 1989, transaction in which Mark Fitzpatrick and Wayne McBean were traded to **NY Islanders** by **Los Angeles** for Kelly Hrudey, May 23, 1989.

CROSSMAN, JEFF

Left wing. shoots left. 6', 200 lbs. Born, Toronto, Ont., December 3, 1967.
(Los Angeles' 10th choice, 191st over-all, in 1984 Entry Draft).

			Regular Season					Playoffs				
Season	Club	Lea	GP	G	A	TP	PIM	GP	G	A	TP	PIM
1982-83	W. Michigan	CCHA	30	3	2	5	43	....	....	....	....	....
1983-84	W. Michigan	CCHA	39	9	12	21	19	....	....	....	....	....
1984-85	W. Michigan	CCHA	35	5	12	17	87	....	....	....	....	....
1985-86	W. Michigan	CCHA	39	13	19	32	154	....	....	....	....	....
1986-87	New Haven	AHL	61	2	3	5	133	2	0	0	0	20
1987-88	Colorado	IHL	60	13	12	25	103	8	0	3	3	23
1988-89	Cape Breton	AHL	2	0	0	0	4	....	....	....	....	....
	Denver	IHL	7	1	2	3	17	....	....	....	....	....

Traded to **NY Rangers** by **Los Angeles** with Marcel Dionne and Los Angeles' third-round choice in 1989 Entry Draft (Draft choice acquired by Minnesota October 12, 1988. Minnesota selected Murray Garbutt.) for Bob Carpenter and Tom Laidlaw, March 10, 1987. Traded to **Edmonton** by **NY Rangers** for Ron Shudra, October 27, 1988.

CROWDER, KEITH SCOTT

Right wing. Shoots right. 6', 190 lbs. Born, Windsor, Ont., January 6, 1959.
(Boston's 4th choice, 57th over-all, in 1979 Entry Draft).

			Regular Season					Playoffs				
Season	Club	Lea	GP	G	A	TP	PIM	GP	G	A	TP	PIM
1976-77	Peterborough	OHA	58	13	19	32	99	4	0	2	2	9
1977-78	Peterborough	OHA	58	30	30	60	139	14	3	5	8	21
1978-79	Peterborough	OHA	42	25	41	66	76	15	12	6	18	40
	Birmingham	WHA	5	1	0	1	17	....	....	....	....	....
1979-80	Binghamton	AHL	13	4	0	4	15	....	....	....	....	....
	Grand Rapids	IHL	20	10	13	23	22	....	....	....	....	....
1980-81	Springfield	AHL	26	12	18	30	34	....	....	....	....	....
	Boston	**NHL**	**47**	**13**	**12**	**25**	**172**	**3**	**2**	**0**	**2**	**9**
1981-82	**Boston**	**NHL**	**71**	**23**	**21**	**44**	**101**	**11**	**2**	**2**	**4**	**14**
1982-83	**Boston**	**NHL**	**74**	**35**	**39**	**74**	**105**	**17**	**1**	**6**	**7**	**54**
1983-84	**Boston**	**NHL**	**63**	**24**	**28**	**52**	**128**	**3**	**0**	**0**	**0**	**7**
1984-85	**Boston**	**NHL**	**79**	**32**	**38**	**70**	**142**	**4**	**3**	**2**	**5**	**19**
1985-86	**Boston**	**NHL**	**78**	**38**	**46**	**84**	**177**	**3**	**2**	**0**	**2**	**21**
1986-87	**Boston**	**NHL**	**58**	**22**	**30**	**52**	**106**	**4**	**0**	**1**	**1**	**4**
1987-88	**Boston**	**NHL**	**68**	**17**	**26**	**43**	**173**	**23**	**3**	**9**	**12**	**44**
1988-89	**Boston**	**NHL**	**69**	**15**	**18**	**33**	**147**	**10**	**0**	**2**	**2**	**37**
	NHL Totals		**607**	**219**	**258**	**477**	**1251**	**78**	**13**	**22**	**35**	**209**

Signed as a free agent by **Los Angeles**, June 28, 1989.

CROWDER, TROY

Right wing. Shoots right. 6'4", 215 lbs. Born, Sudbury, Ont., May 3, 1968.
(New Jersey's 6th choice, 108th overall, in 1986 Entry Draft).

			Regular Season					Playoffs				
Season	Club	Lea	GP	G	A	TP	PIM	GP	G	A	TP	PIM
1985-86	Hamilton	OHL	56	4	4	8	178	....	....	....	....	....
1986-87	North Bay	OHL	56	11	16	27	142	23	3	9	12	99
1987-88	**New Jersey**	**NHL**	....	....	....	....	....	**1**	**0**	**0**	**0**	**12**
	Utica	AHL	3	0	0	0	36	....	....	....	....	....
	Belleville	OHL	55	13	29	42	147	6	2	3	5	24
1988-89	Utica	AHL	62	6	4	10	152	2	0	0	0	25
	NHL Totals		....	....	....	....	....	**1**	**0**	**0**	**0**	**12**

CROWLEY, EDWARD

Defense. Shoots right. 6'2", 190 lbs. Born, Concord, MA, May 3, 1970.
(Toronto's 4th choice, 69th overall, in 1988 Entry Draft).

			Regular Season					Playoffs				
Season	Club	Lea	GP	G	A	TP	PIM	GP	G	A	TP	PIM
1986-87	Lawrence Aca.	HS	....	6	17	23	....	....	....	....	....	....
1987-88	Lawrence Aca.	HS	....	11	23	34	....	....	....	....	....	....
1988-89	U.S. Junior	....	7	1	1	2	0	....	....	....	....	....
	Lawrence Aca.	HS	....	12	24	36	....	....	....	....	....	....

CRUICKSHANK, GORD

Center. Shoots right. 5'11", 185 lbs. Born, Toronto, Ont., May 4, 1965.
(Boston's 8th choice, 178th over-all, in 1985 Entry Draft).

			Regular Season					Playoffs				
Season	Club	Lea	GP	G	A	TP	PIM	GP	G	A	TP	PIM
1982-83	St.Michael's	Jr. B	36	20	24	44	54	....	....	....	....	....
1984-85	Providence	H.E.	40	8	9	17	32	....	....	....	....	....
1985-86a	Providence	H.E.	38	34	18	52	80	....	....	....	....	....
1986-87a	Providence	H.E.	31	27	18	45	38	....	....	....	....	....
1987-88b	Providence	H.E.	36	29	16	45	31	....	....	....	....	....
	Maine	AHL	4	1	1	2	0	....	....	....	....	....
1988-89	Maine	AHL	DID NOT PLAY									

a Hockey East Second All-Star Team (1986, 1987)
b NCAA East Second All-American Team (1988)

CULHANE, JIM

Defense. Shoots left. 6', 195 lbs. Born, Haileybury, Ont., March 13, 1965.
(Hartford's 6th choice, 214th over-all, in 1984 Entry Draft).

			Regular Season					Playoffs				
Season	Club	Lea	GP	G	A	TP	PIM	GP	G	A	TP	PIM
1983-84	W. Michigan	CCHA	42	1	14	15	88	....	....	....	....	....
1984-85	W. Michigan	CCHA	37	2	8	10	84	....	....	....	....	....
1985-86	W. Michigan	CCHA	40	1	21	22	61	....	....	....	....	....
1986-87	W. Michigan	CCHA	43	9	24	33	163	....	....	....	....	....
1987-88	Binghamton	AHL	76	5	17	22	169	4	0	0	0	8
1988-89	Binghamton	AHL	72	6	11	17	200	....	....	....	....	....

CULLEN, JOHN

Center. Shoots right. 5'10", 185 lbs. Born, Puslinch, Ont., August 2, 1964.
(Buffalo's 2nd choice, 10th overall, in 1986 Supplemental Draft).

			Regular Season					Playoffs				
Season	Club	Lea	GP	G	A	TP	PIM	GP	G	A	TP	PIM
1983-84a	Boston U.	H.E.	40	23	33	56	28	....	....	....	....	....
1984-85b	Boston U.	H.E.	41	27	32	59	46	....	....	....	....	....
1985-86bc	Boston U.	H.E.	43	25	49	74	54	....	....	....	....	....
1986-87d	Boston U.	H.E.	36	23	29	52	35	....	....	....	....	....
1987-88efgh	Flint	IHL	81	48	*109	*157	113	16	11	*15	26	16
1988-89	**Pittsburgh**	**NHL**	**79**	**12**	**37**	**49**	**112**	**11**	**3**	**6**	**9**	**28**
	NHL Totals		**79**	**12**	**37**	**49**	**112**	**11**	**3**	**6**	**9**	**28**

a ECAC Rookie of the Year (1984)
b Hockey East First All-Star Team (1985, 1986)
c NCAA East Second All-Star Team (1986)
d Hockey East Second All-Star Team (1987)
e IHL First All-Star Team (1988)
f Won James Gatschene Memorial Trophy (MVP-IHL) (1988)
g Shared Garry F. Longman Memorial Trophy (Top Rookie-IHL) with Ed Belfour (1988)
h Won Leo P. Lamoureux Memorial Trophy (Top Scorer-IHL) (1988)

Signed as a free agent by **Pittsburgh** June 21, 1988.

CUNNEYWORTH, RANDY WILLIAM

Center. Shoots left. 6', 190 lbs. Born, Etobicoke, Ont., May 10, 1961.
(Buffalo's 9th choice, 167th over-all, in 1980 Entry Draft).

			Regular Season					Playoffs				
Season	Club	Lea	GP	G	A	TP	PIM	GP	G	A	TP	PIM
1979-80	Ottawa	OHA	63	16	25	41	145	11	0	1	1	13
1980-81	**Buffalo**	**NHL**	**1**	**0**	**0**	**0**	**2**	....	....	....	....	....
	Rochester	AHL	1	0	1	1	2	....	....	....	....	....
	Ottawa	OHA	67	54	74	128	240	15	5	8	13	35
1981-82	**Buffalo**	**NHL**	**20**	**2**	**4**	**6**	**47**	....	....	....	....	....
	Rochester	AHL	57	12	15	27	86	9	4	0	4	30
1982-83	Rochester	AHL	78	23	33	56	111	16	4	4	8	35
1983-84	Rochester	AHL	54	18	17	35	85	17	5	5	10	55
1984-85	Rochester	AHL	72	30	38	68	148	5	2	1	3	16
1985-86	**Pittsburgh**	**NHL**	**75**	**15**	**30**	**45**	**74**	....	....	....	....	....
1986-87	**Pittsburgh**	**NHL**	**79**	**26**	**27**	**53**	**142**	....	....	....	....	....
1987-88	**Pittsburgh**	**NHL**	**71**	**35**	**39**	**74**	**141**	....	....	....	....	....
1988-89	**Pittsburgh**	**NHL**	**70**	**25**	**19**	**44**	**156**	**11**	**3**	**5**	**8**	**26**
	NHL Totals		**316**	**103**	**119**	**222**	**562**	**11**	**3**	**5**	**8**	**26**

Traded to **Pittsburgh** by **Buffalo** with Mike Moller for Pat Hughes, October 4, 1985. Traded to **Winnipeg** by **Pittsburgh** with Rick Tabaracci and Dave McLlwain for Jim Kyte, Andrew McBain and Randy Gilhen, June 17, 1989.

CURRAN, BRIAN

Defense. Shoots left. 6'3", 215 lbs. Born, Toronto, Ont., November 5, 1963.
(Boston's 2nd choice, 22nd over-all, in 1982 Entry Draft).

			Regular Season					Playoffs				
Season	Club	Lea	GP	G	A	TP	PIM	GP	G	A	TP	PIM
1980-81	Portland	WHL	59	2	28	30	275	7	0	1	1	13
1981-82	Portland	WHL	51	2	16	18	132	14	1	7	8	63
1982-83	Portland	WHL	56	1	30	31	187	14	1	3	4	57
1983-84	Hershey	AHL	23	0	2	2	94	....	....	....	....	....
	Boston	**NHL**	**16**	**1**	**1**	**2**	**57**	**3**	**0**	**0**	**0**	**7**
1984-85	**Boston**	**NHL**	**56**	**0**	**1**	**1**	**158**	....	....	....	....	....
	Hershey	AHL	4	0	0	0	19	....	....	....	....	....
1985-86	**Boston**	**NHL**	**43**	**2**	**5**	**7**	**192**	**2**	**0**	**0**	**0**	**4**
1986-87	**NY Islanders**	**NHL**	**68**	**0**	**10**	**10**	**356**	**8**	**0**	**0**	**0**	**51**
1987-88	**NY Islanders**	**NHL**	**22**	**0**	**1**	**1**	**68**	....	....	....	....	....
	Springfield	AHL	8	1	0	1	43	....	....	....	....	....
	Toronto	**NHL**	**7**	**0**	**1**	**1**	**19**	**6**	**0**	**0**	**0**	**41**
1988-89	**Toronto**	**NHL**	**47**	**1**	**4**	**5**	**185**	....	....	....	....	....
	NHL Totals		**259**	**4**	**23**	**27**	**1035**	**19**	**0**	**0**	**0**	**103**

Signed as a free agent by **NY Islanders**, August 29, 1987. Traded to **Toronto** by **NY Islanders** for Toronto's sixth round choice (Pavel Gross) in 1988 Entry Draft, March 8, 1988

CURRIE, DAN

Left wing. Shoots left. 6′2″, 198 lbs.   Born, Burlington, Ont., March 15, 1968.
(Edmonton's 4th choice, 84th overall, in 1986 Entry Draft).

			Regular Season					Playoffs				
Season	Club	Lea	GP	G	A	TP	PIM	GP	G	A	TP	PIM
1985-86	S.S. Marie	OHL	66	21	24	45	37	....	....	....	....	....
1986-87	S.S. Marie	OHL	66	31	52	83	53	4	2	1	3	2
1987-88	Nova Scotia	AHL	3	4	2	6	0	5	4	3	7	0
	S.S.Marie	OHL	57	50	59	109	53	6	3	9	12	4
1988-89	Cape Breton	AHL	77	29	36	65	29	....	....	....	....	....

CYR, PAUL   (SIHR)

Left wing. Shoots left. 5′10″, 185 lbs.   Born, Port Alberni, B.C., October 31, 1963.
(Buffalo's 2nd choice, 9th over-all, in 1982 Entry Draft).

			Regular Season					Playoffs				
Season	Club	Lea	GP	G	A	TP	PIM	GP	G	A	TP	PIM
1980-81	Victoria	WHL	64	36	23	59	85	14	6	5	11	46
1981-82	Victoria	WHL	58	52	56	108	167	4	3	2	5	12
1982-83	Victoria	WHL	20	21	22	43	61	....	....	....	....	....
	Buffalo	**NHL**	36	15	12	27	59	10	1	3	4	6
1983-84	**Buffalo**	**NHL**	71	16	27	43	52	3	0	1	1	0
1984-85	**Buffalo**	**NHL**	71	22	24	46	63	5	2	2	4	15
1985-86	**Buffalo**	**NHL**	71	20	31	51	120	....	....	....	....	....
1986-87	**Buffalo**	**NHL**	73	11	16	27	122	....	....	....	....	....
1987-88	**Buffalo**	**NHL**	20	1	1	2	38	....	....	....	....	....
	NY Rangers	**NHL**	40	4	13	17	41	....	....	....	....	....
1988-89	**NY Rangers**	**NHL**	1	0	0	0	2	....	....	....	....	....
	NHL Totals		383	89	124	213	497	18	3	6	9	21

Traded to **NY Rangers** by **Buffalo** with Buffalo's tenth round choice (Eric Fenton) in 1988 Entry Draft for Mike Donnelly and Rangers' fifth round choice (Alexander Mogilny) in 1988 Entry Draft, December 31, 1987.

DAGENAIS, MIKE

Defense. Shoots left. 6′3″, 200 lbs.   Born, Gloucester, Ont., July 22, 1969.
(Chicago's 4th choice, 60th overall, in 1987 Entry Draft).

			Regular Season					Playoffs				
Season	Club	Lea	GP	G	A	TP	PIM	GP	G	A	TP	PIM
1985-86	Peterborough	OHL	45	1	3	4	40	....	....	....	....	....
1986-87	Peterborough	OHL	56	1	17	18	66	12	4	1	5	20
1987-88	Peterborough	OHL	66	11	23	34	125	12	1	1	2	31
1988-89	Peterborough	OHL	62	14	23	37	122	13	3	3	6	12

DAHL, KEVIN

Defense. Shoots right. 5′11″, 190 lbs.   Born, Regina, Sask., December 30, 1968.
(Montreal's 12th choice, 230th overall, in 1988 Entry Draft).

			Regular Season					Playoffs				
Season	Club	Lea	GP	G	A	TP	PIM	GP	G	A	TP	PIM
1987-88	Bowling Green	CCHA	44	2	23	25	78	....	....	....	....	....
1988-89	Bowling Green	CCHA	46	9	26	35	51	....	....	....	....	....

DAHLEN, ULF   (DAH lin)

Center. Shoots left. 6′2″, 195 lbs.   Born, Ostersund, Sweden, January 12, 1967.
(NY Rangers' 1st choice, 7th over-all, in 1985 Entry Draft).

			Regular Season					Playoffs				
Season	Club	Lea	GP	G	A	TP	PIM	GP	G	A	TP	PIM
1983-84	Ostersund	Swe.	36	15	11	26	10	....	....	....	....	....
1984-85	Ostersund	Swe.	36	33	26	59	20	....	....	....	....	....
1985-86	Bjorkloven	Swe.	21	4	3	7	8	....	....	....	....	....
1986-87	Bjorkloven	Swe.	31	9	12	21	20	6	6	2	8	4
1987-88	**NY Rangers**	**NHL**	70	29	23	52	26	....	....	....	....	....
	Colorado	IHL	2	2	2	4	0	....	....	....	....	....
1988-89	**NY Rangers**	**NHL**	56	24	19	43	50	4	0	0	0	0
	NHL Totals		126	53	42	95	76	4	0	0	0	0

DAHLQUIST, CHRIS

Defense. Shoots left. 6′1″, 190 lbs.   Born, Fridley, MN, December 14, 1962.

			Regular Season					Playoffs				
Season	Club	Lea	GP	G	A	TP	PIM	GP	G	A	TP	PIM
1981-82	Lake Superior	CCHA	39	4	10	14	62	....	....	....	....	....
1982-83	Lake Superior	CCHA	35	0	12	12	63	....	....	....	....	....
1983-84	Lake Superior	CCHA	40	4	19	23	76	....	....	....	....	....
1984-85	Lake Superior	CCHA	32	4	10	14	18	....	....	....	....	....
1985-86	Baltimore	AHL	65	4	21	25	64	....	....	....	....	....
	Pittsburgh	**NHL**	5	1	2	3	2	....	....	....	....	....
1986-87	**Pittsburgh**	**NHL**	19	0	1	1	20	....	....	....	....	....
	Baltimore	AHL	51	1	16	17	50	....	....	....	....	....
1987-88	**Pittsburgh**	**NHL**	44	3	6	9	69	....	....	....	....	....
1988-89	**Pittsburgh**	**NHL**	43	1	5	6	42	2	0	0	0	0
	Muskegon	IHL	10	3	6	9	14	....	....	....	....	....
	NHL Totals		111	5	14	19	133	2	0	0	0	0

Signed as a free agent by **Pittsburgh**, May, 1985.

DAIGNEAULT, JEAN-JACQUES   (DAYN yoh)

Defense. Shoots left. 5′11″, 185 lbs.   Born, Montreal, Que., October 12, 1965.
(Vancouver's 1st choice, 10th over-all, in 1984 Entry Draft).

			Regular Season					Playoffs				
Season	Club	Lea	GP	G	A	TP	PIM	GP	G	A	TP	PIM
1981-82	Laval	QMJHL	64	4	25	29	41	18	1	3	4	2
1982-83ab	Longueuil	QMJHL	70	26	58	84	58	15	4	11	15	35
1983-84	Cdn. Olympic	....	62	6	15	21	40	....	....	....	....	....
	Longueuil	QMJHL	10	2	11	13	6	14	3	13	16	30
1984-85	**Vancouver**	**NHL**	67	4	23	27	69	....	....	....	....	....
1985-86	**Vancouver**	**NHL**	64	5	23	28	45	3	0	2	2	0
1986-87	**Philadelphia**	**NHL**	77	6	16	22	56	9	1	0	1	0
1987-88	**Philadelphia**	**NHL**	28	2	2	4	12	....	....	....	....	....
	Hershey	AHL	10	1	5	6	8	....	....	....	....	....
1988-89	Hershey	AHL	12	0	10	10	13	....	....	....	....	....
	Sherbrooke	AHL	63	10	33	43	48	6	1	3	4	2
	NHL Totals		236	17	64	81	182	12	1	2	3	0

a QMJHL First All-Star Team (1983)
b Named QMJHL's Top Defenseman (1983)

Traded to **Philadelphia** by **Vancouver** with Vancouver's second-round choice (Kent Hawley) in 1986 Entry Draft for Dave Richter, Rich Sutter and Vancouver's third-round choice (Don Gibson) — acquired earlier — in 1986 Entry Draft, June 6, 1986. Traded to **Montreal** by **Philadelphia** for Scott Sandelin, November 7, 1988.

DALGARNO, BRAD

Right wing. Shoots right. 6′3″, 215 lbs.   Born, Vancouver, B.C., August 11, 1967.
(NY Islanders' 1st choice, 6th over-all, in 1985 Entry Draft).

			Regular Season					Playoffs				
Season	Club	Lea	GP	G	A	TP	PIM	GP	G	A	TP	PIM
1983-84	Markham	OPJHL	40	17	11	28	59	....	....	....	....	....
1984-85	Hamilton	OHL	66	23	30	53	86	17	5	5	10	12
1985-86	**NY Islanders**	**NHL**	2	1	0	1	0	....	....	....	....	....
	Hamilton	OHL	54	22	43	65	79	....	....	....	....	....
1986-87	Hamilton	OHL	60	27	32	59	100	9	4	6	10	11
	NY Islanders	**NHL**	....	....	....	....	....	1	0	1	1	0
1987-88	**NY Islanders**	**NHL**	38	2	8	10	58	4	0	0	0	19
	Springfield	AHL	39	13	11	24	76	....	....	....	....	....
1988-89	**NY Islanders**	**NHL**	55	11	10	21	86	....	....	....	....	....
	NHL Totals		95	14	18	32	144	5	0	1	1	19

DALLMAN, MARTY

Center. Shoots right. 5′10″, 180 lbs.   Born, Niagara Falls, Ont., February 15, 1963.
(Los Angeles' 3rd choice, 81st over-all, in 1981 Entry Draft).

			Regular Season					Playoffs				
Season	Club	Lea	GP	G	A	TP	PIM	GP	G	A	TP	PIM
1980-81	RPI	ECAC	22	8	10	18	6	....	....	....	....	....
1981-82	RPI	ECAC	28	22	18	40	27	....	....	....	....	....
1982-83	RPI	ECAC	27	21	29	50	28	....	....	....	....	....
1983-84a	RPI	ECAC	38	30	24	54	32	....	....	....	....	....
1984-85	New Haven	AHL	78	18	39	57	26	....	....	....	....	....
1985-86	New Haven	AHL	69	23	33	56	92	5	0	4	4	4
1986-87	Newmarket	AHL	42	24	24	48	44	....	....	....	....	....
	Baltimore	AHL	6	0	1	1	0	....	....	....	....	....
1987-88	**Toronto**	**NHL**	2	0	1	1	0	....	....	....	....	....
b	Newmarket	AHL	76	50	39	89	52	....	....	....	....	....
1988-89	**Toronto**	**NHL**	4	0	0	0	0	....	....	....	....	....
	Newmarket	AHL	37	26	20	46	24	....	....	....	....	....
	NHL Totals		6	0	1	1	0	....	....	....	....	....

a ECAC Second All-Star Team (1984)
b AHL Second All-Star Team (1988)

DALLMAN, ROD

Left wing. Shoots left. 5′11″, 185 lbs.   Born, Quesnal, B.C., January 26, 1967.
(NY Islanders' 8th choice, 118th over-all, in 1985 Entry Draft).

			Regular Season					Playoffs				
Season	Club	Lea	GP	G	A	TP	PIM	GP	G	A	TP	PIM
1984-85	Prince Albert	WHL	40	8	11	19	133	12	3	4	7	51
1985-86	Prince Albert	WHL	59	20	21	41	198	....	....	....	....	....
1986-87	Prince Albert	WHL	47	13	21	34	240	5	0	1	1	32
1987-88	**NY Islanders**	**NHL**	3	1	0	1	6	....	....	....	....	....
	Springfield	AHL	59	9	17	26	355	....	....	....	....	....
	Peoria	IHL	8	3	4	7	18	7	0	2	2	65
1988-89	**NY Islanders**	**NHL**	1	0	0	0	15	....	....	....	....	....
	Springfield	AHL	67	12	12	24	360	....	....	....	....	....
	NHL Totals		4	1	0	1	21	....	....	....	....	....

DALY, CRAIG

Defense. Shoots left. 6′3″, 205 lbs.   Born, Plymouth, MA, June 20, 1969.
(Vancouver's 8th choice, 171st overall, in 1987 Entry Draft).

			Regular Season					Playoffs				
Season	Club	Lea	GP	G	A	TP	PIM	GP	G	A	TP	PIM
1986-87	New Hampton	HS	23	10	14	24	....	....	....	....	....	....
1987-88	New Hampton	HS	22	9	18	27	....	....	....	....	....	....
1988-89	U. of Lowell	H.E.	2	0	1	1	2	....	....	....	....	....

DAM, TREVOR

Right wing. Shoots right. 5′10″, 210 lbs.   Born, Scarborough, Ont., April 20, 1970.
(Chicago's 3rd choice, 50th overall, in 1988 Entry Draft).

			Regular Season					Playoffs				
Season	Club	Lea	GP	G	A	TP	PIM	GP	G	A	TP	PIM
1986-87	London	OHL	64	6	17	23	88	....	....	....	....	....
1987-88	London	OHL	66	25	38	63	169	12	0	3	3	19
1988-89	London	OHL	66	33	59	92	111	21	9	11	20	39

DAMPHOUSSE, VINCENT   (dam-FOOSE)

Left wing. Shoots left. 6'1", 190 lbs.   Born, Montreal, Que., December 17, 1967.
(Toronto's 1st choice, 6th over-all, in 1986 Entry Draft).

			Regular Season					Playoffs				
Season	Club	Lea	GP	G	A	TP	PIM	GP	G	A	TP	PIM
1984-85	Laval	QMJHL	68	35	68	103	62	....	....	....	....	....
1985-86a	Laval	QMJHL	69	45	110	155	70	14	9	27	36	12
1986-87	**Toronto**	**NHL**	**80**	**21**	**25**	**46**	**26**	**12**	**1**	**5**	**6**	**8**
1987-88	**Toronto**	**NHL**	**75**	**12**	**36**	**48**	**40**	**6**	**0**	**1**	**1**	**10**
1988-89	**Toronto**	**NHL**	**80**	**26**	**42**	**68**	**75**	....	....	....	....	....
	NHL Totals		**235**	**59**	**103**	**162**	**141**	**18**	**1**	**6**	**7**	**18**

a QMJHL Second All-Star Team (1986)

DANEYKO, KENNETH (KEN)   (DAN ee koh)

Defense. Shoots left. 6', 210 lbs.   Born, Windsor, Ont., April 17, 1964.
(New Jersey's 2nd choice, 18th over-all, in 1982 Entry Draft).

			Regular Season					Playoffs				
Season	Club	Lea	GP	G	A	TP	PIM	GP	G	A	TP	PIM
1980-81	Spokane	WHL	62	6	13	19	40	4	0	0	0	6
1981-82	Spokane	WHL	26	1	11	12	147	....	....	....	....	....
	Seattle	WHL	38	1	22	23	151	14	1	9	10	49
1982-83	Seattle	WHL	69	17	43	60	150	4	1	3	4	14
1983-84	**New Jersey**	**NHL**	**11**	**1**	**4**	**5**	**17**	....	....	....	....	....
	Kamloops	WHL	19	6	28	34	52	17	4	9	13	28
1984-85	**New Jersey**	**NHL**	**1**	**0**	**0**	**0**	**10**	....	....	....	....	....
	Maine	AHL	80	4	9	13	206	11	1	3	4	36
1985-86	**New Jersey**	**NHL**	**44**	**0**	**10**	**10**	**100**	....	....	....	....	....
	Maine	AHL	21	3	2	5	75	....	....	....	....	....
1986-87	**New Jersey**	**NHL**	**79**	**2**	**12**	**14**	**183**	....	....	....	....	....
1987-88	**New Jersey**	**NHL**	**80**	**5**	**7**	**12**	**239**	**20**	**1**	**6**	**7**	**83**
1988-89	**New Jersey**	**NHL**	**80**	**5**	**5**	**10**	**283**	....	....	....	....	....
	NHL Totals		**295**	**13**	**38**	**51**	**832**	**2**	**1**	**6**	**7**	**83**

DANIELS, JEFF

Defense. Shoots left. 6'1", 195 lbs.   Born, Oshawa, Ont., June 24, 1968.
(Pittsburgh's 6th choice, 109th overall, in 1986 Entry Draft).

			Regular Season					Playoffs				
Season	Club	Lea	GP	G	A	TP	PIM	GP	G	A	TP	PIM
1985-86	Oshawa	OHL	62	13	19	32	23	6	0	1	1	0
1986-87	Oshawa	OHL	54	14	9	23	22	15	3	2	5	5
1987-88	Oshawa	OHL	64	29	39	68	59	4	2	3	5	0
1988-89	Muskegon	IHL	58	21	21	42	58	11	3	5	8	11

DAOUST, DANIEL (DAN)   (dow OO)

Center. Shoots left. 5'11", 170 lbs.   Born, Montreal, Que., February 29, 1960.

			Regular Season					Playoffs				
Season	Club	Lea	GP	G	A	TP	PIM	GP	G	A	TP	PIM
1978-79	Cornwall	QJHL	72	42	55	97	85	7	2	4	6	29
1979-80	Cornwall	QJHL	70	40	62	102	82	18	5	9	14	36
1980-81	Nova Scotia	AHL	80	38	60	98	106	6	1	3	4	10
1981-82	Nova Scotia	AHL	61	25	40	65	75	9	5	2	7	11
1982-83a	**Montreal**	**NHL**	**4**	**0**	**1**	**1**	**4**	....	....	....	....	....
	Toronto	**NHL**	**48**	**18**	**33**	**51**	**31**	....	....	....	....	....
1983-84	**Toronto**	**NHL**	**78**	**18**	**56**	**74**	**88**	....	....	....	....	....
1984-85	**Toronto**	**NHL**	**79**	**17**	**37**	**54**	**98**	....	....	....	....	....
1985-86	**Toronto**	**NHL**	**80**	**7**	**13**	**20**	**88**	**10**	**2**	**2**	**4**	**19**
1986-87	**Toronto**	**NHL**	**33**	**4**	**3**	**7**	**35**	**13**	**5**	**2**	**7**	**42**
	Newmarket	AHL	1	0	0	0	4	....	....	....	....	....
1987-88	**Toronto**	**NHL**	**67**	**9**	**8**	**17**	**57**	**4**	**0**	**0**	**0**	**2**
1988-89	**Toronto**	**NHL**	**68**	**7**	**5**	**12**	**54**	....	....	....	....	....
	NHL Totals		**457**	**80**	**156**	**236**	**455**	**27**	**7**	**4**	**11**	**63**

a NHL All-Rookie Team (1983)
Signed as free agent by **Montreal**, March 9, 1981. Traded to **Toronto** by **Montreal** for Toronto's third round choice (Ken Hodge — later transferred to Minnesota) in the 1984 Entry Draft, December 17, 1982.

DARK, MICHAEL

Defense. Shoots right. 6'3", 210 lbs.   Born, Sarnia, Ont., September 17, 1963.
(Montreal's 10th choice, 124th over-all, in 1982 Entry Draft).

			Regular Season					Playoffs				
Season	Club	Lea	GP	G	A	TP	PIM	GP	G	A	TP	PIM
1981-82	Sarnia	SOJL	41	13	30	43	86	....	....	....	....	....
1982-83	RPI	ECAC	29	3	16	18	54	....	....	....	....	....
1983-84	RPI	ECAC	38	2	12	14	60	....	....	....	....	....
1984-85	RPI	ECAC	36	7	26	33	76	....	....	....	....	....
1985-86ab	RPI	ECAC	32	7	29	36	58	....	....	....	....	....
1986-87	**St. Louis**	**NHL**	**13**	**2**	**0**	**2**	**2**	....	....	....	....	....
	Peoria	IHL	42	4	11	15	93	....	....	....	....	....
1987-88	**St. Louis**	**NHL**	**30**	**3**	**6**	**9**	**12**	....	....	....	....	....
	Peoria	IHL	37	21	12	33	97	2	0	0	0	4
1988-89	Salt Lake	IHL	36	3	12	15	57	....	....	....	....	....
	New Haven	AHL	7	0	4	4	4	....	....	....	....	....
	NHL Totals		**43**	**5**	**6**	**11**	**14**	....	....	....	....	....

a NCAA East All-American Team (1986)
b ECAC First All-Star Team (1986)
Traded to **St. Louis** by **Montreal** with Mark Hunter and Montreal's second (Herb Raglan); third (Nelson Emerson); fifth (Dan Brooks); and sixth (Rick Burchill) round choices in 1985 Entry Draft for St. Louis' first (Jose Charbonneau); second (Todd Richard); fourth (Martin Desjardins); fifth (Tom Sagissor); and sixth (Don Dufresne) round choices in 1985 Entry Draft, June 15, 1985. Traded to **Calgary** by **St. Louis** with Mark Hunter, Doug Gilmour and Steve Bozek for Mike Bullard, Craig Coxe and Tim Corkery, September 6, 1988

DAVIDSON, LEE

Center. Shoots left. 5'10", 160 lbs.   Born, Winnipeg, Man., June 30, 1968.
(Washington's 9th choice, 166th overall, in 1986 Entry Draft).

			Regular Season					Playoffs				
Season	Club	Lea	GP	G	A	TP	PIM	GP	G	A	TP	PIM
1985-86	Penticton	BCJHL	46	34	72	106	37	....	....	....	....	....
1986-87	North Dakota	WCHA	41	16	12	28	65	....	....	....	....	....
1987-88	North Dakota	WCHA	40	22	24	46	74	....	....	....	....	....
1988-89	North Dakota	WCHA	41	16	37	53	60	....	....	....	....	....

DAVIDSON, SEAN

Right wing. Shoots right. 5'11", 180 lbs.   Born, Toronto, Ont., April 13, 1968.
(Toronto's 10th choice, 195th overall, in 1986 Entry Draft).

			Regular Season					Playoffs				
Season	Club	Lea	GP	G	A	TP	PIM	GP	G	A	TP	PIM
1985-86	Toronto	OHL	65	18	34	52	23	4	0	1	1	0
1986-87	Toronto	OHL	66	30	32	62	24	....	....	....	....	....
1987-88	Toronto	OHL	66	34	47	81	61	3	3	0	3	2
1988-89	Toronto	OHL	66	32	68	100	70	6	4	3	7	4

DAVIES, CLARK

Defense. Shoots left. 6', 185 lbs.   Born, Yorkton, Sask., June 20, 1967.
(Buffalo's 1st choice, 18th overall, in 1988 Supplemental Draft).

			Regular Season					Playoffs				
Season	Club	Lea	GP	G	A	TP	PIM	GP	G	A	TP	PIM
1986-87	Ferris State	CCHA	42	5	20	25	42	....	....	....	....	....
1987-88	Ferris State	CCHA	40	4	15	19	65	....	....	....	....	....
1988-89	Ferris State	CCHA	32	3	10	13	59	....	....	....	....	....

DAY, JOSEPH (JOE)

Left wing. Shoots left. 5'11", 185 lbs.   Born, Chicago, IL, May 11, 1968.
(Hartford's 8th choice, 186th overall, in 1987 Entry Draft).

			Regular Season					Playoffs				
Season	Club	Lea	GP	G	A	TP	PIM	GP	G	A	TP	PIM
1985-86	St. Michael's	Jr. B	30	23	18	41	69	....	....	....	....	....
1986-87	St. Lawrence	ECAC	33	9	11	20	25	....	....	....	....	....
1987-88	St. Lawrence	ECAC	30	21	16	37	36	....	....	....	....	....
1988-89	St. Lawrence	ECAC	36	21	27	48	44	....	....	....	....	....

DEAN, KEVIN

Defense. Shoots left. 6'1", 195 lbs.   Born, Madison, WI, April 1, 1969.
(New Jersey's 4th choice, 86th overall, in 1987 Entry Draft).

			Regular Season					Playoffs				
Season	Club	Lea	GP	G	A	TP	PIM	GP	G	A	TP	PIM
1985-86	Culver Acad.	HS	35	28	44	72	48	....	....	....	....	....
1986-87	Culver Acad.	HS	25	19	25	44	30	....	....	....	....	....
1987-88	N. Hampshire	H.E.	27	1	6	7	34	....	....	....	....	....
1988-89	N. Hampshire	H.E.	34	1	12	13	28	....	....	....	....	....

DEASLEY, BRYAN

Left wing. Shoots left. 6'3", 205 lbs.   Born, Toronto, Ont., November 26, 1968.
(Calgary's 1st choice, 19th overall, in 1987 Entry Draft).

			Regular Season					Playoffs				
Season	Club	Lea	GP	G	A	TP	PIM	GP	G	A	TP	PIM
1985-86	St.Michael's	Jr. B	30	17	20	37	88	....	....	....	....	....
1986-87	U. of Michigan	CCHA	38	13	11	24	74	....	....	....	....	....
1987-88	U. of Michigan	CCHA	27	18	4	22	38	....	....	....	....	....
1988-89	Cdn. National	....	54	19	19	38	32	....	....	....	....	....
	Salt Lake	IHL						7	3	2	5	25

DeBLOIS, LUCIEN   (DEHB loh wah)

Right wing. Shoots right. 5'11", 200 lbs.   Born, Joliette, Que., June 21, 1957.
(NY Rangers' 1st choice, 8th over-all, in 1977 Amateur Draft).

			Regular Season					Playoffs				
Season	Club	Lea	GP	G	A	TP	PIM	GP	G	A	TP	PIM
1975-76	Sorel	QJHL	70	56	55	111	112	5	1	1	2	32
1976-77	Sorel	QJHL	72	56	78	134	131	....	....	....	....	....
1977-78	**NY Rangers**	**NHL**	**71**	**22**	**8**	**30**	**27**	**3**	**0**	**0**	**0**	**2**
1978-79	New Haven	AHL	7	4	6	10	6	....	....	....	....	....
	NY Rangers	**NHL**	**62**	**11**	**17**	**28**	**26**	**9**	**2**	**0**	**2**	**4**
1979-80	**NY Rangers**	**NHL**	**6**	**3**	**1**	**4**	**7**	....	....	....	....	....
	Colorado	**NHL**	**70**	**24**	**19**	**43**	**36**	....	....	....	....	....
1980-81	**Colorado**	**NHL**	**74**	**26**	**16**	**42**	**78**	....	....	....	....	....
1981-82	**Winnipeg**	**NHL**	**65**	**25**	**27**	**52**	**87**	**4**	**2**	**1**	**3**	**4**
1982-83	**Winnipeg**	**NHL**	**79**	**27**	**27**	**54**	**69**	**3**	**0**	**0**	**0**	**5**
1983-84	**Winnipeg**	**NHL**	**80**	**34**	**45**	**79**	**50**	**3**	**0**	**1**	**1**	**4**
1984-85	**Montreal**	**NHL**	**51**	**12**	**11**	**23**	**20**	**8**	**2**	**4**	**6**	**4**
1985-86	**Montreal**	**NHL**	**61**	**14**	**17**	**31**	**48**	**11**	**0**	**0**	**0**	**7**
1986-87	**NY Rangers**	**NHL**	**40**	**3**	**8**	**11**	**27**	**2**	**0**	**0**	**0**	**2**
1987-88	**NY Rangers**	**NHL**	**74**	**9**	**21**	**30**	**103**	....	....	....	....	....
1988-89	**NY Rangers**	**NHL**	**73**	**9**	**24**	**33**	**107**	**4**	**0**	**0**	**0**	**4**
	NHL Totals		**806**	**219**	**241**	**460**	**685**	**47**	**6**	**6**	**12**	**36**

Traded to **Colorado** by **NY Rangers** with Pat Hickey, Mike McEwen, Dean Turner and future consideration (Bobby Crawford) for Barry Beck, November 2, 1979. Traded to **Winnipeg** by **Colorado** for Brent Ashton and Winnipeg's third-round choice (Dave Kasper) in the 1982 Entry Draft, July 15, 1981. Traded to **Montreal** by **Winnipeg** for Perry Turnbull, June 13, 1984. Signed as a free agent by **Quebec**, August 2, 1989.

DEBOER, PETER

Center/right wing. Shoots right. 6'1", 190 lbs.   Born, Dunnville, Ont., June 13, 1968.
(Toronto's 11th choice, 237th overall, in 1988 Entry Draft).

			Regular Season					Playoffs				
Season	Club	Lea	GP	G	A	TP	PIM	GP	G	A	TP	PIM
1987-88	Windsor	OHL	54	23	18	41	41	12	4	4	8	14
1988-89	Windsor	OHL	65	45	46	91	80	4	2	3	5	0
	Milwaukee	IHL	2	0	1	1	0	1	0	2	2	2

Traded to **Vancouver** by **Toronto** for Paul Lawless, February 27, 1989.

DEBRUSK, LOUIE

Left wing. Shoots left. 6'1", 200 lbs.   Born, Cambridge, Ont., March 19, 1971.
(NY Rangers' 4th choice, 49th overall, in 1989 Entry Draft).

			Regular Season					Playoffs				
Season	Club	Lea	GP	G	A	TP	PIM	GP	G	A	TP	PIM
1987-88	Stratford	OPJHL	43	13	14	27	205	....	....	....	....	....
1988-89	London	OHL	59	11	11	22	149	19	1	1	2	43

de CARLE, MIKE

Left wing. Shoots left. 6', 180 lbs. Born, Covina, CA, August 20, 1966.
(Buffalo's 2nd choice, 6th overall, in 1987 Supplemental Draft).

			Regular Season					Playoffs				
Season	Club	Lea	GP	G	A	TP	PIM	GP	G	A	TP	PIM
1985-86	Lake Superior	CCHA	36	12	21	33	40	....	....	....	....	....
1986-87	Lake Superior	CCHA	38	34	18	52	122	....	....	....	....	....
1987-88ab	Lake Superior	CCHA	43	27	39	66	83	....	....	....	....	....
1988-89	Lake Superior	CCHA	38	20	24	44	76	....	....	....	....	....

a NCAA All-Tournament Team (1988)
b CCHA Second All-Star Team (1988)

DEFREITAS, RICHARD (RICH)

Defense. Shoots left. 6'2", 195 lbs. Born, Manchester, NH, January 28, 1969.
(Washington's 5th choice, 120th overall, in 1987 Entry Draft).

			Regular Season					Playoffs				
Season	Club	Lea	GP	G	A	TP	PIM	GP	G	A	TP	PIM
1986-87	St. Mark's	HS	23	13	32	45	14	....	....	....	....	....
1987-88	St. Mark's	HS	23	12	29	41	....	....	....	....	....	....
1988-89	Harvard	ECAC	5	0	2	2	6	....	....	....	....	....

DeGAETANO, PHIL (DEE-guh-TAN-oh)

Defense. Shoots right. 6'1", 203 lbs. Born, Flushing, NY, August 9, 1963.

			Regular Season					Playoffs				
Season	Club	Lea	GP	G	A	TP	PIM	GP	G	A	TP	PIM
1981-82	N. Michigan	WCHA	36	4	10	14	34	....	....	....	....	....
1982-83	N. Michigan	WCHA	37	5	9	14	56	....	....	....	....	....
1983-84	N. Michigan	WCHA	35	2	9	11	45	....	....	....	....	....
1984-85	N. Michigan	WCHA	40	5	20	25	98	....	....	....	....	....
1985-86	Indianapolis	IHL	80	9	39	48	107	5	2	1	3	15
1986-87	Adirondack	AHL	78	7	23	30	75	10	0	1	1	51
1987-88	Adirondack	AHL	65	4	27	31	105	3	1	1	2	6
1988-89	Maine	AHL	42	3	9	12	156	....	....	....	....	....
	Peoria	IHL	31	4	12	16	55	4	0	1	1	8

Signed as a free agent by **Detroit**, April 8, 1986. Traded to **St. Louis** by **Boston** for Scott Harlow, February 3, 1989.

DEGRAY, DALE EDWARD

Defense. Shoots right. 6', 200 lbs. Born, Oshawa, Ont., September 1, 1963.
(Calgary's 7th choice, 162nd over-all, in 1981 Entry Draft).

			Regular Season					Playoffs				
Season	Club	Lea	GP	G	A	TP	PIM	GP	G	A	TP	PIM
1980-81	Oshawa	OHA	61	11	10	21	93	8	1	1	2	19
1981-82	Oshawa	OHL	66	11	23	34	162	12	3	4	7	49
1982-83	Oshawa	OHL	69	20	30	50	149	17	7	7	14	36
1983-84	Colorado	CHL	67	16	14	30	67	6	1	1	2	2
1984-85a	Moncton	AHL	77	24	37	61	63	....	....	....	....	....
1985-86	**Calgary**	**NHL**	**1**	**0**	**0**	**0**	**0**	....	....	....	....	....
	Moncton	AHL	76	10	31	41	128	6	0	1	1	0
1986-87	**Calgary**	**NHL**	**27**	**6**	**7**	**13**	**29**	....	....	....	....	....
	Moncton	AHL	45	10	22	32	57	5	2	1	3	19
1987-88	**Toronto**	**NHL**	**56**	**6**	**18**	**24**	**63**	**5**	**0**	**1**	**1**	**16**
	Newmarket	AHL	8	2	10	12	8	....	....	....	....	....
1988-89	**Los Angeles**	**NHL**	**63**	**6**	**22**	**28**	**97**	**8**	**1**	**2**	**3**	**12**
	NHL Totals		**147**	**18**	**47**	**65**	**189**	**13**	**1**	**3**	**4**	**28**

a AHL Second All-Star Team (1985)

Traded to **Toronto** by **Calgary** for Toronto's fifth round choice (Scott Matusovich) in 1988 Entry Draft, September 17, 1987. Claimed by **Los Angeles** in NHL Waiver Draft, October 3, 1988.

DELAY, MICHAEL

Defense. Shoots left. 6', 175 lbs. Born, Boston, MA, August 31, 1969.
(Toronto's 8th choice, 174th overall, in 1988 Entry Draft).

			Regular Season					Playoffs				
Season	Club	Lea	GP	G	A	TP	PIM	GP	G	A	TP	PIM
1988-89	Boston College	H.E.	1	1	0	1	0	....	....	....	....	....

DELORME, GILBERT (duh-LOHRM)

Defense. Shoots right. 6'1", 205 lbs. Born, Boucherville, Que., November 25, 1962.
(Montreal's 2nd choice, 18th over-all, in 1981 Entry Draft).

			Regular Season					Playoffs				
Season	Club	Lea	GP	G	A	TP	PIM	GP	G	A	TP	PIM
1979-80	Chicoutimi	QJHL	71	25	86	111	68	12	2	10	12	26
1980-81	Chicoutimi	QJHL	70	27	79	106	77	12	10	12	22	16
1981-82	**Montreal**	**NHL**	**60**	**3**	**8**	**11**	**55**	....	....	....	....	....
1982-83	**Montreal**	**NHL**	**78**	**12**	**21**	**33**	**89**	**3**	**0**	**0**	**0**	**2**
1983-84	**Montreal**	**NHL**	**27**	**2**	**7**	**9**	**8**	....	....	....	....	....
	St. Louis	**NHL**	**44**	**0**	**5**	**5**	**41**	**11**	**1**	**3**	**4**	**11**
1984-85	**St. Louis**	**NHL**	**74**	**2**	**12**	**14**	**53**	**3**	**0**	**0**	**0**	**0**
1985-86	**Quebec**	**NHL**	**64**	**2**	**18**	**20**	**51**	**2**	**0**	**0**	**0**	**5**
1986-87	**Quebec**	**NHL**	**19**	**2**	**0**	**2**	**14**	....	....	....	....	....
	Detroit	**NHL**	**24**	**2**	**3**	**5**	**33**	**16**	**0**	**2**	**2**	**14**
1987-88	**Detroit**	**NHL**	**55**	**2**	**8**	**10**	**81**	**15**	**0**	**3**	**3**	**22**
1988-89	**Detroit**	**NHL**	**42**	**1**	**3**	**4**	**51**	**6**	**0**	**1**	**1**	**2**
	NHL Totals		**487**	**28**	**85**	**113**	**476**	**56**	**1**	**9**	**10**	**56**

Traded to **St. Louis** by **Montreal** with Greg Paslawski and Doug Wickenheiser for Perry Turnbull, December 21, 1983. Traded to **Quebec** by **St. Louis** for Bruce Bell, October 2, 1985. Traded to **Detroit** by **Quebec** with Brent Ashton and Mark Kumpel for Basil McRae, John Ogrodnick and Doug Shedden, January 17, 1987. Signed as a free agent by **Pittsburgh**, June 28, 1989.

DePALMA, LARRY

Left wing. Shoots left. 6', 195 lbs. Born, Trenton, MI, October 27, 1965.

			Regular Season					Playoffs				
Season	Club	Lea	GP	G	A	TP	PIM	GP	G	A	TP	PIM
1984-85	N. Westminster	WHL	65	14	16	30	87	10	1	1	2	25
1985-86	Saskatoon	WHL	65	61	51	112	232	13	7	9	16	58
	Minnesota	**NHL**	**1**	**0**	**0**	**0**	**0**	....	....	....	....	....
1986-87	**Minnesota**	**NHL**	**56**	**9**	**6**	**15**	**219**	....	....	....	....	....
	Springfield	AHL	9	2	2	4	82	....	....	....	....	....
1987-88	**Minnesota**	**NHL**	**7**	**1**	**1**	**2**	**15**	....	....	....	....	....
	Baltimore	AHL	16	8	10	18	121	....	....	....	....	....
	Kalamazoo	IHL	22	6	11	17	215	....	....	....	....	....
1988-89	**Minnesota**	**NHL**	**43**	**5**	**7**	**12**	**102**	**2**	**0**	**0**	**0**	**6**
	NHL Totals		**107**	**15**	**14**	**29**	**336**	**2**	**0**	**0**	**0**	**6**

Signed as a free agent by **Minnesota**, May 12, 1986.

DERKATCH, DALE

Center. Shoots right. 5'5", 170 lbs. Born, Preeceville, Sask., October 17, 1964.
(Edmonton's 6th choice, 140th overall, in 1983 Entry Draft).

			Regular Season					Playoffs				
Season	Club	Lea	GP	G	A	TP	PIM	GP	G	A	TP	PIM
1981-82	Regina	WHL	71	62	80	142	92	19	11	23	34	38
1982-83a	Regina	WHL	67	84	95	17	9	62	55	49	13	
1983-84	Regina	WHL	62	72	87	159	92	23	12	41	53	54
1984-85	Regina	WHL	4	4	7	11	0	7	2	5	7	10
1985-86	Asiago	Italy	28	41	59	100	18	8	10	16	26	12
1986-87	Ilves	Fin.	44	24	31	55	57	....	....	....	....	....
1987-88	Ilves	Fin.	41	28	24	52	24	....	....	....	....	....
1988-89	Ilves	Fin.	44	36	30	66	49	5	2	1	3	4

a WHL First All-Star Team (1983)

DESJARDINS, ERIC (day-jar-DAN)

Defense. Shoots right. 6'1", 185 lbs. Born, Rouyn, Que., June 14, 1969.
(Montreal's 3rd choice, 38th overall, in 1987 Entry Draft).

			Regular Season					Playoffs				
Season	Club	Lea	GP	G	A	TP	PIM	GP	G	A	TP	PIM
1986-87a	Granby	QMJHL	66	14	24	38	178	8	3	2	5	10
1987-88	Sherbrooke	AHL	3	0	0	0	6	4	0	2	2	2
b	Granby	QMJHL	62	18	49	67	138	5	0	3	3	10
1988-89	**Montreal**	**NHL**	**36**	**2**	**12**	**14**	**26**	**14**	**1**	**1**	**2**	**6**
	NHL Totals		**36**	**2**	**12**	**14**	**26**	**14**	**1**	**1**	**2**	**6**

a QMJHL Second All-Star Team (1987)
b QMJHL First All-Star Team (1988)

DESJARDINS, MARTIN

Center. Shoots left. 5'11", 165 lbs. Born, Ste-Rose, Que., January 28, 1967.
(Montreal's 5th choice, 75th over-all, in 1985 Entry Draft).

			Regular Season					Playoffs				
Season	Club	Lea	GP	G	A	TP	PIM	GP	G	A	TP	PIM
1984-85	Trois Rivieres	QMJHL	66	29	34	63	76	7	4	6	10	6
1985-86	Trois Rivieres	QMJHL	71	49	69	118	103	4	2	4	6	4
1986-87	Longueuil	QMJHL	68	39	61	100	89	19	8	10	18	18
1987-88	Sherbrooke	AHL	75	34	36	70	117	5	1	1	2	8
1988-89	Sherbrooke	AHL	70	17	27	44	104	6	2	7	9	21

DESMOND, NED

Defense. Shoots left. 6'3", 205 lbs. Born, New York, NY, February 18, 1966.
(St. Louis' 3rd choice, 54th over-all, in 1985 Entry Draft).

			Regular Season					Playoffs				
Season	Club	Lea	GP	G	A	TP	PIM	GP	G	A	TP	PIM
1985-86	Dartmouth	ECAC	23	4	12	16	4	....	....	....	....	....
1986-87	Dartmouth	ECAC	24	4	9	13	28	....	....	....	....	....
1987-88	Dartmouth	ECAC	DID NOT PLAY — INJURED									
1988-89	Dartmouth	ECAC	17	0	4	4	10	....	....	....	....	....
	Peoria	IHL	9	0	0	0	17	....	....	....	....	....

DEVEREAUX, JOHN

Center. Shoots right. 6', 175 lbs. Born, Scituate, MA, June 8, 1965.
(Hartford's 4th choice, 173rd over-all, in 1984 Entry Draft).

			Regular Season					Playoffs				
Season	Club	Lea	GP	G	A	TP	PIM	GP	G	A	TP	PIM
1984-85	Boston College	H.E.	19	3	3	6	6	....	....	....	....	....
1985-86	Boston College	H.E.	41	8	6	14	24	....	....	....	....	....
1986-87	Boston College	H.E.	39	14	20	34	16	....	....	....	....	....
1987-88	Boston College	H.E.	34	14	24	38	48	....	....	....	....	....
1988-89	Flint	IHL	11	3	1	4	11	....	....	....	....	....

DIDUCK, GERALD

Defense. Shoots right. 6'2", 207 lbs. Born, Edmonton, Alta., April 6, 1965.
(NY Islanders' 2nd choice, 16th over-all, in 1983 Entry Draft).

			Regular Season					Playoffs				
Season	Club	Lea	GP	G	A	TP	PIM	GP	G	A	TP	PIM
1981-82	Lethbridge	WHL	71	1	15	16	81	12	0	3	3	27
1982-83	Lethbridge	WHL	67	8	16	24	151	20	3	12	15	49
1983-84	Lethbridge	WHL	65	10	24	34	133	5	1	4	5	27
	Indianapolis	IHL	....	....	....	....	....	10	1	6	7	19
1984-85	**NY Islanders**	**NHL**	**65**	**2**	**8**	**10**	**80**	....	....	....	....	....
1985-86	**NY Islanders**	**NHL**	**10**	**1**	**2**	**3**	**2**	....	....	....	....	....
	Springfield	AHL	61	6	14	20	173	....	....	....	....	....
1986-87	**NY Islanders**	**NHL**	**30**	**2**	**3**	**5**	**67**	**14**	**0**	**1**	**1**	**35**
	Springfield	AHL	45	6	8	14	120	....	....	....	....	....
1987-88	**NY Islanders**	**NHL**	**68**	**7**	**12**	**19**	**113**	**6**	**1**	**0**	**1**	**42**
1988-89	**NY Islanders**	**NHL**	**65**	**11**	**21**	**32**	**155**	....	....	....	....	....
	NHL Totals		**238**	**23**	**46**	**69**	**417**	**20**	**1**	**1**	**2**	**77**

DIMAIO, ROBERT (ROB)

Center. Shoots right. 5'8", 175 lbs.   Born, Calgary, Alta., February 19, 1968.
(NY Islanders' 6th choice, 118th overall, in 1987 Entry Draft).

			Regular Season					Playoffs				
Season	Club	Lea	GP	G	A	TP	PIM	GP	G	A	TP	PIM
1986-87	Medicine Hat	WHL	70	27	43	70	130	20	7	11	18	46
1987-88	Medicine Hat	WHL	54	47	43	90	120	14	12	19	31	59
1988-89	**NY Islanders**	**NHL**	**16**	**1**	**0**	**1**	**30**	....	....	....	....	....
	Springfield	AHL	40	13	18	31	67	....	....	....	....	....
	NHL Totals		16	1	0	1	30	0	0	0	0	0

DiMUZIO, FRANK

Left wing. Shoots right. 6', 195 lbs.   Born, Toronto, Ont., August 12, 1967.
(Washington's 13th choice, 250th over-all, in 1985 Entry Draft).

			Regular Season					Playoffs				
Season	Club	Lea	GP	G	A	TP	PIM	GP	G	A	TP	PIM
1984-85	Belleville	OHL	68	28	22	50	40	12	4	2	6	8
1985-86	Ottawa	OHL	63	29	26	55	105	....	....	....	....	....
1986-87a	Ottawa	OHL	61	59	30	89	57	7	5	1	6	21
1987-88	Ottawa	OHL	48	51	44	95	96	16	9	11	20	34
1988-89	Baltimore	AHL	33	5	3	8	30	....	....	....	....	....

a OHL Third All-Star Team (1987)

DINEEN, GORDON (GORD)

Defense. Shoots right. 6', 195 lbs.   Born, Quebec City, Que., September 21, 1962.
(NY Islanders' 2nd choice, 42nd over-all, in 1981 Entry Draft).

			Regular Season					Playoffs				
Season	Club	Lea	GP	G	A	TP	PIM	GP	G	A	TP	PIM
1979-80	St. Michael's	Jr. B	42	11	24	35	103	....	....	....	....	....
1980-81	S. S. Marie	OHA	68	4	26	30	158	19	1	7	8	58
1981-82	S. S. Marie	OHL	68	9	45	54	185	13	1	2	3	52
1982-83	**NY Islanders**	**NHL**	**2**	**0**	**0**	**0**	**4**	....	....	....	....	....
abc	Indianapolis	CHL	73	10	47	57	78	13	2	10	12	29
1983-84	Indianapolis	CHL	26	4	13	17	63	....	....	....	....	....
	NY Islanders	**NHL**	**43**	**1**	**11**	**12**	**32**	9	1	1	2	28
1984-85	**NY Islanders**	**NHL**	**48**	**1**	**12**	**13**	**89**	10	0	0	0	26
	Springfield	AHL	25	1	8	9	46	....	....	....	....	....
1985-86	**NY Islanders**	**NHL**	**57**	**1**	**8**	**9**	**81**	3	0	0	0	2
	Springfield	AHL	11	2	3	5	20	....	....	....	....	....
1986-87	**NY Islanders**	**NHL**	**71**	**4**	**10**	**14**	**110**	7	0	4	4	4
1987-88	**NY Islanders**	**NHL**	**57**	**4**	**12**	**16**	**62**	....	....	....	....	....
	Minnesota	**NHL**	**13**	**1**	**1**	**2**	**21**	....	....	....	....	....
1988-89	**Minnesota**	**NHL**	**2**	**0**	**1**	**1**	**2**	....	....	....	....	....
	Kalamazoo	IHL	25	2	6	8	49	....	....	....	....	....
	Pittsburgh	**NHL**	**38**	**1**	**2**	**3**	**42**	11	0	2	2	8
	NHL Totals		331	13	57	70	443	40	1	7	8	68

a CHL First All-Star Team (1983)
b Won Bob Gassoff Trophy (CHL's Most Improved Defenseman) (1983)
c Won Bobby Orr Trophy (CHL's Top Defenseman) (1983)

Traded to **Minnesota** by **NY Islanders** for Chris Pryor and future considerations, March 8, 1988.
Traded to **Pittsburgh** by **Minnesota** with Scott Bjugstad for Ville Siren and Steve Gotaas, December 17, 1988.

DINEEN, KEVIN

Right wing. Shoots right. 5'11", 195 lbs.   Born, Quebec City, Que., October 28, 1963.
(Hartford's 3rd choice, 56th over-all, in 1982 Entry Draft).

			Regular Season					Playoffs				
Season	Club	Lea	GP	G	A	TP	PIM	GP	G	A	TP	PIM
1980-81	St. Michael's	Jr. B	40	15	28	43	167	....	....	....	....	....
1981-82	U. of Denver	WCHA	26	10	10	20	70	....	....	....	....	....
1982-83	U. of Denver	WCHA	36	16	13	29	108	....	....	....	....	....
1983-84	Cdn. Olympic	...	52	5	11	16	2	....	....	....	....	....
1984-85	**Hartford**	**NHL**	**57**	**25**	**16**	**41**	**120**	....	....	....	....	....
	Binghamton	AHL	25	15	8	23	41	....	....	....	....	....
1985-86	**Hartford**	**NHL**	**57**	**33**	**35**	**68**	**124**	10	6	7	13	18
1986-87	**Hartford**	**NHL**	**78**	**40**	**39**	**79**	**110**	6	2	1	3	31
1987-88	**Hartford**	**NHL**	**74**	**25**	**25**	**50**	**217**	6	4	4	8	8
1988-89	**Hartford**	**NHL**	**79**	**45**	**44**	**89**	**167**	4	1	0	1	10
	NHL Totals		345	168	159	327	738	26	13	12	25	67

Played in NHL All-Star Game (1988, 1989)

DINEEN, PETER KEVIN

Defense. Shoots right. 5'11", 190 lbs.   Born, Kingston, Ont., November 19, 1960.
(Philadelphia's 9th choice, 189th over-all, in 1980 Entry Draft).

			Regular Season					Playoffs				
Season	Club	Lea	GP	G	A	TP	PIM	GP	G	A	TP	PIM
1977-78	Seattle	WHL	....	....	....	....	....	2.	0	0	0	0
1978-79	Kingston	OHA	60	7	14	21	70	11	2	6	8	28
1979-80	Kingston	OHA	32	4	10	14	54	3	0	0	0	13
1980-81	Maine	AHL	41	6	7	13	100	16	1	2	3	82
1981-82	Maine	AHL	71	6	14	20	156	3	0	0	0	2
1982-83	Maine	AHL	2	0	0	0	0	....	....	....	....	....
	Moncton	AHL	57	0	10	10	76	....	....	....	....	....
1983-84	Moncton	AHL	63	0	10	10	120	....	....	....	....	....
	Hershey	AHL	12	0	1	1	32	....	....	....	....	....
1984-85	Hershey	AHL	79	4	19	23	144	....	....	....	....	....
1985-86	Binghamton	AHL	11	0	1	1	35	....	....	....	....	....
	Moncton	AHL	55	5	13	18	136	9	1	0	1	9
1986-87	**Los Angeles**	**NHL**	**11**	**0**	**2**	**2**	**8**	....	....	....	....	....
	New Haven	AHL	59	2	17	19	140	7	0	1	1	27
1987-88	Adirondack	AHL	76	8	26	34	137	11	0	2	2	20
1988-89	Adirondack	AHL	32	2	12	14	61	17	2	5	7	22
	NHL Totals		11	0	2	2	8	....	....	....	....	....

Traded to **Edmonton** by **Philadelphia** for Bob Hoffmeyer, October 22, 1982. Signed as a free agent by **Boston**, July 16, 1984. Signed as a free agent by Los Angeles, July 30, 1986.

DIONNE, MARCEL ELPHEGE   (DEE-ahn)

Center. Shoots right. 5'8", 190 lbs.   Born, Drummondville, Que., August 3, 1951.
(Detroit's 1st choice, 2nd over-all, in 1971 Amateur Draft).

			Regular Season					Playoffs				
Season	Club	Lea	GP	G	A	TP	PIM	GP	G	A	TP	PIM
1969-70	St. Catharines	OHA	54	*55	*77	*132	46	....	....	....	....	....
1970-71	St. Catharines	OHA	46	62	81	*143	20	....	....	....	....	....
1971-72	**Detroit**	**NHL**	**78**	**28**	**49**	**77**	**14**	....	....	....	....	....
1972-73	**Detroit**	**NHL**	**77**	**40**	**50**	**90**	**21**	....	....	....	....	....
1973-74	**Detroit**	**NHL**	**74**	**24**	**54**	**78**	**10**	....	....	....	....	....
1974-75a	**Detroit**	**NHL**	**80**	**47**	**74**	**121**	**14**	....	....	....	....	....
1975-76	**Los Angeles**	**NHL**	**80**	**40**	**54**	**94**	**38**	9	6	1	7	0
1976-77ab	**Los Angeles**	**NHL**	**80**	**53**	**69**	**122**	**12**	9	5	9	14	2
1977-78	**Los Angeles**	**NHL**	**70**	**36**	**43**	**79**	**37**	2	0	0	0	0
1978-79cd	**Los Angeles**	**NHL**	**80**	**59**	**71**	**130**	**30**	2	0	1	1	0
1979-80bde	**Los Angeles**	**NHL**	**80**	**53**	**84**	***137**	**32**	4	0	3	3	4
1980-81c	**Los Angeles**	**NHL**	**80**	**58**	**77**	**135**	**70**	4	1	3	4	7
1981-82	**Los Angeles**	**NHL**	**78**	**50**	**67**	**117**	**50**	10	7	4	11	0
1982-83	**Los Angeles**	**NHL**	**80**	**56**	**51**	**107**	**22**	....	....	....	....	....
1983-84	**Los Angeles**	**NHL**	**66**	**39**	**53**	**92**	**28**	....	....	....	....	....
1984-85	**Los Angeles**	**NHL**	**80**	**46**	**80**	**126**	**46**	3	1	2	3	2
1985-86	**Los Angeles**	**NHL**	**80**	**36**	**58**	**94**	**42**	....	....	....	....	....
1986-87	**Los Angeles**	**NHL**	**67**	**24**	**50**	**74**	**54**	....	....	....	....	....
	NY Rangers	**NHL**	**14**	**4**	**6**	**10**	**6**	6	1	1	2	2
1987-88	**NY Rangers**	**NHL**	**67**	**31**	**34**	**65**	**54**	....	....	....	....	....
1988-89	**NY Rangers**	**NHL**	**37**	**7**	**16**	**23**	**20**	....	....	....	....	....
	Denver	IHL	9	0	13	13	6	....	....	....	....	....
	NHL Totals		1348	731	1040	1771	600	49	21	24	45	17

a Won Lady Byng Memorial Trophy (1975, 1977)
b NHL First All-Star Team (1977, 1980)
c NHL Second All-Star Team (1979, 1981)
d Won Lester B. Pearson Memorial Award (1979, 1980)
e Won Art Ross Trophy (1980)

Played in NHL All-Star Game (1975-78, 1980, 1981, 1983, 1985)

Acquired as free agent by **Los Angeles** from **Detroit** with Bart Crashley for Terry Harper, Dan Maloney and Los Angeles' second choice — later transferred to Minnesota (Jimmy Roberts) — in 1976 Amateur Draft, June 23, 1975. Traded to **NY Rangers** by **Los Angeles** with Jeff Crossman and Los Angeles' third-round choice in 1989 Entry Draft (Draft choice acquired by Minnesota, October 12, 1988. **Minnesota** selected Murray Garbutt.) for Bob Carpenter and Tom Laidlaw, March 10, 1987.

DIRK, ROBERT

Defense. Shoots left. 6'4", 205 lbs.   Born, Regina, Sask., August 20, 1966.
(St. Louis' 4th choice, 53rd over-all, in 1984 Entry Draft).

			Regular Season					Playoffs				
Season	Club	Lea	GP	G	A	TP	PIM	GP	G	A	TP	PIM
1982-83	Regina	WHL	1	0	0	0	0	....	....	....	....	....
1983-84	Regina	WHL	62	2	10	12	64	23	1	12	13	24
1984-85	Regina	WHL	69	10	34	44	97	8	0	0	0	4
1985-86	Regina	WHL	72	19	60	79	140	10	3	5	8	8
1986-87	Peoria	IHL	76	5	17	22	155	....	....	....	....	....
1987-88	**St. Louis**	**NHL**	**7**	**0**	**1**	**1**	**16**	6	0	1	1	2
	Peoria	IHL	54	4	21	25	126	....	....	....	....	....
1988-89	**St. Louis**	**NHL**	**9**	**0**	**1**	**1**	**11**	....	....	....	....	....
	Peoria	IHL	22	0	2	2	54	....	....	....	....	....
	NHL Totals		16	0	2	2	27	6	0	1	1	2

DI VITA, DAVID

Defense. Shoots left. 6'2", 205 lbs.   Born, St. Clair Shores, MI, February 3, 1969.
(Buffalo's 6th choice, 106th overall, in 1988 Entry Draft).

			Regular Season					Playoffs				
Season	Club	Lea	GP	G	A	TP	PIM	GP	G	A	TP	PIM
1987-88	Lake Superior	CCHA	26	1	0	1	20	....	....	....	....	....
1988-89	Lake Superior	CCHA	25	1	4	5	28	....	....	....	....	....

DJOOS, PER

Defense. Shoots left. 5'11", 170 lbs.   Born, Mora, Sweden, May 11, 1968.
(Detroit's 7th choice, 127th overall, in 1986 Entry Draft).

			Regular Season					Playoffs				
Season	Club	Lea	GP	G	A	TP	PIM	GP	G	A	TP	PIM
1984-85	Mora	Swe.2	20	2	3	5	2	....	....	....	....	....
1985-86	Mora	Swe.	30	9	5	14	14	....	....	....	....	....
1986-87	Brynas	Swe.	23	1	2	3	16	....	....	....	....	....
1987-88	Brynas	Swe.	34	4	11	15	18	....	....	....	....	....
1988-89	Brynas	Swe.	40	1	17	18	44	....	....	....	....	....

DOBBIN, BRIAN

Right wing. Shoots right. 5'11", 205 lbs.   Born, Petrolia, Ont., August 18, 1966.
(Philadelphia's 6th choice, 100th over-all, in 1984 Entry Draft).

			Regular Season					Playoffs				
Season	Club	Lea	GP	G	A	TP	PIM	GP	G	A	TP	PIM
1983-84	London	OHL	70	30	40	70	70	....	....	....	....	....
1984-85	London	OHL	53	42	57	99	63	8	7	4	11	2
1985-86	London	OHL	59	38	55	93	113	5	2	1	3.	9
1986-87	**Philadelphia**	**NHL**	**12**	**2**	**1**	**3**	**14**	....	....	....	....	....
	Hershey	AHL	52	26	35	61	66	5	4	2	6	15
1987-88	**Philadelphia**	**NHL**	**21**	**3**	**5**	**8**	**6**	....	....	....	....	....
	Hershey	AHL	54	36	47	83	58	12	7	8	15	15
1988-89	**Philadelphia**	**NHL**	**14**	**0**	**1**	**1**	**8**	2	0	0	0	17
a	Hershey	AHL	59	43	48	91	61	11	7	6	13	12
	NHL Totals		47	5	7	12	28	2	0	0	0	17

a AHL First All-Star Team (1989)

DOLLAS, BOBBY

Defense. Shoots left. 6'2", 212 lbs.   Born, Montreal, Que., January 31, 1965.
(Winnipeg's 2nd choice, 14th over-all, in 1983 Entry Draft).

				Regular Season					Playoffs			
Season	Club	Lea	GP	G	A	TP	PIM	GP	G	A	TP	PIM
1981-82	Lac St. Louis	Midget	44	9	31	40	138	....	....	....	....	....
1982-83a	Laval	QMJHL	63	16	45	61	144	11	5	5	10	23
1983-84	**Winnipeg**	**NHL**	**1**	**0**	**0**	**0**	**0**	....	....	....	....	....
	Laval	QMJHL	54	12	33	45	80	14	1	8	9	23
1984-85	**Winnipeg**	**NHL**	**9**	**0**	**0**	**0**	**0**	....	....	....	....	....
	Sherbrooke	AHL	8	1	3	4	4	17	3	6	9	17
1985-86	**Winnipeg**	**NHL**	**46**	**0**	**5**	**5**	**66**	**3**	**0**	**0**	**0**	**2**
	Sherbrooke	AHL	25	4	7	11	29	....	....	....	....	....
1986-87	Sherbrooke	AHL	75	6	18	24	87	16	2	4	6	13
1987-88	**Quebec**	**NHL**	**9**	**0**	**0**	**0**	**2**	....	....	....	....	....
	Moncton	AHL	26	4	10	14	20	....	....	....	....	....
	Fredericton	AHL	33	4	8	12	27	15	2	2	4	24
1988-89	**Quebec**	**NHL**	**16**	**0**	**3**	**3**	**16**	....	....	....	....	....
	Halifax	AHL	57	5	19	24	65	4	1	0	1	14
	NHL Totals		**81**	**0**	**8**	**8**	**84**	**3**	**0**	**0**	**0**	**2**

a QMJHL Second All-Star Team (1983).
Traded to **Quebec** by **Winnipeg** for Stu Kulak, December 17, 1987.

DOMI, TAHIR (TIE)

Right wing. Shoots right. 5'10", 200 lbs.   Born, Windsor, Ont., November 1, 1969.
(Toronto's 2nd choice, 27th overall, in 1988 Entry Draft).

				Regular Season					Playoffs			
Season	Club	Lea	GP	G	A	TP	PIM	GP	G	A	TP	PIM
1986-87	Toronto	OHL	66	21	35	56	65	....	....	....	....	....
1987-88	Peterborough	OHL	60	22	21	43	292	12	3	9	12	24
1988-89	Peterborough	OHL	43	14	16	30	175	17	10	9	19	70

DONATELLI, CLARK

Left wing. Shoots left. 5'10", 190 lbs.   Born, Providence, RI, November 22, 1965.
(NY Ranger's 4th choice, 98th over-all, in 1984 Entry Draft).

				Regular Season					Playoffs			
Season	Club	Lea	GP	G	A	TP	PIM	GP	G	A	TP	PIM
1984-85	Boston U.	H.E.	40	17	18	35	46	....	....	....	....	....
1985-86ab	Boston U.	H.E.	43	28	34	62	30	....	....	....	....	....
1986-87	Boston U.	H.E.	37	15	23	38	46	....	....	....	....	....
1987-88	U.S. National	....	50	11	27	38	26	....	....	....	....	....
	U.S. Olympic	....	6	2	1	3	5	....	....	....	....	....
1988-89						DID NOT PLAY						

a NCAA East Second All-American Team (1986)
b Hockey East Second All-Star Team (1986)
Traded to **Edmonton** by **NY Rangers** with Ville Kentala, Reijo Ruotsalainen and Jim Weimer for Mike Golden, Don Jackson and Miroslav Horava, October 2, 1986.

DONATO, TED

Center. Shoots left. 5'10", 170 lbs.   Born, Dedham, MA, April 28, 1968.
(Boston's 5th choice, 98th overall, in 1987 Entry Draft).

				Regular Season					Playoffs			
Season	Club	Lea	GP	G	A	TP	PIM	GP	G	A	TP	PIM
1986-87	Cath. Memorial	HS	22	29	34	63	30	....	....	....	....	....
1987-88	Harvard	ECAC	28	12	14	26	24	....	....	....	....	....
1988-89	Harvard	ECAC	34	14	37	51	30	....	....	....	....	....

DONNELLY, DAVID (DAVE)

Center. Shoots left. 5'11", 185 lbs.   Born, Edmonton, Alta., February 2, 1962.
(Minnesota's 2nd choice, 27th over-all, in 1981 Entry Draft).

				Regular Season					Playoffs			
Season	Club	Lea	GP	G	A	TP	PIM	GP	G	A	TP	PIM
1979-80	St. Albert	AJHL	59	27	33	60	146	....	....	....	....	....
1980-81	St. Albert	AJHL	53	39	55	94	243	....	....	....	....	....
1981-82	North Dakota	WCHA	38	10	15	25	38	....	....	....	....	....
1982-83	North Dakota	WCHA	34	18	16	34	106	....	....	....	....	....
1983-84	Cdn. Olympic	....	64	17	13	30	52	....	....	....	....	....
	Boston	**NHL**	**16**	**3**	**4**	**7**	**2**	**3**	**0**	**0**	**0**	**0**
1984-85	**Boston**	**NHL**	**38**	**6**	**8**	**14**	**46**	**1**	**0**	**0**	**0**	**0**
	Hershey	AHL	26	11	6	17	28	....	....	....	....	....
1985-86	**Boston**	**NHL**	**8**	**0**	**0**	**0**	**17**	....	....	....	....	....
1986-87	**Chicago**	**NHL**	**71**	**6**	**12**	**18**	**81**	**1**	**0**	**0**	**0**	**0**
1987-88	**Edmonton**	**NHL**	**4**	**0**	**0**	**0**	**4**	....	....	....	....	....
1988-89	Kalpa	Fin.	43	20	22	42	98	....	....	....	....	....
	NHL Totals		**137**	**15**	**24**	**39**	**150**	**5**	**0**	**0**	**0**	**0**

Rights traded to **Boston** by **Minnesota** with Brad Palmer for past considerations, June 9, 1982. Traded to **Detroit** by **Boston** for Dwight Foster, March 11, 1986. Traded to **Edmonton** by **Chicago** for future considerations, October 19, 1987.

DONNELLY, GORDON (GORD)

Right wing. Shoots right. 6'1", 202 lbs.   Born, Montreal, Que., April 5, 1962.
(St. Louis' 3rd choice, 62nd over-all, in 1981 Entry Draft).

				Regular Season					Playoffs			
Season	Club	Lea	GP	G	A	TP	PIM	GP	G	A	TP	PIM
1980-81	Sherbrooke	QMJHL	67	15	23	38	252	14	1	2	3	35
1981-82	Sherbrooke	QMJHL	60	8	41	49	250	22	2	7	9	106
1982-83	Salt Lake	CHL	67	3	12	15	222	6	1	1	2	8
1983-84	**Quebec**	**NHL**	**38**	**0**	**5**	**5**	**60**	....	....	....	....	....
	Fredericton	AHL	30	2	3	5	146	7	1	1	2	43
1984-85	**Quebec**	**NHL**	**22**	**0**	**0**	**0**	**33**	....	....	....	....	....
	Fredericton	AHL	42	1	5	6	134	6	0	1	1	25
1985-86	**Quebec**	**NHL**	**36**	**2**	**2**	**4**	**85**	**1**	**0**	**0**	**0**	**0**
	Fredericton	AHL	38	3	5	8	103	5	0	0	0	33
1986-87	**Quebec**	**NHL**	**38**	**0**	**2**	**2**	**143**	**13**	**0**	**0**	**0**	**53**
1987-88	**Quebec**	**NHL**	**63**	**4**	**3**	**7**	**301**	....	....	....	....	....
1988-89	**Quebec**	**NHL**	**16**	**4**	**0**	**4**	**46**	....	....	....	....	....
	Winnipeg	**NHL**	**57**	**6**	**10**	**16**	**228**	....	....	....	....	....
	NHL Totals		**270**	**16**	**22**	**38**	**896**	**14**	**0**	**0**	**0**	**53**

Rights transferred to **Quebec** by **St. Louis** with rights to Claude Julien when St. Louis signed Jacques Demers as coach, August 19, 1983. Traded to **Winnipeg** by **Quebec** for Mario Marois, December 6, 1988.

DONNELLY, MIKE

Left wing. Shoots left. 5'11", 185 lbs.   Born, Detroit, MI, October 10, 1963.

				Regular Season					Playoffs			
Season	Club	Lea	GP	G	A	TP	PIM	GP	G	A	TP	PIM
1982-83	Michigan State	CCHA	24	7	13	20	8	....	....	....	....	....
1983-84	Michigan State	CCHA	44	18	14	32	40	....	....	....	....	....
1984-85	Michigan State	CCHA	44	26	21	47	48	....	....	....	....	....
1985-86ab	Michigan State	CCHA	44	59	38	97	65	....	....	....	....	....
1986-87	**NY Rangers**	**NHL**	**5**	**1**	**1**	**2**	**0**	....	....	....	....	....
	New Haven	AHL	58	27	34	61	52	7	2	0	2	9
1987-88	**NY Rangers**	**NHL**	**17**	**2**	**2**	**4**	**8**	....	....	....	....	....
	Colorado	IHL	8	7	11	18	15	....	....	....	....	....
	Buffalo	**NHL**	**40**	**6**	**8**	**14**	**44**	....	....	....	....	....
1988-89	**Buffalo**	**NHL**	**22**	**4**	**6**	**10**	**10**	....	....	....	....	....
	Rochester	AHL	53	32	37	69	53	....	....	....	....	....
	NHL Totals		**84**	**13**	**17**	**30**	**62**	....	....	....	....	....

a CCHA First All-Star Team (1986)
b NCAA West First All-American Team (1986)
Signed as a free agent by **NY Rangers**, August 15, 1986. Traded to **Buffalo** by **NY Rangers** with Rangers' fifth round choice (Alexander Mogilny) in 1988 Entry Draft for Paul Cyr and Buffalo's tenth round choice (Eric Fenton) in 1988 Entry Draft, December 31, 1987.

DOOLEY, SEAN

Defense. Shoots left. 6'3", 215 lbs.   Born, Ipswich, MA, March 22, 1969.
(Buffalo's 8th choice, 148th overall, in 1987 Entry Draft).

				Regular Season					Playoffs			
Season	Club	Lea	GP	G	A	TP	PIM	GP	G	A	TP	PIM
1986-87	Groton	HS	23	9	17	26	....	....	....	....	....	....
1987-88	Merrimack	NCAA	3	0	0	0	0	....	....	....	....	....
1988-89	Merrimack	NCAA	19	2	8	10	10	....	....	....	....	....

DORE, DANIEL

Right wing. Shoots right. 6'3", 202 lbs.   Born, St. Jerome, Que., April 9, 1970.
(Quebec's 2nd choice, 5th overall, in 1988 Entry Draft).

				Regular Season					Playoffs			
Season	Club	Lea	GP	G	A	TP	PIM	GP	G	A	TP	PIM
1986-87	Drummondville	QMJHL	68	23	41	64	229	8	0	1	1	18
1987-88	Drummondville	QMJHL	64	24	39	63	218	17	7	11	18	42
1988-89	Drummondville	QMJHL	62	33	58	91	236	4	2	3	5	14

DORION, DAN

Center. Shoots right. 5'9", 180 lbs.   Born, Astoria, NY, March 2, 1963.
(New Jersey's 10th choice, 232nd over-all, in 1982 Entry Draft).

				Regular Season					Playoffs			
Season	Club	Lea	GP	G	A	TP	PIM	GP	G	A	TP	PIM
1981-82	Austin	USHL	48	53	44	97	41	....	....	....	....	....
1982-83	W. Michigan	CCHA	34	11	20	31	23	....	....	....	....	....
1983-84	W. Michigan	CCHA	42	41	50	91	42	....	....	....	....	....
1984-85	W. Michigan	CCHA	39	21	46	67	28	....	....	....	....	....
1985-86abc	W. Michigan	CCHA	42	42	62	104	48	....	....	....	....	....
	New Jersey	**NHL**	**3**	**1**	**1**	**2**	**0**	....	....	....	....	....
	Maine	AHL	....	....	....	....	....	5	2	2	4	0
1986-87	Maine	AHL	70	16	22	38	47	....	....	....	....	....
1987-88	**New Jersey**	**NHL**	**1**	**0**	**0**	**0**	**2**	....	....	....	....	....
	Utica	AHL	65	30	35	65	98	....	....	....	....	....
1988-89	Maine	AHL	16	2	3	5	13	....	....	....	....	....
	Utica	AHL	15	7	4	11	19	....	....	....	....	....
	NHL Totals		**4**	**1**	**1**	**2**	**2**	....	....	....	....	....

a NCAA West First All-American Team (1986)
b CCHA First All-Star Team (1986)
c CCHA Player of the Year (1986)
Traded to **Boston** by **New Jersey** for Jean-Marc Lanthier, December 9, 1988.

DORNIC, IVAN

Left wing. Shoots left. 6', 185 lbs.   Born, Bratislava, Czechoslovakia, June 26, 1962.
(Edmonton's 7th choice, 126th overall, in 1984 Entry Draft).

				Regular Season					Playoffs			
Season	Club	Lea	GP	G	A	TP	PIM	GP	G	A	TP	PIM
1986-87	Bratislava	Czech.	32	15	8	23	....	....	....	....	....	....
1987-88	Bratislava	Czech.	28	6	9	15	....	....	....	....	....	....
1988-89	Bratislava	Czech.	35	6	6	12	....	....	....	....	....	....

DOUCET, WAYNE

Left wing. Shoots left. 6'2", 203 lbs.   Born, Etobicoke, Ont., June 19, 1970.
(New York Islanders' 2nd choice, 29th overall, in 1988 Entry Draft).

				Regular Season					Playoffs			
Season	Club	Lea	GP	G	A	TP	PIM	GP	G	A	TP	PIM
1986-87	Sudbury	OHL	64	20	28	48	85	....	....	....	....	....
1987-88	Hamilton	OHL	60	20	18	38	127	1	0	0	0	8
1988-89	Springfield	AHL	6	2	2	4	4	....	....	....	....	....
	North Bay	OHL	11	3	2	5	58	....	....	....	....	....
	Kingston	OHL	53	22	29	51	193	....	....	....	....	....

DOURIS, PETER

Center. Shoots right. 6'1", 195 lbs.   Born, Toronto, Ont., February 19, 1966.
(Winnipeg's 1st choice, 30th over-all, in 1984 Entry Draft).

				Regular Season					Playoffs			
Season	Club	Lea	GP	G	A	TP	PIM	GP	G	A	TP	PIM
1983-84	N. Hampshire	ECAC	37	19	15	34	14	....	....	....	....	....
1984-85	N. Hampshire	H.E.	42	27	24	51	34	....	....	....	....	....
1985-86	**Winnipeg**	**NHL**	**11**	**0**	**0**	**0**	**0**	....	....	....	....	....
	Cdn. Olympic	....	33	16	7	23	18	....	....	....	....	....
1986-87	**Winnipeg**	**NHL**	**6**	**0**	**0**	**0**	**0**	....	....	....	....	....
	Sherbrooke	AHL	62	14	28	42	24	17	7	15	22	16
1987-88	**Winnipeg**	**NHL**	**4**	**0**	**2**	**2**	**0**	**1**	**0**	**0**	**0**	**0**
	Moncton	AHL	73	42	37	79	53	....	....	....	....	....
1988-89	Peoria	IHL	81	28	41	69	32	4	1	2	3	0
	NHL Totals		**21**	**0**	**2**	**2**	**0**	**1**	**0**	**0**	**0**	**0**

Traded to **St. Louis** by **Winnipeg** for Kent Carlson and St. Louis' twelfth-round choice (Sergei Kharin) in 1989 Entry Draft and St. Louis' fourth-round choice in 1990 Entry Draft, September 29, 1988. Signed as a free agent by **Boston**, June 27, 1989.

DOWD, BRIAN

Defense. Shoots left. 6'1", 190 lbs.   Born, Hamilton, Ont., August 27, 1965.
(Edmonton's 1st choice, 24th overall, in 1988 Supplemental Draft).

			Regular Season					Playoffs				
Season	Club	Lea	GP	G	A	TP	PIM	GP	G	A	TP	PIM
1984-85	Northeastern	H.E.	24	1	8	9	44	....	....	....	....	....
1985-86	Northeastern	H.E.	28	0	3	3	36	....	....	....	....	....
1986-87	Northeastern	H.E.	34	8	13	21	40	....	....	....	....	....
1987-88ab	Northeastern	H.E.	37	6	21	27	52	....	....	....	....	....
1988-89	Fort Wayne	IHL	62	9	24	33	39	6	0	3	3	8

a Hockey East First All-Star Team (1988)
b NCAA East Second All-Star Team (1988)

DOWD, JAMES (JIM)

Right wing. Shoots right. 6'1", 185 lbs.   Born, Brick, NJ, December 25, 1968.
(New Jersey's 7th choice, 149th overall, in 1987 Entry Draft).

			Regular Season					Playoffs				
Season	Club	Lea	GP	G	A	TP	PIM	GP	G	A	TP	PIM
1986-87	Brick	HS	20	62	53	115	....	....	....	....	....	....
1987-88	Lake Superior	CCHA	45	18	27	45	16	....	....	....	....	....
1988-89	Lake Superior	CCHA	46	24	35	59	40	....	....	....	....	....

DOYLE, ROB

Defense. Shoots right. 5'11", 185 lbs.   Born, Lindsay, Ont., February 10, 1964.
(Detroit's 2nd choice, 6th overall, in 1986 Supplemental Draft).

			Regular Season					Playoffs				
Season	Club	Lea	GP	G	A	TP	PIM	GP	G	A	TP	PIM
1983-84	Colorado	WCHA	34	5	29	34	112	....	....	....	....	....
1984-85	Colorado	WCHA	37	11	44	55	136	....	....	....	....	....
1985-86a	Colorado	WCHA	40	18	41	59	73	....	....	....	....	....
1986-87bc	Colorado	WCHA	42	17	37	54	72	....	....	....	....	....
1987-88	Flint	IHL	37	22	22	44	85	....	....	....	....	....
	Adirondack	AHL	40	11	28	39	48	3	0	3	3	2
1988-89	Adirondack	AHL	70	24	52	76	44	17	8	13	21	27

a WCHA Second All-Star Team (1986)
b NCAA West Second All-American Team (1987)
c WCHA First All-Star Team (1987)

DOYLE, SHANE

Defense. Shoots left. 6'1", 200 lbs.   Born, Lindsay, Ont., April 26, 1967.
(Vancouver's 3rd choice, 46th over-all, in 1985 Entry Draft).

			Regular Season					Playoffs				
Season	Club	Lea	GP	G	A	TP	PIM	GP	G	A	TP	PIM
1984-85	Belleville	OHL	59	2	26	28	129	11	1	3	4	11
1985-86	Cornwall	OHL	55	4	28	32	206	6	1	0	1	17
1986-87	Oshawa	OHL	46	9	13	22	168	23	4	4	8	115
1987-88	Utica	AHL	14	0	1	1	38	....	....	....	....	....
	Flint	IHL	13	1	1	2	81	....	....	....	....	....
	Oshawa	OHL	21	3	18	21	66	3	0	2	2	6
1988-89	Indianapolis	IHL	62	4	36	40	224	....	....	....	....	....

Rights traded to **New Jersey** by **Vancouver** for New Jersey's twelfth-round draft choice (Neil Eisenhut) in 1987 Entry Draft, June 1, 1987.

DOYON, MARIO

Defense. Shoots right. 6', 175 lbs.   Born, Quebec City, Que., August 27, 1968.
(Chicago's 5th choice, 119th overall, in 1986 Entry Draft).

			Regular Season					Playoffs				
Season	Club	Lea	GP	G	A	TP	PIM	GP	G	A	TP	PIM
1985-86	Drummondville	QMJHL	71	5	14	19	129	23	5	4	9	32
1986-87	Drummondville	QMJHL	65	18	47	65	150	8	1	3	4	30
1987-88	Drummondville	QMJHL	68	23	54	77	233	17	3	14	17	46
1988-89	**Chicago**	**NHL**	7	1	1	2	6	....	....	....	....	....
	Saginaw	IHL	71	16	32	48	69	6	0	0	0	8
	NHL Totals		7	1	1	2	6	....	....	....	....	....

DRAPER, KRIS

Center. Shoots left. 5'11", 190 lbs.   Born, Toronto, Ont., May 24, 1971.
(Winnipeg's 4th choice, 62nd overall, in 1989 Entry Draft).

			Regular Season					Playoffs				
Season	Club	Lea	GP	G	A	TP	PIM	GP	G	A	TP	PIM
1987-88	Don Mills	Midget	40	35	32	67	46	....	....	....	....	....
1988-89	Cdn. National	....	60	11	15	26	16	....	....	....	....	....

DRIVER, BRUCE

Defense. Shoots left. 6', 185 lbs.   Born, Toronto, Ont., April 29, 1962.
(Colorado's 6th choice, 108th over-all, in 1981 Entry Draft).

			Regular Season					Playoffs				
Season	Club	Lea	GP	G	A	TP	PIM	GP	G	A	TP	PIM
1980-81	U. Wisconsin	WCHA	42	5	15	20	42	....	....	....	....	....
1981-82ab	U. Wisconsin	WCHA	46	7	37	44	84	....	....	....	....	....
1982-83	U. Wisconsin	WCHA	49	19	42	61	100	....	....	....	....	....
1983-84	Cdn. Olympic	...	61	11	17	28	44	....	....	....	....	....
	New Jersey	**NHL**	4	0	2	2	0	....	....	....	....	....
	Maine	AHL	12	2	6	8	15	16	0	10	10	8
1984-85	**New Jersey**	**NHL**	67	9	23	32	36	....	....	....	....	....
1985-86	**New Jersey**	**NHL**	40	3	15	18	32	....	....	....	....	....
	Maine	AHL	15	4	7	11	16	....	....	....	....	....
1986-87	**New Jersey**	**NHL**	74	6	28	34	36	....	....	....	....	....
1987-88	**New Jersey**	**NHL**	74	15	40	55	68	20	3	7	10	14
1988-89	**New Jersey**	**NHL**	27	1	15	16	24	....	....	....	....	....
	NHL Totals		286	34	123	157	196	20	3	7	10	14

a WCHA First All-Team (1982)
b NCAA All-Tournament Team (1982)

DRUCE, JOHN

Right wing. Shoots left. 6'2", 200 lbs.   Born, Peterborough, Ont., February 23, 1966.
(Washington's 2nd choice, 40th over-all, in 1985 Entry Draft).

			Regular Season					Playoffs				
Season	Club	Lea	GP	G	A	TP	PIM	GP	G	A	TP	PIM
1984-85	Peterborough	OHL	54	12	14	26	90	17	6	2	8	21
1985-86	Peterborough	OHL	49	22	24	46	84	16	0	5	5	34
1986-87	Binghamton	AHL	77	13	9	22	131	12	0	3	3	28
1987-88	Binghamton	AHL	68	32	29	61	82	1	0	0	0	0
1988-89	**Washington**	**NHL**	48	8	7	15	62	1	0	0	0	0
	Baltimore	AHL	16	2	11	13	10	....	....	....	....	....
	NHL Totals		48	8	7	15	62	1	0	0	0	0

DRULIA, STAN

Right wing. Shoots right. 5'10", 190 lbs.   Born, Elmira, NY, January 5, 1968.
(Pittsburgh's 11th choice, 214th overall, in 1986 Entry Draft).

			Regular Season					Playoffs				
Season	Club	Lea	GP	G	A	TP	PIM	GP	G	A	TP	PIM
1985-86	Belleville	OHL	66	43	36	79	73	....	....	....	....	....
1986-87	Hamilton	OHL	55	27	51	78	26	....	....	....	....	....
1987-88a	Hamilton	OHL	65	52	69	121	44	14	8	16	24	12
1988-89	Maine	AHL	3	1	1	2	0	....	....	....	....	....
b	Niagara Falls	OHL	47	52	93	145	59	17	11	*6	37	18

a OHL Third All-Star Team (1988)
b OHL First All-Star Team (1989)

DRURY, TED

Center. Shoots left. 6', 185 lbs.   Born, Boston, MA, September 13, 1971.
(Calgary's 2nd choice, 42nd overall, in 1989 Entry Draft).

			Regular Season					Playoffs				
Season	Club	Lea	GP	G	A	TP	PIM	GP	G	A	TP	PIM
1987-88	Fairfield Prep	HS	....	21	28	49	....	....	....	....	....	....
1988-89	Fairfield Prep	HS	....	35	31	66	....	....	....	....	....	....

DUCHESNE, GAETAN

(doo SHAYN)

Left wing. Shoots left. 5'11", 197 lbs.   Born, Quebec City, Que., July 11, 1962.
(Washington's 8th choice, 152nd over-all, in 1981 Entry Draft).

			Regular Season					Playoffs				
Season	Club	Lea	GP	G	A	TP	PIM	GP	G	A	TP	PIM
1979-80	Quebec	QJHL	46	9	28	37	22	5	0	2	2	9
1980-81	Quebec	QJHL	72	27	45	72	63	7	1	4	5	6
1981-82	**Washington**	**NHL**	74	9	14	23	46	....	....	....	....	....
1982-83	Hershey	AHL	1	1	0	1	0	....	....	....	....	....
	Washington	**NHL**	77	18	19	37	52	4	1	1	2	4
1983-84	**Washington**	**NHL**	79	17	19	36	29	8	2	1	3	2
1984-85	**Washington**	**NHL**	67	15	23	38	32	5	0	1	1	7
1985-86	**Washington**	**NHL**	80	11	28	39	32	9	4	3	7	12
1986-87	**Washington**	**NHL**	74	17	35	52	53	7	3	0	3	14
1987-88	**Quebec**	**NHL**	80	24	23	47	83	....	....	....	....	....
1988-89	**Quebec**	**NHL**	70	8	21	29	56	....	....	....	....	....
	NHL Totals		601	119	182	301	383	33	10	6	16	39

Traded to **Quebec** by **Washington** with Alan Haworth and Washington's first-round choice (Joe Sakic) in 1987 Entry Draft for Clint Malarchuk and Dale Hunter, June 13, 1987. Traded to **Minnesota** by **Quebec** for Kevin Kaminsky, June 19, 1989.

DUCHESNE, STEVE

Defense. Shoots left. 5'11", 190 lbs.   Born, Sept-Iles, Que., June 30, 1965.

			Regular Season					Playoffs				
Season	Club	Lea	GP	G	A	TP	PIM	GP	G	A	TP	PIM
1983-84	Drummondville	QMJHL	67	1	34	35	79	....	....	....	....	....
1984-85a	Drummondville	QMJHL	65	22	54	76	94	5	4	7	11	8
1985-86	New Haven	AHL	75	14	35	49	76	5	0	2	2	9
1986-87b	**Los Angeles**	**NHL**	75	13	25	38	74	5	2	2	4	4
1987-88	**Los Angeles**	**NHL**	71	16	39	55	109	5	1	3	4	14
1988-89	**Los Angeles**	**NHL**	79	25	50	75	31	11	4	4	8	12
	NHL Totals		225	54	114	168	214	21	7	9	16	30

a QMJHL First All-Star Team (1985)
b Named to NHL All-Rookie Team (1987)
Played in NHL All-Star Game (1989)
Signed as a free agent by **Los Angeles,** October 1, 1984.

DUCOLON, TOBY

Right wing. Shoots right. 6', 195 lbs.   Born, St. Albans, VT, June 18, 1966.
(St. Louis' 3rd choice, 50th over-all, in 1984 Entry Draft).

			Regular Season					Playoffs				
Season	Club	Lea	GP	G	A	TP	PIM	GP	G	A	TP	PIM
1984-85	U. of Vermont	ECAC	24	7	4	11	14	....	....	....	....	....
1985-86	U. of Vermont	ECAC	30	10	6	16	48	....	....	....	....	....
1986-87	U. of Vermont	ECAC	32	9	11	20	42	....	....	....	....	....
1987-88	U. of Vermont	ECAC	34	21	18	39	62	....	....	....	....	....
1988-89	Peoria	IHL	73	17	33	50	58	4	0	0	0	9

DUFRESNE, DONALD

Defense. Shoots left. 6', 190 lbs.   Born, Quebec City, Que., April 10, 1967.
(Montreal's 8th choice, 117th over-all, in 1985 Entry Draft).

			Regular Season					Playoffs				
Season	Club	Lea	GP	G	A	TP	PIM	GP	G	A	TP	PIM
1983-84	Trois Rivieres	QMJHL	67	7	12	19	97	....	....	....	....	....
1984-85	Trois Rivieres	QMJHL	65	5	30	35	112	7	1	3	4	12
1985-86a	Trois Rivieres	QMJHL	63	8	32	40	160	1	0	0	0	0
1986-87a	Longueuil	QMJHL	67	5	29	34	97	20	1	8	9	38
1987-88	Sherbrooke	AHL	47	1	8	9	107	6	1	0	1	34
1988-89	**Montreal**	**NHL**	13	0	1	1	43	6	1	1	2	4
	Sherbrooke	AHL	47	0	12	12	170	....	....	....	....	....
	NHL Totals		13	0	1	1	43	6	1	1	2	4

a QMJHL Second All-Star Team (1986, 1987).

DUGGAN, KEN

Defense. Shoots left. 6'3", 210 lbs. Born, Toronto, Ont., February 21, 1963.

			Regular Season					Playoffs				
Season	Club	Lea	GP	G	A	TP	PIM	GP	G	A	TP	PIM
1982-83	U. Toronto	OUAA	35	0	5	5	32	....	....	....	....	....
1983-84	U. Toronto	OUAA	47	11	17	28	54	....	....	....	....	....
1984-85	U. Toronto	OUAA	45	6	19	25	105	....	....	....	....	....
1985-86	U. Toronto	OUAA	44	13	41	54	111	....	....	....	....	....
1986-87	Flint	IHL	66	2	23	25	51	....	....	....	....	....
	New Haven	AHL	13	0	1	1	4	....	....	....	....	....
1987-88	**Minnesota**	**NHL**	**1**	**0**	**0**	**0**	**0**	....	....	....	....	....
	Flint	IHL	1	0	0	0	0	....	....	....	....	....
1988-89	Cdn. National	....	3	0	1	1	2	....	....	....	....	....
	NHL Totals		**1**	**0**	**0**	**0**	**0**	....	....	....	....	....

Signed as a free agent by **NY Rangers**, May 22, 1986.

DUGUAY, RONALD (RON) (doo-GAY)

Center. Shoots right. 6'2", 210 lbs. Born, Sudbury, Ont., July 6, 1957.
(NY Rangers' 2nd choice, 13th over-all, in 1977 Amateur Draft).

			Regular Season					Playoffs				
Season	Club	Lea	GP	G	A	TP	PIM	GP	G	A	TP	PIM
1975-76a	Sudbury	OHA	61	42	92	134	101	17	11	9	20	37
1976-77	Sudbury	OHA	61	43	66	109	109	6	4	3	7	5
1977-78	**NY Rangers**	**NHL**	**71**	**20**	**20**	**40**	**43**	**3**	**1**	**1**	**2**	**2**
1978-79	**NY Rangers**	**NHL**	**79**	**27**	**36**	**63**	**35**	**18**	**5**	**4**	**9**	**11**
1979-80	**NY Rangers**	**NHL**	**73**	**28**	**22**	**50**	**37**	**9**	**5**	**2**	**7**	**11**
1980-81	**NY Rangers**	**NHL**	**50**	**17**	**21**	**38**	**83**	**14**	**8**	**9**	**17**	**16**
1981-82	**NY Rangers**	**NHL**	**72**	**40**	**36**	**76**	**82**	**10**	**5**	**1**	**6**	**31**
1982-83	**NY Rangers**	**NHL**	**72**	**19**	**25**	**44**	**58**	**9**	**2**	**2**	**4**	**28**
1983-84	**Detroit**	**NHL**	**80**	**33**	**47**	**80**	**34**	**4**	**2**	**3**	**5**	**2**
1984-85	**Detroit**	**NHL**	**80**	**38**	**51**	**89**	**51**	**3**	**1**	**0**	**1**	**7**
1985-86	**Detroit**	**NHL**	**67**	**19**	**29**	**48**	**26**	....	....	....	....	....
	Pittsburgh	**NHL**	**13**	**6**	**7**	**13**	**6**	....	....	....	....	....
1986-87	**Pittsburgh**	**NHL**	**40**	**5**	**13**	**18**	**30**	....	....	....	....	....
	NY Rangers	**NHL**	**34**	**9**	**12**	**21**	**9**	**6**	**2**	**0**	**2**	**4**
1987-88	**NY Rangers**	**NHL**	**48**	**4**	**4**	**8**	**23**	....	....	....	....	....
	Colorado	IHL	2	0	0	0	0	....	....	....	....	....
	Los Angeles	**NHL**	**15**	**2**	**6**	**8**	**17**	**2**	**0**	**0**	**0**	**0**
1988-89	**Los Angeles**	**NHL**	**70**	**7**	**17**	**24**	**48**	**11**	**0**	**0**	**0**	**6**
	NHL Totals		**864**	**274**	**346**	**620**	**582**	**89**	**31**	**22**	**53**	**118**

a OHA Third All-Star Team (1976)

Played in NHL All-Star Game (1982)

Traded to **Detroit** by **NY Rangers** with Eddie Mio and Eddie Johnstone for Willie Huber, Mark Osborne and Mike Blaisdell, June 13, 1983. Traded to **Pittsburgh** by **Detroit** for Doug Shedden, March 11, 1986. Traded to **NY Rangers** by **Pittsburgh** for Chris Kontos, January 21, 1987. Traded to **Los Angeles** by **NY Rangers** for Mark Hardy, February 23, 1988.

DUMAS, CLAUDE

Center. Shoots right. 6'1", 175 lbs. Born, Thetford Mines, Que., January 10, 1967.
(Washington's 6th choice, 103rd over-all, in 1985 Entry Draft).

			Regular Season					Playoffs				
Season	Club	Lea	GP	G	A	TP	PIM	GP	G	A	TP	PIM
1984-85	Granby	QMJHL	62	19	37	56	34	....	....	....	....	....
1985-86	Granby	QMJHL	64	31	58	89	78	....	....	....	....	....
	Binghamton	AHL	7	2	2	4	0	....	....	....	....	....
1986-87	Granby	QMJHL	67	50	82	132	59	8	6	6	12	2
	Fort Wayne	IHL	3	1	3	4	4	7	4	0	4	0
1987-88	Fort Wayne	IHL	80	28	45	73	32	6	0	2	2	2
1988-89	Baltimore	AHL	1	1	0	1	0	....	....	....	....	....
	Fort Wayne	IHL	71	12	20	32	40	1	0	0	0	0

DUMAS, ROBERT

Defense. Shoots right. 6'1", 200 lbs. Born, Sprint River, Alta., March 19, 1969.
(St. Louis' 9th choice, 180th overall, in 1987 Entry Draft).

			Regular Season					Playoffs				
Season	Club	Lea	GP	G	A	TP	PIM	GP	G	A	TP	PIM
1986-87	Seattle	WHL	72	8	29	37	259	....	....	....	....	....
1987-88	Seattle	WHL	67	12	25	37	218	....	....	....	....	....
1988-89	Peoria	IHL	10	0	0	0	51	4	0	0	0	23
	Seattle	WHL	70	10	27	37	151	....	....	....	....	....

DUMONT, MARC

Left wing. Shoots left. 6', 190 lbs. Born, Beauport, Que., January 28, 1967.

			Regular Season					Playoffs				
Season	Club	Lea	GP	G	A	TP	PIM	GP	G	A	TP	PIM
1984-85	Hull	QMJHL	59	8	13	21	43	5	1	1	2	0
1985-86	Laval	QMJHL	56	14	12	26	65	14	2	7	9	17
1986-87	Laval	QMJHL	67	29	47	76	53	15	10	8	18	6
1987-88	Peoria	IHL	49	5	6	11	31	....	....	....	....	....
1988-89	Flint	IHL	4	1	1	2	0	....	....	....	....	....

Signed as a free agent by **St. Louis**, September 29, 1985.

DUNBAR, DALE

Defense. Shoots left. 6', 200 lbs. Born, Winthrop, MA, October 14, 1961.

			Regular Season					Playoffs				
Season	Club	Lea	GP	G	A	TP	PIM	GP	G	A	TP	PIM
1982-83	Boston U.	ECAC	23	1	7	8	36	....	....	....	....	....
1983-84	Boston U.	ECAC	34	0	15	23	49	....	....	....	....	....
1984-85	Boston U.	H.E.	39	2	19	21	62	....	....	....	....	....
1985-86	**Vancouver**	**NHL**	**1**	**0**	**0**	**0**	**2**	....	....	....	....	....
	Fredericton	AHL	32	2	10	12	26	....	....	....	....	....
1986-87	Peoria	IHL	46	2	8	10	32	....	....	....	....	....
1987-88	Maine	AHL	66	1	7	8	120	9	1	1	2	33
1988-89	**Boston**	**NHL**	**1**	**0**	**0**	**0**	**0**	....	....	....	....	....
	Maine	AHL	65	1	9	10	49	....	....	....	....	....
	NHL Totals		**2**	**0**	**0**	**0**	**2**	....	....	....	....	....

Signed as a free agent by **Vancouver**, May 10, 1985.

DUNCAN, IAIN

Left wing. Shoots left. 6'1", 200 lbs. Born, Weston, Ont., August 4, 1963.
(Winnipeg's 8th choice, 139th over-all, in 1983 Entry Draft).

			Regular Season					Playoffs				
Season	Club	Lea	GP	G	A	TP	PIM	GP	G	A	TP	PIM
1983-84	Bowling Green	CCHA	44	11	20	31	65	....	....	....	....	....
1984-85	Bowling Green	CCHA	37	9	21	30	105	....	....	....	....	....
1985-86	Bowling Green	CCHA	41	26	26	52	124	....	....	....	....	....
1986-87	**Winnipeg**	**NHL**	**6**	**1**	**2**	**3**	**0**	**7**	**0**	**2**	**2**	**6**
a	Bowling Green	CCHA	39	28	40	68	141	....	....	....	....	....
1987-88b	**Winnipeg**	**NHL**	**62**	**19**	**23**	**42**	**73**	**4**	**0**	**1**	**1**	**0**
	Moncton	AHL	8	1	3	4	26	....	....	....	....	....
1988-89	**Winnipeg**	**NHL**	**57**	**14**	**30**	**44**	**74**	....	....	....	....	....
	NHL Totals		**125**	**34**	**55**	**89**	**147**	**11**	**0**	**3**	**3**	**6**

a CCHA First All-Star Team (1987)
b NHL All-Rookie Team (1988)

DUNCANSON, CRAIG

Left wing. Shoots left. 6', 190 lbs. Born, Sudbury, Ont., March 17, 1967.
(Los Angeles' 1st choice, 9th over-all, in 1985 Entry Draft).

			Regular Season					Playoffs				
Season	Club	Lea	GP	G	A	TP	PIM	GP	G	A	TP	PIM
1982-83	St.Michael's	Jr. B	32	14	19	33	68	....	....	....	....	....
1983-84	Sudbury	OHL	62	38	38	76	176	....	....	....	....	....
1984-85a	Sudbury	OHL	53	35	28	63	129	....	....	....	....	....
1985-86	**Los Angeles**	**NHL**	**2**	**0**	**1**	**1**	**0**	....	....	....	....	....
	Cornwall	OHL	61	43	67	110	190	6	4	7	11	2
	New Haven	AHL	....	....	....	....	....	2	0	0	0	5
1986-87	**Los Angeles**	**NHL**	**2**	**0**	**0**	**0**	**24**	....	....	....	....	....
	Cornwall	OHL	52	22	45	67	88	5	4	3	7	20
1987-88	**Los Angeles**	**NHL**	**9**	**0**	**0**	**0**	**12**	....	....	....	....	....
	New Haven	AHL	57	15	25	40	170	....	....	....	....	....
1988-89	**Los Angeles**	**NHL**	**5**	**0**	**0**	**0**	**0**	....	....	....	....	....
	New Haven	AHL	69	25	39	64	200	17	4	8	12	60
	NHL Totals		**18**	**0**	**1**	**1**	**36**	....	....	....	....	....

a OHL Third All-Star Team (1985)

DUNDAS, ROCKY

Right wing. Shoots right. 6', 195 lbs. Born, Regina, Sask., January 30, 1967.
(Montreal's 4th choice, 47th over-all, in 1985 Entry Draft).

			Regular Season					Playoffs				
Season	Club	Lea	GP	G	A	TP	PIM	GP	G	A	TP	PIM
1983-84	Kelowna	WHL	72	15	24	39	57	....	....	....	....	....
1984-85	Kelowna	WHL	71	32	44	76	117	6	1	1	2	14
1985-86	Spokane	WHL	71	31	70	101	160	9	2	5	7	28
1986-87	Spokane	WHL	19	13	17	30	69	....	....	....	....	....
	Medicine Hat	WHL	29	22	24	46	63	20	4	8	12	44
1987-88	Baltimore	AHL	9	0	1	1	46	....	....	....	....	....
	Sherbrooke	AHL	38	9	6	15	104	3	0	0	0	7
1988-89	Sherbrooke	AHL	63	12	29	41	212	2	2	0	2	8

DUNN, RICHARD L. (RICHIE)

Defense. Shoots left. 6', 200 lbs. Born, Boston, MA, May 12, 1957.

			Regular Season					Playoffs				
Season	Club	Lea	GP	G	A	TP	PIM	GP	G	A	TP	PIM
1975-76	Kingston	OHA	61	7	18	25	62	....	....	....	....	....
1976-77	Windsor	OHA	65	5	21	26	98	9	0	5	5	4
1977-78	Hershey	AHL	54	7	22	29	17	....	....	....	....	....
	Buffalo	**NHL**	**25**	**0**	**3**	**3**	**16**	**1**	**0**	**0**	**0**	**2**
1978-79	**Buffalo**	**NHL**	**24**	**0**	**3**	**3**	**14**	....	....	....	....	....
	Hershey	AHL	34	5	18	23	10	4	0	1	1	4
1979-80	**Buffalo**	**NHL**	**80**	**7**	**31**	**38**	**61**	**14**	**2**	**8**	**10**	**8**
1980-81	**Buffalo**	**NHL**	**79**	**7**	**42**	**49**	**34**	**8**	**0**	**5**	**5**	**6**
1981-82	**Buffalo**	**NHL**	**72**	**7**	**19**	**26**	**73**	**4**	**0**	**1**	**1**	**0**
1982-83	**Calgary**	**NHL**	**80**	**3**	**11**	**14**	**47**	**9**	**1**	**1**	**2**	**8**
1983-84	**Hartford**	**NHL**	**63**	**5**	**20**	**25**	**30**	....	....	....	....	....
1984-85	**Hartford**	**NHL**	**13**	**1**	**4**	**5**	**2**	....	....	....	....	....
ab	Binghamton	AHL	64	9	39	48	43	8	2	2	4	8
1985-86	**Buffalo**	**NHL**	**29**	**4**	**5**	**9**	**25**	....	....	....	....	....
	Rochester	AHL	34	6	17	23	12	....	....	....	....	....
1986-87	**Buffalo**	**NHL**	**2**	**0**	**1**	**1**	**2**	....	....	....	....	....
b	Rochester	AHL	64	6	26	32	47	18	1	6	7	6
1987-88	**Buffalo**	**NHL**	**12**	**2**	**0**	**2**	**8**	....	....	....	....	....
c	Rochester	AHL	68	12	35	47	52	7	3	3	6	2
1988-89	**Buffalo**	**NHL**	**4**	**0**	**0**	**0**	**2**	....	....	....	....	....
	Rochester	AHL	69	9	35	44	81	....	....	....	....	....
	NHL Totals		**483**	**36**	**139**	**175**	**314**	**36**	**3**	**15**	**18**	**24**

a Won Eddie Shore Plaque (AHL Outstanding Defenseman 1985)
b AHL First All-Star Team (1985, 1987)
c AHL Second All-Star Team (1988)

Signed as free agent by **Buffalo**, October 3, 1977. Traded to **Calgary** by **Buffalo** with Don Edwards and Buffalo's second round choice (Richard Kromm) in 1982 Entry Draft for Calgary's first round choice (Paul Cyr) and second round choice (Jens Johansson) in the 1982 Entry Draft and Calgary's second round choice (John Tucker) in 1983 Entry Draft, June 9, 1982. In addition, the two clubs exchanged first round draft choices in 1983 — Buffalo claimed Normand Lacombe and Calgary selected Dan Quinn. Traded to **Hartford** by **Calgary** with Joel Quenneville for Mickey Volcan, July 5, 1983. Signed as a free agent by **Buffalo**, July 10, 1986.

DUPUIS, GUY

Defense. Shoots right. 6'2", 200 lbs. Born, Moncton, N.B., May 10, 1970.
(Detroit's 3rd choice, 47th overall, in 1988 Entry Draft).

			Regular Season					Playoffs				
Season	Club	Lea	GP	G	A	TP	PIM	GP	G	A	TP	PIM
1986-87	Hull	QMJHL	69	5	10	15	35	8	1	2	3	2
1987-88	Hull	QMJHL	69	14	34	48	72	19	3	8	11	29
1988-89a	Hull	QMJHL	70	15	56	71	89	9	3	3	6	8

a QMJHL Second All-Star Team (1989)

DUUS, JESPER

Defense. Shoots right. 5'11", 175 lbs.   Born, Rodovre, Denmark, November 24, 1967.
(Edmonton's 12th choice, 241st overall, in 1987 Entry Draft).

			Regular Season					Playoffs				
Season	Club	Lea	GP	G	A	TP	PIM	GP	G	A	TP	PIM
1983-84	Rodovre	Den.	17	0	0	0	0	1	0	0	0	0
1984-85	Rodovre	Den.	14	2	5	7	2	6	0	1	1	4
1985-86	Rodovre	Den.	24	3	5	8	28	6	1	2	3	4
1986-87	Rodovre	Den.	24	6	14	20	14	6	1	3	4	6
1987-88	Farjestad	Swe.	26	2	5	7	8	....	....	....	....	....
1988-89	Farjestad	Swe.	36	4	4	8	10	....	....	....	....	....

DUVAL, MURRAY

Defense. Shoots left. 6'1", 195 lbs.   Born, Thompson, Man., January 22, 1970.
(New York Rangers' 2nd choice, 26th overall, in 1988 Entry Draft).

			Regular Season					Playoffs				
Season	Club	Lea	GP	G	A	TP	PIM	GP	G	A	TP	PIM
1986-87	Spokane	WHL	27	2	6	8	21	....	....	....	....	....
1987-88	Spokane	WHL	70	26	37	63	104	15	5	2	7	22
1988-89	Tri-Cities	WHL	71	14	28	42	144	....	....	....	....	....

DYER, DEAN

Center. Shoots right. 6'3", 195 lbs.   Born, Sherwood Park, Alta., April 11, 1969.
(Hartford's 3rd choice, 74th overall, in 1988 Entry Draft).

			Regular Season					Playoffs				
Season	Club	Lea	GP	G	A	TP	PIM	GP	G	A	TP	PIM
1987-88	Lake Superior	CCHA	45	6	16	22	38	....	....	....	....	....
1988-89	Lake Superior	CCHA	41	4	11	15	52	....	....	....	....	....

DYKSTRA, STEVEN

Defense. Shoots left. 6'2", 210 lbs.   Born, Edmonton, Alta., December 1, 1962.

			Regular Season					Playoffs				
Season	Club	Lea	GP	G	A	TP	PIM	GP	G	A	TP	PIM
1981-82	Seattle	WHL	57	8	26	34	139	10	3	1	4	42
1982-83	Rochester	AHL	70	2	16	18	100	15	0	5	5	27
1983-84	Rochester	AHL	63	3	19	22	141	6	0	0	0	46
1984-85	Flint	IHL	15	1	7	8	36	....	....	....	....	....
	Rochester	AHL	51	9	23	32	113	2	0	1	1	10
1985-86	**Buffalo**	**NHL**	64	4	21	25	108	....	....	....	....	....
1986-87	**Buffalo**	**NHL**	37	0	1	1	179	....	....	....	....	....
	Rochester	AHL	18	0	0	0	77	....	....	....	....	....
1987-88	**Buffalo**	**NHL**	27	1	1	2	91	....	....	....	....	....
	Rochester	AHL	7	0	1	1	33	....	....	....	....	....
	Edmonton	**NHL**	15	2	3	5	39	....	....	....	....	....
1988-89	**Pittsburgh**	**NHL**	65	1	6	7	126	1	0	0	0	2
	NHL Totals		208	8	32	40	543	1	0	0	0	2

Signed as a free agent by **Buffalo**, December 10, 1982. Traded to **Edmonton** by **Buffalo** with Buffalo's seventh round choice (David Payne) in 1989 Entry Draft for Scott Metcalfe and Edmonton's ninth round choice (Donald Audette) in 1989 Entry Draft, February 11, 1988. Claimed by **Pittsburgh** in NHL Waiver Draft, October 3, 1988.

EAGLES, MICHAEL (MIKE)

Center. Shoots left. 5'10", 180 lbs.   Born, Sussex, N.B., March 7, 1963.
(Quebec's 5th choice, 116th over-all, in 1981 Entry Draft).

			Regular Season					Playoffs				
Season	Club	Lea	GP	G	A	TP	PIM	GP	G	A	TP	PIM
1980-81	Kitchener	OHA	56	11	27	38	64	18	4	2	6	36
1981-82	Kitchener	OHL	62	26	40	66	148	15	3	11	14	27
1982-83	**Quebec**	**NHL**	2	0	0	0	2	....	....	....	....	....
	Kitchener	OHL	58	26	36	62	133	12	5	7	12	27
1983-84	Fredericton	AHL	68	13	29	42	85	4	0	0	0	5
1984-85	Fredericton	AHL	36	4	20	24	80	3	0	0	0	2
1985-86	**Quebec**	**NHL**	73	11	12	23	49	3	0	0	0	2
1986-87	**Quebec**	**NHL**	73	13	19	32	55	4	1	0	1	10
1987-88	**Quebec**	**NHL**	76	10	10	20	74	....	....	....	....	....
1988-89	**Chicago**	**NHL**	47	5	11	16	44	....	....	....	....	....
	NHL Totals		271	39	52	91	224	7	1	0	1	12

Traded to **Chicago** by **Quebec** for Bob Mason, July 5, 1988.

EAKINS, DALLAS

Defense. Shoots left. 6'2", 195 lbs.   Born, Dade City, FL, February 27, 1967.
(Washington's 11th choice, 208th over-all, in 1985 Entry Draft).

			Regular Season					Playoffs				
Season	Club	Lea	GP	G	A	TP	PIM	GP	G	A	TP	PIM
1984-85	Peterborough	OHL	48	0	8	8	96	7	0	0	0	18
1985-86	Peterborough	OHL	60	6	16	22	134	16	0	1	1	30
1986-87	Peterborough	OHL	54	3	11	14	145	12	1	4	5	37
1987-88	Peterborough	OHL	64	11	27	38	129	12	3	12	15	16
1988-89	Baltimore	AHL	62	0	10	10	139	....	....	....	....	....

EASTWOOD, MICHAEL

Center. Shoots right. 6'2", 190 lbs.   Born, Ottawa, Ont., July 1, 1967.
(Toronto's 5th choice, 91st overall, in 1987 Entry Draft).

			Regular Season					Playoffs				
Season	Club	Lea	GP	G	A	TP	PIM	GP	G	A	TP	PIM
1987-88	W. Michigan	CCHA	42	5	8	13	14	....	....	....	....	....
1988-89	W. Michigan	CCHA	40	10	13	23	87	....	....	....	....	....

EAVES, MURRAY

Center. Shoots right. 5'10", 185 lbs.   Born, Calgary, Alta., May 10, 1960.
(Winnipeg's 3rd choice, 44th over-all, in 1980 Entry Draft).

			Regular Season					Playoffs				
Season	Club	Lea	GP	G	A	TP	PIM	GP	G	A	TP	PIM
1978-79	U. of Michigan	WCHA	23	12	22	34	14	....	....	....	....	....
1979-80	U. of Michigan	WCHA	33	36	49	85	34	....	....	....	....	....
1980-81	**Winnipeg**	**NHL**	12	1	2	3	5	....	....	....	....	....
	Tulsa	CHL	59	24	34	58	59	8	5	5	10	13
1981-82	**Winnipeg**	**NHL**	2	0	0	0	0	....	....	....	....	....
	Tulsa	CHL	68	30	49	79	33	3	0	2	2	0
1982-83	**Winnipeg**	**NHL**	26	2	7	9	2	....	....	....	....	....
	Sherbrooke	AHL	40	25	34	59	16	....	....	....	....	....
1983-84	Sherbrooke	AHL	78	47	68	115	40	....	....	....	....	....
	Winnipeg	**NHL**	2	0	0	0	0	2	0	0	0	2
1984-85	**Winnipeg**	**NHL**	3	0	3	3	0	2	0	1	1	0
	Sherbrooke	AHL	47	26	42	68	28	15	5	13	18	35
1985-86	**Winnipeg**	**NHL**	4	1	0	1	0	....	....	....	....	....
	Sherbrooke	AHL	68	22	51	73	26	....	....	....	....	....
1986-87	Nova Scotia	AHL	76	26	38	64	46	4	1	1	2	2
1987-88	**Detroit**	**NHL**	7	0	1	1	2	....	....	....	....	....
	Adirondack	AHL	65	39	54	93	65	11	3	*11	14	8
1988-89ab	Adirondack	AHL	80	46	*72	118	11	16	*13	12	25	10
	NHL Totals		56	4	13	17	9	4	0	1	1	2

a AHL Second All-Star Team (1989)
b Won Fred Hunt Award (Sportsmanship-AHL) (1989)

Traded to **Edmonton** by **Winnipeg** for future considerations, July 3, 1986.

EDLUND, PAR

Right wing. Shoots right. 5'11", 180 lbs.   Born, Sweden, April 9, 1967.
(Los Angeles' 3rd choice, 30th over-all, in 1985 Entry Draft).

			Regular Season					Playoffs				
Season	Club	Lea	GP	G	A	TP	PIM	GP	G	A	TP	PIM
1983-84	Bjorkloven	Swe. Jr.	30	14	12	26	10	....	....	....	....	....
1984-85	Bjorkloven	Swe. Jr.	38	30	11	41	16	....	....	....	....	....
1985-86	Bjorkloven	Swe.	6	1	0	1	2	....	....	....	....	....
1986-87	Bjorkloven	Swe.	4	0	0	0	0	....	....	....	....	....
1987-88	Bjorkloven	Swe.	37	6	4	10	14	7	1	0	1	2
1988-89	Bjorkloven	Swe.	18	9	10	19	....	....	....	....	....	....

EHLERS, HEINZ

Center. Shoots left. 5'11", 175 lbs.   Born, Aalborg, Denmark, January 25, 1966.
(NY Rangers' 9th choice, 188th overall, in 1984 Entry Draft).

			Regular Season					Playoffs				
Season	Club	Lea	GP	G	A	TP	PIM	GP	G	A	TP	PIM
1984-85	Leksand	Swe.	31	10	6	16	10	....	....	....	....	....
1985-86	Leksand	Swe.	36	11	16	27	18	....	....	....	....	....
1986-87	Leksand	Swe.	36	14	21	35	32	....	....	....	....	....
1987-88	Leksand	Swe.	35	20	12	32	42	....	....	....	....	....
1988-89	Leksand	Swe.	33	13	27	40	40	3	1	1	2	18

EISENHUT, NEIL

Center. Shoots left. 6'1", 190 lbs.   Born, Oliver, B.C., January 9, 1967.
(Vancouver's 11th choice, 238th overall, in 1987 Entry Draft).

			Regular Season					Playoffs				
Season	Club	Lea	GP	G	A	TP	PIM	GP	G	A	TP	PIM
1986-87	Langley	BCJHL	43	41	34	75	....	....	....	....	....	....
1987-88	North Dakota	WCHA	42	12	20	32	14	....	....	....	....	....
1988-89	North Dakota	WCHA	41	22	16	38	20	....	....	....	....	....

EKLUND, PER-ERIK (PELLE)

Center. Shoots left. 5'10", 175 lbs.   Born, Stockholm, Sweden, March 22, 1963.
(Philadelphia's 8th choice, 167th over-all, in 1983 Entry Draft)

			Regular Season					Playoffs				
Season	Club	Lea	GP	G	A	TP	PIM	GP	G	A	TP	PIM
1981-82	AIK	Swe.	23	2	3	5	2	....	....	....	....	....
1982-83	AIK	Swe.	34	13	17	30	14	3	1	4	5	2
1983-84	AIK	Swe.	35	9	18	27	24	6	6	7	13	2
1984-85	AIK	Swe.	35	16	33	49	10	....	....	....	....	....
1985-86	**Philadelphia**	**NHL**	70	15	51	66	12	5	0	2	2	0
1986-87	**Philadelphia**	**NHL**	72	14	41	55	2	26	7	20	27	2
1987-88	**Philadelphia**	**NHL**	71	10	32	42	12	7	0	3	3	0
1988-89	**Philadelphia**	**NHL**	79	18	51	69	23	19	3	8	11	2
	NHL Totals		292	57	175	232	49	57	10	33	43	4

ELIK, TODD

Center. Shoots left. 6'2", 190 lbs.   Born, Brampton, Ont., April 15, 1966.

			Regular Season					Playoffs				
Season	Club	Lea	GP	G	A	TP	PIM	GP	G	A	TP	PIM
1984-85	Kingston	OHL	34	14	11	25	6	....	....	....	....	....
	North Bay	OHL	23	4	6	10	2	4	2	0	2	0
1985-86	North Bay	OHL	40	12	34	46	20	10	7	6	13	0
1986-87	U. of Regina	CWUAA	27	26	34	60	137	....	....	....	....	....
1987-88	Colorado	IHL	81	44	56	100	83	12	8	12	20	9
1988-89	New Haven	AHL	43	11	25	36	31	17	10	12	22	44
	Denver	IHL	28	20	15	35	22	....	....	....	....	....

Signed as a free agent by **NY Rangers**, February 26, 1988. Traded to **Los Angeles** by **NY Rangers** with Igor Liba, Michael Boyce and future considerations for Dean Kennedy and Denis Larocque, December 12, 1988.

ELLETT, DAVID

Defense. Shoots left. 6'1", 200 lbs. Born, Cleveland, Ohio, March 30, 1964.
(Winnipeg's 4th choice, 75th over-all, in 1982 Entry Draft).

			Regular Season					Playoffs				
Season	Club	Lea	GP	G	A	TP	PIM	GP	G	A	TP	PIM
1982-83	Bowling Green	CCHA	40	4	13	17	34	....	....	....	....	....
1983-84ab	Bowling Green	CCHA	43	15	39	54	96	....	....	....	....	....
1984-85	**Winnipeg**	**NHL**	**80**	**11**	**27**	**38**	**85**	**8**	**1**	**5**	**6**	**4**
1985-86	**Winnipeg**	**NHL**	**80**	**15**	**31**	**46**	**96**	**3**	**0**	**1**	**1**	**0**
1986-87	**Winnipeg**	**NHL**	**78**	**13**	**31**	**44**	**53**	**10**	**0**	**8**	**8**	**2**
1987-88	**Winnipeg**	**NHL**	**68**	**13**	**45**	**58**	**106**	**5**	**1**	**2**	**3**	**10**
1988-89	**Winnipeg**	**NHL**	**75**	**22**	**34**	**56**	**62**	....	....	....	....	....
	NHL Totals		**381**	**74**	**168**	**242**	**402**	**26**	**2**	**16**	**18**	**16**

a CCHA Second All-Star Team (1984).
b Named to NCAA All-Tournament Team (1984).
Played in NHL All-Star Game (1989)

ELLINGSEN, AGE

Defense. Shoots left. 6'5", 210 lbs. Born, Oslo, Norway, November 5, 1962.
(Edmonton's 8th choice, 168th overall, in 1987 Entry Draft).

			Regular Season					Playoffs				
Season	Club	Lea	GP	G	A	TP	PIM	GP	G	A	TP	PIM
1980-81	Furuset	Nor.	35	6	9	15	24	....	....	....	....	....
1981-82	Furuset	Nor.	35	6	8	14	40	....	....	....	....	....
1982-83	Furuset	Nor.	36	18	15	33	40	....	....	....	....	....
1983-84	Storhamar	Nor.	28	8	5	13	32	....	....	....	....	....
1984-85	Storhamar	Nor.	31	24	16	40	42	....	....	....	....	....
1985-86	Storhamar	Nor.	36	22	24	46	36	....	....	....	....	....
1986-87	Storhamar	Nor.	36	13	17	30	53	....	....	....	....	....
1987-88	Bjorkloven	Swe.	40	4	2	6	18	8	1	1	2	6
1988-89	Storhamar	Nor.	37	17	19	36	52	....	....	....	....	....

ELYNUIK, PAT

Right wing. Shoots right. 6', 185 lbs. Born, Foam Lake, Sask., October 30, 1967.
(Winnipeg's 1st choice, 7th over-all, in 1986 Entry Draft).

			Regular Season					Playoffs				
Season	Club	Lea	GP	G	A	TP	PIM	GP	G	A	TP	PIM
1984-85	Prince Albert	WHL	70	23	20	43	54	13	9	3	12	7
1985-86a	Prince Albert	WHL	68	53	53	106	62	20	7	9	16	17
1986-87a	Prince Albert	WHL	64	51	62	113	40	8	5	5	10	12
1987-88	**Winnipeg**	**NHL**	**13**	**1**	**3**	**4**	**12**	....	....	....	....	....
	Moncton	AHL	30	11	18	29	35	....	....	....	....	....
1988-89	**Winnipeg**	**NHL**	**56**	**26**	**25**	**51**	**29**	....	....	....	....	....
	Moncton	AHL	7	8	2	10	2	....	....	....	....	....
	NHL Totals		**69**	**27**	**28**	**55**	**41**	....	....	....	....	....

a WHL East All-Star Team (1986, 1987).

EMERSON, NELSON

Center. Shoots right. 5'11", 165 lbs. Born, Hamilton, Ont., August 17, 1967.
(St. Louis' 2nd choice, 44th over-all, in 1985 Entry Draft).

			Regular Season					Playoffs				
Season	Club	Lea	GP	G	A	TP	PIM	GP	G	A	TP	PIM
1985-86	Stratford	OPJHL	64	54	58	112	....	....	....	....	....	....
1986-87a	Bowling Green	CCHA	45	26	35	61	28	....	....	....	....	....
1987-88bc	Bowling Green	CCHA	45	34	49	83	54	....	....	....	....	....
1988-89d	Bowling Green	CCHA	44	22	46	68	46	....	....	....	....	....

a CCHA Freshman of the Year (1987)
b NCAA West Second All-American Team (1988)
c CCHA First All-Star Team (1988)
d CCHA Second All-Star Team (1989)

EMMONS, GARY

Center. Shoots right. 5'9", 180 lbs. Born, Winnipeg, Man., December 30, 1963.
(NY Rangers' 1st choice, 14th overall, in 1986 Supplemental Draft).

			Regular Season					Playoffs				
Season	Club	Lea	GP	G	A	TP	PIM	GP	G	A	TP	PIM
1983-84	N. Michigan	CCHA	40	28	21	49	42	....	....	....	....	....
1984-85	N. Michigan	CCHA	40	25	28	53	22	....	....	....	....	....
1985-86	N. Michigan	CCHA	36	45	30	75	34	....	....	....	....	....
1986-87	N. Michigan	CCHA	35	32	34	66	59	....	....	....	....	....
1987-88	Milwaukee	IHL	13	3	4	7	4	....	....	....	....	....
	Nova Scotia	AHL	59	18	27	45	22	....	....	....	....	....
1988-89	Cdn. National	....	49	16	26	42	42	....	....	....	....	....

Signed as a free agent by **Edmonton**, July 27, 1987.

ENDEAN, CRAIG

Left wing. Shoots left. 5'11", 170 lbs. Born, Kamloops, B.C., April 13, 1968.
(Winnipeg's 5th choice, 92nd overall, in 1986 Entry Draft).

			Regular Season					Playoffs				
Season	Club	Lea	GP	G	A	TP	PIM	GP	G	A	TP	PIM
1985-86	Seattle	WHL	70	58	70	128	34	5	5	1	6	0
1986-87	Regina	WHL	76	69	77	146	34	3	5	0	5	4
	Winnipeg	**NHL**	**2**	**0**	**1**	**1**	**0**	....	....	....	....	....
1987-88a	Regina	WHL	69	50	86	136	50	4	4	9	13	8
1988-89	Moncton	AHL	18	3	9	12	16	....	....	....	....	....
	Fort Wayne	IHL	34	10	18	28	0	10	4	7	11	6
	NHL Totals		**2**	**0**	**1**	**1**	**0**	....	....	....	....	....

a WHL East All-Star Team (1988)

ENEBAK, JAKE

Left wing. Shoots left. 6'2", 200 lbs. Born, Northfield, MN, December 10, 1968.
(Quebec's 8th choice, 156th overall, in 1987 Entry Draft).

			Regular Season					Playoffs				
Season	Club	Lea	GP	G	A	TP	PIM	GP	G	A	TP	PIM
1986-87	Northfield	HS	22	40	26	66	....	....	....	....	....	....
1987-88	U. Minnesota	WCHA	9	1	1	2	15	....	....	....	....	....
1988-89	U. Minnesota	WCHA	15	1	2	3	26	....	....	....	....	....

ENGEVIK, GLEN

Right wing. Shoots right. 6'1", 205 lbs. Born, Surrey, B.C., October 13, 1965.
(New Jersey's 1st choice, 3rd overall, in 1986 Supplemental Draft).

			Regular Season					Playoffs				
Season	Club	Lea	GP	G	A	TP	PIM	GP	G	A	TP	PIM
1986-87	U. of Denver	WCHA	40	10	8	18	32	....	....	....	....	....
1987-88	U. of Denver	WCHA	38	13	7	20	18	....	....	....	....	....
1988-89	U. of Denver	WCHA	42	12	12	24	33	....	....	....	....	....

ENGLISH, JOHN

Defense. Shoots right. 6'2", 190 lbs. Born, Toronto, Ont., May 13, 1966.
(Los Angeles' 3rd choice, 48th over-all, in 1984 Entry Draft).

			Regular Season					Playoffs				
Season	Club	Lea	GP	G	A	TP	PIM	GP	G	A	TP	PIM
1982-83	St. Michael's	Jr. B	34	2	10	12	92	....	....	....	....	....
1983-84	S. S. Marie	OHL	64	6	11	17	144	16	0	6	6	45
1984-85	S. S. Marie	OHL	15	0	3	3	61	....	....	....	....	....
	Hamilton	OHL	41	2	22	24	105	17	3	3	6	43
1985-86	Ottawa	OHL	54	10	37	47	175	....	....	....	....	....
1986-87	New Haven	AHL	3	0	0	0	6	....	....	....	....	....
	Flint	IHL	18	1	2	3	83	6	1	2	3	12
1987-88	**Los Angeles**	**NHL**	**3**	**1**	**3**	**4**	**4**	**1**	**0**	**0**	**0**	**0**
	New Haven	AHL	65	4	22	26	236	....	....	....	....	....
1988-89	Cape Breton	AHL	13	0	3	3	80	....	....	....	....	....
	New Haven	AHL	49	5	19	24	197	....	....	....	....	....
	NHL Totals		**3**	**1**	**3**	**4**	**4**	**1**	**0**	**0**	**0**	**0**

Traded to **Edmonton** by **Los Angeles** with Brian Wilks for Jim Weimer and Alan May, March 7, 1989.

ENNIS, JIM

Defense. Shoots left. 6', 200 lbs. Born, Sherwood Park, Edmonton, Alta., July 10, 1967.
Last amateur club: Boston University Terriers (H.E.).

			Regular Season					Playoffs				
Season	Club	Lea	GP	G	A	TP	PIM	GP	G	A	TP	PIM
1985-86	Boston U.	H.E.	40	1	4	5	22	....	....	....	....	....
1986-87	Boston U.	H.E.	26	3	4	7	27	....	....	....	....	....
1987-88	**Edmonton**	**NHL**	**5**	**1**	**0**	**1**	**10**	....	....	....	....	....
	Nova Scotia	AHL	59	8	12	20	102	5	0	1	1	16
1988-89	Cape Breton	AHL	67	3	15	18	94	....	....	....	....	....
	NHL Totals		**5**	**1**	**0**	**1**	**10**	....	....	....	....	....

ERICKSON, MICHAEL

Defense. Shoots left. 5'11", 175 lbs. Born, Worcester, MA, March 11, 1969.
(NY Islanders' 11th choice, 223rd overall, in 1987 Entry Draft).

			Regular Season					Playoffs				
Season	Club	Lea	GP	G	A	TP	PIM	GP	G	A	TP	PIM
1986-87	St. John's	HS	20	8	21	29	20	....	....	....	....	....
1987-88	U. of Lowell	H.E.	31	2	4	6	22	....	....	....	....	....
1988-89	U. of Lowell	H.E.	33	4	2	6	50	....	....	....	....	....

ERIKSSON, PATRIK

Center. Shoots left. 5'11", 175 lbs. Born, Gavle, Sweden, March 13, 1969.
(Winnipeg's 2nd choice, 37th overall, in 1987 Entry Draft).

			Regular Season					Playoffs				
Season	Club	Lea	GP	G	A	TP	PIM	GP	G	A	TP	PIM
1986-87	Brynas	Swe.	25	10	5	15	8	....	....	....	....	....
1987-88	Brynas	Swe.	35	14	9	23	6	....	....	....	....	....
1988-89	Brynas	Swe.	33	6	10	16	14	....	....	....	....	....

ERIKSSON, THOMAS

Born, Stockholm, Sweden, October 16, 1959.
Defense. Shoots left. 6'2", 180 lbs.
Last amateur club: Djurgardens IF (Sweden)
(Philadelphia's 6th choice, 98th over-all, in 1979 Entry Draft).

			Regular Season					Playoffs				
Season	Club	Lea	GP	G	A	TP	PIM	GP	G	A	TP	PIM
1979-80	Djurgardens	Swe.	36	12	11	23	63	....	....	....	....	....
	Swe. National	...	22	5	0	5	....	....	....	....	....	....
1980-81	Maine	AHL	54	11	20	31	75	....	....	....	....	....
	Philadelphia	**NHL**	**24**	**1**	**10**	**11**	**14**	**7**	**0**	**2**	**2**	**6**
1981-82	**Philadelphia**	**NHL**	**1**	**0**	**0**	**0**	**4**	....	....	....	....	....
	Djurgardens	Swe.	27	7	5	12	48	....	....	....	....	....
1982-83	Djurgardens	Swe.	32	12	9	21	51	....	....	....	....	....
1983-84a	**Philadelphia**	**NHL**	**68**	**11**	**33**	**44**	**37**	**3**	**0**	**1**	**1**	**0**
1984-85	**Philadelphia**	**NHL**	**72**	**10**	**29**	**39**	**36**	**9**	**0**	**0**	**0**	**6**
1985-86	**Philadelphia**	**NHL**	**43**	**0**	**4**	**4**	**16**	....	....	....	....	....
	NHL Totals		**208**	**22**	**76**	**98**	**107**	**19**	**0**	**3**	**3**	**6**

a Named to NHL All-Rookie Team (1984)

ERIKSSON, PETER (KESSLER)

Left wing. Shoots right. 6'4", 224 lbs. Born, Kramfors, Sweden, July 12, 1965.
(Edmonton's 4th choice, 64th overall, in 1987 Entry Draft).

			Regular Season					Playoffs				
Season	Club	Lea	GP	G	A	TP	PIM	GP	G	A	TP	PIM
1984-85	HV-71	Swe. 2	10	5	2	7	2	....	....	....	....	....
1985-86	HV-71	Swe.	30	7	8	15	18	1	0	0	0	0
1986-87	HV-71	Swe.	36	14	5	19	16	....	....	....	....	....
1987-88	HV-71	Swe.	37	14	9	23	20	2	1	0	1	0
1988-89	HV-71	Swe.	40	10	27	37	48	....	....	....	....	....

ERIKSSON, TOMAZ

Left wing. Shoots left. 6', 195 lbs. Born, Stockholm, Sweden, March 23, 1967.
(Philadelphia's 4th choice, 83rd overall, in 1987 Entry Draft).

			Regular Season					Playoffs				
Season	Club	Lea	GP	G	A	TP	PIM	GP	G	A	TP	PIM
1986-87	Djurgarden	Swe.	20	7	4	11	14	2	2	0	2	0
1987-88	Djurgarden	Swe.	26	4	5	9	16	....	....	....	....	....
1988-89	Djurgarden	Swe.	38	6	13	19	50	....	....	....	....	....

ERIXON, JAN

Right wing. Shoots left. 6', 190 lbs. Born, Skelleftea, Sweden, July 8, 1962.
Last amateur club: Skelleftea (Sweden).

			Regular Season					Playoffs				
Season	Club	Lea	GP	G	A	TP	PIM	GP	G	A	TP	PIM
1979-80	Skelleftea	...	15	1	0	1	2	....	....	....	....	....
1980-81	Skelleftea	...	32	6	6	12	4	3	1	0	1	0
1981-82	Skelleftea	...	30	7	7	14	26	....	....	....	....	....
1982-83	Skelleftea	...	36	10	19	29	32	....	....	....	....	....
1983-84	**NY Rangers**	**NHL**	75	5	25	30	16	5	2	0	2	4
1984-85	**NY Rangers**	**NHL**	66	7	22	29	33	2	0	0	0	2
1985-86	**NY Rangers**	**NHL**	31	2	17	19	4	12	0	1	1	4
1986-87	**NY Rangers**	**NHL**	68	8	18	26	24	6	1	0	1	0
1987-88	**NY Rangers**	**NHL**	70	7	19	26	33	....	....	....	....	....
1988-89	**NY Rangers**	**NHL**	44	4	11	15	27	4	0	1	1	2
	NHL Totals		354	33	112	145	137	29	3	2	5	12

ERREY, BOB   (AIRY)

Left wing. Shoots left. 5'10", 180 lbs. Born, Montreal, Que., September 21, 1964.
(Pittsburgh's 1st choice, 15th over-all, in 1983 Entry Draft).

			Regular Season					Playoffs				
Season	Club	Lea	GP	G	A	TP	PIM	GP	G	A	TP	PIM
1981-82	Peterborough	OHL	68	29	31	60	39	9	3	1	4	9
1982-83a	Peterborough	OHL	67	53	47	100	74	4	1	3	4	7
1983-84	**Pittsburgh**	**NHL**	65	9	13	22	29	....	....	....	....	....
1984-85	**Pittsburgh**	**NHL**	16	0	2	2	7	....	....	....	....	....
	Baltimore	AHL	59	17	24	41	14	8	3	4	7	11
1985-86	**Pittsburgh**	**NHL**	37	11	6	17	8	....	....	....	....	....
	Baltimore	AHL	18	8	7	15	28	....	....	....	....	....
1986-87	**Pittsburgh**	**NHL**	72	16	18	34	46	....	....	....	....	....
1987-88	**Pittsburgh**	**NHL**	17	3	6	9	18	....	....	....	....	....
1988-89	**Pittsburgh**	**NHL**	76	26	32	58	124	11	1	2	3	12
	NHL Totals		283	65	77	142	232	11	1	2	3	12

a OHL First All-Star Team (1983)

ESPE, DAVID

Defense. Shoots left. 6', 185 lbs. Born, St. Paul, MN, November 3, 1966.
(Quebec's 5th choice, 78th over-all, in 1985 Entry Draft).

			Regular Season					Playoffs				
Season	Club	Lea	GP	G	A	TP	PIM	GP	G	A	TP	PIM
1985-86	U. Minnesota	WCHA	27	0	6	6	18	....	....	....	....	....
1986-87	U. Minnesota	WCHA	45	4	8	12	28	....	....	....	....	....
1987-88	U. Minnesota	WCHA	43	4	10	14	68	....	....	....	....	....
1988-89			DID NOT PLAY									

EVANS, DARYL TOMAS

Left wing. Shoots left. 5'9", 185 lbs. Born, Toronto, Ont., January 12, 1961.
(Los Angeles' 11th choice, 178th over-all, in 1980 Entry Draft).

			Regular Season					Playoffs				
Season	Club	Lea	GP	G	A	TP	PIM	GP	G	A	TP	PIM
1979-80	Niagara Falls	OHA	63	43	52	95	47	10	5	13	18	6
1980-81a	Niagara Falls	OHL	5	3	4	7	11	....	....	....	....	....
	Brantford	OHL	58	58	54	112	50	6	4	5	9	6
1981-82	New Haven	AHL	41	14	14	28	10	....	....	....	....	....
	Los Angeles	**NHL**	14	2	6	8	2	10	5	8	13	12
1982-83	**Los Angeles**	**NHL**	80	18	22	40	21	....	....	....	....	....
1983-84	**Los Angeles**	**NHL**	4	0	1	1	0	....	....	....	....	....
	New Haven	AHL	69	51	34	85	14	....	....	....	....	....
1984-85	**Los Angeles**	**NHL**	7	1	0	1	2	....	....	....	....	....
	New Haven	AHL	59	22	24	46	12	....	....	....	....	....
1985-86	**Washington**	**NHL**	6	0	1	1	0	....	....	....	....	....
	Binghamton	AHL	69	40	52	92	50	5	6	2	8	0
1986-87	Newmarket	AHL	74	27	46	73	17	....	....	....	....	....
	Toronto	**NHL**	2	1	0	1	0	1	0	0	0	0
1987-88	Newmarket	AHL	57	29	36	65	10	....	....	....	....	....
1988-89	Newmarket	AHL	64	29	30	59	16	5	1	1	2	0
	NHL Totals		113	22	30	52	25	11	5	8	13	12

a OHL First All-Star Team (1981)
Traded to **Washington** by **Los Angeles** for Glen Currie, September 9, 1985.

EVANS, DOUG

Center. Shoots left. 5'9", 185 lbs. Born, Peterborough, Ont., June 2, 1963.

			Regular Season					Playoffs				
Season	Club	Lea	GP	G	A	TP	PIM	GP	G	A	TP	PIM
1981-82	Peterborough	OHL	56	17	49	66	176	9	0	2	2	41
1982-83	Peterborough	OHL	65	31	55	86	165	4	0	3	3	23
1983-84	Peterborough	OHL	61	45	79	124	98	8	4	12	16	26
1984-85	Peoria	IHL	81	36	61	97	189	20	18	14	32	14
1985-86a	Peoria	IHL	60	46	51	97	179	10	4	6	10	32
	St. Louis	**NHL**	13	1	0	1	2	....	....	....	....	....
1986-87	**St. Louis**	**NHL**	53	3	13	16	91	5	0	0	0	10
	Peoria	IHL	18	10	15	25	39	....	....	....	....	....
1987-88	**St. Louis**	**NHL**	41	5	7	12	49	2	0	0	0	0
	Peoria	IHL	11	4	16	20	64	....	....	....	....	....
1988-89	**St. Louis**	**NHL**	53	7	12	19	81	7	1	2	3	16
	NHL Totals		160	16	32	48	223	14	1	2	3	26

a IHL First All-Star Team (1986)
Signed as a free agent by **St. Louis**, June 10, 1985.

EVANS, SHAWN

Defense. Shoots left. 6'2", 195 lbs. Born, Kingston, Ont., September 7, 1965.
(New Jersey's 2nd choice, 24th over-all, in 1983 Entry Draft).

			Regular Season					Playoffs				
Season	Club	Lea	GP	G	A	TP	PIM	GP	G	A	TP	PIM
1981-82	Kingston	OPJHL	21	9	13	22	55	....	....	....	....	....
1982-83	Peterborough	OHL	58	7	41	48	116	4	2	0	2	12
1983-84a	Peterborough	OHL	67	21	88	109	116	8	1	16	17	8
1984-85b	Peterborough	OHL	66	16	83	99	78	16	6	18	24	6
1985-86	**St. Louis**	**NHL**	7	0	0	0	2	....	....	....	....	....
	Peoria	IHL	55	8	26	34	36	....	....	....	....	....
1986-87	Nova Scotia	AHL	55	7	28	35	29	5	0	4	4	6
1987-88	Nova Scotia	AHL	79	8	62	70	109	5	1	1	2	40
1988-89	Springfield	AHL	68	9	50	59	125	....	....	....	....	....
	NHL Totals		7	0	0	0	2	....	....	....	....	....

a OHL Second All-Star Team (1984)
b OHL Third All-Star Team (1985)
Traded to **St. Louis** by **New Jersey** with New Jersey's fifth-round choice (Michael Wolak) in 1986 Entry Draft for Mark Johnson, September 19, 1985. Traded to **Edmonton** by **St. Louis** for Todd Ewen, October 15, 1986. Signed as a free agent by **NY Islanders**, June 20, 1988.

EVASON, DEAN

Center. Shoots right. 5'10", 180 lbs. Born, Flin Flon, Man., August 22, 1964.
(Washington's 3rd choice, 89th over-all, in 1982 Entry Draft).

			Regular Season					Playoffs				
Season	Club	Lea	GP	G	A	TP	PIM	GP	G	A	TP	PIM
1980-81	Spokane	WHL	3	1	1	2	0	....	....	....	....	....
1981-82	Spokane	WHL	26	8	14	22	65	....	....	....	....	....
	Kamloops	WHL	44	21	55	76	47	4	2	1	3	0
1982-83	Kamloops	WHL	70	71	93	164	102	7	5	7	12	18
1983-84	**Washington**	**NHL**	2	0	0	0	2	....	....	....	....	....
a	Kamloops	WHL	57	49	88	137	89	17	*21	20	41	33
1984-85	**Washington**	**NHL**	15	3	4	7	2	....	....	....	....	....
	Hartford	**NHL**	2	0	0	0	0	....	....	....	....	....
	Binghamton	AHL	65	27	49	76	38	8	3	5	8	9
1985-86	**Hartford**	**NHL**	55	20	28	48	65	10	1	4	5	10
	Binghamton	AHL	26	9	17	26	29	....	....	....	....	....
1986-87	**Hartford**	**NHL**	80	22	37	59	67	5	3	2	5	35
1987-88	**Hartford**	**NHL**	77	10	18	28	115	6	1	1	2	2
1988-89	**Hartford**	**NHL**	67	11	17	28	60	4	1	2	3	10
	NHL Totals		298	66	104	170	311	25	6	9	15	57

a WHL First All-Star Team, West Division (1984)
Traded to **Hartford** by **Washington** with Peter Sidorkiewicz for David Jensen, March 12, 1985.

EVO, MATTHEW (MATT)

Left wing. Shoots left. 6', 185 lbs. Born, Royal Oak, MI, December 31, 1968.
(Vancouver's 12th choice, 234th overall, in 1987 Entry Draft).

			Regular Season					Playoffs				
Season	Club	Lea	GP	G	A	TP	PIM	GP	G	A	TP	PIM
1986-87	Country Day	HS	26	27	32	59	45	....	....	....	....	....
1987-88	Ferris State	CCHA	40	7	8	15	46	....	....	....	....	....
1988-89	Ferris State	CCHA	26	3	4	7	38	....	....	....	....	....

EWEN, DEAN

Left wing. Shoots left. 6'1", 185 lbs. Born, St. Albert, Alta., February 28, 1969.
(NY Islanders' 3rd choice, 55th overall, in 1987 Entry Draft).

			Regular Season					Playoffs				
Season	Club	Lea	GP	G	A	TP	PIM	GP	G	A	TP	PIM
1985-86	N. Westminster	WHL	61	7	15	22	154	....	....	....	....	....
1986-87	N. Westminster	WHL	9	2	3	5	28	....	....	....	....	....
	Spokane	WHL	57	6	11	17	208	5	1	0	1	39
1987-88	Spokane	WHL	49	12	12	24	302	15	1	3	4	49
1988-89	Springfield	AHL	6	0	0	0	26	....	....	....	....	....
	Seattle	WHL	61	22	30	52	307	....	....	....	....	....

EWEN, TODD

Right wing. Shoots right. 6'2", 200 lbs. Born, Saskatoon, Sask., March 26, 1966.
(Edmonton's 9th choice, 168th over-all, in 1984 Entry Draft).

			Regular Season					Playoffs				
Season	Club	Lea	GP	G	A	TP	PIM	GP	G	A	TP	PIM
1982-83	Kamloops	WHL	3	0	0	0	2	2	0	0	0	0
1983-84	N. Westminster	WHL	68	11	13	24	176	7	2	1	3	15
1984-85	N. Westminster	WHL	56	11	20	31	304	10	1	8	9	60
1985-86	N. Westminster	WHL	60	28	24	52	289	....	....	....	....	....
	Maine	AHL	....	....	....	....	....	3	0	0	0	7
1986-87	**St. Louis**	**NHL**	23	2	0	2	84	4	0	0	0	23
	Peoria	IHL	16	3	3	6	110	....	....	....	....	....
1987-88	**St. Louis**	**NHL**	64	4	2	6	227	6	0	0	0	21
1988-89	**St. Louis**	**NHL**	34	4	5	9	171	2	0	0	0	21
	NHL Totals		121	10	7	17	482	12	0	0	0	65

Traded to **St. Louis** by **Edmonton** for Shawn Evans, October 15, 1986.

FABIAN, SEAN

Defense. Shoots left. 6'1", 200 lbs. Born, Minneapolis, MN, May 11, 1969.
(Vancouver's 4th choice, 87th overall, in 1987 Entry Draft).

			Regular Season					Playoffs				
Season	Club	Lea	GP	G	A	TP	PIM	GP	G	A	TP	PIM
1986-87	Hill Murray	HS	26	7	20	27	....	....	....	....	....	....
1987-88	U. Minnesota	WCHA	10	0	1	1	11	....	....	....	....	....
1988-89	U. Minnesota	WCHA	DID NOT PLAY									

FAUSS, TED

Defense. Shoots left. 6'2", 205 lbs. Born, Clark Mills, NY, June 30, 1961.

			Regular Season					Playoffs				
Season	Club	Lea	GP	G	A	TP	PIM	GP	G	A	TP	PIM
1981-82	Clarkson	ECAC	35	3	6	9	79	....	....	....	....	....
1982-83	Clarkson	ECAC	25	4	6	10	60	....	....	....	....	....
1983-84	Nova Scotia	AHL	71	4	11	15	123	7	0	2	2	28
1984-85	Sherbrooke	AHL	77	1	9	10	62	17	2	2	4	27
1985-86			DID NOT PLAY									
1986-87	**Toronto**	**NHL**	**15**	**0**	**1**	**1**	**11**	....	....	....	....	....
	Newmarket	AHL	59	0	5	5	81	....	....	....	....	....
1987-88	**Toronto**	**NHL**	**13**	**0**	**1**	**1**	**4**	....	....	....	....	....
	Newmarket	AHL	49	0	11	11	86	....	....	....	....	....
1988-89	Binghamton	AHL	53	4	11	15	66	....	....	....	....	....
	NHL Totals		**28**	**0**	**2**	**2**	**15**	....	....	....	....	....

Signed as a free agent by **Toronto**, July 21, 1986.

FEATHERSTONE, GLEN

Defense. Shoots left. 6'4", 210 lbs. Born, Toronto, Ont., July 8, 1968.
(St. Louis' 4th choice, 73rd overall, in 1986 Entry Draft).

			Regular Season					Playoffs				
Season	Club	Lea	GP	G	A	TP	PIM	GP	G	A	TP	PIM
1985-86	Windsor	OHL	49	0	6	6	135	14	1	1	2	23
1986-87	Windsor	OHL	47	6	11	17	154	14	2	6	8	19
1987-88	Windsor	OHL	53	7	27	34	201	12	6	9	15	47
1988-89	**St. Louis**	**NHL**	**18**	**0**	**2**	**2**	**22**	**6**	**0**	**0**	**0**	**0**
	Peoria	IHL	37	5	19	24	97	....	....	....	....	....
	NHL Totals		**18**	**0**	**2**	**2**	**22**	**6**	**0**	**0**	**0**	**0**

FEDERKO, BERNARD ALLAN (BERNIE)

Center. Shoots left. 6', 190 lbs. Born, Foam Lake, Sask., May 12, 1956.
(St. Louis' 1st choice, 7th over-all, in 1976 Amateur Draft).

			Regular Season					Playoffs				
Season	Club	Lea	GP	G	A	TP	PIM	GP	G	A	TP	PIM
1973-74	Saskatoon	WHL	68	22	28	50	19	6	0	0	0	2
1974-75	Saskatoon	WHL	66	39	68	107	30	17	*15	7	22	8
1975-76ab	Saskatoon	WHL	72	72	*115	*187	108	20	18	*27	*45	8
1976-77	Kansas City	CHL	42	30	39	69	41	....	....	....	....	....
	St. Louis	**NHL**	**31**	**14**	**9**	**23**	**15**	**4**	**1**	**1**	**2**	**2**
1977-78	**St. Louis**	**NHL**	**72**	**17**	**24**	**41**	**27**	....	....	....	....	....
1978-79	**St. Louis**	**NHL**	**74**	**31**	**64**	**95**	**14**	....	....	....	....	....
1979-80	**St. Louis**	**NHL**	**79**	**38**	**56**	**94**	**24**	**3**	**1**	**0**	**1**	**2**
1980-81	**St. Louis**	**NHL**	**78**	**31**	**73**	**104**	**47**	**11**	**8**	**10**	**18**	**2**
1981-82	**St. Louis**	**NHL**	**74**	**30**	**62**	**92**	**70**	**10**	**3**	**15**	**18**	**10**
1982-83	**St. Louis**	**NHL**	**75**	**24**	**60**	**84**	**24**	**4**	***2**	**3**	**5**	**0**
1983-84	**St. Louis**	**NHL**	**79**	**41**	**66**	**107**	**43**	**11**	**4**	**4**	**8**	**10**
1984-85	**St. Louis**	**NHL**	**76**	**30**	**73**	**103**	**27**	**3**	**0**	**2**	**2**	**4**
1985-86	**St. Louis**	**NHL**	**80**	**34**	**68**	**102**	**34**	**19**	**7**	**14**	**21**	**17**
1986-87	**St. Louis**	**NHL**	**64**	**20**	**52**	**72**	**32**	**6**	**3**	**3**	**6**	**18**
1987-88	**St. Louis**	**NHL**	**79**	**20**	**69**	**89**	**52**	**10**	**2**	**6**	**8**	**18**
1988-89	**St. Louis**	**NHL**	**66**	**22**	**45**	**67**	**54**	**10**	**4**	**8**	**12**	**0**
	NHL Totals		**927**	**352**	**721**	**1073**	**463**	**91**	**35**	**66**	**101**	**83**

a WHL First All-Star Team (1976)
b Named WHL's Most Valuable Player (1976)

Played in NHL All-Star Game (1980, 1981)

Traded to **Detroit** by **St. Louis** with Tony McKegney for Adam Oates and Paul MacLean, June 15, 1989.

FEDYK, BRENT (FED-ick)

Right wing. Shoots right. 6' 190 lbs. Born, Yorkton, Sask., March 8, 1967.
(Detroit's 1st choice, 8th over-all, in 1985 Entry Draft).

			Regular Season					Playoffs				
Season	Club	Lea	GP	G	A	TP	PIM	GP	G	A	TP	PIM
1983-84	Regina	WHL	63	15	28	43	30	23	8	7	15	6
1984-85	Regina	WHL	66	35	35	70	48	8	5	4	9	0
1985-86	Regina	WHL	50	43	34	77	47	5	0	1	1	0
1986-87	Regina	WHL	12	9	6	15	9	....	....	....	....	....
	Seattle	WHL	13	5	11	16	9	....	....	....	....	....
	Portland	WHL	11	5	4	9	6	14	5	6	11	0
1987-88	**Detroit**	**NHL**	**2**	**0**	**1**	**1**	**2**	....	....	....	....	....
	Adirondack	AHL	34	9	11	20	22	5	0	2	2	6
1988-89	**Detroit**	**NHL**	**5**	**2**	**0**	**2**	**0**	....	....	....	....	....
	Adirondack	AHL	66	40	28	68	33	15	7	8	15	23
	NHL Totals		**7**	**2**	**1**	**3**	**2**	....	....	....	....	....

FELIX, CHRIS

Defense. Shoots right. 5'11", 185 lbs. Born, Bramalea, Ont., May 27, 1964.

			Regular Season					Playoffs				
Season	Club	Lea	GP	G	A	TP	PIM	GP	G	A	TP	PIM
1982-83	S.S. Marie	OHL	68	16	57	73	39	16	2	12	14	10
1983-84	S.S. Marie	OHL	70	32	61	93	75	16	3	20	23	16
1984-85	S.S. Marie	OHL	66	29	72	101	89	16	7	21	28	20
1985-86	Cdn. Olympic	...	73	7	33	40	33	....	....	....	....	....
1986-87	Cdn. Olympic	....	78	14	38	52	36	....	....	....	....	....
1987-88	Cdn. National	....	62	6	25	31	66	....	....	....	....	....
	Cdn. Olympic	....	6	1	2	3	2	....	....	....	....	....
	Fort Wayne	IHL	19	5	17	22	24	6	4	4	8	0
	Washington	**NHL**	....	....	....	....	....	**1**	**0**	**0**	**0**	**0**
1988-89	**Washington**	**NHL**	**21**	**0**	**8**	**8**	**8**	**1**	**0**	**1**	**1**	**0**
	Baltimore	AHL	50	8	29	37	44	....	....	....	....	....
	NHL Totals		**21**	**0**	**8**	**8**	**8**	**2**	**0**	**1**	**1**	**0**

Signed as a free agent by **Washington**, March 1, 1987.

FELSNER, DENNY

Left wing. Shoots left. 6', 180 lbs. Born, Warren, MI, April 29, 1970.
(St. Louis' 3rd choice, 55th overall, in 1989 Entry Draft).

			Regular Season					Playoffs				
Season	Club	Lea	GP	G	A	TP	PIM	GP	G	A	TP	PIM
1988-89	U. of Michigan	CCHA	39	30	19	49	22	....	....	....	....	....

FENTON, ERIC

Center. Shoots right. 6'2", 190 lbs. Born, Troy, NY, July 17, 1969.
(NY Rangers' 10th choice, 202nd overall, in 1988 Entry Draft).

			Regular Season					Playoffs				
Season	Club	Lea	GP	G	A	TP	PIM	GP	G	A	TP	PIM
1987-88	Yarmouth Aca.	HS	25	37	33	70	....	....	....	....	....	....
1988-89	U. of Maine	H.E.	DID NOT PLAY									

FENTON, PAUL JOHN

Center. Shoots left. 5'11", 180 lbs. Born, Springfield, MA, December 22, 1959.
Last amateur club: Boston University Terriers (ECAC).

			Regular Season					Playoffs				
Season	Club	Lea	GP	G	A	TP	PIM	GP	G	A	TP	PIM
1979-80	Boston U.	ECAC	24	8	17	25	14	....	....	....	....	....
1980-81	Boston U.	ECAC	5	3	2	5	0	....	....	....	....	....
1981-82	Boston U.	ECAC	28	20	13	33	20	....	....	....	....	....
1982-83	Peoria	IHL	82	60	51	111	53	....	....	....	....	....
	Colorado	CHL	1	0	1	1	0	3	2	0	2	2
1983-84	Binghamton	AHL	78	41	24	65	67	....	....	....	....	....
1984-85	**Hartford**	**NHL**	**33**	**7**	**5**	**12**	**10**	....	....	....	....	....
	Binghamton	AHL	45	26	21	47	18	....	....	....	....	....
1985-86	**Hartford**	**NHL**	**1**	**0**	**0**	**0**	**0**	....	....	....	....	....
a	Binghamton	AHL	75	53	35	88	87	6	2	0	2	2
1986-87	**NY Rangers**	**NHL**	**8**	**0**	**0**	**0**	**2**	....	....	....	....	....
1987-88	**Los Angeles**	**NHL**	**71**	**20**	**23**	**43**	**46**	**5**	**2**	**1**	**3**	**2**
	New Haven	AHL	5	11	5	16	9	....	....	....	....	....
1988-89	**Los Angeles**	**NHL**	**21**	**2**	**3**	**5**	**6**	....	....	....	....	....
	Winnipeg	**NHL**	**59**	**14**	**9**	**23**	**33**	....	....	....	....	....
	NHL Totals		**193**	**43**	**40**	**83**	**97**	**5**	**2**	**1**	**3**	**2**

a AHL First All-Star Team (1986)
b AHL Second All-Star Team (1987)

Signed as free agent by **Hartford**, October 6, 1983. Claimed by **Los Angeles** in NHL Waiver Draft, October 5, 1987. Traded to **Winnipeg** by **Los Angeles** for Gilles Hamel, November 25, 1988.

FENYVES, DAVID (FEHN vuhs)

Defense. Shoots left. 5'11", 192 lbs. Born, Dunnville, Ont., April 29, 1960.

			Regular Season					Playoffs				
Season	Club	Lea	GP	G	A	TP	PIM	GP	G	A	TP	PIM
1978-79	Peterborough	OHA	66	2	23	25	122	19	0	5	5	18
1979-80a	Peterborough	OHA	66	9	36	45	92	14	0	3	3	14
1980-81	Rochester	AHL	77	6	16	22	146	....	....	....	....	....
1981-82	Rochester	AHL	73	3	14	17	68	5	0	1	1	4
1982-83	Rochester	AHL	51	2	19	21	45	....	....	....	....	....
	Buffalo	**NHL**	**24**	**0**	**8**	**8**	**14**	**4**	**0**	**0**	**0**	**0**
1983-84	**Buffalo**	**NHL**	**10**	**0**	**4**	**4**	**9**	**2**	**0**	**0**	**0**	**7**
	Rochester	AHL	70	3	16	19	55	16	1	4	5	22
1984-85	**Buffalo**	**NHL**	**60**	**1**	**8**	**9**	**27**	**5**	**0**	**0**	**0**	**2**
	Rochester	AHL	9	0	3	3	8	....	....	....	....	....
1985-86	**Buffalo**	**NHL**	**47**	**0**	**7**	**7**	**37**	....	....	....	....	....
1986-87	**Buffalo**	**NHL**	**7**	**1**	**0**	**1**	**0**	....	....	....	....	....
1986-87bc	Rochester	AHL	71	6	16	22	57	18	3	12	15	10
1987-88	**Philadelphia**	**NHL**	**5**	**0**	**0**	**0**	**0**	....	....	....	....	....
de	Hershey	AHL	75	11	40	51	47	12	1	8	9	10
1988-89	**Philadelphia**	**NHL**	**1**	**0**	**1**	**1**	**0**	....	....	....	....	....
de	Hershey	AHL	79	15	51	66	41	12	2	6	8	6
	NHL Totals		**154**	**2**	**28**	**30**	**87**	**11**	**0**	**0**	**0**	**9**

a OHA Second All-Star Team (1980)
b AHL Second All-Star Team (1987)
c Named AHL Playoff MVP (1987)
d AHL First All-Star Team, (1988, 1989
e Won Eddie Shore Plaque (Outstanding Defenseman-AHL) (1988, 1989)

Signed as free agent by **Buffalo**, October 31, 1979. Claimed by **Philadelphia** in NHL Waiver Draft, October 5, 1987.

FERGUS, THOMAS JOSEPH (TOM)

Center. Shoots left. 6'3", 210 lbs. Born, Chicago, IL, June 16, 1962.
(Boston's 2nd choice, 60th over-all, in 1980 Entry Draft).

			Regular Season					Playoffs				
Season	Club	Lea	GP	G	A	TP	PIM	GP	G	A	TP	PIM
1979-80	Peterborough	OHA	63	8	6	14	14	14	1	5	6	6
1980-81	Peterborough	OHA	63	43	45	88	33	5	1	4	5	2
1981-82	**Boston**	**NHL**	**61**	**15**	**24**	**39**	**12**	**6**	**3**	**0**	**3**	**0**
1982-83	**Boston**	**NHL**	**80**	**28**	**35**	**63**	**39**	**15**	**2**	**2**	**4**	**15**
1983-84	**Boston**	**NHL**	**69**	**25**	**36**	**61**	**12**	**3**	**2**	**0**	**2**	**9**
1984-85	**Boston**	**NHL**	**79**	**30**	**43**	**73**	**75**	**5**	**0**	**0**	**0**	**4**
1985-86	**Toronto**	**NHL**	**78**	**31**	**42**	**73**	**64**	**10**	**5**	**7**	**12**	**6**
1986-87	**Toronto**	**NHL**	**57**	**21**	**28**	**49**	**57**	**2**	**0**	**1**	**1**	**2**
	Newmarket	AHL	1	0	1	1	0	....	....	....	....	....
1987-88	**Toronto**	**NHL**	**63**	**19**	**31**	**50**	**81**	**6**	**2**	**3**	**5**	**2**
1988-89	**Toronto**	**NHL**	**80**	**22**	**45**	**67**	**48**	....	....	....	....	....
	NHL Totals		**567**	**191**	**284**	**475**	**388**	**47**	**14**	**13**	**27**	**38**

Traded to **Toronto** by **Boston** for Bill Derlago, October 11, 1985.

FERGUSON, JOHN Jr.

Left wing. Shoots left. 6', 175 lbs. Born, Winnipeg, Man., July 7, 1967.
(Montreal's 15th choice, 247th overall, in 1985 Entry Draft).

			Regular Season					Playoffs				
Season	Club	Lea	GP	G	A	TP	PIM	GP	G	A	TP	PIM
1985-86	Providence	H.E.	18	1	2	3	2	....	....	....	....	....
1986-87	Providence	H.E.	23	0	0	0	6	....	....	....	....	....
1987-88	Providence	H.E.	34	0	5	5	31	....	....	....	....	....
1988-89	Providence	H.E.	40	14	15	29	66	....	....	....	....	....

FERNER, MARK

Defense. Shoots left. 6', 193 lbs. Born, Regina, Sask., September 5, 1965.
(Buffalo's 12th choice, 194th over-all, in 1983 Entry Draft).

			Regular Season					Playoffs				
Season	Club	Lea	GP	G	A	TP	PIM	GP	G	A	TP	PIM
1982-83	Kamloops	WHL	69	6	15	21	81	7	0	0	0	7
1983-84	Kamloops	WHL	72	9	30	39	169	14	1	8	9	20
1984-85a	Kamloops	WHL	69	15	39	54	91	15	4	9	13	21
1985-86	Rochester	AHL	63	3	14	17	87	....	....	....	....	....
1986-87	**Buffalo**	**NHL**	**13**	**0**	**3**	**3**	**9**	....	....	....	....	....
	Rochester	AHL	54	0	12	12	157	....	....	....	....	....
1987-88	Rochester	AHL	69	1	25	26	165	7	1	4	5	31
1988-89	**Buffalo**	**NHL**	**2**	**0**	**0**	**0**	**2**	....	....	....	....	....
	Rochester	AHL	55	0	18	18	97	....	....	....	....	....
	NHL Totals		**15**	**0**	**3**	**3**	**11**	....	....	....	....	....

a WHL First All-Star Team, West Division (1985)

Traded to **Washington** by **Buffalo** for Scott McCrory, June 1, 1989.

FERNHOLZ, JAMES (JIM)

Right wing. Shoots right. 6'2", 200 lbs. Born, Minneapolis, MN, March 16, 1969.
(Winnipeg's 9th choice, 184th overall, in 1987 Entry Draft).

			Regular Season					Playoffs				
Season	Club	Lea	GP	G	A	TP	PIM	GP	G	A	TP	PIM
1986-87	White Bear	HS	20	13	17	30	....	....	....	....	....	....
1987-88	U. of Vermont	ECAC	23	3	5	8	12	....	....	....	....	....
1988-89	U. of Vermont	ECAC	28	3	11	14	16	....	....	....	....	....

FERRARO, RAY

Center. Shoots left. 5'10", 185 lbs. Born, Trail, B.C., August 23, 1964.
(Hartford's 5th choice, 88th over-all, in 1982 Entry Draft).

			Regular Season					Playoffs				
Season	Club	Lea	GP	G	A	TP	PIM	GP	G	A	TP	PIM
1981-82	Penticton	BCJHL	52	65	67	132	98	....	....	....	....	....
1982-83	Portland	WHL	50	41	49	90	39	14	14	10	24	13
1983-84a	Brandon	WHL	72	*108	84	*192	84	11	13	15	28	20
1984-85	**Hartford**	**NHL**	**44**	**11**	**17**	**28**	**40**	....	....	....	....	....
	Binghamton	AHL	37	20	13	33	29	....	....	....	....	....
1985-86	**Hartford**	**NHL**	**76**	**30**	**47**	**77**	**57**	**10**	**3**	**6**	**9**	**4**
1986-87	**Hartford**	**NHL**	**80**	**27**	**32**	**59**	**42**	**6**	**1**	**1**	**2**	**8**
1987-88	**Hartford**	**NHL**	**68**	**21**	**29**	**50**	**81**	**6**	**1**	**1**	**2**	**6**
1988-89	**Hartford**	**NHL**	**80**	**41**	**35**	**76**	**86**	**4**	**2**	**0**	**2**	**4**
	NHL Totals		**348**	**130**	**160**	**290**	**306**	**26**	**7**	**8**	**15**	**22**

a WHL First All-Star Team (1984)

FERREIRA, BRIAN

Right wing. Shoots right. 6', 175 lbs. Born, Falmouth, MA. January 2, 1968.
(Boston's 7th choice, 160th overall, in 1986 Entry Draft).

			Regular Season					Playoffs				
Season	Club	Lea	GP	G	A	TP	PIM	GP	G	A	TP	PIM
1985-86	Falmouth	HS	22	40	38	78	18	....	....	....	....	....
1986-87	RPI	ECAC	30	17	15	32	22	....	....	....	....	....
1987-88	RPI	ECAC	32	18	19	37	48	....	....	....	....	....
1988-89	RPI	ECAC	15	3	13	16	28	....	....	....	....	....

FERSOVICH, DARYN

Left wing. Shoots left. 5'11", 175 lbs. Born, Edmonton, Alta., August 7, 1966.
(Philadelphia's 12th choice, 205th overall, in 1984 Entry Draft).

			Regular Season					Playoffs				
Season	Club	Lea	GP	G	A	TP	PIM	GP	G	A	TP	PIM
1986-87	Ohio State	CCHA	43	4	9	13	18	....	....	....	....	....
1987-88	Ohio State	CCHA	40	7	13	20	34	....	....	....	....	....
1988-89	Ohio State	CCHA	39	10	17	27	4	....	....	....	....	....

FETISOV, VIACHESLAV

Defense. Shoots left. 6'1", 205 lbs. Born, Moscow, Soviet Union, May 20, 1958.
(New Jersey's 6th choice, 150th overall, in 1983 Entry Draft).

			Regular Season					Playoffs				
Season	Club	Lea	GP	G	A	TP	PIM	GP	G	A	TP	PIM
1976-77	CSKA	USSR	28	3	4	7	14	....	....	....	....	....
1977-78a	CSKA	USSR	35	9	18	27	46	....	....	....	....	....
1978-79	CSKA	USSR	29	10	19	29	40	....	....	....	....	....
1979-80a	CSKA	USSR	37	10	14	24	46	....	....	....	....	....
1980-81	CSKA	USSR	48	13	16	29	44	....	....	....	....	....
1981-82ac	CSKA	USSR	46	15	26	41	20	....	....	....	....	....
1982-83a	CSKA	USSR	43	6	17	23	46	....	....	....	....	....
1983-84abd	CSKA	USSR	44	19	30	49	38	....	....	....	....	....
1984-85a	CSKA	USSR	20	13	12	25	6	....	....	....	....	....
1985-86abc	CSKA	USSR	40	15	19	34	12	....	....	....	....	....
1986-87ab	CSKA	USSR	39	13	20	33	18	....	....	....	....	....
1987-88	CSKA	USSR	46	18	17	35	26	....	....	....	....	....
1988-89	CSKA	USSR	23	9	8	17	18	....	....	....	....	....

a Soviet National League All-Star Team (1978, 1980, 1982-88)
b Pravda Trophy-Top Scoring Defenseman (1984, 1986-88)
c Soviet Player of the Year (1982, 1986)
d Gold Stick Award-Europe's Top Player (1984)

FINLEY, JEFF

Defense. Shoots left. 6'2", 185 lbs. Born, Edmonton, Alta., April 14, 1967.
(NY Islanders' 4th choice, 55th overall, in 1985 Entry Draft).

			Regular Season					Playoffs				
Season	Club	Lea	GP	G	A	TP	PIM	GP	G	A	TP	PIM
1983-84	Portland	WHL	5	0	0	0	5	5	0	1	1	4
1984-85	Portland	WHL	69	6	44	50	57	6	1	2	3	2
1985-86	Portland	WHL	70	11	59	70	83	15	1	7	8	16
1986-87	Portland	WHL	72	13	53	66	113	20	1	21	22	27
1987-88	**NY Islanders**	**NHL**	**10**	**0**	**5**	**5**	**15**	**1**	**0**	**0**	**0**	**2**
	Springfield	AHL	52	5	18	23	50	....	....	....	....	....
1988-89	**NY Islanders**	**NHL**	**4**	**0**	**0**	**0**	**6**	....	....	....	....	....
	Springfield	AHL	65	3	16	19	55	....	....	....	....	....
	NHL Totals		**14**	**0**	**5**	**5**	**21**	**1**	**0**	**0**	**0**	**2**

FINN, STEVEN

Defense. Shoots left. 6', 198 lbs. Born, Laval, Que., August 20, 1966.
(Quebec's 3rd choice, 57th over-all, in 1984 Entry Draft).

			Regular Season					Playoffs				
Season	Club	Lea	GP	G	A	TP	PIM	GP	G	A	TP	PIM
1982-83	Laval	QMJHL	69	7	30	37	108	6	0	2	2	6
1983-84	Laval	QMJHL	68	7	39	46	159	14	1	6	7	27
1984-85a	Laval	QMJHL	61	20	33	53	169	....	....	....	....	....
	Fredericton	AHL	4	0	0	0	14	6	1	1	2	4
1985-86	**Quebec**	**NHL**	**17**	**0**	**1**	**1**	**28**	....	....	....	....	....
	Laval	QMJHL	29	4	15	19	111	14	6	16	22	57
1986-87	**Quebec**	**NHL**	**36**	**2**	**5**	**7**	**40**	**13**	**0**	**2**	**2**	**29**
	Fredericton	AHL	38	7	19	26	73	....	....	....	....	....
1987-88	**Quebec**	**NHL**	**75**	**3**	**7**	**10**	**198**	....	....	....	....	....
1988-89	**Quebec**	**NHL**	**77**	**2**	**6**	**8**	**235**	....	....	....	....	....
	NHL Totals		**205**	**7**	**19**	**26**	**501**	**13**	**0**	**2**	**2**	**29**

a QMJHL Second All-Star Team (1985).

FIORENTINO, PETER

Defense. Shoots right. 6'1", 200 lbs. Born, Niagara Falls, Ont., December 22, 1968.
(NY Rangers' 11th choice, 215th overall, in 1988 Entry Draft).

			Regular Season					Playoffs				
Season	Club	Lea	GP	G	A	TP	PIM	GP	G	A	TP	PIM
1987-88	S.S. Marie	OHL	65	5	27	32	252	6	2	2	4	21
1988-89	S.S. Marie	OHL	55	5	24	29	220	....	....	....	....	....
	Denver	IHL	10	0	0	0	39	4	0	0	0	24

FISHER, CRAIG

Center. Shoots left. 6'1", 175 lbs. Born, Oshawa, Ont., June 30, 1970.
(Philadelphia's 3rd choice, 56th overall, in 1988 Entry Draft).

			Regular Season					Playoffs				
Season	Club	Lea	GP	G	A	TP	PIM	GP	G	A	TP	PIM
1986-87	Oshawa	OPJHL	34	22	26	48	18	....	....	....	....	....
1987-88	Oshawa	OPJHL	36	42	34	76	48	....	....	....	....	....
1988-89	Miami-Ohio	CCHA	37	22	20	42	37	....	....	....	....	....

FITZGERALD, SEAN

Left wing. Shoots left. 6'1", 210 lbs. Born, W. Seneca, NY, January 12, 1967.
(Los Angeles' 1st choice, 12th overall, in 1988 Supplemental Draft.

			Regular Season					Playoffs				
Season	Club	Lea	GP	G	A	TP	PIM	GP	G	A	TP	PIM
1987-88	Oswego State	NCAA	30	40	36	76	....	....	....	....	....	....
1988-89	Oswego State	NCAA	30	51	26	77	38	....	....	....	....	....

FITZGERALD, TOM

Center. Shoots right. 6'1", 193 lbs. Born, Melrose, MA, August 28, 1968.
(NY Islanders' 1st choice, 17th overall, in 1986 Entry Draft).

			Regular Season					Playoffs				
Season	Club	Lea	GP	G	A	TP	PIM	GP	G	A	TP	PIM
1984-85	Austin Prep	HS	18	20	21	41	....	....	....	....	....	....
1985-86	Austin Prep	HS	24	35	38	73	....	....	....	....	....	....
1986-87	Providence	H.E.	27	8	14	22	22	....	....	....	....	....
1987-88	Providence	H.E.	36	19	15	34	50	....	....	....	....	....
1988-89	**NY Islanders**	**NHL**	**23**	**3**	**5**	**8**	**10**	....	....	....	....	....
	Springfield	AHL	61	24	18	42	43	....	....	....	....	....
	NHL Totals		**23**	**3**	**5**	**8**	**10**	**0**	**0**	**0**	**0**	**0**

FITZPATRICK, ROSS

Center. Shoots left. 6', 195 lbs. Born, Penticton, B.C., October 7, 1960.
(Philadelphia's 7th choice, 147th over-all, in 1980 Entry Draft).

			Regular Season					Playoffs				
Season	Club	Lea	GP	G	A	TP	PIM	GP	G	A	TP	PIM
1978-79	W. Michigan	CCHA	35	16	21	37	31	....	....	....	....	....
1979-80	W. Michigan	CCHA	34	26	33	59	22	....	....	....	....	....
1980-81a	W. Michigan	CCHA	36	28	43	71	22	....	....	....	....	....
1981-82	W. Michigan	CCHA	33	30	28	58	34	....	....	....	....	....
1982-83	**Philadelphia**	**NHL**	**1**	**0**	**0**	**0**	**0**	....	....	....	....	....
	Maine	AHL	66	29	28	57	32	12	5	1	6	12
1983-84	**Philadelphia**	**NHL**	**12**	**4**	**2**	**6**	**0**	....	....	....	....	....
	Springfield	AHL	45	33	30	63	28	4	3	2	5	2
1984-85	**Philadelphia**	**NHL**	**5**	**1**	**0**	**1**	**0**	....	....	....	....	....
	Hershey	AHL	35	26	15	41	8	....	....	....	....	....
1985-86	**Philadelphia**	**NHL**	**2**	**0**	**0**	**0**	**0**	....	....	....	....	....
b	Hershey	AHL	77	50	47	97	28	17	9	7	16	10
1986-87	Hershey	AHL	66	45	40	85	34	5	1	4	5	10
1987-88	Hershey	AHL	35	14	17	31	12	12	*11	4	15	8
1988-89	Hershey	AHL	11	6	9	15	4	9	2	2	4	4
	NHL Totals		**20**	**5**	**2**	**7**	**0**	....	....	....	....	....

a CCHA First All-Star Team (1981)
b AHL Second All-Star Team (1986)

FLAHERTY, JEFF

Right wing. Shoots right. 6'3", 210 lbs. Born, Boston, MA, July 16, 1968.
(Boston's 8th choice, 181st overall, in 1986 Entry Draft).

			Regular Season					Playoffs				
Season	Club	Lea	GP	G	A	TP	PIM	GP	G	A	TP	PIM
1985-86	Weymouth	HS	19	27	23	50	12	....	....	....	....	....
1986-87	U. of Lowell	H.E.	28	4	5	9	37	....	....	....	....	....
1987-88	U. of Lowell	H.E.	34	27	12	39	126	....	....	....	....	....
1988-89	U. of Lowell	H.E.	22	12	11	23	77	....	....	....	....	....

FLANAGAN, JOSEPH

Center. Shoots right. 6', 180 lbs. Born, Arlington, MA, March 5, 1969.
(Los Angeles' 13th choice, 238th overall, in 1988 Entry Draft).

			Regular Season					Playoffs				
Season	Club	Lea	GP	G	A	TP	PIM	GP	G	A	TP	PIM
1987-88	Canterbury	HS	....	55	45	100	....	....	....	....	....	....
1988-89	N. Hampshire	H.E.	23	11	34	45	4	....	....	....	....	....

FLATLEY, PATRICK (FLAT-lee)

Right wing. Shoots right. 6'2", 197 lbs. Born, Toronto, Ont., October 3, 1963.
(NY Islanders' 1st choice, 21st over-all, in 1982 Entry Draft).

			Regular Season					Playoffs				
Season	Club	Lea	GP	G	A	TP	PIM	GP	G	A	TP	PIM
1981-82	U. Wisconsin	WCHA	17	10	9	19	40	....	....	....	....	....
1982-83ab	U. Wisconsin	WCHA	26	17	24	41	48	....	....	....	....	....
1983-84	Cdn. Olympic	....	57	33	17	50	136	....	....	....	....	....
	NY Islanders	**NHL**	**16**	**2**	**7**	**9**	**6**	**21**	**9**	**6**	**15**	**14**
1984-85	**NY Islanders**	**NHL**	**78**	**20**	**31**	**51**	**106**	**4**	**1**	**0**	**1**	**6**
1985-86	**NY Islanders**	**NHL**	**73**	**18**	**34**	**52**	**66**	**3**	**0**	**0**	**0**	**21**
1986-87	**NY Islanders**	**NHL**	**63**	**16**	**35**	**51**	**81**	**11**	**3**	**2**	**5**	**6**
1987-88	**NY Islanders**	**NHL**	**40**	**9**	**15**	**24**	**28**	....	....	....	....	....
1988-89	**NY Islanders**	**NHL**	**41**	**10**	**15**	**25**	**31**	....	....	....	....	....
	Springfield	AHL	2	1	1	2	2	....	....	....	....	....
	NHL Totals		**311**	**75**	**137**	**212**	**318**	**39**	**13**	**8**	**21**	**47**

a WCHA First All-Star Team (1983)
b Named to NCAA All-Tournament Team (1983)

FLETCHER, STEVEN

Left wing. Shoots left. 6'3", 205 lbs. Born, Montreal, Que., March 31, 1962.
Last amateur club: Hull Olympiques (QMJHL).
(Calgary's 11th choice, 202nd overall, in 1980 Entry Draft).

			Regular Season					Playoffs				
Season	Club	Lea	GP	G	A	TP	PIM	GP	G	A	TP	PIM
1981-82	Hull	QMJHL	60	4	20	24	230	....	....	....	....	....
1982-83	Sherbrooke	AHL	36	0	1	1	119	....	....	....	....	....
	Fort Wayne	IHL	34	1	9	10	115	....	....	....	....	....
1983-84	Sherbrooke	AHL	77	3	7	10	208	....	....	....	....	....
1984-85	Sherbrooke	AHL	50	2	4	6	192	13	0	0	0	48
1985-86	Sherbrooke	AHL	64	2	12	14	293	....	....	....	....	....
1986-87	Sherbrooke	AHL	70	15	11	26	261	17	5	5	10	82
1987-88	**Montreal**	**NHL**	....	....	....	....	....	**1**	**0**	**0**	**0**	**5**
	Sherbrooke	AHL	76	8	21	29	338	6	2	1	3	28
1988-89	**Winnipeg**	**NHL**	**3**	**0**	**0**	**0**	**5**	....	....	....	....	....
	Halifax	AHL	29	5	8	13	91	....	....	....	....	....
	Moncton	AHL	23	1	1	2	89	....	....	....	....	....
	NHL Totals		**3**	**0**	**0**	**0**	**5**	**1**	**0**	**0**	**0**	**5**

Signed as a free agent by **Montreal**, August 21, 1984. Traded to **Philadelphia** by **Winnipeg** for future considerations, December 12, 1988.

FLEURY, THEOREN

Center. Shoots right. 5'6", 160 lbs. Born, Oxbow, Sask., June 29, 1968.
(Calgary's 9th choice, 166th overall, in 1987 Entry Draft).

			Regular Season					Playoffs				
Season	Club	Lea	GP	G	A	TP	PIM	GP	G	A	TP	PIM
1986-87	Moose Jaw	WHL	66	61	68	129	110	9	7	9	16	34
1987-88	Moose Jaw	WHL	65	68	92	160	235	....	....	....	....	....
	Salt Lake	IHL	2	3	4	7	7	8	11	5	16	16
1988-89	**Calgary**	**NHL**	**36**	**14**	**20**	**34**	**46**	**22**	**5**	**6**	**11**	**24**
	Salt Lake	IHL	40	37	37	74	81	....	....	....	....	....
	NHL Totals		**36**	**14**	**20**	**34**	**46**	**22**	**5**	**6**	**11**	**24**

FLICHEL, TODD (FLIK-uhl)

Defense. Shoots right. 6'3", 195 lbs. Born, Osgoode, Ont., September 14, 1964.
(Winnipeg's 10th choice, 169th overall, in 1983 Entry Draft).

			Regular Season					Playoffs				
Season	Club	Lea	GP	G	A	TP	PIM	GP	G	A	TP	PIM
1983-84	Bowling Green	CCHA	44	1	3	4	12	....	....	....	....	....
1984-85	Bowling Green	CCHA	42	5	7	12	62	....	....	....	....	....
1985-86	Bowling Green	CCHA	42	3	10	13	84	....	....	....	....	....
1986-87	Bowling Green	CCHA	42	4	15	19	77	....	....	....	....	....
1987-88	**Winnipeg**	**NHL**	**2**	**0**	**0**	**0**	**2**	....	....	....	....	....
	Moncton	AHL	65	5	12	17	102	....	....	....	....	....
1988-89	**Winnipeg**	**NHL**	**1**	**0**	**0**	**0**	**0**	....	....	....	....	....
	Moncton	AHL	74	2	29	31	81	10	1	4	5	25
	NHL Totals		**3**	**0**	**0**	**0**	**2**	....	....	....	....	....

FLOCKHART, RONALD (RON)

Center. Shoots left. 5'11", 185 lbs. Born, Smithers, B.C., October 10, 1960.

			Regular Season					Playoffs				
Season	Club	Lea	GP	G	A	TP	PIM	GP	G	A	TP	PIM
1979-80	Regina	WHL	65	54	76	130	63	17	11	23	34	18
1980-81	Maine	AHL	59	33	33	66	26	....	....	....	....	....
	Philadelphia	**NHL**	**14**	**3**	**7**	**10**	**11**	**3**	**1**	**0**	**1**	**2**
1981-82	**Philadelphia**	**NHL**	**72**	**33**	**39**	**72**	**44**	**4**	**0**	**1**	**1**	**2**
1982-83	**Philadelphia**	**NHL**	**73**	**29**	**31**	**60**	**49**	**2**	**1**	**1**	**2**	**2**
1983-84	**Philadelphia**	**NHL**	**8**	**0**	**3**	**3**	**4**	....	....	....	....	....
	Pittsburgh	**NHL**	**68**	**27**	**18**	**45**	**40**	....	....	....	....	....
1984-85	**Pittsburgh**	**NHL**	**12**	**0**	**5**	**5**	**4**	....	....	....	....	....
	Montreal	**NHL**	**42**	**10**	**12**	**22**	**14**	**2**	**1**	**1**	**2**	**2**
1985-86	**St. Louis**	**NHL**	**79**	**22**	**45**	**67**	**26**	**8**	**1**	**3**	**4**	**6**
1986-87	**St. Louis**	**NHL**	**60**	**16**	**19**	**35**	**12**	....	....	....	....	....
1987-88	**St. Louis**	**NHL**	**21**	**5**	**4**	**9**	**4**	....	....	....	....	....
1988-89	**Boston**	**NHL**	**4**	**0**	**0**	**0**	**0**	....	....	....	....	....
	Maine	AHL	9	5	6	11	0	....	....	....	....	....
	Peoria	IHL	2	0	2	2	2	....	....	....	....	....
	NHL Totals		**453**	**145**	**183**	**328**	**208**	**19**	**4**	**6**	**10**	**14**

Signed as free agent by **Philadelphia**, July 2, 1980. Traded to **Pittsburgh** by **Philadelphia** with Andy Brickley, Mark Taylor and Philadelphia's first round (Roger Belanger) and third round (Mike Stevens - later transferred to Vancouver) choices in 1984 Entry Draft for Rich Sutter and Pittsburgh's second round (Greg Smyth) and third round (David McLay) choices in 1984 Entry Draft, October 23, 1983. Traded to **Montreal** by **Pittsburgh** for John Chabot, November 9, 1984. Traded to **St. Louis** by **Montreal** for Perry Ganchar, August 26, 1985. Traded to **Boston** by **St. Louis** for future considerations, February 13, 1989.

FLORIO, PERRY

Defense. Shoots left. 6', 190 lbs. Born, Glen Cove, NY, July 15, 1967.
(Los Angeles' 5th choice, 72nd overall, in 1985 Entry Draft).

			Regular Season					Playoffs				
Season	Club	Lea	GP	G	A	TP	PIM	GP	G	A	TP	PIM
1984-85	Kent	HS	13	3	12	15	0	....	....	....	....	....
1985-86	Providence	H.E.	38	4	5	9	90	....	....	....	....	....
1986-87	Providence	H.E.	23	1	6	7	58	....	....	....	....	....
1987-88	N. Michigan	WCHA	DID NOT PLAY									
1988-89	N. Michigan	WCHA	10	0	4	4	8	....	....	....	....	....

FLOYD, LARRY DAVID

Center. Shoots left. 5'8", 180 lbs. Born, Peterborough, Ont., May 1, 1961.
Last amateur club: Peterborough Petes (OHL).

			Regular Season					Playoffs				
Season	Club	Lea	GP	G	A	TP	PIM	GP	G	A	TP	PIM
1979-80	Peterborough	OHA	66	21	37	58	54	14	6	9	15	10
1980-81	Peterborough	OHA	44	26	37	63	43	5	2	2	4	0
1981-82	Peterborough	OHL	39	32	37	69	26	9	9	6	15	20
	Rochester	AHL	1	0	2	2	0	7	1	1	2	0
1982-83	**New Jersey**	**NHL**	**5**	**1**	**0**	**1**	**2**	....	....	....	....	....
a	Wichita	CHL	75	40	43	83	16	....	....	....	....	....
1983-84	**New Jersey**	**NHL**	**7**	**1**	**3**	**4**	**7**	....	....	....	....	....
	Maine	AHL	74	37	49	86	40	16	9	8	17	4
1984-85	Maine	AHL	72	30	51	81	24	3	0	1	1	2
1985-86	Maine	AHL	80	29	58	87	25	5	3	3	6	0
1986-87	Maine	AHL	77	30	44	74	50	....	....	....	....	....
1987-88	Utica	AHL	28	21	21	42	14	....	....	....	....	....
1988-89	Cape Breton	AHL	70	16	33	49	40	....	....	....	....	....
	NHL Totals		**12**	**2**	**3**	**5**	**9**	....	....	....	....	....

a Won Ken McKenzie Trophy (CHL's Rookie of the Year) (1983)

Signed as free agent by **New Jersey**, September 16, 1982.

FOGARTY, BRYAN

Defense. Shoots left. 6'2", 198 lbs. Born, Brantford, Ont., June 11, 1969.
(Quebec's 1st choice, 9th overall, in 1987 Entry Draft).

			Regular Season					Playoffs				
Season	Club	Lea	GP	G	A	TP	PIM	GP	G	A	TP	PIM
1985-86	Kingston	OHL	47	2	19	21	14	10	1	3	4	4
1986-87a	Kingston	OHL	56	20	50	70	46	12	2	3	5	5
1987-88	Kingston	OHL	48	11	36	47	50	....	....	....	....	....
1988-89abc	Niagara Falls	OHL	60	47	*108	*155	88	17	10	22	32	36

a OHL First All-Star Team (1987, 1989)
b OHL Player of the Year (1989)
c Canadian Major Junior Player of the Year (1989)

FOLIGNO, MIKE ANTHONY (foh LEE noh)

Right wing. Shoots right. 6'2", 195 lbs. Born, Sudbury, Ont., January 29, 1959.
(Detroit's 1st choice, 3rd over-all, in 1979 Entry Draft).

			Regular Season					Playoffs				
Season	Club	Lea	GP	G	A	TP	PIM	GP	G	A	TP	PIM
1977-78	Sudbury	OHA	67	47	39	86	112	....	....	....	....	....
1978-79a	Sudbury	OHA	68	65	85	*150	98	10	5	5	10	14
1979-80	**Detroit**	**NHL**	**80**	**36**	**35**	**71**	**109**	....	....	....	....	....
1980-81	**Detroit**	**NHL**	**80**	**28**	**35**	**63**	**210**	....	....	....	....	....
1981-82	**Detroit**	**NHL**	**26**	**13**	**13**	**26**	**28**	....	....	....	....	....
	Buffalo	**NHL**	**56**	**20**	**31**	**51**	**149**	**4**	**2**	**0**	**2**	**9**
1982-83	**Buffalo**	**NHL**	**66**	**22**	**25**	**47**	**135**	**10**	**2**	**3**	**5**	**39**
1983-84	**Buffalo**	**NHL**	**70**	**32**	**31**	**63**	**151**	**3**	**2**	**1**	**3**	**19**
1984-85	**Buffalo**	**NHL**	**77**	**27**	**29**	**56**	**154**	**5**	**1**	**3**	**4**	**12**
1985-86	**Buffalo**	**NHL**	**79**	**41**	**39**	**80**	**168**	....	....	....	....	....
1986-87	**Buffalo**	**NHL**	**75**	**30**	**29**	**59**	**176**	....	....	....	....	....
1987-88	**Buffalo**	**NHL**	**74**	**29**	**28**	**57**	**220**	**6**	**3**	**2**	**5**	**31**
1988-89	**Buffalo**	**NHL**	**75**	**27**	**22**	**49**	**156**	**5**	**3**	**1**	**4**	**21**
	NHL Totals		**758**	**305**	**317**	**622**	**1656**	**33**	**13**	**10**	**23**	**131**

a OHL First All-Star Team (1979)

Traded to **Buffalo** by **Detroit** with Dale McCourt and Brent Peterson for Danny Gare, Jim Schoenfeld and Derek Smith, December 2, 1981.

FOOTE, ADAM

Defense. Shoots right. 6'1", 180 lbs. Born, Toronto, Ont., July 10, 1971.
(Quebec's 2nd choice, 22nd overall, in 1989 Entry Draft).

			Regular Season					Playoffs				
Season	Club	Lea	GP	G	A	TP	PIM	GP	G	A	TP	PIM
1987-88	Whitby	Midget	65	25	43	68	108	....	....	....	....	....
1988-89	S.S. Marie	OHL	66	7	32	39	120	....	....	....	....	....

FORREST, PATRIK

Defense. Shoots left. 6'2", 200 lbs. Born, Blaine, MN, April 25, 1968.
(NY Rangers' 8th choice, 173rd overall, in 1988 Entry Draft).

			Regular Season					Playoffs				
Season	Club	Lea	GP	G	A	TP	PIM	GP	G	A	TP	PIM
1987-88	St. Cloud St.	NCAA	24	2	4	6	....	....	....	....	....	....
1988-89	St. Cloud St.	NCAA	DID NOT PLAY									

FORSLUND, THOMAS

Right wing. Shoots left. 6', 185 lbs. Born, Falund, Sweden, November 24, 1968.
(Calgary's 4th choice, 85th overall, in 1988 Entry Draft).

			Regular Season					Playoffs				
Season	Club	Lea	GP	G	A	TP	PIM	GP	G	A	TP	PIM
1986-87	Leksand	Swe.	23	3	5	8	....	....	....	....	....	....
1987-88	Leksand	Swe.	37	9	10	19	....	....	....	....	....	....
1988-89	Leksand	Swe.	39	14	16	30	56	....	....	....	....	....

FORTIER, MARC

Center. Shoots right. 6', 192 lbs. Born, Windsor, Ont., February 26, 1966.

			Regular Season					Playoffs				
Season	Club	Lea	GP	G	A	TP	PIM	GP	G	A	TP	PIM
1983-84	Chicoutimi	QMJHL	67	16	30	46	51	....	....	....	....	....
1984-85	Chicoutimi	QMJHL	68	35	63	98	114	14	8	4	12	16
1985-86	Chicoutimi	QMJHL	71	47	86	133	49	9	2	14	16	12
1986-87	Chicoutimi	QMJHL	65	66	135	201	39	19	11	40	51	20
1987-88	**Quebec**	**NHL**	**27**	**4**	**10**	**14**	**12**	....	....	....	....	....
	Fredericton	AHL	50	26	36	62	48	....	....	....	....	....
1988-89	**Quebec**	**NHL**	**57**	**20**	**19**	**39**	**45**	....	....	....	....	....
	Halifax	AHL	16	11	11	22	14	....	....	....	....	....
	NHL Totals		**84**	**24**	**29**	**53**	**57**	....	....	....	....	....

Signed as a free agent by **Quebec**, February 3, 1987.

FOSTER, COREY

Defense. Shoots left. 6'3", 200 lbs. Born, Ottawa, Ont., October 27, 1969.
(New Jersey's 1st choice, 12th overall, in 1988 Entry Draft).

			Regular Season					Playoffs				
Season	Club	Lea	GP	G	A	TP	PIM	GP	G	A	TP	PIM
1986-87	Peterborough	OHL	30	3	4	7	4	1	0	0	0	0
1987-88	Peterborough	OHL	66	13	31	44	58	11	5	9	14	13
1988-89	**New Jersey**	**NHL**	**2**	**0**	**0**	**0**	**0**	....	....	....	....	....
a	Peterborough	OHL	55	14	42	56	42	17	1	17	18	12
	NHL Totals		**2**	**0**	**0**	**0**	**0**	....	....	....	....	....

a OHL Third All-Star Team (1989)

Traded to **Edmonton** by **New Jersey** for Edmonton's first-round choice (Jason Millar) in 1989 Entry Draft, June 17, 1989.

FOTIU, NICHOLAS EVLAMPIOS (NICK) (foh-TEE-oo)

Left wing. Shoots left. 6'2", 210 lbs. Born, Staten Island, NY, May 25, 1952.

			Regular Season					Playoffs				
Season	Club	Lea	GP	G	A	TP	PIM	GP	G	A	TP	PIM
1971-72	New Hyde Park	MJHA	32	6	17	23	135	....	....	....	....	....
1972-73			DID NOT PLAY									
1973-74	Cape Cod	NAHL	72	12	24	36	371	....	....	....	....	....
1974-75	Cape Cod	NAHL	5	2	1	3	13	....	....	....	....	....
	New England	WHA	61	2	2	4	144	4	2	0	2	27
1975-76	Cape Cod	NAHL	6	2	1	3	15	....	....	....	....	....
	New England	WHA	49	3	2	5	94	16	3	2	5	57
1976-77	**NY Rangers**	**NHL**	**70**	**4**	**8**	**12**	**174**	....	....	....	....	....
1977-78	New Haven	AHL	5	1	1	2	9	....	....	....	....	....
	NY Rangers	**NHL**	**59**	**2**	**7**	**9**	**105**	**3**	**0**	**0**	**0**	**5**
1978-79	**NY Rangers**	**NHL**	**71**	**3**	**5**	**8**	**190**	**4**	**0**	**0**	**0**	**6**
1979-80	**Hartford**	**NHL**	**74**	**10**	**8**	**18**	**107**	**3**	**0**	**0**	**0**	**6**
1980-81	**Hartford**	**NHL**	**42**	**4**	**3**	**7**	**79**	....	....	....	....	....
	NY Rangers	**NHL**	**27**	**5**	**6**	**11**	**91**	**2**	**0**	**0**	**0**	**4**
1981-82	**NY Rangers**	**NHL**	**70**	**8**	**10**	**18**	**151**	**10**	**0**	**2**	**2**	**6**
1982-83	**NY Rangers**	**NHL**	**72**	**8**	**13**	**21**	**90**	**5**	**0**	**1**	**1**	**6**
1983-84	**NY Rangers**	**NHL**	**40**	**7**	**6**	**13**	**115**	....	....	....	....	....
1984-85	**NY Rangers**	**NHL**	**46**	**4**	**7**	**11**	**54**	....	....	....	....	....
1985-86	New Haven	AHL	9	4	2	6	21	....	....	....	....	....
	Calgary	**NHL**	**9**	**0**	**1**	**1**	**21**	**11**	**0**	**1**	**1**	**34**
1986-87	**Calgary**	**NHL**	**42**	**5**	**3**	**8**	**145**	....	....	....	....	....
1987-88	**Philadelphia**	**NHL**	**23**	**0**	**0**	**0**	**40**	....	....	....	....	....
1988-89	**Edmonton**	**NHL**	**1**	**0**	**0**	**0**	**0**	....	....	....	....	....
	NHL Totals		**646**	**60**	**77**	**137**	**1362**	**38**	**0**	**4**	**4**	**67**

Signed as free agent by **NY Rangers**, July 23, 1976. Claimed by **Hartford** from **NY Rangers** in Expansion Draft, June 13, 1979. Traded to **NY Rangers** by **Hartford** for Rangers' fifth round choice (Bill Maguire) in 1981 Entry Draft, January 15, 1981. Traded to **Calgary** by **NY Rangers** for Calgary's sixth-round choice in 1987 Entry Draft, March 11, 1986. Signed as a free agent by **Philadelphia**, October 30, 1987.

FOWLER, DANIEL

Defense. Shoots left. 6'3", 205 lbs. Born, Fredericton, N.B., March 4, 1969.
(St. Louis' 6th choice, 114th overall, in 1988 Entry Draft).

			Regular Season					Playoffs				
Season	Club	Lea	GP	G	A	TP	PIM	GP	G	A	TP	PIM
1987-88	U. of Maine	H.E.	20	1	4	5	20	....	....	....	....	....
1988-89	U. of Maine		DID NOT PLAY									

FOWLER, ROB

Defense. Shoots left. 6'1", 195 lbs. Born, Tewksbury, MA, July 9, 1965.
(Winnipeg's 1st choice, 21st overall, in 1987 Supplemental Draft).

			Regular Season					Playoffs				
Season	Club	Lea	GP	G	A	TP	PIM	GP	G	A	TP	PIM
1983-84	Merrimack	ECAC	28	4	8	12	18	....	....	....	....	....
1984-85	Merrimack	ECAC	32	8	19	27	42	....	....	....	....	....
1985-86	Merrimack	ECAC	32	3	20	23	50	....	....	....	....	....
1986-87a	Merrimack	ECAC	35	2	25	27	49	....	....	....	....	....
1987-88	Moncton	AHL	68	2	11	13	51	....	....	....	....	....
1988-89	Fort Wayne	IHL	67	9	12	21	62	9	1	0	1	8

a NCAA Division III First All-Star Team (1987)

FOX, JAMES CHARLES (JIMMY)

Right wing. Shoots right. 5'8", 185 lbs. Born, Coniston, Ont., May 18, 1960.
(Los Angeles' 2nd choice, 10th over-all, in 1980 Entry Draft).

			Regular Season					Playoffs				
Season	Club	Lea	GP	G	A	TP	PIM	GP	G	A	TP	PIM
1978-79	Ottawa	OHA	53	37	66	103	4	4	2	1	3	2
1979-80ab	Ottawa	OHA	52	65	*101	*166	30	11	6	14	20	2
1980-81	**Los Angeles**	**NHL**	**71**	**18**	**25**	**43**	**8**	**4**	**0**	**1**	**1**	**0**
1981-82	**Los Angeles**	**NHL**	**77**	**30**	**38**	**68**	**23**	**9**	**1**	**4**	**5**	**0**
1982-83	**Los Angeles**	**NHL**	**77**	**28**	**40**	**68**	**8**	....	....	....	....	....
1983-84	**Los Angeles**	**NHL**	**80**	**30**	**42**	**72**	**26**	....	....	....	....	....
1984-85	**Los Angeles**	**NHL**	**79**	**30**	**53**	**83**	**10**	**3**	**0**	**1**	**1**	**0**
1985-86	**Los Angeles**	**NHL**	**39**	**14**	**17**	**31**	**2**	....	....	....	....	....
1986-87	**Los Angeles**	**NHL**	**76**	**19**	**42**	**61**	**48**	**5**	**3**	**2**	**5**	**0**
1987-88	**Los Angeles**	**NHL**	**68**	**16**	**35**	**51**	**18**	**1**	**0**	**0**	**0**	**0**
1988-89	**Los Angeles**	**NHL**	**DID NOT PLAY - INJURED**									
	NHL Totals		**567**	**185**	**292**	**477**	**143**	**22**	**4**	**8**	**12**	**0**

a OHA First All-Star Team (1980)
b Named OHA Most Valuable Player (1980)

FRANCESCHETTI, LOU (FRAN sihs KEH tee)

Right wing. Shoots left. 6', 190 lbs. Born, Toronto, Ont., March 28, 1958.
(Washington's 8th choice, 71st over-all, in 1978 Amateur Draft).

			Regular Season					Playoffs				
Season	Club	Lea	GP	G	A	TP	PIM	GP	G	A	TP	PIM
1976-77	Niagara Falls	OHA	61	23	30	53	80	....	....	....	....	....
1977-78	Niagara Falls	OHA	62	40	50	90	46	....	....	....	....	....
1978-79	Saginaw	IHL	2	1	1	2	0	....	....	....	....	....
	Port Huron	IHL	76	45	58	103	131	....	....	....	....	....
1979-80	Port Huron	IHL	15	3	8	11	31	....	....	....	....	....
	Hershey	AHL	65	27	29	56	58	14	6	9	15	32
1980-81	Hershey	AHL	79	32	36	68	173	10	3	7	10	30
1981-82	Hershey	AHL	50	22	33	55	89	....	....	....	....	....
	Washington	**NHL**	**30**	**2**	**10**	**12**	**23**	....	....	....	....	....
1982-83	Hershey	AHL	80	31	44	75	176	5	1	2	3	16
1983-84	Hershey	AHL	73	26	34	60	130	....	....	....	....	....
	Washington	**NHL**	**2**	**0**	**0**	**0**	**0**	**3**	**0**	**0**	**0**	**8**
1984-85	**Washington**	**NHL**	**22**	**4**	**7**	**11**	**45**	**5**	**1**	**1**	**2**	**15**
	Binghamton	AHL	52	29	43	72	75	....	....	....	....	....
1985-86	**Washington**	**NHL**	**76**	**7**	**14**	**21**	**131**	**8**	**0**	**0**	**0**	**15**
1986-87	**Washington**	**NHL**	**75**	**12**	**9**	**21**	**127**	**7**	**0**	**0**	**0**	**23**
1987-88	**Washington**	**NHL**	**59**	**4**	**8**	**12**	**113**	**4**	**0**	**0**	**0**	**14**
	Binghamton	AHL	6	2	4	6	4	....	....	....	....	....
1988-89	**Washington**	**NHL**	**63**	**7**	**10**	**17**	**123**	**6**	**1**	**0**	**1**	**8**
	Baltimore	AHL	10	8	7	15	30	....	....	....	....	....
	NHL Totals		**327**	**36**	**58**	**94**	**562**	**33**	**2**	**1**	**3**	**83**

Traded to **Toronto** by **Washington** for Toronto's 6th round choice in 1990 Entry Draft, June 29, 1989.

FRANCIS, RONALD (RON)

Center. Shoots left. 6'2", 200 lbs. Born, Sault Ste. Marie, Ont., March 1, 1963.
(Hartford's 1st choice, 4th overall, in 1981 Entry Draft).

			Regular Season					Playoffs				
Season	Club	Lea	GP	G	A	TP	PIM	GP	G	A	TP	PIM
1980-81	S. S. Marie	OHA	64	26	43	69	33	19	7	8	15	34
1981-82	S. S. Marie	OHL	25	18	30	48	46	....	....	....	....	....
	Hartford	**NHL**	**59**	**25**	**43**	**68**	**51**	....	....	....	....	....
1982-83	**Hartford**	**NHL**	**79**	**31**	**59**	**90**	**60**	....	....	....	....	....
1983-84	**Hartford**	**NHL**	**72**	**23**	**60**	**83**	**45**	....	....	....	....	....
1984-85	**Hartford**	**NHL**	**80**	**24**	**57**	**81**	**66**	....	....	....	....	....
1985-86	**Hartford**	**NHL**	**53**	**24**	**53**	**77**	**24**	**10**	**1**	**2**	**3**	**4**
1986-87	**Hartford**	**NHL**	**75**	**30**	**63**	**93**	**45**	**6**	**2**	**2**	**4**	**6**
1987-88	**Hartford**	**NHL**	**80**	**25**	**50**	**75**	**87**	**6**	**2**	**5**	**7**	**2**
1988-89	**Hartford**	**NHL**	**69**	**29**	**48**	**77**	**36**	**4**	**0**	**2**	**2**	**0**
	NHL Totals		**567**	**211**	**433**	**644**	**414**	**26**	**5**	**11**	**16**	**12**

Played in NHL All-Star Game (1983, 1985)

FRASER, CURT M.

Left wing. Shoots left. 6'1" 200 lbs. Born, Cincinnati, OH, January 12, 1958.
(Vancouver's 2nd choice, 22nd over-all, in 1978 Amateur Draft).

			Regular Season					Playoffs				
Season	Club	Lea	GP	G	A	TP	PIM	GP	G	A	TP	PIM
1976-77	Victoria	WHL	60	34	41	75	82	4	4	2	6	4
1977-78	Victoria	WHL	66	48	44	92	256	13	10	7	17	28
1978-79	**Vancouver**	**NHL**	**78**	**16**	**19**	**35**	**116**	**3**	**0**	**2**	**2**	**6**
1979-80	**Vancouver**	**NHL**	**78**	**17**	**25**	**42**	**143**	**4**	**0**	**0**	**0**	**2**
1980-81	**Vancouver**	**NHL**	**77**	**25**	**24**	**49**	**118**	**3**	**1**	**0**	**1**	**2**
1981-82	**Vancouver**	**NHL**	**79**	**28**	**39**	**67**	**175**	**17**	**3**	**7**	**10**	**98**
1982-83	**Vancouver**	**NHL**	**36**	**6**	**7**	**13**	**99**	....	....	....	....	....
	Chicago	**NHL**	**38**	**6**	**13**	**19**	**77**	**13**	**4**	**4**	**8**	**18**
1983-84	**Chicago**	**NHL**	**29**	**5**	**12**	**17**	**28**	**5**	**0**	**0**	**0**	**14**
1984-85	**Chicago**	**NHL**	**73**	**25**	**25**	**50**	**109**	**15**	**6**	**3**	**9**	**36**
1985-86	**Chicago**	**NHL**	**61**	**29**	**39**	**68**	**84**	**3**	**0**	**1**	**1**	**12**
1986-87	**Chicago**	**NHL**	**75**	**25**	**25**	**50**	**182**	**2**	**1**	**1**	**2**	**10**
1987-88	**Chicago**	**NHL**	**27**	**4**	**6**	**10**	**57**	....	....	....	....	....
	Minnesota	**NHL**	**10**	**1**	**1**	**2**	**20**	....	....	....	....	....
1988-89	**Minnesota**	**NHL**	**35**	**5**	**5**	**10**	**76**	....	....	....	....	....
	NHL Totals		**696**	**192**	**240**	**432**	**1284**	**65**	**15**	**18**	**33**	**198**

Traded to **Chicago** by **Vancouver** for Tony Tanti, January 6, 1983. Traded to **Minnesota** by **Chicago** for Dirk Graham, January 4, 1988.

FRASER, JAY

Left wing. Shoots left. 6'1", 200 lbs. Born, St. Lambert, Que., October 26, 1961.
(Philadelphia's 2nd choice, 42nd overall, in 1980 Entry Draft).

			Regular Season					Playoffs				
Season	Club	Lea	GP	G	A	TP	PIM	GP	G	A	TP	PIM
1980-81	Ottawa	OHL	55	17	23	40	204	....	....	....	....	....
1981-82	Toledo	IHL	19	14	8	22	8	....	....	....	....	....
	Maine	AHL	44	5	5	10	116	....	....	....	....	....
1982-83	Carolina	ACHL	68	28	37	65	118	8	2	5	7	20
1983-84	Carolina	ACHL	29	16	29	45	85	....	....	....	....	....
1984-85			DID NOT PLAY									
1985-86	Carolina	ACHL	21	13	14	27	127	....	....	....	....	....
	Rochester	AHL	20	4	5	9	61	....	....	....	....	....
1986-87	Rochester	AHL	36	8	12	20	159	6	0	1	1	17
1987-88	Rochester	AHL	39	5	9	14	98	1	0	0	0	0
1988-89	Maine	AHL	11	2	2	4	14	....	....	....	....	....

Signed as a free agent by **Buffalo**, September 12, 1986.

FRAWLEY, WILLIAM DANIEL (DAN)

Right wing. Shoots right. 6'1", 190 lbs. Born, Sturgeon Falls, Ont., June 2, 1962.
(Chicago's 15th choice, 204th over-all, in 1980 Entry Draft).

			Regular Season					Playoffs				
Season	Club	Lea	GP	G	A	TP	PIM	GP	G	A	TP	PIM
1979-80	Sudbury	OHA	63	21	26	47	67	8	0	1	1	2
1980-81	Cornwall	QMJHL	28	10	14	28	76	18	5	12	17	37
1981-82	Cornwall	OHL	64	27	50	77	239	5	3	8	11	19
1982-83	Springfield	AHL	80	30	27	57	107	....	....	....	....	....
1983-84	**Chicago**	**NHL**	**3**	**0**	**0**	**0**	**0**	....	....	....	....	....
	Springfield	AHL	69	22	34	56	137	4	0	1	1	12
1984-85	**Chicago**	**NHL**	**30**	**4**	**3**	**7**	**64**	**1**	**0**	**0**	**0**	**0**
	Milwaukee	IHL	26	11	12	23	125	....	....	....	....	....
1985-86	**Pittsburgh**	**NHL**	**69**	**10**	**11**	**21**	**174**	....	....	....	....	....
1986-87	**Pittsburgh**	**NHL**	**78**	**14**	**14**	**28**	**218**	....	....	....	....	....
1987-88	**Pittsburgh**	**NHL**	**47**	**6**	**8**	**14**	**152**	....	....	....	....	....
1988-89	**Pittsburgh**	**NHL**	**46**	**3**	**4**	**7**	**66**	....	....	....	....	....
	Muskegon	IHL	24	12	16	28	35	14	6	4	10	31
	NHL Totals		**273**	**37**	**40**	**77**	**674**	**1**	**0**	**0**	**0**	**0**

Claimed by **Pittsburgh** from **Chicago** in NHL Waiver Draft, October 7, 1985.

FREER, MARK

Center. Shoots left. 5'10", 180 lbs. Born, Peterborough, Ont., July 14, 1968.

			Regular Season					Playoffs				
Season	Club	Lea	GP	G	A	TP	PIM	GP	G	A	TP	PIM
1985-86	Peterborough	OHL	65	16	28	44	24	14	3	4	7	13
1986-87	Peterborough	OHL	65	39	43	82	44	12	2	6	8	5
	Philadelphia	**NHL**	**1**	**0**	**1**	**1**	**0**	....	....	....	....	....
1987-88	**Philadelphia**	**NHL**	**1**	**0**	**0**	**0**	**0**	....	....	....	....	....
	Peterborough	OHL	63	38	70	108	63	12	5	12	17	4
1988-89	**Philadelphia**	**NHL**	**5**	**0**	**0**	**0**	**0**	....	....	....	....	....
	Hershey	AHL	75	30	49	79	77	12	4	6	10	2
	NHL Totals		**7**	**0**	**1**	**1**	**0**	....	....	....	....	....

Signed as a free agent by **Philadelphia**, October 7, 1986.

FRYCER, MIROSLAV (FREE-chuhr)

Right wing. Shoots right. 6', 200 lbs. Born, Ostrava, Czechoslovakia, September 27, 1959.

			Regular Season					Playoffs				
Season	Club	Lea	GP	G	A	TP	PIM	GP	G	A	TP	PIM
1979-80	Vitkovice	Czech	44	31	15	46	....	....	....	....	....	....
1980-81	Vitkovice	Czech	34	33	24	57	....	....	....	....	....	....
1981-82	Fredericton	AHL	11	9	5	14	16	....	....	....	....	....
	Quebec	**NHL**	**49**	**20**	**17**	**37**	**47**	....	....	....	....	....
	Toronto	**NHL**	**10**	**4**	**6**	**10**	**31**	....	....	....	....	....
1982-83	**Toronto**	**NHL**	**67**	**25**	**30**	**55**	**90**	**4**	**2**	**5**	**7**	**0**
1983-84	**Toronto**	**NHL**	**47**	**10**	**16**	**26**	**55**	....	....	....	....	....
1984-85	**Toronto**	**NHL**	**65**	**25**	**30**	**55**	**55**	....	....	....	....	....
1985-86	**Toronto**	**NHL**	**73**	**32**	**43**	**75**	**74**	**10**	**1**	**3**	**4**	**10**
1986-87	**Toronto**	**NHL**	**29**	**7**	**8**	**15**	**28**	....	....	....	....	....
1987-88	**Toronto**	**NHL**	**38**	**12**	**20**	**32**	**41**	**3**	**0**	**0**	**0**	**6**
1988-89	**Detroit**	**NHL**	**23**	**7**	**8**	**15**	**47**	....	....	....	....	....
	Edmonton	**NHL**	**14**	**5**	**5**	**10**	**18**	....	....	....	....	....
	NHL Totals		**414**	**146**	**183**	**329**	**486**	**17**	**3**	**8**	**11**	**16**

Played in NHL All-Star Game (1985)

Signed as free agent by **Quebec**, April 21, 1980. Traded to **Toronto** by **Quebec** with Quebec's seventh round choice (Jeff Triano) in 1982 Entry Draft for Wilf Paiement, March 9, 1982. Traded to **Detroit** by **Toronto** for Darren Veitch, June 10, 1988. Traded to **Edmonton** by **Detroit** for Edmonton's tenth-round choice (Rick Judson) in the 1989 Entry Draft, January 3, 1989

GAETZ, LINK

Defense. Shoots left. 6'2", 210 lbs. Born, Vancouver, B.C., October 2, 1968.
(Minnesota's 2nd choice, 40th overall, in 1988 Entry Draft).

			Regular Season					Playoffs				
Season	Club	Lea	GP	G	A	TP	PIM	GP	G	A	TP	PIM
1986-87	N. Westminster	WHL	44	2	7	9	52	....	....	....	....	....
1987-88	Spokane	WHL	59	9	20	29	313	10	2	2	4	70
1988-89	**Minnesota**	**NHL**	**12**	**0**	**2**	**2**	**53**	....	....	....	....	....
	Kalamazoo	IHL	37	3	4	7	192	5	0	0	0	56
	NHL Totals		**12**	**0**	**2**	**2**	**53**	....	....	....	....	....

GAGE, JOSEPH WILLIAM (JODY)

Right wing. Shoots right. 6', 185 lbs. Born, Toronto, Ont., November 29, 1959.
(Detroit's 2nd choice, 45th over-all, in 1979 Entry Draft).

			Regular Season					Playoffs				
Season	Club	Lea	GP	G	A	TP	PIM	GP	G	A	TP	PIM
1977-78	Hamilton	OHA	32	15	18	33	19	....	....	....	....	....
	Kitchener	OHA	36	17	27	44	21	9	4	3	7	4
1978-79	Kitchener	OHA	58	46	43	89	40	10	1	2	3	6
1979-80	Adirondack	AHL	63	25	21	46	15	5	2	1	3	0
1980-81	**Detroit**	**NHL**	**16**	**2**	**2**	**4**	**22**	....	....	....	....	....
	Adirondack	AHL	59	17	31	48	44	17	9	6	15	12
1981-82	Adirondack	AHL	47	21	20	41	21	....	....	....	....	....
	Detroit	**NHL**	**31**	**9**	**10**	**19**	**2**	....	....	....	....	....
1982-83	Adirondack	AHL	65	23	30	53	33	6	1	5	6	8
1983-84	**Detroit**	**NHL**	**3**	**0**	**0**	**0**	**0**	....	....	....	....	....
	Adirondack	AHL	73	40	32	72	32	6	3	4	7	2
1984-85	Adirondack	AHL	78	27	33	60	55	....	....	....	....	....
1985-86	**Buffalo**	**NHL**	**7**	**3**	**2**	**5**	**0**	....	....	....	....	....
a	Rochester	AHL	73	42	57	99	56	....	....	....	....	....
1986-87	Rochester	AHL	70	26	39	65	60	17	14	5	19	24
1987-88	**Buffalo**	**NHL**	**2**	**0**	**0**	**0**	**0**	....	....	....	....	....
ab	Rochester	AHL	76	*60	44	104	46	5	2	5	7	10
1988-89	Rochester	AHL	65	31	38	69	60	....	....	....	....	....
	NHL Totals		**59**	**14**	**14**	**28**	**24**	....	....	....	....	....

a AHL First All-Star Team (1986, 1988)
b Won Les Cunningham Trophy (MVP-AHL) (1988)

Signed as a free agent by **Buffalo**, July 31, 1985

GAGNE, PAUL

Left wing. Shoots left. 5' 10", 180 lbs. Born, Iroquois Falls, Ont., February 6, 1962.
(Colorado's 1st choice, 19th overall, in 1980 Entry Draft).

			Regular Season					Playoffs				
Season	Club	Lea	GP	G	A	TP	PIM	GP	G	A	TP	PIM
1978-79	Windsor	OHA	67	24	18	42	64	7	1	1	2	2
1979-80a	Windsor	OHA	65	48	53	101	87	13	7	8	15	19
1980-81	**Colorado**	**NHL**	**61**	**25**	**16**	**41**	**12**	....	....	....	....	....
1981-82	**Colorado**	**NHL**	**59**	**10**	**12**	**22**	**17**	....	....	....	....	....
1982-83	**New Jersey**	**NHL**	**63**	**14**	**15**	**29**	**13**	....	....	....	....	....
	Wichita	CHL	16	1	9	10	9	....	....	....	....	....
1983-84	**New Jersey**	**NHL**	**66**	**14**	**18**	**32**	**33**	....	....	....	....	....
1984-85	**New Jersey**	**NHL**	**79**	**24**	**19**	**43**	**28**	....	....	....	....	....
1985-86	**New Jersey**	**NHL**	**47**	**19**	**19**	**38**	**14**	....	....	....	....	....
1986-87			DID NOT PLAY — INJURED					....	....	....	....	....
1987-88			DID NOT PLAY — INJURED					....	....	....	....	....
1988-89	**Toronto**	**NHL**	**16**	**3**	**2**	**5**	**6**	....	....	....	....	....
	Newmarket	AHL	56	33	41	74	29	5	4	4	8	5
	NHL Totals		**381**	**109**	**101**	**210**	**123**	....	....	....	....	....

a OHA Second All-Star Team (1980)

Signed as a free agent by **Toronto**, July 28, 1988.

GAGNE, SIMON

Right wing. Shoots right. 6'4", 200 lbs. Born, Montreal, Que., September 29, 1968.
(NY Rangers' 3rd choice, 46th overall, in 1987 Entry Draft).

			Regular Season					Playoffs				
Season	Club	Lea	GP	G	A	TP	PIM	GP	G	A	TP	PIM
1985-86	Laval	QMJHL	71	15	16	31	150	14	2	5	7	37
1986-87	Laval	QMJHL	66	19	35	54	90	15	9	11	20	12
1987-88	Drummondville	QMJHL	68	17	43	60	197	17	3	6	9	94
1988-89	Denver	IHL	69	7	18	25	78	4	1	0	1	7

GAGNE, WAYNE

Defense. Shoots right. 5'9", 180 lbs. Born, Toronto, Ont., June 27, 1964.
(Montreal's 1st choice, 22nd overall, in 1987 Supplemental Draft).

			Regular Season					Playoffs				
Season	Club	Lea	GP	G	A	TP	PIM	GP	G	A	TP	PIM
1983-84	W. Michigan	CCHA	41	8	35	43	32	....	....	....	....	....
1984-85	W. Michigan	CCHA	35	4	29	33	46	....	....	....	....	....
1985-86ab	W. Michigan	CCHA	43	17	59	76	37	....	....	....	....	....
1986-87abc	W. Michigan	CCHA	43	13	76	89	38	....	....	....	....	....
1987-88	Sherbrooke	AHL	14	0	4	4	8	....	....	....	....	....
	Baltimore	AHL	58	8	31	39	30	....	....	....	....	....
	Peoria	IHL	7	1	2	3	8	7	1	4	5	15
1988-89	Peoria	IHL	64	8	41	49	58	4	1	2	3	6

a NCAA West First All-American Team (1986, 1987)
b CCHA First All-Star Team (1986, 1987)
c CCHA Player of the Year (1987)

GAGNER, DAVE

Center. Shoots left. 5'10", 185 lbs. Born, Chatham, Ont., December 11, 1964.
(NY Rangers' 1st choice, 12th over-all, in 1983 Entry Draft).

			Regular Season					Playoffs				
Season	Club	Lea	GP	G	A	TP	PIM	GP	G	A	TP	PIM
1981-82	Brantford	OHL	68	30	46	76	31	11	3	6	9	6
1982-83a	Brantford	OHL	70	55	66	121	57	8	5	5	10	4
1983-84	Cdn. Olympic	...	50	19	18	37	26	....	....	....	....	....
	Brantford	OHL	12	7	13	20	4	6	0	4	4	6
1984-85	**NY Rangers**	**NHL**	**38**	**6**	**6**	**12**	**16**	....	....	....	....	....
	New Haven	AHL	38	13	20	33	23	....	....	....	....	....
1985-86	**NY Rangers**	**NHL**	**32**	**4**	**6**	**10**	**19**	....	....	....	....	....
	New Haven	AHL	16	10	11	21	11	4	1	2	3	2
1986-87	**NY Rangers**	**NHL**	**10**	**1**	**4**	**5**	**12**	....	....	....	....	....
	New Haven	AHL	56	22	41	63	50	7	1	5	6	18
1987-88	**Minnesota**	**NHL**	**51**	**8**	**11**	**19**	**55**	....	....	....	....	....
	Kalamazoo	IHL	14	16	10	26	26	....	....	....	....	....
1988-89	**Minnesota**	**NHL**	**75**	**35**	**43**	**78**	**104**	....	....	....	....	....
	Kalamazoo	IHL	1	0	1	1	4	....	....	....	....	....
	NHL Totals		**206**	**54**	**70**	**124**	**206**	....	....	....	....	....

a OHL Second All-Star Team (1983)

Traded to **Minnesota** by **NY Rangers** with Jay Caulfield for Jari Gronstrand and Paul Boutilier, October 8, 1987.

GAINEY, ROBERT MICHAEL (BOB)

Left wing. Shoots left. 6'2", 200 lbs.   Born, Peterborough, Ont., December 13, 1953.
(Montreal's 1st choice, 8th over-all, in 1973 Amateur Draft).

			Regular Season					Playoffs				
Season	Club	Lea	GP	G	A	TP	PIM	GP	G	A	TP	PIM
1971-72	Peterborough	OHA	4	2	1	3	33	....	....	....	....	....
1972-73	Peterborough	OHA	52	22	21	43	99	....	....	....	....	....
1973-74	Nova Scotia	AHL	6	2	5	7	4	....	....	....	....	....
	Montreal	NHL	66	3	7	10	34	6	0	0	0	6
1974-75	Montreal	NHL	80	17	20	37	49	11	2	4	6	4
1975-76	Montreal	NHL	78	15	13	28	57	13	1	3	4	20
1976-77	Montreal	NHL	80	14	19	33	41	14	4	1	5	25
1977-78a	Montreal	NHL	66	15	16	31	57	15	2	7	9	14
1978-79ab	Montreal	NHL	79	20	18	38	44	16	6	10	16	10
1979-80a	Montreal	NHL	64	14	19	33	32	10	1	1	2	4
1980-81a	Montreal	NHL	78	23	24	47	36	3	0	0	0	2
1981-82	Montreal	NHL	79	21	24	45	24	5	0	1	1	8
1982-83	Montreal	NHL	80	12	18	30	43	3	0	0	0	4
1983-84	Montreal	NHL	77	17	22	39	41	15	1	5	6	9
1984-85	Montreal	NHL	79	19	13	32	40	12	1	3	4	13
1985-86	Montreal	NHL	80	20	23	43	20	20	5	5	10	12
1986-87	Montreal	NHL	47	8	8	16	19	17	1	3	4	6
1987-88	Montreal	NHL	78	11	11	22	14	6	0	1	1	6
1988-89	Montreal	NHL	49	10	7	17	34	16	1	4	5	8
	NHL Totals		1160	239	262	501	585	182	25	48	73	151

a Won Frank J. Selke Trophy (1978, 1979, 1980, 1981)
b Won Conn Smythe Trophy (1979)
Played in NHL All-Star Game (1977, 1978, 1980, 1981)

GALL, WILLIAM (BILL)

Right wing. Shoots right. 6'2", 175 lbs.   Born, Bryn Mawr, PA, May 14, 1968.
(Philadelphia's 5th choice, 104th overall, in 1987 Entry Draft).

			Regular Season					Playoffs				
Season	Club	Lea	GP	G	A	TP	PIM	GP	G	A	TP	PIM
1986-87	New Hampton	HS	26	20	28	48	12	....	....	....	....	....
1987-88	RIT	NCAA	23	8	8	16	4	....	....	....	....	....
1988-89	RIT	NCAA	37	8	19	27	46	....	....	....	....	....

GALLANT, GERARD   (guh-LAHNT)

Left wing. Shoots left. 5'10", 185 lbs.   Born, Summerside, P.E.I., September 2, 1963.
(Detroit's 4th choice, 107th over-all, in 1981 Entry Draft).

			Regular Season					Playoffs				
Season	Club	Lea	GP	G	A	TP	PIM	GP	G	A	TP	PIM
1980-81	Sherbrooke	QMJHL	68	41	59	100	265	14	6	13	19	46
1981-82	Sherbrooke	QMJHL	58	34	58	92	260	22	14	24	38	84
1982-83	St. Jean	QMJHL	33	28	25	53	139	....	....	....	....	....
	Verdun	QMJHL	29	26	49	75	105	15	14	19	33	84
1983-84	Adirondack	AHL	77	31	33	64	195	7	1	3	4	34
1984-85	Detroit	NHL	32	6	12	18	66	3	0	0	0	11
	Adirondack	AHL	46	18	29	47	131	....	....	....	....	....
1985-86	Detroit	NHL	52	20	19	39	106	....	....	....	....	....
1986-87	Detroit	NHL	80	38	34	72	216	16	8	6	14	43
1987-88	Detroit	NHL	73	34	39	73	242	16	6	9	15	55
1988-89a	Detroit	NHL	76	39	54	93	230	6	1	2	3	40
	NHL Totals		313	137	158	295	860	41	15	17	32	149

a NHL Second All-Star Team (1989)

GALLEY, GARRY

Defense. Shoots left. 6', 190 lbs.   Born, Ottawa, Ont., April 16, 1963.
(Los Angeles' 4th choice, 100th over-all, in 1983 Entry Draft).

			Regular Season					Playoffs				
Season	Club	Lea	GP	G	A	TP	PIM	GP	G	A	TP	PIM
1981-82	Bowling Green	CCHA	42	3	36	39	48	....	....	....	....	....
1982-83	Bowling Green	CCHA	40	17	29	46	40	....	....	....	....	....
1983-84ab	Bowling Green	CCHA	44	15	52	67	61	....	....	....	....	....
1984-85	Los Angeles	NHL	78	8	30	38	82	3	1	0	1	2
1985-86	Los Angeles	NHL	49	9	13	22	46	....	....	....	....	....
	New Haven	AHL	4	2	6	8	6	....	....	....	....	....
1986-87	Los Angeles	NHL	30	5	11	16	57	....	....	....	....	....
	Washington	NHL	18	1	10	11	10	2	0	0	0	0
1987-88	Washington	NHL	58	7	23	30	44	13	2	4	6	13
1988-89	Boston	NHL	78	8	21	29	80	9	0	1	1	33
	NHL Totals		311	38	108	146	319	27	3	5	8	48

a CCHA First All-Star Team (1984)
b NCAA All-American (1984)
Traded to **Washington** by **Los Angeles** for Al Jensen, February 14, 1987. Signed as a free agent by **Boston**, July 8, 1988.

GANCHAR, PERRY

Right wing. Shoots right. 5'9", 180 lbs.   Born, Saskatoon, Sask., October 28, 1963.
(St. Louis' 3rd choice, 113th over-all, in 1982 Entry Draft).

			Regular Season					Playoffs				
Season	Club	Lea	GP	G	A	TP	PIM	GP	G	A	TP	PIM
1979-80	Saskatoon	WHL	27	9	14	23	60	....	....	....	....	....
1980-81	Saskatoon	WHL	72	26	53	79	117	....	....	....	....	....
1981-82	Saskatoon	WHL	53	38	52	90	82	5	3	3	6	17
1982-83	Saskatoon	WHL	68	68	48	116	105	6	1	4	5	24
	Salt Lake	CHL	....	....	....	....	....	1	0	1	1	0
1983-84	Montana	CHL	59	23	22	45	77	....	....	....	....	....
	St. Louis	NHL	1	0	0	0	0	7	3	1	4	0
1984-85	St. Louis	NHL	7	0	2	2	0	....	....	....	....	....
a	Peoria	IHL	63	41	29	70	114	20	4	11	15	49
1985-86	Sherbrooke	AHL	75	25	29	54	42	....	....	....	....	....
1986-87	Sherbrooke	AHL	68	22	29	51	64	17	9	8	17	37
1987-88	Montreal	NHL	1	1	0	1	0	....	....	....	....	....
	Sherbrooke	AHL	28	12	18	30	61	....	....	....	....	....
	Pittsburgh	NHL	30	2	5	7	36	....	....	....	....	....
1988-89	Pittsburgh	NHL	3	0	0	0	0	....	....	....	....	....
	Muskegon	IHL	70	39	34	73	114	14	7	8	15	6
	NHL Totals		42	3	7	10	36	7	3	1	4	0

a IHL Second All-Star Team (1985)
Traded to **Montreal** by **St. Louis** for Ron Flockhart, August 26, 1985. Traded to **Pittsburgh** by **Montreal** for future considerations, December 17, 1987.

GARBUTT, MURRAY

Center. Shoots left. 6'1", 205 lbs.   Born, Hanna, Alta., July 29, 1971.
(Minnesota's 3rd choice, 60th overall, in 1989 Entry Draft).

			Regular Season					Playoffs				
Season	Club	Lea	GP	G	A	TP	PIM	GP	G	A	TP	PIM
1987-88	Medicine Hat	WHL	9	2	1	3	15	16	0	1	1	15
1988-89	Medicine Hat	WHL	64	14	24	38	145	3	1	0	1	6

GARDNER, JOEL

Center. Shoots left. 6', 175 lbs.   Born, Petrolia, Ont., September 16, 1967.
(Boston's 10th choice, 244th overall, in 1986 Entry Draft).

			Regular Season					Playoffs				
Season	Club	Lea	GP	G	A	TP	PIM	GP	G	A	TP	PIM
1985-86	Sarnia	OPJHL	42	23	51	74	72	....	....	....	....	....
1986-87	Colgate	ECAC	31	10	20	30	20	....	....	....	....	....
1987-88	Colgate	ECAC	31	14	32	46	24	....	....	....	....	....
1988-89	Colgate	ECAC	30	21	25	46	38	....	....	....	....	....

GARDNER, WILLIAM SCOTT (BILL)

Center. Shoots left. 5'10", 180 lbs.   Born, Toronto, Ont., March 18, 1960.
(Chicago's 3rd choice, 49th over-all, in 1979 Entry Draft).

			Regular Season					Playoffs				
Season	Club	Lea	GP	G	A	TP	PIM	GP	G	A	TP	PIM
1978-79	Peterborough	OHA	68	33	71	104	19	18	4	20	24	6
1979-80a	Peterborough	OHA	59	43	63	106	17	14	13	14	27	8
1980-81	Chicago	NHL	1	0	0	0	0	....	....	....	....	....
	New Brunswick	AHL	48	19	29	48	12	13	5	10	15	0
1981-82	Chicago	NHL	69	8	15	23	20	15	1	4	5	6
1982-83	Chicago	NHL	77	15	25	40	12	13	1	0	1	9
1983-84	Chicago	NHL	79	27	21	48	12	5	0	1	1	0
1984-85	Chicago	NHL	74	17	34	51	12	12	1	3	4	2
1985-86	Chicago	NHL	46	3	10	13	6	....	....	....	....	....
	Hartford	NHL	18	1	8	9	4	....	....	....	....	....
1986-87	Hartford	NHL	8	0	1	1	0	....	....	....	....	....
	Binghamton	AHL	50	17	44	61	18	13	4	8	12	14
1987-88	Chicago	NHL	2	1	0	1	2	....	....	....	....	....
	Saginaw	IHL	54	18	49	67	46	10	4	4	8	14
1988-89	Chicago	NHL	6	1	1	2	0	....	....	....	....	....
	Saginaw	IHL	74	27	45	72	10	6	3	1	4	0
	NHL Totals		380	73	115	188	68	45	3	8	11	17

a OHA Third All-Star Team (1980)
Traded to **Hartford** by **Chicago** for Hartford's third-round choice in 1987 or 1988 Entry Draft, February 3, 1986. Signed as a free agent by **Chicago**, September 25, 1987.

GARPENLOV, JOHAN

Left wing. Shoots left. 5'11", 185 lbs.   Born, Stockholm, Sweden, March 21, 1968.
(Detroit's 5th choice, 85th overall, in 1986 Entry Draft).

			Regular Season					Playoffs				
Season	Club	Lea	GP	G	A	TP	PIM	GP	G	A	TP	PIM
1986-87	Djurgarden	Swe.	29	5	8	13	20	....	....	....	....	....
1987-88	Djurgarden	Swe.	30	7	10	17	12	....	....	....	....	....
1988-89	Djurgarden	Swe.	36	12	19	31	20	....	....	....	....	....

GARTNER, MICHAEL ALFRED (MIKE)

Right wing. Shoots right. 6', 190 lbs.   Born, Ottawa, Ont., October 29, 1959.
(Washington's 1st choice, 4th over-all, in 1979 Entry Draft).

			Regular Season					Playoffs				
Season	Club	Lea	GP	G	A	TP	PIM	GP	G	A	TP	PIM
1976-77	Niagara Falls	OHA	62	33	42	75	125	....	....	....	....	....
1977-78a	Niagara Falls	OHA	64	41	49	90	56	....	....	....	....	....
1978-79	Cincinnati	WHA	78	27	25	52	123	3	0	2	2	2
1979-80	Washington	NHL	77	36	32	68	66	....	....	....	....	....
1980-81	Washington	NHL	80	48	46	94	100	....	....	....	....	....
1981-82	Washington	NHL	80	35	45	80	121	....	....	....	....	....
1982-83	Washington	NHL	73	38	38	76	54	4	0	0	0	4
1983-84	Washington	NHL	80	40	45	85	90	8	3	7	10	16
1984-85	Washington	NHL	80	50	52	102	71	5	4	3	7	9
1985-86	Washington	NHL	74	35	40	75	63	9	2	10	12	4
1986-87	Washington	NHL	78	41	32	73	61	7	4	3	7	14
1987-88	Washington	NHL	80	48	33	81	73	14	3	4	7	14
1988-89	Washington	NHL	56	26	29	55	71	....	....	....	....	....
	Minnesota	NHL	13	7	7	14	2	5	0	0	0	6
	NHL Totals		771	404	399	803	772	52	16	27	43	67

a OHA First All-Star Team (1978)
Played in NHL All-Star Game (1980, 1985, 1986, 1988)
Traded to **Minnesota** by **Washington** with Larry Murphy for Dino Ciccarelli and Bob Rouse, March 7, 1989.

GASSEAU, JAMES

Defense. Shoots right. 6'2", 200 lbs.   Born, Carleton, Que., May 4, 1966.
(Buffalo's 6nd choice, 123rd over-all, in 1984 Entry Draft).

			Regular Season					Playoffs				
Season	Club	Lea	GP	G	A	TP	PIM	GP	G	A	TP	PIM
1983-84	Drummondville	QMJHL	68	6	25	31	72	10	0	4	4	12
1984-85a	Drummondville	QMJHL	64	8	43	51	158	12	1	5	6	34
1985-86	Drummondville	QMJHL	46	20	31	51	155	23	1	13	14	18
1986-87	Rochester	AHL	7	0	2	2	6	....	....	....	....	....
1987-88	Rochester	AHL	75	9	21	30	109	7	2	4	6	24
1988-89	Cdn. National	....	16	2	1	3	14	....	....	....	....	....

a QMJHL Second All-Star Team (1985, 1986)

GAUDREAU, ROBERT

Right wing. Shoots right. 5'11", 185 lbs.   Born, Lincoln, RI, January 20, 1970.
(Pittsburgh's 8th choice, 172nd overall, in 1988 Entry Draft).

			Regular Season					Playoffs				
Season	Club	Lea	GP	G	A	TP	PIM	GP	G	A	TP	PIM
1986-87	Bish. Hendricken HS		33	41	39	80	....	....	....	....	....	....
1987-88	Bish. Hendricken HS		....	52	60	112	....	....	....	....	....	....
1988-89a	Providence	H.E.	42	28	29	57	32	....	....	....	....	....

a Co-winner Hockey East Rookie of the Year (1989)

GAUME, DALLAS
Center. Shoots left. 5'10", 185 lbs.   Born, Innisfal, Alta., August 27, 1963.

					Regular Season					Playoffs			
Season	Club	Lea	GP	G	A	TP	PIM	GP	G	A	TP	PIM
1982-83	Denver	WCHA	37	19	47	66	12	....	....	....	....	....
1983-84	Denver	WCHA	32	12	25	37	22	....	....	....	....	....
1984-85	Denver	WCHA	39	15	48	63	28	....	....	....	....	....
1985-86	Denver	WCHA	47	32	67	99	18	....	....	....	....	....
1986-87	Binghamton	AHL	77	18	39	57	31	12	1	1	2	7
1987-88	Binghamton	AHL	63	24	49	73	39	4	1	2	3	0
1988-89	**Hartford**	**NHL**	**4**	**1**	**1**	**2**	**0**	....	....	....	....	....
	Binghamton	AHL	57	23	43	66	16	....	....	....	....	....
	NHL Totals		**4**	**1**	**1**	**2**	**0**	....	....	....	....	....

Signed as a free agent by **Hartford**, July 10, 1986.

GAUTHIER, DANIEL
Left wing. Shoots left. 6'1", 180 lbs.   Born, Charlemagne, Que., May 17, 1970.
(Pittsburgh's 3rd choice, 62nd overall, in 1988 Entry Draft).

					Regular Season					Playoffs			
Season	Club	Lea	GP	G	A	TP	PIM	GP	G	A	TP	PIM
1986-87	Longueuil	QMJHL	64	23	22	45	23	18	4	5	9	15
1987-88	Victoriaville	QMJHL	66	43	47	90	53	5	2	1	3	0
1988-89	Victoriaville	QMJHL	64	41	75	116	84	16	12	17	29	30

GAUTHIER, LUC
Defense. Shoots right. 5'9", 195 lbs.   Born, Longueuil, Que., April 19, 1964.
Last amateur club: Longueuil Chevaliers (QMJHL).

					Regular Season					Playoffs			
Season	Club	Lea	GP	G	A	TP	PIM	GP	G	A	TP	PIM
1984-85	Longueuil	QMJHL	60	13	47	60	111	....	....	....	....	....
1985-86	Saginaw	IHL	66	9	29	38	160	....	....	....	....	....
1986-87	Sherbrooke	AHL	78	5	17	22	8	17	2	4	6	31
1987-88	Sherbrooke	AHL	61	4	10	14	105	6	0	0	0	18
1988-89	Sherbrooke	AHL	77	8	20	28	178	6	0	0	0	10

Signed as a free agent by **Montreal**, October 7, 1986.

GAVIN, ROBERT (STEWART)
Left wing. Shoots left. 6', 185 lbs.   Born, Ottawa, Ont., March 15, 1960.
(Toronto's 4th choice, 74th over-all, in 1980 Entry Draft).

					Regular Season					Playoffs			
Season	Club	Lea	GP	G	A	TP	PIM	GP	G	A	TP	PIM
1978-79	Toronto	OHA	61	24	25	49	83	3	1	0	1	0
1979-80	Toronto	OHA	68	27	30	57	52	4	1	1	2	2
1980-81	**Toronto**	**NHL**	**14**	**1**	**2**	**3**	**13**	....	....	....	....	....
	New Brunswick	AHL	46	7	12	19	42	13	1	0	1	2
1981-82	**Toronto**	**NHL**	**38**	**5**	**6**	**11**	**29**	....	....	....	....	....
1982-83	St. Catharines	AHL	6	2	4	6	17	....	....	....	....	....
	Toronto	**NHL**	**63**	**6**	**5**	**11**	**44**	**4**	**0**	**0**	**0**	**0**
1983-84	**Toronto**	**NHL**	**80**	**10**	**22**	**32**	**90**	....	....	....	....	....
1984-85	**Toronto**	**NHL**	**73**	**12**	**13**	**25**	**38**	....	....	....	....	....
1985-86	**Hartford**	**NHL**	**76**	**26**	**29**	**55**	**51**	**10**	**4**	**1**	**5**	**13**
1986-87	**Hartford**	**NHL**	**79**	**20**	**21**	**41**	**28**	**6**	**2**	**4**	**6**	**10**
1987-88	**Hartford**	**NHL**	**56**	**11**	**10**	**21**	**59**	**6**	**2**	**2**	**4**	**4**
1988-89	**Hartford**	**NHL**	**73**	**8**	**18**	**26**	**34**	**5**	**3**	**1**	**4**	**10**
	NHL Totals		**552**	**99**	**126**	**225**	**386**	**31**	**11**	**8**	**19**	**37**

Traded to **Hartford** by **Toronto** for Chris Kotsopoulos, October 7, 1985. Claimed by **Minnesota** in NHL Waiver Draft, October 3, 1988.

GAWLICKI, JEFF
Left wing. Shoots left. 6'2", 200 lbs.   Born, Edmonton, Alta., April 15, 1968.
(Los Angeles' 7th choice, 174th overall, in 1987 Entry Draft).

					Regular Season					Playoffs			
Season	Club	Lea	GP	G	A	TP	PIM	GP	G	A	TP	PIM
1986-87	N. Michigan	WCHA	37	7	2	9	61	....	....	....	....	....
1987-88	N. Michigan	WCHA	30	2	3	5	64	....	....	....	....	....
1988-89	N. Michigan	WCHA	45	16	11	27	99	....	....	....	....	....

GEARY, DEREK
Right wing. Shoots right. 6'3", 180 lbs.   Born, Gloucester, MA, February 2, 1970.
(Boston's 5th choice, 123rd overall, in 1988 Entry Draft).

					Regular Season					Playoffs			
Season	Club	Lea	GP	G	A	TP	PIM	GP	G	A	TP	PIM
1987-88	Gloucester	HS	....	26	24	50	....	....	....	....	....	....
1988-89	Andover Aca.	HS	3	1	2	3	0	....	....	....	....	....

GEIST, WILLIAM
Defense. Shoots right. 6'4", 190 lbs.   Born, St. Paul, MN, February 9, 1969.
(Montreal's 10th choice, 164th overall, in 1987 Entry Draft).

					Regular Season					Playoffs			
Season	Club	Lea	GP	G	A	TP	PIM	GP	G	A	TP	PIM
1986-87	St. Paul	HS	21	7	14	21	....	....	....	....	....	....
1987-88	Choate	HS	28	11	16	27	31	....	....	....	....	....
1988-89		DID NOT PLAY										

GELDART, GREGORY
Center. Shoots left. 6'1", 200 lbs.   Born, Edmonton, Alta., May 12, 1968.
(Vancouver's 7th choice, 149th overall, in 1988 Entry Draft).

					Regular Season					Playoffs			
Season	Club	Lea	GP	G	A	TP	PIM	GP	G	A	TP	PIM
1987-88	St. Albert	AJHL	59	38	67	105	78	....	....	....	....	....
1988-89	North Dakota	WCHA	1	0	0	0	0	....	....	....	....	....
	N. Westminster	BCJHL	16	9	10	19	18	....	....	....	....	....

GELINAS, MARTIN
Left wing. Shoots left. 5'11", 195 lbs.   Born, Shawinigan, Que., June 5, 1970.
(Los Angeles' 1st choice, 7th overall, in 1988 Entry Draft).

					Regular Season					Playoffs			
Season	Club	Lea	GP	G	A	TP	PIM	GP	G	A	TP	PIM
1986-87	Magog	Midget	41	36	42	78	36	....	....	....	....	....
1987-88	Hull	QMJHL	65	63	68	131	74	17	15	18	33	32
1988-89	**Edmonton**	**NHL**	**6**	**1**	**2**	**3**	**0**	....	....	....	....	....
	Hull	QMJHL	41	38	39	77	31	9	5	4	9	14
	NHL Totals		**6**	**1**	**2**	**3**	**0**	....	....	....	....	....

Traded to **Edmonton** by **Los Angeles** with Jimmy Carson and Los Angeles' first round choices in 1989, (acquired by New Jersey, June 17, 1989. New Jersey selected Jason Miller), 1991 and 1993 Entry Drafts and cash for Wayne Gretzky, Mike Krushelnyski and Marty McSorley, August 9, 1988.

GERMAIN, ERIC
Defense. Shoots left. 6'1", 195 lbs.   Born, Quebec City, Que., June 26, 1966.

					Regular Season					Playoffs			
Season	Club	Lea	GP	G	A	TP	PIM	GP	G	A	TP	PIM
1983-84	St. Jean	QMJHL	57	2	15	17	60	4	1	0	1	6
1984-85	St. Jean	QMJHL	66	10	31	41	243	5	4	0	4	14
1985-86	St. Jean	QMJHL	66	5	38	43	183	10	0	6	6	56
1986-87	Fredericton	AHL	44	2	8	10	28	....	....	....	....	....
1987-88	**Los Angeles**	**NHL**	**4**	**0**	**1**	**1**	**13**	**1**	**0**	**0**	**0**	**4**
	New Haven	AHL	69	0	10	10	0	....	....	....	....	....
1988-89	New Haven	AHL	55	0	9	9	93	17	0	3	3	23
	NHL Totals		**4**	**0**	**1**	**1**	**13**	**1**	**0**	**0**	**0**	**4**

Signed as a free agent by **Los Angeles**, July 1, 1986.

GERNANDER, KEN
Left wing. Shoots left. 5'10", 175 lbs.   Born, Coleraine, MN, June 30, 1969.
(Winnipeg's 4th choice, 96th overall, in 1987 Entry Draft).

					Regular Season					Playoffs			
Season	Club	Lea	GP	G	A	TP	PIM	GP	G	A	TP	PIM
1986-87	Greenway	HS	26	35	34	69	....	....	....	....	....	....
1987-88	U. Minnesota	WCHA	44	14	14	28	14	....	....	....	....	....
1988-89	U. Minnesota	WCHA	44	9	11	20	2	....	....	....	....	....

GIBSON, DON
Defense. Shoots right. 6'1", 210 lbs.   Born, Deloraine, Man., December 29, 1967.
(Vancouver's 2nd choice, 49th overall, in 1986 Entry Draft).

					Regular Season					Playoffs			
Season	Club	Lea	GP	G	A	TP	PIM	GP	G	A	TP	PIM
1986-87	Michigan State	CCHA	43	3	3	6	74	....	....	....	....	....
1987-88	Michigan State	CCHA	43	7	12	19	118	....	....	....	....	....
1988-89	Michigan State	CCHA	39	7	10	17	107	....	....	....	....	....

GIFFIN, LEE
Right wing. Shoots right. 5'11", 200 lbs.   Born, Chatham, Ont., April 1, 1967.
(Pittsburgh's 2nd choice, 23rd over-all, in 1985 Entry Draft)

					Regular Season					Playoffs			
Season	Club	Lea	GP	G	A	TP	PIM	GP	G	A	TP	PIM
1983-84	Oshawa	OHL	70	23	27	50	88	7	1	4	5	12
1984-85	Oshawa	OHL	62	36	42	78	78	5	1	2	3	2
1985-86	Oshawa	OHL	54	29	37	66	28	6	0	5	5	8
1986-87	**Pittsburgh**	**NHL**	**8**	**1**	**1**	**2**	**0**	....	....	....	....	....
a	Oshawa	OHL	48	31	69	100	46	23	17	19	36	14
1987-88	**Pittsburgh**	**NHL**	**19**	**0**	**2**	**2**	**9**	....	....	....	....	....
	Muskegon	IHL	48	26	37	63	61	6	1	3	4	2
1988-89	Muskegon	IHL	63	30	44	74	93	12	5	7	12	8
	NHL Totals		**27**	**1**	**3**	**4**	**9**	....	....	....	....	....

a OHL First All-Star Team (1987)

GIGUERE, STEPHANE
Left wing. Shoots left. 6', 180 lbs.   Born, Montreal, Que., February 21, 1968.
(Toronto's 6th choice, 111th overall, in 1986 Entry Draft).

					Regular Season					Playoffs			
Season	Club	Lea	GP	G	A	TP	PIM	GP	G	A	TP	PIM
1985-86	St. Jean	QMJHL	71	13	20	33	110	8	0	0	0	7
1986-87	St. Jean	QMJHL	69	45	45	90	129	8	3	5	8	11
1987-88	St. Jean	QMJHL	66	39	48	87	162	....	....	....	....	....
1988-89	Flint	IHL	53	4	10	14	80	....	....	....	....	....

GILBERT, GREGORY SCOTT (GREG)
Left wing. Shoots left. 6'1", 192 lbs.   Born, Mississauga, Ont., January 22, 1962.
(NY Islanders' 5th choice, 80th over-all, in 1980 Entry Draft).

					Regular Season					Playoffs			
Season	Club	Lea	GP	G	A	TP	PIM	GP	G	A	TP	PIM
1980-81	Toronto	OHA	64	30	37	67	73	5	2	6	8	16
1981-82 a	Toronto	OHL	65	41	67	108	119	10	4	12	16	23
	NY Islanders	**NHL**	**1**	**1**	**0**	**1**	**0**	**4**	**1**	**1**	**2**	**2**
1982-83	Indianapolis	CHL	24	11	16	27	23	....	....	....	....	....
	NY Islanders	**NHL**	**45**	**8**	**11**	**19**	**30**	**10**	**1**	**0**	**1**	**14**
1983-84	**NY Islanders**	**NHL**	**79**	**31**	**35**	**66**	**59**	**21**	**5**	**7**	**12**	**39**
1984-85	**NY Islanders**	**NHL**	**58**	**13**	**25**	**38**	**36**	....	....	....	....	....
1985-86	**NY Islanders**	**NHL**	**60**	**9**	**19**	**28**	**82**	**2**	**0**	**0**	**0**	**9**
	Springfield	AHL	2	0	0	0	2	....	....	....	....	....
1986-87	**NY Islanders**	**NHL**	**51**	**6**	**7**	**13**	**26**	**10**	**2**	**2**	**4**	**6**
1987-88	**NY Islanders**	**NHL**	**76**	**17**	**28**	**45**	**46**	**4**	**0**	**0**	**0**	**6**
1988-89	**NY Islanders**	**NHL**	**55**	**8**	**13**	**21**	**45**	....	....	....	....	....
	Chicago	**NHL**	**4**	**0**	**0**	**0**	**0**	**15**	**1**	**5**	**6**	**20**
	NHL Totals		**429**	**93**	**138**	**231**	**324**	**66**	**10**	**15**	**25**	**96**

a OHL Third All-Star Team (1982)

Traded to **Chicago** by **NY Islanders** for Chicago's fifth-round choice (Steve Young) in 1989 Entry Draft, March 7, 1989.

GILCHRIST, BRENT

Center. Shoots left. 5'10", 175 lbs.   Born, Moose Jaw, Sask., April 3, 1967.
(Montreal's 6th choice, 79th overall, in 1985 Entry Draft).

			Regular Season					Playoffs				
Season	Club	Lea	GP	G	A	TP	PIM	GP	G	A	TP	PIM
1983-84	Kelowna	WHL	69	16	11	27	16	....	....	....	....	....
1984-85	Kelowna	WHL	51	35	38	73	58	6	5	2	7	8
1985-86	Spokane	WHL	52	45	45	90	57	9	6	7	13	19
1986-87	Spokane	WHL	46	45	55	100	71	5	2	7	9	6
	Sherbrooke	AHL	....	....	....	....	....	10	2	7	9	2
1987-88	Sherbrooke	AHL	77	26	48	74	83	6	1	3	4	6
1988-89	**Montreal**	**NHL**	49	8	16	24	16	9	1	1	2	10
	Sherbrooke	AHL	7	6	5	11	7	....	....	....	....	....
	NHL Totals		49	8	16	24	16	9	1	1	2	10

GILES, CURT   (JYLES)

Defense. Shoots left. 5'8", 175 lbs.   Born, The Pas, Man., November 30, 1958.
(Minnesota's 4th choice, 54th over-all, in 1978 Amateur Draft).

			Regular Season					Playoffs				
Season	Club	Lea	GP	G	A	TP	PIM	GP	G	A	TP	PIM
1977-78	Minn.-Duluth	WCHA	34	11	36	47	62	....	....	....	....	....
1978-79	Minn.-Duluth	WCHA	30	3	38	41	38	....	....	....	....	....
1979-80	Oklahoma City	CHL	42	4	24	28	35	....	....	....	....	....
	Minnesota	**NHL**	37	2	7	9	31	12	2	4	6	10
1980-81	**Minnesota**	**NHL**	67	5	22	27	56	19	1	4	5	14
1981-82	**Minnesota**	**NHL**	74	3	12	15	87	4	0	0	0	2
1982-83	**Minnesota**	**NHL**	76	2	21	23	70	5	0	2	2	6
1983-84	**Minnesota**	**NHL**	70	6	22	28	59	16	1	3	4	25
1984-85	**Minnesota**	**NHL**	77	5	25	30	49	9	0	0	0	17
1985-86	**Minnesota**	**NHL**	69	6	21	27	30	5	0	1	1	10
1986-87	**Minnesota**	**NHL**	11	0	3	3	4	....	....	....	....	....
	NY Rangers	**NHL**	61	2	17	19	50	5	0	0	0	6
1987-88	**NY Rangers**	**NHL**	13	0	0	0	10	....	....	....	....	....
	Minnesota	**NHL**	59	1	12	13	66	....	....	....	....	....
1988-89	**Minnesota**	**NHL**	76	5	10	15	77	5	0	0	0	4
	NHL Totals		690	37	172	209	589	80	4	14	18	94

Traded to **NY Rangers** by **Minnesota** with Tony McKegney and Minnesota's second-round choice (Troy Mallette) in 1988 Entry Draft for Bob Brooke and NY Rangers' rights to Minnesota's fourth-round choice in (Jeffery Stolp) 1988 Entry Draft previously acquired by NY Rangers in Mark Pavelich deal, November 13, 1986. Traded to **Minnesota** by **NY Rangers** for Byron Lomow and future considerations, November 20, 1987.

GILHEN, RANDY

Left wing. Shoots left. 5'10", 190 lbs.   Born, Zweibrucken, West Germany, June 13, 1963.
(Hartford's 6th choice, 109th over-all, in 1982 Entry Draft).

			Regular Season					Playoffs				
Season	Club	Lea	GP	G	A	TP	PIM	GP	G	A	TP	PIM
1980-81	Saskatoon	WHL	68	10	5	15	154	....	....	....	....	....
1981-82	Saskatoon	WHL	25	15	9	24	45	....	....	....	....	....
	Winnipeg	WHL	36	26	28	54	42	....	....	....	....	....
1982-83	**Hartford**	**NHL**	2	0	1	1	0	....	....	....	....	....
	Winnipeg	WHL	71	57	44	101	84	3	2	2	4	0
1983-84	Binghamton	AHL	73	8	12	20	72	....	....	....	....	....
1984-85	Salt Lake	IHL	57	20	20	40	28	....	....	....	....	....
	Binghamton	AHL	18	3	3	6	9	8	4	1	5	16
1985-86	Fort Wayne	IHL	82	44	40	84	48	15	10	8	18	6
1986-87	**Winnipeg**	**NHL**	2	0	0	0	0	....	....	....	....	....
	Sherbrooke	AHL	75	36	29	65	44	17	7	13	20	10
1987-88	**Winnipeg**	**NHL**	13	3	2	5	15	4	1	0	1	10
	Moncton	AHL	68	40	47	87	51	....	....	....	....	....
1988-89	**Winnipeg**	**NHL**	64	5	3	8	38	....	....	....	....	....
	NHL Totals		81	8	6	14	53	4	1	0	1	10

Traded to **Pittsburgh** by **Winnipeg** with Jim Kyte and Andrew McBain for Randy Cunnyworth, Rick Tabaracci and Dave McLlwain, June 17, 1989.

GILL, TODD

Defense. Shoots left. 6'1", 185 lbs.   Born, Brockville, Ont., November 9, 1965.
(Toronto's 2nd choice, 25th over-all, in 1984 Entry Draft).

			Regular Season					Playoffs				
Season	Club	Lea	GP	G	A	TP	PIM	GP	G	A	TP	PIM
1982-83	Windsor	OHL	70	12	24	36	108	3	0	0	0	11
1983-84	Windsor	OHL	68	9	48	57	184	3	1	1	2	10
1984-85	**Toronto**	**NHL**	10	1	0	1	13	....	....	....	....	....
a	Windsor	OHL	53	17	40	57	148	4	0	1	1	14
1985-86	**Toronto**	**NHL**	15	1	2	3	28	1	0	0	0	0
	St. Catharines	AHL	58	8	25	33	90	10	1	6	7	17
1986-87	**Toronto**	**NHL**	61	4	27	31	92	13	2	2	4	42
	Newmarket	AHL	11	1	8	9	33	....	....	....	....	....
1987-88	**Toronto**	**NHL**	65	8	17	25	131	6	1	3	4	20
	Newmarket	AHL	2	0	1	1	2	....	....	....	....	....
1988-89	**Toronto**	**NHL**	59	11	14	25	72	....	....	....	....	....
	NHL Totals		210	25	60	85	336	20	3	5	8	62

a OHL Third All-Star Team (1985)

GILLIS, PAUL C.

Center. Shoots left. 5'11", 198 lbs.   Born, Toronto, Ont., December 31, 1963.
(Quebec's 2nd choice, 34th over-all, in 1982 Entry Draft).

			Regular Season					Playoffs				
Season	Club	Lea	GP	G	A	TP	PIM	GP	G	A	TP	PIM
1979-80	St. Michael's	Jr. B	41	20	36	56	114	....	....	....	....	....
1980-81	Niagara Falls	OHA	59	14	19	33	165	....	....	....	....	....
1981-82	Niagara Falls	OHL	65	27	62	89	247	5	1	5	6	26
1982-83	**Quebec**	**NHL**	7	0	2	2	2	....	....	....	....	....
	North Bay	OHL	61	34	52	86	151	6	1	3	4	26
1983-84	Fredericton	AHL	18	7	8	15	47	....	....	....	....	....
	Quebec	**NHL**	57	8	9	17	59	1	0	0	0	2
1984-85	**Quebec**	**NHL**	77	14	28	42	168	18	1	7	8	73
1985-86	**Quebec**	**NHL**	80	19	24	43	203	3	0	2	2	14
1986-87	**Quebec**	**NHL**	76	13	26	39	267	13	2	4	6	65
1987-88	**Quebec**	**NHL**	80	7	10	17	164	....	....	....	....	....
1988-89	**Quebec**	**NHL**	79	15	25	40	163	....	....	....	....	....
	NHL Totals		456	76	124	200	1026	35	3	13	16	154

GILMOUR, DOUGLAS (DOUG)

Center. Shoots left. 5'11", 165 lbs.   Born, Kingston, Ont., June 25, 1963.
(St. Louis' 4th choice, 134th over-all, in 1982 Entry Draft).

			Regular Season					Playoffs				
Season	Club	Lea	GP	G	A	TP	PIM	GP	G	A	TP	PIM
1981-82	Cornwall	OHL	67	46	73	119	42	5	6	9	15	2
1982-83ab	Cornwall	OHL	68	70	*107	*177	62	8	8	10	18	16
1983-84	**St. Louis**	**NHL**	80	25	28	53	57	11	2	9	11	10
1984-85	**St. Louis**	**NHL**	78	21	36	57	49	3	1	1	2	2
1985-86	**St. Louis**	**NHL**	74	25	28	53	41	19	9	12	21	25
1986-87	**St. Louis**	**NHL**	80	42	63	105	58	6	2	2	4	16
1987-88	**St. Louis**	**NHL**	72	36	50	86	59	10	3	14	17	18
1988-89	**Calgary**	**NHL**	72	26	59	85	44	22	11	11	22	20
	NHL Totals		456	175	264	439	308	71	28	49	77	91

a OHL First All-Star Team (1983)
b Named OHL's Most Outstanding Player (1983)

Traded to **Calgary** by **St.Louis** with Mark Hunter, Steve Bozek and Michael Dark for Mike Bullard, Craig Coxe and Tim Corkery, September 6, 1988.

GINGRAS, GASTON REGINALD   (JING-rah)

Defense. Shoots left. 6', 190 lbs.   Born, Temiscamingue, Que., February 13, 1959.
(Montreal's 1st choice, 27th over-all, in 1979 Entry Draft).

			Regular Season					Playoffs				
Season	Club	Lea	GP	G	A	TP	PIM	GP	G	A	TP	PIM
1976-77	Kitchener	OHA	59	13	62	75	134	3	0	1	1	6
1977-78	Kitchener	OHA	32	13	24	37	31	....	....	....	....	....
	Hamilton	OHA	29	11	19	30	37	15	3	11	14	13
1978-79	Birmingham	WHA	60	13	21	34	35	....	....	....	....	....
1979-80	Nova Scotia	AHL	30	11	27	38	17	....	....	....	....	....
	Montreal	**NHL**	34	3	7	10	18	10	1	6	7	8
1980-81	**Montreal**	**NHL**	55	5	16	21	22	1	1	0	1	0
1981-82	**Montreal**	**NHL**	34	6	18	24	28	5	0	1	1	0
1982-83	**Montreal**	**NHL**	22	1	8	9	8	....	....	....	....	....
	Toronto	**NHL**	45	10	18	28	10	3	1	2	3	2
1983-84	**Toronto**	**NHL**	59	7	20	27	16	....	....	....	....	....
1984-85	**Toronto**	**NHL**	5	0	2	2	0	....	....	....	....	....
	St. Catharines	AHL	36	7	12	19	13	....	....	....	....	....
	Sherbrooke	AHL	21	3	14	17	6	17	5	4	9	4
1985-86	**Montreal**	**NHL**	34	8	18	26	12	11	2	3	5	4
	Sherbrooke	AHL	42	11	20	31	14	....	....	....	....	....
1986-87	**Montreal**	**NHL**	66	11	34	45	21	5	0	2	2	0
1987-88	**Montreal**	**NHL**	2	0	1	1	2	....	....	....	....	....
	St. Louis	**NHL**	68	7	22	29	18	10	1	3	4	4
1988-89	**St. Louis**	**NHL**	52	3	10	13	6	7	0	1	1	2
	NHL Totals		476	61	174	235	161	52	6	18	24	20

Traded to **Toronto** by **Montreal** for Toronto's second round choice in either 1985 or 1986 Entry Draft, December 17, 1982. Traded to **Montreal** by **Toronto** for Larry Landon, February 14, 1985. Traded to **St. Louis** by **Montreal** for Larry Trader and future considerations, October 13, 1987.

GLASGOW, ROBERT

Right wing. Shoots right. 6', 205 lbs.   Born, Edmonton, Alta., April 22, 1968.
(Hartford's 8th choice, 179th overall, in 1986 Entry Draft).

			Regular Season					Playoffs				
Season	Club	Lea	GP	G	A	TP	PIM	GP	G	A	TP	PIM
1985-86	Sherwood Park	AJHL	52	23	18	41	18	....	....	....	....	....
1986-87	U. Alberta	CWUAA	24	5	4	9	8	....	....	....	....	....
1987-88	U. Alberta	CWUAA	47	21	14	35	24	....	....	....	....	....
1988-89	U. Alberta	CWUAA	38	17	29	46	14	....	....	....	....	....

GLENNON, MATTHEW (MATT)

Left wing. Shoots left. 6', 185 lbs.   Born, Hull, MA, September 20, 1968.
(Boston's 6th choice, 119th overall, in 1987 Entry Draft).

			Regular Season					Playoffs				
Season	Club	Lea	GP	G	A	TP	PIM	GP	G	A	TP	PIM
1986-87	Arch. Williams	HS	18	22	36	58	20	....	....	....	....	....
1987-88	Boston College	H.E.	16	3	3	6	16	....	....	....	....	....
1988-89	Boston College	H.E.	16	1	6	7	4	....	....	....	....	....

GLOVER, MICHAEL

Right wing. Shoots right. 5'11", 195 lbs.   Born, Ottawa, Ont., July 23, 1968.
(Edmonton's 8th choice, 145th overall, in 1988 Entry Draft).

			Regular Season					Playoffs				
Season	Club	Lea	GP	G	A	TP	PIM	GP	G	A	TP	PIM
1985-86	S.S. Marie	OHL	61	14	19	33	133	....	....	....	....	....
1986-87	S.S. Marie	OHL	57	26	22	48	107	4	1	0	1	15
1987-88	S.S. Marie	OHL	63	41	42	83	130	6	3	3	6	14
1988-89	Cape Breton	AHL	61	9	11	20	156	....	....	....	....	....

GLYNN, BRIAN

Defense. Shoots left. 6'4", 215 lbs.   Born, Iserlohn, West Germany, November 23, 1967.
(Calgary's 2nd choice, 37th overall, in 1986 Entry Draft).

			Regular Season					Playoffs				
Season	Club	Lea	GP	G	A	TP	PIM	GP	G	A	TP	PIM
1984-85	Saskatoon	WHL	12	1	0	1	2	3	0	0	0	0
1985-86	Saskatoon	WHL	66	7	25	32	131	13	0	3	3	30
1986-87	Saskatoon	WHL	44	2	26	28	163	11	1	3	4	19
1987-88	**Calgary**	**NHL**	67	5	14	19	87	1	0	0	0	0
1988-89	**Calgary**	**NHL**	9	0	1	1	19	....	....	....	....	....
	Salt Lake	IHL	31	3	10	13	105	14	3	7	10	31
	NHL Totals		76	5	15	20	106	1	0	0	0	0

GOBER, MICHAEL

Left wing. Shoots left. 6'1", 195 lbs.   Born, St. Louis, MO, April 10, 1967.
(Detroit's 8th choice, 137th overall, in 1987 Entry Draft).

			Regular Season					Playoffs				
Season	Club	Lea	GP	G	A	TP	PIM	GP	G	A	TP	PIM
1987-88	Trois-Rivieres	QMJHL	19	5	10	15	96	....	....	....	....	....
1988-89	Adirondack	AHL	41	15	7	22	55	2	0	0	0	4

GOERTZ, DAVE

Defense. Shoots right. 5'11", 210 lbs.   Born, Edmonton, Alta., March 28, 1965.
(Pittsburgh's 10th choice, 212th over-all, in 1983 Entry Draft).

			Regular Season					Playoffs				
Season	Club	Lea	GP	G	A	TP	PIM	GP	G	A	TP	PIM
1981-82	Regina	WHL	67	5	19	24	181	19	1	2	3	61
1982-83	Regina	WHL	69	4	22	26	132	5	0	2	2	9
1983-84	Prince Albert	WHL	60	13	47	60	111	5	2	3	5	0
	Baltimore	AHL	1	0	0	0	2	6	0	0	0	0
1984-85	Prince Albert	WHL	48	3	48	51	62	13	4	14	18	29
1985-86	Baltimore	AHL	74	1	15	16	76	....	....	....	....	....
1986-87	Baltimore	AHL	16	0	3	3	8	....	....	....	....	....
	Muskegon	IHL	44	3	17	20	44	15	0	4	4	14
1987-88	**Pittsburgh**	**NHL**	2	0	0	0	2	....	....	....	....	....
	Muskegon	IHL	73	8	36	44	87	6	0	4	4	14
1988-89	Muskegon	IHL	74	1	32	33	102	14	0	4	4	10
	NHL Totals		2	0	0	0	2	....	....	....	....	....

GOLDEN, MIKE

Center. Shoots right. 6'1", 190 lbs.   Born, Boston, MA, June 14, 1965.
(Edmonton's 2nd choice, 40th overall, in 1983 Entry Draft).

			Regular Season					Playoffs				
Season	Club	Lea	GP	G	A	TP	PIM	GP	G	A	TP	PIM
1985-86	U. of Maine	H.E.	24	3	16	29	10	....	....	....	....	....
1986-87	U. of Maine	H.E.	36	19	23	42	37	....	....	....	....	....
1987-88ab	U. of Maine	H.E.	44	31	44	75	46	....	....	....	....	....
1988-89	Denver	IHL	36	12	10	22	21	3	3	1	4	0

a NCAA East Second All-American Team (1988)
b Hockey East Second All-Star Team (1988)
Traded to **NY Rangers** by **Edmonton** with Miroslav Horava and Don Jackson for Reijo Ruotsalainen, Ville Kentala, Clark Donatelli and Jim Weimer, October 2, 1986.

GOODALL, GLEN

Center. Shoots right. 5'8", 170 lbs.   Born, Fort Nelson, B.C., January 22, 1970.
(Detroit's 9th choice, 206th overall, in 1988 Entry Draft).

			Regular Season					Playoffs				
Season	Club	Lea	GP	G	A	TP	PIM	GP	G	A	TP	PIM
1984-85	Seattle	WHL	59	5	21	26	6	....	....	....	....	....
1985-86	Seattle	WHL	65	13	28	41	53	4	1	1	2	0
1986-87	Seattle	WHL	68	63	49	112	64	....	....	....	....	....
1987-88	Seattle	WHL	70	53	64	117	88	....	....	....	....	....
1988-89	Seattle	WHL	70	52	62	114	58	....	....	....	....	....
	Flint	IHL	9	5	4	9	4	....	....	....	....	....

GORMAN, SEAN

Defense. Shoots left. 6'3", 180 lbs.   Born, Cambridge, MA, February 1, 1969.
(Boston's 12th choice, 245th overall, in 1987 Entry Draft).

			Regular Season					Playoffs				
Season	Club	Lea	GP	G	A	TP	PIM	GP	G	A	TP	PIM
1986-87	Matignon	HS	23	1	9	10	....	....	....	....	....	....
1987-88	Princeton	ECAC	28	0	3	3	6	....	....	....	....	....
1988-89	Princeton	ECAC	17	0	2	2	20	....	....	....	....	....

GOSSELIN, GUY

Defense. Shoots right. 5'11", 190 lbs.   Born, Rochester, MN, January 6, 1964.
(Winnipeg's 6th choice, 159th overall, in 1982 Entry Draft).

			Regular Season					Playoffs				
Season	Club	Lea	GP	G	A	TP	PIM	GP	G	A	TP	PIM
1982-83	Minn.-Duluth	WCHA	4	0	0	0	0	....	....	....	....	....
1983-84	Minn.-Duluth	WCHA	37	3	3	6	26	....	....	....	....	....
1984-85	Minn.-Duluth	WCHA	47	3	7	10	25	....	....	....	....	....
1985-86	Minn.-Duluth	WCHA	39	2	16	18	53	....	....	....	....	....
1986-87a	Minn.-Duluth	WCHA	33	7	8	15	66	....	....	....	....	....
1987-88	**Winnipeg**	**NHL**	5	0	0	0	6	....	....	....	....	....
	U.S. National	....	50	3	19	22	82	....	....	....	....	....
	U.S. Olympic	....	6	0	3	3	2	....	....	....	....	....
1988-89	Moncton	AHL	58	2	8	10	56	10	1	1	2	2
	NHL Totals		5	0	0	0	6	....	....	....	....	....

a WCHA Second All-Star Team (1987)

GOTAAS, STEVE

Center. Shoots right. 5'9", 170 lbs.   Born, Camrose, Alta., May 10, 1967.
(Pittsburgh's 4th choice, 86th overall, in 1985 Entry Draft).

			Regular Season					Playoffs				
Season	Club	Lea	GP	G	A	TP	PIM	GP	G	A	TP	PIM
1983-84	Prince Albert	WHL	65	10	22	32	47	5	0	1	1	0
1984-85	Prince Albert	WHL	72	32	41	73	66	13	3	6	9	17
1985-86	Prince Albert	WHL	61	40	61	101	31	....	....	....	....	....
1986-87	Prince Albert	WHL	68	53	55	108	94	8	5	6	11	16
1987-88	**Pittsburgh**	**NHL**	36	5	6	11	45	....	....	....	....	....
	Muskegon	IHL	34	16	22	38	4	....	....	....	....	....
1988-89	**Minnesota**	**NHL**	12	1	3	4	6	3	0	1	1	5
	Muskegon	IHL	19	9	16	25	34	....	....	....	....	....
	Kalamazoo	IHL	30	24	22	46	12	5	2	3	5	2
	NHL Totals		48	6	9	15	51	3	0	1	1	5

Traded to **Minnesota** by **Pittsburgh** with Ville Siren for Gord Dineen and Scott Bjugstad, December 17, 1988.

GOULD, ROBERT (BOBBY)

Right wing. Shoots right. 6', 195 lbs.   Born, Petrolia, Ont., September 2, 1957.
(Atlanta's 7th choice, 118th over-all, in 1977 Amateur Draft).

			Regular Season					Playoffs				
Season	Club	Lea	GP	G	A	TP	PIM	GP	G	A	TP	PIM
1978-79a	N. Hampshire	ECAC	25	24	17	41	....	....	....	....	....	....
	Tulsa	CHL	5	2	0	2	4	....	....	....	....	....
1979-80	**Atlanta**	**NHL**	1	0	0	0	0	....	....	....	....	....
	Birmingham	CHL	79	27	33	60	73	4	2	4	6	0
1980-81	Birmingham	CHL	58	25	25	50	43	....	....	....	....	....
	Fort Worth	CHL	18	8	6	14	6	5	5	2	7	10
	Calgary	**NHL**	3	0	0	0	0	11	3	1	4	4
1981-82	Oklahoma City	CHL	1	0	1	1	0	....	....	....	....	....
	Calgary	**NHL**	16	3	0	3	4	....	....	....	....	....
	Washington	**NHL**	60	18	13	31	69	....	....	....	....	....
1982-83	**Washington**	**NHL**	80	22	18	40	43	4	5	0	5	4
1983-84	**Washington**	**NHL**	78	21	19	40	74	5	0	2	2	4
1984-85	**Washington**	**NHL**	78	14	19	33	69	5	0	1	1	2
1985-86	**Washington**	**NHL**	79	19	19	38	26	9	4	3	7	11
1986-87	**Washington**	**NHL**	78	23	27	50	74	7	0	3	3	8
1987-88	**Washington**	**NHL**	72	12	14	26	56	14	3	1	4	21
1988-89	**Washington**	**NHL**	75	5	13	18	65	6	0	2	2	0
	NHL Totals		620	137	142	279	480	61	15	13	28	54

a ECAC Second All-Star Team (1979)
Traded to **Washington** by **Calgary** with Randy Holt for Pat Ribble and Washington's second round choice (Todd Francis — later transferred to Montreal in Doug Risebrough deal) in 1983 Entry Draft, November 25, 1981.

GOULET, MICHEL   (goo-LAY)

Left wing. Shoots left. 6'1", 195 lbs.   Born, Peribonka, Que., April 21, 1960.
(Quebec's 1st choice, 20th over-all, in 1979 Entry Draft).

			Regular Season					Playoffs				
Season	Club	Lea	GP	G	A	TP	PIM	GP	G	A	TP	PIM
1976-77	Quebec	QJHL	37	17	18	35	9	14	3	8	11	19
1977-78	Quebec	QJHL	72	73	62	135	109	1	0	1	1	0
1978-79	Birmingham	WHA	78	28	30	58	65	....	....	....	....	....
1979-80	**Quebec**	**NHL**	77	22	32	54	48	....	....	....	....	....
1980-81	**Quebec**	**NHL**	76	32	39	71	45	4	3	4	7	7
1981-82	**Quebec**	**NHL**	80	42	42	84	48	16	8	5	13	6
1982-83a	**Quebec**	**NHL**	80	57	48	105	51	4	0	0	0	6
1983-84b	**Quebec**	**NHL**	75	56	65	121	76	9	2	4	6	17
1984-85	**Quebec**	**NHL**	69	55	40	95	55	17	11	10	21	17
1985-86b	**Quebec**	**NHL**	75	53	51	104	64	3	1	2	3	10
1986-87b	**Quebec**	**NHL**	75	49	47	96	61	13	9	5	14	35
1987-88a	**Quebec**	**NHL**	80	48	58	106	56	....	....	....	....	....
1988-89	**Quebec**	**NHL**	69	26	38	64	67	....	....	....	....	....
	NHL Totals		756	440	460	900	571	66	34	30	64	98

a NHL Second All-Star Team (1983, 1988)
b NHL First All-Star Team (1984, 1986, 1987, 1988)
Played in NHL All-Star Game (1983-86, 1988)

GOVEDARIS, CHRIS

Left wing. Shoots left. 6', 200 lbs.   Born, Toronto, Ont., February 2, 1970.
(Hartford's 1st choice, 11th overall, in 1988 Entry Draft)

			Regular Season					Playoffs				
Season	Club	Lea	GP	G	A	TP	PIM	GP	G	A	TP	PIM
1986-87	Toronto	OHL	64	36	28	64	148	....	....	....	....	....
1987-88	Toronto	OHL	62	42	38	80	118	4	2	1	3	10
1988-89	Toronto	OHL	49	41	38	79	117	6	2	3	5	0

GRAHAM, DIRK MILTON

Right wing. Shoots right. 5'11", 190 lbs.   Born, Regina, Sask., July 29, 1959.
(Vancouver's 5th choice, 89th over-all, in 1979 Entry Draft).

			Regular Season					Playoffs				
Season	Club	Lea	GP	G	A	TP	PIM	GP	G	A	TP	PIM
1975-76	Regina	WHL	2	0	0	0	0	6	1	1	2	5
1976-77	Regina	WHL	65	37	28	65	66	....	....	....	....	....
1977-78	Regina	WHL	72	29	61	110	87	13	15	19	34	37
1978-79	Regina	WHL	71	48	60	108	252	....	....	....	....	....
1979-80	Dallas	CHL	62	17	15	32	96	....	....	....	....	....
1980-81	Fort Wayne	IHL	6	1	2	3	12	....	....	....	....	....
	Toledo	IHL	61	40	45	85	88	....	....	....	....	....
1981-82	Toledo	IHL	72	49	56	105	68	13	10	11	21	8
1982-83a	Toledo	IHL	78	70	55	125	88	11	13	7	20	30
1983-84	**Minnesota**	**NHL**	6	1	1	2	0	1	0	0	0	2
b	Salt Lake	CHL	57	37	57	94	72	5	3	8	11	2
1984-85	**Minnesota**	**NHL**	36	12	11	23	23	9	0	4	4	7
	Springfield	AHL	37	20	28	48	41	....	....	....	....	....
1985-86	**Minnesota**	**NHL**	80	22	33	55	87	5	3	1	4	2
1986-87	**Minnesota**	**NHL**	76	25	29	54	142	....	....	....	....	....
1987-88	**Minnesota**	**NHL**	28	7	5	12	39	....	....	....	....	....
	Chicago	**NHL**	42	17	19	36	32	4	1	2	3	4
1988-89	**Chicago**	**NHL**	80	33	45	78	89	16	2	4	6	38
	NHL Totals		348	117	143	260	412	35	6	11	17	53

a IHL First All-Star Team (1983)
b CHL First All-Star Team (1984)
Signed as free agent by **Minnesota**, August 17, 1983. Traded to **Chicago** by **Minnesota** for Curt Fraser, January 4, 1988.

GRAHAM, ROBB

Right wing. Shoots right. 6'4", 200 lbs.   Born, Bellevue, WA, April 7, 1968.
(NY Rangers' 7th choice, 135th overall, in 1986 Entry Draft).

			Regular Season					Playoffs				
Season	Club	Lea	GP	G	A	TP	PIM	GP	G	A	TP	PIM
1985-86	Guelph	OHL	62	10	18	28	78	20	4	2	6	24
1986-87	Guelph	OHL	45	13	14	27	37	....	....	....	....	....
1987-88	Sudbury	OHL	58	17	17	34	59	....	....	....	....	....
	Colorado	IHL	5	1	1	2	0	6	1	2	3	2
1988-89	Denver	IHL	67	14	22	36	72	1	1	2	3	0

GRANATO, TONY

Center. Shoots right. 5'10", 185 lbs. Born, Downers Grove, IL, July 25, 1964.
(NY Rangers' 5th choice, 120th overall, in 1982 Entry Draft).

			Regular Season					Playoffs				
Season	Club	Lea	GP	G	A	TP	PIM	GP	G	A	TP	PIM
1983-84	U. Wisconsin	WCHA	35	14	17	31	48	....	....	....	....	....
1984-85	U. Wisconsin	WCHA	42	33	34	67	94	....	....	....	....	....
1985-86	U. Wisconsin	WCHA	33	25	24	49	36	....	....	....	....	....
1986-87ab	U. Wisconsin	WCHA	42	28	45	73	64	....	....	....	....	....
1987-88	U.S. National	....	49	40	31	71	55	....	....	....	....	....
	U.S. Olympic	....	6	1	7	8	4	....	....	....	....	....
	Colorado	IHL	22	13	14	27	36	8	9	4	13	16
1988-89c	**NY Rangers**	**NHL**	**78**	**36**	**27**	**63**	**140**	**4**	**1**	**1**	**2**	**21**
	NHL Totals		**78**	**36**	**27**	**63**	**140**	**4**	**1**	**1**	**2**	**21**

a WCHA Second All-Star Team (1987)
b NCAA West Second All-American Team (1987)
c NHL All-Rookie Team (1989)

GRANT, KEVIN

Defense. Shoots right. 6'3", 210 lbs. Born, Toronto, Ont., January 9, 1969.
(Calgary's 3rd choice, 40th overall, in 1987 Entry Draft).

			Regular Season					Playoffs				
Season	Club	Lea	GP	G	A	TP	PIM	GP	G	A	TP	PIM
1985-86	Kitchener	OHL	63	2	15	17	204	5	0	1	1	11
1986-87	Kitchener	OHL	52	5	18	23	125	4	0	1	1	16
1987-88	Kitchener	OHL	48	3	20	23	138	4	0	1	1	4
1988-89	Salt Lake	IHL	3	0	1	1	5	3	0	0	0	12
	Sudbury	OHL	60	9	41	50	106	....	....	....	....	....

GRATTON, DAN

Center. Shoots left. 6', 185 lbs. Born, Brantford, Ont., December 7, 1966.
Last amateur club: Oshawa Generals (OHL).

			Regular Season					Playoffs				
Season	Club	Lea	GP	G	A	TP	PIM	GP	G	A	TP	PIM
1983-84	Oshawa	OHL	65	40	34	74	55	7	2	5	7	15
1984-85	Oshawa	OHL	56	24	48	72	67	5	3	3	6	0
1985-86	Belleville	OHL	54	33	37	70	45	24	20	9	29	16
1986-87	New Haven	AHL	49	6	10	16	45	2	0	0	0	0
1987-88	**Los Angeles**	**NHL**	**7**	**1**	**0**	**1**	**5**	....	....	....	....	....
	New Haven	AHL	57	18	28	46	77	....	....	....	....	....
1988-89	New Haven	AHL	29	5	13	18	41	....	....	....	....	....
	Flint	IHL	20	5	9	14	8	....	....	....	....	....
	NHL Totals		**7**	**1**	**0**	**1**	**5**	....	....	....	....	....

GRAVES, ADAM

Center. Shoots left. 5'11", 200 lbs. Born, Toronto, Ont., April 12, 1968.
(Detroit's 2nd choice, 22nd overall, in 1986 Entry Draft).

			Regular Season					Playoffs				
Season	Club	Lea	GP	G	A	TP	PIM	GP	G	A	TP	PIM
1985-86	Windsor	OHL	62	27	37	64	35	16	5	11	16	10
1986-87	Windsor	OHL	66	45	55	100	70	14	9	8	17	32
	Adirondack	AHL	....	....	....	....	....	5	0	1	1	0
1987-88	**Detroit**	**NHL**	**9**	**0**	**1**	**1**	**8**	....	....	....	....	....
	Windsor	OHL	37	28	32	60	107	12	14	18	32	16
1988-89	**Detroit**	**NHL**	**56**	**7**	**5**	**12**	**60**	**5**	**0**	**0**	**0**	**4**
	Adirondack	AHL	14	10	11	21	28	14	11	7	18	17
	NHL Totals		**65**	**7**	**6**	**13**	**68**	**5**	**0**	**0**	**0**	**4**

GRAVES, STEVE

Center. Shoots left. 5'10", 175 lbs. Born, Trenton, Ont., April 7, 1964.
(Edmonton's 2nd choice, 41st over-all, in 1982 Entry Draft).

			Regular Season					Playoffs				
Season	Club	Lea	GP	G	A	TP	PIM	GP	G	A	TP	PIM
1981-82	S. S. Marie	OHL	66	12	15	27	49	13	8	5	13	14
1982-83	S. S. Marie	OHL	60	21	20	41	48	5	0	0	0	4
1983-84	**Edmonton**	**NHL**	**2**	**0**	**0**	**0**	**0**	....	....	....	....	....
a	S. S. Marie	OHL	67	41	48	89	47	16	6	8	14	8
1984-85	Nova Scotia	AHL	80	17	15	32	20	6	0	1	1	4
1985-86	Nova Scotia	AHL	78	19	18	37	22	....	....	....	....	....
1986-87	**Edmonton**	**NHL**	**12**	**2**	**0**	**2**	**0**	....	....	....	....	....
	Nova Scotia	AHL	59	18	10	28	22	5	1	1	2	2
1987-88	**Edmonton**	**NHL**	**21**	**3**	**4**	**7**	**10**	....	....	....	....	....
	Nova Scotia	AHL	11	6	2	8	4	....	....	....	....	....
1988-89	Cdn. Nationa	....	3	5	1	6	2	....	....	....	....	....
	TPS	Fin.	43	16	12	28	48	10	2	8	10	12
	NHL Totals		**35**	**5**	**4**	**9**	**10**	....	....	....	....	....

a OHL Third All-Star Team (1984)

GREEN, MARK

Center. Shoots right. 6'4", 200 lbs. Born, Watertown, NY, December 26, 1967.
(Winnipeg's 8th choice, 176th overall, in 1986 Entry Draft).

			Regular Season					Playoffs				
Season	Club	Lea	GP	G	A	TP	PIM	GP	G	A	TP	PIM
1987-88	Clarkson	ECAC	18	3	6	9	18	....	....	....	....	....
1988-89	Clarkson	ECAC	30	16	11	27	42	....	....	....	....	....

GREEN, RICHARD DOUGLAS (RICK)

Defense. Shoots left. 6'3", 220 lbs. Born, Belleville, Ont., February 20, 1956.
(Washington's 1st choice and 1st over-all in 1976 Amateur Draft).

			Regular Season					Playoffs				
Season	Club	Lea	GP	G	A	TP	PIM	GP	G	A	TP	PIM
1974-75	London	OHA	65	8	45	53	68	....	....	....	....	....
1975-76ab	London	OHA	61	13	47	60	69	5	1	0	1	4
1976-77	**Washington**	**NHL**	**45**	**3**	**12**	**15**	**16**	....	....	....	....	....
1977-78	**Washington**	**NHL**	**60**	**5**	**14**	**19**	**67**	....	....	....	....	....
1978-79	**Washington**	**NHL**	**71**	**8**	**33**	**41**	**62**	....	....	....	....	....
1979-80	**Washington**	**NHL**	**71**	**4**	**20**	**24**	**52**	....	....	....	....	....
1980-81	**Washington**	**NHL**	**65**	**8**	**23**	**31**	**91**	....	....	....	....	....
1981-82	**Washington**	**NHL**	**65**	**3**	**25**	**28**	**93**	....	....	....	....	....
1982-83	**Montreal**	**NHL**	**66**	**2**	**24**	**26**	**58**	**3**	**0**	**0**	**0**	**2**
1983-84	**Montreal**	**NHL**	**7**	**0**	**1**	**1**	**7**	**15**	**1**	**2**	**3**	**33**
1984-85	**Montreal**	**NHL**	**77**	**1**	**18**	**19**	**30**	**12**	**0**	**3**	**3**	**14**
1985-86	**Montreal**	**NHL**	**46**	**3**	**2**	**5**	**20**	**18**	**1**	**4**	**5**	**8**
1986-87	**Montreal**	**NHL**	**72**	**1**	**9**	**10**	**10**	**17**	**0**	**4**	**4**	**8**
1987-88	**Montreal**	**NHL**	**59**	**2**	**11**	**13**	**33**	**11**	**0**	**2**	**2**	**2**
1988-89	**Montreal**	**NHL**	**72**	**1**	**14**	**15**	**25**	**21**	**1**	**1**	**2**	**6**
	NHL Totals		**776**	**41**	**206**	**247**	**564**	**97**	**3**	**16**	**19**	**73**

a OHA First All-Star Team (1976).
b Named OHA's Most Outstanding Defenseman (1976).

Traded to **Montreal** by **Washington** with Ryan Walter for Brian Engblom, Rod Langway, Doug Jarvis and Craig Laughlin, September 9, 1982.

GREEN, TRAVIS

Center. Shoots right. 6', 195 lbs. Born, Creston, B.C., December 20, 1970.
(NY Islanders' 2nd choice, 23rd overall, in 1989 Entry Draft).

			Regular Season					Playoffs				
Season	Club	Lea	GP	G	A	TP	PIM	GP	G	A	TP	PIM
1985-86	Castlegar	BCJHL	35	30	40	70	41	....	....	....	....	....
1986-87	Spokane	WHL	64	8	17	25	27	3	0	0	0	0
1987-88	Spokane	WHL	72	33	54	87	42	15	10	10	20	13
1988-89	Spokane	WHL	75	51	51	102	79	....	....	....	....	....

GREENLAW, JEFF

Left wing. Shoots left. 6'2", 230 lbs. Born, Toronto, Ont., February 28, 1968.
(Washington's 1st choice, 19th overall, in 1986 Entry Draft).

			Regular Season					Playoffs				
Season	Club	Lea	GP	G	A	TP	PIM	GP	G	A	TP	PIM
1985-86	Cdn. Olympic	...	57	3	16	19	43	....	....	....	....	....
1986-87	**Washington**	**NHL**	**22**	**0**	**3**	**3**	**44**	....	....	....	....	....
	Binghamton	AHL	4	0	2	2	0	....	....	....	....	....
1987-88	**Washington**	**NHL**	...	...	....	....	....	**1**	**0**	**0**	**0**	**19**
	Binghamton	AHL	56	8	7	15	142	1	0	0	0	2
1988-89	Baltimore	AHL	55	12	15	27	115	....	....	....	....	....
	NHL Totals		**22**	**0**	**3**	**3**	**44**	**1**	**0**	**0**	**0**	**19**

GREGG, RANDALL JOHN (RANDY)

Defense. Shoots left. 6'4", 215 lbs. Born, Edmonton, Alta., February 19, 1956.

			Regular Season					Playoffs				
Season	Club	Lea	GP	G	A	TP	PIM	GP	G	A	TP	PIM
1977-78	U. of Alberta	CWUAA	24	7	23	30	37	....	....	....	....	....
1978-79	U. of Alberta	CWUAA	24	5	16	21	47	....	....	....	....	....
1979-80	Cdn. National	...	56	7	17	24	36	....	....	....	....	....
	Cdn. Olympic	...	6	1	1	2	2	....	....	....	....	....
1980-81	Kokuda	Japan	35	12	18	30	30	....	....	....	....	....
1981-82	Kokuda	Japan	36	12	20	32	25	....	....	....	....	....
	Edmonton	**NHL**	....	....	....	....	....	**4**	**0**	**0**	**0**	**0**
1982-83	**Edmonton**	**NHL**	**80**	**6**	**22**	**28**	**54**	**16**	**2**	**4**	**6**	**13**
1983-84	**Edmonton**	**NHL**	**80**	**13**	**27**	**40**	**56**	**19**	**3**	**7**	**10**	**21**
1984-85	**Edmonton**	**NHL**	**57**	**3**	**20**	**23**	**32**	**17**	**0**	**6**	**6**	**12**
1985-86	**Edmonton**	**NHL**	**64**	**2**	**26**	**28**	**47**	**10**	**1**	**0**	**1**	**12**
1986-87	**Edmonton**	**NHL**	**52**	**8**	**16**	**24**	**42**	**18**	**3**	**6**	**9**	**17**
1987-88	**Edmonton**	**NHL**	**15**	**1**	**2**	**3**	**8**	**19**	**1**	**8**	**9**	**24**
	Cdn. National	....	37	2	6	8	37	....	....	....	....	....
	Cdn. Olympic	....	8	1	2	3	8	....	....	....	....	....
1988-89	**Edmonton**	**NHL**	**57**	**3**	**15**	**18**	**28**	**7**	**1**	**0**	**1**	**4**
	NHL Totals		**405**	**36**	**128**	**164**	**267**	**110**	**11**	**31**	**42**	**103**

Signed as a free agent by **Edmonton**, October 18, 1982.

GRESCHNER, RONALD JOHN (RON) (GRESH-nur)

Defense. Shoots left. 6'2", 205 lbs. Born, Goodsoil, Sask., December 22, 1954.
(NY Rangers' 2nd choice, 32nd over-all, in 1974 Amateur Draft).

			Regular Season					Playoffs				
Season	Club	Lea	GP	G	A	TP	PIM	GP	G	A	TP	PIM
1972-73	N. Westminster	WHL	68	22	47	69	169	5	2	4	6	19
1973-74a	N. Westminster	WHL	67	33	70	103	170	11	5	6	11	18
1974-75	Providence	AHL	7	5	6	11	10	....	....	....	....	....
	NY Rangers	**NHL**	**70**	**8**	**37**	**45**	**93**	**3**	**0**	**1**	**1**	**2**
1975-76	**NY Rangers**	**NHL**	**77**	**6**	**21**	**27**	**93**	....	....	....	....	....
1976-77	**NY Rangers**	**NHL**	**80**	**11**	**36**	**47**	**89**	....	....	....	....	....
1977-78	**NY Rangers**	**NHL**	**78**	**24**	**48**	**72**	**100**	**3**	**0**	**0**	**0**	**2**
1978-79	**NY Rangers**	**NHL**	**60**	**17**	**36**	**53**	**66**	**18**	**7**	**5**	**12**	**16**
1979-80	**NY Rangers**	**NHL**	**76**	**21**	**37**	**58**	**103**	**9**	**0**	**6**	**6**	**10**
1980-81	**NY Rangers**	**NHL**	**74**	**27**	**41**	**68**	**112**	**14**	**4**	**8**	**12**	**17**
1981-82	**NY Rangers**	**NHL**	**29**	**5**	**11**	**16**	**16**	....	....	....	....	....
1982-83	**NY Rangers**	**NHL**	**10**	**3**	**5**	**8**	**0**	**8**	**2**	**2**	**4**	**12**
1983-84	**NY Rangers**	**NHL**	**77**	**12**	**44**	**56**	**117**	**2**	**1**	**0**	**1**	**2**
1984-85	**NY Rangers**	**NHL**	**48**	**16**	**29**	**45**	**42**	**2**	**0**	**3**	**3**	**12**
1985-86	**NY Rangers**	**NHL**	**78**	**20**	**28**	**48**	**104**	**5**	**3**	**1**	**4**	**11**
1986-87	**NY Rangers**	**NHL**	**61**	**6**	**34**	**40**	**62**	**6**	**0**	**5**	**5**	**0**
1987-88	**NY Rangers**	**NHL**	**51**	**1**	**5**	**6**	**82**	....	....	....	....	....
1988-89	**NY Rangers**	**NHL**	**58**	**1**	**10**	**11**	**94**	**4**	**0**	**1**	**1**	**6**
	NHL Totals		**927**	**178**	**422**	**600**	**1173**	**74**	**17**	**32**	**49**	**90**

a WHL First All-Star Team (1974)
Played in NHL All-Star Game (1980)

GRETZKY, KEITH (GRETZ-kee)

Center. Shoots left. 5'9", 160 lbs. Born, Brantford, Ont., February 16, 1967.
(Buffalo's 3rd choice, 56th over-all, in 1985 Entry Draft).

			Regular Season					Playoffs				
Season	Club	Lea	GP	G	A	TP	PIM	GP	G	A	TP	PIM
1983-84	Windsor	OHL	70	15	38	53	8	3	0	1	1	2
1984-85	Windsor	OHL	66	31	62	93	12	4	2	2	4	4
1985-86	Belleville	OHL	61	27	47	74	12	24	8	13	21	2
1986-87	Hamilton	OHL	64	35	66	101	18	9	5	9	14	4
1987-88	Rochester	AHL	43	8	24	32	6	....	....	....	....	....
	Flint	IHL	25	9	18	27	0	....	....	....	....	....
1988-89	Rochester	AHL	23	3	13	16	0	....	....	....	....	....
	Flint	IHL	2	0	1	1	0	....	....	....	....	....
	Kettera	Fin.	15	2	11	13	6	....	....	....	....	....

GRETZKY, WAYNE (GRETZ-kee)

Center. Shoots left. 6', 175 lbs. Born, Brantford, Ont., January 26, 1961.

			Regular Season					Playoffs				
Season	Club	Lea	GP	G	A	TP	PIM	GP	G	A	TP	PIM
1976-77	Peterborough	OHA	3	0	3	3	0	....	....	....	....	....
1977-78ab	S. S. Marie	OHA	64	70	112	182	14	13	6	20	26	0
1978-79	Indianapolis	WHA	8	3	3	6	0	....	....	....	....	....
cd	Edmonton	WHA	72	43	61	104	19	13	*10	10	*20	2
1979-80efg	**Edmonton**	**NHL**	**79**	**51**	***86**	***137**	**21**	**3**	**2**	**1**	**3**	**0**
1980-81 ehijk	**Edmonton**	**NHL**	**80**	**55**	***109**	***164**	**28**	**9**	**7**	**14**	**21**	**4**
1981-82 ehijklm	**Edmonton**	**NHL**	**80**	***92**	***120**	***212**	**26**	**5**	**5**	**7**	**12**	**8**
1982-83 ehijmnoq	**Edmonton**	**NHL**	**80**	***71**	***125**	***196**	**59**	**16**	**12**	***26**	***38**	**4**
1983-84 ehimq	**Edmonton**	**NHL**	**74**	***87**	***118**	***205**	**39**	**19**	**13**	***22**	***35**	**12**
1984-85 ehijmnopqr	**Edmonton**	**NHL**	**80**	***73**	***135**	***208**	**52**	**18**	**17**	***30**	***47**	**4**
1985-86 ehijkr	**Edmonton**	**NHL**	**80**	**52**	***163**	***215**	**46**	**10**	**8**	**11**	**19**	**2**
1986-87 ehimqr	**Edmonton**	**NHL**	**79**	***62**	***121**	***183**	**28**	**21**	**5**	***29**	***34**	**6**
1987-88gnp	**Edmonton**	**NHL**	**64**	**40**	***109**	**149**	**24**	**19**	**12**	***31**	***43**	**16**
1988-89egs	**Los Angeles**	**NHL**	**78**	**54**	***114**	**168**	**26**	**11**	**5**	**17**	**22**	**0**
	NHL Totals		**774**	**637**	**1200**	**1837**	**349**	**131**	**86**	**188**	**274**	**56**

a OHA Second All-Star Team (1978)
b Named OHA's Rookie of the Year (1978)
c WHA Second All-Star Team (1979)
d Named WHA's Rookie of the Year (1979)
e Won Hart Trophy (1980, 1981, 1982, 1983, 1984, 1985, 1986, 1987, 1989)
f Won Lady Byng Trophy (1980)
g NHL Second All-Star Team (1980, 1988, 1989)
h NHL First All-Star Team (1981, 1982, 1983, 1984, 1985, 1986, 1987)
i Won Art Ross Trophy (1981, 1982, 1983, 1984, 1985, 1986, 1987)
j NHL record for assists in regular season (1981, 1982, 1983, 1985, 1986)
k NHL record for points in regular season (1981, 1982, 1986)
l NHL record for goals in regular season (1982)
m Won Lester B. Pearson Award (1982, 1983, 1984, 1985, 1987)
n NHL record for assists in one playoff year (1983, 1985, 1988)
o NHL record for points in one playoff year (1983, 1985)
p Won Conn Smythe Trophy (1985, 1988)
q NHL Plus/Minus Leader (1984, 1985, 1987)
r Selected Chrysler-Dodge/NHL Performer of the Year (1985, 1986, 1987)
s Won Dodge Performance of the Year Award (1989)

Played in NHL All-Star Game (1980-1986, 1988-89)

Reclaimed by **Edmonton** as an under-age junior prior to Expansion Draft, June 9, 1979. Claimed as priority selection by **Edmonton**, June 9, 1979. Traded to **Los Angeles** by **Edmonton** with Mike Krushelnyski and Marty McSorley for Jimmy Carson, Martin Gelinas, Los Angeles' first round choices in 1989 (acquired by **New Jersey**, June 17, 1989. **New Jersey** selected Jason Miller), 1991 and 1993 Entry Drafts and cash, August 9, 1988.

GRIBBLE, ANDREW (ANDY)

Right wing. Shoots right. 6', 185 lbs. Born, Toronto, Ont., April 12, 1966.
(Vancouver's 1st choice, 2nd overall, in 1988 Supplemental Draft).

			Regular Season					Playoffs				
Season	Club	Lea	GP	G	A	TP	PIM	GP	G	A	TP	PIM
1984-85	Bowling Green	CCHA	42	12	11	23	8	....	....	....	....	....
1985-86	Bowling Green	CCHA	40	6	17	23	8	....	....	....	....	....
1986-87	Bowling Green	CCHA	45	18	18	36	26	....	....	....	....	....
1987-88	Bowling Green	CCHA	45	31	29	60	22	....	....	....	....	....
1988-89	Flint	IHL	14	1	3	4	4	....	....	....	....	....
	Milwaukee	IHL	27	2	8	10	2	....	....	....	....	....

GRIMSON, STU

Left wing. Shoots left. 6'5", 230 lbs. Born, Kamloops, B.C., May 20, 1965.
(Calgary's 8th choice, 143rd overall, in 1985 Entry Draft).

			Regular Season					Playoffs				
Season	Club	Lea	GP	G	A	TP	PIM	GP	G	A	TP	PIM
1982-83	Regina	WHL	48	0	1	1	105	5	0	0	0	14
1983-84	Regina	WHL	63	8	8	16	131	21	0	1	1	29
1984-85	Regina	WHL	71	24	32	56	248	8	1	2	3	14
1985-86	U. Manitoba	CWUAA	12	7	4	11	113	3	1	1	2	20
1986-87	U. Manitoba	CWUAA	29	8	8	16	67	14	4	2	6	28
1987-88	Salt Lake	IHL	38	9	5	14	268	....	....	....	....	....
1988-89	**Calgary**	**NHL**	**1**	**0**	**0**	**0**	**5**	....	....	....	....	....
	Salt Lake	IHL	72	9	18	27	397	14	2	3	5	86
	NHL Totals		**1**	**0**	**0**	**0**	**5**	....	....	....	....	....

GRONSTRAND, JARI

Defense. Shoots left. 6'3", 195 lbs. Born, Tampere, Finland, November 14, 1962.
(Minnesota's 8th choice, 96th overall, in 1986 Entry Draft).

			Regular Season					Playoffs				
Season	Club	Lea	GP	G	A	TP	PIM	GP	G	A	TP	PIM
1982-83	Tappara	Fin.	35	2	2	4	18	8	0	0	0	4
1983-84	Tappara	Fin.	32	2	4	6	14	9	0	2	2	4
1984-85	Tappara	Fin.	36	1	9	10	27	....	....	....	....	....
1985-86	Tappara	Fin.	36	9	5	14	26	8	1	2	3	4
1986-87	**Minnesota**	**NHL**	**47**	**1**	**6**	**7**	**27**	....	....	....	....	....
1987-88	**NY Rangers**	**NHL**	**62**	**3**	**11**	**14**	**63**	....	....	....	....	....
	Colorado	IHL	3	1	3	4	0	....	....	....	....	....
1988-89	**Quebec**	**NHL**	**25**	**1**	**3**	**4**	**14**	....	....	....	....	....
	Halifax	AHL	8	0	1	1	5	....	....	....	....	....
	NHL Totals		**134**	**5**	**20**	**25**	**104**	....	....	....	....	....

Traded to **NY Rangers** by **Minnesota** with Paul Boutilier for Jay Caulfield and Dave Gagne, October 8, 1987. Traded to **Quebec** by **NY Rangers** with Bruce Bell, Walt Poddubny and NY Rangers' fourth round choice (Eric Dubois) in 1989 Entry Draft for Jason Lafreniere and Normand Rochefort, August 1, 1988.

GROSS, PAVEL

Right wing. Shoots right. 6'3", 195 lbs. Born, Ustin Ogroh, Czechoslovakia, May 11, 1968.
(NY Islanders' 7th choice, 111th overall, in 1988 Entry Draft).

			Regular Season					Playoffs				
Season	Club	Lea	GP	G	A	TP	PIM	GP	G	A	TP	PIM
1987-88	Sparta Praha	Czech	24	3	4	7	0	....	....	....	....	....
1988-89	Sparta Praha	Czech	27	12	13	25	....	....	....	....	....	....

GRUHL, SCOTT KENNETH (GROOL)

Left wing. Shoots left. 5'11", 185 lbs. Born, Port Colborne, Ont., September 13, 1959.

			Regular Season					Playoffs				
Season	Club	Lea	GP	G	A	TP	PIM	GP	G	A	TP	PIM
1978-79	Sudbury	OHA	68	35	49	94	78	10	5	7	12	15
1979-80	Binghamton	AHL	4	1	0	1	0	....	....	....	....	....
	Saginaw	IHL	75	53	40	93	100	7	2	6	8	16
1980-81	Houston	CHL	4	0	0	0	0	....	....	....	....	....
	Saginaw	IHL	77	56	34	90	87	13	11	8	19	12
1981-82	**Los Angeles**	**NHL**	**7**	**2**	**1**	**3**	**2**	....	....	....	....	....
	New Haven	AHL	73	28	41	69	107	4	0	4	4	2
1982-83	**Los Angeles**	**NHL**	**7**	**0**	**2**	**2**	**4**	....	....	....	....	....
	New Haven	AHL	68	25	38	63	114	12	3	3	6	22
1983-84	Muskegon	IHL	56	40	56	96	46	....	....	....	....	....
1984-85a	Muskegon	IHL	82	62	64	126	102	17	7	16	23	25
1985-86b	Muskegon	IHL	82	59	50	109	178	14	7	13	20	22
1986-87	Muskegon	IHL	67	34	39	73	157	15	5	7	12	54
1987-88	**Pittsburgh**	**NHL**	**6**	**1**	**0**	**1**	**0**	....	....	....	....	....
	Muskegon	IHL	55	28	47	75	115	6	5	1	6	12
1988-89	Muskegon	IHL	79	37	55	92	163	14	8	11	19	37
	NHL Totals		**20**	**3**	**3**	**6**	**6**	....	....	....	....	....

a IHL First All-Star Team (1985)
b IHL Second All-Star Team (1986)

Signed as free agent by **Los Angeles**, October 11, 1979. Signed as a free agent by **Pittsburgh**, December 14, 1987.

GUAY, FRANCOIS

Left wing. Shoots left. 6', 185 lbs. Born, Gatineau, Que., June 8, 1968.
(Buffalo's 9th choice, 152nd overall, in 1986 Entry Draft).

			Regular Season					Playoffs				
Season	Club	Lea	GP	G	A	TP	PIM	GP	G	A	TP	PIM
1985-86	Laval	QMJHL	71	19	55	74	46	14	5	6	11	15
1986-87	Laval	QMJHL	63	52	77	129	67	14	5	13	18	18
1987-88	Laval	QMJHL	66	60	84	144	142	14	10	15	25	10
1988-89	Rochester	AHL	45	6	20	26	34	....	....	....	....	....

GUAY, PAUL (GAY)

Right wing. Shoots right. 5'11", 185 lbs. Born, Providence, RI, September 2, 1963.
(Minnesota's 9th choice, 118th over-all, in 1981 Entry Draft).

			Regular Season					Playoffs				
Season	Club	Lea	GP	G	A	TP	PIM	GP	G	A	TP	PIM
1980-81	Mt. St. Charles	R.I.	23	28	38	66	....	....	....	....	....	....
1981-82	Providence	ECAC	33	23	17	40	38	....	....	....	....	....
1982-83a	Providence	ECAC	42	34	31	65	83	....	....	....	....	....
1983-84	U.S. National	...	62	20	18	38	44	....	....	....	....	....
	U.S. Olympic	...	6	1	0	1	8	....	....	....	....	....
	Philadelphia	**NHL**	**14**	**2**	**6**	**8**	**14**	**3**	**0**	**0**	**0**	**4**
1984-85	**Philadelphia**	**NHL**	**2**	**0**	**1**	**1**	**0**	....	....	....	....	....
	Hershey	AHL	74	23	30	53	123	....	....	....	....	....
1985-86	**Los Angeles**	**NHL**	**23**	**3**	**3**	**6**	**18**	....	....	....	....	....
	New Haven	AHL	57	15	36	51	101	5	3	0	3	11
1986-87	New Haven	AHL	6	1	3	4	11	....	....	....	....	....
	Los Angeles	**NHL**	**35**	**2**	**5**	**7**	**16**	**2**	**0**	**0**	**0**	**0**
1987-88	**Los Angeles**	**NHL**	**33**	**4**	**4**	**8**	**40**	**4**	**0**	**1**	**1**	**8**
	New Haven	AHL	42	21	26	47	53	....	....	....	....	....
1988-89	**Los Angeles**	**NHL**	**2**	**0**	**0**	**0**	**2**	....	....	....	....	....
	New Haven	AHL	4	4	6	10	20	....	....	....	....	....
	Boston	**NHL**	**5**	**0**	**2**	**2**	**0**	....	....	....	....	....
	Maine	AHL	61	15	29	44	77	....	....	....	....	....
	NHL Totals		**114**	**11**	**21**	**32**	**90**	**9**	**0**	**1**	**1**	**12**

a ECAC Second All-Star Team (1983)

Rights traded to **Philadelphia** by **Minnesota** with Minnesota's third round choice in 1985 Entry Draft for Paul Holmgren, February 23, 1984. Traded to **Los Angeles** by **Philadelphia** with Philadelphia's fourth-round choice (Sylvain Couturier) in 1986 Entry Draft for Steve Seguin and Los Angeles' second-round choice (Jukka Seppo) in 1986 Entry Draft, October 11, 1985. Traded to **Boston** by **Los Angeles** for the rights to Dave Pasin, November 3, 1988.

GUDEN, DAVE

Left wing. Shoots left. 6'1", 180 lbs. Born, Brighton, MA, April 26, 1968.
(Los Angeles' 4th choice, 86th overall, in 1986 Entry Draft).

			Regular Season					Playoffs				
Season	Club	Lea	GP	G	A	TP	PIM	GP	G	A	TP	PIM
1985-86	Roxbury Latin	HS	15	22	26	48	25	....	....	....	....	....
1986-87	Providence	H.E.	33	4	2	6	22	....	....	....	....	....
1987-88	Providence	H.E.	34	1	5	6	8	....	....	....	....	....
1988-89	Providence	H.E.	31	2	6	8	14	....	....	....	....	....

GUERARD, STEPHANE

Defense. Shoots left. 6'2", 198 lbs. Born, St. Elizabeth, Que., April 12, 1968.
(Quebec's 3rd choice, 41st overall, in 1986 Entry Draft).

			Regular Season					Playoffs				
Season	Club	Lea	GP	G	A	TP	PIM	GP	G	A	TP	PIM
1985-86	Shawinigan	QMJHL	59	4	18	22	167	3	1	1	2	0
1986-87	Shawinigan	QMJHL	31	5	16	21	57	12	2	9	11	36
1987-88	**Quebec**	**NHL**	**30**	**0**	**0**	**0**	**34**	**....**	**....**	**....**	**....**	**....**
1988-89	Halifax	AHL	37	1	9	10	140	4	0	0	0	8
	NHL Totals		**30**	**0**	**0**	**0**	**34**	**....**	**....**	**....**	**....**	**....**

GUERIN, BILL

Right wing. Shoots right. 6'2", 190 lbs. Born, Wilbraham, MA, November 9, 1970.
(New Jersey's 1st choice, 5th overall, in 1989 Entry Draft).

			Regular Season					Playoffs				
Season	Club	Lea	GP	G	A	TP	PIM	GP	G	A	TP	PIM
1985-86	Springfield	USHL	48	26	19	45	71	....	....	....	....	....
1986-87	Springfield	USHL	32	34	20	54	40	....	....	....	....	....
1987-88	Springfield	USHL	38	31	44	75	146	....	....	....	....	....
1988-89	Springfield	USHL	31	32	35	67	90	....	....	....	....	....

GUIDOTTI, VINCE

Left wing. Shoots left. 6', 180 lbs. Born, Sacramento, CA, April 29, 1967.
(St. Louis' 9th choice, 201st overall, in 1985 Entry Draft).

			Regular Season					Playoffs				
Season	Club	Lea	GP	G	A	TP	PIM	GP	G	A	TP	PIM
1985-86	U. of Maine	H.E.	16	0	0	0	8	....	....	....	....	....
1986-87	U. of Maine	H.E.	39	1	3	4	40	....	....	....	....	....
1987-88	U. of Maine	H.E.	44	7	19	26	69	....	....	....	....	....
1988-89	U. of Maine	H.E.	42	7	23	30	76	....	....	....	....	....

GUSAROV, ALEXEI

Defense. Shoots left. 6'2", 170 lbs. Born, Leningrad, Soviet Union, July 8, 1964.
(Quebec's 11th choice, 213th overall, in 1988 Entry Draft).

			Regular Season					Playoffs				
Season	Club	Lea	GP	G	A	TP	PIM	GP	G	A	TP	PIM
1981-82	Leningrad	USSR	20	1	2	3	16	....	....	....	....	....
1982-83	Leningrad	USSR	42	2	1	3	32	....	....	....	....	....
1983-84	Leningrad	USSR	43	2	3	5	32	....	....	....	....	....
1984-85	CSKA	USSR	36	3	2	5	26	....	....	....	....	....
1985-86	CSKA	USSR	40	3	5	8	30	....	....	....	....	....
1986-87	CSKA	USSR	38	4	7	11	24	....	....	....	....	....
1987-88	CSKA	USSR	39	3	2	5	28	....	....	....	....	....
1988-89	CSKA	USSR	42	5	4	9	37	....	....	....	....	....

GUSTAFSSON, BENGT-AKE (GUS tuhf suhn)

Center. Shoots left. 6', 200 lbs. Born, Karlskoga, Sweden, March 23, 1958.
(Washington's 7th choice, 55th over-all, in 1978 Amateur Draft).

			Regular Season					Playoffs				
Season	Club	Lea	GP	G	A	TP	PIM	GP	G	A	TP	PIM
1976-77	Karlskoga	Swe. 2	22	32	18	50	....	....	....	....	....	....
1977-78	Farjestad	Swe.	32	15	10	25	10	....	....	....	....	....
1978-79	Farjestad	Swe.	32	13	12	25	10	3	2	0	2	4
	Edmonton	WHA	....	....	....	....	....	2	1	2	3	0
1979-80	**Washington**	**NHL**	**80**	**22**	**38**	**60**	**17**	**....**	**....**	**....**	**....**	**....**
1980-81	**Washington**	**NHL**	**72**	**21**	**34**	**55**	**26**	**....**	**....**	**....**	**....**	**....**
1981-82	**Washington**	**NHL**	**70**	**26**	**34**	**60**	**40**	**....**	**....**	**....**	**....**	**....**
1982-83	**Washington**	**NHL**	**67**	**22**	**42**	**64**	**16**	**4**	**0**	**1**	**1**	**4**
1983-84	**Washington**	**NHL**	**69**	**32**	**43**	**75**	**16**	**5**	**2**	**3**	**5**	**0**
1984-85	**Washington**	**NHL**	**51**	**14**	**29**	**43**	**8**	**5**	**1**	**3**	**4**	**0**
1985-86	**Washington**	**NHL**	**70**	**23**	**52**	**75**	**26**	**....**	**....**	**....**	**....**	**....**
1986-87	Bofors IK	Swe. 2	28	16	26	42	22	....	....	....	....	....
	Swe. National	....	10	3	8	11	....	....	....	....	....	....
1987-88	**Washington**	**NHL**	**78**	**18**	**36**	**54**	**29**	**14**	**4**	**9**	**13**	**6**
1988-89	**Washington**	**NHL**	**72**	**18**	**51**	**69**	**18**	**4**	**2**	**3**	**5**	**6**
	NHL Totals		**629**	**196**	**359**	**555**	**196**	**32**	**9**	**19**	**28**	**16**

Reclaimed by **Washington** from **Edmonton** prior to Expansion Draft, June 9, 1979.

GUY, KEVAN

Defense. Shoots right. 6'3", 202 lbs. Born, Edmonton, Alta., July 16, 1965.
(Calgary's 5th choice, 71st over-all, in 1983 Entry Draft).

			Regular Season					Playoffs				
Season	Club	Lea	GP	G	A	TP	PIM	GP	G	A	TP	PIM
1982-83	Medicine Hat	WHL	69	7	20	27	89	5	0	3	3	16
1983-84	Medicine Hat	WHL	72	15	42	57	117	14	3	4	7	14
1984-85	Medicine Hat	WHL	31	7	17	24	46	10	1	2	3	2
1985-86	Moncton	AHL	73	4	20	24	56	10	0	2	2	6
1986-87	Moncton	AHL	46	2	10	12	38	....	....	....	....	....
	Calgary	**NHL**	**24**	**0**	**4**	**4**	**19**	**4**	**0**	**1**	**1**	**23**
1987-88	**Calgary**	**NHL**	**11**	**0**	**3**	**3**	**8**	**....**	**....**	**....**	**....**	**....**
	Salt Lake	IHL	61	6	30	36	51	19	1	6	7	26
1988-89	**Vancouver**	**NHL**	**45**	**2**	**2**	**4**	**34**	**1**	**0**	**0**	**0**	**0**
	NHL Totals		**80**	**2**	**9**	**11**	**61**	**5**	**0**	**1**	**1**	**23**

Traded to **Vancouver** by **Calgary** with Brian Bradley and Peter Bakovic for Craig Coxe, March 6, 1988.

HAANPAA, ARI

Right wing. Shoots right. 6'1", 185 lbs. Born, Nokia, Finland, November 28, 1965.
(NY Islanders' 5th choice, 83rd overall, in 1984 Entry Draft).

			Regular Season					Playoffs				
Season	Club	Lea	GP	G	A	TP	PIM	GP	G	A	TP	PIM
1983-84	Ilves	Fin.	27	0	1	1	8	2	0	0	0	2
1984-85	Ilves	Fin.	13	5	0	5	2	9	3	1	4	0
1985-86	Springfield	AHL	20	3	1	4	13	....	....	....	....	....
	NY Islanders	**NHL**	**18**	**0**	**7**	**7**	**20**	**....**	**....**	**....**	**....**	**....**
1986-87	**NY Islanders**	**NHL**	**41**	**6**	**4**	**10**	**17**	**6**	**0**	**0**	**0**	**10**
1987-88	**NY Islanders**	**NHL**	**1**	**0**	**0**	**0**	**0**	**....**	**....**	**....**	**....**	**....**
	Springfield	AHL	61	14	19	33	34	....	....	....	....	....
1988-89	Lukko	Fin.	42	28	19	47	36	....	....	....	....	....
	NHL Totals		**60**	**6**	**11**	**17**	**37**	**6**	**0**	**0**	**0**	**10**

HAAPAKOSKI, MIKKO

Defense. Shoots right. 5'10", 180 lbs. Born, Oulu, Finland, January 19, 1967.
(Detroit's 10th choice, 179th overall, in 1987 Entry Draft).

			Regular Season					Playoffs				
Season	Club	Lea	GP	G	A	TP	PIM	GP	G	A	TP	PIM
1985-86	Karpat	Fin.	17	0	4	4	0	5	1	0	1	6
1986-87	Karpat	Fin.	41	13	15	28	18	9	1	1	2	4
1987-88	Karpat	Fin.	43	7	7	14	40	....	....	....	....	....
1988-89	Karpat	Fin.	40	7	18	25	20	5	1	1	2	2

HAAS, DAVID

Left wing. Shoots left. 6'1", 197 lbs. Born, Toronto, Ont., June 23, 1968.
(Edmonton's 5th choice, 105th overall, in 1986 Entry Draft).

			Regular Season					Playoffs				
Season	Club	Lea	GP	G	A	TP	PIM	GP	G	A	TP	PIM
1985-86	London	OHL	62	4	13	17	91	5	0	1	1	0
1986-87	London	OHL	5	1	0	1	5	....	....	....	....	....
	Kitchener	OHL	4	0	1	1	4	....	....	....	....	....
	Belleville	OHL	55	10	13	23	86	6	3	0	3	13
1987-88a	Windsor	OHL	63	60	47	107	246	11	9	11	20	50
1988-89	Cape Breton	AHL	61	9	9	18	325	....	....	....	....	....

a OHL Second All-Star Team (1988)

HABSCHEID, MARC JOSEPH (HAB-shide)

Center. Shoots right. 6', 185 lbs. Born, Swift Current, Sask., March 1, 1963.
(Edmonton's 6th choice, 113th over-all, in 1981 Entry Draft).

			Regular Season					Playoffs				
Season	Club	Lea	GP	G	A	TP	PIM	GP	G	A	TP	PIM
1980-81	Saskatoon	WHL	72	34	63	97	50	....	....	....	....	....
1981-82	**Edmonton**	**NHL**	**7**	**1**	**3**	**4**	**2**	**....**	**....**	**....**	**....**	**....**
a	Saskatoon	WHL	55	64	87	151	74	5	3	4	7	4
	Wichita	CHL	....	....	....	....	....	3	0	0	0	0
1982-83	Kamloops	WHL	6	7	16	23	8	....	....	....	....	....
	Edmonton	**NHL**	**32**	**3**	**10**	**13**	**14**	**....**	**....**	**....**	**....**	**....**
1983-84	**Edmonton**	**NHL**	**9**	**1**	**0**	**1**	**6**	**....**	**....**	**....**	**....**	**....**
	Moncton	AHL	71	19	37	56	32	....	....	....	....	....
1984-85	**Edmonton**	**NHL**	**26**	**5**	**3**	**8**	**4**	**....**	**....**	**....**	**....**	**....**
	Nova Scotia	AHL	48	29	29	58	65	6	4	3	7	9
1985-86	**Minnesota**	**NHL**	**6**	**2**	**3**	**5**	**0**	**2**	**0**	**0**	**0**	**0**
	Springfield	AHL	41	18	32	50	21	....	....	....	....	....
1986-87	**Minnesota**	**NHL**	**15**	**2**	**0**	**2**	**2**	**....**	**....**	**....**	**....**	**....**
	Cdn. Olympic	....	51	29	32	61	70	....	....	....	....	....
1987-88	**Minnesota**	**NHL**	**16**	**4**	**11**	**15**	**6**	**....**	**....**	**....**	**....**	**....**
	Cdn. National	....	61	19	34	53	42	....	....	....	....	....
	Cdn. Olympic	....	8	5	3	8	6	....	....	....	....	....
1988-89	**Minnesota**	**NHL**	**76**	**23**	**31**	**54**	**40**	**5**	**1**	**3**	**4**	**13**
	NHL Totals		**187**	**41**	**61**	**102**	**74**	**7**	**1**	**3**	**4**	**13**

a WHL Second All-Star Team (1982)

Traded to **Minnesota** by **Edmonton** with Don Barber and Emanuel Viveiros for Gord Sherven and Don Biggs, December 20, 1985. Signed as a free agent by **Detroit**, June 9, 1989.

HAJDU, RICHARD (HI-doo)

Left wing. Shoots left. 6', 185 lbs. Born, Victoria, B.C., May 10, 1965.
(Buffalo's 5th choice, 34th over-all, in 1983 Entry Draft).

			Regular Season					Playoffs				
Season	Club	Lea	GP	G	A	TP	PIM	GP	G	A	TP	PIM
1981-82	Kamloops	WHL	64	19	21	40	50	4	0	0	0	0
1982-83	Kamloops	WHL	70	22	36	58	101	5	0	0	0	4
1983-84	Victoria	WHL	42	17	10	27	106	....	....	....	....	....
1984-85	Victoria	WHL	24	12	16	28	33	....	....	....	....	....
	Rochester	AHL	2	0	2	2	0	....	....	....	....	....
1985-86	**Buffalo**	**NHL**	**3**	**0**	**0**	**0**	**4**	**....**	**....**	**....**	**....**	**....**
	Rochester	AHL	54	10	27	37	95	....	....	....	....	....
1986-87	**Buffalo**	**NHL**	**2**	**0**	**0**	**0**	**0**	**....**	**....**	**....**	**....**	**....**
	Rochester	AHL	58	7	15	22	90	11	1	1	2	9
1987-88	Rochester	AHL	37	7	11	18	24	1	0	0	0	0
	Flint	IHL	17	4	6	10	30	....	....	....	....	....
1988-89	Cdn. National	....	50	14	11	25	22	....	....	....	....	....
	NHL Totals		**5**	**0**	**0**	**0**	**4**	**....**	**....**	**....**	**....**	**....**

HALKIDIS, BOB (hal KEE dihs)

Defense. Shoots left. 5'11", 200 lbs. Born, Toronto, Ont., March 5, 1966.
(Buffalo's 4th choice, 81st over-all, in 1984 Entry Draft).

			Regular Season					Playoffs				
Season	Club	Lea	GP	G	A	TP	PIM	GP	G	A	TP	PIM
1983-84	London	OHL	51	9	22	31	123	8	0	2	2	27
1984-85	**Buffalo**	**NHL**	**....**	**....**	**....**	**....**	**....**	**4**	**0**	**0**	**0**	**19**
ab	London	OHL	62	14	50	64	154	8	3	6	9	22
1985-86	**Buffalo**	**NHL**	**37**	**1**	**9**	**10**	**115**	**....**	**....**	**....**	**....**	**....**
1986-87	**Buffalo**	**NHL**	**6**	**1**	**1**	**2**	**19**	**....**	**....**	**....**	**....**	**....**
	Rochester	AHL	59	1	8	9	144	8	0	0	0	43
1987-88	**Buffalo**	**NHL**	**30**	**0**	**3**	**3**	**115**	**4**	**0**	**0**	**0**	**22**
	Rochester	AHL	15	2	5	7	50	....	....	....	....	....
1988-89	**Buffalo**	**NHL**	**16**	**0**	**1**	**1**	**66**	**....**	**....**	**....**	**....**	**....**
	Rochester	AHL	16	0	6	6	64	....	....	....	....	....
	NHL Totals		**89**	**2**	**14**	**16**	**315**	**8**	**0**	**0**	**0**	**41**

a Named Outstanding Defenseman in OHL (1985)
b OHL First All-Star Team (1985)

HALL, DEAN

Center. Shoots left. 6'1", 175 lbs. Born, Winnipeg, Man., January 14, 1968.
(Boston's 4th choice, 76th overall, in 1986 Entry Draft).

			Regular Season					Playoffs				
Season	Club	Lea	GP	G	A	TP	PIM	GP	G	A	TP	PIM
1986-87	N. Michigan	WCHA	20	4	5	9	16	....	....	....	....	....
1987-88	N. Michigan	WCHA	31	5	6	11	22	....	....	....	....	....
1988-89	N. Michigan	WCHA	2	0	0	0	0	....	....	....	....	....

HALL, TAYLOR

Left wing. Shoots left. 5'11", 180 lbs. Born, Regina, Sask., February 20, 1964.
(Vancouver's 4th choice, 116th over-all, in 1982 Entry Draft).

			Regular Season					Playoffs				
Season	Club	Lea	GP	G	A	TP	PIM	GP	G	A	TP	PIM
1981-82	Regina	WHL	48	14	15	29	43	11	2	3	5	14
1982-83	Regina	WHL	72	37	57	94	78	5	0	3	3	12
1983-84	**Vancouver**	**NHL**	**4**	**1**	**0**	**1**	**0**	....	....	....	....	....
a	Regina	WHL	69	63	79	142	42	23	*21	20	41	26
1984-85	**Vancouver**	**NHL**	**7**	**1**	**4**	**5**	**19**	....	....	....	....	....
1985-86	**Vancouver**	**NHL**	**19**	**5**	**5**	**10**	**6**	....	....	....	....	....
	Fredericton	AHL	45	21	14	35	28	1	0	0	0	0
1986-87	**Vancouver**	**NHL**	**4**	**0**	**0**	**0**	**0**	....	....	....	....	....
	Fredericton	AHL	36	21	20	41	23	....	....	....	....	....
1987-88	**Boston**	**NHL**	**7**	**0**	**0**	**0**	**4**	....	....	....	....	....
	Maine	AHL	71	33	41	74	58	10	1	4	5	21
1988-89	Maine	AHL	8	0	1	1	7	....	....	....	....	....
	Newmarket	AHL	9	5	5	10	14	....	....	....	....	....
	NHL Totals		**41**	**7**	**9**	**16**	**29**	....	....	....	....	....

a WHL First All-Star Team, East Division (1984)

HALLER, KEVIN

Defense. Shoots left. 6'2", 180 lbs. Born, Trochu, Alta., December 5, 1970.
(Buffalo's 1st choice, 14th overall, in 1989 Entry Draft).

			Regular Season					Playoffs				
Season	Club	Lea	GP	G	A	TP	PIM	GP	G	A	TP	PIM
1986-87	Three Hills	Midget	12	10	11	21	8	....	....	....	....	....
1987-88	Olds	AJHL	51	13	31	44	58	....	....	....	....	....
1988-89	Regina	WHL	72	10	31	41	99	....	....	....	....	....

HALWARD, DOUGLAS ROBERT (DOUG) (HALL-ward)

Defense. Shoots left. 6'1", 200 lbs. Born, Toronto, Ont., November 1, 1955.
(Boston's 1st choice, 14th over-all, in 1975 Amateur Draft).

			Regular Season					Playoffs				
Season	Club	Lea	GP	G	A	TP	PIM	GP	G	A	TP	PIM
1973-74	Peterborough	OHA	69	1	15	16	103	....	....	....	....	....
1974-75a	Peterborough	OHA	68	11	52	63	97	3	1	2	3	5
1975-76	**Boston**	**NHL**	**22**	**1**	**5**	**6**	**6**	**1**	**0**	**0**	**0**	**0**
	Rochester	AHL	54	6	11	17	51	4	1	0	1	4
1976-77	Rochester	AHL	54	4	28	32	26	....	....	....	....	....
	Boston	**NHL**	**18**	**2**	**2**	**4**	**6**	**6**	**0**	**0**	**0**	**4**
1977-78	**Boston**	**NHL**	**25**	**0**	**2**	**2**	**2**	....	....	....	....	....
	Rochester	AHL	42	8	14	22	17	6	0	3	3	2
1978-79	Springfield	AHL	14	5	1	6	10	....	....	....	....	....
	Los Angeles	**NHL**	**27**	**1**	**5**	**6**	**13**	**1**	**0**	**0**	**0**	**12**
1979-80	**Los Angeles**	**NHL**	**63**	**11**	**45**	**56**	**52**	**1**	**0**	**0**	**0**	**2**
1980-81	**Los Angeles**	**NHL**	**51**	**4**	**15**	**19**	**96**	....	....	....	....	....
	Vancouver	**NHL**	**7**	**0**	**1**	**1**	**4**	**2**	**0**	**1**	**1**	**6**
1981-82	Dallas	CHL	22	8	18	26	49	....	....	....	....	....
	Vancouver	**NHL**	**37**	**4**	**13**	**17**	**40**	**15**	**2**	**4**	**6**	**44**
1982-83	**Vancouver**	**NHL**	**75**	**19**	**33**	**52**	**83**	**4**	**1**	**0**	**1**	**21**
1983-84	**Vancouver**	**NHL**	**54**	**7**	**16**	**23**	**35**	**4**	**3**	**1**	**4**	**2**
1984-85	**Vancouver**	**NHL**	**71**	**7**	**27**	**34**	**82**	....	....	....	....	....
1985-86	**Vancouver**	**NHL**	**70**	**8**	**25**	**33**	**111**	**3**	**0**	**0**	**0**	**4**
1986-87	**Vancouver**	**NHL**	**10**	**0**	**3**	**3**	**34**	....	....	....	....	....
	Detroit	**NHL**	**11**	**0**	**3**	**3**	**19**	....	....	....	....	....
1987-88	**Detroit**	**NHL**	**70**	**5**	**21**	**26**	**130**	**8**	**1**	**4**	**5**	**18**
1988-89	**Detroit**	**NHL**	**18**	**0**	**1**	**1**	**36**	....	....	....	....	....
	Adirondack	AHL	4	1	0	1	0	....	....	....	....	....
	Edmonton	**NHL**	**24**	**0**	**7**	**7**	**25**	**2**	**0**	**0**	**0**	**0**
	NHL Totals		**653**	**69**	**224**	**293**	**774**	**47**	**7**	**10**	**17**	**113**

a OHA Third All-Star Team (1975)

Traded to **Los Angeles** by **Boston** for future considerations, September 18, 1978. Claimed by **Los Angeles** as fill in Expansion Draft, June 13, 1979. Traded to **Vancouver** by **Los Angeles** for Vancouver's fifth-round choice (Ulf Isaksson) in 1982 Entry Draft, March 8, 1981. Traded to **Detroit** by **Vancouver** for Detroit's sixth-round choice in 1988 Entry Draft, November 21, 1986. Traded to **Edmonton** by **Detroit** for Edmonton's twelfth-round choice (Jason Glickman) in 1989 Entry Draft, January 23, 1989.

HAMALAINEN, ERIK

Defense. Shoots left. 6'1", 190 lbs. Born, Rauma, Finland, April 20, 1965.
(Detroit's 10th choice, 197th overall, in 1985 Entry Draft).

			Regular Season					Playoffs				
Season	Club	Lea	GP	G	A	TP	PIM	GP	G	A	TP	PIM
1982-83	Lukko	Fin.	35	2	1	3	48	....	....	....	....	....
1983-84	Lukko	Fin. 2	36	8	2	10	16	5	1	3	4	10
1984-85	Lukko	Fin.	36	4	3	7	25	....	....	....	....	....
1985-86	Lukko	Fin.	31	13	6	19	32	....	....	....	....	....
1986-87	Lukko	Fin.	44	8	8	16	49	....	....	....	....	....
1987-88	Lukko	Fin.	44	8	4	12	52	8	0	3	3	2
1988-89	Kalpa	Fin.	43	7	4	11	14	2	0	0	0	2

HAMEL, GILLES (ah MEL, zhill)

Left wing. Shoots left. 6', 185 lbs. Born, Asbestos, Que., March 18, 1960.
(Buffalo's 5th choice, 74th over-all, in 1979 Entry Draft).

			Regular Season					Playoffs				
Season	Club	Lea	GP	G	A	TP	PIM	GP	G	A	TP	PIM
1978-79	Laval	QJHL	72	56	55	111	130	....	....	....	....	....
1979-80	Trois Rivieres	QJHL	12	13	8	21	8	....	....	....	....	....
	Chicoutimi	QJHL	57	73	62	135	87	12	10	6	16	20
	Rochester	AHL	....	....	....	....	....	1	0	0	0	0
1980-81	Rochester	AHL	14	8	7	15	7	....	....	....	....	....
	Buffalo	**NHL**	**51**	**10**	**9**	**19**	**53**	**5**	**0**	**1**	**1**	**4**
1981-82	**Buffalo**	**NHL**	**16**	**2**	**7**	**9**	**2**	....	....	....	....	....
	Rochester	AHL	57	31	44	75	55	....	....	....	....	....
1982-83	**Buffalo**	**NHL**	**66**	**22**	**20**	**42**	**26**	**9**	**2**	**2**	**4**	**2**
1983-84	**Buffalo**	**NHL**	**75**	**21**	**23**	**44**	**37**	**3**	**0**	**2**	**2**	**2**
1984-85	**Buffalo**	**NHL**	**80**	**18**	**30**	**48**	**36**	**1**	**0**	**0**	**0**	**0**
1985-86	**Buffalo**	**NHL**	**77**	**19**	**25**	**44**	**61**	....	....	....	....	....
1986-87	**Winnipeg**	**NHL**	**79**	**27**	**21**	**48**	**24**	**8**	**2**	**0**	**2**	**2**
1987-88	**Winnipeg**	**NHL**	**63**	**8**	**11**	**19**	**35**	**1**	**0**	**0**	**0**	**0**
1988-89	**Winnipeg**	**NHL**	**1**	**0**	**0**	**0**	**0**	....	....	....	....	....
	Moncton	AHL	14	7	5	12	10	....	....	....	....	....
	Los Angeles	**NHL**	**11**	**0**	**1**	**1**	**2**	....	....	....	....	....
	New Haven	AHL	34	9	9	18	12	1	0	0	0	0
	NHL Totals		**519**	**127**	**147**	**274**	**276**	**27**	**4**	**5**	**9**	**10**

Traded to **Winnipeg** by **Buffalo** for Scott Arniel, June 21, 1986. Traded to **Los Angeles** by **Winnipeg** for Paul Fenton, November 25, 1988.

HAMILTON, BRAD

Defense. Shoots left. 6', 175 lbs. Born, Calgary, Alta., March 30, 1967.
(Chicago's 10th choice, 200th overall, in 1985 Entry Draft).

			Regular Season					Playoffs				
Season	Club	Lea	GP	G	A	TP	PIM	GP	G	A	TP	PIM
1984-85	Aurora	OPJHL	43	9	29	38	149	....	....	....	....	....
1985-86	Michigan State	CCHA	43	3	10	13	52	....	....	....	....	....
1986-87	Michigan State	CCHA	45	3	29	32	54	....	....	....	....	....
1987-88	Michigan State	CCHA	40	7	22	29	56	....	....	....	....	....
1988-89	Michigan State	CCHA	47	9	20	29	86	....	....	....	....	....

HAMMOND, KEN

Defense. Shoots left. 6'1", 190 lbs. Born, Port Credit, Ont., August 22, 1963.
(Los Angeles' 8th choice, 152nd over-all, in 1983 Entry Draft).

			Regular Season					Playoffs				
Season	Club	Lea	GP	G	A	TP	PIM	GP	G	A	TP	PIM
1982-83	RPI	ECAC	28	17	26	43	8	....	....	....	....	....
1983-84	RPI	ECAC	34	5	11	16	72	....	....	....	....	....
1984-85	**Los Angeles**	**NHL**	**3**	**1**	**0**	**1**	**0**	**3**	**0**	**0**	**0**	**4**
ab	RPI	ECAC	38	11	28	39	90	....	....	....	....	....
1985-86	**Los Angeles**	**NHL**	**3**	**0**	**1**	**1**	**2**	....	....	....	....	....
	New Haven	AHL	67	4	12	16	96	4	0	0	0	7
1986-87	**Los Angeles**	**NHL**	**10**	**0**	**2**	**2**	**11**	....	....	....	....	....
	New Haven	AHL	66	1	15	16	76	6	0	1	1	21
1987-88	**Los Angeles**	**NHL**	**46**	**7**	**9**	**16**	**69**	**2**	**0**	**0**	**0**	**4**
	New Haven	AHL	26	3	8	11	27	....	....	....	....	....
1988-89	**Edmonton**	**NHL**	**5**	**0**	**1**	**1**	**8**	....	....	....	....	....
	NY Rangers	**NHL**	**3**	**0**	**0**	**0**	**0**	....	....	....	....	....
	Denver	IHL	38	5	18	23	24	....	....	....	....	....
	Toronto	**NHL**	**14**	**0**	**2**	**2**	**12**	....	....	....	....	....
	NHL Totals		**84**	**8**	**15**	**23**	**102**	**5**	**0**	**0**	**0**	**8**

a ECAC First All-Star Team (1985)
b Named to NCAA All-American Team (1985)

Claimed by **Edmonton** in NHL Waiver Draft, October 3, 1988. Claimed by **NY Rangers** on waivers from **Edmonton**, November 1, 1988. Traded to **Toronto** by **NY Rangers** for Chris McRae, February 21, 1989.

HANDY, RONALD (RON)

Left wing. Shoots left. 5'11", 175 lbs. Born, Toronto, Ont., January 15, 1963.
(NY Islanders' 3rd choice, 57th over-all, in 1981 Entry Draft).

			Regular Season					Playoffs				
Season	Club	Lea	GP	G	A	TP	PIM	GP	G	A	TP	PIM
1980-81	S. S. Marie	OHA	66	43	43	86	45	18	3	5	8	25
1981-82	S. S. Marie	OHL	20	15	10	25	20	....	....	....	....	....
	Kingston	OHL	44	35	38	73	23	4	1	1	2	16
1982-83	Kingston	OHL	67	52	96	148	64	....	....	....	....	....
	Indianapolis	CHL	9	2	7	9	0	10	3	8	11	18
1983-84a	Indianapolis	CHL	66	29	46	75	40	10	2	5	7	0
1984-85	**NY Islanders**	**NHL**	**10**	**0**	**2**	**2**	**0**	....	....	....	....	....
	Springfield	AHL	69	29	35	64	38	3	2	2	4	0
1985-86	Springfield	AHL	79	31	30	61	66	....	....	....	....	....
1986-87	Indianapolis	IHL	82	55	80	135	57	6	4	3	7	2
1987-88	**St. Louis**	**NHL**	**4**	**0**	**1**	**1**	**0**	....	....	....	....	....
b	Peoria	IHL	78	53	63	116	61	7	2	3	5	4
1988-89	Peoria	IHL	81	43	57	100	24	....	....	....	....	....
	NHL Totals		**14**	**0**	**3**	**3**	**0**	....	....	....	....	....

a CHL Second All-Star Team (1984)
b IHL Second All-Star Team (1988)

HANKINSON, BEN

Center. Shoots right. 6'2", 180 lbs. Born, Edina, MN, January 5, 1969.
(New Jersey's 5th choice, 107th overall, in 1987 Entry Draft).

			Regular Season					Playoffs				
Season	Club	Lea	GP	G	A	TP	PIM	GP	G	A	TP	PIM
1986-87	Edina	HS	46	14	20	34	....	....	....	....	....	....
1987-88	U. Minnesota	WCHA	24	4	7	11	36	....	....	....	....	....
1988-89	U. Minnesota	WCHA	43	7	11	18	115	....	....	....	....	....

HANLEY, TIMOTHY

Right wing. Shoots right. 6', 200 lbs. Born, Greenfield, MN, October 10, 1964.
(Los Angeles' 7th choice, 129th overall, in 1984 Entry Draft).

			Regular Season					Playoffs				
Season	Club	Lea	GP	G	A	TP	PIM	GP	G	A	TP	PIM
1984-85	N. Hampshire	H.E.	42	22	18	40	21	....	....	....	....	....
1985-86	N. Hampshire	H.E.	29	9	13	22	22	....	....	....	....	....
1986-87	N. Hampshire	H.E.	37	11	23	34	34	....	....	....	....	....
1987-88	N. Hampshire	H.E.	30	13	17	30	38	....	....	....	....	....
1988-89	Maine	AHL	4	0	0	0	0	....	....	....	....	....
	Springfield	AHL	33	13	15	28	10	....	....	....	....	....
	New Haven	AHL	1	0	0	0	5	....	....	....	....	....

HANNAN, DAVID (DAVE)

Center. Shoots left. 5'10", 185 lbs. Born, Sudbury, Ont., November 26, 1961.
(Pittsburgh's 9th choice, 196th over-all, in 1981 Entry Draft).

			Regular Season					Playoffs				
Season	Club	Lea	GP	G	A	TP	PIM	GP	G	A	TP	PIM
1979-80	Brantford	OHA	53	16	20	36	57	....	....	....	....	....
1980-81	Brantford	OHA	56	46	35	81	155	6	2	4	6	20
1981-82	**Pittsburgh**	**NHL**	**1**	**0**	**0**	**0**	**0**	....	....	....	....	....
	Erie	AHL	76	33	37	70	129	....	....	....	....	....
1982-83	**Pittsburgh**	**NHL**	**74**	**11**	**22**	**33**	**127**	....	....	....	....	....
	Baltimore	AHL	5	2	2	4	13	....	....	....	....	....
1983-84	**Pittsburgh**	**NHL**	**24**	**2**	**3**	**5**	**33**	....	....	....	....	....
	Baltimore	AHL	47	18	24	42	98	10	2	6	8	27
1984-85	**Pittsburgh**	**NHL**	**30**	**6**	**7**	**13**	**43**	....	....	....	....	....
	Baltimore	AHL	49	20	25	45	91	....	....	....	....	....
1985-86	**Pittsburgh**	**NHL**	**75**	**17**	**18**	**35**	**91**	....	....	....	....	....
1986-87	**Pittsburgh**	**NHL**	**58**	**10**	**15**	**25**	**56**	....	....	....	....	....
1987-88	**Pittsburgh**	**NHL**	**21**	**4**	**3**	**7**	**23**	....	....	....	....	....
	Edmonton	**NHL**	**51**	**9**	**11**	**20**	**43**	**12**	**1**	**1**	**2**	**8**
1988-89	**Pittsburgh**	**NHL**	**72**	**10**	**20**	**30**	**157**	**8**	**0**	**1**	**1**	**4**
	Indianapolis	IHL	3	0	1	1	9	....	....	....	....	....
	NHL Totals		**406**	**69**	**99**	**168**	**573**	**20**	**1**	**2**	**3**	**12**

Traded to **Edmonton** by **Pittsburgh** with Craig Simpson, Moe Mantha and Chris Joseph for Paul Coffey, Dave Hunter and Wayne Van Dorp, November 24, 1987. Claimed by **Pittsburgh** in NHL Waiver Draft, October 3, 1988.

HANUS, TIM

Left wing. Shoots left. 6'1", 185 lbs. Born, Minneapolis, MN, May 12, 1969.
(Quebec's 7th choice, 135th overall, in 1987 Entry Draft).

			Regular Season					Playoffs				
Season	Club	Lea	GP	G	A	TP	PIM	GP	G	A	TP	PIM
1986-87	Minnetonka	HS	20	21	19	40	0	....	....	....	....	....
1987-88	Minnetonka	HS	25	22	29	51	36	....	....	....	....	....
1988-89	St. Cloud	NCAA	33	13	22	35	31	....	....	....	....	....

HARDING, JEFF

Right wing. Shoots right. 6'4", 220 lbs. Born, Toronto, Ont., April 6, 1969.
(Philadelphia's 2nd choice, 30th overall, in 1987 Entry Draft).

			Regular Season					Playoffs				
Season	Club	Lea	GP	G	A	TP	PIM	GP	G	A	TP	PIM
1986-87	St. Michael's	Jr. B	22	22	8	30	97	....	....	....	....	....
1987-88	Michigan State	CCHA	43	17	10	27	129	....	....	....	....	....
1988-89	**Philadelphia**	**NHL**	**6**	**0**	**0**	**0**	**29**	....	....	....	....	....
	Hershey	AHL	34	13	5	18	64	8	1	1	2	33
	NHL Totals		**6**	**0**	**0**	**0**	**29**	....	....	....	....	....

HARDY, MARK LEA

Defense. Shoots left. 5'11", 195 lbs. Born, Semaden, Switzerland, February 1, 1959.
(Los Angeles' 3rd choice, 30th over-all, in 1979 Entry Draft).

			Regular Season					Playoffs				
Season	Club	Lea	GP	G	A	TP	PIM	GP	G	A	TP	PIM
1977-78	Montreal	QJHL	72	25	57	82	150	13	3	10	13	22
1978-79	Montreal	QJHL	67	18	52	70	117	11	5	8	13	40
1979-80	Binghamton	AHL	56	3	13	16	32	....	....	....	....	....
	Los Angeles	**NHL**	**15**	**0**	**1**	**1**	**10**	**4**	**1**	**1**	**2**	**9**
1980-81	**Los Angeles**	**NHL**	**77**	**5**	**20**	**25**	**77**	**4**	**1**	**2**	**3**	**4**
1981-82	**Los Angeles**	**NHL**	**77**	**6**	**39**	**45**	**130**	**10**	**1**	**2**	**3**	**9**
1982-83	**Los Angeles**	**NHL**	**74**	**5**	**34**	**39**	**101**	....	....	....	....	....
1983-84	**Los Angeles**	**NHL**	**79**	**8**	**41**	**49**	**122**	....	....	....	....	....
1984-85	**Los Angeles**	**NHL**	**78**	**14**	**39**	**53**	**97**	**3**	**0**	**1**	**1**	**2**
1985-86	**Los Angeles**	**NHL**	**55**	**6**	**21**	**27**	**71**	....	....	....	....	....
1986-87	**Los Angeles**	**NHL**	**73**	**3**	**27**	**30**	**120**	**5**	**1**	**2**	**3**	**10**
1987-88	**Los Angeles**	**NHL**	**61**	**6**	**22**	**28**	**99**	....	....	....	....	....
	NY Rangers	**NHL**	**19**	**2**	**2**	**4**	**31**	....	....	....	....	....
1988-89	**Minnesota**	**NHL**	**15**	**2**	**4**	**6**	**26**	....	....	....	....	....
	NY Rangers	**NHL**	**45**	**2**	**12**	**14**	**45**	**4**	**0**	**1**	**1**	**31**
	NHL Totals		**668**	**59**	**262**	**321**	**929**	**30**	**4**	**9**	**13**	**65**

Traded to **NY Rangers** by **Los Angeles** for Ron Duguay, February 23, 1988. Traded to **Minnesota** by **NY Rangers** for future considerations (Louie Debrusk) June 13, 1988. Traded to **NY Rangers** by **Minnesota** for Larry Bernard and NY Rangers fifth-round choice (Rhys Hollyman) in 1989 Entry Draft, December 9, 1988).

HARKINS, TODD

Right wing. Shoots right. 6'3", 210 lbs. Born, Cleveland, OH, October 8, 1968.
(Calgary's 2nd choice, 42nd overall, in 1988 Entry Draft).

			Regular Season					Playoffs				
Season	Club	Lea	GP	G	A	TP	PIM	GP	G	A	TP	PIM
1986-87	Aurora	OPJHL	40	19	29	48	102	....	....	....	....	....
1987-88	Miami-Ohio	CCHA	34	9	7	16	133	....	....	....	....	....
1988-89	Miami-Ohio	CCHA	36	8	7	15	77	....	....	....	....	....

HARLOW, SCOTT

Left wing. Shoots left. 6'1", 185 lbs. Born, East Bridgewater, MA, October 11, 1963.
(Montreal's 6th choice, 61st over-all, in 1982 Entry Draft).

			Regular Season					Playoffs				
Season	Club	Lea	GP	G	A	TP	PIM	GP	G	A	TP	PIM
1981-82	S. Shore Braves	Mass	22	58	57	115	0	....	....	....	....	....
1982-83	Boston College	ECAC	24	6	19	25	19	....	....	....	....	....
1983-84	Boston College	ECAC	39	27	20	47	17	....	....	....	....	....
1984-85a	Boston College	ECAC	44	34	38	72	45	....	....	....	....	....
1985-86bcd	Boston College	H.E.	42	38	41	79	48	....	....	....	....	....
1986-87	Sherbrooke	AHL	66	22	26	48	6	15	5	6	11	6
1987-88	**St. Louis**	**NHL**	**1**	**0**	**1**	**1**	**0**	....	....	....	....	....
	Baltimore	AHL	29	24	27	51	21	....	....	....	....	....
1988-89	Maine	AHL	30	16	17	33	8	....	....	....	....	....
	Peoria	IHL	45	16	26	42	22	....	....	....	....	....
	NHL Totals		**1**	**0**	**1**	**1**	**0**	....	....	....	....	....

a Hockey East Second All-Star Team
b NCAA East First All-American Team (1986)
c Hockey East First All-Star Team (1986)
d Hockey East Player of the Year (1986)

Traded to **St. Louis** by **Montreal** for future considerations, January 21, 1988. Traded to **Boston** by **St. Louis** for Phil DeGaetano, February 3, 1989.

HARPER, WARREN

Right wing. Shoots left. 6', 175 lbs. Born, Prince Albert, Sask., May 10, 1963.
(Buffalo's 12th choice, 206th over-all, in 1981 Entry Draft.)

			Regular Season					Playoffs				
Season	Club	Lea	GP	G	A	TP	PIM	GP	G	A	TP	PIM
1980-81	Prince Albert	SJHL	60	35	35	70	158	....	....	....	....	....
1981-82	Prince Albert	SJHL	39	23	29	52	108	....	....	....	....	....
1982-83	Prince Albert	WHL	41	17	15	32	38	....	....	....	....	....
1983-84	Rochester	AHL	78	25	28	53	56	18	3	3	6	11
1984-85	Rochester	AHL	78	29	34	63	43	5	0	2	2	8
1985-86	Rochester	AHL	80	18	30	48	83	....	....	....	....	....
1986-87	Rochester	AHL	61	13	27	40	50	11	1	4	5	18
1987-88	Adirondack	AHL	80	24	33	57	76	10	2	1	3	13
1988-89	Hershey	AHL	66	20	20	40	72	1	0	0	0	0

HARRIS, TIM

Right wing. Shoots right. 6'2", 185 lbs. Born, Uxbridge, Ont., October 16, 1967.
(Calgary's 4th choice, 70th overall, in 1987 Entry Draft).

			Regular Season					Playoffs				
Season	Club	Lea	GP	G	A	TP	PIM	GP	G	A	TP	PIM
1985-86	Pickering	OPJHL	34	13	25	38	91	....	....	....	....	....
1986-87	Pickering	OPJHL	36	20	36	56	142	....	....	....	....	....
1987-88	Lake Superior	CCHA	43	8	10	18	79	....	....	....	....	....
1988-89	Lake Superior	CCHA	29	1	5	6	78	....	....	....	....	....

HARTJE, TODD

Center. Shoots left. 6'1", 180 lbs. Born, Anoka, MN, February 27, 1968.
(Winnipeg's 7th choice, 142nd overall, in 1987 Entry Draft).

			Regular Season					Playoffs				
Season	Club	Lea	GP	G	A	TP	PIM	GP	G	A	TP	PIM
1986-87	Harvard	ECAC	32	3	9	12	36	....	....	....	....	....
1987-88	Harvard	ECAC	32	5	17	22	40	....	....	....	....	....
1988-89	Harvard	ECAC	33	4	17	21	40	....	....	....	....	....

HARTMAN, MIKE

Right wing. Shoots left. 6', 183 lbs. Born, Detroit, MI, February 7, 1967.
(Buffalo's 8th choice, 131st overall, in 1986 Entry Draft).

			Regular Season					Playoffs				
Season	Club	Lea	GP	G	A	TP	PIM	GP	G	A	TP	PIM
1985-86	North Bay	OHL	57	21	17	38	210	10	2	4	6	34
1986-87	**Buffalo**	**NHL**	**17**	**3**	**3**	**6**	**69**	....	....	....	....	....
	North Bay	OHL	32	15	24	39	144	19	7	8	15	88
1987-88	**Buffalo**	**NHL**	**18**	**3**	**1**	**4**	**90**	**6**	**0**	**0**	**0**	**35**
	Rochester	AHL	57	13	14	27	283	4	1	0	1	22
1988-89	**Buffalo**	**NHL**	**70**	**8**	**9**	**17**	**316**	**5**	**0**	**0**	**0**	**34**
	NHL Totals		**105**	**14**	**13**	**27**	**475**	**11**	**0**	**0**	**0**	**69**

HARTSBURG, CRAIG

Defense. Shoots left. 6'1", 200 lbs. Born, Stratford, Ont., June 29, 1959.
(Minnesota's 1st choice, 6th over-all, in 1979 Entry Draft).

			Regular Season					Playoffs				
Season	Club	Lea	GP	G	A	TP	PIM	GP	G	A	TP	PIM
1976-77a	S. S. Marie	OHA	61	29	64	93	142	9	0	11	11	27
1977-78b	S. S. Marie	OHA	36	15	42	57	101	13	4	8	12	24
1978-79	Birmingham	WHA	77	9	40	49	73	....	....	....	....	....
1979-80	**Minnesota**	**NHL**	**79**	**14**	**30**	**44**	**81**	**15**	**3**	**1**	**4**	**17**
1980-81	**Minnesota**	**NHL**	**74**	**13**	**30**	**43**	**124**	**19**	**3**	**12**	**15**	**16**
1981-82	**Minnesota**	**NHL**	**76**	**17**	**60**	**77**	**117**	**4**	**1**	**2**	**3**	**14**
1982-83	**Minnesota**	**NHL**	**78**	**12**	**50**	**62**	**109**	**9**	**3**	**8**	**11**	**7**
1983-84	**Minnesota**	**NHL**	**26**	**7**	**7**	**14**	**37**	....	....	....	....	....
1984-85	**Minnesota**	**NHL**	**32**	**7**	**11**	**18**	**54**	**9**	**5**	**3**	**8**	**14**
1985-86	**Minnesota**	**NHL**	**75**	**10**	**47**	**57**	**127**	**5**	**0**	**1**	**1**	**2**
1986-87	**Minnesota**	**NHL**	**73**	**11**	**50**	**61**	**93**	....	....	....	....	....
1987-88	**Minnesota**	**NHL**	**27**	**3**	**16**	**19**	**29**	....	....	....	....	....
1988-89	**Minnesota**	**NHL**	**30**	**4**	**14**	**18**	**47**	....	....	....	....	....
	NHL Totals		**570**	**98**	**315**	**413**	**818**	**61**	**15**	**27**	**42**	**70**

a OHA Second All-Star Team (1977)
b OHA Third All-Star Team (1978)

Played in NHL All-Star Game (1980, 1982, 1983)

HATCHER, KEVIN

Defense. Shoots right. 6'4", 220 lbs.   Born, Detroit, MI, September 9, 1966.
(Washington's 1st choice, 17th over-all, in 1984 Entry Draft).

			Regular Season					Playoffs				
Season	Club	Lea	GP	G	A	TP	PIM	GP	G	A	TP	PIM
1982-83	Detroit	Midget	75	30	45	75	120	....	....	....	....	....
1983-84	North Bay	OHL	67	10	39	49	61	4	2	2	4	11
1984-85	Washington	NHL	2	1	0	1	0	1	0	0	0	0
a	North Bay	OHL	58	26	37	63	75	8	3	8	11	9
1985-86	Washington	NHL	79	9	10	19	119	9	1	1	2	19
1986-87	Washington	NHL	78	8	16	24	144	7	1	0	1	20
1987-88	Washington	NHL	71	14	27	41	137	14	5	7	12	55
1988-89	Washington	NHL	62	13	27	40	101	6	1	4	5	20
	NHL Totals		292	45	80	125	501	37	8	12	20	114

a OHL Second All-Star Team (1985)

HAWERCHUK, DALE   (HOW-er-chuk)

Center. Shoots left. 5'11", 185 lbs.   Born, Toronto, Ont., April 4, 1963.
(Winnipeg's 1st choice and 1st over-all in 1981 Entry Draft).

			Regular Season					Playoffs				
Season	Club	Lea	GP	G	A	TP	PIM	GP	G	A	TP	PIM
1979-80	Cornwall	QJHL	72	37	66	103	21	18	20	25	45	0
1980-81abc	Cornwall	QJHL	72	81	102	183	69	19	15	20	35	8
1981-82d	Winnipeg	NHL	80	45	58	103	47	4	1	7	8	5
1982-83	Winnipeg	NHL	79	40	51	91	31	3	1	4	5	8
1983-84	Winnipeg	NHL	80	37	65	102	73	3	1	1	2	0
1984-85e	Winnipeg	NHL	80	53	77	130	74	3	2	1	3	4
1985-86	Winnipeg	NHL	80	46	59	105	44	3	0	3	3	0
1986-87	Winnipeg	NHL	80	47	53	100	52	10	5	8	13	4
1987-88	Winnipeg	NHL	80	44	77	121	59	5	3	4	7	16
1988-89	Winnipeg	NHL	75	41	55	96	28	....	....	....	....	....
	NHL Totals		634	353	495	848	408	31	13	28	41	37

a QMJHL First All-Star Team (1981)
b QMJHL Player of the Year (1981)
c Canadian Major Junior Player of the Year (1981)
d Won Calder Memorial Trophy (1982)
e NHL Second All-Star Team (1985)

Played in NHL All-Star Game (1982, 1985, 1986, 1988)

HAWGOOD, GREG

Defense. Shoots left. 5'8", 175 lbs.   Born, Edmonton, Alta., August 10, 1968.
(Boston's 9th choice, 202nd overall, in 1986 Entry Draft).

			Regular Season					Playoffs				
Season	Club	Lea	GP	G	A	TP	PIM	GP	G	A	TP	PIM
1985-86	Kamloops	WHL	71	34	85	119	86	16	9	22	31	16
1986-87a	Kamloops	WHL	61	30	93	123	139	....	....	....	....	....
1987-88	Boston	NHL	1	0	0	0	0	3	1	0	1	0
a	Kamloops	WHL	63	48	85	133	142	16	10	16	26	33
1988-89	Boston	NHL	56	16	24	40	84	10	0	2	2	2
	Maine	AHL	21	2	9	11	41	....	....	....	....	....
	NHL Totals		57	16	24	40	84	13	1	2	3	2

a WHL West All-Star Team (1987, 1988)

HAWKINS, TODD

Right wing. Shoots right. 6'1", 195 lbs.   Born, Kingston, Ont., August 2, 1966.
(Vancouver's 10th choice, 217th overall, in 1986 Entry Draft).

			Regular Season					Playoffs				
Season	Club	Lea	GP	G	A	TP	PIM	GP	G	A	TP	PIM
1984-85	Belleville	OHL	58	7	16	23	117	12	1	0	1	10
1985-86	Belleville	OHL	60	14	13	27	172	24	9	7	16	60
1986-87	Belleville	OHL	60	47	40	87	187	6	3	5	8	16
1987-88	Flint	IHL	50	13	13	26	337	16	3	5	8	174
	Fredericton	AHL	2	0	4	4	11	....	....	....	....	....
1988-89	Vancouver	NHL	4	0	0	0	9	....	....	....	....	....
	Milwaukee	IHL	63	12	14	26	307	9	1	0	1	33
	NHL Totals		4	0	0	0	9	....	....	....	....	....

HAWLEY, KENT

Center. Shoots left. 6'3", 215 lbs.   Born, Kingston, Ont., February 20, 1968.
(Philadelphia's 3rd choice, 28th overall, in 1986 Entry Draft).

			Regular Season					Playoffs				
Season	Club	Lea	GP	G	A	TP	PIM	GP	G	A	TP	PIM
1985-86	Ottawa	OHL	64	21	30	51	96	....	....	....	....	....
1986-87	Ottawa	OHL	64	29	53	82	86	11	0	5	5	43
1987-88	Ottawa	OHL	55	29	48	77	84	16	7	6	13	20
1988-89	Hershey	AHL	54	9	17	26	47	....	....	....	....	....

HAWORTH, ALAN JOSEPH GORDON   (HAW-worth)

Center. Shoots right. 5'10", 190 lbs.   Born, Drummondville, Que., September 1, 1960.
(Buffalo's 6th choice, 95th over-all, in 1979 Entry Draft).

			Regular Season					Playoffs				
Season	Club	Lea	GP	G	A	TP	PIM	GP	G	A	TP	PIM
1976-77	Chicoutimi	QJHL	68	11	18	29	15	....	....	....	....	....
1977-78	Chicoutimi	QJHL	59	17	33	50	40	....	....	....	....	....
1978-79	Sherbrooke	QJHL	70	50	70	120	63	12	6	10	16	8
1979-80	Sherbrooke	QJHL	45	28	36	64	50	15	11	16	27	4
1980-81	Rochester	AHL	21	14	18	32	19	....	....	....	....	....
	Buffalo	NHL	49	16	20	36	34	7	4	4	8	2
1981-82	Rochester	AHL	14	5	12	17	10	....	....	....	....	....
	Buffalo	NHL	57	21	18	39	30	3	0	1	1	2
1982-83	Washington	NHL	74	23	27	50	34	4	0	0	0	2
1983-84	Washington	NHL	75	24	31	55	52	8	3	2	5	4
1984-85	Washington	NHL	76	23	26	49	48	5	1	0	1	0
1985-86	Washington	NHL	71	34	39	73	72	9	4	6	10	11
1986-87	Washington	NHL	50	25	16	41	43	6	0	3	3	7
1987-88	Quebec	NHL	72	23	34	57	112	....	....	....	....	....
1988-89		Switz.	NOT AVAILABLE									
	NHL Totals		524	189	211	400	425	42	12	16	28	0

Traded to **Washington** by **Buffalo** with Buffalo's third round choice (Milan Novy) in 1982 Entry Draft for Washington's second round choice (Mike Anderson) and fourth round choice (Timo Jutila) in 1982 Entry Draft, June 9, 1982. Traded to **Quebec** by **Washington** with Gaetan Duchesne and Washington's first-round choice (Joe Sakic) in 1987 Entry Draft for Clint Malarchuk and Dale Hunter, June 13, 1987.

HAYES, MATTHEW

Defense. Shoots left. 6'2", 180 lbs.   Born, North Andover, MA, November 7, 1969.
(St. Louis' 7th choice, 135th overall, in 1988 Entry Draft).

			Regular Season					Playoffs				
Season	Club	Lea	GP	G	A	TP	PIM	GP	G	A	TP	PIM
1988-89	U. of Lowell	H.E.	30	0	4	4	30	....	....	....	....	....

HAYWARD, RICK

Defense. Shoots left. 6'., 180 lbs.   Born, Toledo, OH, February 25, 1966.
(Montreal's 9th choice, 162nd overall, in 1986 Entry Draft).

			Regular Season					Playoffs				
Season	Club	Lea	GP	G	A	TP	PIM	GP	G	A	TP	PIM
1985-86	Hull	QMJHL	59	3	40	43	354	15	2	11	13	98
1986-87	Sherbrooke	AHL	46	2	3	5	153	3	0	1	1	15
1987-88	Saginaw	IHL	24	3	4	7	129	....	....	....	....	....
	Salt Lake	IHL	17	1	3	4	124	13	0	1	1	120
1988-89	Salt Lake	IHL	72	4	20	24	313	10	4	3	7	42

Traded to **Calgary** by **Montreal** for Martin Nicoletti, February 20, 1988.

HEADON, PETER

Center. Shoots left. 6'1", 180 lbs.   Born, Marystown, Nfld., January 18, 1967.
(Edmonton's 10th choice, 230th overall, in 1985 Entry Draft).
Last amateur club: Brantford Alexanders

			Regular Season					Playoffs				
Season	Club	Lea	GP	G	A	TP	PIM	GP	G	A	TP	PIM
1985-86	Boston U.	H.E.	2	0	0	0	0	....	....	....	....	....
1987-88	Boston U.	H.E.	22	2	3	5	4	....	....	....	....	....
1988-89	Boston U.	H.E.	13	1	2	3	8	....	....	....	....	....

HEDLUND, TOMMY

Defense. Shoots left. 6', 185 lbs.   Born, Stockholm, Sweden, February 9, 1967.
(NY Islanders' 5th choice, 89th overall, in 1985 Entry Draft).

			Regular Season					Playoffs				
Season	Club	Lea	GP	G	A	TP	PIM	GP	G	A	TP	PIM
1988-89	AIK	Swe.	30	3	4	7	28	....	....	....	....	....

HEED, JONAS

Defense. Shoots left. 6', 175 lbs.   Born, Sodertalje, Sweden, January 3, 1967.
(Chicago's 6th choice, 116th overall, in 1985 Entry Draft).

			Regular Season					Playoffs				
Season	Club	Lea	GP	G	A	TP	PIM	GP	G	A	TP	PIM
1984-85	Sodertalje	Swe.	8	0	0	0	0	....	....	....	....	....
1985-86	Sodertalje	Swe.	17	3	2	5	6	....	....	....	....	....
1986-87	Sodertalje	Swe.	24	0	3	3	12	2	0	0	0	0
1987-88	Sodertalje	Swe.	26	1	4	5	12	....	....	....	....	....
1988-89	Sodertalje	Swe.	38	4	9	13	22	....	....	....	....	....

HEINZE, STEPHEN

Center. Shoots right. 5'11", 180 lbs.   Born, Lawrence, MA, January 30, 1970.
(Boston's 2nd choice, 60th overall, in 1988 Entry Draft).

			Regular Season					Playoffs				
Season	Club	Lea	GP	G	A	TP	PIM	GP	G	A	TP	PIM
1986-87	Lawrence	HS	23	26	24	50		....	....	....	....	....
1987-88	Lawrence	HS	23	30	25	55		....	....	....	....	....
1988-89	Boston College	H.E.	36	26	23	49	26	....	....	....	....	....

HEJNA, TONY

Left wing. Shoots left. 6', 190 lbs.   Born, Buffalo, NY, January 8, 1968.
(St. Louis' 3rd choice, 52nd overall, in 1986 Entry Draft).

			Regular Season					Playoffs				
Season	Club	Lea	GP	G	A	TP	PIM	GP	G	A	TP	PIM
1986-87	RPI	ECAC	31	12	18	30	18	....	....	....	....	....
1987-88	RPI	ECAC	32	17	19	36	48	....	....	....	....	....
1988-89	RPI	ECAC	29	12	9	21	14	....	....	....	....	....

HELBER, MICHAEL

Center. Shoots right. 5'11", 175 lbs.   Born, Ann Arbor, MI, June 23, 1970.
(Winnipeg's 11th choice, 178th overall, in 1988 Entry Draft).

			Regular Season					Playoffs				
Season	Club	Lea	GP	G	A	TP	PIM	GP	G	A	TP	PIM
1987-88	Pioneer	HS	28	65	53	118		....	....	....	....	....
1988-89	U. of Michigan	CCHA	35	8	10	18	15	....	....	....	....	....

HELGESON, JON

Center. Shoots right. 6'4", 210 lbs.   Born, Roseau, MN, August 15, 1968.
(Vancouver's 6th choice, 133rd overall, in 1986 Entry Draft).

			Regular Season					Playoffs				
Season	Club	Lea	GP	G	A	TP	PIM	GP	G	A	TP	PIM
1986-87	Roseau	HS	22	28	12	40	....	....	....	....	....	....
1987-88	U. Wisconsin	WCHA	5	0	2	2	2	....	....	....	....	....
1988-89	U. Wisconsin	WCHA	36	7	1	8	28	....	....	....	....	....

HELMINEN, RAIMO ILMARI

Center. Shoots left. 6', 183 lbs.   Born, Tampere, Finland, March 11, 1964.
(New York Rangers' 2nd choice, 35th over-all, in 1984 Entry Draft).

			Regular Season					Playoffs				
Season	Club	Lea	GP	G	A	TP	PIM	GP	G	A	TP	PIM
1983-84	Ilves	Fin.	37	17	13	30	14	....	....	....	....	....
1984-85	Ilves	Fin.	36	21	36	57	20	....	....	....	....	....
1985-86	NY Rangers	NHL	66	10	30	40	10	2	0	0	0	0
1986-87	NY Rangers	NHL	21	2	4	6	2	....	....	....	....	....
	New Haven	AHL	6	0	2	2	0	....	....	....	....	....
	Minnesota	NHL	6	0	1	1	0	....	....	....	....	....
1987-88	Ilves	Fin.	31	20	23	43	42	....	....	....	....	....
1988-89	NY Islanders	NHL	24	1	11	12	4	....	....	....	....	....
	Springfield	AHL	16	6	11	17	0	....	....	....	....	....
	NHL Totals		117	13	46	59	16	2	0	0	0	0

Traded to **Minnesota** by **NY Rangers** for future considerations, March 10, 1987.

HENRY, DALE

Left wing. Shoots left. 6', 205 lbs. Born, Prince Albert, Sask., September 24, 1964.
(New York Islanders' 10th choice, 163rd over-all, in 1983 Entry Draft).

			Regular Season					Playoffs				
Season	Club	Lea	GP	G	A	TP	PIM	GP	G	A	TP	PIM
1981-82	Saskatoon	WHL	32	5	4	9	50	5	0	0	0	0
1982-83	Saskatoon	WHL	63	21	19	40	213	3	0	0	0	12
1983-84	Saskatoon	WHL	71	41	36	77	162	....	....	....	....	....
1984-85	**NY Islanders**	**NHL**	**16**	**2**	**1**	**3**	**19**	....	....	....	....	....
	Springfield	AHL	67	11	20	31	133	4	0	0	0	13
1985-86	**NY Islanders**	**NHL**	**7**	**1**	**3**	**4**	**15**	....	....	....	....	....
	Springfield	AHL	64	14	26	40	162	....	....	....	....	....
1986-87	**NY Islanders**	**NHL**	**19**	**3**	**3**	**6**	**46**	**8**	**0**	**0**	**0**	**2**
	Springfield	AHL	23	9	14	23	49	....	....	....	....	....
1987-88	**NY Islanders**	**NHL**	**48**	**5**	**15**	**20**	**115**	**6**	**1**	**0**	**1**	**17**
	Springfield	AHL	24	9	12	21	103	....	....	....	....	....
1988-89	**NY Islanders**	**NHL**	**22**	**2**	**2**	**4**	**66**	....	....	....	....	....
	Springfield	AHL	50	13	21	34	83	....	....	....	....	....
	NHL Totals		**112**	**13**	**24**	**37**	**261**	**14**	**1**	**0**	**1**	**19**

HENTGES, MATHEW

Defense. Shoots left. 6'5", 200 lbs. Born, St. Paul, MN, December 19, 1969.
(Chicago's 9th choice, 176th overall, in 1988 Entry Draft).

			Regular Season					Playoffs				
Season	Club	Lea	GP	G	A	TP	PIM	GP	G	A	TP	PIM
1987-88	Edina	HS	27	3	18	21	0	....	....	....	....	....
1988-89	Merrimack	NCAA	33	0	16	16	22	....	....	....	....	....

HEPPLE, ALAN

Defense. Shoots left. 5'9", 200 lbs. Born, Blaydon-on-Tyne, England, August 16, 1963.
(New Jersey's 9th choice, 169th over-all, in 1982 Entry Draft).

			Regular Season					Playoffs				
Season	Club	Lea	GP	G	A	TP	PIM	GP	G	A	TP	PIM
1980-81	Ottawa	OHL	64	3	13	16	110	6	0	1	1	2
1981-82	Ottawa	OHL	66	6	22	28	160	17	2	10	12	84
1982-83	Ottawa	OHL	64	10	26	36	168	9	2	1	3	24
1983-84	**New Jersey**	**NHL**	**1**	**0**	**0**	**0**	**7**	....	....	....	....	....
	Maine	AHL	64	4	23	27	117	....	....	....	....	....
1984-85	**New Jersey**	**NHL**	**1**	**0**	**0**	**0**	**0**	....	....	....	....	....
	Maine	AHL	80	7	17	24	125	11	0	3	3	30
1985-86	**New Jersey**	**NHL**	**1**	**0**	**0**	**0**	**0**	....	....	....	....	....
	Maine	AHL	69	4	21	25	104	5	0	0	0	11
1986-87	Maine	AHL	74	6	19	25	137	....	....	....	....	....
1987-88	Utica	AHL	78	3	16	19	213	....	....	....	....	....
1988-89	Newmarket	AHL	72	5	29	34	122	5	0	1	1	23
	NHL Totals		**3**	**0**	**0**	**0**	**7**	....	....	....	....	....

HERNIMAN, STEVE

Defense. Shoots left. 6'4", 210 lbs. Born, Windsor, Ont., June 9, 1968.
(Vancouver's 5th choice, 112th overall, in 1986 Entry Draft).

			Regular Season					Playoffs				
Season	Club	Lea	GP	G	A	TP	PIM	GP	G	A	TP	PIM
1985-86	Cornwall	OHL	55	3	12	15	128	6	0	0	0	2
1986-87	Cornwall	OHL	64	2	8	10	121	3	0	0	0	0
1987-88	Cornwall	OHL	5	1	0	1	8	....	....	....	....	....
	S.S. Marie	OHL	52	3	14	17	111	6	0	1	1	18
1988-89	Kitchener	OHL	61	3	16	19	112	5	0	0	0	4

HEROM, KEVIN

(harem)

Left wing. Shoots left. 5'11", 195 lbs. Born, Regina, Sask., July 6, 1967.
(NY Islanders' 5th choice, 76th overall, in 1985 Entry Draft).

			Regular Season					Playoffs				
Season	Club	Lea	GP	G	A	TP	PIM	GP	G	A	TP	PIM
1984-85	Moose Jaw	WHL	61	20	18	38	44	....	....	....	....	....
1985-86	Moose Jaw	WHL	66	22	18	40	103	13	3	3	6	19
1986-87	Moose Jaw	WHL	72	34	33	67	111	9	3	2	5	24
1987-88	Springfield	AHL	66	9	8	17	14	....	....	....	....	....
	Peoria	IHL	3	0	0	0	19	....	....	....	....	....
1988-89	Indianapolis	IHL	7	0	0	0	21	....	....	....	....	....

HEROUX, YVES

(ay ROO, EEV)

Right wing. Shoots right. 5'11", 185 lbs. Born, Terrebonne, Que., April 27, 1965.
(Quebec's 1st choice, 32nd over-all, in 1983 Entry Draft).

			Regular Season					Playoffs				
Season	Club	Lea	GP	G	A	TP	PIM	GP	G	A	TP	PIM
1981-82	Laurentides	Midget	48	53	53	106	84	....	....	....	....	....
1982-83	Chicoutimi	QMJHL	70	41	40	81	44	5	0	4	4	8
1983-84	Chicoutimi	QMJHL	56	28	25	53	67	....	....	....	....	....
	Fredericton	AHL	4	0	0	0	0	....	....	....	....	....
1984-85	Chicoutimi	QMJHL	66	42	54	96	123	14	5	8	13	16
1985-86	Fredericton	AHL	31	12	10	22	42	2	0	1	1	7
	Muskegon	IHL	42	14	8	22	41	....	....	....	....	....
1986-87	**Quebec**	**NHL**	**1**	**0**	**0**	**0**	**0**	....	....	....	....	....
	Fredericton	AHL	37	8	6	14	13	....	....	....	....	....
	Muskegon	IHL	25	6	8	14	31	2	0	0	0	0
1987-88	Baltimore	AHL	5	0	2	2	2	....	....	....	....	....
1988-89	Flint	IHL	82	43	42	85	98	....	....	....	....	....
	NHL Totals		**1**	**0**	**0**	**0**	**0**	....	....	....	....	....

HERTER, JASON

Defense. Shoots right. 6'1", 180 lbs. Born, Hafford, Sask., October 2, 1970.
(Vancouver's 1st choice, 8th overall, in 1989 Entry Draft).

			Regular Season					Playoffs				
Season	Club	Lea	GP	G	A	TP	PIM	GP	G	A	TP	PIM
1987-88	Notre Dame	SJHL	54	5	3	8	152	....	....	....	....	....
1988-89	North Dakota	WCHA	41	8	24	32	62	....	....	....	....	....

HERVEY, MATT

Defense. Shoots right. 5'11", 205 lbs. Born, Whittier, CA, May 16, 1966.

			Regular Season					Playoffs				
Season	Club	Lea	GP	G	A	TP	PIM	GP	G	A	TP	PIM
1987-88	Moncton	AHL	69	9	20	29	265	....	....	....	....	....
1988-89	**Winnipeg**	**NHL**	**2**	**0**	**0**	**0**	**4**	....	....	....	....	....
	Moncton	AHL	73	8	28	36	295	10	1	2	3	42
	NHL Totals		**2**	**0**	**0**	**0**	**4**	....	....	....	....	....

Signed as a free agent by **Winnipeg**, September 27, 1988.

HEWARD, JAMIE

Right wing. Shoots right. 6'2", 185 lbs. Born, Regina, Sask., March 30, 1971.
(Pittsburgh's 1st choice, 16th overall, in 1989 Entry Draft).

			Regular Season					Playoffs				
Season	Club	Lea	GP	G	A	TP	PIM	GP	G	A	TP	PIM
1987-88	Regina	WHL	68	10	17	27	17	4	1	1	2	2
1988-89	Regina	WHL	52	31	28	59	29	....	....	....	....	....

HIGGINS, TIM RAY

Right wing. Shoots right. 6'1", 185 lbs. Born, Ottawa, Ont., February 7, 1958.
(Chicago's 1st choice, 10th over-all, in 1978 Amateur Draft).

			Regular Season					Playoffs				
Season	Club	Lea	GP	G	A	TP	PIM	GP	G	A	TP	PIM
1976-77	Ottawa	OHA	66	35	52	87	80	19	10	14	24	39
1977-78	Ottawa	OHA	50	41	60	101	99	16	9	13	22	36
1978-79	New Brunswick	AHL	17	3	5	8	14	....	....	....	....	....
	Chicago	**NHL**	**36**	**7**	**16**	**23**	**30**	**4**	**0**	**0**	**0**	**0**
1979-80	**Chicago**	**NHL**	**74**	**13**	**12**	**25**	**50**	**7**	**0**	**3**	**3**	**10**
1980-81	**Chicago**	**NHL**	**78**	**24**	**35**	**59**	**86**	**3**	**0**	**0**	**0**	**0**
1981-82	**Chicago**	**NHL**	**74**	**20**	**30**	**50**	**85**	**12**	**3**	**1**	**4**	**15**
1982-83	**Chicago**	**NHL**	**64**	**14**	**9**	**23**	**63**	**13**	**1**	**3**	**4**	**10**
1983-84	**Chicago**	**NHL**	**32**	**1**	**4**	**5**	**21**	....	....	....	....	....
	New Jersey	**NHL**	**37**	**18**	**10**	**28**	**27**	....	....	....	....	....
1984-85	**New Jersey**	**NHL**	**71**	**19**	**29**	**48**	**30**	....	....	....	....	....
1985-86	**New Jersey**	**NHL**	**59**	**9**	**17**	**26**	**47**	....	....	....	....	....
1986-87	**Detroit**	**NHL**	**77**	**12**	**14**	**26**	**124**	**12**	**0**	**1**	**1**	**16**
1987-88	**Detroit**	**NHL**	**62**	**12**	**13**	**25**	**94**	**13**	**1**	**0**	**1**	**26**
1988-89	**Detroit**	**NHL**	**42**	**5**	**9**	**14**	**62**	**1**	**0**	**0**	**0**	**0**
	Adirondack	AHL	14	7	4	11	24	....	....	....	....	....
	NHL Totals		**706**	**154**	**198**	**352**	**719**	**65**	**5**	**8**	**13**	**77**

Traded to **New Jersey** by **Chicago** for Jeff Larmer, January 11, 1984. Traded to **Detroit** by **New Jersey** for Claude Loiselle, June 25, 1986.

HILDITCH, TODD

Defense. Shoots right. 6'1", 200 lbs. Born, Vancouver, B.C., March 13, 1968.
(Washington's 9th choice, 144th overall, in 1988 Entry Draft).

			Regular Season					Playoffs				
Season	Club	Lea	GP	G	A	TP	PIM	GP	G	A	TP	PIM
1987-88	Penticton	BCJHL	51	24	42	66	98	....	....	....	....	....
1988-89	RPI	ECAC	29	1	1	2	56	....	....	....	....	....

HILL, ALAN DOUGLAS (AL)

Left wing/Center. Shoots left. 6'1", 175 lbs. Born, Nanaimo, B.C., April 22, 1955.
Last amateur club: Victoria Cougars (WHL).

			Regular Season					Playoffs				
Season	Club	Lea	GP	G	A	TP	PIM	GP	G	A	TP	PIM
1974-75	Victoria	WHL	70	21	36	57	75	12	5	2	7	21
1975-76	Victoria	WHL	68	26	40	66	172	15	5	10	15	94
1976-77	**Philadelphia**	**NHL**	**9**	**2**	**4**	**6**	**27**	....	....	....	....	....
	Springfield	AHL	63	13	28	41	125	....	....	....	....	....
1977-78	**Philadelphia**	**NHL**	**3**	**0**	**0**	**0**	**2**	....	....	....	....	....
	Maine	AHL	80	32	59	91	118	12	2	7	9	49
1978-79	Maine	AHL	35	11	14	25	59	....	....	....	....	....
	Philadelphia	**NHL**	**31**	**5**	**11**	**16**	**28**	**7**	**1**	**0**	**1**	**2**
1979-80	**Philadelphia**	**NHL**	**61**	**16**	**10**	**26**	**53**	**19**	**3**	**5**	**8**	**19**
1980-81	**Philadelphia**	**NHL**	**57**	**10**	**15**	**25**	**45**	**12**	**2**	**4**	**6**	**18**
1981-82	**Philadelphia**	**NHL**	**41**	**6**	**13**	**19**	**58**	**3**	**0**	**0**	**0**	**0**
1982-83	Moncton	AHL	78	22	22	44	78	....	....	....	....	....
1983-84	Maine	AHL	51	7	17	24	51	17	6	12	18	22
1984-85	Hershey	AHL	73	11	30	41	77	....	....	....	....	....
1985-86	Hershey	AHL	80	17	40	57	129	18	2	6	8	52
1986-87	**Philadelphia**	**NHL**	**7**	**0**	**2**	**2**	**4**	**9**	**2**	**1**	**3**	**0**
	Hershey	AHL	76	13	35	48	124	5	0	1	1	2
1987-88	**Philadelphia**	**NHL**	**12**	**1**	**0**	**1**	**10**	**1**	**0**	**1**	**1**	**4**
	Hershey	AHL	57	10	21	31	62	10	1	6	7	12
1988-89	Hershey	AHL	62	13	20	33	63	8	2	0	2	10
	NHL Totals		**221**	**40**	**55**	**95**	**227**	**51**	**8**	**11**	**19**	**43**

Signed as a free agent by **Philadelphia**, October 22, 1976. Signed as free agent by **Edmonton**, November 10, 1982. Signed as a free agent by **Philadelphia**, October 8, 1984.

HILL, SEAN

Defense. Shoots right. 6', 185 lbs. Born, Duluth, MN, February 14, 1970.
(Montreal's 9th choice, 167th overall, in 1988 Entry Draft).

			Regular Season					Playoffs				
Season	Club	Lea	GP	G	A	TP	PIM	GP	G	A	TP	PIM
1987-88	Duluth East	HS	24	10	17	27	....	....	....	....	....	....
1988-89	U. Wisconsin	WCHA	45	2	23	25	69	....	....	....	....	....

HILLIER, RANDY GEORGE — (HILL-yer)

Defense. Shoots right. 6'1", 185 lbs.   Born, Toronto, Ont., March 30, 1960.
(Boston's 4th choice, 102nd over-all, in 1980 Entry Draft).

			Regular Season					Playoffs				
Season	Club	Lea	GP	G	A	TP	PIM	GP	G	A	TP	PIM
1978-79	Sudbury	OHA	61	8	25	33	173	10	2	5	7	21
1979-80	Sudbury	OHA	60	16	49	65	143	9	3	6	9	14
1980-81	Springfield	AHL	64	3	17	20	105	6	0	2	2	36
1981-82	Erie	AHL	35	6	13	19	52	....	....	....	....	....
	Boston	**NHL**	25	0	8	8	29	8	0	1	1	16
1982-83	**Boston**	**NHL**	70	0	10	10	99	3	0	0	0	4
1983-84	**Boston**	**NHL**	69	3	12	15	125	....	....	....	....	....
1984-85	**Pittsburgh**	**NHL**	45	2	19	21	56	....	....	....	....	....
1985-86	**Pittsburgh**	**NHL**	28	0	3	3	53	....	....	....	....	....
	Baltimore	AHL	8	0	5	5	14	....	....	....	....	....
1986-87	**Pittsburgh**	**NHL**	55	4	8	12	97	....	....	....	....	....
1987-88	**Pittsburgh**	**NHL**	55	1	12	13	144	....	....	....	....	....
1988-89	**Pittsburgh**	**NHL**	68	1	23	24	141	9	0	1	1	49
	NHL Totals		415	11	95	106	744	20	0	2	2	69

Traded to **Pittsburgh** by **Boston** for Pittsburgh's fourth round choice in 1985 Entry Draft (later traded to Quebec), October 15, 1984.

HILTNER, MICHAEL

Right wing. Shoots right. 6'1", 190 lbs.   Born, St. Cloud, MN, March 22, 1966.
(Quebec's 1st choice, 11th overall, in 1987 Supplemental Draft).

			Regular Season					Playoffs				
Season	Club	Lea	GP	G	A	TP	PIM	GP	G	A	TP	PIM
1987-88	Alaska-Anch.	NCAA	35	28	21	49	123	....	....	....	....	....
1988-89	Fort Wayne	IHL	2	0	0	0	0	....	....	....	....	....
	Kalamazoo	IHL	52	15	17	32	46	2	1	0	1	0

Signed as a free agent by **Minnesota**, November 11, 1988.

HIRTH, MARK

Center. Shoots left. 6'2", 175 lbs.   Born, Ann Arbor, MI, January 7, 1969.
(Hartford's 8th choice, 179th overall, in 1988 Entry Draft).

			Regular Season					Playoffs				
Season	Club	Lea	GP	G	A	TP	PIM	GP	G	A	TP	PIM
1987-88	Michigan State	CCHA	10	0	2	2	0	....	....	....	....	....
1988-89	Michigan State	CCHA	40	6	1	7	8	....	....	....	....	....

HJALM, MICHAEL

Left wing. Shoots left. 6'1", 185 lbs.   Born, Huddinge, Sweden, March 19, 1964.
(Philadelphia's 4th choice, 77th overall, in 1982 Entry Draft).

			Regular Season					Playoffs				
Season	Club	Lea	GP	G	A	TP	PIM	GP	G	A	TP	PIM
1981-82	MoDo	Swe.	27	3	3	6	2	2	0	1	1	6
1982-83	MoDo	Swe.	36	13	24	37	20	....	....	....	....	....
1983-84	MoDo	Swe.	35	17	26	43	24	....	....	....	....	....
	MoDo	Swe.	2				....	2	0	5	5	4
1984-85	Bjorkloven	Swe.	27	5	8	13	16	3	0	0	0	2
1985-86	Bjorkloven	Swe.	35	14	23	37	28	....	....	....	....	....
1986-87	Bjorkloven	Swe.	34	9	13	22	14	....	....	....	....	....
1987-88	MoDo	Swe.	38	13	19	32	20	....	....	....	....	....
1988-89	MoDo	Swe.	38	10	19	29	20	....	....	....	....	....

HOARD, BRIAN

Defense. Shoots right. 6'4", 195 lbs.   Born, Oshawa, Ont., March 10, 1968.
(Toronto's 12th choice, 237th overall, in 1986 Entry Draft).

			Regular Season					Playoffs				
Season	Club	Lea	GP	G	A	TP	PIM	GP	G	A	TP	PIM
1985-86	Hamilton	OHL	34	2	2	4	69	....	....	....	....	....
1986-87	Hamilton	OHL	1	0	1	1	0	....	....	....	....	....
	Belleville	OHL	9	0	0	0	31	....	....	....	....	....
	S.S. Marie	OHL	44	4	8	12	137	4	0	0	0	2
1987-88	S.S. Marie	OHL	59	1	12	13	187	4	1	0	1	18
1988-89	Newmarket	AHL	54	2	5	7	208	2	0	0	0	12

HOBSON, DOUG

Defense. Shoots left. 6', 186 lbs.   Born, Prince Albert, Sask., April 9, 1968.
(Pittsburgh's 7th choice, 130th overall, in 1986 Entry Draft).

			Regular Season					Playoffs				
Season	Club	Lea	GP	G	A	TP	PIM	GP	G	A	TP	PIM
1985-86	Prince Albert	WHL	66	2	17	19	70	20	1	2	3	31
1986-87	Prince Albert	WHL	69	3	20	23	83	8	2	3	5	12
1987-88	Prince Albert	WHL	69	9	26	35	96	10	1	5	6	17
1988-89	Muskegon	IHL	62	5	17	22	82	1	0	1	1	11

HODGE, KENNETH JR. (KEN)

Center. Shoots left. 6'1", 200 lbs.   Born, Windsor, Ont., April 13, 1966.
(Minnesota's 2nd choice, 46th overall, in 1984 Entry Draft).

			Regular Season					Playoffs				
Season	Club	Lea	GP	G	A	TP	PIM	GP	G	A	TP	PIM
1984-85	Boston College	H.E.	41	20	44	64	28	....	....	....	....	....
1985-86	Boston College	H.E.	21	11	17	28	16	....	....	....	....	....
1986-87	Boston College	H.E.	37	29	33	62	30	....	....	....	....	....
1987-88	Kalamazoo	IHL	70	15	35	50	24	....	....	....	....	....
1988-89	**Minnesota**	**NHL**	5	1	1	2	0	....	....	....	....	....
	Kalamazoo	IHL	72	26	45	71	34	6	1	5	6	16
	NHL Totals		5	1	1	2	0	....	....	....	....	0

HODGSON, DANIEL (DAN)

Center. Shoots right. 5'10", 175 lbs.   Born, Fort Vermillion, Alta., August 29, 1965.
(Toronto's 4th choice, 83rd over-all, in 1983 Entry Draft).

			Regular Season					Playoffs				
Season	Club	Lea	GP	G	A	TP	PIM	GP	G	A	TP	PIM
1982-83a	Prince Albert	WHL	72	56	74	130	66	....	....	....	....	....
1983-84b	Prince Albert	WHL	66	62	*119	181	65	5	5	3	8	7
1984-85cd	Prince Albert	WHL	64	70	112	182	86	13	10	26	36	32
1985-86	**Toronto**	**NHL**	40	13	12	25	12	....	....	....	....	....
	St. Catharines	AHL	22	13	16	29	15	13	3	9	12	14
1986-87	Newmarket	AHL	20	7	12	19	16	....	....	....	....	....
	Vancouver	**NHL**	43	9	13	22	25	....	....	....	....	....
1987-88	**Vancouver**	**NHL**	8	3	7	10	2	....	....	....	....	....
	Fredericton	AHL	13	8	18	26	16	....	....	....	....	....
1988-89	**Vancouver**	**NHL**	23	4	13	17	25	....	....	....	....	....
	Milwaukee	IHL	47	27	55	82	47	11	6	7	13	10
	NHL Totals		114	29	45	74	64	....	....	....	....	....

a WHL Rookie of the Year (1983)
b WHL Second Team All-Star (1984)
c WHL First Team All-Star (1985)
d Named WHL Player of the Year (1985)

Traded to **Vancouver** by **Toronto** with Jim Benning for Rick Lanz, December 2, 1986.

HOFFMAN, MICHAEL (MIKE)

Left wing. Shoots left. 5'11", 190 lbs.   Born, Barrie, Ont., February 26, 1963.
(Hartford's 3rd choice, 67th over-all, in 1981 Entry Draft).

			Regular Season					Playoffs				
Season	Club	Lea	GP	G	A	TP	PIM	GP	G	A	TP	PIM
1980-81	Brantford	OHA	68	15	19	34	71	6	1	0	1	5
1981-82	Brantford	OHL	66	34	47	81	169	11	5	8	13	9
1982-83	**Hartford**	**NHL**	2	0	1	1	0	....	....	....	....	....
	Brantford	OHL	63	26	49	75	128	8	5	4	9	18
	Binghamton	AHL	1	0	0	0	0	3	0	1	1	0
1983-84	Binghamton	AHL	64	11	13	24	92	....	....	....	....	....
1984-85	**Hartford**	**NHL**	1	0	0	0	0	....	....	....	....	....
	Binghamton	AHL	76	19	26	45	95	8	4	1	5	23
1985-86	**Hartford**	**NHL**	6	1	2	3	2	....	....	....	....	....
	Binghamton	AHL	40	14	14	28	79	2	1	0	1	2
1986-87	Binghamton	AHL	74	9	32	41	120	13	2	2	4	23
1987-88	Flint	IHL	64	35	28	63	49	14	3	7	10	36
1988-89	Flint	IHL	76	33	39	72	46	....	....	....	....	....
	NHL Totals		9	1	3	4	2	....	....	....	....	....

HOFFORD, JAMES (JIM)

Defense. Shoots right. 6', 190 lbs.   Born, Sudbury, Ont., October 4, 1964.
(Buffalo's 8th choice, 114th over-all, in 1983 Entry Draft).

			Regular Season					Playoffs				
Season	Club	Lea	GP	G	A	TP	PIM	GP	G	A	TP	PIM
1982-83	Windsor	OHL	63	8	20	28	173	3	0	1	1	15
1983-84	Windsor	OHL	1	0	0	0	2	....	....	....	....	....
1984-85	Rochester	AHL	71	2	13	15	166	5	0	0	0	16
1985-86	**Buffalo**	**NHL**	5	0	0	0	5	....	....	....	....	....
	Rochester	AHL	40	2	7	9	148	....	....	....	....	....
1986-87	**Buffalo**	**NHL**	12	0	0	0	40	....	....	....	....	....
	Rochester	AHL	54	1	8	9	204	13	1	0	1	57
1987-88	Rochester	AHL	69	3	15	18	322	7	0	0	0	28
1988-89	**Los Angeles**	**NHL**	1	0	0	0	2	....	....	....	....	....
	Rochester	AHL	34	1	9	10	139	....	....	....	....	....
	NHL Totals		18	0	0	0	47	....	....	....	....	....

Claimed by **Los Angeles** in NHL Waiver Draft, October 3, 1988.

HOGUE, BENOIT — (HOAG)

Center. Shoots left. 5'10", 177 lbs.   Born, Repentigny, Que., October 28, 1966.
(Buffalo's 2nd choice, 35th over-all, in 1985 Entry Draft).

			Regular Season					Playoffs				
Season	Club	Lea	GP	G	A	TP	PIM	GP	G	A	TP	PIM
1983-84	St. Jean	QMJHL	59	14	11	25	42	....	....	....	....	....
1984-85	St. Jean	QMJHL	63	46	44	90	92	....	....	....	....	....
1985-86	St. Jean	QMJHL	65	54	54	108	115	9	6	4	10	26
1986-87	Rochester	AHL	52	14	20	34	52	12	5	4	9	8
1987-88	**Buffalo**	**NHL**	3	1	1	2	0	....	....	....	....	....
	Rochester	AHL	62	24	31	55	141	7	6	1	7	46
1988-89	**Buffalo**	**NHL**	69	14	30	44	120	5	0	0	0	17
	NHL Totals		72	15	31	46	120	5	0	0	0	17

HOLDEN, PAUL

Defense. Shoots left. 6'3", 210 lbs.   Born, Kitchener, Ont., March 15, 1970.
(Los Angeles' 2nd choice, 28th overall, in 1988 Entry Draft).

			Regular Season					Playoffs				
Season	Club	Lea	GP	G	A	TP	PIM	GP	G	A	TP	PIM
1986-87	St. Thomas	SOHL	23	5	11	16	112	....	....	....	....	....
1987-88	London	OHL	65	8	12	20	87	12	1	1	2	10
1988-89	London	OHL	54	11	21	32	90	20	1	3	4	17

HOLIK, ROBERT

Center. Shoots right. 6'1", 185 lbs.   Born, Jihlava, Czechoslovakia, January 1, 1971.
(Hartford's 1st choice, 10th overall, in 1989 Entry Draft).

			Regular Season					Playoffs				
Season	Club	Lea	GP	G	A	TP	PIM	GP	G	A	TP	PIM
1987-88	Jihlava	Czech.	31	5	9	14	....	....	....	....	....	....
1988-89	Jihlava	Czech.	24	7	10	17	....	....	....	....	....	....

HOLLAND, DENNIS

Center. Shoots left. 5'10", 165 lbs.   Born, Vernon, B.C., January 30, 1969.
(Detroit's 4th choice, 52nd overall, in 1987 Entry Draft).

			Regular Season					Playoffs				
Season	Club	Lea	GP	G	A	TP	PIM	GP	G	A	TP	PIM
1986-87a	Portland	WHL	51	43	62	105	40	20	7	14	21	20
1987-88b	Portland	WHL	67	58	86	144	115	....	....	....	....	....
1988-89bc	Portland	WHL	69	*82	85	*167	120	19	15	22	37	18

a WHL Rookie of the Year (1987)
b WHL West All-Star Team (1988, 1989)
c WHL Player of the Year (1989)

HOLLETT, STEVE

Center. Shoots left. 6'1", 200 lbs. Born, St. John's, Nfld., June 12, 1967.
(Washington's 10th choice, 187th overall, in 1985 Entry Draft).

			Regular Season					Playoffs				
Season	Club	Lea	GP	G	A	TP	PIM	GP	G	A	TP	PIM
1984-85	S. S. Marie	OHL	60	12	17	29	25	16	3	4	7	11
1985-86	S. S. Marie	OHL	63	31	34	65	81	....	....	....	....	....
1986-87	S. S. Marie	OHL	65	35	41	76	63	4	0	1	1	7
1987-88	Fort Wayne	IHL	76	42	32	74	56	5	0	2	2	2
1988-89	Fort Wayne	IHL	79	27	21	48	39	10	2	2	4	4

HOLMES, MARK

Right wing. Shoots right. 6'2", 200 lbs. Born, Kingston, Jamaica, June 7, 1964.

			Regular Season					Playoffs				
Season	Club	Lea	GP	G	A	TP	PIM	GP	G	A	TP	PIM
1984-85	Colgate	ECAC	20	3	5	8	12	....	....	....	....	....
1985-86	Colgate	ECAC	30	11	5	16	20	....	....	....	....	....
1986-87	Colgate	ECAC	31	12	14	26	45	....	....	....	....	....
1987-88	Colgate	ECAC	32	11	13	24	28	....	....	....	....	....
1988-89	Salt Lake	IHL	52	6	12	18	46	4	0	2	2	7

Signed as a free agent by **Calgary**, May 1, 1988.

HOOVER, RON

Center. Shoots left. 6'1", 185 lbs. Born, Oakville, Ont., October 28, 1966.
(Hartford's 7th choice, 158th overall, in 1986 Entry Draft).

			Regular Season					Playoffs				
Season	Club	Lea	GP	G	A	TP	PIM	GP	G	A	TP	PIM
1985-86	W. Michigan	CCHA	43	10	23	33	36	....	....	....	....	....
1986-87	W. Michigan	CCHA	34	7	10	17	22	....	....	....	....	....
1987-88a	W. Michigan	CCHA	42	39	23	62	40	....	....	....	....	....
1988-89	W. Michigan	CCHA	42	32	27	59	66	....	....	....	....	....

a CCHA Second All-Star Team (1988)

HOOVER, TIM

Defense. Shoots left. 5'10", 165 lbs. Born, North Bay, Ont., January 9, 1965.
(Buffalo's 11th choice, 174th over-all, in 1983 Entry Draft).

			Regular Season					Playoffs				
Season	Club	Lea	GP	G	A	TP	PIM	GP	G	A	TP	PIM
1982-83	S. S. Marie	OHL	60	6	21	27	53	16	6	5	11	13
1983-84	S. S. Marie	OHL	70	8	34	42	50	16	2	6	8	10
1984-85	S. S. Marie	OHL	49	6	28	34	29	16	0	8	8	10
1985-86	Rochester	AHL	49	2	5	7	34	....	....	....	....	....
1986-87	Flint	IHL	75	3	23	26	26	5	0	4	4	0
1987-88	Baltimore	AHL	73	2	6	8	39	....	....	....	....	....
1988-89	Indianapolis	IHL	3	0	0	0	2	....	....	....	....	....

HOPKINS, DEAN ROBERT

Right wing. Shoots right. 6'1", 210 lbs. Born, Cobourg, Ont., June 6, 1959.
(Los Angeles' 2nd choice, 29th over-all, in 1979 Entry Draft).

			Regular Season					Playoffs				
Season	Club	Lea	GP	G	A	TP	PIM	GP	G	A	TP	PIM
1977-78	London	OHA	67	19	34	53	70	11	1	5	6	24
1978-79	London	OHA	65	37	55	92	149	7	6	0	6	27
1979-80	**Los Angeles**	**NHL**	**60**	**8**	**6**	**14**	**39**	**4**	**0**	**1**	**1**	**5**
1980-81	**Los Angeles**	**NHL**	**67**	**8**	**18**	**26**	**118**	**4**	**1**	**0**	**1**	**9**
1981-82	**Los Angeles**	**NHL**	**41**	**2**	**13**	**15**	**102**	**10**	**0**	**4**	**4**	**15**
1982-83	**Los Angeles**	**NHL**	**49**	**5**	**12**	**17**	**43**	....	....	....	....	....
	New Haven	AHL	20	9	8	17	58	....	....	....	....	....
1983-84	New Haven	AHL	79	35	47	82	162	....	....	....	....	....
1984-85	New Haven	AHL	20	7	10	17	38	....	....	....	....	....
	Nova Scotia	AHL	49	13	17	30	93	6	1	2	3	20
1985-86	**Edmonton**	**NHL**	**1**	**0**	**0**	**0**	**0**	....	....	....	....	....
	Nova Scotia	AHL	60	23	32	55	131	....	....	....	....	....
1986-87	Nova Scotia	AHL	59	20	25	45	84	1	0	0	0	5
1987-88	Nova Scotia	AHL	44	20	22	42	122	5	2	5	7	16
1988-89	**Quebec**	**NHL**	**5**	**0**	**2**	**2**	**4**	....	....	....	....	....
	Halifax	AHL	53	18	31	49	116	3	0	1	1	6
	NHL Totals		**223**	**23**	**51**	**74**	**306**	**18**	**1**	**5**	**6**	**29**

Traded to **Edmonton** by **Los Angeles** for cash, November 27, 1984. Traded to **Los Angeles** by **Edmonton** for future considerations, May 31, 1985. Signed as a free agent by **Edmonton**, September 27, 1985.

HORACEK, TONY

Left wing. Shoots left. 6'4", 210 lbs. Born, Vancouver, B.C., February 3, 1967.
(Philadelphia's 8th choice, 147th overall, in 1985 Entry Draft).

			Regular Season					Playoffs				
Season	Club	Lea	GP	G	A	TP	PIM	GP	G	A	TP	PIM
1984-85	Kelowna	WHL	67	9	18	27	114	6	0	1	1	11
1985-86	Spokane	WHL	64	19	28	47	129	9	4	5	9	29
1986-87	Hershey	AHL	1	0	0	0	0	1	0	0	0	0
	Spokane	WHL	64	23	37	60	177	5	1	3	4	18
1987-88	Hershey	AHL	1	0	0	0	0	....	....	....	....	....
	Kamloops	WHL	50	31	40	71	114	18	6	4	10	73
1988-89	Hershey	AHL	10	0	0	0	38	....	....	....	....	....
	Indianapolis	IHL	43	11	13	24	138	....	....	....	....	....

HORAVA, MIROSLAV

Defense. Shoots left. 6'1", 197 lbs. Born, Kladno, Czechoslovakia, August 14, 1961.
(Edmonton's 8th choice, 176th overall, in 1981 Entry Draft).

			Regular Season					Playoffs				
Season	Club	Lea	GP	G	A	TP	PIM	GP	G	A	TP	PIM
1986-87	Boldi Kladno	Czech.	38	17	26	43	....	....	....	....	....	....
1987-88	Boldi Kladno	Czech.	29	7	11	18	....	....	....	....	....	....
1988-89	Kladno	Czech.	37	10	15	25	....	....	....	....	....	....
	NY Rangers	**NHL**	**6**	**0**	**1**	**1**	**0**	....	....	....	....	....
	NHL Totals		**6**	**0**	**1**	**1**	**0**	....	....	....	....	....

Traded to **NY Rangers** by **Edmonton** with Don Jackson, Mike Golden and future considerations for Reijo Ruotsalainen, Ville Kentala, Clark Donatelli and Jim Wiemer, October 23, 1986.

HORNER, STEVE

Right wing. Shoots right. 6'1", 195 lbs. Born, Cowansville, Que., June 4, 1966.
(Los Angeles' 8th choice, 177th overall, in 1985 Entry Draft).

			Regular Season					Playoffs				
Season	Club	Lea	GP	G	A	TP	PIM	GP	G	A	TP	PIM
1985-86	N. Hampshire	H.E.	30	3	5	8	14	....	....	....	....	....
1986-87	N. Hampshire	H.E.	33	19	17	36	14	....	....	....	....	....
1987-88	N. Hampshire	H.E.	27	10	8	18	10	....	....	....	....	....
1988-89	N. Hampshire	H.E.	32	15	13	28	14	....	....	....	....	....

HOSPODAR, EDWARD DAVID (ED)

Defense. Shoots right. 6'2", 210 lbs. Born, Bowling Green, OH, February 9, 1959.
(NY Rangers' 2nd choice, 34th over-all, in 1979 Entry Draft).

			Regular Season					Playoffs				
Season	Club	Lea	GP	G	A	TP	PIM	GP	G	A	TP	PIM
1977-78	Ottawa	OHA	62	7	26	33	172	16	3	6	9	78
1978-79a	Ottawa	OHA	45	7	16	23	218	1	0	0	0	0
1979-80	New Haven	AHL	25	3	9	12	131	5	0	1	1	39
	NY Rangers	**NHL**	**20**	**0**	**1**	**1**	**76**	**7**	**1**	**0**	**1**	**42**
1980-81	**NY Rangers**	**NHL**	**61**	**5**	**14**	**19**	**214**	**12**	**2**	**0**	**2**	***93**
1981-82	**NY Rangers**	**NHL**	**41**	**3**	**8**	**11**	**152**	....	....	....	....	....
1982-83	**Hartford**	**NHL**	**72**	**1**	**9**	**10**	**199**	....	....	....	....	....
1983-84	**Hartford**	**NHL**	**59**	**0**	**9**	**9**	**163**	....	....	....	....	....
1984-85	**Philadelphia**	**NHL**	**50**	**3**	**4**	**7**	**130**	**18**	**1**	**1**	**2**	**69**
1985-86	**Philadelphia**	**NHL**	**17**	**3**	**1**	**4**	**55**	....	....	....	....	....
	Minnesota	**NHL**	**43**	**0**	**2**	**2**	**91**	**2**	**0**	**0**	**0**	**0**
1986-87	**Philadelphia**	**NHL**	**45**	**2**	**2**	**4**	**136**	**5**	**0**	**0**	**0**	**2**
1987-88	**Buffalo**	**NHL**	**42**	**0**	**1**	**1**	**98**	....	....	....	....	....
1988-89	Rochester	AHL	5	0	0	0	10	....	....	....	....	....
	NHL Totals		**450**	**17**	**51**	**68**	**1314**	**44**	**4**	**1**	**5**	**206**

a OHA Second All-Star Team (1979)

Traded to **Hartford** by **NY Rangers** for Kent-Erik Andersson, October 1, 1982. Signed as free agent by **Philadelphia**, July 25, 1984. Traded to **Minnesota** by **Philadelphia** with Todd Bergen for Bo Berglund and Dave Richter, November 29, 1985. Claimed by **Buffalo** in NHL Waiver Draft, October 5, 1987.

HOSTAK, MARTIN

Center. Shoots left. 6'3", 192 lbs. Born, Hradec Kralove, Czech., November 11, 1967.
(Philadelphia's 3rd choice, 62nd overall, in 1987 Entry Draft).

			Regular Season					Playoffs				
Season	Club	Lea	GP	G	A	TP	PIM	GP	G	A	TP	PIM
1986-87	Sparta Praha	Czech.	34	6	2	8	0	....	....	....	....	....
1987-88	Sparta Praha	Czech	26	8	9	17	0	....	....	....	....	....
1988-89	Sparta Praha	Czech.	35	11	15	26	....	....	....	....	....	....

HOTHAM, GREGORY (GREG) (HOTH-am)

Defense. Shoots right. 5'11", 185 lbs. Born, London, Ont., March 7, 1956.
(Toronto's 5th choice, 84th over-all, in 1976 Amateur Draft).

			Regular Season					Playoffs				
Season	Club	Lea	GP	G	A	TP	PIM	GP	G	A	TP	PIM
1974-75	Kingston	OHA	31	1	14	15	49	8	5	4	9	0
1975-76	Kingston	OHA	49	10	32	42	72	7	1	2	3	10
1976-77	Saginaw	IHL	60	4	33	37	100	....	....	....	....	....
1977-78	Saginaw	IHL	80	13	59	72	56	....	....	....	....	....
	Dallas	CHL	....	....	....	....	....	5	0	2	2	7
1978-79	New Brunswick	AHL	76	9	27	36	86	5	0	2	2	6
1979-80	**Toronto**	**NHL**	**46**	**3**	**10**	**13**	**10**	....	....	....	....	....
	New Brunswick	AHL	21	1	6	7	10	17	2	8	10	26
1980-81	**Toronto**	**NHL**	**11**	**1**	**1**	**2**	**11**	....	....	....	....	....
	New Brunswick	AHL	68	8	48	56	80	11	1	6	7	16
1981-82	**Toronto**	**NHL**	**3**	**0**	**0**	**0**	**0**	....	....	....	....	....
	Cincinnati	CHL	46	10	33	43	94	....	....	....	....	....
	Pittsburgh	**NHL**	**25**	**4**	**6**	**10**	**16**	**5**	**0**	**3**	**3**	**6**
1982-83	**Pittsburgh**	**NHL**	**58**	**2**	**30**	**32**	**39**	....	....	....	....	....
1983-84	**Pittsburgh**	**NHL**	**76**	**5**	**25**	**30**	**59**	....	....	....	....	....
1984-85	**Pittsburgh**	**NHL**	**11**	**0**	**2**	**2**	**4**	....	....	....	....	....
	Baltimore	AHL	44	4	27	31	43	15	4	4	8	34
1985-86	Baltimore	AHL	78	2	26	28	94	....	....	....	....	....
1986-87	Newmarket	AHL	51	4	9	13	60	....	....	....	....	....
1987-88	Newmarket	AHL	78	12	27	39	102	....	....	....	....	....
1988-89	Newmarket	AHL	73	9	42	51	62	5	1	4	5	0
	NHL Totals		**230**	**15**	**74**	**89**	**139**	**5**	**0**	**3**	**3**	**6**

Traded to **Pittsburgh** by **Toronto** for Pittsburgh's sixth round choice (Craig Kales) in 1982 Entry Draft, February 3, 1982.

HOUCK, PAUL (HOWK)

Right wing. Shoots right. 5'11", 185 lbs. Born, North Vancouver, B.C., August 12, 1963.
(Edmonton's 3rd choice, 71st over-all, in 1981 Entry Draft).

			Regular Season					Playoffs				
Season	Club	Lea	GP	G	A	TP	PIM	GP	G	A	TP	PIM
1981-82	U. Wisconsin	WCHA	43	9	16	25	38	....	....	....	....	....
1982-83	U. Wisconsin	WCHA	47	38	33	71	36	....	....	....	....	....
1983-84	U. Wisconsin	WCHA	37	20	20	40	29	....	....	....	....	....
1984-85	U. Wisconsin	WCHA	39	16	24	40	54	....	....	....	....	....
	Nova Scotia	AHL	10	1	0	1	0	....	....	....	....	....
1985-86	**Minnesota**	**NHL**	**3**	**1**	**0**	**1**	**0**	....	....	....	....	....
	Springfield	AHL	61	15	17	32	27	....	....	....	....	....
1986-87	**Minnesota**	**NHL**	**12**	**0**	**2**	**2**	**2**	....	....	....	....	....
	Springfield	AHL	64	29	18	47	58	....	....	....	....	....
1987-88	**Minnesota**	**NHL**	**1**	**0**	**0**	**0**	**0**	....	....	....	....	....
	Kalamazoo	IHL	74	27	29	56	73	7	3	4	7	8
1988-89	Springfield	AHL	2	1	0	1	0	....	....	....	....	....
	Indianapolis	IHL	81	22	37	59	51	....	....	....	....	....
	NHL Totals		**16**	**1**	**2**	**3**	**2**	....	....	....	....	....

Traded to **Minnesota** by **Edmonton** for Gilles Meloche, May 31, 1985.

HOUDA, DOUG (HOO-duh)

Defense. Shoots right. 6'2", 200 lbs. Born, Blairmore, Alta., June 3, 1966.
(Detroit's 2nd choice, 28th over-all, in 1984 Entry Draft).

			Regular Season					Playoffs				
Season	Club	Lea	GP	G	A	TP	PIM	GP	G	A	TP	PIM
1982-83	Calgary	WHL	71	5	23	28	99	16	1	3	4	44
1983-84	Calgary	WHL	69	6	30	36	195	4	0	0	0	7
1984-85a	Calgary	WHL	65	20	54	74	182	8	3	4	7	29
1985-86	**Detroit**	**NHL**	**6**	**0**	**0**	**0**	**4**	....	....	....	....	....
	Medicine Hat	WHL	51	13	33	46	140	25	4	19	23	64
1986-87	Adirondack	AHL	77	6	23	29	142	11	1	8	9	50
1987-88	**Detroit**	**NHL**	**11**	**1**	**1**	**2**	**10**	....	....	....	....	....
b	Adirondack	AHL	71	10	32	42	169	11	0	3	3	44
1988-89	**Detroit**	**NHL**	**57**	**2**	**11**	**13**	**17**	**6**	**0**	**1**	**1**	**0**
	Adirondack	AHL	7	0	3	3	8	....	....	....	....	....
	NHL Totals		**74**	**3**	**12**	**15**	**31**	**6**	**0**	**1**	**1**	**0**

a WHL Second All-Star Team, East Division (1985)
b AHL First All-Star Team (1988)

HOUGH, MIKE (HUHF)

Left wing. Shoots left. 6'1", 192 lbs. Born, Montreal, Que., February 6, 1963.
(Quebec's 7th choice, 181st over-all, in 1982 Entry Draft).

			Regular Season					Playoffs				
Season	Club	Lea	GP	G	A	TP	PIM	GP	G	A	TP	PIM
1981-82	Kitchener	OHL	58	14	14	28	172	14	4	1	5	16
1982-83	Kitchener	OHL	61	17	27	44	156	12	5	4	9	30
1983-84	Fredericton	AHL	69	11	16	27	142	1	0	0	0	7
1984-85	Fredericton	AHL	76	21	27	48	49	6	1	1	2	2
1985-86	Fredericton	AHL	74	21	33	54	68	6	0	3	3	8
1986-87	Fredericton	AHL	10	1	3	4	20	....	....	....	....	....
	Quebec	**NHL**	**56**	**6**	**8**	**14**	**79**	**9**	**0**	**3**	**3**	**26**
1987-88	**Quebec**	**NHL**	**17**	**3**	**2**	**5**	**2**	....	....	....	....	....
	Fredericton	AHL	46	16	25	41	133	15	4	8	12	55
1988-89	**Quebec**	**NHL**	**46**	**9**	**10**	**19**	**39**	....	....	....	....	....
	Halifax	AHL	22	11	10	21	87	....	....	....	....	....
	NHL Totals		**119**	**18**	**20**	**38**	**120**	**9**	**0**	**3**	**3**	**26**

HOULDER, BILL

Defense. Shoots left. 6'3", 210 lbs. Born, Thunder Bay, Ont., March 11, 1967.
(Washington's 4th choice, 82nd overall, in 1985 Entry Draft).

			Regular Season					Playoffs				
Season	Club	Lea	GP	G	A	TP	PIM	GP	G	A	TP	PIM
1984-85	North Bay	OHL	66	4	20	24	37	8	0	0	0	2
1985-86	North Bay	OHL	59	5	30	35	97	10	1	6	7	12
1986-87a	North Bay	OHL	62	17	51	68	68	22	4	19	23	20
1987-88	**Washington**	**NHL**	**30**	**1**	**2**	**3**	**10**	....	....	....	....	....
	Fort Wayne	IHL	43	10	14	24	32	....	....	....	....	....
1988-89	**Washington**	**NHL**	**8**	**0**	**3**	**3**	**4**	....	....	....	....	....
	Baltimore	AHL	65	10	36	46	50	....	....	....	....	....
	NHL Totals		**38**	**1**	**5**	**6**	**14**	....	....	....	....	....

a OHL Third All-Star Team (1987)

HOUSLEY, PHIL (HOWZ-lee)

Defense. Shoots left. 5'10", 180 lbs. Born, St. Paul, MN, March 9, 1964.
(Buffalo's 1st choice, 6th over-all, in 1982 Entry Draft).

			Regular Season					Playoffs				
Season	Club	Lea	GP	G	A	TP	PIM	GP	G	A	TP	PIM
1981-82	South St. Paul	HS	22	31	34	65	18	....	....	....	....	....
1982-83a	**Buffalo**	**NHL**	**77**	**19**	**47**	**66**	**39**	**10**	**3**	**4**	**7**	**2**
1983-84	**Buffalo**	**NHL**	**75**	**31**	**46**	**77**	**33**	**3**	**0**	**0**	**0**	**6**
1984-85	**Buffalo**	**NHL**	**73**	**16**	**53**	**69**	**28**	**5**	**3**	**2**	**5**	**2**
1985-86	**Buffalo**	**NHL**	**79**	**15**	**47**	**62**	**54**	....	....	....	....	....
1986-87	**Buffalo**	**NHL**	**78**	**21**	**46**	**67**	**57**	....	....	....	....	....
1987-88	**Buffalo**	**NHL**	**74**	**29**	**37**	**66**	**96**	**6**	**2**	**4**	**6**	**6**
1988-89	**Buffalo**	**NHL**	**72**	**26**	**44**	**70**	**47**	**5**	**1**	**3**	**4**	**2**
	NHL Totals		**528**	**157**	**320**	**477**	**354**	**29**	**9**	**13**	**22**	**18**

a NHL All-Rookie Team (1983)

Played in NHL All-Star Game (1984, 1989)

HOWARD, SHAWN

Center. Shoots left. 6', 180 lbs. Born, Anchorage, AK, March 20, 1968.
(NY Islanders' 9th choice, 181st overall, in 1987 Entry Draft).

			Regular Season					Playoffs				
Season	Club	Lea	GP	G	A	TP	PIM	GP	G	A	TP	PIM
1986-87	Penticton	BCJHL	51	25	34	59	64	....	....	....	....	....
1987-88	Minn.-Duluth	WCHA	37	13	8	21	42	....	....	....	....	....
1988-89	Minn.-Duluth	WCHA	39	7	9	16	31	....	....	....	....	....

HOWE, MARK STEVEN

Defence. Shoots left. 5'11", 190 lbs. Born, Detroit, Mich., May 28, 1955.
(Boston's 2nd choice, 25th over-all, in 1974 Amateur Draft).

			Regular Season					Playoffs				
Season	Club	Lea	GP	G	A	TP	PIM	GP	G	A	TP	PIM
1972-73	Toronto	OHA	60	38	66	104	27	....	....	....	....	....
1973-74ab	Houston	WHA	76	38	41	79	20	14	9	10	19	4
1974-75	Houston	WHA	74	36	40	76	30	13	*10	12	*22	0
1975-76	Houston	WHA	72	39	37	76	38	17	6	10	16	18
1976-77a	Houston	WHA	57	23	52	75	46	10	4	10	14	2
1977-78	New England	WHA	70	30	61	91	32	14	8	7	15	18
1978-79c	New England	WHA	77	42	65	107	32	6	4	2	6	6
1979-80	**Hartford**	**NHL**	**74**	**24**	**56**	**80**	**20**	**3**	**1**	**2**	**3**	**2**
1980-81	**Hartford**	**NHL**	**63**	**19**	**46**	**65**	**54**	....	....	....	....	....
1981-82	**Hartford**	**NHL**	**76**	**8**	**45**	**53**	**18**	....	....	....	....	....
1982-83d	**Philadelphia**	**NHL**	**76**	**20**	**47**	**67**	**18**	**3**	**0**	**2**	**2**	**4**
1983-84	**Philadelphia**	**NHL**	**71**	**19**	**34**	**53**	**44**	**3**	**0**	**0**	**0**	**2**
1984-85	**Philadelphia**	**NHL**	**73**	**18**	**39**	**57**	**31**	**19**	**3**	**8**	**11**	**6**
1985-86de	**Philadelphia**	**NHL**	**77**	**24**	**58**	**82**	**36**	**5**	**0**	**4**	**4**	**0**
1986-87d	**Philadelphia**	**NHL**	**69**	**15**	**43**	**58**	**37**	**26**	**2**	**10**	**12**	**4**
1987-88	**Philadelphia**	**NHL**	**75**	**19**	**43**	**62**	**62**	**7**	**3**	**6**	**9**	**4**
1988-89	**Philadelphia**	**NHL**	**52**	**9**	**29**	**38**	**45**	**19**	**0**	**15**	**15**	**10**
	NHL Totals		**706**	**175**	**440**	**615**	**365**	**85**	**9**	**47**	**56**	**32**

a WHA Second All-Star Team (1974, 1977)
b Named WHA's Rookie of the Year (1974)
c WHA First All-Star Team (1979)
d NHL First All-Star Team (1983, 1986, 1987)
e NHL Plus/Minus Leader (1986)

Played in NHL All-Star Game (1981, 1983, 1986, 1988)

Reclaimed by **Boston** from **Hartford** prior to Expansion Draft, June 9, 1979. Claimed as priority selection by **Hartford**, June 9, 1979. Traded to **Philadelphia** by **Hartford** with Hartford's third round choice (Derrick Smith) in 1983 Entry Draft for Ken Linseman, Greg Adams and Philadelphia's first (David Jensen) and third round choices (Leif Karlsson) in the 1983 Entry Draft, August 19, 1982.

HRBEK, PETR

Right wing. Shoots right. 5'11", 180 lbs. Born, Prague, Czechoslovakia, April 3, 1969.
(Detroit's 3rd choice, 59th overall, in 1988 Entry Draft).

			Regular Season					Playoffs				
Season	Club	Lea	GP	G	A	TP	PIM	GP	G	A	TP	PIM
1986-87	Sparta Praha	Czech.	11	2	0	2	....	....	....	....	....	....
1987-88	Sparta Praha	Czech.	31	13	9	22	....	....	....	....	....	....
1988-89	Sparta Praha	Czech.	41	10	13	23	....	....	....	....	....	....

HRDINA, JIRI

Center. Shoots right. 5'11", 183 lbs. Born, Mlada Boleslav, Czechoslovakia, January 5, 1958.
(Calgary's 8th choice, 159th overall, in 1984 Entry Draft).

			Regular Season					Playoffs				
Season	Club	Lea	GP	G	A	TP	PIM	GP	G	A	TP	PIM
1985-86	Sparta Praha	Czech.	44	18	19	37	30	....	....	....	....	....
1986-87	Sparta Praha	Czech.	31	18	18	36	24	....	....	....	....	....
1987-88	Sparta Praha	Czech.	22	7	15	22	0	....	....	....	....	....
	Czech Olympic	....	8	2	5	7	4	....	....	....	....	....
	Calgary	**NHL**	**9**	**2**	**5**	**7**	**2**	**1**	**0**	**0**	**0**	**0**
1988-89	**Calgary**	**NHL**	**70**	**22**	**32**	**54**	**26**	**4**	**0**	**0**	**0**	**0**
	NHL Totals		**79**	**24**	**37**	**61**	**28**	**5**	**0**	**0**	**0**	**0**

HRISTICH, DMITRI

Left wing. Shoots right. 6'2", 215 lbs. Born, Kiev, Soviet Union, July 2, 1969.
(Washington's 6th choice, 120th overall, in 1988 Entry Draft).

			Regular Season					Playoffs				
Season	Club	Lea	GP	G	A	TP	PIM	GP	G	A	TP	PIM
1987-88	Sokol Kiev	USSR	37	9	1	10	18	....	....	....	....	....
1988-89	Sokol Kiev	USSR	42	17	8	25	15	....	....	....	....	....

HRKAC, ANTHONY (TONY) (HUHR kuhz)

Center. Shoots left. 5'11", 175 lbs. Born, Thunder Bay, Ont., July 7, 1966.
(St. Louis' 2nd choice, 32nd over-all, in 1984 Entry Draft).

			Regular Season					Playoffs				
Season	Club	Lea	GP	G	A	TP	PIM	GP	G	A	TP	PIM
1983-84	Orillia	OPJHL	42	52	55	107	16	....	....	....	....	....
1984-85	North Dakota	WCHA	36	18	36	54	16	....	....	....	....	....
1985-86	Cdn. Olympic	....	62	19	30	49	36	....	....	....	....	....
1986-87abcd	North Dakota	WCHA	48	46	79	125	48	....	....	....	....	....
	St. Louis	**NHL**	....	....	....	....	....	**3**	**0**	**0**	**0**	**0**
1987-88	**St. Louis**	**NHL**	**67**	**11**	**37**	**48**	**22**	**10**	**6**	**1**	**7**	**4**
1988-89	**St. Louis**	**NHL**	**70**	**17**	**28**	**45**	**8**	**4**	**1**	**1**	**2**	**0**
	NHL Totals		**137**	**28**	**65**	**93**	**30**	**14**	**7**	**2**	**9**	**4**

a WCHA First All-Star Team, Player of the Year (1987)
b NCAA West First All-American Team (1987)
c NCAA All-Tournament Team, Tournament MVP (1987)
d Winner of the 1987 Hobey Baker Memorial Trophy (Top U.S. Collegiate Player) (1987)

HRSTKA, MARTIN

Left wing. Shoots left. 6', 180 lbs. Born, Brno, Czechoslovakia, January 26, 1967.
(Vancouver's 6th choice, 109th overall, in 1985 Entry Draft).

			Regular Season					Playoffs				
Season	Club	Lea	GP	G	A	TP	PIM	GP	G	A	TP	PIM
1986-87	Dukla Trencin	Czech.	26	2	4	6	....	....	....	....	....	....
1987-88	Dukla Trencin	Czech.	22	5	6	11	....	....	....	....	....	....
1988-89	Dukla Trencin	Czech.	25	4	9	13	....	....	....	....	....	....

HRYNEWICH, TIM   (RINN-e-WICK)

Left wing. Shoots left. 5'11", 190 lbs.   Born, Leamington, Ont., October 2, 1963.
(Pittsburgh's 2nd choice, 38th over-all, in 1982 Entry Draft).

			Regular Season					Playoffs				
Season	Club	Lea	GP	G	A	TP	PIM	GP	G	A	TP	PIM
1980-81	Sudbury	OHA	65	25	17	42	104	....	....	....	....	....
1981-82	Sudbury	OHL	64	29	41	70	144	....	....	....	....	....
1982-83	Sudbury	OHL	23	21	16	37	65	....	....	....	....	....
	Pittsburgh	**NHL**	**30**	**2**	**3**	**5**	**48**	....	....	....	....	....
	Baltimore	AHL	9	2	1	3	6	....	....	....	....	....
1983-84	**Pittsburgh**	**NHL**	**25**	**4**	**5**	**9**	**34**	....	....	....	....	....
	Baltimore	AHL	52	13	17	30	65	....	....	....	....	....
1984-85	Baltimore	AHL	21	4	3	7	31	....	....	....	....	....
	Muskegon	IHL	30	10	13	23	42	....	....	....	....	....
1985-86	Muskegon	IHL	67	25	26	51	110	....	....	....	....	....
	Toledo	IHL	13	8	13	21	25	....	....	....	....	....
1986-87	Milwaukee	IHL	82	39	37	76	78	6	2	3	5	2
1987-88	Milwaukee	IHL	28	6	8	14	39	....	....	....	....	....
1988-89	Flint	IHL	5	0	1	1	4	....	....	....	....	....
	Fort Wayne	IHL	4	0	1	1	8	....	....	....	....	....
	NHL Totals		**55**	**6**	**8**	**14**	**82**	....	....	....	....	....

Traded to **Edmonton** by **Pittsburgh** with Marty McSorley for Gilles Meloche, September 12, 1985.

HUDDY, CHARLES WILLIAM (CHARLIE)

Defense. Shoots left. 6', 210 lbs.   Born, Oshawa, Ont., June 2, 1959.

			Regular Season					Playoffs				
Season	Club	Lea	GP	G	A	TP	PIM	GP	G	A	TP	PIM
1977-78	Oshawa	OHA	59	17	18	35	81	6	2	1	3	10
1978-79	Oshawa	OHA	64	20	38	58	108	5	3	4	7	12
1979-80	Houston	CHL	79	14	34	48	46	6	1	0	1	2
1980-81	**Edmonton**	**NHL**	**12**	**2**	**5**	**7**	**6**	....	....	....	....	....
	Wichita	CHL	47	8	36	44	71	17	3	11	14	10
1981-82	Wichita	CHL	32	7	19	26	51	....	....	....	....	....
	Edmonton	**NHL**	**41**	**4**	**11**	**15**	**46**	5	1	2	3	14
1982-83a	**Edmonton**	**NHL**	**76**	**20**	**37**	**57**	**58**	15	1	6	7	10
1983-84	**Edmonton**	**NHL**	**75**	**8**	**34**	**42**	**43**	12	1	9	10	8
1984-85	**Edmonton**	**NHL**	**80**	**7**	**44**	**51**	**46**	18	3	17	20	17
1985-86	**Edmonton**	**NHL**	**76**	**6**	**35**	**41**	**55**	7	0	2	2	0
1986-87	**Edmonton**	**NHL**	**58**	**4**	**15**	**19**	**35**	21	1	7	8	21
1987-88	**Edmonton**	**NHL**	**77**	**13**	**28**	**41**	**71**	13	4	5	9	10
1988-89	**Edmonton**	**NHL**	**76**	**11**	**33**	**44**	**52**	7	2	0	2	4
	NHL Totals		**571**	**75**	**242**	**317**	**412**	**98**	**13**	**48**	**61**	**84**

a NHL Plus/Minus Leader (1983)
Signed as a free agent by **Edmonton**, September 14, 1979.

HUDSON, MIKE

Left wing. Shoots left. 6'1", 185 lbs.   Born, Guelph, Ont., February 6, 1967.
(Chicago's 6th choice, 140th overall, in 1986 Entry Draft).

			Regular Season					Playoffs				
Season	Club	Lea	GP	G	A	TP	PIM	GP	G	A	TP	PIM
1985-86	Sudbury	OHL	66	38	44	82	24	4	2	5	7	7
1986-87	Sudbury	OHL	63	40	57	97	18	....	....	....	....	....
1987-88	Saginaw	IHL	75	18	30	48	44	10	2	3	5	20
1988-89	**Chicago**	**NHL**	**41**	**7**	**16**	**23**	**20**	10	1	2	3	18
	Saginaw	IHL	30	15	17	32	10	....	....	....	....	....
	NHL Totals		**41**	**7**	**16**	**23**	**20**	**10**	**1**	**2**	**3**	**18**

HUFFMAN, KERRY

Defense. Shoots left. 6'2", 200 lbs.   Born, Peterborough, Ont., January 3, 1968.
(Philadelphia's 1st choice, 20th overall, in 1986 Entry Draft).

			Regular Season					Playoffs				
Season	Club	Lea	GP	G	A	TP	PIM	GP	G	A	TP	PIM
1984-85	Peterborough	OPJHL	24	2	5	7	53	....	....	....	....	....
1985-86	Guelph	OHL	56	3	24	27	35	20	1	10	11	10
1986-87	**Philadelphia**	**NHL**	**9**	**0**	**0**	**0**	**2**	....	....	....	....	....
	Hershey	AHL	3	0	1	1	0	4	0	0	0	0
a	Guelph	OHL	44	4	31	35	20	5	0	2	2	8
1987-88	**Philadelphia**	**NHL**	**52**	**6**	**17**	**23**	**34**	2	0	0	0	0
1988-89	**Philadelphia**	**NHL**	**29**	**0**	**11**	**11**	**31**	....	....	....	....	....
	Hershey	AHL	29	2	13	15	16	....	....	....	....	....
	NHL Totals		**90**	**6**	**28**	**34**	**67**	**2**	**0**	**0**	**0**	**0**

a OHL First All-Star Team (1987)

HUGHES, BRENT ALLEN

Left wing. Shoots left. 6', 190 lbs.   Born, New Westminster, B.C., April 5, 1966.

			Regular Season					Playoffs				
Season	Club	Lea	GP	G	A	TP	PIM	GP	G	A	TP	PIM
1983-84	N. Westminster	WHL	67	21	18	39	133	9	2	2	4	27
1984-85	N. Westminster	WHL	64	25	32	57	135	11	2	1	3	37
1985-86	N. Westminster	WHL	71	28	52	80	180	....	....	....	....	....
1986-87	N. Westminster	WHL	8	5	4	9	22	....	....	....	....	....
	Victoria	WHL	61	38	61	99	146	5	4	1	5	8
1987-88	Moncton	AHL	73	13	19	32	206	....	....	....	....	....
1988-89	**Winnipeg**	**NHL**	**28**	**3**	**2**	**5**	**82**	....	....	....	....	....
	Moncton	AHL	54	34	34	68	286	10	9	4	13	40
	NHL Totals		**28**	**3**	**2**	**5**	**82**	....	....	....	....	....

Signed as a free agent by **Winnipeg**, June 13, 1988.

HULL, BRETT

Right wing. Shoots right. 5'11", 195 lbs.   Born, Belleville, Ont., August 9, 1964.
(Calgary's 6th choice, 117th overall, in 1984 Entry Draft).

			Regular Season					Playoffs				
Season	Club	Lea	GP	G	A	TP	PIM	GP	G	A	TP	PIM
1983-84	Penticton	BCJHL	56	105	83	188	20	....	....	....	....	....
1984-85	Minn.-Duluth	WCHA	48	32	28	60	24	....	....	....	....	....
1985-86a	Minn.-Duluth	WCHA	42	52	32	84	46	....	....	....	....	....
	Calgary	**NHL**	**....**	**....**	**....**	**....**	**....**	2	0	0	0	0
1986-87	**Calgary**	**NHL**	**5**	**1**	**0**	**1**	**0**	4	2	1	3	0
bc	Moncton	AHL	67	50	42	92	16	3	2	2	4	2
1987-88	**Calgary**	**NHL**	**52**	**26**	**24**	**50**	**12**	....	....	....	....	....
	St. Louis	**NHL**	**13**	**6**	**8**	**14**	**4**	10	7	2	9	4
1988-89	**St. Louis**	**NHL**	**78**	**41**	**43**	**84**	**33**	10	5	5	10	6
	NHL Totals		**148**	**74**	**75**	**149**	**49**	**26**	**14**	**8**	**22**	**10**

a WCHA First All-Star Team (1986)
b AHL First All-Star Team (1987)
c Won Dudley "Red" Garrett Memorial Trophy (AHL's Top Rookie) (1987)
Played in NHL All-Star Game (1989)
Traded to **St. Louis** by **Calgary** with Steve Bozek for Rob Ramage and Rick Wamsley, March 7, 1988.

HULL, JODY

Right wing. Shoots right. 6'2", 200 lbs.   Born, Cambridge, Ont., February 2, 1969.
(Hartford's 1st choice, 18th overall, in 1987 Entry Draft).

			Regular Season					Playoffs				
Season	Club	Lea	GP	G	A	TP	PIM	GP	G	A	TP	PIM
1985-86	Peterborough	OHL	61	20	22	42	29	16	1	5	6	4
1986-87	Peterborough	OHL	49	18	34	52	22	12	4	9	13	14
1987-88a	Peterborough	OHL	60	50	44	94	33	12	10	8	18	8
1988-89	**Hartford**	**NHL**	**60**	**16**	**18**	**34**	**10**	1	0	0	0	2
	NHL Totals		**60**	**16**	**18**	**34**	**10**	**1**	**0**	**0**	**0**	**2**

a OHL Second All-Star Team (1988)

HULST, KENT

Center. Shoots left. 6', 180 lbs.   Born, St. Thomas, Ont., April 8, 1968.
(Toronto's 4th choice, 69th overall, in 1986 Entry Draft).

			Regular Season					Playoffs				
Season	Club	Lea	GP	G	A	TP	PIM	GP	G	A	TP	PIM
1985-86	Windsor	OHL	60	12	27	39	29	....	....	....	....	....
1986-87	Windsor	OHL	37	18	20	38	49	....	....	....	....	....
	Belleville	OHL	27	13	10	23	17	6	1	1	2	0
1987-88	Belleville	OHL	66	42	43	85	48	6	3	1	4	7
1988-89	Flint	IHL	7	0	1	1	4	....	....	....	....	....
	Newmarket	AHL						2	1	1	2	2
	Belleville	QMJHL	45	21	41	62	43	....	....	....	....	....

HUNT, BRIAN

Center. Shoots left. 6', 200 lbs.   Born, Richmond Hill, Ont., February 12, 1969.
(Winnipeg's 4th choice, 73rd overall, in 1988 Entry Draft).

			Regular Season					Playoffs				
Season	Club	Lea	GP	G	A	TP	PIM	GP	G	A	TP	PIM
1986-87	Oshawa	OHL	61	13	22	35	22	26	5	10	15	13
1987-88	Oshawa	OHL	65	39	56	95	21	7	1	3	4	4
1988-89	Oshawa	OHL	63	30	56	86	36	6	2	2	4	0

HUNT, CURTIS

Defense. Shoots left. 6', 195 lbs.   Born, North Battleford, Sask., January 28, 1967.
(Vancouver's 9th choice, 172nd overall, in 1985 Entry Draft).

			Regular Season					Playoffs				
Season	Club	Lea	GP	G	A	TP	PIM	GP	G	A	TP	PIM
1984-85	Prince Albert	WHL	64	2	13	15	61	13	0	3	3	24
1985-86	Prince Albert	WHL	72	5	29	34	108	18	2	8	10	28
1986-87	Prince Albert	WHL	47	6	31	37	101	8	1	3	4	4
1987-88	Flint	IHL	76	4	17	21	181	2	0	0	0	16
	Fredericton	AHL	1	0	0	0	2	....	....	....	....	....
1988-89	Milwaukee	IHL	65	3	17	20	226	11	1	2	3	43

HUNTER, DALE ROBERT

Center. Shoots left. 5'10", 198 lbs.   Born, Petrolia, Ont., July 31, 1960.
(Quebec's 2nd choice, 41st over-all, in 1979 Entry Draft).

			Regular Season					Playoffs				
Season	Club	Lea	GP	G	A	TP	PIM	GP	G	A	TP	PIM
1978-79	Sudbury	OHA	59	42	68	110	188	10	4	12	16	47
1979-80	Sudbury	OHA	61	34	51	85	189	9	6	9	15	45
1980-81	**Quebec**	**NHL**	**80**	**19**	**44**	**63**	**226**	5	4	2	6	34
1981-82	**Quebec**	**NHL**	**80**	**22**	**50**	**72**	**272**	16	3	7	10	52
1982-83	**Quebec**	**NHL**	**80**	**17**	**46**	**63**	**206**	4	2	1	3	24
1983-84	**Quebec**	**NHL**	**77**	**24**	**55**	**79**	**232**	9	2	3	5	41
1984-85	**Quebec**	**NHL**	**80**	**20**	**52**	**72**	**209**	17	4	6	10	97
1985-86	**Quebec**	**NHL**	**80**	**28**	**42**	**70**	**265**	3	0	0	0	15
1986-87	**Quebec**	**NHL**	**46**	**10**	**29**	**39**	**135**	13	1	7	8	56
1987-88	**Washington**	**NHL**	**79**	**22**	**37**	**59**	**240**	14	7	5	12	98
1988-89	**Washington**	**NHL**	**80**	**20**	**37**	**57**	**219**	6	0	4	4	29
	NHL Totals		**682**	**182**	**392**	**574**	**2004**	**87**	**23**	**35**	**58**	**446**

Traded to **Washington** by **Quebec** with Clint Malarchuk for Gaetan Duchesne, Alan Haworth, and Washington's first-round choice (Joe Sakic) in 1987 Entry Draft, June 13, 1987.

HUNTER, DAVID (DAVE)

Left wing. Shoots left. 5'11", 195 lbs.   Born, Petrolia, Ont., January 1, 1958.
(Montreal's 2nd choice, 17th over-all, in 1978 Amateur Draft).

			Regular Season					Playoffs				
Season	Club	Lea	GP	G	A	TP	PIM	GP	G	A	TP	PIM
1976-77	Sudbury	OHA	62	30	56	86	140	6	1	3	4	9
1977-78	Sudbury	OHA	68	44	44	88	156	....	....	....	....	....
1978-79	Dallas	CHL	6	3	4	7	6	....	....	....	....	....
	Edmonton	WHA	72	7	25	32	134	13	2	3	5	42
1979-80	Edmonton	NHL	80	12	31	43	103	3	0	0	0	7
1980-81	Edmonton	NHL	78	12	16	28	98	9	0	0	0	28
1981-82	Edmonton	NHL	63	16	22	38	63	5	0	1	1	26
1982-83	Edmonton	NHL	80	13	18	31	120	16	4	7	11	60
1983-84	Edmonton	NHL	80	22	26	48	90	17	5	5	10	14
1984-85	Edmonton	NHL	80	17	19	36	122	18	2	5	7	33
1985-86	Edmonton	NHL	62	15	22	37	77	10	2	3	5	23
1986-87	Edmonton	NHL	77	6	9	15	79	21	3	3	6	20
1987-88	Edmonton	NHL	21	3	3	6	6	....	....	....	....	....
	Pittsburgh	NHL	59	11	18	29	77	....	....	....	....	....
1988-89	Winnipeg	NHL	34	3	1	4	61	....	....	....	....	....
	Edmonton	NHL	32	3	5	8	22	6	0	0	0	0
	NHL Totals		746	133	190	323	918	105	16	24	40	211

Claimed by **Edmonton** from **Montreal** in Expansion Draft, June 22, 1979. Traded to **Pittsburgh** by **Edmonton** with Paul Coffey and Wayne Van Dorp for Craig Simpson, Dave Hannan, Moe Mantha and Chris Joseph, November 24, 1987. Acquired by **Edmonton** from **Pittsburgh** as compensation for Pittsburgh's claiming Dave Hannan in NHL Waiver Draft, October 3, 1988. Claimed by **Winnipeg** in NHL Waiver Draft, October 3, 1988. Claimed by **Edmonton** on waivers from **Winnipeg**, January 14, 1989

HUNTER, MARK

Right wing. Shoots right. 6', 205 lbs.   Born, Petrolia, Ont., November 12, 1962.
(Montreal's 1st choice, 7th over-all, in 1981 Entry Draft).

			Regular Season					Playoffs				
Season	Club	Lea	GP	G	A	TP	PIM	GP	G	A	TP	PIM
1979-80	Brantford	OHA	66	34	56	90	171	11	2	8	10	27
1980-81	Brantford	OHA	53	39	40	79	157	6	3	3	6	27
1981-82	Montreal	NHL	71	18	11	29	143	5	0	0	0	20
1982-83	Montreal	NHL	31	8	8	16	73	....	....	....	....	....
1983-84	Montreal	NHL	22	6	4	10	42	14	2	1	3	69
1984-85	Montreal	NHL	72	21	12	33	123	11	0	3	3	13
1985-86	St. Louis	NHL	78	44	30	74	171	19	7	7	14	48
1986-87	St. Louis	NHL	74	36	33	69	167	5	0	3	3	10
1987-88	St. Louis	NHL	66	32	31	63	136	5	2	3	5	24
1988-89	Calgary	NHL	66	22	8	30	194	10	2	2	4	23
	NHL Totals		480	187	137	324	1049	69	13	19	32	207

Played in NHL All-Star Game (1986)

Traded to **St. Louis** by **Montreal** with Michael Dark and Montreal's second (Herb Raglan); third (Nelson Emerson); fifth (Dan Brooks); and sixth (Rick Burchill) round choices in 1985 Entry Draft, for St. Louis' first (Jose Charbonneau); second (Todd Richard); fourth (Martin Desjardins); fifth (Tom Sagissor); and sixth (Don Dufresne) round choices in 1985 Entry Draft, June 15, 1985. Traded to **Calgary** by **St. Louis** with Doug Gilmour, Steve Bozek and Michael Dark for Mike Bullard, Craig Coxe and Tim Corkery, September 6, 1988.

HUNTER, TIMOTHY ROBERT (TIM)

Right wing. Shoots right. 6'2", 202 lbs.   Born, Calgary, Alta., September 10, 1960.
(Atlanta's 4th choice, 54th over-all, in 1979 Entry Draft).

			Regular Season					Playoffs				
Season	Club	Lea	GP	G	A	TP	PIM	GP	G	A	TP	PIM
1979-80	Seattle	WHL	72	14	53	67	311	12	1	2	3	41
1980-81	Birmingham	CHL	58	3	5	8	*236	....	....	....	....	....
	Nova Scotia	AHL	17	0	0	0	62	6	0	1	1	45
1981-82	Calgary	NHL	2	0	0	0	9	....	....	....	....	....
	Oklahoma City	CHL	55	4	12	16	222	....	....	....	....	....
1982-83	Colorado	CHL	46	5	12	17	225	....	....	....	....	....
	Calgary	NHL	16	1	0	1	54	9	1	0	1	70
1983-84	Calgary	NHL	43	4	4	8	130	7	0	0	0	21
1984-85	Calgary	NHL	71	11	11	22	259	4	0	0	0	24
1985-86	Calgary	NHL	66	8	7	15	291	19	0	3	3	108
1986-87	Calgary	NHL	73	6	15	21	361	6	0	0	0	51
1987-88	Calgary	NHL	68	8	5	13	337	9	4	0	4	32
1988-89	Calgary	NHL	75	3	9	12	375	19	0	4	4	32
	NHL Totals		414	41	51	92	1816	73	5	7	12	338

HURD, KELLY

Right wing. Shoots right. 5'11", 185 lbs.   Born, Castlegar, B.C., May 13, 1968.
(Detroit's 6th choice, 143rd overall, in 1988 Entry Draft).

			Regular Season					Playoffs				
Season	Club	Lea	GP	G	A	TP	PIM	GP	G	A	TP	PIM
1987-88	Michigan Tech	WCHA	41	18	22	40	34	....	....	....	....	....
1988-89	Michigan Tech	WCHA	42	18	14	32	36	....	....	....	....	....

HURLBUT, MICHAEL

Defense. Shoots left. 6'2", 200 lbs.   Born, Massena, NY, July 10, 1966.
(NY Rangers' 1st choice, 5th overall, in 1988 Supplemental Draft).

			Regular Season					Playoffs				
Season	Club	Lea	GP	G	A	TP	PIM	GP	G	A	TP	PIM
1985-86	St. Lawrence	ECAC	25	2	10	12	40	....	....	....	....	....
1986-87	St. Lawrence	ECAC	35	8	15	23	44	....	....	....	....	....
1987-88	St. Lawrence	ECAC	38	6	12	18	18	....	....	....	....	....
1988-89a	St. Lawrence	ECAC	36	8	25	33	30	....	....	....	....	....
	Denver	IHL	8	0	2	2	13	4	1	2	3	2

a ECAC First All-Star Team (1989)

HUSCROFT, JAMIE

Defense. Shoots left. 6'2", 200 lbs.   Born, Lister, B.C., January 9, 1967.
(New Jersey's 9th choice, 171st overall, in 1985 Entry Draft).

			Regular Season					Playoffs				
Season	Club	Lea	GP	G	A	TP	PIM	GP	G	A	TP	PIM
1983-84	Seattle	WHL	63	0	12	12	77	5	0	0	0	15
1984-85	Seattle	WHL	69	3	13	16	273	....	....	....	....	....
1985-86	Seattle	WHL	66	6	20	26	394	5	0	1	1	18
1986-87	Seattle	WHL	21	1	18	19	99	....	....	....	....	....
	Medicine Hat	WHL	35	4	21	25	170	20	0	3	3	125
1987-88	Utica	AHL	71	5	7	12	316	....	....	....	....	....
	Flint	IHL	3	1	0	1	2	16	0	1	1	110
1988-89	**New Jersey**	NHL	15	0	2	2	51	....	....	....	....	....
	Utica	AHL	41	2	10	12	215	5	0	0	0	40
	NHL Totals		15	0	2	2	51					

HUSGEN, JAMIE

Defense. Shoots right. 6'3", 205 lbs.   Born, St. Louis, MO, October 13, 1964.
(Winnipeg's 13th choice, 239th overall, in 1983 Entry Draft).

			Regular Season					Playoffs				
Season	Club	Lea	GP	G	A	TP	PIM	GP	G	A	TP	PIM
1983-84	Ill.-Chicago	CCHA	35	6	17	23	76	....	....	....	....	....
1984-85	Ill.-Chicago	CCHA	37	3	7	10	44	....	....	....	....	....
1985-86	Ill.-Chicago	CCHA	29	2	5	7	51	....	....	....	....	....
1986-87	Ill.-Chicago	CCHA	31	2	8	10	59	....	....	....	....	....
	Sherbrooke	AHL	2	0	0	0	0	....	....	....	....	....
1987-88	Moncton	AHL	53	7	12	19	54	....	....	....	....	....
1988-89	Moncton	AHL	35	3	7	10	58	....	....	....	....	....
	Milwaukee	IHL	22	2	12	14	42	4	0	1	1	2

Traded to **Vancouver** by **Winnipeg** for future considerations, February 9, 1989.

HUSS, ANDERS

Center. Shoots right. 5'11", 185 lbs.   Born, Garle, Sweden, April 6, 1964.
(Washington's 8th choice, 225th overall, in 1983 Entry Draft).

			Regular Season					Playoffs				
Season	Club	Lea	GP	G	A	TP	PIM	GP	G	A	TP	PIM
1983-84	Brynas	Swe.	35	13	6	19	18	....	....	....	....	....
1984-85	Brynas	Swe.	35	11	8	19	22	....	....	....	....	....
1985-86	Brynas	Swe.	36	20	7	27	36	3	0	0	0	0
1986-87	Brynas	Swe.	33	12	13	25	40	....	....	....	....	....
1987-88	Brynas	Swe.	40	14	12	26	28	....	....	....	....	....
1988-89	Brynas	Swe.	40	22	17	39	26	....	....	....	....	....

HUTTON, DWAINE

Left wing. Shoots left. 5'11", 180 lbs.   Born, Calgary, Alta., April 18, 1965.
(Washington's 7th choice, 140th over-all, in 1983 Entry Draft).

			Regular Season					Playoffs				
Season	Club	Lea	GP	G	A	TP	PIM	GP	G	A	TP	PIM
1982-83	Kelowna	WHL	65	21	47	68	17	....	....	....	....	....
1983-84	Regina	WHL	14	2	2	4	2	....	....	....	....	....
	Saskatoon	WHL	49	15	32	47	18	....	....	....	....	....
1984-85	Kelowna	WHL	45	35	40	75	34	5	3	1	4	2
1985-86	Spokane	WHL	20	10	21	31	35	....	....	....	....	....
	Cdn. Olympic	....	19	3	4	7	24	....	....	....	....	....
1986-87	Flint	IHL	48	13	24	37	71	....	....	....	....	....
	Milwaukee	IHL	5	2	3	5	0	4	3	0	3	0
1987-88	Milwaukee	IHL	31	6	19	25	6	....	....	....	....	....
	Flint	IHL	40	12	27	39	59	14	8	7	15	19
1988-89	Flint	IHL	14	5	5	10	22	....	....	....	....	....
	Indianapolis	IHL	31	8	5	13	85	....	....	....	....	....

HYNES, GORD

Defense. Shoots left. 6'1", 170 lbs.   Born, Montreal, Que., July 22, 1966.
(Boston's 5th choice, 115th overall, in 1985 Entry Draft).

			Regular Season					Playoffs				
Season	Club	Lea	GP	G	A	TP	PIM	GP	G	A	TP	PIM
1983-84	Medicine Hat	WHL	72	5	14	19	39	14	0	0	0	0
1984-85	Medicine Hat	WHL	70	18	45	63	61	10	6	9	15	17
1985-86	Medicine Hat	WHL	58	22	39	61	45	25	8	15	23	32
1986-87	Moncton	AHL	69	2	19	21	21	4	0	0	0	2
1987-88	Maine	AHL	69	5	30	35	65	7	1	3	4	4
1988-89	Cdn. National	....	61	8	38	46	44	....	....	....	....	....

IAFRATE, AL   (IGH uh FRAY tee)

Defense. Shoots left. 6'3", 215 lbs.   Born, Dearborn, Mich., March 21, 1966.
(Toronto's 1st choice, 4th over-all, in 1984 Entry Draft).

			Regular Season					Playoffs				
Season	Club	Lea	GP	G	A	TP	PIM	GP	G	A	TP	PIM
1982-83	Detroit	Midget	66	30	45	75	90	....	....	....	....	....
1983-84	U.S. National	....	55	4	17	21	26	....	....	....	....	....
	U.S. Olympic	....	6	0	0	0	2	....	....	....	....	....
	Belleville	OHL	10	2	4	6	2	3	0	1	1	5
1984-85	Toronto	NHL	68	5	16	21	51	....	....	....	....	....
1985-86	Toronto	NHL	65	8	25	33	40	10	0	3	3	4
1986-87	Toronto	NHL	80	9	21	30	55	13	1	3	4	11
1987-88	Toronto	NHL	77	22	30	52	80	6	3	4	7	6
1988-89	Toronto	NHL	65	13	20	33	72	....	....	....	....	....
	NHL Totals		355	57	112	169	298	29	4	10	14	21

Played in NHL All-Star Game (1988)

IHNACAK, MIROSLAV (IH nuh chehk)

Left wing. Shoots left. 5'11", 175 lbs. Born, Poprad, Czechoslovakia, November 19, 1962.
(Toronto's 12th choice, 171st over-all, in 1982 Entry Draft).

			Regular Season					Playoffs				
Season	Club	Lea	GP	G	A	TP	PIM	GP	G	A	TP	PIM
1984-85	Kocise	Czech.	43	35	31	66	68	....	....	....	....	....
1985-86	Kocise	Czech	21	16	16	32	....	....	....	....	....	....
	Toronto	**NHL**	**21**	**2**	**4**	**6**	**27**	....	....	....	....	....
	St. Catharines	AHL	13	4	4	8	2	13	8	3	11	10
1986-87	**Toronto**	**NHL**	**34**	**6**	**5**	**11**	**12**	**1**	**0**	**0**	**0**	**0**
	Newmarket	AHL	32	11	17	28	6	....	....	....	....	....
1987-88	Newmarket	AHL	51	11	17	28	24	....	....	....	....	....
1988-89	**Detroit**	**NHL**	**1**	**0**	**0**	**0**	**0**	....	....	....	....	....
	Adirondack	AHL	62	34	37	71	32	13	4	3	7	16
	NHL Totals		**56**	**8**	**9**	**17**	**39**	**1**	**0**	**0**	**0**	**0**

IHNACAK, PETER (IH nuh chehk)

Center. Shoots right. 5'11", 180 lbs. Born, Poprad, Czechoslovakia, May 3, 1957.
(Toronto's 3rd choice, 25th over-all, in 1982 Entry Draft).

			Regular Season					Playoffs				
Season	Club	Lea	GP	G	A	TP	PIM	GP	G	A	TP	PIM
1979-80	Sparta Praha	Czech	44	22	12	34	....	....	....	....	....	....
1980-81	Sparta Praha	Czech	44	23	22	45	....	....	....	....	....	....
1981-82	Sparta Praha	Czech	39	16	22	38	30	....	....	....	....	....
1982-83	**Toronto**	**NHL**	**80**	**28**	**38**	**66**	**44**	....	....	....	....	....
1983-84	**Toronto**	**NHL**	**47**	**10**	**13**	**23**	**24**	....	....	....	....	....
1984-85	**Toronto**	**NHL**	**70**	**22**	**22**	**44**	**24**	....	....	....	....	....
1985-86	**Toronto**	**NHL**	**63**	**18**	**27**	**45**	**16**	**10**	**2**	**3**	**5**	**12**
1986-87	Newmarket	AHL	8	2	6	8	0	....	....	....	....	....
	Toronto	**NHL**	**58**	**12**	**27**	**39**	**16**	**13**	**2**	**4**	**6**	**9**
1987-88	**Toronto**	**NHL**	**68**	**10**	**20**	**30**	**41**	**5**	**0**	**3**	**3**	**4**
1988-89	**Toronto**	**NHL**	**26**	**2**	**16**	**18**	**10**	....	....	....	....	....
	Newmarket	AHL	38	14	16	30	8	....	....	....	....	....
	NHL Totals		**412**	**102**	**163**	**165**	**175**	**28**	**4**	**10**	**14**	**25**

ILJINA, TIMO

Center. Shoots left. 5'11", 175 lbs. Born, Oulu, Finland, June 6, 1966.
(Washington's 6th choice, 143rd overall, in 1984 Entry Draft).

			Regular Season					Playoffs				
Season	Club	Lea	GP	G	A	TP	PIM	GP	G	A	TP	PIM
1984-85	Karpat	Fin.	1	0	0	0	0	....	....	....	....	....
1985-86	Karpat	Fin.	29	1	2	3	12	5	0	0	0	0
1986-87	Karpat	Fin.	28	5	4	9	8	3	0	0	0	0
1987-88	Karpat	Fin.	44	17	15	32	14	....	....	....	....	....
1988-89	Karpat	Fin.	43	8	22	30	20	....	....	....	....	....

INGMAN, JAN

Left wing. Shoots left. 6'2", 190 lbs. Born, Grums, Sweden, November 25, 1961.
(Montreal's 3rd choice, 19th overall, in 1981 Entry Draft).

			Regular Season					Playoffs				
Season	Club	Lea	GP	G	A	TP	PIM	GP	G	A	TP	PIM
1980-81	Farjestad	Swe.	30	13	7	20	12	7	5	0	5	13
1981-82	Farjestad	Swe.	27	7	2	9	6	1	0	0	0	0
1982-83	Farjestad	Swe.	30	13	11	24	20	8	5	0	5	8
1983-84	Farjestad	Swe.	36	14	11	25	36	....	....	....	....	....
1984-85	Farjestad	Swe.	35	19	18	37	14	3	0	0	0	2
1985-86	Farjestad	Swe.	33	19	12	31	20	7	4	1	5	4
1986-87	Farjestad	Swe.	28	9	11	20	14	....	....	....	....	....
1987-88	Farjestad	Swe.	28	6	7	13	14	9	5	3	8	2
1988-89	Farjestad	Swe.	32	15	19	34	24	2	1	1	2	6

Rights traded to **Winnipeg** by **Montreal** with Steve Penney for Brian Hayward, August 19, 1986.

ISSEL, KIM (IS-uhl)

Right wing. Shoots right. 6'4", 200 lbs. Born, Regina, Sask., September 25, 1967.
(Edmonton's 1st choice, 21st over-all, in 1986 Entry Draft).

			Regular Season					Playoffs				
Season	Club	Lea	GP	G	A	TP	PIM	GP	G	A	TP	PIM
1985-86	Prince Albert	WHL	68	29	39	68	41	19	6	7	13	6
1986-87	Prince Albert	WHL	70	31	44	75	55	6	1	2	3	17
1987-88	Nova Scotia	AHL	68	2	25	27	31	2	1	0	1	10
	Peoria	IHL	1	0	0	0	0	....	....	....	....	....
1988-89	**Edmonton**	**NHL**	**4**	**0**	**0**	**0**	**0**	....	....	....	....	....
	Cape Breton	AHL	65	34	28	62	4	....	....	....	....	....
	NHL Totals		**4**	**0**	**0**	**0**	**0**	....	....	....	....	....

JABLONSKI, JEFF

Left wing. Shoots left. 6', 185 lbs. Born, Toledo, OH, June 20, 1967.
(NY Islanders' 11th choice, 185th overall, in 1986 Entry Draft).

			Regular Season					Playoffs				
Season	Club	Lea	GP	G	A	TP	PIM	GP	G	A	TP	PIM
1985-86	London	OPJHL	42	28	32	60	47	....	....	....	....	....
1986-87	Lake Superior	CCHA	40	17	10	27	42	....	....	....	....	....
1987-88	Lake Superior	CCHA	46	13	12	25	54	....	....	....	....	....
1988-89	Lake Superior	CCHA	45	11	12	23	48	....	....	....	....	....

JACKSON, DANE

Right wing. Shoots right. 6'1", 190 lbs. Born, Winnipeg, Man., May 17, 1970.
(Vancouver's 3rd choice, 44th overall, in 1988 Entry Draft).

			Regular Season					Playoffs				
Season	Club	Lea	GP	G	A	TP	PIM	GP	G	A	TP	PIM
1987-88	Vernon	BCJHL	50	28	32	60	99	....	....	....	....	....
1988-89	North Dakota	WCHA	30	4	5	9	33	....	....	....	....	....

JACKSON, JAMES KENNETH (JIM)

Left wing. Shoots right. 5'8", 190 lbs. Born, Oshawa, Ont., February 1, 1960.

			Regular Season					Playoffs				
Season	Club	Lea	GP	G	A	TP	PIM	GP	G	A	TP	PIM
1976-77	Oshawa	OHA	65	13	40	53	26	....	....	....	....	....
1977-78	Oshawa	OHA	68	33	47	80	60	6	2	2	4	26
1978-79	Niagara Falls	OHA	62	26	39	65	73	20	6	9	15	16
1979-80	Niagara Falls	OHA	66	29	57	86	55	10	7	8	15	8
1980-81	Richmond	EHL	58	17	43	60	42	10	1	0	1	4
1981-82	Muskegon	IHL	82	24	51	75	72	....	....	....	....	....
1982-83	Colorado	CHL	30	10	16	26	4	....	....	....	....	....
	Calgary	**NHL**	**48**	**8**	**12**	**20**	**7**	**8**	**2**	**1**	**3**	**2**
1983-84	Colorado	CHL	25	5	27	32	4	....	....	....	....	....
	Calgary	**NHL**	**49**	**6**	**14**	**20**	**13**	**6**	**1**	**1**	**2**	**4**
1984-85	**Calgary**	**NHL**	**10**	**1**	**4**	**5**	**0**	....	....	....	....	....
	Moncton	CHL	24	2	5	7	6	....	....	....	....	....
1985-86	Rochester	AHL	65	16	32	48	10	....	....	....	....	....
1986-87	Rochester	AHL	71	19	38	57	48	16	5	4	9	6
1987-88	**Buffalo**	**NHL**	**5**	**2**	**0**	**2**	**0**	....	....	....	....	....
	Rochester	AHL	74	23	48	71	23	7	2	6	8	4
1988-89	Rochester	AHL	73	19	50	69	14	....	....	....	....	....
	NHL Totals		**112**	**17**	**30**	**47**	**20**	**14**	**3**	**2**	**5**	**6**

Signed as free agent by **Calgary**, October 8, 1982. Signed as a free agent by **Buffalo**, September 26, 1985.

JACKSON, JEFF

Left wing. Shoots left. 6'1", 195 lbs. Born, Dresdan, Ont., April 24, 1965.
(Toronto's 2nd choice, 28th over-all, in 1983 Entry Draft).

			Regular Season					Playoffs				
Season	Club	Lea	GP	G	A	TP	PIM	GP	G	A	TP	PIM
1981-82	Newmarket	OPJHL	45	30	39	69	105	....	....	....	....	....
1982-83	Brantford	OHL	64	18	25	43	63	8	1	1	2	27
1983-84	Brantford	OHL	58	27	42	69	78	2	0	1	1	0
1984-85	**Toronto**	**NHL**	**17**	**0**	**1**	**1**	**24**	....	....	....	....	....
	Hamilton	OHL	20	13	14	27	51	17	8	12	20	26
1985-86	**Toronto**	**NHL**	**5**	**1**	**2**	**3**	**2**	....	....	....	....	....
	St. Catharines	AHL	74	17	28	45	122	13	5	2	7	30
1986-87	**Toronto**	**NHL**	**55**	**8**	**7**	**15**	**64**	....	....	....	....	....
	Newmarket	AHL	7	3	6	9	13	....	....	....	....	....
	NY Rangers	**NHL**	**9**	**5**	**1**	**6**	**15**	**6**	**1**	**1**	**2**	**16**
1987-88	**Quebec**	**NHL**	**68**	**9**	**18**	**27**	**103**	....	....	....	....	....
1988-89	**Quebec**	**NHL**	**33**	**4**	**6**	**10**	**28**	....	....	....	....	....
	NHL Totals		**187**	**27**	**35**	**62**	**236**	**6**	**1**	**1**	**2**	**16**

Traded to **NY Rangers** by **Toronto** with Toronto's third-round choice (Rob Zamuner) in 1989 Entry Draft for Mark Osborne, March 5, 1987. Traded to **Quebec** by **NY Rangers** with Terry Carkner for John Ogrodnick and David Shaw, September, 30, 1987.

JANNEY, CRAIG

Center. Shoots left. 6'11", 190 lbs. Born, Hartford, CT, September 26, 1967.
(Boston's 1st choice, 13th over-all, in 1986 Entry Draft).

			Regular Season					Playoffs				
Season	Club	Lea	GP	G	A	TP	PIM	GP	G	A	TP	PIM
1984-85	Deerfield	HS	17	33	35	68	6	....	....	....	....	....
1985-86	Boston College	H.E.	34	13	14	27	8	....	....	....	....	....
1986-87ab	Boston College	H.E.	37	26	55	81	6	....	....	....	....	....
1987-88	**Boston**	**NHL**	**15**	**7**	**9**	**16**	**0**	**23**	**6**	**10**	**16**	**11**
	U.S. National	....	52	26	44	70	6	....	....	....	....	....
	U.S. Olympic	....	5	3	1	4	2	....	....	....	....	....
1988-89	**Boston**	**NHL**	**62**	**16**	**46**	**62**	**12**	**10**	**4**	**9**	**13**	**21**
	NHL Totals		**77**	**23**	**55**	**78**	**12**	**33**	**10**	**19**	**29**	**32**

a Hockey East First All-Star Team (1987)
b NCAA East First All-American Team (1987)

JANOSTIN, PAT

Defense. Shoots right. 6', 170 lbs. Born, Battleford, Sask., November 17, 1966.
(NY Rangers' 4th choice, 70th over-all, in 1985 Entry Draft).

			Regular Season					Playoffs				
Season	Club	Lea	GP	G	A	TP	PIM	GP	G	A	TP	PIM
1985-86	Minn.-Duluth	WCHA	26	1	2	3	4	....	....	....	....	....
1986-87	Minn.-Duluth	WCHA	22	0	1	1	8	....	....	....	....	....
1987-88	Minn.-Duluth	WCHA	41	1	6	7	12	....	....	....	....	....
1988-89	Minn.-Duluth	WCHA	40	1	6	7	36	....	....	....	....	....

JANSSENS, MARK

Center. Shoots left. 6'3", 200 lbs. Born, Surrey, B.C., May 19, 1968.
(NY Rangers' 4th choice, 72nd overall, in 1986 Entry Draft).

			Regular Season					Playoffs				
Season	Club	Lea	GP	G	A	TP	PIM	GP	G	A	TP	PIM
1985-86	Regina	WHL	71	25	38	63	146	9	0	2	2	17
1986-87	Regina	WHL	68	24	38	62	209	3	0	1	1	14
1987-88	**NY Rangers**	**NHL**	**1**	**0**	**0**	**0**	**0**	....	....	....	....	....
	Colorado	IHL	6	2	2	4	24	12	3	2	5	20
	Regina	WHL	71	39	51	90	202	4	3	4	7	6
1988-89	**NY Rangers**	**NHL**	**5**	**0**	**0**	**0**	**0**	....	....	....	....	....
	Denver	IHL	38	19	19	38	104	4	3	0	3	18
	NHL Totals		**6**	**0**	**0**	**0**	**0**	....	....	....	....	....

JARVENPAA, HANNU

Right wing. Shoots left. 6', 193 lbs. Born, Ii, Finland, May 19, 1963.
(Winnipeg's 4th choice, 71st overall, in 1986 Entry Draft).

			Regular Season					Playoffs				
Season	Club	Lea	GP	G	A	TP	PIM	GP	G	A	TP	PIM
1981-82	Karpat	Fin.	14	11	2	13	18	3	1	1	2	4
1982-83	Karpat	Fin.	34	15	8	23	56	....	....	....	....	....
1983-84	Karpat	Fin.	37	15	13	28	46	10	3	3	6	10
	Fin. Olympic	....	4	1	0	1	4	....	....	....	....	....
1984-85	Karpat	Fin.	34	12	12	24	45	7	2	2	4	2
1985-86	Karpat	Fin.	36	26	9	35	48	5	5	2	7	12
1986-87	**Winnipeg**	**NHL**	**20**	**1**	**8**	**9**	**8**	....	....	....	....	....
1987-88	**Winnipeg**	**NHL**	**41**	**6**	**11**	**17**	**34**	....	....	....	....	....
	Moncton	AHL	5	3	1	4	2	....	....	....	....	....
1988-89	**Winnipeg**	**NHL**	**53**	**4**	**7**	**11**	**41**	....	....	....	....	....
	Moncton	AHL	4	1	0	1	0	....	....	....	....	....
	NHL Totals		**114**	**11**	**26**	**37**	**83**	....	....	....	....	....

JARVI, IIRO

Right wing. Shoots right. 6'1", 198 lbs. Born, Helsinki, Finland, March 23, 1965.
(Quebec's 3rd choice, 54th overall, in 1983 Entry Draft).

			Regular Season					Playoffs				
Season	**Club**	**Lea**	**GP**	**G**	**A**	**TP**	**PIM**	**GP**	**G**	**A**	**TP**	**PIM**
1983-84	IFK Helsinki	Fin.	27	0	6	6	6	....	....	....	....	....
1984-85	IFK Helsinki	Fin.	9	0	1	1	2	....	....	....	....	....
	Kiekkoreipas	Fin.	15	2	3	5	10	....	....	....	....	....
1985-86	IFK Helsinki	Fin.	29	7	6	13	19	10	4	6	10	2
1986-87	IFK Helsinki	Fin.	43	23	30	53	82	5	1	5	6	9
1987-88	IFK Helsinki	Fin.	44	21	20	41	68	5	2	1	3	7
1988-89	**Quebec**	**NHL**	**75**	**11**	**30**	**41**	**40**	....	....	....	....	....
	NHL Totals		**75**	**11**	**30**	**41**	**40**	....	....	....	....	....

JARVIS, WESLEY HERBERT (WES)

Center. Shoots left. 5'11", 185 lbs. Born, Toronto, Ont., May 30, 1958.
(Washington's 18th choice, 213th over-all, in 1978 Amateur Draft).

			Regular Season					Playoffs				
Season	**Club**	**Lea**	**GP**	**G**	**A**	**TP**	**PIM**	**GP**	**G**	**A**	**TP**	**PIM**
1976-77	Sudbury	OHA	65	36	60	96	24	6	3	2	5	7
1977-78	Sudbury	OHA	21	7	16	23	16	....	....	....	....	....
	Windsor	OHA	44	27	51	78	37	6	0	2	2	0
1978-79	Port Huron	IHL	73	44	65	109	39	7	4	4	8	2
1979-80	**Washington**	**NHL**	**63**	**11**	**15**	**26**	**8**	....	....	....	....	....
	Hershey	AHL	16	6	14	20	4	....	....	....	....	....
1980-81	**Washington**	**NHL**	**55**	**9**	**14**	**23**	**30**	....	....	....	....	....
	Hershey	AHL	24	15	25	40	39	10	3	13	16	2
1981-82	**Washington**	**NHL**	**26**	**1**	**12**	**13**	**18**	....	....	....	....	....
	Hershey	AHL	56	31	61	92	44	5	3	4	7	4
1982-83	**Minnesota**	**NHL**	**3**	**0**	**0**	**0**	**2**	....	....	....	....	....
	Birmingham	CHL	75	40	*68	*108	36	13	8	8	16	4
1983-84	**Los Angeles**	**NHL**	**61**	**9**	**13**	**22**	**36**	....	....	....	....	....
1984-85	**Toronto**	**NHL**	**26**	**0**	**1**	**1**	**2**	....	....	....	....	....
	St. Catharines	AHL	52	29	44	73	22	....	....	....	....	....
1985-86	**Toronto**	**NHL**	**2**	**1**	**0**	**1**	**2**	....	....	....	....	....
	St. Catharines	AHL	74	36	60	96	38	13	5	8	13	12
1986-87	**Toronto**	**NHL**	....	....	....	....	....	**2**	**0**	**0**	**0**	**2**
	Newmarket	AHL	70	28	50	78	32	....	....	....	....	....
1987-88	**Toronto**	**NHL**	**1**	**0**	**0**	**0**	**0**	....	....	....	....	....
	Newmarket	AHL	79	25	59	84	48	....	....	....	....	....
1988-89	Newmarket	AHL	52	22	31	53	38	5	2	4	6	4
	NHL Totals		**237**	**31**	**55**	**86**	**98**	**2**	**0**	**0**	**0**	**2**

Traded to **Minnesota** by **Washington** with Rollie Boutin for Robbie Moore and Minnesota's eleventh round choice (Anders Huss) in the 1983 Entry Draft, August 4, 1982. Signed as free agent by **Los Angeles**, August 10, 1983. Signed as a free agent by **Toronto**, October 2, 1984.

JENNINGS, GRANT

Defense. Shoots left. 6'4", 220 lbs. Born, Hudson Bay, Sask., May 5, 1965.

			Regular Season					Playoffs				
Season	**Club**	**Lea**	**GP**	**G**	**A**	**TP**	**PIM**	**GP**	**G**	**A**	**TP**	**PIM**
1983-84	Saskatoon	WHL	64	5	13	18	102	....	....	....	....	....
1984-85	Saskatoon	WHL	47	10	24	34	134	2	1	0	1	2
1985-86	Binghamton	AHL	51	0	4	4	109	....	....	....	....	....
1986-87	Fort Wayne	IHL	3	0	0	0	0	....	....	....	....	....
	Binghamton	AHL	47	1	5	6	125	13	0	2	2	17
1987-88	**Washington**	**NHL**	....	....	....	....	....	**1**	**0**	**0**	**0**	**0**
	Binghamton	AHL	56	2	12	14	195	3	1	0	1	15
1988-89	**Hartford**	**NHL**	**55**	**3**	**10**	**13**	**159**	**4**	**1**	**0**	**1**	**17**
	Binghamton	AHL	2	0	0	0	2	....	....	....	....	....
	NHL Totals		**55**	**3**	**10**	**13**	**159**	**5**	**1**	**0**	**1**	**17**

Signed as a free agent by **Washington**, June 25, 1985. Traded to **Hartford** by **Washington** with Ed Kastelic for Mike Millar and Neil Sheehy, July 6, 1988.

JENSEN, CHRIS

Center. Shoots right. 5'10", 170 lbs. Born, Fort St. John, B.C., October 28, 1963.
(NY Rangers' 4th choice, 78th over-all, in 1982 Entry Draft).

			Regular Season					Playoffs				
Season	**Club**	**Lea**	**GP**	**G**	**A**	**TP**	**PIM**	**GP**	**G**	**A**	**TP**	**PIM**
1981-82	Kelowna	BCJHL	48	46	46	92	212	....	....	....	....	....
1982-83	North Dakota	WCHA	13	3	3	6	28	....	....	....	....	....
1983-84	North Dakota	WCHA	44	24	25	49	100	....	....	....	....	....
1984-85	North Dakota	WCHA	40	25	27	52	80	....	....	....	....	....
1985-86	North Dakota	WCHA	34	25	40	65	53	....	....	....	....	....
	NY Rangers	**NHL**	**9**	**1**	**3**	**4**	**0**	....	....	....	....	....
1986-87	**NY Rangers**	**NHL**	**37**	**6**	**7**	**13**	**21**	....	....	....	....	....
	New Haven	AHL	14	4	9	13	41	....	....	....	....	....
1987-88	**NY Rangers**	**NHL**	**7**	**0**	**1**	**1**	**2**	....	....	....	....	....
	Colorado	IHL	43	10	23	33	68	10	3	7	10	8
1988-89	Hershey	AHL	45	27	31	58	66	10	4	5	9	29
	NHL Totals		**53**	**7**	**11**	**18**	**23**	....	....	....	....	....

Traded to **Philadelphia** by **NY Rangers** for Michael Boyce, September 28, 1988.

JENSEN, CHRISTOPHER (CHRIS)

Defense. Shoots right. 6'2", 190 lbs. Born, Wilmette, IL, June 29, 1968.
(Toronto's 8th choice, 154th overall, in 1987 Entry Draft).

			Regular Season					Playoffs				
Season	**Club**	**Lea**	**GP**	**G**	**A**	**TP**	**PIM**	**GP**	**G**	**A**	**TP**	**PIM**
1986-87	Northwood	HS	29	6	15	21	....	....	....	....	....	....
1987-88	U. Wisconsin	WCHA	7	0	0	0	0	....	....	....	....	....
1988-89	U. Wisconsin	WCHA	2	1	0	1	0	....	....	....	....	....

JENSEN, DAVID A.

Center. Shoots left. 6'1", 195 lbs. Born, Newton, MA, August 19, 1965.
(Hartford's 2nd choice, 20th over-all, in 1983 Entry Draft).

			Regular Season					Playoffs				
Season	**Club**	**Lea**	**GP**	**G**	**A**	**TP**	**PIM**	**GP**	**G**	**A**	**TP**	**PIM**
1982-83	Lawrence Prep.	HS	23	41	48	89	....	....	....	....	....	....
1983-84	U.S. National	....	61	22	56	78	6	....	....	....	....	....
	U.S. Olympic	....	6	2	7	9	0	....	....	....	....	....
1984-85	**Hartford**	**NHL**	**13**	**0**	**4**	**4**	**6**	....	....	....	....	....
	Binghamton	AHL	40	8	9	17	2	....	....	....	....	....
1985-86	**Washington**	**NHL**	**5**	**1**	**0**	**1**	**0**	**4**	**0**	**0**	**0**	**0**
	Binghamton	AHL	41	17	14	31	4	4	2	4	6	0
1986-87	**Washington**	**NHL**	**46**	**8**	**8**	**16**	**12**	**7**	**0**	**0**	**0**	**2**
	Binghamton	AHL	6	2	5	7	0	....	....	....	....	....
1987-88	**Washington**	**NHL**	**5**	**0**	**1**	**1**	**4**	....	....	....	....	....
	Binghamton	AHL	9	5	2	7	2	....	....	....	....	....
	Fort Wayne	IHL	32	10	13	23	8	5	1	1	2	0
1988-89	Maine	AHL	18	12	8	20	2	....	....	....	....	....
	NHL Totals		**69**	**9**	**13**	**22**	**22**	**11**	**0**	**0**	**0**	**2**

Traded to **Washington** by **Hartford** for Dean Evason and Peter Sidorkiewicz, March 12, 1985.

JERRARD, PAUL

Defense. Shoots right. 6'1", 185 lbs. Born, Winnipeg, Man., April 30, 1965.
(NY Rangers' 10th choice, 173rd over-all, in 1983 Entry Draft).

			Regular Season					Playoffs				
Season	**Club**	**Lea**	**GP**	**G**	**A**	**TP**	**PIM**	**GP**	**G**	**A**	**TP**	**PIM**
1983-84	Lake Superior	CCHA	40	8	18	26	48	....	....	....	....	....
1984-85	Lake Superior	CCHA	43	9	25	34	61	....	....	....	....	....
1985-86	Lake Superior	CCHA	38	13	11	24	34	....	....	....	....	....
1986-87	Lake Superior	CCHA	35	10	19	29	56	....	....	....	....	....
1987-88	Colorado	IHL	77	20	28	48	182	11	2	4	6	40
1988-89	**Minnesota**	**NHL**	**5**	**0**	**0**	**0**	**4**	....	....	....	....	....
	Denver	IHL	2	1	1	2	21	....	....	....	....	....
	Kalamazoo	IHL	68	15	25	40	195	6	2	1	3	37
	NHL Totals		**5**	**0**	**0**	**0**	**4**	....	....	....	....	....

Traded to **Minnesota** by **N.Y. Rangers** with Mark Tinordi, the rights to Bret Barnett and Mike Sullivan, and Los Angeles' third-round choice (Murray Garbutt) in 1989 Entry Draft – acquired March 10, 1987 by Minnesota – for Brian Lawton, Igor Liba and the rights to Eric Bennett, October 11, 1988.

JOBE, TREVOR

Left wing. Shoots left. 6'1", 190 lbs. Born, Lethbridge, Alta., May 14, 1967.
(Toronto's 7th choice, 133rd overall, in 1987 Entry Draft).

			Regular Season					Playoffs				
Season	**Club**	**Lea**	**GP**	**G**	**A**	**TP**	**PIM**	**GP**	**G**	**A**	**TP**	**PIM**
1984-85	Calgary	WHL	66	5	19	24	23	8	0	0	0	0
1985-86	Calgary	WHL	7	0	2	2	2	....	....	....	....	....
	Lethbridge	WHL	5	1	0	1	0	....	....	....	....	....
	Spokane	WHL	11	1	4	5	0	....	....	....	....	....
1986-87	Moose Jaw	WHL	58	54	33	87	53	9	4	2	6	4
1987-88	Prince Albert	WHL	72	69	63	132	111	9	6	6	12	41
1988-89	Newmarket	AHL	75	23	24	47	90	5	0	1	1	12

JOHANNESEN, GLENN

Left wing. Shoots right. 6'2", 220 lbs. Born, Lac Laronge, Sask., February 15, 1962.
(NY Islanders' 11th choice, 206th over-all, in 1980 Entry Draft).

			Regular Season					Playoffs				
Season	**Club**	**Lea**	**GP**	**G**	**A**	**TP**	**PIM**	**GP**	**G**	**A**	**TP**	**PIM**
1984-85	Indianapolis	IHL	51	10	19	29	130	....	....	....	....	....
	Springfield	AHL	21	1	3	4	59	....	....	....	....	....
1985-86	Springfield	AHL	78	8	21	29	187	....	....	....	....	....
	NY Islanders	**NHL**	**2**	**0**	**0**	**0**	**0**	....	....	....	....	....
1986-87	Springfield	AHL	54	10	6	16	156	....	....	....	....	....
1987-88	Springfield	AHL	1	0	0	0	0	....	....	....	....	....
	Peoria	IHL	73	24	29	53	172	7	4	3	7	32
1988-89	Springfield	AHL	5	1	1	2	20	....	....	....	....	....
	Indianapolis	IHL	76	18	23	41	235	....	....	....	....	....
	NHL Totals		**2**	**0**	**0**	**0**	**0**	....	....	....	....	....

JOHANSSON, CALLE (yoh-HAN-son)

Defense. Shoots left. 5'11", 200 lbs. Born, Goteborg, Sweden, February 14, 1967.
(Buffalo's 1st choice, 14th overall, in 1985 Entry Draft).

			Regular Season					Playoffs				
Season	**Club**	**Lea**	**GP**	**G**	**A**	**TP**	**PIM**	**GP**	**G**	**A**	**TP**	**PIM**
1983-84	V. Frolunda	Swe.	28	4	4	8	10	....	....	....	....	....
1984-85	V. Frolunda	Swe. 2	25	8	13	21	16	6	1	2	3	4
1985-86	Bjorkloven	Swe.	17	1	2	3	4	....	....	....	....	....
1986-87	Bjorkloven	Swe.	30	2	13	15	20	6	1	3	4	6
1987-88a	**Buffalo**	**NHL**	**71**	**4**	**38**	**42**	**37**	**6**	**0**	**1**	**1**	**0**
1988-89	**Buffalo**	**NHL**	**47**	**2**	**11**	**13**	**33**	....	....	....	....	....
	Washington	**NHL**	**12**	**1**	**7**	**8**	**4**	**6**	**1**	**2**	**3**	**0**
	NHL Totals		**130**	**7**	**56**	**63**	**74**	**12**	**1**	**3**	**4**	**0**

a Named to NHL All-Rookie Team (1988)

Traded to **Washington** by **Buffalo** with Buffalo's second-round choice (Byron Dafoe) in 1989 Entry Draft for Clint Malarchuk, Grant Ledyard and Washington's sixth-round choice in 1991 Entry Draft, March 7, 1989.

JOHANSSON, JAMES (JIM)

Center. Shoots left. 6'2", 200 lbs. Born, Rochester, MN, March 10, 1964.

			Regular Season					Playoffs				
Season	**Club**	**Lea**	**GP**	**G**	**A**	**TP**	**PIM**	**GP**	**G**	**A**	**TP**	**PIM**
1986-87	Landsberg	W.Ger.	57	46	56	102	90	....	....	....	....	....
1987-88	U.S. National	....	47	16	14	30	64	....	....	....	....	....
	U.S. Olympic	....	4	0	1	1	4	....	....	....	....	....
	Salt Lake	IHL	18	14	7	21	50	19	8	15	23	55
1988-89	Salt Lake	IHL	82	35	40	75	87	13	2	5	7	13

Signed as a free agent by **Calgary**, February 25, 1988.

JOHANSSON, ROGER

Defense. Shoots left. 6'1", 180 lbs. Born, Ljungby, Sweden, April 17, 1967.
(Calgary's 5th choice, 80th overall, in 1985 Entry Draft).

			Regular Season					Playoffs				
Season	Club	Lea	GP	G	A	TP	PIM	GP	G	A	TP	PIM
1983-84	Troja	Swe. 2	11	2	2	4	12	....	....	....	....	....
1984-85	Troja	Swe. 2	30	1	6	7	20	9	0	4	4	8
1985-86	Troja	Swe. 2	32	5	16	21	42	....	....	....	....	....
1986-87	Farjestad	Swe.	31	6	11	17	20	7	1	1	2	8
1987-88	Farjestad	Swe.	24	3	11	14	20	....	....	....	....	....
1988-89	Farjestad	Swe.	40	5	15	20	36	....	....	....	....	....

JOHNSON, CHAD

Center. Shoots left. 6', 175 lbs. Born, Grand Forks, ND, January 10, 1970.
(New Jersey's 7th choice, 117th overall, in 1988 Entry Draft).

			Regular Season					Playoffs				
Season	Club	Lea	GP	G	A	TP	PIM	GP	G	A	TP	PIM
1987-88	Rochester	USHL	36	15	26	41	43	....	....	....	....	....
1988-89	Rochester	USHL	34	14	24	38	59	4	1	2	3	2

JOHNSON, GREG

Center. Shoots left. 5'10", 170 lbs. Born, Thunder Bay, Ont., March 16, 1971.
(Philadelphia's 1st choice, 33rd overall, in 1989 Entry Draft).

			Regular Season					Playoffs				
Season	Club	Lea	GP	G	A	TP	PIM	GP	G	A	TP	PIM
1988-89abc	Thunder Bay	USHL	47	32	64	96	4	12	5	13	18	....

a Canadian Junior A Player of the Year (1989)
b USHL First All-Star Team (1989)
c Centennial Cup First All-Star Team (1989)

JOHNSON, JIM

Defense. Shoots left. 6', 190 lbs. Born, New Hope, MI, August 9, 1962.

			Regular Season					Playoffs				
Season	Club	Lea	GP	G	A	TP	PIM	GP	G	A	TP	PIM
1981-82	Minn.-Duluth	WCHA	40	0	10	10	62	....	....	....	....	....
1982-83	Minn.-Duluth	WCHA	44	3	18	21	118	....	....	....	....	....
1983-84	Minn.-Duluth	WCHA	43	3	13	16	116	....	....	....	....	....
1984-85	Minn.-Duluth	WCHA	47	7	29	36	49	....	....	....	....	....
1985-86	**Pittsburgh**	**NHL**	**80**	**3**	**26**	**29**	**115**	....	....	....	....	....
1986-87	**Pittsburgh**	**NHL**	**80**	**5**	**25**	**30**	**116**	....	....	....	....	....
1987-88	**Pittsburgh**	**NHL**	**55**	**1**	**12**	**13**	**87**	....	....	....	....	....
1988-89	**Pittsburgh**	**NHL**	**76**	**2**	**14**	**16**	**163**	**11**	**0**	**5**	**5**	**44**
	NHL Totals		**291**	**11**	**77**	**88**	**481**	**11**	**0**	**5**	**5**	**44**

Signed as a free agent by **Pittsburgh**, June, 1985.

JOHNSON, MARK

Left wing. Shoots left. 5'9", 170 lbs. Born, Madison, WI, September 22, 1957.
(Pittsburgh's 3rd choice, 66th over-all, in 1977 Amateur Draft).

			Regular Season					Playoffs				
Season	Club	Lea	GP	G	A	TP	PIM	GP	G	A	TP	PIM
1977-78a	U. Wisconsin	WCHA	42	*48	38	86	24	....	....	....	....	....
1978-79ab	U. Wisconsin	WCHA	40	*41	49	*90	34	....	....	....	....	....
1979-80	U.S. National	...	53	33	48	81	25	....	....	....	....	....
	U.S. Olympic	...	7	5	6	11	6	....	....	....	....	....
	Pittsburgh	**NHL**	**17**	**3**	**5**	**8**	**4**	**5**	**2**	**2**	**4**	**0**
1980-81	**Pittsburgh**	**NHL**	**73**	**10**	**23**	**33**	**50**	**5**	**2**	**1**	**3**	**6**
1981-82	**Pittsburgh**	**NHL**	**46**	**10**	**11**	**21**	**30**	....	....	....	....	....
	Minnesota	**NHL**	**10**	**2**	**2**	**4**	**10**	**4**	**2**	**0**	**2**	**0**
1982-83	**Hartford**	**NHL**	**73**	**31**	**38**	**69**	**28**	....	....	....	....	....
1983-84	**Hartford**	**NHL**	**79**	**35**	**52**	**87**	**27**	....	....	....	....	....
1984-85	**Hartford**	**NHL**	**49**	**19**	**28**	**47**	**21**	....	....	....	....	....
	St. Louis	**NHL**	**17**	**4**	**6**	**10**	**2**	**3**	**0**	**1**	**1**	**0**
1985-86	**New Jersey**	**NHL**	**80**	**21**	**41**	**62**	**16**	....	....	....	....	....
1986-87	**New Jersey**	**NHL**	**68**	**25**	**26**	**51**	**22**	....	....	....	....	....
1987-88	**New Jersey**	**NHL**	**54**	**14**	**19**	**33**	**14**	**18**	**10**	**8**	**18**	**4**
1988-89	**New Jersey**	**NHL**	**40**	**13**	**25**	**38**	**24**	....	....	....	....	....
	NHL Totals		**606**	**187**	**276**	**463**	**248**	**35**	**16**	**12**	**28**	**10**

a WCHA First All-Star Team (1978, 1979)
b WCHA Player of the Year (1979)

Played in NHL All-Star Game (1984)

Traded to **Minnesota** by **Pittsburgh** for Minnesota's second round choice (Tim Hrynewich) in 1982 Entry Draft, March 2, 1982. Traded to **Hartford** by **Minnesota** with Kent-Erik Andersson for Jordy Douglas and Hartford's fifth round choice (Jiri Poner) in the 1984 Entry Draft, October 1, 1982. Traded to **St. Louis** by **Hartford** with Greg Millen for Mike Liut and Jorgen Pettersson, February 21, 1985. Traded to **New Jersey** by **St. Louis** for Shawn Evans and New Jersey's fifth-round choice (Michael Wolak) in 1986 Entry Draft, September 19, 1985.

JOHNSON, ROSS

Center. Shoots right. 5'11", 180 lbs. Born, Green Bay, WI, August 5, 1967.
(Minnesota's 6th choice, 153rd overall, in 1985 Entry Draft).

			Regular Season					Playoffs				
Season	Club	Lea	GP	G	A	TP	PIM	GP	G	A	TP	PIM
1988-89	North Dakota	WCHA	19	5	7	12	6	....	....	....	....	....

JOHNSON, SCOTT

Left wing. Shoots left. 5'11", 185 lbs. Born, New Hope, MI, October 12, 1963.
Last amateur club: Lake Superior State Lakers (CCHA).

			Regular Season					Playoffs				
Season	Club	Lea	GP	G	A	TP	PIM	GP	G	A	TP	PIM
1982-83	Lake Superior	CCHA	32	2	7	9	9	....	....	....	....	....
1983-84	Lake Superior	CCHA	39	9	13	22	32	....	....	....	....	....
1984-85	Lake Superior	CCHA	44	21	23	44	70	....	....	....	....	....
1985-86	Lake Superior	CCHA	38	21	24	45	55	....	....	....	....	....
1986-87	Baltimore	AHL	63	8	7	15	27	....	....	....	....	....
1987-88	Saginaw	IHL	1	0	0	0	2	....	....	....	....	....
	Muskegon	IHL	51	19	11	30	31	2	0	1	1	33
1988-89	Indianapolis	IHL	2	0	0	0	2	....	....	....	....	....

Signed as a free agent by **Pittsburgh**, July 3, 1986.

JOHNSON, STEVE

Right wing. Shoots right. 6', 190 lbs. Born, Grand Forks, ND, March 3, 1966.
(Vancouver's 1st choice, 3rd overall, in 1987 Supplemental Draft).

			Regular Season					Playoffs				
Season	Club	Lea	GP	G	A	TP	PIM	GP	G	A	TP	PIM
1984-85	North Dakota	WCHA	41	18	16	34	10	....	....	....	....	....
1985-86	North Dakota	WCHA	38	31	28	59	40	....	....	....	....	....
1986-87	North Dakota	WCHA	48	26	44	70	38	....	....	....	....	....
1987-88ab	North Dakota	WCHA	42	34	*51	*85	28	....	....	....	....	....
1988-89	Milwaukee	IHL	64	18	34	52	37	2	0	0	0	0

a WCHA First All-Star Team (1988)
b NCAA West First All-American Team (1988)

JOHNSTON, GREG

Right wing. Shoots right. 6'1", 190 lbs. Born, Barrie, Ont., January 14, 1965.
(Boston's 2nd choice, 42nd over-all, in 1983 Entry Draft).

			Regular Season					Playoffs				
Season	Club	Lea	GP	G	A	TP	PIM	GP	G	A	TP	PIM
1981-82	Barrie	Midget	42	31	46	77	74	....	....	....	....	....
1982-83	Toronto	OHL	58	18	19	37	58	4	1	0	1	4
1983-84	**Boston**	**NHL**	**15**	**2**	**1**	**3**	**2**	....	....	....	....	....
	Toronto	OHL	57	38	35	73	67	9	4	2	6	13
1984-85	**Boston**	**NHL**	**6**	**0**	**0**	**0**	**0**	....	....	....	....	....
	Hershey	AHL	3	1	0	1	0	....	....	....	....	....
	Toronto	OHL	42	22	28	50	55	5	1	3	4	4
1985-86	**Boston**	**NHL**	**20**	**0**	**2**	**2**	**0**	....	....	....	....	....
	Moncton	AHL	60	19	26	45	56	10	4	6	10	4
1986-87	**Boston**	**NHL**	**76**	**12**	**15**	**27**	**79**	**4**	**0**	**0**	**0**	**0**
1987-88	**Boston**	**NHL**	....	....	....	....	....	**3**	**0**	**1**	**1**	**2**
	Maine	AHL	75	21	32	53	106	10	6	4	10	23
1988-89	**Boston**	**NHL**	**57**	**11**	**10**	**21**	**32**	**10**	**1**	**0**	**1**	**6**
	Maine	AHL	15	5	7	12	31	....	....	....	....	....
	NHL Totals		**174**	**25**	**28**	**53**	**113**	**17**	**1**	**1**	**2**	**8**

JONES, BRAD

Center. Shoots left. 6', 195 lbs. Born, Sterling Heights, MI, June 26, 1965.
(Winnipeg's 7th choice, 156th over-all, in 1984 Entry Draft).

			Regular Season					Playoffs				
Season	Club	Lea	GP	G	A	TP	PIM	GP	G	A	TP	PIM
1983-84	U. of Michigan	CCHA	37	8	26	34	32	....	....	....	....	....
1984-85	U. of Michigan	CCHA	34	21	27	48	66	....	....	....	....	....
1985-86a	U. of Michigan	CCHA	36	28	39	67	40	....	....	....	....	....
1986-87bc	U. of Michigan	CCHA	40	32	46	78	64	....	....	....	....	....
	Winnipeg	**NHL**	**4**	**1**	**0**	**1**	**0**	....	....	....	....	....
1987-88	**Winnipeg**	**NHL**	**19**	**2**	**5**	**7**	**15**	**1**	**0**	**0**	**0**	**0**
	U.S. National	....	50	27	23	50	59	....	....	....	....	....
1988-89	**Winnipeg**	**NHL**	**22**	**6**	**5**	**11**	**6**	....	....	....	....	....
	Moncton	AHL	44	20	19	39	62	7	0	1	1	22
	NHL Totals		**45**	**9**	**10**	**19**	**21**	**1**	**0**	**0**	**0**	**0**

a CCHA Second All-Star Team (1986)
b CCHA First All-Star Team (1987)
c NCAA West Second All-American Team (1987)

JONES, CASEY

Center. Shoots left. 5'11", 170 lbs. Born, Temiscaming, Que., May 30, 1968.
(Boston's 10th choice, 230th overall, in 1987 Entry Draft).

			Regular Season					Playoffs				
Season	Club	Lea	GP	G	A	TP	PIM	GP	G	A	TP	PIM
1986-87	Cornell	ECAC	27	6	12	18	38	....	....	....	....	....
1987-88	Cornell	ECAC	27	10	22	32	26	....	....	....	....	
1988-89	Cornell	ECAC	29	8	27	35	22	....	....	....	....	....

JONES, KEITH

Right wing. Shoots right. 6'2", 190 lbs. Born, Brantford, Ont., November 8, 1968.
(Washington's 7th choice, 141st overall, in 1988 Entry Draft).

			Regular Season					Playoffs				
Season	Club	Lea	GP	G	A	TP	PIM	GP	G	A	TP	PIM
1987-88	Niagara Falls	OPJHL	40	50	80	130	....	....	....	....	....	....
1988-89	W. Michigan	CCHA	37	9	12	21	51	....	....	....	....	....

JONSSON, STEFAN

Defense. Shoots left. 6'2", 190 lbs. Born, Sodertalje, Sweden, June 13, 1965.
(Calgary's 11th choice, 221st overall, in 1984 Entry Draft).

			Regular Season					Playoffs				
Season	Club	Lea	GP	G	A	TP	PIM	GP	G	A	TP	PIM
1983-84	Sodertalje	Swe.	11	1	0	1	6	....	....	....	....	....
1984-85	Sodertalje	Swe.	33	3	4	7	24	7	2	3	5	2
1985-86	Sodertalje	Swe.	33	1	1	5	16	7	0	0	0	4
1986-87	Sodertalje	Swe.	35	2	1	3	16	....	....	....	....	....
1987-88	Sodertalje	Swe.	36	4	6	10	24	2	0	0	0	8
1988-89	Sodertalje	Swe.	37	4	2	6	44	....	....	....	....	....

JONSSON, TOMAS (YAHN-suhn)

Defense. Shoots left. 5'10", 185 lbs. Born, Falun, Sweden, April 12, 1960.
(NY Islanders' 2nd choice, 25th over-all, in 1979 Entry Draft).

			Regular Season					Playoffs				
Season	Club	Lea	GP	G	A	TP	PIM	GP	G	A	TP	PIM
1977-78	MoDo AIK	Swe.	35	8	9	17	45	2	0	0	0	4
	Swe. National	....	4	0	0	0	0	....	....	....	....	....
1978-79	MoDo AIK	Swe.	34	11	10	21	77	5	1	2	3	13
	Swe. National	....	15	2	3	5	16	....	....	....	....	....
1979-80	MoDo AIK	Swe.	36	3	12	15	42	....	....	....	....	....
	Swe. National	....	18	2	4	6	24	....	....	....	....	....
1980-81	MoDo AIK	Swe.	35	8	12	20	58	....	....	....	....	....
	Swe. National		19	0	2	2	2	....	....	....	....	....
1981-82	NY Islanders	NHL	70	9	25	34	51	10	0	2	2	21
1982-83	NY Islanders	NHL	72	13	35	48	50	20	2	10	12	18
1983-84	NY Islanders	NHL	72	11	36	47	54	21	3	5	8	22
1984-85	NY Islanders	NHL	69	16	34	50	58	7	1	2	3	10
1985-86	NY Islanders	NHL	77	14	30	44	62	3	0	1	1	4
1986-87	NY Islanders	NHL	47	6	25	31	36	10	1	4	5	6
1987-88	NY Islanders	NHL	72	6	41	47	115	5	2	2	4	10
1988-89	NY Islanders	NHL	53	9	23	32	34	....	....	....	....	....
	Edmonton	NHL	20	1	10	11	22	4	2	0	2	6
	NHL Totals		552	85	259	344	482	80	11	26	37	97

Traded to **Edmonton** by **NY Islanders** for future considerations, February 15, 1989.

JOSEPH, ANTHONY

Right wing. Shoots right. 6'4", 220 lbs. Born, Cornwall, Ont., March 1, 1969.
(Winnipeg's 5th choice, 94th overall, in 1988 Entry Draft).

			Regular Season					Playoffs				
Season	Club	Lea	GP	G	A	TP	PIM	GP	G	A	TP	PIM
1987-88	Oshawa	OHL	49	9	18	27	126	7	0	0	0	9
1988-89	Winnipeg	NHL	2	1	0	1	0	....	....	....	....	....
	Oshawa	OHL	52	20	16	36	105	6	4	2	6	22
	NHL Totals		2	1	0	1	0	....	....	....	....	....

JOSEPH, CHRIS

Defense. Shoots right. 6'2", 210 lbs. Born, Burnaby, B.C., September 10, 1969.
(Pittsburgh's 1st choice, 5th overall, in 1987 Entry Draft).

			Regular Season					Playoffs				
Season	Club	Lea	GP	G	A	TP	PIM	GP	G	A	TP	PIM
1985-86	Seattle	WHL	72	4	8	12	50	5	0	3	3	12
1986-87	Seattle	WHL	67	13	45	58	155	....	....	....	....	....
1987-88	Seattle	WHL	23	5	14	19	49	....	....	....	....	....
	Pittsburgh	NHL	17	0	4	4	12	....	....	....	....	....
	Edmonton	NHL	7	0	4	4	6	....	....	....	....	....
	Nova Scotia	AHL	8	0	2	2	8	4	0	0	0	9
1988-89	Edmonton	NHL	44	4	5	9	54	....	....	....	....	....
	Cape Breton	AHL	5	1	1	2	18	....	....	....	....	....
	NHL Totals		68	4	13	17	72	....	....	....	....	....

Traded to **Edmonton** by **Pittsburgh** with Craig Simpson, Dave Hannan and Moe Mantha for Paul Coffey, Dave Hunter, and Wayne Van Dorp, November 24, 1987.

JOSEPH, FABIAN

Center. Shoots left. 5'8", 165 lbs. Born, Sydney, N.S., December 5, 1965.
(Toronto's 5th choice, 109th over-all, in 1984 Entry Draft).

			Regular Season					Playoffs				
Season	Club	Lea	GP	G	A	TP	PIM	GP	G	A	TP	PIM
1982-83	Victoria	WHL	69	42	48	90	50	12	4	7	11	9
1983-84	Victoria	WHL	72	52	75	127	27	....	....	....	....	....
1984-85	Toronto	OHL	60	32	43	75	16	5	2	4	6	14
1985-86	Cdn. Olympic	....	71	26	18	44	51	....	....	....	....	....
1986-87	Cdn. Olympic	....	74	15	30	45	26	....	....	....	....	....
1987-88	Nova Scotia	AHL	77	31	39	70	20	5	0	3	3	8
1988-89	Cape Breton	AHL	70	32	34	66	30	....	....	....	....	....

JOYCE, ROBERT THOMAS (BOB)

Left wing. Shoots left. 6'1", 195 lbs. Born, St. John, N.B., July 11, 1966.
(Boston's 4th choice, 82nd over-all, in 1984 Entry Draft).

			Regular Season					Playoffs				
Season	Club	Lea	GP	G	A	TP	PIM	GP	G	A	TP	PIM
1984-85	North Dakota	WCHA	41	18	16	34	10	....	....	....	....	....
1985-86	North Dakota	WCHA	38	31	28	59	40	....	....	....	....	....
1986-87abc	North Dakota	WCHA	48	52	37	89	42	....	....	....	....	....
1987-88	Boston	NHL	15	7	5	12	10	23	8	6	14	18
	Cdn. National	....	46	12	10	22	28	....	....	....	....	....
	Cdn. Olympic	....	4	1	0	1	0	....	....	....	....	....
1988-89	Boston	NHL	77	18	31	49	46	9	5	2	7	2
	NHL Totals		92	25	36	61	56	32	13	8	21	20

a WCHA First All-Star Team (1987)
b NCAA West First All-American Team (1987)
c Named to NCAA All-Tournament Team (1987)

JUHLIN, PATRIK

Left wing. Shoots left. 6'0", 185 lbs. Born, Huddinge, Sweden, April 24, 1970.
(Philadelphia's 2nd choice, 34th overall, in 1989 Entry Draft).

			Regular Season					Playoffs				
Season	Club	Lea	GP	G	A	TP	PIM	GP	G	A	TP	PIM
1987-88	Vasteras	Swe.	28	25	10	35	....	....	....	....	....	....
1988-89	Vasteras	Swe.	30	29	13	42	....	....	....	....	....	....

JULIEN, CLAUDE

Defense. Shoots right. 6', 195 lbs. Born, Blind River, Ont., April 23, 1960.

			Regular Season					Playoffs				
Season	Club	Lea	GP	G	A	TP	PIM	GP	G	A	TP	PIM
1979-80	Windsor	OHA	68	14	37	51	148	16	5	11	16	23
1980-81	Windsor	OHA	3	1	1	2	21	....	....	....	....	....
	Port Huron	IHL	77	15	40	55	153	4	1	1	2	4
1981-82	Salt Lake	CHL	70	4	18	22	134	5	1	4	5	0
1982-83	Salt Lake	CHL	76	14	47	61	176	6	3	3	6	16
1983-84	Milwaukee	IHL	5	0	3	3	2	....	....	....	....	....
	Fredericton	AHL	57	7	22	29	58	7	0	4	4	6
1984-85	Quebec	NHL	1	0	0	0	0	....	....	....	....	....
	Fredericton	AHL	77	6	28	34	97	6	2	4	6	13
1985-86	Quebec	NHL	13	0	1	1	25	....	....	....	....	....
	Fredericton	AHL	49	3	18	21	74	6	1	4	5	19
1986-87	Fredericton	AHL	17	1	6	7	22	....	....	....	....	....
	France	....	36	15	50	65	....	....	....	....	....	....
1987-88	Baltimore	AHL	30	6	14	20	22	....	....	....	....	....
	Fredericton	AHL	35	1	14	15	52	13	1	3	4	30
1988-89a	Halifax	AHL	79	8	52	60	72	4	0	2	2	4
	NHL Totals		14	0	1	1	25	....	....	....	....	....

a AHL Second All-Star Team (1989)

Signed as free agent by **St. Louis**, September 28, 1981. Rights transfered to **Quebec** by **St. Louis** with rights to Gord Donnelly when St. Louis signed Jacques Demers as coach, August 19, 1983.

JUNEAU, JOSEPH

Defense. Shoots right. 6'0", 175 lbs. Born, Pont-Rouge, Que., January 5, 1968.
(Boston's 3rd choice, 81st overall, in 1988 Entry Draft).

			Regular Season					Playoffs				
Season	Club	Lea	GP	G	A	TP	PIM	GP	G	A	TP	PIM
1986-87	Levis-Lauzon	Midget	38	27	57	84	....	....	....	....	....	....
1987-88	RPI	ECAC	31	16	29	45	18	....	....	....	....	....
1988-89	RPI	ECAC	30	12	23	35	40	....	....	....	....	....

KACHOWSKI, MARK EDWARD

Left wing. Shoots left. 5'10", 195 lbs. Born, Edmonton, Alta., February 20, 1965.

			Regular Season					Playoffs				
Season	Club	Lea	GP	G	A	TP	PIM	GP	G	A	TP	PIM
1987-88	Pittsburgh	NHL	38	5	3	8	126	....	....	....	....	....
	Muskegon	IHL	25	3	6	9	72	5	0	2	2	11
1988-89	Pittsburgh	NHL	12	1	1	2	43	....	....	....	....	....
	Muskegon	IHL	57	8	8	16	167	8	1	2	3	17
	NHL Totals		50	6	4	10	169	....	....	....	....	....

Signed as a free agent by **Pittsburgh**, August 31, 1987.

KADLEC, ARNOLD

Defense. Shoots left. 6'1", 200 lbs. Born, Most, Czechoslovakia, January 8, 1959.
(Minnesota's 10th choice, 206th overall, in 1982 Entry Draft).

			Regular Season					Playoffs				
Season	Club	Lea	GP	G	A	TP	PIM	GP	G	A	TP	PIM
1986-87	CHZ Litvinov	Czech.	32	9	16	25	....	....	....	....	....	....
1987-88	CHZ Litvinov	Czech.	29	0	13	13	....	....	....	....	....	....
1988-89	CHZ Litvinov	Czech.	34	11	11	22	....	....	....	....	....	....

KADLEC, DRAHOMIR

Defense. Shoots left. 5'11", 200 lbs. Born, Pribram, Czechoslovakia, November 29, 1965.
(Philadelphia's 13th choice, 245th overall, in 1988 Entry Draft).

			Regular Season					Playoffs				
Season	Club	Lea	GP	G	A	TP	PIM	GP	G	A	TP	PIM
1987-88	Dukla Jihlava	Czech.	29	3	7	10	....	....	....	....	....	....
1988-89	Poldi Kladno	Czech.	....	7	14	21	....	....	....	....	....	....

KAESE, TRENT (KASEY)

Right wing. Shoots right. 5'11", 205 lbs. Born, Nanaimo, B.C., September 9, 1967.
(Buffalo's 8th choice, 161st overall, in 1985 Entry Draft).

			Regular Season					Playoffs				
Season	Club	Lea	GP	G	A	TP	PIM	GP	G	A	TP	PIM
1983-84	Lethbridge	WHL	64	6	6	12	33	1	0	0	0	0
1984-85	Lethbridge	WHL	67	20	18	38	107	4	0	1	1	7
1985-86	Lethbridge	WHL	67	24	41	65	67	10	5	3	8	8
1986-87	Swift Current	WHL	2	1	0	1	4	....	....	....	....	....
	Calgary	WHL	68	30	24	54	117	....	....	....	....	....
	Flint	IHL	1	0	0	0	0	6	4	1	5	9
1987-88	Rochester	AHL	37	6	11	17	32	3	1	2	3	2
	Flint	IHL	43	11	26	37	58	12	6	6	12	21
1988-89	Buffalo	NHL	1	0	0	0	0	....	....	....	....	....
	Rochester	AHL	45	9	11	20	68	....	....	....	....	....
	Flint	IHL	9	2	3	5	61	....	....	....	....	....
	NHL Totals		1	0	0	0	0	....	....	....	....	....

KAMENSKY, VALERI

Right wing. Shoots right. 6'0", 170 lbs. Born, Voskresensk, Soviet Union, April 18, 1966.
(Quebec's 8th choice, 129th overall, in 1988 Entry Draft).

			Regular Season					Playoffs				
Season	Club	Lea	GP	G	A	TP	PIM	GP	G	A	TP	PIM
1982-83	Khimik	USSR	5	0	0	0	0	....	....	....	....	....
1983-84	Khimik	USSR	20	2	2	4	6	....	....	....	....	....
1984-85	Khimik	USSR	45	9	3	12	24	....	....	....	....	....
1985-86	CSKA	USSR	40	15	9	24	8	....	....	....	....	....
1986-87	CSKA	USSR	37	13	8	21	16	....	....	....	....	....
1987-88	CSKA	USSR	51	26	20	46	40	....	....	....	....	....
1988-89	CSKA	USSR	40	18	10	28	30	....	....	....	....	....

KAMINSKI, KEVIN

Center. Shoots left. 5'9", 180 lbs.   Born, Churchbridge, Sask., March 13, 1969.
(Minnesota's 3rd choice, 48th overall, in 1987 Entry Draft).

				Regular Season					Playoffs			
Season	Club	Lea	GP	G	A	TP	PIM	GP	G	A	TP	PIM
1986-87	Saskatoon	WHL	67	26	44	70	325	11	5	6	11	45
1987-88	Saskatoon	WHL	55	38	61	99	247	10	5	7	12	37
1988-89	**Minnesota**	**NHL**	1	0	0	0	0	....	....	....	....	....
	Saskatoon	WHL	52	25	43	68	199	8	4	9	13	25
	NHL Totals		1	0	0	0	0	....	....	....	....	....

Traded to **Quebec** by **Minnesota** for Gaetan Duchesne, June 19, 1989.

KAMPERSAL, JEFFREY

Defense. Shoots right. 6'2", 190 lbs.   Born, Beverly, MA, January 27, 1970.
(NY Islanders' 12th choice, 205th overall, in 1988 Entry Draft).

				Regular Season					Playoffs			
Season	Club	Lea	GP	G	A	TP	PIM	GP	G	A	TP	PIM
1987-88	St. John's	HS	....	1	16	17	....	....	....	....	....	....
1988-89	Princeton	ECAC	26	0	3	3	32	....	....	....	....	....

KANE, SHAUN

Defense. Shoots left. 6'2", 180 lbs.   Born, Holyoke, MA, February 24, 1970.
(Minnesota's 3rd choice, 43rd overall, in 1988 Entry Draft).

				Regular Season					Playoffs			
Season	Club	Lea	GP	G	A	TP	PIM	GP	G	A	TP	PIM
1986-87	Springfield	USHL	....	20	36	56	....	....	....	....	....	....
1987-88	Springfield	USHL	....	23	40	63	....	....	....	....	....	....
1988-89	Providence	H.E.	37	2	9	11	54	....	....	....	....	....

KARALIS, TOM

Defense. Shoots left. 6'1", 205 lbs.   Born, Montreal, Que., May 24, 1964.

				Regular Season					Playoffs			
Season	Club	Lea	GP	G	A	TP	PIM	GP	G	A	TP	PIM
1981-82	Shawinigan	QMJHL	42	0	5	5	107	14	2	8	10	29
1982-83	Drummondville	QMJHL	64	6	11	17	218	....	....	....	....	....
1983-84	Drummondville	QMJHL	67	16	37	53	316	10	2	6	8	28
1984-85	Drummondville	QMJHL	64	21	59	80	184	9	0	7	7	12
1985-86	Fredericton	AHL	51	4	8	12	106	....	....	....	....	....
	Muskegon	IHL	21	5	8	13	81	11	1	3	4	32
1986-87	Fredericton	AHL	37	0	3	3	64	....	....	....	....	....
	Muskegon	IHL	28	3	9	12	94	15	2	12	14	28
1987-88	Baltimore	AHL	17	0	2	2	87	....	....	....	....	....
	Flint	IHL	65	5	26	31	268	2	0	0	0	2
1988-89	New Haven	AHL	11	2	3	5	8	....	....	....	....	....
	Flint	IHL	38	1	6	7	170	....	....	....	....	....
	Indianapolis	IHL	26	0	8	8	132	....	....	....	....	....

Signed as a free agent by **Quebec**, June 6, 1985.

KARJALAINEN, KYOSTI

Left wing. Shoots left. 6'1", 185 lbs.   Born, Gavle, Sweden, June 19, 1967.
Last amateur club: Brynas (Sweden).
(Los Angeles' 6th choice, 132nd overall, in 1987 Entry Draft).

				Regular Season					Playoffs			
Season	Club	Lea	GP	G	A	TP	PIM	GP	G	A	TP	PIM
1986-87	Brynas	Swe.	11	3	2	5	0	....	....	....	....	....
1987-88	Brynas	Swe.	20	2	1	3	10	....	....	....	....	....
1988-89	Brynas	Swe.	39	20	17	37	16	....	....	....	....	....

KARLSSON, LARS

Left wing. Shoots left. 5'10", 175 lbs.   Born, Karlstad, Sweden, August 18, 1966.
(Detroit's 7th choice, 152nd overall, in 1984 Entry Draft).

				Regular Season					Playoffs			
Season	Club	Lea	GP	G	A	TP	PIM	GP	G	A	TP	PIM
1986-87	Bjorkloven	Swe.	35	10	24	34	18	....	....	....	....	....
1987-88	Farjestad	Swe.	39	6	13	19	42	....	....	....	....	....
1988-89	Farjestad	Swe.	40	9	9	18	32	2	0	1	1	6

KARLSSON, REINE

Left wing. Shoots left. 6'1", 165 lbs.   Born, Sweden, February 25, 1965.
(Hartford's 12th choice, 193rd overall, in 1983 Entry Draft).

				Regular Season					Playoffs			
Season	Club	Lea	GP	G	A	TP	PIM	GP	G	A	TP	PIM
1982-83	Sodertalje	Swe.	7	1	1	2	2	1	0	0	0	0
1983-84	Sodertalje	Swe.	19	2	2	4	6	3	0	0	0	2
1984-85	Sodertalje	Swe.	33	2	5	7	18	7	1	3	4	6
1985-86	Sodertalje	Swe.	34	6	8	14	28	7	2	1	3	2
1986-87	Sodertalje	Swe.	35	16	5	21	28	....	....	....	....	....
1987-88	Sodertalje	Swe.	26	10	5	15	18	2	0	0	0	0
1988-89	Sodertalje	Swe.	40	17	18	35	52	5	1	3	4	10

KASATONOV, ALEXEI

Defense. Shoots left. 6'1", 210 lbs.   Born, Leningrad, Soviet Union, October 14, 1959.
(New Jersey's 9th choice, 213th overall, in 1983 Entry Draft).

				Regular Season					Playoffs			
Season	Club	Lea	GP	G	A	TP	PIM	GP	G	A	TP	PIM
1976-77	Leningrad	USSR	7	0	0	0	0	....	....	....	....	....
1977-78	Leningrad	USSR	35	4	7	11	15	....	....	....	....	....
1978-79	CSKA	USSR	40	5	14	19	30	....	....	....	....	....
1979-80a	CSKA	USSR	37	5	8	13	26	....	....	....	....	....
1980-81a	CSKA	USSR	47	10	12	22	38	....	....	....	....	....
1981-82a	CSKA	USSR	46	12	27	39	45	....	....	....	....	....
1982-83a	CSKA	USSR	44	12	19	31	37	....	....	....	....	....
1983-84a	CSKA	USSR	39	12	24	36	20	....	....	....	....	....
1984-85a	CSKA	USSR	40	18	18	36	26	....	....	....	....	....
1985-86a	CSKA	USSR	40	6	17	23	27	....	....	....	....	....
1986-87a	CSKA	USSR	40	13	17	30	16	....	....	....	....	....
1987-88a	CSKA	USSR	43	8	12	20	8	....	....	....	....	....
1988-89	CSKA	USSR	41	8	14	22	8	....	....	....	....	....

a Soviet National League All-Star Team (1980-88)

KASPER, STEPHEN NEIL (STEVE)

Center. Shoots left. 5'8", 170 lbs.   Born, Montreal, Que., September 28, 1961.
(Boston's 3rd choice, 81st over-all, in 1980 Entry Draft).

				Regular Season					Playoffs			
Season	Club	Lea	GP	G	A	TP	PIM	GP	G	A	TP	PIM
1978-79	Verdun	QJHL	67	37	67	104	53	11	7	6	13	22
1979-80	Sorel	QJHL	70	57	65	122	117	....	....	....	....	....
1980-81	**Boston**	**NHL**	76	21	35	56	94	3	0	1	1	0
1981-82a	**Boston**	**NHL**	73	20	31	51	72	11	3	6	9	22
1982-83	**Boston**	**NHL**	24	2	6	8	24	12	2	1	3	10
1983-84	**Boston**	**NHL**	27	3	11	14	19	3	0	0	0	7
1984-85	**Boston**	**NHL**	77	16	24	40	33	5	1	0	1	9
1985-86	**Boston**	**NHL**	80	17	23	40	73	3	1	0	1	4
1986-87	**Boston**	**NHL**	79	20	30	50	51	3	0	2	2	0
1987-88	**Boston**	**NHL**	79	26	44	70	35	23	7	6	13	10
1988-89	**Boston**	**NHL**	49	10	16	26	49	....	....	....	....	....
	Los Angeles	**NHL**	29	9	15	24	14	11	1	5	6	10
	NHL Totals		593	144	235	379	464	74	15	21	36	72

a Won Frank J. Selke Trophy (1982)

Traded to **Los Angeles** by **Boston** for Bobby Carpenter, January 23, 1989.

KASTELIC, EDWARD (ED)   (KAS tuh lihk)

Right wing. Shoots right. 6'4", 215 lbs.   Born, Toronto, Ont., January 29, 1964.
(Washington's 4th choice, 110th over-all, in 1982 Entry Draft).

				Regular Season					Playoffs			
Season	Club	Lea	GP	G	A	TP	PIM	GP	G	A	TP	PIM
1981-82	London	OHL	68	5	18	23	63	4	0	1	1	4
1982-83	London	OHL	68	12	11	23	96	3	0	0	0	5
1983-84	London	OHL	68	17	16	33	218	8	0	2	2	41
1984-85	Moncton	AHL	62	5	11	16	187	....	....	....	....	....
	Binghamton	AHL	4	0	0	0	7	....	....	....	....	....
	Fort Wayne	IHL	5	1	0	1	37	....	....	....	....	....
1985-86	**Washington**	**NHL**	15	0	0	0	73	....	....	....	....	....
	Binghamton	AHL	23	7	9	16	76	....	....	....	....	....
1986-87	Binghamton	AHL	48	17	11	28	124	....	....	....	....	....
	Washington	**NHL**	23	1	1	2	83	5	1	0	1	13
1987-88	**Washington**	**NHL**	35	1	0	1	78	1	0	0	0	19
	Binghamton	AHL	6	4	1	5	6	....	....	....	....	....
1988-89	**Hartford**	**NHL**	10	0	2	2	15	....	....	....	....	....
	Binghamton	AHL	35	9	6	15	124	....	....	....	....	....
	NHL Totals		83	2	3	5	249	6	1	0	1	32

Traded to **Hartford** by **Washington** with Grant Jennings for Mike Millar and Neil Sheehy,
July 6, 1988.

KAUTONEN, VELI-PEKKA

Defense. Shoots right. 6'2", 195 lbs.   Born, Helsinki, Finland, May 9, 1970.
(Calgary's 3rd choice, 50th overall, in 1989 Entry Draft).

				Regular Season					Playoffs			
Season	Club	Lea	GP	G	A	TP	PIM	GP	G	A	TP	PIM
1987-88	IFK	Fin.	35	9	11	20	....	....	....	....	....	....
1988-89	IFK	Fin.	36	4	5	9	....	....	....	....	....	....

KEANE, MIKE

Right wing. Shoots right. 6', 180 lbs.   Born, Winnipeg, Man., May 29, 1967.

				Regular Season					Playoffs			
Season	Club	Lea	GP	G	A	TP	PIM	GP	G	A	TP	PIM
1984-85	Moose Jaw	WHL	65	17	26	43	141	....	....	....	....	....
1985-86	Moose Jaw	WHL	67	34	49	83	162	13	6	8	14	9
1986-87	Moose Jaw	WHL	53	25	45	70	107	9	3	9	12	11
	Sherbrooke	AHL	....	....	....	....	....	9	2	2	4	16
1987-88	Sherbrooke	AHL	78	25	43	68	70	6	1	1	2	18
1988-89	**Montreal**	**NHL**	69	16	19	35	69	21	4	3	7	17
	NHL Totals		69	16	19	35	69	21	4	3	7	17

Signed as a free agent by **Montreal**, September 25, 1985.

KECZMER, DAN

Defense. Shoots left. 6'1", 175 lbs.   Born, Mt. Clemens, MI, May 25, 1968.
(Minnesota's 11th choice, 201st overall, in 1986 Entry Draft).

				Regular Season					Playoffs			
Season	Club	Lea	GP	G	A	TP	PIM	GP	G	A	TP	PIM
1986-87	Lake Superior	CCHA	38	3	5	8	26	....	....	....	....	....
1987-88	Lake Superior	CCHA	41	2	15	17	34	....	....	....	....	....
1988-89	Lake Superior	CCHA	46	3	26	29	68	....	....	....	....	....

KELFER, MICHAEL (MIKE)

Center. Shoots right. 5'10", 180 lbs.   Born, Peabody, MA, January 2, 1967.
(Minnesota's 5th choice, 132nd overall, in 1985 Entry Draft).

				Regular Season					Playoffs			
Season	Club	Lea	GP	G	A	TP	PIM	GP	G	A	TP	PIM
1985-86	Boston U.	H.E.	39	13	14	27	40	....	....	....	....	....
1986-87	Boston U.	H.E.	33	21	19	40	20	....	....	....	....	....
1987-88a	Boston U.	H.E.	36	36	27	63	33	....	....	....	....	....
1988-89a	Boston U.	H.E.	33	23	29	52	22	....	....	....	....	....

a Hockey East Second All-Star Team (1988, 1989)

KELLOGG, BOB

Defense. Shoots left. 6'4", 200 lbs.   Born, Springfield, MA, February 16, 1971.
(Chicago's 3rd choice, 48th overall, in 1989 Entry Draft).

				Regular Season					Playoffs			
Season	Club	Lea	GP	G	A	TP	PIM	GP	G	A	TP	PIM
1987-88	Springfield	USHL	....	15	35	50	....	....	....	....	....	....
1988-89	Springfield	USHL	....	13	34	47	....	....	....	....	....	....

KELLY, PAUL

Defense. Shoots left. 6', 190 lbs. Born, Hamilton, Ont., April 17, 1967.
(Los Angeles' 9th choice, 191st overall, in 1986 Entry Draft).

			Regular Season					Playoffs				
Season	Club	Lea	GP	G	A	TP	PIM	GP	G	A	TP	PIM
1985-86	Guelph	OHL	59	26	32	58	95	20	10	7	17	19
1986-87	Guelph	OHL	61	27	48	75	67	5	2	4	6	0
1987-88	New Haven	AHL	60	14	25	39	23	....	....	....	....	....
1988-89	New Haven	AHL	12	4	5	9	22	....	....	....	....	....
	Utica	AHL	34	6	8	14	25	3	0	0	0	6
	Flint	IHL	4	0	1	1	0	....	....	....	....	....

KENNEDY, SHELDON

Right wing. Shoots right. 5'11", 180 lbs. Born, Brandon, Man., June 15, 1969.
(Detroit's 5th choice, 80th overall, in 1988 Entry Draft).

			Regular Season					Playoffs				
Season	Club	Lea	GP	G	A	TP	PIM	GP	G	A	TP	PIM
1986-87	Swift Current	WHL	49	23	41	64	43	4	0	3	3	4
1987-88	Swift Current	WHL	59	53	64	117	45	10	8	9	17	12
1988-89	Swift Current	WHL	51	58	48	106	92	12	9	15	24	22

KENTALA, VILLE

Left wing. Shoots left. 6'2", 180 lbs. Born, Alajarvi, Finland, February 21, 1966.
(NY Rangers' 8th choice, 182nd overall, in 1984 Entry Draft).

			Regular Season					Playoffs				
Season	Club	Lea	GP	G	A	TP	PIM	GP	G	A	TP	PIM
1984-85	IFK Helsinki	Fin. Jr.	26	18	10	28	34	4	2	3	5	4
1986-87	Karhukissat	Fin. 2	37	19	16	35	28	....	....	....	....	....
1986-87	Boston U.	H.E.	35	4	11	15	24	....	....	....	....	....
1987-88	Boston U.	H.E.	32	16	19	35	34	....	....	....	....	....
1988-89	Boston U.	H.E.	34	5	7	12	46	....	....	....	....	....

Traded to **Edmonton** by **NY Rangers** with Reijo Ruotsalainen, Clark Donatelli and Jim Wiemer for Don Jackson, Mike Golden, Miroslav Horava and future considerations, October 23, 1986.

KENNEDY, EDWARD (DEAN)

Defense. Shoots right. 6'2", 190 lbs. Born, Redver, Sask., January 18, 1963.
(Los Angeles' 2nd choice, 39th over-all, in 1981 Entry Draft).

			Regular Season					Playoffs				
Season	Club	Lea	GP	G	A	TP	PIM	GP	G	A	TP	PIM
1980-81	Brandon	WHL	71	3	29	32	157	5	0	2	2	7
1981-82	Brandon	WHL	49	5	38	43	103	....	....	....	....	....
1982-83	Brandon	WHL	14	2	15	17	22	....	....	....	....	....
	Los Angeles	**NHL**	**55**	**0**	**12**	**12**	**97**	**....**	**....**	**....**	**....**	**....**
	Saskatoon	WHL	....	....	....	....	....	4	0	3	3	0
1983-84	**Los Angeles**	**NHL**	**37**	**1**	**5**	**6**	**50**	**....**	**....**	**....**	**....**	**....**
	New Haven	AHL	26	1	7	8	23	....	....	....	....	....
1984-85	New Haven	AHL	76	3	14	17	104	....	....	....	....	....
1985-86	**Los Angeles**	**NHL**	**78**	**2**	**10**	**12**	**132**	**....**	**....**	**....**	**....**	**....**
1986-87	**Los Angeles**	**NHL**	**66**	**6**	**14**	**20**	**91**	**5**	**0**	**2**	**2**	**10**
1987-88	**Los Angeles**	**NHL**	**58**	**1**	**11**	**12**	**158**	**4**	**0**	**1**	**1**	**10**
1988-89	**NY Rangers**	**NHL**	**16**	**0**	**1**	**1**	**40**	**....**	**....**	**....**	**....**	**....**
	Los Angeles	**NHL**	**51**	**3**	**10**	**13**	**63**	**11**	**0**	**2**	**2**	**8**
	NHL Totals		**361**	**13**	**63**	**76**	**631**	**20**	**0**	**5**	**5**	**28**

Traded to **NY Rangers** by **Los Angeles** with Denis Larocque for Igor Liba, Michael Boyce, Todd Elik and future considerations, December 12, 1988. Traded to **Los Angeles** by **NY Rangers** for Los Angeles' fourth-round choice in 1990 Entry Draft, February 3, 1989.

KERR, ALAN

Right wing. Shoots right. 5'11", 195 lbs. Born, Hazelton, B.C., March 28, 1964.
(NY Islanders' 4th choice, 84th over-all, in 1982 Entry Draft).

			Regular Season					Playoffs				
Season	Club	Lea	GP	G	A	TP	PIM	GP	G	A	TP	PIM
1981-82	Seattle	WHL	68	15	18	33	107	10	6	6	12	32
1982-83	Seattle	WHL	71	38	53	91	183	4	2	3	5	0
1983-84a	Seattle	WHL	66	46	66	112	141	5	1	4	5	12
1984-85	**NY Islanders**	**NHL**	**19**	**3**	**1**	**4**	**24**	**4**	**1**	**0**	**1**	**4**
	Springfield	AHL	62	32	27	59	140	4	1	2	3	2
1985-86	**NY Islanders**	**NHL**	**7**	**0**	**1**	**1**	**16**	**1**	**0**	**0**	**0**	**0**
	Springfield	AHL	71	35	36	71	127	....	....	....	....	....
1986-87	**NY Islanders**	**NHL**	**72**	**7**	**10**	**17**	**175**	**14**	**1**	**4**	**5**	**25**
1987-88	**NY Islanders**	**NHL**	**80**	**24**	**34**	**58**	**198**	**6**	**1**	**0**	**1**	**14**
1988-89	**NY Islanders**	**NHL**	**71**	**20**	**18**	**38**	**144**	**....**	**....**	**....**	**....**	**....**
	NHL Totals		**249**	**54**	**64**	**118**	**557**	**25**	**3**	**4**	**7**	**43**

a WHL First All-Star Team, West Division (1984)

KERR, KEVIN

Right wing. Shoots right. 5'10", 170 lbs. Born, North Bay, Ont., September 18, 1967.
(Buffalo's 4th choice, 56th overall, in 1986 Entry Draft).

			Regular Season					Playoffs				
Season	Club	Lea	GP	G	A	TP	PIM	GP	G	A	TP	PIM
1985-86	Windsor	OHL	59	21	51	72	266	16	6	8	14	55
1986-87	Windsor	OHL	63	27	41	68	264	14	3	8	11	45
1987-88	Rochester	AHL	72	18	11	29	352	5	1	3	4	42
1988-89	Rochester	AHL	66	20	18	38	306	....	....	....	....	....

KERR, TIM

Center. Shoots right. 6'3", 230 lbs. Born, Windsor, Ont., January 5, 1960.

			Regular Season					Playoffs				
Season	Club	Lea	GP	G	A	TP	PIM	GP	G	A	TP	PIM
1978-79	Kingston	OHA	57	17	25	42	27	6	1	1	2	2
1979-80	Kingston	OHA	63	40	33	73	39	3	0	1	1	16
	Maine	AHL	7	2	4	6	2	....	....	....	....	....
1980-81	**Philadelphia**	**NHL**	**68**	**22**	**23**	**45**	**84**	**10**	**1**	**3**	**4**	**2**
1981-82	**Philadelphia**	**NHL**	**61**	**21**	**30**	**51**	**138**	**4**	**0**	**2**	**2**	**2**
1982-83	**Philadelphia**	**NHL**	**24**	**11**	**8**	**19**	**6**	**2**	**2**	**0**	**2**	**0**
1983-84	**Philadelphia**	**NHL**	**79**	**54**	**39**	**93**	**29**	**3**	**0**	**0**	**0**	**0**
1984-85	**Philadelphia**	**NHL**	**74**	**54**	**44**	**98**	**57**	**12**	**10**	**4**	**14**	**13**
1985-86	**Philadelphia**	**NHL**	**76**	**58**	**26**	**84**	**79**	**5**	**3**	**3**	**6**	**8**
1986-87a	**Philadelphia**	**NHL**	**75**	**58**	**37**	**95**	**57**	**12**	**8**	**5**	**13**	**2**
1987-88	**Philadelphia**	**NHL**	**8**	**3**	**2**	**5**	**12**	**6**	**1**	**3**	**4**	**4**
1988-89b	**Philadelphia**	**NHL**	**69**	**48**	**40**	**88**	**73**	**19**	**14**	**11**	**25**	**27**
	NHL Totals		**534**	**329**	**249**	**578**	**535**	**73**	**39**	**31**	**70**	**58**

a NHL Second All-Star Team (1987)
b Won Bill Masterton Award (1989)

Played in NHL All-Star Game (1984-86)

Signed as free agent by **Philadelphia**, October 25, 1979.

KESKINEN, ESA

Center. Shoots right. 5'9", 185 lbs. Born, Tampere, Finland, February 3, 1965.
(Calgary's 6th choice, 101st overall, in 1985 Entry Draft).

			Regular Season					Playoffs				
Season	Club	Lea	GP	G	A	TP	PIM	GP	G	A	TP	PIM
1982-83	FoPS	Fin. 2	15	5	14	19	8	4	4	6	10	0
1983-84	TPS	Fin.	31	10	25	35	0	6	0	0	0	0
1984-85	TPS	Fin.	35	11	22	33	6	10	2	3	5	0
1985-86	TPS	Fin.	36	18	28	46	4	7	2	0	2	0
1986-87	TPS	Fin.	46	25	36	61	4	5	1	1	2	0
1987-88	TPS	Fin.	44	14	55	69	14	....	....	....	....	....
1988-89	Lukko	Fin.	41	24	46	70	12	....	....	....	....	....

KIDD, IAN

Defense. Shoots right. 5'11", 195 lbs. Born, Gresham, OR, May 11, 1964.

			Regular Season					Playoffs				
Season	Club	Lea	GP	G	A	TP	PIM	GP	G	A	TP	PIM
1983-84	Penticton	BCJHL	55	31	52	83	188	....	....	....	....	....
1984-85	Penticton	BCJHL	46	31	77	108	177	....	....	....	....	....
1985-86	North Dakota	WCHA	37	6	16	22	65	....	....	....	....	....
1986-87	North Dakota	WCHA	47	13	47	60	58	....	....	....	....	....
1987-88	**Vancouver**	**NHL**	**19**	**4**	**7**	**11**	**25**	**....**	**....**	**....**	**....**	**....**
	Fredericton	AHL	53	1	21	22	70	12	0	4	4	22
1988-89	**Vancouver**	**NHL**	**1**	**0**	**0**	**0**	**0**	**....**	**....**	**....**	**....**	**....**
	Milwaukee	IHL	76	13	40	53	124	4	0	2	2	7
	NHL Totals		**20**	**4**	**7**	**11**	**25**	**....**	**....**	**....**	**....**	**....**

Signed as a free agent by **Vancouver**, July 30, 1987.

KIENE, CHRIS

Defense. Shoots left. 6'6", 225 lbs. Born, So. Windsor, CT, March 6, 1966.
(New Jersey's 12th choice, 231st overall, in 1984 Entry Draft).

			Regular Season					Playoffs				
Season	Club	Lea	GP	G	A	TP	PIM	GP	G	A	TP	PIM
1987-88	Merrimack	NCAA	40	6	34	40	72	....	....	....	....	....
1988-89	Merrimack	NCAA	32	3	25	28	76	....	....	....	....	....

KIHLSTROM, MATS

Defense. Shoots right. 6'2", 198 lbs. Born, Ludvika, Sweden, January 3, 1964.
(Calgary's 8th choice, 118th overall, in 1982 Entry Draft).

			Regular Season					Playoffs				
Season	Club	Lea	GP	G	A	TP	PIM	GP	G	A	TP	PIM
1981-82	Sodertalje	Swe.	25	2	3	5	20	....	....	....	....	....
1982-83	Sodertalje	Swe.	17	5	0	5	35	11	1	3	4	12
1983-84	Sodertalje	Swe.	25	4	3	7	25	3	1	0	1	0
1984-85	Brynas	Swe.	35	4	9	13	14	....	....	....	....	....
1985-86	Brynas	Swe.	35	3	8	11	48	3	1	0	1	4
1986-87	Sodertalje	Swe.	32	2	4	6	28	....	....	....	....	....
1987-88	Sodertalje	Swe.	37	5	7	12	36	2	0	2	2	0
1988-89	Sodertalje	Swe.	39	3	19	22	45	....	....	....	....	....

KIMBLE, DARIN

Right wing. Shoots right. 6'2", 205 lbs. Born, Swift Current, Sask., November 22, 1968.
(Quebec's 5th choice, 66th overall, in 1988 Entry Draft).

			Regular Season					Playoffs				
Season	Club	Lea	GP	G	A	TP	PIM	GP	G	A	TP	PIM
1986-87	Prince Albert	WHL	68	17	13	30	190	....	....	....	....	....
1987-88	Prince Albert	WHL	67	35	36	71	307	10	3	2	5	4
1988-89	**Quebec**	**NHL**	**26**	**3**	**1**	**4**	**149**	**....**	**....**	**....**	**....**	**....**
	Halifax	AHL	39	8	6	14	188	....	....	....	....	....
	NHL Totals		**26**	**3**	**1**	**4**	**149**	**....**	**....**	**....**	**....**	**....**

KING, DEREK

Left wing. Shoots left. 6'1", 203 lbs. Born, Hamilton, Ont., February 11, 1967.
(NY Islanders' 2nd choice, 13th over-all, in 1985 Entry Draft).

			Regular Season					Playoffs				
Season	Club	Lea	GP	G	A	TP	PIM	GP	G	A	TP	PIM
1983-84	Hamilton	OPJHL	37	10	14	24	142	....	....	....	....	....
1984-85a	S.S. Marie	OHL	63	35	38	73	106	16	3	13	16	11
1985-86	Oshawa	OHL	44	20	30	50	48	6	3	2	5	13
1986-87	**NY Islanders**	**NHL**	**2**	**0**	**0**	**0**	**0**	**....**	**....**	**....**	**....**	**....**
b	Oshawa	OHL	57	53	53	106	74	17	14	10	24	40
1987-88	**NY Islanders**	**NHL**	**55**	**12**	**24**	**36**	**30**	**5**	**0**	**2**	**2**	**2**
	Springfield	AHL	10	7	6	13	6	....	....	....	....	....
1988-89	**NY Islanders**	**NHL**	**60**	**14**	**29**	**43**	**14**	**....**	**....**	**....**	**....**	**....**
	Springfield	AHL	4	4	0	4	0	....	....	....	....	....
	NHL Totals		**117**	**26**	**53**	**79**	**44**	**5**	**0**	**2**	**2**	**2**

a OHL Rookie of the Year (1985)
b OHL First All-Star Team (1987)

KING, KRIS

Center. Shoots left. 5'10". 190 lbs. Born, Bracebridge, Ont., February 18, 1966.
(Washington's 4th choice, 80th over-all, in 1984 Entry Draft).

			Regular Season					Playoffs				
Season	Club	Lea	GP	G	A	TP	PIM	GP	G	A	TP	PIM
1983-84	Peterborough	OHL	62	13	18	31	168	8	3	3	6	14
1984-85	Peterborough	OHL	61	18	35	53	222	16	2	8	10	28
1985-86	Peterborough	OHL	58	19	40	59	254	8	4	0	4	21
1986-87	Binghamton	AHL	7	0	0	0	18	....	....	....	....	....
	Peterborough	OHL	46	23	33	56	160	12	5	8	13	41
1987-88	**Detroit**	**NHL**	**3**	**1**	**0**	**1**	**2**	....	....	....	....	....
	Adirondack	AHL	76	21	32	53	337	10	4	4	8	53
1988-89	**Detroit**	**NHL**	**55**	**2**	**3**	**5**	**168**	**2**	**0**	**0**	**0**	**2**
	NHL Totals		**58**	**3**	**3**	**6**	**170**	**2**	**0**	**0**	**0**	**2**

KIRTON, DOUG

Right wing. Shoots right. 6'2", 190 lbs. Born, Penetanguishene, Ont., March 21, 1966.
(New Jersey's 12th choice, 236th overall, in 1986 Entry Draft).

			Regular Season					Playoffs				
Season	Club	Lea	GP	G	A	TP	PIM	GP	G	A	TP	PIM
1985-86	Orillia	OPJHL	46	34	45	79	158	....	....	....	....	....
1986-87	Colorado	WCHA	38	10	10	20	42	....	....	....	....	....
1987-88	Colorado	WCHA	31	11	17	28	42	....	....	....	....	....
1988-89	Colorado	WCHA	38	8	16	24	33	....	....	....	....	....

KIRTON, MARK ROBERT

Center. Shoots left. 5'10", 170 lbs. Born, Regina, Sask., February 3, 1958
(Toronto's 2nd choice, 48th over-all, in 1978 Amateur Draft).

			Regular Season					Playoffs				
Season	Club	Lea	GP	G	A	TP	PIM	GP	G	A	TP	PIM
1976-77	Peterborough	OHA	46	18	24	42	41	4	6	1	7	0
1977-78	Peterborough	OHA	68	27	44	71	29	21	12	14	26	14
1978-79	New Brunswick	AHL	80	20	30	50	14	5	0	0	0	2
1979-80	**Toronto**	**NHL**	**2**	**1**	**0**	**1**	**2**	....	....	....	....	....
	New Brunswick	AHL	61	19	42	61	33	17	7	11	18	16
1980-81	**Toronto**	**NHL**	**11**	**0**	**0**	**0**	**0**	....	....	....	....	....
	Detroit	**NHL**	**50**	**18**	**13**	**31**	**24**	....	....	....	....	....
1981-82	**Detroit**	**NHL**	**74**	**14**	**28**	**42**	**62**	....	....	....	....	....
1982-83	**Detroit**	**NHL**	**10**	**1**	**1**	**2**	**6**	....	....	....	....	....
	Adirondack	AHL	20	6	10	16	12	....	....	....	....	....
	Fredericton	AHL	3	2	0	2	2	....	....	....	....	....
	Vancouver	**NHL**	**31**	**4**	**6**	**10**	**4**	**4**	**1**	**2**	**3**	**7**
1983-84	**Vancouver**	**NHL**	**26**	**2**	**3**	**5**	**2**	....	....	....	....	....
	Fredericton	AHL	35	8	10	18	8	7	2	3	5	6
1984-85	**Vancouver**	**NHL**	**62**	**17**	**5**	**22**	**21**	....	....	....	....	....
	Fredericton	AHL	15	5	9	14	18	....	....	....	....	....
1985-86	Fredericton	AHL	77	23	36	59	33	6	2	2	4	4
1986-87	Fredericton	AHL	80	27	37	64	20	....	....	....	....	....
1987-88	Newmarket	AHL	73	17	30	47	42	....	....	....	....	....
1988-89	Newmarket	AHL	37	4	8	12	18	....	....	....	....	....
	NHL Totals		**266**	**57**	**56**	**113**	**121**	**4**	**1**	**2**	**3**	**7**

Traded to **Detroit** by **Toronto** for Jim Rutherford, December 4, 1980. Traded to **Vancouver** by **Detroit** for Ivan Boldirev, January 17, 1983.

KISIO, KELLY W.

Center. Shoots left. 5'9", 170 lbs. Born, Peace River, Alta., September 18, 1959.

			Regular Season					Playoffs				
Season	Club	Lea	GP	G	A	TP	PIM	GP	G	A	TP	PIM
1978-79	Calgary	WHL	70	60	61	121	73	....	....	....	....	....
1979-80	Calgary	WHL	71	65	73	138	64	....	....	....	....	....
1980-81	Adirondack	AHL	41	10	14	24	43	....	....	....	....	....
	Kalamazoo	IHL	31	27	16	43	48	8	7	7	14	13
1981-82	Dallas	CHL	78	*62	39	101	59	16	*12	*17	*29	38
1982-83	Davos	Swit.	35	40	33	73	....	....	....	....	....	....
	Detroit	**NHL**	**15**	**4**	**3**	**7**	**0**	....	....	....	....	....
1983-84	**Detroit**	**NHL**	**70**	**23**	**37**	**60**	**34**	**4**	**1**	**0**	**1**	**4**
1984-85	**Detroit**	**NHL**	**75**	**20**	**41**	**61**	**56**	**3**	**0**	**2**	**2**	**2**
1985-86	**Detroit**	**NHL**	**76**	**21**	**48**	**69**	**85**	....	....	....	....	....
1986-87	**NY Rangers**	**NHL**	**70**	**24**	**40**	**64**	**73**	**4**	**0**	**1**	**1**	**2**
1987-88	**NY Rangers**	**NHL**	**77**	**23**	**55**	**78**	**88**	....	....	....	....	....
1988-89	**NY Rangers**	**NHL**	**70**	**26**	**36**	**62**	**91**	**4**	**0**	**0**	**0**	**9**
	NHL Totals		**453**	**141**	**260**	**401**	**427**	**15**	**1**	**3**	**4**	**17**

Signed as a free agent by **Detroit**, May 2, 1983. Traded to **NY Rangers** by **Detroit** with Lane Lambert and Jim Leavins for Glen Hanlon and New York's third-round choices in 1987 (Dennis Holland) and 1988 Entry Drafts, July 29, 1986.

KIVELA, TEPPO

Center. Shoots left. 5'11", 180 lbs. Born, Espoo, Finland, November 8, 1969.
(Minnesota's 5th choice, 88th overall, in 1987 Entry Draft).

			Regular Season					Playoffs				
Season	Club	Lea	GP	G	A	TP	PIM	GP	G	A	TP	PIM
1984-85	Jokerit	Fin.	11	1	1	2	2	....	....	....	....	....
1985-86	Jokerit	Fin.	31	2	5	7	6	....	....	....	....	....
1986-87	HPK	Fin.	41	26	38	64	64	6	4	7	11	4
1987-88	HPK	Fin.	36	31	39	70	20	....	....	....	....	....
1988-89	HPK	Fin.	39	20	38	58	54	....	....	....	....	....

KJELLBERG, PATRIK

Left wing. Shoots left. 6'1", 190 lbs. Born, Falun, Sweden, June 17, 1969.
(Montreal's 4th choice, 83rd overall, in 1988 Entry Draft).

			Regular Season					Playoffs				
Season	Club	Lea	GP	G	A	TP	PIM	GP	G	A	TP	PIM
1986-87	Falun	Swe.	27	11	13	24	14	....	....	....	....	....
1987-88	Falun	Swe.	29	15	10	25	18	....	....	....	....	....
1988-89	AIK	Swe.	25	7	9	16	8	....	....	....	....	....

KLEINENDORST, SCOT (KLINE-en-dorst)

Defense. Shoots left. 6'3", 215 lbs. Born, Grand Rapids, MN, January 16, 1960.
(NY Rangers' 5th choice, 98th over-all, in 1980 Entry Draft).

			Regular Season					Playoffs				
Season	Club	Lea	GP	G	A	TP	PIM	GP	G	A	TP	PIM
1978-79	Providence	ECAC	25	4	4	8	27	....	....	....	....	....
1979-80a	Providence	ECAC	30	1	12	13	38	....	....	....	....	....
1980-81	Providence	ECAC	32	3	31	34	75	....	....	....	....	....
1981-82	Providence	ECAC	33	11	27	38	85	....	....	....	....	....
	Springfield	AHL	5	0	4	4	11	....	....	....	....	....
1982-83	Tulsa	CHL	10	0	7	7	2	....	....	....	....	....
	NY Rangers	**NHL**	**30**	**2**	**9**	**11**	**8**	**6**	**0**	**2**	**2**	**2**
1983-84	**NY Rangers**	**NHL**	**23**	**0**	**2**	**2**	**35**	....	....	....	....	....
	Tulsa	CHL	10	4	5	9	4	....	....	....	....	....
1984-85	**Hartford**	**NHL**	**35**	**1**	**8**	**9**	**69**	....	....	....	....	....
	Binghamton	AHL	30	3	7	10	42	....	....	....	....	....
1985-86	**Hartford**	**NHL**	**41**	**2**	**7**	**9**	**62**	**10**	**0**	**1**	**1**	**18**
1986-87	**Hartford**	**NHL**	**66**	**3**	**9**	**12**	**130**	**4**	**1**	**3**	**4**	**20**
1987-88	**Hartford**	**NHL**	**44**	**3**	**6**	**9**	**86**	**3**	**1**	**1**	**2**	**0**
1988-89	**Hartford**	**NHL**	**24**	**0**	**1**	**1**	**36**	....	....	....	....	....
	Binghamton	AHL	4	0	1	1	19	....	....	....	....	....
	Washington	**NHL**	**3**	**0**	**1**	**1**	**10**	....	....	....	....	....
	NHL Totals		**266**	**11**	**43**	**54**	**436**	**23**	**2**	**7**	**9**	**40**

a ECAC Second All-Star Team (1980)

Traded to **Hartford** by **NY Rangers** for Blaine Stoughton, February 27, 1984. Traded to **Washington** by **Hartford** for Jim Thomson, March 6, 1989.

KLIMA, PETR (KLEE-ma)

Left Wing. Shoots left. 6', 190 lbs. Born, Chomulov, Czechoslovakia, December 23, 1964.
(Detroit's 5th choice, 88th overall, in 1983 Entry Draft).

			Regular Season					Playoffs				
Season	Club	Lea	GP	G	A	TP	PIM	GP	G	A	TP	PIM
1982-83	Czech. Jrs.	....	44	19	17	36	74	....	....	....	....	....
1983-84	Dukla Jihlava	Czech.	41	20	16	36	46	....	....	....	....	....
	Czech. Jrs.	....	7	6	5	11	NA	....	....	....	....	....
1984-85	Dukla Jihlava	Czech.	35	23	22	45	NA	....	....	....	....	....
	Czech. Nat'l	....	5	2	1	3	0	....	....	....	....	....
1985-86	**Detroit**	**NHL**	**74**	**32**	**24**	**56**	**16**	....	....	....	....	....
1986-87	**Detroit**	**NHL**	**77**	**30**	**23**	**53**	**42**	**13**	**1**	**2**	**3**	**4**
1987-88	**Detroit**	**NHL**	**78**	**37**	**25**	**62**	**46**	**12**	**10**	**8**	**18**	**10**
1988-89	**Detroit**	**NHL**	**51**	**25**	**16**	**41**	**44**	**6**	**2**	**4**	**6**	**19**
	Adirondack	AHL	5	5	1	6	4	....	....	....	....	....
	NHL Totals		**280**	**124**	**88**	**212**	**148**	**31**	**13**	**14**	**27**	**33**

KLUZAK, GORDON (GORD) (KLOO-zak)

Defense. Shoots left. 6'4", 215 lbs. Born, Climax, Sask., March 4, 1964.
(Boston's 1st choice, 1st over-all, in 1982 Entry Draft).

			Regular Season					Playoffs				
Season	Club	Lea	GP	G	A	TP	PIM	GP	G	A	TP	PIM
1980-81	Billings	WHL	68	4	34	38	160	5	0	1	1	4
1981-82a	Billings	WHL	38	9	24	33	110					
1982-83	**Boston**	**NHL**	**70**	**1**	**6**	**7**	**105**	**17**	**1**	**4**	**5**	**54**
1983-84	**Boston**	**NHL**	**80**	**10**	**27**	**37**	**135**	**3**	**0**	**0**	**0**	**0**
1984-85			DID NOT PLAY — INJURED									
1985-86	**Boston**	**NHL**	**70**	**8**	**31**	**39**	**155**	**3**	**1**	**1**	**2**	**16**
1986-87			DID NOT PLAY — INJURED									
1987-88	**Boston**	**NHL**	**66**	**6**	**31**	**37**	**135**	**23**	**4**	**8**	**12**	**59**
1988-89	**Boston**	**NHL**	**3**	**0**	**1**	**1**	**2**	....	....	....	....	....
	NHL Totals		**289**	**25**	**96**	**121**	**532**	**46**	**6**	**13**	**19**	**129**

a WHL Second All-Star Team (1982)

KOCUR, JOEY (KOH suhr)

Right wing. Shoots right. 6', 195 lbs. Born, Kelvington, Sask., December 21, 1964.
(Detroit's 6th choice, 91st over-all, in 1983 Entry Draft).

			Regular Season					Playoffs				
Season	Club	Lea	GP	G	A	TP	PIM	GP	G	A	TP	PIM
1982-83	Saskatoon	WHL	62	23	17	40	289	6	2	3	5	25
1983-84	Saskatoon	WHL	69	40	41	81	258	....	....	....	....	....
	Adirondack	AHL	....	....	....	....	....	5	0	0	0	20
1984-85	**Detroit**	**NHL**	**17**	**1**	**0**	**1**	**64**	**3**	**1**	**0**	**1**	**5**
	Adirondack	AHL	47	12	7	19	171	....	....	....	....	....
1985-86	**Detroit**	**NHL**	**59**	**9**	**6**	**15**	***377**	....	....	....	....	....
	Adirondack	AHL	9	6	2	8	34	....	....	....	....	....
1986-87	**Detroit**	**NHL**	**77**	**9**	**9**	**18**	**276**	**16**	**2**	**3**	**5**	**71**
1987-88	**Detroit**	**NHL**	**63**	**7**	**7**	**14**	**263**	**10**	**0**	**1**	**1**	**13**
1988-89	**Detroit**	**NHL**	**60**	**9**	**9**	**18**	**213**	**3**	**0**	**1**	**1**	**6**
	NHL Totals		**276**	**35**	**31**	**66**	**1193**	**32**	**3**	**5**	**8**	**95**

KOCUR, KORY

Right wing. Shoots right. 5'11", 190 lbs. Born, Kelvington, Sask., March 6, 1969.
(Detroit's 1st choice, 17th overall, in 1988 Entry Draft).

			Regular Season					Playoffs				
Season	Club	Lea	GP	G	A	TP	PIM	GP	G	A	TP	PIM
1986-87	Saskatoon	WHL	62	13	17	30	98	4	0	0	0	7
1987-88	Saskatoon	WHL	69	34	37	71	95	10	5	4	9	18
1988-89	Saskatoon	WHL	66	45	57	102	111	8	7	11	18	15

KOIVUNEN, PETRO

Center. Shoots right. 6', 175 lbs. Born, Espoo, Finland, May 30, 1970.
(Edmonton's 2nd choice, 39th overall, in 1988 Entry Draft).

			Regular Season					Playoffs				
Season	Club	Lea	GP	G	A	TP	PIM	GP	G	A	TP	PIM
1986-87	K-Espoo	Fin. Jr.	30	22	14	36	26	....	....	....	....	....
1987-88	K-Espoo	Fin. Jr.	31	27	31	58	38	....	....	....	....	....
1988-89	K-Espoo	Fin.	39	32	37	69	42	....	....	....	....	....

KOLSTAD, DEAN

Defense. Shoots left. 6'6", 210 lbs. Born, Edmonton, Alta., June 16, 1968.
(Minnesota's 3rd choice, 33rd overall, in 1986 Entry Draft).

			Regular Season					Playoffs				
Season	Club	Lea	GP	G	A	TP	PIM	GP	G	A	TP	PIM
1985-86	Prince Albert	WHL	70	2	20	22	99	20	5	3	8	26
1986-87	Prince Albert	WHL	72	17	37	54	112	8	1	5	6	8
1987-88	Prince Albert	WHL	72	14	37	51	121	10	0	9	9	20
1988-89	**Minnesota**	**NHL**	**25**	**1**	**5**	**6**	**42**	....	....	....	....	....
	Kalamazoo	IHL	51	10	23	33	91	6	1	0	1	23
	NHL Totals		**25**	**1**	**5**	**6**	**42**	....	....	....	....	....

KONROYD, STEPHEN MARK (STEVE) (KON-royd)

Defense. Shoots left. 6'1", 195 lbs. Born, Scarborough, Ont., February 10, 1961.
(Atlanta's 4th choice, 39th over-all, in 1980 Entry Draft).

			Regular Season					Playoffs				
Season	Club	Lea	GP	G	A	TP	PIM	GP	G	A	TP	PIM
1979-80	Oshawa	OHA	62	11	23	34	133	7	0	2	2	14
1980-81	**Calgary**	**NHL**	**4**	**0**	**0**	**0**	**4**	....	....	....	....	....
a	Oshawa	OHA	59	19	47	68	232	11	3	11	14	35
1981-82	Oklahoma City	CHL	14	2	3	5	15	....	....	....	....	....
	Calgary	**NHL**	**63**	**3**	**14**	**17**	**78**	**3**	**0**	**0**	**0**	**12**
1982-83	**Calgary**	**NHL**	**79**	**4**	**13**	**17**	**73**	**9**	**2**	**1**	**3**	**18**
1983-84	**Calgary**	**NHL**	**80**	**1**	**13**	**14**	**94**	**8**	**1**	**2**	**3**	**8**
1984-85	**Calgary**	**NHL**	**64**	**3**	**23**	**26**	**73**	**4**	**1**	**4**	**5**	**2**
1985-86	**Calgary**	**NHL**	**59**	**7**	**20**	**27**	**64**	....	....	....	....	....
	NY Islanders	**NHL**	**14**	**0**	**5**	**5**	**16**	**3**	**0**	**0**	**0**	**6**
1986-87	**NY Islanders**	**NHL**	**72**	**5**	**16**	**21**	**70**	**14**	**1**	**4**	**5**	**10**
1987-88	**NY Islanders**	**NHL**	**62**	**2**	**15**	**17**	**99**	**6**	**1**	**0**	**1**	**4**
1988-89	**NY Islanders**	**NHL**	**21**	**1**	**5**	**6**	**2**	....	....	....	....	....
	Chicago	**NHL**	**57**	**5**	**7**	**12**	**40**	**16**	**2**	**0**	**2**	**10**
	NHL Totals		**575**	**31**	**131**	**162**	**613**	**63**	**8**	**11**	**19**	**70**

a OHA Second All-Star Team (1981)

Traded to **NY Islanders** by **Calgary** with Richard Kromm for John Tonelli, March 11, 1986. Traded to **Chicago** by **NY Islanders** with Bob Bassen for Marc Bergevin and Gary Nylund, November 25, 1988.

KONTOS, CHRISTOPHER (CHRIS) (KONN-tohs)

Center. Shoots left. 6'1", 195 lbs. Born, Toronto, Ont., December 10, 1963.
(NY Rangers' 1st choice, 15th over-all, in 1982 Entry Draft).

			Regular Season					Playoffs				
Season	Club	Lea	GP	G	A	TP	PIM	GP	G	A	TP	PIM
1980-81	Sudbury	OHA	57	17	27	44	36	....	....	....	....	....
1981-82	Sudbury	OHL	12	6	6	12	18	....	....	....	....	....
	Toronto	OHL	59	36	56	92	68	10	7	9	16	2
1982-83	Toronto	OHL	28	21	33	54	23	....	....	....	....	....
	NY Rangers	**NHL**	**44**	**8**	**7**	**15**	**33**	....	....	....	....	....
1983-84	**NY Rangers**	**NHL**	**6**	**0**	**1**	**1**	**8**	....	....	....	....	....
	Tulsa	CHL	21	5	13	18	8	....	....	....	....	....
1984-85	**NY Rangers**	**NHL**	**28**	**4**	**8**	**12**	**24**	....	....	....	....	....
	New Haven	AHL	48	19	24	43	30	....	....	....	....	....
1985-86	Ilves	Fin.	36	16	15	31	30	....	....	....	....	....
	New Haven	AHL	21	8	15	23	12	5	4	2	6	4
1986-87	**Pittsburgh**	**NHL**	**31**	**8**	**9**	**17**	**6**	....	....	....	....	....
	New Haven	AHL	36	14	17	31	29	....	....	....	....	....
1987-88	**Pittsburgh**	**NHL**	**36**	**1**	**7**	**8**	**12**	....	....	....	....	....
	Muskegon	IHL	10	3	6	9	8	....	....	....	....	....
	Los Angeles	**NHL**	**6**	**2**	**10**	**12**	**2**	**4**	**1**	**0**	**1**	**4**
	New Haven	AHL	16	8	16	24	4	....	....	....	....	....
1988-89	Ilves	Fin.	36	16	15	31	30	....	....	....	....	....
	Los Angeles	**NHL**	**7**	**2**	**1**	**3**	**2**	**11**	**9**	**0**	**9**	**8**
	NHL Totals		**158**	**25**	**43**	**68**	**87**	**15**	**10**	**0**	**10**	**12**

Traded to **Pittsburgh** by **NY Rangers** for Ron Duguay, January 21, 1987. Traded to **Los Angeles** by **Pittsburgh** with Pittsburgh's sixth round choice in 1988 Entry Draft (Micah Aivazoff) for Bryan Erickson, February 5, 1988.

KORDIC, JOHN

Defense. Shoots right. 6'1", 190 lbs. Born, Edmonton, Alta., March 22, 1965.
(Montreal's 6th choice, 80th over-all, in 1984 Entry Draft).

			Regular Season					Playoffs				
Season	Club	Lea	GP	G	A	TP	PIM	GP	G	A	TP	PIM
1982-83	Portland	WHL	72	3	22	25	235	14	1	6	7	30
1983-84	Portland	WHL	67	9	50	59	232	14	0	13	13	56
1984-85a	Seattle	WHL	46	17	36	53	154	....	....	....	....	....
	Portland	WHL	25	6	22	28	73	....	....	....	....	....
	Sherbrooke	AHL	4	0	0	0	4	4	0	0	0	11
1985-86	**Montreal**	**NHL**	**5**	**0**	**1**	**1**	**12**	**18**	**0**	**0**	**0**	**53**
	Sherbrooke	AHL	68	3	14	17	238	....	....	....	....	....
1986-87	**Montreal**	**NHL**	**44**	**5**	**3**	**8**	**151**	**11**	**2**	**0**	**2**	**19**
	Sherbrooke	AHL	10	4	4	8	49	....	....	....	....	....
1987-88	**Montreal**	**NHL**	**60**	**2**	**6**	**8**	**159**	**7**	**2**	**2**	**4**	**26**
1988-89	**Montreal**	**NHL**	**6**	**0**	**0**	**0**	**13**	....	....	....	....	....
	Toronto	**NHL**	**46**	**1**	**2**	**3**	**185**	....	....	....	....	....
	NHL Totals		**161**	**8**	**12**	**20**	**520**	**36**	**4**	**2**	**6**	**98**

a WHL Second All-Star Team, West Division (1985).

Traded to **Toronto** by **Montreal** with Montreal's sixth-round choice (Michael Doers) in 1989 Entry Draft, November 7, 1988.

KORN, JAMES A. (JIM)

Defense. Shoots left. 6'4", 220 lbs. Born, Hopkins, MN, July 28, 1957.
(Detroit's 4th choice, 73rd over-all, in 1977 Amateur Draft).

			Regular Season					Playoffs				
Season	Club	Lea	GP	G	A	TP	PIM	GP	G	A	TP	PIM
1977-78	Providence	ECAC	33	7	14	21	47	....	....	....	....	....
1978-79	Providence	ECAC	27	5	19	24	72	....	....	....	....	....
1979-80	**Detroit**	**NHL**	**63**	**5**	**13**	**18**	**108**	....	....	....	....	....
	Adirondack	AHL	14	2	7	9	40	....	....	....	....	....
1980-81	Adirondack	AHL	9	3	7	10	53	....	....	....	....	....
	Detroit	**NHL**	**63**	**5**	**15**	**20**	**246**	....	....	....	....	....
1981-82	**Detroit**	**NHL**	**59**	**1**	**7**	**8**	**104**	....	....	....	....	....
	Toronto	**NHL**	**11**	**1**	**3**	**4**	**44**	....	....	....	....	....
1982-83	**Toronto**	**NHL**	**80**	**8**	**21**	**29**	**236**	**3**	**0**	**0**	**0**	**26**
1983-84	**Toronto**	**NHL**	**65**	**12**	**14**	**26**	**257**	....	....	....	....	....
1984-85	**Toronto**	**NHL**	**41**	**5**	**5**	**10**	**171**	....	....	....	....	....
1985-86		DID NOT PLAY										
1986-87	**Buffalo**	**NHL**	**52**	**4**	**10**	**14**	**158**	....	....	....	....	....
1987-88	**New Jersey**	**NHL**	**52**	**8**	**13**	**21**	**140**	**9**	**0**	**2**	**2**	**71**
1988-89	**New Jersey**	**NHL**	**65**	**15**	**16**	**31**	**212**	....	....	....	....	....
	NHL Totals		**551**	**64**	**117**	**181**	**1625**	**12**	**0**	**2**	**2**	**97**

Traded to **Toronto** by **Detroit** for Toronto's fourth round choice (Craig Coxe) in 1982 Entry Draft and Toronto's fifth round choice (Joey Kocur) in 1983 Entry Draft, March 8, 1982. Traded to **Calgary** by **Toronto** for Terry Johnson. Traded to **Buffalo** by **Calgary** for Brian Engblom, October 3, 1986. Traded to **New Jersey** by **Buffalo** for Jan Ludwig, May 22, 1987.

KOROL, DAVID

Defense. Shoots right. 6'1", 185 lbs. Born, Winnipeg, Man., March 1, 1965.
(Detroit's 4th choice, 70th over-all, in 1983 Entry Draft).

			Regular Season					Playoffs				
Season	Club	Lea	GP	G	A	TP	PIM	GP	G	A	TP	PIM
1981-82	Winnipeg	WHL	64	4	22	26	55	....	....	....	....	....
1982-83	Winnipeg	WHL	72	14	32	57	90	3	0	1	1	0
1983-84	Winnipeg	WHL	57	15	48	63	49	....	....	....	....	....
	Adirondack	AHL	2	0	4	4	0	3	0	0	0	0
1984-85	Regina	WHL	48	4	30	34	61	3	0	0	0	0
1985-86	Adirondack	AHL	74	3	9	12	56	3	0	1	1	4
1986-87	Adirondack	AHL	48	1	4	5	67	11	2	2	4	21
1987-88	Adirondack	AHL	53	2	17	19	61	10	0	4	4	7
1988-89	Adirondack	AHL	73	3	24	27	57	17	1	2	3	8

KORTKO, ROGER

Center. Shoots left. 5'11", 195 lbs. Born, Hafford, Sask., February 1, 1963.
(NY Islanders' 6th choice, 126th over-all, in 1982 Entry Draft).

			Regular Season					Playoffs				
Season	Club	Lea	GP	G	A	TP	PIM	GP	G	A	TP	PIM
1980-81	Saskatoon	WHL	2	0	1	1	2	....	....	....	....	....
1981-82	Saskatoon	WHL	65	33	51	84	82	4	1	4	5	7
1982-83	Saskatoon	WHL	72	62	99	161	79	1	1	1	2	5
1983-84	Indianapolis	CHL	64	16	27	43	48	9	1	5	6	9
1984-85	**NY Islanders**	**NHL**	**27**	**2**	**9**	**11**	**9**	**10**	**0**	**3**	**3**	**17**
	Springfield	AHL	30	8	30	38	6	....	....	....	....	....
1985-86	**NY Islanders**	**NHL**	**52**	**5**	**8**	**13**	**19**	....	....	....	....	....
	Springfield	AHL	12	2	10	12	10	....	....	....	....	....
1986-87	Springfield	AHL	75	16	30	46	54	....	....	....	....	....
1987-88	Binghamton	AHL	72	26	45	71	46	4	1	1	2	2
1988-89	Binghamton	AHL	79	22	36	58	28	....	....	....	....	....
	NHL Totals		**79**	**7**	**17**	**24**	**28**	**10**	**0**	**3**	**3**	**17**

Signed as a free agent by **Hartford**, September 15, 1987.

KOSTICHKIN, PAVEL

Center. Shoots left. 6'2", 200 lbs. Born, Moscow, Soviet Union, November 9, 1968.
(Winnipeg's 12th choice, 199th overall, in 1988 Entry Draft).

			Regular Season					Playoffs				
Season	Club	Lea	GP	G	A	TP	PIM	GP	G	A	TP	PIM
1985-86	CSKA	USSR	16	5	4	9	12	....	....	....	....	....
1986-87	CSKA	USSR	13	0	3	3	4	....	....	....	....	....
1987-88	CSKA	USSR	40	8	0	8	20	....	....	....	....	....
1988-89	CSKA	USSR	31	4	2	6	16	....	....	....	....	....

KOSTYNSKI, DOUGLAS (DOUG) (kah-STIN-skee)

Center. Shoots right. 6'1", 170 lbs. Born, Castlegar, B.C., February 23, 1963.
(Boston's 9th choice, 186th over-all, in 1982 Entry Draft).

			Regular Season					Playoffs				
Season	Club	Lea	GP	G	A	TP	PIM	GP	G	A	TP	PIM
1979-80	N. Westminster	WHL	11	1	4	5	12	....	....	....	....	....
1980-81	N. Westminster	WHL	64	18	40	58	51	....	....	....	....	....
1981-82	Kamloops	WHL	53	39	42	81	57	3	1	0	1	0
1982-83	Kamloops	WHL	75	57	59	116	55	7	2	7	9	6
1983-84	**Boston**	**NHL**	**9**	**3**	**1**	**4**	**2**	....	....	....	....	....
	Hershey	AHL	67	13	27	40	8	....	....	....	....	....
1984-85	**Boston**	**NHL**	**6**	**0**	**0**	**0**	**2**	....	....	....	....	....
	Hershey	AHL	55	17	27	44	26	....	....	....	....	....
1985-86	Moncton	AHL	72	18	36	54	24	8	3	1	4	9
1986-87	Moncton	AHL	74	21	45	66	22	6	2	1	3	0
1987-88	Adirondack	AHL	10	3	3	6	10	1	0	0	0	2
1988-89	Saipa	Fin.	44	20	32	52	16	....	....	....	....	....
	NHL Totals		**15**	**3**	**1**	**4**	**4**	....	....	....	....	....

KOTSOPOULOS, CHRISTOPHER (CHRIS) (kaht SAH poh LIHZ)

Defense. Shoots right. 6'3", 215 lbs. Born, Scarborough, Ont., November 27, 1958.
Last amateur club: Acadia University Axemen (AUAA)

			Regular Season					Playoffs				
Season	Club	Lea	GP	G	A	TP	PIM	GP	G	A	TP	PIM
1978-79	Toledo	IHL	62	6	22	28	153	6	1	7	8	48
1979-80	New Haven	AHL	75	7	27	34	149	10	4	5	9	28
1980-81	NY Rangers	NHL	54	4	12	16	153	14	0	3	3	63
1981-82	Hartford	NHL	68	13	20	33	147	....	....	....	....	....
1982-83	Hartford	NHL	68	6	24	30	125	....	....	....	....	....
1983-84	Hartford	NHL	72	5	13	18	118	....	....	....	....	....
1984-85	Hartford	NHL	33	5	3	8	53	....	....	....	....	....
1985-86	Toronto	NHL	61	6	11	17	83	10	1	0	1	14
1986-87	Toronto	NHL	43	2	10	12	75	7	0	0	0	14
1987-88	Toronto	NHL	21	2	2	4	19	....	....	....	....	....
1988-89	Toronto	NHL	57	1	14	15	44	....	....	....	....	....
	NHL Totals		477	44	109	153	817	31	1	3	4	91

Signed as a free agent by **NY Rangers**, July 10, 1980. Traded to **Hartford** by **NY Rangers** with Gerry McDonald and Doug Sulliman for Mike Rogers and future considerations, October 2, 1981. Traded to **Toronto** by **Hartford** for Stewart Gavin, October 7, 1985. Signed as a free agent by **Detroit**, June 23, 1989.

KRAKIWSKY, SEAN (kruh-COO-skee)

Right wing. Shoots left. 6', 175 lbs. Born, Calgary, Alta., December 29, 1967.
(Los Angeles' 6th choice, 128th overall, in 1986 Entry Draft).

			Regular Season					Playoffs				
Season	Club	Lea	GP	G	A	TP	PIM	GP	G	A	TP	PIM
1985-86	Calgary	WHL	39	9	32	41	27	....	....	....	....	....
1986-87	Spokane	WHL	57	19	42	61	57	5	2	4	6	4
1987-88	New Haven	AHL	51	17	26	43	18	....	....	....	....	....
1988-89	Cdn. National	....	17	7	10	17	2	....	....	....	....	....

KRAUSS, ROBERT

Defense. Shoots left. 6'2", 210 lbs. Born, Grand Prairie, Alta., October 28, 1969.
(Washington's 5th choice, 78th overall, in 1988 Entry Draft).

			Regular Season					Playoffs				
Season	Club	Lea	GP	G	A	TP	PIM	GP	G	A	TP	PIM
1986-87	Calgary	WHL	70	3	17	20	130	....	....	....	....	....
1987-88	Lethbridge	WHL	69	6	21	27	245	....	....	....	....	....
1988-89	Tri-Cities	WHL	66	4	23	27	257	7	1	2	3	19

KRAYER, ED

Left wing. Shoots left. 6'1", 175 lbs. Born, Acton, MA, June 6, 1967.
(New Jersey's 8th choice, 150th overall, in 1985 Entry Draft).

			Regular Season					Playoffs				
Season	Club	Lea	GP	G	A	TP	PIM	GP	G	A	TP	PIM
1985-86	Harvard	ECAC	34	9	22	31	4	....	....	....	....	....
1986-87	Harvard	ECAC	14	2	9	11	4	....	....	....	....	....
1987-88	Harvard	ECAC	DID NOT PLAY — INJURED									
1988-89	Harvard	ECAC	34	12	14	26	4	....	....	....	....	....

KRENTZ, DALE

Left wing. Shoots left. 5'11", 190 lbs. Born, Steinbach, Man., December 19, 1961.

			Regular Season					Playoffs				
Season	Club	Lea	GP	G	A	TP	PIM	GP	G	A	TP	PIM
1982-83	Michigan State	CCHA	42	11	24	35	50	....	....	....	....	....
1983-84	Michigan State	CCHA	44	12	20	32	34	....	....	....	....	....
1984-85	Michigan State	CCHA	44	24	30	54	26	....	....	....	....	....
1985-86	Adirondack	AHL	79	19	27	46	27	13	2	6	8	9
1986-87	Detroit	NHL	8	0	0	0	0	....	....	....	....	....
	Adirondack	AHL	71	32	39	71	68	11	3	4	7	10
1987-88	Detroit	NHL	6	2	0	2	5	2	0	0	0	0
a	Adirondack	AHL	67	39	43	82	65	8	*11	4	15	8
1988-89	Detroit	NHL	16	3	3	6	4	....	....	....	....	....
	Adirondack	AHL	36	21	20	41	30	....	....	....	....	....
	NHL Totals		30	5	3	8	9	2	0	0	0	0

a AHL Second All-Star Team (1988)

Signed as a free agent by **Detroit**, June 5, 1985.

KRIVOKHIZA, YURI

Defense. Shoots left. 6'2", 185 lbs. Born, Minsk, Soviet Union, March 30, 1968.
(Montreal's 11th choice, 209th overall, in 1988 Entry Draft).

			Regular Season					Playoffs				
Season	Club	Lea	GP	G	A	TP	PIM	GP	G	A	TP	PIM
1988-89	Minsk	USSR	25	2	7	9	22	....	....	....	....	....

KROMM, RICHARD GORDON (RICH)

Left wing. Shoots left. 5'11", 190 lbs. Born, Trail, B.C., March 29, I964.
(Calgary's 2nd choice, 37th over-all, in 1982 Entry Draft).

			Regular Season					Playoffs				
Season	Club	Lea	GP	G	A	TP	PIM	GP	G	A	TP	PIM
1981-82	Portland	WHL	60	16	38	54	30	14	0	3	3	17
1982-83	Portland	WHL	72	35	68	103	64	14	7	13	20	12
1983-84	Portland	WHL	10	10	4	14	13	....	....	....	....	....
	Calgary	NHL	53	11	12	23	27	11	1	1	2	9
1984-85	Calgary	NHL	73	20	32	52	32	3	0	1	1	4
1985-86	Calgary	NHL	63	12	17	29	31	....	....	....	....	....
	NY Islanders	NHL	14	7	7	14	4	3	0	1	1	0
1986-87	NY Islanders	NHL	70	12	17	29	20	14	1	3	4	4
1987-88	NY Islanders	NHL	71	5	10	15	20	5	0	0	0	5
1988-89	NY Islanders	NHL	20	1	6	7	4	....	....	....	....	....
	Springfield	AHL	48	21	26	47	15	....	....	....	....	....
	NHL Totals		364	68	101	169	138	36	2	6	8	22

Traded to **NY Islanders** by **Calgary** with Steve Konroyd for John Tonelli, March 11, 1986.

KRON, ROBERT

Right wing/Center. Shoots right. 5'10", 174 lbs. Born, Brno, Czech., February 27, 1967.
(Vancouver's 5th choice, 88th overall, in 1985 Entry Draft).

			Regular Season					Playoffs				
Season	Club	Lea	GP	G	A	TP	PIM	GP	G	A	TP	PIM
1986-87	Zetor Brno	Czech.	28	14	11	25	....	....	....	....	....	....
1987-88	Zetor Brno	Czech.	32	12	6	18	....	....	....	....	....	....
1988-89	Zetor Brno	Czech.	43	28	19	47	....	....	....	....	....	....

KRUPP, UWE

Defense. Shoots right. 6'6", 230 lbs. Born, Cologne, West Germany, June 24, 1965.
(Buffalo's 13th choice, 214th overall, in 1983 Entry Draft).

			Regular Season					Playoffs				
Season	Club	Lea	GP	G	A	TP	PIM	GP	G	A	TP	PIM
1982-83	KEC	W. Ger.	11	0	0	0	0	....	....	....	....	....
1983-84	KEC	W. Ger.	40	0	4	4	22	....	....	....	....	....
1980-80	KEC	W. Ger.	39	11	8	19	36	....	....	....	....	....
1985-86	KEC	W. Ger.	45	10	21	31	83	....	....	....	....	....
1986-87	Buffalo	NHL	26	1	4	5	23	....	....	....	....	....
	Rochester	AHL	42	3	19	22	50	17	1	11	12	16
1987-88	Buffalo	NHL	75	2	9	11	151	6	0	0	0	15
1988-89	Buffalo	NHL	70	5	13	18	55	5	0	1	1	4
	NHL Totals		171	8	26	34	229	11	0	1	1	19

KRUPPKE, GORD (KRUP-kee)

Defense. Shoots right. 6'1", 200 lbs. Born, Slave Lake, Alta., April 2, 1969.
(Detroit's 2nd choice, 32nd overall, in 1987 Entry Draft).

			Regular Season					Playoffs				
Season	Club	Lea	GP	G	A	TP	PIM	GP	G	A	TP	PIM
1985-87	Prince Albert	WHL	62	1	8	9	81	20	4	4	8	22
1986-87	Prince Albert	WHL	49	2	10	12	129	8	0	0	0	9
1987-88	Prince Albert	WHL	54	8	8	16	113	10	0	0	0	46
1988-89	Prince Albert	WHL	62	6	26	32	254	3	0	0	0	11

KRUSHELNYSKI, MICHAEL (MIKE) (KROO shihl NIH skee)

Center. Shoots left. 6'2", 200 lbs. Born, Montreal, Que., April 27, 1960.
(Boston's 7th choice, 120th over-all, in 1979 Entry Draft).

			Regular Season					Playoffs				
Season	Club	Lea	GP	G	A	TP	PIM	GP	G	A	TP	PIM
1978-79	Montreal	QJHL	46	15	29	44	42	11	3	4	7	8
1979-80	Montreal	QJHL	72	39	60	99	78	6	2	3	5	2
1980-81	Springfield	AHL	80	25	28	53	47	7	1	1	2	29
1981-82	Erie	AHL	62	31	52	83	44	....	....	....	....	....
	Boston	NHL	17	3	3	6	2	1	0	0	0	2
1982-83	Boston	NHL	79	23	42	65	43	17	8	6	14	12
1983-84	Boston	NHL	66	25	20	45	55	2	0	0	0	0
1984-85	Edmonton	NHL	80	43	45	88	60	18	5	8	13	22
1985-86	Edmonton	NHL	54	16	24	40	22	10	4	5	9	16
1986-87	Edmonton	NHL	80	16	35	51	67	21	3	4	7	18
1987-88	Edmonton	NHL	76	20	27	47	64	19	4	6	10	12
1988-89	Los Angeles	NHL	78	26	36	62	110	11	1	4	5	4
	NHL Totals		530	172	232	404	423	99	25	33	58	86

Played in NHL All-Star Game (1985)

Traded to **Edmonton** by **Boston** for Ken Linseman, June 21, 1984. Traded to **Los Angeles** by **Edmonton** with Wayne Gretzky and Marty McSorley for Jimmy Carson, Martin Gelinas, Los Angeles' first round choices in 1989 (acquired by New Jersey, June 17, 1989. New Jersey selected Jason Miller), 1991 and 1993 Entry Drafts and cash, August 9, 1988.

KRUTOV, VLADIMIR

Left wing. Shoots left. 5'9", 195 lbs. Born, Moscow, Soviet Union, June 1, 1960.
(Vancouver's 11th choice, 238th overall, in 1986 Entry Draft).

			Regular Season					Playoffs				
Season	Club	Lea	GP	G	A	TP	PIM	GP	G	A	TP	PIM
1977-78	CSKA	USSR	1	0	0	0	0	....	....	....	....	....
1978-79	CSKA	USSR	25	8	3	11	6	....	....	....	....	....
1979-80	CSKA	USSR	40	30	12	42	16	....	....	....	....	....
1980-81	CSKA	USSR	47	25	15	40	20	....	....	....	....	....
1981-82a	CSKA	USSR	46	37	29	66	30	....	....	....	....	....
1982-83a	CSKA	USSR	44	32	21	53	34	....	....	....	....	....
1983-84a	CSKA	USSR	44	37	20	57	20	....	....	....	....	....
1984-85a	CSKA	USSR	40	23	30	53	26	....	....	....	....	....
1985-86a	CSKA	USSR	40	31	17	48	10	....	....	....	....	....
1986-87a	CSKA	USSR	39	26	24	50	16	....	....	....	....	....
1987-88a	CSKA	USSR	38	19	23	42	20	....	....	....	....	....
1988-89	CSKA	USSR	35	20	21	41	12	....	....	....	....	....

a Soviet National League All-Star

KRYGIER, TODD

Center. Shoots left. 5'11", 180 lbs. Born, Northville, MI, October 12, 1965.
(Hartford's 1st choice, 16th overall, in 1988 Supplemental Draft).

			Regular Season					Playoffs				
Season	Club	Lea	GP	G	A	TP	PIM	GP	G	A	TP	PIM
1987-88	U. Connecticut	NCAA	27	32	39	71	28	....	....	....	....	....
	New Haven	AHL	13	1	5	6	34	....	....	....	....	....
1988-89	Binghamton	AHL	76	26	42	68	77	....	....	....	....	....

KRYS, MARK

Defense. Shoots right. 6'0", 185 lbs. Born, Timmins, Ont., May 29, 1969.
(Boston's 6th choice, 123rd overall, in 1988 Entry Draft).

			Regular Season					Playoffs				
Season	Club	Lea	GP	G	A	TP	PIM	GP	G	A	TP	PIM
1987-88	Boston U.	H.E.	34	0	6	6	40	....	....	....	....	....
1988-89	Boston U.	H.E.	35	0	7	7	54	....	....	....	....	....

KUCERA, FRANTISEK

Defense. Shoots right. 6'2", 205 lbs. Born, Prague, Czechoslovakia, February 3, 1968.
(Chicago's 3rd choice, 77th overall, in 1986 Entry Draft).

			Regular Season					Playoffs				
Season	Club	Lea	GP	G	A	TP	PIM	GP	G	A	TP	PIM
1986-87	Sparta Praha	Czech.	33	7	2	9	....	....	....	....	....	....
1987-88	Sparta Praha	Czech.	34	4	2	6	....	....	....	....	....	....
1988-89	Jihlava	Czech.	45	10	9	19	....	....	....	....	....	....

KUDELSKI, BOB

Center. Shoots right. 6'1", 200 lbs. Born, Feeding Hills, MA, March 3, 1964.
(Los Angeles' 1st choice, 2nd overall, in 1986 Supplemental Draft).

			Regular Season					Playoffs				
Season	Club	Lea	GP	G	A	TP	PIM	GP	G	A	TP	PIM
1983-84	Yale	ECAC	21	14	12	26	12	....	....	....	....	....
1984-85	Yale	ECAC	32	21	23	44	38	....	....	....	....	....
1985-86	Yale	ECAC	31	18	23	41	48	....	....	....	....	....
1986-87a	Yale	ECAC	30	25	22	47	34	....	....	....	....	....
1987-88	**Los Angeles**	**NHL**	**26**	**0**	**1**	**1**	**8**	....	....	....	....	....
	New Haven	AHL	50	15	19	34	41	....	....	....	....	....
1988-89	**Los Angeles**	**NHL**	**14**	**1**	**3**	**4**	**17**	....	....	....	....	....
	New Haven	AHL	60	32	19	51	43	17	8	5	13	12
	NHL Totals		**40**	**1**	**4**	**5**	**25**	....	....	....	....	....

a ECAC First All-Star Team (1987)

KULAK, STUART (STU)

Right wing. Shoots right. 5'10", 180 lbs. Born, Edmonton, Alta., March 10, 1963.
(Vancouver's 5th choice, 115th over-all, in 1981 Entry Draft).

			Regular Season					Playoffs				
Season	Club	Lea	GP	G	A	TP	PIM	GP	G	A	TP	PIM
1979-80	Sherwood Park	AJHL	53	30	23	53	111	....	....	....	....	....
	Victoria	WHL	3	0	0	0	0	....	....	....	....	....
1980-81	Victoria	WHL	72	23	24	47	44	15	3	5	8	19
1981-82	Victoria	WHL	71	38	50	88	92	4	1	2	3	43
1982-83	**Vancouver**	**NHL**	**4**	**1**	**1**	**2**	**0**	....	....	....	....	....
	Victoria	WHL	50	29	33	62	130	10	10	9	19	29
1983-84	Fredericton	AHL	52	12	16	28	55	5	0	0	0	59
1984-85			DID NOT PLAY — INJURED									
1985-86	Fredericton	AHL	3	1	0	1	0	6	2	1	3	0
	Kalamazoo	IHL	30	14	8	22	38	2	2	0	2	0
1986-87	**Vancouver**	**NHL**	**28**	**1**	**1**	**2**	**37**	....	....	....	....	....
	Edmonton	**NHL**	**23**	**3**	**1**	**4**	**41**	....	....	....	....	....
	NY Rangers	**NHL**	**3**	**0**	**0**	**0**	**0**	....	....	....	....	....
1987-88	**Quebec**	**NHL**	**14**	**1**	**1**	**2**	**28**	....	....	....	....	....
	Moncton	AHL	37	9	12	21	58	....	....	....	....	....
1988-89	**Winnipeg**	**NHL**	**18**	**2**	**0**	**2**	**24**	....	....	....	....	....
	Moncton	AHL	51	30	29	59	98	10	5	6	11	16
	NHL Totals		**90**	**8**	**4**	**12**	**130**	....	....	....	....	....

Sold to **Edmonton** by **Vancouver**, December 11, 1986. Acquired by **NY Rangers** from **Edmonton** to complete Reijo Ruotsalanien trade, March 10, 1987. Traded to **Winnipeg** by **Quebec** for Bob Dollas, December 17, 1987. Claimed by **Quebec** in NHL Waiver Draft, October 5, 1987.

KULONEN, TIMO

Defense. Shoots right. 6'4", 210 lbs. Born, Forssa, Finland, November 1, 1967.
(Minnesota's 7th choice, 130th overall, in 1987 Entry Draft).

			Regular Season					Playoffs				
Season	Club	Lea	GP	G	A	TP	PIM	GP	G	A	TP	PIM
1983-84	FoPS	Fin. 2	17	1	0	1	14	....	....	....	....	....
1984-85	FoPS	Fin. 2	42	11	18	29	60	....	....	....	....	....
1985-86	FoPS	Fin. 2	40	14	25	39	48	....	....	....	....	....
1986-87	KalPa	Fin.	39	2	8	10	20	....	....	....	....	....
1987-88	KalPa	Fin.	44	7	15	22	32	....	....	....	....	....
1988-89	Kalpa	Fin.	40	9	16	25	18	2	0	1	1	0

KUMMU, RYAN

Defense. Shoots left. 6'3", 205 lbs. Born, Kitchener, Ont., June 5, 1967.
(Washington's 11th choice, 246th overall, in 1987 Entry Draft).

			Regular Season					Playoffs				
Season	Club	Lea	GP	G	A	TP	PIM	GP	G	A	TP	PIM
1986-87	RPI	ECAC	28	0	2	2	32	....	....	....	....	....
1987-88	RPI	ECAC	29	5	10	15	40	....	....	....	....	....
1988-89	RPI	ECAC	29	2	5	7	28	....	....	....	....	....

KUMPEL, MARK

Right wing. Shoots right. 6', 190 lbs. Born, Wakefield, MA, March 7, 1961.
(Quebec's 4th choice, 108th over-all, in 1980 Entry Draft).

			Regular Season					Playoffs				
Season	Club	Lea	GP	G	A	TP	PIM	GP	G	A	TP	PIM
1979-80	U. of Lowell	ECAC	30	18	18	36	12	....	....	....	....	....
1980-81	U. of Lowell	ECAC	1	2	0	2	0	....	....	....	....	....
1981-82	U. of Lowell	ECAC	35	17	13	30	23	....	....	....	....	....
1982-83	U. of Lowell	ECAC	7	8	5	13	0	....	....	....	....	....
	U.S. National	...	30	14	18	32	6	....	....	....	....	....
1983-84	U.S. National	...	61	14	19	33	19	....	....	....	....	....
	U.S. Olympic	...	6	1	0	1	2	....	....	....	....	....
	Fredericton	AHL	16	1	1	2	5	3	0	0	0	15
1984-85	**Quebec**	**NHL**	**42**	**8**	**7**	**15**	**26**	**18**	**3**	**4**	**7**	**4**
	Fredericton	AHL	18	9	6	15	17	....	....	....	....	....
1985-86	**Quebec**	**NHL**	**47**	**10**	**12**	**22**	**17**	**2**	**1**	**0**	**1**	**0**
	Fredericton	AHL	7	4	2	6	4	....	....	....	....	....
1986-87	**Quebec**	**NHL**	**40**	**1**	**8**	**9**	**16**	....	....	....	....	....
	Detroit	**NHL**	**5**	**0**	**1**	**1**	**0**	**8**	**0**	**0**	**0**	**4**
	Adirondack	AHL	7	2	3	5	0	1	1	0	1	0
1987-88	**Detroit**	**NHL**	**13**	**0**	**2**	**2**	**4**	....	....	....	....	....
	Adirondack	AHL	4	5	0	5	2	....	....	....	....	....
1988-89	**Winnipeg**	**NHL**	**32**	**4**	**4**	**8**	**19**	**4**	**0**	**0**	**0**	**4**
	Moncton	AHL	53	22	23	45	25	10	3	4	7	0
	NHL Totals		**179**	**23**	**34**	**57**	**82**	**32**	**4**	**4**	**8**	**12**

Traded to **Detroit** by **Quebec** with Brent Ashton and Gilbert Delorme for Basil McRae, John Ogrodnick and Doug Shedden, January 17, 1987. Traded to **Winnipeg** by **Detroit** for Jim Nill, January 11, 1988.

KUNDA, DAVID

Defense. Shoots left. 6'1", 210 lbs. Born, Mississauga, Ont., November 23, 1968.
(Montreal's 13th choice, 251st overall, in 1988 Entry Draft).

			Regular Season					Playoffs				
Season	Club	Lea	GP	G	A	TP	PIM	GP	G	A	TP	PIM
1987-88	U. of Guelph	OUAA	8	0	1	1	17	....	....	....	....	....
1988-89	U. of Guelph	OUAA	20	3	7	10	75	....	....	....	....	....

KURRI, JARI (KUHR ree, YAH ree)

Right wing. Shoots right. 6'1", 195 lbs. Born, Helsinki, Finland, May 18, 1960.
(Edmonton's 3rd choice, 69th over-all, in 1980 Entry Draft).

			Regular Season					Playoffs				
Season	Club	Lea	GP	G	A	TP	PIM	GP	G	A	TP	PIM
1977-78	Jokerit	Fin.	29	2	9	11	12	....	....	....	....	....
1978-79	Jokerit	Fin.	33	16	14	30	12	....	....	....	....	....
1979-80	Jokerit	Fin.	33	23	16	39	22	6	7	2	9	13
1980-81	**Edmonton**	**NHL**	**75**	**32**	**43**	**75**	**40**	**9**	**5**	**7**	**12**	**4**
1981-82	**Edmonton**	**NHL**	**71**	**32**	**54**	**86**	**32**	**5**	**2**	**5**	**7**	**10**
1982-83	**Edmonton**	**NHL**	**80**	**45**	**59**	**104**	**22**	**16**	**8**	**15**	**23**	**8**
1983-84a	**Edmonton**	**NHL**	**64**	**52**	**61**	**113**	**14**	**19**	***14**	**14**	**28**	**13**
1984-85bc	**Edmonton**	**NHL**	**73**	**71**	**64**	**135**	**30**	**18**	***19**	**12**	**31**	**6**
1985-86a	**Edmonton**	**NHL**	**78**	***68**	**63**	**131**	**22**	**10**	**2**	**10**	**12**	**4**
1986-87c	**Edmonton**	**NHL**	**79**	**54**	**54**	**108**	**41**	**21**	***15**	**10**	**25**	**20**
1987-88	**Edmonton**	**NHL**	**80**	**43**	**53**	**96**	**30**	**19**	***14**	**17**	**31**	**12**
1988-89	**Edmonton**	**NHL**	**76**	**44**	**58**	**102**	**69**	**7**	**3**	**5**	**8**	**6**
	NHL Totals		**676**	**441**	**509**	**950**	**300**	**124**	**82**	**95**	**177**	**83**

a NHL Second All-Star Team (1984, 1986)
b Won Lady Byng Memorial Trophy (1985)
c NHL First All-Star Team (1985, 1987)

Played in NHL All-Star Game (1983, 1985, 1986, 1988, 1989)

KURVERS, TOM

Defense. Shoots left. 6', 205 lbs. Born, Minneapolis, MN, September 14, 1962.
(Montreal's 10th choice, 145th over-all, in 1981 Entry Draft).

			Regular Season					Playoffs				
Season	Club	Lea	GP	G	A	TP	PIM	GP	G	A	TP	PIM
1980-81	Minn.-Duluth	WCHA	39	6	24	30	48	....	....	....	....	....
1981-82	Minn.-Duluth	WCHA	37	11	31	42	18	....	....	....	....	....
1982-83	Minn.-Duluth	WCHA	26	4	23	27	24	....	....	....	....	....
1983-84ab	Minn.-Duluth	WCHA	43	18	58	76	46	....	....	....	....	....
1984-85	**Montreal**	**NHL**	**75**	**10**	**35**	**45**	**30**	**12**	**0**	**6**	**6**	**6**
1985-86	**Montreal**	**NHL**	**62**	**7**	**23**	**30**	**36**	....	....	....	....	....
1986-87	**Montreal**	**NHL**	**1**	**0**	**0**	**0**	**0**	....	....	....	....	....
	Buffalo	**NHL**	**55**	**6**	**17**	**23**	**22**	....	....	....	....	....
1987-88	**New Jersey**	**NHL**	**56**	**5**	**29**	**34**	**46**	**19**	**6**	**9**	**15**	**38**
1988-89	**New Jersey**	**NHL**	**74**	**16**	**50**	**66**	**38**	....	....	....	....	....
	NHL Totals		**323**	**44**	**154**	**198**	**172**	**31**	**6**	**15**	**21**	**44**

a WCHA First All-Star Team (1984)
b Won Hobey Baker Memorial Trophy (1984)

Traded to **Buffalo** by **Montreal** for Buffalo's second-round choice in 1988 Entry Draft, November 18, 1986. Traded to **New Jersey** by **Buffalo** for the rights to Detroit's third-round choice (Andrew MacVicar) in 1987 Entry Draft previously acquired by New Jersey in Mel Bridgman deal, June 13, 1987.

KURZAWSKI, MARK

Defense. Shoots right. 6'3", 200 lbs. Born, Chicago, IL, February 25, 1968.
(Chicago's 2nd choice, 35th overall, in 1986 Entry Draft).

			Regular Season					Playoffs				
Season	Club	Lea	GP	G	A	TP	PIM	GP	G	A	TP	PIM
1985-86	Windsor	OHL	66	11	25	36	66	16	3	5	8	23
1986-87	Windsor	OHL	65	5	23	28	98	14	3	4	7	38
1987-88	Windsor	OHL	62	8	13	21	150	12	1	2	3	8
1988-89	Saginaw	IHL	75	2	11	13	71	6	0	0	0	12

KUSHNER, DALE

Left wing. Shoots left. 6'1", 205 lbs. Born, Terrace, B.C., June 13, 1966.

			Regular Season					Playoffs				
Season	Club	Lea	GP	G	A	TP	PIM	GP	G	A	TP	PIM
1984-85	Medicine Hat	WHL	67	28	19	47	198	....	....	....	....	....
1985-86	Medicine Hat	WHL	66	25	19	44	218	10	3	3	6	18
1986-87	Medicine Hat	WHL	63	34	34	68	250	25	0	5	5	114
1987-88	Springfield	AHL	68	13	23	36	201	....	....	....	....	....
1988-89	Springfield	AHL	45	5	8	13	132	....	....	....	....	....

Signed as a free agent by **NY Islanders**, April 7, 1987.

KYLLONEN, MARKKU (kill-OH-nen)

Left wing. Shoots left. 6'2", 200 lbs. Born, Joensuu, Finland, February 15, 1962.
(Winnipeg's 8th choice, 163rd overall, in 1987 Entry Draft).

			Regular Season					Playoffs				
Season	Club	Lea	GP	G	A	TP	PIM	GP	G	A	TP	PIM
1980-81	JoKP	Fin. 2	33	7	6	13	12	....	....	....	....	....
1981-82	JoKP	Fin. 2	31	13	16	29	20	....	....	....	....	....
1982-83	JoKP	Fin. 2	35	16	23	39	8	....	....	....	....	....
1983-84	JoKP	Fin. 2	33	16	12	28	4	....	....	....	....	....
1984-85	JoKP	Fin. 2	43	28	27	55	22	....	....	....	....	....
1985-86	JoKP	Fin. 2	34	12	12	24	14	....	....	....	....	....
1986-87	Karpat	Fin.	43	24	16	40	14	9	3	2	5	4
1987-88	Karpat	Fin.	43	8	24	32	32	....	....	....	....	....
1988-89	**Winnipeg**	**NHL**	**9**	**0**	**2**	**2**	**2**	....	....	....	....	....
	Moncton	AHL	60	14	20	34	16	5	1	0	1	0
	NHL Totals		**9**	**0**	**2**	**2**	**2**	....	....	....	....	....

KYPREOS, NICHOLAS (NICK)

Left Wing. Shoots left. 6', 195lbs. Born, Toronto, Ont., June 4, 1966.

			Regular Season					Playoffs				
Season	Club	Lea	GP	G	A	TP	PIM	GP	G	A	TP	PIM
1983-84	North Bay	OHL	51	12	11	23	36	4	3	2	5	9
1984-85	North Bay	OHL	64	41	36	77	71	8	2	2	4	15
1985-86a	North Bay	OHL	64	62	35	97	112	....	....	....	....	....
1986-87	Hershey	AHL	10	0	1	1	4	....	....	....	....	....
b	North Bay	OHL	46	49	41	90	54	24	11	5	16	78
1987-88	Hershey	AHL	71	24	20	44	101	12	0	2	2	17
1988-89	Hershey	AHL	28	12	15	27	19	12	4	5	9	11

a OHL First All-Star Team (1986)
b OHL Second All-Star Team (1987)

Signed as a free agent by **Philadelphia**, September 30, 1984.

KYTE, JAMES (JIM)   (KITE)

Defense. Shoots left. 6'5", 210 lbs.   Born, Ottawa, Ont., March 21, 1964.
(Winnipeg's 1st choice, 12th over-all, in 1982 Entry Draft).

			Regular Season					Playoffs			
Season	Club	Lea	GP	G	A	TP	PIM	GP	G	A	TP	PIM
1981-82	Cornwall	OHL	52	4	13	17	148	5	0	0	0	10
1982-83	**Winnipeg**	**NHL**	2	0	0	0	0	....	....	....	....	....
	Cornwall	OHL	65	6	30	36	195	8	0	2	2	24
1983-84	**Winnipeg**	**NHL**	58	1	2	3	55	3	0	0	0	11
1984-85	**Winnipeg**	**NHL**	71	0	3	3	111	8	0	0	0	14
1985-86	**Winnipeg**	**NHL**	71	1	3	4	126	3	0	0	0	12
1986-87	**Winnipeg**	**NHL**	72	5	5	10	162	10	0	4	4	36
1987-88	**Winnipeg**	**NHL**	51	1	3	4	128	....	....	....	....	....
1988-89	**Winnipeg**	**NHL**	74	3	9	12	190	....	....	....	....	....
	NHL Totals		399	11	25	36	772	24	0	4	4	73

Traded to **Pittsburgh** by **Winnipeg** with Andrew McBain and Randy Gilhen for Randy Cunnyworth, Rick Tabaracci and Dave McLlwain, June 17, 1989.

LACKTEN, KURT

Right wing. Shoots right. 6', 177 lbs.   Born, Kamsack, Sask., May 20, 1967.
(NY Islanders' 9th choice, 139th overall, in 1985 Entry Draft).

			Regular Season					Playoffs			
Season	Club	Lea	GP	G	A	TP	PIM	GP	G	A	TP	PIM
1984-85	Moose Jaw	WHL	66	18	13	31	141	....	....	....	....	....
1985-86	Calgary	WHL	61	5	20	25	112	....	....	....	....	....
1986-87	Swift Current	WHL	65	20	20	40	97	3	0	1	1	4
1987-88	Springfield	AHL	37	1	4	5	64	....	....	....	....	....
	Peoria	IHL	19	0	5	5	20	....	....	....	....	....
1988-89	Indianapolis	IHL	9	1	2	3	11	....	....	....	....	....

LACOMBE, NORMAND

Right wing. Shoots right. 6', 205 lbs.   Born, Pierrefonds, Que., October 18, 1964.
(Buffalo's 2nd choice, 10th over-all, in 1983 Entry Draft).

			Regular Season					Playoffs			
Season	Club	Lea	GP	G	A	TP	PIM	GP	G	A	TP	PIM
1981-82	N. Hampshire	ECAC	35	18	16	34	38	....	....	....	....	....
1982-83	N. Hampshire	ECAC	35	18	25	43	48	....	....	....	....	....
1983-84	Rochester	AHL	44	10	16	26	45	....	....	....	....	....
1984-85	**Buffalo**	**NHL**	30	2	4	6	25	....	....	....	....	....
	Rochester	AHL	33	13	16	29	33	5	3	1	4	4
1985-86	**Buffalo**	**NHL**	25	6	7	13	13	....	....	....	....	....
	Rochester	AHL	32	10	13	23	56	....	....	....	....	....
1986-87	**Buffalo**	**NHL**	39	4	7	11	8	....	....	....	....	....
	Rochester	AHL	13	6	5	11	4	....	....	....	....	....
	Edmonton	**NHL**	1	0	0	0	2	....	....	....	....	....
	Nova Scotia	AHL	10	3	5	8	4	5	1	1	2	6
1987-88	**Edmonton**	**NHL**	53	8	9	17	36	19	3	0	3	28
1988-89	**Edmonton**	**NHL**	64	17	11	28	57	7	2	1	3	21
	NHL Totals		212	37	38	75	141	26	5	1	6	49

Traded to **Edmonton** by **Buffalo** with Wayne Van Dorp and future considerations for Lee Fogolin and Mark Napier, March 6, 1987.

LACOUTURE, BILL

Right wing. Shoots right. 6'2", 190 lbs.   Born, Framingham, MA, May 28, 1968.
(Chicago's 11th choice, 218th overall, in 1987 Entry Draft).

			Regular Season					Playoffs			
Season	Club	Lea	GP	G	A	TP	PIM	GP	G	A	TP	PIM
1985-86	Natick	HS	20	20	18	38	....	....	....	....	....	....
1986-87	Natick	HS	19	15	39	54	....	....	....	....	....	....
1987-88	N. Hampshire	H.E.	13	1	3	4	2	....	....	....	....	....
1988-89	N. Hampshire	H.E.	20	0	1	1	2	....	....	....	....	....

LACROIX, DANIEL

Left wing. Shoots left. 6'2", 185 lbs.   Born, Montreal, Que., March 11, 1969.
(NY Rangers' 2nd choice, 31st overall, in 1987 Entry Draft).

			Regular Season					Playoffs			
Season	Club	Lea	GP	G	A	TP	PIM	GP	G	A	TP	PIM
1986-87	Granby	QMJHL	54	9	16	25	311	8	1	2	3	22
1987-88	Granby	QMJHL	58	24	50	74	468	5	0	4	4	12
1988-89	Granby	QMJHL	70	45	49	94	320	4	1	1	2	57
	Denver	IHL	2	0	1	1	0	2	0	1	1	0

LADOUCEUR, RANDY   (la-da-SEWR)

Defense. Shoots left. 6'2", 220 lbs.   Born, Brockville, Ont., June 30, 1960.

			Regular Season					Playoffs			
Season	Club	Lea	GP	G	A	TP	PIM	GP	G	A	TP	PIM
1978-79	Brantford	OHA	64	3	17	20	141	....	....	....	....	....
1979-80	Brantford	OHA	37	6	15	21	125	8	0	5	5	18
1980-81	Kalamazoo	IHL	80	7	30	37	52	8	1	3	4	10
1981-82	Adirondack	AHL	78	4	28	32	78	5	1	1	2	6
1982-83	**Detroit**	**NHL**	27	0	4	4	16	....	....	....	....	....
	Adirondack	AHL	48	11	21	32	54	....	....	....	....	....
1983-84	Adirondack	AHL	11	3	5	8	12	....	....	....	....	....
	Detroit	**NHL**	71	3	17	20	58	4	1	0	1	6
1984-85	**Detroit**	**NHL**	80	3	27	30	108	3	1	0	1	0
1985-86	**Detroit**	**NHL**	78	5	13	18	196	....	....	....	....	....
1986-87	**Detroit**	**NHL**	34	3	6	9	70	....	....	....	....	....
	Hartford	**NHL**	36	2	3	5	51	6	0	2	2	12
1987-88	**Hartford**	**NHL**	67	1	7	8	91	6	1	1	2	4
1988-89	**Hartford**	**NHL**	75	2	5	7	95	1	0	0	0	10
	NHL Totals		468	19	82	101	685	20	3	3	6	32

Signed as a free agent by **Detroit**, November 1, 1979. Traded to **Hartford** by **Detroit** for Dave Barr, January 12, 1987.

LAFAYETTE, JUSTIN

Left wing. Shoots left. 6'6", 200 lbs.   Born, Vancouver, B.C., January 23, 1970.
(Chicago's 6th choice, 113th overall, in 1988 Entry Draft).

			Regular Season					Playoffs			
Season	Club	Lea	GP	G	A	TP	PIM	GP	G	A	TP	PIM
1987-88	Ferris State	CCHA	34	1	2	3	20	....	....	....	....	....
1988-89	Ferris State	CCHA	36	3	4	7	59	....	....	....	....	....

LAFLEUR, GUY DAMIEN

Right wing. Shoots right. 6', 185 lbs.   Born, Thurso, Que., September 20, 1951.
(Montreal's 1st choice and 1st overall in 1971 Amateur Draft).

			Regular Season					Playoffs			
Season	Club	Lea	GP	G	A	TP	PIM	GP	G	A	TP	PIM
1969-70	Quebec	QJHL	56	*103	67	170	89	15	*25	18	*43	24
1970-71	Quebec	QJHL	62	*130	79	*209	135	14	*22	*21	*43	24
1971-72	**Montreal**	**NHL**	73	29	35	64	48	6	1	4	5	2
1972-73	**Montreal**	**NHL**	69	28	27	55	51	17	3	5	8	9
1973-74	**Montreal**	**NHL**	73	21	35	56	29	6	0	1	1	4
1974-75a	**Montreal**	**NHL**	70	53	66	119	37	11	*12	7	19	15
1975-76ab	**Montreal**	**NHL**	80	56	69	*125	36	13	7	10	17	2
1976-77abcde	**Montreal**	**NHL**	80	56	*80	*135	20	14	9	*17	26	6
1977-78abd	**Montreal**	**NHL**	78	60*	72	*132	26	15	*10	11	*21	16
1978-79a	**Montreal**	**NHL**	80	52	77	129	28	16	10	*13	*23	0
1979-80a	**Montreal**	**NHL**	74	50	75	125	12	3	3	1	4	0
1980-81	**Montreal**	**NHL**	51	27	*43	70	29	3	0	1	1	2
1981-82	**Montreal**	**NHL**	66	27	57	84	24	5	2	1	3	4
1982-83	**Montreal**	**NHL**	68	27	49	76	12	3	0	2	2	2
1983-84	**Montreal**	**NHL**	80	30	40	70	19	12	0	3	3	5
1984-85	**Montreal**	**NHL**	19	2	3	5	10	....	....	....	....	....
1985-86			DID NOT PLAY									
1986-87			DID NOT PLAY									
1987-88f			DID NOT PLAY									
1988-89	**NY Rangers**	**NHL**	67	18	27	45	12	4	1	0	1	0
	NHL Totals		1028	536	755	1291	393	128	58	76	134	67

a NHL First All-Star Team (1975, 1976, 1979, 1980
b Won Art Ross Trophy (1976, 1977, 1978)
c Won Lester B. Pearson Award (1977)
d Won Hart Trophy (1977, 1978)
e Won Conn Smythe Trophy (1977)
f Inducted into Hockey Hall of Fame (1988)

Signed as a free agent by **NY Rangers**, August 19, 1988. Signed as a free agent by **Quebec**, July 14, 1989.

LaFONTAINE, PAT

Center. Shoots right. 5'10", 177 lbs.   Born, St. Louis, MO, February 22, 1965.
(NY Islanders' 1st choice, 3rd over-all, in 1983 Entry Draft).

			Regular Season					Playoffs			
Season	Club	Lea	GP	G	A	TP	PIM	GP	G	A	TP	PIM
1981-82	Detroit Compu.	Midget	79	175	149	324	12	....	....	....	....	....
1982-83abcd	Verdun	QMJHL	70	*104	*130	*234	10	15	11	*24	*35	4
1983-84	U.S. National	...	58	56	55	111	22	....	....	....	....	....
	U.S. Olympic	...	6	5	5	10	0	....	....	....	....	....
	NY Islanders	**NHL**	15	13	6	19	6	16	3	6	9	8
1984-85	**NY Islanders**	**NHL**	67	19	35	54	32	9	1	2	3	4
1985-86	**NY Islanders**	**NHL**	65	30	23	53	43	3	1	0	1	0
1986-87	**NY Islanders**	**NHL**	80	38	32	70	70	14	5	7	12	10
1987-88	**NY Islanders**	**NHL**	75	47	45	92	52	6	4	5	9	8
1988-89	**NY Islanders**	**NHL**	79	45	43	88	26	....	....	....	....	....
	NHL Totals		381	192	184	376	229	48	14	20	34	30

a QMJHL First All-Star Team (1983).
b QMJHL Most Valuable Player (1983).
c QMJHL Most Valuable Player in Playoffs (1983).
d Canadian Major Junior Player of the Year (1983).

Played in NHL All-Star Game (1988, 1989)

LAFORGE, MARC

Defense. Shoots left. 6'2", 200 lbs.   Born, Sudbury, Ont., January 3, 1968.
(Hartford's 2nd choice, 32nd overall, in 1986 Entry Draft).

			Regular Season					Playoffs			
Season	Club	Lea	GP	G	A	TP	PIM	GP	G	A	TP	PIM
1985-86	Kingston	OHL	60	1	13	14	248	10	0	1	1	30
1986-87	Binghamton	AHL	....	....	....	....	....	4	0	0	0	7
	Kingston	OHL	53	2	10	12	224	12	1	0	1	79
1987-88	Sudbury	OHL	14	0	2	2	68	....	....	....	....	....
1988-89	Binghamton	AHL	38	2	2	4	179	....	....	....	....	....
	Indianapolis	IHL	14	0	2	2	138	....	....	....	....	....

LAFRENIERE, JASON

Center. Shoots right. 5'11", 195 lbs.   Born, St. Catharines, Ont., December 6, 1966.
(Quebec's 2nd choice, 36th over-all, in 1985 Entry Draft).

			Regular Season					Playoffs			
Season	Club	Lea	GP	G	A	TP	PIM	GP	G	A	TP	PIM
1983-84	Brantford	OHL	70	24	57	81	4	6	2	4	6	2
1984-85	Hamilton	OHL	59	26	69	95	10	17	12	16	28	0
1985-86a	Belleville	OHL	61	49	82	131	4	23	10	22	32	6
1986-87	**Quebec**	**NHL**	56	13	15	28	8	12	1	5	6	2
	Fredericton	AHL	11	3	11	14	0	....	....	....	....	....
1987-88	**Quebec**	**NHL**	40	10	19	29	4	....	....	....	....	....
	Fredericton	AHL	32	12	19	31	38	....	....	....	....	....
1988-89	**NY Rangers**	**NHL**	38	8	16	24	6	3	0	0	0	17
	Denver	IHL	24	10	19	29	17	....	....	....	....	....
	NHL Totals		134	31	50	81	18	15	1	5	6	19

a OHL First All-Star Team (1986).

Traded to **NY Rangers** by **Quebec** with Normand Rochefort for Bruce Bell, Jari Gronstrand, Walt Poddubny and NY Rangers' fourth round choice (Eric Dubois) in 1989 Entry Draft, August 1, 1988.

LAIDLAW, THOMAS (TOM)

Defense. Shoots left. 6'2", 215 lbs. Born, Brampton, Ont., April 15, 1958.
(NY Rangers' 7th choice, 93rd over-all, in 1978 Amateur Draft).

			Regular Season					Playoffs				
Season	Club	Lea	GP	G	A	TP	PIM	GP	G	A	TP	PIM
1978-79a	N. Michigan	CCHA	29	10	20	30	137	....	....	....	....	....
1979-80ab	N. Michigan	CCHA	39	8	30	38	83	....	....	....	....	....
	New Haven	AHL	1	0	0	0	0	10	1	6	7	27
1980-81	**NY Rangers**	**NHL**	**80**	**6**	**23**	**29**	**100**	**14**	**1**	**4**	**5**	**18**
1981-82	**NY Rangers**	**NHL**	**79**	**3**	**18**	**21**	**104**	**10**	**0**	**3**	**3**	**14**
1982-83	**NY Rangers**	**NHL**	**80**	**0**	**10**	**10**	**75**	**9**	**1**	**1**	**2**	**10**
1983-84	**NY Rangers**	**NHL**	**79**	**3**	**15**	**18**	**62**	**5**	**0**	**0**	**0**	**8**
1984-85	**NY Rangers**	**NHL**	**61**	**1**	**11**	**12**	**52**	**3**	**0**	**2**	**2**	**4**
1985-86	**NY Rangers**	**NHL**	**68**	**6**	**12**	**18**	**103**	**7**	**0**	**2**	**2**	**12**
1986-87	**NY Rangers**	**NHL**	**63**	**1**	**10**	**11**	**65**	....	....	....	....	....
	Los Angeles	**NHL**	**11**	**0**	**3**	**3**	**4**	**5**	**0**	**0**	**0**	**2**
1987-88	**Los Angeles**	**NHL**	**57**	**1**	**12**	**13**	**47**	**5**	**0**	**2**	**2**	**4**
1988-89	**Los Angeles**	**NHL**	**70**	**3**	**17**	**20**	**63**	**11**	**2**	**3**	**5**	**6**
	NHL Totals		**648**	**24**	**131**	**155**	**675**	**59**	**4**	**14**	**18**	**64**

a CCHA First All-Star Team (1979, 1980)
b NCAA All-Tournament Team (1980)

Traded to **Los Angeles** by **NY Rangers** with Bob Carpenter for Jeff Crossman, Marcel Dionne and Los Angeles' third-round choice (Draft choice acquired by Minnesota, June 17, 1989 October 12, 1988. Minnesota selected Murray Garbut.) in 1989 Entry Draft, March 10, 1987.

LAKSO, BOB

Left wing. Shoots left. 5'11", 180 lbs. Born, Baltimore, MD, April 13, 1962.
(Minnesota's 9th choice, 184th over-all, in 1980 Entry Draft).

			Regular Season					Playoffs				
Season	Club	Lea	GP	G	A	TP	PIM	GP	G	A	TP	PIM
1980-81	Minn.-Duluth	WCHA	25	5	3	8	2	....	....	....	....	....
1981-82	Minn.-Duluth	WCHA	22	8	10	18	6	....	....	....	....	....
1982-83	Minn.-Duluth	WCHA	26	11	17	28	4	....	....	....	....	....
1983-84	Minn.-Duluth	WCHA	26	20	18	38	8	....	....	....	....	....
1984-85	Springfield	AHL	8	2	1	3	0	....	....	....	....	....
	Indianapolis	IHL	76	26	32	58	4	6	3	2	5	2
1985-86	Springfield	AHL	17	3	6	9	2	....	....	....	....	....
	Indianapolis	IHL	58	41	35	76	4	5	4	2	6	0
1986-87	Indianapolis	IHL	79	39	55	94	6	6	2	2	4	0
1987-88	Milwaukee	IHL	80	43	28	71	10	....	....	....	....	....
1988-89	Indianapolis	IHL	82	38	34	72	10	....	....	....	....	....

LALA, JIRI

Right wing/Center. Shoots right. 5'10", 181 lbs. Born, Tabor, Czech., August 21, 1959.
(Quebec's 4th choice, 76th overall, in 1982 Entry Draft).

			Regular Season					Playoffs				
Season	Club	Lea	GP	G	A	TP	PIM	GP	G	A	TP	PIM
1986-87	Budejovice	Czech.	31	14	17	31	....	....	....	....	....	....
1987-88	Budejovice	Czech.	28	20	28	48	....	....	....	....	....	....
1988-89	Budejovice	Czech.	45	27	39	66	....	....	....	....	....	....

LALONDE, TODD

Left wing. Shoots left. 6', 190 lbs. Born, Garson, Ont., August 4, 1969.
(Boston's 3rd choice, 56th overall, in 1987 Entry Draft).

			Regular Season					Playoffs				
Season	Club	Lea	GP	G	A	TP	PIM	GP	G	A	TP	PIM
1985-86	Sudbury	OHL	57	17	30	47	43	4	0	1	1	8
1986-87	Sudbury	OHL	29	5	11	16	71	....	....	....	....	....
1987-88	Sudbury	OHL	59	27	43	70	79	....	....	....	....	....
1988-89	Sudbury	OHL	52	32	44	76	57	....	....	....	....	....

LALOR, MIKE

Defense. Shoots left. 6', 190 lbs. Born, Fort Erie, Ont., March 8, 1963.

			Regular Season					Playoffs				
Season	Club	Lea	GP	G	A	TP	PIM	GP	G	A	TP	PIM
1981-82	Brantford	OHL	64	3	13	16	114	11	0	6	6	11
1982-83	Brantford	OHL	65	10	30	40	113	8	1	3	4	20
1983-84	Nova Scotia	AHL	67	5	11	16	80	12	0	2	2	13
1984-85	Sherbrooke	AHL	79	9	23	32	114	17	3	5	8	36
1985-86	**Montreal**	**NHL**	**62**	**3**	**5**	**8**	**56**	**17**	**1**	**2**	**3**	**29**
1986-87	**Montreal**	**NHL**	**57**	**0**	**10**	**10**	**47**	**13**	**2**	**1**	**3**	**29**
1987-88	**Montreal**	**NHL**	**66**	**1**	**10**	**11**	**113**	**11**	**0**	**0**	**0**	**11**
1988-89	**Montreal**	**NHL**	**12**	**1**	**4**	**5**	**15**	....	....	....	....	....
	St. Louis	**NHL**	**36**	**1**	**14**	**15**	**54**	**10**	**1**	**1**	**2**	**14**
	NHL Totals		**233**	**6**	**43**	**49**	**285**	**51**	**4**	**4**	**8**	**83**

Signed as a free agent by **Montreal**, September, 1983. Traded to **St. Louis** by **Montreal** for the option to switch first-round picks in 1990 Entry Draft and St. Louis' third-round choice in the 1991 Entry Draft, January 16, 1989.

LAMB, JEFF

Center. Shoots left. 5'11", 170 lbs. Born, Waterloo, IA, July 14, 1964.
(Pittsburgh's 1st choice, 4th overall, in 1986 Supplemental Draft).

			Regular Season					Playoffs				
Season	Club	Lea	GP	G	A	TP	PIM	GP	G	A	TP	PIM
1983-84	Denver	WCHA	15	0	2	2	8	....	....	....	....	....
1984-85	Denver	WCHA	39	14	25	39	62	....	....	....	....	....
1985-86	Denver	WCHA	45	23	31	54	75	....	....	....	....	....
1986-87	Denver	WCHA	40	10	24	34	58	....	....	....	....	....
1987-88	Maine	AHL	57	7	12	19	96	2	0	0	0	0
1988-89	Maine	AHL	58	11	15	26	64	....	....	....	....	....

LAMB, MARK

Center. Shoots left. 5'9", 180 lbs. Born, Ponteix, Sask., August 3, 1964.
(Calgary's 5th choice, 72nd over-all, in 1982 Entry Draft).

			Regular Season					Playoffs				
Season	Club	Lea	GP	G	A	TP	PIM	GP	G	A	TP	PIM
1981-82	Billings	WHL	72	45	56	101	46	5	4	6	10	4
1982-83	Nanaimo	WHL	30	14	37	51	16	....	....	....	....	....
	Medicine Hat	WHL	46	22	43	65	33	5	3	2	5	4
	Colorado	CHL	....	....	....	....	....	6	0	2	2	0
1983-84a	Medicine Hat	WHL	72	59	77	136	30	14	12	11	23	6
1984-85	Moncton	AHL	80	23	49	72	53	....	....	....	....	....
1985-86	**Calgary**	**NHL**	**1**	**0**	**0**	**0**	**0**	....	....	....	....	....
	Moncton	AHL	79	26	50	76	51	10	2	6	8	17
1986-87	**Detroit**	**NHL**	**22**	**2**	**1**	**3**	**8**	**11**	**0**	**0**	**0**	**11**
	Adirondack	AHL	49	14	36	50	45	....	....	....	....	....
1987-88	**Edmonton**	**NHL**	**2**	**0**	**0**	**0**	**0**	....	....	....	....	....
	Nova Scotia	AHL	69	27	61	88	45	5	0	5	5	6
1988-89	**Edmonton**	**NHL**	**20**	**2**	**8**	**10**	**14**	**6**	**0**	**2**	**2**	**8**
	Cape Breton	AHL	54	33	49	82	29	....	....	....	....	....
	NHL Totals		**45**	**4**	**9**	**13**	**22**	**17**	**0**	**2**	**2**	**19**

a WHL First All-Star Team, East Division (1984)

Claimed by **Edmonton** in NHL Waiver Draft, October 5, 1987.

LAMBERT, LANE (LAM-buhrt)

Right wing. Shoots right. 6', 185 lbs. Born, Melfort, Sask., November 18, 1964.
(Detroit's 2nd choice, 25th over-all, in 1983 Entry Draft).

			Regular Season					Playoffs				
Season	Club	Lea	GP	G	A	TP	PIM	GP	G	A	TP	PIM
1981-82	Saskatoon	WHL	72	45	69	114	111	5	1	1	2	25
1982-83a	Saskatoon	WHL	64	59	60	119	126	6	4	3	7	7
1983-84	**Detroit**	**NHL**	**73**	**20**	**15**	**35**	**115**	**4**	**0**	**0**	**0**	**10**
1984-85	**Detroit**	**NHL**	**69**	**14**	**11**	**25**	**104**	....	....	....	....	....
1985-86	**Detroit**	**NHL**	**34**	**2**	**3**	**5**	**130**	....	....	....	....	....
	Adirondack	AHL	45	16	25	41	69	16	5	5	10	9
1986-87	**NY Rangers**	**NHL**	**18**	**2**	**2**	**4**	**33**	....	....	....	....	....
	New Haven	AHL	11	3	3	6	19	....	....	....	....	....
	Quebec	**NHL**	**15**	**5**	**6**	**11**	**18**	**13**	**2**	**4**	**6**	**30**
1987-88	**Quebec**	**NHL**	**61**	**13**	**28**	**41**	**98**	....	....	....	....	....
1988-89	**Quebec**	**NHL**	**13**	**2**	**2**	**4**	**23**	....	....	....	....	....
	Halifax	AHL	59	25	35	60	162	4	0	2	2	2
	NHL Totals		**283**	**58**	**66**	**124**	**521**	**17**	**2**	**4**	**6**	**40**

a WHL Second All-Star Team (1983)

Traded to **NY Rangers** by **Detroit** with Kelly Kisio and Jim Leavins for Glen Hanlon and New York's third round choices in 1987 (Dennis Holland) and 1988 Entry Drafts, July 29, 1986. Traded to **Quebec** by **NY Rangers** for Pat Price, March 5, 1987.

LAMMENS, HANK

Defense. Shoots left. 6'2", 210 lbs. Born, Brockville, Ont., February 21, 1966.
(NY Islanders' 10th choice, 160th overall, in 1985 Entry Draft).

			Regular Season					Playoffs				
Season	Club	Lea	GP	G	A	TP	PIM	GP	G	A	TP	PIM
1984-85	St. Lawrence	ECAC	21	17	9	26	16	....	....	....	....	....
1985-86	St. Lawrence	ECAC	30	3	14	17	60	....	....	....	....	....
1986-87ab	St. Lawrence	ECAC	35	6	13	19	92	....	....	....	....	....
1987-88a	St. Lawrence	ECAC	32	3	6	9	64	....	....	....	....	....
1988-89	Springfield	AHL	69	1	13	14	55	....	....	....	....	....

a ECAC Second All-Star Team (1987, 1988)
b NCAA East Second All-American Team (1987)

LaMOINE, MIKE

Defense. Shoots left. 6', 190 lbs. Born, Grand Forks, ND, December 1, 1966.
(Detroit's 1st choice, 16th overall, in 1987 Supplemental Draft).

			Regular Season					Playoffs				
Season	Club	Lea	GP	G	A	TP	PIM	GP	G	A	TP	PIM
1985-86	North Dakota	WCHA	13	0	4	4	10	....	....	....	....	....
1986-87	North Dakota	WCHA	47	2	17	19	36	....	....	....	....	....
1987-88	North Dakota	WCHA	40	3	7	10	34	....	....	....	....	....
1988-89	North Dakota	WCHA	40	3	12	15	51	....	....	....	....	....

LAMOUREUX, MITCH (LAM-uh-roo)

Center. Shoots left. 5'6", 175 lbs. Born, Ottawa, Ont., August 22, 1962.
(Pittsburgh's 8th choice, 154th over-all, in 1981 Entry Draft).

			Regular Season					Playoffs				
Season	Club	Lea	GP	G	A	TP	PIM	GP	G	A	TP	PIM
1979-80	Oshawa	OHA	67	28	48	76	63	7	2	1	3	16
1980-81	Oshawa	OHA	63	50	69	119	256	11	11	13	24	57
1981-82a	Oshawa	OHL	66	43	78	121	275	12	4	17	21	68
1982-83bc	Baltimore	AHL	80	57	50	107	107	....	....	....	....	....
1983-84	**Pittsburgh**	**NHL**	**8**	**1**	**1**	**2**	**6**	....	....	....	....	....
	Baltimore	AHL	68	30	38	68	136	9	1	3	4	2
1984-85	**Pittsburgh**	**NHL**	**62**	**10**	**8**	**18**	**53**	....	....	....	....	....
	Baltimore	AHL	18	10	14	24	34	....	....	....	....	....
1985-86	Baltimore	AHL	75	22	31	53	129	....	....	....	....	....
1986-87	Hershey	AHL	78	43	46	89	122	5	1	2	3	8
1987-88	**Philadelphia**	**NHL**	**3**	**0**	**0**	**0**	**0**	....	....	....	....	....
	Hershey	AHL	78	35	52	87	171	12	9	7	*16	48
1988-89	Hershey	AHL	9	9	7	16	14	9	1	4	5	14
	NHL Totals		**73**	**11**	**9**	**20**	**59**	....	....	....	....	....

a OHL Third All-Star Team (1982)
b Won Dudley "Red Garrett Memorial Trophy (AHL's Rookie of the Year) (1983)
c AHL Second All-Star Team (1983)

LANGWAY, ROD CORRY

Defense. Shoots left. 6'4", 220 lbs. Born, Formosa, Taiwan, May 3, 1957.
(Montreal's 3rd choice, 36th over-all, in 1977 Amateur Draft).

			Regular Season					Playoffs				
Season	Club	Lea	GP	G	A	TP	PIM	GP	G	A	TP	PIM
1976-77	N. Hampshire	ECAC	34	10	43	53	52	....	....	....	....	....
1977-78	Hampton	AHL	30	6	16	22	50	....	....	....	....	....
	Birmingham	WHA	52	3	18	21	52	4	0	0	0	9
1978-79	Nova Scotia	AHL	18	6	13	19	29	....	....	....	....	....
	Montreal	**NHL**	45	3	4	7	30	8	0	0	0	16
1979-80	**Montreal**	**NHL**	77	7	29	36	81	10	3	3	6	2
1980-81	**Montreal**	**NHL**	80	11	34	45	120	3	0	0	0	6
1981-82	**Montreal**	**NHL**	66	5	34	39	116	5	0	3	3	18
1982-83ab	**Washington**	**NHL**	80	3	29	32	75	4	0	0	0	0
1983-84ab	**Washington**	**NHL**	80	9	24	33	61	8	0	5	5	7
1984-85c	**Washington**	**NHL**	79	4	22	26	54	5	0	1	1	6
1985-86	**Washington**	**NHL**	71	1	17	18	61	9	1	2	3	6
1986-87	**Washington**	**NHL**	78	2	25	27	53	7	0	1	1	2
1987-88	**Washington**	**NHL**	63	3	13	16	28	6	0	0	0	8
1988-89	**Washington**	**NHL**	76	2	19	21	65	6	0	0	0	6
	NHL Totals		795	50	250	300	744	71	4	15	19	76

a Won James Norris Memorial Trophy (1983, 1984)
b NHL First All-Star Team (1983, 1984)
c NHL Second All-Star Team (1985)

Played in NHL All-Star Game (1981-86)

Claimed by **Montreal** as fill in Expansion Draft, June 13, 1979. Traded to **Washington** by **Montreal** with Doug Jarvis, Craig Laughlin and Brian Engblom for Ryan Walter and Rick Green, September 9, 1982.

LANIEL, MARC

Defense. Shoots left. 6'1", 190 lbs. Born, Oshawa, Ont., January 16, 1968.
(New Jersey's 4th choice, 62nd overall, in 1986 Entry Draft).

			Regular Season					Playoffs				
Season	Club	Lea	GP	G	A	TP	PIM	GP	G	A	TP	PIM
1985-86	Oshawa	OHL	66	9	25	34	27	6	2	3	5	6
1986-87	Oshawa	OHL	63	14	31	45	42	26	3	13	16	20
1987-88	Utica	AHL	2	0	0	0	0	....	....	....	....	....
a	Oshawa	OHL	41	8	32	40	56	7	2	2	4	4
1988-89	Utica	AHL	80	6	28	34	43	5	0	1	1	2

a OHL Third All-Star Team (1988)

LANTHIER, JEAN-MARC (LAN-thee-ay)

Right wing. Shoots right. 6'2", 195 lbs. Born, Montreal, Que., March 27, 1963.
(Vancouver's 2nd choice, 52nd over-all, in 1981 Entry Draft).

			Regular Season					Playoffs				
Season	Club	Lea	GP	G	A	TP	PIM	GP	G	A	TP	PIM
1980-81	Quebec	QMJHL	37	13	32	45	18	....	....	....	....	....
	Sorel	QMJHL	35	6	33	39	29	7	1	4	5	4
1981-82	Laval	QMJHL	60	44	34	78	48	18	8	11	19	8
1982-83	Laval	QMJHL	69	39	71	110	54	12	6	17	23	8
1983-84	**Vancouver**	**NHL**	11	2	1	3	2	....	....	....	....	....
	Fredericton	AHL	60	25	17	42	29	7	4	6	10	0
1984-85	**Vancouver**	**NHL**	27	6	4	10	13	....	....	....	....	....
	Fredericton	AHL	38	8	5	13	15	....	....	....	....	....
1985-86	**Vancouver**	**NHL**	62	7	10	17	12	....	....	....	....	....
	Fredericton	AHL	7	5	5	10	2	....	....	....	....	....
1986-87	Fredericton	AHL	78	15	38	53	24	....	....	....	....	....
1987-88	**Vancouver**	**NHL**	5	1	1	2	2	....	....	....	....	....
	Fredericton	AHL	74	35	71	106	37	15	3	8	11	14
1988-89	Maine	AHL	24	7	16	23	16	....	....	....	....	....
	Utica	AHL	55	23	26	49	22	3	3	0	3	2
	NHL Totals		105	16	16	32	29	....	....	....	....	....

Traded to **New Jersey** bt **Boston** for Dan Dorion, December 9, 1988.

LANZ, RICK ROMAN

Defense. Shoots right. 6'2", 195 lbs. Born, Karlouyvary, Czech., September 16, 1961.
(Vancouver's 1st choice, 7th over-all, in 1980 Entry Draft).

			Regular Season					Playoffs				
Season	Club	Lea	GP	G	A	TP	PIM	GP	G	A	TP	PIM
1978-79	Oshawa	OHA	65	12	47	59	88	5	1	3	4	14
1979-80a	Oshawa	OHA	52	18	38	56	51	7	2	3	5	6
1980-81	**Vancouver**	**NHL**	76	7	22	29	40	3	0	0	0	4
1981-82	**Vancouver**	**NHL**	39	3	11	14	48	....	....	....	....	....
1982-83	**Vancouver**	**NHL**	74	10	38	48	46	4	2	1	3	0
1983-84	**Vancouver**	**NHL**	79	18	39	57	45	4	0	4	4	2
1984-85	**Vancouver**	**NHL**	57	2	17	19	69	....	....	....	....	....
1985-86	**Vancouver**	**NHL**	75	15	38	53	73	3	0	0	0	0
1986-87	**Vancouver**	**NHL**	17	1	6	7	10	....	....	....	....	....
	Toronto	**NHL**	44	2	19	21	32	13	1	3	4	27
1987-88	**Toronto**	**NHL**	75	6	22	28	65	1	0	0	0	2
1988-89	**Toronto**	**NHL**	32	1	9	10	18	....	....	....	....	....
	NHL Totals		568	65	221	286	446	28	3	8	11	35

a OHA Third All-Star Team (1980).

Traded to **Toronto** by **Vancouver** for Jim Benning and Dan Hodgson, December 2, 1986.

LAPPIN, CHRIS

Defense. Shoots right. 6', 190 lbs. Born, St. Charles, IL, August 19, 1967.
(Quebec's 12th choice, 207th overall, in 1986 Entry Draft).

			Regular Season					Playoffs				
Season	Club	Lea	GP	G	A	TP	PIM	GP	G	A	TP	PIM
1987-88	Boston U.	H.E.	31	0	4	4	28	....	....	....	....	....
1988-89	Boston U.	H.E.	27	2	6	8	26	....	....	....	....	....

LAPPIN, MIKE

Center. Shoots left. 5'10", 175 lbs. Born, Chicago, IL, January 1, 1969.
(Chicago's 12th choice, 239th overall, in 1987 Entry Draft).

			Regular Season					Playoffs				
Season	Club	Lea	GP	G	A	TP	PIM	GP	G	A	TP	PIM
1986-87	Northwood	HS	29	20	42	62	....	....	....	....	....	....
1987-88	Boston U.	H.E.	34	12	15	27	40	....	....	....	....	....
1988-89	Boston U.	H.E.	27	11	16	27	43	....	....	....	....	....

LAPPIN, PETER

Center. Shoots right. 5'11", 185 lbs. Born, St. Charles, Ill., December 31, 1965.
(Calgary's 1st choice, 24th overall, in 1987 Supplemental Draft).

			Regular Season					Playoffs				
Season	Club	Lea	GP	G	A	TP	PIM	GP	G	A	TP	PIM
1984-85	St. Lawrence	ECAC	32	10	12	22	22	....	....	....	....	....
1985-86	St. Lawrence	ECAC	30	20	26	46	64	....	....	....	....	....
1986-87ab	St. Lawrence	ECAC	35	34	24	58	32	....	....	....	....	....
1987-88cdef	St. Lawrence	ECAC	30	16	36	52	26	....	....	....	....	....
g	Salt Lake	IHL	3	1	1	2	0	17	*16	12	*28	11
1988-89	Salt Lake	IHL	81	48	42	90	50	14	9	9	18	4

a NCAA East Second All-American Team (1987)
b ECAC Second All-Star Team (1987)
c NCAA East First All-American Team (1988)
d NCAA All-Tournament Team (1988)
e ECAC Player of the Year (1988)
f ECAC First All-Star Team (1988)
g IHL Playoff MVP (1988)

LAPRADE, DOUGLAS

Right wing. Shoots right. 6', 185 lbs. Born, Port Arthur, Ont., October 9, 1968.
(Los Angeles' 12th choice, 217th overall, in 1988 Entry Draft).

			Regular Season					Playoffs				
Season	Club	Lea	GP	G	A	TP	PIM	GP	G	A	TP	PIM
1987-88	Lake Superior	CCHA	30	4	2	6	30	....	....	....	....	....
1988-89	Lake Superior	CCHA	45	4	6	10	48	....	....	....	....	....

LARIONOV, IGOR

Center. Shoots left. 5'9", 165 lbs. Born, Voskresensk, Soviet Union, December 3, 1960.
(Vancouver's 11th choice, 214th overall, in 1988 Entry Draft).

			Regular Season					Playoffs				
Season	Club	Lea	GP	G	A	TP	PIM	GP	G	A	TP	PIM
1977-78	Voskresensk	USSR	6	3	0	3	4	....	....	....	....	....
1978-79	Voskresensk	USSR	32	3	4	7	12	....	....	....	....	
1979-80	Voskresensk	USSR	42	11	7	18	24	....	....	....	....	....
1980-81	Voskresensk	USSR	43	22	23	45	36	....	....	....	....	....
1981-82	CSKA	USSR	46	31	22	53	6	....	....	....	....	....
1982-83a	CSKA	USSR	44	20	19	39	20	....	....	....	....	....
1983-84	CSKA	USSR	43	15	26	41	30	....	....	....	....	....
1984-85	CSKA	USSR	40	18	28	46	20	....	....	....	....	....
1988-86a	CSKA	USSR	40	21	31	52	33	....	....	....	....	....
1986-87a	CSKA	USSR	39	20	26	46	34	....	....	....	....	....
1987-88ab	CSKA	USSR	51	25	32	57	54	....	....	....	....	....
1988-89	CSKA	USSR	31	15	12	27	22	....	....	....	....	....

a Soviet National League All-Star
b Soviet Player of the Year

LARKIN, JAMES

Left wing. Shoots left. 6'0", 165 lbs. Born, Wallingford, VT, April 15, 1970.
(Los Angeles' 10th choice, 175th overall, in 1988 Entry Draft).

			Regular Season					Playoffs				
Season	Club	Lea	GP	G	A	TP	PIM	GP	G	A	TP	PIM
1987-88	Mt. St. Joseph	HS	....	44	41	85	....	....	....	....	....	....
1988-89	U. of Vermont	ECAC	34	16	19	35	8	....	....	....	....	....

LARMER, STEVE DONALD

Right wing. Shoots left. 5'10", 185 lbs. Born, Peterborough, Ont., June 16, 1961.
(Chicago's 11th choice, 120th over-all, in 1980 Entry Draft).

			Regular Season					Playoffs				
Season	Club	Lea	GP	G	A	TP	PIM	GP	G	A	TP	PIM
1979-80	Niagara Falls	OHA	67	45	69	114	71	10	5	9	14	15
1980-81	**Chicago**	**NHL**	4	0	1	1	0	....	....	....	....	....
a	Niagara Falls	OHA	61	55	78	133	73	12	13	8	21	24
1981-82	**Chicago**	**NHL**	3	0	0	0	0	....	....	....	....	....
b	New Brunswick	AHL	74	38	44	82	46	15	6	6	12	0
1982-83cd	**Chicago**	**NHL**	80	43	47	90	28	11	5	7	12	8
1983-84	**Chicago**	**NHL**	80	35	40	75	34	5	2	2	4	7
1984-85	**Chicago**	**NHL**	80	46	40	86	16	15	9	13	22	14
1985-86	**Chicago**	**NHL**	80	31	45	76	47	3	0	3	3	4
1986-87	**Chicago**	**NHL**	80	28	56	84	22	4	0	0	0	2
1987-88	**Chicago**	**NHL**	80	41	48	89	42	5	1	6	7	0
1988-89	**Chicago**	**NHL**	80	43	44	87	54	16	8	9	17	22
	NHL Totals		567	267	321	588	243	59	25	40	65	57

a OHA Second All-Star Team (1981)
b AHL Second All-Star Team (1982)
c Won Calder Trophy (1983)
d NHL All-Rookie Team (1983)

LAROCQUE, DENIS (luh-ROCK)

Defense. Shoots left. 6'1", 195 lbs. Born, Hawkesbury, Ont., October 5, 1967.
(Los Angeles' 2nd choice, 44th overall, in 1986 Entry Draft).

			Regular Season					Playoffs				
Season	Club	Lea	GP	G	A	TP	PIM	GP	G	A	TP	PIM
1984-85	Guelph	OHL	62	1	15	16	67	....	....	....	....	....
1985-86	Guelph	OHL	66	2	17	19	144	....	....	....	....	....
1986-87	Guelph	OHL	45	4	10	14	82	5	0	2	2	9
1987-88	**Los Angeles**	**NHL**	8	0	1	1	18	....	....	....	....	....
	New Haven	AHL	58	4	10	14	154	....	....	....	....	....
1988-89	New Haven	AHL	15	2	2	4	51	....	....	....	....	....
	Denver	IHL	30	2	8	10	39	4	0	2	2	10
	NHL Totals		8	0	1	1	18	0				

Traded to **NY Rangers** by **Los Angeles** with Dean Kennedy for Igor Liba, Michael Boyce, Todd Elik and future considerations, December 12, 1988.

LAROSE, GUY

Center. Shoots left. 5'9", 175 lbs.   Born, Hull, Que., August 31, 1967.
(Buffalo's 11th choice, 224th overall, in 1985 Entry Draft).

			Regular Season					Playoffs				
Season	Club	Lea	GP	G	A	TP	PIM	GP	G	A	TP	PIM
1984-85	Guelph	OHL	58	30	30	60	63	....	....	....	....	....
1985-86	Ottawa	OHL	65	31	61	92	118	....	....	....	....	....
1986-87	Ottawa	OHL	66	28	49	77	77	11	2	8	10	27
1987-88	Moncton	AHL	77	22	31	53	127	....	....	....	....	....
1988-89	**Winnipeg**	**NHL**	3	0	1	1	6	....	....	....	....	....
	Moncton	AHL	72	32	27	59	176	10	4	4	8	37
	NHL Totals		3	0	1	1	6	....	....	....	....	....

Signed as a free agent by **Winnipeg**, July 16, 1987.

LAROUCHE, STEVE

Center. Shoots right. 5'11", 165 lbs.   Born, Rouyn, Que., April 14, 1971.
(Montreal's 3rd choice, 41st overall, in 1989 Entry Draft).

			Regular Season					Playoffs				
Season	Club	Lea	GP	G	A	TP	PIM	GP	G	A	TP	PIM
1987-88	Trois-Rivieres	QMJHL	66	11	29	40	25	....	....	....	....	....
1988-89	Trois-Rivieres	QMJHL	70	51	102	153	53	4	4	2	6	6

LARSON, REED DAVID

Defense. Shoots right. 6', 195 lbs.   Born, Minneapolis, MN, July 30, 1956.
(Detroit's 2nd choice, 22nd over-all, in 1976 Amateur Draft).

			Regular Season					Playoffs				
Season	Club	Lea	GP	G	A	TP	PIM	GP	G	A	TP	PIM
1975-76	U. Minnesota	WCHA	42	13	29	42	94	....	....	....	....	....
1976-77	U. Minnesota	WCHA	21	10	15	25	30	....	....	....	....	....
	Detroit	**NHL**	14	0	1	1	23	....	....	....	....	....
1977-78	**Detroit**	**NHL**	75	19	41	60	95	7	0	2	2	4
1978-79	**Detroit**	**NHL**	79	18	49	67	169	....	....	....	....	....
1979-80	**Detroit**	**NHL**	80	22	44	66	101	....	....	....	....	....
1980-81	**Detroit**	**NHL**	78	27	31	58	153	....	....	....	....	....
1981-82	**Detroit**	**NHL**	80	21	39	60	112	....	....	....	....	....
1982-83	**Detroit**	**NHL**	80	22	52	74	104	....	....	....	....	....
1983-84	**Detroit**	**NHL**	78	23	39	62	122	4	2	0	2	21
1984-85	**Detroit**	**NHL**	77	17	45	62	139	3	1	2	3	20
1985-86	**Detroit**	**NHL**	67	19	41	60	109	....	....	....	....	....
	Boston	**NHL**	13	3	4	7	8	3	1	0	1	6
1986-87	**Boston**	**NHL**	66	12	24	36	95	4	0	2	2	2
1987-88	**Boston**	**NHL**	62	10	24	34	93	8	0	1	1	6
	Maine	AHL	2	2	0	2	4	....	....	....	....	....
1988-89	**Edmonton**	**NHL**	10	2	7	9	15	....	....	....	....	....
	NY Islanders	**NHL**	33	7	13	20	35	....	....	....	....	....
	Minnesota	**NHL**	11	0	9	9	18	3	0	0	0	4
	NHL Totals		903	222	463	685	1391	32	4	7	11	63

Played in NHL All-Star Game (1978, 1980, 1981)

Traded to **Boston** by **Detroit** for Mike O'Connell, March 10, 1986. Traded to **NY Islanders** by **Edmonton** for future considerations, December 6, 1988. Traded to **Minnesota** by NY Islanders for future considerations, March 7, 1989.

LARSSON, ROBERT

Defense. Shoots left. 6'2", 200 lbs.   Born, Stockholm, Sweden, February 20, 1967.
(Los Angeles' 7th choice, 112th overall, in 1988 Entry Draft).

			Regular Season					Playoffs				
Season	Club	Lea	GP	G	A	TP	PIM	GP	G	A	TP	PIM
1987-88	Skelleftea	Swe.	35	6	7	13	49	....	....	....	....	....
1988-89	Skelleftea	Swe.	35	8	6	14	30	....	....	....	....	....

LARTER, TYLER

Center. Shoots left. 5'11", 180 lbs.   Born, Charlottetown, P.E.I., March 12, 1968.
(Washington's 3rd choice, 78th overall, in 1987 Entry Draft).

			Regular Season					Playoffs				
Season	Club	Lea	GP	G	A	TP	PIM	GP	G	A	TP	PIM
1985-86	S.S. Marie	OHL	60	15	40	55	137	....	....	....	....	....
1986-87	S.S. Marie	OHL	59	34	59	93	122	4	0	2	2	8
1987-88	S.S. Marie	OHL	65	44	65	109	155	4	3	9	12	8
1988-89	Baltimore	AHL	71	9	19	28	189	....	....	....	....	....

LATAL, JIRI

Defense. Shoots left. 6', 190 lbs.   Born, Olomouc, Czechoslovakia, February 2, 1967.
(Toronto's 6th choice, 106th overall, in 1985 Entry Draft).

			Regular Season					Playoffs				
Season	Club	Lea	GP	G	A	TP	PIM	GP	G	A	TP	PIM
1984-85	Sparta Praha	Czech.	26	2	2	4	10	....	....	....	....	....
1985-86	Sparta Praha	Czech.	27	3	2	5	....	....	....	....	....	....
1986-87	Sparta Praha	Czech.	9	1	0	2	....	....	....	....	....	....
1987-88	Dukla Trencin	Czech.	43	8	12	20	27	....	....	....	....	....
1988-89	Dukla Trencin	Czech.	45	6	17	23	....	....	....	....	....	....

Traded to **Philadelphia** by **Toronto** for future considerations, August 29, 1989.

LATOS, JAMES

Right wing. Shoots right. 6'1", 200 lbs.   Born, Wakaw, Sask., January 4, 1966.

			Regular Season					Playoffs				
Season	Club	Lea	GP	G	A	TP	PIM	GP	G	A	TP	PIM
1986-87	Portland	WHL	69	27	18	45	210	20	5	3	8	56
1987-88	Colorado	IHL	38	11	12	23	98	....	....	....	....	....
1988-89	**NY Rangers**	**NHL**	1	0	0	0	0	....	....	....	....	....
	Denver	IHL	37	7	5	12	157	4	0	0	0	17
	NHL Totals		1	0	0	0	0	....	....	....	....	....

Signed as a free agent by **NY Rangers**, June 5, 1987.

LATTA, DAVID
(LAT-uh)

Left wing. Shoots left. 6'1", 190 lbs.   Born, Thunder Bay, Ont., January 3, 1967.
(Quebec's 1st choice, 15th over-all, in 1985 Entry Draft).

			Regular Season					Playoffs				
Season	Club	Lea	GP	G	A	TP	PIM	GP	G	A	TP	PIM
1983-84	Kitchener	OHL	66	17	26	43	54	16	3	6	9	9
1984-85	Kitchener	OHL	52	38	27	65	26	4	2	4	6	4
1985-86	**Quebec**	**NHL**	1	0	0	0	0	....	....	....	....	....
	Fredericton	AHL	3	1	0	1	0	5	0	3	3	0
	Kitchener	OHL	55	36	34	70	60	5	7	1	8	15
1986-87a	Kitchener	OHL	50	32	46	78	46	4	0	3	3	2
1987-88	**Quebec**	**NHL**	10	0	0	0	0	....	....	....	....	....
	Fredericton	AHL	34	11	21	32	28	15	9	4	13	24
1988-89	**Quebec**	**NHL**	24	4	8	12	4	....	....	....	....	....
	Halifax	AHL	42	20	26	46	36	4	0	2	2	2
	NHL Totals		35	4	8	12	4	....	....	....	....	....

a OHL Third All-Star Team (1987)

LAUER, BRAD
(LAU-er)

Left wing. Shoots left. 6', 195 lbs.   Born, Humboldt, Sask., October 27, 1966.
(NY Islanders' 3rd choice, 34th over-all, in 1985 Entry Draft).

			Regular Season					Playoffs				
Season	Club	Lea	GP	G	A	TP	PIM	GP	G	A	TP	PIM
1983-84	Regina	WHL	60	5	7	12	51	16	0	1	1	24
1984-85	Regina	WHL	72	33	46	79	57	8	6	6	12	9
1985-86	Regina	WHL	57	36	38	74	69	10	4	5	9	2
1986-87	**NY Islanders**	**NHL**	61	7	14	21	65	6	2	0	2	4
1987-88	**NY Islanders**	**NHL**	69	17	18	35	67	5	3	1	4	4
1988-89	**NY Islanders**	**NHL**	14	3	2	5	2	....	....	....	....	....
	Springfield	AHL	8	1	5	6	0	....	....	....	....	....
	NHL Totals		144	27	34	61	134	11	5	1	6	8

LAUGHLIN, CRAIG
(LOCK-lin)

Right wing. Shoots right. 6', 190 lbs.   Born, Toronto, Ont., September 19, 1957.
(Montreal's 17th choice, 162nd over-all, in 1977 Amateur Draft).

			Regular Season					Playoffs				
Season	Club	Lea	GP	G	A	TP	PIM	GP	G	A	TP	PIM
1976-77	Clarkson	ECAC	33	12	13	25	44	....	....	....	....	....
1977-78	Clarkson	ECAC	30	17	31	48	56	....	....	....	....	....
1978-79	Clarkson	ECAC	30	18	29	47	22	....	....	....	....	....
1979-80	Clarkson	ECAC	34	18	30	48	38	....	....	....	....	....
	Nova Scotia	AHL	2	0	0	0	2	....	....	....	....	....
1980-81	Nova Scotia	AHL	46	32	29	61	15	6	0	1	1	6
1981-82	Nova Scotia	AHL	26	14	15	29	16	....	....	....	....	....
	Montreal	**NHL**	36	12	11	23	33	3	0	1	1	0
1982-83	**Washington**	**NHL**	75	17	27	44	41	4	1	0	1	0
1983-84	**Washington**	**NHL**	80	20	32	52	69	8	4	2	6	6
1984-85	**Washington**	**NHL**	78	16	34	50	38	5	0	0	0	2
1985-86	**Washington**	**NHL**	75	30	45	75	43	9	1	2	3	10
1986-87	**Washington**	**NHL**	80	22	30	52	67	1	0	0	0	0
1987-88	**Washington**	**NHL**	40	5	5	10	26	....	....	....	....	....
	Los Angeles	**NHL**	19	4	8	12	6	3	0	1	1	2
1988-89	**Toronto**	**NHL**	66	10	13	23	41	....	....	....	....	....
	NHL Totals		549	136	205	341	364	33	6	6	12	20

Traded to **Washington** by **Montreal** with Brian Engblom, Doug Jarvis and Rod Langway for Rick Green and Ryan Walter, September 9, 1982. Traded to **Los Angeles** by **Washington** for Grant Ledyard, February 9, 1988.

LAUS, PAUL

Defense. Shoots right. 6'1", 200 lbs.   Born, Beamsville, Ont., September 26, 1970.
(Pittsburgh's 2nd choice, 37th overall, in 1989 Entry Draft).

			Regular Season					Playoffs				
Season	Club	Lea	GP	G	A	TP	PIM	GP	G	A	TP	PIM
1987-88	Hamilton	OHL	56	1	9	10	171	14	0	0	0	28
1988-89	Niagara Falls	OHL	49	1	10	11	225	15	0	5	5	56

LaVARRE, MARK
(la-VAR-ee)

Right wing. Shoots right. 5'11", 170 lbs.   Born, Evanston, IL., February 21, 1965.
(Chicago's 7th choice, 123rd over-all, in 1983 Entry Draft).

			Regular Season					Playoffs				
Season	Club	Lea	GP	G	A	TP	PIM	GP	G	A	TP	PIM
1983-84	North Bay	OHL	41	19	22	41	15	....	....	....	....	....
1984-85	Windsor	OHL	46	15	30	45	30	4	0	0	0	0
1985-86	**Chicago**	**NHL**	2	0	0	0	0	....	....	....	....	....
	Nova Scotia	AHL	62	15	19	34	32	....	....	....	....	....
1986-87	**Chicago**	**NHL**	58	8	15	23	33	....	....	....	....	....
	Nova Scotia	AHL	17	12	8	20	8	....	....	....	....	....
1987-88	**Chicago**	**NHL**	18	1	1	2	25	1	0	0	0	2
	Saginaw	IHL	39	27	18	45	121	5	4	3	7	36
1988-89	Binghamton	AHL	37	20	21	41	70	....	....	....	....	....
	NHL Totals		78	9	16	25	58	1	0	0	0	2

Traded to **Hartford** by **Chicago** for future considerations, October 6, 1988.

LAVIOLETTE, PETER

Defense. Shoots left. 6'2", 190 lbs.   Born, Franklin, MA, July 12, 1964.

			Regular Season					Playoffs				
Season	Club	Lea	GP	G	A	TP	PIM	GP	G	A	TP	PIM
1987-88	U.S. National	....	54	4	20	24	82	....	....	....	....	....
	U.S. Olympic	....	5	0	2	2	4	....	....	....	....	....
	Colorado	IHL	19	2	5	7	27	9	3	5	8	7
1988-89	**NY Rangers**	**NHL**	12	0	0	0	6	....	....	....	....	....
	Denver	IHL	57	6	19	25	120	3	0	0	0	4
	NHL Totals		12	0	0	0	6	....	....	....	....	....

Signed as a free agent by **NY Rangers**, August 12, 1987.

LAVOIE, DOMINIC

Defense. Shoots right. 6'2", 200 lbs. Born, Montreal, Que., November 21, 1967.

			Regular Season					Playoffs				
Season	Club	Lea	GP	G	A	TP	PIM	GP	G	A	TP	PIM
1985-86	St. Jean	QMJHL	70	12	37	49	99	10	2	3	5	20
1986-87	St. Jean	QMJHL	64	12	42	54	97	8	2	7	9	2
1987-88	Peoria	IHL	65	7	26	33	54	7	2	2	4	8
1988-89	St. Louis	NHL	1	0	0	0	0	....	....	....	....	....
	Peoria	IHL	69	11	31	42	98	4	0	0	0	4
	NHL Totals		1	0	0	0	0	....	....	....	....	....

Signed as a free agent by **St. Louis**, September 22, 1986.

LAWLESS, PAUL

Left wing. Shoots left. 6', 185 lbs. Born, Scarborough, Ont., July 2, 1964.
(Hartford's 1st choice, 14th over-all, in 1982 Entry Draft).

			Regular Season					Playoffs				
Season	Club	Lea	GP	G	A	TP	PIM	GP	G	A	TP	PIM
1981-82	Windsor	OHL	68	24	25	49	47	9	1	1	2	4
1982-83	Windsor	OHL	33	15	20	35	25	....	....	....	....	....
	Hartford	NHL	47	6	9	15	4	....	....	....	....	....
1983-84	Hartford	NHL	6	0	3	3	0	....	....	....	....	....
a	Windsor	OHL	55	31	49	80	26	2	0	1	1	0
1984-85	Binghamton	AHL	8	1	1	2	0	....	....	....	....	....
	Salt Lake	IHL	72	49	48	97	14	7	5	3	8	20
1985-86	Hartford	NHL	64	17	21	38	20	1	0	0	0	0
1986-87	Hartford	NHL	60	22	32	54	14	2	0	2	2	2
1987-88	Hartford	NHL	28	4	5	9	16	....	....	....	....	....
	Philadelphia	NHL	8	0	5	5	0	....	....	....	....	....
	Vancouver	NHL	13	0	1	1	0	....	....	....	....	....
1988-89	Toronto	NHL	7	0	0	0	0	....	....	....	....	....
	Milwaukee	IHL	53	30	35	65	58	....	....	....	....	....
	NHL Totals		233	49	76	125	54	3	0	2	2	2

a OHL Second All-Star Team (1984)

Traded to **Philadelphia** by **Hartford** for Lindsay Carson, January 22, 1988. Traded to **Vancouver** by **Philadelphia** with Vancouver's fifth round draft choice (acquired March 7, 1989 by Edmonton, who selected Peter White) in1989 Entry Draft — acquired earlier by Philadelphia — for Willie Huber, March 1, 1988. Traded to **Toronto** by **Vancouver** for the rights to Peter Deboer, February 27, 1989.

LAWRENCE, BRETT

Right wing. Shoots right. 6'2", 180 lbs. Born, Rochester, NY, April 1, 1968.
(Philadelphia's 10th choice, 230th overall, in 1986 Entry Draft).

			Regular Season					Playoffs				
Season	Club	Lea	GP	G	A	TP	PIM	GP	G	A	TP	PIM
1986-87	Colgate	ECAC	33	8	7	15	22	....	....	....	....	....
1987-88	Colgate	ECAC	29	6	5	11	12	....	....	....	....	....
1988-89	Colgate	ECAC	26	2	4	6	10	....	....	....	....	....

LAWTON, BRIAN

Left wing. Shoots left. 6', 190 lbs. Born, New Brunswick, NJ, June 29, 1965.
(Minnesota's 1st choice and 1st over-all in 1983 Entry Draft).

			Regular Season					Playoffs				
Season	Club	Lea	GP	G	A	TP	PIM	GP	G	A	TP	PIM
1981-82	Mt. St. Charles	HS	26	45	43	88	....	....	....	....	....	....
1982-83	Mt. St. Charles	HS	23	40	43	83	....	....	....	....	....	....
1983-84	Minnesota	NHL	58	10	21	31	33	5	0	0	0	10
1984-85	Minnesota	NHL	40	5	6	11	24	....	....	....	....	....
	Springfield	AHL	42	14	28	42	37	4	1	1	2	2
1985-86	Minnesota	NHL	65	18	17	35	36	3	0	1	1	2
1986-87	Minnesota	NHL	66	21	23	44	86	....	....	....	....	....
1987-88	Minnesota	NHL	74	17	24	41	71	....	....	....	....	....
1988-89	NY Rangers	NHL	30	7	10	17	39	....	....	....	....	....
	Hartford	NHL	35	10	16	26	28	3	1	0	1	0
	NHL Totals		368	88	117	205	317	11	1	1	2	12

Traded to **NY Rangers** by **Minnesota** with Igor Liba, and the rights to Eric Bennett for Paul Jerrard and Mark Tinordi, the rights to Bret Barnett and Mike Sullivan, and Los Angeles' third-round choice (Murray Garbutt) in 1989 Entry Draft — acquired March 10, 1987 by Minnesota — October 11, 1988. Traded to **Hartford** by **NY Rangers** with Norm MacIver and Don Maloney for Carrey Wilson and Hartford's fifth-round choice in 1990 Entry Draft, December 26, 1988.

LAXDAL, DEREK

Right wing. Shoots right. 6'1', 175 lbs. Born, St. Boniface, Man., February 21, 1966.
(Toronto's 7th choice, 151st overall, in 1984 Entry Draft).

			Regular Season					Playoffs				
Season	Club	Lea	GP	G	A	TP	PIM	GP	G	A	TP	PIM
1982-83	Portland	WHL	39	4	9	13	27	14	0	2	2	2
1983-84	Brandon	WHL	70	23	20	43	86	12	0	4	4	10
1984-85	Toronto	NHL	3	0	0	0	6	....	....	....	....	....
	Brandon	WHL	69	61	41	102	74	....	....	....	....	....
	St. Catharines	AHL	5	3	2	5	2	....	....	....	....	....
1985-86	N. Westminster	WHL	60	43	41	84	76	....	....	....	....	....
	St. Catharines	AHL	7	0	1	1	15	12	1	1	2	24
1986-87	Toronto	NHL	2	0	0	0	7	....	....	....	....	....
	Newmarket	AHL	78	24	20	44	69	....	....	....	....	....
1987-88	Toronto	NHL	5	0	0	0	6	....	....	....	....	....
	Newmarket	AHL	67	18	25	43	81	....	....	....	....	....
1988-89	Toronto	NHL	41	9	6	15	65	....	....	....	....	....
	Newmarket	AHL	34	22	22	44	53	2	0	2	2	5
	NHL Totals		51	9	6	15	84	....	....	....	....	....

LAYLIN, CORY

Left wing. Shoots left. 5'9", 160 lbs. Born, St. Cloud, MN, January 24, 1970.
(Pittsburgh's 10th choice, 214th overall, in 1988 Entry Draft).

			Regular Season					Playoffs				
Season	Club	Lea	GP	G	A	TP	PIM	GP	G	A	TP	PIM
1987-88	Appollo	HS	21	30	31	61	....	....	....	....	....	....
1988-89	U. Minnesota	WCHA	47	14	10	24	24	....	....	....	....	....

LEACH, JAMIE

Right wing. Shoots right. 6'1", 190 lbs. Born, Philadelphia, PA, August 25, 1969.
(Pittsburgh's 3rd choice, 47th overall, in 1987 Entry Draft).

			Regular Season					Playoffs				
Season	Club	Lea	GP	G	A	TP	PIM	GP	G	A	TP	PIM
1985-86	N. Westminster	WHL	58	8	7	15	20	....	....	....	....	....
1986-87	Hamilton	OHL	64	12	19	31	67	....	....	....	....	....
1987-88	Hamilton	OHL	64	24	19	43	79	14	6	7	13	12
1988-89a	Niagara Falls	OHL	58	45	62	107	47	17	9	11	20	25

a OHL Third All-Star Team (1989)

LEACH, STEPHEN

Right Wing. Shoots right. 5'11", 180 lbs. Born, Cambridge, MA, January 16, 1966.
(Washington's 2nd choice, 34th over-all, in 1984 Entry Draft).

			Regular Season					Playoffs				
Season	Club	Lea	GP	G	A	TP	PIM	GP	G	A	TP	PIM
1982-83	Matignon	HS	23	17	21	39	...	....	....	....	....	....
1983-84	Matignon	HS	21	27	22	49	...	....	....	....	....	....
1984-85	N. Hampshire	H.E.	41	12	25	37	53	....	....	....	....	....
1985-86	Washington	NHL	11	1	1	2	2	6	0	1	1	0
	N. Hampshire	H.E.	25	22	6	28	30	....	....	....	....	....
1986-87	Washington	NHL	15	1	0	1	6	....	....	....	....	....
	Binghamton	AHL	54	18	21	39	39	13	3	1	4	6
1987-88	Washington	NHL	8	1	1	2	17	9	2	1	3	0
	U.S. National	....	49	26	20	46	30	....	....	....	....	....
	U.S. Olympic	....	6	1	2	3	0	....	....	....	....	....
1988-89	Washington	NHL	74	11	19	30	94	6	1	0	1	12
	NHL Totals		108	14	21	35	119	21	3	2	5	12

LEAVINS, JIM (LEH vihns)

Defense. Shoots left. 5'11", 185 lbs. Born, Dinsmore, Sask., July 28, 1960.

			Regular Season					Playoffs				
Season	Club	Lea	GP	G	A	TP	PIM	GP	G	A	TP	PIM
1981-82	Denver	WCHA	41	8	34	42	56	....	....	....	....	....
1982-83	Denver	WCHA	33	16	24	40	20	....	....	....	..	..
1983-84	Denver	WCHA	39	13	26	39	38	....	....	....	....	....
1984-85	Fort Wayne	IHL	76	5	20	25	57	13	3	8	11	10
1985-86	Adirondack	AHL	36	4	21	25	19	....	....	....	....	....
	Detroit	NHL	37	2	11	13	26	....	....	....	....	....
1986-87	NY Rangers	NHL	4	0	1	1	4	....	....	....	....	....
	New Haven	AHL	54	7	21	28	16	7	0	4	4	2
1987-88	New Haven	AHL	11	2	5	7	6	....	....	....	....	....
a	Salt Lake	IHL	68	12	45	57	45	16	5	5	10	8
1988-89	Salt Lake	IHL	25	8	13	21	14	14	2	11	13	6
	Kookoo	Fin.	42	12	11	23	39	....	....	....	....	....
	NHL Totals		41	2	12	14	30	....	....	....	....	....

a IHL Second All-Star Team (1988)

Signed as a free agent by **Detroit**, November 9, 1985. Traded to **NY Rangers** by **Detroit** with Kelly Kisio and Lane Lambert for Glen Hanlon and **New York's** third-round choices in 1987 (Dennis Holland) and 1988 Entry Drafts, July 29, 1986. Traded to **Calgary** by **NY Rangers** for Don Mercier, November 6, 1987.

LEBEAU, BENOIT (luh-BOH)

Left wing. Shoots left. 6'1", 190 lbs. Born, Montreal, Que., June 4, 1968.
(Winnipeg's 6th choice, 101st overall, in 1988 Entry Draft).

			Regular Season					Playoffs				
Season	Club	Lea	GP	G	A	TP	PIM	GP	G	A	TP	PIM
1987-88	Merrimack	NCAA	40	35	38	73	52	....	....	....	....	....
1988-89	Merrimack	NCAA	32	18	20	38	46	....	....	....	....	....

LEBEAU, STEPHAN (luh-BOH)

Center. Shoots right. 5'10", 180 lbs. Born, Sherbrooke, Que., February 28, 1968.

			Regular Season					Playoffs				
Season	Club	Lea	GP	G	A	TP	PIM	GP	G	A	TP	PIM
1984-85	Shawinigan	QMJHL	66	41	38	79	18	9	4	5	9	4
1985-86	Shawinigan	QMJHL	72	69	77	146	22	5	4	2	6	4
1986-87a	Shawinigan	QMJHL	65	77	90	167	60	14	9	20	29	20
1987-88a	Shawinigan	QMJHL	67	*94	94	188	66	11	17	9	26	10
	Sherbrooke	AHL	....	....	....	....	....	1	0	1	1	0
1988-89	Montreal	NHL	1	0	1	1	0	....	....	....	....	....
bcde	Sherbrooke	AHL	78	*70	64	*134	47	6	1	4	5	8
	NHL Totals		1	0	1	1	0	0	0	0	0	0

a QMJHL Second All-Star Team (1987, 1988)
b AHL First All-Star Team (1989)
c Won Dudly "Red" Garrett Memorial Trophy (Top Rookie-AHL) 1989)
d Won John B. Sollenberger Trophy (Top Scorer-AHL) 1989)
e Won Les Cunningham Trophy (MVP-AHL) (1989)

Signed as a free agent by **Montreal**, September 27, 1986.

LeBLANC, JEAN GLENN

Left Wing. Shoots left. 6'1", 195 lbs. Born, Campbellton, N.B., January 21, 1964.

			Regular Season					Playoffs				
Season	Club	Lea	GP	G	A	TP	PIM	GP	G	A	TP	PIM
1983-84	Hull	QMJHL	69	39	35	74	32	....	....	....	....	....
1984-85	New Brunswick	AUAA	24	25	34	59	32	....	....	....	....	....
1985-86a	New Brunswick	AUAA	24	38	28	66	35	....	....	....	....	....
1986-87	Vancouver	NHL	2	1	0	1	0	....	....	....	....	....
	Fredericton	AHL	75	40	30	70	27	....	....	....	....	....
1987-88	Vancouver	NHL	41	12	10	22	18	....	....	....	....	....
	Fredericton	AHL	35	26	25	51	54	15	6	7	13	34
1988-89	Edmonton	NHL	2	1	0	1	0	1	0	0	0	0
	Cape Breton	AHL	3	4	0	4	0	....	....	....	....	....
	Milwaukee	IHL	61	39	31	70	42	....	....	....	....	....
	NHL Totals		45	14	10	24	18	1	0	0	0	0

a Canadian University Player of the Year (1986)

Signed as a free agent by **Vancouver**, April 12, 1986. Traded to **Edmonton** by **Vancouver** with Vancouver's fifth-round choice (Peter White) in 1989 Entry Draft for Doug Smith and Gregory C. Adams, March 7, 1989.

LeBRUN, SEAN

Left wing. Shoots left. 6'2", 200 lbs. Born, Prince George, B.C., May 2, 1969.
(New York Islanders' 3rd choice, 37th overall, in 1988 Entry Draft).

			Regular Season					Playoffs				
Season	Club	Lea	GP	G	A	TP	PIM	GP	G	A	TP	PIM
1986-87	Spokane	WHL	6	2	5	7	9	....	....	....	....	....
	N. Westminster	WHL	55	21	32	53	47	....	....	....	....	....
1987-88a	N. Westminster	WHL	72	36	53	89	59	5	1	3	4	2
1988-89	Tri-Cities	WHL	71	52	73	125	92	5	0	4	4	13

a WHL West Division Second All-Star Team (1988)

LeCLAIR, JOHN

Defense. Shoots left. 6'1", 185 lbs. Born, St. Albans, VT, July 5, 1969.
(Montreal's 2nd choice, 33rd overall, in 1987 Entry Draft).

			Regular Season					Playoffs				
Season	Club	Lea	GP	G	A	TP	PIM	GP	G	A	TP	PIM
1986-87	Bellows	HS	27	44	40	84	30	....	....	....	....	....
1987-88	U. of Vermont	ECAC	31	12	22	34	62	....	....	....	....	....
1988-89	U. of Vermont	ECAC	18	9	12	21	40	....	....	....	....	....

LEDYARD, GRANT

Defense. Shoots left. 6'2", 190 lbs. Born, Winnipeg, Man., November 19, 1961.

			Regular Season					Playoffs				
Season	Club	Lea	GP	G	A	TP	PIM	GP	G	A	TP	PIM
1980-81	Saskatoon	WHL	71	9	28	37	148	....	....	....	....	....
1981-82	Fort Garry	MJHL	63	25	45	70	150	....	....	....	....	....
1982-83	Tulsa	CHL	80	13	29	42	115	....	....	....	....	....
1983-84a	Tulsa	CHL	58	9	17	26	71	9	5	4	9	10
1984-85	**NY Rangers**	**NHL**	**42**	**8**	**12**	**20**	**53**	**3**	**0**	**2**	**2**	**4**
	New Haven	AHL	36	6	20	26	18	....	....	....	....	....
1985-86	**NY Rangers**	**NHL**	**27**	**2**	**9**	**11**	**20**	....	....	....	....	....
	Los Angeles	**NHL**	**52**	**7**	**18**	**25**	**78**	....	....	....	....	....
1986-87	**Los Angeles**	**NHL**	**67**	**14**	**23**	**37**	**93**	**5**	**0**	**0**	**0**	**10**
1987-88	**Los Angeles**	**NHL**	**23**	**1**	**7**	**8**	**52**	....	....	....	....	....
	New Haven	AHL	3	2	1	3	4	....	....	....	....	....
	Washington	**NHL**	**21**	**4**	**3**	**7**	**14**	**14**	**1**	**0**	**1**	**30**
1988-89	**Washington**	**NHL**	**61**	**3**	**11**	**14**	**43**	....	....	....	....	....
	Buffalo	**NHL**	**13**	**1**	**5**	**6**	**8**	**5**	**1**	**2**	**3**	**2**
	NHL Totals		**306**	**40**	**88**	**128**	**361**	**27**	**2**	**4**	**6**	**46**

a Won Bob Gassoff Trophy (CHL's Most Improved Defenseman) (1984)

Signed as a free agent by **NY Rangers**, July 7, 1982. Traded to **Los Angeles** by **NY Rangers** with Roland Melanson for Los Angeles' fourth-round choice in 1987 Entry Draft (Michael Sullivan) and Brian MacLellan, December 7, 1985. Traded to **Washington** by **Los Angeles** for Craig Laughlin, February 9, 1988. Traded to **Buffalo** by **Washington** with Clint Malarchuk and Washington's sixth-round choice in 1991 Entry Draft for Calle Johansson and Buffalo's second-round choice (Byron Dafoe) in 1989 Entry Draft, March 7, 1989.

LEEMAN, GARY

Right wing/Defense. Shoots right. 5'11", 170 lbs. Born, Toronto, Ont., February 19, 1964.
(Toronto's 2nd choice, 24th over-all, in 1982 Entry Draft).

			Regular Season					Playoffs				
Season	Club	Lea	GP	G	A	TP	PIM	GP	G	A	TP	PIM
1981-82	Regina	WHL	72	19	41	60	112	3	2	2	4	0
1982-83ab	Regina	WHL	63	24	62	86	88	5	1	5	6	4
	Toronto	**NHL**	....	....	....	....	....	**2**	**0**	**0**	**0**	**0**
1983-84	**Toronto**	**NHL**	**52**	**4**	**8**	**12**	**31**	....	....	....	....	....
1984-85	**Toronto**	**NHL**	**53**	**5**	**26**	**31**	**72**	....	....	....	....	....
	St. Catharines	AHL	7	2	2	4	11	....	....	....	....	....
1985-86	**Toronto**	**NHL**	**53**	**9**	**23**	**32**	**20**	**10**	**2**	**10**	**12**	**2**
	St. Catharines	AHL	25	15	13	28	6	....	....	....	....	....
1986-87	**Toronto**	**NHL**	**80**	**21**	**31**	**52**	**66**	**5**	**0**	**1**	**1**	**14**
1987-88	**Toronto**	**NHL**	**80**	**30**	**31**	**61**	**62**	**2**	**2**	**0**	**2**	**2**
1988-89	**Toronto**	**NHL**	**61**	**32**	**43**	**75**	**66**	....	....	....	....	....
	NHL Totals		**379**	**101**	**162**	**263**	**317**	**19**	**4**	**11**	**15**	**18**

a WHL First All-Star Team (1983)
b Named WHL's Top Defenseman (1983)

Played in NHL All-Star Game (1989)

LEETCH, BRIAN

Defense. Shoots left. 5'11", 170 lbs. Born, Corpus Christi, TX, March 3, 1968.
(NY Rangers' 1st choice, 9th overall, in 1986 Entry Draft).

			Regular Season					Playoffs				
Season	Club	Lea	GP	G	A	TP	PIM	GP	G	A	TP	PIM
1984-85	Avon O. Farms	HS	26	30	46	76	15	....	....	....	....	....
1985-86	Avon O. Farms	HS	28	40	44	84	18	....	....	....	....	....
1986-87abcd	Boston College	H.E.	37	9	38	47	10	....	....	....	....	....
1987-88	**NY Rangers**	**NHL**	**17**	**2**	**12**	**14**	**0**	....	....	....	....	....
	U.S. National	....	50	13	61	74	38	....	....	....	....	....
	U.S. Olympic	....	6	1	5	6	4	....	....	....	....	....
1988-89ef	**NY Rangers**	**NHL**	**68**	**23**	**48**	**71**	**50**	**4**	**3**	**2**	**5**	**2**
	NHL Totals		**85**	**25**	**60**	**85**	**50**	**4**	**3**	**2**	**5**	**2**

a Hockey East Player of the Year (1987)
b Hockey East Rookie of the Year (1987)
c Hockey East First All-Star Team (1987)
d NCAA East First All-American Team (1987)
e NHL All-Rookie Team (1989)
f Won Calder Memorial Trophy (1989)

LEFEBVRE, SYLVAIN

Defense wing. Shoots left. 6'2", 185 lbs. Born, Richmond, Que., October 14, 1967.

			Regular Season					Playoffs				
Season	Club	Lea	GP	G	A	TP	PIM	GP	G	A	TP	PIM
1984-85	Laval	QMJHL	66	7	5	12	31	....	....	....	....	....
1985-86	Laval	QMJHL	71	8	17	25	48	14	1	0	1	25
1986-87	Laval	QMJHL	70	10	36	46	44	15	1	6	7	12
1987-88	Sherbrooke	AHL	79	3	24	27	73	6	2	3	5	4
1988-89a	Sherbrooke	AHL	77	15	32	47	119	6	1	3	4	4

a AHL Second All-Star Team (1989)

Signed as a free agent by **Montreal**, September 24, 1986.

LEHMANN, TOMMY

Center. Shoots left. 6'1", 185 lbs. Born, Solna, Sweden, February 3, 1964.
(Boston's 11th choice, 228th overall, in 1982 Entry Draft).

			Regular Season					Playoffs				
Season	Club	Lea	GP	G	A	TP	PIM	GP	G	A	TP	PIM
1982-83	AIK	Swe.	28	1	5	6	2	3	0	0	0	0
1983-84	AIK	Swe.	23	4	5	9	6	6	2	2	4	0
1984-85	AIK	Swe.	34	13	13	26	6	....	....	....	....	....
1985-86	AIK	Swe.	35	11	13	24	12	....	....	....	....	....
1986-87	AIK	Swe.	31	25	15	40	12	....	....	....	....	....
1987-88	**Boston**	**NHL**	**9**	**1**	**3**	**4**	**6**	....	....	....	....	....
	Maine	AHL	11	3	5	8	2	....	....	....	....	....
1988-89	**Boston**	**NHL**	**26**	**4**	**2**	**6**	**10**	....	....	....	....	....
	Maine	AHL	26	1	13	14	12	....	....	....	....	....
	NHL Totals		**35**	**5**	**5**	**10**	**16**	....	....	....	....	....

Traded to **Edmonton** by **Boston** for Edmonton's third-round choice (Wes Walz) in 1989 Entry Draft, June 17, 1989.

LEMARQUE, ERIC

Right wing. Shoots right. 5'10", 185 lbs. Born, Canoga Park, CA, July 1, 1969.
(Boston's 11th choice, 224th overall, in 1987 Entry Draft).

			Regular Season					Playoffs				
Season	Club	Lea	GP	G	A	TP	PIM	GP	G	A	TP	PIM
1986-87	N. Michigan	WCHA	38	5	12	17	49	....	....	....	....	....
1987-88	N. Michigan	WCHA	39	8	22	30	54	....	....	....	....	....
1988-89	N. Michigan	WCHA	43	20	17	37	40	....	....	....	....	....

LEMAY, MAURICE (MOE) (le-MAY)

Left wing. Shoots left. 5'11", 185 lbs. Born, Saskatoon, Sask., February 18, 1962.
(Vancouver's 4th choice, 105th over-all, in 1981 Entry Draft).

			Regular Season					Playoffs				
Season	Club	Lea	GP	G	A	TP	PIM	GP	G	A	TP	PIM
1979-80	Ottawa	OHA	62	16	23	39	20	10	2	3	5	19
1980-81	Ottawa	OHA	63	32	45	77	102	7	3	5	8	17
1981-82a	Ottawa	OHL	62	*68	70	138	48	17	9	19	28	18
	Vancouver	**NHL**	**5**	**1**	**2**	**3**	**0**	....	....	....	....	....
1982-83	**Vancouver**	**NHL**	**44**	**11**	**9**	**20**	**41**	....	....	....	....	....
	Fredericton	AHL	26	7	8	15	6	9	0	2	2	10
1983-84	Fredericton	AHL	23	9	7	16	32	....	....	....	....	....
	Vancouver	**NHL**	**56**	**12**	**18**	**30**	**38**	**4**	**0**	**0**	**0**	**12**
1984-85	**Vancouver**	**NHL**	**74**	**21**	**31**	**52**	**68**	....	....	....	....	....
1985-86	**Vancouver**	**NHL**	**48**	**16**	**15**	**31**	**92**	....	....	....	....	....
1986-87	**Vancouver**	**NHL**	**52**	**9**	**17**	**26**	**128**	....	....	....	....	....
	Edmonton	**NHL**	**10**	**1**	**2**	**3**	**36**	**9**	**2**	**1**	**3**	**11**
1987-88	**Edmonton**	**NHL**	**4**	**0**	**0**	**0**	**2**	....	....	....	....	....
	Nova Scotia	AHL	39	14	25	39	89	....	....	....	....	....
	Boston	**NHL**	**2**	**0**	**0**	**0**	**0**	**15**	**4**	**2**	**6**	**32**
	Maine	AHL	11	5	6	11	14	3	2	1	3	22
1988-89	**Boston**	**NHL**	**12**	**0**	**0**	**0**	**23**	....	....	....	....	....
	Maine	AHL	13	6	2	8	32	....	....	....	....	....
	Winnipeg	**NHL**	**10**	**1**	**0**	**1**	**14**	....	....	....	....	....
	Moncton	AHL	16	9	11	20	21	10	3	6	9	25
	NHL Totals		**317**	**72**	**94**	**166**	**442**	**28**	**6**	**3**	**9**	**55**

a OHL First All-Star Team (1982)

Traded to **Edmonton** by **Vancouver** for Raimo Summanen, March 10, 1987. Traded to **Boston** by **Edmonton** for Alan May, March 8, 1988. Traded to **Winnipeg** by **Boston** for Ray Neufeld, December 30, 1988.

LEMIEUX, ALAIN (lehm YUH)

Center. Shoots left. 6', 185 lbs. Born, Montreal, Que., May 24, 1961.
(St. Louis' 4th choice, 96th over-all, in 1980 Entry Draft).

			Regular Season					Playoffs				
Season	Club	Lea	GP	G	A	TP	PIM	GP	G	A	TP	PIM
1979-80	Chicoutimi	QJHL	72	47	95	142	36	12	8	12	20	8
1980-81	Chicoutimi	QJHL	1	0	0	0	2	....	....	....	....	....
	Trois Rivières	QJHL	69	68	98	166	62	19	18	31	49	38
1981-82	**St. Louis**	**NHL**	**3**	**0**	**1**	**1**	**0**	....	....	....	....	....
	Salt Lake	CHL	74	41	42	83	61	10	6	4	10	14
1982-83	Salt Lake	CHL	29	20	24	44	35	....	....	....	....	....
	St. Louis	**NHL**	**42**	**9**	**25**	**34**	**18**	**4**	**0**	**1**	**1**	**0**
1983-84	**St. Louis**	**NHL**	**17**	**4**	**5**	**9**	**6**	....	....	....	....	....
	Montana	CHL	38	28	41	69	36	....	....	....	....	....
	Springfield	AHL	14	11	14	25	18	4	0	3	3	2
1984-85	**St. Louis**	**NHL**	**19**	**4**	**2**	**6**	**0**	....	....	....	....	....
	Peoria	IHL	2	1	0	1	0	....	....	....	....	....
	Quebec	**NHL**	**30**	**11**	**11**	**22**	**12**	**14**	**3**	**3**	**6**	**0**
1985-86	**Quebec**	**NHL**	**7**	**0**	**0**	**0**	**2**	**1**	**1**	**2**	**3**	**0**
	Fredericton	AHL	64	29	45	74	54	5	5	2	7	5
1986-87	**Pittsburgh**	**NHL**	**1**	**0**	**0**	**0**	**0**	....	....	....	....	....
a	Baltimore	AHL	72	41	56	97	62	....	....	....	....	....
1987-88	Hershey	AHL	20	8	10	18	10	....	....	....	....	....
	Baltimore	AHL	16	2	14	16	4	....	....	....	....	....
	Springfield	AHL	15	7	10	17	4	....	....	....	....	....
1988-89	Indianapolis	IHL	29	18	26	44	90	....	....	....	....	....
	Karpat	Fin.	16	4	9	13	16	....	....	....	....	....
	Saipa	Fin.	5	1	4	5	4	....	....	....	....	....
	NHL Totals		**119**	**28**	**44**	**72**	**38**	**19**	**4**	**6**	**10**	**0**

a AHL Second All-Star Team (1987)

Traded to **Quebec** by **St. Louis** for Luc Dufour, January 29, 1985.

LEMIEUX, CLAUDE (lehm YUH)

Right wing. Shoots right. 6'1", 206 lbs. Born, Buckingham, Que., July 16, 1965.
(Montreal's 2nd choice, 26th over-all, in 1983 Entry Draft).

			Regular Season					Playoffs				
Season	Club	Lea	GP	G	A	TP	PIM	GP	G	A	TP	PIM
1981-82	Richelieu	Midget	48	24	48	72	96	....	....	....	....	....
1982-83	Trois Rivières	QMJHL	62	28	38	66	187	4	1	0	1	30
1983-84	**Montreal**	**NHL**	**8**	**1**	**1**	**2**	**12**	....	....	....	....	....
	Verdun	QMJHL	51	41	45	86	225	9	8	12	20	63
	Nova Scotia	AHL	....	....	....	....	....	2	1	0	1	0
1984-85	**Montreal**	**NHL**	**1**	**0**	**1**	**1**	**7**	....	....	....	....	....
ab	Verdun	QMJHL	52	58	66	124	152	14	23	17	40	38
1985-86	**Montreal**	**NHL**	**10**	**1**	**2**	**3**	**22**	**20**	**10**	**6**	**16**	**68**
	Sherbrooke	AHL	58	21	32	53	145	....	....	....	....	....
1986-87	**Montreal**	**NHL**	**76**	**27**	**26**	**53**	**156**	**17**	**4**	**9**	**13**	**41**
1987-88	**Montreal**	**NHL**	**78**	**31**	**30**	**61**	**137**	**11**	**3**	**2**	**5**	**20**
1988-89	**Montreal**	**NHL**	**69**	**29**	**22**	**51**	**136**	**18**	**4**	**3**	**7**	**58**
	NHL Totals		**242**	**89**	**82**	**171**	**470**	**66**	**21**	**20**	**41**	**187**

a Named Most Valuable Player in QMJHL Playoffs (1985).
b QMJHL First All-Star Team (1985).

LEMIEUX, JOCELYN (lehm YUH)

Right wing. Shoots left. 5'10", 200 lbs. Born, Mont Laurier, Que., November 18, 1967.
(St. Louis' 1st choice, 10th overall, in 1986 Entry Draft).

			Regular Season					Playoffs				
Season	Club	Lea	GP	G	A	TP	PIM	GP	G	A	TP	PIM
1984-85	Laval	QMJHL	68	13	19	32	92	....	....	....	....	....
1985-86a	Laval	QMJHL	71	57	68	125	131	14	9	15	24	37
1986-87	**St. Louis**	**NHL**	**53**	**10**	**8**	**18**	**94**	**5**	**0**	**1**	**1**	**6**
1987-88	**St. Louis**	**NHL**	**23**	**1**	**0**	**1**	**42**	**5**	**0**	**0**	**0**	**15**
	Peoria	IHL	8	0	5	5	35	....	....	....	....	....
1988-89	**Montreal**	**NHL**	**1**	**0**	**1**	**1**	**0**	....	....	....	....	....
	Sherbrooke	AHL	73	25	28	53	134	4	3	1	4	6
	NHL Totals		**77**	**11**	**9**	**20**	**136**	**10**	**0**	**1**	**1**	**21**

a QMJHL First All-Star Team (1986).

Traded to **Montreal** by **St. Louis** with Darrell May and St. Louis' second round choice (Patrice Brisbois) in the 1989 Entry Draft for Sergio Momesso and Vincent Riendeau, August 9, 1988.

LEMIEUX, MARIO (lehm YUH)

Center. Shoots right. 6'4", 200 lbs. Born, Montreal, Que., October 5, 1965.
(Pittsburgh's 1st choice and 1st over-all in 1984 Entry Draft).

			Regular Season					Playoffs				
Season	Club	Lea	GP	G	A	TP	PIM	GP	G	A	TP	PIM
1981-82	Laval	QMJHL	64	30	66	96	22	18	5	9	14	31
1982-83a	Laval	QMJHL	66	84	100	184	76	12	14	18	32	18
1983-84bcd	Laval	QMJHL	70	*133	*149	*282	92	14	*29	*23	*52	29
1984-85ef	**Pittsburgh**	**NHL**	**73**	**43**	**57**	**100**	**54**	....	....	....	....	....
1985-86gh	**Pittsburgh**	**NHL**	**79**	**48**	**93**	**141**	**43**	....	....	....	....	....
1986-87g	**Pittsburgh**	**NHL**	**63**	**54**	**53**	**107**	**57**	....	....	....	....	....
1987-88hijklm	**Pittsburgh**	**NHL**	**77**	***70**	**98**	***168**	**92**	....	....	....	....	....
1988-89jkmn	**Pittsburgh**	**NHL**	**76**	***85**	***114**	***199**	**100**	**11**	**12**	**7**	**19**	**16**
	NHL Totals		**368**	**300**	**415**	**715**	**346**	**11**	**12**	**7**	**19**	**16**

a QMJHL Second All-Star Team (1983)
b QMJHL First All-Star Team (1984)
c QMJHL Most Valuable Player (1984)
d Canadian Major Junior Player of the Year (1984)
e Won Calder Memorial Trophy (1985)
f NHL All-Rookie Team (1985)
g NHL Second All-Star Team (1986, 1987)
h Won Lester B. Pearson Award (1986, 1988)
i Won Hart Trophy (1988)
j Won Art Ross Trophy (1988, 1989)
k NHL First All-Star Team (1988, 1989)
l Won Dodge Performance of the Year Award (1988)
m Won Dodge Ram Tough Award (1989)
n Won Dodge Performer of the Year Award (1988, 1989)

Played in NHL All-Star Game (1985, 1986, 1988, 1989)

LENARDON, TIM

Center. Shoots left. 6'2", 185 lbs. Born, Trail, B.C., May 11, 1962.

			Regular Season					Playoffs				
Season	Club	Lea	GP	G	A	TP	PIM	GP	G	A	TP	PIM
1983-84	Brandon U.	CWUAA	24	22	21	43	....	....	....	....	....	....
1984-85	Brandon U.	CWUAA	24	21	39	60	....	....	....	....	....	....
1985-86a	Brandon U.	CWUAA	26	26	40	66	33	....	....	....	....	....
1986-87	**New Jersey**	**NHL**	**7**	**1**	**1**	**2**	**0**	....	....	....	....	....
	Maine	AHL	61	28	35	63	30	....	....	....	....	....
1987-88	Utica	AHL	79	38	53	91	72	....	....	....	....	....
1988-89	Utica	AHL	63	28	27	55	48	....	....	....	....	....
	Milwaukee	IHL	15	6	5	11	27	10	2	3	5	25
	NHL Totals		**7**	**1**	**1**	**2**	**0**	....	....	....	....	....

a Canadian University Player of the Year (1986).

Signed as a free agent by **New Jersey**, August 6, 1986. Traded to **Vancouver** by **New Jersey** for Claude Vilgrain, March 7, 1989.

LEROUX, FRANCOIS

Defense. Shoots left. 6'5", 220 lbs. Born, Ste. Adele, Que., April 18, 1970.
(Edmonton's 1st choice, 19th overall, in 1988 Entry Draft).

			Regular Season					Playoffs				
Season	Club	Lea	GP	G	A	TP	PIM	GP	G	A	TP	PIM
1986-87	Laval-Laur.	Midget	42	5	11	16	76	....	....	....	....	....
1987-88	St. Jean	QMJHL	58	3	8	11	143	7	2	0	2	21
1988-89	St. Jean	QMJHL	57	8	34	42	185	....	....	....	....	....
	Edmonton	**NHL**	**2**	**0**	**0**	**0**	**0**	....	....	....	....	....
	NHL Totals		**2**	**0**	**0**	**0**	**0**	....	....	....	....	....

LESCHYSHYN, CURTIS

Defense. Shoots left. 6'1", 205 lbs. Born, Thompson, Man., September 21, 1969.
(Quebec's 1st choice, 3rd overall, in 1988 Entry Draft).

			Regular Season					Playoffs				
Season	Club	Lea	GP	G	A	TP	PIM	GP	G	A	TP	PIM
1986-87	Saskatoon	WHL	70	14	26	40	107	11	1	5	6	14
1987-88	Saskatoon	WHL	56	14	41	55	86	10	2	5	7	16
1988-89	**Quebec**	**NHL**	**71**	**4**	**9**	**13**	**71**	....	....	....	....	....
	NHL Totals		**71**	**4**	**9**	**13**	**71**	....	....	....	....	....

LESSARD, RICK

Defense. Shoots left. 6'2", 200 lbs. Born, Timmins, Ont., January 9, 1968.
(Calgary's 6th choice, 142nd overall, in 1986 Entry Draft).

			Regular Season					Playoffs				
Season	Club	Lea	GP	G	A	TP	PIM	GP	G	A	TP	PIM
1985-86	Ottawa	OHL	64	1	20	21	231	....	....	....	....	....
1986-87	Ottawa	OHL	66	5	36	41	188	11	1	7	8	30
1987-88	Ottawa	OHL	58	5	34	39	210	16	1	0	1	31
1988-89	**Calgary**	**NHL**	**6**	**0**	**1**	**1**	**2**	....	....	....	....	....
a	Salt Lake	IHL	76	10	42	52	239	14	1	6	7	35
	NHL Totals		**6**	**0**	**1**	**1**	**2**	....	....	....	....	....

a IHL First All-Star Team (1989)

LIBA, IGOR

Left wing. Shoots left. 6', 192 lbs. Born, Presov, Czechoslovakia, November 4, 1960.
(Calgary's 7th choice, 91st overall, in 1983 Entry Draft).

			Regular Season					Playoffs				
Season	Club	Lea	GP	G	A	TP	PIM	GP	G	A	TP	PIM
1986-87	VSZ Kosice	Czech.	39	14	26	40	....	....	....	....	....	....
1987-88	VSZ Kosice	Czech.	31	13	16	29	....	....	....	....	....	....
1988-89	**NY Rangers**	**NHL**	**10**	**2**	**5**	**7**	**15**	....	....	....	....	....
	Los Angeles	**NHL**	**27**	**5**	**13**	**18**	**21**	**2**	**0**	**0**	**0**	**2**
	NHL Totals		**37**	**7**	**18**	**25**	**36**	**2**	**0**	**0**	**0**	**2**

Traded to **Minnesota** by **Calgary** for Minnesota's 5th round draft choice in 1988 Entry Draft (Thomas Forslund), May 20, 1988. Traded to **NY Rangers** by **Minnesota** with Brian Lawton and the rights to Eric Bennett for Paul Jerrard and Mark Tinordi, the rights to Bret Barnett and Mike Sullivan, and Los Angeles' third-round choice (Murray Garbutt) in 1989 Entry Draft — acquired March 10, 1987 by Minnesota — October 11, 1988. Traded to **Los Angeles** by **NY Rangers** with Michael Boyce, Todd Elik and future considerations for Dean Kennedy and Denis Larocque, December 12, 1988.

LIDSTER, DOUG

Defense. Shoots right. 6'1", 200 lbs. Born, Kamloops, B.C., October 18, 1960.
(Vancouver's 6th choice, 133rd over-all, in 1980 Entry Draft).

			Regular Season					Playoffs				
Season	Club	Lea	GP	G	A	TP	PIM	GP	G	A	TP	PIM
1977-78	Seattle	WHL	2	0	0	0	0	....	....	....	....	....
1979-80	Colorado	WCHA	39	18	25	43	52	....	....	....	....	....
1980-81	Colorado	WCHA	36	10	30	40	54	....	....	....	....	....
1981-82	Colorado	WCHA	36	13	22	35	32	....	....	....	....	....
1982-83	Colorado	WCHA	34	15	41	56	30	....	....	....	....	....
1983-84	Cdn. Olympic	...	59	6	20	26	28	....	....	....	....	....
	Vancouver	**NHL**	**8**	**0**	**0**	**0**	**4**	**2**	**0**	**1**	**1**	**0**
1984-85	**Vancouver**	**NHL**	**78**	**6**	**24**	**30**	**55**	....	....	....	....	....
1985-86	**Vancouver**	**NHL**	**78**	**12**	**16**	**28**	**56**	**3**	**0**	**1**	**1**	**2**
1986-87	**Vancouver**	**NHL**	**80**	**12**	**51**	**63**	**40**	....	....	....	....	....
1987-88	**Vancouver**	**NHL**	**64**	**4**	**32**	**36**	**105**	....	....	....	....	....
1988-89	**Vancouver**	**NHL**	**63**	**5**	**17**	**22**	**78**	**7**	**1**	**1**	**2**	**9**
	NHL Totals		**371**	**39**	**140**	**179**	**338**	**12**	**1**	**3**	**4**	**11**

LILLIE, SHAWN

Left wing. Shoots left. 6'0", 180 lbs. Born, Sault Ste. Marie, Ont., August 13, 1967.
(Pittsburgh's 2nd choice, 9th overall, in 1988 Supplemental Draft).

			Regular Season					Playoffs				
Season	Club	Lea	GP	G	A	TP	PIM	GP	G	A	TP	PIM
1986-87	Colgate	ECAC	30	11	10	21	4	....	....	....	....	....
1987 88	Colgate	ECAC	32	12	22	34	12	....	....	....	....	....
1988-89	Colgate	ECAC	31	16	38	54	12	....	....	....	....	....

LINDBERG, CHRIS

Center. Shoots left. 6'1", 185 lbs. Born, Fort Frances, Ont., April 16, 1967.

			Regular Season					Playoffs				
Season	Club	Lea	GP	G	A	TP	PIM	GP	G	A	TP	PIM
1987-88	Minn.-Duluth	WCHA	35	12	10	22	36	....	....	....	....	....
1988-89	Minn.-Duluth	WCHA	36	15	18	33	51	....	....	....	....	....

Signed as a free agent by **Hartford**, March 17, 1989.

LINDEN, TREVOR

Center/Right wing. Shoots right. 6'4", 200 lbs. Born, Medicine Hat, Alta., April 11, 1970.
(Vancouver's 1st choice, 2nd overall, in 1988 Entry Draft).

			Regular Season					Playoffs				
Season	Club	Lea	GP	G	A	TP	PIM	GP	G	A	TP	PIM
1986-87	Medicine Hat	WHL	72	14	22	36	59	20	5	4	9	17
1987-88	Medicine Hat	WHL	67	46	64	110	76	16	13	12	25	19
1988-89a	**Vancouver**	**NHL**	**80**	**30**	**29**	**59**	**41**	**7**	**3**	**4**	**7**	**8**
	NHL Totals		**80**	**30**	**29**	**59**	**41**	**7**	**3**	**4**	**7**	**8**

a NHL All-Rookie Team (1989)

LINDHOLM, MIKAEL

Center. Shoots left. 6'1", 195 lbs. Born, Brynas, Sweden, December 19, 1964.
(Los Angeles' 10th choice, 237th overall, in 1987 Entry Draft).

			Regular Season					Playoffs				
Season	Club	Lea	GP	G	A	TP	PIM	GP	G	A	TP	PIM
1981-82	Gavle GIK	Swe. 2	18	3	3	6	8	....	....	....	....	....
1982-83	Gavle GIK	Swe. 2	27	6	7	13	44	....	....	....	....	....
1983-84	Stromsbro	Swe. 2	20	9	10	19	4	....	....	....	....	....
1984-85	Stromsbro	Swe. 2	30	14	17	31	29	....	....	....	....	....
1985-86	Stromsbro	Swe. 2	32	15	20	35	26	5	2	4	6	6
1986-87	Brynas	Swe.	36	8	9	17	46	....	....	....	....	....
1987-88	Brynas	Swe.	38	9	8	17	56	....	....	....	....	....
1988-89	Brynas	Swe.	40	9	17	26	98	....	....	....	....	....

LINDMAN, MIKAEL

Defense. Shoots left. 6';0", 185 lbs. Born, Bolsaf, Sweden, May 15, 1967.
(Detroit's 12th choice, 239th overall, in 1985 Entry Draft).

			Regular Season					Playoffs				
Season	Club	Lea	GP	G	A	TP	PIM	GP	G	A	TP	PIM
1988-89	Skelleftea	Swe.	38	7	7	14	20	....	....	....	....	....

LINK, ANTHONY (TONY)

Defense. Shoots right. 6'2", 205 lbs. Born, Anchorage, AK, April 3, 1969.
(Philadelphia's 6th choice, 125th overall, in 1987 Entry Draft).

			Regular Season					Playoffs				
Season	Club	Lea	GP	G	A	TP	PIM	GP	G	A	TP	PIM
1986-87	Dimond	HS	20	17	26	43	32	....	....	....	....	....
1987-88	Delta	BCJHL	20	7	12	19	36	....	....	....	....	....
1988-89	U. of Maine	H.E.	22	0	3	3	12	....	....	....	....	....

LINSEMAN, KEN (LIHNS muhn)

Center. Shoots left. 5'11", 180 lbs. Born, Kingston, Ont., August 11, 1958.
(Philadelphia's 2nd choice, 7th over-all, in 1978 Amateur Draft).

			Regular Season					Playoffs				
Season	Club	Lea	GP	G	A	TP	PIM	GP	G	A	TP	PIM
1975-76	Kingston	OHA	65	61	51	112	92	7	5	0	5	18
1976-77a	Kingston	OHA	63	53	74	127	210	10	9	12	21	54
1977-78	Birmingham	WHA	71	38	38	76	126	5	2	2	4	15
1978-79	Maine	AHL	38	17	22	39	106	....	....	....	....	....
	Philadelphia	**NHL**	**30**	**5**	**20**	**25**	**23**	**8**	**2**	**6**	**8**	**22**
1979-80	**Philadelphia**	**NHL**	**80**	**22**	**57**	**79**	**107**	**17**	**4**	***18**	**22**	**40**
1980-81	**Philadelphia**	**NHL**	**51**	**17**	**30**	**47**	**150**	**12**	**4**	**16**	**20**	**67**
1981-82	**Philadelphia**	**NHL**	**79**	**24**	**68**	**92**	**275**	**4**	**1**	**2**	**3**	**6**
1982-83	**Edmonton**	**NHL**	**72**	**33**	**42**	**75**	**181**	**16**	**6**	**8**	**14**	**22**
1983-84	**Edmonton**	**NHL**	**72**	**18**	**49**	**67**	**119**	**19**	**10**	**4**	**14**	**65**
1984-85	**Boston**	**NHL**	**74**	**25**	**49**	**74**	**126**	**5**	**4**	**6**	**10**	**8**
1985-86	**Boston**	**NHL**	**64**	**23**	**58**	**81**	**97**	**3**	**0**	**1**	**1**	**17**
1986-87	**Boston**	**NHL**	**64**	**15**	**34**	**49**	**126**	**4**	**1**	**1**	**2**	**22**
1987-88	**Boston**	**NHL**	**77**	**29**	**45**	**74**	**167**	**23**	**11**	**14**	**25**	**56**
1988-89	**Boston**	**NHL**	**78**	**27**	**45**	**72**	**164**	....	....	....	....	....
	NHL Totals		**741**	**238**	**497**	**735**	**1535**	**111**	**43**	**76**	**119**	**325**

a OHA Second All-Star Team (1977).

Traded to **Hartford** by **Philadelphia** with Greg Adams and Philadelphia's first (David Jensen) and third round choices (Leif Karlsson) in 1983 Entry Draft for Mark Howe and Hartford's third round choice (Derrick Smith) in the 1983 Entry Draft, August 19, 1982. Traded to **Edmonton** by **Hartford** with Don Nachbaur for Risto Siltanen and Brent Loney, August 19, 1982. Traded to **Boston** by **Edmonton** for Mike Krushelnyski, June 21, 1984.

LOACH, LONNIE

Left wing. Shoots left. 5'10", 180 lbs. Born, New Liskeard, Ont., April 14, 1968.
(Chicago's 4th choice, 98th overall, in 1986 Entry Draft).

			Regular Season					Playoffs				
Season	Club	Lea	GP	G	A	TP	PIM	GP	G	A	TP	PIM
1985-86a	Guelph	OHL	65	41	42	83	63	20	7	8	15	16
1986-87	Guelph	OHL	56	31	24	55	42	5	2	1	3	2
1987-88	Guelph	OHL	66	43	49	92	75	....	....	....	....	....
1988-89	Flint	IHL	41	22	26	48	30	....	....	....	....	....
	Saginaw	IHL	32	7	6	13	27	....	....	....	....	....

a OHL Rookie of the Year (1986).

LOCKWOOD, JOE

Right wing. Shoots right. 6', 180 lbs. Born, Milford, MI, March 21, 1965.
(NY Rangers' 1st choice, 15th overall, in 1987 Supplemental Draft).

			Regular Season					Playoffs				
Season	Club	Lea	GP	G	A	TP	PIM	GP	G	A	TP	PIM
1984-85	U. of Michigan	CCHA	38	5	9	14	42	....	....	....	....	....
1985-86	U. of Michigan	CCHA	38	7	6	13	45	....	....	....	....	....
1986-87	U. of Michigan	CCHA	39	13	5	18	62	....	....	....	....	....
1987-88	U. of Michigan	CCHA	32	11	13	24	42	....	....	....	....	....
1988-89	Kalamazoo	IHL	49	14	10	24	27	3	0	0	0	0

LOEWEN, DARCY

Left wing. Shoots left. 5'10", 180 lbs. Born, Calgary, Alta., February 26, 1969.
(Buffalo's 2nd choice, 55th overall, in 1988 Entry Draft).

			Regular Season					Playoffs				
Season	Club	Lea	GP	G	A	TP	PIM	GP	G	A	TP	PIM
1986-87	Spokane	WHL	68	15	25	40	129	5	0	0	0	16
1987-88	Spokane	WHL	72	30	44	74	231	15	7	5	12	54
1988-89	Spokane	WHL	60	31	27	58	194	....	....	....	....	....
	Cdn. National	....	2	0	0	0	0	....	....	....	....	....

LOFTHOUSE, MARK (LOFT-house)

Right wing/Center. Shoots right. 6'2", 195 lbs. Born, New Westminster, B.C., April 21, 1957.
(Washington's 2nd choice, 21st over-all, in 1977 Amateur Draft).

			Regular Season					Playoffs				
Season	Club	Lea	GP	G	A	TP	PIM	GP	G	A	TP	PIM
1974-75	N. Westminster	WHL	61	36	28	64	53	....	....	....	....	....
1975-76	N. Westminster	WHL	72	68	48	116	55	17	9	12	21	22
1976-77	N. Westminster	WHL	70	54	58	112	59	14	10	8	18	19
1977-78	**Washington**	**NHL**	**18**	**2**	**1**	**3**	**8**	....	....	....	....	....
	Hershey	AHL	35	8	6	14	39	....	....	....	....	....
	Salt Lake	CHL	13	0	1	1	4	5	0	1	1	6
1978-79	**Washington**	**NHL**	**52**	**13**	**10**	**23**	**10**	....	....	....	....	....
	Hershey	AHL	16	7	7	14	6	4	0	1	1	2
1979-80	**Washington**	**NHL**	**68**	**15**	**18**	**33**	**20**	....	....	....	....	....
	Hershey	AHL	9	7	3	10	6	....	....	....	....	....
1980-81	**Washington**	**NHL**	**3**	**1**	**1**	**2**	**4**	....	....	....	....	....
ab	Hershey	AHL	72	*48	55	*103	131	10	6	9	15	24
1981-82	**Detroit**	**NHL**	**12**	**3**	**4**	**7**	**13**	....	....	....	....	....
	Adirondack	AHL	69	33	38	71	75	5	2	3	5	2
1982-83	**Detroit**	**NHL**	**28**	**8**	**4**	**12**	**18**	....	....	....	....	....
	Adirondack	AHL	39	27	18	45	20	....	....	....	....	....
1983-84	New Haven	AHL	79	37	64	101	45	....	....	....	....	....
1984-85	New Haven	AHL	12	11	4	15	4	....	....	....	....	....
1985-86	New Haven	AHL	70	32	35	67	56	5	2	1	3	0
1986-87	New Haven	AHL	47	18	27	45	34	4	0	1	1	2
1987-88	Hershey	AHL	51	21	21	42	64	10	6	5	11	6
1988-89	Hershey	AHL	74	32	47	79	71	12	3	4	7	20
	NHL Totals		**181**	**42**	**38**	**80**	**73**	....	....	....	....	....

a AHL First All-Star Team (1981)
b Won John B. Sollenberger Trophy (AHL's leading scorer) (1981)

Traded to **Detroit** by **Washington** for Al Jensen, July 23, 1981. Signed as free agent by **Los Angeles**, August 10, 1983. Signed as a free agent by **Philadelphia**, August 15, 1987.

LOGAN, ROBERT

Right wing. Shoots right. 6', 190 lbs. Born, Montreal, Que., February 22, 1964.
(Buffalo's 8th choice, l00th over-all, in 1982 Entry Draft.)

			Regular Season					Playoffs				
Season	Club	Lea	GP	G	A	TP	PIM	GP	G	A	TP	PIM
1982-83	Yale	ECAC	28	13	12	25	8	....	....	....	....	....
1983-84	Yale	ECAC	22	9	13	22	25	....	....	....	....	....
1984-85	Yale	ECAC	32	19	12	31	18	....	....	....	....	....
1985-86a	Yale	ECAC	27	19	21	40	22	....	....	....	....	....
1986-87	**Buffalo**	**NHL**	**22**	**7**	**3**	**10**	**0**	....	....	....	....	....
	Rochester	AHL	56	30	14	44	27	18	5	10	15	4
1987-88	**Buffalo**	**NHL**	**16**	**3**	**2**	**5**	**0**	....	....	....	....	....
	Rochester	AHL	45	23	15	38	35	....	....	....	....	....
1988-89	**Los Angeles**	**NHL**	**4**	**0**	**0**	**0**	**0**	....	....	....	....	....
	New Haven	AHL	66	21	32	53	27	13	2	3	5	9
	Rochester	AHL	5	2	2	4	2	....	....	....	....	....
	NHL Totals		**42**	**10**	**5**	**15**	**0**	....	....	....	....	....

a ECAC Second All-Star Team (1986).

Traded to **Los Angeles** by **Buffalo** with Buffalo's ninth-round choice (Jim Glacin) in 1989 Entry Draft for Larry Playfair, October 21, 1988.

LOISELLE, CLAUDE (loy ZELL)

Center. Shoots left. 5'11", 195 lbs. Born, Ottawa, Ont., May 29, 1963.
(Detroit's 1st choice, 23rd over-all, in 1981 Entry Draft).

			Regular Season					Playoffs				
Season	Club	Lea	GP	G	A	TP	PIM	GP	G	A	TP	PIM
1980-81	Windsor	OHA	68	38	56	94	103	11	3	3	6	40
1981-82	**Detroit**	**NHL**	**4**	**1**	**0**	**1**	**2**	....	....	....	....	....
	Windsor	OHL	68	36	73	109	192	9	2	10	12	42
1982-83	**Detroit**	**NHL**	**18**	**2**	**0**	**2**	**15**	....	....	....	....	....
	Adirondack	AHL	6	1	7	8	0	6	2	4	6	0
1983-84	**Detroit**	**NHL**	**28**	**4**	**6**	**10**	**32**	....	....	....	....	....
	Adirondack	AHL	29	13	16	29	59	....	....	....	....	....
1984-85	**Detroit**	**NHL**	**30**	**8**	**1**	**9**	**45**	**3**	**0**	**2**	**2**	**0**
	Adirondack	AHL	47	22	29	51	24	....	....	....	....	....
1985-86	**Detroit**	**NHL**	**48**	**7**	**15**	**22**	**142**	....	....	....	....	....
	Adirondack	AHL	21	15	11	26	32	16	5	10	15	38
1986-87	**New Jersey**	**NHL**	**75**	**16**	**24**	**40**	**137**	....	....	....	....	....
1987-88	**New Jersey**	**NHL**	**68**	**17**	**18**	**35**	**121**	**20**	**4**	**6**	**10**	**50**
1988-89	**New Jersey**	**NHL**	**74**	**7**	**14**	**21**	**209**	....	....	....	....	....
	NHL Totals		**345**	**62**	**78**	**140**	**703**	**20**	**4**	**8**	**12**	**50**

Traded to **New Jersey** by **Detroit** for Tim Higgins, June 25, 1986. Traded to **Quebec** by **New Jersey** with Joe Cirella for Walt Poddubny and future considerations, June 17, 1989.

LOMOW, BYRON

Center. Shoots right. 5'11", 180 lbs. Born, Sherwood Park, Alta., April 27, 1965.
Last amateur club: Brandon Wheat Kings (WHL).

			Regular Season					Playoffs				
Season	Club	Lea	GP	G	A	TP	PIM	GP	G	A	TP	PIM
1982-83	Brandon	OHA	62	19	26	45	21	....	....	....	....	....
1983-84	Brandon	WHL	71	44	57	101	44	12	1	5	6	16
1984-85	Brandon	WHL	71	42	70	112	90	....	....	....	....	....
1985-86	Brandon	WHL	72	52	67	119	77	....	....	....	....	....
	Indianapolis	IHL	9	8	3	11	10	5	2	11	3	2
1986-87	Indianapolis	IHL	81	28	43	71	225	6	3	5	8	21
1987-88	Baltimore	AHL	71	14	26	40	77	....	....	....	....	....
	Colorado	IHL	10	2	10	12	7	....	....	....	....	....
1988-89	Fort Wayne	IHL	81	22	35	57	207	11	3	3	6	68

Signed a free agent by **Minnesota**, April 21, 1986. Traded to **NY Rangers** by **Minnesota** with future considerations for Curt Giles, November 20, 1987.

LONEY, TROY

Left wing. Shoots left. 6'3", 210 lbs.   Born, Bow Island, Alta., September 21, 1963.
(Pittsburgh's 3rd choice, 52nd over-all, in 1982 Entry Draft).

			Regular Season					Playoffs				
Season	Club	Lea	GP	G	A	TP	PIM	GP	G	A	TP	PIM
1980-81	Lethbridge	WHL	71	18	13	31	100	9	2	2	5	14
1981-82	Lethbridge	WHL	71	26	33	59	152	12	3	3	6	10
1982-83	Lethbridge	WHL	72	33	34	67	156	20	10	7	17	43
1983-84	Pittsburgh	NHL	13	0	0	0	9	....	....	....	....	....
	Baltimore	AHL	63	18	13	31	147	10	0	2	2	19
1984-85	Pittsburgh	NHL	46	10	8	18	59	....	....	....	....	....
	Baltimore	AHL	15	4	2	6	25	....	....	....	....	....
1985-86	Pittsburgh	NHL	47	3	9	12	95	....	....	....	....	....
	Baltimore	AHL	33	12	11	23	84	....	....	....	....	....
1986-87	Pittsburgh	NHL	23	8	7	15	22	....	....	....	....	....
	Baltimore	AHL	40	13	14	27	134	....	....	....	....	....
1987-88	Pittsburgh	NHL	65	5	13	18	151	....	....	....	....	....
1988-89	Pittsburgh	NHL	69	10	6	16	165	11	1	3	4	24
	NHL Totals		**263**	**36**	**43**	**79**	**501**	**11**	**1**	**3**	**4**	**24**

LOOB, HAKAN

(LOOB, HOH kuhn)

Right wing. Shoots right. 5'9", 180 lbs.   Born, Visby, Sweden, July 3, 1960.
(Calgary's 10th choice, 181st over-all, in 1980 Entry Draft).

			Regular Season					Playoffs				
Season	Club	Lea	GP	G	A	TP	PIM	GP	G	A	TP	PIM
1977-78	Karlskrona	Swe. 2	25	15	4	19	37	....	....	....	....	....
1978-79	Karlskrona	Swe. 2	23	23	9	32	8	....	....	....	....	....
1979-80	Farjestad	Swe.	36	15	4	19	20	....	....	....	....	....
1980-81	Farjestad	Swe.	36	23	6	29	14	7	5	3	8	6
	Swe. National	...	6	0	1	1	0	....	....	....	....	....
1981-82	Farjestad	Swe.	36	26	15	41	28	2	1	0	1	0
	Swe. National	...	21	8	3	11	8	....	....	....	....	....
1982-83	Farjestad	Swe.	36	42	34	76	29	8	10	4	14	6
	Swe. National	...	11	2	2	4	8	....	....	....	....	....
1983-84a	Calgary	NHL	77	30	25	55	22	11	2	3	5	2
1984-85	Calgary	NHL	78	37	35	72	14	4	3	3	6	0
1985-86	Calgary	NHL	68	31	36	67	36	22	4	10	14	6
1986-87	Calgary	NHL	68	18	26	44	26	5	1	2	3	0
1987-88b	Calgary	NHL	80	50	56	106	47	9	8	1	9	4
1988-89	Calgary	NHL	79	27	58	85	44	22	8	9	17	4
	NHL Totals		**450**	**193**	**236**	**429**	**189**	**73**	**26**	**28**	**54**	**16**

a NHL All-Rookie Team (1984)
b NHL First All-Star Team (1988)

LOWE, KEVIN HUGH

(LOH)

Defense. Shoots left. 6'2", 195 lbs.   Born, Lachute, Que., April 15, 1959.
(Edmonton's 1st choice, 21st over-all, in 1979 Entry Draft).

			Regular Season					Playoffs				
Season	Club	Lea	GP	G	A	TP	PIM	GP	G	A	TP	PIM
1977-78	Quebec	QJHL	64	13	52	65	86	4	1	2	3	6
1978-79a	Quebec	QJHL	68	26	60	86	120	6	1	7	8	36
1979-80	Edmonton	NHL	64	2	19	21	70	3	0	1	1	0
1980-81	Edmonton	NHL	79	10	24	34	94	9	0	2	2	11
1981-82	Edmonton	NHL	80	9	31	40	63	5	0	3	3	0
1982-83	Edmonton	NHL	80	6	34	40	43	16	1	8	9	10
1983-84	Edmonton	NHL	80	4	42	46	59	19	3	7	10	16
1984-85	Edmonton	NHL	80	4	21	25	104	16	0	5	5	8
1985-86	Edmonton	NHL	74	2	16	18	90	10	1	3	4	15
1986-87	Edmonton	NHL	77	8	29	37	94	21	2	4	6	22
1987-88	Edmonton	NHL	70	9	15	24	89	19	0	2	2	26
1988-89	Edmonton	NHL	76	7	18	25	98	7	1	2	3	4
	NHL Totals		**760**	**61**	**249**	**310**	**804**	**125**	**8**	**37**	**45**	**112**

a QMJHL Second All-Star Team (1979)
Played in NHL All-Star Game (1984-86, 1988-89.)

LOWRY, DAVE

Left wing. Shoots left. 6'1", 195 lbs.   Born, Sudbury, Ont., January 14, 1965.
(Vancouver's 6th choice, 110th over-all, in 1983 Entry Draft).

			Regular Season					Playoffs				
Season	Club	Lea	GP	G	A	TP	PIM	GP	G	A	TP	PIM
1982-83	London	OHL	42	11	16	27	48	3	0	0	0	14
1983-84	London	OHL	66	29	47	76	125	8	6	6	12	41
1984-85a	London	OHL	61	60	60	120	94	8	6	5	11	10
1985-86	Vancouver	NHL	73	10	8	18	143	3	0	0	0	0
1986-87	Vancouver	NHL	70	8	10	18	176	....	....	....	....	....
1987-88	Vancouver	NHL	22	1	3	4	38	....	....	....	....	....
	Fredericton	AHL	46	18	27	45	59	14	7	3	10	72
1988-89	St. Louis	NHL	21	3	3	6	11	10	0	5	5	4
	Peoria	IHL	58	31	35	66	45	....	....	....	....	....
	NHL Totals		**186**	**22**	**24**	**46**	**368**	**13**	**0**	**5**	**5**	**4**

a OHL First All-Star Team (1985)
Traded to **St. Louis** by **Vancouver** for Ernie Vargas, September 29, 1988.

LUBINA, LADISLAV

Left wing. Shoots left. 5'11", 182 lbs.   Born, Dvur Kralove, Czech., February 11, 1967.
(Minnesota's 9th choice, 216th overall, in 1985 Entry Draft).

			Regular Season					Playoffs				
Season	Club	Lea	GP	G	A	TP	PIM	GP	G	A	TP	PIM
1986-87	Dukla Jihlava	Czech.	34	9	7	16		....				
1987-88	Dukla Jihlava	Czech.	34	12	9	21		....				
1988-89	Dukla Jihlava	Czech.	44	22	16	38		....				

LUDVIG, JAN

(LOOD-vig)

Right wing. Shoots right. 5'10", 190 lbs.   Born, Liberec, Czechoslovakia, September 17, 1961.

			Regular Season					Playoffs				
Season	Club	Lea	GP	G	A	TP	PIM	GP	G	A	TP	PIM
1980-81	CHZ Litvinov	Czech	3	0	0	0	0					
1981-82	St. Albert	AJHL	4	2	4	6	20					
	Kamloops	WHL	37	31	34	65	36	4	2	0	2	7
	Wichita	CHL	....	....	....	....	....	3	2	0	2	0
1982-83	New Jersey	NHL	51	7	10	17	30	....	....	....	....	....
	Wichita	CHL	9	3	0	3	19	....	....	....	....	....
1983-84	New Jersey	NHL	74	22	32	54	70	....	....	....	....	....
1984-85	New Jersey	NHL	74	12	19	31	53	....	....	....	....	....
1985-86	New Jersey	NHL	42	5	9	14	63	....	....	....	....	....
1986-87	New Jersey	NHL	47	7	9	16	98	....	....	....	....	....
	Maine	AHL	14	6	4	10	46	....	....	....	....	....
1987-88	Buffalo	NHL	13	1	6	7	65	....	....	....	....	....
1988-89	Buffalo	NHL	13	0	2	2	39	....	....	....	....	....
	NHL Totals		**314**	**54**	**87**	**141**	**418**	**....**	**....**	**....**	**....**	**....**

Signed as a free agent by **New Jersey**, October 28, 1982. Traded to **Buffalo** by **New Jersey** for Jim Korn, May 22, 1987.

LUDWIG, CRAIG LEE

Defense. Shoots left. 6'3", 215 lbs.   Born, Rinelander, WI, March 15, 1961.
(Montreal's 5th choice, 61st over-all, in 1980 Entry Draft).

			Regular Season					Playoffs				
Season	Club	Lea	GP	G	A	TP	PIM	GP	G	A	TP	PIM
1979-80	North Dakota	WCHA	33	1	8	9	32	....	....	....	....	....
1980-81	North Dakota	WCHA	34	4	8	12	48	....	....	....	....	....
1981-82	North Dakota	WCHA	37	4	17	21	42	....	....	....	....	....
1982-83	Montreal	NHL	80	0	25	25	59	3	0	0	0	2
1983-84	Montreal	NHL	80	7	18	25	52	15	0	3	3	23
1984-85	Montreal	NHL	72	5	14	19	90	12	0	2	2	6
1985-86	Montreal	NHL	69	2	4	6	63	20	0	1	1	48
1986-87	Montreal	NHL	75	4	12	16	105	17	2	3	5	30
1987-88	Montreal	NHL	74	4	10	14	69	11	1	1	2	6
1988-89	Montreal	NHL	74	3	13	16	73	21	0	2	2	24
	NHL Totals		**524**	**25**	**96**	**121**	**511**	**99**	**3**	**12**	**15**	**139**

LUDZIK, STEVE

Center. Shoots left. 5'11", 185 lbs.   Born, Toronto, Ont., April 3, 1962.
(Chicago's 3rd choice, 28th over-all, in 1980 Entry Draft).

			Regular Season					Playoffs				
Season	Club	Lea	GP	G	A	TP	PIM	GP	G	A	TP	PIM
1979-80	Niagara Falls	OHA	67	43	76	119	102	10	6	6	12	16
1980-81	Niagara Falls	OHA	58	50	92	142	108	12	5	9	14	40
1981-82	Chicago	NHL	8	2	1	3	2	....	....	....	....	....
	New Brunswick	AHL	73	21	41	62	142	15	3	7	10	6
1982-83	Chicago	NHL	66	6	19	25	63	13	3	5	8	20
1983-84	Chicago	NHL	80	9	20	29	73	4	0	1	1	9
1984-85	Chicago	NHL	79	11	20	31	86	15	1	1	2	16
1985-86	Chicago	NHL	49	6	5	11	21	3	0	0	0	12
1986-87	Chicago	NHL	52	5	12	17	34	4	0	0	0	0
1987-88	Chicago	NHL	73	6	15	21	40	5	0	1	1	13
1988-89	Chicago	NHL	6	1	0	1	8	....	....	....	....	....
	Saginaw	IHL	65	21	57	78	129	6	0	1	1	17
	NHL Totals		**413**	**46**	**92**	**138**	**327**	**44**	**4**	**8**	**12**	**70**

LUIK, JAAN

Defense. Shoots left. 6'1", 210 lbs.   Born, Scarborough, Ont., January 15, 1970.
(St. Louis' 4th choice, 72nd overall, in 1988 Entry Draft).

			Regular Season					Playoffs				
Season	Club	Lea	GP	G	A	TP	PIM	GP	G	A	TP	PIM
1986-87	Toronto	Midget	66	7	27	34	125	....	....	....	....	....
1987-88	Miami-Ohio	CCHA	35	2	5	7	93	....	....	....	....	....
1988-89	Miami-Ohio	CCHA	33	1	8	9	43	....	....	....	....	....

LUIK, SCOTT

Right wing. Shoots left. 6'1", 210 lbs.   Born, Scarborough, Ont., January 15, 1970.
(New Jersey's 4th choice, 65th overall, in 1988 Entry Draft).

			Regular Season					Playoffs				
Season	Club	Lea	GP	G	A	TP	PIM	GP	G	A	TP	PIM
1986-87	Toronto	Midget	65	34	37	71	102	....	....	....	....	....
1987-88	Miami-Ohio	CCHA	34	4	10	14	47	....	....	....	....	....
1988-89	Miami-Ohio	CCHA	36	13	13	26	92	....	....	....	....	....

LUMME, JYRKI

Defense. Shoots left. 6'1", 190 lbs.   Born, Tampere, Finland, July 16, 1966.
(Montreal's 3rd choice, 57th overall, in 1986 Entry Draft).

			Regular Season					Playoffs				
Season	Club	Lea	GP	G	A	TP	PIM	GP	G	A	TP	PIM
1984-85	KooVee	Fin. 3	30	6	4	10	44	....	....	....	....	....
1985-86	Ilves	Fin.	31	1	4	5	4	....	....	....	....	....
1986-87	Ilves	Fin.	43	12	12	24	52	4	0	1	2	....
1987-88	Ilves	Fin.	43	8	22	30	75	....	....	....	....	....
1988-89	Montreal	NHL	21	1	3	4	10	....	....	....	....	....
	Sherbrooke	AHL	26	4	11	15	10	6	1	3	4	4
	NHL Totals		**21**	**1**	**3**	**4**	**10**	**....**	**....**	**....**	**....**	**....**

LUNDSTROM, MATS

Left wing. Shoots right. 5'10", 185 lbs.   Born, Skelleftea, Sweden, April 23, 1966.
(Detroit's 4th choice, 91st overall, in 1984 Entry Draft).

			Regular Season					Playoffs				
Season	Club	Lea	GP	G	A	TP	PIM	GP	G	A	TP	PIM
1986-87	Skelleftea	Swe.	34	6	7	13	22	....	....	....	....	....
1987-88	Skelleftea	Swe.	39	17	15	32	54	....	....	....	....	....
1988-89	AIK	Swe.	35	17	15	32	24	....	....	....	....	....

LUONGO, CHRISTOPHER (CHRIS)

Defense. Shoots right. 6', 180 lbs. Born, Detroit, MI, March 17, 1967.
(Detroit's 5th choice, 92nd overall, in 1985 Entry Draft).

			Regular Season					Playoffs				
Season	Club	Lea	GP	G	A	TP	PIM	GP	G	A	TP	PIM
1985-86	Michigan State	CCHA	38	1	5	6	29	....	....	....	....	....
1986-87a	Michigan State	CCHA	27	4	16	20	38	....	....	....	....	....
1987-88	Michigan State	CCHA	45	3	15	18	49	....	....	....	....	....
1988-89b	Michigan State	CCHA	47	4	21	25	42	....	....	....	....	....

a Named to NCAA All-Tournament Team (1987)
b CCHA Second All-Star Team (1989)

LYONS, COREY

Right wing. Shoots left. 5'10", 185 lbs. Born, Calgary, Alta., June 13, 1970.
(Calgary's 4th choice, 63rd overall, in 1989 Entry Draft).

			Regular Season					Playoffs				
Season	Club	Lea	GP	G	A	TP	PIM	GP	G	A	TP	PIM
1987-88	Lethbridge	WHL	2	0	0	0	0	....	....	....	....	....
1988-89	Lethbridge	WHL	71	53	59	112	36	8	4	9	13	7

MacARTHUR, KENNETH

Defense. Shoots left. 6'1", 185 lbs. Born, Rossland, B.C., March 15, 1968.
(Minnesota's 5th choice, 148th overall, in 1988 Entry Draft).

			Regular Season					Playoffs				
Season	Club	Lea	GP	G	A	TP	PIM	GP	G	A	TP	PIM
1987-88	U. of Denver	WCHA	38	6	16	22	69	....	....	....	....	....
1988-89	U. of Denver	WCHA	42	11	19	30	77	....	....	....	....	....

MacDERMID, PAUL

Center. Shoots right. 6'1", 205 lbs. Born, Chesley, Ont., April 14, 1963.
(Hartford's 2nd choice, 61st over-all, in 1981 Entry Draft).

			Regular Season					Playoffs				
Season	Club	Lea	GP	G	A	TP	PIM	GP	G	A	TP	PIM
1980-81	Windsor	OHA	68	15	17	32	106	....	....	....	....	....
1981-82	**Hartford**	**NHL**	**3**	**1**	**0**	**1**	**2**	....	....	....	....	....
	Windsor	OHL	65	26	45	71	179	9	6	4	10	17
1982-83	**Hartford**	**NHL**	**7**	**0**	**0**	**0**	**2**	....	....	....	....	....
	Windsor	OHL	42	35	45	80	9	....	....	....	....	....
1983-84	**Hartford**	**NHL**	**3**	**0**	**1**	**1**	**0**	....	....	....	....	....
	Binghamton	AHL	70	31	30	61	130	....	....	....	....	....
1984-85	**Hartford**	**NHL**	**31**	**4**	**7**	**11**	**29**	....	....	....	....	....
	Binghamton	AHL	48	9	31	40	87	....	....	....	....	....
1985-86	**Hartford**	**NHL**	**74**	**13**	**10**	**23**	**160**	**10**	**2**	**1**	**3**	**20**
1986-87	**Hartford**	**NHL**	**72**	**7**	**11**	**18**	**202**	**6**	**2**	**1**	**3**	**34**
1987-88	**Hartford**	**NHL**	**80**	**20**	**15**	**35**	**139**	**6**	**0**	**5**	**5**	**14**
1988-89	**Hartford**	**NHL**	**74**	**17**	**27**	**44**	**141**	**4**	**1**	**1**	**2**	**16**
	NHL Totals		**344**	**62**	**71**	**133**	**675**	**26**	**5**	**8**	**13**	**84**

MacDONALD, BRETT

Defense. Shoots left. 6'1", 205 lbs. Born, Bothwell, Ont., January 5, 1966.
(Vancouver's 7th choice, 94th over-all, in 1984 Entry Draft).

			Regular Season					Playoffs				
Season	Club	Lea	GP	G	A	TP	PIM	GP	G	A	TP	PIM
1983-84	North Bay	OHL	70	8	18	26	83	4	0	1	1	0
1984-85	North Bay	OHL	58	6	27	33	72	8	1	1	2	11
1985-86	North Bay	OHL	15	0	6	6	42	....	....	....	....	....
	Kitchener	OHL	53	10	27	37	52	5	3	7	10	6
1986-87	Fredericton	AHL	49	0	9	9	29	....	....	....	....	....
1987-88	**Vancouver**	**NHL**	**1**	**0**	**0**	**0**	**0**	....	....	....	....	....
	Fredericton	AHL	15	1	5	6	23	....	....	....	....	....
	Flint	IHL	49	2	21	23	43	15	2	2	4	12
1988-89	New Haven	AHL	15	2	4	6	6	....	....	....	....	....
	Flint	IHL	57	3	24	27	53	....	....	....	....	....
	NHL Totals		**1**	**0**	**0**	**0**	**0**	....	....	....	....	....

MacDONALD, BRUCE

Right wing. Shoots left. 6'1", 190 lbs. Born, Utica, NY, December 16, 1967.
(Philadelphia's 9th choice, 188th overall, in 1987 Entry Draft).

			Regular Season					Playoffs				
Season	Club	Lea	GP	G	A	TP	PIM	GP	G	A	TP	PIM
1984-85	Loomis Chaffee	HS	24	23	18	41	18	....	....	....	....	....
1985-86	Loomis Chaffee	HS	28	27	42	69	20	....	....	....	....	....
1986-87	Loomis Chaffee	HS	25	30	33	63	54	....	....	....	....	....
1987-88	N. Hampshire	H.E.	12	0	1	1	8	....	....	....	....	....
1988-89	N. Hampshire	H.E.	21	1	3	4	8	....	....	....	....	....

MacDONALD, LANE

Left wing. Shoots left. 5'11", 190 lbs. Born, Mequon, WI, March 3, 1966.
(Calgary's 4th choice, 58th overall in 1985 Entry Draft).

			Regular Season					Playoffs				
Season	Club	Lea	GP	G	A	TP	PIM	GP	G	A	TP	PIM
1984-85	Harvard	ECAC	24	17	25	42	0	....	....	....	....	....
1985-86	Harvard	ECAC	30	22	24	46	45	....	....	....	....	....
1986-87ab	Harvard	ECAC	34	37	30	67	26	....	....	....	....	....
1987-88	U.S. National	....	50	23	28	51	54	....	....	....	....	....
	U.S. Olympic	....	6	6	1	7	4	....	....	....	....	....
1988-89abcde	Harvard	ECAC	32	31	29	60	42	....	....	....	....	....

a ECAC First All-Star Team (1987, 1989)
b NCAA East First All-American Team (1987, 1989)
c ECAC Player of the Year (1989)
d NCAA All-Tournament Team (1989)
e Won Hobey Baker Memorial Award (Top U.S.Collegiate Player) (1989)

Rights traded to **Hartford** by **Calgary** with Carey Wilson and Neil Sheehy for Dana Murzyn and Shane Churla, January 3, 1988.

MacDOUGALL, JACK

Right wing. Shoots right. 5'11", 185 lbs. Born, Randolph, MA, February 7, 1969.
(Pittsburgh's 9th choice, 173rd overall, in 1987 Entry Draft).

			Regular Season					Playoffs				
Season	Club	Lea	GP	G	A	TP	PIM	GP	G	A	TP	PIM
1988-89	Boston U.	H.E.	24	1	3	4	4	....	....	....	....	....

MacEACHERN, SHANE

Center. Shoots left. 5'11", 180 lbs. Born, Charlottetown, P.E.I., December 14, 1967.

			Regular Season					Playoffs				
Season	Club	Lea	GP	G	A	TP	PIM	GP	G	A	TP	PIM
1985-86	Hull	QMJHL	70	20	45	65	128	15	11	11	22	17
1986-87	Hull	QMJHL	69	43	67	110	105	8	6	7	13	8
1987-88	**St. Louis**	**NHL**	**1**	**0**	**0**	**0**	**0**	....	....	....	....	....
	Peoria	IHL	68	18	30	48	67	7	1	6	7	8
1988-89	Peoria	IHL	73	17	37	54	83	4	0	1	1	2
	NHL Totals		**1**	**0**	**0**	**0**	**0**	....	....	....	....	....

Signed as a free agent by **St. Louis**, September 22, 1986.

MacINNIS, ALLAN

Defense. Shoots right. 6'2", 195 lbs. Born, Inverness, N.S., July 11, 1963.
(Calgary's 1st choice, 15th over-all, in 1981 Entry Draft).

			Regular Season					Playoffs				
Season	Club	Lea	GP	G	A	TP	PIM	GP	G	A	TP	PIM
1980-81	Kitchener	OHA	47	11	28	39	59	18	4	12	16	20
1981-82	**Calgary**	**NHL**	**2**	**0**	**0**	**0**	**0**	....	....	....	....	....
a	Kitchener	OHL	59	25	50	75	145	15	5	10	15	44
1982-83	**Calgary**	**NHL**	**14**	**1**	**3**	**4**	**9**	....	....	....	....	....
a	Kitchener	OHL	51	38	46	84	67	8	3	8	11	9
1983-84	Colorado	CHL	19	5	14	19	22	....	....	....	....	....
	Calgary	**NHL**	**51**	**11**	**34**	**45**	**42**	**11**	**2**	**12**	**14**	**13**
1984-85	**Calgary**	**NHL**	**67**	**14**	**52**	**66**	**75**	**4**	**1**	**2**	**3**	**8**
1985-86	**Calgary**	**NHL**	**77**	**11**	**57**	**68**	**76**	**21**	**4**	**15**	**19**	**30**
1986-87b	**Calgary**	**NHL**	**79**	**20**	**56**	**76**	**97**	**4**	**1**	**0**	**1**	**0**
1987-88	**Calgary**	**NHL**	**80**	**25**	**58**	**83**	**114**	**7**	**3**	**6**	**9**	**18**
1988-89bc	**Calgary**	**NHL**	**79**	**16**	**58**	**74**	**126**	**22**	**7**	***24**	***31**	**46**
	NHL Totals		**449**	**98**	**318**	**416**	**539**	**69**	**18**	**59**	**77**	**115**

a OHL First All-Star Team (1982, 1983)
b NHL Second All-Star Team (1987, 1989)
c Won Conn Smythe Trophy (1989)

Played in NHL All-Star Game (1985, 1988)

MACIVER, NORM

Defense. Shoots left. 5'11", 180 lbs. Born, Thunder Bay, Ont., September 1, 1964.

			Regular Season					Playoffs				
Season	Club	Lea	GP	G	A	TP	PIM	GP	G	A	TP	PIM
1982-83	Minn.Duluth	WCHA	45	1	26	27	40	6	0	2	2	2
1983-84a	Minn.-Duluth	WCHA	31	13	28	41	28	8	1	10	11	8
1984-85bc	Minn.-Duluth	WCHA	47	14	47	61	63	10	3	3	6	6
1985-86bc	Minn.-Duluth	WCHA	42	11	51	62	36	4	2	3	5	2
1986-87	**NY Rangers**	**NHL**	**3**	**0**	**1**	**1**	**0**	....	....	....	....	....
	New Haven	AHL	71	6	30	36	73	7	0	0	0	9
1987-88	**NY Rangers**	**NHL**	**37**	**9**	**15**	**24**	**14**	....	....	....	....	....
	Colorado	IHL	27	6	20	26	22	....	....	....	....	....
1988-89	**NY Rangers**	**NHL**	**26**	**0**	**10**	**10**	**14**	....	....	....	....	....
	Hartford	**NHL**	**37**	**1**	**22**	**23**	**24**	**1**	**0**	**0**	**0**	**2**
	NHL Totals		**103**	**10**	**48**	**58**	**52**	....	....	....	....	....

a WCHA Second All-Star Team (1984)
b WCHA First All-Star Team (1985, 1986)
c NCAA West First All-Star Team (1985, 1986)

Signed as a free agent by **NY Rangers**, September 8, 1986. Traded to **Hartford** by **NY Rangers** with Brian Lawton and Don Maloney for Carey Wilson and Hartford's fifth-round choice in 1990 Entry Draft, December 26, 1988.

MACKEY, DAVID

Left wing. Shoots left. 6'4", 200 lbs. Born, Richmond, B.C., July 24, 1966.
(Chicago's 12th choice, 224th overall, in 1984 Entry Draft).

			Regular Season					Playoffs				
Season	Club	Lea	GP	G	A	TP	PIM	GP	G	A	TP	PIM
1982-83	Victoria	WHL	69	16	16	32	53	12	11	1	2	4
1983-84	Victoria	WHL	69	15	15	30	97	....	....	....	....	....
1984-85	Victoria	WHL	16	5	6	11	45	....	....	....	....	....
	Portland	WHL	56	28	32	60	122	6	2	1	3	13
1985-86	Medicine Hat	WHL	69	28	36	64	180	25	6	3	9	72
1986-87	Saginaw	IHL	81	26	49	75	173	10	5	6	11	22
1987-88	**Chicago**	**NHL**	**23**	**1**	**3**	**4**	**71**	....	....	....	....	....
	Saginaw	IHL	62	29	22	51	211	10	3	7	10	44
1988-89	**Chicago**	**NHL**	**23**	**1**	**2**	**3**	**78**	....	....	....	....	....
	Saginaw	IHL	57	22	23	45	223	....	....	....	....	....
	NHL Totals		**46**	**2**	**5**	**7**	**149**	....	....	....	....	....

MacLEAN, JOHN

Right wing. Shoots right. 6', 200 lbs. Born, Oshawa, Ont., November 20, 1964.
(New Jersey's 1st choice, 6th over-all, in 1983 Entry Draft).

			Regular Season					Playoffs				
Season	Club	Lea	GP	G	A	TP	PIM	GP	G	A	TP	PIM
1981-82	Oshawa	OHL	67	17	22	39	197	12	3	6	9	63
1982-83	Oshawa	OHL	66	47	51	98	138	17	*18	20	*38	35
1983-84	**New Jersey**	**NHL**	**23**	**1**	**0**	**1**	**10**	....	....	....	....	....
	Oshawa	OHL	30	23	36	59	58	7	2	5	7	18
1984-85	**New Jersey**	**NHL**	**61**	**13**	**20**	**33**	**44**	....	....	....	....	....
1985-86	**New Jersey**	**NHL**	**74**	**21**	**36**	**57**	**112**	....	....	....	....	....
1986-87	**New Jersey**	**NHL**	**80**	**31**	**36**	**67**	**120**	....	....	....	....	....
1987-88	**New Jersey**	**NHL**	**76**	**23**	**16**	**39**	**147**	**20**	**7**	**11**	**18**	**60**
1988-89	**New Jersey**	**NHL**	**74**	**42**	**45**	**87**	**127**	....	....	....	....	....
	NHL Totals		**388**	**131**	**153**	**284**	**560**	**20**	**7**	**11**	**18**	**60**

Played in NHL All-Star Game (1989)

MacLEAN, PAUL (muh KLAYN)

Right wing. Shoots right. 6', 190 lbs. Born, Grostenquin, France, March 9, 1958.
(St. Louis' 6th choice, 109th over-all, in 1978 Amateur Draft).

			Regular Season					Playoffs				
Season	Club	Lea	GP	G	A	TP	PIM	GP	G	A	TP	PIM
1977-78	Hull	QJHL	66	38	33	71	125	....	....	....	....	....
1978-79	Dalhousie	AUAA	....	....	....	....	....	....	....	....	....	....
1979-80	Cdn. National	...	50	21	11	32	90	....	....	....	....	....
	Cdn. Olympic	...	6	2	3	5	6	....	....	....	....	....
1980-81	**St. Louis**	**NHL**	**1**	**0**	**0**	**0**	**0**	....	....	....	....	....
	Salt Lake	CHL	80	36	42	78	160	17	11	5	16	47
1981-82	**Winnipeg**	**NHL**	**74**	**36**	**25**	**61**	**106**	**4**	**3**	**2**	**5**	**20**
1982-83	**Winnipeg**	**NHL**	**80**	**32**	**44**	**76**	**121**	**3**	**1**	**2**	**3**	**6**
1983-84	**Winnipeg**	**NHL**	**76**	**40**	**31**	**71**	**155**	**3**	**1**	**0**	**1**	**0**
1984-85	**Winnipeg**	**NHL**	**79**	**41**	**60**	**101**	**119**	**8**	**3**	**4**	**7**	**4**
1985-86	**Winnipeg**	**NHL**	**69**	**27**	**29**	**56**	**74**	**2**	**1**	**0**	**1**	**7**
1986-87	**Winnipeg**	**NHL**	**72**	**32**	**42**	**74**	**75**	**10**	**5**	**2**	**7**	**16**
1987-88	**Winnipeg**	**NHL**	**77**	**40**	**39**	**79**	**76**	**5**	**2**	**0**	**2**	**23**
1988-89	**Detroit**	**NHL**	**76**	**36**	**35**	**71**	**118**	**5**	**1**	**1**	**2**	**8**
	NHL Totals		**604**	**284**	**305**	**589**	**844**	**40**	**17**	**11**	**28**	**84**

Played in NHL All-Star Game (1985)

Traded to **Winnipeg** by **St. Louis** with Bryan Maxwell and Ed Staniowski for Scott Campbell and John Markell, July 3, 1981. Traded to **Detroit** by **Winnipeg** for Brent Ashton, June 13, 1988. Traded to **St. Louis** by **Detroit** with Adam Oates for Bernie Federko and Tony McKegney, June 15, 1989.

MacLEAN, TERRY

Center. Shoots left. 6'1", 180 lbs. Born, Montreal, Que., January 14, 1968.
(St. Louis' 11th choice, 220th overall, in 1986 Entry Draft).

			Regular Season					Playoffs				
Season	Club	Lea	GP	G	A	TP	PIM	GP	G	A	TP	PIM
1985-86	Longueuil	QMJHL	70	36	45	81	18	....	....	....	....	....
1986-87	Trois-Rivieres	QMJHL	69	41	76	117	20	....	....	....	....	....
1987-88	Trois-Rivieres	QMJHL	69	52	91	143	44	....	....	....	....	....
	Peoria	IHL	5	0	1	1	0	....	....	....	....	....
1988-89	Peoria	IHL	73	18	30	48	46	3	1	2	3	2

MacLELLAN, BRIAN

Left wing. Shoots left. 6'3", 215 lbs. Born, Guelph, Ont., October 27, 1958.

			Regular Season					Playoffs				
Season	Club	Lea	GP	G	A	TP	PIM	GP	G	A	TP	PIM
1980-81	Bowling Green	CCHA	37	11	14	25	96	....	....	....	....	....
1981-82	Bowling Green	CCHA	41	11	21	33	109	....	....	....	....	....
1982-83	**Los Angeles**	**NHL**	**8**	**0**	**3**	**3**	**7**	....	....	....	....	....
	New Haven	AHL	71	11	15	26	40	12	5	3	8	4
1983-84	New Haven	AHL	2	0	2	2	0	....	....	....	....	....
	Los Angeles	**NHL**	**72**	**25**	**29**	**54**	**45**	....	....	....	....	....
1984-85	**Los Angeles**	**NHL**	**80**	**31**	**54**	**85**	**53**	**3**	**0**	**1**	**1**	**0**
1985-86	**Los Angeles**	**NHL**	**27**	**5**	**8**	**13**	**19**	....	....	....	....	....
	NY Rangers	**NHL**	**51**	**11**	**21**	**32**	**47**	**16**	**2**	**4**	**6**	**15**
1986-87	**Minnesota**	**NHL**	**76**	**32**	**31**	**63**	**69**	....	....	....	....	....
1987-88	**Minnesota**	**NHL**	**75**	**16**	**32**	**48**	**74**	....	....	....	....	....
1988-89	**Minnesota**	**NHL**	**60**	**16**	**23**	**39**	**104**	....	....	....	....	....
	Calgary	**NHL**	**12**	**2**	**3**	**5**	**14**	**21**	**3**	**2**	**5**	**19**
	NHL Totals		**461**	**138**	**204**	**342**	**432**	**40**	**5**	**7**	**12**	**34**

Signed as a free agent by **Los Angeles,** May 12, 1982. Traded to **NY Rangers** by **Los Angeles** with Los Angeles' fourth-round draft choice in 1987 (Michael Sullivan) for Roland Melanson and Grant Ledyard, December 9, 1985. Traded to **Minnesota** by **NY Rangers** for Minnesota's third-round choice (Simon Gagne) in 1987 Entry Draft, September 8, 1986. Traded to **Calgary** by **Minnesota** with Minnesota's fourth-round choice (Robert Reichel) in 1989 Entry Draft for Shane Churla and Perry Berezan, March 4, 1989.

MACOUN, JAMIE (muh KOW uhn)

Defense. Shoots left. 6'2", 197 lbs. Born, Newmarket, Ont., August 7, 1961.

			Regular Season					Playoffs				
Season	Club	Lea	GP	G	A	TP	PIM	GP	G	A	TP	PIM
1980-81	Ohio State	CCHA	38	9	20	29	83	....	....	....	....	....
1981-82	Ohio State	CCHA	25	2	18	20	89	....	....	....	....	....
1982-83	Ohio State	CCHA	19	6	21	27	54	....	....	....	....	....
	Calgary	**NHL**	**22**	**1**	**4**	**5**	**25**	**9**	**0**	**2**	**2**	**8**
1983-84a	**Calgary**	**NHL**	**72**	**9**	**23**	**32**	**97**	**11**	**1**	**0**	**1**	**0**
1984-85	**Calgary**	**NHL**	**70**	**9**	**30**	**39**	**67**	**4**	**1**	**0**	**1**	**4**
1985-86	**Calgary**	**NHL**	**77**	**11**	**21**	**32**	**81**	**22**	**1**	**6**	**7**	**23**
1986-87	**Calgary**	**NHL**	**79**	**7**	**33**	**40**	**111**	**3**	**0**	**1**	**1**	**8**
1987-88	**Calgary**	**NHL**	DID NOT PLAY — INJURED									
1988-89	**Calgary**	**NHL**	**72**	**8**	**19**	**27**	**76**	**22**	**3**	**6**	**9**	**30**
	NHL Totals		**392**	**45**	**130**	**175**	**457**	**71**	**6**	**15**	**21**	**73**

a NHL All-Rookie Team (1984).

Signed as free agent by **Calgary**, January 31, 1983.

MacPHERSON, DUNCAN A.

Defense. Shoots left. 6'1", 195 lbs. Born, Saskatoon, Sask., February 3, 1966.
(New York Islanders' 1st choice, 20th over-all, in 1984 Entry Draft).

			Regular Season					Playoffs				
Season	Club	Lea	GP	G	A	TP	PIM	GP	G	A	TP	PIM
1982-83	N. Battleford	SJHL	59	6	11	17	215	....	....	....	....	....
1983-84	Saskatoon	WHL	45	0	14	14	74	....	....	....	....	....
1984-85	Saskatoon	WHL	69	9	26	35	116	3	0	0	0	4
1985-86	Saskatoon	WHL	70	10	54	64	147	13	3	8	11	38
1986-87	Springfield	AHL	26	1	0	1	86	....	....	....	....	....
1987-88	Springfield	AHL	74	5	14	19	213	....	....	....	....	....
1988-89	Springfield	AHL	24	1	5	6	69	....	....	....	....	....
	Indianapolis	IHL	33	1	4	5	23	....	....	....	....	....

MacTAVISH, CRAIG

Center. Shoots left. 6'1", 195 lbs. Born, London, Ont., August 15, 1958.
(Boston's 9th choice, 153rd over-all, in 1984 Entry Draft).

			Regular Season					Playoffs				
Season	Club	Lea	GP	G	A	TP	PIM	GP	G	A	TP	PIM
1979-80	Binghamton	AHL	34	17	15	32	29	....	....	....	....	....
	Boston	**NHL**	**46**	**11**	**17**	**28**	**8**	**10**	**2**	**3**	**5**	**7**
1980-81	**Boston**	**NHL**	**24**	**3**	**5**	**8**	**13**	....	....	....	....	....
	Springfield	AHL	53	19	24	43	81	7	5	4	9	8
1981-82	**Boston**	**NHL**	**2**	**0**	**1**	**1**	**0**	....	....	....	....	....
	Erie	AHL	72	23	32	55	37	....	....	....	....	....
1982-83	**Boston**	**NHL**	**75**	**10**	**20**	**30**	**18**	**17**	**3**	**1**	**4**	**18**
1983-84	**Boston**	**NHL**	**70**	**20**	**23**	**43**	**35**	**1**	**0**	**0**	**0**	**0**
1984-85			DID NOT PLAY									
1985-86	**Edmonton**	**NHL**	**74**	**23**	**24**	**47**	**70**	**10**	**4**	**4**	**8**	**11**
1986-87	**Edmonton**	**NHL**	**79**	**20**	**19**	**39**	**55**	**21**	**1**	**9**	**10**	**16**
1987-88	**Edmonton**	**NHL**	**80**	**15**	**17**	**32**	**47**	**19**	**0**	**1**	**1**	**31**
1988-89	**Edmonton**	**NHL**	**80**	**21**	**31**	**52**	**55**	**7**	**0**	**1**	**1**	**8**
	NHL Totals		**530**	**123**	**157**	**280**	**301**	**85**	**10**	**19**	**29**	**91**

Signed as a free agent by **Edmonton,** February 1, 1985.

MacVICAR, ANDREW

Left wing. Shoots left. 6'1", 195 lbs. Born, Dartmouth, N. S., March 12, 1969.
(Buffalo's 3rd choice, 53rd overall, in 1987 Entry Draft).

			Regular Season					Playoffs				
Season	Club	Lea	GP	G	A	TP	PIM	GP	G	A	TP	PIM
1986-87	Peterborough	OHL	64	6	13	19	33	11	2	1	3	7
1987-88	Peterborough	OHL	62	30	51	81	45	12	2	10	12	8
1988-89	Peterborough	OHL	66	25	29	54	56	17	5	6	11	30

MADILL, JEFF

Right wing. Shoots left. 5'11", 195 lbs. Born, Oshawa, Ont., June 21, 1965.
(New Jersey's 2nd choice, 7th overall, in 1987 Supplemental Draft).

			Regular Season					Playoffs				
Season	Club	Lea	GP	G	A	TP	PIM	GP	G	A	TP	PIM
1984-85	Ohio State	CCHA	12	5	6	11	18	....	....	....	....	....
1985-86	Ohio State	CCHA	41	32	25	57	65	....	....	....	....	....
1986-87	Ohio State	CCHA	43	38	32	70	139	....	....	....	....	....
1987-88	Utica	AHL	58	18	15	33	127	....	....	....	....	....
1988-89	Utica	AHL	69	23	25	48	225	4	1	0	1	35

MAGUIRE, KEVIN

Right Wing. Shoots right. 6'2", 200 lbs. Born, Toronto, Ont., January 5, 1963.

			Regular Season					Playoffs				
Season	Club	Lea	GP	G	A	TP	PIM	GP	G	A	TP	PIM
1983-84	Orilla	OPJHL	35	42	77	119	NA	....	....	....	....	....
1984-85	St. Catharines	AHL	76	10	15	25	112	....	....	....	....	....
1985-86	St. Catharines	AHL	61	6	9	15	161	1	0	0	0	0
1986-87	**Toronto**	**NHL**	**17**	**0**	**0**	**0**	**74**	**1**	**0**	**0**	**0**	**0**
	Newmarket	AHL	51	4	2	6	131	....	....	....	....	....
1987-88	**Buffalo**	**NHL**	**46**	**4**	**6**	**10**	**162**	**5**	**0**	**0**	**0**	**50**
1988-89	**Buffalo**	**NHL**	**60**	**8**	**10**	**18**	**241**	**5**	**0**	**0**	**0**	**36**
	NHL Totals		**123**	**12**	**16**	**28**	**477**	**11**	**0**	**0**	**0**	**86**

Signed as a free agent by **Toronto,** October 10, 1984. Claimed by **Buffalo** in NHL Waiver Draft, October, 5, 1987.

MAHONEY, SCOTT

Right wing. Shoots right. 5'10", 190 lbs. Born, Peterborough, Ont., April 19, 1969.
(Calgary's 4th choice, 61st overall, in 1987 Entry Draft).

			Regular Season					Playoffs				
Season	Club	Lea	GP	G	A	TP	PIM	GP	G	A	TP	PIM
1985-86	Peterborough	OHL	31	18	39	57	65	....	....	....	....	....
1986-87	Oshawa	OHL	54	13	9	22	161	22	4	1	5	117
1987-88	Oshawa	OHL	60	10	21	31	272	7	2	4	6	27
1988-89	Oshawa	OHL	56	14	22	36	207	6	1	4	5	18

MAILHOT, JACQUES

Left wing. Shoots left. 6'2", 210 lbs. Born, Shawinigan, Que., December 5, 1961.

			Regular Season					Playoffs				
Season	Club	Lea	GP	G	A	TP	PIM	GP	G	A	TP	PIM
1987-88	Baltimore	AHL	15	2	0	2	167	....	....	....	....	....
	Fredericton	AHL	28	2	6	8	137	8	0	0	0	18
1988-89	**Quebec**	**NHL**	**5**	**0**	**0**	**0**	**33**	....	....	....	....	....
	Halifax	AHL	35	4	1	5	259	1	0	0	0	5
	NHL Totals		**5**	**0**	**0**	**0**	**33**	....	....	....	....	....

Signed as a free agent by **Quebec**, August 15, 1988.

MAJOR, BRUCE

Center. Shoots left. 6'3", 180 lbs. Born, Vernon, B.C., January 3, 1967.
(Quebec's 6th choice, 99th overall, in 1985 Entry Draft).

			Regular Season					Playoffs				
Season	Club	Lea	GP	G	A	TP	PIM	GP	G	A	TP	PIM
1985-86	U. of Maine	H.E.	38	14	14	28	39	....	....	....	....	....
1986-87	U. of Maine	H.E.	37	14	10	24	12	....	....	....	....	....
1987-88	U. of Maine	H.E.	26	0	5	5	14	....	....	....	....	....
1988-89	U. of Maine	H.E.	42	13	11	24	22	....	....	....	....	....

MAJOR, MARK

Left wing. Shoots left. 6'4", 205 lbs. Born, Toronto, Ont., March 20, 1970.
(Pittsburgh's 2nd choice, 25th overall, in 1988 Entry Draft).

			Regular Season					Playoffs				
Season	Club	Lea	GP	G	A	TP	PIM	GP	G	A	TP	PIM
1986-87	Don Mills	Midget	36	12	14	26	81	....	....	....	....	....
1987-88	North Bay	OHL	57	16	17	33	272	4	0	2	2	8
1988-89	North Bay	OHL	11	3	2	5	58	....	....	....	....	....
	Kingston	OHL	53	22	29	51	193	....	....	....	....	....

MAKAROV, SERGEI

Right wing. Shoots left. 5'8", 175 lbs. Born, Chelyabinsk, Soviet Union, June 19, 1958.
(Calgary's 14th choice, 231st overall, in 1983 Entry Draft).

			Regular Season					Playoffs				
Season	Club	Lea	GP	G	A	TP	PIM	GP	G	A	TP	PIM
1976-77	Chelyabinsk	USSR	11	1	0	1	4	....	....	....	....	....
1977-78	Chelyabinsk	USSR	36	18	13	31	10	....	....	....	....	....
1978-79a	CSKA	USSR	44	18	21	39	12	....	....	....	....	....
1979-80abc	CSKA	USSR	44	29	39	68	16	....	....	....	....	....
1980-81ab	CSKA	USSR	49	42	37	79	22	....	....	....	....	....
1981-82ab	CSKA	USSR	46	32	43	75	18	....	....	....	....	....
1982-83a	CSKA	USSR	30	25	17	42	6	....	....	....	....	....
1983-84ab	CSKA	USSR	44	36	37	73	28	....	....	....	....	....
1984-85abc	CSKA	USSR	40	26	39	65	28	....	....	....	....	....
1985-86ab	CSKA	USSR	40	30	32	62	28	....	....	....	....	....
1986-87abc	CSKA	USSR	40	21	32	53	26	....	....	....	....	....
1987-88ab	CSKA	USSR	51	23	45	68	50	....	....	....	....	....
1988-89	CSKA	USSR	44	21	33	54	42	....	....	....	....	....

a Soviet National League All-Star (1979-88)
b Izvestia trophy-leading scorer (1980-82, 1984-88)
c Soviet Player of the Year (1980, 1985, 1987)

MAKELA, MIKKO (MACH-uh-luh)

Right wing. Shoots left. 6'2", 193 lbs. Born, Tampere, Finland, February 28, 1965.
(NY Islanders' 5th choice, 66th over-all, in 1983 Entry Draft).

			Regular Season					Playoffs				
Season	Club	Lea	GP	G	A	TP	PIM	GP	G	A	TP	PIM
1983-84	Ilves	Fin.	35	17	11	28	26	2	0	1	1	0
1984-85a	Ilves	Fin.	36	34	25	59	24	9	4	7	11	10
1985-86	**NY Islanders**	**NHL**	**58**	**16**	**20**	**36**	**28**	....	....	....	....	....
	Springfield	AHL	2	1	1	2	0	....	....	....	....	....
1986-87	**NY Islanders**	**NHL**	**80**	**24**	**33**	**57**	**24**	**11**	**2**	**4**	**6**	**8**
1987-88	**NY Islanders**	**NHL**	**73**	**36**	**40**	**76**	**22**	**6**	**1**	**4**	**5**	**6**
1988-89	**NY Islanders**	**NHL**	**76**	**17**	**28**	**45**	**22**	....	....	....	....	....
	NHL Totals		**287**	**93**	**121**	**214**	**96**	**17**	**3**	**8**	**11**	**14**

a Finnish League First All-Star Team (1985)

MALEY, DAVID

Center. Shoots left. 6'2", 205 lbs. Born, Beaver Dam, WI, April 24, 1963.
(Montreal's 4th choice, 33rd over-all, in 1982 Entry Draft).

			Regular Season					Playoffs				
Season	Club	Lea	GP	G	A	TP	PIM	GP	G	A	TP	PIM
1981-82	Edina	HS	26	22	28	50	26	....	....	....	....	....
1982-83	U. Wisconsin	WCHA	25	4	12	16	4	....	....	....	....	....
1983-84	U. Wisconsin	WCHA	38	10	28	38	56	....	....	....	....	....
1984-85	U. Wisconsin	WCHA	38	19	9	28	86	....	....	....	....	....
1985-86	U. Wisconsin	WCHA	42	20	40	60	135	....	....	....	....	....
	Montreal	**NHL**	**3**	**0**	**0**	**0**	**0**	**7**	**1**	**3**	**4**	**2**
1986-87	**Montreal**	**NHL**	**48**	**6**	**12**	**18**	**55**	....	....	....	....	....
	Sherbrooke	AHL	11	1	5	6	25	12	7	7	14	10
1987-88	**New Jersey**	**NHL**	**44**	**4**	**2**	**6**	**65**	**20**	**3**	**1**	**4**	**80**
	Utica	AHL	9	5	3	8	40	....	....	....	....	....
1988-89	**New Jersey**	**NHL**	**68**	**5**	**6**	**11**	**249**	....	....	....	....	....
	NHL Totals		**163**	**15**	**20**	**35**	**369**	**27**	**4**	**4**	**8**	**82**

Traded to **New Jersey** by **Montreal** for New Jersey's third-round choice (Mathieu Schneider) in 1987 Entry Draft, June 13, 1987.

MALLETTE, TROY

Center. Shoots left. 6'2", 190 lbs. Born, Sudbury, Ont., February 25, 1970.
(New York Rangers' 1st choice, 22nd overall, in 1988 Entry Draft).

			Regular Season					Playoffs				
Season	Club	Lea	GP	G	A	TP	PIM	GP	G	A	TP	PIM
1986-87	S.S. Marie	OHL	65	20	25	45	157	4	0	2	2	12
1987-88	S.S. Marie	OHL	62	18	30	48	186	6	1	3	4	12
1988-89	S.S. Marie	OHL	64	39	37	76	172	0	0	0	0	0

MALLGRAVE, MATTHEW

Right wing. Shoots right. 5'11", 175 lbs. Born, Washington, D.C., May 3, 1970.
(Toronto's 6th choice, 132nd overall, in 1988 Entry Draft).

			Regular Season					Playoffs				
Season	Club	Lea	GP	G	A	TP	PIM	GP	G	A	TP	PIM
1987-88	St. Paul's	HS	....	21	22	43	....	....	....	....	....	....
1988-89	St. Paul's	HS	....	24	14	38	....	....	....	....	....	....

MALONEY, DONALD MICHAEL (DON) (ma-LOAN-ee)

Left wing. Shoots left. 6'1", 190 lbs. Born, Lindsay, Ont., September 5, 1958.
(NY Rangers' 1st choice, 26th over-all, in 1978 Amateur Draft).

			Regular Season					Playoffs				
Season	Club	Lea	GP	G	A	TP	PIM	GP	G	A	TP	PIM
1976-77	Kitchener	OHA	38	22	34	56	126	....	....	....	....	....
1977-78	Kitchener	OHA	62	30	74	104	143	9	4	9	13	40
1978-79	New Haven	AHL	38	18	26	44	62	....	....	....	....	....
	NY Rangers	**NHL**	**28**	**9**	**17**	**26**	**39**	**18**	**7**	***13**	**20**	**19**
1979-80	**NY Rangers**	**NHL**	**79**	**25**	**48**	**73**	**97**	**9**	**0**	**4**	**4**	**10**
1980-81	**NY Rangers**	**NHL**	**61**	**29**	**23**	**52**	**99**	**13**	**1**	**6**	**7**	**13**
1981-82	**NY Rangers**	**NHL**	**54**	**22**	**36**	**58**	**73**	**10**	**5**	**5**	**10**	**10**
1982-83	**NY Rangers**	**NHL**	**78**	**29**	**40**	**69**	**88**	**5**	**0**	**1**	**1**	**0**
1983-84	**NY Rangers**	**NHL**	**79**	**24**	**42**	**66**	**62**	**5**	**1**	**4**	**5**	**0**
1984-85	**NY Rangers**	**NHL**	**37**	**11**	**16**	**27**	**32**	**3**	**4**	**0**	**4**	**2**
1985-86	**NY Rangers**	**NHL**	**68**	**11**	**17**	**28**	**56**	**16**	**2**	**1**	**3**	**31**
1986-87	**NY Rangers**	**NHL**	**72**	**19**	**38**	**57**	**117**	**6**	**2**	**1**	**3**	**6**
1987-88	**NY Rangers**	**NHL**	**66**	**12**	**21**	**33**	**60**	....	....	....	....	....
1988-89	**NY Rangers**	**NHL**	**31**	**4**	**9**	**13**	**16**	....	....	....	....	....
	Hartford	**NHL**	**21**	**3**	**11**	**14**	**23**	**4**	**0**	**0**	**0**	**8**
	NHL Totals		**674**	**198**	**318**	**516**	**762**	**89**	**22**	**35**	**57**	**99**

Played in NHL All-Star Game (1983, 1984)

Traded to **Hartford** by **NY Rangers** with Brian Lawton and Norm MacIver for Carey Wilson and Hartford's fifth-round choice in 1990 Entry Draft, December 26, 1988.

MALTAIS, STEVE

Left wing. Shoots left. 6'2", 195 lbs. Born, Arvida, Que., January 25, 1969.
(Washington's 2nd choice, 57th overall, in 1987 Entry Draft).

			Regular Season					Playoffs				
Season	Club	Lea	GP	G	A	TP	PIM	GP	G	A	TP	PIM
1986-87	Cornwall	OHL	65	32	12	44	29	5	0	0	0	2
1987-88	Cornwall	OHL	59	39	46	85	30	11	9	6	15	33
1988-89	Cornwall	OHL	58	53	70	123	67	18	14	16	30	16
	Fort Wayne	IHL	....	....	....	....	....	4	2	1	3	0

MANDERVILLE, KENT

Left wing. Shoots left. 6'3", 200 lbs. Born, Edmonton, Alta., April 12, 1971.
(Calgary's 1st choice, 24th overall, in 1989 Entry Draft).

			Regular Season					Playoffs				
Season	Club	Lea	GP	G	A	TP	PIM	GP	G	A	TP	PIM
1987-88	Notre Dame	Midget	32	22	18	40	42	....	....	....	....	....
1988-89	Notre Dame	SJHL	58	39	36	75	165	....	....	....	....	....

MANN, JAMES EDWARD (JIMMY)

Right wing. Shoots right. 6', 205 lbs. Born, Montreal, Que., April 17, 1959.
(Winnipeg's 1st choice, 19th over-all, in 1979 Entry Draft).

			Regular Season					Playoffs				
Season	Club	Lea	GP	G	A	TP	PIM	GP	G	A	TP	PIM
1977-78	Sherbrooke	QJHL	67	27	54	81	277	7	3	9	12	14
1978-79	Sherbrooke	QJHL	65	35	47	82	260	12	14	12	26	83
1979-80	**Winnipeg**	**NHL**	**72**	**3**	**5**	**8**	***287**	....	....	....	....	....
1980-81	**Winnipeg**	**NHL**	**37**	**3**	**3**	**6**	**105**	....	....	....	....	....
	Tulsa	CHL	26	4	7	11	175	5	0	0	0	21
1981-82	**Winnipeg**	**NHL**	**37**	**3**	**2**	**5**	**79**	**3**	**0**	**0**	**0**	**7**
1982-83	**Winnipeg**	**NHL**	**40**	**0**	**1**	**1**	**73**	**1**	**0**	**0**	**0**	**0**
1983-84	**Winnipeg**	**NHL**	**16**	**0**	**1**	**1**	**54**	....	....	....	....	....
	Sherbrooke	AHL	20	6	3	9	94	....	....	....	....	....
	Quebec	**NHL**	**22**	**1**	**1**	**2**	**42**	**3**	**0**	**0**	**0**	**22**
1984-85	**Quebec**	**NHL**	**25**	**0**	**4**	**4**	**54**	**13**	**0**	**0**	**0**	**41**
	Fredericton	AHL	13	4	4	8	97	....	....	....	....	....
1985-86	**Quebec**	**NHL**	**35**	**0**	**3**	**3**	**148**	**2**	**0**	**0**	**0**	**19**
1986-87			DID NOT PLAY									
1987-88	**Pittsburgh**	**NHL**	**9**	**0**	**0**	**0**	**53**	....	....	....	....	....
	Muskegon	IHL	10	0	2	2	61	....	....	....	....	....
1988-89	Indianapolis	IHL	38	5	10	15	275	....	....	....	....	....
	NHL Totals		**293**	**10**	**20**	**30**	**895**	**22**	**0**	**0**	**0**	**89**

Traded to **Quebec** by **Winnipeg** for Quebec's fifth round choice (Brent Severyn) in 1984 Entry Draft, February 6, 1984. Signed as a free agent by **Pittsburgh**, June 16, 1987.

MANN, RUSS

Defense. Shoots right. 6'2", 185 lbs. Born, Methuen, MA, July 8, 1967.
(Los Angeles' 10th choice, 212th overall, in 1986 Entry Draft).

			Regular Season					Playoffs				
Season	Club	Lea	GP	G	A	TP	PIM	GP	G	A	TP	PIM
1985-86	St. Lawrence	ECAC	31	3	4	7	44	....	....	....	....	....
1986-87	St. Lawrence	ECAC	34	2	14	16	30	....	....	....	....	....
1987-88	St. Lawrence	ECAC	34	4	9	13	46	....	....	....	....	....
1988-89	St. Lawrence	ECAC	35	7	12	19	44	....	....	....	....	....

MANSON, DAVE

Defense. Shoots left. 6'2", 190 lbs. Born, Prince Albert, Sask., January 27, 1967.
(Chicago's 1st choice, 11th over-all, in 1985 Entry Draft).

			Regular Season					Playoffs				
Season	Club	Lea	GP	G	A	TP	PIM	GP	G	A	TP	PIM
1983-84	Prince Albert	WHL	70	2	7	9	233	5	0	0	0	4
1984-85	Prince Albert	WHL	72	8	30	38	247	13	1	0	1	34
1985-86	Prince Albert	WHL	70	14	34	48	177	20	1	8	9	63
1986-87	**Chicago**	**NHL**	**63**	**1**	**8**	**9**	**146**	**3**	**0**	**0**	**0**	**10**
1987-88	**Chicago**	**NHL**	**54**	**1**	**6**	**7**	**185**	**5**	**0**	**0**	**0**	**27**
	Saginaw	IHL	6	0	3	3	37	....	....	....	....	....
1988-89	**Chicago**	**NHL**	**79**	**18**	**36**	**54**	**352**	**16**	**0**	**8**	**8**	**84**
	NHL Totals		**196**	**20**	**50**	**70**	**683**	**24**	**0**	**8**	**8**	**121**

Played in NHL All-Star Game (1989)

MANTHA, MAURICE WILLIAM (MOE) (MAN-tha)

Defense. Shoots right. 6'2", 210 lbs. Born, Lakewood, OH, January 21, 1961.
(Winnipeg's 2nd choice, 23rd over-all, in 1980 Entry Draft).

			Regular Season					Playoffs				
Season	Club	Lea	GP	G	A	TP	PIM	GP	G	A	TP	PIM
1978-79	Toronto	OHA	68	10	38	48	57	4	0	2	2	11
1979-80	Toronto	OHA	58	8	38	46	86	....	....	....	....	....
1980-81	**Winnipeg**	**NHL**	**58**	**2**	**23**	**25**	**35**	....	....	....	....	....
1981-82	Tulsa	CHL	33	8	15	23	56	....	....	....	....	....
	Winnipeg	**NHL**	**25**	**0**	**12**	**12**	**28**	**4**	**1**	**3**	**4**	**16**
1982-83	Sherbrooke	AHL	13	1	4	5	13	....	....	....	....	....
	Winnipeg	**NHL**	**21**	**2**	**7**	**9**	**6**	**2**	**2**	**2**	**4**	**0**
1983-84	Sherbrooke	AHL	7	1	1	2	10	....	....	....	....	....
	Winnipeg	**NHL**	**72**	**16**	**38**	**54**	**67**	**3**	**1**	**0**	**1**	**0**
1984-85	**Pittsburgh**	**NHL**	**71**	**11**	**40**	**51**	**54**	....	....	....	....	....
1985-86	**Pittsburgh**	**NHL**	**78**	**15**	**52**	**67**	**102**	....	....	....	....	....
1986-87	**Pittsburgh**	**NHL**	**62**	**9**	**31**	**40**	**44**	....	....	....	....	....
1987-88	**Pittsburgh**	**NHL**	**21**	**2**	**8**	**10**	**23**	....	....	....	....	....
	Edmonton	**NHL**	**25**	**0**	**6**	**6**	**26**	....	....	....	....	....
	Minnesota	**NHL**	**30**	**9**	**13**	**22**	**4**	....	....	....	....	....
1988-89	**Minnesota**	**NHL**	**16**	**1**	**6**	**7**	**10**	....	....	....	....	....
	Philadelphia	**NHL**	**30**	**3**	**8**	**11**	**33**	**1**	**0**	**0**	**0**	**0**
	NHL Totals		**509**	**70**	**244**	**314**	**432**	**10**	**4**	**5**	**9**	**16**

Traded to **Pittsburgh** by **Winnipeg**, May 1, 1984 to complete deal of March 6, 1984 when Pittsburgh traded Randy Carlyle to Winnipeg. Traded to **Edmonton** by **Pittsburgh** with Craig Simpson, Dave Hannan, and Chris Joseph for Paul Coffey, Dave Hunter, and Wayne Van Dorp, November 24, 1987. Traded to **Minnesota** by **Edmonton** for Keith Acton, January 22, 1988. Traded to **Philadelphia** by **Minnesota** for Toronto's fifth-round choice (Pat MacLeod) in 1989 Entry Draft, December 8, 1988.

MARCHMENT, BRYAN

Defense. Shoots left. 6'1", 195 lbs.   Born, West Hill-Scarborough, Ont., May 1, 1969.
(Winnipeg's 1st choice, 16th overall, in 1987 Entry Draft).

			Regular Season					Playoffs				
Season	Club	Lea	GP	G	A	TP	PIM	GP	G	A	TP	PIM
1985-86	Belleville	OHL	57	5	15	20	225	21	0	7	7	83
1986-87	Belleville	OHL	52	6	38	44	238	6	0	4	4	17
1987-88	Belleville	OHL	56	7	51	58	200	6	1	3	4	19
1988-89a	Belleville	OHL	43	14	36	50	118	5	0	1	1	12
	Winnipeg	**NHL**	2	0	0	0	2	....	....	....	....	....
	NHL Totals		2	0	0	0	2	....	....	....	....	....

a OHL Second All-Star Team (1989)

MARCIANO, LANCE

Defense. Shoots right. 6'2", 200 lbs.   Born, Mt. Vernon, NY, December 12, 1969.
(NY Rangers' 11th choice, 220th overall, in 1987 Entry Draft).

			Regular Season					Playoffs				
Season	Club	Lea	GP	G	A	TP	PIM	GP	G	A	TP	PIM
1987-88	Yale	ECAC	18	0	2	2	16	....	....	....	....	....
1988-89	Yale	ECAC	24	1	0	1	26	....	....	....	....	....

MARCINYSHYN, DAVID   (mar SIN uh shin)

Defense. Shoots left. 6'3", 210 lbs.   Born, Edmonton, Alta., February 4, 1967.

			Regular Season					Playoffs				
Season	Club	Lea	GP	G	A	TP	PIM	GP	G	A	TP	PIM
1985-86	Kamloops	WHL	57	2	7	9	111	16	1	3	4	12
1986-87	Kamloops	WHL	68	5	27	32	106	13	0	3	3	35
1987-88	Utica	AHL	73	2	7	9	179	....	....	....	....	....
	Flint	IHL	3	0	0	0	4	16	0	2	2	31
1988-89	Utica	AHL	74	4	14	18	101	5	0	0	0	13

Signed as a free agent by **New Jersey**, September 26, 1986.

MARK, GORDON

Defense. Shoots right. 6'4", 210 lbs.   Born, Edmonton, Alta., September 10, 1964.
(New Jersey's 4th choice, 108th over-all, in 1983 Entry Draft).

			Regular Season					Playoffs				
Season	Club	Lea	GP	G	A	TP	PIM	GP	G	A	TP	PIM
1982-83	Kamloops	WHL	71	12	20	32	135	7	1	1	2	8
1983-84	Kamloops	WHL	67	12	30	42	202	17	2	6	8	27
1984-85	Kamloops	WHL	32	11	23	34	68	7	1	2	3	10
1985-86	Maine	AHL	77	9	13	22	134	5	0	1	1	9
1986-87	**New Jersey**	**NHL**	36	3	5	8	82	....	....	....	....	....
	Maine	AHL	29	4	10	14	66	....	....	....	....	....
1987-88	**New Jersey**	**NHL**	19	0	2	2	27	....	....	....	....	....
	Utica	AHL	50	5	21	26	96	....	....	....	....	....
1988-89	Utica	AHL	DID NOT PLAY									
	NHL Totals		55	3	7	10	109	....	....	....	....	....

MARKWART, NEVIN

Left wing. Shoots left. 5'10", 180 lbs.   Born, Toronto, Ont., December 9, 1964.
(Boston's 1st choice, 21st over-all, in 1983 Entry Draft).

			Regular Season					Playoffs				
Season	Club	Lea	GP	G	A	TP	PIM	GP	G	A	TP	PIM
1981-82	Regina	WHL	25	2	12	14	56	20	2	2	4	82
1982-83	Regina	WHL	43	27	39	66	91	1	0	0	0	0
1983-84	**Boston**	**NHL**	70	14	16	30	121	....	....	....	....	....
1984-85	**Boston**	**NHL**	26	0	4	4	36	1	0	0	0	0
	Hershey	AHL	38	13	18	31	79	....	....	....	....	....
1985-86	**Boston**	**NHL**	65	7	15	22	207	....	....	....	....	....
1986-87	**Boston**	**NHL**	64	10	9	19	225	4	0	0	0	9
	Moncton	AHL	3	3	3	6	11	....	....	....	....	....
1987-88	**Boston**	**NHL**	25	1	12	13	85	2	0	0	0	2
1988-89	Maine	AHL	1	0	1	1	0	....	....	....	....	....
	NHL Totals		250	32	56	88	674	7	0	0	0	11

MAROIS, DANIEL

Right wing. Shoots right. 6'1", 180 lbs.   Born, Montreal, Que., October 3, 1968.
(Toronto's 2nd choice, 28th over-all, in 1987 Entry Draft).

			Regular Season					Playoffs				
Season	Club	Lea	GP	G	A	TP	PIM	GP	G	A	TP	PIM
1985-86	Verdun	QMJHL	58	42	35	77	110	5	4	2	6	6
1986-87	Chicoutimi	QMJHL	40	22	26	48	143	16	7	14	21	25
1987-88	**Toronto**	**NHL**	....	....	....	....	....	3	1	0	1	0
	Newmarket	AHL	8	4	4	8	4	....	....	....	....	....
	Verdun	QMJHL	67	52	36	88	153	....	....	....	....	....
1988-89	**Toronto**	**NHL**	76	31	23	54	76	....	....	....	....	....
	NHL Totals		76	31	23	54	76	3	1	0	1	0

MAROIS, MARIO   (MAIR-wah)

Defense. Shoots right. 5'11", 190 lbs.   Born, Ancienne Lorette, Que., December 15, 1957.
(NY Rangers' 5th choice, 62nd over-all, in 1977 Amateur Draft).

			Regular Season					Playoffs				
Season	Club	Lea	GP	G	A	TP	PIM	GP	G	A	TP	PIM
1975-76	Quebec	QJHL	67	11	42	53	270	15	2	3	5	86
1976-77	Quebec	QJHL	72	17	67	84	239	14	1	17	18	75
1977-78	**NY Rangers**	**NHL**	8	1	1	2	15	1	0	0	0	5
	New Haven	AHL	52	8	23	31	147	12	5	3	8	31
1978-79	**NY Rangers**	**NHL**	71	5	26	31	153	18	0	6	6	29
1979-80	**NY Rangers**	**NHL**	79	8	23	31	142	9	0	2	2	8
1980-81	**NY Rangers**	**NHL**	8	1	2	3	46	....	....	....	....	....
	Vancouver	**NHL**	50	4	12	16	115	....	....	....	....	....
	Quebec	**NHL**	11	0	7	7	20	5	0	1	1	6
1981-82	Quebec	NHL	71	11	32	43	161	13	1	2	3	44
1982-83	Quebec	NHL	36	2	12	14	108	....	....	....	....	....
1983-84	Quebec	NHL	80	13	36	49	151	9	1	4	5	6
1984-85	Quebec	NHL	76	6	37	43	91	18	0	8	8	12
1985-86	Quebec	NHL	20	1	12	13	42	....	....	....	....	....
	Winnipeg	**NHL**	56	4	28	32	110	3	1	4	5	6
1986-87	Winnipeg	NHL	79	4	40	44	106	10	1	3	4	23
1987-88	Winnipeg	NHL	79	7	44	51	111	5	0	4	4	6
1988-89	**Winnipeg**	**NHL**	7	1	1	2	17	....	....	....	....	....
	Quebec	**NHL**	42	2	11	13	101	....	....	....	....	....
	NHL Totals		773	70	324	394	1489	91	4	34	38	145

Traded to **Vancouver** by **NY Rangers** with Jim Mayer for Jere Gillis and Jeff Bandura, November 11, 1980. Traded to **Quebec** by **Vancouver** for Garry Lariviere, March 10, 1981. Traded to **Winnipeg** by **Quebec** for Robert Picard, November 27, 1985. Traded to **Quebec** by **Winnipeg** for Gord Donnelly, December 6, 1988.

MARQUETTE, DALE

Left wing. Shoots left. 5'11", 190 lbs.   Born, Prince George, B.C., March 8, 1968.
(Chicago's 10th choice, 197th overall, in 1987 Entry Draft).

			Regular Season					Playoffs				
Season	Club	Lea	GP	G	A	TP	PIM	GP	G	A	TP	PIM
1984-85	Lethbridge	WHL	50	4	4	8	46	2	0	1	1	0
1985-86	Lethbridge	WHL	64	12	14	26	83	10	4	3	7	12
1986-87	Brandon	WHL	68	41	29	70	59	....	....	....	....	....
1987-88	Brandon	WHL	62	51	52	103	48	....	....	....	....	....
	Saginaw	IHL						3	1	0	1	2
1988-89	Saginaw	IHL	46	11	8	19	35	6	1	1	2	2

MARSH, CHARLES BRADLEY (BRAD)

Defense. Shoots left. 6'3", 220 lbs.   Born, London, Ont., March 31, 1958.
(Atlanta's 1st choice, 11th over-all, in 1978 Amateur Draft).

			Regular Season					Playoffs				
Season	Club	Lea	GP	G	A	TP	PIM	GP	G	A	TP	PIM
1976-77a	London	OHA	63	7	33	40	121	20	3	5	8	47
1977-78b	London	OHA	62	8	55	63	192	11	2	10	12	21
1978-79	Atlanta	NHL	80	0	19	19	101	2	0	0	0	17
1979-80	Atlanta	NHL	80	2	9	11	119	4	0	1	1	2
1980-81	Calgary	NHL	80	1	12	13	87	16	0	5	5	8
1981-82	Calgary	NHL	17	0	1	1	10	....	....	....	....	....
	Philadelphia	**NHL**	66	2	22	24	106	4	0	0	0	2
1982-83	Philadelphia	NHL	68	2	11	13	52	2	0	1	1	0
1983-84	Philadelphia	NHL	77	3	14	17	83	3	1	1	2	2
1984-85	Philadelphia	NHL	77	2	18	20	91	19	0	6	6	65
1985-86	Philadelphia	NHL	79	0	13	13	123	5	0	0	0	2
1986-87	Philadelphia	NHL	77	2	9	11	124	26	3	4	7	16
1987-88	Philadelphia	NHL	70	3	9	12	57	7	1	0	1	8
1988-89	**Toronto**	**NHL**	80	1	15	16	79	....	....	....	....	....
	NHL Totals		851	18	152	170	1032	88	5	18	23	122

a OHA Third All-Star Team (1977)
b OHA First All-Star Team (1978)

Claimed by **Atlanta** as fill in Expansion Draft, June 13, 1979. Traded to **Philadelphia** by **Calgary** for Mel Bridgman, November 11, 1981. Claimed by **Toronto** in NHL Waiver Draft, October 3, 1988.

MARSHALL, CHRIS

Left wing. Shoots left. 5'10", 170 lbs.   Born, Quincy, MA, December 12, 1968.
(Buffalo's 6th choice, 106th overall, in 1987 Entry Draft).

			Regular Season					Playoffs				
Season	Club	Lea	GP	G	A	TP	PIM	GP	G	A	TP	PIM
1985-86	B.C. High	HS	18	15	20	35	....	....	....	....	....	....
1986-87	B.C. High	HS	18	22	18	40	50	....	....	....	....	....
1987-88	Michigan State	CCHA	29	0	2	2	27	....	....	....	....	....
1988-89	Michigan State	CCHA	7	0	1	1	11	....	....	....	....	....

MARSHALL, JASON

Defense. Shoots right. 6'2", 185 lbs.   Born, Cranbrook, B.C., February 22, 1971.
(St. Louis' 1st choice, 9th overall, in 1989 Entry Draft).

			Regular Season					Playoffs				
Season	Club	Lea	GP	G	A	TP	PIM	GP	G	A	TP	PIM
1987-88	Columbia Valley	Midget	40	4	28	32	150	....	....	....	....	....
1988-89	Vernon	BCJHL	48	10	30	40	195	....	....	....	....	....

MARSHALL, PAUL

Defense. Shoots right. 6'2", 180 lbs.   Born, Quincy, MA, October 22, 1966.
(Philadelphia's 5th choice, 84th overall, in 1985 Entry Draft).

			Regular Season					Playoffs				
Season	Club	Lea	GP	G	A	TP	PIM	GP	G	A	TP	PIM
1985-86	Boston College	H.E.	40	0	12	12	28	....	....	....	....	....
1986-87	Boston College	H.E.	36	4	10	14	30	....	....	....	....	....
1987-88	Boston College	H.E.	34	12	23	35	50	....	....	....	....	....
1988-89	Boston College	H.E.	40	4	18	22	36	....	....	....	....	....

MARTIN, DONALD

Left wing. Shoots left. 6', 200 lbs. Born, London, Ont., March 29, 1968.
(Edmonton's 6th choice, 103rd overall, in 1988 Entry Draft).

			Regular Season					Playoffs				
Season	Club	Lea	GP	G	A	TP	PIM	GP	G	A	TP	PIM
1985-86	North Bay	OHL	7	0	0	0	21	....	....	....	....	....
	London	OHL	55	7	6	13	112	5	1	0	1	14
1986-87	London	OHL	63	19	38	57	127	....	....	....	....	....
1987-88	London	OHL	57	30	32	62	190	11	6	8	14	50
1988-89	Cape Breton	AHL	3	0	0	0	2	....	....	....	....	....
	Fort Wayne	IHL	40	11	5	16	123	....	....	....	....	....

MARTIN, GRANT MICHAEL

Left wing. Shoots left. 5'10", 190 lbs. Born, Smooth Rock Falls, Ont., March 13, 1962.
(Vancouver's 9th choice, 196th over-all, in 1980 Entry Draft).

			Regular Season					Playoffs				
Season	Club	Lea	GP	G	A	TP	PIM	GP	G	A	TP	PIM
1979-80	Kitchener	OHA	65	31	21	52	62	....	....	....	....	....
1980-81	Kitchener	OHA	66	41	57	98	77	18	9	20	29	42
1981-82	Kitchener	OHL	54	33	63	96	97	12	3	15	18	33
1982-83	Fredericton	AHL	80	19	27	46	73	12	4	1	5	14
1983-84	**Vancouver**	**NHL**	**12**	**0**	**2**	**2**	**6**	....	....	....	....	....
	Fredericton	AHL	57	36	24	60	46	7	4	5	9	16
1984-85	**Vancouver**	**NHL**	**12**	**0**	**1**	**1**	**39**	....	....	....	....	....
	Fredericton	AHL	65	31	47	78	78	6	1	4	5	8
	Salt Lake	IHL	2	0	0	0	0	....	....	....	....	....
1985-86	**Washington**	**NHL**	**11**	**0**	**1**	**1**	**6**	....	....	....	....	....
	Baltimore	AHL	54	27	49	76	97	6	1	3	4	14
1986-87	**Washington**	**NHL**	**9**	**0**	**0**	**0**	**4**	**1**	**1**	**0**	**1**	**2**
	Binghamton	AHL	63	30	23	53	86	12	3	1	4	16
1987-88	Rochester	AHL	22	11	15	26	18	7	4	5	9	17
1988-89	Rochester	AHL	6	7	5	12	6	....	....	....	....	....
	Jyvaskyla	Fin.	43	20	29	49	48	11	1	5	6	11
	NHL Totals		**44**	**0**	**4**	**4**	**55**	**1**	**1**	**0**	**1**	**2**

Signed as a free agent by **Washington**, August 6, 1985.

MARTIN, TOM

Left wing. Shoots left. 6'2", 200 lbs. Born, Kelowna, B.C., May 11, 1964.
(Winnipeg's 2nd choice, 74th over-all, in 1982 Entry Draft).

			Regular Season					Playoffs				
Season	Club	Lea	GP	G	A	TP	PIM	GP	G	A	TP	PIM
1981-82	Kelowna	BCJHL	51	35	45	80	293	....	....	....	....	....
1982-83	U. of Denver	WCHA	37	8	18	26	128	....	....	....	....	....
1983-84	Victoria	WHL	60	30	45	75	261	....	....	....	....	....
	Sherbrooke	AHL	5	0	0	0	16	....	....	....	....	....
1984-85	**Winnipeg**	**NHL**	**8**	**1**	**0**	**1**	**42**	**3**	**0**	**0**	**0**	**2**
	Sherbrooke	AHL	58	4	15	19	212	12	1	1	2	72
1985-86	**Winnipeg**	**NHL**	**5**	**0**	**0**	**0**	**0**	....	....	....	....	....
	Sherbrooke	AHL	69	11	18	29	227	....	....	....	....	....
1986-87	**Winnipeg**	**NHL**	**11**	**1**	**0**	**1**	**49**	....	....	....	....	....
	Adirondack	AHL	18	5	6	11	57	....	....	....	....	....
1987-88	**Hartford**	**NHL**	**5**	**1**	**2**	**3**	**14**	....	....	....	....	....
a	Binghamton	AHL	71	28	61	89	344	3	0	0	0	18
1988-89	**Minnesota**	**NHL**	**4**	**1**	**1**	**2**	**4**	....	....	....	....	....
	Hartford	**NHL**	**38**	**7**	**6**	**13**	**113**	**1**	**0**	**0**	**0**	**4**
	NHL Totals		**71**	**11**	**9**	**20**	**222**	**4**	**0**	**0**	**0**	**6**

a AHL First All-Star Team (1988)

Signed as a free agent by **Hartford**, July 29, 1987. Claimed by **Minnesota** in NHL Waiver Draft, October 3, 1988. Claimed by **Hartford** on waivers from **Minnesota**, December 1988.

MARTINSON, STEVEN

Left wing. Shoots left. 6'1", 205 lbs. Born, Minnetonka, MN, June 21, 1959.

			Regular Season					Playoffs				
Season	Club	Lea	GP	G	A	TP	PIM	GP	G	A	TP	PIM
1982-83	Toledo	IHL	32	9	10	19	111	....	....	....	....	....
	Birmingham	CHL	43	4	5	9	184	13	1	2	3	80
1983-84	Tulsa	CHL	42	3	6	9	240	6	0	0	0	43
1984-85	Toledo	IHL	54	4	10	14	300	2	0	0	0	21
1985-86	Hershey	AHL	69	3	6	9	432	3	0	0	0	56
1986-87	Hershey	AHL	17	0	3	3	85	....	....	....	....	....
	Adirondack	AHL	14	1	1	2	78	11	2	0	2	108
1987-88	**Detroit**	**NHL**	**10**	**1**	**1**	**2**	**84**	....	....	....	....	....
	Adirondack	AHL	32	6	8	14	146	6	1	2	3	66
1988-89	**Montreal**	**NHL**	**25**	**1**	**0**	**1**	**87**	**1**	**0**	**0**	**0**	**10**
	Sherbrooke	AHL	10	5	7	12	61	....	....	....	....	....
	NHL Totals		**35**	**2**	**1**	**3**	**171**	**1**	**0**	**0**	**0**	**10**

Signed as a free agent by **Philadelphia**, September 30, 1985. Signed as a free agent by **Detroit**, October 3, 1987.

MARTTILA, JUKKA

Defense. Shoots left. 6'0", 185 lbs. Born, Tampere, Finland, April 15, 1968.
(Winnipeg's 9th choice, 136th overall, in 1988 Entry Draft).

			Regular Season					Playoffs				
Season	Club	Lea	GP	G	A	TP	PIM	GP	G	A	TP	PIM
1986-87	Tappara	Fin.	33	4	1	5	18	....	....	....	....	....
1987-88	Tappara	Fin.	39	5	7	12	16	....	....	....	....	....
1988-89	Tappara	Fin.	43	11	20	31	32	....	....	....	....	....

MARUK, DENNIS JOHN (muh ROOK)

Center. Shoots left. 5'8", 175 lbs. Born, Toronto, Ont., November 17, 1955.
(California's 2nd choice, 21st over-all, in 1975 Amateur Draft).

			Regular Season					Playoffs				
Season	Club	Lea	GP	G	A	TP	PIM	GP	G	A	TP	PIM
1973-74	London	OHA	67	47	65	112	61	....	....	....	....	....
1974-75	London	OHA	65	66	79	145	53	....	....	....	....	....
1975-76	**California**	**NHL**	**80**	**30**	**32**	**62**	**44**	....	....	....	....	....
1976-77	**Cleveland**	**NHL**	**80**	**28**	**50**	**78**	**68**	....	....	....	....	....
1977-78	**Cleveland**	**NHL**	**76**	**36**	**35**	**71**	**50**	....	....	....	....	....
1978-79	**Minnesota**	**NHL**	**2**	**0**	**0**	**0**	**0**	....	....	....	....	....
	Washington	**NHL**	**76**	**31**	**59**	**90**	**71**	....	....	....	....	....
1979-80	**Washington**	**NHL**	**27**	**10**	**17**	**27**	**8**	....	....	....	....	....
1980-81	**Washington**	**NHL**	**80**	**50**	**47**	**97**	**87**	....	....	....	....	....
1981-82	**Washington**	**NHL**	**80**	**60**	**76**	**136**	**128**	....	....	....	....	....
1982-83	**Washington**	**NHL**	**80**	**31**	**50**	**81**	**71**	**4**	**1**	**1**	**2**	**2**
1983-84	**Minnesota**	**NHL**	**71**	**17**	**43**	**60**	**42**	**16**	**5**	**5**	**10**	**8**
1984-85	**Minnesota**	**NHL**	**71**	**19**	**41**	**60**	**56**	**9**	**4**	**7**	**11**	**12**
1985-86	**Minnesota**	**NHL**	**70**	**21**	**37**	**58**	**67**	**5**	**4**	**9**	**13**	**4**
1986-87	**Minnesota**	**NHL**	**67**	**16**	**30**	**46**	**52**	....	....	....	....	....
1987-88	**Minnesota**	**NHL**	**22**	**7**	**4**	**11**	**15**	....	....	....	....	....
1988-89	**Minnesota**	**NHL**	**6**	**0**	**1**	**1**	**2**	....	....	....	....	....
	Kalamazoo	IHL	5	1	5	6	4	....	....	....	....	....
	NHL Totals		**888**	**356**	**522**	**878**	**761**	**34**	**14**	**22**	**36**	**26**

Played in NHL All-Star Game (1978, 1982)

Protected by **Minnesota** prior to Cleveland-Minnesota Dispersal Draft, June 15, 1978. Traded to **Washington** by **Minnesota** for Pittsburgh's first round choice (Tom McCarthy) in 1979 Entry Draft — Washington's property via earlier deal — October 18, 1978. Traded to **Minnesota** by **Washington** for Minnesota's second round choice (Stephen Leach) in 1984 Entry Draft, July 5, 1983.

MARVIN, DAVID

Defense. Shoots right. 6'1", 180 lbs. Born, Warroad, MN, March 10, 1968.
(St. Louis' 10th choice, 201st overall, in 1987 Entry Draft).

			Regular Season					Playoffs				
Season	Club	Lea	GP	G	A	TP	PIM	GP	G	A	TP	PIM
1987-88	North Dakota	WCHA	35	4	17	21	12	....	....	....	....	....
1988-89	North Dakota	WCHA	38	4	6	10	24	....	....	....	....	....

MATHIAS, SCOTT

Center. Shoots left. 6'1", 175 lbs. Born, Duluth, MN, February 2, 1966.
(Minnesota's 9th choice, 159th overall, in 1986 Entry Draft).

			Regular Season					Playoffs				
Season	Club	Lea	GP	G	A	TP	PIM	GP	G	A	TP	PIM
1985-86	Denver	WCHA	48	12	12	24	0	....	....	....	....	....
1986-87	Denver	WCHA	40	11	13	24	22	....	....	....	....	....
1987-88	Denver	WCHA	37	12	10	22	16	....	....	....	....	....
1988-89	U. of Denver	WCHA	39	8	12	20	38	....	....	....	....	....

MATHIESON, JIM

Defense. Shoots left. 6'1", 210 lbs. Born, Kindersley, Sask., January 24, 1970.
(Washington's 3rd choice, 59th overall, in 1989 Entry Draft).

			Regular Season					Playoffs				
Season	Club	Lea	GP	G	A	TP	PIM	GP	G	A	TP	PIM
1986-87	Regina	WHL	40	0	9	9	40	3	0	1	1	2
1987-88	Regina	WHL	72	3	12	15	115	4	0	2	2	4
1988-89	Regina	WHL	62	5	22	27	151	....	....	....	....	....

MATIKAINEN, PETRI

Defense. Shoots left. 6', 185 lbs. Born, Savonlinna, Finland, January 7, 1967.
(Buffalo's 7th choice, 140th overall, in 1985 Entry Draft).

			Regular Season					Playoffs				
Season	Club	Lea	GP	G	A	TP	PIM	GP	G	A	TP	PIM
1984-85	Sapko	Fin.	24	0	4	4	34	....	....	....	....	....
1985-86	Oshawa	OHL	53	14	42	56	27	....	....	....	....	....
1986-87	Oshawa	OHL	50	8	34	42	53	21	2	12	14	36
1987-88	Tappara	Fin.	41	5	1	6	58	1	0	2	2	4
1988-89	Tappara	Fin.	44	4	13	17	32	8	0	0	0	10

MATILAINEN, ARI

Left wing. Shoots left. 6'2", 185 lbs. Born, Tampere, Finland, January 22, 1966.
(Minnesota's 7th choice, 190th overall, in 1988 Entry Draft).

			Regular Season					Playoffs				
Season	Club	Lea	GP	G	A	TP	PIM	GP	G	A	TP	PIM
1987-88	Assat	Fin.	44	15	23	38	....	....	....	....	....	....
1988-89	Karpat	Fin.	36	11	10	21	28	....	....	....	....	....

MATTEAU, STEPHANE

Left wing. Shoots left. 6'3", 195 lbs. Born, Rouyn-Noranda, Que., September 2, 1969.
(Calgary's 2nd choice, 25th overall, in 1987 Entry Draft).

			Regular Season					Playoffs				
Season	Club	Lea	GP	G	A	TP	PIM	GP	G	A	TP	PIM
1985-86	Hull	QMJHL	60	6	8	14	19	4	0	0	0	0
1986-87	Hull	QMJHL	69	27	48	75	113	8	3	7	10	8
1987-88	Hull	QMJHL	57	17	40	57	179	18	5	14	19	94
1988-89	Hull	QMJHL	59	44	45	89	202	9	8	6	14	30
	Salt Lake	IHL	....	....	....	....	....	9	0	4	4	13

MATULIK, IVAN

Right wing. Shoots left. 6'1", 200 lbs. Born, Nitra, Czechoslovakia, June 17, 1968.
(Edmonton's 7th choice, 147th overall, in 1986 Entry Draft).

			Regular Season					Playoffs				
Season	Club	Lea	GP	G	A	TP	PIM	GP	G	A	TP	PIM
1986-87	Bratislava	Czech.	25	1	3	4	...	....	....	....	....	....
1987-88	Nova Scotia	AHL	46	13	10	23	29	....	....	....	....	....
1988-89	Cape Breton	AHL	1	0	0	0	0	....	....	....	....	....

MATUSOVICH, SCOTT

Defense. Shoots left. 6'2", 205 lbs. Born, Southbury, CT, October 31, 1969.
(Calgary's 5th choice, 90th overall, in 1988 Entry Draft).

			Regular Season					Playoffs				
Season	Club	Lea	GP	G	A	TP	PIM	GP	G	A	TP	PIM
1986-87	Canterbury	HS	....	10	22	32	....	....	....	....	....	....
1987-88	Cantebury	HS	....	20	31	51	....	....	....	....	....	....
1988-89	Yale	ECAC	25	3	11	14	40	....	....	....	....	....

MAY, ALAN

Right wing. Shoots right. 6'1", 200 lbs. Born, Barrhead, Alta., January 14, 1965.

			Regular Season					Playoffs				
Season	Club	Lea	GP	G	A	TP	PIM	GP	G	A	TP	PIM
1984-85	Estevan	SAJHL	64	51	47	98	409	....	....	....	....	....
1985-86	Medicine Hat	WHL	6	1	0	1	25	....	....	....	....	....
	N. Westminster	WHL	32	8	9	17	81	....	....	....	....	....
1986-87	Springfield	AHL	4	0	2	2	11	....	....	....	....	....
	Carolina	ACHL	42	23	14	37	310	5	2	2	4	57
1987-88	Maine	AHL	61	14	11	25	257	....	....	....	....	....
	Boston	**NHL**	**3**	**0**	**0**	**0**	**15**	....	....	....	....	....
	Nova Scotia	AHL	13	4	1	5	54	4	0	0	0	51
1988-89	**Edmonton**	**NHL**	**3**	**1**	**0**	**1**	**7**	....	....	....	....	....
	Cape Breton	AHL	50	12	13	25	214	....	....	....	....	....
	New Haven	AHL	12	2	8	10	99	16	6	3	9	105
	NHL Totals		**6**	**1**	**0**	**1**	**22**	....	....	....	....	....

Signed as a free agent by **Boston**, October 30, 1987. Traded to **Edmonton** by **Boston** for Moe Lemay, March 8, 1988. Traded to **Los Angeles** by **Edmonton** with Jim Weimer for Brian Wilks and John English, March 7, 1989. Traded to **Washington** by **Los Angeles** for Washington's fifth-round choice (Thomas Newman) in 1989 Entry Draft, June 17, 1989.

MAY, ANDY

Center. Shoots left. 6'2", 185 lbs. Born, Orangeville, Ont., May 2, 1968.
(St. Louis' 7th choice, 136th overall, in 1986 Entry Draft).

			Regular Season					Playoffs				
Season	Club	Lea	GP	G	A	TP	PIM	GP	G	A	TP	PIM
1985-86	Bramalea	Jr.B	35	21	26	47	41	....	....	....	....	....
1986-87	Northeastern	H.E.	26	5	5	10	17	....	....	....	....	....
1987-88	Northeastern	H.E.	17	2	5	7	10	....	....	....	....	....
1988-89	Northeastern	H.E.	30	12	14	26	43	....	....	....	....	....

MAYER, DEREK

Defense. Shoots right. 6', 185 lbs. Born, Rossland, B.C., May 21, 1967.
(Detroit's 3rd choice, 43rd overall, in 1986 Entry Draft).

			Regular Season					Playoffs				
Season	Club	Lea	GP	G	A	TP	PIM	GP	G	A	TP	PIM
1985-86	Denver	WCHA	44	2	7	9	42	....	....	....	....	....
1986-87	Denver	WCHA	38	5	17	22	87	....	....	....	....	....
1987-88	Denver	WCHA	34	5	16	21	82	....	....	....	....	....
1988-89	Cdn. National	....	58	3	13	16	81	....	....	....	....	....

MAYER, PATRICK

Defense. Shoots left. 6'3", 225 lbs. Born, Royal Oak, MI, July 24, 1961.

			Regular Season					Playoffs				
Season	Club	Lea	GP	G	A	TP	PIM	GP	G	A	TP	PIM
1985-86	Muskegon	IHL	74	2	15	17	233	13	0	2	2	37
1986-87	Muskegon	IHL	71	4	14	18	387	13	1	0	1	53
1987-88	**Pittsburgh**	**NHL**	**1**	**0**	**0**	**0**	**4**	....	....	....	....	....
	Muskegon	IHL	73	3	10	13	450	5	0	0	0	47
1988-89	New Haven	AHL	6	0	0	0	35	....	....	....	....	....
	Muskegon	IHL	56	0	13	13	314	....	....	....	....	....
	NHL Totals		**1**	**0**	**0**	**0**	**4**	....	....	....	....	....

Signed as a free agent by **Pittsburgh**, July 10, 1987. Traded to **Los Angeles** by **Pittsburgh** for Tim Tookey, March 7, 1989.

MAZUR, JAY

Right wing. Shoots right. 6'2", 205 lbs. Born, Hamilton, Ont., January 22, 1965.
(Vancouver's 12th choice, 230th overall, in 1983 Entry Draft).

			Regular Season					Playoffs				
Season	Club	Lea	GP	G	A	TP	PIM	GP	G	A	TP	PIM
1983-84	Maine	H.E.	34	14	9	23	14	....	....	....	....	....
1984-85	Maine	H.E.	31	0	6	6	20	....	....	....	....	....
1985-86	Maine	H.E.	5	7	12	18	....	....	....	....	....	....
1986-87	Maine	H.E.	39	16	10	26	61	....	....	....	....	....
1987-88	Flint	IHL	39	17	11	28	28	....	....	....	....	....
	Fredericton	AHL	31	14	6	20	28	15	4	2	6	38
1988-89	**Vancouver**	**NHL**	**1**	**0**	**0**	**0**	**0**	....	....	....	....	....
	Milwaukee	IHL	73	33	31	64	86	11	6	5	11	2
	NHL Totals		**1**	**0**	**0**	**0**	**0**	....	....	....	....	....

McBAIN, ANDREW

Right wing. Shoots right. 6'1", 205 lbs. Born, Scarborough, Ont., January 18, 1965.
(Winnipeg's 1st choice, 8th over-all, in 1983 Entry Draft).

			Regular Season					Playoffs				
Season	Club	Lea	GP	G	A	TP	PIM	GP	G	A	TP	PIM
1981-82	Niagara Falls	OHL	68	19	25	44	35	5	0	3	3	4
1982-83a	North Bay	OHL	67	33	87	120	61	8	2	6	8	17
1983-84	**Winnipeg**	**NHL**	**78**	**11**	**19**	**30**	**37**	**3**	**2**	**0**	**2**	**0**
1984-85	**Winnipeg**	**NHL**	**77**	**7**	**15**	**22**	**45**	**7**	**1**	**0**	**1**	**0**
1985-86	**Winnipeg**	**NHL**	**28**	**3**	**3**	**6**	**17**	....	....	....	....	....
1986-87	**Winnipeg**	**NHL**	**71**	**11**	**21**	**32**	**106**	**9**	**0**	**2**	**2**	**10**
1987-88	**Winnipeg**	**NHL**	**74**	**32**	**31**	**63**	**145**	**5**	**2**	**5**	**7**	**29**
1988-89	**Winnipeg**	**NHL**	**80**	**37**	**40**	**77**	**71**	....	....	....	....	....
	NHL Totals		**408**	**101**	**129**	**230**	**421**	**24**	**5**	**7**	**12**	**39**

a OHL Second All-Star Team (1983).

Traded to **Pittsburgh** by **Winnipeg** with Jim Kyte and Randy Gilhen for Randy Cunnyworth, Rick Tabaracci and Dave McLlwain, June 17, 1989.

McBEAN, WAYNE

Defense. Shoots left. 6'2", 185 lbs. Born, Calgary, Alta., February 21, 1969.
(Los Angeles' 1st choice, 4th overall, in 1987 Entry Draft).

			Regular Season					Playoffs				
Season	Club	Lea	GP	G	A	TP	PIM	GP	G	A	TP	PIM
1985-86	Medicine Hat	WHL	67	1	14	15	73	25	1	5	6	36
1986-87a	Medicine Hat	WHL	71	12	41	53	163	20	2	8	10	40
1987-88	**Los Angeles**	**NHL**	**27**	**0**	**1**	**1**	**26**	....	....	....	....	....
	Medicine Hat	WHL	30	15	30	45	48	16	6	17	23	50
1988-89	**Los Angeles**	**NHL**	**33**	**0**	**5**	**5**	**23**	....	....	....	....	....
	New Haven	AHL	7	1	1	2	2	....	....	....	....	....
	NY Islanders	**NHL**	**19**	**0**	**1**	**1**	**12**	....	....	....	....	....
	NHL Totals		**79**	**0**	**7**	**7**	**61**	....	....	....	....	....

a WHL East All-Star Team (1987)

Traded to **NY Islanders** by **Los Angeles** with Mark Fitzpatrick and future considerations (Doug Crossman acquired May 23, 1989) for Kelly Hrudey, February 22, 1989.

McBRIDE, DARYN

Center. Shoots right. 5'9", 180 lbs. Born, Ft. Saskatchewan, Alta., March 29, 1968.
(Pittsburgh's 10th choice, 194th overall, in 1987 Entry Draft).

			Regular Season					Playoffs				
Season	Club	Lea	GP	G	A	TP	PIM	GP	G	A	TP	PIM
1986-87	U. of Denver	WCHA	38	19	13	32	54	....	....	....	....	....
1987-88a	U. of Denver	WCHA	39	30	28	58	122	....	....	....	....	....
1988-89b	U. of Denver	WCHA	42	19	32	51	74	....	....	....	....	....
	Can. National	....	15	3	7	10	6	....	....	....	....	....

a WCHA Second All-Star Team (1988)
b WCHA First All-Star Team (1989)

McCAUGHEY, BRAD

Right wing. Shoots right. 6'2", 195 lbs. Born, Ann Arbor, MI, June 10, 1966.
(Montreal's 10th choice, 158th overall, in 1984 Entry Draft).

			Regular Season					Playoffs				
Season	Club	Lea	GP	G	A	TP	PIM	GP	G	A	TP	PIM
1984-85	U. of Michigan	CCHA	35	16	11	27	49	....	....	....	....	....
1985-86	U. of Michigan	CCHA	32	24	26	50	51	....	....	....	....	....
1986-87	U. of Michigan	CCHA	38	26	23	49	53	....	....	....	....	....
1987-88	U. of Michigan	CCHA	33	20	14	34	36	....	....	....	....	....
1988-89	Sherbrooke	AHL	1	1	0	1	0	....	....	....	....	....
	Peoria	IHL	71	30	38	68	14	4	2	2	4	0

McCLELLAND, KEVIN WILLIAM

Right wing. Shoots right. 6'2", 205 lbs. Born, Oshawa, Ont., July 4, 1962.
(Hartford's 4th choice, 71st over-all, in 1980 Entry Draft).

			Regular Season					Playoffs				
Season	Club	Lea	GP	G	A	TP	PIM	GP	G	A	TP	PIM
1980-81	Niagara Falls	OHA	68	36	72	108	186	12	8	13	21	42
1981-82	Niagara Falls	OHL	46	36	47	83	184	....	....	....	....	....
	Pittsburgh	**NHL**	**10**	**1**	**4**	**5**	**4**	**5**	**1**	**1**	**2**	**5**
1982-83	**Pittsburgh**	**NHL**	**38**	**5**	**4**	**9**	**73**	....	....	....	....	....
1983-84	Baltimore	AHL	3	1	1	2	0	....	....	....	....	....
	Pittsburgh	**NHL**	**24**	**2**	**4**	**6**	**62**	....	....	....	....	....
	Edmonton	**NHL**	**52**	**8**	**20**	**28**	**127**	**18**	**4**	**6**	**10**	**42**
1984-85	**Edmonton**	**NHL**	**62**	**8**	**15**	**23**	**205**	**18**	**1**	**3**	**4**	**75**
1985-86	**Edmonton**	**NHL**	**79**	**11**	**25**	**36**	**266**	**10**	**1**	**0**	**1**	**32**
1986-87	**Edmonton**	**NHL**	**72**	**12**	**13**	**25**	**238**	**21**	**2**	**3**	**5**	**43**
1987-88	**Edmonton**	**NHL**	**74**	**10**	**6**	**16**	**281**	**19**	**2**	**3**	**5**	**68**
1988-89	**Edmonton**	**NHL**	**79**	**6**	**14**	**20**	**161**	**7**	**0**	**2**	**2**	**16**
	NHL Totals		**490**	**63**	**105**	**168**	**1417**	**98**	**11**	**18**	**29**	**281**

Traded to **Pittsburgh** by **Hartford** with Pat Boutette as compensation for Hartford's signing of free agent goaltender Greg Millen, June 29, 1981. Traded to **Edmonton** by **Pittsburgh** with Pittsburgh's sixth round choice (Emanuel Viveiros) in 1984 Entry Draft for Tom Roulston, December 5, 1983.

McCOLGAN, GARY

Left wing. Shoots left. 6', 195 lbs. Born, Scarborough, Ont., March 27, 1966.
(Minnesota's 6th choice, 118th overall in 1984 Entry Draft).

			Regular Season					Playoffs				
Season	Club	Lea	GP	G	A	TP	PIM	GP	G	A	TP	PIM
1983-84	Oshawa	OHL	66	11	28	39	14	....	....	....	....	....
1984-85	Oshawa	OHL	63	29	26	55	17	5	1	3	4	0
1985-86	Oshawa	OHL	57	49	54	103	22	6	7	4	11	2
1986-87	Indianapolis	IHL	75	30	25	55	15	6	0	2	2	0
1987-88	Kalamazoo	IHL	66	17	35	52	13	7	5	4	9	4
1988-89	Kookoo	Fin.	24	2	0	2	22	....	....	....	....	....

McCOOL, STEVE

Defense. Shoots left. 6'2", 195 lbs. Born, Boston, MA, April 28, 1968.
(Montreal's 7th choice, 101st overall, in 1987 Entry Draft).

			Regular Season					Playoffs				
Season	Club	Lea	GP	G	A	TP	PIM	GP	G	A	TP	PIM
1986-87	Hill School	HS	23	14	29	43	24	....	....	....	....	....
1987-88	Boston College	H.E.	19	0	1	1	6	....	....	....	....	....
1988-89	Boston College	H.E.	DID NOT PLAY									

McCORMACK, BRIAN

Defense. Shoots right. 5'10", 170 lbs. Born, Bloomington, MN, November 11, 1969.
(Detroit's 7th choice, 164th overall, in 1988 Entry Draft).

			Regular Season					Playoffs				
Season	Club	Lea	GP	G	A	TP	PIM	GP	G	A	TP	PIM
1987-88	St. Paul's	HS	30	0	24	24	....	....	....	....	....	....
1988-89	Harvard	ECAC	31	0	8	8	16	....	....	....	....	....

McCORMACK, SCOTT

Defense. Shoots right. 6'1", 185 lbs. Born, Minneapolis, MN, September 25, 1967.
(New Jersey's 9th choice, 171st overall, in 1986 Entry Draft).

			Regular Season					Playoffs				
Season	Club	Lea	GP	G	A	TP	PIM	GP	G	A	TP	PIM
1985-86	St. Paul	HS	21	3	17	20	0	....	....	....	....	....
1986-87	Harvard	ECAC	10	1	1	2	0	....	....	....	....	....
1987-88	Harvard	ECAC	31	1	3	4	14	....	....	....	....	....
1988-89	Harvard	ECAC	19	1	8	9	10	....	....	....	....	....

McCORMICK, MICHAEL

Defense. Shoots left. 6'2", 220 lbs. Born, St. Boniface, Man., May 14, 1968.
(Chicago's 6th choice, 113th overall, in 1987 Entry Draft).

			Regular Season					Playoffs				
Season	Club	Lea	GP	G	A	TP	PIM	GP	G	A	TP	PIM
1986-87	Richmond	BCJHL	52	24	26	50	250	17	15	2	17	4
1987-88	North Dakota	WCHA	41	4	0	4	28	....	....	....	....	....
1988-89	North Dakota	WCHA	29	1	4	5	22	....	....	....	....	....

McCRADY, SCOTT

Defense. Shoots right. 6'1", 195 lbs. Born, Calgary, Alta., October 30, 1968.
(Minnesota's 2nd choice, 35th overall, in 1987 Entry Draft).

			Regular Season					Playoffs				
Season	Club	Lea	GP	G	A	TP	PIM	GP	G	A	TP	PIM
1985-86	Medicine Hat	WHL	65	8	25	33	114	25	0	7	7	67
1986-87	Medicine Hat	WHL	70	10	66	76	157	20	2	21	23	30
1987-88a	Medicine Hat	WHL	65	7	70	77	132	16	2	17	19	34
1988-89	Kalamazoo	IHL	73	8	29	37	169	6	0	4	4	24

a WHL East All-Star Team (1988)

McCRIMMON, BYRON (BRAD)

Defense. Shoots left. 5'11", 197 lbs. Born, Dodsland, Sask., March 29, 1959.
(Boston's 2nd choice, 15th over-all, in 1979 Entry Draft).

			Regular Season					Playoffs				
Season	Club	Lea	GP	G	A	TP	PIM	GP	G	A	TP	PIM
1977-78ab	Brandon	WHL	65	19	78	97	245	8	2	11	13	20
1978-79a	Brandon	WHL	66	24	74	98	139	22	9	19	28	34
1979-80	**Boston**	**NHL**	**72**	**5**	**11**	**16**	**94**	**10**	**1**	**1**	**2**	**28**
1980-81	**Boston**	**NHL**	**78**	**11**	**18**	**29**	**148**	**3**	**0**	**1**	**1**	**2**
1981-82	**Boston**	**NHL**	**78**	**1**	**8**	**9**	**83**	**2**	**0**	**0**	**0**	**2**
1982-83	**Philadelphia**	**NHL**	**79**	**4**	**21**	**25**	**61**	**3**	**0**	**0**	**0**	**4**
1983-84	**Philadelphia**	**NHL**	**71**	**0**	**24**	**24**	**76**	**1**	**0**	**0**	**0**	**4**
1984-85	**Philadelphia**	**NHL**	**66**	**8**	**35**	**43**	**81**	**11**	**2**	**1**	**3**	**15**
1985-86	**Philadelphia**	**NHL**	**80**	**13**	**43**	**56**	**85**	**5**	**2**	**0**	**2**	**2**
1986-87	**Philadelphia**	**NHL**	**71**	**10**	**29**	**39**	**52**	**26**	**3**	**5**	**8**	**30**
1987-88cd	**Calgary**	**NHL**	**80**	**7**	**35**	**42**	**98**	**9**	**2**	**3**	**5**	**22**
1988-89	**Calgary**	**NHL**	**72**	**5**	**17**	**22**	**96**	**22**	**0**	**3**	**3**	**30**
	NHL Totals		**747**	**64**	**241**	**305**	**874**	**92**	**10**	**14**	**24**	**139**

a WHL First All-Star Team (1978, 1979)
b Named WHL's Top Defenseman (1978)
c NHL Second All-Star Team (1988)
d NHL Plus/Minus Leader (1988)

Played in NHL All-Star Game (1988)

Traded to **Philadelphia** by **Boston** for Pete Peeters, June 9, 1982. Traded to **Calgary** by **Philadelphia** for Calgary's third round pick in 1988 Entry Draft (Dominic Roussel) and first round pick — acquired March 6, 1988 by Toronto — in 1989 Entry Draft, August 26, 1987. Toronto acquired Calgary's first round pick in 1989 Entry Draft from Philadelphia in deal for Ken Wregget, March 6, 1988. Toronto selected Steve Bancroft.

McCRORY, SCOTT

Center. Shoots right. 5'10", 175 lbs. Born, Sudbury, Ont., February 27, 1967.
(Washington's 13th choice, 250th overall, in 1986 Entry Draft).

			Regular Season					Playoffs				
Season	Club	Lea	GP	G	A	TP	PIM	GP	G	A	TP	PIM
1985-86	Oshawa	OHL	66	52	80	132	40	6	5	8	13	0
1986-87ab	Oshawa	OHL	66	51	99	150	35	24	15	22	37	20
1987-88	Binghamton	AHL	72	18	33	51	29	4	0	1	1	2
1988-89	Baltimore	AHL	80	38	51	89	25	....	....	....	....	....

a OHL Player of the Year (1987)
b OHL First Team All-Star (1987)

Traded to **Buffalo** by **Washington** for Mark Ferner, June 1, 1989.

McCUTCHEON, DARWIN

Defense. Shoots left. 6'4", 210 lbs. Born, Listowel, Ont., April 19, 1962.
(Toronto's 8th choice, 179th overall, in 1980 Entry Draft).

			Regular Season					Playoffs				
Season	Club	Lea	GP	G	A	TP	PIM	GP	G	A	TP	PIM
1984-85	U. of PEI	AUAA	24	5	30	35	73	7	0	0	0	4
1985-86	Moncton	AHL	12	0	2	2	30	9	0	0	0	9
1986-87	Moncton	AHL	69	1	10	11	187	4	0	1	1	51
1987-88	Salt Lake	IHL	64	2	8	10	150	13	0	2	2	94
1988-89	Flint	IHL	37	2	4	6	89	....	....	....	....	....
	Indianapolis	IHL	34	2	6	8	99	....	....	....	....	....

Signed by as a free agent by **Calgary**, March 10, 1986.

McDONALD, LANNY KING

Right wing. Shoots right. 6', 194 lbs. Born, Hanna, Alta., February 16, 1953.
(Toronto's 1st choice, 4th over-all, in 1973 Amateur Draft).

			Regular Season					Playoffs				
Season	Club	Lea	GP	G	A	TP	PIM	GP	G	A	TP	PIM
1971-72	Medicine Hat	WHL	68	50	64	114	54	7	2	2	4	6
1972-73a	Medicine Hat	WHL	68	62	77	139	84	17	*18	19	37	6
1973-74	**Toronto**	**NHL**	**70**	**14**	**16**	**30**	**43**	....	....	....	....	....
1974-75	**Toronto**	**NHL**	**64**	**17**	**27**	**44**	**86**	**7**	**0**	**0**	**0**	**2**
1975-76	**Toronto**	**NHL**	**75**	**37**	**56**	**93**	**70**	**10**	**4**	**4**	**8**	**4**
1976-77b	**Toronto**	**NHL**	**80**	**46**	**44**	**90**	**77**	**9**	**10**	**7**	**17**	**6**
1977-78	**Toronto**	**NHL**	**74**	**47**	**40**	**87**	**54**	**13**	**3**	**4**	**7**	**10**
1978-79	**Toronto**	**NHL**	**79**	**43**	**42**	**85**	**32**	**6**	**3**	**2**	**5**	**0**
1979-80	**Toronto**	**NHL**	**35**	**15**	**15**	**30**	**10**	....	....	....	....	....
	Colorado	**NHL**	**46**	**25**	**20**	**45**	**43**	....	....	....	....	....
1980-81	**Colorado**	**NHL**	**80**	**35**	**46**	**81**	**56**	....	....	....	....	....
1981-82	**Colorado**	**NHL**	**16**	**6**	**9**	**15**	**20**	....	....	....	....	....
	Calgary	**NHL**	**55**	**34**	**33**	**67**	**37**	**3**	**0**	**1**	**1**	**6**
1982-83bc	**Calgary**	**NHL**	**80**	**66**	**32**	**98**	**90**	**7**	**3**	**4**	**7**	**19**
1983-84	**Calgary**	**NHL**	**65**	**33**	**33**	**66**	**64**	**11**	**6**	**7**	**13**	**6**
1984-85	**Calgary**	**NHL**	**43**	**19**	**18**	**37**	**36**	**1**	**0**	**0**	**0**	**0**
1985-86	**Calgary**	**NHL**	**80**	**28**	**43**	**71**	**44**	**22**	**11**	**7**	**18**	**30**
1986-87	**Calgary**	**NHL**	**58**	**14**	**12**	**26**	**54**	**5**	**0**	**0**	**0**	**2**
1987-88d	**Calgary**	**NHL**	**60**	**10**	**13**	**23**	**57**	**9**	**3**	**1**	**4**	**6**
1988-89e	**Calgary**	**NHL**	**51**	**11**	**7**	**18**	**26**	**14**	**1**	**3**	**4**	**29**
	NHL Totals		**1111**	**500**	**506**	**1006**	**899**	**117**	**44**	**40**	**84**	**120**

a WHL First All-Star Team (1973)
b NHL Second All-Star Team (1977, 1983)
c Won Bill Masterton Memorial Trophy (1983)
d Won King Clancy Memorial Trophy (1988)
e Won Bud Man of the Year Award (1989)

Played in NHL All-Star Game (1977, 1978, 1983, 1984)

Traded to **Colorado** by **Toronto** with Joel Quenneville for Pat Hickey and Wilf Paiement, December 29, 1979. Traded to **Calgary** by **Colorado** with Colorado's fourth round choice (Mikko Makela — later transferred to NY Islanders) in 1983 Entry Draft for Bob MacMillan and Don Lever, November 25, 1981.

McDONOUGH, HUBIE

Center. Shoots left 5'9", 180 lbs. Born, Manchester, NH, July 8, 1963.

			Regular Season					Playoffs				
Season	Club	Lea	GP	G	A	TP	PIM	GP	G	A	TP	PIM
1986-87	Flint	IHL	82	27	52	79	59	6	3	2	5	0
1987-88	New Haven	AHL	78	30	29	59	43	....	....	....	....	....
1988-89	**Los Angeles**	**NHL**	**4**	**0**	**1**	**1**	**2**	....	....	....	....	....
	New Haven	AHL	74	37	55	92	41	17	10	21	31	6
	NHL Totals		**4**	**0**	**1**	**1**	**2**	....	....	....	....	....

Signed as a free agent by **Los Angeles**, April 18, 1988.

McEACHERN, SHAWN

Center. Shoots left. 6', 170 lbs. Born, Waltham, MA, February 28, 1969.
(Pittsburgh's 6th choice, 110th overall, in 1987 Entry Draft).

			Regular Season					Playoffs				
Season	Club	Lea	GP	G	A	TP	PIM	GP	G	A	TP	PIM
1985-86	Matignon	HS	20	32	20	52	....	....	....	....	....	....
1986 87	Matignon	HS	16	29	28	57	....	....	....	....	....	....
1987-88	Matignon	HS	....	52	40	92	....	....	....	....	....	....
1988-89	Boston U.	H.E.	36	20	28	48	32	....	....	....	....	....

McGEOUGH, PETER

Defense. Shoots left. 6'1", 190 lbs. Born, Watertown, NY, April 15, 1965.
(NY Islanders' 14th choice, 247th overall, in 1983 Entry Draft).

			Regular Season					Playoffs				
Season	Club	Lea	GP	G	A	TP	PIM	GP	G	A	TP	PIM
1984-85	St. Lawrence	ECAC	32	1	8	9	70	....	....	....	....	....
1985-86	St. Lawrence	ECAC	27	9	8	17	83	....	....	....	....	....
1986-87	St. Lawrence	ECAC	30	7	14	21	90	....	....	....	....	....
1987-88	St. Lawrence	ECAC	34	2	23	25	66	....	....	....	....	....
1988-89	Springfield	AHL	2	0	0	0	0	....	....	....	....	....

McGILL, ROBERT PAUL (BOB)

Defense. Shoot right. 6', 190 lbs. Born, Edmonton, Alta., April 27, 1962.
(Toronto's 2nd choice, 26th over-all, in 1980 Entry Draft).

			Regular Season					Playoffs				
Season	Club	Lea	GP	G	A	TP	PIM	GP	G	A	TP	PIM
1979-80	Victoria	WHL	70	3	18	21	230	15	0	5	5	64
1980-81	Victoria	WHL	66	5	36	41	295	11	1	5	6	67
1981-82	**Toronto**	**NHL**	**68**	**1**	**10**	**11**	**263**	....	....	....	....	....
1982-83	**Toronto**	**NHL**	**30**	**0**	**0**	**0**	**146**	....	....	....	....	....
	St. Catharines	AHL	32	2	5	7	95	....	....	....	....	....
1983-84	**Toronto**	**NHL**	**11**	**0**	**2**	**2**	**51**	....	....	....	....	....
	St. Catharines	AHL	55	1	15	16	217	6	0	0	0	26
1984-85	**Toronto**	**NHL**	**72**	**0**	**5**	**5**	**250**	....	....	....	....	....
1985-86	**Toronto**	**NHL**	**61**	**1**	**4**	**5**	**141**	**9**	**0**	**0**	**0**	**35**
1986-87	**Toronto**	**NHL**	**56**	**1**	**4**	**5**	**103**	**3**	**0**	**0**	**0**	**0**
1987-88	**Chicago**	**NHL**	**67**	**4**	**7**	**11**	**131**	**3**	**0**	**0**	**0**	**2**
1988-89	**Chicago**	**NHL**	**68**	**0**	**4**	**4**	**155**	**16**	**0**	**0**	**0**	**33**
	NHL Totals		**433**	**7**	**36**	**43**	**1240**	**31**	**0**	**0**	**0**	**70**

Traded to **Chicago** by **Toronto** with Steve Thomas and Rick Vaive for Al Secord and Ed Olczyk, September 3, 1987.

McGILL, RYAN

Defense. Shoots right. 6'2", 195 lbs. Born, Sherwood Park, Alta., February 28, 1969.
(Chicago's 2nd choice, 29th overall, in 1987 Entry Draft).

			Regular Season					Playoffs				
Season	Club	Lea	GP	G	A	TP	PIM	GP	G	A	TP	PIM
1985-86	Lethbridge	WHL	64	5	10	15	171	10	0	1	1	9
1986-87	Swift Current	WHL	72	12	36	48	226	4	1	0	1	9
1987-88	Medicine Hat	WHL	67	5	30	35	224	15	7	3	10	47
1988-89	Saginaw	IHL	8	2	0	2	12	6	0	0	0	42
	Medicine Hat	WHL	57	26	45	71	172	3	0	2	2	15

McHUGH, MICHAEL (MIKE)

Left wing. Shoots left. 5'10", 190 lbs. Born, Bowdoin, ME, August 16, 1965.
(Minnesota's 1st choice, 1st overall, in 1988 Supplemental Draft).

			Regular Season					Playoffs				
Season	Club	Lea	GP	G	A	TP	PIM	GP	G	A	TP	PIM
1984-85	U. of Maine	H.E.	25	9	8	17	9	....	....	....	....	....
1985-86	U. of Maine	H.E.	38	9	10	19	24	....	....	....	....	....
1986-87	U. of Maine	H.E.	42	21	29	50	40	....	....	....	....	....
1987-88	U. of Maine	H.E.	44	29	37	66	90	....	....	....	....	....
1988-89	**Minnesota**	**NHL**	**3**	**0**	**0**	**0**	**2**	....	....	....	....	....
	Kalamazoo	IHL	70	17	29	46	89	6	3	1	4	17
	NHL Totals		**3**	**0**	**0**	**0**	**2**	....	....	....	....	....

McINNIS, MARTY

Center. Shoots right. 5'10", 165 lbs. Born, Hingman, MA, June 2, 1970.
(NY Islanders' 10th choice, 163rd overall, in 1988 Entry Draft).

			Regular Season					Playoffs				
Season	Club	Lea	GP	G	A	TP	PIM	GP	G	A	TP	PIM
1987-88	Milton Aca.	HS	....	26	25	51	....	....	....	....	....	....
1988-89	Boston College	H.E.	39	13	19	32	8	....	....	....	....	....

McINTYRE, JOHN

Center. Shoots left. 6'1", 175 lbs. Born, Ravenswood, Ont., April 29, 1969.
(Toronto's 3rd choice, 49th overall, in 1987 Entry Draft).

			Regular Season					Playoffs				
Season	Club	Lea	GP	G	A	TP	PIM	GP	G	A	TP	PIM
1985-86	Guelph	OHL	30	4	6	10	25	20	1	5	6	31
1986-87	Guelph	OHL	47	8	22	30	95	....	....	....	....	....
1987-88	Guelph	OHL	39	24	18	42	109	....	....	....	....	....
1988-89	Newmarket	AHL	3	0	2	2	7	5	1	1	2	20
	Guelph	OHL	52	30	26	56	129	7	5	4	9	25

McKAY, RANDY

Right wing. Shoots right. 6'1", 185 lbs. Born, Montreal, Que., January 25, 1967.
(Detroit's 6th choice, 113th overall, in 1985 Entry Draft).

			Regular Season					Playoffs				
Season	Club	Lea	GP	G	A	TP	PIM	GP	G	A	TP	PIM
1984-85	Michigan Tech	WCHA	25	4	5	9	32	....	....	....	....	....
1985-86	Michigan Tech	WCHA	40	12	22	34	46	....	....	....	....	....
1986-87	Michigan Tech	WCHA	39	5	11	16	46	....	....	....	....	....
1987-88	Michigan Tech	WCHA	41	17	24	41	70	....	....	....	....	....
	Adirondack	AHL	10	0	3	3	12	6	0	4	4	0
1988-89	**Detroit**	**NHL**	**3**	**0**	**0**	**0**	**0**	**2**	**0**	**0**	**0**	**2**
	Adirondack	AHL	58	29	34	63	170	14	4	7	11	60
	NHL Totals		**3**	**0**	**0**	**0**	**0**	**2**	**0**	**0**	**0**	**2**

McKEE, BRIAN

Defense. Shoots left. 5'11", 185 lbs. Born, Willowdale, Ont., December 13, 1964.
(Minnesota's 1st choice, 17th overall, in 1986 Supplemental Draft).

			Regular Season					Playoffs				
Season	Club	Lea	GP	G	A	TP	PIM	GP	G	A	TP	PIM
1984-85	Bowling Green	CCHA	25	3	15	18	62	....	....	....	....	....
1985-86a	Bowling Green	CCHA	42	19	33	52	120	....	....	....	....	....
1986-87a	Bowling Green	CCHA	40	18	31	49	93	....	....	....	....	....
	Indianapolis	IHL	4	0	2	2	4	....	....	....	....	....
1987-88	Saginaw	IHL	18	2	8	10	10	....	....	....	....	....
	Flint	IHL	11	1	6	7	2	....	....	....	....	....
	Milwaukee	IHL	6	1	4	5	2	....	....	....	....	....
1988-89	Fort Wayne	IHL	47	8	22	30	42	11	3	5	8	17

a CCHA Second All-Star Team (1986, 1987)

McKEGNEY, ANTHONY SYIIYD (TONY) (ma-KEG-nee)

Left wing. Shoots left. 6'1", 200 lbs. Born, Montreal, Que., February 15, 1958.
(Buffalo's 2nd choice, 32nd over-all, in 1978 Amateur Draft).

			Regular Season					Playoffs				
Season	Club	Lea	GP	G	A	TP	PIM	GP	G	A	TP	PIM
1976-77a	Kingston	OHA	66	58	77	135	30	14	13	10	23	14
1977-78b	Kingston	OHA	55	43	49	92	19	5	3	3	6	0
1978-79	Hershey	AHL	24	21	18	39	4	1	0	0	0	0
	Buffalo	**NHL**	**52**	**8**	**14**	**22**	**10**	**2**	**0**	**1**	**1**	**0**
1979-80	**Buffalo**	**NHL**	**80**	**23**	**29**	**52**	**24**	**14**	**3**	**4**	**7**	**2**
1980-81	**Buffalo**	**NHL**	**80**	**37**	**32**	**69**	**24**	**8**	**5**	**3**	**8**	**2**
1981-82	**Buffalo**	**NHL**	**73**	**23**	**29**	**52**	**41**	**4**	**0**	**0**	**0**	**2**
1982-83	**Buffalo**	**NHL**	**78**	**36**	**37**	**73**	**18**	**10**	**3**	**1**	**4**	**4**
1983-84	**Quebec**	**NHL**	**75**	**24**	**27**	**51**	**23**	**7**	**0**	**0**	**0**	**0**
1984-85	**Quebec**	**NHL**	**30**	**12**	**9**	**21**	**12**	....	....	....	....	....
	Minnesota	**NHL**	**27**	**11**	**13**	**24**	**4**	**9**	**8**	**6**	**14**	**0**
1985-86	**Minnesota**	**NHL**	**70**	**15**	**25**	**40**	**48**	**5**	**2**	**1**	**3**	**22**
1986-87	**Minnesota**	**NHL**	**11**	**2**	**3**	**5**	**16**	....	....	....	....	....
	NY Rangers	**NHL**	**64**	**29**	**17**	**46**	**56**	**6**	**0**	**0**	**0**	**12**
1987-88	**St. Louis**	**NHL**	**80**	**40**	**38**	**78**	**82**	**9**	**3**	**6**	**9**	**8**
1988-89	**St. Louis**	**NHL**	**71**	**25**	**17**	**42**	**58**	**3**	**0**	**1**	**1**	**0**
	NHL Totals		**791**	**285**	**290**	**575**	**416**	**77**	**24**	**23**	**47**	**52**

a OHA First All-Star Team (1977).
b OHA Second All-Star Team (1978).

Traded to **Quebec** by **Buffalo** with Andre Savard, J.F. Sauve and Buffalo's third round choice (Iirvo Jarvi) in 1983 Entry Draft for Real Cloutier and Quebec's first round choice (Adam Creighton) in 1983 Entry Draft, June 8, 1983. Traded to **Minnesota** by **Quebec** with Bo Berglund for Brent Ashton and Brad Maxwell, December 14, 1984. Traded to **NY Rangers** by **Minnesota** with Curt Giles and Minnesota's second-round (Troy Mallette) choice in 1988 Entry Draft for Bob Brooke and NY Rangers' rights to Minnesota's fourth-round choice (Jeffery Stolp) in 1988 Entry Draft previously acquired by NY Rangers in Mark Pavelich deal, November 13, 1986. Traded to **St. Louis** by **NY Rangers** with Rob Whistle for Bruce Bell and future considerations, May 28, 1987. Traded to **Detroit** by **St. Louis**, with Bernie Federko for Adam Oates and Paul MacLean, June 15, 1989.

McKENNA, SEAN MICHAEL

Right wing. Shoots right. 6', 190 lbs. Born, Asbestos, Que., March 7, 1962.
(Buffalo's 3rd choice, 56th over-all, in 1980 Entry Draft).

			Regular Season					Playoffs				
Season	Club	Lea	GP	G	A	TP	PIM	GP	G	A	TP	PIM
1980-81a	Sherbrooke	QJHL	71	57	47	104	122	14	9	9	18	12
1981-82	**Buffalo**	**NHL**	**3**	**0**	**1**	**1**	**2**	....	....	....	....	....
bc	Sherbrooke	QJHL	59	57	33	90	29	22	26	18	44	28
1982-83	**Buffalo**	**NHL**	**46**	**10**	**14**	**24**	**4**	....	....	....	....	....
	Rochester	AHL	26	16	10	26	14	16	14	8	22	18
1983-84	**Buffalo**	**NHL**	**78**	**20**	**10**	**30**	**45**	**3**	**1**	**0**	**1**	**2**
1984-85	**Buffalo**	**NHL**	**65**	**20**	**16**	**36**	**41**	**5**	**0**	**1**	**1**	**0**
1985-86	**Buffalo**	**NHL**	**45**	**6**	**12**	**18**	**28**	....	....	....	....	....
	Los Angeles	**NHL**	**30**	**4**	**0**	**4**	**7**	....	....	....	....	....
1986-87	**Los Angeles**	**NHL**	**69**	**14**	**19**	**33**	**10**	**5**	**0**	**1**	**1**	**0**
1987-88	**Los Angeles**	**NHL**	**30**	**3**	**2**	**5**	**12**	....	....	....	....	....
	Toronto	**NHL**	**40**	**5**	**5**	**10**	**12**	**2**	**0**	**0**	**0**	**0**
1988-89	**Toronto**	**NHL**	**3**	**0**	**1**	**1**	**0**	....	....	....	....	....
	Newmarket	AHL	61	14	27	41	35	5	1	1	2	4
	NHL Totals		**406**	**82**	**80**	**162**	**161**	**15**	**1**	**2**	**3**	**2**

a QMJHL First All-Star Team (1981)
b QMJHL Second All-Star Team (1982)
c Named Most Valuable Player, 1982 Memorial Cup

Traded to **Los Angeles** by **Buffalo** with Larry Playfair and Ken Baumgartner for Brian Engblom and Doug Smith, January 30, 1986. Traded to **Toronto** by **Los Angeles** for Mike Allison, December 14, 1987.

McKINLEY, JAMIE

Right wing. Shoots right. 6'2", 180 lbs. Born, Moncton, N.B., May 1, 1967.
(New Jersey's 10th choice, 192nd overall, in 1985 Entry Draft).

			Regular Season					Playoffs				
Season	Club	Lea	GP	G	A	TP	PIM	GP	G	A	TP	PIM
1984-85	Guelph	OHL	62	25	23	48	9	....	....	....	....	....
1985-86	Guelph	OHL	66	23	29	52	48	20	9	15	24	12
1986-87	Guelph	OHL	57	23	50	73	109	5	2	3	5	0
1987-88	Guelph	OHL	47	29	28	57	39	....	....	....	....	....
1988-89	Indianapolis	IHL	4	0	0	0	5	....	....	....	....	....

McLAUGHLIN, MICHAEL

Left wing. Shoots right. 6'1", 175 lbs. Born, Longmeadow, MA, March 29, 1970.
(Buffalo's 7th choice, 118th overall, in 1988 Entry Draft).

			Regular Season					Playoffs				
Season	Club	Lea	GP	G	A	TP	PIM	GP	G	A	TP	PIM
1987-88	Choate	HS	18	17	18	35	....	....	....	....	....	....
1988-89	U. of Vermont	ECAC	32	5	6	11	12	....	....	....	....	....

McLAY, DAVID

Left wing. Shoots left. 5'11", 175 lbs. Born, Chilliwack, B.C., May 13, 1966.
(Philadelphia's 4th choice, 43th over-all, in 1984 Entry Draft).

			Regular Season					Playoffs				
Season	Club	Lea	GP	G	A	TP	PIM	GP	G	A	TP	PIM
1983-84	Kelowna	WHL	71	34	34	68	112	....	....	....	....	....
1984-85	Portland	WHL	70	32	36	68	220	6	3	2	5	12
1985-86	Portland	WHL	70	37	49	86	219	15	6	3	9	30
1986-87	Hershey	AHL	7	1	2	3	15	....	....	....	....	....
	Portland	WHL	57	35	42	77	151	18	9	15	24	51
1987-88	Hershey	AHL	37	1	7	8	60	....	....	....	....	....
	Flint	IHL	26	2	10	12	45	....	....	....	....	....
1988-89	Cdn. National	....	4	2	0	2	4	....	....	....	....	....

McLEAN, JOHN

Defense. Shoots right. 6'1", 200 lbs. Born, Wakefield, MA, April 29, 1965.

			Regular Season					Playoffs				
Season	Club	Lea	GP	G	A	TP	PIM	GP	G	A	TP	PIM
1983-84	Boston College	H.E.	16	1	4	5	4	....	....	....	....	....
1984-85	Boston College	H.E.	23	2	7	9	18	....	....	....	....	....
1985-86	Boston College	H.E.	41	5	13	18	20	....	....	....	....	....
1986-87	Boston College	H.E.	37	1	16	17	44	....	....	....	....	....
1987-88	Milwaukee	IHL	20	1	6	7	27	....	....	....	....	....
	Binghamton	AHL	39	0	11	11	32	....	....	....	....	....
1988-89	Maine	AHL	6	0	0	0	0	....	....	....	....	....

Signed as a free agent by **Hartford**, July 20, 1987.

McLELLAN, TODD

Center. Shoots left. 5'11", 185 lbs. Born, Melville, Sask., October 3, 1967.
(NY Islanders' 6th choice, 104th overall, in 1986 Entry Draft).

			Regular Season					Playoffs				
Season	Club	Lea	GP	G	A	TP	PIM	GP	G	A	TP	PIM
1984-85	Saskatoon	WHL	41	15	35	50	33	3	1	0	1	0
1985-86	Saskatoon	WHL	27	9	10	19	13	13	9	3	12	8
1986-87	Saskatoon	WHL	60	34	39	73	66	6	1	1	2	2
1987-88	**NY Islanders**	**NHL**	**5**	**1**	**1**	**2**	**0**	....	....	....	....	....
	Springfield	AHL	70	18	26	44	32	....	....	....	....	....
1988-89	Springfield	AHL	37	7	19	26	17	....	....	....	....	....
	NHL Totals		**5**	**1**	**1**	**2**	**0**	....	....	....	....	....

McLENNAN, DONALD (DON)

Defense. Shoots left. 6'3", 210 lbs. Born, Winnipeg, Man., October 4, 1968.
(Winnipeg's 3rd choice, 79th overall, in 1987 Entry Draft).

			Regular Season					Playoffs				
Season	Club	Lea	GP	G	A	TP	PIM	GP	G	A	TP	PIM
1986-87	U. of Denver	WCHA	35	2	2	4	38	....	....	....	....	....
1987-88	U. of Denver	WCHA	29	0	3	3	24	....	....	....	....	....
1988-89	U. of Denver	WCHA	26	1	3	4	28	....	....	....	....	....

McLLWAIN, DAVE

Right wing. Shoots right. 6', 190 lbs. Born, Seaforth, Ont., June 9, 1967.
(Pittsburgh's 9th choice, 172nd overall, in 1986 Entry Draft).

			Regular Season					Playoffs				
Season	Club	Lea	GP	G	A	TP	PIM	GP	G	A	TP	PIM
1985-86	North Bay	OHL	64	37	35	72	37	10	4	4	8	2
1986-87a	North Bay	OHL	60	46	73	119	35	24	7	18	25	40
1987-88	**Pittsburgh**	**NHL**	**66**	**11**	**8**	**19**	**40**	....	....	....	....	....
1988-89	**Pittsburgh**	**NHL**	**24**	**1**	**2**	**3**	**4**	**3**	**0**	**1**	**1**	**0**
	Muskegon	IHL	46	37	35	72	51	7	8	2	10	6
	NHL Totals		**90**	**12**	**10**	**22**	**44**	**3**	**0**	**1**	**1**	**0**

a OHL Second Team All-Star (1987)

Traded to **Winnipeg** by **Pittsburgh** with Randy Cunnyworth and Rick Tabaracci for Jim Kyte, Andrew McBain and Randy Gilhen, June 17, 1989.

McMURCHY, THOMAS (TOM) (mik-MUR-chee)

Right wing. Shoots left. 5'9", 165 lbs. Born, New Westminster, B.C., December 2, 1963.
(Chicago's 3rd choice, 49th over-all, in 1982 Entry Draft).

			Regular Season					Playoffs				
Season	Club	Lea	GP	G	A	TP	PIM	GP	G	A	TP	PIM
1980-81	Medicine Hat	WHL	14	5	0	5	46	....	....	....	....	....
	Brandon	WHL	46	20	33	53	101	5	2	2	4	4
1981-82	Brandon	WHL	68	59	63	122	179	4	7	3	10	4
1982-83	Brandon	WHL	42	43	38	81	48	....	....	....	....	....
	Springfield	AHL	8	2	2	4	0	....	....	....	....	....
1983-84	**Chicago**	**NHL**	**27**	**3**	**1**	**4**	**42**	....	....	....	....	....
	Springfield	AHL	43	16	14	30	54	4	4	0	4	0
1984-85	**Chicago**	**NHL**	**15**	**1**	**2**	**3**	**13**	....	....	....	....	....
	Milwaukee	IHL	69	30	26	56	61	....	....	....	....	....
1985-86	**Chicago**	**NHL**	**4**	**0**	**0**	**0**	**2**	....	....	....	....	....
	Nova Scotia	AHL	49	26	21	47	73	....	....	....	....	....
	Moncton	AHL	16	7	3	10	27	2	0	1	1	6
1986-87	Nova Scotia	AHL	67	21	35	56	99	4	3	2	5	4
1987-88	**Edmonton**	**NHL**	**9**	**4**	**1**	**5**	**8**	....	....	....	....	....
	Nova Scotia	AHL	61	40	21	61	132	3	2	1	3	4
1988-89	Halifax	AHL	11	10	3	13	18	3	0	2	2	2
	NHL Totals		**55**	**8**	**4**	**12**	**65**	....	....	....	....	....

Traded to **Calgary** by **Chicago** for Rik Wilson, March 11, 1986. Signed as a free agent by **Edmonton,** August 18, 1986.

McNEIL, MICHAEL

Center. Shoots right. 6'1", 175 lbs. Born, Winona, MN, July 22, 1966.
(St. Louis' 1st choice, 14th overall, in 1988 Supplemental Draft).

			Regular Season					Playoffs				
Season	Club	Lea	GP	G	A	TP	PIM	GP	G	A	TP	PIM
1984-85	Notre Dame	ACHA	28	16	26	42	12	....	....	....	....	....
1985-86	Notre Dame	ACHA	34	18	29	47	32	....	....	....	....	....
1986-87	Notre Dame	ACHA	30	21	16	37	24	....	....	....	....	....
1987-88	Notre Dame	ACHA	32	28	44	72	12	....	....	....	....	....
1988-89	Moncton	AHL	1	0	0	0	0	....	....	....	....	....
	Fort Wayne	IHL	75	27	35	62	12	11	1	5	6	2

McPHEE, GEORGE

Left wing. Shoots left. 5'9", 170 lbs. Born, Guelph, Ont., July 2, 1958.

			Regular Season					Playoffs				
Season	Club	Lea	GP	G	A	TP	PIM	GP	G	A	TP	PIM
1978-79ab	Bowling Green	CCHA	43	*40	48	*88	58	....	....	....	....	....
1979-80	Bowling Green	CCHA	34	21	24	45	51	....	....	....	....	....
1980-81b	Bowling Green	CCHA	36	25	29	54	68	....	....	....	....	....
1981-82cde	Bowling Green	CCHA	40	28	52	80	57	....	....	....	....	....
1982-83	Tulsa	CHL	61	17	43	60	145	7	1	1	2	14
	NY Rangers	**NHL**	....	....	....	....	....	**9**	**3**	**3**	**6**	**2**
1983-84	**NY Rangers**	**NHL**	**9**	**1**	**1**	**2**	**11**	....	....	....	....	....
	Tulsa	CHL	49	20	28	48	133	....	....	....	....	....
1984-85	**NY Rangers**	**NHL**	**49**	**12**	**15**	**27**	**139**	**3**	**1**	**0**	**1**	**7**
	New Haven	AHL	3	2	2	4	13	....	....	....	....	....
1985-86	**NY Rangers**	**NHL**	**30**	**4**	**4**	**8**	**63**	**11**	**0**	**0**	**0**	**32**
1986-87	**NY Rangers**	**NHL**	**21**	**4**	**4**	**8**	**34**	**6**	**1**	**0**	**1**	**28**
1987-88	**New Jersey**	**NHL**	**5**	**3**	**0**	**3**	**8**	....	....	....	....	....
1988-89	**New Jersey**	**NHL**	**1**	**0**	**1**	**1**	**2**	....	....	....	....	....
	Utica	AHL	8	3	2	5	31	3	1	0	1	26
	NHL Totals		**115**	**24**	**25**	**49**	**257**	**29**	**5**	**3**	**8**	**69**

a CCHA Rookie of the Year (1979)
b CCHA Second All-Star Team (1979, 1980)
c CCHA First All-Star Team (1982)
d CCHA Player of the Year (1982)
e Winner of the 1982 Hobey Baker Memorial Trophy (Top U.S. College Player).

Signed as a free agent by **NY Rangers,** July 1, 1982. Traded to **Winnipeg** by **NY Rangers** for Winnipeg's fourth round choice (Jim Cummins) in 1989 Entry Draft, September 30, 1987. Traded to **New Jersey** by **Winnipeg** for New Jersey's fourth round choice in 1989 Entry Draft, October 7, 1987.

McPHEE, MICHAEL JOSEPH (MIKE)

Left wing. Shoots left. 6'1", 200 lbs. Born, Rivière Bourgeois, N.S., July 14, 1960.
(Montreal's 8th choice, 124th over-all, in 1980 Entry Draft).

			Regular Season					Playoffs				
Season	Club	Lea	GP	G	A	TP	PIM	GP	G	A	TP	PIM
1980-81	RPI	ECAC	29	28	18	46	22	....	....	....	....	....
1981-82	RPI	ECAC	6	0	3	3	4	....	....	....	....	....
1982-83	Nova Scotia	AHL	42	10	15	25	29	7	1	1	2	14
1983-84	Nova Scotia	AHL	67	22	33	55	101	....	....	....	....	....
	Montreal	**NHL**	**14**	**5**	**2**	**7**	**41**	**15**	**1**	**0**	**1**	**31**
1984-85	**Montreal**	**NHL**	**70**	**17**	**22**	**39**	**120**	**12**	**4**	**1**	**5**	**32**
1985-86	**Montreal**	**NHL**	**70**	**19**	**21**	**40**	**69**	**20**	**3**	**4**	**7**	**45**
1986-87	**Montreal**	**NHL**	**79**	**18**	**21**	**39**	**58**	**17**	**7**	**2**	**9**	**13**
1987-88	**Montreal**	**NHL**	**77**	**23**	**20**	**43**	**53**	**11**	**4**	**3**	**7**	**8**
1988-89	**Montreal**	**NHL**	**73**	**19**	**22**	**41**	**74**	**20**	**4**	**7**	**11**	**30**
	NHL Totals		**383**	**101**	**108**	**209**	**415**	**95**	**23**	**17**	**40**	**159**

Played in NHL All-Star Game (1989)

McPHERSON, DARWIN

Defense. Shoots left. 6'1", 195 lbs. Born, Flin Flon, Man., May 16, 1968.
(Boston's 4th choice, 67th overall, in 1987 Entry Draft).

			Regular Season					Playoffs				
Season	Club	Lea	GP	G	A	TP	PIM	GP	G	A	TP	PIM
1984-85	Brandon	WHL	39	2	0	2	36	....	....	....	....	....
1985-86	N. Westminster	WHL	63	2	8	10	149	....	....	....	....	....
1986-87	N. Westminster	WHL	65	10	22	32	242	....	....	....	....	....
1987-88	N. Westminster	WHL	47	1	17	18	192	5	0	0	0	16
1988-89	Saskatoon	WHL	59	4	13	17	256	8	0	1	1	27

Signed as a free agent by **St. Louis,** August 4, 1989.

McRAE, BASIL PAUL

Left wing. Shoots left. 6'2", 205 lbs. Born, Beaverton, Ont., January 5, 1961.
(Quebec's 3rd choice, 87th over-all, in 1980 Entry Draft).

			Regular Season					Playoffs				
Season	Club	Lea	GP	G	A	TP	PIM	GP	G	A	TP	PIM
1979-80	London	OHA	67	24	36	60	116	5	0	0	0	18
1980-81	London	OHA	65	29	23	52	266	....	....	....	....	....
1981-82	Fredericton	AHL	47	11	15	26	175	....	....	....	....	....
	Quebec	**NHL**	**20**	**4**	**3**	**7**	**69**	**9**	**1**	**0**	**1**	**34**
1982-83	**Quebec**	**NHL**	**22**	**1**	**1**	**2**	**59**	....	....	....	....	....
	Fredericton	AHL	53	22	19	41	146	12	1	5	6	75
1983-84	**Toronto**	**NHL**	**3**	**0**	**0**	**0**	**19**	....	....	....	....	....
	St. Catharines	AHL	78	14	25	39	187	6	0	0	0	40
1984-85	**Toronto**	**NHL**	**1**	**0**	**0**	**0**	**0**	....	....	....	....	....
	St. Catharines	AHL	72	30	25	55	186	....	....	....	....	....
1985-86	**Detroit**	**NHL**	**4**	**0**	**0**	**0**	**5**	....	....	....	....	....
	Adirondack	AHL	69	22	30	52	259	17	5	4	9	101
1986-87	**Detroit**	**NHL**	**36**	**2**	**2**	**4**	**193**	....	....	....	....	....
	Quebec	**NHL**	**33**	**9**	**5**	**14**	**149**	**13**	**3**	**1**	**4**	**99**
1987-88	**Minnesota**	**NHL**	**80**	**5**	**11**	**16**	**382**	....	....	....	....	....
1988-89	**Minnesota**	**NHL**	**78**	**12**	**19**	**31**	**365**	**5**	**0**	**0**	**0**	**58**
	NHL Totals		**277**	**33**	**41**	**74**	**1241**	**27**	**4**	**1**	**5**	**191**

Traded to **Toronto** by **Quebec** for Richard Turmel, August 12, 1983. Signed as a free agent by **Detroit,** July 17, 1985. Traded to **Quebec** by **Detroit** with John Ogrodnick and Doug Shedden for Brent Ashton, Gilbert Delorme and Mark Kumpel, January 17, 1987. Signed as a free agent by **Minnesota,** June 29, 1987.

McRAE, CHRIS

Left wing. Shoots left. 6', 180 lbs. Born, Newmarket, Ont., August 26, 1965.

			Regular Season					Playoffs				
Season	Club	Lea	GP	G	A	TP	PIM	GP	G	A	TP	PIM
1983-84	Sudbury	OHL	62	14	31	45	139	....	....	....	....	....
1984-85	Oshawa	OHL	49	8	9	17	128	5	0	1	1	2
	St. Catharines	AHL	6	4	3	7	24	....	....	....	....	....
1985-86	St. Catharines	AHL	59	1	1	2	233	11	0	1	1	65
1986-87	Newmarket	AHL	51	3	6	9	193	....	....	....	....	....
1987-88	**Toronto**	**NHL**	**11**	**0**	**0**	**0**	**65**	....	....	....	....	....
	Newmarket	AHL	34	7	6	13	165	....	....	....	....	....
1988-89	**Toronto**	**NHL**	**3**	**0**	**0**	**0**	**12**	....	....	....	....	....
	Newmarket	AHL	18	3	1	4	85	....	....	....	....	....
	Denver	IHL	23	1	4	5	121	2	0	0	0	20
	NHL Totals		**14**	**0**	**0**	**0**	**77**	....	....	....	....	....

Signed as a free agent by **Toronto,** October 16, 1985. Traded to **NY Rangers** by **Toronto** for Ken Hammond, February 21, 1989.

McRAE, KEN

Center. Shoots right. 6'1", 195 lbs. Born, Winchester, Ont., April 23, 1968.
(Quebec's 1st choice, 18th overall, in 1986 Entry Draft).

			Regular Season					Playoffs				
Season	Club	Lea	GP	G	A	TP	PIM	GP	G	A	TP	PIM
1985-86	Sudbury	OHL	66	25	49	74	127	4	2	1	3	12
1986-87	Sudbury	OHL	21	12	15	27	40	....	....	....	....	....
	Hamilton	OHL	20	7	12	19	25	7	1	1	2	12
1987-88	**Quebec**	**NHL**	**1**	**0**	**0**	**0**	**0**	....	....	....	....	....
	Fredericton	AHL	....	....	....	....	....	3	0	0	0	8
	Hamilton	OHL	62	30	55	85	158	14	13	9	22	35
1988-89	**Quebec**	**NHL**	**37**	**6**	**11**	**17**	**68**	....	....	....	....	....
	Halifax	AHL	41	20	21	41	87	....	....	....	....	....
	NHL Totals		**38**	**6**	**11**	**17**	**68**	....	....	....	....	....

McREYNOLDS, BRIAN

Center. Shoots left. 6'1", 180 lbs. Born, Penetanguishene, Ont., January 5, 1965.
(NY Rangers' 6th choice, 112th overall, in 1985 Entry Draft).

			Regular Season					Playoffs				
Season	Club	Lea	GP	G	A	TP	PIM	GP	G	A	TP	PIM
1985-86	Michigan State	CCHA	45	14	24	38	78	....	....	....	....	....
1986-87	Michigan State	CCHA	45	16	24	40	68	....	....	....	....	....
1987-88	Michigan State	CCHA	43	10	24	34	50	....	....	....	....	....
1988-89	Cdn. National	....	58	5	25	30	59	....	....	....	....	....

McSORLEY, CHRISTOPHER

Center. Shoots right. 5'11", 185 lbs. Born, Hamilton, Ont., March 22, 1962.

			Regular Season					Playoffs				
Season	Club	Lea	GP	G	A	TP	PIM	GP	G	A	TP	PIM
1984-85	Toledo	IHL	51	15	14	29	285	....	....	....	....	....
1985-86	Toledo	IHL	75	27	28	55	546	....	....	....	....	....
1986-87	New Haven	AHL	22	2	2	4	116	....	....	....	....	....
	Muskegon	IHL	47	18	17	35	293	15	1	3	4	87
1987-88	New Haven	AHL	44	10	9	19	186	....	....	....	....	....
	Flint	IHL	30	5	10	15	222	16	1	7	8	109
1988-89	Springfield	AHL	26	5	8	13	119	....	....	....	....	....
	Indianapolis	IHL	39	2	4	6	222	....	....	....	....	....

Signed as free agent by **Los Angeles,** May 9, 1986.

McSORLEY, MARTIN J. (MARTY)

Defense. Shoots right. 6'2", 220 lbs.   Born, Hamilton, Ont., May 18, 1963.

			Regular Season					Playoffs				
Season	Club	Lea	GP	G	A	TP	PIM	GP	G	A	TP	PIM
1981-82	Belleville	OHL	58	6	13	19	234	....	....	....	....	....
1982-83	Belleville	OHL	70	10	41	51	183	4	0	0	0	7
	Baltimore	AHL	2	0	0	0	22	....	....	....	....	....
1983-84	**Pittsburgh**	**NHL**	72	2	7	9	224	....	....	....	....	....
1984-85	**Pittsburgh**	**NHL**	15	0	0	0	15	....	....	....	....	....
	Baltimore	AHL	58	6	24	30	154	14	0	7	7	47
1985-86	**Edmonton**	**NHL**	59	11	12	23	265	8	0	2	2	50
	Nova Scotia	AHL	9	2	4	6	34	....	....	....	....	....
1986-87	**Edmonton**	**NHL**	41	2	4	6	159	21	4	3	7	65
	Nova Scotia	AHL	7	2	2	4	48	....	....	....	....	....
1987-88	**Edmonton**	**NHL**	60	9	17	26	223	16	0	3	3	67
1988-89	**Los Angeles**	**NHL**	66	10	17	27	350	11	0	2	2	33
	NHL Totals		313	34	57	91	1236	56	4	10	14	215

Signed as free agent by **Pittsburgh**, July 30, 1982. Traded to **Edmonton** by **Pittsburgh** with Tim Hrynewich for Gilles Meloche, September, 12, 1985. Traded to **Los Angeles** by **Edmonton** with Wayne Gretzky and Mike Krushelnyski for Jimmy Carson, Martin Gelinas, Los Angeles' first round choices in 1989 (acquired by New Jersey, June 17, 1989. New Jersey selected Jason Miller), 1991 and 1993 Entry Drafts and cash, August 9, 1988.

McSWEEN, DON

Defense; Shoots left. 5'10", 190 lbs.   Born, Detroit, MI, June 9, 1964.
(Buffalo's 10th choice, 154th overall, in 1983 Entry Draft).

			Regular Season					Playoffs				
Season	Club	Lea	GP	G	A	TP	PIM	GP	G	A	TP	PIM
1983-84	Michigan State	CCHA	46	10	26	36	30	....	....	....	....	....
1984-85	Michigan State	CCHA	44	2	23	25	52	....	....	....	....	....
1985-86a	Michigan State	CCHA	45	9	29	38	18	....	....	....	....	....
1986-87abc	Michigan State	CCHA	45	7	23	30	34	....	....	....	....	....
1987-88	**Buffalo**	**NHL**	5	0	1	1	6	....	....	....	....	....
	Rochester	AHL	63	9	29	38	108	6	0	1	1	15
1988-89	Rochester	AHL	66	7	22	29	45	....	....	....	....	....
	NHL Totals		5	0	1	1	6	....	....	....	....	....

a CCHA First All-Star Team (1986, 1987)
b NCAA West Second All-American Team (1987)
c Named to NCAA All-Tournament Team (1987)

MEAGHER, RICHARD (RICK)   (muh-HAHR)

Center. Shoots left. 5'8", 175 lbs.   Born, Belleville, Ont., November 4, 1953.

			Regular Season					Playoffs				
Season	Club	Lea	GP	G	A	TP	PIM	GP	G	A	TP	PIM
1975-76	Boston U.	ECAC	28	12	25	37	22	....	....	....	....	....
1976-77	Boston U.	ECAC	34	34	46	80	42	....	....	....	....	....
1977-78	Nova Scotia	AHL	57	20	27	47	33	11	5	3	8	11
1978-79	Nova Scotia	AHL	79	35	46	81	57	10	1	6	7	11
1979-80	**Montreal**	**NHL**	2	0	0	0	0	....	....	....	....	....
	Nova Scotia	AHL	64	32	44	76	53	6	3	4	7	2
1980-81	**Hartford**	**NHL**	27	7	10	17	19	....	....	....	....	....
	Binghamton	AHL	50	23	35	58	54	....	....	....	....	....
1981-82	**Hartford**	**NHL**	65	24	19	43	51	....	....	....	....	....
1982-83	**Hartford**	**NHL**	4	0	0	0	0	....	....	....	....	....
	New Jersey	**NHL**	57	15	14	29	11	....	....	....	....	....
1983-84	Maine	AHL	10	6	4	10	2	....	....	....	....	....
	New Jersey	**NHL**	52	14	14	28	16	....	....	....	....	....
1984-85	**New Jersey**	**NHL**	71	11	20	31	22	....	....	....	....	....
1985-86	**St. Louis**	**NHL**	79	11	19	30	28	19	4	4	8	12
1986-87	**St. Louis**	**NHL**	80	18	21	39	54	6	0	0	0	11
1987-88	**St. Louis**	**NHL**	76	18	16	34	76	10	0	0	0	8
1988-89	**St. Louis**	**NHL**	78	15	14	29	53	10	3	2	5	6
	NHL Totals		591	133	147	280	330	45	7	6	13	37

Signed as a free agent by **Montreal**, June 27, 1977. Traded to **Hartford** by **Montreal** with Montreal's third round (Paul MacDermid) and fifth round (Dan Bourbonnais) choices in 1981 Entry Draft for Hartford's third round (Dieter Hegen) and fifth round (Steve Rooney) choices in 1981 Entry Draft, June 5, 1980. Traded to **New Jersey** by **Hartford** with the rights to Garry Howatt for Merlin Malinowski and the rights to Scott Fusco, October 15, 1982. Traded to **St. Louis** by **New Jersey** with New Jersey's 12th round choice (Bill Butler) in 1986 Entry Draft for Perry Anderson, August 29, 1985.

MEASURES, ALLAN

Defense. Shoots left. 5'11", 165 lbs.   Born, Barrhead, Alta., May 8, 1965.
(Vancouver's 9th choice, 170th over-all, in 1983 Entry Draft).

			Regular Season					Playoffs				
Season	Club	Lea	GP	G	A	TP	PIM	GP	G	A	TP	PIM
1982-83	Calgary	WHL	63	5	23	28	43	16	0	5	5	12
1983-84	Calgary	WHL	69	17	36	53	96	4	3	4	7	0
1984-85	Calgary	WHL	65	25	58	83	84	8	2	4	6	11
1985-86	Calgary	WHL	46	23	34	57	50	....	....	....	....	....
1986-87	Fredericton	AHL	29	3	8	11	12	....	....	....	....	....
	Kalamazoo	IHL	37	11	15	26	26	5	1	1	2	0
1987-88	Lukko	Fin.	44	3	13	16	72	....	....	....	....	....
1988-89	Lukko	Fin.	43	3	26	29	46	....	....	....	....	....

MELLANBY, SCOTT

Right wing. Shoots right. 6'1", 206 lbs.   Born, Montreal, Que., June 11, 1966.
(Philadelphia's 2nd choice, 27th over-all, in 1984 Entry Draft).

			Regular Season					Playoffs				
Season	Club	Lea	GP	G	A	TP	PIM	GP	G	A	TP	PIM
1983-84	Henry Carr	HS	39	37	37	74	97	....	....	....	....	....
1984-85	U. Wisconsin	WCHA	40	14	24	38	60	....	....	....	....	....
1985-86	U. Wisconsin	WCHA	32	21	23	44	89	....	....	....	....	....
	Philadelphia	**NHL**	2	0	0	0	0	....	....	....	....	....
1986-87	**Philadelphia**	**NHL**	71	11	21	32	94	24	5	5	10	46
1987-88	**Philadelphia**	**NHL**	75	25	26	51	185	7	0	1	1	16
1988-89	**Philadelphia**	**NHL**	76	21	29	50	183	19	4	5	9	28
	NHL Totals		224	57	76	133	462	50	9	11	20	90

MELNYK, DOUGLAS

Defense. Shoots left. 5'10", 185 lbs.   Born, London, Ont., August 9, 1967.
(NY Islanders' 1st choice, 21st overall, in 1988 Supplemental Draft).

			Regular Season					Playoffs				
Season	Club	Lea	GP	G	A	TP	PIM	GP	G	A	TP	PIM
1986-87	W. Michigan	CCHA	43	2	7	9	40	....	....	....	....	....
1987-88	W. Michigan	CCHA	42	2	16	18	22	....	....	....	....	....
1988-89	W. Michigan	CCHA	30	2	4	6	28	....	....	....	....	....

MELNYK, LARRY JOSEPH   (MEHL-nihk)

Defense. Shoots left. 6', 195 lbs.   Born, Saskatoon, Sask., February 21, 1960.
(Boston's 5th choice, 78th over-all, in 1979 Entry Draft).

			Regular Season					Playoffs				
Season	Club	Lea	GP	G	A	TP	PIM	GP	G	A	TP	PIM
1978-79	N. Westminster	WHL	71	7	33	40	142	8	1	4	5	14
1979-80	N. Westminster	WHL	67	13	38	51	236	....	....	....	....	....
1980-81	**Boston**	**NHL**	26	0	4	4	39	....	....	....	....	....
	Springfield	AHL	47	1	10	11	109	1	0	0	0	0
1981-82	Erie	AHL	10	0	3	3	36	....	....	....	....	....
	Boston	**NHL**	48	0	8	8	84	11	0	3	3	40
1982-83	Baltimore	AHL	72	2	24	26	215	....	....	....	....	....
	Boston	**NHL**	1	0	0	0	0	11	0	0	0	9
1983-84	Hershey	AHL	50	0	18	18	156	....	....	....	....	....
	Moncton	AHL	14	0	3	3	17	....	....	....	....	....
	Edmonton	**NHL**	....	....	....	....	....	6	0	1	1	0
1984-85	**Edmonton**	**NHL**	28	0	11	11	25	12	1	3	4	26
	Nova Scotia	AHL	37	2	10	12	97	....	....	....	....	....
1985-86	**Edmonton**	**NHL**	6	2	3	5	11	....	....	....	....	....
	Nova Scotia	AHL	19	2	8	10	72	....	....	....	....	....
	NY Rangers	**NHL**	46	1	8	9	65	16	1	2	3	46
1986-87	**NY Rangers**	**NHL**	73	3	12	15	182	6	0	0	0	4
1987-88	**NY Rangers**	**NHL**	14	0	1	1	34	....	....	....	....	....
	Vancouver	**NHL**	49	2	3	5	73	....	....	....	....	....
1988-89	**Vancouver**	**NHL**	74	3	11	14	82	4	0	0	0	2
	NHL Totals		365	11	61	72	595	66	2	9	11	127

Traded to **Edmonton** by **Boston** for John Blum, March 6, 1984. Traded to **NY Rangers** by **Edmonton** with Todd Strueby for Mike Rogers, December 20, 1985. Traded to **Vancouver** by **NY Rangers** with Willie Huber for Michel Petit, November 4, 1987.

MELROSE, KEVAN

Defense. Shoots left. 5'10", 180 lbs.   Born, Calgary, Alta., March 28, 1966.
(Calgary's 7th choice, 138th overall in 1984 Entry Draft).

			Regular Season					Playoffs				
Season	Club	Lea	GP	G	A	TP	PIM	GP	G	A	TP	PIM
1983-84	Red Deer	AJHL	42	9	26	35	89	....	....	....	....	....
1984-85			DID NOT PLAY									
1985-86	Penticton	BCJHL	22	18	15	33	56	29	22	25	47	72
1986-87	Cdn. Olympic	....	8	1	0	1	4	....	....	....	....	....
	Red Deer	AJHL	29	15	15	30	171	19	8	16	24	60
1987-88	Harvard	ECAC	31	4	6	10	50	....	....	....	....	....
1988-89	Harvard	ECAC	32	2	13	15	126	....	....	....	....	....

MENDEL, ROBERT (ROB)

Defense. Shoots left. 6'1", 195 lbs.   Born, Los Angeles, CA, September 19, 1968.
(Quebec's 5th choice, 93rd overall, in 1987 Entry Draft).

			Regular Season					Playoffs				
Season	Club	Lea	GP	G	A	TP	PIM	GP	G	A	TP	PIM
1985-86	Edina	HS	21	2	27	29		....	....	....	....	....
1986-87	U. Wisconsin	WCHA	42	1	7	8	26	....	....	....	....	....
1987-88	U. Wisconsin	WCHA	40	0	7	7	22	....	....	....	....	....
1988-89	U. Wisconsin	WCHA	44	1	14	15	37	....	....	....	....	....

MERCIER, DON

Defense. Shoots left. 6'4", 210 lbs.   Born, Grimshaw, Alta., January 21, 1963.

			Regular Season					Playoffs				
Season	Club	Lea	GP	G	A	TP	PIM	GP	G	A	TP	PIM
1982-83	St. Albert	AJHL	28	5	14	19	44	....	....	....	....	....
1983-84	Denver	WCHA	35	2	10	12	44	....	....	....	....	....
1984-85	Denver	WCHA	33	4	12	16	62	....	....	....	....	....
1985-86	Denver	WCHA	48	3	10	13	60	....	....	....	....	....
1986-87	Moncton	AHL	74	5	11	16	107	4	0	0	0	15
1987-88	Salt Lake	IHL	11	0	1	1	16	....	....	....	....	....
	Colorado	IHL	51	3	13	16	137	....	....	....	....	....
1988-89	Denver	IHL	20	0	1	1	20	....	....	....	....	....

Signed as a free agent by **Calgary**, July 17, 1986. Traded to **NY Rangers** by **Calgary** for Jim Leavins, November 6, 1987.

MERKOSKY, GLENN   (mer-KAWS-kee)

Center. Shoots left. 5'10", 175 lbs.   Born, Edmonton, Alta., April 8, 1960.

			Regular Season					Playoffs				
Season	Club	Lea	GP	G	A	TP	PIM	GP	G	A	TP	PIM
1979-80	Calgary	WHL	72	49	40	89	95	7	4	6	10	14
1980-81	Binghamton	AHL	80	26	35	61	61	5	0	2	2	2
1981-82	**Hartford**	**NHL**	7	0	0	0	2	....	....	....	....	....
	Binghamton	AHL	72	29	40	69	83	10	0	2	2	2
1982-83	**New Jersey**	**NHL**	34	4	10	14	20	....	....	....	....	....
	Wichita	CHL	45	26	23	49	15	....	....	....	....	....
1983-84	**New Jersey**	**NHL**	5	1	0	1	0	....	....	....	....	....
	Maine	AHL	75	28	28	56	56	17	11	10	21	20
1984-85a	Maine	AHL	80	38	38	76	19	11	2	3	5	13
1985-86	**Detroit**	**NHL**	17	0	2	2	0	....	....	....	....	....
	Adirondack	AHL	59	24	33	57	22	17	5	7	12	15
1986-87bc	Adirondack	AHL	77	54	31	85	66	11	6	8	14	7
1987-88	Adirondack	AHL	66	34	42	76	34	11	4	6	10	4
1988-89	Adirondack	AHL	76	31	46	77	13	17	8	11	19	10
	NHL Totals		63	5	12	17	22	....	....	....	....	....

a AHL Second All-Star Team (1985)
b AHL First All-Star Team (1987)
c Won Fred T. Hunt Memorial Trophy (Sportsmanship-AHL 1987)

Signed as free agent by **Hartford**, August 10, 1980. Signed as a free agent by **New Jersey**, September 14, 1982. Signed as a free agent by **Detroit**, July 15, 1985.

MERSCH, MIKE

Defense. Shoots left. 6'1", 210 lbs. Born, Skokie, IL, September 29, 1964.

			Regular Season					Playoffs				
Season	Club	Lea	GP	G	A	TP	PIM	GP	G	A	TP	PIM
1983-84	Ill.-Chicago	CCHA	29	0	5	5	18	....	....	....	....	....
1984-85	Ill.-Chicago	CCHA	35	1	14	15	36	....	....	....	....	....
1985-86	Ill.-Chicago	CCHA	36	4	19	23	30	....	....	....	....	....
1986-87	Salt Lake	IHL	43	3	12	15	101	17	0	10	10	14
1987-88	Salt Lake	IHL	1	0	0	0	2	....	....	....	....	....
	Flint	IHL	58	1	14	15	118	16	3	4	7	18
1988-89	New Haven	AHL	1	0	0	0	4	....	....	....	....	....
	Flint	IHL	55	5	20	25	101	....	....	....	....	....
	Muskegon	IHL	16	0	2	2	26	13	0	6	6	38

Signed as a free agent by **Calgary**, April 22, 1986. Signed as a free agent by **Pittsburgh**, August 3, 1989.

MESSIER, MARK DOUGLAS (MEHS-yay)

Center. Shoots left. 6'1", 210 lbs. Born, Edmonton, Alta., January 18, 1961.
(Edmonton's 2nd choice, 48th over-all, in 1979 Entry Draft).

			Regular Season					Playoffs				
Season	Club	Lea	GP	G	A	TP	PIM	GP	G	A	TP	PIM
1977-78	Portland	WHL	....	....	....	....	....	7	4	1	5	2
1978-79	Indianapolis	WHA	5	0	0	0	0	....	....	....	....	....
	Cincinnati	WHA	47	1	10	11	58	....	....	....	....	....
1979-80	Houston	CHL	4	0	3	3	4	....	....	....	....	....
	Edmonton	**NHL**	**75**	**12**	**21**	**33**	**120**	**3**	**1**	**2**	**3**	**2**
1980-81	**Edmonton**	**NHL**	**72**	**23**	**40**	**63**	**102**	**9**	**2**	**5**	**7**	**13**
1981-82a	**Edmonton**	**NHL**	**78**	**50**	**38**	**88**	**119**	**5**	**1**	**2**	**3**	**8**
1982-83a	**Edmonton**	**NHL**	**77**	**48**	**58**	**106**	**72**	**15**	**15**	**6**	**21**	**14**
1983-84bc	**Edmonton**	**NHL**	**73**	**37**	**64**	**101**	**165**	**19**	**8**	**18**	**26**	**19**
1984-85	**Edmonton**	**NHL**	**55**	**23**	**31**	**54**	**57**	**18**	**12**	**13**	**25**	**12**
1985-86	**Edmonton**	**NHL**	**63**	**35**	**49**	**84**	**68**	**10**	**4**	**6**	**10**	**18**
1986-87	**Edmonton**	**NHL**	**77**	**37**	**70**	**107**	**73**	**21**	**12**	**16**	**28**	**16**
1987-88	**Edmonton**	**NHL**	**77**	**37**	**74**	**111**	**103**	**19**	**11**	**23**	**34**	**29**
1988-89	**Edmonton**	**NHL**	**72**	**33**	**61**	**94**	**130**	**7**	**1**	**11**	**12**	**8**
	NHL Totals		**719**	**335**	**506**	**841**	**1009**	**126**	**67**	**102**	**169**	**139**

a NHL First All-Star Team (1982, 1983)
b NHL Second All-Star Team (1984)
c Won Conn Smythe Trophy (1984)

Played in NHL All-Star Game (1982-86, 1988-89)

MESSIER, MITCH

Right wing. Shoots right. 6'2", 205 lbs. Born, Regina, Sask., August 21, 1965.
(Minnesota's 4th choice, 56th overall, in 1983 Entry Draft).

			Regular Season					Playoffs				
Season	Club	Lea	GP	G	A	TP	PIM	GP	G	A	TP	PIM
1983-84	Michigan State	CCHA	37	6	15	21	22	....	....	....	....	....
1984-85	Michigan State	CCHA	42	12	21	33	46	....	....	....	....	....
1985-86	Michigan State	CCHA	38	24	40	64	36	....	....	....	....	....
1986-87ab	Michigan State	CCHA	45	44	48	92	89	....	....	....	....	....
1987-88	**Minnesota**	**NHL**	**13**	**0**	**1**	**1**	**11**	....	....	....	....	....
	Kalamazoo	IHL	69	29	37	66	42	4	2	1	3	0
1988-89	**Minnesota**	**NHL**	**3**	**0**	**1**	**1**	**0**	....	....	....	....	....
	Kalamazoo	IHL	67	34	46	80	71	6	4	3	7	0
	NHL Totals		**16**	**0**	**2**	**2**	**11**	....	....	....	....	....

a CCHA First All-Star Team (1987)
b NCAA West First All-American Team (1987)

METCALFE, SCOTT

Left wing. Shoots left. 6', 195 lbs. Born, Toronto, Ont., January 6, 1967.
(Edmonton's 1st choice, 20th over-all, in 1985 Entry Draft).

			Regular Season					Playoffs				
Season	Club	Lea	GP	G	A	TP	PIM	GP	G	A	TP	PIM
1983-84	Kingston	OHL	68	25	49	74	154	....	....	....	....	....
1984-85	Kingston	OHL	58	27	33	60	100	....	....	....	....	....
1985-86	Kingston	OHL	66	36	43	79	213	10	3	6	9	21
1986-87	Windsor	OHL	57	25	57	82	156	13	5	5	10	27
1987-88	**Edmonton**	**NHL**	**2**	**0**	**0**	**0**	**0**	....	....	....	....	....
	Nova Scotia	AHL	43	9	19	28	87	....	....	....	....	....
	Buffalo	**NHL**	**1**	**0**	**1**	**1**	**0**	....	....	....	....	....
	Rochester	AHL	22	2	13	15	56	7	1	3	4	24
1988-89	**Buffalo**	**NHL**	**9**	**1**	**1**	**2**	**13**	....	....	....	....	....
	Rochester	AHL	60	20	31	51	241	....	....	....	....	....
	NHL Totals		**12**	**1**	**2**	**3**	**13**	....	....	....	....	....

Traded to **Buffalo** by **Edmonton** with Edmonton's ninth round choice (Donald Audette) in 1989 Entry Draft for Steve Dykstra and Buffalo's seventh round choice (David Payne) in 1989 Entry Draft, February 11, 1988.

MEWS, HAROLD RANDALL (HARRY)

Center. Shoots left. 5'11", 175 lbs. Born, Nepean, Ont., February 9, 1967.
(Washington's 1st choice, 20th overall, in 1988 Supplemental Draft).

			Regular Season					Playoffs				
Season	Club	Lea	GP	G	A	TP	PIM	GP	G	A	TP	PIM
1986-87	Northeastern	H.E.	29	10	15	25	70	....	....	....	....	....
1987-88	Northeastern	H.E.	37	16	23	39	82	....	....	....	....	....
1988-89a	Northeastern	H.E.	31	18	24	42	103	....	....	....	....	....

a Hockey East Second All-Star Team (1989)

MICHAYLUK, DAVID (DAVE) (mi-KIE-luck)

Right wing. Shoots left. 5'10", 180 lbs. Born, Wakaw, Sask., May 18, 1962.
(Philadelphia's 5th choice, 65th over-all, in 1981 Entry Draft).

			Regular Season					Playoffs				
Season	Club	Lea	GP	G	A	TP	PIM	GP	G	A	TP	PIM
1980-81	Regina	WHL	72	62	71	133	39	11	5	12	17	8
1981-82	**Philadelphia**	**NHL**	**1**	**0**	**0**	**0**	**0**	....	....	....	....	....
a	Regina	WHL	72	62	111	172	128	12	16	24	*40	23
1982-83	**Philadelphia**	**NHL**	**13**	**2**	**6**	**8**	**8**	....	....	....	....	....
	Maine	AHL	69	32	40	72	16	8	0	2	2	0
1983-84	Springfield	AHL	79	18	44	62	37	4	0	0	0	2
1984-85	Hershey	AHL	3	0	2	2	2	....	....	....	....	....
b	Kalamazoo	IHL	82	66	33	99	49	11	7	7	14	0
1985-86	Nova Scotia	AHL	3	0	1	1	0	....	....	....	....	....
	Muskegon	IHL	77	52	52	104	73	14	6	9	15	12
1986-87c	Muskegon	IHL	82	47	53	100	29	15	2	14	16	8
1987-88c	Muskegon	IHL	81	*56	81	137	46	6	2	0	2	18
1988-89cdef	Muskegon	IHL	80	50	72	*122	84	13	9	12	21	24
	NHL Totals		**14**	**2**	**6**	**8**	**8**	....	....	....	....	....

a WHL Second All-Star Team (1982)
b IHL Second All-Star Team (1985)
c IHL First All-Star Team (1987, 1988, 1989)
d IHL Playoff MVP (1989)
e Won James Gatschene Memorial Trophy (MVP-IHL) 1989
f Won Leo P. Lamoreau Memorial Trophy (Top Scorer-IHL) (1989)

MICK, TROY

Left wing. Shoots left. 5'11", 180 lbs. Born, Burnaby, B.C., March 30, 1969.
(Pittsburgh's 6th choice, 130th overall, in 1988 Entry Draft).

			Regular Season					Playoffs				
Season	Club	Lea	GP	G	A	TP	PIM	GP	G	A	TP	PIM
1986-87	Portland	WHL	57	30	33	63	60	20	8	2	10	40
1987-88a	Portland	WHL	72	63	84	147	78	....	....	....	....	....
1988-89	Portland	WHL	66	49	*87	136	70	19	15	19	34	17

a WHL West All-Star Team (1988)

MIDDENDORF, MAX

Right wing. Shoots right. 6'4", 210 lbs. Born, Syracuse, NY, August 18, 1967.
(Quebec's 3rd choice, 57th overall, in 1985 Entry Draft).

			Regular Season					Playoffs				
Season	Club	Lea	GP	G	A	TP	PIM	GP	G	A	TP	PIM
1984-85	Sudbury	OHL	63	16	28	44	106	....	....	....	....	....
1985-86	Sudbury	OHL	61	40	42	82	71	4	4	2	6	11
1986-87	**Quebec**	**NHL**	**6**	**1**	**4**	**5**	**4**	....	....	....	....	....
	Kitchener	OHL	48	38	44	82	13	4	2	5	7	5
1987-88	**Quebec**	**NHL**	**1**	**0**	**0**	**0**	**0**	....	....	....	....	....
	Fredericton	AHL	38	11	13	24	57	12	4	4	8	18
1988-89	Halifax	AHL	72	41	39	80	85	4	1	2	3	6
	NHL Totals		**7**	**1**	**4**	**5**	**4**	....	....	....	....	....

MIEHM, KEVIN

Centre. Shoots left. 6'2", 190 lbs. Born, Kitchener, Ont., September 10, 1969.
(St. Louis' 2nd choice, 54th overall, in 1987 Entry Draft).

			Regular Season					Playoffs				
Season	Club	Lea	GP	G	A	TP	PIM	GP	G	A	TP	PIM
1986-87	Oshawa	OHL	61	12	27	39	19	26	1	8	9	12
1987-88	Oshawa	OHL	52	16	36	52	30	7	2	5	7	0
1988-89a	Oshawa	OHL	63	43	79	122	19	6	6	6	12	0
	Peoria	IHL	3	1	1	2	0	4	0	2	2	0

a OHL Third All-Star Team (1989)

MILLAR, MIKE (MILLER)

Right wing. Shoots left. 5'10", 170 lbs. Born, St. Catharines, Ont., April 28, 1965.
(Hartford's 2nd choice, 110th over-all, in 1984 Entry Draft).

			Regular Season					Playoffs				
Season	Club	Lea	GP	G	A	TP	PIM	GP	G	A	TP	PIM
1982-83	Brantford	OHL	53	20	29	49	10	8	0	5	5	2
1983-84	Brantford	OHL	69	50	45	95	48	6	4	0	4	2
1984-85	Hamilton	OHL	63	66	60	126	54	17	9	10	19	14
1985-86	Cdn. Olympic	...	69	50	38	88	74	....	....	....	....	....
1986-87	**Hartford**	**NHL**	**10**	**2**	**2**	**4**	**0**	....	....	....	....	....
	Binghamton	AHL	61	45	32	77	38	13	7	4	11	27
1987-88	**Hartford**	**NHL**	**28**	**7**	**7**	**14**	**6**	....	....	....	....	....
	Binghamton	AHL	31	32	17	49	42	....	....	....	....	....
1988-89	**Washington**	**NHL**	**18**	**6**	**3**	**9**	**4**	....	....	....	....	....
a	Baltimore	AHL	53	47	35	82	58	....	....	....	....	....
	NHL Totals		**56**	**15**	**12**	**27**	**10**	....	....	....	....	....

a AHL Second All-Star Team (1989)

Traded to **Washington** by **Hartford** with Neil Sheehy for Grant Jennings and Ed Kastelic, July 6, 1988.

MILLEN, COREY

Center. Shoots right. 5'7", 165 lbs. Born, Cloquet, MN, April 29, 1964.
(NY Rangers' 3rd choice, 57th overall, in 1982 Entry Draft).

			Regular Season					Playoffs				
Season	Club	Lea	GP	G	A	TP	PIM	GP	G	A	TP	PIM
1982-83	U. Minnesota	WCHA	21	14	15	29	18	....	....	....	....	....
1983-84	U.S. Olympic	...	45	15	11	26	10	....	....	....	....	....
1984-85	U. Minnesota	WCHA	38	28	36	64	60	....	....	....	....	....
1985-86ab	U. Minnesota	WCHA	48	41	42	83	64	....	....	....	....	....
1986-87bc	U. Minnesota	WCHA	42	36	29	65	62	....	....	....	....	....
1987-88	U.S. National	....	47	41	43	84	26	....	....	....	....	....
	U.S. Olympic	....	6	6	5	11	4	....	....	....	....	....
1988-89	Ambri	Switz.	36	32	29	61	....	6	4	3	7	....

a NCAA West Second All-American Team (1986)
b WCHA Second All-Star Team (1986, 1987)
c Named to NCAA All-Tournament Team (1987)

MILLER, BRAD

Defense. Shoots left. 6'4", 200 lbs. Born, Edmonton, Alta., July 23, 1969.
(Buffalo's 2nd choice, 22nd overall, in 1987 Entry Draft).

			Regular Season					Playoffs				
Season	Club	Lea	GP	G	A	TP	PIM	GP	G	A	TP	PIM
1985-86	Regina	WHL	71	2	14	16	99	10	1	1	2	4
1986-87	Regina	WHL	67	10	38	48	154	3	0	0	0	6
1987-88	Rochester	AHL	3	0	0	0	4	2	0	0	0	2
	Regina	WHL	61	9	34	43	148	4	1	1	2	12
1988-89	**Buffalo**	**NHL**	**7**	**0**	**0**	**0**	**6**	**....**	**....**	**....**	**....**	**....**
	Regina	WHL	34	8	18	26	95	....	....	....	....	....
	Rochester	AHL	3	0	0	0	4	....	....	....	....	....
	NHL Totals		**7**	**0**	**0**	**0**	**6**	**....**	**....**	**....**	**....**	**....**

MILLER, JAY

Left wing. Shoots left. 6'2", 210 lbs. Born, Wellesley, MA, July 16, 1960.
(Quebec's 2nd choice, 66th overall, in 1980 Entry Draft).

			Regular Season					Playoffs				
Season	Club	Lea	GP	G	A	TP	PIM	GP	G	A	TP	PIM
1981-82	N. Hampshire	ECAC	24	6	4	10	34	....	....	....	....	....
1982-83	N. Hampshire	ECAC	28	6	4	10	28	....	....	....	....	....
1983-84	Toledo	IHL	2	0	0	0	2	....	....	....	....	....
	Maine	AHL	15	1	1	2	27	....	....	....	....	....
1984-85	Muskegon	IHL	56	5	29	34	177	17	1	1	2	56
1985-86	Moncton	AHL	18	4	6	10	113	....	....	....	....	....
	Boston	**NHL**	**46**	**3**	**0**	**3**	**178**	**2**	**0**	**0**	**0**	**17**
1986-87	**Boston**	**NHL**	**55**	**1**	**4**	**5**	**208**	**....**	**....**	**....**	**....**	**....**
1987-88	**Boston**	**NHL**	**78**	**7**	**12**	**19**	**304**	**12**	**0**	**0**	**0**	**124**
1988-89	**Boston**	**NHL**	**37**	**2**	**4**	**6**	**168**	**....**	**....**	**....**	**....**	**....**
	Los Angeles	**NHL**	**29**	**5**	**3**	**8**	**133**	**11**	**0**	**1**	**1**	**63**
	NHL Totals		**245**	**18**	**23**	**41**	**991**	**25**	**0**	**1**	**1**	**204**

Signed as a free agent by **Boston**, October 1, 1985. Traded to **Los Angeles** by **Boston** for future considerations, January 22, 1989.

MILLER, JASON

Center. Shoots left. 6'1", 180 lbs. Born, Edmonton, Alta., March 1, 1971.
(New Jersey's 2nd choice, 18th overall, in 1989 Entry Draft).

			Regular Season					Playoffs				
Season	Club	Lea	GP	G	A	TP	PIM	GP	G	A	TP	PIM
1986-87	Edmonton	Midget	40	38	31	69	76	....	....	....	....	....
1987-88	Medicine Hat	WHL	71	11	18	29	28	15	0	1	1	2
1988-89	Medicine Hat	WHL	72	51	55	106	44	3	1	2	3	2

MILLER, KEITH

Left wing. Shoots left. 6'2", 215 lbs. Born, Toronto, Ont., March 18, 1967.
(Quebec's 10th choice, 165th overall, in 1986 Entry Draft).

			Regular Season					Playoffs				
Season	Club	Lea	GP	G	A	TP	PIM	GP	G	A	TP	PIM
1985-86	Guelph	OHL	61	32	17	49	30	20	8	16	24	6
1986-87	Guelph	OHL	66	50	31	81	44	5	6	2	8	0
1987-88	Baltimore	AHL	21	6	5	11	12	....	....	....	....	....
1988-89	Halifax	AHL	12	6	3	9	6	....	....	....	....	....
	Fort Wayne	IHL	54	35	25	60	13	10	4	3	7	9

MILLER, KELLY

Center. Shoots left. 5'11", 195 lbs. Born, Lansing, MI, March 3, 1963.
(NY Rangers' 9th choice, 183rd over-all, in 1982 Entry Draft).

			Regular Season					Playoffs				
Season	Club	Lea	GP	G	A	TP	PIM	GP	G	A	TP	PIM
1981-82	Michigan State	CCHA	38	11	18	29	17	....	....	....	....	....
1982-83	Michigan State	CCHA	36	16	19	35	12	....	....	....	....	....
1983-84	Michigan State	CCHA	46	28	21	49	12	....	....	....	....	....
1984-85	**NY Rangers**	**NHL**	**5**	**0**	**2**	**2**	**2**	**3**	**0**	**0**	**0**	**2**
ab	Michigan State	CCHA	43	27	23	50	21	....	....	....	....	....
1985-86	**NY Rangers**	**NHL**	**74**	**13**	**20**	**33**	**52**	**16**	**3**	**4**	**7**	**4**
1986-87	**NY Rangers**	**NHL**	**38**	**6**	**14**	**20**	**22**	**....**	**....**	**....**	**....**	**....**
	Washington	**NHL**	**39**	**10**	**12**	**22**	**26**	**7**	**2**	**2**	**4**	**0**
1987-88	**Washington**	**NHL**	**80**	**9**	**23**	**32**	**35**	**14**	**4**	**4**	**8**	**10**
1988-89	**Washington**	**NHL**	**78**	**19**	**21**	**40**	**45**	**6**	**1**	**0**	**1**	**2**
	NHL Totals		**314**	**57**	**92**	**149**	**182**	**46**	**10**	**10**	**20**	**18**

a CCHA First All-Star Team (1985)
b Named to NCAA All-American Team (1985)

Traded to **Washington** by **NY Rangers** with Bob Crawford and Mike Ridley for Bob Carpenter and, Washington's second-round choice (Jason Prosofsky) in 1989 Entry Draft, January 1, 1987.

MILLER, KEVIN

Center. Shoots right. 5'9", 170 lbs. Born, Lansing, MI, August 9, 1965.
(NY Rangers' 10th choice, 202nd overall, in 1984 Entry Draft).

			Regular Season					Playoffs				
Season	Club	Lea	GP	G	A	TP	PIM	GP	G	A	TP	PIM
1984-85	Michigan State	CCHA	44	11	29	40	84	....	....	....	....	....
1985-86	Michigan State	CCHA	45	19	52	71	112	....	....	....	....	....
1986-87	Michigan State	CCHA	42	25	56	81	63	....	....	....	....	....
1987-88	U.S. National	....	48	31	32	63	33	....	....	....	....	....
	U.S. Olympic	....	5	1	3	4	4	....	....	....	....	....
	Michigan State	CCHA	9	6	3	9	18	....	....	....	....	....
1988-89	**NY Rangers**	**NHL**	**24**	**3**	**5**	**8**	**2**	**....**	**....**	**....**	**....**	**....**
	Denver	IHL	55	29	47	76	19	4	2	1	3	2
	NHL Totals		**24**	**3**	**5**	**8**	**2**	**....**	**....**	**....**	**....**	**....**

MILLER, KIP

Center. Shoots left. 5'10", 160 lbs. Born, Lansing, MI, June 11, 1969.
(Quebec's 4th choice, 72nd overall, in 1987 Entry Draft).

			Regular Season					Playoffs				
Season	Club	Lea	GP	G	A	TP	PIM	GP	G	A	TP	PIM
1986-87	Michigan State	CCHA	41	20	19	39	92	....	....	....	....	....
1987-88	Michigan State	CCHA	39	16	25	41	51	....	....	....	....	....
1988-89ab	Michigan State	CCHA	47	32	45	77	94	....	....	....	....	....

a CCHA First All-Star Team (1989)
b NCAA West First All-American Team (1989)

MILLER, KRIS

Defense. Shoots left. 6', 185 lbs. Born, Bemidji, MN, March 30, 1969.
(Montreal's 6th choice, 80th overall, in 1987 Entry Draft).

			Regular Season					Playoffs				
Season	Club	Lea	GP	G	A	TP	PIM	GP	G	A	TP	PIM
1986-87	Greenway	HS	26	10	33	43	....	....	....	....	....	....
1987-88	Minn.-Duluth	WCHA	32	1	6	7	30	....	....	....	....	....
1988-89	Minn.-Duluth	WCHA	39	2	10	12	37	....	....	....	....	....

MILLIER, PIERRE

Defense. Shoots right. 6', 203 lbs. Born, Baie Comeau, Que., January 15, 1968.
(Quebec's 11th choice, 186th overall, in 1986 Entry Draft).

			Regular Season					Playoffs				
Season	Club	Lea	GP	G	A	TP	PIM	GP	G	A	TP	PIM
1985-86	Chicoutimi	QMJHL	67	22	15	37	69	9	1	2	3	8
1986-87	Chicoutimi	QMJHL	68	37	57	94	92	15	5	2	7	42
1987-88	St. Jean	QMJHL	67	33	55	88	187	7	4	3	7	15
1988-89	St. Jean	QMJHL	60	39	47	86	118	....	....	....	....	....

MILLS, CHRIS

Defense. Shoots left. 6'1", 185 lbs. Born, Scarborough, Ont., May 30, 1966.
(Winnipeg's 2nd choice, 68th overall, in 1984 Entry Draft).

			Regular Season					Playoffs				
Season	Club	Lea	GP	G	A	TP	PIM	GP	G	A	TP	PIM
1984-85	Clarkson	ECAC	29	0	1	1	22	....	....	....	....	....
1985-86	Clarkson	ECAC	28	2	3	5	6	....	....	....	....	....
1986-87	Clarkson	ECAC	30	3	14	17	32	....	....	....	....	....
1987-88	Clarkson	ECAC	35	5	15	20	38	....	....	....	....	....
	Moncton	AHL	2	0	0	0	2	....	....	....	....	....
1988-89	Flint	IHL	1	0	0	0	0	....	....	....	....	....

MINER, JOHN

Defense. Shoots right. 5'10", 180 lbs. Born, Moose Jaw, Sask., August 28, 1965.
(Edmonton's 10th choice, 229th over-all, in 1983 Entry Draft).

			Regular Season					Playoffs				
Season	Club	Lea	GP	G	A	TP	PIM	GP	G	A	TP	PIM
1982-83	Regina	WHL	71	11	23	34	126	5	1	1	2	20
1983-84	Regina	WHL	70	27	42	69	132	23	9	25	34	54
1984-85	Regina	WHL	66	30	54	84	128	8	4	10	14	12
1985-86	Nova Scotia	AHL	79	10	33	43	90	....	....	....	....	....
1986-87	Nova Scotia	AHL	45	5	28	33	38	5	0	3	3	4
1987-88	**Edmonton**	**NHL**	**14**	**2**	**3**	**5**	**16**	**....**	**....**	**....**	**....**	**....**
	Nova Scotia	AHL	61	8	26	34	61	....	....	....	....	....
1988-89	New Haven	AHL	7	2	3	5	4	17	3	12	15	40
	NHL Totals		**14**	**2**	**3**	**5**	**16**	**....**	**....**	**....**	**....**	**....**

Traded to **Los Angeles** by **Edmonton** for Craig Redmond, August 10, 1988

MODANO, MICHAEL (MIKE)

Center. Shoots left. 6'3", 190 lbs. Born, Detroit, MI, June 7, 1970.
(Minnesota's 1st choice, 1st overall, in 1988 Entry Draft).

			Regular Season					Playoffs				
Season	Club	Lea	GP	G	A	TP	PIM	GP	G	A	TP	PIM
1986-87	Prince Albert	WHL	70	32	30	62	96	8	1	4	5	4
1987-88	Prince Albert	WHL	65	47	80	127	80	9	7	11	18	18
1988-89a	Prince Albert	WHL	41	39	66	105	74	....	....	....	....	....
	Minnesota	**NHL**	**....**	**....**	**....**	**....**	**....**	**2**	**0**	**0**	**0**	**0**
	NHL Totals		**....**	**....**	**....**	**....**	**....**	**2**	**0**	**0**	**0**	**0**

a WHL East All-Star Team (1989)

MOGILNY, ALEXANDER

Left wing. Shoots left. 5'11", 180 lbs. Born, Khabaravosk, Soviet Union, February 18, 1969.
(Buffalo's 4th choice, 89th overall, in 1988 Entry Draft).

			Regular Season					Playoffs				
Season	Club	Lea	GP	G	A	TP	PIM	GP	G	A	TP	PIM
1986-87	CSKA	USSR	28	15	1	16	4	....	....	....	....	....
1987-88	CSKA	USSR	29	12	8	20	14	....	....	....	....	....
1988-89	CSKA	USSR	31	11	11	22	24	....	....	....	....	....

MOKOSAK, CARL (MOH-ka-sak)

Left wing. Shoots left. 6'1", 180 lbs. Born, Fort Saskatchewan, Alta., September 22, 1962.

			Regular Season					Playoffs				
Season	Club	Lea	GP	G	A	TP	PIM	GP	G	A	TP	PIM
1979-80	Brandon	WHL	61	12	21	33	226	11	0	4	4	66
1980-81	Brandon	WHL	70	28	44	72	363	5	1	3	4	12
1981-82	**Calgary**	**NHL**	**1**	**0**	**1**	**1**	**0**	**....**	**....**	**....**	**....**	**....**
	Brandon	WHL	69	46	61	107	363	4	0	1	1	11
	Oklahoma City	CHL	2	1	1	2	2	4	1	1	2	0
1982-83	**Calgary**	**NHL**	**41**	**7**	**6**	**13**	**87**	**....**	**....**	**....**	**....**	**....**
	Colorado	CHL	28	10	12	22	106	5	1	0	1	12
1983-84	New Haven	AHL	80	18	21	39	206	....	....	....	....	....
1984-85	**Los Angeles**	**NHL**	**30**	**4**	**8**	**12**	**43**	**....**	**....**	**....**	**....**	**....**
	New Haven	AHL	11	6	6	12	26	....	....	....	....	....
1985-86	**Philadelphia**	**NHL**	**1**	**0**	**0**	**0**	**5**	**....**	**....**	**....**	**....**	**....**
	Hershey	AHL	79	30	42	72	312	16	0	4	4	111
1986-87	**Pittsburgh**	**NHL**	**3**	**0**	**0**	**0**	**4**	**....**	**....**	**....**	**....**	**....**
	Baltimore	AHL	67	23	27	50	228	....	....	....	....	....
1987-88	Muskegon	IHL	81	29	37	66	308	6	3	2	5	60
1988-89	**Boston**	**NHL**	**7**	**0**	**0**	**0**	**31**	**1**	**0**	**0**	**0**	**0**
	Maine	AHL	53	20	18	38	337	....	....	....	....	....
	NHL Totals		**83**	**11**	**15**	**26**	**170**	**1**	**0**	**0**	**0**	**0**

Signed as free agent by **Calgary**, July 21, 1981. Traded to **Los Angeles** by **Calgary** with Kevin LaVallee for Steve Bozek, June 20, 1983. Signed as a free agent by **Philadelphia**, July 23, 1985. Signed as a free agent by **Pittsburgh**, July 23, 1986.

MOKOSAK, JOHN · (MOH-ka-sak)

Defense. Shoots left. 5'11", 200 lbs.   Born, Edmonton, Alta., September 7, 1963.
(Hartford's 6th choice, 130th over-all, in 1981 Entry Draft).

			Regular Season					Playoffs				
Season	Club	Lea	GP	G	A	TP	PIM	GP	G	A	TP	PIM
1980-81	Victoria	WHL	71	2	18	20	59	15	0	3	3	53
1981-82	Victoria	WHL	69	6	45	51	102	4	1	1	2	0
1982-83	Victoria	WHL	70	10	33	43	102	12	0	0	0	8
1983-84	Binghamton	AHL	79	3	21	24	80	.....	....	....	....	....
1984-85	Binghamton	AHL	54	1	13	14	109	7	0	0	0	12
	Salt Lake	IHL	22	1	10	11	41	.....	....	....	....	....
1985-86	Binghamton	AHL	64	0	9	9	196	6	0	0	0	6
1986-87	Binghamton	AHL	72	2	15	17	187	9	0	2	2	42
1987-88	Springfield	AHL	77	1	16	17	178	.....	....	....	....	....
1988-89	**Detroit**	**NHL**	**8**	**0**	**1**	**1**	**14**	.....	....	....	....	....
	Adirondack	AHL	65	4	31	35	195	17	0	5	5	49
	NHL Totals		**8**	**0**	**1**	**1**	**14**	.....	....	....	....	....

Signed as a free agent by **Detroit,** August 29, 1988.

MOLLER, MICHAEL JOHN (MIKE) · (MOH-luhr)

Right wing. Shoots right. 6', 194 lbs.   Born, Calgary, Alta., June 16, 1962.
(Buffalo's 2nd choice, 41st over-all, in 1980 Entry Draft).

			Regular Season					Playoffs				
Season	Club	Lea	GP	G	A	TP	PIM	GP	G	A	TP	PIM
1979-80	Lethbridge	WHL	72	30	41	71	55	4	0	6	6	0
1980-81a	Lethbridge	WHL	70	39	69	108	71	9	6	10	16	12
	Buffalo	**NHL**	**5**	**2**	**2**	**4**	**0**	**3**	**0**	**1**	**1**	**0**
1981-82	**Buffalo**	**NHL**	**9**	**0**	**0**	**0**	**0**	.....	....	....	....	....
a	Lethbridge	WHL	49	41	81	122	38	12	5	12	17	9
1982-83	**Buffalo**	**NHL**	**49**	**6**	**12**	**18**	**14**	.....	....	....	....	....
	Rochester	AHL	10	1	6	7	2	11	2	4	6	4
1983-84	**Buffalo**	**NHL**	**59**	**5**	**11**	**16**	**27**	.....	....	....	....	....
1984-85	**Buffalo**	**NHL**	**5**	**0**	**2**	**2**	**0**	.....	....	....	....	....
	Rochester	AHL	73	19	46	65	27	5	1	1	2	0
1985-86	**Edmonton**	**NHL**	**1**	**0**	**0**	**0**	**0**	.....	....	....	....	....
	Nova Scotia	AHL	62	16	15	31	24	.....	....	....	....	....
1986-87	**Edmonton**	**NHL**	**6**	**2**	**1**	**3**	**0**	.....	....	....	....	....
	Nova Scotia	AHL	70	14	33	47	28	1	0	0	0	0
1987-88	Nova Scotia	AHL	60	12	31	43	14	5	3	0	3	0
1988-89	Cdn. National	....	58	18	16	34	18	.....	....	....	....	....
	NHL Totals		**134**	**15**	**28**	**43**	**41**	**3**	**0**	**1**	**1**	**0**

a WHL First All-Star Team (1981, 1982)
Traded to **Pittsburgh** by **Buffalo** with Randy Cunneyworth for Pat Hughes, October 4, 1985.
Traded to **Edmonton** by **Pittsburgh** for Pat Hughes, October 4, 1985.

MOLLER, RANDY

Defense. Shoots right. 6'2", 207 lbs.   Born, Red Deer, Alta., August 23, 1963.
(Quebec's 1st choice, 11th over-all, in 1981 Entry Draft).

			Regular Season					Playoffs				
Season	Club	Lea	GP	G	A	TP	PIM	GP	G	A	TP	PIM
1980-81	Lethbridge	WHL	46	4	21	25	176	9	0	4	4	24
1981-82	**Quebec**	**NHL**	....	....	....	....	....	**1**	**0**	**0**	**0**	**0**
a	Lethbridge	WHL	60	20	55	75	249	12	4	6	10	65
1982-83	**Quebec**	**NHL**	**75**	**2**	**12**	**14**	**145**	**4**	**1**	**0**	**1**	**4**
1983-84	**Quebec**	**NHL**	**74**	**4**	**14**	**18**	**147**	**9**	**1**	**0**	**1**	**45**
1984-85	**Quebec**	**NHL**	**79**	**7**	**22**	**29**	**120**	**18**	**2**	**2**	**4**	**40**
1985-86	**Quebec**	**NHL**	**69**	**5**	**18**	**23**	**141**	**3**	**0**	**0**	**0**	**26**
1986-87	**Quebec**	**NHL**	**71**	**5**	**9**	**14**	**144**	**13**	**1**	**4**	**5**	**23**
1987-88	**Quebec**	**NHL**	**66**	**3**	**22**	**25**	**169**	.....	....	....	....	....
1988-89	**Quebec**	**NHL**	**74**	**7**	**22**	**29**	**136**	.....	....	....	....	....
	NHL Totals		**508**	**33**	**119**	**152**	**1002**	**48**	**5**	**6**	**11**	**138**

a WHL Second All-Star Team (1982)

MOMESSO, SERGIO

Left Wing. Shoots left. 6'3", 200 lbs.   Born, Montreal, Que., September 4, 1965.
(Montreal's 3rd choice, 27th over-all, in 1983 Entry Draft).

			Regular Season					Playoffs				
Season	Club	Lea	GP	G	A	TP	PIM	GP	G	A	TP	PIM
1981-82	Montreal	Midget	45	30	38	68	63	.....	....	....	....	....
1982-83	Shawinigan	QMJHL	70	27	42	69	93	10	5	4	9	55
1983-84	**Montreal**	**NHL**	**1**	**0**	**0**	**0**	**0**	.....	....	....	....	....
	Shawinigan	QMJHL	68	42	88	130	235	6	4	4	8	13
	Nova Scotia	AHL	....	....	....	....	....	8	0	2	2	4
1984-85a	Shawinigan	QMJHL	64	56	90	146	216	8	7	8	15	17
1985-86	**Montreal**	**NHL**	**24**	**8**	**7**	**15**	**46**	.....	....	....	....	....
1986-87	**Montreal**	**NHL**	**59**	**14**	**17**	**31**	**96**	**11**	**1**	**3**	**4**	**31**
	Sherbrooke	AHL	6	1	6	7	10	.....	....	....	....	....
1987-88	**Montreal**	**NHL**	**53**	**7**	**14**	**21**	**101**	**6**	**0**	**2**	**2**	**16**
1988-89	**St. Louis**	**NHL**	**53**	**9**	**17**	**26**	**139**	**10**	**2**	**5**	**7**	**24**
	NHL Totals		**190**	**38**	**55**	**93**	**382**	**27**	**3**	**10**	**13**	**71**

a QMJHL First All-Star Team (1985)
Traded to **St. Louis** by **Montreal** with Vincent Riendeau for Jocelyn Lemieux, Darrell May and St. Louis' second round choice (Patrice Brisebois) in the 1989 Entry Draft, August 9, 1988.

MOORE, JOHN

Center. Shoots right. 6'3", 205 lbs.   Born, Montreal, Que., January 9, 1967.
(Hartford's 7th choice, 165th overall, in 1987 Entry Draft).

			Regular Season					Playoffs				
Season	Club	Lea	GP	G	A	TP	PIM	GP	G	A	TP	PIM
1986-87	Yale	ECAC	30	4	2	6	38	.....	....	....	....	....
1987-88	Yale	ECAC	26	3	18	21	22	.....	....	....	....	....
1988-89	Yale	ECAC	24	3	3	6	38	.....	....	....	....	....

MOORE, STEVE

Defense. Shoots right. 6'2", 185 lbs.   Born, Toronto, Ont., January 21, 1967.
(Boston's 4th choice, 94th overall, in 1985 Entry Draft).

			Regular Season					Playoffs				
Season	Club	Lea	GP	G	A	TP	PIM	GP	G	A	TP	PIM
1984-85	London	OHL	46	12	26	38	112	.....	....	....	....	....
1985-86	RPI	ECAC	24	4	3	7	32	.....	....	....	....	....
1986-87	RPI	ECAC	30	2	15	17	43	.....	....	....	....	....
1987-88	RPI	ECAC	27	3	9	12	26	.....	....	....	....	....
1988-89	RPI	ECAC	32	2	10	12	61	.....	....	....	....	....

MORE, JAYSON

Defense. Shoots right. 6'1", 190 lbs.   Born, Souris, Man., January 12, 1969.
(NY Rangers' 1st choice, 10th overall, in 1987 Entry Draft).

			Regular Season					Playoffs				
Season	Club	Lea	GP	G	A	TP	PIM	GP	G	A	TP	PIM
1984-85	Lethbridge	WHL	71	3	9	12	101	4	1	0	1	7
1985-86	Lethbridge	WHL	61	7	18	25	155	9	0	2	2	36
1986-87	Brandon	WHL	21	4	6	10	62	.....	....	....	....	....
	N. Westminster	WHL	43	4	23	27	155	.....	....	....	....	....
1987-88a	N. Westminster	WHL	70	13	47	60	270	5	0	2	2	26
1988-89	**NY Rangers**	**NHL**	**1**	**0**	**0**	**0**	**0**	.....	....	....	....	....
	Denver	IHL	62	7	15	22	138	3	0	1	1	26
	NHL Totals		**1**	**0**	**0**	**0**	**0**	.....	....	....	....	....

a WHL All-Star Team (1988)

MORIN, STEPHANE

Center. Shoots left. 6'0", 175 lbs.   Born, Montreal, Que., March 27, 1969.
(Quebec's 3rd choice, 43rd overall, in 1989 Entry Draft).

			Regular Season					Playoffs				
Season	Club	Lea	GP	G	A	TP	PIM	GP	G	A	TP	PIM
1987-88	Chicoutimi	QMJHL	68	38	45	83	18	6	3	8	11	2
1988-89ab	Chicoutimi	QMJHL	70	77	*109	*186	71	.....	....	....	....	....

a QMJHL First All-Star Team (1989)
b QMJHL Player of the Year (1989)

MORRIS, JON

Center. Shoots right. 6', 175 lbs.   Born, Lowell, MA, May 6, 1966.
(New Jersey's 5th choice, 86th overall, in 1984 Entry Draft).

			Regular Season					Playoffs				
Season	Club	Lea	GP	G	A	TP	PIM	GP	G	A	TP	PIM
1984-85	Lowell	H.E.	42	29	31	60	16	.....	....	....	....	....
1985-86	Lowell	H.E.	39	25	31	56	52	.....	....	....	....	....
1986-87ab	Lowell	H.E.	35	28	33	61	48	.....	....	....	....	....
1987-88	Lowell	H.E.	37	15	39	54	39	.....	....	....	....	....
1988-89	**New Jersey**	**NHL**	**4**	**0**	**2**	**2**	**0**	.....	....	....	....	....
	NHL Totals		**4**	**0**	**2**	**2**	**0**	.....	....	....	....	....

a Hockey East First All-Star Team (1987)
b NCAA East Second All-American Team (1987)

MORROW, KEN

Defense. Shoots right. 6'4", 210 lbs.   Born, Flint, MI, October 17, 1956.
(NY Islanders' 4th choice, 68th over-all, in 1976 Amateur Draft).

			Regular Season					Playoffs				
Season	Club	Lea	GP	G	A	TP	PIM	GP	G	A	TP	PIM
1978-79ab	Bowling Green	CCHA	45	15	37	52	22	.....	....	....	....	....
1979-80	U.S. National	...	56	4	18	22	6	.....	....	....	....	....
	U.S. Olympic	...	7	1	2	3	6	.....	....	....	....	....
	NY Islanders	**NHL**	**18**	**0**	**3**	**3**	**4**	**20**	**1**	**2**	**3**	**12**
1980-81	**NY Islanders**	**NHL**	**80**	**2**	**11**	**13**	**20**	**18**	**3**	**4**	**7**	**8**
1981-82	**NY Islanders**	**NHL**	**75**	**1**	**18**	**19**	**56**	**19**	**0**	**4**	**4**	**8**
1982-83	**NY Islanders**	**NHL**	**79**	**5**	**11**	**16**	**44**	**19**	**5**	**7**	**12**	**18**
1983-84	**NY Islanders**	**NHL**	**63**	**3**	**11**	**14**	**45**	**20**	**1**	**2**	**3**	**20**
1984-85	**NY Islanders**	**NHL**	**15**	**1**	**7**	**8**	**14**	**10**	**0**	**0**	**0**	**17**
1985-86	**NY Islanders**	**NHL**	**69**	**0**	**12**	**12**	**22**	**2**	**0**	**0**	**0**	**4**
1986-87	**NY Islanders**	**NHL**	**64**	**3**	**8**	**11**	**32**	**13**	**1**	**3**	**4**	**2**
1987-88	**NY Islanders**	**NHL**	**53**	**1**	**4**	**5**	**40**	**6**	**0**	**0**	**0**	**8**
1988-89	**NY Islanders**	**NHL**	**34**	**1**	**3**	**4**	**32**	.....	....	....	....	....
	NHL Totals		**490**	**17**	**88**	**105**	**309**	**127**	**11**	**22**	**33**	**97**

a CCHA First All-Star Team (1979)
b CCHA Player of the Year (1979)

MORROW, SCOTT

Left wing. Shoots left. 6'1", 180 lbs.   Born, Chicago, IL, June 18, 1969.
(Hartford's 4th choice, 95th overall, in 1988 Entry Draft).

			Regular Season					Playoffs				
Season	Club	Lea	GP	G	A	TP	PIM	GP	G	A	TP	PIM
1987-88	Northwood	HS	24	10	13	23	....	.....	....	....	....	....
1988-89	N. Hampshire	H.E.	19	6	7	13	14	.....	....	....	....	....

MORROW, STEVEN

Defense. Shoots left. 6'2", 210 lbs.   Born, Plano, TX, April 3, 1968.
(Philadelphia's 10th choice, 209th overall, in 1987 Entry Draft).

			Regular Season					Playoffs				
Season	Club	Lea	GP	G	A	TP	PIM	GP	G	A	TP	PIM
1986-87	Westminster	HS	20	10	18	28	30	.....	....	....	....	....
1987-88	Northwood	HS	27	4	20	24	....	.....	....	....	....	....
1988-89	N. Hampshire	H.E.	30	0	0	0	28	.....	....	....	....	....

MORTON, DEAN

Defense. Shoots right. 6'1", 195 lbs.   Born, Peterborough, Ont., February 27, 1968.
(Detroit's 8th choice, 148th overall, in 1986 Entry Draft).

			Regular Season					Playoffs				
Season	Club	Lea	GP	G	A	TP	PIM	GP	G	A	TP	PIM
1985-86	Oshawa	OHL	63	5	6	11	117	5	0	0	0	9
1986-87	Oshawa	OHL	62	1	11	12	165	23	3	6	9	112
1987-88	Oshawa	OHL	57	6	19	25	187	7	0	0	0	18
1988-89	Adirondack	AHL	66	2	15	17	186	8	0	1	1	13

MOSCALUK, GARY

Defense. Shoots left. 6'0", 195 lbs.   Born, Waskatenau, Alta., May 23, 1967.

			Regular Season					Playoffs				
Season	Club	Lea	GP	G	A	TP	PIM	GP	G	A	TP	PIM
1987-88	Victoria	WHL	58	9	37	46	118	8	1	3	4	7
1988-89	Saginaw	IHL	68	0	12	12	108	3	0	0	0	0

Signed as a free agent by **Chicago,** October 13, 1988.

MOYLAN, DAVE

Defense. Shoots left. 6'1", 195 lbs. Born, Tillsonburg, Ont., August 13, 1967.
(Buffalo's 4th choice, 77th overall, in 1985 Entry Draft).

			Regular Season					Playoffs				
Season	Club	Lea	GP	G	A	TP	PIM	GP	G	A	TP	PIM
1984-85	Sudbury	OHL	66	1	15	16	108	....	....	....	....	....
1985-86	Sudbury	OHL	52	10	25	35	87	4	0	0	0	15
1986-87	Kitchener	OHL	51	6	13	19	98	3	2	0	2	11
1987-88	Baltimore	AHL	20	4	5	9	35	....	....	....	....	....
	Rochester	AHL	26	0	0	0	2	....	....	....	....	....
	Flint	IHL	9	0	2	2	10	....	....	....	....	....
1988-89	Rochester	AHL	20	0	2	2	15	....	....	....	....	....
	Jokerit	Fin.	15	4	4	8	38	5	0	0	0	2

MULLEN, BRIAN

Left wing. Shoots left. 5'10", 180 lbs. Born, New York, NY, March 16, 1962.
(Winnipeg's 7th choice, 128th over-all, in 1980 Entry Draft).

			Regular Season					Playoffs				
Season	Club	Lea	GP	G	A	TP	PIM	GP	G	A	TP	PIM
1980-81	U. Wisconsin	WCHA	38	11	13	24	28	....	....	....	....	....
1981-82	U. Wisconsin	WCHA	33	20	17	37	10	....	....	....	....	....
1982-83	Winnipeg	NHL	80	24	26	50	14	3	1	0	1	0
1983-84	Winnipeg	NHL	75	21	41	62	28	3	0	3	3	6
1984-85	Winnipeg	NHL	69	32	39	71	32	8	1	2	3	4
1985-86	Winnipeg	NHL	79	28	34	62	38	3	1	2	3	6
1986-87	Winnipeg	NHL	69	19	32	51	20	9	4	2	6	0
1987-88	NY Rangers	NHL	74	25	29	54	42	....	....	....	....	....
1988-89	NY Rangers	NHL	78	29	35	64	60	3	0	1	1	4
	NHL Totals		524	178	236	414	234	29	7	10	17	20

Played in NHL All-Star Game (1989)

Traded to **NY Rangers** by **Winnipeg** with Winnipeg's tenth-round draft choice (Brett Barnett) in 1987 Entry Draft for NY Rangers' fifth-round choice in 1988 Entry Draft (Benoit Lebeau) – acquired earlier by NY Rangers – and NY Rangers' third round choice (Danny Felsher) in 1989 Entry Draft, June 8, 1987.

MULLEN, JOE

Right wing. Shoots right. 5'9", 180 lbs. Born, New York, NY, February 26, 1957.

			Regular Season					Playoffs				
Season	Club	Lea	GP	G	A	TP	PIM	GP	G	A	TP	PIM
1977-78a	Boston College	ECAC	34	34	34	68	12	....	....	....	....	....
1978-79a	Boston College	ECAC	25	32	24	56	8	....	....	....	....	....
1979-80bc	Salt Lake	CHL	75	40	32	72	21	13	*9	11	20	0
	St. Louis	NHL	....	....	....	....	....	1	0	0	0	0
1980-81de	Salt Lake	CHL	80	59	58	*117	8	17	11	9	20	0
1981-82	Salt Lake	CHL	27	21	27	48	12	....	....	....	....	....
	St. Louis	NHL	45	25	34	59	4	10	7	11	18	4
1982-83	St. Louis	NHL	49	17	30	47	6	....	....	....	....	....
1983-84	St. Louis	NHL	80	41	44	85	19	6	2	0	2	0
1984-85	St. Louis	NHL	79	40	52	92	6	3	0	0	0	0
1985-86	St. Louis	NHL	48	28	24	52	10	....	....	....	....	....
	Calgary	NHL	29	16	22	38	11	21	12	7	19	4
1986-87f	Calgary	NHL	79	47	40	87	14	6	2	1	3	0
1987-88	Calgary	NHL	80	40	44	84	30	7	2	4	6	10
1988-89fgh	Calgary	NHL	79	51	59	110	16	21	*16	8	24	4
	NHL Totals		568	305	349	654	116	75	41	31	72	22

a ECAC First All-Star Team (1978, 1979)
b CHL Second All-Star Team (1980)
c Won Ken McKenzie Trophy (CHL's Top Rookie) (1980)
d CHL First All-Star Team (1981)
e Won Tommy Ivan Trophy (CHL's Most Valuable Player) (1981)
f Won Lady Byng Trophy (1987, 1989)
g NHL First All-Star Team (1989)
h NHL Plus/Minus Leader (1989)

Played in NHL All-Star Game (1989)

Signed as a free agent by **St. Louis,** August 16, 1979. Traded to **Calgary** by **St. Louis** with Terry Johnson and Rik Wilson for Ed Beers, Charles Bourgeois and Gino Cavallini, February 1, 1986.

MULLER, KIRK

Center. Shoots left. 6', 205 lbs. Born, Kingston, Ont., February 8, 1966.
(New Jersey's 1st choice, 2nd over-all, in 1984 Entry Draft).

			Regular Season					Playoffs				
Season	Club	Lea	GP	G	A	TP	PIM	GP	G	A	TP	PIM
1981-82	Kingston	OHL	67	12	39	51	27	4	5	1	6	4
1982-83ab	Guelph	OHL	66	52	60	112	41	....	....	....	....	....
1983-84b	Cdn. Olympic	...	21	4	3	7	6	....	....	....	....	....
	Guelph	OHL	49	31	63	94	27	....	....	....	....	....
1984-85	New Jersey	NHL	80	17	37	54	69	....	....	....	....	....
1985-86	New Jersey	NHL	77	25	41	66	45	....	....	....	....	....
1986-87	New Jersey	NHL	79	26	50	76	75	....	....	....	....	....
1987-88	New Jersey	NHL	80	37	57	94	114	20	4	8	12	37
1988-89	New Jersey	NHL	80	31	43	74	119	....	....	....	....	....
	NHL Totals		396	136	228	364	422	20	4	8	12	37

a OHL's Most Gentlemanly Player (1983)
b OHL Third All-Star Team (1983, 1984)

Played in NHL All-Star Game (1985, 1986, 1988)

MULLINS, DWIGHT

Right wing. Shoots right. 5'11", 190 lbs. Born, Calgary, Alta., February 28, 1967.
(Minnesota's 3rd choice, 90th overall, in 1985 Entry Draft).

			Regular Season					Playoffs				
Season	Club	Lea	GP	G	A	TP	PIM	GP	G	A	TP	PIM
1982-83	Lethbridge	WHL	66	5	2	7	71	20	4	6	10	17
1983-84	Lethbridge	WHL	70	20	23	43	101	5	0	0	0	9
1984-85	Lethbridge	WHL	62	21	18	39	94	4	1	2	3	7
1985-86	Lethbridge	WHL	72	52	37	89	99	10	3	4	7	12
1986-87	Calgary	WHL	31	12	8	20	71	....	....	....	....	....
1987-88	Saskatoon	WHL	52	12	17	29	71	10	7	4	11	12
1988-89	Flint	IHL	2	0	0	0	15	....	....	....	....	....

MULLOWNEY, MICHAEL

Defense. Shoots left. 6'1", 190 lbs. Born, Brighton, MA, January 17, 1966.
(Minnesota's 4th choice, 111th overall, in 1985 Entry Draft).

			Regular Season					Playoffs				
Season	Club	Lea	GP	G	A	TP	PIM	GP	G	A	TP	PIM
1985-86	Boston College	H.E.	26	0	2	2	20	....	....	....	....	....
1986-87	Boston College	H.E.	30	0	2	2	22	....	....	....	....	....
1987-88	Boston College	H.E.	25	1	7	8	48	....	....	....	....	....
1988-89	Boston College	H.E.	39	2	7	9	64	....	....	....	....	....

MULVENNA, GLENN

Center. Shoots left. 5'11", 175 lbs. Born, Calgary, Alta., February 18, 1967.

			Regular Season					Playoffs				
Season	Club	Lea	GP	G	A	TP	PIM	GP	G	A	TP	PIM
1986-87	N. Westminster	WHL	53	24	44	68	43	....	....	....	....	....
	Kamloops	WHL	18	13	8	21	18	13	4	6	10	10
1987-88	Kamloops	WHL	38	21	38	59	35	....	....	....	....	....
1988-89	Flint	IHL	32	9	14	23	12	....	....	....	....	....
	Muskegon	IHL	11	3	2	5	0	....	....	....	....	....

Signed as a free agent by **Pittsburgh**, December 3, 1987.

MUNI, CRAIG DOUGLAS (MYEW nee)

Defense. Shoots left. 6'3", 200 lbs. Born, Toronto, Ont., July 19, 1962.
(Toronto's 1st choice, 25th over-all, in 1980 Entry Draft).

			Regular Season					Playoffs				
Season	Club	Lea	GP	G	A	TP	PIM	GP	G	A	TP	PIM
1980-81	Kingston	OHA	38	2	14	16	65	....	....	....	....	....
	Windsor	OHA	25	5	11	16	41	11	1	4	5	14
	New Brunswick	AHL	....	....	....	....	....	2	0	1	1	10
1981-82	Toronto	NHL	3	0	0	0	2	....	....	....	....	....
	Windsor	OHL	49	5	32	37	92	9	2	3	5	16
	Cincinnati	CHL	....	....	....	....	....	3	0	2	2	2
1982-83	Toronto	NHL	2	0	1	1	0	....	....	....	....	....
	St. Catharines	AHL	64	6	32	38	52	....	....	....	....	....
1983-84	St. Catharines	AHL	64	4	16	20	79	7	0	1	1	0
1984-85	Toronto	NHL	8	0	0	0	0	....	....	....	....	....
	St. Catharines	AHL	68	7	17	24	54	....	....	....	....	....
1985-86	Toronto	NHL	6	0	1	1	4	....	....	....	....	....
	St. Catharines	AHL	73	3	34	37	91	13	0	5	5	16
1986-87	Edmonton	NHL	79	7	22	29	85	14	0	2	2	17
1987-88	Edmonton	NHL	72	4	15	19	77	19	0	4	4	31
1988-89	Edmonton	NHL	69	5	13	18	71	7	0	3	3	8
	NHL Totals		239	16	52	68	239	40	0	9	9	56

Signed as a free agent by **Edmonton,** August 18, 1986. Sold to **Buffalo** by **Edmonton**, October 2, 1986. Traded to **Pittsburgh** by **Buffalo** for future considerations, October 3, 1986. Acquired by **Edmonton** from **Pittsburgh** to complete earlier trade for Gilles Meloche, October 6, 1986.

MURANO, ERIC

Center. Shoots right. 6', 190 lbs. Born, Montreal, Que., May 4, 1967.
(Vancouver's 4th choice, 91st overall, in 1986 Entry Draft).

			Regular Season					Playoffs				
Season	Club	Lea	GP	G	A	TP	PIM	GP	G	A	TP	PIM
1985-86	Calgary	AJHL	52	34	41	75	32	....	....	....	....	....
1986-87	U. of Denver	WCHA	31	5	7	12	12	....	....	....	....	....
1987-88	U. of Denver	WCHA	37	8	13	21	26	....	....	....	....	....
1988-89	U. of Denver	WCHA	42	13	16	29	52	....	....	....	....	....

MURPHY, GARY

Defense. Shoots left. 6'1", 175 lbs. Born, Winchester, MA., March 23, 1967.
(Quebec's 12th choice, 225th overall, in 1985 Entry Draft).

			Regular Season					Playoffs				
Season	Club	Lea	GP	G	A	TP	PIM	GP	G	A	TP	PIM
1985-86	U. of Lowell	H.E.	27	0	9	9	32	....	....	....	....	....
1986-87	U. of Lowell	H.E.	21	3	4	7	13	....	....	....	....	....
1987-88	U. of Lowell	H.E.	36	5	10	15	20	....	....	....	....	....
1988-89	U. of Lowell	H.E.	28	4	7	11	51	....	....	....	....	....

MURPHY, GORDON

Defense. Shoots right. 6'2", 190 lbs. Born, Willowdale, Ont., February 23, 1967.
(Philadelphia's 10th choice, 189th overall, in 1985 Entry Draft).

			Regular Season					Playoffs				
Season	Club	Lea	GP	G	A	TP	PIM	GP	G	A	TP	PIM
1984-85	Oshawa	OHL	59	3	12	15	25	....	....	....	....	....
1985-86	Oshawa	OHL	64	7	15	22	56	6	1	1	2	6
1986-87	Oshawa	OHL	56	7	30	37	95	24	6	16	22	22
1987-88	Hershey	AHL	62	8	20	28	44	12	0	8	8	12
1988-89	Philadelphia	NHL	75	4	31	35	68	19	2	7	9	13
	NHL Totals		75	4	31	35	68	19	2	7	9	13

MURPHY, JOE

Center. Shoots left. 6'1", 190 lbs. Born, London, Ont., October 16, 1967.
(Detroit's 1st choice, 1st overall, in 1986 Entry Draft).

			Regular Season					Playoffs				
Season	Club	Lea	GP	G	A	TP	PIM	GP	G	A	TP	PIM
1985-86	Cdn. Olympic	...	8	3	3	6	2	....	....	....	....	....
	Michigan State	CCHA	35	24	37	61	50	....	....	....	....	....
1986-87	Detroit	NHL	5	0	1	1	2	....	....	....	....	....
	Adirondack	AHL	71	21	38	59	61	10	2	1	3	33
1987-88	Detroit	NHL	50	10	9	19	37	8	0	1	1	6
	Adirondack	AHL	6	5	6	11	4	....	....	....	....	....
1988-89	Detroit	NHL	26	1	7	8	28	....	....	....	....	....
	Adirondack	AHL	47	31	35	66	66	16	6	11	17	17
	NHL Totals		81	11	17	28	67	8	0	1	1	6

a CCHA Rookie of the Year (1986)

MURPHY, LAWRENCE THOMAS (LARRY)

Defense. Shoots right. 6'1", 210 lbs.   Born, Scarborough, Ont., March 8, 1961.
(Los Angeles' 1st choice, 4th over-all, in 1980 Entry Draft).

			Regular Season					Playoffs				
Season	Club	Lea	GP	G	A	TP	PIM	GP	G	A	TP	PIM
1978-79	Peterborough	OHA	66	6	21	27	82	19	1	9	10	42
1979-80a	Peterborough	OHA	68	21	68	89	88	14	4	13	17	20
1980-81	Los Angeles	NHL	80	16	60	76	79	4	3	0	3	2
1981-82	Los Angeles	NHL	79	22	44	66	95	10	2	8	10	12
1982-83	Los Angeles	NHL	77	14	48	62	81	....	....	....	....	....
1983-84	Los Angeles	NHL	6	0	3	3	0	....	....	....	....	....
	Washington	NHL	72	13	33	46	50	8	0	3	3	6
1984-85	Washington	NHL	79	13	42	55	51	5	2	3	5	0
1985-86	Washington	NHL	78	21	44	65	50	9	1	5	6	6
1986-87b	Washington	NHL	80	23	58	81	39	7	2	2	4	6
1987-88	Washington	NHL	79	8	53	61	72	13	4	4	8	33
1988-89	Washington	NHL	65	7	29	36	70	....	....	....	....	....
	Minnesota	NHL	13	4	6	10	12	5	0	2	2	8
	NHL Totals		**708**	**141**	**420**	**561**	**599**	**61**	**14**	**27**	**41**	**73**

a OHA First All-Star Team (1980)
b NHL Second All-Star Team (1987)
Traded to **Washington** by **Los Angeles** for Ken Houston and Brian Engblom, October 18, 1983.
Traded to **Minnesota** by **Washington** with Mike Gartner for Dino Ciccarelli and Bob Rouse, March 7, 1989.

MURPHY, ROB

Center. Shoots left. 6'3", 200 lbs.   Born, Hull, Que., April 7, 1968.
(Vancouver's 1st choice, 24th overall, in 1987 Entry Draft).

			Regular Season					Playoffs				
Season	Club	Lea	GP	G	A	TP	PIM	GP	G	A	TP	PIM
1986-87	Laval	QMJHL	70	35	54	89	86	14	3	4	7	15
1987-88	Vancouver	NHL	5	0	0	0	2	....	....	....	....	....
	Laval	QMJHL	26	11	25	36	82	....	....	....	....	....
	Drummondville	QMJHL	33	16	28	44	41	17	4	15	19	45
1988-89	Vancouver	NHL	8	0	1	1	2	....	....	....	....	....
	Milwaukee	IHL	8	4	2	6	4	11	3	5	8	34
	Drummondville	QMJHL	26	13	25	38	16	4	1	3	4	20
	NHL Totals		**13**	**0**	**1**	**1**	**4**	....	....	....	....	....

MURRAY, MIKE

Center. Shoots left. 6', 195 lbs.   Born, Kingston, Ont., August 29, 1966.
(NY Islanders' 6th choice, 104th over-all, in 1984 Entry Draft).

			Regular Season					Playoffs				
Season	Club	Lea	GP	G	A	TP	PIM	GP	G	A	TP	PIM
1983-84	London	OHL	70	8	24	32	14	8	1	4	5	2
1984-85	London	OHL	43	21	35	56	19	....	....	....	....	....
	Guelph	OHL	23	10	9	19	8	....	....	....	....	....
1985-86	Guelph	OHL	56	27	38	65	19	20	7	13	20	0
1986-87	Hershey	AHL	70	8	16	24	10	2	0	0	0	0
1987-88	Philadelphia	NHL	1	0	0	0	0	....	....	....	....	....
	Hershey	AHL	57	14	14	28	34	2	0	0	0	0
1988-89	Hershey	AHL	19	1	2	3	8	....	....	....	....	....
	Indianapolis	IHL	17	5	11	16	2	....	....	....	....	....
	NHL Totals		**1**	**0**	**0**	**0**	**0**	....	....	....	....	....

MURRAY, PAT

Left wing. Shoots left. 6'2", 185 lbs.   Born, Stratford, Ont., August 20, 1969.
(Philadelphia's 2nd choice, 35th overall, in 1988 Entry Draft).

			Regular Season					Playoffs				
Season	Club	Lea	GP	G	A	TP	PIM	GP	G	A	TP	PIM
1986-87	Stratford	SOHL	42	34	75	109	38	....	....	....	....	....
1987-88	Michigan State	CCHA	42	14	21	35	26	....	....	....	....	....
1988-89	Michigan State	CCHA	46	21	41	62	65	....	....	....	....	....

MURRAY, ROB

Left wing. Shoots right. 6'1", 185 lbs.   Born, Toronto, Ont., April 4, 1967.
(Washington's 3rd choice, 61st overall, in 1985 Entry Draft).

			Regular Season					Playoffs				
Season	Club	Lea	GP	G	A	TP	PIM	GP	G	A	TP	PIM
1984-85	Peterborough	OHL	63	12	9	21	155	17	2	7	9	45
1985-86	Peterborough	OHL	52	14	18	32	125	16	1	2	3	50
1986-87	Peterborough	OHL	62	17	37	54	204	3	1	4	5	8
1987-88	Fort Wayne	IHL	80	12	21	33	139	6	0	2	2	16
1988-89	Baltimore	AHL	80	11	23	34	235	....	....	....	....	....

MURRAY, ROBERT FREDERICK (BOB)

Defense. Shoots right. 5'10", 185 lbs.   Born, Kingston, Ont., November 26, 1954.
(Chicago's 3rd choice, 52nd over-all, in 1974 Amateur Draft).

			Regular Season					Playoffs				
Season	Club	Lea	GP	G	A	TP	PIM	GP	G	A	TP	PIM
1972-73	Cornwall	QJHL	32	9	26	35	34	12	1	21	22	43
1973-74	Cornwall	QJHL	63	23	76	99	88	5	0	6	6	6
1974-75	Dallas	CHL	75	14	43	57	130	10	2	6	8	13
1975-76	Chicago	NHL	64	1	2	3	44	....	....	....	....	....
1976-77	Chicago	NHL	77	10	11	21	71	2	0	1	1	2
1977-78	Chicago	NHL	70	14	17	31	41	4	1	4	5	2
1978-79	Chicago	NHL	79	19	32	51	38	4	1	0	1	6
1979-80	Chicago	NHL	74	16	34	50	60	7	2	4	6	6
1980-81	Chicago	NHL	77	13	47	60	93	3	0	0	0	2
1981-82	Chicago	NHL	45	8	22	30	48	15	1	6	7	16
1982-83	Chicago	NHL	79	7	32	39	73	13	2	3	5	10
1983-84	Chicago	NHL	78	11	37	48	78	5	3	1	4	6
1984-85	Chicago	NHL	80	5	38	43	56	15	3	6	9	20
1985-86	Chicago	NHL	80	9	29	38	75	3	0	2	2	0
1986-87	Chicago	NHL	79	6	38	44	80	4	1	0	1	4
1987-88	Chicago	NHL	62	6	20	26	44	5	1	3	4	2
1988-89	Chicago	NHL	15	2	4	6	27	16	2	3	5	22
	Saginaw	IHL	18	3	7	10	14	....	....	....	....	....
	NHL Totals		**959**	**127**	**363**	**490**	**828**	**96**	**17**	**33**	**50**	**98**

Played in NHL All-Star Game (1981, 1983)

MURRAY, TROY NORMAN

Center. Shoots right. 6'1", 195 lbs.   Born, Calgary, Alta., July 31, 1962.
(Chicago's 6th choice, 51st over-all, in 1980 Entry Draft).

			Regular Season					Playoffs				
Season	Club	Lea	GP	G	A	TP	PIM	GP	G	A	TP	PIM
1980-81ab	North Dakota	WCHA	38	33	45	78	28	....	....	....	....	....
1981-82b	North Dakota	WCHA	26	13	17	30	62	....	....	....	....	....
	Chicago	NHL	1	0	0	0	0	7	1	0	1	5
1982-83	Chicago	NHL	54	8	8	16	27	2	0	0	0	0
1983-84	Chicago	NHL	61	15	15	30	45	5	1	0	1	7
1984-85	Chicago	NHL	80	26	40	66	82	15	5	14	19	24
1985-86c	Chicago	NHL	80	45	54	99	94	2	0	0	0	2
1986-87	Chicago	NHL	77	28	43	71	59	4	0	0	0	5
1987-88	Chicago	NHL	79	22	36	58	96	5	1	0	1	8
1988-89	Chicago	NHL	79	21	30	51	113	16	3	6	9	25
	NHL Totals		**511**	**165**	**226**	**391**	**516**	**56**	**11**	**20**	**31**	**76**

a WCHA Rookie of the Year (1981)
b WCHA Second All-Star Team (1981, 1982)
c Won Frank J. Selke Memorial Trophy (1986).

MURZYN, DANA   (MUR zihn)

Defense. Shoots left. 6'2", 200 lbs.   Born, Calgary, Alta., December 9, 1966.
(Hartford's 1st choice, 5th over-all, in 1985 Entry Draft).

			Regular Season					Playoffs				
Season	Club	Lea	GP	G	A	TP	PIM	GP	G	A	TP	PIM
1983-84	Calgary	WHL	65	11	20	31	135	2	0	0	0	10
1984-85a	Calgary	WHL	72	32	60	92	233	8	1	11	12	16
1985-86b	Hartford	NHL	78	3	23	26	125	4	0	0	0	10
1986-87	Hartford	NHL	74	9	19	28	95	6	2	1	3	29
1987-88	Hartford	NHL	33	1	6	7	45	....	....	....	....	....
	Calgary	NHL	41	6	5	11	94	5	2	0	2	13
1988-89	Calgary	NHL	63	3	19	22	142	21	0	3	3	20
	NHL Totals		**289**	**22**	**72**	**94**	**501**	**36**	**4**	**4**	**8**	**72**

a WHL First All-Star Team, East Division (1985).
b NHL All-Rookie Team (1986)
Traded to **Calgary** by **Hartford** with Shane Churla for Neil Sheehy, Carey Wilson and the rights to Lane MacDonald, January 3, 1988.

MUSIL, FRANTISEK

Defense. Shoots left. 6'3", 215 lbs.   Born, Vysoke Myto, Czech., December 17, 1964.
(Minnesota's 3rd choice, 38th overall, in 1983 Entry Draft).

			Regular Season					Playoffs				
Season	Club	Lea	GP	G	A	TP	PIM	GP	G	A	TP	PIM
1985-86	Dukla-Jihlava	Czech.	35	3	7	10	42	....	....	....	....	....
1986-87	Minnesota	NHL	72	2	9	11	148	....	....	....	....	....
1987-88	Minnesota	NHL	80	9	8	17	213	....	....	....	....	....
1988-89	Minnesota	NHL	55	1	19	20	54	5	1	1	2	4
	NHL Totals		**207**	**12**	**36**	**48**	**415**	**5**	**1**	**1**	**2**	**4**

NACHBAUR, DONALD KENNETH (DON)   (NAHK bow uhr)

Center. Shoots left. 6'2", 195 lbs.   Born, Kitimat, B.C., January 30, 1959.
(Hartford's 3rd choice, 60th over-all, in 1979 Entry Draft).

			Regular Season					Playoffs				
Season	Club	Lea	GP	G	A	TP	PIM	GP	G	A	TP	PIM
1977-78	Billings	WHL	68	23	27	50	128	20	*18	7	25	37
1978-79	Billings	WHL	69	44	52	96	175	8	2	3	5	10
1979-80	Springfield	AHL	70	12	17	29	119	....	....	....	....	....
1980-81	Hartford	NHL	77	16	17	33	139	....	....	....	....	....
1981-82	Hartford	NHL	77	5	21	26	117	....	....	....	....	....
1982-83	Moncton	AHL	70	33	32	65	125	....	....	....	....	....
	Edmonton	NHL	4	0	0	0	17	2	0	0	0	7
1983-84	New Haven	AHL	70	33	32	65	194	....	....	....	....	....
1984-85	Hershey	AHL	7	2	3	5	21	....	....	....	....	....
1985-86	Philadelphia	NHL	5	1	1	2	7	....	....	....	....	....
	Hershey	AHL	74	23	24	47	301	18	5	4	9	70
1986-87	Philadelphia	NHL	23	0	2	2	87	7	1	1	2	15
	Hershey	AHL	57	18	17	35	274	5	0	3	3	47
1987-88	Philadelphia	NHL	20	0	4	4	61	2	0	0	0	2
	Hershey	AHL	42	19	21	40	174	8	4	3	7	47
1988-89	Philadelphia	NHL	15	1	0	1	37	....	....	....	....	....
	Hershey	AHL	49	24	31	55	172	12	0	5	5	58
	NHL Totals		**221**	**23**	**45**	**68**	**465**	**11**	**1**	**1**	**2**	**24**

Traded to **Edmonton** by **Hartford** with Ken Linseman for Risto Siltanen and the rights to Brent Loney, August 19, 1982. Claimed by **Los Angeles** from **Edmonton** in NHL Waiver Draft, October 3, 1983. Signed as a free agent by **Philadelphia**, October 4, 1984.

NANNE, MARTY

Right wing. Shoots right. 6', 180 lbs.   Born, Edina, MN, July 21, 1967.
(Chicago's 7th choice, 161st overall, in 1986 Entry Draft).

			Regular Season					Playoffs				
Season	Club	Lea	GP	G	A	TP	PIM	GP	G	A	TP	PIM
1985-86	U. Minnesota	WCHA	19	5	5	10	29	....	....	....	....	....
1986-87	U. Minnesota	WCHA	31	3	4	7	41	....	....	....	....	....
1987-88	U. Minnesota	WCHA	17	1	3	4	16	....	....	....	....	....
1988-89	Saginaw	IHL	36	4	10	14	47	....	....	....	....	....

NAPIER, ROBERT MARK (NAY-pyeer) (MARK)

Right wing. Shoots left. 5'10", 185 lbs.   Born, Toronto, Ont., January 28, 1957.
(Montreal's 1st choice, 10th over-all, in 1977 Amateur Draft).

Season	Club	Lea	GP	G	A	TP	PIM	GP	G	A	TP	PIM
1973-74	Toronto	OHA	70	47	46	93	63	....				
1974-75a	Toronto	OHA	61	66	64	130	106	23	*24	24	*48	13
1975-76b	Toronto	WHA	78	43	50	93	20	....				
1976-77	Birmingham	WHA	80	60	36	96	24	....				
1977-78	Birmingham	WHA	79	33	32	65	9	5	0	2	2	14
1978-79	Montreal	NHL	54	11	20	31	11	12	3	2	5	2
1979-80	Montreal	NHL	76	16	33	49	7	10	2	6	8	0
1980-81	Montreal	NHL	79	35	36	71	24	3	0	0	0	2
1981-82	Montreal	NHL	80	40	41	81	14	5	3	2	5	0
1982-83	Montreal	NHL	73	40	27	67	6	3	0	0	0	0
1983-84	Montreal	NHL	5	3	2	5	0	....				
	Minnesota	NHL	58	13	28	41	17	12	3	2	5	0
1984-85	Minnesota	NHL	39	10	18	28	2	....				
	Edmonton	NHL	33	9	26	35	19	18	5	5	10	7
1985-86	Edmonton	NHL	80	24	32	56	14	10	1	4	5	0
1986-87	Edmonton	NHL	62	8	13	21	2	....				
	Buffalo	NHL	15	5	5	10	0	....				
1987-88	Buffalo	NHL	47	10	8	18	8	6	0	3	3	0
1988-89	Buffalo	NHL	66	11	17	28	33	3	1	0	1	0
	NHL Totals		767	235	306	541	157	82	18	24	42	11

a OHA First All-Star Team (1975)
b Named WHA Rookie of the Year (1976)
Traded to **Minnesota** by **Montreal** with Keith Acton and Toronto's third round choice (Ken Hodge) — Montreal's property via earlier deal — for Bobby Smith, October 28, 1983. Traded to **Edmonton** by **Minnesota** for Gord Sherven and Terry Martin, January 24, 1985. Traded to **Buffalo** by **Edmonton** with Lee Fogolin for Normand Lacombe, Wayne Van Dorp and future considerations, March 6, 1987.

NASLUND, MATS (NAZ-luhnd)

Left wing. Shoots left. 5'7", 160 lbs.   Born, Timra, Sweden, October 31, 1959.
(Montreal's 2nd choice, 37th over-all, in 1979 Entry Draft).

Season	Club	Lea	GP	G	A	TP	PIM	GP	G	A	TP	PIM
1977-78	Timra Swe.	Swe.	35	13	6	19	14	....				
1978-79	Brynas IF	Swe.	36	12	12	24	19	....				
	Swe. National	...	13	8	3	11	12	....				
1979-80	Brynas IF	Swe.	36	18	19	37	34	7	2	2	4	4
	Swe. Olympic	...	7	3	7	10	6	....				
	Swe. National	...	21	3	11	14	10	....				
1980-81	Brynas IF	Swe.	36	17	*25	*42	34	....				
	Swe. National	...	25	4	6	10	20	....				
1981-82	Brynas IF	Swe.	36	24	18	42	16	....				
	Swe. National	...	24	6	9	15	40	....				
1982-83a	Montreal	NHL	74	26	45	71	10	3	1	0	1	0
1983-84	Montreal	NHL	77	29	35	64	4	15	6	8	14	4
1984-85	Montreal	NHL	80	42	37	79	14	12	7	4	11	6
1985-86b	Montreal	NHL	80	43	67	110	16	20	8	11	19	4
1986-87	Montreal	NHL	79	25	55	80	16	17	7	15	22	11
1987-88c	Montreal	NHL	78	24	59	83	14	6	0	7	7	2
1988-89	Montreal	NHL	77	33	51	84	14	21	4	11	15	6
	NHL Totals		545	222	349	571	88	94	33	56	89	33

a Named to NHL All-Rookie Team (1983)
b NHL Second All-Star Team (1986)
c Won Lady Byng Memorial Trophy (1988)
Played in NHL All-Star Game (1984, 1986, 1988)

NATTRESS, ERIC (RIC)

Defense. Shoots right. 6'2", 210 lbs.   Born, Hamilton, Ont., May 25, 1962.
(Montreal's 2nd choice, 27th over-all, in 1980 Entry Draft).

Season	Club	Lea	GP	G	A	TP	PIM	GP	G	A	TP	PIM
1979-80	Brantford	OHA	65	3	21	24	94	11	1	6	7	38
1980-81	Brantford	OHA	51	8	34	42	106	6	1	4	5	19
1981-82	Brantford	OHL	59	11	50	61	126	11	3	7	1	17
	Nova Scotia	AHL	....					5	0	1	1	7
1982-83	Nova Scotia	AHL	9	0	4	4	16	....				
	Montreal	NHL	40	1	3	4	19	3	0	0	0	10
1983-84	Montreal	NHL	34	0	12	12	15	....				
1984-85	Montreal	NHL	5	0	1	1	2	2	0	0	0	2
	Sherbrooke	AHL	72	8	40	48	37	16	4	13	17	20
1985-86	St. Louis	NHL	78	4	20	24	52	18	1	4	5	24
1986-87	St. Louis	NHL	73	6	22	28	24	6	0	0	0	2
1987-88	Calgary	NHL	63	2	13	15	37	6	1	3	4	0
1988-89	Calgary	NHL	38	1	8	9	47	19	0	3	3	20
	NHL Totals		331	14	79	93	196	54	2	10	12	58

Rights sold to **St. Louis** by **Montreal**, October 7, 1985. Traded to **Calgary** by **St. Louis** for Calgary's fourth-round choice (Andy Rymsha) in 1987 Entry Draft and fifth-round choice (Dave Lacouture) in 1988 Entry Draft, June 13, 1987.

NATYSHAK, MIKE (NATT-ee-shak)

Right wing. Shoots right. 6'2", 201 lbs.   Born, Belle River, Ont., November 29, 1963.
(Quebec's 1st choice, 23rd overall, in 1986 Supplemental Draft).

Season	Club	Lea	GP	G	A	TP	PIM	GP	G	A	TP	PIM
1983-84	Bowling Green	CCHA	19	0	0	0	0	....				
1984-85	Bowling Green	CCHA	38	4	9	13	79	....				
1985-86	Bowling Green	CCHA	40	3	5	8	62	....				
1986-87	Bowling Green	CCHA	45	5	10	15	101	....				
1987-88	Quebec	NHL	4	0	0	0	0	....				
	Fredericton	AHL	46	5	9	14	34	6	0	3	3	13
1988-89	Fort Wayne	IHL	48	5	9	14	95	3	0	0	0	0
	NHL Totals		4	0	0	0	0	....				

NAUSS, DARREN

Right wing. Shoots right. 5'11", 180 lbs.   Born, Vancouver, B.C., March 19, 1967.
(Quebec's 11th choice, 198th overall, in 1987 Entry Draft).

Season	Club	Lea	GP	G	A	TP	PIM	GP	G	A	TP	PIM
1986-87	N. Battleford	SJHL	64	58	43	101	....					
1987-88	Minn.-Duluth	WCHA	41	8	13	21	24	....				
1988-89	Minn.-Duluth	WCHA	40	10	4	14	40	....				

NEELY, CAM

Right wing. Shoots right. 6'1", 210 lbs.   Born, Comox, B.C., June 6, 1965.
(Vancouver's 1st choice, 9th over-all, in 1983 Entry Draft).

Season	Club	Lea	GP	G	A	TP	PIM	GP	G	A	TP	PIM
1981-82	Maple Ridge	Midget	64	73	68	141	134	....				
1982-83	Portland	WHL	72	56	64	120	130	14	9	11	20	17
1983-84	Portland	WHL	19	8	18	26	29	....				
	Vancouver	NHL	56	16	15	31	57	4	2	0	2	2
1984-85	Vancouver	NHL	72	21	18	39	137	....				
1985-86	Vancouver	NHL	73	14	20	34	126	3	0	0	0	6
1986-87	Boston	NHL	75	36	36	72	143	4	5	1	6	8
1987-88a	Boston	NHL	69	42	27	69	175	23	9	8	17	51
1988-89	Boston	NHL	74	37	38	75	190	10	7	2	9	8
	NHL Totals		419	166	154	320	828	44	23	11	34	75

a NHL Second All-Star Team (1988)
Played in NHL All-Star Game (1988, 1989)
Traded to **Boston** by **Vancouver** with Vancouver's first-round choice in 1987 (Glen Wesley) for Barry Pederson, June 6, 1986.

NEILL, MIKE

Defense. Shoots left. 6', 190 lbs.   Born, Kenora, Ont., August 6, 1965.
(New York Islanders' 4th choice, 58th over-all, in 1983 Entry Draft).

Season	Club	Lea	GP	G	A	TP	PIM	GP	G	A	TP	PIM
1982-83	S. S. Marie	OHL	65	4	13	17	115	15	0	0	0	22
1983-84	S. S. Marie	OHL	20	2	6	8	42	....				
	Windsor	OHL	49	9	17	26	101	3	1	0	1	2
1984-85	Springfield	AHL	7	0	0	0	16	1	0	0	0	0
	Windsor	OHL	63	3	17	20	143	4	0	1	1	11
1985-86	Springfield	AHL	8	0	2	2	11	....				
	Indianapolis	IHL	71	2	11	13	117	3	0	0	0	4
1986-87	Springfield	AHL	32	3	4	7	67	....				
	Indianapolis	IHL	43	2	10	12	83	....				
1987-88	Springfield	AHL	11	0	1	1	39	....				
	Peoria	IHL	56	4	19	23	148	7	2	0	2	39
1988-89	Maine	AHL	64	0	10	10	200	....				

NELSON, CHRISTOPHER

Defense. Shoots right. 6'2", 190 lbs.   Born, Philadelphia, PA, February 12, 1969.
(New Jersey's 6th choice, 96th overall, in 1988 Entry Draft).

Season	Club	Lea	GP	G	A	TP	PIM	GP	G	A	TP	PIM
1987-88	Rochester	USHL	48	6	29	35	82	....				
1988-89	U. Wisconsin	WCHA	21	1	4	5	24	....				

NEMETH, STEVE

Center. Shoots left. 5'8", 170 lbs.   Born, Calgary, Alta., February 11, 1967.
(NY Rangers' 10th choice, 196th overall, in 1985 Entry Draft).

Season	Club	Lea	GP	G	A	TP	PIM	GP	G	A	TP	PIM
1982-83	Lethbridge	WHL	2	0	1	1	0	....				
1983-84	Lethbridge	WHL	68	22	20	42	33	5	1	1	2	2
1984-85	Lethbridge	WHL	67	39	55	94	39	4	2	3	5	13
1985-86	Lethbridge	WHL	70	42	69	111	47	10	5	5	10	6
1986-87	Kamloops	WHL	10	10	4	14	0	13	11	9	20	12
	Cdn. Olympic	....	43	14	7	21	12	....				
1987-88	NY Rangers	NHL	12	2	0	2	2	....				
	Colorado	IHL	57	13	24	37	28	10	2	1	3	8
1988-89	Cdn. National	....	26	6	10	16	10	....				
	Denver	IHL	11	5	2	7	8	....				
	NHL Totals		12	2	0	2	2	....				

NESICH, JIM

Right wing. Shoots right. 5'11", 170 lbs.   Born, Dearborn, MI, February 22, 1966.
(Montreal's 8th choice, 116th overall, in 1984 Entry Draft).

Season	Club	Lea	GP	G	A	TP	PIM	GP	G	A	TP	PIM
1983-84	Verdun	QMJHL	70	22	24	46	35	10	11	5	16	2
1984-85	Verdun	QMJHL	65	19	33	52	72	14	1	6	7	25
1985-86	Verdun	QMJHL	71	26	55	81	114	5	0	0	0	8
1986-87	Verdun	QMJHL	62	20	50	70	133	....				
1987-88	Sherbrooke	AHL	53	4	10	14	51	4	1	2	3	20
1988-89	Sherbrooke	AHL	74	12	34	46	112	6	1	2	3	10

NEUFELD, RAY MATTHEW (NEW-feld)

Right wing. Shoots right. 6'3", 210 lbs. Born, St. Boniface, Man. April 15, 1959.
(Hartford's 4th choice, 81st over-all, in 1979 Entry Draft).

			Regular Season					Playoffs				
Season	Club	Lea	GP	G	A	TP	PIM	GP	G	A	TP	PIM
1977-78	Flin Flon	WHL	72	23	46	69	224	15	4	4	8	39
1978-79	Edmonton	WHL	57	54	48	102	138	8	5	1	6	2
1979-80	Springfield	AHL	73	23	29	52	51	....	....	....	....	....
	Hartford	NHL	8	1	0	1	0	2	1	0	1	0
1980-81	Hartford	NHL	52	5	10	15	44	....	....	....	....	....
	Binghamton	AHL	25	7	7	14	43	6	2	0	2	0
1981-82	Hartford	NHL	19	4	3	7	4	....	....	....	....	....
	Binghamton	AHL	61	28	31	59	81	15	*9	8	17	10
1982-83	Hartford	NHL	80	26	31	57	86	....	....	....	....	....
1983-84	Hartford	NHL	80	27	42	69	97	....	....	....	....	....
1984-85	Hartford	NHL	76	27	35	62	129	....	....	....	....	....
1985-86	Hartford	NHL	16	5	10	15	40	....	....	....	....	....
	Winnipeg	NHL	60	20	28	48	62	3	2	0	2	10
1986-87	Winnipeg	NHL	80	18	18	36	105	8	1	1	2	30
1987-88	Winnipeg	NHL	78	18	18	36	169	5	2	2	4	6
1988-89	Winnipeg	NHL	31	5	2	7	52	....	....	....	....	....
	Boston	NHL	14	1	3	4	28	10	2	3	5	9
	NHL Totals		594	157	200	357	816	28	8	6	14	55

Traded to **Winnipeg** by **Hartford** for Dave Babych, November 21, 1985. Traded to **Boston** by **Winnipeg** for Moe Lemay, December 30, 1988.

NEURURER, PHILLIP

Defense. Shoots left. 6'2", 195 lbs. Born, Robbinsdale, MA, March 21, 1970.
(NY Islanders' 13th choice, 226th overall, in 1988 Entry Draft).

			Regular Season					Playoffs				
Season	Club	Lea	GP	G	A	TP	PIM	GP	G	A	TP	PIM
1987-88	Osseo	HS	14	0	9	9	0	....	....	....	....	....
1988-89	N. Michigan	WCHA	23	0	1	1	12	....	....	....	....	....

NEZIOL, THOMAS (TOM)

Left wing. Shoots left. 6'1", 190 lbs. Born, Burlington, Ont., August 7, 1967.
(New Jersey's 6th choice, 128th overall, in 1987 Entry Draft).

			Regular Season					Playoffs				
Season	Club	Lea	GP	G	A	TP	PIM	GP	G	A	TP	PIM
1986-87	Miami-Ohio	CCHA	39	11	18	29	80	....	....	....	....	....
1987-88	Miami-Ohio	CCHA	34	13	13	26	52	....	....	....	....	....
1988-89	Miami-Ohio	CCHA	12	5	4	9	14	....	....	....	....	....

NICHOLLS, BERNIE IRVINE (NICK-els)

Center. Shoots right. 6', 185 lbs. Born, Haliburton, Ont., June 24, 1961.
(Los Angeles' 6th choice, 73rd over-all, in 1980 Entry Draft).

			Regular Season					Playoffs				
Season	Club	Lea	GP	G	A	TP	PIM	GP	G	A	TP	PIM
1979-80	Kingston	OHA	68	36	43	79	85	3	1	0	1	10
1980-81	Kingston	OHA	65	63	89	152	109	14	8	10	18	17
1981-82	New Haven	AHL	55	41	30	71	31	....	....	....	....	....
	Los Angeles	NHL	22	14	18	32	27	10	4	0	4	23
1982-83	Los Angeles	NHL	71	28	22	50	124	....	....	....	....	....
1983-84	Los Angeles	NHL	78	41	54	95	83	....	....	....	....	....
1984-85	Los Angeles	NHL	80	46	54	100	76	3	1	1	2	9
1985-86	Los Angeles	NHL	80	36	61	97	78	....	....	....	....	....
1986-87	Los Angeles	NHL	80	33	48	81	101	5	2	5	7	6
1987-88	Los Angeles	NHL	65	32	46	78	114	5	2	6	8	11
1988-89a	Los Angeles	NHL	79	70	80	150	96	11	7	9	16	12
	NHL Totals		555	300	383	683	699	34	16	21	37	61

a NHL Second All-Star Team (1989)
Played in NHL All-Star Game (1984, 1989)

NICHOLS, JAMIE

Left wing. Shoots left. 6', 185 lbs. Born, Vancouver, B.C., March 27, 1968.
(Edmonton's 2nd choice, 42nd overall, in 1986 Entry Draft).

			Regular Season					Playoffs				
Season	Club	Lea	GP	G	A	TP	PIM	GP	G	A	TP	PIM
1985-86	Portland	WHL	65	15	37	52	60	15	2	10	12	7
1986-87	Portland	WHL	59	28	37	65	42	20	6	4	10	17
1987-88	Nova Scotia	AHL	5	2	2	4	0	....	....	....	....	....
	Seattle	WHL	70	34	26	60	43	....	....	....	....	....
1988-89	Cape Breton	AHL	23	3	4	7	18	....	....	....	....	....
	Cdn. National	....	1	0	0	0	0	....	....	....	....	....

NICOLETTI, MARTIN

Right wing. Shoots right. 6', 200 lbs. Born, LaSalle, Que., January 15, 1963.

			Regular Season					Playoffs				
Season	Club	Lea	GP	G	A	TP	PIM	GP	G	A	TP	PIM
1983-84	UQTR	QUAA	24	8	12	20	30	....	....	....	....	....
1984-85	UQTR	QUAA	18	7	8	15	30	....	....	....	....	....
1985-86	UQTR	QUAA	12	5	6	11	25	....	....	....	....	....
1986-87	UQTR	QUAA	18	7	20	27	45	....	....	....	....	....
1987-88	Salt Lake	IHL	49	10	13	23	37	....	....	....	....	....
	Sherbrooke	AHL	18	6	8	14	22	6	1	1	2	11
1988-89	Sherbrooke	AHL	75	15	24	39	148	5	0	0	0	13

Signed as a free agent by **Calgary**, May 19, 1987. Traded to **Montreal** by **Calgary** for Rick Hayward, February 19, 1988.

NIELSON, LEN

Center. Shoots left. 5'9", 170 lbs. Born, Moose Jaw, Sask., March 28, 1967.

			Regular Season					Playoffs				
Season	Club	Lea	GP	G	A	TP	PIM	GP	G	A	TP	PIM
1983-84	Regina	WHL	57	9	15	24	20	23	0	2	2	4
1984-85	Regina	WHL	72	35	74	109	48	8	5	7	12	4
1985-86	Regina	WHL	66	30	77	107	49	10	4	4	8	6
1986-87	Sherbrooke	AHL	3	1	0	1	0	5	1	1	2	0
	Regina	WHL	72	36	100	136	32	3	0	4	4	0
1987-88	Moncton	AHL	66	9	29	38	28	....	....	....	....	....
1988-89	Moncton	AHL	14	4	1	5	4	....	....	....	....	....
	HPK	Fin.	6	0	0	0	2	....	....	....	....	....
	SaPKo	Fin.	15	5	10	15	34	....	....	....	....	....

Signed as a free agent by **Winnipeg**, September 30, 1985.

NIEMAN, THOMAS

Right wing. Shoots right. 6'0", 185 lbs. Born, Winnetka, IL, January 22, 1970.
(Buffalo's 11th choice, 223rd overall, in 1988 Entry Draft).

			Regular Season					Playoffs				
Season	Club	Lea	GP	G	A	TP	PIM	GP	G	A	TP	PIM
1987-88	Choate	HS	....	14	10	24	....	....	....	....	....	....
1988-89	Dartmouth	ECAC	26	7	11	18	38	....	....	....	....	....

NIENHUIS, KRAIG (NEEN-HOWS)

Left wing. Shoots left. 6'2", 205 lbs. Born, Sarnia, Ont., May 9, 1961.

			Regular Season					Playoffs				
Season	Club	Lea	GP	G	A	TP	PIM	GP	G	A	TP	PIM
1982-83	RPI	ECAC	24	9	11	20	34	....	....	....	....	....
1983-84	RPI	ECAC	35	10	12	22	26	....	....	....	....	....
1984-85	RPI	ECAC	36	11	10	21	55	....	....	....	....	....
1985-86	Boston	NHL	70	16	14	30	37	2	0	0	0	14
1986-87	Boston	NHL	16	4	2	6	2	....	....	....	....	....
	Moncton	AHL	54	10	17	27	44	....	....	....	....	....
1987-88	Boston	NHL	1	0	0	0	0	....	....	....	....	....
	Maine	AHL	36	16	17	33	57	....	....	....	....	....
1988-89	Cdn. National	....	4	0	0	0	12	....	....	....	....	....
	Kaufbeuren	WGer.	35	23	28	51	60	12	15	18	33	30
	NHL Totals		87	20	16	36	39	2	0	0	0	14

Signed as a free agent by **Boston**, May 28, 1985.

NIEUWENDYK, JOE (NEW-en-dike)

Center. Shoots left. 6'1", 195 lbs. Born, Oshawa, Ont., September 10, 1966.
(Calgary's 2nd choice, 27th over-all, in 1985 Entry Draft).

			Regular Season					Playoffs				
Season	Club	Lea	GP	G	A	TP	PIM	GP	G	A	TP	PIM
1983-84	Pickering	OPJHL	38	30	28	58	35	....	....	....	....	....
1984-85a	Cornell	ECAC	23	18	21	39	20	....	....	....	....	....
1985-86bc	Cornell	ECAC	21	21	21	42	45	....	....	....	....	....
1986-87	Calgary	NHL	9	5	1	6	0	6	2	2	4	0
bcd	Cornell	ECAC	23	26	26	52	26	....	....	....	....	....
1987-88efg	Calgary	NHL	75	51	41	92	23	8	3	4	7	2
1988-89	Calgary	NHL	77	51	31	82	40	22	10	4	14	10
	NHL Totals		161	107	73	180	63	36	15	10	25	12

a ECAC Rookie of the Year (1985).
b NCAA East First All-American Team (1986, 1987)
c ECAC First All-Star Team (1986, 1987)
d ECAC Player of the Year (1987)
e Won Calder Memorial Trophy (1988)
f NHL All-Rookie Team (1988)
g Won Dodge Ram Tough Award (1988)
Played in NHL All-Star Game (1988, 1989)

NILAN, CHRISTOPHER JOHN (CHRIS) (NIGH-luhn)

Right wing. Shoots right. 6', 205 lbs. Born, Boston, MA, February 9, 1958.
(Montreal's 21st choice, 231st over-all, in 1978 Amateur Draft).

			Regular Season					Playoffs				
Season	Club	Lea	GP	G	A	TP	PIM	GP	G	A	TP	PIM
1978-79	Northeastern	ECAC	32	9	17	26	....	....	....	....	....	....
1979-80	Nova Scotia	AHL	49	15	10	25	*304	....	....	....	....	....
	Montreal	NHL	15	0	2	2	50	5	0	0	0	2
1980-81	Montreal	NHL	57	7	8	15	262	2	0	0	0	0
1981-82	Montreal	NHL	49	7	4	11	204	5	1	1	2	22
1982-83	Montreal	NHL	66	6	8	14	213	3	0	0	0	5
1983-84	Montreal	NHL	76	16	10	26	338	15	1	0	1	81
1984-85	Montreal	NHL	77	21	16	37	358	12	2	1	3	81
1985-86	Montreal	NHL	72	19	15	34	274	18	1	2	3	141
1986-87	Montreal	NHL	44	4	16	20	266	17	3	0	3	75
1987-88	Montreal	NHL	50	7	5	12	209	....	....	....	....	....
	NY Rangers	NHL	22	3	5	8	96	....	....	....	....	....
1988-89	NY Rangers	NHL	38	7	7	14	177	4	0	1	1	38
	NHL Totals		566	97	96	193	2447	81	8	5	13	445

Traded to **NY Rangers** by **Montreal** for a switch of first round choices in 1989 Entry Draft, January 27, 1988.

NILL, JAMES EDWARD (JIM)

Right wing. Shoots right. 6', 185 lbs. Born, Hanna, Alta., April 11, 1958.
(St. Louis' 4th choice, 89th over-all, in 1978 Amateur Draft).

			Regular Season					Playoffs				
Season	Club	Lea	GP	G	A	TP	PIM	GP	G	A	TP	PIM
1975-76	Medicine Hat	WHL	62	5	11	16	69	9	1	1	2	20
1976-77	Medicine Hat	WHL	71	23	24	47	140	4	2	2	4	4
1977-78	Medicine Hat	WHL	72	47	46	93	252	12	8	7	15	37
1978-79	U. of Calgary	CWUAA	20	9	8	17	42	....	....	....	....	....
1979-80	Cdn. National	...	45	13	19	32	54	....	....	....	....	....
	Cdn. Olympic	...	6	1	2	3	4	....	....	....	....	....
1980-81	Salt Lake	CHL	79	28	34	62	222	16	9	8	17	38
1981-82	St. Louis	NHL	61	9	12	21	127	....	....	....	....	....
	Vancouver	NHL	8	1	2	3	5	16	4	3	7	67
1982-83	Vancouver	NHL	65	7	15	22	136	4	0	0	0	6
1983-84	Vancouver	NHL	51	9	6	15	78	....	....	....	....	....
	Boston	NHL	27	3	2	5	81	3	0	0	0	4
1984-85	Boston	NHL	49	1	9	10	62	....	....	....	....	....
	Winnipeg	NHL	20	8	8	16	38	8	0	1	1	28
1985-86	Winnipeg	NHL	61	6	8	14	75	3	0	0	0	4
1986-87	Winnipeg	NHL	36	3	4	7	52	3	0	0	0	7
1987-88	Winnipeg	NHL	24	0	1	1	44	....	....	....	....	....
	Moncton	AHL	3	0	0	0	6	....	....	....	....	....
	Detroit	NHL	36	3	11	14	55	16	6	1	7	62
1988-89	Detroit	NHL	71	8	7	15	83	6	0	0	0	25
	NHL Totals		509	58	85	143	836	59	10	5	15	203

Traded to **Vancouver** by **St. Louis** with Tony Currie, Rick Heinz and St. Louis' fourth round choice (Shawn Kilroy) in 1982 Entry Draft for Glen Hanlon, March 9, 1982. Traded to **Boston** by **Vancouver** for Peter McNab, February 3, 1984. Traded to **Winnipeg** by **Boston** for Morris Lukowich, February 14, 1985. Traded to **Detroit** by **Winnipeg** for Mark Kumpel, January 11, 1988.

NILSSON, PETER

Center. Shoots left. 5'11", 185 lbs. Born, Stockholm, Sweden, June 10, 1962.
(Winnipeg's 7th choice, 127th overall, in 1981 Entry Draft).

			Regular Season					Playoffs				
Season	Club	Lea	GP	G	A	TP	PIM	GP	G	A	TP	PIM
1979-80	Hammarby	Swe. 2	28	6	6	12	12	....	....	....	....	....
1980-81	Hammarby	Swe. 2	29	22	11	33	24	11	4	3	7	4
1981-82	Hammarby	Swe. 2	12	7	8	15	12	10	2	8	10	12
1982-83	Hammarby	Swe.	33	14	7	21	12	....	....	....	....	....
1983-84	Djurgarden	Swe.	34	18	12	30	10	6	0	0	0	2
1984-85	Djurgarden	Swe.	35	18	17	35	8	8	1	4	5	0
1985-86	Djurgarden	Swe.	34	13	11	24	14	....	....	....	....	....
1986-87	Djurgarden	Swe.	33	11	14	25	20	2	1	1	2	2
1987-88	Djurgarden	Swe.	39	14	32	46	22	3	0	2	2	0
1988-89	Djurgarden	Swe.	40	11	20	31	6	8	3	4	7	4

NILSSON, STEFAN

Right wing. Shoots right. 5'11", 170 lbs. Born, Ljungby, Sweden, September 12, 1968.
(Vancouver's 11th choice, 233rd overall, in 1988 Entry Draft).

			Regular Season					Playoffs				
Season	Club	Lea	GP	G	A	TP	PIM	GP	G	A	TP	PIM
1987-88	Troja	Swe.	25	10	11	21	42	....	....	....	....	....
1988-89	Leksand	Swe.	36	7	12	19	48	....	....	....	....	....

NILSSON, STEFAN

Center. Shoots right. 5'11", 170 lbs. Born, Lulea, Sweden, April 5, 1968.
(Washington's 7th choice, 124th overall, in 1986 Entry Draft).

			Regular Season					Playoffs				
Season	Club	Lea	GP	G	A	TP	PIM	GP	G	A	TP	PIM
1985-86	Lulea	Swe.	4	0	0	0	0	....	....	....	....	....
1986-87	Lulea	Swe.	23	3	9	12	14	....	....	....	....	....
1987-88	Lulea	Swe.	31	10	10	20	24	....	....	....	....	....
1988-89	Lulea	Swe.	40	9	22	31	24	....	....	....	....	....

NOBLE, JEFF

Center. Shoots left. 5'10", 170 lbs. Born, Mount Forest, Ont., May 20, 1968.
(Vancouver's 7th choice, 154th overall, in 1986 Entry Draft).

			Regular Season					Playoffs				
Season	Club	Lea	GP	G	A	TP	PIM	GP	G	A	TP	PIM
1985-86	Kitchener	OHL	58	22	33	55	65	5	2	2	4	11
1986-87	Kitchener	OHL	66	29	57	86	55	4	2	0	2	20
1987-88	Kitchener	OHL	55	37	64	101	97	4	3	1	4	4
1988-89	Cdn. National	....	11	2	8	10	6	....	....	....	....	....

NOONAN, BRIAN

Center. Shoots right. 6'1", 180 lbs. Born, Boston, MA, May 29, 1965.
(Chicago's 10th choice, 186th over-all, in 1983 Entry Draft).

			Regular Season					Playoffs				
Season	Club	Lea	GP	G	A	TP	PIM	GP	G	A	TP	PIM
1984-85	N. Westminster	WHL	72	50	66	116	76	11	8	7	15	4
1985-86	Nova Scotia	AHL	2	0	0	0	0	....	....	....	....	....
	Saginaw	IHL	76	39	39	78	69	11	6	3	9	6
1986-87	Nova Scotia	AHL	70	25	26	51	30	5	3	1	4	4
1987-88	**Chicago**	**NHL**	**77**	**10**	**20**	**30**	**44**	**3**	**0**	**0**	**0**	**4**
1988-89	**Chicago**	**NHL**	**45**	**4**	**12**	**16**	**28**	**1**	**0**	**0**	**0**	**0**
	Saginaw	IHL	19	18	13	31	36	1	0	0	0	0
	NHL Totals		**122**	**14**	**32**	**46**	**72**	**4**	**0**	**0**	**0**	**4**

NORDMARK, ROBERT

Defense. Shoots right. 6'1", 190 lbs. Born, Kalix, Sweden, August 20, 1962.
(St. Louis' 3rd choice, 59th overall, in 1987 Entry Draft).

			Regular Season					Playoffs				
Season	Club	Lea	GP	G	A	TP	PIM	GP	G	A	TP	PIM
1979-80	Lulea	Swe. 2	24	4	2	6	16	....	....	....	....	....
1980-81	V. Frolunda	Swe.	34	4	3	7	30	....	....	....	....	....
1981-82	Brynas	Swe.	34	5	5	10	16	....	....	....	....	....
1982-83	Brynas	Swe.	36	8	5	13	32	....	....	....	....	....
1983-84	Brynas	Swe.	32	10	15	25	44	....	....	....	....	....
1984-85	Lulea	Swe.	33	3	9	12	30	....	....	....	....	....
1985-86	Lulea	Swe.	35	9	15	24	48	....	....	....	....	....
1986-87	Lulea	Swe.	32	7	8	15	46	3	0	3	3	4
1987-88	**St. Louis**	**NHL**	**67**	**3**	**18**	**21**	**60**	....	....	....	....	....
1988-89	**Vancouver**	**NHL**	**80**	**6**	**35**	**41**	**97**	**7**	**3**	**2**	**5**	**8**
	NHL Totals		**147**	**9**	**53**	**62**	**157**	**7**	**3**	**2**	**5**	**8**

Traded to **Vancouver** by **St. Louis** for Dave Ritcher and Vancouver's second-round choice in 1990 Entry Draft, September 6, 1988.

NORTON, CHRIS

Defense. Shoots right. 6'2", 200 lbs. Born, Oakville, Ont., April 11, 1965.
(Winnipeg's 11th choice, 228th overall, in 1985 Entry Draft).

			Regular Season					Playoffs				
Season	Club	Lea	GP	G	A	TP	PIM	GP	G	A	TP	PIM
1984-85	Cornell	ECAC	29	4	19	23	34	....	....	....	..	..
1985-86a	Cornell	ECAC	21	8	15	23	56	....	....	....	....	....
1986-87	Cornell	ECAC	24	10	21	31	79	....	....	....	....	....
1987-88a	Cornell	ECAC	27	9	25	34	53	....	....	....	....	....
1988-89	Moncton	AHL	60	1	21	22	49	10	3	2	5	15

a ECAC Second All-Star Team (1986, 1988).

NORTON, D'ARCY

Left wing. Shoots left. 6'1", 180 lbs. Born, Camrose, Alta., May 2, 1967.
(Minnesota's 6th choice, 109th overall, in 1987 Entry Draft).

			Regular Season					Playoffs				
Season	Club	Lea	GP	G	A	TP	PIM	GP	G	A	TP	PIM
1984-85	Lethbridge	WHL	50	4	11	15	49	4	0	0	0	21
1985-86	Lethbridge	WHL	69	19	25	44	69	10	2	7	9	0
1986-87	Kamloops	WHL	71	45	57	102	66	13	7	9	16	15
1987-88	Kamloops	WHL	68	64	43	107	82	18	9	13	22	20
1988-89	Kalamazoo	IHL	75	39	38	77	79	6	2	3	5	15

NORTON, JEFF

Defense. Shoots left. 6'2", 195 lbs. Born, Acton, MA, November 25, 1965.
(NY Islanders' 3rd choice, 62nd overall, in 1984 Entry Draft).

			Regular Season					Playoffs				
Season	Club	Lea	GP	G	A	TP	PIM	GP	G	A	TP	PIM
1984-85	U. of Michigan	CCHA	37	8	16	24	103	....	....	....	....	....
1985-86	U. of Michigan	CCHA	37	15	30	45	99	....	....	....	....	....
1986-87a	U. of Michigan	CCHA	39	12	36	48	92	....	....	....	....	....
1987-88	**NY Islanders**	**NHL**	**15**	**1**	**6**	**7**	**14**	**3**	**0**	**2**	**2**	**13**
	U.S. National	....	54	7	22	29	52	....	....	....	....	....
	U.S. Olympic	....	6	0	4	4	4	....	....	....	....	....
1988-89	**NY Islanders**	**NHL**	**69**	**1**	**30**	**31**	**74**	....	....	....	....	....
	NHL Totals		**84**	**2**	**36**	**38**	**88**	....	....	....	....	....

a CCHA Second All-Star Team (1987)

NORWOOD, LEE CHARLES

Defense. Shoots left. 6', 198 lbs. Born, Oakland, CA, February 2, 1960.
(Quebec's 3rd choice, 62nd over-all, in 1979 Entry Draft).

			Regular Season					Playoffs				
Season	Club	Lea	GP	G	A	TP	PIM	GP	G	A	TP	PIM
1978-79	Oshawa	OHA	61	23	38	61	171	5	2	2	4	17
1979-80	Oshawa	OHA	60	13	39	52	143	6	2	7	9	15
1980-81	Hershey	AHL	52	11	32	43	78	8	0	4	4	14
	Quebec	**NHL**	**11**	**1**	**1**	**2**	**9**	**3**	**0**	**0**	**0**	**2**
1981-82	Fredericton	AHL	29	6	13	19	74	....	....	....	....	....
	Quebec	**NHL**	**2**	**0**	**0**	**0**	**2**	....	....	....	....	....
	Washington	**NHL**	**26**	**7**	**10**	**17**	**125**	....	....	....	....	....
1982-83	**Washington**	**NHL**	**8**	**0**	**1**	**1**	**14**	....	....	....	....	....
	Hershey	AHL	67	12	36	48	90	5	0	1	1	2
1983-84	St. Catharines	AHL	75	13	46	59	91	7	0	5	5	31
1984-85ab	Peoria	IHL	80	17	60	77	229	18	1	11	12	62
1985-86	**St. Louis**	**NHL**	**71**	**5**	**24**	**29**	**134**	**19**	**2**	**7**	**9**	**64**
1986-87	**Detroit**	**NHL**	**57**	**6**	**21**	**27**	**163**	**16**	**1**	**6**	**7**	**31**
	Adirondack	AHL	3	0	3	3	0	....	....	....	....	....
1987-88	**Detroit**	**NHL**	**51**	**9**	**22**	**31**	**131**	**16**	**2**	**6**	**8**	**40**
1988-89	**Detroit**	**NHL**	**66**	**10**	**32**	**42**	**100**	**6**	**1**	**2**	**3**	**16**
	NHL Totals		**292**	**38**	**111**	**149**	**678**	**60**	**6**	**21**	**27**	**153**

a Won Governors' Trophy (IHL's Top Defenseman) 1985
b IHL First All-Star Team (1985)

Traded to **Washington** by **Quebec** for Tim Tookey and Washington's seventh round choice (Daniel Poudrier) in 1982 Entry Draft, February 1, 1982. Traded to **Toronto** by **Washington** for Dave Shand, October 6, 1983. Signed as a free agent by **St. Louis**, August 13, 1985. Traded to **Detroit** by **St. Louis** for Larry Trader, August 7, 1986.

NOVAK, RICHARD

Right wing. Shoots right. 6'1", 170 lbs. Born, Squamish, B.C., February 19, 1966.
(Edmonton's 4th choice, 84th overall, in 1984 Entry Draft).

			Regular Season					Playoffs				
Season	Club	Lea	GP	G	A	TP	PIM	GP	G	A	TP	PIM
1984-85	Michigan Tech	WCHA	40	9	10	19	16	....	....	....	....	..
1985-86	Michigan Tech	WCHA	38	9	20	29	20	....	....	....	....	....
1986-87	Michigan Tech	WCHA	7	0	0	0	4	....	....	....	....	....
1987-88	Michigan Tech	WCHA	40	7	1	8	22	....	....	....	....	....
1988-89	Michigan Tech	WCHA	40	10	11	21	28	....	....	....	....	....

NUMMINEN, TEPPO

Defense. Shoots right. 6'1", 175 lbs. Born, Tampere, Finland, July 3, 1968.
(Winnipeg's 2nd choice, 29th overall, in 1986 Entry Draft).

			Regular Season					Playoffs				
Season	Club	Lea	GP	G	A	TP	PIM	GP	G	A	TP	PIM
1985-86	Tappara	Fin.	31	2	4	6	6	8	0	0	0	0
1986-87	Tappara	Fin.	44	9	9	18	16	9	4	1	5	4
1987-88	Tappara	Fin.	40	10	10	20	29	10	6	6	12	6
1988-89	**Winnipeg**	**NHL**	**69**	**1**	**14**	**15**	**36**	....	....	....	....	....
	NHL Totals		**69**	**1**	**14**	**15**	**36**	....	....	....	....	....

NYLUND, GARY

(NIGH-lund)

Defense. Shoots left. 6'4", 210 lbs. Born, Surrey, B.C., October 28, 1963.
(Toronto's 1st choice, 3rd over-all, in 1982 Entry Draft).

			Regular Season					Playoffs				
Season	Club	Lea	GP	G	A	TP	PIM	GP	G	A	TP	PIM
1979-80	Portland	WHL	72	5	21	26	59	8	0	1	1	2
1980-81a	Portland	WHL	70	6	40	46	186	9	1	7	8	17
1981-82bc	Portland	WHL	65	7	59	66	267	15	3	16	19	74
1982-83	**Toronto**	**NHL**	**16**	**0**	**3**	**3**	**16**	....	....	....	....	....
1983-84	**Toronto**	**NHL**	**47**	**2**	**14**	**16**	**103**	....	....	....	....	....
1984-85	**Toronto**	**NHL**	**76**	**3**	**17**	**20**	**99**	....	....	....	....	....
1985-86	**Toronto**	**NHL**	**79**	**2**	**16**	**18**	**180**	**10**	**0**	**2**	**2**	**25**
1986-87	**Chicago**	**NHL**	**80**	**7**	**20**	**27**	**190**	**4**	**0**	**2**	**2**	**11**
1987-88	**Chicago**	**NHL**	**76**	**4**	**15**	**19**	**208**	**5**	**0**	**0**	**0**	**10**
1988-89	**Chicago**	**NHL**	**23**	**3**	**2**	**5**	**63**	....	....	....	....	....
	NY Islanders	**NHL**	**46**	**4**	**8**	**12**	**74**	....	....	....	....	....
	NHL Totals		**443**	**25**	**95**	**120**	**933**	**19**	**0**	**4**	**4**	**46**

a WHL Second All-Star Team (1981)
b WHL First All-Star Team (1982)
c Named WHL's Top Defenseman (1982)

Signed as a free agent by **Chicago**, August 27, 1987. Traded to **NY Islanders** by **Chicago** with Marc Bergevin for Steve Konroyd and Bob Bassen, November 25, 1988.

OATES, ADAM

Center. Shoots right. 5'11", 190 lbs. Born, Weston, Ont., August 27, 1962.

			Regular Season					Playoffs				
Season	Club	Lea	GP	G	A	TP	PIM	GP	G	A	TP	PIM
1982-83	RPI	ECAC	22	9	33	42	8	....	....	....	....	....
1983-84	RPI	ECAC	38	26	57	83	15	....	....	....	....	....
1984-85ab	RPI	ECAC	38	31	60	91	29	....	....	....	....	....
1985-86	**Detroit**	**NHL**	**38**	**9**	**11**	**20**	**10**	....	....	....	....	....
	Adirondack	AHL	34	18	28	46	4	17	7	14	21	4
1986-87	**Detroit**	**NHL**	**76**	**15**	**32**	**47**	**21**	**16**	**4**	**7**	**11**	**6**
1987-88	**Detroit**	**NHL**	**63**	**14**	**40**	**54**	**20**	**16**	**8**	**12**	**20**	**6**
1988-89	**Detroit**	**NHL**	**69**	**16**	**62**	**78**	**14**	**6**	**0**	**8**	**8**	**2**
	NHL Totals		**246**	**54**	**145**	**199**	**65**	**38**	**12**	**27**	**39**	**14**

a ECAC First All-Star Team (1985)
b Named to NCAA All-American Team (1985)

Signed as a free agent by **Detroit**, June 28, 1985. Traded to **St. Louis** by **Detroit** with Paul MacLean for Bernie Federko and Tony McKegney, June 15, 1989.

O'BRIEN, DAVID

Right wing. Shoots right. 6'1", 180 lbs. Born, Brighton, MA, September 13, 1966.
(St. Louis' 13th choice, 241st overall, in 1986 Entry Draft).

			Regular Season					Playoffs				
Season	Club	Lea	GP	G	A	TP	PIM	GP	G	A	TP	PIM
1985-86	Northeastern	H.E.	39	23	16	39	18	....	....	....	....	....
1986-87	Northeastern	H.E.	35	16	24	40	12	....	....	....	....	....
1987-88a	Northeastern	H.E.	37	18	29	47	18	....	....	....	....	....
1988-89	Binghamton	AHL	53	3	12	15	11	....	....	....	....	....

a Hockey East First All-Star Team (1988)

O'BRIEN, EDWARD

Left wing. Shoots left. 6'0", 175 lbs. Born, Boston, MA, July 22, 1969.
(Philadelphia's 6th choice, 98th overall, in 1988 Entry Draft).

			Regular Season					Playoffs				
Season	Club	Lea	GP	G	A	TP	PIM	GP	G	A	TP	PIM
1987-88	Cushing Aca.	HS	24	16	16	32	....	....	....	....	....	....
1988-89	St. Anselm	NCAA	22	3	9	12	61	....	....	....	....	....

O'BORSKY, ERIC

Center. Shoots left. 6'3", 215 lbs. Born, Los Angeles, CA, June 2, 1968.
(NY Rangers' 5th choice, 94th overall, in 1987 Entry Draft).

			Regular Season					Playoffs				
Season	Club	Lea	GP	G	A	TP	PIM	GP	G	A	TP	PIM
1987-88	Yale	ECAC	14	4	3	7	24	....	....	....	....	....
1988-89	Yale	ECAC	15	0	1	1	27	....	....	....	....	....

O'CALLAHAN, JACK

Defense. Shoots right. 6'1", 190 lbs. Born, Charlestown, MA, July 24, 1957.
(Chicago's 5th choice, 96th over-all, in 1977 Amateur Draft).

			Regular Season					Playoffs				
Season	Club	Lea	GP	G	A	TP	PIM	GP	G	A	TP	PIM
1978-79	Boston U.	ECAC	....	....	....	....	....	....	....	....	....	....
1979-80	U.S. National	...	51	7	29	36	83	....	....	....	....	....
	U.S. Olympic		4	0	1	1	2	....	....	....	....	....
1980-81	New Brunswick	AHL	78	9	25	34	167	13	1	6	7	36
1981-82	New Brunswick	AHL	79	15	33	48	130	15	2	6	8	24
1982-83	Springfield	AHL	35	2	24	26	25	....	....	....	....	....
	Chicago	**NHL**	**39**	**0**	**11**	**11**	**46**	**5**	**0**	**2**	**2**	**2**
1983-84	**Chicago**	**NHL**	**70**	**4**	**13**	**17**	**67**	**2**	**0**	**0**	**0**	**2**
1984-85	**Chicago**	**NHL**	**66**	**6**	**8**	**14**	**105**	**15**	**3**	**5**	**8**	**25**
1985-86	**Chicago**	**NHL**	**80**	**4**	**19**	**23**	**116**	**3**	**0**	**1**	**1**	**4**
1986-87	**Chicago**	**NHL**	**48**	**1**	**13**	**14**	**59**	**2**	**0**	**0**	**0**	**2**
1987-88	**New Jersey**	**NHL**	**50**	**7**	**19**	**26**	**97**	**5**	**1**	**3**	**4**	**6**
1988-89	**New Jersey**	**NHL**	**36**	**5**	**21**	**26**	**51**	....	....	....	....	....
	NHL Totals		**389**	**27**	**104**	**131**	**541**	**32**	**4**	**11**	**15**	**41**

Claimed by **New Jersey** In NHL Waiver Draft, October 5, 1987.

O'CONNELL, MICHAEL THOMAS (MIKE)

Defense. Shoots right. 5'9", 180 lbs. Born, Chicago, IL, November 25, 1955.
(Chicago's 3rd choice, 43rd over-all, in 1975 Amateur Draft).

			Regular Season					Playoffs				
Season	Club	Lea	GP	G	A	TP	PIM	GP	G	A	TP	PIM
1973-74	Kingston	OHA	70	16	43	59	81	....	....	....	....	....
1974-75a	Kingston	OHA	50	18	55	73	47	8	1	3	4	8
1975-76	Dallas	CHL	70	6	37	43	50	10	2	*8	10	8
1976-77	Dallas	CHL	63	15	53	68	30	5	1	4	5	0
1977-78	**Chicago**	**NHL**	**6**	**1**	**1**	**2**	**2**	....	....	....	....	....
	Dallas	CHL	62	6	45	51	75	13	1	*11	12	8
1978-79	New Brunswick	AHL	35	5	19	24	19	....	....	....	....	....
	Chicago	**NHL**	**48**	**4**	**22**	**26**	**20**	**4**	**0**	**0**	**0**	**4**
1979-80	**Chicago**	**NHL**	**78**	**8**	**22**	**30**	**52**	**7**	**0**	**1**	**1**	**0**
1980-81	**Chicago**	**NHL**	**34**	**5**	**16**	**21**	**32**	....	....	....	....	....
	Boston	**NHL**	**48**	**10**	**22**	**32**	**42**	**3**	**1**	**3**	**4**	**2**
1981-82	**Boston**	**NHL**	**80**	**5**	**34**	**39**	**75**	**11**	**2**	**2**	**4**	**20**
1982-83	**Boston**	**NHL**	**80**	**14**	**39**	**53**	**42**	**17**	**3**	**5**	**8**	**12**
1983-84	**Boston**	**NHL**	**75**	**18**	**42**	**60**	**42**	**3**	**0**	**0**	**0**	**0**
1984-85	**Boston**	**NHL**	**78**	**15**	**40**	**55**	**64**	**5**	**1**	**5**	**6**	**0**
1985-86	**Boston**	**NHL**	**63**	**8**	**21**	**29**	**47**	....	....	....	....	....
	Detroit	**NHL**	**13**	**1**	**7**	**8**	**16**	....	....	....	....	....
1986-87	**Detroit**	**NHL**	**77**	**5**	**26**	**31**	**70**	**16**	**1**	**4**	**5**	**14**
1987-88	**Detroit**	**NHL**	**48**	**6**	**13**	**19**	**38**	**10**	**0**	**4**	**4**	**8**
1988-89	**Detroit**	**NHL**	**66**	**1**	**15**	**16**	**41**	**6**	**0**	**0**	**0**	**4**
	NHL Totals		**794**	**101**	**320**	**421**	**583**	**82**	**8**	**24**	**32**	**64**

a OHA First All-Star Team (1975).

Played in NHL All-Star Game (1984)

Traded to **Boston** by **Chicago** for Al Secord, December 18, 1980. Traded to **Detroit** by **Boston** for Reed Larson, March 10, 1986.

O'CONNOR, MYLES

Defense. Shoots left. 5'11", 165 lbs. Born, Calgary, Alta., April 2, 1967.
(New Jersey's 4th choice, 45th overall, in 1985 Entry Draft).

			Regular Season					Playoffs				
Season	Club	Lea	GP	G	A	TP	PIM	GP	G	A	TP	PIM
1985-86	U. of Michigan	CCHA	37	6	19	25	73	....	....	....	....	....
1986-87	U. of Michigan	CCHA	39	15	39	54	111	....	....	....	....	....
1987-88	U. of Michigan	CCHA	40	9	25	34	78	....	....	....	....	....
1988-89ab	U. of Michigan	CCHA	40	3	31	34	91	....	....	....	....	....
	Utica	AHL	1	0	0	0	0	....	....	....	....	....

a CCHA First All-Star Team (1989)
b NCAA West First All-American Team (1989)

ODELEIN, LYLE (OH duh LIGHN)

Center. Shoots left. 5'10", 185 lbs. Born, Quill Lake, Sask., July 21, 1968.
(Montreal's 8th choice, 141st overall, in 1986 Entry Draft).

			Regular Season					Playoffs				
Season	Club	Lea	GP	G	A	TP	PIM	GP	G	A	TP	PIM
1985-86	Moose Jaw	WHL	67	9	37	46	117	13	1	6	7	34
1986-87	Moose Jaw	WHL	59	9	50	59	70	9	2	5	7	26
1987-88	Moose Jaw	WHL	63	15	43	58	166	....	....	....	....	....
1988-89	Sherbrooke	AHL	33	3	4	7	120	3	0	2	2	5
	Peoria	IHL	36	2	8	10	116	....	....	....	....	....

ODELEIN, SELMAR (OH duh LIGHN)

Defense. Shoots right. 6', 205 lbs. Born, Quill Lake, Sask., April 11, 1966.
(Edmonton's 1st choice, 21st over-all, in 1984 Entry Draft).

			Regular Season					Playoffs				
Season	Club	Lea	GP	G	A	TP	PIM	GP	G	A	TP	PIM
1982-83	Regina	Midget	70	30	84	114	38	....	....	....	....	....
1983-84	Regina	WHL	71	9	42	51	45	23	4	11	15	45
1984-85	Regina	WHL	64	24	35	59	121	8	2	2	4	13
1985-86	**Edmonton**	**NHL**	**4**	**0**	**0**	**0**	**0**	....	....	....	....	....
	Regina	WHL	36	13	28	41	57	8	5	2	7	24
1986-87	Nova Scotia	AHL	2	0	1	1	2	....	....	....	....	....
1987-88	**Edmonton**	**NHL**	**12**	**0**	**2**	**2**	**33**	....	....	....	....	....
	Nova Scotia	AHL	43	9	14	23	75	5	0	1	1	31
1988-89	**Edmonton**	**NHL**	**2**	**0**	**0**	**0**	**2**	....	....	....	....	....
	Cape Breton	AHL	63	8	21	29	150	....	....	....	....	....
	NHL Totals		**18**	**0**	**2**	**2**	**35**	....	....	....	....	....

O'DWYER, BILL

Center. Shoots left. 6', 190 lbs. Born, South Boston, MA, January 25, 1960.
(Los Angeles' 10th choice, 157th over-all, in 1980 Entry Draft).

			Regular Season					Playoffs				
Season	Club	Lea	GP	G	A	TP	PIM	GP	G	A	TP	PIM
1978-79	Boston College	ECAC	30	9	30	39	14	....	....	....	....	....
1979-80	Boston College	ECAC	33	20	22	42	22	....	....	....	....	....
1980-81	Boston College	ECAC	31	20	20	40	6	....	....	....	....	....
1981-82	Boston College	ECAC	30	15	26	41	10	....	....	....	....	....
1982-83	New Haven	AHL	77	24	23	47	29	11	3	4	7	9
1983-84	**Los Angeles**	**NHL**	**5**	**0**	**0**	**0**	**0**	....	....	....	....	....
	New Haven	AHL	58	15	42	57	39	....	....	....	....	....
1984-85	**Los Angeles**	**NHL**	**13**	**1**	**0**	**1**	**15**	....	....	....	....	....
	New Haven	AHL	46	19	24	43	27	....	....	....	....	....
1985-86	New Haven	AHL	41	10	15	25	41	5	0	1	1	2
1986-87	New Haven	AHL	65	22	42	64	74	3	0	0	0	14
1987-88	**Boston**	**NHL**	**77**	**7**	**10**	**17**	**83**	**9**	**0**	**0**	**0**	**0**
1988-89	**Boston**	**NHL**	**19**	**1**	**2**	**3**	**8**	....	....	....	....	....
	NHL Totals		**114**	**9**	**12**	**21**	**106**	**9**	**0**	**0**	**0**	**0**

Signed as a free agent by **NY Rangers**, July 13, 1985. Signed as a free agent by **Boston**, August 13, 1987.

OGRODNICK, JOHN ALEXANDER (oh-GRAHD-nik)

Left wing. Shoots left. 6', 205 lbs. Born, Ottawa, Ont., June 20, 1959.
(Detroit's 4th choice, 66th over-all, in 1979 Entry Draft).

			Regular Season					Playoffs				
Season	Club	Lea	GP	G	A	TP	PIM	GP	G	A	TP	PIM
1977-78a	N. Westminster	WHL	72	59	29	88	47	21	14	7	21	14
1978-79	N. Westminster	WHL	72	48	36	84	38	6	2	0	2	4
1979-80	**Detroit**	**NHL**	**41**	**8**	**24**	**32**	**8**	....	....	....	....	....
	Adirondack	AHL	39	13	20	33	21	....	....	....	....	....
1980-81	**Detroit**	**NHL**	**80**	**35**	**35**	**70**	**14**	....	....	....	....	....
1981-82	**Detroit**	**NHL**	**80**	**28**	**26**	**54**	**28**	....	....	....	....	....
1982-83	**Detroit**	**NHL**	**80**	**41**	**44**	**85**	**30**	....	....	....	....	....
1983-84	**Detroit**	**NHL**	**64**	**42**	**36**	**78**	**14**	**4**	**0**	**0**	**0**	**0**
1984-85b	**Detroit**	**NHL**	**79**	**55**	**50**	**105**	**30**	**3**	**1**	**1**	**2**	**0**
1985-86	**Detroit**	**NHL**	**76**	**38**	**32**	**70**	**18**	....	....	....	....	....
1986-87	**Detroit**	**NHL**	**39**	**12**	**28**	**40**	**6**	....	....	....	....	....
	Quebec	**NHL**	**32**	**11**	**16**	**27**	**4**	**13**	**9**	**4**	**13**	**6**
1987-88	**NY Rangers**	**NHL**	**64**	**22**	**32**	**54**	**16**	....	....	....	....	....
1988-89	**NY Rangers**	**NHL**	**60**	**13**	**29**	**42**	**14**	**3**	**2**	**0**	**2**	**0**
	Denver	IHL	3	2	0	2	0	....	....	....	....	....
	NHL Totals		**695**	**305**	**352**	**657**	**182**	**23**	**12**	**5**	**17**	**6**

a Shared WHL Rookie of the Year Award with Keith Brown (Portland) (1978)
b NHL First All-Star Team (1985)

Played in NHL All-Star Game (1981, 1982, 1984-86)

Traded to **Quebec** by **Detroit** with Basil McRae and Doug Shedden for Brent Ashton, Gilbert Delorme and Mark Kumpel, January 17, 1987. Traded to **NY Rangers** by **Quebec** with David Shaw for Jeff Jackson and Terry Carkner, September 30, 1987.

OHLING, JENS

Right wing. Shoots right. 6', 180 lbs. Born, Djurgardens, Sweden, April 3, 1962.
(Boston's 10th choice, 207th overall, in 1980 Entry Draft).

			Regular Season					Playoffs				
Season	Club	Lea	GP	G	A	TP	PIM	GP	G	A	TP	PIM
1977-78	Nacka	Swe. 2	20	4	1	5	2	....	....	....	....	....
1978-79	Nacka	Swe. 2	24	6	6	12	6	....	....	....	....	....
1979-80	Djurgarden	Swe.	2	0	0	0	0	....	....	....	....	....
1980-81	Djurgarden	Swe.	33	10	2	12	10	....	....	....	....	....
1981-82	Djurgarden	Swe.	34	6	4	10	2	6	0	0	0	0
1982-83	Djurgarden	Swe.	35	17	15	32	10	8	2	2	4	0
1983-84	Djurgarden	Swe.	32	14	14	28	6	6	1	1	2	0
1984-85	Djurgarden	Swe.	36	15	16	31	4	8	3	3	6	0
1985-86	Djurgarden	Swe.	35	14	9	23	10	....	....	....	....	....
1986-87	Djurgarden	Swe.	30	4	11	15	4	2	0	0	0	0
1987-88	Djurgarden	Swe.	38	27	19	46	6	3	0	0	0	2
1988-89	Djurgarden	Swe.	38	9	10	19	14	8	6	2	8	2

OHMAN, PAUL

Defense. Shoots left. 6', 185 lbs. Born, Worcester, MA, July 30, 1969.
(Boston's 10th choice, 182nd overall, in 1987 Entry Draft).

			Regular Season					Playoffs				
Season	Club	Lea	GP	G	A	TP	PIM	GP	G	A	TP	PIM
1986-87	St. John	HS	20	10	19	29	....	....	....	....	....	....
1987-88	Brown	ECAC	DID NOT PLAY									
1988-89			DID NOT PLAY									

OHMAN, ROGER

Defense. Shoots left. 6'2", 205 lbs. Born, Stockholm, Sweden, June 5, 1967.
(Winnipeg's 2nd choice, 39th overall, in 1985 Entry Draft).

			Regular Season					Playoffs				
Season	Club	Lea	GP	G	A	TP	PIM	GP	G	A	TP	PIM
1983-84	Leksand	Swe. Jr.	36	31	21	52	80	....	....	....	....	....
1984-85	Leksand	Swe. Jr.	40	32	44	76	60	....	....	....	....	....
	Leksand	Swe.	5	0	0	0	0	....	....	....	....	....
1985-86	V. Frolunda	Swe. 2	32	12	9	21	30	3	1	4	5	0
1986-87	V. Frolunda	Swe.	26	4	10	14	16	2	0	1	1	0
1987-88	Moncton	AHL	67	11	17	28	38	....	....	....	....	....
1988-89	AIK	Swe.	36	11	8	19	20	....	....	....	....	....

OJANEN, JANNE (oh-YAH-nen, YAH-nee)

Center. Shoots left. 6'2", 185 lbs. Born, Tampere, Finland, April 9, 1968.
(New Jersey's 3rd choice, 45th over-all, in 1986 Entry Draft).

			Regular Season					Playoffs				
Season	Club	Lea	GP	G	A	TP	PIM	GP	G	A	TP	PIM
1985-86	Tappara	Fin. Jr.	14	5	17	22	14	5	2	3	5	8
	Taparra	Fin.	3	0	0	0	2	....	....	....	....	....
1986-87	Tappara	Fin.	40	18	13	31	16	9	4	6	10	2
1987-88	Tappara	Fin.	44	21	31	52	30	10	4	4	8	12
1988-89	**New Jersey**	**NHL**	**3**	**0**	**1**	**1**	**2**	....	....	....	....	....
	Utica	AHL	72	23	37	60	10	5	0	3	3	0
	NHL Totals		**3**	**0**	**1**	**1**	**2**	....	....	....	....	....

OLAUSSON, FREDRIK

Defense. Shoots right. 6'2", 200 lbs. Born, Vaxsjo, Sweden, October 5, 1966.
(Winnipeg's 4th choice, 81st overall, in 1985 Entry Draft).

			Regular Season					Playoffs				
Season	Club	Lea	GP	G	A	TP	PIM	GP	G	A	TP	PIM
1982-83	Nybro	Swe. 2	31	4	4	8	12	....	....	....	....	....
1983-84	Nybro	Swe. 2	28	8	14	22	32	....	....	....	....	....
1984-85	Farjestad	Swe.	29	5	12	17	22	3	1	0	1	0
1985-86	Farjestad	Swe.	33	4	12	16	22	8	3	2	5	6
1986-87	**Winnipeg**	**NHL**	**72**	**7**	**29**	**36**	**24**	**10**	**2**	**3**	**5**	**4**
1987-88	**Winnipeg**	**NHL**	**38**	**5**	**10**	**15**	**18**	**5**	**1**	**1**	**2**	**0**
1988-89	**Winnipeg**	**NHL**	**75**	**15**	**47**	**62**	**32**	....	....	....	....	....
	NHL Totals		**185**	**27**	**86**	**113**	**74**	**15**	**3**	**4**	**7**	**4**

OLCZYK, ED (ohl-CHUK)

Right wing. Shoots left. 6'2", 195 lbs. Born, Chicago, IL, August 16, 1966.
(Chicago's 1st choice, 3rd over-all, in 1984 Entry Draft).

			Regular Season					Playoffs				
Season	Club	Lea	GP	G	A	TP	PIM	GP	G	A	TP	PIM
1982-83	Stratford	OPJHL	42	50	92	*141	54	....	....	....	....	....
1983-84	U.S. Olympic	...	62	21	47	68	36	....	....	....	....	....
1984-85	**Chicago**	**NHL**	**70**	**20**	**30**	**50**	**67**	**15**	**6**	**5**	**11**	**11**
1985-86	**Chicago**	**NHL**	**79**	**29**	**50**	**79**	**47**	**3**	**0**	**0**	**0**	**0**
1986-87	**Chicago**	**NHL**	**79**	**16**	**35**	**51**	**119**	**4**	**1**	**1**	**2**	**4**
1987-88	**Toronto**	**NHL**	**80**	**42**	**33**	**75**	**55**	**6**	**5**	**4**	**9**	**2**
1988-89	**Toronto**	**NHL**	**80**	**38**	**52**	**90**	**75**	....	....	....	....	....
	NHL Totals		**388**	**145**	**200**	**345**	**363**	**28**	**12**	**10**	**22**	**17**

Traded to **Toronto** by **Chicago** with Al Secord for Rick Vaive, Steve Thomas and Bob McGill, September 3, 1987.

OLENIUK, DEVON

Defense. Shoots left. 6'1", 193 lbs. Born, Weldon, Sask., March 28, 1968.
(Washington's 6th choice, 141st overall, in 1987 Entry Draft).

			Regular Season					Playoffs				
Season	Club	Lea	GP	G	A	TP	PIM	GP	G	A	TP	PIM
1986-87	Saskatoon	WHL	18	1	3	4	19	....	....	....	....	....
	Kamloops	WHL	37	1	7	8	35	13	0	2	2	19
1987-88	Kamloops	WHL	69	3	11	14	103	18	1	4	5	13
1988-89	Moose Jaw	WHL	68	6	32	38	151	7	0	3	3	10

OLIMB, LAWRENCE

Defense. Shoots left. 5'10", 155 lbs. Born, Warroad, MN, August 11, 1969.
(Minnesota's 10th choice, 193rd overall, in 1987 Entry Draft).

			Regular Season					Playoffs				
Season	Club	Lea	GP	G	A	TP	PIM	GP	G	A	TP	PIM
1986-87	Warroad	HS	26	23	30	53	....	....	....	....	....	....
1987-88	Warroad	HS	27	35	31	66	....	....	....	....	....	....
1988-89	U. Minnesota	WCHA	47	10	29	39	50	....	....	....	....	....

OLSEN, DARRYL

Defense. Shoots left. 6', 180 lbs. Born, Calgary, Alta., October 7, 1966.
(Calgary's 10th choice, 185th overall in 1985 Entry Draft).

			Regular Season					Playoffs				
Season	Club	Lea	GP	G	A	TP	PIM	GP	G	A	TP	PIM
1984-85	St. Albert	AJHL	57	19	48	67	77	....	....	....	....	....
1985-86	N. Michigan	WCHA	37	5	20	25	46	....	....	....	....	....
1986-87	N. Michigan	WCHA	37	5	20	25	46	....	....	....	....	....
1987-88	N. Michigan	WCHA	35	11	20	31	59	....	....	....	....	....
1988-89	Cdn. National	....	3	1	0	1	4	....	....	....	....	....
ab	N. Michigan	WCHA	45	16	26	42	88	....	....	....	....	....

a NCAA West Second All-American Team (1989)
b WCHA First All-Star Team (1989)

OLSEN, MARK

Defense. Shoots left. 6'3", 215 lbs. Born, Irvine, TX, September 6, 1966.
(Calgary's 7th choice, 163rd overall, in 1986 Entry Draft).

			Regular Season					Playoffs				
Season	Club	Lea	GP	G	A	TP	PIM	GP	G	A	TP	PIM
1985-86	Colorado	WCHA	39	2	4	6	48	....	....	....	....	....
1986-87	Colorado	WCHA	42	2	4	6	38	....	....	....	....	....
1987-88	Colorado	WCHA	36	2	11	13	81	....	....	....	....	....
1988-89	Colorado	WCHA	21	5	5	10	28	....	....	....	....	....

OSBORNE, KEITH

Right wing. Shoots right. 6'1", 180 lbs. Born, Toronto, Ont., April 2, 1969.
(St. Louis 1st choice, 12th overall, in 1987 Entry Draft).

			Regular Season					Playoffs				
Season	Club	Lea	GP	G	A	TP	PIM	GP	G	A	TP	PIM
1986-87	North Bay	OHL	61	34	55	89	31	24	11	11	22	25
1987-88	North Bay	OHL	30	14	22	36	20	4	1	5	6	8
1988-89	North Bay	OHL	15	11	15	26	12					
	Niagara Falls	OHL	50	34	49	83	45	17	12	12	25	36

OSBORNE, MARK ANATOLE (AWS-born)

Left wing. Shoots left. 6'2", 205 lbs. Born, Toronto, Ont., August 13, 1961.
(Detroit's 2nd choice, 46th over-all, in 1980 Entry Draft).

			Regular Season					Playoffs				
Season	Club	Lea	GP	G	A	TP	PIM	GP	G	A	TP	PIM
1979-80	Niagara Falls	OHA	52	10	33	43	104	10	2	1	3	23
1980-81	Niagara Falls	OHA	54	39	41	80	140	12	11	10	21	20
	Adirondack	AHL	....	....	....	....	....	13	2	3	5	2
1981-82	**Detroit**	**NHL**	**80**	**26**	**41**	**67**	**61**	....	....	....	....	....
1982-83	**Detroit**	**NHL**	**80**	**19**	**24**	**43**	**83**	....	....	....	....	....
1983-84	**NY Rangers**	**NHL**	**73**	**23**	**28**	**51**	**88**	**5**	**0**	**1**	**1**	**7**
1984-85	**NY Rangers**	**NHL**	**23**	**4**	**4**	**8**	**33**	**3**	**0**	**0**	**0**	**4**
1985-86	**NY Rangers**	**NHL**	**62**	**16**	**24**	**40**	**80**	**15**	**2**	**3**	**5**	**26**
1986-87	**NY Rangers**	**NHL**	**58**	**17**	**15**	**32**	**101**	....	....	....	....	....
	Toronto	**NHL**	**16**	**5**	**10**	**15**	**12**	**9**	**1**	**3**	**4**	**6**
1987-88	**Toronto**	**NHL**	**79**	**23**	**37**	**60**	**102**	**6**	**1**	**3**	**4**	**16**
1988-89	**Toronto**	**NHL**	**75**	**16**	**30**	**46**	**112**	....	....	....	....	....
	NHL Totals		**546**	**149**	**213**	**362**	**672**	**38**	**4**	**10**	**14**	**59**

Traded to **NY Rangers** by **Detroit** with Willie Huber and Mike Blaisdell for Ron Duguay, Eddie Mio and Eddie Johnstone, June 13, 1983. Traded to **Toronto** by **NY Rangers** for Jeff Jackson and Toronto's third-round choice (Rod Zamuner) in 1989 Entry Draft, March 5, 1987.

OSIECKI, MARK

Defense. Shoots right. 6'2", 200 lbs. Born, St. Paul, MN, July 23, 1968.
(Calgary's 10th choice, 187th overall, in 1987 Entry Draft).

			Regular Season					Playoffs				
Season	Club	Lea	GP	G	A	TP	PIM	GP	G	A	TP	PIM
1986-87	U. Wisconsin	WCHA	8	0	1	1	4	....	....	....	....	....
1987-88	U. Wisconsin	WCHA	18	0	1	1	22	....	....	....	....	....
1988-89	U. Wisconsin	WCHA	44	1	3	4	56	....	....	....	....	....

O'TOOLE, MIKE

Right wing. Shoots left. 6'1", 180 lbs. Born, Don Mills, Ont., July 2, 1966.
(St. Louis' 6th choice, 115th overall, in 1986 Entry Draft).

			Regular Season					Playoffs				
Season	Club	Lea	GP	G	A	TP	PIM	GP	G	A	TP	PIM
1986-87	Michigan State	CCHA	43	2	13	15	74	....	....	....	....	....
1987-88	Michigan State	CCHA	44	12	10	22	76	....	....	....	....	....
1988-89	Michigan State	CCHA	24	3	1	4	28	....	....	....	....	....

OTTO, JOEL STUART

Center. Shoots right. 6'4", 220 lbs. Born, Elk River, MN, October 29, 1961.

			Regular Season					Playoffs				
Season	Club	Lea	GP	G	A	TP	PIM	GP	G	A	TP	PIM
1980-81	Bemidji State	NCAA	23	5	11	16	10	....	....	....	....	....
1981-82	Bemidji State	NCAA	31	19	33	52	24	....	....	....	....	....
1982-83	Bemidji State	NCAA	37	33	28	61	68	....	....	....	....	....
1983-84	Bemidji State	NCAA	31	32	43	75	32	....	....	....	....	....
1984-85	**Calgary**	**NHL**	**17**	**4**	**8**	**12**	**30**	**3**	**2**	**1**	**3**	**10**
	Moncton	AHL	56	27	36	63	89	....	....	....	....	....
1985-86	**Calgary**	**NHL**	**79**	**25**	**34**	**59**	**188**	**22**	**5**	**10**	**15**	**80**
1986-87	**Calgary**	**NHL**	**68**	**19**	**31**	**50**	**185**	**2**	**0**	**2**	**2**	**6**
1987-88	**Calgary**	**NHL**	**62**	**13**	**39**	**52**	**194**	**9**	**3**	**2**	**5**	**26**
1988-89	**Calgary**	**NHL**	**72**	**23**	**30**	**53**	**213**	**22**	**6**	**13**	**19**	**46**
	NHL Totals		**298**	**84**	**142**	**226**	**810**	**58**	**16**	**28**	**44**	**168**

Signed as a free agent by **Calgary**, September 11, 1984.

PADDOCK, GORDON

Defense. Shoots right. 6', 180 lbs.   Born, Hamiota, Man., February 15, 1964.
(NY Islanders' 9th choice, 189th over-all, in 1982 Entry Draft).

			Regular Season					Playoffs				
Season	Club	Lea	GP	G	A	TP	PIM	GP	G	A	TP	PIM
1981-82	Saskatoon	WHL	59	8	21	29	232	3	0	0	0	17
1982-83	Saskatoon	WHL	67	4	25	29	158	6	0	2	2	16
1983-84	Brandon	WHL	72	14	37	51	151	12	1	5	6	23
1984-85	Springfield	AHL	12	0	2	2	24	3	0	0	0	6
	Indianapolis	IHL	65	10	21	31	92	7	2	1	3	23
1985-86	Springfield	AHL	20	1	1	2	52	....	....	....	....	....
	Indianapolis	IHL	11	1	1	2	11	....	....	....	....	....
	Muskegon	IHL	47	1	20	21	87	....	....	....	....	....
1986-87	Springfield	AHL	78	6	11	17	127	....	....	....	....	....
1987-88	Springfield	AHL	74	8	26	34	127	....	....	....	....	....
1988-89	Hershey	AHL	75	6	36	42	105	12	0	1	1	17

PAEK, JIM

Defense. Shoots left. 6'1", 190 lbs.   Born, Seoul, Korea, April 7, 1967.
(Pittsburgh's 9th choice, 170th overall in 1985 Entry Draft).

			Regular Season					Playoffs				
Season	Club	Lea	GP	G	A	TP	PIM	GP	G	A	TP	PIM
1983-84	St.Michael's	Jr. B	5	0	2	2	8	....	....	....	....	....
1984-85	Oshawa	OHL	54	2	13	15	57	5	1	0	1	9
1985-86	Oshawa	OHL	64	5	21	26	122	6	0	1	1	9
1986-87	Oshawa	OHL	57	5	17	22	75	26	1	14	15	43
1987-88	Muskegon	IHL	82	7	52	59	141	6	0	0	0	29
1988-89	Muskegon	IHL	80	3	54	57	96	14	1	10	11	24

PALOSAARI, ESA

Right wing. Shoots right. 6'4", 210 lbs.   Born, Oulu, Finland, January 16, 1968.
(Winnipeg's 3rd choice, 50th overall, in 1986 Entry Draft).

			Regular Season					Playoffs				
Season	Club	Lea	GP	G	A	TP	PIM	GP	G	A	TP	PIM
1987-88	Karpat	Fin.	28	1	1	2	10	....	....	....	....	....
	SaPKo	Fin. 2	4	2	0	2	2	....	....	....	....	....
1988-89	Karpat	Fin.	25	3	0	3	12	5	0	0	0	2

PALUCH, SCOTT

Defense. Shoots left. 6'3", 185 lbs.   Born, Chicago, IL, March 9, 1966.
(St. Louis' 7th choice, 92nd overall, in 1984 Entry Draft).

			Regular Season					Playoffs				
Season	Club	Lea	GP	G	A	TP	PIM	GP	G	A	TP	PIM
1984-85	Bowling Green	CCHA	42	11	25	36	64	....	....	....	....	....
1985-86	Bowling Green	CCHA	34	10	11	21	44	....	....	....	....	....
1986-87	Bowling Green	CCHA	45	13	38	51	88	....	....	....	....	....
1987-88bc	Bowling Green	CCHA	44	14	47	61	88	....	....	....	....	....
1988-89	Peoria	IHL	81	10	39	49	92	4	1	1	2	31

a NCAA West First All-American Team (1988)
b CCHA First All-Star Team (1988)

PANCOE, DONALD

Defense. Shoots left. 6'1", 190 lbs.   Born, St. George, Ont., February 23, 1969.
(Pittsburgh's 9th choice, 193rd overall, in 1988 Entry Draft).

			Regular Season					Playoffs				
Season	Club	Lea	GP	G	A	TP	PIM	GP	G	A	TP	PIM
1986-87	Hamilton	OHL	44	4	8	12	120	9	0	1	1	24
1987-88	Hamilton	OHL	60	2	12	14	144	14	0	1	1	55
1988-89	Niagara Falls	OHL	54	1	17	18	167	15	0	2	2	38

PANEK, CHRISTOPHER (CHRIS)

Defense. Shoots left. 6'2", 205 lbs.   Born, Buffalo, NY, October 13, 1966.
(Los Angeles' 1st choice, 11th overall, in 1987 Supplemental Draft).

			Regular Season					Playoffs				
Season	Club	Lea	GP	G	A	TP	PIM	GP	G	A	TP	PIM
1987-88	Plattsburgh	NCAA	33	11	26	37	84	....	....	....	....	....
1988-89	New Haven	AHL	41	4	18	22	13	....	....	....	....	....
	Flint	IHL	8	2	1	3	9	....	....	....	....	....

PARDOSKI, RYAN

Left wing. Shoots left. 6'1", 165 lbs.   Born, Calgary, Alta., August 19, 1968.
(New Jersey's 8th choice, 150th overall, in 1986 Entry Draft).

			Regular Season					Playoffs				
Season	Club	Lea	GP	G	A	TP	PIM	GP	G	A	TP	PIM
1985-86	Calgary	AJHL	50	16	27	43	61	....	....	....	....	....
1986-87	U. of Michigan	CCHA	39	4	9	13	26	....	....	....	....	....
1987-88	U. of Michigan	CCHA	31	4	9	13	36	....	....	....	....	....
1988-89	U. of Michigan	CCHA	38	11	3	14	36	....	....	....	....	....

PARENT, RUSSELL

Defense. Shoots left. 5'9", 180 lbs.   Born, Winnipeg, Man., May 6, 1968.
(NY Rangers' 11th choice, 219th overall, in 1986 Entry Draft).

			Regular Season					Playoffs				
Season	Club	Lea	GP	G	A	TP	PIM	GP	G	A	TP	PIM
1985-86	S. Winnipeg	MJHL	47	16	65	81	106	....	....	....	....	....
1986-87	North Dakota	WCHA	47	2	17	19	50	....	....	....	....	....
1987-88	North Dakota	WCHA	30	4	20	24	38	....	....	....	....	....
1988-89a	North Dakota	WCHA	40	9	28	37	51	....	....	....	....	....

a WCHA Second All-Star Team (1989)

PARKER, JEFF

Center. Shoots left. 6'3", 194 lbs.   Born, St. Paul, MN, September 7, 1964.
(Buffalo's 9th choice, 111th overalll, in 1982 Entry Draft).

			Regular Season					Playoffs				
Season	Club	Lea	GP	G	A	TP	PIM	GP	G	A	TP	PIM
1983-84	Michigan State	CCHA	44	8	13	21	82	....	....	....	....	....
1984-85	Michigan State	CCHA	42	10	12	22	89	....	....	....	....	....
1985-86	Michigan State	CCHA	41	15	20	35	88	....	....	....	....	....
1986-87	**Buffalo**	**NHL**	15	3	3	6	7	....	....	....	....	....
	Rochester	AHL	54	14	8	22	75	14	1	3	4	19
1987-88	**Buffalo**	**NHL**	4	0	2	2	2	....	....	....	....	....
	Rochester	AHL	34	13	31	44	69	2	1	1	2	0
1988-89	**Buffalo**	**NHL**	57	9	9	18	82	5	0	0	0	26
	Rochester	AHL	6	2	4	6	9	....	....	....	....	....
	NHL Totals		**76**	**12**	**14**	**26**	**91**	**5**	**0**	**0**	**0**	**26**

PARKER, JOHN

Center. Shoots right. 6'1", 180 lbs.   Born, St. Paul, MN, March 5, 1968.
(Calgary's 5th choice, 121st overall, in 1986 Entry Draft).

			Regular Season					Playoffs				
Season	Club	Lea	GP	G	A	TP	PIM	GP	G	A	TP	PIM
1985-86	W. B. Lake	HS	24	12	13	25	0	....	....	....	....	....
1986-87	U. Wisconsin	WCHA	8	0	1	1	4	....	....	....	....	....
1987-88	U. Wisconsin	WCHA	4	0	0	0	6	....	....	....	....	....
1988-89	U. Wisconsin	WCHA	20	1	7	8	16	....	....	....	....	....

PASCUCCI, RONALD

Defense. Shoots left. 6'1", 180 lbs.   Born, North Andover, MA, June 9, 1970.
(Washington's 14th choice, 246th overall, in 1988 Entry Draft).

			Regular Season					Playoffs				
Season	Club	Lea	GP	G	A	TP	PIM	GP	G	A	TP	PIM
1987-88	Belmont Hills	HS	....	8	17	25	....	....	....	....	....	....
1988-89	Belmont Hills	HS	....	9	20	29	....	....	....	....	....	....

PASEK, DUSAN

Center. Shoots right. 6'1", 200 lbs.   Born, Bratislava, Czechoslovakia, September 7, 1960.
(Minnesota's 4th choice, 81st overall, in 1982 Entry Draft).

			Regular Season					Playoffs				
Season	Club	Lea	GP	G	A	TP	PIM	GP	G	A	TP	PIM
1986-87	Bratislava	Czech.	32	18	27	45	....	....	....	....	....	....
1987-88	Bratislava	Czech.	28	13	10	23	....	....	....	....	....	....
1988-89	**Minnesota**	**NHL**	48	4	10	14	30	2	1	0	1	0
	NHL Totals		**48**	**4**	**10**	**14**	**30**	**2**	**1**	**0**	**1**	**0**

PASIN, DAVE   (pa-SEEN)

Right wing. Shoots right. 6'1", 205 lbs.   Born, Edmonton, Alta., July 8, 1966.
(Boston's 1st choice, 19th over-all, in 1984 Entry Draft).

			Regular Season					Playoffs				
Season	Club	Lea	GP	G	A	TP	PIM	GP	G	A	TP	PIM
1982-83	Prince Albert	WHL	62	40	42	82	48	....	....	....	....	....
1983-84	Prince Albert	WHL	71	68	54	122	68	5	1	4	5	0
1984-85a	Prince Albert	WHL	65	64	52	116	88	10	10	11	21	10
1985-86	**Boston**	**NHL**	71	18	19	37	50	3	0	1	1	0
1986-87	Moncton	AHL	66	27	25	52	47	6	1	1	2	14
1987-88	Maine	AHL	30	8	14	22	39	8	4	3	7	13
1988-89	Maine	AHL	11	2	5	7	6	....	....	....	....	....
	Los Angeles	**NHL**	5	0	0	0	0	....	....	....	....	....
	New Haven	AHL	48	25	23	48	42	17	8	8	16	47
	NHL Totals		**76**	**18**	**19**	**37**	**50**	**3**	**0**	**1**	**1**	**0**

a WHL Second All-Star Team, East Division (1985).

Rights traded to **Los Angeles** by Boston for Paul Guay, November 3, 1988.

PASLAWSKI, GREGORY STEPHEN (GREG)   (paz-LAWS-kee)

Right wing. Shoots right. 5'11", 190 lbs.   Born, Kindersley, Sask., August 25, 1961.

			Regular Season					Playoffs				
Season	Club	Lea	GP	G	A	TP	PIM	GP	G	A	TP	PIM
1981-82	Nova Scotia	AHL	43	15	11	26	31	....	....	....	....	....
1982-83	Nova Scotia	AHL	75	46	42	88	32	6	1	3	4	8
1983-84	**Montreal**	**NHL**	26	1	4	5	4	....	....	....	....	....
	St. Louis	**NHL**	34	8	6	14	17	9	1	0	1	2
1984-85	**St. Louis**	**NHL**	72	22	20	42	21	3	0	0	0	2
1985-86	**St. Louis**	**NHL**	56	22	11	33	18	17	10	7	17	13
1986-87	**St. Louis**	**NHL**	76	29	35	64	27	6	1	1	2	4
1987-88	**St. Louis**	**NHL**	17	2	1	3	4	3	1	1	2	2
1988-89	**St. Louis**	**NHL**	75	26	26	52	18	9	2	1	3	2
	NHL Totals		**356**	**110**	**103**	**213**	**109**	**47**	**15**	**10**	**25**	**25**

Signed as free agent by **Montreal**, October 5, 1981. Traded to **St. Louis** by **Montreal** with Gilbert Delorme and Doug Wickenheiser for Perry Turnbull, December 21, 1983. Traded to **Winnipeg** by **St. Louis** with St. Louis' third round choice (Kris Draper) in 1989 Entry Draft and second-round choice in1991 Entry Draft, June 17, 1989.

PATERSON, JOSEPH (JOE)

Left wing. Shoots left. 6'2", 205 lbs. Born, Toronto, Ont., June 25, 1960.
(Detroit's 5th choice, 87th over-all, in 1979 Entry Draft).

			Regular Season					Playoffs				
Season	Club	Lea	GP	G	A	TP	PIM	GP	G	A	TP	PIM
1978-79	London	OHA	59	22	19	41	158	7	2	3	5	13
1979-80	London	OHA	62	21	50	71	156	....	....	....	....	....
	Kalamazoo	IHL	4	1	2	3	2	3	2	1	3	11
1980-81	**Detroit**	**NHL**	**38**	**2**	**5**	**7**	**53**	....	....	....	....	....
	Adirondack	AHL	39	9	16	25	68	....	....	....	....	....
1981-82	**Detroit**	**NHL**	**3**	**0**	**0**	**0**	**0**	....	....	....	....	....
	Adirondack	AHL	74	22	28	50	132	5	1	4	5	6
1982-83	**Detroit**	**NHL**	**33**	**2**	**1**	**3**	**14**	....	....	....	....	....
	Adirondack	AHL	36	11	10	21	85	6	1	2	3	21
1983-84	Adirondack	AHL	20	10	15	25	43	....	....	....	....	....
	Detroit	**NHL**	**41**	**2**	**5**	**7**	**148**	**3**	**0**	**0**	**0**	**7**
1984-85	**Philadelphia**	**NHL**	**6**	**0**	**0**	**0**	**31**	**17**	**3**	**4**	**7**	**70**
	Hershey	AHL	67	26	27	53	173	....	....	....	....	....
1985-86	**Philadelphia**	**NHL**	**5**	**0**	**0**	**0**	**12**	....	....	....	....	....
	Hershey	AHL	20	5	10	15	68	....	....	....	....	....
	Los Angeles	**NHL**	**47**	**9**	**18**	**27**	**153**	....	....	....	....	....
1986-87	**Los Angeles**	**NHL**	**45**	**2**	**1**	**3**	**158**	**2**	**0**	**0**	**0**	**0**
	Los Angeles	**NHL**	**32**	**1**	**3**	**4**	**113**	....	....	....	....	....
1987-88	**NY Rangers**	**NHL**	**21**	**1**	**3**	**4**	**63**	....	....	....	....	....
1988-89	**NY Rangers**	**NHL**	**20**	**0**	**1**	**1**	**84**	....	....	....	....	....
	Denver	IHL	9	5	4	9	31	....	....	....	....	....
	NHL Totals		**291**	**19**	**37**	**56**	**829**	**22**	**3**	**4**	**7**	**77**

Traded to **Philadelphia** by **Detroit** with Murray Craven for Darryl Sittler, October 19, 1984. Traded to **Los Angeles** by **Philadelphia** for Philadelphia's fourth-round choice (Mark Bar) — acquired earlier — in 1986 Entry Draft, December 18, 1985. Traded to **NY Rangers** by **Los Angeles** for Gordon Walker and Mike Siltala, January 21, 1988.

PATERSON, MARK

Defense. Shoots left. 5'11", 180 lbs. Born, Ottawa, Ont., February 22, 1964.
(Hartford's 2nd choice, 35th over-all, in 1982 Entry Draft).

			Regular Season					Playoffs				
Season	Club	Lea	GP	G	A	TP	PIM	GP	G	A	TP	PIM
1981-82	Ottawa	OHL	64	4	13	17	59	17	1	5	6	40
1982-83	**Hartford**	**NHL**	**2**	**0**	**0**	**0**	**0**	....	....	....	....	....
	Ottawa	OHL	57	7	14	21	140	9	1	4	5	31
1983-84	**Hartford**	**NHL**	**9**	**2**	**0**	**2**	**4**	....	....	....	....	....
a	Ottawa	OHL	45	8	16	24	114	13	2	7	9	16
1984-85	**Hartford**	**NHL**	**13**	**1**	**3**	**4**	**24**	....	....	....	....	....
	Binghamton	AHL	442	18	20	74		....	....	....	....	
1985-86	**Hartford**	**NHL**	**5**	**0**	**0**	**0**	**5**	....	....	....	....	....
	Binghamton	AHL	67	2	16	18	121	6	0	0	0	6
1986-87	Moncton	AHL	70	6	21	27	112	3	0	0	0	0
1987-88	Saginaw	IHL	23	1	5	6	55	8	0	4	4	15
1988-89	Saginaw	IHL	17	1	3	4	42	....	....	....	....	....
	NHL Totals		**29**	**3**	**3**	**6**	**33**	....	....	....	....	....

a OHL Third Team All-Star (1983, 1984).

Traded to **Calgary** by **Hartford** for Yves Courteau, October 7, 1986.

PATRICK, JAMES

Defense. Shoots right. 6'2", 195 lbs. Born, Winnipeg, Man., June 14, 1963.
(NY Rangers' 1st choice, 9th over-all, in 1981 Entry Draft).

			Regular Season					Playoffs				
Season	Club	Lea	GP	G	A	TP	PIM	GP	G	A	TP	PIM
1980-81ab	Prince Albert	SJHL	59	21	61	82	162	4	1	6	7	....
1981-82cde	North Dakota	WCHA	42	5	24	29	26	....	....	....	....	....
1982-83fg	North Dakota	WCHA	36	12	36	48	29	....	....	....	....	....
1983-84	Cdn. Olympic	....	63	7	24	31	52	....	....	....	....	....
	NY Rangers	**NHL**	**12**	**1**	**7**	**8**	**2**	**5**	**0**	**3**	**3**	**2**
1984-85	**NY Rangers**	**NHL**	**75**	**8**	**28**	**36**	**71**	**3**	**0**	**0**	**0**	**4**
1985-86	**NY Rangers**	**NHL**	**75**	**14**	**29**	**43**	**88**	**16**	**1**	**5**	**6**	**34**
1986-87	**NY Rangers**	**NHL**	**78**	**10**	**45**	**55**	**62**	**6**	**1**	**2**	**3**	**2**
1987-88	**NY Rangers**	**NHL**	**70**	**17**	**45**	**62**	**52**	....	....	....	....	....
1988-89	**NY Rangers**	**NHL**	**68**	**11**	**36**	**47**	**41**	**4**	**0**	**1**	**1**	**2**
	NHL Totals		**378**	**61**	**190**	**251**	**316**	**34**	**2**	**11**	**13**	**44**

a Most Valuable Player, 1981 Centennial Cup Tournament.
b First All-Star Team, 1981 Centennial Cup Tournament.
c WCHA Rookie of the Year (1982)
d WCHA Second All-Star Team (1982)
e Named to NCAA All-Tournament Team (1982)
f WCHA First All-Star Team (1983)
g NCAA All American (West) (1983)

PATTERSON, COLIN

Right wing. Shoots right. 6'2", 195 lbs. Born, Rexdale, Ont., May 11, 1960.

			Regular Season					Playoffs				
Season	Club	Lea	GP	G	A	TP	PIM	GP	G	A	TP	PIM
1980-81	Clarkson	ECAC	34	20	31	51	8	....	....	....	....	....
1981-82	Clarkson	ECAC	34	21	31	52	32	....	....	....	....	....
1982-83	Clarkson	ECAC	31	23	29	52	30	....	....	....	....	....
	Colorado	CHL	7	1	1	2	0	3	0	0	0	15
1983-84	Colorado	CHL	6	2	3	5	9	....	....	....	....	....
	Calgary	**NHL**	**56**	**13**	**14**	**27**	**15**	**11**	**1**	**1**	**2**	**6**
1984-85	**Calgary**	**NHL**	**57**	**22**	**21**	**43**	**5**	**4**	**0**	**0**	**0**	**5**
1985-86	**Calgary**	**NHL**	**61**	**14**	**13**	**27**	**22**	**19**	**6**	**3**	**9**	**10**
1986-87	**Calgary**	**NHL**	**68**	**13**	**13**	**26**	**41**	**6**	**0**	**2**	**2**	**2**
1987-88	**Calgary**	**NHL**	**39**	**7**	**11**	**18**	**28**	**9**	**1**	**0**	**1**	**8**
1988-89	**Calgary**	**NHL**	**74**	**14**	**24**	**38**	**56**	**22**	**3**	**10**	**13**	**24**
	NHL Totals		**355**	**83**	**96**	**179**	**167**	**71**	**11**	**16**	**27**	**55**

Signed as a free agent by **Calgary** March 24, 1983.

PAULETTI, JEFF

Defense. Shoots right. 5'11", 190 lbs. Born, Hastings, MN, January 15, 1968.
(Edmonton's 11th choice, 231st overall, in 1987 Entry Draft).

			Regular Season					Playoffs				
Season	Club	Lea	GP	G	A	TP	PIM	GP	G	A	TP	PIM
1986-87	U. Minnesota	WCHA	4	0	1	1	0	....	....	....	....	....
1987-88	U. Minnesota	WCHA	2	0	0	0	2	....	....	....	....	....
1988-89	U. Minnesota	WCHA	1	0	0	0	0	....	....	....	....	....

PAUNIO, JOEL

Left wing. Shoots left. 6', 180 lbs. Born, Helsinki, Finland, August 16, 1964.
(Calgary's 5th choice, 96th overall, in 1984 Entry Draft)

			Regular Season					Playoffs				
Season	Club	Lea	GP	G	A	TP	PIM	GP	G	A	TP	PIM
1983-84	IFK	Fin.	27	12	21	33	2	2	2	0	2	0
1984-85	IFK	Fin.	20	2	3	5	4	....	....	....	....	....
1985-86	IFK	Fin.	35	3	6	9	6	7	0	0	0	0
1986-87	IFK	Fin.	42	5	4	9	14	3	0	0	0	0
1987-88	IFK	Fin.	43	4	6	10	14	6	1	0	1	0
1988-89	IFK	Fin.	35	3	6	9	6	7	0	0	0	0

PAVESE, JAMES PETER (JIM) (puh VEES)

Defense. Shoots left. 6'2", 205 lbs. Born, New York, NY, May 8, 1962.
(St. Louis' 2nd choice, 54th over-all, in 1980 Entry Draft).

			Regular Season					Playoffs				
Season	Club	Lea	GP	G	A	TP	PIM	GP	G	A	TP	PIM
1980-81	Kitchener	OHA	19	3	12	15	93	....	....	....	....	....
	S.S. Marie	OHA	43	3	25	28	127	19	1	3	4	69
1981-82	S.S. Marie	OHL	26	4	21	25	110	13	2	12	14	38
	St. Louis	**NHL**	**42**	**2**	**9**	**11**	**101**	**3**	**0**	**3**	**3**	**2**
	Salt Lake	CHL	....	....	....	....	....	1	0	0	0	17
1982-83	**St. Louis**	**NHL**	**24**	**0**	**2**	**2**	**45**	**4**	**0**	**0**	**0**	**6**
	Salt Lake	CHL	36	5	6	11	165	4	1	3	4	2
1983-84	**St. Louis**	**NHL**	**4**	**0**	**1**	**1**	**19**	....	....	....	....	....
	Montana	CHL	47	1	19	20	147	....	....	....	....	....
1984-85	**St. Louis**	**NHL**	**51**	**2**	**5**	**7**	**69**	**1**	**0**	**0**	**0**	**5**
1985-86	**St. Louis**	**NHL**	**69**	**4**	**7**	**11**	**116**	**19**	**0**	**2**	**2**	**51**
1986-87	**St. Louis**	**NHL**	**69**	**2**	**9**	**11**	**127**	**2**	**0**	**0**	**0**	**2**
1987-88	**St. Louis**	**NHL**	**4**	**0**	**1**	**1**	**8**	....	....	....	....	....
	NY Rangers	**NHL**	**14**	**0**	**1**	**1**	**48**	....	....	....	....	....
	Colorado	IHL	1	0	0	0	2	....	....	....	....	....
	Detroit	**NHL**	**7**	**0**	**3**	**3**	**21**	**4**	**0**	**1**	**1**	**15**
1988-89	**Detroit**	**NHL**	**39**	**3**	**6**	**9**	**130**	....	....	....	....	....
	Hartford	**NHL**	**5**	**0**	**0**	**0**	**5**	**1**	**0**	**0**	**0**	**0**
	NHL Totals		**328**	**13**	**44**	**57**	**689**	**34**	**0**	**6**	**6**	**81**

Traded to **NY Rangers** by **St. Louis** for future considerations, October 23, 1987. Traded to **Detroit** by **NY Rangers** for future considerations, March 8, 1988. Traded to **Hartford** by **Detroit** for Torrie Robertson, March 7, 1989.

PAVLAS, PETR

Defense. Shoots left. 5'10", 170 lbs. Born, Olomouc, Czechoslovakia, February 4, 1968.
(Washington's 10th choice, 183rd overall, in 1988 Entry Draft).

			Regular Season					Playoffs				
Season	Club	Lea	GP	G	A	TP	PIM	GP	G	A	TP	PIM
1987-88	Dukla Trencin	Czech.	20	4	7	11	....	....	....	....	....	....
1988-89	Dukla Trencin	Czech.	31	14	15	29	....	....	....	....	....	....

PAYNTER, KENT

Defense. Shoots left. 6', 185 lbs. Born, Summerside, PEI, April 17, 1965.
(Chicago's 9th choice, 159th overall, in 1983 Entry Draft).

			Regular Season					Playoffs				
Season	Club	Lea	GP	G	A	TP	PIM	GP	G	A	TP	PIM
1982-83	Kitchener	OHL	65	4	11	15	97	12	1	0	1	20
1983-84	Kitchener	OHL	65	9	27	36	94	16	4	9	13	18
1984-85	Kitchener	OHL	58	7	28	35	93	4	2	1	3	4
1985-86	Nova Scotia	AHL	23	1	2	3	36	....	....	....	....	....
1986-87	Nova Scotia	AHL	66	2	6	8	57	2	0	0	0	0
1987-88	**Chicago**	**NHL**	**2**	**0**	**0**	**0**	**2**	....	....	....	....	....
	Saginaw	IHL	74	8	20	28	141	10	0	1	1	30
1988-89	**Chicago**	**NHL**	**1**	**0**	**0**	**0**	**2**	....	....	....	....	....
	Saginaw	IHL	69	12	14	26	148	6	2	2	4	17
	NHL Totals		**3**	**0**	**0**	**0**	**4**	....	....	....	....	....

PEARSON, ROB

Right wing. Shoots right. 6'1", 175 lbs. Born, Oshawa, Ont., August 3, 1971.
(Toronto's 2nd choice, 12th overall, in 1989 Entry Draft).

			Regular Season					Playoffs				
Season	Club	Lea	GP	G	A	TP	PIM	GP	G	A	TP	PIM
1987-88	Oshawa	Midget	72	68	65	133	188	....	....	....	....	....
1988-89	Belleville	OHL	26	8	12	20	51	....	....	....	....	....

PEARSON, SCOTT

Left wing. Shoots left. 6'1", 205 lbs. Born, Cornwall, Ont., December 19, 1969.
(Toronto's 1st choice, 6th overall, in 1988 Entry Draft).

			Regular Season					Playoffs				
Season	Club	Lea	GP	G	A	TP	PIM	GP	G	A	TP	PIM
1986-87	Kingston	OHL	62	30	24	54	101	9	3	3	6	42
1987-88	Kingston	OHL	46	26	32	58	117	....	....	....	....	....
1988-89	**Toronto**	**NHL**	**9**	**0**	**1**	**1**	**2**	....	....	....	....	....
	Kingston	OHL	13	9	8	17	34	....	....	....	....	....
	Niagara Falls	OHL	32	26	34	60	90	17	14	10	24	53
	NHL Totals		**9**	**0**	**1**	**1**	**2**	....	....	....	....	....

PEDERSEN, ALLEN

Defense. Shoots left. 6'4", 205 lbs. Born, Edmonton, Alta., January 13, 1965.
(Boston's 5th choice, 105th over-all, in 1983 Entry Draft).

			Regular Season					Playoffs				
Season	Club	Lea	GP	G	A	TP	PIM	GP	G	A	TP	PIM
1982-83	Medicine Hat	WHL	63	3	10	13	49	5	0	0	0	7
1983-84	Medicine Hat	WHL	44	0	11	11	47	14	0	2	2	24
1984-85	Medicine Hat	WHL	72	6	16	22	66	10	0	0	0	9
1985-86	Moncton	AHL	59	1	8	9	39	3	0	0	0	0
1986-87	**Boston**	**NHL**	**79**	**1**	**11**	**12**	**71**	**4**	**0**	**0**	**0**	**4**
1987-88	**Boston**	**NHL**	**78**	**0**	**6**	**6**	**90**	**21**	**0**	**0**	**0**	**34**
1988-89	**Boston**	**NHL**	**51**	**0**	**6**	**6**	**69**	**10**	**0**	**0**	**0**	**2**
	NHL Totals		**208**	**1**	**23**	**24**	**230**	**35**	**0**	**0**	**0**	**40**

PEDERSON, BARRY ALAN (PEE-duhr suhn)

Center. Shoots right. 5'11", 185 lbs. Born, Big River, Sask., March 13, 1961.
(Boston's 1st choice, 18th over-all, in 1980 Entry Draft).

			Regular Season					Playoffs				
Season	Club	Lea	GP	G	A	TP	PIM	GP	G	A	TP	PIM
1978-79	Victoria	WHL	72	31	53	84	41	....	....	....	....	....
1979-80	Victoria	WHL	72	52	88	140	50	16	13	14	27	31
1980-81a	Victoria	WHL	55	65	82	147	65	15	15	21	36	10
	Boston	**NHL**	**9**	**1**	**4**	**5**	**6**	....	....	....	....	....
1981-82	**Boston**	**NHL**	**80**	**44**	**48**	**92**	**53**	**11**	**7**	**11**	**18**	**2**
1982-83	**Boston**	**NHL**	**77**	**46**	**61**	**107**	**47**	**17**	**14**	**18**	**32**	**21**
1983-84	**Boston**	**NHL**	**80**	**39**	**77**	**116**	**64**	**3**	**0**	**1**	**1**	**2**
1984-85	**Boston**	**NHL**	**22**	**4**	**8**	**12**	**10**	....	....	....	....	....
1985-86	**Boston**	**NHL**	**79**	**29**	**47**	**76**	**60**	**3**	**1**	**0**	**1**	**0**
1986-87	**Vancouver**	**NHL**	**79**	**24**	**52**	**76**	**50**	....	....	....	....	....
1987-88	**Vancouver**	**NHL**	**76**	**19**	**52**	**71**	**92**	....	....	....	....	....
1988-89	**Vancouver**	**NHL**	**62**	**15**	**26**	**41**	**22**	....	....	....	....	....
	NHL Totals		**564**	**221**	**375**	**596**	**404**	**34**	**22**	**30**	**52**	**25**

a WHL First All-Star Team (1981)

Played in NHL All-Star Game (1983, 1984)

Traded to **Vancouver** by **Boston** for Cam Neely and Vancouver's first-round choice in 1987 Entry Draft (Glen Wesley), June 6, 1986.

PEDERSON, MARK

Left wing. Shoots left. 6'2", 190 lbs. Born, Prelate, Sask., January 14, 1968.
(Montreal's 1st choice, 15th overall, in 1986 Entry Draft).

			Regular Season					Playoffs				
Season	Club	Lea	GP	G	A	TP	PIM	GP	G	A	TP	PIM
1984-85	Medicine Hat	WHL	71	42	40	82	63	10	3	2	5	0
1985-86	Medicine Hat	WHL	72	46	60	106	46	25	12	6	18	25
1986-87a	Medicine Hat	WHL	69	56	46	102	58	20	19	7	26	14
1987-88	Medicine Hat	WHL	62	53	58	111	55	16	*13	6	19	16
1988-89	Sherbrooke	AHL	75	43	38	81	53	6	7	5	12	4

a WHL East All-Star Team (1987)

PEHRSSON, JOAKIM

Left wing. Shoots left. 5'8", 165 lbs. Born, Gavle, Sweden, May 15, 1966.
(Chicago's 10th choice, 195th overall, in 1984 Entry Draft).

			Regular Season					Playoffs				
Season	Club	Lea	GP	G	A	TP	PIM	GP	G	A	TP	PIM
1981-82	Stromsbro	Swe. 2	2	1	1	2	0	....	....	....	....	....
1982-83	Stromsbro	Swe. 2	21	4	7	11	2	....	....	....	....	....
1983-84	Stromsbro	Swe. 2	24	12	17	29	4	....	....	....	....	....
1984-85	Stromsbro	Swe. 2	32	22	26	48	8	....	....	....	....	....
1985-86	Stromsbro	Swe.	35	8	8	13	2	2	0	0	0	0
1986-87	Brynas	Swe.	34	9	8	17	10	....	....	....	....	....
1987-88	Stromsbro	Swe.	37	10	11	21	12	....	....	....	....	....
1988-89	Brynas	Swe.	39	7	10	17	22	....	....	....	....	....

PELLERIN, SCOTT

Left wing. Shoots left. 5'10", 180 lbs. Born, Shediac, N.B., January 9, 1970.
(New Jersey's 4th choice, 47th overall, in 1989 Entry Draft).

			Regular Season					Playoffs				
Season	Club	Lea	GP	G	A	TP	PIM	GP	G	A	TP	PIM
1987-88	Notre Dame	SJHL	57	37	49	86	139	....	....	....	....	....
1988-89a	U. of Maine	H.E.	45	29	33	62	92	....	....	....	....	....

a Co-winner Hockey East Rookie of the Year (1989)

PELTOMAA, TIMO

Right wing. Shoots right. 6'1", 185 lbs. Born, Toijala, Finland, July 26, 1968.
(Los Angeles' 9th choice, 154th overall, in 1988 Entry Draft).

			Regular Season					Playoffs				
Season	Club	Lea	GP	G	A	TP	PIM	GP	G	A	TP	PIM
1987-88	Ilves	Fin.	20	0	1	1	32	....	....	....	....	....
1988-89	Ilves	Fin.	23	4	0	4	16	....	....	....	....	....

PEPLINSKI, JAMES DESMOND (JIM) (peh-PLINS-kee)

Right wing. Shoots right. 6'3", 209 lbs. Born, Renfrew, Ont., October 24, 1960.
(Atlanta's 5th choice, 75th over-all, in 1979 Entry Draft).

			Regular Season					Playoffs				
Season	Club	Lea	GP	G	A	TP	PIM	GP	G	A	TP	PIM
1978-79	Toronto	OHA	66	23	32	55	88	3	0	1	1	0
1979-80	Toronto	OHA	67	35	66	101	89	4	1	2	3	15
1980-81	**Calgary**	**NHL**	**80**	**13**	**25**	**38**	**108**	**16**	**2**	**3**	**5**	**41**
1981-82	**Calgary**	**NHL**	**74**	**30**	**37**	**67**	**115**	**3**	**1**	**0**	**1**	**13**
1982-83	**Calgary**	**NHL**	**80**	**15**	**26**	**41**	**134**	**8**	**1**	**1**	**2**	**45**
1983-84	**Calgary**	**NHL**	**74**	**11**	**22**	**33**	**114**	**11**	**3**	**4**	**7**	**21**
1984-85	**Calgary**	**NHL**	**80**	**16**	**29**	**45**	**111**	**4**	**1**	**3**	**4**	**11**
1985-86	**Calgary**	**NHL**	**77**	**24**	**35**	**59**	**214**	**22**	**5**	**9**	**14**	**107**
1986-87	**Calgary**	**NHL**	**80**	**18**	**32**	**50**	**181**	**6**	**1**	**0**	**1**	**24**
1987-88	**Calgary**	**NHL**	**75**	**20**	**31**	**51**	**234**	**9**	**0**	**5**	**5**	**45**
	Cdn. Olympic	....	7	0	1	1	6	....	....	....	....	....
1988-89	**Calgary**	**NHL**	**79**	**13**	**25**	**38**	**241**	**20**	**1**	**6**	**7**	**75**
	NHL Totals		**699**	**160**	**262**	**422**	**1452**	**99**	**15**	**31**	**46**	**382**

PERGOLA, DAVID

Right wing. Shoots right. 6'1", 185 lbs. Born, Waltham, MA, March 4, 1969.
(Buffalo's 5th choice, 85th overall, in 1987 Entry Draft).

			Regular Season					Playoffs				
Season	Club	Lea	GP	G	A	TP	PIM	GP	G	A	TP	PIM
1986-87	Belmont Hill	HS	23	24	17	41	....	....	....	....	....	....
1987-88	Boston College	H.E.	33	5	7	12	22	....	....	....	....	....
1988-89	Boston College	H.E.	39	12	9	21	16	....	....	....	....	....

PERKINS, TERRY

Right wing. Shoots right. 6'1", 190 lbs. Born, Campbell River, B.C., June 21, 1966.
(Quebec's 4th choice, 78th over-all, in 1984 Entry Draft).

			Regular Season					Playoffs				
Season	Club	Lea	GP	G	A	TP	PIM	GP	G	A	TP	PIM
1983-84	Portland	WHL	30	10	10	20	0	14	8	4	12	2
1984-85	Portland	WHL	63	33	38	71	81	6	0	4	4	5
1985-86	Spokane	WHL	69	71	46	117	74	9	2	5	7	24
1986-87	Fredericton	AHL	44	10	11	21	35	....	....	....	....	....
	Muskegon	IHL	12	4	8	12	31	....	....	....	....	....
1987-88	Baltimore	AHL	65	28	41	69	65	....	....	....	....	....
1988-89	Cdn. National		5	0	2	2	4	....	....	....	....	....

PERSSON, LARS RICKARD

Defense. Shoots left. 6'1", 195 lbs. Born, Ostersund, Sweden, August 24, 1969.
(New Jersey's 2nd choice, 23rd overall, in 1987 Entry Draft).

			Regular Season					Playoffs				
Season	Club	Lea	GP	G	A	TP	PIM	GP	G	A	TP	PIM
1985-86	Ostersund	Swe. 2	24	2	2	4	16	....	....	....	....	....
1986-87	Ostersund	Swe. 2	31	10	11	21	28	....	....	....	....	....
1987-88	Leksand	Swe.	21	2	0	2	8	....	....	....	....	....
1988-89	Leksand	Swe.	33	2	4	6	28	....	....	....	....	....

PESETTI, RON

Defense. Shoots right. 5'11", 190 lbs. Born, Laval, Que., May 3, 1963.
(Winnipeg's 9th choice, 155th overall, in 1983 Entry Draft).

			Regular Season					Playoffs				
Season	Club	Lea	GP	G	A	TP	PIM	GP	G	A	TP	PIM
1982-83	W. Michigan	CCHA	31	2	8	10	34	....	....	....	....	....
1983-84	W. Michigan	CCHA	33	3	11	14	44	....	....	....	....	....
1984-85	W. Michigan	CCHA	29	1	6	7	32	....	....	....	....	....
1985-86	W. Michigan	CCHA	42	8	20	28	62	....	....	....	....	....
1986-87	Fort Wayne	IHL	79	12	39	51	62	5	0	2	2	5
1987-88	Moncton	AHL	60	8	21	29	41	....	....	....	....	....
	Fort Wayne	IHL	3	0	2	2	4	6	2	3	5	2
1988-89	Fort Wayne	IHL	57	3	14	17	29	5	0	0	0	0

PESKLEWIS, MATT

Left wing. Shoots left. 6'2", 185 lbs. Born, Edmonton, Alta., May 21, 1968.
(Boston's 4th choice, 97th overall, in 1986 Entry Draft).

			Regular Season					Playoffs				
Season	Club	Lea	GP	G	A	TP	PIM	GP	G	A	TP	PIM
1985-86	St. Albert	AJHL	51	13	26	39	259	....	....	....	....	....
1986-87	Boston U.	H.E.	24	0	2	2	28	....	....	....	....	....
1987-88	Boston U.	H.E.	28	0	11	11	54	....	....	....	....	....
1988-89	Boston U.	H.E.	12	2	7	9	31	....	....	....	....	....

PETERSON, BRENT RONALD (PEE-ter-son)

Center. Shoots right. 6', 190 lbs. Born, Calgary, Alta., February 15, 1958.
(Detroit's 2nd choice, 12th over-all, in 1978 Amateur Draft).

			Regular Season					Playoffs				
Season	Club	Lea	GP	G	A	TP	PIM	GP	G	A	TP	PIM
1974-75	Edmonton	WHL	66	17	26	43	44	....	....	....	....	....
1975-76	Edmonton	WHL	70	22	39	61	57	5	4	2	6	7
1976-77	Portland	WHL	69	34	78	112	98	10	3	8	11	8
1977-78	Portland	WHL	51	33	50	83	95	3	1	1	2	2
1978-79	Detroit	NHL	5	0	0	0	0	....	....	....	....	....
1979-80	**Detroit**	**NHL**	**18**	**1**	**2**	**3**	**2**	....	....	....	....	....
	Adirondack	AHL	52	9	22	31	61	5	0	0	0	6
1980-81	**Detroit**	**NHL**	**53**	**6**	**18**	**24**	**24**	....	....	....	....	....
	Adirondack	AHL	3	1	0	1	10	....	....	....	....	....
1981-82	**Detroit**	**NHL**	**15**	**1**	**0**	**1**	**6**	....	....	....	....	....
	Buffalo	**NHL**	**46**	**9**	**5**	**14**	**43**	**4**	**1**	**0**	**1**	**12**
1982-83	**Buffalo**	**NHL**	**75**	**13**	**24**	**37**	**38**	**10**	**1**	**2**	**3**	**28**
1983-84	**Buffalo**	**NHL**	**70**	**9**	**12**	**21**	**52**	**3**	**0**	**1**	**1**	**4**
1984-85	**Buffalo**	**NHL**	**74**	**12**	**22**	**34**	**47**	**5**	**0**	**0**	**0**	**6**
1985-86	**Vancouver**	**NHL**	**77**	**8**	**23**	**31**	**94**	**3**	**2**	**0**	**2**	**9**
1986-87	**Vancouver**	**NHL**	**69**	**7**	**15**	**22**	**77**	....	....	....	....	....
1987-88	**Hartford**	**NHL**	**52**	**2**	**7**	**9**	**40**	**4**	**0**	**0**	**0**	**2**
1988-89	**Hartford**	**NHL**	**66**	**4**	**13**	**17**	**61**	**2**	**0**	**1**	**1**	**4**
	NHL Totals		**620**	**72**	**141**	**213**	**484**	**31**	**4**	**4**	**8**	**65**

Traded to **Buffalo** by **Detroit** with Mike Foligno and Dale McCourt for Danny Gare, Jim Schoenfeld and Derek Smith, December 2, 1981. Claimed by **Vancouver** from **Buffalo** in NHL Waiver Draft, October 7, 1985. Claimed by **Hartford** in NHL Waiver Draft, October 5, 1987.

PETERSON, BRETT

Defense. Shoots right. 6'2", 195 lbs. Born, St. Paul, MN, February 1, 1969.
(Calgary's 9th choice, 189th overall, in 1988 Entry Draft).

			Regular Season					Playoffs				
Season	Club	Lea	GP	G	A	TP	PIM	GP	G	A	TP	PIM
1987-88	St. Paul	USHL	37	2	9	11	68	....	....	....	....	....
1988-89	U. of Denver	WCHA	19	0	3	3	4	....	....	....	....	....

PETIT, MICHEL (pih-TEE)

Defense. Shoots right. 6'1", 205 lbs. Born, St. Malo, Que., February 12, 1964.
(Vancouver's 1st choice, 11th over-all, in 1982 Entry Draft).

			Regular Season					Playoffs				
Season	Club	Lea	GP	G	A	TP	PIM	GP	G	A	TP	PIM
1981-82a	Sherbrooke	QMJHL	63	10	39	49	106	22	5	20	25	24
1982-83	**Vancouver**	**NHL**	**2**	**0**	**0**	**0**	**0**	....	....	....	....	....
a	St. Jean	QMJHL	62	19	67	86	196	3	0	0	0	35
1983-84	Cdn. Olympic		19	3	10	13	58	....	....	....	....	....
	Vancouver	**NHL**	**44**	**6**	**9**	**15**	**53**	**1**	**0**	**0**	**0**	**0**
1984-85	**Vancouver**	**NHL**	**69**	**5**	**26**	**31**	**127**	....	....	....	....	....
1985-86	**Vancouver**	**NHL**	**32**	**1**	**6**	**7**	**27**	....	....	....	....	....
	Fredericton	AHL	25	0	13	13	79	....	....	....	....	....
1986-87	**Vancouver**	**NHL**	**69**	**12**	**13**	**25**	**131**	....	....	....	....	....
1987-88	**Vancouver**	**NHL**	**10**	**0**	**3**	**3**	**35**	....	....	....	....	....
	NY Rangers	**NHL**	**64**	**9**	**24**	**33**	**223**	....	....	....	....	....
1988-89	**NY Rangers**	**NHL**	**69**	**8**	**25**	**33**	**156**	**4**	**0**	**2**	**2**	**27**
	NHL Totals		**359**	**41**	**106**	**147**	**752**	**5**	**0**	**2**	**2**	**27**

a QMJHL First All-Star Team (1982, 1983)

Traded to **NY Rangers** by **Vancouver** for Willie Huber and Larry Melnyk, November 4, 1987.

PHAIR, LYLE (FAIR)

Left wing. Shoots left. 6'1", 190 lbs. Born, Pilot Mound, Man., August 31, 1961.

			Regular Season					Playoffs				
Season	Club	Lea	GP	G	A	TP	PIM	GP	G	A	TP	PIM
1981-82	Michigan State	CCHA	42	19	24	43	49	....	....	....	....	....
1982-83	Michigan State	CCHA	42	20	15	35	64	....	....	....	....	....
1983-84	Michigan State	CCHA	45	15	16	31	58	....	....	....	....	....
1984-85	Michigan State	CCHA	43	23	27	50	86	....	....	....	....	....
1985-86	New Haven	AHL	35	9	9	18	15	2	0	0	0	0
	Los Angeles	**NHL**	**15**	**0**	**1**	**1**	**2**	....	....	....	....	....
1986-87	**Los Angeles**	**NHL**	**5**	**2**	**0**	**2**	**2**	....	....	....	....	....
	New Haven	AHL	65	19	27	46	77	7	0	3	3	13
1987-88	**Los Angeles**	**NHL**	**28**	**4**	**6**	**10**	**8**	**1**	**0**	**0**	**0**	**0**
	New Haven	AHL	45	15	12	27	26	....	....	....	....	....
1988-89	New Haven	AHL	11	2	3	5	4	....	....	....	....	....
	Utica	AHL	58	5	19	24	24	3	0	0	0	2
	NHL Totals		**48**	**6**	**7**	**13**	**12**	**1**	**0**	**0**	**0**	**0**

Signed as a free agent by **Los Angeles**, June 7, 1985.

PHILLIPS, GUY

Right wing. Shoots right. 6', 180 lbs. Born, Brooks, Alta., February 13, 1966.

			Regular Season					Playoffs				
Season	Club	Lea	GP	G	A	TP	PIM	GP	G	A	TP	PIM
1984-85	Medicine Hat	WHL	67	16	18	34	46	6	3	3	6	4
1985-86	Medicine Hat	WHL	72	38	55	93	66	25	10	13	23	7
1986-87	Medicine Hat	WHL	44	27	32	59	36	20	10	12	22	16
1987-88	Saginaw	IHL	73	16	30	46	14	8	2	1	3	0
1988-89	Saginaw	IHL	62	20	17	37	31	5	0	0	0	0

Signed as a free agent by **Chicago**, December 30, 1987.

PICARD, ROBERT RENE JOSEPH (PEE-car, roh-BEAR)

Defense. Shoots left. 6'2", 207 lbs. Born, Montreal, Que., May 25, 1957.
(Washington's 1st choice, 3rd over-all, in 1977 Amateur Draft).

			Regular Season					Playoffs				
Season	Club	Lea	GP	G	A	TP	PIM	GP	G	A	TP	PIM
1975-76a	Montreal	QJHL	72	14	67	81	282	6	2	9	11	25
1976-77bc	Montreal	QJHL	70	32	60	92	267	13	2	10	12	20
1977-78	**Washington**	**NHL**	**75**	**10**	**27**	**37**	**101**	....	....	....	....	....
1978-79	**Washington**	**NHL**	**77**	**21**	**44**	**65**	**85**	....	....	....	....	....
1979-80	**Washington**	**NHL**	**78**	**11**	**43**	**54**	**122**	....	....	....	....	....
1980-81	**Toronto**	**NHL**	**59**	**6**	**19**	**25**	**68**	....	....	....	....	....
	Montreal	**NHL**	**8**	**2**	**2**	**4**	**6**	**1**	**0**	**0**	**0**	**0**
1981-82	**Montreal**	**NHL**	**62**	**2**	**26**	**28**	**106**	**5**	**1**	**1**	**2**	**7**
1982-83	**Montreal**	**NHL**	**64**	**7**	**31**	**38**	**60**	**3**	**0**	**0**	**0**	**0**
1983-84	**Montreal**	**NHL**	**7**	**0**	**2**	**2**	**0**	....	....	....	....	....
	Winnipeg	**NHL**	**62**	**6**	**16**	**22**	**34**	**3**	**0**	**0**	**0**	**12**
1984-85	**Winnipeg**	**NHL**	**78**	**12**	**22**	**34**	**107**	**8**	**2**	**2**	**4**	**8**
1985-86	**Winnipeg**	**NHL**	**20**	**2**	**5**	**7**	**17**	....	....	....	....	....
	Quebec	**NHL**	**48**	**7**	**27**	**34**	**36**	**3**	**0**	**2**	**2**	**2**
1986-87	**Quebec**	**NHL**	**78**	**8**	**20**	**28**	**71**	**13**	**2**	**10**	**12**	**10**
1987-88	**Quebec**	**NHL**	**65**	**3**	**13**	**16**	**103**	....	....	....	....	....
1988-89	**Quebec**	**NHL**	**74**	**7**	**14**	**21**	**61**	....	....	....	....	....
	NHL Totals		**855**	**104**	**311**	**415**	**977**	**36**	**5**	**15**	**20**	**39**

a QJHL Second All-Star Team (1976)
b QJHL First All-Star Team (1977)
c Named QJHL's Top Defenseman (1977)

Played in NHL All-Star Game (1980, 1981)

Traded to **Toronto** by **Washington** with Tim Coulis and Washington's second round choice (Bob McGill) in 1980 Entry Draft for Mike Palmateer and Toronto's third round choice (Torrie Robertson) in 1980 Entry Draft, June 11, 1980. Traded to **Montreal** by **Toronto** for Michel Larocque, March 10, 1981. Traded to **Winnipeg** by **Montreal** for Winnipeg's third round choice (Patrick Roy) in 1984 Entry Draft, November 4, 1983. Traded to **Quebec** by **Winnipeg** for Mario Marois, November 27, 1985.

PICHETTE, DAVE (pee-SHETT)

Defense. Shoots left. 6'3", 190 lbs. Born, Grand Falls, Nfld., February 4, 1960.

			Regular Season					Playoffs				
Season	Club	Lea	GP	G	A	TP	PIM	GP	G	A	TP	PIM
1978-79	Quebec	QJHL	57	10	16	26	134	6	1	1	2	35
1979-80	Quebec	QJHL	56	8	19	27	129	5	1	3	4	8
1980-81	Hershey	AHL	20	2	3	5	37	....	....	....	....	....
	Quebec	**NHL**	**46**	**4**	**16**	**20**	**62**	**1**	**0**	**0**	**0**	**14**
1981-82	**Quebec**	**NHL**	**67**	**7**	**30**	**37**	**152**	**16**	**2**	**4**	**6**	**22**
1982-83	Fredericton	AHL	16	3	11	14	14	....	....	....	....	....
	Quebec	**NHL**	**53**	**3**	**21**	**24**	**49**	**2**	**0**	**1**	**1**	**0**
1983-84	**Quebec**	**NHL**	**23**	**2**	**7**	**9**	**12**	....	....	....	....	....
	Fredericton	AHL	10	2	1	3	13	....	....	....	....	....
	St. Louis	**NHL**	**23**	**0**	**11**	**11**	**6**	**9**	**1**	**2**	**3**	**18**
1984-85	**New Jersey**	**NHL**	**71**	**17**	**40**	**57**	**41**	....	....	....	....	....
1985-86	**New Jersey**	**NHL**	**33**	**7**	**12**	**19**	**22**	....	....	....	....	....
	Maine	AHL	25	4	15	19	28	....	....	....	....	....
1986-87	Maine	AHL	61	6	16	22	69	....	....	....	....	....
1987-88	**NY Rangers**	**NHL**	**6**	**1**	**3**	**4**	**4**	....	....	....	....	....
	New Haven	AHL	46	10	21	31	37	....	....	....	....	....
1988-89	Cape Breton	AHL	39	5	21	26	20	....	....	....	....	....
	NHL Totals		**322**	**41**	**140**	**181**	**348**	**28**	**3**	**7**	**10**	**54**

Signed as free agent by **Quebec**, October 31, 1979. Traded to **St. Louis** by **Quebec** for Andre Dore, February 10, 1984. Claimed by **New Jersey** from **St. Louis** in NHL Waiver Draft, October 9, 1984.

PICKELL, DOUG

Left wing. Shoots left. 6'1", 185 lbs. Born, London, Ont., May 7, 1968.
(Calgary's 9th choice, 205th overall, in 1986 Entry Draft).

			Regular Season					Playoffs				
Season	Club	Lea	GP	G	A	TP	PIM	GP	G	A	TP	PIM
1985-86	Kamloops	WHL	70	27	20	47	112	16	1	6	7	25
1986-87	Kamloops	WHL	70	34	24	58	182	13	0	4	4	15
1987-88	Spokane	WHL	67	14	19	33	204	15	5	6	11	34
1988-89	Salt Lake	IHL	47	7	6	13	79	2	0	0	0	0

PIIPARINEN, JARKKO

Left wing. Shoots left. 6'1", 185 lbs. Born, Lahti, Finland, April 18, 1966.
(New Jersey's 11th choice, 211th overall, in 1984 Entry Draft).

			Regular Season					Playoffs				
Season	Club	Lea	GP	G	A	TP	PIM	GP	G	A	TP	PIM
1988-89	Reipas	Fin.	18	5	9	14	22	....	....	....	....	....

PILON, RICHARD

Defense. Shoots left. 6', 202 lbs. Born, Saskatoon, Sask., April 30, 1968.
(NY Islanders' 9th choice, 143rd overall, in 1986 Entry Draft).

			Regular Season					Playoffs				
Season	Club	Lea	GP	G	A	TP	PIM	GP	G	A	TP	PIM
1985-86	Prince Albert	SJHL	35	3	28	31	142	....	....	....	....	....
1986-87	Prince Albert	WHL	68	4	21	25	192	7	1	6	7	17
1987-88	Prince Albert	WHL	65	13	34	47	177	9	0	6	6	38
1988-89	**NY Islanders**	**NHL**	**62**	**0**	**14**	**14**	**242**	....	....	....	....	....
	NHL Totals		**62**	**0**	**14**	**14**	**242**	....	....	....	....	....

PITLICK, LANCE

Defense. Shoots right. 6', 185 lbs. Born, Minneapolis, MN, November 5, 1967.
(Minnesota's 10th choice, 180th overall, in 1986 Entry Draft).

			Regular Season					Playoffs				
Season	Club	Lea	GP	G	A	TP	PIM	GP	G	A	TP	PIM
1985-86	Cooper	HS	47	45	32	77	247	....	....	....	....	....
1986-87	U. Minnesota	WCHA	45	0	9	9	88	....	....	....	....	....
1987-88	U. Minnesota	WCHA	38	3	9	12	76	....	....	....	....	....
1988-89	U. Minnesota	WCHA	47	4	9	13	95	....	....	....	....	....

PIVONKA, MICHAL

Center. Shoots left. 6'2", 200 lbs. Born, Kladno, Czechoslovakia, January 28, 1966.
(Washington's 3rd choice, 59th over-all, in 1984 Entry Draft).

			Regular Season					Playoffs				
Season	Club	Lea	GP	G	A	TP	PIM	GP	G	A	TP	PIM
1985-86	Dukla-Jihlava	Czech.					UNAVAILABLE					
1986-87	**Washington**	**NHL**	**73**	**18**	**25**	**43**	**41**	**7**	**1**	**1**	**2**	**2**
1987-88	**Washington**	**NHL**	**71**	**11**	**23**	**34**	**28**	**14**	**4**	**9**	**13**	**4**
1988-89	**Washington**	**NHL**	**52**	**8**	**19**	**27**	**30**	**6**	**3**	**1**	**4**	**10**
	Baltimore	AHL	31	12	24	36	19	....	....	....	....	....
	NHL Totals		**196**	**37**	**67**	**104**	**99**	**27**	**8**	**11**	**19**	**16**

PLAVSIC, ADRIEN

Defense. Shoots left. 6'1", 190 lbs. Born, Montreal, Que., January 13, 1970.
(St. Louis' 2nd choice, 30th overall, in 1988 Entry Draft).

			Regular Season					Playoffs				
Season	Club	Lea	GP	G	A	TP	PIM	GP	G	A	TP	PIM
1986-87	Lac St. Louis	Midget	42	8	27	35	22	....	....	....	....	....
1987-88	N. Hampshire	H.E.	30	5	6	11	45	....	....	....	....	....
1988-89	Cdn. National	....	62	5	10	15	25	....	....	....	....	....

PLAYFAIR, JAMES (JIM)

Defense. Shoots left. 6'4", 200 lbs. Born, Fort St. James, B.C., May 22, 1964.
(Edmonton's 1st choice, 20th over-all, in 1982 Entry Draft).

			Regular Season					Playoffs				
Season	Club	Lea	GP	G	A	TP	PIM	GP	G	A	TP	PIM
1981-82	Portland	WHL	70	4	13	17	121	15	1	2	3	21
1982-83	Portland	WHL	63	8	27	35	218	14	0	5	5	16
1983-84	**Edmonton**	**NHL**	**2**	**1**	**1**	**2**	**2**	....	....	....	....	....
	Portland	WHL	16	5	6	11	38	....	....	....	....	....
	Calgary	WHL	60	11	15	26	134	4	0	1	1	2
1984-85	Nova Scotia	AHL	41	0	4	4	107	....	....	....	....	....
1985-86	Nova Scotia	AHL	73	2	12	14	160	....	....	....	....	....
1986-87	Nova Scotia	AHL	60	1	21	22	82	....	....	....	....	....
1987-88	**Chicago**	**NHL**	**12**	**1**	**3**	**4**	**21**	....	....	....	....	....
	Saginaw	IHL	50	5	21	26	133	....	....	....	....	....
1988-89	**Chicago**	**NHL**	**7**	**0**	**0**	**0**	**28**	....	....	....	....	....
	Saginaw	IHL	23	3	6	9	73	6	0	2	2	20
	NHL Totals		**21**	**2**	**4**	**6**	**51**	....	....	....	....	....

PLAYFAIR, LARRY WILLIAM

Defense. Shoots left. 6'4", 200 lbs. Born, Fort St. James, B.C., June 23, 1958.
(Buffalo's 1st choice, 13th over-all, in 1978 Amateur Draft).

			Regular Season					Playoffs				
Season	Club	Lea	GP	G	A	TP	PIM	GP	G	A	TP	PIM
1976-77	Portland	WHL	65	2	17	19	199	8	0	0	0	4
1977-78a	Portland	WHL	71	13	19	32	402	8	0	2	2	58
1978-79	**Buffalo**	**NHL**	**26**	**0**	**3**	**3**	**60**	....	....	....	....	....
	Hershey	AHL	45	0	12	12	148	....	....	....	....	....
1979-80	**Buffalo**	**NHL**	**79**	**2**	**10**	**12**	**145**	**14**	**0**	**2**	**2**	**29**
1980-81	**Buffalo**	**NHL**	**75**	**3**	**9**	**12**	**169**	**8**	**0**	**0**	**0**	**26**
1981-82	**Buffalo**	**NHL**	**77**	**6**	**10**	**16**	**258**	**4**	**0**	**0**	**0**	**22**
1982-83	**Buffalo**	**NHL**	**79**	**4**	**13**	**17**	**180**	**5**	**0**	**1**	**1**	**11**
1983-84	**Buffalo**	**NHL**	**76**	**5**	**11**	**16**	**211**	**3**	**0**	**0**	**0**	**0**
1984-85	**Buffalo**	**NHL**	**72**	**3**	**14**	**17**	**157**	**5**	**0**	**3**	**3**	**9**
1985-86	**Buffalo**	**NHL**	**47**	**1**	**2**	**3**	**100**	....	....	....	....	....
	Los Angeles	**NHL**	**14**	**0**	**1**	**1**	**26**	....	....	....	....	....
1986-87	**Los Angeles**	**NHL**	**37**	**2**	**7**	**9**	**181**	....	....	....	....	....
1987-88	**Los Angeles**	**NHL**	**54**	**0**	**7**	**7**	**197**	**3**	**0**	**0**	**0**	**14**
1988-89	**Los Angeles**	**NHL**	**6**	**0**	**3**	**3**	**16**	....	....	....	....	....
	Buffalo	**NHL**	**42**	**0**	**3**	**3**	**110**	**1**	**0**	**0**	**0**	**0**
	NHL Totals		**684**	**26**	**93**	**119**	**1810**	**43**	**0**	**6**	**6**	**111**

a WHL First All-Star Team (1978)

Traded to **Los Angeles** by **Buffalo** with Sean McKenna and Ken Baumgartner for Brian Engblom and Doug Smith, January 30, 1986. Traded to **Buffalo** by **Los Angeles** for Bob Logan and Buffalo's ninth-round choice (Jim Glacin) in 1989 Entry Draft, October 21, 1988

POCHIPINSKI, TREVOR

Defense. Shoots right. 6'2", 190 lbs. Born, Prince Albert, Sask., July 8, 1968.
(Los Angeles' 9th choice, 170th overall, in 1986 Entry Draft).

			Regular Season					Playoffs				
Season	Club	Lea	GP	G	A	TP	PIM	GP	G	A	TP	PIM
1987-88	Colorado	WCHA	37	2	6	8	91	....	....	....	....	....
1988-89	Colorado	WCHA	40	4	10	14	74	....	....	....	....	....

PODDUBNY, WALTER MICHAEL (WALT) (poh DUHB nee)

Center. Shoots left. 6'1", 205 lbs. Born, Thunder Bay, Ont., February 14, 1960.
(Edmonton's 4th choice, 90th over-all, in 1980 Entry Draft).

			Regular Season					Playoffs				
Season	Club	Lea	GP	G	A	TP	PIM	GP	G	A	TP	PIM
1979-80	Kitchener	OHA	19	3	9	12	35	....	....	....	....	....
	Kingston	OHA	43	30	17	47	36	3	0	2	2	0
1980-81	Milwaukee	IHL	5	4	2	6	4	....	....	....	....	....
	Wichita	CHL	70	21	29	50	207	11	1	6	7	26
1981-82	Wichita	CHL	60	35	46	81	79	....	....	....	....	....
	Edmonton	**NHL**	**4**	**0**	**0**	**0**	**0**	....	....	....	....	....
	Toronto	**NHL**	**11**	**3**	**4**	**7**	**8**	....	....	....	....	....
1982-83	**Toronto**	**NHL**	**72**	**28**	**31**	**59**	**71**	**4**	**3**	**1**	**4**	**0**
1983-84	**Toronto**	**NHL**	**38**	**11**	**14**	**25**	**48**	....	....	....	....	....
1984-85	**Toronto**	**NHL**	**32**	**5**	**15**	**20**	**26**	....	....	....	....	....
	St. Catharines	AHL	8	5	7	12	10	....	....	....	....	....
1985-86	**Toronto**	**NHL**	**33**	**12**	**22**	**34**	**25**	**9**	**4**	**1**	**5**	**4**
	St. Catharines	AHL	37	28	27	55	52	....	....	....	....	....
1986-87	**NY Rangers**	**NHL**	**75**	**40**	**47**	**87**	**49**	**6**	**0**	**0**	**0**	**8**
1987-88	**NY Rangers**	**NHL**	**77**	**38**	**50**	**88**	**76**	....	....	....	....	....
1988-89	**Quebec**	**NHL**	**72**	**38**	**37**	**75**	**107**	....	....	....	....	....
	NHL Totals		**414**	**175**	**220**	**395**	**410**	**19**	**7**	**2**	**9**	**12**

Played in NHL All-Star Game (1989)

Traded to **Toronto** by **Edmonton** with Phil Drouilliard for Laurie Boschman, March 28, 1982. Traded to **NY Rangers** by **Toronto** for Mike Allison, August 18, 1986. Traded to **Quebec** by **NY Rangers** with Bruce Bell, Jari Gronstrand and NY Rangers' fourth round choice (Eric Dubois) in 1989 Entry Draft for Jason Lafreniere and Normand Rochefort, August 1, 1988. Traded to **New Jersey** by **Quebec** with future considerations for Joe Cirella and Claude Loiselle, June 17, 1989.

PODEIN, SHJON

Center. Shoots left. 6'2", 200 lbs. Born, Rochester, MN, March 5, 1968.
(Edmonton's 9th choice, 166th overall, in 1988 Entry Draft).

			Regular Season					Playoffs				
Season	Club	Lea	GP	G	A	TP	PIM	GP	G	A	TP	PIM
1987-88	Minn.-Duluth	WCHA	30	4	4	8	48	....	....	....	....	....
1988-89	Minn.-Duluth	WCHA	36	7	5	12	46	....	....	....	....	....

PODLOSKI, RAY

Center. Shoots left. 6'2", 210 lbs. Born, Edmonton, Alta., January 5, 1966.
(Boston's 2nd choice, 40th over-all, in 1984 Entry Draft).

			Regular Season					Playoffs				
Season	Club	Lea	GP	G	A	TP	PIM	GP	G	A	TP	PIM
1982-83	Red Deer	AJHL	59	49	49	97	47	....	....	....	....	....
1983-84	Portland	WHL	66	46	50	96	44	14	8	14	22	14
1984-85	Portland	WHL	67	63	75	138	41	6	3	1	4	7
1985-86	Portland	WHL	66	59	75	134	68	7	1	9	10	8
1986-87	Moncton	AHL	70	23	27	50	12	3	0	0	0	15
1987-88	Maine	AHL	36	12	20	32	12	5	1	2	3	19
1988-89	**Boston**	**NHL**	**8**	**0**	**1**	**1**	**22**	....	....	....	....	....
	Maine	AHL	71	20	34	54	70	....	....	....	....	....
	NHL Totals		**8**	**0**	**1**	**1**	**22**	....	....	....	....	....

POESCHEK, RUDY

Defense. Shoots right. 6'2", 210 lbs. Born, Terrace, B.C., September 29, 1966.
(NY Rangers' 12th choice, 238th overall, in 1985 Entry Draft).

			Regular Season					Playoffs				
Season	Club	Lea	GP	G	A	TP	PIM	GP	G	A	TP	PIM
1983-84	Kamloops	WHL	47	3	9	12	93	8	0	2	2	7
1984-85	Kamloops	WHL	34	6	7	13	100	15	0	3	3	56
1985-86	Kamloops	WHL	32	3	13	16	92	16	3	7	10	40
1986-87	Kamloops	WHL	54	13	18	31	153	15	2	4	6	37
1987-88	**NY Rangers**	**NHL**	**1**	**0**	**0**	**0**	**2**	....	....	....	....	....
	Colorado	IHL	82	7	31	38	210	12	2	2	4	31
1988-89	**NY Rangers**	**NHL**	**52**	**0**	**2**	**2**	**199**	....	....	....	....	....
	Colorado	IHL	2	0	0	0	6	....	....	....	....	....
	NHL Totals		**53**	**0**	**2**	**2**	**201**	....	....	....	....	....

POHL, MICHAEL

Center. Shoots left. 6'2", 185 lbs. Born, Rosenheim, West Germany, January 25, 1968.
(New Jersey's 14th choice, 243rd overall, in 1988 Entry Draft).

			Regular Season					Playoffs				
Season	Club	Lea	GP	G	A	TP	PIM	GP	G	A	TP	PIM
1987-88	Rosenheim	W. Ger.	44	7	9	16	32	....	....	....	....	....
1988-89	Rosenheim	W. Ger.	44	8	14	22	38	....	....	....	....	....

POJAR, JON

Left Wing. Shoots left. 6'0", 180 lbs. Born, St. Paul, MN, May 5, 1970.
(Chicago's 8th choice, 155th overall, in 1988 Entry Draft).

			Regular Season					Playoffs				
Season	Club	Lea	GP	G	A	TP	PIM	GP	G	A	TP	PIM
1987-88	Roseville	HS	19	9	11	20	0	....	....	....	....	....
1988-89	Colorado	WCHA	40	2	3	5	32	....	....	....	....	....

POLILLO, PAUL

Center. Shoots left. 5'11", 175 lbs. Born, Brantford, Ont., April 24, 1967.
(Pittsburgh's 1st choice, 4th overall, in 1988 Supplemental Draft).

			Regular Season					Playoffs				
Season	Club	Lea	GP	G	A	TP	PIM	GP	G	A	TP	PIM
1986-87	W. Michigan	CCHA	42	18	48	66	35	....	....	....	....	....
1987-88a	W. Michigan	CCHA	42	25	60	85	34	....	....	....	....	....
1988-89	W. Michigan	CCHA	41	20	46	66	32	....	....	....	....	....

a CCHA First All-Star Team (1988)

POPOVIC, PETER

Defense. Shoots right. 6'5", 210 lbs. Born, Koping, Sweden, February 10, 1968.
(Montreal's 5th choice, 93rd overall, in 1988 Entry Draft).

			Regular Season					Playoffs				
Season	Club	Lea	GP	G	A	TP	PIM	GP	G	A	TP	PIM
1986-87	VIK	Swe.	24	1	2	3	10	....	....	....	....	....
1987-88	VIK	Swe.	28	3	17	20	....	....	....	....	....	....
1988-89	VIK	Swe.	44	3	8	11	68	....	....	....	....	....

PORTER, DAVID

Left wing. Shoots left. 6'1", 170 lbs. Born, Milford, MI, June 2, 1967.
(NY Rangers' 10th choice, 199th overall, in 1987 Entry Draft).

			Regular Season					Playoffs				
Season	Club	Lea	GP	G	A	TP	PIM	GP	G	A	TP	PIM
1986-87	N. Michigan	WCHA	39	10	12	22	20	....	....	....	....	....
1987-88	N. Michigan	WCHA	38	9	19	28	16	....	....	....	....	....
1988-89	Michigan Tech.	WCHA	31	5	9	14	16	....	....	....	....	....

POSA, VICTOR

Left wing/defense. Shoots left. 6', 195 lbs. Born, Bari, Italy, November 5, 1966.
(Chicago's 7th choice, 137th overall, in 1985 Entry Draft).

			Regular Season					Playoffs				
Season	Club	Lea	GP	G	A	TP	PIM	GP	G	A	TP	PIM
1984-85	U. Wisconsin	WCHA	33	1	5	6	47	....	....	....	....	....
1985-86	Toronto	OHL	48	28	39	62	116	....	....	....	....	....
1986-87	Nova Scotia	AHL	2	1	0	1	2	....	....	....	....	....
	Saginaw	IHL	61	13	27	40	203	7	1	0	1	34
1987-88	Saginaw	IHL	2	0	0	0	0	....	....	....	....	....
	Flint	IHL	9	1	0	1	36	....	....	....	....	....
	Peoria	IHL	10	0	2	2	106	....	....	....	....	....
1988-89	Flint	IHL	3	0	0	0	21	....	....	....	....	....

POSMA, MIKE

Defense. Shoots right. 6'1", 195 lbs. Born, Utica, NY, December 16, 1967.
(St. Louis' 2nd choice, 31st overall, in 1986 Entry Draft).

			Regular Season					Playoffs				
Season	Club	Lea	GP	G	A	TP	PIM	GP	G	A	TP	PIM
1985-86	Buffalo Jr.	Jr. B	40	16	47	63	62	....	....	....	....	....
1986-87	W. Michigan	CCHA	35	12	31	43	42	....	....	....	....	....
1987-88a	W. Michigan	CCHA	42	16	38	54	30	....	....	....	....	....
1988-89	W. Michigan	CCHA	43	7	34	41	58	....	....	....	....	....

a CCHA Second All-Star Team (1988)

POTVIN, MARC

Right wing. Shoots right. 6'1", 185 lbs. Born, Ottawa, Ont., January 29, 1967.
(Detroit's 9th choice, 169th overall, in 1986 Entry Draft).

			Regular Season					Playoffs				
Season	Club	Lea	GP	G	A	TP	PIM	GP	G	A	TP	PIM
1985-86	Stratford	OPJHL	63	5	6	11	117	....	....	....	....	....
1986-87	Bowling Green	CCHA	43	5	15	20	74	....	....	....	....	....
1987-88	Bowling Green	CCHA	45	15	21	36	80	....	....	....	....	....
1988-89	Bowling Green	CCHA	46	23	12	35	63	....	....	....	....	....

POUDRIER, DANIEL (POO dree yay)

Defense. Shoots left. 6'2", 175 lbs. Born, Thetford Mines, Que., February 15, 1964.
(Quebec's 6th choice, 131st over-all, in 1982 Entry Draft).

			Regular Season					Playoffs				
Season	Club	Lea	GP	G	A	TP	PIM	GP	G	A	TP	PIM
1981-82	Shawinigan	QMJHL	64	6	18	24	20	14	1	1	2	2
1982-83	Shawinigan	QMJHL	67	6	28	34	31	10	1	2	3	2
1983-84	Drummondville	QMJHL	64	7	28	35	15	10	2	3	5	4
1984-85	Fredericton	AHL	1	0	0	0	0	....	....	....	....	....
	Muskegon	IHL	82	9	30	39	12	17	2	6	8	2
1985-86	**Quebec**	**NHL**	**13**	**1**	**5**	**6**	**10**	....	....	....	....	....
	Fredericton	AHL	65	5	26	31	9	6	0	3	3	0
1986-87	**Quebec**	**NHL**	**6**	**0**	**0**	**0**	**0**	....	....	....	....	....
	Fredericton	AHL	69	8	18	26	11	....	....	....	....	....
1987-88	**Quebec**	**NHL**	**6**	**0**	**0**	**0**	**0**	....	....	....	....	....
	Fredericton	AHL	66	13	30	43	18	11	2	5	7	2
1988-89	Halifax	AHL	7	2	4	6	2	3	0	0	0	2
	NHL Totals		**25**	**1**	**5**	**6**	**10**	....	....	....	....	....

POULIN, DAVID JAMES (DAVE) (POOL-lihn)

Center. Shoots left. 5'11", 190 lbs. Born, Timmins, Ont., December 17, 1958.

			Regular Season					Playoffs				
Season	Club	Lea	GP	G	A	TP	PIM	GP	G	A	TP	PIM
1978-79	Notre Dame	WCHA	37	28	31	59	32	....	....	....	....	....
1979-80	Notre Dame	WCHA	24	19	24	43	46	....	....	....	....	....
1980-81	Notre Dame	WCHA	35	13	22	35	53	....	....	....	....	....
1981-82a	Notre Dame	CCHA	39	29	30	59	44	....	....	....	....	....
1982-83	Rogle	Swe.	32	35	27	62	64	....	....	....	....	....
	Maine	AHL	16	7	9	16	2	....	....	....	....	....
	Philadelphia	**NHL**	**2**	**2**	**0**	**2**	**2**	**3**	**1**	**3**	**4**	**9**
1983-84	**Philadelphia**	**NHL**	**73**	**31**	**45**	**76**	**47**	**3**	**0**	**0**	**0**	**2**
1984-85	**Philadelphia**	**NHL**	**73**	**30**	**44**	**74**	**59**	**11**	**3**	**5**	**8**	**6**
1985-86	**Philadelphia**	**NHL**	**79**	**27**	**42**	**69**	**49**	**5**	**2**	**0**	**2**	**2**
1986-87b	**Philadelphia**	**NHL**	**75**	**25**	**45**	**70**	**53**	**15**	**3**	**3**	**6**	**14**
1987-88	**Philadelphia**	**NHL**	**68**	**19**	**32**	**51**	**32**	**7**	**2**	**6**	**8**	**4**
1988-89	**Philadelphia**	**NHL**	**69**	**18**	**17**	**35**	**49**	**19**	**6**	**5**	**11**	**16**
	NHL Totals		**439**	**152**	**225**	**377**	**291**	**63**	**17**	**22**	**39**	**53**

a CCHA Second All-Star Team (1982).
b Won Frank J. Selke Trophy (1987).
Played in NHL All-Star Game (1986, 1988)
Signed as free agent by **Philadelphia**, March 8, 1983.

PRAJSLER, PETR

Defense. Shoots left. 6'3", 200 lbs. Born, Hradec Kralove, Czech., September 21, 1965.
(Los Angeles' 5th choice, 93rd overall, in 1985 Entry Draft).

			Regular Season					Playoffs				
Season	Club	Lea	GP	G	A	TP	PIM	GP	G	A	TP	PIM
1986-87	Pardubice	Czech.	41	3	4	7	....	....	....	....	....	....
1987-88	Los Angeles	NHL	7	0	0	0	2	....	....	....	....	....
	New Haven	AHL	41	3	8	11	58	....	....	....	....	....
1988-89	Los Angeles	NHL	2	0	3	3	0	1	0	0	0	0
	New Haven	AHL	43	4	6	10	96	16	3	3	6	34
	NHL Totals		9	0	3	3	2	1	0	0	0	0

PRATT, TOM

Defense. Shoots left. 6'3", 190 lbs. Born, Lake Placid, NY, August 28, 1965.
(Calgary's 12th choice, 191st overall in 1983 Entry Draft).

			Regular Season					Playoffs				
Season	Club	Lea	GP	G	A	TP	PIM	GP	G	A	TP	PIM
1983-84	St. Lawrence	ECAC	32	4	8	12	70	....	....	....	....	....
1984-85	St. Lawrence	ECAC	31	2	4	6	32	....	....	....	....	....
1985-86	Bowling Green	CCHA	38	1	4	5	74	....	....	....	....	....
1986-87	Bowling Green	CCHA	41	1	7	8	46	....	....	....	....	....
1987-88	Salt Lake	IHL	41	2	6	8	146	8	0	0	0	35
1988-89	New Haven	AHL	35	1	7	8	53	....	....	....	....	....
	Flint	IHL	22	1	2	3	38	....	....	....	....	....
	Muskegon	IHL	14	1	3	4	15	2	0	0	0	2

PRAZNIK, JODY

Defense. Shoots right. 6'2", 195 lbs. Born, Winnipeg, Man., June 28, 1969.
(Detroit's 8th choice, 185th overall, in 1988 Entry Draft).

			Regular Season					Playoffs				
Season	Club	Lea	GP	G	A	TP	PIM	GP	G	A	TP	PIM
1987-88	Colorado	WCHA	37	5	10	15	46	....	....	....	....	....
1988-89	Saskatoon	WHL	28	2	9	11	28	8	0	2	2	2

PRESLEY, WAYNE

Right wing. Shoots right. 5'11", 170 lbs. Born, Dearborn, MI, March 23, 1965.
(Chicago's 2nd choice, 39th over-all, in 1983 Entry Draft).

			Regular Season					Playoffs				
Season	Club	Lea	GP	G	A	TP	PIM	GP	G	A	TP	PIM
1981-82	Detroit Little Caesars	Midget	61	38	56	94	146	....	....	....	....	....
1982-83	Kitchener	OHL	70	39	48	87	99	12	1	4	5	9
1983-84a	Kitchener	OHL	70	63	76	139	156	16	12	16	28	38
1984-85	Chicago	NHL	3	0	1	1	0	....	....	....	....	....
	Kitchener	OHL	31	25	21	46	77	....	....	....	....	....
	S.S. Marie	OHL	11	5	9	14	14	16	13	9	22	13
1985-86	Chicago	NHL	38	7	8	15	38	3	0	0	0	0
	Nova Scotia	AHL	29	6	9	15	22	....	....	....	....	....
1986-87	Chicago	NHL	80	32	29	61	114	4	1	0	1	9
1987-88	Chicago	NHL	42	12	10	22	52	5	0	0	0	4
1988-89	Chicago	NHL	72	21	19	40	100	14	7	5	12	18
	NHL Totals		235	72	67	139	304	26	8	5	13	31

a OHL First All-Star Team (1984)

PRIAKIN, SERGEI

Right wing. Shoots left. 6'3", 210 lbs. Born, Moscow, Soviet Union, December 7, 1963.
(Calgary's 12th choice, 252nd overall, in 1988 Entry Draft).

			Regular Season					Playoffs				
Season	Club	Lea	GP	G	A	TP	PIM	GP	G	A	TP	PIM
1987-88	Soviet Wings	USSR	44	10	15	25	16	....	....	....	....	....
1988-89	Soviet Wings	USSR	44	11	15	26	23	....	....	....	....	....
	Calgary	NHL	2	0	0	0	2	1	0	0	0	0
	NHL Totals		2	0	0	0	2	1	0	0	0	0

PRIESTLAY, KEN

Center. Shoots left. 5'10", 187 lbs. Born, Richmond, B.C., August 24, 1967.
(Buffalo's 5th choice, 98th overall, in 1985 Entry Draft).

			Regular Season					Playoffs				
Season	Club	Lea	GP	G	A	TP	PIM	GP	G	A	TP	PIM
1983-84	Victoria	WHL	55	10	18	28	31	....	....	....	....	....
1984-85	Victoria	WHL	50	25	37	62	48	....	....	....	....	....
1985-86	Victoria	WHL	72	73	72	145	45	....	....	....	....	....
	Rochester	AHL	4	0	2	2	0	....	....	....	....	....
1986-87	Buffalo	NHL	34	11	6	17	8	....	....	....	....	....
	Victoria	WHL	33	43	39	82	37	....	....	....	....	....
	Rochester	AHL	....	....	....	....	....	8	3	2	5	4
1987-88	Buffalo	NHL	33	5	12	17	35	6	0	0	0	11
	Rochester	AHL	43	27	24	51	47	....	....	....	....	....
1988-89	Buffalo	NHL	15	2	0	2	2	3	0	0	0	2
	Rochester	AHL	64	56	37	93	60	....	....	....	....	....
	NHL Totals		82	18	18	36	45	9	0	0	0	13

PROBERT, BOB (PROH buhrt)

Left wing. Shoots left. 6'3", 215 lbs. Born, Windsor, Ont., June 5, 1965.
(Detroit's 3rd choice, 46th over-all, in 1983 Entry Draft).

			Regular Season					Playoffs				
Season	Club	Lea	GP	G	A	TP	PIM	GP	G	A	TP	PIM
1982-83	Brantford	OHL	51	12	16	28	133	8	2	2	4	23
1983-84	Brantford	OHL	65	35	38	73	189	6	0	3	3	16
1984-85	S.S. Marie	OHL	44	20	52	72	172	....	....	....	....	....
	Hamilton	OHL	4	0	1	1	21	....	....	....	....	....
1985-86	Detroit	NHL	44	8	13	21	186	....	....	....	....	....
	Adirondack	AHL	32	12	15	27	152	10	2	3	5	68
1986-87	Detroit	NHL	63	13	11	24	221	16	3	4	7	63
	Adirondack	AHL	7	1	4	5	15	....	....	....	....	....
1987-88	Detroit	NHL	74	29	33	62	398	16	8	13	21	51
1988-89	Detroit	NHL	25	4	2	6	106	....	....	....	....	....
	NHL Totals		206	54	59	113	911	32	11	17	28	114

Played in NHL All-Star Game (1988)

PROPP, BRIAN PHILIP

Left wing. Shoots left. 5'10", 195 lbs. Born, Lanigan, Sask., February 15, 1959.
(Philadelphia's 1st choice, 14th over-all, in 1979 Entry Draft).

			Regular Season					Playoffs				
Season	Club	Lea	GP	G	A	TP	PIM	GP	G	A	TP	PIM
1976-77	Brandon	WHL	72	55	80	135	47	16	*14	12	26	5
1977-78a	Brandon	WHL	70	70	*112	*182	200	8	7	6	13	12
1978-79ab	Brandon	WHL	71	*94	*100	*194	127	22	15	23	*38	40
1979-80	Philadelphia	NHL	80	34	41	75	54	19	5	10	15	29
1980-81	Philadelphia	NHL	79	26	40	66	110	12	6	6	12	32
1981-82	Philadelphia	NHL	80	44	47	91	117	4	2	2	4	4
1982-83	Philadelphia	NHL	80	40	42	82	72	3	1	2	3	8
1983-84	Philadelphia	NHL	79	39	53	92	37	3	0	1	1	6
1984-85	Philadelphia	NHL	76	43	53	96	43	19	8	10	18	6
1985-86	Philadelphia	NHL	72	40	57	97	47	5	0	2	2	4
1986-87	Philadelphia	NHL	53	31	36	67	45	26	12	16	28	10
1987-88	Philadelphia	NHL	74	27	49	76	76	7	4	2	6	8
1988-89	Philadelphia	NHL	77	32	46	78	37	18	14	9	23	14
	NHL Totals		750	356	464	820	638	116	52	60	112	121

a WHL First All-Star Team (1978, 1979)
b WHL Player of the Year (1979)

Played in NHL All-Star Game (1980, 1982, 1984, 1986)

PROSOFSKY, JASON

Right wing. Shoots right. 6'4", 220 lbs. Born, Medicine Hat, Alta., May 4, 1971.
(NY Rangers' 2nd choice, 40th overall, in 1989 Entry Draft).

			Regular Season					Playoffs				
Season	Club	Lea	GP	G	A	TP	PIM	GP	G	A	TP	PIM
1987-88	Medicine Hat	WHL	47	6	1	7	94	14	0	0	0	20
1988-89	Medicine Hat	WHL	67	7	16	23	170	3	1	0	1	6

PRYOR, CHRIS

Defense. Shoots right. 6', 200 lbs. Born, St. Paul, MN, January 23, 1961.

			Regular Season					Playoffs				
Season	Club	Lea	GP	G	A	TP	PIM	GP	G	A	TP	PIM
1979-80	N. Hampshire	ECAC	27	9	13	22	27	....	....	....	....	....
1980-81	N. Hampshire	ECAC	33	10	27	37	36	....	....	....	....	....
1981-82	N. Hampshire	ECAC	35	3	16	19	36	....	....	....	....	....
1982-83	N. Hampshire	ECAC	34	4	9	13	23	....	....	....	....	....
1983-84	Salt Lake	CHL	72	7	21	28	215	5	1	2	3	11
1984-85	Minnesota	NHL	4	0	0	0	16	....	....	....	....	....
	Springfield	AHL	77	3	21	24	158	....	....	....	....	....
1985-86	Minnesota	NHL	7	0	1	1	0	....	....	....	....	....
	Springfield	AHL	55	4	16	20	104	....	....	....	....	....
1986-87	Minnesota	NHL	50	1	3	4	49	....	....	....	....	....
	Springfield	AHL	5	0	2	2	17	....	....	....	....	....
1987-88	Minnesota	NHL	3	0	0	0	6	....	....	....	....	....
	NY Islanders	NHL	1	0	0	0	2	....	....	....	....	....
	Kalamazoo	IHL	56	4	16	20	171	....	....	....	....	....
1988-89	NY Islanders	NHL	7	0	0	0	25	....	....	....	....	....
	Springfield	AHL	54	3	6	9	205	....	....	....	....	....
	NHL Totals		72	1	4	5	98	....	....	....	....	....

Signed as a free agent by **Minnesota**, January 10, 1985. Traded to **NY Islanders** by **Minnesota** with future considerations for Gord Dinneen, March 8, 1988.

PURVES, JOHN

Right wing. Shoots right. 6'1", 201 lbs. Born, Toronto, Ont., February 12, 1968.
(Washington's 6th choice, 103rd overall, in 1986 Entry Draft).

			Regular Season					Playoffs				
Season	Club	Lea	GP	G	A	TP	PIM	GP	G	A	TP	PIM
1985-86	Hamilton	OHL	52	16	37	53	42	....	....	....	....	....
1986-87	Hamilton	OHL	28	12	11	23	37	9	2	0	2	12
1987-88	Hamilton	OHL	64	39	44	83	65	14	7	18	25	4
1988-89a	Niagara Falls	OHL	5	5	11	16	2	....	....	....	....	....
	North Bay	OHL	42	34	52	86	38	12	14	12	26	16

a OHL Second All-Star Team (1989)

QUENNEVILLE, JOEL NORMAN (KWEHN vihl)

Defense. Shoots left. 6'1", 200 lbs. Born, Windsor, Ont., September 15, 1958.
(Toronto's 1st choice, 21st over-all, in 1978 Amateur Draft).

			Regular Season					Playoffs				
Season	Club	Lea	GP	G	A	TP	PIM	GP	G	A	TP	PIM
1975-76	Windsor	OHA	66	15	33	48	61	....	....	....	....	....
1976-77	Windsor	OHA	65	19	59	78	169	9	6	5	11	112
1977-78a	Windsor	OHA	66	27	76	103	114	6	2	3	5	17
1978-79	New Brunswick	AHL	16	1	10	11	10	....	....	....	....	....
	Toronto	NHL	61	2	9	11	60	6	0	1	1	4
1979-80	Toronto	NHL	32	1	4	5	24	....	....	....	....	....
	Colorado	NHL	35	5	7	12	26	....	....	....	....	....
1980-81	Colorado	NHL	71	10	24	34	86	....	....	....	....	....
1981-82	Colorado	NHL	64	5	10	15	55	....	....	....	....	....
1982-83	New Jersey	NHL	74	5	12	17	46	....	....	....	....	....
1983-84	Hartford	NHL	80	5	8	13	95	....	....	....	....	....
1984-85	Hartford	NHL	79	6	16	22	96	....	....	....	....	....
1985-86	Hartford	NHL	71	5	20	25	83	10	0	2	2	12
1986-87	Hartford	NHL	37	3	7	10	24	6	0	0	0	0
1987-88	Hartford	NHL	77	1	8	9	44	6	0	2	2	2
1988-89	Hartford	NHL	69	4	7	11	32	4	0	3	3	4
	NHL Totals		750	52	132	184	671	26	0	8	8	22

a OHA Second All-Star Team (1978)

Traded to **Colorado** by **Toronto** with Lanny McDonald for Pat Hickey and Wilf Paiement, December 29, 1979. Traded to **Calgary** by **New Jersey** with Steve Tambellini for Phil Russell and Mel Bridgman, June 20, 1983. Traded to **Hartford** by **Calgary** with Richie Dunn for Mickey Volcan, July 5, 1983.

QUINLAN, CRAIG

Defense. Shoots left. 6'2", 200 lbs. Born, St. Paul, MN, April 9, 1969.
(Detroit's 12th choice, 221st overall, in 1987 Entry Draft).

			Regular Season					Playoffs				
Season	Club	Lea	GP	G	A	TP	PIM	GP	G	A	TP	PIM
1986-87	Hill Murray	HS	27	7	16	23	....	....	....	....	....	....
1987-88	St. Thomas	USHL	7	1	1	2	6	....	....	....	....	....
1988-89					DID NOT PLAY							

QUINN, DAN

Center. Shoots left. 5'10", 175 lbs. Born, Ottawa, Ont., June 1, 1965.
(Calgary's 1st choice, 13th over-all, in 1983 Entry Draft).

			Regular Season					Playoffs				
Season	Club	Lea	GP	G	A	TP	PIM	GP	G	A	TP	PIM
1981-82	Belleville	OHL	67	19	32	51	41	....	....	....	....	....
1982-83	Belleville	OHL	70	59	88	147	27	4	2	6	8	2
1983-84	Belleville	OHL	24	23	36	59	12	....	....	....	....	....
	Calgary	**NHL**	**54**	**19**	**33**	**52**	**20**	**8**	**3**	**5**	**8**	**4**
1984-85	**Calgary**	**NHL**	**74**	**20**	**38**	**58**	**22**	**3**	**0**	**0**	**0**	**0**
1985-86	**Calgary**	**NHL**	**78**	**30**	**42**	**72**	**44**	**18**	**8**	**7**	**15**	**10**
1986-87	**Calgary**	**NHL**	**16**	**3**	**6**	**9**	**14**	....	....	....	....	....
	Pittsburgh	**NHL**	**64**	**28**	**43**	**71**	**40**	....	....	....	....	....
1987-88	**Pittsburgh**	**NHL**	**70**	**40**	**39**	**79**	**50**	....	....	....	....	....
1988-89	**Pittsburgh**	**NHL**	**79**	**34**	**60**	**94**	**102**	**11**	**6**	**3**	**9**	**10**
	NHL Totals		**435**	**174**	**261**	**435**	**292**	**40**	**17**	**15**	**32**	**24**

Traded to **Pittsburgh** by **Calgary** for Mike Bullard, November 12, 1986.

QUINN, JOE

Right wing. Shoots right. 5'11", 185 lbs. Born, Calgary, Alta., February 10, 1967.
(Hartford's 5th choice, 116th overall, in 1986 Entry Draft).

			Regular Season					Playoffs				
Season	Club	Lea	GP	G	A	TP	PIM	GP	G	A	TP	PIM
1985-86	Calgary	AJHL	29	17	24	41	20	....	....	....	....	....
1986-87	Bowling Green	CCHA	39	4	13	17	22	....	....	....	....	....
1987-88	Bowling Green	CCHA	39	14	13	27	24	....	....	....	....	....
1988-89	Cdn. National	....	4	0	1	1	2	....	....	....	....	....
	Bowling Green	CCHA	47	21	20	41	36	....	....	....	....	....

QUINNEY, KEN

Right wing. Shoots right. 5'10", 186 lbs. Born, New Westminster, B.C., May 23, 1965.
(Quebec's 9th choice, 204th over-all, in 1984 Entry Draft).

			Regular Season					Playoffs				
Season	Club	Lea	GP	G	A	TP	PIM	GP	G	A	TP	PIM
1981-82	Calgary	WHL	63	11	17	28	55	2	0	0	0	15
1982-83	Calgary	WHL	71	26	25	51	71	16	6	1	7	46
1983-84	Calgary	WHL	71	64	54	118	38	4	5	2	7	0
1984-85a	Calgary	WHL	56	47	67	114	65	7	6	4	10	15
1985-86	Fredericton	AHL	61	11	26	37	34	6	2	2	4	9
1986-87	**Quebec**	**NHL**	**25**	**2**	**7**	**9**	**16**	....	....	....	....	....
	Fredericton	AHL	48	14	27	41	20	....	....	....	....	....
1987-88	**Quebec**	**NHL**	**15**	**2**	**2**	**4**	**5**	....	....	....	....	....
b	Fredericton	AHL	58	37	39	76	39	13	3	5	8	35
1988-89	Halifax	AHL	72	41	49	90	65	4	3	0	3	0
	NHL Totals		**40**	**4**	**9**	**13**	**21**	....	....	....	....	....

a WHL First All-Star Team, East Division (1985)
b Won Tim Horton Award (Most Three-Star Points-AHL) (1988)

QUINTAL, STEPHANE

Defense. Shoots right. 6'3", 215 lbs. Born, Boucherville, Que., October 22, 1968.
(Boston's 2nd choice, 14th overall, in 1987 Entry Draft).

			Regular Season					Playoffs				
Season	Club	Lea	GP	G	A	TP	PIM	GP	G	A	TP	PIM
1985-86	Granby	QMJHL	67	2	17	19	144	....	....	....	....	....
1986-87a	Granby	QMJHL	67	13	41	54	178	8	0	9	9	10
1987-88	Hull	QMJHL	38	13	23	36	138	19	7	12	19	30
1988-89	**Boston**	**NHL**	**26**	**0**	**1**	**1**	**29**	....	....	....	....	....
	Maine	AHL	16	4	10	14	28	....	....	....	....	....
	NHL Totals		**26**	**0**	**1**	**1**	**29**	....	....	....	....	....

a QMJHL First All-Star Team (1987)

RACINE, YVES

Defense. Shoots left. 6', 185 lbs. Born, Matane, Que., February 7, 1969.
(Detroit's 1st choice, 11th overall, in 1987 Entry Draft).

			Regular Season					Playoffs				
Season	Club	Lea	GP	G	A	TP	PIM	GP	G	A	TP	PIM
1986-87	Longueuil	QMJHL	70	7	43	50	50	20	3	11	14	14
1987-88	Adirondack	AHL	0	0	0	0	0	9	4	2	6	2
a	Victoriaville	QMJHL	69	10	84	94	150	5	0	0	0	13
1988-89a	Victoriaville	QMJHL	63	23	85	108	95	16	3	*30	*33	41
	Adirondack	AHL	....			....	....	2	1	1	2	0

a QMJHL First-All Star Team (1988, 1989)

RAGLAN, HERB

Right wing. Shoots right. 6', 205 lbs. Born, Peterborough, Ont., August 5, 1967.
(St. Louis' 1st choice, 37th over-all, in 1985 Entry Draft).

			Regular Season					Playoffs				
Season	Club	Lea	GP	G	A	TP	PIM	GP	G	A	TP	PIM
1984-85	Peterborough	OHL	58	20	22	42	166	....	....	....	....	....
1985-86	**St. Louis**	**NHL**	**7**	**0**	**0**	**0**	**5**	**10**	**1**	**1**	**2**	**24**
	Kingston	OHL	28	10	9	19	88	10	5	2	7	30
1986-87	**St. Louis**	**NHL**	**62**	**6**	**10**	**16**	**159**	**4**	**0**	**0**	**0**	**2**
1987-88	**St. Louis**	**NHL**	**73**	**10**	**15**	**25**	**190**	**10**	**1**	**3**	**4**	**11**
1988-89	**St. Louis**	**NHL**	**50**	**7**	**10**	**17**	**144**	**8**	**1**	**2**	**3**	**13**
	NHL Totals		**192**	**23**	**35**	**58**	**498**	**32**	**3**	**6**	**9**	**50**

RAMAGE, GEORGE (ROB) (RAM-ihj)

Defense. Shoots right. 6'2", 195 lbs. Born, Byron, Ont., January 11, 1959.
(Colorado's 1st choice and 1st over-all 1979 Entry Draft).

			Regular Season					Playoffs				
Season	Club	Lea	GP	G	A	TP	PIM	GP	G	A	TP	PIM
1975-76	London	OHA	65	12	31	43	113	5	0	1	1	11
1976-77a	London	OHA	65	15	58	73	177	20	3	11	14	55
1977-78b	London	OHA	59	17	48	65	162	11	4	5	9	29
1978-79	Birmingham	WHA	80	12	36	48	165	....	....	....	....	....
1979-80	**Colorado**	**NHL**	**75**	**8**	**20**	**28**	**135**	....	....	....	....	....
1980-81	**Colorado**	**NHL**	**79**	**20**	**42**	**62**	**193**	....	....	....	....	....
1981-82	**Colorado**	**NHL**	**80**	**13**	**29**	**42**	**201**	....	....	....	....	....
1982-83	**St. Louis**	**NHL**	**78**	**16**	**35**	**51**	**193**	**4**	**0**	**3**	**3**	**22**
1983-84	**St. Louis**	**NHL**	**80**	**15**	**45**	**60**	**121**	**11**	**1**	**8**	**9**	**32**
1984-85	**St. Louis**	**NHL**	**80**	**7**	**31**	**38**	**178**	**3**	**1**	**3**	**4**	**6**
1985-86	**St. Louis**	**NHL**	**77**	**10**	**56**	**66**	**171**	**19**	**1**	**10**	**11**	**66**
1986-87	**St. Louis**	**NHL**	**59**	**11**	**28**	**39**	**108**	**6**	**2**	**2**	**4**	**21**
1987-88	**St. Louis**	**NHL**	**67**	**8**	**34**	**42**	**127**	....	....	....	....	....
	Calgary	**NHL**	**12**	**1**	**6**	**7**	**37**	**9**	**1**	**3**	**4**	**21**
1988-89	**Calgary**	**NHL**	**68**	**3**	**13**	**16**	**156**	**20**	**1**	**11**	**12**	**26**
	NHL Totals		**755**	**112**	**339**	**451**	**1620**	**72**	**7**	**40**	**47**	**194**

a OHA Third All-Star Team (1977)
b OHA First All-Star Team (1978)

Played in NHL All-Star Game (1981, 1984, 1986, 1988)

Traded to **St. Louis** by **New Jersey** for St. Louis' first round choice (Rocky Trottier) in 1982 Entry Draft and first round choice (John MacLean) in 1983 Entry Draft, June 9, 1982. Traded to **Calgary** by **St. Louis** with Rick Wamsley for Brett Hull and Steve Bozek, March 7, 1988. Traded to **Toronto** by **Calgary** for Toronto's second-round choice (Kent Manderville) in 1989 Entry Draft, June 16, 1989.

RAMSEY, MICHAEL ALLEN (MIKE)

Defense. Shoots left. 6'3", 190 lbs. Born, Minneapolis, MN, December 3, 1960.
(Buffalo's 1st choice, 11th over-all, in 1979 Entry Draft).

			Regular Season					Playoffs				
Season	Club	Lea	GP	G	A	TP	PIM	GP	G	A	TP	PIM
1978-79	U. Minnesota	WCHA	26	6	11	17	30	....	....	....	....	....
1979-80	U.S. National	...	56	11	22	33	55	....	....	....	....	....
	U.S. Olympic	...	7	0	2	2	8	....	....	....	....	....
	Buffalo	**NHL**	**13**	**1**	**6**	**7**	**6**	**13**	**1**	**2**	**3**	**12**
1980-81	**Buffalo**	**NHL**	**72**	**3**	**14**	**17**	**56**	**8**	**0**	**3**	**3**	**20**
1981-82	**Buffalo**	**NHL**	**80**	**7**	**23**	**30**	**56**	**4**	**1**	**1**	**2**	**14**
1982-83	**Buffalo**	**NHL**	**77**	**8**	**30**	**38**	**55**	**10**	**4**	**4**	**8**	**15**
1983-84	**Buffalo**	**NHL**	**72**	**9**	**22**	**31**	**82**	**3**	**0**	**1**	**1**	**6**
1984-85	**Buffalo**	**NHL**	**79**	**8**	**22**	**30**	**102**	**5**	**0**	**1**	**1**	**23**
1985-86	**Buffalo**	**NHL**	**76**	**7**	**21**	**28**	**117**	....	....	....	....	....
1986-87	**Buffalo**	**NHL**	**80**	**8**	**31**	**39**	**109**	....	....	....	....	....
1987-88	**Buffalo**	**NHL**	**63**	**5**	**16**	**21**	**77**	**6**	**0**	**3**	**3**	**29**
1988-89	**Buffalo**	**NHL**	**56**	**2**	**14**	**16**	**84**	**5**	**1**	**0**	**1**	**11**
	NHL Totals		**668**	**58**	**199**	**257**	**744**	**54**	**7**	**15**	**22**	**130**

Played in NHL All-Star Game (1982, 1983, 1985, 1986)

RANHEIM, PAUL

Center. Shoots right. 6', 195 lbs. Born, St. Louis, MO, January 25, 1966.
(Calgary's 3rd choice, 38th over-all, in 1984 Entry Draft).

			Regular Season					Playoffs				
Season	Club	Lea	GP	G	A	TP	PIM	GP	G	A	TP	PIM
1982-83	Edina	HS	26	12	25	37	4	....	....	....	....	....
1983-84	Edina	HS	26	16	24	40	6	....	....	....	....	....
1984-85	U. Wisconsin	WCHA	42	11	11	22	40	....	....	....	....	....
1985-86	U. Wisconsin	WCHA	33	17	17	34	34	....	....	....	....	....
1986-87a	U. Wisconsin	WCHA	42	24	35	59	54	....	....	....	....	....
1987-88bc	U. Wisconsin	WCHA	44	36	26	62	63	....	....	....	....	....
1988-89	**Calgary**	**NHL**	**5**	**0**	**0**	**0**	**0**	....	....	....	....	....
def	Salt Lake	IHL	75	68	29	97	16	14	5	5	10	8
	NHL Totals		**5**	**0**	**0**	**0**	**0**	....	....	....	....	....

a WCHA Second All-Star Team (1987)
b NCAA West First All-American Team (1988)
c WCHA First All-Star Team (1988)
d IHL Second All-Star Team (1989)
e Won Garry F. Longman Memorial Trophy (Top Rookie-IHL) (1989)
f Won Ken McKenzie Trophy (Outstanding U.S.-born Rookie-NHL) 1989)

RATHBONE, JASON

Right wing. Shoots right. 6', 175 lbs. Born, Brookline, MA, April 13, 1970.
(NY Islanders' 8th choice, 121st overall, in 1988 Entry Draft).

			Regular Season					Playoffs				
Season	Club	Lea	GP	G	A	TP	PIM	GP	G	A	TP	PIM
1987-88	Brookline	HS	....	23	23	46	....	....	....	....	....	....
1988-89	Boston College	H.E.	21	0	3	3	10	....	....	....	....	....

RATUSHNY, DAN

Defense. Shoots right. 6'1", 185 lbs. Born, Nepean, Ont., October 29, 1970.
(Winnipeg's 2nd choice, 25th overall, in 1989 Entry Draft).

			Regular Season					Playoffs				
Season	Club	Lea	GP	G	A	TP	PIM	GP	G	A	TP	PIM
1987-88	Nepean	COJHL	54	8	20	28	116	....	....	....	....	....
1988-89	Cornell	ECAC	28	2	13	15	50	....	....	....	....	....

RAUS, MARTY

Defense. Shoots right. 6'3", 205 lbs. Born, Mississauga, Ont., August 4, 1965.
(St. Louis' 1st choice, 15th overall, in 1986 Supplemental Draft).

			Regular Season					Playoffs				
Season	Club	Lea	GP	G	A	TP	PIM	GP	G	A	TP	PIM
1985-86	Northeastern	H.E.	38	4	21	25	30	....	....	....	....	....
1986-87	Northeastern	H.E.	26	0	7	7	24	....	....	....	....	....
1987-88	Northeastern	H.E.	9	2	3	5	2	....	....	....	....	....
1988-89	Peoria	IHL	7	0	0	0	21	4	0	0	0	2

RAY, DEREK

Right wing. Shoots right. 5'11", 200 lbs.　　Born, Auburn, MA, October 30, 1963.
(Winnipeg's 5th choice, 138th overall, in 1982 Entry Draft).

			Regular Season					Playoffs				
Season	Club	Lea	GP	G	A	TP	PIM	GP	G	A	TP	PIM
1982-83	Clarkson	ECAC	30	1	5	6	50	....	....	....	....	....
1983-84	Clarkson	ECAC	33	12	16	28	102	....	....	....	....	....
1984-85	Clarkson	ECAC	31	6	6	12	94	....	....	....	....	....
1985-86	Clarkson	ECAC	28	8	4	12	142	....	....	....	....	....
1986-87	Fort Wayne	IHL	75	16	23	39	156	11	2	1	3	10
1987-88	Fort Wayne	IHL	56	13	10	23	99	6	2	1	3	34
1988-89	Fort Wayne	IHL	45	12	8	20	72	....	....	....	....	....

RAY, ROBERT

Left wing. Shoots left. 6', 205 lbs.　　Born, Stirling, Ont., June 8, 1968.
(Buffalo's 5th choice, 97th overall, in 1988 Entry Draft).

			Regular Season					Playoffs				
Season	Club	Lea	GP	G	A	TP	PIM	GP	G	A	TP	PIM
1985-86	Cornwall	OHL	53	6	13	19	253	6	0	0	0	26
1986-87	Cornwall	OHL	46	17	20	37	158	5	1	1	2	16
1987-88	Cornwall	OHL	61	11	41	52	179	11	2	3	5	33
1988-89	Rochester	AHL	74	11	18	29	446	....	....	....	....	....

RECCHI, MARK

Right wing. Shoots left. 5'10", 190 lbs.　　Born, Kamloops, B.C., February 1, 1968.
(Pittsburgh's 4th choice, 67th overall, in 1988 Entry Draft).

			Regular Season					Playoffs				
Season	Club	Lea	GP	G	A	TP	PIM	GP	G	A	TP	PIM
1985-86	N. Westminster	WHL	72	21	40	61	55	....	....	....	....	....
1986-87	Kamloops	WHL	40	26	50	76	63	13	3	16	19	17
1987-88a	Kamloops	WHL	62	61	93	154	75	17	10	21	31	18
1988-89	**Pittsburgh**	**NHL**	15	1	1	2	0	....	....	....	....	....
	Muskegon	IHL	63	50	49	99	86	14	7	*14	*21	28
	NHL Totals		15	1	1	2	0	....	....	....	....	....

a WHL West All-Star Team (1988)

REDMOND, CRAIG

Defense. Shoots left. 5'11", 190 lbs.　　Born, Dawson Creek, B.C., September 22, 1965.
(Los Angeles' 1st choice, 6th over-all, in 1984 Entry Draft).

			Regular Season					Playoffs				
Season	Club	Lea	GP	G	A	TP	PIM	GP	G	A	TP	PIM
1982-83ab	U. of Denver	WCHA	34	16	38	54	44	....	....	....	....	....
1983-84	Cdn. Olympic	....	55	10	11	21	38	....	....	....	....	....
1984-85	**Los Angeles**	**NHL**	79	6	33	39	57	3	1	0	1	2
1985-86	**Los Angeles**	**NHL**	73	6	18	24	57	....	....	....	....	....
1986-87	**Los Angeles**	**NHL**	16	1	7	8	8	....	....	....	....	....
	New Haven	AHL	5	2	2	4	6	....	....	....	....	....
1987-88	**Los Angeles**	**NHL**	2	0	0	0	0	....	....	....	....	....
1988-89	Denver	IHL	10	0	13	13	6	....	....	....	....	....
	Edmonton	**NHL**	21	3	10	13	12	....	....	....	....	....
	Cape Breton	AHL	44	13	22	35	28	....	....	....	....	....
	NHL Totals		191	16	68	84	134	3	1	0	1	2

a WCHA Rookie of the Year (1983).
b WCHA Second All-Star Team (1983).
Traded to **Edmonton** by **Los Angeles** for John Miner, August 10, 1988. Claimed by **NY Rangers** in NHL Waiver Draft, October 3, 1988. Claimed on waivers without right of recall by **Edmonton** from **NY Rangers,** November 1, 1988.

REEDS, MARK

Right wing. Shoots right. 5'10", 190 lbs.　　Born, Burlington, Ont., January 24, 1960.
(St. Louis' 3rd choice, 86th over-all, in 1979 Entry Draft).

			Regular Season					Playoffs				
Season	Club	Lea	GP	G	A	TP	PIM	GP	G	A	TP	PIM
1978-79	Peterborough	OHA	66	25	25	50	96	11	0	5	5	19
1979-80	Peterborough	OHA	54	34	45	79	51	14	9	10	19	19
1980-81	Salt Lake	CHL	74	15	45	60	81	17	5	8	13	28
1981-82	Salt Lake	CHL	59	22	24	46	55	....	....	....	....	....
	St. Louis	**NHL**	9	1	3	4	0	10	0	1	1	2
1982-83	Salt Lake	CHL	55	16	26	42	32	....	....	....	....	....
	St. Louis	**NHL**	20	5	14	19	6	4	1	0	1	2
1983-84	**St. Louis**	**NHL**	65	11	14	25	23	11	3	3	6	15
1984-85	**St. Louis**	**NHL**	80	9	30	39	25	3	0	0	0	0
1985-86	**St. Louis**	**NHL**	78	10	28	38	28	19	4	4	8	2
1986-87	**St. Louis**	**NHL**	68	9	16	25	16	6	0	1	1	2
1987-88	**Hartford**	**NHL**	38	0	7	7	31	....	....	....	....	....
1988-89	**Hartford**	**NHL**	7	0	2	2	6	....	....	....	....	....
	Binghamton	AHL	69	26	34	60	18	....	....	....	....	....
	NHL Totals		365	45	114	159	135	53	8	9	17	23

Traded to **Hartford** by **St. Louis** for Hartford's third round choice (Blair Atcheynum) in 1989 Entry Draft, October 5, 1987.

REEKIE, JOE

Defense. Shoots left. 6'3", 215 lbs.　　Born, Petawawa, Ont., February 22, 1965.
(Buffalo's 6th choice, 119th overall, in 1985 Entry Draft)

			Regular Season					Playoffs				
Season	Club	Lea	GP	G	A	TP	PIM	GP	G	A	TP	PIM
1982-83	North Bay	OHL	59	2	9	11	49	8	0	1	1	11
1983-84	Cornwall	OHL	62	7	27	34	184	3	0	0	0	4
1984-85	Cornwall	OHL	65	19	63	82	134	9	4	13	17	18
1985-86	Rochester	AHL	77	3	25	28	178	....	....	....	....	....
	Buffalo	**NHL**	3	0	0	0	14	....	....	....	....	....
1986-87	**Buffalo**	**NHL**	56	1	8	9	82	....	....	....	....	....
	Rochester	AHL	22	0	6	6	52	....	....	....	....	....
1987-88	**Buffalo**	**NHL**	30	1	4	5	68	2	0	0	0	4
1988-89	**Buffalo**	**NHL**	15	1	3	4	26	....	....	....	....	....
	Rochester	AHL	21	1	2	3	56	....	....	....	....	....
	NHL Totals		104	3	15	18	190	2	0	0	0	4

Traded to **NY Islanders** by **Buffalo** for NY Islander's sixth round choice (Bill Pye) in 1989 Entry Draft, June 17, 1989.

REGAN, BRENT

Left wing. Shoots left. 6', 185 lbs.　　Born, Edmonton, Alta., March 4, 1966.
(Hartford's 5th choice, 194th overall, in 1984 Entry Draft).

			Regular Season					Playoffs				
Season	Club	Lea	GP	G	A	TP	PIM	GP	G	A	TP	PIM
1984-85	Bowling Green	CCHA	42	6	18	24	12	....	....	....	....	....
1985-86	Bowling Green	CCHA	32	4	2	6	28	....	....	....	....	....
1986-87	Bowling Green	CCHA	43	12	17	29	22	....	....	....	....	....
1987-88	Bowling Green	CCHA	42	28	22	50	34	....	....	....	....	....
1988-89	Binghamton	AHL	9	0	0	0	2	....	....	....	....	....

REID, DAVID

Left wing. Shoots left. 6', 210 lbs.　　Born, Toronto, Ont., May 15, 1964.
(Boston's 4th choice, 60th over-all, in 1982 Entry Draft).

			Regular Season					Playoffs				
Season	Club	Lea	GP	G	A	TP	PIM	GP	G	A	TP	PIM
1981-82	Peterborough	OHL	68	10	32	42	41	9	2	3	5	11
1982-83	Peterborough	OHL	70	23	34	57	33	4	3	1	4	0
1983-84	**Boston**	**NHL**	8	1	0	1	2	....	....	....	....	....
	Peterborough	OHL	60	33	64	97	12	....	....	....	....	....
1984-85	**Boston**	**NHL**	35	14	13	27	27	5	1	0	1	0
	Hershey	AHL	43	10	14	24	6	....	....	....	....	....
1985-86	**Boston**	**NHL**	37	10	10	20	10	....	....	....	....	....
	Moncton	AHL	26	14	18	32	4	....	....	....	....	....
1986-87	**Boston**	**NHL**	12	3	3	6	0	2	0	0	0	0
	Moncton	AHL	40	12	22	34	23	5	0	1	1	0
1987-88	**Boston**	**NHL**	3	0	0	0	0	....	....	....	....	....
	Maine	AHL	63	21	37	58	40	10	6	7	13	0
1988-89	**Toronto**	**NHL**	77	9	21	30	22	....	....	....	....	....
	NHL Totals		172	37	47	84	61	7	1	0	1	0

REIERSON, DAVID (DAVE)

Defense. Shoots right. 6', 185 lbs.　　Born, Bashaw, Alta., August 30, 1964.
(Calgary's 1st choice, 29th over-all, in 1982 Entry Draft).

			Regular Season					Playoffs				
Season	Club	Lea	GP	G	A	TP	PIM	GP	G	A	TP	PIM
1981-82	Prince Albert	SJHL	60	20	51	71	163	....	....	....	....	....
1982-83	Michigan Tech	CCHA	38	2	14	16	52	....	....	....	....	....
1983-84	Michigan Tech	CCHA	38	4	15	19	63	....	....	....	....	....
1984-85	Michigan Tech	CCHA	36	5	27	32	76	....	....	....	....	....
1985-86	Michigan Tech	WCHA	39	7	16	23	51	....	....	....	....	....
1986-87	Moncton	AHL	....	....	....	....	....	6	0	1	1	12
	Cdn. Olympic	....	61	1	17	18	36	....	....	....	....	....
1987-88	Salt Lake	IHL	48	10	19	29	42	16	2	14	16	30
	Cdn. Olympic	....	32	2	8	10	18	....	....	....	....	....
1988-89	**Calgary**	**NHL**	2	0	0	0	2	....	....	....	....	....
	Salt Lake	IHL	76	7	46	53	70	13	1	8	9	12
	NHL Totals		2	0	0	0	2	....	....	....	....	....

REINHART, PAUL　　　　　　　　　　　　　　　(RINE-hart)

Defense. Shoots left. 5'11", 200 lbs.　　Born, Kitchener, Ont., January 6, 1960.
(Atlanta's 1st choice, 12th over-all, in 1979 Entry Draft).

			Regular Season					Playoffs				
Season	Club	Lea	GP	G	A	TP	PIM	GP	G	A	TP	PIM
1975-76	Kitchener	OHA	53	6	33	39	42	8	1	2	3	4
1976-77	Kitchener	OHA	51	4	14	18	16	3	0	2	2	4
1977-78	Kitchener	OHA	47	17	28	45	15	9	4	6	10	29
1978-79	Kitchener	OHA	66	51	78	129	57	10	3	10	13	16
1979-80	**Atlanta**	**NHL**	79	9	38	47	31	....	....	....	....	....
1980-81	**Calgary**	**NHL**	74	18	49	67	52	16	1	14	15	16
1981-82	**Calgary**	**NHL**	62	13	48	61	17	3	0	1	1	2
1982-83	**Calgary**	**NHL**	78	17	58	75	28	9	6	3	9	2
1983-84	**Calgary**	**NHL**	27	6	15	21	10	11	6	11	17	2
1984-85	**Calgary**	**NHL**	75	23	46	69	18	4	1	1	2	0
1985-86	**Calgary**	**NHL**	32	8	25	33	15	21	5	13	18	4
1986-87	**Calgary**	**NHL**	76	15	53	68	22	4	0	1	1	6
1987-88	**Calgary**	**NHL**	14	0	3	3	10	8	2	7	9	6
1988-89	**Vancouver**	**NHL**	64	7	50	57	44	7	2	3	5	4
	NHL Totals		581	116	386	502	247	83	23	54	77	42

Played in NHL All-Star Game (1985, 1989)

Traded to **Vancouver** by **Calgary** with Steve Bozek for Vancouver's third round pick (Veli-Pekka Kautonen) in 1989 Entry Draft, September 6, 1988.

REISMAN, ERIC

Defense. Shoots left. 6'2", 220 lbs.　　Born, New York, NY, May 19, 1968.
(Boston's 8th choice, 228th overall, in 1988 Entry Draft).

			Regular Season					Playoffs				
Season	Club	Lea	GP	G	A	TP	PIM	GP	G	A	TP	PIM
1987-88	Ohio State	CCHA	29	0	3	3	45	....	....	....	....	....
1988-89	Ohio State	CCHA	38	4	6	10	56	....	....	....	....	....

RENDALL, BRUCE

Left wing. Shoots left. 6'1", 190 lbs.　　Born, Thunder Bay, Ont., April 18, 1967.
(Philadelphia's 2nd choice, 42nd over-all, in 1985 Entry Draft).

			Regular Season					Playoffs				
Season	Club	Lea	GP	G	A	TP	PIM	GP	G	A	TP	PIM
1984-85	Chatham	OPJHL	46	32	33	65	62	....	....	....	....	....
1985-86	Michigan State	CCHA	45	14	18	32	68	....	....	....	....	....
1986-87	Michigan State	CCHA	44	11	14	25	113	....	....	....	....	....
1987-88	Michigan State	CCHA	39	10	2	12	70	....	....	....	....	....
1988-89	Hershey	AHL	37	7	8	15	12	....	....	....	....	....
	Indianapolis	IHL	15	2	2	4	9	....	....	....	....	....

REYNOLDS, BOBBY

Left wing. Shoots left. 5'11", 175 lbs.   Born, Flint, MI, July 14, 1967.
(Toronto's 10th choice, 190th overall, in 1985 Entry Draft).

				Regular Season					Playoffs			
Season	Club	Lea	GP	G	A	TP	PIM	GP	G	A	TP	PIM
1985-86	Michigan State	CCHA	45	9	10	19	26	.....	.....	.....	.....	.....
1986-87	Michigan State	CCHA	40	20	13	33	40	.....	.....	.....	.....	.....
1987-88a	Michigan State	CCHA	46	42	25	67	52	.....	.....	.....	.....	.....
1988-89ab	Michigan State	CCHA	47	36	41	77	78	.....	.....	.....	.....	.....

a CCHA Second All-Star Team (1988, 1989)
b NCAA West First All-American Team (1989)

RICE, STEVEN

Right wing. Shoots right. 6'0", 210 lbs.   Born, Kitchener, Ont., May 26, 1971.
(NY Rangers' 1st choice, 20th overall, in 1989 Entry Draft).

				Regular Season					Playoffs			
Season	Club	Lea	GP	G	A	TP	PIM	GP	G	A	TP	PIM
1987-88	Kitchener	OHL	59	11	14	25	43	4	0	1	1	0
1988-89	Kitchener	OHL	64	36	30	66	42	5	2	1	3	8

RICHARD, JEAN-MARC

Defense. Shoots left. Height 5'11", 172 lbs.   Born, St. Raymond, Que., October 8, 1966.

				Regular Season					Playoffs			
Season	Club	Lea	GP	G	A	TP	PIM	GP	G	A	TP	PIM
1985-86a	Chicoutimi	QMJHL	72	20	87	107	111	9	3	5	8	14
1986-87a	Chicoutimi	QMJHL	67	21	81	102	105	16	6	25	31	28
1987-88	**Quebec**	**NHL**	4	2	1	3	2	.....	.....	.....	.....	.....
	Fredericton	AHL	68	14	42	56	52	7	2	1	3	4
1988-89	Halifax	AHL	57	8	25	33	38	4	1	0	1	4
	NHL Totals		4	2	1	3	2	.....	.....	.....	.....	.....

a QMJHL First All-Star Team (1986, 1987)
Signed as a free agent by **Quebec**, April 13, 1987.

RICHARD, MICHAEL (MIKE)

Center. Shoots right. 5'10", 194 lbs.   Born, Scarborough, Ont., July 9, 1966.

				Regular Season					Playoffs			
Season	Club	Lea	GP	G	A	TP	PIM	GP	G	A	TP	PIM
1983-84	Toronto	OHL	66	19	17	36	12	9	2	1	3	0
1984-85	Toronto	OHL	66	31	41	72	15	5	0	0	0	11
1985-86	Toronto	OHL	63	32	48	80	28	4	1	1	2	2
1986-87	Toronto	OHL	66	57	50	107	38	.....	.....	.....	.....	.....
1987-88a	Binghamton	AHL	72	46	48	94	23	4	0	3	3	4
	Washington	**NHL**	4	0	0	0	0	.....	.....	.....	.....	.....
1988-89	Baltimore	AHL	80	44	63	107	51	.....	.....	.....	.....	.....
	NHL Totals		4	0	0	0	0	.....	.....	.....	.....	.....

a Won Dudley "Red" Garrett Memorial Trophy (Top Rookie - AHL) (1988).
Signed as a free agent by **Washington**, October 9, 1987.

RICHARDS, TODD

Defense. Shoots right. 6', 180 lbs.   Born, Robindale, MN, October, 20, 1966.
(Montreal's 3rd choice, 33rd over-all, in 1985 Entry Draft).

				Regular Season					Playoffs			
Season	Club	Lea	GP	G	A	TP	PIM	GP	G	A	TP	PIM
1984-85	Armstrong	HS	24	10	23	33	24	.....	.....	.....	.....	.....
1985-86	U. Minnesota	WCHA	38	6	23	29	38	.....	.....	.....	.....	.....
1986-87	U. Minnesota	WCHA	49	8	43	51	70	.....	.....	.....	.....	.....
1987-88a	U. Minnesota	WCHA	34	10	30	40	26	.....	.....	.....	.....	.....
1988-89abc	U. Minnesota	WCHA	46	6	32	38	60	.....	.....	.....	.....	.....

a WCHA Second All-Star Team (1988, 1989)
b NCAA West Second All-American Team (1989)
c NCAA All-Tournament Team (1989)

RICHARDS, TRAVIS

Defense. Shoots left. 6'0", 180 lbs.   Born, Robbinsdale, MN, March 22, 1970.
(Minnesota's 6th choice, 169th overall, in 1988 Entry Draft).

				Regular Season					Playoffs			
Season	Club	Lea	GP	G	A	TP	PIM	GP	G	A	TP	PIM
1987-88	Armstrong	HS	24	14	14	28	....	.....	.....	.....	.....	.....
1988-89	U. Minnesota	WCHA		DID NOT PLAY								

RICHARDSON, LUKE

Defense. Shoots left. 6'4", 210 lbs.   Born, Ottawa, Ont., March 26, 1969.
(Toronto's 1st choice, 7th overall, in 1987 Entry Draft).

				Regular Season					Playoffs			
Season	Club	Lea	GP	G	A	TP	PIM	GP	G	A	TP	PIM
1985-86	Peterborough	OHL	63	6	18	24	57	16	2	1	3	50
1986-87	Peterborough	OHL	59	13	32	45	70	12	0	5	5	24
1987-88	**Toronto**	**NHL**	78	4	6	10	90	2	0	0	0	.....
1988-89	**Toronto**	**NHL**	55	2	7	9	106	.....	.....	.....	.....	.....
	NHL Totals		133	6	13	19	196	2	0	0	0	0

RICHER, STEPHANE J. G.   (ree-SHAY)

Defense. Shoots right. 5'11", 200 lbs.   Born, Hull, Que., April 23, 1966.

				Regular Season					Playoffs			
Season	Club	Lea	GP	G	A	TP	PIM	GP	G	A	TP	PIM
1986-87	Hull	QMJHL	33	6	22	28	74	8	3	4	7	17
1987-88	Balimore	AHL	22	0	3	3	6	.....	.....	.....	.....	.....
	Sherbrooke	AHL	41	4	7	11	46	5	1	0	1	10
1988-89	Sherbrooke	AHL	70	7	26	33	158	6	1	2	3	18

Signed as a free agent by **Montreal**, January 9, 1988.

RICHER, STEPHANE J. J.   (ree-SHAY)

Center. Shoots right. 6'2", 200 lbs.   Born, Buckingham, Que., June 7, 1966.
(Montreal's 3rd choice, 29th over-all, in 1984 Entry Draft).

				Regular Season					Playoffs			
Season	Club	Lea	GP	G	A	TP	PIM	GP	G	A	TP	PIM
1982-83	Laval	Midget	48	47	54	101	86	.....	.....	.....	.....	.....
1983-84	Granby	QMJHL	67	39	37	76	58	3	1	1	2	4
1984-85	**Montreal**	**NHL**	1	0	0	0	0	.....	.....	.....	.....	.....
	Sherbrooke	AHL						9	6	3	9	10
a	Chicoutimi	QMJHL	57	61	59	120	71	12	13	13	26	25
1985-86	**Montreal**	**NHL**	65	21	16	37	50	16	4	1	5	23
1986-87	**Montreal**	**NHL**	57	20	19	39	80	5	3	2	5	0
	Sherbrooke	AHL	12	10	4	14	11	.....	.....	.....	.....	.....
1987-88	**Montreal**	**NHL**	72	50	28	78	72	8	7	5	12	6
1988-89	**Montreal**	**NHL**	68	25	35	60	61	21	6	5	11	14
	NHL Totals		263	116	98	214	263	50	20	13	33	43

a QMJHL Second All-Star Team (1985)

RICHMOND, STEVE

Defense. Shoots left. 6'1", 205 lbs.   Born, Chicago, IL, December 11, 1959.

				Regular Season					Playoffs			
Season	Club	Lea	GP	G	A	TP	PIM	GP	G	A	TP	PIM
1978-79	U. of Michigan	CCHA	34	2	5	7	38	.....	.....	.....	.....	.....
1979-80	U. of Michigan	CCHA	38	10	19	29	26	.....	.....	.....	.....	.....
1980-81	U. of Michigan	CCHA	39	22	32	54	56	.....	.....	.....	.....	.....
1981-82a	U. of Michigan	CCHA	38	6	30	36	68	.....	.....	.....	.....	.....
1982-83	Tulsa	CHL	68	5	13	18	187	.....	.....	.....	.....	.....
1983-84	Tulsa	CHL	38	1	17	18	114	.....	.....	.....	.....	.....
	NY Rangers	**NHL**	26	2	5	7	110	4	0	0	0	12
1984-85	**NY Rangers**	**NHL**	34	0	5	5	90	.....	.....	.....	.....	.....
	New Haven	AHL	37	3	10	13	122	.....	.....	.....	.....	.....
1985-86	**NY Rangers**	**NHL**	17	0	2	2	63	.....	.....	.....	.....	.....
	New Haven	AHL	11	2	6	8	32	.....	.....	.....	.....	.....
	Detroit	**NHL**	29	1	2	3	82	.....	.....	.....	.....	.....
	Adirondack	AHL	20	1	7	8	23	17	2	9	11	34
1986-87	**New Jersey**	**NHL**	44	1	7	8	143	.....	.....	.....	.....	.....
1987-88	Utica	AHL	79	6	27	33	141	.....	.....	.....	.....	.....
1988-89	**Los Angeles**	**NHL**	9	0	2	2	26	.....	.....	.....	.....	.....
	New Haven	AHL	49	6	35	41	114	17	3	10	13	84
	NHL Totals		159	4	23	27	514	4	0	0	0	12

a CCHA Second All-Star Team (1982)
Signed as a free agent by **NY Rangers**, June 22, 1982. Traded to **Detroit** by NY Rangers for Mike McEwen, December 26, 1985. Traded to **New Jersey** by Detroit for Sam St. Laurent, August 18, 1986.

RICHTER, DAVE   (RIHK tuhr)

Defense. Shoots right. 6'5", 220 lbs.   Born, St. Boniface, Man., April 8, 1960.
(Minnesota's 10th choice, 205th over-all, in 1980 Entry Draft).

				Regular Season					Playoffs			
Season	Club	Lea	GP	G	A	TP	PIM	GP	G	A	TP	PIM
1980-81	U. of Michigan	WCHA	36	2	13	15	56	.....	.....	.....	.....	.....
1981-82	U. of Michigan	WCHA	36	9	12	21	78	.....	.....	.....	.....	.....
	Nashville	CHL	2	0	1	1	0	.....	.....	.....	.....	.....
	Minnesota	**NHL**	3	0	0	0	11	.....	.....	.....	.....	.....
1982-83	**Minnesota**	**NHL**	6	0	0	0	4	.....	.....	.....	.....	.....
	Birmingham	CHL	69	6	17	23	211	13	3	1	4	36
1983-84	Salt Lake	CHL	10	1	4	5	39	.....	.....	.....	.....	.....
	Minnesota	**NHL**	42	2	3	5	132	8	0	0	0	20
1984-85	**Minnesota**	**NHL**	55	2	8	10	221	9	1	0	1	39
	Springfield	AHL	3	0	0	0	2	.....	.....	.....	.....	.....
1985-86	**Minnesota**	**NHL**	14	0	3	3	29	.....	.....	.....	.....	.....
	Philadelphia	**NHL**	50	0	2	2	138	5	0	0	0	21
1986-87	**Vancouver**	**NHL**	78	2	15	17	172	.....	.....	.....	.....	.....
1987-88	**Vancouver**	**NHL**	49	2	4	6	224	.....	.....	.....	.....	.....
1988-89	**St. Louis**	**NHL**	66	1	5	6	99	.....	.....	.....	.....	.....
	NHL Totals		363	9	40	49	1030	22	1	0	1	80

Traded to **Philadelphia** by **Minnesota** with Bo Berglund for Ed Hospodar and Todd Bergen, November 29, 1985. Traded to **Vancouver** by **Philadelphia** with Rich Sutter and Vancouver's third-round choice (Don Gibson) — acquired earlier — in 1986 Entry Draft fror J.J. Daigneault and Vancouver's second-round choice (Kent Hawley) in 1986 Entry Draft, June 6, 1986. Traded to **St. Louis** by **Vancouver** with Vancouver's second-round choice in 1990 Entry Draft for Robert Nordmark, September 6, 1988.

RIDLEY, MIKE

Center. Shoots left. 6'1", 200 lbs.   Born, Winnipeg, Man., July 8, 1963.

				Regular Season					Playoffs			
Season	Club	Lea	GP	G	A	TP	PIM	GP	G	A	TP	PIM
1983-84a	U. of Manitoba	GPAC	46	39	41	80	....	.....	.....	.....	.....	.....
1984-85b	U. of Manitoba	GPAC	30	29	38	67	48	.....	.....	.....	.....	.....
1985-86c	**NY Rangers**	**NHL**	80	22	43	65	69	16	6	8	14	26
1986-87	**NY Rangers**	**NHL**	38	16	20	36	20	.....	.....	.....	.....	.....
	Washington	**NHL**	40	15	19	34	20	7	2	1	3	6
1987-88	**Washington**	**NHL**	70	28	31	59	22	14	6	5	11	10
1988-89	**Washington**	**NHL**	80	41	48	89	49	6	0	5	5	2
	NHL Totals		310	122	161	283	180	43	14	19	33	44

a Canadian University Player of the Year; CIAU All-Canadian, GPAC MVP and First All-Star Team (1984)
b CIAU All-Canadian, GPAC First All-Star Team (1985)
c NHL All-Rookie Team (1986)
Played in NHL All-Star Game (1989)

Signed as a free agent by **NY Rangers**, September 26, 1985. Traded to **Washington** by **NY Rangers** with Bob Crawford and Kelly Miller for Bob Carpenter and, Washington's second-round choice (Jason Prosofsky) in 1989 Entry Draft, January 1, 1987.

RIIHIJARVI, HEIKKI

Defense. Shoots right. 6'5", 180 lbs. Born, Salla, Finland, April 6, 1966.
(Edmonton's 8th choice, 147th overall, in 1984 Entry Draft).

			Regular Season					Playoffs				
Season	Club	Lea	GP	G	A	TP	PIM	GP	G	A	TP	PIM
1984-85	TPS	Fin.	4	0	0	0	2	....	....	....	....	....
	TPS	Fin. Jr.	28	15	18	33	6	....	....	....	....	....
1985-86	TPS	Fin. Jr.	25	6	8	14	12	....	....	....	....	....
1986-87	Karpat	Fin.	36	4	4	8	10	....	....	....	....	....
1987-88	Karpat	Fin.	21	0	5	5	0	....	....	....	....	....
1988-89	Karpat	Fin.	43	8	11	19	14	5	0	2	2	4

ROBERTS, GARY

Left wing. Shoots left. 6'1", 190 lbs. Born, North York, Ont., May 23, 1966.
(Calgary's 1st choice, 12th over-all, in 1984 Entry Draft).

			Regular Season					Playoffs				
Season	Club	Lea	GP	G	A	TP	PIM	GP	G	A	TP	PIM
1982-83	Ottawa	OHL	53	12	8	20	83	5	1	0	1	19
1983-84	Ottawa	OHL	48	27	30	57	144	13	10	7	17	62
1984-85	Moncton	AHL	7	4	2	6	7	....	....	....	....	....
a	Ottawa	OHL	59	44	62	106	186	5	2	8	10	10
1985-86a	Ottawa	OHL	24	26	25	51	83	....	....	....	....	....
a	Guelph	OHL	23	18	15	33	65	20	18	13	31	43
1986-87	**Calgary**	**NHL**	**32**	**5**	**10**	**15**	**85**	**2**	**0**	**0**	**0**	**4**
	Moncton	AHL	38	20	18	38	72	....	....	....	....	....
1987-88	**Calgary**	**NHL**	**74**	**13**	**15**	**28**	**282**	**9**	**2**	**3**	**5**	**29**
1988-89	**Calgary**	**NHL**	**71**	**22**	**16**	**38**	**250**	**22**	**5**	**7**	**12**	**57**
	NHL Totals		**177**	**40**	**41**	**81**	**617**	**33**	**7**	**10**	**17**	**90**

a OHL Second All-Star Team (1985, 1986)

ROBERTS, GORDON (GORDIE)

Defense. Shoots left. 6'1", 195 lbs. Born, Detroit, MI, October 2, 1957.
(Montreal's 7th choice, 54th over-all, in 1977 Amateur Draft).

			Regular Season					Playoffs				
Season	Club	Lea	GP	G	A	TP	PIM	GP	G	A	TP	PIM
1974-75	Victoria	WHL	53	19	45	64	145	12	1	9	10	42
1975-76	New England	WHA	77	3	19	22	102	17	2	9	11	36
1976-77	New England	WHA	77	13	33	46	169	5	2	2	4	6
1977-78	New England	WHA	78	15	46	61	118	14	0	5	5	29
1978-79	New England	WHA	79	11	46	57	113	10	0	4	4	10
1979-80	**Hartford**	**NHL**	**80**	**8**	**28**	**36**	**89**	**3**	**1**	**1**	**2**	**2**
1980-81	**Hartford**	**NHL**	**27**	**2**	**11**	**13**	**81**	....	....	....	....	....
	Minnesota	**NHL**	**50**	**6**	**31**	**37**	**94**	**19**	**1**	**5**	**6**	**17**
1981-82	**Minnesota**	**NHL**	**79**	**4**	**30**	**34**	**119**	**4**	**0**	**3**	**3**	**27**
1982-83	**Minnesota**	**NHL**	**80**	**3**	**41**	**44**	**103**	**9**	**1**	**5**	**6**	**14**
1983-84	**Minnesota**	**NHL**	**77**	**8**	**45**	**53**	**132**	**15**	**3**	**7**	**10**	**23**
1984-85	**Minnesota**	**NHL**	**78**	**6**	**36**	**42**	**112**	**9**	**1**	**6**	**7**	**6**
1985-86	**Minnesota**	**NHL**	**76**	**2**	**21**	**23**	**101**	**5**	**0**	**4**	**4**	**8**
1986-87	**Minnesota**	**NHL**	**67**	**3**	**10**	**13**	**68**	....	....	....	....	....
1987-88	**Minnesota**	**NHL**	**48**	**1**	**10**	**11**	**103**	....	....	....	....	....
	Philadelphia	**NHL**	**11**	**1**	**2**	**3**	**15**	....	....	....	....	....
	St. Louis	**NHL**	**11**	**1**	**3**	**4**	**25**	**10**	**1**	**2**	**3**	**33**
1988-89	**St. Louis**	**NHL**	**77**	**2**	**24**	**26**	**90**	**10**	**1**	**7**	**8**	**8**
	NHL Totals		**761**	**47**	**292**	**339**	**1132**	**84**	**9**	**40**	**49**	**138**
	WHA Totals		311	42	144	186	502	46	4	20	24	81

Claimed by **Hartford** from **Montreal** in 1979 Expansion Draft, June 22, 1979. Traded to **Minnesota** by **Hartford** for Mike Fidler, December 16, 1980. Traded to **Philadelphia** by **Minnesota** for future considerations, February 8, 1988. Traded to **St. Louis** by **Philadelphia** for future considerations, March 8, 1988.

ROBERTS, TIMOTHY

Center. Shoots left. 6'2", 180 lbs. Born, Boston, MA, March 6, 1969.
(Buffalo's 9th choice, 153rd overall, in 1987 Entry Draft).

			Regular Season					Playoffs				
Season	Club	Lea	GP	G	A	TP	PIM	GP	G	A	TP	PIM
1987-88	RPI	ECAC	28	5	9	14	40	....	....	....	....	....
1988-89	RPI	ECAC	27	4	11	15	50	....	....	....	....	....

ROBERTSON, GEORDIE

Right wing. Shoots right. 6', 165 lbs. Born, Victoria, B.C., August 1, 1959.

			Regular Season					Playoffs				
Season	Club	Lea	GP	G	A	TP	PIM	GP	G	A	TP	PIM
1977-78	Victoria	WHL	61	64	72	136	85	13	15	11	26	42
1978-79	Victoria	WHL	54	31	42	73	94	14	15	10	25	22
1979-80	Rochester	AHL	55	26	26	52	66	4	1	4	5	2
1980-81	Rochester	AHL	20	3	3	6	19	....	....	....	....	....
1981-82	Flint	IHL	11	6	14	20	19	....	....	....	....	....
	Rochester	AHL	46	14	15	29	45	9	1	3	4	13
1982-83	**Buffalo**	**NHL**	**5**	**1**	**2**	**3**	**7**	....	....	....	....	....
	Rochester	AHL	72	46	73	119	83	16	8	6	14	23
1983-84	Rochester	AHL	64	37	54	91	103	18	9	9	18	42
1984-85	Rochester	AHL	70	27	48	75	91	5	0	1	1	4
1985-86	Adirondack	AHL	79	36	56	92	99	15	4	6	10	25
1986-87	Adirondack	AHL	63	28	41	69	94	....	....	....	....	....
1987-88	Adirondack	AHL	30	11	15	26	24	6	1	2	3	14
	Jypht	Fin.	34	14	6	20	28	....	....	....	....	....
1988-89	Rochester	AHL	32	11	12	23	12	....	....	....	....	....
	NHL Totals		**5**	**1**	**2**	**3**	**7**	....	....	....	....	....

Signed as free agent by **Buffalo**, September 5, 1979. Signed as a free agent by **Detroit**, July 9, 1985.

ROBERTSON, TORRIE ANDREW

Left wing. Shoots left. 5'11", 200 lbs. Born, Victoria, B.C., August 2, 1961.
(Washington's 3rd choice, 55th over-all, in 1980 Entry Draft).

			Regular Season					Playoffs				
Season	Club	Lea	GP	G	A	TP	PIM	GP	G	A	TP	PIM
1978-79	Victoria	WHL	69	18	23	41	141	15	1	2	3	29
1979-80	Victoria	WHL	72	23	24	47	298	17	5	7	12	117
1980-81	**Washington**	**NHL**	**3**	**0**	**0**	**0**	**0**	....	....	....	....	....
	Victoria	WHL	59	45	66	111	274	15	10	13	23	55
1981-82	Hershey	AHL	21	5	3	8	60	....	....	....	....	....
	Washington	**NHL**	**54**	**8**	**13**	**21**	**204**	....	....	....	....	....
1982-83	**Washington**	**NHL**	**5**	**2**	**0**	**2**	**4**	....	....	....	....	....
	Hershey	AHL	69	21	33	54	187	5	1	2	3	8
1983-84	**Hartford**	**NHL**	**66**	**7**	**13**	**20**	**198**	....	....	....	....	....
1984-85	**Hartford**	**NHL**	**74**	**11**	**30**	**41**	**337**	....	....	....	....	....
1985-86	**Hartford**	**NHL**	**76**	**13**	**24**	**37**	**358**	**10**	**1**	**0**	**1**	**67**
1986-87	**Hartford**	**NHL**	**20**	**1**	**0**	**1**	**98**	....	....	....	....	....
1987-88	**Hartford**	**NHL**	**63**	**2**	**8**	**10**	**293**	**6**	**0**	**1**	**1**	**6**
1988-89	**Hartford**	**NHL**	**27**	**2**	**4**	**6**	**84**	....	....	....	....	....
	Detroit	**NHL**	**12**	**2**	**2**	**4**	**63**	**6**	**1**	**0**	**1**	**17**
	NHL Totals		**400**	**48**	**94**	**142**	**1639**	**22**	**2**	**1**	**3**	**90**

Traded to **Hartford** by **Washington** for Greg Adams, October 3, 1983. Traded to **Detroit** by **Hartford** for Jim Pavese, March 7, 1989.

ROBISON, JEFF

Defense. Shoots left. 6'1", 175 lbs. Born, Wrentham, MA, June 3, 1970.
(Los Angeles' 5th choice, 91st overall, in 1988 Entry Draft).

			Regular Season					Playoffs				
Season	Club	Lea	GP	G	A	TP	PIM	GP	G	A	TP	PIM
1987-88	Mt. St. Charles	HS	....	5	30	35	....	....	....	....	....	....
1988-89	Providence	H.E.	41	0	5	5	36	....	....	....	....	....

ROBINSON, LARRY CLARK

Defense. Shoots left. 6'3", 220 lbs. Born, Winchester, Ont., June 2, 1951.
(Montreal's 4th choice, 20th over-all, in 1971 Amateur Draft).

			Regular Season					Playoffs				
Season	Club	Lea	GP	G	A	TP	PIM	GP	G	A	TP	PIM
1969-70	Brockville	OHA	40	22	29	51	74	....	....	....	....	....
1970-71	Kitchener	OHA	61	12	39	51	65	....	....	....	....	....
1971-72	Nova Scotia	AHL	74	10	14	24	54	15	2	10	12	31
1972-73	Nova Scotia	AHL	38	6	33	39	33	....	....	....	....	....
	Montreal	**NHL**	**36**	**2**	**4**	**6**	**20**	**11**	**1**	**4**	**5**	**9**
1973-74	**Montreal**	**NHL**	**78**	**6**	**20**	**26**	**66**	**6**	**0**	**1**	**1**	**26**
1974-75	**Montreal**	**NHL**	**80**	**14**	**47**	**61**	**76**	**11**	**0**	**4**	**4**	**27**
1975-76	**Montreal**	**NHL**	**80**	**10**	**30**	**40**	**59**	**13**	**3**	**3**	**6**	**10**
1976-77ab	**Montreal**	**NHL**	**77**	**19**	**66**	**85**	**45**	**14**	**2**	**10**	**12**	**12**
1977-78cd	**Montreal**	**NHL**	**80**	**13**	**52**	**65**	**39**	**15**	**4**	***17**	***21**	**6**
1978-79b	**Montreal**	**NHL**	**67**	**16**	**45**	**61**	**33**	**16**	**6**	**9**	**15**	**8**
1979-80ab	**Montreal**	**NHL**	**72**	**14**	**61**	**75**	**39**	**10**	**0**	**4**	**4**	**2**
1980-81d	**Montreal**	**NHL**	**65**	**12**	**38**	**50**	**37**	**3**	**0**	**1**	**1**	**2**
1981-82	**Montreal**	**NHL**	**71**	**12**	**47**	**59**	**41**	**5**	**0**	**1**	**1**	**8**
1982-83	**Montreal**	**NHL**	**71**	**14**	**49**	**63**	**33**	**3**	**0**	**0**	**0**	**2**
1983-84	**Montreal**	**NHL**	**74**	**9**	**34**	**43**	**39**	**15**	**0**	**5**	**5**	**22**
1984-85	**Montreal**	**NHL**	**76**	**14**	**33**	**47**	**44**	**12**	**3**	**8**	**11**	**8**
1985-86d	**Montreal**	**NHL**	**78**	**19**	**63**	**82**	**39**	**20**	**0**	**13**	**13**	**22**
1986-87	**Montreal**	**NHL**	**70**	**13**	**37**	**50**	**44**	**17**	**3**	**17**	**20**	**6**
1987-88	**Montreal**	**NHL**	**53**	**6**	**34**	**40**	**30**	**11**	**1**	**4**	**5**	**4**
1988-89	**Montreal**	**NHL**	**74**	**4**	**26**	**30**	**22**	**21**	**2**	**8**	**10**	**12**
	NHL Totals		**1202**	**197**	**686**	**883**	**706**	**203**	**25**	**109**	**134**	**186**

a Won James Norris Memorial Trophy (1977, 1980)
b NHL First All-Star Team (1977, 1979, 1980)
c Won Conn Smythe Trophy (1978)
d NHL Second All-Star Team (1978, 1981, 1986)

Played in NHL All-Star Game (1974, 1976-78, 1980, 1982, 1986, 1988, 1989)

Signed as a free agent by **Los Angeles**, July 26, 1989.

ROBINSON, ROBERT

Defense. Shoots left. 6'3", 210 lbs. Born, St. Catharines, Ont., April 19, 1967.
(St. Louis' 6th choice, 117th overall, in 1987 Entry Draft).

			Regular Season					Playoffs				
Season	Club	Lea	GP	G	A	TP	PIM	GP	G	A	TP	PIM
1985-86	Miami-Ohio	CCHA	38	1	9	10	24	....	....	....	....	....
1986-87	Miami-Ohio	CCHA	33	3	5	8	32	....	....	....	....	....
1987-88	Miami-Ohio	CCHA	35	1	3	4	56	....	....	....	....	....
1988-89	Miami-Ohio	CCHA	30	3	4	7	42	....	....	....	....	....
	Peoria	IHL	11	2	0	2	6	....	....	....	....	....

ROBITAILLE, LUC (ROBE-uh-tie)

Left wing. Shoots left. 6', 180 lbs. Born, Montreal, Que., February 17, 1966.
(Los Angeles' 9th choice, 171st over-all, in 1984 Entry Draft).

			Regular Season					Playoffs				
Season	Club	Lea	GP	G	A	TP	PIM	GP	G	A	TP	PIM
1983-84	Hull	QMJHL	70	32	53	85	48	....	....	....	....	....
1984-85a	Hull	QMJHL	64	55	94	149	115	5	4	2	6	27
1985-86bcd	Hull	QMJHL	63	68	123	191	91	15	17	27	44	28
1986-87ef	**Los Angeles**	**NHL**	**79**	**45**	**39**	**84**	**28**	**5**	**1**	**4**	**5**	**2**
1987-88g	**Los Angeles**	**NHL**	**80**	**53**	**58**	**111**	**82**	**5**	**2**	**5**	**7**	**18**
1988-89g	**Los Angeles**	**NHL**	**78**	**46**	**52**	**98**	**65**	**11**	**2**	**6**	**8**	**10**
	NHL Totals		**237**	**144**	**149**	**293**	**175**	**21**	**5**	**15**	**20**	**30**

a QMJHL Second All-Star Team (1985)
bQMJHL First All-Star Team (1986)
c QMJHL Player of the Year (1986)
d Canadian Major Junior Player of the Year (1986)
e Won Calder Memorial Trophy (1987)
f NHL Second All-Star Team (1987)
g NHL First All-Star Team (1988, 1989)

Played in NHL All-Star Game (1988, 1989)

ROCHEFORT, NORMAND (RAHSH fahr)

Defense. Shoots left. 6'1", 211 lbs. Born, Trois Rivieres, Que., January 28, 1961.
(Quebec's 1st choice, 24th over-all, in 1980 Entry Draft).

			Regular Season					Playoffs				
Season	Club	Lea	GP	G	A	TP	PIM	GP	G	A	TP	PIM
1978-79	Trois Rivières	QJHL	72	17	57	74	30	13	3	11	14	17
1979-80	Trois Rivières	QJHL	20	5	25	30	22	....	....	....	....	....
a	Quebec	QJHL	52	8	39	47	68	5	1	3	4	8
1980-81	Quebec	QJHL	9	2	6	8	14	....	....	....	....	....
	Quebec	**NHL**	**56**	**3**	**7**	**10**	**51**	**5**	**0**	**0**	**0**	**4**
1981-82	**Quebec**	**NHL**	**72**	**4**	**14**	**18**	**115**	**16**	**0**	**2**	**2**	**10**
1982-83	**Quebec**	**NHL**	**62**	**6**	**17**	**23**	**40**	**1**	**0**	**0**	**0**	**2**
1983-84	**Quebec**	**NHL**	**75**	**2**	**22**	**24**	**47**	**6**	**1**	**0**	**1**	**6**
1984-85	**Quebec**	**NHL**	**73**	**3**	**21**	**24**	**74**	**18**	**2**	**1**	**3**	**8**
1985-86	**Quebec**	**NHL**	**26**	**5**	**4**	**9**	**30**	....	....	....	....	....
1986-87	**Quebec**	**NHL**	**70**	**6**	**9**	**15**	**46**	**13**	**2**	**1**	**3**	**26**
1987-88	**Quebec**	**NHL**	**46**	**3**	**10**	**13**	**49**	....	....	....	....	....
1988-89	**NY Rangers**	**NHL**	**11**	**1**	**5**	**6**	**18**	....	....	....	....	....
	NHL Totals		**491**	**33**	**109**	**142**	**470**	**59**	**5**	**4**	**9**	**56**

a QMJHL Second All-Star Team (1980)

Traded to **NY Rangers** by **Quebec** with Jason Lafreniere for Bruce Bell, Jari Gronstrand, Walt Poddubny and NY Rangers' fourth round choice (Eric Dubois) in 1989 Entry Draft, August 1, 1988.

ROENICK, JEREMY

Center. Shoots right. 5'11", 170 lbs. Born, Boston, MA, January 17, 1970.
(Chicago's 1st choice, 8th overall, in 1988 Entry Draft).

			Regular Season					Playoffs				
Season	Club	Lea	GP	G	A	TP	PIM	GP	G	A	TP	PIM
1986-87	Thayer Acad.	HS	24	31	34	65	....	....	....	....	....	....
1987-88	Thayer Acad.	HS	24	34	50	84	....	....	....	....	....	....
1988-89	**Chicago**	**NHL**	**20**	**9**	**9**	**18**	**4**	**10**	**1**	**3**	**4**	**7**
a	Hull	QMJHL	28	34	36	70	14	....	....	....	....	....
	NHL Totals		**20**	**9**	**9**	**18**	**4**	**10**	**1**	**3**	**4**	**7**

a QMJHL Second All-Star Team (1989)

ROHLICEK, JEFF (ROW-li-check)

Center. Shoots left. 6', 180 lbs. Born, Park Ridge, IL, January 27, 1966.
(Vancouver's 2nd choice, 31st over-all, in 1984 Entry Draft).

			Regular Season					Playoffs				
Season	Club	Lea	GP	G	A	TP	PIM	GP	G	A	TP	PIM
1982-83	Chicago Jets	Midget	35	57	73	130	...	....	....	....	....	....
	Main West HS	...	25	60	60	120	...	....	....	....	....	....
1983-84	Portland	WHL	71	44	53	97	22	14	13	8	21	10
1984-85a	Kelowna	WHL	65	39	52	91	26	6	3	6	9	2
	Portland	WHL	16	5	13	18	2	....	....	....	....	....
1985-86	Spokane	WHL	57	50	52	102	39	9	6	2	8	16
1986-87	Fredericton	AHL	70	19	37	56	22	....	....	....	....	....
1987-88	**Vancouver**	**NHL**	**7**	**0**	**0**	**0**	**4**	....	....	....	....	....
	Fredericton	AHL	65	26	31	57	50	....	....	....	....	....
1988-89	**Vancouver**	**NHL**	**2**	**0**	**0**	**0**	**4**	....	....	....	....	....
b	Milwaukee	IHL	78	47	63	110	106	11	6	6	12	8
	NHL Totals		**9**	**0**	**0**	**0**	**8**	....	....	....	....	....

a WHL Second All-Star Team, West Division (1985)
b IHL First All-Star Team (1989)

ROHLIK, STEVE

Left wing. Shoots left. 6', 180 lbs. Born, St. Paul, MN, May 15, 1968.
(Pittsburgh's 8th choice, 151st overall, in 1986 Entry Draft).

			Regular Season					Playoffs				
Season	Club	Lea	GP	G	A	TP	PIM	GP	G	A	TP	PIM
1985-86	Hill Murray	HS	27	26	33	59	0	....	....	....	....	....
1986-87	U. Wisconsin	WCHA	31	3	0	3	34	....	....	....	....	....
1987-88	U. Wisconsin	WCHA	44	3	10	13	59	....	....	....	....	....
1988-89	U. of Wisconsin	WCHA	45	11	14	25	44	....	....	....	....	....

ROHLIN, LEIF

Defense. Shoots left. 6'1", 196 lbs. Born, Vasteras, Sweden, February 26, 1968.
Last amateur club: VIK (Sweden).
(Vancouver's 2nd choice, 33rd overall, in 1988 Entry Draft).

			Regular Season					Playoffs				
Season	Club	Lea	GP	G	A	TP	PIM	GP	G	A	TP	PIM
1986-87	VIK	Swe. 2	27	2	5	7	12	12	0	2	2	8
1987-88	VIK	Swe. 2	30	2	15	17	46	10	6	6	12	8
1988-89	Vasteras	Swe.	22	3	7	10	18	....	....	....	....	....

ROHLOFF, JON

Defense. Shoots right. 5'11", 200 lbs. Born, Mankato, MN, October 3, 1969.
(Boston's 7th choice, 186th overall, in 1988 Entry Draft).

			Regular Season					Playoffs				
Season	Club	Lea	GP	G	A	TP	PIM	GP	G	A	TP	PIM
1986-87	Grand Rapids	HS	21	12	23	35	16	....	....	....	....	....
1987-88	Grand Rapids	HS	23	10	13	23	...	....	....	....	....	....
1988-89	Minn.-Duluth	WCHA	9	1	2	3	44	....	....	....	....	....

ROLFE, DANIEL

Defense. Shoots left. 6'4", 200 lbs. Born, Inglewood, CA, December 25, 1967.
(St. Louis' 12th choice, 222nd overall, in 1987 Entry Draft).

			Regular Season					Playoffs				
Season	Club	Lea	GP	G	A	TP	PIM	GP	G	A	TP	PIM
1986-87	Brockville	OPJHL	41	14	23	37	....	....	....	....	....	....
1987-88	Ferris State	CCHA	13	1	1	2	36	....	....	....	....	....
1988-89	Ferris State	CCHA	28	0	2	2	54	....	....	....	....	....

ROMANIUK, RUSSELL

Left wing. Shoots left. 6', 185 lbs. Born, Winnipeg, Man., June 9, 1970.
(Winnipeg's 2nd choice, 31st overall, in 1988 Entry Draft).

			Regular Season					Playoffs				
Season	Club	Lea	GP	G	A	TP	PIM	GP	G	A	TP	PIM
1987-88	St. Boniface	MJHL	38	46	34	80	46	....	....	....	....	....
1988-89	North Dakota	WCHA	39	17	14	31	32	....	....	....	....	....
	Cdn. National	....	3	1	0	1	0	....	....	....	....	....

ROMBERG, PETER

Defense. Shoots left. 6'4", 200 lbs. Born, West Germany, November 2, 1966.
(Calgary's 11th choice, 206th overall, in 1985 Entry Draft).

			Regular Season					Playoffs				
Season	Club	Lea	GP	G	A	TP	PIM	GP	G	A	TP	PIM
1984-85	Essen	W.Ger.2	16	2	7	9	34	....	....	....	....	....
1985-86	Iserlohn	W.Ger.	39	2	0	2	68	....	....	....	....	....
1986-87	Iserlohn	W.Ger.	39	8	10	18	73	....	....	....	....	....
1987-88	Kolner	W.Ger.	44	3	2	5	41	....	....	....	....	....
1988-89	Duisburg	W.Ger.	2	1	4	5	6	....	....	....	....	....

RONAN, EDWARD (ED)

Right wing. Shoots right. 5'11", 170 lbs. Born, Quincy, MA, March 21, 1968.
(Montreal's 13th choice, 227th overall, in 1987 Entry Draft).

			Regular Season					Playoffs				
Season	Club	Lea	GP	G	A	TP	PIM	GP	G	A	TP	PIM
1986-87	Andover	HS	22	12	20	32	10	....	....	....	....	....
1987-88	Boston U.	H.E.	31	2	5	7	20	....	....	....	....	....
1988-89	Boston U.	H.E.	36	4	11	15	34	....	....	....	....	....

RONNING, CLIFF

Center. Shoots left. 5'8", 175 lbs. Born, Vancouver, B.C., October 1, 1965.
(St. Louis' 9th choice, 134th over-all, in 1984 Entry Draft)

			Regular Season					Playoffs				
Season	Club	Lea	GP	G	A	TP	PIM	GP	G	A	TP	PIM
1983-84	N. Westminster	WHL	71	69	67	136	10	9	8	13	21	10
1984-85ab	N. Westminster	WHL	70	89	108	197	20	11	10	14	24	4
1985-86	**St. Louis**	**NHL**	....	....	....	....	....	**5**	**1**	**1**	**2**	**2**
	Cdn. Olympic	...	71	55	63	118	53	....	....	....	....	....
1986-87	**St. Louis**	**NHL**	**42**	**11**	**14**	**25**	**6**	**4**	**0**	**1**	**1**	**0**
	Cdn. Olympic	....	26	16	16	32	12	....	....	....	....	....
1987-88	**St. Louis**	**NHL**	**26**	**5**	**8**	**13**	**12**	....	....	....	....	....
1988-89	**St. Louis**	**NHL**	**64**	**24**	**31**	**55**	**18**	**7**	**1**	**3**	**4**	**0**
	Peoria	IHL	12	11	20	31	8	....	....	....	....	....
	NHL Totals		**132**	**40**	**53**	**93**	**36**	**16**	**2**	**5**	**7**	**2**

a WHL First All-Star Team (1985)
b WHL Most Valuable Player (1985)

ROONEY, LARRY

Defense. Shoots left. 5'11", 165 lbs. Born, Boston, MA, January 30, 1968.
(Buffalo's 6th choice, 89th overall, in 1986 Entry Draft).

			Regular Season					Playoffs				
Season	Club	Lea	GP	G	A	TP	PIM	GP	G	A	TP	PIM
1985-86	Thayer	HS	24	20	35	55	...	....	....	....	....	....
1986-87	Thayer	HS	26	15	26	41	...	....	....	....	....	....
1987-88	Providence	H.E.	33	1	9	10	34	....	....	....	....	....
1988-89	Providence	H.E	10	0	4	4	18	....	....	....	....	....

ROONEY, STEVE

Left wing. Shoots left. 6'2", 195 lbs. Born, Canton, MA, June 28, 1962.
Montreal's 8th choice, 88th over-all, in 1981 Entry Draft)

			Regular Season					Playoffs				
Season	Club	Lea	GP	G	A	TP	PIM	GP	G	A	TP	PIM
1981-82	Providence	ECAC	31	7	10	17	41	....	....	....	....	....
1982-83	Providence	ECAC	42	10	20	30	31	....	....	....	....	....
1983-84	Providence	ECAC	33	11	16	27	46	....	....	....	....	....
1984-85	**Montreal**	**NHL**	**3**	**1**	**0**	**1**	**7**	**11**	**2**	**2**	**4**	**19**
	Providence	H.E.	31	7	10	17	41	....	....	....	....	....
1985-86	**Montreal**	**NHL**	**38**	**2**	**3**	**5**	**114**	**1**	**0**	**0**	**0**	**0**
1986-87	**Montreal**	**NHL**	**2**	**0**	**0**	**0**	**22**	....	....	....	....	....
	Sherbrooke	AHL	22	4	11	15	66	....	....	....	....	....
	Winnipeg	**NHL**	**30**	**2**	**3**	**5**	**57**	**8**	**0**	**0**	**0**	**34**
1987-88	**Winnipeg**	**NHL**	**56**	**7**	**6**	**13**	**217**	**5**	**1**	**0**	**1**	**33**
1988-89	**New Jersey**	**NHL**	**25**	**3**	**1**	**4**	**79**	....	....	....	....	....
	NHL Totals		**154**	**15**	**13**	**28**	**496**	**25**	**3**	**2**	**5**	**86**

Traded to **Winnipeg** by **Montreal** for Winnipeg's third-round choice (Francois Gravel) in 1987 Entry Draft, January 8, 1987. Traded to **New Jersey** by **Winnipeg** with future considerations for Alain Chevrier and New Jersey's seventh round choice (Doug Evans) in the 1989 Entry Draft, July 19, 1988.

ROOT, WILLIAM JOHN (BILL)

Defense. Shoots right. 6', 210 lbs. Born, Toronto, Ont., September 6, 1959.

			Regular Season					Playoffs				
Season	Club	Lea	GP	G	A	TP	PIM	GP	G	A	TP	PIM
1977-78	Niagara Falls	OHA	67	6	11	17	61	....	....	....	....	....
1978-79	Niagara Falls	OHA	67	4	31	35	119	20	4	7	11	42
1979-80	Nova Scotia	AHL	55	4	15	19	57	6	1	1	2	2
1980-81	Nova Scotia	AHL	63	3	12	15	76	6	0	1	1	2
1981-82	Nova Scotia	AHL	77	6	25	31	105	9	1	0	1	4
1982-83	**Montreal**	**NHL**	**46**	**2**	**3**	**5**	**24**	....	....	....	....	....
	Nova Scotia	AHL	24	0	7	7	29	....	....	....	....	....
1983-84	**Montreal**	**NHL**	**72**	**4**	**13**	**17**	**45**	....	....	....	....	....
1984-85	**Toronto**	**NHL**	**35**	**1**	**1**	**2**	**23**	....	....	....	....	....
	St. Catharines	AHL	28	5	9	14	10	....	....	....	....	....
1985-86	**Toronto**	**NHL**	**27**	**0**	**1**	**1**	**29**	**7**	**0**	**2**	**2**	**13**
	St. Catharines	AHL	14	7	4	11	11	....	....	....	....	....
1986-87	**Toronto**	**NHL**	**34**	**3**	**3**	**6**	**37**	**13**	**1**	**0**	**1**	**12**
	Newmarket	AHL	32	4	11	15	23	....	....	....	....	....
1987-88	**St. Louis**	**NHL**	**9**	**0**	**0**	**0**	**6**	....	....	....	....	....
	Philadelphia	**NHL**	**24**	**1**	**2**	**3**	**16**	**2**	**0**	**0**	**0**	**0**
1988-89	Newmarket	AHL	66	10	22	32	39	5	0	0	0	18
	NHL Totals		**247**	**11**	**23**	**34**	**180**	**22**	**1**	**2**	**3**	**25**

Signed as free agent by **Montreal**, October 4, 1979. Traded to **Toronto** by **Montreal** with Montreal's second-round choice (Darryl Shannon) in 1986 Entry Draft for Dom Campedelli, August 21, 1984. Traded to **Hartford** by **Toronto** for Dave Semenko, September 8, 1987. Claimed by **St. Louis** in NHL Waiver Draft, October 5, 1987. Claimed on waivers by **Philadelphia** form **St. Louis**, November 26, 1987. Traded to **Toronto** by **Philadelphia** for Mike Stothers, June 21, 1988.

ROUPE, MAGNUS

Left wing. Shoots left. 6′, 190 lbs.　　Born, Gislaved, Sweden, March 23, 1963.
(Philadelphia's 9th choice, 182nd overall, in 1982 Entry Draft).

				Regular Season					Playoffs			
Season	Club	Lea	GP	G	A	TP	PIM	GP	G	A	TP	PIM
1981-82	Farjestad	Swe.	24	5	3	8	8	2	0	0	0	0
1982-83	Farjestad	Swe.	29	7	4	11	16	6	1	1	2	8
1983-84	Farjestad	Swe.	36	2	3	5	38	....	....	....	....	....
1984-85	Farjestad	Swe.	31	9	6	15	16	3	1	0	1	0
1985-86	Farjestad	Swe.	35	11	10	21	38	8	3	2	5	18
1986-87	Farjestad	Swe.	31	11	6	17	64	7	0	2	2	10
1987-88	**Philadelphia**	**NHL**	33	2	4	6	32	....	....	....	....	....
	Hershey	AHL	23	6	16	22	10	11	3	4	7	31
1988-89	**Philadelphia**	**NHL**	7	1	1	2	10	....	....	....	....	....
	Hershey	AHL	12	2	6	8	17	....	....	....	....	....
	Farjestad	Swe.	18	9	4	13	58	2	0	1	1	6
	NHL Totals		**40**	**3**	**5**	**8**	**42**	....	....	....	....	....

ROUSE, ROBERT (BOB)

Defense. Shoots right. 6′1″, 210 lbs.　　Born, Surrey, B.C., June 18, 1964.
(Minnesota's 3rd choice, 80th over-all, in 1982 Entry Draft).

				Regular Season					Playoffs			
Season	Club	Lea	GP	G	A	TP	PIM	GP	G	A	TP	PIM
1980-81	Billings	WHL	70	0	13	13	116	5	0	0	0	2
1981-82	Billings	WHL	71	7	22	29	209	5	0	2	2	10
1982-83	Nanaimo	WHL	29	7	20	27	86	....	....	....	....	....
	Lethbridge	WHL	42	8	30	38	82	20	2	13	15	55
1983-84	**Minnesota**	**NHL**	1	0	0	0	0	....	....	....	....	....
a	Lethbridge	WHL	71	18	42	60	101	5	0	1	1	28
1984-85	**Minnesota**	**NHL**	63	2	9	11	113	....	....	....	....	....
	Springfield	AHL	8	0	3	3	6	....	....	....	....	....
1985-86	**Minnesota**	**NHL**	75	1	14	15	151	3	0	0	0	0
1986-87	**Minnesota**	**NHL**	72	2	10	12	179	....	....	....	....	....
1987-88	**Minnesota**	**NHL**	74	0	12	12	168	....	....	....	....	....
1988-89	**Minnesota**	**NHL**	66	4	13	17	124	....	....	....	....	....
	Washington	**NHL**	13	0	2	2	36	6	2	0	2	4
	NHL Totals		**364**	**9**	**60**	**69**	**771**	**9**	**2**	**0**	**2**	**6**

a WHL First All-Star Team, East Division (1984)

Traded to **Washington** by **Minnesota** with Dino Ciccarelli for Mike Gartner and Larry Murphy, March 7, 1989.

ROUSSEAU, MARC

Defense. Shoots left. 6′, 185 lbs.　　Born, N. Vancouver, B.C., May 17, 1968.
(Hartford's 4th choice, 102nd overall, in 1987 Entry Draft).

				Regular Season					Playoffs			
Season	Club	Lea	GP	G	A	TP	PIM	GP	G	A	TP	PIM
1986-87	U. of Denver	WCHA	39	3	18	21	70	....	....	....	....	....
1987-88	U. of Denver	WCHA	38	6	22	28	92	....	....	....	....	....
1988-89	U. of Denver	WCHA	43	10	18	28	68	....	....	....	....	....

ROUTHIER, JEAN-MARC

Right wing. Shoots right. 6′2″, 190 lbs.　　Born, Quebec, Que., February 2, 1968.
(Quebec's 2nd choice, 39th overall, in 1986 Entry Draft).

				Regular Season					Playoffs			
Season	Club	Lea	GP	G	A	TP	PIM	GP	G	A	TP	PIM
1985-86	Hull	QMJHL	71	18	16	34	111	15	3	6	9	27
1986-87	Hull	QMJHL	59	17	18	35	98	....	....	....	....	....
1987-88	Victoriaville	QMJHL	57	16	28	44	267	2	0	0	0	5
1988-89	Halifax	AHL	52	13	13	26	189	4	1	1	2	16

ROY, STEPHANE

Center. Shoots left. 6′, 190 lbs.　　Born, Ste. Foy, Que., June 29, 1967.
(Minnesota's 1st choice, 51st overall, in 1985 Entry Draft).

				Regular Season					Playoffs			
Season	Club	Lea	GP	G	A	TP	PIM	GP	G	A	TP	PIM
1984-85	Granby	QMJHL	68	28	53	81	34	....	....	....	....	....
1985-86	Granby	QMJHL	61	33	52	85	68	....	....	....	....	....
	Cdn. Olympic	....	10	0	1	1	4	....	....	....	....	....
1986-87	Granby	QMJHL	45	23	44	67	54	7	2	3	5	50
	Cdn. Olympic	....	9	1	2	3	4	....	....	....	....	....
1987-88	**Minnesota**	**NHL**	12	1	0	1	0	....	....	....	....	....
	Kalamazoo	IHL	58	21	12	33	52	5	1	2	3	11
1988-89	Halifax	AHL	42	8	16	24	28	1	0	0	0	0
	Kalamazoo	IHL	20	5	4	9	27	....	....	....	....	....

Traded to **Quebec** by **Minnesota** for future considerations, December 15, 1988.

RUCHTY, MATTHEW

Left wing. Shoots left. 6′1″, 210 lbs.　　Born, Kitchener, Ont., November 27, 1969.
(New Jersey's 4th choice, 65th overall, in 1988 Entry Draft).

				Regular Season					Playoffs			
Season	Club	Lea	GP	G	A	TP	PIM	GP	G	A	TP	PIM
1987-88	Bowling Green	CCHA	41	6	15	21	78	....	....	....	....	....
1988-89	Bowling Green	CCHA	43	11	21	32	110	....	....	....	....	....

RUCINSKI, MIKE

Center. Shoots left. 5′11″, 190 lbs.　　Born, Wheeling, IL, December 12, 1963.

				Regular Season					Playoffs			
Season	Club	Lea	GP	G	A	TP	PIM	GP	G	A	TP	PIM
1983-84	Ill.-Chicago	CCHA	33	17	26	43	12	....	....	....	....	....
1984-85	Ill.-Chicago	CCHA	40	29	32	61	28	....	....	....	....	....
1985-86	Ill.-Chicago	CCHA	37	16	31	47	18	....	....	....	....	....
1986-87	Moncton	AHL	42	5	9	14	14	....	....	....	....	....
	Salt Lake	IHL	29	16	25	41	19	17	9	18	27	28
1987-88	Saginaw	IHL	44	19	31	50	32	10	1	9	10	10
	Chicago	**NHL**	....	....	....	....	....	2	0	0	0	0
1988-89	**Chicago**	**NHL**	1	0	0	0	0	....	....	....	....	....
	Saginaw	IHL	81	35	72	107	40	6	2	4	6	14
	NHL Totals		**1**	**0**	**0**	**0**	**0**	**2**	**0**	**0**	**0**	**0**

Signed as a free agent by **Calgary**, August 10, 1986.

RUFF, LINDY CAMERON

Defense. Shoots left. 6′2″, 200 lbs.　　Born, Warburg, Alta., February 17, 1960.
(Buffalo's 2nd choice, 32nd over-all, in 1979 Entry Draft).

				Regular Season					Playoffs			
Season	Club	Lea	GP	G	A	TP	PIM	GP	G	A	TP	PIM
1977-78	Lethbridge	WHL	66	9	24	33	219	8	2	8	10	4
1978-79	Lethbridge	WHL	24	9	18	27	108	6	0	1	1	0
1979-80	**Buffalo**	**NHL**	63	5	14	19	38	8	1	1	2	19
1980-81	**Buffalo**	**NHL**	65	8	18	26	121	6	3	1	4	23
1981-82	**Buffalo**	**NHL**	79	16	32	48	194	4	0	0	0	28
1982-83	**Buffalo**	**NHL**	60	12	17	29	130	10	4	2	6	47
1983-84	**Buffalo**	**NHL**	58	14	31	45	101	3	1	0	1	9
1984-85	**Buffalo**	**NHL**	39	13	11	24	45	5	2	4	6	15
1985-86	**Buffalo**	**NHL**	54	20	12	32	158	....	....	....	....	....
1986-87	**Buffalo**	**NHL**	50	6	14	20	74	....	....	....	....	....
1987-88	**Buffalo**	**NHL**	77	2	23	25	179	6	0	2	2	23
1988-89	**Buffalo**	**NHL**	63	6	11	17	86	....	....	....	....	....
	NY Rangers	**NHL**	13	0	5	5	31	2	0	0	0	17
	NHL Totals		**621**	**102**	**188**	**290**	**1157**	**44**	**11**	**10**	**21**	**181**

Traded to **NY Rangers** by **Buffalo** for NY Rangers' fifth-round choice in 1990 Entry Draft, March 7, 1989.

RUMBLE, DARREN

Defense. Shoots left. 6′1″, 200 lbs.　　Born, Barrie, Ont., January 23, 1969.
(Philadelphia's 1st choice, 20th overall, in 1987 Entry Draft).

				Regular Season					Playoffs			
Season	Club	Lea	GP	G	A	TP	PIM	GP	G	A	TP	PIM
1986-87	Kitchener	OHL	64	11	32	43	44	4	0	1	1	9
1987-88	Kitchener	OHL	55	15	50	65	64	....	....	....	....	....
1988-89	Kitchener	OHL	46	11	28	39	25	5	1	0	1	2

RUOTSALINEN, REIJO　　　　　　　　　(ROOTS-a-LAY-nen)

Defense. Shoots right. 5′8″, 170 lbs.　　Born, Oulu, Finland, April 1, 1960.
(NY Rangers' 5th choice, 119th over-all, in 1980 Entry Draft).

				Regular Season					Playoffs			
Season	Club	Lea	GP	G	A	TP	PIM	GP	G	A	TP	PIM
1976-77	Karpat	Fin. 2	36	23	35	58	14	6	2	6	8	0
1977-78	Karpat	Fin.	30	9	14	23	4	....	....	....	....	....
1978-79	Karpat	Fin.	36	14	8	22	47	....	....	....	....	....
1979-80a	Karpat	Fin.	30	15	13	28	31	6	5	2	7	0
1980-81a	Karpat	Fin.	36	28	23	51	28	12	7	4	11	6
1981-82	**NY Rangers**	**NHL**	78	18	38	56	27	10	4	5	9	2
1982-83	**NY Rangers**	**NHL**	77	16	53	69	22	9	4	2	6	6
1983-84	**NY Rangers**	**NHL**	74	20	39	59	26	5	1	1	2	2
1984-85	**NY Rangers**	**NHL**	80	28	45	73	32	3	2	0	2	6
1985-86	**NY Rangers**	**NHL**	80	17	42	59	147	16	0	8	8	6
1986-87	**Edmonton**	**NHL**	16	5	8	13	6	21	2	5	7	10
	Bern	Switz.	36	26	28	54	....	....	....	....	....	....
1987-88	HV71	Swe.	39	10	22	32	26	....	....	....	....	....
1988-89	Bern	Switz.	36	17	30	47	....	9	4	7	11	....
	NHL Totals		**405**	**104**	**225**	**329**	**160**	**64**	**13**	**21**	**34**	**32**

a Named to Finnish League All-Star Team (1980, 1981)

Played in NHL All-Star Game (1986)

Traded to **Edmonton** by **NY Rangers** with Clark Donatelli, Ville Kentala and Jim Weimer for Mike Golden, Don Jackson and Miroslav Horava, October 2, 1986. Claimed by **New Jersey** in NHL Waiver Draft, October 5, 1987.

RUSKOWSKI, TERRY WALLACE

Center. Shoots left. 5′9″, 180 lbs.　　Born, Prince Albert, Sask., December 31, 1954.
(Chicago's 4th choice, 70th over-all, in 1974 Amateur Draft).

				Regular Season					Playoffs			
Season	Club	Lea	GP	G	A	TP	PIM	GP	G	A	TP	PIM
1972-73	Swift Current	WHL	53	25	64	89	136	....	....	....	....	....
1973-74	Swift Current	WHL	68	40	93	133	243	13	5	*23	28	23
1974-75	Houston	WHA	71	10	36	46	134	13	4	2	6	15
1975-76	Houston	WHA	65	14	35	49	100	16	6	10	16	*64
1976-77	Houston	WHA	80	24	60	84	146	11	6	11	17	*67
1977-78	Houston	WHA	78	15	57	72	170	4	1	1	2	5
1978-79	Winnipeg	WHA	75	20	66	86	211	8	1	*12	13	23
1979-80	**Chicago**	**NHL**	74	15	55	70	252	4	0	0	0	22
1980-81	**Chicago**	**NHL**	72	8	51	59	225	3	0	2	2	11
1981-82	**Chicago**	**NHL**	60	7	30	37	120	11	1	2	3	53
1982-83	**Chicago**	**NHL**	5	0	2	2	12	....	....	....	....	....
	Los Angeles	**NHL**	71	14	30	44	127	....	....	....	....	....
1983-84	**Los Angeles**	**NHL**	77	7	25	32	89	....	....	....	....	....
1984-85	**Los Angeles**	**NHL**	78	16	33	49	144	3	0	2	2	0
1985-86	**Pittsburgh**	**NHL**	73	26	37	63	162	....	....	....	....	....
1986-87	**Pittsburgh**	**NHL**	70	14	37	51	145	....	....	....	....	....
1987-88	**Minnesota**	**NHL**	47	5	12	17	76	....	....	....	....	....
1988-89	**Minnesota**	**NHL**	3	1	1	2	2	....	....	....	....	....
	NHL Totals		**630**	**113**	**313**	**426**	**1354**	**21**	**1**	**6**	**7**	**86**

Reclaimed by **Chicago** from **Winnipeg** prior to Expansion Draft, June 9, 1979. Traded to **Los Angeles** by **Chicago** for Larry Goodenough and Los Angeles' third round choice (Trent Yawney) in the 1984 Entry Draft, October 24, 1982. Signed as a free agent by **Pittsburgh**, October 3, 1985.

RUSNAK, DARIUS

Center. Shoots right. 6′1″, 190 lbs.　　Born, Ruzomberok, Czechoslovakia, September 4, 1968.
(Philadelphia's 11th choice, 230th overall, in 1987 Entry Draft).

				Regular Season					Playoffs			
Season	Club	Lea	GP	G	A	TP	PIM	GP	G	A	TP	PIM
1986-87	Bratislava	Czech.	32	15	13	28	....	....	....	....	....	....
1987-88	Dukla Jihlava	Czech.	31	14	23	37	....	....	....	....	....	....
1988-89	Bratislava	Czech.	31	16	15	31	....	....	....	....	....	....

RUSSELL, CAM

Defense. Shoots left. 6'4", 175 lbs.   Born, Halifax, N.S., January 12, 1969.
(Chicago's 3rd choice, 50th overall, in 1987 Entry Draft).

			Regular Season					Playoffs				
Season	Club	Lea	GP	G	A	TP	PIM	GP	G	A	TP	PIM
1985-86	Hull	QMJHL	56	3	4	7	24	15	0	2	2	4
1986-87	Hull	QMJHL	66	3	16	19	119	8	0	1	1	16
1987-88a	Hull	QMJHL	53	9	18	27	141	19	2	5	7	39
1988-89	Hull	QMJHL	66	8	32	40	109	9	2	6	8	6

a QMJHL Third All-Star Team (1988)

RUTHERFORD, PAUL

Center. Shoots left. 6'0", 190 lbs.   Born, Sudbury, Ont., January 1, 1969.
(NY Islanders' 6th choice, 100th overall, in 1988 Entry Draft).

			Regular Season					Playoffs				
Season	Club	Lea	GP	G	A	TP	PIM	GP	G	A	TP	PIM
1987-88	Ohio State	CCHA	40	18	23	41	40	.....	....	....	....	....
1988-89	Ohio State	CCHA	39	16	27	43	52	.....	....	....	....	....

RUSSELL, KERRY

Right wing. Shoots right. 5'11", 165 lbs.   Born, Kamloops, B.C., June 23, 1969.
(Hartford's 6th choice, 137th overall, in 1988 Entry Draft).

			Regular Season					Playoffs				
Season	Club	Lea	GP	G	A	TP	PIM	GP	G	A	TP	PIM
1987-88	Michigan State	CCHA	46	16	23	39	50	.....	....	....	....	....
1988-89	Michigan State	CCHA	46	5	23	28	50	.....	....	....	....	....

RUUTTU, CHRISTIAN   (ROO-TOO)

Center. Shoots left. 5'11", 194 lbs.   Born, Lappeenranta, Finland, February 20, 1964.
(Buffalo's 9th choice, 134th overall, in 1983 Entry Draft).

			Regular Season					Playoffs				
Season	Club	Lea	GP	G	A	TP	PIM	GP	G	A	TP	PIM
1982-83	Assat Pori	Fin.	36	15	18	33	34	.....	....	....	....	....
1983-84	Assat Pori	Fin.	37	18	42	60	72	9	2	5	7	12
1984-85	Assat Pori	Fin.	32	14	32	46	34	8	1	6	7	8
1985-86	IFK Helsinki	Fin.	36	16	38	54	47	10	3	6	9	8
1986-87	Buffalo	NHL	76	22	43	65	62	.....	....	....	....	....
1987-88	Buffalo	NHL	73	26	45	71	85	6	2	5	7	4
1988-89	Buffalo	NHL	67	14	46	60	98	2	0	0	0	2
	NHL Totals		216	62	134	196	245	8	2	5	7	6

Played in NHL All-Star Game (1988)

RUZICKA, VLADIMIR

Center. Shoots left. 6'1", 175 lbs.   Born, Most, Czechoslovakia, June 6, 1963.
(Toronto's 5th choice, 73rd overall, in 1982 Entry Draft).

			Regular Season					Playoffs				
Season	Club	Lea	GP	G	A	TP	PIM	GP	G	A	TP	PIM
1986-87	CHZ Litvinov	Czech.	32	24	15	39		.....	....	....	....	....
1987-88	Dukla Trencin	Czech.	34	32	21	53		.....	....	....	....	....
1988-89	Dukla Trencin	Czech.	45	46	38	84		.....	....	....	....	....

RYCHEL, WARREN

Left wing. Shoots left. 6', 190 lbs.   Born, Tecumseh, Ont., May 12, 1967.

			Regular Season					Playoffs				
Season	Club	Lea	GP	G	A	TP	PIM	GP	G	A	TP	PIM
1985-86	Ottawa	OHL	67	25	23	48	173	.....	....	....	....	....
1986-87	Kitchener	OHL	49	16	12	28	96	4	0	0	0	9
1987-88	Peoria	IHL	7	2	1	3	7	.....	....	....	....	....
	Saginaw	IHL	51	2	7	9	113	1	0	0	0	0
1988-89	Chicago	NHL	2	0	0	0	17	.....	....	....	....	....
	Saginaw	IHL	50	15	14	29	226	6	0	0	0	51
	NHL Totals		2	0	0	0	17	.....	....	....	....	....

Signed as a free agent by **Chicago**, September 19, 1986.

RYMSHA, ANDREW (ANDY)

Defense. Shoots left. 6'3", 210 lbs.   Born, St. Catharines, Ont., December 10, 1968.
(St. Louis' 5th choice, 82nd overall, in 1987 Entry Draft).

			Regular Season					Playoffs				
Season	Club	Lea	GP	G	A	TP	PIM	GP	G	A	TP	PIM
1986-87	W. Michigan	CCHA	41	7	12	19	60	.....	....	....	....	....
1987-88	W. Michigan	CCHA	42	5	6	11	114	.....	....	....	....	....
1988-89	W. Michigan	WCHA	35	3	4	7	139	.....	....	....	....	....

SAATZER, RON

Left wing/center. Shoots left. 6'1", 175 lbs.   Born, Hopkins, MN, October 10, 1966.
(St. Louis' 10th choice, 222nd overall, in 1985 Entry Draft).

			Regular Season					Playoffs				
Season	Club	Lea	GP	G	A	TP	PIM	GP	G	A	TP	PIM
1985-86	Miami-Ohio	CCHA	23	7	9	16	16	.....	....	....	....	....
1986-87	Miami-Ohio	CCHA	27	5	7	12	40	.....	....	....	....	....
1987-88	U. Minnesota	WCHA	DID NOT PLAY									
1988-89	U. Minnesota	WCHA	DID NOT PLAY									

SABOL, SHAWN

Defense. Shoots left. 6'3", 215 lbs.   Born, Fargo, ND, July 13, 1966.
(Philadelphia's 9th choice, 209th overall, in 1986 Entry Draft).

			Regular Season					Playoffs				
Season	Club	Lea	GP	G	A	TP	PIM	GP	G	A	TP	PIM
1986-87	U. Wisconsin	WCHA	40	7	16	23	98	.....	....	....	....	....
1987-88	U. Wisconsin	WCHA	8	4	3	7	10	.....	....	....	....	....
	Hershey	AHL	51	1	9	10	66	2	0	0	0	5
1988-89	Hershey	AHL	58	7	11	18	134	12	0	2	2	35

SABOURIN, KEN

Defense. Shoots left. 6'3", 205 lbs.   Born, Scarborough, Ont. April 28, 1966.
(Calgary's 2nd choice, 33rd over-all, in 1984 Entry Draft).

			Regular Season					Playoffs				
Season	Club	Lea	GP	G	A	TP	PIM	GP	G	A	TP	PIM
1982-83	S.S. Marie	OHL	58	0	8	8	90	10	0	0	0	14
1983-84	S.S. Marie	OHL	63	7	14	21	157	9	0	1	1	25
1984-85	S.S. Marie	OHL	63	5	19	24	139	16	1	4	5	10
1985-86	Moncton	AHL	3	0	0	0	0	6	0	1	1	2
	S.S. Marie	OHL	25	1	5	6	77					
	Cornwall	OHL	37	3	12	15	94	6	1	2	3	6
1986-87	Moncton	AHL	75	1	10	11	166	6	0	1	1	27
1987-88	Salt Lake	IHL	71	2	8	10	186	16	1	6	7	57
1988-89	Calgary	NHL	6	0	1	1	26	1	0	0	0	0
	Salt Lake	IHL	74	2	18	20	197	11	0	1	1	26
	NHL Totals		6	0	1	1	26	1	0	0	0	0

SACCO, DAVID

Defense. Shoots right. 6'1", 180 lbs.   Born, Medford, MA, July 31, 1970.
(Toronto's 9th choice, 195th overall, in 1988 Entry Draft).

			Regular Season					Playoffs				
Season	Club	Lea	GP	G	A	TP	PIM	GP	G	A	TP	PIM
1987-88	Boston U.	H.E.	34	16	20	36	40	.....	....	....	....	....
1988-89	Boston U.	H.E.	35	14	29	43	40	.....	....	....	....	....

SACCO, JOSEPH (JOE)

Right wing. Shoots right. 6'1", 180 lbs.   Born, Medford, MA, February 4, 1969.
(Toronto's 4th choice, 71st overall, in 1987 Entry Draft).

			Regular Season					Playoffs				
Season	Club	Lea	GP	G	A	TP	PIM	GP	G	A	TP	PIM
1986-87	Medford	HS	22	35	45	80	0	.....	....	....	....	....
1987-88	Boston U.	H.E.	34	16	20	36	40	.....	....	....	....	....
1988-89	Boston U.	H.E.	33	21	19	40	66	.....	....	....	....	....

SAGISSOR, THOMAS (TOM)

Center. Shoots left. 5'11", 180 lbs.   Born, Hastings, MN, September 12, 1967.
(Montreal's 7th choice, 96th overall, in 1985 Entry Draft).

			Regular Season					Playoffs				
Season	Club	Lea	GP	G	A	TP	PIM	GP	G	A	TP	PIM
1985-86	Hastings	HS	25	26	38	64	28	.....	....	....	....	....
1986-87	U. Wisconsin	WCHA	41	1	4	5	32	.....	....	....	....	....
1987-88	U. Wisconsin	WCHA	38	4	5	9	65	.....	....	....	....	....
1988-89	U. Wisconsin	WCHA	40	7	11	18	119	.....	....	....	....	....

ST. ARMOUR MARTIN

Left wing. Shoots left. 6'3", 195 lbs.   Born, Montreal, Que., January 30, 1970.
(Montreal's 2nd choice, 34th overall, in 1988 Entry Draft).

			Regular Season					Playoffs				
Season	Club	Lea	GP	G	A	TP	PIM	GP	G	A	TP	PIM
1986-87	Laval-Laur	Midget	42	55	95	150	58	.....	....	....	....	....
1987-88	Verdun	QMJHL	61	20	50	70	111	.....	....	....	....	....
1988-89	Trois-Rivieres	QMJHL	54	27	38	65	156	4	1	2	3	0

ST. CYR, JEFF

Defense. Shoots right. 6'3", 195 lbs.   Born, New Liskeard, Ont., February 16, 1967.
(Hartford's 5th choice, 123rd overall, in 1987 Entry Draft).

			Regular Season					Playoffs				
Season	Club	Lea	GP	G	A	TP	PIM	GP	G	A	TP	PIM
1986-87	Michigan Tech.	WCHA	38	0	2	2	82	.....	....	....	....	....
1987-88	Michigan Tech.	WCHA	40	0	7	7	98	.....	....	....	....	....
1988-89	Michigan Tech.	WCHA	41	0	7	7	79	.....	....	....	....	....

SAKIC, JOE

Center. Shoots left. 5'11", 185 lbs.   Born, Burnaby, B.C., July 7, 1969.
(Quebec's 2nd choice, 15th overall, in 1987 Entry Draft).

			Regular Season					Playoffs				
Season	Club	Lea	GP	G	A	TP	PIM	GP	G	A	TP	PIM
1986-87ab	Swift Current	WHL	72	60	73	133	31	4	0	1	1	0
1987-88acd	Swift Current	WHL	64	*78	82	*160	64	10	11	13	24	12
1988-89	Quebec	NHL	70	23	39	62	24	.....	....	....	....	....
	NHL Totals		70	23	39	62	24	.....	....	....	....	....

a WHL Player of the Year (1987, 1988)
b WHL Rookie of the Year (1987)
c Canadian Major Junior Player of the Year (1988)
d WHL East All-Star Team (1988)

SALLE, JOHAN

Defense. Shoots left. 6'1", 185 lbs.   Born, Orebro, Sweden, February 21, 1967.
(Philadelphia's 9th choice, 161st overall, in 1988 Entry Draft).

			Regular Season					Playoffs				
Season	Club	Lea	GP	G	A	TP	PIM	GP	G	A	TP	PIM
1987-88	Malmo	Swe.	36	9	4	13	48	.....	....	....	....	....
1988-89	Malmo	Swe.	18	6	10	16	32	.....	....	....	....	....

SALMING, ANDERS BORJE (SAHL-ming, BOR-yah)

Defense. Shoots left. 6'1", 185 lbs. Born, Kiruna, Sweden, April 17, 1951.

			Regular Season					Playoffs				
Season	Club	Lea	GP	G	A	TP	PIM	GP	G	A	TP	PIM
1970-71	Brynas	Swe.	27	2	6	8	22	....	....	....	....	....
1971-72	Brynas	Swe.	28	1	5	6	50	....	....	....	....	....
1972-73	Brynas	Swe.	26	5	4	9	34	....	....	....	....	....
1973-74	**Toronto**	**NHL**	**76**	**5**	**34**	**39**	**48**	**4**	**0**	**1**	**1**	**4**
1974-75a	**Toronto**	**NHL**	**60**	**12**	**25**	**37**	**34**	**7**	**0**	**4**	**4**	**6**
1975-76a	**Toronto**	**NHL**	**78**	**16**	**41**	**57**	**70**	**10**	**3**	**4**	**7**	**9**
1976-77b	**Toronto**	**NHL**	**76**	**12**	**66**	**78**	**46**	**9**	**3**	**6**	**9**	**6**
1977-78a	**Toronto**	**NHL**	**80**	**16**	**60**	**76**	**70**	**6**	**2**	**2**	**4**	**6**
1978-79a	**Toronto**	**NHL**	**78**	**17**	**56**	**73**	**76**	**6**	**0**	**1**	**1**	**8**
1979-80a	**Toronto**	**NHL**	**74**	**19**	**52**	**71**	**94**	**3**	**1**	**1**	**2**	**2**
1980-81	**Toronto**	**NHL**	**72**	**5**	**61**	**66**	**154**	**3**	**0**	**2**	**2**	**4**
1981-82	**Toronto**	**NHL**	**69**	**12**	**44**	**56**	**170**	....	....	....	....	....
1982-83	**Toronto**	**NHL**	**69**	**7**	**38**	**45**	**104**	**4**	**1**	**4**	**5**	**10**
1983-84	**Toronto**	**NHL**	**68**	**5**	**38**	**43**	**92**	....	....	....	....	....
1984-85	**Toronto**	**NHL**	**73**	**6**	**33**	**39**	**76**	....	....	....	....	....
1985-86	**Toronto**	**NHL**	**41**	**7**	**15**	**22**	**48**	**10**	**1**	**6**	**7**	**14**
1986-87	**Toronto**	**NHL**	**56**	**4**	**16**	**20**	**42**	**13**	**0**	**3**	**3**	**14**
1987-88	**Toronto**	**NHL**	**66**	**2**	**24**	**26**	**82**	**6**	**1**	**3**	**4**	**8**
1988-89	**Toronto**	**NHL**	**63**	**3**	**17**	**20**	**86**	....	....	....	....	....
	NHL Totals		**1099**	**148**	**620**	**768**	**1292**	**81**	**12**	**37**	**49**	**91**

a NHL Second All-Star Team (1975, 1976, 1978, 1979, 1980)
b NHL First All-Star Team (1977)

Played in NHL All-Star Game (1976-78)

Signed as free agent by **Toronto**, May 12, 1973. Signed as a free agent by **Detroit**, June 12, 1989.

SALO, VESA

Defense. Shoots left. 6'3", 200 lbs. Born, Rauma, Finland, April 17, 1965.
(NY Rangers' 3rd choice, 49th overall, in 1983 Entry Draft).

			Regular Season					Playoffs				
Season	Club	Lea	GP	G	A	TP	PIM	GP	G	A	TP	PIM
1982-83	Lukko	Fin.	36	2	9	11	14	....	....	....	....	....
1983-84	Lukko	Fin.	36	4	15	19	16	5	1	3	4	4
1984-85	Lukko	Fin.	35	13	8	21	20	....	....	....	....	....
1985-86	Lukko	Fin.	30	1	8	9	8	....	....	....	....	....
1986-87	Lukko	Fin.	44	4	22	26	34	....	....	....	....	....
1987-88	Ilves	Fin.	43	8	15	23	42	4	0	1	1	4
1988-89	Tappara	Fin.	42	7	14	21	46	8	0	2	2	8

SAMUELSSON, KJELL (SHELL)

Defense. Shoots right. 6'6", 235 lbs. Born, Tingsryd, Sweden, October 18, 1956.
(NY Rangers' 5th choice, 119th overall, in 1984 Entry Draft).

			Regular Season					Playoffs				
Season	Club	Lea	GP	G	A	TP	PIM	GP	G	A	TP	PIM
1977-78	Tingsryd	Swe. 2	20	3	0	3	41	....	....	....	....	....
1978-79	Tingsryd	Swe. 2	24	3	4	7	67	....	....	....	....	....
1979-80	Tingsryd	Swe. 2	26	5	4	9	45	....	....	....	....	....
1980-81	Tingsryd	Swe. 2	35	6	7	13	61	2	0	1	1	14
1981-82	Tingsryd	Swe. 2	33	11	14	25	68	3	0	2	2	2
1982-83	Tingsryd	Swe. 2	32	11	6	17	57	....	....	....	....	....
1983-84	Leksand	Swe.	36	6	6	12	59	....	....	....	....	....
1984-85	Leksand	Swe.	35	9	5	14	34	....	....	....	....	....
1985-86	New Haven	AHL	56	6	21	27	87	3	0	0	0	10
	NY Rangers	**NHL**	**9**	**0**	**0**	**0**	**10**	**9**	**0**	**1**	**1**	**8**
1986-87	**NY Rangers**	**NHL**	**30**	**2**	**6**	**8**	**50**	....	....	....	....	....
	Philadelphia	**NHL**	**46**	**1**	**6**	**7**	**86**	**26**	**0**	**4**	**4**	**25**
1987-88	**Philadelphia**	**NHL**	**74**	**6**	**24**	**30**	**184**	**7**	**2**	**5**	**7**	**23**
1988-89	**Philadelphia**	**NHL**	**69**	**3**	**14**	**17**	**140**	**19**	**1**	**3**	**4**	**24**
	NHL Totals		**228**	**12**	**50**	**62**	**470**	**61**	**3**	**13**	**16**	**80**

Played in NHL All-Star Game (1988)

Traded to **Philadelphia** by **NY Rangers** with NY Rangers' second-round choice (Patrik Juhlin) in 1989 Entry Draft for Bob Froese, December 18, 1986.

SAMUELSSON, MORGAN

Left wing. Shoots left. 5'9", 165 lbs. Born, Boden, Sweden, April 6, 1968.
(Quebec's 7th choice, 123rd overall, in 1986 Entry Draft).

			Regular Season					Playoffs				
Season	Club	Lea	GP	G	A	TP	PIM	GP	G	A	TP	PIM
1988-89	Lulea	Swe.	36	14	19	33	14	....	....	....	....	....

SAMUELSSON, ULF

Defense. Shoots left. 6'1", 195 lbs. Born, Fagersta, Sweden, March 26, 1964.
(Hartford's 4th choice, 67th over-all, in 1982 Entry Draft).

			Regular Season					Playoffs				
Season	Club	Lea	GP	G	A	TP	PIM	GP	G	A	TP	PIM
1981-82	Leksand	Swe.	31	3	1	4	40	....	....	....	....	....
1982-83	Leksand	Swe.	33	9	6	15	72	....	....	....	....	....
1983-84	Leksand	Swe.	36	5	11	16	53	....	....	....	....	....
1984-85	**Hartford**	**NHL**	**41**	**2**	**6**	**8**	**83**	....	....	....	....	....
	Binghamton	AHL	36	5	11	16	92	....	....	....	....	....
1985-86	**Hartford**	**NHL**	**80**	**5**	**19**	**24**	**174**	**10**	**1**	**2**	**3**	**38**
1986-87	**Hartford**	**NHL**	**78**	**2**	**31**	**33**	**162**	**5**	**0**	**1**	**1**	**41**
1987-88	**Hartford**	**NHL**	**76**	**8**	**33**	**41**	**159**	**5**	**0**	**0**	**0**	**8**
1988-89	**Hartford**	**NHL**	**71**	**9**	**26**	**35**	**181**	**4**	**0**	**2**	**2**	**4**
	NHL Totals		**346**	**26**	**115**	**141**	**759**	**24**	**1**	**5**	**6**	**91**

SANDELIN, SCOTT

Defense. Shoots right. 6', 180 lbs. Born, Hibbing, MN, August 8, 1964.
(Montreal's 5th choice, 48th over-all, in 1982 Entry Draft).

			Regular Season					Playoffs				
Season	Club	Lea	GP	G	A	TP	PIM	GP	G	A	TP	PIM
1981-82	Hibbing	HS	20	5	15	20	30	....	....	....	....	....
1982-83	North Dakota	WCHA	21	0	4	4	10	....	....	....	....	....
1983-84	North Dakota	WCHA	41	4	23	27	24	....	....	....	....	....
1984-85	North Dakota	WCHA	38	4	17	21	30	....	....	....	....	....
1985-86ab	North Dakota	WCHA	40	7	31	38	38	....	....	....	....	....
	Sherbrooke	AHL	6	0	2	2	2	....	....	....	....	....
1986-87	**Montreal**	**NHL**	**1**	**0**	**0**	**0**	**0**	....	....	....	....	....
	Sherbrooke	AHL	74	7	22	29	35	16	2	4	6	2
1987-88	**Montreal**	**NHL**	**8**	**0**	**1**	**1**	**2**	....	....	....	....	....
	Sherbrooke	AHL	58	8	14	22	35	4	0	2	2	0
1988-89	Sherbrooke	AHL	12	0	9	9	8	....	....	....	....	....
	Hershey	AHL	39	6	9	15	38	8	2	1	3	4
	NHL Totals		**9**	**0**	**1**	**1**	**2**	....	....	....	....	....

a NCAA West Second All-Star Team (1986)
b WCHA First All-Star Team (1986).

Traded to **Philadelphia** by **Montreal** for the rights to J.J. Daigneault, November 7, 1988.

SANDLAK, JIM

Right wing. Shoots right. 6'4", 219 lbs. Born, Kitchener, Ont., December 12, 1966.
(Vancouver's 1st choice, 4th over-all, in 1985 Entry Draft)

			Regular Season					Playoffs				
Season	Club	Lea	GP	G	A	TP	PIM	GP	G	A	TP	PIM
1983-84	London	OHL	68	23	18	41	143	8	1	11	12	13
1984-85a	London	OHL	58	40	24	64	128	8	3	2	5	14
1985-86	**Vancouver**	**NHL**	**23**	**1**	**3**	**4**	**10**	**3**	**0**	**1**	**1**	**0**
	London	OHL	16	8	14	22	38	5	2	3	5	24
1986-87b	**Vancouver**	**NHL**	**78**	**15**	**21**	**36**	**66**	....	....	....	....	....
1987-88	**Vancouver**	**NHL**	**49**	**16**	**15**	**31**	**81**					
	Fredericton	AHL	24	10	15	25	47	....	....	....	....	....
1988-89	**Vancouver**	**NHL**	**72**	**20**	**20**	**40**	**99**	**6**	**1**	**1**	**2**	**2**
	NHL Totals		**222**	**52**	**59**	**111**	**256**	**9**	**1**	**2**	**3**	**2**

a OHL Third All-Star Team (1985)
b NHL All-Rookie Team (1987)

SANDSTROM, TOMAS

Right wing. Shoots left. 6'2", 200 lbs. Born, Jakobstad, Finland, September 4, 1964.
(NY Rangers' 2nd choice, 36th over-all, in 1982 Entry Draft).

			Regular Season					Playoffs				
Season	Club	Lea	GP	G	A	TP	PIM	GP	G	A	TP	PIM
1981-82	Fagersta	Swe. 2	32	28	11	39	74	....	....	....	....	....
1982-83	Brynas	Swe.	36	23	14	37	50	....	....	....	....	....
1983-84	Brynas	Swe.	34	19	16	29	81	....	....	....	....	....
1982-83	Brynas	Swe.	36	22	14	36	36	....	....	....	....	....
1983-84	Brynas	Swe.	43	20	10	30	81	....	....	....	....	....
1984-85a	**NY Rangers**	**NHL**	**74**	**29**	**29**	**58**	**51**	**3**	**0**	**2**	**2**	**0**
1985-86	**NY Rangers**	**NHL**	**73**	**25**	**29**	**54**	**109**	**16**	**4**	**6**	**10**	**20**
1986-87	**NY Rangers**	**NHL**	**64**	**40**	**34**	**74**	**60**	**6**	**1**	**2**	**3**	**20**
1987-88	**NY Rangers**	**NHL**	**69**	**28**	**40**	**68**	**95**					
1988-89	**NY Rangers**	**NHL**	**79**	**32**	**56**	**88**	**148**	**4**	**3**	**2**	**5**	**12**
	NHL Totals		**359**	**154**	**188**	**342**	**463**	**29**	**8**	**12**	**20**	**52**

a NHL All-Rookie Team (1985)

Played in NHL All-Star Game (1988)

SANDSTROM, ULF

Right wing. Shoots right. 5'10", 180 lbs. Born, Harnosand, Sweden, April 24, 1967.
(Chicago's 5th choice, 92nd overall, in 1987 Entry Draft).

			Regular Season					Playoffs				
Season	Club	Lea	GP	G	A	TP	PIM	GP	G	A	TP	PIM
1986-87	MoDo	Swe.	25	2	4	6	14	6	3	0	3	0
1987-88	MoDo	Swe.	38	26	9	35	12	....	....	....	....	....
1988-89	MoDo	Swe.	39	19	14	33	16	....	....	....	....	....

SANIPASS, EVERETT

Left wing. Shoots left. 6'1", 190 lbs. Born, Big Cove, N.B., February 13, 1968.
(Chicago's 1st choice, 14th overall, in 1986 Entry Draft).

			Regular Season					Playoffs				
Season	Club	Lea	GP	G	A	TP	PIM	GP	G	A	TP	PIM
1985-86	Verdun	QMJHL	67	23	66	89	320	5	0	2	2	16
1986-87	**Chicago**	**NHL**	**7**	**1**	**3**	**4**	**2**	....	....	....	....	....
a	Granby	QMJHL	35	34	48	82	220	8	6	4	10	48
1987-88	**Chicago**	**NHL**	**57**	**8**	**12**	**20**	**126**	**2**	**2**	**0**	**2**	**2**
1988-89	**Chicago**	**NHL**	**50**	**6**	**9**	**15**	**164**	**3**	**0**	**0**	**0**	**2**
	Saginaw	IHL	23	9	12	21	76	....	....	....	....	....
	NHL Totals		**114**	**15**	**24**	**39**	**292**	**5**	**2**	**0**	**2**	**4**

a QMJHL First All-Star Team (1987)

SAPERGIA, BRENT

Right wing. Shoots right. 5'10", 195 lbs. Born, Moose Jaw, Sask. November 16, 1962.

			Regular Season					Playoffs				
Season	Club	Lea	GP	G	A	TP	PIM	GP	G	A	TP	PIM
1984-85	Salt Lake	IHL	76	47	47	94	36	7	2	7	9	15
1985-86	Salt Lake	IHL	80	58	65	123	127	1	0	1	1	2
1986-87	Kalpa	Fin.	33	25	13	38	117	....	....	....	....	....
	New Haven	AHL	2	0	1	1	0	....	....	....	....	....
1987-88	Salt Lake	IHL	22	10	6	16	22	9	0	1	1	9
1988-89	Indianapolis	IHL	52	43	33	76	246	....	....	....	....	....

Signed as a free agent by **NY Rangers**, March 6, 1987.

SAUNDERS, DAVID

Left wing. Shoots left. 6'1", 195 lbs.   Born, Ottawa, Ont., May 20, 1966.
(Vancouver's 3rd choice, 52nd overall, in 1984 Entry Draft).

			Regular Season					Playoffs				
Season	Club	Lea	GP	G	A	TP	PIM	GP	G	A	TP	PIM
1983-84	St. Lawrence	ECAC	32	10	21	31	24	.....	.....	.....	.....	.....
1984-85	St. Lawrence	ECAC	27	7	9	16	16	.....	.....	.....	.....	.....
1985-86	St. Lawrence	ECAC	29	15	19	34	26	.....	.....	.....	.....	.....
1986-87	St. Lawrence	ECAC	34	18	34	52	44	.....	.....	.....	.....	.....
1987-88	**Vancouver**	**NHL**	56	7	13	20	10	.....	.....	.....	.....	.....
	Fredericton	AHL	14	9	7	16	6	8	1	0	1	12
	Flint	IHL	8	5	5	10	2	.....	.....	.....	.....	.....
1988-89	Milwaukee	IHL	21	6	12	18	21	.....	.....	.....	.....	.....
	Cdn. National	....	6	1	3	4	2	.....	.....	.....	.....	.....
	NHL Totals		56	7	13	20	10	.....	.....	.....	.....	.....

SAVAGE, JOEL

Right wing. Shoots right. 6', 195 lbs.   Born, Surrey, B.C., December 25, 1969.
(Buffalo's 1st choice, 13th overall, in 1988 Entry Draft).

			Regular Season					Playoffs				
Season	Club	Lea	GP	G	A	TP	PIM	GP	G	A	TP	PIM
1986-87	Victoria	WHL	68	14	13	27	48	5	2	0	2	0
1987-88	Victoria	WHL	69	37	32	69	73	.....	.....	.....	.....	.....
1988-89	Victoria	WHL	60	17	30	47	95	6	1	1	2	8

SAVAGE, REGINALD (REGGIE)

Center. Shoots left. 5'10", 180 lbs.   Born, Montreal, Que., May 1, 1970.
(Washington's 1st choice, 15th overall, in 1988 Entry Draft).

			Regular Season					Playoffs				
Season	Club	Lea	GP	G	A	TP	PIM	GP	G	A	TP	PIM
1986-87	Richelieu	Midget	42	82	57	139	44	.....	.....	.....	.....	.....
1987-88	Victoriaville	QMJHL	68	68	54	122	77	5	2	3	5	8
1988-89	Victoriaville	QMJHL	54	58	55	113	178	16	15	13	28	52

SAVARD, DENIS JOSEPH   (sa-VARH, den-NY)

Center. Shoots right. 5'10", 175 lbs.   Born, Pointe Gatineau, Que., February 4, 1961.
(Chicago's 1st choice, 3rd over-all, in 1980 Entry Draft).

			Regular Season					Playoffs				
Season	Club	Lea	GP	G	A	TP	PIM	GP	G	A	TP	PIM
1978-79	Montreal	QJHL	70	46	*112	158	88	11	5	6	11	46
1979-80ab	Montreal	QJHL	72	63	118	181	93	10	7	16	23	8
1980-81	**Chicago**	**NHL**	76	28	47	75	47	3	0	0	0	0
1981-82	**Chicago**	**NHL**	80	32	87	119	82	15	11	7	18	52
1982-83c	**Chicago**	**NHL**	78	35	86	121	99	13	8	9	17	22
1983-84	**Chicago**	**NHL**	75	37	57	94	71	5	1	3	4	9
1984-85	**Chicago**	**NHL**	79	38	67	105	56	15	9	20	29	20
1985-86	**Chicago**	**NHL**	80	47	69	116	111	3	4	1	5	6
1986-87	**Chicago**	**NHL**	70	40	50	90	108	4	1	0	1	12
1987-88	**Chicago**	**NHL**	80	44	87	131	95	5	4	3	7	17
1988-89	**Chicago**	**NHL**	58	23	59	82	110	16	8	11	19	10
	NHL Totals		676	324	609	933	779	79	46	54	100	148

a QMJHL First All-Star Team (1980).
b Named QMJHL's Most Valuable Player (1980).
c NHL Second All-Star Team (1983).
Played in NHL All-Star Game (1982-84, 1986, 1988)

SCHEIFELE, STEVE

Right wing. Shoots right. 6', 185 lbs.   Born, Alexandria, VA, April 18, 1968.
(Philadelphia's 5th choice, 125th overall, in 1986 Entry Draft).

			Regular Season					Playoffs				
Season	Club	Lea	GP	G	A	TP	PIM	GP	G	A	TP	PIM
1985-86	Stratford	OPJHL	40	41	39	80	84	.....	.....	.....	.....	.....
1986-87	Boston College	H.E.	38	13	13	26	28	.....	.....	.....	.....	.....
1987-88	Boston College	H.E.	30	11	16	27	22	.....	.....	.....	.....	.....
1988-89	Boston College	H.E.	40	24	14	38	30	.....	.....	.....	.....	.....

SCHENA, ROB

Defense. Shoots left. 6'1", 190 lbs.   Born, Saugas, MA, February 5, 1967.
(Detroit's 9th choice, 176th overall, in 1985 Entry Draft).

			Regular Season					Playoffs				
Season	Club	Lea	GP	G	A	TP	PIM	GP	G	A	TP	PIM
1986-87	RPI	ECAC	30	1	9	10	32	.....	.....	.....	.....	.....
1987-88	RPI	ECAC	30	5	9	14	56	.....	.....	.....	.....	.....
1988-89	RPI	ECAC	32	7	5	12	64	.....	.....	.....	.....	.....
	Adirondack	AHL	9	1	1	2	2	.....	.....	.....	.....	.....

SCHLEGEL, BRAD

Defense. Shoots right. 5'10", 180 lbs.   Born, Kitchener, Ont., July 22, 1968.
(Washington's 8th choice, 144th overall, in 1988 Entry Draft).

			Regular Season					Playoffs				
Season	Club	Lea	GP	G	A	TP	PIM	GP	G	A	TP	PIM
1986-87	London	OHL	65	4	23	27	24	.....	.....	.....	.....	.....
1987-88a	London	OHL	66	13	63	76	49	12	8	17	25	6
1988-89	Cdn. National	....	60	2	22	24	30	.....	.....	.....	.....	.....

a OHL Second All-Star Team (1988)

SCHMIDT, DONALD (DON)

Defense. Shoots left. 5'10", 185 lbs.   Born, Fort Saskatchewan, Alta., July 13, 1968.
(Minnesota's 8th choice, 151st overall, in 1987 Entry Draft).

			Regular Season					Playoffs				
Season	Club	Lea	GP	G	A	TP	PIM	GP	G	A	TP	PIM
1984-85	Prince Albert	WHL	52	3	14	17	159	5	0	0	0	8
1985-86	Prince Albert	WHL	14	0	2	2	48	.....	.....	.....	.....	.....
	Kamloops	WHL	29	2	5	7	168	12	0	4	4	57
1986-87	Prince Albert	WHL	49	5	21	26	248	13	2	2	4	34
1987-88	Kamloops	WHL	54	5	28	33	208	16	6	7	13	52
1988-89	Kamloops	WHL	35	5	9	14	135	.....	.....	.....	.....	.....

SCHNEIDER, MATHIEU

Defense. Shoots left. 5'11", 180 lbs.   Born, Woonsockett, RI, June 12, 1969.
(Montreal's 4th choice, 44th overall, in 1987 Entry Draft).

			Regular Season					Playoffs				
Season	Club	Lea	GP	G	A	TP	PIM	GP	G	A	TP	PIM
1986-87	Cornwall	OHL	63	7	29	36	75	5	0	0	0	22
1987-88	**Montreal**	**NHL**	4	0	0	0	2	.....	.....	.....	.....	.....
	Sherbrooke	AHL	.....	.....	.....	.....	.....	3	0	3	3	12
a	Cornwall	OHL	48	21	40	61	83	11	2	6	8	14
1988-89	Cornwall	OHL	59	16	57	73	96	18	7	20	27	30
	NHL Totals		4	0	0	0	2	.....	.....	.....	.....	.....

a OHL First All-Star Team (1988)

SCHNEIDER, SCOTT

Center. Shoots right. 6'1", 175 lbs.   Born, Rochester, MN, May 18, 1965.
(Winnipeg's 4th choice, 93rd overall, in 1984 Entry Draft).

			Regular Season					Playoffs				
Season	Club	Lea	GP	G	A	TP	PIM	GP	G	A	TP	PIM
1983-84	Colorado	WCHA	35	19	14	33	24	.....	.....	.....	.....	.....
1984-85	Colorado	WCHA	33	16	13	29	60	.....	.....	.....	.....	.....
1985-86	Colorado	WCHA	40	16	22	38	32	.....	.....	.....	.....	.....
1986-87	Colorado	WCHA	42	21	22	43	36	.....	.....	.....	.....	.....
1987-88	Moncton	AHL	68	12	23	35	28	.....	.....	.....	.....	.....
1988-89	Moncton	AHL	64	29	36	65	51	6	2	6	8	4

SCHOFIELD, DAVID

Center. Shoots right. 6'1", 185 lbs.   Born Wayland, MA, February 17, 1965.
(Minnesota's 2nd choice, 6th overall, in 1988 Supplemental Draft).

			Regular Season					Playoffs				
Season	Club	Lea	GP	G	A	TP	PIM	GP	G	A	TP	PIM
1984-85	Merrimack	NCAA	31	5	19	24	24	.....	.....	.....	.....	.....
1985-86	Merrimack	NCAA	12	3	5	8	18	.....	.....	.....	.....	.....
1986-87	Merrimack	NCAA	14	4	10	14	14	.....	.....	.....	.....	.....
1987-88	Merrimack	NCAA	40	12	40	52	76	.....	.....	.....	.....	.....
1988-89	Kalamazoo	IHL	24	1	6	7	30	.....	.....	.....	.....	.....

SCHREIBER, WALLY

Right wing. Shoots right. 5'11", 180 lbs.   Born, Edmonton, Alta., April 15, 1962.
(Washington's 5th choice, 152nd overall, in 1982 Entry Draft).

			Regular Season					Playoffs				
Season	Club	Lea	GP	G	A	TP	PIM	GP	G	A	TP	PIM
1981-82	Regina	WHL	68	56	68	124	68	20	12	12	24	34
1982-83	Fort Wayne	IHL	67	24	34	58	23	.....	.....	.....	.....	.....
1983-84	Fort Wayne	IHL	82	47	66	113	44	6	3	3	6	6
1984-85	Fort Wayne	IHL	81	51	58	109	45	13	3	7	10	10
1985-86	Fort Wayne	IHL	72	35	51	86	35	15	10	8	18	6
1986-87	Cdn. Olympic	....	70	40	37	77	27	.....	.....	.....	.....	.....
1987-88	**Minnesota**	**NHL**	16	6	5	11	2	.....	.....	.....	.....	.....
	Cdn. National	....	61	24	15	39	34	.....	.....	.....	.....	.....
	Cdn. Olympic	....	8	1	2	3	2	.....	.....	.....	.....	.....
1988-89	**Minnesota**	**NHL**	25	2	5	7	10	.....	.....	.....	.....	.....
	Fort Wayne	IHL	32	15	16	31	51	.....	.....	.....	.....	.....
	Kalamazoo	IHL	5	5	7	12	2	.....	.....	.....	.....	.....
	NHL Totals		41	8	10	18	12	.....	.....	.....	.....	.....

Signed as a free agent by **Minnesota**, May 26, 1987.

SCOTT, KEVIN

Center. Shoots left. 5'10", 170 lbs.   Born, Vernon, B.C., November 3, 1967.
(Detroit's 9th choice, 158th overall, in 1987 Entry Draft).

			Regular Season					Playoffs				
Season	Club	Lea	GP	G	A	TP	PIM	GP	G	A	TP	PIM
1986-87	Vernon	BCJHL	38	56	70	126	50	.....	.....	.....	.....	.....
1987-88	N. Michigan	WCHA	36	9	12	21	42	.....	.....	.....	.....	.....
1988-89	N. Michigan	WCHA	40	11	14	25	36	.....	.....	.....	.....	.....

SCREMIN, CLAUDIO

Defense. Shoots right. 6'2", 205 lbs.   Born, Burnaby, B.C., May 28, 1968.
(Washington's 12th choice, 204th overall, in 1988 Entry Draft).

			Regular Season					Playoffs				
Season	Club	Lea	GP	G	A	TP	PIM	GP	G	A	TP	PIM
1986-87	U. of Maine	H.E.	15	0	1	1	2	.....	.....	.....	.....	.....
1987-88	U. of Maine	H.E.	44	6	18	24	22	.....	.....	.....	.....	.....
1988-89	U. of Maine	H.E.	45	5	24	29	42	.....	.....	.....	.....	.....

Traded to **Minnesota** by **Washington** for Don Beaupre, November 1, 1988.

SEABROOKE, GLEN

Center. Shoots left. 6', 190 lbs.   Born, Peterborough, Ont., September 11, 1967.
(Philadelphia's 1st choice, 21st over-all, in 1985 Entry Draft).

			Regular Season					Playoffs				
Season	Club	Lea	GP	G	A	TP	PIM	GP	G	A	TP	PIM
1983-84	Peterborough	Midget	29	36	31	67	31	.....	.....	.....	.....	.....
1984-85	Peterborough	OHL	45	21	13	34	49	16	3	5	8	4
1985-86	Peterborough	OHL	19	8	12	20	33	14	9	7	16	14
1986-87	**Philadelphia**	**NHL**	10	1	4	5	2	.....	.....	.....	.....	.....
	Peterborough	OHL	48	30	39	69	29	4	3	3	6	6
1987-88	**Philadelphia**	**NHL**	6	0	1	1	2	.....	.....	.....	.....	.....
	Hershey	AHL	73	32	46	78	39	7	4	5	9	2
1988-89	**Philadelphia**	**NHL**	3	0	1	1	0	.....	.....	.....	.....	.....
	Hershey	AHL	51	23	15	38	19	.....	.....	.....	.....	.....
	NHL Totals		19	1	6	7	4	.....	.....	.....	.....	.....

SECORD, ALAN WILLIAM (AL) **(SEE-cord)**

Left wing. Shoots left. 6'1", 205 lbs. Born, Sudbury, Ont., March 3, 1958.
(Boston's 1st choice, 16th over-all, in 1978 Amateur Draft).

			Regular Season					Playoffs				
Season	**Club**	**Lea**	**GP**	**G**	**A**	**TP**	**PIM**	**GP**	**G**	**A**	**TP**	**PIM**
1976-77	St. Catharines	OHA	57	32	34	66	343	14	4	3	7	46
1977-78	Hamilton	OHA	59	28	22	50	185	20	8	11	19	71
1978-79	Rochester	AHL	4	4	2	6	40	....	....	....	....	....
	Boston	**NHL**	**71**	**16**	**7**	**23**	**125**	**4**	**0**	**0**	**0**	**4**
1979-80	**Boston**	**NHL**	**77**	**23**	**16**	**39**	**170**	**10**	**0**	**3**	**3**	**65**
1980-81	Springfield	AHL	8	3	5	8	21	....	....	....	....	....
	Boston	**NHL**	**18**	**0**	**3**	**3**	**42**	....	....	....	....	....
	Chicago	**NHL**	**41**	**13**	**9**	**22**	**145**	**3**	**4**	**0**	**4**	**14**
1981-82	**Chicago**	**NHL**	**80**	**44**	**31**	**75**	**303**	**15**	**2**	**5**	**7**	**61**
1982-83	**Chicago**	**NHL**	**80**	**54**	**32**	**86**	**180**	**12**	**4**	**7**	**11**	**66**
1983-84	**Chicago**	**NHL**	**14**	**4**	**4**	**8**	**77**	**5**	**3**	**4**	**7**	**28**
1984-85	**Chicago**	**NHL**	**51**	**15**	**11**	**26**	**193**	**15**	**7**	**9**	**16**	**42**
1985-86	**Chicago**	**NHL**	**80**	**40**	**36**	**76**	**201**	**2**	**0**	**2**	**2**	**26**
1986-87	**Chicago**	**NHL**	**77**	**29**	**29**	**58**	**196**	**4**	**0**	**0**	**0**	**21**
1987-88	**Toronto**	**NHL**	**74**	**15**	**27**	**42**	**221**	**6**	**1**	**0**	**1**	**16**
1988-89	**Toronto**	**NHL**	**40**	**5**	**10**	**15**	**71**	....	....	....	....	....
	Philadelphia	**NHL**	**20**	**1**	**0**	**1**	**38**	**14**	**0**	**4**	**4**	**31**
	NHL Totals		**723**	**259**	**215**	**474**	**1962**	**90**	**21**	**34**	**55**	**374**

Played in NHL All-Star Game (1982, 1983)

Traded to **Chicago** by **Boston** for Mike O'Connell, December 18, 1980. Traded to **Tornoto** by **Chicago** with Ed Olczyk for Rick Vaive, Steve Thomas and Bob McGill, September 3, 1987. Traded to **Philadelphia** by **Toronto** for Philadelphia's fifth-round choice (Keith Carney) in 1989 Entry Draft, February 7, 1989. Signed as a free agent by **Chicago**, August 7, 1989.

SEFTEL, STEVE

Left wing. Shoots left. 6'3", 200 lbs. Born, Kitchener, Ont., May 14, 1968.
(Washington's 2nd choice, 40th overall, in 1986 Entry Draft).

			Regular Season					Playoffs				
Season	**Club**	**Lea**	**GP**	**G**	**A**	**TP**	**PIM**	**GP**	**G**	**A**	**TP**	**PIM**
1985-86	Kingston	OHL	42	11	16	27	53	....	....	....	....	....
1986-87	Kingston	OHL	54	21	43	64	55	12	1	4	5	9
1987-88	Binghamton	AHL	3	0	0	0	2	....	....	....	....	....
	Kingston	OHL	66	32	43	75	51					
1988-89	Binghamton	AHL	58	12	15	27	70	....	....	....	....	....

SEJBA, JIRI

Left wing. Shoots left. 5'10", 185 lbs. Born, Pardubice, Czech., July 22, 1962.
(Buffalo's 9th choice, 182nd overall, in 1985 Entry Draft).

			Regular Season					Playoffs				
Season	**Club**	**Lea**	**GP**	**G**	**A**	**TP**	**PIM**	**GP**	**G**	**A**	**TP**	**PIM**
1986-87	Pardubice	Czech.	34	23	11	34	....	....	....	....	....	
1987-88	Pardubice	Czech.	23	10	15	25	....	....	....	....	....	....
1988-89	Pardubice	Czech.	44	38	21	59	68	....	....	....	....	....

SELANNE, TEEMU

Right wing. Shoots right. 6', 175 lbs. Born, Helsinki, Finland, March 7, 1970.
(Winnipeg's 1st choice, 10th overall, in 1988 Entry Draft).

			Regular Season					Playoffs				
Season	**Club**	**Lea**	**GP**	**G**	**A**	**TP**	**PIM**	**GP**	**G**	**A**	**TP**	**PIM**
1986-87	Jokerit	Fin. Jr.	33	10	12	22	8	....	....	....	....	....
1987-88	Jokerit	Fin. Jr.	33	43	23	66	18	5	4	3	7	2
	Jokerit	Fin. 2	5	1	1	2	0	....	....	....	....	....
1988-89	Jokerit	Fin.	34	35	33	68	12	5	7	3	10	4

SEMAK, ALEXANDER

Center. Shoots left. 5'9", 190 lbs. Born, Ufa, Soviet Union, February 11, 1968.
(New Jersey's 12th choice, 207th overall, in 1988 Entry Draft).

			Regular Season					Playoffs				
Season	**Club**	**Lea**	**GP**	**G**	**A**	**TP**	**PIM**	**GP**	**G**	**A**	**TP**	**PIM**
1987-88	Moscow D'amo	USSR	47	21	14	35	40	....	....	....	....	....
1988-89	Moscow D'amo	USSR	44	18	10	28	22	....	....	....	....	....

SEPPO, JUKKA PEKKA

Center/left wing. Shoots left. 6'2", 190 lbs. Born, Vaasa, Finland, January 22, 1968.
(Philadelphia's 2nd choice, 23rd overall, in 1986 Entry Draft).

			Regular Season					Playoffs				
Season	**Club**	**Lea**	**GP**	**G**	**A**	**TP**	**PIM**	**GP**	**G**	**A**	**TP**	**PIM**
1985-86	Vaasa Sport	Fin.	21	20	30	50	46	....	....	....	....	....
1986-87	Tappara	Fin.	39	11	16	27	50	....	....	....	....	....
1987-88	Vaasa Sport	Fin.	42	28	37	65	78	....	....	....	....	....
1988-89	IFK Helsinki	Fin.	35	7	13	20	28	....	....	....	....	....

SEROWICK, JEFF

Defense. Shoots right. 6', 190 lbs. Born, Manchester, NH, October 1, 1967.
(Toronto's 5th choice, 85th overall, in 1985 Entry Draft).

			Regular Season					Playoffs				
Season	**Club**	**Lea**	**GP**	**G**	**A**	**TP**	**PIM**	**GP**	**G**	**A**	**TP**	**PIM**
1986-87	Providence	H.E.	33	3	8	11	22	....	....	....	....	....
1987-88	Providence	H.E.	33	3	9	12	44	....	....	....	....	....
1988-89	Providence	H.E.	35	3	14	17	48	....	....	....	....	....

SEVCIK, JAROSLAV **(SEV-chik, YAR-o-slav)**

Left wing. Shoots right. 5'9", 170 lbs. Born, Brno, Czechoslovakia, May 15, 1965.
(Quebec's 9th choice, 177th overall, in 1987 Entry Draft).

			Regular Season					Playoffs				
Season	**Club**	**Lea**	**GP**	**G**	**A**	**TP**	**PIM**	**GP**	**G**	**A**	**TP**	**PIM**
1986-87	Zetor Brno	Czech.	34	12	5	17	....	....	....	....	....	....
1987-88	Fredericton	AHL	32	9	7	16	6	....	....	....	....	....
1988-89	Halifax	AHL	78	17	41	58	17	4	1	1	2	2

SEVERYN, BRENT

Defense. Shoots left. 6'2", 210 lbs. Born, Vegreville, Alta., February 22, 1966.

			Regular Season					Playoffs				
Season	**Club**	**Lea**	**GP**	**G**	**A**	**TP**	**PIM**	**GP**	**G**	**A**	**TP**	**PIM**
1987-88	U. of Alberta	CWUAA	46	21	29	50	178	....	....	....	....	....
1988-89	Halifax	AHL	47	2	12	14	141	....	....	....	....	....

Signed as a free agent by **Quebec**, July 15, 1988.

SEVIGNY, PIERRE

Left wing. Shoots left. 5'11", 180 lbs. Born, Trois-Rivieres, Que., September 8, 1971.
(Montreal's 4th choice, 51st overall, in 1989 Entry Draft).

			Regular Season					Playoffs				
Season	**Club**	**Lea**	**GP**	**G**	**A**	**TP**	**PIM**	**GP**	**G**	**A**	**TP**	**PIM**
1987-88	Magog	Midget	40	43	78	121	72	....	....	....	....	....
1988-89	Verdun	QMJHL	67	27	43	70	88	....	....	....	....	....

SEXSMITH, DEAN

Center. Shoots left. 6'1", 190 lbs. Born, Virden, Man., May 13, 1968.
(NY Islanders' 5th choice, 101st overall, in 1986 Entry Draft).

			Regular Season					Playoffs				
Season	**Club**	**Lea**	**GP**	**G**	**A**	**TP**	**PIM**	**GP**	**G**	**A**	**TP**	**PIM**
1985-86	Brandon	WHL	65	13	23	36	34	....	....	....	....	....
1986-87	Seattle	WHL	65	14	24	38	46	....	....	....	....	....
1987-88	Saskatoon	WHL	74	25	35	60	47	10	0	3	3	0
1988-89	Spokane	WHL	59	26	36	62	71	....	....	....	....	....

SHANAHAN, BRENDAN

Center. Shoots right. 6'3", 205 lbs. Born, Mimico, Ont., January 23, 1969.
(New Jersey's 1st choice, 2nd overall, in 1987 Entry Draft).

			Regular Season					Playoffs				
Season	**Club**	**Lea**	**GP**	**G**	**A**	**TP**	**PIM**	**GP**	**G**	**A**	**TP**	**PIM**
1985-86	London	OHL	59	28	34	62	70	5	5	5	10	5
1986-87	London	OHL	56	39	53	92	92	....	....	....	....	....
1987-88	**New Jersey**	**NHL**	**65**	**7**	**19**	**26**	**131**	**12**	**2**	**1**	**3**	**44**
1988-89	**New Jersey**	**NHL**	**68**	**22**	**28**	**50**	**115**	....	....	....	....	....
	NHL Totals		**133**	**29**	**47**	**76**	**246**	**12**	**2**	**1**	**3**	**44**

SHANK, DANIEL

Right wing. Shoots right. 5'10", 190 lbs. Born, Montreal, Que., May 12, 1967.

			Regular Season					Playoffs				
Season	**Club**	**Lea**	**GP**	**G**	**A**	**TP**	**PIM**	**GP**	**G**	**A**	**TP**	**PIM**
1986-87	Hull	QMJHL	46	26	43	69	325	....	....	....	....	....
1987-88	Hull	QMJHL	42	23	34	57	274	5	3	2	5	16
1988-89	Adirondack	AHL	42	5	20	25	113	17	11	8	19	102

Signed as a free agent by **Detroit**, May 26, 1989.

SHANNON, DARRIN

Left wing. Shoots left. 6'2", 190 lbs. Born, Barrie, Ont., December 8, 1969.
(Pittsburgh's 1st choice, 4th overall, in 1988 Entry Draft).

			Regular Season					Playoffs				
Season	**Club**	**Lea**	**GP**	**G**	**A**	**TP**	**PIM**	**GP**	**G**	**A**	**TP**	**PIM**
1986-87	Windsor	OHL	60	16	67	83	116	14	4	6	10	8
1987-88	Windsor	OHL	43	33	41	74	49	12	6	12	18	9
1988-89	Windsor	OHL	54	33	48	81	47	4	1	6	7	2
	Buffalo	**NHL**	**3**	**0**	**0**	**0**	**0**	**2**	**0**	**0**	**0**	**0**
	NHL Totals		**3**	**0**	**0**	**0**	**0**	**2**	**0**	**0**	**0**	**0**

Traded to **Buffalo** by **Pittsburgh** with Doug Bodger for Tom Barrasso and Buffalo's third-round choice in 1990 Entry Draft, November 12, 1988.

SHANNON, DARRYL

Defense. Shoots left. 6'2", 190 lbs. Born, Barrie, Ont., June 21, 1968.
(Toronto's 2nd choice, 36th over-all, in 1986 Entry Draft).

			Regular Season					Playoffs				
Season	**Club**	**Lea**	**GP**	**G**	**A**	**TP**	**PIM**	**GP**	**G**	**A**	**TP**	**PIM**
1985-86	Windsor	OHL	57	6	21	27	52	16	5	6	11	22
1986-87a	Windsor	OHL	64	23	27	50	83	14	4	8	12	18
1987-88b	Windsor	OHL	60	16	67	83	116	12	3	8	11	17
1988-89	**Toronto**	**NHL**	**14**	**1**	**3**	**4**	**6**	....	....	....	....	....
	Newmarket	AHL	61	5	24	29	37	5	0	3	3	10
	NHL Totals		**14**	**1**	**3**	**4**	**6**	....	....	....	....	....

a OHL Second All-Star Team
b OHL First All-Star Team (1988)

SHARPLES, JEFF

Defense. Shoots left. 6'1", 195 lbs. Born, Terrace, B.C., July 28, 1967.
(Detroit's 2nd choice, 29th over-all, in 1985 Entry Draft)

			Regular Season					Playoffs				
Season	**Club**	**Lea**	**GP**	**G**	**A**	**TP**	**PIM**	**GP**	**G**	**A**	**TP**	**PIM**
1983-84	Kelowna	WHL	72	9	24	33	51	....	....	....	....	....
1984-85a	Kelowna	WHL	72	12	41	53	90	6	0	1	1	6
1985-86	Portland	WHL	22	2	6	8	48	15	2	6	8	6
1986-87	**Detroit**	**NHL**	**3**	**0**	**1**	**1**	**2**	**2**	**0**	**0**	**0**	**2**
	Portland	WHL	44	25	35	60	92	20	7	15	22	23
1987-88	**Detroit**	**NHL**	**56**	**10**	**25**	**35**	**42**	**4**	**0**	**3**	**3**	**4**
	Adirondack	AHL	4	2	1	3	4					
1988-89	**Detroit**	**NHL**	**46**	**4**	**9**	**13**	**26**	**1**	**0**	**0**	**0**	**0**
	Adirondack	AHL	10	0	4	4	8	....	....	....	....	....
	NHL Totals		**105**	**14**	**35**	**49**	**70**	**7**	**0**	**3**	**3**	**6**

a WHL Second All-Star Team, West Division (1985)

SHAUNESSY, SCOTT

Left wing. Shoots left. 6'4", 220 lbs. Born, Newport, RI, January 22, 1964.
(Quebec's 9th choice, 192nd over-all, in 1983 Entry Draft).

			Regular Season					Playoffs				
Season	Club	Lea	GP	G	A	TP	PIM	GP	G	A	TP	PIM
1983-84	Boston U.	H.E.	40	6	22	28	48	....	....	....	....	....
1984-85	Boston U.	H.E.	42	7	15	22	87	....	....	....	....	....
1985-86a	Boston U.	H.E.	38	16	13	29	31	....	....	....	....	....
1986-87	**Quebec**	**NHL**	**3**	**0**	**0**	**0**	**7**	....	....	....	....	....
	Boston U.	H.E.	32	2	13	15	71	....	....	....	....	....
1987-88	Fredericton	AHL	60	0	9	9	257	1	0	0	0	2
1988-89	Boston U.	H.E.	11	0	2	2	36	....	....	....	....	....
	Quebec	**NHL**	**4**	**0**	**0**	**0**	**16**	....	....	....	....	....
	Halifax	AHL	41	3	10	13	106	....	....	....	....	....
	NHL Totals		**7**	**0**	**0**	**0**	**23**	....	....	....	....	....

a Hockey East First All-Star Team (1986)

SHAW, BRAD

Defense. Shoots right. 5'11", 170 lbs. Born, Cambridge, Ont., April 28, 1964.
(Detroit's 5th choice, 86th over-all, in 1982 Entry Draft).

			Regular Season					Playoffs				
Season	Club	Lea	GP	G	A	TP	PIM	GP	G	A	TP	PIM
1981-82	Ottawa	OHL	68	13	59	72	24	15	1	13	14	4
1982-83	Ottawa	OHL	63	12	66	78	24	9	2	9	11	4
1983-84a	Ottawa	OHL	68	11	71	82	75	13	2	*27	29	9
1984-85	Binghamton	AHL	24	1	10	11	4	8	1	8	9	6
	Salt Lake	IHL	44	3	29	32	25	....	....	....	....	....
1985-86	**Hartford**	**NHL**	**8**	**0**	**2**	**2**	**4**	....	....	....	....	....
	Binghamton	AHL	64	10	44	54	33	5	0	2	2	6
1986-87	**Hartford**	**NHL**	**2**	**0**	**0**	**0**	**0**	....	....	....	....	....
bc	Binghamton	AHL	77	9	30	39	43	12	1	8	9	2
1987-88	**Hartford**	**NHL**	**1**	**0**	**0**	**0**	**0**	....	....	....	....	....
b	Binghamton	AHL	73	12	50	62	50	4	0	5	5	4
1988-89	Cdn. National	....	4	1	0	1	2	....	....	....	....	....
	Hartford	**NHL**	**3**	**1**	**0**	**1**	**0**	**3**	**1**	**0**	**1**	**0**
	NHL Totals		**14**	**1**	**2**	**3**	**4**	**3**	**1**	**0**	**1**	**0**

a OHL First All-Star Team (1984)
b AHL First All-Star Team (1987, 1988)
c Won Eddie Shore Plaque (AHL Outstanding Defenseman) (1987)

Rights traded to **Hartford** by **Detroit** for Hartford's eighth round choice (Urban Nordin) in 1984 Entry Draft, May 29, 1984.

SHAW, DAVID

Defense. Shoots right. 6'1", 190 lbs. Born, St. Thomas, Ont., May 25, 1964.
(Quebec's 1st choice, 13th over-all, in 1982 Entry Draft).

			Regular Season					Playoffs				
Season	Club	Lea	GP	G	A	TP	PIM	GP	G	A	TP	PIM
1981-82	Kitchener	OHL	68	6	25	31	94	15	2	2	4	51
1982-83	**Quebec**	**NHL**	**2**	**0**	**0**	**0**	**0**	....	....	....	....	....
	Kitchener	OHL	57	18	56	74	78	12	2	10	12	18
1983-84	**Quebec**	**NHL**	**3**	**0**	**0**	**0**	**0**	....	....	....	....	....
a	Kitchener	OHL	58	14	34	48	73	16	4	9	13	12
1984-85	**Quebec**	**NHL**	**14**	**0**	**0**	**0**	**11**	....	....	....	....	....
	Fredericton	AHL	48	7	6	13	73	2	0	0	0	7
1985-86	**Quebec**	**NHL**	**73**	**7**	**19**	**26**	**78**	....	....	....	....	....
1986-87	**Quebec**	**NHL**	**75**	**0**	**19**	**19**	**69**	....	....	....	....	....
1987-88	**NY Rangers**	**NHL**	**68**	**7**	**25**	**32**	**100**	....	....	....	....	....
1988-89	**NY Rangers**	**NHL**	**63**	**6**	**11**	**17**	**88**	**4**	**0**	**2**	**2**	**30**
	NHL Totals		**296**	**20**	**74**	**94**	**346**	**4**	**0**	**2**	**2**	**30**

a OHL First All-Star Team (1984).

Traded to **NY Rangers** by **Quebec** with John Ogrodnick for Jeff Jackson and Terry Carkner, September 30, 1987.

SHEDDEN, DOUGLAS ARTHUR (DOUG)

Center. Shoots right. 6', 185 lbs. Born, Wallaceburg, Ont., April 29, 1961.
(Pittsburgh's 5th choice, 93rd over-all, in 1980 Entry Draft).

			Regular Season					Playoffs				
Season	Club	Lea	GP	G	A	TP	PIM	GP	G	A	TP	PIM
1979-80	Kitchener	OHA	16	10	16	26	26	....	....	....	....	....
	S. S. Marie	OHA	45	30	44	74	59	....	....	....	....	....
1980-81	S. S. Marie	OHA	66	51	72	123	114	19	16	22	38	10
1981-82	Erie	AHL	17	4	6	10	14	....	....	....	....	....
	Pittsburgh	**NHL**	**38**	**10**	**15**	**25**	**12**	....	....	....	....	....
1982-83	**Pittsburgh**	**NHL**	**80**	**24**	**43**	**67**	**54**	....	....	....	....	....
1983-84	**Pittsburgh**	**NHL**	**67**	**22**	**35**	**57**	**20**	....	....	....	....	....
1984-85	**Pittsburgh**	**NHL**	**80**	**35**	**32**	**67**	**30**	....	....	....	....	....
1985-86	**Pittsburgh**	**NHL**	**67**	**32**	**34**	**66**	**32**	....	....	....	....	....
	Detroit	**NHL**	**11**	**2**	**3**	**5**	**2**	....	....	....	....	....
1986-87	**Detroit**	**NHL**	**33**	**6**	**12**	**18**	**6**	....	....	....	....	....
	Adirondack	AHL	5	2	2	4	4	....	....	....	....	....
	Quebec	**NHL**	**16**	**0**	**2**	**2**	**8**	....	....	....	....	....
	Fredericton	AHL	15	12	6	18	0	....	....	....	....	....
1987-88	Baltimore	AHL	80	37	51	88	32	....	....	....	....	....
1988-89	**Toronto**	**NHL**	**1**	**0**	**0**	**0**	**2**	....	....	....	....	....
	Newmarket	AHL	29	14	26	40	6	....	....	....	....	....
	NHL Totals		**393**	**131**	**176**	**307**	**166**	....	....	....	....	....

Traded to **Detroit** by **Pittsburgh** for Ron Duguay, March 11, 1986. Traded to **Quebec** by **Detroit** with Basil McRae and John Ogrodnick for Brent Ashton, Gilbert Delorme and Mark Kumpel, January 17, 1987. Signed as a free agent by **Toronto**, August 4, 1988.

SHEEHY, NEIL

Defense. Shoots right. 6'2", 210 lbs. Born, International Falls, MN, February 9, 1960.

			Regular Season					Playoffs				
Season	Club	Lea	GP	G	A	TP	PIM	GP	G	A	TP	PIM
1979-80	Harvard	ECAC	13	0	0	0	10	....	....	....	....	....
1980-81	Harvard	ECAC	26	4	8	12	22	....	....	....	....	....
1981-82	Harvard	ECAC	30	7	11	18	46	....	....	....	....	....
1982-83	Harvard	ECAC	34	5	13	18	48	....	....	....	....	....
1983-84	**Calgary**	**NHL**	**1**	**1**	**0**	**1**	**2**	**4**	**0**	**0**	**0**	**4**
	Colorado	CHL	74	5	18	23	151	....	....	....	....	....
1984-85	**Calgary**	**NHL**	**31**	**3**	**4**	**7**	**109**	....	....	....	....	....
	Moncton	AHL	34	6	9	15	101	....	....	....	....	....
1985-86	**Calgary**	**NHL**	**65**	**2**	**16**	**18**	**271**	**22**	**0**	**2**	**2**	**79**
	Moncton	AHL	4	1	1	2	21	....	....	....	....	....
1986-87	**Calgary**	**NHL**	**54**	**4**	**6**	**10**	**151**	**6**	**0**	**0**	**0**	**21**
1987-88	**Calgary**	**NHL**	**36**	**2**	**6**	**8**	**73**	....	....	....	....	....
	Hartford	**NHL**	**26**	**1**	**4**	**5**	**116**	**1**	**0**	**0**	**0**	**7**
1988-89	**Washington**	**NHL**	**72**	**3**	**4**	**7**	**179**	**6**	**0**	**0**	**0**	**19**
	NHL Totals		**285**	**16**	**40**	**56**	**901**	**39**	**0**	**2**	**2**	**130**

Signed as free agent by **Calgary**, August 16, 1983. Traded to **Hartford** by **Calgary** with Carey Wilson and the rights to Lane MacDonald for Dana Murzyn and Shane Churla, January 3, 1988. Traded to **Washington** by **Hartford** with Mike Millar for Grant Jennings and Ed Kastelic, July 6, 1988.

SHEPPARD, RAY

Right wing. Shoots right. 6'1", 180 lbs. Born, Pembroke, Ont., May 27, 1966.
(Buffalo's 3rd choice, 60th over-all, in 1984 Entry Draft).

			Regular Season					Playoffs				
Season	Club	Lea	GP	G	A	TP	PIM	GP	G	A	TP	PIM
1983-84	Cornwall	OHL	68	44	36	80	69	....	....	....	....	....
1984-85	Cornwall	OHL	49	25	33	58	51	9	2	12	14	4
1985-86ab	Cornwall	OHL	63	81	61	142	25	6	7	4	11	0
1986-87	Rochester	AHL	55	18	13	31	11	15	12	3	15	2
1987-88c	**Buffalo**	**NHL**	**74**	**38**	**27**	**65**	**14**	**6**	**1**	**1**	**2**	**2**
1988-89	**Buffalo**	**NHL**	**67**	**22**	**21**	**43**	**15**	**1**	**0**	**1**	**1**	**0**
	NHL Totals		**141**	**60**	**48**	**108**	**29**	**7**	**1**	**2**	**3**	**2**

a OHL Player of the Year (1986)
b OHL First All-Star Team (1986)
c NHL All-Rookie Team (1988)

SHIELDS, DAVID (DAVE)

Center. Shoots right. 5'9", 175 lbs. Born, Calgary, Alta., April 24, 1967.
(Minnesota's 12th choice, 235th overall, in 1987 Entry Draft).

			Regular Season					Playoffs				
Season	Club	Lea	GP	G	A	TP	PIM	GP	G	A	TP	PIM
1986-87	U. of Denver	WCHA	40	18	30	48	8	....	....	....	....	....
1987-88	U. of Denver	WCHA	21	10	7	17	2	....	....	....	....	....
1988-89	U. of Denver	WCHA	43	12	28	40	12	....	....	....	....	....

SHOEBOTTOM, BRUCE

Defense, Shoots left. 6'2", 200 lbs. Born, Windsor, Ont., August 20, 1965.
(Los Angeles' 1st choice, 47th over-all, in 1983 Entry Draft).

			Regular Season					Playoffs				
Season	Club	Lea	GP	G	A	TP	PIM	GP	G	A	TP	PIM
1982-83	Peterborough	OHL	34	2	10	12	106	....	....	....	....	....
1983-84	Peterborough	OHL	16	0	5	5	73	....	....	....	....	....
1984-85	Perterborough	OHL	60	2	15	17	143	17	0	4	4	26
1985-86	New Haven	AHL	6	2	0	2	12	....	....	....	....	....
	Binghamton	AHL	62	7	5	12	249	....	....	....	....	....
1986-87	Fort Wayne	IHL	75	2	10	12	309	10	0	0	0	31
1987-88	**Boston**	**NHL**	**3**	**0**	**1**	**1**	**0**	**4**	**1**	**0**	**1**	**42**
	Maine	AHL	70	2	12	14	338	....	....	....	....	....
1988-89	**Boston**	**NHL**	**29**	**1**	**3**	**4**	**44**	**10**	**0**	**2**	**2**	**35**
	Maine	AHL	44	0	8	8	265	....	....	....	....	....
	NHL Totals		**32**	**1**	**4**	**5**	**44**	**14**	**1**	**2**	**3**	**77**

Traded to **Washington** by **Los Angeles** for Bryan Erickson, October 31, 1985.

SHUCHUK, GARY

Center. Shoots right. 5'10", 185 lbs. Born, Edmonton, Alta., February 17, 1967.
(Detroit's 1st choice, 22nd overall, in 1988 Supplemental Draft).

			Regular Season					Playoffs				
Season	Club	Lea	GP	G	A	TP	PIM	GP	G	A	TP	PIM
1986-87	U. Wisconsin	WCHA	42	19	11	30	72	....	....	....	....	....
1987-88	U. Wisconsin	WCHA	44	7	22	29	70	....	....	....	....	....
1988-89	U. Wisconsin	WCHA	46	18	19	37	102	....	....	....	....	....

SHUDRA, RON

Defense. Shoots left. 6'2", 192 lbs. Born, Winnipeg, Man., November 28, 1967.
(Edmonton's 3rd choice, 63rd over-all, in 1986 Entry Draft).

			Regular Season					Playoffs				
Season	Club	Lea	GP	G	A	TP	PIM	GP	G	A	TP	PIM
1985-86a	Kamloops	WHL	72	10	40	50	81	16	1	11	12	11
1986-87	Kamloops	WHL	71	49	70	119	68	11	7	3	10	10
1987-88	**Edmonton**	**NHL**	**10**	**0**	**5**	**5**	**6**	....	....	....	....	....
	Nova Scotia	AHL	49	7	15	22	21	....	....	....	....	....
1988-89	Cape Breton	AHL	5	0	0	0	0	....	....	....	....	....
	Denver	IHL	64	11	14	25	44	2	0	0	0	0
	NHL Totals		**10**	**0**	**5**	**5**	**6**	....	....	....	....	....

a WHL Rookie of the Year (1986)

Traded to **NY Rangers** by **Edmonton** for Jeff Crossman, October 27, 1988.

SILLINGER, MIKE

Center. Shoots right. 5'10", 190 lbs. Born, Regina, Sask., June 29, 1971.
(Detroit's 1st choice, 11th overall, in 1989 Entry Draft).

			Regular Season					Playoffs				
Season	Club	Lea	GP	G	A	TP	PIM	GP	G	A	TP	PIM
1987-88	Regina	WHL	67	18	25	43	17	4	2	2	4	0
1988-89	Regina	WHL	72	53	78	131	52	....	....	....	....	....

SIM, TREVOR

Center. Shoots right. 6'2", 180 lbs. Born, Calgary, Alta., June 9, 1970.
(Edmonton's 2nd choice, 53rd overall, in 1988 Entry Draft).

			Regular Season					Playoffs				
Season	Club	Lea	GP	G	A	TP	PIM	GP	G	A	TP	PIM
1985-86	Ottawa W.	Midget	37	15	35	50	30	....	....	....	....	....
	Peterborough	OHL	23	7	16	23	46	....	....	....	....	....
1986-87	Calgary	AJHL	57	38	50	88	48	....	....	....	....	....
1987-88	Seattle	WHL	67	17	18	35	87	....	....	....	....	....
1988-89	Swift Current	WHL	63	20	27	47	117	11	10	6	16	20

SIMARD, MARTIN

Right wing. Shoots right. 6'3", 215 lbs. Born, Montreal, Que., June 25, 1966.

			Regular Season					Playoffs				
Season	Club	Lea	GP	G	A	TP	PIM	GP	G	A	TP	PIM
1984-85	Granby	QMJHL	58	22	31	53	78	8	3	7	10	21
1985-86	Granby	QMJHL	54	32	28	69	129	....	....	....	....	....
	Hull	QMJHL	14	8	8	16	55	14	8	19	27	19
1986-87	Granby	QMJHL	41	30	47	77	105	8	3	7	10	21
1987-88	Salt Lake	IHL	82	8	23	31	281	19	6	3	9	100
1988-89	Salt Lake	IHL	71	13	15	28	221	14	4	0	4	45

Signed as a free agent by **Calgary**, May 19, 1987.

SIMPSON, CRAIG

Center. Shoots right. 6'2", 195 lbs. Born, London, Ont., February 15, 1967.
(Pittsburgh's 1st choice, 2nd over-all, in 1985 Entry Draft)

			Regular Season					Playoffs				
Season	Club	Lea	GP	G	A	TP	PIM	GP	G	A	TP	PIM
1983-84	Michigan State	CCHA	46	14	43	57	38	....	....	....	....	....
1984-85ab	Michigan State	CCHA	42	31	53	84	33	....	....	....	....	....
1985-86	**Pittsburgh**	**NHL**	**76**	**11**	**17**	**28**	**49**	....	....	....	....	....
1986-87	**Pittsburgh**	**NHL**	**72**	**26**	**25**	**51**	**57**	....	....	....	....	....
1987-88	**Pittsburgh**	**NHL**	**21**	**13**	**13**	**26**	**34**	....	....	....	....	....
	Edmonton	**NHL**	**59**	**43**	**21**	**64**	**43**	**19**	**13**	**6**	**19**	**26**
1988-89	**Edmonton**	**NHL**	**66**	**35**	**41**	**76**	**80**	**7**	**2**	**0**	**2**	**10**
	NHL Totals		**294**	**128**	**117**	**245**	**263**	**26**	**15**	**6**	**21**	**36**

a CCHA First All-Star Team (1985)
b NCAA All-American (1985)

Traded to **Edmonton** by **Pittsburgh** with Dave Hannan, Moe Mantha and Chris Joseph for Paul Coffey, Dave Hunter and Wayne Van Dorp, November 24, 1987.

SINISALO, ILKKA (sin-i-SAL-oh)

Left wing. Shoots left. 6', 200 lbs. Born, Valeakoski, Finland, July 10, 1958.

			Regular Season					Playoffs				
Season	Club	Lea	GP	G	A	TP	PIM	GP	G	A	TP	PIM
1976-77	PiTa	Fin. 2	35	22	16	38	8	....	....	....	....	....
1977-78	IFK	Fin.	36	9	3	12	18	....	....	....	....	....
1978-79	IFK	Fin.	30	6	4	10	16	6	0	5	5	25
1979-80	IFK	Fin.	35	16	9	25	16	7	1	3	4	12
1980-81	IFK	Fin.	36	27	17	44	14	6	5	3	8	4
1981-82	**Philadelphia**	**NHL**	**66**	**15**	**22**	**37**	**22**	**4**	**0**	**2**	**2**	**0**
1982-83	**Philadelphia**	**NHL**	**61**	**21**	**29**	**50**	**16**	**3**	**1**	**1**	**2**	**0**
1983-84	**Philadelphia**	**NHL**	**73**	**29**	**17**	**46**	**29**	**2**	**2**	**0**	**2**	**0**
1984-85	**Philadelphia**	**NHL**	**70**	**36**	**37**	**73**	**16**	**19**	**6**	**1**	**7**	**0**
1985-86	**Philadelphia**	**NHL**	**74**	**39**	**37**	**76**	**31**	**5**	**2**	**2**	**4**	**2**
1986-87	**Philadelphia**	**NHL**	**42**	**10**	**21**	**31**	**8**	**18**	**5**	**1**	**6**	**4**
1987-88	**Philadelphia**	**NHL**	**68**	**25**	**17**	**42**	**30**	**7**	**4**	**2**	**6**	**0**
1988-89	**Philadelphia**	**NHL**	**13**	**1**	**6**	**7**	**2**	**8**	**1**	**1**	**2**	**0**
	NHL Totals		**467**	**176**	**186**	**362**	**154**	**66**	**21**	**10**	**31**	**6**

Signed as free agent by **Philadelphia**, February 14, 1981.

SIREN, VILLE

Defense. Shoots left. 6'1", 185 lbs. Born, Tampere, Finland, February 10, 1964.
(Hartford's 3rd choice, 23rd overall, in 1983 Entry Draft).

			Regular Season					Playoffs				
Season	Club	Lea	GP	G	A	TP	PIM	GP	G	A	TP	PIM
1982-83	Ilves	Fin.	29	3	2	5	42	8	1	3	4	8
1983-84	Ilves	Fin.	36	1	10	11	40	2	0	0	0	2
	Fin. Olympic	....	2	0	0	0	0	....	....	....	....	....
1984-85	Ilves	Fin	36	11	13	24	24	9	0	2	2	10
1985-86	**Pittsburgh**	**NHL**	**60**	**4**	**8**	**12**	**32**	....	....	....	....	....
1986-87	**Pittsburgh**	**NHL**	**69**	**5**	**17**	**22**	**50**	....	....	....	....	....
1987-88	**Pittsburgh**	**NHL**	**58**	**1**	**20**	**21**	**62**	....	....	....	....	....
1988-89	**Pittsburgh**	**NHL**	**12**	**1**	**0**	**1**	**14**	....	....	....	....	....
	Minnesota	**NHL**	**38**	**2**	**10**	**12**	**58**	**4**	**0**	**0**	**0**	**4**
	NHL Totals		**237**	**13**	**55**	**68**	**216**	**4**	**0**	**0**	**0**	**4**

Traded to **Pittsburgh** by **Hartford** for Pat Boutette, November 16, 1984. Traded to **Minnesota** by **Pittsburgh** with Steve Gotaas for Gord Dineen and Scott Bjugstad, December 17, 1988.

SJODIN, TOMMY

Defense. Shoots right. 5'11", 180 lbs. Born, Sundsvall, Sweden, August 13, 1965.
(Minnesota's 10th choice, 237th overall, in 1985 Entry Draft).

			Regular Season					Playoffs				
Season	Club	Lea	GP	G	A	TP	PIM	GP	G	A	TP	PIM
1983-84	Timra	Swe. 2	16	4	4	8	6	6	0	0	0	4
1984-85	Timra	Swe. 2	23	8	11	19	14	....	....	....	....	....
1985-86	Timra	Swe. 2	32	13	12	25	40	....	....	....	....	....
1986-87	Brynas	Swe.	29	0	4	4	24	....	....	....	....	....
1987-88	Brynas	Swe.	40	6	9	15	28	....	....	....	....	....
1988-89	Brynas	Swe.	40	8	11	19	54	....	....	....	....	....

SJOGREN, THOMAS

Right wing. Shoots right. 5'9", 180 lbs. Born, Teg, Sweden, June 8, 1968.
(Washington's 7th choice, 162nd overall, in 1987 Entry Draft).

			Regular Season					Playoffs				
Season	Club	Lea	GP	G	A	TP	PIM	GP	G	A	TP	PIM
1986-87	V. Frolunda	Swe. 2	25	23	10	33	10	2	1	2	3	0
1987-88	V. Frolunda	Swe. 2	36	36	27	63	42	10	6	6	12	8
1988-89	Sodertalje	Swe.	40	23	19	42	22	....	....	....	....	....

SKALDE, JARROD

Center. Shoots left. 6'0", 180 lbs. Born, Niagara Falls, Ont., February 26, 1971.
(New Jersey's 3rd choice, 26th overall, in 1989 Entry Draft).

			Regular Season					Playoffs				
Season	Club	Lea	GP	G	A	TP	PIM	GP	G	A	TP	PIM
1986-87	Fort Erie	OPJHL	41	27	34	61	36	....	....	....	....	....
1987-88	Oshawa	OHL	60	12	16	28	24	7	2	1	3	2
1988-89	Oshawa	OHL	65	38	38	76	36	6	1	5	6	2

SKARDA, RANDY

Defense. Shoots right. 6'1", 195 lbs. Born, St. Paul, MN, May 5, 1968.
(St. Louis' 8th choice, 157th overall, in 1986 Entry Draft).

			Regular Season					Playoffs				
Season	Club	Lea	GP	G	A	TP	PIM	GP	G	A	TP	PIM
1985-86	St. Thomas	HS	23	15	27	42	0	....	....	....	....	....
1986-87	U. Minnesota	WCHA	43	3	10	13	77	....	....	....	....	....
1987-88ab	U. Minnesota	WCHA	42	19	26	45	102	....	....	....	....	....
1988-89	U. Minnesota	WCHA	43	6	24	30	91	....	....	....	....	....

a NCAA West Second All-American Team (1988)
b WCHA First All-Star Team (1988)

SKRIKO, PETRI

Right wing. Shoots left. 5'10", 170 lbs. Born, Lappeenreenta, Finland, March 12, 1962.
(Vancouver's 7th choice, 157th over-all, in 1981 Entry Draft)

			Regular Season					Playoffs				
Season	Club	Lea	GP	G	A	TP	PIM	GP	G	A	TP	PIM
1979-80	SaiPa	Fin. 2	36	25	20	45	8	....	....	....	....	....
1980-81	Saipa	Fin.	36	20	13	33	14	....	....	....	....	....
1981-82	Saipa	Fin.	33	19	27	46	24	....	....	....	....	....
1982-83	Saipa	Fin.	36	23	12	35	12	....	....	....	....	....
1983-84	Saipa	Fin.	32	25	26	51	13	....	....	....	....	....
	Fin. Olympic	....	7	1	1	2	0	....	....	....	....	....
1984-85	**Vancouver**	**NHL**	**72**	**21**	**14**	**35**	**10**	....	....	....	....	....
1985-86	**Vancouver**	**NHL**	**80**	**38**	**40**	**78**	**34**	**3**	**0**	**0**	**0**	**0**
1986-87	**Vancouver**	**NHL**	**76**	**33**	**41**	**74**	**44**	....	....	....	....	....
1987-88	**Vancouver**	**NHL**	**73**	**30**	**34**	**64**	**32**	....	....	....	....	....
1988-89	**Vancouver**	**NHL**	**74**	**30**	**36**	**66**	**57**	**7**	**1**	**5**	**6**	**0**
	NHL Totals		**375**	**152**	**165**	**317**	**177**	**10**	**1**	**5**	**6**	**0**

SKRUDLAND, BRIAN (SKROOD-luhnd)

Center. Shoots left. 6', 188 lbs. Born, Peace River, Alta., July 31, 1963.

			Regular Season					Playoffs				
Season	Club	Lea	GP	G	A	TP	PIM	GP	G	A	TP	PIM
1980-81	Saskatoon	WHL	66	15	27	42	97	....	....	....	....	....
1981-82	Saskatoon	WHL	71	27	29	56	135	5	0	1	1	2
1982-83	Saskatoon	WHL	71	35	59	94	42	6	1	3	4	19
1983-84	Nova Scotia	AHL	56	13	12	25	55	12	2	8	10	14
1984-85	Sherbrooke	AHL	70	22	28	50	109	17	9	8	17	23
1985-86	**Montreal**	**NHL**	**65**	**9**	**13**	**22**	**57**	**20**	**2**	**4**	**6**	**76**
1986-87	**Montreal**	**NHL**	**79**	**11**	**17**	**28**	**107**	**14**	**1**	**5**	**6**	**29**
1987-88	**Montreal**	**NHL**	**79**	**12**	**24**	**36**	**112**	**11**	**1**	**5**	**6**	**24**
1988-89	**Montreal**	**NHL**	**71**	**12**	**29**	**41**	**84**	**21**	**3**	**7**	**10**	**40**
	NHL Totals		**294**	**44**	**83**	**127**	**360**	**66**	**7**	**21**	**28**	**169**

Signed as a free agent by **Montreal**, September 13, 1983.

SLANINA, PETER

Defense. Shoots right. 6'2", 185 lbs. Born, Czechoslovakia, December 16, 1959.
(Toronto's 11th choice, 233rd overall, in 1984 Entry Draft).

			Regular Season					Playoffs				
Season	Club	Lea	GP	G	A	TP	PIM	GP	G	A	TP	PIM
1986-87	VSZ Kosice	Czech.	33	11	7	18	....	....	....	....	....	....
1987-88	VSZ Kosice	Czech.	34	7	15	22	....	....	....	....	....	....
1988-89	VSZ Kosice	Czech.	42	12	24	36	....	....	....	....	....	....

SLATALLA, DANIEL

Left wing. Shoots left. 6'1", 185 lbs. Born, Lake Havasu, AZ, November 3, 1968.
(Hartford's 11th choice, 242nd overall, in 1988 Entry Draft).

			Regular Season					Playoffs				
Season	Club	Lea	GP	G	A	TP	PIM	GP	G	A	TP	PIM
1987-88	Deerfield Aca.	HS	35	15	14	29	0	....	....	....	....	....
1988-89	Princeton	ECAC	11	0	5	5	10	....	....	....	....	....

SLIFSTIEN, KEITH

Right wing. Shoots right. 6'0", 190 lbs. Born, Hyde Park, NY, January 2, 1969.
(NY Rangers' 12th choice, 236th overall, in 1988 Entry Draft).

			Regular Season					Playoffs				
Season	Club	Lea	GP	G	A	TP	PIM	GP	G	A	TP	PIM
1987-88	Choate	HS	23	12	16	28		....	....	....	....	....
1988-89	Northeastern	H.E.			DID NOT PLAY							

SMAIL, DOUGLAS (DOUG)

Left wing. Shoots left. 5'9", 175 lbs. Born, Moose Jaw, Sask., September 2, 1957.

			Regular Season					Playoffs				
Season	Club	Lea	GP	G	A	TP	PIM	GP	G	A	TP	PIM
1978-79	North Dakota	WCHA	35	24	34	58	46	....	....	....	....	....
1979-80ab	North Dakota	WCHA	40	43	44	87	70	....	....	....	....	....
1980-81	**Winnipeg**	**NHL**	**30**	**10**	**8**	**18**	**45**	....	....	....	....	....
1981-82	**Winnipeg**	**NHL**	**72**	**17**	**18**	**35**	**55**	**4**	**0**	**0**	**0**	**0**
1982-83	**Winnipeg**	**NHL**	**80**	**15**	**29**	**44**	**32**	**3**	**0**	**0**	**0**	**6**
1983-84	**Winnipeg**	**NHL**	**66**	**20**	**17**	**37**	**62**	**3**	**0**	**1**	**1**	**7**
1984-85	**Winnipeg**	**NHL**	**80**	**31**	**35**	**66**	**45**	**8**	**2**	**1**	**3**	**4**
1985-86	**Winnipeg**	**NHL**	**73**	**16**	**26**	**42**	**32**	**3**	**1**	**0**	**1**	**0**
1986-87	**Winnipeg**	**NHL**	**78**	**25**	**18**	**43**	**36**	**10**	**4**	**0**	**4**	**10**
1987-88	**Winnipeg**	**NHL**	**71**	**15**	**16**	**31**	**34**	**5**	**1**	**0**	**1**	**22**
1988-89	**Winnipeg**	**NHL**	**47**	**14**	**15**	**29**	**52**	....	....	....	....	....
	NHL Totals		**597**	**163**	**182**	**345**	**393**	**36**	**8**	**2**	**10**	**49**

a WCHA Second All-Star Team (1980).
b Most Valuable Player, NCAA Tournament (1980).

Signed as free agent by **Winnipeg**, May 22, 1980.

SMITH, DARIN

Left wing. Shoots left. 6'2", 205 lbs. Born, Vineland Station, Ont., February 20, 1967.
(St. Louis' 4th choice, 75th overall, in 1987 Entry Draft).

			Regular Season					Playoffs				
Season	Club	Lea	GP	G	A	TP	PIM	GP	G	A	TP	PIM
1986-87	North Bay	OHL	59	22	25	47	142	23	3	8	11	84
1987-88	Peoria	IHL	81	21	23	44	144	7	1	2	3	16
1988-89	Peoria	IHL	62	13	17	30	127	4	1	0	1	7

SMITH, DENNIS

Defense. Shoots left. 5'11", 190 lbs. Born, Detroit, MI, July 27, 1964.

			Regular Season					Playoffs				
Season	Club	Lea	GP	G	A	TP	PIM	GP	G	A	TP	PIM
1981-82	Kingston	OHL	48	2	24	26	84	4	0	2	2	0
1982-83	Kingston	OHL	58	6	30	36	100	....	....	....	....	....
1983-84	Kingston	OHL	62	10	41	51	165	....	....	....	....	....
1984-85	Osby	Swe.	30	15	15	30	74	....	....	....	....	....
1985-86	Peoria	IHL	70	5	15	20	102	10	0	2	2	18
1986-87	Adirondack	AHL	64	4	24	28	120	6	0	0	0	8
1987-88	Adirondack	AHL	75	6	24	30	213	11	2	2	4	47
1988-89	Adirondack	AHL	75	5	35	40	176	17	1	6	7	47

Signed as a free agent by **Detroit**, December 2, 1986. Signed as a gree agent by **Washington**, July 25, 1989.

SMITH, DERRICK

Left wing. Shoots left. 6'2", 215 lbs. Born, Scarborough, Ont., January 22, 1965.
(Philadelphia's 2nd choice, 44th over-all, in 1983 Entry Draft).

			Regular Season					Playoffs				
Season	Club	Lea	GP	G	A	TP	PIM	GP	G	A	TP	PIM
1982-83	Peterborough	OHL	70	16	19	35	47	....	....	....	....	....
1983-84	Peterborough	OHL	70	30	36	66	31	8	4	4	8	7
1984-85	**Philadelphia**	**NHL**	**77**	**17**	**22**	**39**	**31**	**19**	**2**	**5**	**7**	**16**
1985-86	**Philadelphia**	**NHL**	**69**	**6**	**6**	**12**	**57**	**4**	**0**	**0**	**0**	**10**
1986-87	**Philadelphia**	**NHL**	**71**	**11**	**21**	**32**	**34**	**26**	**6**	**4**	**10**	**26**
1987-88	**Philadelphia**	**NHL**	**76**	**16**	**8**	**24**	**104**	**7**	**0**	**0**	**0**	**6**
1988-89	**Philadelphia**	**NHL**	**74**	**16**	**14**	**30**	**43**	**19**	**5**	**2**	**7**	**12**
	NHL Totals		**367**	**66**	**71**	**137**	**269**	**75**	**13**	**11**	**24**	**70**

SMITH, DOUGLAS ERIC (DOUG)

Center. Shoots right. 5'11", 186 lbs. Born, Ottawa, Ont., May 17, 1963.
(Los Angeles' 1st choice, 2nd over-all, in 1981 Entry Draft).

			Regular Season					Playoffs				
Season	Club	Lea	GP	G	A	TP	PIM	GP	G	A	TP	PIM
1979-80	Ottawa	OHA	64	23	34	57	45	11	2	0	2	33
1980-81	Ottawa	OHA	54	45	56	101	61	7	5	6	11	13
1981-82	**Los Angeles**	**NHL**	**80**	**16**	**14**	**30**	**64**	**10**	**3**	**2**	**5**	**11**
1982-83	**Los Angeles**	**NHL**	**42**	**11**	**11**	**22**	**12**	....	....	....	....	....
1983-84	**Los Angeles**	**NHL**	**72**	**16**	**20**	**36**	**28**	....	....	....	....	....
1984-85	**Los Angeles**	**NHL**	**62**	**21**	**20**	**41**	**58**	**3**	**1**	**0**	**1**	**4**
1985-86	**Los Angeles**	**NHL**	**48**	**8**	**9**	**17**	**56**	....	....	....	....	....
	Buffalo	**NHL**	**30**	**10**	**11**	**21**	**73**	....	....	....	....	....
1986-87	**Buffalo**	**NHL**	**62**	**16**	**24**	**40**	**106**	....	....	....	....	....
	Rochester	AHL	15	5	6	11	35	....	....	....	....	....
1987-88	**Buffalo**	**NHL**	**70**	**9**	**19**	**28**	**117**	**1**	**0**	**0**	**0**	**0**
1988-89	**Edmonton**	**NHL**	**19**	**1**	**1**	**2**	**9**	....	....	....	....	....
	Cape Breton	AHL	24	11	11	22	69	....	....	....	....	....
	Vancouver	**NHL**	**10**	**3**	**4**	**7**	**4**	**4**	**0**	**0**	**0**	**6**
	NHL Totals		**495**	**111**	**133**	**244**	**527**	**18**	**4**	**2**	**6**	**21**

Traded to **Buffalo** by **Los Angeles** with Brian Engblom for Sean McKenna, Larry Playfair and Ken Baumgartner, January 30, 1986. Claimed by **Edmonton** in NHL Waiver Draft, October 3, 1988. Traded to **Vancouver** by **Edmonton** with Gregory C. Adams for Jean LeBlanc and Vancouver's fifth round choice (Peter White) in 1989 Entry Draft, March 7, 1989.

SMITH, JAMES STEPHEN (STEVE)

Defense. Shoots left. 6'4", 215 lbs. Born, Glasgow, Scotland, April 30, 1963.
(Edmonton's 5th choice, 111th over-all, in 1981 Entry Draft).

			Regular Season					Playoffs				
Season	Club	Lea	GP	G	A	TP	PIM	GP	G	A	TP	PIM
1980-81	London	OHA	62	4	12	16	141	....	....	....	....	....
1981-82	London	OHL	58	10	36	46	207	4	1	2	3	13
1982-83	Moncton	AHL	2	0	0	0	0	....	....	....	....	....
	London	OHL	50	6	35	41	133	3	1	0	1	10
1983-84	Moncton	AHL	64	1	8	9	176	....	....	....	....	....
1984-85	**Edmonton**	**NHL**	**2**	**0**	**0**	**0**	**2**	....	....	....	....	....
	Nova Scotia	AHL	68	2	28	30	161	5	0	3	3	40
1985-86	**Edmonton**	**NHL**	**55**	**4**	**20**	**24**	**166**	**6**	**0**	**1**	**1**	**14**
	Nova Scotia	AHL	4	0	2	2	11	....	....	....	....	....
1986-87	**Edmonton**	**NHL**	**62**	**7**	**15**	**22**	**165**	**15**	**1**	**3**	**4**	**45**
1987-88	**Edmonton**	**NHL**	**79**	**12**	**43**	**55**	**286**	**19**	**1**	**11**	**12**	**55**
1988-89	**Edmonton**	**NHL**	**35**	**3**	**19**	**22**	**97**	**7**	**2**	**2**	**4**	**20**
	NHL Totals		**233**	**26**	**97**	**123**	**716**	**47**	**4**	**17**	**21**	**134**

SMITH, NATHAN (NATE)

Defense. Shoots left. 6'1", 190 lbs. Born, Brunswick, ME, July 13, 1967.
(Calgary's 9th choice, 164th overall in 1985 Entry Draft).

			Regular Season					Playoffs				
Season	Club	Lea	GP	G	A	TP	PIM	GP	G	A	TP	PIM
1984-85	Lawrence	HS	24	5	19	24	4	....	....	....	....	....
1985-86	Lawrence	HS	22	10	21	31	22	....	....	....	....	....
1986-87	Princeton	ECAC	25	0	3	3	10	....	....	....	....	....
1987-88	Princeton	ECAC	27	0	6	6	6	....	....	....	....	....
1988-89	Princeton	ECAC	24	1	5	6	12	....	....	....	....	....

SMITH, RANDY

Center. Shoots left. 6'4", 200 lbs. Born, Saskatoon, Sask., July 7, 1965.

			Regular Season					Playoffs				
Season	Club	Lea	GP	G	A	TP	PIM	GP	G	A	TP	PIM
1983-84	Saskatoon	WHL	69	19	21	40	53	....	....	....	....	....
1984-85	Saskatoon	WHL	71	34	51	85	26	8	4	3	7	0
1985-86	Saskatoon	WHL	70	60	86	146	44	9	4	9	13	4
	Minnesota	**NHL**	**1**	**0**	**0**	**0**	**0**	....	....	....	....	....
1986-87	**Minnesota**	**NHL**	**2**	**0**	**0**	**0**	**0**	....	....	....	....	....
	Springfield	AHL	75	20	44	64	24	....	....	....	....	....
1987-88	Kalamazoo	IHL	77	13	43	56	54	6	0	8	8	2
1988-89	Maine	AHL	33	9	16	25	34	....	....	....	....	....
	Kalamazoo	IHL	23	4	9	13	2	....	....	....	....	....
	NHL Totals		**3**	**0**	**0**	**0**	**0**	....	....	....	....	....

Signed as a free agent by **Minnesota**, May 12, 1986.

SMITH, ROBERT DAVID (BOBBY)

Center. Shoots left. 6'4", 210 lbs. Born, North Sydney, N.S., February 12, 1958.
(Minnesota's 1st choice and 1st over-all in 1978 Amateur Draft).

			Regular Season					Playoffs				
Season	Club	Lea	GP	G	A	TP	PIM	GP	G	A	TP	PIM
1976-77a	Ottawa	OHA	64	*65	70	135	52	19	16	16	32	29
1977-78bc	Ottawa	OHA	61	69	*123	*192	44	16	15	15	30	10
1978-79d	**Minnesota**	**NHL**	**80**	**30**	**44**	**74**	**39**	....	....	....	....	....
1979-80	**Minnesota**	**NHL**	**61**	**27**	**56**	**83**	**24**	**15**	**1**	**13**	**14**	**9**
1980-81	**Minnesota**	**NHL**	**78**	**29**	**64**	**93**	**73**	**19**	**8**	**17**	**25**	**13**
1981-82	**Minnesota**	**NHL**	**80**	**43**	**71**	**114**	**82**	**4**	**2**	**4**	**6**	**5**
1982-83	**Minnesota**	**NHL**	**77**	**24**	**53**	**77**	**81**	**9**	**6**	**4**	**10**	**17**
1983-84	**Minnesota**	**NHL**	**10**	**3**	**6**	**9**	**9**	....	....	....	....	....
	Montreal	**NHL**	**70**	**26**	**37**	**63**	**62**	**15**	**2**	**7**	**9**	**8**
1984-85	**Montreal**	**NHL**	**65**	**16**	**40**	**56**	**59**	**12**	**5**	**6**	**11**	**30**
1985-86	**Montreal**	**NHL**	**79**	**31**	**55**	**86**	**55**	**20**	**7**	**8**	**15**	**22**
1986-87	**Montreal**	**NHL**	**80**	**28**	**47**	**75**	**72**	**17**	**9**	**9**	**18**	**19**
1987-88	**Montreal**	**NHL**	**78**	**27**	**66**	**93**	**78**	**11**	**3**	**4**	**7**	**8**
1988-89	**Montreal**	**NHL**	**80**	**32**	**51**	**83**	**69**	**21**	**11**	**8**	**19**	**46**
	NHL Totals		**838**	**316**	**590**	**906**	**703**	**143**	**54**	**80**	**134**	**177**

a OHA Second All-Star Team (1977)
b OHA First All-Star Team (1978)
c Named Canadian Major Junior Player of the Year (1978).
d Won Calder Memorial Trophy (1979)

Played in NHL All-Star Game (1981, 1982, 1989)

Traded to **Montreal** by **Minnesota** for Keith Acton, Mark Napier and Toronto's third round choice (Ken Hodge) in 1984 Entry Draft — Montreal's property via earlier deal — October 28, 1983.

SMITH, SANDY

Center. Shoots right. 5'11", 185 lbs. Born, Brainerd, MN, October 23, 1967.
(Pittsburgh's 5th choice, 88th overall, in 1986 Entry Draft).

			Regular Season					Playoffs				
Season	Club	Lea	GP	G	A	TP	PIM	GP	G	A	TP	PIM
1985-86	Brainerd	HS	17	28	22	50	0	....	....	....	....	....
1986-87	Minn.-Duluth	WCHA	35	3	3	6	26	....	....	....	....	....
1987-88	Minn.-Duluth	WCHA	41	22	9	31	47	....	....	....	....	....
1988-89	Minn.-Duluth	WCHA	40	6	16	22	75	....	....	....	....	....

SMITH, STEVE

Defense. Shoots left. 5'9", 195 lbs. Born, Trenton, Ont., April 4, 1963.
(Philadelphia's 1st choice, 16th over-all, in 1981 Entry Draft).

			Regular Season					Playoffs				
Season	Club	Lea	GP	G	A	TP	PIM	GP	G	A	TP	PIM
1980-81a	S. S. Marie	OHA	61	3	37	40	143	19	0	6	6	60
1981-82b	**Philadelphia**	**NHL**	**8**	**0**	**1**	**1**	**0**	....	....	....	....	....
	S. S. Marie	OHL	50	7	20	27	179	12	0	2	2	23
1982-83b	S. S. Marie	OHL	55	11	33	44	139	16	0	8	8	28
1983-84	Springfield	AHL	70	4	25	29	77	4	0	0	0	0
1984-85	**Philadelphia**	**NHL**	**2**	**0**	**0**	**0**	**7**	....	....	....	....	....
	Hershey	AHL	65	10	20	30	83	....	....	....	....	....
1985-86	**Philadelphia**	**NHL**	**2**	**0**	**0**	**0**	**2**	....	....	....	....	....
	Hershey	AHL	49	1	11	12	96	16	2	4	6	43
1986-87	**Philadelphia**	**NHL**	**2**	**0**	**0**	**0**	**6**	....	....	....	....	....
	Hershey	AHL	66	11	26	37	191	5	0	2	2	8
1987-88	Hershey	AHL	66	10	19	29	132	12	2	10	12	35
1988-89	Rochester	AHL	48	2	12	14	79	....	....	....	....	....
	NHL Totals		**14**	**0**	**1**	**1**	**15**	....	....	....	....	....

a OHA Second All-Star Team (1981).
b OHL Second All-Star Team (1982, 1983).

Claimed by **Buffalo** in NHL Waiver Draft, October 3, 1988.

SMITH, VERN

Defense. Shoots left. 6'1", 190 lbs. Born, Winnipeg, Man., May 30, 1964.
(NY Islanders' 2nd choice, 42nd over-all, in 1982 Entry Draft).

			Regular Season					Playoffs				
Season	Club	Lea	GP	G	A	TP	PIM	GP	G	A	TP	PIM
1981-82	Lethbridge	WHL	72	5	38	43	73	12	0	2	2	8
1982-83	Lethbridge	WHL	30	2	10	12	54	....	....	....	....	....
	Nanaimo	WHL	42	6	21	27	62	....	....	....	....	....
1983-84	N. Westminster	WHL	69	13	44	57	94	9	6	6	12	12
1984-85	**NY Islanders**	**NHL**	**1**	**0**	**0**	**0**	**0**	....	....	....	....	....
	Springfield	AHL	76	6	20	26	115	4	0	2	2	9
1985-86	Springfield	AHL	55	3	11	14	83	....	....	....	....	....
1986-87	Springfield	AHL	41	1	10	11	58	....	....	....	....	....
1987-88	Springfield	AHL	64	5	22	27	78	....	....	....	....	....
1988-89	Springfield	AHL	80	3	26	29	121	....	....	....	....	....
	NHL Totals		**1**	**0**	**0**	**0**	**0**	....	....	....	....	....

SMYL, STANLEY PHILLIP (STAN) (SMEEL)

Right wing. Shoots right. 5'8", 190 lbs. Born, Glendon, Alta., January 28, 1958.
(Vancouver's 3rd choice, 40th over-all, in 1978 Amateur Draft).

			Regular Season					Playoffs				
Season	Club	Lea	GP	G	A	TP	PIM	GP	G	A	TP	PIM
1975-76	N. Westminster	WHL	72	32	42	74	169	19	8	6	14	58
1976-77	N. Westminster	WHL	72	36	31	66	200	13	6	7	13	51
1977-78	N. Westminster	WHL	53	29	47	76	211	20	14	21	35	43
1978-79	Dallas	CHL	3	1	1	2	9	....	....	....	....	....
	Vancouver	NHL	62	14	24	38	89	2	1	1	2	0
1979-80	Vancouver	NHL	77	31	47	78	204	4	0	2	2	14
1980-81	Vancouver	NHL	80	25	38	63	171	3	1	2	3	0
1981-82	Vancouver	NHL	80	34	44	78	144	17	9	9	18	25
1982-83	Vancouver	NHL	74	38	50	88	114	4	3	2	5	12
1983-84	Vancouver	NHL	80	24	43	67	136	4	2	1	3	4
1984-85	Vancouver	NHL	80	27	37	64	100	....	....	....	....	....
1985-86	Vancouver	NHL	73	27	35	62	144	....	....	....	....	....
1986-87	Vancouver	NHL	66	20	23	43	84	....	....	....	....	....
1987-88	Vancouver	NHL	57	12	25	37	110	....	....	....	....	....
1988-89	Vancouver	NHL	75	7	18	25	102	7	0	0	0	9
	NHL Totals		804	259	384	643	1398	41	16	17	33	64

SMYTH, GREG (smith)

Defense. Shoots right. 6'3", 194 lbs. Born, Oakville, Ont., April 23, 1966.
(Philadelphia's 1st choice, 22nd over-all, in 1984 Entry Draft).

			Regular Season					Playoffs				
Season	Club	Lea	GP	G	A	TP	PIM	GP	G	A	TP	PIM
1983-84	London	OHL	64	4	21	25	252	6	1	0	1	24
1984-85	London	OHL	47	7	16	23	188	8	2	2	4	27
1985-86	Hershey	AHL	2	0	1	1	5	8	0	0	0	60
a	London	OHL	46	12	42	54	199	4	1	2	3	28
1986-87	Philadelphia	NHL	1	0	0	0	0	1	0	0	0	2
	Hershey	AHL	35	0	2	2	158	2	0	0	0	19
1987-88	Philadelphia	NHL	48	1	6	7	192	5	0	0	0	38
	Hershey	AHL	21	0	10	10	102	....	....	....	....	....
1988-89	Quebec	NHL	10	0	1	1	70	....	....	....	....	....
	Halifax	AHL	43	3	9	12	310	4	0	1	1	35
	NHL Totals		59	1	7	8	262	6	0	0	0	40

a OHL Second All-Star Team (1986).

Traded to **Quebec** by **Philadelphia** with Philadelphia's third round choice (John Tanner) in the 1989 Entry Draft for Terry Carkner, July 25, 1988.

SNEPSTS, HAROLD JOHN (SNEHPS)

Defense. Shoots left. 6'3", 210 lbs. Born, Edmonton, Alta., October 24, 1954.
(Vancouver's 3rd choice, 59th over-all, in 1974 Amateur Draft).

			Regular Season					Playoffs				
Season	Club	Lea	GP	G	A	TP	PIM	GP	G	A	TP	PIM
1972-73	Edmonton	WHL	68	2	24	26	155	11	0	1	1	54
1973-74	Edmonton	WHL	68	8	41	49	239	....	....	....	....	....
1974-75	Seattle	CHL	19	1	6	7	58	....	....	....	....	....
	Vancouver	NHL	27	1	2	3	30	....	....	....	....	....
1975-76	Vancouver	NHL	78	3	15	18	125	2	0	0	0	4
1976-77	Vancouver	NHL	79	4	18	22	149	....	....	....	....	....
1977-78	Vancouver	NHL	75	4	16	20	118	....	....	....	....	....
1978-79	Vancouver	NHL	76	7	24	31	130	3	0	0	0	0
1979-80	Vancouver	NHL	79	3	20	23	202	4	0	2	2	8
1980-81	Vancouver	NHL	76	3	16	19	212	3	0	0	0	8
1981-82	Vancouver	NHL	68	3	14	17	153	17	0	4	4	50
1982-83	Vancouver	NHL	46	2	8	10	80	4	1	1	2	8
1983-84	Vancouver	NHL	79	4	16	20	152	4	0	1	1	15
1984-85	Minnesota	NHL	71	0	7	7	232	9	0	0	0	24
1985-86	Detroit	NHL	35	0	6	6	75	....	....	....	....	....
1986-87	Detroit	NHL	54	1	13	14	129	11	0	2	2	18
1987-88	Detroit	NHL	31	1	4	5	67	10	0	0	0	40
	Adirondack	AHL	3	0	2	2	14	....	....	....	....	....
1988-89	Vancouver	NHL	59	0	8	8	69	7	0	1	1	6
	NHL Totals		933	36	187	223	1923	74	1	11	12	181

Played in NHL All-Star Game (1977, 1982)

Traded to **Minnesota** by **Vancouver** for Al MacAdam, June 21, 1984. Signed as a free agent by **Detroit**, July 31, 1985.

SNUGGERUD, DAVE

Left wing. Shoots left. 6', 170 lbs. Born, Minnetonka, MN. June 20, 1966.
(Buffalo's 1st choice, 1st overall, in 1987 Supplemental Draft).

			Regular Season					Playoffs				
Season	Club	Lea	GP	G	A	TP	PIM	GP	G	A	TP	PIM
1985-86	U. Minnesota	WCHA	42	14	18	32	47	....	....	....	....	....
1986-87	U. Minnesota	WCHA	39	30	29	59	38	....	....	....	....	....
1987-88	U.S. National	....	51	14	21	35	26	....	....	....	....	....
	U.S. Olympic	....	6	3	2	5	4	....	....	....	....	....
1988-89ab	U. Minnesota	WCHA	45	29	20	49	39	....	....	....	....	....

a WCHA Second All-Star Team (1989)
b NCAA West Second All-American Team (1989)

SOBERLAK, PETER

Center. Shoots left. 6'3", 205 lbs. Born, Kamloops, B.C., May 12, 1969.
(Edmonton's 1st choice, 21st overall, in 1987 Entry Draft).

			Regular Season					Playoffs				
Season	Club	Lea	GP	G	A	TP	PIM	GP	G	A	TP	PIM
1985-86	Kamloops	WHL	55	10	11	21	46	3	1	1	2	9
1986-87	Swift Current	WHL	68	33	42	75	45	....	....	....	....	....
1987-88	Swift Current	WHL	67	43	56	99	47	10	5	7	12	14
1988-89	Swift Current	WHL	37	25	33	58	21	12	5	11	16	11

SOCHA, GARY

Center. Shots left. 6'4", 175 lbs. Born, North Attleboro, MA, December 30, 1969.
(Calgary's 3rd choice, 84th overall, in 1988 Entry Draft).

			Regular Season					Playoffs				
Season	Club	Lea	GP	G	A	TP	PIM	GP	G	A	TP	PIM
1987-88	Tabor	HS	....	25	15	40	....	....	....	....	....	....
1988-89	Tabor	HS	30	20	22	42	....	....	....	....	....	....

SORENSEN, MARK

Defense. Shoots left. 6'0", 180 lbs. Born Newmarket, Ont. March 27, 1969.
(Washington's 11th choice, 192nd overall, in 1988 Entry Draft).

			Regular Season					Playoffs				
Season	Club	Lea	GP	G	A	TP	PIM	GP	G	A	TP	PIM
1987-88	U. of Michigan	CCHA	39	3	9	12	77	....	....	....	....	....
1988-89	U. of Michigan	CCHA	33	1	5	6	33	....	....	....	....	....

SOULES, JASON

Defense. Shoots left. 6'2", 210 lbs. Born, Hamilton, Ont., March 14, 1971.
(Edmonton's 1st choice, 15th overall, in 1989 Entry Draft).

			Regular Season					Playoffs				
Season	Club	Lea	GP	G	A	TP	PIM	GP	G	A	TP	PIM
1987-88	Hamilton	OHL	19	1	1	2	56	4	0	0	0	13
1988-89	Niagara Falls	OHL	57	3	8	11	187	....	....	....	....	....

SPANGLER, KEN

Defense. Shoots right. 5'11", 190 lbs. Born, Edmonton, Alta., May 2, 1967.
(Toronto's 2nd choice, 22nd over-all, in 1985 Entry Draft).

			Regular Season					Playoffs				
Season	Club	Lea	GP	G	A	TP	PIM	GP	G	A	TP	PIM
1983-84	Calgary	WHL	71	1	12	13	119	4	0	0	0	6
1984-85	Calgary	WHL	71	5	30	35	251	8	6	2	8	18
1985-86a	Calgary	WHL	66	19	36	55	237	....	....	....	....	....
	St. Catharines	AHL	7	0	0	0	16	2	0	0	0	15
1986-87	Calgary	WHL	49	12	24	36	185	....	....	....	....	....
1987-88	Newmarket	AHL	64	3	6	9	128	....	....	....	....	....
1988-89	Baltimore	AHL	12	0	3	3	33	....	....	....	....	....
	Flint	IHL	37	4	15	19	97	....	....	....	....	....

a WHL East All-Star Team (1986)

SPEER, MICHAEL

Defense. Shoots left. 6'2", 200 lbs. Born, Toronto, Ont., March 26, 1971.
(Chicago's 2nd choice, 27th overall, in 1989 Entry Draft).

			Regular Season					Playoffs				
Season	Club	Lea	GP	G	A	TP	PIM	GP	G	A	TP	PIM
1987-88	Guelph	OHL	53	4	10	14	60	....	....	....	....	....
1988-89	Guelph	OHL	65	9	31	40	185	7	2	4	6	23

SPROTT, JIM

Defense. Shoots left. 6'1", 198 lbs. Born, Oakville, Ont., April 11, 1969.
(Quebec's 3rd choice, 51st overall, in 1987 Entry Draft).

			Regular Season					Playoffs				
Season	Club	Lea	GP	G	A	TP	PIM	GP	G	A	TP	PIM
1986-87	London	OHL	66	8	30	38	153	....	....	....	....	....
1987-88	London	OHL	65	8	23	31	211	12	1	6	7	8
1988-89a	London	OHL	64	15	42	57	236	21	4	17	21	68

a OHL Second All-Star Team (1989)

SRSEN, TOMAS

Left wing. Shoots left. 5'11", 180 lbs. Born, Olomouc, Czechoslovakia, August 25, 1966.
(Edmonton's 7th choice, 147th overall, in 1987 Entry Draft).

			Regular Season					Playoffs				
Season	Club	Lea	GP	G	A	TP	PIM	GP	G	A	TP	PIM
1986-87	Zetor Brno	Czech.	34	13	7	20	....	....	....	....	....	....
1987-88	Zetor Brno	Czech.	34	14	5	19	....	....	....	....	....	....
1988-89	Zetor Brno	Czech.	42	19	11	30	....	....	....	....	....	....

STAMBERT, ORWAR

Defense. Shoots left. 5'11", 190 lbs. Born, Stockholm, Sweden, September 30, 1960.
(Buffalo's 8th choice, 165th overall, in 1984 Entry Draft).

			Regular Season					Playoffs				
Season	Club	Lea	GP	G	A	TP	PIM	GP	G	A	TP	PIM
1979-80	Hammarby	Swe. 2	31	3	5	8	20	6	0	0	0	2
1980-81	Hammarby	Swe. 2	27	3	10	13	32	11	2	2	4	10
1981-82	Hammarby	Swe. 2	33	5	9	14	16	10	2	3	5	12
1982-83	Hammarby	Swe. 2	34	7	4	11	22	....	....	....	....	....
1983-84	Djurgarden	Swe.	35	4	15	19	24	6	0	0	0	0
1984-85	Djurgarden	Swe.	36	5	10	15	22	8	0	1	1	6
1985-86	Djurgarden	Swe.	36	4	11	15	30	....	....	....	....	....
1986-87	Djurgarden	Swe.	34	7	4	11	22	2	0	0	0	4
1987-88	Djurgarden	Swe.	38	5	18	23	24	3	0	1	1	6
1988-89	Djurgarden	Swe.	40	5	10	15	20	8	4	3	7	4

STANLEY, DARYL

Left Wing. Shoots left. 6'2", 200 lbs. Born, Winnipeg, Man., December 2, 1962.
Last amateur club: Saskatoon Blades (WHL).

			Regular Season					Playoffs				
Season	Club	Lea	GP	G	A	TP	PIM	GP	G	A	TP	PIM
1980-81	N. Westminster	WHL	66	7	27	34	127	....	....	....	....	....
1981-82	Saskatoon	WHL	65	7	25	32	175	5	1	1	2	14
	Maine	AHL	....	....	....	....	....	2	0	2	2	2
1982-83	Maine	AHL	44	2	5	7	95	2	0	0	0	0
1983-84	Springfield	AHL	51	4	10	14	122	....	....	....	....	....
	Philadelphia	NHL	23	1	4	5	71	3	0	0	0	19
1984-85	Hershey	AHL	24	0	7	7	33	....	....	....	....	....
1985-86	Philadelphia	NHL	33	0	2	2	69	1	0	0	0	2
	Hershey	AHL	27	0	4	4	88	....	....	....	....	....
1986-87	Philadelphia	NHL	33	1	2	3	76	13	0	0	0	9
1987-88	Vancouver	NHL	57	2	7	9	151	....	....	....	....	....
1988-89	Vancouver	NHL	20	3	1	4	14	....	....	....	....	....
	NHL Totals		166	7	16	23	381	17	0	0	0	30

Signed as a free agent by **Philadelphia**, October 9, 1981. Traded to **Vancouver** by **Philadelphia** with Darren Jensen for Wendell Young and Vancouver's third round pick in the 1990 Entry Draft, August 31, 1987.

STANTON, PAUL

Defense. Shoots right. 6', 175 lbs.   Born, Boston, MA, June 22, 1967.
(Pittsburgh's 8th choice, 149th overall, in 1985 Entry Draft).

			Regular Season					Playoffs			
Season	Club	Lea	GP	G	A	TP	PIM	GP	G	A	TP	PIM
1985-86	U. Wisconsin	WCHA	36	4	6	10	16	....	....	....	....	....
1986-87	U. Wisconsin	WCHA	41	5	17	22	70	....	....	....	....	....
1987-88ab	U. Wisconsin	WCHA	45	9	38	47	98	....	....	....	....	....
1988-89c	U. Wisconsin	WCHA	45	7	29	36	126	....	....	....	....	....

a NCAA West First All-American Team (1988)
b WCHA Second All-Star Team (1988)
c WCHA First All-Star Team (1989)

STAPLETON, MIKE

Center. Shoots right. 5'10", 165 lbs.   Born, Sarnia, Ont., May 5, 1966.
(Chicago's 7th choice, 132nd over-all, in 1984 Entry Draft).

			Regular Season					Playoffs			
Season	Club	Lea	GP	G	A	TP	PIM	GP	G	A	TP	PIM
1983-84	Cornwall	OHL	70	24	45	69	94	3	1	2	3	4
1984-85	Cornwall	OHL	56	41	44	85	68	9	2	4	6	23
1985-86	Cornwall	OHL	56	39	64	103	74	6	2	3	5	2
1986-87	Chicago	NHL	39	3	6	9	6	4	0	0	0	2
	Cdn. Olympic	....	21	2	4	6	4	....	....	....	....	....
1987-88	Chicago	NHL	53	2	9	11	59	....	....	....	....	....
	Saginaw	IHL	31	11	19	30	52	10	5	6	11	10
1988-89	Chicago	NHL	7	0	1	1	7	....	....	....	....	....
	Saginaw	IHL	69	21	47	68	162	6	1	3	4	4
	NHL Totals		99	5	16	21	72	4	0	0	0	2

STARIKOV, SERGEI

Defense. Shoots left. 5'10", 215 lbs.   Born, Chelyabinsk, Soviet Union, December 4, 1958.
(New Jersey's 7th choice, 152nd overall, in 1989 Entry Draft).

			Regular Season					Playoffs			
Season	Club	Lea	GP	G	A	TP	PIM	GP	G	A	TP	PIM
1976-77	Chelyabinsk	USSR	35	2	4	6	28	....	....	....	....	....
1977-78	Chelyabinsk	USSR	36	3	5	8	26	....	....	....	....	....
1978-79	Chelyabinsk	USSR	44	6	8	14	34	....	....	....	....	....
1979-80	CSKA	USSR	39	10	8	18	14	....	....	....	....	....
1980-81	CSKA	USSR	49	4	8	12	26	....	....	....	....	....
1981-82	CSKA	USSR	40	1	4	5	14	....	....	....	....	....
1982-83	CSKA	USSR	44	6	14	20	14	....	....	....	....	....
1983-84	CSKA	USSR	44	11	7	18	20	....	....	....	....	....
1984-85	CSKA	USSR	40	3	10	13	12	....	....	....	....	....
1985-86	CSKA	USSR	37	3	2	5	6	....	....	....	....	....
1986-87	CSKA	USSR	34	4	2	6	8	....	....	....	....	....
1987-88	CSKA	USSR	38	2	11	13	12	....	....	....	....	....
1988-89	CSKA	USSR	30	3	3	6	4	....	....	....	....	....

STARK, JAY

Defense. Shoots right. 6', 190 lbs.   Born, Vernon, B.C., February 29, 1968.
(Detroit's 5th choice, 106th overall, in 1986 Entry Draft).

			Regular Season					Playoffs			
Season	Club	Lea	GP	G	A	TP	PIM	GP	G	A	TP	PIM
1985-86	Portland	WHL	69	2	13	15	115	15	1	5	6	10
1986-87	Portland	WHL	70	2	14	16	321	20	0	6	6	58
1987-88	Seattle	WHL	64	1	9	10	254	....	....	....	....	....
1988-89	Flint	IHL	12	0	1	1	14	....	....	....	....	....
	Seattle	WHL	71	3	11	14	212	....	....	....	....	....

STASTNY, ANTON   (SHTAHSH nee)

Left wing. Shoots left. 6', 188 lbs.   Born, Bratislava, Czechoslovakia, August 5, 1959.
(Quebec's 4th choice, 83rd over-all, in 1979 Entry Draft).

			Regular Season					Playoffs			
Season	Club	Lea	GP	G	A	TP	PIM	GP	G	A	TP	PIM
1978-79	Slovan	Czech.	44	32	19	51		....	....	....	....	....
1979-80	Slovan	Czech.	40	30	30	60		....	....	....	....	....
	Czech. Olympic	....	6	4	4	8	2	....	....	....	....	....
1980-81	Quebec	NHL	80	39	46	85	12	5	4	3	7	2
1981-82	Quebec	NHL	68	26	46	72	16	16	5	10	15	10
1982-83	Quebec	NHL	79	32	60	92	25	4	2	2	4	0
1983-84	Quebec	NHL	69	25	37	62	14	9	2	5	7	7
1984-85	Quebec	NHL	79	38	42	80	30	16	3	3	6	6
1985-86	Quebec	NHL	74	31	43	74	19	3	1	1	2	0
1986-87	Quebec	NHL	77	27	35	62	8	13	3	8	11	6
1987-88	Quebec	NHL	69	27	45	72	14	....	....	....	....	....
1988-89	Quebec	NHL	55	7	30	37	12	....	....	....	....	....
	Halifax	AHL	16	9	5	14	4	....	....	....	....	....
	NHL Totals		650	252	384	636	150	66	20	32	52	31

STASTNY, PETER   (SHTAHSH nee)

Center. Shoots left. 6'1", 199 lbs.   Born, Bratislava, Czechoslovakia, September 18, 1956.

			Regular Season					Playoffs			
Season	Club	Lea	GP	G	A	TP	PIM	GP	G	A	TP	PIM
1978-79	Slovan	Czech.	44	32	23	55		....	....	....	....	....
1979-80a	Slovan	Czech.	40	30	30	60		....	....	....	....	....
	Czech. Olympic	....	16	7	7	14	6	....	....	....	....	....
1980-81bcd	Quebec	NHL	77	39	70	109	37	5	2	8	10	7
1981-82	Quebec	NHL	80	46	93	139	91	12	7	11	18	10
1982-83	Quebec	NHL	75	47	77	124	78	4	3	2	5	10
1983-84	Quebec	NHL	80	46	73	119	73	9	2	7	9	31
1984-85	Quebec	NHL	75	32	68	100	95	18	4	19	23	24
1985-86	Quebec	NHL	76	41	81	122	60	3	0	1	1	2
1986-87	Quebec	NHL	64	24	53	77	43	13	6	9	15	12
1987-88	Quebec	NHL	76	46	65	111	69	....	....	....	....	....
1988-89	Quebec	NHL	72	35	50	85	117	....	....	....	....	....
	NHL Totals		675	356	630	986	663	64	24	57	81	96

a Czechoslovakian League Player of the Year (1980)
b Won Calder Memorial Trophy (1981)
c NHL record for assists by a rookie (1981)
d NHL record for points by a rookie (1981)
Played in NHL All-Star Game (1981, 1982-84, 1986, 1988)
Signed as free agent by **Quebec**, August 26, 1980.

STAVJANA, ANTONIN

Defense. Shoots right. 6', 190 lbs.   Born, Gottwaldov, Czechoslovakia, February 10, 1963.
(Calgary's 11th choice, 247th overall, in 1986 Entry Draft).

			Regular Season					Playoffs			
Season	Club	Lea	GP	G	A	TP	PIM	GP	G	A	TP	PIM
1986-87	Gottwaldov	Czech.	33	11	7	18		....	....	....	....	....
1987-88	Gottwaldov	Czech.	28	5	11	16		....	....	....	....	....
1988-89	Gottwaldov	Czech.	43	11	12	23		....	....	....	....	....

STEEN, THOMAS

Center. Shoots left. 5'10", 195 lbs.   Born, Tocksmark, Sweden, June 8, 1960.
(Winnipeg's 5th choice, 103rd over-all, in 1979 Entry Draft).

			Regular Season					Playoffs			
Season	Club	Lea	GP	G	A	TP	PIM	GP	G	A	TP	PIM
1976-77	Leksand	Swe.	2	1	1	2	2	....	....	....	....	....
1977-78	Leksand	Swe.	35	5	6	11	30	....	....	....	....	....
1978-79	Leksand	Swe.	23	13	4	17	35	2	0	0	0	0
	Swe. National	...	2	0	0	0	0	....	....	....	....	....
1979-80	Leksand	Swe.	18	7	7	14	14	2	0	0	0	6
1980-81	Farjestad	Swe.	32	16	23	39	30	7	4	2	6	8
	Swe. National		19	2	5	7	12	....	....	....	....	....
1981-82	Winnipeg	NHL	73	15	29	44	42	4	0	4	4	2
1982-83	Winnipeg	NHL	75	26	33	59	60	3	0	2	2	0
1983-84	Winnipeg	NHL	78	20	45	65	69	3	0	1	1	9
1984-85	Winnipeg	NHL	79	30	54	84	80	8	2	3	5	17
1985-86	Winnipeg	NHL	78	17	47	64	76	3	1	1	2	4
1986-87	Winnipeg	NHL	75	17	33	50	59	10	3	4	7	8
1987-88	Winnipeg	NHL	76	16	38	54	53	5	1	5	6	2
1988-89	Winnipeg	NHL	80	27	61	88	80	....	....	....	....	....
	NHL Totals		614	168	340	508	519	36	7	20	27	42

STEPAN, BRAD

Left wing. Shoots left. 5'11", 195 lbs.   Born, Hastings, MN, August 27, 1967.
(NY Rangers' 5th choice, 91st overall, in 1985 Entry Draft).

			Regular Season					Playoffs			
Season	Club	Lea	GP	G	A	TP	PIM	GP	G	A	TP	PIM
1986-87	Windsor	OHL	54	18	21	39	58	13	2	5	7	14
1987-88	Windsor	OHL	3	2	2	4	9	....	....	....	....	....
	S.S. Marie	OHL	56	34	31	65	68	6	3	4	7	12
1988-89	Denver	IHL	55	13	11	24	112	3	0	0	0	6

STERN, RONALD (RONNIE)

Right wing. Shoots right. 6', 195 lbs.   Born, Ste. Agathe, Que., January 11, 1967.
(Vancouver's 3rd choice, 70th overall, in 1986 Entry Draft).

			Regular Season					Playoffs			
Season	Club	Lea	GP	G	A	TP	PIM	GP	G	A	TP	PIM
1984-85	Longueuil	QMJHL	67	6	14	20	176	....	....	....	....	....
1985-86	Longueuil	QMJHL	70	39	33	72	317	....	....	....	....	....
1986-87	Longueuil	QMJHL	56	32	39	71	266	19	11	9	20	55
1987-88	Vancouver	NHL	15	0	0	0	52	....	....	....	....	....
	Flint	IHL	55	14	19	33	294	16	8	8	16	94
1988-89	Vancouver	NHL	17	1	0	1	49	3	0	1	1	17
	Milwaukee	IHL	45	19	23	42	280	5	1	0	1	11
	NHL Totals		17	1	0	1	49	3	0	1	1	17

STEVENS, JOHN

Defense. Shoots left. 6'1", 195 lbs.   Born, Campleton, N.B., May 4, 1966.
(Philadelphia's 5th choice, 47th over-all, in 1984 Entry Draft).

			Regular Season					Playoffs			
Season	Club	Lea	GP	G	A	TP	PIM	GP	G	A	TP	PIM
1983-84	Oshawa	OHL	70	1	10	11	71	7	0	1	1	6
1984-85	Oshawa	OHL	44	2	10	12	61	5	0	2	2	4
	Hershey	AHL	3	0	0	0	0	....	....	....	....	....
1985-86	Kalamazoo	IHL	6	0	1	1	8	6	0	3	3	9
	Oshawa	OHL	65	1	7	8	146	6	0	2	2	14
1986-87	Philadelphia	NHL	6	0	2	2	14	....	....	....	....	....
	Hershey	AHL	63	1	15	16	131	3	0	0	0	7
1987-88	Philadelphia	NHL	3	0	0	0	0	....	....	....	....	....
	Hershey	AHL	59	1	15	16	108	....	....	....	....	....
1988-89	Hershey	AHL	78	3	13	16	129	12	1	1	2	29
	NHL Totals		9	0	2	2	14	....	....	....	....	....

STEVENS, KEVIN

Center. Shoots left. 6'3", 210 lbs.   Born, Brockton, MA April 15, 1965.
(Los Angeles' 6th choice, 108th overall, in 1983 Entry Draft).

			Regular Season					Playoffs			
Season	Club	Lea	GP	G	A	TP	PIM	GP	G	A	TP	PIM
1983-84	Boston College	ECAC	37	6	14	20	36	....	....	....	....	....
1984-85	Boston College	H.E.	40	13	23	36	36	....	....	....	....	....
1985-86	Boston College	H.E.	42	17	27	44	56	....	....	....	....	....
1986-87ab	Boston College	H.E.	39	35	35	70	54	....	....	....	....	....
1987-88	Pittsburgh	NHL	16	5	2	7	8	....	....	....	....	....
	U.S. National	....	44	22	23	45	52	....	....	....	....	....
	U.S. Olympic	....	5	1	3	4	2	....	....	....	....	....
1988-89	Pittsburgh	NHL	24	12	3	15	19	11	3	7	10	16
	Muskegon	IHL	45	24	41	65	113	....	....	....	....	....
	NHL Totals		40	17	5	22	27	11	3	7	10	16

a Hockey East First All-Star Team (1987)
b NCAA East Second All-American Team (1987)
Rights traded to **Pittsburgh** by **Los Angeles** for Anders Hakansson, September 9, 1983.

STEVENS, MIKE

Left wing. Shoots left. 5'11", 195 lbs. Born, Kitchener, Ont., December 30, 1965.
(Vancouver's 5th choice, 58th over-all, in 1984 Entry Draft).

			Regular Season					Playoffs				
Season	Club	Lea	GP	G	A	TP	PIM	GP	G	A	TP	PIM
1982-83	Kitchener	OHL	13	0	4	4	16	12	0	1	1	9
1983-84	Kitchener	OHL	66	19	21	40	109	16	10	7	17	40
1984-85	Vancouver	NHL	6	0	3	3	6	....	....	....	....	....
	Kitchener	OHL	37	17	18	35	121	4	1	1	2	8
1985-86	Fredericton	AHL	79	12	19	31	208	6	1	1	2	35
1986-87	Fredericton	AHL	71	7	18	25	258	....	....	....	....	....
1987-88	Boston	NHL	7	0	1	1	9	....	....	....	....	....
	Maine	AHL	63	30	25	55	265	7	1	2	3	37
1988-89	NY Islanders	NHL	9	1	0	1	14	....	....	....	....	....
	Springfield	AHL	42	17	13	30	120	....	....	....	....	....
	NHL Totals		22	1	4	5	29	....	....	....	....	....

Traded to **Boston** by **Vancouver** for cash, October 6, 1987.

STEVENS, SCOTT

Defense. Shoots left. 6'1", 215 lbs. Born, Kitchener, Ont., April 1, 1964.
(Washington's 1st choice, 5th over-all, in 1982 Entry Draft).

			Regular Season					Playoffs				
Season	Club	Lea	GP	G	A	TP	PIM	GP	G	A	TP	PIM
1980-81	Kitchener	OPJHL	39	7	33	40	82	....	....	....	....	....
	Kitchener	OHA	1	0	0	0	0	....	....	....	....	....
1981-82	Kitchener	OHL	68	6	36	42	158	15	1	10	11	71
1982-83a	Washington	NHL	77	9	16	25	195	4	1	0	1	26
1983-84	Washington	NHL	78	13	32	45	201	8	1	8	9	21
1984-85	Washington	NHL	80	21	44	65	221	5	0	1	1	20
1985-86	Washington	NHL	73	15	38	53	165	9	3	8	11	12
1986-87	Washington	NHL	77	10	51	61	283	7	0	5	5	19
1987-88b	Washington	NHL	80	12	60	72	184	13	1	11	12	46
1988-89	Washington	NHL	80	7	61	68	225	6	1	4	5	11
	NHL Totals		545	87	302	389	1474	52	7	37	44	155

a NHL All-Rookie Team (1983)
b NHL First All-Star Team (1988)

Played in NHL All-Star Game (1985, 1989)

STEVENSON, SHAYNE

Right wing. Shoots right. 6'1", 190 lbs. Born, London, Ont., October 26, 1970.
(Boston's 1st choice, 17th overall, in 1989 Entry Draft).

			Regular Season					Playoffs				
Season	Club	Lea	GP	G	A	TP	PIM	GP	G	A	TP	PIM
1987-88	Kitchener	OHL	66	24	50	74	104	4	1	1	2	4
1988-89	Kitchener	OHL	56	25	50	75	86	5	2	3	5	4

STEWART, ALLAN

Left wing. Shoots left. 6', 195 lbs. Born, Grande Centre, Alta., January 31, 1964.
(New Jersey's 9th choice, 213th over-all, in 1983 Entry Draft).

			Regular Season					Playoffs				
Season	Club	Lea	GP	G	A	TP	PIM	GP	G	A	TP	PIM
1982-83	Prince Albert	WHL	70	25	34	59	272	....	....	....	....	....
1983-84	Prince Albert	WHL	67	44	39	83	216	5	1	2	3	29
	Maine	AHL	....	....	....	....	....	3	0	0	0	0
1984-85	Maine	AHL	75	8	11	19	241	11	1	2	3	58
1985-86	New Jersey	NHL	4	0	0	0	21	....	....	....	....	....
	Maine	AHL	58	7	12	19	181	....	....	....	....	....
1986-87	New Jersey	NHL	7	1	0	1	26	....	....	....	....	....
	Maine	AHL	74	14	24	38	143	....	....	....	....	....
1987-88	New Jersey	NHL	1	0	0	0	0	....	....	....	....	....
	Utica	AHL	49	8	17	25	129	....	....	....	....	....
1988-89	New Jersey	NHL	6	0	2	2	15	....	....	....	....	....
	Utica	AHL	72	9	23	32	110	5	1	0	1	4
	NHL Totals		18	1	2	3	62	....	....	....	....	....

STEWART, RYAN

Center. Shoots right. 6'1", 175 lbs. Born, Houston, B.C., June 1, 1967.
(Winnipeg's 1st choice, 18th over-all, in 1985 Entry Draft).

			Regular Season					Playoffs				
Season	Club	Lea	GP	G	A	TP	PIM	GP	G	A	TP	PIM
1983-84	Kamloops	WHL	69	31	38	69	88	16	7	7	14	19
1984-85	Kamloops	WHL	54	33	37	70	92	11	6	6	12	34
1985-86	Winnipeg	NHL	3	1	0	1	0	....	....	....	....	....
	Prince Albert	WHL	62	52	44	96	82	15	7	8	15	21
1986-87	Brandon	WHL	15	7	9	16	15	....	....	....	....	....
	Portland	WHL	7	5	2	7	12	17	7	11	18	34
1987-88	Moncton	AHL	48	5	18	23	83	....	....	....	....	....
1988-89	Maine	AHL	7	1	0	1	7	....	....	....	....	....
	Moncton	AHL	1	0	0	0	0	....	....	....	....	....
	NHL Totals		3	1	0	1	0	....	....	....	....	....

STIENBURG, TREVOR

Right wing. Shoots right. 6'1", 200 lbs. Born, Kingston, Ont., May 13, 1966.
(Quebec's 1st choice, 15th over-all, in 1984 Entry Draft).

			Regular Season					Playoffs				
Season	Club	Lea	GP	G	A	TP	PIM	GP	G	A	TP	PIM
1982-83	Brockville	OPJHL	47	39	30	69	182	....	....	....	....	....
1983-84	Guelph	OHL	65	33	18	51	104	....	....	....	....	....
1984-85	Guelph	OHL	18	7	12	19	38	....	....	....	....	....
	London	OHL	22	9	11	20	45	8	1	3	4	22
1985-86	Quebec	NHL	2	1	0	1	0	1	0	0	0	0
	London	OHL	31	12	18	30	88	5	0	0	0	20
1986-87	Quebec	NHL	6	1	0	1	12	....	....	....	....	....
	Fredericton	AHL	48	14	12	26	123	....	....	....	....	....
1987-88	Quebec	NHL	8	0	1	1	24	....	....	....	....	....
	Fredericton	AHL	55	12	24	36	279	13	3	3	6	115
1988-89	Quebec	NHL	55	6	3	9	125	....	....	....	....	....
	NHL Totals		71	8	4	12	161	1	0	0	0	0

STOLK, DARREN

Defense. Shoots left. 6'4", 205 lbs. Born, Taber, Alta., July 22, 1968.
(Pittsburgh's 11th choice, 235th overall, in 1988 Entry Draft).

			Regular Season					Playoffs				
Season	Club	Lea	GP	G	A	TP	PIM	GP	G	A	TP	PIM
1986-87	Brandon	WHL	71	3	9	12	60	....	....	....	....	....
1987-88	Lethbridge	WHL	60	3	10	13	79	....	....	....	....	....
1988-89	Medicine Hat	WHL	65	8	31	39	141	3	0	0	0	2

STONE, DONALD

Center. Shoots left. 5'11", 165 lbs. Born, Detroit, MI, May 6, 1969.
(Detroit's 11th choice, 248th overall, in 1988 Entry Draft).

			Regular Season					Playoffs				
Season	Club	Lea	GP	G	A	TP	PIM	GP	G	A	TP	PIM
1987-88	U. of Michigan	CCHA	38	18	19	37	22	....	....	....	....	....
1988-89	U. of Michigan	CCHA	40	24	17	41	19	....	....	....	....	....

STOTHERS, MICHAEL PATRICK (MIKE)

Defense. Shoots left. 6'4", 210 lbs. Born, Toronto, Ont., February 22, 1962.
(Philadelphia's 1st choice, 21st over-all, in 1980 Entry Draft).

			Regular Season					Playoffs				
Season	Club	Lea	GP	G	A	TP	PIM	GP	G	A	TP	PIM
1979-80	Kingston	OHA	66	4	23	27	137	....	....	....	....	....
1980-81	Kingston	OHA	65	4	22	26	237	14	0	3	3	27
1981-82	Kingston	OHL	61	1	20	21	203	4	0	1	1	8
	Maine	AHL	5	0	0	0	4	1	0	0	0	0
1982-83	Maine	AHL	80	2	16	18	139	12	0	0	0	21
1983-84	Maine	AHL	61	2	10	12	109	17	0	1	1	34
1984-85	Philadelphia	NHL	1	0	0	0	0	....	....	....	....	....
	Hershey	AHL	59	8	18	26	142	....	....	....	....	....
1985-86	Philadelphia	NHL	6	0	1	1	6	3	0	0	0	4
1986-87	Philadelphia	NHL	2	0	0	0	4	2	0	0	0	7
	Hershey	AHL	75	5	11	16	283	5	0	0	0	10
1987-88	Philadelphia	NHL	3	0	0	0	13	....	....	....	....	....
	Hershey	AHL	13	3	2	5	55	....	....	....	....	....
	Toronto	NHL	18	0	1	1	42	....	....	....	....	....
	Newmarket	AHL	38	1	9	10	69	....	....	....	....	....
1988-89	Hershey	AHL	76	4	11	15	262	9	0	2	2	29
	NHL Totals		30	0	2	2	65	5	0	0	0	11

Traded to **Toronto** by **Philadelphia** for future considerations, December 4, 1987. Traded to **Philadelphia** by **Toronto** for Bill Root, June 21, 1988.

STRAPON, MARK

Defense. Shoots left. 6'3", 205 lbs. Born, Hayward, WI, July 15, 1969.
(Philadelphia's 7th choice, 146th overall, in 1987 Entry Draft).

			Regular Season					Playoffs				
Season	Club	Lea	GP	G	A	TP	PIM	GP	G	A	TP	PIM
1986-87	Hayward	HS	19	16	22	38	54	....	....	....	....	....
1987-88	St. Paul	USHL	48	4	12	16	34	....	....	....	....	....
1988-89	St. Paul	USHL	38	16	29	45	81	....	....	....	....	....

STREET, KEITH

Center. Shoots left. 6'1", 170 lbs. Born, Moose Jaw, Sask., March 18, 1965.

			Regular Season					Playoffs				
Season	Club	Lea	GP	G	A	TP	PIM	GP	G	A	TP	PIM
1985-86	Alaska-Fair.	NCAA	25	12	18	30	14	....	....	....	....	....
1986-87	Alaska-Fair.	NCAA	35	19	25	44	20	....	....	....	....	....
1987-88	Alaska-Fair.	NCAA	31	37	46	83	30	....	....	....	....	....
1988-89	Milwaukee	IHL	40	10	11	21	22	....	....	....	....	....

Signed as a free agent by **Vancouver**, July 22, 1988.

STROMBACK, DOUG

Right wing. Shoots right. 6', 175 lbs. Born, Farmington, MI, March 3, 1967.
(Washington's 7th choice, 124th overall, in 1985 Entry Draft).

			Regular Season					Playoffs				
Season	Club	Lea	GP	G	A	TP	PIM	GP	G	A	TP	PIM
1984-85	Kitchener	OHL	66	20	24	44	48	4	2	1	3	0
1985-86	North Bay	OHL	63	26	32	58	63	10	0	0	0	14
1986-87	Belleville	OHL	65	32	46	78	23	6	2	2	4	10
1987-88	Belleville	OHL	60	27	35	62	19	5	3	0	3	4
1988-89	Flint	IHL	2	0	0	0	0	....	....	....	....	....

STRUEBY, TODD KENNETH (STROO-bee)

Left wing. Shoots left. 6'1", 185 lbs. Born, Lannigan, Sask., June 15, 1963.
(Edmonton's 2nd choice, 29th over-all, in 1981 Entry Draft).

			Regular Season					Playoffs				
Season	Club	Lea	GP	G	A	TP	PIM	GP	G	A	TP	PIM
1980-81	Regina	WHL	71	18	27	45	99	11	3	6	9	19
1981-82a	Saskatoon	WHL	61	60	58	118	160	5	2	2	4	6
	Edmonton	NHL	3	0	0	0	0	....	....	....	....	....
1982-83	Edmonton	NHL	1	0	0	0	0	....	....	....	....	....
b	Saskatoon	WHL	65	40	70	110	119	6	3	3	6	19
1983-84	Edmonton	NHL	1	0	1	1	2	....	....	....	....	....
	Moncton	AHL	72	17	25	42	38	....	....	....	....	....
1984-85	Nova Scotia	AHL	38	2	3	5	29	....	....	....	....	....
	Muskegon	IHL	27	19	12	31	55	17	4	10	14	27
1985-86	Muskegon	IHL	58	25	40	65	191	14	7	5	12	51
1986-87	Muskegon	IHL	82	28	41	69	208	13	4	6	10	53
1987-88	Fort Wayne	IHL	68	29	27	56	211	4	0	0	0	14
1988-89	Cdn. National	....	61	18	20	38	112	....	....	....	....	....
	NHL Totals		5	0	1	1	2	....	....	....	....	....

a WHL First All-Star Team (1982)
b WHL Second All-Star Team (1983)

Traded to **NY Rangers** by **Edmonton** with Larry Melnyk for Mike Rogers, December 20, 1985.

SUCHANEK, RUDOLF

Defense. Shoots right. 6'3", 215 lbs.   Born, Ceske Budejovice, Czech., January 27, 1962.
(Calgary's 12th choice, 241st overall, in 1984 Entry Draft).

			Regular Season					Playoffs				
Season	Club	Lea	GP	G	A	TP	PIM	GP	G	A	TP	PIM
1986-87	Budejovice	Czech.	30	3	6	9	....	....	....	....	....	....
1987-88	Budejovice	Czech.	33	3	18	21	....	....	....	....	....	....
1988-89	Budejovice	Czech.	45	7	24	31	60	....	....	....	....	....

SULLIMAN, SIMON DOUGLAS (DOUG)

Right wing. Shoots left. 6'2", 210 lbs.   Born, Glace Bay, N.S., August 29, 1959.
(NY Rangers' 1st choice, 13th over-all, in 1979 Entry Draft).

			Regular Season					Playoffs				
Season	Club	Lea	GP	G	A	TP	PIM	GP	G	A	TP	PIM
1977-78	Kitchener	OHA	68	50	39	89	87	9	5	7	12	24
1978-79	Kitchener	OHA	68	38	77	115	88	10	5	7	12	7
1979-80	NY Rangers	NHL	31	4	7	11	2	....	....	....	....	....
	New Haven	AHL	31	9	7	16	9	....	....	....	....	....
1980-81	New Haven	AHL	45	10	16	26	18	1	0	0	0	0
	NY Rangers	NHL	32	4	1	5	32	3	1	0	1	0
1981-82	Hartford	NHL	77	29	40	69	39	....	....	....	....	....
1982-83	Hartford	NHL	77	22	19	41	14	....	....	....	....	....
1983-84	Hartford	NHL	67	6	13	19	20	....	....	....	....	....
1984-85	New Jersey	NHL	57	22	16	38	4	....	....	....	....	....
1985-86	New Jersey	NHL	73	21	22	43	20	....	....	....	....	....
1986-87	New Jersey	NHL	78	27	26	53	14	....	....	....	....	....
1987-88	New Jersey	NHL	59	16	14	30	22	9	0	3	3	2
1988-89	Philadelphia	NHL	52	6	6	12	8	4	0	0	0	0
	NHL Totals		603	157	164	321	175	16	1	3	4	2

Traded to Hartford by NY Rangers with Chris Kotsopoulos and Gerry McDonald for Mike Rogers and NY Rangers' tenth round choice (Simo Saarinen) in 1982 Entry Draft, October 2, 1981. Signed as free agent by New Jersey, July 11, 1984. Claimed by Philadelphia in NHL Waiver Draft, October 3, 1988.

SULLIVAN, BRIAN

Right wing. Shoots right. 6'4", 195 lbs.   Born, South Windsor, CT, April 23, 1969.
(New Jersey's 3rd choice, 65th overall, in 1987 Entry Draft).

			Regular Season					Playoffs				
Season	Club	Lea	GP	G	A	TP	PIM	GP	G	A	TP	PIM
1986-87	Springfield	USHL	42	30	35	65	50	....	....	....	....	....
1987-88	Northeastern	H.E.	37	20	12	32	18	....	....	....	....	....
1988-89	Northeastern	H.E.	34	13	14	27	65	....	....	....	....	....

SULLIVAN, KEVIN

Right wing. Shoots right. 6'2", 180 lbs.   Born, Hartford, CT, May 16, 1968.
(Hartford's 9th choice, 228th overall, in 1987 Entry Draft).

			Regular Season					Playoffs				
Season	Club	Lea	GP	G	A	TP	PIM	GP	G	A	TP	PIM
1986-87	Princeton	ECAC	25	1	0	1	10	....	....	....	....	....
1987-88	Princeton	ECAC	22	0	3	3	8	....	....	....	....	....
1988-89	Princeton	ECAC	26	7	7	14	58	....	....	....	....	....

SULLIVAN, MICHAEL

Center. Shoots left. 6'2", 185 lbs.   Born, Marshfield, MA, February 27, 1968.
(NY Rangers' 4th choice, 69th overall, in 1987 Entry Draft).

			Regular Season					Playoffs				
Season	Club	Lea	GP	G	A	TP	PIM	GP	G	A	TP	PIM
1986-87	Boston U.	H.E.	37	13	18	31	18	....	....	....	....	....
1987-88	Boston U.	H.E.	30	18	22	40	30	....	....	....	....	....
1988-89	Boston U.	H.E.	36	19	17	36	30	....	....	....	....	....

Rights traded to Minnesota by NY Rangers with Paul Jerrard, the rights to Bret Barnett, and Los Angeles' third-round choice (Murray Garbutt) in 1989 Entry Draft — acquired March 10, 1987 by Minnesota — for Brian Lawton, Igor Liba and the rights to Eric Bennett, October 11, 1988.

SUMMANEN, RAIMO   (SOO-ma-nen, RYE-moh)

Left wing. Shoots left. 5'11", 185 lbs.   Born, Jyvaskyla, Finland, March 2, 1962.
(Edmonton's 6th choice, 125th over-all, in 1982 Entry Draft).

			Regular Season					Playoffs				
Season	Club	Lea	GP	G	A	TP	PIM	GP	G	A	TP	PIM
1981-82	Kiekkoreipas	Fin.	36	15	6	21	17	2	2	0	2	0
1982-83	Ilves	Fin.	36	45	15	60	36	8	7	3	10	2
1983-84	Ilves	Fin.	37	28	19	47	26	....	....	....	....	....
	Edmonton	NHL	2	1	4	5	2	5	1	4	5	0
1984-85	Edmonton	NHL	9	0	4	4	0	....	....	....	....	....
	Nova Scotia	AHL	66	20	33	53	2	5	1	2	3	0
1985-86	Edmonton	NHL	73	19	18	37	16	5	1	1	2	0
1986-87	Edmonton	NHL	48	10	7	17	15	....	....	....	....	....
	Vancouver	NHL	10	4	4	8	0	....	....	....	....	....
1987-88	Vancouver	NHL	9	2	3	5	2	....	....	....	....	....
	Fredericton	AHL	20	7	15	22	38	....	....	....	....	....
	Flint	IHL	7	1	1	2	0	....	....	....	....	....
1988-89	Ilves	Fin.	44	35	46	81	22	5	4	3	7	6
	NHL Totals		151	36	40	76	35	10	2	5	7	0

Traded to Vancouver by Edmonton for Moe Lemay, March 10, 1987.

SUNDIN, MATS

Center/right wing. Shoots right. 6'3", 185 lbs.   Born, Sollentuna, Sweden, February 13, 1971.
(Quebec's 1st choice, 1st overall, in 1989 Entry Draft).

			Regular Season					Playoffs				
Season	Club	Lea	GP	G	A	TP	PIM	GP	G	A	TP	PIM
1988-89	Nacka	Swe.	25	10	8	18	18	....	....	....	....	....

SUNDSTROM, PATRIK

Center/Right wing. Shoots left. 6', 195 lbs.   Born, Skelleftea, Sweden, December 14, 1961.
(Vancouver's 8th choice, 175th over-all, in 1980 Entry Draft).

			Regular Season					Playoffs				
Season	Club	Lea	GP	G	A	TP	PIM	GP	G	A	TP	PIM
1978-79	Bjorkloven	Swe.	1	0	0	0	0	....	....	....	....	....
1979-80	Bjorkloven	Swe.	26	5	7	12	20	3	1	0	1	4
1980-81	Bjorkloven	Swe.	36	10	18	28	30	3	1	0	1	4
	Swe. National		15	4	2	6	6	....	....	....	....	....
1981-82	Bjorkloven	Swe.	36	22	13	35	38	7	3	4	7	6
	Swe. National		36	17	7	24	24	....	....	....	....	....
1982-83	Vancouver	NHL	74	23	23	46	30	4	0	0	0	2
1983-84	Vancouver	NHL	78	38	53	91	37	4	0	1	1	7
1984-85	Vancouver	NHL	71	25	43	68	46	....	....	....	....	....
1985-86	Vancouver	NHL	79	18	48	66	28	3	1	0	1	0
1986-87	Vancouver	NHL	72	29	42	71	40	....	....	....	....	....
1987-88	New Jersey	NHL	78	15	36	51	42	18	7	13	20	14
1988-89	New Jersey	NHL	65	28	41	69	36	....	....	....	....	....
	NHL Totals		517	176	286	462	259	29	8	14	22	23

Traded to New Jersey by Vancouver with Vancouver's fourth round choice (Matt Ruchty) in 1988 Entry Draft for Kirk McLean and Greg Adams, September 15, 1987.

SUNDSTROM, PETER

Left wing. Shoots left. 6', 180 lbs.   Born, Skelleftea, Sweden, December 14, 1961.
(New York Rangers' 3rd choice, 50th over-all, in 1981 Entry Draft).

			Regular Season					Playoffs				
Season	Club	Lea	GP	G	A	TP	PIM	GP	G	A	TP	PIM
1978-79	Bjorkloven	Swe.	1	0	0	0	0	....	....	....	....	....
1979-80	Bjorkloven	Swe.	8	0	0	0	2	....	....	....	....	....
1980-81	Bjorkloven	Swe.	29	7	2	9	8	....	....	....	....	....
1981-82	Bjorkloven	Swe.	35	10	14	24	18	7	2	1	3	0
1982-83	Bjorkloven	Swe.	33	14	11	25	3	2	0	2	0	4
1983-84	NY Rangers	NHL	77	22	22	44	24	5	1	3	4	0
1984-85	NY Rangers	NHL	76	18	25	43	34	3	0	0	0	0
1985-86	NY Rangers	NHL	53	8	15	23	12	1	0	0	0	2
	New Haven	AHL	8	3	6	9	4	....	....	....	....	....
1986-87	Bjorkloven	Swe.	36	22	16	38	44	6	2	5	7	8
1987-88	Washington	NHL	76	8	17	25	34	14	2	0	2	6
1988-89	Washington	NHL	35	4	2	6	12	....	....	....	....	....
	NHL Totals		317	60	81	141	116	23	3	3	6	8

Traded by NY Rangers to Washington for Washington's fifth round selection in the 1988 Entry Draft, August 27, 1987. Traded to Washington by NY Rangers for Washington's fifth round choice (Martin Bergeron) in 1988 Entry Draft, August 28, 1987. Traded to New Jersey by Washington for New Jersey's 10th round choice in 1990 Entry Draft, June 19, 1989.

SUTER, GARY

Defense. Shoots left. 6', 190 lbs.   Born, Madison, WI, June 24, 1964.
(Calgary's 10th choice, 180th over-all, in 1984 Entry Draft).

			Regular Season					Playoffs				
Season	Club	Lea	GP	G	A	TP	PIM	GP	G	A	TP	PIM
1983-84	U. Wisconsin	WCHA	35	4	18	22	32	....	....	....	....	....
1984-85	U. Wisconsin	WCHA	39	12	39	51	110	....	....	....	....	....
1985-86ab	Calgary	NHL	80	18	50	68	141	10	2	8	10	8
1986-87	Calgary	NHL	68	9	40	49	70	6	0	3	3	10
1987-88c	Calgary	NHL	75	21	70	91	126	9	1	9	10	6
1988-89	Calgary	NHL	63	13	49	62	78	5	0	3	3	10
	NHL Totals		286	61	209	270	415	30	3	23	26	28

a Won Calder Memorial Trophy (1986)
b NHL All-Rookie Team (1986)
c NHL Second All-Star Team (1988)
Played in NHL All-Star Game (1986, 1988, 1989)

SUTTER, BRENT COLIN   (SUH tuhr)

Center. Shoots right. 5'11", 180 lbs.   Born, Viking, Alta., June 10, 1962.
(NY Islanders' 1st choice, 17th over-all, in 1980 Entry Draft).

			Regular Season					Playoffs				
Season	Club	Lea	GP	G	A	TP	PIM	GP	G	A	TP	PIM
1979-80	Red Deer	AJHL	59	70	101	171	....	....	....	....	....	....
	Lethbridge	WHL	5	1	0	1	2	....	....	....	....	....
1980-81	NY Islanders	NHL	3	2	2	4	0	....	....	....	....	....
	Lethbridge	WHL	68	54	54	108	116	9	6	4	10	51
1981-82	Lethbridge	WHL	34	46	33	79	162	....	....	....	....	....
	NY Islanders	NHL	43	21	22	43	114	19	2	6	8	36
1982-83	NY Islanders	NHL	80	21	19	40	128	20	10	11	21	26
1983-84	NY Islanders	NHL	69	34	15	49	69	20	4	10	14	18
1984-85	NY Islanders	NHL	72	42	60	102	51	10	3	3	6	14
1985-86	NY Islanders	NHL	61	24	31	55	74	3	0	1	1	2
1986-87	NY Islanders	NHL	69	27	36	63	73	5	1	0	1	4
1987-88	NY Islanders	NHL	70	29	31	60	55	6	2	1	3	18
1988-89	NY Islanders	NHL	77	29	34	63	77	....	....	....	....	....
	NHL Totals		544	229	250	479	641	83	22	32	54	118

Played in NHL All-Star Game (1985)

SUTTER, DUANE CALVIN (SUH tuhr)

Right wing. Shoots right. 6'1", 185 lbs. Born, Viking, Alta., March 16, 1960.
(NY Islanders' 1st choice, 17th over-all, in 1979 Entry Draft).

			Regular Season					Playoffs				
Season	**Club**	**Lea**	**GP**	**G**	**A**	**TP**	**PIM**	**GP**	**G**	**A**	**TP**	**PIM**
1976-77	Lethbridge	WHL	1	0	1	1	2	8	0	1	1	15
1977-78	Lethbridge	WHL	5	1	5	6	19	8	1	4	5	10
1978-79	Lethbridge	WHL	71	50	75	125	212	19	11	12	23	43
1979-80	Lethbridge	WHL	21	18	16	34	74	....	....	....	....	....
	NY Islanders	**NHL**	**56**	**15**	**9**	**24**	**55**	**21**	**3**	**7**	**10**	**74**
1980-81	**NY Islanders**	**NHL**	**23**	**7**	**11**	**18**	**26**	**12**	**3**	**1**	**4**	**10**
1981-82	**NY Islanders**	**NHL**	**77**	**18**	**35**	**53**	**100**	**19**	**5**	**5**	**10**	**57**
1982-83	**NY Islanders**	**NHL**	**75**	**13**	**19**	**32**	**118**	**20**	**9**	**12**	**21**	**43**
1983-84	**NY Islanders**	**NHL**	**78**	**17**	**23**	**40**	**94**	**21**	**1**	**3**	**4**	**48**
1984-85	**NY Islanders**	**NHL**	**78**	**17**	**24**	**41**	**174**	**10**	**0**	**2**	**2**	**47**
1985-86	**NY Islanders**	**NHL**	**80**	**20**	**33**	**53**	**157**	**3**	**0**	**0**	**0**	**16**
1986-87	**NY Islanders**	**NHL**	**80**	**14**	**17**	**31**	**169**	**14**	**1**	**0**	**1**	**26**
1987-88	**Chicago**	**NHL**	**37**	**7**	**9**	**16**	**70**	**5**	**0**	**0**	**0**	**21**
1988-89	**Chicago**	**NHL**	**75**	**7**	**9**	**16**	**214**	**16**	**3**	**1**	**4**	**15**
	NHL Totals		**659**	**135**	**189**	**324**	**1177**	**141**	**25**	**31**	**56**	**357**

Traded to **Chicago** by **NY Islanders** for Chicago's second round choice (Wayne Doucet) in 1988 Entry Draft, September 9, 1987.

SUTTER, RICHARD (RICH) (SUH tuhr)

Right wing. Shoots right. 5'11", 165 lbs. Born, Viking, Alta., December 2, 1963.
(Pittsburgh's 1st choice, 10th over-all, in 1982 Entry Draft).

			Regular Season					Playoffs				
Season	**Club**	**Lea**	**GP**	**G**	**A**	**TP**	**PIM**	**GP**	**G**	**A**	**TP**	**PIM**
1980-81	Lethbridge	WHL	72	23	18	41	255	9	3	1	4	35
1981-82	Lethbridge	WHL	57	38	31	69	263	12	3	3	6	55
1982-83	**Pittsburgh**	**NHL**	**4**	**0**	**0**	**0**	**0**	....	....	....	....	....
	Lethbridge	WHL	64	37	30	67	200	17	14	9	23	43
1983-84	Baltimore	AHL	2	0	1	1	0	....	....	....	....	....
	Pittsburgh	**NHL**	**5**	**0**	**0**	**0**	**0**	....	....	....	....	....
	Philadelphia	**NHL**	**70**	**16**	**12**	**28**	**93**	**3**	**0**	**0**	**0**	**15**
1984-85	**Philadelphia**	**NHL**	**56**	**6**	**10**	**16**	**89**	**11**	**3**	**0**	**3**	**10**
	Hershey	AHL	13	3	7	10	14	....	....	....	....	....
1985-86	**Philadelphia**	**NHL**	**78**	**14**	**25**	**39**	**199**	**5**	**2**	**0**	**2**	**19**
1986-87	**Vancouver**	**NHL**	**74**	**20**	**22**	**42**	**113**	....	....	....	....	....
1987-88	**Vancouver**	**NHL**	**80**	**15**	**15**	**30**	**165**	....	....	....	....	....
1988-89	**Vancouver**	**NHL**	**75**	**17**	**15**	**32**	**122**	**7**	**2**	**1**	**3**	**12**
	NHL Totals		**442**	**88**	**99**	**187**	**781**	**26**	**7**	**1**	**8**	**56**

Traded to **Philadelphia** by **Pittsburgh** with Pittsburgh's second round (Greg Smyth) and third round (David McLay) choices in 1984 Entry Draft for Andy Brickley, Mark Taylor, Ron Flockhart, Philadelphia's first round (Roger Belanger) and third round (Mike Stevens — later transferred to Vancouver) choices in 1984 Entry Draft, October 23, 1983. Traded to **Vancouver** by **Philadelphia**, with Dave Richter and Vancouver's third-round choice (Don Gibson) in 1986 Entry Draft — acquired earlier — for J.J. Daigneault and Vancouver's second-round choice (Kent Hawley) in 1986 Entry Draft, June 6, 1986.

SUTTER, RONALD (RON) (SUH tuhr)

Center. Shoots right. 6', 180 lbs. Born, Viking, Alta., December 2, 1963.
(Philadelphia's 1st choice, 4th over-all, in 1982 Entry Draft).

			Regular Season					Playoffs				
Season	**Club**	**Lea**	**GP**	**G**	**A**	**TP**	**PIM**	**GP**	**G**	**A**	**TP**	**PIM**
1980-81	Lethbridge	WHL	72	13	32	45	152	9	2	5	7	29
1981-82	Lethbridge	WHL	59	38	54	92	207	12	6	5	11	28
1982-83	**Philadelphia**	**NHL**	**10**	**1**	**1**	**2**	**9**	....	....	....	....	....
	Lethbridge	WHL	58	35	48	83	98	20	22	19	41	45
1983-84	**Philadelphia**	**NHL**	**79**	**19**	**32**	**51**	**101**	**3**	**0**	**0**	**0**	**22**
1984-85	**Philadelphia**	**NHL**	**73**	**16**	**29**	**45**	**94**	**19**	**4**	**8**	**12**	**28**
1985-86	**Philadelphia**	**NHL**	**75**	**18**	**42**	**60**	**159**	**5**	**0**	**2**	**2**	**10**
1986-87	**Philadelphia**	**NHL**	**39**	**10**	**17**	**27**	**69**	**16**	**1**	**7**	**8**	**12**
1987-88	**Philadelphia**	**NHL**	**69**	**8**	**25**	**33**	**146**	**7**	**0**	**1**	**1**	**26**
1988-89	**Philadelphia**	**NHL**	**55**	**26**	**22**	**48**	**80**	**19**	**1**	**9**	**10**	**51**
	NHL Totals		**400**	**98**	**168**	**266**	**658**	**69**	**6**	**27**	**33**	**149**

SUTTON, BOYD

Center/Left wing. Shoots left. 5'10", 175 lbs. Born, Anchorage, AK, December 6, 1966.
(Buffalo's 10th choice, 203rd overall, in 1985 Entry Draft).

			Regular Season					Playoffs				
Season	**Club**	**Lea**	**GP**	**G**	**A**	**TP**	**PIM**	**GP**	**G**	**A**	**TP**	**PIM**
1985-86	Miami-Ohio	CCHA	33	8	13	21	24	....	....	....	....	....
1986-87	Miami-Ohio	CCHA	39	19	18	37	44	....	....	....	....	....
1987-88	Miami-Ohio	CCHA	37	17	16	33	34	....	....	....	....	....
1988-89	Miami-Ohio	CCHA	37	16	23	39	24	....	....	....	....	....

SVEEN, JEFF

Center. Shoots right. 5'11", 176 lbs. Born, Barrhead, Alta., February 5, 1967.
(NY Islanders' 7th choice, 97th overall, in 1985 Entry Draft).

			Regular Season					Playoffs				
Season	**Club**	**Lea**	**GP**	**G**	**A**	**TP**	**PIM**	**GP**	**G**	**A**	**TP**	**PIM**
1984-85	Boston U.	H.E.	42	14	10	24	10	....	....	....	....	....
1985-86	Boston U.	H.E.	35	15	8	23	18	....	....	....	....	....
1986-87	Boston U.	H.E.	34	8	6	14	32	....	....	....	....	....
1987-88	Boston U.	H.E.	17	6	5	11	14	....	....	....	....	....
1988-89	Cdn. National	....	4	0	0	0	0	....	....	....	....	....

SVENSSON, MAGNUS

Defense. Shoots left. 5'11", 170 lbs. Born, Leksand, Sweden, March 1, 1963.
(Calgary's 13th choice, 250th overall, in 1987 Entry Draft).

			Regular Season					Playoffs				
Season	**Club**	**Lea**	**GP**	**G**	**A**	**TP**	**PIM**	**GP**	**G**	**A**	**TP**	**PIM**
1983-84	Leksand	Swe.	35	3	8	11	20	....	....	....	....	....
1984-85	Leksand	Swe.	35	8	7	15	22	....	....	....	....	....
1985-86	Leksand	Swe.	36	6	9	15	62	....	....	....	....	....
1986-87	Leksand	Swe.	33	8	16	24	42	....	....	....	....	....
1987-88	Leksand	Swe.	40	12	11	23	20	....	....	....	....	....
1988-89	Leksand	Swe.	39	15	22	37	40	10	3	5	8	8

SVETLOV, SERGEI

Right wing. Shoots left. 6'1", 195 lbs. Born, Penza, Soviet Union, January 17, 1961.
(New Jersey's 10th choice, 180th overall, in 1988 Entry Draft).

			Regular Season					Playoffs				
Season	**Club**	**Lea**	**GP**	**G**	**A**	**TP**	**PIM**	**GP**	**G**	**A**	**TP**	**PIM**
1987-88	Moscow D'amo	USSR	35	12	18	30	14	....	....	....	....	....
1988-89	Moscow D'amo	USSR	31	12	10	22	21	....	....	....	....	....

SVITEK, VLADIMIR

Right wing. Shoots left. 6'2", 180 lbs. Born, Banska Bystrica, Czech., October 19, 1962.
(Philadelphia's 9th choice, 137th overall, in 1981 Entry Draft).

			Regular Season					Playoffs				
Season	**Club**	**Lea**	**GP**	**G**	**A**	**TP**	**PIM**	**GP**	**G**	**A**	**TP**	**PIM**
1986-87	VSZ Kosice	Czech.	22	4	8	12	....	....	....	....	....	....
1987-88	VSZ Kosice	Czech.	21	13	8	21	....	....	....	....	....	....
1988-89	VSZ Kosice	Czech.	45	13	24	37	....	....	....	....	....	....

SVOBODA, PETR (svah BOH duh)

Defense. Shoots left. 6'1", 170 lbs. Born, Most, Czechoslovakia, February 14, 1966.
(Montreal's 1st choice, 5th over-all, in 1984 Entry Draft).

			Regular Season					Playoffs				
Season	**Club**	**Lea**	**GP**	**G**	**A**	**TP**	**PIM**	**GP**	**G**	**A**	**TP**	**PIM**
1983-84	Czech. Jrs.	...	40	15	21	36	14	....	....	....	....	....
1984-85	**Montreal**	**NHL**	**73**	**4**	**27**	**31**	**65**	**7**	**1**	**1**	**2**	**12**
1985-86	**Montreal**	**NHL**	**73**	**1**	**18**	**19**	**93**	**8**	**0**	**0**	**0**	**21**
1986-87	**Montreal**	**NHL**	**70**	**5**	**17**	**22**	**63**	**14**	**0**	**5**	**5**	**10**
1987-88	**Montreal**	**NHL**	**69**	**7**	**22**	**29**	**149**	**10**	**0**	**5**	**5**	**12**
1988-89	**Montreal**	**NHL**	**71**	**8**	**37**	**45**	**147**	**21**	**1**	**11**	**12**	**16**
	NHL Totals		**356**	**25**	**121**	**146**	**517**	**60**	**2**	**22**	**24**	**71**

SWEENEY, DON

Defense. Shoots left. 5'11", 170 lbs. Born, St. Stephen, N.B., August 17, 1966.
(Boston's 8th choice, 166th overall, in 1984 Entry Draft).

			Regular Season					Playoffs				
Season	**Club**	**Lea**	**GP**	**G**	**A**	**TP**	**PIM**	**GP**	**G**	**A**	**TP**	**PIM**
1984-85	Harvard	ECAC	29	3	7	10	30	....	....	....	....	....
1985-86	Harvard	ECAC	31	4	5	9	12	....	....	....	....	....
1986-87	Harvard	ECAC	34	7	4	11	22	....	....	....	....	....
1987-88ab	Harvard	ECAC	30	6	23	29	37	....	....	....	....	....
	Maine	AHL	....	....	....	....	....	6	1	3	4	0
1988-89	**Boston**	**NHL**	**36**	**3**	**5**	**8**	**20**	....	....	....	....	....
	Maine	AHL	42	8	17	25	24	....	....	....	....	....
	NHL Totals		**36**	**3**	**5**	**8**	**20**	....	....	....	....	....

a NCAA East All-American Team (1988)
b ECAC First All-Star Team (1988)

SWEENEY, ROBERT (BOB)

Center. Shoots right. 6'3", 200 lbs. Born, Concord, MA, January 25, 1964.
(Boston's 6th choice, 123rd over-all, in 1982 Entry Draft).

			Regular Season					Playoffs				
Season	**Club**	**Lea**	**GP**	**G**	**A**	**TP**	**PIM**	**GP**	**G**	**A**	**TP**	**PIM**
1982-83	Boston College	ECAC	30	17	11	28	10	....	....	....	....	....
1983-84	Boston College	ECAC	23	14	7	21	10	....	....	....	....	....
1984-85a	Boston College	ECAC	44	32	32	64	43	....	....	....	....	....
1985-86	Boston College	H.E.	41	15	24	39	52	....	....	....	....	....
1986-87	**Boston**	**NHL**	**14**	**2**	**4**	**6**	**21**	**3**	**0**	**0**	**0**	**0**
	Moncton	AHL	58	29	26	55	81	4	0	2	2	13
1987-88	**Boston**	**NHL**	**80**	**22**	**23**	**45**	**73**	**23**	**6**	**8**	**14**	**66**
1988-89	**Boston**	**NHL**	**75**	**14**	**14**	**28**	**99**	**10**	**2**	**4**	**6**	**19**
	NHL Totals		**169**	**38**	**41**	**79**	**193**	**36**	**8**	**12**	**20**	**85**

a ECAC Second Team All-Star (1985)

SWEENEY, TIM

Center. Shoots left. 5'11", 180 lbs. Born, Boston. MA, April 12, 1967.
(Calgary's 7th choice, 122nd over-all, in 1985 Entry Draft).

			Regular Season					Playoffs				
Season	**Club**	**Lea**	**GP**	**G**	**A**	**TP**	**PIM**	**GP**	**G**	**A**	**TP**	**PIM**
1985-86	Boston College	H.E.	32	8	4	12	8	....	....	....	....	....
1986-87	Boston College	H.E.	38	31	18	49	28	....	....	....	....	....
1987-88	Boston College	H.E.	18	9	11	20	18	....	....	....	....	....
1988-89ab	Boston College	H.E.	39	29	44	73	26	....	....	....	....	....

a Hockey East First All-Star Team (1989)
b NCAA East Second All-American Team (1989)

SYKES, PHIL

Left wing. Shoots left. 6', 185 lbs. Born, Dawson Creek, B.C., May 18, 1959.

			Regular Season					Playoffs				
Season	**Club**	**Lea**	**GP**	**G**	**A**	**TP**	**PIM**	**GP**	**G**	**A**	**TP**	**PIM**
1979-80	North Dakota	WCHA	37	22	27	49	34	....	....	....	....	....
1980-81	North Dakota	WCHA	38	28	34	62	22	....	....	....	....	....
1981-82abc	North Dakota	WCHA	37	22	27	49	34	....	....	....	....	....
1982-83	**Los Angeles**	**NHL**	**7**	**2**	**0**	**2**	**2**	....	....	....	....	....
	New Haven	AHL	71	19	26	45	111	12	2	2	4	21
1983-84	**Los Angeles**	**NHL**	**3**	**0**	**0**	**0**	**2**	....	....	....	....	....
	New Haven	AHL	77	29	37	66	101	....	....	....	....	....
1984-85	**Los Angeles**	**NHL**	**79**	**17**	**15**	**32**	**38**	**3**	**0**	**1**	**1**	**4**
1985-86	**Los Angeles**	**NHL**	**76**	**20**	**24**	**44**	**97**	....	....	....	....	....
1986-87	**Los Angeles**	**NHL**	**58**	**6**	**15**	**21**	**133**	**5**	**0**	**1**	**1**	**8**
1987-88	**Los Angeles**	**NHL**	**40**	**9**	**12**	**21**	**82**	**4**	**0**	**0**	**0**	**0**
1988-89	**Los Angeles**	**NHL**	**23**	**0**	**1**	**1**	**8**	**3**	**0**	**0**	**0**	**8**
	New Haven	AHL	34	9	17	26	23	....	....	....	....	....
	NHL Totals		**286**	**54**	**67**	**121**	**362**	**15**	**0**	**2**	**2**	**20**

a WCHA First All-Star Team (1982)
b Named WCHA Player of the Year (1982)
c Named Most Valuable Player, NCAA Tournament (1982)

Signed as a free agent by **Los Angeles**, April 5, 1982.

TAGLIANETTI, PETER

Defense. Shoots left. 6'2", 195 lbs. Born, Framingham, MA, August 15, 1963.
(Winnipeg's 4th choice, 43rd over-all, in 1983 Entry Draft).

			Regular Season					Playoffs				
Season	Club	Lea	GP	G	A	TP	PIM	GP	G	A	TP	PIM
1981-82	Providence	ECAC	2	0	0	0	2	....	....	....	....	....
1982-83	Providence	ECAC	43	4	17	21	68	....	....	....	....	....
1983-84	Providence	ECAC	30	4	25	29	68	....	....	....	....	....
1984-85	**Winnipeg**	**NHL**	**1**	**0**	**0**	**0**	**0**	**1**	**0**	**0**	**0**	**0**
a	Providence	H.E.	35	6	18	24	32	....	....	....	....	....
1985-86	**Winnipeg**	**NHL**	**18**	**0**	**0**	**0**	**48**	**3**	**0**	**0**	**0**	**2**
	Sherbrooke	AHL	24	1	18	9	75	....	....	....	....	....
1986-87	**Winnipeg**	**NHL**	**3**	**0**	**0**	**0**	**12**	....	....	....	....	....
	Sherbrooke	AHL	54	5	14	19	104	10	2	5	7	25
1987-88	**Winnipeg**	**NHL**	**70**	**6**	**17**	**23**	**182**	**5**	**1**	**1**	**2**	**12**
1988-89	**Winnipeg**	**NHL**	**66**	**1**	**14**	**15**	**226**	....	....	....	....	....
	NHL Totals		**158**	**7**	**31**	**38**	**468**	**9**	**1**	**1**	**2**	**14**

a Hockey East First All-Star Team (1985).

TANTI, TONY (TAN-tee)

Right wing. Shoots left. 5'9", 190 lbs. Born, Toronto, Ont., September 7, 1963.
(Chicago's 1st choice, 12th over-all, in 1981 Entry Draft).

			Regular Season					Playoffs				
Season	Club	Lea	GP	G	A	TP	PIM	GP	G	A	TP	PIM
1979-80	St. Michael's	Jr. B	37	31	27	50	67	....	....	....	....	....
1980-81a	Oshawa	OHA	67	81	69	150	197	11	7	8	15	41
1981-82	**Chicago**	**NHL**	**2**	**0**	**0**	**0**	**0**	....	....	....	....	....
b	Oshawa	OHL	57	62	64	126	138	12	14	12	26	15
1982-83	Oshawa	OHL	30	34	28	62	35	....	....	....	....	....
	Chicago	**NHL**	**1**	**1**	**0**	**1**	**0**	....	....	....	....	....
	Vancouver	**NHL**	**39**	**8**	**8**	**16**	**16**	**4**	**0**	**1**	**1**	**0**
1983-84	**Vancouver**	**NHL**	**79**	**45**	**41**	**86**	**50**	**4**	**1**	**2**	**3**	**0**
1984-85	**Vancouver**	**NHL**	**68**	**39**	**20**	**59**	**45**	....	....	....	....	....
1985-86	**Vancouver**	**NHL**	**77**	**39**	**33**	**72**	**85**	**3**	**0**	**1**	**1**	**11**
1986-87	**Vancouver**	**NHL**	**77**	**41**	**38**	**79**	**84**	....	....	....	....	....
1987-88	**Vancouver**	**NHL**	**73**	**40**	**37**	**77**	**90**	....	....	....	....	....
1988-89	**Vancouver**	**NHL**	**77**	**24**	**25**	**49**	**69**	**7**	**0**	**5**	**5**	**4**
	NHL Totals		**493**	**237**	**202**	**439**	**439**	**18**	**1**	**9**	**10**	**15**

a OHA First All-Star Team (1981)
b OHL Second All-Star Team (1982)

Played in NHL All-Star Game (1986)

Traded to **Vancouver** by **Chicago** for Curt Fraser, January 6, 1983.

TARRANT, JERRY

Defense. Shoots left. 6'2", 190 lbs. Born, Burlington, VT, April 3, 1966.
(Calgary's 1st choice, 26th overall, in 1988 Supplemental Draft).

			Regular Season					Playoffs				
Season	Club	Lea	GP	G	A	TP	PIM	GP	G	A	TP	PIM
1985-86	U. of Vermont	ECAC	23	0	4	4	22	....	....	....	....	....
1986-87	U. of Vermont	ECAC	32	3	9	12	34	....	....	....	....	....
1987-88	U. of Vermont	ECAC	31	2	8	10	28	....	....	....	....	....
1988-89	U. of Vermont	ECAC	34	3	19	22	54	....	....	....	....	....

TAYLOR, DARREN

Center. Shoots left. 6'1", 170 lbs. Born, Calgary, Alta., May 28, 1967.
(Vancouver's 12th choice, 235th over-all, in 1985 Entry Draft).

			Regular Season					Playoffs				
Season	Club	Lea	GP	G	A	TP	PIM	GP	G	A	TP	PIM
1984-85	Calgary	WHL	72	11	5	16	54	7	1	0	1	10
1985-86	Seattle	WHL	68	11	19	30	137	5	0	0	0	8
1986-87	Seattle	WHL	60	13	13	26	112	....	....	....	....	....
1988-89	Peoria	IHL	40	6	6	12	149	....	....	....	....	....

TAYLOR, DAVID ANDREW (DAVE)

Right wing. Shoots right. 6', 200 lbs. Born, Levack, Ont., December 4, 1955.
(Los Angeles' 14th choice, 210th over-all, in 1975 Amateur Draft).

			Regular Season					Playoffs				
Season	Club	Lea	GP	G	A	TP	PIM	GP	G	A	TP	PIM
1976-77	Clarkson	ECAC	34	41	67	108	....	....	....	....	....	....
	Fort Worth	CHL	7	2	4	6	6	....	....	....	....	....
1977-78	**Los Angeles**	**NHL**	**64**	**22**	**21**	**43**	**47**	**2**	**0**	**0**	**0**	**5**
1978-79	**Los Angeles**	**NHL**	**78**	**43**	**48**	**91**	**124**	**2**	**0**	**0**	**0**	**2**
1979-80	**Los Angeles**	**NHL**	**61**	**37**	**53**	**90**	**72**	**4**	**2**	**1**	**3**	**4**
1980-81a	**Los Angeles**	**NHL**	**72**	**47**	**65**	**112**	**130**	**4**	**2**	**2**	**4**	**10**
1981-82	**Los Angeles**	**NHL**	**78**	**39**	**67**	**106**	**130**	**10**	**4**	**6**	**10**	**20**
1982-83	**Los Angeles**	**NHL**	**46**	**21**	**37**	**58**	**76**	....	....	....	....	....
1983-84	**Los Angeles**	**NHL**	**63**	**20**	**49**	**69**	**91**	....	....	....	....	....
1984-85	**Los Angeles**	**NHL**	**79**	**41**	**51**	**92**	**132**	**3**	**2**	**2**	**4**	**8**
1985-86	**Los Angeles**	**NHL**	**76**	**33**	**38**	**71**	**110**	....	....	....	....	....
1986-87	**Los Angeles**	**NHL**	**67**	**18**	**44**	**62**	**84**	**5**	**2**	**3**	**5**	**6**
1987-88	**Los Angeles**	**NHL**	**68**	**26**	**41**	**67**	**129**	**5**	**3**	**3**	**6**	**6**
1988-89	**Los Angeles**	**NHL**	**70**	**26**	**37**	**63**	**80**	**11**	**1**	**5**	**6**	**19**
	NHL Totals		**822**	**373**	**551**	**924**	**1205**	**46**	**16**	**22**	**38**	**80**

a NHL Second All-Star Team (1981)

Played in NHL All-Star Game (1981, 1982, 1986)

TAYLOR, RANDY

Defense. Shoots right. 6'2", 195 lbs. Born, Cornwall, Ont., July 30, 1965.
(Pittsburgh's 2nd choice, 9th overall, in 1986 Supplemental Draft).

			Regular Season					Playoffs				
Season	Club	Lea	GP	G	A	TP	PIM	GP	G	A	TP	PIM
1983-84	Harvard	ECAC	23	0	3	3	4	....	....	....	....	....
1984-85	Harvard	ECAC	30	6	30	36	12	....	....	....	....	....
1985-86a	Harvard	ECAC	33	5	20	25	30	....	....	....	....	....
1986-87b	Harvard	ECAC	34	3	35	38	30	....	....	....	....	....
1987-88	Peoria	IHL	27	1	7	8	22	7	0	1	1	8
	Muskegon	IHL	37	0	14	14	14	....	....	....	....	....
1988-89	Flint	IHL	31	2	6	8	11	....	....	....	....	....
	Indianapolis	IHL	44	2	15	17	31	....	....	....	....	....

a ECAC Second All-Star Team (1986)
b ECAC First All-Star Team (1987)

TAYLOR, SCOTT

Defense. Shoots right. 6', 180 lbs. Born, Toronto, Ont., March 23, 1968.
(Toronto's 5th choice, 90th overall, in 1986 Entry Draft).

			Regular Season					Playoffs				
Season	Club	Lea	GP	G	A	TP	PIM	GP	G	A	TP	PIM
1985-86	Kitchener	OHL	59	4	13	17	211	4	1	0	1	6
1986-87	Kitchener	OHL	53	6	16	22	123	4	0	0	0	9
1987-88	Belleville	OHL	48	5	12	17	165	....	....	....	....	....
1988-89	Flint	IHL	7	0	2	2	22	....	....	....	....	....

TAYLOR, TIM

Center. Shoots left. 5'11", 170 lbs. Born, Stratford, Ont., February 6, 1969.
(Washington's 2nd choice, 36th overall, in 1988 Entry Draft).

			Regular Season					Playoffs				
Season	Club	Lea	GP	G	A	TP	PIM	GP	G	A	TP	PIM
1986-87	London	OHL	34	7	9	16	11	....	....	....	....	....
1987-88	London	OHL	64	46	50	96	66	12	9	9	18	26
1988-89	London	OHL	61	34	80	114	93	21	*21	25	*46	58

TEEVENS, MARK

Right wing. Shoots left. 6', 180 lbs. Born, Ottawa, Ont., June 17, 1966.
(Pittsburgh's 4th choice, 64th over-all, in 1984 Entry Draft).

			Regular Season					Playoffs				
Season	Club	Lea	GP	G	A	TP	PIM	GP	G	A	TP	PIM
1983-84	Peterborough	OHL	70	27	37	64	70	8	3	4	7	4
1984-85	Peterborough	OHL	65	43	90	133	70	17	10	12	22	24
1985-86	Peterborough	OHL	50	31	50	81	106	16	4	21	25	19
1986-87	Baltimore	AHL	71	15	16	31	34	....	....	....	....	....
1987-88	Muskegon	IHL	53	17	26	43	39	....	....	....	....	....
1988-89	Indianapolis	IHL	78	30	22	52	51	....	....	....	....	....

TEPPER, STEPHEN

Right wing. Shoots right. 6'4", 220 lbs. Born, Westboro, MA, March 10, 1969.
(Chicago's 7th choice, 134th overall, in 1987 Entry Draft).

			Regular Season					Playoffs				
Season	Club	Lea	GP	G	A	TP	PIM	GP	G	A	TP	PIM
1987-88	Westboro	HS	24	39	24	63	....	....	....	....	....	....
1988-89	U. of Maine	H.E.	26	3	9	12	32	....	....	....	....	....

TERRION, GREG PATRICK (TAIR ee yahn)

Left wing. Shoots left. 5'11", 190 lbs. Born, Marmora, Ont., May 2, 1960.
(Los Angeles' 3rd choice, 33rd over-all, in 1980 Entry Draft).

			Regular Season					Playoffs				
Season	Club	Lea	GP	G	A	TP	PIM	GP	G	A	TP	PIM
1978-79	Brantford	OHA	59	27	28	55	48	....	....	....	....	....
1979-80	Brantford	OHA	67	44	78	122	13	11	4	7	11	14
1980-81	**Los Angeles**	**NHL**	**73**	**12**	**25**	**37**	**99**	**3**	**1**	**0**	**1**	**4**
1981-82	**Los Angeles**	**NHL**	**61**	**15**	**22**	**37**	**23**	....	....	....	....	....
1982-83	New Haven	AHL	4	0	1	1	7	....	....	....	....	....
	Toronto	**NHL**	**74**	**16**	**16**	**32**	**59**	**4**	**1**	**2**	**3**	**2**
1983-84	**Toronto**	**NHL**	**79**	**15**	**24**	**39**	**36**	....	....	....	....	....
1984-85	**Toronto**	**NHL**	**72**	**14**	**17**	**31**	**20**	....	....	....	....	....
1985-86	**Toronto**	**NHL**	**76**	**10**	**22**	**32**	**31**	**10**	**0**	**3**	**3**	**17**
1986-87	**Toronto**	**NHL**	**67**	**7**	**8**	**15**	**6**	**13**	**0**	**2**	**2**	**14**
1987-88	**Toronto**	**NHL**	**59**	**4**	**16**	**20**	**65**	**5**	**0**	**2**	**2**	**4**
	Newmarket	AHL	4	1	3	4	6	....	....	....	....	....
1988-89	Newmarket	AHL	60	15	34	49	64	4	0	1	1	2
	NHL Totals		**556**	**93**	**150**	**243**	**339**	**35**	**2**	**9**	**11**	**41**

Traded to **Toronto** by **Los Angeles** for Toronto's fourth round choice (David Korol) in 1983 Entry Draft (later transferred to Detroit), October 19, 1982.

TERWILLIGER, TOM

Defense. Shoots right. 6'2", 185 lbs. Born, Denver, CO, September 1, 1965.
(Minnesota's 11th choice, 222nd overall, in 1984 Entry Draft).

			Regular Season					Playoffs				
Season	Club	Lea	GP	G	A	TP	PIM	GP	G	A	TP	PIM
1984-85	Miami-Ohio	CCHA	29	2	3	5	18	....	....	....	....	....
1985-86	Miami-Ohio	CCHA	32	1	3	4	35	....	....	....	....	....
1986-87	Miami-Ohio	CCHA	26	2	1	3	24	....	....	....	....	....
1987-88	Miami-Ohio	CCHA	35	1	4	5	53	....	....	....	....	....
1988-89			DID NOT PLAY									

THAYER, CHRIS

Center. Shoots right. 6'2", 190 lbs. Born, Exeter, NH, November 9, 1967.
(Chicago's 10th choice, 224th overall, in 1986 Entry Draft).

			Regular Season					Playoffs				
Season	Club	Lea	GP	G	A	TP	PIM	GP	G	A	TP	PIM
1985-86	Kent	HS	25	7	16	23	3	....	....	....	....	....
1986-87	Kent	HS	22	15	22	37	0	....	....	....	....	....
1987-88	N. Hampshire	H.E.	18	0	0	0	8	....	....	....	....	....
1988-89	N. Hampshire	H.E.	DID NOT PLAY									

THELVEN, MICHAEL (tell-VAIN)

Defense. Shoots right. 5'11", 185 lbs. Born, Stockholm, Sweden, January 7, 1961.
(Boston's 8th choice, 186th over-all, in 1980 Entry Draft).

			Regular Season					Playoffs				
Season	Club	Lea	GP	G	A	TP	PIM	GP	G	A	TP	PIM
1978-79	Djurgarden	Swe.	10	0	1	1	8	....	....	....	....	....
1980-81	Djurgarden	Swe.	28	2	4	6	38	....	....	....	....	....
1981-82	Djurgarden	Swe.	34	5	3	8	53	6	2	1	3	2
1982-83	Djurgarden	Swe.	30	3	14	17	50	7	1	2	3	12
1983-84	Djurgarden	Swe.	27	6	8	14	51	5	1	1	2	6
1984-85	Djurgarden	Swe.	33	8	13	21	54	8	0	2	2	2
1985-86	**Boston**	**NHL**	**60**	**6**	**20**	**26**	**48**	**3**	**0**	**0**	**0**	**0**
1986-87	**Boston**	**NHL**	**34**	**5**	**15**	**20**	**18**	....	....	....	....	....
1987-88	**Boston**	**NHL**	**67**	**6**	**25**	**31**	**57**	**21**	**3**	**3**	**6**	**26**
1988-89	**Boston**	**NHL**	**40**	**3**	**18**	**21**	**71**	**10**	**1**	**7**	**8**	**8**
	NHL Totals		**201**	**20**	**78**	**98**	**194**	**34**	**4**	**10**	**14**	**34**

THIBAUDEAU, GILLES (TIB ah doh)

Center. Shoots left. 5'10", 165 lbs. Born, Montreal, Que., March 4, 1963.

			Regular Season					Playoffs				
Season	Club	Lea	GP	G	A	TP	PIM	GP	G	A	TP	PIM
1983-84	St. Antoine	Jr. B	38	63	77	140	146	....	....	....	....	....
1984-85	Sherbrooke	AHL	7	2	4	6	0	....	....	....	....	....
	Flint	IHL	71	52	45	97	81	....	....	....	....	....
1985-86	Sherbrooke	AHL	61	15	23	38	20	....	....	....	....	....
1986-87	**Montreal**	**NHL**	**9**	**1**	**3**	**4**	**0**	....	....	....	....	....
	Sherbrooke	AHL	62	27	40	67	26	....	....	....	....	....
1987-88	**Montreal**	**NHL**	**17**	**5**	**6**	**11**	**0**	**8**	**3**	**3**	**6**	**2**
	Sherbrooke	AHL	59	39	57	96	45	....	....	....	....	....
1988-89	**Montreal**	**NHL**	**32**	**6**	**6**	**12**	**6**	....	....	....	....	....
	NHL Totals		**49**	**11**	**12**	**23**	**6**	**8**	**3**	**3**	**6**	**2**

Signed as a free agent by **Montreal**, October 9, 1984.

THOMAS, JOHN (SCOTT)

Right wing. Shoots right. 6'2", 195 lbs. Born, Buffalo, NY, January 18, 1970.
(Buffalo's 2nd choice, 56th overall, in 1989 Entry Draft).

			Regular Season					Playoffs				
Season	Club	Lea	GP	G	A	TP	PIM	GP	G	A	TP	PIM
1987-88	Nichols	HS	16	23	39	63	82	....	....	....	....	....
1988-89	Nichols	HS	....	38	52	90	....	....	....	....	....	....

THOMAS, STEVE

Left Wing. Shoots left. 5'10", 180 lbs. Born, Stockport, England, July 15, 1963.

			Regular Season					Playoffs				
Season	Club	Lea	GP	G	A	TP	PIM	GP	G	A	TP	PIM
1983-84	Toronto	OHL	70	51	54	105	77	....	....	....	....	....
1984-85	**Toronto**	**NHL**	**18**	**1**	**1**	**2**	**2**	....	....	....	....	....
ab	St. Catharines	AHL	64	42	48	90	56	....	....	....	....	....
1985-86	**Toronto**	**NHL**	**65**	**20**	**37**	**57**	**36**	**10**	**6**	**8**	**14**	**9**
	St. Catharines	AHL	19	18	14	32	35	....	....	....	....	....
1986-87	**Toronto**	**NHL**	**78**	**35**	**27**	**62**	**114**	**13**	**2**	**3**	**5**	**13**
1987-88	**Chicago**	**NHL**	**30**	**13**	**13**	**26**	**40**	**3**	**1**	**2**	**3**	**6**
1988-89	**Chicago**	**NHL**	**45**	**21**	**19**	**40**	**69**	**12**	**3**	**5**	**8**	**10**
	NHL Totals		**236**	**90**	**97**	**187**	**261**	**38**	**12**	**18**	**30**	**38**

a Won AHL Rookie of the Year (1985)
b AHL First All-Star Team (1985)

Signed as a free agent by **Toronto,** May 12, 1984. Traded to **Chicago** by **Toronto** with Rick Vaive and Bob McGill for Al Secord and Ed Olczyk, September 3, 1987.

THOMLINSON, DAVE

Left wing. Shoots left. 6'1", 185 lbs. Born, Edmonton, Alta., October 22, 1966.
(Toronto's 3rd choice, 43rd overall, in 1985 Entry Draft).

			Regular Season					Playoffs				
Season	Club	Lea	GP	G	A	TP	PIM	GP	G	A	TP	PIM
1984-85	Brandon	WHL	26	13	14	27	70	....	....	....	....	....
1985-86	Brandon	WHL	53	25	20	45	116	....	....	....	....	....
1986-87	Brandon	WHL	2	0	1	1	9	....	....	....	....	....
	Moose Jaw	WHL	70	44	36	80	117	9	7	3	10	19
1987-88	Peoria	IHL	74	27	30	57	56	7	4	3	7	11
1988-89	Peoria	IHL	64	27	29	56	154	3	0	1	1	8

THOMPSON, BRENT

Defense. Shoots left. 6'2", 175 lbs. Born, Calgary, Alta., January 9, 1971.
(Los Angeles' 1st choice, 39th overall, in 1989 Entry Draft).

			Regular Season					Playoffs				
Season	Club	Lea	GP	G	A	TP	PIM	GP	G	A	TP	PIM
1987-88	Calgary	Midget	25	0	13	13	33	....	....	....	....	....
1988-89	Medicine Hat	WHL	72	3	10	13	160	3	0	0	0	2

THOMSON, JIM

Right Wing. Shoots right. 6'1", 205 lbs. Born, Edmonton, Alta., December 30, 1965.
(Washington's 9th choice, 185th over-all, in 1984 Entry Draft).

			Regular Season					Playoffs				
Season	Club	Lea	GP	G	A	TP	PIM	GP	G	A	TP	PIM
1983-84	Toronto	OHL	60	10	18	28	68	9	1	0	1	26
1984-85	Toronto	OHL	63	23	28	51	122	5	3	1	4	25
	Binghamton	AHL	4	0	0	0	2	....	....	....	....	....
1985-86	Binghamton	AHL	59	15	9	24	195	....	....	....	....	....
1986-87	**Washington**	**NHL**	**10**	**0**	**0**	**0**	**35**	....	....	....	....	....
	Binghamton	AHL	57	13	10	23	360	10	0	1	1	40
1987-88	Binghamton	AHL	25	8	9	17	64	4	1	2	3	7
1988-89	**Washington**	**NHL**	**14**	**2**	**0**	**2**	**53**	....	....	....	....	....
	Hartford	**NHL**	**5**	**0**	**0**	**0**	**14**	....	....	....	....	....
	Baltimore	AHL	41	25	16	41	129	....	....	....	....	....
	NHL Totals		**29**	**2**	**0**	**2**	**102**	....	....	....	....	....

Traded to **Hartford** by **Washington** for Scot Kleinendorst, March 6, 1989.

THORNTON, SCOTT

Center. Shoots left. 6'2", 200 lbs. Born, London, Ont., January 9, 1971.
(Toronto's 1st choice, 3rd overall, in 1989 Entry Draft).

			Regular Season					Playoffs				
Season	Club	Lea	GP	G	A	TP	PIM	GP	G	A	TP	PIM
1987-88	Belleville	OHL	62	11	19	30	54	6	0	1	1	2
1988-89	Belleville	OHL	59	28	34	62	103	5	1	1	2	6

TIKKANEN, ESA (TEE kuh nehn)

Left Wing. Shoots left. 6'1", 200 lbs. Born, Helsinki, Finland, January 25, 1965.
(Edmonton's 4th choice, 82nd over-all, in 1983 Entry Draft).

			Regular Season					Playoffs				
Season	Club	Lea	GP	G	A	TP	PIM	GP	G	A	TP	PIM
1981-82	Regina	WHL	2	0	0	0	0	....	....	....	....	....
1982-83	IFK	Fin. Jr.	30	34	31	65	104	4	4	3	7	10
	IFK	Fin.	....	....	....	....	....	1	0	0	0	2
1983-84	IFK	Fin. Jr.	6	5	9	14	13	4	4	3	7	8
	IFK	Fin.	36	19	11	30	30	2	0	0	0	0
1984-85	IFK	Fin.	36	21	33	54	42	....	....	....	....	....
	Edmonton	**NHL**	....	....	....	....	....	**3**	**0**	**0**	**0**	**2**
1985-86	**Edmonton**	**NHL**	**35**	**7**	**6**	**13**	**28**	**8**	**3**	**2**	**5**	**7**
	Nova Scotia	AHL	15	4	8	12	17	....	....	....	....	....
1986-87	**Edmonton**	**NHL**	**76**	**34**	**44**	**78**	**120**	**21**	**7**	**2**	**9**	**22**
1987-88	**Edmonton**	**NHL**	**80**	**23**	**51**	**74**	**153**	**19**	**10**	**17**	**27**	**72**
1988-89	**Edmonton**	**NHL**	**67**	**31**	**47**	**78**	**92**	**7**	**1**	**3**	**4**	**12**
	NHL Totals		**258**	**95**	**148**	**243**	**393**	**58**	**21**	**24**	**45**	**115**

TILLEY, TOM

Defense. Shoots right. 6', 180 lbs. Born, Trenton, Ont., March 28, 1965.
(St. Louis' 13th choice, 196th overall, in 1984 Entry Draft).

			Regular Season					Playoffs				
Season	Club	Lea	GP	G	A	TP	PIM	GP	G	A	TP	PIM
1984-85	Michigan State	CCHA	37	1	5	6	58	....	....	....	....	....
1985-86	Michigan State	CCHA	42	9	25	34	48	....	....	....	....	....
1986-87	Michigan State	CCHA	42	7	14	21	48	....	....	....	....	....
1987-88a	Michigan State	CCHA	46	8	18	26	44	....	....	....	....	....
1988-89	**St. Louis**	**NHL**	**70**	**1**	**22**	**23**	**47**	**10**	**1**	**2**	**3**	**17**
	NHL Totals		**70**	**1**	**22**	**23**	**47**	**10**	**1**	**2**	**3**	**17**

a CCHA First All-Star Team (1988)

TINORDI, MARK

Defense. Shoots left. 6'4", 205 lbs. Born, Red Deer, Alta., May 9, 1966.

			Regular Season					Playoffs				
Season	Club	Lea	GP	G	A	TP	PIM	GP	G	A	TP	PIM
1982-83	Lethbridge	WHL	64	0	4	4	50	20	1	1	2	6
1983-84	Lethbridge	WHL	72	5	14	19	53	5	0	1	1	7
1984-85	Lethbridge	WHL	58	10	15	25	134	4	0	2	2	12
1985-86	Lethbridge	WHL	58	8	30	38	139	8	1	3	4	15
1986-87	Calgary	WHL	61	29	37	66	148	....	....	....	....	....
	New Haven	AHL	2	0	0	0	2	2	0	0	0	0
1987-88	**NY Rangers**	**NHL**	**24**	**1**	**2**	**3**	**50**	....	....	....	....	....
	Colorado	IHL	41	8	19	27	150	11	1	5	6	31
1988-89	**Minnesota**	**NHL**	**47**	**2**	**3**	**5**	**107**	**5**	**0**	**0**	**0**	**0**
	Kalamazoo	IHL	10	0	0	0	35	....	....	....	....	....
	NHL Totals		**71**	**3**	**5**	**8**	**157**	**5**	**0**	**0**	**0**	**0**

Signed as a free agent by **NY Rangers**, January 4, 1987.

Traded to **Minnesota** by **NY Rangers** with Paul Jerrard, the rights to Bret Barnett and Mike Sullivan, and Los Angeles' third-round choice (Murray Garbutt) in 1989 Entry Draft — acquired March 10, 1987 by Minnesota — for Brian Lawton, Igor Liba and the rights to Eric Bennett, October 11, 1988.

TIPPETT, DAVE (TIP-it)

Center. Shoots left. 5'10", 180 lbs. Born, Moosomin, Sask., August 25, 1961.

			Regular Season					Playoffs				
Season	Club	Lea	GP	G	A	TP	PIM	GP	G	A	TP	PIM
1981-82	North Dakota	WCHA	43	13	28	41	20	....	....	....	....	....
1982-83	North Dakota	WCHA	36	15	31	46	24	....	....	....	....	....
1983-84	Cdn. Olympic	...	66	14	19	33	24	....	....	....	....	....
	Hartford	**NHL**	**17**	**4**	**2**	**6**	**2**	....	....	....	....	....
1984-85	**Hartford**	**NHL**	**80**	**7**	**12**	**19**	**12**	....	....	....	....	....
1985-86	**Hartford**	**NHL**	**80**	**14**	**20**	**34**	**18**	**10**	**2**	**2**	**4**	**4**
1986-87	**Hartford**	**NHL**	**80**	**9**	**22**	**31**	**42**	**6**	**0**	**2**	**2**	**4**
1987-88	**Hartford**	**NHL**	**80**	**16**	**21**	**37**	**32**	**6**	**0**	**0**	**0**	**2**
1988-89	**Hartford**	**NHL**	**80**	**17**	**24**	**41**	**45**	**4**	**0**	**1**	**1**	**0**
	NHL Totals		**417**	**67**	**101**	**168**	**151**	**26**	**2**	**5**	**7**	**10**

Signed as free agent by **Hartford**, February 29, 1984.

TIRKKONEN, PEKKA

Center. Shoots left. 6'1", 195 lbs. Born, Savonlinna, Finland, July 17, 1968.
(Boston's 2nd choice, 34th overall, in 1986 Entry Draft).

			Regular Season					Playoffs				
Season	Club	Lea	GP	G	A	TP	PIM	GP	G	A	TP	PIM
1984-85	Sapko	Fin.	21	3	5	8	0	6	6	0	6.	0
1985-86	Sapko	Fin.	40	14	13	27	12	....	....	....	....	....
1986-87	Sapko	Fin.	40	15	21	36	10	....	....	....	....	....
1987-88	T.P.S.	Fin.	44	11	12	23	4	....	....	....	....	....
1988-89	T.P.S.	Fin.	42	11	15	26	8	10	1	2	3	0

TISDALE, TIMOTHY

Center. Shoots right. 6'1", 190 lbs. Born, Shaunavon, Sask., May 28, 1965.
(Edmonton's 13th choice, 250th overall, in 1988 Entry Draft).

			Regular Season					Playoffs				
Season	Club	Lea	GP	G	A	TP	PIM	GP	G	A	TP	PIM
1987-88	Swift Current	WHL	32	11	15	26	45	....	....	....	....	....
1988-89	Swift Current	WHL	68	57	82	139	89	12	17	15	32	22

TKACHUK, GRANT (kuh-CHUK)

Left wing. Shoots left. 5'10", 180 lbs. Born, Lac La Biche, Alta., September 24, 1968.
(Buffalo's 9th choice, 169th overall, in 1987 Entry Draft).

			Regular Season					Playoffs				
Season	Club	Lea	GP	G	A	TP	PIM	GP	G	A	TP	PIM
1984-85	Saskatoon	WHL	71	8	16	24	55	3	0	1	1	2
1985-86	Saskatoon	WHL	52	18	27	45	82	12	1	3	4	15
1986-87	Saskatoon	WHL	71	46	36	82	108	11	4	3	7	12
1987-88a	Saskatoon	WHL	70	51	46	97	126	6	3	6	9	8
1988-89	Rochester	AHL	64	12	13	25	26	....	....	....	....	....

a WHL East All-Star Team (1988)

TOCCHET, RICK (TAHK-iht)

Right wing. Shoots right. 6', 195 lbs.   Born, Scarborough, Ont., April 9, 1964.
(Philadelphia's 5th choice, 121st over-all, in 1983 Entry Draft).

			Regular Season					Playoffs				
Season	Club	Lea	GP	G	A	TP	PIM	GP	G	A	TP	PIM
1980-81	St.Michael's	Jr. B.	5	1	1	2	2	....	....	....	....	....
1981-82	S. S. Marie	OHL	59	7	15	22	184	11	1	1	2	28
1982-83	S. S. Marie	OHL	66	32	34	66	146	16	4	13	17	67
1983-84	S. S. Marie	OHL	64	44	64	108	209	16	*22	14	*36	41
1984-85	Philadelphia	NHL	75	14	25	39	181	19	3	4	7	72
1985-86	Philadelphia	NHL	69	14	21	35	284	5	1	2	3	26
1986-87	Philadelphia	NHL	69	21	26	47	288	26	11	10	21	72
1987-88	Philadelphia	NHL	65	31	33	64	301	5	1	4	5	55
1988-89	Philadelphia	NHL	66	45	36	81	183	16	6	6	12	69
	NHL Totals		344	125	141	266	1237	71	22	26	48	294

Played in NHL All-Star Game (1989)

TODD, KEVIN

Center. Shoot left. 5'10", 180 lbs.   Born, Winnipeg, Man., May 4, 1968.
(New Jersey's 7th choice, 129th overall, in 1986 Entry Draft).

			Regular Season					Playoffs				
Season	Club	Lea	GP	G	A	TP	PIM	GP	G	A	TP	PIM
1985-86	Prince Albert	WHL	55	14	25	39	19	20	7	6	13	29
1986-87	Prince Albert	WHL	71	39	46	85	92	8	2	5	7	17
1987-88	Prince Albert	WHL	72	49	72	121	83	10	8	11	19	27
1988-89	New Jersey	NHL	1	0	0	0	0	....	....	....	....	....
	Utica	AHL	78	26	45	71	62	4	2	0	2	6
	NHL Totals		1	0	0	0	0	....	....	....	....	....

TOIVOLA, TERO

Left wing. Shoots left. 5'11", 155 lbs.   Born, Tampere, Finland, July 22, 1968.
(Washington's 10th choice, 187th overall, in 1986 Entry Draft).

			Regular Season					Playoffs				
Season	Club	Lea	GP	G	A	TP	PIM	GP	G	A	TP	PIM
1985-86	Tappara	Fin. Jr.	24	8	21	29	59	5	1	2	3	16
1986-87	Tappara	Fin.	11	0	0	0	0	9	0	0	0	0
1987-88	Tappara	Fin.	31	6	8	14	18	7	0	1	1	12
1988-89	Tappara	Fin.	32	7	14	21	16	5	2	1	3	4

TOMLINSON, KIRK

Center. Shoots left. 5'10", 175 lbs.   Born, Toronto, Ont., May 2, 1968.
(Minnesota's 7th choice, 75th overall, in 1986 Entry Draft).

			Regular Season					Playoffs				
Season	Club	Lea	GP	G	A	TP	PIM	GP	G	A	TP	PIM
1985-86	Hamilton	OHL	58	28	23	51	230	....	....	....	....	....
1986-87	Hamilton	OHL	65	33	37	70	169	9	4	6	10	28
1987-88	Minnesota	NHL	1	0	0	0	0	....	....	....	....	....
	Oshawa	OHL	49	20	31	51	200	6	4	4	8	16
1988-89	Kalamazoo	IHL	3	0	0	0	12	....	....	....	....	....
	NHL Totals		1	0	0	0	0	....	....	....	....	....

TONELLI, JOHN (tah-NEL-ee)

Left wing. Shoots left. 6'1", 200 lbs.   Born, Milton, Ont., March 23, 1957.
(NY Islanders' 2nd choice, 33rd over-all, in 1977 Amateur Draft).

			Regular Season					Playoffs				
Season	Club	Lea	GP	G	A	TP	PIM	GP	G	A	TP	PIM
1973-74	Toronto	OHA	69	18	37	55	62	....	....	....	....	....
1974-75a	Toronto	OHA	70	49	86	135	85	....	....	....	....	....
1975-76	Houston	WHA	79	17	14	31	66	17	7	7	14	18
1976-77	Houston	WHA	80	24	31	55	109	11	3	4	7	12
1977-78	Houston	WHA	65	23	41	64	103	6	1	3	4	8
1978-79	NY Islanders	NHL	73	17	39	56	44	10	1	6	7	0
1979-80	NY Islanders	NHL	77	14	30	44	49	21	7	9	16	18
1980-81	NY Islanders	NHL	70	20	32	52	57	16	5	8	13	16
1981-82b	NY Islanders	NHL	80	35	58	93	57	19	6	10	16	18
1982-83	NY Islanders	NHL	76	31	40	71	55	20	7	11	18	20
1983-84	NY Islanders	NHL	73	27	40	67	66	17	1	3	4	31
1984-85b	NY Islanders	NHL	80	42	58	100	95	10	1	8	9	10
1985-86	NY Islanders	NHL	65	20	41	61	50	....	....	....	....	....
	Calgary	NHL	9	3	4	7	10	22	7	9	16	49
1986-87	Calgary	NHL	78	20	31	51	72	3	0	0	0	4
1987-88	Calgary	NHL	74	17	41	58	84	6	2	5	7	8
1988-89	Los Angeles	NHL	77	31	33	64	110	6	0	0	0	8
	NHL Totals		832	277	447	724	749	150	37	69	106	182

a OHA First All-Star Team (1975)
b NHL Second Team All-Star (1982, 1985)
Played in NHL All-Star Game (1982, 1985)
Traded to **Calgary** by **NY Islanders** for Richard Kromm and Steve Konroyd, March 11, 1986.

TOOKEY, TIMOTHY RAYMOND (TIM)

Center. Shoots left. 5'11", 180 lbs.   Born, Edmonton, Alta., August 29, 1960.
(Washington's 4th choice, 88th over-all, in 1979 Entry Draft).

			Regular Season					Playoffs				
Season	Club	Lea	GP	G	A	TP	PIM	GP	G	A	TP	PIM
1977-78	Portland	WHL	72	16	15	31	55	8	2	2	4	5
1978-79	Portland	WHL	56	33	47	80	55	25	6	14	20	6
1979-80	Portland	WHL	70	58	83	141	55	8	2	5	7	4
1980-81	Washington	NHL	29	10	13	23	18	....	....	....	....	....
	Hershey	AHL	47	20	38	58	129	....	....	....	....	....
1981-82	Washington	NHL	28	8	8	16	35	....	....	....	....	....
	Hershey	AHL	14	4	9	13	10	....	....	....	....	....
	Fredericton	AHL	16	6	10	16	16	....	....	....	....	....
1982-83	Quebec	NHL	12	1	6	7	4	....	....	....	....	....
	Fredericton	AHL	53	24	43	67	24	9	5	4	9	0
1983-84	Pittsburgh	NHL	8	0	2	2	2	....	....	....	....	....
	Baltimore	AHL	58	16	28	44	25	8	1	1	2	2
1984-85	Baltimore	AHL	74	25	43	68	74	15	8	10	18	13
1985-86ab	Hershey	AHL	69	35	62	97	66	18	11	8	19	10
1986-87	Philadelphia	NHL	2	0	0	0	0	10	1	3	4	2
cde	Hershey	AHL	80	51	73	124	45	5	4	5	9	0
1987-88	Los Angeles	NHL	20	1	6	7	8	....	....	....	....	....
	New Haven	AHL	11	6	7	13	2	....	....	....	....	....
1988-89	Los Angeles	NHL	7	2	1	3	4	....	....	....	....	....
	New Haven	AHL	33	11	18	29	30	....	....	....	....	....
	Muskegon	IHL	18	7	14	21	7	8	2	9	11	4
	NHL Totals		106	22	36	58	71	10	1	3	4	2

a AHL Second All-Star Team (1986)
b AHL Playoff MVP (1986)
c AHL First All-Star Team (1987)
d Won Les Cunningham Plaque (MVP-AHL 1987)
e Won John B. Sollenberger Trophy (Top Scorer–AHL 1987)
Traded to **Quebec** by **Washington** with Washington's seventh round choice (Daniel Poudrier) in 1982 Entry Draft for Lee Norwood and Quebec's sixth round choice (Mats Kihlstron) —later transferred to Calgary— in 1982 Entry Draft, February 1, 1982. Signed as free agent by **Pittsburgh**, September 12, 1983. Signed as a free agent by **Philadelphia**, July 23, 1985. Claimed by **Los Angeles** in NHL Waiver Draft, October 5, 1987. Traded to **Pittsburgh** by **Los Angeles** for Patrick Mayer, March 7, 1989.

TOOMEY, SEAN

Left wing. Shoots left. 6'1", 200 lbs.   Born, St. Paul, MN, June 27, 1965.
(Minnesota's 8th choice, 136th overall, in 1983 Entry Draft).

			Regular Season					Playoffs				
Season	Club	Lea	GP	G	A	TP	PIM	GP	G	A	TP	PIM
1983-84	Minn.-Duluth	WCHA	29	3	5	8	8	....	....	....	....	....
1984-85	Minn.-Duluth	WCHA	43	6	7	13	14	....	....	....	....	....
1985-86	Minn.-Duluth	WCHA	33	23	11	34	10	....	....	....	....	....
1986-87	Minnesota	NHL	1	0	0	0	0	....	....	....	....	....
	Minn.-Duluth	WCHA	39	26	17	43	34	....	....	....	....	....
	Indianapolis	IHL	13	3	3	6	0	5	2	2	4	2
1987-88	Baltimore	AHL	49	15	18	33	12	....	....	....	....	....
	Kalamazoo	IHL	23	12	5	17	2	4	1	3	4	0
1988-89	Assat	Fin.	34	14	13	27	18	5	3	0 *	3	0
	NHL Totals		1	0	0	0	0	....	....	....	....	....

TORKKI, JARI

Left wing. Shoots left. 5'11", 165 lbs.   Born, Rauma, Finland, August 11, 1965.
(Chicago's 6th choice, 115th overall, in 1983 Entry Draft).

			Regular Season					Playoffs				
Season	Club	Lea	GP	G	A	TP	PIM	GP	G	A	TP	PIM
1981-82	Lukko	Fin.	1	0	0	0	0	....	....	....	....	....
1982-83	Lukko	Fin.	34	13	17	30	34	....	....	....	....	....
1983-84	Lukko	Fin. 2	36	41	25	66	70	5	4	1	5	8
1984-85	Lukko	Fin.	36	25	21	46	40	....	....	....	....	....
1985-86	Lukko	Fin.	32	22	18	40	40	....	....	....	....	....
1986-87	Lukko	Fin.	44	27	8	35	42	....	....	....	....	....
1987-88	Lukko	Fin.	43	23	24	47	54	8	4	3	7	12
1988-89	Chicago	NHL	4	1	0	1	0	....	....	....	....	....
	Saginaw	IHL	72	30	42	72	22	6	2	1	3	4
	NHL Totals		4	1	0	1	0	....	....	....	....	....

TORREL, DOUGLAS

Center. Shoots right. 6'2", 175 lbs.   Born, Hibbing, MN, April 29, 1969.
(Vancouver's 3rd choice, 66th overall, in 1987 Entry Draft).

			Regular Season					Playoffs				
Season	Club	Lea	GP	G	A	TP	PIM	GP	G	A	TP	PIM
1986-87	Hibbing	HS	20	22	21	43		....	....	....	....	....
1987-88	Hibbing	HS	20	22	16	38	38	....	....	....	....	....
1988-89	Minn.-Duluth	WCHA	40	4	6	10	36	....	....	....	....	....

TORY, PAUL

Right wing. Shoots right. 6', 175 lbs.   Born, Coquitlam, B.C., January 13, 1966.
(Hartford's 8th choice, 194th overall, in 1985 Entry Draft).

			Regular Season					Playoffs				
Season	Club	Lea	GP	G	A	TP	PIM	GP	G	A	TP	PIM
1984-85	Ill.-Chicago	CCHA	40	13	14	27	60	....	....	....	....	....
1985-86	Ill.-Chicago	CCHA	40	21	14	35	45	....	....	....	....	....
1986-87	Ill.-Chicago	CCHA	34	17	21	38	73	....	....	....	....	....
1988-89	Ill.-Chicago	CCHA	21	5	8	13	33	....	....	....	....	....

TRADER, LARRY

Defense. Shoots left. 6'1", 180 lbs.   Born, Barry's Bay, Ont., July 7, 1963.
(Detroit's 3rd choice, 86th over-all, in 1981 Entry Draft).

			Regular Season					Playoffs			
Season	Club	Lea	GP	G	A	TP	PIM	GP	G	A	TP	PIM
1980-81	London	OHA	68	5	23	28	132	....	....	....	....	....
1981-82	London	OHL	68	19	37	56	161	4	0	1	1	6
1982-83	**Detroit**	**NHL**	15	0	2	2	6	....	....	....	....	....
	London	OHL	39	16	28	44	67	3	0	1	1	6
	Adirondack	AHL	6	2	2	4	4	6	2	1	3	10
1983-84	Adirondack	AHL	80	13	28	41	89	6	1	1	2	4
1984-85	**Detroit**	**NHL**	40	3	7	10	39	3	0	0	0	0
	Adirondack	AHL	6	0	4	4	0	....	....	....	....	....
1985-86a	Adirondack	AHL	64	10	46	56	77	17	6	16	22	14
1986-87	**St. Louis**	**NHL**	5	0	0	0	8	....	....	....	....	....
	Cdn. Olympic	....	48	4	16	20	56	....	....	....	....	....
1987-88	**St. Louis**	**NHL**	1	0	0	0	2	....	....	....	....	....
	Montreal	**NHL**	30	2	4	6	19	....	....	....	....	....
	Sherbrooke	AHL	11	2	2	4	25	....	....	....	....	....
1988-89	Binghamton	AHL	65	11	40	51	72	....	....	....	....	....
	NHL Totals		**91**	**5**	**13**	**18**	**74**	**3**	**0**	**0**	**0**	**0**

a AHL Second All-Star Team (1986)
Traded to **St. Louis** by **Detroit** for Lee Norwood, August 7, 1986. Traded to **Montreal** by **St. Louis** with future considerations for Gaston Gingras, October 13, 1987. Signed as a free agent by **Hartford**, August 3, 1988.

TRESL, LADISLAV

Center. Shoots left. 6'1", 170 lbs.   Born, Brno, Czechoslovakia, July 30, 1961.
(Quebec's 10th choice, 183rd overall, in 1987 Entry Draft)

			Regular Season					Playoffs			
Season	Club	Lea	GP	G	A	TP	PIM	GP	G	A	TP	PIM
1986-87	Zetor Brno	Czech.	33	13	11	24	....	....	....	....	....	....
1987-88	Fredericton	AHL	30	6	16	22	16	....	....	....	....	....
1988-89	Halifax	AHL	67	24	35	59	28	4	0	1	1	4

TRETOWICZ, DAVID

Defense. Shoots left. 5'11", 185 lbs.   Born, Liverpool, NY, March 15, 1969.
(Calgary's 11th choice, 231st overall, in 1988 Entry Draft).

			Regular Season					Playoffs			
Season	Club	Lea	GP	G	A	TP	PIM	GP	G	A	TP	PIM
1987-88	Clarkson	ECAC	35	8	14	22	28	....	....	....	....	....
1988-89	Clarkson	ECAC	32	6	17	23	22	....	....	....	....	....

TROTTIER, BRYAN JOHN   (TRAHT chay)

Center. Shoots left. 5'11", 195 lbs.   Born, Val Marie, Sask., July 17, 1956.
(NY Islanders' 2nd choice, 22nd over-all, in 1974 Amateur Draft).

			Regular Season					Playoffs			
Season	Club	Lea	GP	G	A	TP	PIM	GP	G	A	TP	PIM
1972-73	Swift Current	WHL	67	16	29	45	10	....	....	....	....	....
1973-74	Swift Current	WHL	68	41	71	112	76	13	7	8	15	8
1974-75ab	Lethbridge	WHL	67	46	*98	144	103	6	2	5	7	14
1975-76c	NY Islanders	NHL	80	32	63	95	21	13	1	7	8	8
1976-77	NY Islanders	NHL	76	30	42	72	34	12	2	8	10	2
1977-78d	NY Islanders	NHL	77	46	*77	123	46	7	0	3	3	4
1978-79def	NY Islanders	NHL	76	47	*87	*134	50	10	2	4	6	13
1979-80g	NY Islanders	NHL	78	42	62	104	68	21	*12	17	*29	16
1980-81	NY Islanders	NHL	73	31	72	103	74	18	11	18	29	34
1981-82h	NY Islanders	NHL	80	50	79	129	88	19	6	*23	*29	40
1982-83	NY Islanders	NHL	80	34	55	89	68	17	8	12	20	18
1983-84h	NY Islanders	NHL	68	40	71	111	59	21	8	6	14	49
1984-85	NY Islanders	NHL	68	28	31	59	47	10	4	2	6	8
1985-86	NY Islanders	NHL	78	37	59	96	72	3	1	1	2	2
1986-87	NY Islanders	NHL	80	23	64	87	50	14	8	5	13	12
1987-88i	NY Islanders	NHL	77	30	52	82	48	6	0	0	0	10
1988-89j	NY Islanders	NHL	73	17	28	45	44	....	....	....	....	....
	NHL Totals		**1064**	**487**	**842**	**1329**	**769**	**171**	**63**	**106**	**169**	**216**

a WHL Most Valuable Player (1975)
b WHL First All-Star Team (1975)
c Won Calder Memorial Trophy (1976)
d NHL First All-Star Team (1978, 1979)
e Won Art Ross Trophy (1979)
f Won Hart Trophy (1979)
g Won Conn Smythe Trophy (1980)
h NHL Second All-Star Team (1982, 1984)
i Named Budweiser/NHL Man of the Year (1988)
j Won King Clancy Memorial Trophy (1989)
Played in NHL All-Star Game (1976, 1978, 1980, 1982, 1983, 1985, 1986)

TRUE, SOREN

Center. Shoots left. 6', 175 lbs.   Born, Aarhus, Denmark, February 9, 1968.
(NY Rangers' 12th choice, 240th overall, in 1986 Entry Draft).

			Regular Season					Playoffs			
Season	Club	Lea	GP	G	A	TP	PIM	GP	G	A	TP	PIM
1988-89	Humboldt	SJHL	63	45	68	113	75	....	....	....	....	....

TSUJIURA, STEVE   (tah-JUR-a)

Center. Shoots left. 5'5", 155 lbs.   Born, Goaldale, Alta., February 28, 1962.
(Philadelphia's 10th choice, 205th over-all, in 1981 Entry Draft).

			Regular Season					Playoffs			
Season	Club	Lea	GP	G	A	TP	PIM	GP	G	A	TP	PIM
1978-79	Medicine Hat	WHL	62	24	45	69	14	....	....	....	....	....
1979-80	Medicine Hat	WHL	72	25	77	102	36	16	9	4	13	14
1980-81	Medicine Hat	WHL	72	55	84	139	60	5	4	4	8	0
1981-82	U. of Calgary	CWUAA	37	26	53	79	33	....	....	....	....	....
1982-83	Maine	AHL	78	15	51	66	46	14	3	4	7	8
1983-84	Springfield	AHL	78	24	56	80	27	4	4	3	7	2
1984-85	Maine	AHL	69	28	38	66	40	11	3	8	11	14
1985-86a	Maine	AHL	80	31	55	86	34	5	2	3	5	2
1986-87	Maine	AHL	80	24	41	65	73	....	....	....	....	....
1987-88	Utica	AHL	54	15	32	47	55	....	....	....	....	....
	Maine	AHL	12	2	8	10	10	10	2	4	6	24
1988-89	Maine	AHL	79	15	41	56	67	....	....	....	....	....

a AHL Most Sportsmanlike Player of the Year (1986)
Signed as free agent by **New Jersey**, July 15, 1984. Traded to **Boston** by **New Jersey** for Boston's tenth round choice (Alexander Semak) in 1988 Entry Draft, March 8, 1988.

TUCKER, JOHN

Center. Shoots right. 6', 197 lbs.   Born, Windsor, Ont., September 29, 1964.
(Buffalo's 4th choice, 31st over-all, in 1983 Entry Draft).

			Regular Season					Playoffs			
Season	Club	Lea	GP	G	A	TP	PIM	GP	G	A	TP	PIM
1981-82	Kitchener	OHL	67	16	32	48	32	15	2	3	5	2
1982-83	Kitchener	OHL	70	60	80	140	33	11	5	9	14	10
1983-84ab	**Buffalo**	**NHL**	21	12	4	16	4	3	1	0	1	0
	Kitchener	OHL	39	40	60	100	25	12	12	18	30	8
1984-85	**Buffalo**	**NHL**	64	22	27	49	21	5	1	5	6	0
1985-86	**Buffalo**	**NHL**	75	31	34	65	39	....	....	....	....	....
1986-87	**Buffalo**	**NHL**	54	17	34	51	21	....	....	....	....	....
1987-88	**Buffalo**	**NHL**	45	19	19	38	20	6	7	3	10	18
1988-89	**Buffalo**	**NHL**	60	13	31	44	31	3	0	3	3	0
	NHL Totals		**319**	**114**	**149**	**263**	**136**	**17**	**9**	**11**	**20**	**18**

a OHL First All-Star Team (1984)
b OHL Player of the Year (1984)

TUER, ALLAN (AL)

Defense. Shoots left. 6', 190 lbs.   Born, North Battleford, Sask., July 19, 1963.
(Los Angeles' 8th choice, 186th over-all, in 1981 Entry Draft).

			Regular Season					Playoffs			
Season	Club	Lea	GP	G	A	TP	PIM	GP	G	A	TP	PIM
1980-81	Regina	WHL	31	0	7	7	58	8	0	1	1	37
1981-82	Regina	WHL	63	2	18	20	*486	13	0	3	3	117
1982-83	Regina	WHL	71	3	27	30	229	5	0	0	0	37
1983-84	New Haven	AHL	78	0	20	20	195	....	....	....	....	....
1984-85	New Haven	AHL	56	0	7	7	241	....	....	....	....	....
1985-86	**Los Angeles**	**NHL**	45	0	1	1	150	....	....	....	....	....
	New Haven	AHL	8	1	0	1	53	....	....	....	....	....
1986-87	New Haven	AHL	69	1	14	15	273	5	0	1	1	48
1987-88	**Minnesota**	**NHL**	6	1	0	1	29	....	....	....	....	....
	Kalamazoo	IHL	68	2	15	17	303	7	0	0	0	34
1988-89	**Hartford**	**NHL**	4	0	0	0	23	....	....	....	....	....
	Binghamton	AHL	43	1	7	8	234	....	....	....	....	....
	NHL Totals		**55**	**1**	**1**	**2**	**202**					

Signed as a free agent by **Edmonton**, August 18, 1986. Claimed by **Minnesota** in NHL Waiver Draft, October 5, 1987.

TURCOTTE, ALFIE

Center. Shoots left. 5'9", 170 lbs.   Born, Gary, IN, June 5, 1965.
(Montreal's 1st choice, 17th over-all, in 1983 Entry Draft).

			Regular Season					Playoffs			
Season	Club	Lea	GP	G	A	TP	PIM	GP	G	A	TP	PIM
1981-82	Detroit Compu.	Midget	93	131	152	283	40	....	....	....	....	....
1982-83	Nanaimo	WHL	36	23	27	50	22	....	....	....	....	....
	Portland	WHL	39	26	51	77	26	14	14	18	32	9
1983-84	Portland	WHL	32	22	41	63	39	....	....	....	....	....
	Montreal	**NHL**	30	7	7	14	10	....	....	....	....	....
1984-85	**Montreal**	**NHL**	53	8	16	24	35	5	0	0	0	0
1985-86	**Montreal**	**NHL**	2	0	0	0	2	....	....	....	....	....
	Sherbrooke	AHL	75	29	36	65	60	....	....	....	....	....
1986-87	Nova Scotia	AHL	70	27	41	68	37	5	2	4	6	2
1987-88	**Winnipeg**	**NHL**	3	0	0	0	0	....	....	....	....	....
a	Baltimore	AHL	33	21	33	54	42	....	....	....	....	....
	Moncton	AHL	25	12	25	37	18	....	....	....	....	....
	Sherbrooke	AHL	8	3	8	11	4	....	....	....	....	....
1988-89	**Winnipeg**	**NHL**	14	1	3	4	2	....	....	....	....	....
	Moncton	AHL	54	27	39	66	74	10	3	9	12	17
	NHL Totals		**102**	**16**	**26**	**42**	**49**	**5**	**0**	**0**	**0**	**0**

a AHL Second All-Star team (1988)
Traded to **Edmonton** by **Montreal** for future considerations, June 25, 1986. Sold to **Montreal** by **Edmonton**, May 14, 1987. Traded to **Winnipeg** by **Montreal** for future considerations, January 14, 1988. Signed as a free agent by **Boston**, June 27, 1989.

TURCOTTE, DARREN

Center. Shoots left. 6', 185 lbs.   Born, Boston, MA, March 2, 1968.
(NY Rangers' 6th choice, 114th overall, in 1986 Entry Draft).

			Regular Season					Playoffs			
Season	Club	Lea	GP	G	A	TP	PIM	GP	G	A	TP	PIM
1985-86	North Bay	OHL	62	35	37	72	35	10	3	4	7	8
1986-87	North Bay	OHL	55	30	48	78	20	18	12	8	20	6
1987-88	Colorado	IHL	8	4	3	7	9	6	2	6	8	8
	North Bay	OHL	32	30	33	63	16	4	3	0	3	4
1988-89	**NY Rangers**	**NHL**	20	7	3	10	4	1	0	0	0	0
	Denver	IHL	40	21	28	49	32	....	....	....	....	....
	NHL Totals		**20**	**7**	**3**	**10**	**4**	**1**	**0**	**0**	**0**	**0**

TURGEON, PIERRE

Center. Shoots left. 6'1", 200 lbs.   Born, Rouyn, Que., August 29, 1969.
(Buffalo's 1st choice, 1st overall, in 1987 Entry Draft).

			Regular Season					Playoffs				
Season	Club	Lea	GP	G	A	TP	PIM	GP	G	A	TP	PIM
1985-86	Granby	QMJHL	69	47	67	114	31	....	....	....	....	....
1986-87	Granby	QMJHL	58	69	85	154	8	7	9	6	15	15
1987-88	Buffalo	NHL	76	14	28	42	34	6	4	3	7	4
1988-89	Buffalo	NHL	80	34	54	88	26	5	3	5	8	2
	NHL Totals		156	48	82	130	60	11	7	8	15	6

TURGEON, SYLVAIN

Left wing. Shoots left. 6', 195 lbs.   Born, Noranda, Que., January 17, 1965.
(Hartford's 1st choice, 2nd over-all, in 1983 Entry Draft).

			Regular Season					Playoffs				
Season	Club	Lea	GP	G	A	TP	PIM	GP	G	A	TP	PIM
1981-82	Hull	QMJHL	57	33	40	73	78	14	11	11	22	16
1982-83a	Hull	QMJHL	67	54	109	163	103	7	8	7	15	10
1983-84b	Hartford	NHL	76	40	32	72	55	....	....	....	....	....
1984-85	Hartford	NHL	64	31	31	62	67	....	....	....	....	....
1985-86	Hartford	NHL	76	45	34	79	88	9	2	3	5	4
1986-87	Hartford	NHL	41	23	13	36	45	6	1	2	3	4
1987-88	Hartford	NHL	71	23	26	49	71	6	0	0	0	4
1988-89	Hartford	NHL	42	16	14	30	40	4	0	2	2	4
	NHL Totals		370	178	150	328	366	25	3	7	10	16

a QMJHL First All-Star Team (1983).
b NHL All-Rookie Team (1984).
Played in NHL All-Star Game (1986)
Traded to **New Jersey** by **Hartford** for Pat Verbeek, June 17, 1989.

TURNER, BRAD

Defense. Shoots right. 6'2", 190 lbs.   Born, Winnipeg, Man., May 25, 1968.
(Minnesota's 6th choice, 58th overall, in 1986 Entry Draft).

			Regular Season					Playoffs				
Season	Club	Lea	GP	G	A	TP	PIM	GP	G	A	TP	PIM
1985-86	Calgary	AJHL	54	14	21	35	109	....	....	....	....	....
1986-87	U. of Michigan	CCHA	40	3	10	13	40	....	....	....	....	....
1986-87	U. of Michigan	CCHA	40	3	10	13	40	....	....	....	....	....
1987-88	U. of Michigan	CCHA	39	3	11	14	52	....	....	....	....	....
1988-89	U. of Michigan	CCHA	33	3	8	11	38	....	....	....	....	....

TUTT, BRIAN

Defense. Shoots left. 6'1", 195 lbs.   Born, Small Well, Alta., June 9, 1962.
(Philadelphia's 6th choice, 126th over-all, in 1980 Entry Draft).

			Regular Season					Playoffs				
Season	Club	Lea	GP	G	A	TP	PIM	GP	G	A	TP	PIM
1979-80	Calgary	WHL	2	0	0	0	2	4	0	1	1	6
1980-81	Calgary	WHL	72	10	41	51	111	22	3	11	14	30
1981-82	Calgary	WHL	40	2	16	18	85	9	2	2	4	22
1982-83	Maine	AHL	31	0	0	0	28	....	....	....	....	....
	Toledo	IHL	23	5	10	15	26	11	1	7	8	16
1983-84	Springfield	AHL	1	0	0	0	2	....	....	....	....	....
a	Toledo	IHL	82	7	44	51	79	13	0	6	6	16
1984-85	Hershey	AHL	3	0	0	0	8	....	....	....	....	....
a	Kalamazoo	IHL	80	8	45	53	62	11	2	4	6	19
1985-86	Kalamazoo	IHL	82	11	39	50	129	6	1	6	7	11
1986-87	Maine	AHL	41	6	15	21	19	....	....	....	....	....
	Kalamazoo	IHL	19	2	7	9	10	....	....	....	....	....
1987-88	New Haven	AHL	32	1	12	13	33	....	....	....	....	....
1988-89	Baltimore	AHL	6	1	5	6	6	....	....	....	....	....
	Cdn. National	....	63	0	19	19	87	....	....	....	....	....

a IHL Second All-Star Team (1984, 1985)
Signed as a free agent by **Washington**, July 25, 1989.

TUTTLE, STEVE

Right wing. Shoots right. 6'1", 180 lbs.   Born, Vancouver, B.C., January 5, 1966.
(St. Louis' 8th choice, 113th overall, in 1984 Entry Draft).

			Regular Season					Playoffs				
Season	Club	Lea	GP	G	A	TP	PIM	GP	G	A	TP	PIM
1984-85	U. Wisconsin	WCHA	28	3	4	7	0	....	....	....	....	....
1985-86	U. Wisconsin	WCHA	32	2	10	12	2	....	....	....	....	....
1986-87	U. Wisconsin	WCHA	42	31	21	52	14	....	....	....	....	....
1987-88ab	U. Wisconsin	WCHA	45	27	39	66	18	....	....	....	....	....
1988-89	St. Louis	NHL	53	13	12	25	6	6	1	2	3	0
	NHL Totals		53	13	12	25	6	6	1	2	3	0

a NCAA West Second All-American Team (1988)
b WCHA Second All-Star Team (1988)
Rangers (OHL)

TWIST, ANTHONY

Defense. Shoots left. 6'0", 210 lbs.   Born, Sherwood Park, Alta., May 9, 1968.
(St. Louis' 9th choice, 177th overall, in 1988 Entry Draft).

			Regular Season					Playoffs				
Season	Club	Lea	GP	G	A	TP	PIM	GP	G	A	TP	PIM
1987-88	Saskatoon	WHL	55	1	8	9	226	10	1	1	2	6
1988-89	Peoria	IHL	67	3	8	11	312	....	....	....	....	....

URBAN, JEFF

Left wing. Shoots left. 6'2", 200 lbs.   Born, Edina, MN, March 23, 1967.
(St. Louis' 8th choice, 180th overall, in 1985 Entry Draft).

			Regular Season					Playoffs				
Season	Club	Lea	GP	G	A	TP	PIM	GP	G	A	TP	PIM
1985-86	U. of Michigan	CCHA	36	9	6	15	23	....	....	....	....	....
1986-87	U. of Michigan	CCHA	28	3	4	7	18	....	....	....	....	....
1987-88	U. of Michigan	CCHA	23	1	3	4	24	....	....	....	....	....
1988-89	U. of Michigan	CCHA	31	4	6	10	20	....	....	....	....	....

UVIRA, EDWARD

Defense. Shoots right. 6', 207 lbs.   Born, Opava, Czechoslovakia, July 12, 1961.
(Toronto's 6th choice, 86th overall, in 1982 Entry Draft).

			Regular Season					Playoffs				
Season	Club	Lea	GP	G	A	TP	PIM	GP	G	A	TP	PIM
1986-87	Bratislava	Czech.	29	4	9	13		....	....	....	....	....
1987-88	Bratislava	Czech.	25	0	6	6		....	....	....	....	....
1988-89	Bratislava	Czech.	26	2	2	4		....	....	....	....	....

VAIVE, RICHARD CLAUDE (RICK)   (VIHV)

Right wing. Shoots right. 6', 180 lbs.   Born, Ottawa, Ont., May 14, 1959.
(Vancouver's 1st choice, 5th over-all, in 1979 Entry Draft).

			Regular Season					Playoffs				
Season	Club	Lea	GP	G	A	TP	PIM	GP	G	A	TP	PIM
1976-77	Sherbrooke	QJHL	67	51	59	110	91	18	10	13	23	78
1977-78	Sherbrooke	QJHL	68	76	79	155	199	9	8	4	12	38
1978-79	Birmingham	WHA	75	26	33	59	*248	....	....	....	....	....
1979-80	Vancouver	NHL	47	13	8	21	111	....	....	....	....	....
	Toronto	NHL	22	9	7	16	77	3	1	0	1	11
1980-81	Toronto	NHL	75	33	29	62	229	3	1	0	1	4
1981-82	Toronto	NHL	77	54	35	89	157	....	....	....	....	....
1982-83	Toronto	NHL	78	51	28	79	105	4	2	5	7	6
1983-84	Toronto	NHL	76	52	41	93	114	....	....	....	....	....
1984-85	Toronto	NHL	72	35	33	68	112	....	....	....	....	....
1985-86	Toronto	NHL	61	33	31	64	85	9	6	2	8	9
1986-87	Toronto	NHL	73	32	34	66	61	13	4	2	6	23
1987-88	Chicago	NHL	76	43	26	69	108	5	6	2	8	38
1988-89	Chicago	NHL	30	12	13	25	60	....	....	....	....	....
	Buffalo	NHL	28	19	13	32	64	5	2	1	3	8
	NHL Totals		715	386	298	684	1283	42	22	12	34	99

Played in NHL All-Star Game (1982-84)
Traded to **Toronto** by **Vancouver** with Bill Derlago for Dave Williams and Jerry Butler, February 18, 1980. Traded to **Chicago** by **Toronto** with Steve Thomas and Bob McGill for Al Secord and Ed Olczyk, September 3, 1987. Traded to **Buffalo** by **Chicago** for Adam Creighton, December 26, 1988.

VALEK, OLDRICH

Right wing. Shoots right. 6'2", 216 lbs.   Born, Opava, Czechoslovakia, March 9, 1960.
(Minnesota's 12th choice, 212th overall, in 1983 Entry Draft).

			Regular Season					Playoffs				
Season	Club	Lea	GP	G	A	TP	PIM	GP	G	A	TP	PIM
1986-87	Dukla Jihlava	Czech.	28	17	9	26		....	....	....	....	....
1987-88	Dukla Jihlava	Czech.	31	14	23	37		....	....	....	....	....
1988-89	Dukla Jihlava	Czech.	44	22	23	45	73	....	....	....	....	....

VALIMONT, CARL

Defense. Shoots left. 6'1", 180 lbs.   Born, Southington, CT, March 1, 1966.
(Vancouver's 10th choice, 193rd overall, in 1985 Entry Draft).

			Regular Season					Playoffs				
Season	Club	Lea	GP	G	A	TP	PIM	GP	G	A	TP	PIM
1984-85	Lowell	H.E.	40	4	11	15	24	....	....	....	....	....
1985-86	Lowell	H.E.	26	1	9	10	12	....	....	....	....	....
1986-87	Lowell	H.E.	36	8	9	17	36	....	....	....	....	....
1987-88a	Lowell	H.E.	38	6	26	32	59	....	....	....	....	....
1988-89	Milwaukee	IHL	79	4	33	37	56	11	2	8	10	12

a Hockey East Second All-Star Team (1988)

VALK, GARRY

Right wing. Shoots right. 6'1", 190 lbs.   Born, Edmonton, Alta., November 27, 1967.
(Vancouver's 5th choice, 108th overall, in 1987 Entry Draft).

			Regular Season					Playoffs				
Season	Club	Lea	GP	G	A	TP	PIM	GP	G	A	TP	PIM
1986-87	Sherwood Park	AJHL	59	42	44	86	204	....	....	....	....	....
1987-88	North Dakota	WCHA	38	23	12	35	64	....	....	....	....	....
1988-89	North Dakota	WCHA	40	14	17	31	71	....	....	....	....	....

VALLIS, LINDSAY

Right wing. Shoots right. 6'2", 200 lbs.   Born, Winnipeg, Man., January 12, 1971.
(Montreal's 1st choice, 13th overall, in 1989 Entry Draft).

			Regular Season					Playoffs				
Season	Club	Lea	GP	G	A	TP	PIM	GP	G	A	TP	PIM
1987-88	Seattle	WHL	68	31	45	76	65	....	....	....	....	....
1988-89	Seattle	WHL	63	21	32	53	48	....	....	....	....	....

VAN ALLEN, SHAUN

Center. Shoots right. 6'1", 205 lbs.   Born, Shaunavon, Sask., August 29, 1967.
(Edmonton's 7th choice, 147th overall, in 1987 Entry Draft).

			Regular Season					Playoffs				
Season	Club	Lea	GP	G	A	TP	PIM	GP	G	A	TP	PIM
1985-86	Saskatoon	WHL	55	12	11	23	43	13	4	8	12	28
1986-87	Saskatoon	WHL	72	38	59	97	116	11	4	6	10	24
1987-88	Milwaukee	IHL	40	14	28	42	34	....	....	....	....	....
	Nova Scotia	AHL	19	4	10	14	17	4	1	1	2	4
1988-89	Cape Breton	AHL	76	32	42	74	81	....	....	....	....	....

VAN DORP, WAYNE

Left wing. Shoots left. 6'4", 225 lbs. Born, Vancouver, B.C., May 19, 1961.

			Regular Season					Playoffs				
Season	Club	Lea	GP	G	A	TP	PIM	GP	G	A	TP	PIM
1979-80	Seattle	WHL	68	8	13	21	195	12	3	1	4	33
1980-81	Seattle	WHL	63	22	30	52	242	5	1	0	1	10
1984-85	GIJS Groningen	Neth.	29	38	46	84	112	6	6	2	8	23
	Erie	ACHL	7	9	8	17	21	10	0	2	6	2
1985-86a	GIJS Groningen	Neth.	29	19	24	43	81	8	9	12*	21	6
1986-87	Rochester	AHL	47	7	3	10	192	....	....	....	....	....
	Nova Scotia	AHL	11	2	3	5	37	5	0	0	0	56
	Edmonton	**NHL**	**3**	**0**	**0**	**0**	**25**	**3**	**0**	**0**	**0**	**2**
1987-88	**Pittsburgh**	**NHL**	**25**	**1**	**3**	**4**	**75**	....	....	....	....	....
	Nova Scota	AHL	12	2	2	4	87	....	....	....	....	....
1988-89	**Chicago**	**NHL**	**8**	**0**	**0**	**0**	**23**	**16**	**0**	**1**	**1**	**17**
	Rochester	AHL	28	3	6	9	202	....	....	....	....	....
	Saginaw	IHL	11	4	3	7	60	....	....	....	....	....
	NHL Totals		**36**	**1**	**3**	**4**	**123**	**19**	**0**	**1**	**1**	**19**

a Named playoff MVP (1986)

Signed as a free agent by **Edmonton**, March 7, 1987. Traded to **Pittsburgh** by **Edmonton** with Paul Coffey and Dave Hunter for Craig Simpson, Dave Hannan, Moe Mantha, and Chris Joseph, November 24, 1987. Traded to **Buffalo** by **Pittsburgh** for future considerations, September 30, 1988. Traded to **Chicago** by **Buffalo** for Chicago's seventh-round choice in 1990 Entry Draft, February 16, 1989.

VANIK, MILOS

Center. Shoots right. 5'11" 179 lbs. Born, Prague, Czechoslavakia, March 29, 1968.
(Washington's 9th choice, 225th overall, in 1987 Entry Draft).

			Regular Season					Playoffs				
Season	Club	Lea	GP	G	A	TP	PIM	GP	G	A	TP	PIM
1986-87	EHC Freiberg	W.Ger.	34	4	9	13	....	....	....	....	....	....
1987-88	Kaufbeuren	W.Ger.	37	8	11	19	27	....	....	....	....	....
1988-89	Kaufbeuren	W. Ger.	36	10	8	18	34	....	....	....	....	....

VAN KESSEL, JOHN

Right wing. Shoots right. 6'4", 180 lbs. Born, Bridgewater, N.S., December 19, 1969.
(Los Angeles' 3rd choice, 49th overall, in 1988 Entry Draft).

			Regular Season					Playoffs				
Season	Club	Lea	GP	G	A	TP	PIM	GP	G	A	TP	PIM
1986-87	Belleville	OHL	61	1	10	11	58	....	....	....	....	....
1987-88	North Bay	OHL	50	13	16	29	214	4	1	1	2	16
1988-89	North Bay	OHL	50	7	13	20	218	11	2	4	6	31

VARGAS, ERNIE

Center. Shoots left. 6'1", 180 lbs. Born, St. Paul, MN, March 1, 1964.
(Montreal's 9th choice, 117th over-all, in 1982 Entry Draft).

			Regular Season					Playoffs				
Season	Club	Lea	GP	G	A	TP	PIM	GP	G	A	TP	PIM
1982-83	U. of Wisconsin	WCHA	25	1	4	5	30	....	....	....	....	....
1983-84	U. of Wisconsin	WCHA	36	5	15	20	32	....	....	....	....	....
1984-85	U. of Wisconsin	WCHA	42	8	16	24	68	....	....	....	....	....
1985-86	U. of Wisconsin	WCHA	41	20	23	43	67	....	....	....	....	....
1986-87	Sherbrooke	AHL	69	22	32	54	52	16	6	3	9	13
1987-88	Baltimore	AHL	5	1	0	1	2	....	....	....	....	....
	Sherbrooke	AHL	31	6	21	27	48	....	....	....	....	....
	Peoria	IHL	31	9	13	22	26	7	1	3	4	15
1988-89	Milwaukee	IHL	61	16	35	51	89	8	1	0	1	6

Traded to **St. Louis** by **Montreal** for future considerations, February 2, 1988. Traded to **Vancouver** by **St. Louis** for Dave Lowry, September 29, 1988.

VASKE, DENNIS

Defense. Shoots left. 6'2", 210 lbs. Born, Rockford, IL., October 11, 1967.
(NY Islanders' 2nd choice, 38th overall, in 1986 Entry Draft).

			Regular Season					Playoffs				
Season	Club	Lea	GP	G	A	TP	PIM	GP	G	A	TP	PIM
1984-85	Armstrong	HS	22	5	18	23	....	....	....	....	....	....
1985-86	Armstrong	HS	20	9	13	22	30	....	....	....	....	....
1986-87	Minn.-Duluth	WCHA	33	0	2	2	40	....	....	....	....	....
1987-88	Minn.-Duluth	WCHA	39	1	6	7	90	....	....	....	....	....
1988-89	Minn.-Duluth	WCHA	37	9	19	28	86	....	....	....	....	....

VEILLEUX, STEVE

Defense. Shoots right. 6', 190 lbs. Born, Lachenaie, Que., March 9, 1969.
(Vancouver's 2nd choice, 45th overall, in 1987 Entry Draft).

			Regular Season					Playoffs				
Season	Club	Lea	GP	G	A	TP	PIM	GP	G	A	TP	PIM
1985-86	Trois Rivieres	QMJHL	67	1	20	21	132	5	0	0	0	13
1986-87	Trois Rivieres	QMJHL	62	6	22	28	227	....	....	....	....	....
1987-88a	Trois Rivieres	QMJHL	63	7	25	32	150	....	....	....	....	....
1988-89a	Trois Rivieres	QMJHL	49	5	28	33	149	4	0	0	0	10
	Milwaukee	IHL	1	0	0	0	0	4	0	0	0	13

a QMJHL Second All-Star Team (1988, 1989)

VEITCH, DARREN WILLIAM (VEECH)

Defense. Shoots right. 6', 190 lbs. Born, Saskatoon, Sask., April 24, 1960.
(Washington's 1st choice, 5th over-all, in 1980 Entry Draft).

			Regular Season					Playoffs				
Season	Club	Lea	GP	G	A	TP	PIM	GP	G	A	TP	PIM
1976-77	Regina	WHL	1	0	0	0	0	....	....	....	....	....
1977-78	Regina	WHL	71	13	32	45	135	9	0	2	2	4
1978-79	Regina	WHL	51	11	36	47	80	....	....	....	....	....
1979-80a	Regina	WHL	71	29	*93	122	118	18	13	18	31	13
1980-81	**Washington**	**NHL**	**59**	**4**	**21**	**25**	**46**	....	....	....	....	....
	Hershey	AHL	26	6	22	28	12	10	6	3	9	15
1981-82	Hershey	AHL	10	5	10	15	16	....	....	....	....	....
	Washington	**NHL**	**67**	**9**	**44**	**53**	**54**	....	....	....	....	....
1982-83	**Washington**	**NHL**	**10**	**0**	**8**	**8**	**0**	....	....	....	....	....
	Hershey	AHL	5	0	1	1	2	....	....	....	....	....
1983-84	Hershey	AHL	11	1	6	7	4	....	....	....	....	....
	Washington	**NHL**	**46**	**6**	**18**	**24**	**17**	**5**	**0**	**1**	**1**	**15**
1984-85	**Washington**	**NHL**	**75**	**3**	**18**	**21**	**37**	**5**	**0**	**1**	**1**	**4**
1985-86	**Washington**	**NHL**	**62**	**3**	**9**	**12**	**27**	....	....	....	....	....
	Detroit	**NHL**	**13**	**0**	**5**	**5**	**2**	....	....	....	....	....
1986-87	**Detroit**	**NHL**	**77**	**13**	**45**	**58**	**52**	**12**	**3**	**4**	**7**	**8**
1987-88	**Detroit**	**NHL**	**63**	**7**	**33**	**40**	**45**	**11**	**1**	**5**	**6**	**6**
1988-89	**Toronto**	**NHL**	**37**	**3**	**7**	**10**	**16**	....	....	....	....	....
	Newmarket	AHL	33	5	19	24	29	5	0	4	4	4
	NHL Totals		**509**	**48**	**208**	**256**	**296**	**33**	**4**	**11**	**15**	**33**

a WHL First All-Star Team (1980)

Traded to **Detroit** by **Washington** for John Barrett and Greg Smith, March 10, 1986. Traded to **Toronto** by **Detroit** for Miroslav Frycer, June 10, 1988.

VELISCHEK, RANDY

Defense. Shoots left. 6', 200 lbs. Born, Montreal, Que., February 10, 1962.
(Minnesota's 3rd choice, 53rd over-all, in 1980 Entry Draft).

			Regular Season					Playoffs				
Season	Club	Lea	GP	G	A	TP	PIM	GP	G	A	TP	PIM
1979-80	Providence	ECAC	31	5	5	10	20	....	....	....	....	....
1980-81	Providence	ECAC	33	3	12	15	26	....	....	....	....	....
1981-82a	Providence	ECAC	33	1	14	15	38	....	....	....	....	....
1982-83bc	Providence	ECAC	41	18	34	52	50	....	....	....	....	....
	Minnesota	**NHL**	**3**	**0**	**0**	**0**	**2**	**9**	**0**	**0**	**0**	**0**
1983-84	Salt Lake	CHL	43	7	21	28	54	5	0	3	3	2
	Minnesota	**NHL**	**33**	**2**	**2**	**4**	**10**	**1**	**0**	**0**	**0**	**0**
1984-85	**Minnesota**	**NHL**	**52**	**4**	**9**	**13**	**26**	**9**	**2**	**3**	**5**	**8**
	Springfield	AHL	26	2	7	9	22	....	....	....	....	....
1985-86	**New Jersey**	**NHL**	**47**	**2**	**7**	**9**	**39**	....	....	....	....	....
	Maine	AHL	21	0	4	4	4	....	....	....	....	....
1986-87	**New Jersey**	**NHL**	**64**	**2**	**16**	**18**	**52**	....	....	....	....	....
1987-88	**New Jersey**	**NHL**	**51**	**3**	**9**	**12**	**66**	**19**	**0**	**2**	**2**	**20**
1988-89	**New Jersey**	**NHL**	**80**	**4**	**14**	**18**	**70**	....	....	....	....	....
	NHL Totals		**330**	**17**	**57**	**74**	**265**	**38**	**2**	**5**	**7**	**28**

a ECAC Second All-Star Team (1982)
b ECAC First All-Star Team (1983)
c Named ECAC Player of the Year (1983)

Claimed by **New Jersey** from **Minnesota** in NHL Waiver Draft, October 7, 1985

VELLUCCI, MIKE

Defense. Shoots left. 6'1", 180 lbs. Born, Farmington, MI, August 11, 1966.
(Hartford's 3rd choice, 131st overall, in 1984 Entry Draft).

			Regular Season					Playoffs				
Season	Club	Lea	GP	G	A	TP	PIM	GP	G	A	TP	PIM
1983-84	Belleville	OHL	67	2	20	22	83	3	1	0	1	6
1984-85			DID NOT PLAY — INJURED									
1985-86	Belleville	OHL	64	11	32	43	154	24	2	5	7	45
1986-87	Salt Lake	IHL	60	5	30	35	94	....	....	....	....	....
1987-88	**Hartford**	**NHL**	**2**	**0**	**0**	**0**	**11**	....	....	....	....	....
	Binghamton	AHL	3	0	0	0	2	....	....	....	....	....
	Milwaukee	IHL	66	7	18	25	202	....	....	....	....	....
1988-89	Binghamton	AHL	37	9	9	18	59	....	....	....	....	....
	Indianapolis	IHL	12	1	2	3	43	....	....	....	....	....
	NHL Totals		**2**	**0**	**0**	**0**	**11**	....	....	....	....	....

VENKUS, CHRISTOPHER

Right wing. Shoots right. 5'11", 190 lbs. Born, Hinsdale, IL, April 14, 1969.
(Washington's 13th choice, 225th overall, in 1988 Entry Draft).

			Regular Season					Playoffs				
Season	Club	Lea	GP	G	A	TP	PIM	GP	G	A	TP	PIM
1987-88	W. Michigan	CCHA	42	8	9	17	76	....	....	....	....	....
1988-89	W. Michigan	CCHA	42	2	11	13	66	....	....	....	....	....

VENNE, STEPHANE

Defense. Shoots right. 6'3", 210 lbs. Born, Montreal, Que., April 29, 1969.
(Quebec's 6th choice, 87th overall, in 1988 Entry Draft).

			Regular Season					Playoffs				
Season	Club	Lea	GP	G	A	TP	PIM	GP	G	A	TP	PIM
1987-88	U. of Vermont	ECAC	29	9	12	21	52	....	....	....	....	....
1988-89	U. of Vermont	ECAC	19	4	5	9	35	....	....	....	....	....

VERBEEK, BRIAN (vuhr-BEEK)

Center. Shoots left. 5'9",195 lbs. Born, Wyoming, Ont., October 22, 1966.
(Hartford's 11th choice, 242nd overall, in 1986 Entry Draft).

			Regular Season					Playoffs				
Season	Club	Lea	GP	G	A	TP	PIM	GP	G	A	TP	PIM
1985-86	Kingston	OHL	62	50	40	90	132	10	3	4	7	34
1986-87	Salt Lake	IHL	52	22	15	37	119	....	....	....	....	....
1987-88	Kookoo	Fin.	2	0	0	0	9	....	....	....	....	....
1988-89	Binghamton	AHL	27	9	3	12	50	....	....	....	....	....

VERBEEK, PATRICK (PAT)   (vuhr-BEEK)

Center. Shoots right. 5'9", 190 lbs.   Born, Sarnia, Ont., May 24, 1964.
(New Jersey's 3rd choice, 43rd over-all, in 1982 Entry Draft).

			Regular Season					Playoffs			
Season	Club	Lea	GP	G	A	TP	PIM	GP	G	A	TP	PIM
1980-81	Petrolia	OPJHL	42	44	44	88	155	.....	.....	.....	.....	.....
1981-82	Sudbury	OHL	66	37	51	88	180	.....	.....	.....	.....	.....
1982-83	Sudbury	OHL	61	40	67	107	184	.....	.....	.....	.....	.....
	New Jersey	NHL	6	3	2	5	8	.....	.....	.....	.....	.....
1983-84	New Jersey	NHL	79	20	27	47	158	.....	.....	.....	.....	.....
1984-85	New Jersey	NHL	78	15	18	33	162	.....	.....	.....	.....	.....
1985-86	New Jersey	NHL	76	25	28	53	79	.....	.....	.....	.....	.....
1986-87	New Jersey	NHL	74	35	24	59	120	.....	.....	.....	.....	.....
1987-88	New Jersey	NHL	73	46	31	77	227	20	4	8	12	51
1988-89	New Jersey	NHL	77	26	21	47	189	.....	.....	.....	.....	.....
	NHL Totals		**463**	**170**	**151**	**321**	**943**	**20**	**4**	**8**	**12**	**51**

Traded to **Hartford** by **New Jersey** for Sylvian Turgeon, June 17, 1989.

VERMETTE, MARK

Right wing. Shoots right. 6'1", 203 lbs.   Born, Cochenour, Ont., October 3, 1967.
(Quebec's 8th choice, 134th overall, in 1986 Entry Draft).

			Regular Season					Playoffs			
Season	Club	Lea	GP	G	A	TP	PIM	GP	G	A	TP	PIM
1985-86	Lake Superior	CCHA	32	1	4	5	7	.....	.....	.....	.....	.....
1986-87	Lake Superior	CCHA	38	19	17	36	59	.....	.....	.....	.....	.....
1987-88abc	Lake Superior	CCHA	46	*45	30	75	154	.....	.....	.....	.....	.....
1988-89	**Quebec**	NHL	12	0	4	4	7	.....	.....	.....	.....	.....
	Halifax	AHL	52	12	16	28	30	1	0	0	0	0
	NHL Totals		**12**	**0**	**4**	**4**	**7**	.....	.....	.....	.....	.....

a NCAA West All-American Team (1988)
b CCHA Player of the Year (1988)
c CCHA First All-Star Team (1988)

VESEY, JIM

Center. Shoots right. 6'1", 200 lbs..   Born, Boston, MA, September 29, 1965.
(St. Louis' 11th choice, 155th over-all, in 1984 Entry Draft).

			Regular Season					Playoffs			
Season	Club	Lea	GP	G	A	TP	PIM	GP	G	A	TP	PIM
1984-85	Merrimack	NCAA	33	19	11	30	28	.....	.....	.....	.....	.....
1985-86	Merrimack	NCAA	32	29	32	61	67	.....	.....	.....	.....	.....
1986-87	Merrimack	NCAA	35	22	36	58	57	.....	.....	.....	.....	.....
1987-88	Merrimack	NCAA	33	33	50	83	....	.....	.....	.....	.....	.....
1988-89	**St. Louis**	NHL	5	1	1	2	7	.....	.....	.....	.....	.....
a	Peoria	IHL	76	47	46	93	137	4	1	2	3	6
	NHL Totals		**5**	**1**	**1**	**2**	**7**	.....	.....	.....	.....	.....

a IHL First All-Star Team (1989)

VIAL, DENNIS

Defense. Shoots left. 6'1", 190 lbs.   Born, Sault Ste. Marie, Ont., April 10, 1969.
(NY Rangers' 5th choice, 110th overall, in 1988 Entry Draft).

			Regular Season					Playoffs			
Season	Club	Lea	GP	G	A	TP	PIM	GP	G	A	TP	PIM
1986-87	Hamilton	OHL	53	1	8	9	194	8	0	0	0	8
1987-88	Hamilton	OHL	52	3	17	20	229	13	2	2	4	49
1988-89	Niagara Falls	OHL	50	10	27	37	227	15	1	7	8	44

VICHOREK, MARK   (vuh-CHORE-ik)

Defense. Shoots right. 6'3", 200 lbs.   Born, Moose Lake, MN, August 11, 1966.
(Philadelphia's 12th choice, 245th overall, in 1982 Entry Draft).

			Regular Season					Playoffs			
Season	Club	Lea	GP	G	A	TP	PIM	GP	G	A	TP	PIM
1981-82	Sioux City	USHL	48	11	27	38	111	.....	.....	.....	.....	.....
1982-83	Lake Superior	CCHA	36	2	13	15	24	.....	.....	.....	.....	.....
1983-84	Lake Superior	CCHA	40	3	8	11	14	.....	.....	.....	.....	.....
1984-85	Lake Superior	CCHA	44	4	11	15	36	.....	.....	.....	.....	.....
1985-86	Lake Superior	CCHA	41	9	11	20	40	.....	.....	.....	.....	.....
1986-87	Binghamton	AHL	64	1	12	13	63	.....	.....	.....	.....	.....
	Salt Lake	IHL	16	1	0	1	32	17	0	8	8	23
1987-88	Binghamton	AHL	26	0	4	4	48	.....	.....	.....	.....	.....
	Milwaukee	IHL	49	4	5	9	67	.....	.....	.....	.....	.....
1988-89	New Haven	AHL	23	1	5	6	26	17	2	4	6	57
	Flint	IHL	44	4	9	13	47	.....	.....	.....	.....	.....

VILGRAIN, CLAUDE

Right wing. Shoots right. 6'1", 195 lbs.   Born, Port-au-Prince, Haiti, March 1, 1963.
(Detroit's 6th choice, 107th overall, in 1982 Entry Draft).

			Regular Season					Playoffs			
Season	Club	Lea	GP	G	A	TP	PIM	GP	G	A	TP	PIM
1983-84	U. of Moncton	AUAA	20	11	20	31	8	.....	.....	.....	.....	.....
1984-85	U. of Moncton	AUAA	24	35	28	63	20	.....	.....	.....	.....	.....
1985-86	U. of Moncton	AUAA	19	17	20	37	25	.....	.....	.....	.....	.....
1986-87	Cdn. Olympic	...	78	28	42	70	38	.....	.....	.....	.....	.....
1987-88	**Vancouver**	NHL	6	1	1	2	0	.....	.....	.....	.....	.....
	Cdn. National		61	21	20	41	41	.....	.....	.....	.....	.....
	Cdn. Olympic	.....	6	0	0	0	0	.....	.....	.....	.....	.....
1988-89	Utica	AHL	55	23	30	53	41	5	0	2	2	2
	Milwaukee	IHL	23	9	13	22	26	.....	.....	.....	.....	.....
	NHL Totals		**6**	**1**	**1**	**2**	**0**	.....	.....	.....	.....	.....

Signed as a free agent by **Vancouver**, June 18, 1987. Traded to **New Jersey** by **Vancouver** for Tim Lenardon, March 7, 1989.

VINCELETTE, DANIEL

Left wing. Shoots left. 6'1", 200 lbs.   Born, Verdun, Que., August 1, 1967.
(Chicago's 3rd choice, 74th over-all, in 1985 Entry Draft).

			Regular Season					Playoffs			
Season	Club	Lea	GP	G	A	TP	PIM	GP	G	A	TP	PIM
1984-85	Drummondville	QMJHL	64	11	24	35	124	12	0	1	1	11
1985-86	Drummondville	QMJHL	70	37	47	84	234	22	11	14	25	40
1986-87	Drummondville	QMJHL	50	34	35	69	288	8	6	5	11	17
1987-88	**Chicago**	NHL	69	6	11	17	109	4	0	0	0	0
1988-89	**Chicago**	NHL	66	11	4	15	119	5	0	0	0	4
	Saginaw	IHL	2	0	0	0	14	.....	.....	.....	.....	.....
	NHL Totals		**135**	**17**	**15**	**32**	**228**	**9**	**0**	**0**	**0**	**4**

VIRTA, HANNU   (VIR-ta HAN-oo)

Defense. Shoots left. 6', 180 lbs.   Born, Turku, Finland, March 22, 1963.
(Buffalo's 2nd choice, 38th over-all, in 1981 Entry Draft).

			Regular Season					Playoffs			
Season	Club	Lea	GP	G	A	TP	PIM	GP	G	A	TP	PIM
1980-81a	T.P.S.	Fin.	1	0	1	1	0	4	0	1	1	4
1981-82b	T.P.S.	Fin.	36	5	12	17	6	7	1	1	2	2
	Buffalo	NHL	3	0	1	1	4	4	0	1	1	0
1982-83	**Buffalo**	NHL	74	13	24	37	18	10	1	2	3	4
1983-84	**Buffalo**	NHL	70	6	30	36	12	3	0	0	0	2
1984-85	**Buffalo**	NHL	51	1	23	24	16	.....	.....	.....	.....	.....
1985-86	**Buffalo**	NHL	47	5	23	28	16	.....	.....	.....	.....	.....
1986-87c	T.P.S.	Fin.	41	13	30	43	20	5	0	3	3	2
1987-88	T.P.S.	Fin.	44	10	28	38	20	.....	.....	.....	.....	.....
1988-89	T.P.S.	Fin.	43	7	25	32	30	10	1	7	8	0
	NHL Totals		**245**	**25**	**101**	**126**	**66**	**17**	**1**	**3**	**4**	**6**

a Named to All-Star Team, 1981 European Junior Championships
b Named Rookie of the Year in Finnish National League (1982)
c Finnish League First All-Star Team (1987)

VITOLINSH, HARIJS

Center. Shoots left. 6'2", 205 lbs.   Born, Riga, Soviet Union, April 30, 1968.
(Montreal's 10th choice, 188th overall, in 1988 Entry Draft).

			Regular Season					Playoffs			
Season	Club	Lea	GP	G	A	TP	PIM	GP	G	A	TP	PIM
1987-88	Dynamo Riga	USSR	25	2	2	4	22	.....	.....	.....	.....	.....
1988-89	Dynamo Riga	USSR	36	3	2	5	16	.....	.....	.....	.....	.....

VIVEIROS, EMANUEL   (VEE VEH ROHZ)

Defense. Shoots left. 6', 175 lbs.   Born, St. Albert, Alta., January 8, 1966.
(Edmonton's 6th choice, 106th over-all, in 1984 Entry Draft).

			Regular Season					Playoffs			
Season	Club	Lea	GP	G	A	TP	PIM	GP	G	A	TP	PIM
1982-83	Prince Albert	WHL	59	6	26	32	55	.....	.....	.....	.....	.....
1983-84	Prince Albert	WHL	67	15	94	109	48	2	0	3	3	6
1984-85a	Prince Albert	WHL	68	17	71	88	94	13	2	9	11	14
1985-86	**Minnesota**	NHL	4	0	1	1	0	.....	.....	.....	.....	.....
bc	Prince Albert	WHL	57	22	70	92	30	20	4	24	28	4
1986-87	**Minnesota**	NHL	1	0	1	1	0	.....	.....	.....	.....	.....
	Springfield	AHL	76	7	35	42	38	.....	.....	.....	.....	.....
1987-88	**Minnesota**	NHL	24	1	9	10	6	.....	.....	.....	.....	.....
	Kalamazoo	IHL	57	15	48	63	41	.....	.....	.....	.....	.....
1988-89	Kalamazoo	IHL	54	11	29	40	37	.....	.....	.....	.....	.....
	NHL Totals		**29**	**1**	**11**	**12**	**6**	.....	.....	.....	.....	.....

a WHL Second All-Star Team, East Division (1985)
b WHL East All-Star Team (1986)
c WHL Player of the Year (1986)

Traded to **Minnesota** by **Edmonton** with Marc Habscheid, Don Barber for Gord Sherven and Don Biggs, December 20, 1985.

VLACH, ROSTISLAV

Center/left wing. Shoots left. 6', 170 lbs.   Born, Gottwaldov, Czech., July 3, 1962.
(Los Angeles' 9th choice, 216th overall, in 1987 Entry Draft).

			Regular Season					Playoffs			
Season	Club	Lea	GP	G	A	TP	PIM	GP	G	A	TP	PIM
1986-87	Gottwaldov	Czech.	34	24	12	36	8	.....	.....	.....	.....	.....
1987-88	Gottwaldov	Czech.	30	15	14	29	4	.....	.....	.....	.....	.....
1988-89	Gottwaldov	Czech.	41	20	18	38	83	.....	.....	.....	.....	.....

VLK, PETER

Left wing. Shoots left. 6', 180 lbs.   Born, Havlicek Brod, Czechoslovakia, January 7, 1964.
(NY Islanders' 5th choice, 97th overall, in 1987 Entry Draft).

			Regular Season					Playoffs			
Season	Club	Lea	GP	G	A	TP	PIM	GP	G	A	TP	PIM
1986-87	Dukla Jihlava	Czech.	33	17	8	25	.....	.....	.....	.....	.....	.....
1987-88	Dukla Jihlava	Czech.	18	6	3	9	.....	.....	.....	.....	.....	.....
1988-89	Dukla Jihlava	Czech.	33	11	8	19	66	.....	.....	.....	.....	.....

VOLEK, DAVID

Right wing/right wing. Shoots left. 6', 185 lbs.   Born, Prague, Czechoslovakia, June 18, 1966.
(NY Islanders' 11th choice, 208th overall, in 1984 Entry Draft).

			Regular Season					Playoffs			
Season	Club	Lea	GP	G	A	TP	PIM	GP	G	A	TP	PIM
1986-87	Sparta Praha	Czech.	39	27	25	52	.....	.....	.....	.....	.....	.....
1987-88	Sparta Praha	Czech.	30	18	12	30	.....	.....	.....	.....	.....	.....
1988-89a	**NY Islanders**	NHL	77	25	34	59	24	.....	.....	.....	.....	.....
	NHL Totals		**77**	**25**	**34**	**59**	**24**	.....	.....	.....	.....	.....

a NHL All-Rookie Team (1989)

VOLHOFFER, TROY

Right wing. Shoots left. 5'11", 185 lbs.   Born, Regina, Sask., February 9, 1966.

			Regular Season					Playoffs				
Season	Club	Lea	GP	G	A	TP	PIM	GP	G	A	TP	PIM
1983-84	Winnipeg	WHL	66	22	37	59	92	....	....	....	....	....
1984-85	Saskatoon	WHL	62	21	31	52	82	....	....	....	....	....
1985-86	Saskatoon	WHL	72	55	55	110	118	13	8	10	18	20
1986-87	Baltimore	AHL	67	11	25	36	90	....	....	....	....	....
1987-88	New Haven	AHL	18	2	6	8	30	....	....	....	....	....
	Muskegon	IHL	33	4	13	17	54	....	....	....	....	....
1988-89	Flint	IHL	63	6	23	29	186	....	....	....	....	....
	Muskegon	IHL	2	0	0	0	9	....	....	....	....	....

Signed as a free agent by **Pittsburgh**, December 9, 1986.

VON STEFENELLI, PHILIP

Defense. Shoots left. 6'1", 183 lbs.   Born, Vancouver, B.C., April 10, 1969.
(Vancouver's 5th choice, 122nd overall, in 1988 Entry Draft).

			Regular Season					Playoffs				
Season	Club	Lea	GP	G	A	TP	PIM	GP	G	A	TP	PIM
1987-88	Boston U.	H.E.	34	3	13	16	38	....	....	....	....	....
1988-89	Boston U.	H.E.	33	2	6	8	34	....	....	....	....	....

VUKONICH, MICHAEL

Center. Shoots left. 6'1", 190 lbs.   Born, Duluth, MN, May 11, 1968.
(Los Angeles' 4th choice, 90th overall, in 1987 Entry Draft).

			Regular Season					Playoffs				
Season	Club	Lea	GP	G	A	TP	PIM	GP	G	A	TP	PIM
1986-87	Duluth Denfield	HS	22	30	23	53	....	....	....	....	....	....
1987-88	Harvard	ECAC	32	9	14	23	24	....	....	....	....	....
1988-89	Harvard	ECAC	27	11	8	19	12	....	....	....	....	....

VUKOTA, MICK

Right wing. Shoots right. 6'2", 195 lbs.   Born, Saskatoon, Sask., September 14, 1966.

			Regular Season					Playoffs				
Season	Club	Lea	GP	G	A	TP	PIM	GP	G	A	TP	PIM
1985-86	Spokane	WHL	64	19	14	33	369	9	6	4	10	68
1986-87	Spokane	WHL	61	25	28	53	337	4	0	0	0	40
1987-88	Springfield	AHL	52	7	9	16	375	....	....	....	....	....
	NY Islanders	**NHL**	17	1	0	1	82	2	0	0	0	23
1988-89	**NY Islanders**	**NHL**	48	2	2	4	237	....	....	....	....	....
	Springfield	AHL	3	1	0	1	33	....	....	....	....	....
	NHL Totals		65	3	2	5	319	2	0	0	0	23

Signed as a free agent by **NY Islanders**, March 2, 1987.

VYAZMIKIN, IGOR

Right wing. Shoots left. 6'1", 195 lbs.   Born, Soviet Union, January 8, 1966.
(Edmonton's 13th choice, 252nd overall, in 1987 Entry Draft).

			Regular Season					Playoffs				
Season	Club	Lea	GP	G	A	TP	PIM	GP	G	A	TP	PIM
1983-84	CSKA	USSR	38	8	12	20	4	....	....	....	....	....
1984-85	CSKA	USSR	26	6	5	11	6	....	....	....	....	....
1985-86	CSKA	USSR	19	7	6	13	6	....	....	....	....	....
1986-87	CSKA	USSR	4	0	0	0	0	....	....	....	....	....
1987-88	CSKA	USSR	8	1	0	1	16	....	....	....	....	....
1988-89	CSKA	USSR	30	10	7	17	20	....	....	....	....	....

WAHLSTEN, SAMI

Left wing. Shoots left. 6', 175 lbs.   Born, Turku, Finland, November 25, 1967.
(Philadelphia's 6th choice, 146th overall, in 1986 Entry Draft).

			Regular Season					Playoffs				
Season	Club	Lea	GP	G	A	TP	PIM	GP	G	A	TP	PIM
1984-85	Fussen	W.Ger.2	51	36	50	86	38	....	....	....	....	....
1985-86	T.P.S.	Fin.	30	8	4	12	13	7	1	2	3	0
1986-87	T.P.S.	Fin.	40	15	13	28	22	5	2	2	4	4
1987-88	T.P.S.	Fin.	43	11	8	19	23	....	....	....	....	....
1988-89	Jokerit	Fin.	44	27	30	57	24	5	1	1	2	0

WALKER, GORD

Left wing. Shoots left. 6', 175 lbs.   Born, Castlegar, B.C., August 12, 1965.
(New York Rangers' 3rd choice, 54th over-all, in 1983 Entry Draft).

			Regular Season					Playoffs				
Season	Club	Lea	GP	G	A	TP	PIM	GP	G	A	TP	PIM
1982-83	Portland	WHL	66	24	30	54	95	14	5	8	13	12
1983-84	Portland	WHL	58	28	41	69	65	14	8	11	19	18
1984-85a	Kamloops	WHL	66	67	67	134	76	15	13	14	27	34
1985-86	New Haven	AHL	46	11	28	39	66	....	....	....	....	....
1986-87	**NY Rangers**	**NHL**	1	1	0	1	4	....	....	....	....	....
	New Haven	AHL	59	24	20	44	58	7	3	2	5	0
1987-88	**NY Rangers**	**NHL**	18	1	4	5	17	....	....	....	....	....
	New Haven	AHL	14	10	9	19	17	....	....	....	....	....
	Colorado	IHL	16	4	9	13	4	....	....	....	....	....
1988-89	**Los Angeles**	**NHL**	11	1	0	1	2	....	....	....	....	....
	New Haven	AHL	60	21	25	46	50	17	7	8	15	23
	NHL Totals		30	3	4	7	23	....	....	....	....	....

a WHL First All-Star Team (1985)
Traded to **Los Angeles** by **NY Rangers** with Mike Siltala for Joe Paterson, January 21, 1988.

WALKER, JOHN

Left wing. Shoots left. 6'4", 195 lbs.   Born, Iserlohn, West Germany, January 22, 1964.
(New Jersey's 1st choice, 2nd overall, in 1987 Supplemental Draft).

			Regular Season					Playoffs				
Season	Club	Lea	GP	G	A	TP	PIM	GP	G	A	TP	PIM
1985-86	N. Alberta	ACAC	40	42	23	65	15	....	....	....	....	....
1986-87	N. Alberta	ACAC	39	33	29	62	14	....	....	....	....	....
1987-88	Utica	AHL	65	11	11	22	15	....	....	....	....	....
1988-89	Utica	AHL	14	2	5	7	11	....	....	....	....	....

WALLWORK, ROBERT

Center. Shoots left. 5'11", 180 lbs.   Born, Boston, Mass., March, 15, 1968.
(Buffalo's 12th choice, 244th overall, in 1988 Entry Draft).

			Regular Season					Playoffs				
Season	Club	Lea	GP	G	A	TP	PIM	GP	G	A	TP	PIM
1987-88	Miami-Ohio	CCHA	36	6	24	30	59	....	....	....	....	....
1988-89	Miami-Ohio	CCHA	19	1	8	9	30	....	....	....	....	....

WALSH, MIKE

Left wing. Shoots right. 6'2", 195 lbs.   Born, New York, N.Y., April 3, 1962.

			Regular Season					Playoffs				
Season	Club	Lea	GP	G	A	TP	PIM	GP	G	A	TP	PIM
1980-81	Colgate	ECAC	35	10	15	25	62	....	....	....	....	....
1981-82	Colgate	ECAC	26	2	7	9	42	....	....	....	....	....
1982-83	Colgate	ECAC	24	9	14	23	36	....	....	....	....	....
1983-84	Colgate	ECAC	35	16	17	33	94	....	....	....	....	....
1984-85			DID NOT PLAY									
1985-86	Malmo	Swe.	42	52	27	79	....	....	....	....	....	....
1986-87	Springfield	AHL	67	20	26	46	32	....	....	....	....	....
1987-88	**NY Islanders**	**NHL**	1	0	0	0	0	....	....	....	....	....
	Springfield	AHL	77	27	23	50	48	....	....	....	....	....
1988-89	**NY Islanders**	**NHL**	13	2	0	2	4	....	....	....	....	....
	Springfield	AHL	68	31	34	65	73	....	....	....	....	....
	NHL Totals		14	2	0	2	4	....	....	....	....	....

Signed as a free agent by **NY Islanders**, August, 1986.

WALTER, BRET

Center. Shoots right. 6'1", 195 lbs.   Born, Calgary, Alta., April 28, 1968.
(NY Rangers' 2nd choice, 51st over-all, in 1986 Entry Draft).

			Regular Season					Playoffs				
Season	Club	Lea	GP	G	A	TP	PIM	GP	G	A	TP	PIM
1984-85	Ft. Sask.	Midget	32	38	39	77	44	....	....	....	....	....
1985-86	U. of Alberta	CWUAA	37	8	17	25	10	....	....	....	....	....
1986-87	U. of Alberta	CWUAA	43	17	17	34	24	....	....	....	....	....
	Cdn. Olympic	....	2	0	0	0	0	....	....	....	....	....
1987-88	U. of Alberta	CWUAA	21	7	10	17	18	....	....	....	....	....
1988-89	Denver	IHL	47	12	10	22	41	2	0	0	0	0

WALTER, RYAN WILLIAM

Center/Left wing. Shoots left. 6', 195 lbs.   Born, New Westminster, B.C., April 23, 1958.
(Washington's 1st choice, 2nd over-all, in 1978 Amateur Draft).

			Regular Season					Playoffs				
Season	Club	Lea	GP	G	A	TP	PIM	GP	G	A	TP	PIM
1974-75	Kamloops	WHL	9	8	4	12	2	2	1	1	2	2
1975-76	Kamloops	WHL	72	35	49	84	96	12	3	9	12	10
1976-77	Kamloops	WHL	71	41	58	99	100	5	1	3	4	11
1977-78abc	Seattle	WHL	62	54	71	125	148	....	....	....	....	....
1978-79	**Washington**	**NHL**	69	28	28	56	70	....	....	....	....	....
1979-80	**Washington**	**NHL**	80	24	42	66	106	....	....	....	....	....
1980-81	**Washington**	**NHL**	80	24	44	68	150	....	....	....	....	....
1981-82	**Washington**	**NHL**	78	38	49	87	142	....	....	....	....	....
1982-83	**Montreal**	**NHL**	80	29	46	75	40	3	0	0	0	11
1983-84	**Montreal**	**NHL**	73	20	29	49	83	15	2	1	3	4
1984-85	**Montreal**	**NHL**	72	19	19	38	59	12	2	7	9	13
1985-86	**Montreal**	**NHL**	69	15	34	49	45	5	0	1	1	2
1986-87	**Montreal**	**NHL**	76	23	23	46	34	17	7	12	19	10
1987-88	**Montreal**	**NHL**	61	13	23	36	39	11	2	4	6	6
1988-89	**Montreal**	**NHL**	78	14	17	31	48	21	3	5	8	6
	NHL Totals		816	247	354	601	816	84	16	30	46	52

a WHL Most Valuable Player (1978)
b WHL Player of the Year (1978)
c WHL First All-Star Team (1978)
Played in NHL All-Star Game (1983)
Traded to **Montreal** by **Washington** with Rick Green for Rod Langway, Brian Engblom, Doug Jarvis and Craig Laughlin, September 9, 1982.

WALZ, WES

Center. Shoots right. 5'10", 180 lbs.   Born, Calgary, Alta., May 15, 1970.
(Boston's 3rd choice, 57th overall, in 1989 Entry Draft).

			Regular Season					Playoffs				
Season	Club	Lea	GP	G	A	TP	PIM	GP	G	A	TP	PIM
1988-89a	Lethbridge	WHL	63	29	75	104	32	8	1	5	6	6

a WHL Rookie of the Year (1989)

WARD, DIXON

Right wing. Shoots right. 6', 195 lbs.   Born, Leduc, Alta., September 23, 1968.
(Vancouver's 6th choice, 128th overall, in 1988 Entry Draft).

			Regular Season					Playoffs				
Season	Club	Lea	GP	G	A	TP	PIM	GP	G	A	TP	PIM
1986-87	Red Deer	AJHL	59	46	40	86	....	....	....	....	....	....
1987-88	Red Deer	AJHL	50	60	71	131	....	....	....	....	....	....
1988-89	North Dakota	WCHA	37	8	9	17	26	....	....	....	....	....

WARD, EDWARD

Right wing. Shoots right. 6'3", 190 lbs.   Born, Edmonton, Alta., November 10, 1969.
(Quebec's 7th choice, 108th overall, in 1988 Entry Draft).

			Regular Season					Playoffs				
Season	Club	Lea	GP	G	A	TP	PIM	GP	G	A	TP	PIM
1986-87	Sherwood Park	AJHL	60	18	28	46	272	....	....	....	....	....
1987-88	N. Michigan	WCHA	25	0	2	2	40	....	....	....	....	....
1988-89	N. Michigan	WCHA	42	5	15	20	36	....	....	....	....	....

WARE, MICHAEL

Defense. Shoots right. 6'5", 205 lbs. Born, York, Ont., March 22, 1967.
(Edmonton's 3rd choice, 62nd over-all, in 1985 Entry Draft).

			Regular Season					Playoffs				
Season	Club	Lea	GP	G	A	TP	PIM	GP	G	A	TP	PIM
1984-85	Hamilton	OHL	57	4	14	18	225	12	0	1	1	29
1985-86	Hamilton	OHL	44	8	11	19	155	....	....	....	....	....
1986-87	Cornwall	OHL	50	5	19	24	173	5	0	1	1	10
1987-88	Nova Scotia	AHL	52	0	8	8	253	3	0	0	0	16
1988-89	**Edmonton**	**NHL**	**2**	**0**	**1**	**1**	**11**	....	....	....	....	....
	Cape Breton	AHL	48	1	11	12	317	....	....	....	....	....
	NHL Totals		**2**	**0**	**1**	**1**	**11**	....	....	....	....	....

WARUS, MIKE

Right wing. Shoots right. 6'1", 190 lbs. Born, Sudbury, Ont., January 16, 1964.
(Winnipeg's 10th choice, 218th over-all, in 1984 Entry Draft).

			Regular Season					Playoffs				
Season	Club	Lea	GP	G	A	TP	PIM	GP	G	A	TP	PIM
1983-84	Lake Superior	CCHA	35	6	4	10	33	....	....	....	....	....
1984-85	Lake Superior	CCHA	43	4	11	15	36	....	....	....	....	....
1985-86	Lake Superior	CCHA	38	5	6	11	85	....	....	....	....	....
1986-87	Lake Superior	CCHA	38	6	15	21	113	....	....	....	....	....
1987-88	Moncton	AHL	38	11	9	20	63	....	....	....	....	....
1988-89	Moncton	AHL	35	6	8	14	127	....	....	....	....	....

WAVER, JEFF

Defense. Shoots left. 5'11", 190 lbs. Born, St. Boniface, Man., September 28, 1968.
(Pittsburgh's 5th choice, 89th overall, in 1987 Entry Draft).

			Regular Season					Playoffs				
Season	Club	Lea	GP	G	A	TP	PIM	GP	G	A	TP	PIM
1986-87	Hamilton	OHL	63	12	28	40	132	9	0	5	5	23
1987-88	Hamilton	OHL	64	27	34	61	134	14	6	7	13	24
1988-89a	Kingston	OHL	55	30	43	73	95	....	....	....	....	....
	Muskegon	IHL	3	0	1	1	0	1	0	0	0	0

a OHL Third All-Star Team (1989)

WASLEN, GERARD

Right wing. Shoots right. 6', 190 lbs. Born, Humboldt, Sask., October 5, 1962.

			Regular Season					Playoffs				
Season	Club	Lea	GP	G	A	TP	PIM	GP	G	A	TP	PIM
1982-83	Colgate	ECAC	28	17	38	55	10	....	....	....	....	....
1983-84	Colgate	ECAC	35	28	33	61	64	....	....	....	....	....
1984-85	Colgate	ECAC	28	10	20	30	55	....	....	....	....	....
1985-86a	Colgate	ECAC	21	14	21	35	36	....	....	....	....	....
1986-87	Newmarket	AHL	79	22	30	52	64	....	....	....	....	....
1987-88	Newmarket	AHL	71	26	36	62	58	....	....	....	....	....
1988-89	Newmarket	AHL	18	4	1	5	11	....	....	....	....	....
	Flint	IHL	13	4	7	11	7	....	....	....	....	....

a ECAC Second All-Star Team (1986)

Signed as a free agent by **Toronto**, June 27, 1986.

WATSON, WILLIAM (BILL)

Right wing. Shoots right. 6', 185 lbs. Born, Pine Falls, Man., March 30, 1964.
(Chicago's 4th choice, 70th over-all, in 1982 Entry Draft).

			Regular Season					Playoffs				
Season	Club	Lea	GP	G	A	TP	PIM	GP	G	A	TP	PIM
1980-81	Prince Albert	SJHL	54	30	39	69	27	....	....	....	....	....
1981-82	Prince Albert	SJHL	47	43	41	84	37	....	....	....	....	....
1982-83	Minn.-Duluth	WCHA	22	5	10	15	10	....	....	....	....	....
1983-84a	Minn.-Duluth	WCHA	40	35	51	86	12	....	....	....	....	....
1984-85b	Minn.-Duluth	WCHA	42	46	54	100	46	....	....	....	....	....
1985-86	**Chicago**	**NHL**	**52**	**8**	**16**	**24**	**2**	**2**	**0**	**1**	**1**	**0**
1986-87	**Chicago**	**NHL**	**51**	**13**	**19**	**32**	**6**	**4**	**0**	**1**	**1**	**0**
1987-88	**Chicago**	**NHL**	**9**	**2**	**0**	**2**	**0**	....	....	....	....	....
	Saginaw	IHL	35	15	20	35	10	....	....	....	....	....
1988-89	**Chicago**	**NHL**	**3**	**0**	**1**	**1**	**4**	....	....	....	....	....
	Saginaw	IHL	42	26	24	50	18	3	1	0	1	2
	NHL Totals		**115**	**23**	**36**	**59**	**12**	**6**	**0**	**2**	**2**	**0**

a WCHA First All-Star Team (1984)
b Named winner of 1985 Hobey Baker Trophy (Top U.S. Collegiate Player)

WATTERS, TIMOTHY J. (TIM)

Defense. Shoots left. 5'11", 180 lbs. Born, Kamloops, B.C., July 25, 1959.
(Winnipeg's 6th choice, 124th over-all, in 1979 Entry Draft).

			Regular Season					Playoffs				
Season	Club	Lea	GP	G	A	TP	PIM	GP	G	A	TP	PIM
1978-79	Michigan Tech	WCHA	38	6	21	27	48	....	....	....	....	....
1979-80	Cdn. National	...	56	8	21	29	43	....	....	....	....	....
	Cdn. Olympic	...	6	1	1	2	0	....	....	....	....	....
1980-81ab	Michigan Tech	WCHA	43	12	38	50	36	....	....	....	....	....
1981-82	Tulsa	CHL	5	1	2	3	0	....	....	....	....	....
	Winnipeg	**NHL**	**69**	**2**	**22**	**24**	**97**	**4**	**0**	**1**	**1**	**8**
1982-83	**Winnipeg**	**NHL**	**77**	**5**	**18**	**23**	**98**	**3**	**0**	**0**	**0**	**2**
1983-84	**Winnipeg**	**NHL**	**74**	**3**	**20**	**23**	**169**	**3**	**1**	**0**	**1**	**2**
1984-85	**Winnipeg**	**NHL**	**63**	**2**	**20**	**22**	**74**	**8**	**0**	**1**	**1**	**16**
1985-86	**Winnipeg**	**NHL**	**56**	**6**	**8**	**14**	**97**	....	....	....	....	....
1986-87	**Winnipeg**	**NHL**	**63**	**3**	**13**	**16**	**119**	**10**	**0**	**0**	**0**	**21**
1987-88	**Winnipeg**	**NHL**	**36**	**0**	**0**	**0**	**106**	**4**	**0**	**0**	**0**	**4**
	Cdn. National	....	8	0	1	1	2	....	....	....	....	....
	Cdn. Olympic	....	2	0	2	2	0	....	....	....	....	....
1988-89	**Los Angeles**	**NHL**	**76**	**3**	**18**	**21**	**168**	**11**	**0**	**1**	**1**	**6**
	NHL Totals		**514**	**24**	**119**	**143**	**928**	**43**	**1**	**3**	**4**	**59**

a WCHA First All-Star Team (1981)
b Named to NCAA All-Tournament Team (1981)

Signed as a free agent by **Los Angeles**, June 27, 1988.

WEINRICH, ERIC (WINE-rich)

Defense. Shoots left. 6'1", 190 lbs. Born, Roanoke, VA, December 19, 1966.
(New Jersey's 3rd choice, 32nd over-all, in 1985 Entry Draft).

			Regular Season					Playoffs				
Season	Club	Lea	GP	G	A	TP	PIM	GP	G	A	TP	PIM
1983-84	N. Yarmouth	Mass.	17	23	33	56	32	....	....	....	....	....
1984-85	N. Yarmouth	Mass.	20	6	21	27	28	....	....	....	....	....
1985-86	U. of Maine	H.E.	34	0	15	15	26	....	....	....	....	....
1986-87ab	U. of Maine	H.E.	41	12	32	44	59	....	....	....	....	....
1987-88	U. of Maine	H.E.	8	4	7	11	22	....	....	....	....	....
	U.S. National	....	38	3	9	12	24	....	....	....	....	....
	U.S. Olympic	....	3	0	0	0	0	....	....	....	....	....
1988-89	**New Jersey**	**NHL**	**2**	**0**	**0**	**0**	**0**	....	....	....	....	....
	Utica	AHL	80	17	27	44	70	5	0	1	1	4
	NHL Totals		**2**	**0**	**0**	**0**	**0**	....	....	....	....	....

a Hockey East First All-Star Team (1987)
b NCAA East Second All-American Team (1987)

WEISBROD, JOHN

Center. Shoots right. 6'1", 185 lbs. Born, Syosset, NY, October 8, 1968.
(Minnesota's 4th choice, 73rd overall, in 1987 Entry Draft).

			Regular Season					Playoffs				
Season	Club	Lea	GP	G	A	TP	PIM	GP	G	A	TP	PIM
1985-86	Choate Acad.	HS	26	21	25	46	....	....	....	....	....	....
1986-87	Choate Acad.	HS	23	13	14	27	....	....	....	....	....	....
1987-88	Harvard	ECAC	22	8	11	19	16	....	....	....	....	....
1988-89	Harvard	ECAC	31	22	13	35	61	....	....	....	....	....

WELLS, GORDON (JAY)

Defense. Shoots left. 6'1", 210 lbs. Born, Paris, Ont., May 18, 1959.
(Los Angeles' 1st choice, 16th over-all, in 1979 Entry Draft).

			Regular Season					Playoffs				
Season	Club	Lea	GP	G	A	TP	PIM	GP	G	A	TP	PIM
1977-78	Kingston	OHA	68	9	13	22	195	5	1	2	3	6
1978-79a	Kingston	OHA	48	6	21	27	100	11	2	7	9	29
1979-80	Binghamton	AHL	28	0	6	6	48	....	....	....	....	....
	Los Angeles	**NHL**	**43**	**0**	**0**	**0**	**113**	**4**	**0**	**0**	**0**	**11**
1980-81	**Los Angeles**	**NHL**	**72**	**5**	**13**	**18**	**155**	**4**	**0**	**0**	**0**	**27**
1981-82	**Los Angeles**	**NHL**	**60**	**1**	**8**	**9**	**145**	**10**	**1**	**3**	**4**	**41**
1982-83	**Los Angeles**	**NHL**	**69**	**3**	**12**	**15**	**167**	....	....	....	....	....
1983-84	**Los Angeles**	**NHL**	**69**	**3**	**18**	**21**	**141**	....	....	....	....	....
1984-85	**Los Angeles**	**NHL**	**77**	**2**	**9**	**11**	**185**	**3**	**0**	**1**	**1**	**0**
1985-86	**Los Angeles**	**NHL**	**79**	**11**	**31**	**42**	**226**	....	....	....	....	....
1986-87	**Los Angeles**	**NHL**	**77**	**7**	**29**	**36**	**155**	**5**	**1**	**2**	**3**	**10**
1987-88	**Los Angeles**	**NHL**	**58**	**2**	**23**	**25**	**159**	**5**	**1**	**2**	**3**	**21**
1988-89	**Philadelphia**	**NHL**	**67**	**2**	**19**	**21**	**184**	**18**	**0**	**2**	**2**	**51**
	NHL Totals		**671**	**36**	**162**	**198**	**1630**	**49**	**3**	**10**	**13**	**161**

a OHA First All-Star Team (1979)

Traded to **Philadelphia** by **Los Angeles** for Doug Crossman, September 29, 1988.

WENAAS, JEFF

Center. Shoots left. 6', 200 lbs. Born, Eastend, Sask., September 1, 1967.
(Calgary's 3rd choice, 38th over-all, in 1985 Entry Draft).

			Regular Season					Playoffs				
Season	Club	Lea	GP	G	A	TP	PIM	GP	G	A	TP	PIM
1984-85	Medicine Hat	WHL	70	27	27	54	70	9	2	5	7	7
1985-86	Medicine Hat	WHL	65	20	26	46	57	25	7	10	17	20
1986-87	Medicine Hat	WHL	70	42	29	71	68	17	9	9	18	28
1987-88	Salt Lake	IHL	80	23	39	62	109	17	5	2	7	25
1988-89	Salt Lake	IHL	17	2	8	10	6	....	....	....	....	....
	Cdn. National	....	21	2	3	5	17	....	....	....	....	....

WENSLEY, DAVID

Right wing. Shoots right. 6', 180 lbs. Born, North Vancouver, B.C., August 29, 1964.

			Regular Season					Playoffs				
Season	Club	Lea	GP	G	A	TP	PIM	GP	G	A	TP	PIM
1984-85	Maine	H.E.	42	17	17	34	36	....	....	....	....	....
1985-86	Maine	H.E.	40	13	18	31	30	....	....	....	....	....
1986-87	Maine	H.E.	31	16	17	33	22	....	....	....	....	....
1987-88	Maine	H.E.	43	24	20	44	40	....	....	....	....	....
1988-89	Baltimore	AHL	2	0	1	1	0	....	....	....	....	....
	Fort Wayne	IHL	11	1	2	3	4	....	....	....	....	....

Signed as a free agent by **Washington**, June 16, 1988.

WERENKA, BRAD

Defense. Shoots left. 6'2", 205 lbs. Born, Two Hills, Alta., February 12, 1969.
(Edmonton's 2nd choice, 42nd overall, in 1987 Entry Draft).

			Regular Season					Playoffs				
Season	Club	Lea	GP	G	A	TP	PIM	GP	G	A	TP	PIM
1986-87	N. Michigan	WCHA	30	4	4	8	35	....	....	....	....	....
1987-88	N. Michigan	WCHA	34	7	23	30	26	....	....	....	....	....
1988-89	N. Michigan	WCHA	28	7	13	20	16	....	....	....	....	....

WERNESS, LANCE

Right wing. Shoots right. 6', 175 lbs. Born, Burnsville, MN, March 28, 1969.
(Chicago's 9th choice, 176th overall, in 1987 Entry Draft).

			Regular Season					Playoffs				
Season	Club	Lea	GP	G	A	TP	PIM	GP	G	A	TP	PIM
1986-87	Burnsville	HS	26	17	29	46	....	....	....	....	....	....
1987-88	U. Minnesota	WCHA	27	8	5	13	20	....	....	....	....	....
1988-89	U. Minnesota	WCHA	13	2	4	6	12	....	....	....	....	....

WESLEY, GLEN

Defense. Shoots left. 6'1", 195 lbs. Born, Red Deer, Alta., October 2, 1968.
(Boston's 1st choice, 3rd overall, in 1987 Entry Draft).

			Regular Season					Playoffs				
Season	Club	Lea	GP	G	A	TP	PIM	GP	G	A	TP	PIM
1983-84	Portland	WHL	3	1	2	3	0	....	....	....	....	....
1984-85	Portland	WHL	67	16	52	68	76	6	1	6	7	8
1985-86a	Portland	WHL	69	16	75	91	96	15	3	11	14	29
1986-87a	Portland	WHL	63	16	46	62	72	20	8	18	26	27
1987-88b	**Boston**	**NHL**	**79**	**7**	**30**	**37**	**69**	**23**	**6**	**8**	**14**	**22**
1988-89	**Boston**	**NHL**	**77**	**19**	**35**	**54**	**61**	**10**	**0**	**2**	**2**	**4**
	NHL Totals		**156**	**26**	**65**	**91**	**130**	**33**	**6**	**10**	**16**	**26**

a WHL West All-Star Team (1986, 1987).
b NHL All-Rookie Team (1988)
Played in NHL All-Star Game (1989)

WHEELDON, SIMON

Center. Shoots left. 5'11", 170 lbs. Born, Vancouver, B.C., August 30, 1966.
(Edmonton's 11th choice, 231st over-all, in 1984 Entry Draft).

			Regular Season					Playoffs				
Season	Club	Lea	GP	G	A	TP	PIM	GP	G	A	TP	PIM
1983-84	Victoria	WHL	56	14	24	38	43	....	....	....	....	....
1984-85a	Victoria	WHL	67	50	76	126	78	....	....	....	....	....
	Nova Scotia	AHL	4	0	1	1	0	1	0	0	0	0
1985-86	Victoria	WHL	70	61	96	157	85	....	....	....	....	....
1986-87	Flint	IHL	41	17	53	70	20	....	....	....	....	....
	New Haven	AHL	38	11	28	39	39	5	0	0	0	6
1987-88	**NY Rangers**	**NHL**	**5**	**0**	**1**	**1**	**4**	....	....	....	....	....
b	Colorado	IHL	69	45	54	99	80	13	8	11	19	12
1988-89	**NY Rangers**	**NHL**	**6**	**0**	**1**	**1**	**2**	....	....	....	....	....
b	Denver	IHL	74	50	56	106	77	4	0	2	2	6
	NHL Totals		**11**	**0**	**2**	**2**	**6**	....	....	....	....	....

a WHL Second All-Star Team, West Division (1985)
b IHL Second All-Star Team (1988, 1989)

WHISTLE, ROB

Defense. Shoots right. 6'2", 195 lbs. Born, Thunder Bay, Ont., April 4, 1961.

			Regular Season					Playoffs				
Season	Club	Lea	GP	G	A	TP	PIM	GP	G	A	TP	PIM
1982-83	Laurier	OUAA	24	6	14	20	12	....	....	....	....	....
1983-84	Laurier	OUAA	24	9	15	24	42	....	....	....	....	....
1984-85a	Laurier	OUAA	24	5	22	27	31	....	....	....	....	....
1985-86b	New Haven	AHL	20	1	4	5	5	....	....	....	....	....
	NY Rangers	**NHL**	**32**	**4**	**2**	**6**	**10**	**3**	**0**	**0**	**0**	**2**
1986-87	New Haven	AHL	55	4	12	16	30	7	1	1	2	7
1987-88	**St. Louis**	**NHL**	**19**	**3**	**3**	**6**	**6**	**1**	**0**	**0**	**0**	**0**
	Peoria	IHL	39	5	21	26	21	....	....	....	....	....
1988-89	Baltimore	AHL	61	2	24	26	30	....	....	....	....	....
	Peoria	IHL	4	0	1	1	4	....	....	....	....	....
	NHL Totals		**51**	**7**	**5**	**12**	**16**	**4**	**0**	**0**	**0**	**2**

a Canadian University Player of the Year, CIAU All-Canadian (1985)
b OUAA 1st All-Star Team (1985)
Signed as a free agent by **NY Rangers**, August 13, 1985. Traded to **St. Louis** by **NY Rangers** with Tony McKegney for Bruce Bell and future considerations, May 28, 1987. Traded to **Washington** by **St. Louis** for Washington's sixth-round choice (Derek Frenette) in 1989 Entry Draft, October 19, 1988.

WHITE, ROBERT

Defense. Shoots right. 6', 185 lbs. Born, Brockville, Ont., March 9, 1968.
(Hartford's 10th choice, 221st overall, in 1988 Entry Draft).

			Regular Season					Playoffs				
Season	Club	Lea	GP	G	A	TP	PIM	GP	G	A	TP	PIM
1986-87	St. Lawrence	ECAC	30	2	9	11	52	....	....	....	....	....
1987-88	St. Lawrence	ECAC	31	4	16	20	29	....	....	....	....	....
1988-89	St. Lawrence	ECAC	35	5	19	24	64	....	....	....	....	....

WHITE, SCOTT

Defense. Shoots right. 6', 190 lbs. Born, Ormstown, Que., April 21, 1968.
(Quebec's 6th choice, 117th overall, in 1986 Entry Draft).

			Regular Season					Playoffs				
Season	Club	Lea	GP	G	A	TP	PIM	GP	G	A	TP	PIM
1985-86	Michigan Tech	WCHA	40	3	15	18	58	....	....	....	....	....
1986-87	Michigan Tech	WCHA	36	4	15	19	58	....	....	....	....	....
1987-88	Michigan Tech	WCHA	40	7	25	32	32	....	....	....	....	....
1988-89	Michigan Tech	WCHA	38	6	18	24	38	....	....	....	....	....

WHITHAM, SHAWN

Defense. Shoots left. 5'11", 175 lbs. Born, Verdun, Que., March 13, 1967.
(Buffalo's 10th choice, 173rd overall, in 1986 Entry Draft).

			Regular Season					Playoffs				
Season	Club	Lea	GP	G	A	TP	PIM	GP	G	A	TP	PIM
1985-86	Providence	H.E.	38	10	14	24	91	....	....	....	....	....
1986-87	Providence	H.E.	31	9	11	20	57	....	....	....	....	....
1987-88	Providence	H.E.	29	8	17	25	71	....	....	....	....	....
1988-89	Rochester	AHL	46	4	15	19	75	....	....	....	....	....
	Flint	IHL	17	3	13	16	18	....	....	....	....	....

WHITTEMORE, TODD

Forward. Shoots right. 6'1", 175 lbs. Born, Taunton, MA, June 20, 1967.
(Toronto's 9th choice, 169th overall, in 1985 Entry Draft).

			Regular Season					Playoffs				
Season	Club	Lea	GP	G	A	TP	PIM	GP	G	A	TP	PIM
1986-87	Providence	H.E.	29	1	4	5	12	....	....	....	....	....
1987-88	Providence	H.E.	34	5	10	15	38	....	....	....	....	....
1988-89	Providence	H.E.	29	7	1	8	28	....	....	....	....	....

WICKENHEISER, DOUGLAS PETER (DOUG) (WIHK ehn HIGH zuhr)

Center. Shoots left. 6'1", 200 lbs. Born, Regina, Sask., March 30, 1961.
(Montreal's 1st choice and 1st over-all in 1980 Entry Draft).

			Regular Season					Playoffs				
Season	Club	Lea	GP	G	A	TP	PIM	GP	G	A	TP	PIM
1977-78	Regina	WHL	68	37	51	88	49	13	4	5	9	4
1978-79	Regina	WHL	68	32	62	94	141	....	....	....	....	....
1979-80abc	Regina	WHL	71	*89	81	*170	99	18	14	*26	*40	20
1980-81	**Montreal**	**NHL**	**41**	**7**	**8**	**15**	**20**	....	....	....	....	....
1981-82	**Montreal**	**NHL**	**56**	**12**	**23**	**35**	**43**	....	....	....	....	....
1982-83	**Montreal**	**NHL**	**78**	**25**	**30**	**55**	**49**	....	....	....	....	....
1983-84	**Montreal**	**NHL**	**27**	**5**	**5**	**10**	**6**	....	....	....	....	....
	St. Louis	**NHL**	**46**	**7**	**21**	**28**	**19**	**11**	**2**	**2**	**4**	**2**
1984-85	**St. Louis**	**NHL**	**68**	**23**	**20**	**43**	**36**	....	....	....	....	....
1985-86	**St. Louis**	**NHL**	**36**	**8**	**11**	**19**	**16**	**19**	**2**	**5**	**7**	**12**
1986-87	**St. Louis**	**NHL**	**80**	**13**	**15**	**28**	**37**	**6**	**0**	**0**	**0**	**2**
1987-88	**Vancouver**	**NHL**	**80**	**7**	**19**	**26**	**36**	....	....	....	....	....
1988-89	**NY Rangers**	**NHL**	**1**	**1**	**0**	**1**	**0**	....	....	....	....	....
	Flint	IHL	21	9	7	16	18	....	....	....	....	....
	Cdn. National	....	26	7	15	22	40	....	....	....	....	....
	Washington	**NHL**	**16**	**2**	**5**	**7**	**4**	**5**	**0**	**0**	**0**	**2**
	Baltimore	AHL	2	0	5	5	0	....	....	....	....	....
	NHL Totals		**529**	**110**	**157**	**267**	**266**	**41**	**4**	**7**	**11**	**18**

a WHL First All-Star Team (1980)
b WHL Most Valuable Player (1980)
c Named Canadian Major Junior Player of the Year (1980)
Traded to **St. Louis** by **Montreal** with Gilbert Delorme and Greg Paslawski for Perry Turnbull, December 21, 1983. Claimed by **Hartford** in NHL Waiver Draft, October 5, 1987. Claimed by **Vancouver** in NHL Waiver Draft, October 5, 1987.

WIEBE, DANIEL

Right wing. Shoots left. 6'4", 190 lbs. Born, Manning, Alta., April 3, 1969.
(Quebec's 10th choice, 171st overall, in 1988 Entry Draft).

			Regular Season					Playoffs				
Season	Club	Lea	GP	G	A	TP	PIM	GP	G	A	TP	PIM
1987-88	U. of Alberta	CWUAA	25	6	4	10	....	....	....	....	....	....
1988-89	U. of Alberta	CWUAA	40	5	8	13	56	....	....	....	....	....

WIEGAND, CHARLES

Center. Shoots left. 6'1", 175 lbs. Born, Burlington, VT, December 28, 1968.
(NY Rangers 8th choice, 157th overall, in 1987 Entry Draft).

			Regular Season					Playoffs				
Season	Club	Lea	GP	G	A	TP	PIM	GP	G	A	TP	PIM
1987-88	New Hampton	HS	25	15	10	25	....	....	....	....	....	....
1988-89	Ferris State	CCHA	36	5	5	10	44	....	....	....	....	....

WIEMER, JAMES DUNCAN (JIM) (WEE-mer)

Defense. Shoots left. 6'4", 208 lbs. Born, Sudbury, Ont., January 9, 1961.
(Buffalo's 5th choice, 83rd over-all, in 1980 Entry Draft).

			Regular Season					Playoffs				
Season	Club	Lea	GP	G	A	TP	PIM	GP	G	A	TP	PIM
1978-79	Peterborough	OHA	61	15	12	27	50	18	4	4	8	15
1979-80	Peterborough	OHA	53	17	32	49	63	14	6	9	15	19
1980-81	Peterborough	OHA	65	41	54	95	102	5	1	2	3	15
1981-82	Rochester	AHL	74	19	26	45	57	9	0	4	4	2
1982-83	**Buffalo**	**NHL**	....	....	....	....	....	**1**	**0**	**0**	**0**	**0**
	Rochester	AHL	74	15	44	59	43	15	5	15	20	22
1983-84	**Buffalo**	**NHL**	**64**	**5**	**15**	**20**	**48**	....	....	....	....	....
	Rochester	AHL	12	4	11	15	11	18	3	13	16	20
1984-85	**Buffalo**	**NHL**	**10**	**3**	**2**	**5**	**4**	....	....	....	....	....
	Rochester	AHL	13	1	9	10	24	....	....	....	....	....
	NY Rangers	**NHL**	**22**	**4**	**3**	**7**	**30**	**1**	**0**	**0**	**0**	**0**
	New Haven	AHL	33	9	27	36	39	....	....	....	....	....
1985-86	**NY Rangers**	**NHL**	**7**	**3**	**0**	**3**	**2**	**8**	**1**	**0**	**1**	**6**
ab	New Haven	AHL	73	24	49	73	108	....	....	....	....	....
1986-87	New Haven	AHL	6	0	7	7	6	....	....	....	....	....
	Nova Scotia	AHL	59	9	25	34	72	5	0	4	4	2
1987-88	**Edmonton**	**NHL**	**12**	**1**	**2**	**3**	**15**	**2**	**0**	**0**	**0**	**2**
	Nova Scotia	AHL	57	11	32	43	99	5	1	1	2	14
1988-89	Cape Breton	AHL	51	12	29	41	80	....	....	....	....	....
	Los Angeles	**NHL**	**9**	**2**	**3**	**5**	**20**	**10**	**2**	**1**	**3**	**19**
	New Haven	AHL	3	1	1	2	2	7	2	3	5	2
	NHL Totals		**124**	**18**	**25**	**43**	**119**	**22**	**3**	**1**	**4**	**27**

a AHL First All-Star Team (1986)
b AHL Defenseman of the Year (1986)
Traded to **NY Rangers** by **Buffalo** with Steve Patrick for Dave Maloney and Chris Renaud, December 6, 1984. Traded to **Los Angeles** by **Edmonton** with Alan May for Brian Wilks and John English, March 7, 1989.

WIKBERG, ANDERS

Left wing. Shoots left. 6', 180 lbs. Born, Timra, Sweden, January 17, 1963.
(Buffalo's 6th choice, 83rd overall, in 1981 Entry Draft).

			Regular Season					Playoffs				
Season	Club	Lea	GP	G	A	TP	PIM	GP	G	A	TP	PIM
1981-82	Timra	Swe. 2	24	2	2	4	14	....	....	....	....	....
1982-83	Timra	Swe. 2	29	5	10	15	4	5	4	1	5	2
1983-84	Timra	Swe. 2	31	12	21	33	18	....	....	....	....	....
1984-85	Modo	Swe. 2	26	25	25	50	18	....	....	....	....	....
1985-86	Modo	Swe.	35	11	11	22	16	6	3	1	4	2
1986-87	Modo	Swe.	32	22	9	31	8	6	3	1	4	2
1987-88	Modo	Swe.	30	15	8	23	2	....	....	....	....	....
1988-89	Orebro	Swe.	17	21	16	37	....	....	....	....	....	....

WILKIE, BOB

Defense. Shoots right. 6'2", 200 lbs. Born, Calgary, Alta., February 11, 1969.
(Detroit's 3rd choice, 41st overall, in 1987 Entry Draft).

			Regular Season					Playoffs				
Season	Club	Lea	GP	G	A	TP	PIM	GP	G	A	TP	PIM
1985-86	Calgary	Midget	63	8	19	27	56	....	....	....	....	....
1986-87	Swift Current	WHL	65	12	38	50	50	4	1	3	4	2
1987-88	Swift Current	WHL	67	12	68	80	124	10	4	12	16	8
1988-89	Swift Current	WHL	62	18	67	85	89	12	1	11	12	47

WILKINSON, NEIL

Defense. Shoots right. 6'3", 180 lbs. Born, Selkirk, Man., August 16, 1967.
(Minnesota's 2nd choice, 30th overall, in 1986 Entry Draft).

			Regular Season					Playoffs				
Season	Club	Lea	GP	G	A	TP	PIM	GP	G	A	TP	PIM
1985-86	Selkirk	MJHL	42	14	35	49	91	....	....	....	....	....
1986-87	Michigan State	CCHA	19	3	4	7	18	....	....	....	....	....
1987-88	Medicine Hat	WHL	55	11	21	32	157	5	1	0	1	2
1988-89	Kalamazoo	IHL	39	5	15	20	96	....	....	....	....	....

WILKS, BRIAN

Center. Shoots right. 5'11", 175 lbs. Born, North York, Ont., February 27, 1966.
(Los Angeles' 2nd choice, 24th over-all, in 1984 Entry Draft).

			Regular Season					Playoffs				
Season	Club	Lea	GP	G	A	TP	PIM	GP	G	A	TP	PIM
1982-83	Kitchener	OHL	69	6	17	23	25	1	0	0	0	0
1983-84	Kitchener	OHL	64	21	54	75	36	16	6	14	20	9
1984-85	Los Angeles	NHL	2	0	0	0	0	....	....	....	....	....
	Kitchener	OHL	58	30	63	93	52	4	2	4	6	2
1985-86	Los Angeles	NHL	43	4	8	12	25	....	....	....	....	....
1986-87	Los Angeles	NHL	1	0	0	0	0	....	....	....	....	....
	New Haven	AHL	43	16	20	36	23	7	1	3	4	7
1987-88	New Haven	AHL	18	4	8	12	26	....	....	....	....	....
1988-89	Cape Breton	AHL	12	4	11	15	27	....	....	....	....	....
	Los Angeles	NHL	2	0	0	0	2	....	....	....	....	....
	New Haven	AHL	44	15	19	34	48	....	....	....	....	....
	NHL Totals		48	4	8	12	27	....	....	....	....	....

Traded to **Edmonton by Los Angeles** with John English for Jim Weimer and Alan May, March 7, 1989.

WILLIAMS, DAVID

Defense. Shoots right. 6'2", 195 lbs. Born, Plainfield, NJ, August 25, 1967.
(New Jersey's 12th choice, 234th overall, in 1985 Entry Draft).

			Regular Season					Playoffs				
Season	Club	Lea	GP	G	A	TP	PIM	GP	G	A	TP	PIM
1986-87	Dartmouth	ECAC	23	2	19	21	20	....	....	....	....	....
1987-88	Dartmouth	ECAC	25	8	14	22	30	....	....	....	....	....
1988-89ab	Dartmouth	ECAC	25	4	11	15	28	....	....	....	....	....

a ECAC First All-Star Team (1989)
b NCAA East Second All-American Team (1989)

WILLIAMS, SEAN

Center. Shoots left. 6'1", 180 lbs. Born, Oshawa, Ont., January 28, 1968.
(Chicago's 11th choice, 245th overall, in 1986 Entry Draft).

			Regular Season					Playoffs				
Season	Club	Lea	GP	G	A	TP	PIM	GP	G	A	TP	PIM
1984-85	Oshawa	OHL	40	6	7	13	28	5	1	0	1	0
1985-86	Oshawa	OHL	55	15	23	38	23	6	2	3	5	4
1986-87	Oshawa	OHL	62	21	23	44	32	25	7	5	12	19
1987-88a	Oshawa	OHL	65	*58	65	123	38	7	3	3	6	6
1988-89	Saginaw	IHL	77	32	27	59	75	6	0	3	3	0

a OHL First All-Star Team (1988)

WILSON, BEHN BEVAN

Defense. Shoots left 6'3", 210 lbs. Born. Toronto, Ont., December 19, 1958.
(Philadelphia's 1st choice, 6th over-all, in 1978 Amateur Draft).

			Regular Season					Playoffs				
Season	Club	Lea	GP	G	A	TP	PIM	GP	G	A	TP	PIM
1975-76	Ottawa	OHA	63	5	16	21	131	12	3	2	5	46
1976-77	Ottawa	OHA	31	8	29	37	115	....	....	....	....	....
	Windsor	OHA	17	4	16	20	38	....	....	....	....	....
	Kalamazoo	IHL	13	2	7	9	40	....	....	....	....	....
1977-78	Kingston	OHA	52	18	58	76	186	2	1	3	4	21
1978-79	Philadelphia	NHL	80	13	36	49	197	5	1	0	1	8
1979-80	Philadelphia	NHL	61	9	25	34	212	19	4	9	13	66
1980-81	Philadelphia	NHL	77	16	47	63	237	12	2	10	12	36
1981-82	Philadelphia	NHL	59	13	23	36	135	4	1	4	5	10
1982-83	Philadelphia	NHL	62	8	24	32	92	3	0	1	1	2
1983-84	Chicago	NHL	59	10	22	32	143	4	0	0	0	0
1984-85	Chicago	NHL	76	10	23	33	185	15	4	5	9	60
1985-86	Chicago	NHL	69	13	37	50	113	2	0	0	0	2
1986-87	Chicago	NHL	DID NOT PLAY — INJURED									
1987-88	Chicago	NHL	58	6	23	29	166	3	0	0	0	6
1988-89	Chicago	NHL	DID NOT PLAY — INJURED									
	NHL Totals		601	98	260	358	1480	67	12	29	41	190

Claimed by **Vancouver** in NHL Waiver Draft, October 3, 1988.

WILSON, CAREY

Center. Shoots right. 6'2", 205 lbs. Born, Winnipeg, Man., May 19, 1962.
(Chicago's 8th choice, 67th over-all, in 1980 Entry Draft).

			Regular Season					Playoffs				
Season	Club	Lea	GP	G	A	TP	PIM	GP	G	A	TP	PIM
1979-80	Dartmouth	ECAC	31	16	22	38	20	....	....	....	....	....
1980-81	Dartmouth	ECAC	24	9	13	22	52	....	....	....	....	....
1981-82	Helsinki	Fin.	29	15	17	32	58	7	1	4	5	6
1982-83	Helsinki	Fin.	36	16	24	40	62	9	1	3	4	12
1983-84	Cdn. Olympic	...	56	19	24	43	34	....	....	....	....	....
	Calgary	NHL	15	2	5	7	2	6	3	1	4	2
1984-85	Calgary	NHL	74	24	48	72	27	4	0	0	0	0
1985-86	Calgary	NHL	76	29	29	58	24	9	0	2	2	2
1986-87	Calgary	NHL	80	20	36	56	42	6	1	1	2	6
1987-88	Calgary	NHL	34	9	21	30	18	....	....	....	....	....
	Hartford	NHL	36	18	20	38	22	6	2	4	6	2
1988-89	Hartford	NHL	34	11	11	22	14	....	....	....	....	....
	NY Rangers	NHL	41	21	34	55	45	4	1	2	3	2
	NHL Totals		390	134	204	338	194	35	7	10	17	14

Rights traded to **Calgary** by **Chicago** for Denis Cyr, November 8, 1982. Traded to **Hartford** by **Calgary** with Neil Sheehy and the rights to Lane MacDonald for Dana Murzyn and Shane Churla, January 3, 1988. Traded by **NY Rangers** by **Hartford** with Hartford's fifth-round choice in 1990 Entry Draft for Brian Lawton, Norm MacIver and Don Maloney, December 26, 1988.

WILSON, DOUGLAS, JR. (DOUG)

Defense. Shoots left. 6'1", 185 lbs. Born, Ottawa, Ont., July 5, 1957.
(Chicago's 1st choice, 6th over-all, in 1977 Amateur Draft).

			Regular Season					Playoffs				
Season	Club	Lea	GP	G	A	TP	PIM	GP	G	A	TP	PIM
1975-76	Ottawa	OHA	58	26	62	88	142	12	5	10	15	24
1976-77a	Ottawa	OHA	43	25	54	79	85	19	4	20	24	34
1977-78	Chicago	NHL	77	14	20	34	72	4	0	0	0	0
1978-79	Chicago	NHL	56	5	21	26	37	....	....	....	....	....
1979-80	Chicago	NHL	73	12	49	61	70	7	2	8	10	6
1980-81	Chicago	NHL	76	12	39	51	80	3	0	3	3	2
1981-82bc	Chicago	NHL	76	39	46	85	54	15	3	10	13	32
1982-83	Chicago	NHL	74	18	51	69	58	13	4	11	15	12
1983-84	Chicago	NHL	66	13	45	58	64	5	0	3	3	2
1984-85d	Chicago	NHL	78	22	54	76	44	12	3	10	13	12
1985-86	Chicago	NHL	79	17	47	64	80	3	1	1	2	2
1986-87	Chicago	NHL	69	16	32	48	36	4	0	0	0	0
1987-88	Chicago	NHL	27	8	24	32	28	....	....	....	....	....
1988-89	Chicago	NHL	66	15	47	62	69	4	1	2	3	0
	NHL Totals		817	191	475	666	692	70	14	48	62	68

a OHA First All-Star Team (1977)
b Won James Norris Memorial Trophy (1982)
c NHL First All-Star Team (1982)
d NHL Second All-Star Team (1985)

Played in NHL All-Star Game (1982-86)

WILSON, MITCH

Center. Shoots right. 5'8", 190 lbs. Born, Kelowna, B.C., February 15, 1962.

			Regular Season					Playoffs				
Season	Club	Lea	GP	G	A	TP	PIM	GP	G	A	TP	PIM
1980-81	Seattle	WHL	64	8	23	31	253	5	3	0	3	31
1981-82	Seattle	WHL	60	18	17	35	436	10	3	7	10	55
1982-83	Wichita	CHL	55	4	6	10	186	....	....	....	....	....
1983-84	Maine	AHL	71	6	8	14	349	17	3	6	9	98
1984-85	New Jersey	NHL	9	0	2	2	21	....	....	....	....	....
	Maine	AHL	51	6	3	9	220	2	0	0	0	32
1985-86	Maine	AHL	64	4	3	7	217	3	0	0	0	2
1986-87	Pittsburgh	NHL	17	2	1	3	83	....	....	....	....	....
	Baltimore	AHL	58	8	9	17	353	....	....	....	....	....
1987-88	Muskegon	IHL	68	27	25	52	400	5	1	0	1	23
1988-89	Muskegon	IHL	61	16	34	50	382	11	4	5	9	83
	NHL Totals		26	2	3	5	104	....	....	....	....	....

Signed as a free agent by **New Jersey**, October 12, 1982.

WILSON, RICHARD WILLIAM (RIK)

Defense. Shoots right. 6', 180 lbs. Born, Long Beach, CA, June 17, 1962.
(St. Louis' 1st choice, 12th over-all, in 1980 Entry Draft).

			Regular Season					Playoffs				
Season	Club	Lea	GP	G	A	TP	PIM	GP	G	A	TP	PIM
1980-81a	Kingston	OHA	68	30	70	100	108	13	1	9	10	18
	Salt Lake	CHL	....	....	....	....	....	4	1	1	2	2
1981-82	Kingston	OHL	16	9	10	19	38	....	....	....	....	....
	St. Louis	NHL	48	3	18	21	24	9	0	3	3	14
1982-83	St. Louis	NHL	56	3	11	14	50	....	....	....	....	....
	Salt Lake	CHL	4	0	0	0	0	....	....	....	....	....
1983-84	Montana	CHL	6	0	3	3	2	....	....	....	....	....
	St. Louis	NHL	48	7	11	18	53	11	0	0	0	9
1984-85	St. Louis	NHL	51	8	16	24	39	2	0	1	1	0
1985-86	St. Louis	NHL	32	0	4	4	48	....	....	....	....	....
	Calgary	NHL	2	0	0	0	0	....	....	....	....	....
	Nova Scotia	AHL	13	4	5	9	11	....	....	....	....	....
	Moncton	AHL	8	3	3	6	2	....	....	....	....	....
1986-87	Nova Scotia	AHL	45	8	13	21	109	5	1	3	4	20
1987-88	Chicago	NHL	14	4	5	9	6	....	....	....	....	....
	Saginaw	IHL	33	4	5	9	105	....	....	....	....	....
1988-89	Villach	Aus.	45	17	43	60	110	....	....	....	....	....
	NHL Totals		251	25	65	90	220	22	0	4	4	23

a OHA First All-Star Team (1981)

Traded to **Calgary** by **St. Louis** with Joe Mullen and Terry Johnson for Ed Beers, Charles Bourgeois and Gino Cavallini, February 1, 1986. Traded to **Chicago** by **Calgary** for Tom McMurchy, March 11, 1986. Signed as a free agent by **St. Louis**, July 19, 1989.

WILSON, ROB

Defense. Shoots left. 6'3", 190 lbs. Born, Toronto, Ont., July 18, 1968.
(Pittsburgh's 12th choice, 235th overall, in 1986 Entry Draft).

			Regular Season					Playoffs				
Season	Club	Lea	GP	G	A	TP	PIM	GP	G	A	TP	PIM
1985-86	Sudbury	OHL	61	1	5	6	93	4	0	2	2	10
1986-87	Sudbury	OHL	58	1	27	28	135	....	....	....	....	....
1987-88	Sudbury	OHL	42	3	15	18	93	....	....	....	....	....
1988-89	Peterborough	OHL	63	4	14	18	146	17	2	7	9	29

WILSON, RONALD LEE (RON)

Left wing. Shoots left. 5'9", 170 lbs. Born, Toronto, Ont., May 13, 1956.
(Montreal's 15th choice, 133rd over-all, in 1976 Amateur Draft).

			Regular Season					Playoffs				
Season	**Club**	**Lea**	**GP**	**G**	**A**	**TP**	**PIM**	**GP**	**G**	**A**	**TP**	**PIM**
1974-75	Toronto	OHA	16	6	12	18	6	23	9	17	26	6
1975-76	St. Catharines	OHA	64	37	62	99	44	4	1	6	7	7
1976-77	Nova Scotia	AHL	67	15	21	36	18	6	0	0	0	0
1977-78	Nova Scotia	AHL	59	15	25	40	17	11	4	4	8	9
1978-79	Nova Scotia	AHL	77	33	42	75	91	10	5	6	11	14
1979-80	**Winnipeg**	**NHL**	**79**	**21**	**36**	**57**	**28**	....	....	....	....	....
1980-81	**Winnipeg**	**NHL**	**77**	**18**	**33**	**51**	**55**	....	....	....	....	....
1981-82	**Winnipeg**	**NHL**	**39**	**3**	**13**	**16**	**49**	....	....	....	....	....
	Tulsa	CHL	41	20	38	58	22	3	1	0	1	2
1982-83	Sherbrooke	AHL	65	30	55	85	71	....	....	....	....	....
	Winnipeg	**NHL**	**12**	**6**	**3**	**9**	**4**	**3**	**2**	**2**	**4**	**2**
1983-84	**Winnipeg**	**NHL**	**51**	**3**	**12**	**15**	**12**	....	....	....	....	....
	Sherbrooke	AHL	22	10	30	40	16	....	....	....	....	....
1984-85	**Winnipeg**	**NHL**	**75**	**10**	**9**	**19**	**31**	**8**	**4**	**2**	**6**	**2**
1985-86	**Winnipeg**	**NHL**	**54**	**6**	**7**	**13**	**16**	**1**	**0**	**0**	**0**	**0**
	Sherbrooke	AHL	10	9	8	17	9	....	....	....	....	....
1986-87	**Winnipeg**	**NHL**	**80**	**3**	**13**	**16**	**13**	**10**	**1**	**2**	**3**	**0**
1987-88	**Winnipeg**	**NHL**	**69**	**5**	**8**	**13**	**28**	**1**	**0**	**0**	**0**	**2**
1988-89a	Moncton	AHL	80	31	61	92	110	8	1	4	5	20
	NHL Totals		**536**	**75**	**134**	**209**	**236**	**23**	**7**	**6**	**13**	**6**

a AHL Second All-Star Team (1989)

Sold to **Winnipeg** by **Montreal**, October 4, 1979.

WILSON, ROSS

Right wing. Shoots right. 6'3", 195 lbs. Born, Val Caron, Ont., June 26, 1969.
(Los Angeles' 3rd choice, 43rd overall, in 1987 Entry Draft).

			Regular Season					Playoffs				
Season	**Club**	**Lea**	**GP**	**G**	**A**	**TP**	**PIM**	**GP**	**G**	**A**	**TP**	**PIM**
1986-87	Peterborough	OHL	66	28	11	39	91	12	3	5	8	16
1987-88	Peterborough	OHL	66	29	30	59	114	12	2	9	11	15
1988-89	Peterborough	OHL	64	48	41	89	90	15	10	13	23	23

WINNES, CHRISTOPHER (CHRIS)

Right wing. Shoots right. 6', 170 lbs. Born, Ridgefield, CT, February 12, 1968.
(Boston's 9th choice, 161st overall, in 1987 Entry Draft).

			Regular Season					Playoffs				
Season	**Club**	**Lea**	**GP**	**G**	**A**	**TP**	**PIM**	**GP**	**G**	**A**	**TP**	**PIM**
1986-87	Northwood	HS	27	25	25	50	....	....	....	....	....	....
1987-88	N. Hampshire	H.E.	30	17	19	36	28	....	....	....	....	....
1988-89	N. Hampshire	H.E.	30	11	20	31	22	....	....	....	....	....

WOLAK, MICHAEL

Center. Shoots left. 5'10", 185 lbs. Born, Utica, NY, April 29, 1968.
(St. Louis' 5th choice, 87th overall, in 1986 Entry Draft).

			Regular Season					Playoffs				
Season	**Club**	**Lea**	**GP**	**G**	**A**	**TP**	**PIM**	**GP**	**G**	**A**	**TP**	**PIM**
1985-86	Kitchener	OHL	62	24	44	68	48	5	0	9	9	2
1986-87	Kitchener	OHL	9	3	6	9	6	....	....	....	....	....
	Belleville	OHL	25	20	16	36	18	....	....	....	....	....
	Windsor	OHL	26	7	14	21	26	14	2	7	9	2
1987-88	Windsor	OHL	63	42	72	114	86	9	7	4	11	22
1988-89	Flint	IHL	2	0	1	1	4	....	....	....	....	....
	Windsor	OHL	35	19	38	57	56	4	5	4	9	4
	Peoria	IHL	8	2	4	6	16	1	0	0	0	0

WOLANIN, CHRISTOPHER

Defense. Shoots left. 6'2", 205 lbs. Born, Detroit, MI, September 12, 1968.
(Vancouver's 10th choice, 212th overall, in 1988 Entry Draft).

			Regular Season					Playoffs				
Season	**Club**	**Lea**	**GP**	**G**	**A**	**TP**	**PIM**	**GP**	**G**	**A**	**TP**	**PIM**
1987-88	Ill-Chicago	CCHA	37	1	6	7	38	....	....	....	....	....
1988-89	Ill-Chicago	CCHA	30	1	9	10	33	....	....	....	....	....

WOLANIN, CRAIG

Defense. Shoots left. 6'3", 210 lbs. Born, Grosse Pointe, MI, July 27, 1967.
(New Jersey's 1st choice, 3rd over-all, in 1985 Entry Draft).

			Regular Season					Playoffs				
Season	**Club**	**Lea**	**GP**	**G**	**A**	**TP**	**PIM**	**GP**	**G**	**A**	**TP**	**PIM**
1983-84	Detroit Compu.	Midget	69	8	42	50	86	....	....	....	....	....
1984-85	Kitchener	OHL	60	5	16	21	95	4	1	1	2	2
1985-86	**New Jersey**	**NHL**	**44**	**2**	**16**	**18**	**74**	....	....	....	....	....
1986-87	**New Jersey**	**NHL**	**68**	**4**	**6**	**10**	**109**	....	....	....	....	....
1987-88	**New Jersey**	**NHL**	**78**	**6**	**25**	**31**	**170**	**18**	**2**	**5**	**7**	**51**
1988-89	**New Jersey**	**NHL**	**56**	**3**	**8**	**11**	**69**	....	....	....	....	....
	NHL Totals		**246**	**15**	**55**	**70**	**422**	**18**	**2**	**5**	**7**	**51**

WOLF, GREGORY (GREGG)

Defense. Shoots left. 6'1", 200 lbs. Born, Buffalo, NY, August 20, 1969.
(Hartford's 6th choice, 144th overall, in 1987 Entry Draft).

			Regular Season					Playoffs				
Season	**Club**	**Lea**	**GP**	**G**	**A**	**TP**	**PIM**	**GP**	**G**	**A**	**TP**	**PIM**
1987-88	Colgate	ECAC	32	0	7	7	66	....	....	....	....	....
1988-89	Colgate	ECAC	13	1	3	4	20	....	....	....	....	....

WOLF, TODD

Defense. Shoots left. 6'2", 215 lbs. Born, East Aurora, NY, November 5, 1967.
(Chicago's 1st choice, 13th overall, in 1988 Supplemental Draft).

			Regular Season					Playoffs				
Season	**Club**	**Lea**	**GP**	**G**	**A**	**TP**	**PIM**	**GP**	**G**	**A**	**TP**	**PIM**
1985-86	Colgate	ECAC	32	0	2	2	22	....	....	....	....	....
1986-87	Colgate	ECAC	33	1	15	16	44	....	....	....	....	....
1987-88	Colgate	ECAC	29	2	12	14	76	....	....	....	....	....
1988-89	Colgate	ECAC	29	1	13	14	58	....	....	....	....	....

WOOD, RANDY

Left wing. Shoots left. 6', 195 lbs. Born, Princeton, NJ, October 12, 1963.

			Regular Season					Playoffs				
Season	**Club**	**Lea**	**GP**	**G**	**A**	**TP**	**PIM**	**GP**	**G**	**A**	**TP**	**PIM**
1983-84	Yale	ECAC	18	7	7	14	10	....	....	....	....	....
1984-85a	Yale	ECAC	32	25	28	53	23	....	....	....	....	....
1985-86bc	Yale	ECAC	31	25	30	55	26	....	....	....	....	....
1986-87	Springfield	AHL	75	23	24	47	57	....	....	....	....	....
	NY Islanders	**NHL**	**6**	**1**	**0**	**1**	**4**	**13**	**1**	**3**	**4**	**14**
1987-88	**NY Islanders**	**NHL**	**75**	**22**	**16**	**38**	**80**	**5**	**1**	**0**	**1**	**6**
	Springfield	AHL	1	0	1	1	0	....	....	....	....	....
1988-89	**NY Islanders**	**NHL**	**77**	**15**	**13**	**28**	**44**	....	....	....	....	....
	Springfield	AHL	1	1	1	2	0	....	....	....	....	....
	NHL Totals		**158**	**38**	**29**	**67**	**128**	**18**	**2**	**3**	**5**	**20**

a ECAC Second All-Star Team (1985)
b ECAC First All-Star Team (1986)
c NCAA East Second All-Star Team (1986)

Signed as a free agent by **NY Islanders**, September 17, 1986.

WOODCROFT, CRAIG

Left wing. Shoots left. 6'1", 185 lbs. Born, Toronto, Ont., December 3, 1969.
(Chicago's 7th choice, 134th overall, in 1988 Entry Draft).

			Regular Season					Playoffs				
Season	**Club**	**Lea**	**GP**	**G**	**A**	**TP**	**PIM**	**GP**	**G**	**A**	**TP**	**PIM**
1987-88	Colgate	ECAC	29	7	10	17	28	....	....	....	....	....
1988-89	Colgate	ECAC	29	20	29	49	62	....	....	....	....	....
	Cdn. National	....	2	0	0	0	4	....	....	....	....	....

WOODLEY, DAN

Center. Shoots right. 5'11", 185 lbs. Born, Oklahoma City, OK, December 29, 1967.
(Vancouver's 1st choice, 7th overall, in 1986 Entry Draft).

			Regular Season					Playoffs				
Season	**Club**	**Lea**	**GP**	**G**	**A**	**TP**	**PIM**	**GP**	**G**	**A**	**TP**	**PIM**
1984-85	Portland	WHL	63	21	36	57	108	1	0	0	0	0
1985-86	Portland	WHL	62	45	47	92	100	12	0	8	8	31
1986-87	Portland	WHL	47	30	50	80	81	19	19	17	36	52
1987-88	**Vancouver**	**NHL**	**5**	**2**	**0**	**2**	**17**	....	....	....	....	....
a	Flint	IHL	69	29	37	66	104	9	1	3	4	26
1988-89	Milwaukee	IHL	30	9	12	21	48	....	....	....	....	....
	Sherbrooke	AHL	30	9	16	25	69	4	1	6	7	5
	NHL Totals		**5**	**2**	**0**	**2**	**17**	....	....	....	....	....

a Won Ken McKenzie Trophy (American Rookie of the Year-IHL) (1988)

Traded to **Montreal** by **Vancouver** for Jose Charbonneau, January 25, 1989.

WOODS, ROBERT

Defense. Shoots left. 6'0", 170 lbs. Born, Leroy, Sask., January 24, 1968.
(New Jersey's 11th choice, 201st overall, in 1988 Entry Draft).

			Regular Season					Playoffs				
Season	**Club**	**Lea**	**GP**	**G**	**A**	**TP**	**PIM**	**GP**	**G**	**A**	**TP**	**PIM**
1986-87	Nipawin	SJHL	63	22	48	70	78	....	....	....	....	....
1987-88	Brandon	WHL	72	21	56	77	84	4	1	5	6	9
1988-89	Brandon	WHL	68	26	50	76	100	....	....	....	....	....
	Utica	AHL	11	0	1	1	2	4	0	0	0	2

WOODWARD, ROBERT

Left wing. Shoots left. 6'4", 220 lbs. Born, Evanston, IL, January 15, 1971.
(Vancouver's 2nd choice, 29th overall, in 1989 Entry Draft).

			Regular Season					Playoffs				
Season	**Club**	**Lea**	**GP**	**G**	**A**	**TP**	**PIM**	**GP**	**G**	**A**	**TP**	**PIM**
1987-88	Deerfield	HS	25	36	55	91	....	....	....	....	....	....
1988-89	Deerfield	HS	29	46	71	117	12	....	....	....	....	....

WOOLLEY, JASON

Defense. Shoots left. 6'0", 185 lbs. Born, Toronto, Ont., July 27, 1969.
(Washington's 4th choice, 61st overall, in 1989 Entry Draft).

			Regular Season					Playoffs				
Season	**Club**	**Lea**	**GP**	**G**	**A**	**TP**	**PIM**	**GP**	**G**	**A**	**TP**	**PIM**
1987-88	St. Michael's	Jr. B.	31	19	37	56	22	....	....	....	....	....
1988-89	Michigan State	CCHA	40	12	25	37	26	....	....	....	....	....

YAKE, TERRY

Center. Shoots right. 5'11", 185 lbs. Born, New Westminster, B.C., October 22, 1968.
(Hartford's 3rd choice, 81st overall, in 1987 Entry Draft).

			Regular Season					Playoffs				
Season	**Club**	**Lea**	**GP**	**G**	**A**	**TP**	**PIM**	**GP**	**G**	**A**	**TP**	**PIM**
1984-85	Brandon	WHL	11	1	1	2	0	....	....	....	....	....
1985-86	Brandon	WHL	72	26	26	52	49	....	....	....	....	....
1986-87	Brandon	WHL	71	44	58	102	64	....	....	....	....	....
1987-88	Brandon	WHL	72	55	85	140	59	3	4	2	6	7
1988-89	**Hartford**	**NHL**	**2**	**0**	**0**	**0**	**0**	....	....	....	....	....
	Binghamton	AHL	75	39	56	95	57	....	....	....	....	....
	NHL Totals		**2**	**0**	**0**	**0**	**0**	....	....	....	....	....

YAREMCHUK, GARY (yuh RHEM chuhk)

Center. Shoots left. 6', 185 lbs. Born, Edmonton, Alta., August 15, 1961.
(Toronto's 2nd choice, 24th over-all, in 1981 Entry Draft).

			Regular Season					Playoffs				
Season	Club	Lea	GP	G	A	TP	PIM	GP	G	A	TP	PIM
1979-80	Portland	WHL	41	21	34	55	23	6	1	4	5	2
1980-81	Portland	WHL	72	56	79	135	121	....	....	....	....	....
1981-82	**Toronto**	**NHL**	**18**	**0**	**3**	**3**	**10**	....	....	....	....	....
	Cincinnati	CHL	53	21	35	56	101	4	0	2	2	4
1982-83	**Toronto**	**NHL**	**3**	**0**	**0**	**0**	**2**	....	....	....	....	....
	St. Catharines	AHL	61	17	28	45	72	....	....	....	....	....
1983-84	**Toronto**	**NHL**	**1**	**0**	**0**	**0**	**0**	....	....	....	....	....
	St. Catharines	AHL	73	24	37	61	84	7	5	1	6	2
1984-85	**Toronto**	**NHL**	**12**	**1**	**1**	**2**	**16**	....	....	....	....	....
	St. Catharines	AHL	66	17	47	64	75	....	....	....	....	....
1985-86	Adirondack	AHL	60	12	32	44	90	1	1	0	1	0
1986-87	Jokerit	Fin.	20	7	21	28	116	....	....	....	....	....
1987-88	Karpat	Fin.	36	16	27	43	92	....	....	....	....	....
1988-89	Kookoo	Fin.	44	12	27	39	50	....	....	....	....	....
	NHL Totals		**34**	**1**	**4**	**5**	**28**	....	....	....	....	....

Signed as a free agent by **Detroit**, August 13, 1985.

YAREMCHUK, KEN (yuh REHM chuhk)

Center. Shoots right. 5'11", 185 lbs. Born, Edmonton, Alta., January 1, 1964.
(Chicago's 1st choice, 7th over-all, in 1982 Entry Draft).

			Regular Season					Playoffs				
Season	Club	Lea	GP	G	A	TP	PIM	GP	G	A	TP	PIM
1980-81	Portland	WHL	72	35	72	107	105	9	2	8	10	24
1981-82a	Portland	WHL	72	58	99	157	181	15	10	21	31	12
1982-83b	Portland	WHL	66	51	109	160	76	14	11	15	26	12
1983-84	**Chicago**	**NHL**	**47**	**6**	**7**	**13**	**19**	**1**	**0**	**0**	**0**	**0**
1984-85	**Chicago**	**NHL**	**63**	**10**	**16**	**26**	**16**	**15**	**5**	**5**	**10**	**37**
	Milwaukee	IHL	7	4	6	10	9	....	....	....	....	....
1985-86	**Chicago**	**NHL**	**78**	**14**	**20**	**34**	**43**	**3**	**1**	**1**	**2**	**2**
1986-87	**Toronto**	**NHL**	**20**	**3**	**8**	**11**	**16**	**6**	**0**	**0**	**0**	**0**
	Newmarket	AHL	14	2	4	6	21	....	....	....	....	....
1987-88	**Toronto**	**NHL**	**16**	**2**	**5**	**7**	**10**	**6**	**0**	**2**	**2**	**10**
	Cdn. National	....	38	15	18	33	63	....	....	....	....	....
	Cdn. Olympic	....	8	3	3	6	2	....	....	....	....	....
1988-89	**Toronto**	**NHL**	**11**	**1**	**0**	**1**	**2**	....	....	....	....	....
	Newmarket	AHL	55	25	33	58	145	5	7	7	14	12
	NHL Totals		**235**	**36**	**56**	**92**	**106**	**31**	**6**	**8**	**14**	**49**

a WHL First All-Star Team (1982)
b WHL Second All-Star Team (1983)

Acquired by **Toronto** from **Chicago** with Jerome Dupont and Chicago's fourth-round choice in 1987 Entry Draft (Joe Sacco) as compensation for signing of free agent Gary Nylund, September 6, 1986.

YAWNEY, TRENT

Defense. Shoots left. 6'3", 185 lbs. Born, Hudson Bay, Sask., September 29, 1965.
(Chicago's 2nd choice, 45th over-all, in 1984 Entry Draft).

			Regular Season					Playoffs				
Season	Club	Lea	GP	G	A	TP	PIM	GP	G	A	TP	PIM
1982-83	Saskatoon	WHL	59	6	31	37	44	6	0	2	2	0
1983 84	Saskatoon	WHL	73	13	46	59	81	....	....	....	....	....
1984-85	Saskatoon	WHL	72	16	51	67	158	3	1	6	7	7
1985-86	Cdn. Olympic	...	73	6	15	21	60	....	....	....	....	....
1986-87	Cdn. Olympic	....	51	4	15	19	37	....	....	....	....	....
1987-88	**Chicago**	**NHL**	**15**	**2**	**8**	**10**	**15**	**5**	**0**	**4**	**4**	**8**
	Cdn. National	....	60	4	12	16	81	....	....	....	....	....
	Cdn. Olympic	....	8	1	1	2	6	....	....	....	....	....
1988-89	**Chicago**	**NHL**	**69**	**5**	**19**	**24**	**116**	**15**	**3**	**6**	**9**	**20**
	NHL Totals		**84**	**7**	**27**	**34**	**131**	**20**	**3**	**10**	**13**	**28**

YOUNG, SCOTT

Right wing. Shoots right. 6', 190 lbs. Born, Clinton, MA, October 1, 1967.
(Hartford's 1st choice, 11th overall, in 1986 Entry Draft).

			Regular Season					Playoffs				
Season	Club	Lea	GP	G	A	TP	PIM	GP	G	A	TP	PIM
1985-86a	Boston U.	H.E.	38	16	13	29	31	....	....	....	....	....
1986-87	Boston U.	H.E.	33	15	21	36	24	....	....	....	....	....
1987-88	**Hartford**	**NHL**	**7**	**0**	**0**	**0**	**2**	**4**	**1**	**0**	**1**	**0**
	U.S. National	....	56	11	47	58	31	....	....	....	....	....
	U.S. Olympic	....	6	2	6	8	4	....	....	....	....	....
1988-89	**Hartford**	**NHL**	**76**	**19**	**40**	**59**	**27**	**4**	**2**	**0**	**2**	**4**
	NHL Totals		**83**	**19**	**40**	**59**	**29**	**8**	**3**	**0**	**3**	**4**

a Hockey East Rookie of the Year (1986)

YSEBAERT, PAUL

Center. Shoots left. 6'1", 185 lbs. Born, Sarnia, Ont., May 15, 1966.
(New Jersey's 4th choice, 74th overall, in 1984 Entry Draft).

			Regular Season					Playoffs				
Season	Club	Lea	GP	G	A	TP	PIM	GP	G	A	TP	PIM
1984-85	Bowling Green	CCHA	42	23	32	55	54	....	....	....	....	....
1985-86a	Bowling Green	CCHA	42	23	45	68	50	....	....	....	....	....
1986-87a	Bowling Green	CCHA	45	27	58	85	44	....	....	....	....	....
	Cdn. Olympic	....	5	1	0	1	4	....	....	....	....	....
1987-88	Utica	AHL	78	30	49	79	60	....	....	....	....	....
1988-89	**New Jersey**	**NHL**	**5**	**0**	**4**	**4**	**0**	....	....	....	....	....
	Utica	AHL	56	36	44	80	22	5	0	1	1	4
	NHL Totals		**5**	**0**	**4**	**4**	**0**	....	....	....	....	....

a CCHA Second All-Star Team (1986, 1987)

YZERMAN, STEVE (IGH zur muhn)

Center. Shoots right. 5'11", 185 lbs. Born, Cranbrook, B.C., May 9, 1965.
(Detroit's 1st choice, 4th over-all, in 1983 Entry Draft).

			Regular Season					Playoffs				
Season	Club	Lea	GP	G	A	TP	PIM	GP	G	A	TP	PIM
1981-82	Peterborough	OHL	58	21	43	64	65	6	0	1	1	16
1982-83	Peterborough	OHL	56	42	49	91	33	4	1	4	5	0
1983-84a	**Detroit**	**NHL**	**80**	**39**	**48**	**87**	**33**	**4**	**3**	**3**	**6**	**0**
1984-85	**Detroit**	**NHL**	**80**	**30**	**59**	**89**	**58**	**3**	**2**	**1**	**3**	**2**
1985-86	**Detroit**	**NHL**	**51**	**14**	**28**	**42**	**16**	....	....	....	....	....
1986-87	**Detroit**	**NHL**	**80**	**31**	**59**	**90**	**43**	**16**	**5**	**13**	**18**	**8**
1987-88	**Detroit**	**NHL**	**64**	**50**	**52**	**102**	**44**	**3**	**1**	**3**	**4**	**6**
1988-89b	**Detroit**	**NHL**	**80**	**65**	**90**	**155**	**61**	**6**	**5**	**5**	**10**	**2**
	NHL Totals		**435**	**229**	**336**	**565**	**255**	**32**	**16**	**25**	**41**	**18**

a NHL All-Rookie Team (1984)
b Won Lester B. Pearson Award (1989)

Played in NHL All-Star Game (1984-88, 1988-89)

ZALAPSKI, ZARLEY

Defense. Shoots left. 6'1", 204 lbs. Born, Edmonton, Alta., April 22, 1968.
(Pittsburgh's 1st choice, 4th overall, in 1986 Entry Draft).

			Regular Season					Playoffs				
Season	Club	Lea	GP	G	A	TP	PIM	GP	G	A	TP	PIM
1985-86	Cdn. Olympic	...	59	22	37	59	56	....	....	....	....	....
1986-87	Cdn. Olympic	....	74	11	29	40	28	....	....	....	....	....
1987-88	**Pittsburgh**	**NHL**	**15**	**3**	**8**	**11**	**7**	....	....	....	....	....
	Cdn. National	....	47	3	13	16	32	....	....	....	....	....
	Cdn. Olympic	....	8	1	3	4	2	....	....	....	....	....
1988-89a	**Pittsburgh**	**NHL**	**58**	**12**	**33**	**45**	**57**	**11**	**1**	**8**	**9**	**13**
	NHL Totals		**73**	**15**	**41**	**56**	**64**	**11**	**1**	**8**	**9**	**13**

a NHL All-Rookie Team (1989)

ZEMLAK, RICHARD ANDREW

Center. Shoots right. 6'2", 190 lbs. Born, Wynard, Sask., March 3, 1963.
(St. Louis' 9th choice, 209th over-all, in 1981 Entry Draft).

			Regular Season					Playoffs				
Season	Club	Lea	GP	G	A	TP	PIM	GP	G	A	TP	PIM
1980-81	Spokane	WHL	72	19	19	38	132	4	1	1	2	6
1981-82	Spokane	WHL	26	9	20	29	113	....	....	....	....	....
	Winnipeg	WHL	2	1	2	3	0	....	....	....	....	....
	Medicine Hat	WHL	41	11	20	31	70	....	....	....	....	....
	Salt Lake	CHL	6	0	0	0	2	1	0	0	0	0
1982-83	Medicine Hat	WHL	51	20	17	37	119	....	....	....	....	....
	Nanaimo	WHL	18	2	8	10	50	....	....	....	....	....
1983-84	Montana	CHL	14	2	2	4	17	....	....	....	....	....
	Toledo	IHL	45	8	19	27	101	....	....	....	....	....
1984-85	Muskegon	IHL	64	19	18	37	223	17	5	4	9	68
	Fredericton	AHL	16	3	4	7	59	....	....	....	....	....
1985-86	Fredericton	AHL	58	6	5	11	305	3	0	0	0	49
	Muskegon	IHL	3	1	2	3	36	....	....	....	....	....
1986-87	**Quebec**	**NHL**	**20**	**0**	**2**	**2**	**47**	....	....	....	....	....
	Fredericton	AHL	29	9	6	15	201	....	....	....	....	....
1987-88	**Minnesota**	**NHL**	**54**	**1**	**4**	**5**	**307**	....	....	....	....	....
1988-89	**Minnesota**	**NHL**	**3**	**0**	**0**	**0**	**13**	....	....	....	....	....
	Kalamazoo	IHL	2	1	3	4	22	....	....	....	....	....
	Pittsburgh	**NHL**	**31**	**0**	**0**	**0**	**135**	**1**	**0**	**0**	**0**	**10**
	Muskegon	IHL	18	5	4	9	55	8	1	1	2	35
	NHL Totals		**108**	**1**	**6**	**7**	**502**	**1**	**0**	**0**	**0**	**10**

Rights sold to **Quebec** by **St. Louis** with rights to Dan Wood and Roger Hagglund, June 22, 1984. Claimed by **Minnesota** in NHL Waiver Draft, October 5, 1987. Traded to **Pittsburgh** by **Minnesota** for the rights to Rob Gaudreau, November 1, 1988.

ZAMUNER, ROB

Center. Shoots left. 6'2", 200 lbs. Born, Oakville, Ont., September 17, 1969.
(NY Rangers' 3rd choice, 45th overall, in 1989 Entry Draft).

			Regular Season					Playoffs				
Season	Club	Lea	GP	G	A	TP	PIM	GP	G	A	TP	PIM
1987-88	Guelph	OHL	58	20	41	61	18	....	....	....	....	....
1988-89a	Guelph	OHL	66	46	65	111	38	7	5	5	10	9

a OHL Third All-Star Team (1989)

ZENT, JASON

Left wing. Shoots left. 5'11", 180 lbs. Born, Buffalo, NY, April 15, 1971.
(NY Islanders' 3rd choice, 44th overall, in 1989 Entry Draft).

			Regular Season					Playoffs				
Season	Club	Lea	GP	G	A	TP	PIM	GP	G	A	TP	PIM
1987-88	Nichols	HS	21	20	16	36	28	....	....	....	....	....
1988-89	Nichols	HS	29	49	32	81	26	....	....	....	....	....

ZETTLER, ROB

Defense. Shoots left. 6'3", 190 lbs. Born, Sept Iles, Que., March 8, 1968.
(Minnesota's 5th choice, 55th overall, in 1986 Entry Draft).

			Regular Season					Playoffs				
Season	Club	Lea	GP	G	A	TP	PIM	GP	G	A	TP	PIM
1985-86	S.S. Marie	OHL	57	5	23	28	92	....	....	....	....	....
1986-87	S.S. Marie	OHL	64	13	22	35	89	4	0	0	0	0
1986-87	S.S. Marie	OHL	64	13	22	35	89	4	0	0	0	0
1987-88	Kalamazoo	IHL	2	0	1	1	0	7	0	2	2	2
	S.S.Marie	OHL	64	7	41	48	77	6	2	2	4	9
1988-89	**Minnesota**	**NHL**	**2**	**0**	**0**	**0**	**0**	....	....	....	....	....
	Kalamazoo	IHL	80	5	21	26	79	6	0	1	1	26
	NHL Totals		**2**	**0**	**0**	**0**	**0**	....	....	....	....	....

ZEZEL, PETER
(ZEH zuhl)

Center. Shoots left. 5'9", 200 lbs.   Born, Toronto, Ont., April 22, 1965.
(Philadelphia's 1st choice, 41st over-all, in 1983 Entry Draft).

			Regular Season					Playoffs				
Season	Club	Lea	GP	G	A	TP	PIM	GP	G	A	TP	PIM
1981-82	Don Mills	Midget	40	43	51	94	36	....	....	....	....	....
1982-83	Toronto	OHL	66	35	39	74	28	4	2	4	6	0
1983-84	Toronto	OHL	68	47	86	133	31	9	7	5	12	4
1984-85	**Philadelphia**	**NHL**	65	15	46	61	26	19	1	8	9	28
1985-86	**Philadelphia**	**NHL**	79	17	37	54	76	5	3	1	4	4
1986-87	**Philadelphia**	**NHL**	71	33	39	72	71	25	3	10	13	10
1987-88	**Philadelphia**	**NHL**	69	22	35	57	42	7	3	2	5	7
1988-89	**Philadelphia**	**NHL**	26	4	13	17	15	....	....	....	....	....
	St. Louis	NHL	52	17	36	53	27	10	6	6	12	4
	NHL Totals		362	108	206	314	257	66	16	27	43	53

Traded to **St. Louis** by **Philadelphia** for Mike Bullard, November 29, 1988.

ZMOLEK, DOUG

Defense. Shoots left. 6'1", 195 lbs.   Born, Rochester, MN, November 3, 1970.
(Minnesota's 1st choice, 7th overall, in 1989 Entry Draft).

			Regular Season					Playoffs				
Season	Club	Lea	GP	G	A	TP	PIM	GP	G	A	TP	PIM
1987-88	John Marshall	HS	27	4	32	36		....	....	....	....	....
1988-89	John Marshall	HS	29	17	41	58		....	....	....	....	....

ZOMBO, RICHARD (RICK)

Defense. Shoots right. 6'1", 195 lbs.   Born, Des Plaines, IL., May 8, 1963.
(Detroit's 6th choice, 149th over-all, in 1981 Entry Draft).

			Regular Season					Playoffs				
Season	Club	Lea	GP	G	A	TP	PIM	GP	G	A	TP	PIM
1983-84	North Dakota	WCHA	34	7	24	31	40	....	....	....	....	....
1984-85	**Detroit**	**NHL**	1	0	0	0	0	....	....	....	....	....
	Adirondack	AHL	56	3	32	35	70	....	....	....	....	....
1985-86	**Detroit**	**NHL**	14	0	1	1	16	....	....	....	....	....
	Adirondack	AHL	69	7	34	41	94	17	0	4	4	40
1986-87	**Detroit**	**NHL**	44	1	4	5	59	7	0	1	1	9
	Adirondack	AHL	25	0	6	6	22	....	....	....	....	....
1987-88	**Detroit**	**NHL**	62	3	14	17	96	16	0	6	6	55
1988-89	**Detroit**	**NHL**	75	1	20	21	106	6	0	1	1	16
	NHL Totals		196	5	39	44	277	29	0	8	8	80

*Despite missing 20 games due to injury, Bruins'
captain Ray Bourque recorded 61 points in the
regular season and was selected to the
Second All-Star Team.*

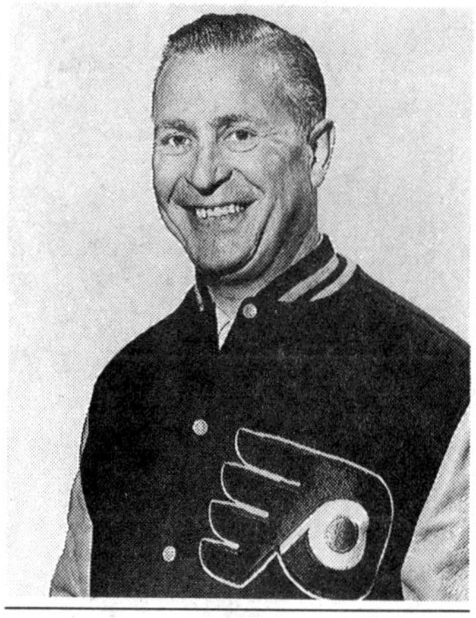

Keith Allen

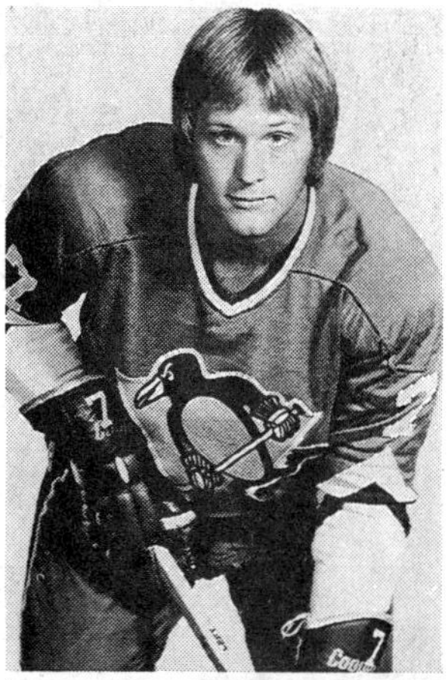

Russ Anderson

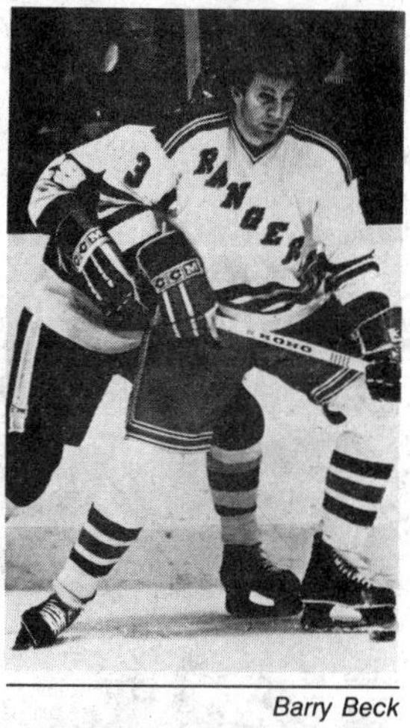

Barry Beck

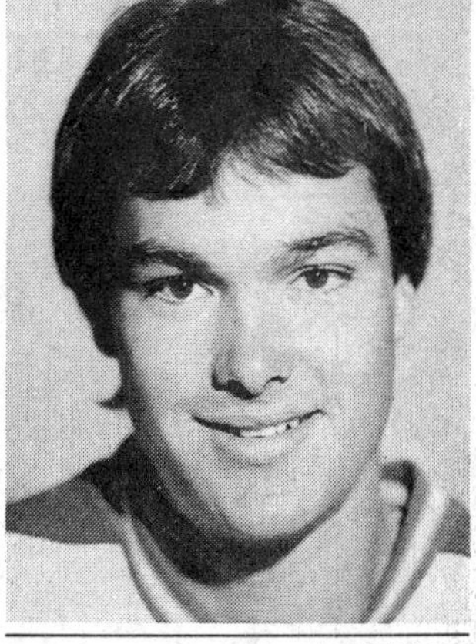

Ed Beers

Retired NHL Player Index

Abbreviations: Teams/Cities: — **Atl.** – Atlanta, **Bos.** – Boston; **Buf.** – Buffalo; **Cal.** – California; **Cgy.** – Calgary; **Chi.** – Chicago; **Cle.** – Cleveland; **Col.** – Colorado; **Det.** – Detroit; **Edm.** – Edmonton; **Ham.** – Hamilton; **Hfd.** – Hartford; **L.A.** – Los Angeles; **Min.** – Minnesota; **Mtl.** – Montreal; **Mtl.M.** – Montreal Maroons; **Mtl.W.** – Montreal Wanderers; **N.J.** – New Jersey; **NY** – New York; **NYA** – NY Americans; **NYI** – New York Islanders; **NYR** – New York Rangers; **Oak.** – Oakland; **Ott.** – Ottawa; **Phi.** – Philadelphia; **Pit.** – Pittsburgh; **Que.** – Quebec; **St.L.** – St. Louis; **Tor.** – Toronto; **Van.** – Vancouver; **Wpg.** – Winnipeg; **Wsh.** – Washington.

Total seasons are rounded off to the nearest full season. **A** – assists; **G** – goals; **GP** – games played; **PIM** – penalties in minutes; **TP** – total points. Assists not recorded prior to 1926.

			Regular Schedule					Playoffs					First	Last
Name	**NHL Teams**	**NHL Seasons**	**GP**	**G**	**A**	**TP**	**PIM**	**GP**	**G**	**A**	**TP**	**PIM**	**NHL Season**	**NHL Season**
A														
Abbott, Reg	Mtl.	1	3	0	0	0	0	....	....	....	....	....	1952-53	1952-53
Abel, Gerry	Det.	1	1	0	0	0	0	....	....	....	....	....	1966-67	1966-67
Abel, Sid	Det., Chi.	14	613	189	283	472	376	96	28	30	58	77	1938-39	1953-54
Abel, Clarence	NYR, Chi.	8	332	18	18	36	359	38	1	1	2	56	1926-27	1933-34
Abgrall, Dennis	L.A.	1	13	0	2	2	4	....	....	....	....	....	1975-76	1975-76
Abrahamsson, Thommy	Hfd.	1	32	6	11	17	16	....	....	....	....	....	1980-81	1980-81
Achtymichuk, Gene	Mtl., Det.	4	32	3	5	8	2	....	....	....	....	....	1951-52	1958-59
Acomb, Doug	Tor.	1	2	0	1	1	0	....	....	....	....	....	1969-70	1969-70
Adam, Douglas	NYR	1	4	0	1	1	0	....	....	....	....	....	1949-50	1949-50
Adam, Russ	Tor.	1	8	1	2	3	11	....	....	....	....	....	1982-83	1982-83
Adams, Jack J.	Tor., Ott.	7	173	82	29	111	292	12	3	0	3	9	1917-18	1926-27
Adams, Jack	Mtl.	1	42	6	12	18	11	3	0	0	0	0	1940-41	1940-41
Adams, Stuart	Chi., Tor.	4	106	9	26	35	60	11	3	3	6	14	1929-30	1932-33
Adduono, Rick	Bos., Atl.	2	4	0	0	0	2	....	....	....	....	....	1975-76	1979-80
Affleck, Bruce	St.L., Van., NYI	7	280	14	66	80	86	8	0	0	0	0	1974-75	1983-84
Ahern, Fred	Cal., Cle., Col.	2	146	31	30	61	130	2	0	1	1	2	1974-75	1980-81
Ahlin	Chi.	1	1	0	0	0	0	....	....	....	....	....	1937-38	1937-38
Ahrens, Chris	Min.	1	52	0	3	3	84	1	0	0	0	0	1977-78	1977-78
Albright, Clint	NYR	1	59	14	5	19	19	....	....	....	....	....	1948-49	1948-49
Aldcorn, Gary	Tor., Det., Bos.	4	226	41	56	97	78	6	1	2	3	4	1956-57	1960-61
Alexander, Claire	Tor., Van.	4	155	18	47	65	36	16	2	4	6	4	1974-75	1977-78
Alexandre, Art	Mtl.	2	11	0	2	2	8	4	0	0	0	0	1931-32	1932-33
Allen, George	NYR, Chi., Mtl.	8	339	82	115	197	179	41	9	10	19	32	1938-39	1946-47
Allen, Jeff	Cle.	1	4	0	0	0	2	....	....	....	....	....	1977-78	1977-78
Allen, Keith	Det.	2	28	0	4	4	8	5	0	0	0	0	1953-54	1954-55
Allen, Viv	NYA	1	6	0	1	1	0	....	....	....	....	....	1940-41	1940-41
Alley, Steve	Hfd.	2	15	3	3	6	11	3	0	1	1	0	1979-80	1980-81
Allison, Dave	Mtl.	1	3	0	0	0	12	....	....	....	....	....	1983-84	1983-84
Allison, Ray	Hfd., Phi.	7	238	64	93	157	223	12	2	3	5	20	1979-80	1986-87
Allsby, Lloyd	NYR	1	3	0	0	0	2	....	....	....	....	....	1951-52	1951-52
Allum, Bill	NYR	1	1	0	1	1	0	....	....	....	....	....	1940-41	1940-41
Amadio, Dave	Det., L.A.	2	125	11	16	27	163	16	1	2	3	18	1957-58	1968-69
Amodeo, Mike	Wpg.	1	19	0	0	0	2	....	....	....	....	....	1979-80	1979-80
Anderson, Bill	Bos.	1	1	0	0	0	0	....	....	....	....	....	1942-43	1942-43
Anderson, Dale	Det.	1	13	0	0	0	6	2	0	0	0	0	1956-57	1956-57
Anderson, Doug	Mtl.	1	....	....	....	....	....	2	0	0	0	0	1952-53	1952-53
Anderson, Earl	Det., Bos.	2	109	19	19	38	22	5	0	1	1	0	1974-75	1976-77
Anderson, Jim	L.A.	2	7	1	2	3	2	4	0	0	0	2	1967-68	1968-69
Anderson, Murray	Wsh.	1	40	0	1	1	68	....	....	....	....	....	1974-75	1974-75
Anderson, Ron C.	Det., L.A., St.L., Buf.	4	251	28	30	58	146	1	0	0	0	0	1967-68	1971-72
Anderson, Ron H.	Wsh.	1	28	9	7	16	8	....	....	....	....	....	1974-75	1974-75
Anderson, Russ	Pit., Hfd., L.A.	10	519	22	99	121	1086	10	0	3	3	28	1976-77	1984-85
Anderson, Tom	Det., NYA	8	319	62	127	189	190	16	2	7	9	62	1934-35	1941-42
Andersson Kent-Erik	Min., NYR	7	456	72	103	175	78	50	4	11	15	4	1977-78	1983-84
Andersson, Peter	Wsh., Que.	3	172	10	41	51	80	7	0	2	2	2	1983-84	1985-86
Andrascik, Steve	NYR	1	....	....	....	....	....	1	0	0	0	0	1971-72	1971-72
Andrea, Paul	NYR, Pit., Cal., Buf.	3	150	31	49	80	10	....	....	....	....	....	1965-66	1970-71
Andrews, Lloyd	Tor.	4	53	8	5	13	10	7	2	0	2	5	1921-22	1924-25
Andruff, Ron	Mtl., Col.,	5	153	19	36	55	54	2	0	0	0	0	1974-75	1978-79
Angotti, Lou	NYR, Chi., Phi., Pit., St.L.	10	653	103	186	289	228	65	8	8	16	17	1964-65	1973-74
Anholt, Darrel	Chi.	1	1	0	0	0	0	....	....	....	....	....	1983-84	1983-84
Anslow, Bert	NYR	1	2	0	0	0	0	....	....	....	....	....	1947-48	1947-48
Antonovich, Mike	Min., Hfd., N.J.	5	87	10	15	25	37	....	....	....	....	....	1975-76	1983-84
Apps, Syl (Jr.)	NYR, Pit., L.A.	9	727	183	423	606	311	23	5	5	10	23	1970-71	1979-80
Apps, Syl (Sr.)	Tor.	10	423	201	231	432	56	69	25	28	53	16	1936-37	1947-48
Arbour, Al	Det., Chi., Tor., St.L.	11	626	12	58	70	617	86	1	8	9	92	1953-54	1970-71
Arbour, Amos	Mtl., Ham., Tor.	6	109	51	13	64	66	....	....	....	....	....	1918-19	1923-24
Arbour, Jack	Det., Tor.	2	47	5	1	6	56	....	....	....	....	....	1926-27	1928-29
Arbour, John	Bos., Pit., Van., St.L.	6	106	1	9	10	149	5	0	0	0	0	1965-66	1971-72
Arbour, Ty	Pit., Chi.	5	207	28	28	56	112	11	2	0	2	6	1926-27	1930-31
Archambault, Michel	Chi.	1	3	0	0	0	0	....	....	....	....	....	1976-77	1976-77
Archibald, Jim	Min.	3	16	1	2	3	45	....	....	....	....	....	1984-85	1986-87
Areshenkoff, Ronald	Edm.	1	4	0	0	0	0	....	....	....	....	....	1979-80	1979-80
Armstrong, Bob	Bos.	10	542	13	86	99	671	42	1	7	8	28	1950-51	1961-62
Armstrong, George	Tor.	20	1187	296	417	713	721	110	26	34	60	52	1949-50	1970-71
Armstrong, Murray	Tor., NYA, Det.,	8	270	67	121	188	72	30	4	6	10	2	1937-38	1945-46
Armstrong, Red	Tor.	1	7	1	1	2	2	....	....	....	....	....	1962-63	1962-63
Arnason, Chuck	Mtl., Atl., Pit., K.C., Col., Clev., Min., Wsh.	6	401	109	90	199	122	9	2	4	6	4	1971-72	1978-79
Arthur, Fred	Hfd., Phi.	3	80	1	8	9	49	4	0	0	0	2	1980-81	1982-83
Arundel, John	Tor.	1	3	0	0	0	0	....	....	....	....	....	1949-50	1949-50
Ashbee, Barry	Bos., Phi.	5	284	15	70	85	291	17	0	4	4	22	1965-66	1973-74
Ashby, Don	Tor., Col., Edm.	3	188	40	56	96	40	12	1	0	1	4	1975-76	1980-81
Ashworth, Frank	Chi.	1	18	5	4	9	2	....	....	....	....	....	1946-47	1946-47
Asmundson, Oscar	NYR, Det., St.L., NYA, Mtl.	5	112	11	23	34	30	9	0	2	2	4	1932-33	1937-38
Atanas, Walt	NYR	1	49	13	8	21	40	....	....	....	....	....	1944-45	1944-45
Atkinson, Steve	Bos., Buf., Wsh.	1	302	60	51	111	104	1	0	0	0	0	1968-69	1974-75
Attwell, Bob	Col.	2	22	1	5	6	0	....	....	....	....	....	1979-80	1980-81
Attwell, Ron	St.L., NYR	1	21	1	7	8	8	....	....	....	....	....	1967-68	1967-68
Aubin, Norm	Tor.	2	69	18	13	31	30	1	0	0	0	0	1981-82	1982-83
Aubry, Pierre	Que., Det.	5	202	24	26	50	133	20	1	1	2	32	1980-81	1984-85
Aubuchon, Ossie	Bos., NYR	2	50	19	12	31	4	6	1	0	1	0	1942-43	1943-44
Auge, Les	Col.	1	6	0	3	3	4	....	....	....	....	....	1980-81	1980-81
Aurie, Larry	Det.	16	979	31	158	189	1065	24	6	9	15	10	1927-28	1938-39
Awrey, Don	Bos., St.L., Mtl., Pit., NYR	15	923	30	154	184	1047	71	0	18	18	150	1963-64	1978-79
Ayres, Vern	NYA, Mtl.W., St.L., NYR	6	211	6	14	20	350	....	....	....	....	....	1930-31	1935-36
B														
Babando, Pete	Bos., Det., Chi., NYR	6	351	86	73	159	194	17	3	3	6	6	1947-48	1952-83
Babin, Mitch	St.L.	1	8	0	0	0	0	....	....	....	....	....	1975-76	1975-76
Baby, John	Cle., Min.	2	26	2	8	10	26	....	....	....	....	....	1977-78	1978-79
Babych, Wayne	St.L., Pit., Que., Hfd.	9	519	192	246	438	498	41	7	9	16	25	1978-79	1986-87
Backman, Mike	NYR	3	18	1	6	7	18	10	2	2	4	2	1981-82	1983-84
Backor, Peter	Tor.	1	36	4	5	9	6	....	....	....	....	....	1944-45	1944-45
Backstrom, Ralph	Mtl., L.A., Chi.	16	1032	278	361	639	386	116	27	32	59	68	1956-57	1972-73
Bailey, Ace (I.)	Tor.	8	314	111	82	193	472	20	3	4	7	12	1926-27	1933-34
Bailey, Ace (G.)	Bos., Det., St.L., Wsh.	10	568	107	171	278	633	15	2	4	6	28	1968-69	1977-78
Bailey, Bob	Tor., Det., Chi.	4	150	15	21	36	207	15	0	4	4	22	1953-54	1957-58
Bailey, Reid	Phi., Tor., Hfd.	4	40	1	3	4	105	16	0	2	2	25	1980-81	1983-84
Baird, Ken	Cal.	1	10	0	2	2	15	....	....	....	....	....	1971-72	1971-72
Baker, Bill	Mtl., Col., St.L., NYR	3	143	7	25	32	175	6	0	0	0	0	1980-81	1982-83
Baldwin, Doug	Tor., Det., Chi.	3	24	0	1	1	8	....	....	....	....	....	1945-46	1947-48
Balfour, Earl	Tor., Chi.,	5	288	30	22	52	78	26	0	3	3	4	1951-52	1960-61
Balfour, Murray	Mtl., Chi., Bos.	6	306	67	90	157	391	40	9	10	19	45	1956-57	1964-65
Ball, Terry	Phi., Buf.	3	74	7	19	26	26	....	....	....	....	....	1967-68	1971-72
Balon, Dave	NYR, Mtl., Min., Van.	14	775	192	222	414	607	78	14	21	35	109	1959-60	1972-73
Baluik, Stanley	Bos.	1	7	0	0	0	2	....	....	....	....	....	1959-60	1959-60

			Regular Schedule					Playoffs					First	Last
Name	NHL Teams	NHL Seasons	GP	G	A	TP	PIM	GP	G	A	TP	PIM	NHL Season	NHL Season
Bandura, Jeff	NYR	1	2	0	1	1	0	....	....	....	....	....	1980-81	1980-81
Barbe, Andy	Tor.	1	1	0	0	0	2	....	....	....	....	....	1950-51	1950-51
Barber, Bill	Phi.	13	903	420	463	883	623	129	53	55	108	109	1972-73	1984-85
Bergland, Bob	Phi.	3	130	28	39	67	40	....	....	....	....	....	1983-84	1985-86
Barilko, Bill	Tor.	5	252	26	36	62	456	47	5	7	12	104	1946-47	1950-51
Barkley, Doug	Chi., Det.	6	253	24	80	104	382	30	0	9	9	63	1957-58	1965-66
Barlow, Bob	Min.	1	77	16	17	33	10	6	2	2	4	6	1970-71	1970-71
Barnes, Blair	L.A.	1	1	0	0	0	0	....	....	....	....	....	1982-83	1982-83
Barnes, Norm	Phi., Hfd.	5	156	6	38	44	178	12	0	0	0	8	1976-77	1981-82
Brennan, Dan	L.A.	2	8	0	1	1	9	....	....	....	....	....	1983-84	1985-86
Baron, Normand	Mtl., St.L.	2	27	2	0	2	51	3	0	0	0	22	1983-84	1985-86
Barrett, Fred	Min., L.A.	13	745	25	123	148	67	44	0	2	2	60	1970-71	1983-84
Barrett, John	Det., Wsh., Min.	8	488	20	77	97	644	16	2	2	4	50	1980-81	1987-88
Barrie, Doug	Pit., Buf., L.A.	3	158	10	42	52	268	....	....	....	....	....	1968-69	1971-72
Baltimore, Byron	Edm.	1	2	0	0	0	4	....	....	....	....	....	1979-80	1979-80
Barry, Ed	Bos.	1	19	1	3	4	2	....	....	....	....	....	1946-47	1946-47
Barry, Marty	NYA, Bos., Det., Mtl.	12	509	195	192	387	205	43	15	18	33	34	1927-28	1939-40
Barry, Ray	Bos.	1	18	1	2	3	6	....	....	....	....	....	1951-52	1951-52
Bartel, Robin	Cgy., Van.	2	41	0	1	1	14	6	0	0	0	16	1985-86	1986-87
Bartlett, Jim	Mtl., NYR, Bos.	3	191	34	23	57	273	2	0	0	0	0	1954-55	1960-61
Barton, Cliff	Pit., Phi., NYR	3	85	10	9	19	22	....	....	....	....	....	1929-30	1939-40
Bathe, Frank	Det., Phi.,	9	224	3	28	31	542	27	1	3	4	42	1974-75	1983-84
Bathgate, Andy	NYR, Tor., Det., Pit.	16	1069	349	624	973	624	54	21	14	35	76	1952-53	1970-71
Bathgate, Frank	NYR	1	2	0	0	0	2	....	....	....	....	....	1952-53	1952-53
Baumgartner, Mike	K.C.	1	17	0	0	0	0	....	....	....	....	....	1974-75	1974-75
Baun, Bob	Tor., Oak., Det.	16	964	37	187	224	1493	96	3	12	15	171	1956-57	1972-73
Bauer, Bobby	Bos.	7	327	123	137	260	36	48	11	8	19	6	1935-36	1951-52
Baxter, Paul	Que., Pit., Cgy.	8	472	48	121	169	1564	40	0	5	5	162	1979-80	1986-87
Beadle, Sandy	Wpg.	1	6	1	0	1	2	....	....	....	....	....	1980-81	1980-81
Beaton, Frank	NYR	2	25	1	1	2	43	....	....	....	....	....	1978-79	1979-80
Beattle, Red	Bos., Det., NYA	9	335	62	85	147	137	22	4	2	6	6	1930-31	1938-39
Beaudin, Norm	St.L., Min.	2	25	1	2	3	4	....	....	....	....	....	1967-68	1970-71
Beaudoin, Serge	Atl.	1	3	0	0	0	0	....	....	....	....	....	1979-80	1979-80
Beaudoin, Yves	Wsh.	3	11	0	0	0	5	....	....	....	....	....	1985-86	1987-88
Beck, Barry	Col., NYR	9	563	103	244	347	963	51	10	23	33	77	1977-78	1985-86
Beckett, Bob	Bos.	2	68	7	6	13	18	....	....	....	....	....	1956-57	1963-64
Bedard, James	Chi.	2	22	1	1	2	8	....	....	....	....	....	1949-50	1950-51
Belnarski, John	NYR, Edm.	4	100	2	18	20	114	1	0	0	0	0	1974-75	1979-80
Beers, Eddy	Cgy., St.L.	5	250	94	116	210	256	41	7	10	17	47	1981-82	1985-86
Behling, Dick	Det.	2	5	1	0	1	2	....	....	....	....	....	1940-41	1942-43
Beisler, Frank	NYA	2	0	0	0	0	0	....	....	....	....	....	1936-37	1939-40
Belanger, Alain	Tor.	1	9	0	1	1	6	....	....	....	....	....	1977-78	1977-78
Belanger, Roger	Pit.	1	44	3	5	8	32	....	....	....	....	....	1984-85	1984-85
Belisle, Danny	NYR	1	4	2	0	2	0	....	....	....	....	....	1960-61	1960-61
Beliveau, Jean	Mtl.	20	1125	507	712	1219	1029	162	79	97	176	211	1950-51	1970-71
Bell, Billy	Mtl.W, Mtl., Ott.	6	61	3	1	4	4	9	0	0	0	0	1917-18	1923-24
Bell, Harry	NYR	1	1	0	1	1	0	....	....	....	....	....	1946-47	1946-47
Bell, Joe	NYR	2	62	8	9	17	18	....	....	....	....	....	1942-43	1946-47
Belland, Neil	Van., Pit.	6	109	13	32	45	54	21	2	9	11	23	1981-82	1986-87
Bellefeuille, Pete	Tor., Det.	4	92	26	4	30	58	....	....	....	....	....	1925-26	1929-30
Bellemer, Andy	Mtl.M	1	15	0	0	0	0	....	....	....	....	....	1932-33	1932-33
Bend, Lin	NYR	1	8	3	1	4	2	....	....	....	....	....	1942-43	1942-43
Bennett, Bill	Bos., Hfd.	2	31	4	7	11	65	....	....	....	....	....	1978-79	1979-80
Bennett, Curt	St.L., NYR, Atl.	10	580	152	182	334	347	21	1	1	2	57	1970-71	1979-80
Bennett, Frank	Det.	1	7	0	1	1	2	....	....	....	....	....	1943-44	1943-44
Bennett, Harvey	Pit., Wsh., Phi., Min., St.L.	5	268	44	46	90	340	4	0	0	0	2	1974-75	1978-79
Bennett, Max	Mtl.	1	1	0	0	0	0	....	....	....	....	....	1935-36	1935-36
Benoit, Joe	Mtl.	5	185	75	69	144	94	11	6	3	9	11	1940-41	1946-47
Benson, Bill	NYA	2	67	11	25	36	35	....	....	....	....	....	1940-41	1941-42
Benson, Bobby	Bos.	1	8	0	1	1	4	....	....	....	....	....	1924-25	1924-25
Bentley, Doug	Chi., NYR	13	566	219	324	543	217	23	9	8	17	8	1939-40	1953-54
Bentley, Max	Chi., Tor., NYR	12	646	245	299	544	179	52	18	27	45	14	1940-41	1953-54
Bentley, Reggie	Chi.	1	11	1	2	3	2	....	....	....	....	....	1942-43	1942-43
Berenson, Red	Mtl., St.L., Det., NYR	17	987	261	397	658	305	85	23	14	37	49	1961-62	1977-78
Bergdinon, Fred	Bos.	1	2	0	0	0	0	....	....	....	....	....	1925-26	1925-26
Bergen, Todd	Phi.	1	14	11	5	16	4	17	4	9	13	8	1984-85	1984-85
Bergeron, Michel	Det., NYI, Wsh.	5	229	80	58	138	165	....	....	....	....	....	1974-75	1978-79
Bergeron, Yves	Pit.	2	3	0	0	0	0	....	....	....	....	....	1974-75	1976-77
Bergloff, Bob	Min.	1	2	0	0	0	5	....	....	....	....	....	1982-83	1982-83
Bergman, Gary	Det., Min., K.C.	12	838	68	299	367	1249	21	0	5	5	20	1964-65	1975-76
Bergman, Thommie	Det.	6	246	21	44	65	243	7	0	2	2	2	1972-73	1979-80
Berlinquette, Louis	Mtl.	5	193	44	29	73	111	16	1	1	2	0	1917-18	1925-26
Bernier, Serge	Phi., L.A., Que.	5	302	78	119	197	234	5	1	1	2	0	1968-69	1980-81
Berry, Bob	Mtl., L.A.	8	541	159	191	350	344	26	2	6	8	6	1968-69	1976-77
Berry, Doug	Col.	2	121	10	33	43	25	....	....	....	....	....	1979-80	1980-81
Berglund, Bo	**Que., Min., Phi.**	**3**	**130**	**28**	**39**	**67**	**40**	9	2	0	2	6	1983-84	1985-86
Berry, Fred	Det.	1	3	0	0	0	0	....	....	....	....	....	1976-77	1976-77
Besler, Phil	Bos., Chi., Det.	2	30	1	4	5	18	....	....	....	....	....	1935-36	1938-39
Bessone, Pete	Det.	1	6	0	1	1	6	....	....	....	....	....	1937-38	1937-38
Bethel, John	Wpg.	1	17	0	2	2	4	....	....	....	....	....	1979-80	1979-80
Bettio, Sam	Bos.	1	44	9	12	21	32	....	....	....	....	....	1949-50	1949-50
Beverley, Nick	Bos., Pit., NYR, Min., L.A., Col.	11	502	18	94	112	156	7	0	1	1	0	1966-67	1979-80
Bialowas, Dwight	Atl., Min.	4	164	11	46	57	46	....	....	....	....	....	1973-74	1976-77
Bianchin, Wayne	Pit., Edm.	7	276	68	41	109	137	3	0	1	1	6	1973-74	1979-80
Bidner, Todd	Wsh.	1	12	2	1	3	7	....	....	....	....	....	1981-82	1981-82
Biggs, Don	Min.	1	1	0	0	0	0	....	....	....	....	....	1984-85	1984-85
Bignell, Larry	Pit.	2	20	0	3	3	2	3	0	0	0	2	1973-74	1974-75
Bilodeau, Gilles	Que.	1	9	0	1	1	25	....	....	....	....	....	1979-80	1979-80
Bionda, Jack	Tor., Bos.	4	93	3	9	12	113	11	0	1	1	14	1955-56	1958-59
Black, Stephen	Det., Chi.	2	113	11	20	31	77	13	0	0	0	13	1949-50	1950-51
Blackburn, Bob	Nyr., Pit.	3	135	8	12	20	105	6	0	0	0	4	1968-69	1970-71
Blackburn, Don	Bos., Phi., NYR, NYI, Min.	6	185	23	44	67	87	12	3	0	3	10	1962-63	1972-73
Blade, Hank	Chi.	2	24	2	3	5	2	....	....	....	....	....	1946-47	1947-48
Bladon, Tom	Phi., Pit., Edm., Wpg., Det.	9	610	73	197	270	392	86	8	29	37	70	1972-73	1980-81
Blaine, Gary	Mtl.	1	1	0	0	0	0	....	....	....	....	....	1954-55	1954-55
Blair, Andy	Tor., Chi.	9	402	74	86	160	323	38	6	6	12	32	1928-29	1936-37
Blair, Chuck	Tor.	2	3	0	0	0	0	....	....	....	....	....	1948-49	1950-51
Blair, George	Tor.	1	2	0	0	0	0	....	....	....	....	....	1950-51	1950-51
Blake, Mickey	St.L., Bos., Tor.	2	16	1	1	2	4	....	....	....	....	....	1934-35	1935-36
Blake, Toe	Mtl.M, Mtl.	15	578	235	292	527	272	57	25	37	62	23	1932-33	1947-48
Blight, Rick	Van., L.A.	7	326	96	125	221	170	5	0	5	5	2	1975-76	1982-83
Blinco, Russ	Mtl.M, Chi.	6	268	59	66	125	24	19	3	3	6	4	1933-34	1938-39
Block, Ken	Van.	1	1	0	0	0	0	....	....	....	....	....	1970-71	1970-71
Blomqvist, Timo	Wsh., N.J.	5	243	4	53	57	293	13	0	0	0	24	1981-82	1986-87
Bloom, Mike	Wsh., Det.	3	201	30	47	77	215	....	....	....	....	....	1974-75	1976-77
Boddy, Gregg	Van.	5	273	23	44	67	263	3	0	0	0	0	1971-72	1975-76
Bodnar, Gus	Tor., Chi., Bos.	12	667	142	254	396	207	32	4	3	7	10	1943-44	1954-55
Boehm, Ron	Oak.	1	16	2	1	3	10	....	....	....	....	....	1967-68	1967-68
Boesch, Garth	Tor.	4	197	9	28	37	205	34	2	5	7	18	1946-47	1949-50
Boh, Rick	Min.	1	8	2	1	3	4	....	....	....	....	....	1987-88	1987-88
Boileau, Marc	Det.	1	54	5	6	11	8	....	....	....	....	....	1961-62	1961-62
Boileau, Rene	NYA	1	7	0	0	0	0	....	....	....	....	....	1925-26	1925-26
Boimistruck, Fred	Tor.	2	83	4	14	18	45	....	....	....	....	....	1981-82	1982-83
Boisvert, Serge	Tor., Mtl.	5	46	5	7	12	8	23	3	7	10	4	1982-83	1987-88
Boivin, Leo	Tor., Bos., Det., Pit., Min.	19	1150	72	250	322	1192	54	3	10	13	59	1951-52	1969-70
Boland, Mike A.	Phi.	1	2	0	0	0	0	....	....	....	....	....	1974-75	1974-75
Boland, Mike J.	K.C., Buf.	2	23	1	2	3	29	3	1	0	1	2	1974-75	1978-79
Boldirev, Ivan	Bos., Cal., Chi., Atl., Van., Det.	15	1052	361	505	866	507	48	13	20	33	14	1970-71	1984-85
Bolduc, Danny	Det., Cgy.	3	102	22	19	41	33	1	0	0	0	0	1978-79	1983-84
Bolduc, Michel	Que.	2	10	0	0	0	6	....	....	....	....	....	1981-82	1982-83
Boll, Buzz	Tor., NYA, Bos.	11	436	133	130	263	148	29	7	3	10	13	1933-34	1943-44
Bolonchuk, Larry	Van., Wsh.	4	74	3	9	12	97	....	....	....	....	....	1972-73	1977-78
Bolton, Hughie	Tor.	8	235	10	51	61	221	17	0	5	5	14	1949-50	1956-57
Bonar, Dan	L.A.	3	170	25	39	64	208	14	3	4	7	22	1980-81	1982-83
Bonin, Marcel	Det., Bos., Mtl.	9	454	97	175	272	336	50	11	14	25	51	1952-53	1961-62
Boo, Jim	Min.	1	6	0	0	0	22	....	....	....	....	....	1977-78	1977-78
Boone, Buddy	Bos.	2	34	5	3	8	28	22	2	1	3	25	1956-57	1957-58
Boothman, George	Tor.	2	58	17	19	36	18	5	2	1	3	2	1942-43	1943-44

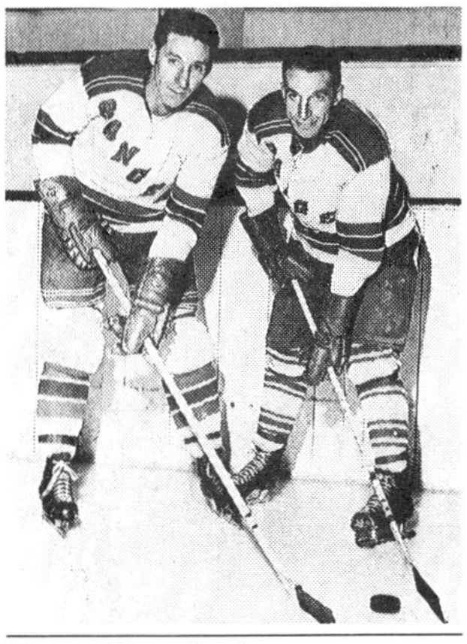

Max and Doug Bentley

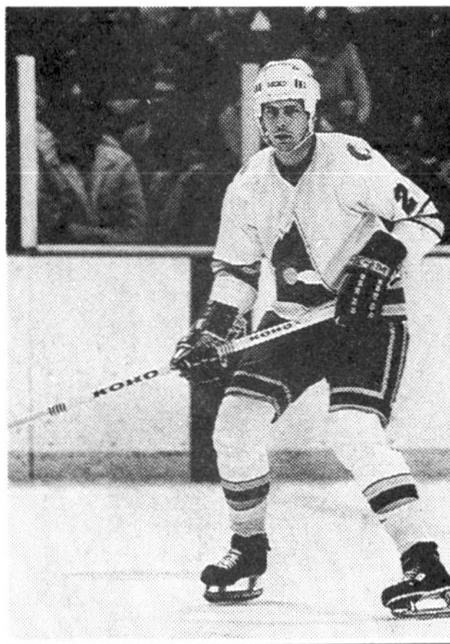

Nick Beverley

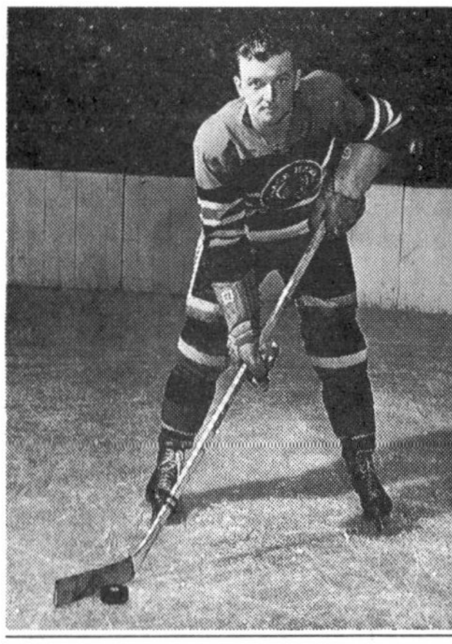

Gus Bodnar

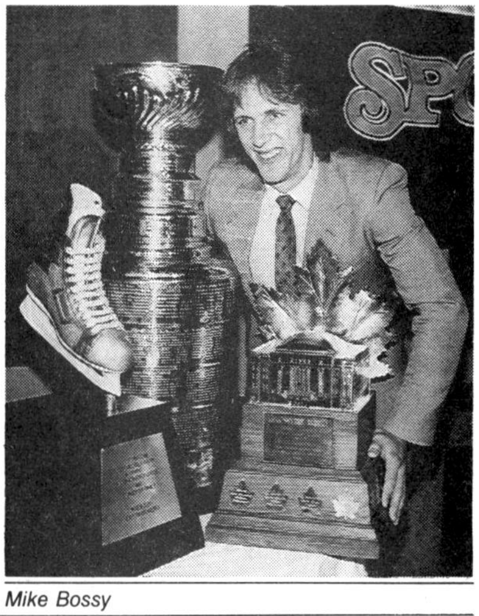

Mike Bossy

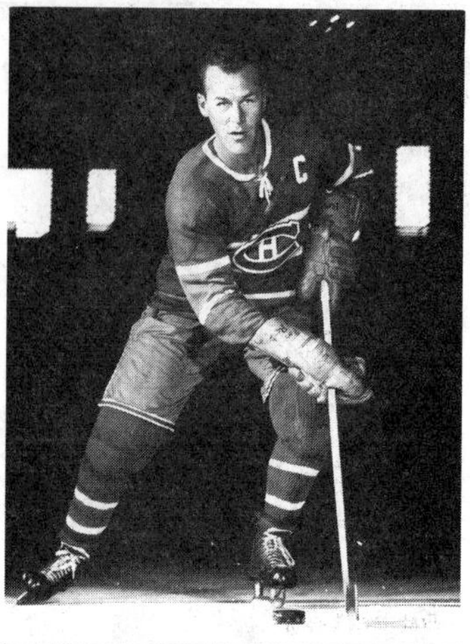

Emile Bouchard

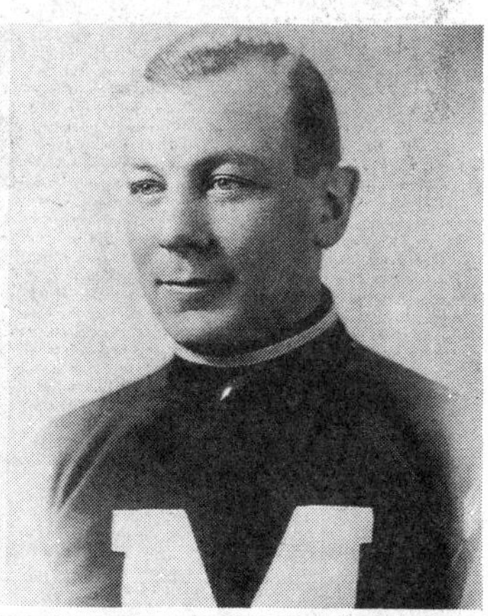

Harry Broadbent

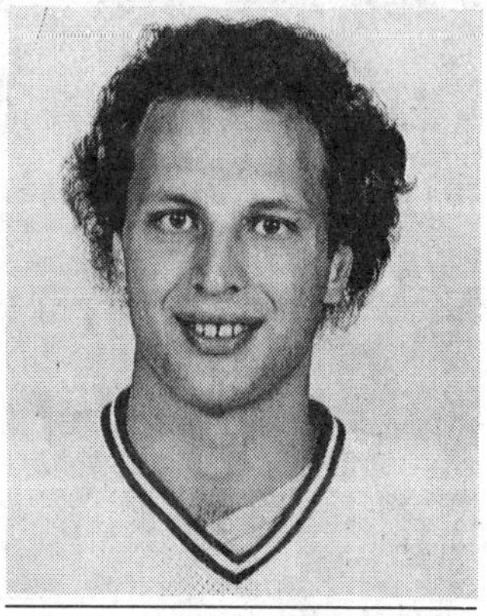

Jeff Brownschidle

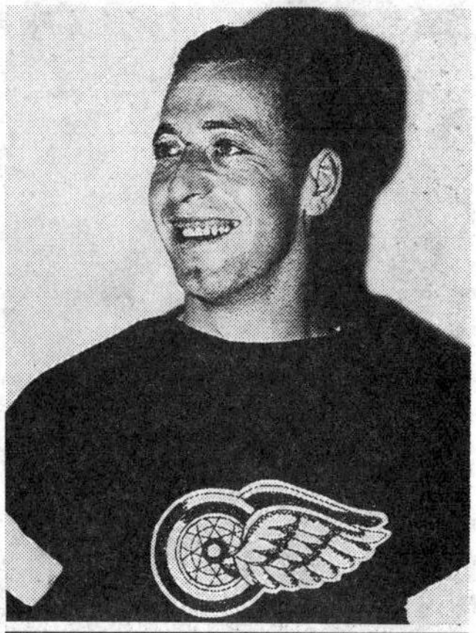

Mud Bruneteau

			Regular Schedule					Playoffs					First	Last
Name	NHL Teams	NHL Seasons	GP	G	A	TP	PIM	GP	G	A	TP	PIM	NHL Season	NHL Season
Bordeleau, Chris.	Mtl., St.L., Chi.,	4	205	38	65	103	82	19	4	7	11	17	1968-69	1971-72
Bordeleau, J. P.	Chi.	9	519	97	126	223	143	48	3	6	9	12	1971-72	1979-80
Bordeleau, Paulin	Van.	3	183	33	56	89	47	5	2	1	3	0	1973-74	1975-76
Borotsik, Jack	St.L.	1	1	0	0	0	0	....	....	....	....	....	1974-75	1974-75
Bossy, Mike	NYI	10	752	573	553	1126	210	129	85	75	160	38	1977-78	1986-87
Bostrom, Helge	Chi.	4	96	3	3	6	58	13	0	0	0	16	1929-30	1932-33
Botell, Mark	Phi.	1	32	4	10	14	31	....	....	....	....	....	1981-82	1981-82
Botting, Cam	Atl.	1	2	0	1	1	0	....	....	....	....	....	1975-76	1975-76
Boucha, Henry	Det., Min., K.C., Col.	6	247	53	49	102	157	....	....	....	....	....	1971-72	1976-77
Bouchard, Emile (Butch)	Mtl.	15	785	49	144	193	863	113	11	21	32	121	1941-42	1955-56
Bouchard, Dick	NYR	1	1	0	0	0	0	....	....	....	....	....	1954-55	1954-55
Bouchard, Edmond	Mtl., Ham., NYA, Pit.	8	223	19	20	39	105	....	....	....	....	....	1921-22	1928-29
Bouchard, Pierre	Mtl., Wsh.	12	595	24	82	106	233	76	3	10	13	56	1970-71	1981-82
Boucher, Billy	Mtl., Bos., NYA.	7	213	93	35	128	391	21	9	3	12	35	1921-22	1927-28
Boucher, Frank	Ott., NYR	14	557	161	262	423	118	56	16	18	34	12	1921-22	1943-44
Boucher, George	Ott., Mtl.M, Chi.	15	457	122	62	184	712	44	11	4	15	84	1917-18	1931-32
Boucher, Robert	Mtl.	1	12	0	0	0	0	....	....	....	....	....	1923-24	1923-24
Boudrias, Andre	Mtl., Min., St.L. Van.	12	662	151	340	491	218	34	6	10	16	12	1963-64	1975-76
Boughner, Barry	Oak., Cal.	2	20	0	0	0	11	....	....	....	....	....	1969-70	1970-71
Bourbonnais, Dan	Hfd.	2	59	3	25	28	11	....	....	....	....	....	1981-82	1983-84
Bourbonnais, Rick	St.L.	3	71	9	15	24	29	4	0	1	1	0	1975-76	1977-78
Bourcier, Conrad	Mtl.	1	9	0	1	1	0	....	....	....	....	....	1935-36	1935-36
Bourcier, Jean	Mtl.	1	6	0	0	0	0	....	....	....	....	....	1935-36	1935-36
Bourgeault, Leo	Tor. NYR, Ott., Mtl.	8	307	24	20	44	269	24	1	1	2	18	1926-27	1934-35
Bourne, Bob	NYI, L.A.	14	964	258	324	582	605	139	40	56	96	108	1974-75	1987-88
Boutette, Pat	Tor., Hfd., Pit.	10	756	171	282	453	1354	46	10	14	24	109	1975-76	1984-85
Bowcher, Clarence	NYA	2	47	2	2	4	110	....	....	....	....	....	1926-27	1927-28
Bowman, Kirk	Chi.	2	88	11	17	28	19	7	1	0	1	0	1976-77	1978-79
Bowman, Ralph	Ott., St.L., Det.	7	274	8	17	25	260	22	2	2	4	6	1933-34	1939-40
Bownass, Jack	Mtl., NYR	4	80	3	8	11	58	....	....	....	....	....	1957-58	1961-62
Bowness, Rick	Atl., Det., St. L, Wpg.	7	173	18	37	55	191	5	0	0	0	2	1975-76	1981-82
Boyd, Bill	NYR, NYA	4	138	15	7	22	72	9	0	0	0	2	1926-27	1929-30
Boyd, Irwin	Bos., Det.	4	97	18	19	37	51	15	0	1	1	4	1931-32	1943-44
Boyer, Wally	Tor., Chi., Oak. Pit.	7	365	54	105	159	163	15	1	3	4	0	1965-66	1971-72
Brackenborough, John	Bos.	1	7	0	0	0	0	....	....	....	....	....	1925-26	1925-26
Brackenbury, Curt	Que., Edm., St.L.	4	141	9	17	26	226	2	0	0	0	0	1979-80	1982-83
Bradley, Barton	Bos.	1	1	0	0	0	0	....	....	....	....	....	1949-50	1949-50
Bradley, Walter	Cal. Cle.	2	6	1	0	1	2	....	....	....	....	....	1973-74	1976-77
Bragnalo, Rick	Wsh.	4	145	15	35	50	46	....	....	....	....	....	1975-76	1978-79
Brannigan, Andy	NYA	2	26	1	2	3	31	....	....	....	....	....	1940-41	1941-42
Brasar, Per-Olov	Min., Van.	5	348	64	142	206	33	13	1	2	3	0	1977-78	1981-82
Brayshaw, Russ	Chi.	1	43	5	9	14	24	....	....	....	....	....	1944-45	1944-45
Breitenbach, Ken	Buf.	3	68	1	13	14	49	7	0	1	1	4	1975-76	1978-79
Brennan, Doug	NYR	3	123	9	7	16	152	16	1	0	1	21	1931-32	1933-34
Brennan, Tom	Bos.	2	22	2	2	4	2	....	....	....	....	....	1943-44	1944-45
Brenneman, John	Chi., NYR, Tor., Det., Oak.	5	152	21	19	40	46	....	....	....	....	....	1964-65	1968-69
Bretto, Joe	Chi.	1	3	0	0	0	4	....	....	....	....	....	1944-45	1944-45
Brewer, Carl	Tor., Det., St.L.	12	604	25	198	223	1037	72	3	17	20	146	1957-58	1979-80
Briden, Archie	Det., Pit.	2	72	9	5	14	56	....	....	....	....	....	1926-27	1929-30
Briere, Michel	Pit.	1	76	12	32	44	20	10	5	3	8	17	1969-70	1969-70
Brindley, Doug	Tor.	1	3	0	0	0	0	....	....	....	....	....	1970-71	1970-71
Brink, Milt	Chi.	1	5	0	0	0	0	....	....	....	....	....	1936-37	1936-37
Brisson, Gerry	Mtl.	1	4	0	2	2	4	....	....	....	....	....	1962-63	1962-63
Britz, Greg	Tor., Hfd.	3	8	0	0	0	4	....	....	....	....	....	1983-84	1986-87
Broadbent, Harry	Ott. Mt.M, NYA	11	302	122	45	167	553	41	13	3	16	69	1918-19	1928-29
Broden, Connie	Mtl.	2	6	2	1	3	2	7	0	1	1	0	1955-56	1957-58
Brooks, Gord	St.L., Wsh.	3	70	7	18	25	37	....	....	....	....	....	1971-72	1974-75
Brophy, Bernie	Mtl.M, Det.	3	62	4	4	8	25	2	0	0	0	2	1925-26	1929-30
Brossart, Willie	Phi., Tor., Wsh.	6	129	1	14	15	88	1	0	0	0	0	1970-71	1975-76
Brown, Adam	Det. Chi. Bos.	9	391	104	113	217	333	22	2	4	6	4	1941-42	1951-52
Brown, Arnie	Tor. NYR, Det., NYI, Atl.	12	681	44	141	185	738	22	0	6	6	23	1961-62	1974-75
Brown, Connie	Det.	5	91	15	24	39	12	14	2	3	5	0	1938-39	1942-43
Brown, Fred	Mtl.M	1	19	1	0	1	0	9	0	0	0	0	1927-28	1927-28
Brown, George	Mtl.	3	79	6	22	28	34	7	0	0	0	2	1936-37	1938-39
Brown, Gerry	Det.	2	23	4	5	9	2	12	2	1	3	4	1941-42	1945-46
Brown, Harold	NYR	1	13	2	1	3	2	....	....	....	....	....	1945-46	1945-46
Brown, Jim	L.A.	1	3	0	1	1	5	....	....	....	....	....	1982-83	1982-83
Brown, Larry	NYR, Det., Phi., L.A.	9	455	7	53	60	180	35	0	4	4	10	1969-70	1977-78
Brown, Stan	NYR, Det.	2	48	8	2	10	18	2	0	0	0	0	1926-27	1927-28
Brown, Wayne	Bos.	1	4	0	0	0	2	....	....	....	....	....	1953-54	1953-54
Browne, Cecil	Chi.	1	13	2	0	2	4	....	....	....	....	....	1927-28	1927-28
Brownschidle, Jack	St.L., Hfd.	9	494	39	162	201	151	26	0	5	5	18	1977-78	1985-86
Brownschidle, Jeff	Hfd.	2	7	0	1	1	2	....	....	....	....	....	1981-82	1982-83
Bruce, Gordie	Bos.	3	28	4	9	13	13	7	2	3	5	4	1940-41	1945-46
Bruce, Morley	Ott.	4	72	8	1	9	27	12	0	0	0	3	1917-18	1921-22
Bruneteau, Eddie	Det.	7	180	40	42	82	35	26	7	6	13	0	1940-41	1948-49
Bruneteau, Mud	Det.	11	411	139	138	277	80	77	23	14	37	22	1935-36	1945-46
Brydge, Bill	Tor., Det., NYA	9	368	26	52	78	506	2	0	0	0	4	1926-27	1935-36
Brydson, Glenn	Mtl.M, St.L., NYR, Chi.	8	299	56	79	135	203	11	0	0	0	8	1930-31	1937-38
Brydson, Gord	Tor.	1	8	2	0	2	8	....	....	....	....	....	1929-30	1929-30
Bubla, Jiri	Van.	5	256	17	101	118	202	6	0	0	0	7	1981-82	1985-86
Buchanan, Al	Tor.	2	4	0	1	1	2	....	....	....	....	....	1948-49	1949-50
Buchanan, Bucky	NYR	1	2	0	0	0	0	....	....	....	....	....	1948-49	1948-49
Buchanan, Mike	Chi.	1	1	0	0	0	0	....	....	....	....	....	1966-67	1969-70
Buchanan, Ron	Bos., St.L.	2	58	0	0	0	0	....	....	....	....	....	1966-67	1969-70
Bucyk, John	Det., Bos.,	23	1540	556	813	1369	497	124	41	64	103	42	1955-56	1977-78
Buhr, Doug	K.C.	1	6	0	2	2	4	....	....	....	....	....	1974-75	1974-75
Bukovich, Tony	Det.	2	44	7	3	10	6	6	0	1	1	0	1943-44	1944-45
Buller, Hy	Det., NYR	5	188	22	58	80	215	....	....	....	....	....	1943-44	1953-54
Bulley, Ted	Chi., Wsh., Pit.	8	414	101	113	214	704	29	5	5	10	24	1976-77	1983-84
Burch, Billy	Ham., NYA, Bos., Chi.	11	390	137	53	190	251	2	0	0	0	0	1922-23	1932-33
Burchell, Fred	Mtl.	2	4	0	0	0	2	....	....	....	....	....	1950-51	1953-54
Burdon, Glen	K.C.	1	11	0	2	2	0	....	....	....	....	....	1974-75	1974-75
Burega, Bill	Bos.	1	4	0	1	1	4	....	....	....	....	....	1955-56	1955-56
Burke, Eddie	Bos., NYA	4	106	29	20	49	55	....	....	....	....	....	1931-32	1934-35
Burke, Marty	Mtl., Pit., Ott., Chi.	11	494	19	47	66	560	31	2	4	6	44	1927-28	1937-38
Burmeister, Roy	NYA	3	67	4	3	7	2	....	....	....	....	....	1929-30	1931-32
Burnett, Kelly	NYR	1	3	1	0	1	0	....	....	....	....	....	1952-53	1952-53
Burns, Bobby	Chi.	3	20	1	0	1	8	....	....	....	....	....	1927-28	1929-30
Burns, Charlie	Det., Bos., Oak., Pit., Min.	11	749	106	198	304	252	31	5	4	9	4	1958-59	1972-73
Burns, Gary	NYR	2	11	2	2	4	18	5	0	0	0	6	1980-81	1981-82
Burns, Norm	NYR	1	11	0	4	4	2	....	....	....	....	....	1941-42	1941-42
Burns, Robin	Pit., K.C.	5	190	31	38	69	139	....	....	....	....	....	1970-71	1975-76
Burrows, Dave	Pit., Tor.	10	724	29	135	164	377	29	1	5	6	25	1971-72	1980-81
Burry, Bert	Ott.	1	4	0	0	0	0	....	....	....	....	....	1932-33	1932-33
Burton, Cummy	Det.	3	43	0	2	2	21	3	0	0	0	0	1955-56	1958-59
Burton, Nelson	Wsh.	2	8	1	0	1	21	....	....	....	....	....	1977-78	1978-79
Bush, Eddie	Det.	2	27	4	6	10	50	12	1	6	7	23	1938-39	1941-42
Busniuk, Mike	Phi.	2	143	3	23	26	297	25	2	5	7	34	1979-80	1980-81
Busniuk, Ron	Buf.	2	6	0	3	3	4	....	....	....	....	....	1972-73	1973-74
Buswell, Walt	Det., Mtl.	8	368	10	40	50	164	24	2	1	3	10	1932-33	1939-40
Butler, Dick	Chi.	1	7	2	0	2	0	....	....	....	....	....	1947-48	1947-48
Butler, Jerry	Tor., Van., Wpg., NYR, St.L.	11	641	99	120	219	515	48	3	3	6	79	1972-73	1982-83
Butters, Bill	Min.	2	72	1	4	5	77	....	....	....	....	....	1977-78	1978-79
Buttrey, Gord	Chi.	1	10	0	0	0	0	10	0	0	0	0	1943-44	1943-44
Buynak, Gordon	St. L	1	4	0	0	0	2	....	....	....	....	....	1974-75	1974-75
Byers, Gord	Bos.	1	1	0	1	1	0	....	....	....	....	....	1949-50	1949-50
Byers, Jerry	Min., Atl, NYR	4	43	3	4	7	10	....	....	....	....	....	1972-73	1977-78
Byers, Mike	Tor., Phi., Buf., L.A.	4	166	42	34	76	39	4	0	1	1	0	1967-68	1971-72

C

Caffery, Jack	Tor., Bos.	3	57	3	2	5	22	10	1	0	1	4	1954-55	1957-58
Caffery, Terry	Chi., Min.	2	14	0	0	0	0	1	0	0	0	0	1969-70	1970-71
Cahan, Larry	Tor., NYR, Oak., L.A.	13	665	38	92	130	700	29	1	1	2	38	1954=55	1970-71
Cahill, Chuck	Bos.	1	31	0	1	1	4	....	....	....	....	....	1925-26	1925-26
Cain, Herbert	Mtl.M, Mtl., Bos.	13	571	206	194	400	178	64	16	13	29	13	1933-34	1945-46

Name	NHL Teams	NHL Seasons	Regular Schedule GP	G	A	TP	PIM	Playoffs GP	G	A	TP	PIM	First NHL Season	Last NHL Season
Cain, Jim	Mtl.M, Tor.	2	61	4	0	4	35	....	....	....	....	....	1924-25	1925-26
Cairns, Don	K.C., Col.	2	9	0	1	1	2	....	....	....	....	....	1975-76	1976-77
Calder, Eric	Wsh.	2	2	0	0	0	0	....	....	....	....	....	1981-82	1982-83
Calladine, Norm	Bos.	3	63	19	29	48	8	....	....	....	....	....	1942-43	1944-45
Callander, Drew	Phi., Van.	4	39	6	2	8	7	....	....	....	....	....	1976-77	1979-80
Callighen, Brett	Edm.	3	160	56	89	145	132	14	4	6	10	8	1979-80	1981-82
Callighen, Patsy	NYR	1	36	0	0	0	32	9	0	0	0	0	1927-28	1927-28
Camazzola, James	Chi.	2	3	0	0	0	0	....	....	....	....	....	1983-84	1986-87
Camazzola, Tony	Wsh.	1	3	0	0	0	4	....	....	....	....	....	1981-82	1981-82
Cameron, Al	Det., Wpg.	6	282	11	44	55	356	7	0	1	1	2	1975-76	1980-81
Cameron, Scotty	NYR	1	35	8	11	19	0	....	....	....	....	....	1942-43	1942-43
Cameron, Billy	Mtl., NYA	2	39	0	0	0	2	6	0	0	0	0	1923-24	1925-26
Cameron, Craig	Det., St.L., Min., NYI	9	552	87	65	152	202	27	3	1	4	17	1966-67	1975-76
Cameron, Dave	Col., N.J.	3	168	25	28	53	238	....	....	....	....	....	1981-82	1983-84
Cameron, Harry	Tor., Ott., Mtl.	6	127	85	32	117	120	20	7	3	10	29	1917-18	1922-23
Campbell, Bryan	L.A., Chi.	5	260	35	71	106	74	22	3	4	7	2	1967-68	1971-72
Campbell, Colin	Pit., Col., Edm., Van., Det.	11	636	25	103	128	1292	45	4	10	14	181	1974-75	1984-85
Campbell, Dave	Mtl.	1	3	0	0	0	0	....	....	....	....	....	1920-21	1920-21
Campbell, Don	Chi.	1	17	1	3	4	8	....	....	....	....	....	1943-44	1943-44
Campbell, Scott	Wpg., St.L.	3	80	4	21	25	243	....	....	....	....	....	1979-80	1981-82
Campbell, Spiff	Ott., NYA	3	77	5	1	6	12	6	0	0	0	0	1923-24	1925-26
Campbell, Wade	Wpg., Bos.	6	213	9	27	36	305	10	0	0	0	20	1982-83	1987-88
Campeau, Tod	Mtl.	3	42	5	9	14	16	1	0	0	0	0	1943-44	1948-49
Campedelli, Dom	Mtl.	1	2	0	0	0	0	....	....	....	....	....	1985-86	1985-86
Carbol, Leo	Chi.	1	6	0	1	1	4	....	....	....	....	....	1942-43	1942-43
Cardin, Claude	St.L.	1	1	0	0	0	0	....	....	....	....	....	1967-68	1967-68
Cardwell, Steve	Pit.	3	53	9	11	20	35	4	0	0	0	2	1970-71	1972-73
Carey, George	Que, Ham., Tor.	5	72	22	8	30	14	....	....	....	....	....	1919-20	1923-24
Carleton, Wayne	Tor., Bos., Cal.	7	278	55	73	128	172	18	2	4	6	14	1965-66	1971-72
Carlin, Brian	L.A.	1	5	1	0	1	0	....	....	....	....	....	1971-72	1971-72
Carlson, Jack	Min., St.L.	5	236	30	15	45	404	25	1	2	3	72	1978-79	1983-84
Carlson, Steve	L.A.	1	52	9	12	21	23	4	1	1	2	7	1979-80	1979-80
Caron, Alain	Oak., Mtl.	2	60	9	13	22	18	....	....	....	....	....	1967-68	1968-69
Carpenter, Eddie	Que, Ham.	2	44	10	4	14	23	....	....	....	....	....	1919-20	1920-21
Carr, Al	Tor.	1	5	0	1	1	4	....	....	....	....	....	1943-44	1943-44
Carr, Gene	St.L., NYR, Atl., Pit., L.A.	8	465	79	136	215	365	35	5	8	13	66	1971-72	1978-79
Carr, Lorne	NYR, NYA, Tor.	13	580	194	222	416	132	53	10	9	19	13	1933-34	1945-46
Carriere, Larry	Buf. Atl, Van., L.A., Tor.	7	416	17	83	100	517	27	0	3	3	42	1972-73	1979-80
Carrigan, Gene	NYR, StL, Det.	3	37	2	1	3	13	4	0	0	0	0	1930-31	1934-35
Carroll, Billy	NYI, Edm., Det.	7	322	30	54	84	113	71	6	12	18	18	1980-81	1986-87
Carroll, George	Mtl.M, Bos.	1	15	0	0	0	9	....	....	....	....	....	1924-25	1924-25
Carroll, Greg	Wsh., Det., Hfd.	2	131	20	34	54	44	....	....	....	....	....	1978-79	1979-80
Carruthers, Dwight	Det. Phi.	2	2	0	0	0	0	....	....	....	....	....	1965-66	1967-68
Carse, Bill	NYR, Chi.	4	124	28	43	71	38	16	3	2	5	0	1938-39	1941-42
Carse, Bob	Chi., Mtl.	5	167	32	55	87	52	10	0	2	2	2	1939-40	1947-48
Carson, Bill	Tor., Bos.	4	159	54	24	78	156	11	3	0	3	14	1926-27	1929-30
Carson, Frank	Mtl.M., NYA, Det.	7	248	42	48	90	166	22	0	2	2	9	1925-26	1933-34
Carson, Gerry	Mtl., NYR, Mtl.M.	6	261	12	11	23	205	22	0	0	0	12	1928-29	1936-37
Carter, Billy	Mtl., Bos.	3	16	0	0	0	6	....	....	....	....	....	1957-58	1961-62
Carter, Ron	Edm.	1	2	0	0	0	0	....	....	....	....	....	1979-80	1981-82
Carveth, Joe	Det., Bos., Mtl.	11	504	150	189	339	81	69	21	16	37	28	1940-41	1950-51
Cashman, Wayne	Bos.	17	1027	277	516	893	1041	145	31	57	88	250	1964-65	1982-83
Cassidy, Tom	Pit.	1	26	3	4	7	15	....	....	....	....	....	1977-78	1977-78
Cassolato, Tony	Wsh.	3	23	1	6	7	4	....	....	....	....	....	1979-80	1981-82
Ceresino, Ray	Tor.	1	12	1	1	2	2	....	....	....	....	....	1948-49	1948-49
Cernik, Frantisek	Det.	1	49	5	4	9	13	....	....	....	....	....	1984-85	1984-85
Chad John	Chi.	3	80	15	22	37	29	10	0	1	1	2	1939-40	1945-46
Chalmers, Bill	NYR	1	1	0	0	0	0	....	....	....	....	....	1953-54	1953-54
Chalupa, Milan	Det.	1	14	0	5	5	6	....	....	....	....	....	1984-85	1984-85
Chamberlain, Murph	Tor., Mtl., NYA, Bos.	12	510	100	175	275	769	66	14	17	31	96	1937-38	1948-49
Champagne, Andre	Tor.	1	2	0	0	0	0	....	....	....	....	....	1962-63	1962-63
Chapman, Art	Bos., NYA	10	438	62	174	236	140	25	1	5	6	9	1930-31	1939-40
Chapman, Blair	Pit., St.L.	7	402	106	125	231	158	25	4	6	10	15	1976-77	1982-83
Charlebois, Bob	Min.	1	7	1	0	1	0	....	....	....	....	....	1967-68	1967-68
Charron, Guy	Mtl., Det., K.C., Wsh.	12	734	221	309	530	218	....	....	....	....	....	1969-70	1980-81
Chartier, Dave	Wpg.	1	1	0	0	0	0	....	....	....	....	....	1980-81	1980-81
Chartraw, Rick	Mtl., L.A., NYR, Edm.	10	420	28	64	92	399	75	7	9	16	80	1974-75	1983-84
Check, Lude	Det., Chi.	2	27	6	2	8	4	....	....	....	....	....	1943-44	1944-45
Chernoff, Mike	Min.	1	1	0	0	0	0	....	....	....	....	....	1968-69	1968-69
Cherry, Dick	Bos., Phi.	3	145	12	10	22	45	4	1	0	1	4	1956-57	1969-70
Cherry, Don	Bos.	1	1	0	0	0	0	....	....	....	....	....	1954-55	1954-55
Chevrefils, Real	Bos., Det.	8	387	104	97	201	185	30	5	4	9	20	1951-52	1958-59
Chicoine, Dan	Cle. Min.	3	31	1	2	3	12	1	0	0	0	0	1977-78	1979-80
Chinnick, Rick	Edm., Que.	2	4	0	2	2	0	....	....	....	....	....	1973-74	1974-75
Chipperfield, Ron	Edm., Que.,	3	83	22	24	46	34	....	....	....	....	....	1979-80	1980-81
Chisholm, Art	Bos.	1	3	0	0	0	0	....	....	....	....	....	1960-61	1960-61
Chisholm, Colin	Min.	1	1	0	0	0	0	....	....	....	....	....	1986-87	1986-87
Chisholm, Lex	Tor.	2	54	10	8	18	19	3	1	0	1	0	1939-40	1940-41
Chorney, Marc	Pit. L.A.	4	210	8	27	35	209	7	0	1	1	2	1980-81	1983-84
Chouinard, Gene	Ott.	1	8	0	0	0	0	....	....	....	....	....	1927-28	1927-28
Chouinard, Guy	Atl, Cgy., St.L.	10	578	205	370	575	120	46	9	28	37	12	1974-75	1983-84
Christie, Mike	Cal. Cle., Col., Van.	7	412	15	101	116	550	2	0	0	0	0	1974-75	1980-81
Christoff, Steve	Min. Cgy., L.A.	5	248	77	64	141	108	35	16	12	28	25	1979-80	1983-84
Chrystal, Bob	NYR	2	132	11	14	25	112	....	....	....	....	....	1953-54	1954-55
Church, Jack	Tor., NYA., Bos.	6	145	5	22	27	164	25	1	1	2	18	1938-39	1945-46
Ciesla, Hank	Chi., NYR	4	269	26	51	77	87	6	0	2	2	0	1955-56	1958-59
Clackson, Kim	Pit., Que.	2	106	0	8	8	37	8	0	0	0	70	1979-80	1980-81
Clancy, Francis (King)	Ott., Tor.	16	592	137	143	280	904	61	9	8	17	92	1921-22	1936-37
Clancy, Terry	Oak., Tor.	4	93	6	6	12	39	....	....	....	....	....	1967-68	1972-73
Clapper, Dit	Bos.	20	833	228	246	474	462	86	13	17	30	50	1927-28	1946-47
Clark, Andy	Bos.	1	5	0	0	0	0	....	....	....	....	....	1927-28	1927-28
Clark, Dan	NYR	1	4	0	1	1	6	....	....	....	....	....	1978-79	1978-79
Clark, Dean	Edm.	1	1	0	0	0	0	....	....	....	....	....	1983-84	1983-84
Clark, Gordie	Bos.	2	8	0	1	1	0	1	0	0	0	0	1974-75	1975-76
Clarke, Bobby	Phi.	15	1144	358	852	1210	1453	136	42	77	119	152	1969-70	1983-84
Cleghorn, Odie	Mtl., Pit.	10	180	95	29	124	147	23	9	2	11	2	1918-19	1927-28
Cleghorn, Sprague	Ott. Tor. Mtl., Bos.	10	256	84	39	123	489	37	7	8	15	48	1918-19	1927-28
Clement, Bill	Phi., Wsh., Atl., Cgy.	11	719	148	208	356	383	50	5	3	8	26	1971-72	1981-82
Cline, Bruce	NYR	1	30	2	3	5	10	....	....	....	....	....	1956-57	1956-57
Clippingdale, Steve	L.A., Wsh.	2	19	1	2	3	9	1	0	0	0	0	1976-77	1979-80
Cloutier, Real	Que. Buf.	6	317	146	198	344	119	25	7	5	12	20	1979-80	1984-85
Cloutier, Rejean	Det.	1	3	0	1	1	0	....	....	....	....	....	1979-80	1979-80
Cloutier, Roland	Det., Que.	3	34	8	9	17	2	....	....	....	....	....	1977-78	1979-80
Clune, Wally	Mtl.	1	5	0	0	0	6	....	....	....	....	....	1955-56	1955-56
Coalter, Gary	Cal., K.C.	2	34	2	4	6	2	....	....	....	....	....	1973-74	1974-75
Coates, Steve	Det.	1	5	1	0	1	24	....	....	....	....	....	1976-77	1976-77
Coflin, Hughie	Chi.	1	31	0	3	3	33	....	....	....	....	....	1950-51	1950-51
Colley, Tom	Min.	1	1	0	0	0	2	....	....	....	....	....	1974-75	1974-75
Collings, Norm	Mtl.	1	1	0	1	1	0	....	....	....	....	....	1934-35	1934-35
Collins, Bill	Min., Mtl., Det., St. L, NYR, Phi., Wsh.	11	768	157	154	311	415	18	3	5	8	12	1967-68	1977-78
Collins, Gary	Tor.	1	2	0	0	0	0	....	....	....	....	....	1958-59	1958-59
Collyard, Bob	St.L.	1	10	1	3	4	4	....	....	....	....	....	1973-74	1973-74
Colville, Mac	NYR	9	353	71	104	175	132	40	9	10	19	14	1935-36	1946-47
Colville, Neil	NYR	12	464	99	166	265	213	46	7	19	26	33	1935-36	1948-49
Colwill, Les	NYR	1	69	7	6	13	16	....	....	....	....	....	1958-59	1958-59
Comeau, Rey	Mtl., Atl, Col.	9	564	98	141	239	175	9	2	1	3	8	1971-72	1979-80
Conacher, Brian	Tor., Det.	5	154	28	28	56	84	12	3	2	5	21	1961-62	1971-72
Conacher, Charlie	Tor., Det., NYA	12	460	225	173	398	516	49	17	18	35	53	1929-30	1940-41
Conacher, Jim	Det., Chi., NYR	8	328	85	117	202	91	19	5	2	7	4	1945-46	1952-53
Conacher, Lionel	Pit., NYA, Mtl.M., Chi.	12	500	80	105	185	882	35	2	2	4	34	1925-26	1936-37
Conacher, Pete	Chi., NYR, Tor.	6	229	47	39	86	57	7	0	0	0	0	1951-52	1957-58
Conacher, Roy	Bos., Det., Chi.	11	490	226	200	426	90	42	15	15	30	14	1938-39	1951-52
Conn, Hugh	NYA	2	96	9	28	37	22	....	....	....	....	....	1933-34	1934-35
Connelly, Wayne	Mtl., Bos., Min., Det., St. L, Van.	10	543	133	174	307	156	24	11	7	18	4	1960-61	1971-72
Connolly, Bert	NYR, Chi.	3	87	13	15	28	37	14	1	0	1	0	1934-35	1937-38
Connor, Cam	Mtl., Edm., NYR	5	89	9	22	31	256	20	5	0	5	6	1978-79	1982-83
Connor, Harry	Bos., NYA, Ott.	4	134	16	5	21	139	10	0	0	0	2	1927-28	1930-31

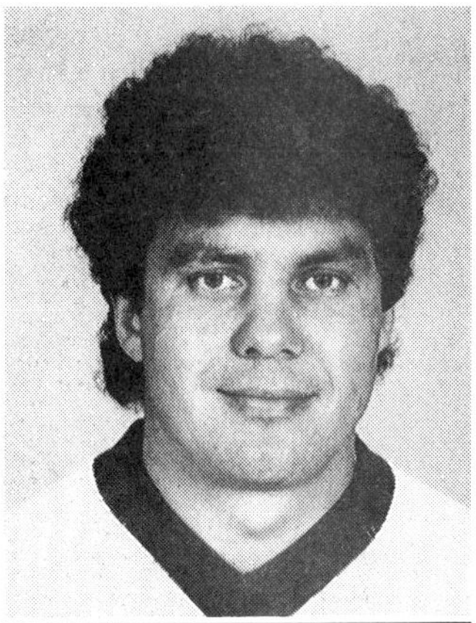

Frantisek Cernik

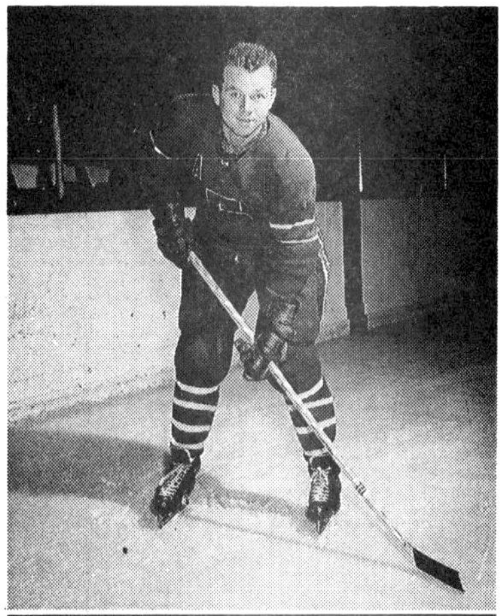

Don Cherry

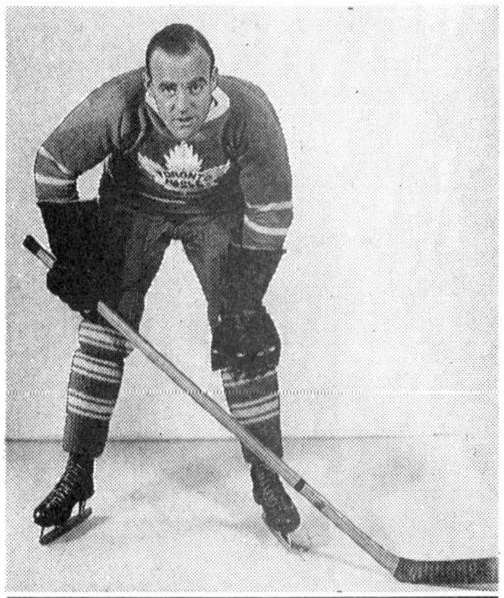

King Clancy

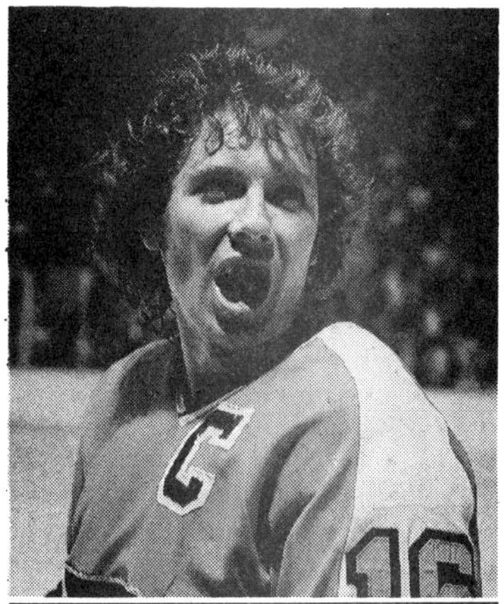

Bobby Clarke

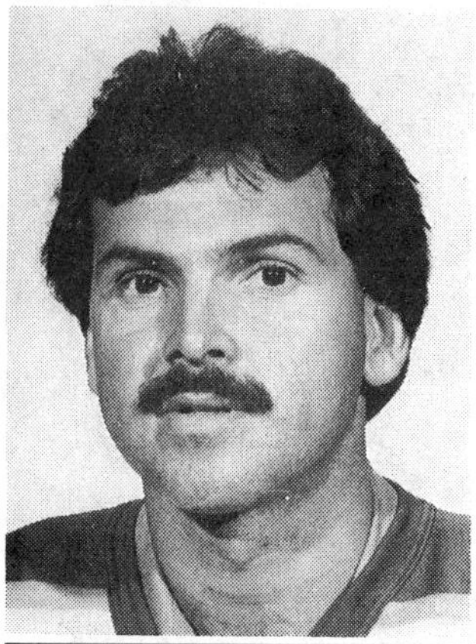

Real Cloutier

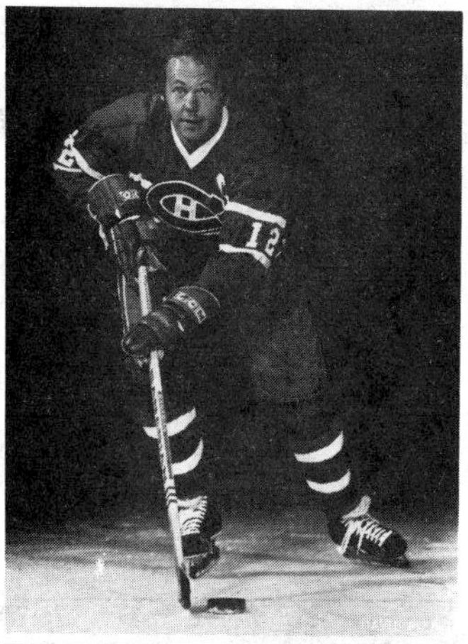

Yvan Cournoyer

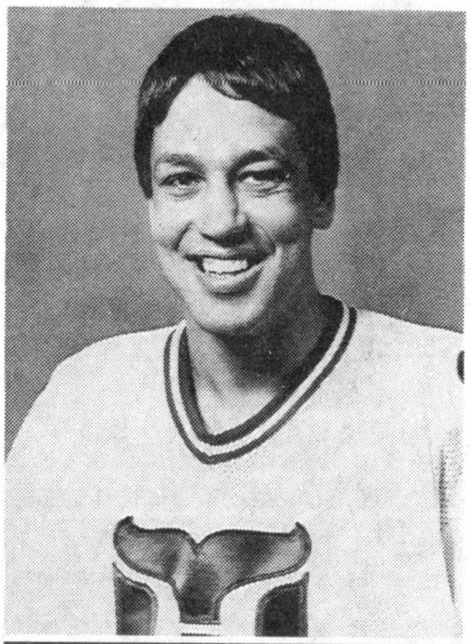

Mike Crombeen

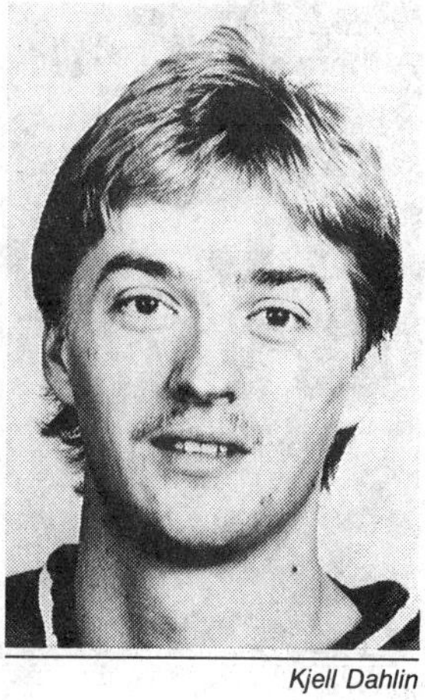

Kjell Dahlin

Name	NHL Teams	NHL Seasons	Regular Schedule					Playoffs					First NHL Season	Last NHL Season
			GP	G	A	TP	PIM	GP	G	A	TP	PIM		
Connors, Bobby	NYA, Det.	3	78	17	10	27	110	2	0	0	0	10	1926-27	1929-30
Contini, Joe	Col., Min.	3	68	17	21	38	34	2	0	0	0	0	1977-78	1980-81
Convey, Eddie	NYR	3	36	1	1	2	33	....	....	....	....	....	1930-31	1932-33
Cook, Bill	NYR	11	452	223	132	355	386	46	13	12	25	66	1926-27	1936-37
Cook, Bob	Van., Det., NYI, Min.	4	72	13	9	22	22	....	....	....	....	....	1970-71	1974-75
Cook, Bud	Bos., Ott., St.L.	3	51	5	4	9	22	....	....	....	....	....	1931-32	1934-35
Cook, Bun	NYR, Bos.	11	473	158	144	302	427	46	15	3	18	57	1926-27	1936-37
Cook, Lloyd	Bos.	1	4	1	0	1	0	....	....	....	....	....	1924-25	1924-25
Cook, Tom	Chi., Mtl.M.	8	311	72	89	161	169	24	2	4	6	17	1929-30	1937-38
Cooper, Carson	Bos., Mtl., Det.	8	278	110	57	167	111	4	0	0	0	2	1924-25	1931-32
Cooper, Ed	Col.	2	49	8	7	15	46	....	....	....	....	....	1980-81	1981-82
Cooper, Hal	NYR	1	8	0	0	0	2	....	....	....	....	....	1944-45	1944-45
Cooper, Joe	NYR, CHI	11	420	30	66	96	442	32	3	5	8	6	1935-36	1946-47
Copp, Bob	Tor.	2	40	3	9	12	26	....	....	....	....	....	1942-43	1950-51
Corbeau, Bert	Mtl.. Ham., Tor.,	10	257	65	33	98	589	14	2	0	2	10	1917-18	1926-27
Corbett, Michael	L.A.	1	2	0	1	1	2	....	....	....	....	....	1967-68	1967-68
Corcoran, Norm	Bos., Det., Chi.	4	29	1	3	4	21	4	0	0	0	6	1949-50	1955-56
Cormier, Roger	Mtl.	1	0	0	0	0	0	....	....	....	....	....	1925-26	1925-26
Corrigan, Charlie	Tor., NYA	2	19	2	2	4	2	....	....	....	....	....	1937-38	1940-41
Corrigan, Mike	L.A., Van., Pit.	10	594	152	195	347	698	17	2	3	5	20	1967-68	1977-78
Corriveau, Fred	Mtl.	1	3	0	1	1	0	....	....	....	....	....	1953-54	1953-54
Cory, Ross	Wpg.	2	51	2	10	12	41	....	....	....	....	....	1979-80	1980-81
Cossete, Jacques	Pit.	3	64	8	6	14	29	3	0	1	1	4	1975-76	1978-79
Costello, Les	Tor.	3	15	2	3	5	11	6	2	2	4	2	1947-48	1949-50
Costello, Murray	Chi., Bos., Det.	4	162	13	19	32	54	5	0	0	0	2	1953-54	1956-57
Costello, Rich	Tor.	2	12	2	2	4	2	....	....	....	....	....	1983-84	1985-86
Cotch, Charlie	Ham.	1	11	1	0	1	0	....	....	....	....	....	1924-25	1924-25
Cote, Ray	Edm.	3	15	0	0	0	4	14	3	2	5	0	1982-83	1984-85
Cotton, Baldy	Pit., Tor., NYA	12	500	101	103	204	419	43	4	9	13	46	1925-26	1936-37
Coughlin, Jack	Tor., Que, Mtl., Ham.	3	19	2	0	2	0	....	....	....	....	....	1917-18	1920-21
Coulis, Tim	Wsh., Min.	4	47	4	5	9	138	3	1	0	1	2	1979-80	1985-86
Coulson, D'arcy	Phi.	1	28	0	0	0	103	....	....	....	....	....	1930-31	1930-31
Coulter, Art	Chi., NYR	11	465	30	82	112	563	49	4	5	9	61	1931-32	1941-42
Coulter, Neal	NYI	3	26	5	5	10	11	1	0	0	0	0	1985-86	1987-88
Coulter, Tommy	Chi.	1	2	0	0	0	0	....	....	....	....	....	1933-34	1933-34
Cournoyer, Yvan	Mtl.	16	968	428	435	863	255	147	64	63	127	47	1963-64	1978-79
Courteau, Yves	Cgy., Hfd.	3	22	2	5	7	4	1	0	0	0	0	1984-85	1986-87
Couture, Billy	Mtl., Ham., Bos.	10	239	33	18	51	350	32	2	0	2	42	1917-18	1926-27
Couture, Gerry	Det., Mtl., Chi.,	10	385	86	70	156	89	45	9	7	16	4	1944-45	1953-54
Couture, Rosie	Chi., Mtl.	8	304	48	56	104	184	23	1	5	6	15	1928-29	1935-36
Cowan, Tommy	Phi.	1	1	0	0	0	0	....	....	....	....	....	1930-31	1930-31
Cowick, Bruce	Phi., Wsh., St.L.	3	70	5	6	11	43	8	0	0	0	9	1973-74	1975-76
Cowley, Bill	St.L., Bos.	13	549	195	353	548	174	64	13	33	46	22	1934-35	1946-47
Cox, Danny	Tor., Ott., Det., NYR, St.L.	9	329	47	49	96	110	10	0	1	1	6	1926-27	1934-35
Crashley, Bart	Det., K.C., L.A.	6	140	7	36	43	50	....	....	....	....	....	1965-66	1975-76
Crawford, Bob	St.L., Hfd., NYR, Wsh.	7	246	71	71	142	72	11	0	1	1	8	1986-87	1986-87
Crawford, Bobby	Col., Det.	2	16	1	3	4	6	....	....	....	....	....	1980-81	1982-83
Crawford, John	Bos.	13	547	38	140	178	202	66	4	13	17	36	1937-38	1949-50
Crawford, Marc	Van.	6	176	19	31	50	229	20	1	2	3	44	1981-82	1986-87
Crawford, Rusty	Ott., Tor.,	2	38	10	3	13	51	2	2	1	3	0	1917-18	1918-19
Creighton, Dave	Bos., Chi., Tor., NYR	12	615	140	174	314	223	51	11	13	24	20	1948-49	1959-60
Creighton, Jimmy	Det.,	1	11	1	0	1	2	....	....	....	....	....	1930-31	1930-31
Cressman, Dave	Min.	2	85	6	8	14	37	....	....	....	....	....	1974-75	1975-76
Cressman, Glen	Mtl.	1	4	0	0	0	2	....	....	....	....	....	1956-57	1956-57
Crisp, Terry	Bos., St.L., Phi., NYI	11	536	67	134	201	135	110	15	28	43	40	1965-66	1976-77
Croghen, Maurice	Mtl.M.	1	16	0	0	0	4	....	....	....	....	....	1937-38	1937-38
Crombeen, Mike	Cle., St.L., Hfd.	8	475	55	68	123	218	27	6	2	8	32	1977-78	1984-85
Crossett, Stan	Phi.,	1	21	0	0	0	10	....	....	....	....	....	1930-31	1930-31
Croteau, Gary	L.A., Det., Cal., K.C., Col.	12	684	144	175	319	143	11	3	2	5	8	1968-69	1979-80
Crowder, Bruce	Bos., Pit.	4	243	47	51	98	156	31	8	4	12	41	1981-82	1984-85
Crozier, Joe	Tor.,	1	5	0	3	3	2	....	....	....	....	....	1959-60	1959-60
Crutchfield, Wels	Mtl.	1	41	5	5	10	20	2	0	1	1	22	1934-35	1954-55
Cullen, Barry	Tor., Det.	5	219	32	52	84	111	6	0	0	0	2	1955-56	1959-60
Cullen, Brian	Tor., NYR	7	326	56	100	156	92	19	3	0	3	2	1954-55	1960-61
Cullen, Ray	NYR, Det., Min., Van.	6	313	92	123	215	120	20	3	10	13	2	1965-66	1970-71
Cummins, Barry	Cal.	1	36	1	2	3	39	....	....	....	....	....	1973-74	1973-74
Cunningham, Bob	NYR	2	4	0	1	1	0	....	....	....	....	....	1960-61	1961-62
Cunningham, Jim	Phi.	1	1	0	0	0	4	....	....	....	....	....	1977-78	1977-78
Cunningham, Les	NYA, Chi.	2	60	7	19	26	21	1	0	0	0	2	1936-37	1939-40
Cupolo, Bill	Bos.	1	47	11	13	24	10	7	1	2	3	0	1944-45	1944-45
Currie, Glen	L.A.	8	326	39	79	118	100	12	1	3	4	4	1979-80	1987-88
Currie, Hugh	Mtl.	1	1	0	0	0	0	....	....	....	....	....	1950-51	1950-51
Currie, Tony	St.L., Hfd., Van.	8	300	92	119	211	83	16	4	12	16	14	1977-78	1984-85
Curry, Floyd	Mtl.	11	601	105	99	204	147	91	23	17	40	38	1947-48	1957-58
Curtale, Tony	Cgy.	1	2	0	0	0	0	....	....	....	....	....	1980-81	1980-81
Curtis, Paul	Mtl., L.A., St.L.	4	185	3	34	37	151	5	0	0	0	2	1969-70	1972-73
Cushenan, Ian	Chi., Mtl., NYR, Det.	5	129	3	11	14	134	....	....	....	....	....	1956-57	1963-64
Cusson, Jean	Oak.	1	2	0	0	0	0	....	....	....	....	....	1967-68	1967-68
Cyr, Denis	Cgy., Chi., St.L.	6	193	41	43	84	36	4	0	0	0	0	1980-81	1985-86

D

Dahlin, Kjell	Mtl.	3	166	57	59	116	10	35	6	11	17	6	1985-86	1987-88
Dahlstrom, Cully	Chi.	8	342	88	118	206	58	29	6	8	14	4	1937-38	1944-45
Daigle, Alain	Chi.	6	389	56	50	106	122	17	0	1	1	0	1974-75	1979-80
Dailey, Bob	Van., Phi.	9	561	94	231	325	814	63	12	34	46	106	1973-74	1981-82
Daley, Frank	Det.	1	5	0	0	0	0	2	0	0	0	0	1928-29	1928-29
Daley, Pat	Wpg.	2	12	1	0	1	13	....	....	....	....	....	1979-80	1980-81
Dame, Bunny	Mtl.	1	34	2	5	7	4	....	....	....	....	....	1941-42	1941-42
Damore, Hank	NYR	1	4	1	0	1	2	....	....	....	....	....	1943-44	1943-44
Darragh, Harry	Pit., Phi., Bos., Tor.	8	308	68	49	117	50	16	1	3	4	4	1925-26	1932-33
Darragh, Jack	Ott.	6	120	68	21	89	84	21	14	2	16	7	1917-18	1923-24
David, Richard	Que.	3	31	4	4	8	10	1	0	0	0	0	1979-80	1982-83
Davidson, Bob	Tor.,	12	491	94	160	254	398	82	5	17	22	79	1934-35	1945-46
Davidson, Gord	NYR	2	51	3	6	9	8	....	....	....	....	....	1942-43	1942-43
Davie, Bob	Bos.	3	41	0	1	1	25	....	....	....	....	....	1933-34	1935-36
Davies, Ken	NYR	1	1	0	0	0	0	....	....	....	....	....	1947-48	1947-48
Davis, Bob	Det.	1	3	0	0	0	0	....	....	....	....	....	1932-33	1932-33
Davis, Kim	Pit., Tor.	4	36	5	7	12	12	4	0	0	0	0	1977-78	1980-81
Davis, Lorne	Mtl., Chi., Det., Bos.	5	95	8	12	20	20	18	3	1	4	10	1951-52	1959-60
Davis, Mal	Det., Buf.	5	100	31	22	53	34	7	1	0	1	0	1980-81	1985-86
Davison, Murray	Bos.	1	1	0	0	0	0	....	....	....	....	....	1965-66	1965-66
Dawes, Robert	Tor., Mtl.	4	32	2	7	4	6	10	0	0	0	2	1946-47	1950-51
Day, Hap	Tor., NYA	14	581	86	116	202	596	53	4	7	11	56	1924-25	1937-38
Dea, Billy	Chi., NYR, Det., Pit.	7	397	67	54	121	44	11	2	0	2	6	1953-54	1970-71
Deacon, Don	Det.	3	30	6	4	10	6	2	2	1	3	0	1936-37	1939-40
Deadmarsh, Butch	Buf., ATL, K.C.	5	137	12	5	17	155	4	0	0	0	17	1970-71	1974-75
Dean, Barry	Col., Phi.	3	165	25	56	81	146	....	....	....	....	....	1976-77	1978-79
Debenedet, Nelson	Det., Pit.	2	46	10	4	14	13	....	....	....	....	....	1973-74	1974-75
Debol, David	Hfd.	2	92	26	26	52	4	3	0	0	0	0	1979-80	1980-81
Defazio, Dean	Pit.	1	22	0	2	2	28	....	....	....	....	....	1983-84	1983-84
Delmonte, Armand	Bos.	1	1	0	0	0	0	....	....	....	....	....	1945-46	1945-46
Delorme, Ron	Col., Van.	9	524	83	83	166	667	25	1	2	3	59	1976-77	1984-85
Delory, Valentine	NYR	1	0	0	0	0	0	....	....	....	....	....	1948-49	1948-49
Delparte, Guy	Col.	1	48	1	8	9	18	....	....	....	....	....	1976-77	1976-77
Delvecchio, Alex	Det.	24	1549	456	825	1281	383	121	35	69	104	29	1950-51	1973-74
DeMarco, Ab	Chi., Tor., Bos., NYR	7	209	72	93	165	53	11	3	0	3	2	1938-39	1946-47
DeMarco, Albert	NYR, St.L., Pit., Van., L.A., Bos.	9	344	44	80	124	75	25	1	2	3	17	1969-70	1978-79
DeMeres, Tony	Mtl., NYR	6	83	20	22	42	23	3	0	0	0	0	1937-38	1943-44
Denis, Johnny	NYR	2	10	0	2	2	2	....	....	....	....	....	1946-47	1949-50
Denis, Lulu	Mtl.	2	3	0	1	1	0	....	....	....	....	....	1949-50	1950-51
Denneny, Corbett	Tor., Ham., Chi.	9	175	99	29	128	130	15	7	4	11	6	1917-18	1927-28
Denneny, Cy	Ott., Bos.	12	326	250	69	319	176	37	18	3	21	31	1917-18	1928-29
Dennis, Norm	St.L.	4	12	3	0	3	11	5	0	0	0	2	1968-69	1971-72
Denoird, Gerry	Tor.	1	15	0	0	0	0	....	....	....	....	....	1922-23	1922-23
Derlago, Bill	Van., Bos., Wpg., Que., Tor.	9	555	189	227	416	247	13	5	0	5	8	1978-79	1986-87
Desaulniers, Gerard	Mtl.	3	8	0	2	2	4	....	....	....	....	....	1950-51	1953-54

			Regular Schedule					Playoffs					Last	Last
Name	NHL Teams	NHL Seasons	GP	G	A	TP	PIM	GP	G	A	TP	PIM	NHL Season	Pro Season
Desilets, Joffre	Mtl., Chi.	5	192	37	45	82	57	7	1	0	1	7	1935-36	1939-40
Desjardins, Vic	Chi., NYR	2	87	6	15	21	27	16	0	0	0	0	1930-31	1931-32
Deslauriers, Jacques	Mtl.	1	2	0	0	0	0	....	....	....	....	....	1955-56	1955-56
Devine, Kevin	NYI	1	2	0	1	1	8	....	....	....	....	....	1982-83	1982-83
Dewar, Tom	NYR	1	9	0	2	2	4	....	....	....	....	....	1943-44	1943-44
Dewsbury, Al	Det., Chi.	9	347	30	78	108	365	14	1	5	6	60	1946-47	1955-56
Deziel, Michel	Buf.	1	0	0	0	0	0	1	0	0	0	0	1974-75	1974-75
Dheere, Marcel	Mtl.	1	11	1	2	3	2	5	0	0	0	6	1942-43	1942-43
Diachuk, Edward	Det.	1	12	0	0	0	19	....	....	....	....	....	1960-61	1960-61
Dick, Harry	Chi.	1	12	0	1	1	12	....	....	....	....	....	1946-47	1946-47
Dickens, Ernie	Tor., Chi.	6	278	12	44	56	48	13	0	0	0	4	1941-42	1950-51
Dickenson, Herb	NYR	2	48	18	17	35	10	....	....	....	....	....	1951-52	1952-53
Dietrich, Don	Chi., N.J.	2	28	0	7	7	10	....	....	....	....	....	1983-84	1985-86
Dill, Bob	NYR	2	76	15	15	30	135	....	....	....	....	....	1943-44	1944-45
Dillabough, Bob	Det., Bos., Pit., Oak.	7	283	32	54	86	76	17	3	0	3	0	1961-62	1969-70
Dillon, Cecil	NYR, Det.	10	453	167	131	298	105	43	14	9	23	14	1930-31	1939-40
Dillon, Gary	Col.	1	13	1	1	2	29	....	....	....	....	....	1980-81	1980-81
Dillon, Wayne	NYR, Wpg.	4	229	43	66	109	60	3	0	1	1	0	1975-76	1979-80
Dineen, Bill	Det., Chi.	5	323	51	44	95	122	37	1	1	2	18	1953-54	1957-58
Dineen, Gary	Min.	1	4	0	1	1	0	....	....	....	....	....	1968-69	1968-69
Dinsmore, Chuck	Mtl.M	4	100	6	2	8	44	12	1	0	1	6	1924-25	1929-30
Doak, Gary	Det., Bos., Van., NYR	16	789	23	107	130	908	78	2	4	6	121	1965-66	1980-81
Dobson, Jim	Min., Col.	3	11	0	0	0	6	....	....	....	....	....	1979-80	1981-82
Doherty, Fred	Mtl.	1	3	0	0	0	0	....	....	....	....	....	1918-19	1918-19
Donaldson, Gary	Chi.	1	1	0	0	0	0	....	....	....	....	....	1973-74	1973-74
Donnelly, Babe	Mtl.M.	1	34	0	1	1	14	2	0	0	0	0	1926-27	1926-27
Doran, Red (I.)	Det.	1	24	3	2	5	10	....	....	....	....	....	1946-47	1946-47
Doran, Red (J.)	NYA., Det., Mtl.	5	98	5	10	15	110	3	0	0	0	0	1933-34	1939-40
Doraty, Ken	Chi., Tor., Det.	5	103	15	26	41	24	15	7	2	9	2	1926-27	1937-38
Dore, Andre	NYR, St.L., Que.	7	257	14	81	95	261	23	1	2	3	32	1978-79	1984-85
Dorey, Jim	Tor., NYR	4	232	25	74	99	553	11	0	2	2	40	1968-69	1971-72
Dornhoefer, Gary	Bos., Phi.	14	787	214	328	542	1291	80	17	19	36	203	1963-64	1977-78
Dorohoy, Eddie	Mtl.	1	16	0	0	0	6	....	....	....	....	....	1948-49	1948-49
Douglas, Jordy	Hfd., Min., Wpg.	6	268	76	62	138	160	6	0	0	0	4	1979-80	1984-85
Douglas, Kent	Tor., Oak., Det.	7	428	33	115	148	631	19	1	3	4	33	1962-63	1968-69
Douglas, Les	Det.	4	52	6	12	18	8	10	3	2	5	0	1940-41	1946-47
Downie, Dave	Tor.	1	11	0	1	1	2	....	....	....	....	....	1932-33	1932-33
Draper, Bruce	Tor.	1	1	0	0	0	0	....	....	....	....	....	1962-63	1962-63
Drillon, Gordie	Tor., Mtl.	7	311	155	139	294	56	50	26	15	41	10	1936-37	1942-43
Driscoll, Pete	Edm.	2	60	3	8	11	97	3	0	0	0	0	1979-80	1980-81
Drolet, Rene	Phi., Det.	2	2	0	0	0	0	....	....	....	....	....	1971-72	1974-75
Drouillard, Clarence	Det.	1	10	0	1	1	0	....	....	....	....	....	1937-38	1937-38
Drouin, Jude	Mtl., Min., NYI, Wpg.	12	666	151	305	456	346	72	27	41	68	33	1968-69	1980-81
Drouin, Polly	Mtl.	6	173	27	57	84	80	5	0	1	1	5	1935-36	1940-41
Drummond, John	NYR	1	2	0	0	0	0	....	....	....	....	....	1944-45	1944-45
Drury, Herb	Pit., Phi.	6	213	24	13	37	203	4	1	1	2	0	1925-26	1930-31
Dube, Gilles	Mtl.., Det.	2	12	1	2	3	2	2	0	0	0	0	1949-50	1953-54
Dube, Norm	K.C.	2	57	8	10	18	54	....	....	....	....	....	1974-75	1975-76
Dudley, Rick	Buf., Wpg.	6	309	75	99	174	292	25	7	2	9	69	1972-73	1980-81
Duff, Dick	Tor., NYR, Mtl., L.A., Buf.	18	1030	283	289	572	743	114	30	49	79	78	1954-55	1971-72
Dufour, Luc	Bos., Que., St.L.	3	167	23	21	44	199	18	1	0	1	32	1982-83	1984-85
Dufour, Marc	NYR, L.A.	3	14	1	0	1	2	....	....	....	....	....	1963-64	1968-69
Duggan, Jack	Ott.	1	27	0	0	0	0	2	0	0	0	0	1925-26	1925-26
Duguid, Lorne	Mtl.M, Det., Bos.	6	135	9	15	24	57	2	0	0	0	4	1931-32	1936-37
Dumart, Woodie	Bos.	16	771	211	218	429	99	82	12	15	27	23	1935-36	1953-54
Duncan, Art	Det., Tor.	5	156	18	16	34	225	5	0	0	0	4	1926-27	1932-33
Dunlap, Frank	Tor.	1	15	0	1	1	2	....	....	....	....	....	1943-44	1943-44
Dunlop, Blake	Min., Phi., St.L., Det.	11	550	130	274	404	172	40	4	10	14	18	1973-74	1983-84
Dunn, Dave	Van., Tor., Wpg.	3	184	14	41	55	313	10	1	1	2	41	1973-74	1975-76
Dupere, Denis	Tor., Wsh., St.L., K.C., Col.	8	421	80	99	179	66	16	1	0	1	0	1970-71	1977-78
Dupont, Andre	NYR, St.L., Phi., Que.	13	810	59	185	244	1986	140	14	18	32	352	1970-71	1982-83
Dupont, Jerome	Chi., Tor.	6	214	7	29	36	468	20	0	2	2	56	1981-82	1986-87
Dupont, Norm	Mtl., Wpg., Hfd.	5	256	55	85	140	52	13	4	2	6	0	1979-80	1983-84
Durbano, Steve	St.L., Pit., K.C., Col., St.L.	6	220	13	60	73	1127	5	0	2	2	8	1972-73	1978-79
Duris, Vitezslav	Tor.	2	89	3	20	23	62	3	0	1	1	2	1980-81	1982-83
Dussault, Norm	Mtl.	4	206	31	62	93	47	7	3	1	4	0	1947-48	1950-51
Dutkowski, Duke	Chi., NYA, NYR	5	200	16	30	46	172	6	0	0	0	6	1926-27	1933-34
Dutton, Red	Mtl.M, NYA	10	449	29	67	96	871	18	1	0	1	33	1926-27	1935-36
Dvorak, Miroslav	Phi.	3	193	11	74	85	51	18	0	2	2	6	1982-83	1984-85
Dwyer, Mike	Col., Cgy.	4	31	2	6	8	25	1	1	0	1	0	1978-79	1981-82
Dyck, Henry	NYR	1	1	0	0	0	0	....	....	....	....	....	1943-44	1943-44
Dye, Babe	Tor., Ham., Chi., NYA	11	271	200	41	241	200	15	11	2	13	11	1919-20	1930-31
Dyte, John	Chi.	1	27	1	0	1	31	....	....	....	....	....	1943-44	1943-44

E

Eakin, Bruce	Cgy., Det.	4	13	2	2	4	4	....	....	....	....	....	1981-82	1985-86
Eatough, Jeff	Buf.	1	1	0	0	0	0	....	....	....	....	....	1981-82	1981-82
Eaves, Mike	Min., Cgy.	8	324	83	143	226	80	43	7	10	17	14	1978-79	1985-86
Ecclestone, Tim	St.L., Det., Tor., Atl.	11	692	126	233	359	346	48	6	11	17	76	1967-68	1977-78
Edberg, Rolf	Wsh.	3	184	45	58	103	24	....	....	....	....	....	1978-79	1980-81
Eddolls, Frank	Mtl., NYR	8	317	23	43	66	114	31	0	2	2	10	1944-45	1951-52
Edestrand, Darryl	St.L., Phi., Pit., Bos., L.A.	10	455	34	90	124	404	42	3	9	12	57	1967-68	1978-79
Edmundson, Garry	Mtl., Tor.	3	43	4	6	10	49	11	0	1	1	8	1951-52	1960-61
Edur, Tom	Col., Pit	2	158	17	70	87	67	....	....	....	....	....	1976-77	1977-78
Egan, Pat	NYA, Det., Bos., NYR	11	554	77	153	230	776	44	9	4	13	44	1939-40	1950-51
Egers, Jack	NYR, St.L., Wsh.	7	284	64	69	133	154	32	5	6	11	32	1969-70	1975-76
Ehman, Gerry	Bos., Det., Tor., Dak, Cal.	9	429	96	118	214	100	41	10	10	20	12	1957-58	1970-71
Eldebrink, Anders	Van., Que.	2	55	3	11	14	29	14	0	0	0	0	1981-82	1982-83
Elik, Boris	Det.	1	3	0	0	0	0	....	....	....	....	....	1962-63	1962-63
Elliot, Fred	Ott.	1	43	2	0	2	6	....	....	....	....	....	1928-29	1928-29
Ellis, Ron	Tor.	16	1034	332	308	640	207	70	18	8	26	20	1963-64	1980-81
Eloranta, Kari	Cgy., St.L.	4	254	12	97	109	146	20	1	5	6	19	1981-82	1984-85
Emberg, Eddie	Mtl.	1	2	1	0	1	0	....	....	....	....	....	1944-45	1944-45
Emms, Hap	Mtl.M, NYA, Det., Bos.	10	320	37	53	90	311	14	0	0	0	12	1926-27	1937-38
Engblom, Brian	Mtl., Wsh., L.A., Buf., Cgy.	11	659	29	177	206	599	48	3	9	12	43	1976-77	1986-87
Engele, Jerry	Min.	3	100	2	13	15	162	2	0	1	1	0	1975-76	1977-78
Erickson, Aut	Bos., Chi., Oak., Tor.	7	227	7	84	31	182	7	0	0	0	2	1959-60	1969-70
Erickson, Bryan	Wsh., L.A., Pit.	5	278	74	102	176	121	11	3	4	7	7	1983-84	1987-88
Erickson, Grant	Bos., Min.	2	6	1	0	1	4	....	....	....	....	....	1968-69	1969-70
Eriksson, Rolie	Min., Van.	3	193	48	95	143	26	2	1	0	1	0	1976-77	1978-79
Esposito, Phi.	Chi., Bos., NYR	18	1282	717	873	1590	910	130	61	76	137	137	1963-64	1980-81
Evans, Chris	Tor., Buf., St.L., Det., K.C.	5	241	19	42	61	143	12	1	1	2	8	1969-70	1974-75
Evans, Jack	NYR, Chi.	14	752	19	80	99	989	56	2	2	4	97	1948-49	1962-63
Evans, John	Phi.	3	103	14	25	39	34	1	0	0	0	0	1978-79	1982-83
Evans, Paul	Tor.	2	11	1	1	2	21	2	0	0	0	0	1976-77	1977-78
Evans, Stewart	Det., Mtl., Mtl.M	8	367	28	49	77	425	26	0	0	0	20	1930-31	1938-39
Ezinicki, Bill	Tor., Bos., NYR	9	368	79	105	184	713	40	5	8	13	87	1944-45	1954-55

F

Fahey, Trevor	NYR	1	1	0	0	0	0	....	....	....	....	....	1964-65	1964-65
Fairbairn, Bill	NYR, Min. St.L.	11	658	162	261	423	173	54	13	22	35	42	1968-69	1978-79
Falkenberg, Bob	Det.	5	54	1	5	6	26	....	....	....	....	....	1966-67	1971-72
Farrant, Walt	Chi.	1	1	0	0	0	0	....	....	....	....	....	1943-44	1943-44
Farrish, Dave	NYR, Que, Tor.	7	430	17	110	127	440	14	0	2	2	24	1976-77	1983-84
Fashoway, Gordie	Chi.	1	13	3	2	5	14	....	....	....	....	....	1950-51	1950-51
Faubert, Mario	Pit.	7	231	21	90	111	292	10	2	2	4	6	1974-75	1981-82
Faulkner, Alex	Tor., Det.	3	101	15	17	32	15	12	5	0	5	2	1961-62	1963-64
Feamster, Dave	Chi.	4	169	13	24	37	155	33	3	5	8	61	1981-82	1984-85
Featherstone, Tony	Oak., Cal., Min.	3	130	17	21	38	65	2	0	0	0	0	1969-70	1973-74
Feltrin, Tony	Pit., NYR	4	48	3	3	6	65	....	....	....	....	....	1980-81	1985-86
Ferguson	Chi.	1	1	0	0	0	0	....	....	....	....	....	1939-40	1939-40
Ferguson, George	Tor., Pit, Min	12	797	160	238	398	431	86	14	23	37	44	1972-73	1983-84
Ferguson, John	Mtl.	8	500	145	158	303	1214	85	20	18	38	260	1963-64	1970-71
Ferguson, Lorne	Bos., Det., Chi.	8	422	82	80	162	193	31	6	3	9	24	1949-50	1958-59

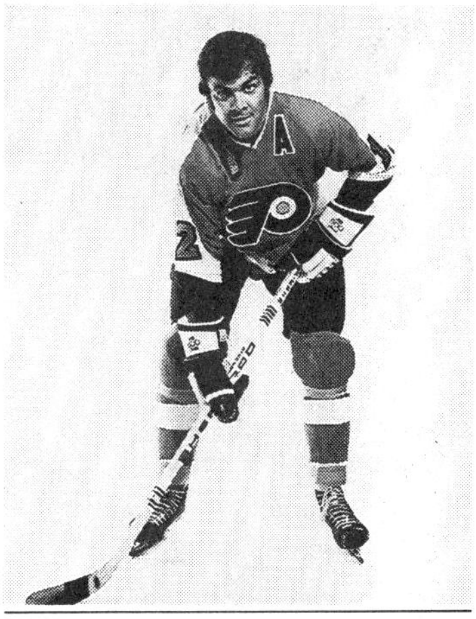
Gary Dornhoefer

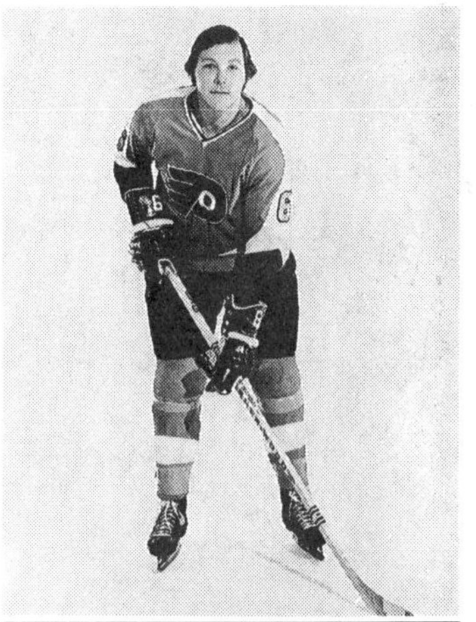
Andre Dupont

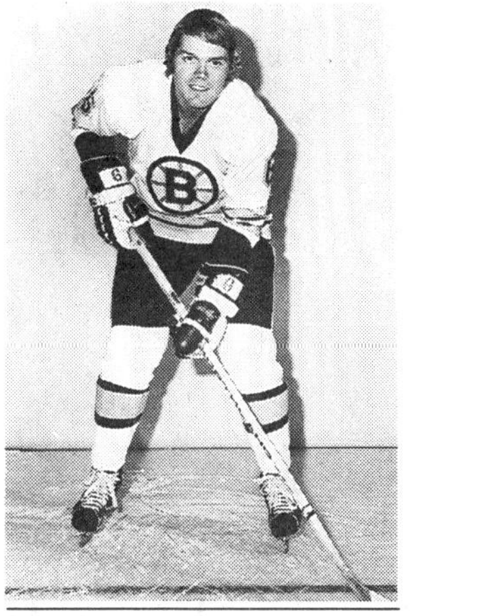
Darryl Edestrand

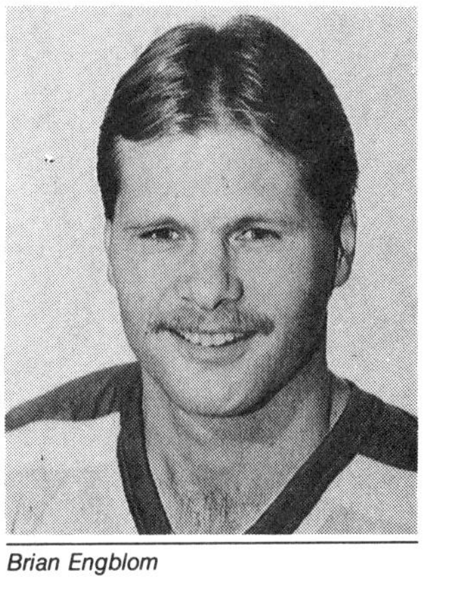
Brian Engblom

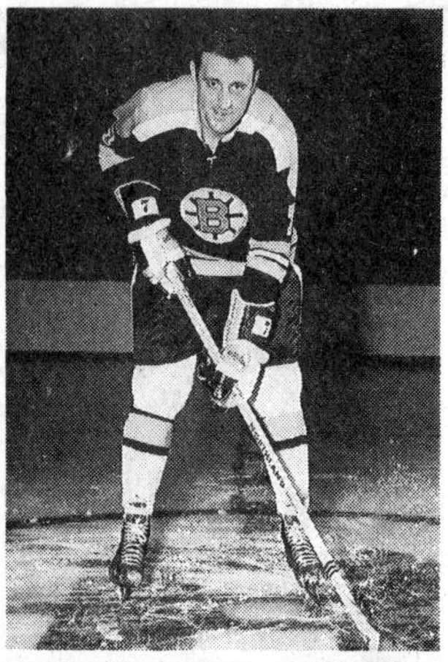

Phil Esposito

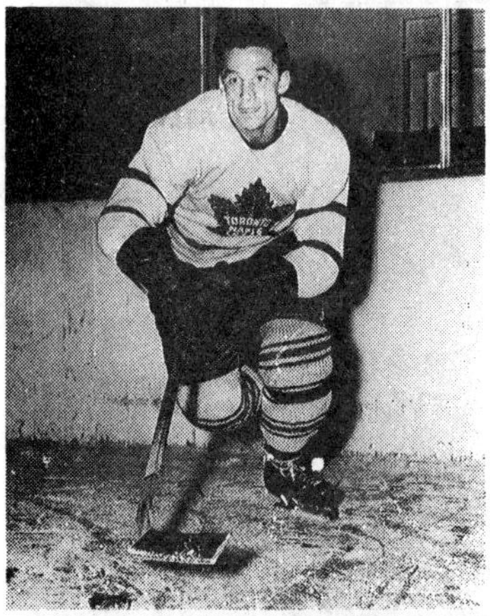

Bill Ezinicki

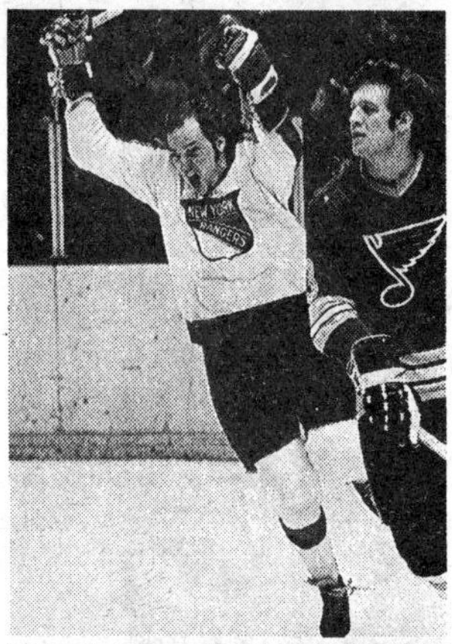

Dave Farrish

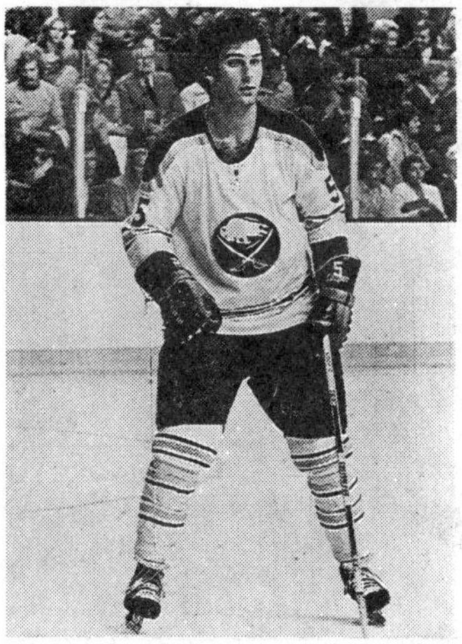

Lee Fogolin

Name	NHL Teams	NHL Seasons	Regular Schedule GP	G	A	TP	PIM	Playoffs GP	G	A	TP	PIM	First NHL Season	Last NHL Season
Ferguson, Norm	Oak., Cal.	4	279	73	66	139	72	10	1	4	5	7	1968-69	1971-72
Ferner, Mark	Buf.	1	13	0	3	3	9	....	....	....	....	....	1986-87	1986-87
Fidler, Mike	Cle., Min, Hfd., Chi.	7	271	84	97	181	124	....	....	....	....	....	1976-77	1982-83
Field, Wilf	NYA, Mtl., Chi.	6	218	17	25	42	151	3	0	0	0	0	1936-37	1944-45
Fielder, Guyle	Det., Chi.	4	36	0	0	0	2	6	0	0	0	2	1950-51	1957-58
Fillion, Bob	Mtl.	7	327	37	61	98	84	33	7	4	11	10	1943-44	1949-50
Fillion, Marcel	Bos.	1	1	0	0	0	0	....	....	....	....	....	1944-45	1944-45
Filmore, Tommy	Det., NYA, Bos.	4	116	15	12	27	33	....	....	....	....	....	1930-31	1933-34
Finkbeiner, Lloyd	NYA	1	1	0	0	0	0	....	....	....	....	....	1940-41	1940-41
Finney, Sid	Chi.	3	59	10	7	17	4	7	0	0	0	2	1951-52	1953-54
Finnigan, Ed	Bos.	1	3	0	0	0	0	....	....	....	....	....	1935-36	1935-36
Finnigan, Frank	Ott., Tor., St.L.	14	555	115	88	203	405	39	6	9	15	22	1923-24	1936-37
Fischer, Ron	Buf.	2	18	0	7	7	6	....	....	....	....	....	1981-82	1982-83
Fisher, Alvin	Tor.	1	9	1	0	1	4	....	....	....	....	....	1924-25	1924-25
Fisher, Dunc	NYR, Bos., Det.	7	275	45	70	115	10	21	4	4	8	14	1947-48	1958-59
Fisher, Joe	Det.	4	66	8	12	20	13	15	2	1	3	6	1939-40	1942-43
Fitchner, Dave	Que	2	78	12	20	32	59	3	0	0	0	10	1979-80	1980-81
Fitzpatrick, Sandy	NYR, Min.	2	22	3	6	9	8	12	0	0	0	0	1964-65	1967-68
Flaman, Fern	Bos., Tor.	17	910	34	174	208	1370	63	4	8	12	93	1944-45	1960-61
Fleming, Reggie	Mtl., Chi., Bos., NYR, Phi., Buf.	12	749	108	132	240	1468	50	3	6	9	106	1959-60	1970-71
Flesch	Ham.	1	1	0	0	0	0	....	....	....	....	....	1920-21	1920-21
Flesch, John	Min, Pit, Col.	4	124	18	23	41	117	....	....	....	....	....	1974-75	1979-80
Flett, Bill	L.A., Phi., Tor., Atl, Edm.	11	689	202	215	417	501	52	7	16	23	42	1967-68	1979-80
Flockhart, Rob	Van., Min	5	55	2	5	7	14	1	1	0	1	2	1976-77	1980-81
Floyd, Larry	N.J.	2	12	2	3	5	9	....	....	....	....	....	1982-83	1983-84
Fogolin, Lee	Buf., Edm.	13	924	44	195	239	1318	108	5	19	24	173	1974-75	1986-87
Fogolin, Lidio (Lee)	Det., Chi.	9	427	10	48	58	575	28	0	2	2	30	1947-48	1955-56
Folco, Peter	Van.	1	2	0	0	0	0	....	....	....	....	....	1973-74	1973-74
Foley, Gerry	Tor., NYR, L.A.	4	142	9	14	23	99	9	0	1	1	2	1954-55	1957-58
Foley, Rick	Chi., Phi., Det.	3	67	11	26	37	180	4	0	1	1	4	1970-71	1973-74
Folk, Bill	Det.	2	12	0	0	0	4	....	....	....	....	....	1951-52	1952-53
Fontaine, Len	Det.	2	46	8	11	19	10	....	....	....	....	....	1972-73	1973-74
Fontas, Jon	Min.	2	2	0	0	0	0	....	....	....	....	....	1979-80	1980-81
Fonteyne, Val	Det., NYR, Pit.	13	820	75	154	229	26	59	3	10	13	8	1959-60	1971-72
Fontinato, Louie	NYR, Mtl.	9	535	26	78	104	1247	21	0	2	2	42	1954-55	1962-63
Forbes, Dave	Bos., Wsh.	6	363	64	64	128	341	45	1	4	5	13	1973-74	1978-79
Forbes, Mike	Bos., Edm.	3	50	1	11	12	41	....	....	....	....	....	1977-78	1979-80
Forey, Connie	St.L.	1	4	0	0	0	2	....	....	....	....	....	1973-74	1973-74
Forsey, Jack	Tor.	1	19	7	9	16	10	3	0	1	1	0	1942-43	1942-43
Forslund, Gus	Ott.	1	48	4	9	13	2	....	....	....	....	....	1932-33	1932-33
Forsyth, Alex	Wsh.	1	1	0	0	0	0	....	....	....	....	....	1976-77	1976-77
Fortier, Charles	Mtl.	1	1	0	0	0	0	....	....	....	....	....	1923-24	1923-24
Fortier, Dave	Tor., NYI, Van.	4	205	8	21	29	335	20	0	2	2	33	1972-73	1976-77
Fortin, Ray	St.L.	3	92	2	6	8	33	6	0	0	0	8	1967-68	1969-70
Foster, Dwight	Bos., Col., N.J., Det.	10	541	111	163	274	420	35	5	12	17	4	1977-78	1986-87
Foster, Herb	NYR	2	5	1	0	1	5	....	....	....	....	....	1940-41	1947-48
Foster, Harry	NYR, Bos., Det.	4	83	3	2	5	32	....	....	....	....	....	1929-31	1934-35
Fowler, Jimmy	Tor.	3	135	18	29	47	39	18	0	3	3	2	1936-37	1938-39
Fowler, Tom	Chi.	1	24	0	1	1	18	....	....	....	....	....	1946-47	1946-47
Fox, Greg	Atl, Chi., Pit.	8	494	14	92	106	637	44	1	9	10	67	1977-78	1984-85
Foyston, Frank	Det.	2	64	17	7	24	32	....	....	....	....	....	1926-27	1927-28
Frampton, Bob	Mtl.	1	2	0	0	0	0	3	0	0	0	0	1949-50	1949-50
Francis, Bobby	Det.	1	14	2	0	2	0	....	....	....	....	....	1982-83	1982-83
Fraser, Archie	NYR	1	3	0	1	1	0	....	....	....	....	....	1943-44	1943-44
Fraser, Gord	Chi., Det., Mtl., Pit., Phi.	5	144	24	12	36	224	2	1	0	1	6	1926-27	1930-31
Fraser, Harry	Chi.	1	21	5	4	9	0	....	....	....	....	....	1944-45	1944-45
Fraser, Jack	Ham.	1	1	0	0	0	0	....	....	....	....	....	1923-24	1923-24
Frederickson, Frank	Det., Bos., Pit.	5	165	39	34	73	206	10	2	5	7	26	1926-27	1930-31
Frew, Irv	Mtl.M, St.L., Mtl.	3	95	2	5	7	146	4	0	0	0	6	1933-34	1935-36
Friday, Tim	Det.	1	23	0	3	3	6	....	....	....	....	....	1985-86	1985-86
Fridgen, Dan	Hfd.	2	13	2	3	5	2	....	....	....	....	....	1981-82	1982-83
Friest, Ron	Min.	3	64	7	7	14	191	6	1	0	1	7	1980-81	1982-83
Frig, Len	Chi., Cal., Cle., St.L.	7	311	13	51	64	479	14	2	1	3	0	1972-73	1979-89
Frost, Harry	Bos.	1	3	0	0	0	0	1	0	0	0	0	1938-39	1938-39
Fryday, Bob	Mtl.	2	5	1	0	1	0	....	....	....	....	....	1949-50	1951-52
Ftorek, Robbie	Det., Que, NYR	8	334	77	150	227	262	19	9	6	15	28	1972-73	1984-85
Fullin, Lawrence	Wsh.	1	4	1	0	1	0	....	....	....	....	....	1974-75	1974-75
Fusco, Mark	Hfd.	2	80	3	12	15	42	....	....	....	....	....	1983-84	1984-85

G

Name	NHL Teams	NHL Seasons	Regular Schedule GP	G	A	TP	PIM	Playoffs GP	G	A	TP	PIM	First NHL Season	Last NHL Season
Gadsby, Bill	Chi., NYR, Det.	20	1248	130	437	567	1539	67	4	23	27	92	1946-47	1965-66
Gagne, Art	Mtl., Bos., Ott., Det.	6	228	67	33	100	257	11	2	1	3	20	1926-27	1931-32
Gagne, Pierre	Bos.	1	2	0	0	0	0	....	....	....	....	....	1959-60	1959-60
Gagnon, Germaine	Mtl., NYI, Chi., K.C.	5	259	40	101	141	72	49	2	3	5	2	1971-72	1975-76
Gagnon, Johnny	Mtl., Bos., NYA	10	454	120	141	265	295	32	12	12	24	37	1930-31	1939-40
Gainor, Dutch	Bos., NYR, Ott., Mtl.M	7	243	51	56	107	129	25	2	1	3	14	1927-28	1934-35
Galarneau, Michel	Hfd.	3	78	7	10	17	34	....	....	....	....	....	1980-81	1982-83
Galbraith, Percy	Bos., Ott.	8	347	29	31	60	223	31	4	7	11	24	1926-27	1933-34
Gallagher, John	Mtl.M, Det., NYA	7	204	14	19	33	153	22	2	3	5	27	1930-31	1938-39
Gallimore, Jamie	Min.	1	2	0	0	0	0	....	....	....	....	....	1977-78	1977-78
Gallinger, Don	Bos.	5	222	65	88	153	89	23	5	5	10	19	1942-43	1947-48
Gamble, Dick	Mtl., Chi., Tor.	8	195	41	41	82	66	14	1	2	3	4	1950-51	1966-67
Gambucci, Gary	Min.	2	51	2	7	9	9	....	....	....	....	....	1971-72	1973-74
Gans, Dave	L.A.	2	6	0	0	0	2	....	....	....	....	....	1982-83	1985-86
Gardiner, Herb	Mtl., Chi.	3	101	10	9	19	52	7	0	1	1	14	1926-27	1928-29
Gardner, Cal	NYR, Tor., Chi., Bos.	12	696	154	238	392	517	61	7	10	17	20	1945-46	1956-57
Gardner, Dave	Mtl., St.L., Cal., Cle., Phi.	7	350	75	115	190	41	....	....	....	....	....	1972-73	1979-80
Gardner, Paul	Col., Tor., Pit., Wsh., Buf.	7	447	201	201	402	207	16	2	6	8	14	1976-77	1985-86
Gare, Danny	Buf., Det., Edm.	13	827	354	331	685	1285	64	25	21	46	195	1974-75	1986-87
Gariepy, Ray	Bos., Tor.	2	36	1	6	7	43	....	....	....	....	....	1953-54	1955-56
Garland, Scott	Tor., L.A.	3	91	13	24	37	115	7	1	2	3	35	1975-76	1978-79
Garner, Bob	Pit.	1	1	0	0	0	0	....	....	....	....	....	1982-83	1982-83
Garrett, Red	NYR	1	23	1	1	2	18	....	....	....	....	....	1942-43	1942-43
Gassoff, Bob	St.L.	4	245	11	47	58	866	9	0	1	1	16	1973-74	1976-77
Gassoff, Brad	Van.	4	122	19	17	36	163	3	0	0	0	0	1975-76	1978-79
Gatzos, Steve	Pit.	4	89	15	20	35	83	1	0	0	0	0	1981-82	1984-85
Gaudreault, Armand	Bos.	1	44	15	9	24	27	7	0	2	2	8	1944-45	1944-45
Gaudreault, Leo	Mtl.	3	67	8	4	12	30	....	....	....	....	....	1927-28	1932-33
Gaulin, Jean-Marc	Que.	4	26	4	3	7	8	1	0	0	0	0	1982-83	1985-86
Gauthier, Art	Mtl.	1	13	0	0	0	0	1	0	0	0	0	1926-27	1926-27
Gauthier, Fern	NYR, Mtl., Det.	6	229	46	50	96	35	22	5	1	6	7	1943-44	1948-49
Gauthier, Jean	Mtl., Phi., Bos.	10	166	6	29	35	150	14	1	3	4	22	1960-61	1969-70
Gauvreau, Jocelyn	Mtl.	1	2	0	0	0	0	....	....	....	....	....	1983-84	1983-84
Geale, Bob	Pit.	1	1	0	0	0	2	....	....	....	....	....	1984-85	1984-85
Gee, George	Chi., Det.	9	551	135	183	318	245	41	6	13	19	32	1945-46	1953-54
Geldart, Gary	Min.	1	4	0	0	0	5	....	....	....	....	....	1970-71	1970-71
Gendron, Jean-Guy	NYR, Mtl., Bos., Phi.	14	863	182	201	383	701	42	7	4	11	47	1955-56	1971-72
Geoffrion, Bernie	Mtl., NYR	16	883	393	429	822	689	132	58	60	118	88	1950-51	1967-68
Geoffrion, Danny	Mtl., Wpg., Que.	3	111	20	32	52	99	2	0	0	0	7	1979-80	1981-82
Geran, Gerry	Mtl.W., Bos.	2	37	5	1	6	6	....	....	....	....	....	1917-18	1925-26
Gerard, Eddie	Ott.	6	128	50	30	80	99	26	7	3	10	51	1917-18	1922-23
Getliffe, Ray	Bos., Mtl.	10	393	136	137	273	280	45	9	10	19	30	1935-36	1944-45
Giallonardo, Mario	Col.	2	23	0	3	3	6	....	....	....	....	....	1979-80	1980-81
Gibbs, Barry	Bos., Min., Atl., St.L., L.A.	13	797	58	224	282	945	36	4	2	6	67	1967-68	1979-80
Gibson, Doug	Bos., Wsh.	3	63	9	19	28	0	1	0	0	0	0	1973-74	1977-78
Gibson, John	L.A., Wpg.	3	48	0	2	2	120	....	....	....	....	....	1980-81	1983-84
Giesebrecht, Gus	Det.	4	135	27	51	78	13	17	2	3	5	0	1938-39	1941-42
Gilbert, Ed	K.C., Pit.	3	166	21	31	52	22	....	....	....	....	....	1974-75	1976-77
Gilbert, Jean	Bos.	2	9	0	0	0	4	....	....	....	....	....	1962-63	1964-65
Gilbert, Rod	NYR	18	1065	406	615	1021	508	79	34	33	67	43	1960-61	1977-78
Gilbertson, Stan	Wsh., Pit., Cal., St.L.	6	428	85	89	174	148	3	1	1	2	2	1971-72	1976-77
Gillen, Don	Phi., Hfd.	2	35	2	4	6	22	....	....	....	....	....	1979-80	1981-82
Gillie, Ferrand	Det.	1	1	0	0	0	0	....	....	....	....	....	1928-29	1928-29
Gillies, Clark	NYI, Buf.	14	958	319	378	697	1023	164	47	47	94	287	1974-75	1987-88
Gillis, Jere	Que., Buf., Phi., Van., NYR	9	386	78	95	173	230	19	4	7	11	9	1977-78	1986-87
Gillis, Mike	Col., Bos.	6	246	33	43	76	186	27	2	5	7	10	1983-84	1983-84

			Regular Schedule					Playoffs					First	Last
Name	NHL Teams	NHL Seasons	GP	G	A	TP	PIM	GP	G	A	TP	PIM	First NHL Season	Last NHL Season
Girard, Bob	Wsh., Cal., Cle.	5	305	45	69	114	140	....	....	....	....	....	1975-79	1979-80
Girard, Kenny	Tor.	3	7	0	1	1	2	....	....	....	....	....	1956-57	1959-60
Giroux, Art	Det., Mtl., Bos.	3	54	6	4	10	14	2	0	0	0	0	1932-33	1935-36
Giroux, Larry	Det., Hfd., St.L., K.C.	7	274	15	74	89	333	5	0	0	0	4	1973-74	1979-80
Giroux, Pierre	L.A.	1	6	1	0	1	17	....	....	....	....	....	1982-83	1982-83
Gladney, Bob	L.A., Pit.	2	14	1	5	6	4	....	....	....	....	....	1982-83	1983-84
Gladu, Jean	Bos.	1	40	6	14	20	2	7	2	2	4	0	1944-45	1944-45
Glennie, Brian	Tor., L.A.	10	572	14	100	114	621	32	0	1	1	66	1969-70	1978-79
Gloeckner, Lorry	Det.	1	13	0	2	2	6	....	....	....	....	....	1978-79	1978-79
Gloor, Dan	Van.	1	2	0	0	0	0	....	....	....	....	....	1973-74	1973-74
Glover, Fred	Det., Chi.	4	92	13	11	24	62	3	0	0	0	0	1948-49	1952-53
Glover, Howie	Chi., Det., NYR, Mtl.	5	144	29	17	46	101	11	1	2	3	2	1958-59	1967-68
Godden, Ernie	Tor.	1	5	1	1	2	6	....	....	....	....	....	1981-82	1981-82
Godfrey, Warren	Bos., Det.	16	786	32	125	157	752	52	1	4	5	42	1952-53	1967-68
Godin, Eddy	Wsh.	2	27	3	6	9	12	....	....	....	....	....	1977-78	1978-79
Godin, Sammy	Ott., Mtl.	3	83	4	3	7	36	....	....	....	....	....	1927-28	1933-34
Goegan, Peter	Det., NYR, Min.	11	383	19	67	86	365	33	1	3	4	61	1957-58	1967-68
Goldham, Bob	Tor., Chi., Det.	12	650	28	143	171	400	66	3	14	17	53	1941-42	1955-56
Goldsworthy, Bill	Bos., Min., NYR	14	771	283	258	541	793	40	18	19	37	30	1964-65	1977-78
Goldsworthy, Leroy	NYR, Det., Chi., Mtl., Bos., NYA	9	337	66	57	123	79	22	1	0	1	4	1929-30	1938-39
Goldup, Glenn	Mtl., L.A.	9	291	52	67	119	303	16	4	3	7	22	1973-74	1981-82
Goldup, Hank	Tor., NYR	6	181	57	76	133	95	26	5	1	6	6	1939-40	1945-46
Gooden, Bill	NYR	2	53	9	11	20	15	....	....	....	....	....	1942-43	1943-44
Goodenough, Larry	Phi., Van.	6	242	22	77	99	179	22	3	15	18	10	1974-75	1979-80
Goodfellow, Ebbie	Det.	14	554	134	190	324	516	45	8	8	16	65	1929-30	1942-43
Gordon, Fred	Det., Bos.	2	77	8	7	15	68	1	0	0	0	0	1926-27	1927-28
Gordon, Jackie	NYR	3	36	3	10	13	0	9	1	1	2	7	1948-49	1950-51
Gorence, Tom	Phi., Edm.	6	303	58	53	111	89	37	9	6	15	47	1978-79	1983-84
Goring, Butch	L.A., NYI, Bos.	16	1107	375	513	888	102	134	38	50	88	32	1969-70	1984-85
Gorman, Dave	Atl.	1	3	0	0	0	0	....	....	....	....	....	1979-80	1979-80
Gorman, Ed	Ott., Tor.	4	111	14	5	19	108	8	0	0	0	2	1924-25	1927-28
Gosselin, Benoit	NYR	1	7	0	0	0	33	....	....	....	....	....	1977-78	1977-78
Gottselig, Johnny	Chi.	16	589	177	195	372	225	43	13	13	26	20	1928-29	1944-45
Gould, John	Buf., Van., Atl.	9	504	131	138	269	113	14	3	2	5	4	1971-72	1979-80
Gould, Larry	Van.	1	2	0	0	0	0	....	....	....	....	....	1973-74	1973-74
Goupille, Red	Mtl.	8	222	12	28	40	256	8	2	0	2	6	1935-36	1942-43
Goyer, Gerry	Chi.	1	40	1	2	3	4	3	0	0	0	2	1967-68	1967-68
Goyette, Phil	Mtl., NYR, St.L., Buf.	16	941	207	467	674	131	94	17	29	46	26	1956-57	1971-72
Graboski, Tony	Mtl.	3	66	6	10	16	18	2	0	0	0	0	1940-41	1942-43
Gracie, Bob	Tor., Bos., NYA, Mtl., Mtl.M., Chi.	9	378	82	109	191	207	33	4	7	11	4	1930-31	1938-39
Gradin, Thomas	Van., Bos.	9	677	209	384	593	298	42	17	25	42	20	1978-79	1986-87
Graham, Leth	Ott., Ham.	6	26	3	0	3	0	1	0	0	0	0	1920-21	1925-26
Graham, Pat	Pit., Tor.	3	103	11	17	28	136	4	0	0	0	2	1981-82	1983-84
Graham, Rod	Bos.	1	14	2	1	3	7	....	....	....	....	....	1974-75	1974-75
Graham, Ted	Chi., Mtl.M., Det., St.L., Bos., NYA	9	343	14	25	39	300	23	3	1	4	34	1927-28	1936-37
Grant, Danny	Mtl., Det., Min., L.A.	13	736	263	273	536	239	43	10	14	24	19	1965-66	1978-79
Gratton, Norm	NYR, Atl., Buf., Min.	5	201	39	44	83	64	6	0	1	1	2	1971-72	1975-76
Gravelle, Leo	Mtl., Det.	5	223	44	34	78	42	17	4	1	5	2	1946-47	1950-51
Graves, Hilliard	Cal., Atl., Van., Wpg.	9	556	118	163	281	209	2	0	0	0	0	1970-71	1979-80
Gray, Alex	NYR, Tor.	2	50	7	0	7	30	13	1	0	1	0	1927-28	1928-29
Gray, Terry	Bos., Mtl., L.A., St.L.	6	147	26	28	54	64	35	5	5	10	22	1961-62	1970-71
Green	Det.	1	2	0	0	0	0	....	....	....	....	....	1928-29	1928-29
Green, Red	Ham., NYA, Bos., Det.	6	195	59	13	72	261	....	....	....	....	....	1923-24	1928-29
Green, Ted	Bos.	11	620	48	206	254	1029	31	4	8	12	54	1960-61	1971-72
Green, Wilf	Ham., NYA	4	103	33	8	41	151	....	....	....	....	....	1923-24	1926-27
Greig, Bruce	Cal.	2	9	0	1	1	46	....	....	....	....	....	1973-74	1974-75
Grenier, Lucien	Mtl., L.A.	4	151	14	14	28	18	2	0	0	0	0	1968-69	1971-72
Grenier, Richard	NYI	1	10	1	1	2	2	....	....	....	....	....	1972-73	1972-73
Grigor, George	Chi.	1	2	1	0	1	0	1	0	0	0	0	1943-44	1943-44
Grisdale, John	Tor., Van.	6	250	4	39	43	346	10	0	1	1	15	1972-73	1978-79
Gronsdahl, Lloyd	Bos.	1	10	1	2	3	0	....	....	....	....	....	1941-42	1941-42
Gross, Llyod	Tor., NYA, Bos., Det.	3	62	11	5	16	20	1	0	0	0	0	1926-27	1934-35
Grosso, Don	Det., Chi., Bos.	9	334	86	116	202	90	50	14	12	26	46	1938-39	1946-47
Grosvenar, Len	Ott., NYA, Mtl.	6	147	9	11	20	78	4	0	0	0	2	1927-28	1932-33
Groulx, Wayne	Que.	1	1	0	0	0	0	....	....	....	....	....	1984-85	1984-85
Gruen, Danny	Det., Col.	3	49	9	13	22	19	....	....	....	....	....	1972-73	1976-77
Gryp, Bob	Bos., Wsh.	3	74	11	13	24	33	....	....	....	....	....	1973-74	1975-76
Guevremont, Jocelyn	Van., Buf., NYR	9	571	84	223	307	319	40	4	17	21	18	1971-72	1979-80
Guidolin, Aldo	NYR	4	182	9	15	24	117	....	....	....	....	....	1952-53	1955-56
Guidolin, Bep	Bos., Det., Chi.	9	519	107	171	278	606	24	5	7	12	35	1942-43	1951-52
Guindon, Bobby	Wpg.	1	6	0	1	1	0	....	....	....	....	....	1979-80	1979-80
Gustavsson, Peter	Col.	1	2	0	0	0	0	....	....	....	....	....	1981-82	1981-82

H

Hachborn, Len	Phi., L.A.	3	102	20	39	59	29	7	0	3	3	7	1983-84	1985-86
Haddon, Llyod	Det.	1	8	0	0	0	2	1	0	0	0	0	1959-60	1959-60
Hadfield, Vic	NYR, Pit.	16	1002	323	389	712	1154	73	27	21	48	117	1961-62	1976-77
Haggarty, Jim	Mtl.	1	5	1	1	2	0	3	2	1	3	0	1941-42	1941-42
Hagman, Matti	Bos., Edm.	4	237	56	89	145	36	20	5	2	7	6	1976-77	1981-82
Haidy, Adam	Det.	1	....	....	....	....	....	1	0	0	0	0	1949-50	1949-50
Hajt, Bill	Buf.	14	854	42	202	244	433	80	2	16	18	70	1973-74	1986-87
Hakansson, Anders	Min., Pit., L.A.	5	330	52	46	98	141	6	0	0	0	2	1981-82	1985-86
Halderson, Slim	Det., Tor.	1	44	3	2	5	65	....	....	....	....	....	1926-27	1926-27
Hale, Larry	Phi.	4	196	5	37	42	90	8	0	0	0	12	1968-69	1971-72
Haley, Len	Det.	2	30	2	2	4	14	6	1	3	4	6	1959-60	1960-61
Hall, Bob	NYA	1	8	0	0	0	0	....	....	....	....	....	1925-26	1925-26
Hall, Del	Cal.	3	9	2	0	2	2	....	....	....	....	....	1971-72	1973-74
Hall, Gary	NYR	1	4	0	0	0	0	....	....	....	....	....	1960-61	1960-61
Hall, Joe	Mtl.	2	37	15	1	16	85	12	0	2	2	0	1917-18	1918-19
Hall, Murray	Chi., Det., Min., Van.	7	164	35	48	83	46	6	0	0	0	0	1961-62	1971-72
Halliday, Milt	Ott.	3	67	1	0	1	6	6	0	0	0	0	1926-27	1928-29
Hallin, Mats	NYI, Min.	5	152	17	14	31	193	15	1	0	1	13	1982-83	1986-87
Hamel, Herb	Tor.	1	2	0	0	0	14	....	....	....	....	....	1930-31	1930-31
Hamel, Jean	St.L., Det., Que., Mtl.	12	699	26	95	121	766	33	0	2	2	44	1972-73	1983-84
Hamel, Pierre	Wpg.	1	35	0	2	2	10	....	....	....	....	....	1979-80	1979-80
Hamill, Red	Bos., Chi.	12	442	128	94	222	160	13	1	2	3	12	1937-38	1950-51
Hamilton, Al	NYR, Buf., Edm.	7	257	10	78	88	258	7	0	0	0	2	1965-66	1979-80
Hamilton, Chuck	Mtl., St.L.	2	4	0	2	2	2	....	....	....	....	....	1961-62	1972-73
Hamilton, Jack	Tor.	3	138	31	48	79	76	11	2	1	3	0	1942-43	1945-46
Hamilton, Jim	Pit.	8	95	14	18	32	28	6	3	0	3	0	1977-78	1984-85
Hamilton, Reg	Tor., Chi.	12	387	18	71	89	412	64	6	6	12	54	1935-36	1946-47
Hammarstrom, Inge	Tor., St.L.	6	427	116	123	239	86	13	2	3	5	4	1973-74	1978-79
Hampson, Gord	Cgy.	1	4	0	0	0	5	....	....	....	....	....	1982-83	1982-83
Hampson, Ted	Tor., NYR, Det., Oak., Cal., Min.	12	676	108	245	353	94	35	7	10	17	2	1959-60	1971-72
Hampton, Rick	Cal., Cle., L.A.	6	337	59	113	172	147	2	0	0	0	0	1974-75	1979-80
Hamway, Mark	NYI	3	53	5	13	18	9	1	0	0	0	0	1984-85	1986-87
Hangsleben, Al	Hfd., Wsh., L.A.	3	185	21	48	69	396	....	....	....	....	....	1979-80	1981-82
Hanna, John	NYR, Mtl., Phi.	5	198	6	26	32	206	....	....	....	....	....	1958-59	1967-68
Hannigan, Gord	Tor.	4	161	29	31	60	117	9	2	0	2	8	1952-53	1955-56
Hannigan, Pat	Tor., NYR, Phi.	5	182	30	39	69	116	11	1	2	3	11	1959-60	1968-69
Hannigan, Ray	Tor.	1	3	0	0	0	2	....	....	....	....	....	1948-49	1948-49
Hansen, Ritchie	NYI, St.L.	4	20	2	8	10	6	....	....	....	....	....	1976-77	1981-82
Hanson, Dave	Det., Min.	2	33	1	1	2	65	....	....	....	....	....	1978-79	1979-80
Hanson, Emil	Det.	1	7	0	0	0	6	....	....	....	....	....	1932-33	1932-33
Hanson, Keith	Cgy.	1	25	0	2	2	77	....	....	....	....	....	1983-84	1983-84
Hanson, Ossie	Chi.	1	7	0	0	0	0	....	....	....	....	....	1937-38	1937-38
Harbaruk, Nick	Pit., St.L.	5	364	45	75	120	273	14	3	1	4	20	1969-70	1973-74
Hardy, Joe	Oak., Cal.	2	63	9	14	23	51	4	0	0	0	0	1969-70	1970-71
Hargreaves, Jim	Van.	2	66	1	7	8	105	....	....	....	....	....	1970-71	1972-73
Harmon, Glen	Mtl.	9	452	50	96	146	334	53	5	10	15	37	1942-43	1950-51
Harms, John	Chi.	2	44	5	5	10	21	3	3	0	3	2	1943-44	1944-45
Harnott, Happy	Bos.	1	6	0	0	0	6	....	....	....	....	....	1933-34	1933-34
Harper, Terry	Mtl., L.A., Det., St.L., Col.	19	1066	35	221	256	1362	112	4	13	17	140	1962-63	1980-81
Harrer, Tim	Cgy.	1	3	0	0	0	2	....	....	....	....	....	1982-83	1982-83
Harrington, Hago	Bos., Mtl.	3	72	9	3	12	15	4	1	0	1	2	1925-26	1932-33
Harris, Billy	Tor., Oak., Cal., Pit.	12	769	126	219	345	205	62	8	10	18	30	1955-56	1968-69

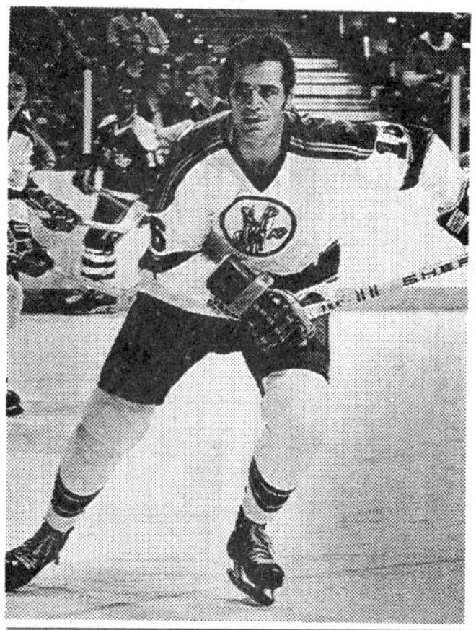
Germain Gagnon

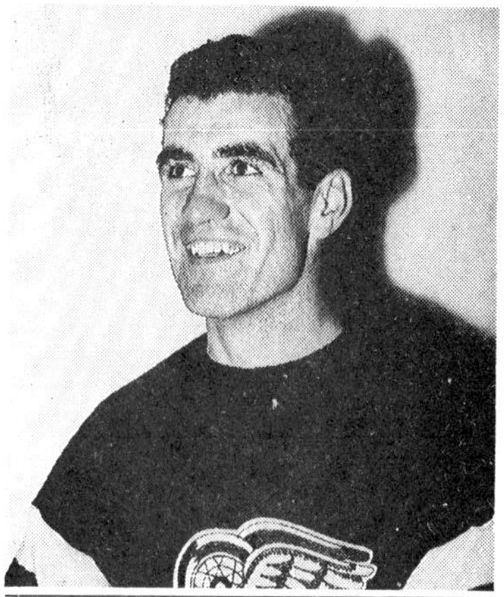
Fern Gauthier

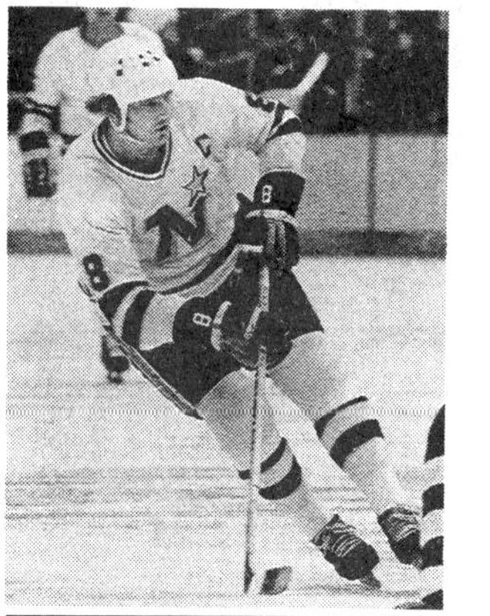
Bill Goldsworthy

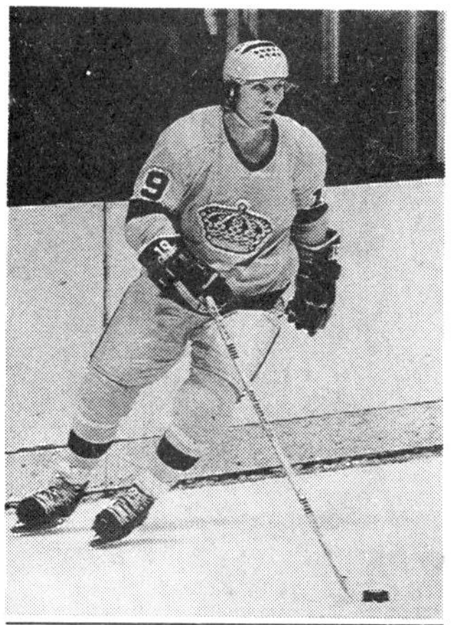
Butch Goring

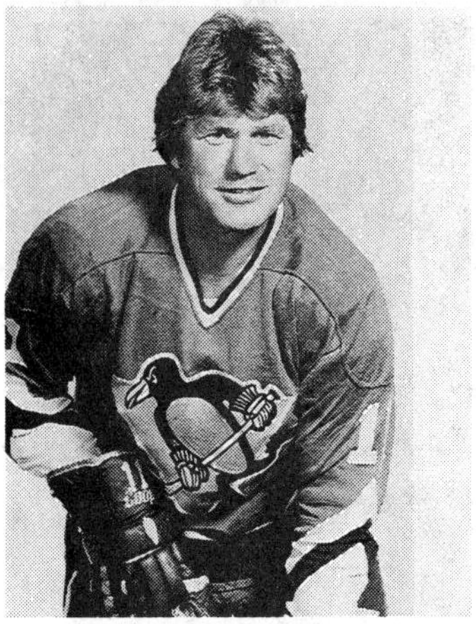

Vic Hadfield

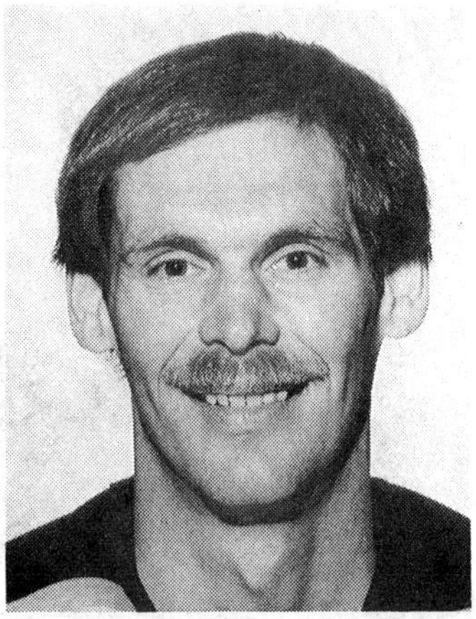

Bill Hajt

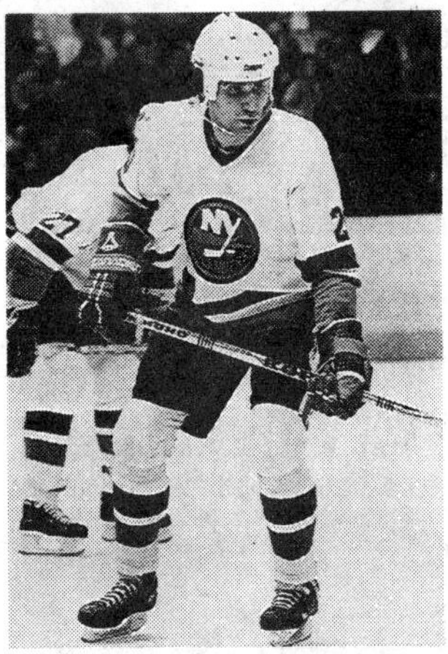

Mats Hallin

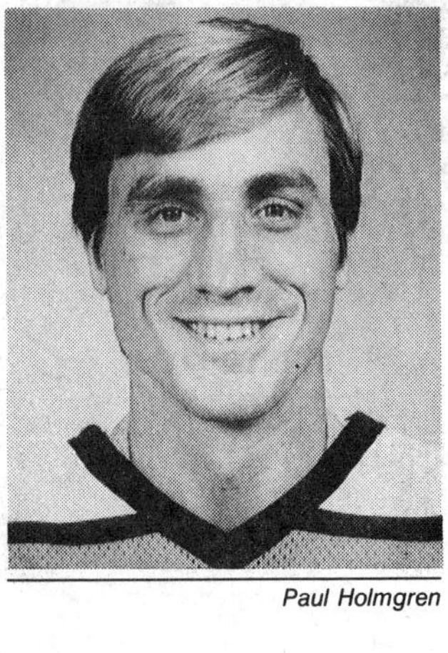

Paul Holmgren

			Regular Schedule					Playoffs					First	Last
Name	**NHL Teams**	**NHL Seasons**	**GP**	**G**	**A**	**TP**	**PIM**	**GP**	**G**	**A**	**TP**	**PIM**	**NHL Season**	**NHL Season**
Harris, Billy	NYI, L.A., Tor.	12	897	231	327	558	394	71	19	19	38	48	1972-73	1983-84
Harris, Duke	Min., Tor.	1	26	1	4	5	4	....	....	....	....	....	1967-68	1967-68
Harris, Hugh	Buf.	1	60	12	26	38	17	3	0	0	0	0	1972-73	1972-73
Harris, Ron	Det., Oak., Atl., NYR	12	476	20	91	111	484	28	4	3	7	33	1962-63	1975-76
Harris, Smokey	Bos.	1	6	3	1	4	8	....	....	....	....	....	1924-25	1924-25
Harris, Ted	Mtl., Min., Det., St.L., Phi.	12	788	30	168	198	1000	100	1	22	23	230	1963-64	1974-75
Harrison, Fran	Bos., NYR	4	194	27	24	51	53	9	1	0	1	2	1947-48	1950-51
Harrison, Jim	Bos., Tor., Chi., Edm.	8	324	67	86	153	435	13	1	1	2	43	1968-69	1979-80
Hart, Gerry	Det., NYI, Que., St.L.	15	730	29	150	179	1240	78	3	12	15	175	1968-69	1982-83
Hart, Gizzy	Det., Mtl.	3	100	6	8	14	12	8	0	1	1	0	1926-27	1932-33
Harvey, Doug	Mtl., NYR, Det., St.L.	19	1113	88	452	540	1216	137	8	64	72	152	1947-48	1968-69
Harvey, Fred	Min., Atl., K.C., Det.	6	407	90	118	208	131	14	0	2	2	8	1970-71	1976-77
Harvey, Lionel	K.C.	2	18	1	1	2	4	....	....	....	....	....	1974-75	1974-75
Hassard, Bob	Tor., Chi.	5	126	9	28	37	22	....	....	....	....	....	1949-50	1954-55
Hatoum, Ed	Det., Van.	3	47	3	6	9	25	....	....	....	....	....	1968-69	1970-71
Haworth, Alan	Buf., Wsh., Que.	8	524	189	211	400	425	42	12	16	28	28	1980-81	1987-88
Haworth, Gord	NYR	1	2	0	1	1	0	....	....	....	....	....	1952-53	1952-53
Hawryliw, Neil	NYI	1	1	0	0	0	0	....	....	....	....	....	1981-82	1981-82
Hay, Billy	Chi.	8	506	113	273	386	244	67	15	21	36	62	1959-60	1966-67
Hay, George	Chi., Det.	7	242	74	60	134	84	8	2	3	5	14	1926-27	1933-34
Hay, Jim	Det.	3	75	1	5	6	22	9	1	0	1	2	1952-53	1954-55
Hayek, Peter	Min.	1	1	0	0	0	0	....	....	....	....	....	1981-82	1981-82
Hayes, Chris	Bos.	1	....	....	....	....	....	1	0	0	0	0	1971-72	1971-72
Haynes, Paul	Mtl.M., Bos., Mtl.	11	390	61	134	195	164	25	2	8	10	13	1930-31	1940-41
Hazlett, Steve	Van.	1	1	0	0	0	0	....	....	....	....	....	1979-80	1979-80
Head, Galen	Bos.	1	1	0	0	0	0	....	....	....	....	....	1967-68	1967-68
Headley, Fern	Bos., Mtl.	1	27	1	1	2	6	5	0	0	0	0	1924-25	1924-25
Healey, Dick	Det.	1	1	0	0	0	2	....	....	....	....	....	1960-61	1960-61
Heaslip, Mark	NYR, L.A.	3	117	10	19	29	110	5	0	0	0	2	1976-77	1978-79
Heath, Randy	NYR	2	13	2	4	6	15	....	....	....	....	....	1984-85	1985-86
Hebenton, Andy	NYR, Bos.	9	630	189	202	391	83	22	6	5	11	8	1955-56	1963-64
Hedberg, Anders	NYR	7	465	172	225	397	144	58	22	24	46	31	1978-79	1984-85
Heffernan, Frank	Tor.	1	17	0	0	0	4	....	....	....	....	....	1919-20	1919-20
Heffernan, Gerry	Mtl.	3	83	33	35	68	27	11	3	3	6	8	1941-42	1943-44
Heidt, Mike	L.A.	1	6	0	1	1	7	....	....	....	....	....	1983-84	1983-84
Heindl, Bill	Min., NYR	3	18	2	1	3	0	....	....	....	....	....	1970-71	1972-73
Heinrich, Lionel	Bos.	1	35	1	1	2	33	....	....	....	....	....	1955-56	1955-56
Heiskala, Earl	Phi.	3	127	13	11	24	294	....	....	....	....	....	1968-69	1970-71
Helander, Peter	L.A.	1	7	0	1	1	0	....	....	....	....	....	1982-83	1982-83
Heller, Ott.	NYR	15	647	55	176	231	465	61	6	8	14	61	1931-32	1945-46
Helman, Harry	Ott.	3	42	1	0	1	7	5	0	0	0	0	1922-23	1924-25
Hemmerling, Tony	NYA	2	24	3	3	6	4	....	....	....	....	....	1935-36	1936-37
Henderson, Archie	Wsh., Min., Hfd.	3	23	3	1	4	92	....	....	....	....	....	1980-81	1982-83
Henderson, Murray	Bos.	8	405	24	62	86	305	41	2	3	5	23	1944-45	1951-52
Henderson, Paul	Det., Tor., Atl.	13	707	236	241	477	304	56	11	14	25	28	1962-63	1979-80
Hendrickson, John	Det.	3	5	0	0	0	4	....	....	....	....	....	1957-58	1961-62
Henning, Lorne	NYI	9	544	73	111	184	102	81	7	7	14	8	1972-73	1980-81
Henry, Camille	NYR, Chi., St.L.	14	727	279	249	528	88	47	6	12	18	7	1953-54	1969-70
Hepple, Alan	N.J.	3	3	0	0	0	7	....	....	....	....	....	1983-84	1985-86
Herberts, Jimmy	Bos., Tor., Det.	6	206	83	29	112	250	9	3	0	3	35	1924-25	1929-30
Herchenratter, Art	Det.	1	10	1	2	3	2	....	....	....	....	....	1940-41	1940-41
Hergerts, Fred	NYA	2	19	2	4	6	2	....	....	....	....	....	1934-35	1935-36
Hergesheimer, Philip	Chi., Bos.	4	125	21	41	62	19	7	0	0	0	2	1939-40	1942-43
Hergesheimer, Wally	NYR, Chi.	7	351	114	85	199	106	5	1	0	1	0	1951-52	1958-59
Heron, Red	Tor., NYA, Mtl.	4	106	21	19	40	38	16	2	2	4	55	1938-39	1941-42
Hess, Bob	St.L., Buf., Hfd.	8	329	27	95	122	178	4	1	1	2	2	1974-75	1983-84
Heximer, Orville	NYR, Bos., NYA	3	85	13	7	20	28	5	0	0	0	2	1929-30	1934-35
Hextall, Bryan Sr.	NYR	11	447	188	175	363	221	37	8	9	17	19	1936-37	1947-48
Hextall, Bryan Jr.	NYR, Pit., Atl., Det., Min.	8	549	99	161	260	738	18	0	4	4	59	1962-63	1975-76
Hextall, Dennis	NYR, L.A., Cal., Min., Det., Wsh.	13	681	153	350	503	1398	22	3	3	6	45	1968-69	1979-80
Heyliger, Vic	Chi.	2	34	2	3	5	2	....	....	....	....	....	1937-38	1943-44
Hicke, Bill	Mtl., NYR, Oak.	14	729	168	234	402	395	42	3	10	13	41	1958-59	1971-72
Hicke, Ernie	Cal., Atl., NYI, Min., L.A.	8	520	132	140	272	407	2	1	0	1	0	1970-71	1977-78
Hickey, Greg	NYR	1	1	0	0	0	0	....	....	....	....	....	1977-78	1977-78
Hickey, Pat	NYR, Col., Tor., Que., St.L.	10	646	192	212	404	351	55	5	11	16	37	1975-76	1984-85
Hicks, Doug	Min., Chi., Edm., Wsh.	9	561	37	131	168	442	....	....	....	....	....	1974-75	1982-83
Hicks, Glenn	Det.	2	108	6	12	18	127	....	....	....	....	....	1979-80	1980-81
Hicks, Hal	Mtl.M., Det.	3	110	7	2	9	72	....	....	....	....	....	1928-29	1930-31
Hicks, Wayne	Chi., Bos., Mtl., Phi., Pit.	5	115	13	23	36	22	2	0	1	1	2	1959-60	1967-68
Hidi, Andre	Wsh.	2	7	2	1	3	9	2	0	0	0	0	1983-84	1984-85
Hiemer, Ullie	N.J.	3	143	19	54	73	176	....	....	....	....	....	1984-85	1986-87
Higgins, Paul	Tor.	2	25	0	0	0	152	1	0	0	0	0	1981-82	1982-83
Hildebrand, Ike	NYR, Chi.	2	41	7	11	18	16	....	....	....	....	....	1953-54	1954-55
Hill, Brian	Hfd.	1	19	1	1	2	4	....	....	....	....	....	1979-80	1979-80
Hill, Mel	Bos., NYA, Tor.	9	323	89	109	198	128	43	12	7	19	18	1937-38	1945-46
Hiller, Dutch	NYR, Det., Bos., Mtl.	9	385	91	113	204	163	48	9	8	17	21	1937-38	1945-46
Hillman, Floyd	Bos.	1	6	0	0	0	10	....	....	....	....	....	1956-57	1956-57
Hillman, Larry	Det., Bos., Tor., Min., Mtl., Phi., L.A., Buf.	19	790	36	196	232	579	74	2	9	11	30	1954-55	1972-73
Hillman, Wayne	Chi., NYR, Min., Phi.	13	691	18	86	104	534	28	0	3	3	19	1960-61	1972-73
Hilworth, John	Det.	3	57	1	1	2	89	....	....	....	....	....	1977-78	1979-80
Himes, Normie	NYA	9	402	106	113	219	127	2	0	0	0	0	1926-27	1934-35
Hindmarch, Dave	Cgy.	4	99	21	17	38	25	10	0	0	0	6	1981-83	1981-84
Hinse, Andre	Tor.	1	4	0	0	0	0	....	....	....	....	....	1967-68	1967-68
Hinton, Dan	Chi.	1	14	0	0	0	16	....	....	....	....	....	1976-77	1976-77
Hirsch, Tom	Min.	3	31	1	7	8	30	12	0	0	0	6	1983-84	1987-88
Hirschfeld, Bert	Mtl.	2	33	1	4	5	2	5	1	0	1	0	1949-50	1950-51
Hirsh, Tom	Min.	2	31	1	7	8	30	12	0	0	0	6	1983-84	1984-85
Hislop, Jamie	Que., Cgy.	5	345	75	103	178	86	28	3	2	5	11	1979-80	1983-84
Hitchman, Lionel	Ott., Bos.	12	413	28	33	61	523	40	4	1	5	77	1922-23	1933-34
Hlinka, Ivan	Van.	2	137	42	81	123	28	16	3	10	13	8	1981-82	1982-83
Hodge, Ken	Chi., Bos., NYR	13	881	328	472	800	779	97	34	47	81	120	1965-66	1977-78
Hodgson, Rick	Hfd.	1	6	0	0	0	6	1	0	0	0	0	1979-80	1979-80
Hodgson, Ted	Bos.	1	4	0	0	0	0	....	....	....	....	....	1966-67	1966-67
Hoekstra, Cecil	Mtl.	1	4	0	0	0	0	....	....	....	....	....	1959-60	1959-60
Hoekstra, Ed	Phi.	1	70	15	21	36	6	7	0	1	1	0	1967-68	1967-68
Hoene, Phi.	L.A.	3	37	2	4	6	22	....	....	....	....	....	1972-73	1974-75
Hoffinger, Vic	Chi.	2	28	0	1	1	30	....	....	....	....	....	1927-28	1928-29
Hoffman, Mike	Hfd.	3	9	1	3	4	2	....	....	....	....	....	1982-83	1985-86
Hoffmeyer, Bob	Chi., Phi., N.J.	6	198	14	52	66	325	3	0	1	1	25	1977-78	1984-85
Hogaboam, Bill	Atl., Det., Min.	8	332	80	109	189	100	2	0	0	0	0	1972-73	1979-80
Hoganson, Dale	L.A., Mtl., Que.	7	343	13	77	90	186	11	0	3	3	12	1969-70	1981-82
Holbrook, Terry	Min.	2	43	3	6	9	4	6	0	0	0	0	1972-73	1973-74
Holland, Jerry	NYR	2	37	8	4	12	6	....	....	....	....	....	1974-75	1975-76
Hollett, Frank	Tor., Ott., Bos., Det.	13	565	132	181	313	378	79	8	26	34	38	1933-34	1945-46
Hollingworth, Gord	Chi., Det.	4	163	4	14	18	201	3	0	0	0	2	1954-55	1957-58
Holmes, Bill	Mtl., NYA.	2	51	6	4	10	35	....	....	....	....	....	1925-26	1929-30
Holmes, Chuck	Det.	2	23	1	3	4	10	....	....	....	....	....	1958-59	1961-62
Holmes, Lou	Chi.	2	59	1	4	5	6	2	0	0	0	2	1931-32	1932-33
Holmes, Warren	L.A.	3	45	8	18	26	7	....	....	....	....	....	1981-82	1983-84
Holmgren, Paul	Phi., Min.	10	527	144	179	323	1684	82	19	32	51	195	1975-76	1984-85
Holota, John	Det.	2	15	2	0	2	0	....	....	....	....	....	1942-43	1945-46
Holloway, Bruce	Van.	1	2	0	0	0	0	....	....	....	....	....	1984-85	1984-85
Holst, Greg	NYR	3	11	0	0	0	0	....	....	....	....	....	1975-76	1977-78
Holt, Gary	Cal., Clev., St.L.	5	101	13	11	24	183	....	....	....	....	....	1973-74	1977-78
Holt, Randy	Chi., Clev., Van., L.A., Cgy., Wsh., Phi.	10	395	4	37	41	1438	21	2	3	5	83	1974-75	1983-84
Holway, Albert	Tor., Mtl.M., Pit.	5	117	7	2	9	48	8	0	0	0	2	1923-24	1928-29
Homenuke, Ron	Van.	1	1	0	0	0	0	....	....	....	....	....	1972-73	1972-73
Hopkins, Dean	L.A., Edm.	5	218	23	49	72	302	18	1	5	6	29	1979-80	1985-86
Hopkins, Larry	Tor., Wpg.	4	60	13	16	29	26	6	0	0	0	2	1977-78	1982-83
Horbul, Doug	K.C.	1	4	1	0	1	2	....	....	....	....	....	1974-75	1974-75
Hordy, Mike	NYI	2	11	0	0	0	7	....	....	....	....	....	1978-79	1979-80
Horeck, Pete	Chi., Det., Bos.	8	426	106	118	224	340	34	6	8	14	43	1944-45	1951-52
Horne, George	Mtl.M, Tor.	3	54	9	3	12	34	4	0	0	0	4	1925-26	1928-29
Horner, Red	Tor.	12	490	42	110	152	1264	71	7	10	17	166	1928-29	1939-40
Hornung, Larry	St.L.	2	48	2	9	11	10	11	0	2	2	2	1970-71	1971-72

Name	NHL Teams	NHL Seasons	Regular Schedule GP	G	A	TP	PIM	Playoffs GP	G	A	TP	PIM	First NHL Season	Last NHL Season
Horton, Tim	Tor., NYR, Buf., Pit.	24	1446	115	403	518	1611	126	11	39	50	183	1949-50	1973-74
Horvath, Bronco	NYR, Mtl., Bos., Chi., Tor., Min.	9	434	141	185	326	319	36	12	9	21	18	1955-56	1967-68
Hotham, Greg	Tor., Pit.	6	230	15	74	89	139	5	0	3	3	6	1979-80	1984-85
Houde, Claude	K.C.	2	59	3	6	9	40	....	....	....	....	....	1974-75	1975-76
Houle, Rejean	Mtl.	11	635	161	247	408	395	90	14	34	48	66	1969-70	1982-83
Houston, Ken	Atl., Cgy., Wsh., L.A.	9	570	161	167	328	624	35	10	9	19	66	1975-76	1983-84
Howard, Frank	Tor.	1	2	0	0	0	0	....	....	....	....	....	1936-37	1936-37
Howatt, Garry	NYI, Hfd., N.J.	12	720	112	156	268	1836	87	12	14	26	289	1972-73	1983-84
Howe, Gordie	Det., Hfd.	26	1767	801	1049	1850	1685	157	68	92	160	220	1946-47	1979-80
Howe, Marty	Hfd., Bos.	6	197	2	29	31	99	15	1	2	3	9	1979-80	1984-85
Howe, Syd	Ott., Phi., Tor., St.L., Det.	17	691	237	291	528	214	70	17	27	44	10	1929-30	1945-46
Howe, Vic	NYR	3	33	3	4	7	10	....	....	....	....	....	1950-51	1954-55
Howell, Harry	NYR, Oak., L.A.	21	1411	94	324	418	1298	38	3	3	6	32	1952-53	1972-73
Howell, Ron	NYR	2	4	0	0	0	4	....	....	....	....	....	1954-55	1955-56
Howson, Scott	NYI	2	18	5	3	8	4	....	....	....	....	....	1984-85	1985-86
House, Don	L.A.	1	33	2	5	7	6	2	0	0	0	0	1979-80	1979-80
Hoyda, Dave	Phi., Wpg.	4	132	6	17	23	299	12	0	0	0	17	1977-78	1980-81
Hrechkosy, Dave	Cal., St.L.	4	140	42	24	66	41	3	1	0	1	2	1973-74	1976-77
Hrycuik, Jim	Wsh.	1	21	5	5	10	12	....	....	....	....	....	1974-75	1974-75
Hrymnak, Steve	Chi., Det.	2	18	2	1	3	4	2	0	0	0	0	1951-52	1952-53
Hrynewich, Tim	Pit.	2	55	6	8	14	82	....	....	....	....	....	1982-83	1983-84
Huard, Rolly	Tor.	1	1	1	0	1	0	....	....	....	....	....	1930-31	1930-31
Huber, Willie	Det., NYR, Van., Phi.	10	655	104	217	321	950	33	5	5	10	35	1978-79	1987-88
Hubick, Greg	Tor., Van.	2	77	6	9	15	10	....	....	....	....	....	1975-76	1979-80
Huck, Fran	Mtl., St.L.	3	94	24	30	54	38	11	3	4	7	2	1969-70	1972-73
Hucul, Fred	Chi., St.L.	5	164	11	30	41	113	6	1	0	1	10	1950-51	1967-68
Hudson, Dave	NYI, K.C., Col.	6	409	59	124	183	89	2	1	1	2	0	1972-73	1977-78
Hudson, Lex	Pit.	1	2	0	0	0	0	2	0	0	0	0	1978-79	1978-79
Hudson, Ron	Det.	2	34	5	2	7	2	....	....	....	....	....	1937-38	1939-40
Huggins, Al	Mtl.M	1	20	1	1	2	2	....	....	....	....	....	1930-31	1930-31
Hughes, Al	NYA	2	60	6	8	14	22	....	....	....	....	....	1930-31	1931-32
Hughes, Brent	L.A., Phi., St.L., Det., K.C.	8	435	15	117	132	440	22	1	3	4	53	1967-68	1974-75
Hughes, Frank	Cal.	1	5	0	0	0	0	....	....	....	....	....	1971-72	1971-72
Hughes, Howie	L.A.	3	168	25	32	57	30	14	2	0	2	2	1967-68	1969-70
Hughes, Jack	Col.	2	46	2	5	7	104	....	....	....	....	....	1980-81	1981-82
Hughes, John	Van., Edm., NYR	3	70	2	14	16	211	7	0	1	1	16	1979-80	1980-81
Hughes, Pat	Mtl., Pit., Edm., Buf., St.L., Hfd.	10	573	130	128	258	653	71	8	25	33	77	1977-78	1986-87
Hughes, Rusty	Det.	1	40	0	1	1	48	....	....	....	....	....	1929-30	1929-30
Hull, Bobby	Chi., Wpg., Hfd.	16	1063	610	560	1170	640	119	62	67	129	102	1957-58	1979-80
Hull, Dennis	Chi., Det.	14	959	303	351	654	261	104	33	34	67	30	1964-65	1977-78
Hunt, Fred	NYA, NYR	2	59	15	14	29	6	....	....	....	....	....	1940-41	1944-45
Huras, Larry	NYR	1	1	0	0	0	0	....	....	....	....	....	1976-77	1976-77
Hurlburt, Bob	Van.	1	1	0	0	0	2	....	....	....	....	....	1974-75	1974-75
Hurley, Paul	Bos.	1	1	0	1	1	0	....	....	....	....	....	1968-69	1968-69
Hurst, Ron	Tor.	2	64	9	7	16	7	3	0	2	2	4	1955-56	1956-57
Huston, Ron	Cal.	2	79	15	31	46	8	....	....	....	....	....	1973-74	1974-75
Hutchinson, Ronald	NYR	1	9	0	0	0	0	....	....	....	....	....	1960-61	1960-61
Hutchison, Dave	L.A., Tor., Chi., N.J.	10	584	19	97	116	1550	48	2	12	14	149	1974-75	1983-84
Hutton, William	Bos., Ott., Phi.	2	64	3	2	5	8	2	0	0	0	0	1929-30	1930-31
Hyland, Harry	Mtl.W, Ott.	1	16	14	0	14	0	....	....	....	....	....	1917-18	1917-18
Hynes, Dave	Bos.	2	22	4	0	4	2	....	....	....	....	....	1973-74	1974-75

I

Name	NHL Teams	NHL Seasons	Regular Schedule GP	G	A	TP	PIM	Playoffs GP	G	A	TP	PIM	First NHL Season	Last NHL Season
Imlach, Brent	Tor.	2	3	0	0	0	2	....	....	....	....	....	1965-66	1966-67
Ingarfield, Earl	NYR, Pit., Oak., Cal.	13	746	179	226	405	239	21	9	8	17	10	1958-59	1970-71
Ingarfield, Earl Jr.	Atl., Cgy., Det.	2	39	4	4	8	22	2	0	1	1	0	1979-80	1980-81
Inglis, Bill	L.A., Buf.	3	36	1	3	4	4	11	1	2	3	4	1967-68	1970-71
Ingoldsby, Johnny	Tor.	2	29	5	1	6	15	....	....	....	....	....	1942-43	1943-44
Ingram, Frank	Bos., Chi.	4	102	24	16	40	69	11	0	1	1	2	1924-25	1931-32
Ingram, Ron	Chi., Det., NYR	3	114	5	15	20	81	2	0	0	0	0	1956-57	1964-65
Irvin, Dick	Chi.	3	94	29	23	52	76	2	2	0	2	4	1926-27	1928-29
Irvine, Ted	Bos., L.A., NYR, St.L.	11	724	154	177	331	657	83	16	24	40	115	1963-64	1976-77
Irwin, Ivan	Mtl., NYR	5	155	2	27	29	214	5	0	0	0	8	1952-53	1957-58
Isaksson, Ulf	L.A.	1	50	7	15	22	10	....	....	....	....	....	1982-83	1982-83

J

Name	NHL Teams	NHL Seasons	Regular Schedule GP	G	A	TP	PIM	Playoffs GP	G	A	TP	PIM	First NHL Season	Last NHL Season
Jackson, Art	Tor., Bos., NYA.	11	466	116	175	291	144	51	8	12	20	27	1934-35	1944-45
Jackson, Harvey	Bos.	15	636	241	234	475	437	71	18	12	30	53	1929-30	1943-44
Jackson, Don	Min., Edm., NYR	10	311	16	52	68	640	53	4	5	9	147	1977-78	1986-87
Jackson, Hal	Chi., Det.	8	222	17	34	51	208	31	1	2	3	33	1936-37	1946-47
Jackson, John	Chi.	1	48	2	5	7	38	....	....	....	....	....	1946-47	1946-47
Jackson, Lloyd	NYA	1	14	1	1	2	0	....	....	....	....	....	1936-37	1936-37
Jackson, Stan	Tor., Bos., Ott.	5	84	9	4	13	74	....	....	....	....	....	1921-22	1926-27
Jackson, Walt	NYA	3	82	16	11	27	18	....	....	....	....	....	1932-33	1934-35
Jacobs, Paul	Tor.	1	1	0	0	0	0	....	....	....	....	....	1918-19	1918-19
Jacobs, Tim	Cal.	1	46	0	10	10	35	....	....	....	....	....	1975-76	1975-76
Jalo, Risto	Edm.	1	3	0	3	3	0	....	....	....	....	....	1985-86	1985-86
Jalonen, Kari	Cgy.	1	25	9	3	12	4	5	1	0	1	0	1982-83	1982-83
James, Gerry	Tor.	5	149	14	26	40	257	15	1	0	1	8	1954-55	1959-60
James, Val	Buf., Tor.	2	11	0	0	0	30	....	....	....	....	....	1981-82	1986-87
Jamieson, Jim	NYR	1	1	0	1	1	0	....	....	....	....	....	1943-44	1943-44
Jankowski, Lou	Det., Chi.	4	127	19	18	37	15	1	0	0	0	0	1950-51	1954-55
Jarrett, Doug	Chi., NYR	13	775	38	182	220	631	99	7	16	23	82	1964-65	1976-77
Jarrett, Gary	Tor., Det., Oak., Cal.	7	341	72	92	164	131	11	3	1	4	9	1960-61	1971-72
Jarry, Pierre	NYR, Tor., Det., Min.	7	344	88	117	205	142	5	0	1	1	0	1971-72	1977-78
Jarvis, Doug	Mtl., Wsh., Hfd.	13	964	139	264	403	263	105	14	27	41	42	1975-76	1987-88
Jarvis, Jim	Pit., Phi., Tor.	3	108	17	15	32	62	....	....	....	....	....	1929-30	1936-37
Jeffrey, Larry	Det., Tor., NYR	8	368	39	62	101	293	38	4	10	14	42	1961-62	1968-69
Jenkins, Dean	L.A.	1	5	0	0	0	2	....	....	....	....	....	1983-84	1983-84
Jenkins, Roger	Tor., Chi., Mtl., Bos., Mtl.M., NYA	8	328	15	39	54	279	25	1	7	8	12	1930-31	1938-39
Jennings, Bill	Det., Bos.	5	108	32	33	65	45	20	4	4	8	6	1940-41	1944-45
Jensen, David H.	Min.	3	18	0	2	2	11	....	....	....	....	....	1983-84	1985-86
Jensen, Steve	Min., L.A.	7	439	113	107	220	318	12	0	3	3	9	1975-76	1981-82
Jeremiah, Ed	NYA, Bos.	1	15	0	1	1	0	....	....	....	....	....	1931-32	1931-32
Jerwa, Frank	Bos., St.L.	4	91	11	16	27	53	....	....	....	....	....	1931-32	1934-35
Jerwa, Joe	NYR, Bos., NYA	7	233	29	58	87	315	17	2	3	5	20	1930-31	1938-39
Jirik, Jaroslav	St.L.	1	3	0	0	0	0	....	....	....	....	....	1969-70	1969-70
Joanette, Rosario	Mtl.	1	2	0	1	1	4	....	....	....	....	....	1944-45	1944-45
Jodzio, Rick	Col., Clev.	1	70	2	8	10	71	....	....	....	....	....	1977-78	1977-78
Johansen, Trevor	Tor., Col., L.A.	5	286	11	46	57	282	13	0	3	3	21	1977-78	1981-82
Johansson, Bjorn	Clev.	2	15	1	1	2	10	....	....	....	....	....	1976-77	1977-78
Johannson, John	N.J.	1	5	0	0	0	0	....	....	....	....	....	1983-84	1983-84
Johns, Don	NYR, Mtl., Min.	6	153	2	21	23	76	....	....	....	....	....	1960-61	1967-68
Johnson, Al	Mtl., Det.	4	105	21	28	49	30	11	2	2	4	6	1956-57	1962-63
Johnson, Brian	Det.	1	3	0	0	0	5	....	....	....	....	....	1983-84	1983-84
Johnson, Ivan	NYR, NYA	12	435	38	48	86	808	60	5	2	7	161	1926-27	1937-38
Johnson, Danny	Tor., Van., Det.	3	121	18	19	37	24	....	....	....	....	....	1969-70	1971-72
Johnson, Earl	Det.	1	1	0	0	0	0	....	....	....	....	....	1953-54	1953-54
Johnson, Jim	NYR, Phi., L.A.	8	302	75	111	186	73	7	0	2	2	2	1964-65	1971-72
Johnson, Norm	Bos., Chi.	3	61	5	20	25	41	14	4	0	4	6	1957-58	1959-60
Johnson, Terry	Que., St.L., Cgy., Tor.	9	285	3	24	27	580	38	0	4	4	118	1979-80	1987-88
Johnson, Tom	Mtl., Bos.	16	978	51	213	264	960	111	8	15	23	109	1947-48	1964-65
Johnson, Virgil	Chi.	3	75	2	9	11	27	19	0	3	3	4	1937-38	1944-45
Johnson, William	Tor.	1	1	0	0	0	0	....	....	....	....	....	1949-50	1949-50
Johnston, Bernie	Hfd.	2	57	12	24	36	44	3	0	1	1	0	1979-80	1980-81
Johnston, George	Chi.	4	58	20	12	32	2	....	....	....	....	....	1941-42	1946-47
Johnston, Jay	Wsh.	2	8	0	0	0	13	....	....	....	....	....	1980-81	1981-82
Johnston, Joey	Min., Cal., Chi.	6	332	85	106	191	320	....	....	....	....	....	1968-69	1975-76
Johnston, Larry	L.A., Det., K.C., Col.	7	320	9	64	73	580	....	....	....	....	....	1967-68	1976-77
Johnston, Marshall	Min., Cal.	7	251	14	52	66	58	6	0	0	0	2	1967-68	1973-74
Johnston, Randy	NYI	1	4	0	0	0	4	....	....	....	....	....	1979-80	1979-80
Johnstone, Eddie	NYR, Det.	10	426	122	136	258	375	55	13	10	23	83	1975-76	1986-87
Johnstone, Ross	Tor.	2	42	5	4	9	14	3	0	0	0	0	1943-44	1944-45
Joliat, Aurel	Mtl.	16	654	270	190	460	757	54	14	19	33	89	1922-23	1937-38

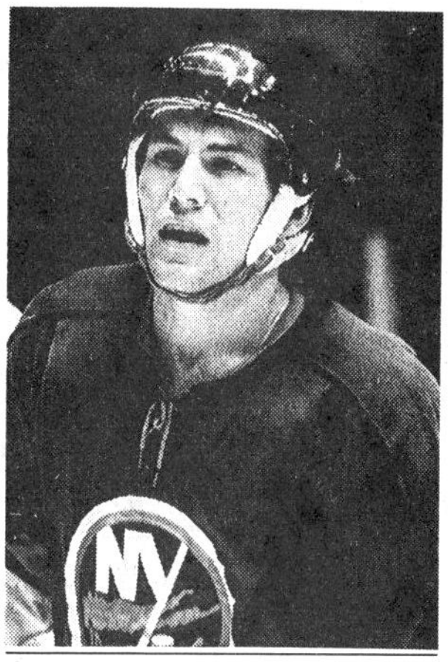

Gary Howatt

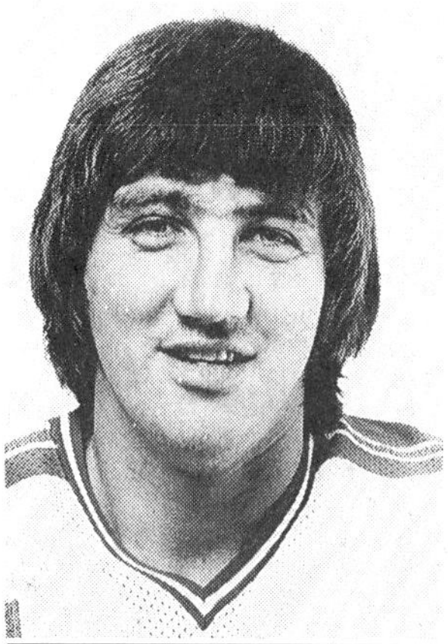

Ed Johnstone

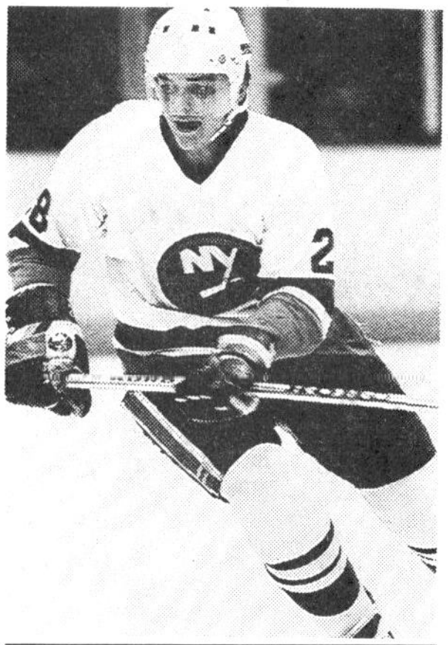

Anders Kallur

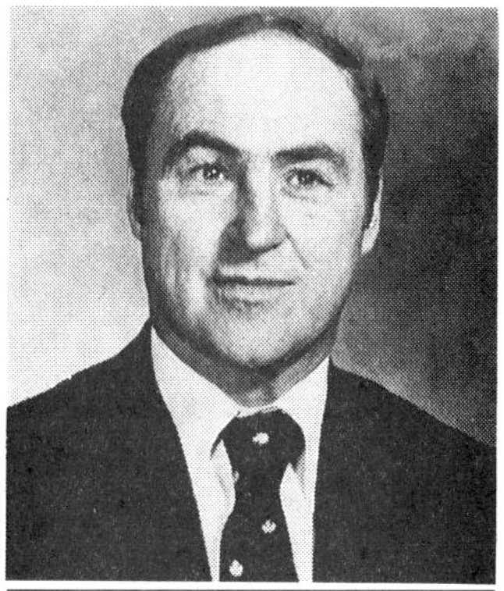

Red Kelly

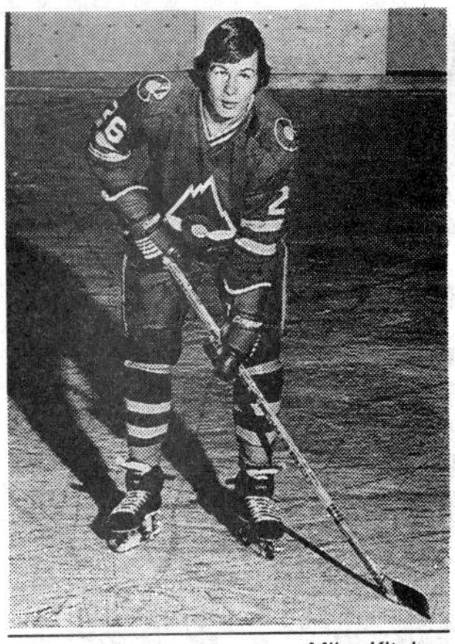

Mike Kitchen

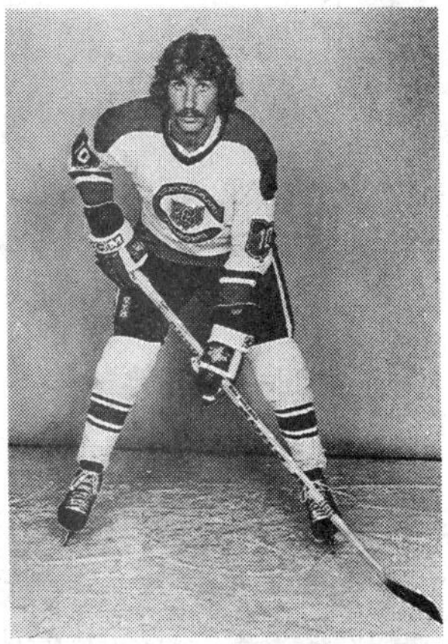

Ralph Klassen

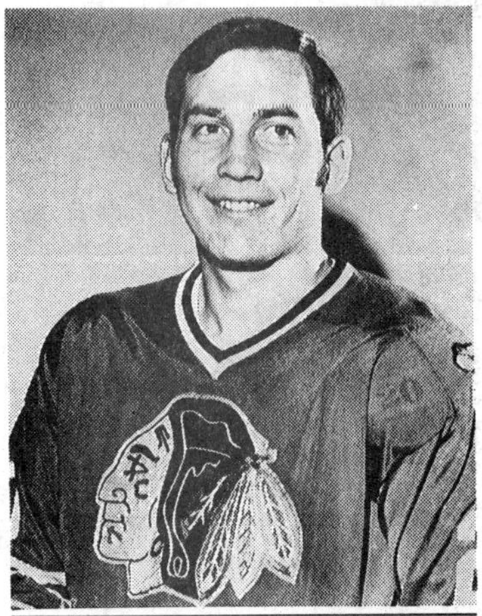

Cliff Koroll

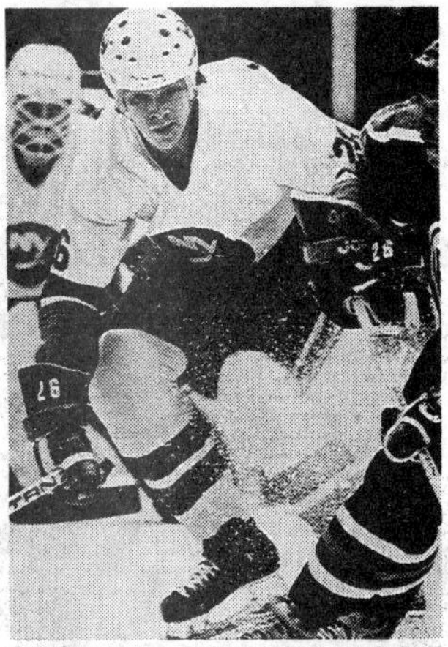

Dave Langevin

			Regular Schedule					Playoffs					First	Last
Name	NHL Teams	NHL Seasons	GP	G	A	TP	PIM	GP	G	A	TP	PIM	NHL Season	NHL Season
Joliat, Bobby	Mtl.	1	1	0	0	0	0	....	....	....	....	....	1924-25	1924-25
Joly, Greg	Wsh., Det.	9	365	21	76	97	250	5	0	0	0	8	1974-75	1982-83
Joly, Yvan	Mtl.	3	2	0	0	0	0	10	0	0	0	0	1979-80	1982-83
Jonathon, Stan	Bos., Pit.	8	411	91	110	201	751	63	8	4	12	137	1975-76	1982-83
Jones, Bob	NYR	1	2	0	0	0	0	....	....	....	....	....	1968-69	1968-69
Jones, Buck	Det., Tor.	4	50	2	2	4	36	12	0	1	1	18	1938-39	1942-43
Jones, Jim	Cal.	1	2	0	0	0	0	....	....	....	....	....	1971-72	1971-72
Jones, Jimmy	Tor.	3	148	13	18	31	68	19	1	5	6	11	1977-78	1979-80
Jones, Ron	Bos., Pit., Wsh.	5	54	1	4	5	31	....	....	....	....	....	1971-72	1975-76
Joyal, Eddie	Det., Tor., L.A., Phi.	9	466	128	134	262	103	50	11	8	19	18	1962-63	1971-72
Juckes, Bing	NYR	2	16	2	1	3	6	....	....	....	....	....	1947-48	1949-50
Jutila, Timo	Buf.	1	10	1	5	6	13	....	....	....	....	....	1984-85	1984-85
Juzda, Bill	NYR, Tor.	9	393	14	54	68	398	42	0	3	3	46	1940-41	1951-52

K

Kabel, Bob	NYR	2	48	5	13	18	34	....	....	....	....	....	1959-60	1960-61
Kachur, Ed	Chi.	2	96	10	14	24	35	....	....	....	....	....	1956-57	1957-58
Kaiser, Vern	Mtl.	1	50	7	5	12	33	2	0	0	0	0	1950-51	1950-51
Kalbfleish, Jeff	Ott., St.L., NYA, Bos.	4	36	0	4	4	32	5	0	0	0	2	1933-34	1936-37
Kaleta, Alex	Chi., NYR	7	387	92	121	213	190	17	1	6	7	2	1941-42	1950-51
Kallur, Anders	NYI	6	383	101	110	211	149	78	12	23	35	32	1979-80	1984-85
Kaminsky, Max	Ott., St.L., Bos., Mtl.M.	4	130	22	34	56	38	4	0	0	0	0	1933-34	1936-37
Kampman, Bingo	Tor.	5	189	14	30	44	287	47	1	4	5	38	1937-38	1941-42
Kane, Frank	Det.	1	2	0	0	0	0	....	....	....	....	....	1943-44	1943-44
Kannegiesser, Gord	St.L.	2	23	0	1	1	15	....	....	....	....	....	1967-68	1971-72
Kannegiesser, Sheldon	Pit., NYR, L.A., Van.	8	366	14	67	81	202	18	0	2	2	10	1970-71	1977-78
Karlander, Al	Det.	4	212	36	56	92	70	4	0	1	1	0	1969-70	1972-73
Kaszycki, Mike	NYI, Wsh., Tor.	5	226	42	80	122	108	19	2	6	8	10	1977-78	1982-83
Kea, Ed	Atl., St.L.	10	583	30	145	175	508	32	2	4	6	39	1973-74	1982-83
Kearns, Dennis	Van.	10	677	31	290	321	386	11	1	2	3	8	1971-72	1980-81
Keating, Jack	NYA	2	35	5	5	10	17	....	....	....	....	....	1931-32	1932-33
Keating, John	Det.	2	11	2	1	3	4	....	....	....	....	....	1938-39	1939-40
Keating, Mike	NYR	1	1	0	0	0	0	....	....	....	....	....	1977-78	1977-78
Keats, Duke	Det., Chi.	3	80	3	19	49	113	....	....	....	....	....	1926-27	1928-29
Keeling, Butch	Tor., NYR	12	528	157	63	220	331	47	11	11	22	32	1926-27	1937-38
Keenan, Larry	Tor., St.L., Buf., Phi.	6	233	38	64	102	28	46	15	16	31	12	1961-62	1971-72
Kehoe, Rick	Tor., Pit.	14	906	371	396	767	120	39	4	17	21	4	1971-72	1984-85
Keller, Ralph	NYR	1	3	1	0	1	6	....	....	....	....	....	1962-63	1962-63
Kellgren, Christer	Col.	1	5	0	0	0	0	....	....	....	....	....	1981-82	1981-82
Kelly, Bob	St.L., Pit., Chi.	6	425	87	109	196	687	23	6	3	9	40	1973-74	1978-79
Kelly, Bob	Phi., Wsh.	12	837	154	208	362	1454	101	9	14	23	172	1970-71	1981-82
Kelly, Dave	Det.	1	16	2	0	2	4	....	....	....	....	....	1976-77	1976-77
Kelly, John Paul	L.A.	7	400	54	70	124	366	18	1	1	2	41	1979-80	1985-86
Kelly, Reg	Tor., Chi., NYA	8	289	74	53	127	105	39	7	6	13	10	1934-35	1941-42
Kelly, Pete	St.L., Det., NYA	7	180	21	38	59	68	19	3	1	4	8	1934-35	1941-42
Kelly, Red	Det., Tor.	20	1316	281	542	823	327	164	33	59	92	51	1947-48	1966-67
Kemp, Kevin	Hfd.	1	3	0	0	0	4	....	....	....	....	....	1980-81	1980-81
Kemp, Stan	Tor.	1	1	0	0	0	2	....	....	....	....	....	1948-49	1948-49
Kendall, William	Chi., Tor.	5	132	16	10	26	28	5	0	0	0	0	1933-34	1937-38
Kennedy, Forbes	Chi., Det., Bos., Phi., Tor.	11	603	70	108	178	988	12	2	4	6	64	1956-57	1968-69
Kennedy, Ted	Tor.	14	696	231	329	560	432	78	29	31	60	32	1942-43	1956-57
Kenny, Eddie	NYR, Chi.	2	11	0	0	0	18	....	....	....	....	....	1930-31	1934-35
Keon, Dave	Tor., Hfd.	18	1296	396	590	986	117	92	32	36	68	6	1960-61	1981-82
Kerr, Reg	Cle., Chi., Edm.	6	263	66	94	160	169	7	1	0	1	7	1977-78	1983-84
Kessell, Rick	Pit., Cal.	5	135	4	24	28	6	....	....	....	....	....	1969-70	1973-74
Ketola, Veli-Pekka	Col.	1	44	9	5	14	4	....	....	....	....	....	1981-82	1981-82
Ketter, Kerry	Atl.	1	41	0	2	2	58	....	....	....	....	....	1972-73	1972-73
Kiessling, Udo	Min.	1	1	0	0	0	2	....	....	....	....	....	1981-82	1981-82
Kilrea, Brian	Det., L.A.	2	26	3	5	8	12	....	....	....	....	....	1957-58	1967-68
Kilrea, Hec	Ott., Det., Tor.	15	633	167	129	296	438	48	8	7	15	18	1925-26	1939-40
Kilrea, Ken	Det.	5	88	16	23	39	8	10	2	2	4	4	1938-39	1943-44
Kilrea, Wally	Ott., Phi., NYA, Mtl.M., Det.	9	315	35	58	93	87	25	2	4	6	6	1929-30	1937-38
Kindrachuk, Orest	Phi., Pit., Wsh.	10	508	118	261	379	648	76	20	20	40	53	1972-73	1981-82
King, Frank	Mtl.	1	10	1	0	1	2	....	....	....	....	....	1950-51	1950-51
King, Wayne	Cal.	3	73	5	18	23	34	....	....	....	....	....	1973-74	1975-76
Kinsella, Brian	Wsh.	2	10	0	1	1	0	....	....	....	....	....	1975-76	1976-77
Kinsella, Ray	Ott.	1	14	0	0	0	0	....	....	....	....	....	1930-31	1930-31
Kirk, Bobby	NYR	1	39	4	8	12	14	....	....	....	....	....	1937-38	1937-38
Kirkpatrick, Bob	NYR	1	49	12	12	24	6	....	....	....	....	....	1942-43	1942-43
Kirton, Mark	Van., Det., Tor.	6	266	57	56	113	121	4	1	2	3	7	1979-80	1984-85
Kitchen, Bill	Mtl., Tor.	4	41	1	4	5	40	3	0	1	1	0	1981-82	1984-85
Kitchen, Hobie	Mtl.M., Det.	2	47	5	4	9	58	....	....	....	....	....	1925-26	1926-27
Kitchen, Mike	Col., N.J.	8	474	12	62	74	370	2	0	0	0	2	1976-77	1983-84
Klassen, Ralph	Cal., Clev., Col., St.L.	9	497	52	93	145	120	26	4	2	6	12	1975-76	1983-84
Klein, Jim	Bos., NYA	8	169	30	24	54	68	5	0	0	0	2	1928-29	1937-38
Klingbeil, Ike	Chi.	1	5	1	2	3	2	....	....	....	....	....	1936-37	1936-37
Klukay, Joe	Tor., Bos.	10	566	109	127	236	189	71	13	10	23	23	1946-47	1955-56
Knibbs, Bill	Bos.	1	53	7	10	17	4	....	....	....	....	....	1964-65	1964-65
Knott, Bill	NYA	1	14	3	1	4	9	....	....	....	....	....	1941-42	1941-42
Knox, Bill	Tor.	1	1	0	0	0	0	....	....	....	....	....	1954-55	1954-55
Komadoski, Neil	L.A., St.L.	8	502	16	76	92	632	23	0	2	2	47	1972-73	1979-80
Konik, George	Pit.	1	52	7	8	15	26	....	....	....	....	....	1967-68	1967-68
Kopak, Russ	Bos.	1	24	7	9	16	0	....	....	....	....	....	1943-44	1943-44
Korab, Jerry	Chi., Van., Buf., L.A.	15	975	114	341	455	1629	93	8	18	26	201	1970-71	1984-85
Korney, Mike	Det., NYR	4	77	9	10	19	59	....	....	....	....	....	1973-74	1978-79
Koroll, Cliff	Chi.	11	814	208	254	462	376	85	19	29	48	67	1969-70	1979-80
Kortko, Roger	NYI	2	79	7	17	24	28	10	0	3	3	17	1984-85	1985-86
Kostynski, Doug	Bos.	2	15	3	1	4	4	....	....	....	....	....	1983-84	1984-85
Kotanen, Dick	Det., NYR	2	2	0	1	1	0	....	....	....	....	....	1948-49	1950-51
Kowal, Joe	Buf.	2	22	0	5	5	13	2	0	0	0	0	1976-77	1977-78
Kozak, Don	L.A., Van.	7	437	96	86	182	480	29	7	2	9	69	1972-73	1978-79
Kozak, Les	Tor.	1	12	1	0	1	2	....	....	....	....	....	1961-62	1961-62
Kraftcheck, Stephen	Bos., NYR, Tor.	4	157	11	18	29	83	6	0	0	0	7	1950-51	1958-59
Krake, Skip	Bos., L.A., Buf.	7	249	23	40	63	182	10	1	0	1	17	1963-64	1970-71
Krol, Joe	NYR, NYA	3	26	10	4	14	8	....	....	....	....	....	1936-37	1941-42
Krook, Kevin	Col.	1	3	0	0	0	2	....	....	....	....	....	1978-79	1978-79
Krulicki, Jim	NYR, Det.	1	41	0	3	3	6	....	....	....	....	....	1970-71	1970-71
Kryskow, Dave	Chi., Wsh., Det., Atl.	4	231	33	56	89	174	12	2	0	2	4	1972-73	1975-76
Kryznowski, Edward	Bos., Chi.	5	237	15	22	37	65	18	0	1	1	4	1948-49	1952-53
Kuhn, Gord	NYA	1	12	1	1	2	4	....	....	....	....	....	1932-33	1932-33
Kukulowicz, Adolph	NYR	2	4	1	0	1	0	....	....	....	....	....	1952-53	1953-54
Kullman, Arnie	Bos.	2	13	0	1	1	11	....	....	....	....	....	1947-48	1949-50
Kullman, Eddie	NYR	6	343	56	70	126	298	6	1	0	1	2	1947-48	1953-54
Kuntz, Alan	NYR	2	45	10	12	22	12	6	1	0	1	2	1941-42	1945-46
Kuntz, Murray	St.L.	1	7	1	2	3	0	....	....	....	....	....	1974-75	1974-75
Kurtenbach, Orland	NYR, Bos., Tor., Van.	13	639	119	213	332	628	19	2	4	6	70	1960-61	1973-74
Kuryluk, Mervin	Chi.	1	2	0	0	0	0	....	....	....	....	....	1961-62	1961-62
Kuzyk, Ken	Clev.	2	41	5	9	14	8	....	....	....	....	....	1976-77	1977-78
Kwong, King	NYR	1	1	0	0	0	0	....	....	....	....	....	1947-48	1947-48
Kyle, Bill	NYR	2	3	0	3	3	0	....	....	....	....	....	1949-50	1950-51
Kyle, Gus	NYR, Bos.	3	203	6	20	26	362	14	1	2	3	34	1949-50	1951-52

L

Labadie, Mike	NYR	1	3	0	0	0	0	....	....	....	....	....	1952-53	1952-53
Labatte, Neil	St.L.	2	26	0	2	2	19	....	....	....	....	....	1978-79	1981-82
L'abbe, Moe	Chi.	1	5	0	1	1	0	....	....	....	....	....	1972-73	1972-73
Labine, Leo	Bos., Det.	11	643	128	193	321	730	60	11	12	23	82	1951-52	1961-62
Labossierre, Gord	NYR, L.A., Min.	6	215	44	62	106	75	10	2	3	5	28	1963-64	1971-72
Labovitch, Max	NYR	1	5	0	0	0	4	....	....	....	....	....	1943-44	1943-44
Labraaten, Dan	Det., Cgy.	4	268	71	73	144	47	5	1	0	1	4	1978-79	1981-82
Labre, Yvon	Pit., Wsh.	9	317	14	87	101	788	....	....	....	....	....	1970-71	1980-81
Labrie, Guy	Bos., NYR	2	42	4	9	13	16	....	....	....	....	....	1943-44	1944-45
Lach, Elmer	Mtl.	14	664	215	408	623	478	76	19	45	64	36	1940-41	1953-54
Lachance, Earl	Mtl.	1	1	0	0	0	0	....	....	....	....	....	1926-27	1926-27

Name	NHL Teams	NHL Seasons	Regular Schedule					Playoffs					First NHL Season	Last NHL Season
			GP	G	A	TP	PIM	GP	G	A	TP	PIM		
Lachance, Michel	Col.	1	21	0	4	4	22	....	....	....	....	....	1978-79	1978-79
Lacombe, Francois	Oak., Buf., Que.	4	78	2	17	19	54	3	1	0	1	0	1968-69	1979-80
Lacroix, Andre	Phi., Chi., Hfd.	6	325	79	119	198	44	16	2	5	7	0	1967-68	1979-80
Lacroix, Pierre	Que., Hfd.	4	274	24	108	132	197	8	0	2	2	10	1979-80	1982-83
Lafleur, Rene	Mtl.	1	0	0	0	0	0	....	....	....	....	....	1924-25	1924-25
Laforce, Ernie	Mtl.	1	0	0	0	0	0	....	....	....	....	....	1942-43	1942-43
LaForest, Bob	L.A.	1	5	1	0	1	2	....	....	....	....	....	1983-84	1983-84
Laforge, Claude	Mtl., Det., Phi.	8	192	24	33	57	82	5	1	2	3	15	1967-68	1967-68
Laframboise, Pete	Cal., Wsh., Pit.	4	227	33	55	88	70	9	1	0	1	0	1971-72	1974-75
Lafrance, Adie	Mtl.	1	3	0	0	0	2	2	0	0	0	0	1933-34	1933-34
Lafrance, Leo	Mtl., Chi.	2	33	2	0	2	6	....	....	....	....	....	1926-27	1927-28
Lafreniere, Roger	Det., St.L.	2	13	0	0	0	4	....	....	....	....	....	1962-63	1972-73
Lagace, Jean-Guy	Pit., Buf., K.C.	6	187	9	39	48	251	....	....	....	....	....	1968-69	1975-76
Lagace, Michel	Pit.	1	17	0	1	1	14	....	....	....	....	....	1968-69	1968-69
Laird, Robbie	Min.	1	1	0	0	0	0	....	....	....	....	....	1979-80	1979-80
Lajeunesse, Serge	Det., Phi.	5	103	1	4	5	103	7	1	2	3	4	1970-71	1974-75
Lalande, Hec	Chi., Det.	4	151	21	39	60	120	....	....	....	....	....	1953-54	1957-58
Lalonde, Bobby	Van., Atl., Bos., Cgy.	11	641	124	210	334	298	16	4	2	6	6	1971-72	1981-82
Lalonde, Edouard	Mtl., NYA	6	99	124	27	154	122	12	22	1	23	0	1917-18	1926-27
Lalonde, Ron	Pit., Wsh.	7	397	45	78	123	106	....	....	....	....	....	1972-73	1978-79
Lamb, Joe	Mtl.M., Ott., NYA, Bos., Mtl., St.L., Det.	11	444	108	101	209	601	18	1	1	2	51	1927-28	1937-38
Lambert, Yvon	Mtl., Buf.	10	683	206	273	479	340	90	27	22	49	67	1972-73	1981-82
Lamby, Dick	St.L.	3	22	0	5	5	22	....	....	....	....	....	1978-79	1980-81
Lamirande, Jean-Paul	NYR, Mtl.	4	49	5	5	10	26	8	0	0	0	4	1946-47	1954-55
Lamoureux, Leo	Mtl.	6	235	19	79	98	145	28	1	6	7	16	1941-42	1946-47
Lampman, Mike	St.L., Van., Wsh.	4	96	17	20	37	34	....	....	....	....	....	1972-73	1976-77
Lancien, Jack	NYR	4	63	1	5	6	35	6	0	1	1	2	1946-47	1950-51
Landon, Larry	Mtl., Tor.	2	9	0	0	0	2	....	....	....	....	....	1983-84	1984-85
Lane, Gord	Wsh., NYI	10	539	19	94	113	1228	75	3	14	17	214	1975-76	1984-85
Lane, Myles	NYR, Bos.	3	60	4	1	5	41	10	0	0	0	0	1928-29	1933-34
Langdon, Steve	Bos.	3	7	0	1	1	2	4	0	0	0	2	1974-75	1977-78
Langelle, Pete	Tor.	4	137	22	51	73	11	41	5	9	14	4	1938-39	1941-42
Langevin, Chris	Buf.	2	22	3	1	4	22	....	....	....	....	....	1983-84	1985-86
Langevin, Dave	NYI, Min., L.A.	8	513	12	107	119	530	87	2	15	17	106	1979-80	1986-87
Langlais, Joseph	Min.	2	25	4	4	8	10	....	....	....	....	....	1973-74	1974-75
Langlois, Al	Mtl., NYR, Det., Bos.	9	448	21	91	112	488	53	1	5	6	60	1957-58	1965-66
Langlois, Charlie	Ham., NYA., Pit., Mtl.	4	151	22	3	25	201	2	0	0	0	0	1924-25	1927-28
Lanyon, Ted	Pit.	1	5	0	0	0	4	....	....	....	....	....	1967-68	1967-68
Laperriere, Jacques	Mtl.	12	691	40	242	282	674	88	9	22	31	101	1962-63	1973-74
Lapointe, Guy	Mtl., St.L., Bos.	16	884	171	451	622	893	123	26	44	70	138	1968-69	1983-84
Lapointe, Rick	Det., Phi., St.L., Que., L.A.	11	664	44	176	220	831	46	2	7	9	64	1975-76	1985-86
Laprade, Edgar	NYR	10	501	108	172	280	42	18	4	9	13	4	1945-46	1954-55
LaPrairie, Ben	Chi.	1	7	0	0	0	0	....	....	....	....	....	1936-37	1936-37
Lariviere, Garry	Que., Edm.	4	219	6	57	63	167	14	0	5	5	8	1979-80	1982-83
Larmer, Jeff	Col., N.J., Chi.	5	158	37	51	88	57	5	1	0	1	2	1981-82	1985-86
Larochelle, Wildor	Mtl., Chi.	12	474	92	74	166	211	34	6	4	10	24	1925-26	1936-37
Larose, Charles	Bos.	1	6	0	0	0	0	....	....	....	....	....	1925-26	1925-26
Larose, Claude	Mtl., Min., St.L.	16	943	226	257	483	887	97	14	18	32	143	1962-63	1977-78
Larose, Claude	NYR	2	25	4	7	11	2	2	0	0	0	0	1979-80	1981-82
Larouche, Pierre	Pit., Mtl., Hfd., NYR	14	812	395	427	822	237	64	20	34	54	16	1974-75	1987-88
Larson, Norman	NYA., NYR	3	89	25	18	43	12	....	....	....	....	....	1940-41	1946-47
Latreille, Phi.	NYR	1	4	0	0	0	2	....	....	....	....	....	1960-61	1960-61
Lauder, Marty	Bos.	1	3	0	0	0	2	....	....	....	....	....	1927-28	1927-28
Laughton, Mike	Oak., Cal.	4	189	39	48	87	101	11	2	4	6	0	1967-68	1970-71
Laurence, Red	Atl., St.L.	2	79	15	22	37	14	....	....	....	....	....	1978-79	1979-80
LaVallee, Kevin	Cgy., L.A., St.L., Pit.	7	366	110	125	235	85	32	5	8	13	24	1980-81	1986-87
Laven, Mike	Wpg.	1	4	0	1	1	0	....	....	....	....	....	1983-84	1983-84
Lavender, Brian	St.L., NYI, Det., Cal.	4	184	16	26	42	174	3	0	0	0	2	1971-72	1974-75
Laviolette, Jack	Mtl.	1	18	2	....	2	....	2	0	....	0	....	1917-18	1917-18
Lawson, Danny	Det., Min., Buf.	5	219	28	29	57	61	16	0	1	1	2	1967-68	1971-72
Laycoe, Hal	NYR, Mtl., Bos.	11	531	25	77	102	292	40	2	5	7	39	1945-46	1955-56
Leach, Larry	Bos.	3	126	13	29	42	91	7	1	1	2	8	1958-59	1961-62
Leach, Reggie	Bos., Cal., Phi., Det.	13	934	381	285	666	387	94	47	22	69	22	1970-71	1982-83
Leavins, Jim	Det., NYR	2	41	2	12	14	30	....	....	....	....	....	1985-86	1986-87
LeBlanc, Fern	Det.	3	34	5	6	11	0	....	....	....	....	....	1976-77	1978-79
LeBlanc, J.P.	Chi., Det.	5	153	14	30	44	87	2	0	0	0	0	1968-69	1978-79
LeBrun, Al	NYR	2	6	0	2	2	4	....	....	....	....	....	1960-61	1965-66
Lecaine, Bill	Pit.	1	4	0	0	0	0	....	....	....	....	....	1968-69	1968-69
Leclair, Jackie	Mtl.,	3	160	20	40	60	56	20	6	0	7	6	1954-55	1956-57
Leclerc, Rene	Det.	2	87	10	11	21	105	....	....	....	....	....	1968-69	1970-71
Lecuyer, Doug	Chi., Wpg., Pit.	4	126	11	31	42	178	7	4	0	4	15	1978-79	1982-83
Ledingham, Walt	Chi., NYI	3	15	0	2	2	4	....	....	....	....	....	1972-73	1976-77
LeDuc, Albert	Mtl., Ott., NYR	10	383	57	35	92	614	31	5	6	11	32	1925-26	1934-35
LeDuc, Rich	Bos., Que.	4	130	28	38	66	55	5	0	0	0	9	1972-73	1980-81
Lee, Bobby	Mtl.	1	1	0	0	0	0	....	....	....	....	....	1942-43	1942-43
Lee, Edward	Que.	1	2	0	0	0	5	....	....	....	....	....	1984-85	1984-85
Lee, Peter	Pit.	6	431	114	131	245	257	19	0	8	8	4	1977-78	1982-83
Lefley, Bryan	N.Y.I., K.C., Col.	5	228	7	29	36	101	2	0	0	0	0	1972-73	1977-78
Lefley, Chuck	Mtl., St.L.	9	407	128	164	292	137	29	5	8	13	10	1970-71	1980-81
Leger, Roger	NYR, Mtl.	5	187	18	53	71	71	20	0	7	7	14	1943-44	1949-50
Legge, Barry	Que., Wpg.	3	107	1	11	12	144	....	....	....	....	....	1979-80	1981-82
Legge, Randy	NYR	1	12	0	2	2	2	....	....	....	....	....	1972-80	1972-73
Lehtonen, Antero	Wsh.	1	65	9	12	21	14	....	....	....	....	....	1979-80	1979-80
Lehvonen, Henri	K.C.	1	4	0	0	0	0	....	....	....	....	....	1974-75	1974-75
Leier, Edward	Chi.	2	16	2	1	3	2	....	....	....	....	....	1949-50	1950-51
Leinonen, Mikko	NYR, Wsh.	4	162	31	78	109	71	20	2	11	13	28	1981-82	1984-85
Leiter, Bobby	Bos., Pit., Atl.	10	447	98	126	224	144	8	3	0	3	2	1962-63	1975-76
Lemaire, Jacques	Mtl.	12	853	366	469	835	217	145	61	78	139	63	1967-68	1978-79
Lemelin, Roger	K.C.	2	19	0	1	1	6	....	....	....	....	....	1974-75	1975-76
Lemieux, Jacques	L.A.	2	91	11	32	43	76	1	0	0	0	0	1967-68	1968-69
Lemieux, Jean	L.A., Atl., Wsh.	6	204	23	63	86	39	3	1	1	2	0	1969-70	1977-78
Lemieux, Real	Det., L.A., NYR, Buf.	7	381	40	75	115	184	18	2	4	6	10	1966-67	1973-74
Lemieux, Richard	Van., St.L., K.C., Atl.	5	274	39	82	121	132	2	0	0	0	0	1971-72	1975-76
Lepine, Hec	Mtl.	1	33	5	2	7	2	....	....	....	....	....	1925-26	1925-26
Lepine, Pit	Mtl.	13	526	143	98	241	392	41	7	5	12	26	1925-26	1937-38
Leroux, Gaston	Mtl.	1	2	0	0	0	0	....	....	....	....	....	1935-36	1935-36
Lesieur, Art	Mtl., Chi.	4	100	4	2	6	50	14	0	0	0	4	1928-29	1935-36
Lesuk, Bill	Bos., Phi., L.A., Wsh., Wpg.	8	388	44	63	107	368	9	1	0	1	12	1968-69	1979-78
Leswick, Jack	Chi.	1	47	1	7	8	16	....	....	....	....	....	1933-34	1933-34
Leswick, Peter	NYA, Bos.	2	3	1	0	1	0	....	....	....	....	....	1936-37	1944-45
Leswick, Tony	NYR, Det., Chi.	12	740	165	159	324	900	59	13	10	23	91	1945-46	1957-58
Levandoski, Joseph	NYR	1	8	1	1	2	0	....	....	....	....	....	1946-47	1946-47
Leveille, Norm	Bos.	2	75	17	25	42	49	....	....	....	....	....	1981-82	1982-83
Lever, Don	Van., Atl., Cgy., Col., N.J., Buf.	15	1020	313	367	680	593	30	7	10	17	26	1972-73	1986-87
Levie, Craig	Wpg., Min., Van., St.L.	6	183	22	53	75	177	16	2	3	5	32	1981-82	1986-87
Levinsky, Alex	Tor., Chi., NYR	9	367	23	56	79	287	34	2	1	3	2	1930-31	1938-39
Levo, Tapio	Col., N.J.,	2	107	16	53	69	36	....	....	....	....	....	1981-82	1982-83
Lewicki, Danny	Tor., NYR, Chi.	9	461	105	135	240	177	28	0	4	4	8	1950-51	1958-59
Lewis, Bob	NYR	1	8	0	0	0	0	....	....	....	....	....	1975-76	1975-76
Lewis, Dave	NYI, L.A., N.J., Det.	15	1008	36	187	223	953	91	1	20	21	143	1973-74	1987-88
Lewis, Douglas	Mtl..	1	3	0	0	0	0	....	....	....	....	....	1946-47	1946-47
Lewis, Herbie	Det.	11	483	148	161	309	248	38	13	10	23	6	1928-29	1938-39
Ley, Rick	Tor., Hfd.	6	310	12	72	84	528	14	0	2	2	20	1968-69	1980-81
Libett, Nick	Det., K.C., Pit.	14	982	237	268	505	472	16	6	2	8	2	1967-68	1980-81
Licari, Anthony	Det.	1	9	0	1	1	0	....	....	....	....	....	1946-47	1946-47
Liddington, Bob	Tor.	1	11	0	1	1	2	....	....	....	....	....	1970-71	1970-71
Lindgren, Lars	Van., Min.	6	394	25	113	138	325	40	5	6	11	20	1978-79	1983-84
Lindsay, Ted	Det., Chi.	17	1068	379	472	851	1808	133	47	49	96	194	1944-45	1964-65
Lindstrom, Willy	Wpg., Edm., Pit.	8	582	161	162	323	200	57	14	18	32	24	1979-80	1986-87
Liscombe, Carl	Det.	9	383	137	140	277	133	59	22	19	41	20	1937-38	1945-46
Litzenberger, Ed	Mtl., Chi., Det., Tor.	12	618	178	238	416	283	40	5	13	18	34	1952-53	1963-64
Locas, Jacques	Mtl..	2	59	7	8	15	66	....	....	....	....	....	1947-48	1948-49
Lochead, Bill	NYR, Det., Col.	6	330	69	62	131	180	7	3	0	3	6	1974-75	1979-80
Locking, Norm	Chi.	2	48	2	6	8	26	1	0	0	0	0	1934-35	1935-36
Lofthouse, Mark	Wsh., Det.	6	181	42	38	80	73	....	....	....	....	....	1977-78	1982-83
Logan, Dave	Chi., Van.	6	218	5	29	34	470	12	0	0	0	10	1975-76	1980-81
Long, Barry	L.A., Det., Wpg.	5	280	11	58	79	250	5	0	1	1	18	1972-73	1981-82

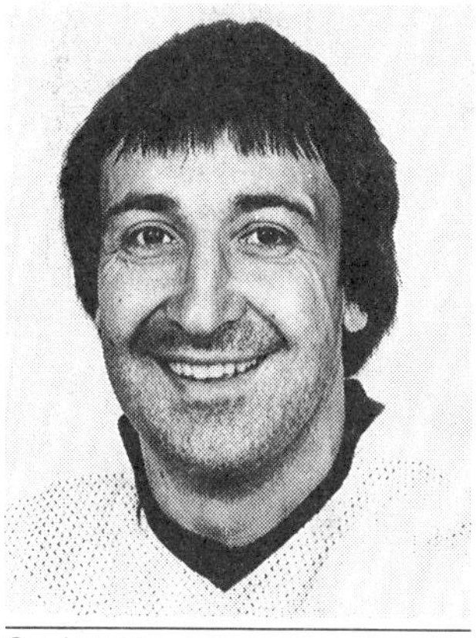

Guy Lapointe

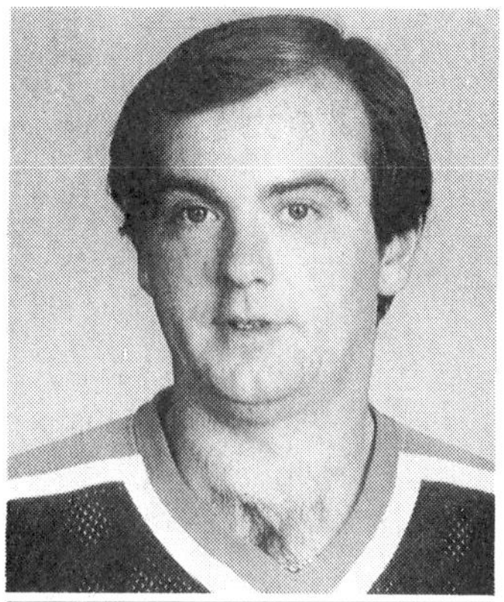

Garry Lariviere

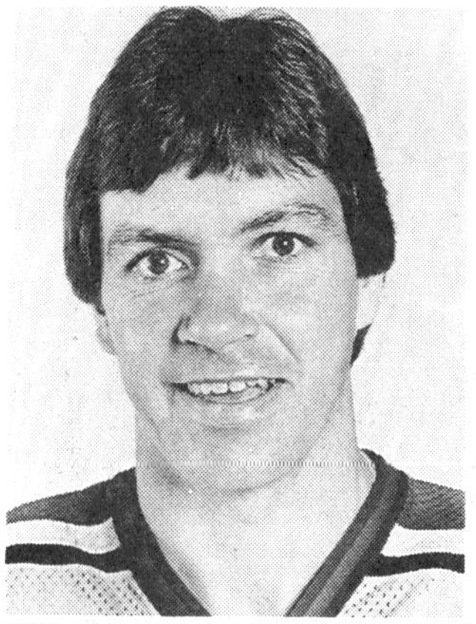

Don Lever

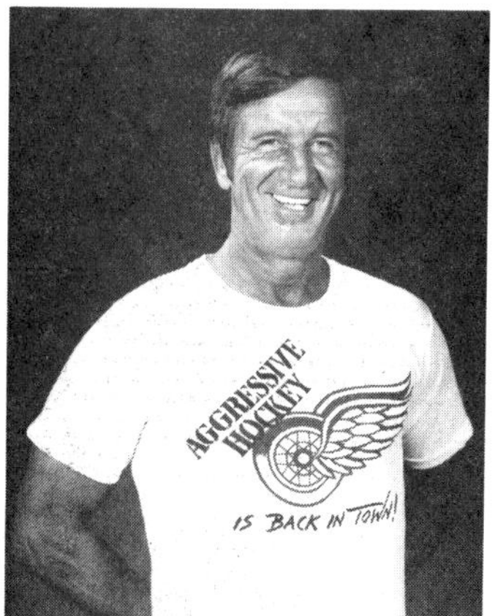

Ted Lindsay

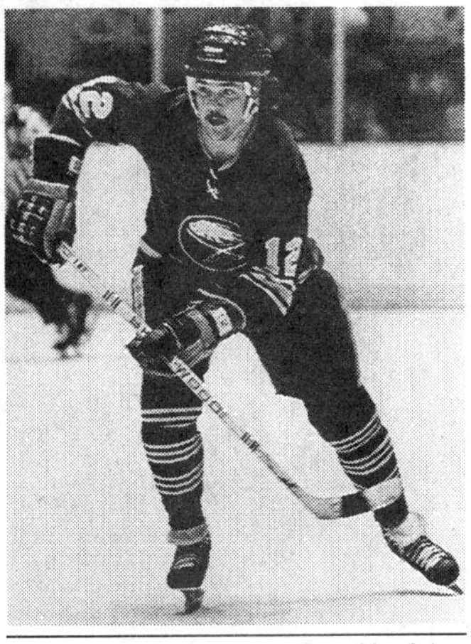

Gary MacAdam

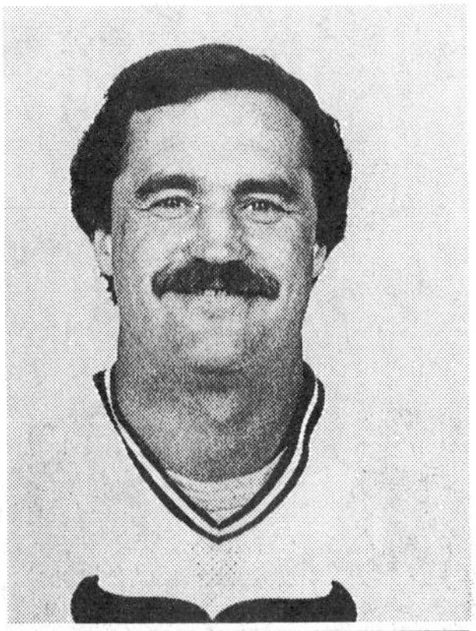

Rick MacLeish

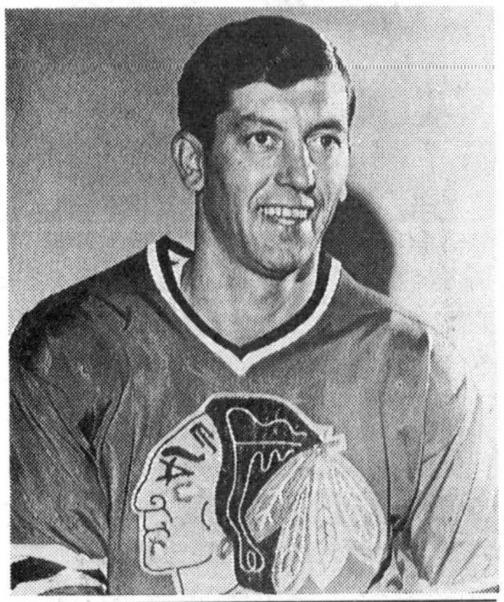

Chico Maki

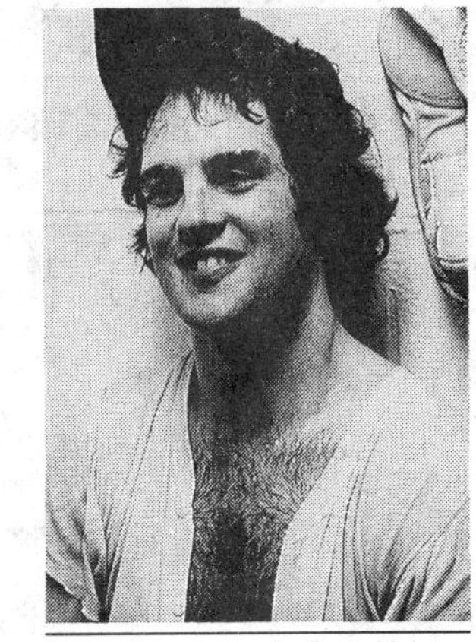

Dave Maloney

Name	NHL Teams	NHL Seasons	Regular Schedule					Playoffs					First NHL Season	Last NHL Season
			GP	G	A	TP	PIM	GP	G	A	TP	PIM		
Long, Stanley	Mtl..	1	3	0	0	0	0	....	....	....	....	....	1951-52	1951-52
Lonsberry, Ross	Phi., Pit., Bos., L.A.	15	968	256	310	566	806	100	21	25	46	87	1966-67	1980-81
Lorentz, Jim	NYR, Buf., Bos., St.L.	10	659	161	238	399	208	54	12	10	22	30	1968-69	1977-78
Lorimer, Bob	NYI, Col., N.J.	10	529	22	90	112	431	49	3	10	13	83	1976-77	1985-86
Lorraine, Rod	Mtl..	6	179	28	39	67	30	11	0	3	3	0	1935-36	1941-42
Loughlin, Clem	Det., Chi.	3	101	8	6	14	77	....	....	....	....	....	1926-27	1928-29
Loughlin, Wilf	Tor.	1	14	0	0	0	2	....	....	....	....	....	1923-24	1923-24
Lowdermilk, Dwayne	Wsh.	1	2	0	1	1	2	....	....	....	....	....	1980-81	1980-81
Lowe, Darren	Pit.	1	8	1	2	3	0	....	....	....	....	....	1983-84	1983-84
Lowe, Norm	NYR	2	4	1	1	2	0	....	....	....	....	....	1948-49	1949-50
Lowe, Ross	Bos., Mtl..	3	77	6	8	14	82	2	0	0	0	0	1949-50	1951-52
Lowery, Fred	Mtl.M., Pit.	2	54	1	0	1	10	2	0	0	0	6	1924-25	1925-26
Lowrey, Eddie	Ott., Ham.	3	24	2	0	2	3	....	....	....	....	....	1917-18	1920-21
Lowrey, Gerry	Chi., Ott., Tor., Phi., Pit.	6	209	48	48	96	148	2	1	0	1	2	1927-28	1932-33
Lucas, Danny	Phi.	1	6	1	0	1	0	....	....	....	....	....	1978-79	1978-79
Lucas, Dave	Det.	1	1	0	0	0	0	....	....	....	....	....	1962-63	1962-63
Luce, Don	NYR, Det., Buf., L.A., Tor.	13	894	225	329	554	364	71	17	22	39	52	1969-70	1981-82
Lukowich, Bernie	Pit., St.L.	2	79	13	15	28	34	2	0	0	0	0	1973-74	1974-75
Lukowich, Morris	Wpg., Bos., L.A.	8	582	199	219	418	584	11	0	2	2	24	1979-80	1986-87
Luksa, Charlie	Hfd.	1	8	0	1	1	4	....	....	....	....	....	1979-80	1979-80
Lumley, Dave	Mtl., Edm., Hfd.	9	437	98	160	258	680	61	6	8	14	131	1978-79	1986-87
Lund, Pentti	NYR, Bos.	7	259	44	55	99	40	18	7	5	12	0	1946-47	1952-53
Lundberg, Brian	Pit.	1	1	0	0	0	2	....	....	....	....	....	1982-83	1982-83
Lunde, Len	Min., Van., Det., Chi.	8	321	39	83	122	75	20	3	2	5	2	1958-59	1970-71
Lundholm, Bengt	Wpg.	5	275	48	95	143	72	14	3	4	7	14	1981-82	1985-86
Lundrigan, Joe	Tor., Wsh.	2	52	2	8	10	22	....	....	....	....	....	1972-73	1974-75
Lundstrom, Tord	Det.	1	11	1	1	2	0	....	....	....	....	....	1973-74	1973-74
Lundy, Pat	Det. Chi.	5	150	37	32	69	31	9	1	1	2	2	1945-46	1950-51
Lupien, Gilles	Mtl., Pit., Hfd.	5	226	5	25	30	416	25	0	0	0	21	1977-78	1981-82
Lupul, Gary	Van.	7	293	70	75	145	243	25	4	7	11	11	1979-80	1985-86
Lyle, George	Det., Hfd.	4	99	24	38	62	51	....	....	....	....	....	1979-80	1982-83
Lynch, Jack	Pit., Det., Wsh.	7	382	24	106	130	336	....	....	....	....	....	1972-73	1978-79
Lynn, Vic	Det., Mtl., Tor., Bos., Chi.	10	326	49	76	125	274	47	7	10	17	46	1943-44	1954-55
Lyon, Steve	Pit.	1	3	0	0	0	2	....	....	....	....	....	1976-77	1976-77
Lyons, Ron	Bos., Phi.	1	36	2	4	6	29	5	0	0	0	0	1930-31	1930-31
Lysiak, Tom	Atl., Chi.	13	919	292	551	843	567	78	25	38	63	49	1973-74	1985-86

M

Name	NHL Teams	NHL Seasons	GP	G	A	TP	PIM	GP	G	A	TP	PIM	First NHL Season	Last NHL Season
MacAdam, Al	Phi., Cal., Cle., Min., Van.	12	864	240	351	591	509	64	20	24	44	21	1973-74	1984-85
MacDonald, Blair	Edm., Van.	4	219	91	100	191	65	11	0	6	6	2	1979-80	1982-83
MacDonald, Kilby	NYR	4	151	36	34	70	47	15	1	2	3	4	1939-40	1944-45
MacDonald, Lowell	Det., L.A., Pit.	13	506	180	210	390	92	30	11	11	22	12	1961-62	1977-78
MacDonald, Parker	Tor., NYR, Det., Bos., Min.	14	676	144	179	323	253	75	14	14	28	20	1952-53	1968-69
MacDougall, Kim	Min.	1	1	0	0	0	0	....	....	....	....	....	1974-75	1974-75
Macey, Hubert	NYR, Mtl.	3	30	6	9	15	0	8	0	0	0	0	1941-42	1946-47
MacGregor, Bruce	Det., NYR	14	893	213	257	470	217	107	19	28	47	44	1960-61	1973-74
MacGregor, Randy	Hfd.	1	2	1	1	2	2	....	....	....	....	....	1981-82	1981-82
MacGuigan, Garth	NYR	1	2	0	0	0	0	....	....	....	....	....	1979-80	1979-80
MacIntosh, Ian	NYR	1	4	0	0	0	4	....	....	....	....	....	1952-53	1952-53
MacIver, Don	Wpg.	1	6	0	0	0	2	....	....	....	....	....	1979-80	1979-80
MacKasey, Blair	Tor.	1	1	0	0	0	2	....	....	....	....	....	1976-77	1976-77
MacKay, Calum	Det., Mtl.	7	237	50	55	105	214	38	5	13	18	20	1946-47	1954-55
MacKay, Dave	Chi.	1	29	3	0	3	26	5	0	1	1	2	1940-41	1940-41
MacKay, Mickey	Chi., Pit., Bos.	4	151	44	19	63	79	11	0	0	0	6	1926-27	1929-30
MacKay, Murdo	Mtl.	3	19	0	3	3	0	15	1	2	3	0	1945-46	1947-48
Mackell, Fleming	Tor., Bos.	13	665	149	220	369	562	80	22	41	63	75	1947-48	1959-60
MacKenzie, Barry	Min.	1	6	0	1	1	6	....	....	....	....	....	1968-69	1968-69
MacKenzie, Bill	Chi., Mtl.(M),Mtl., NYR	7	266	15	14	29	133	19	1	1	2	11	1932-33	1939-40
MacKey, Reggie	NYR	1	34	0	0	0	16	1	0	0	0	0	1926-27	1926-27
Mackie, Howie	Det.	2	20	1	0	1	4	8	0	0	0	0	1936-37	1937-38
MacKinnon, Paul	Wsh.	5	147	5	23	28	91	....	....	....	....	....	1979-80	1983-84
MacLeish, Rick	Phi., Hfd., Pit., Det.	14	846	349	410	759	434	114	54	53	107	38	1970-71	1983-84
MacMillan, Billy	Tor., Atl., NYI	7	446	74	77	151	184	53	6	6	12	40	1970-71	1976-77
MacMillan, Bob	NYR, St.L., Atl., Cgy., Col., N.J., Chi.	11	753	228	349	577	260	31	8	11	19	16	1974-75	1984-85
MacMillan, John	Tor., Det.	5	104	5	10	15	32	12	0	1	1	2	1960-61	1963-64
MacNeil, Al	Tor., Mtl., Chi., NYR, Pit.	11	524	17	75	92	617	37	0	4	4	67	1955-56	1967-68
MacNeil, Bernie	St.L.	1	4	0	0	0	0	....	....	....	....	....	1973-74	1973-74
Macoun, Jamie	Cgy.	5	320	37	111	148	381	49	3	9	12	43	1982-83	1986-87
MacPherson, Bud	Mtl.	7	259	5	33	38	233	29	0	3	3	21	1948-49	1956-57
MacSweyn, Ralph	Phi.	4	47	0	5	5	10	8	0	0	0	6	1967-68	1971-72
Madigan, Connie	St.L.	1	20	0	3	3	25	5	0	0	0	4	1972-73	1972-73
Magee, Dean	Min.	1	7	0	0	0	4	....	....	....	....	....	1977-78	1977-78
Maggs, Daryl	Chi., Cal., Tor.	3	135	14	19	33	54	4	0	0	0	0	1971-72	1979-80
Magnan, Marc	Tor.	1	4	0	1	1	5	....	....	....	....	....	1982-83	1982-83
Magnuson, Keith	Chi.	11	589	14	125	139	1442	68	3	9	12	164	1969-70	1979-80
Mahaffy, John	Mtl., NYR	3	37	11	25	36	4	1	0	1	1	0	1942-43	1944-45
Mahovlich, Frank	Tor., Det., Mtl.	18	1181	533	570	1103	1056	137	51	67	118	163	1956-57	1973-74
Mahovlich, Pete	Det., Mtl., Pit.	16	884	288	485	773	916	88	30	42	72	134	1965-66	1980-81
Mailley, Frank	Mtl.	1	1	0	0	0	0	....	....	....	....	....	1942-43	1942-43
Mair, Jim	Phi., NYI, Van.	5	76	4	15	19	49	3	1	2	3	4	1970-71	1974-75
Majeau, Fern	Mtl.	2	56	22	24	466	43	1	0	0	0	0	1943-44	1944-45
Maki, Chico	Chi.	15	841	143	292	435	345	113	17	36	53	43	1960-61	1975-76
Maki, Wayne	Chi., St.L., Van.	6	246	57	79	136	184	2	1	0	1	2	1967-68	1972-73
Makkonen, Karl	Edm.	1	9	2	2	4	0	....	....	....	....	....	1979-80	1979-80
Malinowski, Merlin	Col., N.J., Hfd.	5	282	54	111	165	121	....	....	....	....	....	1978-79	1982-83
Malone, Cliff	Mtl.	1	3	0	0	0	0	....	....	....	....	....	1951-52	1951-52
Malone, Greg	Pit., Hfd., Que.	11	704	191	310	501	661	20	3	5	8	32	1976-77	1986-87
Malone, Joe	Mtl., Que., Ham.	7	125	146	21	167	23	9	5	0	5	0	1917-18	1923-24
Maloney, Dan	Chi., L.A., Det., Tor.	11	737	192	259	451	1489	40	4	7	11	35	1970-71	1981-82
Maloney, Dave	NYR, Buf.	11	657	71	246	317	1154	49	7	17	24	91	1974-75	1984-85
Maloney, Phi.	Bos., Tor., Chi.	5	158	28	43	71	16	6	0	0	0	0	1949-50	1959-60
Maluta, Ray	Bos.	2	25	2	3	5	6	2	0	0	0	0	1975-76	1976-77
Manastersky, Tom	Mtl.	1	6	0	0	0	11	....	....	....	....	....	1950-51	1950-51
Mancuso, Gus	Mtl., NYR	4	42	7	9	16	17	....	....	....	....	....	1937-38	1942-43
Mandich, Dan	Min.	4	111	5	11	16	303	7	0	0	0	2	1982-83	1985-86
Manery, Kris	Van., Wpg., Clev., Min.	4	250	63	64	127	91	....	....	....	....	....	1977-78	1980-81
Manery, Randy	L.A., Det., Atl.	10	582	50	206	256	415	13	0	2	2	12	1970-71	1979-80
Mann, Jack	NYR	2	9	3	4	7	0	....	....	....	....	....	1943-44	1944-45
Mann, Ken	Det.	1	1	0	0	0	0	....	....	....	....	....	1975-76	1975-76
Mann, Norm	Tor.	2	31	0	3	3	4	1	0	0	0	0	1938-39	1940-41
Manners, Rennison	Pit., Phi.	2	37	3	2	5	14	....	....	....	....	....	1929-30	1930-31
Manno, Bob	Van., Tor., Det.	8	371	41	131	172	274	17	2	4	6	12	1976-77	1984-85
Manson, Ray	Bos., NYR	2	2	0	1	1	0	....	....	....	....	....	1947-48	1948-49
Mantha, Georges	Mtl..	13	498	89	102	181	148	36	6	2	8	16	1928-29	1940-41
Mantha, Sylvio	Mtl., Bos.	14	543	63	72	135	667	46	5	4	9	66	1923-24	1936-37
Maracle, Buddy	NYR	1	11	1	3	4	4	4	0	0	0	0	1930-31	1930-31
Marcetta, Milan	Tor., Min.	3	54	7	15	22	10	17	7	7	14	4	1966-67	1968-69
March, Mush	Chi.	17	758	153	233	386	523	48	12	15	27	41	1928-29	1944-45
Marchinko, Brian	Tor., NYI	4	47	2	6	8	0	....	....	....	....	....	1970-71	1973-74
Marcon, Lou	Det.	3	70	0	4	4	42	....	....	....	....	....	1958-59	1962-63
Marcotte, Don	Bos.	15	868	230	254	484	317	132	34	27	61	81	1965-66	1981-82
Marini, Hector	NYR, N.J.	5	154	27	46	73	246	10	3	6	9	14	1978-79	1983-84
Mario, Frank	Bos.	2	53	9	19	28	24	....	....	....	....	....	1941-42	1944-45
Mariucci, John	Chi.	5	223	11	34	45	308	8	0	3	3	26	1940-41	1947-48
Markell, John	Wpg.	2	52	11	10	21	36	....	....	....	....	....	1979-80	1980-81
Marker, Gus	Det., Mtl.M., Tor., NYA	10	336	64	69	133	136	45	6	8	14	36	1932-33	1941-42
Markham, Ray	NYR	1	14	1	1	2	21	7	1	0	1	24	1979-80	1979-80
Markle, Jack	Tor.	1	8	0	1	1	0	....	....	....	....	....	1935-36	1935-36
Marks, Jack	Mtl.W, Tor., Que.	2	7	0	0	0	4	....	....	....	....	....	1917-18	1919-20
Marks, John	Chi.	10	648	112	163	275	330	57	5	9	14	60	1972-73	1981-82
Marotte, Gilles	Bos., Chi., L.A., NYR, St.L.	12	808	56	265	321	872	29	3	3	6	26	1965-66	1976-77
Marquess, Mark	Bos.	1	27	5	4	9	27	4	0	0	0	0	1946-47	1946-47
Marsh, Gary	Det., Tor.	2	7	1	3	4	4	....	....	....	....	....	1967-68	1968-69
Marsh, Peter	Wpg., Chi.	5	279	48	71	119	224	26	1	5	6	33	1979-80	1983-84
Marshall, Bert	Det., Oak., Cal., NYR, NYI	14	868	17	181	198	296	72	4	22	26	99	1965-66	1978-79

			Regular Schedule					Playoffs					First	Last
Name	NHL Teams	NHL Seasons	GP	G	A	TP	PIM	GP	G	A	TP	PIM	NHL Season	NHL Season
Marshall, Don	Mtl., NYR, Buf., Tor.	19	1176	265	324	589	127	94	8	15	23	14	1951-52	1971-72
Marshall, Paul	Pit., Tor., Hfd.	4	95	15	18	33	17	1	0	0	0	0	1979-80	1982-83
Marshall, Willie	Tor.	4	33	1	15	16	2	....	....	....	....	....	1952-53	1958-59
Marson, Mike	Wsh., L.A.	6	196	24	24	48	233	....	....	....	....	....	1974-75	1979-80
Martin, Clare	Bos., Det., Chi., NYR	6	237	12	28	40	78	22	0	2	2	6	1941-42	1951-52
Martin, Frank	Bos., Chi.	6	282	11	46	57	122	10	0	1	1	2	1952-53	1957-58
Martin, Grant	Van., Wsh.	4	44	0	4	4	55	1	1	0	1	2	1983-84	1986-87
Martin, Jack	Tor.	1	1	0	0	0	0	....	....	....	....	....	1960-61	1960-61
Martin, Pit	Det., Bos., Chi., Van.	17	1101	324	485	809	609	100	27	31	58	56	1961-62	1978-79
Martin, Rick	Buf., L.A.	11	685	384	317	701	477	63	24	29	53	74	1971-72	1981-82
Martin, Ron	NYA	2	94	13	16	29	36	....	....	....	....	....	1932-33	1933-34
Martin, Terry	Buf., Que., Tor., Edm., Min.	10	479	104	101	205	202	21	4	2	6	26	1975-76	1984-85
Martin, Tom	Tor.	1	3	1	0	1	0	....	....	....	....	....	1967-68	1968-68
Martineau, Don	Atl., Min., Det.	4	90	6	10	16	63	....	....	....	....	....	1973-74	1976-77
Maruk, Dennis	Cal., Clev., Min., Wsh.	13	882	356	521	877	759	34	14	22	36	26	1975-76	1987-88
Masnick, Paul	Mtl., Chi., Tor.	6	232	18	41	59	139	33	4	5	9	27	1950-51	1957-58
Mason, Charley	NYR, NYA, Det., Chi.	4	95	7	18	25	44	4	0	1	1	0	1934-35	1938-39
Massecar, George	NYA	3	100	12	11	23	46	....	....	....	....	....	1929-30	1931-32
Masters, Jamie	St.L.	3	33	1	13	14	2	2	0	0	0	0	1975-76	1976-77
Masterton, Bill	Min.	1	38	4	8	12	4	....	....	....	....	....	1967-68	1967-68
Mathers, Frank	Tor.	3	23	1	3	4	4	....	....	....	....	....	1948-49	1951-52
Mathiasen, Dwight	Pit.	3	33	1	7	8	18	....	....	....	....	....	1985-86	1987-88
Matte, Joe	Tor., Ham., Bos., Mtl.	4	64	18	14	32	43	....	....	....	....	....	1919-20	1925-26
Matte, Joe	Chi.	1	12	0	1	1	0	....	....	....	....	....	1942-43	1942-43
Matte, Roland	Det.	1	12	0	1	1	0	....	....	....	....	....	1929-30	1929-30
Mattiussi, Dick	Pit., Oak., Cal.	4	200	8	31	39	124	8	0	1	1	6	1967-68	1970-71
Matz, Johnny	Mtl.	1	30	3	2	5	0	5	0	0	0	2	1924-25	1924-25
Maxner, Wayne	Bos.	2	62	8	9	17	48	....	....	....	....	....	1964-65	1965-66
Maxwell, Brad	Min., Que., Tor., Van., NYR	10	612	98	270	368	1270	79	12	49	61	178	1977-78	1986-87
Maxwell, Bryan	Min., St.L., Wpg., Pit.	8	331	18	77	95	745	15	1	1	2	86	1977-78	1984-85
Maxwell, Kevin	Min., Col., N.J.	3	66	6	15	21	61	16	3	4	7	24	1980-81	1983-84
Maxwell, Wally	Tor.	1	2	0	0	0	0	....	....	....	....	....	1952-53	1952-53
Mayer, Jim	NYR	1	4	0	0	0	0	....	....	....	....	....	1979-80	1979-80
Mayer, Shep	Tor.	1	12	1	2	3	4	....	....	....	....	....	1942-43	1942-43
Mazur, Eddie	Mtl., Chi.	6	107	8	20	28	120	25	4	5	9	22	1950-51	1956-57
McAdam, Gary	Buf., Pit., Det., Cal., Wsh., N.J., Tor.	11	534	96	132	228	243	30	6	5	11	16	1975-76	1985-86
McAdam, Sam	NYR	1	5	0	0	0	0	....	....	....	....	....	1930-31	1930-31
McAndrew, Hazen	NYA	1	7	0	1	1	6	....	....	....	....	....	1941-42	1941-42
McAneeley, Ted	Cal.	3	158	8	35	43	141	....	....	....	....	....	1972-73	1974-75
McAtee, Jud	Det.	3	46	15	13	28	6	14	2	1	3	0	1942-43	1944-45
McAtee, Norm	Bos.	1	13	0	1	1	0	....	....	....	....	....	1946-47	1946-47
McAvoy, George	Mtl.	1	4	0	0	0	0	....	....	....	....	....	1954-55	1954-55
McBride, Cliff	Mtl.M., Tor.	2	2	0	0	0	0	....	....	....	....	....	1928-29	1929-30
McBurney, Jim	Chi.	1	1	0	1	1	0	....	....	....	....	....	1952-53	1952-53
McCabe, Stan	Det., Mtl.M.	4	78	9	4	13	49	....	....	....	....	....	1929-30	1933-34
McCaffrey, Bert	Tor., Pit., Mtl.	7	260	42	30	72	202	8	2	1	3	12	1924-25	1930-31
McCahill, John	Col.	1	1	0	0	0	0	....	....	....	....	....	1977-78	1977-78
McCaig, Douglas	Det., Chi.	7	263	8	21	29	255	17	0	1	1	8	1941-42	1950-51
McCallum, Dunc	NYR, Pit.	5	187	14	35	49	230	10	1	2	3	12	1965-66	1970-71
McCalmon, Eddie	Chi., Phi.	2	39	5	0	5	14	....	....	....	....	....	1927-28	1930-31
McCann, Rick	Det.	6	43	1	4	5	6	....	....	....	....	....	1967-68	1974-75
McCarthy, Dan	NYR	1	5	4	0	4	4	....	....	....	....	....	1980-81	1980-81
McCarthy, Kevin	Phi., Van., Pit.	10	537	67	191	258	527	21	2	3	5	20	1977-78	1986-87
McCarthy, Tom	Det., Bos.	4	60	8	9	17	8	....	....	....	....	....	1956-57	1960-61
McCarthy, Tom	Que., Ham.	2	34	19	3	22	10	....	....	....	....	....	1919-20	1920-21
McCarthy, Tom	Min., Bos.	9	460	178	221	399	330	68	12	26	38	67	1979-80	1987-88
McCartney, Walt	Mtl.	1	2	0	0	0	0	....	....	....	....	....	1932-33	1932-33
McCaskill, Ted	Min.	1	4	0	2	2	0	....	....	....	....	....	1967-68	1967-68
McClanahan, Rob	Buf., Hfd., NYR	5	224	38	63	101	126	34	4	12	16	31	1979-80	1983-84
McCord, Bob	Bos., Det., Min., St.L.	7	316	58	68	126	262	14	2	5	7	10	1963-64	1972-73
McCord, Dennis	Van.	1	3	0	0	0	0	....	....	....	....	....	1973-74	1973-74
McCormack, John	Tor., Mtl., Chi.	8	311	25	49	74	35	22	1	1	2	0	1947-48	1954-55
McCourt, Dale	Det., Buf., Tor.	7	532	194	284	478	124	21	9	7	16	6	1977-78	1983-84
McCreary, Bill E.	NYR, Det., Mtl., St.L.	10	309	53	62	115	108	48	6	16	22	14	1953-54	1970-71
McCreary, Bill	Tor.	1	12	1	0	1	4	....	....	....	....	....	1980-81	1980-81
McReavy, Keith	Pit., Atl.	8	532	131	112	243	294	16	0	4	4	6	1967-68	1974-75
McReavy, Pat	Bos., Det.	4	55	5	10	15	4	20	3	3	6	9	1938-39	1941-42
McCreedy, Johnny	Tor.	2	64	17	12	29	25	21	4	3	7	16	1941-42	1944-45
McCrimmon, Jim	St.L.	1	2	0	0	0	0	....	....	....	....	....	1974-75	1974-75
McCulley, Bob	Mtl.	1	1	0	0	0	0	....	....	....	....	....	1934-35	1934-35
McCutcheon, Brian	Det.	3	37	3	1	4	7	....	....	....	....	....	1974-75	1976-77
McDill, Jeff	Chi.	1	1	0	0	0	0	....	....	....	....	....	1976-77	1976-77
McDonagh, Bill	NYR	1	4	0	0	0	2	....	....	....	....	....	1949-50	1949-50
McDonald, Ab	Mtl., Chi., Bos., Det., Pit., St.L.	15	762	182	248	430	200	84	21	29	50	42	1957-58	1973-74
McDonald, Brian	Chi., Buf.	2	12	0	0	0	29	8	0	0	0	2	1967-68	1970-71
McDonald, Bucko	Det., Tor., NYR	11	448	35	88	123	206	63	6	1	7	24	1934-35	1944-45
McDonald, Butch	Det., Chi.	2	66	8	20	28	2	5	0	2	2	10	1939-40	1944-45
McDonald, Gerry	Hfd.	1	3	0	0	0	0	....	....	....	....	....	1981-82	1981-82
McDonald, Jack	Mtl.W, Mtl., Que., Tor.	5	73	27	11	38	13	12	2	0	2	0	1917-18	1921-22
McDonald, John	NYR	1	43	10	9	19	6	....	....	....	....	....	1943-44	1943-44
McDonald, Robert	NYR	1	1	0	0	0	0	....	....	....	....	....	1943-44	1943-44
McDonald, Terry	K.C.	1	8	0	1	1	6	....	....	....	....	....	1975-76	1975-76
McDonnell, Joe	Van., Pit.	3	50	2	10	12	34	....	....	....	....	....	1981-82	1985-86
McDonnell, Moylan	Ham.	1	20	1	1	2	0	....	....	....	....	....	1920-21	1920-21
McDonough, Al	L.A., Pit., Atl., Det.	5	237	73	88	161	73	8	0	1	1	2	1970-71	1977-78
McDougal, Mike	NYR, Hfd.	4	61	8	10	18	43	....	....	....	....	....	1978-79	1982-83
McElmury, Jim	Min., K.C., Col.	5	180	14	47	61	49	....	....	....	....	....	1972-73	1977-78
McEwen, Mike	NYR, Col., NYI, L.A., Wsh., Det., Hfd.	12	716	108	296	404	460	78	12	36	48	48	1976-77	1987-88
McFadden, Jim	Det., Chi.	7	412	100	126	226	89	49	10	9	19	30	1947-48	1953-54
McFall, Dan	Wpg.	2	9	0	1	1	0	....	....	....	....	....	1984-85	1985-86
McFadyen, Don	Chi.	4	179	12	33	45	77	12	2	2	4	5	1932-33	1935-36
McFarland, George	Chi.	1	2	0	0	0	0	....	....	....	....	....	1926-27	1926-27
McGeough, Jim	Wsh., Pit.	4	57	7	10	17	32	....	....	....	....	....	1981-82	1986-87
McGibbon, John	Mtl.	1	1	0	0	0	2	....	....	....	....	....	1942-43	1942-43
McGill, Jack	Mtl.	3	134	27	10	37	71	3	2	0	2	0	1934-35	1936-37
McGill, Jack G.	Bos.	4	97	23	36	59	42	27	7	4	11	17	1941-42	1946-47
McGregor, Sandy	NYR	1	2	0	0	0	2	....	....	....	....	....	1963-64	1963-64
McGuire, Mickey	Pit.	2	36	3	0	3	6	....	....	....	....	....	1926-27	1927-28
McCurry, Duke	Pit.	4	148	21	11	32	119	4	0	2	2	4	1925-26	1928-29
McIlhargey, Jack	Phi., Van., Hfd.	8	393	11	36	47	1102	27	0	3	3	68	1974-75	1981-82
McInenly, Bert	Det., NYA, Ott., Bos.	6	166	19	15	34	144	4	0	0	0	2	1930-31	1935-36
McIntosh, Bruce	Min.	1	2	0	0	0	0	....	....	....	....	....	1972-73	1972-73
McIntosh, Paul	Buf.	2	48	0	0	2	66	2	0	0	0	7	1974-75	1975-76
McIntyre, Jack	Bos., Chi., Det.	10	499	109	102	211	173	29	7	6	13	4	1949-50	1959-60
McIntyre, Larry	Tor.	2	41	0	3	3	26	....	....	....	....	....	1969-70	1972-73
McKay, Doug	Det.	1	....	....	....	....	....	1	0	0	0	0	1949-50	1949-50
McKay, Ray	Chi., Buf., Cal.	6	140	2	16	18	102	1	0	0	0	0	1968-69	1973-74
McKechnie, Walt	Min., Cal., Bos., Det., Wsh., Clev., Tor., Col.	16	955	214	392	606	469	15	7	5	12	9	1967-68	1982-83
McKegney, Ian	Chi.	1	3	0	0	0	2	....	....	....	....	....	1976-77	1976-77
McKell, Jack	Ott.	2	42	4	1	5	42	9	0	0	0	0	1919-20	1920-21
McKendry, Alex	NYI, Cgy.	4	46	3	6	9	21	6	2	2	4	0	1977-78	1980-81
McKenney, Don	Bos., NYR, Tor., Det., St.L.	13	798	237	345	582	211	58	18	29	47	10	1954-55	1967-68
McKenny, Jim	Tor., Min.	14	604	82	247	329	294	37	7	9	16	10	1965-66	1978-79
McKenzie, Brian	Pit.	1	6	1	1	2	4	....	....	....	....	....	1971-72	1971-72
McKenzie, John	Chi., Det., NYR, Bos.	12	691	206	268	474	917	69	15	32	47	133	1958-59	1971-72
McKinnon, Alex	Ham., NYA, Chi.	5	194	19	10	29	235	....	....	....	....	....	1924-25	1928-29
McKinnon, Bob	Chi.	1	2	0	0	0	0	....	....	....	....	....	1928-29	1928-29
McKinnon, John	Mtl., Pit., Phi.	6	218	28	11	39	224	2	0	0	0	4	1925-26	1930-31
McLean, Don	Wsh.	1	9	0	0	0	6	....	....	....	....	....	1975-76	1975-76
McLean, Fred	Que., Ham.	2	9	0	0	0	2	....	....	....	....	....	1919-20	1920-21
McLean, Jack	Tor.	3	67	14	24	38	76	13	2	2	4	8	1942-43	1944-45
McLellan, John	Tor.	1	2	0	0	0	0	....	....	....	....	....	1951-52	1951-52
McLellan, Scott	Bos.	1	2	0	0	0	0	....	....	....	....	....	1982-83	1982-83
McLenahan, Roly	Det.	1	9	2	1	3	10	2	0	0	0	0	1945-46	1945-46
McLeod, Al	Det.	1	26	2	2	4	24	....	....	....	....	....	1973-74	1973-74
McLeod, Jackie	NYR	5	106	14	23	37	12	7	0	0	0	0	1949-50	1954-55

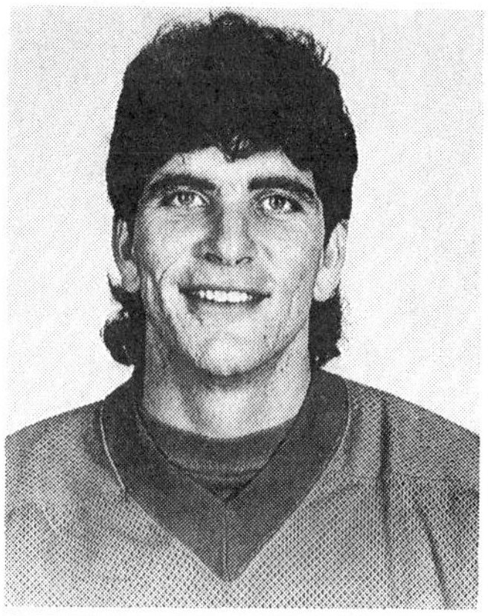
Bob Manno

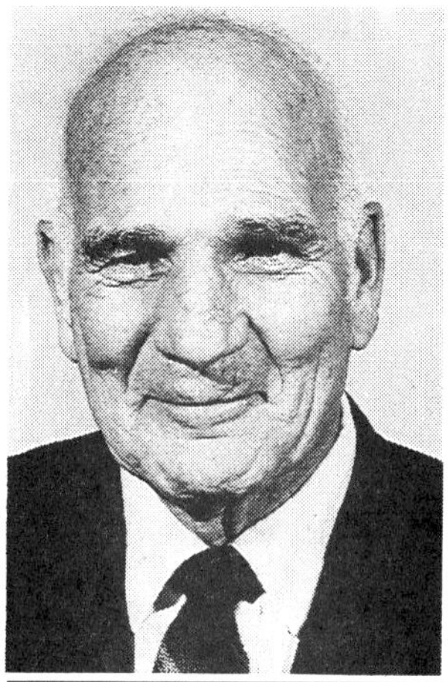
John Mariucci

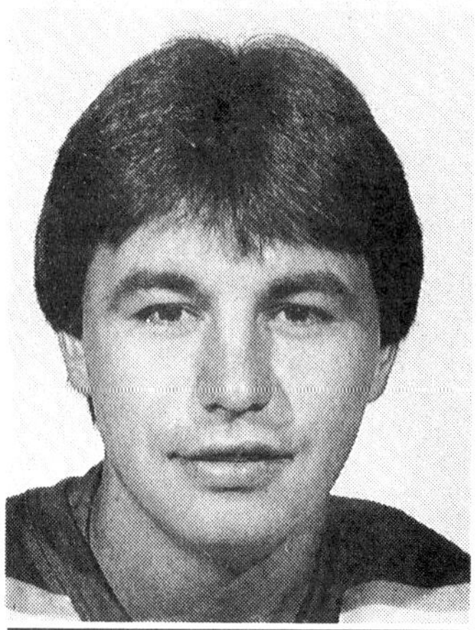
Dale McCourt

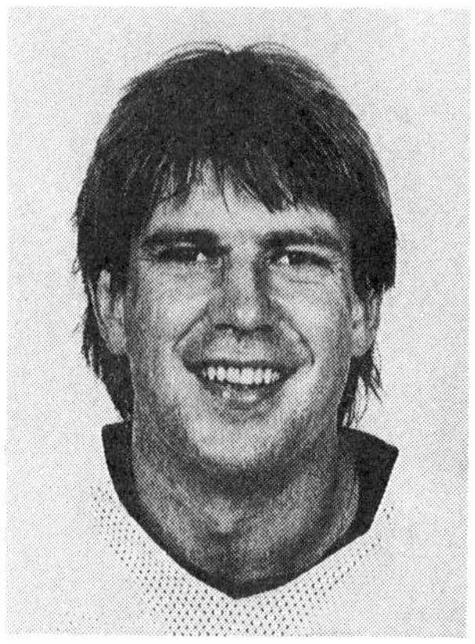
Peter McNab

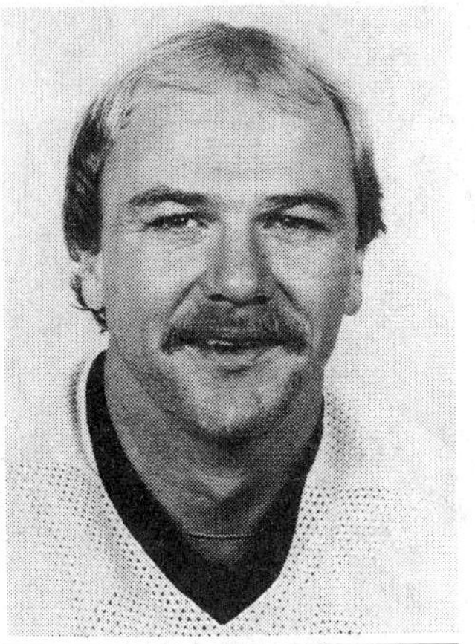
Rick Middleton

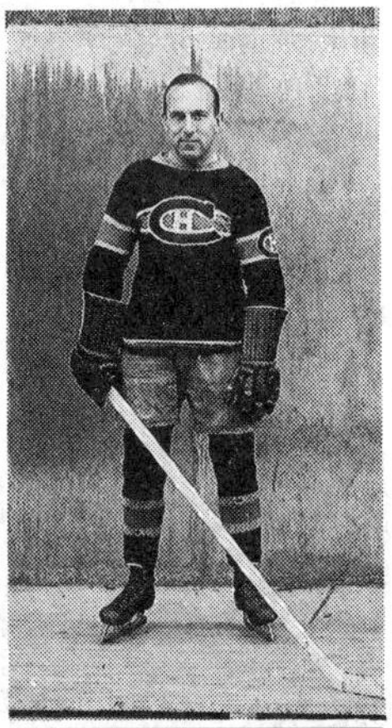
Howie Morenz

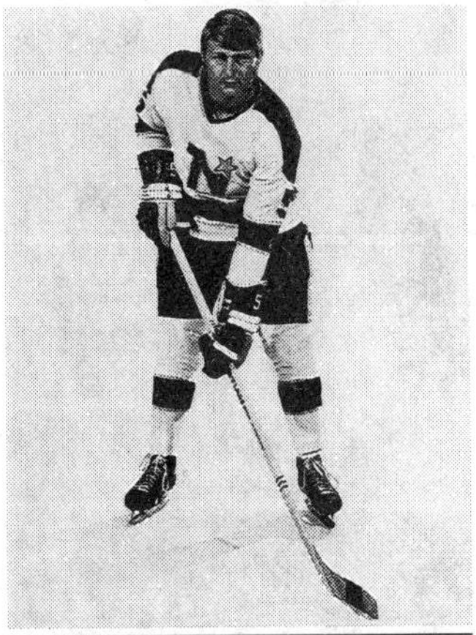
Dennis O'Brien

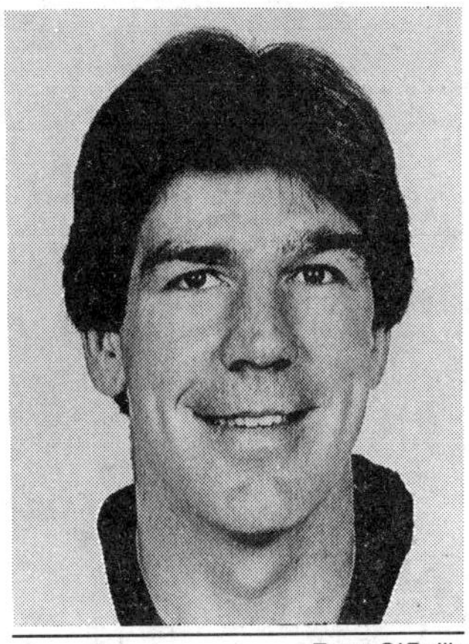
Terry O'Reilly

			Regular Schedule					Playoffs					First	Last
Name	NHL Teams	NHL Seasons	GP	G	A	TP	PIM	GP	G	A	TP	PIM	NHL Season	NHL Season
McMahon, Mike	NYR, Min., Chi., Det., Pit., Buf.	8	224	15	68	83	171	14	3	7	10	4	1963-64	1971-72
McMahon, Mike C.	Mtl., Bos.	3	57	7	18	25	102	13	1	2	3	30	1942-43	1945-46
McManama, Bob	Pit.	3	99	11	25	36	28	8	0	1	1	6	1973-74	1975-76
McManus, Sammy	Mtl.M., Bos.	2	26	0	1	1	8	1	0	0	0	0	1934-35	1936-37
McNab, Max	Det.	4	128	16	19	35	24	25	1	0	1	4	1947-48	1950-51
McNab, Peter	Buf., Bos., Van., N.J.	14	954	363	450	813	179	107	40	42	82	20	1973-74	1986-87
McNabney, Sid	Mtl.	1	5	0	1	1	2	....	....	....	....	....	1950-51	1950-51
McNamara, Howard	Mtl.	1	11	1	0	1	2	....	....	....	....	....	1919-20	1919-20
McNaughton, George	Que.	1	1	0	0	0	0	....	....	....	....	....	1919-20	1919-20
McNeill, Billy	Det.	6	257	21	46	67	142	4	1	1	2	4	1956-57	1963-64
McNeill, Stu	Det.	3	10	1	1	2	2	....	....	....	....	....	1957-58	1959-60
McSheffrey, Bryan	Van., Buf.	3	90	13	7	20	44	....	....	....	....	....	1972-73	1974-75
McTaggart, Jim	Wsh.	2	71	3	10	13	205	....	....	....	....	....	1980-81	1981-82
McTavish, Gordon	St.L., Wpg.	2	11	1	3	4	2	....	....	....	....	....	1978-79	1979-80
McVeigh, Charley	Chi., NYA	9	397	84	88	172	138	4	0	0	0	2	1926-27	1934-35
McVicar, Jack	Mtl.	2	88	2	4	6	63	2	0	0	0	2	1930-31	1931-32
Meehan, Gerry	Tor., Phi., Buf., Van., Atl., Wsh.	10	670	180	243	423	111	10	0	1	1	0	1968-69	1978-79
Meeke, Brent	Cal., Clev.	5	75	9	22	31	8	....	....	....	....	....	1972-73	1976-77
Meeker, Howie	Tor.	8	346	83	102	185	329	42	6	9	15	50	1946-47	1953-54
Meeker, Mike	Pit.	1	4	0	0	0	5	....	....	....	....	....	1978-79	1978-79
Meeking, Harry	Tor., Det., Bos.	3	63	18	3	21	42	14	4	2	6	0	1917-18	1926-27
Meger, Paul	Mtl.	6	212	39	52	91	112	35	3	8	11	16	1949-50	1954-55
Meighan, Ron	Min., Pit.	2	48	3	7	10	18	....	....	....	....	....	1981-82	1982-83
Meissner, Barrie	Min.	2	6	0	1	1	4	....	....	....	....	....	1967-68	1968-69
Meissner, Dick	Bos., NYR	5	171	11	15	26	37	....	....	....	....	....	1959-60	1964-65
Melametsa, Anssi	Wpg.	1	27	0	3	3	2	....	....	....	....	....	1985-86	1985-86
Melin, Roger	Min.	2	3	0	0	0	0	....	....	....	....	....	1980-81	1981-82
Mellor, Tom	Det.	2	26	2	4	6	25	....	....	....	....	....	1973-74	1974-75
Melnyk, Gerry	Det., Chi., St.L.	6	269	39	77	116	34	53	6	6	12	6	1955-56	1967-68
Melrose, Barry	Wpg., Tor., Det.	6	300	10	23	33	728	7	0	2	2	38	1979-80	1985-86
Menard, Hillary	Chi.	1	1	0	0	0	0	....	....	....	....	....	1953-54	1953-54
Menard, Howie	Det., L.A., Chi., Oak.	4	151	23	42	65	87	19	3	7	10	36	1963-64	1969-70
Mercredi, Vic	Atl.	1	2	0	0	0	0	....	....	....	....	....	1974-75	1974-75
Meredith, Greg	Cgy.	2	38	6	4	10	8	5	3	1	4	4	1980-81	1982-83
Merkosky, Glenn	Hfd., N.J., Det.	4	63	5	12	17	22	....	....	....	....	....	1981-82	1985-86
Meronek, Bill	Mtl.	2	19	5	8	13	0	1	0	0	0	0	1939-40	1942-43
Merrick, Wayne	St.L., Cal., Clev., NYI	12	774	191	265	456	303	102	19	30	49	30	1972-73	1983-84
Merrill, Horace	Ott.	2	11	0	0	0	0	....	....	....	....	....	1917-18	1919-20
Messier, Paul	Col.	1	9	0	0	0	4	....	....	....	....	....	1978-79	1978-79
Metz, Don	Tor.	7	172	20	35	55	42	47	7	8	15	10	1934-40	1948-49
Metz, Nick	Tor.	12	518	131	119	250	149	76	19	20	39	31	1934-35	1947-48
Michaluk, Art	Chi.	1	5	0	0	0	0	....	....	....	....	....	1947-48	1947-48
Michaluk, John	Chi.	1	1	0	0	0	0	....	....	....	....	....	1950-51	1950-51
Michayluk, Dave	Phi.	2	14	2	6	8	8	....	....	....	....	....	1981-82	1982-83
Micheletti, Joe	St.L., Col.	3	158	11	60	71	114	11	1	11	12	10	1979-80	1981-82
Micheletii, Pat	Min.	1	12	2	0	2	8	....	....	....	....	....	1987-88	1987-88
Mickey, Larry	Chi., NYR, Tor., Mtl., L.A., Phi., Buf.	11	292	39	53	92	160	9	1	0	1	10	1964-65	1974-75
Mickoski, Nick	NYR, Chi., Det., Bos.	13	703	158	184	342	319	18	1	6	7	6	1947-48	1959-60
Middleton, Rick	NYR, Bos.	14	1005	448	540	988	157	114	45	55	100	19	1974-75	1987-88
Migay, Rudy	Tor.	10	418	59	92	151	293	15	1	0	1	20	1949-50	1959-60
Mikita, Stan	Chi.	22	1394	541	926	1467	1270	155	59	91	150	169	1958-59	1979-80
Mikkelson, Bill	L.A., N.Y.I., Wsh.	4	147	4	18	22	105	....	....	....	....	....	1971-72	1976-77
Mikol, Jim	Tor., NYR	2	34	1	4	5	8	....	....	....	....	....	1962-63	1964-65
Milbury, Mike	Bos.	12	754	49	189	238	1552	86	4	24	28	219	1975-76	1986-87
Milks, Hib	Pit., Phi., NYR, Ott.	8	314	87	41	128	179	10	0	0	0	2	1925-26	1932-33
Millar, Hugh	Det.	1	4	0	0	0	0	1	0	0	0	0	1946-47	1946-47
Miller, Bill	Mtl.M., Mtl.	3	95	7	3	10	16	12	0	0	0	0	1934-35	1936-37
Miller, Bob	Bos., Col.	5	341	71	103	174	185	34	4	6	10	27	1977-78	1981-82
Miller, Earl	Chi., Tor.	5	116	19	14	33	124	10	1	0	1	6	1927-28	1931-32
Miller, Jack	Chi.	2	17	0	0	0	4	....	....	....	....	....	1949-50	1950-51
Miller, Paul	Col.	1	3	0	3	3	0	....	....	....	....	....	1981-82	1981-82
Miller, Perry	Det.	4	217	10	51	61	387	....	....	....	....	....	1977-78	1980-81
Miller, Tom	Det., NYI	4	118	16	25	41	34	....	....	....	....	....	1970-71	1974-75
Miller, Warren	NYR, Hfd.	4	262	40	50	90	137	6	1	0	1	0	1979-80	1982-83
Minor, Gerry	Van.	5	140	11	21	32	173	12	1	3	4	25	1979-80	1983-84
Miszuk, John	Det., Chi., Phi., Min.	6	237	7	39	46	232	19	0	3	3	19	1963-64	1969-70
Mitchell, Bill	Dot.	1	1	0	0	0	0	....	....	....	....	....	1963-64	1963-64
Mitchell, Herb	Bos.	2	53	6	0	6	38	....	....	....	....	....	1924-25	1925-26
Mitchell, Red	Chi.	3	83	4	5	9	67	....	....	....	....	....	1941-42	1944-45
Moe, Billy	NYR	5	261	11	42	53	163	1	0	0	0	0	1944-45	1948-49
Moffat, Lyle	Tor., Wpg.	3	97	12	16	28	51	....	....	....	....	....	1972-73	1979-80
Moffat, Ron	Det.	3	36	1	1	2	8	7	0	0	0	0	1932-33	1934-35
Moher, Mike	N.J.	1	9	0	1	1	28	....	....	....	....	....	1982-83	1982-83
Mohns, Doug	Bos., Chi., Min., Atl., Wsh.	22	1390	248	462	710	1250	94	14	36	50	122	1953-54	1974-75
Mohns, Lloyd	NYR	1	1	0	0	0	0	....	....	....	....	....	1943-44	1943-44
Molin, Lars	Van.	3	172	33	65	98	37	19	2	9	11	7	1981-82	1983-84
Molyneaux, Larry	NYR	2	45	0	1	1	20	3	0	0	0	8	1937-38	1938-39
Monahan, Garry	Mtl., Det., L.A., Tor., Van.	12	748	116	169	285	484	22	3	1	4	13	1967-68	1978-79
Monahan, Hartland	Cal., NYR, Wsh., Pit., L.A., St.L.	7	334	61	80	141	163	6	0	0	0	4	1973-74	1980-81
Mondou, Armand	Mtl.	12	385	47	71	118	99	35	3	5	8	12	1928-29	1939-40
Mondou, Pierre	Mtl.	9	548	194	262	456	179	69	17	28	45	26	1976-77	1984-85
Mongrain, Bob	Buf., L.A.	6	83	13	14	27	14	11	1	2	3	2	1979-80	1985-86
Monteith, Hank	Det.	3	77	5	12	17	6	4	0	0	0	0	1968-69	1970-71
Moore, Dickie	Mtl., Tor., St.L.	14	719	261	347	608	652	135	46	64	110	122	1951-52	1967-68
Moran, Amby	Mtl., Chi.	2	35	1	1	2	24	....	....	....	....	....	1926-27	1927-28
Morenz, Howie	Mtl., Chi., NYR	14	550	273	197	470	563	47	21	11	32	68	1923-24	1936-37
Moretto, Angelo	Clev.	1	5	1	2	3	2	....	....	....	....	....	1976-77	1976-77
Morin, Pete	Mtl.	1	31	10	12	22	7	1	0	0	0	0	1941-42	1941-42
Morris, Bernie	Bos.	1	6	2	0	2	0	....	....	....	....	....	1924-25	1924-25
Morris, Elwyn	Tor., NYR	4	135	13	29	42	58	18	4	2	6	16	1943-44	1948-49
Morrison, Dave	L.A., Van.	4	39	3	3	6	4	....	....	....	....	....	1980-81	1984-85
Morrison, Don	Det., Chi.	3	112	18	28	46	12	3	0	1	1	0	1947-48	1950-51
Morrison, Doug	Bos.	4	23	7	3	10	15	....	....	....	....	....	1979-80	1984-85
Morrison, Gary	Phi.	3	43	1	15	16	70	5	0	1	1	2	1979-80	1981-82
Morrison, George	St.L.	2	115	17	21	38	13	3	0	0	0	0	1970-71	1971-72
Morrison, Jim	Bos., Tor., Det., NYR, Pit.	12	704	40	160	200	542	36	0	12	12	38	1951-52	1970-71
Morrison, John	NYA	1	18	0	0	0	0	....	....	....	....	....	1925-26	1925-26
Morrison, Kevin	Col.	1	41	4	11	15	23	....	....	....	....	....	1979-80	1979-80
Morrison, Lew	Phi., Atl., Wsh., Pit.	9	564	39	52	91	107	17	0	0	0	2	1969-70	1977-78
Morrison, Mark	NYR	2	10	1	1	2	0	....	....	....	....	....	1981-82	1983-84
Morrison, Roderick	Det.	1	34	8	7	15	4	3	0	0	0	0	1947-48	1947-48
Mortson, Gus	Tor., Chi., Det.	13	797	46	152	198	1380	54	5	8	13	68	1946-47	1958-59
Mosdell, Kenny	NYA, Mtl., Chi.	16	693	141	168	309	475	79	16	13	29	48	1941-42	1958-59
Mosienko, Bill	Chi.	14	711	258	282	540	117	22	10	4	14	15	1941-42	1954-55
Mott, Morris	Cal.	3	199	18	32	50	49	....	....	....	....	....	1972-73	1974-75
Motter, Alex	Bos., Det.	8	267	39	64	103	135	40	3	9	12	41	1934-35	1942-43
Moxey, Jim	Cal., Clev., L.A.	3	127	22	27	49	59	....	....	....	....	....	1974-75	1976-77
Mulhern, Richard	Atl., L.A., Tor., Wpg.	6	303	27	93	120	217	7	0	3	3	5	1975-76	1980-81
Muloin, Wayne	Det., Oak., Cal., Min.	3	147	3	21	24	93	11	0	0	0	2	1963-64	1970-71
Mulvey, Grant	Chi., N.J.	10	586	149	135	284	816	42	10	5	15	70	1974-75	1983-84
Mulvey, Paul	Wsh., Pit., L.A.	4	225	30	51	81	613	....	....	....	....	....	1978-79	1983-84
Mummery, Harry	Tor., Que., Mtl., Ham.	6	106	33	13	46	161	7	1	4	5	0	1917-18	1921-22
Munro, Dunc	Mtl.	8	239	28	18	46	170	25	3	2	5	24	1924-25	1931-32
Munro, Gerry	Mtl., Tor.	2	33	1	0	1	22	....	....	....	....	....	1924-25	1925-26
Murdoch, Bob L.	Cal., Clev., St.L.	4	260	72	85	157	127	....	....	....	....	....	1975-76	1978-79
Murdoch, Bob J.	Mtl., L.A., Atl., Cgy.	12	757	60	218	278	764	69	4	18	22	92	1970-71	1981-82
Murdoch, Don	NYR, Edm., Det.	6	320	121	117	238	155	24	10	8	18	16	1976-77	1981-82
Murdoch, Murray	NYR	11	508	67	112	179	184	66	10	15	25	30	1926-27	1936-37
Murphy, Brian	Det.	1	1	0	0	0	0	....	....	....	....	....	1974-75	1974-75
Murphy, Mike	St.L. NYR, L.A.	12	831	238	318	556	514	66	13	23	36	54	1971-72	1982-83
Murphy, Ron	NYR, Chi., Det., Bos.	18	889	205	274	479	460	53	7	8	15	26	1952-53	1969-70
Murray, Allan	NYA	7	277	5	9	14	163	14	0	0	0	8	1933-34	1939-40
Murray, Bob J.	Atl., Van.	4	194	6	16	22	98	9	1	1	2	15	1973-74	1976-77
Murray, Jim	L.A.	1	30	0	2	2	14	....	....	....	....	....	1967-68	1967-68
Murray, Ken	Tor., N.Y.I., Det., K.C.	5	106	1	10	11	135	....	....	....	....	....	1969-70	1975-76
Murray, Leo	Mtl.	1	6	0	0	0	2	....	....	....	....	....	1932-33	1932-33
Murray, Randy	Tor.	1	3	0	0	0	2	....	....	....	....	....	1969-70	1969-70

Name	NHL Teams	NHL Seasons	Regular Schedule GP	G	A	TP	PIM	Playoffs GP	G	A	TP	PIM	First NHL Season	Last NHL Season
Murray, Terry	Cal., Phi., Det., Wsh.	8	302	4	76	80	199	18	2	2	4	10	1972-73	1981-82
Myers, Hap	Buf.	1	13	0	0	0	6	....	....	....	....	....	1970-71	1970-71
Myles, Vic	NYR	1	45	6	9	15	57	....	....	....	....	....	1942-43	1942-43

N

Name	NHL Teams	NHL Seasons	GP	G	A	TP	PIM	GP	G	A	TP	PIM	First NHL Season	Last NHL Season
Nahrgang, Jim	Det.	3	57	5	12	17	34	....	....	....	....	....	1974-75	1976-77
Nanne, Lou	Min.	11	635	68	157	225	356	32	4	10	14	9	1967-68	1977-78
Nantais, Richard	Min.	3	63	5	4	9	79	....	....	....	....	....	1974-75	1976-77
Nattrass, Ralph	Chi.	4	223	18	38	56	308	....	....	....	....	....	1946-47	1949-50
Nechaev, Victor	L.A.	1	3	1	0	1	0	....	....	....	....	....	1982-83	1982-83
Nedomansky, Vaclav	St.L., Det., NYR	6	421	122	156	278	88	7	3	5	8	0	1977-78	1982-83
Neely, Bob	Tor., Col.	5	283	39	59	98	266	26	5	7	12	15	1973-74	1977-78
Neilsen, Jim	NYR, Cal., Clev.	16	1023	69	299	368	904	65	1	17	18	61	1962-63	1977-78
Nelson, Gordie	Tor.	1	3	0	0	0	11	....	....	....	....	....	1969-70	1969-70
Nesterenko, Eric	Tor., Chi.	21	1219	250	324	574	1273	124	13	24	37	127	1951-52	1971-72
Nethery, Lance	NYR, Edm.	2	41	11	14	25	14	14	5	3	8	9	1980-81	1981-82
Neville, Mike	Tor.	3	62	6	3	9	14	2	0	0	0	0	1917-18	1925-26
Nevin, Bob	Tor., NYR, Min., L.A.	18	1128	307	419	726	211	84	16	18	34	24	1957-58	1975-76
Newberry, John	Mtl., Hfd.	4	22	0	4	4	6	2	0	0	0	0	1982-83	1985-86
Newell, Rick	Det.	2	7	0	0	0	0	....	....	....	....	....	1972-73	1973-74
Newman, Dan	NYR, Mtl., Edm.	4	126	17	24	41	63	3	0	0	0	4	1976-77	1979-80
Newman, John	Det.	1	8	1	1	2	0	....	....	....	....	....	1930-31	1930-31
Nicholson, Al	Bos.	2	19	0	1	1	4	....	....	....	....	....	1955-56	1956-57
Nicholson, Edward	Det.	1	1	0	0	0	0	....	....	....	....	....	1947-48	1947-48
Nicholson, Graeme	Bos., Col., NYR	3	52	2	7	9	60	....	....	....	....	....	1978-79	1982-83
Nicholson, John	Chi.	1	2	1	0	1	0	....	....	....	....	....	1937-38	1937-38
Nicholson, Neil	Oak., N.Y.I.	4	39	3	1	4	23	2	0	0	0	0	1969-70	1977-78
Nicholson, Paul	Wsh.	3	62	4	8	12	18	....	....	....	....	....	1974-75	1976-77
Niekamp, Jim	Det.	2	29	0	2	2	27	....	....	....	....	....	1970-71	1971-72
Nighbor, Frank	Ott., Tor.	13	348	135	61	196	255	36	11	9	20	27	1917-18	1929-30
Nigro, Frank	Tor.	2	68	8	18	26	39	3	0	0	0	2	1982-83	1983-84
Nilsson, Kent	Atl., Cgy., Min., Edm.	8	547	263	422	685	116	59	11	41	52	14	1979-80	1986-87
Nilsson, Ulf	NYR	4	170	57	112	169	85	25	8	14	22	27	1978-79	1982-83
Nistico, Lou	Col.	1	3	0	0	0	0	....	....	....	....	....	1977-78	1977-78
Noble, Reg	Tor., Mtl.M., Det.	16	526	167	79	246	807	32	4	5	9	39	1917-18	1932-33
Noel, Claude	Wsh.	1	7	0	0	0	0	....	....	....	....	....	1979-80	1979-80
Nolan, Pat	Tor.	1	2	0	0	0	0	....	....	....	....	....	1921-22	1921-22
Nolan, Ted	Det., Pit.	3	78	6	16	22	105	....	....	....	....	....	1981-82	1985-86
Nolet, Simon	Phi., K.C., Pit., Col.	10	562	150	182	332	187	34	6	3	9	8	1967-68	1976-77
Noris, Joe	Pit., St.L., Buf.	3	55	2	5	7	22	....	....	....	....	....	1971-72	1973-74
Norrish, Rod	Min.	2	21	3	3	6	2	....	....	....	....	....	1973-74	1974-75
Northcott, Baldy	Mtl.M., Chi.	11	446	133	112	245	273	31	8	5	13	14	1928-29	1938-39
Norwich, Craig	Wpg., St.L., Col.	2	104	17	58	75	60	....	....	....	....	....	1979-80	1980-81
Novy, Milan	Wsh.	1	73	18	30	48	16	2	0	0	0	0	1982-83	1982-83
Nowak, Hank	Pit., Det., Bos.	4	180	26	29	55	161	13	1	0	1	8	1973-74	1976-77
Nykoluk, Mike	Tor.	1	32	3	1	4	20	....	....	....	....	....	1956-57	1956-57
Nyrop, Bill	Mtl., Min.	4	207	12	51	63	101	35	1	7	8	22	1975-76	1981-82
Nystrom, Bob	NYI	14	900	235	278	513	1248	157	39	44	83	236	1972-73	1985-86

O

Name	NHL Teams	NHL Seasons	GP	G	A	TP	PIM	GP	G	A	TP	PIM	First NHL Season	Last NHL Season
Oatman, Russell	Det., Mtl.M., NYR	3	124	20	9	29	100	17	1	0	1	18	1926-27	1928-29
O'Brien, Dennis	Min., Col., Clev., Bos.	10	592	31	91	122	1017	34	1	2	3	101	1970-71	1979-80
O'Brien, Obie	Bos.	1	2	0	0	0	0	....	....	....	....	....	1955-56	1955-56
O'Connor, Buddy	Mtl., NYR	10	509	140	257	397	34	53	15	21	36	6	1941-42	1950-51
Oddleifson, Chris	Bos., Van.	9	524	95	191	286	464	14	1	6	7	8	1972-73	1980-81
O'Donnell, Fred	Bos.	2	115	15	11	26	98	5	0	1	1	5	1972-73	1973-74
O'Donoghue, Don	Oak., Cal.	3	125	18	17	35	35	3	0	0	0	0	1969-70	1971-72
Odrowski, Gerry	Det., Oak., St.L.	6	299	12	19	31	111	30	0	1	1	16	1960-61	1971-72
O'Flaherty, Gerry	Tor., Van., Atl.	8	438	99	95	194	168	7	2	2	4	6	1971-72	1978-79
O'Flaherty, John	NYA	2	21	5	1	6	0	....	....	....	....	....	1940-41	1941-42
Ogilvie, Brian	Chi., St.L.	6	90	15	21	36	29	....	....	....	....	....	1972-73	1978-79
O'Grady, George	Mtl.M.	1	4	0	0	0	0	....	....	....	....	....	1917-18	1917-18
Okerlund, Todd	NYI	1	4	0	0	0	2	....	....	....	....	....	1987-88	1987-88
Oliver, Harry	Bos., NYA	11	473	127	85	212	147	35	10	6	16	22	1926-27	1936-37
Oliver, Murray	Det., Bos., Tor., Min.	17	1127	274	454	728	319	35	9	16	25	10	1957-58	1974-75
Olmstead, Bert	Chi., Mtl., Tor.	14	848	181	421	602	884	115	16	42	58	101	1948-49	1961-62
Olson, Dennis	Det.	1	4	0	0	0	0	....	....	....	....	....	1957-58	1957-58
O'Neil, Paul	Van., Bos.	2	6	0	0	0	0	....	....	....	....	....	1973-74	1975-76
O'Neill, Jim	Bos., Mtl.	6	165	6	30	36	109	11	1	1	2	13	1933-34	1941-42
O'Neill, Tom	Tor.	2	66	10	12	22	53	4	0	0	0	6	1943-44	1944-45
O'Regan, Tom	Pit.	3	60	5	12	17	10	....	....	....	....	....	1983-84	1985-86
Orban, Bill	Chi., Min.	3	114	8	15	23	67	3	0	0	0	0	1967-68	1969-70
O'Ree, Willie	Bos.	2	45	4	10	14	26	....	....	....	....	....	1957-58	1960-61
O'Reilly, Terry	Bos.	14	891	204	402	606	2095	108	25	42	67	335	1971-72	1984-85
Orlando, Gaetano	Buf.	3	98	18	26	44	51	5	0	4	4	14	1984-85	1986-87
Orlando, Jimmy	Det.	6	200	7	24	31	375	36	0	9	9	105	1936-37	1942-43
Orleski, Dave	Mtl.	2	2	0	0	0	0	....	....	....	....	....	1980-81	1981-82
Orr, Bobby	Bos., Chi.	12	657	270	645	915	953	74	26	66	92	107	1966-67	1978-79
Osburn, Randy	Tor., Phi.	2	27	0	2	2	0	....	....	....	....	....	1972-73	1974-75
O'Shea, Danny	Min., Chi., St.L.	5	369	64	115	179	265	39	3	7	10	62	1968-69	1972-73
O'Shea, Kevin	Buf., St.L.	3	134	13	18	31	85	12	2	1	3	10	1970-71	1972-73
Ouelette, Eddie	Chi.	1	43	3	2	5	11	1	0	0	0	0	1935-36	1935-36
Ouelette, Gerry	Bos.	1	39	5	4	9	0	....	....	....	....	....	1960-61	1960-61
Owchar, Dennis	Pit., Col.	6	288	30	85	115	200	10	1	1	2	8	1974-75	1979-80
Owen, George	Bos.	5	192	44	33	77	151	21	2	5	7	25	1928-29	1932-33

P

Name	NHL Teams	NHL Seasons	GP	G	A	TP	PIM	GP	G	A	TP	PIM	First NHL Season	Last NHL Season
Pachal, Clayton	Bos., Col.	3	35	2	3	5	95	....	....	....	....	....	1976-77	1978-79
Paddock, John	Wsh., Phi., Que.	5	87	8	14	22	86	5	2	0	2	0	1975-76	1982-83
Paiement, Rosaire	Phi., Van.	5	190	48	52	100	343	3	3	0	3	0	1967-68	1971-72
Paiement, Wilf	K.C., Col., Tor., Que., NYR, Buf., Pit.	14	946	356	458	814	1757	69	18	17	35	185	1974-75	1987-88
Palangio, Peter	Mtl., Det., Chi.	5	71	13	10	23	28	7	0	0	0	0	1926-27	1937-38
Palazzari, Aldo	Bos., NYR	1	35	8	3	11	4	....	....	....	....	....	1943-44	1943-44
Palazzari, Doug	St.L.	4	108	18	20	38	23	2	0	0	0	0	1974-75	1978-79
Palmer, Brad	Min., Bos.	3	168	32	38	70	58	29	9	5	14	16	1980-81	1982-83
Palmer, Rob H.	L.A., N.J.	7	320	9	101	110	115	8	1	2	3	6	1977-78	1983-84
Palmer, Rob R.	Chi.	3	16	0	3	3	2	....	....	....	....	....	1973-74	1975-76
Panagabko, Ed	Bos.	2	29	0	3	3	38	....	....	....	....	....	1955-56	1956-57
Papike, Joe	Chi.	3	21	3	3	6	4	5	0	2	2	0	1940-41	1944-45
Pappin, Jim	Tor., Chi., Cal., Clev.	14	767	278	295	573	667	92	33	34	67	101	1963-64	1976-77
Paradise, Bob	Min., Atl., Pit., Wsh.	8	368	8	54	62	393	12	0	1	1	19	1971-72	1978-79
Pargeter, George	Mtl.	1	4	0	0	0	0	....	....	....	....	....	1946-47	1946-47
Parise, J.P.	Bos., Tor., Min., NYI, Clev.	14	890	238	356	594	706	86	27	31	58	87	1965-66	1978-79
Parizeau, Michel	St.L., Phi.	1	58	3	14	17	18	....	....	....	....	....	1971-72	1971-72
Park, Brad	NYR, Bos., Det.	17	1113	213	683	896	1429	161	35	90	125	217	1968-69	1984-85
Parkes, Ernie	Mtl.M.	1	17	0	0	0	2	....	....	....	....	....	1924-25	1924-25
Parsons, George	Tor.	3	64	12	13	25	17	7	3	2	5	11	1936-37	1938-39
Paterson, Mark	Hfd.	4	29	3	3	6	33	....	....	....	....	....	1982-83	1985-86
Paterson, Rick	Chi.	9	430	50	43	93	136	61	7	10	17	51	1978-79	1986-87
Patey, Doug	Wsh.	3	45	4	2	6	8	....	....	....	....	....	1976-77	1978-79
Patey, Larry	Cal., St.L., NYR	12	717	153	163	316	631	40	8	10	18	57	1973-74	1984-85
Patrick, Craig	Cal., St.L., K.C., Min., Wsh.	8	401	72	91	163	61	2	0	1	1	0	1971-72	1978-79
Patrick, Glenn	St.L., Cal., Clev.	3	38	2	3	5	72	....	....	....	....	....	1973-74	1976-77
Patrick, Lester	NYR	1	1	0	0	0	0	....	....	....	....	....	1926-27	1926-27
Patrick, Lynn	NYR	10	455	145	190	335	270	44	10	6	16	22	1934-35	1945-46
Patrick, Muzz	NYR	5	166	5	26	31	133	25	4	0	4	34	1937-38	1945-46
Patrick, Steve	Buf., NYR, Que.	6	250	40	68	108	242	12	0	1	1	12	1980-81	1985-86
Patterson, Dennis	K.C., Phi.	3	138	6	22	28	67	....	....	....	....	....	1974-75	1979-80
Patterson, Pat	Bos., Det., St.L., Tor., Mtl., NYA	9	289	51	27	78	221	3	0	0	0	2	1926-27	1934-35
Paul, Arthur	Det.	1	3	0	0	0	0	....	....	....	....	....	1964-65	1964-65
Paulus, Rollie	Mtl.	1	33	0	0	0	0	....	....	....	....	....	1925-26	1925-26

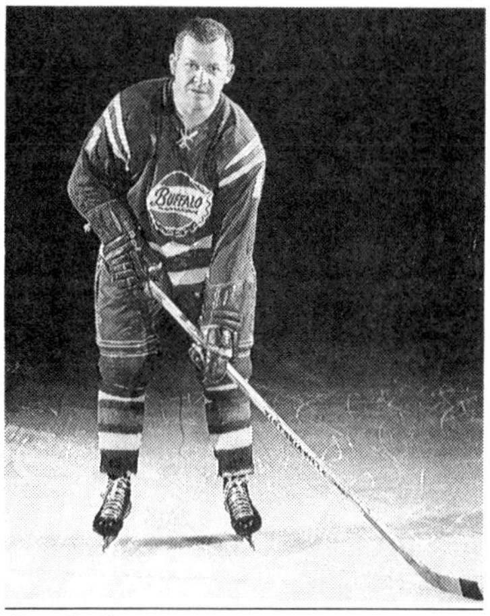

Gary Ouellette

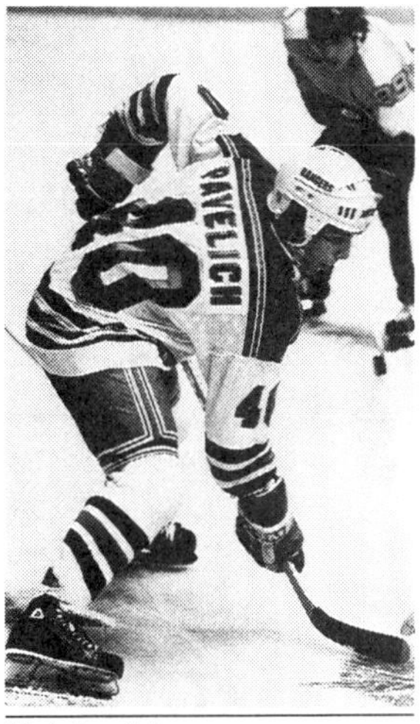

Mark Pavelich

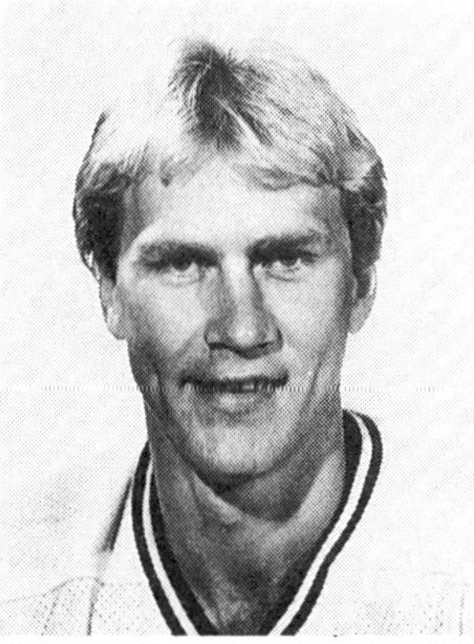
Willi Plett

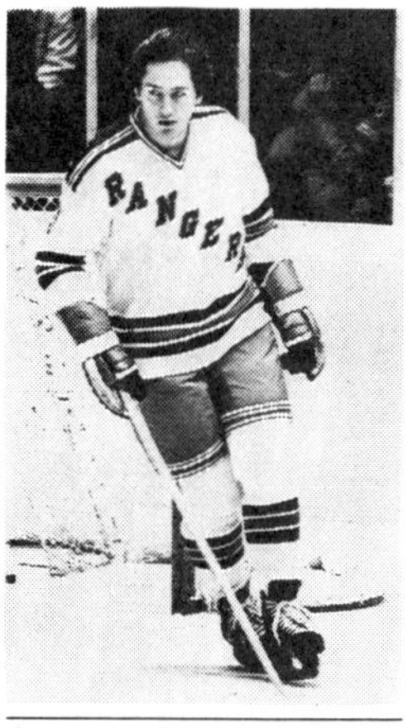

Greg Polis

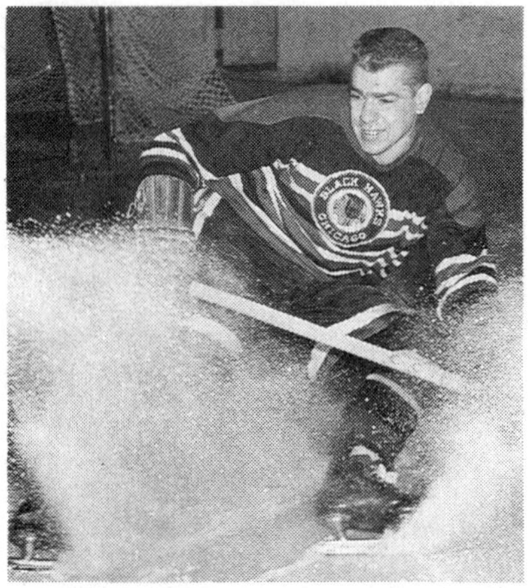

Metro Prystai

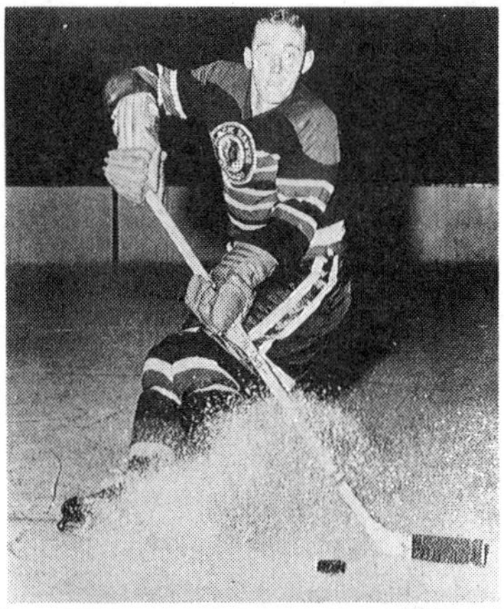

Clare Raglan

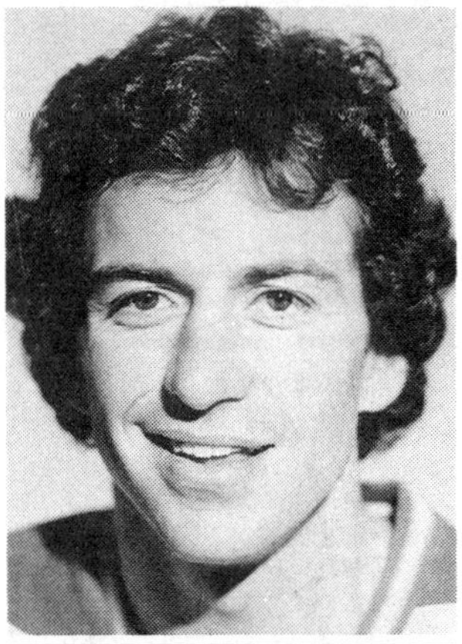

Doug Risebrough

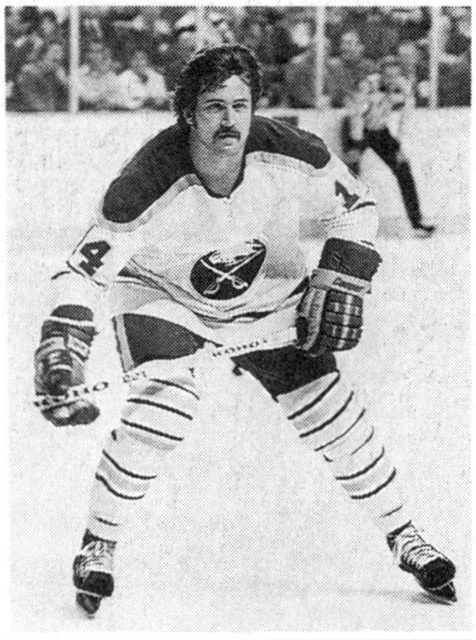

Rene Robert

Name	NHL Teams	NHL Seasons	Regular Schedule					Playoffs					First NHL Season	Last NHL Season
			GP	G	A	TP	PIM	GP	G	A	TP	PIM		
Pavelich, Mark	NYR, Min.	6	353	137	191	328	336	23	7	17	24	14	1981-82	1986-87
Pavelich, Marty	Det.	10	634	93	159	252	454	91	13	15	28	74	1947-48	1956-57
Payer, Evariste	Mtl.	1	1	0	0	0	0	....	....	....	....	....	1917-18	1917-18
Payne, Steve	Min.	10	613	228	238	466	435	71	35	35	70	60	1978-79	1987-88
Pearson, Mel	NYR, Pit.	5	38	2	6	8	25	....	....	....	....	....	1949-50	1967-68
Peer, Bert	Det.	1	1	0	0	0	0	....	....	....	....	....	1939-40	1939-40
Peirson, Johnny	Bos.	11	545	153	173	326	315	49	9	17	26	26	1946-47	1957-58
Pelensky, Perry	Chi.	1	4	0	0	0	5	....	....	....	....	....	1983-84	1983-84
Peloffy, Andre	Wsh.	1	9	0	0	0	2	....	....	....	....	....	1974-75	1974-75
Pelyk, Mike	Tor.	9	441	26	88	114	566	40	0	3	3	41	1967-68	1977-78
Pennington, Cliff	Mtl., Bos.	3	101	17	42	59	6	....	....	....	....	....	1960-61	1962-63
Perlini, Fred	Tor.	2	8	2	3	5	0	....	....	....	....	....	1981-82	1983-84
Perreault, Fern	NYR	2	3	0	0	0	0	....	....	....	....	....	1947-48	1949-50
Perreault, Gilbert	Buf.	17	1191	512	814	1326	500	90	33	70	103	44	1970-71	1986-87
Perry, Brian	Oak., Buf.	3	96	16	29	45	24	8	1	1	2	4	1968-69	1970-71
Persson, Stefan	NYI	9	622	52	317	369	574	102	7	50	57	69	1977-78	1985-86
Pesut, George	Cal.	2	92	3	22	25	130	....	....	....	....	....	1974-75	1975-76
Peters, Frank	NYR	1	43	0	0	0	59	4	0	0	0	2	1930-31	1930-31
Peters, Garry	Mtl., NYR, Phi., Bos.	8	331	34	34	68	261	9	2	2	4	31	1964-65	1971-72
Peters, Jim	Det., Chi., Mtl., Bos.	9	574	125	150	275	186	60	5	9	14	22	1945-46	1953-54
Peters, Jimmy	Det., L.A.	9	309	37	36	73	48	11	0	2	2	2	1964-65	1974-75
Peters, Steve	Col.	1	2	0	1	1	0	....	....	....	....	....	1979-80	1979-80
Pettersson, Jorgen	St.L., Hfd., Wsh.	6	435	174	192	366	117	44	15	12	27	4	1980-81	1985-86
Pettinger, Eric	Ott., Bos., Tor.	3	97	7	12	19	83	4	1	0	1	8	1928-29	1930-31
Pettinger, Gord	Det., NYR, Bos.	8	292	42	74	116	77	49	4	5	9	11	1932-33	1939-40
Phillipoff, Harold	Atl., Chi.,	3	141	26	57	83	267	6	0	2	2	9	1977-78	1979-80
Phillips, Bat	Mtl.M.	1	27	1	1	2	6	4	0	0	0	2	1929-30	1929-30
Phillips, Bill	Mtl.M., NYA.	8	302	52	31	83	232	28	6	2	8	19	1925-26	1932-33
Phillips, Charlie	Mtl.	1	17	0	0	0	6	....	....	....	....	....	1942-43	1942-43
Picard, Adrien	St.L.	1	15	2	2	4	21	....	....	....	....	....	1967-68	1967-68
Picard, Noel	Atl., Mtl., St.L.	7	335	12	63	75	616	50	2	11	13	167	1964-65	1972-73
Picketts, Hal	NYA.	1	48	3	1	4	32	....	....	....	....	....	1933-34	1933-34
Pidhirny, Harry	Bos.	1	2	0	0	0	0	....	....	....	....	....	1957-58	1957-58
Pierce, Randy	Col., N.J., Hfd.	8	277	62	76	138	223	2	0	0	0	0	1977-78	1984-85
Pike, Alf	NYR	6	234	42	77	119	145	21	4	2	6	12	1939-40	1946-47
Pilote, Pierre	Chi., Tor.	14	890	80	418	498	1251	86	8	53	61	102	1955-56	1968-69
Pinder, Gerry	Chi., Cal.	3	223	55	69	124	135	17	0	4	4	6	1969-70	1971-72
Pirus, Alex	Min., Det.	4	159	30	28	58	94	2	0	1	1	2	1976-77	1979-80
Pitre, Didier	Mtl.	6	127	64	17	81	50	14	2	2	4	0	1917-18	1922-23
Plager, Barclay	St.L.	10	614	44	187	231	1115	68	3	20	23	182	1967-68	1976-77
Plager, Bob	NYR, St.L.	14	644	20	126	146	802	74	2	17	19	195	1964-65	1977-78
Plager, William	Min., St.L., Atl.	9	263	4	34	38	292	31	0	2	2	26	1967-68	1975-76
Plamondon, Gerry	Mtl.	5	74	7	13	20	10	11	5	2	7	2	1945-46	1950-51
Plante, Cam	Tor.	1	2	0	0	0	0	....	....	....	....	....	1984-85	1984-85
Plante, Pierre	NYR, Que., Phi., St.L., Chi.	9	599	125	172	297	599	33	2	6	8	51	1971-72	1979-80
Plantery, Mark	Wpg.	1	25	1	5	6	14	....	....	....	....	....	1980-81	1980-81
Plaxton, Hugh	Mtl.M.	1	15	1	2	3	4	....	....	....	....	....	1932-33	1932-33
Pleau, Larry	Mtl.	3	94	9	15	24	27	4	0	0	0	0	1969-70	1971-72
Plett, Willi	Atl., Cgy., Min., Bos.	13	834	222	215	437	2572	83	24	22	46	466	1975-76	1987-88
Plumb, Rob	Det.	1	7	2	1	3	0	....	....	....	....	....	1977-78	1977-78
Plumb, Ron	Hfd.	1	26	3	4	7	14	....	....	....	....	....	1979-80	1979-80
Pocza, Harvie	Wsh.	2	3	0	0	0	0	....	....	....	....	....	1979-80	1981-82
Podolsky, Nels	Det.	1	1	0	0	0	0	7	0	0	0	4	1948-49	1948-49
Poeta, Anthony	Chi.	1	1	0	0	0	0	....	....	....	....	....	1951-52	1951-52
Poile, Bud	NYR, Bos., Det., Tor., Chi.,	7	311	107	122	229	91	23	4	4	8	8	1942-43	1949-50
Poile, Don	Det.	2	66	7	9	16	12	4	0	0	0	0	1954-55	1957-58
Poirer, Gordie	Mtl.	1	10	0	1	1	0	....	....	....	....	....	1939-40	1939-40
Polanic, Tom	Min.	2	19	0	2	2	53	5	1	1	2	4	1969-70	1970-71
Polich, John	NYR	2	3	0	1	1	0	....	....	....	....	....	1939-40	1940-41
Polich, Mike	Mtl., Min.	5	226	24	29	53	57	23	2	1	3	2	1976-77	1980-81
Polis, Greg	Pit., St.L., NYR, Wsh.	10	615	174	169	343	391	7	0	2	2	6	1970-71	1979-80
Poliziani, Daniel	Bos.	1	1	0	0	0	0	3	0	0	0	0	1958-59	1958-59
Polonich, Dennis	Det.	8	390	59	82	141	1242	7	1	0	1	19	1974-75	1982-83
Pooley, Paul	Wpg.	2	15	0	3	3	0	....	....	....	....	....	1984-85	1985-86
Popein, Larry	NYR, Oak.	8	449	80	141	221	162	16	1	4	5	6	1954-55	1967-68
Popiel, Paul	Bos., L.A., Det., Van., Edm.	7	224	13	41	54	210	4	1	0	1	4	1965-66	1979-80
Portland, Jack	Chi., Mtl., Bos.	10	381	15	56	71	323	33	1	3	4	25	1933-34	1942-43
Posavad, Mike	St.L.	2	8	0	0	0	0	....	....	....	....	....	1985-86	1986-87
Porvari, Jukka	Col., N.J.	2	39	3	9	12	4	....	....	....	....	....	1981-82	1982-83
Potvin, Denis	NYI	15	1060	310	742	1052	1356	185	56	108	164	253	1973-74	1987-88
Potvin, Jean	L.A., Min., Phi., NYI, Cle.	11	613	63	224	287	478	39	2	9	11	17	1970-71	1980-81
Poulin, Dan	Min., Phi.	2	5	3	1	4	4	....	....	....	....	....	1981-82	1982-83
Pouzar, Jaroslav	Edm.	4	186	34	48	82	136	29	6	4	10	16	1982-83	1986-87
Powell, Ray	Chi.	1	31	7	15	22	2	....	....	....	....	....	1950-51	1950-51
Powis, Jeff	Chi.	1	2	0	0	0	0	....	....	....	....	....	1967-68	1967-68
Powis, Lynn	Chi., K.C.	2	130	19	33	52	25	1	0	0	0	0	1973-74	1974-75
Pratt, Babe	Bos., NYR, Tor.	12	517	83	209	292	473	63	12	17	29	90	1935-36	1946-47
Pratt, Jack	Bos.	2	37	2	0	2	42	4	0	0	0	0	1930-31	1931-32
Pratt, Kelly	Pit.	1	22	0	6	6	15	....	....	....	....	....	1974-75	1974-75
Pratt, Tracy	Van., Col., Buf., Pit. Tor., Oak.	10	580	17	97	114	1026	25	0	1	1	62	1967-68	1976-77
Prentice, Dean	Pit., Min., Det., NYR, Bos.	22	1378	391	469	860	484	54	13	17	30	38	1952-53	1973-74
Prentice, Eric	Tor.	1	5	0	0	0	4	....	....	....	....	....	1943-44	1943-44
Preston, Rich	Chi., N.J.	8	580	127	164	291	348	47	4	18	22	56	1979-80	1986-87
Preston, Yves	Phi.	2	28	7	3	10	4	....	....	....	....	....	1978-79	1980-81
Price, Bob	Ott.	1	1	0	0	0	0	....	....	....	....	....	1919-20	1919-20
Price, Jack	Chi.	3	57	4	6	10	24	4	0	0	0	0	1951-52	1953-54
Price, Noel	Pit., L.A., Det., Tor., NYR, Mtl., Atl.	14	499	14	114	128	333	12	0	1	1	8	1957-58	1975-76
Price, Pat	NYI, Edm., Pit., Que., NYR, Min.	13	726	43	218	261	1456	74	2	10	12	195	1975-76	1987-88
Price, Tom	Cal., Clev., Pit.	5	29	0	2	2	12	....	....	....	....	....	1974-75	1978-79
Primeau, Joe	Tor.	9	310	66	177	243	111	38	5	18	23	12	1927-28	1935-36
Primeau, Kevin	Van.	1	2	0	0	0	4	....	....	....	....	....	1980-81	1980-81
Pringle, Ellie	NYA	1	6	0	0	0	0	....	....	....	....	....	1930-31	1930-31
Prodgers, Goldie	Tor., Ham.	6	110	63	22	85	33	....	....	....	....	....	1919-20	1924-25
Pronovost, Andre	Det., Min., Mtl., Bos.	10	556	94	104	198	408	70	11	11	22	58	1956-57	1957-58
Pronovost, Jean	Wsh., Pit., Atl.	14	998	391	383	774	413	35	11	9	20	14	1968-69	1981-82
Pronovost, Marcel	Det., Tor.	21	1206	88	257	345	851	134	8	23	31	104	1950-51	1969-70
Provost, Claude	Mtl.	15	1005	254	335	589	469	126	25	38	63	86	1955-56	1969-70
Prystai, Metro	Chi., Det.	11	674	151	179	330	231	43	12	14	26	8	1947-48	1957-58
Pudas, Al	Tor.	1	3	0	0	0	0	....	....	....	....	....	1926-27	1926-27
Pulford, Bob	Tor., L.A.	16	1079	281	362	643	792	89	25	26	51	126	1956-57	1971-72
Pulkkinen, Dave	NYI	1	2	0	0	0	0	....	....	....	....	....	1972-73	1972-73
Purpur, Cliff	Det., Chi., St.L.	5	144	26	34	60	46	16	1	2	3	4	1934-35	1944-45
Pusie, Jean	Mtl., NYR, Bos.	5	61	1	4	5	28	7	0	0	0	0	1930-31	1935-36
Pyatt, Nelson	Det., Wsh., Col.	7	296	71	63	134	67	....	....	....	....	....	1973-74	1979-80

Q

Quackenbush, Bill	Det., Bos.	14	774	62	222	284	95	79	2	19	21	8	1942-43	1955-56
Quackenbush, Max	Bos., Chi.,	2	61	4	7	11	30	6	0	0	0	4	1950-51	1951-52
Quenneville, Leo	NYR	1	25	0	3	3	10	3	0	0	0	0	1929-30	1929-30
Quilty, John	Mtl., Bos.	4	125	36	34	70	81	13	3	5	8	9	1940-41	1947-48
Quinn, Pat	Tor., Van., Atl.	9	606	18	113	131	950	11	0	1	1	21	1968-69	1976-77

R

Radley, Yip	NYA, Mtl.M.	2	18	0	1	1	13	....	....	....	....	....	1930-31	1936-37
Raglan, Clare	Det., Chi.	3	100	4	9	13	52	3	0	0	0	0	1950-51	1952-53
Raleigh, Don	NYR	10	535	101	219	320	96	18	6	5	11	6	1943-44	1955-56
Ramsay, Beattie	Tor.,	1	43	0	2	2	10	....	....	....	....	....	1927-28	1927-28
Ramsay, Craig	Buf.	14	1070	252	420	672	201	89	17	31	48	27	1971-72	1984-85
Ramsay, Les	Chi.	1	11	2	2	4	2	....	....	....	....	....	1944-45	1944-45
Ramsay, Wayne	Buf.	1	2	0	0	0	0	....	....	....	....	....	1977-78	1977-78
Randall, Ken	Tor., Ham., NYA	10	217	67	28	95	360	13	3	1	4	19	1917-18	1926-27
Ranieri, George	Bos.	1	2	0	0	0	0	....	....	....	....	....	1956-57	1956-57
Ratelle, Jean	NYR, Bos.	21	1281	491	776	1267	276	123	32	66	98	24	1960-61	1980-81
Rathwell, John	Bos.	1	1	0	0	0	0	....	....	....	....	....	1974-75	1974-75

			Regular Schedule					Playoffs					First	Last
Name	NHL Teams	NHL Seasons	GP	G	A	TP	PIM	GP	G	A	TP	PIM	NHL Season	NHL Season
Rausse, Errol	Wsh.	3	31	7	3	10	0	....	....	....	....	....	1979-80	1981-82
Rautakallio, Pekka	Atl., Cgy.	3	235	33	121	154	122	23	2	5	7	8	1979-80	1981-82
Ravlich, Matt	Bos., Chi., Det., L.A.	9	410	12	78	90	364	24	1	5	6	16	1962-63	1972-73
Raymond, Armand	Mtl.	2	22	0	2	2	10	....	....	....	....	....	1937-38	1939-40
Raymond, Paul	Mtl.	4	76	2	3	5	6	5	0	0	0	2	1932-33	1937-38
Read, Mel	NYR	1	1	0	0	0	0	....	....	....	....	....	1946-47	1946-47
Reardon, Ken	Mtl.	7	341	26	96	122	604	31	2	5	7	62	1940-41	1949-50
Reardon, Terry	Bos., Mtl.	7	193	47	53	100	73	30	8	10	18	12	1938-39	1946-47
Reaume, Marc	Tor., Det., Mtl., Van.	9	344	8	43	51	273	21	0	2	2	8	1954-55	1970-71
Reay, Billy	Det., Mtl.	10	479	105	162	267	202	63	13	16	29	43	1943-44	1952-53
Redahl, Gord	Bos.	1	18	0	1	1	2	....	....	....	....	....	1958-59	1958-59
Redding, George	Bos.	2	35	3	2	5	10	....	....	....	....	....	1924-25	1925-26
Redmond, Dick	Min., Cal., Chi., St.L., Atl., Bos.	13	771	133	312	445	504	66	9	22	31	27	1969-70	1981-82
Redmond, Mickey	Mtl., Det.	9	538	233	195	428	219	16	2	3	5	2	1967-68	1975-76
Regan, Bill	NYR, NYA	3	67	3	2	5	67	8	0	0	0	2	1929-30	1932-33
Regan, Larry	Bos., Tor.,	5	280	41	95	136	71	42	7	14	21	18	1956-57	1960-61
Regier, Darcy	Clev., NYI	3	26	0	2	2	35	....	....	....	....	....	1977-78	1983-84
Reibel, Earl	Det., Chi., Bos.	6	409	84	161	245	75	39	6	14	20	4	1953-54	1958-59
Reid, Dave	Tor.	3	7	0	0	0	0	....	....	....	....	....	1952-53	1955-56
Reid, Gerry	Det.	1	2	0	0	0	2	....	....	....	....	....	1948-49	1948-49
Reid, Gordie	NYA	1	1	0	0	0	2	....	....	....	....	....	1936-37	1936-37
Reid, Reg	Tor.	2	40	2	0	2	4	2	0	0	0	0	1924-25	1925-26
Reid, Tom	Chi., Min.	11	701	17	113	130	654	42	1	13	14	49	1967-68	1977-78
Reigle, Ed	Bos.	1	17	0	2	2	25	....	....	....	....	....	1950-51	1950-51
Reinikka, Ollie	NYR	1	16	0	0	0	0	....	....	....	....	....	1926-27	1926-27
Reise, Leo Jr.	Chi., Det., NYR	9	494	28	81	109	399	52	8	5	13	68	1945-46	1953-54
Reise, Leo Sr.	Ham., NYA, NYR	8	199	36	29	65	177	6	0	0	0	16	1920-21	1929-30
Renaud, Mark	Hfd., Buf.	5	152	6	50	56	86	....	....	....	....	....	1979-80	1983-84
Ribble, Pat	Atl., Chi., Tor., Wsh., Cgy.	8	349	19	60	79	365	8	0	1	1	12	1975-76	1982-83
Richard, Henri	Mtl.	20	1256	358	688	1046	928	180	49	80	129	181	1955-56	1974-75
Richard, Jacques	Alt., Buf., Que.	10	556	160	187	347	307	35	5	5	10	34	1972-73	1982-83
Richard, Maurice	Mtl.	18	978	544	421	965	1285	133	82	44	126	188	1942-43	1959-60
Richardson, Dave	NYR, Chi., Det.	4	45	3	2	5	27	....	....	....	....	....	1963-64	1967-68
Richardson, Glen	Van.	1	24	3	6	9	19	....	....	....	....	....	1975-76	1975-76
Richardson, Ken	St.L.	3	49	8	13	21	16	....	....	....	....	....	1974-75	1978-79
Richer, Bob	Buf.	1	3	0	0	0	0	....	....	....	....	....	1972-73	1972-73
Riley, Bill	Wsh., Wpg.	5	139	31	30	61	320	....	....	....	....	....	1974-75	1979-80
Riley, Jack	Det., Mtl., Bos.,	4	104	10	22	32	8	4	0	3	3	0	1932-33	1935-36
Riley, Jim	Det.	1	17	0	2	2	14	....	....	....	....	....	1926-27	1926-27
Riopellie, Howard	Mtl.	3	169	27	16	43	73	8	1	1	2	2	1947-48	1949-50
Rioux, Gerry	Wpg.	1	8	0	0	0	6	....	....	....	....	....	1979-80	1979-80
Rioux, Pierre	Cgy.	1	14	1	2	3	4	....	....	....	....	....	1982-83	1982-83
Ripley, Vic	Chi., Bos., NYR, St.L.	7	278	51	49	100	173	20	4	1	5	10	1928-29	1934-35
Risebrough, Doug	Mtl., Cgy.	14	740	185	286	471	1542	124	21	37	58	238	1974-75	1986-87
Rissling, Gary	Wsh., Pit.	7	221	23	30	53	1008	5	0	1	1	4	1978-79	1984-85
Ritchie, Bob	Phi., Det.	2	29	8	4	12	10	....	....	....	....	....	1976-77	1977-78
Ritchie, Dave	Mtl.W, Ott., Tor., Que., Mtl.	6	54	15	3	18	27	1	0	0	0	0	1917-18	1925-26
Ritson, Alex	NYR	1	1	0	0	0	0	....	....	....	....	....	1944-45	1944-45
Rittinger, Alan	Bos.	1	19	3	7	10	0	....	....	....	....	....	1943-44	1943-44
Rivard, Bob	Pit.	1	27	5	12	17	4	....	....	....	....	....	1967-68	1967-68
Rivers, Gus	Mtl.	3	88	4	5	9	12	16	2	0	2	2	1929-30	1931-32
Rivers, Wayne	Det., Bos., St.L., NYR	7	108	15	30	45	94	....	....	....	....	....	1961-62	1968-69
Rizzuto, Garth	Van.	1	37	3	4	7	16	....	....	....	....	....	1970-71	1970-71
Roach, Mickey	Tor., Ham., NYA	8	209	75	27	102	41	....	....	....	....	....	1919-20	1926-27
Robert, Claude	Mtl.	1	23	1	0	1	9	....	....	....	....	....	1950-51	1950-51
Robert, Rene	Tor., Pit., Buf., Col.	12	744	284	418	702	597	50	22	19	41	73	1970-71	1981-82
Robert, Sammy	Ott.	1	1	0	0	0	0	....	....	....	....	....	1917-18	1917-18
Roberto, Phil	Mtl., St.L., Det., K.C., Col., Clev.	8	385	75	106	181	464	31	9	8	17	69	1969-70	1976-77
Roberts, Doug	Det., Oak., Cal., Bos.	10	419	43	104	147	342	16	2	3	5	46	1965-66	1974-75
Roberts, Jim	Mtl., St.L.	15	1006	126	194	320	621	153	20	16	36	160	1963-64	1977-78
Roberts, Jimmy	Min.	3	106	17	23	40	33	2	0	0	0	0	1976-77	1978-79
Robertson, Fred	Tor., Det.,	2	34	1	0	1	35	7	0	0	0	0	1931-32	1933-34
Robertson, Geordie	Buf.	1	5	1	2	3	7	....	....	....	....	....	1982-83	1982-83
Robertson, George	Mtl.	2	31	2	5	7	6	....	....	....	....	....	1947-48	1948-49
Robidoux, Florent	Chi.	3	52	7	4	11	75	....	....	....	....	....	1980-81	1983-84
Robinson, Doug	Chi., NYR, L.A.	7	239	44	67	111	34	11	4	3	7	0	1963-64	1970-71
Robinson, Earl	Mtl.M., Chi., Mtl.	11	418	83	98	181	133	25	5	4	9	0	1928-29	1939-40
Robinson, Moe	Mtl.	1	1	0	0	0	0	....	....	....	....	....	1979-80	1979-80
Robitaille, Mike	NYR, Det., Buf., Van.	8	382	23	105	128	280	13	0	1	1	4	1969-70	1976-77
Roche, Michel	Mtl.M., Ott., St.L., Mtl., Det.	4	112	20	18	38	44	....	....	....	....	....	1930-31	1934-35
Roche, Earl	Mtl.M., Bos., Ott., St.L., Det.	4	146	25	27	52	48	2	0	0	0	0	1930-31	1934-35
Roche, Ernest	Mtl.	1	4	0	0	0	2	....	....	....	....	....	1950-51	1950-51
Rochefort, Dave	Det.	1	1	0	0	0	0	....	....	....	....	....	1966-67	1966-67
Rochefort, Leon	NYR, Mtl., Phi., L.A., Det., Atl., Van.	15	617	121	147	268	93	39	4	4	8	16	1960-61	1975-76
Rockburn, Harvey	Det., Ott.	3	94	4	2	6	254	....	....	....	....	....	1929-30	1932-33
Rodden, Eddie	Chi., Tor., Bos., NYR	4	98	6	14	20	152	2	0	1	1	0	1926-27	1930-31
Rogers, Alfred	Min.	2	14	2	4	6	0	....	....	....	....	....	1973-74	1974-75
Rogers, Mike	Hfd., NYR, Edm.	7	484	202	317	519	184	17	1	13	14	6	1979-80	1985-86
Rolfe, Dale	Bos., L.A., Det., NYR	9	509	25	125	150	556	71	5	24	29	89	1959-60	1974-75
Romanchych, Larry	Chi., Atl	6	298	68	97	165	102	7	2	2	4	4	1970-71	1976-77
Rombough, Doug	Buf., NYI, Min.	4	150	24	27	51	80	....	....	....	....	....	1972-73	1975-76
Romnes, Doc	Chi., Tor., NYA	10	359	67	137	204	42	43	7	18	25	4	1930-31	1939-40
Honan, Skene	Ott.	1	11	0	0	0	0	....	....	....	....	....	1918-19	1918-19
Ronson, Len	NYR, Oak.	2	18	2	1	3	10	....	....	....	....	....	1960-61	1968-69
Ronty, Paul	Bos., NYR, Mtl.	8	488	101	211	312	103	21	1	7	8	6	1947-48	1954-55
Ross, Art	Mtl.W	1	3	1	0	1	0	....	....	....	....	....	1917-18	1917-18
Ross, Jim	NYR	2	62	2	11	13	29	....	....	....	....	....	1951-52	1952-53
Rossignol, Roland	Det., Mtl.	3	14	3	5	8	6	1	0	0	0	2	1943-44	1945-46
Rota, Darcy	Chi., Atl., Van.	11	794	256	239	495	973	60	14	7	21	147	1973-74	1983-84
Rota, Randy	Mtl., L.A., K.C., Col.	5	212	38	39	77	60	5	0	1	1	0	1972-73	1976-77
Rothschild, Sam	Mtl.M., NYA	4	99	8	6	14	24	10	0	0	0	0	1924-25	1927-28
Roulston, Rolly	Det.	3	24	0	6	6	10	....	....	....	....	....	1935-36	1937-38
Roulston, Tom	Edm., Pit.	6	195	47	49	96	74	21	2	2	4	2	1980-81	1985-86
Rousseau, Bobby	Mtl., Min., NYR	15	942	245	458	703	359	128	27	57	84	69	1960-61	1974-75
Rousseau, Guy	Mtl.	2	4	0	1	1	0	....	....	....	....	....	1954-55	1965-66
Rousseau, Roland	Mtl.	1	2	0	0	0	0	....	....	....	....	....	1952-53	1952-53
Rowe, Bobby	Bos.	1	4	1	0	1	0	....	....	....	....	....	1924-25	1924-25
Rowe, Mike	Pit.	3	11	0	0	0	11	....	....	....	....	....	1984-85	1986-87
Rowe, Ron	NYR	1	5	1	0	1	0	....	....	....	....	....	1947-48	1947-48
Rowe, Tom	Wsh., Hfd., Det.	7	357	85	100	185	615	3	2	0	2	0	1976-77	1982-83
Rozzini, Gino	Bos.	1	31	5	10	15	20	6	1	2	3	6	1944-45	1944-45
Ruelle, Bernard	Det.	1	2	1	0	1	0	....	....	....	....	....	1943-44	1943-44
Ruhnke, Kent	Bos.	1	2	0	1	1	0	....	....	....	....	....	1975-76	1975-76
Rundqvist, Thomas	Mtl.	1	2	0	1	1	0	....	....	....	....	....	1984-85	1984-85
Runge, Paul	Bos., Mtl.M., Mtl.	7	143	18	22	40	57	7	0	0	0	6	1930-31	1937-38
Ruotsalinen, Reijo	NYR, Edm.	6	405	104	225	329	160	64	13	21	34	32	1981-82	1986-87
Rupp, Duane	NYR, Tor., Min., Pit.	10	374	24	93	117	220	10	2	2	4	8	1962-63	1972-73
Russell, Churchill	NYR	3	90	20	16	36	12	....	....	....	....	....	1945-46	1947-48
Russell, Phi.	Chi., Atl., Cgy., N.J., Buf.	15	1016	99	325	424	2038	73	4	22	26	202	1972-73	1986-87

S

Saarinen, Simo	NYR	1	8	0	0	0	0	....	....	....	....	....	1984-85	1984-85
Sabourin, Bob	Tor.	1	1	0	0	0	2	....	....	....	....	....	1951-52	1951-52
Sabourin, Gary	St.L., Tor., Cal., Clev.	10	627	169	188	357	397	62	19	11	30	58	1967-68	1976-77
Sacharuk, Larry	NYR, St.L.	5	151	29	33	62	42	2	1	1	2	2	1972-73	1976-77
Saganiuk, Rocky	Tor., Pit.	6	259	57	65	122	201	6	1	0	1	15	1978-79	1983-84
St. Laurent, Andre	NYI, Det., L.A., Pit.	11	644	129	187	316	749	59	8	12	20	48	1973-74	1983-84
St. Laurent, Dollard	Mtl., Chi.	12	652	29	133	162	496	92	2	22	24	87	1950-51	1961-62
St. Marseille, Frank	St.L., L.A.	10	707	140	285	425	242	88	20	25	45	18	1967-68	1976-77
St. Sauveur, Claude	Atl.	1	79	24	24	48	23	2	0	0	0	0	1975-76	1975-76
Saleski, Don	Phi., Col.	9	543	128	125	253	629	82	13	17	30	131	1971-72	1979-80
Salovaara, John	Det.	2	90	2	13	15	70	....	....	....	....	....	1974-75	1975-76
Salvian, Dave	NYI	1	1	0	1	1	2	....	....	....	....	....	1976-77	1976-77
Samis, Phi.	Tor.	2	2	0	0	0	0	5	0	1	1	2	1947-48	1949-50
Sampson, Gary	Wsh.	4	105	13	22	35	25	12	1	0	1	0	1983-84	1986-87
Sanderson, Derek	Bos., NYR, St.L., Van., Pit.	13	598	202	250	452	911	56	18	12	30	187	1965-66	1977-78

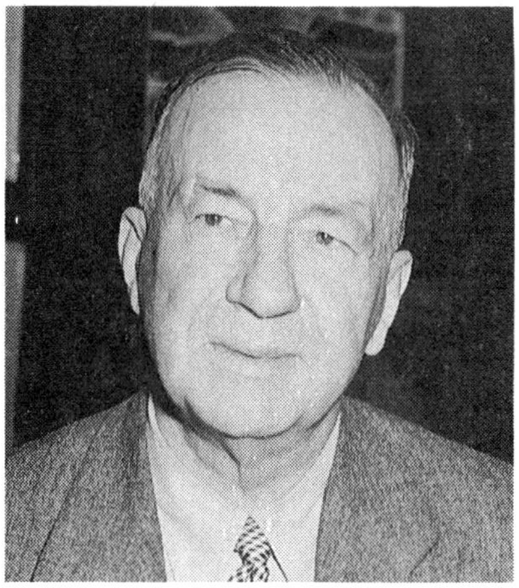
Art Ross

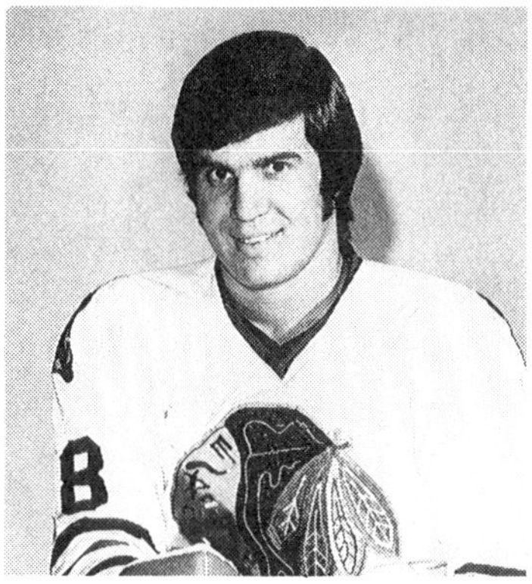
Darcy Rota

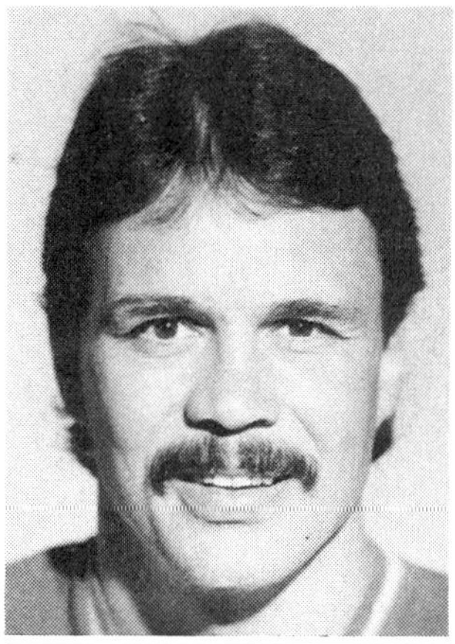
Phil Russell

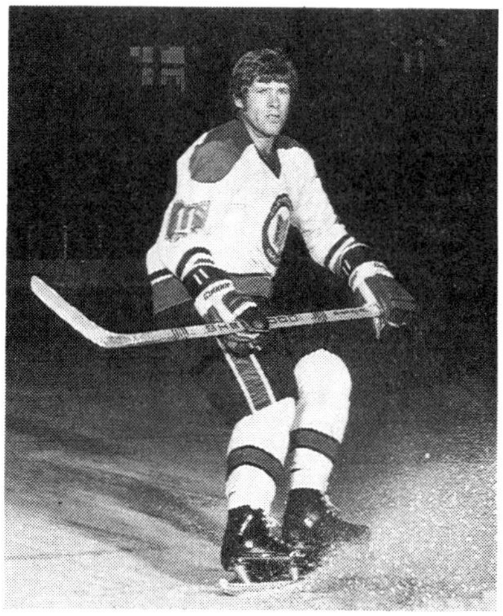
Garry Sabourin

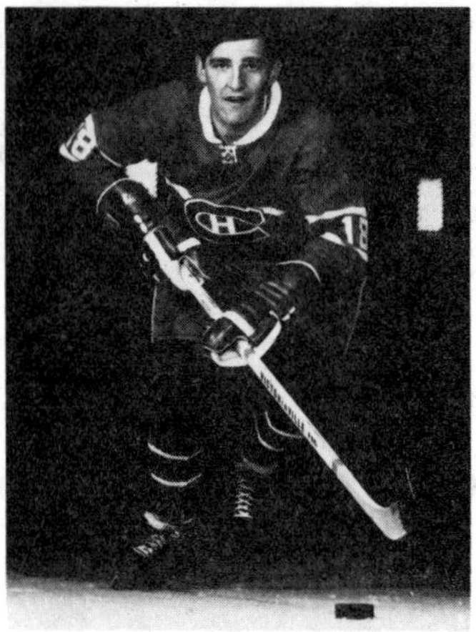

Serge Savard

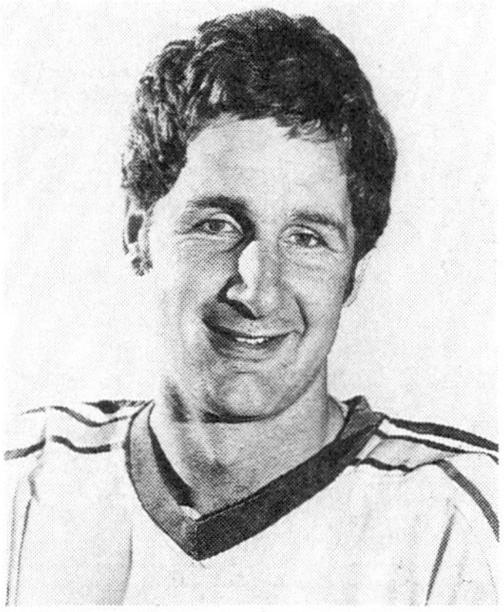

Rod Seiling

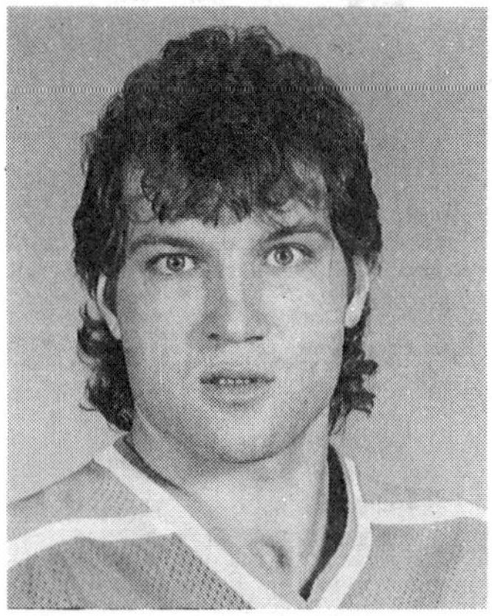

Dave Semenko

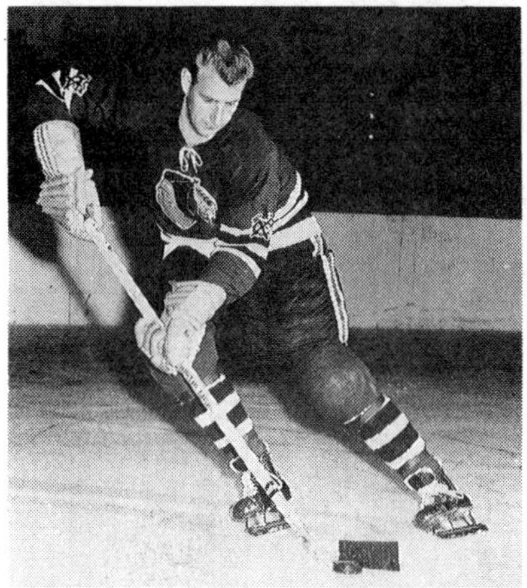

Glen Skov

			Regular Schedule					Playoffs					First	Last
Name	NHL Teams	NHL Seasons	GP	G	A	TP	PIM	GP	G	A	TP	PIM	NHL Season	NHL Season
Sandford, Ed	Bos., Det., Chi.	9	502	106	145	251	355	42	12	11	24	27	1947-48	1955-56
Sands, Charlie	Tor., Bos., Mtl., NYR	12	432	99	109	208	58	44	6	6	12	4	1932-33	1943-44
Sargent, Gary	L.A., Min.	8	402	61	161	222	273	20	5	7	12	8	1975-76	1982-83
Sarner, Craig	Bos.	1	7	0	0	0	0	....	....	....	....	....	1974-75	1974-75
Sarrazin, Dick	Phi.	3	100	20	35	55	22	4	0	0	0	0	1968-69	1971-72
Saskamoose, Fred	Chi.	1	11	0	0	0	6	....	....	....	....	....	1953-54	1953-54
Sasser, Grant	Pit.	1	3	0	0	0	0	....	....	....	....	....	1983-84	1983-84
Sather, Glen	Bos., Pit., NYR, St.L., Mtl., Min.	10	658	80	113	193	724	72	1	5	6	86	1966-67	1975-76
Saunders, Bernie	Que.	2	10	0	1	1	8	....	....	....	....	....	1979-80	1980-81
Saunders, Bud	Ott.	1	19	1	3	4	4	....	....	....	....	....	1933-34	1933-34
Sauve, Jenn F.	Buf., Que.	7	290	65	138	203	117	36	9	12	21	10	1980-81	1986-87
Savage, Tony	Bos., Mtl.	1	49	1	5	6	6	2	0	0	0	0	1934-35	1934-35
Savard, Andre	Bos., Buf., Que.	12	790	211	271	482	411	85	13	18	31	77	1973-74	1984-85
Savard, Jean	Chi., Hfd.	3	43	7	12	19	29	....	....	....	....	....	1977-78	1979-80
Savard, Serge	Mtl., Wpg.	17	1040	106	333	439	592	130	19	49	68	88	1966-67	1982-83
Scamurra, Peter	Wsh.	4	132	8	25	33	59	....	....	....	....	....	1975-76	1979-80
Sceviour, Darin	Chi.	1	1	0	0	0	0	....	....	....	....	....	1986-87	1986-87
Schaeffer, Butch	Chi.,	1	5	0	0	0	6	....	....	....	....	....	1936-37	1936-37
Schamehorn, Kevin	Det., L.A.	3	10	0	0	0	17	....	....	....	....	....	1976-77	1980-81
Schella, John	Van.	2	115	2	18	20	224	....	....	....	....	....	1970-71	1971-72
Scherza, Chuck	Bos., NYR	2	56	6	6	12	35	....	....	....	....	....	1943-44	1944-45
Schinkel, Ken	NYR, Pit.	12	636	127	198	325	163	19	7	2	9	4	1959-60	1972-73
Schliebener, Andy	Van.	3	84	2	11	13	74	6	0	0	0	0	1981-82	1984-85
Schmautz, Bobby	Chi., Bos., Edm., Col., Van.	13	764	271	286	557	988	73	28	33	61	92	1967-68	1980-81
Schmautz, Cliff	Buf., Phi.	1	56	13	19	32	33	....	....	....	....	....	1970-71	1970-71
Schmidt, Clarence	Bos.,	1	7	1	0	1	2	....	....	....	....	....	1943-44	1943-44
Schmidt, Jackie	Bos.	1	45	6	7	13	6	5	0	0	0	0	1942-43	1942-43
Schmidt, Joseph	Bos.	1	2	0	0	0	0	....	....	....	....	....	1943-44	1943-44
Schmidt, Milt	Bos.	16	778	229	346	575	466	86	24	25	49	60	1936-37	1954-55
Schmidt, Norm	Pit.	4	125	23	33	56	73	....	....	....	....	....	1983-84	1987-88
Schnarr, Werner	Bos.	2	25	0	0	0	0	....	....	....	....	....	1924-25	1925-26
Schock, Danny	Bos., Phi.	2	20	1	2	3	0	1	0	0	0	0	1969-70	1970-71
Schock, Ron	Bos., St.L., Pit., Buf.	15	909	166	351	517	260	55	4	16	20	29	1963-64	1977-78
Schoenfeld, Jim	Buf., Det., Bos.	13	719	51	204	255	1132	75	3	13	16	151	1972-73	1984-85
Schofield, Dwight	Det., Mtl., St.L., Wsh., Pit., Wpg.	7	211	8	22	30	631	9	0	0	0	55	1976-77	1987-88
Schriner, Sweeny	NYA, Tor.	11	484	206	204	410	148	60	18	11	29	54	1934-35	1945-46
Schultz, Dave	Phi., L.A., Pit., Buf.	9	535	79	121	200	2294	73	8	12	20	412	1971-72	1979-80
Schurman, Maynard	Hfd.	1	7	0	0	0	0	....	....	....	....	....	1979-80	1979-80
Schutt, Rod	Mtl., Pit., Tor.	8	286	77	92	169	177	22	8	6	14	26	1977-78	1985-86
Sclisizzi, Enio	Det., Chi.	6	81	12	11	23	26	13	0	0	0	6	1946-47	1952-53
Scott, Ganton	Tor., Ham., Mtl.M.	3	53	1	1	2	0	....	....	....	....	....	1922-23	1924-25
Scott, Laurie	NYA, NYR	2	62	6	3	9	28	....	....	....	....	....	1926-27	1927-28
Scruton, Howard	L.A.	1	4	0	4	4	9	....	....	....	....	....	1982-83	1982-83
Sedlbauer, Ron	Van., Chi., Tor.	7	430	143	86	229	210	19	1	3	4	27	1974-75	1980-81
Seguin, Dan	Min., Van.	2	37	2	6	8	50	....	....	....	....	....	1970-71	1973-74
Seguin, Steve	L.A.	1	5	0	0	0	9	....	....	....	....	....	1984-85	1984-85
Seibert, Earl	NYR, Chi., Det.	15	89	187	276	768	66	11	8	9	19	66	1931-32	1945-46
Seiling, Ric	Buf., Det.	10	738	179	208	387	573	62	14	14	28	36	1977-78	1986-87
Seiling, Rod	Tor., NYR, Wsh., St.L., Atl.	17	979	62	269	331	603	77	4	8	12	55	1962-63	1978-79
Selby, Brit	Tor., Phi., St.L.	8	350	55	62	117	163	16	1	1	2	8	1964-65	1971-72
Self, Steve	Wsh.	1	3	0	0	0	0	....	....	....	....	....	1976-77	1976-77
Selwood, Brad	Tor., L.A.	3	163	7	40	47	153	6	0	0	0	4	1970-71	1979-80
Semenko, Dave	Edm., Hfd., Tor.	9	575	65	88	153	1175	73	6	6	12	208	1979-80	1987-88
Senick, George	NYR	1	13	2	3	5	8	....	....	....	....	....	1952-53	1952-53
Seppa, Jyrki	Wpg.	1	13	0	2	2	6	....	....	....	....	....	1983-84	1983-84
Serafini, Ron	Cal.	1	2	0	0	0	2	....	....	....	....	....	1973-74	1973-74
Servinis, George	Min.	1	5	0	0	0	0	....	....	....	....	....	1987-88	1987-88
Shack, Eddie	NYR, Tor., Bos., L.A., Buf., Pit.	17	1047	239	226	465	1437	74	6	7	13	151	1957-58	1974-75
Shack, Joe	NYR	2	70	23	13	36	20	....	....	....	....	....	1942-43	1944-45
Shakes, Paul	Cal.	1	21	0	4	4	12	....	....	....	....	....	1973-74	1973-74
Shanahan, Sean	Mtl., Col., Bos.	3	40	1	3	4	47	....	....	....	....	....	1975-76	1977-78
Shand, Dave	Atl., Tor., Wsh.	8	421	19	84	103	544	26	1	2	3	83	1976-77	1984-85
Shannon, Charles	NYA	1	4	0	0	0	2	....	....	....	....	....	1939-40	1939-40
Shannon, Gerry	Ott., St.L., Bos., Mtl.M.	5	183	23	29	52	121	9	0	1	1	2	1933-34	1937-38
Sharpley, Glen	Min., Chi.	6	389	117	161	278	199	27	7	11	18	24	1976-77	1981-82
Shaunessy, Scott	Que.	1	3	0	0	0	7	....	....	....	....	....	1986-87	1986-87
Shay, Norman	Bos., Tor.	2	53	5	2	7	34	....	....	....	....	....	1924-25	1925-26
Shea, Pat	Chi.	1	14	0	1	1	0	....	....	....	....	....	1931-32	1931-32
Sheehan, Bobby	Mtl., Cal., Chi., Det., NYR, Col., L.A.	9	310	48	63	111	50	25	4	3	7	8	1969-70	1980-82
Sheehy, Tim	Det., Hfd.	2	27	2	1	3	0	....	....	....	....	....	1977-78	1979-80
Shelton, Doug	Chi.	1	5	0	1	1	0	....	....	....	....	....	1967-68	1967-68
Sheppard, Frank	Det.	1	8	1	1	2	0	....	....	....	....	....	1927-28	1927-28
Sheppard, Gregg	Bos., Pit.	10	657	205	293	498	243	92	32	40	72	31	1972-73	1981-82
Sheppard, Johnny	Det., NYA, Bos., Chi.	8	311	68	58	126	224	10	0	0	0	0	1926-27	1933-34
Sherf, John	Det.	5	19	0	0	0	8	8	0	1	1	2	1935-36	1943-44
Shero, Fred	NYR	3	145	6	14	20	137	13	0	2	2	8	1947-48	1949-50
Sherritt, Gordon	Det.	1	8	0	0	0	12	....	....	....	....	....	1943-44	1987-88
Sherven, Gord	Edm., Min., Hfd.	5	97	13	22	35	33	3	0	0	0	0	1983-84	1987-88
Shewchuck, Jack	Bos.	6	187	9	19	28	160	20	0	1	1	19	1938-39	1944-45
Shibicky, Alex	NYR	8	317	110	91	201	161	40	12	12	24	12	1935-36	1945-46
Shields, Al	Ott., Phi., NYA, Mtl.M., Bos.	11	460	39	49	88	637	17	0	1	1	14	1927-28	1937-38
Shill, Bill	Bos.	3	79	21	13	34	18	7	1	2	3	2	1942-43	1946-47
Shill, Jack	Tor., Bos., NYA, Chi.	6	163	15	20	35	70	27	1	6	7	13	1933-34	1938-39
Shinske, Rick	Clev., St.L.	3	63	5	16	21	10	....	....	....	....	....	1970-71	1972-73
Shires, Jim	Det., St.L., Pit.	3	56	3	6	9	32	....	....	....	....	....	1968-69	1981-82
Shmyr, Paul	Chi., Cal., Min., Hfd.	7	343	13	72	85	528	34	3	3	6	44	1981-82	1981-82
Shore, Eddie	Bos., NYA	14	553	105	179	284	1047	55	6	13	19	187	1926-27	1939-40
Shore, Hamby	Ott.	1	18	3	0	3	0	....	....	....	....	....	1917-18	1917-18
Shores, Aubry	Phi.	1	1	0	0	0	0	....	....	....	....	....	1930-31	1930-31
Short, Steve	L.A., Det.	2	6	0	0	0	2	....	....	....	....	....	1977-78	1978-79
Shutt, Steve	Mtl., L.A.	13	930	424	393	817	410	99	50	48	98	65	1972-73	1984-85
Siebert, Babe	Mtl.M., NYR, Bos., Mtl.	14	593	140	156	296	982	54	8	7	15	62	1925-26	1938-39
Silk, Dave	NYR, Bos., Wpg., Det.	7	249	54	59	113	271	13	2	4	6	13	1979-80	1985-86
Siltala, Mike	Wsh., NYR	3	7	1	0	1	2	....	....	....	....	....	1981-82	1987-88
Siltanen, Risto	Edm., Hfd., Que.	8	562	90	265	355	266	32	6	12	18	30	1979-80	1986-87
Simonetti, Frank	Bos.	4	115	5	8	13	76	12	0	1	1	8	1984-85	1987-88
Simmer, Charlie	Cal., Clev., L.A., Bos., Pit.	14	712	342	369	711	544	24	9	9	18	32	1974-75	1987-88
Simmons, Al	Cal., Bos.	3	11	0	1	1	21	1	0	0	0	0	1971-72	1975-76
Simon, Cully	Det., Chi.	3	130	4	11	15	121	14	0	1	1	6	1942-43	1944-45
Simon, Thain	Det.	1	3	0	0	0	0	....	....	....	....	....	1946-47	1946-47
Simpson, Bobby	Atl., St.L., Pit.	5	175	35	29	64	98	6	0	1	1	2	1976-77	1982-83
Simpson, Cliff	Det.	2	6	0	1	1	0	2	0	0	0	0	1946-47	1947-48
Simpson, Joe	NYA	6	228	21	19	40	156	2	0	0	0	0	1925-26	1930-31
Sims, Al	Bos., Hfd., L.A.	9	475	49	116	165	286	41	0	2	2	14	1973-74	1981-82
Sinclair, Reg	NYR, Det.	3	208	49	43	92	139	3	1	0	1	0	1950-51	1952-53
Singbush, Alex	Mtl.	1	32	0	5	5	15	3	0	0	0	4	1940-41	1940-41
Sirois, Bob	Phi., Wsh.	6	286	92	120	212	42	....	....	....	....	....	1974-75	1979-80
Sittler, Darryl	Tor., Phi., Det.	15	1096	484	637	1121	948	76	29	45	74	137	1970-71	1984-85
Sjoberg, Lars-Erik	Wpg.	1	79	7	27	34	48	....	....	....	....	....	1979-80	1979-80
Skaare, Bjorne	Det.	1	1	0	0	0	0	....	....	....	....	....	1978-79	1978-79
Skilton, Raymie	Mtl.W	1	1	1	0	1	0	....	....	....	....	....	1917-18	1917-18
Skinner, Alf	Tor., Bos., Mtl.M., Pit.	4	70	26	4	30	56	7	8	1	9	0	1917-18	1925-26
Skinner, Larry	Col.	4	47	10	12	22	8	2	0	0	0	0	1976-77	1979-80
Skov, Glen	Det., Chi., Mtl.	12	650	106	136	242	413	53	7	7	14	48	1949-50	1960-61
Sleaver, John	Chi.	2	24	2	0	2	6	....	....	....	....	....	1953-54	1956-57
Sleigher, Louis	Que., Bos.	6	194	46	53	99	146	17	1	1	2	64	1979-80	1985-86
Sloan, Tod	Tor., Chi.	13	745	220	262	482	781	47	9	12	21	47	1947-48	1960-61
Slobodzian, Peter	NYA	1	41	3	2	5	54	....	....	....	....	....	1940-41	1940-41
Slowinski, Eddie	NYR	6	291	58	74	132	63	16	2	6	8	6	1947-48	1952-53
Sly, Darryl	Tor., Min., Van.	4	79	1	2	3	20	....	....	....	....	....	1965-66	1970-71
Smart, Alec	Mtl.	1	8	2	5	7	0	....	....	....	....	....	1942-43	1942-43
Smedsmo, Dale	Tor.	1	4	0	0	0	0	....	....	....	....	....	1972-73	1972-73
Smillie, Don	Bos.	1	12	2	2	4	4	....	....	....	....	....	1933-34	1933-34
Smith, Alex	Ott., Det., Bos., NYA	11	443	41	50	91	643	19	0	2	2	40	1924-25	1934-35
Smith, Arthur	Tor., Ott.	4	137	15	10	25	249	4	1	1	2	8	1927-28	1930-31
Smith, Barry	Bos., Col.	3	114	7	7	14	10	....	....	....	....	....	1975-76	1980-81
Smith, Brad	Van., Atl., Cgy., Det., Tor.	9	222	28	34	62	591	20	3	3	6	49	1978-79	1986-87
Smith, Brian D.	L.A., Min.	2	67	10	10	20	33	7	0	0	0	0	1967-68	1968-69

Name	NHL Teams	NHL Seasons	Regular Schedule GP	G	A	TP	PIM	Playoffs GP	G	A	TP	PIM	First NHL Season	Last NHL Season
Smith, Brian S.	Det.	3	61	2	8	10	12	5	0	0	0	0	1957-58	1960-61
Smith, Carl	Det.	1	7	1	1	2	2	....	....	....	....	....	1943-44	1943-44
Smith, Clint	NYR, Chi.	11	483	161	236	397	24	44	10	14	24	2	1936-37	1946-47
Smith, Dallas	Bos., NYR	16	890	55	252	307	959	86	3	29	32	128	1959-60	1977-78
Smith, Dalton	NYA, Det.	2	11	1	2	3	0	....	....	....	....	....	1936-37	1943-44
Smith, Derek	Buf., Det.	8	335	78	116	194	60	30	9	14	23	13	1975-76	1982-83
Smith, Des	Mtl.M., Mtl., Chi., Bos.	5	195	22	25	47	236	25	1	4	5	18	1937-38	1941-42
Smith, Don	Mtl.	1	10	1	0	1	4	....	....	....	....	....	1919-20	1919-20
Smith, Don A.	NYR	1	11	1	1	2	0	1	0	0	0	0	1949-50	1949-50
Smith, Floyd	Bos., NYR, Det., Tor., Buf.	13	616	129	178	307	207	48	12	11	23	16	1954-55	1971-72
Smith, George	Tor.	1	9	0	0	0	0	....	....	....	....	....	1921-22	1921-22
Smith, Glen	Chi.	1	2	0	0	0	0	....	....	....	....	....	1950-51	1950-51
Smith, Glenn	Tor.	1	9	0	0	0	0	....	....	....	....	....	1922-23	1922-23
Smith, Gord	Wsh., Wpg.	6	299	9	30	39	284	....	....	....	....	....	1974-75	1979-80
Smith, Greg	Cal., Clev., Min., Det., Wsh.	13	829	56	232	288	1110	63	4	7	11	106	1975-76	1987-88
Smith, Hooley	Ott., Mtl.M., Bos., NYA	17	715	200	215	415	1013	54	11	8	19	109	1924-25	1940-41
Smith, Kenny	Bos.	7	331	78	93	171	49	30	8	13	21	6	1944-45	1950-51
Smith, Randy	Min.	2	3	0	0	0	0	....	....	....	....	....	1985-86	1986-87
Smith, Rick	Bos., Cal., St.L., Det., Wsh.	13	687	52	167	219	560	78	3	23	26	73	1968-69	1980-81
Smith, Roger	Pit., Phi.	6	210	20	4	24	172	4	3	0	3	0	1925-26	1930-31
Smith, Ron	NYI	1	11	1	1	2	14	....	....	....	....	....	1972-73	1972-73
Smith, Sid	Tor.	12	601	186	183	369	94	44	17	10	27	2	1946-47	1957-58
Smith, Stan	NYR	2	9	2	1	3	0	....	....	....	....	....	1939-40	1940-41
Smith, Stu E.	Mtl.	2	17	2	4	6	2	....	....	....	....	....	1940-41	1941-42
Smith, Stu G.	Hfd.	4	77	2	10	12	95	....	....	....	....	....	1979-80	1982-83
Smith, Tommy	Que.	1	10	0	0	0	9	....	....	....	....	....	1919-20	1919-20
Smith, Wayne	Chi.	1	2	1	1	2	2	1	0	0	0	0	1966-67	1966-67
Smith, Vern	NYI	1	1	0	0	0	0	....	....	....	....	....	1984-85	1984-85
Smrke, John	St.L., Que.	3	103	11	17	28	33	....	....	....	....	....	1977-78	1979-80
Smrke, Stan	Mtl.	2	9	0	3	3	0	....	....	....	....	....	1956-57	1957-58
Smylie, Rod	Tor., Ott.	6	76	4	1	5	10	9	1	2	3	2	1920-21	1925-26
Snell, Ron	Pit.	2	7	3	2	5	6	....	....	....	....	....	1968-69	1969-70
Snell, Ted	Pit., K.C., Det.	2	104	7	18	25	22	....	....	....	....	....	1973-74	1974-75
Snow, Sandy	Det.	1	3	0	0	0	2	....	....	....	....	....	1968-69	1968-69
Sobchuk, Denis	Det., Que.	2	35	5	6	11	2	....	....	....	....	....	1979-80	1982-83
Sobchuk, Gene	Van.	1	1	0	0	0	0	....	....	....	....	....	1973-74	1973-74
Solheim, Ken	Chi., Min., Det.	5	135	19	20	39	34	3	1	1	2	2	1980-81	1985-86
Solinger, Bob	Tor., Det.	5	99	10	11	21	19	....	....	....	....	....	1951-52	1959-60
Somers, Art	Chi., NYR	6	222	33	56	89	189	30	1	5	6	20	1929-30	1934-35
Sommer, Roy	Edm.	1	3	1	0	1	7	....	....	....	....	....	1980-81	1980-81
Songin, Tom	Bos.	3	43	5	5	10	22	....	....	....	....	....	1978-79	1980-81
Sonmor, Glen	NYR	2	28	2	0	2	21	....	....	....	....	....	1953-54	1954-55
Sorrell, John	Det., NYA	11	490	127	119	246	100	42	12	15	27	10	1930-31	1940-41
Sparrow, Emory	Bos.	1	6	0	0	0	4	....	....	....	....	....	1924-25	1924-25
Speck, Fred	Det., Van.	3	28	1	2	3	2	....	....	....	....	....	1968-69	1971-72
Speer, Bill	Pit., Bos.	4	130	5	20	25	79	8	1	0	1	4	1967-68	1970-71
Speers, Ted	Det.	1	4	1	1	2	0	....	....	....	....	....	1985-86	1985-86
Spencer, Brian	Tor., NYI, Buf., Pit.	10	553	80	143	223	634	37	1	5	6	29	1969-70	1978-79
Spencer, Irv	NYR, Bos., Det.	8	230	12	38	50	127	16	0	0	0	8	1959-60	1967-68
Speyer, Chris	Tor.	2	5	0	0	0	0	....	....	....	....	....	1923-24	1924-25
Spring, Don	Wpg.	4	259	1	52	55	80	6	0	0	0	10	1980-81	1983-84
Spring, Frank	Bos., St.L., Cal., Clev.	5	61	14	20	34	12	....	....	....	....	....	1976-77	1976-77
Spring, Jesse	Ham., Pit., Tor., NYA	6	137	11	2	13	62	2	0	2	2	2	1923-24	1929-30
Spruce, Andy	Van., Col.	3	172	31	42	73	111	2	0	2	2	2	1976-77	1978-79
Stackhouse, Ron	Cal., Det., Pit.	12	889	87	372	459	824	32	5	8	13	38	1970-71	1981-82
Stackhouse, Ted	Tor.	1	12	0	0	0	2	5	0	0	0	0	1921-22	1921-22
Stahan, Butch	Mtl.	1	3	0	1	1	2	....	....	....	....	....	1944-45	1944-45
Staley, Al	NYR	1	1	0	1	1	0	....	....	....	....	....	1948-49	1948-49
Stamler, Lorne	L.A., Tor., Wpg.	4	116	14	11	25	16	....	....	....	....	....	1976-77	1979-80
Standing, George	Min.	1	2	0	0	0	0	....	....	....	....	....	1967-68	1967-68
Stanfield, Fred	Chi., Bos., Min., Buf.	14	914	211	405	616	134	106	21	35	56	10	1964-65	1977-78
Stanfield, Jack	Chi.	1	1	0	0	0	0	....	....	....	....	....	1965-66	1965-66
Stanfield, Jim	L.A.	3	7	0	1	1	0	....	....	....	....	....	1969-70	1971-72
Stankiewicz, Edward	Det.	2	6	0	0	0	2	....	....	....	....	....	1953-54	1955-56
Stankiewicz, Myron	St.L., Phi.	1	35	0	7	7	36	1	0	0	0	0	1968-69	1968-69
Stanley, Allan	NYR, Chi., Bos., Tor., Phi.	21	1244	100	333	433	792	109	7	36	43	80	1948-49	1968-69
Stanley, Barney	Chi.	1	1	0	0	0	0	....	....	....	....	....	1927-28	1927-28
Stanowski, Wally	Tor., NYR	10	428	23	88	111	160	60	3	14	17	13	1939-40	1950-51
Stapleton, Brian	Wsh.	1	1	0	0	0	0	....	....	....	....	....	1975-76	1975-76
Stapleton, Pat	Bos., Chi.	10	635	43	294	337	353	65	10	39	49	38	1961-62	1972-73
Starr, Harold	Ott., Mtl.M., Mtl., NYR	7	203	6	5	11	186	17	1	0	1	2	1929-30	1935-36
Starr, Wilf	NYA, Det.	4	89	8	6	14	25	7	0	2	2	2	1932-33	1935-36
Stasiuk, Vic	Chi., Det., Bos.	14	745	183	254	437	669	69	16	18	34	40	1949-50	1962-63
Stastny, Marian	Que., Tor.	5	322	121	173	294	110	32	5	17	22	7	1980-81	1985-86
Staszak, Ray	Det.	1	4	0	1	1	7	....	....	....	....	....	1985-86	1985-86
Steele, Frank	Det.	1	1	0	0	0	0	....	....	....	....	....	1930-31	1930-31
Steen, Anders	Wpg.	1	42	5	11	16	22	....	....	....	....	....	1980-81	1980-81
Stefaniw, Morris	Atl.	1	13	1	1	2	2	....	....	....	....	....	1972-73	1972-73
Stefanski, Bud	NYR	1	1	0	0	0	0	....	....	....	....	....	1977-78	1977-78
Stemkowski, Pete	Tor., Det., NYR, L.A.	15	967	206	349	555	866	83	25	29	54	136	1963-64	1977-78
Stenlund, Ken	Clev.	1	4	0	0	0	0	....	....	....	....	....	1976-77	1976-77
Stephens, Phi.	Mtl.W	1	25	1	0	1	0	....	....	....	....	....	1917-18	1917-18
Stephenson, Bob	Hfd., Tor.	1	18	2	3	5	4	....	....	....	....	....	1979-80	1979-80
Sterner, Ulf	NYR	1	4	0	0	0	0	....	....	....	....	....	1964-65	1964-65
Stevens, Paul	Bos.	1	17	0	0	0	0	....	....	....	....	....	1925-26	1925-26
Stewart, Bill	Buf., St.L.	8	261	7	64	71	424	13	1	3	4	11	1977-78	1985-86
Stewart, Blair	Det., Wsh., Que.	7	229	34	44	78	326	....	....	....	....	....	1973-74	1979-80
Stewart, Gaye	Tor., Chi., Det., NYR, Mtl.	10	502	185	159	344	274	25	2	9	11	16	1941-42	1953-54
Stewart, Jack	Det., Chi.	12	565	31	84	115	765	80	5	14	19	143	1938-39	1951-52
Stewart, John	Pit., Atl., Cal., Que.	5	258	58	60	118	158	4	0	0	0	10	1970-71	1974-75
Stewart, Ken	Chi.	1	6	1	1	2	2	....	....	....	....	....	1941-42	1941-42
Stewart, Nels	Mtl.M., Bos., NYA	15	651	324	191	515	953	54	15	13	28	61	1925-26	1939-40
Stewart, Paul	Que.	1	21	2	0	2	74	....	....	....	....	....	1979-80	1979-80
Stewart, Ralph	Van., NYI	7	252	57	73	130	28	19	4	4	8	2	1970-71	1977-78
Stewart, Robert	Bos., Cal., Clev., St.L., Pit.	9	510	27	101	128	809	5	1	1	2	2	1971-72	1979-80
Stewart, Ron	Tor., Bos., St.L., NYR, Van., NYI	21	1353	276	253	529	560	119	14	21	35	60	1952-53	1972-73
Stiles, Tony	Cgy.	1	30	2	7	9	20	....	....	....	....	....	1983-84	1983-84
Stoddard, Jack	NYR	2	80	16	15	31	31	....	....	....	....	....	1951-52	1952-53
Stoltz, Roland	Wsh.	1	14	2	2	4	14	....	....	....	....	....	1981-82	1981-82
Stone, Steve	Van.	1	2	0	0	0	0	....	....	....	....	....	1973-74	1973-74
Stoughton, Blaine	Pit., Tor., Hfd., NYR	8	526	258	191	449	204	8	4	2	6	2	1973-74	1983-84
Stoyanovich, Steve	Hfd.	1	23	3	5	8	11	....	....	....	....	....	1983-84	1983-84
Strain, Neil	NYR	1	52	11	13	24	12	....	....	....	....	....	1952-53	1952-53
Strate, Gord	Det.	3	61	0	0	0	34	....	....	....	....	....	1956-57	1958-59
Stratton, Art	NYR, Det., Chi., Pit., Phi.	4	95	18	33	51	24	5	0	0	0	0	1959-60	1967-68
Strobel, Art	NYR	1	7	0	0	0	0	....	....	....	....	....	1943-44	1943-44
Strong, Ken	Tor.	3	15	2	2	4	6	....	....	....	....	....	1982-83	1984-85
Strueby, Todd	Edm.	3	5	0	1	1	2	....	....	....	....	....	1981-82	1983-84
Stuart, Billy	Tor., Bos.	7	193	30	17	47	145	17	1	0	1	12	1920-21	1926-27
Stumpf, Robert	St.L., Pit.	1	10	1	1	2	20	....	....	....	....	....	1974-75	1974-75
Sturgeon, Peter	Col.	2	6	0	1	1	2	....	....	....	....	....	1979-80	1980-81
Suikkanen, Kai	Buf.	2	2	0	0	0	0	....	....	....	....	....	1981-82	1982-83
Sullivan, Barry	Det.	1	1	0	0	0	0	....	....	....	....	....	1947-48	1947-48
Sullivan, Bob	Hfd.	1	62	18	19	37	18	....	....	....	....	....	1982-83	1982-83
Sullivan, Frank	Tor., Chi.	4	8	0	0	0	2	....	....	....	....	....	1949-50	1955-56
Sullivan, Peter	Wpg.	2	126	28	54	82	40	....	....	....	....	....	1979-80	1980-81
Sullivan, Red	Bos., Chi., NYR	10	557	107	239	346	441	18	1	2	3	7	1949-50	1960-61
Summerhill, Bill	Mtl., NYA	3	72	14	17	31	70	3	0	0	0	2	1938-39	1941-42
Suomi, Al	Chi.	1	5	0	0	0	0	....	....	....	....	....	1936-37	1936-37
Sutherland, Bill	Mtl., Phi., Tor., St.L., Det.	6	250	70	58	128	99	14	2	4	6	0	1962-63	1971-72
Sutherland, Ron	Bos.	1	2	0	0	0	0	....	....	....	....	....	1931-32	1931-32
Sutter, Brian	St.L.	12	779	303	333	636	1786	65	21	21	42	249	1976-77	1987-88
Sutter, Darryl	Chi.	8	406	161	118	279	288	51	24	19	43	26	1979-80	1986-87
Suzor, Mark	Phi., Col.	2	64	4	16	20	60	....	....	....	....	....	1976-77	1977-78
Svensson, Leif	Wsh.	2	121	6	40	46	49	....	....	....	....	....	1978-79	1979-80
Swain, Garry	Pit.	1	9	1	1	2	0	....	....	....	....	....	1968-69	1968-69
Swarbrick, George	Oak., Pit., Phi.	4	132	17	25	42	173	....	....	....	....	....	1967-68	1970-71
Sweeny, Bill	NYR	1	4	1	0	1	0	....	....	....	....	....	1959-60	1959-60

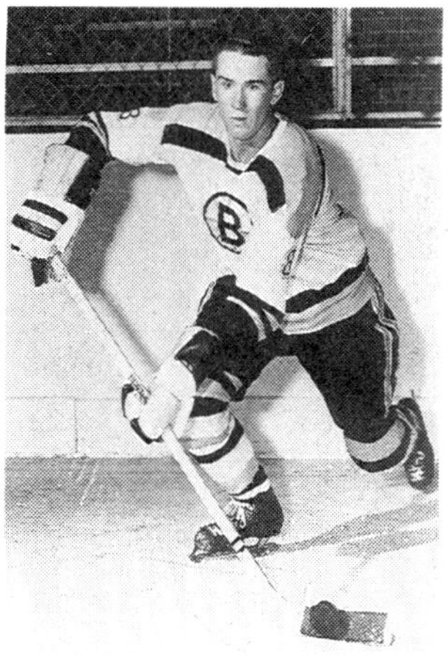

Dallas Smith

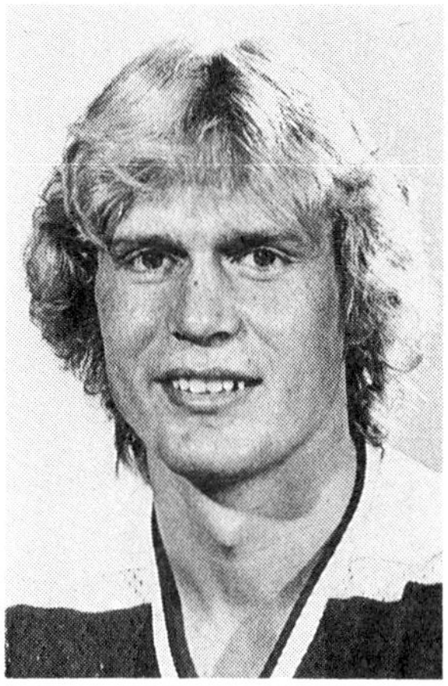

Ken Solheim

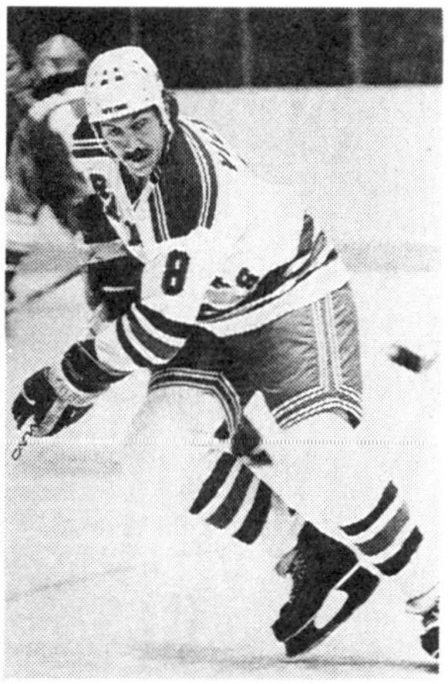

Walt Tkaczuk

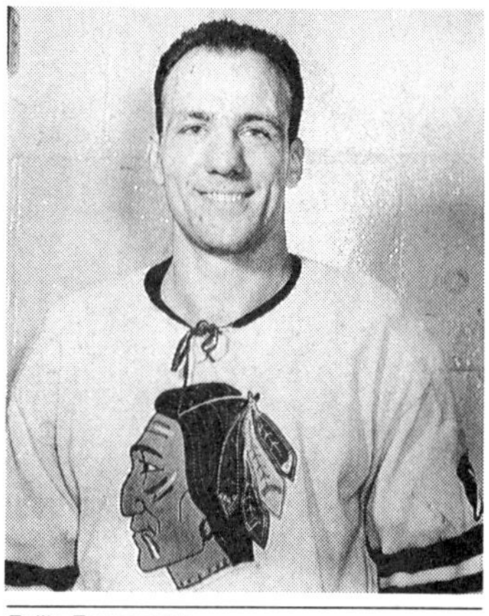

Zellio Toppazzini

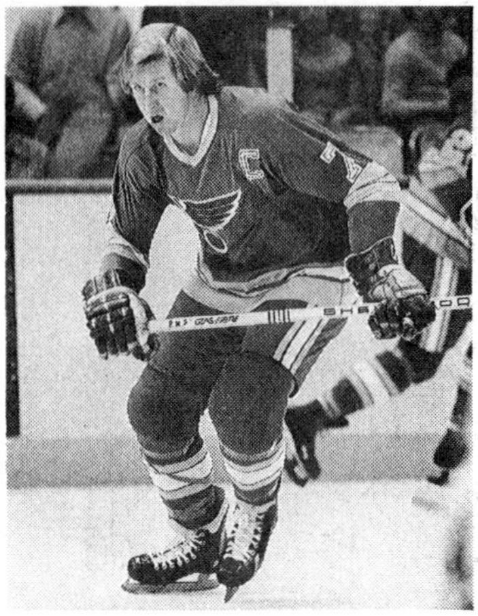

Garry Unger

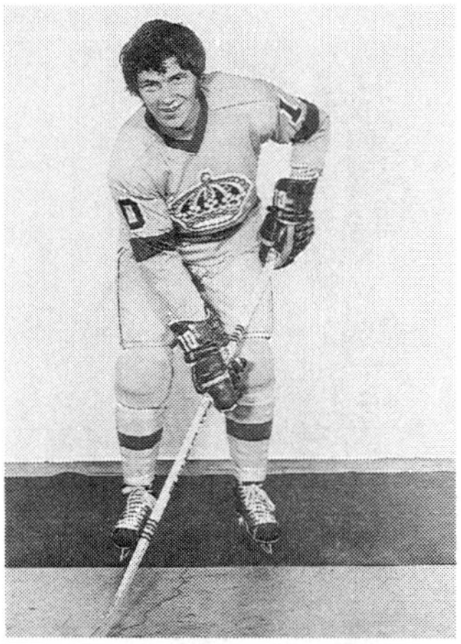

Vic Venasky

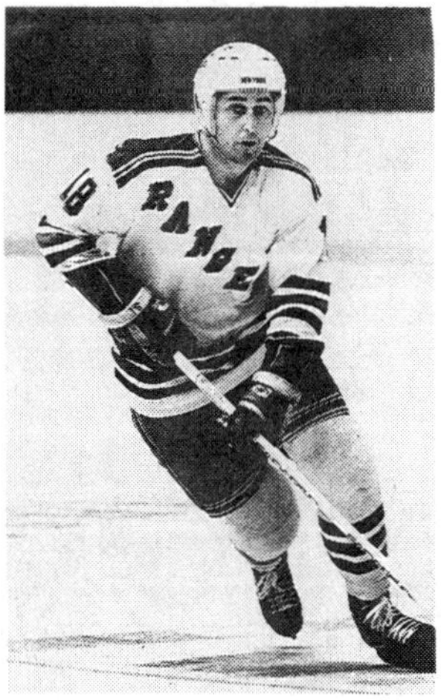

Steve Vickers

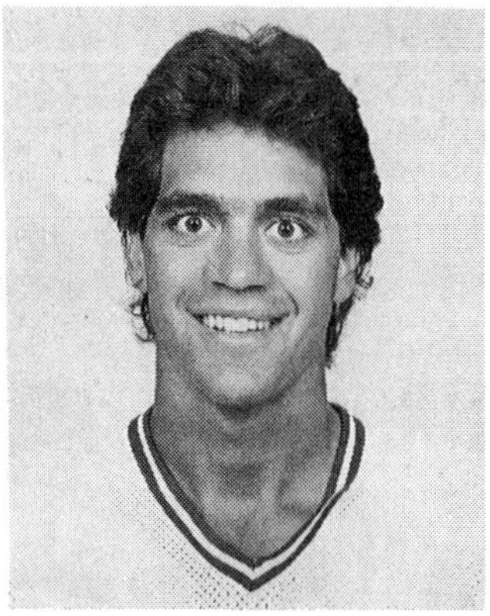

Mickey Volcan

Name	NHL Teams	NHL Seasons	Regular Schedule GP	G	A	TP	PIM	Playoffs GP	G	A	TP	PIM	First NHL Season	Last NHL Season
Sykes, Bob	Tor.	1	2	0	0	0	0	....	....	....	....	....	1974-75	1974-75
Szura, Joe	Oak.	2	90	10	15	25	30	7	2	3	5	2	1967-68	1968-69
T														
Taft, John	Det.	1	15	0	2	2	4	....	....	....	....	....	1978-79	1978-79
Talafous, Dean	Atl., Min., NYR	8	479	104	154	258	163	21	4	7	11	11	1974-75	1981-82
Talakoski, Ron	NYR	2	9	0	1	1	33	....	....	....	....	....	1986-87	1987-88
Talbot, Jean-Guy	Mtl., Min., Det., St.L., Buf.	17	1056	43	242	285	1006	150	4	26	30	142	1954-55	1970-71
Tallon, Dale	Van., Chi., Pit.	10	642	98	238	336	568	33	2	10	12	45	1970-71	1979-80
Tambellini, Steve	NYI, Col., N.J., Cgy., Van.	10	553	160	150	310	105	2	0	1	1	0	1978-79	1987-88
Tanguay, Chris	Que.	1	2	0	0	0	0	....	....	....	....	....	1981-82	1981-82
Tannahill, Don	Van.	2	111	30	33	63	25	....	....	....	....	....	1972-73	1973-74
Tardif, Marc	Mtl., Que.	8	517	194	207	401	443	62	13	15	28	75	1969-70	1982-83
Taylor, Billy	Tor., Det., Bos., NYR	7	323	87	180	267	120	33	6	18	24	13	1939-40	1947-48
Taylor, Billy	NYR	1	2	0	0	0	0	....	....	....	....	....	1964-65	1964-65
Taylor, Bob	Bos.	1	8	0	0	0	6	....	....	....	....	....	1929-30	1929-30
Taylor, Ted	NYR, Det., Min., Van.	6	166	23	35	58	181	....	....	....	....	....	1964-65	1971-72
Taylor, Harry	Tor., Chi.	3	66	5	10	15	30	1	0	0	0	0	1946-47	1951-52
Taylor, Mark	Phi., Pit., Wsh.	5	209	42	68	110	73	6	0	0	0	0	1981-82	1985-86
Taylor, Ralph	Chi., NYR	3	99	4	1	5	169	4	0	0	0	10	1927-28	1929-30
Teal, Jeff	Mtl.	1	6	0	1	1	0	....	....	....	....	....	1984-85	1984-85
Teal, Skip	Bos.	1	1	0	0	0	0	....	....	....	....	....	1954-55	1954-55
Teal, Victor	NYI	1	1	0	0	0	0	....	....	....	....	....	1973-74	1973-74
Tebbutt, Greg	Que., Pit.	2	26	0	3	3	35	....	....	....	....	....	1979-80	1983-84
Terbenche, Paul	Chi., Buf.	5	189	5	26	31	28	12	0	0	0	0	1967-68	1973-74
Terry, Bill	Min.	1	5	0	0	0	0	....	....	....	....	....	1987-88	1987-88
Tessier, Orval	Mtl., Bos.	3	59	5	7	12	6	....	....	....	....	....	1954-55	1960-61
Thatchell, Spence	NYR	1	1	0	0	0	0	....	....	....	....	....	1942-43	1942-43
Theberge, Greg	Wsh.	5	153	15	63	78	73	4	0	1	1	0	1979-80	1983-84
Therrien, Gaston	Que.	3	22	0	8	8	12	9	0	1	1	4	1980-81	1982-83
Thelin, Mats	Bos.	3	163	8	19	27	107	5	0	0	0	6	1984-85	1986-87
Thibeault, Laurence	Det., Mtl.	2	5	0	2	2	0	....	....	....	....	....	1944-45	1945-46
Thiffault, Leo	Min.	1	....	....	....	....	....	5	0	0	0	0	1967-68	1967-68
Thomson, Jack	NYA	1	3	0	0	0	0	....	....	....	....	....	1940-41	1940-41
Thomas, Cy	Chi., Tor.	1	14	2	2	4	12	....	....	....	....	....	1947-48	1947-48
Thomas, Reg	Que.	1	39	9	7	16	6	....	....	....	....	....	1979-80	1979-80
Thompson, Cliff	Bos.	2	13	0	1	1	2	....	....	....	....	....	1941-42	1948-49
Thompson, Errol	Tor., Det., Pit.	10	599	208	185	393	184	34	7	5	12	11	1970-71	1980-81
Thompson, Kenneth	Mtl.W	1	1	0	0	0	0	....	....	....	....	....	1917-18	1917-18
Thompson, Paul	NYR, Chi.	13	586	153	179	332	336	48	11	11	22	54	1926-27	1938-39
Thoms, Bill	Tor., Chi., Bos.	13	549	135	206	341	176	44	6	10	16	6	1932-33	1944-45
Thomson, Bill	Det., Chi.	2	10	2	2	4	0	2	0	0	0	0	1938-39	1943-44
Thomson, Floyd	St.L.	8	411	56	97	153	341	10	0	2	2	6	1971-72	1979-80
Thomson, Jimmy	Tor., Chi.	13	787	19	215	234	920	63	2	13	15	135	1945-46	1957-58
Thomson, Rhys	Mtl., Tor.	2	25	0	2	2	38	....	....	....	....	....	1939-40	1942-43
Thornbury, Tom	Pit.	1	14	1	8	9	16	....	....	....	....	....	1983-84	1983-84
Thorsteinson, Joe	NYA	1	4	0	0	0	0	....	....	....	....	....	1932-33	1932-33
Thurier, Fred	NYA, NYR	3	80	25	27	52	18	....	....	....	....	....	1940-41	1944-45
Thurlby, Tom	Oak.	1	20	1	2	3	4	....	....	....	....	....	1967-68	1967-68
Tidey, Alex	Buf., Edm.	3	9	0	0	0	8	2	0	0	0	0	1976-77	1979-80
Timgren, Ray	Tor., Chi.	6	251	14	44	58	70	30	3	9	12	6	1948-49	1954-55
Titanic, Morris	Buf.	2	19	0	0	0	0	....	....	....	....	....	1974-75	1975-76
Tkaczuk, Walt	NYR	14	945	227	451	678	556	93	19	32	51	119	1967-68	1980-81
Toal, Mike	Edm.	1	3	0	0	0	0	....	....	....	....	....	1979-80	1979-80
Tomalty, Glenn	Wpg.	1	1	0	0	0	0	....	....	....	....	....	1979-80	1979-80
Tomson, John	NYA	2	8	1	1	2	0	2	0	0	0	0	1938-39	1939-40
Toppazzini, Jerry	Bos., Chi., Det.	12	783	163	244	407	436	40	13	9	22	13	1952-53	1963-64
Toppazzini, Zellio	Bos., NYR, Chi.	5	123	21	22	43	49	2	0	0	0	0	1948-49	1956-57
Toupey, Bill	Mtl.M., Ott., Bos.	7	280	65	40	105	107	2	1	0	1	0	1927-28	1933-34
Toupin, Jaques	Chi.	1	8	1	2	3	0	4	0	0	0	0	1943-44	1943-44
Townsend, Art	Chi.	1	5	0	0	0	0	....	....	....	....	....	1926-27	1926-27
Trainor, Wes	NYR	1	17	1	2	3	6	....	....	....	....	....	1948-49	1948-49
Trapp, Bobby	Chi.	2	82	4	4	8	129	2	0	0	0	4	1926-27	1927-28
Trapp, Doug	Buf.	1	2	0	0	0	0	....	....	....	....	....	1986-87	1986-87
Traub, Percy	Chi., Det.	3	130	3	3	6	214	4	0	0	0	6	1926-27	1928-29
Tredway, Brock	L.A.	1	1	0	0	0	0	....	....	....	....	....	1981-82	1981-82
Tremblay, Brent	Wsh.	2	10	1	0	1	6	....	....	....	....	....	1978-79	1979-80
Tremblay, Gilles	Mtl.	9	509	168	162	330	161	48	9	14	23	4	1960-61	1968-69
Tremblay, J.C.	Mtl.	13	794	57	306	363	204	108	14	51	65	58	1959-60	1971-72
Tremblay, Marcel	Mtl.	1	10	0	2	2	0	....	....	....	....	....	1938-39	1938-39
Tremblay, Mario	Mtl.	12	852	258	326	584	1043	100	20	29	49	187	1974-75	1985-86
Tremblay, Nels	Mtl.	2	3	0	1	1	0	2	0	0	0	0	1944-45	1945-46
Trimper, Tim	Chi., Wpg., Min.	6	190	30	36	66	153	2	0	0	0	2	1979-80	1984-85
Trottier, Dave	Mtl.M., Det.	11	446	121	113	234	508	31	4	3	7	41	1928-29	1938-39
Trottier, Guy	NYR, Tor.	3	115	28	17	45	37	9	1	0	1	16	1968-69	1971-72
Trottier, Rocky	N.J.	2	38	6	4	10	2	....	....	....	....	....	1983-84	1984-85
Trudel, Louis	Chi., Mtl.	8	306	49	69	118	122	24	1	3	4	6	1933-34	1940-41
Trudell, Rene	NYR	3	129	24	28	52	72	5	0	0	0	2	1945-46	1947-48
Tudin, Connie	Mtl.	1	4	0	1	1	4	....	....	....	....	....	1941-42	1941-42
Tudor, Rob	Van., St.L.	3	28	4	4	8	19	3	0	0	0	0	1978-79	1982-83
Turlick, Gord	Bos.	1	2	0	0	0	2	....	....	....	....	....	1959-60	1959-60
Turnbull, Ian	Tor., L.A., Pit.	10	628	123	317	440	753	55	13	32	45	94	1973-74	1982-83
Turnbull, Perry	St.L., Mtl., Wpg.	9	608	188	163	351	1245	34	6	7	13	86	1979-80	1987-88
Turnbull, Randy	Cgy.	1	1	0	0	0	2	....	....	....	....	....	1981-82	1981-82
Turner, Bob	Mtl., Chi.	8	478	19	51	70	307	68	1	4	5	44	1955-56	1962-63
Turner, Dean	NYR, Col., L.A.	4	35	1	0	1	59	....	....	....	....	....	1978-79	1982-83
Tustin, Norman	NYR	1	18	2	4	6	0	....	....	....	....	....	1941-42	1941-42
Tuten, Audley	Chi.	2	39	4	8	12	48	....	....	....	....	....	1941-42	1942-43
UV														
Ubriaco, Gene	Pit., Oak., Chi.	3	177	39	35	74	50	11	2	0	2	4	1967-68	1969-70
Ullman, Norm	Det., Tor.	20	1410	490	739	1229	712	106	30	53	83	67	1955-56	1974-75
Unger, Garry	Tor., Det., St.L., Atl., L.A., Edm.	16	1105	413	391	804	1075	52	12	18	30	105	1967-68	1982-83
Vadnais, Carol	Mtl., Oak., Cal., Bos., NYR, N.J.	17	1087	169	418	587	1813	106	10	40	50	185	1966-67	1982-83
Vail, Eric	Atl, Cgy., Det.	9	591	216	260	476	281	20	5	6	11	6	1973-74	1981-82
Vail, Melville	NYR	2	50	4	1	5	18	10	0	0	0	2	1928-29	1929-30
Valentine, Chris	Wsh.	3	105	43	52	95	127	2	0	0	0	4	1981-82	1983-84
Valiquette, Jack	Tor., Col.	7	350	84	134	218	79	23	3	6	9	4	1974-75	1980-81
Van Boxmeer, John	Mtl., Col., Buf., Que.	11	588	84	274	358	465	38	5	15	20	37	1973-74	1983-84
Van Impe, Ed	Chi., Phi., Pit.	11	700	27	126	153	1025	66	1	12	13	131	1966-67	1976-77
Vasko, Elmer	Chi., Min.	13	786	34	166	200	719	78	2	7	9	73	1956-57	1969-70
Vasko, Rick	Det.	3	31	3	7	10	29	....	....	....	....	....	1977-78	1980-81
Vautour, Yvon	NYI, Col., N.J., Que.	6	204	26	33	59	401	....	....	....	....	....	1979-80	1984-85
Vaydik, Greg	Chi.	1	5	0	0	0	0	....	....	....	....	....	1976-77	1976-77
Venasky, Vic	L.A.	7	430	61	101	162	66	21	1	5	6	12	1972-73	1978-79
Veneruzzo, Gary	St.L.	2	7	1	1	2	0	9	0	2	2	2	1967-68	1971-72
Verret, Claude	Buf.	2	14	2	5	7	2	....	....	....	....	....	1983-84	1984-85
Verstraete, Leigh	Tor.	3	8	0	1	1	14	....	....	....	....	....	1982-83	1987-88
Ververgaert, Dennis	Van., Phi., Wsh.	8	583	176	216	392	247	8	1	2	3	6	1973-74	1980-81
Veysey, Sid	Van.	1	1	0	0	0	0	....	....	....	....	....	1977-78	1977-78
Vickers, Steve	NYR	10	698	246	340	586	330	68	24	25	49	58	1972-73	1981-82
Vigneault, Alain	St.L.	2	42	2	5	7	82	4	0	1	1	26	1981-82	1982-83
Vipond, Pete	Cal.	1	3	0	0	0	0	....	....	....	....	....	1972-73	1972-73
Vokes, Ed	Chi.	1	5	0	0	0	0	....	....	....	....	....	1930-31	1930-31
Volcan, Mickey	Hfd., Cgy.	4	162	8	33	41	146	....	....	....	....	....	1980-81	1983-84
Volmar, Doug	Det., L.A.	4	62	13	8	21	26	2	1	0	1	0	1969-70	1972-73
Voss, Carl	Tor., NYR, Det., Ott., St.L., Mtl.M., NYA, Chi.	8	261	34	70	104	50	24	5	3	8	0	1926-27	1937-38
W														
Waddell, Don	L.A.	1	1	0	0	0	0	....	....	....	....	....	1980-81	1980-81
Waite, Frank	NYR	1	17	1	3	4	4	....	....	....	....	....	1930-31	1930-31
Walker, Howard	Wsh., Cal.	3	83	2	13	15	133	....	....	....	....	....	1980-81	1982-83

Name	NHL Teams	NHL Seasons	Regular Schedule GP	G	A	TP	PIM	Playoffs GP	G	A	TP	PIM	First NHL Season	Last NHL Season
Walker, Jack	Det.	2	80	5	8	13	18	....	....	....	....	....	1926-27	1927-28
Walker, Kurt	Tor.	3	71	4	5	9	152	16	0	0	0	34	1975-76	1977-78
Walker, Russ	L.A.	2	17	1	0	1	41	....	....	....	....	....	1976-77	1977-78
Wall, Bob	Det., L.A., St.L.	8	322	30	55	85	155	22	0	3	3	2	1964-65	1971-72
Wallin, Peter	NYR	2	52	3	14	17	14	14	2	6	8	6	1980-81	1981-82
Walsh, Jim	Buf.	1	4	0	1	1	4	....	....	....	....	....	1981-82	1981-82
Walton, Bobby	Mtl.	1	4	0	0	0	0	....	....	....	....	....	1943-44	1943-44
Walton, Mike	Tor., Bos., Van., Chi., St.L.	12	588	201	247	448	357	47	14	10	24	45	1965-66	1978-79
Wappel, Gord	Atl., Cgy.	3	20	1	1	2	10	2	0	0	0	4	1979-80	1981-82
Ward, Don	Chi., Bos.	2	34	0	1	1	160	....	....	....	....	....	1957-58	1959-60
Ward, Jimmy	Mtl.M., Mtl.	12	532	147	127	274	455	31	4	4	8	18	1927-28	1938-39
Ward, Joe	Col.	1	4	0	0	0	2	....	....	....	....	....	1980-81	1980-81
Ward, Ron	Tor., Van.	2	89	2	5	7	6	....	....	....	....	....	1969-70	1971-72
Wares, Eddie	NYR, Det., Chi.	9	291	60	102	162	161	45	5	7	12	34	1936-37	1946-47
Warner, Bob	Tor.	2	10	1	1	2	4	4	0	0	0	0	1975-76	1976-77
Warner, Jim	Hfd.	1	32	0	3	3	10	....	....	....	....	....	1979-80	1979-80
Warwick, Bill	NYR	2	14	3	3	6	16	....	....	....	....	....	1942-43	1943-44
Warwick, Grant	NYR, Bos., Mtl.	9	395	147	142	289	220	16	2	4	6	6	1941-42	1949-50
Wasnie, Nick	Chi., Mtl., NYA, Ott., St.L.	7	248	57	34	91	176	14	6	3	9	20	1927-28	1934-35
Watson, Bryan	Mtl., Oak., Pit., Det., St.L., Wsh.	16	878	17	135	152	2212	32	2	0	2	70	1963-64	1978-79
Watson, Dave	Col.	2	18	0	1	1	10	....	....	....	....	....	1979-80	1980-81
Watson, Harry	NYA, Det., Tor., Chi.	14	805	236	207	443	150	62	16	9	25	27	1941-42	1956-57
Watson, Jim	Det., Buf.	7	221	4	19	23	345	....	....	....	....	....	1963-64	1971-72
Watson, Jimmy	Phi.	10	613	38	148	186	492	101	5	34	39	89	1972-73	1981-82
Watson, Joe	Bos., Phi., Col.	14	835	38	178	216	447	84	3	12	15	82	1964-65	1978-79
Watson, Phil	NYR, Mtl.	13	590	144	265	409	532	45	10	25	35	67	1935-36	1947-48
Watts, Brian	Det.	1	4	0	0	0	0	....	....	....	....	....	1975-76	1975-76
Webster, Aubrey	Phi., Mtl.M.	2	5	0	0	0	0	....	....	....	....	....	1930-31	1934-35
Webster, Don	Tor.	1	27	7	6	13	28	5	0	0	0	12	1943-44	1943-44
Webster, John	NYR	1	14	0	0	0	4	....	....	....	....	....	1949-50	1949-50
Webster, Tom	Bos., Det., Cal.	5	102	33	42	75	61	1	0	0	0	0	1968-69	1979-80
Weiland, Cooney	Bos., Ott., Det.	11	508	173	160	333	147	45	12	10	22	12	1928-29	1938-39
Weir, Stan	Cal., Tor., Edm., Col., Det.	10	642	139	207	346	183	37	6	5	11	4	1972-73	1982-83
Weir, Wally	Que., Hfd., Pit.	6	320	21	45	66	625	23	0	1	1	96	1979-80	1984-85
Wellington, Duke	Que.	1	1	0	0	0	0	....	....	....	....	....	1919-20	1919-20
Wensink, John	Bos., Que., Col., N.J., St.L.	8	403	70	68	138	840	43	2	6	8	86	1973-74	1982-83
Wentworth, Cy	Chi., Mtl.M., Mtl.	13	578	39	68	107	355	35	5	6	11	22	1927-28	1939-40
Wesley, Blake	Phi., Hfd., Que., Tor.	7	298	18	46	64	486	19	2	2	4	30	1979-80	1985-86
Westfall, Ed	Bos., NYI	18	1227	231	394	625	544	95	22	37	59	41	1961-62	1978-79
Wharram, Kenny	Chi.	14	766	252	281	533	222	80	16	27	43	38	1951-52	1968-69
Wharton, Len	NYR	1	1	0	0	0	0	....	....	....	....	....	1944-45	1944-45
Wheldon, Donald	St.L.	1	2	0	0	0	0	....	....	....	....	....	1974-75	1974-75
Whelton, Bill	Wpg.	1	2	0	0	0	0	....	....	....	....	....	1980-81	1980-81
White, Bill	L.A., Chi.	9	604	50	215	265	495	91	7	32	39	76	1967-68	1975-76
White, Moe	Mtl.	1	4	0	1	1	2	....	....	....	....	....	1945-46	1945-46
White, Sherman	NYR	2	4	0	2	2	0	....	....	....	....	....	1946-47	1949-50
White, Tex	Pit., NYA	5	194	30	12	42	139	4	0	0	0	2	1925-26	1929-30
White, Tony	Wsh., Min.	5	164	37	28	65	104	....	....	....	....	....	1974-75	1979-80
Whitelaw, Bob	Det.	2	32	0	2	2	2	8	0	0	0	0	1940-41	1941-42
Whitlock, Bob	Min.	1	1	0	0	0	0	....	....	....	....	....	1969-70	1969-70
Widing, Juha	NYR, L.A., Clev.	8	575	144	226	370	208	8	1	2	3	2	1969-70	1976-77
Wiebe, Art	Chi.	11	411	14	27	41	209	31	1	3	4	8	1932-33	1943-44
Wilcox, Archie	Mtl.M., Bos., St.L.	6	212	8	14	22	158	12	1	0	1	10	1929-30	1934-35
Wilcox, Barry	Van.	2	33	3	2	5	15	....	....	....	....	....	1972-73	1974-75
Wilder, Arch	Det.	1	18	0	2	2	2	....	....	....	....	....	1940-41	1940-41
Wiley, Jim	Pit., Van.	5	63	4	10	14	8	....	....	....	....	....	1972-73	1976-77
Wilkins, Barry	Bos., Van., Pit.	9	418	27	125	152	663	6	0	1	1	4	1966-67	1975-76
Wilkinson, John	Bos.	1	9	0	0	0	3	....	....	....	....	....	1943-44	1943-44
Willard, Rod	Tor.	1	1	0	0	0	0	....	....	....	....	....	1982-83	1982-83
Williams, Burr	Det., St.L., Bos.	3	19	0	1	1	28	2	0	0	0	8	1933-34	1936-37
Williams, Dave	Tor., Van., Det., L.A., Hfd.	14	962	241	272	513	3966	83	12	23	35	455	1974-75	1987-88
Williams, Fred	Det.	1	44	2	5	7	10	....	....	....	....	....	1976-77	1976-77
Williams, Gord	Phi.	2	2	0	0	0	2	....	....	....	....	....	1981-82	1982-83
Williams, Tom	Bos., Min., Cal., Wsh.	13	663	161	269	430	177	10	2	5	7	2	1961-62	1975-76
Williams, Tommy	NYR, L.A.	8	397	115	138	253	73	29	8	7	15	4	1971-72	1978-79
Williams, Warren	St.L., Cal.	3	108	14	35	49	131	....	....	....	....	....	1973-74	1975-76
Willson, Don	Mtl.	2	22	2	7	9	0	3	0	0	0	0	1937-38	1938-39
Wilson, Bert	NYR, L.A., St.L., Cgy.	8	478	37	44	81	646	21	0	2	2	42	1973-74	1980-81
Wilson, Bob	Chi.	1	1	0	0	0	0	....	....	....	....	....	1953-54	1953-54
Wilson, Cully	Tor., Mtl., Ham., Chi.	5	125	60	23	83	232	2	1	0	1	6	1919-20	1926-27
Wilson, Gord	Bos.	1	2	0	0	0	0	....	....	....	....	....	1954-55	1954-55
Wilson, Hub	NYA	1	2	0	0	0	0	....	....	....	....	....	1931-32	1931-32
Wilson, Jerry	Mtl.	1	3	0	0	0	2	....	....	....	....	....	1956-57	1956-57
Wilson, Johnny	Det., Chi., Tor., NYR	12	688	161	171	332	190	66	14	13	27	11	1949-50	1961-62
Wilson, Larry	Det., Chi.	6	152	21	48	69	75	4	0	0	0	0	1949-50	1955-56
Wilson, Murray	Mtl., L.A.	7	386	94	95	189	162	53	5	14	19	32	1972-73	1978-79
Wilson, Rick	Mtl., St.L., Det.	4	239	6	26	32	165	3	0	0	0	0	1973-74	1976-77
Wilson, Roger	Chi.	1	7	0	2	2	6	....	....	....	....	....	1974-75	1974-75
Wilson, Ron	Tor., Min.	6	164	22	59	81	66	11	3	7	10	6	1977-78	1987-88
Wilson, Wally	Bos.	1	53	11	8	19	18	1	0	0	0	0	1947-48	1947-48
Wing, Murray	Det.	1	1	0	1	1	0	....	....	....	....	....	1973-74	1973-74
Wiseman, Eddie	Det., NYA, Bos.	10	454	115	164	279	137	45	10	10	20	16	1932-33	1941-42
Wiste, Jim	Chi., Van.	3	52	1	10	11	8	....	....	....	....	....	1968-69	1970-71
Witherspoon, Jim	L.A.	1	2	0	0	0	0	....	....	....	....	....	1975-76	1975-76
Witiuk, Steve	Chi.	1	33	3	8	11	14	....	....	....	....	....	1951-52	1951-52
Woit, Benny	Det., Chi.	7	334	7	26	33	170	41	2	6	8	18	1950-51	1956-57
Wojciechowski, Steven	Det.	2	54	19	20	39	17	6	0	1	1	0	1944-45	1946-47
Wolf, Bennett	Pit.	3	30	0	1	1	133	....	....	....	....	....	1980-81	1982-83
Wong, Mike	Det.	1	22	1	1	2	12	....	....	....	....	....	1975-76	1975-76
Wood, Robert	NYR	1	1	0	0	0	0	....	....	....	....	....	1950-51	1950-51
Woods, Paul	Det.	7	501	72	124	196	276	7	0	5	5	4	1977-78	1983-84
Woytowich, Bob	Bos., Min., Pit., L.A.	8	503	32	126	158	352	24	1	3	4	20	1964-65	1971-72
Wright, John	Van., St.L., K.C.	3	127	16	36	52	67	....	....	....	....	....	1972-73	1974-75
Wright, Keith	Phi.	1	1	0	0	0	0	....	....	....	....	....	1967-68	1967-68
Wright, Larry	Phi., Cal., Det.	5	106	4	8	12	19	....	....	....	....	....	1971-72	1977-78
Wycherley, Ralph	NYA	2	28	4	7	11	6	....	....	....	....	....	1940-41	1941-42
Wylie, Duane	Chi.	2	14	3	3	6	2	....	....	....	....	....	1974-75	1976-77
Wylie, William	NYR	1	1	0	0	0	0	....	....	....	....	....	1950-51	1950-51
Wyrozub, Randy	Buf.	4	100	8	10	18	10	....	....	....	....	....	1970-71	1973-74

YZ

Name	NHL Teams	NHL Seasons	Regular Schedule GP	G	A	TP	PIM	Playoffs GP	G	A	TP	PIM	First NHL Season	Last NHL Season
Yackel, Ken	Bos.	1	6	0	0	0	2	2	0	0	0	0	1958-59	1958-59
Yaremchuk, Gary	Tor.	4	34	1	4	5	28	....	....	....	....	....	1981-82	1984-85
Yates, Ross	Hfd.	1	7	1	1	2	4	....	....	....	....	....	1983-84	1983-84
Young, Brian	Chi.	1	8	0	2	2	6	....	....	....	....	....	1980-81	1980-81
Young, Douglas	Mtl., Det.	10	391	35	45	80	303	28	1	5	6	16	1931-32	1940-41
Young, Howie	Det., Chi., Van.	8	336	12	62	74	851	19	2	4	6	46	1960-61	1970-71
Young, Tim	Min., Wpg., Phi.	10	620	195	341	536	438	36	7	24	31	27	1975-76	1984-85
Young, Warren	Min., Pit., Det.	7	236	72	77	149	472	....	....	....	....	....	1981-82	1987-88
Younghans, Tom	Min., NYR	6	429	44	41	85	373	24	2	1	3	21	1976-77	1981-82
Zabroski, Marty	Chi.	1	1	0	0	0	0	....	....	....	....	....	1944-45	1944-45
Zaharko, Miles	Atl., Chi.	4	129	5	32	37	84	3	0	0	0	0	1977-78	1981-82
Zaine, Rod	Pit., Buf.	2	61	10	6	16	25	....	....	....	....	....	1970-71	1971-72
Zanussi, Joe	NYR, Bos., St.L.	3	87	1	13	14	46	4	0	1	1	2	1974-75	1976-77
Zanussi, Ron	Min., Tor.	5	299	52	83	135	373	17	0	4	4	17	1977-78	1981-82
Zeidel, Larry	Det., Chi., Phi.	5	158	3	16	19	198	12	0	1	1	12	1951-52	1968-69
Zeniuk, Ed	Det.	1	2	0	0	0	0	....	....	....	....	....	1954-55	1954-55
Zetterstrom, Lars	Van.	1	14	0	1	1	2	....	....	....	....	....	1978-79	1978-79
Zuke, Mike	St.L., Hfd.	8	421	86	196	282	220	26	6	6	12	12	1978-79	1985-86
Zunich, Ruby	Det.	1	2	0	0	0	2	....	....	....	....	....	1943-44	1943-44

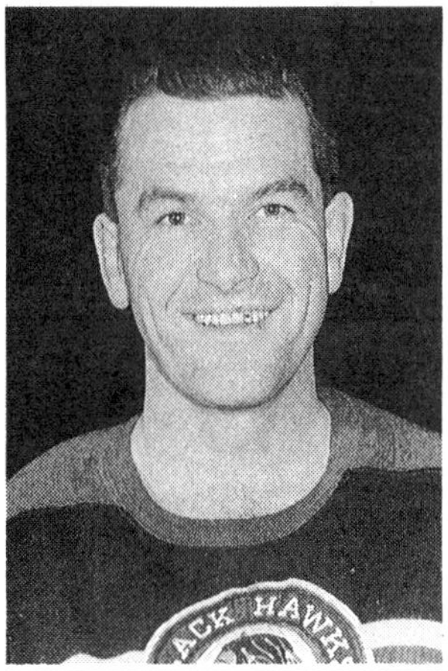
Harry Watson

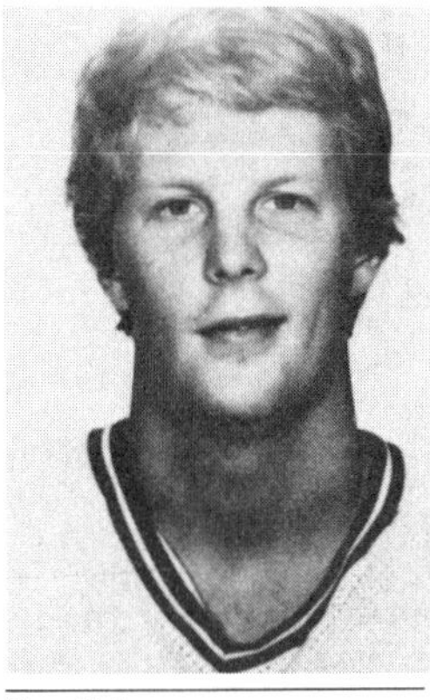
Ross Yates

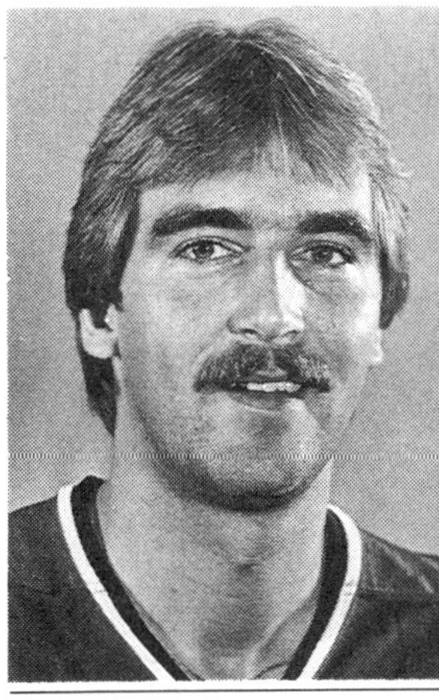
Miles Zaharko

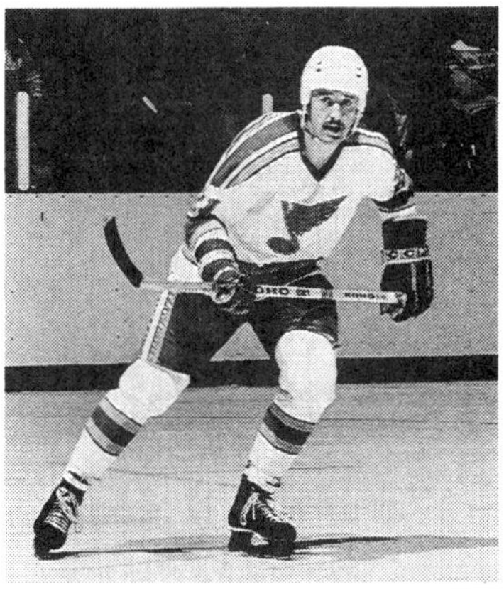
Mike Zuke

Jeff Reese

Brian Hayward

Sean Burke

1989-90 Goaltender Register

Note: The 1989-90Goaltender Register lists every goaltender who appeared in an NHL game in the 1988-89 season, every goaltender drafted in the first two rounds of the 1988 and 1989 Entry Drafts and other goaltenders on NHL Reserve Lists.

Trades and roster changes are current as of August 10, 1989.

To calculate a goaltender's goals-against-per-game average **(Avg)**, divide goals against **(GA)** by minutes played **(Mins)** and multiply this result by **60**.

Abbreviations: A list of league names can be found at the beginning of the Player Register. **Avg** – goals against per game average; **GA** – goals against; **GP** – games played; **L** – losses; **Lea** – league; **SO** – shutouts; **T** – ties; **W** – wins.

Player Register begins on page 207.

ANDERSON, DEAN

Goaltender. Catches left. 5'10", 175 lbs. Born, Oshawa, Ont., July 14, 1966.
(Toronto's 1st choice, 11th overall, in 1988 Supplemental Draft).

			Regular Season								Playoffs						
Season	Club	Lea	GP	W	L	T	Mins	GA	SO	Avg	GP	W	L	Mins	GA	SO	Avg
1984-85	U. Wisconsin	WCHA	36	21	13	0	2072	148	0	4.29	....	....	....	....	....	....	....
1985-86	U. Wisconsin	WCHA	20	13	6	0	1128	80	0	4.25	....	....	....	....	....	....	....
1986-87	U. Wisconsin	WCHA	9	4	2	0	409	27	0	3.96	....	....	....	....	....	....	....
1987-88a	U. Wisconsin	WCHA	45	30	13	2	2718	148	2	3.27	....	....	....	....	....	....	....
1988-89	Newmarket	AHL	2	0	1	0	38	4	0	6.32	1	0	1	30	1	0	2.00
	Flint	IHL	16	1	12	0	770	82	1	6.39	....	....	....	....	....	....	....

a WCHA Second All-Star Team (1988)

BARRASSO, TOM (bahr AH soh)

Goaltender. Catches right. 6'3", 207 lbs. Born, Boston, MA, March 31, 1965.
(Buffalo's 1st choice, 5th over-all, in 1983 Entry Draft).

			Regular Season								Playoffs						
Season	Club	Lea	GP	W	L	T	Mins	GA	SO	Avg	GP	W	L	Mins	GA	SO	Avg
1981-82	Acton-Boxboro	Mass.	23	....	....	....	1035	32	7	1.39	....	....	....	....	....	....	....
1982-83	Acton-Boxboro	Mass.	23	....	....	....	1035	17	10	0.73	....	....	....	....	....	....	....
1983-84abcd	**Buffalo**	**NHL**	**42**	**26**	**12**	**3**	**2475**	**117**	**2**	**2.84**	**3**	**0**	**2**	**139**	**8**	**0**	**3.45**
1984-85ef	**Buffalo**	**NHL**	**54**	**25**	**18**	**10**	**3248**	**144**	***5**	**2.66**	**5**	**2**	**3**	**300**	**22**	**0**	**4.40**
	Rochester	AHL	5	3	1	1	267	6	1	1.35	....	....	....	....	....	....	....
1985-86	**Buffalo**	**NHL**	**60**	**29**	**24**	**5**	**3561**	**214**	**2**	**3.61**	....	....	....	....	....	....	....
1986-87	**Buffalo**	**NHL**	**46**	**17**	**23**	**2**	**2501**	**152**	**2**	**3.65**	....	....	....	....	....	....	....
1987-88	**Buffalo**	**NHL**	**54**	**25**	**18**	**8**	**3133**	**173**	**2**	**3.31**	**4**	**1**	**3**	**224**	**16**	**0**	**4.29**
1988-89	**Buffalo**	**NHL**	**10**	**2**	**7**	**0**	**545**	**45**	**0**	**4.95**	....	....	....	....	....	....	....
	Pittsburgh	**NHL**	**44**	**18**	**15**	**7**	**2406**	**162**	**0**	**4.04**	**11**	**7**	**4**	**631**	**40**	**0**	**3.80**
	NHL Totals		**310**	**142**	**117**	**35**	**17869**	**1007**	**13**	**3.38**	**23**	**10**	**12**	**1294**	**86**	**0**	**3.99**

a NHL First All-Star Team (1984)
b Won Vezina Trophy (1984)
c Won Calder Memorial Trophy (1984)
d NHL All-Rookie Team (1984)
e NHL Second All-Star Team (1985)
f Shared William Jennings Trophy with Bob Sauve (1985)

Played in NHL All-Star Game (1985)

Traded to **Pittsburgh** by **Buffalo** with Buffalo's third-round choice in 1990 Entry Draft for Doug Bodger and Darrin Shannon, November 12, 1988.

BEALS, DARREN

Goaltender. Catches right. 6', 200 lbs. Born, Dartmouth, N.S., August 28, 1968.

			Regular Season								Playoffs						
Season	Club	Lea	GP	W	L	T	Mins	GA	SO	Avg	GP	W	L	Mins	GA	SO	Avg
1985-86	Ottawa	OHL	45	12	29	2	2622	233	1	5.33	....	....	....	....	....	....	....
1986-87	Kitchener	OHL	49	20	16	3	2582	190	1	4.42	2	0	2	120	9	0	4.50
1987-88	Kitchener	OHL	38	14	18	1	2063	169	0	4.92	1	0	1	21	7	0	20.00
1988-89	Cape Breton	AHL	14	3	10	1	738	65	0	5.28	....	....	....	....	....	....	....

Signed as a free agent by **Edmonton**, September 26, 1986.

BEAUPRE, DONALD WILLIAM (DON) (boh-PRAY)

Goaltender. Catches left. 5'9", 165 lbs. Born, Waterloo, Ont., September 19, 1961.
(Minnesota's 2nd choice, 37th over-all, in 1980 Entry Draft).

			Regular Season								Playoffs						
Season	Club	Lea	GP	W	L	T	Mins	GA	SO	Avg	GP	W	L	Mins	GA	SO	Avg
1978-79	Sudbury	OHA	54	....	....	....	3248	260	2	4.78	10	....	....	600	44	0	4.20
1979-80a	Sudbury	OHA	59	28	29	2	3447	248	0	4.32	9	5	4	552	38	0	4.13
1980-81	**Minnesota**	**NHL**	**44**	**18**	**14**	**11**	**2585**	**138**	**0**	**3.20**	**6**	**4**	**2**	**360**	**26**	**0**	**4.33**
1981-82	Nashville	CHL	5	2	3	0	299	25	0	5.02	....	....	....	....	....	....	....
	Minnesota	**NHL**	**29**	**11**	**8**	**9**	**1634**	**101**	**0**	**3.71**	**2**	**0**	**1**	**60**	**4**	**0**	**4.00**
1982-83	Birmingham	CHL	10	8	2	0	599	31	0	3.11	....	....	....	....	....	....	....
	Minnesota	**NHL**	**36**	**19**	**10**	**5**	**2011**	**120**	**0**	**3.58**	**4**	**2**	**2**	**245**	**20**	**0**	**4.90**
1983-84	Salt Lake	CHL	7	2	5	0	419	30	0	4.30	....	....	....	....	....	....	....
	Minnesota	**NHL**	**33**	**16**	**13**	**2**	**1791**	**123**	**0**	**4.12**	**13**	**6**	**7**	**782**	**40**	**1**	**3.07**
1984-85	**Minnesota**	**NHL**	**31**	**10**	**17**	**3**	**1770**	**109**	**1**	**3.69**	**4**	**1**	**1**	**184**	**12**	**0**	**3.91**
1985-86	**Minnesota**	**NHL**	**52**	**25**	**20**	**6**	**3073**	**182**	**1**	**3.55**	**5**	**2**	**3**	**300**	**17**	**0**	**3.40**
1986-87	**Minnesota**	**NHL**	**47**	**17**	**20**	**6**	**2622**	**174**	**1**	**3.98**	....	....	....	....	....	....	....
1987-88	**Minnesota**	**NHL**	**43**	**10**	**22**	**3**	**2288**	**161**	**0**	**4.22**	....	....	....	....	....	....	....
1988-89	**Minnesota**	**NHL**	**1**	**0**	**1**	**0**	**59**	**3**	**0**	**3.05**	....	....	....	....	....	....	....
	Kalamazoo	IHL	3	1	2	0	179	9	1	3.02	....	....	....	....	....	....	....
	Washington	**NHL**	**11**	**5**	**4**	**0**	**578**	**28**	**1**	**2.91**	....	....	....	....	....	....	....
	Baltimore	AHL	30	14	12	2	1715	102	0	3.57	....	....	....	....	....	....	....
	NHL Totals		**327**	**131**	**129**	**45**	**18411**	**1139**	**4**	**3.71**	**34**	**15**	**16**	**1931**	**119**	**1**	**3.70**

a OHA First All-Star Team (1980)

Played in NHL All-Star Game (1981)

Traded to **Washington** by **Minnesota** for rights to Claudio Scremin, November 1, 1988.

BEAUREGARD, STEPHANE

Goaltender. Catches right. 5'11", 185 lbs. Born, Cowansville, Que., January 10, 1968.
(Winnipeg's 3rd choice, 52nd overall, in 1988 Entry Draft).

			Regular Season								Playoffs						
Season	Club	Lea	GP	W	L	T	Mins	GA	SO	Avg	GP	W	L	Mins	GA	SO	Avg
1986-87	St. Jean	QMJHL	13	6	7	0	785	58	0	4.43	5	1	3	260	26	0	6.00
1987-88a	St. Jean	QMJHL	66	38	20	3	3766	229	2	3.65	7	3	4	423	34	0	4.82
1988-89	Fort Wayne	IHL	16	9	5	0	830	43	0	3.10	9	4	4	484	21	*1	*2.60

a QMJHL First All-Star Team (1988)

BEEDON, ROGER

Goaltender. Catches left. 6', 175 lbs. Born, Marysville, MI, May 30, 1967.
(Montreal's 11th choice, 184th over-all, in 1985 Entry Draft).

			Regular Season								Playoffs						
Season	Club	Lea	GP	W	L	T	Mins	GA	SO	Avg	GP	W	L	Mins	GA	SO	Avg
1985-86	Ohio State	CCHA	27	12	11	0	1393	115	0	4.95	....	....	....	....	....	....	....
1986-87	Ohio State	CCHA	24	8	13	1	1322	114	1	5.17	....	....	....	....	....	....	....
1988-89	Ohio State	CCHA	12	0	7	1	496	54	0	6.53	....	....	....	....	....	....	....

BELFOUR, ED

Goaltender. Catches left. 6', 175 lbs. Born, Carmen, Man., April 21, 1965.

			Regular Season								Playoffs						
Season	Club	Lea	GP	W	L	T	Mins	GA	SO	Avg	GP	W	L	Mins	GA	SO	Avg
1986-87a	North Dakota	WCHA	34	29	4	0	2049	81	3	2.43	....	....	....	....	....	....	....
1987-88bc	Saginaw	IHL	61	32	25	0	3446	183	3	3.19	9	4	5	561	33	0	3.53
1988-89	**Chicago**	**NHL**	**23**	**4**	**12**	**3**	**1148**	**74**	**0**	**3.87**	....	....	....	....	....	....	....
	Saginaw	IHL	29	12	10	0	1760	92	0	3.10	5	2	3	298	14	0	2.82
	NHL Totals		**23**	**4**	**12**	**3**	**1148**	**74**	**0**	**3.87**	....	....	....	....	....	....	....

a WCHA First All-Star Team (1987)
b IHL First All-Star Team (1988)
c Shared Garry F. Longman Memorial Trophy (Top Rookie - IHL) (1988)

Signed as a free agent by **Chicago**, September 25, 1987.

BERGERON, JEAN-CLAUDE

Goaltender. Catches left. 6'2", 180 lbs. Born, Hauterive, Que., October 14, 1968.
(Montreal's 6th choice, 104th overall, in 1988 Entry Draft).

			Regular Season								Playoffs						
Season	Club	Lea	GP	W	L	T	Mins	GA	SO	Avg	GP	W	L	Mins	GA	SO	Avg
1987-88	Verdun	QMJHL	49	13	31	3	2715	265	0	5.86	....	....	....	....	....	....	....
1988-89	Verdun	QMJHL	44	8	34	1	2417	199	0	4.94	....	....	....	....	....	....	....
	Sherbrooke	AHL	19	12	4	1	1075	60	2	3.35	....	....	....	....	....	....	....

BERNHARDT, TIMOTHY JOHN (TIM) (burn-HEART)

Goaltender. Catches left. 5'9", 160 lbs. Born, Sarnia, Ont., January 17, 1958.
(Atlanta's 2nd choice, 47th over-all, in 1978 Amateur Draft).

			Regular Season								Playoffs						
Season	Club	Lea	GP	W	L	T	Mins	GA	SO	Avg	GP	W	L	Mins	GA	SO	Avg
1976-77a	Cornwall	QJHL	44	....	....	....	2497	151	0	3.63	12	....	....	720	47	0	3.92
1977-78a	Cornwall	QJHL	54	....	....	....	3165	179	2	3.39	9	....	....	540	27	2	3.00
1978-79	Tulsa	CHL	46	....	....	....	2705	191	0	4.24	....	....	....	....	....	....	....
1979-80	Birmingham	CHL	34	15	16	1	1933	122	1	3.79	3	....	....	160	17	0	6.38
1980-81	Birmingham	CHL	29	11	13	2	1598	106	1	3.98	....	....	....	....	....	....	....
1981-82	Oklahoma City	CHL	10	1	8	0	526	45	0	5.13	....	....	....	....	....	....	....
	Rochester	AHL	29	15	10	.2	1586	95	0	3.59	9	4	3	527	29	0	3.30
1982-83	**Calgary**	**NHL**	**6**	**0**	**5**	**0**	**280**	**21**	**0**	**4.50**	....	....	....	....	....	....	....
	Colorado	CHL	34	19	11	1	1896	122	0	3.86	5	2	3	304	19	0	3.75
1983-84	St. Catharines	AHL	42	25	13	4	2461	154	0	3.75	5	2	3	288	17	0	3.54
1984-85	**Toronto**	**NHL**	**37**	**13**	**19**	**4**	**2182**	**136**	**0**	**3.74**	....	....	....	....	....	....	....
	St. Catharines	AHL	14	5	7	2	801	55	0	412	....	....	....	....	....	....	....
1985-86	**Toronto**	**NHL**	**23**	**4**	**12**	**3**	**1266**	**107**	**0**	**5.07**	....	....	....	....	....	....	....
	St.Catharines	AHL	14	6	4	2	776	38	1	2.94	3	0	3	140	12	0	5.14
1986-87	**Toronto**	**NHL**	**1**	**0**	**0**	**0**	**20**	**3**	**0**	**9.00**	....	....	....	....	....	....	....
	Newmarket	AHL	31	6	17	0	1705	117	1	4.12	....	....	....	....	....	....	....
1987-88	Newmarket	AHL	49	22	19	4	2704	166	0	3.68	....	....	....	....	....	....	....
1988-89	Newmarket	AHL	37	17	16	2	2004	145	1	4.34	....	....	....	....	....	....	....
	NHL Totals		**67**	**17**	**36**	**7**	**3748**	**267**	**0**	**4.27**	....	....	....	....	....	....	....

a QMJHL First All-Star Team (1977, 1978)

Signed as a free agent by **Toronto**, December 5, 1984.

BERTHIAUME, DANIEL

Goaltender. Catches left. 5'9", 150 lbs. Born, Longueuil, Que., January 26, 1966.
(Winnipeg's 3rd choice, 60th over-all, in 1985 Entry Draft).

			Regular Season								Playoffs						
Season	Club	Lea	GP	W	L	T	Mins	GA	SO	Avg	GP	W	L	Mins	GA	SO	Avg
1984-85	Chicoutimi	QMJHL	59	40	11	2	2177	149	0	4.11	14	8	6	770	51	0	3.97
1985-86	Chicoutimi	QMJHL	66	34	29	3	3718	286	1	4.62	9	4	5	580	36	0	3.72
	Winnipeg	**NHL**	....	....	....	....	....	....	....	....	**1**	**0**	**1**	**68**	**4**	**0**	**3.53**
1986-87	**Winnipeg**	**NHL**	**31**	**18**	**7**	**3**	**1758**	**93**	**1**	**3.17**	**8**	**4**	**4**	**439**	**21**	**0**	**2.87**
	Sherbrooke	AHL	7	4	3	0	420	23	0	3.29	....	....	....	....	....	....	....
1987-88	**Winnipeg**	**NHL**	**56**	**22**	**19**	**7**	**3010**	**176**	**2**	**3.51**	**5**	**1**	**4**	**300**	**25**	**0**	**5.00**
1988-89	**Winnipeg**	**NHL**	**9**	**0**	**8**	**0**	**443**	**44**	**0**	**5.96**	....	....	....	....	....	....	....
	Moncton	AHL	21	6	9	2	1083	76	0	4.21	3	1	2	180	11	0	3.67
	NHL Totals		**96**	**40**	**34**	**10**	**5211**	**313**	**3**	**3.60**	**14**	**5**	**9**	**807**	**50**	**0**	**3.72**

BESTER, ALLAN J.

Goaltender. Catches left. 5'7", 150 lbs. Born, Hamilton, Ont., March 26, 1964.
(Toronto's 3rd choice, 48th over-all, in 1983 Entry Draft).

			Regular Season								Playoffs						
Season	Club	Lea	GP	W	L	T	Mins	GA	SO	Avg	GP	W	L	Mins	GA	SO	Avg
1981-82	Brantford	OHL	19	4	11	0	970	68	0	4.21	....	....	....	....	....	....	....
1982-83a	Brantford	OHL	56	29	21	3	3210	188	0	3.51	8	3	3	480	20	*1	*2.50
1983-84	**Toronto**	**NHL**	**32**	**11**	**16**	**4**	**1848**	**134**	**0**	**4.35**	....	....	....	....	....	....	....
	Brantford	OHL	23	12	9	1	1271	71	1	3.35	1	0	1	60	5	0	5.00
1984-85	**Toronto**	**NHL**	**15**	**3**	**9**	**1**	**767**	**54**	**1**	**4.22**	....	....	....	....	....	....	....
	St. Catharines	AHL	30	9	18	1	1669	133	0	4.78	....	....	....	....	....	....	....
1985-86	**Toronto**	**NHL**	**1**	**0**	**0**	**0**	**20**	**2**	**0**	**6.00**	....	....	....	....	....	....	....
	St.Catharines	AHL	50	23	23	3	2855	173	1	3.64	11	7	3	637	27	0	2.54
1986-87	**Toronto**	**NHL**	**36**	**10**	**14**	**3**	**1808**	**110**	**2**	**3.65**	**1**	**0**	**0**	**39**	**1**	**0**	**1.54**
	Newmarket	AHL	3	1	0	0	190	6	0	1.89	....	....	....	....	....	....	....
1987-88	**Toronto**	**NHL**	**30**	**8**	**12**	**5**	**1607**	**102**	**2**	**3.81**	**5**	**2**	**3**	**253**	**21**	**0**	**4.98**
1988-89	**Toronto**	**NHL**	**43**	**17**	**20**	**3**	**2460**	**156**	**2**	**3.80**	....	....	....	....	....	....	....
	NHL Totals		**157**	**49**	**71**	**16**	**8510**	**558**	**7**	**3.93**	**6**	**2**	**3**	**292**	**22**	**0**	**4.52**

a OHL First All-Star Team (1983)

BILLINGTON, CRAIG

Goaltender. Catches left. 5'10", 165 lbs. Born, London, Ont., September 11, 1966.
(New Jersey's 2nd choice, 23rd over-all, in 1984 Entry Draft).

			Regular Season								Playoffs						
Season	Club	Lea	GP	W	L	T	Mins	GA	SO	Avg	GP	W	L	Mins	GA	SO	Avg
1982-83	London	OPJHL	23	....	....	....	1338	76	0	3.39	....	....	....	....	....	....	....
1983-84	Belleville	OHL	44	20	19	0	2335	162	1	4.16	1	0	0	30	3	0	6.00
1984-85a	Belleville	OHL	47	26	19	0	2544	180	1	4.25	14	7	5	761	47	1	3.71
1985-86	**New Jersey**	**NHL**	**18**	**4**	**9**	**1**	**901**	**77**	**0**	**5.13**	....	....	....	....	....	....	....
	Belleville	OHL	3	2	1	0	180	11	0	3.67	20	9	6	1133	68	0	3.60
1986-87	**New Jersey**	**NHL**	**22**	**4**	**13**	**2**	**1114**	**89**	**0**	**4.79**	....	....	....	....	....	....	....
	Maine	AHL	20	9	8	2	1151	70	0	3.65	....	....	....	....	....	....	....
1987-88	Utica	AHL	59	22	27	8	3404	208	1	3.67	....	....	....	....	....	....	....
1988-89	**New Jersey**	**NHL**	**3**	**1**	**1**	**0**	**140**	**11**	**0**	**4.71**	....	....	....	....	....	....	....
	Utica	AHL	41	17	18	6	2432	150	2	3.70	4	1	3	220	18	0	4.91
	NHL Totals		**43**	**9**	**23**	**3**	**2155**	**177**	**0**	**4.93**	....	....	....	....	....	....	....

a OHL First All-Star Team (1985)

BLUE, JOHN

Goaltender. Catches left. 5'10", 185 lbs. Born, Huntington Beach, CA, February 19, 1966.
(Winnipeg's 9th choice, 197th overall, in 1986 Entry Draft).

			Regular Season								Playoffs						
Season	Club	Lea	GP	W	L	T	Mins	GA	SO	Avg	GP	W	L	Mins	GA	SO	Avg
1984-85	U. Minnesota	WCHA	34	23	10	0	1964	111	2	3.39	...	...	...	...	...	...	...
1985-86a	U. Minnesota	WCHA	29	20	6	0	1588	80	2	3.02	...	...	...	...	...	...	...
1986-87	U. Minnesota	WCHA	33	21	9	1	1889	99	3	3.14	...	...	...	...	...	...	...
1987-88	Kalamazoo	IHL	15	3	8	4	847	65		4.60	1	0	1	40	6		9.00
	U.S. National	....	13	3	4	1	588	33	0	3.37	....	....	....	....	....	....	....
1988-89	Kalamazoo	IHL	17	8	6	0	970	69	0	4.27	....	....	....	....	....	....	....

a WCHA First All-Star Team (1986)

Traded to **Minnesota** by **Winnipeg** for Winnipeg's seventh round choice in 1988 Entry Draft (Markus Akerblom), March 7, 1988.

BRADLEY, JOHN

Goaltender. Catches left. 6', 165 lbs. Born, Pawtucket, RI, February 6, 1968.
(Buffalo's 4th choice, 84th overall, in 1987 Entry Draft).

			Regular Season								Playoffs						
Season	Club	Lea	GP	W	L	T	Mins	GA	SO	Avg	GP	W	L	Mins	GA	SO	Avg
1987-88	Boston U.	H.E.	9	4	4	0	528	40	0	4.53	....	....	....	....	....	....	....
1988-89	Boston U.	H.E.	11	5	4	1	584	53	0	5.45	....	....	....	....	....	....	....

BRODEUR, RICHARD (broh-DYEWR)

Goaltender. Catches left. 5'7", 160 lbs. Born, Longueuil, Que., September 15, 1952.
(NY Islanders' 7th choice, 97th over-all, in 1972 Amateur Draft).

			Regular Season								Playoffs						
Season	Club	Lea	GP	W	L	T	Mins	GA	SO	Avg	GP	W	L	Mins	GA	SO	Avg
1970-71	Verdun	QJHL	6	....	....	....	360	47	0	7.83	....	....	....	....	....	....	....
	Cornwall	QJHL	35	....	....	....	2102	144	0	4.11	....	....	....	....	....	....	....
1971-72	Cornwall	QJHL	58	....	....	....	3481	170	5	2.93	16	....	....	960	44	0	2.75
1972-73	Quebec	WHA	24	....	....	....	1288	102	0	4.75	....	....	....	....	....	....	....
1973-74	Quebec	WHA	30	....	....	....	1607	89	1	3.32	....	....	....	....	....	....	....
	Maine	NAHL	16	....	....	....	927	47	0	3.04	....	....	....	....	....		....
1974-75	Quebec	WHA	51	....	....	....	2938	188	0	3.84	15	....	....	906	48	1	3.18
1975-76	Quebec	WHA	69	....	....	....	3967	244	2	3.69	5	....	....	299	22	0	4.41
1976-77	Quebec	WHA	53	....	....	....	2906	167	2	3.45	17	....	....	1007	55	*1	3.28
1977-78	Quebec	WHA	36	18	15	2	1962	121	0	3.70	11	....	....	622	38	*1	3.67
1978-79	Quebec	WHA	42	....	....	....	2433	126	*3	3.11	3	....	....	114	14	0	7.37
1979-80	**NY Islanders**	**NHL**	**2**	**1**	**1**	**0**	**80**	**6**	**0**	**4.50**	....	....	....	....	....	....	....
ab	Indianapolis	CHL	46	22	19	5	2722	131	*4	*2.88	6	3	3	357	12	*1	*2.02
1980-81	**Vancouver**	**NHL**	**52**	**17**	**18**	**16**	**3024**	**177**	**0**	**3.51**	**3**	**0**	**3**	**185**	**13**	**0**	**4.22**
1981-82	**Vancouver**	**NHL**	**52**	**20**	**18**	**12**	**3010**	**168**	**2**	**3.35**	**17**	**11**	**6**	**1089**	**49**	**0**	**2.70**
1982-83	**Vancouver**	**NHL**	**58**	**21**	**26**	**8**	**3291**	**208**	**0**	**3.79**	**3**	**0**	**3**	**193**	**13**	**0**	**4.04**
1983-84	**Vancouver**	**NHL**	**36**	**10**	**21**	**5**	**2110**	**141**	**1**	**4.01**	**4**	**1**	**3**	**222**	**12**	**1**	**3.24**
1984-85	**Vancouver**	**NHL**	**51**	**16**	**27**	**6**	**2930**	**228**	**0**	**4.67**	....	....	....	....	....	....	....
	Fredericton	AHL	4	3	0	1	249	13	0	3.13	....	....	....	....	....	....	....
1985-86	**Vancouver**	**NHL**	**64**	**19**	**32**	**8**	**3541**	**240**	**2**	**4.07**	**2**	**0**	**2**	**120**	**12**	**0**	**6.00**
1986-87	**Vancouver**	**NHL**	**53**	**20**	**25**	**5**	**2972**	**178**	**1**	**3.59**	....	....	....	....	....	....	....
1987-88	**Vancouver**	**NHL**	**11**	**3**	**6**	**2**	**670**	**49**	**0**	**4.39**	....	....	....	....	....	....	....
	Fredericton	AHL	2	0	1	0	99	8	0	4.85	....	....	....	....	....	....	....
	Hartford	**NHL**	**6**	**4**	**2**	**0**	**340**	**15**	**0**	**2.65**	**4**	**1**	**3**	**200**	**12**	**0**	**3.60**
1988-89	Binghamton	AHL	6	1	2	0	222	21	0	5.68	....	....	....	....	....	....	....
	NHL Totals		**385**	**131**	**176**	**62**	**21968**	**1410**	**6**	**3.85**	**33**	**13**	**20**	**2009**	**111**	**1**	**3.32**

a CHL First All-Star Team (1980)
b Shared Terry Sawchuk Trophy (CHL's Leading Goaltenders) with Jim Park (1980)

Reclaimed by **NY Islanders** from **Quebec** prior to Expansion Draft, June 9, 1979. Traded to **Vancouver** by **NY Islanders** with NY Islanders' fifth-round choice (Moe Lemay) in 1981 Entry Draft for Vancouver's fifth-round choice (Jacques Sylvestre) in the 1981 Entry Draft, October 6, 1980. Traded to **Hartford** by **Vancouver** for Steve Weeks, March 8, 1988.

BROWER, SCOTT

Goaltender. Catches left. 6', 185 lbs. Born, Viking, Alta., September 26, 1964.
(NY Rangers' 12th choice, 243rd over-all, in 1984 Entry Draft).

			Regular Season								Playoffs						
Season	Club	Lea	GP	W	L	T	Mins	GA	SO	Avg	GP	W	L	Mins	GA	SO	Avg
1984-85	North Dakota	WCHA	31	15	12	2	1808	99	0	3.28	....	....	....	....	....	....	....
1985-86	North Dakota	WCHA	20	11	6	0	1096	67	0	3.47	....	....	....	....	....	....	....
1986-87	North Dakota	WCHA	15	11	4	0	803	44	0	3.29	....	....	....	....	....	....	....
1987-88	North Dakota	WCHA	23	10	12	0	1450	88	1	3.64	....	....	....	....	....	....	....
1988-89	Flint	IHL	5	1	2	0	235	22	0	5.62	....	....	....	....	....	....	....
	Denver	IHL	20	3	5	0	938	82	0	5.25	1	0	0	31	1	0	1.94

BRUNETTA, MARIO

Goaltender. Catches right. 6'3", 180 lbs. Born, Quebec City, Que., January 25, 1967.
(Quebec's 9th choice, 162nd over-all, in 1985 Entry Draft).

			Regular Season								Playoffs						
Season	Club	Lea	GP	W	L	T	Mins	GA	SO	Avg	GP	W	L	Mins	GA	SO	Avg
1984-85	Quebec	QMJHL	45	20	21	1	2255	192	0	5.11	2	0	2	120	13	0	6.50
1985-86	Laval	QMJHL	63	30	25	1	3383	279	0	4.95	14	9	5	834	60	0	4.32
1986-87	Laval	QMJHL	59	27	25	4	3469	261	1	4.51	14	8	6	820	63	0	4.61
1987-88	**Quebec**	**NHL**	**29**	**10**	**12**	**1**	**1550**	**96**	**0**	**3.72**	....	....	....	....	....	....	....
	Fredericton	AHL	5	4	1	0	300	24	0	4.80	....	....	....	....	....	....	....
1988-89	**Quebec**	**NHL**	**5**	**1**	**3**	**0**	**226**	**19**	**0**	**5.04**	....	....	....	....	....	....	....
	Halifax	AHL	36	14	14	5	1898	124	0	3.92	3	0	2	142	12	0	5.07
	NHL Totals		**34**	**11**	**15**	**1**	**1776**	**115**	**0**	**3.89**	....	....	....	....	....	....	....

BURCHILL, RICH

Goaltender. Catches right. 6', 180 lbs. Born, Boston, MA, January 3, 1967.
(St. Louis' 5th choice, 121st overall, in 1985 Entry Draft).

			Regular Season								Playoffs						
Season	Club	Lea	GP	W	L	T	Mins	GA	SO	Avg	GP	W	L	Mins	GA	SO	Avg
1987-88	Northeastern	H.E.	6	3	2	0	323	22	0	4.08	....	....	....	....	....	....	....
1988-89	Northeastern	H.E.	30	16	12	2	1815	118	0	3.90	....	....	....	....	....	....	....

BURKE, SEAN

Goaltender. Catches left. 6'3", 205 lbs. Born, Windsor, Ont., January 29, 1967.
(New Jersey's 2nd choice, 24th over-all, in 1985 Entry Draft).

			Regular Season								Playoffs						
Season	Club	Lea	GP	W	L	T	Mins	GA	SO	Avg	GP	W	L	Mins	GA	SO	Avg
1984-85	Toronto	OHL	49	25	21	3	2987	211	0	4.24	5	1	3	266	25	0	5.64
1985-86	Toronto	OHL	47	16	27	3	2840	233	0	4.92	4	0	4	238	24	0	6.05
1986-87	Can. Olympic	....	42	27	13	2	2550	130	0	3.05	....	....	....	....	....	....	....
1987-88	**New Jersey**	**NHL**	**13**	**10**	**1**	**0**	**689**	**35**	**1**	**3.05**	**17**	**9**	**8**	**1001**	**57**	***1**	**3.42**
	Cdn. National	....	37	19	9	2	1962	92	1	2.81	....	....	....	....	....	....	....
	Cdn. Olympic	....	4	1	2	1	238	12		3.02	....	....	....	....	....	....	....
1988-89	**New Jersey**	**NHL**	**62**	**22**	**31**	**9**	**3590**	**230**	**3**	**3.84**	....	....	....	....	....	....	....
	NHL Totals		**75**	**32**	**32**	**9**	**4289**	**265**	**4**	**3.71**	**17**	**9**	**8**	**1001**	**57**	**1**	**3.42**

Played in NHL All-Star Game (1989)

CAPRICE, FRANK (kuh-PREEZ)

Goaltender. Catches left. 5'9", 150 lbs. Born, Hamilton, Ont., May 2, 1962.
(Vancouver's 8th choice, 178th over-all, in 1981 Entry Draft).

			Regular Season								Playoffs						
Season	Club	Lea	GP	W	L	T	Mins	GA	SO	Avg	GP	W	L	Mins	GA	SO	Avg
1979-80	London	OHA	18	3	7	3	919	74	1	4.84	3	1	1	94	10	0	6.38
1980-81	London	OHA	42	11	26	0	2171	190	0	5.25	....	....	....	....	....	....	....
1981-82a	London	OHL	45	24	17	2	2614	196	0	4.50	4	1	3	240	18	0	4.50
	Dallas	CHL	3	0	3	0	178	19	0	6.40	....	....	....	....	....	....	....
1982-83	**Vancouver**	**NHL**	**1**	**0**	**0**	**0**	**20**	**3**	**0**	**9.09**	....	....	....	....	....	....	....
	Fredericton	AHL	14	5	8	1	819	50	0	3.67	....	....	....	....	....	....	....
1983-84	**Vancouver**	**NHL**	**19**	**8**	**2**	**2**	**1098**	**62**	**1**	**3.39**	....	....	....	....	....	....	....
	Fredericton	AHL	18	11	5	2	1089	49	2	2.70	....	....	....	....	....	....	....
1984-85	**Vancouver**	**NHL**	**28**	**8**	**14**	**3**	**1523**	**122**	**0**	**4.81**	....	....	....	....	....	....	....
1985-86	**Vancouver**	**NHL**	**7**	**0**	**3**	**2**	**308**	**28**	**0**	**5.46**	....	....	....	....	....	....	....
	Fredericton	AHL	26	12	11	2	1526	109	0	4.29	6	2	4	333	22	0	3.96
1986-87	**Vancouver**	**NHL**	**25**	**8**	**11**	**2**	**1390**	**89**	**0**	**3.84**	....	....	....	....	....	....	....
	Fredericton	AHL	12	5	5	0	686	47	0	4.11	....	....	....	....	....	....	....
1987-88	**Vancouver**	**NHL**	**22**	**7**	**10**	**2**	**1250**	**87**	**0**	**4.18**	....	....	....	....	....	....	....
1988-89	Milwaukee	IHL	39	24	12	0	2204	143	2	3.89	2	0	1	91	5	0	3.30
	NHL Totals		**102**	**31**	**40**	**11**	**5589**	**391**	**1**	**4.20**	....	....	....	....	....	....	....

a OHL Third All-Star Team (1982).

Traded to **Boston** by **Vancouver** for Boston's twelfth-round choice (Jan Bergman) in 1989 Entry Draft, June 17, 1989.

CASEY, JON

Goaltender. Catches right. 5'9", 155 lbs. Born, Grand Rapids, Minn., August 29, 1962.

			Regular Season								Playoffs						
Season	Club	Lea	GP	W	L	T	Mins	GA	SO	Avg	GP	W	L	Mins	GA	SO	Avg
1980-81	North Dakota	WCHA	5	3	1	0	300	19	0	3.80	....	....	....	....	....	....	....
1981-82	North Dakota	WCHA	18	15	3	0	1038	48	1	2.77	....	....	....	....	....	....	....
1982-83	North Dakota	WCHA	17	9	6	2	1020	42	0	2.51	....	....	....	....	....	....	....
1983-84	North Dakota	WCHA	37	25	10	2	2180	115	2	3.13	....	....	....	....	....	....	....
	Minnesota	**NHL**	**2**	**1**	**0**	**0**	**84**	**6**	**0**	**4.29**	....	....	....	....	....	....	....
1984-85ab	Baltimore	AHL	46	30	11	4	2646	116	4	2.63	13	8	3	689	38	0	3.31
1985-86	**Minnesota**	**NHL**	**26**	**11**	**11**	**1**	**1402**	**91**	**0**	**3.89**	....	....	....	....	....	....	....
	Springfield	AHL	9	4	3	1	464	30	0	3.88	....	....	....	....	....	....	....
1986-87	Springfield	AHL	13	1	8	0	770	56	0	4.36	....	....	....	....	....	....	....
	Indianapolis	IHL	31	14	15	0	1794	133	0	4.45	....	....	....	....	....	....	....
1987-88	**Minnesota**	**NHL**	**14**	**1**	**7**	**4**	**663**	**41**	**0**	**3.71**	....	....	....	....	....	....	....
	Kalamazoo	IHL	42	24	13	5	2541	154		3.64	7	3	3	382	26		4.08
1988-89	**Minnesota**	**NHL**	**55**	**18**	**17**	**12**	**2961**	**151**	**1**	**3.06**	**4**	**1**	**3**	**211**	**16**	**0**	**4.55**
	NHL Totals		**100**	**31**	**35**	**17**	**5110**	**289**	**1**	**3.39**	**4**	**1**	**3**	**211**	**16**	**0**	**4.55**

a Won Baz Bastien Trophy (AHL Most Valuable Goaltender) (1985)
b AHL First All-Star Team (1985)

Signed as a free agent by **Minnesota**, April 1, 1984.

CHABOT, FREDERIC

Goaltender. Catches right. 5'10", 170 lbs. Born, Hebertville, Que., February 12, 1968.
(New Jersey's 10th choice, 192nd overall, in 1986 Entry Draft).

			Regular Season								Playoffs						
Season	Club	Lea	GP	W	L	T	Mins	GA	SO	Avg	GP	W	L	Mins	GA	SO	Avg
1986-87	Drummondville	QMJHL	62	31	29	0	3508	293	1	5.01	8	2	6	481	40	0	4.99
1987-88	Drummondville	QMJHL	58	27	24	4	3276	237	1	4.34	16	10	6	1019	56	*1	*3.30
1988-89a	Prince Albert	WHL	54	21	29	0	2957	202	2	4.10	4	1	1	199	16	0	4.82

a WHL East All-Star Team (1989)

CHEVELDAE, TIM (CHEV-uhl-day)

Goaltender. Catches left. 5'11", 175 lbs. Born, Melville, Sask., February 15, 1968.
(Detroit's 4th choice, 64th overall, in 1986 Entry Draft).

			Regular Season								Playoffs						
Season	Club	Lea	GP	W	L	T	Mins	GA	SO	Avg	GP	W	L	Mins	GA	SO	Avg
1985-86	Saskatoon	WHL	36	21	10	3	2030	165	0	4.88	8	6	2	480	29	0	3.63
1986-87	Saskatoon	WHL	33	20	11	0	1909	133	2	4.18	5	4	1	308	20	0	3.90
1987-88a	Saskatoon	WHL	66	44	19	3	3798	235	1	3.71	6	4	2	364	27	0	4.45
1988-89	**Detroit**	**NHL**	**2**	**0**	**2**	**0**	**122**	**9**	**0**	**4.43**	....	....	....	....	....	....	....
	Adirondack	AHL	30	20	8	0	1694	98	1	3.47	2	1	0	99	9	0	5.45
	NHL Totals		**2**	**0**	**2**	**0**	**122**	**9**	**0**	**4.43**	....	....	....	....	....	....	....

a WHL East All-Star Team (1988)

CHEVRIER, ALAIN

Goaltender. Catches left. 5'8", 180 lbs. Born, Cornwall Ont., April 23, 1961.

			Regular Season								Playoffs						
Season	Club	Lea	GP	W	L	T	Mins	GA	SO	Avg	GP	W	L	Mins	GA	SO	Avg
1982-83	Miami-Ohio	CCHA	33	15	16	1	1894	125	0	3.96	....	....	....	....	....	....	....
1983-84	Miami-Ohio	CCHA	32	9	19	1	1509	123	0	4.89	....	....	....	....	....	....	....
1984-85	Fort Wayne	IHL	56	26	21	7	3219	194	0	3.62	9	5	4	556	28	0	3.02
1985-86	**New Jersey**	**NHL**	**37**	**11**	**18**	**2**	**1862**	**143**	**0**	**4.61**	....	....	....	....	....	....	....
1986-87	**New Jersey**	**NHL**	**58**	**24**	**26**	**2**	**3153**	**227**	**0**	**4.32**	....	....	....	....	....	....	....
1987-88	**New Jersey**	**NHL**	**45**	**18**	**19**	**3**	**2354**	**148**	**1**	**3.77**	....	....	....	....	....	....	....
1988-89	**Winnipeg**	**NHL**	**22**	**8**	**8**	**2**	**1092**	**78**	**1**	**4.29**	....	....	....	....	....	....	....
	Chicago	**NHL**	**27**	**13**	**11**	**2**	**1573**	**92**	**0**	**3.51**	**16**	**9**	**7**	**1013**	**44**	**0**	**2.61**
	NHL Totals		**189**	**74**	**82**	**11**	**10034**	**688**	**2**	**4.11**	**16**	**9**	**7**	**1013**	**44**	**0**	**2.61**

Signed as a free agent by **New Jersey**, May 31, 1985. Traded to **Winnipeg** by **New Jersey** with New Jersey's seventh round (Doug Evans) choice in the 1989 Entry Draft for Steve Rooney and future considerations, July 19, 1988. Traded to **Chicago** by **Winnipeg** for Chicago's fourth-round choice (Allain Roy) in the 1989 Entry Draft, January 19, 1989.

CLIFFORD, CHRIS

Goaltender. Catches left. 5'9", 150 lbs. Born, Kingston, Ont., May 26, 1966.
(Chicago's 6th choice, 111th over-all, in 1984 Entry Draft).

			Regular Season								Playoffs						
Season	Club	Lea	GP	W	L	T	Mins	GA	SO	Avg	GP	W	L	Mins	GA	SO	Avg
1983-84	Kingston	OHL	50	16	28	0	2808	229	2	4.89	....	....	....	....	....	....	....
1984-85	Kingston	OHL	52	15	34	0	2768	241	0	5.22	....	....	....	....	....	....	....
1985-86	Kingston	OHL	50	26	21	3	2988	178	1	3.57	10	5	5	564	31	1	3.30
1986-87	Kingston	OHL	44	18	25	0	2596	191	1	4.41	12	6	6	730	42	0	3.45
1987-88	Saginaw	IHL	22	9	7	2	1146	80		4.19	....	....	....	....	....	....	....
1988-89	**Chicago**	**NHL**	**1**	**0**	**0**	**0**	**4**	**0**	**0**	**0.00**	....	....	....	....	....	....	....
	Saginaw	IHL	7	4	2	0	321	23	0	4.30	....	....	....	....	....	....	....
	NHL Totals		**1**	**0**	**0**	**0**	**4**	**0**	**0**	**0.00**	....	....	....	....	....	....	....

CLOUTIER, JACQUES (clootz-YAY)

Goaltender. Catches left. 5'7", 167 lbs. Born, Noranda, Que., January 3, 1960.
(Buffalo's 4th choice, 55th over-all, in 1979 Entry Draft).

			Regular Season								Playoffs						
Season	Club	Lea	GP	W	L	T	Mins	GA	SO	Avg	GP	W	L	Mins	GA	SO	Avg
1977-78	Trois Rivières	QJHL	71	....	....	....	4134	240	*4	3.48	13	....	....	779	40	1	3.08
1978-79a	Trois Rivières	QJHL	72	....	....	....	4168	218	*3	*3.14	13	....	....	780	36	0	*2.77
1979-80	Trois Rivières	QJHL	55	27	20	7	3222	231	2	4.30	7	3	4	420	33	0	4.71
1980-81	Rochester	AHL	61	27	27	6	3478	209	1	3.61	....	....	....	....	....	....	....
1981-82	Rochester	AHL	23	14	7	2	1366	64	0	2.81	....	....	....	....	....	....	....
	Buffalo	**NHL**	**7**	**5**	**1**	**0**	**311**	**13**	**0**	**2.51**	....	....	....	....	....	....	....
1982-83	**Buffalo**	**NHL**	**25**	**10**	**7**	**6**	**1390**	**81**	**0**	**3.50**	....	....	....	....	....	....	....
	Rochester	AHL	13	7	3	1	634	42	0	3.97	16	12	4	992	47	0	2.84
1983-84	Rochester	AHL	51	26	22	1	2841	172	1	3.63	18	9	9	1145	68	0	3.56
1984-85	**Buffalo**	**NHL**	**1**	**0**	**0**	**1**	**65**	**4**	**0**	**3.69**	....	....	....	....	....		
	Rochester	AHL	14	10	2	1	803	36	0	2.69	....	....	....	....	....	....	....
1985-86	**Buffalo**	**NHL**	**15**	**5**	**9**	**1**	**872**	**49**	**1**	**3.37**	....	....	....	....	....	....	....
	Rochester	AHL	14	10	2	2	835	38	1	2.73	....	....	....	....	....	....	....
1986-87	**Buffalo**	**NHL**	**40**	**11**	**19**	**5**	**2167**	**137**	**0**	**3.79**	....	....	....	....	....	....	....
1987-88	**Buffalo**	**NHL**	**20**	**4**	**8**	**2**	**851**	**67**	**0**	**4.72**	....	....	....	....	....	....	....
1988-89	**Buffalo**	**NHL**	**36**	**15**	**14**	**0**	**1786**	**108**	**0**	**3.63**	**4**	**1**	**3**	**238**	**10**	**1**	**2.52**
	Rochester	AHL	11	2	7	0	527	41	0	4.67	....	....	....	....	....	....	....
	NHL Totals		**144**	**50**	**58**	**15**	**7442**	**459**	**1**	**3.70**	**4**	**1**	**3**	**238**	**10**	**1**	**2.52**

a QMJHL First All-Star Team (1979)

CONNELL, PAUL

Goaltender. Catches left. 5'8", 160 lbs. Born, Cranston, RI, March 19, 1967.
(Philadelphia's 1st choice, 19th overall, in 1988 Supplemental Draft).

			Regular Season								Playoffs						
Season	Club	Lea	GP	W	L	T	Mins	GA	SO	Avg	GP	W	L	Mins	GA	SO	Avg
1986-87	Bowling Green	CCHA	7	4	1	0	324	23	0	4.26	....	....	....	....	....	....	....
1987-88	Bowling Green	CCHA	39	27	10	2	2322	155	0	4.00	....	....	....	....	....	....	....
1988-89	Bowling Green	CCHA	41	21	16	3	2439	140	0	3.44	....	....	....	....	....	....	....

COOPER, JEFFREY

Goaltender. Catches right. 5'10", 170 lbs. Born, Ottawa, Ont., June 12, 1962.

			Regular Season								Playoffs						
Season	Club	Lea	GP	W	L	T	Mins	GA	SO	Avg	GP	W	L	Mins	GA	SO	Avg
1982-83	Colgate	ECAC	26	12	10	2	1486	100	0	4.04	....	....	....	....	....	....	....
1983-84	Colgate	ECAC	32	18	12	1	1874	121	1	*3.87	....	....	....	....	....	....	....
1984-85	Colgate	ECAC	31	13	18	0	1778	110	3	3.71	....	....	....	....	....	....	....
1985-86	Baltimore	AHL	23	6	13	0	1099	77	2	4.20	....	....	....	....	....	....	....
1986-87a	Muskegon	IHL	45	23	21	1	2673	147	2	3.30	1	0	1	8	1	0	7.50
1987-88	New Haven	AHL	9	1	6	0	485	37	0	4.58	....	....	....	....	....	....	....
	Muskegon	IHL	21	11	5	4	1195	80		4.02	5	1	3	236	16		4.07
1988-89	Saginaw	IHL	4	1	3	0	226	16	0	4.25	....	....	....	....	....	....	....
	Muskegon	IHL	7	3	2	0	428	31	0	4.35	....	....	....	....	....	....	....
	Indianapolis	IHL	9	3	6	0	491	32	0	3.91	....	....	....	....	....	....	....

a IHL First All-Star Team (1987)

Signed as a free agent by **Pittsburgh**, April 6, 1985.

COWLEY, WAYNE

Goaltender. Catches left. 6'0", 185 lbs. Born, Scarborough, Ont., December 4, 1964.

			Regular Season								Playoffs						
Season	Club	Lea	GP	W	L	T	Mins	GA	SO	Avg	GP	W	L	Mins	GA	SO	Avg
1985-86	Colgate	ECAC	7	2	2	0	313	23	1	4.42	....	....	....	....	....	....	....
1986-87	Colgate	ECAC	31	21	8	1	1805	106	0	3.52	....	....	....	....	....	....	....
1987-88	Colgate	ECAC	20	11	7	1	1162	58	1	2.99	....	....	....	....	....	....	....
1988-89	Salt Lake	IHL	29	17	7	1	1423	94	0	3.96	2	1	0	69	6	0	5.22

Signed as a free agent by **Calgary**, May 1, 1988.

DADSWELL, DOUG

Goaltender. Catches left. 5'10", 180 lbs. Born, Scarborough, Ont., February 7, 1964.

			Regular Season								Playoffs						
Season	Club	Lea	GP	W	L	T	Mins	GA	SO	Avg	GP	W	L	Mins	GA	SO	Avg
1985-86	Cornell	ECAC	30	20	7	3	1815	92	1	3.04	...	...	...	...	...	...	...
1986-87	**Calgary**	**NHL**	**2**	**0**	**1**	**1**	**125**	**10**	**0**	**4.80**	...	...	...	...	...	...	...
	Moncton	AHL	42	23	12	0	2276	138	1	3.64	6	2	4	326	23	0	4.23
1987-88	**Calgary**	**NHL**	**25**	**8**	**7**	**2**	**1221**	**89**	**0**	**4.37**	....	....	....	....	....	....	....
1988-89	Salt Lake	IHL	32	15	10	0	1723	110	0	3.83	....	....	....	....	....	....	....
	Indianapolis	IHL	24	4	15	0	1207	122	0	6.06	....	....	....	....	....	....	....
	NHL Totals		**27**	**8**	**8**	**3**	**1346**	**99**	**0**	**4.41**	....	....	....	....	....	....	....

a ECAC Second All-Star Team (1986)
b NCAA East First All-Star Team (1986)

Signed as a free agent by **Calgary**, August 6, 1986.

DAFOE, BYRON

Goaltender. Catches left. 5'11", 175 lbs. Born, Duncan, B.C., February 25, 1971.
(Washington's 2nd choice, 35th overall, in 1989 Entry Draft).

			Regular Season								Playoffs						
Season	Club	Lea	GP	W	L	T	Mins	GA	SO	Avg	GP	W	L	Mins	GA	SO	Avg
1988-89	Portland	WHL	59	29	24	3	3279	291	1	5.32	*18	10	8	*1091	81	*1	4.45

D'ALESSIO, CORRIE

Goaltender. Catches left. 5'11", 155 lbs. Born, Cornwall, Ont., September 9, 1969.
(Vancouver's 4th choice, 107th overall, in 1988 Entry Draft).

			Regular Season								Playoffs						
Season	Club	Lea	GP	W	L	T	Mins	GA	SO	Avg	GP	W	L	Mins	GA	SO	Avg
1987-88a	Cornell	ECAC	25	17	8	0	1457	67	0	2.76	....	....	....	....	....	....	....
1988-89	Cornell	ECAC	29	15	13	1	1684	96	1	3.42	....	....	....	....	....	....	....

a ECAC All-Rookie Team (1988)

D'AMOUR, MARC

Goaltender. Catches left. 5'9", 185 lbs. Born, Sudbury, Ont., April 29, 1961.

			Regular Season								Playoffs						
Season	Club	Lea	GP	W	L	T	Mins	GA	SO	Avg	GP	W	L	Mins	GA	SO	Avg
1979-80	S. S. Marie	OHA	33	16	15	0	1429	117	0	4.91	....	....	....	....	....	....	....
1980-81	S. S. Marie	OHA	16	7	1	1	653	38	0	3.49	14	5	4	683	41	0	3.60
1981-82a	S. S. Marie	OHL	41	28	12	1	3284	130	1	*3.27	10	3	2	504	30	0	3.57
1982-83	Colorado	CHL	42	16	21	2	2373	153	1	3.87	1	....	....	59	4	0	4.08
1983-84	Colorado	CHL	36	18	12	1	1917	131	0	4.10	1	0	0	20	0	0	0.00
1984-85	Moncton	AHL	37	18	14	2	2051	115	0	3.36	....	....	....	....	....	....	....
	Salt Lake	IHL	12	7	2	2	694	33	0	2.85	....	....	....	....	....	....	....
1985-86	**Calgary**	**NHL**	**15**	**2**	**4**	**2**	**560**	**32**	**0**	**3.43**	**....**	**....**	**....**	**....**	**....**	**....**	**....**
	Moncton	AHL	21	6	9	3	1129	72	0	3.83	5	1	4	296	20	0	4.05
1986-87	Binghamton	AHL	8	5	3	0	461	30	0	3.90	....	....	....	....	....	....	....
	Salt Lake	IHL	10	3	6	0	523	37	0	4.24	....	....	....	....	....	....	....
	Can. Olympic	....	1	0	0	0	30	4	0	8.00	....	....	....	....	....	....	....
1987-88	Salt Lake	IHL	62	26	19	5	3245	177		3.27	*19	*12	7	*1123	67		3.58
1988-89	**Philadelphia**	**NHL**	**1**	**0**	**0**	**0**	**19**	**0**	**0**	**0.00**	**....**	**....**	**....**	**....**	**....**	**....**	**....**
	Hershey	AHL	39	19	13	3	2174	127	0	3.51	....	....	....	....	....	....	....
	Indianapolis	IHL	6	2	3	0	324	20	0	3.70	....	....	....	....	....	....	....
	NHL Totals		**16**	**2**	**4**	**2**	**579**	**32**	**0**	**3.32**	**....**	**....**	**....**	**....**	**....**	**....**	**....**

a OHL First All-Star Team (1982)

Signed as free agent by **Calgary**, June 7, 1982.

DASKALAKIS, CLEON

Goaltender. Catches left. 5'9", 175 lbs. Born, Boston, MA, September 29, 1962.

			Regular Season								Playoffs						
Season	Club	Lea	GP	W	L	T	Mins	GA	SO	Avg	GP	W	L	Mins	GA	SO	Avg
1980-81	Boston U.	ECAC	8	4	2	0	399	24	0	3.61	....	....	....	....	....	....	....
1981-82	Boston U.	ECAC	20	9	6	3	1101	59	3	3.22	....	....	....	....	....	....	....
1982-83	Boston U.	ECAC	24	15	7	1	1398	78	1	3.35	....	....	....	....	....	....	....
1983-84	Boston U.	ECAC	35	25	10	0	1972	96	0	2.92	....	....	....	....	....	....	....
1984-85	**Boston**	**NHL**	**8**	**1**	**2**	**1**	**289**	**24**	**0**	**4.98**	**....**	**....**	**....**	**....**	**....**	**....**	**....**
	Hershey	AHL	30	9	13	4	1614	119	0	4.42	....	....	....	....	....	....	....
1985-86	**Boston**	**NHL**	**2**	**0**	**2**	**0**	**120**	**10**	**0**	**5.00**	**....**	**....**	**....**	**....**	**....**	**....**	**....**
	Moncton	AHL	41	19	14	6	2343	141	0	3.61	6	4	1	372	13	....	2.10
1986-87	**Boston**	**NHL**	**2**	**2**	**0**	**0**	**97**	**7**	**0**	**4.33**	**....**	**....**	**....**	**....**	**....**	**....**	**....**
	Moncton	AHL	27	8	14	0	1452	118	0	4.88	1	0	0	36	2	0	3.33
1987-88	Hershey	AHL	3	1	1	0	122	9	0	4.43	....	....	....	....	....	....	....
	Binghamton	AHL	6	2	2	1	344	27	0	4.71	....	....	....	....	....	....	....
	Rochester	AHL	8	4	3	0	382	22	0	3.46	....	....	....	....	....	....	....
	Milwaukee	IHL	9	1	5	3	483	47		5.84	....	....	....	....	....	....	....
1988-89	U.S. National	....	1	0	0	0	20	1	0	3.20	....	....	....	....	....	....	....
	NHL Totals		**12**	**3**	**4**	**1**	**506**	**41**	**0**	**4.86**	**....**	**....**	**....**	**....**	**....**	**....**	**....**

Signed as a free agent by **Boston,** June 1, 1984.

DELGUIDICE, MATT

Goaltender. Catches right. 5'9", 170 lbs. Born, West Haven, CT, March 5, 1967.
(Boston's 4th choice, 77th overall, in 1987 Entry Draft).

			Regular Season								Playoffs						
Season	Club	Lea	GP	W	L	T	Mins	GA	SO	Avg	GP	W	L	Mins	GA	SO	Avg
1987-88					DID NOT PLAY												
1988-89	U. of Maine	H.E.	20	16	4	0	1090	57	1	3.14	....	....	....	....	....	....	....

DELIANIEDIS, DANIEL JAMES (DAN) (duh-lan-dis)

Goaltender. Catches left. 5'9", 185 lbs. Born, Worcester, MA, July 3, 1964.

			Regular Season								Playoffs						
Season	Club	Lea	GP	W	L	T	Mins	GA	SO	Avg	GP	W	L	Mins	GA	SO	Avg
1982-83	Colgate	ECAC	6	3	0	1	221	14	0	3.80	....	....	....	....	....	....	....
1983-84	Colgate	ECAC	6	2	2	0	260	28	0	6.46	....	....	....	....	....	....	....
1984-85	Colgate	ECAC	5	1	0	0	160	10	0	3.76	....	....	....	....	....	....	....
1985-86	Colgate	ECAC	26	13	12	1	1470	110	0	4.49	....	....	....	....	....	....	....
1986-87a	Mohawk Valley	ACHL	35	....	....	....	1943	161	0	4.97	12	7	5	714	43	0	3.61
1987-88	Utica	AHL	22	7	7	3	1048	73	0	4.18	....	....	....	....	....	....	....
1988-89	Utica	AHL	3	0	1	0	94	8	0	5.11	....	....	....	....	....	....	....

a ACHL Second All-Star Team (1987)

Signed as a free agent by **New Jersey**, October 20, 1987.

DERKSEN, DUANE

Goaltender. Catches left. 6'1", 180 lbs. Born, St. Boniface, Man., July 7, 1968.
(Washington's 4th choice, 57th overall, in 1988 Entry Draft).

			Regular Season								Playoffs						
Season	Club	Lea	GP	W	L	T	Mins	GA	SO	Avg	GP	W	L	Mins	GA	SO	Avg
1986-87	Winkler	MJHL	48	....	....	....	2140	171	1	4.80	....	....	....	....	....	....	....
1987-88	Winkler	MJHL	38	....	....	....	2294	198	0	5.20	....	....	....	....	....	....	....
1988-89	U. Wisconsin	WCHA	11	4	5	0	561	37	1	3.96	....	....	....	....	....	....	....

DRAPER, TOM

Goaltender. Catches left. 5'11", 180 lbs. Born, Outremont, Que., November 20, 1966.
(Winnipeg's 8th choice, 165th overall, in 1985 Entry Draft).

			Regular Season								Playoffs						
Season	Club	Lea	GP	W	L	T	Mins	GA	SO	Avg	GP	W	L	Mins	GA	SO	Avg
1983-84	U. of Vermont	ECAC	20	8	12	0	1205	82	0	4.08	...	...	...	...	...	...	...
1984-85	U. of Vermont	ECAC	24	5	17	0	1316	90	0	4.11	...	...	...	...	...	...	...
1985-86	U. of Vermont	ECAC	29	15	12	1	1697	87	1	3.08	...	...	...	...	...	...	...
1986-87a	U. of Vermont	ECAC	29	16	13	0	1662	96	2	3.47	...	...	...	...	...	...	...
1987-88	Tappara	Fin.	28	16	3	9	1619	87	0	3.22	....	....	....	....	....	....	....
1988-89	**Winnipeg**	**NHL**	**2**	**1**	**1**	**0**	**120**	**12**	**0**	**6.00**	**....**	**....**	**....**	**....**	**....**	**....**	**....**
b	Moncton	AHL	*54	27	17	5	*2962	171	2	3.46	7	5	2	419	24	0	3.44
	NHL Totals		**2**	**1**	**1**	**0**	**120**	**12**	**0**	**6.00**	**....**	**....**	**....**	**....**	**....**	**....**	**....**

a ECAC First All-Star Team (1987).
b AHL Second All-Star Team (1989)

ELIOT, DARREN

Goaltender. Catches right. 6'1", 175 lbs. Born, Hamilton, Ont., November 26, 1961.
(Los Angeles' 8th choice, 115th over-all, in 1980 Entry Draft).

			Regular Season								Playoffs						
Season	Club	Lea	GP	W	L	T	Mins	GA	SO	Avg	GP	W	L	Mins	GA	SO	Avg
1979-80	Cornell	ECAC	26	14	8	0	1362	94	0	4.10	5	3	2	300	20	0	4.00
1980-81	Cornell	ECAC	18	8	7	0	912	52	1	3.29	3	1	1	119	7	0	2.33
1981-82	Cornell	ECAC	7	1	3	0	337	25	0	4.44	....	....	....	....	....	....	....
1982-83ab	Cornell	ECAC	26	13	10	3	1606	100	1	3.66	....	....	....	....	....	....	....
1983-84	Cdn. Olympic	...	31	....	....	....	1676	111	0	3.97	....	....	....	....	....	....	....
	New Haven	AHL	7	4	1	0	365	30	0	4.93	....	....	....	....	....	....	....
1984-85	**Los Angeles**	**NHL**	**33**	**12**	**11**	**6**	**1882**	**137**	**0**	**4.37**	**....**	**....**	**....**	**....**	**....**	**....**	**....**
1985-86	**Los Angeles**	**NHL**	**27**	**5**	**17**	**3**	**1481**	**121**	**0**	**4.90**	**....**	**....**	**....**	**....**	**....**	**....**	**....**
	New Haven	AHL	3	1	2	1	180	19	0	6.33	1	0	1	60	4	0	4.00
1986-87	**Los Angeles**	**NHL**	**24**	**8**	**13**	**2**	**1404**	**103**	**1**	**4.40**	**1**	**0**	**0**	**40**	**7**	**0**	**10.50**
	New Haven	AHL	4	2	2	0	239	15	0	3.77	....	....	....	....	....	....	....
1987-88	**Detroit**	**NHL**	**3**	**0**	**0**	**1**	**97**	**9**	**0**	**5.57**	**....**	**....**	**....**	**....**	**....**	**....**	**....**
	Adirondack	AHL	43	23	11	7	2445	136	0	3.34	10	4	6	614	45	0	4.40
1988-89	**Buffalo**	**NHL**	**2**	**0**	**0**	**0**	**67**	**7**	**0**	**6.27**	**....**	**....**	**....**	**....**	**....**	**....**	**....**
	Rochester	AHL	23	8	6	2	969	59	0	3.65	....	....	....	....	....	....	....
	NHL Totals		**89**	**25**	**41**	**12**	**4931**	**377**	**1**	**4.59**	**1**	**0**	**0**	**40**	**7**	**0**	*****

a ECAC First All-Star Team (1983)
b NCAA All-American Team (1983)

Signed as a free agent by **Detroit**, June 30, 1987.

ERICKSON, CHAD

Goaltender. Catches right. 5'9", 175 lbs. Born, Minneapolis, MN, August 21, 1970.
(New Jersey's 8th choice, 138th overall, in 1988 Entry Draft).

			Regular Season								Playoffs						
Season	Club	Lea	GP	W	L	T	Mins	GA	SO	Avg	GP	W	L	Mins	GA	SO	Avg
1987-88	Warroad	HS	24	....	....	....	1080	33	7	1.38	....	....	....	....	....	....	....
1988-89	Minn.-Duluth	WCHA	15	5	7	1	821	49	0	3.58	....	....	....	....	....	....	....

ESSENSA, BOB (ESS en sa)

Goaltender. Catches left. 6', 160 lbs. Born, Toronto, Ont., January 14, 1965.
(Winnipeg's 5th choice, 71st over-all, in 1983 Entry Draft).

			Regular Season								Playoffs						
Season	Club	Lea	GP	W	L	T	Mins	GA	SO	Avg	GP	W	L	Mins	GA	SO	Avg
1983-84	Michigan State	CCHA	17	11	4	0	946	44	2	2.79	....	....	....	....	....	....	....
1984-85	Michigan State	CCHA	18	15	2	0	1059	29	2	1.64	....	....	....	....	....	....	....
1985-86a	Michigan State	CCHA	23	17	4	1	1333	74	1	3.33	....	....	....	....	....	....	....
1986-87	Michigan State	CCHA	25	19	3	1	1383	64	2	2.78	....	....	....	....	....	....	....
1987-88	Moncton	AHL	27	7	11	1	1287	100	1	4.66	....	....	....	....	....	....	....
1988-89	**Winnipeg**	**NHL**	**20**	**6**	**8**	**3**	**1102**	**68**	**1**	**3.70**	**....**	**....**	**....**	**....**	**....**	**....**	**....**
	Fort Wayne	IHL	22	14	7	0	1287	70	0	3.26	....	....	....	....	....	....	....
	NHL Totals		**20**	**6**	**8**	**3**	**1102**	**68**	**1**	**3.70**	**....**	**....**	**....**	**....**	**....**	**....**	**....**

a CCHA Second All-Star Team (1986).

EVOY, SEAN

Goaltender. Catches left. 6', 190 lbs. Born, Sudbury, Ont., February 11, 1966.
(Hartford's 9th choice, 220th overall, in 1986 Entry Draft).

			Regular Season								Playoffs						
Season	Club	Lea	GP	W	L	T	Mins	GA	SO	Avg	GP	W	L	Mins	GA	SO	Avg
1985-86	Sudbury	OHL	21	13	6	1	1212	69	0	3.42	...	...	...	...	...	...	...
	Cornwall	OHL	27	11	11	0	1391	122	1	5.26	5	1	3	300	27	0	5.40
1986-87a	Oshawa	OHL	31	23	3	1	1702	89	2	3.14	14	8	3	720	31	2	2.58
1987-88	Milwaukee	IHL	17	7	8	1	933	71		4.57	....	....	....	....	....	....	....
1988-89	Binghamton	AHL	9	1	6	0	472	45	0	5.72	....	....	....	....	....	....	....

a OHL Third All-Star Team (1987).

EXELBY, RANDY

Goaltender. Catches left. 5'9", 170 lbs. Born, Toronto, Ont., August 13, 1965.
(Montreal's 1st choice, 20th overall, in 1986 Supplemental Draft).

			Regular Season								Playoffs						
Season	Club	Lea	GP	W	L	T	Mins	GA	SO	Avg	GP	W	L	Mins	GA	SO	Avg
1983-84	Lake Superior	CCHA	21	6	10	0	905	75	0	4.97	...	...	...	...	...	...	...
1984-85	Lake Superior	CCHA	36	22	11	1	1999	112	0	3.36	...	...	...	...	...	...	...
1985-86	Lake Superior	CCHA	28	14	11	1	1625	98	0	3.61	...	...	...	...	...	...	...
1987-87	Lake Superior	CCHA	28	12	9	1	1357	91	0	4.02	...	...	...	...	...	...	...
1987-88	Sherbrooke	AHL	19	7	10	0	1050	49	0	2.80	4	2	2	212	13	0	3.68
1988-89	**Montreal**	**NHL**	**1**	**0**	**0**	**0**	**3**	**0**	**0**	**0.00**	**....**	**....**	**....**	**....**	**....**	**....**	**...**
abc	Sherbrooke	AHL	52	*31	13	6	2935	146	*6	*2.98	6	1	4	329	24	0	4.38
	NHL Totals		**1**	**0**	**0**	**0**	**3**	**0**	**0**	**0.00**	**....**	**....**	**....**	**....**	**....**	**....**	**....**

a AHL First All-Star Team (1989)
b Shared Harry "Hap Holmes Trophy (fewest goals-against-AHL) with Francois Gravel (1989)
c Won Baz Bastien Award (Top Goaltender-AHL) (1989)

FANNING, TODD

Goaltender. Catches left. 5'11", 175 lbs. Born, Winnipeg, Man., February 12, 1968.
(Vancouver's 6th choice, 129th overall, in 1987 Entry Draft).

			Regular Season								Playoffs						
Season	Club	Lea	GP	W	L	T	Mins	GA	SO	Avg	GP	W	L	Mins	GA	SO	Avg
1986-87	Ohio State	CCHA	24	11	10	0	1276	97	0	4.56	....	....	....	....	....	....	....
1987-88	Ohio State	CCHA	28	8	11	3	1290	104	0	4.84	....	....	....	....	....	....	....
1988-89	Ohio State	CCHA	33	9	19	4	1894	154	0	4.88	....	....	....	....	....	....	....

FELICIO, MARC

Goaltender. Catches left. 5'7", 170 lbs. Born, Woonsockett, RI, December 1, 1968.
(Minnesota's 11th choice, 214th overall, in 1987 Entry Draft).

			Regular Season								Playoffs						
Season	Club	Lea	GP	W	L	T	Mins	GA	SO	Avg	GP	W	L	Mins	GA	SO	Avg
1987-88	Ferris State	CCHA	18	4	9	0	806	74	0	5.50	....	....	....	....	....	....	....
1988-89	Ferris State	CCHA	19	6	9	1	1045	85	0	4.88	....	....	....	....	....	....	....

FISET, STEPHANE

Goaltender. Catches left. 6', 175 lbs. Born, Montreal, Que., June 17, 1970.
(Quebec's 3rd choice, 24th overall, in 1988 Entry Draft).

			Regular Season								Playoffs						
Season	Club	Lea	GP	W	L	T	Mins	GA	SO	Avg	GP	W	L	Mins	GA	SO	Avg
1987-88	Victoriaville	QMJHL	40	15	17	4	2221	146	1	3.94	2	0	2	163	10	0	3.68
1988-89a	Victoriaville	QMJHL	43	25	14	0	2401	138	1	*3.45	12	*9	2	711	33	0	*2.78

a QMJHL First All-Star Team (1989)

FISH, PETER

Goaltender. Catches left. 5'9", 165 lbs. Born, East Greenwich, RI, January 3, 1966.
(Montreal's 1st choice, 25th overall, in 1988 Supplemental Draft).

			Regular Season								Playoffs						
Season	Club	Lea	GP	W	L	T	Mins	GA	SO	Avg	GP	W	L	Mins	GA	SO	Avg
1985-86	Boston U.	H.E.	1	1	0	0	60	5	0	5.00	....	....	....	....	....	....	....
1986-87	Boston U.	H.E.	5	4	1	0	285	17	0	3.58	....	....	....	....	....	....	....
1987-88	Boston U.	H.E.	37	10	13	3	1550	114	1	4.41	....	....	....	....	....	....	....
1988-89	Boston U.	H.E.	17	6	10	0	1005	64	2	3.82	....	....	....	....	....	....	....

FITZPATRICK, MARK

Goaltender. Catches right. 6'2", 190 lbs. Born, Toronto, Ont., November 13, 1968.
(Los Angeles' 2nd choice, 27th overall, in 1987 Entry Draft).

			Regular Season								Playoffs						
Season	Club	Lea	GP	W	L	T	Mins	GA	SO	Avg	GP	W	L	Mins	GA	SO	Avg
1985-86	Medicine Hat	WHL	41	26	6	1	2074	99	1	2.86	19	12	5	986	58	0	3.53
1986-87	Medicine Hat	WHL	50	31	11	4	2844	159	4	3.35	20	12	8	1224	71	1	3.48
1987-88	Medicine Hat	WHL	63	36	15	6	3600	194	2	3.23	16	12	4	959	52	*1	*3.25
1988-89	**Los Angeles**	**NHL**	**17**	**6**	**7**	**3**	**957**	**64**	**0**	**4.01**	....	....	....	....	....	....	....
	New Haven	AHL	18	10	5	1	980	54	1	3.31	....	....	....	....	....	....	....
	NY Islanders	**NHL**	**11**	**3**	**5**	**2**	**627**	**41**	**0**	**3.92**	....	....	....	....	....	....	....
	NHL Totals		**28**	**9**	**12**	**5**	**1584**	**105**	**0**	**3.98**	....	....	....	....	....	....	....

Traded to **NY Islanders** by **Los Angeles** with Wayne McBean and future (Doug Crossman, acquired May 23, 1989) considerations for Kelly Hrudey, February 22, 1989.

FLETCHER, JOHN

Goaltender. Catches right. 5'7", 165 lbs. Born, Holden, MA, October 14, 1967.
(Vancouver's 9th choice, 192nd overall, in 1987 Entry Draft).

			Regular Season								Playoffs						
Season	Club	Lea	GP	W	L	T	Mins	GA	SO	Avg	GP	W	L	Mins	GA	SO	Avg
1986-87a	Clarkson	ECAC	23	11	8	1	1240	62	4	2.99	....	....	....	....	....	....	....
1987-88bc	Clarkson	ECAC	33	16	11	3	1820	97	1	3.19	....	....	....	....	....	....	....
1988-89	Clarkson	ECAC	23	9	8	2	1146	79	0	4.13	....	....	....	....	....	....	....

a ECAC Rookie of the Year (1987)
b ECAC First All-Star Team (1988)
c NCAA East Second All-American Team (1988)

FORD, BRIAN

Goaltender. Catches left. 5'10", 170 lbs. Born, Edmonton, Alta., September 22, 1961.

			Regular Season								Playoffs						
Season	Club	Lea	GP	W	L	T	Mins	GA	SO	Avg	GP	W	L	Mins	GA	SO	Avg
1980-81	Billings	WHL	44	14	26	0	2435	204	0	5.03	3	....	....	143	15	0	4.66
1981-82	Billings	WHL	53	19	26	1	2791	256	0	5.50	5	....	....	226	26	0	5.86
1982-83	Carolina	ACHL	4	....	....	....	203	7	0	2.07	....	....	....	....	....	....	....
	Fredericton	AHL	27	14	7	2	1443	84	0	3.49	1	0	0	11	1	0	5.56
1983-84	**Quebec**	**NHL**	**3**	**1**	**1**	**0**	**123**	**13**	**0**	**6.34**	....	....	....	....	....	....	....
a	Fredericton	AHL	36	17	17	1	2132	105	2	2.96	4	1	3	223	18	0	4.84
1984-85	**Pittsburgh**	**NHL**	**8**	**2**	**6**	**0**	**457**	**48**	**0**	**6.30**	....	....	....	....	....	....	....
	Baltimore	AHL	6	3	3	0	363	21	0	3.47	....	....	....	....	....	....	....
	Muskegon	IHL	22	17	5	0	1321	59	1	2.68	....	....	....	....	....	....	....
1985-86	Baltimore	AHL	39	12	20	4	2230	136	1	3.66	....	....	....	....	....	....	....
	Muskegon	IHL	9	4	4	0	513	33	0	3.06	13	12	1	793	41	0	3.10
1986-87	Baltimore	AHL	32	10	11	0	1541	99	0	3.85	....	....	....	....	....	....	....
1987-88	Springfield	AHL	35	12	15	4	1898	118	0	3.73	....	....	....	....	....	....	....
1988-89	Rochester	AHL	19	12	4	1	1075	60	2	3.35	....	....	....	....	....	....	....
	NHL Totals		**11**	**3**	**7**	**0**	**580**	**61**	**0**	**6.31**	....	....	....	....	....	....	....

a Won Harry (Hap) Holmes Memorial Trophy (AHL's leading goaltender) (1984)

Signed as a free agent by **Quebec**, August 1, 1982. Traded to **Pittsburgh** by **Quebec** for Tom Thornbury, December 6, 1984.

FOSTER, NORM

Goaltender. Catches left. 5'9", 175 lbs. Born, Vancouver, B.C., February 10, 1965.
(Boston's 11th choice, 222nd over-all, in 1983 Entry Draft).

			Regular Season								Playoffs						
Season	Club	Lea	GP	W	L	T	Mins	GA	SO	Avg	GP	W	L	Mins	GA	SO	Avg
1984-85	Michigan State	CCHA	26	22	4	0	1531	67	0	2.63	....	....	....	....	....	....	....
1985-86	Michigan State	CCHA	24	17	5	1	1414	87	0	3.69	....	....	....	....	....	....	....
1986-87	Michigan State	CCHA	24	14	7	1	1383	90	1	3.90	....	....	....	....	....	....	....
1987-88	Milwaukee	IHL	38	10	22	1	2001	170		5.10	....	....	....	....	....	....	....
1988-89	Maine	AHL	47	16	17	6	2411	156	1	3.88	....	....	....	....	....	....	....

FOURNIER, ROB

Goaltender. Catches left. 6', 190 lbs. Born, Sudbury, Ont., April 8, 1969.
(St. Louis' 3rd choice, 51st overall, in 1988 Entry Draft).

			Regular Season								Playoffs						
Season	Club	Lea	GP	W	L	T	Mins	GA	SO	Avg	GP	W	L	Mins	GA	SO	Avg
1986-87	North Bay	OHL	25	13	6	1	1281	72	2	3.37	....	....	....	....	....	....	....
1987-88a	North Bay	OHL	61	30	23	5	3601	210	1	3.50	4	0	4	255	21	0	4.94
1988-89	North Bay	OHL	9	0	7	1	582	99	0	10.20	....	....	....	....	....	....	....
	Niagara Falls	OHL	32	11	5	0	1293	104	0	4.83	7	0	3	154	20	0	7.79

a OHL Second All-Star Team (1988)

FRANCIS, MICHAEL

Goaltender. Catches left. 6', 165 lbs. Born, Braintree, MA, November 19, 1969.
(St. Louis' 12th choice, 240th overall, in 1988 Entry Draft).

			Regular Season								Playoffs						
Season	Club	Lea	GP	W	L	T	Mins	GA	SO	Avg	GP	W	L	Mins	GA	SO	Avg
1987-88	Harvard	ECAC	10	6	3	0	580	25	0	2.59	....	....	....	....	....	....	....
1988-89	Harvard	ECAC	3	2	0	0	140	2	0	0.86	....	....	....	....	....	....	....

FROESE, ROBERT GLENN (BOB) (FROHZ)

Goaltender. Catches left. 5'11", 180 lbs. Born, St. Catharines, Ont., June 30, 1958.
(St. Louis' 11th choice, 160th over-all, in 1978 Amateur Draft).

			Regular Season								Playoffs						
Season	Club	Lea	GP	W	L	T	Mins	GA	SO	Avg	GP	W	L	Mins	GA	SO	Avg
1975-76	St. Catharines	OHA	39	....	....	....	1976	193	0	5.83	4	....	....	240	20	0	5.00
1976-77	Niagara Falls	OHA	39	....	....	....	2063	162	2	4.68	....	....	....	....	....	....	....
1977-78	Niagara Falls	OHA	52	....	....	....	3128	249	0	4.71	3	....	....	236	17	0	4.36
1978-79	Saginaw	IHL	21	....	....	....	1050	58	0	3.31	....	....	....	....	....	....	....
	Milwaukee	IHL	14	....	....	....	715	42	1	3.52	7	....	....	334	23	0	4.14
1979-80	Maine	AHL	1	0	1	0	60	5	0	5.00	....	....	....	....	....	....	....
	Saginaw	IHL	52	....	....	....	2827	178	0	3.78	4	....	....	213	13	0	3.66
1980-81	Saginaw	IHL	43	....	....	....	2298	114	3	2.98	13	....	....	806	29	*2	*2.16
1981-82	Maine	AHL	33	16	11	4	1900	104	2	3.28	....	....	....	....	....	....	....
1982-83	Maine	AHL	33	18	11	3	1966	110	2	3.36	....	....	....	....	....	....	....
	Philadelphia	**NHL**	**25**	**17**	**4**	**2**	**1407**	**59**	**4**	**2.52**	....	....	....	....	....	....	....
1983-84	**Philadelphia**	**NHL**	**48**	**28**	**13**	**7**	**2863**	**150**	**2**	**3.14**	**3**	**0**	**2**	**154**	**11**	**0**	**4.28**
1984-85	**Philadelphia**	**NHL**	**17**	**13**	**2**	**0**	**923**	**37**	**1**	**2.41**	**4**	**0**	**1**	**146**	**11**	**0**	**4.52**
	Hershey	AHL	4	1	2	1	245	15	0	3.67	....	....	....	....	....	....	....
1985-86a	**Philadelphia**	**NHL**	**51**	**31**	**10**	**3**	**2728**	**116**	**5**	**2.55**	**5**	**2**	**3**	**293**	**15**	**0**	**3.07**
1986-87	**Philadelphia**	**NHL**	**3**	**3**	**0**	**0**	**180**	**8**	**0**	**2.67**	....	....	....	....	....	....	....
	NY Rangers	**NHL**	**28**	**14**	**11**	**0**	**1474**	**92**	**0**	**3.74**	**4**	**1**	**1**	**165**	**10**	**0**	**3.64**
1987-88	**NY Rangers**	**NHL**	**25**	**8**	**11**	**3**	**1443**	**85**	**0**	**3.53**	....	....	....	....	....	....	....
1988-89	**NY Rangers**	**NHL**	**30**	**9**	**14**	**4**	**1621**	**102**	**1**	**3.78**	**2**	**0**	**2**	**72**	**8**	**0**	**6.67**
	NHL Totals		227	123	65	19	12639	649	13	3.08	18	3	9	830	55	0	3.98

a NHL Second All-Star Team (1986)

Played in NHL All-Star Game (1986)

Signed as a free agent by **Philadelphia**, June 18, 1981. Traded to **NY Rangers** by **Philadelphia** for Kjell Samuelsson and NY Rangers' second round choice (Patrik Juhlin) in 1989 Entry Draft, December 18, 1986.

FUHR, GRANT (FYOOR)

Goaltender. Catches right. 5'10", 189 lbs. Born, Spruce Grove, Alta., September 28, 1962.
(Edmonton's 1st choice, 8th over-all, in 1981 Entry Draft).

			Regular Season								Playoffs						
Season	Club	Lea	GP	W	L	T	Mins	GA	SO	Avg	GP	W	L	Mins	GA	SO	Avg
1979-80ab	Victoria	WHL	43	30	12	0	2488	130	2	3.14	8	5	3	465	22	0	2.84
1980-81a	Victoria	WHL	59	48	9	1	3448	160	*4	*2.78	15	12	3	899	45	*1	*3.00
1981-82c	**Edmonton**	**NHL**	**48**	**28**	**5**	**14**	**2847**	**157**	**0**	**3.31**	**5**	**2**	**3**	**309**	**26**	**0**	**5.05**
1982-83	Moncton	AHL	10	4	5	1	604	40	0	3.98	....	....	....	....	....	....	....
	Edmonton	**NHL**	**32**	**13**	**12**	**5**	**1803**	**129**	**0**	**4.29**	**1**	**0**	**0**	**11**	**0**	**0**	**0.00**
1983-84	**Edmonton**	**NHL**	**45**	**30**	**10**	**4**	**2625**	**171**	**1**	**3.91**	**16**	**11**	**4**	**883**	**44**	**1**	**2.99**
1984-85	**Edmonton**	**NHL**	**46**	**26**	**8**	**7**	**2559**	**165**	**1**	**3.87**	**18**	**15**	**3**	**1064**	**55**	**0**	**3.10**
1985-86	**Edmonton**	**NHL**	**40**	**29**	**8**	**0**	**2184**	**143**	**0**	**3.93**	**9**	**5**	**4**	**541**	**28**	**0**	**3.11**
1986-87	**Edmonton**	**NHL**	**44**	**22**	**13**	**3**	**2388**	**137**	**0**	**3.44**	**19**	**14**	**5**	**1148**	**47**	**0**	**2.46**
1987-88de	**Edmonton**	**NHL**	***75**	***40**	**24**	**9**	***4304**	**246**	***4**	**3.43**	***19**	***16**	**2**	***1136**	**55**	**0**	**2.90**
1988-89	**Edmonton**	**NHL**	**59**	**23**	**26**	**6**	**3341**	**213**	**1**	**3.83**	**7**	**3**	**4**	**417**	**24**	**1**	**3.45**
	NHL Totals		389	211	106	48	22051	1361	7	3.70	94	66	25	5509	279	2	3.04

a WHL First All-Star Team (1980, 1981)
b WHL Rookie of the Year (1980)
c NHL Second All-Star Team (1982)
d NHL First All-Star Team (1988)
e Won Vezina Trophy (1988)

Played in NHL All-Star Game (1982, 1984-86, 1988-89)

FURLAN, FRANK

Goaltender. Catches left. 5'9", 174 lbs. Born, Nanaimo, B.C., March 8, 1968.
(Winnipeg's 7th choice, 155th overall, in 1986 Entry Draft).

			Regular Season								Playoffs						
Season	Club	Lea	GP	W	L	T	Mins	GA	SO	Avg	GP	W	L	Mins	GA	SO	Avg
1986-87	Michigan Tech	WCHA	11	1	10	0	623	66	0	6.36	....	....	....	....	....	....	....
1987-88	Michigan Tech	WCHA	16	4	10	0	864	87	0	6.04	....	....	....	....	....	....	....
1988-89	Tri-Cities	WHL	46	17	23	3	2662	191	1	4.31	3	0	1	67	7	0	6.27

GAMBLE, TROY

Goaltender. Catches left. 5'11", 190 lbs. Born, New Glasgow, N.S., April 7, 1967.
(Vancouver's 2nd choice, 25th over-all, in 1985 Entry Draft).

			Regular Season								Playoffs						
Season	Club	Lea	GP	W	L	T	Mins	GA	SO	Avg	GP	W	L	Mins	GA	SO	Avg
1984-85a	Medicine Hat	WHL	37	27	6	2	2095	100	3	2.86	2	1	1	120	9	0	4.50
1985-86	Medicine Hat	WHL	45	28	11	0	2264	142	0	3.76	11	5	4	530	31	0	3.51
1986-87	**Vancouver**	**NHL**	**1**	**0**	**1**	**0**	**60**	**4**	**0**	**4.00**	....	....	....	....	....	....	....
	Spokane	WHL	38	17	17	1	2155	163	0	4.54	5	0	5	298	35	0	7.05
	Medicine Hat	WHL	11	7	3	0	646	46	0	4.27	....	....	....	....	....	....	....
1987-88b	Spokane	WHL	67	36	26	1	3824	235	0	3.69	15	7	8	875	56	1	3.84
1988-89	**Vancouver**	**NHL**	**5**	**2**	**3**	**0**	**302**	**12**	**0**	**2.38**	....	....	....	....	....	....	....
	Milwaukee	IHL	42	23	9	0	2198	138	0	3.77	11	5	5	640	35	0	3.28
	NHL Totals		**6**	**2**	**4**	**0**	**362**	**16**	**0**	**2.65**	....	....	....	....	....	....	....

a WHL First All-Star Team, East Division (1985)
b WHL First All-Star Team, West Division (1988)

GILMOUR, DARRYL

Goaltender. Shoots left. 6', 171 lbs. Born, Winnipeg, Man., February 13, 1967.
(Philadelphia's 3rd choice, 48th over-all, in 1985 Entry Draft).

			Regular Season								Playoffs						
Season	Club	Lea	GP	W	L	T	Mins	GA	SO	Avg	GP	W	L	Mins	GA	SO	Avg
1984-85	Moose Jaw	WHL	58	15	35	0	3004	297	0	5.93	....	....	....	....	....	....	....
1985-86a	Moose Jaw	WHL	62	19	34	3	3482	276	1	4.76	9	4	4	490	48	0	5.88
1986-87	Moose Jaw	WHL	31	14	13	2	1776	123	2	4.16	....	....	....	....	....	....	....
	Portland	WHL	24	15	7	1	1460	111	0	4.56	19	12	7	1167	83	1	4.27
1987-88	Hershey	AHL	25	14	7	0	1273	78	1	3.68	....	....	....	....	....	....	....
1988-89	Hershey	AHL	38	16	14	5	2093	144	0	4.13	....	....	....	....	....	....	....

a WHL First All-Star Team, East Division (1986).

GORDON, SCOTT

Goaltender. Catches left. 5'10", 175 lbs. Born, Brockton, MA, February 6, 1963.

			Regular Season								Playoffs						
Season	Club	Lea	GP	W	L	T	Mins	GA	SO	Avg	GP	W	L	Mins	GA	SO	Avg
1982-83	Boston College	ECAC	9	3	3	0	371	15	0	2.43	....	....	....	....	....	....	....
1983-84	Boston College	ECAC	35	21	13	0	2034	127	1	3.75	....	....	....	....	....	....	....
1984-85	Boston College	H.E.	36	23	11	2	2179	131	1	3.61	....	....	....	....	....	....	....
1985-86a	Boston College	H.E.	32	17	8	1	1852	112	2	3.63	....	....	....	....	....	....	....
1986-87	Fredericton	AHL	32	9	12	2	1616	120	0	4.46	....	....	....	....	....	....	....
1987-88	Baltimore	AHL	34	7	17	3	1638	145	0	5.31	....	....	....	....	....	....	....
1988-89	Halifax	AHL	2	0	2	0	116	10	0	5.17	....	....	....	....	....	....	....

a Hockey East First All-Star Team (1986)

Signed as a free agent by **Quebec**, October 2, 1986.

GOSSELIN, MARIO

Goaltender. Catches left. 5'8", 165 lbs. Born, Thetford Mines, Que., June 15, 1963.
(Quebec's 3rd choice, 55th over-all, in 1982 Entry Draft).

			Regular Season								Playoffs						
Season	Club	Lea	GP	W	L	T	Mins	GA	SO	Avg	GP	W	L	Mins	GA	SO	Avg
1980-81	Shawinigan	QMJHL	21	4	9	0	907	75	0	4.96	1	0	0	20	2	0	6.00
1981-82a	Shawinigan	QMJHL	60	....	....	....	3404	2496	0	4.05	14	....	....	788	58	0	4.42
1982-83	Shawinigan	QMJHL	46	32	9	1	2496	133	3	3.12	8	5	3	457	29	0	3.81
1983-84	Cdn. Olympic	...	36	....	....	....	2007	126	0	3.77	....	....	....	....	....	....	....
	Quebec	NHL	3	2	0	0	148	3	1	1.21	....	....	....	....	....	....	....
1984-85	Quebec	NHL	35	19	10	3	1960	109	1	3.34	17	9	8	1059	54	0	3.06
1985-86	Quebec	NHL	31	14	14	1	1726	111	2	3.86	1	0	1	40	5	0	7.50
	Fredericton	AHL	5	2	2	1	304	15	0	2.96	....	....	....	....	....	....	....
1986-87	Quebec	NHL	30	13	11	1	1625	86	0	3.18	11	7	4	654	37	0	3.39
1987-88	Quebec	NHL	54	20	28	4	3002	189	2	3.78	....	....	....	....	....	....	....
1988-89	Quebec	NHL	39	11	19	3	2064	146	0	4.24	....	....	....	....	....	....	....
	Halifax	AHL	3	3	0	0	183	9	0	2.95	....	....	....	....	....	....	....
	NHL Totals		192	79	82	12	10525	644	6	3.67	29	16	13	1753	96	0	3.29

a QMJHL Second All-Star Team (1982)

Played in NHL All-Star Game (1986)

GRAVEL, FRANCOIS (gruh-VEL)

Goaltender. Catches right. 6'2", 185 lbs. Born, Ste. Foy, Que., October 21, 1968.
(Montreal's 5th choice, 58th overall, in 1987 Entry Draft).

			Regular Season								Playoffs						
Season	Club	Lea	GP	W	L	T	Mins	GA	SO	Avg	GP	W	L	Mins	GA	SO	Avg
1985-86	St. Jean	QMJHL	42	13	15	2	1827	151	0	4.96	5	3	2	307	38	0	7.42
1986-87	Shawinigan	QMJHL	40	18	17	5	2415	194	0	4.82	11	8	3	678	47	0	4.16
1987-88	Shawinigan	QMJHL	44	19	20	2	2499	200	1	4.80	8	4	4	488	39	0	4.80
1988-89a	Sherbrooke	AHL	33	12	10	3	1625	95	2	3.51	1	1	0	40	3	0	4.50

a Shared Harry "Hap" Holmes Trophy (fewest goals-against-AHL) with Randy Exelby (1989)

GREENLAY, MIKE

Goaltender. Catches left. 6'3", 200 lbs. Born, Calgary, Alta., September 15, 1968.
(Edmonton's 9th choice, 189th overall, in 1986 Entry Draft).

			Regular Season								Playoffs						
Season	Club	Lea	GP	W	L	T	Mins	GA	SO	Avg	GP	W	L	Mins	GA	SO	Avg
1986-87	Lake Superior	CCHA	17	7	5	0	744	44	0	3.54	....	....	....	....	....	....	....
1987-88	Lake Superior	CCHA	19	10	3	3	1023	57	0	3.34	....	....	....	....	....	....	....
1988-89	Saskatoon	WHL	20	10	8	1	1128	86	0	4.57	6	2	0	174	16	0	5.52
	Lake Superior	CCHA	2	1	1	0	85	6	0	4.23	....	....	....	....	....	....	....

GUENETTE, STEVE

Goaltender. Catches left. 5'9", 170 lbs. Born, Gloucester Ont., November 13, 1965.

			Regular Season								Playoffs						
Season	Club	Lea	GP	W	L	T	Mins	GA	SO	Avg	GP	W	L	Mins	GA	SO	Avg
1983-84	Guelph	OHL	38	9	18	2	1808	155	0	5.14	....	....	....	....	....	....	....
1984-85	Guelph	OHL	47	16	22	4	2593	200	1	4.63	....	....	....	....	....	....	....
1985-86a	Guelph	OHL	48	26	20	1	2908	165	3	3.40	20	15	3	1167	54	1	2.77
1986-87	Pittsburgh	NHL	2	0	2	0	113	8	0	4.25	....	....	....	....	....	....	....
	Baltimore	AHL	54	21	23	0	3035	157	5	3.10	....	....	....	....	....	....	....
1987-88	Pittsburgh	NHL	19	12	7	0	1092	61	1	3.35	....	....	....	....	....	....	....
bc	Muskegon	IHL	33	23	4	5	1943	91		*2.81	....	....	....	....	....	....	....
1988-89	Pittsburgh	NHL	11	5	6	0	574	41	0	4.29	....	....	....	....	....	....	....
	Muskegon	IHL	10	6	4	0	597	39	0	3.92	....	....	....	....	....	....	....
c	Salt Lake	IHL	30	24	5	0	1810	82	2	2.72	*13	*8	5	*782	44	0	3.38
	NHL Totals		32	17	15	0	1779	110	1	3.71	....	....	....	....	....	....	....

a OHL Second All-Star Team (1986)
b Won James Norris Memorial Trophy (IHL Top Goaltender) (1988, 1989)
c IHL Second All-Star Team (1988)

Signed as a free agent by **Pittsburgh**, April 6, 1985. Traded to **Calgary** by **Pittsburgh** for Calgary's sixth-round choice (Mike Needham) in 1989 Entry Draft, January 9, 1989.

HACKETT, JEFF

Goaltender. Catches left. 6'1", 175 lbs. Born, London, Ont., June 1, 1968.
(NY Islanders's 2nd choice, 34th overall, in 1987 Entry Draft).

			Regular Season								Playoffs						
Season	Club	Lea	GP	W	L	T	Mins	GA	SO	Avg	GP	W	L	Mins	GA	SO	Avg
1986-87	Oshawa	OHL	31	18	9	2	1672	85	2	3.05	15	8	7	895	40	0	2.68
1987-88a	Oshawa	OHL	53	30	21	2	3165	205	0	3.89	7	3	4	438	31	0	4.25
1988-89	NY Islanders	NHL	13	4	7	0	662	39	0	3.53	....	....	....	....	....	....	....
	Springfield	AHL	29	12	14	2	1677	116	0	4.15	....	....	....	....	....	....	....
	NHL Totals		13	4	7	0	662	39	0	3.53	....	....	....	....	....	....	....

a OHL Third All-Star Team (1988)

HANLON, GLEN

Goaltender. Catches right. 6', 185 lbs. Born, Brandon, Man., February 20, 1957.
(Vancouver's 3rd choice, 40th over-all, in 1977 Amateur Draft).

			Regular Season								Playoffs						
Season	Club	Lea	GP	W	L	T	Mins	GA	SO	Avg	GP	W	L	Mins	GA	SO	Avg
1974-75	Brandon	WHL	43	....	....	....	2498	176	0	4.22	5	....	....	284	29	0	6.12
1975-76a	Brandon	WHL	64	....	....	....	3523	234	4	3.99	5	....	....	300	33	0	6.60
1976-77a	Brandon	WHL	65	....	....	....	3784	195	*4	*3.09	16	....	....	914	53	0	3.48
1977-78	Vancouver	NHL	4	1	2	1	200	9	0	2.70	....	....	....	....	....	....	....
bc	Tulsa	CHL	53	....	....	....	3123	160	*3	3.07	2	....	....	120	5	0	*2.50
1978-79	Vancouver	NHL	31	12	13	5	1821	94	3	3.10	....	....	....	....	....	....	....
1979-80	Vancouver	NHL	57	17	29	10	3341	193	0	3.47	2	0	0	60	3	0	3.00
1980-81	Vancouver	NHL	17	5	8	0	798	59	1	4.44	....	....	....	....	....	....	....
	Dallas	CHL	4	3	1	0	239	8	1	2.01	....	....	....	....	....	....	....
1981-82	Vancouver	NHL	28	8	14	5	1610	106	1	3.95	....	....	....	....	....	....	....
	St. Louis	NHL	2	0	1	0	76	8	0	6.30	3	0	2	109	9	0	4.95
1982-83	St. Louis	NHL	14	3	8	1	671	50	0	4.47	....	....	....	....	....	....	....
	NY Rangers	NHL	21	9	10	1	1173	67	0	3.43	1	0	1	60	5	0	5.00
1983-84	NY Rangers	NHL	50	28	14	4	2837	166	1	3.51	5	2	3	308	13	1	2.53
1984-85	NY Rangers	NHL	44	14	20	7	2510	175	0	4.18	3	0	3	168	14	0	5.00
1985-86	NY Rangers	NHL	23	5	12	1	1170	65	0	3.33	3	0	0	75	6	0	4.80
	Adirondack	AHL	10	5	4	1	605	33	0	3.27	....	....	....	....	....	....	....
	New Haven	AHL	5	3	2	0	279	22	0	4.73	....	....	....	....	....	....	....
1986-87	Detroit	NHL	36	11	16	5	1963	104	1	3.18	8	5	2	467	13	2	1.67
1987-88	Detroit	NHL	47	22	17	5	2623	141	*4	3.23	8	4	3	431	22	*1	3.06
1988-89	Detroit	NHL	39	13	14	8	2092	124	1	3.56	2	0	1	78	7	0	5.38
	NHL Totals		413	148	178	53	22885	1361	12	3.57	35	11	14	1756	92	4	3.14

a WHL First All-Star Team (1976, 1977)
b CHL Rookie of the Year (1978)
c CHL First All-Star Team (1978)

Traded to **St. Louis** by **Vancouver** for Tony Currie, Jim Nill, Rick Heinz and St. Louis' fourth round choice (Shawn Kilroy) in 1982 Entry Draft, March 9, 1982. Traded to **NY Rangers** by **St. Louis** with Vaclav Nedomansky for Andre Dore, January 4, 1983. Traded to **Detroit** by **NY Rangers** with New York's third round choices in 1987 (Dennis Holland) and 1988 (Guy Dupuis) Entry Drafts for Kelly Kisio, Lane Lambert and Jim Leavins, July 29, 1986.

HANSCH, RANDY

Goaltender. Catches right. 5'11", 165 lbs. Born, Edmonton, Alta., February 8, 1966.
(Detroit's 5th choice, 112th overall, in 1984 Entry Draft).

			Regular Season								Playoffs						
Season	Club	Lea	GP	W	L	T	Mins	GA	SO	Avg	GP	W	L	Mins	GA	SO	Avg
1983-84	Victoria	WHL	36	12	19	0	1894	144	0	4.56	....	....	....	....	....	....	....
1984-85	Victoria	WHL	52	17	28	3	3021	260	0	5.16	....	....	....	....	....	....	....
1985-86	Kamloops	WHL	31	10	21	0	1821	172	0	5.67	14	11	2	820	36	1	2.63
1986-87	Kalamazoo	IHL	16	8	7	0	926	60	2	3.88	....	....	....	....	....	....	....
	Adirondack	AHL	10	6	4	0	544	36	0	3.97	10	5	4	579	34	0	3.52
1987-88			DID NOT PLAY-INJURED														
1988-89	Cdn. National	....	29	9	12	4	1489	96	0	3.86	....	....	....	....	....	....	....

HARRIS, PETER

Goaltender. Catches left. 6'2", 210 lbs. Born, Haverhill, MA, April 22, 1968.
(NY Islanders' 8th choice, 164th overall, in 1986 Entry Draft).

			Regular Season								Playoffs						
Season	Club	Lea	GP	W	L	T	Mins	GA	SO	Avg	GP	W	L	Mins	GA	SO	Avg
1986-87	U. of Lowell	H.E.	6	1	2	1	279	22	0	4.73	....	....	....	....	....	....	....
1987-88	U. of Lowell	H.E.	DID NOT PLAY														
1988-89	U. of Lowell	H.E.	9	1	2	0	401	29	0	4.34	....	....	....	....	....	....	....

HARVEY, CHRIS

Goaltender. Catches left. 6'1", 180 lbs. Born, Cambridge, MA, December 8, 1967.
(Boston's 1st choice, 23rd overall, in 1988 Supplemental Draft).

			Regular Season								Playoffs						
Season	Club	Lea	GP	W	L	T	Mins	GA	SO	Avg	GP	W	L	Mins	GA	SO	Avg
1986-87	Brown	ECAC	22	9	13	0	1241	88	0	4.26	....	....	....	....	....	....	....
1987-88	Brown	ECAC	21	3	17	1	1235	104	0	5.05	....	....	....	....	....	....	....
1988-89	Brown	ECAC	23	1	22	0	1327	131	0	5.92	....	....	....	....	....	....	....

HAYWARD, BRIAN

Goaltender. Catches left. 5'10", 175 lbs. Born, Georgetown, Ont., June 25, 1960.

			Regular Season								Playoffs						
Season	Club	Lea	GP	W	L	T	Mins	GA	SO	Avg	GP	W	L	Mins	GA	SO	Avg
1978-79	Cornell	ECAC	25	18	6	0	1469	95	0	3.88	3	2	1	179	14	0	4.66
1979-80	Cornell	ECAC	12	2	7	0	508	52	0	6.02	....	....	....	....	....	....	....
1980-81	Cornell	ECAC	19	11	4	1	967	58	1	3.54	4	2	1	181	18	0	4.50
1981-82ab	Cornell	ECAC	22	11	10	1	1320	68	0	3.09	....	....	....	....	....	....	....
1982-83	Sherbrooke	AHL	22	6	11	3	1208	89	1	4.42	....	....	....	....	....	....	....
	Winnipeg	NHL	24	10	12	2	1440	89	1	3.71	3	0	3	160	14	0	5.24
1983-84	Winnipeg	NHL	28	7	18	2	1530	124	0	4.86	....	....	....	....	....	....	....
	Sherbrooke	AHL	15	4	8	0	781	69	0	5.30	....	....	....	....	....	....	....
1984-85	Winnipeg	NHL	61	33	17	7	3416	220	0	3.86	6	2	4	309	23	0	4.47
1985-86	Winnipeg	NHL	52	13	28	5	2721	217	0	4.79	2	0	1	68	6	0	5.29
	Sherbrooke	AHL	3	2	0	1	185	5	0	1.62	....	....	....	....	....	....	....
1986-87c	Montreal	NHL	37	19	13	4	2178	102	1	2.81	13	6	5	708	32	0	2.71
1987-88c	Montreal	NHL	39	22	10	4	2247	107	2	2.86	4	2	2	230	9	0	2.35
1988-89c	Montreal	NHL	36	20	13	3	2091	101	1	2.90	2	1	1	124	7	0	3.39
	NHL Totals		277	124	111	27	15623	960	5	3.69	30	11	16	1599	91	0	3.41

a ECAC First All-Star Team (1982)
b NCAA All-America Team (1982)
c Shared William Jennings Trophy with Patrick Roy (1987, 1988, 1989)

Signed as a free agent by **Winnipeg**, May 5, 1982. Traded to **Montreal** by **Winnipeg** for Steve Penney and the rights to Jan Ingman, August 19, 1986

HEALY, GLEN

Goaltender. Catches left. 5'10", 185 lbs. Born, Pickering, Ont., August 23, 1962.

			Regular Season								Playoffs						
Season	Club	Lea	GP	W	L	T	Mins	GA	SO	Avg	GP	W	L	Mins	GA	SO	Avg
1981-82	W. Michigan	CCHA	27	7	19	1	1569	116	0	4.44	....	....	....	....	....	....	....
1982-83	W. Michigan	CCHA	30	8	19	2	1732	116	0	4.01	....	....	....	....	....	....	....
1983-84	W. Michigan	CCHA	38	19	16	3	2241	146	0	3.90	....	....	....	....	....	....	....
1984-85	W. Michigan	CCHA	37	21	14	2	2171	118	0	3.26	....	....	....	....	....	....	....
1985-86	New Haven	AHL	43	21	15	4	2410	160	0	3.98	2	0	2	49	11	0	5.55
	Los Angeles	NHL	1	0	0	0	51	6	0	7.06	....	....	....	....	....	....	....
1986-87	New Haven	AHL	47	21	15	0	2828	173	1	3.67	7	3	4	427	19	0	2.67
1987-88	Los Angeles	NHL	34	12	18	1	1869	135	1	4.33	4	1	3	240	20	0	5.00
1988-89	Los Angeles	NHL	48	25	19	7	2699	192	0	4.27	....	....	....	....	....	....	....
	NHL Totals		83	37	37	8	4619	333	1	4.33	4	1	3	240	20	0	5.00

Signed as a free agent by **Los Angeles**, June 13, 1985.

HEBERT, GUY

Goaltender. Catches left. 5'8", 180 lbs. Born, Troy, NY, January 7, 1967.
(St. Louis' 8th choice, 159th overall, in 1987 Entry Draft).

			Regular Season								Playoffs						
Season	Club	Lea	GP	W	L	T	Mins	GA	SO	Avg	GP	W	L	Mins	GA	SO	Avg
1986-87	Hamilton Col.	NCAA	18	12	5	0	1070	40	0	2.19	....	....	....	....	....	....	....
1987-88	Hamilton Col.	NCAA	8	5	3	0	450	19	0	2.53	....	....	....	....	....	....	....
1988-89	Hamilton Col.	NCAA	25	18	7	0	1453	62	0	2.56	....	....	....	....	....	....	....

HEXTALL, RON

Goaltender. Catches left. 6'3", 192 lbs. Born, Winnipeg, Man., May 3, 1964.
(Philadelphia's 6th choice, 119th over-all, in 1982 Entry Draft).

			Regular Season								Playoffs						
Season	Club	Lea	GP	W	L	T	Mins	GA	SO	Avg	GP	W	L	Mins	GA	SO	Avg
1981-82	Brandon	WHL	30	12	11	0	1398	133	0	5.71	3	0	2	103	16	0	9.32
1982-83	Brandon	WHL	44	13	30	0	2589	249	0	5.77	....	....	....	....	....	....	....
1983-84	Brandon	WHL	46	29	13	2	2670	190	0	4.27	10	5	5	592	37	0	3.75
1984-85	Hershey	AHL	11	4	6	0	555	34	0	3.68	....	....	....	....	....	....	....
	Kalamazoo	IHL	19	6	11	1	1103	80	0	4.35	....	....	....	....	....	....	....
1985-86ab	Hershey	AHL	53	30	19	2	3061	174	5	3.41	13	5	7	780	42	1	3.23
1986-87cdef	**Philadelphia**	**NHL**	**66**	**37**	**21**	**6**	**3799**	**190**	**1**	**3.00**	**26**	**15**	**11**	**1540**	**71**	**2**	**2.77**
1987-88g	**Philadelphia**	**NHL**	**62**	**30**	**22**	**7**	**3561**	**208**	**0**	**3.50**	**7**	**2**	**4**	**379**	**30**	**0**	**4.75**
1988-89h	**Philadelphia**	**NHL**	***64**	**30**	**28**	**6**	***3756**	**202**	**0**	**3.23**	**15**	**8**	**7**	**886**	**49**	**0**	**3.32**
	NHL Totals		**192**	**97**	**71**	**19**	**11116**	**600**	**1**	**3.24**	**48**	**25**	**22**	**2805**	**150**	**2**	**3.21**

a AHL First All-Star Team (1986)
b AHL Rookie of the Year (1986)
c NHL First All-Star Team (1987)
d Won Vezina Trophy (1987)
e Won Conn Smyth Trophy (1987)
f NHL All-Rookie Team (1987)
g Scored a goal vs. Boston, December 8, 1987
h Scored a goal in playoffs vs. Washington, April 11, 1989

Played in NHL All-Star Game (1988)

HORN, BILL

Goaltender. Catches left. 5'8", 150 lbs. Born, Regina, Sask., April 16, 1967.
(Hartford's 4th choice, 95th overall, in 1986 Entry Draft).

			Regular Season								Playoffs						
Season	Club	Lea	GP	W	L	T	Mins	GA	SO	Avg	GP	W	L	Mins	GA	SO	Avg
1985-86a	W. Michigan	CCHA	30	25	5	0	1797	114	0	3.81	....	....	....	....	....	....	....
1986-87b	W. Michigan	CCHA	36	19	16	0	2065	136	2	3.95	....	....	....	....	....	....	....
1987-88	W. Michigan	CCHA	33	15	13	2	1889	139	1	4.42	....	....	....	....	....	....	....
1988-89	W. Michigan	CCHA	37	12	19	6	2181	153	0	4.21	....	....	....	....	....	....	....

a NCAA West Second All-Star Team (1986)
b CCHA Second All-Star Team (1987)

HRIVNAK, JIM

Goaltender. Catches left. 6'2", 185 lbs. Born, Montreal, Que., May 28, 1968.
(Edmonton's 4th choice, 61st overall, in 1986 Entry Draft).

			Regular Season								Playoffs						
Season	Club	Lea	GP	W	L	T	Mins	GA	SO	Avg	GP	W	L	Mins	GA	SO	Avg
1985-86	Merrimack	NCAA	21	12	8	0	1230	75	0	3.66	....	....	....	....	....	....	....
1986-87	Merrimack	NCAA	34	27	7	0	1618	58	3	2.14	....	....	....	....	....	....	....
1987-88	Merrimack	NCAA	37	31	6	0	2119	84	4	2.38	....	....	....	....	....	....	....
1988-89	Baltimore	AHL	10	1	8	0	502	55	0	6.57	....	....	....	....	....	....	....

HRUDEY, KELLY STEPHEN (ROO-dee)

Goaltender. Catches left. 5'10", 180 lbs. Born, Edmonton, Alta., January 13, 1961.
(NY Islanders' 2nd choice, 38th over-all, in 1980 Entry Draft).

			Regular Season								Playoffs						
Season	Club	Lea	GP	W	L	T	Mins	GA	SO	Avg	GP	W	L	Mins	GA	SO	Avg
1978-79	Medicine Hat	WHL	57	12	34	7	3093	318	0	6.17	....	....	....	....	....	....	....
1979-80	Medicine Hat	WHL	57	25	23	4	3049	212	1	4.17	13	6	6	638	48	0	4.51
1980-81a	Medicine Hat	WHL	55	32	19	1	3023	200	4	3.97	4	....	....	244	17	0	4.18
	Indianapolis	CHL	....	....	....	....	....	....	....	....	2	....	....	135	8	0	3.56
1981-82bc	Indianapolis	CHL	51	27	19	4	3033	149	1	*2.95	13	11	2	842	34	*1	*2.42
1982-83bcd	Indianapolis	CHL	47	26	17	1	2744	139	2	3.04	10	7	3	637	28	0	2.64
1983-84	Indianapolis	CHL	6	3	2	1	370	21	0	3.40	....	....	....	....	....	....	....
	NY Islanders	**NHL**	**12**	**7**	**2**	**0**	**535**	**28**	**0**	**3.14**	....	....	....	....	....	....	....
1984-85	**NY Islanders**	**NHL**	**41**	**19**	**17**	**3**	**2335**	**141**	**2**	**3.62**	**5**	**1**	**3**	**281**	**8**	**0**	**1.71**
1985-86	**NY Islanders**	**NHL**	**45**	**19**	**15**	**8**	**2563**	**137**	**1**	**3.21**	**2**	**0**	**2**	**120**	**6**	**0**	**3.00**
1986-87	**NY Islanders**	**NHL**	**46**	**21**	**15**	**7**	**2634**	**145**	**0**	**3.30**	**14**	**7**	**7**	**842**	**38**	**0**	**2.71**
1987-88	**NY Islanders**	**NHL**	**47**	**22**	**17**	**5**	**2751**	**153**	**3**	**3.34**	**6**	**2**	**4**	**381**	**23**	**0**	**3.62**
1988-89	**NY Islanders**	**NHL**	**50**	**18**	**24**	**3**	**2800**	**183**	**0**	**3.92**	....	....	....	....	....	....	....
	Los Angeles	**NHL**	**16**	**10**	**4**	**2**	**974**	**47**	**1**	**2.90**	**10**	**4**	**6**	**566**	**35**	**0**	**3.71**
	NHL Totals		**257**	**116**	**94**	**28**	**14592**	**834**	**7**	**3.43**	**37**	**14**	**22**	**2190**	**110**	**0**	**3.01**

a WHL Second All-Star Team (1981)
b CHL First All-Star Team (1982, 1983)
c Shared Terry Sawchuk Trophy (CHL's Leading Goaltenders) with Rob Holland (1982, 1983)
d Won Tommy Ivan Trophy (CHL's Most Valuable Player) (1983)

Traded to **Los Angeles** by **NY Islanders** for Mark Fitzpatrick, Wayne McBean and future considerations (Doug Crossman, acquired May 23, 1989) February 22, 1989.

HUGHES, CHARLES

Goaltender. Catches right. 5'8", 165 lbs. Born, Quincy, MA, January 30, 1970.
(New Jersey's 13th choice, 222nd overall, in 1988 Entry Draft).

			Regular Season								Playoffs						
Season	Club	Lea	GP	W	L	T	Mins	GA	SO	Avg	GP	W	L	Mins	GA	SO	Avg
1988-89	Harvard	ECAC	17	15	1	0	990	46	1	2.79	....	....	....	....	....	....	....

HYDUKE, JOHN

Goaltender. Catches left. 5'10", 155 lbs. Born, Hibbing, MN, June 23, 1967.
(Los Angeles' 8th choice, 156th over-all, in 1985 Entry Draft).

			Regular Season								Playoffs						
Season	Club	Lea	GP	W	L	T	Mins	GA	SO	Avg	GP	W	L	Mins	GA	SO	Avg
1985-86	Minn-Duluth	WCHA	24	14	17	3	1401	84	0	3.60	....	....	....	....	....	....	....
1986-87	Minn-Duluth	WCHA	23	7	15	0	1359	99	0	4.37	....	....	....	....	....	....	....
1987-88	Minn-Duluth	WCHA	31	14	15	2	1883	127	0	4.05	....	....	....	....	....	....	....
1988-89	Minn.-Duluth	WCHA	28	10	16	1	1622	103	0	3.81	....	....	....	....	....	....	....

ING, PETER

Goaltender. Catches left. 6'2", 165 lbs. Born, Toronto, Ont., April 28, 1969.
(Toronto's 3rd choice, 48th overall, in 1988 Entry Draft).

			Regular Season								Playoffs						
Season	Club	Lea	GP	W	L	T	Mins	GA	SO	Avg	GP	W	L	Mins	GA	SO	Avg
1986-87	Windsor	OHL	28	13	11	3	1615	105	0	3.90	5	4	0	161	9	0	3.35
1987-88	Windsor	OHL	43	30	7	1	2422	125	2	3.10	3	2	0	225	7	0	1.87
1988-89	Windsor	OHL	19	7	7	3	1043	76	*1	4.37	....	....	....	....	....	....	....
a	London	OHL	32	18	11	2	1848	104	*2	3.38	21	11	9	1093	82	0	4.50

a OHL Third All-Star Team (1989)

JABLONSKI, PAT

Goaltender. Catches right. 6', 175 lbs. Born, Toledo, OH, June 20, 1967.
(St. Louis' 6th choice, 138th over-all, in 1985 Entry Draft).

			Regular Season								Playoffs						
Season	Club	Lea	GP	W	L	T	Mins	GA	SO	Avg	GP	W	L	Mins	GA	SO	Avg
1985-86	Windsor	OHL	29	6	16	4	1600	119	1	4.46	6	0	3	263	20	0	4.56
1986-87	Windsor	OHL	41	22	14	2	2328	128	3	3.30	12	8	4	710	38	0	3.21
1987-88	Peoria	IHL	5	2	2	1	285	17		3.58	....	....	....	....	....	....	....
	Windsor	OHL	18	14	3	0	994	48	2	2.90	9	*8	0	537	28	0	3.13
1988-89	Peoria	IHL	35	11	20	0	2051	163	1	4.77	3	0	2	130	13	0	6.00

JANECYK, ROBERT (BOB) (JAN uh sehk)

Goaltender. Catches left. 6'1", 180 lbs. Born, Chicago, IL., May 18, 1957.

			Regular Season								Playoffs						
Season	Club	Lea	GP	W	L	T	Mins	GA	SO	Avg	GP	W	L	Mins	GA	SO	Avg
1979-80	Flint	IHL	2	....	....	....	119	5	0	2.53	....	....	....	....	....	....	....
a	Fort Wayne	IHL	42	....	....	....	2327	133	1	3.43	3	....	....	89	4	0	2.70
1980-81	New Brunswick	AHL	34	11	18	1	1915	131	0	4.10	....	....	....	....	....	....	....
1981-82bc	New Brunswick	AHL	53	32	13	7	3224	153	2	2.85	14	11	2	818	32	*1	*2.35
1982-83b	Springfield	AHL	47	....	....	....	2754	167	3	3.64	....	....	....	....	....	....	....
1983-84	**Chicago**	**NHL**	**8**	**2**	**3**	**1**	**412**	**28**	**0**	**4.08**	....	....	....	....	....	....	....
	Springfield	AHL	30	14	11	4	1664	94	0	3.39	....	....	....	....	....	....	....
1984-85	**Los Angeles**	**NHL**	**51**	**22**	**21**	**8**	**3002**	**183**	**2**	**3.66**	**3**	**0**	**3**	**184**	**10**	**0**	**3.26**
1985-86	**Los Angeles**	**NHL**	**38**	**14**	**16**	**4**	**2083**	**162**	**0**	**4.67**	....	....	....	....	....	....	....
1986-87	**Los Angeles**	**NHL**	**7**	**4**	**3**	**0**	**420**	**34**	**0**	**4.86**	....	....	....	....	....	....	....
1987-88	**Los Angeles**	**NHL**	**5**	**1**	**4**	**0**	**303**	**23**	**0**	**4.55**	....	....	....	....	....	....	....
	New Haven	AHL	37	19	13	3	2162	125	1	3.47	....	....	....	....	....	....	....
1988-89	**Los Angeles**	**NHL**	**1**	**0**	**0**	**0**	**30**	**2**	**0**	**4.00**	....	....	....	....	....	....	....
	New Haven	AHL	34	14	13	6	1992	131	1	3.95	....	....	....	....	....	....	....
	NHL Totals		**110**	**43**	**47**	**13**	**6250**	**432**	**2**	**4.15**	**3**	**0**	**3**	**184**	**10**	**0**	**3.26**

a IHL Second All-Star Team (1980)
b AHL First All-Star Team (1982, 1983)
c Shared Harry "Hap" Holmes Memorial Trophy (AHL's Leading Goaltenders) with Warren Skorodenski (1982)

Signed as free agent by **Chicago**, June 3, 1980. Traded to **Los Angeles** by **Chicago** with Chicago's first round (Craig Redmond), third round (John English) and fourth round (Thomas Glavine) choices in 1984 Entry Draft for Los Angeles' first round (Ed Olczyk) and fourth round (Tommy Eriksson) choices in 1984 Entry Draft, June 9, 1984.

JEFFREY, MIKE

Goaltender. Catches right. 6'3", 195 lbs. Born, Kamloops, B.C., April 6, 1965.
(Boston's 1st choice, 19th overall, in 1987 Supplemental Draft).

			Regular Season								Playoffs						
Season	Club	Lea	GP	W	L	T	Mins	GA	SO	Avg	GP	W	L	Mins	GA	SO	Avg
1984-85	N. Michigan	WCHA	12	7	3	0	573	44	0	4.61	....	....	....	....	....	....	....
1985-86	N. Michigan	WCHA	15	5	6	0	743	58	0	4.69	....	....	....	....	....	....	....
1986-87	N. Michigan	WCHA	28	13	12	1	1601	102	0	3.82	....	....	....	....	....	....	....
1987-88	N. Michigan	WCHA	30	13	13	4	1801	107	0	3.56	....	....	....	....	....	....	....
1988-89	Maine	AHL	44	16	22	2	2368	148	1	3.75	....	....	....	....	....	....	....

JENSEN, DARREN AKSEL

Goaltender. Catches left. 5'9", 165 lbs. Born, Creston, B.C., May 27, 1960.
(Hartford's 5th choice, 92nd over-all, in 1980 Entry Draft).

			Regular Season								Playoffs						
Season	Club	Lea	GP	W	L	T	Mins	GA	SO	Avg	GP	W	L	Mins	GA	SO	Avg
1979-80	North Dakota	WCHA	15	....	....	....	890	33	1	2.22	....	....	....	....	....	....	....
1980-81	North Dakota	WCHA	25	....	....	....	1510	110	0	4.37	....	....	....	....	....	....	....
1981-82	North Dakota	WCHA	16	....	....	....	909	45	1	2.96	....	....	....	....	....	....	....
1982-83	North Dakota	WCHA	15	....	....	....	905	45	0	2.98	....	....	....	....	....	....	....
1983-84abc	Fort Wayne	IHL	56	40	12	3	3325	162	*4	*2.92	6	2	4	358	21	0	3.52
1984-85	**Philadelphia**	**NHL**	**1**	**0**	**1**	**0**	**60**	**7**	**0**	**7.00**	....	....	....	....	....	....	....
	Hershey	AHL	39	12	20	6	2263	150	1	3.98	....	....	....	....	....	....	....
1985-86d	**Philadelphia**	**NHL**	**29**	**15**	**9**	**1**	**1436**	**88**	**2**	**3.68**	....	....	....	....	....	....	....
	Hershey	AHL	14	11	1	1	795	38	1	2.87	7	5	1	365	19	0	3.12
1986-87	Hershey	AHL	60	26	26	0	3429	215	0	3.76	4	1	2	203	15	0	4.43
1987-88	Fredericton	AHL	42	18	19	4	2459	158	0	3.86	12	7	5	715	40	0	3.36
1988-89	Milwaukee	IHL	11	7	2	0	555	36	0	3.89	....	....	....	....	....	....	....
	NHL Totals		**30**	**15**	**10**	**1**	**1496**	**95**	**2**	**3.81**	....	....	....	....	....	....	....

a IHL First All-Star Team (1984)
b IHL Most Valuable Player (1984)
c IHL Rookie of the Year (1984)
d Shared William Jennings Trophy with Bob Froese (1986)

Signed as free agent by **Philadelphia**, May 1, 1984. Traded to **Vancouver** by **Philadelphia** with Daryl Stanley for Wendell Young and Vancouver's third round pick in 1990 Entry Draft, August 28, 1987.

JOSEPH, CURTIS

Goaltender. Catches left. 5'10", 170 lbs. Born, Keswick, Ont., April 29, 1967.

			Regular Season								Playoffs						
Season	Club	Lea	GP	W	L	T	Mins	GA	SO	Avg	GP	W	L	Mins	GA	SO	Avg
1987-88	Notre Dame	SJHL	36	25	4	7	2174	94	1	2.59	....	....	....	....	....	....	....
1988-89abc	U. Wisconsin	WCHA	38	21	11	5	2267	94	1	2.49	....	....	....	....	....	....	....

Signed as a free agent by **St. Louis**, June 16, 1989.

a WCHA First All-Star Team (1989)
b WCHA Player of the Year (1989)
c WCHA Rookie of the Year (1989)

KEANS, DOUGLAS FREDERICK (DOUG)

Goaltender. Catches left. 5'7", 185 lbs. Born, Pembroke, Ont., January 7, 1958.
(Los Angeles' 2nd choice, 94th over-all, in 1978 Amateur Draft).

			Regular Season								Playoffs						
Season	**Club**	**Lea**	**GP**	**W**	**L**	**T**	**Mins**	**GA**	**SO**	**Avg**	**GP**	**W**	**L**	**Mins**	**GA**	**SO**	**Avg**
1976-77	Oshawa	OHA	48	....	....	....	2632	291	0	6.63	....	....	....	....	....	....	....
1977-78	Oshawa	OHA	42	....	....	....	2500	173	1	4.12	5	....	....	299	23	0	4.63
1978-79	Saginaw	IHL	59	....	....	....	3207	217	0	4.06	2	....	....	120	10	0	5.05
1979-80	Binghamton	AHL	7	3	3	2	429	25	0	3.50	....	....	....	....	....	....	....
	Saginaw	IHL	22	....	....	....	1070	67	1	3.76	....	....	....	....	....	....	....
	Los Angeles	**NHL**	**10**	**3**	**3**	**3**	**559**	**23**	**0**	**2.47**	**1**	**0**	**1**	**40**	**7**	**0**	**10.50**
1980-81	**Los Angeles**	**NHL**	**9**	**2**	**3**	**1**	**454**	**37**	**0**	**4.89**	....	....	....	....	....	....	....
	Houston	CHL	11	3	4	4	699	27	0	2.32	....	....	....	....	....	....	....
	Oklahoma City	CHL	9	3	5	0	492	32	1	3.90	....	....	....	....	....	....	....
1981-82	New Haven	AHL	13	5	5	1	686	33	2	2.89	....	....	....	....	....	....	....
	Los Angeles	**NHL**	**31**	**8**	**10**	**7**	**1436**	**103**	**0**	**4.30**	**2**	**0**	**1**	**32**	**1**	**0**	**1.88**
1982-83	**Los Angeles**	**NHL**	**6**	**0**	**2**	**2**	**304**	**24**	**0**	**4.73**	....	....	....	....	....	....	....
	New Haven	AHL	30	13	13	2	1724	125	0	4.35	....	....	....	....	....	....	....
1983-84	**Boston**	**NHL**	**33**	**19**	**8**	**3**	**1779**	**92**	**2**	**3.10**	....	....	....	....	....	....	....
1984-85	**Boston**	**NHL**	**25**	**16**	**6**	**3**	**1497**	**82**	**1**	**3.29**	**4**	**2**	**2**	**240**	**15**	**0**	**3.75**
1985-86	**Boston**	**NHL**	**30**	**14**	**13**	**3**	**1757**	**107**	**0**	**3.65**	....	....	....	....	....	....	....
1986-87	**Boston**	**NHL**	**36**	**18**	**8**	**4**	**1942**	**108**	**0**	**3.34**	**2**	**0**	**2**	**120**	**11**	**0**	**5.50**
1987-88	**Boston**	**NHL**	**30**	**16**	**11**	**0**	**1660**	**90**	**1**	**3.25**	....	....	....	....	....	....	....
	Maine	AHL	10	8	2	0	600	34	0	3.40	10	5	5	617	42	0	4.08
1988-89	Baltimore	AHL	4	1	3	0	239	17	0	4.27	....	....	....	....	....	....	....
	Springfield	AHL	32	11	16	2	1737	124	0	4.28	....	....	....	....	....	....	....
	NHL Totals		**210**	**96**	**64**	**26**	**11388**	**666**	**4**	**3.51**	**9**	**2**	**6**	**432**	**34**	**0**	**4.72**

Claimed on waivers by **Boston** from **Los Angeles**, May 24, 1983.

KING, SCOTT

Goaltender. Catches left. 6'1", 170 lbs. Born, Thunder Bay, Ont., June 25, 1967.
(Detroit's 10th choice, 190th overall, in 1986 Entry Draft).

			Regular Season								Playoffs						
Season	**Club**	**Lea**	**GP**	**W**	**L**	**T**	**Mins**	**GA**	**SO**	**Avg**	**GP**	**W**	**L**	**Mins**	**GA**	**SO**	**Avg**
1985-86	Vernon	BCJHL	29	17	9	0	1718	134	0	4.68	....	....	....	....	....	....	....
1986-87	U. of Maine	H.E.	21	11	6	1	1111	58	0	3.13	....	....	....	....	....	....	....
1987-88a	U. of Maine	H.E.	33	25	5	1	1761	91	0	3.10	....	....	....	....	....	....	....
1988-89a	U. of Maine	H.E.	27	13	8	0	1394	83	0	3.57	....	....	....	....	....	....	....

a Hockey East Second All-Star Team (1988, 1989)

KNICKLE, RICHARD (RICK)

Goaltender. Catches left. 5'10", 155 lbs. Born, Chatham, N.B., February 26, 1960.
(Buffalo's 7th choice, 116th over-all, in 1979 Entry Draft).

			Regular Season								Playoffs						
Season	**Club**	**Lea**	**GP**	**W**	**L**	**T**	**Mins**	**GA**	**SO**	**Avg**	**GP**	**W**	**L**	**Mins**	**GA**	**SO**	**Avg**
1977-78	Brandon	WHL	49	34	5	7	2806	182	0	3.89	8	....	....	450	36	0	4.82
1978-79a	Brandon	WHL	38	26	3	8	2240	118	1	*3.16	16	12	3	886	41	*1	*2.78
1979-80	Brandon	WHL	33	11	14	1	1604	125	0	4.68	....	....	....	....	....	....	....
	Muskegon	IHL	16	....	....	....	829	52	0	3.76	3	....	....	156	17	0	6.54
1980-81b	Erie	EHL	43	....	....	....	2347	125	1	*3.20	8	....	....	446	14	0	*1.88
1981-82	Rochester	AHL	31	10	12	5	1753	108	1	3.70	3	0	2	125	7	0	3.37
1982-83	Flint	IHL	27	....	....	....	1638	92	2	3.37	3	....	....	193	10	0	3.11
1983-84c	Flint	IHL	60	32	21	5	3518	203	3	3.46	8	8	0	480	24	0	3.00
1984-85	Sherbrooke	AHL	14	7	6	0	780	53	0	4.08	....	....	....	....	....	....	....
	Flint	IHL	36	18	11	3	2018	115	2	3.42	7	3	4	401	27	0	4.04
1985-86	Saginaw	IHL	39	16	15	0	2235	135	2	3.62	3	2	1	193	12	0	3.73
1986-87	Saginaw	IHL	26	9	13	0	1413	113	0	4.80	5	1	4	329	21	0	3.83
1987-88	Flint	IHL	1	0	1	0	60	4		4.00	....	....	....	....	....	....	....
	Peoria	IHL	13	2	8	1	705	58		4.94	6	3	3	294	20		4.08
1988-89de	Fort Wayne	IHL	47	22	16	0	2716	141	1	*3.11	4	1	2	173	15	0	5.20

a WHL First All-Star Team (1979)
b EHL First All-Star Team (1981)
c IHL Second All-Star Team (1984)
d IHL First All-Star Team (1989)
e Won James Norris Memorial Trophy (Top Goaltender-IHL) (1989)

Signed as a free agent by **Montreal,** February 8, 1985.

KOLZIG, OLAF

Goaltender. Catches left. 6'3", 205 lbs. Born, Johannesburg, South Africa, April 6, 1970.
(Washington's 1st choice, 19th overall, in 1989 Entry Draft).

			Regular Season								Playoffs						
Season	**Club**	**Lea**	**GP**	**W**	**L**	**T**	**Mins**	**GA**	**SO**	**Avg**	**GP**	**W**	**L**	**Mins**	**GA**	**SO**	**Avg**
1987-88	N. Westminster	WHL	15	6	5	0	650	48	1	4.43	3	....	....	149	11	0	4.43
1988-89	Tri-Cities	WHL	30	16	10	2	1671	97	1	*3.48	....	....	....	....	....	....	....

KRUESEL, JEFFREY

Goaltender. Catches right. 5'11", 180 lbs. Born, Rochester, MN, June 1, 1970.
(Los Angeles' 8th choice, 133rd overall, in 1988 Entry Draft).

			Regular Season								Playoffs						
Season	**Club**	**Lea**	**GP**	**W**	**L**	**T**	**Mins**	**GA**	**SO**	**Avg**	**GP**	**W**	**L**	**Mins**	**GA**	**SO**	**Avg**
1987-88	John Marshall	HS	19	....	....	....	855	31	4	1.67	....	....	....	....	....	....	....
1988-89	St. Cloud St.	NCAA	DID NOT PLAY														

KRUZICH, GARY

Goaltender. Catches left. 5'5", 175 lbs. Born, Oak Lawn, IL, April 22, 1965.
(NY Islanders' 1st choice, 22nd overall, in 1986 Supplemental Draft).

			Regular Season								Playoffs						
Season	**Club**	**Lea**	**GP**	**W**	**L**	**T**	**Mins**	**GA**	**SO**	**Avg**	**GP**	**W**	**L**	**Mins**	**GA**	**SO**	**Avg**
1983-84a	Bowling Green	CCHA	28	21	5	2	1725	83	0	2.89	....	....	....	....	....	....	....
1984-85	Bowling Green	CCHA	31	16	12	0	1739	115	0	3.79	....	....	....	....	....	....	....
1985-86bc	Bowling Green	CCHA	35	23	11	0	2089	124	0	3.56	....	....	....	....	....	....	....
1986-87bc	Bowling Green	WCHA	38	27	7	2	2229	123	0	3.31	....	....	....	....	....	....	....
1987-88	Flint	IHL	27	14	5	1	1315	91		4.15	2	0	0	43	2		2.79
1988-89	Flint	IHL	30	9	17	0	1637	132	1	4.84	....	....	....	....	....	....	....

a NCAA Tournament MVP (1984)
b CCHA First All-Star Team (1986, 1987)
c NCAA West First All-American Team (1986, 1987)

KUNTAR, LES

Goaltender. Catches left. 6'2", 194 lbs. Born, Buffalo, NY, July 28, 1969.
(Montreal's 8th choice, 122nd overall, in 1987 Entry Draft).

			Regular Season								Playoffs						
Season	**Club**	**Lea**	**GP**	**W**	**L**	**T**	**Mins**	**GA**	**SO**	**Avg**	**GP**	**W**	**L**	**Mins**	**GA**	**SO**	**Avg**
1987-88	St. Lawrence	ECAC	10	6	1	0	488	27	0	3.31	....	....	....	....	....	....	....
1988-89	St. Lawrence	ECAC	14	11	2	0	786	31	0	2.37	....	....	....	....	....	....	....

LaFOREST, MARK ANDREW

Goaltender. Catches left. 5'11", 190 lbs. Born, Welland, Ont., July 10, 1962.

			Regular Season								Playoffs						
Season	**Club**	**Lea**	**GP**	**W**	**L**	**T**	**Mins**	**GA**	**SO**	**Avg**	**GP**	**W**	**L**	**Mins**	**GA**	**SO**	**Avg**
1981-82	Niagara Falls	OHL	24	10	13	1	1365	105	1	4.62	5	1	2	300	19	0	3.80
1982-83	North Bay	OHL	54	34	17	1	3140	195	0	3.73	8	4	4	474	31	0	3.92
1983-84	Adirondack	AHL	7	3	3	1	351	29	0	4.96	....	....	....	....	....	....	....
	Kalamazoo	IHL	13	4	5	2	718	48	1	4.01	....	....	....	....	....	....	....
1984-85	Adirondack	AHL	11	2	3	1	430	35	0	488	....	....	....	....	....	....	....
1985-86	**Detroit**	**NHL**	**28**	**4**	**21**	**0**	**1383**	**114**	**1**	**4.95**	....	....	....	....	....	....	....
	Adirondack	AHL	19	13	5	1	1142	57	0	2.99	17	12	5	1075	58	0	3.24
1986-87	**Detroit**	**NHL**	**5**	**2**	**1**	**0**	**219**	**12**	**0**	**3.29**	....	....	....	....	....	....	....
a	Adirondack	AHL	37	23	8	0	2229	105	3	2.83	....	....	....	....	....	....	....
1987-88	**Philadelphia**	**NHL**	**21**	**5**	**9**	**2**	**972**	**60**	**1**	**3.70**	**2**	**1**	**0**	**48**	**1**	**0**	**1.25**
	Hershey	AHL	5	2	1	2	309	13	0	2.52	....	....	....	....	....	....	....
1988-89	**Philadelphia**	**NHL**	**17**	**5**	**7**	**2**	**933**	**64**	**0**	**4.12**	....	....	....	....	....	....	....
	Hershey	AHL	3	2	0	0	185	9	0	2.92	12	7	5	744	27	1	2.18
	NHL Totals		**71**	**16**	**38**	**4**	**3507**	**250**	**2**	**4.28**	**2**	**1**	**0**	**48**	**1**	**0**	**1.25**

a Won Baz Bastien Trophy (AHL Most Valuable Goaltender) (1987)

Signed as free agent by **Detroit**, April 29, 1983. Traded to **Philadelphia** by **Detroit** for Philadelphia's second-round choice (Bob Wilkie) in 1987 Entry Draft, June 13, 1987.

LAFORT, BRYAN

Goaltender. Catches left. 6'1", 195 lbs. Born, Potsdam, NY, June 30, 1970.
(New Jersey's 9th choice, 159th overall, in 1988 Entry Draft).

			Regular Season								Playoffs						
Season	**Club**	**Lea**	**GP**	**W**	**L**	**T**	**Mins**	**GA**	**SO**	**Avg**	**GP**	**W**	**L**	**Mins**	**GA**	**SO**	**Avg**
1988-89	Boston U.	H.E.	11	3	7	0	585	48	1	4.93	....	....	....	....	....	....	....

LAURIN, STEVE

Goaltender. Catches left. 5'10", 150 lbs. Born, Barrie, Ont., December 2, 1967.
(Hartford's 10th choice, 249th overall, in 1987 Entry Draft).

			Regular Season								Playoffs						
Season	**Club**	**Lea**	**GP**	**W**	**L**	**T**	**Mins**	**GA**	**SO**	**Avg**	**GP**	**W**	**L**	**Mins**	**GA**	**SO**	**Avg**
1986-87	Dartmouth	ECAC	15	0	14	0	883	75	0	5.09	....	....	....	....	....	....	....
1987-88a	Dartmouth	ECAC	16	4	9	1	874	59	1	4.05	....	....	....	....	....	....	....
1988-89	Dartmouth	ECAC	13	2	9	1	747	57	0	4.57	....	....	....	....	....	....	....

a ECAC Second All-Star Team (1988)

LEHKONEN, TIMO

Goaltender. Catches left. 5'11", 170 lbs. Born, Helsinki, Finland, January 8, 1966.
(Chicago's 4th choice, 90th overall, in 1984 Entry Draft).

			Regular Season								Playoffs						
Season	**Club**	**Lea**	**GP**	**W**	**L**	**T**	**Mins**	**GA**	**SO**	**Avg**	**GP**	**W**	**L**	**Mins**	**GA**	**SO**	**Avg**
1988-89	TPS	Fin.	12	8	4	0	644	25	0	2.33	....	....	....	....	....	....	....

LEMELIN, REJEAN (REGGIE) (LEHM uh lihn)

Goaltender. Catches left. 5'11", 170 lbs. Born, Quebec City, Que. November 19, 1954.
(Philadelphia's 6th choice, 125th over-all, in 1974 Amateur Draft).

			Regular Season								Playoffs						
Season	**Club**	**Lea**	**GP**	**W**	**L**	**T**	**Mins**	**GA**	**SO**	**Avg**	**GP**	**W**	**L**	**Mins**	**GA**	**SO**	**Avg**
1972-73	Sherbrooke	QJHL	28	....	....	....	1681	146	0	5.21	2	....	....	120	12	0	6.00
1973-74	Sherbrooke	QJHL	35	....	....	....	2061	158	0	4.60	1	....	....	60	3	0	3.00
1974-75	Philadelphia	NAHL	43	....	....	....	2277	131	3	3.45	....	....	....	....	....	....	....
1975-76	Philadelphia	NAHL	29	....	....	....	1601	97	1	3.63	3	....	....	171	15	0	5.26
1976-77	Springfield	AHL	3	2	1	0	180	10	0	3.33	....	....	....	....	....	....	....
	Philadelphia	NAHL	51	26	19	1	2763	170	1	3.61	3	....	....	191	14	0	4.40
1977-78a	Philadelphia	AHL	60	31	21	7	3585	177	4	2.96	2	0	2	119	12	0	6.05
1978-79	Philadelphia	AHL	13	3	9	1	780	36	0	2.77	....	....	....	....	....	....	....
	Atlanta	**NHL**	**18**	**8**	**8**	**1**	**994**	**55**	**0**	**3.32**	**1**	**0**	**0**	**20**	**0**	**0**	**0.00**
1979-80	**Atlanta**	**NHL**	**3**	**0**	**2**	**0**	**150**	**15**	**0**	**6.00**	....	....	....	....	....	....	....
	Birmingham	CHL	38	13	21	2	2188	137	0	3.76	2	0	1	79	5	0	3.80
1980-81	Birmingham	CHL	13	3	8	2	757	56	0	4.44	....	....	....	....	....	....	....
	Calgary	**NHL**	**29**	**14**	**6**	**7**	**1629**	**88**	**2**	**3.24**	**6**	**3**	**3**	**366**	**22**	**0**	**3.61**
1981-82	**Calgary**	**NHL**	**34**	**10**	**5**	**6**	**1866**	**135**	**0**	**4.34**	....	....	....	....	....	....	....
1982-83	**Calgary**	**NHL**	**39**	**16**	**12**	**8**	**2211**	**133**	**0**	**3.61**	**7**	**3**	**3**	**327**	**27**	**0**	**4.95**
1983-84	**Calgary**	**NHL**	**51**	**21**	**12**	**9**	**2568**	**150**	**0**	**3.50**	**8**	**4**	**4**	**448**	**32**	**0**	**4.29**
1984-85	**Calgary**	**NHL**	**56**	**30**	**12**	**10**	**3176**	**183**	**1**	**3.46**	**4**	**1**	**3**	**248**	**15**	**1**	**3.63**
1985-86	**Calgary**	**NHL**	**60**	**29**	**24**	**4**	**3369**	**229**	**1**	**4.08**	**3**	**0**	**1**	**109**	**7**	**0**	**3.85**
1986-87	**Calgary**	**NHL**	**34**	**16**	**9**	**1**	**1735**	**94**	**2**	**3.25**	**2**	**0**	**1**	**101**	**6**	**0**	**3.56**
1987-88	**Boston**	**NHL**	**49**	**24**	**17**	**6**	**2828**	**138**	**3**	**2.93**	**17**	**11**	**6**	**1027**	**45**	***1**	***2.63**
1988-89	**Boston**	**NHL**	**40**	**19**	**15**	**6**	**2392**	**120**	**0**	**3.01**	**4**	**1**	**3**	**252**	**16**	**0**	**3.81**
	NHL Totals		**413**	**187**	**122**	**58**	**22918**	**1340**	**9**	**3.51**	**52**	**23**	**24**	**2898**	**170**	**2**	**3.52**

a AHL First All-Star Team (1978)

Played in NHL All-Star Game (1989)

Signed as free agent by **Atlanta**, August 17, 1978. Signed as a free agent by **Boston**, August 13, 1987.

LINDFORS, SAKARI

Goaltender. Catches left. 5'7", 150 lbs. Born, Helsinki, Finland, April 27, 1966.
(Quebec's 9th choice, 150th overall, in 1988 Entry Draft).

			Regular Season								Playoffs						
Season	**Club**	**Lea**	**GP**	**W**	**L**	**T**	**Mins**	**GA**	**SO**	**Avg**	**GP**	**W**	**L**	**Mins**	**GA**	**SO**	**Avg**
1988-89	IFK Helsinki	Fin.	24	11	11	2	1433	89	1	3.75	....	....	....	....	....	....	....

LITTMAN, DAVID

Goaltender. Catches left. 6', 175 lbs. Born, Cranston, RI, June 13, 1967.
(Buffalo's 12th choice, 211th overall, in 1987 Entry Draft).

			Regular Season								Playoffs						
Season	**Club**	**Lea**	**GP**	**W**	**L**	**T**	**Mins**	**GA**	**SO**	**Avg**	**GP**	**W**	**L**	**Mins**	**GA**	**SO**	**Avg**
1985-86	Boston College	H.E.	7	4	0	1	312	18	0	3.46	....	....	....	....	....	....	....
1986-87	Boston College	H.E.	21	15	5	0	1182	68	0	3.45	....	....	....	....	....	....	....
1987-88a	Boston College	H.E.	30	11	16	2	1726	116	0	4.03	....	....	....	....	....	....	....
1988-89bc	Boston College	H.E.	32	19	9	4	1945	107	0	3.30	....	....	....	....	....	....	....

a Hockey East Second All-Star Team (1988)
b Hockey East First All-Star Team (1989)
c NCAA East Second All-American Team (1989)

LIUT, MICHAEL (MIKE) (lee-OOT)

Goaltender. Catches left. 6'2", 195 lbs. Born, Weston, Ont., January 7, 1956.
(St. Louis' 5th choice, 56th over-all, in 1976 Amateur Draft).

			Regular Season								Playoffs						
Season	Club	Lea	GP	W	L	T	Mins	GA	SO	Avg	GP	W	L	Mins	GA	SO	Avg
1973-74	Bowling Green	CCHA	24	10	12	0	1272	88	1	4.15	....	....	....	....	....	....	....
1974-75	Bowling Green	CCHA	20	12	6	1	1174	78	0	3.99	....	....	....	....	....	....	....
1975-76	Bowling Green	CCHA	21	13	5	0	1171	50	2	2.56	....	....	....	....	....	....	....
1976-77	Bowling Green	CCHA	24	18	4	0	1346	61	2	2.72	....	....	....	....	....	....	....
1977-78	Cincinnati	WHA	27	8	12	0	1215	86	0	4.25	....	....	....	....	....	....	....
1978-79	Cincinnati	WHA	54	23	27	4	3181	184	*3	3.47	3	1	2	179	12	0	4.02
1979-80	**St. Louis**	**NHL**	**64**	**32**	**23**	**9**	**3661**	**194**	**2**	**3.18**	**3**	**0**	**3**	**193**	**12**	**0**	**3.73**
1980-81ab	**St. Louis**	**NHL**	**61**	**33**	**14**	**13**	**3570**	**199**	**1**	**3.34**	**11**	**5**	**6**	**685**	**50**	**0**	**4.38**
1981-82	**St. Louis**	**NHL**	**64**	**28**	**28**	**7**	**3691**	**250**	**2**	**4.06**	**10**	**5**	**3**	**494**	**27**	**0**	**3.28**
1982-83	**St. Louis**	**NHL**	**68**	**21**	**27**	**13**	**3794**	**235**	**1**	**3.72**	**4**	**1**	**3**	**240**	**15**	**0**	**3.75**
1983-84	**St. Louis**	**NHL**	**58**	**25**	**29**	**4**	**3425**	**197**	**3**	**3.45**	**11**	**6**	**5**	**714**	**29**	**1**	**2.44**
1984-85	**St. Louis**	**NHL**	**32**	**12**	**12**	**6**	**1869**	**119**	**1**	**3.82**	....	....	....	....	....	....	....
	Hartford	**NHL**	**12**	**4**	**7**	**1**	**731**	**36**	**1**	**2.95**	....	....	....	....	....	....	....
1985-86	**Hartford**	**NHL**	**57**	**27**	**23**	**4**	**3282**	**198**	**2**	**3.62**	**8**	**5**	**2**	**441**	**14**	**1**	**1.90**
1986-87c	**Hartford**	**NHL**	**59**	**31**	**22**	**5**	**3476**	**187**	**4**	**3.23**	**6**	**2**	**4**	**332**	**25**	**0**	**4.52**
1987-88	**Hartford**	**NHL**	**60**	**25**	**28**	**5**	**3532**	**187**	**2**	**3.18**	**3**	**1**	**1**	**160**	**11**	**0**	**4.13**
1988-89	**Hartford**	**NHL**	**35**	**13**	**19**	**1**	**2006**	**142**	**1**	**4.25**	....	....	....	....	....	....	....
	NHL Totals		**570**	**251**	**232**	**68**	**33037**	**1944**	**20**	**3.53**	**56**	**25**	**27**	**3259**	**183**	**2**	**3.37**

a NHL First All-Star Team (1981)
b Won Lester B. Pearson Award (1981)
c NHL Second All-Star Team (1987)

Played in NHL All-Star Game (1981)

Reclaimed by **St. Louis** from Cincinnati (WHA) prior to Expansion Draft, June 9, 1979. Traded to **Hartford** by **St. Louis** with Jorgen Pettersson for Mark Johnson and Greg Millen, February 21, 1985.

LORENZ, DANNY

Goaltender. Catches left. 5'10", 170 lbs. Born, Murrayville, BC, December 12, 1969.
(NY Islander's 4th choice, 58th overall, in 1988 Entry Draft).

			Regular Season								Playoffs						
Season	Club	Lea	GP	W	L	T	Mins	GA	SO	Avg	GP	W	L	Mins	GA	SO	Avg
1986-87	Seattle	WHL	38	12	21	2	2103	199	0	5.68	....	....	....	....	....	....	....
1987-88	Seattle	WHL	62	20	37	2	3302	314	0	5.71	....	....	....	....	....	....	....
1988-89	Springfield	AHL	4	2	1	0	210	12	0	3.43	....	....	....	....	....	....	....
ab	Seattle	WHL	*68	31	33	4	*4003	240	*3	3.60	....	....	....	....	....	....	....

a WHL West All-Star Team (1989)
b WHL Top Goaltender (1989)

MALARCHUK, CLINT

Goaltender. Catches left. 6', 190 lbs. Born, Grande, Prairie, Alta. May 1, 1961.
(Quebec's 3rd choice, 74th over-all, in 1981 Entry Draft).

			Regular Season								Playoffs						
Season	Club	Lea	GP	W	L	T	Mins	GA	SO	Avg	GP	W	L	Mins	GA	SO	Avg
1979-80	Portland	WHL	37	21	10	0	1948	147	0	4.53	1	0	0	40	3	0	4.50
1980-81	Portland	WHL	38	28	8	0	2235	142	3	3.81	4	....	....	307	21	0	4.10
1981-82	**Quebec**	**NHL**	**2**	**0**	**1**	**1**	**120**	**14**	**0**	**7.00**	....	....	....	....	....	....	....
	Fredericton	AHL	51	15	34	2	2906	247	0	5.10	....	....	....	....	....	....	....
1982-83	Fredericton	AHL	25	....	....	....	1506	78	0	3.11	....	....	....	....	....	....	....
	Quebec	**NHL**	**15**	**8**	**5**	**2**	**900**	**71**	**0**	**4.73**	....	....	....	....	....	....	....
1983-84	Fredericton	AHL	11	5	5	1	663	40	0	3.62	....	....	....	....	....	....	....
	Quebec	**NHL**	**23**	**10**	**9**	**2**	**1215**	**80**	**0**	**3.95**	**1**	**0**	**0**	**0**	**0**	**0**	**0.00**
1984-85	Fredericton	AHL	56	26	25	4	3347	198	2	3.55	6	2	4	379	20	0	3.17
1985-86	**Quebec**	**NHL**	**46**	**26**	**12**	**4**	**2657**	**142**	**4**	**3.21**	**3**	**0**	**2**	**143**	**11**	**0**	**4.62**
1986-87	**Quebec**	**NHL**	**54**	**18**	**26**	**9**	**3092**	**175**	**1**	**3.40**	**3**	**0**	**2**	**140**	**8**	**0**	**3.43**
1987-88	**Washington**	**NHL**	**54**	**24**	**20**	**4**	**2926**	**154**	***4**	**3.16**	**4**	**0**	**2**	**193**	**15**	**0**	**4.66**
1988-89	**Washington**	**NHL**	**42**	**16**	**18**	**7**	**2428**	**141**	**1**	**3.48**	**1**	**0**	**1**	**59**	**5**	**0**	**5.08**
	Buffalo	**NHL**	**7**	**3**	**1**	**1**	**326**	**13**	**1**	**2.39**	....	....	....	....	....	....	....
	NHL Totals		**243**	**105**	**92**	**30**	**13664**	**790**	**11**	**3.47**	**11**	**0**	**6**	**476**	**34**	**0**	**4.29**

Traded to **Washington** by **Quebec** with Dale Hunter for Gaetan Duchesne, Alan Haworth, and Washington's first-round choice (Joe Sakic) in 1987 Entry Draft, June 13, 1987. Traded to **Buffalo** by **Washington** with Grant Ledyard and Washington's sixth-round choice in 1991 Entry Draft for Calle Johansson and Buffalo's second-round choice (Byron Dafoe) in 1989 Entry Draft, March 7, 1989.

MANELUK, GEORGE

Goaltender. Catches left. 5'11", 185 lbs. Born, Winnipeg, Man., July 25, 1967.
(NY Islanders' 4th choice, 76th overall, in 1987 Entry Draft).

			Regular Season								Playoffs						
Season	Club	Lea	GP	W	L	T	Mins	GA	SO	Avg	GP	W	L	Mins	GA	SO	Avg
1986-87	Brandon	WHL	58	16	35	4	3258	315	0	5.80	....	....	....	....	....	....	....
1987-88	Brandon	WHL	64	24	33	3	3651	297	0	4.88	4	1	3	271	22	0	4.87
	Springfield	AHL	2	0	1	1	125	9	0	4.32	....	....	....	....	....	....	....
	Peoria	IHL	3	1	2	0	148	14	0	5.68	1	0	1	60	5	0	5.00
1988-89	Springfield	AHL	24	7	13	0	1202	84	0	4.19	....	....	....	....	....	....	....

MASON, BOB

Goaltender. Catches right. 6'1", 180 lbs. Born, International Falls, MN, April 22, 1961.

			Regular Season								Playoffs						
Season	Club	Lea	GP	W	L	T	Mins	GA	SO	Avg	GP	W	L	Mins	GA	SO	Avg
1981-82	Minn.-Duluth	WCHA	26	....	....	....	1401	115	0	4.45	....	....	....	....	....	....	....
1982-83	Minn.-Duluth	WCHA	43	....	....	....	2593	151	1	3.49	....	....	....	....	....	....	....
1983-84	U.S. National	...	33	....	....	....	1895	89	0	2.82	....	....	....	....	....	....	....
	U.S. Olympic	...	3	....	....	....	160	10	0	3.75	....	....	....	....	....	....	....
	Hershey	AHL	5	1	4	0	282	26	0	5.53	....	....	....	....	....	....	....
	Washington	**NHL**	**2**	**2**	**0**	**0**	**120**	**3**	**0**	**1.50**	....	....	....	....	....	....	....
1984-85	**Washington**	**NHL**	**12**	**8**	**2**	**1**	**661**	**31**	**1**	**2.81**	....	....	....	....	....	....	....
	Binghamton	AHL	20	10	6	1	1052	58	1	3.31	....	....	....	....	....	....	....
1985-86	**Washington**	**NHL**	**1**	**1**	**0**	**0**	**16**	**0**	**0**	**0.00**	....	....	....	....	....	....	....
	Binghamton	AHL	34	20	11	2	1940	126	0	3.90	3	1	1	124	9	0	4.35
1986-87	**Washington**	**NHL**	**45**	**20**	**18**	**5**	**2536**	**137**	**0**	**3.24**	**4**	**2**	**2**	**309**	**9**	**1**	**1.75**
1987-88	**Chicago**	**NHL**	**41**	**13**	**18**	**8**	**2312**	**160**	**0**	**4.15**	**1**	**0**	**1**	**60**	**3**	**0**	**3.00**
1988-89	**Quebec**	**NHL**	**22**	**5**	**14**	**1**	**1168**	**92**	**0**	**4.73**	....	....	....	....	....	....	....
	Halifax	AHL	23	11	7	1	1278	73	1	3.43	2	0	2	97	9	0	5.57
	NHL Totals		**123**	**49**	**52**	**15**	**6813**	**423**	**1**	**3.73**	**5**	**2**	**3**	**369**	**12**	**1**	**1.95**

Signed as a free agent by **Washington**, February 21, 1984. Traded to **Quebec** by **Chicago** for Mike Eagles, July 5, 1988. Traded to **Washington** by **Quebec** for future considerations, June 17, 1989.

MAY, DARRELL GERALD

Goaltender. Catches left. 6', 175 lbs. Born, Edmonton, Alta., March 6, 1962.
(Vancouver's 4th choice, 91st over-all, in 1980 Entry Draft).

			Regular Season								Playoffs						
Season	Club	Lea	GP	W	L	T	Mins	GA	SO	Avg	GP	W	L	Mins	GA	SO	Avg
1978-79	Portland	WHL	21	12	2	2	1113	64	0	3.45	2	1	0	80	7	0	5.25
1979-80	Portland	WHL	43	32	8	1	2416	143	1	3.55	8	3	5	439	27	0	3.69
1980-81	Portland	WHL	36	28	7	1	2128	122	3	3.44	4	....	....	243	21	0	5.19
1981-82	Portland	WHL	52	31	20	2	3097	226	0	4.38	15	....	....	851	59	0	4.16
1982-83	Fort Wayne	IHL	46	....	....	....	2584	177	0	4.11	2	....	....	120	13	0	6.50
1983-84	Erie	ACHL	43	21	16	2	2404	163	1	4.07	....	....	....	....	....	....	....
1984-85	Peoria	IHL	19	13	4	2	1133	56	1	2.97	10	6	4	609	33	0	3.25
1985-86	**St. Louis**	**NHL**	**3**	**1**	**2**	**0**	**184**	**13**	**0**	**4.24**	....	....	....	....	....	....	....
	Peoria	IHL	56	33	21	0	3321	179	1	3.23	11	6	5	634	38	1	3.60
1986-87a	Peoria	IHL	58	26	31	1	3420	214	2	3.75	....	....	....	....	....	....	....
1987-88	**St. Louis**	**NHL**	**3**	**0**	**3**	**0**	**180**	**18**	**0**	**6.00**	....	....	....	....	....	....	....
	Peoria	IHL	48	22	19	5	2754	162		3.53	....	....	....	....	....	....	....
1988-89	Peoria	IHL	52	20	22	0	2908	202	0	4.17	2	0	2	137	13	0	5.69
	NHL Totals		**6**	**1**	**5**	**0**	**364**	**31**	**0**	**5.11**	....	....	....	....	....	....	....

a IHL First All-Star Team (1987)

Traded to **Montreal** by **St. Louis** with Jocelyn Lemieux and St. Louis' second round choice (Patrice Brisebois) in the 1989 Entry Draft for Sergio Momesso and Vincent Riendeau, August 9, 1988.

McKAY, ROSS LEE

Goaltender. Catches right. 5'11", 175 lbs. Born, Edmonton, Alta., March 3, 1964.

			Regular Season								Playoffs						
Season	Club	Lea	GP	W	L	T	Mins	GA	SO	Avg	GP	W	L	Mins	GA	SO	Avg
1988-89	Binghamton	AHL	19	5	9	2	938	81	1	5.18	....	....	....	....	....	....	....
	Indianapolis	IHL	5	1	3	0	187	18	0	5.78	....	....	....	....	....	....	....

Signed as a free agent by **Hartford**, May 2, 1988.

McKICHAN, STEVE

Goaltender. Catches left. 5'11", 180 lbs. Born, Strathroy, Ont., May 29, 1967.
(Vancouver's 2nd choice, 7th overall, in 1988 Supplemental Draft).

			Regular Season								Playoffs						
Season	Club	Lea	GP	W	L	T	Mins	GA	SO	Avg	GP	W	L	Mins	GA	SO	Avg
1986-87	Miami-Ohio	CCHA	28	3	19	0	1351	130	0	5.77	....	....	....	....	....	....	....
1987-88	Miami-Ohio	CCHA	34	12	17	1	1767	140	1	4.75	....	....	....	....	....	....	....
1988-89	Miami-Ohio	CCHA	21	4	15	0	1014	85	0	5.02	....	....	....	....	....	....	....

McLEAN, KIRK

Goaltender. Catches left. 6', 175 lbs. Born, Willowdale, Ont., June 26, 1966.
(New Jersey's 6th choice, 107th over-all, in 1984 Entry Draft).

			Regular Season								Playoffs						
Season	Club	Lea	GP	W	L	T	Mins	GA	SO	Avg	GP	W	L	Mins	GA	SO	Avg
1983-84	Oshawa	OHL	17	5	9	0	940	67	0	4.28	....	....	....	....	....	....	....
1984-85	Oshawa	OHL	47	23	17	2	2581	143	1	3.32	5	1	3	271	21	0	4.65
1985-86	**New Jersey**	**NHL**	**2**	**1**	**1**	**0**	**111**	**11**	**0**	**5.95**	....	....	....	....	....	....	....
	Oshawa	OHL	51	24	21	2	2830	169	1	3.58	4	1	2	201	18	0	5.37
1986-87	**New Jersey**	**NHL**	**4**	**1**	**1**	**0**	**160**	**10**	**0**	**3.75**	....	....	....	....	....	....	....
	Maine	AHL	45	15	23	4	2606	140	1	3.22	....	....	....	....	....	....	....
1987-88	**Vancouver**	**NHL**	**41**	**11**	**27**	**3**	**2380**	**147**	**1**	**3.71**	....	....	....	....	....	....	....
1988-89	**Vancouver**	**NHL**	**42**	**20**	**17**	**3**	**2477**	**127**	**4**	**3.08**	**5**	**2**	**3**	**302**	**18**	**0**	**3.58**
	NHL Totals		**89**	**33**	**46**	**6**	**5128**	**295**	**5**	**3.45**	**5**	**2**	**3**	**302**	**18**	**0**	**3.58**

Traded to **Vancouver** by **New Jersey** with Greg Adams for Patrik Sundstrom and Vancouver's fourth round choice (Matt Ruchty) in 1988 Entry Draft, September 15, 1987.

MELANSON, ROLAND JOSEPH (ROLLIE) (mel-AWN-son)

Goaltender. Catches left. 5'10", 180 lbs. Born, Moncton, N.B., June 28, 1960.
(NY Islanders' 4th choice, 59th over-all, in 1979 Entry Draft).

			Regular Season								Playoffs						
Season	Club	Lea	GP	W	L	T	Mins	GA	SO	Avg	GP	W	L	Mins	GA	SO	Avg
1978-79a	Windsor	OHA	58	....	....	....	3468	258	1	4.41	7	....	....	392	31	0	4.75
1979-80	Windsor	OHA	22	11	8	0	1099	90	0	4.91	....	....	....	....	....	....	....
	Oshawa	OHA	38	26	12	0	2240	136	3	3.64	7	3	4	420	32	0	4.57
1980-81bc	Indianapolis	CHL	52	31	16	3	3056	131	2	*2.57	....	....	....	....	....	....	....
	NY Islanders	**NHL**	**11**	**8**	**1**	**1**	**620**	**32**	**0**	**3.10**	**3**	**1**	**0**	**92**	**6**	**0**	**3.91**
1981-82	**NY Islanders**	**NHL**	**36**	**22**	**7**	**6**	**2115**	**114**	**0**	**3.23**	**3**	**0**	**1**	**64**	**5**	**0**	**4.69**
1982-83de	**NY Islanders**	**NHL**	**44**	**24**	**12**	**5**	**2460**	**109**	**1**	**2.66**	**5**	**2**	**2**	**238**	**10**	**0**	**2.52**
1983-84	**NY Islanders**	**NHL**	**37**	**20**	**11**	**2**	**2019**	**110**	**0**	**3.27**	**6**	**0**	**1**	**87**	**5**	**0**	**3.45**
1984-85	**NY Islanders**	**NHL**	**8**	**3**	**3**	**0**	**425**	**35**	**0**	**4.94**	....	....	....	....	....	....	....
	Minnesota	**NHL**	**20**	**5**	**10**	**3**	**1142**	**78**	**0**	**4.10**	....	....	....	....	....	....	....
1985-86	**Minnesota**	**NHL**	**6**	**2**	**1**	**2**	**325**	**24**	**0**	**4.43**	....	....	....	....	....	....	....
	Los Angeles	**NHL**	**22**	**4**	**16**	**1**	**1246**	**87**	**0**	**4.19**	....	....	....	....	....	....	....
	New Haven	AHL	3	1	2	0	179	13	0	4.36	....	....	....	....	....	....	....
1986-87	**Los Angeles**	**NHL**	**46**	**18**	**21**	**6**	**2734**	**168**	**1**	**3.69**	**5**	**1**	**4**	**260**	**24**	**0**	**5.54**
1987-88	**Los Angeles**	**NHL**	**47**	**17**	**20**	**7**	**2676**	**195**	**2**	**4.37**	**1**	**0**	**1**	**60**	**9**	**0**	**9.00**
1988-89	**Los Angeles**	**NHL**	**4**	**1**	**1**	**0**	**178**	**19**	**0**	**6.40**	....	....	....	....	....	....	....
	New Haven	AHL	29	11	15	3	1734	106	1	3.67	*17	9	8	*1019	74	1	4.36
	NHL Totals		**281**	**124**	**103**	**33**	**15940**	**971**	**4**	**3.65**	**23**	**4**	**9**	**801**	**59**	**0**	**4.42**

a OHA Second All-Star Team (1979)
b CHL First All-Star Team (1981)
c Won Ken McKenzie Trophy (CHL's Rookie of the Year) (1981)
d Shared William Jennings Trophy with Billy Smith (1983)
e NHL Second All-Star Team (1983)

Traded to **Minnesota** by **NY Islanders** for Minnesota's first round choice in 1985 Entry draft (Brad Dalgarno), November 19, 1984. Traded to **NY Rangers** by **Minnesota** for New York's second round draft choice in 1986 (Neil Wilkinson) and fourth round choice in 1987 (John Weisbrod), December 9, 1985. Traded to **Los Angeles** by **NY Rangers** with Grant Ledyard for Brian MacLellan and Los Angeles' fourth round draft choice in 1987 (Michael Sullivan), December 9, 1985. Signed as a free agent by **New Jersey** August 10, 1989.

MERTEN, MATT

Goaltender. Catches left. 6'3", 190 lbs. Born, Milford, MA, June 29, 1967.
(Vancouver's 8th choice, 175th overall, in 1986 Entry Draft).

			Regular Season								Playoffs						
Season	Club	Lea	GP	W	L	T	Mins	GA	SO	Avg	GP	W	L	Mins	GA	SO	Avg
1986-87	Providence	H.E.	24	6	14	2	1455	104	0	4.29	....	....	....	....	....	....	....
1987-88	Providence	H.E.	25	8	11	1	1328	100	0	4.52	....	....	....	....	....	....	....
1988-89	Providence	H.E.	20	7	8	1	1067	69	0	3.88	....	....	....	....	....	....	....

MILLEN, GREG H.

Goaltender. Catches right. 5'9", 175 lbs. Born, Toronto, Ont., June 25, 1957.
(Pittsburgh's 4th choice, 102nd over-all, in 1977 Amateur Draft).

			Regular Season								Playoffs						
Season	Club	Lea	GP	W	L	T	Mins	GA	SO	Avg	GP	W	L	Mins	GA	SO	Avg
1976-77	Peterborough	OHA	59	....	....	....	3457	244	0	4.23	4	....	....	240	23	0	5.75
1977-78	Kalamazoo	IHL	3	....	....	....	180	14	0	4.67	....	....	....	....	....	....	....
	S. S. Marie	OHA	25	....	....	....	1449	105	1	4.29	13	....	....	774	61	0	4.73
1978-79	**Pittsburgh**	**NHL**	28	14	11	1	1532	86	2	3.37	....	....	....	....	....	....	....
1979-80	**Pittsburgh**	**NHL**	44	18	18	7	2586	157	2	3.64	5	2	3	300	21	0	4.20
1980-81	**Pittsburgh**	**NHL**	63	25	27	10	3721	258	0	4.16	5	2	3	325	19	0	3.51
1981-82	**Hartford**	**NHL**	55	11	30	12	3201	229	0	4.29	....	....	....	....	....	....	....
1982-83	**Hartford**	**NHL**	60	14	38	6	3520	282	1	4.81	....	....	....	....	....	....	....
1983-84	**Hartford**	**NHL**	60	21	30	9	3583	221	2	3.70	....	....	....	....	....	....	....
1984-85	**Hartford**	**NHL**	44	16	22	6	2659	187	1	4.22	....	....	....	....	....	....	....
	St. Louis	**NHL**	10	2	7	1	607	35	0	3.46	1	0	1	60	2	0	2.00
1985-86	**St. Louis**	**NHL**	36	14	16	6	2168	129	1	3.57	10	6	3	586	29	0	2.97
1986-87	**St. Louis**	**NHL**	42	15	18	9	2482	146	0	3.53	4	1	3	250	10	0	2.40
1987-88	**St. Louis**	**NHL**	48	21	19	7	2854	167	1	3.51	10	5	5	600	38	0	3.80
1988-89	**St. Louis**	**NHL**	52	22	20	7	3019	170	*6	3.38	10	5	5	649	34	0	3.14
	NHL Totals		542	193	256	81	31932	2067	16	3.88	45	21	23	2770	153	0	3.31

Signed as free agent by **Hartford**, June 15, 1981. As compensation, **Pittsburgh** received Pat Boutette and the rights to Kevin McLelland, June 29, 1981. Traded to **St. Louis** by **Hartford** with Mark Johnson for Mike Liut and Jorgen Pettersson, February 21, 1985.

MOOG, DONALD ANDREW (ANDY) (MOHG)

Goaltender. Catches left. 5'8", 170 lbs. Born, Penticton, B.C., February 18, 1960.
(Edmonton's 6th choice, 132nd over-all, in 1980 Entry Draft).

			Regular Season								Playoffs						
Season	Club	Lea	GP	W	L	T	Mins	GA	SO	Avg	GP	W	L	Mins	GA	SO	Avg
1978-79	Billings	WHL	26	13	5	4	1306	90	4	4.13	5	1	3	229	21	0	5.50
1979-80a	Billings	WHL	46	23	14	1	2435	149	1	3.67	3	2	1	190	10	0	3.16
1980-81	**Edmonton**	**NHL**	7	3	3	0	313	20	0	3.83	9	5	4	526	32	0	3.65
	Wichita	CHL	29	14	13	1	1602	89	0	3.33	5	3	2	300	16	0	3.20
1981-82	**Edmonton**	**NHL**	8	3	5	0	399	32	0	4.81	....	....	....	....	....	....	....
b	Wichita	CHL	40	23	13	3	2391	119	1	2.99	7	3	4	434	23	0	3.18
1982-83	**Edmonton**	**NHL**	50	33	8	7	2833	167	1	3.54	16	11	5	949	48	0	3.03
1983-84	**Edmonton**	**NHL**	38	27	8	1	2212	139	1	3.77	7	4	0	263	12	0	2.74
1984-85	**Edmonton**	**NHL**	39	22	9	3	2019	111	1	3.30	2	0	0	20	0	0	0.00
1985-86	**Edmonton**	**NHL**	47	27	9	7	2664	164	1	3.69	1	1	0	60	1	0	1.00
1986-87	**Edmonton**	**NHL**	46	28	11	3	2461	144	0	3.51	2	2	0	120	8	0	4.00
1987-88	**Boston**	**NHL**	6	4	2	0	360	17	1	2.83	7	1	4	354	25	0	4.24
	Cdn. National	....	27	10	7	5	1438	86	0	3.58	....	....	....	....	....	....	....
	Cdn. Olympic	....	4	4	0	0	240	9		2.25	....	....	....	....	....	....	....
1988-89	**Boston**	**NHL**	41	18	14	8	2482	133	1	3.22	6	4	2	359	14	0	2.34
	NHL Totals		282	165	69	29	15743	927	6	3.53	50	28	15	2651	140	0	3.17

a WHL Second All-Star Team (1980)
b CHL Second All-Star Team (1982)

Played in NHL All-Star Game (1985, 1986)

Traded to **Boston** by **Edmonton** for Geoff Courtnall and Bill Ranford, March 8, 1988.

MUZZATTI, JASON

Goaltender. Catches left. 6'1", 190 lbs. Born, Toronto, Ont., February 3, 1970.
(Calgary's 1st choice, 21st overall, in 1988 Entry Draft).

			Regular Season								Playoffs						
Season	Club	Lea	GP	W	L	T	Mins	GA	SO	Avg	GP	W	L	Mins	GA	SO	Avg
1986-87	St. Michael's	Jr. B.	20	10	5	2	1054	69	1	3.93	....	....	....	....	....	....	....
1987-88a	Michigan State	CCHA	33	19	9	3	1915	109	0	3.41	....	....	....	....	....	....	....
1988-89	Michigan State	WCHA	42	32	9	1	2515	127	3	3.03	....	....	....	....	....	....	....

a CCHA Second All-Star Team (1988)

MYLLYS, JARMO

Goaltender. Catches right. 5'8", 150 lbs. Born, Sovanlinna, Finland, May 29, 1965.
(Minnesota's 9th choice, 172nd overall, in 1987 Entry Draft).

			Regular Season								Playoffs						
Season	Club	Lea	GP	W	L	T	Mins	GA	SO	Avg	GP	W	L	Mins	GA	SO	Avg
1987-88	Lukko	Fin.	43	....	....	....	2580	160	....	3.72	....	....	....	....	....	....	....
1988-89	**Minnesota**	**NHL**	6	1	4	0	238	22	0	5.55	....	....	....	....	....	....	....
	Kalamazoo	IHL	28	13	8	4	1523	93	0	3.66	6	2	4	419	22	0	3.15
	NHL Totals		6	1	4	0	238	22	0	5.55	....	....	....	....	....	....	....

MYLNIKOV, SERGEI

Goaltender. Catches left. 5'10", 175 lbs. Born, Chelyabinsk, Soviet Union, October 6, 1958.
(Quebec's 9th choice, 127th overall, in 1989 Entry Draft).

			Regular Season								Playoffs						
Season	Club	Lea	GP	W	L	T	Mins	GA	SO	Avg	GP	W	L	Mins	GA	SO	Avg
1976-77	Chelyabinsk	USSR	2	....	....	....	120	2	....	1.00	....	....	....	....	....	....	....
1977-78	Chelyabinsk	USSR	22	....	....	....	1320	71	....	3.22	....	....	....	....	....	....	....
1978-79	Chelyabinsk	USSR	32	....	....	....	1862	90	....	2.90	....	....	....	....	....	....	....
1979-80	Chelyabinsk	USSR	17	....	....	....	1023	58	....	3.40	....	....	....	....	....	....	....
1980-81	Leningrad	USSR	40	....	....	....	2415	157	....	3.90	....	....	....	....	....	....	....
1981-82	Leningrad	USSR	42	....	....	....	2310	132	....	3.42	....	....	....	....	....	....	....
1982-83	Chelyabinsk	USSR	37	....	....	....	1954	124	....	3.80	....	....	....	....	....	....	....
1983-84	Chelyabinsk	USSR	37	....	....	....	2173	91	....	2.51	....	....	....	....	....	....	....
1984-85	Chelyabinsk	USSR	28	....	....	....	1360	74	....	3.26	....	....	....	....	....	....	....
1985-86	Chelyabinsk	USSR	37	....	....	....	2126	96	....	2.70	....	....	....	....	....	....	....
1986-87	Chelyabinsk	USSR	36	....	....	....	2059	103	....	3.00	....	....	....	....	....	....	....
1987-88	Chelyabinsk	USSR	28	....	....	....	1559	69	....	2.65	....	....	....	....	....	....	....
1988-89	Chelyabinsk	USSR	33	....	....	....	1980	85	....	2.58	....	....	....	....	....	....	....

O'NEILL, MICHAEL (MIKE)

Goaltender. Catches left. 5'7", 160 lbs. Born, LaSalle, Que., November 3, 1967.
(Winnipeg's 1st choice, 15th overall, in 1988 Supplemental Draft).

			Regular Season								Playoffs						
Season	Club	Lea	GP	W	L	T	Mins	GA	SO	Avg	GP	W	L	Mins	GA	SO	Avg
1985-86	Yale	ECAC	6	3	1	0	389	17	0	3.53	....	....	....	....	....	....	....
1986-87a	Yale	ECAC	16	9	6	1	964	55	2	3.42	....	....	....	....	....	....	....
1987-88	Yale	ECAC	24	6	17	0	1385	101	0	4.37	....	....	....	....	....	....	....
1988-89ab	Yale	ECAC	25	10	14	1	1490	93	0	3.74	....	....	....	....	....	....	....

a ECAC First All-Star Team (1987, 1989)
b NCAA East First All-American Team (1989)

PANG, DARREN

Goaltender. Catches left. 5'5" 155 lbs. Born, Meaford, Ont. Feb. 17, 1964

			Regular Season								Playoffs						
Season	Club	Lea	GP	W	L	T	Mins	GA	SO	Avg	GP	W	L	Mins	GA	SO	Avg
1982-83	Belleville	OHL	12	....	....	....	570	44	0	4.63	....	....	....	....	....	....	....
	Ottawa	OHL	47	....	....	....	2729	166	1	3.65	9	5	4	510	33	0	3.88
1983-84	Ottawa	OHL	43	....	....	....	2318	117	2	3.03	....	....	....	....	....	....	....
1984-85	Milwaukee	IHL	53	19	29	3	3129	226	0	4.33	....	....	....	....	....	....	....
	Chicago	**NHL**	1	0	1	0	60	4	0	4.00	....	....	....	....	....	....	....
1985-86	Saginaw	IHL	44	21	21	0	2638	148	2	3.37	8	3	5	492	32	0	3.90
1986-87	Nova Scotia	AHL	7	4	2	0	389	21	0	3.24	3	1	2	200	11	0	3.30
1986-87a	Saginaw	IHL	44	25	16	0	2500	151	0	3.62	....	....	....	....	....	....	....
1987-88b	**Chicago**	**NHL**	45	17	23	1	2548	163	0	3.84	4	1	3	240	18	0	4.50
1988-89	**Chicago**	**NHL**	35	10	11	6	1644	120	0	4.38	2	0	0	10	0	0	0.00
	Saginaw	IHL	2	1	0	0	89	6	0	4.04	....	....	....	....	....	....	....
	NHL Totals		81	27	35	7	4252	287	0	4.05	6	1	3	250	18	0	4.32

a IHL Second All-Star Team (1987)
b NHL All-Rookie Team (1988)

Signed as a free agent by **Chicago**, August 15, 1984.

PARSON, MIKE

Goaltender. Catches left. 6'0", 170 lbs. Born, Listowel, Ont., March 12, 1970.
(Boston's 2nd choice, 38th overall, in 1989 Entry Draft).

			Regular Season								Playoffs						
Season	Club	Lea	GP	W	L	T	Mins	GA	SO	Avg	GP	W	L	Mins	GA	SO	Avg
1987-88	Guelph	OHL	31	9	17	2	1703	135	0	4.76	....	....	....	....	....	....	....
1988-89	Guelph	OHL	53	25	22	5	3047	194	0	3.82	7	3	4	421	29	0	4.13

PEETERS, PETER (PETE)

Goaltender. Catches left. 6'1", 195 lbs. Born, Edmonton, Alta., August 17, 1957.
(Philadelphia's 9th choice, 135th over-all, in 1977 Amateur Draft).

			Regular Season								Playoffs						
Season	Club	Lea	GP	W	L	T	Mins	GA	SO	Avg	GP	W	L	Mins	GA	SO	Avg
1975-76	Medicine Hat	WHL	37	....	....	....	2074	147	0	4.25	....	....	....	....	....	....	....
1976-77	Medicine Hat	WHL	62	....	....	....	3423	232	1	4.07	4	....	....	204	17	0	5.00
1977-78	Milwaukee	IHL	32	....	....	....	1698	93	1	3.29	....	....	....	....	....	....	....
	Maine	AHL	17	....	....	....	855	40	1	2.80	11	....	....	562	25	*1	2.67
1978-79	**Philadelphia**	**NHL**	5	1	2	1	280	16	0	3.43	....	....	....	....	....	....	....
ab	Maine	AHL	35	25	6	3	2067	100	*2	*2.90	6	5	0	329	15	0	2.74
1979-80	**Philadelphia**	**NHL**	40	29	5	5	2373	108	1	2.73	13	8	5	799	37	1	2.78
1980-81	**Philadelphia**	**NHL**	40	22	12	5	2333	115	2	2.96	3	2	1	180	12	0	4.00
1981-82	**Philadelphia**	**NHL**	44	23	18	3	2591	160	0	3.71	4	1	2	220	17	0	4.64
1982-83cd	**Boston**	**NHL**	62	40	11	9	*3611	142	*8	*2.36	17	9	8	1024	61	1	3.57
1983-84	**Boston**	**NHL**	50	29	16	2	2868	151	0	3.16	3	0	3	180	10	0	3.33
1984-85	**Boston**	**NHL**	51	19	26	4	2975	172	1	3.47	1	0	1	60	4	0	4.00
1985-86	**Boston**	**NHL**	8	3	4	1	485	31	0	3.84	....	....	....	....	....	....	....
	Washington	**NHL**	34	19	11	3	2021	113	1	3.35	9	5	4	544	24	0	2.65
1986-87	**Washington**	**NHL**	37	17	11	4	2002	107	0	3.21	3	1	2	180	9	0	3.00
	Binghamton	AHL	4	3	0	0	245	4	1	0.98	....	....	....	....	....	....	....
1987-88	**Washington**	**NHL**	35	14	12	5	1896	88	2	*2.78	12	7	5	654	34	0	3.12
1988-89	**Washington**	**NHL**	33	20	7	3	1854	88	4	2.85	6	2	4	359	24	0	4.01
	NHL Totals		439	236	135	45	25289	1291	19	3.06	71	35	35	4200	232	2	3.31

a AHL Second All-Star Team (1979)
b Shared Harry "Hap" Holmes Memorial Trophy (AHL's Leading Goaltenders) with Robbie Moore (1979)
c NHL First All-Star Team (1983)
d Won Vezina Trophy (1983)

Played in NHL All-Star Game (1980, 1981, 1983, 1984)

Traded to **Boston** by **Philadelphia** for Brad McCrimmon, June 9, 1982. Traded to **Washington** by **Boston** for Pat Riggin, November 14, 1985. Signed as a free agent by **Philadelphia,** June 17,1989.

PERREAULT, JOCELYN

Goaltender. Catches right. 6'4", 210 lbs. Born, Montreal, Que., January 8, 1966.

			Regular Season								Playoffs						
Season	Club	Lea	GP	W	L	T	Mins	GA	SO	Avg	GP	W	L	Mins	GA	SO	Avg
1985-86	St. Laurent	CEGEP	11	7	2	0	582	30	0	3.09	...	...	...	...	...	...	...
1986-87	Sherbrooke	AHL	13	8	4	0	722	40	0	3.32	6	3	0	258	9	0	2.09
1987-88a	Sherbrooke	AHL	25	8	11	1	1244	77	0	3.71	1	0	0	30	2	0	4.00
1988-89	Hershey	AHL	8	3	3	1	394	22	0	3.35	....	....	....	....	....	....	....
	Indianapolis	IHL	5	0	3	0	214	22	0	6.17	....	....	....	....	....	....	....

a Shared Harry "Hap" Holmes Memorial Trophy (AHL Leading Goaltender) with Vincent Riendeau (1988)

Signed as a free agent by **Montreal**, September 30, 1986.

PERRY, ALAN

Goaltender. Catches right. 5'8", 155 lbs. Born, Providence, RI, August 30, 1966.
(St. Louis' 5th choice, 56th over-all, in 1984 Entry Draft).

			Regular Season								Playoffs						
Season	Club	Lea	GP	W	L	T	Mins	GA	SO	Avg	GP	W	L	Mins	GA	SO	Avg
1984-85	Windsor	OHL	34	15	17	0	1905	135	1	4.25	2	0	2	120	14	0	7.00
1985-86	Windsor	OHL	42	28	10	2	2424	131	3	3.24	13	8	5	697	51	0	4.39
1986-87	Peoria	IHL	6	0	5	0	312	36	0	6.92	....	....	....	....	....	....	....
	Belleville	OHL	15	7	7	1	843	64	0	4.56	6	2	4	367	18	1	2.94
1987-88	Peoria	IHL	20	7	10	0	1069	77		4.32	2	0	1	68	6		5.29
1988-89	Indianapolis	IHL	47	14	22	0	2266	195	0	5.16	....	....	....	....	....	....	....

PIETRANGELO, FRANK (peter-AN-gelo)

Goaltender. Catches left. 5'10", 182 lbs. Born, Niagara Falls, Ont., December 17, 1964.
(Pittsburgh's 4th choice, 64th over-all, in 1983 Entry Draft).

			Regular Season								Playoffs						
Season	Club	Lea	GP	W	L	T	Mins	GA	SO	Avg	GP	W	L	Mins	GA	SO	Avg
1982-83	U. Minnesota	WCHA	25	15	6	1	1348	80	1	3.55	....	....	....	....	....	....	....
1983-84	U. Minnesota	WCHA	20	13	7	0	1141	66	0	3.47	....	....	....	....	....	....	....
1984-85	U. Minnesota	WCHA	17	8	3	3	912	52	0	3.42	....	....	....	....	....	....	....
1985-86	U. Minnesota	WCHA	23	15	7	0	1284	76	0	3.55	....	....	....	....	....	....	....
1986-87	Muskegon	IHL	35	23	11	0	2090	119	2	3.42	15	10	4	923	46	0	2.99
1987-88	**Pittsburgh**	**NHL**	21	9	11	0	1207	80	1	3.98	....	....	....	....	....	....	....
	Muskegon	IHL	15	11	3	1	868	43		2.97	....	....	....	....	....	....	....
1988-89	**Pittsburgh**	**NHL**	15	5	3	0	669	45	0	4.04	....	....	....	....	....	....	....
	Muskegon	IHL	13	10	1	0	760	38	1	3.00	9	*8	1	566	29	0	3.07
	NHL Totals		36	14	14	0	1876	125	1	4.00	....	....	....	....	....	....	....

PUPPA, DAREN (POO puh)

Goaltender. Catches right. 6'3", 191 lbs. Born, Kirkland Lake, Ont., March 23, 1963.
(Buffalo's 7th choice, 76th over-all, in 1983 Entry Draft).

			Regular Season								Playoffs						
Season	Club	Lea	GP	W	L	T	Mins	GA	SO	Avg	GP	W	L	Mins	GA	SO	Avg
1983-84	RPI	ECAC	32	24	6	0	....	....	....	2.94	....	....	....	....	....	....	....
1984-85	RPI	ECAC	32	31	1	0	1830	78	0	2.56	....	....	....	....	....	....	....
1985-86	**Buffalo**	**NHL**	**7**	**3**	**4**	**0**	**401**	**21**	**1**	**3.14**	....	....	....	....	....	....	....
	Rochester	AHL	20	8	11	0	1092	79	0	4.34	....	....	....	....	....	....	....
1986-87	**Buffalo**	**NHL**	**3**	**0**	**2**	**1**	**185**	**13**	**0**	**4.22**	....	....	....	....	....	....	....
1986-87a	Rochester	AHL	57	33	14	0	3129	146	1	2.80	16	10	6	944	48	1	3.05
1987-88	**Buffalo**	**NHL**	**17**	**8**	**6**	**1**	**874**	**61**	**0**	**4.19**	**3**	**1**	**1**	**142**	**11**	**0**	**4.65**
	Rochester	AHL	26	14	8	2	1415	65	2	2.76	2	0	1	108	5	0	2.78
1988-89	**Buffalo**	**NHL**	**37**	**17**	**10**	**6**	**1908**	**107**	**1**	**3.36**	....	....	....	....	....	....	....
	NHL Totals		**64**	**28**	**22**	**8**	**3368**	**202**	**2**	**3.60**	**3**	**1**	**1**	**142**	**11**	**0**	**4.65**

a AHL First All-Star Team (1987)

RACINE, BRUCE

Goaltender. Catches left. 6', 160 lbs. Born, Cornwall, Ont., August 9, 1966.
(Pittsburgh's 3rd choice, 58th over-all, in 1985 Entry Draft).

			Regular Season								Playoffs						
Season	Club	Lea	GP	W	L	T	Mins	GA	SO	Avg	GP	W	L	Mins	GA	SO	Avg
1984-85	Northeastern	H.E.	26	11	14	1	1615	103	1	3.83	....	....	....	....	....	....	....
1985-86	Northeastern	H.E.	32	17	14	1	1920	147	0	4.56	....	....	....	....	....	....	....
1986-87ab	Northeastern	H.E.	33	12	18	3	1966	133	0	4.06	....	....	....	....	....	....	....
1987-88b	Northeastern	H.E.	30	15	11	4	1808	108	1	3.58	....	....	....	....	....	....	....
1988-89	Muskegon	IHL	51	*37	11	0	*3039	184	*3	3.63	5	4	1	300	15	0	3.00

a Hockey East First All-Star Team (1987)
b NCAA East First All-American Team (1987, 1988)

RALPH, JAMES RICHARD (JIM)

Goaltender. Catches right. 5'11", 165 lbs. Born, Sault Ste. Marie, Ont., May 13 1962.
(Chicago's 12th choice, 162nd over-all, in 1980 Entry Draft).

			Regular Season								Playoffs						
Season	Club	Lea	GP	W	L	T	Mins	GA	SO	Avg	GP	W	L	Mins	GA	SO	Avg
1979-80	Ottawa	OHA	45	26	12	2	2451	171	0	4.19	4	1	1	210	17	0	4.86
1980-81a	Ottawa	OHA	57	38	14	2	3266	202	*2	3.71	7	2	4	367	23	0	3.77
1981-82b	Ottawa	OHL	53	35	16	2	3211	185	1	3.45	17	8	8	999	67	0	4.02
1982-83	Springfield	AHL	26	....	....	....	1498	105	0	4.21	....	....	....	....	....	....	....
	Colorado	CHL	5	3	2	0	300	18	0	3.60	....	....	....	....	....	....	....
1983-84	Springfield	AHL	9	5	3	0	479	42	0	5.26	....	....	....	....	....	....	....
	Baltimore	AHL	25	12	10	2	1455	87	0	3.59	2	....	....	82	6	0	4.38
1984-85	Milwaukee	IHL	19	3	13	2	1072	78	0	4.37	....	....	....	....	....	....	....
1985-86	Nova Scotia	AHL	9	2	5	2	549	46	0	5.03	....	....	....	....	....	....	....
	Milwaukee	IHL	14	7	6	0	819	58	1	4.25	....	....	....	....	....	....	....
1986-87	Milwaukee	IHL	2	0	2	0	120	9	0	4.50	....	....	....	....	....	....	....
1987-88	Newmarket	AHL	14	1	6	1	550	45	0	4.91	....	....	....	....	....	....	....
1988-89	Newmarket	AHL	17	4	5	1	721	48	0	3.99	5	1	3	269	23	0	5.13

a OHA First All-Star Team (1981)
b OHL Second All-Star Team (1982)

RANFORD, BILL

Goaltender. Catches left. 5'10", 170 lbs. Born, Brandon, Man., December 14, 1966.
(Boston's 2nd choice, 52nd overall, in 1985 Entry Draft).

			Regular Season								Playoffs						
Season	Club	Lea	GP	W	L	T	Mins	GA	SO	Avg	GP	W	L	Mins	GA	SO	Avg
1983-84	N. Westminster	WHL	27	10	14	0	1450	130	0	5.38	1	0	0	27	2	0	4.44
1984-85	N. Westminster	WHL	38	19	17	0	2034	142	0	4.19	7	2	3	309	26	0	5.05
1985-86	N. Westminster	WHL	53	17	29	1	2791	225	0	4.84	....	....	....	....	....	....	....
	Boston	**NHL**	**4**	**3**	**1**	**0**	**240**	**10**	**0**	**2.50**	**2**	**0**	**2**	**120**	**7**	**0**	**3.50**
1986-87	**Boston**	**NHL**	**41**	**16**	**20**	**2**	**2234**	**124**	**3**	**3.33**	**2**	**0**	**2**	**123**	**8**	**0**	**3.90**
	Moncton	AHL	3	3	0	0	180	6	0	2.00	....	....	....	....	....	....	....
1987-88	**Edmonton**	**NHL**	**6**	**3**	**0**	**2**	**325**	**16**	**0**	**2.95**	....	....	....	....	....	....	....
	Maine	AHL	51	27	16	6	2856	165	1	3.47	....	....	....	....	....	....	....
1988-89	**Edmonton**	**NHL**	**29**	**15**	**8**	**2**	**1509**	**88**	**1**	**3.50**	....	....	....	....	....	....	....
	NHL Totals		**80**	**37**	**29**	**6**	**4308**	**238**	**4**	**3.31**	**4**	**0**	**4**	**243**	**15**	**0**	**3.70**

Traded to **Edmonton** by **Boston** with Geoff Courtnall and future considerations for Andy Moog, March 8, 1988.

RAYMOND, ALAIN

Goaltender. Catches left. 5'10", 177 lbs. Born, Rimouski, Que., June 24, 1965.
(Washington's 11th choice, 224th over-all, in 1983 Entry Draft).

			Regular Season								Playoffs						
Season	Club	Lea	GP	W	L	T	Mins	GA	SO	Avg	GP	W	L	Mins	GA	SO	Avg
1983-84	Trois Rivières	QMJHL	53	18	25	0	2725	223	3	4.91	....	....	....	....	....	....	....
1984-85a	Trois Rivères	QMJHL	58	29	26	1	3295	220	2	4.01	7	3	5	438	32	0	4.38
1985-86	Cdn. Olympic	....	46	25	18	3	2571	151	4	3.52	....	....	....	....	....	....	....
1986-87b	Fort Wayne	IHL	45	23	16	0	2433	134	1	3.30	6	2	3	320	23	0	4.31
1987-88	**Washington**	**NHL**	**1**	**0**	**1**	**0**	**40**	**2**	**0**	**3.00**	....	....	....	....	....	....	....
	Fort Wayne	IHL	40	20	15	3	2271	142		3.75	2	0	1	67	7		6.27
1988-89	Baltimore	AHL	41	14	22	2	2301	162	0	4.22	....	....	....	....	....	....	....
	NHL Totals		**1**	**0**	**1**	**0**	**40**	**2**	**0**	**3.00**	....	....	....	....	....	....	....

a QMJHL Second All-Star Team (1985).
b Shared James Norris Memorial Trophy (IHL's Top Goaltender) with Michel Dufour (1987)

REAUGH, DARYL (RAY)

Goaltender. Catches left. 6'4", 200 lbs. Born, Prince George, B.C., February 13, 1965.
(Edmonton's 2nd choice, 42nd over-all, in 1984 Entry Draft).

			Regular Season								Playoffs						
Season	Club	Lea	GP	W	L	T	Mins	GA	SO	Avg	GP	W	L	Mins	GA	SO	Avg
1982-83	Cowichan	BCJHL	32	....	....	....	1673	191	0	5.96	....	....	....	....	....	....	....
1983-84	Kamloops	WHL	55	....	....	....	2748	199	1	4.34	17	....	....	972	57	0	3.52
1984-85	**Edmonton**	**NHL**	**1**	**0**	**1**	**0**	**60**	**5**	**0**	**5.00**	....	....	....	....	....	....	....
a	Kamloops	WAL	49	....	....	....	2749	170	2	3.71	14	....	....	787	56	0	4.27
1985-86	Nova Scotia	AHL	38	15	18	4	2205	156	0	4.24	....	....	....	....	....	....	....
1986-87	Nova Scotia	AHL	46	19	22	0	2637	163	1	3.71	2	0	2	120	13	0	6.50
1987-88	**Edmonton**	**NHL**	**6**	**1**	**1**	**0**	**176**	**14**	**0**	**4.77**	....	....	....	....	....	....	....
	Nova Scotia	AHL	8	2	5	0	443	33	0	4.47	....	....	....	....	....	....	....
	Milwaukee	IHL	9	0	8	0	493	44		5.35	....	....	....	....	....	....	....
1988-89	Cape Breton	AHL	13	3	10	0	778	72	0	5.55	....	....	....	....	....	....	....
	NHL Totals		**7**	**1**	**2**	**0**	**236**	**19**	**0**	**4.83**	....	....	....	....	....	....	....

a WHL First All-Star Team, West Division (1985).

REDDICK, ELDON

Goaltender. Catches left. 5'8", 170 lbs. Born, Halifax, N.S., October 6, 1964.

			Regular Season								Playoffs						
Season	Club	Lea	GP	W	L	T	Mins	GA	SO	Avg	GP	W	L	Mins	GA	SO	Avg
1982-83	Nanaimo	WHL	66	19	38	1	3549	383	0	6.46	....	....	....	....	....	....	....
1983-84	N. Westminster	WHL	50	24	22	2	2930	215	0	4.40	9	4	5	542	53	0	5.87
1984-85	Brandon	WHL	47	14	30	1	2585	243	0	5.64	....	....	....	....	....	....	....
1985-86	Fort Wayne	IHL	29	15	11	0	1674	86	3	3.00	....	....	....	....	....	....	....
1986-87	**Winnipeg**	**NHL**	**48**	**21**	**21**	**4**	**2762**	**149**	**0**	**3.24**	**3**	**0**	**2**	**166**	**10**	**0**	**3.61**
1987-88	**Winnipeg**	**NHL**	**28**	**9**	**13**	**3**	**1487**	**102**	**0**	**4.12**	....	....	....	....	....	....	....
	Moncton	AHL	9	2	6	1	545	26	0	2.86	....	....	....	....	....	....	....
1988-89	**Winnipeg**	**NHL**	**41**	**11**	**17**	**7**	**2109**	**144**	**0**	**4.10**	....	....	....	....	....	....	....
	NHL Totals		**117**	**41**	**51**	**14**	**6358**	**395**	**0**	**3.73**	**3**	**0**	**2**	**166**	**10**	**0**	**3.61**

Signed as a free agent by **Winnipeg**, September 27, 1985.

REESE, JEFF

Goaltender. Catches right. 5'9", 150 lbs. Born, Brantford, Ont., March 24, 1966.
(Toronto's 3rd choice, 67th over-all, in 1984 Entry Draft).

			Regular Season								Playoffs						
Season	Club	Lea	GP	W	L	T	Mins	GA	SO	Avg	GP	W	L	Mins	GA	SO	Avg
1983-84	London	OHL	43	18	19	0	2308	173		4.50	6	3	3	327	27	0	4.95
1984-85	London	OHL	50	31	15	1	2878	186	1	3.88	8	5	2	440	20	1	2.73
1985-86	London	OHL	57	25	26	3	3281	215	0	3.93	5	0	4	299	25	0	5.02
1986-87	Newmarket	AHL	50	11	29	0	2822	193	1	4.10	....	....	....	....	....	....	....
1987-88	**Toronto**	**NHL**	**5**	**1**	**2**	**1**	**249**	**17**	**0**	**4.10**	....	....	....	....	....	....	....
	Newmarket	AHL	28	10	14	3	1587	103	0	3.89	....	....	....	....	....	....	....
1988-89	**Toronto**	**NHL**	**10**	**2**	**6**	**1**	**486**	**40**	**0**	**4.94**	....	....	....	....	....	....	....
	Newmarket	AHL	37	17	14	3	2072	132	0	3.82	....	....	....	....	....	....	....
	NHL Totals		**15**	**3**	**8**	**2**	**735**	**57**	**0**	**4.65**	....	....	....	....	....	....	....

REID, JOHN

Goaltender. Catches right. 5'11", 202 lbs. Born, Windsor, Ont., February 18, 1967.
(Chicago's 8th choice, 158th over-all, in 1985 Entry Draft).

			Regular Season								Playoffs						
Season	Club	Lea	GP	W	L	T	Mins	GA	SO	Avg	GP	W	L	Mins	GA	SO	Avg
1984-85	Belleville	OHL	31	16	6	0	1443	92	0	3.83	2	1	0	79	4	0	3.04
1985-86	North Bay	OHL	47	28	14	2	2627	164	1	3.75	10	5	4	577	37	0	3.85
1986-87	North Bay	OHL	47	33	12	1	2737	142	1	3.11	24	14	10	1496	92	0	3.69
1987-88	Colorado	IHL	32	15	14	1	1673	117		4.20	....	....	....	....	....	....	....
	Saginaw	IHL	5	3	1	0	260	11		2.54	1	0	1	58	5		5.17
1988-89	Indianapolis	IHL	5	2	2	0	244	16	0	3.93	....	....	....	....	....	....	....
	Saginaw	IHL	12	6	3	0	633	37	0	3.51	....	....	....	....	....	....	....

REIMER, MARK (RIGH-mur)

Goaltender. Catches left. 5'11", 170 lbs. Born, Calgary, Alta., March 23, 1967.
(Detroit's 5th choice, 74th overall, in 1987 Entry Draft).

			Regular Season								Playoffs						
Season	Club	Lea	GP	W	L	T	Mins	GA	SO	Avg	GP	W	L	Mins	GA	SO	Avg
1984-85	Saskatoon	WHL	2	2	0	0	120	7	0	3.50	....	....	....	....	....	....	....
1985-86	Saskatoon	WHL	41	17	18	3	2362	192	0	4.88	5	....	....	300	25	0	5.00
1986-87	Saskatoon	WHL	42	24	15	2	2442	141	1	3.46	6	....	....	360	20	0	3.33
1987-88	Portland	WHL	38	13	23	2	2268	208	0	5.50	....	....	....	....	....	....	....
	Flint	IHL	5	0	3	0	169	22	0	7.86	....	....	....	....	....	....	....
	Adirondack	AHL	8	6	1	0	459	24	0	3.14	1	0	0	20	0	0	0.00
1988-89	Adirondack	AHL	18	5	6	3	900	64	0	4.27	....	....	....	....	....	....	....
	Flint	IHL	17	5	8	0	1022	83	0	4.87	....	....	....	....	....	....	....

REIN, KENTON (RIGHN)

Goaltender. Catches left. 5'11', 195 lbs. Born, Saskatoon, Sask., September 12, 1967.
(Buffalo's 11th choice, 194th overall, in 1986 Entry Draft).

			Regular Season								Playoffs						
Season	Club	Lea	GP	W	L	T	Mins	GA	SO	Avg	GP	W	L	Mins	GA	SO	Avg
1985-86	Prince Albert	WHL	23	18	3	0	1302	71	0	3.27	6	5	0	308	4	2	.78
1986-87a	Prince Albert	WHL	51	29	18	3	2996	159	0	3.18	8	3	5	443	31	0	4.20
1987-88	Flint	IHL	1	0	1	0	20	3		9.00	....	....	....	....	....	....	....
1988-89	Rochester	AHL	15	5	6	2	676	39	2	3.46	....	....	....	....	....	....	....
	Flint	IHL	8	1	6	0	439	29	0	3.96	....	....	....	....	....	....	....

a WHL First All-Star Team (1987)

RHODES, DAMIAN

Goaltender. Catches left. 6', 165 lbs. Born, St. Paul, MN, May 28, 1969.
(Toronto's 6th choice, 112th overall, in 1987 Entry Draft).

			Regular Season								Playoffs						
Season	Club	Lea	GP	W	L	T	Mins	GA	SO	Avg	GP	W	L	Mins	GA	SO	Avg
1987-88	Michigan Tech	WCHA	29	16	10	1	1625	114	0	4.20	....	....	....	....	....	....	....
1988-89	Michigan Tech	WCHA	37	15	22	0	2216	163	0	4.41	....	....	....	....	....	....	....

RICHTER, MIKE

Goaltender. Catches left. 5'11", 185 lbs. Born, Philadelphia, PA, September 22, 1966.
(NY Rangers' 2nd choice, 28th over-all, in 1985 Entry Draft.)

			Regular Season								Playoffs						
Season	Club	Lea	GP	W	L	T	Mins	GA	SO	Avg	GP	W	L	Mins	GA	SO	Avg
1985-86a	U. Wisconsin	WCHA	24	14	9	0	1394	92	1	3.96	....	....	....	....	....	....	....
1986-87b	U. Wisconsin	WCHA	36	19	16	1	2136	126	0	3.54	....	....	....	....	....	....	....
1987-88	Colorado	IHL	22	16	5	0	1298	68		3.14	10	5	3	536	35		3.92
	U.S. National	....	29	17	7	2	1559	86	0	3.31	....	....	....	....	....	....	....
	U.S. Olympic	....	4	2	2	0	230	15	0	3.91	....	....	....	....	....	....	....
1988-89	Denver	IHL	*57	23	26	0	3031	217	1	4.30	4	0	4	210	21	0	6.00

a WCHA Rookie of the Year (1986)

RIENDEAU, VINCENT (ree-en-DOH)

Goaltender. Catches left. 5'10", 185 lbs. Born, St. Hyacinthe, Que., April 20, 1966.

			Regular Season								Playoffs						
Season	Club	Lea	GP	W	L	T	Mins	GA	SO	Avg	GP	W	L	Mins	GA	SO	Avg
1985-86a	Drummondville	QMJHL	57	33	20	3	3336	215	2	3.87	23	10	13	1271	106	1	5.00
1986-87b	Sherbrooke	AHL	41	25	14	0	2363	114	2	2.89	13	8	5	742	47	0	3.80
1987-88	**Montreal**	**NHL**	**1**	**0**	**0**	**0**	**36**	**5**	**0**	**8.33**	....	....	....	....	....	....	....
c	Sherbrooke	AHL	44	27	13	3	2521	112	*4	*2.67	2	0	2	127	7	0	3.31
1988-89	**St. Louis**	**NHL**	**32**	**11**	**15**	**5**	**1842**	**108**	**0**	**3.52**	....	....	....	....	....	....	....
	NHL Totals		**33**	**11**	**15**	**5**	**1878**	**113**	**0**	**3.61**	....	....	....	....	....	....	....

a QMJHL Second All-Star Team (1986)
b Won Harry "Hap" Holmes Memorial Trophy (AHL Leading Goaltender) (1987)
c Shared Harry "Hap" Holmes Memorial Trophy (AHL Leading Goaltender) with Jocelyn Perreault (1988)

Signed as a free agent by **Montreal**, October 9, 1985. Traded to **St. Louis** by **Montreal** with Sergio Momesso for Jocelyn Lemieux, Darrell May and St. Louis' second round choice (Patrice Brisebois) in the 1989 Entry Draft, August 9, 1988.

ROSATI, MICHAEL

Goaltender. Catches left. 5'10", 170 lbs. Born, Toronto, Ont., January 7, 1968.
(N Y Rangers' 6th choice, 131st overall, in 1988 Entry Draft).

			Regular Season								Playoffs						
Season	Club	Lea	GP	W	L	T	Mins	GA	SO	Avg	GP	W	L	Mins	GA	SO	Avg
1987-88	Hamilton	OHL	62	29	25	3	3468	233	1	4.03	14	8	6	833	66	0	4.75
1988-89	Niagara Falls	OHL	52	*28	15	2	2339	174	1	4.45	16	10	4	861	62	0	4.32

ROUSSEL, DOMINIC

Goaltender. Catches left. 6'1", 190 lbs. Born, Hull, Que., February 22, 1970.
(Philadelphia's 4th choice, 63rd overall, in 1988 Entry Draft).

			Regular Season								Playoffs						
Season	Club	Lea	GP	W	L	T	Mins	GA	SO	Avg	GP	W	L	Mins	GA	SO	Avg
1987-88	Trois Rivieres	QMJHL	51	18	25	4	2905	251	0	5.18	...	....	....	....	....	....	....
1988-89	Shawinigan	QMJHL	46	24	15	2	2555	171	0	4.02	10	6	4	638	36	0	3.39

ROY, PATRICK (roo AH)

Goaltender. Catches left. 6', 174 lbs. Born, Quebec City, Que., October 5, 1965.
(Montreal's 4th choice, 51st over-all, in 1984 Entry Draft).

			Regular Season								Playoffs						
Season	Club	Lea	GP	W	L	T	Mins	GA	SO	Avg	GP	W	L	Mins	GA	SO	Avg
1982-83	Granby	QMJHL	54	....	....	....	2808	293	0	6.26	....	....	....	....	....	....	....
1983-84	Granby	QMJHL	61	29	29	1	3585	265	0	4.44	4	0	4	244	22	0	5.41
1984-85	Granby	QMJHL	44	16	25	1	2463	228	0	5.55	....	....	....	....	....	....	....
	Sherbrooke	AHL	1	1	0	0	60	4	0	4.00	12	10	3	769	37	0	2.89
	Montreal	**NHL**	**1**	**1**	**0**	**0**	**20**	**0**	**0**	**0.00**	....	....	....	....	....	....	....
1985-86ab	**Montreal**	**NHL**	**47**	**23**	**19**	**3**	**2651**	**148**	**1**	**3.35**	**20**	**15**	**5**	**1218**	**39**	**1**	**1.92**
1986-87c	**Montreal**	**NHL**	**46**	**22**	**16**	**6**	**2686**	**131**	**1**	**2.93**	**6**	**4**	**2**	**330**	**22**	**0**	**4.00**
1987-88cd	**Montreal**	**NHL**	**45**	**23**	**12**	**9**	**2586**	**125**	**3**	**2.90**	**8**	**3**	**4**	**430**	**24**	**0**	**3.35**
1988-89cefg	**Montreal**	**NHL**	**48**	**33**	**5**	**6**	**2744**	**113**	**4**	***2.47**	**19**	**13**	**6**	**1206**	**42**	**2**	***2.09**
	NHL Totals		**187**	**102**	**52**	**24**	**10687**	**519**	**9**	**2.91**	**53**	**35**	**17**	**3184**	**127**	**3**	**2.39**

a Won Conn Smythe Trophy (1986)
b NHL All-Rookie Team (1986)
c Shared William Jennings Trophy with Brian Hayward (1987, 1988, 1989)
d NHL Second All-Star Team (1988)
e Won Vezina Trophy (1989)
f NHL First All-Star Team (1989)
g Won Trico Goaltending Award (1989)

Played in NHL All-Star Game (1988)

ST. LAURENT, SAM (sa luh RAH)

Goaltender. Catches left. 5'10", 190 lbs. Born, Arvida, Que., February 16, 1959.

			Regular Season								Playoffs						
Season	Club	Lea	GP	W	L	T	Mins	GA	SO	Avg	GP	W	L	Mins	GA	SO	Avg
1977-78	Chicoutimi	QJHL	60	....	....	....	3251	351	0	6.46	....	....	....	....	....	....	....
1978-79	Chicoutimi	QJHL	70	....	....	....	3806	290	0	4.57	1	....	....	47	8	0	10.21
1979-80	Maine	AHL	5	2	1	0	229	17	0	4.45	....	....	....	....	....	....	....
	Toledo	IHL	38	....	....	....	2143	138	2	3.86	4	....	....	239	24	0	6.03
1980-81	Maine	AHL	7	3	3	0	363	28	0	4.63	....	....	....	....	....	....	....
	Toledo	IHL	30	....	....	....	1614	113	1	4.20	....	....	....	....	....	....	....
1981-82	Toledo	IHL	4	....	....	....	248	11	0	2.66	....	....	....	....	....	....	....
	Maine	AHL	25	15	7	1	1396	76	0	3.27	4	1	3	240	18	0	4.50
1982-83	Maine	AHL	30	....	....	....	1739	109	0	3.76	17	....	....	1012	54	0	3.20
1983-84	Maine	AHL	38	14	18	4	2158	145	0	4.03	12	9	2	708	32	1	2.71
1984-85a	Maine	AHL	55	26	22	7	3245	168	4	3.11	10	5	5	656	45	0	4.12
1985-86	**New Jersey**	**NHL**	**4**	**2**	**1**	**0**	**188**	**13**	**1**	**4.15**	....	....	....	....	....	....	....
	Maine	AHL	50	24	20	4	2862	161	1	3.38	....	....	....	....	....	....	....
1986-87	**Detroit**	**NHL**	**6**	**1**	**2**	**2**	**342**	**16**	**0**	**2.81**	....	....	....	....	....	....	....
	Adirondack	AHL	25	7	13	0	1397	98	1	4.21	3	0	2	105	10	0	5.71
1987-88	**Detroit**	**NHL**	**6**	**2**	**2**	**0**	**294**	**16**	**0**	**3.27**	**1**	**0**	**0**	**10**	**1**	**0**	**6.00**
	Adirondack	AHL	32	12	14	4	1826	104	2	3.42	1	0	1	59	6	0	6.10
1988-89	**Detroit**	**NHL**	**4**	**1**	**1**	**0**	**141**	**9**	**0**	**3.83**	....	....	....	....	....	....	....
b	Adirondack	AHL	34	20	11	3	2054	113	0	3.30	16	*11	5	956	47	*2	*2.95
	NHL Totals		**20**	**6**	**6**	**2**	**965**	**54**	**1**	**3.36**	**1**	**0**	**0**	**10**	**1**	**0**	**6.00**

a AHL Second All-Star Team (1985)
b Won Jack Butterfield Trophy (Playoff MVP-AHL) (1989)

Signed as a free agent by **Philadelphia**, October 10, 1979. Traded to **Detroit** by **New Jersey** for Steve Richmond, August 18, 1986.

SANDS, MICHAEL (MIKE)

Goaltender. Catches left. 5'9", 170 lbs. Born, Mississauga, Ont., April 6, 1963.
(Minnesota's 3rd choice, 31st over-all, in 1981 Entry Draft).

			Regular Season								Playoffs						
Season	Club	Lea	GP	W	L	T	Mins	GA	SO	Avg	GP	W	L	Mins	GA	SO	Avg
1980-81	Sudbury	OHA	50	15	28	2	2789	236	0	5.08	....	....	....	....	....	....	....
1981-82	Sudbury	OHL	53	13	33	1	2854	265	1	5.57	....	....	....	....	....	....	....
	Nashville	CHL	7	3	3	1	380	26	0	4.11	....	....	....	....	....	....	....
1982-83	Sudbury	OHL	43	11	27	0	2320	204	1	5.28	....	....	....	....	....	....	....
	Birmingham	CHL	4	0	4	0	169	14	0	4.97	....	....	....	....	....	....	....
1983-84	Salt Lake	CHL	23	7	12	1	1145	93	0	4.87	....	....	....	....	....	....	....
1984-85	**Minnesota**	**NHL**	**3**	**0**	**3**	**0**	**139**	**14**	**0**	**6.04**	....	....	....	....	....	....	....
	Springfield	AHL	46	23	17	3	2589	140	2	3.24	3	0	3	130	15	0	6.92
1985-86	Springfield	AHL	27	8	15	1	1490	94	0	3.79	....	....	....	....	....	....	....
1986-87	**Minnesota**	**NHL**	**3**	**0**	**2**	**0**	**163**	**12**	**0**	**4.42**	....	....	....	....	....	....	....
	Springfield	AHL	19	4	10	0	1048	77	0	4.41	....	....	....	....	....	....	....
1987-88	Baltimore	AHL	4	0	4	0	185	22	0	7.14	....	....	....	....	....	....	....
	Kalamazoo	IHL	3	0	2	1	184	16		5.22	....	....	....	....	....	....	....
1988-89	Cdn. National	....	21	6	13	1	1012	75	0	4.45	....	....	....	....	....	....	....
	NHL Totals		**6**	**0**	**5**	**0**	**302**	**26**	**0**	**5.17**	....	....	....	....	....	....	....

SAUVE, ROBERT (SOH-vay)

Goaltender. Catches left. 5'8", 175 lbs. Born, Ste. Genevieve, Que., June 17, 1955.
(Buffalo's 1st choice, 17th over-all, in 1975 Amateur Draft).

			Regular Season								Playoffs						
Season	Club	Lea	GP	W	L	T	Mins	GA	SO	Avg	GP	W	L	Mins	GA	SO	Avg
1973-74	Laval	QJHL	61	....	....	....	3621	341	0	5.65	5	....	....	300	19	0	3.80
1974-75	Laval	QJHL	57	....	....	....	3403	287	0	5.06	16	....	....	960	81	0	5.06
1975-76	Providence	AHL	14	....	....	....	848	44	0	3.11	....	....	....	....	....	....	....
	Charlotte	SHL	17	....	....	....	979	36	2	2.21	7	....	....	420	10	*2	*1.43
1976-77	Rhode Island	AHL	25	....	....	....	1346	94	0	4.14	....	....	....	....	....	....	....
	Buffalo	**NHL**	**4**	**1**	**2**	**0**	**184**	**11**	**0**	**3.59**	....	....	....	....	....	....	....
	Hershey	AHL	9	....	....	....	539	38	0	4.23	....	....	....	....	....	....	....
1977-78	**Buffalo**	**NHL**	**11**	**6**	**2**	**0**	**480**	**20**	**0**	**2.50**	....	....	....	....	....	....	....
	Hershey	AHL	16	....	....	....	872	59	0	4.05	....	....	....	....	....	....	....
1978-79	Hershey	AHL	5	....	....	....	278	14	0	3.02	....	....	....	....	....	....	....
	Buffalo	**NHL**	**29**	**10**	**10**	**7**	**1610**	**100**	**0**	**3.73**	**3**	**1**	**2**	**181**	**9**	**0**	**2.98**
1979-80a	**Buffalo**	**NHL**	**32**	**20**	**8**	**4**	**1880**	**74**	**4**	***2.36**	**8**	**6**	**2**	**501**	**17**	***2**	***2.04**
1980-81	**Buffalo**	**NHL**	**35**	**16**	**10**	**9**	**2100**	**111**	**2**	**3.17**	....	....	....	....	....	....	....
1981-82	**Buffalo**	**NHL**	**14**	**6**	**1**	**5**	**760**	**35**	**0**	**2.76**	....	....	....	....	....	....	....
	Detroit	**NHL**	**41**	**11**	**25**	**4**	**2365**	**165**	**0**	**4.19**	....	....	....	....	....	....	....
1982-83	**Buffalo**	**NHL**	**54**	**25**	**20**	**7**	**3110**	**179**	**1**	**3.45**	**10**	**6**	**4**	**545**	**28**	***2**	**3.08**
1983-84	**Buffalo**	**NHL**	**40**	**22**	**13**	**4**	**2375**	**138**	**0**	**3.49**	**2**	**0**	**1**	**41**	**5**	**0**	**7.32**
1984-85b	**Buffalo**	**NHL**	**27**	**13**	**10**	**3**	**1564**	**84**	**0**	**3.22**	....	....	....	....	....	....	....
1985-86	**Chicago**	**NHL**	**38**	**19**	**13**	**2**	**2099**	**138**	**0**	**3.95**	**2**	**0**	**2**	**99**	**8**	**0**	**4.85**
1986-87	**Chicago**	**NHL**	**46**	**19**	**19**	**5**	**2660**	**159**	**1**	**3.59**	**4**	**0**	**4**	**245**	**15**	**0**	**3.67**
1987-88	**New Jersey**	**NHL**	**34**	**10**	**16**	**3**	**1804**	**107**	**0**	**3.56**	**5**	**2**	**1**	**238**	**13**	**0**	**3.28**

a Shared Vezina Trophy with Don Edwards (1980)
b Shared Jennings Trophy with Tom Barrasso (1985)

Traded to **Detroit** by **Buffalo** for future considerations, December 2, 1981. Signed as free agent by **Buffalo**, June 1, 1982. Traded to **Chicago** by **Buffalo** for Chicago's third round draft choice in 1986 (Kevin Kerr), October 15, 1985. Signed as a free agent by **New Jersey**, July 10, 1987.

SCOTT, RON

Goaltender. Catches left. 5'8", 155 lbs. Born, Guelph, Ont., July 21, 1960.

			Regular Season								Playoffs						
Season	Club	Lea	GP	W	L	T	Mins	GA	SO	Avg	GP	W	L	Mins	GA	SO	Avg
1980-81	Michigan State	WCHA	33	11	21	1	1899	123	2	3.89	....	....	....	....	....	....	....
1981-82	Michigan State	CCHA	39	24	13	1	2298	109	2	2.85	....	....	....	....	....	....	....
1982-83a	Michigan State	CCHA	40	29	9	1	2273	100	2	2.64	....	....	....	....	....	....	....
1983-84	**NY Rangers**	**NHL**	**9**	**2**	**3**	**3**	**485**	**29**	**0**	**3.59**	....	....	....	....	....	....	....
b	Tulsa	CHL	29	13	13	3	1717	109	0	3.81	5	....	....	280	20	0	4.28
1984-85	New Haven	AHL	36	13	18	4	2047	130	0	3.81	....	....	....	....	....	....	....
1985-86	**NY Rangers**	**NHL**	**4**	**0**	**3**	**0**	**156**	**11**	**0**	**4.23**	....	....	....	....	....	....	....
	New Haven	AHL	19	8	8	1	1069	66	1	3.70	2	1	1	143	8	0	3.36
1986-87	**NY Rangers**	**NHL**	**1**	**0**	**0**	**1**	**65**	**5**	**0**	**4.62**	....	....	....	....	....	....	....
	New Haven	AHL	29	16	7	0	1744	107	2	3.68	....	....	....	....	....	....	....
1987-88	**NY Rangers**	**NHL**	**2**	**1**	**1**	**0**	**90**	**6**	**0**	**4.00**	....	....	....	....	....	....	....
	New Haven	AHL	17	8	7	1	963	49	0	3.05	....	....	....	....	....	....	....
	Colorado	IHL	8	3	4	0	395	33	0	5.01	5	1	4	259	16		3.71
1988-89	Denver	IHL	18	7	11	0	990	79	0	4.79	....	....	....	....	....	....	....
	NHL Totals		**16**	**3**	**7**	**4**	**796**	**51**	**0**	**3.84**	....	....	....	....	....	....	....

a CCHA First All-Star Team (1983)
b Shared Terry Sawchuk Trophy (CHL's leading goaltenders) with John Vanbiesbrouck (1984)

Signed as a free agent by **NY Rangers**, May 25, 1983.

SHARPLES, WARREN

Goaltender. Catches left. 6', 180 lbs. Born, Calgary, Alta., March 1, 1968.
(Calgary's 8th choice, 184th overall, in 1986 Entry Draft).

			Regular Season								Playoffs						
Season	Club	Lea	GP	W	L	T	Mins	GA	SO	Avg	GP	W	L	Mins	GA	SO	Avg
1986-87	U. of Michigan	CCHA	32	12	16	1	1720	148	1	5.14	...	...	...	...	...	...	...
1987-88	U. of Michigan	CCHA	33	18	15	0	1930	132	0	4.10	....	....	....	....	....	....	....
1988-89	U. of Michigan	CCHA	33	17	11	2	1887	116	0	3.69	....	....	....	....	....	....	....

SIDORKIEWICZ, PETER (suh-DORK-oh-WITZ)

Goaltender. Catches left. 5'9", 180 lbs. Born, Dabrown Bialostocka, Poland, June 29, 1963.
(Washington's 5th choice, 91st over-all, in 1981 Entry Draft).

			Regular Season								Playoffs						
Season	Club	Lea	GP	W	L	T	Mins	GA	SO	Avg	GP	W	L	Mins	GA	SO	Avg
1980-81	Oshawa	OHA	7	3	3	0	308	24	0	4.68	5	2	2	266	20	0	4.52
1981-82	Oshawa	OHL	29	14	11	1	1553	123	*2	4.75	1	0	0	13	1	0	4.62
1982-83	Oshawa	OHL	60	36	20	3	3536	213	0	3.61	17	15	1	1020	60	0	3.53
1983-84a	Oshawa	OHL	52	28	21	1	2966	250	1	4.15	7	3	4	420	27	*1	3.86
1984-85	Binghamton	AHL	45	31	9	5	2691	137	3	3.05	8	4	4	481	31	0	3.87
	Fort Worth	IHL	10	4	4	2	590	43	0	4.37	....	....	....	....	....	....	....
1985-86	Binghamton	AHL	49	21	22	3	2819	150	2	3.19	4	1	3	235	12	0	3.06
1986-87b	Binghamton	AHL	57	23	16	0	3304	161	4	2.92	13	6	7	794	36	0	2.72
1987-88	**Hartford**	**NHL**	**1**	**0**	**1**	**0**	**60**	**6**	**0**	**6.00**	....	....	....	....	....	....	....
	Binghamton	AHL	42	19	17	3	2345	144	0	3.68	3	0	2	147	8	0	3.27
1988-89c	**Hartford**	**NHL**	**44**	**22**	**18**	**4**	**2635**	**133**	**4**	**3.03**	**2**	**0**	**2**	**124**	**8**	**0**	**3.87**
	NHL Totals		**45**	**22**	**19**	**4**	**2695**	**139**	**4**	**3.09**	**2**	**0**	**2**	**124**	**8**	**0**	**3.87**

a OHL Third All-Star Team (1984).
b AHL Second All-Star Team (1987)
c NHL All-Rookie Team (1989)

Traded to **Hartford** by **Washington** with Dean Evason for David Jensen, March 12, 1985.

SIMPSON, SHAWN

Goaltender. Catches left. 5'11", 180 lbs. Born, Gloucester Ont., August 10, 1968.
(Washington's 3rd choice, 60th over-all, in 1986 Entry Draft).

			Regular Season								Playoffs						
Season	Club	Lea	GP	W	L	T	Mins	GA	SO	Avg	GP	W	L	Mins	GA	SO	Avg
1985-86	S.S. Marie	OHL	42	10	26	1	2213	217	1	5.88	....	....	....	....	....	....	....
1986-87a	S.S. Marie	OHL	46	20	22	2	2673	184	0	4.13	4	0	4	243	17	0	4.20
1987-88	S.S. Marie	OHL	57	26	29	1	3214	234	2	4.37	6	2	4	401	27	0	4.04
1988-89	Baltimore	AHL	1	0	1	0	60	7	0	7.00	....	....	....	....	....	....	....
	Oshawa	OHL	33	18	10	3	1818	131	0	4.32	6	2	4	368	23	1	3.75

a OHL Second All-Star Team (1987)

SKORODENSKI, WARREN

Goaltender. Catches left. 6'1", 180 lbs. Born, Winnipeg, Man., March 22, 1960.

			Regular Season								Playoffs						
Season	Club	Lea	GP	W	L	T	Mins	GA	SO	Avg	GP	W	L	Mins	GA	SO	Avg
1977-78	Calgary	WHL	53	8	22	10	2460	213	1	5.20	....	....	....	....	....	....	....
1978-79	Calgary	WHL	66	26	31	5	3595	309	1	5.16	15	7	8	884	61	0	4.14
1979-80	Calgary	WHL	66	39	23	2	3724	261	1	4.21	7	3	4	357	29	0	4.87
1980-81	New Brunswick	AHL	2	0	1	0	124	9	0	4.35	....	....	....	....	....	....	....
	Flint	IHL	47	....	....	....	2602	189	2	4.36	6	....	....	301	18	0	3.58
1981-82	**Chicago**	**NHL**	**1**	**0**	**1**	**0**	**60**	**5**	**0**	**5.00**	....	....	....	....	....	....	....
a	New Brunswick	AHL	28	16	8	4	1644	70	*3	*2.55	2	0	2	90	6	0	4.00
1982-83	Springfield	AHL	13	....	....	....	592	49	0	4.97	....	....	....	....	....	....	....
	Birmingham	CHL	25	11	11	1	1450	81	1	3.35	5	....	....	195	19	0	5.85
1983-84	Sherbrooke	AHL	19	5	10	2	1048	88	0	5.04	....	....	....	....	....	....	....
	Springfield	AHL	14	3	11	0	756	67	0	5.32	2	0	2	124	13	0	6.28
1984-85	**Chicago**	**NHL**	**27**	**11**	**9**	**3**	**1396**	**75**	**2**	**3.22**	**2**	**0**	**0**	**33**	**6**	**0**	**10.91**
1985-86	**Chicago**	**NHL**	**1**	**0**	**1**	**0**	**60**	**6**	**0**	**6.00**	....	....	....	....	....	....	....
	Nova Scotia	AHL	32	11	14	2	1716	109	0	3.81	....	....	....	....	....	....	....
1986-87	**Chicago**	**NHL**	**3**	**1**	**0**	**1**	**155**	**7**	**0**	**2.71**	....	....	....	....	....	....	....
	Nova Scotia	AHL	32	10	15	0	1813	121	2	4.00	....	....	....	....	....	....	....
	Saginaw	IHL	6	4	1	0	319	21	0	3.95	6	3	2	304	24	0	4.74
1987-88	**Edmonton**	**NHL**	**3**	**0**	**0**	**0**	**61**	**7**	**0**	**6.89**	....	....	....	....	....	....	....
	Nova Scotia	AHL	46	25	15	5	2746	171	0	3.74	5	1	4	305	22	0	4.33
1988-89	Cape Breton	AHL	25	11	13	1	1497	111	0	4.45	....	....	....	....	....	....	....
	Cdn. National	....	22	8	9	1	1160	82	0	4.24	....	....	....	....	....	....	....
	NHL Totals		**35**	**12**	**11**	**4**	**1732**	**100**	**2**	**3.46**	**2**	**0**	**0**	**33**	**6**	**0**	*****

a Shared Harry "Hap" Holmes Memorial Trophy with Bob Janecyk (1982)

Signed as a free agent by **Chicago**, August 12, 1979. Signed as a free agent by **Edmonton**, October 8, 1987.

SMITH, WILLIAM JOHN (BILL)

Goaltender. Catches left. 5'10", 185 lbs. Born, Perth, Ont., December 12, 1950.
(Los Angeles' 3rd choice, 59th over-all, in 1970 Amateur Draft).

			Regular Season								Playoffs						
Season	Club	Lea	GP	W	L	T	Mins	GA	SO	Avg	GP	W	L	Mins	GA	SO	Avg
1969-70	Cornwall	QJHL	55	....	....	....	3305	249	1	4.52	6	....	....	360	14	1	2.33
1970-71	Springfield	AHL	49	....	....	....	2728	160	2	3.51	12	....	....	682	29	1	*2.56
1971-72	**Los Angeles**	**NHL**	**5**	**1**	**3**	**1**	**300**	**23**	**0**	**4.60**	....	....	....	....	....	....	....
	Springfield	AHL	28	....	....	....	1649	77	*4	2.80	4	....	....	192	13	0	4.06
1972-73	**NY Islanders**	**NHL**	**37**	**7**	**24**	**3**	**2122**	**147**	**0**	**4.16**	....	....	....	....	....	....	....
1973-74	**NY Islanders**	**NHL**	**46**	**9**	**23**	**12**	**2615**	**134**	**0**	**3.07**	....	....	....	....	....	....	....
1974-75	**NY Islanders**	**NHL**	**58**	**21**	**18**	**17**	**3368**	**156**	**3**	**2.78**	**6**	**1**	**4**	**333**	**23**	**0**	**4.14**
1975-76	**NY Islanders**	**NHL**	**39**	**19**	**10**	**9**	**2254**	**98**	**3**	**2.61**	**8**	**4**	**3**	**437**	**21**	**0**	**2.88**
1976-77	**NY Islanders**	**NHL**	**36**	**21**	**8**	**6**	**2089**	**87**	**2**	**2.50**	**10**	**7**	**3**	**580**	**27**	**0**	**2.79**
1977-78	**NY Islanders**	**NHL**	**38**	**20**	**8**	**8**	**2154**	**95**	**2**	**2.65**	**1**	**0**	**0**	**47**	**1**	**0**	**1.28**
1978-79	**NY Islanders**	**NHL**	**40**	**25**	**8**	**4**	**2261**	**108**	**1**	**2.87**	**5**	**4**	**1**	**315**	**10**	***1**	***1.90**
1979-80a	**NY Islanders**	**NHL**	**38**	**15**	**14**	**7**	**2114**	**104**	**2**	**2.95**	**20**	**15**	**4**	**1198**	**56**	**1**	**2.80**
1980-81	**NY Islanders**	**NHL**	**41**	**22**	**10**	**8**	**2363**	**129**	**2**	**3.28**	**17**	**14**	**3**	**994**	**42**	**0**	***2.54**
1981-82bc	**NY Islanders**	**NHL**	**46**	**32**	**9**	**4**	**2685**	**133**	**0**	**2.97**	**18**	**15**	**3**	**1120**	**47**	***1**	**2.52**
1982-83de	**NY Islanders**	**NHL**	**41**	**18**	**14**	**7**	**2340**	**112**	**1**	**2.87**	**17**	**13**	**3**	**962**	**43**	***2**	***2.68**
1983-84	**NY Islanders**	**NHL**	**42**	**23**	**13**	**2**	**2279**	**130**	**2**	**3.42**	**21**	**12**	**8**	**1190**	**54**	**0**	**2.72**
1984-85	**NY Islanders**	**NHL**	**37**	**18**	**14**	**3**	**2090**	**133**	**0**	**3.82**	**6**	**3**	**3**	**342**	**19**	**0**	**3.33**
1985-86	**NY Islanders**	**NHL**	**41**	**20**	**14**	**4**	**2308**	**143**	**1**	**3.72**	**1**	**0**	**1**	**60**	**4**	**0**	**4.00**
1986-87	**NY Islanders**	**NHL**	**40**	**14**	**18**	**5**	**2252**	**132**	**1**	**3.52**	**2**	**0**	**0**	**67**	**1**	**0**	**0.90**
1987-88	**NY Islanders**	**NHL**	**38**	**17**	**14**	**5**	**2107**	**113**	**2**	**3.22**	....	....	....	....	....	....	....
1988-89	**NY Islanders**	**NHL**	**17**	**3**	**11**	**0**	**730**	**54**	**0**	**4.44**	....	....	....	....	....	....	....
	NHL Totals		**680**	**305**	**233**	**105**	**38426**	**2031**	**22**	**3.17**	**132**	**88**	**36**	**7645**	**348**	**5**	**2.73**

a Credited with a goal against Colorado Rockies (November 28, 1979).
b Won Vezina Trophy (1982)
c NHL First All-Star Team (1982)
d Won Conn Smythe Trophy (1983)
e Shared William Jennings Trophy with Roland Melanson (1983)

Played in NHL All-Star Game (1978)

Claimed by **NY Islanders** from **Los Angeles** in Expansion Draft, June 6, 1972.

SNOW, GARTH

Goaltender. Catches left. 6'3", 200 lbs. Born, Wrentham, MA, July 28, 1969.
(Quebec's 6th choice, 114th overall, in 1987 Entry Draft).

			Regular Season								Playoffs						
Season	Club	Lea	GP	W	L	T	Mins	GA	SO	Avg	GP	W	L	Mins	GA	SO	Avg
1988-89	U. of Maine	H.E.	5	2	2	0	241	14	1	3.49	....	....	....	....	....	....	....

STAUBER, ROBB

Goaltender. Catches left. 5'10", 165 lbs. Born, Duluth, MN, November 25, 1967.
(Los Angeles' 5th choice, 107th overall, in 1986 Entry Draft).

			Regular Season								Playoffs						
Season	Club	Lea	GP	W	L	T	Mins	GA	SO	Avg	GP	W	L	Mins	GA	SO	Avg
1986-87	U. Minnesota	WCHA	20	13	5	0	1072	63	0	3.53	....	....	....	....	....	....	....
1987-88abcd	U. Minnesota	WCHA	44	34	10	0	2621	119	5	2.72	....	....	....	....	....	....	....
1988-89e	U. Minnesota	WCHA	34	26	8	0	2024	82	0	2.43	....	....	....	....	....	....	....

a Won Hobey Baker Memorial Award (Top U.S. Collegiate Player) (1988)
b NCAA West First All-American Team (1988)
c WCHA Player of the Year (1988)
d WCHA First All-Star Team (1988)
e WCHA Second All-Star Team (1989)

STEFAN, GREGORY STEVEN (GREG) (STEH fihn)

Goaltender. Catches left. 5'11", 180 lbs. Born, Brantford, Ont., February 11, 1961.
(Detroit's 5th choice, 128th over-all, in 1981 Entry Draft).

			Regular Season								Playoffs						
Season	Club	Lea	GP	W	L	T	Mins	GA	SO	Avg	GP	W	L	Mins	GA	SO	Avg
1979-80	Oshawa	OHA	17	8	6	0	897	58	0	3.88	....	....	....	....	....	....	....
1980-81	Oshawa	OHA	46	23	14	3	2407	174	0	4.34	6	2	3	298	20	0	4.02
1981-82	**Detroit**	**NHL**	**2**	**0**	**2**	**0**	**120**	**10**	**0**	**5.00**	....	....	....	....	....	....	....
	Adirondack	AHL	29	11	13	3	1571	99	2	3.78	1	0	0	20	0	0	0.00
1982-83	**Detroit**	**NHL**	**35**	**6**	**16**	**9**	**1847**	**139**	**0**	**4.52**	....	....	....	....	....	....	....
1983-84	**Detroit**	**NHL**	**50**	**19**	**22**	**2**	**2600**	**152**	**2**	**3.51**	**3**	**1**	**2**	**210**	**8**	**0**	**2.29**
1984-85	**Detroit**	**NHL**	**46**	**21**	**19**	**3**	**2635**	**190**	**0**	**4.33**	**3**	**0**	**3**	**138**	**17**	**0**	**7.39**
1985-86	**Detroit**	**NHL**	**37**	**10**	**20**	**5**	**2068**	**155**	**1**	**4.50**	....	....	....	....	....	....	....
1986-87	**Detroit**	**NHL**	**43**	**20**	**17**	**3**	**2351**	**135**	**1**	**3.45**	**9**	**4**	**5**	**508**	**24**	**0**	**2.83**
1987-88	**Detroit**	**NHL**	**33**	**17**	**9**	**5**	**1854**	**96**	**1**	**3.11**	**10**	**5**	**4**	**531**	**32**	**1**	**3.62**
1988-89	**Detroit**	**NHL**	**46**	**21**	**17**	**3**	**2499**	**167**	**0**	**4.01**	**5**	**2**	**3**	**294**	**18**	**0**	**3.67**
	NHL Totals		**292**	**114**	**122**	**30**	**15974**	**1044**	**5**	**3.92**	**30**	**12**	**17**	**1681**	**99**	**1**	**3.53**

STOLP, JEFFREY

Goaltender. Catches left. 6'0", 170 lbs. Born, Hibbing, MN, June 20, 1970.
(Minnesota's 4th choice, 64th overall, in 1988 Entry Draft).

			Regular Season								Playoffs						
Season	Club	Lea	GP	W	L	T	Mins	GA	SO	Avg	GP	W	L	Mins	GA	SO	Avg
1987-88	Greenway	HS	22	....	....	....	990	52	0	2.51	....	....	....	....	....	....	....
1988-89	U. Minnesota	WCHA	16	7	2	3	742	45	0	3.64	....	....	....	....	....	....	....

TABARACCI, RICHARD

Goaltender. Catches left. 5'10", 185 lbs. Born, Toronto, Ont., January 2, 1969.
(Pittsburgh's 2nd choice, 26th overall, in 1987 Entry Draft).

			Regular Season								Playoffs						
Season	Club	Lea	GP	W	L	T	Mins	GA	SO	Avg	GP	W	L	Mins	GA	SO	Avg
1986-87	Cornwall	OHL	59	23	32	3	3347	290	1	5.20	5	1	4	303	26	0	3.17
1987-88a	Cornwall	OHL	58	33	18	6	3448	200	3	3.48	11	5	6	642	37	0	3.46
	Muskegon	IHL	...	...	...	...	....	....	...	....	1	0	0	13	1		4.62
1988-89	**Pittsburgh**	**NHL**	**1**	**0**	**0**	**0**	**33**	**4**	**0**	**7.27**	....	....	....	....	....	....	....
b	Cornwall	OHL	47	18	18	4	2449	163	1	3.99	18	10	8	1080	65	*1	3.61
	NHL Totals		**1**	**0**	**0**	**0**	**33**	**4**	**0**	**7.27**	....	....	....	....	....	....	....

a OHL First All-Star Team (1988)
b OHL Second All-Star Team (1989)

Traded to **Winnipeg** by **Pittsburgh** with Randy Cunnyworth and Dave McLlwain for Jim Kyte, Andrew McBain and Randy Gilhen, June 17, 1989.

TAILLEFER, TERRY

Goaltender. Catches left. 6', 162 lbs. Born, Edmonton, Alta., July 23, 1965.
(Boston's 6th choice, 122nd over-all, in 1983 Entry Draft).

			Regular Season								Playoffs						
Season	Club	Lea	GP	W	L	T	Mins	GA	SO	Avg	GP	W	L	Mins	GA	SO	Avg
1983-84	Boston U.	ECAC	10	3	1	1	412	20	0	2.91	....	....	....	....	....	....	....
1984-85	Boston U.	H.E.	15	9	4	2	938	47	0	3.01	....	....	....	....	....	....	....
1985-86a	Boston U.	H.E.	20	11	5	2	1113	65	1	3.50	....	....	....	....	....	....	....
1986-87	Boston U.	H.E.	22	10	10	1	1260	82	0	3.90	....	....	....	....	....	....	....
1987-88	Maine	AHL	12	4	3	0	506	28	0	3.32	....	....	....	....	....	....	....
1988-89	Maine	AHL	3	0	1	0	71	11	0	9.30	....	....	....	....	....	....	....

a Hockey East Second All-Star Team (1986)

TAKKO, KARI (TAH koh)

Goaltender. Catches left. 6'2", 185 lbs. Born, Uusikaupunki, Finland, June 23, 1963.
(Minnesota's 5th choice, 97th over-all, in 1984 Entry Draft).

			Regular Season								Playoffs						
Season	Club	Lea	GP	W	L	T	Mins	GA	SO	Avg	GP	W	L	Mins	GA	SO	Avg
1985-86	Springfield	AHL	43	18	19	3	2286	161	1	4.05	....	....	....	....	....	....	....
	Minnesota	**NHL**	**1**	**0**	**1**	**0**	**60**	**3**	**0**	**3.00**	....	....	....	....	....	....	....
1986-87	**Minnesota**	**NHL**	**38**	**13**	**18**	**4**	**2075**	**119**	**0**	**3.44**	....	....	....	....	....	....	....
	Springfield	AHL	5	3	2	0	300	16	1	3.20	....	....	....	....	....	....	....
1987-88	**Minnesota**	**NHL**	**37**	**8**	**19**	**6**	**1919**	**143**	**1**	**4.47**	....	....	....	....	....	....	....
1988-89	**Minnesota**	**NHL**	**32**	**8**	**15**	**4**	**1603**	**93**	**0**	**3.48**	**3**	**0**	**1**	**105**	**7**	**0**	**4.00**
	NHL Totals		**108**	**29**	**53**	**14**	**5657**	**358**	**1**	**3.80**	**3**	**0**	**1**	**105**	**7**	**0**	**4.00**

TANNER, JOHN

Goaltender. Catches left. 6'3", 180 lbs. Born, Cambridge, Ont., March 17, 1971.
(Quebec's 4th choice, 54th overall, in 1989 Entry Draft).

			Regular Season								Playoffs						
Season	Club	Lea	GP	W	L	T	Mins	GA	SO	Avg	GP	W	L	Mins	GA	SO	Avg
1987-88a	Peterborough	OHL	26	18	4	3	1532	88	0	3.45	2	....	....	98	3	0	1.84
1988-89	Peterborough	OHL	34	22	10	0	1923	107	2	*3.34	8	4	3	369	23	0	3.74

a Won Dave Pinkey Trophy - Top Team Goaltending OHL shared with Todd Bojcun (1989)

TERRERI, CHRIS

Goaltender. Catches left. 5'9", 160 lbs. Born, Providence, RI, November 15, 1964.
(New Jersey's 3rd choice, 87th over-all, in 1983 Entry Draft).

			Regular Season								Playoffs						
Season	Club	Lea	GP	W	L	T	Mins	GA	SO	Avg	GP	W	L	Mins	GA	SO	Avg
1982-83	Providence	ECAC	11	7	1	0	528	17	2	1.93	....	....	....	....	....	....	....
1983-84	Providence	ECAC	10	4	2	0	391	20	0	3.07	....	....	....	....	....	....	....
1984-85abc	Providence	H.E.	33	15	13	5	1956	116	1	3.35	....	....	....	....	....	....	....
1985-86	Providence	H.E.	22	6	16	0	1320	84	0	3.74	....	....	....	....	....	....	....
1986-87	**New Jersey**	**NHL**	**7**	**0**	**3**	**1**	**286**	**21**	**0**	**4.41**	....	....	....	....	....	....	....
	Maine	AHL	14	4	9	1	765	57	0	4.47	....	....	....	....	....	....	....
1987-88	Utica	AHL	7	5	1	0	399	18	0	2.71	....	....	....	....	....	....	....
	U.S. National	....	26	17	7	2	1430	81	0	3.40	....	....	....	....	....	....	....
	U.S. Olympic	....	3	1	1	0	128	14	0	6.56	....	....	....	....	....	....	....
1988-89	**New Jersey**	**NHL**	**8**	**0**	**4**	**2**	**402**	**18**	**0**	**2.69**	....	....	....	....	....	....	....
	Utica	AHL	39	20	15	3	2314	132	0	3.42	2	0	1	80	6	0	4.50
	NHL Totals		**15**	**0**	**7**	**3**	**688**	**39**	**0**	**3.40**	....	....	....	....	....	....	....

a Hockey East All-Star Team
b Hockey East Player of the Year (1985)
c NCAA All-American Team (1985)

TUGNUTT, RON

Goaltender. Catches left. 5′11″, 155 lbs. Born, Scarborough, Ont., October 22, 1967.
(Quebec's 4th choice, 81st overall, in 1986 Entry Draft).

			Regular Season								Playoffs						
Season	Club	Lea	GP	W	L	T	Mins	GA	SO	Avg	GP	W	L	Mins	GA	SO	Avg
1984-85	Peterborough	OHL	18	7	4	2	938	59	0	3.77	....	....	....	....	....	....	....
1985-86	Peterborough	OHL	26	18	7	0	1543	74	1	2.88	3	2	0	133	6	0	2.71
1986-87a	Peterborough	OHL	31	21	7	2	1891	88	2	2.79	6	3	3	374	21	1	3.37
1987-88	Quebec	NHL	6	2	3	0	284	16	0	3.38	....	....	....	....	....	....	....
	Fredericton	AHL	34	20	9	4	1964	118	1	3.60	4	1	2	204	11	0	3.24
1988-89	Quebec	NHL	26	10	10	3	1367	82	0	3.60	....	....	....	....	....	....	....
	Halifax	AHL	24	14	7	2	1368	79	1	3.46	....	....	....	....	....	....	....
	NHL Totals		32	12	13	3	1651	98	0	3.56	....	....	....	....	....	....	....

a OHL First All-Star Team (1987)

VANBIESBROUCK, JOHN (van BEES bruhk)

Goaltender. Catches left. 5′7″, 175 lbs. Born, Detroit, MI, September 4, 1963.
(NY Rangers' 5th choice, 72nd over-all, in 1981 Entry Draft).

			Regular Season								Playoffs						
Season	Club	Lea	GP	W	L	T	Mins	GA	SO	Avg	GP	W	L	Mins	GA	SO	Avg
1980-81a	S.S. Marie	OHA	56	31	16	1	2941	203	0	4.14	11	3	3	457	24	1	3.15
1981-82	NY Rangers	NHL	1	1	0	0	60	1	0	1.00	....	....	....	....	....	....	....
	S.S. Marie	OHL	31	12	12	2	1686	102	0	3.62	7	1	4	276	20	0	4.35
1982-83b	S.S. Marie	OHL	62	39	21	1	3471	209	0	3.61	16	7	6	944	56	*1	3.56
1983-84	NY Rangers	NHL	3	2	1	0	180	10	0	3.33	1	0	0	1	0	0	0.00
cde	Tulsa	CHL	37	20	13	2	2153	124	*3	3.46	4	4	0	240	10	0	*2.50
1984-85	NY Rangers	NHL	42	12	24	3	2358	166	1	4.22	1	0	0	20	0	0	0.00
1985-86fg	NY Rangers	NHL	61	31	21	5	3326	184	3	3.32	16	8	8	899	49	1	3.27
1986-87	NY Rangers	NHL	50	18	20	5	2656	161	0	3.64	4	1	3	195	11	1	3.38
1987-88	NY Rangers	NHL	56	27	22	7	3319	187	2	3.38	....	....	....	....	....	....	....
1988-89	NY Rangers	NHL	56	28	21	4	3207	197	0	3.69	2	0	1	107	6	0	3.36
	NHL Totals		269	119	109	24	15106	906	6	3.60	24	9	12	1222	66	2	3.24

a OHA Third All-Star Team (1981).
b OHL Second All-Star Team (1983).
c CHL First All-Star Team (1984)
d Shared Terry Sawchuk Trophy (CHL's leading goaltenders) with Ron Scott (1984)
e Shared Tommy Ivan Trophy (CHL's Most Valuable Player) with Bruce Affleck of Indianapolis (1984)
f Won Vezina Trophy (1986)
g NHL First All-Star Team (1986)

VERNON, MICHAEL (MIKE)

Goaltender. Catches left. 5′9″, 170 lbs. Born, Calgary, Alta., February 24, 1963.
(Calgary's 2nd choice, 56th over-all, in 1981 Entry Draft).

			Regular Season								Playoffs						
Season	Club	Lea	GP	W	L	T	Mins	GA	SO	Avg	GP	W	L	Mins	GA	SO	Avg
1980-81	Calgary	WHL	59	33	17	1	3154	198	1	3.77	22	....	....	1271	82	1	3.87
1981-82ab	Calgary	WHL	42	22	14	2	2329	143	3	3.68	9	....	....	527	30	0	3.42
	Oklahoma City	CHL	....	....	....	....	....	....	....	....	1	0	1	70	4	0	3.43
1982-83	Calgary	NHL	2	0	2	0	100	11	0	6.59	....	....	....	....	....	....	....
ab	Calgary	WHL	50	19	18	2	2856	155	3	3.26	16	9	7	925	60	0	3.89
1983-84	Calgary	NHL	1	0	1	0	11	4	0	22.22	....	....	....	....	....	....	....
c	Colorado	CHL	46	30	13	2	2648	148	1	*3.35	6	2	4	347	21	0	3.63
1984-85	Moncton	AHL	41	10	20	4	2050	134	0	3.92	....	....	....	....	....	....	....
1985-86	Calgary	NHL	18	9	3	3	921	52	1	3.39	21	12	9	1229	60	0	2.93
	Moncton	AHL	6	3	1	2	374	21	0	3.37	....	....	....	....	....	....	....
	Salt Lake	IHL	10	....	....	....	600	34	1	3.40	....	....	....	....	....	....	....
1986-87	Calgary	NHL	54	30	21	1	2957	178	1	3.61	5	2	3	263	16	0	3.65
1987-88	Calgary	NHL	64	39	16	7	3565	210	1	3.53	9	4	4	515	34	0	3.96
1988-89d	Calgary	NHL	52	*37	6	5	2938	130	0	2.65	*22	*16	5	*1381	52	*3	2.26
	NHL Totals		191	115	49	16	10492	585	3	3.35	57	34	21	3388	162	3	2.87

a WHL First All-Star Team (1982, 1983)
b WHL Most Valuable Player (1982, 1983)
c CHL Second All-Star Team (1984)
d NHL Second All-Star Team (1989)

Played in NHL All-Star Game (1988, 1989)

WAITE, JIMMY

Goaltender. Catches right. 6′, 165 lbs. Born, Sherbrooke, Que., April 15, 1969.
(Chicago's 1st choice, 8th overall, in 1987 Entry Draft).

			Regular Season								Playoffs						
Season	Club	Lea	GP	W	L	T	Mins	GA	SO	Avg	GP	W	L	Mins	GA	SO	Avg
1986-87a	Chicoutimi	QMJHL	50	23	17	3	2569	209	2	4.48	11	4	6	576	54	1	5.63
1987-88	Chicoutimi		36	17	16	1	2000	150	0	4.50	4	1	2	222	17	0	4.59
1988-89	Chicago	NHL	11	0	7	1	494	43	0	5.22	....	....	....	....	....	....	....
	Saginaw	IHL	5	3	1	0	304	10	0	1.97	....	....	....	....	....	....	....
	NHL Totals	QMJHL	11	0	7	1	494	43	0	5.22	....	....	....	....	....	....	....

a QMJHL Second All-Star Team (1987)

WAKALUK, DARCY (WAUK-a-luk)

Goaltender. Catches left. 5′11″, 180 lbs. Born, Pincher Creek, Alta., March 14, 1966.
(Buffalo's 7th choice, 144th over-all, in 1984 Entry Draft).

			Regular Season								Playoffs						
Season	Club	Lea	GP	W	L	T	Mins	GA	SO	Avg	GP	W	L	Mins	GA	SO	Avg
1983-84	Kelowna	WHL	31	....	....	....	1555	163	0	6.29	....	....	....	....	....	....	....
1984-85	Kelowna	WHL	54	19	30	4	3094	244	0	4.73	5	1	4	282	22	0	4.68
1985-86	Spokane	WHL	47	21	22	1	2562	224	1	5.25	7	3	4	419	37	0	5.30
1986-87	Rochester	AHL	11	2	2	0	545	26	0	2.86	5	2	0	141	11	0	4.68
1987-88	Rochester	AHL	55	27	16	3	2763	159	0	3.45	6	3	3	328	22	0	4.02
1988-89	Buffalo	NHL	6	1	3	0	214	15	0	4.21	....	....	....	....	....	....	....
	Rochester	AHL	33	11	14	0	1566	97	1	3.72	....	....	....	....	....	....	....
	NHL Totals		6	1	3	0	214	15	0	4.21	....	....	....	....	....	....	....

WAMSLEY, RICHARD (RICK) (WAHMS-lee)

Goaltender. Catches left. 5′11″, 185 lbs. Born, Simcoe, Ont., May 25, 1959.
(Montreal's 5th choice, 58th over-all, in 1979 Entry Draft).

			Regular Season								Playoffs						
Season	Club	Lea	GP	W	L	T	Mins	GA	SO	Avg	GP	W	L	Mins	GA	SO	Avg
1977-78	Hamilton	OHA	25	....	....	....	1495	74	2	2.97	....	....	....	....	....	....	....
1978-79	Brantford	OHA	24	....	....	....	1444	128	0	5.32	....	....	....	....	....	....	....
1979-80	Nova Scotia	AHL	40	19	16	2	2305	125	2	3.25	3	1	1	143	12	0	5.03
1980-81	Montreal	NHL	5	3	0	1	253	8	1	1.90	....	....	....	....	....	....	....
	Nova Scotia	AHL	43	17	19	3	2372	155	0	3.92	4	2	1	199	6	*1	1.81
1981-82a	Montreal	NHL	38	23	7	7	2206	101	2	2.75	5	2	3	300	11	0	*2.20
1982-83	Montreal	NHL	46	27	12	5	2583	151	0	3.51	3	0	3	152	7	0	2.77
1983-84	Montreal	NHL	42	19	17	3	2333	144	2	3.70	1	0	1	32	0	0	0.00
1984-85	St. Louis	NHL	40	23	12	5	2319	126	0	3.26	2	0	2	120	7	0	3.50
1985-86	St. Louis	NHL	42	22	16	3	2517	144	1	3.43	10	4	6	569	29	0	3.90
1986-87	St. Louis	NHL	41	17	15	6	2410	142	0	3.54	2	1	1	120	5	0	2.50
1987-88	St. Louis	NHL	31	13	16	1	1818	103	2	3.40	....	....	....	....	....	....	....
	Calgary	NHL	2	1	0	0	73	5	0	4.11	1	0	1	33	2	0	3.64
1988-89	Calgary	NHL	35	17	11	4	1927	95	2	2.96	1	0	1	20	2	0	6.00
	NHL Totals		322	165	109	35	18439	1019	10	3.32	25	7	18	1346	63	0	2.81

a Shared Williams Jennings Trophy with Denis Herron (1982)

Traded to **St. Louis** by **Montreal** with Hartford's second round choice (Brian Benning); — Montreal property via earlier deal — Montreal's second round choice (Anthony Hrkac) and third round choice (Robert Dirk), all in the 1984 Entry Draft, for St. Louis' first (Shayne Corson) and second round (Stephane Richer) choices in the 1984 Entry Draft, June 9, 1984. Traded to **Calgary** by **St. Louis** with Rob Ramage for Brett Hull and Steve Bozek, March 7, 1988.

WEEKS, STEPHEN (STEVE)

Goaltender. Catches left. 5′11″, 165 lbs. Born, Scarborough, Ont., June 30, 1958.
(NY Rangers' 12th choice, 176th over-all, in 1978 Amateur Draft).

			Regular Season								Playoffs						
Season	Club	Lea	GP	W	L	T	Mins	GA	SO	Avg	GP	W	L	Mins	GA	SO	Avg
1977-78	N. Michigan	CCHA	19	....	....	....	1015	56	1	3.31	....	....	....	....	....	....	....
1978-79	N. Michigan	CCHA	25	....	....	....	1437	82	0	3.42	....	....	....	....	....	....	....
1979-80	N. Michigan	CCHA	36	29	6	1	2133	105	0	2.95	....	....	....	....	....	....	....
1980-81	New Haven	AHL	36	14	17	3	2065	142	1	4.04	....	....	....	....	....	....	....
	NY Rangers	NHL	1	0	1	0	60	2	0	2.00	1	0	0	14	1	0	4.29
1981-82	NY Rangers	NHL	49	23	16	9	2852	179	1	3.77	4	1	2	127	9	0	4.25
1982-83	NY Rangers	NHL	18	9	5	3	1040	68	0	3.92	....	....	....	....	....	....	....
	Tulsa	CHL	19	8	10	0	1116	60	0	3.23	....	....	....	....	....	....	....
1983-84	NY Rangers	NHL	26	10	11	2	1361	90	0	3.97	....	....	....	....	....	....	....
	Tulsa	CHL	3	3	0	0	180	7	0	2.33	....	....	....	....	....	....	....
1984-85	Hartford	NHL	24	10	12	2	1457	93	2	3.82	....	....	....	....	....	....	....
	Binghamton	AHL	5	5	0	0	303	13	0	2.57	....	....	....	....	....	....	....
1985-86	Hartford	NHL	27	13	13	0	1544	99	1	3.85	3	1	2	169	8	0	2.84
1986-87	Hartford	NHL	25	12	8	2	1367	78	1	3.42	1	0	0	36	1	0	1.67
1987-88	Hartford	NHL	18	6	7	2	918	55	0	3.59	....	....	....	....	....	....	....
	Vancouver	NHL	9	4	3	2	550	31	0	3.38	....	....	....	....	....	....	....
1988-89	Vancouver	NHL	35	11	19	5	2056	102	0	2.98	3	1	1	140	8	0	3.43
	NHL Totals		232	98	95	27	13205	797	5	3.62	12	3	5	486	27	0	3.33

Traded to **Vancouver** by **Hartford** for Richard Brodeur, March 8, 1988.

WHITMORE, KAY

Goaltender. Catches left. 5′11″, 175 lbs. Born, Sudbury, Ont., April 10, 1967.
(Hartford's 2nd choice, 26th over-all, in 1985 Entry Draft).

			Regular Season								Playoffs						
Season	Club	Lea	GP	W	L	T	Mins	GA	SO	Avg	GP	W	L	Mins	GA	SO	Avg
1983-84	Peterborough	OHL	29	17	8	0	1471	110	0	4.49	....	....	....	....	....	....	....
1984-85a	Peterborough	OHL	53	35	16	2	3077	172	2	3.35	17	10	4	1020	58	0	3.41
1985-86b	Peterborough	OHL	41	27	12	2	2467	114	3	2.77	14	8	5	837	40	0	2.87
1986-87	Peterborough	OHL	36	14	17	5	2159	118	1	3.28	7	3	3	366	17	1	2.79
1987-88	Binghamton	AHL	38	17	15	4	2137	121	3	3.40	2	0	2	118	10	0	5.08
1988-89	Hartford	NHL	3	2	1	0	180	10	0	3.33	2	0	2	135	10	0	4.44
	Binghamton	AHL	56	21	29	4	3200	241	1	4.52	....	....	....	....	....	....	....
	NHL Totals		3	2	1	0	180	10	0	3.33	2	0	2	135	10	0	4.44

a OHL Third All-Star Team (1985).
b OHL First All-Star Team (1986).

WILLIAMS, MIKE

Goaltender. Catches left. 6′, 185 lbs. Born, Woodhaven, MI, April 16, 1967.
(Quebec's 12th choice, 219th overall, in 1987 Entry Draft).

			Regular Season								Playoffs						
Season	Club	Lea	GP	W	L	T	Mins	GA	SO	Avg	GP	W	L	Mins	GA	SO	Avg
1986-87	Ferris State	CCHA	17	4	9	0	846	65	0	4.61	....	....	....	....	....	....	....
1987-88	Ferris State	CCHA	30	11	11	5	1671	122	0	4.38	....	....	....	....	....	....	....
1988-89	Ferris State	CCHA	25	6	13	5	1394	84	0	3.62	....	....	....	....	....	....	....

WREGGET, KEN

Goaltender. Catches left. 6′1″, 195 lbs. Born, Brandon, Man., March 25, 1964.
(Toronto's 4th choice, 45th over-all, in 1982 Entry Draft).

			Regular Season								Playoffs						
Season	Club	Lea	GP	W	L	T	Mins	GA	SO	Avg	GP	W	L	Mins	GA	SO	Avg
1981-82	Lethbridge	WHL	36	19	12	0	1713	118	0	4.13	3	....	....	84	3	0	2.14
1982-83	Lethbridge	WHL	48	26	17	1	2696	157	0	3.49	20	14	5	1154	58	1	3.02
1983-84	Toronto	NHL	3	1	1	1	165	14	0	5.09	....	....	....	....	....	....	....
a	Lethbridge	WHL	53	32	20	0	3053	161	0	*3.16	4	1	3	210	18	0	5.14
1984-85	Toronto	NHL	23	2	15	3	1278	103	0	4.84	....	....	....	....	....	....	....
	St. Catharines	AHL	12	2	8	1	688	48	0	4.19	....	....	....	....	....	....	....
1985-86	Toronto	NHL	30	9	13	4	1566	113	0	4.33	10	6	4	607	32	1	3.16
	St. Catharines	AHL	18	8	9	0	1058	78	1	4.42	....	....	....	....	....	....	....
1986-87	Toronto	NHL	56	22	28	3	3026	200	0	3.97	13	7	6	761	29	1	2.29
1987-88	Toronto	NHL	56	12	35	4	3000	222	2	4.44	2	0	1	108	11	0	6.11
1988-89	Toronto	NHL	32	9	20	2	1888	139	0	4.42	....	....	....	....	....	....	....
	Philadelphia	NHL	3	1	1	0	130	13	0	6.00	5	2	2	268	10	1	2.24
	NHL Totals		203	56	113	17	11053	804	2	4.36	30	15	13	1744	82	3	2.82

a WHL First All-Star Team, East Division (1984).

Traded to **Philadelphia** by **Toronto** for Philadelphia's first-round choice (Rob Peterson) and Calgary's first-round choice (Steve Bancroft) — acquired by Philadelphia in the Brad McCrimmon trade — in 1989 Entry Draft, March 6, 1989.

YOUNG, WENDELL

Goaltender. Catches left. 5'9", 185 lbs.   Born, Halifax, N.S., August 1, 1963.
(Vancouver's 3rd choice, 73rd over-all, in 1981 Entry Draft).

| | | | | | Regular Season | | | | | | | | Playoffs | | | | |
Season	Club	Lea	GP	W	L	T	Mins	GA	SO	Avg	GP	W	L	Mins	GA	SO	Avg
1980-81	Kitchener	OHA	42	19	15	0	2215	164	1	4.44	14	9	1	800	42	*1	3.15
1981-82	Kitchener	OHL	60	38	17	2	3470	195	1	3.37	15	12	1	900	35	*1	*2.33
1982-83a	Kitchener	OHL	61	41	19	0	3611	231	1	3.84	12	6	5	720	43	0	3.58
1983-84	Fredericton	AHL	11	7	3	0	569	39	1	4.11	....	....	....	....	....	....	....
	Milwaukee	IHL	6	....	....	....	339	17	0	3.01	....	....	....	....	....	....	....
	Salt Lake	CHL	20	11	6	0	1094	80	0	4.39	4	0	2	122	11	0	5.42
1984-85	Fredericton	AHL	22	7	11	3	1242	83	0	4.01	....	....	....	....	....	....	....
1985-86	**Vancouver**	**NHL**	22	4	9	3	1023	61	0	3.58	1	0	1	60	5	0	5.00
	Fredericton	AHL	24	12	8	4	1457	78	0	3.21	....	....	....	....	....	....	....
1986-87	**Vancouver**	**NHL**	8	1	6	1	420	35	0	5.00	....	....	....	....	....	....	....
	Fredericton	AHL	30	11	16	0	1676	118	0	4.22	....	....	....	....	....	....	....
1987-88bcd	**Philadelphia**	**NHL**	6	3	2	0	320	20	0	3.75	....	....	....	....	....	....	....
	Hershey	AHL	51	*33	15	1	2922	135	1	2.77	12	*12	0	767	28	1	*2.19
1988-89	**Pittsburgh**	**NHL**	22	12	9	0	1150	92	0	4.80	1	0	0	39	1	0	1.54
	NHL Totals		58	20	26	4	2913	208	0	4.28	2	0	1	99	6	0	3.64

a OHL Third All-Star Team (1983).
b AHL First All-Star Team (1988).
c Won Baz Bastien Award (AHL Most Valuable Goaltender) (1988).
d Won Jack Butterfield Trophy (AHL Playoff MVP) (1988).

Traded to **Philadelphia** by **Vancouver** with Vancouver's third round pick in 1990 Entry Draft for
Daryl Stanley, August 28, 1987. Traded to **Pittsburgh** by **Philadelphia** with Philadelphia's
seventh-round choice in 1990 Entry Draft for Pittsburgh's third-round choice in 1990 Entry Draft,
Steptember 1, 1988.

Kay Whitmore

Johnny Bower

Gary Edwards

Gilles Meloche

Jim Craig

Tony Esposito

Chuck Rayner

Roger Crozier

Ed Giacomin

Garry Smith

Gerry Desjardins

Harry Lumley

Gilles Villemure

Retired NHL Goaltender Index

Abbreviations: Teams/Cities:—**Atl.**-Atlanta; **Bos.**-Boston; **Buf.**-Buffalo; **Cal.**-California; **Cgy.**-Calgary; **Chi.**-Chicago; **Cle.**-Cleveland; **Col.**-Colorado; **Det.**-Detroit; **Edm.**-Edmonton; **Ham.**-Hamilton; **Hfd.**-Hartford; **L.A.**-Los Angeles; **Min.**-Minnesota; **Mtl.**-Montreal; **Mtl. M.**-Montreal Maroons; **Mtl. W.**-Montreal Wanderers; **N.J.**-New Jersey; **NY**-New York; **NYA**-NY Americans; **NYI**-New York Islanders; **NYR**-New York Rangers; **Oak.**-Oakland; **Ott.**-Ottawa; **Phi.**-Philadelphia; **Pit.**-Pittsburgh; **Que.**-Quebec; **St. L.**-St. Louis; **Tor.**-Toronto; **Van.**-Vancouver; **Wpg.**-Winnipeg; **Wsh.**-Washington.

Avg – goals against per 60 minutes played; **GA** – goals against; **GP** – games played; **Mins** – minutes played; **SO** – shutouts.

			Regular Schedule								Playoffs									
Name	**NHL Teams**	**NHL Seasons**	**GP**	**W**	**L**	**T**	**Mins**	**GA**	**SO**	**Avg**	**GP**	**W**	**L**	**T**	**Mins**	**GA**	**SO**	**Avg**	**First NHL Season**	**Last NHL Season**
Abbott, George	Bos.	1	1	0	1	0	60	7	0	7.00	....	....	....	....	....	....	....	....	1943-44	1943-44
Adams, John	Bos., Wsh.	2	22	9	10	1	1180	85	1	4.32	....	....	....	....	....	....	....	....	1972-73	1974-75
Aiken, Don	Mtl.	1	1	0	1	0	34	6	0	10.59	....	....	....	....	....	....	....	....	1957-58	1957-58
Aitkenhead, Andy	NYR	3	106	47	43	16	6570	257	11	2.35	10	6	3	1	608	15	3	1.48	1932-33	1934-35
Almas, Red	Det., Chi.	3	3	0	2	1	180	13	0	4.33	5	1	3	....	263	13	0	2.97	1946-47	1952-53
Anderson, Lorne	NYR	1	3	1	2	0	180	18	0	6.00	....	....	....	....	....	....	....	....	1951-52	1951-52
Astrom, Hardy	NYR, Col.	3	83	17	44	12	4456	277	0	3.73	....	....	....	....	....	....	....	....	1977-78	1980-81
Baker, Steve	NYR	4	67	20	20	20	3081	190	3	3.70	14	7	7	....	826	55	0	4.00	1979-80	1982-83
Bannerman, Murray	Van., Chi.	8	289	116	125	33	16470	1051	8	3.83	40	20	18	....	2322	165	0	4.26	1977-78	1986-87
Baron, Marco	Bos., L.A., Edm.	6	86	34	39	9	4822	292	1	3.63	1	0	1	....	20	3	0	9.00	1979-80	1984-85
Bassen, Hank	Chi., Det., Pit.	9	157	47	66	31	8829	441	5	2.99	5	1	4	....	274	11	0	2.41	1954-55	1967-68
Bastien, Baz	Tor.	1	5	0	4	1	300	20	0	4.00	....	....	....	....	....	....	....	....	1945-46	1945-46
Bauman, Gary	Mtl., Min.	3	35	6	18	6	1718	102	0	3.56	....	....	....	....	....	....	....	....	1966-67	1968-69
Bedard, Jim	Wsh.	2	73	17	40	13	4232	278	1	3.94	....	....	....	....	....	....	....	....	1977-78	1977-78
Behrend, Marc	Wpg.	3	36	12	19	0	1946	160	1	4.93	7	1	3	....	312	19	0	3.65	1983-84	1985-86
Belanger, Yves	St.L., Atl., Bos.	6	78	27	36	6	4134	259	2	3.76	....	....	....	....	....	....	....	....	1974-75	1979-80
Belhumeur, Michel	Phi., Wsh.	3	65	9	36	7	3306	254	0	4.61	1	0	0	....	10	1	0	6.00	1972-73	1975-76
Bell, Gordie	Tor., NYR	2	8	3	5	0	480	31	0	3.88	2	1	1	....	120	9	0	4.50	1945-46	1955-56
Benedict, Clint	Ott., Mtl.M.	13	362	190	43	28	22321	863	57	2.32	48	25	18	4	2907	87	15	1.80	1917-18	1929-30
Bennett, Harvey	Bos.	1	24	10	12	2	1470	106	0	4.33	....	....	....	....	....	....	....	....	1944-45	1944-45
Beveridge, Bill	Det., Ott., St.L., Mtl.M., NYR	9	297	87	166	42	18375	879	18	2.87	5	2	3	....	300	11	0	2.20	1929-30	1942-43
Bibeault, Paul	Mtl., Tor., Bos., Chi.	7	213	68	82	21	12780	785	10	3.69	20	6	14	....	1237	71	2	3.44	1940-41	1946-47
Binette, Andre	Mtl.	1	1	1	0	0	60	4	0	4.00	....	....	....	....	....	....	....	....	1954-55	1954-55
Binkley, Les	Pit.	5	196	58	94	34	11046	575	11	3.12	7	5	2	....	428	15	0	2.10	1967-68	1971-72
Bittner, Richard	Bos.	1	1	0	0	1	60	3	0	3.00	....	....	....	....	....	....	....	....	1949-50	1949-50
Blake, Mike	L.A.	3	40	13	5	15	2117	150	0	4.25	....	....	....	....	....	....	....	....	1981-82	1983-84
Boisvert, Gilles	Det.	1	3	0	3	0	180	9	0	3.00	....	....	....	....	....	....	....	....	1959-60	1959-60
Bouchard, Dan	Atl., Cgy., Que., Wpg.	14	655	286	232	113	37919	2061	27	3.26	43	13	30	....	2549	147	1	3.46	1972-73	1985-86
Bourque, Claude	Mtl., Det.	2	62	16	38	8	3830	192	5	3.01	3	1	2	....	188	8	1	2.55	1938-39	1939-40
Boutin, Rollie	Wsh.	3	22	7	10	1	1137	75	0	3.96	....	....	....	....	....	....	....	....	1978-79	1980-81
Bouvrette, Lionel	NYR	1	1	0	1	0	60	6	0	6.00	....	....	....	....	....	....	....	....	1942-43	1942-43
Bower, Johnny	NYR, Tor.	15	552	251	196	90	32077	1347	37	2.52	74	34	35	....	4350	184	5	2.54	1953-54	1969-70
Brannigan, Andy	NYA	1	1	0	0	0	7	0	0	0.00	....	....	....	....	....	....	....	....	1940-41	1940-41
Brimsek, Frank	Bos., Chi.	10	514	252	182	80	31210	1404	40	2.70	68	32	36	....	4365	186	2	2.56	1938-39	1949-50
Broda, Turk	Tor.	14	628	302	224	101	37680	1605	62	2.56	101	58	42	....	6348	211	13	1.99	1936-37	1951-52
Broderick, Ken	Min., Bos.	*3	27	11	12	1	1464	74	2	3.03	....	....	....	....	....	....	....	....	1969-70	1974-75
Broderick, Len	Mtl.	1	1	1	0	0	60	2	0	2.00	....	....	....	....	....	....	....	....	1957-58	1957-58
Bromley, Gary	Buf., Van.	6	136	54	44	28	7427	425	7	3.43	7	2	5	....	360	25	0	4.17	1973-74	1980-81
Brooks, Arthur	Tor.	1	4	2	1	0	220	23	0	5.75	....	....	....	....	....	....	....	....	1917-18	1917-18
Brooks, Ross	Bos.	3	54	37	7	6	3047	134	4	2.64	1	0	0	....	20	3	0	9.00	1972-73	1974-75
Brophy, Frank	Que.	1	21	3	18	0	1247	148	0	7.05	....	....	....	....	....	....	....	....	1919-20	1919-20
Brown, Andy	Det., Pit.	3	62	22	26	9	3373	213	1	3.79	....	....	....	....	....	....	....	....	1971-72	1973-74
Brown, Ken	Chi.	1	1	0	0	0	18	1	0	3.33	....	....	....	....	....	....	....	....	1970-71	1970-71
Bullock, Bruce	Van.	3	16	3	9	3	427	74	0	4.79	....	....	....	....	....	....	....	....	1972-73	1976-77
Buzinski, Steve	NYR	1	9	2	6	1	560	55	0	5.89	....	....	....	....	....	....	....	....	1942-43	1942-43
Caley, Don	St.L.	1	1	0	0	0	30	3	0	6.00	....	....	....	....	....	....	....	....	1967-68	1967-68
Caron, Jacques	L.A., St.L., Van.	5	72	24	29	11	3846	211	2	3.29	12	4	7	....	639	34	0	3.19	1967-68	1973-74
Carter, Lyle	Cal.	1	15	4	7	0	721	50	0	4.16	....	....	....	....	....	....	....	....	1971-72	1971-72
Chabot, Lorne	NYR, Tor., Mtl., Chi., Mtl.M., NYA	11	411	206	140	65	25309	861	0	2.04	37	13	17	6	2558	64	5	1.50	1926-27	1936-37
Chadwick, Ed	Tor., Bos.	6	184	57	92	35	10980	551	14	3.01	....	....	....	....	....	....	....	....	1955-56	1961-62
Champoux, Bob	Det., Cal.	2	17	2	11	3	923	80	0	5.20	1	0	0	....	40	4	0	6.00	1963-64	1973-74
Cheevers, Gerry	Tor., Bos.	13	418	230	94	74	24394	1175	26	2.89	88	47	35	....	5396	242	8	3.30	1961-62	1979-80
Clancy, Frank	Tor.	1	1	0	0	0	1	0	0	0.00	....	....	....	....	....	....	....	....	1931-32	1931-32
Cleghorn, Odie	Pit.	1	1	1	0	0	60	2	0	2.00	....	....	....	....	....	....	....	....	1925-26	1925-26
Colvin, Les	Bos.	1	1	0	1	0	60	4	0	4.00	....	....	....	....	....	....	....	....	1948-49	1948-49
Conacher, Charlie	Tor., Det.	13	3	0	0	0	9	0	0	0.00	....	....	....	....	....	....	....	....	1929-30	1940-41
Connell, Alex	Ott., Det., NYA, Mtl.M.	12	416	199	155	59	26030	837	80	2.01	21	9	5	7	1309	26	4	1.19	1924-25	1936-37
Corsi, Jim	Edm.	1	26	8	14	3	1366	83	0	3.65	....	....	....	....	....	....	....	....	1979-80	1979-80
Courteau, Maurice	Bos.	1	6	2	4	0	360	33	0	5.50	....	....	....	....	....	....	....	....	1943-44	1943-44
Cox, Abbie	Mtl.M., Det., NYA, Mtl.	3	5	1	1	2	263	11	0	2.51	....	....	....	....	....	....	....	....	1929-30	1935-36
Craig, Jim	Atl., Bos., Min.	2	27	10	9	7	1478	91	0	3.69	....	....	....	....	....	....	....	....	1979-80	1980-81
Crha, Jiri	Tor.	2	69	28	27	11	3942	261	0	3.97	5	0	4	....	186	21	0	6.77	1979-80	1980-81
Crozier, Roger	Det., Buf., Wsh.	14	518	206	197	74	28567	1446	30	3.04	31	14	15	....	1798	82	1	2.75	1963-64	1976-77
Cude, Wilf	Phi., Bos., Chi., Det., Mtl.	10	282	100	129	49	17486	796	24	2.73	19	7	11	1	1317	51	1	2.32	1930-31	1940-41
Cutts, Don	Edm.	1	6	1	2	1	269	16	0	3.57	....	....	....	....	....	....	....	....	1979-80	1979-80
Cyr, Claude	Mtl.	1	1	0	0	0	20	1	0	3.00	....	....	....	....	....	....	....	....	1958-59	1958-59
Daley, Joe	Pit., Buf., Det.	4	105	34	44	19	5836	326	3	3.35	....	....	....	....	....	....	....	....	1968-69	1971-72
Damore, Nick	Bos.	1	1	0	1	0	60	3	0	3.00	....	....	....	....	....	....	....	....	1941-42	1941-42
D'Amour, Mark	Cgy.	1	15	2	4	2	560	32	0	3.43	....	....	....	....	....	....	....	....	1985-86	1985-86
Davidson, John	St.L., NYR	10	301	123	124	39	17109	1004	7	3.52	31	16	14	....	1862	77	1	248	1973-74	1982-83
Decourcy, Robert	NYR	1	1	0	1	0	29	6	0	12.41	....	....	....	....	....	....	....	....	1947-48	1947-48
Defelice, Norman	Bos.	1	10	3	5	2	600	30	0	3.00	....	....	....	....	....	....	....	....	1956-57	1956-57
DeJordy, Denis	Chi., L.A., Mtl., Det.	11	316	124	127	51	17798	929	15	3.13	18	6	.9	....	946	55	0	3.49	1962-63	1973-74
Desjardins, Gerry	L.A., Chi., NYI, Buf.	10	331	122	153	44	19014	1042	12	3.29	35	15	15	....	1874	108	0	3.46	1968-69	1977-78
Dickie, Bill	Chi.	1	1	1	0	0	60	3	0	3.00	....	....	....	....	....	....	....	....	1941-42	1941-42
Dion, Connie	Det.	2	38	23	11	4	2280	119	0	3.13	5	1	4	....	300	17	0	3.40	1943-44	1944-45
Dion, Michel	Que., Wpg., Pit.	6	227	60	118	32	12695	8982	2	4.24	5	2	3	....	304	22	0	4.34	1979-80	1984-85
Dolson, Clarence	Det.	3	93	35	44	13	5820	192	16	1.98	2	0	2	....	120	7	0	3.50	1929-30	1930-31
Dowie, Bruce	Tor.	1	2	0	1	0	72	4	0	3.33	....	....	....	....	....	....	....	....	1983-84	1983-84
Dryden, Dave	NYR, Chi., Buf., Edm.	9	203	48	57	24	10424	555	9	3.19	3	0	2	....	133	9	0	4.06	1961-62	1979-80
Dryden, Ken	Mtl.	8	397	258	57	74	23352	870	46	2.24	112	80	32	....	6841	274	10	2.40	1970-71	1978-79
Dumas, Michel	Chi.	2	8	2	1	2	362	24	0	3.98	1	0	0	....	19	1	0	3.16	1974-75	1976-77
Dupuis, Bob	Edm.	1	1	0	1	0	60	4	0	4.00	....	....	....	....	....	....	....	....	1979-80	1979-80
Durnan, Bill	Mtl.	7	383	208	112	62	22945	901	34	2.36	45	27	18	....	2851	99	2	2.08	1943-44	1949-50
Dyck, Ed	Van.	3	49	8	28	5	2453	178	1	4.35	....	....	....	....	....	....	....	....	1971-72	1973-74
Edwards, Don	Buf., Cgy., Tor.	10	459	208	155	77	26181	1449	16	3.32	42	16	21	....	2302	132	1	3.44	1976-77	1985-86
Edwards, Gary	St.L., L.A., Clev., Min., Edm., Pit.	13	286	88	125	43	16002	973	11	3.65	11	5	4	....	537	34	0	3.80	1968-69	1981-82
Edwards, Marv	Pit., Tor., Cal.	4	61	15	34	7	3467	218	2	3.77	....	....	....	....	....	....	....	....	1968-69	1973-74
Edwards, Roy	Det., Pit.	7	236	92	88	38	13109	637	12	2.92	4	0	3	....	206	11	0	3.20	1967-68	1973-74
Ellacott, Ken	Van.	1	12	2	3	4	555	41	0	4.43	....	....	....	....	....	....	....	....	1982-83	1982-83
Esposito, Tony	Mtl., Chi.	16	886	423	307	151	52585	2563	76	2.92	....	....	....	....	....	....	....	....	1968-69	1983-84
Evans, Claude	Mtl., Bos.	2	5	2	2	1	280	16	0	3.43	....	....	....	....	....	....	....	....	1954-55	1957-58
Farr, Rocky	Buf.	3	19	2	6	3	722	42	0	3.49	....	....	....	....	....	....	....	....	1972-73	1974-75
Favell, Doug	Phi., Tor., Col.	12	373	123	153	69	20771	1096	18	3.17	21	5	16	....	1270	66	1	3.12	1967-68	1978-79
Forbes, Jake	Tor., Ham., NYA, Phi.	13	210	84	114	11	12922	594	19	2.76	2	0	2	....	120	7	0	3.50	1919-20	1932-33
Ford, Brian	Que., Pit.	2	11	3	7	0	580	61	0	6.31	....	....	....	....	....	....	....	....	1983-84	1984-85
Fowler, Hec	Bos.	1	7	1	6	0	420	43	0	6.14	....	....	....	....	....	....	....	....	1924-25	1924-25

Name	NHL Teams	NHL Seasons	Regular Schedule								Playoffs								First NHL Season	Last NHL Season
			GP	W	L	T	Mins	GA	SO	Avg	GP	W	L	T	Mins	GA	SO	Avg		
Francis, Emile	Chi., NYR	6	95	31	52	11	5700	355	1	3.74	....	....	....	....	....	....	....	....	1946-47	1951-52
Franks, Jim	Det., NYR, Bos.	4	43	12	23	7	2580	185	1	4.30	1	0	1	....	30	2	0	4.00	1936-37	1943-44
Frederick, Ray	Chi.	1	5	0	4	1	300	22	0	4.40	....	....	....	....	....	....	....	....	1954-55	1954-55
Friesen, Karl	N.J.	1	4	0	2	1	130	16	0	7.38	....	....	....	....	....	....	....	....	1986-87	1986-87
Gamble, Bruce	NYR, Bos., Tor., Phi.	10	327	109	139	47	18442	992	22	3.23	5	0	4	....	206	25	0	7.29	1958-59	1971-72
Gardiner, Bert	NYR, Mtl., Chi., Bos.	6	144	49	68	27	8760	554	3	3.79	9	4	5	....	647	20	0	1.85	1935-36	1943-44
Gardiner, Chuck	Chi.	7	316	112	152	52	19687	664	42	2.02	21	12	6	3	1532	35	5	1.37	1927-28	1933-34
Gardner, George	Det., Van.	5	66	16	30	6	3313	207	0	3.75	....	....	....	....	....	....	....	....	1965-66	1971-72
Garrett, John	Hfd., Que., Van.	6	207	68	91	37	11763	837	1	4.27	9	4	3	....	461	33	0	4.30	1979-80	1984-85
Gatherum, Dave	Det.	1	3	2	0	1	180	3	1	1.00	....	....	....	....	....	....	....	....	1953-54	1953-54
Gauthier, Paul	Mtl.	1	1	0	0	1	70	2	0	1.71	....	....	....	....	....	....	....	....	1937-38	1937-38
Gelineau, Jack	Bos., Chi.	4	143	46	64	33	8580	447	7	3.12	4	2	2	....	260	7	1	1.62	1948-49	1953-54
Giacomin, Ed	NYR, Det.	13	610	289	206	97	35693	1675	54	2.82	65	29	35	....	3834	180	1	2.82	1965-66	1977-78
Gilbert, Gilles	Min., Bos., Det.	14	416	182	148	60	23677	1290	18	3.27	32	17	15	....	1919	97	3	3.03	1969-70	1962-63
Gill, Andre	Bos.	1	5	3	2	0	270	13	1	2.89	....	....	....	....	....	....	....	....	1967-68	1967-68
Goodman, Paul	Chi.	3	52	23	20	9	3240	117	6	2.17	3	0	3	....	187	10	0	3.21	1937-38	1940-41
Grahame, Ron	Bos., L.A., Que.	4	114	50	43	15	6472	409	5	3.79	4	2	1	....	202	7	0	2.08	1977-78	1980-81
Grant, Ben	Tor., NYA., Bos.	6	50	17	26	4	2990	188	4	3.77	....	....	....	....	....	....	....	....	1928-29	1943-44
Grant, Doug	Det., St.L.	7	77	27	34	8	4199	280	2	4.00	....	....	....	....	....	....	....	....	1973-74	1979-80
Gratton, Gilles	St.L., NYR	2	47	13	18	9	2299	154	0	4.02	....	....	....	....	....	....	....	....	1975-76	1976-77
Gray, Gerry	Det., NYI	2	8	1	5	1	440	35	0	4.77	....	....	....	....	....	....	....	....	1970-71	1972-73
Gray, Harrison	Det.	1	1	0	0	0	40	5	0	730	....	....	....	....	....	....	....	....	1963-64	1963-64
Hainsworth, George	Mtl., Tor.	11	465	247	146	74	29415	937	94	1.91	52	21	20	5	3486	112	8	1.93	1926-27	1936-37
Hall, Glenn	Det., Chi., St.L.	18	906	407	327	165	53484	2239	84	2.51	115	49	65	....	6899	321	6	2.79	1952-53	1970-71
Hamel, Pierre	Tor., Wpg.	4	69	13	41	7	3766	276	0	4.40	....	....	....	....	....	....	....	....	1974-75	1980-81
Harrison, Paul	Min., Tor., Pit., Buf.	7	109	28	53	8	5806	408	2	4.22	4	0	1	....	157	9	0	3.44	1975-76	1981-82
Head, Don	Bos.	1	38	9	26	3	3280	161	2	4.24	....	....	....	....	....	....	....	....	1961-62	1961-62
Hebert, Sammy	Tor., Ott.	2	4	1	3	0	200	19	0	5.70	....	....	....	....	....	....	....	....	1917-18	1923-24
Heinz, Rick	St.L., Van.	5	49	14	19	5	2356	159	2	4.05	....	....	....	....	....	....	....	....	1980-81	1984-85
Henderson, John	Bos.	2	46	15	15	15	2700	113	5	2.51	2	0	2	....	120	8	0	4.00	1954-55	1955-56
Henry, Gord	Bos.	4	3	1	2	0	180	5	1	1.67	5	0	4	....	283	21	0	4.45	1948-49	1952-53
Henry, Jim	NYR, Chi., Bos.	9	404	159	178	67	24240	1166	28	2.88	29	11	18	....	1741	81	2	2.79	1941-42	1954-55
Herron, Denis	Pit., K.C., Mtl.	14	462	146	203	76	25608	1579	10	3.70	15	5	10	....	901	50	0	3.30	1972-73	1985-86
Highton, Hec	Chi.	1	24	10	14	0	1440	108	0	4.50	....	....	....	....	....	....	....	....	1943-44	1943-44
Himes, Normie	NYA	2	2	0	0	1	79	3	0	2.28	....	....	....	....	....	....	....	....	1927-28	1928-29
Hodge, Charlie	Mtl., Oak., Van.	13	358	152	124	60	20593	927	24	2.70	16	6	8	....	803	32	2	2.39	1954-55	1970-71
Hoganson, Paul	Pit.	1	2	0	1	0	57	7	0	7.37	....	....	....	....	....	....	....	....	1970-71	1970-71
Hogosta, Goran	NYI, Que.	2	22	5	12	3	1208	83	1	4.12	....	....	....	....	....	....	....	....	1977-78	1979-80
Holden, Mark	Mtl., Wpg.	4	8	2	2	1	372	25	0	4.03	....	....	....	....	....	....	....	....	1981-82	1984-85
Holland, Ken	Hfd.	1	1	0	1	0	60	7	0	7.00	....	....	....	....	....	....	....	....	1980-81	1980-81
Holland, Robbie	Pit.	2	44	11	22	9	2513	171	1	4.06	....	....	....	....	....	....	....	....	1979-80	1980-81
Holmes, Harry	Tor., Det.	4	105	41	54	10	6510	264	17	2.43	7	4	3	....	420	26	0	3.71	1917-18	1927-28
Horner, Red	Tor.	1	1	0	0	0	1	1	0	60.00	....	....	....	....	....	....	....	....	1932-33	1932-33
Inness, Gary	Pit., Phi., Wsh.	7	162	58	61	27	8710	494	2	3.40	9	5	4	....	540	24	0	2.67	1973-74	1980-81
Ireland, Randy	Buf.	1	2	0	0	0	30	3	0	6.00	....	....	....	....	....	....	....	....	1978-79	1978-79
Irons, Robbie	St.L.	1	1	0	0	0	3	0	0	0.00	....	....	....	....	....	....	....	....	1968-69	1968-69
Ironstone, Joe	NYA, Tor.	2	2	1	1	0	110	3	0	1.64	....	....	....	....	....	....	....	....	1925-26	1927-28
Jackson, Doug	Chi.	1	6	2	3	1	360	42	0	7.00	....	....	....	....	....	....	....	....	1947-48	1947-48
Jackson, Percy	Bos., NYA, NYR	4	7	1	3	1	392	26	0	3.98	....	....	....	....	....	....	....	....	1931-32	1935-36
Janaszak, Steve	Min., Col.	2	3	0	1	1	160	15	0	5.63	....	....	....	....	....	....	....	....	1979-80	1981-82
Jenkins, Roger	NYA	1	1	0	1	0	30	7	0	14.00	....	....	....	....	....	....	....	....	1938-39	1938-39
Jensen, Al	Det., Wsh., L.A.	7	179	95	53	18	9974	557	8	3.35	12	5	5	....	598	32	0	3.21	1980-81	1986-87
Jensen, Darren	Phi.	2	30	15	10	1	1496	95	2	3.81	....	....	....	....	....	....	....	....	1984-85	1985-86
Johnson, Bob	St.L., Pit.	2	24	9	9	1	1059	66	0	3.74	....	....	....	....	....	....	....	....	1972-73	1974-75
Johnston, Eddie	Bos., Tor., St.L., Chi.	16	592	236	256	87	34209	1855	32	3.25	18	7	10	....	1023	57	1	3.34	1962-63	1977-78
Junkin, Joe	Bos.	1	1	0	0	0	8	0	0	0.00	....	....	....	....	....	....	....	....	1968-69	1968-69
Kaarela, Jari	Col.	1	5	2	2	0	220	22	0	6.00	....	....	....	....	....	....	....	....	1980-81	1980-81
Kampurri, Hannu	N.J.	1	13	1	10	1	645	54	0	5.02	....	....	....	....	....	....	....	....	1984-85	1984-85
Karakas, Mike	Chi., Mtl.	8	336	114	169	53	20616	1002	28	2.92	23	11	12	....	1434	72	3	3.01	1935-36	1945-46
Keenan, Don	Bos.	1	1	0	1	0	60	4	0	4.00	....	....	....	....	....	....	....	....	1958-59	1958-59
Kerr, Dave	Mtl.M., NYA, NYR	11	426	203	148	75	26519	960	51	2.17	40	18	19	3	2616	76	8	1.74	1930-31	1940-41
Kleisinger, Terry	NYR	1	4	0	2	0	191	14	0	4.40	....	....	....	....	....	....	....	....	1985-86	1985-86
Klymkiw, Julian	NYR	1	1	0	0	0	19	2	0	6.32	....	....	....	....	....	....	....	....	1958-59	1958-59
Kurt, Gary	Cal.	1	16	1	7	5	838	60	0	4.30	....	....	....	....	....	....	....	....	1971-72	1971-72
Lacroix, Al	Mtl.	1	5	1	4	0	280	16	0	3.20	....	....	....	....	....	....	....	....	1925-26	1925-26
LaFerriere, Rick	Col.	1	1	0	0	0	20	1	0	3.00	....	....	....	....	....	....	....	....	1981-82	1981-82
Larocque, Michel	Mtl., Tor., Phi., St.L.	11	312	160	89	45	17615	178	17	3.33	14	6	6	....	978	37	1	2.92	1973-74	1983-84
Laskowski, Gary	L.A.	2	59	19	27	5	2942	228	0	4.65	....	....	....	....	....	....	....	....	1982-83	1983-84
Laxton, Gord	Pit.	4	17	4	9	0	800	74	0	5.55	....	....	....	....	....	....	....	....	1975-76	1978-79
LeDuc, Albert	Mtl.	1	1	0	0	0	2	1	0	30.00	....	....	....	....	....	....	....	....	1931-32	1931-32
Legris, Claude	Det.	2	4	0	1	1	91	4	0	2.64	....	....	....	....	....	....	....	....	1980-81	1981-82
Lehman, Hugh	Chi.	2	48	20	24	4	3047	136	6	2.68	2	0	1	1	120	10	0	5.00	1926-27	1927-28
Lessard, Mario	L.A.	6	240	92	97	39	13529	843	9	3.74	20	6	12	....	1136	83	0	4.38	1978-79	1983-84
Levasseur, Louis	Min.	1	1	0	1	0	60	7	0	7.00	....	....	....	....	....	....	....	....	1979-80	1979-80
Levinsky, Alex	Tor.	1	1	0	0	0	1	1	0	60.00	....	....	....	....	....	....	....	....	1932-33	1932-33
Lindbergh, Pelle	Phi.	5	157	87	49	15	9151	503	7	3.30	23	12	10	....	1214	63	3	3.11	1981-82	1985-86
Lindsay, Bert	Mtl.W., Tor.	2	20	6	14	0	2219	118	0	3.19	....	....	....	....	....	....	....	....	1917-18	1918-19
Lockett, Ken	Van.	2	55	13	15	8	2348	131	2	3.35	1	0	1	...	60	6	0	6.00	1974-75	1975-76
Lockhart, Howie	Tor., Que., Ham., Bos.	5	57	17	39	0	3371	282	1	5.02	....	....	....	....	....	....	....	....	1919-20	1924-25
Lopresti, Pete	Min., Edm.	6	175	43	102	20	9858	668	5	4.07	2	0	2	....	77	6	0	4.68	1974-75	1980-81
Lopresti, Sam	Chi.	2	74	30	38	6	4530	236	4	3.13	8	3	5	....	530	17	1	1.92	1940-41	1941-42
Loustel, Ron	Wpg.	1	1	0	1	0	60	10	0	10.00	....	....	....	....	....	....	....	....	1980-81	1980-81
Low, Ron	Tor., Wsh., Det., Que., Edm., NJ	11	382	102	203	37	20502	1463	4	4.28	7	1	6	....	452	29	0	3.85	1972-73	1984-85
Lozinski, Pete	Det.	1	30	6	11	7	1459	105	0	4.32	....	....	....	....	....	....	....	....	1980-81	1980-81
Lumley, Harry	Det., NYR, Chi., Tor., Bos.	16	804	332	324	143	48107	2210	71	2.76	76	29	47	....	4759	199	7	2.51	1943-44	1959-60
MacKenzie, Shawn	N.J.	1	4	0	1	0	130	15	0	6.91	....	....	....	....	....	....	....	....	1982-83	1982-83
Maniago, Cesare	Tor., Mtl., NYR, Min., Van.	15	568	189	261	96	32570	1774	30	3.27	36	15	21	....	2245	100	3	2.67	1960-61	1977-78
Marios, Jean	Tor., Chi.	2	3	1	2	0	180	15	0	5.00	....	....	....	....	....	....	....	....	1943-44	1953-54
Martin, Seth	St.L.	1	30	8	10	7	1552	67	1	2.59	2	0	0	....	73	5	0	4.11	1967-68	1967-68
Mattson, Markus	Wpg., Min., L.A.	4	92	21	46	14	5007	343	6	4.11	....	....	....	....	....	....	....	....	1979-80	1983-84
Mayer, Gilles	Tor.	4	9	1	7	1	540	25	0	2.78	....	....	....	....	....	....	....	....	1949-50	1955-56
McAuley, Ken	NYR	2	96	17	64	15	5740	537	1	5.61	....	....	....	....	....	....	....	....	1943-44	1944-45
McCartan, Jack	NYR	2	12	3	7	2	680	43	1	3.79	....	....	....	....	....	....	....	....	1959-60	1960-61
McCool, Frank	Tor.	2	72	34	31	7	4320	242	4	3.36	13	8	5	....	807	30	4	2.23	1944-45	1945-46
McDuffe, Pete	St.L., NYR, K.C., Det.	5	57	11	36	6	3207	218	0	4.08	1	0	1	....	60	7	0	7.00	1971-72	1975-76
McGrattan, Tom	Det.	1	1	0	0	0	8	0	0	0.00	....	....	....	....	....	....	....	....	1947-48	1947-48
McKenzie, Bill	Det., K.C., Col.	6	91	18	49	13	4776	326	2	4.10	....	....	....	....	....	....	....	....	1973-74	1979-80
McLachlan, Murray	Tor.	1	2	0	1	0	25	4	0	9.60	....	....	....	....	....	....	....	....	1970-71	1970-71
McLelland, Dave	Van.	1	2	1	1	0	120	10	0	5.00	....	....	....	....	....	....	....	....	1972-73	1972-73
McLeod, Don	Det., Phi.	2	18	3	10	1	879	74	0	5.05	....	....	....	....	....	....	....	....	1970-71	1971-72
McLeod, Jim	St.L.	1	16	6	6	4	880	44	0	3.00	....	....	....	....	....	....	....	....	1971-72	1971-72
McNamara, Gerry	Tor.	2	7	2	2	1	323	15	0	2.79	....	....	....	....	....	....	....	....	1960-61	1969-70
McNeil, Gerry	Mtl.	7	276	119	105	52	16535	650	28	2.36	35	17	18	....	2288	72	5	1.89	1947-48	1956-57
McRae, Gord	Tor.	5	71	21	32	10	3799	221	1	3.49	8	2	5	....	454	22	0	2.91	1972-73	1977-78
Meloche, Gilles	Chi., Cal., Cle., Min., Pit.	18	788	270	351	131	45401	2756	20	3.64	45	21	19	....	2464	143	2	3.48	1970-71	1987-88
Micalef, Corrado	Det.	5	113	26	59	15	5794	409	2	4.24	....	....	....	....	....	....	....	....	1981-82	1985-86
Middlebrook, Lindsay	Wpg., Min., N.J., Edm.	4	37	3	23	6	1845	152	0	4.94	....	....	....	....	....	....	....	....	1979-80	1982-83
Millar, Joe	Bos.	1	6	1	3	2	360	25	0	4.17	....	....	....	....	....	....	....	....	1957-58	1957-58
Miller, Joe	NYA, Pit., Phi.	4	130	24	90	16	7981	386	16	2.90	3	2	1	....	180	3	1	1.00	1927-28	1930-31
Mio, Eddie	Edm., NYR, Det.	7	192	83	85	31	12299	822	6	4.01	17	9	7	....	986	63	0	3.83	1979-80	1985-86

Name	NHL Teams	NHL Seasons	Regular Schedule GP	W	L	T	Mins	GA	SO	Avg	Playoffs GP	W	L	T	Mins	GA	SO	Avg	First NHL Season	Last NHL Season
Mitchell, Ivan	Tor.	3	21	11	9	0	1232	93	0	4.53	....	....	....	....	....	....	....	....	1919-20	1921-22
Moffatt, Mike	Bos.	3	19	7	7	2	979	70	0	4.29	11	6	5	....	663	38	0	3.44	1918-82	1983-84
Moore, Alfie	NYA, Det., Chi.,	3	21	7	14	0	1290	81	1	3.77	3	1	2	....	180	7	0	2.33	1936-37	1939-40
Moore, Robbie	Phi., Wsh.	2	6	3	1	1	257	8	2	1.87	5	3	2	....	268	18	0	4.03	1978-79	1982-83
Morisette, Jean	Mtl.	1	1	0	1	0	36	4	0	6.67	....	....	....	....	....	....	....	....	1963-64	1963-64
Mowers, Johnny	Det.	4	152	65	55	25	9350	399	15	2.56	32	19	13	....	2000	85	2	2.55	1940-41	1946-47
Mrazek, Jerry	Phi.	1	1	0	0	0	6	1	0	10.00	....	....	....	....	....	....	....	....	1975-76	1975-76
Mummery, Harry	Que., Ham.	2	4	2	1	0	191	20	0	6.28	....	....	....	....	....	....	....	....	1919-20	1921-22
Murphy, Hal	Mtl.	1	1	1	0	0	60	4	0	4.00	....	....	....	....	....	....	....	....	1952-53	1952-53
Murray, Tom	Mtl.	1	1	0	1	0	60	4	0	4.00	....	....	....	....	....	....	....	....	1929-30	1929-30
Myre, Phil	Mtl., Atl., St.L., Phi., Col., Buf.	14	439	149	198	76	25220	1482	14	3.53	12	6	5	....	747	41	1	3.29	1969-70	1982-83
Newton, Lam	Pit.	2	16	4	7	1	814	51	0	3.76	....	....	....	....	....	....	....	....	1970-71	1972-73
Norris, Jack	Bos., Chi., L.A.	4	58	19	26	4	3119	202	2	3.89	....	....	....	....	....	....	....	....	1964-65	1970-71
Oleschuk, Bill	K.C., Col.	4	55	7	28	10	2835	188	1	3.98	....	....	....	....	....	....	....	....	1975-76	1979-80
Olesevich, Dan	NYR	1	1	0	0	1	40	2	0	3.00	....	....	....	....	....	....	....	....	1961-62	1961-62
Ouimet, Ted	St.L.	1	1	0	1	0	60	2	0	2.00	....	....	....	....	....	....	....	....	1968-69	1968-69
Pagean, Paul	L.A.	1	1	0	1	0	60	8	0	8.00	....	....	....	....	....	....	....	....	1980-81	1980-81
Paille, Marcel	NYR	7	107	33	52	21	6342	362	2	3.42	....	....	....	....	....	....	....	....	1957-58	1964-65
Palmateer, Mike	Tor., Wsh.	8	356	149	138	52	20131	1183	17	3.53	29	12	17	....	1765	89	2	3.03	1976-77	1983-84
Parent, Bernie	Bos., Tor., Phi.	13	608	270	197	121	35136	1493	55	2.55	71	38	33	....	4302	174	6	2.43	1965-66	1978-79
Parent, Bob	Tor.	2	3	0	2	0	160	15	0	5.63	....	....	....	....	....	....	....	....	1981-82	1982-83
Parro, Dave	Wsh.	4	77	21	36	10	4015	274	2	4.09	....	....	....	....	....	....	....	....	1980-81	1983-84
Patrick, Lester	NYR	....	....	....	....	....	....	....	....	....	1	1	0	0	46	1	0	1.30	1927-28	1927-28
Pelletier, Marcel	Chi., NYR	2	8	1	6	1	395	33	0	5.01	....	....	....	....	....	....	....	....	1950-51	1962-63
Penney, Steve	Mtl., Wpg.	5	91	35	38	12	5194	313	1	3.62	27	15	12	....	1604	72	4	2.69	1983-84	1987-88
Perreault, Robert	Mtl., Det., Bos.	3	31	8	16	6	1860	106	2	3.42	....	....	....	....	....	....	....	....	1955-56	1962-63
Pettie, Jim	Bos.	3	21	9	7	2	1157	71	1	3.68	....	....	....	....	....	....	....	....	1976-77	1978-79
Plante, Jacques	Mtl., NYR, St.L., Tor., Bos.	18	837	434	246	137	49633	1965	82	2.37	112	71	37	....	6651	241	15	2.17	1952-53	1972-73
Plasse, Michel	Mtl., St.L., K.C., Pit., Col., Que.	11	299	92	136	54	16760	1058	2	3.79	4	1	2	....	195	9	1	2.77	1970-71	1981-82
Plaxton, Hugh	Mtl.M.	1	1	0	1	0	59	5	0	1.02	....	....	....	....	....	....	....	....	1932-33	1932-33
Pronovost, Claude	Bos., Mtl.	2	3	1	1	0	120	7	1	3.50	....	....	....	....	....	....	....	....	1955-56	1958-59
Pusey, Chris	Det.	1	1	0	0	0	40	3	0	4.50	....	....	....	....	....	....	....	....	1985-86	1986-86
Rayner, Chuck	NYA, NYR	10	424	138	209	77	25384	1294	25	3.06	18	9	9	....	1134	46	1	2.43	1940-41	1952-53
Redquest, Greg	Pit.	1	1	0	0	0	13	3	0	1385	....	....	....	....	....	....	....	....	1977-78	1977-78
Reece, Dave	Bos.	1	14	7	5	2	777	43	2	3.32	....	....	....	....	....	....	....	....	1975-76	1975-76
Resch, Glenn	NYI, Col., N.J., Phi.	14	571	231	224	82	32279	1761	26	3.27	41	17	17	....	2044	85	2	2.50	1973-74	1986-87
Rheaume, Herb	Mtl.	1	31	10	19	1	1889	92	0	2.97	....	....	....	....	....	....	....	....	1925-26	1925-26
Ricci, Nick	Pit.	4	19	7	12	0	1087	79	0	4.36	....	....	....	....	....	....	....	....	1979-80	1982-83
Richardson, Terry	Det., St.L.	5	20	3	11	0	906	85	0	5.63	....	....	....	....	....	....	....	....	1973-74	1978-79
Ridley, Curt	NYR, Van., Tor.	6	104	27	47	16	5498	355	1	3.87	2	0	2	....	120	8	0	4.00	1974-75	1980-81
Riggin, Denis	Det.	2	18	5	10	2	985	54	1	3.29	....	....	....	....	....	....	....	....	1959-60	1962-63
Riggin, Pat	Atl., Cgy., Wsh., Bos., Pit.	9	350	153	120	52	19872	1135	11	3.43	25	8	13	....	1336	72	0	3.23	1979-80	1987-88
Ring, Bob	Bos.	1	1	0	0	0	34	4	0	7.06	....	....	....	....	....	....	....	....	1965-66	1965-66
Rivard, Fern	Min.	4	55	9	20	7	2865	190	2	3.98	....	....	....	....	....	....	....	....	1968-69	1974-75
Roach, John	Tor., NYR, Det.	14	491	218	204	69	30423	1246	58	2.46	34	15	16	3	2206	69	8	1.88	1921-22	1934-35
Roberts, Moe	Bos., NYA, Chi.	4	10	2	5	0	506	31	0	3.68	....	....	....	....	....	....	....	....	1925-26	1951-52
Robertson, Earl	NYA, Det.	6	190	60	95	34	11820	575	16	2.92	15	6	7	....	995	29	2	1.75	1936-37	1941-42
Rollins, Al	Tor., Chi., NYR	9	430	138	205	84	25717	1196	28	2.79	13	6	7	....	755	30	0	2.38	1949-50	1959-60
Romano, Roberto	Pit., Bos.	5	125	45	64	7	7046	474	4	4.04	....	....	....	....	....	....	....	....	1982-83	1986-87
Rupp, Pat	Det.	1	1	0	1	0	60	4	0	4.00	....	....	....	....	....	....	....	....	1963-64	1963-64
Rutherford, Jim	Det., Pit., Tor., L.A.	13	457	150	227	59	25895	1576	14	3.65	8	2	5	....	440	28	0	3.82	1970-71	1982-83
Rutledge, Wayne	L.A.	3	82	22	30	5	4325	241	2	3.34	8	2	2	....	378	20	0	3.17	1967-68	1969-70
St.Croix, Rick	Phi., Tor.	8	129	49	54	18	7275	450	2	3.71	11	4	6	....	562	29	1	3.10	1977-78	1984-85
Sands, Charlie	Mtl.	1	1	0	0	0	25	5	0	5.00	....	....	....	....	....	....	....	....	1939-40	1939-40
Sands, Mike	Min.	2	6	0	5	0	302	26	0	5.17	....	....	....	....	....	....	....	....	1984-85	1986-87
Sawchuk, Terry	Det., Bos., Tor., L.A., NYR	21	971	435	337	188	57205	2401	103	2.52	106	54	48	....	6291	267	12	2.64	1949-50	1969-70
Schaefer, Joe	NYR	2	2	0	1	0	86	8	0	5.58	....	....	....	....	....	....	....	....	1959-60	1960-61
Sevigny, Richard	Mtl., Que.	8	176	90	44	20	9485	507	5	3.21	6	0	3	....	208	13	0	3.75	1979-80	1986-87
Shields, Al	NYA	1	2	0	0	0	41	9	0	13.17	....	....	....	....	....	....	....	....	1931-32	1931-32
Simmons, Don	Bos., Tor., NYR	11	247	100	104	39	14435	705	20	2.93	24	13	11	....	1436	64	2	2.67	1956-57	1968-69
Simmons, Gary	Cal., Clev., L.A.	4	107	30	57	15	6162	366	5	3.56	1	0	0	....	20	1	0	3.00	1974-75	1977-78
Skidmore, Paul	St.L.	1	2	1	1	0	120	6	0	3.00	....	....	....	....	....	....	....	....	1981-82	1981-82
Smith, Al	Tor., Pit., Det., Buf., Hfd., Col.	10	233	68	99	36	12752	735	10	3.46	6	1	4	....	317	21	0	3.97	1965-66	1980-81
Smith, Gary	Tor., Oak., Cal., Chi., Van., Wsh., Min., Wpg.	14	532	152	237	67	29619	1675	26	3.39	20	5	13	....	1153	62	1	3.23	1965-66	1979-80
Smith, Norman	Mtl.M., Det.	8	199	81	83	35	12297	475	17	2.32	12	9	2	....	880	18	3	1.23	1931-32	1944-45
Sneddon, Bob	Cal.	1	5	0	2	0	225	21	0	5.60	....	....	....	....	....	....	....	....	1970-71	1970-71
Soetaert, Doug	NYR, Wpg., Mtl.	12	284	110	103	44	15583	1030	6	3.97	5	1	2	....	180	14	0	4.67	1975-76	1986-87
Spooner, Reo	Pit.	1	1	0	1	0	60	6	0	6.00	....	....	....	....	....	....	....	....	1929-30	1929-30
Staniowski, Ed	St.L., Wpg., Hfd.	10	219	67	104	21	12075	818	2	4.06	8	1	6	....	428	28	0	3.92	1975-76	1984-85
Starr, Harold	Mtl.M.	1	1	0	0	0	3	0	0	0.00	....	....	....	....	....	....	....	....	1931-32	1931-32
Stein, Phi.	Tor.	1	1	0	0	1	70	2	0	1.71	....	....	....	....	....	....	....	....	1939-40	1939-40
Stephenson, Wayne	St.L., Phi., Wsh.	10	328	146	93	46	18343	937	14	3.06	26	11	12	....	1522	79	2	3.11	1971-72	1980-81
Stevenson, Doug	NYR, Chi.	2	8	2	6	0	480	39	0	4.88	....	....	....	....	....	....	....	....	1944-45	1945-46
Stewart, Charles	Bos.	3	77	31	41	5	4737	194	10	2.46	....	....	....	....	....	....	....	....	1924-25	1926-27
Stewart, Jim	Bos.	1	1	0	1	0	20	5	0	15.00	....	....	....	....	....	....	....	....	1979-80	1979-80
Stuart, Herb	Det.	1	3	0	1	0	180	5	0	1.67	....	....	....	....	....	....	....	....	1926-27	1926-27
Sylvestri, Don	Bos.	1	3	0	0	2	102	6	0	3.53	....	....	....	....	....	....	....	....	1984-85	1984-85
Tataryn, Dave	NYR	1	2	1	1	0	80	10	0	7.50	....	....	....	....	....	....	....	....	1976-77	1976-77
Taylor, Bobby	Phi., Pit.	5	46	15	17	6	2268	155	0	4.10	....	....	....	....	....	....	....	....	1971-72	1975-76
Teno, Harvey	Det.	1	5	2	3	0	3.00	15	0	3.00	....	....	....	....	....	....	....	....	1938-39	1938-39
Thomas, Wayne	Mtl., Tor., NYR	8	243	103	93	34	13768	766	10	3.34	15	6	8	....	849	50	1	3.53	1972-73	1980-81
Thompson, Tiny	Bos., Det.	12	553	284	194	75	34174	1183	81	2.08	44	20	22	....	2970	93	7	1.88	1924-25	1939-40
Tremblay, Vince	Tor., Pit.	5	58	12	26	8	2785	223	1	4.80	....	....	....	....	....	....	....	....	1979-80	1983-84
Tucker, Ted	Cal.	1	5	1	1	1	177	10	0	3.39	....	....	....	....	....	....	....	....	1973-74	1973-74
Turner, Joe	Det.	1	1	0	0	1	60	3	0	3.00	....	....	....	....	....	....	....	....	1941-42	1941-42
Vachon, Rogatien	Mtl., L.A., Det., Bos.	16	785	355	291	115	46298	2310	51	2.99	48	23	23	....	2876	133	2	2.77	1966-67	1981-82
Veisor, Mike	Chi., Hfd., Wpg.	10	139	41	62	26	7806	532	5	4.09	4	0	2	....	180	15	0	5.00	1973-74	1983-84
Vezina, Georges	Mtl.	9	191	105	80	5	11564	633	13	3.28	26	19	6	....	1596	74	4	2.78	1917-18	1925-26
Villemure, Gilles	NYR, Chi.	10	205	98	65	27	11581	542	13	2.81	14	5	5	....	656	32	0	2.93	1963-64	1974-75
Wakely, Ernie	Mtl., St.L.	5	113	41	42	17	6344	290	8	2.79	10	2	6	....	509	37	1	4.36	1962-63	1971-72
Walsh, James	Mtl.M., NYA	7	108	48	43	16	6461	250	12	2.32	8	2	4	2	570	16	2	1.68	1926-27	1932-33
Watt, Jim	St.L.	1	1	0	0	0	20	2	0	6.00	....	....	....	....	....	....	....	....	1973-74	1973-74
Wetzel, Carl	Det., Min.	2	7	1	3	1	302	22	0	4.37	....	....	....	....	....	....	....	....	1964-65	1967-68
Wilson, Dunc	Phi., Van., Tor., NYR, Pit.	10	287	80	150	33	15851	988	8	3.74	....	....	....	....	....	....	....	....	1969-70	1978-79
Wilson, Lefty	Det., Tor., Bos.	3	3	0	0	1	85	1	0	0.71	....	....	....	....	....	....	....	....	1953-54	1957-58
Winkler, Hal	NYR, Bos.	2	75	35	26	14	4739	126	21	1.60	10	2	3	5	640	18	2	1.69	1926-27	1927-28
Wolfe, Bernie	Wsh.	4	120	20	61	21	6104	424	1	4.17	....	....	....	....	....	....	....	....	1975-76	1978-79
Woods, Alec	NYA	1	1	0	1	0	70	3	0	2.57	....	....	....	....	....	....	....	....	1936-37	1936-37
Worsley, Gump	NYR, Mtl., Min.	21	860	335	353	150	50201	2432	43	2.91	70	41	25	....	4080	192	5	2.82	1952-53	1973-74
Worters, Roy	Pit., NYA, Mtl.	12	484	171	233	68	30175	1143	66	2.27	11	3	6	2	690	24	3	2.09	1925-26	1936-37
Worthy, Chris	Oak., Cal.	3	26	5	10	4	1326	98	0	4.43	....	....	....	....	....	....	....	....	1968-69	1970-71
Young, Doug	Det.	1	1	0	0	0	21	1	0	2.86	....	....	....	....	....	....	....	....	1933-34	1933-34
Zanier, Mike	Edm.	1	3	1	1	1	185	12	0	3.89	....	....	....	....	....	....	....	....	1984-85	1984-85

Notes

Notes

1988-89 Transactions

September, 1988

1 - **Wendell Young** traded to Pittsburgh by Philadelphia with Philadelphia's seventh round choice in 1990 Entry Draft for Pittsburgh's third round choice in 1990 Entry Draft.

6 - **Steve Bozek, Michael Dark, Doug Gilmour** and **Mark Hunter** traded to Calgary by St. Louis for **Mike Bullard, Tim Corkery** and **Craig Coxe**.

- **Steve Bozek** and **Paul Reinhart** traded to Vancouver by Calgary for Vancouver's third round choice (**Veli-Pekka Kautonen**) in 1989 Entry Draft.

- **Robert Nordmark** traded to Vancouver by St. Louis for **Dave Richter** and Vancouver's fourth round choice in 1990 Entry Draft.

28 - **Michael Boyce** traded to NY Rangers by Philadelphia for **Chris Jensen**.

29 - **Doug Crossman** traded to Los Angeles by Philadelphia for **Jay Wells**.

29 - **Kent Carlson** traded to Winnipeg by St. Louis with St. Louis' twelfth round choice (**Sergei Kharin**) in 1989 Entry Draft and St. Louis' fourth round choice in 1990 Entry Draft for **Peter Douris**.

29 - **Dave Lowry** traded to St. Louis by Vancouver for **Ernie Vargas**.

30 - **Wayne Van Dorp** traded to Buffalo by Pittsburgh for future considerations.

October

3 - NHL Waiver Draft:

Stu Gavin	Minnesota
Behn Wilson	Vancouver
Steve Dykstra	Pittsburgh
Craig Redmond	NY Rangers
Tom Martin	Minnesota
Risto Siltanen	Vancouver
Jay Caufield	Pittsburgh
Andy Brickley	Boston
Ken Hammond	Edmonton
Ken Leiter	Minnesota
Dave Hannan	Pittsburgh
Dave Hunter	Winnipeg
Jim Hofford	Los Angeles
Steve Smith	Buffalo
Doug Sulliman	Philadelphia
Doug Smith	Edmonton
Brad Marsh	Toronto
Dale Degray	Los Angeles

6 - **Mark LaVarre** traded to Hartford by Chicago for future considerations.

11 - **Brian Lawton, Igor Liba** and the rights to **Eric Bennett** traded to NY Rangers by Minnesota for **Paul Jerrard** and **Mark Tinordi**, the rights to **Bret Barnett** and **Mike Sullivan** and Los Angeles' third round choice (**Murray Garbutt**) in 1989 Entry Draft, — obtained previously by NY Rangers.

11 - **Kent Carlson** traded to Washington by Winnipeg for future considerations.

19 - **Rob Whistle** traded to Washington by St. Louis for Washington's sixth round choice (**Derek Frenette**) in 1989 entry Draft.

21 - **Larry Playfair** traded to Buffalo by Los Angeles for Buffalo's ninth round choice (**Jim Glacin**) in 1989 Entry Draft.

27 - **Jeff Crossman** traded to Edmonton by NY Rangers for **Ron Shudra**.

November

1 - **Ken Hammond** claimed on waivers without right of recall by NY Rangers from Edmonton.

- **Craig Redmond** claimed on waivers without right of recall by Edmonton from NY Rangers.

- **Don Beaupre** traded to Washington by Minnesota for the rights to **Claudio Scremin.**

- **Richard Zemlak** traded to Pittsburgh by Minnesota for the rights to **Rob Gaudreau.**

3 - **Paul Guay** traded to Boston by Los Angeles for the rights to **Dave Pasin.**

7 - **J.J. Daigneault** traded to Montreal by Philadelphia for **Scott Sandelin.**

- **Russ Courtnall** traded to Montreal by Toronto for **John Kordic** and Montreal's sixth round choice (**Michael Doers**) in 1989 Entry Draft.

- **Glen Cochrane** claimed on waivers by Edmonton from Chicago.

12 - **Tom Barrasso** traded to Pittsburgh by Buffalo with Buffalo's third round choice in 1990 Entry Draft for **Doug Bodger** and **Darrin Shannon.**

25 - **Paul Fenton** traded to Winnipeg by Los Angeles for **Gilles Hamel.**

25 - **Bob Bassen** and **Steve Konroyd** traded to Chicago by NY Islanders for **Marc Bergevin** and **Gary Nylund.**

29 - **Mike Bullard** traded to Philadelphia by St. Louis for **Peter Zezel.**

December

6 - **Gord Donnelly** traded to Winnipeg by Quebec for **Mario Marois.**

- **Reed Larson** traded to NY Islanders by Edmonton for future considerations.

8 - **Moe Mantha** traded to Minnesota by Philadelphia for Toronto's fifth round choice (**Pat MacLeod**) in 1989 Entry Draft — aquired earlier by Philadelphia.

9 - **Dan Dorion** traded to Boston by New Jersey for **Jean-Marc Lanthier.**

10 - **Steve Fletcher** traded to Philadelphia by Winnipeg for future considerations.

12 - **Michael Boyce, Todd Elik** and **Igor Liba** and future considerations traded to Los Angeles by NY Rangers for **Dean Kennedy** and **Denis Larocque.**

- **Tommy Albelin** traded to New Jersey by Quebec for New Jersey's fourth round choice (**Niclas Andersson**) in 1989 Entry Draft.

15 - **Stephane Roy** traded to Quebec by Minnesota for future considerations.

17 - **Scott Bjugstad** and **Gord Dineen** traded to Pittsburgh by Minnesota for **Steve Gotaas** and **Ville Siren.**

26 - **Brian Lawton, Norm Maciver** and **Don Maloney** traded to Hartford by NY Rangers for **Carey Wilson** and Hartford's fifth round choice in 1990 Entry Draft.

26 - **Adam Creighton** traded to Chicago by Buffalo for **Rick Vaive.**

30 - **Moe Lemay** traded to Boston by Winnipeg for **Ray Neufeld.**

January 1989

3 - **Miroslav Frycer** traded to Edmonton by Detroit for Edmonton's tenth round choice (**Rick Judson**) in 1989 Entry Draft.

9 - **Steve Guenette** traded to Calgary by Pittsburgh for Calgary's sixth round choice (**Mike Needham**) in 1989 Entry Draft.

16 - **Mike Lalor** traded to St. Louis by Montreal for the option to switch first round choices in 1990 Entry Draft and St. Louis' third round choice in 1991 Entry Draft.

19 - **Alain Chevrier** traded to Chicago by Winnipeg for Chicago's fourth round choice (**Allain Roy**) in 1989 Entry Draft.

22 - **Jay Miller** traded to Los Angeles by Boston for future considerations.

23 - **Doug Halward** traded to Edmonton by Detroit for Edmonton's twelfth round choice (**Jason Glickman**) in 1989 Entry Draft.

- **Bobby Carpenter** traded to Boston by Los Angeles for **Steve Kasper.**

25 - **Jose Charbonneau** traded to Vancouver by Montreal for **Dan Woodley.**

February

3 - **Phil DeGaetano** traded to St. Louis by Boston for **Scott Harlow.**

- **Dean Kennedy** traded to Los Angeles by NY Rangers for Los Angeles' fourth round choice in 1990 Entry Draft.

7 - **Al Secord** traded to Philadelphia by Toronto for Philadelphia's fifth round choice (**Keith Carney**) in 1989 Entry Draft.

- **Keith Acton** traded to Philadelphia by Edmonton with Philadelphia's fifth round choice in 1991 Entry Draft for **Dave Brown.**

9 - **Jamie Husgen** traded to Vancouver by Winnipeg for future considerations.

13 - **Ron Flockhart** traded to Boston by St. Louis for future considerations.

15 - **Tomas Jonsson** traded to Edmonton by NY Islanders for future considerations.

16 - **Wayne Van Dorp** traded to Chicago by Buffalo for Chicago's seventh round choice in 1990 Entry Draft.

21 - **Ken Hammond** traded to Toronto by NY Rangers for **Chris McRae.**

22 - **Mark Fitzpatrick, Wayne McBean** and future considerations traded to NY Islanders by Los Angeles for **Kelly Hrudey.**

27 - **Paul Lawless** traded to Toronto by Vancouver for the rights to **Peter Deboer.**

March

4 - **Perry Berezan** and **Shane Churla** traded to Minnesota by Calgary for **Brian MacLellan** and Minnesota's fourth round choice (**Robert Reichel**) in 1989 Entry Draft.

6 - **Ken Wregget** traded to Philadelphia by Toronto for Philadelphia's first round choice (**Rob Pearson**) and Calgary's first round choice (**Steve Bancroft**) in 1989 Entry Draft — obtained previously by Philadelphia in the Brad McCrimmon trade.

- **Scot Kleinendorst** traded to Washington by Hartford for **Jim Thomson.**

- **Patrick Mayer** traded to Los Angeles by Pittsburgh for **Tim Tookey.**

7 - **Calle Johannson** traded to Washington by Buffalo with Buffalo's second round choice (**Byron Dafoe**) in 1989 Entry Draft for **Grant Ledyard, Clint Malarchuk** and Washington's sixth round choice in 1991 Entry Draft.

- **Lindy Ruff** traded to NY Rangers by Buffalo for NY Rangers' fifth round choice in 1990 Entry Draft.

- **Jim Pavese** traded to Hartford by Detroit for **Torrie Robertson.**

- **Reed Larson** traded to Minnesota by NY Islanders for future considerations.

- **Tim Lenardon** traded to Vancouver by New Jersey for **Claude Vilgrain.**

- **John English** and **Brian Wilks** traded to Edmonton by Los Angeles for **Alan May** and **Jim Wiemer.**

- **Greg Gilbert** traded to Chicago by NY Islanders for Chicago's fifth round choice (**Steve Young**) in 1989 Entry Draft.

- **Dino Ciccarelli** and **Bob Rouse** traded to Washington by Minnesota for **Mike Gartner** and **Larry Murphy.**

- **Greg Adams** and **Doug Smith** traded to Vancouver by Edmonton for **Jean LeBlanc** and Vancouver's fifth round choice (**Peter White**) in 1989 Entry Draft.

June

1 - **Mark Ferner** traded to Washington by Buffalo for **Scott McCrory.**

15 - **Adam Oates** and **Paul MacLean** traded to St. Louis by Detroit for **Bernie Federko** and **Tony McKegney.**

16 - NHL Supplemental Draft:

Quebec	**Dave Depinto** (Ill.-Chicago)
NY Islanders	**Rob Vanderydt** (Miami-Ohio)
Toronto	**David Tomlinson** (Boston College)
Winnipeg	**Peter Hankinson** (U. Minnesota)
New Jersey	**C.J. Young** (Harvard)
Quebec	**Rick Berens** (U. of Denver)
NY Islanders	**Brad Mattson** (St. Mary's)
Toronto	**Mike Moes** (U. of Michigan)
Winnipeg	**Jon Anderson** (U. Minnesota)
New Jersey	**Mark Romaine** (Providence)
Chicago	**Alex Roberts** (U. of Michigan)
Minnesota	**Jamie Loewen** (Alaska-Fair.)
Vancouver	**Jeff Napierala** (Lake Superior)
St. Louis	**Rob Tustian** (Michigan Tech)
Hartford	**Chris Tancill** (U. Wisconsin)
Detroit	**Brad Kreick** (Brown)
Philadelphia	**Jamie Baker** (U. of Windsor)
NY Rangers	**Anthony Polumbo** (Lake Superior)
Buffalo	**Ian Boyce** (Vermont)
Edmonton	**David Aiken** (N. Hampshire)
Pittsburgh	**John Depourcq** (Ferris State)
Boston	**Jeff Schulman** (Vermont)
Los Angeles	**Carl Repp** (U.B.C.)
Washington	**Karl Clauss** (Colgate)
Montreal	**Graig Charron** (Lowell)
Calgary	**Shawn Heaphy** (Michigan State)

- **Rob Ramage** traded to Toronto by Calgary for Toronto's second round choice (**Kent Manderville**) in 1989 Entry Draft.

17 - **Greg Paslawski** traded to Winnipeg by St. Louis with St. Louis' third round choice (**Kris Draper**) in 1989 Entry Draft for Winnipeg's third round choice (**Denny Felsner**) in 1989 Entry Draft and second round choice in 1991 Entry Draft.

- **Randy Cunneyworth, Dave McLlwain** and **Rick Tabaracci** traded to Winnipeg by Pittsburgh for **Randy Gilhen, Jim Kyte** and **Andrew McBain.**

- **Bob Mason** traded to Washington by Quebec for future considerations.

- **Frank Caprice** traded to Boston by Vancouver for Boston's twelfth round choice (**Jan Bergman**) in 1989 Entry Draft.

- **Tommy Lehman** traded to Edmonton by Boston for Edmonton's third round choice (**Wes Walz**) in 1989 Entry Draft.

- **Corey Foster** traded to Edmonton by New Jersey for Edmonton's first round choice (**Jason Miller**) in 1989 Entry Draft.

- **Alan May** traded to Washington by Los Angeles for Washington's fifth round choice (**Tomas Newman**) in 1989 Entry Draft.

- **Joe Cirella** and **Claude Loiselle** traded to Quebec by New Jersey for **Walt Poddubny** and future considerations.

- **Sylvain Turgeon** traded to New Jersey by Hartford for **Pat Verbeek.**

- **Joe Reekie** traded to NY Islanders by Buffalo for NY Islanders sixth round choice (**Bill Pye**) in 1989 Entry Draft.

19 - **Kevin Kaminsky** traded to Quebec by Minnesota for **Gaetan Duchesne.**

- **Peter Sundstrom** traded to New Jersey by Washington for New Jersey's tenth round choice in 1991 Entry Draft.

29 - **Lou Franceschetti** traded to Toronto by Washington for Toronto's sixth round choice in the 1990 Entry Draft.

July

21 - **Shawn Cronin** traded to Winnipeg by Philadelphia for future considerations.

NHL Schedule 1989-90 continued from inside front cover

* Afternoon Game

Game #	Visitor	Home
Sun. Dec. 3		
284	Boston	Philadelphia
285	St Louis	Buffalo
286	Toronto	Edmonton
287	Detroit	Chicago
288	Minnesota	Vancouver
Tues. Dec. 5		
289	Boston	Quebec
290	Buffalo	NY Islanders
291	Washington	Philadelphia
292	St Louis	Detroit
Wed. Dec. 6		
293	NY Islanders	Hartford
294	Montreal	Minnesota
295	New Jersey	NY Rangers
296	Washington	Pittsburgh
297	Toronto	Chicago
298	Winnipeg	Calgary
299	Vancouver	Los Angeles
Thur. Dec. 7		
300	Hartford	Boston
301	Buffalo	Philadelphia
302	Toronto	St Louis
Fri. Dec. 8		
303	Montreal	Winnipeg
304	Pittsburgh	New Jersey
305	Minnesota	Detroit
306	Los Angeles	Edmonton
Sat. Dec. 9		
307	*Washington	Boston
308	New Jersey	Hartford
309	Montreal	Toronto
310	*Philadelphia	Quebec
311	NY Rangers	NY Islanders
312	Chicago	Pittsburgh
313	Detroit	Minnesota
314	Vancouver	St Louis
Sun. Dec. 10		
315	Washington	Buffalo
316	*Los Angeles	Quebec
317	Philadelphia	NY Rangers
318	Vancouver	Chicago
319	*Calgary	Winnipeg
Mon. Dec. 11		
320	Los Angeles	Montreal
321	St Louis	Toronto
322	Calgary	Edmonton
Tues. Dec. 12		
323	Boston	Pittsburgh
324	New Jersey	NY Islanders
325	Vancouver	Minnesota
Wed. Dec. 13		
326	Boston	Buffalo
327	Los Angeles	Hartford
328	Chicago	Montreal
329	Quebec	Edmonton
330	NY Islanders	New Jersey
331	St Louis	NY Rangers
332	Toronto	Detroit
333	Vancouver	Winnipeg
Thur. Dec. 14		
334	Hartford	Philadelphia
335	Quebec	Calgary
336	Pittsburgh	Minnesota
Fri. Dec. 15		
337	NY Islanders	Washington
338	Los Angeles	New Jersey
339	Chicago	Detroit
340	Winnipeg	Vancouver
Sat. Dec. 16		
341	*Buffalo	Boston
342	Washington	Hartford
343	Detroit	Montreal
344	NY Rangers	NY Islanders
345	Los Angeles	Philadelphia
346	Pittsburgh	Calgary
347	Minnesota	Toronto
348	Edmonton	St Louis
Sun. Dec. 17		
349	Boston	New Jersey
350	Philadelphia	Buffalo
351	Montreal	NY Rangers
352	Quebec	Vancouver
353	Edmonton	Chicago
Mon. Dec. 18		
354	St Louis	Toronto
Tues. Dec. 19		
355	Hartford	Pittsburgh
356	New Jersey	NY Islanders
357	Washington	Philadelphia
358	Edmonton	Minnesota
359	Winnipeg	Los Angeles
360	Calgary	Vancouver
Wed. Dec. 20		
361	Boston	Hartford
362	Buffalo	NY Rangers
363	Toronto	Detroit
364	St Louis	Chicago
365	Vancouver	Calgary
Thur. Dec. 21		
366	Minnesota	Boston
367	Quebec	Los Angeles
368	Washington	Pittsburgh
369	Winnipeg	Edmonton
Fri. Dec. 22		
370	Montreal	Buffalo
371	New Jersey	Philadelphia
372	Toronto	Chicago
Sat. Dec. 23		
373	*Detroit	Boston
374	Minnesota	Hartford
375	Buffalo	Quebec
376	Philadelphia	Montreal
377	*Pittsburgh	NY Islanders
378	NY Rangers	Washington
379	St Louis	New Jersey
380	Chicago	Toronto
381	Calgary	Edmonton
382	Vancouver	Los Angeles
Tues. Dec. 26		
383	Toronto	Boston
384	Hartford	Quebec
385	Detroit	Buffalo
386	New Jersey	NY Rangers
387	Pittsburgh	Washington
388	Chicago	St Louis
389	Minnesota	Winnipeg
Wed. Dec. 27		
390	Montreal	Vancouver
391	NY Rangers	Pittsburgh
392	Washington	New Jersey
393	Philadelphia	Edmonton
394	Detroit	Toronto
395	Calgary	Los Angeles
Thur. Dec. 28		
396	St Louis	NY Islanders
397	Minnesota	Chicago
Fri. Dec. 29		
398	Boston	Buffalo
399	Montreal	Edmonton
400	NY Rangers	New Jersey
401	Detroit	Washington
402	Winnipeg	Calgary
Sat. Dec. 30		
403	Boston	Toronto
404	Hartford	Chicago
405	Montreal	Calgary
406	NY Islanders	Quebec
407	Philadelphia	Los Angeles
408	Minnesota	St Louis
Sun. Dec. 31		
409	NY Islanders	Buffalo
410	*Pittsburgh	NY Rangers
411	New Jersey	Detroit
412	Philadelphia	Vancouver
413	St Louis	Minnesota
414	*Edmonton	Winnipeg
Mon. Jan. 1		
415	*Los Angeles	Washington
Tues. Jan. 2		
416	Boston	Pittsburgh
417	Buffalo	New Jersey
418	Los Angeles	NY Islanders
419	Philadelphia	Calgary
420	Vancouver	Detroit
421	Edmonton	St Louis
Wed. Jan. 3		
422	Winnipeg	Hartford
423	Quebec	Toronto
424	Washington	NY Rangers
425	Edmonton	Chicago
Thur. Jan. 4		
426	Winnipeg	Boston
427	Quebec	Detroit
428	NY Rangers	Minnesota
429	Los Angeles	New Jersey
430	Philadelphia	St Louis
431	Vancouver	Pittsburgh
Fri. Jan. 5		
432	Hartford	Calgary
433	Vancouver	Washington
Sat. Jan. 6		
434	Washington	Boston
435	Hartford	Edmonton
436	Buffalo	Montreal
437	Quebec	NY Islanders
438	NY Rangers	St Louis
439	Philadelphia	Chicago
440	Winnipeg	Pittsburgh
441	Los Angeles	Toronto
442	Detroit	Minnesota
Sun. Jan. 7		
443	Boston	Buffalo
444	Vancouver	Montreal
445	Calgary	Edmonton
Mon. Jan. 8		
446	Pittsburgh	NY Rangers
447	Winnipeg	New Jersey
448	Washington	Toronto
Tues. Jan. 9		
449	Montreal	Quebec
450	Minnesota	Detroit
451	St Louis	Los Angeles
452	Edmonton	Calgary
Wed. Jan. 10		
453	Hartford	Vancouver
454	NY Islanders	Toronto
455	Chicago	NY Rangers
456	Pittsburgh	New Jersey
457	Washington	Winnipeg
Thur. Jan. 11		
458	Quebec	Boston
459	Buffalo	Calgary
460	NY Islanders	Minnesota
461	Chicago	Philadelphia
462	Edmonton	Los Angeles
Fri. Jan. 12		
463	Montreal	New Jersey
464	Pittsburgh	Washington
465	Detroit	Winnipeg
466	St Louis	Vancouver
Sat. Jan. 13		
467	*NY Rangers	Boston
468	Hartford	Los Angeles
469	Buffalo	Vancouver
470	Philadelphia	Montreal
471	New Jersey	Quebec
472	Washington	NY Islanders
473	Calgary	Toronto
474	Detroit	Minnesota
Sun. Jan. 14		
475	Philadelphia	NY Rangers
476	Calgary	Chicago
477	St Louis	Winnipeg
Mon. Jan. 15		
478	Hartford	Boston
479	Minnesota	Montreal
480	Chicago	Toronto
Tues. Jan. 16		
481	Buffalo	Los Angeles
482	Quebec	Winnipeg
483	Vancouver	NY Islanders
484	New Jersey	Washington
485	Philadelphia	Pittsburgh
486	Detroit	Edmonton
487	Calgary	St Louis
Wed. Jan. 17		
488	Boston	Hartford
489	NY Islanders	Montreal
490	Minnesota	Chicago
491	Winnipeg	Edmonton
Thur. Jan. 18		
492	Calgary	Boston
493	Quebec	Minnesota
494	NY Rangers	Pittsburgh
495	Vancouver	Philadelphia
496	Toronto	St Louis
497	Detroit	Los Angeles
Fri. Jan. 19		
498	Calgary	Hartford
499	Washington	Buffalo
500	NY Islanders	Winnipeg
501	Vancouver	Chicago
Sun. Jan. 21		
All-Star Game at Pittsburgh		
Tues. Jan. 23		
502	Boston	Quebec
503	NY Islanders	Hartford
504	Buffalo	Philadelphia
505	NY Rangers	Edmonton
506	New Jersey	Pittsburgh
507	Winnipeg	Washington
508	St Louis	Detroit
509	Los Angeles	Vancouver
Wed. Jan. 24		
510	Buffalo	Chicago
511	Quebec	Montreal
512	Washington	New Jersey
513	Minnesota	Toronto
Thur. Jan. 25		
514	NY Islanders	Boston
515	Hartford	St Louis
516	NY Rangers	Calgary
517	Winnipeg	Philadelphia
518	Pittsburgh	Detroit
519	Los Angeles	Edmonton
Fri. Jan. 26		
520	Chicago	Buffalo
521	Montreal	Washington
522	Toronto	New Jersey
523	Minnesota	Vancouver
Sat. Jan. 27		
524	*Philadelphia	Boston
525	Chicago	Hartford
526	Montreal	Toronto
527	Detroit	Quebec
528	*Pittsburgh	NY Islanders
529	NY Rangers	Los Angeles
530	Winnipeg	St Louis
531	Minnesota	Calgary
532	Vancouver	Edmonton
Sun. Jan. 28		
533	*Pittsburgh	Buffalo
534	*New Jersey	NY Islanders
535	*Philadelphia	Washington
Mon. Jan. 29		
536	Boston	Montreal
537	Winnipeg	Minnesota
Tues. Jan. 30		
538	Edmonton	Hartford
539	Buffalo	Quebec
540	St Louis	NY Islanders
541	New Jersey	Los Angeles
542	Philadelphia	Pittsburgh
543	Calgary	Vancouver
Wed. Jan. 31		
544	Quebec	Buffalo
545	St Louis	NY Rangers
546	Washington	Minnesota
547	Toronto	Winnipeg
548	Edmonton	Detroit
Thur. Feb. 1		
549	Montreal	Boston
550	Hartford	Philadelphia
551	Chicago	Los Angeles
552	Vancouver	Calgary
Fri. Feb. 2		
553	Washington	NY Islanders
554	Edmonton	Pittsburgh
555	Toronto	Detroit
556	Vancouver	Winnipeg
Sat. Feb. 3		
557	*NY Rangers	Boston
558	*Hartford	Quebec
559	Buffalo	Montreal
560	*Minnesota	Philadelphia
561	Pittsburgh	Toronto
562	Detroit	St Louis
563	Calgary	Los Angeles
Sun. Feb. 4		
564	*Boston	Quebec
565	Hartford	Montreal
566	NY Islanders	Buffalo
567	Minnesota	NY Rangers
568	New Jersey	Vancouver
569	*Edmonton	Washington
570	Chicago	Winnipeg
Tues. Feb. 6		
571	Boston	Detroit
572	Quebec	Washington
573	NY Islanders	Pittsburgh
574	Edmonton	New Jersey
575	Toronto	St Louis
576	Winnipeg	Vancouver
577	Los Angeles	Calgary
Wed. Feb. 7		
578	Hartford	Minnesota
579	Montreal	Buffalo
580	Edmonton	NY Rangers
581	St Louis	Toronto
Thur. Feb. 8		
582	Quebec	Boston
583	NY Islanders	Philadelphia
584	Washington	Pittsburgh
585	Chicago	Detroit
586	Winnipeg	Los Angeles